Collins

SCRUBBLE™
BRAND Crossword Game
WORD CHECKER

HarperCollins Publishers
Westerhill Road
Bishopbriggs
Glasgow
G64 2QT

Second Edition 2012
Published 2008 and 2012 as
Collins Scrabble Dictionary. Reissued
2013 as *Collins Scrabble Word Checker*.

Reprint 10 9 8 7 6 5 4 3 2 1 0

© HarperCollins Publishers 2008,
2012, 2013

ISBN 978-0-00-753794-5

Collins® is a registered trademark
of HarperCollins Publishers Limited

Scrabble® is a registered trademark
of J.W. Spear & Sons Ltd, a subsidiary
of Mattel, Inc. © 2012 Mattel

www.collins.co.uk
www.collinsdictionary.com

A catalogue record for this book is
available from the British Library

Typeset by Davidson Publishing
Solutions, Glasgow

Printed in Great Britain by Clays Ltd,
St Ives plc

Acknowledgements
We would like to thank those
authors and publishers who kindly
gave permission for copyright
material to be used in the Collins
Corpus. We would also like to thank
Times Newspapers Ltd for providing
valuable data.

Contents

EDITORIAL STAFF

Introduction

Collins Scrabble Word Checker – Every Word Counts

The *Collins Scrabble Word Checker* is the ideal reference book for people who play Scrabble for enjoyment, in a social or family setting. This dictionary doesn't include every word eligible for Scrabble, but does contain the most commonly used of the 270,000 words in *Collins Official Scrabble Words 2011*, the definitive Scrabble wordlist. The concise definitions in the *Scrabble Word Checker* allow players to check the meaning of words, as well as to use the book for settling arguments during games.

The *Collins Scrabble Word Checker* contains words of up to 7 letters in length. However, references to longer words playable in Scrabble are included. These longer words output in bold, and are introduced by a chevron symbol (>). Because this dictionary is designed for family play, it does not include offensive terms. Such words are, on the other hand, included in the *Collins Official Scrabble Words 2011*, the complete wordlist for tournaments and club competitions, along with words of 8–15 letters.

In the *Collins Scrabble Word Checker*, all words are listed in alphabetical order, rather than some being grouped at the base form as in a conventional dictionary. Where words are inflections of a base form, only the base form has a definition, but the inflections are listed alphabetically as individual entries for easy reference during a game. A black triangle symbol (▶) is used to refer readers to another related entry in the dictionary.

Two-letter words

A sound knowledge of the 124 two-letter words is crucial to success in Scrabble, not least because they are so useful in enabling 'tagging plays', as explained below in the Forming Words section. For this reason, these are supplied in a separate list on pages 13–16 as well as being included in the body of the text.

Special Scrabble Words

To help family players learn and use some of the most useful words in the game, the *Collins Scrabble Word Checker* includes a number of special panel entries, drawing attention to more than 200 words of particular interest or utility. For the most part these are words which are less likely to form part of a novice player's natural vocabulary, and the emphasis is on particularly useful three-letter words, on high probability seven-letter bonus words, on words that are especially useful when you have either too many vowels on your rack or too many consonants, and on selected shorter words that use the high value consonants **J**, **K**, **Q**, **X** and **Z**. But just for fun we have also featured a few of the unusual and exciting words of the kind that Scrabble players dream about. Realistically, you may well never get the chance to play words like **ZOOTAXY**, **TZADDIQ** and **QUETZAL**. But imagine the thrill (and the score!) if you did...

There are also panel entries at the start of every letter section, which offer advice on useful words beginning with that letter.

The *Collins Scrabble Word Checker* is designed to be useful to new players and Scrabble veterans alike – we hope you enjoy using it!

Forming Words

The key to successful Scrabble is constant awareness of the opportunities for forming words on the board. The obvious way to play a new word is to place it so that it intersects with a word already on the board through a common letter:

			D_2		
			O_1		
	L_1	U_1	C_3	K_5	
			T_1		
			O_1		
			R_1		

The common letter is known as a floater, in this case the floater being **C**. Skilful players are occasionally able to play through two or more floaters, whether the floating letters are adjacent or (even more difficult!) separated. A good deal of Scrabble skill revolves around using floaters, and on denying the use of floaters to your opponent.

Other methods of forming words, however, create more than one new word in the process, giving a higher score. The two main ways of doing this are 'hooking' and 'tagging'.

Hooking

Hooking involves 'hanging' one word on another – the word already on the board acts as a 'hook' on which the other word can be hung – changing the first word in the process. When you form a word by hooking, you add a letter to the beginning or end of a word on the board, transforming it into a longer word as you do so:

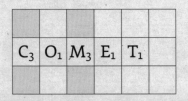

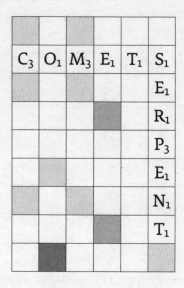

In this example, you get the points for **COMETS** as well as for **SERPENTS**. Plurals ending in **S** provide some of the most obvious – and useful – end-hooks. But there are plenty of other end-hooks as well. There are also lots of useful front-hooks. Consider the following example:

If you happened to have **C**, **E**, **F**, **I**, **K** and **L** among the letters on your rack, you could play the following, taking full advantage of the valuable **X** played by your opponent:

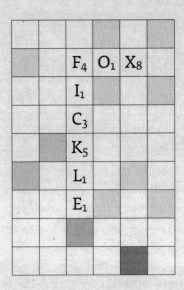

Here you get the 13 points for **FOX** as well as those for **FICKLE**. So you can see that hooking is generally a much more profitable method of word-formation than simply playing a word through one that is already on the board.

Obviously, not all words provide hooks. Some words cannot form other words by having a letter added to either their front or their back; these are known as 'blockers', as they prevent other players from adding words by hooking.

Tagging

Playing a word parallel to one already on the board, so that one or more tiles are in contact, is known as tagging. Tagging is more difficult than hooking because you need to form one additional word for each tile in contact with the word on the board. In most circumstances, these will be two-letter words, which is why these words are so vital to the game. The more two-letter words you know, the greater your opportunities for fitting words onto the board through tagging – and of running up some impressive scores! Very skilful players have even been known to make 7-letter parallel plays!

For example, consider the following situation (your opponent has started the game with **SHAM** and you have **E,E,H,I,S,T** and **X** on your rack):

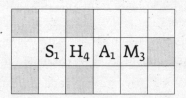

You could play **HEXES** so that it also forms **SH**, **HE**, **AX** and **ME** (all valid two-letter words), thus adding the scores for these three words to the points you make from **HEXES**:

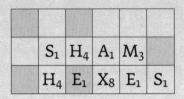

A particular advantage of tagging is that it allows you to benefit from valuable tiles twice in one go, as in the example above where **X** is used in both **HEXES** and **AX**.

Other Word Forming Techniques

There are other ways of forming new words from letters already on the board. For example, it is sometimes possible to 'infill' between existing letters, or to extend existing words at the front or back by the addition of more than one letter. Thus, if your opponent opens with **COVER**, placing the **C** on the double-letter square, you may be able to prefix it with **DIS** making **DISCOVER** and earning a triple-word score. But hooking and tagging are by far the most common techniques.

Two-letter Words

Where many inexperienced Scrabble players go wrong is
that they think the longer a word is, the better it is to know,
as it's likely to score more. In fact, the key to a good Scrabble
vocabulary is a good knowledge of short words.

The reason for that is you can use the short words to 'hook'
the word you want to play on to the board, allowing you to
play parallel to another word, rather than always going
through it crosswise. That way you will usually make more
than one word each shot, gaining you a higher score.

8 POINTS = BAD PLAY

25 POINTS = GOOD PLAY

Notice how by using the same letters from your rack, you
have scored seventeen more points. But notice also that little
word **FA** which enabled you to fit the play in. And there we
have the first, essential thing you have to know to improve

your game: **all the allowable two letter words**.
Yes, all of them.

There are 124 of these to learn, but to make the list more manageable, you can divide them into three groups:

1. The ones you already know.

2. The ones you already know, but may not have realized were words.

3. The ones you probably don't know.

There are thirty-seven two-letter words which most people would know and which would appear in most dictionaries:

AH	AM	AN	AS	AT	AX	AY	BE	BY	DO	EH
GO	HA	HE	HI	HO	IF	IN	IS	IT	LA	LO
MA	ME	MY	NO	OF	OH	ON	OR	OX	PA	SO
TO	UP	US	WE							

So straight away you only have eighty-seven new ones to learn. But it's not even as bad as that, because now we move on to the second group: the ones you know, but don't know you know.

These include:

Contractions

AD (advertisement)   **PO** (chamberpot)

BI (bisexual)   **RE** (regarding)

MO (moment)   **TA** (thank you)

OP (operation)

Interjections and exclamations

AW	ER	HM	MM	OI	OW	OY
SH	ST	UH	UM	UR	YA	YO

Letters of the alphabet

AR	EF	EL	EM	EN	ES	EX

Then add in **ID** (the psychiatric term), **PI** (the Greek letter and mathematical term), and **YE** (the old form of **YOU**), and that's another thirty-one taken care of with no trouble at all.

Fifty-six to go. These are the ones you probably don't know, so let's set them out where you can get the measure of them:

AA	AB	AE	AG	AI	AL	BA	BO	CH	DA	DE
DI	EA	ED	EE	ET	FA	FE	FY	GI	GU	IO
JA	JO	KA	KI	KO	KY	LI	MI	MU	NA	NE
NU	NY	OB	OD	OE	OM	OO	OS	OU	PE	QI
SI	TE	TI	UG	UN	UT	WO	XI	XU	YU	ZA
ZO										

If all this looks a bit gobbledygookish, you may be surprised to know that even some of these are more familiar to you than you might realize. An **AB** is an abdominal muscle, as in toning up your abs and your pecs. **MU**, **NU**, and **XI** are Greek letters (and **PE** and **TE** are letters from our alphabet). **OM** is what Buddhists chant as part of their prayers.

Having said that, it can't be denied that some of the definitions are genuinely obscure. To go from start to finish, **AA** is a word from Hawaiian, meaning a rough volcanic rock. And a **ZO** is a Himalayan cross-breed of a yak and a cow, also spelt **ZHO**, **DZO**, **DZHO**, or **DSO**.

Now, where else but in Scrabble can you go from Hawaii to the Himalayas in one step? Have a look at the two-letter words every so often. Once you're happy with the first two groups (i.e. the common ones, the contractions, the interjections, the letters, plus **ID**, **PI**, and **YE**), have a real go at mastering the unusual ones. They really are the essential first step to improving your game.

Abbreviations

adj	adjective
adv	adverb
conj	conjunction
det	determiner
interj	interjection
n	noun
pl	plural
prep	preposition
pron	pronoun
vb	verb

Aa

A forms a two-letter word when followed by any one of **A, B, D, E, G, H, I, L, M, N, R, S, T, W, X** and **Y** - 16 letters out of 26 - so it's a really useful tile. There are also a number of short high-scoring words beginning with **A**. **Axe** (10 points) and **adze** (14 points) are good examples, but don't forget their US variants, **ax** (9 points) and **adz** (13 points). Also remember their plurals and the verb form **axed** (12 points). **Aye** (6) and **ay** (5) are handy for tight corners.

AA *n* volcanic rock consisting of angular blocks of lava with a very rough surface

AAH *vb* exclaim in pleasure or surprise

AAHED ▶ aah

AAHING ▶ aah

AAHS ▶ aah

AAL *n* Asian shrub or tree

> An **aal** is an East Indian shrub, useful for getting rid of annoying multiples of A.

AALII *n* bushy sapindaceous shrub with small greenish flowers and sticky foliage

> An **aalii** is a tropical tree, great for getting rid of surplus As and Is.

AALIIS ▶ aalii

AALS ▶ aal

AARGH ▶ argh

AARRGH ▶ argh

AARRGHH ▶ argh

AARTI *n* Hindu ceremony in which lights with wicks soaked in ghee are lit and offered up to one or more deities

AARTIS ▶ aarti

AAS ▶ aa

AB *n* abdominal muscle

ABA *n* type of cloth from Syria, made of goat hair or camel hair

ABAC *n* mathematical diagram

ABACA *n* Philippine plant, related to the banana

ABACAS ▶ abaca

ABACI ▶ abacus

ABACK *adv* towards the back; backwards

ABACS ▶ abac

ABACTOR *n* cattle thief

ABACUS *n* beads on a wire frame, used for doing calculations

ABAFT *adv* closer to the rear of (a ship) ▷ *adj* closer to the stern of a ship

ABAKA *n* abaca

ABAKAS ▶ abaka

ABALONE *n* edible sea creature with a shell lined with mother of pearl

ABAMP *same as* > **abampere**

ABAMPS ▶ abamp

ABAND *vb* abandon

ABANDED ▶ aband

ABANDON *vb* desert or leave (one's wife, children, etc) ▷ *n* lack of inhibition

ABANDS ▶ aband

ABAS ▶ aba

ABASE *vb* humiliate or degrade (oneself)

ABASED ▶ abase

ABASER ▶ abase

ABASERS ▶ abase

ABASES ▶ abase

ABASH *vb* cause to feel ill at ease, embarrassed, or confused

ABASHED *adj* embarrassed and ashamed

ABASHES ▶ abash

ABASIA *n* disorder affecting ability to walk

ABASIAS ▶ abasia

ABASING ▶ abase

ABASK *adv* in pleasant warmth

ABATE *vb* make or become less strong

ABATED ▶ abate

ABATER ▶ abate

ABATERS ▶ abate

ABATES ▶ abate

ABATING ▶ abate

ABATIS *n* rampart of felled trees bound together, placed with their branches outwards

ABATOR *n* person who effects an abatement

ABATORS ▶ abator

ABATTIS *same as* ▶ **abatis**

ABATTU *adj* dejected

ABATURE *n* trail left by hunted stag

ABAXIAL *adj* facing away from the axis, as the surface of a leaf

ABAXILE *adj* away from the axis

ABAYA *n* Arab outer garment

ABAYAS ▶ abaya

ABB *n* yarn used in weaving

ABBA *n* title for a bishop in the Coptic Church

ABBACY *n* office or jurisdiction of an abbot or abbess

ABBAS ▶ abba

ABBE *n* French abbot

ABBED *adj* displaying well-developed abdominal muscles

ABBES ▶ abbe

ABBESS *n* nun in charge of a convent

ABBEY *n* dwelling place of, or a church belonging to, a community of monks or nuns

A

ABBEYS ▸ abbey
ABBOT n head of an abbey of monks
ABBOTCY ▸ abbot
ABBOTS ▸ abbot
ABBS ▸ abb
ABCEE n alphabet
ABCEES ▸ abcee
ABDABS n highly nervous state
ABDOMEN n part of the body containing the stomach and intestines
ABDUCE vb abduct
ABDUCED ▸ abduce
ABDUCES ▸ abduce
ABDUCT vb carry off, kidnap
ABDUCTS ▸ abduct
ABEAM adj at right angles to the length of a ship or aircraft
ABEAR vb bear or behave
ABEARS ▸ abear
ABED adv in bed
ABEIGH adv aloof
ABELE n white poplar tree
ABELES ▸ abele
ABELIA n garden plant with pink or white flowers
ABELIAN ▸ abelia
ABELIAS ▸ abelia
ABET vb help or encourage in wrongdoing
ABETS ▸ abet
ABETTAL ▸ abet
ABETTED ▸ abet
ABETTER ▸ abet
ABETTOR ▸ abet
ABEYANT > abeyance
ABFARAD n cgs unit of capacitance in the electromagnetic system
ABHENRY n cgs unit of inductance in the electromagnetic system
ABHOR vb detest utterly
ABHORS ▸ abhor
ABID ▸ abide
ABIDDEN ▸ abide
ABIDE vb endure, put up with
ABIDED ▸ abide
ABIDER ▸ abide
ABIDERS ▸ abide
ABIDES ▸ abide
ABIDING adj lasting ▷ n action of one who abides
ABIES n fir tree
ABIETIC adj as in **abietic acid** a yellowish powder used in lacquers, varnishes, and soap
ABIGAIL n maid for a lady

ABILITY n competence, power
ABIOSES ▸ abiosis
ABIOSIS n absence of life
ABIOTIC ▸ abiosis
ABITUR n German final-year school examination
ABITURS ▸ abitur
ABJECT adj utterly miserable ▷ vb throw down
ABJECTS ▸ abject
ABJOINT vb cut off
ABJURE vb deny or renounce on oath
ABJURED ▸ abjure
ABJURER ▸ abjure
ABJURES ▸ abjure
ABLATE vb remove by ablation
ABLATED ▸ ablate
ABLATES ▸ ablate
ABLATOR n heat shield of a space vehicle, which melts or wears away during re-entry into the earth's atmosphere
ABLAUT n vowel gradation, esp in Indo-European languages
ABLAUTS ▸ ablaut
ABLAZE adj burning fiercely ▷ adv on fire
ABLE adj capable, competent ▷ vb enable
ABLED adj having a range of physical powers as specified
ABLEISM n discrimination against disabled or handicapped people
ABLEIST ▸ ableism
ABLER ▸ able
ABLES ▸ able
ABLEST ▸ able
ABLET n freshwater fish
ABLETS ▸ ablet
ABLING ▸ able
ABLINGS adv possibly
ABLINS adv Scots word meaning perhaps
ABLOOM adj in flower
ABLOW adj blooming
ABLUENT n substance used for cleansing
ABLUSH adj blushing
ABLUTED adj washed thoroughly
ABLY adv competently or skilfully
ABMHO n unit of electrical conductance
ABMHOS ▸ abmho

ABOARD adv on, in, onto, or into (a ship, train, or plane) ▷ adj on, in, onto, or into (a ship, plane, or train)
ABODE n home, dwelling ▷ vb forebode
ABODED ▸ abode
ABODES ▸ abode
ABODING ▸ abode
ABOHM n cgs unit of resistance in the electromagnetic system: equivalent to 10^{-9} ohm
ABOHMS ▸ abohm
ABOIL adj boiling
ABOLISH vb do away with
ABOLLA n Roman cloak
ABOLLAE ▸ abolla
ABOLLAS ▸ abolla
ABOMA n South American snake
ABOMAS ▸ aboma
ABOMASA ▸ abomasum
ABOMASI > abomasus
ABOON Scots word for ▸ above
ABORAL adj away from or opposite the mouth
ABORD vb accost
ABORDED ▸ abord
ABORDS ▸ abord
ABORE ▸ abear
ABORNE adj Shakespearean form of auburn
ABORT vb have an abortion or perform an abortion on ▷ n premature termination or failure of (a space flight, military operation, etc)
ABORTED ▸ abort
ABORTEE n woman having an abortion
ABORTER ▸ abort
ABORTS ▸ abort
ABORTUS n aborted fetus
ABOUGHT ▸ aby
ABOULIA same as ▸ abulia
ABOULIC ▸ aboulia
ABOUND vb be plentiful
ABOUNDS ▸ abound
ABOUT adv nearly, approximately
ABOUTS prep about
ABOVE adv over or higher (than) ▷ n something that is or appears above
ABOVES ▸ above
ABRADE vb scrape away or wear down by friction
ABRADED ▸ abrade
ABRADER ▸ abrade
ABRADES ▸ abrade
ABRAID vb awake

ABRAIDS ▸ abraid

ABRAM *adj* auburn

ABRASAX *same as*
▸ **abraxas**

ABRAXAS *n* ancient charm composed of Greek letters: believed to have magic powers; from the second century AD personified by Gnostics as a deity

ABRAY *vb* awake

ABRAYED ▸ abray

ABRAYS ▸ abray

ABRAZO *n* embrace

ABRAZOS ▸ abrazo

ABREACT *vb* alleviate (emotional tension) through abreaction

ABREAST *adj* side by side

ABREGE *n* abridgment

ABREGES ▸ abrege

ABRI *n* shelter or place of refuge, esp in wartime

ABRIDGE *vb* shorten by using fewer words

ABRIM *adj* full to the brim

ABRIN *n* poisonous compound

ABRINS ▸ abrin

ABRIS ▸ abri

ABROACH *adj* (of a cask, barrel, etc) tapped

ABROAD *adv* in a foreign country ▷ *adj* (of news, rumours, etc) in general circulation ▷ *n* foreign place

ABROADS ▸ abroad

ABROOKE *vb* bear or tolerate

ABROSIA *n* condition involving refusal to eat

ABRUPT *adj* sudden, unexpected ▷ *n* abyss

ABRUPTS ▸ abrupt

ABS ▸ ab

ABSCESS *n* inflamed swelling containing pus ▷ *vb* form a swelling containing pus

ABSCIND *vb* cut off

ABSCISE *vb* separate or be separated by abscission

ABSCISS *n* cutting off

ABSCOND *vb* leave secretly

ABSEIL *vb* go down a steep drop by a rope fastened at the top and tied around one's body ▷ *n* instance of abseiling

ABSEILS ▸ abseil

ABSENCE *n* being away

ABSENT *adj* not present

▷ *vb* stay away

ABSENTS ▸ absent

ABSEY *n* alphabet

ABSEYS ▸ absey

ABSINTH *same as*
> **absinthe**

ABSIT *n* overnight leave from college

ABSITS ▸ absit

ABSOLVE *vb* declare to be free from blame or sin

ABSORB *vb* soak up (a liquid)

ABSORBS ▸ absorb

ABSTAIN *vb* choose not to do something

ABSURD *adj* incongruous or ridiculous ▷ *n* conception of the world, esp in Existentialist thought, as neither designed nor predictable but irrational and meaningless

ABSURDS ▸ absurd

ABTHANE *n* ancient Scottish church territory

ABUBBLE *adj* bubbling

ABULIA *n* pathological inability to take decisions

ABULIAS ▸ abulia

ABULIC ▸ abulia

ABUNA *n* male head of Ethiopian family

ABUNAS ▸ abuna

ABUNE *Scots word for*
▸ **above**

ABURST *adj* bursting

ABUSAGE *n* wrong use

ABUSE *vb* use wrongly ▷ *n* prolonged ill-treatment

ABUSED ▸ abuse

ABUSER ▸ abuse

ABUSERS ▸ abuse

ABUSES ▸ abuse

ABUSING ▸ abuse

ABUSION *n* wrong use or deception

ABUSIVE *adj* rude or insulting

ABUT *vb* be next to or touching

ABUTS ▸ abut

ABUTTAL *same as*
> **abutment**

ABUTTED ▸ abut

ABUTTER *n* owner of adjoining property

ABUZZ *adj* noisy, busy with activity etc

ABVOLT *n* cgs unit of potential difference in the electromagnetic system

ABVOLTS ▸ abvolt

ABWATT *n* cgs unit of power in the electromagnetic system, equal to the power dissipated when a current of 1 abampere flows across a potential difference of 1 abvolt: equivalent to 10^{-7} watt

ABWATTS ▸ abwatt

ABY *vb* pay the penalty for

> If someone plays this word, remember that it can be expanded to **baby** and **gaby** and also to **abye** and **abys**.

ABYE *same as* ▸ **aby**

ABYEING ▸ abye

ABYES ▸ abye

ABYING ▸ aby

ABYS ▸ aby

ABYSM *archaic word for*
▸ **abyss**

ABYSMAL *adj* extremely bad, awful

ABYSMS ▸ abysm

ABYSS *n* very deep hole or chasm

ABYSSAL *adj* of or belonging to the ocean depths, esp below 2000 metres (6500 feet)

ABYSSES ▸ abyss

ACACIA *n* tree or shrub with yellow or white flowers

ACACIAS ▸ acacia

ACADEME *n* place of learning

ACADEMY *n* society to advance arts or sciences

ACAI *n* berry found in Brazilian rainforest

ACAIS ▸ acai

ACAJOU *n* type of mahogany used by cabinet-makers in France

ACAJOUS ▸ acajou

ACALEPH *n* invertebrate of the former taxonomic group which included the jellyfishes

ACANTH *n* acanthus

ACANTHA *n* thorn or prickle

ACANTHI > acanthus

ACANTHS ▸ acanth

ACAPNIA *n* lack of carbon dioxide

ACARI ▸ acarus

ACARIAN ▸ acarus

ACARID *n* member of the group of small arachnids which includes the ticks and mites ▷ *adj* of or relating to these arachnids

ACARIDS ▶ acarid
ACARINE n acarid
ACAROID adj resembling a mite or tick
ACARUS n type of mites which is a serious pests of stored flour, grain, etc
ACATER n buyer of provisions
ACATERS ▶ acater
ACATES n provisions
ACATOUR n buyer of provisions
ACAUDAL adj having no tail
ACCA n academic
ACCABLE adj dejected or beaten
ACCAS ▶ acca
ACCEDE vb consent or agree (to)
ACCEDED ▶ accede
ACCEDER ▶ accede
ACCEDES ▶ accede
ACCEND vb set alight
ACCENDS ▶ accend
ACCENT n distinctive style of pronunciation of a local, national, or social group ▷ vb place emphasis on
ACCENTS ▶ accent
ACCEPT vb receive willingly
ACCEPTS ▶ accept
ACCESS n means of or right to approach or enter ▷ vb obtain (data) from a computer
ACCIDIA same as ▶ accidie
ACCIDIE n spiritual sloth
ACCINGE vb put a belt around
ACCITE vb summon
ACCITED ▶ accite
ACCITES ▶ accite
ACCLAIM vb applaud, praise ▷ n enthusiastic approval
ACCLOY vb choke or clog
ACCLOYS ▶ accloy
ACCOAST vb accost
ACCOIED ▶ accoy
ACCOIL n welcome ▷ vb gather together
ACCOILS ▶ accoil
ACCOMPT vb account
ACCORD n agreement, harmony ▷ vb fit in with
ACCORDS ▶ accord
ACCOST vb approach and speak to, often aggressively ▷ n greeting
ACCOSTS ▶ accost
ACCOUNT n report, description ▷ vb judge to be
ACCOURT vb entertain

ACCOY vb soothe
ACCOYED ▶ accoy
ACCOYLD ▶ accoil
ACCOYS ▶ accoy
ACCRETE vb grow or cause to grow together
ACCREW vb accrue
ACCREWS ▶ accrew
ACCRUAL n act of accruing
ACCRUE vb increase gradually
ACCRUED ▶ accrue
ACCRUES ▶ accrue
ACCURSE vb curse
ACCURST same as ▷ accursed
ACCUSAL n accusation
ACCUSE vb charge with wrongdoing
ACCUSED n person or people accused of a crime in a court
ACCUSER ▶ accuse
ACCUSES ▶ accuse
ACE n playing card with one symbol on it ▷ adj excellent ▷ vb serve an ace in racquet sports
ACED ▶ ace
ACEDIA same as ▶ accidie
ACEDIAS ▶ acedia
ACEQUIA n irrigation ditch
ACER n type of tree cultivated for its brightly coloured foliage
ACERATE same as ▷ acerated
ACERB adj bitter
ACERBER ▶ acerb
ACERBIC adj harsh or bitter
ACEROLA n cherry-like fruit
ACEROSE adj shaped like a needle, as pine leaves
ACEROUS same as ▶ acerose
ACERS ▶ acer
ACES ▶ ace
ACETA ▶ acetum
ACETAL n 1,1-diethoxyethane, a colourless volatile liquid used as a solvent and in perfumes
ACETALS ▶ acetal
ACETATE n salt or ester of acetic acid
ACETIC adj of or involving vinegar
ACETIFY vb become or cause to become acetic acid or vinegar
ACETIN n type of acetate
ACETINS ▶ acetin

ACETONE n colourless liquid used as a solvent
ACETOSE same as ▶ acetous
ACETOUS adj containing, producing, or resembling acetic acid or vinegar
ACETUM n solution that has dilute acetic acid as solvent
ACETYL n of, consisting of, or containing the monovalent group CH_3CO-
ACETYLS ▶ acetyl
ACH interj Scots expression of surprise
ACHAGE n pain
ACHAGES ▶ achage
ACHAR n spicy pickle made from mango
ACHARNE adj furiously violent
ACHARS ▶ achar
ACHARYA n prominent religious teacher and spiritual guide
ACHATES same as ▶ acates
ACHE n dull continuous pain ▷ vb be in or cause continuous dull pain
ACHED ▶ ache
ACHENE n dry one-seeded indehiscent fruit with the seed distinct from the fruit wall. It may be smooth, as in the buttercup, or feathery, as in clematis
ACHENES ▶ achene
ACHENIA ▶ achenium
ACHES ▶ ache
ACHIER ▶ achy
ACHIEST ▶ achy
ACHIEVE vb gain by hard work or ability
ACHING ▶ ache
ACHINGS ▶ ache
ACHIOTE n annatto
ACHIRAL adj of a tuber producing arrowroot
ACHKAN n man's coat in India
ACHKANS ▶ achkan
ACHOLIA n condition involving lack of bile secretion
ACHOO interj sound of a sneeze
ACHY adj affected by a continuous dull pain
ACICULA n needle-shaped part, such as a spine, prickle, or crystal
ACID n one of a class of compounds, corrosive and sour when dissolved in

water, that combine with a base to form a salt ▷ *adj* containing acid

ACIDER ▸ acid

ACIDEST ▸ acid

ACIDIC *adj* containing acid

ACIDIER ▸ acid

ACIDIFY *vb* convert into acid

ACIDITY *n* quality of being acid

ACIDLY ▸ acid

ACIDS ▸ acid

ACIDY ▸ acid

ACIFORM *adj* shaped like a needle

ACINAR *adj* of small sacs

ACING ▸ ace

ACINI ▸ acinus

ACINIC ▸ acinus

ACINOSE ▸ acinus

ACINOUS ▸ acinus

ACINUS *n* any of the terminal saclike portions of a compound gland

ACKEE *n* tropical African tree cultivated in the Caribbean for its edible fruit

ACKEES ▸ ackee

ACKER *same as* **▸ acca**

ACKERS ▸ acker

ACKNEW ▸ acknow

ACKNOW *vb* recognize

ACKNOWN ▸ acknow

ACKNOWS ▸ acknow

ACLINIC *adj* unbending

ACMATIC *adj* highest or ultimate

ACME *n* highest point of achievement or excellence

ACMES ▸ acme

ACMIC *same as* **▸ acmatic**

ACMITE *n* chemical with pyramid-shaped crystals

ACMITES ▸ acmite

ACNE *n* pimply skin disease

ACNED *adj* marked by acne

ACNES ▸ acne

ACNODAL ▸ acnode

ACNODE *n* point whose coordinates satisfy the equation of a curve although it does not lie on the curve

ACNODES ▸ acnode

ACOCK *adv* cocked

ACOLD *adj* feeling cold

ACOLYTE *n* follower or attendant

ACOLYTH *n* acolyte

ACONITE *n* poisonous plant with hoodlike flowers

ACORN *n* nut of the oak tree

ACORNED *adj* covered with acorns

ACORNS ▸ acorn

ACOUCHI *n* South American rodent with a white-tipped tail

ACOUCHY *same as* **▸ acouchi**

ACQUEST *n* something acquired

ACQUIRE *vb* gain, get

ACQUIS *n as in* **acquis communautaire** body of law accumulated by the European Union

ACQUIST *n* acquisition

ACQUIT *vb* pronounce (someone) innocent

ACQUITE *vb* acquit

ACQUITS ▸ acquit

ACRASIA *n* lack of willpower

ACRASIN *n* chemical produced by slime moulds

ACRATIC ▸ acrasia

ACRAWL *adv* crawling

ACRE *n* measure of land, 4840 square yards (4046.86 square metres)

ACREAGE *n* land area in acres ▷ *adj* of or relating to a large allotment of land, esp in a rural area

ACRED *adj* having acres of land

ACRES ▸ acre

ACRID *adj* pungent, bitter

ACRIDER ▸ acrid

ACRIDIN *n* acridine

ACRIDLY ▸ acrid

ACROBAT *n* person skilled in gymnastic feats requiring agility and balance

ACROGEN *n* any flowerless plant, such as a fern or moss, in which growth occurs from the tip of the main stem

ACROMIA ▸ acromion

ACRONIC *adj* acronical

ACRONYM *n* word formed from the initial letters of other words, such as NASA

ACROSS *adv* from side to side (of)

ACROTER *n* plinth bearing a statue, etc, at either end or at the apex of a pediment

ACROTIC *adj* of a surface

ACRYLIC *adj* (synthetic fibre, paint, etc) made from acrylic acid ▷ *n* man-made fibre used for clothes and blankets

ACRYLYL *n* type of monovalent group

ACT *n* thing done ▷ *vb* do something

ACTA *n* minutes of meeting

ACTABLE ▸ act

ACTANT *n* (in valency grammar) a noun phrase functioning as the agent of the main verb of a sentence

ACTANTS ▸ actant

ACTED ▸ act

ACTIN *n* protein that participates in many kinds of cell movement, including muscle contraction, during which it interacts with filaments of a second protein, myosin

ACTINAL *adj* of or denoting the oral part of a radiate animal, such as a jellyfish, sea anemone, or sponge, from which the rays, tentacles, or arms grow

ACTING *n* art of an actor ▷ *adj* temporarily performing the duties of

ACTINGS ▸ acting

ACTINIA *n* type of sea anemone common in rock pools

ACTINIC *adj* (of radiation) producing a photochemical effect

ACTINON *same as* **▸ actinide**

ACTINS ▸ actin

ACTION *n* process of doing something ▷ *vb* put into effect

ACTIONS ▸ action

ACTIVE *adj* moving, working ▷ *n* active form of a verb

ACTIVES ▸ active

ACTON *n* jacket or jerkin, originally of quilted cotton, worn under a coat of mail

ACTONS ▸ acton

ACTOR *n* person who acts in a play, film, etc

ACTORLY *adj* of or relating to an actor

ACTORS ▸ actor

ACTRESS *n* woman who acts in a play, film, broadcast, etc

ACTS ▸ act

ACTUAL *adj* existing in reality

ACTUALS *pl n* commercial commodities that can be

A

bought and used

ACTUARY *n* statistician who calculates insurance risks

ACTUATE *vb* start up (a device)

ACTURE *n* action

ACTURES ▸ **acture**

ACUATE *adj* sharply pointed

ACUITY *n* keenness of vision or thought

ACULEI ▸ **aculeus**

ACULEUS *n* prickle or spine, such as the thorn of a rose

ACUMEN *n* ability to make good judgments

ACUMENS ▸ **acumen**

ACUSHLA *n* Irish endearment

ACUTE *adj* severe ▷ *n* accent (´) over a letter to indicate the quality or length of its sound, as in café

ACUTELY ▸ **acute**

ACUTER ▸ **acute**

ACUTES ▸ **acute**

ACUTEST ▸ **acute**

ACYCLIC *adj* not cyclic

ACYL *n* member of the monovalent group of atoms RCO-

ACYLATE *vb* introduce an acyl group into a compound

ACYLOIN *n* organic chemical compound

ACYLS ▸ **acyl**

AD *n* advertisement

ADAGE *n* wise saying, proverb

ADAGES ▸ **adage**

ADAGIAL ▸ **adage**

ADAGIO *adv* (piece to be played) slowly and gracefully ▷ *n* movement or piece to be performed slowly

ADAGIOS ▸ **adagio**

ADAMANT *adj* unshakable in determination or purpose ▷ *n* any extremely hard or apparently unbreakable substance

ADAPT *vb* alter for new use or new conditions

ADAPTED ▸ **adapt**

ADAPTER *same as* ▸ **adaptor**

ADAPTOR *n* device for connecting several electrical appliances to a single socket

ADAPTS ▸ **adapt**

ADAW *vb* subdue

ADAWED ▸ **adaw**

ADAWING ▸ **adaw**

ADAWS ▸ **adaw**

ADAXIAL *adj* facing towards the axis, as the surface of a leaf that faces the stem

ADAYS *adv* daily

ADD *vb* combine (numbers or quantities)

ADDABLE ▸ **add**

ADDAX *n* N African light-coloured antelope with ribbed spiralled horns

ADDAXES ▸ **addax**

ADDED ▸ **add**

ADDEDLY ▸ **add**

ADDEEM *vb* adjudge

ADDEEMS ▸ **addeem**

ADDEND *n* any of a set of numbers that is to be added

ADDENDA > **addendum**

ADDENDS ▸ **addend**

ADDER *n* small poisonous snake

ADDERS ▸ **adder**

ADDIBLE *adj* addable

ADDICT *n* person who is unable to stop taking drugs ▷ *vb* cause (someone or oneself) to become dependent (on something, esp a narcotic drug)

ADDICTS ▸ **addict**

ADDIES ▸ **addy**

ADDING *n* act or instance of addition ▷ *adj* of, for, or relating to addition

ADDINGS ▸ **adding**

ADDIO *interj* farewell ▷ *n* cry of addio

ADDLE *vb* make or become confused or muddled ▷ *adj* indicating a confused or muddled state

ADDLED ▸ **addle**

ADDLES ▸ **addle**

ADDLING ▸ **addle**

ADDOOM *vb* adjudge

ADDOOMS ▸ **addoom**

ADDRESS *n* place where a person lives ▷ *vb* mark the destination, as on an envelope

ADDREST ▸ **address**

ADDS ▸ **add**

ADDUCE *vb* mention something as evidence or proof

ADDUCED ▸ **adduce**

ADDUCER ▸ **adduce**

ADDUCES ▸ **adduce**

ADDUCT *vb* (of a muscle) to draw or pull (a leg, arm, etc)

towards the median axis of the body ▷ *n* compound formed by direct combination of two or more different compounds or elements

ADDUCTS ▸ **adduct**

ADDY *n* e-mail address

ADEEM *vb* cancel

ADEEMED ▸ **adeem**

ADEEMS ▸ **adeem**

ADENINE *n* purine base present in tissues of all living organisms as a constituent of the nucleic acids DNA and RNA and of certain coenzymes

ADENOID *adj* of or resembling a gland

ADENOMA *n* tumour, usually benign, occurring in glandular tissue

ADENYL *n* enzyme

ADENYLS ▸ **adenyl**

ADEPT *n* very skilful (person) ▷ *adj* proficient in something requiring skill

ADEPTER ▸ **adept**

ADEPTLY ▸ **adept**

ADEPTS ▸ **adept**

ADERMIN *n* vitamin

ADHAN *n* call to prayer

ADHANS ▸ **adhan**

ADHARMA *n* wickedness

ADHERE *vb* stick (to)

ADHERED ▸ **adhere**

ADHERER ▸ **adhere**

ADHERES ▸ **adhere**

ADHIBIT *vb* administer or apply

ADIEU *n* goodbye

> This French word for farewell is very appropriate when you want to say goodbye to a surplus of vowels. And remember that its plural can be either **adieus** or **adieux**.

ADIEUS ▸ **adieu**

ADIEUX ▸ **adieu**

ADIOS *sentence substitute* Spanish for goodbye

ADIPIC *adj as in* **adipic acid** colourless crystalline solid used in the preparation of nylon

ADIPOSE *adj* of or containing fat ▷ *n* animal fat

ADIPOUS *adj* made of fat

ADIPSIA *n* complete lack of thirst

ADIT *n* almost horizontal shaft into a mine, for access or drainage

ADITS ▸ adit

ADJIGO *n* SW Australian yam plant with edible tubers

ADJIGOS ▸ adjigo

ADJOIN *vb* be next to

ADJOINS ▸ adjoin

ADJOINT *n* type of mathematical matrix

ADJOURN *vb* close (a court) at the end of a session

ADJUDGE *vb* declare (to be)

ADJUNCT *n* something incidental added to something else

ADJURE *vb* command (to do)

ADJURED ▸ adjure

ADJURER ▸ adjure

ADJURES ▸ adjure

ADJUROR ▸ adjure

ADJUST *vb* adapt to new conditions

ADJUSTS ▸ adjust

ADLAND *n* advertising industry and the people who work in it

ADLANDS ▸ adland

ADMAN *n* man who works in advertising

ADMASS *n* mass advertising

ADMEN ▸ adman

ADMIN *n* administration

ADMINS ▸ admin

ADMIRAL *n* highest naval rank

ADMIRE *vb* regard with esteem and approval

ADMIRED ▸ admire

ADMIRER ▸ admire

ADMIRES ▸ admire

ADMIT *vb* confess, acknowledge

ADMITS ▸ admit

ADMIX *vb* mix or blend

ADMIXED ▸ admix

ADMIXES ▸ admix

ADMIXT ▸ admix

ADNATE *adj* growing closely attached to an adjacent part or organ

ADNEXA *pl n* organs adjoining the uterus

ADNEXAL ▸ adnexa

ADNOUN *n* adjective used as a noun

ADNOUNS ▸ adnoun

ADO *n* fuss, trouble

ADOBE *n* sun-dried brick

ADOBES ▸ adobe

ADOBO *n* Philippine dish

ADOBOS ▸ adobo

ADONIS *n* beautiful young man

ADONISE *vb* adorn

ADONIZE *vb* adorn

ADOORS *adv* at the door

ADOPT *vb* take (someone else's child) as one's own

ADOPTED *adj* having been adopted

ADOPTEE *n* one who has been adopted

ADOPTER *n* person who adopts

ADOPTS ▸ adopt

ADORE *vb* love intensely

ADORED ▸ adore

ADORER ▸ adore

ADORERS ▸ adore

ADORES ▸ adore

ADORING ▸ adore

ADORN *vb* decorate, embellish

ADORNED ▸ adorn

ADORNER ▸ adorn

ADORNS ▸ adorn

ADOS ▸ ado

ADOWN *adv* down

ADOZE *adv* asleep

ADPRESS *vb* press together

ADRAD *adj* afraid

ADREAD *vb* dread

ADREADS ▸ adread

ADRED *adj* filled with dread

ADRENAL *adj* near the kidneys ▷ *n* adrenal gland

ADRIFT *adv* drifting

ADROIT *adj* quick and skilful

ADRY *adj* dry

ADS ▸ ad

ADSORB *vb* (of a gas or vapour) condense and form a thin film on a surface

ADSORBS ▸ adsorb

ADSUKI *same as* ▸ **adzuki**

ADSUKIS ▸ adsuki

ADSUM *sentence substitute* I am present

ADUKI *same as* ▸ **adzuki**

ADUKIS ▸ aduki

ADULATE *vb* flatter or praise obsequiously

ADULT *adj* fully grown, mature ▷ *n* adult person or animal

ADULTLY ▸ adult

ADULTS ▸ adult

ADUNC *adj* hooked

ADUST *vb* dry up or darken by heat

ADUSTED ▸ adust

ADUSTS ▸ adust

ADVANCE *vb* go or bring forward ▷ *n* forward movement ▷ *adj* done or happening before an event

ADVECT *vb* move horizontally in air

ADVECTS ▸ advect

ADVENE *vb* add as extra

ADVENED ▸ advene

ADVENES ▸ advene

ADVENT *n* arrival

ADVENTS ▸ advent

ADVERB *n* word that adds information about a verb, adjective, or other adverb

ADVERBS ▸ adverb

ADVERSE *adj* unfavourable

ADVERT *n* advertisement ▷ *vb* draw attention (to)

ADVERTS ▸ advert

ADVEW *vb* look at

ADVEWED ▸ advew

ADVEWS ▸ advew

ADVICE *n* recommendation as to what to do

ADVICES ▸ advice

ADVISE *vb* offer advice to

ADVISED *adj* considered, thought-out

ADVISEE *n* person receiving advice

ADVISER *n* person who offers advice, e.g. on careers to students or school pupils

ADVISES ▸ advise

ADVISOR *same as* ▸ **adviser**

ADWARD *vb* award

ADWARDS ▸ adward

ADWARE *n* type of computer software that collects information about a user's browsing patterns in order to display relevant advertisements in his or her Web browser

ADWARES ▸ adware

ADWOMAN *n* woman working in advertising

ADWOMEN ▸ adwoman

ADYTA ▸ adytum

ADYTUM *n* most sacred place of worship in an ancient temple from which the laity was prohibited

ADZ *same as* ▸ **adze**

This is the American spelling of **adze**, and is one of the essential short words to know for using the Z.

ADZE *n* tool with an arched

A

blade at right angles to the handle ▷ *vb* use an adze
ADZED ▸ **adze**
ADZES ▸ **adze**
ADZING ▸ **adze**
ADZUKI *n* type of leguminous plant with yellow flowers and pods containing edible brown seeds
ADZUKIS ▸ **adzuki**
AE *determiner* one
AECIA ▸ **aecium**
AECIAL ▸ **aecium**
AECIDIA > **aecidium**
AECIUM *n* globular or cup-shaped structure in some rust fungi in which aeciospores are produced
AEDES *n* type of mosquito which transmits yellow fever and dengue
AEDILE *n* magistrate of ancient Rome in charge of public works, games, buildings, and roads
AEDILES ▸ **aedile**
AEDINE *adj* of a species of mosquito
AEFALD *adj* single
AEFAULD *adj* single
AEGIS *n* sponsorship, protection
AEGISES ▸ **aegis**
AEMULE *vb* emulate
AEMULED ▸ **aemule**
AEMULES ▸ **aemule**
AENEOUS *adj* brass-coloured or greenish-gold
AENEUS *n* aquarium fish
AEOLIAN *adj* of or relating to the wind
AEON *n* immeasurably long period of time

> Meaning a long period of time, this little word often gets played as a rack-balancing move when you have too many vowels. And it has a partner **eoan**, meaning of the dawn: beware though that this, unlike **aeon**, does not take a plural S.

AEONIAN *adj* everlasting
AEONIC ▸ **aeon**
AEONS ▸ **aeon**
AERATE *vb* put gas into (a liquid), as when making a fizzy drink
AERATED ▸ **aerate**
AERATES ▸ **aerate**

AERATOR ▸ **aerate**
AERIAL *adj* in, from, or operating in the air ▷ *n* metal pole, wire, etc, for receiving or transmitting radio or TV signals
AERIALS ▸ **aerial**
AERIE *a variant spelling (esp US) of* ▸ **eyrie**

> This word for an eagle's nest is a great one for dealing with a surplus of vowels. And it has several variants: **aery, aiery, ayrie, eyrie** and **eyry**.

AERIED *adj* in a very high place
AERIER ▸ **aery**
AERIES ▸ **aerie**
AERIEST ▸ **aery**
AERIFY *vb* change or cause to change into a gas
AERILY ▸ **aery**
AERO *n* of or relating to aircraft or aeronautics
AEROBAT *n* person who does stunt flying
AEROBE *n* organism that requires oxygen to survive
AEROBES ▸ **aerobe**
AEROBIA > **aerobium**
AEROBIC *adj* designed for or relating to aerobics
AEROBOT *n* unmanned aircraft used esp in space exploration
AEROGEL *n* colloid that has a continuous solid phase containing dispersed gas
AEROS ▸ **aero**
AEROSAT *n* communications satellite
AEROSOL *n* pressurized can from which a substance can be dispensed as a fine spray
AERUGO *(esp of old bronze)* another name for > **verdigris**
AERUGOS ▸ **aerugo**
AERY *adj* lofty, insubstantial, or visionary
AESC *n* rune
AESCES ▸ **aesc**
AESIR *n* chief of the Norse gods
AETHER *same as* ▸ **ether**
AETHERS ▸ **aether**
AFALD *adj* single
AFAR *adv* at, from, or to a great distance ▷ *n* great distance
AFARA *n* African tree
AFARAS ▸ **afara**
AFARS ▸ **afar**

AFAWLD *adj* single
AFEAR *vb* frighten
AFEARD *an archaic or dialect word for* ▸ **afraid**
AFEARED *same as* ▸ **afeard**
AFEARS ▸ **afear**
AFF *adv* off
AFFABLE *adj* friendly and easy to talk to
AFFABLY ▸ **affable**
AFFAIR *n* event or happening
AFFAIRE *n* love affair
AFFAIRS *pl n* personal or business interests
AFFEAR *vb* frighten
AFFEARD ▸ **affear**
AFFEARE *vb* frighten
AFFEARS ▸ **affear**
AFFECT *vb* act on, influence ▷ *n* emotion associated with an idea or set of ideas
AFFECTS ▸ **affect**
AFFEER *vb* assess
AFFEERS ▸ **affeer**
AFFIANT *n* person who makes an affidavit
AFFICHE *n* poster or advertisement, esp one drawn by an artist, as for the opening of an exhibition
AFFIED ▸ **affy**
AFFIES ▸ **affy**
AFFINAL ▸ **affine**
AFFINE *adj* of, characterizing, or involving transformations which preserve collinearity, esp in classical geometry, those of translation, rotation and reflection in an axis ▷ *n* relation by marriage
AFFINED *adj* closely related
AFFINES ▸ **affine**
AFFIRM *vb* declare to be true
AFFIRMS ▸ **affirm**
AFFIX *vb* attach or fasten ▷ *n* word or syllable added to a word to change its meaning
AFFIXAL ▸ **affix**
AFFIXED ▸ **affix**
AFFIXER ▸ **affix**
AFFIXES ▸ **affix**
AFFLICT *vb* give pain or grief to
AFFLUX *n* flowing towards a point
AFFOORD *vb* consent
AFFORCE *vb* strengthen
AFFORD *vb* have enough

money to buy

AFFORDS ▸ **afford**

AFFRAP vb strike

AFFRAPS ▸ **affrap**

AFFRAY n noisy fight, brawl ▹ vb frighten

AFFRAYS ▸ **affray**

AFFRET n furious attack

AFFRETS ▸ **affret**

AFFRONT n insult ▹ vb hurt someone's pride or dignity

AFFY vb trust

AFFYDE ▸ **affy**

AFFYING ▸ **affy**

AFGHAN n type of biscuit

AFGHANI n standard monetary unit of Afghanistan, divided into 100 puli

AFGHANS ▸ **afghan**

AFIELD adj away from one's usual surroundings or home

AFIRE adj on fire

AFLAJ ▸ **falaj**

AFLAME adj burning

AFLOAT adj floating ▹ adv floating

AFOOT adj happening, in operation ▹ adv happening

AFORE adv before

AFOUL adj in or into a state of difficulty, confusion, or conflict (with)

AFRAID adj frightened

AFREET n powerful evil demon or giant monster

AFREETS ▸ **afreet**

AFRESH adv again, anew

AFRIT same as ▸ **afreet**

AFRITS ▸ **afrit**

AFRO n bush-like frizzy hairstyle

AFRONT adv in front

AFROS ▸ **afro**

AFT adv at or towards the rear of a ship or aircraft ▹ adj at or towards the rear of a ship or aircraft

AFTER adv at a later time

AFTERS n sweet course of a meal

AFTMOST adj furthest towards rear

AFTOSA n foot-and-mouth disease

AFTOSAS ▸ **aftosa**

AG n agriculture

AGA n title of respect, often used with the title of a senior position

AGACANT adj irritating

AGAIN adv once more

AGAINST prep in opposition or contrast to

AGAMA n type of small terrestrial lizard which inhabits warm regions of the Old World

AGAMAS ▸ **agama**

AGAMETE n reproductive cell, such as the merozoite of some protozoans, that develops into a new form without fertilization

AGAMI n South American bird

AGAMIC adj asexual

AGAMID same as ▸ **agama**

AGAMIDS ▸ **agamid**

AGAMIS ▸ **agami**

AGAMOID n lizard of the agamid type

AGAMONT another name for > **schizont**

AGAMOUS adj without sex

AGAPAE ▸ **agape**

AGAPAI ▸ **agape**

AGAPE adj (of the mouth) wide open ▹ n love feast among the early Christians

AGAPEIC ▸ **agape**

AGAPES ▸ **agape**

AGAR n jelly-like substance obtained from seaweed and used as a thickener in food

AGARIC n fungus with gills on the underside of the cap, such as a mushroom

AGARICS ▸ **agaric**

AGAROSE n gel used in chemistry

AGARS ▸ **agar**

AGAS ▸ **aga**

AGAST adj aghast

AGATE n semiprecious form of quartz with striped colouring ▹ adv on the way

AGATES ▸ **agate**

AGATISE same as ▸ **agatize**

AGATIZE vb turn into agate

AGATOID adj like agate

AGAVE n tropical American plant with tall flower stalks and thick leaves

AGAVES ▸ **agave**

AGAZE adj gazing at something

AGAZED adj amazed

AGE n length of time a person or thing has existed ▹ vb make or grow old

AGED adj old

AGEDLY ▸ **aged**

AGEE adj awry, crooked, or ajar ▹ adv awry

AGEING n fact or process of growing old ▹ adj becoming or appearing older

AGEINGS ▸ **ageing**

AGEISM n discrimination against people on the grounds of age

AGEISMS ▸ **ageism**

AGEIST ▸ **ageism**

AGEISTS ▸ **ageism**

AGELAST n someone who never laughs

AGELESS adj apparently never growing old

AGELONG adj lasting for a very long time

AGEMATE n person the same age as another person

AGEN archaic form of ▸ **again**

AGENCY n organization providing a service

AGENDA n list of things to be dealt with, esp at a meeting

AGENDAS same as ▸ **agenda**

AGENDUM same as ▸ **agenda**

AGENE n chemical used to whiten flour

AGENES ▸ **agene**

AGENISE same as ▸ **agenize**

AGENIZE vb whiten using agene

AGENT n person acting on behalf of another ▹ vb act as an agent

AGENTED ▸ **agent**

AGENTRY n acting as agent

AGENTS ▸ **agent**

AGER n something that ages

AGERS ▸ **ager**

AGES ▸ **age**

AGEUSIA n lack of the sense of taste

AGGADA n explanation in Jewish literature

AGGADAH same as ▸ **aggada**

AGGADAS ▸ **aggada**

AGGADIC adj of aggada

AGGADOT ▸ **aggada**

AGGER n earthwork or mound forming a rampart, esp in a Roman military camp

AGGERS adj aggressive

AGGIE n American agricultural student

AGGIES ▸ **aggie**

AGGRACE vb add grace to

A

AGGRADE vb build up the level of (any land surface) by the deposition of sediment

AGGRATE vb gratify

AGGRESS vb attack first or begin a quarrel

AGGRI adj of African beads

AGGRO n aggressive behaviour

AGGROS ▸ aggro

AGGRY adj of African beads

AGHA same as ▸ **aga**

AGHAS ▸ agha

AGHAST adj overcome with amazement or horror

AGILA n eaglewood

AGILAS ▸ agila

AGILE adj nimble, quick-moving

AGILELY ▸ agile

AGILER ▸ agile

AGILEST ▸ agile

AGILITY ▸ agile

AGIN prep against, opposed to

AGING same as ▸ **ageing**

AGINGS ▸ aging

AGINNER n someone who is against something

AGIO n difference between the nominal and actual values of a currency

AGIOS ▸ agio

AGISM same as ▸ **ageism**

AGISMS ▸ agism

AGIST vb care for and feed (cattle or horses) for payment

AGISTED ▸ agist

AGISTER n person who grazes cattle for money

AGISTOR n person who grazes cattle for money

AGISTS ▸ agist

AGITA n acid indigestion

AGITANS adj as in **paralysis agitans** Parkinson's disease

AGITAS ▸ agita

AGITATE vb disturb or excite

AGITATO adv (to be performed) in an agitated manner

AGITPOP n use of pop music to promote political propaganda

AGLARE adj glaring

AGLEAM adj glowing

AGLEE same as ▸ **agley**

AGLET n metal sheath or tag at the end of a shoelace, ribbon, etc

AGLETS ▸ aglet

AGLEY adj awry

AGLOO same as ▸ **aglu**

AGLOOS ▸ agloo

AGLOW adj glowing

AGLU n breathing hole made in ice by a seal

AGLUS ▸ aglu

AGLY Scots word for ▸ **wrong**

AGLYCON n chemical compound

AGMA n symbol used to represent a velar nasal consonant

AGMAS ▸ agma

AGNAIL another name for ▸ **hangnail**

AGNAILS ▸ agnail

AGNAME n name additional to first name and surname

AGNAMED adj having an agname

AGNAMES ▸ agname

AGNATE adj related by descent from a common male ancestor ▹ n male or female descendant by male links from a common male ancestor

AGNATES ▸ agnate

AGNATIC ▸ agnate

AGNISE vb acknowledge

AGNISED ▸ agnise

AGNISES ▸ agnise

AGNIZE vb acknowledge

AGNIZED ▸ agnize

AGNIZES ▸ agnize

AGNOMEN n fourth name or second cognomen occasionally acquired by an ancient Roman

AGNOSIA n loss or diminution of the power to recognize familiar objects or people, usually as a result of brain damage

AGNOSIC ▸ agnosia

AGO adv in the past

AGOG adj eager or curious

AGOGE n ancient Greek tempo

AGOGES ▸ agoge

AGOGIC n musical accent

AGOGICS ▸ agogic

AGOING adj moving

AGON n (in ancient Greece) a festival at which competitors contended for prizes. Among the best known were the Olympic, Pythian, Nemean, and Isthmian Games

AGONAL adj of agony

AGONE an archaic word for ▸ **ago**

AGONES ▸ agon

AGONIC adj forming no angle

AGONIES ▸ agony

AGONISE same as ▸ **agonize**

AGONIST n any muscle that is opposed in action by another muscle

AGONIZE vb worry greatly

AGONS ▸ agon

AGONY n extreme physical or mental pain

AGOOD adv seriously or earnestly

AGORA n marketplace in Athens, used for popular meetings, or any similar place of assembly in ancient Greece

AGORAE ▸ agora

AGORAS ▸ agora

AGOROT ▸ agora

AGOROTH n agorot

AGOUTA n Haitian rodent

AGOUTAS ▸ agouta

AGOUTI n rodent of Central and South America and the Caribbean with long legs and hooflike claws, valued for its meat

AGOUTIS ▸ agouti

AGOUTY n agouti

AGRAFE same as ▸ **agraffe**

AGRAFES ▸ agrafe

AGRAFFE n fastening consisting of a loop and hook, formerly used in armour and clothing

AGRAPHA > agraphon

AGRASTE ▸ aggrace

AGRAVIC adj of zero gravity

AGREE vb be of the same opinion

AGREED adj determined by common consent

AGREES ▸ agree

AGREGE n winner in examination for university teaching post.

AGREGES ▸ agrege

AGRIA n appearance of pustules

AGRIAS ▸ agria

AGRIN adv grinning

AGRISE vb fill with fear

AGRISED ▸ agrise

AGRISES ▸ agrise

AGRIZE vb fill with fear

AGRIZED ▸ agrize

AGRIZES ▸ agrize

AGROUND adv onto the

A

bottom of shallow water ▷ *adj* on or onto the ground or bottom, as in shallow water

AGRYZE *vb* fill with fear

AGRYZED ▶ **agryze**

AGRYZES ▶ **agryze**

AGS ▶ **ag**

AGUE *n* periodic fever with shivering

AGUED *adj* suffering from fever

AGUES ▶ **ague**

AGUISE *vb* dress

AGUISED ▶ **aguise**

AGUISES ▶ **aguise**

AGUISH ▶ **ague**

AGUIZE *vb* dress

AGUIZED ▶ **aguize**

AGUIZES ▶ **aguize**

AGUNA *n* (in Jewish law) woman whose husband will not grant her a divorce

AGUNAH ▶ **aguna**

AGUNOT ▶ **aguna**

AGUTI *n* agouti

AGUTIS ▶ **aguti**

AH *interj* exclamation expressing surprise, joy etc ▷ *vb* say ah

AHA *interj* exclamation expressing triumph, surprise, etc, according to the intonation of the speaker

AHCHOO *interj* sound made by someone sneezing

AHEAD *adv* in front

AHEAP *adv* in a heap

AHED ▶ **ah**

AHEIGHT *adv* at height

AHEM *interj* clearing of the throat in order to attract attention

AHENT *adv* behind

AHI *n* yellowfin tuna

▎ You will be surprised how many times you want to catch this Hawaiian fish!

AHIGH *adv* at height

AHIMSA *n* (in Hindu, Buddhist, and Jainist philosophy) the law of reverence for, and nonviolence to, every form of life

AHIMSAS ▶ **ahimsa**

AHIND *adv* behind

AHING ▶ **ah**

AHINT *adv* behind

AHIS ▶ **ahi**

AHOLD *n* holding

AHOLDS ▶ **ahold**

AHORSE *adv* on horseback

AHOY *interj* hail used to call a ship

AHS ▶ **ah**

AHULL *adv* with sails furled

AHUNGRY *adj* very hungry

AHURU *n* type of small pink cod of SW Pacific waters

AHURUS ▶ **ahuru**

AI *n* shaggy-coated slow-moving animal of South America

AIA *n* female servant in East

AIAS ▶ **aia**

AIBLINS *Scots word for* ▶ **perhaps**

AID *n* (give) assistance or support ▷ *vb* help financially or in other ways

AIDA *n* cotton fabric with a natural mesh

AIDANCE *n* help

AIDANT *adj* helping

AIDAS ▶ **aida**

AIDE *n* assistant

AIDED ▶ **aid**

AIDER ▶ **aid**

AIDERS ▶ **aid**

AIDES ▶ **aid**

AIDFUL *adj* helpful

AIDING ▶ **aid**

AIDLESS *adj* without help

AIDMAN *n* military medical assistant

AIDMEN ▶ **aidman**

AIDOI *adj* of the genitals

AIDOS *Greek word for* ▶ **shame**

AIDS ▶ **aid**

AIERIES ▶ **aiery**

AIERY *n* eyrie

AIGA *n* Maori word for family

AIGAS ▶ **aiga**

AIGHT *adv* all right

AIGLET *same as* ▶ **aglet**

AIGLETS ▶ **aiglet**

AIGRET *same as* > **aigrette**

AIGRETS ▶ **aigret**

AIKIDO *n* Japanese system of self-defence employing similar principles to judo, but including blows from the hands and feet

AIKIDOS ▶ **aikido**

AIKONA *interj* South African expression meaning no

AIL *vb* trouble, afflict

AILANTO *n* Asian tree

AILED ▶ **ail**

AILERON *n* movable flap on an aircraft wing which controls rolling

AILETTE *n* shoulder armour

AILING *adj* sickly

AILMENT *n* illness

AILS ▶ **ail**

AIM *vb* point (a weapon or missile) or direct (a blow or remark) at a target ▷ *n* aiming

AIMED ▶ **aim**

AIMER ▶ **aim**

AIMERS ▶ **aim**

AIMFUL *adj* with purpose or intention

AIMING ▶ **aim**

AIMLESS *adj* having no purpose

AIMS ▶ **aim**

AIN *same as* ▶ **ayin**

AINE *adj* French word for elder (male)

▎ This is a word of French origin meaning elder, one of those words that doesn't score much but is useful to remember when you have too many vowels and are trying to balance your rack. And it can be extended to **ainee**, the feminine form.

AINEE *adj* French word for elder (female)

AINGA *n* Maori word for village

AINGAS ▶ **ainga**

AINS ▶ **ain**

AINSELL *n* Scots word meaning own self

AIOLI *n* garlic mayonnaise

AIOLIS ▶ **aioli**

AIR *n* mixture of gases forming the earth's atmosphere ▷ *vb* make known publicly

AIRBAG *n* safety device in a car, consisting of a bag that inflates automatically in an accident to protect the driver or passenger

AIRBAGS ▶ **airbag**

AIRBASE *n* centre from which military aircraft operate

AIRBOAT *n* shallow-draught boat powered by an aeroplane engine on a raised structure for use in swamps

AIRBUS *n* commercial passenger aircraft

AIRCON *n* air conditioner

AIRCONS ▶ **aircon**

A

AIRCREW n crew of an aircraft

AIRDATE n date of a programme broadcast

AIRDROP n delivery of supplies, troops, etc, from an aircraft by parachute ▷ vb deliver (supplies, etc) by an airdrop

AIRED ▸ **air**

AIRER n device on which clothes are hung to dry

AIRERS ▸ **airer**

AIREST ▸ **air**

AIRFARE n money for an aircraft ticket

AIRFLOW n flow of air in a wind tunnel or past a moving aircraft, car, train, etc

AIRFOIL same as > **aerofoil**

AIRGAP n gap between parts in an electrical machine

AIRGAPS ▸ **airgap**

AIRGLOW n faint light from the upper atmosphere in the night sky, esp in low latitudes

AIRGUN n gun fired by compressed air

AIRGUNS ▸ **airgun**

AIRHEAD n person who is stupid or incapable of serious thought

AIRHOLE n hole that allows the passage of air

AIRIER ▸ **airy**

AIRIEST ▸ **airy**

AIRILY adv in a light-hearted and casual manner

AIRING n exposure to air for drying or ventilation

AIRINGS ▸ **airing**

AIRLESS adj stuffy

AIRLIFT n transport of troops or cargo by aircraft when other routes are blocked ▷ vb transport by airlift

AIRLIKE ▸ **air**

AIRLINE n company providing scheduled flights for passengers and cargo

AIRLOCK n air bubble blocking the flow of liquid in a pipe

AIRMAIL n system of sending mail by aircraft ▷ adj of, used for, or concerned with airmail ▷ vb send by airmail

AIRMAN n member of the air force

AIRMEN ▸ **airman**

AIRN Scots word for ▸ **iron**

AIRNED ▸ **airn**

AIRNING ▸ **airn**

AIRNS ▸ **airn**

AIRPARK n car park at airport

AIRPLAY n broadcast performances of a record on radio

AIRPORT n airfield for civilian aircraft, with facilities for aircraft maintenance and passengers

AIRPOST n system of delivering mail by air

AIRPROX n near collision involving aircraft

AIRS pl n manners put on to impress people

AIRSHED n air over a particular geographical area

AIRSHIP n lighter-than-air self-propelled aircraft

AIRSHOT n (in golf) shot that misses the ball completely, but counts as a stroke

AIRSHOW n occasion when an air base is open to the public and a flying display and, usually, static exhibitions are held

AIRSICK adj nauseated from travelling in an aircraft

AIRSIDE n part of an airport nearest the aircraft

AIRSTOP n helicopter landing-place

AIRT n direction or point of the compass, esp the direction of the wind ▷ vb direct

AIRTED ▸ **airt**

AIRTH same as ▸ **airt**

AIRTHED ▸ **airth**

AIRTHS ▸ **airth**

AIRTIME n time allocated to a particular programme, topic, or type of material on radio or television

AIRTING ▸ **airt**

AIRTS ▸ **airt**

AIRWARD adj into air

AIRWAVE n radio wave used in radio and television broadcasting

AIRWAY n air route used regularly by aircraft

AIRWAYS ▸ **airway**

AIRWISE adv towards the air

AIRY adj well-ventilated

AIS ▸ **ai**

AISLE n passageway separating seating areas in a church, theatre, etc, or row of shelves in a supermarket

AISLED ▸ **aisle**

AISLES ▸ **aisle**

AISLING Irish word for ▸ **dream**

AIT n islet, esp in a river

AITCH n letter h or the sound represented by it

AITCHES ▸ **aitch**

AITS ▸ **ait**

AITU n half-human half-divine being

This Polynesian word for a demigod is frequently played to dispose of an excess of vowels.

AITUS ▸ **aitu**

AIVER n a working horse

AIVERS ▸ **aiver**

AIZLE n Scots word for hot ashes

AIZLES ▸ **aizle**

AJAR adv (of a door) partly open ▷ adj not in harmony

AJEE same as ▸ **agee**

This Scots word meaning ajar is often useful for disposing of the J. It has an alternative spelling **agee**.

AJIVA n Jainist term for non-living thing

AJIVAS ▸ **ajiva**

AJOWAN n plant related to caraway

AJOWANS ▸ **ajowan**

AJUGA n garden plant

AJUGAS ▸ **ajuga**

AJUTAGE n nozzle

AJWAN n plant related to caraway

AJWANS ▸ **ajwan**

AKA n type of New Zealand vine

This New Zealand vine is one of the key short words when it comes to using the K.

AKAS ▸ **aka**

AKATEA n New Zealand vine with white flowers

AKATEAS ▸ **akatea**

AKE vb old spelling of ache

AKEAKE n New Zealand tree

AKEAKES ▸ akeake
AKED ▸ ake
AKEDAH n binding of Isaac in Bible
AKEDAHS ▸ akedah
AKEE same as ▸ **ackee**
AKEES ▸ akee
AKELA n adult leader of a pack of Cub Scouts
AKELAS ▸ akela
AKENE same as ▸ **achene**
AKENES ▸ akene
AKENIAL ▸ achene
AKES ▸ ake
AKHARA n (in India) gymnasium
AKHARAS ▸ akhara
AKIMBO adj as in **with arms akimbo** with hands on hips and elbows projecting outwards
AKIN adj related by blood
AKING ▸ ake
AKIRAHO n small New Zealand shrub with white flowers
AKITA n large powerfully-built dog of a Japanese breed with erect ears, a typically white coat, and a large full tail carried curled over its back
AKITAS ▸ akita
AKKAS slang word for ▸ **money**
AKRASIA n weakness of will
AKRATIC ▸ akrasia
AKVAVIT same as ▸ **aquavit**
AL same as ▸ **aal**
ALA n wing or flat winglike process or structure, such as a part of some bones and cartilages
ALAAP n part of raga in Indian music
ALAAPS ▸ alaap
ALACK archaic or poetic word for ▸ **alas**
ALAE ▸ ala
ALALIA n complete inability to speak
ALALIAS ▸ alalia
ALAMEDA n public walk or promenade lined with trees, often poplars
ALAMO n poplar tree
ALAMODE n soft light silk used for shawls and dresses, esp in the 19th century
ALAMORT adj exhausted and downcast
ALAMOS ▸ alamo

ALAN n member of ancient European nomadic people
ALAND vb come onto land
ALANDS ▸ aland
ALANE Scots word for ▸ **alone**
ALANG n type of grass in Malaysia
ALANGS ▸ alang
ALANIN n alanine
ALANINE n nonessential aliphatic amino acid that occurs in many proteins
ALANINS ▸ alanin
ALANNAH interj my child: used as a term of address or endearment ▷ n cry of alannah
ALANS ▸ alan
ALANT n flowering plant used in herbal medicine
ALANTS ▸ alant
ALANYL n chemical found in proteins
ALANYLS ▸ alanyl
ALAP n Indian vocal music without words
ALAPA n part of raga in Indian music
ALAPAS ▸ alapa
ALAPS ▸ alap
ALAR adj relating to, resembling, or having wings or alae
ALARM n sudden fear caused by awareness of danger ▷ vb fill with fear
ALARMED ▸ alarm
ALARMS ▸ alarm
ALARUM n alarm, esp a call to arms ▷ vb raise the alarm
ALARUMS ▸ alarum
ALARY adj of, relating to, or shaped like wings
ALAS adv unfortunately, regrettably
ALASKA n dessert made of cake and ice cream
ALASKAS ▸ alaska
ALASTOR n avenging demon
ALATE adj having wings or winglike extensions ▷ n winged insect
ALATED adj having wings
ALATES ▸ alate
ALATION n state of having wings
ALAY vb allay
ALAYED ▸ alay
ALAYING ▸ alay
ALAYS ▸ alay

ALB n long white robe worn by a Christian priest
ALBA n song of lament
ALBAS ▸ alba
ALBATA n variety of German silver consisting of nickel, copper, and zinc
ALBATAS ▸ albata
ALBE old word for ▸ **albeit**
ALBEDO n ratio of the intensity of light reflected from an object, such as a planet, to that of the light it receives from the sun
ALBEDOS ▸ albedo
ALBEE archaic form of ▸ **albeit**
ALBEIT conj even though
ALBERGO n Italian word for inn
ALBERT n kind of watch chain usually attached to a waistcoat
ALBERTS ▸ albert
ALBINAL ▸ albino
ALBINIC ▸ albino
ALBINO n person or animal with white skin and hair and pink eyes
ALBINOS ▸ albino
ALBITE n colourless, milky-white, yellow, pink, green, or black mineral
ALBITES ▸ albite
ALBITIC ▸ albite
ALBIZIA n mimosa
ALBS ▸ alb
ALBUGO n opacity of the cornea
ALBUGOS ▸ albugo
ALBUM n book with blank pages for keeping photographs or stamps in
ALBUMEN ▸ albumin
ALBUMIN n protein found in blood plasma, egg white, milk, and muscle
ALBUMS ▸ album
ALCADE same as ▸ **alcalde**
ALCADES ▸ alcade
ALCAIC n verse consisting of strophes with four tetrametric lines
ALCAICS ▸ alcaic
ALCAIDE n commander of a fortress or castle
ALCALDE n (in Spain and Spanish America) the mayor or chief magistrate in a town
ALCAYDE n alcaide
ALCAZAR n any of various palaces or fortresses built in

Spain by the Moors

ALCHEMY n medieval form of chemistry concerned with trying to turn base metals into gold and to find the elixir of life

ALCHERA n (in the mythology of Australian Aboriginal peoples) mythical Golden Age of the past

ALCHYMY old spelling of ▶ **alchemy**

ALCID n bird of the auk family

ALCIDS ▶ **alcid**

ALCO same as ▶ **alko**

ALCOHOL n colourless flammable liquid present in intoxicating drinks

ALCOOL n form of pure grain spirit distilled in Quebec

ALCOOLS ▶ **alcool**

ALCOPOP n alcoholic drink that tastes like a soft drink

ALCORZA n Spanish sweet

ALCOS ▶ **alco**

ALCOVE n recess in the wall of a room

ALCOVED adj with or in an alcove

ALCOVES ▶ **alcove**

ALDEA n Spanish village

ALDEAS ▶ **aldea**

ALDER n tree related to the birch

ALDERN adj made of alder wood

ALDERS ▶ **alder**

ALDOL n colourless or yellowish oily liquid

ALDOLS ▶ **aldol**

ALDOSE n sugar that contains the aldehyde group or is a hemiacetal

ALDOSES ▶ **aldose**

ALDRIN n brown to white poisonous crystalline solid

ALDRINS ▶ **aldrin**

ALE n kind of beer

ALEC same as ▶ **aleck**

ALECK n irritatingly oversmart person

ALECKS ▶ **aleck**

ALECOST another name for ▶ **costmary**

ALECS ▶ **alec**

ALEE adj on or towards the lee

ALEF n first letter of Hebrew alphabet

ALEFS ▶ **alef**

ALEFT adv at or to left

ALEGAR n malt vinegar

ALEGARS ▶ **alegar**

ALEGGE vb alleviate

ALEGGED ▶ **alegge**

ALEGGES ▶ **alegge**

ALEMBIC n anything that distils or purifies, esp an obsolete vessel used for distillation

ALENCON n elaborate lace worked on a hexagonal mesh

ALENGTH adv at length

ALEPH n first letter in the Hebrew alphabet

ALEPHS ▶ **aleph**

ALEPINE n type of cloth

ALERCE n wood of the sandarac tree

ALERCES ▶ **alerce**

ALERION n eagle in heraldry

ALERT adj watchful, attentive ▶ n warning of danger ▶ vb warn of danger

ALERTED ▶ **alert**

ALERTER ▶ **alert**

ALERTLY ▶ **alert**

ALERTS ▶ **alert**

ALES ▶ **ale**

ALETHIC adj of or relating to such philosophical concepts as truth, necessity, possibility, contingency, etc

ALEURON n outer protein-rich layer of certain seeds, esp of cereal grains

ALEVIN n young fish, esp a young salmon or trout

ALEVINS ▶ **alevin**

ALEW n cry to call hunting hounds

ALEWIFE n North American fish

ALEWS ▶ **alew**

ALEXIA n disorder of the central nervous system characterized by impaired ability to read

ALEXIAS ▶ **alexia**

ALEXIC ▶ **alexia**

ALEXIN n complement

ALEXINE same as ▶ **alexin**

ALEXINS ▶ **alexin**

ALEYE vb allay

ALEYED ▶ **aleye**

ALEYES ▶ **aleye**

ALEYING ▶ **aleye**

ALF n uncultivated Australian

ALFA n type of grass

ALFAKI n expert in Muslim law

ALFAKIS ▶ **alfaki**

ALFALFA n kind of plant used to feed livestock

ALFAQUI n expert in Muslim law

ALFAS ▶ **alfa**

ALFEREZ n Spanish standard-bearer

ALFORJA n saddlebag made of leather or canvas

ALFREDO adj cooked with a cheese and egg sauce

ALFS ▶ **alf**

ALGA n unicellular or multicellular organism formerly classified as a plant

ALGAE ▶ **alga**

ALGAL ▶ **alga**

ALGAS ▶ **alga**

ALGATE adv anyway

ALGATES adv anyway

ALGEBRA n branch of mathematics using symbols to represent numbers

ALGESES ▶ **algesis**

ALGESIA n capacity to feel pain

ALGESIC ▶ **algesia**

ALGESIS n feeling of pain

ALGETIC ▶ **algesia**

ALGID adj chilly or cold

ALGIN n gelatinous solution obtained as a by-product in the extraction of iodine from seaweed

ALGINIC adj as in **alginic acid** powdery substance extracted from kelp

ALGINS ▶ **algin**

ALGOID adj resembling or relating to algae

ALGOR n chill

ALGORS ▶ **algor**

ALGUM n type of wood mentioned in Bible

ALGUMS ▶ **algum**

ALIAS adv also known as ▶ n false name

ALIASES ▶ **alias**

ALIBI n plea of being somewhere else when a crime was committed ▶ vb provide someone with an alibi

ALIBIED ▶ **alibi**

ALIBIES ▶ **alibi**

ALIBIS ▶ **alibi**

ALIBLE adj nourishing

ALICANT n wine from Alicante in Spain

ALIDAD same as ▶ **alidade**

ALIDADE n surveying instrument used in plane-tabling for drawing lines of sight on a distant object and taking angular measurements

ALIDADS ▶ alidad

ALIEN adj foreign ▷ n foreigner ▷ vb transfer (property, etc) to another

ALIENED ▶ alien

ALIENEE n person to whom a transfer of property is made

ALIENER ▶ alien

ALIENLY ▶ alien

ALIENOR n person who transfers property to another

ALIENS ▶ alien

ALIF n first letter of Arabic alphabet

ALIFORM adj wing-shaped

ALIFS ▶ alif

ALIGHT vb step out of (a vehicle) ▷ adj on fire ▷ adv on fire

ALIGHTS ▶ alight

ALIGN vb bring (a person or group) into agreement with the policy of another

ALIGNED ▶ align

ALIGNER ▶ align

ALIGNS ▶ align

ALIKE adj like, similar ▷ adv in the same way

ALIMENT n something that nourishes or sustains the body or mind ▷ vb support or sustain

ALIMONY n allowance paid under a court order to a separated or divorced spouse

ALINE a rare spelling of ▶ align

ALINED ▶ aline

ALINER ▶ aline

ALINERS ▶ aline

ALINES ▶ aline

ALINING ▶ aline

ALIPED n animal, like the bat, whose toes are joined by a membrane that serves as a wing ▷ adj (of bats and similar animals) having the digits connected by a winglike membrane

ALIPEDS ▶ aliped

ALIQUOT adj of or denoting an exact divisor of a number ▷ n exact divisor

ALISMA n marsh plant

ALISMAS ▶ alisma

ALISON same as ▶ alyssum

ALISONS ▶ alison

ALIST adj leaning over

ALIT rare past tense and past participle of ▶ alight

ALIUNDE adj from a source extrinsic to the matter, document, or instrument under consideration

ALIVE adj living, in existence

ALIYA n immigration to Holy Land

ALIYAH n immigration to the Holy Land

ALIYAHS ▶ aliyah

ALIYAS ▶ aliya

ALIYOS n remission of sin in Jewish faith

ALIYOT ▶ aliyah

ALIYOTH ▶ aliyah

ALIZARI n madder from Middle East

ALKALI n substance which combines with acid and neutralizes it to form a salt

ALKALIC adj (of igneous rocks) containing large amounts of alkalis, esp sodium and potassium

ALKALIN adj leaning over

ALKALIS ▶ alkali

ALKANE n any saturated hydrocarbon with the general formula $CnH_{2}n+2$

ALKANES ▶ alkane

ALKANET n European plant whose roots yield a red dye

ALKENE n type of unsaturated hydrocarbon

ALKENES ▶ alkene

ALKIE same as ▶ alky

ALKIES ▶ alky

ALKINE n alkyne

ALKINES ▶ alkine

ALKO n heavy drinker or alcoholic

ALKOS ▶ alko

ALKOXY adj of type of chemical compound containing oxygen

ALKY n heavy drinker or alcoholic

ALKYD n synthetic resin

ALKYDS ▶ alkyd

ALKYL n of or containing the monovalent group $CnH_{2}n+1$

ALKYLIC ▶ alkyl

ALKYLS ▶ alkyl

ALKYNE n any unsaturated aliphatic hydrocarbon

ALKYNES ▶ alkyne

ALL adj whole quantity or number (of) ▷ adv wholly, entirely ▷ n entire being, effort, or property

ALLAY vb reduce (fear or anger)

ALLAYED ▶ allay

ALLAYER ▶ allay

ALLAYS ▶ allay

ALLEDGE vb allege

ALLEE n avenue

ALLEES ▶ allee

ALLEGE vb state without proof

ALLEGED adj stated but not proved

ALLEGER ▶ allege

ALLEGES ▶ allege

ALLEGGE vb alleviate

ALLEGRO adv (piece to be played) in a brisk lively manner ▷ n piece or passage to be performed in a brisk lively manner

ALLEL n form of gene

ALLELE n any of two or more genes that are responsible for alternative characteristics, such as smooth or wrinkled seeds in peas

ALLELES ▶ allele

ALLELIC ▶ allele

ALLELS ▶ allel

ALLERGY n extreme sensitivity to a substance, which causes the body to react to it

ALLEY n narrow street or path

ALLEYED adj having alleys

ALLEYS ▶ alley

ALLHEAL n any of several plants reputed to have healing powers, such as selfheal and valerian

ALLICE n species of fish

ALLICES ▶ allice

ALLICIN n chemical found in garlic

ALLIED adj joined, as by treaty, agreement, or marriage

ALLIES ▶ ally

ALLIS n species of fish

ALLISES ▶ allis

ALLIUM n type of plant of the family including the onion, garlic, shallot, leek, and chive

ALLIUMS ▶ allium

ALLNESS n being all

ALLOBAR n form of element

A

ALLOD same as ▸ **allodium**
ALLODIA ▸ **allodium**
ALLODS ▸ **allod**
ALLONGE n paper extension to bill of exchange
ALLONS interj French word meaning let's go
ALLONYM n name, often one of historical significance or that of another person, assumed by a person, esp an author
ALLOT vb assign as a share or for a particular purpose
ALLOTS ▸ **allot**
ALLOVER n fabric completely covered with a pattern
ALLOW vb permit
ALLOWED ▸ **allow**
ALLOWS ▸ **allow**
ALLOXAN n chemical found in uric acid
ALLOY n mixture of two or more metals ▹ vb mix (metals)
ALLOYED ▸ **alloy**
ALLOYS ▸ **alloy**
ALLS ▸ **all**
ALLSEED n any of several plants that produce many seeds, such as knotgrass
ALLUDE vb refer indirectly to
ALLUDED ▸ **allude**
ALLUDES ▸ **allude**
ALLURE n attractiveness ▹ vb entice or attract
ALLURED ▸ **allure**
ALLURER ▸ **allure**
ALLURES ▸ **allure**
ALLUVIA ▸ **alluvium**
ALLY vb unite or be united, esp formally, as by a treaty, confederation, or marriage ▹ n country, person, or group allied with another
ALLYING ▸ **ally**
ALLYL n of, consisting of, or containing the monovalent group CH_2:$CHCH_2^-$
ALLYLIC ▸ **allyl**
ALLYLS ▸ **allyl**
ALLYOU pron all of you
ALMA n Egyptian dancing girl
ALMAH n Egyptian dancing girl
ALMAHS ▸ **almah**
ALMAIN n German dance
ALMAINS ▸ **almain**
ALMANAC n yearly calendar with detailed information

on anniversaries, phases of the moon, etc
ALMAS ▸ **alma**
ALME n Egyptian dancing girl
ALMEH n Egyptian dancing girl
ALMEHS ▸ **almeh**
ALMEMAR n (in Ashkenazic usage) the raised platform in a synagogue on which the reading desk stands
ALMERY n cupboard for church vessels
ALMES ▸ **alme**
ALMIRAH n cupboard
ALMNER n almoner
ALMNERS ▸ **almoner**
ALMOND n edible oval-shaped nut which grows on a small tree
ALMONDS ▸ **almond**
ALMONDY ▸ **almond**
ALMONER n formerly, a hospital social worker
ALMONRY n house of an almoner, usually the place where alms were given
ALMOST adv very nearly
ALMOUS Scots word for ▸ **alms**
ALMS pl n gifts to the poor
ALMSMAN n person who gives or receives alms
ALMSMEN ▸ **almsman**
ALMUCE n fur-lined hood or cape formerly worn by members of certain religious orders, more recently by canons of France
ALMUCES ▸ **almuce**
ALMUD n Spanish unit of measure
ALMUDE n Spanish unit of measure
ALMUDES ▸ **almude**
ALMUDS ▸ **almud**
ALMUG n type of wood mentioned in Bible
ALMUGS ▸ **almug**
ALNAGE n measurement in ells
ALNAGER n inspector of cloth
ALNAGES ▸ **alnage**
ALNICO n alloy of various metals including iron, nickel, and cobalt
ALNICOS ▸ **alnico**
ALOD n feudal estate with no superior
ALODIA ▸ **alodium**

ALODIAL ▸ **alodium**
ALODIUM same as ▸ **allodium**
ALODS ▸ **alod**
ALOE n plant with fleshy spiny leaves
ALOED adj containing aloes
ALOES another name for ▸ **eaglewood**
ALOETIC ▸ **aloe**
ALOFT adv in the air ▹ adj in or into a high or higher place
ALOGIA n inability to speak
ALOGIAS ▸ **alogia**
ALOHA a Hawaiian word for ▸ **hello**
ALOHAS ▸ **aloha**
ALOIN n bitter crystalline compound derived from various species of aloe: used as a laxative and flavouring agent
ALOINS ▸ **aloin**
ALONE adv without anyone or anything else
ALONELY ▸ **alone**
ALONG adv forward
ALONGST adv along
ALOO n (in Indian cookery) potato
ALOOF adj distant or haughty in manner
ALOOFLY ▸ **aloof**
ALOOS ▸ **aloo**
ALOUD adv in an audible voice ▹ adj in a normal voice
ALOW adj in or into the lower rigging of a vessel, near the deck
ALOWE Scots word for ▸ **ablaze**
ALP n high mountain
ALPACA n Peruvian llama
ALPACAS ▸ **alpaca**
ALPACCA same as ▸ **alpaca**
ALPEEN n Irish cudgel
ALPEENS ▸ **alpeen**
ALPHA n first letter in the Greek alphabet
ALPHAS ▸ **alpha**
ALPHORN n wind instrument used in the Swiss Alps, consisting of a very long tube of wood or bark with a cornet-like mouthpiece
ALPHYL n univalent radical
ALPHYLS ▸ **alphyl**
ALPINE adj of high mountains ▹ n mountain plant

ALPINES ▸ alpine

ALPS ▸ alp

ALREADY *adv* before the present time

ALRIGHT *adj* all right

ALS ▸ al

ALSIKE *n* clover native to Europe and Asia

ALSIKES ▸ alsike

ALSO *adv* in addition, too

ALSOON *same as* ▸ **alsoone**

ALSOONE *adv* as soon

ALT *n* octave directly above the treble staff

ALTAR *n* table used for Communion in Christian churches

ALTARS ▸ altar

ALTER *vb* make or become different

ALTERED ▸ alter

ALTERER ▸ alter

ALTERN *adj* alternate

ALTERNE *n* neighbouring but different plant group

ALTERS ▸ alter

ALTESSE *n* French word for highness

ALTEZA *n* Spanish word for highness

ALTEZAS ▸ alteza

ALTEZZA *n* Italian word for highness

ALTHAEA *n* plant such as the hollyhock, having tall spikes of showy white, yellow, or red flowers

ALTHEA *same as* ▸ **althaea**

ALTHEAS ▸ althea

ALTHO *conj* short form of although

ALTHORN *n* valved brass musical instrument belonging to the saxhorn or flügelhorn families

ALTO *n* (singer with) the highest adult male voice ▹ *adj* denoting such an instrument, singer, or voice

ALTOIST *n* person who plays the alto saxophone

ALTOS ▸ alto

ALTS ▸ alt

ALU ▸ aloo

ALUDEL *n* pear-shaped vessel, open at both ends, formerly used with similar vessels for collecting condensates, esp for subliming mercury

ALUDELS ▸ aludel

ALULA *n* tuft of feathers attached to the first digit of a bird

ALULAE ▸ alula

ALULAR ▸ alula

ALULAS ▸ alula

ALUM *n* double sulphate of aluminium and potassium

ALUMIN *n* aluminium oxide

ALUMINA *n* aluminium oxide

ALUMINE *n* French word for alumina

ALUMINS ▸ alumin

ALUMISH *adj* like alum

ALUMIUM *old name for* > **aluminium**

ALUMNA *n* female graduate of a school, college, etc

ALUMNAE ▸ alumna

ALUMNI ▸ alumnus

ALUMNUS *n* graduate of a college

ALUMS ▸ alum

ALUNITE *n* white, grey, or reddish mineral

ALURE *n* area behind battlements

ALURES ▸ alure

ALUS ▸ alu

ALVEARY *n* beehive

ALVEOLE *n* alveolus

ALVEOLI ▸ alveolus

ALVINE *adj* of or relating to the intestines or belly

ALWAY *same as* ▸ **always**

ALWAYS *adv* at all times

ALYSSUM *n* garden plant with small yellow or white flowers

AM *see* ▸ **be**

AMA *n* vessel for water

AMABILE *adj* sweet

AMADODA *pl n* grown men

AMADOU *n* spongy substance made from certain fungi, used as tinder to light fires and in medicine to stop bleeding

AMADOUS ▸ amadou

AMAH *n* (in the East, formerly) a nurse or maidservant

AMAHS ▸ amah

AMAIN *adv* with great strength, speed, or haste

AMAKOSI ▸ inkhosi

AMALGAM *n* blend or combination

AMANDLA *n* political slogan calling for power to the Black population

AMANITA *n* type of fungus

AMARANT *n* amaranth

AMARNA *adj* pertaining to the reign of the Pharaoh Akhenaton

AMARONE *n* strong dry red Italian wine

AMAS ▸ ama

AMASS *vb* collect or accumulate

AMASSED ▸ amass

AMASSER ▸ amass

AMASSES ▸ amass

AMATE *vb* match

AMATED ▸ amate

AMATES ▸ amate

AMATEUR *n* person who engages in a sport or activity as a pastime rather than as a profession ▹ *adj* not professional

AMATING ▸ amate

AMATION *n* lovemaking

AMATIVE *a rare word for* ▸ **amorous**

AMATOL *n* explosive mixture of ammonium nitrate and TNT, used in shells and bombs

AMATOLS ▸ amatol

AMATORY *adj* relating to romantic or sexual love

AMAUT *n* hood on an Inuit woman's parka for carrying a child

AMAUTS ▸ amaut

AMAZE *vb* surprise greatly, astound

AMAZED ▸ amaze

AMAZES ▸ amaze

AMAZING *adj* causing wonder or astonishment

AMAZON *n* any tall, strong, or aggressive woman

AMAZONS ▸ amazon

AMBACH *same as* ▸ **ambatch**

AMBAGE *n* ambiguity

AMBAGES ▸ ambage

AMBAN *n* Chinese official

AMBANS ▸ amban

AMBARI *same as* ▸ **ambary**

AMBARIS ▸ ambari

AMBARY *n* tropical Asian plant that yields a fibre similar to jute

AMBASSY *n* embassy

AMBATCH *n* tree or shrub of the Nile Valley, valued for its light-coloured wood

AMBEER *n* saliva coloured by tobacco juice

AMBEERS ▸ ambeer

AMBER *n* clear yellowish

A

fossil resin ▷ *adj* brownish-yellow

AMBERED *adj* fixed in amber

AMBERS ▷ amber

AMBERY *adj* like amber

AMBIENT *adj* surrounding ▷ *n* ambient music

AMBIT *n* limits or boundary

AMBITS ▷ ambit

AMBITTY *adj* crystalline and brittle

AMBLE *vb* walk at a leisurely pace ▷ *n* leisurely walk or pace

AMBLED ▷ amble

AMBLER ▷ amble

AMBLERS ▷ amble

AMBLES ▷ amble

AMBLING *n* walking at a leisurely pace

AMBO *n* either of two raised pulpits from which the gospels and epistles were read in early Christian churches

AMBOINA *same as* ▷ amboyna

AMBONES ▷ ambo

AMBOS ▷ ambo

AMBOYNA *n* mottled curly-grained wood of an Indonesian tree, used in making furniture

AMBRIES ▷ ambry

AMBROID *same as* > amberoid

AMBRY *n* recessed cupboard in the wall of a church near the altar, used to store sacred vessels, etc

AMBSACE *n* double ace, the lowest throw at dice

AMBUSH *n* act of waiting in a concealed position to make a surprise attack ▷ *vb* attack from a concealed position

AME *n* soul

AMEARST *old form of* ▷ amerce

AMEBA *same as* ▷ amoeba

AMEBAE ▷ ameba

AMEBAN ▷ ameba

AMEBAS ▷ ameba

AMEBEAN *same as* > amoebean

AMEBIC ▷ ameba

AMEBOID *same as* > amoeboid

AMEER *n* (formerly) the ruler of Afghanistan

AMEERS ▷ ameer

AMELIA *n* congenital absence of arms or legs

AMELIAS ▷ amelia

AMEN *n* term used at the end of a prayer or religious statement ▷ *vb* say amen

AMENAGE *vb* tame

AMEND *vb* make small changes to correct or improve (something)

AMENDE *n* public apology and reparation made to satisfy the honour of the person wronged

AMENDED ▷ amend

AMENDER ▷ amend

AMENDES ▷ amende

AMENDS *n* recompense or compensation given or gained for some injury, insult, etc

AMENE *adj* pleasant

AMENED ▷ amen

AMENING ▷ amen

AMENITY *n* useful or enjoyable feature

AMENS ▷ amen

AMENT *n* mentally deficient person

AMENTA ▷ amentum

AMENTAL ▷ amentum

AMENTIA *n* severe mental deficiency, usually congenital

AMENTS ▷ ament

AMENTUM *same as* ▷ ament

AMERCE *vb* punish by a fine

AMERCED ▷ amerce

AMERCER ▷ amerce

AMERCES ▷ amerce

AMES ▷ ame

AMESACE *same as* ▷ ambsace

AMI *n* male friend

AMIA *n* species of fish

AMIABLE *adj* friendly, pleasant-natured

AMIABLY ▷ amiable

AMIAS ▷ amia

AMICE *n* rectangular piece of white linen worn by priests around the neck and shoulders under the alb or, formerly, on the head

AMICES ▷ amice

AMICI ▷ amicus

AMICUS *n* Latin for friend

AMID *prep* in the middle of, among ▷ *n* amide

AMIDASE *n* enzyme

AMIDE *n* any organic compound containing the group $-CONH_2$

AMIDES ▷ amide

AMIDIC ▷ amide

AMIDIN *n* form of starch

AMIDINE *n* crystalline compound

AMIDINS ▷ amidin

AMIDO *adj* containing amide

AMIDOL *n* chemical used in developing photographs

AMIDOLS ▷ amidol

AMIDONE *n* pain-killing drug

AMIDS *same as* ▷ amid

AMIDST *same as* ▷ amid

AMIE *n* female friend

AMIES ▷ amie

AMIGA *n* Spanish female friend

AMIGAS ▷ amiga

AMIGO *n* friend

AMIGOS ▷ amigo

AMILDAR *n* manager in India

AMIN *same as* ▷ amine

AMINE *n* organic base formed by replacing one or more of the hydrogen atoms of ammonia by organic groups

AMINES ▷ amine

AMINIC ▷ amine

AMINITY *n* amenity

AMINO *n* of, consisting of, or containing the group of atoms $-NH_2$

AMINS ▷ amin

AMIR *n* (formerly) the ruler of Afghanistan

AMIRATE ▷ amir

AMIRS ▷ amir

AMIS ▷ ami

AMISES ▷ ami

AMISS *adv* wrongly, badly ▷ *adj* wrong, faulty ▷ *n* evil deed

AMISSES ▷ amiss

AMITIES ▷ amity

AMITY *n* friendship

AMLA *n* species of Indian tree

AMLAS ▷ amla

AMMAN *same as* ▷ amtman

AMMANS ▷ amman

AMMETER *n* instrument for measuring electric current

AMMINE *n* compound that has molecules containing one or more ammonia molecules bound to another molecule, group, or atom by coordinate bonds

AMMINES ▸ ammine

AMMINO *adj* containing ammonia molecules

AMMIRAL old word for ▸ **admiral**

AMMO *n* ammunition

AMMON *n* Asian wild sheep

AMMONAL *n* explosive made by mixing TNT, ammonium nitrate, and aluminium powder

AMMONIA *n* strong-smelling alkaline gas containing hydrogen and nitrogen

AMMONIC *adj* of or concerned with ammonia or ammonium compounds

AMMONO *adj* using ammonia

AMMONS ▸ ammon

AMMOS ▸ ammo

AMNESIA *n* loss of memory

AMNESIC ▸ amnesia

AMNESTY *n* general pardon for offences against a government ▷ *vb* overlook or forget (an offence)

AMNIA ▸ amnion

AMNIC *adj* relating to amnion

AMNIO *n* amniocentesis

AMNION *n* innermost of two membranes enclosing an embryo

AMNIONS ▸ amnion

AMNIOS ▸ amnio

AMNIOTE *n* any vertebrate animal, such as a reptile, bird, or mammal, that possesses an amnion, chorion, and allantois during embryonic development

AMOEBA *n* microscopic single-celled animal able to change its shape

AMOEBAE ▸ amoeba

AMOEBAN ▸ amoeba

AMOEBAS ▸ amoeba

AMOEBIC ▸ amoeba

AMOK *n* state of murderous frenzy, originally observed among Malays

AMOKS ▸ amok

AMOKURA *n* type of white tropical sea bird with a red beak and long red tail feathers

AMOLE *n* American plant

AMOLES ▸ amole

AMOMUM *n* plant of ginger family

AMOMUMS ▸ amomum

AMONG *prep* in the midst of

AMONGST same as ▸ **among**

AMOOVE *vb* stir someone's emotions

AMOOVED ▸ amoove

AMOOVES ▸ amoove

AMORAL *adj* without moral standards

AMORANT > amorance

AMORCE *n* small percussion cap

AMORCES ▸ amorce

AMORET *n* sweetheart

AMORETS ▸ amoret

AMORINI ▸ amorino

AMORINO same as > **amoretto**

AMORISM ▸ amorist

AMORIST *n* lover or a writer about love

AMOROSA *n* lover

AMOROSO *adv* (to be played) lovingly ▷ *n* rich sweetened sherry of a dark colour

AMOROUS *adj* feeling, showing, or relating to sexual love

AMORT *adj* in low spirits

AMOSITE *n* form of asbestos

AMOTION *n* act of removing

AMOUNT *n* extent or quantity ▷ *vb* be equal or add up to

AMOUNTS ▸ amount

AMOUR *n* (secret) love affair

AMOURS ▸ amour

AMOVE *vb* stir someone's emotions

AMOVED ▸ amove

AMOVES ▸ amove

AMOVING ▸ amove

AMOWT same as ▸ **amaut**

AMOWTS ▸ amowt

AMP *n* ampere ▷ *vb* excite or become excited

AMPASSY *n* ampersand

AMPED ▸ amp

AMPERE *n* basic unit of electric current

AMPERES ▸ ampere

AMPHORA *n* two-handled ancient Greek or Roman jar

AMPING ▸ amp

AMPLE *adj* more than sufficient

AMPLER ▸ ample

AMPLEST ▸ ample

AMPLIFY *vb* increase the strength of (a current or sound signal)

AMPLY *adv* fully or generously

AMPOULE *n* small sealed glass vessel containing liquid for injection

AMPS ▸ amp

AMPUL *n* ampoule

AMPULE same as ▸ **ampoule**

AMPULES ▸ ampule

AMPULLA *n* dilated end part of certain tubes in the body

AMPULS ▸ ampul

AMPUTEE *n* person who has had a limb amputated

AMREETA same as ▸ **amrita**

AMRIT *n* sanctified solution of sugar and water used in the Amrit Ceremony

AMRITA *n* ambrosia of the gods that bestows immortality

AMRITAS ▸ amrita

AMRITS ▸ amrit

AMTMAN *n* magistrate in parts of Europe

AMTMANS ▸ amtman

AMTRAC *n* amphibious tracked vehicle

AMTRACK *n* amphibious tracked vehicle

AMTRACS ▸ amtrac

AMU *n* unit of mass

AMUCK same as ▸ **amok**

AMUCKS ▸ amuck

AMULET *n* something carried or worn as a protection against evil

AMULETS ▸ amulet

AMUS ▸ amu

AMUSE *vb* cause to laugh or smile

AMUSED ▸ amuse

AMUSER ▸ amuse

AMUSERS ▸ amuse

AMUSES ▸ amuse

AMUSIA *n* inability to recognize musical tones

AMUSIAS ▸ amusia

AMUSIC ▸ amusia

AMUSING *adj* mildly entertaining

AMUSIVE *adj* deceptive

AMYGDAL *n* almond

AMYL *n* of, consisting of, or containing any of eight isomeric forms of the monovalent group $C_5H_{11}-$

AMYLASE *n* enzyme, present in saliva, that helps to change starch into sugar

A

AMYLENE another name (no longer in technical usage) for ▶ **pentene**

AMYLIC adj of or derived from amyl

AMYLOID n complex protein resembling starch, deposited in tissues in some degenerative diseases ▷ adj starchlike

AMYLOSE n minor component (about 20 per cent) of starch, consisting of long unbranched chains of glucose units. It is soluble in water and gives an intense blue colour with iodine

AMYLS ▶ amyl

AMYLUM another name for ▶ **starch**

AMYLUMS ▶ amylum

AN adj form of **a** used before vowels, and sometimes before 'h' ▷ n an additional consideration or condition, as in 'ifs and ans'

ANA adv (of ingredients in a prescription) in equal quantities ▷ n collection of reminiscences, sketches, etc, of or about a person or place

ANABAS n type of fish

ANADEM n garland for the head

ANADEMS ▶ anadem

ANAEMIA n deficiency in the number of red blood cells

ANAEMIC adj having anaemia

ANAGOGE n allegorical or spiritual interpretation, esp of sacred works such as the Bible

ANAGOGY same as ▶ anagoge

ANAGRAM n word or phrase made by rearranging the letters of another word or phrase

ANAL adj of the anus

ANALGIA same as > **analgesia**

ANALITY n quality of being psychologically anal

ANALLY ▶ anal

ANALOG same as > **analogue**

ANALOGA > **analogon**

ANALOGS ▶ analog

ANALOGY n similarity in some respects

ANALYSE vb make an analysis of (something)

ANALYST n person skilled in analysis

ANALYTE n substance that is being analyzed

ANALYZE same as ▶ **analyse**

ANAN interj expression of failure to understand

ANANA n pineapple

> More than two As on your rack is not good news, but fortunately there are a number of short words that use three of them, of which this word for the pineapple plant is one.

ANANAS n plant related to the pineapple

ANANKE n unalterable necessity

ANANKES ▶ ananke

ANAPEST same as > **anapaest**

ANAPHOR n word referring back to a previous word

ANARCH n instigator or personification of anarchy

ANARCHS ▶ anarch

ANARCHY n lawlessness and disorder

ANAS ▶ ana

ANATA n (in Theravada Buddhism) the belief that since all things are constantly changing, there can be no such thing as a permanent, unchanging self

ANATAS ▶ anata

ANATASE n rare blue or black mineral

ANATMAN same as ▶ anata

ANATOMY n science of the structure of the body

ANATTA n annatto

ANATTAS ▶ anatta

ANATTO same as ▶ annatto

ANATTOS ▶ anatto

ANAXIAL adj asymmetrical

ANBURY n soft spongy tumour occurring in horses and oxen

ANCE dialect form of ▶ once

ANCHO n chili pepper

ANCHOR n heavy hooked device attached to a boat by a cable and dropped overboard to fasten the ship to the sea bottom ▷ vb fasten with or as if with an anchor

ANCHORS pl n brakes of a motor vehicle

ANCHOS ▶ ancho

ANCHOVY n small strong-tasting fish

ANCHUSA n Eurasian plant with rough hairy stems and leaves and blue flowers

ANCIENT adj dating from very long ago ▷ n member of a civilized nation in the ancient world, esp a Greek, Roman, or Hebrew

ANCILE n mythical Roman shield

ANCILIA ▶ ancile

ANCILLA n Latin word for servant

ANCLE old spelling of ▶ ankle

ANCLES ▶ ancle

ANCOME n inflammation

ANCOMES ▶ ancome

ANCON n projecting bracket or console supporting a cornice

ANCONAL ▶ ancon

ANCONE same as ▶ ancon

ANCONES ▶ ancone

ANCORA adv Italian for encore

ANCRESS n female anchorite

AND n additional matter or problem

ANDANTE adv (piece to be played) moderately slowly ▷ n passage or piece to be performed moderately slowly

ANDIRON n iron stand for supporting logs in a fireplace

ANDRO n type of sex hormone

ANDROID n robot resembling a human ▷ adj resembling a human being

ANDROS ▶ andro

ANDS ▶ and

ANDVILE old form of ▶ anvil

ANE Scots word for ▶ one

ANEAR adv nearly ▷ vb approach

ANEARED ▶ anear

ANEARS ▶ anear

ANEATH Scots word for ▶ **beneath**

ANELACE same as ▶ anlace

ANELE vb anoint, esp to give extreme unction to

ANELED ▶ anele

ANELES ▶ anele

ANELING ▶ anele

ANELLI *pl n* pasta shaped like small rings

ANEMIA *n* anaemia

ANEMIAS *same as* ▸ **anemia**

ANEMIC *same as* ▸ **anaemic**

ANEMONE *n* plant with white, purple, or red flowers

ANENST *dialect word for* ▸ **against**

ANENT *prep* lying against

ANERGIA *n* anergy

ANERGIC ▸ **anergy**

ANERGY *n* lack of energy

ANERLY *Scots word for* ▸ **only**

ANEROID *adj* not containing a liquid ▷ *n* barometer that does not contain liquid

Referring to a kind of barometer, this is one of the most commonly played of all 7-letter bonus words.

ANES ▸ **ane**

ANESTRA > **anestrus**

ANESTRI > **anestrus**

ANETHOL *n* substance derived from oil of anise

ANETIC *adj* medically soothing

ANEURIN *a less common name for* ▸ **thiamine**

ANEW *adv* once more

ANGA *n* a part in Indian music

ANGAKOK *n* Inuit shaman

ANGARIA *n* species of shellfish

ANGARY *n* right of a belligerent state to use the property of a neutral state or to destroy it if necessary, subject to payment of full compensation to the owners

ANGAS ▸ **anga**

ANGEKOK *n* Inuit shaman

ANGEL *n* spiritual being believed to be an attendant or messenger of God ▷ *vb* provide financial support for

ANGELED ▸ **angel**

ANGELIC *adj* very kind, pure, or beautiful

ANGELS ▸ **angel**

ANGELUS *n* series of prayers recited in the morning, at midday, and in the evening, commemorating the Annunciation and Incarnation

ANGER *n* fierce displeasure or extreme annoyance ▷ *vb* make (someone) angry

ANGERED ▸ **anger**

ANGERLY *adv* old form of angrily

ANGERS ▸ **anger**

ANGICO *n* South American tree

ANGICOS ▸ **angico**

ANGINA *n* heart disorder causing sudden severe chest pains

ANGINAL ▸ **angina**

ANGINAS ▸ **angina**

ANGIOMA *n* tumour consisting of a mass of blood vessels or lymphatic vessels

ANGLE *n* space between or shape formed by two lines or surfaces that meet ▷ *vb* bend or place (something) at an angle

ANGLED ▸ **angle**

ANGLER *n* person who fishes with a hook and line

ANGLERS ▸ **angler**

ANGLES ▸ **angle**

ANGLICE *adv* in English

ANGLIFY *same as* > **anglicize**

ANGLING *n* art or sport of fishing with a hook and line

ANGLIST *same as* > **anglicist**

ANGLO *n* White inhabitant of the US not of Latin extraction

ANGLOS ▸ **anglo**

ANGOLA *same as* ▸ **angora**

ANGORA *n* variety of goat, cat, or rabbit with long silky hair

ANGORAS ▸ **angora**

ANGRIER ▸ **angry**

ANGRIES ▸ **angry**

ANGRILY ▸ **angry**

ANGRY *adj* full of anger ▷ *n* angry person

ANGST *n* feeling of anxiety

ANGSTS ▸ **angst**

ANGSTY *adj* displaying or feeling angst, esp in a self-conscious manner

ANGUINE *adj* of, relating to, or similar to a snake

ANGUISH *n* great mental pain ▷ *vb* afflict or be afflicted with anguish

ANGULAR *adj* (of a person) lean and bony

ANHINGA *n* type of bird

ANI *n* tropical American bird

with black plumage, a long square-tipped tail, and a hooked bill

ANICCA *n* (in Theravada Buddhism) the belief that all things, including the self, are impermanent and constantly changing: the first of the three basic characteristics of existence

ANICCAS ▸ **anicca**

ANICUT *n* dam in India

ANICUTS ▸ **anicut**

ANIGH *adv* near

ANIGHT *adv* at night

ANIL *n* West Indian shrub, from which indigo is obtained

ANILE *adj* of or like a feeble old woman

ANILIN *n* aniline

ANILINE *n* colourless oily liquid obtained from coal tar and used for making dyes, plastics, and explosives

ANILINS ▸ **anilin**

ANILITY ▸ **anile**

ANILS ▸ **anil**

ANIMA *n* feminine principle as present in the male unconscious

ANIMACY *n* state of being animate

ANIMAL *n* living creature with specialized sense organs and capable of voluntary motion, esp one other than a human being ▷ *adj* of animals

ANIMALS ▸ **animal**

ANIMAS ▸ **anima**

ANIMATE *vb* give life to ▷ *adj* having life

ANIMATO *adv* (to be performed) in a lively manner

ANIME *n* type of Japanese animated film with themes and styles similar to manga comics

ANIMES ▸ **anime**

ANIMI ▸ **animus**

ANIMIS ▸ **animi**

ANIMISM *n* belief that natural objects possess souls

ANIMIST ▸ **animism**

ANIMUS *n* hatred, animosity

ANION *n* ion with negative charge

ANIONIC ▸ **anion**

A

ANIONS ▶ anion

ANIS ▶ ani

ANISE n plant with liquorice-flavoured seeds

ANISEED n liquorice-flavoured seeds of the anise plant

ANISES ▶ anise

ANISIC ▶ anise

ANISOLE n colourless pleasant-smelling liquid used as a solvent

ANKER n old liquid measure for wine

ANKERS ▶ anker

ANKH n T-shaped cross with a loop on the top, which symbolized eternal life in ancient Egypt

ANKHS ▶ ankh

ANKLE n joint between the foot and leg ▷ vb move

ANKLED ▶ ankle

ANKLES ▶ ankle

ANKLET n ornamental chain worn round the ankle

ANKLETS ▶ anklet

ANKLING ▶ ankle

ANKLONG n Asian musical instrument

ANKLUNG n Asian musical instrument

ANKUS n stick used, esp in India, for goading elephants

ANKUSES ▶ ankus

ANKUSH n Indian weapon

ANLACE n medieval short dagger with a broad tapering blade

ANLACES ▶ anlace

ANLAGE n organ or part in the earliest stage of development

ANLAGEN ▶ anlage

ANLAGES ▶ anlage

ANLAS same as ▶ anlace

ANLASES ▶ anlas

ANN n old Scots word for a widow's pension

ANNA n former Indian coin worth one sixteenth of a rupee

ANNAL n recorded events of one year

ANNALS ▶ annal

ANNAS ▶ anna

ANNAT n singular of annates

ANNATES pl n first year's revenue of a see, an abbacy, or a minor benefice, paid to the pope

ANNATS ▶ annat

ANNATTA n annatto

ANNATTO n small tropical American tree with red or pinkish flowers and seeds that yield a dye

ANNEAL vb toughen (metal or glass) by heating and slow cooling ▷ n act of annealing

ANNEALS ▶ anneal

ANNELID n type of worm with a segmented body, such as an earthworm

ANNEX vb seize (territory)

ANNEXE n extension to a building

ANNEXED ▶ annex

ANNEXES ▶ annexe

ANNICUT n dam in India

ANNO adv Latin for in the year

ANNONA n American tree or shrub

ANNONAS ▶ annona

ANNOY vb irritate or displease

ANNOYED ▶ annoy

ANNOYER ▶ annoy

ANNOYS ▶ annoy

ANNS ▶ ann

ANNUAL adj happening once a year ▷ n plant that completes its life cycle in a year

ANNUALS ▶ annual

ANNUITY n fixed sum paid every year

ANNUL vb declare (something, esp a marriage) invalid

ANNULAR adj ring-shaped ▷ n ring finger

ANNULET n moulding in the form of a ring, as at the top of a column adjoining the capital

ANNULI ▶ annulus

ANNULS ▶ annul

ANNULUS n area between two concentric circles

ANOA n type of small cattle

ANOAS ▶ anoa

ANOBIID n any type of beetle

ANODAL ▶ anode

ANODE n positive electrode in a battery, valve, etc

ANODES ▶ anode

ANODIC ▶ anode

ANODISE same as ▶ anodize

ANODIZE vb coat (metal) with a protective oxide film by electrolysis

ANODYNE n something that relieves pain or distress ▷ adj relieving pain or distress

ANOESES ▶ anoesis

ANOESIS n feeling without understanding

ANOETIC ▶ anoesis

ANOINT vb smear with oil as a sign of consecration

ANOINTS ▶ anoint

ANOLE n type of lizard

ANOLES ▶ anole

ANOLYTE n part of electrolyte around anode

ANOMALY n something that deviates from the normal, irregularity

ANOMIC ▶ anomie

ANOMIE n lack of social or moral standards

ANOMIES ▶ anomie

ANOMY same as ▶ anomie

ANON adv in a short time, soon

ANONYM n anonymous person or publication

ANONYMA n promiscuous woman

ANONYMS ▶ anonym

ANOPIA n inability to see

ANOPIAS ▶ anopia

ANOPSIA n squint in which the eye turns upwards

ANORAK n light waterproof hooded jacket

ANORAKS ▶ anorak

ANOREXY old name for ▶ anorexia

ANOSMIA n loss of the sense of smell, usually as the result of a lesion of the olfactory nerve, disease in another organ or part, or obstruction of the nasal passages

ANOSMIC ▶ anosmia

ANOTHER adj one more

ANOUGH adj enough

ANOW adj old form of enough

ANOXIA n lack or absence of oxygen

ANOXIAS ▶ anoxia

ANOXIC ▶ anoxia

ANS pl n as in **ifs and ans** things that might have happened, but which did not

ANSA n either end of Saturn's rings

ANSAE ▶ ansa

ANSATE adj having a handle or handle-like part

ANSATED adj ansate

ANSWER n reply to a question, request, letter, etc ▷ vb give an answer (to)

ANSWERS ▶ answer

ANT n small insect living in highly-organized colonies

ANTA n pilaster attached to the end of a side wall or sometimes to the side of a doorway

ANTACID n substance that counteracts acidity, esp in the stomach ▷ adj having the properties of this substance

ANTAE ▶ anta

ANTAR old word for ▶ cave

ANTARA n South American panpipes

ANTARAS ▶ antara

ANTARS ▶ antar

ANTAS ▶ anta

ANTBEAR n aardvark

ANTBIRD n any of various dull-coloured South American passerine birds that typically feed on ants

ANTE n player's stake in poker ▷ vb place (one's stake) in poker

ANTED ▶ ante

ANTEED ▶ ante

ANTEFIX n carved ornament at the eaves of a roof to hide the joint between the tiles

ANTEING ▶ ante

ANTENNA n insect's feeler

ANTES ▶ ante

ANTHEM n song of loyalty, esp to a country ▷ vb provide with an anthem

ANTHEMS ▶ anthem

ANTHER n part of a flower's stamen containing pollen

ANTHERS ▶ anther

ANTHILL n mound of soil, leaves, etc, near the entrance of an ants' nest, carried and deposited there by the ants while constructing the nest

ANTHOID adj resembling a flower

ANTHRAX n dangerous disease of cattle and sheep, communicable to humans

ANTI adj opposed (to) ▷ n opponent of a party, policy, or attitude

ANTIAIR adj countering attack by aircraft or missile

ANTIAR another name for ▶ upas

ANTIARS ▶ antiar

ANTIBUG adj acting against computer bugs

ANTIC n actor in a ludicrous or grotesque part ▷ adj fantastic

ANTICAL adj (of the position of plant parts) in front of or above another part

ANTICAR n opposed to cars

ANTICK vb perform antics

ANTICKE adj old form of antique

ANTICKS ▶ antick

ANTICLY adv grotesquely

ANTICS pl n absurd acts or postures

ANTIENT old spelling of ▶ ancient

ANTIFAT adj acting to remove or prevent fat

ANTIFLU adj acting against influenza

ANTIFOG adj preventing the buildup of moisture on a surface

ANTIFUR adj opposed to the wearing of fur garments

ANTIGAY adj hostile to homosexuals

ANTIGEN n substance causing the blood to produce antibodies

ANTIGUN adj opposed to the possession of guns

ANTIJAM adj preventing jamming

ANTILOG n number whose logarithm to a given base is a given number

ANTIMAN adj opposed to men

ANTING n placing or rubbing of ants by birds on their feathers. The body fluids of the ants are thought to repel parasites

ANTINGS ▶ anting

ANTIPOT adj opposed to illegal use of marijuana

ANTIQUE n object of an earlier period, valued for its beauty, workmanship, or age ▷ adj made in an earlier period ▷ vb give an antique appearance to

ANTIRED adj of a particular colour of antiquark

ANTIS ▶ anti

ANTISAG adj preventing sagging

ANTISEX adj opposed to sexual activity

ANTITAX adj opposed to taxation

ANTIWAR adj opposed to war

ANTLER n branched horn of a male deer

ANTLERS ▶ antler

ANTLIA n butterfly proboscis

ANTLIAE ▶ antlia

ANTLIKE adj of or like an ant or ants

ANTLION n type of insect resembling a dragonfly, mostly found in tropical regions

ANTONYM n word that means the opposite of another

ANTRA ▶ antrum

ANTRAL ▶ antrum

ANTRE n cavern or cave

ANTRES ▶ antre

ANTRUM n natural cavity, esp in a bone

ANTRUMS ▶ antrum

ANTS ▶ ant

ANTSIER ▶ antsy

ANTSY adj restless, nervous, and impatient

ANURAL adj without a tail

ANURAN n type of tailless amphibian with very long hind legs specialized for hopping, such as frogs and toads

ANURANS ▶ anuran

ANURIA n complete suppression of urine formation, often as the result of a kidney disorder

ANURIAS ▶ anuria

ANURIC ▶ anuria

ANUROUS adj lacking a tail

ANUS n opening at the end of the alimentary canal, through which faeces are discharged

ANUSES ▶ anus

ANVIL n heavy iron block on which metals are hammered into particular shapes ▷ vb forge on an anvil

ANVILED ▶ anvil

ANVILS ▶ anvil

ANXIETY n state of being anxious

ANXIOUS *adj* worried and tense

ANY *adj* one or some, no matter which ▷ *adv* at all

ANYBODY *n* any person at random

ANYHOW *adv* anyway

ANYMORE *adv* at present

ANYON *n* (in mathematics) projective representation of a Lie group

ANYONE *pron* any person ▷ *n* any person at random

ANYONES ▶ **anyone**

ANYONS ▶ **anyon**

ANYROAD *a northern English dialect word for* ▶ **anyway**

ANYTIME *adv* at any time

ANYWAY *adv* at any rate, nevertheless

ANYWAYS *nonstandard word for* ▶ **anyway**

ANYWHEN *adv* at any time

ANYWISE *adv* in any way or manner

ANZIANI *n* Italian word for councillors

AORIST *n* tense of the verb in classical Greek and in certain other inflected languages, indicating past action without reference to whether the action involved was momentary or continuous

AORISTS ▶ **aorist**

AORTA *n* main artery of the body, carrying oxygen-rich blood from the heart

AORTAE ▶ **aorta**

AORTAL ▶ **aorta**

AORTAS ▶ **aorta**

AORTIC ▶ **aorta**

AOUDAD *n* N African wild mountain sheep with curved horns and long hair covering the neck and forelegs

AOUDADS ▶ **aoudad**

APACE *adv* swiftly

APACHE *n* Parisian gangster or ruffian

APACHES ▶ **apache**

APADANA *n* ancient Persian palace hall

APAGE *interj* Greek word meaning go away

APAGOGE *n* reduction to absurdity

APAID ▶ **apay**

APANAGE *same as* > **appanage**

APAREJO *n* kind of packsaddle made of stuffed leather cushions

APART *adv* to pieces or in pieces

APATHY *n* lack of interest or enthusiasm

APATITE *n* pale green to purple mineral, found in igneous rocks

APAY *vb* old word meaning satisfy

APAYD ▷ **apay**

APAYING ▶ **apay**

APAYS ▶ **apay**

APE *n* tailless monkey such as the chimpanzee or gorilla ▷ *vb* imitate

APEAK *adj* in a vertical or almost vertical position

APED ▶ **ape**

APEDOM *n* state of being an ape

APEDOMS ▶ **apedom**

APEEK *adv* nautical word meaning vertically

APEHOOD *n* state of being ape

APELIKE ▶ **ape**

APEMAN *n* extinct primate thought to have been the forerunner of true humans

APEMEN ▶ **apeman**

APEPSIA *n* digestive disorder

APEPSY *n* apepsia

APER *n* person who apes

APERCU *n* outline

APERCUS ▶ **apercu**

APERIES ▶ **apery**

APERS ▶ **aper**

APERT *adj* open

APERY *n* imitative behaviour

APES ▶ **ape**

APETALY > **apetalous**

APEX *n* highest point

APEXES ▶ **apex**

APGAR *n as in* **apgar score** system for determining the condition of an infant at birth

APHAGIA *n* refusal or inability to swallow

APHAKIA *n* absence of the lens of an eye, congenital or otherwise

APHASIA *n* disorder of the central nervous system that affects the ability to speak and understand words

APHASIC ▶ **aphasia**

APHELIA > **aphelion**

APHESES ▶ **aphesis**

APHESIS *n* gradual disappearance of an unstressed vowel at the beginning of a word

APHETIC ▶ **aphesis**

APHID *n* small insect which sucks the sap from plants

APHIDES ▶ **aphis**

APHIDS ▶ **aphid**

APHIS *n* type of aphid such as the blackfly

APHONIA *n* loss of the voice caused by damage to the vocal tract

APHONIC *adj* affected with aphonia ▷ *n* person affected with aphonia

APHONY *same as* ▶ **aphonia**

APHOTIC *adj* characterized by or growing in the absence of light

APHTHA *n* small ulceration on a mucous membrane, as in thrush, caused by a fungal infection

APHTHAE ▶ **aphtha**

APHYLLY > **aphyllous**

APIAN *adj* of, relating to, or resembling bees

APIARY *n* place where bees are kept

APICAL *adj* of, at, or being an apex ▷ *n* sound made with the tip of the tongue

APICALS ▶ **apical**

APICES *plural of* ▶ **apex**

APICIAN *adj* of fine or dainty food

APICULI > **apiculus**

APIECE *adv* each

APIEZON *adj as in* **apiezon oil** oil left by distillation

APING ▶ **ape**

APIOL *n* substance formerly used to assist menstruation

APIOLS ▶ **apiol**

APISH *adj* stupid or foolish

APISHLY ▶ **apish**

APISM *n* behaviour like an ape

APISMS ▶ **apism**

APLANAT *n* aplanatic lens

APLASIA *n* congenital absence or abnormal development of an organ or part

APLENTY *adv* in plenty

APLITE *n* light-coloured fine-grained acid igneous rock with a sugary texture, consisting of quartz and feldspars

APLITES ▸ aplite

APLITIC ▸ aplite

APLOMB n calm self-possession

APLOMBS ▸ aplomb

APNEA same as ▸ **apnoea**

APNEAL ▸ apnea

APNEAS ▸ apnea

APNEIC ▸ apnea

APNOEA n temporary inability to breathe

APNOEAL ▸ apnoea

APNOEAS ▸ apnoea

APNOEIC ▸ apnoea

APO n type of protein

APOCARP n apocarpous gynoecium or fruit

APOCOPE n omission of the final sound or sounds of a word

APOD n animal without feet

APODAL adj (of snakes, eels, etc) without feet

APODE n animal without feet

APODES ▸ apode

APODOUS same as ▸ **apodal**

APODS ▸ apod

APOGAMY n type of reproduction, occurring in some ferns, in which the sporophyte develops from the gametophyte without fusion of gametes

APOGEAL ▸ apogee

APOGEAN ▸ apogee

APOGEE n point of the moon's or a satellite's orbit that is farthest from the earth

APOGEES ▸ apogee

APOGEIC ▸ apogee

APOLLO n strikingly handsome youth

APOLLOS ▸ apollo

APOLOG same as > **apologue**

APOLOGS ▸ apolog

APOLOGY n expression of regret for wrongdoing

APOLUNE n point in a lunar orbit when a spacecraft is at its greatest distance from the moon

APOMICT n organism, esp a plant, produced by apomixis

APOOP adv on the poop deck

APOPLEX vb afflict with apoplexy

APORIA n doubt, real or professed, about what to do or say

APORIAS ▸ aporia

APORT adj on or towards the port side

APOS ▸ apo

APOSTIL n marginal note

APOSTLE n one of the twelve disciples chosen by Christ to preach his gospel

APOTHEM n perpendicular line or distance from the centre of a regular polygon to any of its sides

APOZEM n medicine dissolved in water

APOZEMS ▸ apozem

APP n application program

APPAID ▸ appay

APPAIR vb old form of impair

APPAIRS ▸ appair

APPAL vb dismay, terrify

APPALL same as ▸ **appal**

APPALLS ▸ appall

APPALS ▸ appal

APPALTI ▸ appalto

APPALTO n Italian word for contact

APPARAT n Communist Party organization in the former Soviet Union and other states

APPAREL n clothing ▷ vb clothe, adorn, etc

APPAY old word for ▸ **satisfy**

APPAYD ▸ appay

APPAYS ▸ appay

APPEACH old word for ▸ **accuse**

APPEAL vb make an earnest request ▷ n earnest request

APPEALS ▸ appeal

APPEAR vb become visible or present

APPEARS ▸ appear

APPEASE vb pacify (a person) by yielding to his or her demands

APPEL n stamp of the foot, used to warn of one's intent to attack

APPELS ▸ appel

APPEND vb join on, add

APPENDS ▸ append

APPERIL old word for ▸ **peril**

APPLAUD vb show approval of by clapping one's hands

APPLE n round firm fleshy fruit that grows on trees

APPLES ▸ apple

APPLET n computing program that runs within a page on the World Wide Web

APPLETS ▸ applet

APPLEY adj resembling or tasting like an apple

APPLIED adj (of a skill, science, etc) put to practical use

APPLIER ▸ apply

APPLIES ▸ apply

APPLY vb make a formal request

APPOINT vb assign to a job or position

APPORT n production of objects by apparently supernatural means at a spiritualists' seance

APPORTS ▸ apport

APPOSE vb place side by side or near to each other

APPOSED ▸ appose

APPOSER ▸ appose

APPOSES ▸ appose

APPRESS vb press together

APPRISE vb make aware (of)

APPRIZE same as ▸ **apprise**

APPRO n approval

APPROOF old word for ▸ **trial**

APPROS ▸ appro

APPROVE vb consider good or right

APPS ▸ app

APPUI n support

APPUIED ▸ appuy

APPUIS ▸ appui

APPULSE n very close approach of two celestial bodies so that they are in conjunction but no eclipse or occultation occurs

APPUY vb support

APPUYED ▸ appuy

APPUYS ▸ appuy

APRAXIA n disorder of the central nervous system caused by brain damage and characterized by impaired ability to carry out purposeful muscular movements

APRAXIC ▸ apraxia

APRES prep French word for after

APRICOT n yellowish-orange juicy fruit like a small peach ▷ adj yellowish-orange

APRON n garment worn over the front of the body to protect the clothes ▷ vb equip with an apron

APRONED ▸ apron

APRONS ▸ apron

APROPOS adv appropriate(ly)

APROTIC adj (of solvents) neither accepting nor donating hydrogen ions

APSARAS n Hindu water sprite

APSE n arched or domed recess, esp in a church

APSES ▷ apse

APSIDAL ▷ apsis

APSIDES ▷ apsis

APSIS n either of two points lying at the extremities of the elliptical orbit of a planet or satellite

APSO n Tibetan terrier

APSOS ▷ apso

APT adj having a specified tendency ▷ vb be fitting

APTAMER n artificially-created DNA or RNA molecule with therapeutic properties

APTED ▷ apt

APTER ▷ apt

APTERAL adj (esp of a classical temple) not having columns at the sides

APTERIA > apterium

APTERYX n kiwi (the bird)

APTEST ▷ apt

APTING ▷ apt

APTLY ▷ apt

APTNESS ▷ apt

APTOTE n noun without inflections

APTOTES ▷ aptote

APTOTIC ▷ aptote

APTS ▷ apt

APYRASE n enzyme

AQUA n water

This Latin word for water, together with its plural **aquae** or **aquas**, comes up over and over again.

AQUAE ▷ aqua

AQUAFER n aquifer

AQUAFIT n type of aerobic exercise done in water

AQUARIA > aquarium

AQUAS ▷ aqua

AQUATIC adj living in or near water ▷ n marine or freshwater animal or plant

AQUAVIT n grain- or potato-based spirit from the Scandinavian countries, flavoured with aromatic seeds and spices, esp caraway

AQUEOUS adj of, like, or containing water

AQUIFER n deposit of rock, such as sandstone, containing water that can be used to supply wells

AQUILON n name for the north wind

AQUIVER adv quivering

AR n letter R

ARAARA another name for > trevally

ARAARAS ▷ araara

ARABA n Asian carriage

This word for a kind of Russian wagon is another of the short words that can help you to deal with a surplus of As.

ARABAS ▷ araba

ARABESK same as > arabesque

ARABIC adj as in **gum arabic** gum exuded by certain acacia trees

ARABICA n high-quality coffee bean

ARABIN n essence of gum arabic

ARABINS ▷ arabin

ARABIS n type of plant which forms low-growing mats with downy grey foliage and white flowers

ARABISE vb make or become Arab

ARABIZE vb make or become Arab

ARABLE adj suitable for growing crops on ▷ n arable land or farming

ARABLES ▷ arable

ARACHIS n Brazilian plant

ARAISE vb old form of raise

ARAISED ▷ araise

ARAISES ▷ araise

ARAK same as ▷ arrack

ARAKS ▷ arak

ARALIA n type of plant grown in greenhouses or as a house plant for its decorative evergreen foliage

ARALIAS ▷ aralia

ARAME n Japanese edible seaweed

ARAMES ▷ arame

ARAMID n synthetic fibre

ARAMIDS ▷ aramid

ARANEID n type of arachnid of the order which comprises the spiders

ARAR n African tree

ARAROBA n Brazilian leguminous tree

ARARS ▷ arar

ARAYSE vb old form of raise

ARAYSED ▷ arayse

ARAYSES ▷ arayse

ARB short for > arbitrage

ARBA n Asian carriage

ARBAS ▷ arba

ARBITER n person empowered to judge in a dispute

ARBLAST n arbalest

ARBOR n revolving shaft or axle in a machine

ARBORED adj having arbors

ARBORES ▷ arbor

ARBORET n old name for an area planted with shrubs

ARBORIO n as in **arborio rice** variety of round-grain rice used for making risotto

ARBORS ▷ arbor

ARBOUR n glade sheltered by trees

ARBOURS ▷ arbour

ARBS ▷ arb

ARBUTE old name for ▷ arbutus

ARBUTES ▷ arbute

ARBUTUS n evergreen shrub with strawberry-like berries

ARC n part of a circle or other curve ▷ vb form an arc

ARCADE n covered passageway lined with shops ▷ vb provide with an arcade

ARCADED ▷ arcade

ARCADES ▷ arcade

ARCADIA n traditional idealized rural setting

ARCANA n either of the two divisions of a pack of tarot cards

ARCANAS ▷ arcana

ARCANE adj mysterious and secret

ARCANUM n profound secret or mystery known only to initiates

ARCED ▷ arc

ARCH n curved structure supporting a bridge or roof ▷ vb (cause to) form an arch ▷ adj superior, knowing

ARCHAEA n order of prokaryotic microorganisms

ARCHAEI > archaeus

ARCHAIC adj ancient

ARCHEAN > archaean
ARCHED *adj* provided with or spanned by an arch or arches
ARCHEI ▸ archeus
ARCHER *n* person who shoots with a bow and arrow
ARCHERS ▸ archer
ARCHERY *n* art or sport of shooting with a bow and arrow
ARCHES ▸ arch
ARCHEST ▸ arch
ARCHEUS *n* spirit believed to inhabit a living thing
ARCHFOE *n* chief enemy
ARCHIL *a variant spelling of* ▸ orchil
ARCHILS ▸ archil
ARCHINE *n* Russian unit of length equal to about 71 cm
ARCHING ▸ arch
ARCHIVE *n* collection of records or documents ▷ *vb* store (documents, data, etc) in an archive or other repository
ARCHLET *n* small arch
ARCHLY ▸ arch
ARCHON *n* (in ancient Athens) one of the nine chief magistrates
ARCHONS ▸ archon
ARCHWAY *n* passageway under an arch
ARCING ▸ arc
ARCINGS ▸ arc
ARCKED ▸ arc
ARCKING ▸ arc
ARCMIN *n* 1/60 of a degree of an angle
ARCMINS ▸ arcmin
ARCO *adv* musical direction meaning with bow ▷ *n* bow of a stringed instrument
ARCOS ▸ arco
ARCS ▸ arc
ARCSEC *n* 1/3600 of a degree of an angle
ARCSECS ▸ arcsec
ARCSINE *n* trigonometrical function
ARCTIC *adj* very cold ▷ *n* high waterproof overshoe with buckles
ARCTICS ▸ arctic
ARCTIID *n* type of moth of the family which includes the ermine and tiger moths
ARCTOID *adj* like a bear
ARCUATE *adj* shaped or bent like an arc or bow

ARCUS *n* circle around the cornea of the eye
ARCUSES ▸ arcus
ARD *n* primitive plough
ARDEB *n* unit of dry measure used in Egypt and other Middle Eastern countries. In Egypt it is approximately equal to 0.195 cubic metres
ARDEBS ▸ ardeb
ARDENCY ▸ ardent
ARDENT *adj* passionate
ARDOR *same as* ▸ ardour
ARDORS ▸ ardor
ARDOUR *n* passion
ARDOURS ▸ ardour
ARDRI *n* Irish high king
ARDRIGH *n* Irish high king
ARDRIS ▸ ardri
ARDS ▸ ard
ARDUOUS *adj* hard to accomplish, strenuous
ARE *n* unit of measure, 100 square metres ▷ *vb* used as the singular form with you
AREA *n* part or region
AREACH *vb* old form of reach
AREAD *vb* old word meaning declare
AREADS ▸ aread
AREAE ▸ area
AREAL ▸ area
AREALLY ▸ area
AREAR *n* old form of arrear
AREAS ▸ area
AREAWAY *n* passageway between parts of a building or between different buildings
ARECA *n* tall SE Asian palm tree with white flowers and orange or red egg-shaped nuts
ARECAS ▸ areca
ARED ▸ aread
AREDD ▸ aread
AREDE *vb* old word meaning declare
AREDES ▸ arede
AREDING ▸ arede
AREFIED ▸ arefy
AREFIES ▸ arefy
AREFY *vb* dry up
AREG *a plural of* ▸ erg
AREIC *adj* relating to area
ARENA *n* seated enclosure for sports events
ARENAS ▸ arena
ARENE *n* aromatic hydrocarbon
ARENES ▸ arene

ARENITE *n* any arenaceous rock
ARENOSE *adj* sandy
ARENOUS *adj* sandy
AREOLA *n* small circular area, such as the coloured ring around the human nipple
AREOLAE ▸ areola
AREOLAR ▸ areola
AREOLAS ▸ areola
AREOLE *n* space outlined on a surface, such as an area between veins on a leaf or on an insect's wing
AREOLES ▸ areole
AREPA *n* Colombian cornmeal cake
AREPAS ▸ arepa
ARERE *adv* old word meaning backwards
ARES ▸ are
ARET *vb* old word meaning entrust
ARETE *n* sharp ridge separating two cirques or glacial valleys in mountainous regions
ARETES ▸ arete
ARETS ▸ aret
ARETT *vb* old word meaning entrust
ARETTED ▸ arett
ARETTS ▸ arett
AREW *adv* old word meaning in a row
ARF *n* barking sound
ARFS ▸ arf
ARGAL *same as* ▸ argali
ARGALA *n* Indian stork
ARGALAS ▸ argala
ARGALI *n* large wild sheep of central Asia, the male of which has massive curving horns
ARGALIS ▸ argali
ARGALS ▸ argal
ARGAN *n* Moroccan tree
ARGAND *n* lamp with a hollow circular wick
ARGANDS ▸ argand
ARGANS ▸ argan
ARGENT *n* silver
ARGENTS ▸ argent
ARGH *interj* cry of pain
ARGHAN *n* agave plant
ARGHANS ▸ arghan
ARGIL *n* clay, esp potters' clay
ARGILS ▸ argil
ARGLE *vb* quarrel
ARGLED ▸ argle
ARGLES ▸ argle

ARGLING ▸ argle

ARGOL n crude potassium hydrogentartrate, deposited as a crust on the sides of wine vats

ARGOLS ▸ argol

ARGON n inert gas found in the air

ARGONON n inert gas

ARGONS ▸ argon

ARGOSY n large merchant ship

ARGOT n slang or jargon

ARGOTIC ▸ argot

ARGOTS ▸ argot

ARGUE vb try to prove by giving reasons

ARGUED ▸ argue

ARGUER ▸ argue

ARGUERS ▸ argue

ARGUES ▸ argue

ARGUFY vb argue or quarrel, esp over something trivial

ARGUING ▸ argue

ARGULI ▸ argulus

ARGULUS n parasite on fish

ARGUS n any of various brown butterflies

ARGUSES ▸ argus

ARGUTE adj shrill or keen

ARGYLE adj made of knitted or woven material with a diamond-shaped pattern of two or more colours ▷ n sock made of this

ARGYLES ▸ argyle

ARGYLL n sock with diamond pattern

ARGYLLS ▸ argyll

ARGYRIA n staining of skin by exposure to silver

ARHAT n Buddhist, esp a monk who has achieved enlightenment and at death passes to nirvana

ARHATS ▸ arhat

ARIA n elaborate song for solo voice, esp one from an opera

ARIARY n currency of Madagascar

ARIAS ▸ aria

ARID adj parched, dry

ARIDER ▸ arid

ARIDEST ▸ arid

ARIDITY ▸ arid

ARIDLY ▸ arid

ARIEL n type of Arabian gazelle

ARIELS ▸ ariel

ARIETTA n short relatively uncomplicated aria

ARIETTE same as ▸ arietta

ARIGHT adv rightly

ARIKI n first-born male or female in a notable family

ARIKIS ▸ ariki

ARIL n appendage on certain seeds, such as those of the yew and nutmeg, developed from or near the funicle of the ovule and often brightly coloured and fleshy

ARILED adj having an aril

ARILLI ▸ arillus

ARILLUS n aril

ARILS ▸ aril

ARIOSE adj songlike

ARIOSI ▸ arioso

ARIOSO n recitative with the lyrical quality of an aria

ARIOSOS ▸ arioso

ARIOT adv riotously

ARIPPLE adv in ripples

ARISE vb come about

ARISEN ▸ arise

ARISES ▸ arise

ARISH n field that has been mown

ARISHES ▸ arish

ARISING ▸ arise

ARISTA n stiff bristle such as the awn of some grasses and cereals

ARISTAE ▸ arista

ARISTAS ▸ arista

ARISTO n aristocrat

ARISTOS ▸ aristo

ARK n boat built by Noah, which survived the Flood ▷ vb place in an ark

ARKED ▸ ark

ARKING ▸ ark

ARKITE n passenger in ark

ARKITES ▸ arkite

ARKOSE n sandstone consisting of grains of feldspar and quartz cemented by a mixture of quartz and clay minerals

ARKOSES ▸ arkose

ARKOSIC ▸ arkose

ARKS ▸ ark

ARLE vb make downpayment

ARLED ▸ arle

ARLES ▸ arle

ARLING ▸ arle

ARM n either of the upper limbs from the shoulder to the wrist ▷ vb supply with weapons

ARMADA n large number of warships

ARMADAS ▸ armada

ARMBAND n band of material worn round the arm, such as one bearing an identifying mark, etc, or a black one indicating mourning

ARMED adj equipped with or supported by arms, armour, etc

ARMER ▸ arm

ARMERS ▸ arm

ARMET n close-fitting medieval visored helmet with a neck guard

ARMETS ▸ armet

ARMFUL n as much as can be held in the arms

ARMFULS ▸ armful

ARMHOLE n opening in a garment through which the arm passes

ARMIES ▸ army

ARMIGER n person entitled to bear heraldic arms, such as a sovereign or nobleman

ARMIL n bracelet

ARMILLA n bracelet

ARMILS ▸ armil

ARMING n act of taking arms or providing with arms

ARMINGS ▸ arming

ARMLESS ▸ arm

ARMLET n band worn round the arm

ARMLETS ▸ armlet

ARMLIKE ▸ arm

ARMLOAD n amount carried in the arms

ARMLOCK vb grip someone's arms

ARMOIRE n large cabinet, originally used for storing weapons

ARMOR same as ▸ armour

ARMORED same as ▸ armoured

ARMORER same as ▸ armourer

ARMORS ▸ armor

ARMORY same as ▸ armoury

ARMOUR n metal clothing formerly worn to protect the body in battle ▷ vb equip or cover with armour

ARMOURS ▸ armour

ARMOURY n place where weapons are stored

ARMPIT n hollow under the arm at the shoulder

ARMPITS ▸ armpit

ARMREST n part of a chair or sofa that supports the arm

ARMS ▸ arm

ARMSFUL ▸ armful

ARMURE n silk or wool fabric with a small cobbled pattern

ARMURES ▸ armure

ARMY n military land forces of a nation

ARNA n Indian water buffalo

ARNAS ▸ arna

ARNATTO n annatto

ARNICA n N temperate or arctic plant typically having yellow flowers

ARNICAS ▸ arnica

ARNOTTO n annatto

ARNUT n plant with edible tubers

ARNUTS ▸ arnut

AROBA n Asian carriage

AROBAS ▸ aroba

AROHA n love, compassion, or affection

AROHAS ▸ aroha

AROID n type of plant of the family which includes the arum, calla, and anthurium

AROIDS ▸ aroid

AROINT vb drive away

AROINTS ▸ aroint

AROLLA n European pine tree

AROLLAS ▸ arolla

AROMA n pleasant smell

AROMAS ▸ aroma

AROSE past tense of ▸ **arise**

AROUND adv on all sides (of)

AROUSAL ▸ arouse

AROUSE vb stimulate, make active

AROUSED ▸ arouse

AROUSER ▸ arouse

AROUSES ▸ arouse

AROW adv in a row

AROYNT vb old word meaning to drive away

AROYNTS ▸ aroynt

ARPA n website concerned with structure of the internet

ARPAS ▸ arpa

ARPEN n old French measure of land

ARPENS ▸ arpen

ARPENT n former French unit of length equal to 190 feet (approximately 58 metres)

ARPENTS ▸ arpent

ARRACK n alcoholic drink distilled from grain or rice

ARRACKS ▸ arrack

ARRAH interj Irish exclamation

ARRAIGN vb bring (a prisoner) before a court to answer a charge

ARRANGE vb plan

ARRANT adj utter, downright

ARRAS n tapestry wall-hanging

ARRASED adj having an arras

ARRASES ▸ arras

ARRAY n impressive display or collection ▷ vb arrange in order

ARRAYAL ▸ array

ARRAYED ▸ array

ARRAYER ▸ array

ARRAYS ▸ array

ARREAR n singular of arrears

ARREARS pl n money owed

ARRECT adj pricked up

ARREEDE vb old word meaning declare

ARREST vb take (a person) into custody ▷ n act of taking a person into custody

ARRESTS ▸ arrest

ARRET n judicial decision

ARRETS ▸ arret

ARRIAGE n Scottish feudal service

ARRIBA interj exclamation of pleasure or approval

ARRIDE vb old word meaning gratify

ARRIDED ▸ arride

ARRIDES ▸ arride

ARRIERE adj French word meaning old-fashioned

ARRIERO n Spanish word for mule driver

ARRIS n sharp edge at the meeting of two surfaces at an angle with one another, as at two adjacent sides of a stone block

ARRISES ▸ arris

ARRISH n corn stubble

ARRIVAL n arriving

ARRIVE vb reach a place or destination

ARRIVED ▸ arrive

ARRIVER ▸ arrive

ARRIVES ▸ arrive

ARROBA n unit of weight used in some Spanish-speaking countries

ARROBAS ▸ arroba

ARROW n pointed shaft shot from a bow

ARROWED adj having an arrow pattern

ARROWS ▸ arrow

ARROWY adj like an arrow

ARROYO n steep-sided stream bed that is usually dry except after heavy rain

ARROYOS ▸ arroyo

ARS ▸ ar

ARSENAL n place where arms and ammunition are made or stored

ARSENIC n toxic grey element ▷ adj of or containing arsenic

ARSENO adj containing arsenic

ARSHEEN n old measure of length in Russia

ARSHIN n old measure of length in Russia

ARSHINE n old measure of length in Russia

ARSHINS ▸ arshin

ARSINE n colourless poisonous gas used in the manufacture of organic compounds, to dope transistors, and as a military poisonous gas

ARSINES ▸ arsine

ARSINO adj containing arsine

ARSIS n (in classical prosody) the long syllable or part on which the ictus falls in a metrical foot

ARSON n crime of intentionally setting property on fire

ARSONS ▸ arson

ART n creation of works of beauty, esp paintings or sculpture

ARTAL a plural of ▸ **rotl**

ARTEL n (in the former Soviet Union) a cooperative union or organization, esp of producers, such as peasants

ARTELS ▸ artel

ARTERY n one of the tubes carrying blood from the heart

ARTFUL adj cunning, wily

ARTI n ritual performed in homes and temples in which incense and light are offered to a deity

ARTIC *n* articulated vehicle

ARTICLE *n* written piece in a magazine or newspaper ▷ *vb* bind by a written contract

ARTICS ▸ artic

ARTIER ▸ arty

ARTIES ▸ arty

ARTIEST ▸ arty

ARTILY ▸ arty

ARTIS ▸ arti

ARTISAN *n* skilled worker, craftsman

ARTIST *n* person who produces works of art, esp paintings or sculpture

ARTISTE *n* professional entertainer such as a singer or dancer

ARTISTS ▸ artist

ARTLESS *adj* free from deceit or cunning

ARTS ▸ art

ARTSIER ▸ artsy

ARTSIES ▸ artsy

ARTSMAN *old word for* **> craftsman**

ARTSMEN ▸ artsman

ARTSY *adj* interested in the arts ▷ *n* person interested in the arts

ARTWORK *n* all the photographs and illustrations in a publication

ARTY *adj* having an affected interest in art ▷ *n* person interested in art

ARUGOLA *n* salad plant

ARUGULA *another name for* **▸ rocket**

ARUHE *n* edible root of a fern

ARUHES ▸ aruhe

ARUM *n* type of plant with arrow-shaped leaves and a typically white spathe

ARUMS ▸ arum

ARUSPEX *variant spelling of* **> haruspex**

ARVAL *adj* of ploughed land

ARVO *n* afternoon

ARVOS ▸ arvo

ARY *dialect form of* **▸ any**

ARYL *n* of, consisting of, or containing an aromatic group

ARYLS ▸ aryl

AS *adv* used to indicate amount or extent in comparisons ▷ *n* ancient Roman unit of weight

ASANA *n* any of various postures in yoga

ASANAS ▸ asana

ASAR ▸ as

ASARUM *n* dried strong-scented root of the wild ginger plant: a flavouring agent and source of an aromatic oil used in perfumery, formerly used in medicine

ASARUMS ▸ asarum

ASCARED *adj* afraid

ASCARID *n* type of parasitic nematode worm, such as the common roundworm

ASCARIS ▸ ascarid

ASCAUNT *adv* old word meaning slantwise

ASCEND *vb* go or move up

ASCENDS ▸ ascend

ASCENT *n* ascending

ASCENTS ▸ ascent

ASCESES ▸ ascesis

ASCESIS *n* exercise of self-discipline

ASCETIC *adj* (person) abstaining from worldly pleasures and comforts ▷ *n* person who abstains from worldly comforts and pleasures

ASCI ▸ ascus

ASCIAN *n* person living in the tropics

ASCIANS ▸ ascian

ASCIDIA > ascidium

ASCITES *n* accumulation of serous fluid in the peritoneal cavity

ASCITIC ▸ ascites

ASCONCE *adv* old form of askance

ASCOT *n* cravat with wide square ends, usually secured with an ornamental stud

ASCOTS ▸ ascot

ASCRIBE *vb* attribute, as to a particular origin

ASCUS *n* saclike structure that produces (usually) eight ascospores during sexual reproduction in ascomycetous fungi such as yeasts and mildews

ASDIC *an early form of* **▸ sonar**

ASDICS ▸ asdic

ASEA *adv* towards the sea

ASEITY *n* existence derived from itself, having no other source

ASEPSES ▸ asepsis

ASEPSIS *n* aseptic condition

ASEPTIC *adj* free from harmful bacteria ▷ *n* aseptic substance

ASEXUAL *adj* without sex

ASH *n* powdery substance left when something is burnt ▷ *vb* reduce to ashes

ASHAKE *adv* shaking

ASHAME *vb* make ashamed

ASHAMED *adj* feeling shame

ASHAMES ▸ ashame

ASHCAKE *n* cornmeal bread

ASHCAN *n* large metal dustbin

ASHCANS ▸ ashcan

ASHED ▸ ash

ASHEN *adj* pale with shock

ASHERY *n* place where ashes are made

ASHES ▸ ash

ASHET *n* shallow oval dish or large plate

ASHETS ▸ ashet

ASHFALL *n* dropping of ash from a volcano

ASHIER ▸ ashy

ASHIEST ▸ ashy

ASHINE *adv* old word meaning shining

ASHING ▸ ash

ASHIVER *adv* shivering

ASHKEY *n* winged fruit of the ash

ASHKEYS ▸ ashkey

ASHLAR *n* square block of hewn stone used in building ▷ *vb* build with ashlars

ASHLARS ▸ ashlar

ASHLER *same as* **▸ ashlar**

ASHLERS ▸ ashler

ASHLESS ▸ ash

ASHMAN *n* man who shovels ashes

ASHMEN ▸ ashman

ASHORE *adv* towards or on land ▷ *adj* on land, having come from the water

ASHRAF ▸ sherif

ASHRAM *n* religious retreat where a Hindu holy man lives

ASHRAMA *n* stage in Hindu spiritual life

ASHRAMS ▸ ashram

ASHTRAY *n* receptacle for tobacco ash and cigarette butts

ASHY *adj* pale greyish

ASIAGO *n* either of two

varieties (ripened or fresh) of a cow's-milk cheese produced in NE Italy

ASIAGOS ▸ **asiago**

ASIDE *adv* one side ▷ *n* remark not meant to be heard by everyone present

ASIDES ▸ **aside**

ASINICO *n* old Spanish word for fool

ASININE *adj* stupid, idiotic

ASK *vb* say or write (something) in a form that requires an answer

ASKANCE *adv* with an oblique glance ▷ *vb* turn aside

ASKANT *same as* ▸ **askance**

ASKANTS ▸ **askant**

ASKARI *n* (in East Africa) a soldier or policeman

ASKARIS ▸ **askari**

ASKED ▸ **ask**

ASKER ▸ **ask**

ASKERS ▸ **ask**

ASKESES ▸ **askesis**

ASKESIS *n* practice of self-discipline

ASKEW *adj* one side, crooked

ASKING ▸ **ask**

ASKINGS ▸ **ask**

ASKLENT *Scots word for* ▸ **aslant**

ASKOI ▸ **askos**

ASKOS *n* ancient Greek vase

ASKS ▸ **ask**

ASLAKE *vb* slake

ASLAKED ▸ **aslake**

ASLAKES ▸ **aslake**

ASLANT *adv* at a slant (to), slanting (across)

ASLEEP *adj* sleeping

ASLOPE *adj* sloping

ASLOSH *adj* awash

ASMEAR *adj* smeared

ASOCIAL *n* person who avoids social contact

ASP *n* small poisonous snake

ASPECT *n* feature or element ▷ *vb* look at

ASPECTS ▸ **aspect**

ASPEN *n* kind of poplar tree ▷ *adj* trembling

ASPENS ▸ **aspen**

ASPER *n* former Turkish monetary unit, a silver coin, worth 1/120 of a piastre

ASPERGE *vb* sprinkle

ASPERS ▸ **asper**

ASPERSE *vb* spread false rumours about

ASPHALT *n* black hard tarlike substance used for road surfaces etc ▷ *vb* cover with asphalt

ASPHYXY *n* > **asphyxia**

ASPIC *n* savoury jelly used to coat meat, eggs, fish, etc

ASPICK *old word for* ▸ **asp**

ASPICKS ▸ **aspick**

ASPICS ▸ **aspic**

ASPIDIA > **aspidium**

ASPINE *old word for* ▸ **aspen**

ASPINES ▸ **aspine**

ASPIRE *vb* yearn (for), hope (to do or be)

ASPIRED ▸ **aspire**

ASPIRER ▸ **aspire**

ASPIRES ▸ **aspire**

ASPIRIN *n* drug used to relieve pain and fever

ASPIS *n* horned viper

ASPISES ▸ **aspis**

ASPISH *adj* like an asp

ASPORT *vb* old word meaning take away

ASPORTS ▸ **asport**

ASPOUT *adv* spouting

ASPRAWL *adv* sprawling

ASPREAD *adv* spreading

ASPRO *n* associate professor at an academic institution

ASPROS ▸ **aspro**

ASPROUT *adv* sprouting

ASPS ▸ **asp**

ASQUAT *adv* squatting

ASQUINT *adj* with a glance from the corner of the eye, esp a furtive one

ASRAMA *n* stage in Hindu spiritual life

ASRAMAS ▸ **asrama**

ASS *n* donkey

ASSAGAI *same as* ▸ **assegai**

ASSAI *adv* (usually preceded by a musical direction) very ▷ *n* Brazilian palm tree with small dark purple fleshy edible fruit

ASSAIL *vb* attack violently

ASSAILS ▸ **assail**

ASSAIS ▸ **assai**

ASSAM *n* (in Malaysia) tamarind as used in cooking

ASSAMS ▸ **assam**

ASSART *vb* clear ground for cultivation

ASSARTS ▸ **assart**

ASSAULT *n* violent attack ▷ *vb* attack violently

ASSAY *n* analysis of a substance, esp a metal, to ascertain its purity ▷ *vb*

make such an analysis

ASSAYED ▸ **assay**

ASSAYER ▸ **assay**

ASSAYS ▸ **assay**

ASSEGAI *n* slender spear used in S Africa ▷ *vb* spear with an assegai

ASSENT *n* agreement or consent ▷ *vb* agree or consent

ASSENTS ▸ **assent**

ASSERT *vb* declare forcefully

ASSERTS ▸ **assert**

ASSES ▸ **ass**

ASSESS *vb* judge the worth or importance of

ASSET *n* valuable or useful person or thing

ASSETS ▸ **asset**

ASSEVER *vb* old form of asseverate

ASSEZ *adv* (as part of a musical direction) fairly

ASSIEGE *vb* old form of besiege

ASSIGN *vb* appoint (someone) to a job or task ▷ *n* person to whom property is assigned

ASSIGNS ▸ **assign**

ASSIST *vb* give help or support ▷ *n* pass by a player which enables another player to score a goal

ASSISTS ▸ **assist**

ASSIZE *n* sitting of a legislative assembly or administrative body

ASSIZED ▸ **assize**

ASSIZER *n* weights and measures official

ASSIZES ▸ **assize**

ASSLIKE ▸ **ass**

ASSOIL *vb* absolve

ASSOILS ▸ **assoil**

ASSORT *vb* arrange or distribute into groups of the same type

ASSORTS ▸ **assort**

ASSOT *vb* old word meaning make infatuated

ASSOTS ▸ **assot**

ASSOTT *vb* besot

ASSUAGE *vb* relieve (pain, grief, thirst, etc)

ASSUME *vb* take to be true without proof

ASSUMED *adj* false

ASSUMER ▸ **assume**

ASSUMES ▸ **assume**

ASSURE *vb* promise or guarantee

ASSURED adj confident ▷ n beneficiary under a life assurance policy
ASSURER ▸ assure
ASSURES ▸ assure
ASSUROR ▸ assure
ASSWAGE old spelling of ▸ assuage
ASTABLE adj not stable
ASTARE adv staring
ASTART old word for ▸ start
ASTARTS ▸ astart
ASTASIA n inability to stand
ASTATIC adj not static
ASTATKI n fuel derived from petroleum
ASTEISM n use of irony
ASTELIC ▸ astely
ASTELY n lack of central cylinder in plants
ASTER n plant with daisy-like flowers
ASTERIA n gemstone with starlike light effect
ASTERID n variety of flowering plant
ASTERN adv at or towards the stern of a ship ▷ adj at or towards the stern of a ship
ASTERS ▸ aster
ASTERT vb start
ASTERTS ▸ astert
ASTHENY same as ▸ asthenia
ASTHMA n illness causing difficulty in breathing
ASTHMAS ▸ asthma
ASTHORE n Irish endearment
ASTILBE n E Asian and N American plant cultivated for its ornamental spikes of pink or white flowers
ASTIR adj out of bed
ASTONE vb old form of ▸ astonish
ASTONED ▸ astone
ASTONES ▸ astone
ASTONY vb old form of ▸ astonish
ASTOOP adv stooping
ASTOUND vb overwhelm with amazement
ASTRAL adj of stars ▷ n oil lamp
ASTRALS ▸ astral
ASTRAND adv on shore
ASTRAY adv off the right path
ASTRICT vb bind, confine, or constrict

ASTRIDE adv with a leg on either side (of) ▷ adj with a leg on either side
ASTROID n hypocycloid having four cusps
ASTRUT adv old word meaning in a protruding way
ASTUN vb old form of astonish
ASTUNS ▸ astun
ASTUTE adj perceptive or shrewd
ASTUTER ▸ astute
ASTYLAR adj without columns or pilasters
ASUDDEN adv old form of suddenly
ASUNDER adv into parts or pieces ▷ adj into parts or pieces
ASWARM adj filled, esp with moving things
ASWAY adv swaying
ASWIM adv floating
ASWING adv swinging
ASWIRL adv swirling
ASWOON adv swooning
ASYLA ▸ asylum
ASYLEE n person who is granted asylum
ASYLEES ▸ asylee
ASYLUM n refuge or sanctuary
ASYLUMS ▸ asylum
AT n Laotian monetary unit worth one hundredth of a kip
ATAATA n grazing marine gastropod
ATAATAS ▸ ataata
ATABAL n N African drum
ATABALS ▸ atabal
ATABEG n Turkish ruler
ATABEGS ▸ atabeg
ATABEK n Turkish ruler
ATABEKS ▸ atabek
ATABRIN n drug formerly used for treating malaria
ATACTIC adj (of a polymer) having a random sequence of the stereochemical arrangement of groups on carbon atoms in the chain
ATAGHAN same as ▸ yataghan
ATALAYA n watchtower in Spain
ATAMAN n elected leader of the Cossacks
ATAMANS ▸ ataman
ATAP n palm tree of S Asia
ATAPS ▸ atap

ATARAXY same as ▸ ataraxia
ATAVIC ▸ atavism
ATAVISM n recurrence of a trait present in distant ancestors
ATAVIST ▸ atavism
ATAXIA n lack of muscular coordination
ATAXIAS ▸ ataxia
ATAXIC ▸ ataxia
ATAXICS ▸ ataxia
ATAXIES ▸ ataxy
ATAXY same as ▸ ataxia
ATE past tense of ▸ eat
ATEBRIN n drug formerly used to treat malaria
ATELIC adj of action without end
ATELIER n workshop, artist's studio
ATEMOYA n tropical fruit tree
ATES n shop selling confectionery
ATHAME n (in Wicca) witch's ceremonial knife, usually with a black handle, used in rituals rather than for cutting or carving
ATHAMES ▸ athame
ATHANOR n alchemist's furnace
ATHEISE vb speak atheistically
ATHEISM n belief that there is no God
ATHEIST ▸ atheism
ATHEIZE vb speak atheistically
ATHEOUS adj without a belief in god
ATHIRST adj having an eager desire
ATHLETA n old form of ▸ athlete
ATHLETE n person trained in or good at athletics
ATHODYD another name for ▸ ramjet
ATHRILL adv feeling thrills
ATHROB adv throbbing
ATHWART adv transversely
ATIGI n type of parka worn by the Inuit in Canada
ATIGIS ▸ atigi
ATILT adj in a tilted or inclined position
ATIMIES ▸ atimy
ATIMY n loss of honour
ATINGLE adv tingling
ATISHOO n sound of a sneeze

ATLAS n book of maps
ATLASES ▸ **atlas**
ATLATL n Native American throwing stick
ATLATLS ▸ **atlatl**
ATMA same as ▸ **atman**
ATMAN n personal soul or self
ATMANS ▸ **atman**
ATMAS ▸ **atma**
ATOC n skunk
ATOCIA n inability to have children
ATOCIAS ▸ **atocia**
ATOCS ▸ **atoc**
ATOK n skunk
ATOKAL adj having no children
ATOKE n part of a worm
ATOKES ▸ **atoke**
ATOKOUS adj having no children
ATOKS ▸ **atok**
ATOLL n ring-shaped coral reef enclosing a lagoon
ATOLLS ▸ **atoll**
ATOM n smallest unit of matter which can take part in a chemical reaction
ATOMIC adj of or using atomic bombs or atomic energy
ATOMICS n science of atoms
ATOMIES ▸ **atomy**
ATOMISE same as ▸ **atomize**
ATOMISM n ancient philosophical theory that the ultimate constituents of the universe are atoms
ATOMIST ▸ **atomism**
ATOMIZE vb reduce to atoms or small particles
ATOMS ▸ **atom**
ATOMY n atom or minute particle
ATONAL adj (of music) not written in an established key
ATONE vb make amends (for sin or wrongdoing)
ATONED ▸ **atone**
ATONER ▸ **atone**
ATONERS ▸ **atone**
ATONES ▸ **atone**
ATONIA n lack of normal muscle tone
ATONIAS ▸ **atonia**
ATONIC adj (of a syllable, word, etc) carrying no stress ▷ n unaccented or unstressed syllable, word
ATONICS ▸ **atonic**

ATONIES ▸ **atony**

> The plural of **atony**, this is another of the most frequently played 7-letter bonus words that it is essential to know.

ATONING ▸ **atone**
ATONY n lack of normal tone or tension, as in muscles
ATOP adv on top
ATOPIC adj of or relating to hereditary hypersensitivity to certain allergens
ATOPIES ▸ **atopy**
ATOPY n hereditary tendency to be hypersensitive to certain allergens
ATRESIA n absence of or unnatural narrowing of a body channel
ATRESIC ▸ **atresia**
ATRETIC ▸ **atresia**
ATRIA ▸ **atrium**
ATRIAL ▸ **atrium**
ATRIP adj (of an anchor) no longer caught on the bottom
ATRIUM n upper chamber of either half of the heart
ATRIUMS ▸ **atrium**
ATROPHY n wasting away of an organ or part ▷ vb (cause to) waste away
ATROPIA n atropine
ATROPIN same as > **atropine**
ATS ▸ **at**
ATT n old Siamese coin
ATTABOY sentence substitute expression of approval or exhortation
ATTACH vb join, fasten, or connect
ATTACHE n a specialist attached to a diplomatic mission
ATTACK vb launch a physical assault (against) ▷ n act of attacking
ATTACKS ▸ **attack**
ATTAIN vb achieve or accomplish (a task or aim)
ATTAINS ▸ **attain**
ATTAINT vb pass judgment of death or outlawry upon (a person) ▷ n dishonour
ATTAP n palm tree of South Asia
ATTAPS ▸ **attap**
ATTAR n fragrant oil made from roses

ATTARS ▸ **attar**
ATTASK old word for > **criticize**
ATTASKS ▸ **attask**
ATTASKT ▸ **attask**
ATTEMPT vb try, make an effort ▷ n effort or endeavour
ATTEND vb be present at
ATTENDS ▸ **attend**
ATTENT old word for > **attention**
ATTENTS ▸ **attent**
ATTEST vb affirm the truth of, be proof of
ATTESTS ▸ **attest**
ATTIC n space or room within the roof of a house
ATTICS ▸ **attic**
ATTIRE n fine or formal clothes ▷ vb dress, esp in fine elegant clothes
ATTIRED ▸ **attire**
ATTIRES ▸ **attire**
ATTONCE adv old word for at once
ATTONE vb old word meaning appease
ATTONED ▸ **attone**
ATTONES ▸ **attone**
ATTORN vb acknowledge a new owner of land as one's landlord
ATTORNS ▸ **attorn**
ATTRACT vb arouse the interest or admiration of
ATTRAP vb adorn
ATTRAPS ▸ **attrap**
ATTRIST vb old word meaning to sadden
ATTRIT vb wear down or dispose of gradually
ATTRITE vb wear down
ATTRITS ▸ **attrit**
ATTUENT adj carrying out attuition
ATTUITE vb perceive by attuition
ATTUNE vb adjust or accustom (a person or thing)
ATTUNED ▸ **attune**
ATTUNES ▸ **attune**
ATUA n spirit or demon
ATUAS ▸ **atua**
ATWAIN adv old word meaning into two parts
ATWEEL Scots word for ▸ **well**
ATWEEN an archaic or Scots word for ▸ **between**
ATWIXT old word for ▸ **between**
ATYPIC adj not typical

A

AUA n yellow-eye mullet
This Maori word for a kind of mullet is very often played to balance a rack by getting rid of a surplus of vowels.

AUAS ▸ aua

AUBADE n song or poem appropriate to or greeting the dawn

AUBADES ▸ aubade

AUBERGE n inn or tavern

AUBURN adj (of hair) reddish-brown ▷ n moderate reddish-brown colour

AUBURNS ▸ auburn

AUCEPS n old word meaning person who catches hawks

AUCTION n public sale in which articles are sold to the highest bidder ▷ vb sell by auction

AUCUBA n Japanese laurel

AUCUBAS ▸ aucuba

AUDAD n wild African sheep

AUDADS ▸ audad

AUDIAL adj of sound

AUDIBLE adj loud enough to be heard ▷ n change of playing tactics called by the quarterback when the offence is lined up at the line of scrimmage ▷ vb call an audible

AUDIBLY ▸ audible

AUDIENT n person who hears

AUDILE n person who possesses a faculty for auditory imagery that is more distinct than his visual or other imagery ▷ adj of or relating to such a person

AUDILES ▸ audile

AUDING n practice of listening to try to understand

AUDINGS ▸ auding

AUDIO adj of sound or hearing ▷ n of or relating to sound or hearing

AUDIOS ▸ audio

AUDIT n official examination of business accounts ▷ vb examine (business accounts) officially

AUDITED ▸ audit

AUDITEE n one who is audited

AUDITOR n person qualified to audit accounts

AUDITS ▸ audit

AUE interj Maori exclamation
This is another of those Maori words, an exclamation of pain or distress, so useful for getting rid of surplus vowels. But remember that unlike **aua** it does not take an S.

AUF old word for ▸ oaf

AUFGABE n word used in psychology to mean task

AUFS ▸ auf

AUGEND n number to which another number, the addend, is added

AUGENDS ▸ augend

AUGER n tool for boring holes

AUGERS ▸ auger

AUGHT adv in any least part ▷ n less common word for nought (zero)

AUGHTS ▸ aught

AUGITE n black or greenish-black mineral

AUGITES ▸ augite

AUGITIC ▸ augite

AUGMENT vb increase or enlarge ▷ n (in Greek and Sanskrit grammar) a vowel or diphthong prefixed to a verb to form a past tense

AUGUR vb be a sign of (future events) ▷ n (in ancient Rome) a religious official who observed and interpreted omens and signs to help guide the making of public decisions

AUGURAL ▸ augur

AUGURED ▸ augur

AUGURER old word for ▸ augur

AUGURS ▸ augur

AUGURY n foretelling of the future

AUGUST adj dignified and imposing ▷ n auguste

AUGUSTE n type of circus clown who usually wears battered ordinary clothes and is habitually maladroit or unlucky

AUGUSTS ▸ august

AUK n northern sea bird with short wings and black-and-white plumage

AUKLET n type of small auk

AUKLETS ▸ auklet

AUKS ▸ auk

AULA n hall

AULAS ▸ aula

AULD a Scots word for ▸ old

AULDER ▸ auld

AULDEST ▸ auld

AULIC adj relating to a royal court

AULNAGE n measurement in ells

AULOI ▸ aulos

AULOS n ancient Greek pipes

AUMAIL old word for ▸ enamel

AUMAILS ▸ aumail

AUMBRY same as ▸ ambry

AUMIL n manager in India

AUMILS ▸ aumil

AUNE n old French measure of length

AUNES ▸ aune

AUNT n father's or mother's sister

AUNTER old word for > adventure

AUNTERS ▸ aunter

AUNTIE n aunt

AUNTIES ▸ aunty

AUNTLY adj of or like an aunt

AUNTS ▸ aunt

AUNTY same as ▸ auntie

AURA n distinctive air or quality of a person or thing

AURAE ▸ aura

AURAL adj of or using the ears or hearing

AURALLY ▸ aural

AURAR plural of ▸ eyrir

AURAS ▸ aura

AURATE n salt of auric acid

AURATED adj combined with auric acid

AURATES ▸ aurate

AUREATE adj covered with gold, gilded

AUREI ▸ aureus

AUREITY n attributes of gold

AURELIA n large jellyfish

AUREOLA same as ▸ aureole

AUREOLE n halo

AURES ▸ auris

AUREUS n gold coin of the Roman Empire

AURIC adj of or containing gold in the trivalent state

AURICLE n upper chamber of the heart

AURIFY vb turn into gold

AURIS n medical word for ear

AURIST a former name for > **audiology**

AURISTS ▸ aurist

AUROCHS n recently extinct European wild ox

AURORA n bands of light sometimes seen in the sky in polar regions

AURORAE ▸ aurora

AURORAL ▸ aurora

AURORAS ▸ aurora

AUROUS adj of or containing gold, esp in the monovalent state

AURUM n gold

AURUMS ▸ aurum

AUSFORM vb temper steel

AUSPEX same as ▸ **augur**

AUSPICE n patronage or guidance

AUSTERE adj stern or severe

AUSTRAL adj southern ▷ n former monetary unit of Argentina equal to 100 centavos, replaced by the peso

AUSUBO n tropical tree

AUSUBOS ▸ ausubo

AUTARCH n absolute ruler

AUTARKY n policy of economic self-sufficiency

AUTEUR n director whose creative influence on a film is so great as to be considered its author

AUTEURS ▸ auteur

AUTHOR n writer of a book etc ▷ vb write or originate

AUTHORS ▸ author

AUTISM n disorder characterized by lack of response to people and limited ability to communicate

AUTISMS ▸ autism

AUTIST n autistic person

AUTISTS ▸ autist

AUTO n automobile ▷ vb travel in an automobile

AUTOBUS n motor bus

AUTOCAR n motor car

AUTOCUE n electronic television prompting device

AUTOED ▸ auto

AUTOING ▸ auto

AUTOMAN n car manufacturer

AUTOMAT n vending machine

AUTOMEN ▸ automan

AUTONYM n writing published under the real name of an author

AUTOPEN n mechanical device used to produce imitation signatures

AUTOPSY n examination of a corpse to determine the cause of death

AUTOPUT n motorway in the former Yugoslavia

AUTOS ▸ auto

AUTOVAC n vacuum pump in a car petrol tank

AUTUMN n season between summer and winter

AUTUMNS ▸ autumn

AUTUMNY adj like autumn

AUXESES ▸ auxesis

AUXESIS n growth in animal or plant tissues resulting from an increase in cell size without cell division

AUXETIC n something that promotes growth

AUXIN n any of various plant hormones, such as indoleacetic acid, that promote growth and control fruit and flower development. Synthetic auxins are widely used in agriculture and horticulture

AUXINIC ▸ auxin

AUXINS ▸ auxin

AVA adv at all ▷ n Polynesian shrub

AVAIL vb be of use or advantage (to) ▷ n use or advantage

AVAILE old word for ▸ **lower**

AVAILED ▸ avail

AVAILES ▸ availe

AVAILS ▸ avail

AVAL adj of a grandparent

AVALE old word for ▸ **lower**

AVALED ▸ avale

AVALES ▸ avale

AVALING ▸ avale

AVANT prep before

AVANTI interj forward!

AVARICE n greed for wealth

AVAS ▸ ava

AVAST sentence substitute stop! cease!

AVATAR n appearance of a god in animal or human form

AVATARS ▸ avatar

AVAUNT sentence substitute go away! depart! ▷ vb go away; depart

AVAUNTS ▸ avaunt

AVE n expression of welcome or farewell

AVEL same as ▸ **ovel**

AVELLAN adj of hazelnuts

AVELS ▸ avel

AVENGE vb take revenge in retaliation for (harm done) or on behalf of (a person harmed)

AVENGED ▸ avenge

AVENGER ▸ avenge

AVENGES ▸ avenge

AVENIR n future

AVENIRS ▸ avenir

AVENS n any of several temperate or arctic rosaceous plants

AVENSES ▸ avens

AVENTRE old word for ▸ **thrust**

AVENUE n wide street

AVENUES ▸ avenue

AVER vb state to be true

AVERAGE n typical or normal amount or quality ▷ adj usual or typical ▷ vb calculate the average of

AVERRED ▸ aver

AVERS ▸ aver

AVERSE adj disinclined or unwilling

AVERT vb turn away

AVERTED ▸ avert

AVERTER ▸ avert

AVERTS ▸ avert

AVES ▸ ave

AVGAS n aviation fuel

AVGASES ▸ avgas

AVIAN adj of or like a bird ▷ n bird

AVIANS ▸ avian

AVIARY n large cage or enclosure for birds

AVIATE vb pilot or fly in an aircraft

AVIATED ▸ aviate

AVIATES ▸ aviate

AVIATIC adj pertaining to aviation

AVIATOR n pilot of an aircraft

AVID adj keen or enthusiastic

AVIDER ▸ avid

AVIDEST ▸ avid

AVIDIN n protein, found in egg-white, that combines with biotin to form a stable compound that cannot be absorbed, leading to a biotin deficiency in the consumer

AVIDINS ▸ avidin
AVIDITY n quality or state of being avid
AVIDLY ▸ avid
AVIETTE n aeroplane driven by human strength
AVIFORM adj like a bird
AVINE adj of birds
AVION n aeroplane
AVIONIC > avionics
AVIONS ▸ avion
AVISE old word for ▸ advise
AVISED ▸ avise
AVISES ▸ avise
AVISING ▸ avise
AVISO n boat carrying messages
AVISOS ▸ aviso
AVITAL adj of a grandfather
AVIZE old word for ▸ advise
AVIZED ▸ avize
AVIZES ▸ avize
AVIZING ▸ avize
AVO n Macao currency unit
AVOCADO n pear-shaped tropical fruit with a leathery green skin and yellowish-green flesh
AVOCET n long-legged wading bird with a long slender upward-curving bill
AVOCETS ▸ avocet
AVODIRE n African tree
AVOID vb prevent from happening
AVOIDED ▸ avoid
AVOIDER ▸ avoid
AVOIDS ▸ avoid
AVOS ▸ avo
AVOSET n avocet
AVOSETS ▸ avoset
AVOUCH vb vouch for
AVOURE old word for ▸ avowal
AVOURES ▸ avoure
AVOUTRY old word for > adultery
AVOW vb state or affirm
AVOWAL ▸ avow
AVOWALS ▸ avow
AVOWED ▸ avow
AVOWER ▸ avow
AVOWERS ▸ avow
AVOWING ▸ avow
AVOWRY old word for ▸ avowal
AVOWS ▸ avow
AVOYER n former Swiss magistrate
AVOYERS ▸ avoyer
AVRUGA n herring roe with a smoky flavour, sometimes used as a less expensive

alternative to caviar
AVRUGAS ▸ avruga
AVULSE vb take away by force
AVULSED ▸ avulse
AVULSES ▸ avulse
AVYZE old word for ▸ advise
AVYZED ▸ avyze
AVYZES ▸ avyze
AVYZING ▸ avyze
AW same as ▸ all
AWA adv away
AWAIT vb wait for
AWAITED ▸ await
AWAITER ▸ await
AWAITS ▸ await
AWAKE vb emerge or rouse from sleep ▷ adj not sleeping
AWAKED ▸ awake
AWAKEN vb awake
AWAKENS ▸ awaken
AWAKES ▸ awake
AWAKING ▸ awake
AWARD vb give (something, such as a prize) formally ▷ n something awarded, such as a prize
AWARDED ▸ award
AWARDEE ▸ award
AWARDER ▸ award
AWARDS ▸ award
AWARE adj having knowledge, informed
AWARER ▸ aware
AWAREST ▸ aware
AWARN vb old form of warn
AWARNED ▸ awarn
AWARNS ▸ awarn
AWASH adv washed over by water ▷ adj washed over by water
AWATCH adv watching
AWATO n New Zealand caterpillar
AWATOS ▸ awato
AWAVE adv in waves
AWAY adv from a place ▷ adj not present ▷ n game played or won at an opponent's ground
AWAYDAY n day trip taken for pleasure
AWAYES old word for ▸ away
AWAYS ▸ away
AWDL n traditional Welsh poem
AWDLS ▸ awdl
AWE n wonder and respect mixed with dread ▷ vb fill with awe
AWEARY old form of ▸ weary
AWED ▸ awe

AWEE adv for a short time
AWEEL interj Scots word meaning well
AWEIGH adj (of an anchor) no longer hooked onto the bottom
AWEING ▸ awe
AWELESS ▸ awe
AWES ▸ awe
AWESOME adj inspiring awe
AWETO n New Zealand caterpillar
AWETOS ▸ aweto
AWFUL adj very bad or unpleasant ▷ adv very
AWFULLY adv in an unpleasant way
AWFY adv (Scots) awfully, extremely
AWHAPE old word for ▸ amaze
AWHAPED ▸ awhape
AWHAPES ▸ awhape
AWHATO n New Zealand caterpillar
AWHATOS ▸ awhato
AWHEEL adv on wheels
AWHEELS same as ▸ awheel
AWHETO n New Zealand caterpillar
AWHETOS ▸ awheto
AWHILE adv for a brief time
AWHIRL adv whirling
AWING ▸ awe
AWK n type of computer programming language

This computer language provides a useful high-scoring outlet for what can be the awkward letters W and K.

AWKS ▸ awk
AWKWARD adj clumsy or ungainly
AWL n pointed tool for piercing wood, leather, etc
AWLBIRD n woodpecker
AWLESS ▸ awe
AWLS ▸ awl
AWLWORT n type of small stemless aquatic plant of the N hemisphere, with slender sharp-pointed leaves and minute white flowers
AWMOUS Scots word for ▸ alms
AWMRIE n cupboard for church vessels
AWMRIES ▸ awmrie
AWMRY n cupboard for

church vessels

AWN n any of the bristles growing from the flowering parts of certain grasses and cereals

AWNED ▸ awn

AWNER n machine for removing awns

AWNERS ▸ awner

AWNIER ▸ awny

AWNIEST ▸ awny

AWNING n canvas roof supported by a frame to give protection against the weather

AWNINGS ▸ awning

AWNLESS ▸ awn

AWNS ▸ awn

AWNY adj having awns

AWOKE past tense of ▸ awake

AWOKEN ▸ awake

AWOL n person who is absent without leave

AWOLS ▸ awol

AWORK adv old word meaning at work

AWRACK adv in wrecked condition

AWRONG adv old word meaning wrongly

AWRY adj with a twist to one side, askew

AWSOME adj old form of awesome

AX same as ▸ axe

AXAL adj of an axis

AXE n tool with a sharp blade for felling trees or chopping wood ▷ vb dismiss (employees), restrict (expenditure), or terminate (a project)

AXEBIRD n nightjar of northern Queensland and New Guinea with a cry that sounds like a chopping axe

AXED ▸ axe

AXEL n jump in which the skater takes off from the forward outside edge of one skate, makes one and a half, two and a half, or three and a half turns in the air, and lands on the backward outside edge of the other skate

AXELS ▸ axel

AXEMAN n man who wields an axe, esp to cut down trees

AXEMEN ▸ axeman

AXENIC adj (of a biological culture or culture medium)

free from other microorganisms

AXES ▸ axis

AXIAL adj forming or of an axis

AXIALLY ▸ axial

AXIL n angle where the stalk of a leaf joins a stem

AXILE adj of, relating to, or attached to the axis

AXILLA n area on the undersurface of a bird's wing corresponding to the armpit

AXILLAE ▸ axilla

AXILLAR same as > axillary

AXILLAS ▸ axilla

AXILS ▸ axil

AXING ▸ axe

AXINITE n crystalline substance

AXIOM n generally accepted principle

AXIOMS ▸ axiom

AXION n type of hypothetical elementary particle

AXIONS ▸ axion

AXIS n (imaginary) line round which a body can rotate or about which an object or geometrical figure is symmetrical

AXISED adj having an axis

AXISES ▸ axis

AXITE n type of gunpowder

AXITES ▸ axite

AXLE n shaft on which a wheel or pair of wheels turns

AXLED adj having an axle

AXLES ▸ axle

AXLIKE ▸ ax

AXMAN same as ▸ axeman

AXMEN ▸ axman

AXOID n type of curve

AXOIDS ▸ axoid

AXOLOTL n aquatic salamander of central America

AXON n long threadlike extension of a nerve cell that conducts nerve impulses from the cell body

AXONAL ▸ axon

AXONE same as ▸ axon

AXONEME n part of cell consisting of proteins

AXONES ▸ axone

AXONIC ▸ axon

AXONS ▸ axon

AXSEED n crown vetch

AXSEEDS ▸ axseed

AY adv ever ▷ n expression of agreement

AYAH n (in parts of the former British Empire) a native maidservant or nursemaid

AYAHS ▸ ayah

AYE n affirmative vote or voter ▷ adv always

AYELP adv yelping

AYES ▸ aye

AYGRE old word for ▸ eager

AYIN n 16th letter in the Hebrew alphabet

AYINS ▸ ayin

AYONT adv beyond

AYRE old word for ▸ air

AYRES ▸ ayre

AYRIE old word for ▸ eyrie

AYRIES ▸ ayrie

AYS ▸ ay

AYU n small Japanese fish

This small Japanese fish comes up more times than you might think, being an extension of both **ay** and **yu**, which illustrates how important it is to know those little 'hook' words.

AYUS ▸ ayu

AYWORD n old word meaning byword

AYWORDS ▸ ayword

AZALEA n garden shrub grown for its showy flowers

AZALEAS ▸ azalea

AZAN n call to prayer five times a day, usually by a muezzin from a minaret

AZANS ▸ azan

AZERTY n common European version of typewriter keyboard layout with the characters a, z, e, r, t, and y positioned on the top row of alphabetic characters at the left side of the keyboard

AZIDE n type of chemical compound

AZIDES ▸ azide

AZIDO adj containing an azide

AZIMUTH n arc of the sky between the zenith and the horizon

AZINE n any organic compound having a six-membered ring containing at least one nitrogen atom

AZINES ▸ azine

A

AZIONE n musical drama
AZIONES ▸ azione
AZLON n fibre made from protein
AZLONS ▸ azlon
AZO adj of, consisting of, or containing the divalent group -N:N-

> **Azo** is a chemical term that you will want to play very often, but remember that it does not take an S. It does however take an N to form **azon**.

AZOIC adj without life
AZOLE n organic five-membered ring compound containing one or more atoms in the ring, the number usually being specified by a prefix
AZOLES ▸ azole
AZOLLA n tropical water fern
AZOLLAS ▸ azolla
AZON n type of drawing paper

AZONAL adj not divided into zones
AZONIC adj not confined to a zone
AZONS ▸ azon
AZOTE an obsolete name for > **nitrogen**
AZOTED ▸ azote
AZOTES ▸ azote
AZOTH n panacea postulated by Paracelsus
AZOTHS ▸ azoth
AZOTIC adj of, containing, or concerned with nitrogen
AZOTISE same as ▸ **azotize**
AZOTIZE vb combine or treat with nitrogen or a nitrogen compound
AZOTOUS adj containing nitrogen
AZUKI same as ▸ **adzuki**
AZUKIS ▸ azuki
AZULEJO n Spanish porcelain tile

> An **azulejo** is a kind of brightly coloured tile, beautiful in its combination of the J and Z.

AZURE n (of) the colour of a clear blue sky ▷ adj deep blue
AZUREAN adj azure
AZURES ▸ azure
AZURINE n blue dye
AZURITE n azure-blue mineral associated with copper deposits
AZURN old word for ▸ **azure**
AZURY adj bluish
AZYGIES ▸ azygy
AZYGOS n biological structure not in a pair
AZYGOUS adj developing or occurring singly
AZYGY n state of not being joined in a pair
AZYM n unleavened bread
AZYME n unleavened bread
AZYMES ▸ azyme
AZYMITE n member of a church using unleavened bread in the Eucharist
AZYMOUS adj unleavened
AZYMS ▸ azym

Bb

B forms a two-letter word before every vowel except **U** - and with **Y** as well. With a **B** in your rack, you can play lots of short words that will give you relatively high scores. The best of these are **box** (12 points), **bez** (14 points) and **biz** (14 points), but don't forget **bay** (8), **by** (7), **bow** (8), **boy** (8), **buy** (8) and **bye** (8).

BA n symbol for the soul in Ancient Egyptian religion

BAA vb make the characteristic bleating sound of a sheep ▷ n cry made by a sheep

BAAED ▶ baa

BAAING ▶ baa

BAAINGS ▶ baa

BAAL n any false god or idol

BAALIM ▶ baal

BAALISM ▶ baal

BAALS ▶ baal

BAAS South African word for ▶ **boss**

BAASES ▶ baas

BAASKAP n (in South Africa) control by Whites of non-Whites

BABA n small cake of leavened dough, sometimes mixed with currants and usually soaked in rum

BABACO n greenish-yellow egg-shaped fruit

BABACOS ▶ babaco

BABALAS adj drunk

BABAS ▶ baba

BABASSU n Brazilian palm tree with hard edible nuts that yield an oil used to make soap, margarine, etc

BABBITT vb line (a bearing) or face (a surface) with Babbitt metal or a similar soft alloy

BABBLE vb talk excitedly or foolishly ▷ n muddled or foolish speech

BABBLED ▶ babble

BABBLER n person who babbles

BABBLES ▶ babble

BABBLY ▶ babble

BABE n baby

BABEL n confused mixture of noises or voices

BABELS ▶ babel

BABES ▶ babe

BABESIA n parasite causing infection in cattle

BABICHE n thongs or lacings of rawhide

BABIED ▶ baby

BABIER ▶ baby

BABIES ▶ baby

BABIEST ▶ baby

BABKA n cake

BABKAS ▶ babka

BABLAH n type of acacia

BABLAHS ▶ bablah

BABOO same as ▶ **babu**

BABOOL n type of acacia

BABOOLS ▶ babool

BABOON n large monkey with a pointed face and a long tail

BABOONS ▶ baboon

BABOOS ▶ baboo

BABOOSH same as > **babouche**

BABU n title or form of address used in India

BABUCHE same as > **babouche**

BABUDOM ▶ babu

BABUISM ▶ babu

BABUL n N African and Indian tree with small yellow flowers, which is a source of gum arabic, tannin, and hardwood

BABULS ▶ babul

BABUS ▶ babu

BABY n very young child or animal ▷ adj comparatively small of its type ▷ vb treat as a baby

BABYING ▶ baby

BABYISH ▶ baby

BABYSAT ▶ babysit

BABYSIT vb look after a child in its parents' absence

BAC n baccalaureate

BACALAO n dried salt cod

BACCA n berry

BACCAE ▶ bacca

BACCARA same as > **baccarat**

BACCARE same as ▶ **backare**

BACCAS ▶ bacca

BACCATE adj like a berry in form, texture, etc

BACCHIC adj riotously drunk

BACCHII > **bacchius**

BACCIES ▶ baccy

BACCO n tobacco

BACCOES ▶ bacco

BACCOS ▶ bacco

BACCY n tobacco

BACH same as ▶ **batch**

BACHA n Indian English word for young child

BACHAS ▶ bacha

BACHCHA n Indian English word for young child

BACHED ▶ bach

BACHES ▶ bach

BACHING ▶ bach

BACHS ▶ bach

BACILLI > **bacillus**

BACK n rear part of the human body, from the neck to the pelvis ▷ vb (cause to) move backwards ▷ adj situated behind ▷ adv at, to, or towards the rear

BACKARE interj instruction to keep one's distance; back off

BACKBIT > **backbite**

BACKED adj having a back or backing

B

BACKER n person who gives financial support

BACKERS ▸ backer

BACKET n shallow box

BACKETS ▸ backet

BACKFIT vb overhaul nuclear power plant

BACKHOE n digger ▷ vb dig with a backhoe

BACKIE n ride on the back of someone's bicycle

BACKIES ▸ backie

BACKING n support

BACKLIT adj illuminated from behind

BACKLOG n accumulation of things to be dealt with

BACKLOT n area outside a film or television studio used for outdoor filming

BACKOUT n instance of withdrawing (from an agreement, etc)

BACKRA n white person

BACKRAS ▸ backra

BACKS ▸ back

BACKSAW n small handsaw stiffened along its upper edge by a metal section

BACKSET n reversal

BACKSEY n sirloin

BACKUP n support or reinforcement

BACKUPS ▸ backup

BACLAVA same as ▸ baklava

BACON n salted or smoked pig meat

BACONER n pig that weighs between 83 and 101 kg, from which bacon is cut

BACONS ▸ bacon

BACS ▸ bac

BACULA ▸ baculum

BACULUM n bony support in the penis of certain mammals, esp the carnivores

BAD adj not good ▷ n unfortunate or unpleasant events collectively ▷ adv badly

BADDER ▸ bad

BADDEST ▸ bad

BADDIE n bad character in a story, film, etc, esp an opponent of the hero

BADDIES ▸ baddy

BADDISH ▸ bad

BADDY same as ▸ baddie

BADE ▸ bid

BADGE n emblem worn to show membership, rank, etc ▷ vb put a badge on

BADGED ▸ badge

BADGER n nocturnal burrowing mammal of Europe, Asia, and N America with a black and white head ▷ vb pester or harass

BADGERS ▸ badger

BADGES ▸ badge

BADGING ▸ badge

BADIOUS adj chestnut; brownish-red

BADLAND > badlands

BADLY adv poorly

BADMAN n hired gunman, outlaw, or criminal

BADMASH n evil-doer ▷ adj naughty or bad ▷ n hooligan

BADMEN ▸ badman

BADNESS ▸ bad

BADS ▸ bad

BADWARE n software designed to harm a computer system

BAEL n type of spiny Indian tree

BAELS ▸ bael

BAETYL n magical meteoric stone

BAETYLS ▸ baetyl

BAFF vb strike ground with golf club

BAFFED ▸ baff

BAFFIES pl n slippers

BAFFING ▸ baff

BAFFLE vb perplex or puzzle ▷ n device to limit or regulate the flow of fluid, light, or sound

BAFFLED ▸ baffle

BAFFLER ▸ baffle

BAFFLES ▸ baffle

BAFFS ▸ baff

BAFFY n golf club

BAFT n coarse fabric

BAFTS ▸ baft

BAG n flexible container with an opening at one end ▷ vb put into a bag

BAGARRE n brawl

BAGASS same as ▸ bagasse

BAGASSE n pulp remaining after the extraction of juice from sugar cane or similar plants: used as fuel and for making paper, etc

BAGEL n hard ring-shaped bread roll

BAGELS ▸ bagel

BAGFUL n amount (of something) that can be held in a bag

BAGFULS ▸ bagful

BAGGAGE n suitcases packed for a journey

BAGGED ▸ bag

BAGGER n person who packs groceries

BAGGERS ▸ bagger

BAGGIE n plastic bag

BAGGIER ▸ baggy

BAGGIES ▸ baggy

BAGGILY ▸ baggy

BAGGING ▸ bag

BAGGIT n unspawned salmon

BAGGITS ▸ baggit

BAGGY same as ▸ bagie

BAGH n (in India and Pakistan) a garden

BAGHS ▸ bagh

BAGIE n turnip

BAGIES ▸ bagie

BAGLESS adj (esp of a vacuum cleaner) not containing a bag

BAGLIKE ▸ bag

BAGMAN n travelling salesman

BAGMEN ▸ bagman

BAGNIO n brothel

BAGNIOS ▸ bagnio

BAGPIPE vb play the bagpipes

BAGS ▸ bag

BAGSFUL ▸ bagful

BAGUET same as > baguette

BAGUETS ▸ baguet

BAGUIO n hurricane

BAGUIOS ▸ baguio

BAGWASH n laundry that washes clothes without drying or pressing them

BAGWIG n 18th-century wig with hair pushed back into a bag

BAGWIGS ▸ bagwig

BAGWORM n type of moth

BAH interj expression of contempt or disgust

BAHADA same as ▸ bajada

BAHADAS ▸ bahada

BAHADUR n title formerly conferred by the British on distinguished Indians

BAHT n standard monetary unit of Thailand, divided into 100 satang

BAHTS ▸ baht

BAHU n (in India) daughter-in-law

BAHUS ▸ bahu

BAHUT n decorative cabinet

BAHUTS ▸ bahut

BAIL n money deposited

with a court as security for a person's reappearance in court ▷ *vb* pay bail for (a person)

BAILED ▸ **bail**

BAILEE *n* person to whom the possession of goods is transferred under a bailment

BAILEES ▸ **bailee**

BAILER ▸ **bail**

BAILERS ▸ **bail**

BAILEY *n* outermost wall or court of a castle

BAILEYS ▸ **bailey**

BAILIE *n* (in Scotland) a municipal magistrate

BAILIES ▸ **bailie**

BAILIFF *n* sheriff's officer who serves writs and summonses

BAILING ▸ **bail**

BAILLI *n* magistrate

BAILLIE *same as* ▸ **bailie**

BAILLIS ▸ **bailli**

BAILOR *n* person who retains ownership of goods but entrusts possession of them to another under a bailment

BAILORS ▸ **bailor**

BAILOUT *n* instance of helping (a person, organization, etc) out of a predicament

BAILS ▸ **bail**

BAININ *n* Irish collarless jacket made of white wool

BAININS ▸ **bainin**

BAINITE *n* mixture of iron and iron carbide found in incompletely hardened steels, produced when austenite is transformed at temperatures between the pearlite and martensite ranges

BAIRN *n* child

BAIRNLY ▸ **bairn**

BAIRNS ▸ **bairn**

BAIT *n* piece of food on a hook or in a trap to attract fish or animals ▷ *vb* put a piece of food on or in (a hook or trap)

BAITED ▸ **bait**

BAITER ▸ **bait**

BAITERS ▸ **bait**

BAITH *adj* both

BAITING ▸ **bait**

BAITS ▸ **bait**

BAIZA *n* Omani unit of currency

BAIZAS ▸ **baiza**

BAIZE *n* woollen fabric used to cover billiard and card tables ▷ *vb* line or cover with such fabric

BAIZED ▸ **baize**

BAIZES ▸ **baize**

BAIZING ▸ **baize**

BAJADA *n* sloping surface formed from rock deposits

BAJADAS ▸ **bajada**

BAJAN *n* freshman at Aberdeen University

BAJANS ▸ **bajan**

BAJRA *n* Indian millet

BAJRAS ▸ **bajra**

BAJREE *same as* ▸ **bajra**

BAJREES ▸ **bajree**

BAJRI *same as* ▸ **bajra**

BAJRIS ▸ **bajri**

BAJU *n* Malay jacket

BAJUS ▸ **baju**

BAKE *vb* cook by dry heat as in an oven ▷ *n* party at which the main dish is baked

BAKED ▸ **bake**

BAKEN ▸ **bake**

BAKEOFF *n* baking competition

BAKER *n* person whose business is to make or sell bread, cakes, etc

BAKERS ▸ **baker**

BAKERY *n* place where bread, cakes, etc are baked or sold

BAKES ▸ **bake**

BAKGAT *adj* fine, excellent, marvellous

BAKING *n* process of cooking bread, cakes, etc ▷ *adj* (esp of weather) very hot and dry

BAKINGS ▸ **baking**

BAKKIE *n* small truck

BAKKIES ▸ **bakkie**

BAKLAVA *n* rich cake of Middle Eastern origin consisting of thin layers of pastry filled with nuts and honey

BAKLAWA *same as* ▸ **baklava**

BAKRA *n* White person, esp one from Britain ▷ *adj* (of people) White, esp British

BAKRAS ▸ **bakra**

BAL *n* balmoral

BALADIN *n* dancer

BALANCE *n* stability of mind or body ▷ *vb* weigh in a balance

BALAS *n* red variety of spinel, used as a gemstone

BALASES ▸ **balas**

BALATA *n* tropical American tree yielding a latex-like sap

BALATAS ▸ **balata**

BALBOA *n* standard currency unit of Panama, divided into 100 centesimos

BALBOAS ▸ **balboa**

BALCONY *n* platform on the outside of a building with a rail along the outer edge

BALD *adj* having little or no hair on the scalp ▷ *vb* make bald

BALDED ▸ **bald**

BALDER ▸ **bald**

BALDEST ▸ **bald**

BALDIE ▸ **baldy**

BALDIER ▸ **baldy**

BALDIES ▸ **baldy**

BALDING *adj* becoming bald

BALDISH ▸ **bald**

BALDLY ▸ **bald**

BALDRIC *n* wide silk sash or leather belt worn over the right shoulder to the left hip for carrying a sword, etc

BALDS ▸ **bald**

BALDY *adj* bald ▷ *n* bald person

BALE *same as* ▸ **bail**

BALED ▸ **bale**

BALEEN *n* whalebone

BALEENS ▸ **baleen**

BALEFUL *adj* vindictive or menacing

BALER ▸ **bail**

BALERS ▸ **bail**

BALES ▸ **bale**

BALING ▸ **bale**

BALISE *n* electronic beacon used on a railway

BALISES ▸ **balise**

BALISTA *same as* ▸ **ballista**

BALK *vb* stop short, esp suddenly or unexpectedly ▷ *n* roughly squared heavy timber beam

BALKED ▸ **balk**

BALKER ▸ **balk**

BALKERS ▸ **balk**

BALKIER ▸ **balky**

BALKILY ▸ **balky**

BALKING ▸ **balk**

BALKS ▸ **balk**

BALKY *adj* inclined to stop abruptly and unexpectedly

BALL *n* round or nearly round object, esp one used in games ▷ *vb* form into a ball

B

BALLAD *n* narrative poem or song ▷ *vb* sing or write a ballad

BALLADE *n* verse form consisting of three stanzas and an envoy, all ending with the same line

BALLADS ▸ ballad

BALLAN *n* species of fish

BALLANS ▸ ballan

BALLANT *vb* write a ballad

BALLAST *n* substance, such as sand, used to stabilize a ship when it is not carrying cargo ▷ *vb* give stability or weight to

BALLAT *vb* write a ballad

BALLATS ▸ ballat

BALLED ▸ ball

BALLER *n* ball-game player

BALLERS ▸ baller

BALLET *n* classical style of expressive dancing based on conventional steps

BALLETS ▸ ballet

BALLIES ▸ bally

BALLING ▸ ball

BALLIUM *same as* ▸ **bailey**

BALLON *n* light, graceful quality

BALLONS ▸ ballon

BALLOON *n* inflatable rubber bag used as a plaything or decoration ▷ *vb* fly in a balloon

BALLOT *n* method of voting ▷ *vb* vote or ask for a vote from

BALLOTS ▸ ballot

BALLOW *n* heavy club

BALLOWS ▸ ballow

BALLUTE *n* inflatable balloon parachute

BALLY *another word for* > **ballyhoo**

BALM *n* aromatic substance used for healing and soothing ▷ *vb* apply balm to

BALMED ▸ balm

BALMIER ▸ balmy

BALMILY ▸ balmy

BALMING ▸ balm

BALMS ▸ balm

BALMY *adj* (of weather) mild and pleasant

BALNEAL *adj* of or relating to baths or bathing

BALONEY *n* foolish talk; nonsense

BALOO *n* bear

BALOOS ▸ baloo

BALS ▸ bal

BALSA *n* very light wood from a tropical American tree

BALSAM *n* type of fragrant balm ▷ *vb* embalm

BALSAMS ▸ balsam

BALSAMY ▸ balsam

BALSAS ▸ balsa

BALTI *n* spicy Indian dish served in a metal dish

BALTIC *adj* very cold

BALTIS ▸ balti

BALU *same as* ▸ **baloo**

BALUN *n* device for coupling two electrical circuit elements, such as an aerial and its feeder cable, where one is balanced and the other is unbalanced

BALUNS ▸ balun

BALUS ▸ balu

BAM *vb* cheat

BAMBI *n* born-again middle-aged biker: an affluent middle-aged man who rides a powerful motorbike

BAMBINI ▸ bambino

BAMBINO *n* young child, esp an Italian one

BAMBIS ▸ bambi

BAMBOO *n* tall treelike tropical grass with hollow stems

BAMBOOS ▸ bamboo

BAMMED ▸ bam

BAMMER ▸ bam

BAMMERS ▸ bam

BAMMING ▸ bam

BAMPOT *n* fool

BAMPOTS ▸ bampot

BAMS ▸ bam

BAN *vb* prohibit or forbid officially ▷ *n* official prohibition

BANAK *n* type of Central American tree

BANAKS ▸ banak

BANAL *adj* ordinary and unoriginal

BANALER ▸ banal

BANALLY ▸ banal

BANANA *n* yellow crescent-shaped fruit

BANANAS *adj* crazy

BANC *n as in* **in banc** sitting as a full court

BANCO *n* call made in gambling games

BANCOS ▸ banco

BANCS ▸ banc

BAND *n* group of musicians playing together ▷ *vb* unite

BANDA *n* African thatched hut

BANDAGE *n* piece of material used to cover a wound or wrap an injured limb ▷ *vb* cover with a bandage

BANDAID *adj* (of a solution or remedy) temporary

BANDANA *same as* > **bandanna**

BANDAR *n* species of monkey

BANDARI *n* Indian English word for female monkey

BANDARS ▸ bandar

BANDAS ▸ banda

BANDBOX *n* lightweight usually cylindrical box for hats

BANDEAU *n* narrow ribbon worn round the head

BANDED ▸ band

BANDER ▸ band

BANDERS ▸ band

BANDH *n* (in India) a general strike

BANDHS ▸ bandh

BANDIED ▸ bandy

BANDIER ▸ bandy

BANDIES ▸ bandy

BANDING *n* practice of grouping schoolchildren according to ability to ensure a balanced intake at different levels of ability to secondary school

BANDIT *n* robber, esp a member of an armed gang

BANDITO *n* Mexican bandit

BANDITS ▸ bandit

BANDOG *n* ferocious dog

BANDOGS ▸ bandog

BANDOOK *same as* ▸ **bundook**

BANDORA *same as* ▸ **bandore**

BANDORE *n* 16th-century plucked musical instrument resembling a lute but larger and fitted with seven pairs of metal strings

BANDROL *same as* > **banderole**

BANDS ▸ band

BANDSAW *n* power saw with continuous blade

BANDURA *n* type of lute

BANDY *adj* having legs curved outwards at the knees ▷ *vb* exchange (words) in a heated manner

BANE n person or thing that causes misery or distress ▷ vb cause harm or distress to (someone)

BANED ▸ bane

BANEFUL adj destructive, poisonous, or fatal

BANES ▸ bane

BANG vb make a short explosive noise

BANGED ▸ bang

BANGER n old decrepit car

BANGERS ▸ banger

BANGING ▸ bang

BANGKOK n type of straw hat

BANGLE n bracelet worn round the arm or the ankle

BANGLED ▸ bangle

BANGLES ▸ bangle

BANGS ▸ bang

BANI ▸ ban

BANIA same as ▸ banyan

BANIAN same as ▸ banyan

BANIANS ▸ banian

BANIAS ▸ bania

BANING ▸ bane

BANISH vb send (someone) into exile

BANJAX vb ruin; destroy
Meaning to ruin or confound, this is a great word to remember, with its high-scoring combination of J and X.

BANJO n guitar-like musical instrument with a circular body

BANJOES ▸ banjo

BANJOS ▸ banjo

BANK n institution offering services such as the safekeeping and lending of money ▷ vb deposit (cash or cheques) in a bank

BANKED ▸ bank

BANKER n manager or owner of a bank

BANKERS ▸ banker

BANKET n gold-bearing conglomerate found in South Africa

BANKETS ▸ banket

BANKING same as ▸ bank

BANKIT same as
> banquette

BANKITS ▸ bankit

BANKS ▸ bank

BANKSIA n Australian evergreen tree or shrub

BANNED ▸ ban

BANNER n long strip of cloth displaying a slogan, advertisement, etc ▷ vb (of a newspaper headline) to display (a story) prominently ▷ adj outstandingly successful

BANNERS ▸ banner

BANNET n bonnet

BANNETS ▸ bannet

BANNING ▸ ban

BANNOCK n round flat cake made from oatmeal or barley

BANNS pl n public declaration, esp in a church, of an intended marriage

BANOFFI same as
> banoffee

BANQUET n elaborate formal dinner ▷ vb hold or take part in a banquet

BANS same as ▸ banns

BANSELA same as ▸ bonsela

BANSHEE n (in Irish folklore) female spirit whose wailing warns of a coming death

BANSHIE same as ▸ banshee

BANT n string ▷ vb tie with string

BANTAM n small breed of chicken

BANTAMS ▸ bantam

BANTED ▸ bant

BANTENG n wild ox

BANTER vb tease jokingly ▷ n teasing or joking conversation

BANTERS ▸ banter

BANTIES ▸ banty

BANTING ▸ bant

BANTS ▸ bant

BANTY n bantam

BANYA n traditional Russian steam bath

BANYAN n Indian tree whose branches grow down into the soil forming additional trunks

BANYANS ▸ banyan

BANYAS ▸ banya

BANZAI interj patriotic cheer, battle cry, or salutation

BANZAIS ▸ banzai

BAOBAB n African tree with a thick trunk and angular branches

BAOBABS ▸ baobab

BAP n large soft bread roll

BAPS ▸ bap

BAPTISE same as ▸ baptize

BAPTISM n Christian religious ceremony in which a person is immersed in or sprinkled with water as a sign of being cleansed from sin and accepted into the Church

BAPTIST n one who baptizes

BAPTIZE vb perform baptism on

BAPU n spiritual father

BAPUS ▸ bapu

BAR n rigid usually straight length of metal, wood, etc, that is longer than it is wide or thick, used esp as a barrier or as a structural or mechanical part ▷ vb fasten or secure with a bar

BARACAN same as
> barracan

BARAZA n place where public meetings are held

BARAZAS ▸ baraza

BARB n cutting remark ▷ vb provide with a barb or barbs

BARBAL adj of a beard

BARBATE adj having tufts of long hairs

BARBE n Waldensian missionary

BARBED ▸ barb

BARBEL n long thin growth that hangs from the jaws of certain fishes, such as the carp

BARBELL n long metal rod to which heavy discs are attached at each end for weightlifting

BARBELS ▸ barbel

BARBER n person who cuts men's hair and shaves beards ▷ vb cut the hair of

BARBERS ▸ barber

BARBES ▸ barbe

BARBET n type of small tropical brightly coloured bird with short weak wings and a sharp stout bill

BARBETS ▸ barbet

BARBIE short for > barbecue

BARBIES ▸ barbie

BARBING ▸ barb

BARBOLA n small models of flowers, etc made from plastic paste

BARBS ▸ barb

BARBULE n very small barb

BARBUT n open-faced helmet

BARBUTS ▸ barbut

BARBY > barbecue

B

BARCA n boat

BARCAS ▷ barca

BARCHAN n crescent-shaped shifting sand dune, convex on the windward side and steeper and concave on the leeward

BARCODE n machine-readable code printed on goods

BARD n poet ▷ vb place a piece of pork fat on

BARDASH n kept boy in a homosexual relationship

BARDE same as ▶ bard

BARDED ▶ barde

BARDES ▶ barde

BARDIC ▶ bard

BARDIE n type of Australian grub

BARDIER ▶ bard

BARDIES ▶ bardie

BARDING ▶ bard

BARDISM ▶ bard

BARDO n (in Tibetan Buddhism) the state of the soul between its death and its rebirth

BARDOS ▶ bardo

BARDS ▶ bard

BARDY ▶ bard

BARE adj unclothed, naked ▷ vb uncover

BARED ▶ bare

BAREFIT ▷ barefoot

BAREGE n light silky gauze fabric made of wool ▷ adj made of such a fabric

BAREGES ▶ barege

BARELY adv only just

BARER ▶ bare

BARES ▶ bare

BAREST ▶ bare

BARF vb vomit ▷ n act of vomiting

BARFED ▶ barf

BARFING ▶ barf

BARFLY n person who frequents bars

BARFS ▶ barf

BARFUL adj presenting difficulties

BARGAIN n agreement establishing what each party will give, receive, or perform in a transaction ▷ vb negotiate the terms of an agreement

BARGE n flat-bottomed boat used to transport freight ▷ vb push violently

BARGED ▶ barge

BARGEE n person in charge of a barge

BARGEES ▶ bargee

BARGES ▶ barge

BARGEST same as > barghest

BARGING ▶ barge

BARGOON Canadian word for ▶ bargain

BARHOP vb visit several bars in succession

BARHOPS ▶ barhop

BARIC adj of or containing barium

BARILLA n impure mixture of sodium carbonate and sodium sulphate obtained from the ashes of certain plants, such as the saltworts

BARING ▶ bare

BARISH adj quite thinly covered

BARISTA n person who makes and sells coffee in a coffee bar

BARITE n colourless or white mineral consisting of barium sulphate in orthorhombic crystalline form, occurring in sedimentary rocks and with sulphide ores: a source of barium

BARITES ▶ barite

BARIUM n soft white metallic element

BARIUMS ▶ barium

BARK vb (of a dog) make its typical loud abrupt cry

BARKAN same as ▶ barchan

BARKANS ▶ barkan

BARKED ▶ bark

BARKEEP n barkeeper

BARKEN vb become dry with a bark-like outer layer

BARKENS ▶ barken

BARKER n person at a fairground who calls loudly to passers-by in order to attract customers

BARKERS ▶ barker

BARKHAN same as ▶ barchan

BARKIER ▶ barky

BARKING adj mad ▷ adv extremely

BARKS ▶ bark

BARKY adj having the texture or appearance of bark

BARLESS ▶ bar

BARLEY n tall grasslike plant cultivated for grain ▷ sentence substitute cry for truce or respite from the rules of a game

BARLEYS ▶ barley

BARLOW n type of strong knife

BARLOWS ▶ barlow

BARM n yeasty froth on fermenting malt liquors

BARMAID n woman who serves in a pub

BARMAN same as > bartender

BARMEN ▶ barman

BARMIE same as ▶ barmy

BARMIER ▶ barmy

BARMKIN n protective wall around castle

BARMPOT n foolish or deranged person

BARMS ▶ barm

BARMY adj insane

BARN n large building on a farm used for storing grain ▷ vb keep in a barn

BARNED ▶ barn

BARNET n hair

BARNETS ▶ barnet

BARNEY n noisy fight or argument ▷ vb argue or quarrel

BARNEYS ▶ barney

BARNIER ▶ barny

BARNING ▶ barn

BARNS ▶ barn

BARNY adj reminiscent of a barn

BAROCCO same as ▶ baroque

BAROCK same as ▶ baroque

BAROCKS ▶ barock

BAROLO n red Italian wine

BAROLOS ▶ barolo

BARON n member of the lowest rank of nobility

BARONET n commoner who holds the lowest hereditary British title

BARONG n broad-bladed cleaver-like knife used in the Philippines

BARONGS ▶ barong

BARONNE n baroness

BARONS ▶ baron

BARONY n domain or rank of a baron

BAROQUE n highly ornate style of art, architecture, or music from the late 16th to the early 18th century ▷ adj ornate in style

BARP n hillock or bank of stones

BARPS ▸ barp

BARQUE n sailing ship, esp one with three masts

BARQUES ▸ barque

BARRA n barramundi

BARRACE n record of teams entering a sports contest

BARRACK vb criticize loudly or shout against (a team or speaker)

BARRAGE n continuous delivery of questions, complaints, etc ▷ vb attack or confront with a barrage

BARRAS ▸ barra

BARRAT n fraudulent dealings

BARRATS ▸ barrat

BARRE n rail at hip height used for ballet practice ▷ vb execute guitar chords by laying the index finger over some or all of the strings so that the pitch of each stopped string is simultaneously raised ▷ adv by using the barre

BARRED ▸ bar

BARREED ▸ barre

BARREL n cylindrical container with rounded sides and flat ends ▷ vb put in a barrel

BARRELS ▸ barrel

BARREN adj (of a woman or female animal) incapable of producing offspring

BARRENS pl n (in North America) a stretch of usually level land that is sparsely vegetated or barren

BARRES ▸ barre

BARRET n small flat cap resembling a biretta

BARRETS ▸ barret

BARRICO n small container for liquids

BARRIE adj very good

BARRIER n anything that prevents access, progress, or union ▷ vb create or form a barrier

BARRIES ▸ barry

BARRING ▸ bar

BARRIO n Spanish-speaking quarter in a town or city, esp in the US

BARRIOS ▸ barrio

BARRO adj embarrassing

BARROOM n room or building where alcoholic drinks are served over a counter

BARROW n wheelbarrow

BARROWS ▸ barrow

BARRY n mistake or blunder

BARS ▸ bar

BARTEND vb serve drinks from a bar

BARTER vb trade (goods) in exchange for other goods ▷ n trade by the exchange of goods

BARTERS ▸ barter

BARTON n farmyard

BARTONS ▸ barton

BARTSIA n type of semiparasitic plant

BARWARE n glasses, etc used in a bar

BARWOOD n red wood from small African tree

BARYE n unit of pressure in the cgs system equal to one dyne per square centimetre. 1 barye is equivalent to 1 microbar

BARYES ▸ barye

BARYON n elementary particle that has a mass greater than or equal to that of the proton

BARYONS ▸ baryon

BARYTA same as ▸ barite

BARYTAS ▸ baryta

BARYTE same as ▸ baryta

BARYTES ▸ baryte

BARYTIC ▸ baryta

BARYTON n bass viol with sympathetic strings as well as its six main strings

BAS ▸ ba

BASAL adj of, at, or constituting a base

BASALLY ▸ basal

BASALT n dark volcanic rock

BASALTS ▸ basalt

BASAN n sheepskin tanned in bark

BASANS ▸ basan

BASANT n Pakistani spring festival

BASANTS ▸ basant

BASCULE n drawbridge that operates by a counterbalanced weight

BASE n bottom or supporting part of anything ▷ vb use as a basis (for) ▷ adj dishonourable or immoral

BASED ▸ base

BASEEJ pl n Iranian volunteer militia

BASELY ▸ base

BASEMAN n fielder positioned near a base

BASEMEN ▸ baseman

BASEN Spencerian spelling of ▸ basin

BASENJI n small smooth-haired breed of dog of African origin having a tightly curled tail and an inability to bark

BASER ▸ base

BASES ▸ basis

BASEST ▸ base

BASH vb hit violently or forcefully ▷ n heavy blow

BASHAW n important or pompous person

BASHAWS ▸ bashaw

BASHED ▸ bash

BASHER ▸ bash

BASHERS ▸ bash

BASHES ▸ bash

BASHFUL adj shy or modest

BASHING ▸ bash

BASHLIK n Caucasian hood

BASHLYK same as ▸ bashlik

BASHO n grand tournament in sumo wrestling

BASIC adj of or forming a base or basis ▷ n fundamental principle, fact, etc

BASICS ▸ basic

BASIDIA > basidium

BASIFY vb make basic

BASIJ ▸ baseej

BASIL n aromatic herb used in cooking

BASILAR adj of or situated at a base

BASILIC > basilica

BASILS ▸ basil

BASIN n round open container

BASINAL ▸ basin

BASINED ▸ basin

BASINET n close-fitting medieval helmet of light steel usually with a visor

BASING ▸ base

BASINS ▸ basin

BASION n (in anatomy) midpoint on the forward border of the foramen magnum

BASIONS ▸ basion

BASIS n fundamental principles etc from which something is started or developed

BASK vb lie in or be exposed to something, esp pleasant warmth

BASKED ▸ bask

B

BASKET n container made of interwoven strips of wood or cane

BASKETS ▸ basket

BASKING ▸ bask

BASKS ▸ bask

BASMATI n variety of long-grain rice with slender aromatic grains, used for savoury dishes

BASNET same as ▸ basinet

BASNETS ▸ basnet

BASOCHE n society of medieval French lawyers who performed comic plays

BASON same as ▸ basin

BASONS ▸ bason

BASQUE n tight-fitting bodice for women

BASQUED ▸ basque

BASQUES ▸ basque

BASS vb speak or sing in a low pitch

BASSE same as ▸ bass

BASSED ▸ bass

BASSER ▸ bass

BASSES ▸ bass

BASSEST ▸ bass

BASSET n long low smooth-haired breed of hound with short strong legs and long ears ▷ vb outcrop

BASSETS ▸ basset

BASSETT same as ▸ basset

BASSI ▸ basso

BASSIER ▸ bassy

BASSING ▸ bass

BASSIST n player of a double bass, esp in a jazz band

BASSLY ▸ bass

BASSO n singer with a bass voice

BASSOON n low-pitched woodwind instrument

BASSOS ▸ basso

BASSY adj manifesting strong bass tones

BAST n fibrous material obtained from the phloem of jute, hemp, flax, lime, etc, used for making rope, matting, etc

BASTA interj enough; stop

BASTE vb moisten (meat) during cooking with hot fat

BASTED ▸ baste

BASTER ▸ baste

BASTERS ▸ baste

BASTES ▸ baste

BASTI n (in India) a slum inhabited by poor people

BASTIDE n small isolated house in France

BASTILE same as ▸ bastille

BASTING n loose temporary stitches

BASTION n projecting part of a fortification

BASTIS ▸ basti

BASTLE n fortified house

BASTLES ▸ bastle

BASTO n ace of clubs in certain card games

BASTOS ▸ basto

BASTS ▸ bast

BASUCO n cocaine-based drug

BASUCOS ▸ basuco

BAT n any of various types of club used to hit the ball in certain sports ▷ vb strike with or as if with a bat

BATABLE ▸ bat

BATATA n sweet potato

BATATAS ▸ batata

BATAVIA n variety of lettuce with smooth pale green leaves

BATBOY n boy who works at baseball games

BATBOYS ▸ batboy

BATCH n group of people or things dealt with at the same time ▷ vb group (items) for efficient processing

BATCHED ▸ batch

BATCHER ▸ batch

BATCHES ▸ batch

BATE vb (of hawks) to jump violently from a perch or the falconer's fist, often hanging from the leash while struggling to escape

BATEAU n light flat-bottomed boat used on rivers in Canada and the northern US

BATEAUX ▸ bateau

BATED ▸ bate

BATES ▸ bate

BATFISH n type of angler fish with a flattened scaleless body

BATFOWL vb catch birds by temporarily blinding them with light

BATGIRL n girl who works at baseball games

BATH n large container in which to wash the body ▷ vb wash in a bath

BATHE vb swim in open water for pleasure

BATHED ▸ bathe

BATHER ▸ bathe

BATHERS pl n swimming costume

BATHES ▸ bathe

BATHING ▸ bathe

BATHMAT n mat to stand on after a bath

BATHMIC > bathmism

BATHOS n sudden ludicrous change in speech or writing from a serious subject to a trivial one

BATHS ▸ bath

BATHTUB n bath, esp one not permanently fixed

BATHYAL adj denoting or relating to an ocean depth of between 200 and 2000 metres (about 100 and 1000 fathoms), corresponding to the continental slope

BATIK n process of printing fabric using wax to cover areas not to be dyed ▷ vb treat material with this process

BATIKED ▸ batik

BATIKS ▸ batik

BATING ▸ bate

BATISTE n fine plain-weave cotton fabric: used esp for shirts and dresses

BATLER n flat piece of wood for beating clothes, etc before washing

BATLERS ▸ batler

BATLET same as ▸ batler

BATLETS ▸ batlet

BATLIKE ▸ bat

BATMAN n officer's servant in the armed forces

BATMEN ▸ batman

BATON n thin stick used by the conductor of an orchestra ▷ vb carry or wave a baton

BATONED ▸ baton

BATONS ▸ baton

BATOON same as ▸ baton

BATOONS ▸ batoon

BATS ▸ bat

BATSMAN n person who bats or specializes in batting

BATSMEN ▸ batsman

BATT ▸ bat

BATTA n soldier's allowance

BATTAS ▸ batta

BATTEAU same as ▸ bateau

BATTED ▸ bat

BATTEL vb make fertile

BATTELS ▸ battel

BATTEN n strip of wood fixed to something, esp to hold it in place ▷ vb strengthen or fasten with battens

BATTENS ▸ batten

BATTER vb hit repeatedly ▷ n mixture of flour, eggs, and milk, used in cooking

BATTERO n heavy club

BATTERS ▸ batter

BATTERY n device that produces electricity in a torch, radio, etc ▷ adj kept in series of cages for intensive rearing

BATTIER ▸ batty

BATTIES ▸ batty

BATTIK same as ▸ batik

BATTIKS ▸ battik

BATTILL old spelling of ▸ battle

BATTING ▸ bat

BATTLE n fight between large armed forces ▷ vb struggle

BATTLED ▸ battle

BATTLER ▸ battle

BATTLES ▸ battle

BATTS ▸ batt

BATTU adj (in ballet) involving a beating movement

BATTUE n beating of woodland or cover to force game to flee in the direction of hunters

BATTUES ▸ battue

BATTUTA n (in music) a beat

BATTUTO n (in Italian cookery) selection of chopped herbs

BATTY adj eccentric or crazy ▷ n bottom; bum

BATWING adj shaped like the wings of a bat, as a black tie, collar, etc

BAUBEE same as ▸ bawbee

BAUBEES ▸ baubee

BAUBLE n trinket of little value

BAUBLES ▸ bauble

BAUCHLE vb shuffle along

BAUD n unit used to measure the speed of transmission of electronic data

BAUDRIC same as ▸ baldric

BAUDS ▸ baud

BAUERA n small evergreen Australian shrub

BAUERAS ▸ bauera

BAUK same as ▸ balk

BAUKED ▸ bauk

BAUKING ▸ bauk

BAUKS ▸ bauk

BAULK ▸ balk

BAULKED ▸ balk

BAULKER ▸ balk

BAULKS ▸ balk

BAULKY same as ▸ balky

BAUR n humorous anecdote; joke

BAURS ▸ baur

BAUSOND adj (of animal) dappled with white spots

BAUXITE n claylike substance that is the chief source of aluminium

BAVIN n impure limestone

BAVINS ▸ bavin

BAWBEE n former Scottish silver coin

BAWBEES ▸ bawbee

BAWBLE same as ▸ bauble

BAWBLES ▸ bawble

BAWCOCK n fine fellow

BAWD n person who runs a brothel, esp a woman

BAWDIER ▸ bawdy

BAWDIES ▸ bawdy

BAWDILY ▸ bawdy

BAWDKIN same as > baldachin

BAWDRIC n heavy belt to support sword

BAWDRY n obscene talk or language

BAWDS ▸ bawd

BAWDY adj (of writing etc) containing humorous references to sex ▷ n obscenity or eroticism, esp in writing or drama

BAWL vb shout or weep noisily ▷ n loud shout or cry

BAWLED ▸ bawl

BAWLER ▸ bawl

BAWLERS ▸ bawl

BAWLEY n small fishing boat

BAWLEYS ▸ bawley

BAWLING ▸ bawl

BAWLS ▸ bawl

BAWN n fortified enclosure

BAWNEEN same as ▸ bainin

BAWNS ▸ bawn

BAWR same as ▸ baur

BAWRS ▸ bawr

BAWSUNT adj black and white in colour

BAWTIE n name for a dog

BAWTIES ▸ bawtie

BAWTY same as ▸ bawtie

BAXTER old variant of ▸ baker

BAXTERS ▸ baxter

BAY n wide semicircular indentation of a shoreline ▷ vb howl in deep tones

BAYAMO n Cuban strong wind

BAYAMOS ▸ bayamo

BAYARD n bay horse

BAYARDS ▸ bayard

BAYE vb bathe

BAYED ▸ bay

BAYES ▸ baye

BAYING ▸ bay

BAYLE n barrier

BAYLES ▸ bayle

BAYMAN n fisherman

BAYMEN ▸ bayman

BAYONET n sharp blade that can be fixed to the end of a rifle ▷ vb stab with a bayonet

BAYOU n (in the southern US) a sluggish marshy tributary of a lake or river

BAYOUS ▸ bayou

BAYS ▸ bay

BAYT same as ▸ bate

BAYTED ▸ bayt

BAYTING ▸ bayt

BAYTS ▸ bayt

BAYWOOD n light soft wood of a tropical American mahogany tree

BAYYAN n Islamic declaration

BAYYANS ▸ bayyan

BAZAAR n sale in aid of charity

BAZAARS ▸ bazaar

BAZAR same as ▸ bazaar

BAZARS ▸ bazar

BAZAZZ same as ▸ pizzazz

BAZOO a US slang word for ▸ mouth

BAZOOKA n portable rocket launcher that fires an armour-piercing projectile

BAZOOS ▸ bazoo

BAZOUKI same as > bouzouki

BAZZAZZ ▸ pizzazz

BE vb exist or live

BEACH n area of sand or pebbles on a shore ▷ vb run or haul (a boat) onto a beach

BEACHED ▸ beach

BEACHES ▸ beach

BEACHY adj with gentle sandy slopes

BEACON n fire or light on a hill or tower, used as a

B

warning ▷ vb guide or warn
BEACONS ▸ **beacon**
BEAD n small piece of plastic, wood, etc, pierced for threading on a string to form a necklace etc ▷ vb decorate with beads
BEADED ▸ **bead**
BEADER n person making things with beads
BEADERS ▸ **beader**
BEADIER ▸ **beady**
BEADILY ▸ **beady**
BEADING n strip of moulding used for edging furniture
BEADLE n (formerly) a minor parish official who acted as an usher
BEADLES ▸ **beadle**
BEADMAN same as > **beadsman**
BEADMEN ▸ **beadman**
BEADS ▸ **bead**
BEADY adj small, round, and glittering
BEAGLE n small hound with short legs and drooping ears ▷ vb hunt with beagles, normally on foot
BEAGLED ▸ **beagle**
BEAGLER n person who hunts with beagles
BEAGLES ▸ **beagle**
BEAK n projecting horny jaws of a bird ▷ vb strike with the beak
BEAKED ▸ **beak**
BEAKER n large drinking cup
BEAKERS ▸ **beaker**
BEAKIER ▸ **beak**
BEAKS ▸ **beak**
BEAKY ▸ **beak**
BEAM n broad smile ▷ vb smile broadly
BEAMED ▸ **beam**
BEAMER n full-pitched ball bowled at the batsman's head
BEAMERS ▸ **beamer**
BEAMIER ▸ **beam**
BEAMILY ▸ **beam**
BEAMING ▸ **beam**
BEAMISH adj smiling
BEAMLET n small beam
BEAMS ▸ **beam**
BEAMY ▸ **beam**
BEAN n seed or pod of various plants, eaten as a vegetable or used to make coffee etc ▷ vb strike on the head

BEANBAG n small cloth bag filled with dried beans and thrown in games
BEANED ▸ **bean**
BEANERY n cheap restaurant
BEANIE n close-fitting woollen hat
BEANIES ▸ **beany**
BEANING ▸ **bean**
BEANO n celebration or party
BEANOS ▸ **beano**
BEANS ▸ **bean**
BEANY same as ▸ **beanie**
BEAR vb support or hold up (something) ▷ n type of omnivorous mammal with a large head, long shaggy coat, and strong claws
BEARCAT n lesser panda
BEARD n hair growing on the lower parts of a man's face ▷ vb oppose boldly
BEARDED ▸ **beard**
BEARDIE n another name for bearded loach
BEARDS ▸ **beard**
BEARDY adj having a beard
BEARE same as ▸ **bear**
BEARED ▸ **bear**
BEARER n person who carries, presents, or upholds something
BEARERS ▸ **bearer**
BEARES ▸ **beare**
BEARHUG n wrestling hold in which the arms are locked tightly round an opponent's chest and arms
BEARING ▸ **bear**
BEARISH adj like a bear
BEARS ▸ **bear**
BEAST n large wild animal ▷ vb torture someone using excessive physical exercise
BEASTED ▸ **beast**
BEASTIE n small animal
BEASTLY adj unpleasant or disagreeable ▷ adv extremely
BEASTS ▸ **beast**
BEAT vb strike with or as if with a series of violent blows; dash or pound repeatedly (against) ▷ n stroke or blow ▷ adj totally exhausted
BEATBOX n drum machine simulated by a human voice
BEATEN ▸ **beat**
BEATER n device used for beating

BEATERS ▸ **beater**
BEATH vb dry; heat
BEATHED ▸ **beath**
BEATHS ▸ **beath**
BEATIER ▸ **beaty**
BEATIFY vb declare (a dead person) to be among the blessed in heaven: the first step towards canonization
BEATING ▸ **beat**
BEATNIK n young person in the late 1950s who rebelled against conventional attitudes etc
BEATS ▸ **beat**
BEATY adj (of music) having a strong rhythm
BEAU n boyfriend or admirer
BEAUFET same as ▸ **buffet**
BEAUFIN same as ▸ **biffin**
BEAUISH adj vain and showy
BEAUS ▸ **beau**
BEAUT n person or thing that is outstanding or distinctive ▷ adj good or excellent ▷ interj exclamation of joy or pleasure
BEAUTS ▸ **beaut**
BEAUTY n combination of all the qualities of a person or thing that delight the senses and mind ▷ interj expression of approval or agreement ▷ vb make beautiful
BEAUX ▸ **beau**
BEAVER n amphibious rodent with a big flat tail ▷ vb work steadily or assiduously
BEAVERS ▸ **beaver**
BEAVERY n place for keeping beavers
BEBEERU n tropical American tree
BEBLOOD vb stain with blood
BEBOP same as ▸ **bop**
BEBOPS ▸ **bebop**
BEBUNG n vibrato effect on clavichord
BEBUNGS ▸ **bebung**
BECALL vb use insulting words about someone
BECALLS ▸ **becall**
BECALM vb make calm
BECALMS ▸ **becalm**
BECAME ▸ **become**
BECAP vb put cap on
BECAPS ▸ **becap**
BECASSE n woodcock

BECAUSE conj on account of the fact that; on account of being; since

BECHALK vb mark with chalk

BECHARM vb delight

BECK n stream ▷ vb attract someone's attention by nodding or gesturing

BECKE same as ▸ beak

BECKED ▸ beck

BECKES ▸ becke

BECKET n clevis forming part of one end of a sheave, used for securing standing lines by means of a thimble

BECKETS ▸ becket

BECKING ▸ beck

BECKON vb summon with a gesture ▷ n summoning gesture

BECKONS ▸ beckon

BECKS ▸ beck

BECLASP vb embrace

BECLOAK vb dress in cloak

BECLOG vb put clogs on

BECLOGS ▸ beclog

BECLOUD vb cover or obscure with a cloud

BECLOWN vb clown around

BECOME vb come to be

BECOMES ▸ become

BECRAWL vb crawl all over

BECRIME vb make someone guilty of a crime

BECROWD vb crowd with something

BECRUST vb cover with crust

BECURL vb curl

BECURLS ▸ becurl

BECURSE vb curse

BECURST ▸ becurse

BED n piece of furniture on which to sleep ▷ vb plant in a bed

BEDAD interj by God (oath)

BEDAMN vb damn

BEDAMNS ▸ bedamn

BEDASH vb sprinkle with liquid

BEDAUB vb smear with something sticky or dirty

BEDAUBS ▸ bedaub

BEDAWIN same as ▸ bedouin

BEDAZE vb daze

BEDAZED ▸ bedaze

BEDAZES ▸ bedaze

BEDBATH n washing of a sick person in bed

BEDBUG n small blood-sucking wingless insect that infests dirty houses

BEDBUGS ▸ bedbug

BEDDED ▸ bed

BEDDER n (at some universities) a college servant employed to keep students' rooms in order

BEDDERS ▸ bedder

BEDDING ▸ bed

BEDE n prayer

BEDECK vb cover with decorations

BEDECKS ▸ bedeck

BEDEL archaic spelling of ▸ beadle

BEDELL ▸ beadle

BEDELLS ▸ bedell

BEDELS ▸ bedel

BEDEMAN same as ▸ beadsman

BEDEMEN ▸ bedeman

BEDERAL same as ▸ bedral

BEDES ▸ bede

BEDEVIL vb harass, confuse, or torment

BEDEW vb wet or cover with or as if with drops of dew

BEDEWED ▸ bedew

BEDEWS ▸ bedew

BEDFAST an archaic word for ▸ bedridden

BEDGOWN n night dress

BEDHEAD n untidy state of hair, esp caused by sleeping

BEDIDE ▸ bedye

BEDIGHT vb array or adorn ▷ adj adorned or bedecked

BEDIM vb make dim or obscure

BEDIMS ▸ bedim

BEDIRTY vb make dirty

BEDIZEN vb dress or decorate gaudily or tastelessly

BEDLAM n noisy confused situation

BEDLAMP n bedside light

BEDLAMS ▸ bedlam

BEDLESS ▸ bed

BEDLIKE adj like a bed

BEDMATE n person who shares a bed

BEDOUIN n member of any of the nomadic tribes of Arabs inhabiting the deserts of Arabia, Jordan, and Syria, as well as parts of the Sahara

BEDPAN n shallow bowl used as a toilet by bedridden people

BEDPANS ▸ bedpan

BEDPOST n vertical support on a bedstead

BEDRAIL n rail or board along the side of a bed that connects the headboard with the footboard

BEDRAL n minor church official

BEDRALS ▸ bedral

BEDRAPE vb adorn

BEDRID same as ▸ bedridden

BEDRITE ▸ bedright

BEDROCK n solid rock beneath the surface soil

BEDROLL n portable roll of bedding, such as a sleeping bag, used esp for sleeping in the open

BEDROOM n room used for sleeping ▷ adj containing references to sex

BEDROP vb drop on

BEDROPS ▸ bedrop

BEDROPT ▸ bedrop

BEDRUG vb drug excessively

BEDRUGS ▸ bedrug

BEDS ▸ bed

BEDSIDE n area beside a bed ▷ adj placed at or near the side of the bed

BEDSIT n furnished sitting room with a bed

BEDSITS ▸ bedsit

BEDSORE n ulcer on the skin, caused by a lengthy period of lying in bed due to illness

BEDTICK n case containing stuffing in mattress

BEDTIME n time when one usually goes to bed

BEDU adj relating to beduins

BEDUCK vb duck under water

BEDUCKS ▸ beduck

BEDUIN same as ▸ bedouin

BEDUINS ▸ beduin

BEDUMB vb make dumb

BEDUMBS ▸ bedumb

BEDUNCE vb cause to look or feel foolish

BEDUNG vb spread with dung

BEDUNGS ▸ bedung

BEDUST vb cover with dust

BEDUSTS ▸ bedust

BEDWARD adj towards bed

BEDWARF vb hamper growth of

BEDYDE ▸ bedye

BEDYE vb dye

B

BEDYED ▸ bedye

BEDYES ▸ bedye

BEE n insect that makes wax and honey

BEEBEE n air rifle

BEEBEES ▸ beebee

BEECH n tree with a smooth greyish bark

BEECHEN ▸ beech

BEECHES ▸ beech

BEECHY ▸ beech

BEEDI n Indian cigarette

BEEDIE ▸ beedi

BEEDIES ▸ beedi

BEEF n flesh of a cow, bull, or ox ▸ vb complain

BEEFALO n cross between cow and buffalo

BEEFED ▸ beef

BEEFIER ▸ beefy

BEEFILY ▸ beefy

BEEFING ▸ beef

BEEFS ▸ beef

BEEFY adj like beef

BEEGAH same as ▸ bigha

BEEGAHS ▸ beegah

BEEHIVE n structure in which bees live

BEELIKE ▸ bee

BEELINE n most direct route between two places ▸ adj make a beeline for (something)

BEEN ▸ be

BEENAH n understanding; insight

BEENAHS ▸ beenah

BEENTO n person who has resided in Britain, esp during part of his education ▸ adj of, relating to, or characteristic of such a person

BEENTOS ▸ beento

BEEP n high-pitched sound, like that of a car horn ▸ vb (cause to) make this noise

BEEPED ▸ beep

BEEPER ▸ beep

BEEPERS ▸ beep

BEEPING ▸ beep

BEEPS ▸ beep

BEER n alcoholic drink brewed from malt and hops

BEERAGE n brewing industry

BEERIER ▸ beery

BEERILY ▸ beery

BEERS ▸ beer

BEERY adj smelling or tasting of beer

BEES ▸ bee

BEESOME same as ▸ bisson

BEESWAX n wax secreted by bees, used in polishes etc ▸ vb polish with such wax

BEET n plant with an edible root and leaves ▸ vb improve or make better

BEETED ▸ beet

BEETFLY n type of fly which is a common pest of beets and mangel-wurzels

BEETING ▸ beet

BEETLE n insect with a hard wing cover on its back ▸ adj overhang or jut ▸ vb scuttle or scurry

BEETLED ▸ beetle

BEETLER n one who operates a beetling machine

BEETLES ▸ beetle

BEETS ▸ beet

BEEVES ▸ beef

BEEYARD n place where bees are kept

BEEZER n person or chap ▸ adj excellent

BEEZERS ▸ beezer

BEFALL vb happen to (someone)

BEFALLS ▸ befall

BEFANA n Italian gift-bearing good fairy

BEFANAS ▸ befana

BEFELD ▸ befall

BEFELL ▸ befall

BEFFANA same as ▸ befana

BEFIT vb be appropriate or suitable for

BEFITS ▸ befit

BEFLAG vb decorate with flags

BEFLAGS ▸ beflag

BEFLEA vb infect with fleas

BEFLEAS ▸ beflea

BEFLECK vb fleck

BEFLUM vb fool; deceive

BEFLUMS ▸ beflum

BEFOAM vb cover with foam

BEFOAMS ▸ befoam

BEFOG vb surround with fog

BEFOGS ▸ befog

BEFOOL vb make a fool of

BEFOOLS ▸ befool

BEFORE adv indicating something earlier in time, in front of, or preferred to ▸ prep preceding in space or time

BEFOUL vb make dirty or foul

BEFOULS ▸ befoul

BEFRET vb fret about something

BEFRETS ▸ befret

BEG vb solicit (money, food, etc), esp in the street

BEGAD interj emphatic exclamation

BEGALL vb make sore by rubbing

BEGALLS ▸ begall

BEGAN ▸ begin

BEGAR n compulsory labour

BEGARS ▸ begar

BEGAT ▸ beget

BEGAZE vb gaze about or around

BEGAZED ▸ begaze

BEGAZES ▸ begaze

BEGEM vb decorate with gems

BEGEMS ▸ begem

BEGET vb cause or create

BEGETS ▸ beget

BEGGAR n person who begs, esp one who lives by begging ▸ vb be beyond the resources of

BEGGARS ▸ beggar

BEGGARY n extreme poverty or need

BEGGED ▸ beg

BEGGING ▸ beg

BEGHARD n member of a Christian brotherhood that was founded in Flanders in the 13th century and followed a life based on that of the Beguines

BEGIFT vb give gift or gifts to

BEGIFTS ▸ begift

BEGILD vb gild

BEGILDS ▸ begild

BEGILT ▸ begild

BEGIN vb start

BEGINNE same as ▸ beginning

BEGINS ▸ begin

BEGIRD vb surround

BEGIRDS ▸ begird

BEGIRT ▸ begird

BEGLAD vb make glad

BEGLADS ▸ beglad

BEGLOOM vb make gloomy

BEGNAW vb gnaw at

BEGNAWS ▸ begnaw

BEGO vb harrass; beset

BEGOES ▸ bego

BEGOING ▸ bego

BEGONE ▸ bego

BEGONIA n tropical plant with waxy flowers

BEGORAH same as ▸ begorra

BEGORED adj smear with gore

BEGORRA interj emphatic exclamation, regarded as a characteristic utterance of Irishmen

BEGOT past participle of ▸ **beget**

BEGRIM same as ▸ **begrime**

BEGRIME vb make dirty

BEGRIMS ▸ **begrim**

BEGROAN vb groan at

BEGS ▸ **beg**

BEGUILE vb cheat or mislead

BEGUIN another name for ▸ **beghard**

BEGUINE n S American dance

BEGUINS ▸ **beguin**

BEGULF vb overwhelm

BEGULFS ▸ **begulf**

BEGUM n Muslim woman of high rank

BEGUMS ▸ **begum**

BEGUN past participle of ▸ **begin**

BEGUNK vb delude; trick

BEGUNKS ▸ **begunk**

BEHALF n interest, part, benefit, or respect

BEHAVE vb act or function in a particular way

BEHAVED ▸ **behave**

BEHAVER ▸ **behave**

BEHAVES ▸ **behave**

BEHEAD vb remove the head from

BEHEADS ▸ **behead**

BEHELD ▸ **behold**

BEHEST n order or earnest request

BEHESTS ▸ **behest**

BEHIGHT vb entrust

BEHIND adv indicating position to the rear, lateness, responsibility, etc ▸ n buttocks ▸ prep in or to a position further back than ▸ adj in a position further back

BEHINDS ▸ **behind**

BEHOLD vb look (at)

BEHOLDS ▸ **behold**

BEHOOF n advantage or profit

BEHOOFS ▸ **behoof**

BEHOOVE same as ▸ **behove**

BEHOTE same as ▸ **behight**

BEHOTES ▸ **behote**

BEHOVE vb be necessary or fitting for

BEHOVED ▸ **behove**

BEHOVES ▸ **behove**

BEHOWL vb howl at

BEHOWLS ▸ **behowl**

BEIGE adj pale brown ▸ n very light brown, sometimes with a yellowish tinge, similar to the colour of undyed wool

BEIGEL same as ▸ **bagel**

BEIGELS ▸ **beigel**

BEIGER ▸ **beige**

BEIGES ▸ **beige**

BEIGIER ▸ **beige**

BEIGNE same as ▸ **beignet**

BEIGNES ▸ **beigne**

BEIGNET n square deep-fried pastry served hot and sprinkled with icing sugar

BEIGY ▸ **beige**

BEIN adj financially comfortable

BEING ▸ **be**

BEINGS ▸ **be**

BEINKED adj daubed with ink

BEJADE vb jade; tire

BEJADED ▸ **bejade**

BEJADES ▸ **bejade**

BEJANT same as ▸ **bajan**

BEJANTS ▸ **bejant**

BEJESUS interj exclamation of surprise ▸ n as in **the bejesus** mild expletive

BEJEWEL vb decorate with or as if with jewels

BEKAH n half shekel

BEKAHS ▸ **bekah**

BEKISS vb smother with kisses

BEKNAVE vb treat as a knave

BEKNOT vb tie a knot or knots in

BEKNOTS ▸ **beknot**

BEKNOWN adj known about

BEL n unit for comparing two power levels or measuring the intensity of a sound, equal to 10 decibels

BELABOR same as ▸ **belabour**

BELACE vb decorate with lace

BELACED ▸ **belace**

BELACES ▸ **belace**

BELADY vb call a lady

BELAH n Australian tree which yields a useful timber

BELAHS ▸ **belah**

BELAMY n close friend

BELAR same as ▸ **belah**

BELARS ▸ **belar**

BELATE vb cause to be late

BELATED adj late or too late

BELATES ▸ **belate**

BELAUD vb praise highly

BELAUDS ▸ **belaud**

BELAY vb secure a line to a pin or cleat ▸ n attachment (of a climber) to a mountain by tying the rope off round a rock spike, piton, nut, etc, to safeguard the party in the event of a fall

BELAYED ▸ **belay**

BELAYER ▸ **belay**

BELAYS ▸ **belay**

BELCH vb expel wind from the stomach noisily through the mouth ▸ n act of belching

BELCHED ▸ **belch**

BELCHER ▸ **belch**

BELCHES ▸ **belch**

BELDAM n old woman, esp an ugly or malicious one

BELDAME same as ▸ **beldam**

BELDAMS ▸ **beldam**

BELEAP vb leap over

BELEAPS ▸ **beleap**

BELEAPT ▸ **beleap**

BELEE vb put on sheltered side

BELEED ▸ **belee**

BELEES ▸ **belee**

BELFRY n part of a tower where bells are hung

BELGA n former Belgian monetary unit worth five francs

BELGARD n kind gaze

BELGAS ▸ **belga**

BELIE vb show to be untrue

BELIED ▸ **belie**

BELIEF n faith or confidence

BELIEFS ▸ **belief**

BELIER ▸ **belie**

BELIERS ▸ **belie**

BELIES ▸ **belie**

BELIEVE vb accept as true or real

BELIKE adv perhaps

BELIVE adv speedily

BELL n hollow, usu metal, cup-shaped instrument that emits a ringing sound when struck ▸ vb utter (such a sound)

BELLBOY n man or boy employed in a hotel, club, etc, to carry luggage and answer calls for service

BELLE n beautiful woman, esp the most attractive woman at a function

B

BELLED ▸ bell

BELLEEK *n* kind of thin fragile porcelain with a lustrous glaze

BELLES ▸ belle

BELLHOP *same as* ▸ **bellboy**

BELLIED ▸ belly

BELLIES ▸ belly

BELLING ▸ bell

BELLMAN *n* man who rings a bell, esp (formerly) a town crier

BELLMEN ▸ bellman

BELLOCK *vb* shout

BELLOW *vb* make a low deep cry like that of a bull ▷ *n* loud deep roar

BELLOWS *pl n* instrument for pumping a stream of air into something

BELLS ▸ bell

BELLY *n* part of the body of a vertebrate which contains the intestines ▷ *vb* (cause to) swell out

BELON *n* type of oyster

BELONG *vb* be the property of

BELONGS ▸ belong

BELONS ▸ belon

BELOVE *vb* love

BELOVED *adj* dearly loved ▷ *n* person dearly loved

BELOVES ▸ belove

BELOW *adv* at or to a position lower than, under ▷ *prep* at or to a position lower than

BELOWS *same as* ▸ **bellows**

BELS ▸ bel

BELT *n* band of cloth, leather, etc, worn usu around the waist ▷ *vb* fasten with a belt

BELTED ▸ belt

BELTER *n* outstanding person or event

BELTERS ▸ belter

BELTING *n* material used to make a belt or belts ▷ *adj* excellent

BELTMAN *n* (formerly) the member of a beach life-saving team who swam out with a line attached to his belt

BELTMEN ▸ beltman

BELTS ▸ belt

BELTWAY *n* people and institutions located in the area bounded by the Washington Beltway, taken to be politically and socially out of touch with the rest of America and much given to political intrigue

BELUGA *n* large white sturgeon of the Black and Caspian Seas, from which caviar and isinglass are obtained

BELUGAS ▸ beluga

BELYING ▸ belie

BEMA *n* speaker's platform in the assembly in ancient Athens

BEMAD *vb* cause to become mad

BEMADAM *vb* call a person madam

BEMADS ▸ bemad

BEMAS ▸ bema

BEMATA ▸ bema

BEMAUL *vb* maul

BEMAULS ▸ bemaul

BEMAZED *adj* amazed

BEMBEX *n* type of wasp

BEMBIX *same as* ▸ **bembex**

BEMEAN *a less common word for* ▸ **demean**

BEMEANS ▸ bemean

BEMEANT ▸ bemean

BEMEDAL *vb* decorate with medals

BEMETE *vb* measure

BEMETED ▸ bemete

BEMETES ▸ bemete

BEMIRE *vb* soil with or as if with mire

BEMIRED ▸ bemire

BEMIRES ▸ bemire

BEMIST *vb* cloud with mist

BEMISTS ▸ bemist

BEMIX *vb* mix thoroughly

BEMIXED ▸ bemix

BEMIXES ▸ bemix

BEMIXT ▸ bemix

BEMOAN *vb* express sorrow or dissatisfaction about

BEMOANS ▸ bemoan

BEMOCK *vb* mock

BEMOCKS ▸ bemock

BEMOIL *vb* soil with mud

BEMOILS ▸ bemoil

BEMOUTH *vb* endow with a mouth

BEMUD *vb* cover with mud

BEMUDS ▸ bemud

BEMUSE *vb* confuse

BEMUSED *adj* puzzled or confused

BEMUSES ▸ bemuse

BEN *n* mountain peak ▷ *adv* in ▷ *adj* inner

BENAME *an archaic word for* ▸ **name**

BENAMED ▸ bename

BENAMES ▸ bename

BENCH *n* long seat ▷ *vb* put a person on a bench

BENCHED ▸ bench

BENCHER *n* member of the governing body of one of the Inns of Court, usually a judge or a Queen's Counsel

BENCHES ▸ bench

BENCHY *adj* (of a hillside) hollowed out in benches

BEND *vb* (cause to) form a curve ▷ *n* curved part

BENDAY *vb* (printing) reproduce using Benday technique

BENDAYS ▸ benday

BENDED ▸ bend

BENDEE *same as* ▸ **bendy**

BENDEES ▸ bendee

BENDER *n* drinking bout

BENDERS ▸ bender

BENDIER ▸ bendy

BENDING ▸ bend

BENDLET *n* narrow diagonal stripe on heraldic shield

BENDS ▸ bend

BENDY *adj* flexible or pliable ▷ *n* okra

BENDYS ▸ bendy

BENE *n* blessing

BENEATH *prep* below ▷ *adv* below

BENEFIC *adj* a rare word for beneficent

BENEFIT *n* something that improves or promotes ▷ *vb* do or receive good

BENEMPT *a past participle of* ▸ **name**

BENES ▸ bene

BENET *vb* trap (something) in a net

BENETS ▸ benet

BENGA *n* type of Kenyan popular music featuring guitars

BENGAS ▸ benga

BENI *n* sesame plant

BENIGHT *vb* shroud in darkness

BENIGN *adj* showing kindliness

BENIS ▸ beni

BENISON *n* blessing, esp a spoken one

BENJ *another word for* ▸ **bhang**

BENJES ▸ benj

BENNE *another name for* ▸ **sesame**

B

BENNES ▸ benne

BENNET n Eurasian and N African plant with yellow flowers

BENNETS ▸ bennet

BENNI n sesame

BENNIES ▸ benny

BENNIS ▸ benni

BENNY n amphetamine tablet, esp benzedrine: a stimulant

BENOMYL n fungicide, derived from imidazole, used on cereal and fruit crops: suspected of being carcinogenic

BENS ▸ ben

BENT adj not straight ▷ n personal inclination, propensity, or aptitude

BENTHAL ▸ benthos

BENTHIC ▸ benthos

BENTHON same as ▸ benthos

BENTHOS n animals and plants living at the bottom of a sea or lake

BENTIER ▸ benty

BENTO n thin lightweight box divided into compartments, which contain small separate dishes comprising a Japanese meal

BENTOS ▸ bento

BENTS ▸ bent

BENTY adj covered with bentgrass

BENUMB vb make numb or powerless

BENUMBS ▸ benumb

BENZAL n transparent crystalline substance

BENZALS ▸ benzal

BENZENE n flammable poisonous liquid used as a solvent, insecticide, etc

BENZIL n yellow compound radical

BENZILS ▸ benzil

BENZIN same as ▸ benzine

BENZINE n volatile liquid used as a solvent

BENZINS ▸ benzine

BENZOIC adj of, containing, or derived from benzoic acid or benzoin

BENZOIN n gum resin obtained from various Javanese and Sumatran trees, used in ointments, perfume, etc

BENZOL n crude form of benzene, containing toluene, xylene, and other hydrocarbons, obtained from coal tar or coal gas and used as a fuel

BENZOLE same as ▸ benzol

BENZOLS ▸ benzol

BENZOYL n of, consisting of, or containing the monovalent group C_6H_5CO-

BENZYL n of, consisting of, or containing the monovalent group $C_6H_5CH_2-$

BENZYLS ▸ benzyl

BEPAINT vb dye; paint

BEPAT vb pat

BEPATS ▸ bepat

BEPEARL vb decorate with pearls

BEPELT vb pelt energetically

BEPELTS ▸ bepelt

BEPITY vb feel great pity for

BEPROSE vb (of poetry) reduce to prose

BEPUFF vb puff up

BEPUFFS ▸ bepuff

BEQUEST n legal gift of money or property by someone who has died

BERAKE vb rake thoroughly

BERAKED ▸ berake

BERAKES ▸ berake

BERATE vb scold harshly

BERATED ▸ berate

BERATES ▸ berate

BERAY vb soil; defile

BERAYED ▸ beray

BERAYS ▸ beray

BERBERE n hot-tasting Ethiopian paste made from garlic, cayenne pepper, coriander, and other spices, often used in stews

BERBICE n as in **berbice chair** large armchair with long arms that can be folded inwards to act as leg rests

BERCEAU n arched trellis for climbing plants

BERDASH same as > berdache

BERE n barley

BEREAVE vb deprive (of) something or someone valued, esp through death

BEREFT adj deprived

BERES ▸ bere

BERET n round flat close-fitting brimless cap

BERETS ▸ beret

BERETTA n type of pistol

BERG n iceberg

BERGAMA n type of Turkish rug

BERGEN n large rucksack with a capacity of over 50 litres

BERGENS ▸ bergen

BERGERE n type of French armchair

BERGS ▸ berg

BERGYLT n large northern marine food fish

BERHYME vb mention in poetry

BERIME same as ▸ berhyme

BERIMED ▸ berime

BERIMES ▸ berime

BERK n stupid person

BERKO adj berserk

BERKS ▸ berk

BERLEY n bait scattered on water to attract fish ▷ vb scatter (bait) on water

BERLEYS ▸ berley

BERLIN n fine wool yarn used for tapestry work, etc

BERLINE same as ▸ berlin

BERLINS ▸ berlin

BERM n narrow grass strip between the road and the footpath in a residential area ▷ vb create a berm

BERME same as ▸ berm

BERMED ▸ berm

BERMES ▸ berme

BERMING ▸ berm

BERMS ▸ berm

BEROB vb rob

BEROBED adj wearing a robe

BEROBS ▸ berob

BERRET same as ▸ beret

BERRETS ▸ berret

BERRIED ▸ berry

BERRIES ▸ berry

BERRY n small soft stoneless fruit ▷ vb bear or produce berries

BERSEEM n Mediterranean clover grown as a forage crop and to improve the soil

BERSERK adj frenziedly violent or destructive ▷ n member of a class of ancient Norse warriors who worked themselves into a frenzy before battle and fought with insane fury and courage

BERTH n bunk in a ship or train ▷ vb dock (a ship)

BERTHA n wide deep capelike collar, often of

B

lace, usually to cover up a low neckline
BERTHAS ▸ bertha
BERTHE n type of lace collar
BERTHED ▸ berth
BERTHES ▸ berthe
BERTHS ▸ berth
BERYL n hard transparent mineral
BERYLS ▸ beryl
BES same as ▸ **beth**
BESAINT vb give saint status to
BESANG ▸ besing
BESAT ▸ besit
BESAW ▸ besee
BESCOUR vb scour thoroughly
BESEE vb provide for; mind
BESEECH vb ask earnestly
BESEEKE same as ▸ **beseech**
BESEEM vb be suitable for
BESEEMS ▸ beseem
BESEEN ▸ besee
BESEES ▸ besee
BESES ▸ bes
BESET vb trouble or harass constantly
BESETS ▸ beset
BESHAME vb cause to feel shame
BESHINE vb illuminate
BESHONE ▸ beshine
BESHOUT vb shout about
BESHREW vb wish evil on
BESIDE prep at, by, or to the side of
BESIDES prep in addition ▷ adv in addition
BESIEGE vb surround with military forces
BESIGH vb sigh for
BESIGHS ▸ besigh
BESING vb sing about joyfully
BESINGS ▸ besing
BESIT vb suit; fit
BESITS ▸ besit
BESLAVE vb treat as slave
BESLIME vb cover with slime
BESMEAR vb smear over
BESMILE vb smile on
BESMOKE vb blacken with smoke
BESMUT vb blacken with smut
BESMUTS ▸ besmut
BESNOW vb cover with snow
BESNOWS ▸ besnow
BESOIN n need
BESOINS ▸ besoin

BESOM n broom made of twigs ▷ vb sweep with a besom
BESOMED ▸ besom
BESOMS ▸ besom
BESORT vb fit
BESORTS ▸ besort
BESOT vb make stupid or muddled
BESOTS ▸ besot
BESPAKE ▸ bespoke
BESPAT ▸ bespit
BESPATE ▸ bespit
BESPEAK vb indicate or suggest
BESPED ▸ bespeed
BESPEED vb get on with (doing something)
BESPICE vb flavour with spices
BESPIT vb cover with spittle
BESPITS ▸ bespit
BESPOKE adj (esp of a suit) made to the customer's specifications
BESPORT vb amuse oneself
BESPOT vb mark with spots
BESPOTS ▸ bespot
BESPOUT vb speak pretentiously
BEST adj most excellent of a particular group etc ▷ adv in a manner surpassing all others ▷ n utmost effort ▷ vb defeat
BESTAD same as ▸ **bestead**
BESTAIN vb stain
BESTAR vb decorate with stars
BESTARS ▸ bestar
BESTEAD vb serve; assist
BESTED ▸ best
BESTI Indian English word for ▸ **shame**
BESTIAL adj brutal or savage
BESTICK vb cover with sharp points
BESTILL vb cause to be still
BESTING ▸ best
BESTIR vb cause (oneself) to become active
BESTIRS ▸ bestir
BESTIS ▸ besti
BESTORM vb assault
BESTOW vb present (a gift) or confer (an honour)
BESTOWS ▸ bestow
BESTREW vb scatter or lie scattered over (a surface)
BESTRID > bestride
BESTROW same as ▸ **bestrew**
BESTS ▸ best

BESTUCK ▸ bestick
BESTUD vb set with, or as with studs
BESTUDS ▸ bestud
BESUNG ▸ besing
BESWARM vb swarm over
BET n agreement between two parties that a sum of money or other stake will be paid by the loser to the party who correctly predicts the outcome of an event ▷ vb make or place a bet with (a person or persons)
BETA n second letter in the Greek alphabet, a consonant, transliterated as b
BETAINE n sweet-tasting alkaloid that occurs in the sugar beet
BETAKE vb as in betake oneself go
BETAKEN ▸ betake
BETAKES ▸ betake
BETAS ▸ beta
BETAXED adj burdened with taxes
BETCHA interj bet you
BETE same as ▸ **beet**
BETED ▸ bete
BETEEM vb accord
BETEEME same as ▸ **beteem**
BETEEMS ▸ beteem
BETEL n Asian climbing plant, the leaves and nuts of which can be chewed
BETELS ▸ betel
BETES ▸ bete
BETH n second letter of the Hebrew alphabet transliterated as b
BETHANK vb thank
BETHEL n seaman's chapel
BETHELS ▸ bethel
BETHINK vb cause (oneself) to consider or meditate
BETHORN vb cover with thorns
BETHS ▸ beth
BETHUMB vb (of books) wear by handling
BETHUMP vb thump hard
BETID ▸ betide
BETIDE vb happen (to)
BETIDED ▸ betide
BETIDES ▸ betide
BETIGHT ▸ betide
BETIME vb befall
BETIMED ▸ betime
BETIMES ▸ betime
BETING ▸ bete

BETISE n folly or lack of perception

BETISES ▸ betise

BETITLE vb give title to

BETOIL vb tire through hard work

BETOILS ▸ betoil

BETOKEN vb indicate or signify

BETON n concrete

BETONS ▸ beton

BETONY n North American plant

BETOOK the past tense of ▸ betake

BETOSS vb toss about

BETRAY vb hand over or expose (one's nation, friend, etc) treacherously to an enemy

BETRAYS ▸ betray

BETREAD vb tread over

BETRIM vb decorate

BETRIMS ▸ betrim

BETROD ▸ betread

BETROTH vb promise to marry or to give in marriage

BETS ▸ bet

BETTA n fighting fish

BETTAS ▸ betta

BETTED ▸ bet

BETTER adj more excellent than others ▷ adv in a more excellent manner ▷ pl n one's superiors ▷ vb improve upon

BETTERS ▸ better

BETTIES ▸ betty

BETTING ▸ bet

BETTONG n short-nosed rat kangaroo

BETTOR n person who bets

BETTORS ▸ bettor

BETTY n type of short crowbar

BETWEEN adv indicating position in the middle, alternatives, etc ▷ prep at a point intermediate to two other points in space, time, etc

BETWIXT adv between

BEURRE n butter

BEURRES ▸ beurre

BEVEL n slanting edge ▷ vb slope

BEVELED ▸ bevel

BEVELER ▸ bevel

BEVELS ▸ bevel

BEVER n snack

BEVERS ▸ bever

BEVIES ▸ bevy

BEVOMIT vb vomit over

BEVOR n armour protecting lower part of face

BEVORS ▸ bevor

BEVUE n careless error

BEVUES ▸ bevue

BEVVIED ▸ bevvy

BEVVIES ▸ bevvy

BEVVY n alcoholic drink ▷ vb drink alcohol

BEVY n flock or group

BEWAIL vb express great sorrow over

BEWAILS ▸ bewail

BEWARE vb be on one's guard (against)

BEWARED ▸ beware

BEWARES ▸ beware

BEWEARY vb cause to be weary

BEWEEP vb express grief through weeping

BEWEEPS ▸ beweep

BEWENT ▸ bego

BEWEPT ▸ beweep

BEWET vb make wet

BEWETS ▸ bewet

BEWHORE vb treat as a whore

BEWIG vb adorn with a wig

BEWIGS ▸ bewig

BEWITCH vb attract and fascinate

BEWORM vb fill with worms

BEWORMS ▸ beworm

BEWORRY vb beset with worry

BEWRAP vb wrap up

BEWRAPS ▸ bewrap

BEWRAPT ▸ bewrap

BEWRAY an obsolete word for ▸ betray

BEWRAYS ▸ bewray

BEY n (in the Ottoman empire) a title given to senior officers, provincial governors, and certain other officials

A **bey** was an official in the Ottoman empire. If someone plays this remember that you can of course put an O in front of it to make **obey**.

BEYLIC n province ruled over by a bey

BEYLICS ▸ beylic

BEYLIK same as ▸ beylic

BEYLIKS ▸ beylik

BEYOND prep at or to a point on the other side of ▷ adv at or to the far side of something ▷ n unknown, esp life after death

BEYONDS ▸ beyond

BEYS ▸ bey

BEZ n part of deer's horn

This word for the tine of a deer's horn is one of the essential short words for using the Z.

BEZANT n medieval Byzantine gold coin

BEZANTS ▸ bezant

BEZAZZ another word for ▸ pizzazz

BEZEL n sloping edge of a cutting tool

BEZELS ▸ bezel

BEZES ▸ bez

BEZIL archaic word for > alcoholic

BEZILS ▸ bezil

BEZIQUE n card game for two or more players

This card game played with two decks of cards combines the Q and Z and would make a wonderful bonus word.

BEZOAR n hard mass, such as a stone or hairball, in the stomach and intestines of animals, esp ruminants, and man: formerly thought to be an antidote to poisons

BEZOARS ▸ bezoar

BEZZANT same as ▸ bezant

BEZZAZZ ▸ bezazz

BEZZLE vb drink to excess

BEZZLED ▸ bezzle

BEZZLES ▸ bezzle

BHAGEE same as ▸ bhaji

BHAGEES ▸ bhagee

BHAI n Indian form of address for a man

BHAIS ▸ bhai

BHAJAN n singing of devotional songs and hymns

BHAJANS ▸ bhajan

BHAJEE same as ▸ bhaji

BHAJEES ▸ bhajee

BHAJI n Indian deep-fried savoury of chopped vegetables in spiced batter

BHAJIA ▸ bhaji

BHAJIS ▸ bhaji

BHAKTA n Hindu term for devotee of God

BHAKTAS ▸ bhakta

BHAKTI n loving devotion to God leading to nirvana

BHAKTIS ▸ bhakti

BHANG n preparation of Indian hemp used as a narcotic and intoxicant

B

BHANGRA *n* type of traditional Punjabi folk music combined with elements of Western pop music

BHANGS ▸ bhang

BHARAL *n* wild Himalayan sheep with a bluish-grey coat and round backward-curving horns

BHARALS ▸ bharal

BHAT *n* currency of Thailand

BHAVAN *n* (in India) a large house or building

BHAVANS ▸ bhavan

BHAWAN *same as* ▸ **bhavan**

BHAWANS ▸ bhawan

BHEESTY ▸ bhishti

BHEL *same as* ▸ **bael**

BHELS ▸ bhel

BHIKHU *n* fully ordained Buddhist monk

BHIKHUS ▸ bhikhu

BHINDI *same as* ▸ **bindhi**

BHINDIS ▸ bhindi

BHISHTI *n* (formerly in India) a water-carrier

BHISTEE *same as* ▸ **bhishti**

BHISTI *same as* ▸ **bhishti**

BHISTIE *same as* ▸ **bhishti**

BHISTIS ▸ bhisti

BHOONA ▸ bhuna

BHOONAS ▸ bhoona

BHOOT *same as* ▸ **bhut**

BHOOTS ▸ bhoot

BHUNA *n* Indian sauce

BHUNAS ▸ bhuna

BHUT *n* Hindu term for type of ghost

BHUTS ▸ bhut

BI *short for* ▸ **bisexual**

BIALI *same as* ▸ **bialy**

BIALIES ▸ bialy

BIALIS ▸ biali

BIALY *n* type of bagel

BIALYS ▸ bialy

BIAS *n* mental tendency, esp prejudice ▷ *vb* cause to have a bias ▷ *adj* slanting obliquely ▷ *adv* obliquely

BIASED ▸ bias

BIASES ▸ bias

BIASING ▸ bias

BIASSED ▸ bias

BIASSES ▸ bias

BIAXIAL *same as* ▸ **biaxial**

BIAXIAL *adj* (esp of a crystal) having two axes

BIB *same as* ▸ **bibcock**

BIBASIC *adj* with two bases

BIBB *n* wooden support on a mast for the trestletrees

BIBBED ▸ bib

BIBBER *n* drinker

BIBBERS ▸ bibber

BIBBERY *n* drinking to excess

BIBBING ▸ bib

BIBBLE *n* pebble

BIBBLES ▸ bibble

BIBBS ▸ bibb

BIBCOCK *n* tap with a nozzle bent downwards

BIBELOT *n* attractive or curious trinket

BIBFUL *n as in* **spill a bibful** to divulge secrets

BIBFULS ▸ bibful

BIBLE *n* any book containing the sacred writings of a religion

BIBLES ▸ bible

BIBLESS ▸ bib

BIBLIKE ▸ bib

BIBLIST *same as* > **biblicist**

BIBS ▸ bib

BICARB *n* bicarbonate of soda

BICARBS ▸ bicarb

BICCIES ▸ biccy

BICCY *n* biscuit

BICE *n* medium blue colour

BICEP *same as* ▸ **biceps**

BICEPS *n* muscle with two origins, esp the muscle that flexes the forearm

BICES ▸ bice

BICHIR *n* African freshwater fish with an elongated body

BICHIRS ▸ bichir

BICHORD *adj* having two strings for each note

BICKER *vb* argue over petty matters ▷ *n* petty squabble

BICKERS ▸ bicker

BICKIE *short for* ▸ **biscuit**

BICKIES ▸ bickie

BICOLOR *same as* > **bicolour**

BICORN *adj* having two horns or hornlike parts

BICORNE *same as* ▸ **bicorn**

BICORNS ▸ bicorn

BICRON *n* billionth part of a metre

BICRONS ▸ bicron

BICYCLE *n* vehicle with two wheels, one behind the other, pedalled by the rider ▷ *vb* ride a bicycle

BID *vb* offer (an amount) in attempting to buy something, esp in competition with others as at an auction ▷ *n* offer of a specified amount, as at an auction

BIDARKA *n* canoe covered in animal skins, esp sealskin, used by the Inuit of Alaska

BIDDEN ▸ bid

BIDDER ▸ bid

BIDDERS ▸ bid

BIDDIES ▸ biddy

BIDDING ▸ bid

BIDDY *n* woman, esp an old gossipy one

BIDE *vb* stay or continue

BIDED ▸ bide

BIDENT *n* instrument with two prongs

BIDENTS ▸ bident

BIDER ▸ bide

BIDERS ▸ bide

BIDES ▸ bide

BIDET *n* low basin for washing the genital area

BIDETS ▸ bidet

BIDI *same as* ▸ **beedi**

BIDING ▸ bide

BIDINGS ▸ bide

BIDIS ▸ bidi

BIDON *n* oil drum

BIDONS ▸ bidon

BIDS ▸ bid

BIELD *n* shelter ▷ *vb* shelter or take shelter

BIELDED ▸ bield

BIELDS ▸ bield

BIELDY *adj* sheltered

BIEN *adv* well

BIENNIA > **biennium**

BIER *n* stand on which a corpse or coffin rests before burial

BIERS ▸ bier

BIFACE *n* prehistoric stone tool

BIFACES ▸ biface

BIFF *n* blow with the fist ▷ *vb* give (someone) such a blow

BIFFED ▸ biff

BIFFER *n* someone, such as a sportsperson, who has a reputation for hitting hard

BIFFERS ▸ biffer

BIFFIES ▸ biffy

BIFFIN *n* variety of red cooking apple

BIFFING ▸ biff

BIFFINS ▸ biffin

BIFFO *n* fighting or aggressive behaviour ▷ *adj* aggressive

BIFFOS ▸ biffo

BIFFS ▸ biff

BIFFY *n* outdoor toilet

BIFID *adj* divided into two by

a cleft in the middle
BIFIDLY ▶ **bifid**
BIFILAR adj having two parallel threads, as in the suspension of certain measuring instruments
BIFLEX adj bent or flexed in two places
BIFOCAL adj having two different focuses
BIFOLD adj that can be folded in two places
BIFORM adj having or combining the characteristics of two forms, as a centaur
BIFTAH n ▶ **bifter**
BIFTAHS ▶ **biftah**
BIFTER n cannabis cigarette
BIFTERS ▶ **bifter**
BIG adj of considerable size, height, number, or capacity ▷ adv on a grand scale ▷ vb build
BIGA n chariot drawn by two horses
BIGAE ▶ **biga**
BIGAMY n crime of marrying a person while still legally married to someone else
BIGENER n hybrid between individuals of different genera
BIGEYE n type of tropical or subtropical red marine fish with very large eyes and rough scales
BIGEYES ▶ **bigeye**
BIGFEET ▶ **bigfoot**
BIGFOOT n yeti ▷ vb throw one's weight around
BIGG n type of barley
BIGGED ▶ **big**
BIGGER ▶ **big**
BIGGEST ▶ **big**
BIGGETY same as ▶ **biggity**
BIGGIE n something big or important
BIGGIES ▶ **biggie**
BIGGIN n plain close-fitting cap, often tying under the chin, worn in the Middle Ages and by children in the 17th century
BIGGING ▶ **big**
BIGGINS ▶ **biggin**
BIGGISH ▶ **big**
BIGGITY adj conceited
BIGGON same as ▶ **biggin**
BIGGONS ▶ **biggon**
BIGGS ▶ **bigg**
BIGGY same as ▶ **biggie**

BIGHA n in India, unit for measuring land
BIGHAS ▶ **bigha**
BIGHEAD n conceited person
BIGHORN n large wild mountain sheep of N America and NE Asia, the male of which has massive curved horns
BIGHT n long curved shoreline ▷ vb fasten or bind with a bight
BIGHTED ▶ **bight**
BIGHTS ▶ **bight**
BIGLY ▶ **big**
BIGNESS ▶ **big**
BIGOS n Polish stew
BIGOSES ▶ **bigos**
BIGOT n person who is intolerant, esp regarding religion or race
BIGOTED ▶ **bigot**
BIGOTRY n attitudes, behaviour, or way of thinking of a bigot
BIGOTS ▶ **bigot**
BIGS ▶ **big**
BIGTIME adj important
BIGWIG n important person
BIGWIGS ▶ **bigwig**
BIJOU adj (of a house) small but elegant ▷ n something small and delicately worked

> A **bijou** is a French word for a jewel, and it is indeed a jewel to play, getting rid of awkward letters for a good score. And remember that the plural can be **bijous** or **bijoux**.

BIJOUS ▶ **bijou**
BIJOUX ▶ **bijou**
BIKE same as ▶ **bicycle**
BIKED ▶ **bike**
BIKER n person who rides a motorcycle
BIKERS ▶ **biker**
BIKES ▶ **bike**
BIKEWAY n cycle lane
BIKIE n member of a motorcycle gang
BIKIES ▶ **bikie**
BIKING ▶ **bike**
BIKINGS ▶ **bike**
BIKINI n woman's brief two-piece swimming costume
BIKINIS ▶ **bikini**
BIKKIE slang word for ▶ **biscuit**
BIKKIES ▶ **bikkie**

BILAYER n part of cell membrane
BILBIES ▶ **bilby**
BILBO n (formerly) a sword with a marked temper and elasticity
BILBOA same as ▶ **bilbo**
BILBOAS ▶ **bilboa**
BILBOES ▶ **bilbo**
BILBOS ▶ **bilbo**
BILBY n Australian marsupial with long pointed ears and grey fur
BILE n bitter yellow fluid secreted by the liver ▷ vb boil
BILED ▶ **bile**
BILES ▶ **bile**
BILEVEL n hairstyle with two different lengths
BILGE n nonsense ▷ vb (of a vessel) to take in water at the bilge
BILGED ▶ **bilge**
BILGES ▶ **bilge**
BILGIER ▶ **bilge**
BILGING ▶ **bilge**
BILGY ▶ **bilge**
BILIAN n type of tree used for its wood
BILIANS ▶ **bilian**
BILIARY adj of bile, the ducts that convey bile, or the gall bladder ▷ n disease found in dogs
BILIMBI n type of fruit-bearing tree
BILING ▶ **bile**
BILIOUS adj sick, nauseous
BILK vb cheat, esp by not paying ▷ n swindle or cheat
BILKED ▶ **bilk**
BILKER ▶ **bilk**
BILKERS ▶ **bilk**
BILKING ▶ **bilk**
BILKS ▶ **bilk**
BILL n money owed for goods or services supplied ▷ vb to send or present an account for payment to (a person)
BILLBUG n type of weevil
BILLED ▶ **bill**
BILLER n stem of a plant
BILLERS ▶ **biller**
BILLET vb assign a lodging to (a soldier) ▷ n accommodation for a soldier in civil lodgings
BILLETS ▶ **billet**
BILLIE same as ▶ **billy**
BILLIES ▶ **billy**
BILLING n relative

importance of a performer or act as reflected in the prominence given in programmes, advertisements, etc

BILLION n one thousand million ▷ determiner amounting to a billion

BILLMAN n person who uses a billhook

BILLMEN ▸ billman

BILLON n alloy consisting of gold or silver and a base metal, usually copper, used esp for coinage

BILLONS ▸ billon

BILLOW n large sea wave ▷ vb rise up or swell out

BILLOWS ▸ billow

BILLOWY adj full of or forming billows

BILLS ▸ bill

BILLY n metal can or pot for cooking on a camp fire

BILLYO n as in like billyo phrase used to emphasize or intensify something

BILLYOH same as ▸ billyo

BILLYOS ▸ billyo

BILOBAR same as ▸ bilobate

BILOBED same as ▸ bilobate

BILSTED n American gum tree

BILTONG n strips of dried meat

BIMA same as ▸ bema

BIMAH same as ▸ bema

BIMAHS ▸ bimah

BIMANAL same as ▸ bimanous

BIMAS ▸ bima

BIMBLE n as in bimble box type of dense Australian tree

BIMETAL n material made from two sheets of metal

BIMODAL adj having two modes

BIMORPH n assembly of two piezoelectric crystals cemented together so that an applied voltage causes one to expand and the other to contract, converting electrical signals into mechanical energy. Conversely, bending can generate a voltage: used in loudspeakers, gramophone pick-ups, etc

BIN n container for rubbish or for storing grain, coal,

etc ▷ vb put in a rubbish bin

BINAL adj twofold

BINARY adj composed of, relating to, or involving two ▷ n something composed of two parts or things

BINATE adj occurring in two parts or in pairs

BIND vb make secure with or as if with a rope ▷ n annoying situation

BINDER n firm cover for holding loose sheets of paper together

BINDERS ▸ binder

BINDERY n bookbindery

BINDHI same as ▸ bindi

BINDHIS ▸ bindhi

BINDI n decorative dot worn in the middle of the forehead, esp by Hindu women

BINDING ▸ bind

BINDIS ▸ bindi

BINDLE n small packet

BINDLES ▸ bindle

BINDS ▸ bind

BINE n climbing or twining stem of any of various plants, such as the woodbine or bindweed

BINER n clip used by climbers

BINERS ▸ biner

BINES ▸ bine

BING n heap or pile, esp of spoil from a mine

BINGE n bout of excessive indulgence, esp in drink ▷ vb indulge in a binge (esp of eating or drinking)

BINGED ▸ binge

BINGER n person who is addicted to crack cocaine

BINGERS ▸ binger

BINGES ▸ binge

BINGIES ▸ bingy

BINGING ▸ binge

BINGLE n minor crash or upset, as in a car or on a surfboard ▷ vb layer (hair)

BINGLED ▸ bingle

BINGLES ▸ bingle

BINGO n gambling game in which numbers are called out and covered by the players on their individual cards ▷ sentence substitute cry by the winner of a game of bingo

BINGOES ▸ bingo

BINGOS ▸ bingo

BINGS ▸ bing

BINGY Australian slang for ▸ stomach

BINIOU n small high-pitched Breton bagpipe

BINIOUS ▸ biniou

BINIT n (computing) early form of bit

BINITS ▸ binit

BINK n ledge

BINKS ▸ bink

BINMAN another name for ▸ dustman

BINMEN ▸ binman

BINNED ▸ bin

BINNING ▸ bin

BINOCLE n binocular-style telescope

BINOCS > binocular

BINS ▸ bin

BIO short for > biography

BIOBANK n large store of human samples for medical research

BIOCHIP n small glass or silicon plate containing an array of biochemical molecules or structures, used as a biosensor or in gene sequencing

BIOCIDE n substance used to destroy living things

BIODATA n information regarding an individual's education and work history, esp in the context of a selection process

BIODOT n temperature-sensitive device stuck to the skin in order to monitor stress

BIODOTS ▸ biodot

BIOFACT n item of biological information

BIOFILM n thin layer of living organisms

BIOFUEL n gaseous, liquid, or solid substance of biological origin that is used as a fuel ▷ vb fuel (a vehicle, etc) using biofuel

BIOG short form of > biography

BIOGAS n gaseous fuel produced by the fermentation of organic waste

BIOGEN n hypothetical protein assumed to be the basis of the formation and functioning of body cells and tissues

BIOGENS ▸ biogen

BIOGENY n principle that a living organism must originate from a parent form similar to itself

BIOGS ▶ biog

BIOHERM n mound of material laid down by sedentary marine organisms, esp a coral reef

BIOLOGY n study of living organisms

BIOMASS n total number of living organisms in a given area

BIOME n major ecological community, extending over a large area and usually characterized by a dominant vegetation

BIOMES ▶ biome

BIONIC adj having a part of the body that is operated electronically

BIONICS n study of biological functions in order to develop electronic equipment that operates similarly

BIONOMY n laws of life

BIONT n living thing

BIONTIC ▶ biont

BIONTS ▶ biont

BIOPHOR n hypothetical material particle

BIOPIC n film based on the life of a famous person

BIOPICS ▶ biopic

BIOPSIC ▶ biopsy

BIOPSY n examination of tissue from a living body ▷ vb perform a biopsy on

BIOPTIC ▶ biopsy

BIOS ▶ bio

BIOTA n plant and animal life of a particular region or period

BIOTAS ▶ biota

BIOTECH n biotechnology

BIOTIC adj of or relating to living organisms ▷ n living organism

BIOTICS ▶ biotic

BIOTIN n vitamin of the B complex, abundant in egg yolk and liver

BIOTINS ▶ biotin

BIOTITE n black or dark green mineral of the mica group

BIOTOPE n small area, such as the bark of a tree, that supports its own distinctive community

BIOTRON n climate-control chamber

BIOTYPE n group of genetically identical plants within a species, produced by apomixis

BIPACK n obsolete filming process

BIPACKS ▶ bipack

BIPARTY adj involving two parties

BIPED n animal with two feet ▷ adj having two feet

BIPEDAL adj having two feet

BIPEDS ▶ biped

BIPLANE n aeroplane with two sets of wings, one above the other

BIPOD n two-legged support or stand

BIPODS ▶ bipod

BIPOLAR adj having two poles

BIPRISM n prism having a highly obtuse angle to facilitate beam splitting

BIRCH n tree with thin peeling bark ▷ vb flog with a birch

BIRCHED ▶ birch

BIRCHEN ▶ birch

BIRCHES ▶ birch

BIRCHIR ▶ bichir

BIRD n creature with feathers and wings, most types of which can fly ▷ vb hunt for birds

BIRDDOG n dog used or trained to retrieve game birds

BIRDED ▶ bird

BIRDER n birdwatcher

BIRDERS ▶ birder

BIRDIE n score of one stroke under par for a hole ▷ vb play (a hole) in one stroke under par

BIRDIED ▶ birdie

BIRDIES ▶ birdie

BIRDING ▶ bird

BIRDMAN n man concerned with birds, such as a fowler or ornithologist

BIRDMEN ▶ birdman

BIRDS ▶ bird

BIREME n ancient galley having two banks of oars

BIREMES ▶ bireme

BIRETTA n stiff square cap worn by the Catholic clergy

BIRIANI same as ▶ biryani

BIRK n birch tree ▷ adj consisting or made of birch

BIRKEN adj relating to the birch tree

BIRKIE n spirited or lively person ▷ adj lively

BIRKIER ▶ birkie

BIRKIES ▶ birkie

BIRKS ▶ birk

BIRL same as ▶ burl

BIRLE same as ▶ burl

BIRLED ▶ birl

BIRLER ▶ birl

BIRLERS ▶ birl

BIRLES ▶ birle

BIRLING ▶ birl

BIRLINN n small Scottish boat

BIRLS ▶ birl

BIRO n tradename of a kind of ballpoint pen

BIROS ▶ biro

BIRR vb make or cause to make a whirring sound ▷ n whirring sound

BIRRED ▶ birr

BIRRING ▶ birr

BIRRS ▶ birr

BIRSE n bristle

BIRSES ▶ birse

BIRSIER ▶ birsy

BIRSLE vb roast

BIRSLED ▶ birsle

BIRSLES ▶ birsle

BIRSY adj bristly

BIRTH n process of bearing young ▷ vb give birth to

BIRTHED ▶ birth

BIRTHS ▶ birth

BIRYANI n any of a variety of Indian dishes made with rice, highly flavoured and coloured with saffron or turmeric, mixed with meat or fish

BIS adv twice ▷ sentence substitute encore! again!

BISCUIT n small flat dry sweet or plain cake ▷ adj pale brown

BISE n cold dry northerly wind in Switzerland and the neighbouring parts of France and Italy, usually in the spring

BISECT vb divide into two equal parts

BISECTS ▶ bisect

BISES ▶ bise

BISH n mistake

BISHES ▶ bish

BISHOP n clergyman who governs a diocese ▷ vb make a bishop

BISHOPS ▸ bishop

BISK *a less common spelling of* ▸ **bisque**

BISKS ▸ bisk

BISMAR *n* type of weighing scale

BISMARS ▸ bismar

BISMUTH *n* pinkish-white metallic element

BISNAGA *n* type of cactus

BISOM ▸ besom

BISOMS ▸ bisom

BISON *same as* ▸ **buffalo**

BISONS ▸ bison

BISQUE *n* thick rich soup made from shellfish

BISQUES ▸ bisque

BISSON *adj* blind

BIST *a form of the second person singular of* ▸ **be**

BISTATE *adj* involving two states

BISTER *same as* ▸ **bestir**

BISTERS ▸ bister

BISTORT *n* Eurasian plant with a spike of small pink flowers

BISTRE *n* transparent water-soluble brownish-yellow pigment made by boiling the soot of wood, used for pen and wash drawings

BISTRED ▸ bistre

BISTRES ▸ bistre

BISTRO *n* small restaurant

BISTROS ▸ bistro

BIT *n* small piece, portion, or quantity

BITABLE ▸ bite

BITCH *n* female dog, fox, or wolf ▷ *vb* complain or grumble

BITCHED ▸ bitch

BITCHEN *same as* > **bitching**

BITCHES ▸ bitch

BITCHY *adj* spiteful or malicious

BITE *vb* grip, tear, or puncture the skin, as with the teeth or jaws ▷ *n* act of biting

BITER ▸ bite

BITERS ▸ bite

BITES ▸ bite

BITING ▸ bite

BITINGS ▸ bite

BITLESS *adj* without a bit

BITMAP *n* picture created by colour or shading on a visual display unit ▷ *vb* create a bitmap of

BITMAPS ▸ bitmap

BITO *n* African and Asian tree

BITONAL *adj* consisting of black and white tones

BITOS ▸ bito

BITOU *n as in* **bitou bush** type of sprawling woody shrub

BITS ▸ bit

BITSER *n* mongrel dog

BITSERS ▸ bitser

BITSIER ▸ bitsy

BITSY *adj* very small

BITT *n* one of a pair of strong posts on the deck of a ship for securing mooring and other lines ▷ *vb* secure (a line) by means of a bitt

BITTE *interj* you're welcome

BITTED ▸ bitt

BITTEN ▸ bite

BITTER *adj* having a sharp unpleasant taste ▷ *n* beer with a slightly bitter taste ▷ *adv* very ▷ *vb* make or become bitter

BITTERN *n* wading marsh bird with a booming call

BITTERS *pl n* bitter-tasting spirits flavoured with plant extracts

BITTIE *n* small piece

BITTIER ▸ bitty

BITTIES ▸ bittie

BITTING ▸ bitt

BITTOCK *n* small amount

BITTOR *n* bittern

BITTORS ▸ bittor

BITTOUR *same as* ▸ **bittor**

BITTS ▸ bitt

BITTUR *same as* ▸ **bittor**

BITTURS ▸ bittur

BITTY *adj* lacking unity, disjointed

BITUMED *adj* covered with bitumen

BITUMEN *n* black sticky substance obtained from tar or petrol

BIVALVE *adj* (marine mollusc) with two hinged segments to its shell ▷ *n* sea creature, such as an oyster or mussel, that has a shell consisting of two hinged valves and breathes through gills

BIVIA ▸ bivium

BIVINYL *another word for* > **butadiene**

BIVIOUS *adj* offering a choice of two different ways

BIVIUM *n* parting of ways

BIVOUAC *n* temporary camp in the open air ▷ *vb* camp in a bivouac

BIVVIED ▸ bivvy

BIVVIES ▸ bivvy

BIVVY *n* small tent or shelter ▷ *vb* camp in a bivouac

BIZ *n* business

BIZARRE *adj* odd or unusual ▷ *n* bizarre thing

BIZARRO *n* bizarre person

BIZAZZ *same as* ▸ **pizazz**

BIZE *n* dry, cold wind in France

BIZES ▸ bize

BIZNAGA *same as* ▸ **bisnaga**

BIZONAL ▸ bizone

BIZONE *n* place comprising two zones

BIZONES ▸ bizone

BIZZES ▸ biz

BIZZIES ▸ bizzy

BIZZO *n* empty and irrelevant talk or ideas

BIZZOS ▸ bizzo

BIZZY *n* policeman

BLAB *vb* reveal (secrets) indiscreetly

BLABBED ▸ blab

BLABBER *vb* talk without thinking ▷ *n* person who blabs

BLABBY *adj* talking too much; indiscreet

BLABS ▸ blab

BLACK *adj* of the darkest colour, like coal ▷ *n* darkest colour ▷ *vb* make black

BLACKED ▸ black

BLACKEN *vb* make or become black

BLACKER ▸ black

BLACKLY ▸ black

BLACKS ▸ black

BLAD *same as* ▸ **blaud**

BLADDED ▸ blad

BLADDER *n* sac in the body where urine is held

BLADE *n* cutting edge of a weapon or tool

BLADED ▸ blade

BLADER *n* person skating with in-line skates

BLADERS ▸ blader

BLADES ▸ blade

BLADIER ▸ blady

BLADING *n* act or instance of skating with in-line skates

BLADS ▸ blad

BLADY *adj as in* **blady grass**

coarse leafy Australasian grass

BLAE *adj* bluish-grey

BLAER ▸ **blae**

BLAES *n* hardened clay or shale, esp when crushed and used to form the top layer of a sports pitch: bluish-grey or reddish in colour

BLAEST ▸ **blae**

BLAFF *n* West Indian stew

BLAFFS ▸ **blaff**

BLAG *vb* obtain by wheedling or cadging ▸ *n* robbery, esp with violence

BLAGGED ▸ **blag**

BLAGGER ▸ **blag**

BLAGS ▸ **blag**

BLAGUE *n* pretentious but empty talk

BLAGUER ▸ **blague**

BLAGUES ▸ **blague**

BLAH *n* worthless or silly talk ▸ *adj* uninteresting ▸ *vb* talk nonsense or boringly

BLAHED ▸ **blah**

BLAHING ▸ **blah**

BLAHS ▸ **blah**

BLAIN *n* blister, blotch, or sore on the skin

BLAINS ▸ **blain**

BLAISE *same as* ▸ **blaes**

BLAIZE *same as* ▸ **blaes**

BLAM *n* representation of the sound of a bullet being fired

BLAME *vb* consider (someone) responsible ▸ *n* responsibility for something that is wrong

BLAMED *euphemistic word for* ▸ **damned**

BLAMER ▸ **blame**

BLAMERS ▸ **blame**

BLAMES ▸ **blame**

BLAMING ▸ **blame**

BLAMS ▸ **blam**

BLANCH *vb* become white or pale

BLANCO *n* whitening substance ▸ *vb* whiten (something) with blanco

BLANCOS ▸ **blanco**

BLAND *adj* dull and uninteresting ▸ *n* bland thing ▸ *vb as in* **bland out** to become bland

BLANDED ▸ **bland**

BLANDER ▸ **bland**

BLANDLY ▸ **bland**

BLANDS ▸ **bland**

BLANK *adj* not written on ▸ *n* empty space ▸ *vb* cross out, blot, or obscure

BLANKED ▸ **blank**

BLANKER ▸ **blank**

BLANKET *n* large thick cloth used as covering for a bed ▸ *adj* applying to a wide group of people, situations, conditions, etc ▸ *vb* cover as with a blanket

BLANKLY ▸ **blank**

BLANKS ▸ **blank**

BLARE *vb* sound loudly and harshly ▸ *n* loud harsh noise

BLARED ▸ **blare**

BLARES ▸ **blare**

BLARING ▸ **blare**

BLARNEY *n* flattering talk ▸ *vb* cajole with flattery

BLART *vb* sound loudly and harshly

BLARTED ▸ **blart**

BLARTS ▸ **blart**

BLASE *adj* indifferent or bored through familiarity

BLASH *n* splash

BLASHES ▸ **blash**

BLASHY *adj* windy and rainy

BLAST *n* explosion ▸ *vb* blow up (a rock etc) with explosives ▸ *interj* expression of annoyance

BLASTED *adv* extreme or extremely ▸ *adj* blighted or withered

BLASTER ▸ **blast**

BLASTIE *n* ugly creature

BLASTS ▸ **blast**

BLASTY *adj* gusty

BLAT *vb* cry out or bleat like a sheep

BLATANT *adj* glaringly obvious

BLATE *adj* shy; ill at ease

BLATER ▸ **blate**

BLATEST ▸ **blate**

BLATHER *vb* speak foolishly ▸ *n* foolish talk

BLATS ▸ **blat**

BLATT *n* newspaper

BLATTED ▸ **blat**

BLATTER *n, vb* prattle

BLATTS ▸ **blatt**

BLAUBOK *n* South African antelope

BLAUD *vb* slap

BLAUDED ▸ **blaud**

BLAUDS ▸ **blaud**

BLAW *vb* blow

BLAWED ▸ **blaw**

BLAWING ▸ **blaw**

BLAWN ▸ **blaw**

BLAWORT *n* harebell

BLAWS ▸ **blaw**

BLAY *n* small river fish

BLAYS ▸ **blay**

BLAZAR *n* type of active galaxy

BLAZARS ▸ **blazar**

BLAZE *n* strong fire or flame ▸ *vb* burn or shine brightly

BLAZED ▸ **blaze**

BLAZER *n* lightweight jacket, often in the colours of a school etc

BLAZERS ▸ **blazer**

BLAZES *pl n* hell

BLAZING ▸ **blaze**

BLAZON *vb* proclaim publicly ▸ *n* coat of arms

BLAZONS ▸ **blazon**

BLEACH *vb* make or become white or colourless ▸ *n* bleaching agent

BLEAK *adj* exposed and barren ▸ *n* type of slender silvery European fish found in slow-flowing rivers

BLEAKER ▸ **bleak**

BLEAKLY ▸ **bleak**

BLEAKS ▸ **bleak**

BLEAKY *same as* ▸ **bleak**

BLEAR *vb* make (eyes or sight) dim with or as if with tears ▸ *adj* bleary

BLEARED ▸ **blear**

BLEARER ▸ **blear**

BLEARS ▸ **blear**

BLEARY *adj* with eyes dimmed, as by tears or tiredness

BLEAT *vb* (of a sheep, goat, or calf) utter its plaintive cry ▸ *n* cry of sheep, goats, and calves

BLEATED ▸ **bleat**

BLEATER ▸ **bleat**

BLEATS ▸ **bleat**

BLEB *n* fluid-filled blister on the skin

BLEBBY ▸ **bleb**

BLEBS ▸ **bleb**

BLED ▸ **bleed**

BLEE *n* complexion; hue

BLEED *vb* lose or emit blood

BLEEDER *n* despicable person

BLEEDS ▸ **bleed**

BLEEP *n* high-pitched signal or beep ▸ *vb* make such a noise

BLEEPED ▸ **bleep**

BLEEPER *n* small portable

B

radio receiver that makes a bleeping signal

BLEEPS ▸ bleep

BLEES ▸ blee

BLELLUM n babbler; blusterer

BLEMISH n defect or stain ▹vb spoil or tarnish

BLENCH vb shy away, as in fear

BLEND vb mix or mingle (components or ingredients) ▹n mixture

BLENDE n mineral consisting mainly of zinc sulphide

BLENDED ▸ blend

BLENDER n electrical appliance for puréeing vegetables etc

BLENDES ▸ blende

BLENDS ▸ blend

BLENNY n small fish with a tapering scaleless body

BLENT a past participle of ▸ blend

BLERT n foolish person

BLERTS ▸ blert

BLESBOK n S African antelope with a deep reddish-brown coat and a white blaze between the eyes

BLESS vb make holy by means of a religious rite

BLESSED ▸ bless

BLESSER ▸ bless

BLESSES ▸ bless

BLEST ▸ bless

BLET n state of softness or decay in certain fruits, such as the medlar, brought about by overripening ▹vb go soft

BLETHER same as ▸ blather

BLETS ▸ blet

BLETTED ▸ blet

BLEW ▸ blow

BLEWART same as ▸ blawort

BLEWITS n type of edible fungus with a pale brown cap and a bluish stalk

BLEY same as ▸ blay

BLEYS ▸ bley

BLIGHT n person or thing that spoils or prevents growth ▹vb cause to suffer a blight

BLIGHTS ▸ blight

BLIGHTY n home country; home leave

BLIKSEM interj South

African expression of surprise

BLIMEY interj exclamation of surprise or annoyance

BLIMP n small airship

BLIMPS ▸ blimp

BLIMY same as ▸ blimey

BLIN Scots word for ▸ blind

BLIND adj unable to see ▹vb deprive of sight ▹n covering for a window

BLINDED ▸ blind

BLINDER same as ▸ blind

BLINDLY ▸ blind

BLINDS ▸ blind

BLING adj flashy ▹n ostentatious jewellery

BLINGER ▸ bling

BLINGS ▸ bling

BLINGY same as ▸ bling

BLINI pl n Russian pancakes made of buckwheat flour and yeast

BLINIS same as ▸ blini

BLINK vb close and immediately reopen (the eyes) ▹n act of blinking

BLINKED ▸ blink

BLINKER vb provide (a horse) with blinkers ▹n flashing light for sending messages, etc, such as a direction indicator on a road vehicle

BLINKS ▸ blink

BLINNED ▸ blin

BLINS ▸ blin

BLINTZ n thin pancake folded over a filling usually of apple, cream cheese, or meat

BLINTZE same as ▸ blintz

BLINY same as ▸ blini

BLIP n spot of light on a radar screen indicating the position of an object ▹vb produce such a noise

BLIPPED ▸ blip

BLIPS ▸ blip

BLISS n perfect happiness ▹vb make or become perfectly happy

BLISSED ▸ bliss

BLISSES ▸ bliss

BLIST archaic form of ▸ blessed

BLISTER n small bubble on the skin ▹vb (cause to) have blisters

BLIT vb move or copy (a block of data) from one location to another in a

computer's memory

BLITE n type of herb

BLITES ▸ blite

BLITHE adj casual and indifferent

BLITHER same as ▸ blether

BLITS ▸ blit

BLITTED ▸ blit

BLITTER n circuit that transfers large amounts of data within a computer's memory

BLITZ n violent and sustained attack by aircraft ▹vb attack suddenly and intensively

BLITZED ▸ blitz

BLITZER ▸ blitz

BLITZES ▸ blitz

BLIVE same as ▸ belive

BLOAT vb cause to swell, as with liquid or air ▹n abnormal distention of the abdomen in cattle, sheep, etc, caused by accumulation of gas in the stomach

BLOATED adj swollen, as with a liquid, air, or wind

BLOATER n salted smoked herring

BLOATS ▸ bloat

BLOB n soft mass or drop ▹vb put blobs, as of ink or paint, on

BLOBBED ▸ blob

BLOBBY ▸ blob

BLOBS ▸ blob

BLOC n people or countries combined by a common interest

BLOCK n large solid piece of wood, stone, etc ▹vb obstruct or impede by introducing an obstacle

BLOCKED adj functionally impeded by amphetamine

BLOCKER n person or thing that blocks

BLOCKIE n owner of a small property, esp a farm

BLOCKS ▸ block

BLOCKY adj like a block, esp in shape and solidity

BLOCS ▸ bloc

BLOG n journal written on-line and accessible to users of the internet ▹vb write a blog

BLOGGED ▸ blog

BLOGGER ▸ blog

BLOGS ▸ blog

BLOKART n single-seat

three-wheeled vehicle propelled by the wind

BLOKE n man

BLOKES ▸ bloke

BLOKEY same as ▸ blokeish

BLOKIER ▸ blokey

BLOKISH same as ▸ blokeish

BLOND adj (of men's hair) of a light colour ▷ n person, esp a man, having light-coloured hair and skin

BLONDE n fair-haired (person) ▷ adj (of hair) fair

BLONDER ▸ blonde

BLONDES ▸ blonde

BLONDS ▸ blond

BLOOD n red fluid that flows around the body ▷ vb initiate (a person) to war or hunting

BLOODED adj (of horses, cattle, etc) of good breeding

BLOODS ▸ blood

BLOODY adj covered with blood ▷ adv extreme or extremely ▷ vb stain with blood

BLOOEY adj out of order; faulty

BLOOIE same as ▸ blooey

BLOOK n book published on a blog

BLOOKS ▸ blook

BLOOM n blossom on a flowering plant ▷ vb (of flowers) open

BLOOMED adj (of a lens) coated with a thin film of magnesium fluoride or some other substance to reduce the amount of light lost by reflection

BLOOMER n stupid mistake

BLOOMS ▸ bloom

BLOOMY adj having a fine whitish coating on the surface, such as on the rind of a cheese

BLOOP vb (baseball) hit a ball into air beyond infield

BLOOPED ▸ bloop

BLOOPER n stupid mistake

BLOOPS ▸ bloop

BLOOSME same as ▸ blossom

BLORE n strong blast of wind

BLORES ▸ blore

BLOSSOM n flowers of a plant ▷ vb (of plants) flower

BLOT n spot or stain ▷ vb cause a blemish in or on

BLOTCH n discoloured area or stain ▷ vb become or cause to become marked by such discoloration

BLOTCHY adj covered in or marked by blotches

BLOTS ▸ blot

BLOTTED ▸ blot

BLOTTER n sheet of blotting paper

BLOTTO adj extremely drunk

BLOTTY adj covered in blots

BLOUBOK same as ▸ blaubok

BLOUSE n woman's shirtlike garment ▷ vb hang or cause to hang in full loose folds

BLOUSED ▸ blouse

BLOUSES ▸ blouse

BLOUSON n short loose jacket with a tight waist

BLOUSY adj loose; blouse-like

BLOW vb (of air, the wind, etc) move ▷ n hard hit

BLOWBY n leakage of gas past the piston of an engine at maximum pressure

BLOWBYS ▸ blowby

BLOWED ▸ blow

BLOWER n mechanical device, such as a fan, that blows

BLOWERS ▸ blower

BLOWFLY n fly that lays its eggs in meat

BLOWGUN same as ▸ blowpipe

BLOWIE n bluebottle

BLOWIER ▸ blowy

BLOWIES ▸ blowie

BLOWING n moving of air

BLOWN ▸ blow

BLOWOFF n discharge of a surplus fluid

BLOWOUT n sudden loss of air in a tyre

BLOWS ▸ blow

BLOWSE n large, red-faced woman

BLOWSED same as ▸ blowsy

BLOWSES ▸ blowse

BLOWSY adj fat, untidy, and red-faced

BLOWUP n fit of temper

BLOWUPS ▸ blowup

BLOWY adj windy

BLOWZE same as ▸ blowse

BLOWZED same as ▸ blowsy

BLOWZES ▸ blowze

BLOWZY same as ▸ blowsy

BLUB a slang word for ▸ blubber

BLUBBED ▸ blub

BLUBBER n, vb sob without restraint ▷ adj swollen or fleshy ▷ n fat of whales, seals, etc

BLUBS ▸ blub

BLUCHER n high shoe with laces over the tongue

BLUDE Scots form of ▸ blood

BLUDES ▸ blude

BLUDGE vb evade work ▷ n easy task

BLUDGED ▸ bludge

BLUDGER n person who scrounges

BLUDGES ▸ bludge

BLUDIE Scots form of ▸ bloody

BLUDIER ▸ bludie

BLUDY same as ▸ bludie

BLUE n colour of a clear unclouded sky ▷ adj of the colour blue ▷ vb make or become blue

BLUECAP another name for ▸ bluetit

BLUED ▸ blue

BLUEFIN another name for ▸ tunny

BLUEGUM n tall fast-growing widely cultivated Australian tree with aromatic leaves, bark that peels off in shreds, and hard timber

BLUEING ▸ blue

BLUEISH same as ▸ bluish

BLUEJAY n common N American jay with bright blue plumage and greyish-white underparts

BLUELY ▸ blue

BLUER ▸ blue

BLUES pl n type of music

BLUEST ▸ blue

BLUESY ▸ blues

BLUET n N American plant with small four-petalled blue flowers

BLUETIT n small European bird with a blue crown, wings, and tail and yellow underparts

BLUETS ▸ bluet

BLUETTE n short, brilliant piece of music

BLUEY adj bluish ▷ n informal Australian word meaning blanket

BLUEYS ▸ bluey

BLUFF vb pretend to be

confident in order to influence (someone) ▷ *n* act of bluffing ▷ *adj* good-naturedly frank and hearty

BLUFFED ▸ **bluff**

BLUFFER ▸ **bluff**

BLUFFLY ▸ **bluff**

BLUFFS ▸ **bluff**

BLUGGY *same as* ▸ **bloody**

BLUID *Scots word for* ▸ **blood**

BLUIDS ▸ **bluid**

BLUIDY ▸ **bluid**

BLUIER ▸ **bluey**

BLUIEST ▸ **bluey**

BLUING ▸ **blue**

BLUINGS ▸ **blue**

BLUISH *adj* slightly blue

BLUME *Scots word for* ▸ **bloom**

BLUMED ▸ **blume**

BLUMES ▸ **blume**

BLUMING ▸ **blume**

BLUNDER *n* clumsy mistake ▷ *vb* make a blunder

BLUNGE *vb* mix (clay or a similar substance) with water in order to form a suspension for use in ceramics

BLUNGED ▸ **blunge**

BLUNGER *n* large vat in which the contents, esp clay and water, are mixed by rotating arms

BLUNGES ▸ **blunge**

BLUNK *vb* ruin; botch

BLUNKED ▸ **blunk**

BLUNKER ▸ **blunk**

BLUNKS ▸ **blunk**

BLUNT *adj* not having a sharp edge or point ▷ *vb* make less sharp ▷ *n* cannabis cigarette

BLUNTED ▸ **blunt**

BLUNTER ▸ **blunt**

BLUNTLY ▸ **blunt**

BLUNTS ▸ **blunt**

BLUR *vb* make or become vague or less distinct ▷ *n* something vague, hazy, or indistinct

BLURB *n* promotional description, as on the jacket of a book ▷ *vb* describe or recommend in a blurb

BLURBED ▸ **blurb**

BLURBS ▸ **blurb**

BLURRED ▸ **blur**

BLURRY ▸ **blur**

BLURS ▸ **blur**

BLURT *vb* utter suddenly and involuntarily

BLURTED ▸ **blurt**

BLURTER ▸ **blurt**

BLURTS ▸ **blurt**

BLUSH *vb* become red in the face, esp from embarrassment or shame ▷ *n* reddening of the face

BLUSHED ▸ **blush**

BLUSHER *n* cosmetic for giving the cheeks a rosy colour

BLUSHES ▸ **blush**

BLUSHET *n* modest young woman

BLUSTER *vb* speak loudly or in a bullying way ▷ *n* empty threats or protests

BLYPE *n* piece of skin peeled off after sunburn

BLYPES ▸ **blype**

BO *interj* exclamation uttered to startle or surprise someone, esp a child in a game ▷ *n* fellow, buddy

BOA *n* large nonvenomous snake

BOAB *short for* ▸ **baobab**

BOABS ▸ **boab**

BOAK *same as* ▸ **boke**

BOAKED ▸ **boak**

BOAKING ▸ **boak**

BOAKS ▸ **boak**

BOAR *n* uncastrated male pig

BOARD *n* long flat piece of sawn timber ▷ *vb* go aboard (a train, aeroplane, etc)

BOARDED ▸ **board**

BOARDER *n* person who pays rent in return for accommodation in someone else's home

BOARDS ▸ **board**

BOARISH *adj* coarse, cruel, or sensual

BOARS ▸ **boar**

BOART *same as* ▸ **bort**

BOARTS ▸ **boart**

BOAS ▸ **boa**

BOAST *vb* speak too proudly about one's talents etc ▷ *n* bragging statement

BOASTED ▸ **boast**

BOASTER ▸ **boast**

BOASTS ▸ **boast**

BOAT *n* small vehicle for travelling across water ▷ *vb* travel in a boat

BOATED ▸ **boat**

BOATEL *n* waterside hotel catering for boating people

BOATELS ▸ **boatel**

BOATER *n* flat straw hat

BOATERS ▸ **boater**

BOATFUL ▸ **boat**

BOATIE *n* boating enthusiast

BOATIES ▸ **boatie**

BOATING *n* rowing, sailing, or cruising in boats as a form of recreation

BOATMAN *n* man who works on, hires out, or repairs boats

BOATMEN ▸ **boatman**

BOATS ▸ **boat**

BOB *vb* move or cause to move up and down repeatedly, as while floating in water ▷ *n* short abrupt movement, as of the head

BOBA *n* type of Chinese tea

BOBAC *same as* ▸ **bobak**

BOBACS ▸ **bobac**

BOBAK *n* type of marmot

BOBAKS ▸ **bobak**

BOBAS ▸ **boba**

BOBBED ▸ **bob**

BOBBER *n* type of float for fishing

BOBBERS ▸ **bobber**

BOBBERY *n* mixed pack of hunting dogs, often not belonging to any of the hound breeds ▷ *adj* noisy or excitable

BOBBIES ▸ **bobby**

BOBBIN *n* reel on which thread is wound

BOBBING ▸ **bob**

BOBBINS ▸ **bobbin**

BOBBISH ▸ **cheery**

BOBBITT *vb* sever the penis of

BOBBLE *n* small ball of material, usu for decoration ▷ *vb* (of a ball) to bounce erratically because of an uneven playing surface

BOBBLED ▸ **bobble**

BOBBLES ▸ **bobble**

BOBBLY *adj* (of fabric) covered in small balls; worn

BOBBY *n* policeman

BOBCAT *n* N American feline mammal with reddish-brown fur with dark spots or stripes, tufted ears, and a short tail

BOBCATS ▸ **bobcat**

BOBECHE *n* candle drip-catcher

BOBLET n two-man bobsleigh
BOBLETS ▶ boblet
BOBOL n fraud carried out by one or more persons with access to public funds in collusion with someone in a position of authority ▷ vb commit a bobol
BOBOLS ▶ bobol
BOBOTIE n dish of curried mince
BOBS ▶ bob
BOBSLED same as ▶ bobsleigh
BOBSTAY n strong stay between a bowsprit and the stem of a vessel for holding down the bowsprit
BOBTAIL n docked tail ▷ adj having the tail cut short ▷ vb dock the tail of
BOBWIG n type of short wig
BOBWIGS ▶ bobwig
BOCAGE n wooded countryside characteristic of northern France, with small irregular-shaped fields and many hedges and copses
BOCAGES ▶ bocage
BOCCA n mouth
BOCCAS ▶ bocca
BOCCE same as ▶ boccie
BOCCES ▶ bocce
BOCCI same as ▶ boccie
BOCCIA same as ▶ boccie
BOCCIAS ▶ boccia
BOCCIE n Italian version of bowls played on a lawn smaller than a bowling green
BOCCIES ▶ boccie
BOCCIS ▶ bocci
BOCK a variant spelling of ▶ boke
BOCKED ▶ bock
BOCKEDY adj (of a structure, piece of furniture, etc) unsteady
BOCKING ▶ bock
BOCKS ▶ bock
BOD n person
BODACH n old man
BODACHS ▶ bodach
BODDLE same as ▶ bodle
BODDLES ▶ boddle
BODE vb portend or presage
BODED ▶ bode
BODEFUL adj portentous
BODEGA n shop in a Spanish-speaking country that sells wine

BODEGAS ▶ bodega
BODES ▶ bode
BODGE vb make a mess of
BODGED ▶ bodge
BODGER adj worthless or second-rate
BODGERS ▶ bodger
BODGES ▶ bodge
BODGIE n unruly or uncouth young man, esp in the 1950s ▷ adj inferior
BODGIER ▶ bodgie
BODGIES ▶ bodgie
BODGING ▶ bodge
BODHI n as in bodhi tree holy tree of Buddhists
BODHRAN n shallow one-sided drum popular in Irish and Scottish folk music
BODICE n upper part of a dress
BODICES ▶ bodice
BODIED ▶ body
BODIES ▶ body
BODIKIN n little body
BODILY adj relating to the body ▷ adv by taking hold of the body
BODING ▶ bode
BODINGS ▶ bode
BODKIN n blunt large-eyed needle
BODKINS ▶ bodkin
BODLE n small obsolete Scottish coin
BODLES ▶ bodle
BODRAG n enemy attack
BODRAGS ▶ bodrag
BODS ▶ bod
BODY n entire physical structure of an animal or human
BODYING ▶ body
BOEP n South African word for a big belly
BOEPS ▶ boep
BOERBUL n crossbred mastiff used esp as a watchdog
BOET n brother
BOETS ▶ boet
BOEUF n as in boeuf bourguignon casserole of beef, vegetables, herbs, etc, cooked in red wine
BOFF n boffin ▷ vb hit
BOFFED ▶ boff
BOFFIN n scientist or expert
BOFFING ▶ boff
BOFFINS ▶ boffin
BOFFO adj very good
BOFFOLA n great success
BOFFOS ▶ boffo

BOFFS ▶ boff
BOG n wet spongy ground ▷ vb mire or delay
BOGAN n youth who dresses and behaves rebelliously
BOGANS ▶ bogan
BOGART vb monopolize or keep (something, esp a marijuana cigarette) to oneself selfishly
BOGARTS ▶ bogart
BOGBEAN same as ▶ buckbean
BOGEY n evil or mischievous spirit ▷ vb play (a hole) in one stroke over par
BOGEYED ▶ bogey
BOGEYS ▶ bogey
BOGGARD same as ▶ boggart
BOGGART n ghost or poltergeist
BOGGED ▶ bog
BOGGER n lavatory
BOGGERS ▶ bogger
BOGGIER ▶ bog
BOGGING ▶ bog
BOGGISH ▶ bog
BOGGLE vb be surprised, confused, or alarmed
BOGGLED ▶ boggle
BOGGLER ▶ boggle
BOGGLES ▶ boggle
BOGGY ▶ bog
BOGIE same as ▶ bogey
BOGIED ▶ bogie
BOGIES ▶ bogy
BOGLAND n area of wetland
BOGLE n rhythmic dance performed to ragga music ▷ vb to perform such a dance
BOGLED ▶ bogle
BOGLES ▶ bogle
BOGLING ▶ bogle
BOGMAN n body of a person found preserved in a peat bog
BOGMEN ▶ bogman
BOGOAK n oak or other wood found preserved in peat bogs; bogwood
BOGOAKS ▶ bogoak
BOGONG n large nocturnal Australian moth
BOGONGS ▶ bogong
BOGS ▶ bog
BOGUS adj not genuine
BOGUSLY ▶ bogus
BOGWOOD same as ▶ bogoak

B

BOGY same as ▸ **bogey**

BOGYISM same as > **bogeyism**

BOGYMAN same as > **bogeyman**

BOGYMEN ▸ **bogyman**

BOH same as ▸ **bo**

BOHEA n black Chinese tea, once regarded as the choicest, but now as an inferior grade

BOHEAS ▸ **bohea**

BOHEMIA n area frequented by unconventional (esp creative) people

BOHO short for > **bohemian**

BOHOS ▸ **boho**

BOHRIUM n element artificially produced in minute quantities

BOHS ▸ **boh**

BOI n lesbian who dresses like a boy

BOIL vb (cause to) change from a liquid to a vapour so quickly that bubbles are formed ▷ n state or action of boiling

BOILED ▸ **boil**

BOILER n piece of equipment which provides hot water

BOILERS ▸ **boiler**

BOILERY n place where water is boiled to extract salt

BOILING adj very hot ▷ n sweet

BOILOFF n quantity of liquified gases lost in evaporation

BOILS ▸ **boil**

BOING vb rebound making a noise

BOINGED ▸ **boing**

BOINGS ▸ **boing**

BOINK same as ▸ **boing**

BOINKED ▸ **boink**

BOINKS ▸ **boink**

BOIS ▸ **boi**

BOITE n artist's portfolio

BOITES ▸ **boite**

BOK n S African antelope

> This useful K word, meaning an antelope, can take quite a number of front extensions, forming words like **blesbok, reitbok, rhebok,** and even, if you are lucky, **jambok** or **sjambok**.

BOKE vb retch or vomit ▷ n retch

BOKED ▸ **boke**

BOKES ▸ **boke**

BOKING ▸ **boke**

BOKO slang word for ▸ **nose**

BOKOS ▸ **boko**

BOKS ▸ **bok**

BOLA n missile used by gauchos and Indians of South America, consisting of two or more heavy balls on a cord. It is hurled at a running quarry, such as an ox or rhea, so as to entangle its legs

BOLAR adj relating to clay

BOLAS same as ▸ **bola**

BOLASES ▸ **bolas**

BOLD adj confident and fearless ▷ n boldface

BOLDEN vb make bold

BOLDENS ▸ **bolden**

BOLDER ▸ **bold**

BOLDEST ▸ **bold**

BOLDLY ▸ **bold**

BOLDS ▸ **bold**

BOLE n tree trunk

BOLERO n (music for) traditional Spanish dance

BOLEROS ▸ **bolero**

BOLES ▸ **bole**

BOLETE n type of fungus

BOLETES ▸ **bolete**

BOLETI ▸ **boletus**

BOLETUS n type of fungus, often edible, with a brownish umbrella-shaped cap

BOLIDE n large exceptionally bright meteor that often explodes

BOLIDES ▸ **bolide**

BOLINE n (in Wicca) a knife, usually sickle-shaped and with a white handle, used for gathering herbs and carving symbols

BOLINES ▸ **boline**

BOLIVAR n standard monetary unit of Venezuela, equal to 100 céntimos

BOLIVIA n type of woollen fabric

BOLL n rounded seed capsule of cotton, flax, etc ▷ vb form into a boll

BOLLARD n short thick post used to prevent the passage of motor vehicles

BOLLED ▸ **boll**

BOLLEN ▸ **boll**

BOLLING ▸ **boll**

BOLLS ▸ **boll**

BOLO n large single-edged knife, originating in the Philippines

BOLOGNA n type of sausage

BOLONEY a variant spelling of ▸ **baloney**

BOLOS ▸ **bolo**

BOLSHIE adj difficult or rebellious ▷ n any political radical

BOLSHY same as ▸ **bolshie**

BOLSON n desert valley surrounded by mountains, with a shallow lake at the centre

BOLSONS ▸ **bolson**

BOLSTER vb support or strengthen ▷ n long narrow pillow

BOLT n sliding metal bar for fastening a door etc ▷ vb run away suddenly

BOLTED ▸ **bolt**

BOLTER ▸ **bolt**

BOLTERS ▸ **bolt**

BOLTING ▸ **bolt**

BOLTS ▸ **bolt**

BOLUS same as ▸ **bole**

BOLUSES ▸ **bolus**

BOMA n enclosure, esp a palisade or fence of thorn bush, set up to protect a camp, herd of animals, etc

BOMAS ▸ **boma**

BOMB n container fitted with explosive material ▷ vb attack with bombs

BOMBARD vb attack with heavy gunfire or bombs ▷ n ancient type of cannon that threw stone balls

BOMBAST n pompous language ▷ vb speak pompous language

BOMBAX n type of S American tree

BOMBE n dessert of ice cream lined or filled with custard, cake crumbs, etc ▷ adj (of furniture) having a projecting swollen shape

BOMBED ▸ **bomb**

BOMBER n aircraft that drops bombs

BOMBERS ▸ **bomber**

BOMBES ▸ **bombe**

BOMBING ▸ **bomb**

BOMBLET n small bomb

BOMBO n inferior wine

BOMBORA n submerged reef

BOMBOS ▸ bombo
BOMBS ▸ bomb
BOMBYX n type of moth
BOMMIE n outcrop of coral reef
BOMMIES ▸ bommie
BON adj good
BONA n goods
BONACI n type of fish
BONACIS ▸ bonaci
BONAMIA n parasite
BONANZA n sudden good luck or wealth
BONASUS n European bison
BONBON n sweet
BONBONS ▸ bonbon
BONCE n head
BONCES ▸ bonce
BOND n something that binds, fastens or holds together ▸ vb bind
BONDAGE n slavery
BONDED adj consisting of, secured by, or operating under a bond or bonds
BONDER same as ▸ bondstone
BONDERS ▸ bonder
BONDING n process by which individuals become emotionally attached to one another
BONDMAN same as ▸ bondsman
BONDMEN ▸ bondman
BONDS ▸ bond
BONDUC n type of North American tree
BONDUCS ▸ bonduc
BONE n any of the hard parts in the body that form the skeleton ▸ vb remove the bones from (meat for cooking etc)
BONED ▸ bone
BONER n blunder
BONERS ▸ boner
BONES ▸ bone
BONESET n N American plant with flat clusters of small white flowers
BONEY same as ▸ bony
BONEYER ▸ boney
BONFIRE n large outdoor fire
BONG n deep reverberating sound, as of a large bell ▸ vb make a deep reverberating sound
BONGED ▸ bong
BONGING ▸ bong
BONGO n small drum played with the fingers

BONGOES ▸ bongo
BONGOS ▸ bongo
BONGS ▸ bong
BONHAM n piglet
BONHAMS ▸ bonham
BONIATO n sweet potato
BONIE same as ▸ bonny
BONIER ▸ bony
BONIEST ▸ bony
BONING ▸ bone
BONINGS ▸ bone
BONISM n doctrine that the world is good, although not the best of all possible worlds
BONISMS ▸ bonism
BONIST ▸ bonism
BONISTS ▸ bonism
BONITA slang term for ▸ heroin
BONITAS ▸ bonita
BONITO n small tunny-like marine food fish
BONITOS ▸ bonito
BONJOUR interj hello
BONK vb have sex with
BONKED ▸ bonk
BONKERS adj crazy
BONKING ▸ bonk
BONKS ▸ bonk
BONNE n housemaid or female servant
BONNES ▸ bonne
BONNET n metal cover over a vehicle's engine ▸ vb place a bonnet on
BONNETS ▸ bonnet
BONNIE same as ▸ bonny
BONNIER ▸ bonny
BONNIES ▸ bonny
BONNILY ▸ bonny
BONNOCK n thick oatmeal cake
BONNY adj beautiful ▸ adv agreeably or well
BONOBO n type of anthropoid ape of central W Africa
BONOBOS ▸ bonobo
BONSAI n ornamental miniature tree or shrub
BONSELA n small gift of money
BONSOIR interj good evening
BONUS n something given, paid, or received above what is due or expected
BONUSES ▸ bonus
BONXIE n great skua
BONXIES ▸ bonxie
BONY adj having many bones

BONZA same as ▸ bonzer
BONZE n Chinese or Japanese Buddhist priest or monk
BONZER adj excellent
BONZES ▸ bonze
BOO interj shout of disapproval ▸ vb shout 'boo' to show disapproval
BOOAI ▸ boohai
BOOAIS ▸ boohai
BOOAY ▸ boohai
BOOAYS ▸ booay
BOOB n foolish mistake ▸ vb make a foolish mistake ▸ adj of poor quality, similar to that provided in prison
BOOBED ▸ boob
BOOBIES ▸ booby
BOOBING ▸ boob
BOOBIRD n person who boos
BOOBISH ▸ booby
BOOBOO n blunder
BOOBOOK n small spotted Australian brown owl
BOOBOOS ▸ booboo
BOOBS ▸ boob
BOOBY n foolish person
BOOCOO same as ▸ beaucoup
BOOCOOS ▸ boocoo
BOODIE n type of kangaroo
BOODIED ▸ boody
BOODIES ▸ boody
BOODLE n money or valuables, esp when stolen, counterfeit, or used as a bribe ▸ vb give or receive money corruptly or illegally
BOODLED ▸ boodle
BOODLER ▸ boodle
BOODLES ▸ boodle
BOODY vb sulk
BOOED ▸ boo
BOOFIER ▸ boofy
BOOFY adj muscular and strong but stupid
BOOGER n dried mucous from the nose
BOOGERS ▸ booger
BOOGEY same as ▸ boogie
BOOGEYS ▸ boogey
BOOGIE vb dance to fast pop music ▸ n session of dancing to pop music
BOOGIED ▸ boogie
BOOGIES ▸ boogie
BOOGY same as ▸ boogie
BOOH same as ▸ boo
BOOHAI n as in up the boohai thoroughly lost
BOOHAIS ▸ boohai

B

BOOHED ▸ booh
BOOHING ▸ booh
BOOHOO vb sob or pretend to sob noisily ▷ n distressed or pretended sobbing
BOOHOOS ▸ boohoo
BOOHS ▸ booh
BOOING ▸ boo
BOOJUM n American tree
BOOJUMS ▸ boojum
BOOK n number of pages bound together between covers ▷ vb reserve (a place, passage, etc) in advance
BOOKED ▸ book
BOOKEND n one of a pair of usually ornamental supports for holding a row of books upright
BOOKER ▸ book
BOOKERS ▸ book
BOOKFUL ▸ book
BOOKIE short for
> **bookmaker**
BOOKIER ▸ booky
BOOKIES ▸ bookie
BOOKING n reservation, as of a table or seat
BOOKISH adj fond of reading
BOOKLET n thin book with paper covers
BOOKMAN n learned person
BOOKMEN ▸ bookman
BOOKOO same as ▸ **boocoo**
BOOKOOS ▸ bookoo
BOOKS ▸ book
BOOKSIE same as ▸ **booksy**
BOOKSY adj inclined to be bookish or literary
BOOKY adj bookish
BOOL n bowling bowl ▷ vb play bowls
BOOLED ▸ bool
BOOLING ▸ bool
BOOLS ▸ bool
BOOM vb make a loud deep echoing sound ▷ n loud deep echoing sound
BOOMBOX n portable stereo system
BOOMED ▸ boom
BOOMER n large male kangaroo
BOOMERS ▸ boomer
BOOMIER ▸ boomy
BOOMING ▸ boom
BOOMKIN n short boom projecting from the deck of a ship, used to secure the main-brace blocks or to

extend the lower edge of the foresail
BOOMLET n small boom in business, birth rate, etc
BOOMS ▸ boom
BOOMY adj characterized by heavy bass sound
BOON n something extremely useful, helpful, or beneficial
BOONER n young working-class person from Canberra
BOONERS ▸ booner
BOONIES short form of
> **boondocks**
BOONS ▸ boon
BOOR n rude or insensitive person
BOORD obsolete spelling of
▸ **board**
BOORDE obsolete spelling of
▸ **board**
BOORDES ▸ boorde
BOORDS ▸ boord
BOORISH adj ill-mannered, clumsy, or insensitive
BOORKA same as ▸ **burka**
BOORKAS ▸ boorka
BOORS ▸ boor
BOOS ▸ boo
BOOSE same as ▸ **booze**
BOOSED ▸ boose
BOOSES ▸ boose
BOOSHIT adj very good
BOOSING ▸ boose
BOOST n encouragement or help ▷ vb improve
BOOSTED ▸ boost
BOOSTER n small additional injection of a vaccine
BOOSTS ▸ boost
BOOT n outer covering for the foot that extends above the ankle ▷ vb kick
BOOTCUT adj (of trousers) slightly flared at the bottom of the legs to fit over boots
BOOTED adj wearing boots
BOOTEE n baby's soft shoe
BOOTEES ▸ bootee
BOOTERY n shop where boots and shoes are sold
BOOTH n small partly enclosed cubicle
BOOTHS ▸ booth
BOOTIE n Royal Marine
BOOTIES ▸ booty
BOOTING ▸ boot
BOOTLEG adj produced, distributed, or sold illicitly

▷ vb make, carry, or sell (illicit goods) ▷ n something made or sold illicitly, such as alcohol during Prohibition in the US
BOOTS ▸ boot
BOOTY n valuable articles obtained as plunder
BOOZE n (consume) alcoholic drink ▷ vb drink alcohol, esp in excess
BOOZED ▸ booze
BOOZER n person who is fond of drinking
BOOZERS ▸ boozer
BOOZES ▸ booze
BOOZEY same as ▸ **boozy**
BOOZIER ▸ boozy
BOOZILY ▸ boozy
BOOZING ▸ booze
BOOZY adj inclined to or involving excessive drinking of alcohol
BOP vb dance to pop music ▷ n form of jazz with complex rhythms and harmonies
BOPEEP n quick look; peek
BOPEEPS ▸ bopeep
BOPPED ▸ bop
BOPPER ▸ bop
BOPPERS ▸ bop
BOPPING ▸ bop
BOPS ▸ bop
BOR n neighbour
BORA n Aboriginal ceremony
BORACES ▸ borax
BORACIC same as ▸ **boric**
BORAGE n Mediterranean plant with star-shaped blue flowers
BORAGES ▸ borage
BORAK n rubbish
BORAKS ▸ borak
BORAL n type of fine powder
BORALS ▸ boral
BORANE n any compound of boron and hydrogen, used in the synthesis of other boron compounds and as high-energy fuels
BORANES ▸ borane
BORAS ▸ bora
BORATE n salt or ester of boric acid. Salts of boric acid consist of BO_3 and BO_4 units linked together ▷ vb treat with borax, boric acid, or borate
BORATED ▸ borate
BORATES ▸ borate

BORAX n soluble white mineral occurring in alkaline soils and salt deposits

BORAXES ▸ borax

BORAZON n extremely hard form of boron nitride

BORD obsolete spelling of ▸ board

BORDAR n smallholder who held cottage in return for menial work

BORDARS ▸ bordar

BORDE obsolete spelling of ▸ board

BORDEL same as ▸ bordello

BORDELS ▸ bordel

BORDER n dividing line between political or geographical regions ▷ vb provide with a border

BORDERS ▸ border

BORDES ▸ borde

BORDS ▸ bord

BORDURE n outer edge of a shield, esp when decorated distinctively

BORE vb make (someone) weary by being dull

BOREAL adj of or relating to the north or the north wind

BOREAS n name for the north wind

BORED ▸ bore

BOREDOM n state of being bored

BOREE same as ▸ myall

BOREEN n country lane or narrow road

BOREENS ▸ boreen

BOREES ▸ boree

BOREL adj unlearned

BORER n machine or hand tool for boring holes

BORERS ▸ borer

BORES ▸ bear

BORGO n small attractive medieval village

BORGOS ▸ borgo

BORIC adj of or containing boron

BORIDE n compound in which boron is the most electronegative element, esp a compound of boron and a metal

BORIDES ▸ boride

BORING n act or process of making or enlarging a hole ▷ adj dull

BORINGS ▸ boring

BORK vb dismiss from job unfairly

BORKED ▸ bork

BORKING ▸ bork

BORKS ▸ bork

BORM vb smear with paint, oil, etc

BORMED ▸ borm

BORMING ▸ borm

BORMS ▸ borm

BORN adj possessing certain qualities from birth

BORNA n as in **borna disease** viral disease found in mammals, esp horses

BORNE ▸ bear

BORNEOL n white solid terpene alcohol

BORNITE n mineral consisting of a sulphide of copper and iron that tarnishes to purple

BORNYL n as in **bornyl alcohol** white solid alcohol from a Malaysian tree

BORNYLS ▸ bornyl

BORON n element used in hardening steel

BORONIA n Australian aromatic flowering shrub

BORONIC ▸ boron

BORONS ▸ boron

BOROUGH n town or district with its own council

BORREL adj ignorant

BORRELL same as ▸ borrel

BORROW vb obtain (something) temporarily

BORROWS ▸ borrow

BORS ▸ bor

BORSCH same as ▸ borscht

BORSCHT n Russian soup based on beetroot

BORSHCH same as ▸ borscht

BORSHT same as ▸ borscht

BORSHTS ▸ borsht

BORSIC n strong light composite material of boron fibre and silicon carbide used in aviation

BORSICS ▸ borsic

BORSTAL n (formerly in Britain) prison for young criminals

BORT n inferior grade of diamond used for cutting and drilling or, in powdered form, as an industrial abrasive

BORTIER ▸ bort

BORTS ▸ bort

BORTSCH same as ▸ borscht

BORTY ▸ bort

BORTZ same as ▸ bort

BORTZES ▸ bortz

BORZOI n tall dog with a long silky coat

BORZOIS ▸ borzoi

BOS ▸ bo

BOSBOK same as > bushbuck

BOSBOKS ▸ bosbok

BOSCAGE n mass of trees and shrubs

BOSH n empty talk, nonsense

BOSHBOK same as > bushbuck

BOSHES ▸ bosh

BOSHTA same as ▸ boshter

BOSHTER adj excellent

BOSIE n (in cricket) another term for googly

BOSIES ▸ bosie

BOSK n small wood of bushes and small trees

BOSKAGE same as ▸ boscage

BOSKER adj excellent

BOSKET n clump of small trees or bushes

BOSKETS ▸ bosket

BOSKIER ▸ bosky

BOSKS ▸ bosk

BOSKY adj containing or consisting of bushes or thickets

BOSOM n chest of a person, esp the female breasts ▷ adj very dear ▷ vb embrace

BOSOMED ▸ bosom

BOSOMS ▸ bosom

BOSOMY adj (of a woman) having large breasts

BOSON n any of a group of elementary particles, such as a photon or pion, that has zero or integral spin and obeys the rules of Bose-Einstein statistics

BOSONIC ▸ boson

BOSONS ▸ boson

BOSQUE same as ▸ bosk

BOSQUES ▸ bosque

BOSQUET same as ▸ bosket

BOSS n raised knob or stud ▷ vb employ, supervise, or be in charge of ▷ adj excellent

BOSSBOY n Black African foreman of a gang of workers

BOSSDOM n bosses collectively

BOSSED ▸ boss

BOSSER ▸ boss

BOSSES ▸ boss

B

BOSSEST ▸ boss

BOSSET n either of the rudimentary antlers found in young deer

BOSSETS ▸ bosset

BOSSIER ▸ bossy

BOSSIES ▸ bossy

BOSSILY ▸ bossy

BOSSING n act of shaping malleable metal, such as lead cladding, with mallets to fit a surface

BOSSISM n domination or the system of domination of political organizations by bosses

BOSSY same as ▸ **boss**

BOSTON n card game for four, played with two packs

BOSTONS ▸ boston

BOSTRYX n phenomenon in which flowers develop on one side only

BOSUN same as > **boatswain**

BOSUNS ▸ bosun

BOT n larva of a botfly, which typically develops inside the body of a horse, sheep, or man

BOTA n leather container

BOTANIC same as > **botanical**

BOTANY n study of plants

BOTARGO n relish consisting of the roe of mullet or tunny, salted and pressed into rolls

BOTAS ▸ bota

BOTCH vb spoil through clumsiness ▷ n badly done piece of work or repair

BOTCHED ▸ botch

BOTCHER ▸ botch

BOTCHES ▸ botch

BOTCHY adj clumsily done or made

BOTE n compensation given for injury or damage to property

BOTEL same as ▸ **boatel**

BOTELS ▸ botel

BOTES ▸ bote

BOTFLY n type of stout-bodied hairy fly, the larvae of which are parasites of man, sheep, and horses

BOTH pron two considered together ▷ adj two considered together ▷ determiner two

BOTHAN n unlicensed drinking house

BOTHANS ▸ bothan

BOTHER vb take the time or trouble ▷ n trouble, fuss, or difficulty ▷ interj exclamation of slight annoyance

BOTHERS ▸ bother

BOTHIE same as ▸ **bothy**

BOTHIES ▸ bothy

BOTHOLE n hole made by the larva of the botfly

BOTHRIA > bothrium

BOTHY n hut used for temporary shelter

BOTNET n network of infected computers

BOTNETS ▸ botnet

BOTONE adj having lobes at the ends

BOTONEE same as ▸ **botone**

BOTS n digestive disease of horses and some other animals caused by the presence of botfly larvae in the stomach

BOTT same as ▸ **bot**

BOTTE n thrust or hit

BOTTED ▸ bot

BOTTEGA n workshop; studio

BOTTES ▸ botte

BOTTIES ▸ botty

BOTTINE n light boot for women or children

BOTTING ▸ bot

BOTTLE n container for holding liquids ▷ vb put in a bottle

BOTTLED ▸ bottle

BOTTLER n exceptional person or thing

BOTTLES ▸ bottle

BOTTOM n lowest, deepest, or farthest removed part of a thing ▷ adj lowest or last ▷ vb provide with a bottom

BOTTOMS ▸ bottom

BOTTONY same as ▸ **botone**

BOTTS ▸ bott

BOTTY n diminutive for bottom

BOTULIN n potent toxin produced by a bacterium in imperfectly preserved food, etc, which causes botulism

BOUBOU n long flowing garment worn by men and women in Mali, Nigeria, Senegal, and some other parts of Africa

BOUBOUS ▸ boubou

BOUCHE n notch cut in top corner of shield

BOUCHEE n small pastry case filled with a savoury mixture, served hot with cocktails or as an hors d'oeuvre

BOUCHES ▸ bouche

BOUCLE n looped yarn giving a knobbly effect ▷ adj of or designating such a yarn or fabric

BOUCLEE n support for a cue in billiards formed by doubling the first finger so that its tip is aligned with the thumb at its second joint, to form a loop through which the cue may slide

BOUCLES ▸ boucle

BOUDIN n French version of a black pudding

BOUDINS ▸ boudin

BOUDOIR n woman's bedroom or private sitting room

BOUFFE n type of light or satirical opera common in France during the 19th century

BOUFFES ▸ bouffe

BOUGE vb move

BOUGED ▸ bouge

BOUGES ▸ bouge

BOUGET n budget

BOUGETS ▸ bouget

BOUGH n large branch of a tree

BOUGHED ▸ bough

BOUGHS ▸ bough

BOUGHT ▸ buy

BOUGHTS ▸ buy

BOUGIE n long slender semiflexible cylindrical instrument for inserting into body passages, such as the rectum or urethra, to dilate structures, introduce medication, etc

BOUGIES ▸ bougie

BOUGING ▸ bouge

BOUILLI n stew

BOUK n bulk; volume

BOUKS ▸ bouk

BOULDER n large rounded rock ▷ vb convert into boulders

BOULE same as ▸ **boulle**

BOULES n game, popular in France, in which metal bowls are thrown to land as close as possible to a target ball

BOULLE adj denoting or relating to a type of marquetry of patterned inlays of brass and tortoiseshell, occasionally with other metals such as pewter, much used on French furniture from the 17th century ▷ n something ornamented with such marquetry

BOULLES ▸ boulle

BOULT same as ▸ bolt

BOULTED ▸ boult

BOULTER ▸ bolt

BOULTS ▸ boult

BOUN vb prepare to go out

BOUNCE vb (of a ball etc) rebound from an impact ▷ n act of rebounding

BOUNCED ▸ bounce

BOUNCER n person employed at a disco etc to remove unwanted people

BOUNCES ▸ bounce

BOUNCY adj lively, exuberant, or self-confident

BOUND ▸ bind

BOUNDED adj (of a set) having a bound, esp where a measure is defined in terms of which all the elements of the set, or the differences between all pairs of members, are less than some value, or else all its members lie within some other well-defined set

BOUNDEN adj morally obligatory

BOUNDER n morally reprehensible person

BOUNDS pl n limit

BOUNED ▸ boun

BOUNING ▸ boun

BOUNS ▸ boun

BOUNTY n generosity

BOUQUET n bunch of flowers

BOURBON n whiskey made from maize

BOURD n prank

BOURDER n prankster

BOURDON n 16-foot organ stop of the stopped diapason type

BOURDS ▸ bourd

BOURG n French market town, esp one beside a castle

BOURGS ▸ bourg

BOURKHA same as ▸ burka

BOURLAW same as ▸ byrlaw

BOURN n (in S Britain) stream

BOURNE same as ▸ bourn

BOURNES ▸ bourne

BOURNS ▸ bourn

BOURREE n traditional French dance in fast duple time

BOURSE n stock exchange of continental Europe, esp Paris

BOURSES ▸ bourse

BOURSIN n tradename of a smooth white creamy cheese, often flavoured with garlic

BOUSE vb raise or haul with a tackle

BOUSED ▸ bouse

BOUSES ▸ bouse

BOUSIER ▸ bousy

BOUSING ▸ bouse

BOUSY adj drunken; boozy

BOUT n period of activity or illness

BOUTADE n outburst

BOUTON n knob-shaped contact between nerve fibres

BOUTONS ▸ bouton

BOUTS ▸ bout

BOUVIER n large powerful dog of a Belgian breed, having a rough shaggy coat: used esp for cattle herding and guarding

BOVATE n obsolete measure of land

BOVATES ▸ bovate

BOVID n type of ruminant, hollow-horned mammal such as sheep, goats, cattle, antelopes, and buffalo

BOVIDS ▸ bovid

BOVINE n domesticated bovine mammal

BOVINES ▸ bovine

BOVVER n rowdiness, esp caused by gangs of teenage youths

BOVVERS ▸ bovver

BOW vb lower (one's head) or bend (one's knee or body) as a sign of respect or shame ▷ n movement made when bowing

BOWAT n lamp

BOWATS ▸ bowat

BOWBENT adj bent; bow-like

BOWED adj lowered, bent

forward, or curved

BOWEL n intestine, esp the large intestine ▷ vb remove the bowels

BOWELED ▸ bowel

BOWELS ▸ bowel

BOWER n shady leafy shelter ▷ vb surround as with a bower

BOWERED ▸ bower

BOWERS ▸ bower

BOWERY ▸ bower

BOWES ▸ bough

BOWET same as ▸ bowat

BOWETS ▸ bowet

BOWFIN n primitive N American freshwater bony fish with an elongated body and a very long dorsal fin

BOWFINS ▸ bowfin

BOWGET obsolete variant of ▸ budget

BOWGETS ▸ bowget

BOWHEAD n type of large-mouthed arctic whale

BOWIE n as in bowie knife type of hunting knife

BOWING n technique of using the bow in playing a violin, viola, cello, or related instrument

BOWINGS ▸ bowing

BOWKNOT n decorative knot usually having two loops and two loose ends

BOWL n round container with an open top ▷ vb roll smoothly along the ground

BOWLDER same as ▸ boulder

BOWLED ▸ bowl

BOWLEG n a leg curving outwards like a bow between the ankle and the thigh

BOWLEGS ▸ bowleg

BOWLER n player who sends (a ball) towards the batsman

BOWLERS ▸ bowler

BOWLESS ▸ bow

BOWLFUL same as ▸ bowl

BOWLIKE ▸ bow

BOWLINE n line used to keep the sail taut against the wind

BOWLING n game in which bowls are rolled at a group of pins

BOWLS n game played on a very smooth area of grass in which opponents roll

B

biased wooden bowls as near a small bowl (the jack) as possible
BOWMAN n archer
BOWMEN ▸ bowman
BOWNE same as ▸ boun
BOWNED ▸ bowne
BOWNES ▸ bowne
BOWNING ▸ bowne
BOWPOT same as > boughpot
BOWPOTS ▸ bowpot
BOWR n muscle
BOWRS ▸ bowr
BOWS ▸ bow
BOWSAW n saw with a thin blade in a bow-shaped frame
BOWSAWS ▸ bowsaw
BOWSE same as ▸ bouse
BOWSED ▸ bowse
BOWSER n tanker containing fuel for aircraft, military vehicles, etc
BOWSERS ▸ bowser
BOWSES ▸ bowse
BOWSEY ▸ bowsie
BOWSEYS ▸ bowsey
BOWSHOT n distance an arrow travels from the bow
BOWSIE n low-class, mean or obstreperous person
BOWSIES ▸ bowsie
BOWSING ▸ bowse
BOWWOW n imitation of the bark of a dog ▷ vb make a noise like a dog
BOWWOWS ▸ bowwow
BOWYANG n band worn round trouser leg below knee
BOWYER n person who makes or sells archery bows
BOWYERS ▸ bowyer
BOX n container with a firm flat base and sides ▷ vb put into a box
BOXBALL n street ball game
BOXCAR n closed railway freight van
BOXCARS ▸ boxcar
BOXED ▸ box
BOXEN ▸ box
BOXER n person who participates in the sport of boxing
BOXERS ▸ boxer
BOXES ▸ box
BOXFISH another name for > trunkfish
BOXFUL same as ▸ box
BOXFULS ▸ box
BOXHAUL vb bring (a

square-rigger) onto a new tack by backwinding the foresails and steering hard round
BOXIER ▸ boxy
BOXIEST ▸ boxy
BOXILY ▸ boxy
BOXING n sport of fighting with the fists
BOXINGS ▸ boxing
BOXLIKE ▸ box
BOXPLOT n (in statistics) type of graph
BOXROOM n small room in which boxes, cases, etc may be stored
BOXTIES n Irish potato cakes
BOXTY n type of Irish potato pancake
BOXWOOD n hard yellow wood of the box tree, used to make tool handles, etc
BOXY adj squarish or chunky
BOY n male child ▷ vb act the part of a boy in a play
BOYAR n member of an old order of Russian nobility, ranking immediately below the princes: abolished by Peter the Great
BOYARD same as ▸ boyar
BOYARDS ▸ boyard
BOYARS ▸ boyar
BOYAU n connecting trench
BOYAUX ▸ boyau
BOYCHIK n young boy
BOYCOTT vb refuse to deal with (an organization or country) ▷ n instance of boycotting
BOYED ▸ boy
BOYF n boyfriend
BOYFS ▸ boyf
BOYG n troll-like mythical creature
BOYGS ▸ boyg
BOYHOOD n state or time of being a boy
BOYING ▸ boy
BOYISH adj of or like a boy in looks, behaviour, or character, esp when regarded as attractive or endearing
BOYKIE n chap or fellow
BOYKIES ▸ boykie
BOYLA n Australian Aboriginal word for magician
BOYLAS ▸ boyla
BOYO n boy or young man:

often used in direct address
BOYOS ▸ boyo
BOYS ▸ boy
BOYSIER ▸ boysy
BOYSY adj suited to or typical of boys or young men
BOZO n man, esp a stupid one
BOZOS ▸ bozo
BRA same as > brassiere
BRAAI vb grill or roast (meat) over open coals
BRAAIED ▸ braai
BRAAIS ▸ braai
BRAATA n small portion added to a purchase of food by a market vendor, to encourage the customer to return
BRAATAS same as ▸ braata
BRABBLE rare word for > squabble
BRACCIA ▸ braccio
BRACCIO n former unit of measurement; length of man's arm
BRACE n object fastened to something to straighten or support it ▷ vb steady or prepare (oneself) for something unpleasant
BRACED ▸ brace
BRACER n person or thing that braces
BRACERO n Mexican World War II labourer
BRACERS ▸ bracer
BRACES pl n pair of straps worn over the shoulders for holding up the trousers
BRACH n bitch hound
BRACHAH n blessing
BRACHES ▸ brach
BRACHET same as ▸ brach
BRACHIA > brachium
BRACHOT ▸ brachah
BRACHS ▸ brach
BRACING adj refreshing and invigorating ▷ n system of braces used to strengthen or support
BRACK same as > barmbrack
BRACKEN n large fern
BRACKET n pair of characters used to enclose a section of writing ▷ vb put in brackets
BRACKS ▸ brack
BRACT n leaf at the base of a flower
BRACTED ▸ bract
BRACTS ▸ bract

B

BRAD *n* small tapered nail with a small head
BRADAWL *n* small boring tool
BRADDED ▸ brad
BRADOON *same as* ▸ bridoon
BRADS ▸ brad
BRAE *n* hill or slope
BRAES ▸ brae
BRAG *vb* speak arrogantly and boastfully ▸ *n* boastful talk or behaviour
BRAGGED ▸ brag
BRAGGER ▸ brag
BRAGGY *adj* boastful
BRAGLY ▸ brag
BRAGS ▸ brag
BRAHMA *n* heavy breed of domestic fowl with profusely feathered legs and feet
BRAHMAN *n* member of highest Hindu caste
BRAHMAS ▸ brahma
BRAHMIN *same as* ▸ brahman
BRAID *vb* interweave (hair, thread, etc) ▸ *n* length of hair etc that has been braided ▸ *adj* broad ▸ *adv* broadly
BRAIDE *adj* given to deceit
BRAIDED *adj* (of a river or stream) flowing in several shallow interconnected channels separated by banks of deposited material
BRAIDER ▸ braid
BRAIDS ▸ braid
BRAIL *n* one of several lines fastened to the leech of a fore-and-aft sail to aid in furling it ▸ *vb* furl (a fore-and-aft sail) using brails
BRAILED ▸ brail
BRAILLE *n* system of writing for the blind consisting of raised dots that can be interpreted by touch ▸ *vb* print or write using this method
BRAILS ▸ brail
BRAIN *n* soft mass of nervous tissue in the head ▸ *vb* hit (someone) hard on the head
BRAINED ▸ brain
BRAINS ▸ brain
BRAINY *adj* clever
BRAIRD *vb* appear as shoots
BRAIRDS ▸ braird

BRAISE *vb* cook slowly in a covered pan with a little liquid
BRAISED ▸ braise
BRAISES ▸ braise
BRAIZE *same as* ▸ braise
BRAIZES ▸ braize
BRAK *n* crossbred dog ▸ *adj* (of water) slightly salty
BRAKE *same as* ▸ bracken
BRAKED ▸ brake
BRAKES ▸ brake
BRAKIER ▸ braky
BRAKING ▸ brake
BRAKS ▸ brak
BRAKY *adj* brambly
BRALESS ▸ bra
BRAMBLE *n* Scots word for blackberry
BRAMBLY ▸ bramble
BRAME *n* powerful feeling of emotion
BRAMES ▸ brame
BRAN *n* husks of cereal grain
BRANCH *n* secondary stem of a tree ▸ *vb* (of stems, roots, etc) divide, then develop in different directions
BRANCHY ▸ branch
BRAND *n* particular product ▸ *vb* mark with a brand
BRANDED *adj* identifiable as being the product of a particular manufacturer or marketing company
BRANDER ▸ brand
BRANDS ▸ brand
BRANDY *n* alcoholic spirit distilled from wine ▸ *vb* give brandy to
BRANE *n* hypothetical component of string theory
BRANES ▸ brane
BRANGLE *vb* quarrel noisily
BRANK *vb* walk with swaggering gait
BRANKED ▸ brank
BRANKS *pl n* (formerly) iron bridle used to restrain scolding women
BRANKY *adj* ostentatious
BRANLE *n* old French country dance performed in a linked circle
BRANLES ▸ branle
BRANNED ▸ bran
BRANNER *n* person or machine that treats metal with bran
BRANNY *adj* having the appearance or texture of bran

BRANS ▸ bran
BRANSLE *another word for* ▸ brantle
BRANT *n* type of small goose of northern coastal regions, with dark grey plumage and a short neck
BRANTLE *n* French country dance
BRANTS ▸ brant
BRAS ▸ bra
BRASCO *n* lavatory
BRASCOS ▸ brasco
BRASERO *n* metal grid for burning coals
BRASES ▸ bra
BRASH *adj* offensively loud, showy, or self-confident ▸ *n* loose rubbish, such as broken rock, hedge clippings, etc ▸ *vb* assault
BRASHED ▸ brash
BRASHER ▸ brash
BRASHES ▸ brash
BRASHLY ▸ brash
BRASHY *adj* loosely fragmented
BRASIER *same as* ▸ brazier
BRASIL *same as* ▸ brazil
BRASILS ▸ brasil
BRASS *n* alloy of copper and zinc ▸ *vb* make irritated or annoyed
BRASSED ▸ brass
BRASSES ▸ brass
BRASSET *same as* > brassart
BRASSIE *n* former name for a club, a No. 2 wood, originally having a brass-plated sole and with a shallower face than a driver to give more loft
BRASSY *same as* ▸ brassie
BRAST *same as* ▸ burst
BRASTS ▸ brast
BRAT *n* unruly child
BRATS ▸ brat
BRATTLE *vb* make a rattling sound
BRATTY ▸ brat
BRAUNCH *old variant of* ▸ branch
BRAVA *n* professional assassin
BRAVADO *n* showy display of self-confidence ▸ *vb* behave with bravado
BRAVAS ▸ brava
BRAVE *adj* having or showing courage, resolution, and daring ▸ *n* Native American warrior ▸ *vb* confront with

resolution or courage
BRAVED ▸ brave
BRAVELY ▸ brave
BRAVER ▸ brave
BRAVERS ▸ brave
BRAVERY ▸ brave
BRAVES ▸ brave
BRAVEST ▸ brave
BRAVI ▸ bravo
BRAVING ▸ brave
BRAVO *interj* well done! ▷ *n* cry of 'bravo' ▷ *vb* cry or shout 'bravo'
BRAVOED ▸ bravo
BRAVOES ▸ bravo
BRAVOS ▸ bravo
BRAVURA *n* display of boldness or daring
BRAVURE ▸ bravura
BRAW *adj* fine or excellent, esp in appearance or dress ▷ *pl n* best clothes
BRAWER ▸ braw
BRAWEST ▸ braw
BRAWL *n* noisy fight ▷ *vb* fight noisily
BRAWLED ▸ brawl
BRAWLER ▸ brawl
BRAWLIE *adj* in good health
BRAWLS ▸ brawl
BRAWLY ▸ braw
BRAWN *n* physical strength
BRAWNED ▸ brawn
BRAWNS ▸ brawn
BRAWNY *adj* muscular and strong
BRAWS *n* fine apparel
BRAXIES ▸ braxy
BRAXY *n* acute and usually fatal bacterial disease of sheep
BRAY *vb* (of a donkey) utter its loud harsh sound ▷ *n* donkey's loud harsh sound
BRAYED ▸ bray
BRAYER ▸ bray
BRAYERS ▸ bray
BRAYING ▸ bray
BRAYS ▸ bray
BRAZA *n* Spanish unit of measurement
BRAZAS ▸ braza
BRAZE *vb* join (two metal surfaces) with brass ▷ *n* high-melting solder or alloy used in brazing
BRAZED ▸ braze
BRAZEN *adj* shameless and bold ▷ *vb* face and overcome boldly or shamelessly
BRAZENS ▸ brazen
BRAZER ▸ braze

BRAZERS ▸ braze
BRAZES ▸ braze
BRAZIER *n* portable container for burning charcoal or coal
BRAZIL *n* red wood obtained from various tropical leguminous trees, used for cabinetwork
BRAZILS ▸ brazil
BRAZING ▸ braze
BREACH *n* breaking of a promise, obligation, etc ▷ *vb* break (a promise, law, etc)
BREAD *n* food made by baking a mixture of flour and water or milk ▷ *vb* cover (food) with breadcrumbs before cooking
BREADED ▸ bread
BREADS ▸ bread
BREADTH *n* extent of something from side to side
BREADY *adj* having the appearance or texture of bread
BREAK ▸ bracken
BREAKER *n* large wave
BREAKS ▸ bracken
BREAKUP *n* separation or disintegration
BREAM *n* Eurasian freshwater fish with a compressed body covered with silvery scales ▷ *vb* clean debris (from the bottom of a vessel)
BREAMED ▸ bream
BREAMS ▸ bream
BREARE *same as* ▸ **brier**
BREARES ▸ breare
BREAST *n* either of the (two soft fleshy milk-secreting glands on a woman's chest ▷ *vb* reach the summit of
BREASTS ▸ breast
BREATH *n* taking in and letting out of air during breathing
BREATHE *vb* take in oxygen and give out carbon dioxide
BREATHS ▸ breath
BREATHY *adj* (of the speaking voice) accompanied by an audible emission of breath
BRECCIA *n* rock consisting of angular fragments embedded in a finer matrix, formed by erosion, impact, volcanic activity, etc

BRECHAM *n* straw horse-collar
BRECHAN *same as* ▸ **brecham**
BRED *n* person who lives in a small remote place
BREDE *archaic spelling of* ▸ **braid**
BREDED ▸ brede
BREDES ▸ brede
BREDIE *n* meat and vegetable stew
BREDIES ▸ bredie
BREDING ▸ brede
BREDREN > brethren
BREDRIN > brethren
BREDS ▸ bred
BREE *n* broth, stock, or juice
BREECH *n* buttocks ▷ *vb* fit (a gun) with a breech
BREED *vb* produce new or improved strains of (domestic animals or plants) ▷ *n* group of animals etc within a (species that have certain clearly defined characteristics
BREEDER *n* person who breeds plants or animals
BREEDS ▸ breed
BREEKS *pl n* trousers
BREEM *same as* ▸ **breme**
BREENGE *vb* lunge forward ▷ *n* violent movement
BREER *another word for* ▸ **braird**
BREERED ▸ breer
BREERS ▸ breer
BREES ▸ bree
BREESE *same as* ▸ **breeze**
BREESES ▸ breese
BREEST ▸ breast
BREESTS ▸ breast
BREEZE *n* gentle wind ▷ *vb* move quickly or casually
BREEZED ▸ breeze
BREEZES ▸ breeze
BREEZY *adj* windy
BREGMA *n* point on the top (of the skull where the coronal and sagittal sutures meet: in infants this corresponds to the anterior fontanelle
BREHON *n* (formerly) judge in Ireland
BREHONS ▸ brehon
BREI *vb* speak with a uvular r, esp in Afrikaans
BREID *n* bread
BREIDS ▸ breid
BREIING ▸ brei

BREINGE *same as* ▶ **breenge**
BREIS ▶ **brei**
BREIST *Scots word for* ▶ **breast**
BREISTS ▶ **breist**
BREKKY *slang word for* > **breakfast**
BREME *adj* well-known
BREN *n* type of machine gun
BRENNE *vb* burn
BRENNES ▶ **brenne**
BRENS ▶ **bren**
BRENT *n* type of goose ▷ *adj* steep
BRENTER ▶ **brent**
BRENTS ▶ **brent**
BRER *n* brother: usually prefixed by a name
BRERE *same as* ▶ **brier**
BRERES ▶ **brere**
BRERS ▶ **brer**
BRETON *n* hat with an upturned brim and a rounded crown
BRETONS ▶ **breton**
BREVE *n* accent (˘), placed over a vowel to indicate that it is short or is pronounced in a specified way
BREVES ▶ **breve**
BREVET *n* document entitling a commissioned officer to hold temporarily a higher military rank without the appropriate pay and allowances ▷ *vb* promote by brevet
BREVETE *adj* patented
BREVETS ▶ **brevet**
BREVIER *n* (formerly) size of printer's type approximately equal to 8 point
BREVIS *same as* ▶ **brewis**
BREVITY *n* shortness
BREW *vb* make (beer etc) by steeping, boiling, and fermentation ▷ *n* beverage produced by brewing
BREWAGE *n* product of brewing
BREWED ▶ **brew**
BREWER ▶ **brew**
BREWERS ▶ **brew**
BREWERY *n* place where beer etc is brewed
BREWING *n* quantity of a beverage brewed at one time
BREWIS *n* bread soaked in broth, gravy, etc
BREWPUB *n* pub that incorporates a brewery on its premises
BREWS ▶ **brew**
BREWSKI *n* beer
BREY *same as* ▶ **brei**
BREYED ▶ **brey**
BREYING ▶ **brey**
BREYS ▶ **brey**
BRIAR *n* S European shrub with a hard woody root (briarroot)
BRIARD *n* medium-sized dog of an ancient French sheep-herding breed having a long rough coat of a single colour
BRIARDS ▶ **briard**
BRIARED ▶ **briar**
BRIARS ▶ **briar**
BRIARY ▶ **briar**
BRIBE *vb* offer or give something to someone to gain favour, influence, etc ▷ *n* something given or offered as a bribe
BRIBED ▶ **bribe**
BRIBEE *n* one who is bribed
BRIBEES ▶ **bribee**
BRIBER ▶ **bribe**
BRIBERS ▶ **bribe**
BRIBERY *n* process of giving or taking bribes
BRIBES ▶ **bribe**
BRIBING ▶ **bribe**
BRICHT *Scots word for* ▶ **bright**
BRICK *n* (rectangular block of) baked clay used in building ▷ *vb* build, enclose, or fill with bricks
BRICKED ▶ **brick**
BRICKEN *adj* made of brick
BRICKIE *n* bricklayer
BRICKLE *same as* ▶ **brittle**
BRICKS ▶ **brick**
BRICKY *same as* ▶ **brickie**
BRICOLE *n* shot in which the cue ball touches a cushion after striking the object ball and before touching another ball
BRIDAL *adj* of a bride or a wedding ▷ *n* wedding or wedding feast
BRIDALS ▶ **bridal**
BRIDE *n* woman who has just been or is about to be married
BRIDED ▶ **bride**
BRIDES ▶ **bride**
BRIDGE *n* structure for crossing a river etc ▷ *vb* build a bridge over (something)
BRIDGED ▶ **bridge**
BRIDGES ▶ **bridge**
BRIDIE *n* semicircular pie containing meat and onions
BRIDIES ▶ **bridie**
BRIDING ▶ **bride**
BRIDLE *n* headgear for controlling a horse ▷ *vb* show anger or indignation
BRIDLED ▶ **bridle**
BRIDLER ▶ **bridle**
BRIDLES ▶ **bridle**
BRIDOON *n* horse's bit: small snaffle used in double bridles
BRIE *same as* ▶ **bree**
BRIEF *adj* short in duration ▷ *n* condensed statement or written synopsis ▷ *vb* give information and instructions to (a person)
BRIEFED ▶ **brief**
BRIEFER ▶ **brief**
BRIEFLY ▶ **brief**
BRIEFS *pl n* men's or women's underpants without legs
BRIER *same as* ▶ **briar**
BRIERED ▶ **brier**
BRIERS ▶ **brier**
BRIERY ▶ **brier**
BRIES ▶ **brie**
BRIG *n* two-masted square-rigged ship
BRIGADE *n* army unit smaller than a division ▷ *vb* organize into a brigade
BRIGAND *n* bandit
BRIGHT *adj* emitting or reflecting much light ▷ *adv* brightly
BRIGHTS *pl n* high beam of the headlights of a motor vehicle
BRIGS ▶ **brig**
BRIGUE *vb* solicit
BRIGUED ▶ **brigue**
BRIGUES ▶ **brigue**
BRIK *n* Tunisian deep-fried spicy pastry filled with fish or meat and sometimes an egg
BRIKI *same as* ▶ **cezve**
BRIKIS ▶ **briki**
BRIKS ▶ **brik**
BRILL *n* type of European flatfish popular as a food fish
BRILLER ▶ **brill**
BRILLO *n* tradename for a type of scouring pad impregnated with a detergent

B

BRILLOS ▸ brillo

BRILLS ▸ brill

BRIM n upper rim of a vessel ▷ vb fill or be full to the brim

BRIMFUL adj completely filled with

BRIMING n phosphorescence of sea

BRIMMED ▸ brim

BRIMMER n vessel, such as a glass or bowl, filled to the brim

BRIMS ▸ brim

BRIN n thread of silk from silkworm

BRINDED adj streaky or patchy

BRINDLE n brindled animal

BRINE n salt water ▷ vb soak in or treat with brine

BRINED ▸ brine

BRINER ▸ brine

BRINERS ▸ brine

BRINES ▸ brine

BRING vb carry, convey, or take to a designated place or person

BRINGER ▸ bring

BRINGS ▸ bring

BRINIER ▸ briny

BRINIES ▸ briny

BRINING ▸ brine

BRINISH ▸ brine

BRINJAL n dark purple tropical fruit, cooked and eaten as a vegetable

BRINK n edge of a steep place

BRINKS ▸ brink

BRINNY n stone, esp when thrown

BRINS ▸ brin

BRINY adj very salty

BRIO n liveliness

BRIOCHE n soft roll or loaf made from a very light yeast dough, sometimes mixed with currants

BRIONY same as ▸ **bryony**

BRIOS ▸ brio

BRIQUET same as > **briquette**

BRIS n ritual circumcision of male babies, usually at eight days old, regarded as the formal entry of the child to the Jewish community

BRISANT > **brisance**

BRISE n type of jump

BRISES ▸ bris

BRISK adj lively and quick ▷ vb enliven

BRISKED ▸ brisk

BRISKEN vb make or become more lively or brisk

BRISKER ▸ brisk

BRISKET n beef from the breast of a cow

BRISKLY ▸ brisk

BRISKS ▸ brisk

BRISKY another word for ▸ **brisk**

BRISS same as ▸ **bris**

BRISSES ▸ bris

BRISTLE n short stiff hair ▷ vb (cause to) stand up like bristles

BRISTLY ▸ bristle

BRISTOL n as in **bristol board** type of heavy cardboard

BRISURE n mark of cadency in heraldry

BRIT n young of a herring, sprat, or similar fish

BRITH same as ▸ **bris**

BRITHS ▸ brith

BRITS ▸ brit

BRITSKA same as ▸ **britzka**

BRITT n young herring or sprat

BRITTLE adj hard but easily broken ▷ n crunchy sweet made with treacle and nuts

BRITTLY ▸ brittle

BRITTS ▸ britt

BRITZKA n long horse-drawn carriage with a folding top over the rear seat and a rear-facing front seat

BRIZE same as ▸ **breeze**

BRIZES ▸ brize

BRO n family member

BROACH vb introduce (a topic) for discussion ▷ n spit for roasting meat

BROAD adj having great breadth or width ▷ n woman

BROADAX same as > **broadaxe**

BROADEN vb make or become broad or broader

BROADER ▸ broad

BROADLY ▸ broad

BROADS ▸ broad

BROCADE n rich fabric woven with a raised design ▷ vb weave with such a design

BROCAGE another word for > **brokerage**

BROCARD n basic principle of civil law

BROCH n (in Scotland) a circular dry-stone tower large enough to serve as a fortified home

BROCHAN n type of thin porridge

BROCHE adj woven with a raised design, as brocade

BROCHED ▸ broche

BROCHES ▸ broche

BROCHO same as ▸ **brachah**

BROCHOS ▸ brocho

BROCHS ▸ broch

BROCK n badger

BROCKED adj having different colours

BROCKET n small tropical American deer with small unbranched antlers

BROCKIT same as ▸ **brocked**

BROCKS ▸ brock

BROCOLI same as > **broccoli**

BROD vb prod

BRODDED ▸ brod

BRODDLE vb poke or pierce (something)

BRODKIN same as > **brodekin**

BRODS ▸ brod

BROG n bradawl

BROGAN n heavy laced, usually ankle-high, work boot

BROGANS ▸ brogan

BROGGED ▸ brog

BROGH same as ▸ **broch**

BROGHS ▸ brogh

BROGS ▸ brog

BROGUE n sturdy walking shoe

BROGUES ▸ brogue

BROIDER archaic word for > **embroider**

BROIL vb cook by direct heat under a grill ▷ n process of broiling

BROILED ▸ broil

BROILER n young tender chicken for roasting

BROILS ▸ broil

BROKAGE another word for > **brokerage**

BROKE vb negotiate or deal

BROKED ▸ broke

BROKEN ▸ bracken

BROKER n agent who buys or sells goods, securities, etc ▷ vb act as a broker (in)

BROKERS ▸ broker

BROKERY n work done by a broker

BROKES ▸ broke

BROKING ▸ broke

BROLGA n large grey

Australian crane with a trumpeting call

BROLGAS ▸ brolga

BROLLY n umbrella

BROMAL n yellowish oily synthetic liquid formerly used medicinally as a sedative and hypnotic

BROMALS ▸ bromal

BROMATE same as > brominate

BROME n type of grass

BROMES ▸ brome

BROMIC adj of or containing bromine in the trivalent or pentavalent state

BROMID same as ▸ bromide

BROMIDE n chemical compound used in medicine and photography

BROMIDS ▸ bromid

BROMIN same as ▸ bromine

BROMINE n dark red liquid element that gives off a pungent vapour

BROMINS ▸ bromin

BROMISE same as ▸ bromize

BROMISM n poisoning caused by the excessive intake of bromine or compounds containing bromine

BROMIZE vb treat with bromine

BROMMER n S African word for bluebottle

BROMO n something that contains bromide

BROMOS ▸ bromo

BRONC same as ▸ bronco

BRONCHI > bronchus

BRONCHO same as ▸ bronco

BRONCO n (in the US) wild or partially tamed pony

BRONCOS ▸ bronco

BRONCS ▸ bronc

BROND n old form of brand

BRONDS ▸ brond

BRONZE n alloy of copper and tin ▷ adj made of, or coloured like, bronze ▷ vb (esp of the skin) make or become brown

BRONZED ▸ bronze

BRONZEN adj made of or the colour of bronze

BRONZER n cosmetic applied to the skin to simulate a sun tan

BRONZES ▸ bronze

BRONZY ▸ bronze

BROO n brow of hill

BROOCH n ornament with a pin, worn fastened to clothes ▷ vb decorate with a brooch

BROOD n number of birds produced at one hatching ▷ vb (of a bird) sit on or hatch eggs

BROODED ▸ brood

BROODER n enclosure or other structure, usually heated, used for rearing young chickens or other fowl

BROODS ▸ brood

BROODY adj moody and sullen

BROOK n small stream ▷ vb bear or tolerate

BROOKED ▸ brook

BROOKIE n brook trout

BROOKS ▸ brook

BROOL n low roar

BROOLS ▸ brool

BROOM n long-handled sweeping brush ▷ vb sweep with a broom

BROOMED ▸ broom

BROOMS ▸ broom

BROOMY adj covered with growth of broom

BROOS ▸ broo

BROOSE n race at country wedding

BROOSES ▸ broose

BROS ▸ bro

BROSE n oatmeal or pease porridge, sometimes with butter or fat added

BROSES ▸ brose

BROSIER ▸ brosy

BROSY adj smeared with porridge

BROTH n soup, usu containing vegetables

BROTHEL n house where men pay to have sex with prostitutes

BROTHER n boy or man with the same parents as another person ▷ interj exclamation of amazement, disgust, surprise, disappointment, etc ▷ vb treat someone like a brother

BROTHS ▸ broth

BROTHY adj having appearance or texture of broth

BROUGH same as ▸ broch

BROUGHS ▸ brough

BROUGHT ▸ bring

BROUZE same as ▸ broose

BROUZES ▸ brouze

BROW n part of the face (from the eyes to the hairline)

BROWED adj having a brow

BROWN n colour of earth or wood ▷ adj (of bread) made from wheatmeal or wholemeal flour ▷ vb make or become brown

BROWNED ▸ brown

BROWNER ▸ brown

BROWNIE n small square nutty chocolate cake

BROWNS ▸ brown

BROWNY ▸ brown

BROWS ▸ brow

BROWSE vb look through (a book or articles for sale) in a casual manner ▷ n instance of browsing

BROWSED ▸ browse

BROWSER n software package that enables a user to read hypertext, esp on the Internet

BROWSES ▸ browse

BROWST n brewing (of ale, tea)

BROWSTS ▸ browst

BROWSY ▸ browse

BRR same as ▸ brrr

This is useful if your consonant-heavy rack is giving you the shivers. And if you are even colder, **brrr** is available.

BRRR interj used to suggest shivering

BRU South African word for ▸ friend

BRUCHID n type of beetle

BRUCIN same as ▸ brucine

BRUCINE n bitter poisonous alkaloid resembling strychnine

BRUCINS ▸ brucin

BRUCITE n white translucent mineral

BRUCKLE adj brittle

BRUGH n large house

BRUGHS ▸ brugh

BRUHAHA same as > brouhaha

BRUIN n name for a bear, used in children's tales, fables, etc

BRUINS ▸ bruin

BRUISE n discoloured area on the skin caused by an injury ▷ vb cause a bruise on

BRUISED ▸ bruise

BRUISER n strong tough person

BRUISES ▸ bruise

BRUIT vb report ▷ n abnormal sound heard within the body during auscultation, esp a heart murmur

BRUITED ▸ bruit

BRUITER ▸ bruit

BRUITS ▸ bruit

BRULE n shortened form of the archaic word for a mixed-race person of Canadian Indian and White (usually French-Canadian) ancestry

BRULES ▸ brule

BRULOT n coffee-based alcoholic drink, served flaming

BRULOTS ▸ brulot

BRULYIE same as ▸ brulzie

BRULZIE n noisy dispute

BRUMAL adj of, characteristic of, or relating to winter

BRUMBY n wild horse

BRUME n heavy mist or fog

BRUMES ▸ brume

BRUMMER same as ▸ brommer

BRUMOUS ▸ brume

BRUNCH n breakfast and lunch combined ▷ vb eat brunch

BRUNET adj dark brown

BRUNETS ▸ brunet

BRUNG ▸ bring

BRUNT n main force or shock of a blow, attack, etc ▷ vb suffer the main force or shock of a blow, attack, etc

BRUNTED ▸ brunt

BRUNTS ▸ brunt

BRUS ▸ bru

BRUSH n device made of bristles, wires, etc used for cleaning, painting, etc ▷ vb clean, scrub, or paint with a brush

BRUSHED adj treated with a brushing process to raise the nap and give a softer and warmer finish

BRUSHER ▸ brush

BRUSHES ▸ brush

BRUSHUP n the act or an instance of tidying one's appearance

BRUSHY adj like a brush

BRUSK same as ▸ brusque

BRUSKER ▸ brusk

BRUSQUE adj blunt or curt in manner or speech

BRUSSEN adj bold

BRUST same as ▸ burst

BRUSTS ▸ brust

BRUT adj (of champagne or sparkling wine) very dry ▷ n very dry champagne

BRUTAL adj cruel and vicious

BRUTE n brutal person ▷ adj wholly instinctive or physical, like an animal

BRUTED ▸ brute

BRUTELY ▸ brute

BRUTER n diamond cutter

BRUTERS ▸ bruter

BRUTES ▸ brute

BRUTIFY less common word for ▸ brutalize

BRUTING n diamond cutting

BRUTISH adj of or like an animal

BRUTISM n stupidity; vulgarity

BRUTS ▸ brut

BRUX vb grind one's teeth

BRUXED ▸ brux

BRUXES ▸ brux

BRUXING ▸ brux

BRUXISM n habit of grinding the teeth, esp unconsciously

BRYONY n wild climbing hedge plant

BUAT same as ▸ bowat

BUATS ▸ buat

BUAZE n fibrous African plant

BUAZES ▸ buaze

BUB n youngster

BUBA another name for ▸ yaws

BUBAL n any of various antelopes, esp an extinct N African variety of hartebeest

BUBALE n large antelope

BUBALES ▸ bubale

BUBALIS same as ▸ bubal

BUBALS ▸ bubal

BUBAS ▸ buba

BUBBA n ordinary American person

BUBBAS ▸ bubba

BUBBLE n ball of air in a liquid or solid ▷ vb form bubbles

BUBBLED ▸ bubble

BUBBLER n drinking fountain in which the water

is forced in a stream from a small vertical nozzle

BUBBLES ▸ bubble

BUBBLY adj excited and lively ▷ n champagne

BUBINGA n reddish-brown wood from African tree

BUBKES n very small amount

BUBKIS n nothing

BUBO n inflammation and swelling of a lymph node, esp in the armpit or groin

BUBOED ▸ bubo

BUBOES ▸ bubo

BUBONIC ▸ bubo

BUBS ▸ bub

BUBU same as ▸ boubou

BUBUKLE n red spot on skin

BUBUS ▸ bubu

BUCARDO n type of Spanish mountain goat, recently extinct

BUCCAL adj of or relating to the cheek

BUCCINA n curved Roman horn

BUCHU n S African shrub whose leaves are used as an antiseptic and diuretic

BUCHUS ▸ buchu

BUCK n male of the goat, hare, kangaroo, rabbit, and reindeer ▷ vb (of a horse etc) jump with legs stiff and back arched

BUCKED ▸ buck

BUCKEEN n (in Ireland) poor young man who aspires to the habits and dress of the wealthy

BUCKER ▸ buck

BUCKERS ▸ buck

BUCKET vb open-topped roughly cylindrical container ▷ vb rain heavily

BUCKETS ▸ bucket

BUCKEYE n N American tree with erect clusters of white or red flowers and prickly fruits

BUCKIE n whelk or its shell

BUCKIES ▸ buckie

BUCKING ▸ buck

BUCKISH ▸ buck

BUCKLE n clasp for fastening a belt or strap ▷ vb fasten or be fastened with a buckle

BUCKLED ▸ buckle

BUCKLER n small round shield worn on the forearm ▷ vb defend

B

B

BUCKLES ▸ buckle

BUCKO *n* lively young fellow: often a term of address

BUCKOES ▸ bucko

BUCKOS ▸ bucko

BUCKRAM *n* cotton or linen cloth stiffened with size, etc, used in lining or stiffening clothes, bookbinding, etc ▷ *vb* stiffen with buckram

BUCKS ▸ buck

BUCKSAW *n* woodcutting saw having its blade set in a frame and tensioned by a turnbuckle across the back of the frame

BUCKSOM *same as* ▸ **buxom**

BUCKU *same as* ▸ **buchu**

BUCKUS ▸ bucku

BUCOLIC *adj* of the countryside or country life ▷ *n* pastoral poem

BUD *n* swelling on a plant that develops into a leaf or flower ▷ *vb* produce buds

BUDDED ▸ bud

BUDDER ▸ bud

BUDDERS ▸ bud

BUDDHA *n* person who has achieved a state of perfect enlightenment

BUDDHAS ▸ buddha

BUDDIED ▸ buddy

BUDDIER ▸ buddy

BUDDIES ▸ buddy

BUDDING ▸ buddy

BUDDLE *n* sloping trough in which ore is washed ▷ *vb* wash (ore) in a buddle

BUDDLED ▸ buddle

BUDDLES ▸ buddle

BUDDY *n* friend ▷ *vb* act as a friend to ▷ *adj* friendly

BUDGE *vb* move slightly ▷ *n* lambskin dressed for the fur to be worn on the outer side

BUDGED ▸ budge

BUDGER ▸ budge

BUDGERO *same as* > **budgerow**

BUDGERS ▸ budge

BUDGES ▸ budge

BUDGET *n* financial plan for a period of time ▷ *vb* plan the expenditure of (money or time) ▷ *adj* cheap

BUDGETS ▸ budget

BUDGIE *n* short form of budgerigar

BUDGIES ▸ budgie

BUDGING ▸ budge

BUDLESS ▸ bud

BUDLIKE ▸ bud

BUDMASH ▸ badmash

BUDO *n* combat and spirit in martial arts

BUDOS ▸ budo

BUDS ▸ bud

BUDWORM *n* pest that eats tree leaves and buds

BUFF *n* soft flexible undyed leather ▷ *adj* dull yellowish-brown ▷ *vb* clean or polish with soft material

BUFFA ▸ buffo

BUFFALO *n* member of the cattle tribe with upward-curving horns, mostly found in game reserves in S and E Africa ▷ *vb* confuse

BUFFE ▸ buffo

BUFFED ▸ buff

BUFFEL *adj as in* **buffel grass** grass used for pasture in Africa, India, and Australia

BUFFER *same as* ▸ **buff**

BUFFERS ▸ buffer

BUFFEST ▸ buff

BUFFET *n* counter where drinks and snacks are served ▷ *vb* knock against or about

BUFFETS ▸ buffet

BUFFI ▸ buffo

BUFFIER ▸ buffy

BUFFING ▸ buff

BUFFO *n* (in Italian opera of the 18th century) comic part, esp one for a bass

BUFFOON *n* clown or fool

BUFFOS ▸ buffo

BUFFS ▸ buff

BUFFY *adj* having appearance or texture of buff

BUFO *n* type of toad

BUFOS ▸ bufo

BUG *n* insect ▷ *vb* irritate

BUGABOO *n* imaginary source of fear

BUGBANE *n* European plant whose flowers are reputed to repel insects

BUGBEAR *n* thing that causes obsessive anxiety

BUGEYE *n* oyster-dredging boat

BUGEYES ▸ bugeye

BUGGAN *n* evil spirit

BUGGANE *same as* ▸ **buggan**

BUGGANS ▸ buggan

BUGGED ▸ bug

BUGGERY *n* anal intercourse

BUGGIER ▸ buggy

BUGGIES ▸ buggy

BUGGIN *same as* ▸ **buggan**

BUGGING ▸ bug

BUGGINS ▸ buggin

BUGGY *n* light horse-drawn carriage having two or four wheels ▷ *adj* infested with bugs

BUGLE *n* instrument like a small trumpet ▷ *vb* play or sound (on) a bugle

BUGLED ▸ bugle

BUGLER ▸ bugle

BUGLERS ▸ bugle

BUGLES ▸ bugle

BUGLET *n* small bugle

BUGLETS ▸ buglet

BUGLING ▸ bugle

BUGLOSS *n* hairy Eurasian plant with clusters of blue flowers

BUGONG *same as* ▸ **bogong**

BUGONGS ▸ bugong

BUGOUT *n* act of running away

BUGOUTS ▸ bugout

BUGS ▸ bug

BUGSEED *n* form of tumbleweed

BUGSHA *same as* ▸ **buqsha**

BUGSHAS ▸ bugsha

BUGWORT *another name for* ▸ **bugbane**

BUHL *same as* ▸ **boulle**

BUHLS ▸ buhl

BUHR ▸ burr

BUHRS ▸ burr

BUHUND *n* type of Norwegian dog

BUHUNDS ▸ buhund

BUIBUI *n* piece of black cloth worn as a shawl by Muslim women, esp on the E African coast

BUIBUIS ▸ buibui

BUIK *same as* ▸ **book**

BUIKS ▸ buik

BUILD *vb* make, construct, or form by joining parts or materials ▷ *n* shape of the body

BUILDED ▸ build

BUILDER *n* person who constructs houses and other buildings

BUILDS ▸ build

BUILDUP *n* gradual approach to a climax or critical point

BUILT ▸ build

BUIRDLY adj well-built

BUIST vb brand sheep with identification mark

BUISTED ▸ buist

BUISTS ▸ buist

BUKE same as ▸ **book**

BUKES ▸ buke

BUKKAKE n type of sexual practice

BUKSHEE n person in charge of paying wages

BUKSHI same as ▸ **bukshee**

BUKSHIS ▸ bukshi

BULB n onion-shaped root which grows into a flower or plant ▷ vb form into the shape of a bulb

BULBAR adj of or relating to a bulb, esp the medulla oblongata

BULBED ▸ bulb

BULBEL same as ▸ **bulbil**

BULBELS ▸ bulbel

BULBIL n small bulblike organ of vegetative reproduction growing in leaf axils or on flower stalks of plants such as the onion and tiger lily

BULBILS ▸ bulbil

BULBING ▸ bulb

BULBLET n small bulb at base of main bulb

BULBOUS adj round and fat

BULBS ▸ bulb

BULBUL n songbird of tropical Africa and Asia, with brown plumage and often a distinct crest

BULBULS ▸ bulbul

BULGE n swelling on a normally flat surface ▷ vb swell outwards

BULGED ▸ bulge

BULGER ▸ bulge

BULGERS ▸ bulge

BULGES ▸ bulge

BULGHUR same as ▸ **bulgur**

BULGIER ▸ bulge

BULGINE same as > **bullgine**

BULGING ▸ bulge

BULGUR n kind of dried cracked wheat

BULGURS ▸ bulgur

BULGY ▸ bulge

BULIMIA n disorder characterized by compulsive overeating followed by vomiting

BULIMIC ▸ bulimia

BULIMUS ▸ bulimia

BULIMY ▸ bulimia

BULK n volume, size, or magnitude of something ▷ vb cohere or cause to cohere in a mass

BULKAGE ▸ bulk

BULKED ▸ bulk

BULKER n ship that carries unpackaged cargo, usually consisting of a single dry commodity, such as coal or grain

BULKERS ▸ bulker

BULKIER ▸ bulky

BULKILY ▸ bulky

BULKING n expansion of excavated material to a volume greater than that of the excavation from which it came

BULKS ▸ bulk

BULKY adj very large and massive, esp so as to be unwieldy

BULL adj any male bovine animal, esp one that is sexually mature

BULLA n a leaden seal affixed to a papal bull, having a representation of Saints Peter and Paul on one side and the name of the reigning pope on the other

BULLACE n small Eurasian tree of which the damson is the cultivated form

BULLAE ▸ bulla

BULLARY n boilery for preparing salt

BULLATE adj puckered or blistered in appearance

BULLBAT another name for > **nighthawk**

BULLDOG n thickset dog with a broad head and a muscular body

BULLED ▸ bull

BULLER vb make bubbling sound

BULLERS ▸ buller

BULLET n small piece of metal fired from a gun ▷ vb move extremely quickly

BULLETS ▸ bullet

BULLIED ▸ bully

BULLIER ▸ bully

BULLIES ▸ bully

BULLING ▸ bull

BULLION n gold or silver in the form of bars

BULLISH adj like a bull

BULLOCK n castrated bull ▷ vb work hard and long

BULLOSA adj as in **epidermolysis bullosa**

type of genetic skin disorder

BULLOUS adj blistered

BULLPEN n large cell where prisoners are confined together temporarily

BULLS ▸ bull

BULLY n person who hurts, persecutes, or intimidates weaker people ▷ vb hurt, intimidate, or persecute (a weaker or smaller person), esp to make him do something ▷ adj dashing

BULRUSH n tall stiff reed

BULSE n purse or bag for diamonds

BULSES ▸ bulse

BULWARK n wall used as a fortification ▷ vb defend or fortify with or as if with a bulwark

BUM n buttocks or anus ▷ vb get by begging ▷ adj of poor quality

BUMALO same as > **bummalo**

BUMBAG n small bag attached to a belt and worn round the waist

BUMBAGS ▸ bumbag

BUMBAZE vb confuse; bewilder

BUMBLE vb speak, do, or move in a clumsy way ▷ n blunder or botch

BUMBLED ▸ bumble

BUMBLER ▸ bumble

BUMBLES ▸ bumble

BUMBO n drink with gin or rum, nutmeg, lemon juice, etc

BUMBOAT n any small boat used for ferrying supplies or goods for sale to a ship at anchor or at a mooring

BUMBOS ▸ bumbo

BUMELIA n thorny shrub

BUMF n official documents or forms

BUMFS ▸ bumf

BUMKIN same as ▸ **bumpkin**

BUMKINS ▸ bumkin

BUMMALO n Bombay duck

BUMMED ▸ bum

BUMMEL n stroll

BUMMELS ▸ stroll

BUMMER n unpleasant or disappointing experience

BUMMERS ▸ bummer

BUMMEST ▸ bum

BUMMING ▸ bum

BUMMLE Scots variant of

▶ **bumble**

BUMMLED ▶ bummle

BUMMLES ▶ bummle

BUMMOCK n submerged mass of ice projecting downwards

BUMP vb knock or strike with a jolt ▷ n dull thud from an impact or collision

BUMPED ▶ bump

BUMPER n bar on the front and back of a vehicle to protect against damage ▷ adj unusually large or abundant ▷ vb toast with a bumper

BUMPERS ▶ bumper

BUMPH same as ▶ bumf

BUMPHS ▶ bumph

BUMPIER ▶ bumpy

BUMPILY ▶ bumpy

BUMPING ▶ bump

BUMPKIN n awkward simple country person

BUMPS ▶ bump

BUMPY adj having an uneven surface

BUMS ▶ bum

BUMSTER adj (of trousers) cut low so as to reveal the top part of the buttocks

BUN n small sweet bread roll or cake

BUNA n synthetic rubber formed by polymerizing butadiene or by copolymerizing it with such compounds as acrylonitrile or styrene

BUNAS ▶ buna

BUNCE n windfall; boom ▷ vb charge someone too much money

BUNCED ▶ bunce

BUNCES ▶ bunce

BUNCH n number of things growing, fastened, or grouped together ▷ vb group or be grouped together in a bunch

BUNCHED ▶ bunch

BUNCHES pl n hairstyle in which hair is tied into two sections on either side of the head at the back

BUNCHY adj composed of or resembling bunches

BUNCING ▶ bunce

BUNCO n swindle, esp one by confidence tricksters ▷ vb swindle

BUNCOED ▶ bunco

BUNCOS ▶ bunco

BUND n embankment or German federation ▷ vb form into an embankment

BUNDE ▶ bund

BUNDED ▶ bund

BUNDH same as ▶ bandh

BUNDHS ▶ bundh

BUNDIED ▶ bundy

BUNDIES ▶ bundy

BUNDING ▶ bund

BUNDIST ▶ bund

BUNDLE n number of things gathered loosely together ▷ vb cause to go roughly or unceremoniously

BUNDLED ▶ bundle

BUNDLER ▶ bundle

BUNDLES ▶ bundle

BUNDOOK n rifle

BUNDS ▶ bund

BUNDT n type of sweet cake

BUNDTS ▶ bundt

BUNDU n largely uninhabited wild region far from towns

BUNDUS ▶ bundu

BUNDY n time clock at work ▷ vb register arrival or departure from work on a time clock

BUNG n stopper for a cask etc ▷ vb close with a bung

BUNGED ▶ bung

BUNGEE n strong elastic cable

BUNGEES ▶ bungee

BUNGER n firework

BUNGERS ▶ bunger

BUNGEY same as ▶ bungee

BUNGEYS ▶ bungey

BUNGIE same as ▶ bungee

BUNGIES ▶ bungy

BUNGING ▶ bung

BUNGLE vb spoil through incompetence ▷ n blunder or muddle

BUNGLED ▶ bungle

BUNGLER ▶ bungle

BUNGLES ▶ bungle

BUNGS ▶ bung

BUNGY ▶ bungee

BUNIA same as ▶ bunnia

BUNIAS ▶ bunia

BUNION n inflamed swelling on the big toe

BUNIONS ▶ bunion

BUNJE same as ▶ bungee

BUNJEE same as ▶ bungee

BUNJEES ▶ bunjee

BUNJES ▶ bunje

BUNJIE same as ▶ bungee

BUNJIES ▶ bunjie

BUNJY same as ▶ bungee

BUNK n narrow shelflike bed ▷ vb prepare to sleep

BUNKED ▶ bunk

BUNKER n sand-filled hollow forming an obstacle on a golf course ▷ vb drive (the ball) into a bunker

BUNKERS ▶ bunker

BUNKING ▶ bunk

BUNKO same as ▶ bunco

BUNKOED ▶ bunko

BUNKOS ▶ bunko

BUNKS ▶ bunk

BUNKUM n nonsense

BUNKUMS ▶ bunkum

BUNN same as ▶ bun

BUNNET same as ▶ bonnet

BUNNETS ▶ bunnet

BUNNIA n Hindu shopkeeper

BUNNIAS ▶ bunnia

BUNNIES ▶ bunny

BUNNS ▶ bunn

BUNNY n child's word for a rabbit

BUNRAKU n Japanese form of puppet theatre in which the puppets are usually about four feet high, with moving features as well as limbs and each puppet is manipulated by up to three puppeteers who remain onstage

BUNS pl n buttocks

BUNSEN n as in **bunsen burner** gas burner used in scientific labs

BUNSENS ▶ bunsen

BUNT vb (of an animal) butt (something) with the head or horns ▷ n act or an instance of bunting

BUNTAL n straw obtained from leaves of the talipot palm

BUNTALS ▶ buntal

BUNTED ▶ bunt

BUNTER n batter who deliberately taps ball lightly

BUNTERS ▶ bunter

BUNTIER ▶ bunt

BUNTING n decorative flags

BUNTS ▶ bunt

BUNTY ▶ bunt

BUNYA n tall dome-shaped Australian coniferous tree

BUNYAS ▶ bunya

BUNYIP n legendary monster said to live in swamps and lakes

BUNYIPS ▶ bunyip

BUOY n floating marker

·anchored in the sea ▷ *vb* prevent from sinking

BUOYAGE *n* system of buoys

BUOYANT *adj* able to float

BUOYED ▶ **buoy**

BUOYING ▶ **buoy**

BUOYS ▶ **buoy**

BUPKES *same as* ▶ **bubkes**

BUPKIS ▶ **bubkis**

BUPKUS *same as* ▶ **bubkes**

BUPPIE *n* affluent young Black person

BUPPIES ▶ **buppy**

BUPPY *same as* ▶ **buppie**

BUQSHA *n* former Yemeni coin

BUQSHAS ▶ **buqsha**

BUR ▶ **burr**

BURA *same as* ▶ **buran**

BURAN *n* blizzard, with the wind blowing from the north and reaching gale force

BURANS ▶ **buran**

BURAS ▶ **bura**

BURB *n* suburb

BURBLE *vb* make a bubbling sound ▷ *n* bubbling or gurgling sound

BURBLED ▶ **burble**

BURBLER ▶ **burble**

BURBLES ▶ **burble**

BURBLY *adj* burbling

BURBOT *n* freshwater fish of the cod family that has barbels around its mouth

BURBOTS ▶ **burbot**

BURBS ▶ **burb**

BURD *Scots form of* ▶ **bird**

BURDASH *n* fringed sash worn over coat

BURDEN *n* heavy load ▷ *vb* put a burden on

BURDENS ▶ **burden**

BURDIE *Scots form of* ▶ **birdie**

BURDIES ▶ **burdie**

BURDOCK *n* weed with prickly burrs

BURDS ▶ **burd**

BUREAU *n* office that provides a service

BUREAUS ▶ **bureau**

BUREAUX ▶ **bureau**

BURET *same as* ▶ **burette**

BURETS ▶ **buret**

BURETTE *n* glass tube for dispensing known volumes of fluids

BURG *n* fortified town

BURGAGE *n* (in England) tenure of land or tenement

in a town or city, which originally involved a fixed money rent

BURGEE *n* triangular or swallow-tailed flag flown from the mast of a merchant ship for identification and from the mast of a yacht to indicate its owner's membership of a particular yacht club

BURGEES ▶ **burgee**

BURGEON *vb* develop or grow rapidly ▷ *n* bud of a plant

BURGER *n* hamburger

BURGERS ▶ **burger**

BURGESS *n* (in England) citizen or freeman of a borough

BURGH *n* Scottish borough

BURGHAL ▶ **burgh**

BURGHER *n* citizen

BURGHS ▶ **burgh**

BURGHUL *same as* ▶ **bulgur**

BURGLAR *n* person who enters a building to commit a crime, esp theft ▷ *vb* burgle

BURGLE *vb* break into (a house, shop, etc)

BURGLED ▶ **burgle**

BURGLES ▶ **burgle**

BURGOO *n* porridge

BURGOOS ▶ **burgoo**

BURGOUT *same as* ▶ **burgoo**

BURGS ▶ **burg**

BURHEL *same as* ▶ **bharal**

BURHELS ▶ **burhel**

BURIAL *n* burying of a dead body

BURIALS ▶ **burial**

BURIED ▶ **bury**

BURIER *n* person or thing that buries

BURIERS ▶ **burier**

BURIES ▶ **bury**

BURIN *n* steel chisel used for engraving metal, wood, or marble

BURINS ▶ **burin**

BURITI *n* type of palm tree

BURITIS ▶ **buriti**

BURK *same as* ▶ **berk**

BURKA *same as* ▶ **burqa**

BURKAS ▶ **burka**

BURKE *vb* murder in such a way as to leave no marks on the body, usually by suffocation

BURKED ▶ **burke**

BURKER ▶ **burke**

BURKERS ▶ **burke**

BURKES ▶ **burke**

BURKHA *n* all-enveloping garment worn by Muslim women

BURKHAS ▶ **burkha**

BURKING ▶ **burke**

BURKITE ▶ **burke**

BURKS ▶ **burk**

BURL *n* small knot or lump in wool ▷ *vb* remove the burls from (cloth)

BURLAP *n* coarse fabric woven from jute, hemp, or the like

BURLAPS ▶ **burlap**

BURLED ▶ **burl**

BURLER ▶ **burl**

BURLERS ▶ **burl**

BURLESK *same as* > burlesque

BURLEY *same as* ▶ **berley**

BURLEYS ▶ **burley**

BURLIER ▶ **burly**

BURLILY ▶ **burly**

BURLING ▶ **burl**

BURLS ▶ **burl**

BURLY *adj* (of a person) broad and strong

BURN *vb* be or set on fire ▷ *n* injury or mark caused by fire or exposure to heat

BURNED ▶ **burn**

BURNER *n* part of a stove or lamp that produces the flame

BURNERS ▶ **burner**

BURNET *n* type of rose

BURNETS ▶ **burnet**

BURNIE *n* sideburn

BURNIES ▶ **burnie**

BURNING ▶ **burn**

BURNISH *vb* make smooth and shiny by rubbing ▷ *n* shiny finish

BURNOUS *n* long circular cloak with a hood, worn esp by Arabs

BURNOUT *n* failure of a mechanical device from excessive heating

BURNS ▶ **burn**

BURNT ▶ **burn**

BUROO *n* government office from which unemployment benefit is distributed

BUROOS ▶ **buroo**

BURP *n* belch ▷ *vb* belch

BURPED ▶ **burp**

BURPEE *n* type of physical exercise movement

BURPEES ▶ **burpee**

BURPING ▶ **burp**

BURPS ▸ burp

BURQA n long enveloping garment worn by Muslim women in public, covering all but the wearer's eyes

> This Arab woman's garment, illustrates the fact that Q doesn't always have to be followed by U. It has several variants including **burka** and **burkha**.

BURQAS as ▸ **burqa**

BURR n small power-driven hand-operated rotary file, esp for removing burrs or for machining recesses ▷ vb form a rough edge on (a workpiece)

BURRED ▸ burr

BURREL same as ▸ **bharal**

BURRELL same as ▸ **bharal**

BURRELS ▸ burrel

BURRER n person who removes burrs

BURRERS ▸ burrer

BURRHEL same as ▸ **burrel**

BURRIER ▸ burry

BURRING ▸ burr

BURRITO n tortilla folded over a filling of minced beef, chicken, cheese, or beans

BURRO n donkey, esp one used as a pack animal

BURROS ▸ burro

BURROW n hole dug in the ground by a rabbit etc ▷ vb dig holes in the ground

BURROWS ▸ burrow

BURRS ▸ burr

BURRY adj full of or covered in burs

BURS ▸ burr

BURSA n small fluid-filled sac that reduces friction between movable parts of the body, esp at joints

BURSAE ▸ bursa

BURSAL ▸ bursa

BURSAR n treasurer of a school, college, or university

BURSARS ▸ bursar

BURSARY n scholarship

BURSAS ▸ bursa

BURSATE ▸ bursa

BURSE n flat case used at Mass as a container for the corporal

BURSEED n type of plant

BURSERA adj of a type of gum tree

BURSES ▸ burse

BURST vb break or cause to break open or apart suddenly and noisily, esp from internal pressure ▷ n sudden breaking open or apart ▷ adj broken apart

BURSTED ▸ burst

BURSTEN ▸ burst

BURSTER ▸ burst

BURSTS ▸ burst

BURTHEN archaic word for ▸ **burden**

BURTON n type of hoisting tackle

BURTONS ▸ burton

BURWEED n any of various plants that bear burs, such as the burdock

BURY vb place in a grave

BURYING ▸ bury

BUS n large motor vehicle for carrying passengers between stops ▷ vb travel by bus

BUSBAR n electrical conductor, maintained at a specific voltage and capable of carrying a high current, usually used to make a common connection between several circuits in a system

BUSBARS ▸ busbar

BUSBIES ▸ busby

BUSBOY n waiter's assistant

BUSBOYS ▸ busboy

BUSBY n tall fur hat worn by some soldiers

BUSED ▸ bus

BUSERA n Ugandan alcoholic drink made from millet: sometimes mixed with honey

BUSERAS ▸ busera

BUSES ▸ bus

BUSGIRL n waiter's assistant

BUSH n dense woody plant, smaller than a tree ▷ vb fit a bush to (a casing or bearing)

BUSHED adj extremely tired

BUSHEL n obsolete unit of measure equal to 8 gallons (36.4 litres) ▷ vb alter or mend (a garment)

BUSHELS ▸ bushel

BUSHER ▸ bush

BUSHERS ▸ bush

BUSHES ▸ bush

BUSHFLY n small black Australian fly that breeds in faeces and dung

BUSHIDO n feudal code of the Japanese samurai, stressing self-discipline, courage and loyalty

BUSHIE same as ▸ **bushy**

BUSHIER ▸ bushy

BUSHIES ▸ bushy

BUSHILY ▸ bushy

BUSHING same as ▸ **bush**

BUSHMAN n person who lives or travels in the bush

BUSHMEN ▸ bushman

BUSHPIG n wild brown or black forest pig of tropical Africa and Madagascar

BUSHTIT n small grey active North American songbird

BUSHWA n nonsense

BUSHWAH same as ▸ **bushwa**

BUSHWAS ▸ bushwa

BUSHY adj (of hair) thick and shaggy ▷ n person who lives in the bush

BUSIED ▸ busy

BUSIER ▸ busy

BUSIES ▸ busy

BUSIEST ▸ busy

BUSILY adv in a busy manner

BUSING ▸ bus

BUSINGS ▸ bus

BUSK vb act as a busker ▷ n strip of whalebone, wood, steel, etc, inserted into the front of a corset to stiffen it

BUSKED ▸ busk

BUSKER ▸ busk

BUSKERS ▸ busk

BUSKET n bouquet

BUSKETS ▸ busket

BUSKIN n (formerly) sandal-like covering for the foot and leg, reaching the calf and usually laced

BUSKING ▸ busk

BUSKINS ▸ buskin

BUSKS ▸ busk

BUSKY same as ▸ **bosky**

BUSLOAD n number of people bus carries

BUSMAN n person who drives a bus

BUSMEN ▸ busman

BUSS archaic or dialect word for ▸ **kiss**

BUSSED ▸ bus

BUSSES ▸ bus

BUSSING ▸ bus

BUSSU n type of palm tree

BUSSUS ▸ bussu

B

BUST n chest of a human being, esp a woman's bosom ▷ adj broken ▷ vb burst or break

BUSTARD n bird with long strong legs, a heavy body, a long neck, and speckled plumage

BUSTED ▸ bust

BUSTEE same as ▸ basti

BUSTEES ▸ bustee

BUSTER n person or thing destroying something as specified

BUSTERS ▸ buster

BUSTI same as ▸ basti

BUSTIC n type of small American tree

BUSTICS ▸ bustic

BUSTIER n close-fitting strapless women's top

BUSTING ▸ bust

BUSTIS ▸ busti

BUSTLE vb hurry with a show of activity or energy ▷ n energetic and noisy activity

BUSTLED ▸ bustle

BUSTLER ▸ bustle

BUSTLES ▸ bustle

BUSTS ▸ bust

BUSTY adj (of a woman) having a prominent bust

BUSUUTI n long garment with short sleeves and a square neckline, worn by Ugandan women, esp in S Uganda

BUSY adj actively employed ▷ vb keep (someone, esp oneself) busy

BUSYING ▸ busy

BUT prep except ▷ adv only ▷ n outer room of a two-roomed cottage: usually the kitchen

BUTANE n gas used for fuel

BUTANES ▸ butane

BUTANOL n colourless substance

BUTCH adj markedly or aggressively masculine ▷ n lesbian who is noticeably masculine

BUTCHER n person who slaughters animals or sells their meat ▷ vb kill and prepare (animals) for meat

BUTCHES ▸ butch

BUTE n drug used illegally to dope horses

BUTENE n pungent colourless gas

BUTENES ▸ butene

BUTEO n type of American hawk

BUTEOS ▸ buteo

BUTES ▸ bute

BUTLE vb act as butler

BUTLED ▸ butle

BUTLER n chief male servant ▷ vb act as a butler

BUTLERS ▸ butler

BUTLERY n butler's room

BUTLES ▸ butle

BUTLING ▸ butle

BUTMENT same as > abutment

BUTS ▸ but

BUTT n thicker or blunt end of something, such as the end of the stock of a rifle ▷ vb strike or push with the head or horns

BUTTALS n abuttal

BUTTE n isolated steep flat-topped hill

BUTTED ▸ butt

BUTTER n edible fatty yellow solid made form cream ▷ vb put butter on

BUTTERS ▸ butter

BUTTERY n (in some universities) room in which food and drink are sold to students ▷ adj containing, like, or coated with butter

BUTTES ▸ butte

BUTTIES ▸ butty

BUTTING ▸ butt

BUTTLE vb act as butler

BUTTLED ▸ buttle

BUTTLES ▸ buttle

BUTTOCK n either of the two fleshy masses that form the human rump ▷ vb perform a kind of wrestling manoeuvre on a person

BUTTON n small disc or knob sewn to clothing, which can be passed through a slit in another piece of fabric to fasten them ▷ vb fasten with buttons

BUTTONS n page boy

BUTTONY ▸ button

BUTTS ▸ butt

BUTTY n sandwich

BUTUT n Gambian monetary unit worth one hundredth of a dalasi

BUTUTS ▸ butut

BUTYL adj of or containing any of four isomeric forms of the group C_4H_9— ▷ n of, consisting of, or containing any of four isomeric forms of the group C_4H_9—

BUTYLS ▸ butyl

BUTYRAL n type of resin

BUTYRIC adj as in **butyric acid** type of acid

BUTYRIN n colourless liquid ester or oil found in butter. It is formed from butyric acid and glycerine

BUTYRYL n radical of butyric acid

BUVETTE n roadside café

BUXOM adj (of a woman) healthily plump and full-bosomed

BUXOMER ▸ buxom

BUXOMLY ▸ buxom

BUY vb acquire by paying money for ▷ n thing acquired through payment

BUYABLE ▸ buy

BUYBACK n repurchase by a company of some or all of its shares from an investor, who acquired them by putting venture capital into the company when it was formed

BUYER n customer

BUYERS ▸ buyer

BUYING n as in **panic buying** the buying up of large quantities of something feared to be scarce

BUYINGS ▸ buying

BUYOFF n purchase

BUYOFFS ▸ buyoff

BUYOUT n purchase of a company, esp by its former management or staff

BUYOUTS ▸ buyout

BUYS ▸ buy

BUZUKI same as > bouzouki

BUZUKIA ▸ buzuki

BUZUKIS ▸ buzuki

BUZZ n rapidly vibrating humming sound ▷ vb make a humming sound

BUZZARD n bird of prey of the hawk family

BUZZCUT n very short haircut

BUZZED ▸ buzz

BUZZER n electronic device that produces a buzzing sound as a signal

BUZZERS ▸ buzzer

BUZZES ▸ buzz

BUZZIER ▸ buzzy

BUZZING ▸ buzz

B

BUZZWIG n bushy wig
BUZZY adj making a buzzing sound
BWANA n (in E Africa) master, often used as a respectful form of address
BWANAS ▸ bwana
BWAZI same as ▸ buaze
BWAZIS ▸ bwazi
BY prep indicating the doer of an action, nearness, movement past, time before or during which, etc ▷ adv near ▷ n a pass to the next round (of a competition, etc)
BYCATCH n unwanted fish and other sea animals caught in a fishing net along with the desired kind of fish
BYCOKET n former Italian high-crowned hat
BYDE same as ▸ bide
BYDED ▸ byde
BYDES ▸ byde
BYDING ▸ byde
BYE n situation where a player or team wins a round by having no opponent ▷ interj goodbye ▷ sentence substitute goodbye
BYELAW n rule made by a local authority for the regulation of its affairs or management of the area it governs
BYELAWS ▸ byelaw
BYES ▸ bye
BYGONE adj past
BYGONES ▸ bygone
BYKE ▸ bicycle
BYKED ▸ bicycle

BYKES ▸ bicycle
BYKING ▸ bicycle
BYLANE n side lane or alley off a road
BYLANES ▸ bylane
BYLAW n rule made by a local authority
BYLAWS ▸ bylaw
BYLINE n line under the title of a newspaper or magazine article giving the author's name ▷ vb give a byline to
BYLINED ▸ byline
BYLINER ▸ byline
BYLINES ▸ byline
BYLIVE same as ▸ belive
BYNAME n nickname
BYNAMES ▸ byname
BYNEMPT ▸ bename
BYPASS n main road built to avoid a city ▷ vb go round or avoid
BYPAST ▸ bypass
BYPATH n little-used path or track, esp in the country
BYPATHS ▸ bypath
BYPLACE n private place
BYPLAY n secondary action or talking carried on apart while the main action proceeds, esp in a play
BYPLAYS ▸ byplay
BYRE n shelter for cows
BYREMAN n man who works in byre
BYREMEN ▸ byreman
BYRES ▸ byre
BYRL same as ▸ birl
BYRLADY interj short for By Our Lady
BYRLAW same as ▸ bylaw
BYRLAWS ▸ byrlaw
BYRLED ▸ byrl

BYRLING ▸ byrl
BYRLS ▸ byrl
BYRNIE n archaic word for coat of mail
BYRNIES ▸ byrnie
BYROAD n secondary or side road
BYROADS ▸ byroad
BYROOM n private room
BYROOMS ▸ byroom
BYS ▸ by
BYSSAL adj of mollusc's byssus
BYSSI ▸ byssus
BYSSINE adj made from flax
BYSSOID adj consisting of fine fibres
BYSSUS n mass of strong threads secreted by a sea mussel or similar mollusc that attaches the animal to a hard fixed surface
BYTALK n trivial conversation
BYTALKS ▸ bytalk
BYTE n group of bits processed as one unit of data
BYTES ▸ byte
BYWAY n minor road
BYWAYS ▸ byway
BYWONER n poor tenant-farmer
BYWORD n person or thing regarded as a perfect example of something
BYWORDS ▸ byword
BYWORK n work done outside usual working hours
BYWORKS ▸ bywork
BYZANT same as ▸ bezant
BYZANTS ▸ byzant

Cc

C can be a tricky letter to use, especially as it only forms a single two-letter word **ch**. But if you remember this, you won't waste time racking your brains for two-letter words. There are, however, plenty of good three-letter words beginning with **C**. **Cox** scores 12 points, while **caw, cow** and **coy** are each worth 8 and **caz, coz** and **cuz** are worth 14. It's also a good idea to remember the short words starting with **C** that don't contain any vowels: **cly** and **cwm** as well as **ch**.

CAA *a Scots word for* ▸ **call**

CAAED ▸ **caa**

CAAING ▸ **caa**

CAAS ▸ **caa**

CAB *n* taxi ▷ *vb* take a taxi

CABA *same as* ▸ **cabas**

CABAL *n* small group of political plotters ▷ *vb* form a cabal

CABALA *a variant spelling of* > **kabbalah**

CABALAS ▸ **cabala**

CABALS ▸ **cabal**

CABANA *n* tent used as a dressing room by the sea

CABANAS ▸ **cabana**

CABARET *n* dancing and singing show in a nightclub

CABAS *n* reticule

CABBAGE *n* vegetable with a large head of green leaves ▷ *vb* steal

CABBAGY ▸ **cabbage**

CABBALA *a variant spelling of* > **kabbalah**

CABBED ▸ **cab**

CABBIE *n* taxi driver

CABBIES ▸ **cabbie**

CABBING ▸ **cab**

CABBY *same as* ▸ **cabbie**

CABER *n* tree trunk tossed in competition at Highland games

CABERS ▸ **caber**

CABEZON *n* large food fish of N American Pacific coastal waters, with greenish flesh

CABILDO *n* Spanish municipal council

CABIN *n* compartment in a ship or aircraft ▷ *vb* confine in a small space

CABINED ▸ **cabin**

CABINET *n* piece of furniture with drawers or shelves

CABINS ▸ **cabin**

CABLE *n* strong thick rope; a wire or bundle of wires that conduct electricity ▷ *vb* send (someone) a message by cable

CABLED ▸ **cable**

CABLER *n* cable broadcasting company

CABLERS ▸ **cabler**

CABLES ▸ **cable**

CABLET *n* small cable, esp a cable-laid rope that has a circumference of less than 25 centimetres (ten inches)

CABLETS ▸ **cablet**

CABLING ▸ **cable**

CABMAN *n* driver of a cab

CABMEN ▸ **cabman**

CABOB *vb* roast on a skewer

CABOBS ▸ **cabob**

CABOC *n* type of Scottish cheese

CABOCS ▸ **caboc**

CABOMBA *n* type of aquatic plant

CABOOSE *n* guard's van on a train

CABOVER *adj* of or denoting a truck or lorry in which the cab is over the engine

CABRE *adj* heraldic term designating an animal rearing

CABRIE *n* pronghorn antelope

CABRIES ▸ **cabrie**

CABRIO *short for* > **cabriolet**

CABRIOS ▸ **cabrio**

CABRIT *n* pronghorn antelope

CABRITS ▸ **cabrit**

CABS ▸ **cab**

CACA *n* heroin

CACAO *same as* ▸ **cocoa**

CACAOS ▸ **cocoa**

CACAS ▸ **caca**

CACHACA *n* white Brazilian rum made from sugar cane

CACHE *n* hidden store of weapons or treasure ▷ *vb* store in a cache

CACHED ▸ **cache**

CACHES ▸ **cache**

CACHET *n* prestige, distinction ▷ *vb* apply a commemorative design to an envelope, as a first-day cover

CACHETS ▸ **cachet**

CACHEXY *same as* > **cachexia**

CACHING ▸ **cache**

CACHOU *same as* ▸ **catechu**

CACHOUS ▸ **catechu**

CACIQUE *n* American Indian chief in a Spanish-speaking region

CACKIER ▸ **cacky**

CACKLE *vb* laugh shrilly ▷ *n* cackling noise

CACKLED ▸ **cackle**

CACKLER ▸ **cackle**

CACKLES ▸ **cackle**

CACKY *adj* of or like excrement

CACODYL *n* oily poisonous liquid with a strong garlic smell

CACOEPY *n* bad or mistaken pronunciation

CACOLET n seat fitted to the back of a mule

CACONYM n erroneous name

CACOON n large seed of the sword-bean

CACOONS ▸ cacoon

CACTI ▸ cactus

CACTOID adj resembling a cactus

CACTUS n fleshy desert plant with spines but no leaves

CACUMEN n apex

CAD n dishonourable man

CADAGA n eucalyptus tree of tropical and subtropical Australia with a smooth green trunk

CADAGAS ▸ cadaga

CADAGI same as ▸ cadaga

CADAGIS ▸ cadagi

CADAVER n corpse

CADDICE same as ▸ caddis

CADDIE n person who carries a golfer's clubs ▷ vb act as a caddie

CADDIED ▸ caddie

CADDIES ▸ caddie

CADDIS n type of coarse woollen yarn, braid, or fabric

CADDISH ▸ cad

CADDY same as ▸ caddie

CADDYSS ▸ caddis

CADE n juniper tree ▷ adj (of a young animal) left by its mother and reared by humans, usually as a pet

CADEAU n present

CADEAUX ▸ cadeau

CADEE old form of ▸ cadet

CADEES ▸ cadee

CADELLE n type of beetle that feeds on flour, grain, and other stored foods

CADENCE n rise and fall in the pitch of the voice ▷ vb modulate musically

CADENCY same as ▸ cadence

CADENT adj having cadence

CADENZA n complex solo passage in a piece of music

CADES ▸ cade

CADET n young person training for the armed forces or police

CADETS ▸ cadet

CADGE vb get (something) by taking advantage of someone's generosity

CADGED ▸ cadge

CADGER n person who cadges

CADGERS ▸ cadger

CADGES ▸ cadge

CADGIER ▸ cadgy

CADGING ▸ cadge

CADGY adj cheerful

CADI n judge in a Muslim community

CADIE n messenger

CADIES ▸ cadie

CADIS ▸ cadi

CADMIC ▸ cadmium

CADMIUM n bluish-white metallic element used in alloys

CADRANS n instrument used in gemcutting

CADRE n small group of people selected and trained to form the core of a political organization or military unit

CADRES ▸ cadre

CADS ▸ cad

CADUAC n windfall

CADUACS ▸ caduac

CADUCEI > caduceus

CAECA ▸ caecum

CAECAL ▸ caecum

CAECUM n pouch at the beginning of the large intestine

CAEOMA n aecium in some rust fungi that has no surrounding membrane

CAEOMAS ▸ caeoma

CAERULE same as ▸ cerule

CAESAR n any emperor, autocrat, dictator, or other powerful ruler

CAESARS ▸ caesar

CAESE interj Shakespearean interjection

CAESIUM n silvery-white metallic element used in photocells

CAESTUS same as ▸ cestus

CAESURA n pause in a line of verse

CAFARD n feeling of severe depression

CAFARDS ▸ cafard

CAFE n small or inexpensive restaurant serving light refreshments

CAFES ▸ cafe

CAFF n café

CAFFEIN same as > caffeine

CAFFILA n caravan train

CAFFS ▸ caff

CAFILA same as ▸ caffila

CAFILAS ▸ cafila

CAFTAN same as ▸ kaftan

CAFTANS ▸ caftan

CAG same as ▸ cagoule

CAGANER n figure of a squatting defecating person, a traditional character in Catalan Christmas crèche scenes

CAGE n enclosure of bars or wires, for keeping animals or birds ▷ vb confine in a cage

CAGED ▸ cage

CAGEFUL n amount which fills a cage to capacity

CAGER n basketball player

CAGERS ▸ cager

CAGES ▸ cage

CAGEY adj reluctant to go into details

CAGIER ▸ cagey

CAGIEST ▸ cagey

CAGILY ▸ cagey

CAGING ▸ cage

CAGMAG adj done shoddily ▷ vb chat idly

CAGMAGS ▸ cagmag

CAGOT n member of a class of French outcasts

CAGOTS ▸ cagot

CAGOUL same as ▸ cagoule

CAGOULE n lightweight hooded waterproof jacket

CAGOULS ▸ cagoul

CAGS ▸ cag

CAGY same as ▸ cagey

CAHIER n notebook

CAHIERS ▸ cahier

CAHOOT n partnership

CAHOOTS ▸ cahoot

CAHOW n Bermuda petrel

CAHOWS ▸ cahow

CAID n Moroccan district administrator

CAIDS ▸ caid

CAILLE n quail

CAILLES ▸ caille

CAIMAC same as > caimacam

CAIMACS ▸ caimac

CAIMAN same as ▸ cayman

CAIMANS ▸ caiman

CAIN n (in Scotland and Ireland) payment in kind, usually farm produce paid as rent

CAINS ▸ cain

CAIQUE n long narrow light rowing skiff used on the Bosporus

CAIQUES ▸ caique

CAIRD n travelling tinker

CAIRDS ▸ caird**

CAIRN n mound of stones erected as a memorial or marker

CAIRNED adj marked by a cairn

CAIRNS ▸ cairn

CAIRNY adj covered with cairns

CAISSON > cofferdam

CAITIFF n cowardly or base person ▷ adj cowardly

CAITIVE n captive

CAJAPUT same as ▸ cajuput

CAJEPUT same as ▸ cajuput

CAJOLE vb persuade by flattery

CAJOLED ▸ cajole

CAJOLER ▸ cajole

CAJOLES ▸ cajole

CAJON n Peruvian wooden box used as a drum

CAJONES ▸ cajon

CAJUN n music of the Cajun people, combining blues and European folk music

CAJUPUT n small tree or shrub native to the East Indies and Australia, with whitish flowers and leaves

CAKE n sweet food baked from a mixture of flour, eggs, etc ▷ vb form into a hardened mass or crust

CAKED ▸ cake

CAKES ▸ cake

CAKEY ▸ cake

CAKIER ▸ cake

CAKIEST ▸ cake

CAKING ▸ cake

CAKINGS ▸ cake

CAKY ▸ cake

CALALOO same as ▸ calalu

CALALU n edible leaves of various plants, used as greens or in making thick soups

CALALUS ▸ calalu

CALAMAR n any member of the squid family

CALAMI ▸ calamus

CALAMUS n tropical Asian palm, some species of which are a source of rattan and canes

CALANDO adv (to be performed) with gradually decreasing tone and speed

CALASH n horse-drawn carriage with low wheels and a folding top

CALATHI > calathus

CALCAR n spur or spurlike process, as on the leg of a

bird or the corolla of a flower

CALCARS ▸ calcar

CALCED adj wearing shoes

CALCES ▸ calx

CALCIC adj of, containing, or concerned with lime or calcium

CALCIFY vb harden by the depositing of calcium salts

CALCINE vb oxidize (a substance) by heating

CALCITE n colourless or white form of calcium carbonate

CALCIUM n silvery-white metallic element found in bones, teeth, limestone, and chalk

CALCULI > calculus

CALDERA n large basin-shaped crater at the top of a volcano, formed by the collapse or explosion of the cone

CALDRON same as > cauldron

CALECHE same as ▸ calash

CALEFY vb to make warm

CALENDS pl n first day of each month in the ancient Roman calendar

CALESA n horse-drawn buggy

CALESAS ▸ calesa

CALF n young cow, bull, elephant, whale, or seal

CALFS ▸ calf

CALIBER same as ▸ calibre

CALIBRE n person's ability or worth

CALICES ▸ calix

CALICHE n bed of sand or clay in arid regions cemented by calcium carbonate, sodium chloride, and other soluble minerals

CALICLE same as ▸ calycle

CALICO n white cotton fabric

CALICOS ▸ calico

CALID adj warm

CALIF same as ▸ caliph

CALIFS ▸ calif

CALIGO n speck on the cornea causing poor vision

CALIGOS ▸ caligo

CALIMA n Saharan dust-storm

CALIMAS ▸ calima

CALIPEE n yellow glutinous edible part of the turtle

found next to the lower shell, considered a delicacy

CALIPER same as > calliper

CALIPH n Muslim ruler

CALIPHS ▸ caliph

CALIVER n type of musket

CALIX n cup

CALK same as ▸ caulk

CALKED ▸ calk

CALKER ▸ calk

CALKERS ▸ calk

CALKIN ▸ calk

CALKING ▸ calk

CALKINS ▸ calk

CALKS ▸ calk

CALL vb name ▷ n cry, shout

CALLA n S African plant with a white funnel-shaped spathe enclosing a yellow spadix

CALLAIS n green stone found as beads and ornaments in the late Neolithic and early Bronze Age of W Europe

CALLAN same as ▸ callant

CALLANS ▸ callan

CALLANT n youth

CALLAS ▸ calla

CALLBOY n person who notifies actors when it is time to go on stage

CALLED ▸ call

CALLEE n computer function being used

CALLEES ▸ callee

CALLER n person or thing that calls, esp a person who makes a brief visit ▷ adj (of food, esp fish) fresh

CALLERS ▸ caller

CALLET n scold

CALLETS ▸ callet

CALLID adj cunning

CALLING n vocation, profession

CALLOP n edible Australian freshwater fish, often golden or pale yellow in colour

CALLOPS ▸ callop

CALLOSE n carbohydrate, a polymer of glucose, found in plants, esp in the sieve tubes

CALLOUS adj showing no concern for other people's feelings ▷ vb make or become callous

CALLOW adj young and inexperienced ▷ n someone young and inexperienced

CALLOWS ▶ callow

CALLS ▶ call

CALLUNA n type of heather

CALLUS n area of thick hardened skin ▷ vb produce or cause to produce a callus

CALM adj not agitated or excited ▷ n peaceful state ▷ vb make or become calm

CALMANT n sedative

CALMED ▶ calm

CALMER ▶ calm

CALMEST ▶ calm

CALMIER ▶ calmy

CALMING ▶ calm

CALMLY ▶ calm

CALMS ▶ calm

CALMY adj tranquil

CALO n military servant

CALOMEL n colourless tasteless powder

CALORIC adj of heat or calories ▷ n hypothetical elastic fluid formerly postulated as the embodiment of heat

CALORIE n unit of measurement for the energy value of food

CALORY same as ▶ calorie

CALOS ▶ calo

CALOTTE n skullcap worn by Roman Catholic clergy

CALOYER n monk of the Greek Orthodox Church, esp of the Basilian Order

CALP n type of limestone

CALPA n Hindu unit of time

CALPAC n large black brimless hat made of sheepskin or felt, worn by men in parts of the Near East

CALPACK same as ▶ calpac

CALPACS ▶ calpac

CALPAIN n type of enzyme

CALPAS ▶ calpa

CALPS ▶ calp

CALQUE ▶ caulk

CALQUED ▶ calque

CALQUES ▶ calque

CALTHA n marsh marigold

CALTHAS ▶ caltha

CALTRAP same as ▶ caltrop

CALTROP n floating Asian plant

CALUMBA n Mozambiquan root used for medicinal purposes

CALUMET n peace pipe

CALUMNY n false or malicious statement

CALVARY n representation of Christ's crucifixion, usually sculptured and in the open air

CALVE vb give birth to a calf

CALVED ▶ calve

CALVER vb prepare fish for cooking

CALVERS ▶ calver

CALVES ▶ calf

CALVING ▶ calve

CALX n powdery metallic oxide formed when an ore or mineral is roasted

CALXES ▶ calx

CALYCES ▶ calyx

CALYCLE n cup-shaped structure, as in the coral skeleton

CALYPSO n West Indian song with improvised topical lyrics

CALYX n outer leaves that protect a flower bud

CALYXES ▶ calyx

CALZONE n folded pizza filled with cheese, tomatoes, etc

CALZONI ▶ calzone

CAM n device that converts a circular motion to a to-and-fro motion ▷ vb furnish (a machine) with a cam

CAMA n hybrid offspring of a camel and a llama

CAMAIEU n cameo

CAMAIL n neck and shoulders covering of mail worn with and laced to the basinet

CAMAILS ▶ camail

CAMAN n wooden stick used to hit the ball in shinty

CAMANS ▶ caman

CAMARON n shrimp

CAMAS same as ▶ camass

CAMASES ▶ camas

CAMASH same as ▶ camass

CAMASS n type of North American plant

CAMBER n slight upward curve to the centre of a surface ▷ vb form or be formed with a surface that curves upwards to its centre

CAMBERS ▶ camber

CAMBIA ▶ cambium

CAMBIAL ▶ cambium

CAMBISM ▶ cambist

CAMBIST n dealer or expert in foreign exchange

CAMBIUM n meristem that increases the girth of stems and roots by producing additional xylem and phloem

CAMBOGE n type of gum resin

CAMBREL same as ▶ gambrel

CAMBRIC n fine white linen fabric

CAME ▶ come

CAMEL n humped mammal that can survive long periods without food or water in desert regions

CAMELIA same as ▶ camellia

CAMELID adj of or relating to camels ▷ n any animal of the camel family

CAMELOT n supposedly idyllic period or age

CAMELRY n troops mounted on camels

CAMELS ▶ camel

CAMEO n brooch or ring with a profile head carved in relief ▷ vb to appear in a brief role

CAMEOED ▶ cameo

CAMEOS ▶ cameo

CAMERA n apparatus used for taking photographs or pictures for television or cinema

CAMERAE ▶ camera

CAMERAL adj of or relating to a judicial or legislative chamber

CAMERAS ▶ camera

CAMES ▶ canvas

CAMESE same as ▶ camise

CAMESES ▶ camese

CAMION n lorry, or, esp formerly, a large dray

CAMIONS ▶ camion

CAMIS n light robe

CAMISA n smock

CAMISAS ▶ camisa

CAMISE n loose light shirt, smock, or tunic originally worn in the Middle Ages

CAMISES ▶ camise

CAMISIA n surplice

CAMLET n tough waterproof cloth

CAMLETS ▶ camlet

CAMMED ▶ cam

CAMMIE n webcam award

CAMMIES ▶ cammie

CAMMING ▶ cam

CAMO n short for camouflage

C

CAMOGIE n form of hurling played by women

CAMOODI a Caribbean name for ▷ **anaconda**

CAMORRA n secret criminal group

CAMOS ▷ **camo**

CAMOTE n type of sweet potato

CAMOTES ▷ **camote**

CAMP vb stay in a camp ▷ adj effeminate or homosexual ▷ adj (place for) temporary lodgings consisting of tents, huts, or cabins

CAMPANA n bell or bell shape

CAMPED ▷ **camp**

CAMPER n person who lives or temporarily stays in a tent, cabin, etc

CAMPERS ▷ **camper**

CAMPERY n campness

CAMPEST ▷ **camp**

CAMPHOL another word for ▷ **borneol**

CAMPHOR n aromatic crystalline substance used medicinally and in mothballs

CAMPI ▷ **campo**

CAMPIER ▷ **campy**

CAMPILY ▷ **campy**

CAMPING ▷ **camp**

CAMPION n red, pink, or white wild flower

CAMPLE vb to argue

CAMPLED ▷ **cample**

CAMPLES ▷ **cample**

CAMPLY ▷ **camp**

CAMPO n level or undulating savanna country, esp in the uplands of Brazil

CAMPONG n in Malaysia, a village

CAMPOS ▷ **campo**

CAMPOUT n camping trip

CAMPS ▷ **camp**

CAMPUS n grounds of a university or college ▷ vb to restrict a student to campus, as a punishment

CAMPY adj effeminate

CAMS ▷ **cam**

CAMSHO adj crooked

CAMUS n type of loose robe

CAMUSES ▷ **camus**

CAMWOOD n W African leguminous tree whose hard wood was formerly used to make a red dye

CAN vb be able to ▷ n metal container for food or liquids

CANADA n canada goose

CANADAS ▷ **canada**

CANAKIN same as ▷ **cannikin**

CANAL n artificial waterway ▷ vb. dig a canal through

CANALED ▷ **canal**

CANALS ▷ **canal**

CANAPE n small piece of bread or toast with a savoury topping

CANAPES ▷ **canape**

CANARD n false report

CANARDS ▷ **canard**

CANARY n small yellow songbird often kept as a pet ▷ vb perform a dance called the canary

CANASTA n card game like rummy, played with two packs

CANBANK n container for receiving cans for recycling

CANCAN n lively high-kicking dance performed by a female group

CANCANS ▷ **cancan**

CANCEL vb stop (something that has been arranged) from taking place ▷ n new leaf or section of a book replacing a defective one, one containing errors, or one that has been omitted

CANCELS ▷ **cancel**

CANCER n serious disease resulting from a malignant growth or tumour

CANCERS ▷ **cancer**

CANCHA n toasted maize

CANCHAS ▷ **cancha**

CANDELA n unit of luminous intensity

CANDENT adj emitting light as a result of being heated to a high temperature

CANDID adj honest and straightforward ▷ n unposed photograph

CANDIDA n yeastlike parasitic fungus which causes thrush

CANDIDS ▷ **candid**

CANDIE n South Indian unit of weight

CANDIED adj coated with sugar

CANDIES ▷ **candy**

CANDIRU n parasitic

freshwater catfish of the Amazon region

CANDLE n stick of wax enclosing a wick, which is burned to produce light ▷ vb test by holding up to a candle

CANDLED ▷ **candle**

CANDLER ▷ **candle**

CANDLES ▷ **candle**

CANDOCK n type of water lily, or horsetail

CANDOR same as ▷ **candour**

CANDORS ▷ **candor**

CANDOUR n honesty and straightforwardness

CANDY n sweet or sweets ▷ vb make sweet

CANE n stem of the bamboo or similar plant ▷ vb beat with a cane

CANED ▷ **cane**

CANEH n Hebrew unit of length

CANEHS ▷ **caneh**

CANELLA n fragrant cinnamon-like inner bark of a W Indian tree, used as a spice and in medicine

CANER ▷ **cane**

CANERS ▷ **cane**

CANES ▷ **cane**

CANFUL n amount a can will hold

CANFULS ▷ **canful**

CANG same as ▷ **cangue**

CANGLE vb to wrangle

CANGLED ▷ **cangle**

CANGLES ▷ **cangle**

CANGS ▷ **cang**

CANGUE n (formerly in China) a large wooden collar worn by petty criminals as a punishment

CANGUES ▷ **cangue**

CANID n animal of the dog family

CANIDS ▷ **canid**

CANIER ▷ **cany**

CANIEST ▷ **cany**

CANIKIN same as ▷ **cannikin**

CANINE adj of or like a dog ▷ n sharp pointed tooth between the incisors and the molars

CANINES ▷ **canine**

CANING n beating with a cane as a punishment

CANINGS ▷ **caning**

CANKER n ulceration, ulcerous disease ▷ vb infect or become infected with or as if with canker

CANKERS ▸ canker
CANKERY *adj* like a canker
CANN *vb* direct a ship's steering
CANNA *n* type of tropical plant with broad leaves, cultivated for its red or yellow showy flowers
CANNACH *n* cotton grass
CANNAE *vb* can not
CANNAS ▸ canna
CANNED ▸ can
CANNEL *n* type of dull coal
CANNELS ▸ cannel
CANNER *n* person or organization whose job is to can foods
CANNERS ▸ canner
CANNERY *n* factory where food is canned
CANNIE *same as* ▸ **canny**
CANNIER ▸ canny
CANNILY ▸ canny
CANNING ▸ can
CANNOLI *n* Sicilian pudding of pasta shells filled with sweetened ricotta
CANNON *n* gun of large calibre ▹ *vb* to collide (with)
CANNONS ▸ cannon
CANNOT *vb* can not
CANNS ▸ cann
CANNULA *n* narrow tube for insertion into a bodily cavity, as for draining off fluid, introducing medication, etc
CANNY *adj* shrewd, cautious ▹ *adv* quite
CANOE *n* light narrow open boat propelled by a paddle or paddles ▹ *vb* use a canoe
CANOED ▸ canoe
CANOER ▸ canoe
CANOERS ▸ canoe
CANOES ▸ canoe
CANOLA *n* cooking oil extracted from a variety of rapeseed developed in Canada
CANOLAS ▸ canola
CANON *n* priest serving in a cathedral
CANONIC *same as* > **canonical**
CANONRY *n* office, benefice, or status of a canon
CANONS ▸ canon
CANOPIC *adj* of ancient Egyptian vase
CANOPY *n* covering above a bed, door, etc ▹ *vb* cover

with or as if with a canopy
CANS ▸ can
CANSFUL ▸ canful
CANSO *n* love song
CANSOS ▸ canso
CANST *vb* form of 'can' used with the pronoun *thou* or its relative form
CANT *n* insincere talk ▹ *vb* use cant ▹ *adj* oblique
CANTAL *n* French cheese
CANTALA *n* tropical American plant, the agave
CANTALS ▸ cantal
CANTAR *variant form of* ▸ **kantar**
CANTARS ▸ cantar
CANTATA *n* musical work consisting of arias, duets, and choruses
CANTATE *n* 98th psalm sung as a nonmetrical hymn
CANTDOG *same as* > **canthook**
CANTED ▸ cant
CANTEEN *n* restaurant attached to a workplace or school
CANTER *vb* move at gait between trot and gallop
CANTERS ▸ canter
CANTEST ▸ cant
CANTHAL ▸ canthus
CANTHI ▸ canthus
CANTHUS *n* inner or outer corner or angle of the eye, formed by the natural junction of the eyelids
CANTIC ▸ cant
CANTICO *vb* to dance as part of an act of worship
CANTIER ▸ canty
CANTILY ▸ canty
CANTINA *n* bar or wine shop, esp in a Spanish-speaking country
CANTING ▸ cant
CANTION *n* song
CANTLE *n* back part of a saddle that slopes upwards ▹ *vb* to set up, or stand, on high
CANTLED ▸ cantle
CANTLES ▸ cantle
CANTLET *n* piece
CANTO *same as* ▸ **cantus**
CANTON *n* political division of a country, esp Switzerland ▹ *vb* divide into cantons
CANTONS ▸ canton
CANTOR *n* man employed

to lead services in a synagogue
CANTORS ▸ cantor
CANTOS ▸ canto
CANTRAP *same as* > **cantraip**
CANTRED *n* district comprising a hundred villages
CANTREF *same as* ▸ **cantred**
CANTRIP *n* magic spell ▹ *adj* (of an effect) produced by black magic
CANTS ▸ cant
CANTUS *n* medieval form of church singing
CANTY *adj* lively
CANULA *same as* ▸ **cannula**
CANULAE ▸ canula
CANULAR *adj* shaped like a cannula
CANULAS ▸ canula
CANVAS *n* heavy coarse cloth used for sails and tents, and for oil painting ▹ *vb* to cover with, or be applied to, canvas
CANVASS *vb* try to get votes or support (from) ▹ *n* canvassing
CANY *adj* cane-like
CANYON *n* deep narrow valley
CANYONS ▸ canyon
CANZONA *n* type of 16th- or 17th-century contrapuntal music, usually for keyboard, lute, or instrumental ensemble
CANZONE *n* Provençal or Italian lyric, often in praise of love or beauty
CANZONI ▸ canzone
CAP *n* soft close-fitting covering for the head ▹ *vb* cover or top with something
CAPA *n* type of Spanish cloak
CAPABLE *adj* having the ability (for)
CAPABLY ▸ capable
CAPAS ▸ capa
CAPE *n* short cloak ▹ *vb* to cut and remove the hide of an animal
CAPED ▸ cape
CAPELAN *another word for* ▸ **capelin**
CAPELET *n* small cape
CAPELIN *n* type of small marine food fish occurring in northern and Arctic seas

CAPER n high-spirited prank ⊳ vb skip about

CAPERED ▶ caper

CAPERER ▶ caper

CAPERS pl n pickled flower buds of a Mediterranean shrub used in sauces

CAPES ▶ cape

CAPEX n capital expenditure

CAPEXES ▶ capex

CAPFUL n quantity held by a (usually bottle) cap

CAPFULS ▶ capful

CAPH n letter of the Hebrew alphabet

CAPHS ▶ caph

CAPI ▶ capo

CAPIAS n (formerly) a writ directing a sheriff or other officer to arrest a named person

CAPING ▶ cape

CAPITA ▶ caput

CAPITAL n chief city of a country ⊳ adj involving or punishable by death

CAPITAN another name for ▶ hogfish

CAPITOL n (in America) building housing the state legislature

CAPIZ n bivalve shell of a mollusc found esp in the Philippines, used in jewellery, ornaments, lampshades, etc

CAPIZES ▶ capiz

CAPLE n horse

CAPLES ▶ caple

CAPLESS ▶ cap

CAPLET n medicinal tablet, usually oval in shape, coated in a soluble substance

CAPLETS ▶ caplet

CAPLIN same as ▶ capelin

CAPLINS ▶ caplin

CAPO n device fitted across the strings of a guitar or similar instrument so as to raise the pitch

CAPON n castrated cock fowl fattened for eating

CAPONS ▶ capon

CAPORAL n strong coarse dark tobacco

CAPOS ▶ capo

CAPOT n winning of all the tricks by one player ⊳ vb score a capot (against)

CAPOTE n long cloak or soldier's coat, usually with a hood

CAPOTES ▶ capote

CAPOTS ▶ capot

CAPOUCH same as ▶ capuche

CAPPED ▶ cap

CAPPER ▶ cap

CAPPERS ▶ cap

CAPPING ▶ cap

CAPRATE n any salt of capric acid

CAPRIC adj (of a type of acid) smelling of goats

CAPRICE same as ▶ capriccio

CAPRID n any member of the goat family

CAPRIDS ▶ caprid

CAPRIFY vb induce figs to ripen

CAPRINE adj of or resembling a goat

CAPRIS pl n women's tight-fitting trousers

CAPROCK n layer of rock that overlies a salt dome

CAPROIC adj as in **caproic acid** oily acid found in milk

CAPS ▶ cap

CAPSID n outer protein coat of a mature virus

CAPSIDS ▶ capsid

CAPSIZE vb (of a boat) overturn accidentally

CAPSTAN n rotating cylinder round which a ship's rope is wound

CAPSULE n soluble gelatine case containing a dose of medicine ⊳ adj very concise ⊳ vb to contain within a capsule

CAPTAIN n commander of a ship or civil aircraft ⊳ vb be captain of

CAPTAN n type of fungicide

CAPTANS ▶ captan

CAPTION n title or explanation accompanying an illustration ⊳ vb provide with a caption

CAPTIVE n person kept in confinement ⊳ adj kept in confinement ⊳ vb to take prisoner

CAPTOR n person who captures a person or animal

CAPTORS ▶ captor

CAPTURE vb take by force ⊳ n capturing

CAPUCHE n large hood or cowl, esp that worn by Capuchin friars

CAPUERA same as

> capoeira

CAPUL same as ▶ caple

CAPULS ▶ capul

CAPUT n main or most prominent part of an organ or structure

CAR n motor vehicle designed to carry a small number of people

CARABAO n water buffalo

CARABID n type of usu dark-coloured beetle such as the bombardier and other ground beetles

CARABIN same as ▶ carbine

CARACAL n lynx, which inhabits reddish fur, which inhabits deserts of N Africa and S Asia

CARACK same as ▶ carrack

CARACKS ▶ carack

CARACOL same as

> caracole

CARACT n sign or symbol

CARACTS ▶ caract

CARACUL n black loosely curled fur obtained from the skins of newly born lambs of the karakul sheep

CARAFE n glass bottle for serving water or wine

CARAFES ▶ carafe

CARAMBA n Spanish interjection similar to 'wow!'

CARAMEL n chewy sweet made from sugar and milk ⊳ vb to turn into caramel

CARANNA n gumlike substance

CARAP n crabwood

CARAPAX n carapace

CARAPS ▶ carap

CARAT n unit of weight of precious stones

CARATE n tropical disease

CARATES ▶ carate

CARATS ▶ carat

CARAUNA same as

▶ caranna

CARAVAN n large enclosed vehicle for living in, designed to be towed by a car or horse ⊳ vb travel or have a holiday in a caravan

CARAVEL n two- or three-masted sailing ship, esp one with a broad beam, high-poop deck, and lateen rig that was used by the Spanish and Portuguese in the 15th and 16th centuries

CARAWAY n plant whose

seeds are used as a spice

CARB n carbohydrate

CARBARN n streetcar depot

CARBEEN n Australian eucalyptus tree with drooping branches and grey bark

CARBENE n neutral divalent free radical, such as methylene: CH_2

CARBIDE n compound of carbon with a metal

CARBIES ▶ carby

CARBINE n light automatic rifle

CARBO n carbohydrate

CARBON n nonmetallic element occurring as charcoal, graphite, and diamond, found in all organic matter

CARBONS ▶ carbon

CARBORA n former name for the koala

CARBOS ▶ carbo

CARBOY n large bottle with a protective casing

CARBOYS ▶ carboy

CARBS ▶ carb

CARBY n short for carburettor

CARCAKE n (formerly, in Scotland) a cake traditionally made for Shrove Tuesday

CARCASE ▶ carcass

CARCASS n dead body of an animal ▷ vb to make a carcass of

CARCEL n French unit of light

CARCELS ▶ carcel

CARD n piece of thick stiff paper or cardboard used for identification, reference, or sending greetings or messages ▷ vb comb out fibres of wool or cotton before spinning

CARDAN n as in cardan joint type of universal joint

CARDECU n old French coin (a quarter of a crown)

CARDED ▶ card

CARDER ▶ card

CARDERS ▶ card

CARDI n cardigan

CARDIA n lower oesophageal sphincter

CARDIAC adj of the heart ▷ n person with a heart disorder

CARDIAE ▶ cardia

CARDIAS ▶ cardia

CARDIE short for ▶ cardigan

CARDIES ▶ cardie

CARDING ▶ card

CARDIO adj exercising heart ▷ n cardiovascular exercise

CARDIOS ▶ cardio

CARDIS ▶ cardi

CARDON n variety of cactus

CARDONS ▶ cardon

CARDOON n thistle-like S European plant with spiny leaves, purple flowers, and an edible leafstalk

CARDS ▶ card

CARDUUS n thistle

CARDY same as ▶ cardie

CARE vb be concerned ▷ n careful attention, caution

CARED ▶ care

CAREEN vb tilt over to one side

CAREENS ▶ careen

CAREER n series of jobs in a profession or occupation that a person has through their life ▷ vb rush in an uncontrolled way ▷ adj having chosen to dedicate his or her life to a particular occupation

CAREERS ▶ career

CAREFUL adj cautious in attitude or action

CAREME n period of Lent

CAREMES ▶ careme

CARER n person who looks after someone who is ill or old, often a relative

CARERS ▶ carer

CARES ▶ care

CARESS n gentle affectionate touch or embrace ▷ vb touch gently and affectionately

CARET n symbol indicating a place in written or printed matter where something is to be inserted

CARETS ▶ caret

CAREX n any member of the sedge family

CARFARE n fare that a passenger is charged for a ride on a bus, etc

CARFAX n place where principal roads or streets intersect, esp a place in a town where four roads meet

CARFOX same as ▶ carfax

CARFUL n maximum number of people a car will hold

CARFULS ▶ carful

CARGO n goods carried by a ship, aircraft, etc ▷ vb to load

CARGOED ▶ cargo

CARGOES ▶ cargo

CARGOS ▶ cargo

CARHOP n waiter or waitress at a drive-in restaurant ▷ vb work as a carhop

CARHOPS ▶ carhop

CARIAMA another word for ▶ seriema

CARIBE n piranha

CARIBES ▶ caribe

CARIBOU n large N American reindeer

CARICES ▶ carex

CARIED adj (of teeth) decayed

CARIERE obsolete word for ▶ career

CARIES n tooth decay

CARINA n keel-like part or ridge, as in the breastbone of birds or the fused lower petals of a leguminous flower

CARINAE ▶ carina

CARINAL adj keel-like

CARINAS ▶ carina

CARING adj feeling or showing care and compassion for other people ▷ n practice or profession of providing social or medical care

CARINGS ▶ caring

CARIOCA n Brazilian dance similar to the samba

CARIOLE n small open two-wheeled horse-drawn vehicle

CARIOSE same as ▶ carious

CARIOUS adj (of teeth or bone) affected with caries

CARITAS n divine love; charity

CARJACK vb attack (a car driver) to rob them or to steal the car ▷ vb to steal a car, by force, from a person who is present

CARK vb break down

CARKED ▶ cark

CARKING ▶ cark

CARKS ▶ cark

CARL another word for ▶ churl

CARLE same as ▶ carl

C

CARLES ▸ carle
CARLESS ▸ car
CARLIN ▸ carling
CARLINE same as ▸ **carling**
CARLING n fore-and-aft beam in a vessel, used for supporting the deck, esp around a hatchway or other opening
CARLINS ▸ carling
CARLISH adj churlish
CARLOAD n amount that can be carried by a car
CARLOCK n type of Russian isinglass
CARLOT n boor
CARLOTS ▸ carlot
CARLS ▸ carl
CARMAN n man who drives a car or cart
CARMEN ▸ carman
CARMINE adj vivid red ▷ n vivid red colour, sometimes with a purplish tinge
CARN n cairn
CARNAGE n extensive slaughter of people
CARNAL adj of a sexual or sensual nature ▷ vb act in a carnal manner
CARNALS ▸ carnal
CARNET n customs licence permitting motorists to take their cars across certain frontiers
CARNETS ▸ carnet
CARNEY same as ▸ **carny**
CARNEYS ▸ carney
CARNIE same as ▸ **carny**
CARNIED ▸ carny
CARNIER ▸ carny
CARNIES ▸ carny
CARNIFY vb (esp of lung tissue, as the result of pneumonia) to be altered so as to resemble skeletal muscle
CARNOSE adj fleshy
CARNS ▸ carn
CARNY vb coax or cajole or act in a wheedling manner ▷ n person who works in a carnival ▷ adj sly
CARNYX n bronze Celtic war trumpet
CAROACH same as ▸ **caroche**
CAROB n pod of a Mediterranean tree, used as a chocolate substitute
CAROBS ▸ carob
CAROCH same as ▸ **caroche**
CAROCHE n stately

ceremonial carriage used in the 16th and 17th centuries
CAROL n joyful Christmas hymn ▷ vb sing carols
CAROLED ▸ carol
CAROLER ▸ carol
CAROLI ▸ carolus
CAROLS ▸ carol
CAROLUS n any of several coins struck in the reign of a king called Charles, esp an English gold coin from the reign of Charles I
CAROM n shot in which the cue ball is caused to contact one object ball after another ▷ vb to carambole
CAROMED ▸ carom
CAROMEL vb to turn into caramel
CAROMS ▸ carom
CARON n inverted circumflex
CARONS ▸ caron
CAROTID n either of the two arteries supplying blood to the head ▷ adj of either of these arteries
CAROTIN same as > **carotene**
CAROUSE vb have a merry drinking party
CARP n large freshwater fish ▷ vb complain, find fault
CARPAL n wrist bone
CARPALE same as ▸ **carpal**
CARPALS ▸ carpal
CARPED ▸ carp
CARPEL n female reproductive organ of a flowering plant
CARPELS ▸ carpel
CARPER ▸ carp
CARPERS ▸ carp
CARPET n heavy fabric for covering floors ▷ vb cover with a carpet
CARPETS ▸ carpet
CARPI ▸ carpus
CARPING adj tending to make petty complaints ▷ n petty complaint
CARPOOL vb (of a group of people) to share the use of a single car to travel to work or school
CARPORT n shelter for a car, consisting of a roof supported by posts
CARPS ▸ carp
CARPUS n set of eight bones of the wrist

CARR n area of bog or fen in which scrub, esp willow, has become established
CARRACK n galleon sailed in the Mediterranean as a merchantman in the 15th and 16th centuries
CARRACT same as ▸ **carrack**
CARRAT same as ▸ **carat**
CARRATS ▸ carrat
CARRECT same as ▸ **carrack**
CARREL n small individual study room or private desk, often in a library, where a student or researcher can work undisturbed
CARRELL same as ▸ **carrel**
CARRELS ▸ carrel
CARRICK n as in **carrick bend** type of knot
CARRIED ▸ carry
CARRIER n person or thing that carries something
CARRIES ▸ carry
CARRION n dead and rotting flesh
CARROCH same as ▸ **caroche**
CARROM ▸ carom
CARROMS ▸ carom
CARRON n as in **carron oil** ointment of limewater and linseed oil
CARROT n long tapering orange root vegetable
CARROTS ▸ carrot
CARROTY adj (of hair) reddish-orange
CARRS ▸ carr
CARRY vb take from one place to another
CARRYON n fuss or commotion
CARS ▸ car
CARSE n riverside area of flat fertile alluvium
CARSES ▸ carse
CARSEY slang word for ▸ **toilet**
CARSEYS ▸ carsey
CARSICK adj nauseated from riding in a car
CART n open two-wheeled horse-drawn vehicle for carrying goods or passengers ▷ vb carry, usu with some effort
CARTA n charter
CARTAGE n process or cost of carting
CARTAS ▸ carta
CARTE n fencing position
CARTED ▸ cart
CARTEL n association of

competing firms formed to fix prices

CARTELS ▸ cartel

CARTER ▸ cart

CARTERS ▸ cart

CARTES ▸ carte

CARTFUL n amount a cart can hold

CARTING ▸ cart

CARTON n container made of cardboard or waxed paper ▷ vb enclose (goods) in a carton

CARTONS ▸ carton

CARTOON n humorous or satirical drawing ▷ vb to depict in a cartoon

CARTOP adj designed to be transported on top of a vehicle

CARTS ▸ cart

CARTWAY n way by which carts travel

CARVE vb cut to form an object

CARVED ▸ carve

CARVEL same as ▸ caravel

CARVELS ▸ carvel

CARVEN an archaic or literary past participle of ▸ carve

CARVER n carving knife

CARVERS ▸ carver

CARVERY n restaurant where customers pay a set price for unrestricted helpings of carved meat and other food

CARVES ▸ carve

CARVIES ▸ carvy

CARVING n figure or design produced by carving stone or wood

CARVY n caraway seed

CARWASH n drive-through structure containing automated equipment for washing cars

CASA n house

CASABA n kind of winter muskmelon having a yellow rind and sweet juicy flesh

CASABAS ▸ casaba

CASAS ▸ casa

CASAVA same as ▸ cassava

CASAVAS ▸ casava

CASBAH n citadel of a N African city

CASBAHS ▸ casbah

CASCADE n waterfall ▷ vb flow or fall in a cascade

CASCARA n bark of a N American shrub, used as a laxative

CASCO n Argentinian homestead

CASCOS ▸ casco

CASE n instance, example ▷ vb inspect (a building) with the intention of burgling it

CASEASE n proteolytic enzyme formed by certain bacteria that activates the solution of albumin and casein in milk and cheese

CASEATE vb undergo caseation

CASED ▸ case

CASEFY vb make or become similar to cheese

CASEIC adj relating to cheese

CASEIN n a phosphoprotein, precipitated from milk by the action of rennin, forming the basis of cheese: used in the manufacture of plastics and adhesives

CASEINS ▸ casein

CASEMAN n in printing, a person who sets and corrects type

CASEMEN ▸ caseman

CASEMIX n mix or type of patients treated by a hospital or medical unit

CASEOSE n peptide produced by the peptic digestion of casein

CASEOUS adj of or like cheese

CASERN n (formerly) a billet or accommodation for soldiers in a town

CASERNE same as ▸ casern

CASERNS ▸ casern

CASES ▸ case

CASETTE same as > **cassette**

CASEVAC vb evacuate (a casualty) from a combat zone, usu by air

CASH n banknotes and coins ▷ adj of, for, or paid in cash ▷ vb obtain cash for

CASHAW n winter squash

CASHAWS ▸ cashaw

CASHBOX n box for holding cash

CASHED ▸ cash

CASHES ▸ cash

CASHEW n edible kidney-shaped nut

CASHEWS ▸ cashew

CASHIER n person responsible for handling cash in a bank, shop, etc

▷ vb dismiss with dishonour from the armed forces

CASHING ▸ cash

CASHOO n catechu

CASHOOS ▸ cashoo

CASING n protective case, covering

CASINGS ▸ casing

CASINI ▸ casino

CASINO n public building or room where gambling games are played

CASINOS ▸ casino

CASITA n small house

CASITAS ▸ casita

CASK n barrel used to hold alcoholic drink ▷ vb to put into a cask

CASKED ▸ cask

CASKET n small box for valuables ▷ vb to put into a casket

CASKETS ▸ casket

CASKIER ▸ casky

CASKING ▸ cask

CASKS ▸ cask

CASKY adj (of wine) having a musty smell due to resting too long in the cask

CASPASE n type of enzyme

CASQUE n helmet or a helmet-like process or structure, as on the bill of most hornbills

CASQUED ▸ casque

CASQUES ▸ casque

CASSABA same as ▸ casaba

CASSATA n ice cream, originating in Italy, usually containing nuts and candied fruit

CASSAVA n starch obtained from the roots of a tropical American plant, used to make tapioca

CASSENA same as ▸ cassina

CASSENE same as ▸ cassina

CASSIA n tropical plant whose pods yield a mild laxative

CASSIAS ▸ cassia

CASSINA n American tree

CASSINE same as ▸ cassina

CASSINO n card game for two to four players in which players pair cards from their hands with others exposed on the table

CASSIS n blackcurrant cordial

CASSOCK n long tunic, usu black, worn by priests

CASSONE n highly-decorated Italian dowry chest

CASSPIR n armoured military vehicle

CAST n actors in a play or film collectively ▷ vb select (an actor) to play a part in a play or film

CASTE n any of the hereditary classes into which Hindu society is divided

CASTED adj having a caste

CASTER n person or thing that casts

CASTERS ▸ caster

CASTES ▸ caste

CASTING ▸ cast

CASTLE n large fortified building, often built as a ruler's residence ▷ vb (in chess) move (the king) two squares laterally on the first rank and place the nearest rook on the square passed over by the king

CASTLED adj like a castle in construction

CASTLES ▸ castle

CASTOCK n kale stalk

CASTOFF n person or thing that has been discarded or abandoned

CASTOR same as ▸ caster

CASTORS ▸ castor

CASTORY n dye derived from beaver pelts

CASTRAL adj relating to camps

CASTS ▸ cast

CASUAL adj careless, nonchalant ▷ n occasional worker

CASUALS ▸ casual

CASUIST n person, esp a theologian, who attempts to resolve moral dilemmas by the application of general rules and the careful distinction of special cases

CASUS n event

CAT n small domesticated furry mammal ▷ vb flog with a cat-'o-nine-tails

CATALO same as ▸ cattalo

CATALOG same as ▸ catalogue

CATALOS ▸ catalo

CATALPA n tree of N America and Asia with bell-shaped whitish flowers

CATAPAN n governor in the Byzantine Empire

CATARRH n excessive mucus in the nose and throat, during or following a cold

CATASTA n platform on which slaves were presented for sale

CATAWBA n type of red North American grape

CATBIRD n North American songbird whose call resembles the mewing of a cat

CATBOAT n sailing vessel with a single mast, set well forward and often unstayed, and a large sail, usually rigged with a gaff

CATCALL n derisive whistle or cry ▷ vb utter such a call (at)

CATCH vb seize, capture ▷ n device for fastening a door, window, etc

CATCHED rarely used past tense of ▸ catch

CATCHEN same as ▸ catch

CATCHER n person or thing that catches, esp in a game or sport

CATCHES ▸ catch

CATCHT same as ▸ catched

CATCHUP a variant spelling (esp US) of ▸ ketchup

CATCHY adj (of a tune) pleasant and easily remembered

CATCLAW n type of shrub; black bear

CATCON n catalytic converter

CATCONS ▸ catcon

CATE n delicacy

CATECHU n astringent resinous substance obtained from certain tropical plants, used in medicine, tanning, and ·dyeing

CATELOG obsolete word for > catalogue

CATENA n connected series, esp of patristic comments on the Bible

CATENAE ▸ catena

CATENAS ▸ catena

CATER vb provide what is needed or wanted, esp food or services

CATERAN n (formerly) a member of a band of

brigands and marauders in the Scottish highlands

CATERED ▸ cater

CATERER n person whose job is to provide food for social events such as parties and weddings

CATERS ▸ cater

CATES pl n choice dainty food

CATFACE n deformity of the surface of a tree trunk, caused by fire or disease

CATFALL n line used as a tackle for hoisting an anchor to the cathead

CATFISH n fish with whisker-like barbels round the mouth

CATFLAP n small flap in a door to let a cat go through

CATGUT n strong cord used to string musical instruments and sports rackets

CATGUTS ▸ catgut

CATHEAD n fitting at the bow of a vessel for securing the anchor when raised

CATHECT vb to invest mental or emotional energy in

CATHODE n negative electrode, by which electrons leave a circuit

CATHOLE n hole in a ship through which ropes are passed

CATHOOD n state of being a cat

CATION n positively charged ion

CATIONS ▸ cation

CATJANG n tropical shrub

CATKIN n drooping flower spike of certain trees

CATKINS ▸ catkin

CATLIKE ▸ cat

CATLIN same as ▸ catling

CATLING n long double-edged surgical knife for amputations

CATLINS ▸ catlin

CATMINT n Eurasian plant with scented leaves that attract cats

CATNAP vb doze ▷ n short sleep or doze

CATNAPS ▸ catnap

CATNEP same as ▸ catmint

CATNEPS ▸ catnep

CATNIP same as ▸ catmint

CATNIPS ▸ catmint

CATS ▸ cat

CATSKIN n skin and/or fur of a cat

CATSPAW n person used by another as a tool

CATSUIT n one-piece usually close-fitting trouser suit

CATSUP a variant (esp US) of ▸ **ketchup**

CATSUPS ▸ catsup

CATTABU n cross between common cattle and zebu

CATTAIL n reed mace

CATTALO n hardy breed of cattle developed by crossing the American bison with domestic cattle

CATTED ▸ cat

CATTERY n place where cats are bred or looked after

CATTIE same as ▸ **catty**

CATTIER ▸ catty

CATTIES ▸ catty

CATTILY ▸ catty

CATTING ▸ cat

CATTISH ▸ cat

CATTLE pl n domesticated cows and bulls

CATTY adj spiteful ▷ n unit of weight, used esp in China, equal to about one and a half pounds or about 0.67 kilogram

CATWALK n narrow pathway or platform

CATWORM n type of carnivorous worm about 10cm (4in) long, often dug for bait

CAUCUS n local committee or faction of a political party ▷ vb hold a caucus

CAUDA n area behind the anus of an animal

CAUDAD adv towards the tail or posterior part

CAUDAE ▸ cauda

CAUDAL adj at or near an animal's tail

CAUDATE adj having a tail or a tail-like appendage ▷ n lizard-like amphibian

CAUDEX n thickened persistent stem base of some herbaceous perennial plants

CAUDLE n hot spiced wine drink made with gruel, formerly used medicinally ▷ vb make such a drink

CAUDLED ▸ caudle

CAUDLES ▸ caudle

CAUDRON Spenserian spelling of ▸ **cauldron**

CAUF n cage for holding live fish in the water

CAUGHT ▸ catch

CAUK n type of barite

CAUKER n one who caulks

CAUKERS ▸ cauker

CAUKS ▸ cauk

CAUL n membrane sometimes covering a child's head at birth

CAULD a Scots word for ▸ **cold**

CAULDER ▸ cauld

CAULDS ▸ cauld

CAULES ▸ caulis

CAULINE adj relating to or growing from a plant stem

CAULIS n main stem of a plant

CAULK vb fill in (cracks) with paste etc

CAULKED ▸ caulk

CAULKER ▸ caulk

CAULKS ▸ caulk

CAULOME n plant's stem structure, considered as a whole

CAULS ▸ caul

CAUM same as ▸ **cam**

CAUMED ▸ caum

CAUMING ▸ caum

CAUMS ▸ caum

CAUP n type of quaich

CAUPS ▸ caup

CAUSA n reason or cause

CAUSAE ▸ causa

CAUSAL adj of or being a cause ▷ n something that suggests a cause

CAUSALS ▸ causal

CAUSE n something that produces a particular effect ▷ vb be the cause of

CAUSED ▸ cause

CAUSEN old infinitive of ▸ **cause**

CAUSER ▸ cause

CAUSERS ▸ cause

CAUSES ▸ cause

CAUSEY n cobbled street ▷ vb cobble

CAUSEYS ▸ causey

CAUSING ▸ cause

CAUSTIC adj capable of burning by chemical action ▷ n caustic substance

CAUTEL n craftiness

CAUTELS ▸ cautel

CAUTER n cauterising instrument

CAUTERS ▸ cauter

CAUTERY n coagulation of blood or destruction of body tissue by cauterizing

CAUTION n care, esp in the face of danger ▷ vb warn, advise

CAUVES ▸ cauf

CAVA n Spanish sparkling wine produced by a method similar to that used for champagne

CAVALLA n type of tropical fish

CAVALLY same as ▸ **cavalla**

CAVALRY n part of the army orig. on horseback, but now often using fast armoured vehicles

CAVAS ▸ cava

CAVASS n Turkish armed police officer

CAVE n hollow in the side of a hill or cliff ▷ vb hollow out

CAVEAT n warning ▷ vb to introduce a caveat

CAVEATS ▸ caveat

CAVED ▸ cave

CAVEL n drawing of lots among miners for an easy and profitable place at the coalface

CAVELS ▸ cavel

CAVEMAN n prehistoric cave dweller

CAVEMEN ▸ caveman

CAVER ▸ caving

CAVERN n large cave ▷ vb shut in or as if in a cavern

CAVERNS ▸ cavern

CAVERS ▸ caving

CAVES ▸ cave

CAVETTI ▸ cavetto

CAVETTO n concave moulding, shaped to a quarter circle in cross section

CAVIAR n salted sturgeon roe, regarded as a delicacy

CAVIARE same as ▸ **caviar**

CAVIARS ▸ caviar

CAVIE n hen coop

CAVIER same as ▸ **caviar**

CAVIERS ▸ cavier

CAVIES ▸ cavy

CAVIL vb make petty objections ▷ n petty objection

CAVILED ▸ cavil

CAVILER ▸ cavil

CAVILS ▸ cavil

CAVING n sport of exploring caves

CAVINGS ▸ caving

C

CAVITY n hollow space

CAVORT vb skip about

CAVORTS ▸ cavort

CAVY n type of small S American rodent with a thickset body and a very small tail

CAW n cry of a crow, rook, or raven ▷ vb make this cry

CAWED ▸ caw

CAWING ▸ caw

CAWINGS ▸ caw

CAWK same as ▸ cauk

CAWKER n metal projection on a horse's shoe to prevent slipping

CAWKERS ▸ cawker

CAWKS ▸ cawk

CAWS ▸ caw

CAXON n type of wig

CAXONS ▸ caxon

CAY n low island or bank composed of sand and coral fragments

CAYENNE n very hot condiment, bright red in colour, made from dried capsicums

CAYMAN n S American reptile similar to an alligator

CAYMANS ▸ cayman

CAYS ▸ cay

CAYUSE n small American Indian pony used by cowboys

CAYUSES ▸ cayuse

CAZ short for ▸ casual

> Caz is slang for casual, and is one of the essential short words for using the Z.

CAZIQUE same as ▸ cacique

> This word means an American Indian chief, and its plural **caziques** was once played as a 9-timer (that is, a word spanning two triple-word squares) earning the highest score for a single word ever officially recorded in a game of Scrabble, 392 points.

CEAS same as ▸ caese

CEASE vb bring or come to an end

CEASED ▸ cease

CEASES ▸ cease

CEASING ▸ cease

CEAZE obsolete spelling of ▸ seize

CEAZED ▸ ceaze

CEAZES ▸ ceaze

CEAZING ▸ ceaze

CEBID n any member of the Cebidae family of New World monkeys

CEBIDS ▸ cebid

CEBOID same as ▸ cebid

CEBOIDS ▸ ceboid

CECA ▸ cecum

CECAL ▸ cecum

CECALLY ▸ cecum

CECILS pl n fried meatballs

CECITIS n inflammation of the c(a)ecum

CECITY n rare word for blindness

CECUM same as ▸ caecum

CEDAR n evergreen coniferous tree ▷ adj made of the wood of a cedar tree

CEDARED adj covered with cedars

CEDARN adj relating to cedar

CEDARS ▸ cedar

CEDARY adj like cedar

CEDE vb surrender (territory or legal rights)

CEDED ▸ cede

CEDER ▸ cede

CEDERS ▸ cede

CEDES ▸ cede

CEDI n standard monetary unit of Ghana, divided into 100 pesewas

CEDILLA n character placed under a c in some languages, to show that it is pronounced s, not k

CEDING ▸ cede

CEDIS ▸ cedi

CEDRATE n citron

CEDRINE adj relating to cedar

CEDULA n form of identification in Spanish-speaking countries

CEDULAS ▸ cedula

CEE n third letter of the alphabet

CEES ▸ cee

CEIBA n type of tropical tree

CEIBAS ▸ ceiba

CEIL vb line (a ceiling) with plaster, boarding, etc

CEILED ▸ ceil

CEILER ▸ ceil

CEILERS ▸ ceil

CEILI variant spelling of ▸ ceilidh

CEILIDH n informal social gathering for singing and dancing, esp in Scotland

CEILING n inner upper surface of a room ▷ vb make a ceiling

CEILIS ▸ ceili

CEILS ▸ ceil

CEL short for ▸ celluloid

CELADON n type of porcelain having a greyish-green glaze: mainly Chinese

CELEB n celebrity

CELEBS ▸ celeb

CELERY n vegetable with long green crisp edible stalks

CELESTA n instrument like a small piano in which key-operated hammers strike metal plates

CELESTE same as ▸ celesta

CELIAC same as ▸ coeliac

CELIACS ▸ celiac

CELL n smallest unit of an organism that is able to function independently

CELLA n inner room of a classical temple, esp the room housing the statue of a deity

CELLAE ▸ cella

CELLAR n underground room for storage ▷ vb store in a cellar

CELLARS ▸ cellar

CELLED adj cellular

CELLI ▸ cello

CELLING n formation of cells

CELLIST ▸ cello

CELLO n large low-pitched instrument of the violin family

CELLOS ▸ cello

CELLOSE n a disaccharide obtained by the hydrolysis of cellulose by cellulase

CELLS ▸ cell

CELLULE n very small cell

CELOM same as ▸ coelom

CELOMIC ▸ celom

CELOMS ▸ celom

CELOSIA same as ▸ cockscomb

CELOTEX n tradename for a type of insulation board

CELS ▸ cel

CELT n stone or metal axelike instrument with a bevelled edge

CELTS ▸ celt

CEMBALI ▸ cembalo

CEMBALO n harpsichord

CEMBRA *n* Swiss pine
CEMBRAS ▸ **cembra**
CEMENT *n* fine grey powder mixed with water and sand to make mortar or concrete ▷ *vb* join, bind, or cover with cement
CEMENTA > **cementum**
CEMENTS ▸ **cement**
CENACLE *n* supper room, esp one on an upper floor
CENDRE *adj* ash-blond
CENOTE *n* (esp in the Yucatán peninsula) a natural well formed by the collapse of an overlying limestone crust: often used as a sacrificial site by the Mayas
CENOTES ▸ **cenote**
CENS *n* type of annual property rent
CENSE *vb* burn incense near or before (an altar, shrine, etc)
CENSED ▸ **cense**
CENSER *n* container for burning incense
CENSERS ▸ **censer**
CENSES ▸ **cense**
CENSING ▸ **cense**
CENSOR *n* person authorized to examine films, books, etc, to ban or cut anything considered obscene or objectionable ▷ *vb* ban or cut parts of (a film, book, etc)
CENSORS ▸ **censor**
CENSUAL ▸ **census**
CENSURE *n* severe disapproval ▷ *vb* criticize severely
CENSUS *n* official count of a population ▷ *vb* to conduct a census
CENT *n* hundredth part of a monetary unit such as the dollar or euro
CENTAGE *n* rate per hundred
CENTAI ▸ **centas**
CENTAL *n* unit of weight equal to 100 pounds (45.3 kilograms)
CENTALS ▸ **cental**
CENTARE *same as* > **centiare**
CENTAS *n* monetary unit of Lithuania, worth one hundredth of a litas
CENTAUR *n* mythical creature with the head, arms, and torso of a man, and the lower body and legs of a horse
CENTAVO *n* monetary unit worth one hundredth of the main unit of currency in Portugal and many Latin American countries
CENTER *same as* ▸ **centre**
CENTERS ▸ **center**
CENTILE *n* one of 99 actual or notional values of a variable dividing its distribution into 100 groups with equal frequencies
CENTIME *n* monetary unit worth one hundredth of a franc
CENTIMO *n* monetary unit of Costa Rica, Paraguay, Peru, and Venezuela. It is worth one hundredth of their respective standard currency units
CENTNER *n* unit of weight equivalent to 100 pounds (45.3 kilograms)
CENTO *n* piece of writing, esp a poem, composed of quotations from other authors
CENTOS ▸ **cento**
CENTRA ▸ **centrum**
CENTRAL *adj* of, at, or forming the centre ▷ *n* workplace serving as a telecommunications facility
CENTRE *n* middle point or part ▷ *vb* put in the centre of something
CENTRED *adj* mentally and emotionally confident, focused, and well-balanced
CENTRES ▸ **centre**
CENTRIC *adj* being central or having a centre
CENTRUM *n* main part or body of a vertebra
CENTRY *obsolete variant of* ▸ **sentry**
CENTS ▸ **cent**
CENTU *n* Lithuanian money unit
CENTUM *adj* denoting or belonging to the Indo-European languages in which original velar stops (k) were not palatalized ▷ *n* hundred
CENTUMS ▸ **centum**
CENTURY *n* period of 100 years

CEORL *n* freeman of the lowest class in Anglo-Saxon England
CEORLS ▸ **ceorl**
CEP *another name for* ▸ **porcino**
CEPAGE *n* grape variety or type of wine
CEPAGES ▸ **cepage**
CEPE *another spelling of* ▸ **cep**
CEPES ▸ **cepe**
CEPHEID *n* type of variable star with a regular cycle of variations in luminosity
CEPS ▸ **cep**
CERAMAL *same as* ▸ **cermet**
CERAMIC *n* hard brittle material made by heating clay to a very high temperature ▷ *adj* made of ceramic
CERASIN *n* meta-arabinic acid
CERATE *n* hard ointment or medicated paste consisting of lard or oil mixed with wax or resin
CERATED *adj* (of certain birds, such as the falcon) having a cere
CERATES ▸ **cerate**
CERATIN *same as* ▸ **keratin**
CERCAL *adj* of or relating to a tail
CERCI ▸ **cercus**
CERCIS *n* type of tree or shrub of the genus which includes the redbud and Judas tree
CERCUS *n* one of a pair of sensory appendages at the tip of the abdomen of some insects and other arthropods
CERE *n* soft waxy swelling, containing the nostrils, at the base of the upper beak of a parrot ▷ *vb* wrap (a corpse) in a cerecloth
CEREAL *n* grass plant with edible grain, such as oat or wheat
CEREALS ▸ **cereal**
CEREBRA > **cerebrum**
CERED ▸ **cere**
CEREOUS *adj* waxlike
CERES ▸ **cere**
CERESIN *n* white wax extracted from ozocerite
CEREUS *n* type of tropical American cactus
CERGE *n* large altar candle
CERGES ▸ **cerge**

CERIA n ceric oxide

CERIAS ▸ ceria

CERIC adj of or containing cerium in the tetravalent state

CERING ▸ cere

CERIPH same as ▸ serif

CERIPHS ▸ ceriph

CERISE adj cherry-red ▷ n moderate to dark red colour

CERISES ▸ cerise

CERITE n hydrous silicate of cerium

CERITES ▸ cerite

CERIUM n steel-grey metallic element

CERIUMS ▸ cerium

CERMET n any of several materials consisting of a metal matrix with ceramic particles disseminated through it. They are hard and resistant to high temperatures

CERMETS ▸ cermet

CERNE obsolete variant of > encircle

CERNED ▸ cerne

CERNES ▸ cerne

CERNING ▸ cerne

CERO n type of large spiny-finned food fish of warm American coastal regions of the Atlantic

CEROON n hide-covered bale

CEROONS ▸ ceroon

CEROS ▸ cero

CEROTIC adj as in **cerotic acid** white insoluble odourless wax

CEROUS adj of or containing cerium in the trivalent state

CERRADO n vast area of tropical savanna in Brazil

CERRIAL adj relating to the cerris

CERRIS n Turkey oak

CERT n certainty

CERTAIN adj positive and confident

CERTES adv with certainty

CERTIE n as in **by my certie** assuredly

CERTIFY vb confirm, attest to

CERTS ▸ cert

CERTY n as in **by my certy** assuredly

CERULE adj sky-blue

CERUMEN n soft

brownish-yellow wax secreted by glands in the auditory canal of the external ear

CERUSE n white lead

CERUSES ▸ ceruse

CERVEZA n Spanish word for beer

CERVID n type of ruminant mammal such as the deer, characterized by the presence of antlers

CERVIDS ▸ cervid

CERVINE adj resembling or relating to a deer

CERVIX n narrow entrance of the womb

CESIOUS same as > caesious

CESIUM same as ▸ caesium

CESIUMS ▸ cesium

CESS n any of several special taxes, such as a land tax in Scotland ▷ vb tax or assess for taxation

CESSE obsolete variant of ▸ cease

CESSED ▸ cess

CESSER n coming to an end of a term interest or annuity

CESSERS ▸ cesser

CESSES ▸ cess

CESSING ▸ cess

CESSION n ceding

CESSPIT same as > cesspool

CESTA n in jai alai, the basket used to throw and catch the pelota

CESTAS ▸ cesta

CESTI ▸ cestus

CESTODE n type of parasitic flatworm such as the tapeworms

CESTOI ▸ cestos

CESTOID adj (esp of tapeworms and similar animals) ribbon-like in form ▷ n ribbon-like worm

CESTOS same as ▸ cestus

CESTUI n "the one (who)", legal term, used in certain phrases, to designate a person

CESTUIS ▸ cestui

CESTUS n girdle of Aphrodite (Venus) decorated to cause amorousness

CESURA a variant spelling of ▸ caesura

CESURAE ▸ cesura

CESURAL ▸ cesura

CESURAS ▸ cesura

CESURE same as ▸ caesura

CESURES ▸ cesure

CETANE n colourless liquid hydrocarbon, used as a solvent

CETANES ▸ cetane

CETE n group of badgers

CETES ▸ cete

CETYL n univalent alcohol radical

CETYLS ▸ cetyl

CEVICHE n Peruvian seafood dish

CEZVE n small metal pot for brewing coffee

CEZVES ▸ cezve

CH pron obsolete from of I

CHA n tea

CHABLIS n dry white French wine

CHABOUK n type of whip

CHABUK same as ▸ chabouk

CHABUKS ▸ chabuk

CHACE obsolete variant of ▸ chase

CHACED ▸ chace

CHACES ▸ chace

CHACHKA n cheap trinket

CHACING ▸ chace

CHACK vb to bite

CHACKED ▸ chack

CHACKS ▸ chack

CHACMA n type of baboon with coarse greyish hair, occurring in S and E Africa

CHACMAS ▸ chacma

CHACO same as ▸ shako

CHACOES ▸ chaco

CHACOS ▸ chaco

CHAD n small pieces removed during the punching of holes in punch cards, printer paper, etc

CHADAR same as ▸ chuddar

CHADARS ▸ chadar

CHADDAR same as ▸ chuddar

CHADDOR same as ▸ chuddar

CHADO n Japanese tea ceremony

CHADOR same as ▸ chuddar

CHADORS ▸ chador

CHADOS ▸ chado

CHADRI n shroud which covers the body from head to foot, usually worn by females in Islamic countries

CHADS ▸ chad

CHAEBOL n large, usually family-owned, business group in South Korea

CHAETA n any of the

C

chitinous bristles on the body of such annelids as the earthworm and the lugworm: used in locomotion
CHAETAE ▸ chaeta
CHAETAL ▸ chaeta
CHAFE vb make sore or worn by rubbing
CHAFED ▸ chafe
CHAFER n large beetle
CHAFERS ▸ chafer
CHAFES ▸ chafe
CHAFF n grain husks ▷ vb tease good-naturedly
CHAFFED ▸ chaff
CHAFFER vb haggle
CHAFFS ▸ chaff
CHAFFY ▸ chaff
CHAFING ▸ chafe
CHAFT n jaw
CHAFTS ▸ chaft
CHAGAN n Mongolian royal or imperial title
CHAGANS ▸ chagan
CHAGRIN n annoyance and disappointment ▷ vb embarrass and annoy
CHAI n tea, esp as made in India with added spices
CHAIN n flexible length of connected metal links ▷ vb restrict or fasten with or as if with a chain
CHAINE adj (of a dance turn) producing a full rotation for every two steps taken ▷ vb produce a full rotation for every two steps taken
CHAINED ▸ chain
CHAINES ▸ chaine
CHAINS ▸ chain
CHAIR n seat with a back, for one person ▷ vb preside over (a meeting)
CHAIRED ▸ chair
CHAIRS ▸ chair
CHAIS ▸ chai
CHAISE n light horse-drawn carriage
CHAISES ▸ chaise
CHAKRA n (in yoga) any of the seven major energy centres in the body
CHAKRAS ▸ chakra
CHAL n in Romany, person or fellow
CHALAH same as ▸ challah
CHALAHS ▸ chalah
CHALAN vb (in India) to cause an accused person to appear before a magistrate
CHALANS ▸ chalan

CHALAZA n one of a pair of spiral threads of albumen holding the yolk of a bird's egg in position
CHALCID n type of tiny hymenopterous insect whose larvae are parasites of other insects
CHALDER n former Scottish dry measure
CHALEH same as ▸ challah
CHALEHS ▸ chaleh
CHALET n kind of Swiss wooden house with a steeply sloping roof
CHALETS ▸ chalet
CHALICE n large goblet
CHALK n soft white rock consisting of calcium carbonate ▷ vb draw or mark with chalk
CHALKED ▸ chalk
CHALKS ▸ chalk
CHALKY ▸ chalk
CHALLA same as ▸ challah
CHALLAH n bread, usually in the form of a plaited loaf, traditionally eaten by Jews to celebrate the Sabbath
CHALLAN same as ▸ chalan
CHALLAS ▸ challa
CHALLIE same as ▸ challis
CHALLIS n lightweight plain-weave fabric of wool, cotton, etc, usually with a printed design
CHALLOT ▸ challah
CHALLY same as ▸ challis
CHALONE n any internal secretion that inhibits a physiological process or function
CHALOT ▸ chalah
CHALOTH ▸ chalah
CHALS ▸ chal
CHALUPA n Mexican dish
CHALUTZ n member of an organization of immigrants to Israeli agricultural settlements
CHAM an archaic word for ▸ khan
CHAMADE n (formerly) a signal by drum or trumpet inviting an enemy to a parley
CHAMBER n hall used for formal meetings ▷ vb act lasciviously
CHAMBRE adj (of wine) at room temperature
CHAMETZ n leavened food which may not be eaten

during Passover
CHAMFER same as ▸ chase
CHAMISA n American shrub
CHAMISE same as ▸ chamiso
CHAMISO n fourwing saltbush
CHAMLET same as ▸ camlet
CHAMMY same as ▸ chamois
CHAMOIS n small mountain antelope or a pice of leather from its skin, used for polishing ▷ vb polish with a chamois
CHAMOIX same as ▸ chamois
CHAMP vb chew noisily
CHAMPAC n type of tree of India and the E Indies, whose yellow flowers yield an oil used in perfumes
CHAMPAK same as ▸ champac
CHAMPED ▸ champ
CHAMPER ▸ champ
CHAMPS ▸ champ
CHAMPY adj (of earth) churned up (by cattle, for example)
CHAMS ▸ cham
CHANA n (in Indian cookery) chickpeas
CHANAS ▸ chana
CHANCE n likelihood, probability ▷ vb risk, hazard
CHANCED ▸ chance
CHANCEL n part of a church containing the altar and choir
CHANCER n unscrupulous or dishonest opportunist who is prepared to try any dubious scheme for making money or furthering his own ends
CHANCES ▸ chance
CHANCEY same as ▸ chancy
CHANCRE n small hard growth which is the first sign of syphilis
CHANCY adj uncertain, risky
CHANG n loud discordant noise
CHANGA interj in Indian English, an expression of approval or agreement
CHANGE n becoming different ▷ vb make or become different
CHANGED ▸ change
CHANGER ▸ change

CHANGES ▸ change

CHANGS ▸ chang

CHANK n shell of several types of sea conch, used to make bracelets

CHANKS ▸ chank

CHANNEL n band of broadcasting frequencies ▷ vb direct or convey through a channel

CHANNER n gravel

CHANOYO same as ▸ chado

CHANOYU same as ▸ chado

CHANSON n song

CHANT vb utter or sing (a slogan or psalm) ▷ n rhythmic or repetitious slogan

CHANTED ▸ chant

CHANTER n (on bagpipes) pipe on which the melody is played

CHANTEY the usual US spelling of ▸ shanty

CHANTIE n chamber pot

CHANTOR same as ▸ chanter

CHANTRY n endowment for the singing of Masses for the soul of the founder or others designated by him

CHANTS ▸ chant

CHANTY same as ▸ shanty

CHAO n Vietnamese rice porridge

CHAOS n complete disorder or confusion

CHAOSES ▸ chaos

CHAOTIC ▸ chaos

CHAP n man or boy ▷ vb (of the skin) to make or become raw and cracked, esp by exposure to cold

CHAPATI n (in Indian cookery) flat thin unleavened bread

CHAPE n metal tip or trimming for a scabbard

CHAPEAU n hat

CHAPEL n place of worship with its own altar, within a church

CHAPELS ▸ chapel

CHAPES ▸ chape

CHAPESS n woman

CHAPKA same as ▸ czapka

CHAPKAS ▸ chapka

CHAPLET n garland for the head ▷ vb create a garland

CHAPMAN n travelling pedlar

CHAPMEN ▸ chapman

CHAPPAL n one of a pair of sandals, usually of leather, worn in India

CHAPPED ▸ chap

CHAPPIE n man or boy

CHAPPY adj (of skin) chapped

CHAPS ▸ chap

CHAPT adj chapped

CHAPTER n division of a book ▷ vb divide into chapters

CHAR vb blacken by partial burning ▷ n charwoman

CHARA n type of green freshwater algae

CHARACT n distinctive mark

CHARADE n absurd pretence

CHARAS another name for ▸ hashish

CHARD n variety of beet with large succulent leaves and thick stalks, used as a vegetable

CHARDS ▸ chard

CHARE same as ▸ char

CHARED ▸ char

CHARES ▸ char

CHARET obsolete variant of ▸ chariot

CHARETS ▸ charet

CHARGE vb ask as a price ▷ n price charged

CHARGED ▸ charge

CHARGER n device for charging an accumulator

CHARGES ▸ charge

CHARIER ▸ chary

CHARILY adv cautiously

CHARING ▸ char

CHARIOT n two-wheeled horse-drawn vehicle used in ancient times in wars and races ▷ vb to ride in a chariot

CHARISM same as > charisma

CHARITY n organization that gives help, such as money or food, to those in need

CHARK vb to char

CHARKA same as ▸ charkha

CHARKAS ▸ charka

CHARKED ▸ chark

CHARKHA n (in India) a spinning wheel, esp for cotton

CHARKS ▸ chark

CHARLEY n as in charley horse muscle stiffness after strenuous exercise

CHARLIE n fool

CHARM n attractive quality ▷ vb attract, delight

CHARMED adj delighted or fascinated

CHARMER n attractive person

CHARMS ▸ charm

CHARNEL adj ghastly ▷ n ghastly thing

CHARPAI same as ▸ charpoy

CHARPIE n lint pieces used to make surgical dressings

CHARPOY n bedstead of woven webbing or hemp stretched on a wooden frame on four legs, common in India

CHARQUI n meat, esp beef, cut into strips and dried

CHARR same as ▸ char

CHARRED ▸ char

CHARRO n Mexican cowboy

CHARROS ▸ charro

CHARRS ▸ charr

CHARRY adj of or relating to charcoal

CHARS ▸ char

CHART n graph, table, or diagram showing information ▷ vb plot the course of

CHARTA n charter

CHARTAS ▸ charta

CHARTED ▸ chart

CHARTER n document granting or demanding certain rights ▷ vb hire by charter

CHARTS ▸ chart

CHARY adj wary, careful

CHAS ▸ cha

CHASE vb run after quickly in order to catch or drive away ▷ n chasing, pursuit

CHASED ▸ chase

CHASER n milder drink drunk after another stronger one

CHASERS ▸ chaser

CHASES ▸ chase

CHASING ▸ chase

CHASM n deep crack in the earth ▷ vb create a chasm

CHASMAL ▸ chasm

CHASMED ▸ chasm

CHASMIC ▸ chasm

CHASMS ▸ chasm

CHASMY adj full of chasms

CHASSE n one of a series of gliding steps in ballet in which the same foot always leads ▷ *vb* perform either of these steps

CHASSED ▸ **chasse**

CHASSES ▸ **chasse**

CHASSIS *n* frame, wheels, and mechanical parts of a vehicle

CHASTE *adj* abstaining from sex outside marriage or altogether

CHASTEN *vb* subdue by criticism

CHASTER ▸ **chaste**

CHAT *n* informal conversation ▷ *vb* have an informal conversation

CHATBOT *n* computer program in the form of a virtual e-mail correspondent that can reply to messages from computer users

CHATEAU *n* French castle

CHATON *n* in jewellery, a stone with a reflective metal foil backing

CHATONS ▸ **chaton**

CHATS ▸ **chat**

CHATTA *n* umbrella

CHATTAS ▸ **chatta**

CHATTED ▸ **chat**

CHATTEL *n* item of movable personal property

CHATTER *vb* speak quickly and continuously about unimportant things ▷ *n* idle talk

CHATTI *n* (in India) an earthenware pot

CHATTIS ▸ **chatti**

CHATTY *adj* (of a person) fond of friendly, informal conversation

CHAUFE *obsolete variant of* ▸ **chafe**

CHAUFED ▸ **chaufe**

CHAUFER *same as* > **chauffer**

CHAUFES ▸ **chaufe**

CHAUFF *obsolete variant of* ▸ **chafe**

CHAUFFS ▸ **chauff**

CHAUMER *n* chamber

CHAUNCE *archaic variant of* ▸ **chance**

CHAUNGE *archaic variant of* ▸ **change**

CHAUNT *a less common variant of* ▸ **chant**

CHAUNTS ▸ **chaunt**

CHAUVIN *n* chauvinist

CHAVE *vb* old dialect term for "I have"

CHAW *vb* chew (tobacco), esp without swallowing it ▷ *n* something chewed, esp a plug of tobacco

CHAWED ▸ **chaw**

CHAWER ▸ **chaw**

CHAWERS ▸ **chaw**

CHAWING ▸ **chaw**

CHAWK *n* jackdaw

CHAWKS ▸ **chawk**

CHAWS ▸ **chaw**

CHAY *n* plant of the madder family

CHAYA *same as* ▸ **chay**

CHAYAS ▸ **chaya**

CHAYOTE *n* tropical American climbing plant with edible pear-shaped fruit enclosing a single huge seed

CHAYS ▸ **chay**

CHAZAN *same as* ▸ **cantor**

CHAZANS ▸ **chazan**

CHAZZAN *same as* ▸ **chazan**

CHAZZEN *same as* ▸ **chazzan**

CHE *pron* dialectal form meaning "I"

CHEAP *adj* costing relatively little ▷ *adv* at very little cost ▷ *n* bargain ▷ *vb* take the cheapest option

CHEAPED ▸ **cheap**

CHEAPEN *vb* lower the reputation of

CHEAPER ▸ **cheap**

CHEAPIE *n* something inexpensive

CHEAPLY ▸ **cheap**

CHEAPO *n* very cheap and possibly shoddy thing

CHEAPOS ▸ **cheapo**

CHEAPS ▸ **cheap**

CHEAPY *same as* ▸ **cheapie**

CHEAT *vb* act dishonestly to gain profit or advantage ▷ *n* person who cheats

CHEATED ▸ **cheat**

CHEATER ▸ **cheat**

CHEATS ▸ **cheat**

CHEBEC *n* type of boat

CHEBECS ▸ **chebec**

CHECHIA *n* Berber skullcap

CHECK *vb* examine or investigate ▷ *n* control designed to ensure accuracy

CHECKED ▸ **check**

CHECKER *same as* ▸ **chequer**

CHECKS ▸ **check**

CHECKUP *n* thorough medical examination ▷ *vb* investigate or make an inquiry into (a person's character, evidence, etc), esp when suspicions have been aroused

CHECKY *adj* having squares of alternating tinctures or furs

CHEDDAR *n* type of smooth hard yellow or whitish cheese

CHEDER *n* (in Western countries) elementary religious education classes, usually outside normal school hours

CHEDERS ▸ **cheder**

CHEDITE *same as* > **cheddite**

CHEEK *n* either side of the face below the eye ▷ *vb* speak impudently to

CHEEKED ▸ **cheek**

CHEEKS ▸ **cheek**

CHEEKY *adj* impudent, disrespectful

CHEEP *n* young bird's high-pitched cry ▷ *vb* utter a cheep

CHEEPED ▸ **cheep**

CHEEPER ▸ **cheep**

CHEEPS ▸ **cheep**

CHEER *vb* applaud or encourage with shouts ▷ *n* shout of applause or encouragement

CHEERED ▸ **cheer**

CHEERER ▸ **cheer**

CHEERIO *interj* goodbye ▷ *n* small red cocktail sausage ▷ *sentence substitute* farewell greeting

CHEERLY *adv* cheerful or cheerfully

CHEERO *same as* ▸ **cheerio**

CHEEROS ▸ **cheero**

CHEERS *interj* drinking toast ▷ *sentence substitute* drinking toast

CHEERY *adj* cheerful

CHEESE *n* food made from coagulated milk curd ▷ *vb* stop

CHEESED ▸ **cheese**

CHEESES ▸ **cheese**

CHEESY *adj* like cheese

CHEETAH *n* large fast-running spotted African wild cat

CHEF *n* cook in a restaurant ▷ *vb* to work as a chef

CHEFDOM *n* state or condition of being a chef

CHEFED ▸ **chef**

CHEFFED ▸ chef
CHEFING ▸ chef
CHEFS ▸ chef
CHEGOE *same as* ▸ **chigger**
CHEGOES ▸ chigger
CHEKA *n* secret police set up in Russia in 1917
CHEKAS ▸ cheka
CHEKIST *n* member of the cheka
CHELA *n* disciple of a religious teacher
CHELAE ▸ chela
CHELAS ▸ chela
CHELATE *n* coordination compound in which a metal atom or ion is bound to a ligand at two or more points on the ligand, so as to form a heterocyclic ring containing a metal atom ▸ *adj* of or possessing chelae ▸ *vb* form a chelate
CHELLUP *n* noise
CHELOID *a variant spelling of* ▸ **keloid**
CHELONE *n* hardy N American plant grown for its white, rose, or purple flower spikes
CHELP *vb* (esp of women or children) to chatter or speak out of turn
CHELPED ▸ chelp
CHELPS ▸ chelp
CHEMIC *vb* to bleach ▸ *n* chemist
CHEMICS ▸ chemic
CHEMISE *n* woman's loose-fitting slip
CHEMISM *n* chemical action
CHEMIST *n* shop selling medicines and cosmetics
CHEMMY *n* gambling card game
CHEMO *n* short form of chemotherapy
CHEMOS ▸ chemo
CHENAR *n* oriental plane tree
CHENARS ▸ chenar
CHENET *another word for* ▸ **genip**
CHENETS ▸ chenet
CHENIX *n* ancient measure, slightly more than a quart
CHEQUE *n* written order to one's bank to pay money from one's account
CHEQUER *n* piece used in Chinese chequers ▸ *vb* make irregular in colour or character

CHEQUES ▸ cheque
CHEQUY *same as* ▸ **checky**
CHER *adj* dear or expensive
CHERE *feminine variant of* ▸ **cher**
CHERISH *vb* cling to (an idea or feeling)
CHEROOT *n* cigar with both ends cut flat
CHERRY *n* small red or black fruit with a stone ▸ *adj* deep red ▸ *vb* to cheer
CHERT *n* microcrystalline form of silica usually occurring as bands or layers of pebbles in sedimentary rock. Formula: SiO$_2$. Varieties include flint, lyddite (Lydian stone)
CHERTS ▸ chert
CHERTY ▸ chert
CHERUB *n* angel, often represented as a winged child
CHERUBS ▸ cherub
CHERUP *same as* ▸ **chirrup**
CHERUPS ▸ cherup
CHERVIL *n* aniseed-flavoured herb
CHESIL *n* gravel or shingle
CHESILS ▸ chesil
CHESNUT *rare variant of* > **chestnut**
CHESS *n* game for two players with 16 pieces each, played on a chequered board of 64 squares
CHESSEL *n* mould used in cheese-making
CHESSES ▸ chess
CHEST *n* front of the body, from neck to waist ▸ *vb* to hit with the chest, as with a ball in football
CHESTED ▸ chest
CHESTS ▸ chest
CHESTY *adj* symptomatic of chest disease
CHETAH *same as* ▸ **cheetah**
CHETAHS ▸ chetah
CHETH *same as* ▸ **heth**
CHETHS ▸ cheth
CHETNIK *n* member of a Serbian nationalist paramilitary group
CHETRUM *n* monetary unit in Bhutan
CHEVAL *n as in* **cheval glass** full-length mirror that can swivel
CHEVEN *n* chub
CHEVENS ▸ cheven
CHEVET *n* semicircular or

polygonal east end of a church, esp a French Gothic church, often with a number of attached apses
CHEVETS ▸ chevet
CHEVIED ▸ chevy
CHEVIES ▸ chevy
CHEVIN *same as* ▸ **cheven**
CHEVINS ▸ chevin
CHEVIOT *n* type of British sheep reared for its wool
CHEVRE *n* any cheese made from goats' milk
CHEVRES ▸ chevre
CHEVRET *n* type of goats' cheese
CHEVRON *n* V-shaped pattern, esp on the sleeve of a military uniform to indicate rank ▸ *vb* make a chevron
CHEVY *same as* ▸ **chivy**
CHEW *vb* grind (food) between the teeth ▸ *n* act of chewing
CHEWED ▸ chew
CHEWER ▸ chew
CHEWERS ▸ chew
CHEWET *n* type of meat pie
CHEWETS ▸ chewet
CHEWIE *n* chewing gum
CHEWIER ▸ chewy
CHEWIES ▸ chewy
CHEWING ▸ chew
CHEWINK *n* towhee
CHEWS ▸ chew
CHEWY *adj* requiring a lot of chewing ▸ *n* dog's rubber toy
CHEZ *prep* at the home of
CHI *n* 22nd letter of the Greek alphabet, a consonant, transliterated as *ch* or rarely *kh*

> **Chi** is a letter of the Greek alphabet, and can also be spelt **khi**.

CHIA *n* plant of the mint family
CHIACK *vb* tease or banter ▸ *n* good-humoured banter
CHIACKS ▸ chiack
CHIANTI *n* dry red Italian wine
CHIAO *n* Chinese coin equal to one tenth of one yuan
CHIAS ▸ chia
CHIASM *same as* ▸ **chiasma**
CHIASMA *n* cross-shaped connection produced by the crossing over of pairing chromosomes during meiosis

CHIASMI > **chiasmus**
CHIASMS > **chiasma**
CHIAUS same as > **chouse**
CHIB vb in Scots English, stab or slash with a sharp weapon ▷ n sharp weapon
CHIBBED ▶ **chib**
CHIBOL n spring onion
CHIBOLS ▶ **chibol**
CHIBOUK n Turkish tobacco pipe with an extremely long stem
CHIBS ▶ **chib**
CHIC adj stylish, elegant ▷ n stylishness, elegance
CHICA n Spanish young girl
CHICANA n female chicano
CHICANE n obstacle in a motor-racing circuit ▷ vb deceive or trick by chicanery
CHICANO n American citizen of Mexican origin
CHICAS ▶ **chica**
CHICER ▶ **chic**
CHICEST ▶ **chic**
CHICH another word for > **chickpea**
CHICHA n Andean drink made from fermented maize
CHICHAS ▶ **chicha**
CHICHES > **chickpea**
CHICHI adj affectedly pretty or stylish ▷ n quality of being affectedly pretty or stylish
CHICHIS ▶ **chichi**
CHICK n baby bird
CHICKEE n opensided, thatched building on stilts
CHICKEN n domestic fowl ▷ adj cowardly ▷ vb to lose one's nerve
CHICKS ▶ **chick**
CHICLE n gumlike substance obtained from the sapodilla
CHICLES ▶ **chicle**
CHICLY ▶ **chic**
CHICO n spiny chenopodiaceous shrub
CHICON same as ▶ **chicory**
CHICONS ▶ **chicon**
CHICORY n plant whose leaves are used in salads
CHICOS ▶ **chico**
CHICS ▶ **chic**
CHID ▶ **chide**
CHIDDEN ▶ **chide**
CHIDE vb rebuke, scold
CHIDED ▶ **chide**
CHIDER ▶ **chide**

CHIDERS ▶ **chide**
CHIDES ▶ **chide**
CHIDING ▶ **chide**
CHIEF n head of a group of people ▷ adj most important
CHIEFER ▶ **chief**
CHIEFLY adv especially ▷ adj of or relating to a chief or chieftain
CHIEFRY same as > **chiefery**
CHIEFS ▶ **chief**
CHIEL n young man
CHIELD same as ▶ **chiel**
CHIELDS ▶ **chiel**
CHIELS ▶ **chiel**
CHIFFON n fine see-through fabric ▷ adj made of chiffon
CHIGGER n parasitic larva of any of various mites, which causes intense itching of human skin
CHIGNON n knot of hair pinned up at the back of the head ▷ vb make a chignon
CHIGOE same as ▶ **chigger**
CHIGOES ▶ **chigoe**
CHIGRE same as ▶ **chigger**
CHIGRES ▶ **chigre**
CHIK n slatted blind
CHIKARA n Indian seven-stringed musical instrument
CHIKHOR same as ▶ **chukar**
CHIKOR same as ▶ **chukar**
CHIKORS ▶ **chikor**
CHIKS ▶ **chik**
CHILD n young human being, boy or girl ▷ vb to give birth
CHILDE n young man of noble birth
CHILDED ▶ **child**
CHILDER dialect variant of > **children**
CHILDES ▶ **childe**
CHILDLY ▶ **child**
CHILDS ▶ **child**
CHILE a variant spelling of ▶ **chilli**
CHILES ▶ **chile**
CHILI same as ▶ **chilli**
CHILIAD n group of one thousand
CHILIES ▶ **chili**
CHILIS ▶ **chili**
CHILL n feverish cold ▷ vb make (something) cool or cold ▷ adj unpleasantly cold
CHILLED ▶ **chill**
CHILLER n cooling or refrigerating device

CHILLI n small red or green hot-tasting capsicum pod, used in cooking
CHILLIS ▶ **chilli**
CHILLS ▶ **chill**
CHILLUM n short pipe, usually of clay, used esp for smoking cannabis
CHILLY adj moderately cold
CHIMAR same as ▶ **chimere**
CHIMARS ▶ **chimar**
CHIMB same as ▶ **chime**
CHIMBLY same as ▶ **chimney**
CHIMBS ▶ **chime**
CHIME n musical ringing sound of a bell or clock ▷ vb make a musical ringing sound
CHIMED ▶ **chime**
CHIMER ▶ **chime**
CHIMERA n unrealistic hope or idea
CHIMERE n sleeveless red or black gown, part of a bishop's formal dress though not a vestment
CHIMERS ▶ **chime**
CHIMES ▶ **chime**
CHIMING ▶ **chime**
CHIMLA same as ▶ **chimney**
CHIMLAS ▶ **chimla**
CHIMLEY same as ▶ **chimney**
CHIMNEY n hollow vertical structure for carrying away smoke from a fire ▷ vb to climb two vertical, parallel, chimney-like rock faces
CHIMO interj Inuit greeting and toast
CHIMP n chimpanzee
CHIMPS ▶ **chimp**
CHIN n part of the face below the mouth ▷ vb hit someone in the chin
CHINA n fine earthenware or porcelain
CHINAR same as ▶ **chenar**
CHINARS ▶ **chenar**
CHINAS ▶ **china**
CHINCH another name for a ▶ **bedbug**
CHINCHY adj tightfisted
CHINDIT n Allied soldier fighting behind the Japanese lines in Burma during World War II
CHINE same as ▶ **chime**
CHINED ▶ **chine**
CHINES ▶ **chine**
CHINESE adj of or relating to China

CHINING ▸ chine

CHINK n small narrow opening ▷ vb make a light ringing sound

CHINKED ▸ chink

CHINKS ▸ chink

CHINKY ▸ chink

CHINNED ▸ chin

CHINO n durable cotton twill cloth

CHINONE n benzoquinone

CHINOOK n warm dry southwesterly wind blowing down the eastern slopes of the Rocky Mountains

CHINOS pl n trousers made of a kind of hard-wearing cotton

CHINS ▸ chin

CHINTS obsolete variant of ▸ chintz

CHINTZ n printed cotton fabric with a glazed finish

CHINTZY adj of or covered with chintz

CHINWAG n chat

CHIP n strip of potato, fried in deep fat ▷ vb break small pieces from

CHIPPED ▸ chip

CHIPPER vb chirp or chatter

CHIPPIE same as ▸ chippy

CHIPPY n fish-and-chip shop ▷ adj resentful or oversensitive about being perceived as inferior

CHIPS ▸ chip

CHIPSET n highly integrated circuit on the motherboard of a computer that controls many of its data transfer functions

CHIRAL > chirality

CHIRK vb to creak, like a door ▷ adj spritely; high-spirited

CHIRKED ▸ chirk

CHIRKER ▸ chirk

CHIRKS ▸ chirk

CHIRL vb to warble

CHIRLED ▸ chirl

CHIRLS ▸ chirl

CHIRM n chirping of birds ▷ vb (esp of a bird) to chirp

CHIRMED ▸ chirm

CHIRMS ▸ chirm

CHIRO n an informal name for chiropractor

CHIROS ▸ chiro

CHIRP vb (of a bird or insect) make a short high-pitched sound ▷ n chirping sound

CHIRPED ▸ chirp

CHIRPER ▸ chirp

CHIRPS ▸ chirp

CHIRPY adj lively and cheerful

CHIRR vb (esp of certain insects, such as crickets) to make a shrill trilled sound ▷ n sound of chirring

CHIRRE same as ▸ chirr

CHIRRED ▸ chirr

CHIRREN n dialect form of children

CHIRRES ▸ chirre

CHIRRS ▸ chirr

CHIRRUP vb (of some birds) to chirp repeatedly ▷ n chirruping sound

CHIRT vb to squirt

CHIRTED ▸ chirt

CHIRTS ▸ chirt

CHIRU n Tibetan antelope with a dense woolly pinkish-brown fleece, prized as the source of shahtoosh wool

CHIRUS ▸ chiru

CHIS ▸ chi

CHISEL n metal tool with a sharp end for shaping wood or stone ▷ vb carve or form with a chisel

CHISELS ▸ chisel

CHIT n short official note, such as a receipt ▷ vb to sprout

CHITAL n type of deer

CHITALS ▸ chital

CHITIN n tough substance forming the outer layer of the bodies of arthropods

CHITINS ▸ chitin

CHITLIN n pig intestine cooked and served as a dish

CHITON n (in ancient Greece and Rome) a loose woollen tunic worn knee length by men and full length by women

CHITONS ▸ chiton

CHITS ▸ chit

CHITTED ▸ chit

CHITTER vb twitter or chirp

CHITTY adj childish ▷ vb sprout

CHIV n knife ▷ vb stab (someone)

CHIVARI same as > charivari

CHIVE n small Eurasian purple-flowered plant whose long slender hollow leaves are used in cooking ▷ vb file or cut off

CHIVED ▸ chive

CHIVES same as ▸ chive

CHIVIED ▸ chivy

CHIVIES ▸ chivy

CHIVING ▸ chive

CHIVS ▸ chiv

CHIVVED ▸ chiv

CHIVVY same as ▸ chivvy

CHIVY vb harass or nag ▷ n hunt

CHIZ n cheat ▷ vb cheat

CHIZZ same as ▸ chiz

CHIZZED ▸ chiz

CHIZZES ▸ chiz

CHLAMYS n woollen cloak worn by ancient Greek soldiers

CHLORAL n colourless oily liquid with a pungent odour, made from chlorine and acetaldehyde and used in preparing chloral hydrate and DDT

CHLORIC adj of or containing chlorine in the pentavalent state

CHLORID n type of chlorine compound

CHLORIN same as > chlorine

CHOANA n posterior nasal aperture

CHOANAE ▸ choana

CHOBDAR n in India and Nepal, king's macebearer or attendant

CHOC short form of > chocolate

CHOCCY n chocolate ▷ adj made of, tasting of, smelling of, or resembling chocolate

CHOCHO same as ▸ chayote

CHOCHOS ▸ chocho

CHOCK n block or wedge used to prevent a heavy object from moving ▷ vb secure by a chock ▷ adv as closely or tightly as possible

CHOCKED ▸ chock

CHOCKER adj full up

CHOCKO same as ▸ choco

CHOCKOS ▸ chocko

CHOCKS ▸ chock

CHOCO n member of the Australian army

CHOCOS ▸ choco

CHOCS ▸ choc

CHOCTAW n turn from the inside edge of one skate to the outside edge of the other or vice versa

CHODE ▸ chide

CHOENIX same as ▸ chenix

CHOG n core of a piece of fruit

CHOGS ▸ chog

CHOICE n choosing ▷ adj of high quality

CHOICER ▸ choice

CHOICES ▸ choice

CHOIR n organized group of singers, esp in church ▷ vb to sing in chorus

CHOIRED ▸ choir

CHOIRS ▸ choir

CHOKE vb hinder or stop the breathing of (a person) by strangling or smothering ▷ n device controlling the amount of air that is mixed with the fuel in a petrol engine

CHOKED adj disappointed or angry

CHOKER n tight-fitting necklace

CHOKERS ▸ choker

CHOKES ▸ choke

CHOKEY n a slang word for prison ▷ adj involving, caused by, or causing choking

CHOKEYS ▸ chokey

CHOKIER ▸ chokey

CHOKIES ▸ chokey

CHOKING ▸ choke

CHOKO n pear-shaped fruit of a tropical American vine, eaten as a vegetable

CHOKOS ▸ choko

CHOKRA n in India, a boy or young man

CHOKRAS ▸ chokra

CHOKRI n in India, a girl or young woman

CHOKRIS ▸ chokri

CHOKY same as ▸ chokey

CHOLA n Hispanic girl

CHOLAS ▸ chola

CHOLATE n salt of cholic acid

CHOLENT n meal usually consisting of a stew of meat, potatoes, and pulses prepared before the Sabbath on Friday and left to cook until eaten for Sabbath lunch

CHOLER n bad temper

CHOLERA n serious infectious disease causing severe vomiting and diarrhoea

CHOLERS ▸ choler

CHOLI n short-sleeved bodice, as worn by Indian women

CHOLIC adj as in cholic acid crystalline acid found in bile

CHOLINE n colourless viscous soluble alkaline substance present in animal tissues, esp as a constituent of lecithin: used as a supplement to the diet of poultry and in medicine for preventing the accumulation of fat in the liver

CHOLIS ▸ choli

CHOLLA n type of spiny cactus of the southwestern US and Mexico, with cylindrical stem segments

CHOLLAS ▸ cholla

CHOLO n chicano gangster

CHOLOS ▸ cholo

CHOLTRY n caravanserai

CHOMETZ same as ▸ chametz

CHOMMIE n (in informal South African English) friend

CHOMP vb chew noisily ▷ n act or sound of chewing in this manner

CHOMPED ▸ chomp

CHOMPER ▸ chomp

CHOMPS ▸ chomp

CHON n North and South Korean monetary unit worth one hundredth of a won

CHONDRE another word for ▸ chondrule

CHONDRI ▸ chondrus

CHOOF vb go away

CHOOFED ▸ choof

CHOOFS ▸ choof

CHOOK n hen or chicken ▷ vb make the sound of a hen of chicken

CHOOKED ▸ chook

CHOOKIE same as ▸ chook

CHOOKS ▸ chook

CHOOM n Englishman

CHOOMS ▸ choom

CHOON n slang term for music that one likes

CHOONS ▸ choon

CHOOSE vb select from a number of alternatives

CHOOSER ▸ choose

CHOOSES ▸ choose

CHOOSEY same as ▸ choosy

CHOOSY adj fussy, hard to please

CHOP vb cut with a blow from an axe or knife ▷ n cutting or sharp blow

CHOPIN same as ▸ chopine

CHOPINE n sandal-like shoe on tall wooden or cork bases popular in the 18th century

CHOPINS ▸ chopin

CHOPPED ▸ chop

CHOPPER n helicopter ▷ vb travel by helicopter

CHOPPY adj (of the sea) fairly rough

CHOPS ▸ chop

CHORAGI > choragus

CHORAL adj of a choir

CHORALE n slow stately hymn tune

CHORALS ▸ choral

CHORD n straight line joining two points on a curve ▷ vb provide (a melodic line) with chords

CHORDA n in anatomy, a cord

CHORDAE ▸ chorda

CHORDAL ▸ chord

CHORDED ▸ chord

CHORDEE n painful penile erection, a symptom of gonorrhoea

CHORDS ▸ chord

CHORE n routine task ▷ vb to carry out chores

CHOREA n disorder of the nervous system characterized by uncontrollable brief jerky movements

CHOREAL ▸ chorea

CHOREAS ▸ chorea

CHORED ▸ chore

CHOREE n trochee

CHOREES ▸ choree

CHOREGI > choregus

CHOREIC ▸ chorea

CHORES ▸ chore

CHOREUS same as ▸ choree

CHORIA ▸ chorion

CHORIAL ▸ chorion

CHORIC adj of, like, for, or in the manner of a chorus, esp of singing, dancing, or the speaking of verse

CHORINE n chorus girl

CHORING ▸ chore

CHORION n outer of two membranes that form a sac around the embryonic reptile, bird, or mammal

CHORISM > chorisis

CHORIST n choir member

CHORIZO n kind of highly seasoned pork sausage of Spain or Mexico

CHOROID adj resembling the chorion, esp in being vascular ▷ n brownish vascular membrane of the eyeball between the sclera and the retina

CHORRIE n dilapidated old car

CHORTEN n Buddhist shrine

CHORTLE vb chuckle in amusement ▷ n amused chuckle

CHORUS n large choir ▷ vb sing or say together

CHOSE ▸ choose

CHOSEN ▸ choose

CHOSES ▸ choose

CHOTA adj (in British Empire Indian usage) small

CHOTT a variant spelling of ▸ shott

CHOTTS ▸ chott

CHOU n type of cabbage

CHOUGH n large black Eurasian and N African bird of the crow family

CHOUGHS ▸ chough

CHOUSE vb to cheat

CHOUSED ▸ chouse

CHOUSER ▸ chouse

CHOUSES ▸ chouse

CHOUSH n Turkish messenger

CHOUT n blackmail

CHOUTS ▸ chout

CHOUX ▸ chou

CHOW n thick-coated dog with a curled tail, orig. from China ▷ vb eat

CHOWDER n thick soup containing clams or fish ▷ vb to make a chowder of

CHOWED ▸ chow

CHOWING ▸ chow

CHOWK n marketplace or market area

CHOWKS ▸ chowk

CHOWRI n fly-whisk

CHOWRIS ▸ chowri

CHOWRY same as ▸ chowri

CHOWS ▸ chow

CHOWSE same as ▸ chouse

CHOWSED ▸ chowse

CHOWSES ▸ chowse

CHRISM n consecrated oil used for anointing in some churches

CHRISMA > chrismon

CHRISMS ▸ chrism

CHRISOM same as ▸ chrism

CHRISTY n skiing turn for stopping or changing direction quickly

CHROMA n attribute of a colour that enables an observer to judge how much chromatic colour it contains irrespective of achromatic colour present

CHROMAS ▸ chroma

CHROME n anything plated with chromium ▷ vb plate with chromium ▷ vb to chromium-plate ▷ adj of or having the appearance of chrome

CHROMED ▸ chrome

CHROMEL n nickel-based alloy containing about 10 per cent chromium, used in heating elements

CHROMES ▸ chrome

CHROMIC adj of or containing chromium in the trivalent state

CHROMO n picture produced by the process of making coloured prints by lithography

CHROMOS ▸ chromo

CHROMY ▸ chrome

CHROMYL n of, consisting of, or containing the divalent radical CrO_2

CHRONIC adj (of an illness) lasting a long time ▷ n chronically-ill patient

CHRONON n unit of time equal to the time that a photon would take to traverse the diameter of an electron: about 10^{-24} seconds

CHUB n European freshwater fish of the carp family

CHUBBY adj plump and round

CHUBS ▸ chub

CHUCK vb throw ▷ n cut of beef from the neck to the shoulder

CHUCKED ▸ chuck

CHUCKER n person who throws something

CHUCKIE n small stone

CHUCKLE vb laugh softly ▷ n soft laugh

CHUCKS ▸ chuck

CHUCKY same as ▸ chuckie

CHUDDAH same as ▸ chuddar

CHUDDAR n large shawl or veil worn by Muslim or Hindu women that covers them from head to foot

CHUDDER same as ▸ chuddar

CHUDDY n chewing gum

CHUFA n type of sedge of warm regions of the Old World, with nutlike edible tubers

CHUFAS ▸ chufa

CHUFF vb (of a steam engine) move while making a puffing sound ▷ n puffing sound of or as if of a steam engine ▷ adj boorish

CHUFFED adj very pleased

CHUFFER ▸ chuff

CHUFFS ▸ chuff

CHUFFY adj boorish and surly

CHUG n short dull sound like the noise of an engine ▷ vb operate or move with this sound

CHUGGED ▸ chug

CHUGGER ▸ chug

CHUGS ▸ chug

CHUKAR n common Indian partridge with red legs and bill and a black-barred sandy plumage

CHUKARS ▸ chukar

CHUKKA n period of play in polo

CHUKKAR same as ▸ chukka

CHUKKAS ▸ chukka

CHUKKER same as ▸ chukka

CHUKOR same as ▸ chukar

CHUKORS ▸ chukor

CHUM n close friend ▷ vb be or become an intimate friend (of)

CHUMASH n printed book containing one of the Five Books of Moses

CHUMLEY same as ▸ chimney

CHUMMED ▸ chum

CHUMMY adj friendly ▷ n chum

CHUMP n stupid person ▷ vb chew noisily

CHUMPED ▸ chump

CHUMPS ▸ chump

CHUMS ▸ chum

CHUNDER vb vomit ▷ n vomit

CHUNK n thick solid piece ▷ vb to break up into chunks

CHUNKED ▸ chunk

CHUNKS ▸ chunk

CHUNKY adj (of a person)

broad and heavy

CHUNNEL n rail tunnel beneath the English Channel, linking England and France

CHUNNER same as ▸ **chunter**

CHUNTER vb mutter or grumble incessantly in a meaningless fashion

CHUPATI same as > **chupatti**

CHUPPA same as ▸ **chuppah**

CHUPPAH n canopy under which a marriage is performed

CHUPPAS ▸ **chuppa**

CHUPPOT ▸ **chuppah**

CHUR interj expression of agreement

CHURCH n building for public Christian worship ▹vb bring (someone, esp a woman after childbirth) to church for special ceremonies

CHURCHY adj like a church, church service, etc

CHURL n surly ill-bred person

CHURLS ▸ **churl**

CHURN n machine in which cream is shaken to make butter ▹vb stir (cream) vigorously to make butter

CHURNED ▸ **churn**

CHURNER ▸ **churn**

CHURNS ▸ **churn**

CHURR same as ▸ **chirr**

CHURRED ▸ **churr**

CHURRO n Spanish dough stick snack

CHURROS ▸ **churro**

CHURRS ▸ **churr**

CHURRUS n hemp resin

CHUSE obsolete variant of ▸ **choose**

CHUSES ▸ **chuse**

CHUSING ▸ **chuse**

CHUT interj expression of surprise or annoyance ▹vb make such an expression

CHUTE n steep slope down which things may be slid ▹vb to descend by a chute

CHUTED ▸ **chute**

CHUTES ▸ **chute**

CHUTING ▸ **chute**

CHUTIST ▸ **chute**

CHUTNEE same as ▸ **chutney**

CHUTNEY n pickle made from fruit, vinegar, spices, and sugar

CHUTZPA same as > **chutzpah**

CHYACK same as ▸ **chiack**

CHYACKS ▸ **chyack**

CHYLDE archaic word for ▸ **child**

CHYLE n milky fluid formed in the small intestine during digestion

CHYLES ▸ **chyle**

CHYLIFY vb to be turned into chyle

CHYLOUS ▸ **chyle**

CHYME n thick fluid mass of partially digested food that leaves the stomach

CHYMES ▸ **chyme**

CHYMIC same as ▸ **chemic**

CHYMICS ▸ **chymic**

CHYMIFY vb to form into chyme

CHYMIST same as ▸ **chemist**

CHYMOUS ▸ **chyme**

CHYND adj chined

CHYPRE n perfume made from sandalwood

CHYPRES ▸ **chypre**

CHYTRID n variety of fungus

CIAO an informal word for ▸ **hello**

CIBOL same as ▸ **chibol**

CIBOLS ▸ **cibol**

CIBORIA > **ciborium**

CIBOULE same as ▸ **chibol**

CICADA n large insect that makes a high-pitched drone

CICADAE ▸ **cicada**

CICADAS ▸ **cicada**

CICALA same as ▸ **cicada**

CICALAS ▸ **cicala**

CICALE ▸ **cicala**

CICELY n type of plant

CICERO n measure for type that is somewhat larger than the pica

CICEROS ▸ **cicero**

CICHLID n type of tropical freshwater fish popular in aquariums

CICOREE same as ▸ **chicory**

CICUTA n spotted hemlock

CICUTAS ▸ **cicuta**

CID n leader

CIDARIS n sea urchin

CIDE Shakespearean variant of ▸ **decide**

CIDED ▸ **cide**

CIDER n alcoholic drink made from fermented apple juice

CIDERS ▸ **cider**

CIDERY ▸ **cider**

CIDES ▸ **cide**

CIDING ▸ **cide**

CIDS ▸ **cid**

CIEL same as ▸ **ceil**

CIELED ▸ **ciel**

CIELING ▸ **ciel**

CIELS ▸ **ciel**

CIERGE same as ▸ **cerge**

CIERGES ▸ **cierge**

CIG same as > **cigarette**

CIGAR n roll of cured tobacco leaves for smoking

CIGARET same as > **cigarette**

CIGARS ▸ **cigar**

CIGGIE same as > **cigarette**

CIGGIES ▸ **ciggie**

CIGGY ▸ **cigarette**

CIGS ▸ **cig**

CILIA ▸ **cilium**

CILIARY adj of or relating to cilia

CILIATE n type of protozoan

CILICE n haircloth fabric or garment

CILICES ▸ **cilice**

CILIUM n short thread projecting from a cell, whose rhythmic beating causes movement

CILL a variant spelling (used in the building industry) for ▸ **sill**

CILLS ▸ **cill**

CIMAR same as ▸ **cymar**

CIMARS ▸ **cimar**

CIMELIA n (especially, ecclesiastical) treasures

CIMEX n type of heteropterous insect, esp the bedbug

CIMICES ▸ **cimex**

CIMIER n crest of a helmet

CIMIERS ▸ **cimier**

CINCH n easy task ▹vb fasten a girth around (a horse)

CINCHED ▸ **cinch**

CINCHES ▸ **cinch**

CINCT adj encircled

CINDER n piece of material that will not burn, left after burning coal ▹vb burn to cinders

CINDERS ▸ **cinder**

CINDERY ▸ **cinder**

CINE n as in **cine camera** camera able to film moving pictures

CINEAST same as > **cineaste**

CINEMA n place for showing films

CINEMAS ▸ **cinema**

CINEOL n colourless oily

C

liquid with a camphor-like odour and a spicy taste
CINEOLE same as ▸ **cineol**
CINEOLS ▸ **cineol**
CINEREA n grey matter of the brain and nervous system
CINERIN n either of two organic compounds used as insecticides
CINES ▸ **cine**
CINGULA > **cingulum**
CINQUE n number five in cards, dice, etc
CINQUES ▸ **cinque**
CION same as ▸ **scion**
CIONS ▸ **cion**
CIPHER n system of secret writing ▸ vb put (a message) into secret writing
CIPHERS ▸ **cipher**
CIPHONY n ciphered telephony; process of enciphering audio information, producing encrypted speech
CIPOLIN n Italian marble with alternating white and green streaks
CIPPI ▸ **cippus**
CIPPUS n pillar bearing an inscription
CIRCA prep approximately, about
CIRCAR n in India, part of a province
CIRCARS ▸ **circar**
CIRCLE n perfectly round geometric figure, line, or shape ▸ vb move in a circle (round)
CIRCLED ▸ **circle**
CIRCLER ▸ **circle**
CIRCLES ▸ **circle**
CIRCLET n circular ornament worn on the head
CIRCLIP n flat spring ring split at one point so that it can be sprung open, passed over a shaft or spindle, and allowed to close into a closely fitting annular recess to form a collar on the shaft. A similar design can be closed to pass into a bore and allowed to spring out into an annular recess to form a shoulder in the bore
CIRCS pl n circumstances
CIRCUIT n complete route

or course, esp a circular one ▸ vb make or travel in a circuit around (something)
CIRCUS n (performance given by) a travelling company of acrobats, clowns, performing animals, etc
CIRCUSY ▸ **circus**
CIRE adj (of fabric) treated with a heat or wax process to make it smooth ▸ n such a surface on a fabric
CIRES ▸ **cire**
CIRL n bird belonging to the bunting family
CIRLS ▸ **cirl**
CIRQUE n steep-sided semicircular hollow found in mountainous areas
CIRQUES ▸ **cirque**
CIRRATE adj bearing or resembling cirri
CIRRI ▸ **cirrus**
CIRROSE same as ▸ **cirrate**
CIRROUS same as ▸ **cirrate**
CIRRUS n high wispy cloud
CIRSOID adj resembling a varix
CIS adj having two groups of atoms on the same side of a double bond
CISCO n whitefish, esp the lake herring of cold deep lakes of North America
CISCOES ▸ **cisco**
CISCOS ▸ **cisco**
CISSIER ▸ **cissy**
CISSIES ▸ **cissy**
CISSING n appearance of pinholes, craters, etc, in paintwork due to poor adhesion of the paint to the surface
CISSOID n geometric curve whose two branches meet in a cusp at the origin and are asymptotic to a line parallel to the y-axis
CISSUS n type of climbing plant sometimes grown as a greenhouse or house plant for its shiny green or mottled leaves
CISSY same as ▸ **sissy**
CIST n wooden box for holding ritual objects used in ancient Rome and Greece ▸ vb make a cist
CISTED ▸ **cist**
CISTERN n water tank, esp one that holds water for flushing a toilet

CISTIC adj cist-like
CISTRON n section of a chromosome that encodes a single polypeptide chain
CISTS ▸ **cist**
CISTUS n type of plant
CIT n pejorative term for a town dweller
CITABLE ▸ **cite**
CITADEL n fortress in a city
CITAL n court summons
CITALS ▸ **cital**
CITATOR n legal publication listing cases and statutes, their history and current status
CITE vb quote, refer to
CITED ▸ **cite**
CITER ▸ **cite**
CITERS ▸ **cite**
CITES ▸ **cite**
CITESS n female cit
CITHARA n stringed musical instrument of ancient Greece and elsewhere, similar to the lyre and played with a plectrum
CITHER same as ▸ **cittern**
CITHERN ▸ **cittern**
CITHERS ▸ **cither**
CITHREN same as ▸ **cithara**
CITIED adj having cities
CITIES ▸ **city**
CITIFY vb cause to conform to or adopt the customs, habits, or dress of city people
CITING ▸ **cite**
CITIZEN n native or naturalized member of a state or nation
CITO adv swiftly
CITOLA n type of medieval stringed instrument
CITOLAS ▸ **citola**
CITOLE a rare word for ▸ **cittern**
CITOLES ▸ **citole**
CITRAL n yellow volatile liquid with a lemon-like odour, found in oils of lemon grass, orange, and lemon and used in perfumery
CITRALS ▸ **citral**
CITRATE n any salt or ester of citric acid
CITRIC adj of or derived from citrus fruits or citric acid
CITRIN n vitamin P
CITRINE n brownish-yellow variety of quartz: a gemstone

CITRINS ▸ citrin

CITRON n lemon-like fruit of a small Asian tree

CITRONS ▸ citron

CITROUS same as ▸ citrus

CITRUS n type of tropical or subtropical tree or shrub of the genus which includes the orange, lemon, lime, and grapefruit

CITRUSY same as ▸ citrussy

CITS ▸ cit

CITTERN n medieval stringed instrument resembling a lute but having wire strings and a flat back

CITY n large or important town

CITYFY same as ▸ citify

CIVE same as ▸ chive

CIVES ▸ cive

CIVET n spotted catlike African mammal

CIVETS ▸ civet

CIVIC adj of a city or citizens

CIVICS n study of the rights and responsibilities of citizenship

CIVIE same as ▸ civvy

CIVIES ▸ civie

CIVIL adj relating to the citizens of a state as opposed to the armed forces or the Church

CIVILLY ▸ civil

CIVILS ▸ civil

CIVISM n good citizenship

CIVISMS ▸ civism

CIVVIES ▸ civvy

CIVVY n civilian

CIZERS archaic spelling of ▸ scissors

CLABBER vb to cover with mud

CLACH n stone

CLACHAN n small village

CLACHS ▸ clach

CLACK n sound made by two hard objects striking each other ▷ vb make this sound

CLACKED ▸ clack

CLACKER n object that makes a clacking sound

CLACKS ▸ clack

CLAD vb bond a metal to (another metal), esp to form a protective coat

CLADDED adj covered with cladding

CLADDER ▸ clad

CLADDIE another name for ▸ korari

CLADE n group of organisms considered as having evolved from a common ancestor

CLADES ▸ clade

CLADISM ▸ cladist

CLADIST n proponent of cladistics: a method of grouping animals that makes use of lines of descent rather than structural similarities

CLADODE n flattened stem resembling and functioning as a leaf, as in butcher's-broom

CLADS ▸ clad

CLAES Scots word for ▸ clothes

CLAG n sticky mud ▷ vb stick, as mud

CLAGGED ▸ clag

CLAGGY adj stickily clinging, as mud

CLAGS ▸ clag

CLAIM vb assert as a fact ▷ n assertion that something is true

CLAIMED ▸ claim

CLAIMER ▸ claim

CLAIMS ▸ claim

CLAM n edible shellfish with a hinged shell ▷ vb gather clams

CLAMANT adj noisy

CLAMBE old variant of ▸ climb

CLAMBER vb climb awkwardly ▷ n climb performed in this manner

CLAME archaic variant of ▸ claim

CLAMES ▸ claim

CLAMMED ▸ clam

CLAMMER n person who gathers clams

CLAMMY adj unpleasantly moist and sticky

CLAMOR same as ▸ clamour

CLAMORS ▸ clamor

CLAMOUR n loud protest ▷ vb make a loud noise or outcry

CLAMP n tool with movable jaws for holding things together tightly ▷ vb fasten with a clamp

CLAMPED ▸ clamp

CLAMPER n spiked metal frame fastened to the sole of a shoe to prevent slipping on ice ▷ vb to tread heavily

CLAMPS ▸ clamp

CLAMS ▸ clam

CLAN n group of families with a common ancestor, esp among Scottish Highlanders

CLANG vb make a loud ringing metallic sound ▷ n ringing metallic sound

CLANGED ▸ clang

CLANGER n obvious mistake

CLANGOR same as ▸ clangour

CLANGS ▸ clang

CLANK n harsh metallic sound ▷ vb make such a sound

CLANKED ▸ clank

CLANKS ▸ clank

CLANKY adj making clanking sounds

CLANS ▸ clan

CLAP vb applaud by hitting the palms of one's hands sharply together ▷ n act or sound of clapping

CLAPNET n net that can be closed instantly by pulling a string

CLAPPED ▸ clap

CLAPPER n piece of metal inside a bell, which causes it to sound when struck against the side ▷ vb make a sound like a clapper

CLAPS ▸ clap

CLAPT ▸ clap

CLAQUE n group of people hired to applaud

CLAQUER same as ▸ claqueur

CLAQUES ▸ claque

CLARAIN n one of the four major lithotypes of banded coal

CLARET n dry red wine from Bordeaux ▷ adj purplish-red ▷ vb to drink claret

CLARETS ▸ claret

CLARIES ▸ clary

CLARIFY vb make (a matter) clear and unambiguous

CLARINI ▸ clarino

CLARINO adj of or relating to a high passage for the trumpet in 18th-century music ▷ n high register of the trumpet

CLARION n obsolete high-pitched trumpet ▷ adj clear and ringing ▷ vb

C

proclaim loudly

CLARITY n clearness

CLARKIA n N American plant cultivated for its red, purple, or pink flowers

CLARO n mild light-coloured cigar

CLAROES ▸ claro

CLAROS ▸ claro

CLART vb to dirty

CLARTED ▸ clart

CLARTS pl n lumps of mud, esp on shoes

CLARTY adj dirty, esp covered in mud

CLARY n European plant with aromatic leaves and blue flowers

CLASH vb come into conflict ▸ n fight, argument

CLASHED ▸ clash

CLASHER ▸ clash

CLASHES ▸ clash

CLASP n device for fastening things ▸ vb grasp or embrace firmly

CLASPED ▸ clasp

CLASPER ▸ clasp

CLASPS ▸ clasp

CLASPT old inflection of ▸ clasp

CLASS n group of people sharing a similar social position ▸ vb place in a class

CLASSED ▸ class

CLASSER ▸ class

CLASSES ▸ classis

CLASSIC adj being a typical example of something ▸ n author, artist, or work of art of recognized excellence

CLASSIS n governing body of elders or pastors

CLASSON n elementary atomic particle

CLASSY adj stylish and elegant

CLAST n fragment of a clastic rock

CLASTIC adj (of sedimentary rock, etc) composed of fragments of pre-existing rock that have been transported some distance from their points of origin ▸ n clast

CLASTS ▸ clast

CLAT n irksome or troublesome task ▸ vb to scrape

CLATCH vb to move making a squelching sound

CLATS ▸ clat

CLATTED ▸ clat

CLATTER n (make) a rattling noise ▸ vb make a rattling noise, as when hard objects hit each other

CLAUCHT vb to seize by force

CLAUGHT ▸ claucht

CLAUSAL ▸ clause

CLAUSE n section of a legal document

CLAUSES ▸ clause

CLAUT same as ▸ clat

CLAUTED ▸ claut

CLAUTS ▸ claut

CLAVATE adj shaped like a club with the thicker end uppermost

CLAVE n one of a pair of hardwood sticks struck together to make a hollow sound, esp to mark the beat of Latin-American dance music

CLAVER vb talk idly ▸ n idle talk

CLAVERS ▸ claver

CLAVES ▸ clave

CLAVI ▸ clavus

CLAVIE n tar-barrel traditionally set alight in Moray in Scotland on Hogmanay

CLAVIER n any keyboard instrument

CLAVIERS ▸ clavie

CLAVIS n key

CLAVUS n corn on the toe

CLAW n sharp hooked nail of a bird or beast ▸ vb tear with claws or nails

CLAWED ▸ claw

CLAWER ▸ claw

CLAWERS ▸ claw

CLAWING ▸ claw

CLAWS ▸ claw

CLAXON same as ▸ klaxon

CLAXONS ▸ claxon

CLAY n fine-grained earth, soft when moist and hardening when baked, used to make bricks and pottery ▸ vb cover or mix with clay

CLAYED ▸ clay

CLAYEY ▸ clay

CLAYIER ▸ clay

CLAYING ▸ clay

CLAYISH ▸ clay

CLAYPAN n layer of stiff impervious clay situated just below the surface of

the ground, which holds water after heavy rain

CLAYS ▸ clay

CLEAN adj free from dirt or impurities ▸ vb make (something) free from dirt ▸ adv completely

CLEANED ▸ clean

CLEANER n person or thing that removes dirt

CLEANLY adv easily or smoothly ▸ adj habitually clean or neat

CLEANS ▸ clean

CLEANSE vb make clean

CLEANUP n process of cleaning up or eliminating something

CLEAR adj free from doubt or confusion ▸ adv in a clear or distinct manner ▸ vb make or become clear

CLEARED ▸ clear

CLEARER ▸ clear

CLEARLY adv in a clear, distinct, or obvious manner

CLEARS ▸ clear

CLEAT n wedge ▸ vb supply or support with a cleat or cleats

CLEATED ▸ cleat

CLEATS ▸ cleat

CLEAVE vb split apart ▸ n split

CLEAVED ▸ cleave

CLEAVER n butcher's heavy knife with a square blade

CLEAVES ▸ cleave

CLECHE adj (in heraldry) voided so that only a narrow border is visible

CLECK vb (of birds) to hatch ▸ n piece of gossip

CLECKED ▸ cleck

CLECKS ▸ cleck

CLECKY ▸ cleck

CLEEK n large hook, such as one used to land fish ▸ vb to seize

CLEEKED ▸ cleek

CLEEKIT ▸ cleek

CLEEKS ▸ cleek

CLEEP same as ▸ clepe

CLEEPED ▸ cleep

CLEEPS ▸ cleep

CLEEVE n cliff

CLEEVES ▸ cleeve

CLEF n symbol at the beginning of a stave to show the pitch

CLEFS ▸ clef

CLEFT ▸ cleave

CLEFTED ▸ cleave

CLEFTS ▸ cleave

CLEG another name for a
> horsefly

CLEGS ▸ cleg

CLEIK same as ▸ cleek

CLEIKS ▸ cleek

CLEM vb be hungry or cause
to be hungry

CLEMENT adj (of weather)
mild

CLEMMED ▸ clem

CLEMS ▸ clem

CLENCH vb close or squeeze
(one's teeth or fist) tightly
▷ n firm grasp or grip

CLEOME n type of
herbaceous or shrubby
plant cultivated for
its clusters of white or
purplish flowers

CLEOMES ▸ cleome

CLEPE vb call by the name of

CLEPED ▸ clepe

CLEPES ▸ clepe

CLEPING ▸ clepe

CLEPT ▸ clepe

CLERGY n priests and
ministers as a group

CLERIC n member of the
clergy

CLERICS ▸ cleric

CLERID n beetle that preys
on other insects

CLERIDS ▸ clerid

CLERISY n learned or
educated people

CLERK n employee in an
office, bank, or court who
keeps records, files, and
accounts ▷ vb work as a
clerk

CLERKED ▸ clerk

CLERKLY adj of or like a
clerk ▷ adv in the manner of
a clerk

CLERKS ▸ clerk

CLERUCH n settler in a
cleruchy

CLEUCH same as ▸ clough

CLEUCHS ▸ cleuch

CLEUGH same as ▸ clough

CLEUGHS ▸ cleugh

CLEVE same as ▸ cleeve

CLEVER adj intelligent,
quick at learning

CLEVES ▸ cleeve

CLEVIS n U-shaped
component of a shackle for
attaching a drawbar to a
plough or similar
implement

CLEW n ball of thread, yarn,
or twine ▷ vb coil or roll

into a ball

CLEWED ▸ clew

CLEWING ▸ clew

CLEWS ▸ clew

CLICHE n expression or idea
that is no longer effective
because of overuse ▷ vb
use a cliché (in speech or
writing)

CLICHED ▸ cliche

CLICHES ▸ cliche

CLICK n short sharp sound
▷ vb make this sound

CLICKED ▸ click

CLICKER ▸ click

CLICKET vb make a click

CLICKS ▸ click

CLIED ▸ cly

CLIENT n person who uses
the services of a
professional person or
company

CLIENTS ▸ client

CLIES ▸ cly

CLIFF n steep rock face, esp
along the sea shore ▷ vb
scale a cliff

CLIFFED ▸ cliff

CLIFFS ▸ cliff

CLIFFY ▸ cliff

CLIFT same as ▸ cliff

CLIFTED ▸ cliff

CLIFTS ▸ cliff

CLIFTY ▸ cliff

CLIMATE n typical weather
conditions of an area ▷ vb
acclimatize

CLIMAX n most intense
point of an experience,
series of events, or story
▷ vb reach a climax

CLIMB vb go up, ascend ▷ n
climbing

CLIMBED ▸ climb

CLIMBER n person or thing
that climbs

CLIMBS ▸ climb

CLIME n place or its climate

CLIMES ▸ clime

CLINAL ▸ cline

CLINCH vb settle (an
argument or agreement)
decisively ▷ n movement in
which one competitor
holds on to the other to
avoid punches

CLINE n continuous
variation in form between
members of a species
having a wide variable
geographical or ecological
range

CLINES ▸ cline

CLING vb hold tightly or
stick closely ▷ n tendency
of cotton fibres in a sample
to stick to each other

CLINGED ▸ cling

CLINGER ▸ cling

CLINGS ▸ cling

CLINGY ▸ cling

CLINIC n building where
outpatients receive medical
treatment or advice

CLINICS ▸ clinic

CLINK n (make) a light sharp
metallic sound ▷ vb make a
light sharp metallic sound

CLINKED ▸ clink

CLINKER n fused coal left
over in a fire or furnace ▷ vb
form clinker during burning

CLINKS ▸ clink

CLINT n section of a
limestone pavement
separated from adjacent
sections by solution fissures

CLINTS ▸ clint

CLIP vb cut with shears or
scissors ▷ n short extract of
a film

CLIPART n large collection
of simple drawings stored
in a computer

CLIPE same as ▸ clype

CLIPED ▸ clipe

CLIPES ▸ clipe

CLIPING ▸ clipe

CLIPPED ▸ clip

CLIPPER n fast commercial
sailing ship

CLIPPIE n bus conductress

CLIPS ▸ clip

CLIPT old inflection of ▸ clip

CLIQUE n small exclusive
group ▷ vb to form a clique

CLIQUED ▸ clique

CLIQUES ▸ clique

CLIQUEY adj exclusive,
confined to a small group

CLIQUY same as ▸ cliquey

CLIT > clitoris

CLITIC adj (of a word)
incapable of being stressed,
usually pronounced as if
part of the word that
follows or precedes it ▷ n
clitic word

CLITICS ▸ clitic

CLITS ▸ clit

CLITTER vb to stridulate

CLIVERS same as > cleavers

CLIVIA n plant belonging to
the Amaryllid family

CLIVIAS ▸ clivia

CLOACA n cavity in most

C

animals, except higher mammals, into which the alimentary canal and the genital and urinary ducts open

CLOACAE ▸ cloaca
CLOACAL ▸ cloaca
CLOACAS ▸ cloaca
CLOAK n loose sleeveless outer garment ▷ vb cover or conceal
CLOAKED ▸ cloak
CLOAKS ▸ cloak
CLOAM adj made of clay or earthenware ▷ n clay or earthenware pots, dishes, etc, collectively
CLOAMS ▸ cloam
CLOBBER vb hit ▷ n belongings, esp clothes
CLOCHE n cover to protect young plants
CLOCHES ▸ cloche
CLOCK n instrument for showing the time ▷ vb record (time) with a stopwatch
CLOCKED ▸ clock
CLOCKER ▸ clock
CLOCKS ▸ clock
CLOD n lump of earth ▷ vb pelt with clods
CLODDED ▸ clod
CLODDY ▸ clod
CLODLY ▸ clod
CLODS ▸ clod
CLOFF n cleft of a tree
CLOFFS ▸ cloff
CLOG vb obstruct ▷ n. wooden or wooden-soled shoe
CLOGGED ▸ clog
CLOGGER n clogmaker
CLOGGY ▸ clog
CLOGS ▸ clog
CLOISON n partition
CLOKE same as ▸ cloak
CLOKED ▸ cloke
CLOKES ▸ cloke
CLOKING ▸ cloke
CLOMB a past tense and past participle of ▸ climb
CLOMP same as ▸ clump
CLOMPED ▸ clomp
CLOMPS ▸ clomp
CLON same as ▸ clone
CLONAL ▸ clone
CLONE n animal or plant produced artificially from the cells of another animal or plant, and identical to the original ▷ vb produce as a clone

CLONED ▸ clone
CLONER ▸ clone
CLONERS ▸ clone
CLONES ▸ clone
CLONIC ▸ clonus
CLONING ▸ clone
CLONISM n series of clonic spasms
CLONK vb make a loud dull thud ▷ n loud thud
CLONKED ▸ clonk
CLONKS ▸ clonk
CLONS ▸ clon
CLONUS n type of convulsion characterized by rapid contraction and relaxation of a muscle
CLOOP n sound made when a cork is drawn from a bottle
CLOOPS ▸ cloop
CLOOT n hoof
CLOOTIE adj as in **clootie dumpling** kind of dumpling
CLOOTS ▸ cloot
CLOP vb make or move along with a sound as of a horse's hooves striking the ground ▷ n sound of this nature
CLOPPED ▸ clop
CLOPS ▸ clop
CLOQUE n fabric with an embossed surface
CLOQUES ▸ cloque
CLOSE vb shut ▷ n end, conclusion ▷ adj near ▷ adv closely, tightly ▷ n passageway leading to a tenement building
CLOSED ▸ close
CLOSELY ▸ close
CLOSER ▸ close
CLOSERS ▸ close
CLOSES ▸ close
CLOSEST ▸ close
CLOSET n cupboard ▷ adj private, secret ▷ vb shut (oneself) away in private
CLOSETS ▸ closet
CLOSEUP n photo taken close to subject
CLOSING ▸ close
CLOSURE n closing ▷ vb (in a deliberative body) to end (debate) by closure
CLOT n soft thick lump formed from liquid ▷ vb form soft thick lumps
CLOTBUR n burdock
CLOTE n burdock
CLOTES ▸ clote
CLOTH n (piece of) woven fabric

CLOTHE vb put clothes on
CLOTHED ▸ clothe
CLOTHES n garments
CLOTHS ▸ cloth
CLOTS ▸ clot
CLOTTED ▸ clot
CLOTTER vb to clot
CLOTTY adj full of clots
CLOTURE n closure in the US Senate ▷ vb end (debate) in the US Senate by cloture
CLOU n crux; focus
CLOUD n mass of condensed water vapour floating in the sky ▷ vb become cloudy
CLOUDED ▸ cloud
CLOUDS ▸ cloud
CLOUDY adj having a lot of clouds
CLOUGH n gorge or narrow ravine
CLOUGHS ▸ clough
CLOUR vb to thump or dent
CLOURED ▸ clour
CLOURS ▸ clour
CLOUS ▸ clou
CLOUT n hard blow ▷ vb hit hard
CLOUTED ▸ clout
CLOUTER ▸ clout
CLOUTS ▸ clout
CLOVE n tropical evergreen myrtaceous tree
CLOVEN ▸ cleave
CLOVER n plant with three-lobed leaves
CLOVERS ▸ clover
CLOVERY ▸ clover
CLOVES ▸ clove
CLOVIS n as in **clovis point** flint projectile dating from the 10th millennium bc
CLOW n clove
CLOWDER n collective term for a group of cats
CLOWN n comic entertainer in a circus ▷ vb behave foolishly
CLOWNED ▸ clown
CLOWNS ▸ clown
CLOWS ▸ clow
CLOY vb make weary or cause weariness through an excess of something initially pleasurable or sweet
CLOYE vb to claw
CLOYED ▸ cloy
CLOYES ▸ cloye
CLOYING adj sickeningly sweet

CLOYS ▸ cloy

CLOZE adj as in **cloze test** test of the ability to understand text

CLOZES ▸ cloze

CLUB n association of people with common interests ▷ vb hit with a club

CLUBBED ▸ club

CLUBBER n person who regularly frequents nightclubs and similar establishments

CLUBBY adj sociable, esp effusively so

CLUBMAN n man who is an enthusiastic member of a club or clubs

CLUBMEN ▸ clubman

CLUBS ▸ club

CLUCK n low clicking noise made by a hen ▷ vb make this noise

CLUCKED ▸ cluck

CLUCKS ▸ cluck

CLUCKY adj wishing to have a baby

CLUDGIE n toilet

CLUE n something that helps to solve a mystery or puzzle ▷ vb help solve a mystery or puzzle

CLUED ▸ clue

CLUEING ▸ clue

CLUES ▸ clue

CLUING ▸ clue

CLUMBER n type of thickset spaniel

CLUMP n small group of things or people ▷ vb walk heavily

CLUMPED ▸ clump

CLUMPER ▸ clump

CLUMPS ▸ clump

CLUMPY ▸ clump

CLUMSY adj lacking skill or physical coordination

CLUNCH n hardened clay

CLUNG ▸ cling

CLUNK n dull metallic sound ▷ vb make such a sound

CLUNKED ▸ clunk

CLUNKER n dilapidated old car or other machine

CLUNKS ▸ clunk

CLUNKY adj making a clunking noise

CLUPEID n type of widely distributed soft-finned fish, typically with oily flesh, such as the herrings,

sardines, and shad

CLUSIA n tree of the tropical American genus Clusia

CLUSIAS ▸ clusia

CLUSTER n small close group ▷ vb gather in clusters

CLUTCH vb grasp tightly ▷ n device enabling two revolving shafts to be connected and disconnected, esp in a motor vehicle

CLUTCHY adj (of a person) tending to cling

CLUTTER vb scatter objects about (a place) untidily ▷ n untidy mess

CLY vb to steal or seize

> A little word meaning to seize or steal, this can be useful when you are short of vowels.

CLYING ▸ cly

CLYPE vb tell tales ▷ n person who tells tales

CLYPEAL ▸ clypeus

CLYPED ▸ clype

CLYPEI ▸ clypeus

CLYPES ▸ clype

CLYPEUS n cuticular plate on the head of some insects between the labrum and the frons

CLYPING ▸ clype

CLYSTER a former name for an ▸ **enema**

CNEMIAL ▸ cnemis

CNEMIS n shin or tibia

CNIDA n nematocyst

CNIDAE ▸ cnida

COACH n long-distance bus ▷ vb train, teach

COACHED ▸ coach

COACHEE n person who receives training from a coach, esp in business or office practice

COACHER ▸ coach

COACHES ▸ coach

COACHY n coachman ▷ adj resembling or pertaining to a coach

COACT vb to act together

COACTED ▸ coact

COACTOR ▸ coact

COACTS ▸ coact

COADMIT vb to admit together

COAEVAL n contemporary

COAGENT > **coagency**

COAGULA > **coagulum**

COAITA n spider monkey

COAITAS ▸ coaita

COAL n black rock consisting mainly of carbon, used as fuel ▷ vb take in, or turn into coal

COALA same as ▸ **koala**

COALAS ▸ coala

COALBIN n bin for holding coal

COALBOX n box for holding coal

COALED ▸ coal

COALER n ship, train, etc, used to carry or supply coal

COALERS ▸ coaler

COALIER ▸ coal

COALIFY vb to turn into coal

COALING ▸ coal

COALISE vb to form a coalition

COALIZE same as ▸ **coalise**

COALMAN n man who delivers coal

COALMEN ▸ coalman

COALPIT n pit from which coal is extracted

COALS ▸ coal

COALY ▸ coal

COAMING n raised frame round a ship's hatchway for keeping out water

COANNEX vb to annex with something else

COAPT vb to secure

COAPTED ▸ coapt

COAPTS ▸ coapt

COARB n spiritual successor

COARBS ▸ coarb

COARSE adj rough in texture

COARSEN vb make or become coarse

COARSER ▸ coarse

COAST n place where the land meets the sea ▷ vb move by momentum, without the use of power

COASTAL ▸ coast

COASTED ▸ coast

COASTER n small mat placed under a glass

COASTS ▸ coast

COAT n outer garment with long sleeves ▷ vb cover with a layer

COATE same as ▸ **quote**

COATED adj covered with an outer layer, film, etc

COATEE n short coat, esp for a baby

COATEES ▸ coatee

COATER n machine that applies a coating to something

COATERS ▸ coater
COATES ▸ coate
COATI n type of omnivorous mammal of Central and S America, with a long flexible snout and a brindled coat
COATING n covering layer
COATIS ▸ coati
COATS ▸ coat
COAX vb persuade gently
COAXAL same as ▸ coaxial
COAXED ▸ coax
COAXER ▸ coax
COAXERS ▸ coax
COAXES ▸ coax
COAXIAL adj (of a cable) transmitting by means of two concentric conductors separated by an insulator
COAXING ▸ coax
COB n stalk of an ear of maize ▷ vb beat, esp on the buttocks
COBAEA n tropical American climbing shrub grown for its large trumpet-shaped purple or white flowers
COBAEAS ▸ cobaea
COBALT n brittle silvery-white metallic element
COBALTS ▸ cobalt
COBB same as ▸ cob
COBBED ▸ cob
COBBER n friend
COBBERS ▸ cobber
COBBIER ▸ cobby
COBBING ▸ cob
COBBLE n cobblestone ▷ vb pave (a road) with cobblestones
COBBLED ▸ cobble
COBBLER n shoe mender
COBBLES pl n coal in small rounded lumps
COBBS ▸ cobb
COBBY adj short and stocky
COBIA n large dark-striped game fish of tropical and subtropical seas
COBIAS ▸ cobia
COBLE n small single-masted flat-bottomed fishing boat
COBLES ▸ coble
COBLOAF n round loaf of bread
COBNUT another name for ▸ hazelnut
COBNUTS ▸ cobnut
COBRA n venomous

hooded snake of Asia and Africa
COBRAS ▸ cobra
COBRIC ▸ cobra
COBS ▸ cob
COBURG n rounded loaf with a cross cut on the top
COBURGS ▸ coburg
COBWEB n spider's web
COBWEBS ▸ cobweb
COBZA n Romanian lute
COBZAS ▸ cobza
COCA n dried leaves of a S American shrub which contain cocaine
COCAIN same as ▸ cocaine
COCAINE n addictive drug used as a narcotic and as an anaesthetic
COCAINS ▸ cocain
COCAS ▸ coca
COCCAL ▸ coccus
COCCI ▸ coccus
COCCIC ▸ coccus
COCCID n type of homopterous insect of the family which includes the scale insects
COCCIDS ▸ coccid
COCCO n taro
COCCOID ▸ coccus
COCCOS ▸ cocco
COCCOUS ▸ coccus
COCCUS n any spherical or nearly spherical bacterium, such as a staphylococcus
COCCYX n bone at the base of the spinal column
COCH obsolete variant of ▸ coach
COCHAIR vb to chair jointly
COCHES ▸ coch
COCHIN n large breed of domestic fowl
COCHINS ▸ cochin
COCHLEA n spiral tube in the internal ear, which converts sound vibrations into nerve impulses
COCK n male bird, esp of domestic fowl ▷ vb draw back (the hammer of a gun) to firing position
COCKADE n feather or rosette worn on a hat as a badge
COCKED ▸ cock
COCKER n devotee of cockfighting ▷ vb pamper or spoil by indulgence
COCKERS ▸ cocker
COCKET n document issued by a customs officer

COCKETS ▸ cocket
COCKEYE n eye affected with strabismus or one that squints
COCKIER ▸ cocky
COCKIES ▸ cocky
COCKILY ▸ cocky
COCKING ▸ cock
COCKISH adj wanton
COCKLE n edible shellfish ▷ vb fish for cockles
COCKLED ▸ cockle
COCKLER n person employed to gather cockles
COCKLES ▸ cockle
COCKNEY n native of London, esp of its East End ▷ adj characteristic of cockneys or their dialect
COCKPIT n pilot's compartment in an aircraft
COCKS ▸ cock
COCKSHY n target aimed at in throwing games
COCKSY adj cocky
COCKUP n something done badly ▷ vb ruin or spoil
COCKUPS ▸ cockup
COCKY adj conceited and overconfident ▷ n farmer whose farm is regarded as small or of little account
COCO n coconut palm
COCOA n powder made from the seed of the cacao tree
COCOAS ▸ cocoa
COCOMAT n mat made from coconut fibre
COCONUT n large hard fruit of a type of palm tree
COCOON n silky protective covering of a silkworm ▷ vb wrap up tightly for protection
COCOONS ▸ cocoon
COCOPAN n (in South Africa) a small wagon running on narrow-gauge railway lines used in mines
COCOS ▸ coco
COCOTTE n small fireproof dish in which individual portions of food are cooked
COCOYAM n either of two food plants of West Africa, the taro or the yantia, both of which have edible underground stems
COCTILE adj made by exposing to heat
COCTION n boiling
COD n large food fish of the

North Atlantic ▷ adj having the character of an imitation or parody ▷ vb make fun of

CODA n final part of a musical composition

CODABLE adj capable of being coded

CODAS ▶ coda

CODDED ▶ cod

CODDER n cod fisherman or his boat

CODDERS ▶ codder

CODDING ▶ cod

CODDLE vb pamper, overprotect ▷ n stew made from ham and bacon scraps

CODDLED, ▶ coddle

CODDLER ▶ coddle

CODDLES ▶ coddle

CODE n system of letters, symbols, or prearranged signals by which messages can be communicated secretly or briefly ▷ vb put into code

CODEC n set of equipment that encodes an analogue speech or video signal into digital form for transmission purposes and at the receiving end decodes the digital signal into a form close to its original

CODECS ▶ codec

CODED ▶ code

CODEIA n codeine

CODEIAS ▶ codeia

CODEIN same as ▶ codeine

CODEINA obsolete variant of ▶ codeine

CODEINE n drug used as a painkiller

CODEINS ▶ codein

CODEN n unique six-character code assigned to a publication for identification purposes

CODENS ▶ coden

CODER n person or thing that codes

CODERS ▶ coder

CODES ▶ code

CODETTA n short coda

CODEX n volume of manuscripts of an ancient text

CODFISH n cod

CODGER n old man

CODGERS ▶ codger

CODICES ▶ codex

CODICIL n addition to a will

CODIFY vb organize (rules or procedures) systematically

CODILLA n coarse tow of hemp and flax

CODILLE n in the card game ombre, term indicating that the game is won

CODING ▶ code

CODINGS ▶ code

CODIST n codifier

CODISTS ▶ codist

CODLIN same as ▶ codling

CODLING n young cod

CODLINS ▶ codlin

CODON n unit that consists of three adjacent bases on a DNA molecule and that determines the position of a specific amino acid in a protein molecule during protein synthesis

CODONS ▶ codon

CODRIVE vb take alternate turns driving a car with another person

CODROVE ▶ codrive

CODS ▶ cod

COED adj educating both sexes together ▷ n school or college that educates both sexes together

COEDIT vb edit (a book, newspaper, etc) jointly

COEDITS ▶ coedit

COEDS ▶ coed

COEHORN n type of small artillery mortar

COELIAC adj of or relating to the abdomen ▷ n person who has coeliac disease

COELOM n body cavity of many multicellular animals, situated in the mesoderm and containing the digestive tract and other visceral organs

COELOME same as ▶ coelom

COELOMS ▶ coelom

COEMPT vb buy up something in its entirety

COEMPTS ▶ coempt

COENACT vb to enact jointly

COENURE variant form of > coenurus

COENURI > coenurus

COEQUAL n equal ▷ adj of the same size, rank, etc

COERCE vb compel, force

COERCED ▶ coerce

COERCER ▶ coerce

COERCES ▶ coerce

COERECT vb to erect together

COESITE n polymorph of silicon dioxide

COEVAL n contemporary ▷ adj contemporary

COEVALS ▶ coeval

COEXERT vb to exert together

COEXIST vb exist together, esp peacefully despite differences

COFF vb buy

COFFED ▶ coff

COFFEE n drink made from the roasted and ground seeds of a tropical shrub ▷ adj medium-brown

COFFEES ▶ coffee

COFFER n chest, esp for storing valuables ▷ vb store

COFFERS > cofferdam

COFFIN n box in which a corpse is buried or cremated ▷ vb place in or as in a coffin

COFFING ▶ coff

COFFINS ▶ coffin

COFFLE n (esp formerly) a line of slaves, beasts, etc, fastened together ▷ vb to fasten together in a coffle

COFFLED ▶ coffle

COFFLES ▶ coffle

COFFRET n small coffer

COFFS ▶ coff

COFOUND vb to found jointly

COFT ▶ coff

COG n one of the teeth on the rim of a gearwheel ▷ vb roll (cast-steel ingots) to convert them into blooms

COGENCE ▶ cogent

COGENCY ▶ cogent

COGENER n congener

COGENT adj forcefully convincing

COGGED ▶ cog

COGGER n deceiver

COGGERS ▶ cogger

COGGIE n quaich or drinking cup

COGGIES ▶ coggie

COGGING ▶ cog

COGGLE vb wobble or rock

COGGLED ▶ coggle

COGGLES ▶ coggle

COGGLY ▶ coggle

COGIE same as ▶ coggie

COGIES ▶ cogie

COGITO n philosophical theory that one must exist

because one is capable of thought

COGITOS ▸ cogito
COGNAC n French brandy
COGNACS ▸ cognac
COGNATE adj derived from a common original form ▷ n cognate word or language
COGNISE same as ▸ **cognize**
COGNIZE vb perceive, become aware of, or know
COGON n type of coarse tropical grass used for thatching
COGONS ▸ cogon
COGS ▸ cog
COGUE n wooden pail or drinking vessel
COGUES ▸ cogue
COGWAY n rack railway
COGWAYS ▸ cogway
COHAB n cohabitor
COHABIT vb live together as husband and wife without being married
COHABS ▸ cohab
COHEAD vb to head jointly
COHEADS ▸ cohead
COHEIR n person who inherits jointly with others
COHEIRS ▸ coheir
COHEN ▸ kohen
COHENS ▸ cohen
COHERE vb hold or stick together
COHERED ▸ cohere
COHERER n electrical component formerly used to detect radio waves, consisting of a tube containing loosely packed metal particles. The waves caused the particles to cohere, thereby changing the current through the circuit
COHERES ▸ cohere
COHIBIT vb to restrain
COHO n type of Pacific salmon
COHOE same as ▸ **coho**
COHOES ▸ coho
COHOG n quahog, an edible clam
COHOGS ▸ cohog
COHORN same as ▸ **coehorn**
COHORNS ▸ coehorn
COHORT n band of associates
COHORTS ▸ cohort
COHOS ▸ coho
COHOSH n type of North

American plant
COHOST vb to host jointly
COHOSTS ▸ cohost
COHUNE n tropical American feather palm whose large nuts yield an oil similar to coconut oil
COHUNES ▸ cohune
COIF vb arrange the hair of ▷ n close-fitting cap worn in the Middle Ages
COIFED adj wearing a coif
COIFFE vb to coiffure
COIFFED ▸ coif
COIFFES ▸ coiffe
COIFING ▸ coif
COIFS ▸ coif
COIGN vb wedge ▷ n quoin
COIGNE same as ▸ **coign**
COIGNED ▸ coign
COIGNES ▸ coigne
COIGNS ▸ coign
COIL vb wind in loops ▷ n something coiled
COILED ▸ coil
COILER ▸ coil
COILERS ▸ coil
COILING ▸ coil
COILS ▸ coil
COIN n piece of metal money ▷ vb invent (a word or phrase)
COINAGE n coins collectively
COINED ▸ coin
COINER ▸ coin
COINERS ▸ coin
COINFER vb infer jointly
COINING ▸ coin
COINOP adj (of a machine) operated by putting a coin in a slot
COINS ▸ coin
COINTER vb to inter together
COIR n coconut fibre, used for matting
COIRS ▸ coir
COIT n buttocks
COITAL ▸ coitus
COITION same as ▸ **coitus**
COITS ▸ coit
COITUS n sexual intercourse
COJOIN vb to conjoin
COJOINS ▸ cojoin
COJONES pl n testicles
COKE n solid fuel left after gas has been distilled from coal ▷ vb become or convert into coke
COKED ▸ coke
COKES n fool
COKESES ▸ cokes

COKIER ▸ coky
COKIEST ▸ coky
COKING ▸ coke
COKY adj like coke
COL n high mountain pass
COLA n dark brown fizzy soft drink
COLAS ▸ cola
COLBIES ▸ colby
COLBY n type of mild-tasting hard cheese
COLBYS ▸ colby
COLD adj lacking heat ▷ n lack of heat
COLDER ▸ cold
COLDEST ▸ cold
COLDIE n cold can or bottle of beer
COLDIES ▸ coldie
COLDISH ▸ cold
COLDLY ▸ cold
COLDS ▸ cold
COLE same as ▸ **cabbage**
COLEAD vb to lead together
COLEADS ▸ colead
COLED ▸ colead
COLES ▸ cole
COLETIT n coal tit
COLEUS n Old World plant cultivated for its variegated leaves, typically marked with red, yellow, or white
COLEY same as ▸ **coalfish**
COLEYS ▸ coley
COLIBRI n hummingbird
COLIC n severe pains in the stomach and bowels
COLICIN n bactericidal protein
COLICKY adj relating to or suffering from colic
COLICS ▸ colic
COLIES ▸ coly
COLIN n quail
COLINS ▸ colin
COLITIC ▸ colitis
COLITIS n inflammation of the colon
COLL vb to embrace
COLLAGE n art form in which various materials or objects are glued onto a surface ▷ vb to make a collage
COLLAR n part of a garment round the neck ▷ vb seize, arrest
COLLARD n variety of the cabbage with a crown of edible leaves
COLLARS ▸ collar
COLLATE vb gather together, examine, and put

in order

COLLECT vb gather together ▷ n short prayer

COLLED ▸ coll

COLLEEN n girl

COLLEGE n place of higher education

COLLET n (in a jewellery setting) a band or coronet-shaped claw that holds an individual stone ▷ vb mount in a collet

COLLETS ▸ collet

COLLIDE vb crash together violently

COLLIE n silky-haired sheepdog

COLLIED ▸ colly

COLLIER n coal miner

COLLIES ▸ colly

COLLING n embrace

COLLINS n tall fizzy iced drink made with gin, vodka, rum, etc, mixed with fruit juice, soda water, and sugar

COLLOID n suspension of particles in a solution ▷ adj of or relating to the gluelike translucent material found in certain degenerating tissues

COLLOP n small slice of meat

COLLOPS ▸ collop

COLLS ▸ coll

COLLUDE vb act in collusion

COLLY n soot or grime, such as coal dust ▷ vb begrime

COLOBI ▸ colobus

COLOBID ▸ colobus

COLOBUS n type of leaf-eating arboreal Old World monkey of W and central Africa, with a slender body, long silky fur, and a long tail

COLOG n logarithm of the reciprocal of a number

COLOGNE n mild perfume

COLOGS ▸ colog

COLON n punctuation mark (:)

COLONE same as ▸ colon

COLONEL n senior commissioned army or air-force officer

COLONES ▸ colone

COLONI ▸ colonus

COLONIC adj of or relating to the colon ▷ n irrigation of the colon by injecting large amounts of fluid high into the colon

COLONS ▸ colon

COLONUS n ancient Roman farmer

COLONY n group of people who settle in a new country but remain under the rule of their homeland

COLOR same as ▸ colour

COLORED US spelling of ▸ coloured

COLORER ▸ color

COLORS ▸ color

COLORY same as ▸ coloury

COLOSSI ▸ colossus

COLOUR n appearance of things as a result of reflecting light ▷ vb apply colour to

COLOURS ▸ colour

COLOURY adj possessing colour

COLS ▸ col

COLT n young male horse ▷ vb to fool

COLTAN n metallic ore found esp in the E Congo, consisting of columbite and tantalite and used as a source of tantalum

COLTANS ▸ coltan

COLTED ▸ colt

COLTER same as ▸ coulter

COLTERS ▸ coulter

COLTING ▸ colt

COLTISH adj inexperienced

COLTS ▸ colt

COLUGO n flying lemur

COLUGOS ▸ colugo

COLUMEL n in botany, the central column in a capsule

COLUMN n pillar ▷ vb create a column

COLUMNS ▸ column

COLURE n either of two great circles on the celestial sphere, one of which passes through the celestial poles and the equinoxes and the other through the poles and the solstices

COLURES ▸ colure

COLY n S African arboreal bird with a soft hairlike plumage, crested head, and very long tail

COLZA n oilseed rape, a Eurasian plant with bright yellow flowers

COLZAS ▸ colza

COMA n state of deep unconsciousness

COMADE ▸ comake

COMAE ▸ coma

COMAKE vb to make together

COMAKER ▸ comake

COMAKES ▸ comake

COMAL ▸ coma

COMARB same as ▸ coarb

COMARBS ▸ comarb

COMART n covenant

COMARTS ▸ comart

COMAS ▸ coma

COMATE adj having tufts of hair ▷ n companion

COMATES ▸ comate

COMATIC ▸ coma

COMATIK same as ▸ komatik

COMB n toothed implement for arranging the hair ▷ vb use a comb on

COMBAT vb fight, struggle ▷ n fight or struggle

COMBATS ▸ combat

COMBE same as ▸ comb

COMBED ▸ comb

COMBER n long curling wave

COMBERS ▸ comber

COMBES ▸ combe

COMBI n combination boiler

COMBIER ▸ comby

COMBIES ▸ comby

COMBINE vb join together ▷ n association of people or firms for a common purpose

COMBING ▸ comb

COMBIS ▸ combi

COMBLE n apex; zenith

COMBLES ▸ comble

COMBO n small group of jazz musicians

COMBOS ▸ combo

COMBS ▸ comb

COMBUST adj (of a star or planet) invisible for a period between 24 and 30 days each year due to its proximity to the sun ▷ vb burn

COMBY adj comb-like ▷ n combination boiler

COME vb move towards a place, arrive

COMEDIC adj of or relating to comedy

COMEDO the technical name for ▸ blackhead

COMEDOS ▸ comedo

COMEDY n humorous play, film, or programme

COMELY adj nice-looking

COMER n person who comes

COMERS ▶ comer

COMES ▶ come

COMET n heavenly body with a long luminous tail

COMETH ▶ come

COMETIC ▶ comet

COMETS ▶ comet

COMFIER ▶ comfy

COMFIT n sugar-coated sweet

COMFITS ▶ comfit

COMFORT n physical ease or wellbeing ▷ vb soothe, console

COMFREY n tall plant with bell-shaped flowers

COMFY adj comfortable

COMIC adj humorous, funny ▷ n comedian

COMICAL adj amusing

COMICE n kind of pear

COMICES ▶ comice

COMICS ▶ comic

COMING ▶ come

COMINGS ▶ come

COMIQUE n comic actor

COMITAL adj relating to a count or earl

COMITIA n ancient Roman assembly that elected officials and exercised judicial and legislative authority

COMITY n friendly politeness, esp between different countries

COMIX n comic books in general

COMM n as in comm badge small wearable badge-shaped radio transmitter and receiver

COMMA n punctuation mark (,)

COMMAND vb order ▷ n authoritative instruction that something must be done

COMMAS ▶ comma

COMMATA ▶ comma

COMMEND vb praise

COMMENT n remark ▷ vb make a comment

COMMER same as ▶ comer

COMMERE n female compere

COMMERS ▶ commer

COMMIE adj communist

COMMIES ▶ commie

COMMIS n apprentice waiter or chef ▷ adj (of a waiter or chef) apprentice

COMMIT vb perform (a crime or error)

COMMITS ▶ commit

COMMIX a rare word for ▶ mix

COMMIXT ▶ commix

COMMO short for ▷ communist

COMMODE n seat with a hinged flap concealing a chamber pot

COMMODO same as ▷ comodo

COMMON adj occurring often ▷ n area of grassy land belonging to a community ▷ vb sit at table with strangers

COMMONS n people not of noble birth viewed as forming a political order

COMMOS ▶ commo

COMMOT n in medieval Wales, a division of land

COMMOTE same as ▷ commot

COMMOTS ▶ commot

COMMOVE vb disturb

COMMS pl n communications

COMMUNE n group of people who live together and share everything ▷ vb feel very close (to)

COMMUTE vb travel daily to and from work ▷ n journey made by commuting

COMMY same as ▶ commie

COMODO adv (to be performed) at a convenient relaxed speed

COMOSE another word for ▶ comate

COMOUS adj hairy

COMP n person who sets and corrects type ▷ vb set or correct type

COMPACT adj closely packed ▷ n small flat case containing a mirror and face powder ▷ vb pack closely together

COMPAGE obsolete form of ▷ compages

COMPAND vb (of a transmitter signal) to compress before, and expand after, transmission

COMPANY n business organization ▷ vb associate or keep company with someone

COMPARE vb examine (things) and point out the resemblances or differences

COMPART vb to divide into parts

COMPAS n rhythm in flamenco

COMPASS n instrument for showing direction, with a needle that points north ▷ vb encircle or surround

COMPAST adj rounded

COMPEAR vb in Scots law, to appear in court

COMPED ▶ comp

COMPEER n person of equal rank, status, or ability ▷ vb to equal

COMPEL vb force (to be or do)

COMPELS ▶ compel

COMPEND n compendium

COMPER n person who regularly enters competitions in newspapers, magazines, etc, esp competitions offering consumer goods as prizes

COMPERE n person who presents a stage, radio, or television show ▷ vb be the compere of

COMPERS ▶ comper

COMPETE vb try to win or achieve (a prize, profit, etc)

COMPILE vb collect and arrange (information), esp to make a book

COMPING ▶ comp

COMPLEX adj made up of parts ▷ n whole made up of parts ▷ vb to form a complex

COMPLIN same as ▷ compline

COMPLOT n plot or conspiracy ▷ vb plot together

COMPLY vb act in accordance (with)

COMPO n mixture of materials, such as mortar, plaster, etc ▷ adj intended to last for several days

COMPONE same as ▶ compony

COMPONY adj made up of alternating metal and colour, colour and fur, or fur and metal

COMPORT vb behave (oneself) in a specified way

COMPOS ▶ compo

COMPOSE vb put together

COMPOST n decayed plants used as a fertilizer ▷ vb make (vegetable matter) into compost

COMPOT same as ▶ compote

COMPOTE n fruit stewed with sugar

COMPOTS ▸ compot

COMPS ▸ comp

COMPT obsolete variant of ▸ count

COMPTED ▸ compt

COMPTER n formerly, a prison

COMPTS ▸ count

COMPUTE vb calculate, esp using a computer ▹ n calculation

COMRADE n fellow member of a union or socialist political party

COMS pl n one-piece woollen undergarment with long sleeves and legs

COMTE n European nobleman

COMTES ▸ comte

COMUS n wild party

COMUSES ▸ comus

CON vb deceive, swindle ▹ n convict ▹ prep with

CONACRE n farming land let for a season or for eleven months ▹ vb to let conacre

CONARIA > conarium

CONATUS n effort or striving of natural impulse

CONCAVE adj curving inwards ▹ vb make concave

CONCEAL vb cover and hide

CONCEDE vb admit to be true

CONCEDO interj I allow; I concede (a point)

CONCEIT n too high an opinion of oneself ▹ vb like or be able to bear (something, such as food or drink)

CONCENT n concord, as of sounds, voices, etc

CONCEPT n abstract or general idea

CONCERN n anxiety, worry ▹ vb worry (someone)

CONCERT n musical entertainment

CONCH same as ▸ concha

CONCHA n any bodily organ or part resembling a shell in shape, such as the external ear

CONCHAE ▸ concha

CONCHAL ▸ concha

CONCHAS ▸ concha

CONCHE vb (in chocolate-making) to use a conche (machine which mixes and smooths the chocolate mass)

CONCHED ▸ conche

CONCHES ▸ conche

CONCHIE n conscientious objector

CONCHO n American metal ornament

CONCHOS ▸ concho

CONCHS ▸ conch

CONCHY same as ▸ conchie

CONCISE adj brief and to the point ▹ vb mutilate

CONCOCT vb make up (a story or plan)

CONCORD n state of peaceful agreement, harmony ▹ vb to agree

CONCREW vb to grow together

CONCUPY n concupiscence

CONCUR vb agree

CONCURS ▸ concur

CONCUSS vb injure (the brain) by a fall or blow

COND old inflection of ▸ con

CONDEMN vb express disapproval of

CONDER n person who directs the steering of a vessel

CONDERS ▸ conder

CONDIE n culvert; tunnel

CONDIES ▸ condie

CONDIGN adj (esp of a punishment) fitting

CONDO n condominium

CONDOES ▸ condo

CONDOLE vb express sympathy with someone in grief, pain, etc

CONDOM n rubber sheath worn on the penis or in the vagina during sexual intercourse to prevent conception or infection

CONDOMS ▸ condom

CONDONE vb overlook or forgive (wrongdoing)

CONDOR n large vulture of S America

CONDORS ▸ condor

CONDOS ▸ condo

CONDUCE vb lead or contribute (to a result)

CONDUCT n management of an activity ▹ vb carry out (a task)

CONDUIT n channel or tube for fluid or cables

CONDYLE n rounded projection on the articulating end of a bone, such as the ball portion of a ball-and-socket joint

CONE n object with a circular base, tapering to a point ▹ vb shape like a cone or part of a cone

CONED ▸ cone

CONES ▸ cone

CONEY same as ▸ cony

CONEYS ▸ coney

CONF n online forum

CONFAB n conversation ▹ vb converse

CONFABS ▸ confab

CONFECT vb prepare by combining ingredients

CONFER vb discuss together

CONFERS ▸ confer

CONFESS vb admit (a fault or crime)

CONFEST adj admitted

CONFIDE vb tell someone (a secret)

CONFINE vb keep within bounds ▹ n limit

CONFIRM vb prove to be true

CONFIT n preserve

CONFITS ▸ confit

CONFIX vb to fasten

CONFLUX n merging or following togther, especially of rivers

CONFORM vb comply with accepted standards or customs

CONFS ▸ conf

CONFUSE vb mix up

CONFUTE vb prove wrong

CONGA n dance performed by a number of people in single file ▹ vb dance the conga

CONGAED ▸ conga

CONGAS ▸ conga

CONGE n permission to depart or dismissal, esp when formal ▹ vb to take one's leave

CONGEAL vb (of a liquid) become thick and sticky

CONGED ▸ conge

CONGEE same as ▸ conge

CONGEED ▸ congee

CONGEES ▸ congee

CONGER n large sea eel

CONGERS ▸ conger

CONGES ▸ conge

CONGEST vb crowd or become crowded to excess

CONGII ▸ congius

CONGIUS n unit of liquid measure equal to 1 Imperial gallon

CONGO same as ▸ congou

C

CONGOES ▸ congou
CONGOS ▸ congo
CONGOU n kind of black tea from China
CONGOUS ▸ congou
CONGREE vb to agree
CONGRUE vb to agree
CONI ▸ conus
CONIA same as ▸ **coniine**
CONIAS ▸ coniine
CONIC adj having the shape of a cone
CONICAL adj cone-shaped
CONICS n branch of geometry concerned with the parabola, ellipse, and hyperbola
CONIDIA > conidium
CONIES ▸ cony
CONIFER n cone-bearing tree, such as the fir or pine
CONIINE n colourless poisonous soluble liquid alkaloid found in hemlock
CONIMA n gum resin from the conium hemlock tree
CONIMAS ▸ conima
CONIN same as ▸ **coniine**
CONINE same as ▸ **coniine**
CONINES ▸ conine
CONING ▸ cone
CONINS ▸ conin
CONIUM n N temperate umbelliferous plant, esp hemlock
CONIUMS ▸ conium
CONJECT vb to conjecture
CONJEE vb prepare as, or in, a conjee (a gruel of boiled rice and water)
CONJEED ▸ conjee
CONJEES ▸ conjee
CONJOIN vb join or become joined
CONJURE vb perform tricks that appear to be magic
CONJURY n magic
CONK n nose ▷ vb strike (someone) on the head or nose
CONKED ▸ conk
CONKER n nut of the horse chestnut
CONKERS n game played with conkers tied on strings
CONKIER ▸ conky
CONKING ▸ conk
CONKS ▸ conk
CONKY adj affected by the timber disease, conk
CONN same as ▸ **con**
CONNATE adj existing in a person or thing from birth

CONNE same as ▸ **con**
CONNECT vb join together
CONNED ▸ con
CONNER same as ▸ **conder**
CONNERS ▸ conner
CONNES ▸ conne
CONNIE n tram or bus conductor
CONNIES ▸ connie
CONNING ▸ con
CONNIVE vb allow (wrongdoing) by ignoring it
CONNOTE vb (of a word, phrase, etc) to imply or suggest (associations or ideas) other than the literal meaning
CONNS ▸ conn
CONOID n geometric surface formed by rotating a parabola, ellipse, or hyperbola about one axis ▷ adj conical, cone-shaped
CONOIDS ▸ conoid
CONQUER vb defeat
CONS ▸ con
CONSEIL n advice
CONSENT n agreement, permission ▷ vb permit, agree to
CONSIGN vb put somewhere
CONSIST vb be composed (of)
CONSOL n consolidated annuity, a British government bond
CONSOLE vb comfort in distress ▷ n panel of controls for electronic equipment
CONSOLS pl n irredeemable British government securities carrying annual interest rates of two and a half or four per cent
CONSORT vb keep company (with) ▷ n husband or wife of a monarch
CONSPUE vb spit on with contempt
CONSTER obsolete variant of > **construe**
CONSUL n official representing a state in a foreign country
CONSULS ▸ consul
CONSULT vb go to for advice or information
CONSUME vb eat or drink
CONTACT n communicating ▷ vb get in touch with ▷ interj (formerly) a call made by

the pilot to indicate that an aircraft's ignition is switched on and that the engine is ready for starting by swinging the propeller
CONTAIN vb hold or be capable of holding
CONTE n tale or short story, esp of adventure
CONTECK n contention
CONTEMN vb regard with contempt
CONTEND vb deal with
CONTENT n meaning or substance of a piece of writing ▷ adj satisfied with things as they are ▷ vb make (someone) content
CONTES ▸ conte
CONTEST n competition or struggle ▷ vb dispute, object to
CONTEXT n circumstances of an event or fact
CONTO n former Portuguese monetary unit worth 1000 escudos
CONTORT vb twist out of shape
CONTOS ▸ conto
CONTOUR n outline ▷ vb shape so as to form or follow the contour of something
CONTRA n counter-argument
CONTRAS ▸ contra
CONTRAT old form of > **contract**
CONTROL n power to direct something ▷ vb have power over
CONTUND vb to pummel
CONTUSE vb injure (the body) without breaking the skin
CONURE n small American parrot
CONURES ▸ conure
CONUS n any of several cone-shaped structures, such as the conus medullaris, the lower end of the spinal cord
CONVECT vb to circulate hot air by convection
CONVENE vb gather or summon for a formal meeting
CONVENT n building where nuns live ▷ vb to summon
CONVERT vb change in form, character, or function ▷ n person who has

converted to a different belief or religion

CONVEX adj curving outwards ▷ vb make convex

CONVEY vb communicate (information)

CONVEYS ▶ convey

CONVICT vb declare guilty ▷ n person serving a prison sentence ▷ adj convicted

CONVIVE vb to feast together

CONVO n conversation

CONVOKE vb call together

CONVOS ▶ convo

CONVOY n group of vehicles or ships travelling together ▷ vb escort while in transit

CONVOYS ▶ convoy

CONY n rabbit

COO vb (of a dove or pigeon) make a soft murmuring sound ▷ n sound of cooing ▷ interj exclamation of surprise, awe, etc

COOCOO old spelling of ▶ cuckoo

COOED ▶ coo

COOEE interj call to attract attention ▷ vb utter this call ▷ n calling distance

COOEED ▶ cooee

COOEES ▶ cooee

COOER ▶ coo

COOERS ▶ coo

COOEY same as ▶ cooee

COOEYED ▶ cooey

COOEYS ▶ cooey

COOF n simpleton

COOFS ▶ coof

COOING ▶ coo

COOINGS ▶ coo

COOK vb prepare (food) by heating ▷ n person who cooks food

COOKED ▶ cook

COOKER n apparatus for cooking heated by gas or electricity

COOKERS ▶ cooker

COOKERY n art of cooking

COOKEY same as ▶ cookie

COOKEYS ▶ cookey

COOKIE n biscuit

COOKIES ▶ cookie

COOKING ▶ cook

COOKOFF n cookery competition

COOKOUT n party where a meal is cooked and eaten out of doors

COOKS ▶ cook

COOKTOP n flat unit for cooking in saucepans or the top part of a stove

COOKY same as ▶ cookie

COOL adj moderately cold ▷ vb make or become cool ▷ n coolness

COOLANT n fluid used to cool machinery while it is working

COOLED ▶ cool

COOLER n container for making or keeping things cool

COOLERS ▶ cooler

COOLEST ▶ cool

COOLIE n unskilled Oriental labourer

COOLIES ▶ coolie

COOLING n as in **regenerative cooling** a method of cooling rocket combustion chambers

COOLISH ▶ cool

COOLLY ▶ cool

COOLS ▶ cool

COOLTH n coolness

COOLTHS ▶ coolth

COOLY same as ▶ coolie

COOM n waste material, such as dust from coal, grease from axles, etc ▷ vb to blacken

COOMB same as ▶ comb

COOMBE ▶ comb

COOMBES ▶ coombe

COOMBS ▶ coomb

COOMED ▶ coom

COOMIER ▶ coomy

COOMING ▶ coom

COOMS ▶ coom

COOMY adj grimy

COON n raccoon

COONCAN n card game for two players, similar to rummy

COONDOG n dog trained to hunt raccoons

COONS ▶ coon

COONTIE n evergreen plant of S Florida, with large dark green leathery leaves

COONTY same as ▶ coontie

COOP n cage or pen for poultry ▷ vb confine in a restricted area

COOPED ▶ coop

COOPER n person who makes or repairs barrels ▷ vb make or mend (barrels, casks, etc)

COOPERS ▶ cooper

COOPERY same as > cooperage

COOPING ▶ coop

COOPS ▶ coop

COOPT vb add (someone) to a group by the agreement of the existing members

COOPTED ▶ coopt

COOPTS ▶ coopt

COORIE same as ▶ courie

COORIED ▶ coorie

COORIES ▶ coorie

COOS ▶ coo

COOSEN same as ▶ cozen

COOSENS ▶ coosen

COOSER n stallion

COOSERS ▶ cooser

COOSIN same as ▶ cozen

COOSINS ▶ coosin

COOST Scots form of ▶ cast

COOT n small black water bird

COOTCH n hiding place ▷ vb hide

COOTER n type of freshwater turtle

COOTERS ▶ cooter

COOTIE ▶ louse

COOTIES ▶ cootie

COOTS ▶ coot

COP same as ▶ copper

COPAIBA n resin obtained from certain tropical S American trees, used in varnishes and ointments

COPAIVA same as ▶ copaiba

COPAL n resin used in varnishes

COPALM n aromatic brown resin obtained from the sweet gum tree

COPALMS ▶ copalm

COPALS ▶ copal

COPAY n amount payable for treatment by person with medical insurance

COPAYS ▶ copay

COPE vb deal successfully (with) ▷ n large ceremonial cloak worn by some Christian priests

COPECK same as ▶ kopeck

COPECKS ▶ copeck

COPED ▶ cope

COPEN n shade of blue

COPENS ▶ copen

COPEPOD n type of minute crustacean of marine and fresh waters, which is an important constituent of plankton

COPER n horse-dealer ▷ vb smuggle liquor to deep-sea fishermen

COPERED ▶ coper

COPERS ▶ coper

COPES ▸ cope

COPIED ▸ copy

COPIER n machine that copies

COPIERS ▸ copier

COPIES ▸ copy

COPIHUE n Chilean bellflower

COPILOT n second pilot of an aircraft

COPING n sloping top row of a wall

COPINGS ▸ coping

COPIOUS adj abundant, plentiful

COPITA n tulip-shaped sherry glass

COPITAS ▸ copita

COPLOT vb plot together

COPLOTS ▸ coplot

COPOUT n act of avoiding responsibility

COPOUTS ▸ copout

COPPED ▸ copper

COPPER n soft reddish-brown metal ▷ adj reddish-brown ▷ vb coat or cover with copper

COPPERS ▸ copper

COPPERY ▸ copper

COPPICE n small group of trees growing close together ▷ vb trim back (trees or bushes) to form a coppice

COPPIES ▸ coppy

COPPIN n ball of thread

COPPING ▸ copper

COPPINS ▸ coppin

COPPLE n hill rising to a point

COPPLES ▸ copple

COPPRA same as ▸ copra

COPPRAS ▸ coppra

COPPY n small wooden stool

COPRA n dried oil-yielding kernel of the coconut

COPRAH same as ▸ copra

COPRAHS ▸ coprah

COPRAS ▸ copra

COPS ▸ copper

COPSE same as ▸ coppice

COPSED ▸ copse

COPSES ▸ copse

COPSHOP n police station

COPSIER ▸ copsy

COPSING ▸ copse

COPSY adj having copses

COPTER n helicopter

COPTERS ▸ copter

COPULA n verb used to link the subject and complement of a sentence

COPULAE ▸ copula

COPULAR ▸ copula

COPULAS ▸ copula

COPY n thing made to look exactly like another ▷ vb make a copy of

COPYBOY n formerly, in journalism, boy who carried copy and ran errands

COPYCAT n person who imitates or copies someone ▷ vb to imitate with great attention to detail

COPYING ▸ copy

COPYISM n slavish copying

COPYIST n person who makes written copies

COQUET vb behave flirtatiously

COQUETS ▸ coquet

COQUINA n soft limestone consisting of shells, corals, etc, that occurs in parts of the US

COQUITO n Chilean palm tree yielding edible nuts and a syrup

COR interj exclamation of surprise, amazement, or admiration

CORACLE n small round boat of wicker covered with skins

CORAL n hard substance formed from the skeletons of very small sea animals ▷ adj orange-pink

CORALLA > corallum

CORALS ▸ coral

CORAM prep before, in the presence of

CORANTO same as > courante

CORBAN n gift to God

CORBANS ▸ corban

CORBE obsolete variant of ▸ corbel

CORBEAU n blackish green colour

CORBEIL n carved ornament in the form of a basket of fruit, flowers, etc

CORBEL n stone or timber support sticking out of a wall ▷ vb lay (a stone or brick) so that it forms a corbel

CORBELS ▸ corbel

CORBES ▸ corbe

CORBIE n raven or crow

CORBIES ▸ corbie

CORBINA n type of North American whiting

CORBY same as ▸ corbie

CORCASS n in Ireland, marshland

CORD n thin rope or thick string ▷ adj (of fabric) ribbed ▷ vb bind or furnish with a cord or cords

CORDAGE n lines and rigging of a vessel

CORDATE adj heart-shaped

CORDED adj tied or fastened with cord

CORDER ▸ cord

CORDERS ▸ cord

CORDIAL adj warm and friendly ▷ n drink with a fruit base

CORDING ▸ cord

CORDITE n explosive used in guns and bombs

CORDOBA n standard monetary unit of Nicaragua, divided into 100 centavos

CORDON n chain of police, soldiers, etc, guarding an area ▷ vb put or form a cordon (around)

CORDONS ▸ cordon

CORDS pl n trousers made of corduroy

CORE n central part of certain fruits, containing the seeds ▷ vb remove the core from

CORED ▸ core

COREIGN vb to reign jointly

CORELLA n white Australian cockatoo

COREMIA > coremium

CORER ▸ core

CORERS ▸ core

CORES ▸ core

CORF n wagon or basket used formerly in mines

CORGI n short-legged sturdy dog

CORGIS ▸ corgi

CORIA ▸ corium

CORIES ▸ cory

CORING ▸ core

CORIOUS adj leathery

CORIUM n deep inner layer of the skin, beneath the epidermis, containing connective tissue, blood vessels, and fat

CORIUMS ▸ corium

CORIVAL same as > corrival

CORIXID n type of water bug

CORK n thick light bark of a

Mediterranean oak ▷ *vb* seal with a cork ▷ *adj* made of cork

CORKAGE *n* restaurant's charge for serving wine bought elsewhere

CORKED *adj* (of wine) spoiled through having a decayed cork

CORKER *n* splendid or outstanding person or thing

CORKERS ▶ corker

CORKIER ▶ corky

CORKING *adj* excellent

CORKIR *n* lichen from which red or purple dye is made

CORKIRS ▶ corkir

CORKS ▶ cork

CORKY same as ▶ corked

CORM *n* bulblike underground stem of certain plants

CORMEL *n* new small corm arising from the base of a fully developed one

CORMELS ▶ cormel

CORMOID *adj* like a corm

CORMOUS ▶ corm

CORMS ▶ corm

CORMUS *n* corm

CORN *n* cereal plant such as wheat or oats ▷ *vb* feed (animals) with corn, esp oats

CORNAGE *n* rent fixed according to the number of horned cattle pastured

CORNCOB *n* core of an ear of maize, to which the kernels are attached

CORNEA *n* transparent membrane covering the eyeball

CORNEAE ▶ cornea

CORNEAL ▶ cornea

CORNEAS ▶ cornea

CORNED *adj* (esp of beef) cooked and then preserved or pickled in salt or brine, now often canned

CORNEL *n* type of plant such as the dogwood and dwarf cornel

CORNELS ▶ cornel

CORNER *n* area or angle where two converging lines or surfaces meet ▷ *vb* force into a difficult or inescapable position

CORNERS ▶ corner

CORNET same as ▶ cornett

CORNETS ▶ cornet

CORNETT *n* musical instrument consisting of a straight or curved tube of wood or ivory having finger holes like a recorder and a cup-shaped mouthpiece like a trumpet

CORNFED *adj* fed on corn

CORNFLY *n* small fly whose larvae cause swollen, gouty stems in cereal crops

CORNI ▶ corno

CORNICE *n* decorative moulding round the top of a wall ▷ *vb* furnish or decorate with or as if with a cornice

CORNIER ▶ corny

CORNIFY *vb* turn soft tissue hard

CORNILY ▶ corny

CORNING ▶ corn

CORNIST *n* horn-player

CORNO *n* French horn

CORNROW *n* hairstyle in which the hair is plaited in close parallel rows ▷ *vb* style the hair in a cornrow

CORNS ▶ corn

CORNU *n* part or structure resembling a horn or having a hornlike pattern, such as a cross section of the grey matter of the spinal cord

CORNUA ▶ cornu

CORNUAL ▶ cornu

CORNUS *n* any member of the genus Cornus, such as dogwood

CORNUTE *adj* having or resembling cornua ▷ *vb* to make a cuckold of

CORNUTO *n* cuckold

CORNY *adj* unoriginal or oversentimental

CORODY *n* (originally) the right of a lord to receive free quarters from his vassal

COROLLA *n* petals of a flower collectively

CORONA *n* ring of light round the moon or sun

CORONAE ▶ corona

CORONAL *n* circlet for the head ▷ *adj* of or relating to a corona or coronal

CORONAS ▶ corona

CORONEL *n* iron head of a tilting spear

CORONER *n* official responsible for the investigation of violent, sudden, or suspicious deaths

CORONET *n* small crown

CORONIS *n* in Greek grammar, symbol placed over a contracted syllable

COROZO *n* tropical American palm whose seeds yield a useful oil

COROZOS ▶ corozo

CORPORA ▶ corpus

CORPS *n* military unit with a specific function

CORPSE *n* dead body ▷ *vb* laugh or cause to laugh involuntarily or inopportunely while on stage

CORPSED ▶ corpse

CORPSES ▶ corpse

CORPUS *n* collection of writings, esp by a single author

CORRADE *vb* (of rivers, streams, etc) to erode (land) by the abrasive action of rock particles

CORRAL *n* enclosure for cattle or horses ▷ *vb* put in a corral

CORRALS ▶ corral

CORREA *n* Australian evergreen shrub with large showy tubular flowers

CORREAS ▶ correa

CORRECT *adj* free from error, true ▷ *vb* put right

CORRIDA *the Spanish word for* ▶ bullfight

CORRIE same as ▶ cirque

CORRIES ▶ corrie

CORRODE *vb* eat or be eaten away by chemical action or rust

CORRODY same as ▶ corody

CORRUPT *adj* open to or involving bribery ▷ *vb* make corrupt

CORS ▶ cor

CORSAC *n* type of fox of central Asia

CORSACS ▶ corsac

CORSAGE *n* small bouquet worn on the bodice of a dress

CORSAIR *n* pirate

CORSE *n* corpse

CORSES ▶ corse

CORSET *n* women's close-fitting undergarment worn to shape the torso ▷ *vb* dress or enclose in, or as in, a corset

CORSETS ▸ corset

CORSEY n pavement or pathway

CORSEYS ▸ corsey

CORSIVE n corrodent

CORSLET same as ▸ **corselet**

CORSNED n ordeal whereby an accused person had to eat a morsel of bread; swallowing it freely indicated innocence; choking, guilt

CORSO n promenade

CORSOS ▸ corso

CORTEGE n funeral procession

CORTEX n outer layer of the brain or other internal organ

CORTILE n open, internal courtyard

CORTILI ▸ cortile

CORTIN n adrenal cortex extract containing cortisone and other hormones

CORTINA n weblike part of certain mushrooms

CORTINS ▸ cortin

CORULER n joint ruler

CORVEE n day's unpaid labour owed by a feudal vassal to his lord

CORVEES ▸ corvee

CORVES ▸ corf

CORVET same as ▸ **curvet**

CORVETS ▸ corvet

CORVID n any member of the crow family

CORVIDS ▸ corvid

CORVINA same as ▸ **corbina**

CORVINE adj of, relating to, or resembling a crow

CORVUS n type of ancient hook

CORY n catfish belonging to the South American Corydoras genus

CORYLUS n hazel genus

CORYMB n flat-topped flower cluster with the stems growing progressively shorter towards the centre ▸ vb be corymb-like

CORYMBS ▸ corymb

CORYPHE n coryphaeus

CORYZA n acute inflammation of the mucous membrane of the nose, with discharge of mucus

CORYZAL ▸ coryza

CORYZAS ▸ coryza

COS same as ▸ **cosine**

COSE vb get cosy

COSEC same as ▸ **cosecant**

COSECH n hyperbolic cosecant

COSECHS ▸ cosech

COSECS ▸ cosec

COSED ▸ cose

COSES ▸ cose

COSET n mathematical set

COSETS ▸ coset

COSEY n tea cosy

COSEYS ▸ cosey

COSH n heavy blunt weapon ▸ vb hit with a cosh

COSHED ▸ cosh

COSHER vb pamper or coddle

COSHERS ▸ cosher

COSHERY n Irish chief's right to lodge at his tenants' houses

COSHES ▸ cosh

COSHING ▸ cosh

COSIE same as ▸ **cosy**

COSIED ▸ cosy

COSIER n cobbler

COSIERS ▸ cosier

COSIES ▸ cosy

COSIEST ▸ cosy

COSIGN vb to sign jointly

COSIGNS ▸ cosign

COSILY ▸ cosy

COSINE n (in trigonometry) ratio of the length of the adjacent side to that of the hypotenuse in a right-angled triangle

COSINES ▸ cosine

COSING ▸ cose

COSMEA n plant of the genus Cosmos

COSMEAS ▸ cosmea

COSMIC adj of the whole universe

COSMID n segment of DNA

COSMIDS ▸ cosmid

COSMIN same as ▸ **cosmine**

COSMINE n substance resembling dentine, forming the outer layer of cosmoid scales

COSMINS ▸ cosmin

COSMISM n Russian cultural and philosophical movement

COSMIST ▸ cosmism

COSMOID adj (of the scales of coelacanths and lungfish) consisting of two inner bony layers and an outer layer of cosmine

COSMOS n universe

COSS another name for ▸ **kos**

COSSACK n Slavonic warrior-peasant who served in the Russian cavalry under the tsars

COSSES ▸ coss

COSSET vb pamper ▸ n any pet animal, esp a lamb

COSSETS ▸ cosset

COSSIE n informal name for a swimming costume

COSSIES ▸ cossie

COST n amount of money, time, labour, etc, required for something ▸ vb have as its cost

COSTA n riblike part, such as the midrib of a plant leaf

COSTAE ▸ costa

COSTAL n strengthening rib of an insect's wing

COSTALS ▸ costal

COSTAR n actor who shares the billing with another ▸ vb share the billing with another actor

COSTARD n English variety of apple tree

COSTARS ▸ costar

COSTATE adj having ribs

COSTE vb to draw near

COSTEAN vb to mine for lodes

COSTED ▸ cost

COSTER n person who sells fruit, vegetables etc from a barrow

COSTERS ▸ coster

COSTES ▸ coste

COSTING n as in **marginal costing** a method of cost accounting

COSTIVE adj having or causing constipation

COSTLY adj expensive

COSTREL n flask, usually of earthenware or leather

COSTS ▸ cost

COSTUME n style of dress of a particular place or time, or for a particular activity ▸ vb provide with a costume

COSTUS n Himalayan herb with an aromatic root

COSY adj warm and snug ▸ n cover for keeping things warm ▸ vb to make oneself snug and warm

COSYING ▸ cosy

COT n baby's bed with high sides ▸ vb entangle or become entangled

COTAN same as ▸ **cotangent**
COTANS ▸ **cotangent**
COTE ▸ **cot**
COTEAU n hillside
COTEAUX ▸ **coteau**
COTED ▸ **cot**
COTERIE n exclusive group, clique
COTES ▸ **cote**
COTH n hyperbolic cotangent
COTHS ▸ **coth**
COTHURN same as ▸ **cothurnus**
COTIDAL adj (of a line on a tidal chart) joining points at which high tide occurs simultaneously
COTING ▸ **cot**
COTINGA n tropical American bird such as the umbrella bird and the cock-of-the-rock, with a broad slightly hooked bill
COTISE same as ▸ **cottise**
COTISED ▸ **cotise**
COTISES ▸ **cotise**
COTLAND n grounds that belong to a cotter
COTS ▸ **cot**
COTT same as ▸ **cot**
COTTA n short form of surplice
COTTAE ▸ **cotta**
COTTAGE n small house in the country ▸ vb engage in homosexual activity in a public lavatory
COTTAR same as ▸ **cotter**
COTTARS ▸ **cottar**
COTTAS ▸ **cotta**
COTTED ▸ **cot**
COTTER n pin or wedge used to secure machine parts ▸ vb secure (two parts) with a cotter
COTTERS ▸ **cottier**
COTTID n type of fish typically with a large head, tapering body, and spiny fins
COTTIDS ▸ **cottid**
COTTIER same as ▸ **cotter**
COTTING ▸ **cot**
COTTISE n type of heraldic decoration ▸ vb (in heraldry) decorate with a cottise
COTTOID adj resembling a fish of the genus Cottus
COTTON n white downy fibre covering the seeds of a tropical plant ▸ vb take a liking

COTTONS ▸ **cotton**
COTTONY ▸ **cotton**
COTTOWN Scots variant of ▸ **cotton**
COTTS ▸ **cott**
COTTUS n type of fish with four yellowish knobs on its head
COTWAL n Indian police officer
COTWALS ▸ **cotwal**
COTYLAE ▸ **cotyle**
COTYLE n cuplike cavity
COTYLES ▸ **cotyle**
COTYPE n additional type specimen from the same brood as the original type specimen
COTYPES ▸ **cotype**
COUCAL n type of ground-living bird of Africa, S Asia, and Australia, with long strong legs
COUCALS ▸ **coucal**
COUCH n piece of upholstered furniture for seating more than one person ▸ vb express in a particular way
COUCHE adj in heraldry (of a shield), tilted
COUCHED ▸ **couch**
COUCHEE n reception held late at night
COUCHER ▸ **couch**
COUCHES ▸ **couch**
COUDE adj (of a reflecting telescope) having plane mirrors positioned to reflect light from the primary mirror along the axis onto a detector
COUGAN n drunk and rowdy person
COUGANS ▸ **cougan**
COUGAR n puma
COUGARS ▸ **cougar**
COUGH vb expel air from the lungs abruptly and noisily ▸ n act or sound of coughing
COUGHED ▸ **cough**
COUGHER ▸ **cough**
COUGHS ▸ **cough**
COUGUAR same as ▸ **cougar**
COULD ▸ **can**
COULDST vb form of 'could' used with the pronoun thou or its relative form
COULEE n flow of molten lava
COULEES ▸ **coulee**

COULIS n thin purée of vegetables or fruit, usually served as a sauce surrounding a dish
COULOIR n deep gully on a mountain side, esp in the French Alps
COULOMB n SI unit of electric charge
COULTER n blade at the front of a ploughshare
COUNCIL n group meeting for discussion or consultation ▸ adj of or by a council
COUNSEL n advice or guidance ▸ vb give guidance to
COUNT vb say numbers in order ▸ n counting
COUNTED ▸ **count**
COUNTER n long flat surface in a bank or shop, on which business is transacted ▸ vb oppose, retaliate against ▸ adv in the opposite direction
COUNTRY n nation
COUNTS ▸ **count**
COUNTY n (in some countries) division of a country ▸ adj upper-class
COUP n successful action ▸ vb turn or fall over
COUPE n sports car with two doors and a sloping fixed roof
COUPED ▸ **coup**
COUPEE n (in dance) a forward movement on one leg, with the other slightly bent and raised
COUPEES ▸ **coupee**
COUPER n dealer
COUPERS ▸ **couper**
COUPES ▸ **coupe**
COUPING ▸ **coup**
COUPLE n two people who are married or romantically involved ▸ vb connect, associate
COUPLED ▸ **couple**
COUPLER n link or rod transmitting power between two rotating mechanisms or a rotating part and a reciprocating part
COUPLES ▸ **couple**
COUPLET n two consecutive lines of verse, usu rhyming and of the same metre
COUPON n piece of paper

entitling the holder to a discount or gift

COUPONS ▶ coupon

COUPS ▶ coup

COUPURE n entrenchment made by beseiged forces behind a breach in their defences

COUR obsolete variant of ▶ cover

COURAGE n ability to face danger or pain without fear

COURANT n courante ▷ adj (of an animal) running

COURB vb to bend

COURBED ▶ courb

COURBS ▶ courb

COURD obsolete variant of ▶ covered

COURE obsolete variant of ▶ cover

COURED ▶ coure

COURES ▶ coure

COURIE vb nestle or snuggle

COURIED ▶ courie

COURIER n person employed to look after holiday-makers ▷ vb send (a parcel, letter, etc) by courier

COURIES ▶ courie

COURING ▶ cour

COURLAN another name for ▶ limpkin

COURS ▶ cour

COURSE n series of lessons or medical treatment ▷ vb (of liquid) run swiftly

COURSED ▶ course

COURSER n swift horse

COURSES another word for ▶ menses

COURT n body which decides legal cases ▷ vb try to gain the love of

COURTED ▶ court

COURTER n suitor

COURTLY adj ceremoniously polite

COURTS ▶ court

COUSIN n child of one's uncle or aunt

COUSINS ▶ cousin

COUTA n traditional Australian sailing boat

COUTAS ▶ couta

COUTEAU n large two-edged knife used formerly as a weapon

COUTER n armour designed to protect the elbow

COUTERS ▶ couter

COUTH adj refined ▷ n refinement

COUTHER ▶ couth

COUTHIE adj sociable

COUTHS ▶ couth

COUTHY same as ▶ couthie

COUTIL n type of tightly-woven twill cloth

COUTILS ▶ coutil

COUTURE n high-fashion designing and dressmaking ▷ adj relating to high fashion design and dress-making

COUVADE n custom in certain cultures of treating the husband of a woman giving birth as if he were bearing the child

COUVERT another word for ▶ cover

COUZIN n South African word for a friend

COUZINS ▶ couzin

COVARY vb vary together maintaining a certain mathematical relationship

COVE n small bay or inlet ▷ vb form an architectural cove in

COVED ▶ cove

COVELET n small cove

COVEN n meeting of witches

COVENS ▶ coven

COVENT same as ▶ convent

COVENTS ▶ covent

COVER vb place something over, to protect or conceal ▷ n anything that covers

COVERED ▶ cover

COVERER ▶ cover

COVERS ▶ cover

COVERT adj concealed, secret ▷ n thicket giving shelter to game birds or animals

COVERTS ▶ covert

COVERUP n concealment of a mistake, crime, etc

COVES ▶ cove

COVET vb long to possess (what belongs to someone else)

COVETED ▶ covet

COVETER ▶ covet

COVETS ▶ covet

COVEY n small flock of grouse or partridge

COVEYS ▶ covey

COVIN n conspiracy between two or more persons to act to the detriment or injury of another

COVING same as ▶ cove

COVINGS ▶ coving

COVINS ▶ covin

COVYNE same as ▶ covin

COVYNES ▶ covyne

COW n mature female of cattle and of certain other mammals, such as the elephant or seal ▷ vb intimidate, subdue

COWAGE n tropical climbing plant whose bristly pods cause severe itching and stinging

COWAGES ▶ cowage

COWAL n shallow lake or swampy depression supporting vegetation

COWALS ▶ cowal

COWAN n drystone waller

COWANS ▶ cowan

COWARD n person who lacks courage ▷ vb show (someone) up to be a coward

COWARDS ▶ coward

COWBANE n N temperate poisonous marsh plant with clusters of small white flowers

COWBELL n bell hung around a cow's neck

COWBIND n any of various bryony plants, esp the white bryony

COWBIRD n American oriole with a dark plumage and short bill

COWBOY n (in the US) ranch worker who herds and tends cattle, usu on horseback ▷ vb work or behave as a cowboy

COWBOYS ▶ cowboy

COWED ▶ cow

COWEDLY ▶ cow

COWER vb cringe in fear

COWERED ▶ cower

COWERS ▶ cower

COWFISH n type of trunkfish with hornlike spines over the eyes

COWFLAP n cow dung

COWFLOP n foxglove

COWGIRL n female cowboy

COWHAGE same as ▶ cowage

COWHAND same as ▶ cowboy

COWHEEL n heel of a cow, used as cooking ingredient

COWHERB n European plant with clusters of pink flowers

COWHERD n person employed to tend cattle
COWHIDE n hide of a cow ▷ vb to lash with a cowhide whip
COWIER ▸ cowy
COWIEST ▸ cowy
COWING ▸ cow
COWISH adj cowardly
COWITCH another name for ▸ cowage
COWK vb retch or feel nauseated
COWKED ▸ cowk
COWKING ▸ cowk
COWKS ▸ cowk
COWL same as ▸ cowling
COWLED adj wearing a cowl
COWLICK n tuft of hair over the forehead
COWLING n cover on an engine
COWLS ▸ cowl
COWMAN n man who owns cattle
COWMEN ▸ cowman
COWP same as ▸ coup
COWPAT n pool of cow dung
COWPATS ▸ cowpat
COWPEA n type of tropical climbing plant producing long pods with edible pealike seeds
COWPEAS ▸ cowpea
COWPED ▸ cowp
COWPIE n cowpat
COWPIES ▸ cowpie
COWPING ▸ cowp
COWPLOP n cow dung
COWPOKE n cowboy
COWPOX n disease of cows, the virus of which is used in the smallpox vaccine
COWPS ▸ cowp
COWRIE n brightly-marked sea shell
COWRIES ▸ cowrie
COWRITE vb to write jointly
COWROTE ▸ cowrite
COWRY same as ▸ cowrie
COWS ▸ cow
COWSHED n byre
COWSKIN same as ▸ cowhide
COWSLIP n small yellow wild European flower
COWTREE n South American tree that produces latex
COWY adj cowlike
COX n coxswain ▷ vb act as cox of (a boat)
COXA n technical name for the hipbone or hip joint

COXAE ▸ coxa
COXAL ▸ coxa
COXALGY same as ▸ coxalgia
COXCOMB same as ▸ cockscomb
COXED ▸ cox
COXES ▸ cox
COXIB n anti-inflammatory drug used to treat osteoarthritis
COXIBS ▸ coxib
COXIER ▸ coxy
COXIEST ▸ coxy
COXING ▸ cox
COXITIS n inflammation of the hip joint
COXLESS ▸ cox
COXY adj cocky
COY adj affectedly shy or modest ▷ vb to caress
COYDOG n cross between a coyote and a dog
COYDOGS ▸ coydog
COYED ▸ coy
COYER ▸ coy
COYEST ▸ coy
COYING ▸ coy
COYISH ▸ coy
COYLY ▸ coy
COYNESS ▸ coy
COYOTE n prairie wolf of N America
COYOTES ▸ coyote
COYPOU same as ▸ coypu
COYPOUS ▸ coypou
COYPU n beaver-like aquatic rodent native to S America, bred for its fur
COYPUS ▸ coypu
COYS ▸ coy
COZ archaic word for ▸ cousin

> **Coz** is an old word for **cousin**, and a good one to know for using the Z.

COZE vb to chat
COZED ▸ coze
COZEN vb cheat, trick
COZENED ▸ cozen
COZENER ▸ cozen
COZENS ▸ cozen
COZES ▸ coze
COZEY n tea cosy
COZEYS ▸ cozey
COZIE same as ▸ cozey
COZIED ▸ cosy
COZIER n cobbler
COZIERS ▸ cozier
COZIES ▸ cozey
COZIEST ▸ cozy
COZILY ▸ cozy
COZING ▸ coze
COZY ▸ cosy

COZYING ▸ cozy
COZZES ▸ coz
CRAAL vb to enclose in a craal (or kraal)
CRAALED ▸ craal
CRAALS ▸ craal
CRAB n edible shellfish with ten legs, the first pair modified into pincers
CRABBED ▸ crab
CRABBER n crab fisherman
CRABBIT adj bad-tempered
CRABBY adj bad-tempered
CRABS ▸ crab
CRACK vb break or split partially ▷ n sudden sharp noise ▷ adj first-rate, excellent
CRACKED adj damaged by cracking ▷ n sharp noise
CRACKER n thin dry biscuit
CRACKET n low stool, often one with three legs
CRACKLE vb make small sharp popping noises ▷ n crackling sound
CRACKLY adj making a cracking sound
CRACKS ▸ crack
CRACKUP n physical or mental breakdown
CRACKY adj full of cracks
CRACOWE n medieval shoe with a sharply pointed toe
CRADLE n baby's bed on rockers ▷ vb hold gently as if in a cradle
CRADLED ▸ cradle
CRADLER ▸ cradle
CRADLES ▸ cradle
CRAFT n occupation requiring skill with the hands ▷ vb make skilfully
CRAFTED ▸ craft
CRAFTER n person doing craftwork
CRAFTS ▸ craft
CRAFTY adj skilled in deception
CRAG n steep rugged rock
CRAGGED same as ▸ craggy
CRAGGY adj having many crags
CRAGS ▸ crag
CRAIC n Irish word meaning fun
CRAICS ▸ craic
CRAIG a Scots word for ▸ crag
CRAIGS ▸ craig
CRAKE n bird of the rail family, such as the corncrake ▷ vb to boast
CRAKED ▸ crake**

CRAKES ▸ crake

CRAKING ▸ crake

CRAM vb force into too small a space ▷ n act or condition of cramming

CRAMBE n any plant of the genus Crambe

CRAMBES ▸ crambe

CRAMBO n word game in which one team says a rhyme or rhyming line for a word or line given by the other team

CRAMBOS ▸ crambo

CRAME n merchant's booth or stall

CRAMES ▸ crame

CRAMESY same as ▸ cramoisy

CRAMMED ▸ cram

CRAMMER n person or school that prepares pupils for an examination

CRAMP n painful muscular contraction ▷ vb affect with a cramp

CRAMPED adj closed in

CRAMPER n spiked metal plate used as a brace for the feet in throwing the stone

CRAMPET n cramp iron

CRAMPIT same as ▸ crampet

CRAMPON n spiked plate strapped to a boot for climbing on ice ▷ vb climb using crampons

CRAMPS ▸ cramp

CRAMPY adj affected with cramp

CRAMS ▸ cram

CRAN n unit of capacity used for measuring fresh herring, equal to 37.5 gallons

CRANAGE n use of a crane

CRANCH vb to crunch

CRANE n machine for lifting and moving heavy weights ▷ vb stretch (one's neck) to see something

CRANED ▸ crane

CRANES ▸ crane

CRANIA ▸ cranium

CRANIAL adj of or relating to the skull

CRANING ▸ crane

CRANIUM n skull

CRANK n arm projecting at right angles from a shaft, for transmitting or converting motion ▷ vb turn with a crank ▷ adj (of a

sailing vessel) easily keeled over by the wind

CRANKED ▸ crank

CRANKER ▸ crank

CRANKLE vb to bend or wind

CRANKLY adj vigorously

CRANKS ▸ crank

CRANKY same as ▸ crank

CRANNOG n ancient Celtic lake or bog dwelling dating from the late Bronze Age to the 16th century AD

CRANNY n narrow opening ▷ vb to become full of crannies

CRANS ▸ cran

CRANTS n garland carried in front of a maiden's bier

CRAP n rubbish, nonsense ▷ vb defecate

CRAPAUD n frog or toad

CRAPE same as ▸ crepe

CRAPED ▸ crape

CRAPES ▸ crape

CRAPIER ▸ crape

CRAPING ▸ crape

CRAPLE same as ▸ grapple

CRAPLES ▸ craple

CRAPOLA n rubbish

CRAPPED ▸ crap

CRAPPIE n N American freshwater fish

CRAPPY adj worthless, lousy

CRAPS ▸ crap

CRAPY ▸ crape

CRARE n type of trading vessel

CRARES ▸ crare

CRASES ▸ crasis

CRASH n collision involving a vehicle or vehicles ▷ vb (cause to) collide violently with a vehicle, a stationary object, or the ground ▷ adj requiring or using great effort in order to achieve results quickly

CRASHED ▸ crash

CRASHER ▸ crash

CRASHES ▸ crash

CRASIS n fusion or contraction of two adjacent vowels into one

CRASS adj stupid and insensitive

CRASSER ▸ crass

CRASSLY ▸ crass

CRATCH n rack for holding fodder for cattle, etc

CRATE n large wooden container for packing goods ▷ vb put in a crate

CRATED ▸ crate

CRATER n bowl-shaped opening at the top of a volcano ▷ vb make or form craters

CRATERS ▸ crater

CRATES ▸ crate

CRATHUR n ▸ cratur

CRATING ▸ crate

CRATON n stable part of the earth's continental crust or lithosphere that has not been deformed significantly for many millions, even hundreds of millions, of years

CRATONS ▸ craton

CRATUR n whisky or whiskey

CRATURS ▸ cratur

CRAUNCH same as ▸ crunch

CRAVAT n man's scarf worn like a tie ▷ vb wear a cravat

CRAVATS ▸ cravat

CRAVE vb desire intensely

CRAVED ▸ crave

CRAVEN adj cowardly ▷ n coward ▷ vb to make cowardly

CRAVENS ▸ craven

CRAVER ▸ crave

CRAVERS ▸ crave

CRAVES ▸ crave

CRAVING n intense desire or longing

CRAW n pouchlike part of a bird's oesophagus

CRAWDAD n crayfish

CRAWL vb move on one's hands and knees ▷ n crawling motion or pace

CRAWLED ▸ crawl

CRAWLER n servile flatterer

CRAWLS ▸ crawl

CRAWLY adj feeling or causing a sensation like creatures crawling on one's skin

CRAWS ▸ craw

CRAY n crayfish

CRAYER same as ▸ crare

CRAYERS ▸ crayer

CRAYON n a stick or pencil of coloured wax or clay ▷ vb draw or colour with a crayon

CRAYONS ▸ crayon

CRAYS ▸ cray

CRAZE n short-lived fashion or enthusiasm ▷ vb make mad

CRAZED adj wild and uncontrolled

CRAZES ▸ craze

CRAZIER ▸ crazy

CRAZIES ▸ crazy

CRAZILY ▸ crazy

CRAZING ▸ craze

CRAZY adj ridiculous ▷ n crazy person ▷ n crazy person

CREACH same as ▸ **creagh**

CREACHS ▸ creach

CREAGH n foray

CREAGHS ▸ creagh

CREAK n (make) a harsh squeaking sound ▷ vb make or move with a harsh squeaking sound

CREAKED ▸ creak

CREAKS ▸ creak

CREAKY ▸ creak

CREAM n fatty part of milk ▷ adj yellowish-white ▷ vb beat to a creamy consistency

CREAMED ▸ cream

CREAMER n powdered milk substitute for use in coffee

CREAMS ▸ cream

CREAMY adj resembling cream in colour, taste, or consistency

CREANCE n long light cord used in falconry

CREANT adj formative

CREASE n line made by folding or pressing ▷ vb crush or line

CREASED ▸ crease

CREASER ▸ crease

CREASES ▸ crease

CREASY ▸ crease

CREATE vb make, cause to exist

CREATED ▸ create

CREATES ▸ create

CREATIC adj relating to flesh or meat

CREATIN same as ▸ **creatine**

CREATOR n person who creates

CRECHE n place where small children are looked after while their parents are working, shopping, etc

CRECHES ▸ creche

CRED n short for credibility

CREDAL ▸ creed

CREDENT adj believing or believable

CREDIT n system of allowing customers to receive goods and pay later ▷ vb enter as a credit in an account

CREDITS pl n list of people responsible for the production of a film, programme, or record

CREDO n creed

CREDOS ▸ credo

CREDS ▸ cred

CREE vb to soften grain by boiling or soaking

CREED n statement or system of (Christian) beliefs or principles

CREEDAL ▸ creed

CREEDS ▸ creed

CREEING ▸ cree

CREEK n narrow inlet or bay

CREEKS ▸ creek

CREEKY adj abounding in creeks

CREEL n wicker basket used by anglers ▷ vb to fish using creels

CREELED ▸ creel

CREELS ▸ creel

CREEP vb move quietly and cautiously ▷ n creeping movement

CREEPED ▸ creep

CREEPER n creeping plant ▷ vb train a plant to creep

CREEPIE n low stool

CREEPS ▸ creep

CREEPY adj causing a feeling of fear or disgust

CREES ▸ cree

CREESE ▸ kris

CREESED ▸ creese

CREESES ▸ creese

CREESH vb to lubricate

CREESHY adj greasy

CREM n crematorium

CREMANT adj (of wine) moderately sparkling

CREMATE vb burn (a corpse) to ash

CREME n cream ▷ adj (of a liqueur) rich and sweet

CREMES ▸ creme

CREMINI n variety of mushroom

CREMONA same as ▸ **cromorna**

CREMOR n cream

CREMORS ▸ cremor

CREMS ▸ crem

CREMSIN same as ▸ **cremosin**

CRENA n cleft or notch

CRENAS ▸ crena

CRENATE adj having a scalloped margin, as certain leaves

CRENEL n any of a set of openings formed in the top of a wall or parapet and having slanting sides, as in a battlement ▷ vb to crenelate

CRENELS ▸ crenel

CREOLE n language developed from a mixture of languages ▷ adj of or relating to a creole

CREOLES ▸ creole

CREOSOL n colourless or pale yellow insoluble oily liquid with a smoky odour and a burning taste

CREPE n fabric or rubber with a crinkled texture ▷ vb cover or drape with crepe ▷ vb to crimp or frizz

CREPED ▸ crepe

CREPES ▸ crepe

CREPEY same as ▸ **crepy**

CREPIER ▸ crepy

CREPING ▸ crepe

CREPON n thin material made of fine wool and/or silk

CREPONS ▸ crepon

CREPS pl n slang term for training shoes

CREPT ▸ creep

CREPY adj (esp of the skin) having a dry wrinkled appearance like crepe

CRESOL n aromatic compound derived from phenol, existing in three isomeric forms: found in coal tar and creosote and used in making synthetic resins and as an antiseptic and disinfectant

CRESOLS ▸ cresol

CRESS n plant with strong-tasting leaves, used in salads

CRESSES ▸ cress

CRESSET n metal basket mounted on a pole in which oil or pitch was burned for illumination

CRESSY ▸ cress

CREST n top of a mountain, hill, or wave ▷ vb come to or be at the top of

CRESTA adj as in cresta run high-speed tobogganing down a steep narrow passage of compacted snow and ice

CRESTAL ▸ crest

CRESTED ▸ crest

CRESTON n hogback

CRESTS ▸ crest

CRESYL n tolyl

CRESYLS ▸ cresyl

CRETIC n metrical foot consisting of three syllables,

the first long, the second short, and the third long

CRETICS ▶ **cretic**

CRETIN n stupid person

CRETINS ▶ **cretin**

CRETISM n lying

CRETONS pl n spread made from pork fat and onions

CREVICE n narrow crack or gap in rock

CREW n people who work on a ship or aircraft ▷ vb serve as a crew member (on)

CREWCUT n very short haircut

CREWE n type of pot

CREWED ▶ **crew**

CREWEL n fine worsted yarn used in embroidery ▷ vb to embroider in crewel

CREWELS ▶ **crewel**

CREWES ▶ **crewe**

CREWING ▶ **crew**

CREWMAN n member of a ship's crew

CREWMEN ▶ **crewman**

CREWS ▶ **crew**

CRIA n baby llama, alpaca, or vicu

CRIANT adj garish

CRIAS ▶ **cria**

CRIB n piece of writing stolen from elsewhere ▷ vb copy (someone's work) dishonestly

CRIBBED ▶ **crib**

CRIBBER ▶ **crib**

CRIBBLE vb to sift

CRIBLE adj dotted

CRIBS ▶ **crib**

CRICK n muscle spasm or cramp in the back or neck ▷ vb cause a crick in

CRICKED ▶ **crick**

CRICKET n outdoor game played with bats, a ball, and wickets by two teams of eleven ▷ vb play cricket

CRICKEY same as ▶ **crikey**

CRICKS ▶ **crick**

CRICKY same as ▶ **crikey**

CRICOID adj of or relating to the ring-shaped lowermost cartilage of the larynx ▷ n this cartilage

CRIED ▶ **cry**

CRIER n (formerly) official who made public announcements

CRIERS ▶ **crier**

CRIES ▶ **cry**

CRIKEY interj expression of surprise

CRIM short for ▶ **criminal**

CRIME n unlawful act ▷ vb charge with a crime

CRIMED ▶ **crime**

CRIMEN n crime

CRIMES ▶ **crime**

CRIMINA ▶ **crimen**

CRIMINE interj expression of surprise

CRIMING ▶ **crime**

CRIMINI ▶ **crimine**

CRIMINY interj cry of surprise

CRIMMER a variant spelling of ▶ **krimmer**

CRIMP vb fold or press into ridges ▷ n act or result of crimping

CRIMPED ▶ **crimp**

CRIMPER ▶ **crimp**

CRIMPLE vb crumple, wrinkle, or curl

CRIMPS ▶ **crimp**

CRIMPY ▶ **crimp**

CRIMS ▶ **crim**

CRIMSON adj deep purplish-red ▷ n deep or vivid red colour ▷ vb make or become crimson

CRINAL adj relating to the hair

CRINATE adj having hair

CRINE vb to shrivel

CRINED ▶ **crine**

CRINES ▶ **crine**

CRINGE vb flinch in fear ▷ n act of cringing

CRINGED ▶ **cringe**

CRINGER ▶ **cringe**

CRINGES ▶ **cringe**

CRINGLE n eye at the edge of a sail, usually formed from a thimble or grommet

CRINING ▶ **crine**

CRINITE adj covered with soft hairs or tufts ▷ n sedimentary rock

CRINKLE n wrinkle, crease, or fold ▷ vb become slightly creased or folded

CRINKLY adj wrinkled ▷ n old person

CRINOID n type of primitive echinoderm with delicate feathery arms radiating from a central disc, such as feather stars and sea lilies

CRINOSE adj hairy

CRINUM n type of mostly tropical plant with straplike leaves and clusters of lily-like flowers

CRINUMS ▶ **crinum**

CRIOLLO n native or inhabitant of Latin America of European descent, esp of Spanish descent ▷ adj of, relating to, or characteristic of a criollo or criollos

CRIOS n multicoloured woven woollen belt traditionally worn by men in the Aran Islands

CRIOSES ▶ **crios**

CRIPE same as ▶ **cripes**

CRIPES interj expression of surprise

CRIPPLE n offensive word for a person who is lame or disabled ▷ vb make lame or disabled

CRIS same as ▶ **kris**

CRISE n crisis

CRISES ▶ **crisis**

CRISIC adj relating to a crisis

CRISIS n crucial stage, turning point

CRISP adj fresh and firm ▷ n very thin slice of potato fried till crunchy ▷ vb make or become crisp

CRISPED same as ▶ **crispate**

CRISPEN vb to make crisp

CRISPER n compartment in a refrigerator for storing salads, vegetables, etc, in order to keep them fresh

CRISPIN n cobbler

CRISPLY ▶ **crisp**

CRISPS ▶ **crisp**

CRISPY adj hard and crunchy

CRISSA ▶ **crissum**

CRISSAL ▶ **crissum**

CRISSUM n area or feathers surrounding the cloaca of a bird

CRISTA n structure resembling a ridge or crest, such as that formed by folding of the inner membrane of a mitochondrion

CRISTAE ▶ **crista**

CRIT abbreviation of ▶ **criticism**

CRITH n unit of weight for gases

CRITHS ▶ **crith**

CRITIC n professional judge of any of the arts

CRITICS ▶ **critic**

CRITS ▶ **crit**

CRITTER a dialect word for ▶ **creature**

CRITTUR same as ▶ **critter**

CRIVENS interj expression of surprise

CROAK vb (of a frog or crow) give a low hoarse cry ▷ n low hoarse sound

CROAKED ▶ **croak**

CROAKER n animal, bird, etc, that croaks

CROAKS ▶ **croak**

CROAKY ▶ **croak**

CROC short for ▶ **crocodile**

CROCEIN n any one of a group of red or orange acid azo dyes

CROCHE n knob at the top of a deer's horn

CROCHES ▶ **croche**

CROCHET vb make by looping and intertwining yarn with a hooked needle ▷ n work made in this way

CROCI ▶ **crocus**

CROCINE adj relating to the crocus

CROCK n earthenware pot or jar ▷ vb become or cause to become weak or disabled

CROCKED adj injured

CROCKET n carved ornament in the form of a curled leaf or cusp, used in Gothic architecture

CROCKS ▶ **crock**

CROCS ▶ **croc**

CROCUS n flowering plant

CROFT n small farm worked by one family in Scotland ▷ vb farm land as a croft

CROFTED ▶ **croft** vb

CROFTER n owner or tenant of a small farm, esp in Scotland or northern England

CROFTS ▶ **croft**

CROG vb ride on a bicycle as a passenger

CROGGED ▶ **crog**

CROGGY n ride on a bicycle as a passenger

CROGS ▶ **crog**

CROJIK n triangular sail

CROJIKS ▶ **crojik**

CROMACK same as > **crummock**

CROMB same as ▶ **crome**

CROMBEC n African Old World warbler with colourful plumage

CROMBED ▶ **cromb**

CROMBS ▶ **cromb**

CROME n hook ▷ vb use a crome

CROMED ▶ **crome**

CROMES ▶ **crome**

CROMING ▶ **crome**

CRONE n witchlike old woman

CRONES ▶ **crone**

CRONET n hair which grows over the top of a horse's hoof

CRONETS ▶ **cronet**

CRONIES ▶ **crony**

CRONISH ▶ **crone**

CRONK adj unfit

CRONKER ▶ **cronk**

CRONY n close friend

CROODLE vb to nestle close

CROOK n dishonest person ▷ vb bend or curve

CROOKED adj bent or twisted

CROOKER ▶ **crook**

CROOKS ▶ **crook**

CROOL vb spoil

CROOLED ▶ **crool**

CROOLS ▶ **crool**

CROON vb sing, hum, or speak in a soft low tone ▷ n soft low singing or humming

CROONED ▶ **croon**

CROONER ▶ **croon**

CROONS ▶ **croon**

CROOVE n animal enclosure

CROOVES ▶ **croove**

CROP n cultivated plant ▷ vb cut very short

CROPFUL n quantity that can be held in the craw

CROPPED ▶ **crop**

CROPPER n person who cultivates or harvests a crop

CROPPIE same as ▶ **croppy**

CROPPY n rebel in the Irish rising of 1798

CROPS ▶ **crop**

CROQUET n game played on a lawn in which balls are hit through hoops ▷ vb drive away (another player's ball) by hitting one's own ball when the two are in contact

CROQUIS n rough sketch

CRORE n (in Indian English) ten million

CRORES ▶ **crore**

CROSIER n staff surmounted by a crook or cross, carried by bishops as a symbol of pastoral office ▷ vb bear or carry such a cross

CROSS vb move or go across (something) ▷ n structure, symbol, or mark of two intersecting lines ▷ adj angry, annoyed

CROSSE n light staff with a triangular frame to which a network is attached, used in playing lacrosse

CROSSED ▶ **cross**

CROSSER ▶ **cross**

CROSSES ▶ **cross**

CROSSLY ▶ **cross**

CROST ▶ **cross**

CROTAL n any of various lichens used in dyeing wool, esp for the manufacture of tweeds

CROTALA > **crotalum**

CROTALS ▶ **crotal**

CROTCH n part of the body between the tops of the legs ▷ vb have crotch (usu of a piece of clothing) removed

CROTON n type of shrub or tree, the seeds of which yield croton oil

CROTONS ▶ **croton**

CROTTLE same as ▶ **crotal**

CROUCH vb bend low with the legs and body close ▷ n this position

CROUP n throat disease of children, with a cough ▷ vb have croup

CROUPE same as ▶ **croup**

CROUPED ▶ **croup**

CROUPER obsolete variant of ▶ **crupper**

CROUPES ▶ **croupe**

CROUPON n type of highly-polished flexible leather

CROUPS ▶ **croup**

CROUPY ▶ **croup**

CROUSE adj lively, confident, or saucy

CROUT n sauerkraut

CROUTE n small round of toasted bread on which a savoury mixture is served

CROUTES ▶ **croute**

CROUTON n small piece of fried or toasted bread served in soup

CROUTS ▶ **crout**

CROW n large black bird with a harsh call ▷ vb (of a cock) make a shrill squawking sound

CROWBAR n iron bar used as a lever ▷ vb use a crowbar to lever (something)

CROWD n large group of people or things ▷ vb gather together in large numbers

CROWDED ▸ crowd

CROWDER ▸ crowd

CROWDIE n porridge of meal and water

CROWDS ▸ crowd

CROWDY same as ▸ **crowdie**

CROWEA n Australian shrub with pink flowers

CROWEAS ▸ crowea

CROWED ▸ crow

CROWER ▸ crow

CROWERS ▸ crow

CROWING ▸ crow

CROWN n monarch's headdress of gold and jewels ▷ vb put a crown on the head of (someone) to proclaim him or her monarch

CROWNED ▸ crown

CROWNER n promotional label consisting of a shaped printed piece of card or paper attached to a product on display

CROWNET n coronet

CROWNS ▸ crown

CROWS ▸ crow

CROZE n recess cut at the end of a barrel or cask to receive the head

CROZER n machine which cuts grooves in cask staves

CROZERS ▸ crozer

CROZES ▸ croze

CROZIER same as ▸ **crosier**

CRU n (in France) a vineyard, group of vineyards, or wine-producing region

CRUBEEN n pig's trotter

CRUCES ▸ crux

CRUCIAL adj very important

CRUCIAN n European fish with a dark-green back, a golden-yellow undersurface, and reddish dorsal and tail fins, popular in aquariums

CRUCIFY vb put to death by fastening to a cross

CRUCK n one of a pair of curved wooden timbers supporting the end of the roof in certain types of building

CRUCKS ▸ cruck

CRUD n sticky or encrusted substance ▷ interj expression of disgust, disappointment, etc ▷ vb cover with a sticky or encrusted substance

CRUDDED ▸ crud

CRUDDLE vb to curdle

CRUDDY adj dirty or unpleasant

CRUDE adj rough and simple ▷ n crude oil

CRUDELY ▸ crude

CRUDER ▸ crude

CRUDES ▸ crude

CRUDEST ▸ crude

CRUDITY ▸ crude

CRUDS ▸ crud

CRUDY adj raw

CRUE obsolete variant of ▸ **crew**

CRUEL adj delighting in others' pain

CRUELER ▸ cruel

CRUELLS same as ▸ **cruels**

CRUELLY ▸ cruel

CRUELS n disease of cattle and sheep

CRUELTY n deliberate infliction of pain or suffering

CRUES ▸ crew

CRUET n small container for salt, pepper, etc, at table

CRUETS ▸ cruet

CRUISE n sail for pleasure ▷ vb sail from place to place for pleasure

CRUISED ▸ cruise

CRUISER n fast warship

CRUISES ▸ cruise

CRUISIE same as ▸ **cruizie**

CRUIVE n animal enclosure

CRUIVES ▸ cruive

CRUIZIE n oil lamp

CRULLER n light sweet ring-shaped cake, fried in deep fat

CRUMB n small fragment of bread or other dry food ▷ vb prepare or cover (food) with breadcrumbs ▷ adj (esp of pie crusts) made with a mixture of biscuit crumbs, sugar, etc

CRUMBED ▸ crumb

CRUMBER ▸ crumb

CRUMBLE vb break into fragments ▷ n pudding of stewed fruit with a crumbly topping

CRUMBLY adj easily crumbled or crumbling

CRUMBS interj expression of dismay or surprise

CRUMBUM n rogue

CRUMBY adj full of crumbs

CRUMEN n deer's larmier or tear-pit

CRUMENS ▸ crumen

CRUMMIE n cow with a crumpled horn

CRUMMY adj of poor quality ▷ n lorry that carries loggers to work from their camp

CRUMP vb thud or explode with a loud dull sound ▷ n crunching, thudding, or exploding noise ▷ adj crooked

CRUMPED ▸ crump

CRUMPER ▸ crump

CRUMPET n round soft yeast cake, eaten buttered

CRUMPLE vb crush, crease ▷ n untidy crease or wrinkle

CRUMPLY ▸ crumple

CRUMPS ▸ crump

CRUMPY adj crisp

CRUNCH vb bite or chew with a noisy crushing sound ▷ n crunching sound

CRUNCHY ▸ crunch

CRUNK n form of hip-hop music originating in the Southern US

CRUNKED adj excited or intoxicated

CRUNKLE Scots variant of ▸ **crinkle**

CRUNKS ▸ crunk

CRUNODE n point at which two branches of a curve intersect, each branch having a distinct tangent

CRUOR n blood clot

CRUORES ▸ cruor

CRUORS ▸ cruor

CRUPPER n strap that passes from the back of a saddle under a horse's tail

CRURA ▸ crus

CRURAL adj of or relating to the leg or thigh

CRUS n leg, esp from the knee to the foot

CRUSADE n medieval Christian war to recover the Holy Land from the Muslims ▷ vb take part in a crusade

CRUSADO n former gold or silver coin of Portugal bearing on its reverse the figure of a cross

CRUSE n small earthenware jug or pot

CRUSES ▸ cruse

CRUSET n goldsmith's crucible

CRUSETS ▸ cruset

CRUSH vb compress so as to injure, break, or crumple ▷ n dense crowd

CRUSHED ▸ crush

CRUSHER ▸ crush

CRUSHES ▸ crush

CRUSIAN same as ▸ **crucian**

CRUSIE same as ▸ **cruizie**

CRUSIES ▸ crusie

CRUSILY adj (in heraldry) strewn with crosses

CRUST n hard outer part of something, esp bread ▷ vb cover with or form a crust

CRUSTA n hard outer layer

CRUSTAE ▸ crusta

CRUSTAL adj of or relating to the earth's crust

CRUSTED ▸ crust

CRUSTS ▸ crust

CRUSTY adj having a crust ▷ n dirty type of punk or hippy whose lifestyle involves travelling and squatting

CRUSY same as ▸ **cruizie**

CRUTCH n long sticklike support with a rest for the armpit, used by a lame person ▷ vb support or sustain (a person or thing) as with a crutch

CRUVE same as ▸ **cruive**

CRUVES ▸ cruve

CRUX n crucial or decisive point

CRUXES ▸ crux

CRUZADO same as ▸ **crusado**

CRUZIE same as ▸ **cruizie**

CRUZIES ▸ cruizie

CRWTH n ancient stringed instrument of Celtic origin similar to the cithara but bowed in later types

> This old Celtic musical instrument makes a fine tune when your rack is all consonants.

CRWTHS ▸ crwth

CRY vb shed tears ▷ n fit of weeping

CRYBABY n person, esp a child, who cries too readily

CRYING ▸ cry

CRYINGS ▸ cry

CRYOGEN n substance used to produce low temperatures

CRYONIC > cryonics

CRYPT n vault under a church, esp one used as a burial place

CRYPTAL ▸ crypt

CRYPTIC adj obscure in meaning, secret

CRYPTO n person who is a secret member of an organization or sect

CRYPTON n krypton

CRYPTOS ▸ crypto

CRYPTS ▸ crypt

CRYSTAL n (single grain of) a symmetrically shaped solid formed naturally by some substances ▷ adj bright and clear

CSARDAS n type of Hungarian folk dance

CTENE n locomotor organ found in ctenophores (or comb jellies)

CTENES ▸ ctene

CTENOID adj toothed like a comb, as the scales of perches

CUATRO n four-stringed guitar

CUATROS ▸ cuatro

CUB n young wild animal such as a bear or fox ▷ adj young or inexperienced ▷ vb give birth to cubs

CUBAGE same as > **cubature**

CUBAGES > cubature

CUBANE n rare octahedral hydrocarbon

CUBANES ▸ cubane

CUBBED ▸ cub

CUBBIER ▸ cubby

CUBBIES ▸ cubby

CUBBING ▸ cub

CUBBISH ▸ cub

CUBBY n a cubbyhole ▷ adj short and plump

CUBE n object with six equal square sides ▷ vb cut into cubes

CUBEB n SE Asian woody climbing plant with brownish berries

CUBEBS ▸ cubeb

CUBED ▸ cube

CUBER ▸ cube

CUBERS ▸ cube

CUBES ▸ cube

CUBHOOD n state of being a cub

CUBIC adj having three dimensions ▷ n cubic equation

CUBICA n fine shalloon-like fabric

CUBICAL adj of or related to volume

CUBICAS ▸ cubica

CUBICLE n enclosed part of a large room, screened for privacy

CUBICLY ▸ cubic

CUBICS ▸ cubic

CUBING ▸ cube

CUBISM n style of art in which objects are represented by geometrical shapes

CUBISMS ▸ cubism

CUBIST ▸ cubism

CUBISTS ▸ cubism

CUBIT n old measure of length based on the length of the forearm

CUBITAL adj of or relating to the forearm

CUBITI ▸ cubitus

CUBITS ▸ cubit

CUBITUS n elbow

CUBLESS adj having no cubs

CUBOID adj shaped like a cube ▷ n geometric solid whose six faces are rectangles

CUBOIDS ▸ cuboid

CUBS ▸ cub

CUCKING adj as in **cucking stool** stool to which suspected witches, etc, were tied and pelted or ducked into water as punishment

CUCKOLD n man whose wife has been unfaithful ▷ vb be unfaithful to (one's husband)

CUCKOO n migratory bird with a characteristic two-note call, which lays its eggs in the nests of other birds ▷ adj insane or foolish ▷ interj imitation or representation of the call of a cuckoo ▷ vb repeat over and over

CUCKOOS ▸ cuckoo

CUD n partially digested food which a ruminant brings back into its mouth to chew again

CUDBEAR another name for ▸ **orchil**

CUDDEN n young coalfish

CUDDENS ▸ cudden

CUDDIE same as ▸ **cuddy**

CUDDIES ▸ cuddy

CUDDIN same as ▸ **cudden**

CUDDINS ▸ cuddin

CUDDLE n hug ▷ vb hold (another person or thing) close or (of two people, etc) to hold each other close, as for affection, comfort, or warmth

CUDDLED ▸ cuddle

CUDDLER ► cuddle

CUDDLES ► cuddle

CUDDLY ► cuddle

CUDDY n small cabin in a boat

CUDGEL n short thick stick used as a weapon ▷ vb use a cudgel

CUDGELS ► cudgel

CUDS ► cud

CUDWEED n type of temperate woolly plant with clusters of whitish or yellow flowers

CUE n signal to an actor or musician to begin speaking or playing ▷ vb give a cue to

CUED ► cue

CUEING > foldback

CUEINGS ► cueing

CUEIST n snooker or billiards player

CUEISTS ► cueist

CUES ► cue

CUESTA n long low ridge with a steep scarp slope and a gentle back slope, formed by the differential erosion of strata of differing hardness

CUESTAS ► cuesta

CUFF n end of a sleeve ▷ vb hit with an open hand

CUFFED ► cuff

CUFFIN n man

CUFFING ► cuff

CUFFINS ► cuffin

CUFFLE vb scuffle

CUFFLED ► cuffle

CUFFLES ► cuffle

CUFFO adv free of charge

CUFFS ► cuff

CUIF same as ► coof

CUIFS ► cuif

CUING ► cue

CUIRASS n piece of armour, of leather or metal covering the chest and back ▷ vb equip with a cuirass

CUISH same as ► cuisse

CUISHES ► cuish

CUISINE n style of cooking

CUISSE n piece of armour for the thigh

CUISSER same as ► cooser

CUISSES ► cuisse

CUIT n ankle

CUITER vb to pamper

CUITERS ► cuiter

CUITS ► cuit

CUITTLE vb to wheedle

CUKE n cucumber

CUKES ► cuke

CULCH n mass of broken stones, shells, and gravel that forms the basis of an oyster bed

CULCHES ► culch

CULCHIE n rough or unsophisticated country-dweller from outside Dublin

CULET n flat face at the bottom of a gem

CULETS ► culet

CULEX n type of mosquito

CULEXES ► culex

CULICES ► culex

CULICID n type of dipterous insect of the family which comprises the mosquitoes

CULL vb choose, gather ▷ n culling

CULLAY n soapbark tree

CULLAYS ► cullay

CULLED ► cull

CULLER n person employed to cull animals

CULLERS ► culler

CULLET n waste glass for melting down to be reused

CULLETS ► cullet

CULLIED ► cully

CULLIES ► cully

CULLING ► cull

CULLION n rascal

CULLIS same as > coulisse

CULLS ► cull

CULLY n pal ▷ vb to trick

CULM n coal-mine waste ▷ vb to form a culm or grass stem

CULMED ► culm

CULMEN n summit

CULMINA ► culmen

CULMING ► culm

CULMS ► culm

CULOTTE > culottes

CULPA n act of neglect

CULPAE ► culpa

CULPRIT n person guilty of an offence or misdeed

CULT n specific system of worship ▷ adj very popular among a limited group of people

CULTCH same as ► culch

CULTER same as ► coulter

CULTERS ► culter

CULTI ► cultus

CULTIC adj of or relating to a religious cult

CULTIER ► culty

CULTISH adj intended to appeal to a small group of fashionable people

CULTISM ► cult

CULTIST ► cult

CULTS ► cult

CULTURE n ideas, customs, and art of a particular society ▷ vb grow (bacteria) for study

CULTUS another word for ► cult

CULTY same as ► cultish

CULVER an archaic or poetic name for ► pigeon

CULVERS ► culver

CULVERT n drain under a road or railway

CUMARIC ► cumarin

CUMARIN same as > coumarin

CUMBENT adj lying down

CUMBER vb obstruct or hinder ▷ n hindrance or burden

CUMBERS ► cumber

CUMBIA n Colombian style of music

CUMBIAS ► cumbia

CUMEC n unit of volumetric rate of flow

CUMECS ► cumec

CUMIN n sweet-smelling seeds of a Mediterranean plant, used in cooking

CUMINS ► cumin

CUMMER n gossip

CUMMERS ► cummer

CUMMIN same as ► cumin

CUMMINS ► cummin

CUMQUAT same as ► kumquat

CUMSHAW n (used, esp formerly, by beggars in Chinese ports) a present or tip

CUMULET n variety of domestic fancy pigeon, pure white or white with light red markings

CUMULI ► cumulus

CUMULUS n thick white or dark grey cloud

CUNDIES ► cundy

CUNDUM n early form of condom

CUNDUMS ► cundum

CUNDY n sewer

CUNEAL same as > cuneiform

CUNEATE adj wedge-shaped: cuneate leaves are attached at the narrow end

CUNEI ► cuneus

CUNETTE n small trench dug in the main ditch of a fortification

CUNEUS n small wedge-shaped area of the cerebral cortex

CUNNER n fish of the wrasse family

CUNNERS ▸ **cunner**

CUNNING adj clever at deceiving ▷ n cleverness at deceiving

CUP n small bowl-shaped drinking container with a handle ▷ vb form (one's hands) into the shape of a cup

CUPCAKE n small cake baked in a cup-shaped foil or paper case

CUPEL n refractory pot in which gold or silver is refined ▷ vb refine (gold or silver) by means of cupellation

CUPELED ▸ **cupel**

CUPELER ▸ **cupel**

CUPELS ▸ **cupel**

CUPFUL n amount a cup will hold

CUPFULS ▸ **cupful**

CUPGALL n gall found on oakleaves

CUPHEAD n type of bolt or rivet with a cup-shaped head

CUPID n figure representing the Roman god of love

CUPIDS ▸ **cupid**

CUPLIKE ▸ **cup**

CUPMAN n drinking companion

CUPMEN ▸ **cupman**

CUPOLA n domed roof or ceiling ▷ vb to provide with a cupola

CUPOLAR ▸ **cupola**

CUPOLAS ▸ **cupola**

CUPPA n cup of tea

CUPPAS ▸ **cuppa**

CUPPED ▸ **cup**

CUPPER same as ▸ **cuppa**

CUPPERS ▸ **cupper**

CUPPIER ▸ **cuppy**

CUPPING ▸ **cup**

CUPPY adj cup-shaped

CUPRIC adj of or containing copper in the divalent state

CUPRITE n red secondary mineral

CUPROUS adj of or containing copper in the monovalent state

CUPRUM an obsolete name for ▸ **copper**

CUPRUMS ▸ **cuprum**

CUPS ▸ **cup**

CUPSFUL ▸ **cupful**

CUPULA n dome-shaped structure, esp the sensory structure within the semicircular canals of the ear

CUPULAE ▸ **cupula**

CUPULAR same as ▸ **cupulate**

CUPULE n cup-shaped part or structure, such as the cup around the base of an acorn

CUPULES ▸ **cupule**

CUR n mongrel dog

CURABLE adj capable of being cured

CURABLY ▸ **curable**

CURACAO n orange-flavoured liqueur

CURACOA same as ▸ **curacao**

CURACY n work or position of a curate

CURAGH same as ▸ **currach**

CURAGHS ▸ **curagh**

CURARA same as ▸ **curare**

CURARAS ▸ **curara**

CURARE n poisonous resin of a S American tree, used as a muscle relaxant in medicine

CURARES ▸ **curare**

CURARI same as ▸ **curare**

CURARIS ▸ **curari**

CURAT n cuirass

CURATE n clergyman who assists a parish priest ▷ vb be in charge of (an art exhibition or museum) ▷ vb to act as a curator

CURATED ▸ **curate**

CURATES ▸ **curate**

CURATOR n person in charge of a museum or art gallery

CURATS ▸ **curat**

CURB n something that restrains ▷ vb control, restrain

CURBED ▸ **curb**

CURBER ▸ **curb**

CURBERS ▸ **curb**

CURBING the US spelling of ▸ **kerbing**

CURBS ▸ **curb**

CURCH n woman's plain cap or kerchief

CURCHEF same as ▸ **curch**

CURCHES ▸ **curch**

CURCUMA n type of tropical Asian tuberous plant

CURD n coagulated milk, used to make cheese ▷ vb turn into or become curd

CURDED ▸ **curd**

CURDIER ▸ **curd**

CURDING ▸ **curd**

CURDLE vb turn into curd, coagulate

CURDLED ▸ **curdle**

CURDLER ▸ **curdle**

CURDLES ▸ **curdle**

CURDS ▸ **curd**

CURDY ▸ **curd**

CURE vb get rid of (an illness or problem) ▷ n (treatment causing) curing of an illness or person

CURED ▸ **cure**

CURER ▸ **cure**

CURERS ▸ **cure**

CURES ▸ **cure**

CURET same as ▸ **curette**

CURETS ▸ **curet**

CURETTE n surgical instrument for scraping tissue from body cavities ▷ vb scrape with a curette

CURF n type of limestone

CURFEW n law ordering people to stay inside their homes after a specific time at night

CURFEWS ▸ **curfew**

CURFS ▸ **curf**

CURIA n papal court and government of the Roman Catholic Church

CURIAE ▸ **curia**

CURIAL ▸ **curia**

CURIAS ▸ **curia**

CURIE n standard unit of radioactivity

CURIES ▸ **curie**

CURIET n cuirass

CURIETS ▸ **curiet**

CURING ▸ **cure**

CURIO n rare or unusual object valued as a collector's item

CURIOS ▸ **curio**

CURIOSA n curiosities

CURIOUS adj eager to learn or know

CURITE n oxide of uranium and lead

CURITES ▸ **curite**

CURIUM n radioactive element artificially produced from plutonium

CURIUMS ▸ **curium**

CURL n curved piece of hair ▷ vb make (hair) into curls or (of hair) grow in curls

CURLED ▸ **curl**

CURLER n pin or small tube for curling hair

CURLERS ▸ curler
CURLEW n long-billed wading bird
CURLEWS ▸ curlew
CURLI pl n curled hairlike processes on the surface of the E. coli bacterium, by means of which it adheres to and infects wounds
CURLIER ▸ curly
CURLIES pl n as in **have by the short and curlies** have completely in one's power
CURLILY ▸ curly
CURLING n game like bowls, played with heavy stones on ice
CURLS ▸ curl
CURLY adj tending to curl
CURN n grain (of corn etc)
CURNEY same as ▸ **curny**
CURNIER ▸ curny
CURNS ▸ curn
CURNY adj granular
CURPEL same as ▸ **crupper**
CURPELS ▸ curpel
CURR vb to purr
CURRACH a Scots or Irish name for ▸ **coracle**
CURRAGH same as ▸ **currach**
CURRAN n black bun
CURRANS ▸ curran
CURRANT n small dried grape
CURRED ▸ curr
CURRENT adj of the immediate present ▷ n flow of water or air in one direction
CURRIE same as ▸ **curry**
CURRIED ▸ curry
CURRIER n person who curries leather
CURRIES ▸ curry
CURRING ▸ curr
CURRISH adj of or like a cur
CURRS ▸ curr
CURRY n Indian dish of meat or vegetables in a hot spicy sauce ▷ vb prepare (food) with curry powder
CURS ▸ cur
CURSAL ▸ cursus
CURSE vb swear (at) ▷ n swearword
CURSED ▸ curse
CURSER ▸ curse
CURSERS ▸ curse
CURSES ▸ curse
CURSI ▸ cursus
CURSING ▸ curse
CURSIVE n (handwriting) done with joined letters ▷ adj of handwriting or print in which letters are joined in a flowing style
CURSOR n movable point of light that shows a specific position on a visual display unit
CURSORS ▸ cursor
CURSORY adj quick and superficial
CURST ▸ curse
CURSUS n Neolithic parallel earthworks
CURT adj brief and rather rude
CURTAIL vb cut short
CURTAIN n piece of cloth hung at a window or opening as a screen ▷ vb provide with curtains
CURTAL adj cut short ▷ n animal whose tail has been docked
CURTALS ▸ curtal
CURTANA n unpointed sword carried before an English sovereign at a coronation as an emblem of mercy
CURTATE adj shortened
CURTAXE same as > **curtalaxe**
CURTER ▸ curt
CURTEST ▸ curt
CURTESY n widower's life interest in his wife's estate
CURTLY ▸ curt
CURTSEY same as ▸ **curtsy**
CURTSY n woman's gesture of respect made by bending the knees and bowing the head ▷ vb make a curtsy
CURULE adj (in ancient Rome) of the highest rank, esp one entitled to use a curule chair
CURVATE adj curved
CURVE n continuously bending line with no straight parts ▷ vb form or move in a curve
CURVED ▸ curve
CURVES ▸ curve
CURVET n horse's low leap with all four feet off the ground ▷ vb make such a leap
CURVETS ▸ curvet
CURVEY same as ▸ **curvy**
CURVIER ▸ curve
CURVING ▸ curve
CURVITY n curvedness

CURVY ▸ curve
CUSCUS n large Australian nocturnal possum
CUSEC n unit of flow equal to 1 cubic foot per second
CUSECS ▸ cusec
CUSH n cushion
CUSHAT n wood pigeon
CUSHATS ▸ cushat
CUSHAW same as ▸ **cashaw**
CUSHAWS ▸ cushaw
CUSHES ▸ cush
CUSHIE same as ▸ **cushat**
CUSHIER ▸ cushy
CUSHIES ▸ cushie
CUSHILY ▸ cushy
CUSHION n bag filled with soft material, to make a seat more comfortable ▷ vb lessen the effects of
CUSHTY interj exclamation of pleasure, agreement, approval, etc
CUSHY adj easy
CUSK n type of food fish of northern coastal waters, with a single long dorsal fin
CUSKS ▸ cusk
CUSP n pointed end, esp on a tooth
CUSPAL ▸ cusp
CUSPATE adj having a cusp or cusps
CUSPED same as ▸ **cuspate**
CUSPID n tooth having one point
CUSPIDS ▸ cuspid
CUSPIER ▸ cuspy
CUSPIS n in anatomy, tapering structure
CUSPS ▸ cusp
CUSPY adj (of a computer program) well-designed and user-friendly
CUSS n curse, oath ▷ vb swear (at)
CUSSED adj obstinate
CUSSER same as ▸ **cooser**
CUSSERS ▸ cusser
CUSSES ▸ cuss
CUSSING ▸ cuss
CUSSO n tree of the rose family
CUSSOS ▸ cusso
CUSTARD n sweet yellow sauce made from milk and eggs
CUSTOCK same as ▸ **castock**
CUSTODE n custodian
CUSTODY n protective care
CUSTOM n long-established

activity or action ▷ *adj* made to the specifications of an individual customer

CUSTOMS *n* duty charged on imports or exports

CUSTOS *n* superior in the Franciscan religious order

CUSTREL *n* knave

CUSUM *n* analysis technique used in statistics

CUSUMS ▸ **cusum**

CUT *vb* open up, penetrate, wound, or divide with a sharp instrument ▷ *n* act of cutting

CUTAWAY *adj* (of a drawing or model) having part of the outside omitted to reveal the inside ▷ *n* man's coat cut diagonally from the front waist to the back of the knees

CUTBACK *n* decrease or reduction ▷ *vb* shorten by cutting

CUTBANK *n* steep banking at a bend in a river

CUTCH *same as* ▸ **catechu**

CUTCHA *adj* crude

CUTCHES ▸ **cutch**

CUTDOWN *n* decrease

CUTE *adj* appealing or attractive

CUTELY ▸ **cute**

CUTER ▸ **cute**

CUTES ▸ **cutis**

CUTESIE *same as* ▸ **cutesy**

CUTEST ▸ **cute**

CUTESY *adj* affectedly cute or coy

CUTEY *same as* ▸ **cutie**

CUTEYS ▸ **cutey**

CUTICLE *n* skin at the base of a fingernail or toenail

CUTIE *n* person regarded as appealing or attractive, esp a girl or woman

CUTIES ▸ **cutie**

CUTIKIN *same as* > **cootikin**

CUTIN *n* waxy waterproof substance, consisting of derivatives of fatty acids, that is the main constituent of the plant cuticle

CUTINS ▸ **cutin**

CUTIS *a technical name for the* ▸ **skin**

CUTISES ▸ **cutis**

CUTLAS *same as* ▸ **cutlass**

CUTLASS *n* curved one-edged sword formerly used by sailors

CUTLER *n* maker of cutlery

CUTLERS ▸ **cutler**

CUTLERY *n* knives, forks, and spoons

CUTLET *n* small piece of meat like a chop

CUTLETS ▸ **cutlet**

CUTLINE *n* caption

CUTOFF *n* limit or termination

CUTOFFS ▸ **cutoff**

CUTOUT *n* something that has been cut out from something else

CUTOUTS ▸ **cutout**

CUTOVER *n* transitional period in IT system changeover, during which old and new systems are working concurrently

CUTS ▸ **cut**

CUTTAGE *n* propagation by using parts taken from growing plants

CUTTER *n* person or tool that cuts

CUTTERS ▸ **cutter**

CUTTIER ▸ **cutty**

CUTTIES ▸ **cutty**

CUTTING ▸ **cut**

CUTTLE *vb* to whisper

CUTTLED ▸ **cuttle**

CUTTLES ▸ **cuttle**

CUTTO *n* large knife

CUTTOE *same as* ▸ **cutto**

CUTTOES ▸ **cutto**

CUTTY *adj* short or cut short ▷ *n* something cut short, such as a spoon or short-stemmed tobacco pipe

CUTUP *n* joker or prankster

CUTUPS ▸ **cutup**

CUTWORK *n* openwork embroidery in which the pattern is cut away from the background

CUTWORM *n* caterpillar of various types of moth, a pest of young crop plants in N America

CUVEE *n* individual batch or blend of wine

CUVEES ▸ **cuvee**

CUVETTE *n* shallow dish or vessel for holding liquid

CUZ *n* cousin

> **Cuz** is another word for **cousin**, great for using the Z.

CUZZES ▸ **cuz**

CUZZIE *n* close friend or family member

CUZZIES ▸ **cuzzie**

CWM *same as* ▸ **cirque**

> **Cwm** is a Welsh word meaning a valley, a useful one to remember because it doesn't contain any vowels.

CWMS ▸ **cwm**

CWTCH *vb* be snuggled up

> This delightful Welsh word meaning to cuddle is not likely to come up, but might just help you out of a tight spot one day when your rack is all consonants.

CWTCHED ▸ **cwtch**

CWTCHES ▸ **cwtch**

CYAN *n* highly saturated green-blue that is the complementary colour of red and forms, with magenta and yellow, a set of primary colours ▷ *adj* of this colour

CYANATE *n* any salt or ester of cyanic acid

CYANIC *adj as in* **cyanic acid** colourless poisonous volatile liquid acid

CYANID *same as* ▸ **cyanide**

CYANIDE *n* extremely poisonous chemical compound ▷ *vb* treat with cyanide

CYANIDS ▸ **cyanid**

CYANIN *same as* ▸ **cyanine**

CYANINE *n* blue dye used to extend the sensitivity of photographic emulsions to colours other than blue and ultraviolet

CYANINS ▸ **cyanin**

CYANISE *vb* to turn into cyanide

CYANITE *a variant spelling of* ▸ **kyanite**

CYANIZE *same as* ▸ **cyanise**

CYANO *adj* containing cyanogen

CYANS ▸ **cyan**

CYATHI ▸ **cyathus**

CYATHIA > **cyathium**

CYATHUS *n* ancient measure of wine

CYBER *adj* involving computers

CYBORG *n* (in science fiction) a living being whose powers are enhanced by computer implants

CYBORGS ▸ **cyborg**

CYBRID *n* cytoplasmic hybrid (hybrid resulting from the fusion of a cytoplast and a whole cell)

CYBRIDS ▸ cybrid

CYCAD n type of tropical or subtropical plant with an unbranched stem and fernlike leaves crowded at the top

CYCADS ▸ cycad

CYCAS n palm tree of the genus Cycas

CYCASES ▸ cycas

CYCASIN n glucoside, toxic to mammals, occurring in cycads

CYCLASE n enzyme which acts as a catalyst in the formation of a cyclic compound

CYCLE vb ride a bicycle ▷ n bicycle

CYCLED ▸ cycle

CYCLER same as ▸ **cyclist**

CYCLERS ▸ cyclist

CYCLERY n business dealing in bicycles and bicycle accessories

CYCLES ▸ cycle

CYCLIC adj recurring or revolving in cycles

CYCLIN n type of protein

CYCLING ▸ cycle

CYCLINS ▸ cyclin

CYCLISE same as ▸ **cyclize**

CYCLIST n person who rides a bicycle

CYCLIZE vb be cyclical

CYCLO n type of rickshaw

CYCLOID adj resembling a circle ▷ n curve described by a point on the circumference of a circle as the circle rolls along a straight line

CYCLONE n violent wind moving round a central area

CYCLOPS n type of copepod characterized by having one eye

CYCLOS ▸ cyclo

CYCLUS n cycle

CYDER same as ▸ **cider**

CYDERS ▸ cyder

CYESES ▸ cyesis

CYESIS the technical name for ▸ **pregnancy**

CYGNET n young swan

CYGNETS ▸ cygnet

CYLICES ▸ cylix

CYLIX same as ▸ **kylix**

CYMA n moulding with a double curve, part concave

and part convex

CYMAE ▸ cyma

CYMAR n woman's short fur-trimmed jacket, popular in the 17th and 18th centuries

CYMARS ▸ cymar

CYMAS ▸ cyma

CYMATIA ▸ cymatium

CYMBAL n percussion instrument consisting of a brass plate which is struck against another or hit with a stick

CYMBALO another name for ▸ **dulcimer**

CYMBALS ▸ cymbal

CYME n flower cluster which has a single flower on the end of each stem and of which the central flower blooms first

CYMENE n colourless insoluble liquid with an aromatic odour that exists in three isomeric forms

CYMENES ▸ cymene

CYMES ▸ cyme

CYMLIN same as ▸ **cymling**

CYMLING n pattypan squash

CYMLINS ▸ cymlin

CYMOID adj resembling a cyme or cyma

CYMOL same as ▸ **cymene**

CYMOLS ▸ cymol

CYMOSE adj having the characteristics of a cyme

CYMOUS adj relating to a cyme

CYNIC n person who believes that people always act selfishly ▷ adj of or relating to Sirius, the Dog Star

CYNICAL adj believing that people always act selfishly

CYNICS ▸ cynic

CYPHER same as ▸ **cipher**

CYPHERS ▸ cypher

CYPRES n legal doctrine stating that a testator's intentions should be carried out as closely as possible

CYPRESS n evergreen tree with dark green leaves

CYPRIAN n prostitute or dancer

CYPRID n cypris

CYPRIDS ▸ cyprid

CYPRINE adj relating to carp

CYPRIS n member of the genus Cypris (small bivalve freshwater crustaceans)

CYPRUS same as ▸ **cypress**

CYPSELA n dry one-seeded fruit of the daisy and related plants, which resembles an achene but is surrounded by a calyx sheath

CYST n (abnormal) sac in the body containing fluid or soft matter

CYSTEIN same as > **cysteine**

CYSTIC adj of, relating to, or resembling a cyst

CYSTID n cystidean

CYSTIDS ▸ cystid

CYSTINE n sulphur-containing amino acid

CYSTOID adj resembling a cyst or bladder ▷ n tissue mass, such as a tumour, that resembles a cyst but lacks an outer membrane

CYSTS ▸ cyst

CYTASE n cellulose-dissolving enzyme

CYTASES ▸ cytase

CYTE n biological cell

CYTES ▸ cyte

CYTISI ▸ cytisus

CYTISUS n any plant of the broom genus, Cytisus

CYTODE n mass of protoplasm without a nucleus

CYTODES ▸ cytode

CYTOID adj resembling a cell

CYTON n main part of a neuron

CYTONS ▸ cyton

CYTOSOL n solution of proteins and metabolites inside a biological cell, in which the organelles are suspended

CZAPKA n leather and felt peaked military helmet of Polish origin

CZAPKAS ▸ czapka

CZAR same as ▸ **tsar**

CZARDAS n Hungarian national dance of alternating slow and fast sections

CZARDOM ▸ czar

CZARINA variant spellings (esp US) of ▸ **tsarina**

CZARISM a variant spelling (esp US) of ▸ **tsarism**

CZARIST ▸ czarism

CZARS ▸ czar

Dd

D forms a two-letter word before every vowel except **U**. There are plenty of good three-letter words beginning with **D**, particularly those with a **Y** or **W**: **day**, **dye** and **dew** are worth 7 points each, for example. And don't forget **dex** and **dux** for 11 points each and the invaluable **dzo** for 13 points.

DA n Burmese knife

DAAL n (in Indian cookery) split pulses

DAALS ▸ daal

DAB vb pat lightly ▷ n small amount of something soft or moist

DABBA n in Indian cookery, round metal box used to transport hot food

DABBAS ▸ dabba

DABBED ▸ dab

DABBER n pad used by printers for applying ink by hand

DABBERS ▸ dabber

DABBING ▸ dab

DABBITY n temporary tattoo

DABBLE vb be involved in something superficially

DABBLED ▸ dabble

DABBLER ▸ dabble

DABBLES ▸ dabble

DABS ▸ dab

DABSTER n incompetent or amateurish worker

DACE n small European freshwater fish

DACES ▸ dace

DACHA n country cottage in Russia

DACHAS ▸ dacha

DACITE n volcanic rock

DACITES ▸ dacite

DACK vb remove the trousers from (someone) by force

DACKED ▸ dack

DACKER vb walk slowly

DACKERS ▸ dacker

DACKING ▸ dack

DACKS ▸ dack

DACOIT n (in India and Myanmar) a member of a gang of armed robbers

DACOITS ▸ dacoit

DACOITY n (in India and Myanmar) robbery by an armed gang

DACRON n US tradename for a synthetic polyester fibre or fabric characterized by lightness and crease resistance

DACRONS ▸ dacron

DACTYL n metrical foot of three syllables, one long followed by two short

DACTYLI > dactylus

DACTYLS ▸ dactyl

DAD n father ▷ vb act or treat as a father

DADA n nihilistic artistic movement of the early 20th century

DADAH n illegal drugs

DADAHS ▸ dadah

DADAISM same as ▸ dada

DADAIST ▸ dada

DADAS ▸ dada

DADDED ▸ dad

DADDIES ▸ daddy

DADDING ▸ dad

DADDLE vb walk unsteadily

DADDLED ▸ daddle

DADDLES ▸ daddle

DADDOCK n core of a dead tree

DADDY n father

DADGUM mild form of ▸ damned

DADO n lower part of an interior wall, below a rail, decorated differently from the upper part ▷ vb provide with a dado

DADOED ▸ dado

DADOES ▸ dado

DADOING ▸ dado

DADOS ▸ dado

DADS ▸ dad

DAE a Scots word for ▸ do

DAEDAL adj skilful or intricate

DAEING ▸ dae

DAEMON same as ▸ demon

DAEMONS ▸ daemon

DAES ▸ dae

DAFF vb frolic

DAFFED ▸ daff

DAFFIER ▸ daffy

DAFFIES ▸ daffy

DAFFILY ▸ daffy

DAFFING ▸ daff

DAFFS ▸ daff

DAFFY another word for ▸ daft

DAFT adj foolish or crazy

DAFTAR Indian word for ▸ office

DAFTARS ▸ daftar

DAFTER ▸ daft

DAFTEST ▸ daft

DAFTIE n foolish person

DAFTIES ▸ daftie

DAFTLY ▸ daft

DAG n character ▷ vb cut daglocks from sheep

DAGABA n shrine for Buddhist relics

DAGABAS ▸ dagaba

DAGGA n cannabis

DAGGAS ▸ dagga

DAGGED ▸ dag

DAGGER ▸ dag

DAGGERS ▸ dag

DAGGIER ▸ daggy

DAGGING ▸ dag

DAGGLE vb trail through water

DAGGLED ▸ daggle

DAGGLES ▸ daggle

DAGGY adj amusing

DAGLOCK n dung-caked

lock of wool around the hindquarters of a sheep

DAGOBA n dome-shaped shrine containing relics of the Buddha or a Buddhist saint

DAGOBAS ▶ dagoba

DAGS ▶ dag

DAGWOOD n European shrub

DAH n long sound used in combination with the short sound in the spoken representation of Morse and other telegraphic codes

DAHL same as ▶ dhal

DAHLIA n brightly coloured garden flower

DAHLIAS ▶ dahlia

DAHLS ▶ dahl

DAHOON n evergreen shrub

DAHOONS ▶ dahoon

DAHS ▶ dah

DAIDLE vb waddle about

DAIDLED ▶ daidle

DAIDLES ▶ daidle

DAIKER vb walk slowly

DAIKERS ▶ daiker

DAIKO n Japanese drum

DAIKON another name for ▶ mooli

DAIKONS ▶ daikon

DAIKOS ▶ daiko

DAILIES ▶ daily

DAILY adj occurring every day or every weekday ▷ adv every day ▷ n daily newspaper

DAIMEN adj occasional

DAIMIO same as ▶ daimyo

DAIMIOS ▶ daimio

DAIMOKU n Nichiren Buddhist chant

DAIMON same as ▶ demon

DAIMONS ▶ daimon

DAIMYO n (in Japan) one of the territorial magnates who dominated much of the country from about the 11th to the 19th century

DAIMYOS ▶ daimyo

DAINE vb condescend

DAINED ▶ daine

DAINES ▶ daine

DAINING ▶ daine

DAINT adj dainty

DAINTY adj delicate or elegant ▷ n small cake or sweet

DAIRIES ▶ dairy

DAIRY n place for the processing or sale of milk and its products ▷ adj of

milk or its products

DAIS n raised platform in a hall, used by a speaker

DAISES ▶ dais

DAISIED ▶ daisy

DAISIES ▶ daisy

DAISY n small wild flower with a yellow centre and white petals

DAK n system of mail delivery or passenger transport by relays of bearers or horses stationed at intervals along a route

> A **dak** is an old mail or transport system, often useful for disposing of the K.

DAKER vb walk slowly

DAKERED ▶ daker

DAKERS ▶ daker

DAKOIT same as ▶ dacoit

DAKOITI same as ▶ dakoit

DAKOITS ▶ dakoit

DAKOITY n armed robbery

DAKS an informal name for > trousers

DAL same as > decalitre

DALAPON n herbicide

DALASI n standard monetary unit of The Gambia, divided into 100 bututs

DALASIS ▶ dalasi

DALE n (esp in N England) valley

DALED same as ▶ daleth

DALEDH n letter of Hebrew alphabet

DALEDHS ▶ daledh

DALEDS ▶ daled

DALES ▶ dale

DALETH n fourth letter of the Hebrew alphabet, transliterated as d or, when final, dh

DALETHS ▶ daleth

DALGYTE another name for ▶ bilby

DALI n type of tree

DALIS ▶ dali

DALLE ▶ dalles

DALLES pl n stretch of a river between high rock walls, with rapids and dangerous currents

DALLIED ▶ dally

DALLIER ▶ dally

DALLIES ▶ dally

DALLOP n semisolid lump

DALLOPS ▶ dallop

DALLY vb waste time

DALS ▶ dal

DALT n foster child

DALTON n atomic mass unit

DALTONS ▶ dalton

DALTS ▶ dalt

DAM n barrier built across a river to create a lake ▷ vb build a dam across (a river)

DAMAGE vb harm, spoil ▷ n harm to a person or thing

DAMAGED ▶ damage

DAMAGER ▶ damage

DAMAGES pl n money awarded as compensation for injury or loss

DAMAN n the Syrian rock hyrax

DAMANS ▶ daman

DAMAR same as ▶ dammar

DAMARS ▶ dammar

DAMASK n fabric with a pattern woven into it, used for tablecloths etc ▷ vb ornament (metal) by etching or inlaying, usually with gold or silver

DAMASKS ▶ damask

DAMBROD n draughtboard

DAME n woman

DAMES ▶ dame

DAMFOOL adj foolish

DAMIANA n herbal medicine

DAMMAR n any of various resins obtained from SE Asian trees used for varnishes, lacquers, bases for oil paints, etc

DAMMARS ▶ dammar

DAMME interj exclamation of surprise

DAMMED ▶ dam

DAMMER same as ▶ dammar

DAMMERS ▶ dammer

DAMMING ▶ dam

DAMMIT interj exclamation of surprise

DAMN interj exclamation of annoyance ▷ adj extreme(ly) ▷ vb condemn as bad or worthless

DAMNED adj condemned to hell ▷ adv extreme or extremely

DAMNER n person who damns

DAMNERS ▶ damner

DAMNIFY vb cause loss or damage to (a person)

DAMNING ▶ damn

DAMNS ▶ damn

DAMOSEL same as ▶ damsel

DAMOZEL same as ▶ damsel

DAMP *adj* slightly wet ▷ *n* slight wetness, moisture ▷ *vb* make damp

DAMPED ▸ damp

DAMPEN *vb* reduce the intensity of

DAMPENS ▸ dampen

DAMPER *n* movable plate to regulate the draught in a fire

DAMPERS ▸ damper

DAMPEST ▸ damp

DAMPIER ▸ dampy

DAMPING *n* moistening or wetting

DAMPISH ▸ damp

DAMPLY ▸ damp

DAMPS ▸ damp

DAMPY *adj* damp

DAMS ▸ dam

DAMSEL *n* young woman

DAMSELS ▸ damsel

DAMSON *n* small blue-black plumlike fruit

DAMSONS ▸ damson

DAN *n* in judo, any of the 10 black-belt grades of proficiency

DANAZOL *n* type of drug

DANCE *vb* move the feet and body rhythmically in time to music ▷ *n* series of steps and movements in time to music

DANCED ▸ dance

DANCER ▸ dance

DANCERS ▸ dance

DANCES ▸ dance

DANCEY *adj* of, relating to, or resembling dance music

DANCIER ▸ dancey

DANCING ▸ dance

DANCY *adj* (of music) appropriate for dancing

DANDER *n* stroll ▷ *vb* stroll

DANDERS ▸ dander

DANDIER ▸ dandy

DANDIES ▸ dandy

DANDIFY *vb* dress like or cause to resemble a dandy

DANDILY ▸ dandy

DANDLE *vb* move (a child) up and down on one's knee

DANDLED ▸ dandle

DANDLER ▸ dandle

DANDLES ▸ dandle

DANDY *n* man who is overconcerned with the elegance of his appearance ▷ *adj* very good

DANELAW *n* Danish law and customs of northern, central, and eastern parts

of Anglo-Saxon England

DANG *a euphemistic word for* ▸ **damn**

DANGED ▸ dang

DANGER *n* possibility of being injured or killed ▷ *vb* in archaic usage, endanger

DANGERS ▸ danger

DANGING ▸ dang

DANGLE *vb* hang loosely ▷ *n* act of dangling or something that dangles

DANGLED ▸ dangle

DANGLER ▸ dangle

DANGLES ▸ dangle

DANGLY ▸ dangle

DANGS ▸ dang

DANIO *n* type of brightly coloured tropical freshwater fish popular in aquariums

DANIOS ▸ danio

DANISH *n* sweet pastry

DANK *adj* unpleasantly damp and chilly ▷ *n* unpleasant damp and chilliness

DANKER ▸ dank

DANKEST ▸ dank

DANKISH ▸ dank

DANKLY ▸ dank

DANKS ▸ dank

DANNIES ▸ danny

DANNY *n* hand (used esp when addressing children)

DANS ▸ dan

DANSEUR *n* male ballet dancer

DANT *vb* intimidate

DANTED ▸ dant

DANTING ▸ dant

DANTON *same as* ▸ **daunton**

DANTONS ▸ danton

DANTS ▸ dant

DAP *vb* fish with a natural or artificial fly on a floss silk line so that the wind makes the fly bob on and off the surface of the water

DAPHNE *n* ornamental Eurasian shrub with shiny evergreen leaves and clusters of small bell-shaped flowers

DAPHNES ▸ daphne

DAPHNIA *n* type of water flea with a rounded body in a transparent shell

DAPHNID *n* water flea

DAPPED ▸ dap

DAPPER *adj* (of a man) neat in appearance ▷ *n*

fisherman or -woman who uses a bobbing bait

DAPPERS ▸ dapper

DAPPING ▸ dap

DAPPLE *vb* mark or become marked with spots or patches of a different colour ▷ *n* mottled or spotted markings ▷ *adj* marked with dapples or spots

DAPPLED ▸ dapple

DAPPLES ▸ dapple

DAPS ▸ dap

DAPSONE *n* antimicrobial drug used to treat leprosy and certain types of dermatitis

DAQUIRI *n* rum cocktail

DARAF *n* unit of elastance equal to a reciprocal farad

DARAFS ▸ daraf

DARB *n* something excellent

DARBAR *n* hall in Sikh temple

DARBARS ▸ darbar

DARBIES > handcuffs

DARBS ▸ darb

DARCIES ▸ darcy

DARCY *n* unit expressing the permeability coefficient of rock

DARCYS ▸ darcy

DARE *vb* be courageous enough to try (to do something) ▷ *n* challenge to do something risky

DARED ▸ dare

DAREFUL *adj* daring

DARER ▸ dare

DARERS ▸ dare

DARES ▸ dare

DARESAY *vb* venture to say

DARG *n* day's work

DARGA *n* Muslim shrine

DARGAH *n* tomb of a Muslim saint

DARGAHS ▸ dargah

DARGAS ▸ darga

DARGLE *n* wooded hollow

DARGLES ▸ dargle

DARGS ▸ darg

DARI *n* variety of sorghum

DARIC *n* gold coin of ancient Persia

DARICS ▸ daric

DARING *adj* willing to take risks ▷ *n* courage to do dangerous things

DARINGS ▸ daring

DARIOLE *n* small cup-shaped mould used for

D

making individual sweet or savoury dishes

DARIS ▸ **dari**

DARK adj having little or no light ▷ vb in archaic usage, darken

DARKED ▸ **dark**

DARKEN vb make or become dark or darker

DARKENS ▸ **darken**

DARKER ▸ **dark**

DARKEST ▸ **dark**

DARKING ▸ **dark**

DARKISH ▸ **dark**

DARKLE vb grow dark

DARKLED ▸ **darkle**

DARKLES ▸ **darkle**

DARKLY ▸ **dark**

DARKNET n covert communication network on the Internet

DARKS ▸ **dark**

DARLING n much-loved person ▷ adj much-loved

DARN vb mend (a garment) with a series of interwoven stitches ▷ n patch of darned work

DARNED adj damned

DARNEL n weed that grows in grain fields

DARNELS ▸ **darnel**

DARNER ▸ **darn**

DARNERS ▸ **darn**

DARNING ▸ **darn**

DARNS ▸ **darn**

DAROGHA n in India, manager

DARRAIN vb clear of guilt

DARRAYN vb clear of guilt

DARRE vb dare

DARRED ▸ **darre**

DARRES ▸ **darre**

DARRING ▸ **darre**

DARSHAN n Hindu blessing

DART n small narrow pointed missile that is thrown or shot, esp in the game of darts ▷ vb move or direct quickly and suddenly

DARTED ▸ **dart**

DARTER n type of aquatic bird of tropical and subtropical inland waters, with a long slender neck and bill

DARTERS ▸ **darter**

DARTING ▸ **dart**

DARTLE vb move swiftly

DARTLED ▸ **dartle**

DARTLES ▸ **dartle**

DARTRE n skin disease

DARTRES ▸ **dartre**

DARTS n game in which darts are thrown at a dartboard

DARZI n tailor in India

DARZIS ▸ **darzi**

DAS ▸ **da**

DASH vb move quickly ▷ n sudden quick movement

DASHED ▸ **dash**

DASHEEN another name for ▸ **taro**

DASHEKI n upper garment

DASHER n one of the boards surrounding an ice-hockey rink

DASHERS ▸ **dasher**

DASHES ▸ **dash**

DASHI n clear stock made from dried fish and kelp

DASHIER ▸ **dashy**

DASHIKI n large loose-fitting buttonless upper garment worn esp by Blacks in the US, Africa, and the Caribbean

DASHING adj stylish and attractive

DASHIS ▸ **dashi**

DASHPOT n device for damping vibrations

DASHY adj showy

DASSIE n type of hoofed rodent-like animal

DASSIES ▸ **dassie**

DASTARD n contemptible sneaking coward

DASYPOD n armadillo

DASYURE n small marsupial of Australia, New Guinea, and adjacent islands

DATA n information consisting of observations, measurements, or facts

DATABLE ▸ **date**

DATABUS n computing term

DATAL adj slow-witted ▷ n day labour

DATALS ▸ **datal**

DATARIA n Roman Catholic office

DATARY n head of the dataria, the papal office that assesses candidates for benefices reserved to the Holy See

DATCHA same as ▸ **dacha**

DATCHAS ▸ **datcha**

DATE n specified day of the month ▷ vb mark with the date

DATED adj old-fashioned

DATEDLY ▸ **dated**

DATER n person who dates

DATERS ▸ **dater**

DATES ▸ **date**

DATING n any of several techniques, such as radioactive dating, dendrochronology, or varve dating, for establishing the age of rocks, palaeontological or archaeological specimens, etc

DATINGS ▸ **dating**

DATIVAL ▸ **dative**

DATIVE adj denoting a case of nouns, pronouns, and adjectives used to express the indirect object ▷ n this grammatical case

DATIVES ▸ **dative**

DATO n chief of any of certain Muslim tribes in the Philippine Islands

DATOS ▸ **dato**

DATTO n Datsun car

DATTOS ▸ **datto**

DATUM n single piece of information in the form of a fact or statistic

DATUMS ▸ **datum**

DATURA n type of chiefly Indian plant with large trumpet-shaped flowers, prickly pods, and narcotic properties

DATURAS ▸ **datura**

DATURIC ▸ **datura**

DAUB vb smear or spread quickly or clumsily ▷ n crude or badly done painting

DAUBE n braised meat stew

DAUBED ▸ **daub**

DAUBER ▸ **daub**

DAUBERS ▸ **daub**

DAUBERY n act or an instance of daubing

DAUBES ▸ **daube**

DAUBIER ▸ **daub**

DAUBING ▸ **daub**

DAUBRY n unskilful painting

DAUBS ▸ **daub**

DAUBY ▸ **daub**

DAUD n lump or chunk of something ▷ vb (in dialect) whack

DAUDED ▸ **daud**

DAUDING ▸ **daud**

DAUDS ▸ **daud**

DAULT n foster child

DAULTS ▸ dault
DAUNDER vb stroll
DAUNER vb stroll
DAUNERS ▸ dauner
DAUNT vb intimidate
DAUNTED ▸ daunt
DAUNTER ▸ daunt
DAUNTON vb dishearten
DAUNTS ▸ daunt
DAUPHIN n (formerly) eldest son of the king of France
DAUR a Scots word for ▸ **dare**
DAURED ▸ daur
DAURING ▸ daur
DAURS ▸ daur
DAUT vb fondle
DAUTED ▸ daut
DAUTIE n darling
DAUTIES ▸ dautie
DAUTING ▸ daut
DAUTS ▸ daut
DAVEN vb pray
DAVENED ▸ daven
DAVENS ▸ daven
DAVIDIA n Chinese shrub
DAVIES ▸ davy
DAVIT n crane, usu one of a pair, at a ship's side, for lowering and hoisting a lifeboat
DAVITS ▸ davit
DAVY n miner's safety lamp
DAW n an archaic, dialect, or poetic name for a jackdaw ▷ vb old word for dawn

> This is another name for a **jackdaw**. It is worth remembering that not only does this little word take D, K, N, S and T at the back, to make **dawd, dawk, dawn, daws** and **dawt**, but you can put an A on the front of it to make **adaw**.

DAWAH n practice of educating non-Muslims about the message of Islam
DAWAHS ▸ dawah
DAWBAKE n foolish or slow-witted person
DAWBRY n unskilful painting
DAWCOCK n male jackdaw
DAWD vb thump
DAWDED ▸ dawd
DAWDING ▸ dawd
DAWDLE vb walk slowly, lag behind
DAWDLED ▸ dawdle
DAWDLER ▸ dawdle
DAWDLES ▸ dawdle

DAWDS ▸ dawd
DAWED ▸ daw
DAWEN ▸ daw
DAWING ▸ daw
DAWISH ▸ daw
DAWK same as ▸ **dak**
DAWKS ▸ dawk
DAWN n daybreak ▷ vb begin to grow light
DAWNED ▸ dawn
DAWNER vb stroll
DAWNERS ▸ dawner
DAWNEY adj (of a person) dull or slow
DAWNING ▸ dawn
DAWNS ▸ dawn
DAWS ▸ daw
DAWT vb fondle
DAWTED ▸ dawt
DAWTIE n darling
DAWTIES ▸ dawtie
DAWTING ▸ dawt
DAWTS ▸ dawt
DAY n period of 24 hours
DAYAN n senior rabbi, esp one who sits in a religious court
DAYANIM ▸ dayan
DAYANS ▸ dayan
DAYBED n narrow bed with a head piece and sometimes a foot piece and back, for day use
DAYBEDS ▸ daybed
DAYBOAT n small sailing boat with no sleeping accommodation
DAYBOOK n book in which the transactions of each day are recorded as they occur
DAYBOY n boy who attends a boarding school daily, but returns home each evening
DAYBOYS ▸ dayboy
DAYCARE n occupation, treatment, or supervision during the working day for people who might be at risk if left on their own, or whose usual carers need daytime relief
DAYCH vb thatch
DAYCHED ▸ daych
DAYCHES ▸ daych
DAYFLY another name for ▸ **mayfly**
DAYGIRL n a girl who attends boarding school during the day but returns home in the evening
DAYGLO n fluorescent colours

DAYGLOW n fluorescent colours
DAYLILY n any of various plants having lily-like flowers that typically last only one day before being succeeded by others
DAYLIT ▸ daylight
DAYLONG adv lasting the entire day
DAYMARE n bad dream during the day
DAYMARK n navigation aid
DAYNT adj dainty
DAYPACK n small rucksack
DAYROOM n communal living room in a residential institution
DAYS adv during the day, esp regularly
DAYSACK n rucksack
DAYSIDE n side of a planet nearest the sun
DAYSMAN n umpire
DAYSMEN ▸ daysman
DAYSTAR a poetic word for ▸ **sun**
DAYTALE n day labour
DAYTIME n time from sunrise to sunset
DAYWEAR n clothes for everyday or informal wear
DAYWORK n daytime work
DAZE vb. stun, by a blow or shock ▷ n state of confusion or shock
DAZED ▸ daze
DAZEDLY ▸ daze
DAZER ▸ daze
DAZERS ▸ daze
DAZES ▸ daze
DAZING ▸ daze
DAZZLE vb impress greatly ▷ n bright light that dazzles
DAZZLED ▸ dazzle
DAZZLER ▸ dazzle
DAZZLES ▸ dazzle
DE prep of or from
DEACON n ordained minister ranking immediately below a priest ▷ vb make a deacon of
DEACONS ▸ deacon
DEAD adj no longer alive ▷ n period during which coldness or darkness is most intense ▷ adv extremely ▷ vb in archaic usage, die or kill
DEADBOY ▸ deadman
DEADED ▸ dead
DEADEN vb make less intense

DEADENS ▸ deaden
DEADER ▸ dead
DEADERS ▸ dead
DEADEST ▸ dead
DEADEYE n either of a pair of disclike wooden blocks, supported by straps in grooves around them, between which a line is rove so as to draw them together to tighten a shroud
DEADING ▸ dead
DEADLY adj likely to cause death ▷ adv extremely
DEADMAN n heavy plate, wall, or block buried in the ground that acts as an anchor for a retaining wall, sheet pile, etc, by a tie connecting the two
DEADMEN ▸ deadman
DEADPAN adv showing no emotion or expression ▷ adj deliberately emotionless ▷ n deadpan expression or manner
DEADS ▸ dead
DEAF adj unable to hear
DEAFEN vb make deaf, esp temporarily
DEAFENS ▸ deafen
DEAFER ▸ deaf
DEAFEST ▸ deaf
DEAFISH ▸ deaf
DEAFLY ▸ deaf
DEAIR vb reove air from
DEAIRED ▸ deair
DEAIRS ▸ deair
DEAL n agreement or transaction ▷ vb inflict (a blow) on ▷ adj of fir or pine
DEALATE adj (of ants and other insects) having lost their wings, esp by biting or rubbing them off after mating ▷ n insect that has shed its wings
DEALER n person whose business involves buying and selling
DEALERS ▸ dealer
DEALING ▸ deal
DEALS ▸ deal
DEALT ▸ deal
DEAN n chief administrative official of a college or university faculty ▷ vb punish (a student) by sending them to the dean
DEANED ▸ dean
DEANER n shilling
DEANERS ▸ deaner

DEANERY n office or residence of a dean
DEANING ▸ dean
DEANS ▸ dean
DEAR n someone regarded with affection ▷ adj much-loved
DEARE vb harm
DEARED ▸ deare
DEARER ▸ dear
DEARES ▸ dear
DEAREST ▸ dear
DEARIE same as ▸ deary
DEARIES ▸ deary
DEARING ▸ deare
DEARLY adv very much
DEARN vb hide
DEARNLY ▸ dearn
DEARNS ▸ dearn
DEARS ▸ dear
DEARTH n inadequate amount, scarcity
DEARTHS ▸ dearth
DEARY n term of affection: now often sarcastic or facetious
DEASH vb remove ash from
DEASHED ▸ deash
DEASHES ▸ deash
DEASIL adv in the direction of the apparent course of the sun ▷ n motion in this direction
DEASILS ▸ deasil
DEASIUL n motion towards the sun
DEASOIL n motion towards the sun
DEATH n permanent end of life in a person or animal
DEATHLY adv like death ▷ adj resembling death
DEATHS ▸ death
DEATHY ▸ death
DEAVE vb deafen
DEAVED ▸ deave
DEAVES ▸ deave
DEAVING ▸ deave
DEAW n dew
DEAWIE ▸ deaw
DEAWS ▸ deaw
DEAWY ▸ deaw
DEB n debutante
DEBACLE n disastrous failure
DEBAG vb remove the trousers from (someone) by force
DEBAGS ▸ debag
DEBAR vb prevent, bar
DEBARK vb remove the bark from (a tree)
DEBARKS ▸ debark

DEBARS ▸ debar
DEBASE vb lower in value, quality, or character
DEBASED ▸ debase
DEBASER ▸ debase
DEBASES ▸ debase
DEBATE n discussion ▷ vb discuss formally
DEBATED ▸ debate
DEBATER ▸ debate
DEBATES ▸ debate
DEBAUCH vb make (someone) bad or corrupt, esp sexually ▷ n instance or period of extreme dissipation
DEBBIER ▸ debby
DEBBIES ▸ debby
DEBBY n debutante ▷ adj of, or resembling a debutante
DEBE n tin
DEBEAK vb remove part of the beak of poultry to reduce the risk of such habits as feather-picking or cannibalism
DEBEAKS ▸ debeak
DEBEARD vb remove beard from mussel
DEBEL vb beat in war
DEBELS ▸ debel
DEBES ▸ debe
DEBILE adj lacking strength
DEBIT n acknowledgment of a sum owing by entry on the left side of an account ▷ vb charge (an account) with a debt
DEBITED ▸ debit
DEBITOR n person in debt
DEBITS ▸ debit
DEBONE vb remove bones from
DEBONED ▸ debone
DEBONER ▸ debone
DEBONES ▸ debone
DEBOSH vb debauch
DEBOSS vb carve a design into
DEBOUCH vb move out from a narrow place to a wider one ▷ n outlet or passage, as for the exit of troops
DEBRIDE vb remove dead tissue from
DEBRIEF vb receive a report from (a soldier, diplomat, etc) after an event
DEBRIS n fragments of something destroyed
DEBS ▸ deb

DEBT *n* something owed, esp money
DEBTED *adj* in debt
DEBTEE *n* person owed a debt
DEBTEES ▸ debtee
DEBTOR *n* person who owes money
DEBTORS ▸ debtor
DEBTS ▸ debt
DEBUD *same as* ▸ **disbud**
DEBUDS ▸ debud
DEBUG *vb* find and remove defects in (a computer program) ▷ *n* something, esp a computer program, that locates and removes defects in a device, system, etc
DEBUGS ▸ debug
DEBUNK *vb* expose the falseness of
DEBUNKS ▸ debunk
DEBUR *vb* remove burs from (a piece of machined metal)
DEBURR *vb* remove burrs from (a workpiece)
DEBURRS ▸ deburr
DEBURS ▸ debur
DEBUS *vb* unload (goods) or (esp of troops) to alight from a motor vehicle
DEBUSED ▸ debus
DEBUSES ▸ debus
DEBUT *n* first public appearance of a performer ▷ *vb* make a debut
DEBUTED ▸ debut
DEBUTS ▸ debut
DEBYE *n* unit of electric dipole moment
DEBYES ▸ debye
DECAD *n* ten years
DECADAL ▸ decade
DECADE *n* period of ten years
DECADES ▸ decade
DECADS ▸ decad
DECAF *n* decaffeinated coffee ▷ *adj* decaffeinated
DECAFF *n* decaffeinated coffee
DECAFFS ▸ decaff
DECAFS ▸ decaf
DECAGON *n* geometric figure with ten faces
DECAL *vb* transfer (a design) by decalcomania
DECALED ▸ decal
DECALOG *same as* > **decalogue**
DECALS ▸ decal
DECAMP *vb* depart secretly or suddenly

DECAMPS ▸ decamp
DECANAL *adj* of or relating to a dean or deanery
DECANE *n* liquid alkane hydrocarbon
DECANES ▸ decane
DECANI *adv* be sung by the decanal side of a choir
DECANT *vb* pour (a liquid) from one container to another
DECANTS ▸ decant
DECAPOD *n* creature, such as a crab, with five pairs of walking limbs ▷ *adj* of, relating to, or belonging to these creatures
DECARB *vb* decoke
DECARBS ▸ decarb
DECARE *n* ten ares or 1000 square metres
DECARES ▸ decare
DECAY *vb* become weaker or more corrupt ▷ *n* process of decaying
DECAYED ▸ decay
DECAYER ▸ decay
DECAYS ▸ decay
DECCIE *n* decoration
DECCIES ▸ deccie
DECEASE *n* death
DECEIT *n* behaviour intended to deceive
DECEITS ▸ deceit
DECEIVE *vb* mislead by lying
DECENCY *n* conformity to the prevailing standards of what is right
DECENT *adj* (of a person) polite and morally acceptable
DECERN *vb* decree or adjudge
DECERNS ▸ decern
DECIARE *n* one tenth of an are or 10 square metres
DECIBEL *n* unit for measuring the intensity of sound
DECIDE *vb* (cause to) reach a decision
DECIDED *adj* unmistakable
DECIDER *n* point, goal, game, etc, that determines who wins a match or championship
DECIDES ▸ decide
DECIDUA *n* specialized mucous membrane that lines the uterus of some mammals during pregnancy: is shed, with the placenta, at parturition

DECILE *n* one of nine actual or notional values of a variable dividing its distribution into ten groups with equal frequencies: the ninth decile is the value below which 90% of the population lie
DECILES ▸ decile
DECIMAL *n* fraction written in the form of a dot followed by one or more numbers ▷ *adj* relating to or using powers of ten
DECIME *n* a former French coin
DECIMES ▸ decime
DECK *n* area of a ship that forms a floor ▷ *vb* dress or decorate
DECKED *adj* having a wooden deck or platform
DECKEL *same as* ▸ **deckle**
DECKELS ▸ deckel
DECKER ▸ deck
DECKERS ▸ deck
DECKING *n* wooden platform in a garden
DECKLE *n* frame used to contain pulp on the mould in the making of handmade paper
DECKLED ▸ deckle
DECKLES ▸ deckle
DECKO *n* look ▷ *vb* have a look
DECKOED ▸ decko
DECKOS ▸ decko
DECKS ▸ deck
DECLAIM *vb* speak loudly and dramatically
DECLARE *vb* state firmly and forcefully
DECLASS *vb* lower in social status or position
DECLAW *vb* remove claws from
DECLAWS ▸ declaw
DECLINE *vb* become smaller, weaker, or less important ▷ *n* gradual weakening or loss
DECO *adj* as in **art deco** style of art, jewellery, design, etc
DECOCT *vb* extract the essence from (a substance) by boiling
DECOCTS ▸ decoct
DECODE *vb* convert from code into ordinary language
DECODED ▸ decode

DECODER ▸ decode
DECODES ▸ decode
DECOKE n decarbonize
DECOKED ▸ decoke
DECOKES ▸ decoke
DECOLOR vb bleach
DECOR n style in which a room or house is decorated
DECORS ▸ decor
DECORUM n polite and socially correct behaviour
DECOS ▸ deco
DECOY n person or thing used to lure someone into danger ▷ vb lure away by means of a trick
DECOYED ▸ decoy
DECOYER ▸ decoy
DECOYS ▸ decoy
DECREE n law made by someone in authority ▷ vb order by decree
DECREED ▸ decree
DECREER ▸ decree
DECREES ▸ decree
DECREET n final judgment or sentence of a court
DECREW vb decrease
DECREWS ▸ decrew
DECRIAL ▸ decry
DECRIED ▸ decry
DECRIER ▸ decry
DECRIES ▸ decry
DECROWN vb depose
DECRY vb express disapproval of
DECRYPT vb decode (a message) with or without previous knowledge of its key
DECTET n ten musicians
DECTETS ▸ dectet
DECUMAN n large wave
DECUPLE vb increase by ten times ▷ n amount ten times as large as a given reference ▷ adj increasing tenfold
DECURIA n group of ten
DECURVE vb curve downwards
DECURY n (in ancient Rome) a body of ten men
DEDAL same as ▸ daedal
DEDANS n open gallery at the server's end of the court
DEDIMUS n legal term
DEDUCE vb reach (a conclusion) by reasoning from evidence
DEDUCED ▸ deduce
DEDUCES ▸ deduce
DEDUCT vb subtract

DEDUCTS ▸ deduct
DEE a Scots word for ▸ die
DEED n something that is done ▷ vb convey or transfer (property) by deed ▷ adj Scots form of dead
DEEDED ▸ deed
DEEDER ▸ deed
DEEDEST ▸ deed
DEEDFUL adj full of exploits
DEEDIER ▸ deedy
DEEDILY ▸ deedy
DEEDING ▸ deed
DEEDS ▸ deed
DEEDY adj hard-working
DEEING ▸ dee
DEEJAY n disc jockey ▷ vb work or act as a disc jockey
DEEJAYS ▸ deejay
DEEK vb look at
DEELY adj as in **deely boppers** hairband with two bobbing antennae-like attachments
DEEM vb consider, judge
DEEMED ▸ deem
DEEMING ▸ deem
DEEMS ▸ deem
DEEN n din
DEENS ▸ deen
DEEP adj extending or situated far down, inwards, backwards, or sideways ▷ n any deep place on land or under water
DEEPEN vb make or become deeper or more intense
DEEPENS ▸ deepen
DEEPER ▸ deep
DEEPEST ▸ deep
DEEPIE n 3D film
DEEPIES ▸ deepie
DEEPLY ▸ deep
DEEPS ▸ deep
DEER n large wild animal, the male of which has antlers
DEERE adj serious
DEERFLY n insect related to the horsefly
DEERLET n ruminant mammal
DEERS ▸ deer
DEES ▸ dee
DEET n insect-repellent
DEETS ▸ deet
DEEV n mythical monster
DEEVE vb deafen
DEEVED ▸ deeve
DEEVES ▸ deeve
DEEVING ▸ deeve
DEEVS ▸ deev
DEEWAN n chief of a village in India

DEEWANS ▸ deewan
DEF adj very good
DEFACE vb deliberately spoil the appearance of
DEFACED ▸ deface
DEFACER ▸ deface
DEFACES ▸ deface
DEFAME vb attack the good reputation of
DEFAMED ▸ defame
DEFAMER ▸ defame
DEFAMES ▸ defame
DEFANG vb remove the fangs of
DEFANGS ▸ defang
DEFAST adj defaced
DEFASTE adj defaced
DEFAT vb remove fat from
DEFATS ▸ defat
DEFAULT n failure to do something ▷ vb fail to fulfil an obligation
DEFEAT vb win a victory over ▷ n defeating
DEFEATS ▸ defeat
DEFECT n imperfection, blemish ▷ vb desert one's cause or country to join the opposing forces
DEFECTS ▸ defect
DEFENCE n resistance against attack
DEFEND vb protect from harm or danger
DEFENDS ▸ defend
DEFENSE same as ▸ defence
DEFER vb delay (something) until a future time
DEFERS ▸ defer
DEFFER ▸ def
DEFFEST ▸ def
DEFFLY archaic word meaning the same as ▸ deftly
DEFFO interj definitely: an expression of agreement or consent
DEFI n challenge
DEFIANT adj marked by resistance or bold opposition, as to authority
DEFICIT n amount by which a sum of money is too small
DEFIED ▸ defy
DEFIER ▸ defy
DEFIERS ▸ defy
DEFIES ▸ defy
DEFILE vb treat (something sacred or important) without respect ▷ n narrow valley or pass
DEFILED ▸ defile
DEFILER ▸ defile
DEFILES ▸ defile

DEFINE vb state precisely the meaning of
DEFINED ▸ define
DEFINER ▸ define
DEFINES ▸ define
DEFIS ▸ defi
DEFLATE vb (cause to) collapse through the release of air
DEFLEA vb remove fleas from
DEFLEAS ▸ deflea
DEFLECT vb (cause to) turn aside from a course
DEFLEX vb turn downwards
DEFO interj (slang) definitely
DEFOAM vb remove foam from
DEFOAMS ▸ defoam
DEFOCUS vb put out of focus
DEFOG vb clear of vapour
DEFOGS ▸ defog
DEFORCE vb withhold (property, esp land) wrongfully or by force from the rightful owner
DEFORM vb put out of shape or spoil the appearance of
DEFORMS ▸ deform
DEFOUL vb defile
DEFOULS ▸ defoul
DEFRAG vb defragment
DEFRAGS ▸ defrag
DEFRAUD vb cheat out of money, property, etc
DEFRAY vb provide money for (costs or expenses)
DEFRAYS ▸ defray
DEFROCK vb deprive (a priest) of priestly status
DEFROST vb make or become free of ice
DEFROZE > defreeze
DEFT adj quick and skilful in movement
DEFTER ▸ deft
DEFTEST ▸ deft
DEFTLY ▸ deft
DEFUEL vb remove fuel from
DEFUELS ▸ defuel
DEFUNCT adj no longer existing or operative ▷ n deceased person
DEFUND vb stop funds to
DEFUNDS ▸ defund
DEFUSE vb remove the fuse of (an explosive device)
DEFUSED ▸ defuse
DEFUSER ▸ defuse
DEFUSES ▸ defuse

DEFUZE same as ▸ defuse
DEFUZED ▸ defuze
DEFUZES ▸ defuze
DEFY vb resist openly and boldly
DEFYING ▸ defy
DEG vb water (a plant, etc)
DEGAGE adj unconstrained in manner
DEGAME n tree of South and Central America
DEGAMES ▸ degame
DEGAMI same as ▸ degame
DEGAMIS ▸ degami
DEGAS vb remove gas from (a container, vacuum tube, liquid, adsorbent, etc)
DEGASES ▸ degas
DEGAUSS n demagnetize
DEGERM vb remove germs from
DEGERMS ▸ degerm
DEGGED ▸ deg
DEGGING ▸ deg
DEGLAZE vb dilute meat sediments in (a pan) in order to make a sauce or gravy
DEGOUT n disgust
DEGOUTS ▸ degout
DEGRADE vb reduce to dishonour or disgrace
DEGRAS n emulsion used for dressing hides
DEGREE n stage in a scale of relative amount or intensity
DEGREED adj having a degree
DEGREES ▸ degree
DEGS ▸ deg
DEGU n small S American rodent
DEGUM vb remove gum from
DEGUMS ▸ degum
DEGUS ▸ degu
DEGUST vb taste, esp with care or relish
DEGUSTS ▸ degust
DEHISCE vb (of the seed capsules of some plants) to burst open spontaneously
DEHORN vb remove or prevent the growth of the horns of (cattle, sheep, or goats)
DEHORNS ▸ dehorn
DEHORT vb dissuade
DEHORTS ▸ dehort
DEI ▸ deus
DEICE vb to free or be freed of ice

DEICED ▸ deice
DEICER ▸ deice
DEICERS ▸ deice
DEICES ▸ deice
DEICIDE n act of killing a god
DEICING ▸ deice
DEICTIC adj proving by direct argument
DEID a Scots word for ▸ dead
DEIDER ▸ deid
DEIDEST ▸ deid
DEIDS ▸ deid
DEIF a Scots word for ▸ deaf
DEIFER ▸ deif
DEIFEST ▸ deif
DEIFIC adj making divine or exalting to the position of a god
DEIFIED ▸ deify
DEIFIER ▸ deify
DEIFIES ▸ deify
DEIFORM adj having the form or appearance of a god
DEIFY vb treat or worship as a god
DEIGN vb agree (to do something), but as if doing someone a favour
DEIGNED ▸ deign
DEIGNS ▸ deign
DEIL a Scots word for ▸ devil
DEILS ▸ deil
DEINDEX vb cause to become no longer index-linked
DEISEAL n clockwise motion
DEISM n belief in God but not in divine revelation
DEISMS ▸ deism
DEIST ▸ deism
DEISTIC ▸ deism
DEISTS ▸ deism
DEITIES ▸ deity
DEITY n god or goddess
DEIXES ▸ deixis
DEIXIS n use or reference of a deictic word
DEJECT vb have a depressing effect on ▷ adj downcast
DEJECTA pl n waste products excreted through the anus
DEJECTS ▸ deject
DEJEUNE n lunch
DEKARE n unit of measurement equal to ten ares
DEKARES ▸ dekare
DEKE vb (in ice hockey or box lacrosse) to draw (a

D

defending player) out of position by faking a shot or movement ▷ *n* such a shot or movement

DEKED ▶ **deke**

DEKEING ▶ **deke**

DEKES ▶ **deke**

DEKING ▶ **deke**

DEKKO *n* look ▷ *vb* have a look

DEKKOED ▶ **dekko**

DEKKOS ▶ **dekko**

DEL *n* differential operator

DELAINE *n* sheer wool or wool and cotton fabric

DELAPSE *vb* be inherited

DELATE *vb* (formerly) to bring a charge against

DELATED ▶ **delate**

DELATES ▶ **delate**

DELATOR ▶ **delate**

DELAY *vb* put off to a later time ▷ *n* act of delaying

DELAYED ▶ **delay**

DELAYER ▶ **delay**

DELAYS ▶ **delay**

DELE *n* sign indicating that typeset matter is to be deleted ▷ *vb* mark (matter to be deleted) with a dele

DELEAD *vb* remove lead from

DELEADS ▶ **delead**

DELEAVE *vb* separate copies

DELEBLE *adj* able to be deleted

DELED ▶ **dele**

DELEING ▶ **dele**

DELENDA *pl n* items for deleting

DELES ▶ **dele**

DELETE *vb* remove (something written or printed)

DELETED ▶ **delete**

DELETES ▶ **delete**

DELF *n* kind of earthenware

DELFS ▶ **delf**

DELFT *n* tin-glazed earthenware, typically having blue designs on white

DELFTS ▶ **delft**

DELI *n* delicatessen

DELIBLE *adj* able to be deleted

DELICE *n* delicacy

DELICES ▶ **delice**

DELICT *n* wrongful act for which the person injured has the right to a civil remedy

DELICTS ▶ **delict**

DELIGHT *n* (source of) great pleasure ▷ *vb* please greatly

DELIME *vb* remove lime from

DELIMED ▶ **delime**

DELIMES ▶ **delime**

DELIMIT *vb* mark or lay down the limits of

DELIRIA ▶ **delirium**

DELIS ▶ **deli**

DELISH *adj* delicious

DELIST *vb* remove from a list

DELISTS ▶ **delist**

DELIVER *vb* carry (goods etc) to a destination

DELL *n* small wooded hollow

DELLIES ▶ **delly**

DELLS ▶ **dell**

DELLY *n* delicatessen

DELO *an informal word for* ▶ **delegate**

DELOPE *vb* shoot into the air

DELOPED ▶ **delope**

DELOPES ▶ **delope**

DELOS ▶ **delo**

DELOUSE *vb* rid (a person or animal) of lice

DELPH *n* kind of earthenware

DELPHIC *adj* obscure or ambiguous

DELPHIN *n* fatty substance from dolphin oil

DELPHS ▶ **delph**

DELS ▶ **del**

DELT *n* deltoid muscle

DELTA *n* fourth letter in the Greek alphabet

DELTAIC ▶ **delta**

DELTAS ▶ **delta**

DELTIC ▶ **delta**

DELTOID *n* thick muscle forming the rounded contour of the outer edge of the shoulder and acting to raise the arm ▷ *adj* shaped like a Greek capital delta

DELTS ▶ **delt**

DELUDE *vb* deceive

DELUDED ▶ **delude**

DELUDER ▶ **delude**

DELUDES ▶ **delude**

DELUGE *n* great flood ▷ *vb* flood

DELUGED ▶ **deluge**

DELUGES ▶ **deluge**

DELUXE *adj* rich, elegant, superior, or sumptuous

DELVE *vb* research deeply (for information)

DELVED ▶ **delve**

DELVER ▶ **delve**

DELVERS ▶ **delve**

DELVES ▶ **delve**

DELVING ▶ **delve**

DEMAGOG *same as* ▶ **demagogue**

DEMAIN *n* demesne

DEMAINE *n* demesne

DEMAINS ▶ **demain**

DEMAN *vb* reduce the workforce of (a plant, industry, etc)

DEMAND *vb* request forcefully ▷ *n* forceful request

DEMANDS ▶ **demand**

DEMANS ▶ **deman**

DEMARK *vb* demarcate

DEMARKS ▶ **demark**

DEMAST *vb* remove the mast from

DEMASTS ▶ **demast**

DEMAYNE *n* demesne

DEME *n* (in preclassical Greece) the territory inhabited by a tribe

DEMEAN *vb* lower (oneself) in dignity, status, or character

DEMEANE *n* demesne

DEMEANS ▶ **demean**

DEMENT *vb* deteriorate mentally, esp because of old age

DEMENTI *n* denial

DEMENTS ▶ **dement**

DEMERGE *vb* separate a company from another with which it was previously merged

DEMERIT *n* fault, disadvantage ▷ *vb* deserve

DEMERSE *vb* immerse

DEMES ▶ **deme**

DEMESNE *n* land surrounding a house

DEMETON *n* insecticide

DEMIC *adj* of population

DEMIES ▶ **demy**

DEMIGOD *n* being who is part mortal, part god

DEMIREP *n* woman of bad repute, esp a prostitute

DEMISE *n* eventual failure (of something successful) ▷ *vb* transfer for a limited period

DEMISED ▶ **demise**

DEMISES ▶ **demise**

DEMISS *adj* humble

DEMIST vb remove condensation from (a windscreen)

DEMISTS ▸ demist

DEMIT vb resign (an office, position, etc)

DEMITS ▸ demit

DEMIVEG n person who eats poultry and fish, but no red meat ▹ adj denoting a person who eats poultry and fish, but no red meat

DEMO n demonstration, organized expression of public opinion ▹ vb demonstrate

DEMOB vb demobilize

DEMOBS ▸ demob

DEMODE adj out of fashion

DEMODED adj out of fashion

DEMOED ▸ demo

DEMOING ▸ demo

DEMON n evil spirit

DEMONIC adj evil

DEMONRY ▸ demon

DEMONS ▸ demon

DEMOS n people of a nation regarded as a political unit

DEMOSES ▸ demos

DEMOTE vb reduce in status or rank

DEMOTED ▸ demote

DEMOTES ▸ demote

DEMOTIC adj of the common people ▹ n demotic script of ancient Egypt

DEMOUNT vb remove (a motor, gun, etc) from its mounting or setting

DEMPT ▸ deem

DEMUR vb raise objections or show reluctance ▹ n act of demurring

DEMURE adj quiet, reserved, and rather shy ▹ vb archaic for look demure ▹ n archaic for demure look

DEMURED ▸ demure

DEMURER ▸ demure

DEMURES ▸ demure

DEMURS ▸ demur

DEMY n size of printing paper, 17½ by 22½ inches (444.5 x 571.5 mm)

DEN n home of a wild animal ▹ vb live in or as if in a den

DENAR n standard monetary unit of Macedonia, divided into 100 deni

DENARI ▸ denar

DENARII ▸ denarius

DENARS ▸ denar

DENARY adj calculated by tens

DENAY vb deny

DENAYED ▸ denay

DENAYS ▸ denay

DENDRON same as ▸ dendrite

DENE n narrow wooded valley

DENES ▸ dene

DENET vb remove from the Net Book Agreement

DENETS ▸ denet

DENGUE n viral disease transmitted by mosquitoes, characterized by headache, fever, pains in the joints, and a rash

DENGUES ▸ dengue

DENI n monetary unit of the Former Yugoslav Republic of Macedonia, worth one hundredth of a denar

DENIAL n statement that something is not true

DENIALS ▸ denial

DENIED ▸ deny

DENIER n unit of weight used to measure the fineness of nylon or silk

DENIERS ▸ denier

DENIES ▸ deny

DENIM n hard-wearing cotton fabric, usu blue

DENIMED adj wearing denim

DENIMS pl n jeans or overalls made of denim

DENIS ▸ deni

DENIZEN n inhabitant ▹ vb make a denizen

DENNED ▸ den

DENNET n carriage for one horse

DENNETS ▸ dennet

DENNING ▸ den

DENOTE vb be a sign of

DENOTED ▸ denote

DENOTES ▸ denote

DENS ▸ den

DENSE adj closely packed

DENSELY ▸ dense

DENSER ▸ dense

DENSEST ▸ dense

DENSIFY vb make or become dense

DENSITY n degree to which something is filled or occupied

DENT n hollow in the surface of something, made by hitting it ▹ vb make a dent in

DENTAL adj of teeth or dentistry ▹ n dental consonant

DENTALS ▸ dental

DENTARY n lower jawbone with teeth

DENTATE adj having teeth or teethlike notches

DENTED ▸ dent

DENTEL n architectural term

DENTELS ▸ dentel

DENTEX n large predatory fish of Mediterranean and E Atlantic waters, with long sharp teeth and powerful jaws

DENTIL n one of a set of small square or rectangular blocks evenly spaced to form an ornamental row, usually under a classical cornice on a building, piece of furniture, etc

DENTILS ▸ dentil

DENTIN same as ▸ dentine

DENTINE n hard dense tissue forming the bulk of a tooth

DENTING ▸ dent

DENTINS ▸ dentin

DENTIST n person qualified to practise dentistry

DENTOID adj resembling a tooth

DENTS ▸ dent

DENTURE n false tooth

DENUDE vb remove the covering or protection from

DENUDED ▸ denude

DENUDER ▸ denude

DENUDES ▸ denude

DENY vb declare to be untrue

DENYING ▸ deny

DEODAND n (formerly) a thing that had caused a person's death and was forfeited to the crown for a charitable purpose: abolished 1862

DEODAR n Himalayan cedar with drooping branches

DEODARA same as ▸ deodar

DEODARS ▸ deodar

DEODATE n offering to God

DEONTIC adj of or relating to such ethical concepts as obligation and permissibility

DEORBIT vb go out of orbit
DEOXY adj having less oxygen than a specified related compound
DEPAINT vb depict
DEPART vb leave
DEPARTS ▸ depart
DEPECHE n message
DEPEND vb put trust (in)
DEPENDS ▸ depend
DEPERM vb demagnetize
DEPERMS ▸ deperm
DEPICT vb produce a picture of
DEPICTS ▸ depict
DEPLANE vb disembark from an aeroplane
DEPLETE vb use up
DEPLORE vb condemn strongly
DEPLOY vb organize (troops or resources) into a position ready for immediate action
DEPLOYS ▸ deploy
DEPLUME vb deprive of feathers
DEPONE vb declare (something) under oath
DEPONED ▸ depone
DEPONES ▸ depone
DEPORT vb remove forcibly from a country
DEPORTS ▸ deport
DEPOSAL n deposition; giving of testimony under oath
DEPOSE vb remove from an office or position of power
DEPOSED ▸ depose
DEPOSER ▸ depose
DEPOSES ▸ depose
DEPOSIT vb put down ▸ n sum of money paid into a bank account
DEPOT n building where goods or vehicles are kept when not in use ▸ adj (of a drug or drug dose) designed for gradual release from the site of an injection so as to act over a long period
DEPOTS ▸ depot
DEPRAVE vb make morally bad
DEPRESS vb make sad
DEPRIVE vb prevent from (having or enjoying)
DEPSIDE n any ester formed by the condensation of the carboxyl group of one phenolic carboxylic acid with the hydroxyl group of another, found in plant cells

DEPTH n distance downwards, backwards, or inwards
DEPTHS ▸ depth
DEPUTE vb appoint (someone) to act on one's behalf ▸ n deputy
DEPUTED ▸ depute
DEPUTES ▸ depute
DEPUTY n person appointed to act on behalf of another
DEQUEUE vb remove (an item) from a queue of computing tasks
DERAIGN vb contest (a claim, suit, etc)
DERAIL vb cause (a train) to go off the rails ▸ n device designed to make rolling stock or locomotives leave the rails to avoid a collision or accident
DERAILS ▸ derail
DERANGE vb disturb the order or arrangement of
DERAT vb remove rats from
DERATE vb assess the value of (some types of property, such as agricultural land) at a lower rate than others for local taxation
DERATED ▸ derate
DERATES ▸ derate
DERATS ▸ derat
DERAY vb go mad
DERAYED ▸ deray
DERAYS ▸ deray
DERBIES ▸ derby
DERBY n bowler hat
DERE vb injure
DERED ▸ dere
DERES ▸ dere
DERHAM same as ▸ dirham
DERHAMS ▸ derham
DERIDE vb treat with contempt or ridicule
DERIDED ▸ deride
DERIDER ▸ deride
DERIDES ▸ deride
DERIG vb remove equipment, e.g. from stage set
DERIGS ▸ derig
DERING ▸ dere
DERIVE vb take or develop (from)
DERIVED ▸ derive
DERIVER ▸ derive
DERIVES ▸ derive
DERM same as ▸ derma
DERMA n beef or fowl intestine used as a casing

for certain dishes, esp kishke
DERMAL adj of or relating to the skin
DERMAS ▸ derma
DERMIC ▸ dermis
DERMIS another name for ▸ corium
DERMOID adj of or resembling skin ▸ n congenital cystic tumour whose walls are lined with epithelium
DERMS ▸ derm
DERN n concealment
DERNFUL adj sorrowful
DERNIER adj last
DERNLY adv sorrowfully
DERNS ▸ dern
DERO n tramp or derelict
DEROS ▸ dero
DERRICK n simple crane ▸ vb raise or lower the jib of (a crane)
DERRIES ▸ derry
DERRIS n E Indian woody climbing plant
DERRO n vagrant
DERROS ▸ derro
DERRY n derelict house, esp one used by tramps, drug addicts, etc
DERTH same as ▸ dearth
DERTHS ▸ derth
DERV n diesel oil, when used for road transport
DERVISH n member of a Muslim religious order noted for a frenzied whirling dance
DERVS ▸ derv
DESALT vb desalinate
DESALTS ▸ desalt
DESAND vb remove sand from
DESANDS ▸ desand
DESCALE vb remove a hard coating from inside (a kettle or pipe)
DESCANT n tune played or sung above a basic melody ▸ adj denoting the highest member in a family of musical instruments ▸ vb compose or perform a descant (for a piece of music)
DESCEND vb move down (a slope etc)
DESCENT n descending
DESCRY vb catch sight of
DESEED vb to remove the seeds from (eg a fruit)

DESEEDS ▸ deseed

DESERT n region with little or no vegetation because of low rainfall ▷vb abandon (a person or place) without intending to return

DESERTS ▸ desert

DESERVE vb be entitled to or worthy of

DESEX n desexualize

DESEXED ▸ desex

DESEXES ▸ desex

DESHI same as ▸ desi

DESI adj in Indian English, indigenous or local

DESIGN vb work out the structure or form of (something), by making a sketch or plans ▷n preliminary drawing

DESIGNS ▸ design

DESINE same as ▸ design

DESINED ▸ desine

DESINES ▸ desine

DESIRE vb want very much ▷n wish, longing

DESIRED ▸ desire

DESIRER ▸ desire

DESIRES ▸ desire

DESIST vb stop (doing something)

DESISTS ▸ desist

DESK n piece of furniture with a writing surface and drawers

DESKILL vb mechanize or computerize (a job) thereby reducing the skill required to do it

DESKING n desks and related furnishings in a given space, eg an office

DESKMAN n police officer in charge in police station

DESKMEN ▸ deskman

DESKS ▸ desk

DESKTOP adj (of a computer) small enough to use at a desk ▷n denoting a computer system, esp for word processing, that is small enough to use at a desk

DESMAN n either of two molelike amphibious mammals

DESMANS ▸ desman

DESMID n type of mainly unicellular freshwater green alga

DESMIDS ▸ desmid

DESMINE n type of mineral

DESMOID adj resembling a tendon or ligament ▷n very firm tumour of connective tissue

DESNOOD vb remove the snood of a turkey poult to reduce the risk of cannibalism

DESORB vb change from an adsorbed state on a surface to a gaseous or liquid state

DESORBS ▸ desorb

DESOXY same as ▸ deoxy

DESPAIR n total loss of hope ▷vb lose hope

DESPISE vb regard with contempt

DESPITE prep in spite of ▷n contempt ▷vb show contempt for

DESPOIL vb plunder

DESPOND vb lose heart or hope

DESPOT n person in power who acts unfairly or cruelly

DESPOTS ▸ despot

DESSE n desk

DESSERT n sweet course served at the end of a meal

DESSES ▸ desse

DESTAIN vb remove stain from

DESTINE vb set apart or appoint (for a certain purpose or person, or to do something)

DESTINY n future marked out for a person or thing

DESTOCK vb (of a retailer) to reduce the amount of stock held or cease to stock certain products

DESTROY vb ruin, demolish

DESUGAR vb remove sugar from

DESYNE same as ▸ design

DESYNED ▸ desyne

DESYNES ▸ desyne

DETACH vb disengage and separate

DETAIL n individual piece of information ▷vb list fully

DETAILS ▸ detail

DETAIN vb delay (someone)

DETAINS ▸ detain

DETECT vb notice

DETECTS ▸ detect

DETENT n locking piece of a mechanism, often spring-loaded to check the movement of a wheel in one direction only

DETENTE n easing of tension between nations

DETENTS ▸ detent

DETENU n prisoner

DETENUE n female prisoner

DETENUS ▸ detenu

DETER vb discourage (someone) from doing something by instilling fear or doubt

DETERGE vb wash or wipe away

DETERS ▸ deter

DETEST vb dislike intensely

DETESTS ▸ detest

DETICK vb remove ticks from

DETICKS ▸ detick

DETINUE n action brought by a plaintiff to recover goods wrongfully detained

DETORT vb pervert

DETORTS ▸ detort

DETOUR n route that is not the most direct one ▷vb deviate or cause to deviate from a direct route or course of action

DETOURS ▸ detour

DETOX n treatment to rid the body of poisonous substances ▷vb undergo treatment to rid the body of poisonous substances, esp alcohol and drugs

DETOXED ▸ detox

DETOXES ▸ detox

DETRACT vb make (something) seem less good

DETRAIN vb leave or cause to leave a railway train, as passengers, etc

DETRUDE vb force down or thrust away or out

DETUNE vb change pitch of (stringed instrument)

DETUNED ▸ detune

DETUNES ▸ detune

DEUCE vb score deuce in tennis ▷n score of forty all

DEUCED adj damned

DEUCES ▸ deuce

DEUCING ▸ deuce

DEUS n god

DEUTON old form of ▸ deuteron

DEUTONS ▸ deuton

DEUTZIA n shrub with clusters of pink or white flowers

DEV same as ▸ deva

Dev is a Sanskrit word for a good spirit; related words are **deev** and **deva**

DEVA n (in Hinduism and Buddhism) divine being or god

DEVALL vb stop

DEVALLS ▶ **devall**

DEVALUE vb reduce the exchange value of (a currency)

DEVAS ▶ **deva**

DEVEIN vb remove vein from

DEVEINS ▶ **devein**

DEVEL same as ▶ **devvel**

DEVELED ▶ **devel**

DEVELOP vb grow or bring to a later, more elaborate, or more advanced stage

DEVELS ▶ **devel**

DEVEST variant spelling of ▶ **divest**

DEVESTS ▶ **devest**

DEVIANT adj (person) deviating from what is considered acceptable behaviour ▷ n person whose behaviour deviates from what is considered to be acceptable

DEVIATE vb differ from others in belief or thought

DEVICE n machine or tool used for a specific task

DEVICES ▶ **device**

DEVIL n evil spirit ▷ vb prepare (food) with a highly flavoured spiced mixture

DEVILED ▶ **devil**

DEVILET n young devil

DEVILRY n mischievousness

DEVILS ▶ **devil**

DEVIOUS adj insincere and dishonest

DEVISAL n act of inventing, contriving, or devising

DEVISE vb work out (something) in one's mind ▷ n disposition of property by will

DEVISED ▶ **devise**

DEVISEE n person to whom property, esp realty, is devised by will

DEVISER ▶ **devise**

DEVISES ▶ **devise**

DEVISOR n person who devises property, esp realty, by will

DEVLING n young devil

DEVOICE vb make (a voiced speech sound) voiceless

DEVOID adj completely lacking (in)

DEVOIR n duty

DEVOIRS ▶ **devoir**

DEVOLVE vb pass (power or duties) or (of power or duties) be passed to a successor or substitute

DEVON n bland processed meat in sausage form, eaten cold in slices

DEVONS ▶ **devon**

DEVORE n velvet fabric with a raised pattern created by disintegrating some of the pile with chemicals

DEVORES ▶ **devore**

DEVOT n devotee

DEVOTE vb apply or dedicate to a particular purpose

DEVOTED adj showing loyalty or devotion

DEVOTEE n person who is very enthusiastic about something

DEVOTES ▶ **devote**

DEVOTS ▶ **devot**

DEVOUR vb eat greedily

DEVOURS ▶ **devour**

DEVOUT adj deeply religious

DEVS ▶ **dev**

DEVVEL vb strike with blow

DEVVELS ▶ **devvel**

DEW n drops of water that form on the ground at night from vapour in the air ▷ vb moisten with or as with dew

DEWAN n (formerly in India) the chief minister or finance minister of a state ruled by an Indian prince

DEWANI n post of dewan

DEWANIS ▶ **dewani**

DEWANNY same as ▶ **dewani**

DEWANS ▶ **dewan**

DEWAR n as in **dewar flask** type of vacuum flask

DEWARS ▶ **dewar**

DEWATER vb remove water from

DEWAX vb remove wax from

DEWAXED ▶ **dewax**

DEWAXES ▶ **dewax**

DEWCLAW n nonfunctional claw on a dog's leg

DEWDROP n drop of dew

DEWED ▶ **dew**

DEWFALL n formation of dew

DEWFULL obsolete form of ▶ **due**

DEWIER ▶ **dewy**

DEWIEST ▶ **dewy**

DEWILY ▶ **dewy**

DEWING ▶ **dew**

DEWITT vb kill, esp hang unlawfully

DEWITTS ▶ **dewitt**

DEWLAP n loose fold of skin hanging under the throat in dogs, cattle, etc

DEWLAPS ▶ **dewlap**

DEWLAPT ▶ **dewlap**

DEWLESS ▶ **dew**

DEWOOL vb remove wool from

DEWOOLS ▶ **dewool**

DEWORM vb rid of worms

DEWORMS ▶ **deworm**

DEWS ▶ **dew**

DEWY adj moist with or as with dew

DEX n dextroamphetamine

Short for Dexedrine®, a stimulant drug, this is another of the key words to know for using the X. It can be extended to **dexy** or **dexie**.

DEXES ▶ **dex**

DEXIE n pill containing dextroamphetamine

DEXIES ▶ **dexie**

DEXTER adj of or on the right side of a shield, etc, from the bearer's point of view ▷ n small breed of red or black beef cattle, originally from Ireland

DEXTERS ▶ **dexter**

DEXTRAL adj of, relating to, or located on the right side, esp of the body

DEXTRAN n polysaccharide produced by the action of bacteria on sucrose: used as a substitute for plasma in blood transfusions

DEXTRIN n sticky substance obtained from starch, used as a thickening agent in food

DEXTRO adj dextrorotatory or rotating to the right

DEXY same as ▶ **dexie**

DEY n title given to commanders or (from 1710) governors of the Janissaries of Algiers (1671–1830)

DEYS ▶ **dey**

DEZINC vb remove zinc from

DEZINCS ▶ **dezinc**

DHAK n tropical Asian tree with bright red flowers,

which yields a red resin used as an astringent

DHAKS ▸ dhak

DHAL n curry made from lentils or beans

DHALS ▸ dhal

DHAMMA same as ▸ **dharma**

DHAMMAS ▸ dhamma

DHANSAK n any of a variety of Indian dishes consisting of meat or vegetables braised with water or stock and lentils

DHARMA n moral law or behaviour

DHARMAS ▸ dharma

DHARMIC ▸ dharma

DHARNA n (in India) a method of obtaining justice, as the payment of a debt, by sitting, fasting, at the door of the person from whom reparation is sought

DHARNAS ▸ dharna

DHIMMI n non-Muslim living in a state governed by sharia law

DHIMMIS ▸ dhimmi

DHOBI n (in India, Malaya, East Africa, etc, esp formerly) a washerman

DHOBIS ▸ dhobi

DHOL n type of Indian drum

DHOLE n fierce canine mammal of the forests of central and SE Asia, with a reddish-brown coat and rounded ears

DHOLES ▸ dhole

DHOLL same as ▸ **dhal**

DHOLLS ▸ dholl

DHOLS ▸ dhol

DHOOLY same as ▸ **doolie**

DHOORA same as ▸ **durra**

DHOORAS ▸ dhoora

DHOOTI same as ▸ **dhoti**

DHOOTIE same as ▸ **dhoti**

DHOOTIS ▸ dhooti

DHOTI n long loincloth worn by men in India

DHOTIS ▸ dhoti

DHOURRA same as ▸ **durra**

DHOW n Arab sailing ship

DHOWS ▸ dhow

DHURNA same as ▸ **dharna**

DHURNAS ▸ dhurna

DHURRA same as ▸ **durra**

DHURRAS ▸ dhurra

DHURRIE same as ▸ **durrie**

DHUTI same as ▸ **dhoti**

DHUTIS ▸ dhuti

DI ▸ deus

DIABASE n altered dolerite

DIABLE n type of sauce

DIABLES ▸ diable

DIABOLO n game in which one throws and catches a spinning top on a cord fastened to two sticks held in the hands

DIACID n lead plaster

DIACIDS ▸ diacid

DIACT n two-rayed

DIADEM n crown ▷ vb adorn or crown with or as with a diadem

DIADEMS ▸ diadem

DIADROM n complete course of pendulum

DIAGRAM n sketch showing the form or workings of something ▷ vb show in or as if in a diagram

DIAGRID n diagonal structure network

DIAL n face of a clock or watch ▷ vb operate the dial or buttons on a telephone in order to contact (a number)

DIALECT n form of a language spoken in a particular area

DIALED ▸ dial

DIALER ▸ dial

DIALERS ▸ dial

DIALING ▸ dial

DIALIST n dial-maker

DIALLED ▸ dial

DIALLEL n interbreeding among a group of parents

DIALLER ▸ dial

DIALOG same as > **dialogue**

DIALOGS ▸ dialog

DIALS ▸ dial

DIALYSE vb separate by dialysis

DIALYZE same as ▸ **dialyse**

DIAMIDE n compound containing two amido groups

DIAMIN same as ▸ **diamine**

DIAMINE n any chemical compound containing two amino groups in its molecules

DIAMINS ▸ diamin

DIAMOND n exceptionally hard, usu colourless, precious stone ▷ adj (of an anniversary) the sixtieth ▷ vb stud or decorate with diamonds

DIAMYL adj with two amyl groups

DIANDRY n practice of having two husbands

DIANE adj as in **steak diane** kind of steak

DIANOIA n perception and experience regarded as lower modes of knowledge

DIAPASE same as > **diapason**

DIAPER n nappy ▷ vb decorate with a geometric pattern

DIAPERS ▸ diaper

DIAPIR n anticlinal fold in which the brittle overlying rock has been pierced by material, such as salt, from beneath

DIAPIRS ▸ diapir

DIAPSID n reptile with two holes in rear of skull

DIARCH adj (of a vascular bundle) having two strands of xylem

DIARCHY n government by two states, individuals, etc

DIARIAL ▸ diary

DIARIAN ▸ diary

DIARIES ▸ diary

DIARISE same as ▸ **diarize**

DIARIST n person who writes a diary

DIARIZE vb record in diary

DIARY n (book for) a record of daily events, appointments, or observations

DIASCIA n S African plant, usu with pink flowers

DIASTEM same as > **diastema**

DIASTER n stage in cell division at which the chromosomes are in two groups at the poles of the spindle before forming daughter nuclei

DIATOM n microscopic unicellular alga

DIATOMS ▸ diatom

DIATRON n circuit that uses diodes

DIAXON n bipolar cell

DIAXONS ▸ diaxon

DIAZIN same as ▸ **diazine**

DIAZINE n organic compound

DIAZINS ▸ diazin

DIAZO adj of, or relating to the reproduction of documents using the bleaching action of ultraviolet radiation on diazonium salts ▷ *n* document produced by this method

DIAZOES ▸ **diazo**

DIAZOLE *n* type of organic compound

DIAZOS ▸ **diazo**

DIB *vb* fish by allowing the bait to bob and dip on the surface

DIBASIC *adj* (of an acid, such as sulphuric acid, H_2SO_4) containing two acidic hydrogen atoms

DIBBED ▸ **dib**

DIBBER *same as* ▸ **dibble**

DIBBERS ▸ **dibber**

DIBBING ▸ **dib**

DIBBLE *n* small hand tool used to make holes in the ground for seeds or plants ▷ *vb* make a hole in (the ground) with a dibble

DIBBLED ▸ **dibble**

DIBBLER ▸ **dibble**

DIBBLES ▸ **dibble**

DIBBS *n* money

DIBBUK *variant spelling of* ▸ **dybbuk**

DIBBUKS ▸ **dibbuk**

DIBS ▸ **dib**

DIBUTYL *adj* with two butyl groups

DICAMBA *n* type of weedkiller

DICAST *n* (in ancient Athens) a juror in the popular courts chosen by lot from a list of citizens

DICASTS ▸ **dicast**

DICE *n* small cube each of whose sides has a different number of spots (1 to 6), used in games of chance ▷ *vb* cut (food) into small cubes

DICED ▸ **dice**

DICER ▸ **dice**

DICERS ▸ **dice**

DICES ▸ **dice**

DICEY *adj* dangerous or risky

DICH *interj* archaic expression meaning "may it do"

DICHORD *n* two-stringed musical instrument

DICHT *vb* wipe

DICHTED ▸ **dicht**

DICHTS ▸ **dicht**

DICIER ▸ **dicey**

DICIEST ▸ **dicey**

DICING ▸ **dice**

DICINGS ▸ **dice**

DICKENS *n* euphemism for devil

DICKER *vb* trade (goods) by bargaining ▷ *n* petty bargain or barter

DICKERS ▸ **dicker**

DICKEY *same as* ▸ **dicky**

DICKEYS ▸ **dickey**

DICKIE *same as* ▸ **dicky**

DICKIER ▸ **dicky**

DICKIES ▸ **dicky**

DICKTY *same as* ▸ **dicty**

DICKY *n* false shirt front ▷ *adj* shaky or weak

DICLINY > **diclinous**

DICOT *n* type of flowering plant

DICOTS ▸ **dicot**

DICOTYL *n* a type of flowering plant; dicotyledon

DICT *vb* dictate

DICTA ▸ **dictum**

DICTATE *vb* say aloud for someone else to write down ▷ *n* authoritative command

DICTED ▸ **dict**

DICTIER ▸ **dicty**

DICTING ▸ **dict**

DICTION *n* manner of pronouncing words and sounds

DICTS ▸ **dict**

DICTUM *n* formal statement

DICTUMS ▸ **dictum**

DICTY *adj* conceited; snobbish

DICYCLY > **dicyclic**

DID ▸ **do**

DIDACT *n* instructive person

DIDACTS ▸ **didact**

DIDAKAI *same as* ▸ **didicoy**

DIDAKEI *same as* ▸ **didicoy**

DIDDER *vb* shake with fear

DIDDERS ▸ **didder**

DIDDIER ▸ **diddy**

DIDDIES ▸ **diddy**

DIDDLE *vb* swindle

DIDDLED ▸ **diddle**

DIDDLER ▸ **diddle**

DIDDLES ▸ **diddle**

DIDDLEY *n* worthless amount

DIDDLY *n* worthless amount

DIDDY *n* female breast or nipple ▷ *adj* of or relating to a diddy

DIDICOI *same as* ▸ **didicoy**

DIDICOY *n* (in Britain) one

of a group of caravan-dwelling roadside people who live like Gypsies but are not true Romanies

DIDIE *same as* ▸ **didy**

DIDIES ▸ **didy**

DIDO *n* antic

DIDOES ▸ **dido**

DIDOS ▸ **dido**

DIDST *form of the past tense of* ▸ **do**

DIDY *n* woman's breast

DIE *vb* (of a person, animal, or plant) cease all biological activity permanently ▷ *n* shaped block used to cut or form metal

DIEB *n* N African jackal

DIEBACK *n* disease of trees and shrubs characterized by death of the young shoots, which spreads to the larger branches: caused by injury to the roots or attack by bacteria or fungi ▷ *vb* (of plants) to suffer from dieback

DIEBS ▸ **dieb**

DIED ▸ **die**

DIEDRAL *same as* > **dihedral**

DIEDRE *n* large shallow groove or corner in a rock face

DIEDRES ▸ **diedre**

DIEHARD *n* person who resists change or who holds on to an outdated attitude

DIEING ▸ **die**

DIEL *n* 24-hour period

DIENE *n* hydrocarbon that contains two carbon-to-carbon double bonds in its molecules

DIENES ▸ **diene**

DIEOFF *n* process of dying in large numbers

DIEOFFS ▸ **dieoff**

DIES ▸ **die**

DIESEL *vb* drive diesel-fueled vehicle ▷ *n* diesel engine

DIESELS ▸ **diesel**

DIESES ▸ **diesis**

DIESIS *n* (in ancient Greek theory) any interval smaller than a whole tone, esp a semitone in the Pythagorean scale

DIESTER *n* synthetic lubricant

DIET *n* food that a person or animal regularly eats ▷ *vb* follow a special diet so as to lose weight ▷ *adj* (of food) suitable for a weight-reduction diet

DIETARY *adj* of or relating to a diet ▷ *n* regulated diet

DIETED ▸ **diet**

DIETER ▸ **diet**

DIETERS ▸ **diet**

DIETHER *n* chemical compound

DIETHYL *adj as in* **diethyl ether** ether

DIETINE *n* low-ranking diet

DIETING ▸ **diet**

DIETIST *another word for* > **dietitian**

DIETS ▸ **diet**

DIF *same as* ▸ **diff**

DIFF *n* (slang) difference

DIFFER *vb* be unlike

DIFFERS ▸ **differ**

DIFFORM *adj* irregular in form

DIFFS ▸ **diff**

DIFFUSE *vb* spread over a wide area ▷ *adj* widely spread

DIFS ▸ **dif**

DIG *vb* cut into, break up, and turn over or remove (earth), esp with a spade ▷ *n* digging

DIGAMMA *n* letter of the Greek alphabet that became obsolete before the classical period of the language.

DIGAMY *n* second marriage contracted after the termination of the first by death or divorce

DIGEST *vb* subject to a process of digestion ▷ *n* shortened version of a book, report, or article

DIGESTS ▸ **digest**

DIGGED *a past tense of* ▸ **dig**

DIGGER *n* machine used for digging

DIGGERS ▸ **digger**

DIGGING ▸ **dig**

DIGHT *vb* adorn or equip, as for battle

DIGHTED ▸ **dight**

DIGHTS ▸ **dight**

DIGICAM *n* digital camera

DIGIT *n* finger or toe

DIGITAL *adj* displaying information as numbers rather than with hands and a dial ▷ *n* one of the keys on the manuals of an organ or on a piano, harpsichord, etc

DIGITS ▸ **digit**

DIGLOT *n* bilingual book

DIGLOTS ▸ **diglot**

DIGLYPH *n* ornament in Doric frieze with two grooves

DIGNIFY *vb* add distinction to

DIGNITY *n* serious, calm, and controlled behaviour or manner

DIGONAL *adj* of or relating to a symmetry operation in which the original figure is reconstructed after a 180° turn about an axis

DIGOXIN *n* glycoside extracted from the leaves of the woolly foxglove

DIGRAPH *n* two letters used to represent a single sound, such as *gh* in *tough*

DIGRESS *vb* depart from the main subject in speech or writing

DIGS ▸ **dig**

DIHEDRA ▸ **dihedron**

DIKA *n* wild mango

DIKAS ▸ **dika**

DIKAST *same as* ▸ **dicast**

DIKASTS ▸ **dikast**

DIKDIK *n* small African antelope

DIKDIKS ▸ **dikdik**

DIKE *same as* ▸ **dyke**

DIKED ▸ **dike**

DIKER *n* builder of dikes

DIKERS ▸ **diker**

DIKES ▸ **dike**

DIKING ▸ **dike**

DIKKOP *n* type of brownish shore bird with a large head and eyes

DIKKOPS ▸ **dikkop**

DIKTAT *n* dictatorial decree

DIKTATS ▸ **diktat**

DILATE *vb* make or become wider or larger

DILATED ▸ **dilate**

DILATER *same as* ▸ **dilator**

DILATES ▸ **dilate**

DILATOR *n* something that dilates an object, esp a surgical instrument for dilating a bodily cavity

DILDO *n* object used as a substitute for an erect penis

DILDOE *same as* ▸ **dildo**

DILDOES ▸ **dildoe**

DILDOS ▸ **dildo**

DILEMMA *n* situation offering a choice between two equally undesirable alternatives

DILL *vb* flavour with dill ▷ *n* sweet-smelling herb

DILLED ▸ **dill**

DILLI *n* dilly bag; small bag, esp one made of plaited grass and used for carrying food

DILLIER ▸ **dilly**

DILLIES ▸ **dilly**

DILLING ▸ **dill**

DILLIS ▸ **dilli**

DILLS ▸ **dill**

DILLY *adj* foolish ▷ *n* person or thing that is remarkable

DILUENT *adj* causing dilution or serving to dilute ▷ *n* substance used for or causing dilution

DILUTE *vb* make (a liquid) less concentrated, esp by adding water ▷ *adj* (of a liquid) thin and watery

DILUTED ▸ **dilute**

DILUTEE ▸ **dilute**

DILUTER ▸ **dilute**

DILUTES ▸ **dilute**

DILUTOR *n* thing intended to have a diluting effect

DILUVIA > **diluvium**

DIM *adj* badly lit ▷ *vb* make or become dim

DIMBLE *n* wooded hollow; dingle

DIMBLES ▸ **dimble**

DIME *n* coin of the US and Canada, worth ten cents

DIMER *n* molecule made up of two identical molecules bonded together

DIMERIC *adj* of a dimer

DIMERS ▸ **dimer**

DIMES ▸ **dime**

DIMETER *n* line of verse consisting of two metrical feet or a verse written in this metre

DIMITY *n* light strong cotton fabric with woven stripes or squares

DIMLY ▸ **dim**

DIMMED ▸ **dim**

DIMMER ▸ **dim**

DIMMERS ▸ **dim**

DIMMEST ▸ **dim**

DIMMING *n as in* **global dimming** decrease in the amount of sunlight reaching the earth

DIMMISH ▸ **dim**

DIMNESS ▸ **dim**

DIMORPH *n* either of two forms of a substance that exhibits dimorphism

DIMOUT n reduction of lighting

DIMOUTS ▸ dimout

DIMP n in Northern English dialect, a cigarette butt

DIMPLE n small natural dent, esp in the cheeks or chin ▷ vb produce dimples by smiling

DIMPLED ▸ dimple

DIMPLES ▸ dimple

DIMPLY ▸ dimple

DIMPS ▸ dimp

DIMPSY n twilight

DIMS ▸ dim

DIMWIT n stupid person

DIMWITS ▸ dimwit

DIN n loud unpleasant confused noise ▷ vb instil (something) into someone by constant repetition

DINAR n monetary unit of various Balkan, Middle Eastern, and North African countries

DINARS ▸ dinar

DINDLE another word for ▸ dinnle

DINDLED ▸ dindle

DINDLES ▸ dindle

DINE vb eat dinner

DINED ▸ dine

DINER n person eating a meal

DINERIC adj of or concerned with the interface between immiscible liquids

DINERO n money

DINEROS ▸ dinero

DINERS ▸ diner

DINES ▸ dine

DINETTE n alcove or small area for use as a dining room

DINFUL adj noisy

DING n small dent in a vehicle ▷ vb ring or cause to ring, esp with tedious repetition

DINGBAT n any unnamed object, esp one used as a missile

DINGE n dent ▷ vb make a dent in (something)

DINGED ▸ dinge

DINGER n (in baseball) home run

DINGERS ▸ dinger

DINGES n jocular word for something whose name is unknown or forgotten

DINGEY same as ▸ dinghy

DINGEYS ▸ dingey

DINGHY n small boat, powered by sails, oars, or a motor ▷ vb ignore or avoid a person or event

DINGIED ▸ dingey

DINGIER ▸ dingy

DINGIES ▸ dingy

DINGILY ▸ dingy

DINGING ▸ dinge

DINGLE n small wooded hollow or valley

DINGLES ▸ dingle

DINGO n Australian wild dog ▷ vb act in a cowardly manner

DINGOED ▸ dingo

DINGOES ▸ dingo

DINGS ▸ ding

DINGUS same as ▸ dinges

DINGY adj lacking light ▷ vb ignore or avoid a person or event

DINIC n remedy for vertigo

DINICS ▸ dinic

DINING ▸ dine

DINITRO adj containing two nitro groups

DINK adj neat or neatly dressed ▷ vb carry (a second person) on a horse, bicycle, etc ▷ n ball struck delicately

DINKED ▸ dink

DINKER ▸ dink

DINKEST ▸ dink

DINKEY n small locomotive

DINKEYS ▸ dinkey

DINKIE n affluent married childless person ▷ adj designed for or appealing to dinkies

DINKIER ▸ dinky

DINKIES ▸ dinkie

DINKING ▸ dink

DINKLY adj neat

DINKS ▸ dink

DINKUM n truth or genuineness

DINKUMS ▸ dinkum

DINKY adj small and neat

DINMONT n neutered sheep

DINNA vb a Scots word for do not

DINNAE vb (Scots) do not

DINNED ▸ din

DINNER vb dine ▷ n main meal of the day, eaten either in the evening or at midday

DINNERS ▸ dinner

DINNING ▸ din

DINNLE vb shake

DINNLED ▸ dinnle

DINNLES ▸ dinnle

DINO n dinosaur

DINOS ▸ dino

DINS ▸ din

DINT same as ▸ dent

DINTED ▸ dint

DINTING ▸ dint

DINTS ▸ dint

DIOBOL n ancient Greek coin

DIOBOLS ▸ diobol

DIOCESE n district over which a bishop has control

DIODE n semiconductor device for converting alternating current to direct current

DIODES ▸ diode

DIOECY n state of being dioecious

DIOL n any of a class of alcohols that have two hydroxyl groups in each molecule

DIOLS ▸ diol

DIOPTER same as ▸ dioptre

DIOPTRE n unit for measuring the refractive power of a lens

DIORAMA n miniature three-dimensional scene, in which models of figures are seen against a three-dimensional background

DIORISM n definition; clarity

DIORITE n dark coarse-grained igneous plutonic rock consisting of plagioclase feldspar and ferromagnesian minerals such as hornblende

DIOTA n type of ancient vase

DIOTAS ▸ diota

DIOXAN n colourless insoluble toxic liquid made by heating ethanediol with sulphuric acid

DIOXANE same as ▸ dioxan

DIOXANS ▸ dioxan

DIOXID same as ▸ dioxide

DIOXIDE n oxide containing two oxygen atoms per molecule

DIOXIDS ▸ dioxid

DIOXIN n any of a number of mostly poisonous chemical by-products of certain weedkillers

DIOXINS ▸ dioxin

DIP vb plunge quickly or briefly into to a liquid ▷ n dipping

DIPHASE adj of, having, or concerned with two phases

DIPHONE n combination of two speech sounds

DIPLEX adj (in telecommunications) permitting the transmission of simultaneous signals in both directions

DIPLOE n spongy bone separating the two layers of compact bone of the skull

DIPLOES ▸ diploe

DIPLOIC adj relating to diploe

DIPLOID adj denoting a cell or organism with pairs of homologous chromosomes ▷ n diploid cell or organism

DIPLOMA vb bestow diploma on ▷ n qualification awarded by a college on successful completion of a course

DIPLON another name for > **deuteron**

DIPLONS ▸ diplon

DIPLONT n animal or plant that has the diploid number of chromosomes in its somatic cells

DIPNET vb fish using fishing net on pole

DIPNETS ▸ dipnet

DIPNOAN n lungfish

DIPODIC ▸ dipody

DIPODY n metrical unit consisting of two feet

DIPOLAR ▸ dipole

DIPOLE n two equal but opposite electric charges or magnetic poles separated by a small distance

DIPOLES ▸ dipole

DIPPED ▸ dip

DIPPER n ladle used for dipping

DIPPERS ▸ dipper

DIPPIER ▸ dippy

DIPPING ▸ dip

DIPPY adj odd, eccentric, or crazy

DIPS ▸ dip

DIPSAS n type of snake

DIPSHIT n stupid person

DIPSO n (slang) dipsomaniac or alcoholic

DIPSOS ▸ dipso

DIPT ▸ dip

DIPTERA n order of insects with two wings

DIPTYCA same as ▸ diptych

DIPTYCH n painting on two hinged panels

DIQUARK n low-energy configuration of two quarks attracted to one another by virtue of having antisymmetric colours and spins

DIQUAT n type of herbicide

DIQUATS ▸ diquat

DIRAM n money unit of Tajikistan

DIRAMS ▸ diram

DIRDAM same as ▸ dirdum

DIRDAMS ▸ dirdam

DIRDUM n tumult

DIRDUMS ▸ dirdum

DIRE adj disastrous, urgent, or terrible

DIRECT adj (of a route) shortest, straight ▷ adv in a direct manner ▷ vb lead and organize

DIRECTS ▸ direct

DIREFUL same as ▸ dire

DIRELY ▸ dire

DIREMPT vb separate with force

DIRER ▸ dire

DIREST ▸ dire

DIRGE n slow sad song of mourning

DIRGES ▸ dirge

DIRHAM n standard monetary unit of Morocco, divided into 100 centimes

DIRHAMS ▸ dirham

DIRHEM same as ▸ dirham

DIRHEMS ▸ dirhem

DIRIGE n dirge

DIRIGES ▸ dirige

DIRK n dagger, formerly worn by Scottish Highlanders ▷ vb stab with a dirk

DIRKE same as ▸ dirk

DIRKED ▸ dirk

DIRKES ▸ dirke

DIRKING ▸ dirk

DIRKS ▸ dirk

DIRL vb tingle; vibrate

DIRLED ▸ dirl

DIRLING ▸ dirl

DIRLS ▸ dirl

DIRNDL n full gathered skirt originating from Tyrolean peasant wear

DIRNDLS ▸ dirndl

DIRT vb soil ▷ n unclean substance, filth

DIRTBAG n filthy person

DIRTED ▸ dirt

DIRTIED ▸ dirty

DIRTIER ▸ dirty

DIRTIES ▸ dirty

DIRTILY ▸ dirty

DIRTING ▸ dirt

DIRTS ▸ dirt

DIRTY adj covered or marked with dirt ▷ vb make dirty

DIS same as ▸ diss

DISA n type of orchid

DISABLE vb make ineffective, unfit, or incapable

DISALLY vb separate

DISARM vb deprive of weapons

DISARMS ▸ disarm

DISAS ▸ disa

DISAVOW vb deny connection with or responsibility for

DISBAND vb (cause to) cease to function as a group

DISBAR vb deprive (a barrister) of the right to practise

DISBARK same as > **disembark**

DISBARS ▸ disbar

DISBUD vb remove superfluous buds, flowers, or shoots from (a plant, esp a fruit tree)

DISBUDS ▸ disbud

DISC n flat circular object ▷ vb work (land) with a disc harrow

DISCAGE vb release from cage

DISCAL adj relating to or resembling a disc

DISCANT same as ▸ descant

DISCARD vb get rid of (something or someone) as useless or undesirable ▷ n person or thing that has been cast aside

DISCASE vb remove case from

DISCED ▸ disc

DISCEPT vb discuss

DISCERN vb see or be aware of (something) clearly

DISCERP vb divide

DISCI ▸ discus

DISCIDE vb split

DISCING ▸ disc

DISCO vb go to a disco ▷ n nightclub where people dance to amplified pop records

DISCOED ▸ **disco**

DISCOER ▸ **disco**

DISCOID adj like a disc ▷ n disclike object

DISCORD n lack of agreement or harmony between people ▷ vb disagree

DISCOS ▸ **disco**

DISCS ▸ **disc**

DISCURE old form of > **discover**

DISCUS n heavy disc-shaped object thrown in sports competitions

DISCUSS vb consider (something) by talking it over

DISDAIN n feeling of superiority and dislike ▷ vb refuse with disdain

DISEASE vb make uneasy ▷ n illness, sickness

DISEDGE vb render blunt

DISEUR same as ▸ **diseuse**

DISEURS ▸ **diseur**

DISEUSE n (esp formerly) an actress who presents dramatic recitals, usually sung accompanied by music

DISFAME n discredit

DISFORM vb change form of

DIGEST vb digest

DISGOWN vb remove gown from

DISGUST n great loathing or distaste ▷ vb sicken, fill with loathing

DISH n shallow container used for holding or serving food ▷ vb put into a dish

DISHED adj shaped like a dish

DISHELM vb remove helmet from

DISHES ▸ **dish**

DISHFUL n the amount that a dish is able to hold

DISHIER ▸ **dishy**

DISHING ▸ **dish**

DISHOME vb deprive of home

DISHORN vb remove horns from

DISHPAN n large pan for washing dishes, pots, etc

DISHRAG n dishcloth

DISHY adj good-looking

DISJECT vb break apart

DISJOIN vb disconnect or become disconnected

DISJUNE n breakfast

DISK same as ▸ **disc**

DISKED ▸ **disk**

DISKING ▸ **disk**

DISKS ▸ **disk**

DISLEAF vb remove leaf or leaves from

DISLEAL archaic form of > **disloyal**

DISLIKE vb consider unpleasant or disagreeable ▷ n feeling of not liking something or someone

DISLIMB vb remove limbs from

DISLIMN vb efface

DISLINK vb disunite

DISLOAD vb unload

DISMAL adj gloomy and depressing

DISMALS pl n gloomy state of mind

DISMAN vb remove men from

DISMANS ▸ **disman**

DISMASK vb remove mask from

DISMAST vb break off the mast or masts of (a sailing vessel)

DISMAY vb fill with alarm or depression ▷ n alarm mixed with sadness

DISMAYD ▸ **dismay**

DISMAYL vb remove a coat of mail from

DISMAYS ▸ **dismay**

DISME old form of ▸ **dime**

DISMES ▸ **disme**

DISMISS vb remove (an employee) from a job ▷ sentence substitute order to end an activity or give permission to disperse

DISNEST vb remove from nest

DISOBEY vb neglect or refuse to obey

DISOMIC adj having an extra chromosome in the haploid state that is homologous to an existing chromosome in this set

DISOMY ▸ **disomic**

DISOWN vb deny any connection with (someone)

DISOWNS ▸ **disown**

DISPACE vb move or travel about

DISPARK vb release

DISPART vb separate

DISPEL vb destroy or remove

DISPELS ▸ **dispel**

DISPEND vb spend

DISPLAY vb make visible or noticeable ▷ n displaying

DISPLE vb punish

DISPLED ▸ **disple**

DISPLES ▸ **disple**

DISPONE vb transfer ownership

DISPORT vb indulge (oneself) in pleasure ▷ n amusement

DISPOSE vb place in a certain order

DISPOST vb remove from post

DISPRAD old form of > **dispread**

DISPRED old spelling of > **dispread**

DISPUTE n disagreement, argument ▷ vb argue about (something)

DISRANK vb demote

DISRATE vb punish (an officer) by lowering in rank

DISROBE vb undress

DISROOT vb uproot

DISRUPT vb interrupt the progress of

DISS vb treat (a person) with contempt

DISSAVE vb spend savings

DISSEAT vb unseat

DISSECT vb cut open (a corpse) to examine it

DISSED ▸ **diss**

DISSENT vb disagree ▷ n disagreement

DISSERT n give or make a dissertation; dissertate

DISSES ▸ **diss**

DISSING ▸ **diss**

DISTAFF n rod on which wool etc is wound for spinning

DISTAIN vb stain; tarnish

DISTAL adj (of a muscle, bone, limb, etc) situated farthest from the centre, median line, or point of attachment or origin

DISTANT adj far apart

DISTEND vb (of part of the body) swell

DISTENT adj bloated; swollen

DISTICH n unit of two verse lines

DISTIL vb subject to or obtain by distillation

DISTILL same as ▸ **distil**

DISTILS ▸ **distil**

DISTOME n parasitic flatworm

DISTORT vb misrepresent (the truth or facts)

DISTRIX n splitting of the ends of hairs

DISTUNE vb cause to be out of tune

DISTURB vb intrude on

DISTYLE n temple with two columns

DISUSE vb stop using ▷ n state of being no longer used

DISUSED adj no longer used

DISUSES ▸ disuse

DISYOKE vb unyoke

DIT vb stop something happening ▷ n short sound used, in combination with the long sound in the spoken representation of Morse and other telegraphic codes

DITA n tropical African and Asian shrub with large shiny whorled leaves and medicinal bark

DITAL n key for raising pitch of lute string

DITALS ▸ dital

DITAS ▸ dita

DITCH n narrow channel dug in the earth for drainage or irrigation ▷ vb abandon

DITCHED ▸ ditch

DITCHER ▸ ditch

DITCHES ▸ ditch

DITE vb set down in writing

DITED ▸ dite

DITES ▸ dite

DITHER vb be uncertain or indecisive ▷ n state of indecision or agitation

DITHERS ▸ dither

DITHERY ▸ dither

DITHIOL n chemical compound

DITING ▸ dite

DITONE n interval of two tones

DITONES ▸ ditone

DITS ▸ dit

DITSIER ▸ ditsy

DITSY same as ▸ ditzy

DITT same as ▸ dit

DITTANY n aromatic Cretan plant with pink drooping flowers, formerly credited with great medicinal properties

DITTAY n accusation; charge

DITTAYS ▸ dittay

DITTED ▸ dit

DITTIED ▸ ditty

DITTIES ▸ ditty

DITTING ▸ dit

DITTIT ▸ dit

DITTO n same ▷ adv in the same way ▷ sentence substitute used to avoid repeating or to confirm agreement with an immediately preceding sentence ▷ vb copy

DITTOED ▸ ditto

DITTOS ▸ ditto

DITTS ▸ ditt

DITTY vb set to music ▷ n short simple poem or song

DITZ n silly scatterbrained person

DITZES ▸ ditz

DITZIER ▸ ditzy

DITZY adj silly and scatterbrained

DIURNAL adj happening during the day or daily ▷ n service book containing all the canonical hours except matins

DIURON n type of herbicide

DIURONS ▸ diuron

DIV n stupid or foolish person

DIVA n distinguished female singer

DIVAN n low backless bed

DIVANS ▸ divan

DIVAS ▸ diva

DIVE vb plunge headfirst into water ▷ n diving

DIVED ▸ dive

DIVER n person who works or explores underwater

DIVERGE vb separate and go in different directions

DIVERS adj various ▷ determiner various

DIVERSE vb turn away ▷ adj having variety, assorted

DIVERT vb change the direction of

DIVERTS ▸ divert

DIVES ▸ dive

DIVEST vb strip (of clothes)

DIVESTS ▸ divest

DIVI alternative spelling of ▸ divvy

DIVIDE vb separate into parts ▷ n division, split

DIVIDED adj split

DIVIDER n screen used to divide a room into separate areas

DIVIDES ▸ divide

DIVIED ▸ divvied

DIVINE adj of God or a god ▷ vb discover (something) by intuition or guessing ▷ n priest who is learned in theology

DIVINED ▸ divine

DIVINER ▸ divine

DIVINES ▸ divine

DIVING ▸ dive

DIVINGS ▸ dive

DIVIS ▸ divi

DIVISIM adv separately

DIVISOR n number to be divided into another number

DIVNA vb do not

DIVO n male diva

DIVORCE n legal ending of a marriage ▷ vb legally end one's marriage (to)

DIVOS ▸ divo

DIVOT n small piece of turf

DIVOTS ▸ divot

DIVS ▸ div

DIVULGE vb make known, disclose

DIVULSE vb tear apart

DIVVIED ▸ divvy

DIVVIER ▸ divvy adj

DIVVIES ▸ divvy

DIVVY vb divide and share ▷ adj stupid ▷ n stupid person

DIVVYING > divvying

DIWAN same as ▸ dewan

DIWANS ▸ diwan

DIXI interj I have spoken

DIXIE n large metal pot for cooking, brewing tea, etc

DIXIES ▸ dixie

DIXIT n statement

DIXITS ▸ dixit

DIXY same as ▸ dixie

DIYA n small oil lamp, usu made from clay

DIYAS ▸ diya

DIZAIN n ten-line poem

DIZAINS ▸ dizain

DIZEN archaic word for ▸ bedizen

DIZENED ▸ dizen

DIZENS ▸ dizen

DIZZARD n dunce

DIZZIED ▸ dizzy

DIZZIER ▸ dizzy

DIZZIES ▸ dizzy

DIZZILY ▸ dizzy

DIZZY adj having or causing a whirling sensation ▷ vb make dizzy

DJEBEL a variant spelling of ▸ jebel

DJEBELS ▶ djebel

DJEMBE *n* W African drum played by beating with the hand

DJEMBES ▶ djembe

DJIBBAH *same as* ▶ **jubbah**

DJIN *same as* ▶ **jinn**

DJINN *same as* ▶ **jinn**

DJINNI *same as* ▶ **jinni**

DJINNS ▶ djinn

DJINNY *same as* ▶ **jinni**

DJINS ▶ djin

DO *vb* perform or complete (a deed or action) ▷ *n* party, celebration

DOAB *n* alluvial land between two converging rivers, esp the area between the Ganges and Jumna in N India

DOABLE *adj* capable of being done

DOABS ▶ doab

DOAT *same as* ▶ **dote**

DOATED ▶ doat

DOATER ▶ doat

DOATERS ▶ doat

DOATING ▶ doat

DOATS ▶ doat

DOB *vb* *as in* **dob in** inform against or report

DOBBED ▶ dob

DOBBER *n* informant or traitor

DOBBERS ▶ dobber

DOBBIE *same as* ▶ **dobby**

DOBBIES ▶ dobby

DOBBIN *n* name for a horse, esp a workhorse, often used in children's tales, etc

DOBBING ▶ dob

DOBBINS ▶ dobbin

DOBBY *n* attachment to a loom, used in weaving small figures

DOBHASH *n* interpreter

DOBIE *n* cannabis

DOBIES ▶ dobie

DOBLA *n* medieval Spanish gold coin, probably worth 20 maravedis

DOBLAS ▶ dobla

DOBLON *a variant spelling of* > **doubloon**

DOBLONS ▶ doblon

DOBRA *n* standard monetary unit of São Tomé e Principe, divided into 100 cêntimos

DOBRAS ▶ dobra

DOBRO *n* tradename for a type of acoustic guitar having a metal resonator

built into the body

DOBROS ▶ dobro

DOBS ▶ dob

DOBSON *n* larva of dobsonfly

DOBSONS ▶ dobson

DOBY *same as* ▶ **dobie**

DOC *same as* ▶ **doctor**

DOCENT *n* voluntary worker who acts as a guide in a museum, art gallery, etc

DOCENTS ▶ docent

DOCETIC *adj* believer in docetism: a heresy that the humanity of Christ was apparent rather than real

DOCHMII > dochmius

DOCHT ▶ dow

DOCIBLE *adj* easily tamed

DOCILE *adj* (of a person or animal) easily controlled

DOCILER ▶ docile

DOCK *n* enclosed area of water where ships are loaded, unloaded, or repaired ▷ *vb* bring or be brought into dock

DOCKAGE *n* charge levied upon a vessel for using a dock

DOCKED ▶ dock

DOCKEN *n* something of no value or importance

DOCKENS ▶ docken

DOCKER *n* person employed to load and unload ships

DOCKERS ▶ docker

DOCKET *n* label on a package or other delivery, stating contents, delivery instructions, etc ▷ *vb* fix a docket to (a package or other delivery)

DOCKETS ▶ docket

DOCKING ▶ dock

DOCKISE *same as* ▶ **dockize**

DOCKIZE *vb* convert into docks

DOCKS ▶ dock

DOCO *n* (slang) documentary

DOCOS ▶ doco

DOCQUET *same as* ▶ **docket**

DOCS ▶ doc

DOCTOR *n* person licensed to practise medicine ▷ *vb* alter in order to deceive

DOCTORS ▶ doctor

DOD *vb* clip

DODDARD *adj* archaic word for missing branches; rotten

DODDED ▶ dod

DODDER *vb* move unsteadily ▷ *n* type of rootless parasitic plant whose twining stems have suckers for drawing nourishment from the host plant

DODDERS ▶ dodder

DODDERY ▶ dodder

DODDIER ▶ doddy

DODDIES ▶ doddy

DODDING ▶ dod

DODDLE *n* something easily accomplished

DODDLES ▶ doddle

DODDY *n* bad mood ▷ *adj* sulky

DODGE *vb* avoid (a blow, being seen, etc) by moving suddenly ▷ *n* cunning or deceitful trick

DODGED ▶ dodge

DODGEM *n* bumper car

DODGEMS ▶ dodgem

DODGER *n* person who evades a responsibility or duty

DODGERS ▶ dodger

DODGERY *n* deception

DODGES ▶ dodge

DODGIER ▶ dodgy

DODGING ▶ dodge

DODGY *adj* dangerous, risky

DODKIN *n* coin of little value

DODKINS ▶ dodkin

DODMAN *n* snail

DODMANS ▶ dodman

DODO *n* large flightless extinct bird

DODOES ▶ dodo

DODOISM ▶ dodo

DODOS ▶ dodo

DODS ▶ dod

DOE *n* female deer, hare, or rabbit

DOEK *n* square of cloth worn on the head by women

DOEKS ▶ doek

DOEN ▶ do

DOER *n* active or energetic person

DOERS ▶ doer

DOES ▶ do

DOESKIN *n* skin of a deer, lamb, or sheep

DOEST ▶ do

DOETH ▶ do

DOF *informal South African word for* ▶ **stupid**

DOFF *vb* take off or lift (one's

hat) in polite greeting

DOFFED ▸ doff

DOFFER ▸ doff

DOFFERS ▸ doff

DOFFING ▸ doff

DOFFS ▸ doff

DOG *n* domesticated four-legged mammal of many different breeds ▷ *vb* follow (someone) closely

DOGATE *n* office of doge

DOGATES ▸ dogate

DOGBANE *n* N American plant with bell-shaped white or pink flowers, thought to be poisonous to dogs

DOGBOLT *n* bolt on cannon

DOGCART *n* light horse-drawn two-wheeled cart

DOGDOM *n* world of dogs

DOGDOMS ▸ dogdom

DOGE *n* (formerly) chief magistrate of Venice or Genoa

DOGEAR *vb* fold down the corner of (a page) ▷ *n* folded-down corner of a page

DOGEARS ▸ dogear

DOGEATE *n* office of doge

DOGEDOM *n* domain of doge

DOGES ▸ doge

DOGEY *same as* ▸ dogie

DOGEYS ▸ dogey

DOGFACE *n* WW2 US soldier

DOGFISH *n* small shark

DOGFOX *n* male fox

DOGGED ▸ dog

DOGGER *n* Dutch fishing vessel with two masts

DOGGERS ▸ dogger

DOGGERY *n* surly behaviour

DOGGESS *n* female dog

DOGGIE *same as* ▸ doggy

DOGGIER ▸ doggy

DOGGIES ▸ doggy

DOGGING ▸ dog

DOGGISH *adj* of or like a dog

DOGGO *adv* in hiding and keeping quiet

DOGGONE *interj* exclamation of annoyance, disappointment, etc ▷ *vb* damn ▷ *adj* damnedest

DOGGREL *same as* > doggerel

DOGGY *n* child's word for a dog ▷ *adj* of or like a dog

DOGHOLE *n* squalid dwelling place

DOGIE *n* motherless calf

DOGIES ▸ dogy

DOGLEG *n* sharp bend ▷ *vb* go off at an angle ▷ *adj* of or with the shape of a dogleg

DOGLEGS ▸ dogleg

DOGLIKE ▸ dog

DOGMA *n* doctrine or system of doctrines proclaimed by authority as true

DOGMAN *n* person who directs the operation of a crane whilst riding on an object being lifted by it

DOGMAS ▸ dogma

DOGMATA ▸ dogma

DOGMEN ▸ dogman

DOGNAP *vb* carry off and hold (a dog), usually for ransom

DOGNAPS ▸ dognap

DOGS ▸ dog

DOGSHIP *n* condition of being a dog

DOGSKIN *n* leather from dog's skin

DOGSLED *n* sleigh drawn by dogs

DOGTOWN *n* community of prairie dogs

DOGTROT *n* gently paced trot

DOGVANE *n* light windvane consisting of a feather or a piece of cloth or yarn mounted on the side of a vessel

DOGWOOD *n* type of tree or shrub, esp a European species with clusters of small white flowers and black berries

DOGY *same as* ▸ dogie

DOH *n* in tonic sol-fa, first degree of any major scale ▷ *interj* exclamation of annoyance when something goes wrong

| This is one of the very useful short words denoting a note of the musical scale.

DOHS ▸ doh

DOHYO *n* sumo wrestling ring

DOHYOS ▸ dohyo

DOILED *same as* ▸ doilt

DOILIES ▸ doily

DOILT *adj* foolish

DOILTER ▸ doilt

DOILY *n* decorative lacy paper mat, laid on a plate

DOING ▸ do

DOINGS *pl n* deeds or actions

DOIT *n* former small copper coin of the Netherlands

DOITED *adj* foolish or childish, as from senility

DOITIT *same as* ▸ doited

DOITKIN *same as* ▸ doit

DOITS ▸ doit

DOJO *n* room or hall for the practice of martial arts

DOJOS ▸ dojo

DOL *n* unit of pain intensity, as measured by dolorimetry

DOLCE *n* dessert ▷ *adv* (to be performed) gently and sweetly

DOLCES ▸ dolce

DOLCI ▸ dolce

DOLE *n* money received from the state while unemployed ▷ *vb* distribute in small quantities

DOLED ▸ dole

DOLEFUL *adj* dreary, unhappy

DOLENT *adj* sad

DOLENTE *adv* (to be performed) in a sorrowful manner

DOLES ▸ dole

DOLIA ▸ dolium

DOLINA *same as* ▸ doline

DOLINAS ▸ dolina

DOLINE *n* shallow usually funnel-shaped depression of the ground surface formed by solution in limestone regions

DOLINES ▸ doline

DOLING ▸ dole

DOLIUM *n* genus of molluscs

DOLL *n* small model of a human being, used as a toy ▷ *vb* as in **doll up** dress up

DOLLAR *n* standard monetary unit of many countries

DOLLARS ▸ dollar

DOLLDOM ▸ doll

DOLLED ▸ doll

DOLLIED ▸ dolly

DOLLIER *n* person who operates a dolly

DOLLIES ▸ dolly

DOLLING ▸ doll

DOLLISH ▸ doll

DOLLOP *n* lump (of food) ▷ *vb* serve out (food)

DOLLOPS ▸ dollop

DOLLS ▸ doll

D

DOLLY adj attractive and unintelligent ▷ n wheeled support on which a camera may be mounted; shaped block of lead used to hammer dents out of sheet metal ▷ vb wheel (a camera) backwards or forwards on a dolly

DOLMA n vine leaf stuffed with a filling of meat and rice

DOLMAN n long Turkish outer robe

DOLMANS ▶ dolman

DOLMAS ▶ dolma

DOLMEN n prehistoric monument consisting of a horizontal stone supported by vertical stones

DOLMENS ▶ dolmen

DOLOR same as ▶ dolour

DOLORS ▶ dolor

DOLOS n knucklebone of a sheep, buck, etc, used esp by diviners

DOLOSSE ▶ dolos

DOLOUR n grief or sorrow

DOLOURS ▶ dolour

DOLPHIN n sea mammal of the whale family, with a beaklike snout

DOLS ▶ dol

DOLT n stupid person

DOLTISH ▶ dolt

DOLTS ▶ dolt

DOM n title given to Benedictine, Carthusian, and Cistercian monks and to certain of the canons regular

DOMAIN n field of knowledge or activity

DOMAINE n French estate where wine is made

DOMAINS ▶ domain

DOMAL adj of a house

DOMATIA ▶ domatium

DOME n rounded roof built on a circular base ▷ vb cover with or as if with a dome

DOMED ▶ dome

DOMES ▶ dome

DOMETT n wool and cotton cloth

DOMETTS ▶ domett

DOMIC adj dome-shaped

DOMICAL ▶ dome

DOMICIL same as > domicile

DOMIER ▶ domy

DOMIEST ▶ domy

DOMINE n clergyman

DOMINEE n minister of the Dutch Reformed Church

DOMINES ▶ domine

DOMING ▶ dome

DOMINIE n minister or clergyman: also used as a term of address

DOMINO n small rectangular block marked with dots, used in dominoes

DOMINOS ▶ domino

DOMOIC adj as in **domoic acid** kind of amino acid

DOMS ▶ dom

DOMY adj having a dome or domes

DON vb put on (clothing) ▷ n member of the teaching staff at a university or college

DONA n Spanish lady

DONAH n woman

DONAHS ▶ donah

DONARY n thing given for holy use

DONAS ▶ dona

DONATE vb give, esp to a charity or organization

DONATED ▶ donate

DONATES ▶ donate

DONATOR ▶ donate

DONDER vb beat (someone) up ▷ n wretch

DONDERS ▶ donder

DONE ▶ do

DONEE n person who receives a gift

DONEES ▶ donee

DONER n as in **doner kebab** grilled meat and salad served in pitta bread with chilli sauce

DONG n deep reverberating sound of a large bell ▷ vb (of a bell) to make a deep reverberating sound

DONGA n steep-sided gully created by soil erosion

DONGAS ▶ donga

DONGED ▶ dong

DONGING ▶ dong

DONGLE n electronic device that accompanies a software item to prevent the unauthorized copying of programs

DONGLES ▶ dongle

DONGOLA n leather tanned using a particular method

DONGS ▶ dong

DONING n act of giving blood

DONINGS ▶ doning

DONJON n heavily fortified central tower of a castle

DONJONS ▶ donjon

DONKEY n long-eared member of the horse family

DONKEYS ▶ donkey

DONKO n tearoom or cafeteria in a factory, wharf area, etc

DONKOS ▶ donko

DONNA n Italian lady

DONNARD same as ▶ donnert

DONNART same as ▶ donnert

DONNAS ▶ donna

DONNAT n lazy person

DONNATS ▶ donnat

DONNE same as ▶ donnee

DONNED ▶ don

DONNEE n subject or theme

DONNEES ▶ donnee

DONNERD adj stupid

DONNERT adj stunned

DONNES ▶ donne

DONNIES ▶ donny

DONNING ▶ don

DONNISH adj serious and academic

DONNISM n loftiness

DONNOT n lazy person

DONNOTS ▶ donnot

DONNY same as ▶ danny

DONOR n person who gives blood or organs for use in the treatment of another person

DONORS ▶ donor

DONS ▶ don

DONSHIP n state or condition of being a don

DONSIE adj rather unwell

DONSIER ▶ donsie

DONSY same as ▶ donsie

DONUT same as > doughnut

DONUTS ▶ donut

DONZEL n man of high birth

DONZELS ▶ donzel

DOO a Scots word for ▶ dove

DOOB n cannabis cigarette

DOOBIE same as ▶ doob

DOOBIES ▶ doobie

DOOBREY n thingumabob

DOOBRIE ▶ doobrey

DOOBS ▶ doob

DOOCE vb dismiss (an employee) because of comments they have posted on the Internet

DOOCED ▶ dooce

DOOCES ▶ dooce

DOOCING ▶ dooce

DOOCOT n dovecote
DOOCOTS ▷ **doocot**
DOODAD same as ▷ **doodah**
DOODADS ▷ **doodad**
DOODAH n unnamed thing, esp an object the name of which is unknown or uncertain
DOODAHS ▷ **doodah**
DOODIES ▷ **doody**
DOODLE vb scribble or draw aimlessly ▷ n shape or picture drawn aimlessly
DOODLED ▷ **doodle**
DOODLER ▷ **doodle**
DOODLES ▷ **doodle**
DOODOO n excrement
DOODOOS n **doodoo**
DOODY same as ▷ **doodoo**
DOOFER n thingamajig
DOOFERS ▷ **doofer**
DOOFUS n slow-witted or stupid person
DOOK n wooden plug driven into a wall to hold a nail, screw, etc ▷ vb dip or plunge
DOOKED ▷ **dook**
DOOKET n dovecote
DOOKETS ▷ **dooket**
DOOKING ▷ **dook**
DOOKS ▷ **dook**
DOOL n boundary marker
DOOLAN n Roman Catholic
DOOLANS ▷ **doolan**
DOOLE same as ▷ **dool**
DOOLEE same as ▷ **doolie**
DOOLEES ▷ **doolee**
DOOLES ▷ **doole**
DOOLIE n enclosed couch on poles for carrying passengers
DOOLIES ▷ **doolie**
DOOLS ▷ **dool**
DOOLY same as ▷ **doolie**
DOOM n death or a terrible fate ▷ vb destine to or condemn to death or a terrible fate
DOOMED ▷ **doom**
DOOMFUL ▷ **doom**
DOOMIER ▷ **doomy**
DOOMILY ▷ **doomy**
DOOMING ▷ **doom**
DOOMS ▷ **doom**
DOOMY adj despondent or pessimistic
DOON same as ▷ **down**
DOONA n large quilt used as a bed cover in place of the top sheet and blankets
DOONAS ▷ **doona**
DOOR n hinged or sliding

panel for closing the entrance to a building, room, etc
DOORMAN n man employed to be on duty at the entrance to a large public building
DOORMAT n mat for wiping dirt from shoes before going indoors
DOORMEN ▷ **doorman**
DOORN n thorn
DOORNS ▷ **doorn**
DOORS ▷ **door**
DOORWAY n opening into a building or room
DOOS ▷ **doo**
DOOSRA n in cricket, a delivery, bowled by an off-spinner, that turns the opposite way from an off-break
DOOSRAS ▷ **doosra**
DOOWOP n style of singing in harmony
DOOWOPS ▷ **doowop**
DOOZER same as ▷ **doozy**
DOOZERS ▷ **doozer**
DOOZIE same as ▷ **doozy**
DOOZIES ▷ **doozie**
DOOZY n something excellent
DOP vb curtsy ▷ n tot or small drink, usually alcoholic ▷ vb fail to reach the required standard in (an examination, course, etc)
DOPA n precursor to dopamine
DOPANT n element or compound used to dope a semiconductor
DOPANTS ▷ **dopant**
DOPAS ▷ **dopa**
DOPATTA n headscarf
DOPE n illegal drug, usu cannabis ▷ vb give a drug to, esp in order to improve performance in a race ▷ adj excellent
DOPED ▷ **dope**
DOPER n person who administers dope
DOPERS ▷ **doper**
DOPES ▷ **dope**
DOPEY adj half-asleep, drowsy
DOPIAZA n Indian meat or fish dish cooked in onion sauce
DOPIER ▷ **dopy**
DOPIEST ▷ **dopy**
DOPILY ▷ **dopey**

DOPING ▷ **dope**
DOPINGS ▷ **dope**
DOPPED ▷ **dop**
DOPPER n member of an Afrikaner church who practises a strict Calvinism
DOPPERS ▷ **dopper**
DOPPIE n cartridge case
DOPPIES ▷ **doppie**
DOPPING ▷ **dop**
DOPPIO n double measure, esp of espresso coffee
DOPPIOS ▷ **doppio**
DOPS ▷ **dop**
DOPY same as ▷ **dopey**
DOR n European dung beetle that makes a droning sound when it flies
DORAD n South American river fish
DORADO n large marine percoid fish
DORADOS ▷ **dorado**
DORADS ▷ **dorad**
DORB same as ▷ **dorba**
DORBA n stupid, inept, or clumsy person
DORBAS ▷ **dorba**
DORBS ▷ **dorb**
DORBUG n type of beetle
DORBUGS ▷ **dorbug**
DORE n walleye fish
DOREE n type of fish
DOREES ▷ **doree**
DORES ▷ **dore**
DORHAWK n nightjar
DORIC adj rustic
DORIES ▷ **dory**
DORIS n woman
DORISE same as ▷ **dorize**
DORISED ▷ **dorise**
DORISES ▷ **dorise**
DORIZE vb become Doric
DORIZED ▷ **dorize**
DORIZES ▷ **dorize**
DORK n stupid person.
DORKIER ▷ **dork**
DORKISH adj stupid or contemptible
DORKS ▷ **dork**
DORKY ▷ **dork**
DORLACH n quiver of arrows
DORM same as > **dormitory**
DORMANT n supporting beam ▷ adj temporarily quiet, inactive, or not being used
DORMER n window that sticks out from a sloping roof
DORMERS ▷ **dormer**
DORMICE > **dormouse**

DORMIE adj (of a player or side) as many holes ahead of an opponent as there are still to play

DORMIN n hormone found in plants

DORMINS ▶ dormin

DORMS ▶ dorm

DORMY same as ▶ dormie

DORNECK same as ▶ dornick

DORNICK n heavy damask cloth, formerly used for vestments, curtains, etc

DORNOCK n type of coarse fabric

DORP n small town

DORPER n breed of sheep

DORPERS ▶ dorper

DORPS ▶ dorp

DORR same as ▶ dor

DORRED ▶ dor

DORRING ▶ dor

DORRS ▶ dorr

DORS ▶ dor

DORSA ▶ dorsum

DORSAD adj towards the back or dorsal aspect

DORSAL adj of or on the back ▷ n dorsal fin

DORSALS ▶ dorsal

DORSE n type of small fish

DORSEL another word for ▶ dossal

DORSELS ▶ dorsel

DORSER n hanging tapestry

DORSERS ▶ dorser

DORSES ▶ dorse

DORSUM n the back

DORT vb sulk

DORTED ▶ dort

DORTER n dormitory

DORTERS ▶ dorter

DORTIER ▶ dorty

DORTING ▶ dort

DORTOUR same as ▶ dorter

DORTS ▶ dort

DORTY adj haughty, or sullen

DORY n spiny-finned edible sea fish

DOS ▶ do

DOSAGE same as ▶ dose

DOSAGES ▶ dosage

DOSE n specific quantity of a medicine taken at one time ▷ vb give a dose to

DOSED ▶ dose

DOSEH n former Egyptian religious ceremony

DOSEHS ▶ doseh

DOSER ▶ dose

DOSERS ▶ dose

DOSES ▶ dose

DOSH n money

DOSHES ▶ dosh

DOSING ▶ dose

DOSS vb sleep, esp in a dosshouse ▷ n bed, esp in a dosshouse

DOSSAL n ornamental hanging, placed at the back of an altar or at the sides of a chancel

DOSSALS ▶ dossal

DOSSED ▶ doss

DOSSEL same as ▶ dossal

DOSSELS ▶ dossel

DOSSER n bag or basket for carrying objects on the back

DOSSERS ▶ dosser

DOSSES ▶ doss

DOSSIER n collection of documents about a subject or person

DOSSIL n lint for dressing wound

DOSSILS ▶ dossil

DOSSING ▶ doss

DOST a singular form of the present tense (indicative mood) of ▶ do

DOT n small round mark ▷ vb mark with a dot

DOTAGE n weakness as a result of old age

DOTAGES ▶ dotage

DOTAL ▶ dot

DOTANT another word for ▶ dotard

DOTANTS ▶ dotant

DOTARD n person who is feeble-minded through old age

DOTARDS ▶ dotard

DOTCOM n company that does most of its business on the Internet

DOTCOMS ▶ dotcom

DOTE vb love to an excessive or foolish degree

DOTED ▶ dote

DOTER ▶ dote

DOTERS ▶ dote

DOTES ▶ dote

DOTH a singular form of the present tense of ▶ do

DOTIER ▶ doty

DOTIEST ▶ doty

DOTING ▶ dote

DOTINGS ▶ dote

DOTISH adj foolish

DOTS ▶ dot

DOTTED ▶ dot

DOTTEL same as ▶ dottle

DOTTELS ▶ dottel

DOTTER ▶ dot

DOTTERS ▶ dot

DOTTIER ▶ dotty

DOTTILY ▶ dotty

DOTTING ▶ dot

DOTTLE n tobacco left in a pipe after smoking ▷ adj relating to dottle

DOTTLED adj foolish

DOTTLER ▶ dottle

DOTTLES ▶ dottle

DOTTREL same as > dotterel

DOTTY adj rather eccentric

DOTY adj (of wood) rotten

DOUANE n customs house

DOUANES ▶ douane

DOUAR same as ▶ duar

DOUARS ▶ douar

DOUBLE adj as much again in number, amount, size, etc ▷ adv twice over ▷ n twice the number, amount, size, etc ▷ vb make or become twice as much or as many

DOUBLED ▶ double

DOUBLER ▶ double

DOUBLES n game between two pairs of players

DOUBLET n man's close-fitting jacket, with or without sleeves

DOUBLY adv in a greater degree, quantity, or measure

DOUBT n uncertainty about the truth, facts, or existence of something ▷ vb question the truth of

DOUBTED ▶ doubt

DOUBTER ▶ doubt

DOUBTS ▶ doubt

DOUC n Old World monkey of SE Asia with a bright yellow face surrounded by reddish-brown fur, a white tail, and white hindquarters

DOUCE adj quiet

DOUCELY ▶ douce

DOUCER ▶ douce

DOUCEST ▶ douce

DOUCET n former flute-like instrument

DOUCETS ▶ doucet

DOUCEUR n gratuity, tip, or bribe

DOUCHE n (instrument for applying) a stream of water directed onto or into the body for cleansing or medical purposes ▷ *vb* cleanse or treat by means of a douche

DOUCHED ▸ **douche**

DOUCHES ▸ **douche**

DOUCINE *n* type of moulding for cornice

DOUCS ▸ **douc**

DOUGH *n* thick mixture of flour and water or milk, used for making bread etc

DOUGHS ▸ **dough**

DOUGHT ▸ **dow**

DOUGHTY *adj* brave and determined

DOUGHY *adj* resembling dough in consistency, colour, etc

DOUK *same as* ▸ **dook**

DOUKED ▸ **douk**

DOUKING ▸ **douk**

DOUKS ▸ **douk**

DOULA *n* woman who is trained to provide support to women and their families during pregnancy, childbirth, and the period of time following the birth

DOULAS ▸ **doula**

DOULEIA *same as* ▸ **dulia**
This word refers to the inferior veneration accorded to saints and angels, as distinct from **latria**, the veneration accorded to God alone, and is another of the few seven-letter words that use all five vowels. It's surprising how often you want to do this!

DOUM *n as in* **doum palm** variety of palm tree

DOUMA *same as* ▸ **duma**

DOUMAS ▸ **douma**

DOUMS ▸ **doum**

DOUN *same as* ▸ **down**

DOUP *n* bottom

DOUPS ▸ **doup**

DOUR *adj* sullen and unfriendly

DOURA *same as* ▸ **durra**

DOURAH *same as* ▸ **durra**

DOURAHS ▸ **dourah**

DOURAS ▸ **doura**

DOURER ▸ **dour**

DOUREST ▸ **dour**

DOURINE *n* infectious venereal disease of horses

DOURLY ▸ **dour**

DOUSE *vb* drench with water or other liquid ▷ *n* immersion

DOUSED ▸ **douse**

DOUSER ▸ **douse**

DOUSERS ▸ **douse**

DOUSES ▸ **douse**

DOUSING ▸ **douse**

DOUT *vb* extinguish

DOUTED ▸ **dout**

DOUTER ▸ **dout**

DOUTERS ▸ **dout**

DOUTING ▸ **dout**

DOUTS ▸ **dout**

DOUX *adj* sweet

DOVE *vb* be semi-conscious ▷ *n* bird with a heavy body, small head, and short legs

DOVECOT *same as* > **dovecote**

DOVED ▸ **dove**

DOVEISH *adj* dovelike

DOVEKEY *same as* ▸ **dovekie**

DOVEKIE *n* small short-billed auk

DOVELET *n* small dove

DOVEN *vb* pray

DOVENED ▸ **doven**

DOVENS ▸ **doven**

DOVER *vb* doze ▷ *n* doze

DOVERED ▸ **dover**

DOVERS ▸ **dover**

DOVES ▸ **dove**

DOVIE *Scots word for* ▸ **stupid**

DOVIER ▸ **dovie**

DOVIEST ▸ **dovie**

DOVING ▸ **dovie**

DOVISH ▸ **dove**

DOW *vb* archaic word meaning be of worth

DOWABLE *adj* capable of being endowed

DOWAGER *n* widow possessing property or a title obtained from her husband

DOWAR *same as* ▸ **duar**

DOWARS ▸ **dowar**

DOWD *n* woman who wears unfashionable clothes

DOWDIER ▸ **dowdy**

DOWDIES ▸ **dowdy**

DOWDILY ▸ **dowdy**

DOWDS ▸ **dowd**

DOWDY *adj* dull and old-fashioned ▷ *n* dowdy woman

DOWED ▸ **dow**

DOWEL *n* wooden or metal peg that fits into two corresponding holes to join two adjacent parts ▷ *vb* join pieces of wood using dowels

DOWELED ▸ **dowel**

DOWELS ▸ **dowel**

DOWER *n* life interest in a part of her husband's estate allotted to a widow by law ▷ *vb* endow

DOWERED ▸ **dower**

DOWERS ▸ **dower**

DOWERY *same as* ▸ **dowry**

DOWF *adj* dull; listless

DOWIE *adj* dull and dreary

DOWIER ▸ **dowie**

DOWIEST ▸ **dowie**

DOWING ▸ **dow**

DOWL *n* fluff

DOWLAS *n* coarse fabric

DOWLE *same as* ▸ **dowl**

DOWLES ▸ **dowle**

DOWLIER ▸ **dowly**

DOWLNE *obsolete form of* ▸ **down**

DOWLNES ▸ **dowlne**

DOWLNEY ▸ **dowlne**

DOWLS ▸ **dowl**

DOWLY *adj* dull

DOWN *adv* indicating movement to or position in a lower place ▷ *adj* depressed, unhappy ▷ *vb* drink quickly ▷ *n* soft fine feathers

DOWNA *obsolete Scots form of* ▸ **cannot**

DOWNBOW *n* (in music) a downward stroke of the bow across the strings

DOWNED ▸ **down**

DOWNER *n* barbiturate, tranquillizer, or narcotic

DOWNERS ▸ **downer**

DOWNIER ▸ **downy**

DOWNING ▸ **down**

DOWNS *pl n* low grassy hills, esp in S England

DOWNY *adj* covered with soft fine hair or feathers

DOWP *same as* ▸ **doup**

DOWPS ▸ **dowp**

DOWRIES ▸ **dowry**

DOWRY *n* property brought by a woman to her husband at marriage

DOWS ▸ **dow**

DOWSE *same as* ▸ **douse**

DOWSED ▸ **dowse**

DOWSER ▸ **dowse**

DOWSERS ▸ **dowse**

DOWSES ▸ **dowse**

DOWSET *same as* ▸ **doucet**

DOWSETS ▸ **dowset**

DOWSING ▸ **dowse**

DOWT *n* cigarette butt

DOWTS ▸ **dowt**

DOXIE same as ▸ **doxy**

DOXIES ▸ **doxy**

DOXY n opinion or doctrine, esp concerning religious matters

DOY n beloved person: used esp as an endearment

DOYEN n senior member of a group, profession, or society

DOYENNE ▸ **doyen**

DOYENS ▸ **doyen**

DOYLEY same as ▸ **doily**

DOYLEYS ▸ **doyley**

DOYLIES ▸ **doyly**

DOYLY same as ▸ **doily**

DOYS ▸ **doy**

DOZE vb sleep lightly or briefly ▷ n short sleep

DOZED adj (of timber or rubber) rotten or decayed

DOZEN vb stun

DOZENED ▸ **dozen**

DOZENS ▸ **dozen**

DOZENTH ▸ **dozen**

DOZER ▸ **doze**

DOZERS ▸ **doze**

DOZES ▸ **doze**

DOZIER ▸ **dozy**

DOZIEST ▸ **dozy**

DOZILY ▸ **dozy**

DOZING ▸ **doze**

DOZINGS ▸ **doze**

DOZY adj feeling sleepy

DRAB adj dull and dreary ▷ n light olive-brown colour ▷ vb consort with prostitutes

DRABBED ▸ **drab**

DRABBER n one who frequents low women

DRABBET n yellowish-brown fabric of coarse linen

DRABBLE vb make or become wet or dirty

DRABBY adj promiscuous

DRABLER same as ▸ **drabble**

DRABLY ▸ **drab**

DRABS ▸ **drab**

DRAC same as ▸ **drack**

DRACENA same as ▸ **dracaena**

DRACHM same as ▸ **dram**

DRACHMA n former monetary unit of Greece

DRACHMS ▸ **drachm**

DRACK adj (esp of a woman) unattractive

DRACO n as in draco lizard . flying lizard

DRACONE n large flexible cylindrical container towed by a ship, used for transporting liquids

DRAD ▸ **dread**

DRAFF n residue of husks after fermentation of the grain used in brewing, used as a food for cattle

DRAFFS ▸ **draff**

DRAFFY ▸ **draff**

DRAFT same as ▸ **draught**

DRAFTED ▸ **draft**

DRAFTEE n conscript

DRAFTER ▸ **draft**

DRAFTS ▸ **draft**

DRAFTY same as ▸ **draughty**

DRAG vb pull with force, esp along the ground ▷ n person or thing that slows up progress

DRAGEE n sweet made of a nut, fruit, etc, coated with a hard sugar icing

DRAGEES ▸ **dragee**

DRAGGED ▸ **drag**

DRAGGER ▸ **drag**

DRAGGLE vb make or become wet or dirty by trailing on the ground

DRAGGY adj slow or boring

DRAGNET n net used to scour the bottom of a pond or river to search for something

DRAGON n mythical fire-breathing monster like a huge lizard

DRAGONS ▸ **dragon**

DRAGOON n heavily armed cavalryman ▷ vb coerce, force

DRAGS ▸ **drag**

DRAIL n weighted hook used in trolling ▷ vb fish with a drail

DRAILED ▸ **drail**

DRAILS ▸ **drail**

DRAIN n pipe or channel that carries off water or sewage ▷ vb draw off or remove liquid from

DRAINED ▸ **drain**

DRAINER n person or thing that drains

DRAINS ▸ **drain**

DRAKE n male duck

DRAKES ▸ **drake**

DRAM n small amount of a strong alcoholic drink, esp whisky ▷ vb drink a dram

DRAMA n serious play for theatre, television, or radio

DRAMADY same as ▸ **dramedy**

DRAMAS ▸ **drama**

DRAMEDY n television or film drama in which there are important elements of comedy

DRAMMED ▸ **dram**

DRAMS ▸ **dram**

DRANK ▸ **drink**

DRANT vb drone

DRANTED ▸ **drant**

DRANTS ▸ **drant**

DRAP a Scots word for ▸ **drop**

DRAPE vb cover with material, usu in folds ▷ n piece of cloth hung at a window or opening as a screen

DRAPED ▸ **drape**

DRAPER n person who sells fabrics and sewing materials

DRAPERS ▸ **draper**

DRAPERY n fabric or clothing arranged and draped

DRAPES pl n material hung at an opening or window to shut out light or to provide privacy

DRAPET n cloth

DRAPETS ▸ **drapet**

DRAPEY adj hanging in loose folds

DRAPIER n draper

DRAPING ▸ **drape**

DRAPPED ▸ **drap**

DRAPPIE n little drop, esp a small amount of spirits

DRAPPY n drop (of liquid)

DRAPS ▸ **drap**

DRASTIC n strong purgative ▷ adj strong and severe

DRAT interj exclamation of annoyance ▷ vb curse

DRATS ▸ **drat**

DRATTED adj wretched

DRAUGHT vb make preliminary plan ▷ n current of cold air, esp in an enclosed space ▷ adj (of an animal) used for pulling heavy loads

DRAUNT same as ▸ **drant**

DRAUNTS ▸ **draunt**

DRAVE archaic past of ▸ **drive**

DRAW vb sketch (a figure, picture, etc) with a pencil or pen ▷ n raffle or lottery

DRAWBAR n strong metal bar on a tractor, locomotive, etc, bearing a hook or link and pin to attach a trailer, wagon, etc

DRAWEE n person or organization on which a cheque or other order for payment is drawn

DRAWEES ▸ drawee

DRAWER n sliding box-shaped part of a piece of furniture, used for storage

DRAWERS pl n undergarment worn on the lower part of the body

DRAWING ▸ draw

DRAWL vb speak slowly, with long vowel sounds ▷ n drawling manner of speech

DRAWLED ▸ drawl

DRAWLER ▸ drawl

DRAWLS ▸ drawl

DRAWLY ▸ drawl

DRAWN ▸ draw

DRAWS ▸ draw

DRAY vb pull using cart ▷ n low cart used for carrying heavy loads

DRAYAGE n act of transporting something a short distance by lorry or other vehicle

DRAYED ▸ dray

DRAYING ▸ dray

DRAYMAN n driver of a dray

DRAYMEN ▸ drayman

DRAYS ▸ dray

DRAZEL n low woman

DRAZELS ▸ drazel

DREAD vb anticipate with apprehension or fear ▷ n great fear ▷ adj awesome

DREADED ▸ dread

DREADER ▸ dread

DREADLY ▸ dread

DREADS ▸ dread

DREAM n imagined series of events experienced in the mind while asleep ▷ vb see imaginary pictures in the mind while asleep ▷ adj ideal

DREAMED ▸ dream

DREAMER n person who dreams habitually

DREAMS ▸ dream

DREAMT ▸ dream

DREAMY adj vague or impractical

DREAR same as ▸ dreary

DREARE obsolete form of ▸ drear

DREARER ▸ drear

DREARES ▸ dreare

DREARS ▸ drear

DREARY adj dull, boring ▷ n a dreary thing or person

DRECK n rubbish

DRECKS ▸ dreck

DRECKY ▸ dreck

DREDGE vb clear or search (a river bed or harbour) by removing silt or mud ▷ n machine used to scoop or suck up silt or mud from a river bed or harbour

DREDGED ▸ dredge

DREDGER same as ▸ dredge

DREDGES ▸ dredge

DREE vb endure

DREED ▸ dree

DREEING ▸ dree

DREES ▸ dree

DREG n small quantity

DREGGY adj like or full of dregs

DREGS pl n solid particles that settle at the bottom of some liquids

DREICH adj dreary

DREIDEL n spinning top

DREIDL same as ▸ dreidel

DREIDLS ▸ dreidl

DREIGH same as ▸ dreich

DREK same as ▸ dreck

DREKS ▸ drek

DRENCH vb make completely wet ▷ n act or an instance of drenching

DRENT ▸ drench

DRERE obsolete form of ▸ drear

DRERES ▸ drere

DRESS n one-piece garment for a woman or girl, consisting of a skirt and bodice and sometimes sleeves ▷ vb put clothes on ▷ adj suitable for a formal occasion

DRESSED ▸ dress

DRESSER n piece of furniture with shelves and with cupboards, for storing or displaying dishes

DRESSES ▸ dress

DRESSY adj (of clothes) elegant

DREST ▸ dress

DREVILL n offensive person

DREW ▸ draw

DREY n squirrel's nest

DREYS ▸ drey

DRIB vb flow in drops

DRIBBED ▸ drib

DRIBBER ▸ drib

DRIBBLE vb (allow to) flow in drops ▷ n small quantity of liquid falling in drops

DRIBBLY ▸ dribble

DRIBLET n small amount

DRIBS ▸ drib

DRICE n pellets of frozen carbon dioxide

DRICES ▸ drice

DRIED ▸ dry

DRIEGH adj tedious

DRIER ▸ dry

DRIERS ▸ dry

DRIES ▸ dry

DRIEST ▸ dry

DRIFT vb be carried along by currents of air or water ▷ n something piled up by the wind or current, such as a snowdrift

DRIFTED ▸ drift

DRIFTER n person who moves aimlessly from place to place or job to job

DRIFTS ▸ drift

DRIFTY ▸ drift

DRILL n tool or machine for boring holes ▷ vb bore a hole in (something) with or as if with a drill

DRILLED ▸ drill

DRILLER ▸ drill

DRILLS ▸ drill

DRILY adv in a dry manner

DRINK vb swallow (a liquid) ▷ n (portion of) a liquid suitable for drinking

DRINKER n person who drinks, esp a person who drinks alcohol habitually

DRINKS ▸ drink

DRIP vb (let) fall in drops ▷ n falling of drops of liquid

DRIPPED ▸ drip

DRIPPER ▸ drip

DRIPPY adj mawkish, insipid, or inane

DRIPS ▸ drip

DRIPT ▸ drip

DRIVE vb guide the movement of (a vehicle) ▷ n journey by car, van, etc

DRIVEL n foolish talk ▷ vb speak foolishly

DRIVELS ▸ drivel

DRIVEN ▸ drive

DRIVER n person who drives a vehicle

DRIVERS ▸ driver

DRIVES ▸ drive

DRIVING ▸ drive

DRIZZLE n very light rain ▷ vb rain lightly

DRIZZLY ▸ drizzle

DROGER n W Indian boat

DROGERS ▸ droger

DROGHER *same as* ▸ **droger**

DROGUE *n* any funnel-like device, esp one of canvas, used as a sea anchor

DROGUES ▸ drogue

DROGUET *n* woollen fabric

DROICH *n* dwarf

DROICHS ▸ droich

DROICHY *adj* dwarfish

DROID *same as* ▸ **android**

DROIDS ▸ droid

DROIL *vb* carry out boring menial work

DROILED ▸ droil

DROILS ▸ droil

DROIT *n* legal or moral right or claim

DROITS ▸ droit

DROLE *adj* amusing ▷ *n* scoundrel

DROLER ▸ drole

DROLES ▸ drole

DROLEST ▸ drole

DROLL *vb* speak wittily ▷ *adj* quaintly amusing

DROLLED ▸ droll

DROLLER ▸ droll

DROLLS ▸ droll

DROLLY ▸ droll

DROME > aerodrome

DROMES ▸ drome

DROMIC *adj* relating to running track

DROMOI ▸ dromos

DROMON *same as* ▸ **dromond**

DROMOND *n* large swift sailing vessel of the 12th to 15th centuries

DROMONS ▸ dromon

DROMOS *n* Greek passageway

DRONE *n* male bee ▷ *vb* make a monotonous low dull sound

DRONED ▸ drone

DRONER ▸ drone

DRONERS ▸ drone

DRONES ▸ drone

DRONGO *n* tropical songbird with a glossy black plumage, a forked tail, and a stout bill

DRONGOS ▸ drongo

DRONIER ▸ drony

DRONING ▸ drone

DRONISH ▸ drone

DRONY *adj* monotonous

DROOB *n* pathetic person

DROOBS ▸ droob

DROOG *n* ruffian

DROOGS ▸ droog

DROOK *same as* ▸ **drouk**

DROOKED ▸ drook

DROOKIT *same as* ▸ **droukit**

DROOKS ▸ drook

DROOL *vb* show excessive enthusiasm (for)

DROOLED ▸ drool

DROOLS ▸ drool

DROOLY *adj* tending to drool

DROOME *obsolete form of* ▸ **drum**

DROOMES ▸ drum

DROOP *vb* hang downwards loosely ▷ *n* act or state of drooping

DROOPED ▸ droop

DROOPS ▸ droop

DROOPY *adj* hanging or sagging downwards

DROP *vb* (allow to) fall vertically ▷ *n* small quantity of liquid forming a round shape

DROPFLY *n* (angling) artificial fly

DROPLET *n* very small drop of liquid

DROPOUT *n* person who rejects conventional society ▷ *vb* abandon or withdraw (from an institution or group)

DROPPED ▸ drop

DROPPER *n* small tube with a rubber part at one end for drawing up and dispensing drops of liquid

DROPPLE *n* trickle

DROPS ▸ drop

DROPSY *n* illness in which watery fluid collects in the body

DROPT ▸ drop

DROSERA *n* insectivorous plant

DROSHKY *n* open four-wheeled horse-drawn passenger carriage, formerly used in Russia

DROSKY *same as* ▸ **droshky**

DROSS *n* scum formed on the surfaces of molten metals

DROSSES ▸ dross

DROSSY ▸ dross

DROSTDY *n* office of landdrost

DROUGHT *n* prolonged shortage of rainfall

DROUK *vb* drench

DROUKED ▸ drouk

DROUKIT *adj* drenched

DROUKS ▸ drouk

DROUTH *same as* ▸ **drought**

DROUTHS ▸ drouth

DROUTHY *adj* thirsty or dry

DROVE ▸ drive

DROVED ▸ drive

DROVER *n* person who drives sheep or cattle

DROVERS ▸ drover

DROVES ▸ drive

DROVING ▸ drive

DROW *n* sea fog

DROWN *vb* die or kill by immersion in liquid

DROWND *dialect form of* ▸ **drown**

DROWNDS ▸ drownd

DROWNDS ▸ drown

DROWNER ▸ drown

DROWNS ▸ drown

DROWS ▸ drow

DROWSE *vb* be sleepy, dull, or sluggish ▷ *n* state of being drowsy

DROWSED ▸ drowse

DROWSES ▸ drowse

DROWSY *adj* feeling sleepy

DRUB *vb* beat as with a stick ▷ *n* blow, as from a stick

DRUBBED ▸ drub

DRUBBER ▸ drub

DRUBS ▸ drub

DRUCKEN *adj* drunken

DRUDGE *n* person who works hard at uninteresting tasks ▷ *vb* work at such tasks

DRUDGED ▸ drudge

DRUDGER ▸ drudge

DRUDGES ▸ drudge

DRUG *n* substance used in the treatment or prevention of disease ▷ *vb* give a drug to (a person or animal) to cause sleepiness or unconsciousness

DRUGGED ▸ drug

DRUGGER *n* druggist

DRUGGET *n* coarse fabric used as a protective floor-covering, etc

DRUGGIE *n* drug addict

DRUGGY ▸ drug

DRUGS ▸ drug

DRUID *n* member of an ancient order of priests in Gaul, Britain, and Ireland in the pre-Christian era

DRUIDIC ▸ druid

DRUIDRY ▸ druid

DRUIDS ▸ druid

DRUM *n* percussion instrument sounded by

striking a membrane stretched across the opening of a hollow cylinder ▷ *vb* play (music) on a drum

DRUMBLE *vb* be inactive

DRUMLIN *n* streamlined mound of glacial drift, rounded or elongated in the direction of the original flow of ice

DRUMLY *adj* dismal; dreary

DRUMMED ▸ **drum**

DRUMMER *n* person who plays a drum or drums

DRUMMY *n* (in South Africa) drum majorette

DRUMS ▸ **drum**

DRUNK ▸ **drink**

DRUNKEN *adj* drunk or frequently drunk

DRUNKER ▸ **drink**

DRUNKS ▸ **drink**

DRUPE *n* fleshy fruit with a stone, such as the peach or cherry

DRUPEL *same as* ▸ **drupelet**

DRUPELS ▸ **drupel**

DRUPES ▸ **drupe**

DRUSE *n* aggregate of small crystals within a cavity, esp those lining a cavity in a rock or mineral

DRUSEN *pl n* small deposits of material on the retina

DRUSES ▸ **druse**

DRUSIER ▸ **drusy**

DRUSY *adj* made of tiny crystals

DRUXIER ▸ **druxy**

DRUXY *adj* (of wood) having decayed white spots

DRY *adj* lacking moisture ▷ *vb* make or become dry

DRYABLE ▸ **dry**

DRYAD *n* wood nymph

DRYADES ▸ **dryad**

DRYADIC ▸ **dryad**

DRYADS ▸ **dryad**

DRYBEAT *vb* beat severely

DRYER ▸ **dry**

DRYERS ▸ **dry**

DRYEST ▸ **dry**

DRYING ▸ **dry**

DRYINGS ▸ **dry**

DRYISH *adj* fairly dry

DRYLAND *adj* of an arid area

DRYLOT *n* livestock enclosure

DRYLOTS ▸ **drylot**

DRYLY *same as* ▸ **drily**

DRYNESS ▸ **dry**

DRYS ▸ **dry**

DRYSUIT *n* waterproof rubber suit for wearing in esp cold water

DRYWALL *n* wall built without mortar ▷ *vb* build a wall without mortar

DRYWELL *n* type of sewage disposal system

DSO *same as* ▸ **zho**

⎸ A **dso** is a kind of Himalayan ox; the other forms are **dzo, zho, dzho** and **zo** and it's worth remembering all of them.

DSOBO *same as* ▸ **zobo**

DSOBOS ▸ **dsobo**

DSOMO *same as* ▸ **zhomo**

DSOMOS ▸ **dsomo**

DSOS ▸ **dso**

DUAD *a rare word for* ▸ **pair**

DUADS ▸ **duad**

DUAL *adj* having two parts, functions, or aspects ▷ *n* dual number ▷ *vb* make (a road) into a dual carriageway

DUALIN *n* explosive substance

DUALINS ▸ **dualin**

DUALISE *same as* ▸ **dualize**

DUALISM *n* state of having or being believed to have two distinct parts or aspects

DUALIST ▸ **dualism**

DUALITY *n* state or quality of being two or in two parts

DUALIZE *vb* cause to have two parts

DUALLED ▸ **dual**

DUALLY ▸ **dual**

DUALS ▸ **dual**

DUAN *n* poem

DUANS ▸ **duan**

DUAR *n* Arab camp

DUARCHY *same as* ▸ **diarchy**

DUARS ▸ **duar**

DUB *vb* give (a person or place) a name or nickname ▷ *n* style of reggae record production involving exaggeration of instrumental parts, echo, etc

DUBBED ▸ **dub**

DUBBER ▸ **dub**

DUBBERS ▸ **dub**

DUBBIN *n* thick grease applied to leather to soften and waterproof it

DUBBING ▸ **dub**

DUBBINS ▸ **dubbin**

DUBBO *adj* stupid ▷ *n* stupid person

DUBBOS ▸ **dubbo**

DUBIETY *n* state of being doubtful

DUBIOUS *adj* feeling or causing doubt

DUBNIUM *n* element produced in minute quantities by bombarding plutonium with high-energy neon ions

DUBS ▸ **dub**

DUBSTEP *n* genre of electronic music

DUCAL *adj* of a duke

DUCALLY ▸ **ducal**

DUCAT *n* former European gold or silver coin

DUCATS ▸ **ducat**

DUCDAME *interj* Shakespearean nonsense word

DUCE *n* leader

DUCES ▸ **duce**

DUCHESS *n* woman who holds the rank of duke ▷ *vb* overwhelm with flattering attention

DUCHIES ▸ **duchy**

DUCHY *n* territory of a duke or duchess

DUCI ▸ **duce**

DUCK *n* water bird with short legs, webbed feet, and a broad blunt bill ▷ *vb* move (the head or body) quickly downwards, to avoid being seen or to dodge a blow

DUCKED ▸ **duck**

DUCKER ▸ **duck**

DUCKERS ▸ **duck**

DUCKIE *same as* ▸ **ducky**

DUCKIER ▸ **ducky**

DUCKIES ▸ **ducky**

DUCKING ▸ **duck**

DUCKPIN *n* short bowling pin

DUCKS ▸ **duck**

DUCKY *n* darling or dear: used as a term of endearment among women, but now often used in imitation of the supposed usage of homosexual men ▷ *adj* delightful

DUCT *vb* convey via a duct ▷ *n* tube, pipe, or channel through which liquid or gas is conveyed

DUCTAL ▸ duct
DUCTED ▸ duct
DUCTILE adj (of a metal) able to be shaped into sheets or wires
DUCTING ▸ duct
DUCTS ▸ duct
DUCTULE n small duct
DUD n ineffectual person or thing ▷ adj bad or useless
DUDDER n door-to-door salesman
DUDDERS ▸ dudder
DUDDERY n place where old clothes are sold
DUDDIE adj ragged
DUDDIER ▸ duddie
DUDDY same as ▸ duddie
DUDE vb dress fashionably ▷ n man
DUDED ▸ dude
DUDEEN n clay pipe with a short stem
DUDEENS ▸ dudeen
DUDES ▸ dude
DUDGEON n anger or resentment
DUDHEEN n type of pipe
DUDING ▸ dude
DUDISH ▸ dude
DUDISM n being a dude
DUDISMS ▸ dudism
DUDS ▸ dud
DUE vb supply with ▷ adj expected or scheduled to be present or arrive ▷ n something that is owed or required ▷ adv directly or exactly
DUED ▸ due
DUEFUL adj proper
DUEL n formal fight with deadly weapons between two people, to settle a quarrel ▷ vb fight in a duel
DUELED ▸ duel
DUELER ▸ duel
DUELERS ▸ duel
DUELING ▸ duel
DUELIST ▸ duel
DUELLED ▸ duel
DUELLER ▸ duel
DUELLI ▸ duello
DUELLO n art of duelling
DUELLOS ▸ duello
DUELS ▸ duel
DUENDE n Spanish goblin
DUENDES ▸ duende
DUENESS ▸ due
DUENNA n (esp in Spain) elderly woman acting as chaperone to a young woman

DUENNAS ▸ duenna
DUES pl n membership fees paid to a club or organization
DUET n piece of music for two performers ▷ vb perform a duet
DUETED ▸ duet
DUETING ▸ duet
DUETS ▸ duet
DUETT same as ▸ duet
DUETTED ▸ duet
DUETTI ▸ duetto
DUETTO same as ▸ duet
DUETTOS ▸ duetto
DUETTS ▸ duett
DUFF adj broken or useless ▷ vb change the appearance of or give a false appearance to (old or stolen goods) ▷ n rump or buttocks
DUFFED ▸ duff
DUFFEL n heavy woollen cloth with a thick nap
DUFFELS ▸ duffel
DUFFER n dull or incompetent person
DUFFERS ▸ duffer
DUFFEST ▸ duff
DUFFING ▸ duff
DUFFLE same as ▸ duffel
DUFFLES ▸ duffle
DUFFS ▸ duff
DUFUS same as ▸ doofus
DUFUSES ▸ dufus
DUG ▸ dig
DUGITE n medium-sized Australian venomous snake
DUGITES ▸ dugite
DUGONG n whalelike mammal of tropical waters
DUGONGS ▸ dugong
DUGOUT n (at a sports ground) covered bench where managers and substitutes sit
DUGOUTS ▸ dugout
DUGS ▸ dig
DUH interj ironic response to a question or statement, implying that the speaker is stupid or that the reply is obvious

┃ This word provides a useful front hook to **uh**.

DUHKHA same as ▸ dukkha
DUHKHAS ▸ duhkha
DUI ▸ duo
DUIKER n small African antelope
DUIKERS ▸ duiker
DUING ▸ due

DUIT n former Dutch coin
DUITS ▸ duit
DUKA n shop
DUKAS ▸ duka
DUKE vb fight with fists ▷ n nobleman of the highest rank
DUKED ▸ duke
DUKEDOM n title, rank, or position of a duke
DUKERY n duke's domain
DUKES pl n fists
DUKING ▸ duke
DUKKA n mix of ground roast nuts and spices, originating in Egypt, and used for sprinkling on meat or as a dip
DUKKAH same as ▸ dukka
DUKKAHS ▸ dukkah
DUKKAS ▸ dukka
DUKKHA n (in Theravada Buddhism) the belief that all things are suffering, due to the desire to seek permanence or recognise the self when neither exist: one of the three basic characteristics of existence
DUKKHAS ▸ dukkha
DULCET adj (of a sound) soothing or pleasant ▷ n soft organ stop
DULCETS ▸ dulcet
DULCIAN n precursor to the bassoon
DULCIFY vb make pleasant or agreeable
DULCITE n sweet substance
DULCOSE another word for ▸ dulcite
DULE n suffering; misery
DULES ▸ dule
DULIA n veneration accorded to saints in the Roman Catholic and Eastern Churches, as contrasted with hyperdulia and latria
DULIAS ▸ dulia
DULL adj not interesting ▷ vb make or become dull
DULLARD n dull or stupid person
DULLED ▸ dull
DULLER ▸ dull
DULLEST ▸ dull
DULLIER ▸ dull
DULLING ▸ dull
DULLISH ▸ dull
DULLS ▸ dull
DULLY ▸ dull
DULNESS ▸ dull

DULOSES ▸ dulosis

DULOSIS n practice of some ants, in which one species forces members of a different species to do the work of the colony

DULOTIC ▸ dulosis

DULSE n seaweed with large red edible fronds

DULSES ▸ dulse

DULY adv in a proper manner

DUMA n elective legislative assembly established by Tsar Nicholas II in 1905: overthrown by the Bolsheviks in 1917

DUMAIST n member of duma

DUMAS ▸ duma

DUMB vb silence ▷ adj lacking the power to speak

DUMBED ▸ dumb

DUMBER ▸ dumb

DUMBEST ▸ dumb

DUMBING ▸ dumb

DUMBLY ▸ dumb

DUMBO n slow-witted unintelligent person

DUMBOS ▸ dumbo

DUMBS ▸ dumb

DUMDUM n soft-nosed bullet that expands on impact and causes serious wounds

DUMDUMS ▸ dumdum

DUMELA sentence substitute hello

DUMKA n Slavonic lyrical song

DUMKY ▸ dumka

DUMMIED ▸ dummy

DUMMIER ▸ dummy

DUMMIES ▸ dummy

DUMMY adj sham ▷ n figure representing the human form, used for displaying clothes etc ▷ adj imitation, substitute ▷ vb prepare a dummy of (a proposed book, page, etc)

DUMOSE adj bushlike

DUMOUS same as ▸ dumose

DUMP vb drop or let fall in a careless manner ▷ n place where waste materials are left

DUMPBIN n free-standing unit in a bookshop in which a particular publisher's books are displayed

DUMPED ▸ dump

DUMPEE n person dumped from a relationship

DUMPEES ▸ dumpee

DUMPER ▸ dump

DUMPERS ▸ dump

DUMPIER ▸ dumpy

DUMPIES ▸ dumpy

DUMPILY ▸ dumpy

DUMPING ▸ dump

DUMPISH same as ▸ dumpy

DUMPLE vb form into dumpling shape

DUMPLED ▸ dumple

DUMPLES ▸ dumple

DUMPS pl n state of melancholy or depression

DUMPY n dumpy person ▷ adj short and plump

DUN adj brownish-grey ▷ vb demand payment from (a debtor) ▷ n demand for payment

DUNAM n unit of area measurement

DUNAMS ▸ dunam

DUNCE n person who is stupid or slow to learn

DUNCERY n duncelike behaviour

DUNCES ▸ dunce

DUNCH vb push against gently

DUNCHED ▸ dunch

DUNCHES ▸ dunch

DUNCISH adj duncelike

DUNDER n cane juice lees

DUNDERS ▸ dunder

DUNE n mound or ridge of drifted sand

DUNES ▸ dune

DUNG n faeces from animals such as cattle ▷ vb cover (ground) with manure

DUNGED ▸ dung

DUNGEON vb hold captive in dungeon ▷ n underground prison cell

DUNGER n old decrepit car

DUNGERS ▸ dunger

DUNGIER ▸ dung

DUNGING ▸ dung

DUNGS ▸ dung

DUNGY ▸ dung

DUNITE n ultrabasic igneous rock consisting mainly of olivine

DUNITES ▸ dunite

DUNITIC ▸ dunite

DUNK vb dip (a biscuit or bread) in a drink or soup before eating it

DUNKED ▸ dunk

DUNKER ▸ dunk

DUNKERS ▸ dunk

DUNKING ▸ dunk

DUNKS ▸ dunk

DUNLIN n small sandpiper with a brown back found in northern regions

DUNLINS ▸ dunlin

DUNNAGE n loose material used for packing cargo

DUNNART n type of mouselike insectivorous marsupial of Australia and New Guinea

DUNNED ▸ dun

DUNNER ▸ dun

DUNNESS ▸ dun

DUNNEST ▸ dun

DUNNIER ▸ dunny

DUNNIES ▸ dunny

DUNNING ▸ dun

DUNNISH ▸ dun

DUNNITE n explosive containing ammonium picrate

DUNNO vb slang for don't know

DUNNOCK n hedge sparrow

DUNNY n in Australia, toilet ▷ adj relating to dunny

DUNS ▸ dun

DUNSH same as ▸ dunch

DUNSHED ▸ dunsh

DUNSHES ▸ dunsh

DUNT n blow ▷ vb strike or hit

DUNTED ▸ dunt

DUNTING ▸ dunt

DUNTS ▸ dunt

DUO same as ▸ duet

DUODENA ▸ duodenum

DUOLOG same as ▸ duologue

DUOLOGS ▸ duolog

DUOMI ▸ duomo

DUOMO n cathedral in Italy

DUOMOS ▸ duomo

DUOPOLY n situation in which control of a commodity or service in a particular market is vested in just two producers or suppliers

DUOS ▸ duo

DUOTONE n process for producing halftone illustrations using two shades of a single colour or black and a colour

DUP vb open

DUPABLE ▸ dupe

DUPATTA n scarf worn in India

DUPE vb deceive or cheat ▷ n person who is easily deceived
DUPED ▸ dupe
DUPER ▸ dupe
DUPERS ▸ dupe
DUPERY ▸ dupe
DUPES ▸ dupe
DUPING ▸ dupe
DUPION n silk fabric made from the threads of double cocoons
DUPIONS ▸ dupion
DUPLE adj having two beats in a bar
DUPLET n pair of electrons shared between two atoms in a covalent bond
DUPLETS ▸ duplet
DUPLEX vb duplicate ▷ n apartment on two floors ▷ adj having two parts
DUPLIED ▸ duply
DUPLIES ▸ duply
DUPLY vb give a second reply
DUPPED ▸ dup
DUPPIES ▸ duppy
DUPPING ▸ dup
DUPPY n spirit or ghost
DUPS ▸ dup
DURA same as ▸ durra
DURABLE adj long-lasting
DURABLY ▸ durable
DURAL n alloy of aluminium and copper
DURALS ▸ dural
DURAMEN another name for > heartwood
DURANCE n imprisonment
DURANT n tough, leathery cloth
DURANTS ▸ durant
DURAS ▸ dura
DURBAR n (formerly) the court of a native ruler or a governor in India
DURBARS ▸ durbar
DURDUM same as ▸ dirdum
DURDUMS ▸ durdum
DURE vb endure
DURED ▸ dure
DUREFUL adj lasting
DURES ▸ dure
DURESS n compulsion by use of force or threats
DURESSE same as ▸ duress
DURGAH same as ▸ dargah
DURGAHS ▸ durgah
DURGAN n dwarf
DURGANS ▸ durgan
DURGIER ▸ durgy
DURGY adj dwarflike

DURIAN n SE Asian tree whose very large oval fruits have a hard spiny rind and an evil smell
DURIANS ▸ durian
DURING prep throughout or within the limit of (a period of time)
DURION same as ▸ durian
DURIONS ▸ durion
DURMAST n large Eurasian oak tree with lobed leaves
DURN ▸ darn
DURNED ▸ durn
DURNING ▸ durn
DURNS ▸ durn
DURO n silver peso of Spain or Spanish America
DUROC n breed of pig
DUROCS ▸ duroc
DUROS ▸ duro
DUROY n coarse woollen fabric
DUROYS ▸ duroy
DURR same as ▸ durra
DURRA n Old World variety of sorghum with hairy flower spikes and round seeds, cultivated for grain and fodder
DURRAS ▸ durra
DURRIE n cotton carpet made in India, often in rectangular pieces fringed at the ends: sometimes used as a sofa cover, wall hanging, etc
DURRIES ▸ durry
DURRS ▸ durr
DURRY n cigarette
DURST a past tense of ▸ dare
DURUM n variety of wheat cultivated mainly in the Mediterranean region, used chiefly to make pastas
DURUMS ▸ durum
DURZI n Indian tailor
DURZIS ▸ durzi
DUSH vb strike hard
DUSHED ▸ dush
DUSHES ▸ dush
DUSHING ▸ dush
DUSK n time just before nightfall, when it is almost dark ▷ adj shady ▷ vb make or become dark
DUSKED ▸ dusk
DUSKEN vb grow dark
DUSKENS ▸ dusken
DUSKER ▸ dusk
DUSKEST ▸ dusk
DUSKIER ▸ dusky
DUSKILY ▸ dusky

DUSKING ▸ dusk
DUSKISH ▸ dusk
DUSKLY ▸ dusk
DUSKS ▸ dusk
DUSKY adj dark in colour
DUST n small dry particles of earth, sand, or dirt ▷ vb remove dust from (furniture) by wiping
DUSTBIN n large container for household rubbish
DUSTED ▸ dust
DUSTER n cloth used for dusting
DUSTERS ▸ duster
DUSTIER ▸ dusty
DUSTILY ▸ dusty
DUSTING ▸ dust
DUSTMAN n man whose job is to collect household rubbish
DUSTMEN ▸ dustman
DUSTOFF n casualty evacuation helicopter
DUSTPAN n short-handled shovel into which dust is swept from floors
DUSTRAG n cloth for dusting
DUSTS ▸ dust
DUSTUP n quarrel, fight, or argument
DUSTUPS ▸ dustup
DUSTY adj covered with dust
DUTCH n wife
DUTCHES ▸ dutch
DUTEOUS adj dutiful or obedient
DUTIED adj liable for duty
DUTIES ▸ duty
DUTIFUL adj doing what is expected
DUTY n work or a task performed as part of one's job
DUUMVIR n one of two coequal magistrates or officers
DUVET same as ▸ doona
DUVETS ▸ duvet
DUVETYN n soft napped velvety fabric of cotton, silk, wool, or rayon
DUX n (in Scottish and certain other schools) the top pupil in a class or school
A **dux** is a leader, and is often useful for disposing of the X.
DUXES ▸ dux
DUYKER same as ▸ duiker
DUYKERS ▸ duyker

DVANDVA *n* class of compound words consisting of two elements having a coordinate relationship as if connected by *and*

DVORNIK *n* Russian doorkeeper

DWAAL *n* state of absent-mindedness

DWAALS ▶ dwaal

DWALE *n* deadly nightshade

DWALES ▶ dwale

DWALM *vb* faint

DWALMED ▶ dwalm

DWALMS ▶ dwalm

DWAM *n* stupor or daydream ▷ *vb* faint or fall ill

DWAMMED ▶ dwam

DWAMS ▶ dwam

DWANG *n* short piece of wood inserted in a timber-framed wall

DWANGS ▶ dwang

DWARF *adj* undersized ▷ *n* person who is smaller than average ▷ *adj* (of an animal or plant) much smaller than the usual size for the species ▷ *vb* cause (someone or something) to seem small by being much larger

DWARFED ▶ dwarf

DWARFER ▶ dwarf

DWARFS ▶ dwarf

DWARVES ▶ dwarf

DWAUM *same as* **▶ dwam**

DWAUMED ▶ dwaum

DWAUMS ▶ dwaum

DWEEB *n* stupid or uninteresting person

DWEEBS ▶ dweeb

DWEEBY *adj* like or typical of a dweeb

DWELL *vb* live, reside ▷ *n* regular pause in the operation of a machine

DWELLED ▶ dwell

DWELLER ▶ dwell

DWELLS ▶ dwell

DWELT ▶ dwell

DWILE *n* floor cloth

DWILES ▶ dwile

DWINDLE *vb* grow less in size, strength, or number

DWINE *vb* languish

DWINED ▶ dwine

DWINES ▶ dwine

DWINING ▶ dwine

DYABLE ▶ dye

DYAD *n* operator that is the unspecified product of two vectors. It can operate on a vector to produce either a scalar or vector product

DYADIC *adj* of or relating to a dyad ▷ *n* sum of a particular number of dyads

DYADICS ▶ dyadic

DYADS ▶ dyad

DYARCHY *same as* **▶ diarchy**

DYBBUK *n* (in the folklore of the cabala) the soul of a dead sinner that has transmigrated into the body of a living person

DYBBUKS ▶ dybbuk

DYE *n* colouring substance ▷ *vb* colour (hair or fabric) by applying a dye

DYEABLE ▶ dye

DYED ▶ dye

DYEING ▶ dye

DYEINGS ▶ dye

DYELINE *same as* **▶ diazo**

DYER ▶ dye

DYERS ▶ dye

DYES ▶ dye

DYESTER *n* dyer

DYEWEED *n* plant that produces dye

DYEWOOD *n* any wood, such as brazil, from which dyes and pigments can be obtained

DYING ▶ die

DYINGLY ▶ die

DYINGS ▶ die

DYKE *n* wall built to prevent flooding ▷ *vb* embankment or wall built to confine a river to a particular course

DYKED ▶ dyke

DYKES ▶ dyke

DYKING ▶ dyke

DYKON *n* celebrity admired by lesbians

DYKONS ▶ dykon

DYNAMIC *adj* full of energy, ambition, and new ideas ▷ *n* energetic or driving force

DYNAMO *n* device for converting mechanical energy into electrical energy

DYNAMOS ▶ dynamo

DYNAST *n* hereditary ruler

DYNASTS ▶ dynast

DYNASTY *n* sequence of hereditary rulers

DYNE *n* cgs unit of force

DYNEIN *n* class of proteins

DYNEINS ▶ dynein

DYNEL *n* trade name for synthetic fibre

DYNELS ▶ dynel

DYNES ▶ dyne

DYNODE *n* electrode onto which a beam of electrons can fall, causing the emission of a greater number of electrons by secondary emission. They are used in photomultipliers to amplify the signal

DYNODES ▶ dynode

DYSLOGY *n* uncomplimentary remarks

DYSODIL *n* yellow or green mineral

DYSPNEA *same as* **> dyspnoea**

DYSURIA *n* difficult or painful urination

DYSURIC ▶ dysuria

DYSURY *same as* **▶ dysuria**

DYVOUR *n* debtor

DYVOURS ▶ dyvour

DYVOURY *n* bankruptcy

DZEREN *n* Chinese yellow antelope

DZERENS ▶ dzeren

DZHO *same as* **▶ zho**

DZHOS ▶ dzho

DZO *a variant spelling of* **▶ zo**

DZOS ▶ zo

Ee

E is the most common tile in the game and, while it is only worth one point, as the most frequent letter in English it is extremely useful, especially when it comes to forming bonus words scoring an extra 50 points. Many words contain two or more **E**s, so, unlike many tiles, it does no harm to have two **E**s on your rack and even three can be manageable. Keep in mind three-letter words formed by an **E** on either side of a consonant, like **eye**, **ewe** and **eve** (6 points each), and **eke** (7). **E** can also be handy for getting rid of double consonants: think of words like **egg** or **ebb** (each 5 points). **E** also combines well with **K**: as well as **eke**, we have **elk** and **eek** (both 7), and **ewk** (10). If you have an **X** on your rack, **E** offers you all kinds of options: just think of all the words that begin with **ex-**, like **exhaust** (17), which will give you a 50-point bonus if you use all of your tiles to form it. And don't forget **ex** itself, a nice little word that earns you 9 points, and also the very useful **exo** for 10 points. Just as important are **jee** for 10 points, **zee** for 12 points and **zed** for 13 points.

EA *n* river

EACH *pron* every (one) taken separately ▷ *determiner* every (one) of two or more considered individually ▷ *adv* for, to, or from each one

EADISH *n* aftermath

EAGER *adj* showing or feeling great desire, keen ▷ *n* eagre

EAGERER ▸ **eager**

EAGERLY ▸ **eager**

EAGERS ▸ **eager**

EAGLE *n* bird of prey ▷ *vb* in golf, score two strokes under par for a hole

EAGLED ▸ **eagle**

EAGLES ▸ **eagle**

EAGLET *n* young eagle

EAGLETS ▸ **eaglet**

EAGLING ▸ **eagle**

EAGRE *n* tidal bore, esp of the Humber or Severn estuaries

EAGRES ▸ **eagre**

EALE *n* beast in Roman legend

EALES ▸ **eale**

EAN *vb* give birth

EANED ▸ **ean**

EANING ▸ **ean**

EANLING *n* newborn lamb

EANS ▸ **ean**

EAR *n* organ of hearing, esp the external part of it ▷ *vb* (of cereal plants) to develop such parts

EARACHE *n* pain in the ear

EARBALL *n* (in acupressure) a small ball kept in position in the ear and pressed when needed to relieve stress

EARBASH *vb* talk incessantly

EARBOB *n* earring

EARBOBS ▸ **earbob**

EARBUD *n* small earphone

EARBUDS ▸ **earbud**

EARCON *n* sound representing object or event

EARCONS ▸ **earcon**

EARD *vb* bury

EARDED ▸ **eard**

EARDING ▸ **eard**

EARDROP *n* pendant earring

EARDRUM *n* thin piece of skin inside the ear which enables one to hear sounds

EARDS ▸ **eard**

EARED *adj* having an ear or ears

EARFLAP *n* either of two pieces of fabric or fur attached to a cap, which can be let down to keep the ears warm

EARFUL *n* scolding or telling-off

EARFULS ▸ **earful**

EARING *n* line fastened to a corner of a sail for reefing

EARINGS ▸ **earing**

EARL *n* British nobleman ranking next below a marquess

EARLAP *same as* ▸ **earflap**

EARLAPS ▸ **earlap**

EARLDOM *n* rank, title, or dignity of an earl or countess

EARLESS ▸ **ear**

EARLIER ▸ **early**

EARLIES ▸ **early**

EARLIKE ▸ **ear**

EARLOBE *n* fleshy lower part of the outer ear

EARLOCK *n* curl of hair close to ear

EARLS ▸ **earl**

EARLY *adv* before the expected or usual time ▷ *adj* occurring or arriving before the correct or expected time ▷ *n* something which is early

EARMARK *vb* set (something) aside for a specific purpose ▷ *n* distinguishing mark

EARMUFF n one of a pair of pads of fur or cloth, joined by a headband, for keeping the ears warm

EARN vb obtain by work or merit

EARNED ▸ earn

EARNER ▸ earn

EARNERS ▸ earn

EARNEST adj serious and sincere ▷ n part payment given in advance, esp to confirm a contract

EARNING ▸ earn

EARNS ▸ earn

EARPICK n instrument for removing ear wax

EARPLUG n piece of soft material placed in the ear to keep out water or noise

EARRING n ornament for the lobe of the ear

EARS ▸ ear

EARSHOT n hearing range

EARST adv first; previously

EARTH n planet that we live on ▷ vb connect (a circuit) to earth

EARTHED ▸ earth

EARTHEN adj made of baked clay or earth

EARTHLY adj conceivable or possible ▷ n a chance

EARTHS ▸ earth

EARTHY adj coarse or crude

EARWAX nontechnical name for ▸ cerumen

EARWIG n small insect with a pincer-like tail ▷ vb eavesdrop

EARWIGS ▸ earwig

EARWORM n irritatingly catchy tune

EAS ▸ ea

EASE n freedom from difficulty, discomfort, or worry ▷ vb give bodily or mental ease to

EASED ▸ ease

EASEFUL adj characterized by or bringing ease

EASEL n frame to support an artist's canvas or a blackboard

EASELED adj mounted on easel

EASELS ▸ easel

EASER ▸ ease

EASERS ▸ ease

EASES ▸ ease

EASIED ▸ easy

EASIER ▸ easy

EASIES ▸ easy

EASIEST ▸ easy

EASILY adv without difficulty

EASING n as in **quantitative easing** increasing the supply of money to stimulate the economy

EASINGS ▸ easing

EASLE n hot ash

EASLES ▸ easle

EASSEL adv easterly

EASSIL adv easterly

EAST n (direction towards) the part of the horizon where the sun rises ▷ adj in the east ▷ adv in, to, or towards the east ▷ vb move or turn east

EASTED ▸ east

EASTER n most important festival of the Christian Church, commemorating the Resurrection of Christ

EASTERN adj situated in or towards the east

EASTERS ▸ easter

EASTING n net distance eastwards made by a vessel moving towards the east

EASTLIN adj easterly

EASTS ▸ east

EASY adj not needing much work or effort ▷ vb stop rowing

EASYING ▸ easy

EAT vb take (food) into the mouth and swallow it

EATABLE adj fit or suitable for eating

EATAGE n grazing rights

EATAGES ▸ eatage

EATCHE n adze

EATCHES ▸ eatche

EATEN ▸ eat

EATER ▸ eat

EATERIE same as ▸ eatery

EATERS ▸ eat

EATERY n restaurant or eating house

EATH adj easy

EATHE same as ▸ eath

EATHLY ▸ eath

EATING ▸ eat

EATINGS ▸ eat

EATS ▸ eat

EAU same as ▸ ea

EAUS ▸ eau

EAUX ▸ eau

EAVE n overhanging edge of a roof

EAVED adj having eaves

EAVES ▸ eave

EBAUCHE n rough sketch

EBAYER n any person who buys or sells using the internet auction site, eBay

EBAYERS ▸ ebayer

EBAYING n buying or selling using the internet auction site eBay

EBB vb (of tide water) flow back ▷ n flowing back of the tide

EBBED ▸ ebb

EBBET n type of newt

EBBETS ▸ ebbet

EBBING ▸ ebb

EBBLESS ▸ ebb

EBBS ▸ ebb

EBON poetic word for ▸ ebony

EBONICS n dialect used by African-Americans

EBONIES ▸ ebony

EBONISE same as ▸ ebonize

EBONIST n carver of ebony

EBONITE another name for > vulcanite

EBONIZE vb stain or otherwise finish in imitation of ebony

EBONS ▸ ebon

EBONY n hard black wood ▷ adj deep black

EBOOK n book in electronic form

EBOOKS ▸ ebook

EBRIATE adj drunk

EBRIETY n drunkenness

EBRIOSE adj drunk

ECAD n organism whose form has been affected by its environment

ECADS ▸ ecad

ECARTE n card game for two, played with 32 cards and king high

ECARTES ▸ ecarte

ECBOLE n digression

ECBOLES ▸ ecbole

ECBOLIC adj hastening labour or abortion ▷ n drug or agent that hastens labour or abortion

ECCE interj behold

ECCO interj look there

ECCRINE adj of or denoting glands that secrete externally, esp the numerous sweat glands on the human body

ECDEMIC adj not indigenous or endemic

ECDYSES ▸ ecdysis

ECDYSIS n periodic

shedding of the cuticle in insects and other arthropods or the outer epidermal layer in reptiles

ECDYSON ▶ ecdysone

ECESIC ▶ ecesis

ECESIS n establishment of a plant in a new environment

ECH same as ▶ **eche**

ECHAPPE n leap in ballet

ECHARD n water that is present in the soil but cannot be absorbed or otherwise utilized by plants

ECHARDS ▶ echard

ECHE vb eke out

ECHED ▶ eche

ECHELLE n ladder; scale

ECHELON n level of power or responsibility ▷ vb assemble in echelon

ECHES ▶ eche

ECHIDNA n Australian spiny egg-laying mammal

ECHING ▶ eche

ECHINI ▶ echinus

ECHINUS n ovolo moulding between the shaft and the abacus of a Doric column

ECHIUM n type of Eurasian and African plant

ECHIUMS ▶ echium

ECHO n repetition of sounds by reflection of sound waves off a surface ▷ vb repeat or be repeated as an echo

ECHOED ▶ echo

ECHOER ▶ echo

ECHOERS ▶ echo

ECHOES ▶ echo

ECHOEY adj producing echoes

ECHOIC adj characteristic of or resembling an echo

ECHOIER ▶ echoey

ECHOING ▶ echo

ECHOISE same as ▶ **echoize**

ECHOISM n onomatopoeia as a source of word formation

ECHOIST ▶ echoism

ECHOIZE vb repeat like echo

ECHOS ▶ echo

ECHT adj real

ECLAIR n finger-shaped pastry filled with cream and covered with chocolate

ECLAIRS ▶ eclair

ECLAT n brilliant success

ECLATS ▶ eclat

ECLIPSE n temporary obscuring of one star or

planet by another ▷ vb surpass or outclass

ECLOGUE n pastoral or idyllic poem, usually in the form of a conversation or soliloquy

ECLOSE vb emerge

ECLOSED ▶ eclose

ECLOSES ▶ eclose

ECO n ecology activist

ECOCIDE n total destruction of an area of the natural environment, esp by human agency

ECOD same as ▶ **egad**

ECOLOGY n study of the relationships between living things and their environment

ECOMAP n diagram showing the relationships between an individual and their community

ECOMAPS ▶ ecomap

ECONOMY n system of interrelationship of money, industry, and employment in a country ▷ adj denoting a class of air travel that is cheaper than first-class

ECONUT n environmentalist

ECONUTS ▶ econut

ECORCHE n anatomical figure without the skin, so that the muscular structure is visible

ECOS ▶ eco

ECOTAGE n sabotage for ecological motives

ECOTONE n zone between two major ecological communities

ECOTOUR n holiday taking care not to damage environment

ECOTYPE n group of organisms within a species that is adapted to particular environmental conditions and therefore exhibits behavioural, structural, or physiological differences from other members of the species

ECRU adj pale creamy-brown ▷ n greyish-yellow to a light greyish colour

ECRUS ▶ ecru

ECSTASY n state of intense delight

ECTASES ▶ ectasis

ECTASIA n distension or

dilation of a duct, vessel, or hollow viscus

ECTASIS same as ▶ **ectasia**

ECTATIC ▶ ectasia

ECTHYMA n local inflammation of the skin characterized by flat ulcerating pustules

ECTOPIA n congenital displacement or abnormal positioning of an organ or part

ECTOPIC ▶ ectopia

ECTOPY same as ▶ **ectopia**

ECTOZOA > ectozoon

ECTYPAL ▶ ectype

ECTYPE n copy as distinguished from a prototype

ECTYPES ▶ ectype

ECU n any of various former French gold or silver coins

ECUELLE n covered soup bowl with handles

ECURIE n team of motor-racing cars

ECURIES ▶ ecurie

ECUS ▶ ecu

ECZEMA n skin disease causing intense itching

ECZEMAS ▶ eczema

ED n education

EDACITY > edacious

EDAMAME n immature soybeans boiled in the pod

EDAPHIC adj of or relating to the physical and chemical conditions of the soil, esp in relation to the plant and animal life it supports

EDDIED ▶ eddy

EDDIES ▶ eddy

EDDISH n pasture grass

EDDO same as ▶ **taro**

EDDOES ▶ eddo

EDDY n circular movement of air, water, etc ▷ vb move with a circular motion

EDDYING ▶ eddy

EDEMA same as ▶ **oedema**

EDEMAS ▶ edema

EDEMATA ▶ edema

EDENIC adj delightful, like the Garden of Eden

EDENTAL adj having few or no teeth

EDGE n border or line where something ends or begins ▷ vb provide an edge or border for

EDGED ▶ edge

EDGER ▶ edge

EDGERS ▸ edge
EDGES ▸ edge
EDGIER ▸ edgy
EDGIEST ▸ edgy
EDGILY ▸ edgy
EDGING *n* anything placed along an edge to finish it ▷ *adj* relating to or used for making an edge
EDGINGS ▸ edging
EDGY *adj* nervous or irritable
EDH *n* character of the runic alphabet used to represent the voiced dental fricative
EDHS ▸ edh
EDIBLE *adj* fit to be eaten
EDIBLES *pl n* articles fit to eat
EDICT *n* order issued by an authority
EDICTAL ▸ edict
EDICTS ▸ edict
EDIFICE *n* large building
EDIFIED ▸ edify
EDIFIER ▸ edify
EDIFIES ▸ edify
EDIFY *vb* improve morally by instruction
EDILE *variant spelling of* ▸ aedile
EDILES ▸ edile
EDIT *vb* prepare (a book, film, etc) for publication or broadcast ▷ *n* act of editing
EDITED ▸ edit
EDITING ▸ edit
EDITION *n* number of copies of a new publication printed at one time ▷ *vb* produce multiple copies of (an original work of art)
EDITOR *n* person who edits
EDITORS ▸ editor
EDITRIX *n* female editor
EDITS ▸ edit
EDS ▸ ed
EDUCATE *vb* teach
EDUCE *vb* evolve or develop, esp from a latent or potential state
EDUCED ▸ educe
EDUCES ▸ educe
EDUCING ▸ educe
EDUCT *n* substance separated from another substance without chemical change
EDUCTOR ▸ educe
EDUCTS ▸ educt
EE *Scots word for* ▸ eye
EECH *same as* ▸ eche
EECHED ▸ eech

EECHES ▸ eech
EECHING ▸ eech
EEJIT *Scots and Irish word for* ▸ idiot
EEJITS ▸ eejit
EEK *interj* indicating shock or fright
EEL *n* snakelike fish
EELFARE *n* young eel
EELIER ▸ eel
EELIEST ▸ eel
EELLIKE *adj* resembling an eel
EELPOUT *n* marine eel-like blennioid fish
EELS ▸ eel
EELWORM *n* any of various nematode worms, esp the wheatworm and the vinegar eel
EELY ▸ eel
EEN ▸ ee
EERIE *adj* uncannily frightening or disturbing
EERIER ▸ eerie
EERIEST ▸ eerie
EERILY ▸ eerie
EERY *same as* ▸ eerie
EEVEN *n* evening
EEVENS ▸ eeven
EEVN *n* evening
EEVNING *n* evening
EEVNS ▸ eevn
EF *n* the letter F
EFF *vb* say the word 'fuck'
EFFABLE *adj* capable of being expressed in words
EFFACE *vb* remove by rubbing
EFFACED ▸ efface
EFFACER ▸ efface
EFFACES ▸ efface
EFFECT *n* change or result caused by someone or something ▷ *vb* cause to happen, accomplish
EFFECTS *pl n* personal belongings
EFFED ▸ eff
EFFEIR *vb* suit
EFFEIRS ▸ effeir
EFFENDI *n* (in the Ottoman Empire) a title of respect used to address men of learning or social standing
EFFERE *same as* ▸ effeir
EFFERED ▸ effere
EFFERES ▸ effere
EFFETE *adj* powerless, feeble
EFFIGY *n* image or likeness of a person
EFFING ▸ eff

EFFINGS ▸ eff
EFFLUX *same as* > effluence
EFFORCE *vb* force
EFFORT *n* physical or mental exertion
EFFORTS ▸ effort
EFFRAY *same as* ▸ affray
EFFRAYS ▸ effray
EFFS ▸ eff
EFFULGE *vb* radiate
EFFUSE *vb* pour or flow out ▷ *adj* (esp of an inflorescence) spreading out loosely
EFFUSED ▸ effuse
EFFUSES ▸ effuse
EFS ▸ ef
EFT *n* dialect or archaic name for a newt ▷ *adv* again
EFTEST *adj* nearest at hand
EFTS ▸ eft
EFTSOON > eftsoons
EGAD *n* mild oath or expression of surprise
EGADS ▸ egad
EGAL *adj* equal
EGALITE *n* equality
EGALITY *n* equality
EGALLY ▸ egal
EGENCE *n* need
EGENCES ▸ egence
EGENCY *same as* ▸ egence
EGER *same as* ▸ eagre
EGERS ▸ eger
EGEST *vb* excrete (waste material)
EGESTA *pl n* anything egested, as waste material from the body
EGESTED ▸ egest
EGESTS ▸ egest
EGG *n* oval or round object laid by the females of birds and other creatures, containing a developing embryo ▷ *vb* urge or incite, esp to daring or foolish acts
EGGAR *same as* ▸ egger
EGGARS ▸ eggar
EGGCUP *n* cup for holding a boiled egg
EGGCUPS ▸ eggcup
EGGED ▸ egg
EGGER *n* any of various widely distributed moths having brown bodies and wings
EGGERS ▸ egger
EGGERY *n* place where eggs are laid
EGGHEAD *n* intellectual person

EGGIER ▸ eggy
EGGIEST ▸ eggy
EGGING ▸ egg
EGGLER n egg dealer: sometimes itinerant
EGGLERS ▸ eggler
EGGLESS ▸ egg
EGGMASS n intelligentsia
EGGNOG n drink made of raw eggs, milk, sugar, spice, and brandy or rum
EGGNOGS ▸ eggnog
EGGS ▸ egg
EGGWASH n beaten egg for brushing on pastry
EGGY adj soaked in or tasting of egg
EGIS rare spelling of ▸ **aegis**
EGISES ▸ egis
EGMA mispronunciation of ▸ **enigma**
EGMAS ▸ egma
EGO n conscious mind of an individual
EGOISM n excessive concern for one's own interests
EGOISMS ▸ egoism
EGOIST n person who is preoccupied with his own interests
EGOISTS ▸ egoist
EGOITY n essence of the ego
EGOLESS adj without an ego
EGOS ▸ ego
EGOTISE same as ▸ **egotize**
EGOTISM n concern only for one's own interests and feelings
EGOTIST n conceited boastful person
EGOTIZE vb talk or write in self-important way
EGRESS same as ▸ **emersion**
EGRET n lesser white heron
EGRETS ▸ egret
EH interj exclamation of surprise or inquiry, or to seek confirmation of a statement or question ▷ vb say 'eh'
EHED ▸ eh
EHING ▸ eh
EHS ▸ eh
EIDE ▸ eidos
EIDENT adj diligent
EIDER n Arctic duck
EIDERS ▸ eider
EIDETIC adj (of visual, or sometimes auditory, images) exceptionally vivid and allowing detailed recall

of something previously perceived ▷ n person with eidetic ability
EIDOLA ▸ eidolon
EIDOLIC ▸ eidolon
EIDOLON n unsubstantial image
EIDOS n intellectual character of a culture or a social group
EIGHT n one more than seven ▷ adj amounting to eight
EIGHTH n (of) number eight in a series ▷ adj coming after the seventh and before the ninth in numbering or counting order, position, time, etc ▷ adv after the seventh person, position, event, etc
EIGHTHS ▸ eighth
EIGHTS ▸ eight
EIGHTVO another word for ▸ **octavo**
EIGHTY n eight times ten ▷ adj amounting to eighty ▷ determiner amounting to eighty
EIGNE adj firstborn
EIK variant form of ▸ **eke**
EIKED ▸ eik
EIKING ▸ eik
EIKON variant spelling of ▸ **icon**
EIKONES ▸ eikon
EIKONS ▸ eikon
EIKS ▸ eik
EILD n old age
EILDING n fuel
EILDS ▸ eild
EINA interj exclamation of pain
EINE pl n eyes
EINKORN n variety of wheat of Greece and SW Asia
EIRACK n young hen
EIRACKS ▸ eirack
EIRENIC variant spelling of ▸ **irenic**
EISEL n vinegar
EISELL same as ▸ **eisel**
EISELLS ▸ eisell
EISELS ▸ eisel
EISH interj South African exclamation expressive of surprise, agreement, disapproval, etc
EISWEIN n wine made from grapes frozen on the vine
EITHER pron one or the other (of two) ▷ adv

likewise ▷ determiner one or the other (of two)
EJECT vb force out, expel
EJECTA pl n matter thrown out of a crater by an erupting volcano or during a meteorite impact
EJECTED ▸ eject
EJECTOR n person or thing that ejects
EJECTS ▸ eject
EKE vb increase, enlarge, or lengthen
EKED ▸ eke
EKES ▸ eke
EKING ▸ eke
EKISTIC > ekistics
EKKA n type of one-horse carriage
EKKAS ▸ ekka
EKPWELE n former monetary unit of Equatorial Guinea
EKUELE same as ▸ **ekpwele**
EL n American elevated railway
ELAIN same as > **triolein**
ELAINS ▸ elain
ELAN n style and vigour
ELANCE vb throw a lance
ELANCED ▸ elance
ELANCES ▸ elance
ELAND n large antelope of southern Africa
ELANDS ▸ eland
ELANET n bird of prey
ELANETS ▸ elanet
ELANS ▸ elan
ELAPID n mostly tropical type of venomous snake
ELAPIDS ▸ elapid
ELAPINE adj of or like an elapid
ELAPSE vb (of time) pass by
ELAPSED ▸ elapse
ELAPSES ▸ elapse
ELASTIC adj resuming normal shape after distortion ▷ n tape or fabric containing interwoven strands of flexible rubber
ELASTIN n fibrous scleroprotein constituting the major part of elastic tissue, such as the walls of arteries
ELATE vb fill with high spirits, exhilaration, pride or optimism
ELATED adj extremely happy and excited
ELATER n elaterid beetle
ELATERS ▸ elater

ELATES ▸ elate

ELATING ▸ elate

ELATION n feeling of great happiness and excitement

ELATIVE adj (in the grammar of Finnish and other languages) denoting a case of nouns expressing a relation of motion or direction ▷ n elative case

ELBOW n joint between the upper arm and the forearm ▷ vb shove or strike with the elbow

ELBOWED ▸ elbow

ELBOWS ▸ elbow

ELCHEE n ambassador

ELCHEES ▸ elchee

ELCHI same as ▸ elchee

ELCHIS ▸ elchi

ELD n old age

ELDER adj older ▷ n older person

ELDERLY adj (fairly) old

ELDERS ▸ elder

ELDEST adj oldest

ELDIN n fuel

ELDING same as ▸ eldin

ELDINGS ▸ elding

ELDINS ▸ eldin

ELDRESS n woman elder

ELDRICH same as > eldritch

ELDS ▸ eld

ELECT vb choose by voting ▷ adj appointed but not yet in office

ELECTED ▸ elect

ELECTEE n someone who is elected

ELECTOR n someone who has the right to vote in an election

ELECTRO vb (in printing) make a metallic copy of a page

ELECTS ▸ elect

ELEGANT adj pleasing or graceful in dress, style, or design

ELEGIAC adj mournful or plaintive ▷ n elegiac couplet or stanza

ELEGIES ▸ elegy

ELEGISE same as ▸ elegize

ELEGIST ▸ elegize

ELEGIT n writ delivering debtor's property to plaintiff

ELEGITS ▸ elegit

ELEGIZE vb compose an elegy or elegies (in memory of)

ELEGY n mournful poem,

esp a lament for the dead

ELEMENT n component part

ELEMI n fragrant resin obtained from various tropical trees, used to make varnishes, ointments, inks, etc

ELEMIS ▸ elemi

ELENCH n refutation in logic

ELENCHI > elenchus

ELENCHS ▸ elench

ELEVATE vb raise in rank or status

ELEVEN n one more than ten ▷ adj amounting to eleven ▷ determiner amounting to eleven

ELEVENS ▸ eleven

ELEVON n aircraft control surface that combines the functions of an elevator and aileron, usually fitted to tailless or delta-wing aircraft

ELEVONS ▸ elevon

ELF n (in folklore) small mischievous fairy ▷ vb entangle (esp hair)

ELFED ▸ elf

ELFHOOD ▸ elf

ELFIN adj small and delicate ▷ n young elf

ELFING ▸ elf

ELFINS ▸ elfin

ELFISH adj of, relating to, or like an elf or elves ▷ n supposed language of elves

ELFLAND another name for > fairyland

ELFLIKE ▸ elf

ELFLOCK n lock of hair, fancifully regarded as having been tangled by the elves

ELFS ▸ elf

ELHI adj informal word for or relating to elementary high school

ELIAD n glance

ELIADS ▸ eliad

ELICHE n pasta in the form of spirals

ELICHES ▸ eliche

ELICIT vb bring about (a response or reaction)

ELICITS ▸ elicit

ELIDE vb omit (a vowel or syllable) from a spoken word

ELIDED ▸ elide

ELIDES ▸ elide

ELIDING ▸ elide

ELINT n electronic intelligence

ELINTS ▸ elint

ELISION n omission of a syllable or vowel from a spoken word

ELITE n most powerful, rich, or gifted members of a group ▷ adj of, relating to, or suitable for an elite

ELITES ▸ elite

ELITISM n belief that society should be governed by a small group of superior people

ELITIST ▸ elitism

ELIXIR n imaginary liquid that can prolong life or turn base metals into gold

ELIXIRS ▸ elixir

ELK n large deer of N Europe and Asia

ELKHORN n as in **elkhorn fern** fern with a large leaf like an elk's horn

ELKS ▸ elk

ELL n obsolete unit of length equal to approximately 45 inches

ELLAGIC adj of an acid derived from gallnuts

ELLIPSE n oval shape

ELLOPS same as ▸ elops

ELLS ▸ ell

ELLWAND n stick for measuring lengths

ELM n tree with serrated leaves

ELMEN adj of or relating to elm trees

ELMIER ▸ elmy

ELMIEST ▸ elmy

ELMS ▸ elm

ELMWOOD n wood from an elm tree

ELMY adj of or relating to elm trees

ELOCUTE vb speak as if practising elocution

ELODEA n type of American plant

ELODEAS ▸ elodea

ELOGE same as ▸ eulogy

ELOGES ▸ eloge

ELOGIES ▸ elogy

ELOGIST ▸ elogy

ELOGIUM same as ▸ eulogy

ELOGY same as ▸ eulogy

ELOIGN vb remove (oneself, one's property, etc) to a distant place

ELOIGNS ▸ eloign

ELOIN same as ▸ eloign

ELOINED ▸ eloin

ELOINER ▸ eloign

ELOINS ▸ eloin

ELOPE vb (of two people) run away secretly to get married

ELOPED ▸ elope

ELOPER ▸ elope

ELOPERS ▸ elope

ELOPES ▸ elope

ELOPING ▸ elope

ELOPS n type of fish

ELOPSES ▸ elops

ELPEE n LP, long-playing record

ELPEES ▸ elpee

ELS ▸ el

ELSE adv in addition or more

ELSHIN n cobbler's awl

ELSHINS ▸ elshin

ELSIN same as ▸ **elshin**

ELSINS ▸ elsin

ELT n young female pig

ELTCHI same as ▸ **elchee**

ELTCHIS ▸ eltchi

ELTS ▸ elt

ELUANT same as ▸ **eluent**

ELUANTS ▸ eluant

ELUATE n solution of adsorbed material in the eluent obtained during the process of elution

ELUATES ▸ eluate

ELUDE vb escape from by cleverness or quickness

ELUDED ▸ elude

ELUDER ▸ elude

ELUDERS ▸ elude

ELUDES ▸ elude

ELUDING ▸ elude

ELUENT n solvent used for eluting

ELUENTS ▸ eluent

ELUSION ▸ elude

ELUSIVE adj difficult to catch or remember

ELUSORY adj avoiding the issue

ELUTE vb wash out (a substance) by the action of a solvent, as in chromatography

ELUTED ▸ elute

ELUTES ▸ elute

ELUTING ▸ elute

ELUTION ▸ elute

ELUTOR ▸ elute

ELUTORS ▸ elute

ELUVIA ▸ eluvium

ELUVIAL ▸ eluvium

ELUVIUM n mass of sand, silt, etc: a product of the erosion of rocks that has

remained in its place of origin

ELVAN n type of rock

ELVANS ▸ elvan

ELVER n young eel

ELVERS ▸ elver

ELVES ▸ elf

ELVISH same as ▸ **elfish**

ELYSIAN adj delightful, blissful

ELYTRA ▸ elytrum

ELYTRAL ▸ elytron

ELYTRON n either of the horny front wings of beetles and some other insects, which cover and protect the hind wings

ELYTRUM same as ▸ **elytron**

EM n square of a body of any size of type, used as a unit of measurement

EMACS n powerful computer program used for creating and editing text

EMACSEN ▸ emacs

EMAIL n electronic mail ▷ vb send a message by electronic mail

EMAILED ▸ email

EMAILER ▸ email

EMAILS ▸ email

EMANANT ▸ emanate

EMANATE vb issue, proceed from a source

EMBACE same as ▸ **embase**

EMBACES ▸ embace

EMBAIL vb enclose in a circle

EMBAILS ▸ embail

EMBALE vb bind

EMBALED ▸ embale

EMBALES ▸ embale

EMBALL vb enclose in a circle

EMBALLS ▸ emball

EMBALM vb preserve (a corpse) from decay by the use of chemicals etc

EMBALMS ▸ embalm

EMBANK vb protect, enclose, or confine (a waterway, road, etc) with an embankment

EMBANKS ▸ embank

EMBAR vb close in with bars

EMBARGO n order by a government prohibiting trade with a country ▷ vb put an embargo on

EMBARK vb board a ship or aircraft

EMBARKS ▸ embark

EMBARS ▸ embar

EMBASE vb degrade or debase

EMBASED ▸ embase

EMBASES ▸ embase

EMBASSY n offices or official residence of an ambassador

EMBASTE ▸ embase

EMBATHE vb bathe with water

EMBAY vb form into a bay

EMBAYED ▸ embay

EMBAYLD ▸ embail

EMBAYS ▸ embay

EMBED vb fix firmly in something solid ▷ n journalist accompanying an active military unit

EMBEDS ▸ embed

EMBER n glowing piece of wood or coal in a dying fire

EMBERS ▸ ember

EMBLAZE vb cause to light up

EMBLEM n object or design that symbolizes a quality, type, or group ▷ vb represent or signify

EMBLEMA n mosaic decoration

EMBLEMS ▸ emblem

EMBLIC n type of Indian tree

EMBLICS ▸ emblic

EMBLOOM vb adorn with blooms

EMBODY vb be an example or expression of

EMBOG vb sink down into a bog

EMBOGS ▸ embog

EMBOGUE vb go out through a narrow channel or passage

EMBOIL vb enrage or be enraged

EMBOILS ▸ emboil

EMBOLI ▸ embolus

EMBOLIC adj of or relating to an embolus or embolism

EMBOLUS n material, such as a blood clot, that blocks a blood vessel

EMBOLY n infolding of the outer layer of cells of an organism or part of an organism so as to form a pocket in the surface

EMBOSK vb hide or cover

EMBOSKS ▸ embosk

EMBOSOM vb enclose or envelop, esp protectively

EMBOSS vb mould or carve a decoration on (a surface)

so that it stands out from the surface

EMBOST ▸ emboss

EMBOUND vb surround or encircle

EMBOW vb design or create (a structure) in the form of an arch or vault

EMBOWED ▸ embow

EMBOWEL vb bury or embed deeply

EMBOWER vb enclose in or as in a bower

EMBOWS ▸ embow

EMBOX vb put in a box

EMBOXED ▸ embox

EMBOXES ▸ embox

EMBRACE vb clasp in the arms, hug ▷ n act of embracing

EMBRAID vb braid or interweave

EMBRAVE vb adorn or decorate

EMBREAD vb braid

EMBROIL vb involve (a person) in problems

EMBROWN vb make or become brown

EMBRUE variant spelling of ▸ imbrue

EMBRUED ▸ embrue

EMBRUES ▸ embrue

EMBRUTE same as ▸ imbrute

EMBRYO n unborn creature in the early stages of development

EMBRYON same as ▸ embryo

EMBRYOS ▸ embryo

EMBUS vb cause (troops) to board or (of troops) to board a transport vehicle

EMBUSED ▸ embus

EMBUSES ▸ embus

EMBUSY vb keep occupied

EMCEE n master of ceremonies ▷ vb act as master of ceremonies (for or at)

EMCEED ▸ emcee

EMCEES ▸ emcee

EMDASH n long dash in punctuation

EME n uncle

EMEER same as ▸ emir

EMEERS ▸ emeer

EMEND vb remove errors from

EMENDED ▸ emend

EMENDER ▸ emend

EMENDS ▸ emend

EMERALD n bright green precious stone ▷ adj bright green

EMERGE vb come into view

EMERGED ▸ emerge

EMERGES ▸ emerge

EMERIED ▸ emery

EMERIES ▸ emery

EMERITA adj retired, but retaining an honorary title ▷ n woman who is retired, but retains an honorary title

EMERITI ▷ emeritus

EMEROD n haemorrhoid

EMERODS ▸ emerod

EMEROID same as ▸ emerod

EMERSE ▸ emersed

EMERSED adj (of the leaves or stems of aquatic plants) protruding above the surface of the water

EMERY n hard mineral used for smoothing and polishing ▷ vb apply emery to

EMES ▸ eme

EMESES ▸ emesis

EMESIS technical name for ▷ **vomiting**

EMETIC n substance that causes vomiting ▷ adj causing vomiting

EMETICS ▸ emetic

EMETIN same as ▸ emetine

EMETINE n white bitter poisonous alkaloid

EMETINS ▸ emetin

EMEU same as ▸ emu

EMEUS ▸ emeu

EMEUTE n uprising or rebellion

EMEUTES ▸ emeute

EMIC adj of or relating to a significant linguistic unit

EMICANT ▸ emicate

EMICATE vb twinkle

EMIGRE n someone who has left his native country for political reasons

EMIGRES ▸ emigre

EMINENT adj distinguished, well-known

EMIR n Muslim ruler

EMIRATE n emir's country

EMIRS ▸ emir

EMIT vb give out

EMITS ▸ emit

EMITTED ▸ emit

EMITTER n person or thing that emits

EMLETS pl n as in **blood-drop emlets**

Chilean plant with red-spotted yellow flowers

EMMA n former communications code for the letter A

EMMAS ▸ emma

EMMER n variety of wheat grown in mountainous parts of Europe

EMMERS ▸ emmer

EMMESH same as ▸ enmesh

EMMET n tourist or holiday-maker

EMMETS ▸ emmet

EMMEW vb restrict

EMMEWED ▸ emmew

EMMEWS ▸ emmew

EMMOVE vb cause emotion in

EMMOVED ▸ emmove

EMMOVES ▸ emmove

EMMY n (in the US) one of the gold-plated statuettes awarded annually for outstanding television performances and productions

EMMYS ▸ emmy

EMO n type of music combining hard rock with emotional lyrics

EMODIN n type of chemical compound

EMODINS ▸ emodin

EMONG same as ▸ among

EMONGES same as ▸ among

EMONGST same as ▸ amongst

EMOS ▸ emo

EMOTE vb display exaggerated emotion, as if acting

EMOTED ▸ emote

EMOTER ▸ emote

EMOTERS ▸ emote

EMOTES ▸ emote

EMOTING ▸ emote

EMOTION n strong feeling

EMOTIVE adj tending to arouse emotion

EMOVE vb cause to feel emotion

EMOVED ▸ emove

EMOVES ▸ emove

EMOVING ▸ emove

EMPAIRE same as ▸ impair

EMPALE less common spelling of ▸ impale

EMPALED ▸ empale

EMPALER ▸ empale

EMPALES ▸ empale

EMPANEL vb enter on a list (names of persons to be

E

E

summoned for jury service)
EMPARE same as ▸ **impair**
EMPARED ▸ **empare**
EMPARES ▸ **empare**
EMPARL same as ▸ **imparl**
EMPARLS ▸ **emparl**
EMPART same as ▸ **impart**
EMPARTS ▸ **empart**
EMPATHY n ability to understand someone else's feelings as if they were one's own
EMPAYRE same as ▸ **impair**
EMPEACH same as ▸ **impeach**
EMPERCE same as > **empierce**
EMPEROR n ruler of an empire
EMPERY n dominion or power
EMPIGHT adj attached or positioned
EMPIRE n group of territories under the rule of one state or person
EMPIRES ▸ **empire**
EMPIRIC n person who relies on empirical methods
EMPLACE vb put in place or position
EMPLANE vb board or put on board an aeroplane
EMPLOY vb engage or make use of the services of (a person) in return for money ▸ n state of being employed
EMPLOYE same as > **employee**
EMPLOYS ▸ **employ**
EMPLUME vb put a plume on
EMPORIA > **emporium**
EMPOWER vb enable, authorize
EMPRESS n woman who rules an empire
EMPRISE n chivalrous or daring enterprise
EMPRIZE same as ▸ **emprise**
EMPT vb empty
EMPTED ▸ **empt**
EMPTIED ▸ **empty**
EMPTIER ▸ **empty**
EMPTIES ▸ **empty**
EMPTILY ▸ **empty**
EMPTING ▸ **empt**
EMPTINS pl n liquid leavening agent made from potatoes
EMPTION n process of buying something
EMPTS ▸ **empt**

EMPTY adj containing nothing ▸ vb make or become empty ▸ n empty container, esp a bottle
EMPUSA n goblin in Greek mythology
EMPUSAS ▸ **empusa**
EMPUSE same as ▸ **empusa**
EMPUSES ▸ **empuse**
EMPYEMA n collection of pus in a body cavity, esp in the chest
EMS ▸ **em**
EMU n large Australian flightless bird with long legs
EMULATE vb attempt to equal or surpass by imitating
EMULE same as ▸ **emulate**
EMULED ▸ **emule**
EMULES ▸ **emule**
EMULGE vb remove liquid from
EMULGED ▸ **emulge**
EMULGES ▸ **emulge**
EMULING ▸ **emule**
EMULOUS adj desiring or aiming to equal or surpass another
EMULSIN n enzyme that is found in almonds
EMULSOR n device that emulsifies
EMUNGE vb clean or clear out
EMUNGED ▸ **emunge**
EMUNGES ▸ **emunge**
EMURE same as ▸ **immure**
EMURED ▸ **emure**
EMURES ▸ **emure**
EMURING ▸ **emure**
EMUS ▸ **emu**
EMYD n freshwater tortoise or terrapin
EMYDE same as ▸ **emyd**
EMYDES ▸ **emyde**
EMYDS ▸ **emyd**
EMYS n freshwater tortoise or terrapin
EN n unit of measurement, half the width of an em
ENABLE vb provide (a person) with the means, opportunity, or authority (to do something)
ENABLED ▸ **enable**
ENABLER ▸ **enable**
ENABLES ▸ **enable**
ENACT vb establish by law
ENACTED ▸ **enact**
ENACTOR ▸ **enact**
ENACTS ▸ **enact**
ENAMEL n glasslike coating

applied to metal etc to preserve the surface ▸ vb cover with enamel
ENAMELS ▸ **enamel**
ENAMINE n type of unsaturated compound
ENAMOR same as ▸ **enamour**
ENAMORS ▸ **enamor**
ENAMOUR vb inspire with love
ENARCH same as ▸ **inarch**
ENARM vb provide with arms
ENARMED ▸ **enarm**
ENARMS ▸ **enarm**
ENATE adj growing out or outwards ▸ n relative on the mother's side
ENATES ▸ **enate**
ENATIC adj related on one's mother's side
ENATION ▸ **enate**
ENCAGE vb confine in or as in a cage
ENCAGED ▸ **encage**
ENCAGES ▸ **encage**
ENCALM vb becalm, settle
ENCALMS ▸ **encalm**
ENCAMP vb set up in a camp
ENCAMPS ▸ **encamp**
ENCASE vb enclose or cover completely
ENCASED ▸ **encase**
ENCASES ▸ **encase**
ENCASH vb exchange (a cheque) for cash
ENCAVE same as ▸ **incave**
ENCAVED ▸ **encave**
ENCAVES ▸ **encave**
ENCHAFE vb heat up
ENCHAIN vb bind with chains
ENCHANT vb delight and fascinate
ENCHARM vb enchant
ENCHASE less common word for ▸ **chase**
ENCHEER vb cheer up
ENCINA n type of oak
ENCINAL ▸ **encina**
ENCINAS ▸ **encina**
ENCLASP vb clasp
ENCLAVE n part of a country entirely surrounded by foreign territory ▸ vb hold in an enclave
ENCLOSE vb surround completely
ENCLOUD vb hide with clouds
ENCODE vb convert (a

message) into code

ENCODED ▸ encode

ENCODER ▸ encode

ENCODES ▸ encode

ENCOMIA > encomium

ENCORE *interj* again, once more ▷ *n* extra performance due to enthusiastic demand ▷ *vb* demand an extra or repeated performance of (a work, piece of music, etc) by (a performer)

ENCORED ▸ encore

ENCORES ▸ encore

ENCRATY *n* control of one's desires, actions, etc

ENCRUST *vb* cover with a layer of something

ENCRYPT *vb* put (a message) into code

ENCYST *vb* enclose or become enclosed by a cyst, thick membrane, or shell

ENCYSTS ▸ encyst

END *n* furthest point or part ▷ *vb* bring or come to a finish

ENDARCH *adj* (of a xylem strand) having the first-formed xylem internal to that formed later

ENDART *same as* ▸ indart

ENDARTS ▸ endart

ENDASH *n* short dash in punctuation

ENDEAR *vb* cause to be liked

ENDEARS ▸ endear

ENDED ▸ end

ENDEMIC *adj* present within a localized area or peculiar to a particular group of people ▷ *n* endemic disease or plant

ENDER ▸ end

ENDERON *same as* ▸ andiron

ENDERS ▸ end

ENDEW *same as* ▸ endue

ENDEWED ▸ endew

ENDEWS ▸ endew

ENDGAME *n* closing stage of a game of chess, in which only a few pieces are left on the board

ENDGATE *n* tailboard of a vehicle

ENDING *n* last part or conclusion of something

ENDINGS ▸ ending

ENDIRON *same as* ▸ andiron

ENDITE *same as* ▸ indict

ENDITED ▸ endite

ENDITES ▸ endite

ENDIVE *n* curly-leaved plant used in salads

ENDIVES ▸ endive

ENDLANG *same as* ▸ endlong

ENDLEAF *n* endpaper in a book

ENDLESS *adj* having no end

ENDLONG *adv* lengthways or on end

ENDMOST *adj* nearest the end

ENDNOTE *n* note at the end of a section of writing

ENDOGEN *n* plant that increases in size by internal growth

ENDOPOD *n* inner branch of a two-branched crustacean

ENDORSE *vb* give approval to

ENDOSS *vb* endorse

ENDOW *vb* provide permanent income for

ENDOWED ▸ endow

ENDOWER ▸ endow

ENDOWS ▸ endow

ENDOZOA > endozoon

ENDPLAY *n* way of playing the last few tricks in a hand so that an opponent is forced to make a particular lead ▷ *vb* force (an opponent) to make a particular lead near the end of a hand

ENDRIN *n* type of insecticide

ENDRINS ▸ endrin

ENDS ▸ end

ENDSHIP *n* small village

ENDUE *vb* invest or provide, as with some quality or trait

ENDUED ▸ endue

ENDUES ▸ endue

ENDUING ▸ endue

ENDURE *vb* bear (hardship) patiently

ENDURED ▸ endure

ENDURER ▸ endure

ENDURES ▸ endure

ENDURO *n* long-distance race for vehicles, intended to test endurance

ENDUROS ▸ enduro

ENDWAYS *adv* having the end forwards or upwards ▷ *adj* vertical or upright

ENDWISE *same as* ▸ endways

ENDYSES ▸ endysis

ENDYSIS *n* formation of new layers of integument after ecdysis

ENDZONE *n* (in American football) area at either end of the playing field

ENE *same as* ▸ even

ENEMA *n* medicine injected into the rectum to empty the bowels

ENEMAS ▸ enema

ENEMATA ▸ enema

ENEMIES ▸ enemy

ENEMY *n* hostile person or nation, opponent ▷ *adj* of or belonging to an enemy

ENERGIC ▸ energy

ENERGID *n* nucleus and the cytoplasm associated with it in a syncytium

ENERGY *n* capacity for intense activity

ENERVE *vb* enervate

ENERVED ▸ enerve

ENERVES ▸ enerve

ENES ▸ ene

ENEW *vb* force a bird into water

ENEWED ▸ enew

ENEWING ▸ enew

ENEWS ▸ enew

ENFACE *vb* write, print, or stamp (something) on the face of (a document)

ENFACED ▸ enface

ENFACES ▸ enface

ENFANT *n* French child

ENFANTS ▸ enfant

ENFELON *vb* infuriate

ENFEOFF *vb* invest (a person) with possession of a freehold estate in land

ENFEVER *vb* make feverish

ENFILED *adj* passed through

ENFIRE *vb* set alight

ENFIRED ▸ enfire

ENFIRES ▸ enfire

ENFIX *same as* ▸ infix

ENFIXED ▸ enfix

ENFIXES ▸ enfix

ENFLAME *same as* ▸ inflame

ENFLESH *vb* make flesh

ENFOLD *vb* cover by wrapping something around

ENFOLDS ▸ enfold

ENFORCE *vb* impose obedience (to a law etc)

ENFORM *same as* ▸ inform

E

ENFORMS ▸ enform
ENFRAME vb put inside a frame
ENFREE vb release, make free
ENFREED ▸ enfree
ENFREES ▸ enfree
ENFROZE ▸ enfreeze
ENG another name for ▸ **agma**
ENGAGE vb take part, participate ▷ adj (of a writer or artist, esp a man) morally or politically committed to some ideology
ENGAGED adj pledged to be married
ENGAGEE adj (of a female writer or artist) morally or politically committed to some ideology
ENGAGER ▸ engage
ENGAGES ▸ engage
ENGAOL vb put into gaol
ENGAOLS ▸ engaol
ENGILD vb cover with or as if with gold
ENGILDS ▸ engild
ENGILT ▸ engild
ENGINE n any machine which converts energy into mechanical work ▷ vb put an engine in
ENGINED ▸ engine
ENGINER ▸ engine
ENGINES ▸ engine
ENGIRD vb surround
ENGIRDS ▸ engird
ENGIRT ▸ engird
ENGLISH vb put a spinning movement on a billiard ball
ENGLOBE vb surround as if in a globe
ENGLOOM vb make dull or dismal
ENGLUT vb devour ravenously
ENGLUTS ▸ englut
ENGOBE n liquid put on pottery before glazing
ENGOBES ▸ engobe
ENGORE vb pierce or wound
ENGORED ▸ engore
ENGORES ▸ engore
ENGORGE vb clog with blood
ENGRACE vb give grace to
ENGRAFF same as ▸ **engraft**
ENGRAFT vb graft (a shoot, bud, etc) onto a stock
ENGRAIL vb decorate or mark (the edge of) (a coin)

with small carved notches
ENGRAIN variant spelling of ▸ **ingrain**
ENGRAM n physical basis of an individual memory in the brain
ENGRAMS ▸ engram
ENGRASP vb grasp or seize
ENGRAVE vb carve (a design) onto a hard surface
ENGROSS vb occupy the attention of (a person) completely
ENGS ▸ eng
ENGUARD vb protect or defend
ENGULF vb cover or surround completely
ENGULFS ▸ engulf
ENGULPH same as ▸ **engulf**
ENHALO vb surround with or as if with a halo
ENHALOS ▸ enhalo
ENHANCE vb increase in quality, value, or attractiveness
ENIAC n early type of computer built in the 1940s
ENIACS ▸ eniac
ENIGMA n puzzling thing or person
ENIGMAS ▸ enigma
ENISLE vb put on or make into an island
ENISLED ▸ enisle
ENISLES ▸ enisle
ENJAMB vb (of a line of verse) run over into the next line
ENJAMBS ▸ enjamb
ENJOIN vb order (someone) to do something
ENJOINS ▸ enjoin
ENJOY vb take joy in
ENJOYED ▸ enjoy
ENJOYER ▸ enjoy
ENJOYS ▸ enjoy
ENLACE vb bind or encircle with or as with laces
ENLACED ▸ enlace
ENLACES ▸ enlace
ENLARD vb put lard on
ENLARDS ▸ enlard
ENLARGE vb make or grow larger
ENLEVE adj having been abducted
ENLIGHT vb light up
ENLINK vb link together
ENLINKS ▸ enlink
ENLIST vb enter the armed forces
ENLISTS ▸ enlist

ENLIT ▸ enlight
ENLIVEN vb make lively or cheerful
ENLOCK vb lock or secure
ENLOCKS ▸ enlock
ENMESH vb catch or involve in or as if in a net or snare
ENMEW same as ▸ **emmew**
ENMEWED ▸ enmew
ENMEWS ▸ enmew
ENMITY n ill will, hatred
ENMOVE same as ▸ **emmove**
ENMOVED ▸ enmove
ENMOVES ▸ enmove
ENNAGE n total number of ens in a piece of matter to be set in type
ENNAGES ▸ ennage
ENNEAD n group or series of nine
ENNEADS ▸ ennead
ENNOBLE vb make noble, elevate
ENNOG n back alley
ENNOGS ▸ ennog
ENNUI n boredom, dissatisfaction ▷ vb bore
ENNUIED ▸ ennui
ENNUIS ▸ ennui
ENNUYE adj bored
ENNUYED ▸ ennui
ENNUYEE same as ▸ **ennuye**
ENODAL adj having no nodes
ENOKI same as > **enokitake**
ENOKIS ▸ enoki
ENOL n any organic compound containing the group -CH:CO-, often existing in chemical equilibrium with the corresponding keto form
ENOLASE n type of enzyme
ENOLIC ▸ enol
ENOLOGY usual US spelling of > **oenology**
ENOLS ▸ enol
ENOMOTY n division of the Spartan army in ancient Greece
ENORM same as > **enormous**
ENOSES ▸ enosis
ENOSIS n union of Greece and Cyprus
ENOUGH adj as much as or many as necessary ▷ n sufficient quantity ▷ adv sufficiently
ENOUGHS ▸ enough
ENOUNCE vb enunciate
ENOW archaic word for ▸ **enough**

ENOWS ▸ enow

ENPLANE vb board an aircraft

ENPRINT n standard photographic print produced from a negative

ENQUEUE vb add (an item) to a queue of computing tasks

ENQUIRE same as ▸ **inquire**

ENQUIRY ▸ enquire

ENRACE vb bring in a race of people

ENRACED ▸ enrace

ENRACES ▸ enrace

ENRAGE vb make extremely angry

ENRAGED ▸ enrage

ENRAGES ▸ enrage

ENRANGE vb arrange, organize

ENRANK vb put in a row

ENRANKS ▸ enrank

ENRAPT > enrapture

ENRHEUM vb pass a cold on to

ENRICH vb improve in quality

ENRING vb put a ring round

ENRINGS ▸ enring

ENRIVEN adj ripped

ENROBE vb dress in or as if in a robe

ENROBED ▸ enrobe

ENROBER ▸ enrobe

ENROBES ▸ enrobe

ENROL vb (cause to) become a member

ENROLL same as ▸ **enrol**

ENROLLS ▸ enroll

ENROLS ▸ enrol

ENROOT vb establish (plants) by fixing their roots in the earth

ENROOTS ▸ enroot

ENROUGH vb roughen

ENROUND vb encircle

ENS n being or existence in the most general abstract sense

ENSATE adj shaped like a sword

ENSEAL vb seal up

ENSEALS ▸ enseal

ENSEAM vb put a seam on

ENSEAMS ▸ enseam

ENSEAR vb dry

ENSEARS ▸ ensear

ENSERF vb enslave

ENSERFS ▸ enserf

ENSEW same as ▸ **ensue**

ENSEWED ▸ ensew

ENSEWS ▸ ensew

ENSHELL same as ▸ **inshell**

ENSIGN n naval flag ⊳vb mark with a sign

ENSIGNS ▸ ensign

ENSILE vb store and preserve (green fodder) in an enclosed pit or silo

ENSILED ▸ ensile

ENSILES ▸ ensile

ENSKIED ▸ ensky

ENSKIES ▸ ensky

ENSKY vb put in the sky

ENSKYED ▸ ensky

ENSLAVE vb make a slave of (someone)

ENSNARE vb catch in or as if in a snare

ENSNARL vb become tangled in

ENSOUL vb endow with a soul

ENSOULS ▸ ensoul

ENSTAMP vb imprint with a stamp

ENSTEEP vb soak in water

ENSTYLE vb give a name to

ENSUE vb come next, result

ENSUED ▸ ensue

ENSUES ▸ ensue

ENSUING adj following subsequently or in order

ENSURE vb make certain or sure

ENSURED ▸ ensure

ENSURER ▸ ensure

ENSURES ▸ ensure

ENSWEEP vb sweep across

ENSWEPT ▸ ensweep

ENTAIL vb bring about or impose inevitably ⊳n restriction imposed by entailing an estate

ENTAILS ▸ entail

ENTAME vb make tame

ENTAMED ▸ entame

ENTAMES ▸ entame

ENTASES ▸ entasis

ENTASIA same as ▸ **entasis**

ENTASIS n slightly convex curve given to the shaft of a column, pier, or similar structure, to correct the illusion of concavity produced by a straight shaft

ENTAYLE same as ▸ **entail**

ENTENTE n friendly understanding between nations

ENTER vb come or go in

ENTERA ▸ enteron

ENTERAL same as ▸ **enteric**

ENTERED ▸ enter

ENTERER ▸ enter

ENTERIC adj intestinal ⊳n infectious disease of the intestines

ENTERON n alimentary canal, esp of an embryo or a coelenterate

ENTERS ▸ enter

ENTETE adj obsessed

ENTETEE same as ▸ **entete**

ENTHRAL vb hold the attention of

ENTHUSE vb (cause to) show enthusiasm

ENTIA ▸ ens

> This means entities, and because of the common letters it uses is one of the most frequently played five-letter words, at least towards the end of the game.

ENTICE vb attract by exciting hope or desire, tempt

ENTICED ▸ entice

ENTICER ▸ entice

ENTICES ▸ entice

ENTIRE adj including every detail, part, or aspect of something ⊳n state of being entire

ENTIRES ▸ entire

ENTITLE vb give a right to

ENTITY n separate distinct thing

ENTOIL archaic word for ▸ **ensnare**

ENTOILS ▸ entoil

ENTOMB vb place (a corpse) in a tomb

ENTOMBS ▸ entomb

ENTOMIC adj denoting or relating to insects

ENTOPIC adj situated in its normal place or position

ENTOTIC adj of or relating to the inner ear

ENTOZOA > entozoon

ENTRAIL vb twist or entangle

ENTRAIN vb board or put aboard a train

ENTRALL same as ▸ **entrails**

ENTRANT n person who enters a university, contest, etc

ENTRAP vb trick into difficulty etc

ENTRAPS ▸ entrap

ENTREAT vb ask earnestly

ENTREE n dish served before a main course

ENTREES ▸ entree
ENTREZ interj enter
ENTRIES ▸ entry
ENTRISM same as
▸ entryism
ENTRIST ▸ entryism
ENTROLD adj surrounded
ENTROPY n lack of
organization
ENTRUST vb put into the
care or protection of
ENTRY n entrance ▷ adj
necessary in order to enter
something
ENTWINE vb twist together
or around
ENTWIST vb twist together
or around
ENUF common intentional
literary misspelling of
▸ enough
ENURE variant spelling of
▸ inure
ENURED ▸ enure
ENURES ▸ enure
ENURING ▸ enure
ENURN ▸ inurn
ENURNED ▸ inurned
ENURNS ▸ inurns
ENVAULT vb enclose in a
vault; entomb
ENVELOP vb wrap up,
enclose
ENVENOM vb fill or
impregnate with venom
ENVIED ▸ envy
ENVIER ▸ envy
ENVIERS ▸ envy
ENVIES ▸ envy
ENVIOUS adj full of envy
ENVIRO n environmentalist
ENVIRON vb encircle or
surround
ENVIROS ▸ enviro
ENVOI same as ▸ envoy
ENVOIS ▸ envoi
ENVOY n messenger
ENVOYS ▸ envoy
ENVY n feeling of discontent
aroused by another's good
fortune ▷ vb grudge
(another's good fortune,
success, or qualities)
ENVYING ▸ envy
ENWALL vb wall in
ENWALLS ▸ enwall
ENWHEEL archaic word for
▸ encircle
ENWIND vb wind or coil
around
ENWINDS ▸ enwind
ENWOMB vb enclose in or
as if in a womb

ENWOMBS ▸ enwomb
ENWOUND ▸ enwind
ENWRAP vb wrap or cover
up
ENWRAPS ▸ enwrap
ENZIAN n gentian violet
ENZIANS ▸ enzian
ENZONE vb enclose in a
zone
ENZONED ▸ enzone
ENZONES ▸ enzone
ENZYM same as ▸ enzyme
ENZYME n any of a group of
complex proteins that act
as catalysts in specific
biochemical reactions
ENZYMES ▸ enzyme
ENZYMIC ▸ enzyme
ENZYMS ▸ enzym
EOAN adj of or relating to
the dawn
EOBIONT n hypothetical
chemical precursor of a
living cell
EOCENE adj of, denoting, or
formed in the second epoch
of the Tertiary period
EOLIAN adj of or relating to
the wind

> 6-letter words tend to be
> among the least known
> and least used, because
> they leave you at the
> mercy of the tile bag
> without scoring that
> extra 50 points you
> would get for using all 7
> letters. This word,
> meaning related to the
> wind, often comes in
> useful for dumping a
> surplus of vowels. And its
> alternative spelling
> **aeolian** is even better for
> this and what's more will
> get you a bonus!

EOLITH n stone, usually
crudely broken, used as a
primitive tool in Eolithic
times
EOLITHS ▸ eolith
EON n longest division of
geological time, comprising
two or more eras
EONIAN adj of or relating to
an eon
EONISM n adoption of
female dress and behaviour
by a male
EONISMS ▸ eonism
EONS ▸ eon
EORL n Anglo-Saxon
nobleman

EORLS ▸ eorl
EOSIN n red crystalline
water-insoluble derivative
of fluorescein
EOSINE same as ▸ eosin
EOSINES ▸ eosine
EOSINIC ▸ eosin
EOSINS ▸ eosin
EOTHEN adv from the East
EPACRID n type of
heath-like plant
EPACRIS n genus of the
epacrids
EPACT n difference in time,
about 11 days, between the
solar year and the lunar
year
EPACTS ▸ epact
EPAGOGE n inductive
reasoning
EPARCH n bishop or
metropolitan in charge of
an eparchy
EPARCHS ▸ eparch
EPARCHY n diocese of the
Eastern Christian Church
EPATANT adj startling or
shocking, esp through
being unconventional
EPAULE n shoulder of a
fortification
EPAULES ▸ epaule
EPAULET same as
> epaulette
EPAXIAL adj above the axis
EPAZOTE n type of herb
EPEE n straight-bladed
sword used in fencing
EPEEIST n one who uses or
specializes in using an epee
EPEES ▸ epee
EPEIRA same as ▸ epeirid
EPEIRAS ▸ epeira
EPEIRIC adj in, of, or relating
to a continent
EPEIRID n type of spider
EPERDU adj distracted
EPERDUE adj distracted
EPERGNE n ornamental
centrepiece for a table: a
stand with holders for
sweetmeats, fruit, flowers,
etc
EPHA same as ▸ ephah
EPHAH n Hebrew unit of dry
measure equal to
approximately one bushel
or about 33 litres
EPHAHS ▸ ephah
EPHAS ▸ epha
EPHEBE n (in ancient
Greece) youth about to
enter full citizenship, esp

one undergoing military training

EPHEBES ► ephebe

EPHEBI ► ephebe

EPHEBIC ► ephebe

EPHEBOI ► ephebos

EPHEBOS *same as* ► **ephebe**

EPHEBUS *same as* ► **ephebe**

EPHEDRA *n* gymnosperm shrub of warm regions of America and Eurasia

EPHELIS *n* freckle

EPHOD *n* embroidered vestment believed to resemble an apron with shoulder straps, worn by priests in ancient Israel

EPHODS ► ephod

EPHOR *n* (in ancient Greece) one of a board of senior magistrates in any of several Dorian states, esp the five Spartan ephors, who were elected by the vote of all full citizens and who wielded effective power

EPHORAL ► ephor

EPHORI ► ephor

EPHORS ► ephor

EPIBLEM *n* outermost cell layer of a root

EPIBOLY *n* process that occurs during gastrulation in vertebrates, in which cells on one side of the blastula grow over and surround the remaining cells and yolk and eventually form the ectoderm

EPIC *n* long poem, book, or film about heroic events or actions ▷ *adj* very impressive or ambitious

EPICAL ► epic

EPICARP *n* outermost layer of the pericarp of fruits: forms the skin of a peach or grape

EPICEDE *same as* > **epicedium**

EPICENE *adj* having the characteristics of both sexes; hermaphroditic ▷ *n* epicene person or creature

EPICIER *n* grocer

EPICISM *n* style or trope characteristic of epics

EPICIST *n* writer of epics

EPICS ► epic

EPICURE *n* person who enjoys good food and drink

EPIDERM *same as* > **epidermis**

EPIDOTE *n* green mineral consisting of hydrated calcium iron aluminium silicate in monoclinic crystalline form: common in metamorphic rocks

EPIGEAL *adj* of or relating to seed germination in which the cotyledons appear above the ground because of the growth of the hypocotyl

EPIGEAN *same as* ► **epigeal**

EPIGEIC *same as* ► **epigeal**

EPIGENE *adj* formed or taking place at or near the surface of the earth

EPIGON *same as* ► **epigone**

EPIGONE *n* inferior follower or imitator

EPIGONI ► epigone

EPIGONS ► epigon

EPIGRAM *n* short witty remark or poem

EPIGYNY > epigynous

EPILATE *vb* remove hair from

EPILOG *same as* > **epilogue**

EPILOGS ► epilog

EPIMER *n* isomer

EPIMERE *n* dorsal part of the mesoderm of a vertebrate embryo, consisting of a series of segments

EPIMERS ► epimer

EPINAOI ► epinaos

EPINAOS *n* rear vestibule

EPISCIA *n* creeping plant

EPISODE *n* incident in a series of incidents

EPISOME *n* unit of genetic material (DNA) in bacteria, such as a plasmid, that can either replicate independently or can be integrated into the host chromosome

EPISTLE *n* letter, esp of an apostle ▷ *vb* preface

EPITAPH *n* commemorative inscription on a tomb ▷ *vb* compose an epitaph

EPITAXY *n* growth of a thin layer on the surface of a crystal so that the layer has the same structure as the underlying crystal

EPITHEM *n* external topical application

EPITHET *n* descriptive word

or name ▷ *vb* name

EPITOME *n* typical example

EPITOPE *n* site on an antigen at which a specific antibody becomes attached

EPIZOA ► epizoon

EPIZOAN *same as* ► **epizoon**

EPIZOIC *adj* (of an animal or plant) growing or living on the exterior of a living animal

EPIZOON *n* animal, such as a parasite, that lives on the body of another animal

EPOCH *n* period of notable events

EPOCHA *same as* ► **epoch**

EPOCHAL ► epoch

EPOCHAS ► epocha

EPOCHS ► epoch

EPODE *n* part of a lyric ode that follows the strophe and the antistrophe

EPODES ► epode

EPODIC ► epode

EPONYM *n* name, esp a place name, derived from the name of a real or mythical person

EPONYMS ► eponym

EPONYMY *n* derivation of names of places, etc, from those of persons

EPOPEE *n* epic poem

EPOPEES ► epopee

EPOPT *n* one initiated into mysteries

EPOPTS ► epopt

EPOS *n* body of poetry in which the tradition of a people is conveyed, esp a group of poems concerned with a common epic theme

EPOSES ► epos

EPOXIDE *n* compound containing an oxygen atom joined to two different groups that are themselves joined to other groups

EPOXIED ► epoxy

EPOXIES ► epoxy

EPOXY *adj* of or containing an oxygen atom joined to two different groups that are themselves joined to other groups ▷ *n* epoxy resin ▷ *vb* glue with epoxy resin

EPOXYED ► epoxy

EPRIS *adj* enamoured

EPRISE *feminine form of* ► **epris**

EPSILON n fifth letter of the Greek alphabet, a short vowel, transliterated as e

EPUISE adj exhausted

EPUISEE feminine form of ▸ epuise

EPULARY adj of or relating to feasting

EPULIS n swelling of the gum, usually as a result of fibrous hyperplasia

EPURATE vb purify

EPYLLIA > epyllion

EQUABLE adj even-tempered

EQUABLY ▸ equable

EQUAL adj identical in size, quantity, degree, etc ▷ n person or thing equal to another ▷ vb be equal to

EQUALED ▸ equal

EQUALI pl n pieces for a group of instruments of the same kind

EQUALLY ▸ equal

EQUALS ▸ equal

EQUANT n circle in which a planet was formerly believed to move

EQUANTS ▸ equant

EQUATE vb make or regard as equivalent

EQUATED ▸ equate

EQUATES ▸ equate

EQUATOR n imaginary circle round the earth, equidistant from the poles

EQUERRY n officer who acts as an attendant to a member of a royal family

EQUID n any animal of the horse family

EQUIDS ▸ equid

EQUINAL same as ▸ equine

EQUINE adj of or like a horse ▷ n any animal of the horse family

EQUINES ▸ equine

EQUINIA n glanders

EQUINOX n time of year when day and night are of equal length

EQUIP vb provide with supplies, components, etc

EQUIPE n (esp in motor racing) team

EQUIPES ▸ equipe

EQUIPS ▸ equip

EQUITES pl n cavalry

EQUITY n fairness

ER interj sound made when hesitating in speech

ERA n period of time

considered as distinctive

ERAS ▸ era

ERASE vb destroy all traces of

ERASED ▸ erase

ERASER n object for erasing something written

ERASERS ▸ eraser

ERASES ▸ erase

ERASING ▸ erase

ERASION n act of erasing

> This means the state of being erased: not an exciting word, but its combination of common letters makes it one of the most frequently played of 7-letter bonus words.

ERASURE n erasing

ERATHEM n stratum of rocks representing a specific geological era

ERBIA n oxide of erbium

ERBIAS ▸ erbia

ERBIUM n metallic element of the lanthanide series

ERBIUMS ▸ erbium

ERE prep before ▷ vb plough

ERECT vb build ▷ adj upright

ERECTED ▸ erect

ERECTER same as ▸ erector

ERECTLY ▸ erect

ERECTOR n any muscle that raises a part or makes it erect

ERECTS ▸ erect

ERED ▸ ere

ERELONG adv before long

EREMIC adj of or relating to deserts

EREMITE n Christian hermit

EREMURI > eremurus

ERENOW adv long before the present

EREPSIN n mixture of proteolytic enzymes secreted by the small intestine

ERES ▸ ere

ERETHIC > erethism

EREV n day before

EREVS ▸ erev

ERF n plot of land, usually urban, marked off for building purposes

ERG same as > ergometer

ERGATE n worker ant

ERGATES ▸ ergate

ERGO same as > ergometer

ERGODIC adj of or relating to the probability that any state will recur

ERGON n work

ERGONS ▸ ergon

ERGOS ▸ ergo

ERGOT n fungal disease of cereal

ERGOTIC ▸ ergot

ERGOTS ▸ ergot

ERGS ▸ erg

ERHU n Chinese two-stringed violin

ERHUS ▸ erhu

ERIACH same as ▸ eric

ERIACHS ▸ eriach

ERIC n (in old Irish law) fine paid by a murderer to the family of his victim

ERICA n genus of plants including heathers

ERICAS ▸ erica

ERICK same as ▸ eric

ERICKS ▸ erick

ERICOID adj (of leaves) small and tough, resembling those of heather

ERICS ▸ eric

ERING ▸ ere

ERINGO same as ▸ eryngo

ERINGOS ▸ eringo

ERINITE n arsenate of copper

ERINUS n type of plant

ERISTIC adj of, relating, or given to controversy or logical disputation, esp for its own sake ▷ n person who engages in logical disputes

ERK n aircraftman or naval rating

ERKS ▸ erk

ERLANG n unit of traffic intensity in a telephone system equal to the intensity for a specific period when the average number of simultaneous calls is unity

ERLANGS ▸ erlang

ERLKING n malevolent spirit who carries off children

ERM interj expression of hesitation

ERMELIN n ermine

ERMINE n stoat in northern regions, where it has a white winter coat with a black-tipped tail

ERMINED adj clad in the fur of the ermine

ERMINES ▸ ermine

ERN archaic variant of ▸ earn

ERNE n fish-eating (European) sea eagle

ERNED ▸ ern

ERNES ▸ erne

ERNING ▸ ern

ERNS ▸ ern

ERODE vb wear away

ERODED ▸ erode

ERODENT ▸ erode

ERODES ▸ erode

ERODING ▸ erode

ERODIUM n type of geranium

EROS n lust

EROSE adj jagged or uneven, as though gnawed or bitten

EROSELY ▸ erose

EROSES ▸ eros

EROSION n wearing away of rocks or soil by the action of water, ice, or wind

EROSIVE ▸ erosion

EROTEMA n rhetorical question

EROTEME same as ▸ erotema

EROTIC adj relating to sexual pleasure or desire ▷ n person who has strong sexual desires or is especially responsive to sexual stimulation

EROTICA n sexual literature or art

EROTICS ▸ erotic

EROTISE same as ▸ erotize

EROTISM same as > eroticism

EROTIZE vb make erotic

ERR vb make a mistake

ERRABLE adj capable of making a mistake

ERRANCY n state or an instance of erring or a tendency to err

ERRAND n short trip to do something for someone

ERRANDS ▸ errand

ERRANT adj behaving in a manner considered to be unacceptable ▷ n knight-errant

ERRANTS ▸ errant

ERRATA ▸ erratum

ERRATAS informal variant of ▸ errata

ERRATIC adj irregular or unpredictable ▷ n rock that has been transported by glacial action

ERRATUM n error in writing or printing

ERRED ▸ err

ERRHINE adj causing nasal secretion ▷ n errhine drug or agent

ERRING ▸ err

ERRINGS ▸ err

ERROR n mistake, inaccuracy, or misjudgment

ERRORS ▸ error

ERRS ▸ err

ERS same as ▸ ervil

ERSATZ adj made in imitation ▷ n ersatz substance or article

ERSES ▸ ers

ERST adv long ago

ERUCIC adj as in **erucic acid** crystalline fatty acid derived from rapeseed, mustard seed and wallflower seed

ERUCT vb belch

ERUCTED ▸ eruct

ERUCTS ▸ eruct

ERUDITE adj having great academic knowledge ▷ n erudite person

ERUGO n verdigris

ERUGOS ▸ erugo

ERUPT vb eject (steam, water, or volcanic material) violently

ERUPTED ▸ erupt

ERUPTS ▸ erupt

ERUV n area, circumscribed by a symbolic line, within which certain activities forbidden to Orthodox Jews on the Sabbath are permitted

ERUVIM ▸ eruv

ERUVIN ▸ eruv

ERUVS ▸ eruv

ERVEN ▸ erf

ERVIL n type of vetch

ERVILS ▸ ervil

ERYNGO n type of plant with toothed or lobed leaves, such as the sea holly

ERYNGOS ▸ eryngo

ES n letter S

ESCALOP another word for ▸ scallop

ESCAPE vb get free (of) ▷ n act of escaping

ESCAPED ▸ escape

ESCAPEE n person who has escaped

ESCAPER ▸ escape

ESCAPES ▸ escape

ESCAR same as ▸ esker

ESCARP n inner side of the ditch separating besiegers and besieged ▷ vb make into a slope

ESCARPS ▸ escarp

ESCARS ▸ escar

ESCHAR n dry scab or slough, esp one following a burn or cauterization of the skin

ESCHARS ▸ eschar

ESCHEAT n private possessions that become state property in the absence of an heir ▷ vb attain such property

ESCHEWS ▸ eschew

ESCHEW vb abstain from, avoid

ESCHEWS ▸ eschew

ESCOLAR n slender spiny-finned fish

ESCORT n people or vehicles accompanying another person for protection or as an honour ▷ vb act as an escort to

ESCORTS ▸ escort

ESCOT vb maintain

ESCOTED ▸ escot

ESCOTS ▸ escot

ESCRIBE vb draw (a circle) so that it is tangential to one side of a triangle and to the other two sides produced

ESCROC n conman

ESCROCS ▸ escroc

ESCROL same as ▸ escroll

ESCROLL n scroll

ESCROLS ▸ escrol

ESCROW n money, goods, or a written document, such as a contract bond, delivered to a third party and held by him pending fulfilment of some condition ▷ vb place (money, a document, etc) in escrow

ESCROWS ▸ escrow

ESCUAGE (in medieval Europe) another word for ▸ scutage

ESCUDO n former monetary unit of Portugal

ESCUDOS ▸ escudo

ESERINE n crystalline alkaloid

ESES ▸ es

ESILE n vinegar

ESILES ▸ esile

ESKAR same as ▸ esker

ESKARS ▸ eskar

ESKER n long winding ridge of gravel, sand, etc,

E

originally deposited by a
meltwater stream running
under a glacier
ESKERS ▶ esker
ESKIES ▶ esky
ESKY n portable insulated
container for keeping food
and drink cool
ESLOIN same as ▶ **eloign**
ESLOINS ▶ esloin
ESLOYNE same as ▶ **eloign**
ESNE n household slave
ESNECY n right of the eldest
daughter to make the first
choice when dividing
inheritance
ESNES ▶ esne
ESOTERY > esoteric
ESPADA n sword
ESPADAS ▶ espada
ESPANOL n Spanish person
ESPARTO n grass of S
Europe and N Africa used
for making rope etc
ESPIAL n act or fact of being
seen or discovered
ESPIALS ▶ espial
ESPIED ▶ espy
ESPIER ▶ espy
ESPIERS ▶ espy
ESPIES ▶ espy
ESPOUSE vb adopt or give
support to (a cause etc)
ESPRIT n spirit, liveliness, or
wit
ESPRITS ▶ esprit
ESPY vb catch sight of
ESPYING ▶ espy
ESQUIRE n courtesy title
placed after a man's name
▷ vb escort
ESS n letter S
ESSAY n short literary
composition ▷ vb attempt
ESSAYED ▶ essay
ESSAYER ▶ essay
ESSAYS ▶ essay
ESSE n existence
ESSENCE n most important
feature of a thing which
determines its identity
ESSES ▶ ess
ESSIVE n grammatical case
ESSIVES ▶ essive
ESSOIN n excuse
ESSOINS ▶ essoin
ESSOYNE same as ▶ **essoin**
EST n treatment intended to
help people towards
psychological growth, in
which they spend many
hours in large groups,
deprived of food and water

and hectored by stewards
ESTATE n landed property
▷ vb provide with an estate
ESTATED ▶ estate
ESTATES ▶ estate
ESTEEM n high regard ▷ vb
think highly of
ESTEEMS ▶ esteem
ESTER n compound
produced by the reaction
between an acid and an
alcohol
ESTERS ▶ ester
ESTHETE US spelling of
> **aesthete**
ESTIVAL usual US spelling of
> **aestival**
ESTOC n short stabbing
sword
ESTOCS ▶ estoc
ESTOILE n heraldic star with
wavy points
ESTOP vb preclude by
estoppel
ESTOPS ▶ estop
ESTOVER same as
> **estovers**
ESTRADE n dais or raised
platform
ESTRAL US spelling of
▶ **oestral**
ESTRAY n stray domestic
animal of unknown
ownership ▷ vb stray
ESTRAYS ▶ estray
ESTREAT n true copy of or
extract from a court record
▷ vb enforce (a
recognizance that has been
forfeited) by sending an
extract of the court record
to the proper authority
ESTREPE vb lay waste
ESTRICH n ostrich
ESTRIN US spelling of
▶ **oestrin**
ESTRINS ▶ estrin
ESTRIOL usual US spelling of
> **oestriol**
ESTRO n poetic inspiration
ESTRONE usual US spelling of
> **oestrone**
ESTROS ▶ estro
ESTROUS ▶ estrus
ESTRUAL ▶ estrus
ESTRUM usual US spelling of
▶ **oestrum**
ESTRUMS ▶ estrum
ESTRUS usual US spelling of
▶ **oestrus**
ESTS ▶ est
ESTUARY n mouth of a river
ET dialect past tense of ▶ **eat**

ETA n seventh letter in the
Greek alphabet, a long
vowel sound
ETACISM n pronunciation of
eta as a long vowel sound
ETAERIO n aggregate fruit,
as one consisting of drupes
(raspberry) or achenes
(traveller's joy)

This strange-looking
word is a botanical term
for a type of fruit, and
because it uses the
commonest letters is,
along with **otarine**, the
most frequently played
of all bonus words.

ETAGE n floor in a
multi-storey building
ETAGERE n stand with open
shelves for displaying
ornaments, etc
ETAGES ▶ etage
ETALAGE n display
ETALON n device used in
spectroscopy to measure
wavelengths by
interference effects
produced by multiple
reflections between parallel
half-silvered glass or quartz
plates
ETALONS ▶ etalon
ETAMIN same as ▶ **etamine**
ETAMINE n cotton or
worsted fabric of loose
weave, used for clothing,
curtains, etc
ETAMINS ▶ etamin
ETAPE n public storehouse
ETAPES ▶ etape
ETAS ▶ eta
ETAT n state
ETATISM same as
> **etatisme**
ETATIST > etatisme
ETATS ▶ etat
ETCH vb wear away or cut
the surface of (metal, glass,
etc) with acid
ETCHANT n any acid or
corrosive used for etching
ETCHED ▶ etch
ETCHER ▶ etch
ETCHERS ▶ etch
ETCHES ▶ etch
ETCHING n picture printed
from an etched metal plate
ETEN n giant
ETENS ▶ eten
ETERNAL adj without
beginning or end ▷ n
eternal thing

ETERNE archaic or poetic word for ▸ **eternal**

ETESIAN adj (of NW winds) recurring annually in the summer in the E Mediterranean ▷ n etesian wind

ETH same as ▸ **edh**

ETHAL n cetyl alcohol

ETHANAL n colourless volatile pungent liquid

ETHANE n odourless flammable gas obtained from natural gas and petroleum

ETHANES ▸ ethane

ETHANOL same as ▸ **alcohol**

ETHE adj easy

ETHENE same as > **ethylene**

ETHENES ▸ ethene

ETHER n colourless sweet-smelling liquid used as an anaesthetic

ETHERIC ▸ ether

ETHERS ▸ ether

ETHIC n moral principle

ETHICAL adj of or based on a system of moral beliefs about right and wrong ▷ n drug available only by prescription

ETHICS n code of behaviour

ETHINYL same as ▸ **ethynyl**

ETHION n type of pesticide

ETHIONS ▸ ethion

ETHIOPS n dark-coloured chemical compound

ETHMOID adj denoting or relating to a bone of the skull that forms part of the eye socket and the nasal cavity ▷ n ethmoid bone

ETHNIC adj relating to a people or group that shares a culture, religion, or language ▷ n member of an ethnic group, esp a minority group

ETHNICS ▸ ethnic

ETHNOS n ethnic group

ETHOS n distinctive spirit and attitudes of a people, culture, etc

ETHOSES ▸ ethos

ETHOXY ▸ ethoxyl

ETHOXYL n univalent radical

ETHS ▸ eth

ETHYL adj type of chemical hydrocarbon group

ETHYLIC ▸ ethyl

ETHYLS ▸ ethyl

ETHYNE another name for > **acetylene**

ETHYNES ▸ ethyne

ETHYNYL n univalent radical

ETIC adj (in linguistics) of or relating to items analyzed without consideration of their structural function

ETIOLIN n yellow pigment

ETNA n container used to heat liquids

ETNAS ▸ etna

ETOILE n star

ETOILES ▸ etoile

ETOURDI adj foolish

ETRENNE n New Year's gift

ETRIER n short portable ladder or set of webbing loops that can be attached to a karabiner or fifi hook

ETRIERS ▸ etrier

ETTIN n giant

ETTINS ▸ ettin

ETTLE vb intend

ETTLED ▸ ettle

ETTLES ▸ ettle

ETTLING ▸ ettle

ETUDE n short musical composition for a solo instrument, esp intended as a technical exercise

ETUDES ▸ etude

ETUI n small usually ornamented case for holding needles, cosmetics, or other small articles

ETUIS ▸ etui

ETWEE same as ▸ **etui**

E is a very desirable letter, but sometimes you can have too much of even this good thing. This word for a needle-case, a variant of **etui**, can help you dispose of a few of them.

ETWEES ▸ etui

ETYMA ▸ etymon

ETYMIC ▸ etymon

ETYMON n earliest form of a word or morpheme, or a reconstructed form, from which another word or morpheme is derived

ETYMONS ▸ etymon

ETYPIC n unable to conform to type

EUCAIN same as ▸ **eucaine**

EUCAINE n crystalline optically active substance formerly used as a local anaesthetic

EUCAINS ▸ eucain

EUCHRE n US and Canadian card game similar to écarté for two to four players, using a poker pack with joker ▷ vb prevent (a player) from making his contracted tricks

EUCHRED ▸ euchre

EUCHRES ▸ euchre

EUCLASE n brittle green gem

EUCRITE n type of stony meteorite

EUDEMON n benevolent spirit or demon

EUGARIE another name for ▸ **pipi**

EUGE interj well done!

EUGENIA n plant of the clove family

EUGENIC > eugenics

EUGENOL n colourless or pale yellow oily liquid substance with a spicy taste and an odour of cloves, used in perfumery

EUGH archaic form of ▸ **yew**

EUGHEN archaic form of ▸ **yew**

EUGHS ▸ eugh

EUGLENA n type of freshwater unicellular organism

EUK vb itch

EUKED ▸ euk

EUKING ▸ euk

EUKS ▸ euk

EULOGIA n blessed bread distributed to members of the congregation after the liturgy, esp to those who have not communed

This means blessed bread and is one of the few 7-letter words that use all the vowels. What's more, it can take a plural in E as well as S, giving **eulogiae**, which can be even better for getting you out of vowel trouble.

EULOGY n speech or writing in praise of a person

EUMONG same as ▸ **eumung**

EUMONGS ▸ eumong

EUMUNG n any of various Australian acacias

EUMUNGS ▸ eumung

EUNUCH n castrated man, esp (formerly) a guard in a harem

EUNUCHS ▸ eunuch

EUOI n cry of Bacchic frenzy
This is a cry expressing Bacchic frenzy, and is forever coming in useful to dispose of a surplus of vowels. It has the less commonly played but still useful variants **evoe**, **evhoe** and **evohe**.

EUOUAE n a mnemonic used to recall the sequence of tones in a particular passage of the Gloria
This word is remarkable in containing no consonants. You will be surprised at how often you will be glad to play it!

EUOUAES ▸ euouae
EUPAD n antiseptic powder
EUPADS ▸ eupad
EUPEPSY same as ▸ eupepsia
EUPHON n glass harmonica
EUPHONS ▸ euphon
EUPHONY n pleasing sound
EUPHORY same as ▸ euphoria
EUPHROE n wooden block with holes through which the lines of a crowfoot are rove
EUPLOID adj having chromosomes present in an exact multiple of the haploid number ▷ n euploid cell or individual
EUPNEA same as ▸ eupnoea
EUPNEAS ▸ eupnea
EUPNEIC ▸ eupnoea
EUPNOEA n normal relaxed breathing
EUREKA n exclamation of triumph at finding something
EUREKAS ▸ eureka
EURIPI ▸ euripus
EURIPUS n strait or channel with a strong current or tide
EURO n unit of the single currency of the European Union
EUROKY n ability of an organism to live under different conditions
EUROPOP n type of pop music by European artists
EUROS ▸ euro
EURYOKY same as ▸ euroky
EUSOL n solution of eupad in water

EUSOLS ▸ eusol
EUSTACY > eustatic
EUSTASY > eustatic
EUSTELE n central cylinder of a seed plant
EUSTYLE n building with columns optimally spaced
EUTAXIA n condition of being easily melted
EUTAXY n good order
EUTEXIA same as ▸ eutaxia
EUTROPY n regular variation of the crystalline structure of a series of compounds according to atomic number
EVACUEE n person evacuated from a place of danger, esp in wartime
EVADE vb get away from or avoid
EVADED ▸ evade
EVADER ▸ evade
EVADERS ▸ evade
EVADES ▸ evade
EVADING ▸ evade
EVANGEL n gospel of Christianity
EVANISH poetic word for ▸ vanish
EVASION n act of evading something, esp a duty or responsibility, by cunning or illegal means
EVASIVE adj not straightforward
EVE n evening or day before some special event
EVEJAR n nightjar
EVEJARS ▸ evejar
EVEN adj flat or smooth ▷ adv equally ▷ vb make even ▷ n eve
EVENED ▸ even
EVENER ▸ even
EVENERS ▸ even
EVENEST ▸ even
EVENING n end of the day or early part of the night ▷ adj of or in the evening
EVENLY ▸ even
EVENS adv (of a bet) winning the same as the amount staked if successful
EVENT n anything that takes place ▷ vb take part or ride (a horse) in eventing
EVENTED ▸ event
EVENTER ▸ eventing
EVENTS ▸ event
EVER adv at any time
EVERNET n hypothetical form of internet that is

continuously accessible using a wide variety of devices
EVERT vb turn (an eyelid, the intestines, or some other bodily part) outwards or inside out
EVERTED ▸ evert
EVERTOR n any muscle that turns a part outwards
EVERTS ▸ evert
EVERY adj each without exception
EVES ▸ eve
EVET n eft
EVETS ▸ evet
EVHOE interj cry of Bacchic frenzy
EVICT vb legally expel (someone) from his or her home
EVICTED ▸ evict
EVICTEE ▸ evict
EVICTOR ▸ evict
EVICTS ▸ evict
EVIDENT adj easily seen or understood ▷ n item of evidence
EVIL n wickedness ▷ adj harmful ▷ adv in an evil manner
EVILER ▸ evil
EVILEST ▸ evil
EVILLER ▸ evil
EVILLY ▸ evil
EVILS ▸ evil
EVINCE vb make evident
EVINCED ▸ evince
EVINCES ▸ evince
EVIRATE vb castrate
EVITATE archaic word for ▸ avoid
EVITE archaic word for ▸ avoid
EVITED ▸ evite
EVITES ▸ evite
EVITING ▸ evite
EVO informal word for ▸ evening
EVOCATE vb evoke
EVOE interj cry of Bacchic frenzy
EVOHE interj cry of Bacchic frenzy
EVOKE vb call or summon up (a memory, feeling, etc)
EVOKED ▸ evoke
EVOKER ▸ evoke
EVOKERS ▸ evoke
EVOKES ▸ evoke
EVOKING ▸ evoke
EVOLUE n (in the African former colonies of Belgium

and France) African person educated according to European principles

EVOLUES ▸ evolue

EVOLUE n geometric curve that describes the locus of the centres of curvature of another curve ▷ adj having the margins rolled outwards ▷ vb evolve

EVOLVE vb develop gradually

EVOLVED ▸ evolve

EVOLVER ▸ evolve

EVOLVES ▸ evolve

EVOS ▸ evo

EVOVAE n a mnemonic used to recall the sequence of tones in a particular passage of the Gloria Patri

EVOVAES ▸ evovae

EVULSE vb extract by force

EVULSED ▸ evulse

EVULSES ▸ evulse

EVZONE n soldier in an elite Greek infantry regiment

EVZONES ▸ evzone

EWE n female sheep

EWER n large jug with a wide mouth

EWERS ▸ ewer

EWES ▸ ewe

EWEST Scots word for ▸ **near**

EWFTES Spenserian plural of ▸ **eft**

EWGHEN archaic form of ▸ **yew**

EWHOW interj expression of pity or regret

EWK vb itch

> Ewk is a dialect word for itch. It's a handy little word and a good one to remember in case you end up with both K and W, and remember that it's a verb so you can have **ewks, ewked** and **ewking**. It's also worth knowing its variants **euk, yeuk, youk, yuck** and **yuke**!

EWKED ▸ ewk

EWKING ▸ ewk

EWKS ▸ ewk

EWT archaic form of ▸ **newt**

EWTS ▸ ewt

EX prep not including ▷ n a former husband, wife etc ▷ vb cross out or delete

EXABYTE n very large unit of computer memory

EXACT adj correct and complete in every detail ▷ vb demand (payment or obedience)

EXACTA n horse-racing bet in which the first and second horses must be named in the correct order

EXACTAS ▸ exacta

EXACTED ▸ exact

EXACTER ▸ exact

EXACTLY adv precisely, in every respect ▷ interj just so! precisely!

EXACTOR ▸ exact

EXACTS ▸ exact

EXACUM n type of tropical plant often grown as a greenhouse plant for its bluish-purple platter-shaped flowers

EXACUMS ▸ exacum

EXALT vb praise highly

EXALTED adj high or elevated in rank, position, dignity, etc

EXALTER ▸ exalt

EXALTS ▸ exalt

EXAM n examination

EXAMEN n examination of conscience, usually made daily by Jesuits and others

EXAMENS ▸ examen

EXAMINE vb look at closely

EXAMPLE n specimen typical of its group

EXAMS ▸ exam

EXAPTED adj biologically adapted

EXARATE adj (of the pupa of such insects as ants and bees) having legs, wings, antennae, etc, free and movable

EXARCH n head of certain autonomous Orthodox Christian Churches, such as that of Bulgaria and Cyprus ▷ adj (of a xylem strand) having the first-formed xylem external to that formed later

EXARCHS ▸ exarch

EXARCHY same as > **exarchate**

EXCAMB vb exchange

EXCAMBS ▸ excamb

EXCEED vb be greater than

EXCEEDS ▸ exceed

EXCEL vb be superior to

EXCELS ▸ excel

EXCEPT prep other than, not including ▷ vb leave out; omit; exclude

EXCEPTS ▸ except

EXCERPT n passage taken from a book, speech, etc ▷ vb take a passage from a book, speech, etc

EXCESS n state or act of exceeding the permitted limits ▷ vb make (a position) redundant

EXCHEAT same as ▸ **escheat**

EXCIDE vb cut out

EXCIDED ▸ excide

EXCIDES ▸ excide

EXCIMER n excited dimer formed by the association of excited and unexcited molecules, which would remain dissociated in the ground state

EXCIPLE n part of a lichen

EXCISE n tax on goods produced for the home market ▷ vb cut out or away

EXCISED ▸ excise

EXCISES ▸ excise

EXCITE vb arouse to strong emotion

EXCITED adj emotionally aroused, esp to pleasure or agitation

EXCITER n person or thing that excites

EXCITES ▸ excite

EXCITON n mobile neutral entity in a crystalline solid consisting of an excited electron bound to the hole produced by its excitation

EXCITOR n nerve that, when stimulated, causes increased activity in the organ or part it supplies

EXCLAIM vb speak suddenly, cry out

EXCLAVE n part of a country entirely surrounded by foreign territory: viewed from the position of the home country

EXCLUDE vb keep out, leave out

EXCRETA n excrement

EXCRETE vb discharge (waste matter) from the body

EXCUDIT sentence substitute (named person) made this

EXCURSE vb wander

EXCUSAL ▸ excuse

EXCUSE n explanation offered to justify (a fault etc) ▷ vb put forward a

E

reason or justification for (a fault etc)

EXCUSED ▸ excuse

EXCUSER ▸ excuse

EXCUSES ▸ excuse

EXEAT n leave of absence from school or some other institution

EXEATS ▸ exeat

EXEC n executive

EXECS ▸ exec

EXECUTE vb put (a condemned person) to death

EXED ▸ ex

EXEDRA n building, room, portico, or apse containing a continuous bench, used in ancient Greece and Rome for holding discussions

EXEDRAE ▸ exedra

EXEEM same as ▸ **exeme**

EXEEMED ▸ exeem

EXEEMS ▸ exeem

EXEGETE n person who practises exegesis

EXEME vb set free

EXEMED ▸ exeme

EXEMES ▸ exeme

EXEMING ▸ exeme

EXEMPLA > **exemplum**

EXEMPLE same as ▸ **example**

EXEMPT adj not subject to an obligation etc ▷ vb release from an obligation etc ▷ n person who is exempt from an obligation, tax, etc

EXEMPTS ▸ exempt

EXEQUY n funeral rite

> Meaning a funeral rite, this word combines X and Q. Even better is its plural **exequies**, which would earn an extra 50 points for using all your tiles.

EXERGUE n space on the reverse of a coin or medal below the central design, often containing the date, place of minting, etc

EXERGY n maximum amount of useful work obtainable from a system

EXERT vb use (influence, authority, etc) forcefully or effectively

EXERTED ▸ exert

EXERTS ▸ exert

EXES ▸ ex

EXEUNT vb (they) go out

EXHALE vb breathe out

EXHALED ▸ exhale

EXHALES ▸ exhale

EXHAUST vb tire out ▷ n gases ejected from an engine as waste products

EXHEDRA same as ▸ **exedra**

EXHIBIT vb display to the public ▷ n object exhibited to the public

EXHORT vb urge earnestly

EXHORTS ▸ exhort

EXHUME vb dig up (something buried, esp a corpse)

EXHUMED ▸ exhume

EXHUMER ▸ exhume

EXHUMES ▸ exhume

EXIES n hysterics

EXIGENT adj urgent ▷ n emergency

EXILE n prolonged, usu enforced, absence from one's country ▷ vb expel from one's country

EXILED ▸ exile

EXILER ▸ exile

EXILERS ▸ exile

EXILES ▸ exile

EXILIAN ▸ exile

EXILIC ▸ exile

EXILING ▸ exile

EXILITY n poverty or meagreness

EXINE n outermost coat of a pollen grain or a spore

EXINES ▸ exine

EXING ▸ ex

EXIST vb have being or reality

EXISTED ▸ exist

EXISTS ▸ exist

EXIT n way out ▷ vb go out

EXITED ▸ exit

EXITING ▸ exit

EXITS ▸ exit

EXO informal word for > **excellent**

> Exo is an informal Australian way of saying excellent. This is a great little word as it allows you to combine X with two of the most common tiles in the game, E and O.

EXOCARP same as ▸ **epicarp**

EXODE n exodus

EXODERM same as > **ectoderm**

EXODES ▸ exode

EXODIC ▸ exode

EXODIST ▸ exodus

EXODOI ▸ exodos

EXODOS n processional song performed at the end of a play

EXODUS n departure of a large number of people

EXOGAMY n custom or an act of marrying a person belonging to another tribe, clan, or similar social unit

EXOGEN n plant with a stem that develops through the growth of new layers on its outside

EXOGENS ▸ exogen

EXOMION same as ▸ **exomis**

EXOMIS n sleeveless jacket

EXON n one of the four officers who command the Yeomen of the Guard

EXONIC ▸ exon

EXONS ▸ exon

EXONYM n name given to a place by foreigners

EXONYMS ▸ exonym

EXOPOD same as > **exopodite**

EXOPODS ▸ exopod

EXORDIA ▸ exordium

EXOSMIC > **exosmosis**

EXOTIC adj having a strange allure or beauty ▷ n non-native plant

EXOTICA pl n (collection of) exotic objects

EXOTICS ▸ exotic

EXOTISM ▸ exotic

EXPAND vb make or become larger

EXPANDS ▸ expand

EXPANSE n uninterrupted wide area

EXPAT n short for

EXPATS ▸ expat

EXPECT vb regard as probable

EXPECTS ▸ expect

EXPEL vb drive out with force

EXPELS ▸ expel

EXPEND vb spend, use up

EXPENDS ▸ expend

EXPENSE n cost

EXPERT n person with extensive skill or knowledge in a particular field ▷ adj skilful or knowledgeable ▷ vb experience

EXPERTS ▸ expert

EXPIATE vb make amends for

EXPIRE vb finish or run out

EXPIRED ▸ expire

EXPIRER ▸ expire
EXPIRES ▸ expire
EXPIRY n end, esp of a contract period
EXPLAIN vb make clear and intelligible
EXPLANT vb transfer (living tissue) from its natural site to a new site or to a culture medium ▷ n piece of tissue treated in this way
EXPLODE vb burst with great violence, blow up
EXPLOIT vb take advantage of for one's own purposes ▷ n notable feat or deed
EXPLORE vb investigate
EXPO n exposition, large public exhibition
EXPORT n selling or shipping of goods to a foreign country ▷ vb sell or ship (goods) to a foreign country
EXPORTS ▸ export
EXPOS ▸ expo
EXPOSAL ▸ expose
EXPOSE vb uncover or reveal ▷ n bringing of a crime, scandal, etc to public notice
EXPOSED adj not concealed
EXPOSER ▸ expose
EXPOSES ▸ expose
EXPOSIT vb state
EXPOUND vb explain in detail
EXPRESS vb put into words ▷ adj explicitly stated ▷ n fast train or bus stopping at only a few stations ▷ adv by express delivery
EXPUGN vb storm
EXPUGNS ▸ expugn
EXPULSE vb expel
EXPUNCT vb expunge
EXPUNGE vb delete, erase, blot out
EXPURGE vb purge
EXSCIND vb cut off or out
EXSECT vb cut out
EXSECTS ▸ exsect
EXSERT vb thrust out ▷ adj protruded, stretched out, or (esp of stamens) projecting beyond the corolla of a flower
EXSERTS ▸ exsert
EXTANT adj still existing
EXTASY same as ▸ ecstasy
EXTATIC same as ▸ ecstatic
EXTEND vb draw out or be drawn out, stretch

EXTENDS ▸ extend
EXTENSE adj extensive
EXTENT n range over which something extends, area
EXTENTS ▸ extent
EXTERN n person, such as a physician at a hospital, who has an official connection with an institution but does not reside in it
EXTERNE same as ▸ extern
EXTERNS ▸ extern
EXTINCT adj having died out ▷ vb extinguish
EXTINE same as ▸ exine
EXTINES ▸ extine
EXTIRP vb extirpate
EXTIRPS ▸ extirp
EXTOL vb praise highly
EXTOLD archaic past participle of ▸ extol
EXTOLL same as ▸ extol
EXTOLLS ▸ extoll
EXTOLS ▸ extol
EXTORT vb get (something) by force or threats
EXTORTS ▸ extort
EXTRA adj more than is usual, expected or needed ▷ n additional person or thing ▷ adv unusually or exceptionally
EXTRACT vb pull out by force ▷ n something extracted, such as a passage from a book etc
EXTRAIT n extracts
EXTRAS ▸ extra
EXTREAT n extraction
EXTREMA ▸ extremum
EXTREME adj of a high or the highest degree or intensity ▷ n either of the two limits of a scale or range
EXTRUDE vb squeeze or force out
EXUDATE same as ▸ exudation
EXUDE vb (of a liquid or smell) seep or flow out slowly and steadily
EXUDED ▸ exude
EXUDES ▸ exude
EXUDING ▸ exude
EXUL n exile
EXULS ▸ exul
EXULT vb be joyful or jubilant
EXULTED ▸ exult
EXULTS ▸ exult
EXURB n residential area beyond suburbs

EXURBAN ▸ exurbia
EXURBIA n region outside the suburbs of a city, consisting of residential areas that are occupied predominantly by rich commuters
EXURBS ▸ exurb
EXUVIA n cast-off exoskeleton of animal
EXUVIAE ▸ exuvia
EXUVIAL ▸ exuvia
EXUVIUM n cast-off exoskeleton of animal
EYALET n province of Ottoman Empire
EYALETS ▸ eyalet
EYAS n nestling hawk or falcon, esp one reared for training in falconry
EYASES ▸ eyas
EYASS same as ▸ eyas
EYASSES ▸ eyass
EYE n organ of sight ▷ vb look at carefully or warily
EYEABLE adj pleasant to look at
EYEBALL n ball-shaped part of the eye ▷ vb eye
EYEBANK n place in which corneas are stored for use in corneal grafts
EYEBAR n bar with flattened ends with holes for connecting pins
EYEBARS ▸ eyebar
EYEBATH same as ▸ eyecup
EYEBEAM n glance
EYEBOLT n threaded bolt, the head of which is formed into a ring or eye for lifting, pulling, or securing
EYEBROW n line of hair on the bony ridge above the eye ▷ vb equip with artificial eyebrows
EYECUP same as ▸ eyebath
EYECUPS ▸ eyecup
EYED ▸ eye
EYEFOLD n fold of skin above eye
EYEFUL n view
EYEFULS ▸ eyeful
EYEHOLE n hole through which something, such as a rope, hook, or bar, is passed
EYEHOOK n hook attached to a ring at the extremity of a rope or chain
EYEING ▸ eye
EYELASH n short hair that grows out from the eyelid
EYELESS ▸ eye

E

E

EYELET *n* small hole for a lace or cord to be passed through ▷ *vb* supply with an eyelet or eyelets

EYELETS ▸ **eyelet**

EYELIAD *same as* > **oeillade**

EYELID *n* fold of skin that covers the eye when it is closed

EYELIDS ▸ **eyelid**

EYELIFT *n* cosmetic surgery for eyes

EYELIKE ▸ **eye**

EYEN *pl n* eyes

EYER *n* someone who eyes

EYERS ▸ **eyer**

EYES ▸ **eye**

EYESHOT *n* range of vision

EYESOME *adj* attractive

EYESORE *n* ugly object

EYESPOT *n* small area of light-sensitive pigment in some protozoans, algae, and other simple organisms

EYEWASH *n* nonsense

EYEWEAR *n* spectacles; glasses

EYEWINK *n* wink of the eye; instant

EYING ▸ **eye**

EYLIAD *same as* > **oeillade**

EYLIADS ▸ **eyliad**

EYNE *poetic plural of* ▸ **eye**

EYOT *n* island

EYOTS ▸ **eyot**

EYRA *n* reddish-brown variety of the jaguarondi

EYRAS ▸ **eyra**

EYRE *n* any of the circuit courts held in each shire from 1176 until the late 13th century

EYRES ▸ **eyre**

EYRIE *n* nest of an eagle

EYRIES ▸ **eyrie**

EYRIR *n* Icelandic monetary unit worth one hundredth of a krona

EYRY *same as* ▸ **eyrie**

Ff

F is a useful letter in Scrabble: it begins three two-letter words (**fa**, **fe** and **fy**). There are also quite a few words that combine **F** with **X** or **Z**, allowing high scores, particularly if you can hit a bonus square with them. **Fax**, **fix** and **fox** are good examples (13 points each), and don't forget **fez** and **fiz** (15 points each). **Fay**, **fey**, **fly**, **foy** and **fry** can also be useful (9 each).

F

FA same as ▸ **fah**
FAA Scots word for ▸ **fall**
FAAING ▸ **faa**
FAAN ▸ **faa**
FAAS ▸ **faa**
FAB adj excellent ▸ n fabrication
FABBER ▸ **fab**
FABBEST ▸ **fab**
FABBIER ▸ **fabby**
FABBY same as ▸ **fab** adj
FABLE n story with a moral ▸ vb relate or tell (fables)
FABLED adj made famous in legend
FABLER ▸ **fable**
FABLERS ▸ **fable**
FABLES ▸ **fable**
FABLIAU n comic usually ribald verse tale, of a kind popular in France in the 12th and 13th centuries
FABLING ▸ **fable**
FABRIC n knitted or woven cloth ▸ vb to build
FABRICS ▸ **fabric**
FABS ▸ **fab**
FABULAR adj relating to fables
FACADE n front of a building
FACADES ▸ **facade**
FACE n front of the head ▸ vb look or turn towards
FACEBAR n wrestling hold in which a wrestler stretches the skin on his opponent's face backwards
FACED ▸ **face**
FACEMAN n miner who works at the coalface
FACEMEN ▸ **faceman**
FACER n difficulty or problem
FACERS ▸ **facer**

FACES ▸ **face**
FACET n aspect ▸ vb cut facets in (a gemstone)
FACETE adj witty and humorous
FACETED ▸ **facet**
FACETS ▸ **facet**
FACEUP adj with the face or surface exposed
FACIA same as ▸ **fascia**
FACIAE ▸ **facia**
FACIAL adj of or relating to the face ▸ n beauty treatment for the face
FACIALS ▸ **facial**
FACIAS ▸ **facia**
FACIEND n multiplicand
FACIES n general form and appearance of an individual or a group of plants or animals
FACILE adj (of a remark, argument, etc) superficial and showing lack of real thought
FACING n lining or covering for decoration or reinforcement
FACINGS ▸ **facing**
FACONNE adj denoting a fabric with the design woven in ▸ n such a fabric
FACT n event or thing known to have happened or existed
FACTFUL ▸ **fact**
FACTICE n soft rubbery material made by reacting sulphur or sulphur chloride with vegetable oil
FACTION n (dissenting) minority group within a larger body
FACTIS same as ▸ **factice**

FACTIVE adj (of a linguistic context) giving rise to the presupposition that a sentence occurring in that context is true, as John regrets that Mary did not attend
FACTOID n piece of unreliable information believed to be true because of the way it is presented or repeated in print
FACTOR n element contributing to a result ▸ vb engage in the business of a factor
FACTORS ▸ **factor**
FACTORY n building where goods are manufactured
FACTS ▸ **fact**
FACTUAL adj concerning facts rather than opinions or theories
FACTUM n something done, deed
FACTUMS ▸ **factum**
FACTURE n construction
FACULA n any of the bright areas on the sun's surface, usually appearing just before a sunspot and subject to the same 11-year cycle
FACULAE ▸ **facula**
FACULAR ▸ **facula**
FACULTY n physical or mental ability
FAD n short-lived fashion
FADABLE ▸ **fade**
FADAISE n silly remark
FADDIER ▸ **faddy**
FADDISH ▸ **fad**
FADDISM ▸ **fad**
FADDIST ▸ **fad**

FADDLE vb mess around, toy with
FADDLED ▸ faddle
FADDLES ▸ faddle
FADDY adj unreasonably fussy, particularly about food
FADE vb (cause to) lose brightness, colour, or strength ▷ n act or an instance of fading
FADED ▸ fade
FADEDLY ▸ fade
FADEIN n gradual appearance of image on film
FADEINS ▸ fadein
FADEOUT n gradual disappearance of image on film
FADER ▸ fade
FADERS ▸ fade
FADES ▸ fade
FADEUR n blandness, insipidness
FADEURS ▸ fadeur
FADGE vb agree ▷ n package of wool in a wool-bale that weighs less than 100 kilograms
FADGED ▸ fadge
FADGES ▸ fadge
FADGING ▸ fadge
FADIER ▸ fady
FADIEST ▸ fady
FADING n variation in the strength of received radio signals due to variations in the conditions of the transmission medium
FADINGS ▸ fading
FADLIKE ▸ fad
FADO n type of melancholy Portuguese folk song
FADOS ▸ fado
FADS ▸ fad
FADY adj faded
FAE Scots word for ▸ from
FAECAL adj of, relating to, or consisting of faeces
FAECES pl n waste matter discharged from the anus
FAENA n matador's final series of passes with sword and cape before the kill
FAENAS ▸ faena
FAERIE n land of fairies
FAERIES ▸ faery
FAERY same as ▸ faerie
FAFF vb dither or fuss
FAFFED ▸ faff
FAFFING ▸ faff
FAFFS ▸ faff

FAG same as ▸ faggot
FAGGED ▸ fag
FAGGING ▸ fag
FAGGOT n ball of chopped liver, herbs, and bread ▷ vb collect into a bundle or bundles
FAGGOTS ▸ faggot
FAGIN n criminal
FAGINS ▸ fagin
FAGOT same as ▸ faggot
FAGOTED ▸ fagot
FAGOTER ▸ fagot
FAGOTS ▸ fagot
FAGOTTI ▸ fagotto
FAGOTTO n bassoon
FAGS ▸ fag
FAH n (in tonic sol-fa) fourth degree of any major scale
FAHLERZ n copper ore
FAHLORE n copper ore
FAHS ▸ fah
FAIBLE same as ▸ foible
FAIBLES ▸ faible
FAIENCE n tin-glazed earthenware
FAIK vb grasp
FAIKED ▸ faik
FAIKES ▸ faik
FAIKING ▸ faik
FAIKS ▸ faik
FAIL vb be unsuccessful ▷ n instance of not passing an exam or test
FAILED ▸ fail
FAILING n weak point ▷ prep in the absence of
FAILLE n soft light ribbed fabric of silk, rayon, or taffeta
FAILLES ▸ faille
FAILS ▸ fail
FAILURE n act or instance of failing
FAIN adv gladly ▷ adj willing or eager
FAINE same as ▸ fain
FAINED ▸ fain
FAINER ▸ fain
FAINES ▸ faine
FAINEST ▸ fain
FAINING ▸ fain
FAINLY ▸ fain
FAINNE n small ring-shaped metal badge worn by advocates of the Irish language
FAINNES ▸ fainne
FAINS same as > fainites
FAINT adj lacking clarity, brightness, or volume ▷ vb lose consciousness temporarily ▷ n temporary

loss of consciousness
FAINTED ▸ faint
FAINTER ▸ faint
FAINTLY ▸ faint
FAINTS ▸ faint
FAINTY ▸ faint
FAIR adj unbiased and reasonable ▷ adv fairly ▷ n travelling entertainment with sideshows, rides, and amusements ▷ vb join together so as to form a smooth or regular shape or surface
FAIRED ▸ fair
FAIRER ▸ fair
FAIREST ▸ fair
FAIRIES ▸ fairy
FAIRILY ▸ fairy
FAIRING n curved metal structure fitted round part of a car, aircraft, etc to reduce drag
FAIRISH adj moderately good, well, etc
FAIRLY adv moderately
FAIRS ▸ fair
FAIRWAY n smooth area between the tee and the green
FAIRY n imaginary small creature with magic powers
FAITH n strong belief, esp without proof
FAITHED adj having faith or a faith
FAITHER Scots word for ▸ father
FAITHS ▸ faith
FAITOR n traitor, impostor
FAITORS ▸ faitor
FAITOUR n impostor
FAIX interj have faith
FAJITA ▸ fajitas
FAJITAS pl n Mexican dish of soft tortillas wrapped around fried strips of meat or vegetables
FAKE vb cause something not genuine to appear real or more valuable by fraud ▷ n person, thing, or act that is not genuine ▷ adj not genuine
FAKED ▸ fake
FAKEER same as ▸ fakir
FAKEERS ▸ fakeer
FAKER ▸ fake
FAKERS ▸ fake
FAKERY ▸ fake
FAKES ▸ fake

FAKEY *adj, adv* (of a skateboarding or snowboarding manoeuvre) performed with the board facing backwards

FAKIE ▸ **fakey**

FAKIER ▸ **fakey**

FAKIES ▸ **fakie**

FAKIEST ▸ **fakey**

FAKING ▸ **fake**

FAKIR *n* Muslim who spurns worldly possessions

FAKIRS ▸ **fakir**

FALAFEL *n* ball or cake of ground spiced chickpeas, deep-fried and often served with pitta bread

FALAJ *n* kind of irrigation channel in ancient Oman

FALBALA *n* gathered flounce, frill, or ruffle

FALCADE *n* movement of a horse

FALCATE *adj* shaped like a sickle

FALCES ▸ **falx**

FALCON *n* small bird of prey

FALCONS ▸ **falcon**

FALCULA *n* sharp curved claw, esp of a bird

FALDAGE *n* feudal right

FALL *vb* drop from a higher to a lower place through the force of gravity ▸ *n* falling

FALLACY *n* false belief

FALLAL *n* showy ornament, trinket, or article of dress

FALLALS ▸ **fallal**

FALLEN ▸ **fall**

FALLER *n* any device that falls or operates machinery by falling, as in a spinning machine

FALLERS ▸ **faller**

FALLING ▸ **fall**

FALLOFF *n* decline or drop

FALLOUT *n* radioactive particles spread as a result of a nuclear explosion ▸ *vb* disagree and quarrel ▸ *sentence substitute* order to leave a parade or disciplinary formation

FALLOW *adj* (of land) ploughed but left unseeded to regain fertility ▸ *n* land treated in this way ▸ *vb* leave (land) unseeded after ploughing and harrowing it

FALLOWS ▸ **fallow**

FALLS ▸ **fall**

FALSE *adj* not true or correct

▸ *adv* in a false or dishonest manner ▸ *vb* falsify

FALSED ▸ **false**

FALSELY ▸ **false**

FALSER ▸ **false**

FALSERS *n* colloquial term for false teeth

FALSES ▸ **false**

FALSEST ▸ **false**

FALSIE *n* pad used to enlarge breast shape

FALSIES ▸ **falsie**

FALSIFY *vb* alter fraudulently

FALSING ▸ **false**

FALSISH ▸ **false**

FALSISM ▸ **false**

FALSITY *n* state of being false

FALTER *vb* be hesitant, weak, or unsure ▸ *n* uncertainty or hesitancy in speech or action

FALTERS ▸ **falter**

FALX *n* sickle-shaped anatomical structure

FAME *n* state of being widely known or recognized ▸ *vb* make known or famous

FAMED ▸ **fame**

FAMES ▸ **fame**

FAMILLE *n* type of Chinese porcelain

FAMILY *n* group of parents and their children ▸ *adj* suitable for parents and children together

FAMINE *n* severe shortage of food

FAMINES ▸ **famine**

FAMING ▸ **fame**

FAMISH *vb* be or make very hungry or weak

FAMOUS *adj* very well-known ▸ *vb* make famous

FAMULI ▸ **famulus**

FAMULUS *n* (formerly) the attendant of a sorcerer or scholar

FAN *n* hand-held or mechanical object used to create a current of air for ventilation or cooling ▸ *vb* blow or cool with a fan

FANAL *n* lighthouse

FANALS ▸ **fanal**

FANATIC *n* person who is excessively enthusiastic about something ▸ *adj* excessively enthusiastic

FANBASE *n* body of

admirers of a particular pop singer, sports team, etc

FANBOY *n* obsessive fan of a subject or hobby

FANBOYS ▸ **fanboy**

FANCIED *adj* imaginary

FANCIER *n* person who is interested in and often breeds plants or animals

FANCIES ▸ **fancy**

FANCIFY *vb* make more beautiful

FANCILY ▸ **fancy**

FANCY *adj* elaborate, not plain ▸ *n* sudden irrational liking or desire ▸ *vb* be sexually attracted to

FAND *vb* try

FANDED ▸ **fand**

FANDING ▸ **fand**

FANDOM *n* collectively, the fans of a sport, pastime or person

FANDOMS ▸ **fandom**

FANDS ▸ **fand**

FANE *n* temple or shrine

FANEGA *n* Spanish unit of measurement

FANEGAS ▸ **fanega**

FANES ▸ **fane**

FANFARE *n* short loud tune played on brass instruments ▸ *vb* perform a fanfare

FANFIC *n* fiction written around previously established characters invented by other authors

FANFICS ▸ **fanfic**

FANFOLD *vb* fold (paper) like a fan

FANG *n* snake's tooth which injects poison ▸ *vb* seize

FANGA *same as* ▸ **fanega**

FANGAS ▸ **fanga**

FANGED ▸ **fang**

FANGING ▸ **fang**

FANGLE *vb* fashion

FANGLED ▸ **fangle**

FANGLES ▸ **fangle**

FANGO *n* mud from thermal springs in Italy, used in the treatment of rheumatic disease

FANGOS ▸ **fango**

FANGS ▸ **fang**

FANION *n* small flag used by surveyors to mark stations

FANIONS ▸ **fanion**

FANJET *same as* ▸ **turbofan**

FANJETS ▸ **fanjet**

FANK *n* sheep pen

FANKLE *vb* entangle ▸ *n* tangle

FANKLED ▸ fankle
FANKLES ▸ fankle
FANKS ▸ fank
FANLIKE ▸ fan
FANNED ▸ fan
FANNEL n ecclesiastical vestment
FANNELL same as ▸ **fannel**
FANNELS ▸ fannel
FANNER ▸ fan
FANNERS ▸ fan
FANNING ▸ fan
FANO same as ▸ **fanon**
FANON n collar-shaped vestment worn by the pope when celebrating mass
FANONS ▸ fanon
FANOS ▸ fano
FANS ▸ fan
FANSITE n website aimed at fans of a celebrity, film, etc
FANSUB n fan-produced subtitling of films
FANSUBS ▸ fansub
FANTAD n nervous, agitated state
FANTADS ▸ fantad
FANTAIL n small New Zealand bird with a tail like a fan
FANTASM archaic spelling of > **phantasm**
FANTAST n dreamer or visionary
FANTASY n far-fetched notion ▷ adj of a competition in which a participant selects players for an imaginary, ideal team and points are awarded according to the actual performances of the chosen players ▷ vb fantasize
FANTEEG n nervous, agitated state
FANTOD n crotchety or faddish behaviour
FANTODS ▸ fantod
FANTOM archaic spelling of ▸ **phantom**
FANTOMS ▸ fantom
FANUM n temple
FANUMS ▸ fanum
FANWISE adj like a fan
FANWORT n aquatic plant
FANZINE n magazine produced by fans of a specific interest, soccer club, etc, for fellow fans
FAP adj drunk
FAQIR same as ▸ **fakir**

Meaning a Hindu ascetic; this is one of those invaluable words allowing you to play the Q without a U. It can also be spelt **fakeer, fakir** and **faquir**.

FAQIRS ▸ faqir
FAQUIR same as ▸ **faqir**
FAQUIRS ▸ faquir
FAR adv at, to, or from a great distance ▷ adj remote in space or time ▷ vb go far
FARAD n unit of electrical capacitance
FARADAY n quantity of electricity, used in electrochemical calculations
FARADIC adj of or concerned with an intermittent asymmetric alternating current such as that induced in the secondary winding of an induction coil
FARADS ▸ farad
FARAND adj pleasant or attractive in manner or appearance
FARAWAY adj very distant
FARCE n boisterous comedy ▷ vb enliven (a speech, etc) with jokes
FARCED ▸ farce
FARCER same as ▸ **farceur**
FARCERS ▸ farcer
FARCES ▸ farce
FARCEUR n writer of or performer in farces
FARCI adj (of food) stuffed
FARCIE same as ▸ **farci**
FARCIED adj afflicted with farcy
FARCIES ▸ farcy
FARCIFY vb turn into a farce
FARCIN n equine disease
FARCING ▸ farce
FARCINS ▸ farcin
FARCY n form of glanders, a bacterial disease of horses
FARD n paint for the face, esp white paint ▷ vb paint (the face) with fard
FARDAGE n material laid beneath or between cargo
FARDED ▸ fard
FARDEL n bundle or burden
FARDELS ▸ fardel
FARDEN n farthing
FARDENS ▸ farden
FARDING ▸ fard
FARDS ▸ fard

FARE n charge for a passenger's journey ▷ vb get on (as specified)
FAREBOX n box where money for bus fares is placed
FARED ▸ fare
FARER ▸ fare
FARERS ▸ fare
FARES ▸ fare
FARFAL same as ▸ **felafel**
FARFALS ▸ farfal
FARFEL same as ▸ **felafel**
FARFELS same as ▸ **farfel**
FARFET adj far-fetched
FARINA n flour or meal made from any kind of cereal grain
FARINAS ▸ farina
FARING ▸ fare
FARINHA n cassava meal
FARL n thin cake of oatmeal, often triangular in shape
FARLE same as ▸ **farl**
FARLES ▸ farle
FARLS ▸ farl
FARM n area of land for growing crops or rearing livestock ▷ vb cultivate (land)
FARMED adj (of fish or game) reared on a farm rather than caught in the wild
FARMER n person who owns or runs a farm
FARMERS ▸ farmer
FARMERY n farm buildings
FARMING n business or skill of agriculture
FARMOST ▸ far
FARMS ▸ farm
FARNESS ▸ far
FARO n gambling game in which players bet against the dealer on what cards he will turn up
FAROS ▸ faro
FARRAGO n jumbled mixture of things
FARRAND same as ▸ **farand**
FARRANT same as ▸ **farand**
FARRED ▸ far
FARREN n allotted ground
FARRENS ▸ farren
FARRIER n person who shoes horses
FARRING ▸ far
FARROW n litter of piglets ▷ vb (of a sow) give birth ▷ adj (of a cow) not calving in a given year

FARROWS ▸ farrow
FARRUCA n flamenco dance performed by men
FARS ▸ far
FARSE vb insert into
FARSED ▸ farse
FARSES ▸ farse
FARSIDE n part of the Moon facing away from the Earth
FARSING ▸ farse
FARTHEL same as ▸ **farl**
FARTHER ▸ far
FARTLEK n in sport, another name for interval training
FAS ▸ fa
FASCES pl n (in ancient Rome) a bundle of rods containing an axe with its blade pointing out
FASCI ▸ fascio
FASCIA n outer surface of a dashboard
FASCIAE ▸ fascia
FASCIAL ▸ fascia
FASCIAS ▸ fascia
FASCINE n bundle of long sticks used for filling in ditches and in the construction of embankments, roads, fortifications, etc
FASCIO n political group
FASCIS ▸ fasces
FASCISM n right-wing totalitarian political system characterized by state control and extreme nationalism
FASCIST n adherent or practitioner of fascism ▷ adj characteristic of or relating to fascism
FASH n worry ▷ vb trouble
FASHED ▸ fash
FASHERY n difficulty, trouble
FASHES ▸ fash
FASHING ▸ fash
FASHION n style in clothes, hairstyle, etc, popular at a particular time ▷ vb form or make into a particular shape
FAST adj (capable of) acting or moving quickly ▷ adv quickly ▷ vb go without food, esp for religious reasons ▷ n period of fasting
FASTED ▸ fast
FASTEN vb make or become firmly fixed or joined

FASTENS ▸ fasten
FASTER ▸ fast
FASTERS ▸ fast
FASTEST ▸ fast
FASTI pl n in ancient Rome, days when business could legally be carried out
FASTIE n deceitful act
FASTIES ▸ fastie
FASTING ▸ fast
FASTISH ▸ fast
FASTLY ▸ fast
FASTS ▸ fast
FAT adj having excess flesh on the body ▷ n extra flesh on the body
FATAL adj causing death or ruin
FATALLY adv resulting in death or disaster
FATBACK n fat, usually salted, from the upper part of a side of pork
FATBIRD n nocturnal bird
FATE n power supposed to predetermine events ▷ vb predetermine
FATED adj destined
FATEFUL adj having important, usu disastrous, consequences
FATES ▸ fate
FATHEAD n stupid person
FATHER n male parent ▷ vb be the father of (offspring)
FATHERS ▸ father
FATHOM n unit of length, used in navigation, equal to six feet (1.83 metres) ▷ vb understand
FATHOMS ▸ fathom
FATIDIC adj prophetic
FATIGUE n extreme physical or mental tiredness ▷ vb tire out
FATING ▸ fate
FATLESS ▸ fat
FATLIKE ▸ fat
FATLING n young farm animal fattened for killing
FATLY ▸ fat
FATNESS ▸ fat
FATS ▸ fat
FATSIA n type of shrub with large deeply palmate leaves and umbels of white flowers
FATSIAS ▸ fatsia
FATTED ▸ fat
FATTEN vb (cause to) become fat
FATTENS ▸ fatten
FATTER ▸ fat

FATTEST ▸ fat
FATTIER ▸ fatty
FATTIES ▸ fatty
FATTILY ▸ fatty
FATTING ▸ fat
FATTISH ▸ fat
FATTISM n discrimination on the basis of weight, esp prejudice against those considered to be overweight
FATTIST ▸ fattism
FATTY adj containing fat ▷ n fat person
FATUITY n foolish thoughtlessness
FATUOUS adj foolish
FATWA n religious decree issued by a Muslim leader ▷ vb issue a fatwa
FATWAH same as ▸ **fatwa**
FATWAHS ▸ fatwah
FATWAS ▸ fatwa
FATWOOD n wood used for kindling
FAUCAL adj of or relating to the fauces
FAUCALS ▸ faucal
FAUCES n area between the cavity of the mouth and the pharynx, including the surrounding tissues
FAUCET n tap
FAUCETS ▸ faucet
FAUCHON same as > **fauchion**
FAUCIAL same as ▸ **faucal**
FAUGH interj exclamation of disgust, scorn, etc
FAULD n piece of armour
FAULDS ▸ fauld
FAULT n responsibility for something wrong ▷ vb criticize or blame
FAULTED ▸ fault
FAULTS ▸ fault
FAULTY adj badly designed or not working properly
FAUN n (in Roman legend) creature with a human face and torso and a goat's horns and legs
FAUNA n animals of a given place or time
FAUNAE ▸ fauna
FAUNAL ▸ fauna
FAUNAS ▸ fauna
FAUNIST ▸ fauna
FAUNS ▸ fauna
FAUNULA n fauna of a small single environment
FAUNULE same as ▸ **faunula**
FAUR Scots word for ▸ **far**

FAURD adj favoured

FAURER ▸ faur

FAUREST ▸ faur

FAUT Scots word for ▸ fault

FAUTED ▸ faut

FAUTING ▸ faut

FAUTOR n patron

FAUTORS ▸ fautor

FAUTS ▸ faut

FAUVE adj of the style of the Fauve art movement ▷ n member of the Fauve art movement

FAUVES ▸ fauve

FAUVISM ▸ fauve

FAUVIST n artist following the Fauve style of painting

FAUX adj false

FAVA n type of bean

FAVAS ▸ fava

FAVE short for > favourite

FAVEL adj (of a horse) dun-coloured

FAVELA n (in Brazil) a shanty or shantytown

FAVELAS ▸ favela

FAVELL same as ▸ favel

FAVELLA n group of spores

FAVER ▸ fave

FAVES ▸ fave

FAVEST ▸ fave

FAVICON n icon displayed before a website's URL

FAVISM n type of anaemia

FAVISMS ▸ favism

FAVOR same as ▸ favour

FAVORED ▸ favor

FAVORER ▸ favour

FAVORS same as ▸ favours

FAVOSE same as > faveolate

FAVOUR n approving attitude ▷ vb prefer

FAVOURS pl n sexual intimacy, as when consented to by a woman

FAVOUS adj resembling honeycomb

FAVRILE n type of iridescent glass

FAVUS n infectious fungal skin disease of man and some domestic animals, characterized by formation of a honeycomb-like mass of roundish dry cup-shaped crusts

FAVUSES ▸ favus

FAW n gypsy

> A **faw** is a gypsy, a good word for taking advantage of a nearby bonus square.

FAWN n young deer ▷ adj light yellowish-brown ▷ vb seek attention from (someone) by insincere flattery

FAWNED ▸ fawn

FAWNER ▸ fawn

FAWNERS ▸ fawn

FAWNIER ▸ fawny

FAWNING ▸ fawn

FAWNS ▸ fawn

FAWNY adj of a fawn colour

FAWS ▸ faw

FAX n electronic system for sending facsimiles of documents by telephone ▷ vb send (a document) by this system

FAXED ▸ fax

FAXES ▸ fax

FAXING ▸ fax

FAY n fairy or sprite ▷ adj of or resembling a fay ▷ vb fit or be fitted closely or tightly

> A **fay** is a fairy but it can also be a verb, meaning to fit closely. It has a variant **fey**. Both are useful high-scoring short words.

FAYED ▸ fay

FAYENCE same as ▸ faience

FAYER ▸ fay

FAYEST ▸ fay

FAYING ▸ fay

FAYNE vb pretend

FAYNED ▸ fayne

FAYNES ▸ fayne

FAYNING ▸ fayne

FAYRE pseudo-archaic spelling of ▸ fair

FAYRES ▸ fayre

FAYS ▸ fay

FAZE vb disconcert or fluster

FAZED adj worried or disconcerted

FAZENDA n large estate or ranch

FAZES ▸ faze

FAZING ▸ faze

FE n variant of Hebrew letter pe, transliterated as f

FEAGUE vb whip or beat

FEAGUED ▸ feague

FEAGUES ▸ feague

FEAL vb conceal

FEALED ▸ feal

FEALING ▸ feal

FEALS ▸ feal

FEALTY n (in feudal society) subordinate's loyalty to his ruler or lord

FEAR n distress or alarm caused by impending danger or pain ▷ vb be afraid of (something or someone)

FEARE n companion, spouse

FEARED ▸ fear

FEARER ▸ fear

FEARERS ▸ fear

FEARES ▸ feare

FEARFUL adj feeling fear

FEARING ▸ fear

FEARS ▸ fear

FEART adj (Scots) afraid

FEASE vb perform an act

FEASED ▸ fease

FEASES ▸ fease

FEASING ▸ fease

FEAST n lavish meal ▷ vb eat a feast

FEASTED ▸ feast

FEASTER ▸ feast

FEASTS ▸ feast

FEAT n remarkable, skilful, or daring action

FEATED ▸ feat

FEATER ▸ feat

FEATEST ▸ feat

FEATHER n one of the barbed shafts forming the plumage of birds ▷ vb fit or cover with feathers

FEATING ▸ feat

FEATLY ▸ feat

FEATOUS same as > feateous

FEATS ▸ feat

FEATURE n part of the face, such as the eyes ▷ vb have as a feature or be a feature in

FEAZE same as ▸ feeze

FEAZED ▸ feaze

FEAZES ▸ feaze

FEAZING ▸ feaze

FEBRILE adj very active and nervous

FECAL same as ▸ faecal

FECES same as ▸ faeces

FECHT Scots word for ▸ fight

FECHTER ▸ fecht

FECHTS ▸ fecht

FECIAL adj heraldic

FECIALS ▸ fecial

FECIT vb (he or she) made it: used formerly on works of art next to the artist's name

FECULA n starch obtained by washing the crushed parts of plants, such as the potato

FECULAE ▸ fecula

FECULAS ▸ fecula

FECUND adj fertile

FED n FBI agent

FEDARIE n accomplice

FEDAYEE n (in Arab states) a commando, esp one fighting against Israel

FEDERAL adj of a system in which power is divided between one central government and several regional governments ▷ n supporter of federal union or federation

FEDEX vb send by FedEx

FEDEXED ▸ fedex

FEDEXES ▸ fedex

FEDORA n man's soft hat with a brim

FEDORAS ▸ fedora

FEDS ▸ fed

FEE n charge paid to be allowed to do something ▷ vb pay a fee to

FEEB n contemptible person

FEEBLE adj lacking physical or mental power ▷ vb make feeble

FEEBLED ▸ feeble

FEEBLER ▸ feeble

FEEBLES ▸ feeble

FEEBLY ▸ feeble

FEEBS ▸ feeb

FEED vb give food to ▷ n act of feeding

FEEDBAG n any bag in which feed for livestock is sacked

FEEDBOX n trough, manger

FEEDER n baby's bib

FEEDERS ▸ feeder

FEEDING ▸ feed

FEEDLOT n area or building where livestock are fattened rapidly for market

FEEDS ▸ feed

FEEING ▸ fee

FEEL vb have a physical or emotional sensation of ▷ n act of feeling

FEELBAD n something inducing depression

FEELER n organ of touch in some animals

FEELERS ▸ feeler

FEELESS ▸ fee

FEELING ▸ feel

FEELS ▸ feel

FEEN n in Irish dialect, an informal word for 'man'

FEENS ▸ feen

FEER vb make a furrow

FEERED ▸ feer

FEERIE n fairyland

FEERIES ▸ feerie

FEERIN n furrow

FEERING ▸ feer

FEERINS ▸ feerin

FEERS ▸ feer

FEES ▸ fee

FEESE vb perturb

FEESED ▸ feese

FEESES ▸ feese

FEESING ▸ feese

FEET ▸ foot

FEEZE vb beat ▷ n rush

FEEZED ▸ feeze

FEEZES ▸ feeze

FEEZING ▸ feeze

FEG same as ▸ fig

FEGARY same as ▸ vagary

FEGS ▸ feg

FEH ▸ fe

FEHM n medieval German court

FEHME ▸ fehm

FEHMIC ▸ fehm

FEHS ▸ feh

FEIGN vb pretend

FEIGNED ▸ feign

FEIGNER ▸ feign

FEIGNS ▸ feign

FEIJOA n evergreen myrtaceous shrub of S America

FEIJOAS ▸ feijoa

FEINT n sham attack or blow meant to distract an opponent ▷ vb make a feint ▷ adj printing term meaning ruled with faint lines

FEINTED ▸ feint

FEINTER ▸ feint

FEINTS pl n leavings of the second distillation of Scotch malt whisky

FEIRIE adj nimble

FEIRIER ▸ feirie

FEIS n Irish music and dance festival

FEIST n small aggressive dog

FEISTS ▸ feist

FEISTY adj showing courage or spirit

FELAFEL same as ▸ falafel

FELICIA n type of African herb

FELID n any animal belonging to the cat family

FELIDS ▸ felid

FELINE adj of cats ▷ n member of the cat family

FELINES ▸ feline

FELL vb cut or knock down ▷ adj cruel or deadly

FELLA nonstandard variant of ▸ fellow

FELLAH n peasant in Arab countries

FELLAHS ▸ fellah

FELLAS ▸ fella

FELLATE vb perform fellatio on (a person)

FELLED ▸ fell

FELLER n person or thing that fells

FELLERS ▸ feller

FELLEST ▸ fell

FELLIES ▸ felly

FELLING ▸ fell

FELLOE n (segment of) the rim of a wheel

FELLOES ▸ felloe

FELLOW n man or boy ▷ adj in the same group or condition

FELLOWS ▸ fellow

FELLS ▸ fell

FELLY same as ▸ felloe

FELON n (formerly) person guilty of a felony ▷ adj evil

FELONRY n felons collectively

FELONS ▸ felon

FELONY n serious crime

FELSIC adj relating to igneous rock

FELSITE n any fine-grained igneous rock consisting essentially of quartz and feldspar

FELSPAR same as ▸ feldspar

FELT n matted fabric ▷ vb become matted

FELTED ▸ felt

FELTER vb mat together

FELTERS ▸ felter

FELTIER ▸ felt

FELTING n felted material

FELTS ▸ felt

FELTY ▸ felt

FELUCCA n narrow lateen-rigged vessel of the Mediterranean

FELWORT n type of plant of Europe and SW China with purple flowers and rosettes of leaves

FEM n passive homosexual

FEMAL adj effeminate ▷ n effeminate person

FEMALE adj of the sex which bears offspring ▷ n female person or animal

FEMALES ▸ female

FEMALS ▸ femal

FEME n woman or wife

FEMES ▸ feme

FEMINAL adj feminine, female

FEMINIE n women collectively

FEMITER same as > **fumitory**

FEMME n woman or wife

FEMMES ▸ **femme**

FEMMIER ▸ **femmy**

FEMMY adj markedly or exaggeratedly feminine in appearance, manner, etc

FEMORA ▸ **femur**

FEMORAL adj of the thigh

FEMS ▸ **fem**

FEMUR n thighbone

FEMURS ▸ **femur**

FEN n low-lying flat marshy land

FENAGLE same as ▸ **finagle**

FENCE n barrier of posts linked by wire or wood, enclosing an area ▷ vb enclose with or as if with a fence

FENCED ▸ **fence**

FENCER n person who fights with a sword, esp one who practises the art of fencing

FENCERS ▸ **fencer**

FENCES ▸ **fence**

FENCING n sport of fighting with swords

FEND vb give support (to someone, esp oneself) ▷ n shift or effort

FENDED ▸ **fend**

FENDER n low metal frame in front of a fireplace

FENDERS ▸ **fender**

FENDIER ▸ **fendy**

FENDING ▸ **fend**

FENDS ▸ **fend**

FENDY adj thrifty

FENI n Goan alcoholic drink

FENIS ▸ **feni**

FENITAR same as > **fumitory**

FENKS n whale blubber

FENLAND ▸ **fen**

FENMAN ▸ **fen**

FENMEN ▸ **fen**

FENNEC n type of very small nocturnal desert fox of N Africa and Arabia, with pale fur and enormous ears

FENNECS ▸ **fennec**

FENNEL n fragrant plant whose seeds, leaves, and root are used in cookery

FENNELS ▸ **fennel**

FENNIER ▸ **fenny**

FENNIES ▸ **fenny**

FENNISH ▸ **fen**

FENNY adj boggy or marshy ▷ n feni

FENS ▸ **fen**

FENT n piece of waste fabric

FENTS ▸ **fent**

FENURON n type of herbicide

FEOD same as ▸ **feud**

FEODAL ▸ **feod**

FEODARY ▸ **feod**

FEODS ▸ **feod**

FEOFF same as ▸ **fief**

FEOFFED ▸ **feoff**

FEOFFEE n (in feudal society) a vassal granted a fief by his lord

FEOFFER ▸ **feoff**

FEOFFOR ▸ **feoff**

FEOFFS ▸ **feoff**

FER same as ▸ **far**

FERAL adj wild ▷ n person who displays such tendencies and appearance

FERALS ▸ **feral**

FERBAM n black slightly water-soluble fluffy powder used as a fungicide

FERBAMS ▸ **ferbam**

FERE n companion ▷ adj fierce

FERER ▸ **fere**

FERES ▸ **fere**

FEREST ▸ **fere**

FERIA n weekday, other than Saturday, on which no feast occurs

FERIAE ▸ **feria**

FERIAL adj of or relating to a feria

FERIAS ▸ **feria**

FERINE same as ▸ **feral**

FERITY ▸ **feral**

FERLIE same as ▸ **ferly**

FERLIED ▸ **ferly**

FERLIER ▸ **ferly**

FERLIES ▸ **ferly**

FERLY adj wonderful ▷ n wonder ▷ vb wonder

FERM same as ▸ **farm**

FERMATA another word for ▸ **pause**

FERMATE ▸ **fermata**

FERMENT n any agent that causes fermentation ▷ vb (cause to) undergo fermentation

FERMI n unit of length used in nuclear physics equal to 10^{-15} metre

FERMION n any of a group of elementary particles, such as a nucleon, that has half-integral spin and obeys

Fermi-Dirac statistics

FERMIS ▸ **fermi**

FERMIUM n element artificially produced by neutron bombardment of plutonium

FERMS ▸ **ferm**

FERN n flowerless plant with fine fronds

FERNERY n place where ferns are grown

FERNIER ▸ **fern**

FERNING n production of a fern-like pattern

FERNS ▸ **fern**

FERNY ▸ **fern**

FERRATE n type of salt

FERREL same as ▸ **ferrule**

FERRELS ▸ **ferrel**

FERRET n tamed polecat used to catch rabbits or rats ▷ vb hunt with ferrets

FERRETS ▸ **ferret**

FERRETY ▸ **ferret**

FERRIC adj of or containing iron

FERRIED ▸ **ferry**

FERRIES ▸ **ferry**

FERRITE n any of a group of ferromagnetic highly resistive ceramic compounds

FERROUS adj of or containing iron in the divalent state

FERRUGO n disease affecting plants

FERRULE n metal cap to strengthen the end of a stick ▷ vb equip (a stick, etc) with a ferrule

FERRUM Latin word for ▸ **iron**

FERRUMS ▸ **ferrum**

FERRY n boat for transporting people and vehicles ▷ vb carry by ferry

FERTILE adj capable of producing young, crops, or vegetation

FERULA n large Mediterranean plant with thick stems and dissected leaves, cultivated for its strongly-scented gum resin

FERULAE ▸ **ferula**

FERULAS ▸ **ferula**

FERULE same as ▸ **ferrule**

FERULED ▸ **ferule**

FERULES ▸ **ferule**

FERVENT adj intensely passionate and sincere

FERVID same as ▸ **fervent**

FERVOR same as ▸ **fervour**

FERVORS ▸ **fervor**

FERVOUR n intensity of feeling

FES ▸ **fe**

FESCUE n pasture and lawn grass with stiff narrow leaves

FESCUES ▸ **fescue**

FESS same as ▸ **fesse**

FESSE n ordinary consisting of a horizontal band across a shield, conventionally occupying a third of its length and being wider than a bar

FESSED ▸ **fess**

FESSES ▸ **fesse**

FESSING ▸ **fess**

FEST n event at which the emphasis is on a particular activity

FESTA n festival

FESTAL adj festive ▷ n festivity

FESTALS ▸ **festal**

FESTAS ▸ **festa**

FESTER vb grow worse and increasingly hostile ▷ n small ulcer or sore containing pus

FESTERS ▸ **fester**

FESTIER ▸ **festy**

FESTIVE adj of or like a celebration

FESTOON vb hang decorations in loops ▷ n decorative chain of flowers or ribbons suspended in loops

FESTS ▸ **fest**

FESTY adj dirty

FET vb fetch

FETA n white salty Greek cheese

FETAL adj of, relating to, or resembling a fetus

FETAS ▸ **feta**

FETCH vb go after and bring back ▷ n ghost or apparition of a living person

FETCHED ▸ **fetch**

FETCHER n person or animal that fetches

FETCHES ▸ **fetch**

FETE n gala, bazaar, etc, usu held outdoors ▷ vb honour or entertain regally

FETED ▸ **fete**

FETES ▸ **fete**

FETIAL n (in ancient Rome) any of the 20 priestly heralds involved in

declarations of war and in peace negotiations ▷ adj of or relating to the fetiales

FETIALS ▸ **fetial**

FETICH same as ▸ **fetish**

FETICHE same as ▸ **fetich**

FETID adj stinking

FETIDER ▸ **fetid**

FETIDLY ▸ **fetid**

FETING ▸ **fete**

FETISH n form of behaviour in which sexual pleasure is derived from looking at or handling an inanimate object

FETLOCK n projection behind and above a horse's hoof

FETOR n offensive stale or putrid odour

FETORS ▸ **fetor**

FETS ▸ **fet**

FETT same as ▸ **fet**

FETTA same as ▸ **feta**

FETTAS ▸ **fetta**

FETTED ▸ **fet**

FETTER n chain or shackle for the foot ▷ vb restrict

FETTERS ▸ **fetter**

FETTING ▸ **fet**

FETTLE same as ▸ **fettling**

FETTLED ▸ **fettle**

FETTLER n person employed to maintain railway tracks

FETTLES ▸ **fettle**

FETTS ▸ **fett**

FETUS n embryo of a mammal in the later stages of development

FETUSES ▸ **fetus**

FETWA same as ▸ **fatwa**

FETWAS ▸ **fetwa**

FEU n (in Scotland) right of use of land in return for a fixed annual payment

FEUAR n tenant of a feu

FEUARS ▸ **feuar**

FEUD n long bitter hostility between two people or groups ▷ vb carry on a feud

FEUDAL adj of or like feudalism

FEUDARY n holder of land through feudal right

FEUDED ▸ **feud**

FEUDING ▸ **feud**

FEUDIST n person who takes part in a feud or quarrel

FEUDS ▸ **feud**

FEUED ▸ **feu**

FEUING ▸ **feu**

FEUS ▸ **feu**

FEUTRE vb place in a resting position

FEUTRED ▸ **feutre**

FEUTRES ▸ **feutre**

FEVER n (illness causing) high body temperature ▷ vb affect with or as if with fever

FEVERED ▸ **fever**

FEVERS ▸ **fever**

FEW adj not many as in **the few** small number of people considered as a class

FEWER ▸ **few**

FEWEST ▸ **few**

FEWMET same as ▸ **fumet**

FEWMETS ▸ **fewmet**

FEWNESS ▸ **few**

FEWS ▸ **few**

FEWTER same as ▸ **feutre**

FEWTERS ▸ **feutre**

FEY adj whimsically strange ▷ vb clean out

FEYED ▸ **fey**

FEYER ▸ **fey**

FEYEST ▸ **fey**

FEYING ▸ **fey**

FEYLY ▸ **fey**

FEYNESS ▸ **fey**

FEYS ▸ **fey**

FEZ n brimless tasselled cap, orig. from Turkey

FEZES ▸ **fez**

FEZZED adj wearing a fez

FEZZES ▸ **fez**

FEZZY ▸ **fez**

FIACRE n small four-wheeled horse-drawn carriage, usually with a folding roof

FIACRES ▸ **fiacre**

FIANCE n man engaged to be married

FIANCEE n woman who is engaged to be married

FIANCES ▸ **fiance**

FIAR n property owner

FIARS n legally fixed price of corn

FIASCHI ▸ **fiasco**

FIASCO n ridiculous or humiliating failure

FIASCOS ▸ **fiasco**

FIAT n arbitrary order ▷ vb issue a fiat

FIATED ▸ **fiat**

FIATING ▸ **fiat**

FIATS ▸ **fiat**

FIAUNT n fiat

FIAUNTS ▸ **fiaunt**

FIB n trivial lie ▷ vb tell a lie

FIBBED ▸ **fib**

FIBBER ▸ **fib**

F

F

FIBBERS ▸ fib
FIBBERY ▸ fib
FIBBING ▸ fib
FIBER *same as* **▸ fibre**
FIBERED ▸ fibre
FIBERS ▸ fiber
FIBRATE *n* drug used to lower fat levels in the body
FIBRE *n* thread that can be spun into yarn
FIBRED ▸ fibre
FIBRES ▸ fibre
FIBRIL *n* small fibre
FIBRILS ▸ fibril
FIBRIN *n* white insoluble elastic protein formed when blood clots
FIBRINS ▸ fibrin
FIBRO *n* mixture of cement and asbestos fibre, used in sheets for building
FIBROID *adj* (of structures or tissues) containing or resembling fibres ▷ *n* benign tumour composed of fibrous connective tissue
FIBROIN *n* tough elastic protein that is the principal component of spiders' webs and raw silk
FIBROMA *n* benign tumour derived from fibrous connective tissue
FIBROS ▸ fibro
FIBROSE *vb* become fibrous
FIBROUS *adj* consisting of, containing, or resembling fibres
FIBS ▸ fib
FIBSTER *n* fibber
FIBULA *n* slender outer bone of the lower leg
FIBULAE ▸ fibula
FIBULAR ▸ fibula
FIBULAS ▸ fibula
FICE *n* small aggressive dog
FICES ▸ fice
FICHE *n* sheet of film for storing publications in miniaturized form
FICHES ▸ fiche
FICHU *n* woman's shawl or scarf of some light material, worn esp in the 18th century
FICHUS ▸ fichu
FICIN *n* enzyme
FICINS ▸ ficin
FICKLE *adj* changeable, inconstant ▷ *vb* puzzle
FICKLED ▸ fickle
FICKLER ▸ fickle
FICKLES ▸ fickle

FICKLY ▸ fickle
FICO *n* worthless trifle
FICOES ▸ fico
FICOS ▸ fico
FICTILE *adj* moulded or capable of being moulded from clay
FICTION *n* literary works of the imagination, such as novels
FICTIVE *adj* of, relating to, or able to create fiction
FICTOR *n* sculptor
FICTORS ▸ fictor
FICUS *n* type of plant such as the edible fig, often grown as a greenhouse or house plant
FICUSES ▸ ficus
FID *n* spike for separating strands of rope in splicing
FIDDLE *n* violin ▷ *vb* play the violin
FIDDLED ▸ fiddle
FIDDLER *n* person who plays the fiddle
FIDDLES ▸ fiddle
FIDDLEY *n* vertical space above a vessel's engine room extending into its stack
FIDDLY *adj* awkward to do or use
FIDEISM *n* theological doctrine that religious truth is a matter of faith and cannot be established by reason
FIDEIST ▸ fideism
FIDES *n* faith or trust
FIDGE *obsolete word for* **▸ fidget**
FIDGED ▸ fidge
FIDGES ▸ fidge
FIDGET *vb* move about restlessly ▷ *n* person who fidgets
FIDGETS ▸ fidget
FIDGETY ▸ fidget
FIDGING ▸ fidge
FIDIBUS *n* spill for lighting a candle or pipe
FIDO *n* generic term for a dog
FIDOS ▸ fido
FIDS ▸ fid
FIE ▸ fey
FIEF *n* land granted by a lord in return for war service
FIEFDOM *n* (in Feudal Europe) the property owned by a lord
FIEFS ▸ fief

FIELD *n* piece of land, usu enclosed with a fence or hedge, and used for pasture or growing crops ▷ *vb* stop, catch, or return (the ball) as a fielder
FIELDED ▸ field
FIELDER *n* (in certain sports) player whose task is to field the ball
FIELDS ▸ field
FIEND *n* evil spirit
FIENDS ▸ fiend
FIENT *n* fiend
FIENTS ▸ fient
FIER *same as* **▸ fere**
FIERCE *adj* wild or aggressive
FIERCER ▸ fierce
FIERE ▸ fere
FIERES ▸ fere
FIERIER ▸ fiery
FIERILY ▸ fiery
FIERS ▸ fier
FIERY *adj* consisting of or like fire
FIEST ▸ fie
FIESTA *n* religious festival, carnival
FIESTAS ▸ fiesta
FIFE *n* small high-pitched flute ▷ *vb* play (music) on a fife
FIFED ▸ fife
FIFER ▸ fife
FIFERS ▸ fife
FIFES ▸ fife
FIFING ▸ fife
FIFTEEN *n* five and ten ▷ *adj* amounting to fifteen ▷ *determiner* amounting to fifteen
FIFTH *n* (of) number five in a series ▷ *adj* of or being number five in a series ▷ *adv* after the fourth person, position, event, etc
FIFTHLY *same as* **▸ fifth**
FIFTHS ▸ fifth
FIFTIES ▸ fifty
FIFTY *n* five times ten ▷ *adj* amounting to fifty ▷ *determiner* amounting to fifty
FIG *n* soft pear-shaped fruit ▷ *vb* dress (up) or rig (out)
FIGGED ▸ fig
FIGGERY *n* adornment, ornament
FIGGING ▸ fig
FIGHT *vb* struggle (against) in battle or physical combat ▷ *n* aggressive conflict

between two (groups of) people

FIGHTER n boxer

FIGHTS ▸ fight

FIGJAM n very conceited person

FIGJAMS ▸ figjam

FIGMENT n fantastic notion, invention, or fabrication

FIGO same as ▸ fico

FIGOS ▸ figo

FIGS ▸ fig

FIGURAL adj composed of or relating to human or animal figures

FIGURE n numerical symbol ▷ vb calculate (sums or amounts)

FIGURED adj decorated with a design

FIGURER ▸ figure

FIGURES ▸ figure

FIGWORT n N temperate plant with square stems and small brown or greenish flowers

FIKE vb fidget

FIKED ▸ fike

FIKERY n fuss

FIKES ▸ fike

FIKIER ▸ fiky

FIKIEST ▸ fiky

FIKING ▸ fike

FIKISH adj fussy

FIKY adj fussy

FIL same as ▸ fils

FILA ▸ filum

FILABEG same as ▸ filibeg

FILACER n formerly, English legal officer

FILAR adj of thread

FILAREE n type of storksbill, a weed

FILARIA n type of parasitic nematode worm transmitted to vertebrates by insects, the cause of filariasis

FILASSE n vegetable fibre such as jute

FILAZER same as ▸ filacer

FILBERD same as ▸ filbert

FILBERT n hazelnut

FILCH vb steal (small amounts)

FILCHED ▸ filch

FILCHER ▸ filch

FILCHES ▸ filch

FILE n box or folder used to keep documents in order ▷ vb place (a document) in a file

FILED ▸ file

FILEMOT n type of brown colour

FILER ▸ file

FILERS ▸ file

FILES ▸ file

FILET same as ▸ fillet

FILETED ▸ filet

FILETS ▸ filet

FILFOT same as ▸ fylfot

FILFOTS ▸ filfot

FILIAL adj of or befitting a son or daughter

FILIATE vb fix judicially the paternity of (a child, esp one born out of wedlock)

FILIBEG n kilt worn by Scottish Highlanders

FILII ▸ filius

> This plural of **filius**, a Latin word for son, is the only 5-letter word that lets you get rid of three Is!

FILING ▸ file

FILINGS pl n shavings removed by a file

FILIUS n son

FILL vb make or become full

FILLE n girl

FILLED ▸ fill

FILLER n substance that fills a gap or increases bulk

FILLERS ▸ filler

FILLES ▸ fille

FILLET n boneless piece of meat or fish ▷ vb remove the bones from

FILLETS ▸ fillet

FILLIES ▸ filly

FILLING n substance that fills a gap or cavity, esp in a tooth ▷ adj (of food) substantial and satisfying

FILLIP n something that adds stimulation or enjoyment ▷ vb stimulate or excite

FILLIPS ▸ fillip

FILLO same as ▸ filo

FILLOS ▸ fillo

FILLS ▸ fill

FILLY n young female horse

FILM n sequence of images projected on a screen, creating the illusion of movement ▷ vb photograph with a movie or video camera ▷ adj connected with films or the cinema

FILMDOM n cinema industry

FILMED ▸ film

FILMER n film-maker

FILMERS ▸ filmer

FILMI adj in Indian English, of or relating to the Indian film industry or Indian films

FILMIC adj of or suggestive of films or the cinema

FILMIER ▸ filmy

FILMILY ▸ filmy

FILMING ▸ film

FILMIS ▸ filmi

FILMISH ▸ film

FILMS ▸ film

FILMSET vb set (type matter) by filmsetting

FILMY adj very thin, delicate

FILO n type of flaky Greek pastry in very thin sheets

FILOS ▸ filo

FILOSE adj resembling or possessing a thread or threadlike process

FILS n fractional monetary unit of Bahrain, Iraq, Jordan, and Kuwait, worth one thousandth of a dinar

FILTER n material or device permitting fluid to pass but retaining solid particles ▷ vb remove impurities from (a substance) with a filter

FILTERS ▸ filter

FILTH n disgusting dirt

FILTHS ▸ filth

FILTHY adj characterized by or full of filth ▷ adv extremely

FILTRE adj as in cafe filtre a strong black filtered coffee

FILUM n any threadlike structure or part

FIMBLE n male plant of the hemp, which matures before the female plant

FIMBLES ▸ fimble

FIMBRIA n fringe or fringelike margin or border, esp at the opening of the Fallopian tubes

FIN n any of the firm appendages that are the organs of locomotion and balance in fishes and some other aquatic mammals ▷ vb provide with fins

FINABLE adj liable to a fine

FINAGLE vb get or achieve by craftiness or trickery

FINAL adj at the end ▷ n deciding contest between winners of previous rounds in a competition

FINALE n concluding part of a dramatic performance or musical work

FINALES ▸ finale

FINALIS n musical finishing note

FINALLY adv after a long delay

FINALS pl n deciding part of a competition

FINANCE vb provide or obtain funds for ▹ n system of money, credit, and investment

FINBACK another name for ▸ rorqual

FINCA n Spanish villa

FINCAS ▸ finca

FINCH n small songbird with a short strong beak

FINCHED adj with streaks or spots on the back

FINCHES ▸ finch

FIND vb discover by chance ▹ n person or thing found, esp when valuable

FINDER n small telescope fitted to a larger one

FINDERS ▸ finder

FINDING ▸ find

FINDRAM same as ▸ finnan

FINDS ▸ find

FINE adj very good ▹ n payment imposed as a penalty ▹ vb impose a fine on

FINED ▸ fine

FINEER same as ▸ veneer

FINEERS ▸ fineer

FINEISH ▸ fine

FINELY adv into small pieces

FINER ▸ fine

FINERS ▸ fine

FINERY n showy clothing

FINES ▸ fine

FINESSE n delicate skill ▹ vb bring about with finesse

FINEST ▸ fine

FINFISH n fish with fins, as opposed to shellfish

FINFOOT n type of tropical and subtropical aquatic bird with broadly lobed toes, a long slender head and neck, and pale brown plumage

FINGAN same as ▸ finjan

FINGANS ▸ fingan

FINGER n one of the four long jointed parts of the hand ▹ vb touch or handle with the fingers

FINGERS ▸ finger

FINI n end; finish

FINIAL n ornament at the apex of a gable or spire

FINIALS ▸ finial

FINICAL another word for ▸ finicky

FINICKY adj excessively particular, fussy

FINIKIN same as ▸ finicky

FINING n process of removing undissolved gas bubbles from molten glass

FININGS ▸ fining

FINIS ▸ fini

FINISES ▸ finis

FINISH vb bring to an end, stop ▹ n end, last part

FINITE adj having limits in space, time, or size ▹ n a verb limited by person, number, tense or mood

FINITES ▸ finite

FINITO adj finished

FINJAN n small, handleless coffee cup

FINJANS ▸ finjan

FINK n strikebreaker ▹ vb inform (on someone), as to the police

FINKED ▸ fink

FINKING ▸ fink

FINKS ▸ fink

FINLESS ▸ fin

FINLIKE ▸ fin

FINMARK n monetary unit of Finland

FINNAC same as ▸ finnock

FINNACK same as ▸ finnock

FINNACS ▸ finnac

FINNAN n smoked haddock

FINNANS ▸ finnan

FINNED ▸ fin

FINNER another name for ▸ rorqual

FINNERS ▸ finner

FINNIER ▸ finny

FINNING ▸ fin

FINNOCK n young sea trout on its first return to fresh water

FINNSKO same as ▸ finnesko

FINNY adj relating to or containing many fishes

FINO n very dry sherry

FINOS ▸ fino

FINS ▸ fin

FINSKO same as ▸ finnesko

FIORD same as ▸ fjord

FIORDS ▸ fiord

FIORIN n type of temperate perennial grass

FIORINS ▸ fiorin

FIPPLE n wooden plug forming a flue in the end of a pipe, as the mouthpiece of a recorder

FIPPLES ▸ fipple

FIQH n Islamic jurisprudence

FIQHS ▸ fiqh

FIQUE n hemp

FIQUES ▸ fique

FIR n pyramid-shaped tree with needle-like leaves and erect cones

FIRE n state of combustion producing heat, flames, and smoke ▹ vb operate (a weapon) so that a bullet or missile is released

FIREARM n rifle, pistol, or shotgun

FIREBOX n furnace chamber of a boiler in a steam locomotive

FIREBUG n person who deliberately sets fire to property

FIRED ▸ fire

FIREDOG n either of a pair of decorative metal stands used to support logs in an open fire

FIREFLY n beetle that glows in the dark

FIRELIT adj lit by firelight

FIREMAN n man whose job is to put out fires and rescue people endangered by them

FIREMEN ▸ fireman

FIREPAN n metal container for a fire in a room

FIREPOT n Chinese fondue-like cooking pot

FIRER ▸ fire

FIRERS ▸ fire

FIRES ▸ fire

FIRIE n in Australian English, informal word for a firefighter

FIRIES ▸ firie

FIRING n discharge of a firearm

FIRINGS ▸ firing

FIRK vb beat

FIRKED ▸ firk

FIRKIN n small wooden barrel or similar container

FIRKING ▸ firk

FIRKINS ▸ firkin

FIRKS ▸ firk

FIRLOT n unit of measurement for grain

FIRLOTS ▸ firlot
FIRM *adj* not soft or yielding ▷ *adv* in an unyielding manner ▷ *vb* make or become firm ▷ *n* business company
FIRMAN *n* edict of an Oriental sovereign
FIRMANS ▸ firman
FIRMED ▸ firm
FIRMER ▸ firm
FIRMERS ▸ firm
FIRMEST ▸ firm
FIRMING ▸ firm
FIRMLY ▸ firm
FIRMS ▸ firm
FIRN *another name for* ▸ **neve**
FIRNS ▸ firn
FIRRIER ▸ firry
FIRRING *n* wooden battens used in building construction
FIRRY *adj* of, relating to, or made from fir trees
FIRS ▸ fir
FIRST *adj* earliest in time or order ▷ *n* person or thing coming before all others ▷ *adv* before anything else
FIRSTLY *adv* coming before other points, questions, etc
FIRSTS *pl n* saleable goods of the highest quality
FIRTH *n* narrow inlet of the sea, esp in Scotland
FIRTHS ▸ firth
FIRWOOD *n* wood of the fir tree
FISC *n* state or royal treasury
FISCAL *adj* of government finances, esp taxes ▷ *n* (in some countries) a public prosecutor
FISCALS ▸ fiscal
FISCS ▸ fisc
FISGIG *same as* ▸ **fishgig**
FISGIGS ▸ fisgig
FISH *n* cold-blooded vertebrate with gills, that lives in water ▷ *vb* try to catch fish
FISHED ▸ fish
FISHER *n* fisherman
FISHERS ▸ fisher
FISHERY *n* area of the sea used for fishing
FISHES ▸ fish
FISHEYE *n* in photography, a lens of small focal length, having a highly curved protruding front element, that covers an angle of view

of almost 180°
FISHFUL *adj* teeming with fish
FISHGIG *n* pole with barbed prongs for impaling fish
FISHIER ▸ fishy
FISHIFY *vb* change into fish
FISHILY ▸ fishy
FISHING *n* job or pastime of catching fish
FISHNET *n* open mesh fabric resembling netting
FISHWAY *n* fish ladder
FISHY *adj* of or like fish
FISK *vb* frisk
FISKED ▸ fisk
FISKING ▸ fisk
FISKS ▸ fisk
FISSATE ▸ fissile
FISSILE *adj* capable of undergoing nuclear fission
FISSION *n* splitting
FISSIVE ▸ fissile
FISSLE *vb* rustle
FISSLED ▸ fissle
FISSLES ▸ fissle
FISSURE *n* long narrow cleft or crack ▷ *vb* crack or split apart
FIST *n* clenched hand ▷ *vb* hit with the fist
FISTED ▸ fist
FISTFUL *n* quantity that can be held in a fist or hand
FISTIC *adj* of or relating to fisticuffs or boxing
FISTIER ▸ fist
FISTING ▸ fist
FISTS ▸ fist
FISTULA *n* long narrow ulcer
FISTY ▸ fist
FIT *vb* be appropriate or suitable for ▷ *adj* appropriate ▷ *n* way in which something fits
FITCH *n* fur of the polecat or ferret
FITCHE *adj* pointed
FITCHEE *same as* ▸ **fitche**
FITCHES ▸ fitch
FITCHET *same as* ▸ **fitch**
FITCHEW *archaic name for* ▸ **polecat**
FITCHY *same as* ▸ **fitche**
FITFUL *adj* occurring in irregular spells
FITLIER ▸ fitly
FITLY *adv* in a proper manner or place or at a proper time
FITMENT *n* accessory attached to a machine

FITNA *n* state of trouble or chaos
FITNAS ▸ fitna
FITNESS *n* state of being fit
FITS ▸ fit
FITT *n* song
FITTE *same as* ▸ **fitt**
FITTED ▸ fit
FITTER ▸ fit
FITTERS ▸ fit
FITTES ▸ fitte
FITTEST ▸ fit
FITTING ▸ fit
FITTS ▸ fitt
FIVE *n* one more than four ▷ *adj* amounting to five ▷ *determiner* amounting to five
FIVEPIN ▸ fivepins
FIVER *n* five-pound note
FIVERS ▸ fiver
FIVES *n* ball game resembling squash but played with bats or the hands
FIX *vb* make or become firm, stable, or secure ▷ *n* difficult situation
FIXABLE ▸ fix
FIXATE *vb* become or cause to become fixed
FIXATED ▸ fixate
FIXATES ▸ fixate
FIXATIF *same as* ▸ **fixative**
FIXED *adj* attached or placed so as to be immovable
FIXEDLY ▸ fixed
FIXER *n* solution used to make a photographic image permanent
FIXERS ▸ fixer
FIXES ▸ fix
FIXING *n* means of attaching one thing to another, as a pipe to a wall, slate to a roof, etc
FIXINGS *pl n* apparatus or equipment
FIXIT *n* solution to a complex problem
FIXITY *n* state or quality of a person's gaze, attitude, or concentration not changing or weakening
FIXIVE ▸ fix
FIXT *adj* fixed
FIXTURE *n* permanently fitted piece of household equipment
FIXURE *n* firmness
FIXURES ▸ fixure
FIZ *same as* ▸ **fizz**

FIZGIG vb inform on someone to the police

FIZGIGS ▸ fizgig

FIZZ vb make a hissing or bubbling noise ▷ n hissing or bubbling noise

FIZZED ▸ fizz

FIZZEN same as ▸ **foison**

FIZZENS ▸ fizzen

FIZZER n anything that fizzes

FIZZERS ▸ fizzer

FIZZES ▸ fizz

FIZZIER ▸ fizz

FIZZING ▸ fizz

FIZZLE vb make a weak hissing or bubbling sound ▷ n hissing or bubbling sound

FIZZLED ▸ fizzle

FIZZLES ▸ fizzle

FIZZY ▸ fizz

FJELD n high rocky plateau with little vegetation in Scandinavian countries

FJELDS ▸ fjeld

FJORD n long narrow inlet of the sea between cliffs, esp in Norway

FJORDIC ▸ fjord

FJORDS ▸ fjord

FLAB n unsightly body fat

FLABBY adj having flabby flesh

FLABS ▸ flab

FLACCID adj soft and limp

FLACK vb flutter

FLACKED ▸ flack

FLACKER vb flutter like a bird

FLACKET n flagon

FLACKS ▸ flack

FLACON n small stoppered bottle or flask, such as one used for perfume

FLACONS ▸ flacon

FLAFF vb flap

FLAFFED ▸ flaff

FLAFFER vb flutter

FLAFFS ▸ flaff

FLAG n piece of cloth attached to a pole as an emblem or signal ▷ vb mark with a flag or sticker

FLAGGED ▸ flag

FLAGGER ▸ flag

FLAGGY adj drooping

FLAGMAN n person who has charge of, carries, or signals with a flag, esp a railway employee

FLAGMEN ▸ flagman

FLAGON n wide bottle for wine or cider

FLAGONS ▸ flagon

FLAGS ▸ flag

FLAIL vb wave about wildly ▷ n tool formerly used for threshing grain by hand

FLAILED ▸ flail

FLAILS ▸ flail

FLAIR n natural ability

FLAIRS ▸ flair

FLAK n anti-aircraft fire

FLAKE n small thin piece, esp chipped off something ▷ vb peel off in flakes

FLAKED ▸ flake

FLAKER ▸ flake

FLAKERS ▸ flake

FLAKES ▸ flake

FLAKEY same as ▸ **flaky**

FLAKIER ▸ flaky

FLAKIES n dandruff

FLAKILY ▸ flaky

FLAKING ▸ flake

FLAKS ▸ flak

FLAKY adj like or made of flakes

FLAM n falsehood, deception, or sham ▷ vb cheat or deceive

FLAMBE vb cook or serve (food) in flaming brandy ▷ adj (of food, such as steak or pancakes) served in flaming brandy

FLAMBEE same as ▸ **flambe**

FLAMBES ▸ flambe

FLAME n luminous burning gas coming from burning material ▷ vb burn brightly

FLAMED ▸ flame

FLAMEN n (in ancient Rome) any of 15 priests who each served a particular deity

FLAMENS ▸ flamen

FLAMER ▸ flame

FLAMERS ▸ flame

FLAMES ▸ flame

FLAMFEW n fantastic trifle

FLAMIER ▸ flame

FLAMING adj burning with flames ▷ adv extremely

FLAMM same as ▸ **flam**

FLAMMED ▸ flam

FLAMMS ▸ flamm

FLAMS ▸ flam

FLAMY ▸ flame

FLAN n open sweet or savoury tart

FLANCH same as ▸ **flaunch**

FLANES n arrows

FLANEUR n idler or loafer

FLANGE n projecting rim or collar ▷ vb attach or provide (a component) with a flange

FLANGED ▸ flange

FLANGER ▸ flange

FLANGES ▸ flange

FLANK n part of the side between the hips and ribs ▷ vb be at or move along the side of

FLANKED ▸ flank

FLANKEN n cut of beef

FLANKER n one of a detachment of soldiers detailed to guard the flanks, esp of a formation

FLANKS ▸ flank

FLANNEL n small piece of cloth for washing the face ▷ vb talk evasively

FLANNEN adj made of flannel

FLANNIE ▸ flanny

FLANNY n a shirt made of flannel

FLANS ▸ flan

FLAP vb move back and forwards or up and down ▷ n action or sound of flapping

FLAPPED ▸ flap

FLAPPER n (in the 1920s) a lively young woman who dressed and behaved unconventionally

FLAPPY adj loose

FLAPS ▸ flap

FLARE vb blaze with a sudden unsteady flame ▷ n sudden unsteady flame

FLARED ▸ flare

FLARES pl n trousers with legs that widen below the knee

FLAREUP n outbreak of something

FLARIER ▸ flare

FLARING ▸ flare

FLARY ▸ flare

FLASER n type of sedimentary structure in rock

FLASERS ▸ flaser

FLASH n sudden burst of light or flame ▷ adj vulgarly showy ▷ vb (cause to) burst into flame

FLASHED ▸ flash

FLASHER n man who exposes himself indecently

FLASHES ▸ flash

FLASHY adj showy in a vulgar way

FLASK n flat bottle for carrying alcoholic drink in the pocket

FLASKET n long shallow basket

FLASKS ▶ flask

FLAT adj level and horizontal ▷ adv in or into a flat position ▷ n flat surface ▷ vb live in a flat

FLATBED n printing machine on which the type forme is carried on a flat bed under a revolving paper-bearing cylinder

FLATCAP n Elizabethan man's hat with a narrow down-turned brim

FLATCAR n flatbed

FLATLET n small flat

FLATLY ▶ flat

FLATS ▶ flat

FLATTED ▶ flat

FLATTEN vb make or become flat or flatter

FLATTER vb praise insincerely

FLATTIE n flat tyre

FLATTOP n informal name for an aircraft carrier

FLATTY n flat shoe

FLATUS n gas generated in the alimentary canal

FLAUGHT vb flutter

FLAUNCH n cement or mortar slope around a chimney top, manhole, etc, to throw off water ▷ vb cause to slope in this manner

FLAUNE same as ▶ flam

FLAUNES ▶ flaune

FLAUNT vb display (oneself or one's possessions) arrogantly ▷ n act of flaunting

FLAUNTS ▶ flaunt

FLAUNTY adj characterized by or inclined to ostentatious display or flaunting

FLAUTA n tortilla rolled around a filling

FLAUTAS ▶ flauta

FLAVA n individual style

FLAVAS ▶ flava

FLAVIN n heterocyclic ketone

FLAVINE same as ▶ flavin

FLAVINS ▶ flavin

FLAVONE n crystalline compound occurring in plants

FLAVOR same as ▶ flavour

FLAVORS ▶ flavor

FLAVORY adj flavoursome

FLAVOUR n distinctive taste ▷ vb give flavour to

FLAW n imperfection or blemish ▷ vb make or become blemished, defective, or imperfect

FLAWED ▶ flaw

FLAWIER ▶ flaw

FLAWING ▶ flaw

FLAWN same as ▶ flam

FLAWNS ▶ flawn

FLAWS ▶ flaw

FLAWY ▶ flaw

FLAX n plant grown for its stem fibres and seeds

FLAXEN adj (of hair) pale yellow

FLAXES ▶ flax

FLAXIER ▶ flaxy

FLAXY same as ▶ flaxen

FLAY same as ▶ fley

FLAYED ▶ flay

FLAYER ▶ flay

FLAYERS ▶ flay

FLAYING ▶ flay

FLAYS ▶ flay

FLEA n small wingless jumping bloodsucking insect

FLEABAG n dirty or unkempt person, esp a woman

FLEADH n festival of Irish music, dancing, and culture

FLEADHS ▶ fleadh

FLEAM n lancet used for letting blood

FLEAMS ▶ fleam

FLEAPIT n shabby cinema or theatre

FLEAS ▶ flea

FLECHE n slender spire, esp over the intersection of the nave and transept ridges of a church roof

FLECHES ▶ fleche

FLECK n small mark, streak, or speck ▷ vb speckle

FLECKED ▶ fleck

FLECKER same as ▶ fleck

FLECKS ▶ fleck

FLECKY ▶ fleck

FLED ▶ flee

FLEDGE vb feed and care for (a young bird) until it is able to fly

FLEDGED ▶ fledge

FLEDGES ▶ fledge

FLEDGY adj feathery or feathered

FLEE vb run away (from)

FLEECE n sheep's coat of wool ▷ vb defraud or overcharge

FLEECED ▶ fleece

FLEECER ▶ fleece

FLEECES ▶ fleece

FLEECH vb flatter

FLEECIE n person who collects fleeces after shearing and prepares them for baling

FLEECY adj made of or like fleece ▷ n person who collects fleeces after shearing and prepares them for baling

FLEEING ▶ flee

FLEER vb grin or laugh at ▷ n derisory glance or grin

FLEERED ▶ fleer

FLEERER ▶ fleer

FLEERS ▶ fleer

FLEES ▶ flee

FLEET n number of warships organized as a unit ▷ adj swift in movement ▷ vb move rapidly

FLEETED ▶ fleet

FLEETER ▶ fleet

FLEETLY ▶ fleet

FLEETS ▶ fleet

FLEG vb scare

FLEGGED ▶ fleg

FLEGS ▶ fleg

FLEHMEN vb (of mammal) grimace

FLEME vb drive out

FLEMES ▶ fleme

FLEMING n native or inhabitant of Flanders or a Flemish-speaking Belgian

FLEMISH vb stow (a rope) in a Flemish coil

FLEMIT ▶ fleme

FLENCH same as ▶ flense

FLENSE vb strip (a whale, seal, etc) of (its blubber or skin)

FLENSED ▶ flense

FLENSER ▶ flense

FLENSES ▶ flense

FLESH n soft part of a human or animal body

FLESHED ▶ flesh

FLESHER n person or machine that fleshes hides or skins

FLESHES ▶ flesh

FLESHLY adj carnal

FLESHY adj plump

FLETCH same as ▶ fledge

FLETTON n type of brick

FLEURET *same as*
> **fleurette**
FLEURON *n* decorative
piece of pastry
FLEURY *same as* > **flory**
FLEW > **fly**
FLEWED *adj* having large
flews
FLEWS *pl n* fleshy hanging
upper lip of a bloodhound
or similar dog
FLEX *n* flexible insulated
electric cable ▷ *vb* bend
FLEXED > **flex**
FLEXES > **flex**
FLEXILE *same as* > **flexible**
FLEXING > **flex**
FLEXION *n* act of bending a
joint or limb
FLEXO *n, adj, adv*
flexography
FLEXOR *n* any muscle
whose contraction serves
to bend a joint or limb
FLEXORS > **flexor**
FLEXOS > **flexo**
FLEXURE *n* act of flexing or
the state of being flexed
FLEY *vb* be afraid or cause to
be afraid
FLEYED > **fley**
FLEYING > **fley**
FLEYS > **fley**
FLIC *n* French police officer
FLICK *vb* touch or move
with the finger or hand in a
quick movement ▷ *n* tap or
quick stroke
FLICKED > **flick**
FLICKER *vb* shine unsteadily
or intermittently ▷ *n*
unsteady brief light
FLICKS > **flick**
FLICS > **flic**
FLIED > **fly**
FLIER > **fly**
FLIERS > **fly**
FLIES > **fly**
FLIEST > **fly**
FLIGHT *n* journey by air ▷ *vb*
cause (a ball, dart, etc) to
float slowly or deceptively
towards its target
FLIGHTS > **flight**
FLIGHTY *adj* frivolous and
fickle
FLIM *n* five-pound note
FLIMP *vb* steal
FLIMPED > **flimp**
FLIMPS > **flimp**
FLIMS > **flim**
FLIMSY *adj* not strong or
substantial ▷ *n* thin paper

used for making carbon
copies of a letter, etc
FLINCH *same as* > **flense**
FLINDER *n* fragment
FLING *vb* throw, send, or
move forcefully or hurriedly
▷ *n* spell of self-indulgent
enjoyment
FLINGER > **fling**
FLINGS > **fling**
FLINT *n* hard grey stone
▷ *vb* fit or provide with a
flint
FLINTED > **flint**
FLINTS > **flint**
FLINTY *adj* cruel
FLIP *vb* throw (something
small or light) carelessly ▷ *n*
snap or tap ▷ *adj* flippant
FLIPPED > **flip**
FLIPPER *n* limb of a sea
animal adapted for
swimming
FLIPPY *adj* (of clothes)
tending to move to and fro
as the wearer walks
FLIPS > **flip**
FLIR *n* forward looking
infrared radar
FLIRS > **flir**
FLIRT *vb* behave as if
sexually attracted to
someone ▷ *n* person who
flirts
FLIRTED > **flirt**
FLIRTER > **flirt**
FLIRTS > **flirt**
FLIRTY > **flirt**
FLISK *vb* skip
FLISKED > **flisk**
FLISKS > **flisk**
FLISKY > **flisk**
FLIT *vb* move lightly and
rapidly ▷ *n* act of flitting
FLITCH *n* side of pork salted
and cured ▷ *vb* cut (a tree
trunk) into flitches
FLITE *vb* scold or rail at ▷ *n*
dispute or scolding
FLITED > **flite**
FLITES > **flite**
FLITING > **flite**
FLITS > **flit**
FLITT *adj* fleet
FLITTED > **flit**
FLITTER > **flit**
FLIVVER *n* old, cheap, or
battered car
FLIX *n* fur ▷ *vb* have fur
FLIXED > **flix**
FLIXES > **flix**
FLIXING > **flix**
FLOAT *vb* rest on the surface

of a liquid ▷ *n* light object
used to help someone or
something float
FLOATED > **float**
FLOATEL *same as* > **flotel**
FLOATER *n* person or thing
that floats
FLOATS *pl n* footlights
FLOATY *adj* filmy and light
FLOB *vb* spit
FLOBBED > **flob**
FLOBS > **flob**
FLOC *same as* > **flock**
FLOCCED > **floc**
FLOCCI > **floccus**
FLOCCUS *n* downy or
woolly covering, as on the
young of certain birds ▷ *adj*
(of a cloud) having the
appearance of woolly tufts
at odd intervals in its
structure
FLOCK *n* number of animals
of one kind together ▷ *vb*
gather in a crowd ▷ *adj* (of
wallpaper) with a velvety
raised pattern
FLOCKED > **flock**
FLOCKS > **flock**
FLOCKY > **flock**
FLOCS > **floc**
FLOE *n* sheet of floating ice
FLOES > **floe**
FLOG *vb* beat with a whip or
stick
FLOGGED > **flog**
FLOGGER > **flog**
FLOGS > **flog**
FLOKATI *n* Greek
hand-woven shaggy
woollen rug
FLONG *n* material, usually
pulped paper or cardboard,
used for making moulds in
stereotyping
FLONGS > **flong**
FLOOD *n* overflow of water
onto a normally dry area
▷ *vb* cover or become
covered with water
FLOODED > **flood**
FLOODER > **flood**
FLOODS > **flood**
FLOOEY *adj* awry
FLOOIE *same as* > **flooey**
FLOOR *n* lower surface of a
room ▷ *vb* knock down
FLOORED > **floor**
FLOORER *n* coup de grâce
FLOORS > **floor**
FLOOSIE *same as* > **floozy**
FLOOSY *same as* > **floosie**
FLOOZIE *same as* > **floozy**

FLOOZY n disreputable woman

FLOP vb bend, fall, or collapse loosely or carelessly ▷ n failure

FLOPPED ▸ flop

FLOPPER ▸ flop

FLOPPY adj hanging downwards, loose ▷ n floppy disk

FLOPS ▸ flop

FLOR n yeast formed on the surface of sherry after fermentation

FLORA n plants of a given place or time

FLORAE ▸ flora

FLORAL adj consisting of or decorated with flowers ▷ n class of perfume

FLORALS ▸ floral

FLORAS ▸ flora

FLOREAT vb may (a person, institution, etc) flourish

FLORET n small flower forming part of a composite flower head

FLORETS ▸ floret

FLORID adj with a red or flushed complexion

FLORIER ▸ flory

FLORIN n former British and Australian coin

FLORINS ▸ florin

FLORIST n seller of flowers

FLORS ▸ flor

FLORUIT prep (he or she) flourished: used to indicate the period when a historical figure, whose birth and death dates are unknown, was most active ▷ n such a period in a person's life

FLORULA n flora of a small single environment

FLORULE same as ▸ florula

FLORY adj containing a fleur-de-lys

FLOSH n hopper-shaped box

FLOSHES ▸ flosh

FLOSS n fine silky fibres ▷ vb clean (between the teeth) with dental floss

FLOSSED ▸ floss

FLOSSER ▸ floss

FLOSSES ▸ floss

FLOSSIE same as ▸ flossy

FLOSSY adj consisting of or resembling floss ▷ n floozy

FLOTA n formerly, Spanish commercial fleet

FLOTAGE n act or state of floating

FLOTANT adj in heraldry, flying in the air

FLOTAS ▸ flota

FLOTE n aquatic perennial grass

FLOTEL n (in the oil industry) an oil rig or boat used as accommodation for workers in off-shore oil fields

FLOTELS ▸ flotel

FLOTES ▸ flote

FLOTSAM n floating wreckage

FLOUNCE vb go with emphatic movements ▷ n flouncing movement

FLOUNCY ▸ flounce

FLOUR n powder made by grinding grain, esp wheat ▷ vb sprinkle with flour

FLOURED ▸ flour

FLOURS ▸ flour

FLOURY ▸ flour

FLOUSE vb splash

FLOUSED ▸ flouse

FLOUSES ▸ flouse

FLOUSH same as ▸ flouse

FLOUT vb deliberately disobey (a rule, law, etc)

FLOUTED ▸ flout

FLOUTER ▸ flout

FLOUTS ▸ flout

FLOW vb (of liquid) move in a stream ▷ n act, rate, or manner of flowing

FLOWAGE n act of flowing or overflowing or the state of having overflowed

FLOWED ▸ flow

FLOWER n part of a plant that produces seeds ▷ vb produce flowers, bloom

FLOWERS ▸ flower

FLOWERY adj decorated with a floral design

FLOWING ▸ flow

FLOWN ▸ fly

FLOWS ▸ flow

FLOX adj as in **flox silk** type of silk

FLU n any of various viral infections, esp a respiratory or intestinal infection

FLUATE n fluoride

FLUATES ▸ fluate

FLUB vb bungle

FLUBBED ▸ flub

FLUBBER ▸ flub

FLUBDUB n bunkum

FLUBS ▸ flub

FLUE n passage or pipe for smoke or hot air

FLUED adj having a flue

FLUENCE ▸ fluency

FLUENCY n quality of being fluent, esp facility in speech or writing

FLUENT adj able to speak or write with ease ▷ n variable quantity in fluxions

FLUENTS ▸ fluent

FLUERIC adj of or relating to fluidics

FLUES ▸ flue

FLUEY adj involved in, caused by, or like influenza

FLUFF n soft fibres ▷ vb make or become soft and puffy

FLUFFED ▸ fluff

FLUFFER n person employed on a pornographic film set to ensure that male actors are kept aroused

FLUFFS ▸ fluff

FLUFFY adj of, resembling, or covered with fluff

FLUGEL n grand piano or harpsichord

FLUGELS ▸ flugel

FLUID n substance able to flow and change its shape ▷ adj able to flow or change shape easily

FLUIDAL ▸ fluid

FLUIDIC > fluidics

FLUIDLY ▸ fluid

FLUIDS ▸ fluid

FLUIER ▸ fluey

FLUIEST ▸ fluey

FLUISH ▸ flu

FLUKE n accidental stroke of luck ▷ vb gain, make, or hit by a fluke

FLUKED ▸ fluke

FLUKES ▸ fluke

FLUKEY same as ▸ fluky

FLUKIER ▸ fluky

FLUKILY ▸ fluky

FLUKING ▸ fluke

FLUKY adj done or gained by an accident, esp a lucky one

FLUME n narrow sloping channel for water ▷ vb transport (logs) in a flume

FLUMED ▸ flume

FLUMES ▸ flume

FLUMING ▸ flume

FLUMMOX vb puzzle or confuse

FLUMP vb move or fall heavily

FLUMPED ▸ flump

FLUMPS ▸ flump
FLUNG ▸ fling
FLUNK vb fail ▹ n low grade below the pass standard
FLUNKED ▸ flunk
FLUNKER ▸ flunk
FLUNKEY same as ▸ **flunky**
FLUNKIE same as ▸ **flunky**
FLUNKS ▸ flunk
FLUNKY n servile person
FLUOR ▸ fluorspar
FLUORIC adj of, concerned with, or produced from fluorine or fluorspar
FLUORID same as ▹ **fluoride**
FLUORIN same as ▹ **fluorine**
FLUORS ▸ fluor
FLURR vb scatter
FLURRED ▸ flurr
FLURRS ▸ flurr
FLURRY n sudden commotion ▹ vb confuse
FLUS ▸ flu
FLUSH vb blush or cause to blush ▹ n blush ▹ adj level with the surrounding surface ▹ adv so as to be level
FLUSHED ▸ flush
FLUSHER ▸ flush
FLUSHES ▸ flush
FLUSHY adj ruddy
FLUSTER vb make nervous or upset ▹ n nervous or upset state
FLUTE n wind instrument consisting of a tube with sound holes and a mouth hole in the side ▹ vb utter in a high-pitched tone
FLUTED adj having decorative grooves
FLUTER n craftsman who makes flutes or fluting
FLUTERS ▸ fluter
FLUTES ▸ flute
FLUTEY ▸ flute
FLUTIER ▸ flute
FLUTINA n type of accordion
FLUTING n design of decorative grooves
FLUTIST same as ▸ **flautist**
FLUTTER vb wave rapidly ▹ n flapping movement
FLUTY ▸ flute
FLUVIAL adj of rivers
FLUX n constant change or instability ▹ vb make or become fluid
FLUXED ▸ flux
FLUXES ▸ flux
FLUXING ▸ flux

FLUXION n rate of change of a function, especially the instantaneous velocity of a moving body
FLUXIVE ▸ flux
FLUYT n Dutch sailing ship
FLUYTS ▸ fluyt
FLY vb move through the air on wings or in an aircraft ▹ n fastening at the front of trousers ▹ adj sharp and cunning
FLYABLE ▸ fly
FLYAWAY adj (of hair) very fine and soft ▹ n person who is frivolous or flighty
FLYBACK n fast return of the spot on a cathode-ray tube after completion of each trace
FLYBANE n type of campion
FLYBELT n strip of tsetse-infested land
FLYBLEW ▸ flyblow
FLYBLOW vb contaminate, esp with the eggs or larvae of the blowfly ▹ n egg or young larva of a blowfly, deposited on meat, paper, etc
FLYBOAT n any small swift boat
FLYBOOK n small case or wallet used by anglers for storing artificial flies
FLYBOY n air force pilot
FLYBOYS ▸ flyboy
FLYBY n flight past a particular position or target, esp the close approach of a spacecraft to a planet or satellite for investigation of conditions
FLYBYS ▸ flyby
FLYER ▸ fly
FLYERS ▸ fly
FLYEST ▸ fly
FLYHAND n device for transferring printed sheets from the press to a flat pile
FLYING ▸ fly
FLYINGS ▸ fly
FLYLEAF n blank leaf at the beginning or end of a book
FLYLESS ▸ fly
FLYMAN n stagehand who operates the scenery, curtains, etc, in the flies
FLYMEN ▸ flyman
FLYOFF n total volume of water transferred from the earth to the atmosphere
FLYOFFS ▸ flyoff

FLYOVER n road passing over another by a bridge
FLYPAST n ceremonial flight of aircraft over a given area
FLYPE vb fold back
FLYPED ▸ flype
FLYPES ▸ flype
FLYPING ▸ flype
FLYSCH n marine sedimentary facies consisting of a sequence of sandstones, conglomerates, marls, shales, and clays that were formed by erosion during a period of mountain building and subsequently deformed as the mountain building continued
FLYTE same as ▸ **flite**
FLYTED ▸ flyte
FLYTES ▸ flyte
FLYTIER n person who makes his own fishing flies
FLYTING ▸ flyte
FLYTRAP n any of various insectivorous plants, esp Venus's flytrap
FLYWAY n usual route used by birds when migrating
FLYWAYS ▸ flyway
FOAL n young of a horse or related animal ▹ vb give birth to a foal
FOALED ▸ foal
FOALING ▸ foal
FOALS ▸ foal
FOAM n mass of small bubbles on a liquid ▹ vb produce foam
FOAMED ▸ foam
FOAMER n (possibly obsessive) enthusiast
FOAMERS ▸ foamer
FOAMIER ▸ foamy
FOAMILY ▸ foamy
FOAMING ▸ foam
FOAMS ▸ foam
FOAMY adj of, resembling, consisting of, or covered with foam
FOB n short watch chain ▹ vb cheat
FOBBED ▸ fob
FOBBING ▸ fob
FOBS ▸ fob
FOCAL adj of or at a focus
FOCALLY ▸ focal
FOCI ▸ focus
FOCUS n point at which light or sound waves converge ▹ vb bring or come into focus

FOCUSED ▸ focus
FOCUSER ▸ focus
FOCUSES ▸ focus
FODDER n feed for livestock ▷ vb supply (livestock) with fodder
FODDERS ▸ fodder
FODGEL adj buxom
FOE n enemy, opponent
FOEHN same as ▸ fohn
FOEHNS ▸ foehn
FOEMAN n enemy in war
FOEMEN ▸ foeman
FOEN ▸ foe
FOES ▸ foe
FOETAL same as ▸ fetal
FOETID same as ▸ fetid
FOETOR same as ▸ fetor
FOETORS ▸ foetor
FOETUS same as ▸ fetus
FOG n mass of condensed water vapour in the lower air, often greatly reducing visibility ▷ vb cover with steam
FOGASH n type of Hungarian pike perch
FOGBOW n faint arc of light sometimes seen in a fog bank
FOGBOWS ▸ fogbow
FOGDOG n whitish spot sometimes seen in fog near the horizon
FOGDOGS ▸ fogdog
FOGEY n old-fashioned person
FOGEYS ▸ fogey
FOGGAGE n grass grown for winter grazing
FOGGED ▸ fog
FOGGER n device that generates a fog
FOGGERS ▸ fogger
FOGGIER ▸ fog
FOGGILY ▸ fog
FOGGING ▸ fog
FOGGY ▸ fog
FOGHORN n large horn sounded to warn ships in fog
FOGIE same as ▸ fogey
FOGIES ▸ fogie
FOGLE n silk handkerchief
FOGLES ▸ fogle
FOGLESS ▸ fog
FOGMAN n person in charge of railway fog-signals
FOGMEN ▸ fogman
FOGOU n man-made subterranean passage or chamber found in Cornwall

FOGOUS ▸ fogou
FOGRAM n fogey
FOGRAMS ▸ fogram
FOGS ▸ fog
FOGY same as ▸ fogey
FOGYDOM ▸ fogy
FOGYISH ▸ fogy
FOGYISM ▸ fogy
FOH interj expression of disgust
FOHN n warm dry wind blowing down the northern slopes of the Alps
FOHNS ▸ fohn
FOIBLE n minor weakness or slight peculiarity
FOIBLES ▸ foible
FOID n rock-forming mineral similar to feldspar
FOIDS ▸ foid
FOIL vb ruin (someone's plan) ▷ n metal in a thin sheet, esp for wrapping food
FOILED ▸ foil
FOILING ▸ foil
FOILS ▸ foil
FOIN n thrust or lunge with a weapon ▷ vb thrust with a weapon
FOINED ▸ foin
FOINING ▸ foin
FOINS ▸ foin
FOISON n plentiful supply or yield
FOISONS ▸ foison
FOIST vb force or impose on
FOISTED ▸ foist
FOISTER ▸ foist
FOISTS ▸ foist
FOLACIN n folic acid
FOLATE n folic acid
FOLATES ▸ folic
FOLD vb bend so that one part covers another ▷ n folded piece or part
FOLDED ▸ fold
FOLDER n piece of folded cardboard for holding loose papers
FOLDERS ▸ folder
FOLDING ▸ fold
FOLDOUT another name for > gatefold
FOLDS ▸ fold
FOLDUP n something that folds up
FOLDUPS ▸ foldup
FOLEY n footsteps editor
FOLEYS ▸ foley
FOLIA ▸ folium
FOLIAGE n leaves
FOLIAR adj of or relating to

a leaf or leaves
FOLIATE adj relating to, possessing, or resembling leaves ▷ vb ornament with foliage or with leaf forms such as foils
FOLIC adj as in **folic acid** any of a group of vitamins of the B complex, including pteroylglutamic acid and its derivatives: used in the treatment of megaloblastic anaemia
FOLIE n madness
FOLIES ▸ folie
FOLIO n sheet of paper folded in half to make two leaves of a book ▷ adj of or made in the largest book size, common esp in early centuries of European printing ▷ vb number the leaves of (a book) consecutively
FOLIOED ▸ folio
FOLIOLE n part of a compound leaf
FOLIOS ▸ folio
FOLIOSE adj (of a tree) leaf-bearing
FOLIOUS adj foliose
FOLIUM n plane geometrical curve consisting of a loop whose two ends, intersecting at a node, are asymptotic to the same line
FOLIUMS ▸ folium
FOLK n people in general ▷ adj originating from or traditional to the common people of a country
FOLKIE n devotee of folk music ▷ adj of or relating to folk music
FOLKIER ▸ folkie
FOLKIES ▸ folkie
FOLKISH ▸ folk
FOLKMOT same as > folkmoot
FOLKS ▸ folk
FOLKSY adj simple and unpretentious
FOLKWAY singular form of > folkways
FOLKY same as ▸ folkie
FOLLES ▸ follis
FOLLIED ▸ folly
FOLLIES ▸ folly
FOLLIS n Roman coin
FOLLOW vb go or come after
FOLLOWS ▸ follow

FOLLY *n* foolishness ▷ *vb* behave foolishly

FOMENT *vb* encourage or stir up (trouble)

FOMENTS ▶ **foment**

FOMES *n* any material, such as bedding or clothing, that may harbour pathogens and therefore convey disease

FOMITE ▶ **fomes**

FOMITES ▶ **fomes**

FON *vb* compel

FOND *adj* tender, loving ▷ *n* background of a design, as in lace ▷ *vb* dote

FONDA *n* Spanish hotel

FONDANT *n* (sweet made from) flavoured paste of sugar and water ▷ *adj* (of a colour) soft

FONDAS ▶ **fonda**

FONDED ▶ **fond**

FONDER ▶ **fond**

FONDEST ▶ **fond**

FONDING ▶ **fond**

FONDLE *vb* caress

FONDLED ▶ **fondle**

FONDLER ▶ **fondle**

FONDLES ▶ **fondle**

FONDLY ▶ **fond**

FONDS ▶ **fond**

FONDU *n* ballet movement, lowering the body by bending the leg(s)

FONDUE *n* Swiss dish of a hot melted cheese sauce into which pieces of bread are dipped ▷ *vb* cook and serve (food) as a fondue

FONDUED ▶ **fondue**

FONDUES ▶ **fondue**

FONDUS ▶ **fondu**

FONE *same as* ▶ **foe**

FONLY *adv* foolishly

FONNED ▶ **fon**

FONNING ▶ **fon**

FONS ▶ **fon**

FONT *n* bowl in a church for baptismal water

FONTAL ▶ **font**

FONTINA *n* semihard, pale yellow, mild Italian cheese made from cow's milk

FONTLET ▶ **font**

FONTS ▶ **font**

FOOBAR *same as* ▶ **fubar**

FOOD *n* what one eats; solid nourishment

FOODFUL *adj* supplying abundant food

FOODIE *n* gourmet

FOODIES ▶ **foodie**

FOODISM *n* enthusiasm for and interest in the preparation and consumption of good food

FOODS ▶ **food**

FOODY *same as* ▶ **foodie**

FOOL *n* person lacking sense or judgment ▷ *vb* deceive (someone)

FOOLED ▶ **fool**

FOOLERY *n* foolish behaviour

FOOLING ▶ **fool**

FOOLISH *adj* unwise, silly, or absurd

FOOLS ▶ **fool**

FOOT *n* part of the leg below the ankle ▷ *vb* kick

FOOTAGE *n* amount of film used

FOOTBAG *n* sport of keeping small round object off the ground by kicking it

FOOTBAR *n* any bar designed as a footrest or to be operated by the foot

FOOTBOY *n* boy servant

FOOTED ▶ **foot**

FOOTER *n* person who goes on foot ▷ *vb* potter

FOOTERS ▶ **footer**

FOOTIE *same as* ▶ **footy**

FOOTIER ▶ **footy**

FOOTIES ▶ **footie**

FOOTING *n* basis or foundation

FOOTLE *vb* loiter aimlessly ▷ *n* foolishness

FOOTLED ▶ **footle**

FOOTLER ▶ **footle**

FOOTLES ▶ **footle**

FOOTMAN *n* male servant in uniform

FOOTMEN ▶ **footman**

FOOTPAD *n* highwayman, on foot rather than horseback

FOOTRA *same as* ▶ **foutra**

FOOTRAS ▶ **footra**

FOOTS *pl n* sediment that accumulates at the bottom of a vessel containing any of certain liquids, such as vegetable oil or varnish

FOOTSIE *n* flirtation involving the touching together of feet

FOOTSY *same as* ▶ **footsie**

FOOTWAY *n* way or path for pedestrians, such as a raised walk along the edge of a bridge

FOOTY *n* football ▷ *adj* mean

FOOZLE *vb* bungle (a shot) ▷ *n* bungled shot

FOOZLED ▶ **foozle**

FOOZLER ▶ **foozle**

FOOZLES ▶ **foozle**

FOP *n* man excessively concerned with fashion ▷ *vb* act like a fop

FOPLING *n* vain affected dandy

FOPPED ▶ **fop**

FOPPERY *n* clothes, affectations, obsessions, etc, of or befitting a fop

FOPPING ▶ **fop**

FOPPISH ▶ **fop**

FOPS ▶ **fop**

FOR *prep* indicating a person intended to benefit from or receive something, span of time or distance, person or thing represented by someone, etc

FORA ▶ **forum**

FORAGE *vb* search about (for) ▷ *n* food for cattle or horses

FORAGED ▶ **forage**

FORAGER ▶ **forage**

FORAGES ▶ **forage**

FORAM *n* a marine protozoan

FORAMEN *n* natural hole, esp one in a bone through which nerves pass

FORAMS ▶ **foram**

FORANE *adj as in* **vicar forane** in the Roman Catholic church, vicar or priest appointed to act in a certain area of the diocese

FORAY *n* brief raid or attack ▷ *vb* raid or ravage (a town, district, etc)

FORAYED ▶ **foray**

FORAYER ▶ **foray**

FORAYS ▶ **foray**

FORB *n* any herbaceous plant that is not a grass

FORBAD ▶ **forbid**

FORBADE ▶ **forbid**

FORBARE ▶ **forbear**

FORBEAR *vb* cease or refrain (from doing something)

FORBID *vb* prohibit, refuse to allow

FORBIDS ▶ **forbid**

FORBODE *vb* obsolete word meaning forbid ▷ *n* obsolete word meaning forbidding

FORBORE *past tense of*

▶ **forbear**

FORBS ▶ **forb**

FORBY adv besides

FORBYE same as ▶ **forby**

FORCAT n convict or galley slave

FORCATS ▶ **forcat**

FORCE n strength or power ▷ vb compel, make (someone) do something

FORCED adj compulsory

FORCEPS pl n surgical pincers

FORCER ▶ **force**

FORCERS ▶ **force**

FORCES ▶ **force**

FORCING ▶ **force**

FORD n shallow place where a river may be crossed ▷ vb cross (a river) at a ford

FORDED ▶ **ford**

FORDID ▶ **fordo**

FORDING ▶ **ford**

FORDO vb destroy

FORDOES ▶ **fordo**

FORDONE ▶ **fordo**

FORDS ▶ **ford**

FORE adj in, at, or towards the front ▷ n front part ▷ interj golfer's shouted warning to a person in the path of a ball

FOREARM n arm from the wrist to the elbow ▷ vb prepare beforehand

FOREBAY n reservoir or canal

FOREBY same as ▶ **forby**

FOREBYE same as ▶ **forby**

FORECAR n three-wheeled passenger vehicle attached to a motorcycle

FOREDID ▶ **foredo**

FOREDO same as ▶ **fordo**

FOREGO same as ▶ **forgo**

FOREGUT n anterior part of the digestive tract of vertebrates, between the buccal cavity and the bile duct

FOREIGN adj not of, or in, one's own country

FOREL n type of parchment

FORELAY archaic word for ▶ **ambush**

FORELEG n either of the front legs of an animal

FORELIE vb lie in front of

FORELS ▶ **forel**

FOREMAN n person in charge of a group of workers

FOREMEN ▶ **foreman**

FOREPAW n either of the front feet of a land mammal that does not have hooves

FORERAN ▶ **forerun**

FORERUN vb serve as a herald for

FORES ▶ **fore**

FORESAW ▶ **foresee**

FORESAY vb foretell

FORESEE vb see or know beforehand

FOREST n large area with a thick growth of trees ▷ vb create a forest (in)

FORESTS ▶ **forest**

FORETOP n platform at the top of the foremast

FOREVER adv without end

FOREX n foreign exchange

FOREXES ▶ **forex**

FORFAIR vb perish

FORFEIT n thing lost or given up as a penalty for a fault or mistake ▷ vb lose as a forfeit ▷ adj lost as a forfeit

FORFEND vb protect or secure

FORFEX n pair of pincers, esp the paired terminal appendages of an earwig

FORGAT past tense of ▶ **forget**

FORGAVE ▶ **forgive**

FORGE n place where metal is worked, smithy ▷ vb make a fraudulent imitation of (something)

FORGED ▶ **forge**

FORGER ▶ **forge**

FORGERS ▶ **forge**

FORGERY n illegal copy of something

FORGES ▶ **forge**

FORGET vb fail to remember

FORGETS ▶ **forget**

FORGING n process of producing a metal component by hammering

FORGIVE vb cease to blame or hold resentment against, pardon

FORGO vb do without or give up

FORGOER ▶ **forgo**

FORGOES ▶ **forgo**

FORGONE ▶ **forgo**

FORGOT past tense of ▶ **forget**

FORHENT same as > **forehent**

FORHOO vb forsake

FORHOOS ▶ **forhoo**

FORHOW same as ▶ **forhoo**

FORHOWS ▶ **forhow**

FORINT n standard monetary unit of Hungary, divided into 100 fillér

FORINTS ▶ **forint**

FORK n tool for eating food, with prongs and a handle ▷ vb pick up, dig, etc with a fork

FORKED adj having a fork or forklike parts

FORKER ▶ **fork**

FORKERS ▶ **fork**

FORKFUL ▶ **fork**

FORKIER ▶ **forky**

FORKING ▶ **fork**

FORKS ▶ **fork**

FORKY adj forked

FORLANA n Venetian dance

FORLEND same as > **forlend**

FORLENT ▶ **forlend**

FORLORN adj lonely and unhappy ▷ n forsaken person

FORM n shape or appearance ▷ vb give a (particular) shape to or take a (particular) shape

FORMAL adj of or characterized by established conventions of ceremony and behaviour

FORMALS ▶ **formal**

FORMANT n any of several frequency ranges within which the partials of a sound, esp a vowel sound, are at their strongest, thus imparting to the sound its own special quality, tone colour, or timbre

FORMAT n size and shape of a publication ▷ vb arrange in a format

FORMATE n any salt or ester of formic acid containing the ion $HCOO^-$ or the group $HCOO-$ ▷ vb fly aircraft in formation

FORMATS ▶ **format**

FORME n type matter, blocks, etc, assembled in a chase and ready for printing

FORMED ▶ **form**

FORMEE n type of heraldic cross

FORMER adj of an earlier time, previous ▷ n person or thing that forms or shapes

F

FORMERS ▸ former
FORMES ▸ forme
FORMFUL adj imaginative
FORMIC adj of, relating to, or derived from ants
FORMICA n tradename for any of various laminated plastic sheets, containing melamine, used esp for heat-resistant surfaces that can be easily cleaned
FORMING ▸ form
FORMOL same as ▸ **formalin**
FORMOLS ▸ formol
FORMS ▸ form
FORMULA n group of numbers, letters, or symbols expressing a scientific or mathematical rule
FORMYL n of, consisting of, or containing the monovalent group HCO-
FORMYLS ▸ formyl
FORNENT same as ▸ **fornenst**
FORNIX n any archlike structure, esp the arched band of white fibres at the base of the brain
FORPET n quarter of a peck (measure)
FORPETS ▸ forpet
FORPINE vb waste away
FORPIT same as ▸ **forpet**
FORPITS ▸ forpit
FORRAD adv forward
FORRAY archaic variant of ▸ **foray**
FORRAYS ▸ forray
FORREN adj foreign
FORRIT adv forward(s)
FORSAID ▸ forsay
FORSAKE vb withdraw support or friendship from
FORSAY vb renounce
FORSAYS ▸ forsay
FORSLOE same as ▸ **forslow**
FORSLOW vb hinder
FORSOOK past tense of ▸ **forsake**
FORT n fortified building or place ▷ vb fortify
FORTE n thing at which a person excels ▷ adv loudly
FORTED ▸ fort
FORTES ▸ fortis
FORTH adv forwards, out, or away ▷ prep out of
FORTHY adv therefore
FORTIES ▸ forty
FORTIFY vb make (a place)

defensible, as by building walls
FORTING ▸ fort
FORTIS adj (of a consonant) articulated with considerable muscular tension of the speech organs or with a great deal of breath pressure or plosion ▷ n consonant, such as English p or f, pronounced with considerable muscular force or breath pressure
FORTLET ▸ fort
FORTS ▸ fort
FORTUNE n luck, esp when favourable ▷ vb befall
FORTY n four times ten ▷ adj amounting to forty ▷ determiner amounting to forty
FORUM n meeting or medium for open discussion or debate
FORUMS ▸ forum
FORWARD same as ▸ **forwards**
FORWARN archaic word for ▸ **forbid**
FORWENT past tense of ▸ **forgo**
FORWHY adv for what reason
FORWORN adj weary
FORZA n force
FORZATI ▸ forzato
FORZATO same as ▸ **forzando**
FORZE ▸ forza
FOSS same as ▸ **fosse**
FOSSA n anatomical depression, trench, or hollow area
FOSSAE ▸ fossa
FOSSAS ▸ fossa
FOSSATE adj having cavities or depressions
FOSSE n ditch or moat, esp one dug as a fortification
FOSSED adj having a ditch or moat
FOSSES ▸ fosse
FOSSICK vb search, esp for gold or precious stones
FOSSIL n hardened remains of a prehistoric animal or plant preserved in rock ▷ adj of, like, or being a fossil
FOSSILS ▸ fossil
FOSSOR n grave digger
FOSSORS ▸ fossor

FOSSULA n small fossa
FOSTER vb promote the growth or development of ▷ adj of or involved in fostering a child
FOSTERS ▸ foster
FOTHER vb stop a leak in a ship's hull
FOTHERS ▸ fother
FOU adj full ▷ n bushel
FOUAT n succulent pink-flowered plant
FOUATS ▸ fouat
FOUD n sheriff in Orkney and Shetland
FOUDRIE n foud's district or office
FOUDS ▸ foud
FOUER ▸ fou
FOUEST ▸ fou
FOUET n archaic word for a whip
FOUETS ▸ fouet
FOUETTE n step in ballet in which the dancer stands on one foot and makes a whiplike movement with the other
FOUGADE n booby-trapped pit or type of mine
FOUGHT ▸ fight
FOUGHTY adj musty
FOUL adj loathsome or offensive ▷ n violation of the rules ▷ vb make dirty or polluted
FOULARD n soft light fabric of plain-weave or twill-weave silk or rayon, usually with a printed design
FOULDER vb flash like lightning
FOULE n type of woollen cloth
FOULED ▸ foul
FOULER ▸ foul
FOULES ▸ foule
FOULEST ▸ foul
FOULIE n bad mood
FOULIES ▸ foulie
FOULING ▸ foul
FOULLY ▸ foul
FOULS ▸ foul
FOUMART former name for the ▸ **polecat**
FOUND vb set up or establish (an institution, etc)
FOUNDED ▸ found
FOUNDER vb break down or fail ▷ n person who establishes an institution,

company, society, etc

FOUNDRY n place where metal is melted and cast

FOUNDS ▸ found

FOUNT same as ▸ font

FOUNTS ▸ fount

FOUR n one more than three ▸ adj amounting to four ▸ determiner amounting to four

FOURGON n long covered wagon, used mainly for carrying baggage, supplies, etc

FOURS ▸ four

FOURSES n snack eaten at four o'clock

FOURTH n (of) number four in a series ▸ adj of or being number four ▸ adv after the third person, position, event, etc

FOURTHS ▸ fourth

FOUS ▸ fou

FOUSSA n Madagascan civet-like animal

FOUSSAS ▸ foussa

FOUSTY archaic variant of ▸ fusty

FOUTER same as ▸ footer

FOUTERS ▸ fouter

FOUTH n abundance

FOUTHS ▸ fouth

FOUTRA n fig; expression of contempt

FOUTRAS ▸ foutra

FOUTRE vb footer

FOUTRED ▸ foutre

FOUTRES ▸ foutre

FOVEA n any small pit or depression in the surface of a bodily organ or part

FOVEAE ▸ fovea

FOVEAL ▸ fovea

FOVEAS ▸ fovea

FOVEATE ▸ fovea

FOVEOLA n small fovea

FOVEOLE same as ▸ foveola

FOWL n domestic cock or hen ▸ vb hunt or snare wild birds

FOWLED ▸ fowl

FOWLER ▸ fowling

FOWLERS ▸ fowling

FOWLING n shooting or trapping of birds for sport or as a livelihood

FOWLPOX n viral infection of poultry and other birds

FOWLS ▸ fowl

FOWTH same as ▸ fouth

FOWTHS ▸ fowth

FOX n reddish-brown

bushy-tailed animal of the dog family ▸ vb perplex or deceive

FOXED ▸ fox

FOXES ▸ fox

FOXFIRE n luminescent glow emitted by certain fungi on rotting wood

FOXFISH n type of shark

FOXHOLE n small pit dug for protection

FOXHUNT n hunting of foxes with hounds ▸ vb hunt foxes with hounds

FOXIE n fox terrier

FOXIER ▸ foxy

FOXIES ▸ foxie

FOXIEST ▸ foxy

FOXILY ▸ foxy

FOXING n piece of leather used to reinforce or trim part of the upper of a shoe

FOXINGS ▸ foxing

FOXLIKE ▸ fox

FOXSHIP n cunning

FOXSKIN adj made from the skin of a fox ▸ n skin of a fox

FOXTAIL n European, Asian, and S American grass with soft cylindrical spikes of flowers, cultivated as a pasture grass

FOXTROT n ballroom dance with slow and quick steps ▸ vb perform this dance

FOXY adj of or like a fox, esp in craftiness

FOY n loyalty

> This unusual word for loyalty can be a good scorer.

FOYBOAT n small rowing boat

FOYER n entrance hall in a theatre, cinema, or hotel

FOYERS ▸ foyer

FOYLE same as ▸ foil

FOYLED ▸ foyle

FOYLES ▸ foyle

FOYLING ▸ foyle

FOYNE same as ▸ foin

FOYNED ▸ foyne

FOYNES ▸ foyne

FOYNING ▸ foyne

FOYS ▸ foy

FOZIER ▸ fozy

FOZIEST ▸ fozy

FOZY adj spongy

FRA n brother: a title given to an Italian monk or friar

FRAB vb nag

FRABBED ▸ frab

FRABBIT adj peevish

FRABS ▸ frab

FRACAS n noisy quarrel

FRACK adj bold

FRACT vb break

FRACTAL n figure or surface generated by successive subdivisions of a simpler polygon or polyhedron, according to some iterative process ▸ adj of, relating to, or involving such a process

FRACTED ▸ fract

FRACTI ▸ fractus

FRACTS ▸ fract

FRACTUR same as ▸ fraktur

FRACTUS n ragged-shaped cloud formation

FRAE Scots word for ▸ from

FRAENA ▸ fraenum

FRAENUM n fold of membrane or skin, such as the fold beneath the tongue, that supports an organ

FRAG vb kill or wound (a fellow soldier or superior officer) deliberately with an explosive device

FRAGGED ▸ frag

FRAGILE adj easily broken or damaged

FRAGOR n sudden sound

FRAGORS ▸ fragor

FRAGS ▸ frag

FRAIL adj physically weak ▸ n rush basket for figs or raisins

FRAILER ▸ frail

FRAILLY ▸ frail

FRAILS ▸ frail

FRAILTY n physical or moral weakness

FRAIM n stranger

FRAIMS ▸ fraim

FRAISE n neck ruff worn during the 16th century ▸ vb provide a rampart with a palisade

FRAISED ▸ fraise

FRAISES ▸ fraise

FRAKTUR n style of typeface, formerly used in German typesetting for many printed works

FRAME n structure giving shape or support ▸ vb put together, construct

FRAMED ▸ frame

FRAMER ▸ frame

FRAMERS ▸ frame

FRAMES ▸ frame

FRAMING n frame, framework, or system of frames

F

FRAMPAL same as
> **frampold**
FRANC n monetary unit of
Switzerland, various
African countries, and
formerly of France and
Belgium
FRANCO adj post-free
FRANCS ▸ **franc**
FRANGER n condom
FRANION n lover, paramour
FRANK adj honest and
straightforward in speech
or attitude ▷ n official mark
on a letter permitting
delivery ▷ vb put such a
mark on (a letter)
FRANKED ▸ **frank**
FRANKER ▸ **frank**
FRANKLY adv in truth
FRANKS ▸ **frank**
FRANTIC adj distracted
with rage, grief, joy, etc
FRANZY adj irritable
FRAP vb lash down or
together
FRAPE adj tightly bound
FRAPPE adj (of drinks)
chilled ▷ n drink consisting
of a liqueur, etc, poured
over crushed ice
FRAPPED ▸ **frap**
FRAPPEE ▸ **frappe**
FRAPPES ▸ **frappe**
FRAPS ▸ **frap**
FRAS ▸ **fra**
FRASS n excrement or other
refuse left by insects and
insect larvae
FRASSES ▸ **frass**
FRAT n member of a
fraternity
FRATCH n quarrel
FRATCHY adj quarrelsome
FRATE n friar
FRATER n mendicant friar
or a lay brother in a
monastery or priory
FRATERS ▸ **frater**
FRATERY ▸ **frater**
FRATI ▸ **frate**
FRATRY ▸ **frater**
FRATS ▸ **frat**
FRAU n married German
woman
FRAUD n (criminal)
deception, swindle
FRAUDS ▸ **fraud**
FRAUGHT adj tense or
anxious ▷ vb archaic word
for load ▷ n archaic word
for freight
FRAUS ▸ **frau**

FRAWZEY n celebration
FRAY n noisy quarrel or
conflict ▷ vb make or
become ragged at the edge
FRAYED ▸ **fray**
FRAYING ▸ **fray**
FRAYS ▸ **fray**
FRAZIL n small pieces of ice
that form in water moving
turbulently enough to
prevent the formation of a
sheet of ice
FRAZILS ▸ **frazil**
FRAZZLE n exhausted state
▷ vb tire out
FREAK n abnormal person
or thing ▷ adj abnormal
▷ vb streak with colour
FREAKED ▸ **freak**
FREAKS ▸ **freak**
FREAKY adj weird, peculiar
FRECKLE n small brown
spot on the skin ▷ vb mark
or become marked with
freckles
FRECKLY ▸ **freckle**
FREE adj able to act at will,
not compelled or restrained
▷ vb release, liberate
FREEBEE same as ▸ **freebie**
FREEBIE n something
provided without charge
▷ adj without charge
FREED ▸ **free**
FREEDOM n being free
FREEGAN n person who
avoids buying consumer
goods, recycling discarded
goods instead
FREEING ▸ **free**
FREELY ▸ **free**
FREEMAN n person who
has been given the freedom
of a city
FREEMEN ▸ **freeman**
FREER n liberator
FREERS ▸ **freer**
FREES ▸ **free**
FREESIA n plant with
fragrant tubular flowers
FREEST ▸ **free**
FREET n omen or
superstition
FREETS ▸ **freet**
FREETY adj superstitious
FREEWAY n motorway
FREEZE vb change from a
liquid to a solid by the
reduction of temperature,
as water to ice ▷ n period of
very cold weather
FREEZER n insulated
cabinet for cold-storage of

perishable foods
FREEZES ▸ **freeze**
FREIGHT n commercial
transport of goods ▷ vb
send by freight
FREIT same as ▸ **freet**
FREITS ▸ **freit**
FREITY adj superstitious
FREMD adj, n alien or
strange (person or thing)
FREMDS ▸ **fremd**
FREMIT same as ▸ **fremd**
FREMITS ▸ **fremit**
FRENA ▸ **frenum**
FRENCH vb (of food) cut
into thin strips
FRENNE same as ▸ **fremd**
FRENNES ▸ **frenne**
FRENULA > **frenulum**
FRENUM same as
▸ **fraenum**
FRENUMS ▸ **frenum**
FRENZY n violent mental
derangement ▷ vb make
frantic
FRERE n friar
FRERES ▸ **frere**
FRESCO n watercolour
painting done on wet
plaster on a wall ▷ vb paint
a fresco
FRESCOS ▸ **fresco**
FRESH adj newly made,
acquired, etc ▷ adv recently
▷ vb freshen
FRESHED ▸ **fresh**
FRESHEN vb make or
become fresh or fresher
FRESHER n first-year
student
FRESHES ▸ **fresh**
FRESHET n sudden
overflowing of a river
FRESHIE n in Indian English,
new immigrant to the UK
from the Asian
subcontinent
FRESHLY ▸ **fresh**
FRESNEL n unit of
frequency equivalent to 10^{12}
hertz
FRET vb be worried ▷ n
worried state
FRETFUL adj irritable
FRETS ▸ **fret**
FRETSAW n fine saw with a
narrow blade, used for
fretwork
FRETTED ▸ **fret**
FRETTER ▸ **fret**
FRETTY adj decorated with
frets
FRIABLE adj easily crumbled

FRIAND n small almond cake

FRIANDE same as ▶ **friand**

FRIANDS ▶ **friand**

FRIAR n member of a male Roman Catholic religious order

FRIARLY ▶ **friar**

FRIARS ▶ **friar**

FRIARY n house of friars

FRIB n short heavy-conditioned piece of wool removed from a fleece during classing

FRIBBLE vb fritter away ▷ n wasteful or frivolous person or action ▷ adj frivolous

FRIBS ▶ **frib**

FRICHT vb frighten

FRICHTS ▶ **fricht**

FRIDGE n apparatus in which food and drinks are kept cool ▷ vb archaic word for chafe

FRIDGED ▶ **fridge**

FRIDGES ▶ **fridge**

FRIED ▶ **fry**

FRIEND n person whom one knows well and likes ▷ vb befriend

FRIENDS ▶ **friend**

FRIER same as ▶ **fryer**

FRIERS ▶ **frier**

FRIES ▶ **fry**

FRIEZE n ornamental band on a wall ▷ vb give a nap to (cloth)

FRIEZED ▶ **frieze**

FRIEZES ▶ **frieze**

FRIGATE n medium-sized fast warship

FRIGHT n sudden fear or alarm

FRIGHTS ▶ **fright**

FRIGID adj (of a woman) sexually unresponsive

FRIGOT same as ▶ **frigate**

FRIGOTS ▶ **frigot**

FRIJOL n variety of bean, esp the French bean, extensively cultivated for food in Mexico

FRIJOLE same as ▶ **frijol**

FRILL n gathered strip of fabric attached at one edge ▷ vb adorn or fit with a frill or frills

FRILLED ▶ **frill**

FRILLER ▶ **frill**

FRILLS ▶ **frill**

FRILLY adj with a frill or frills

FRINGE n hair cut short and hanging over the forehead

▷ vb decorate with a fringe ▷ adj (of theatre) unofficial or unconventional

FRINGED ▶ **fringe**

FRINGES ▶ **fringe**

FRINGY adj having a fringe

FRIPON n rogue

FRIPONS ▶ **fripon**

FRIPPER n dealer in old clothes

FRIPPET n frivolous or flamboyant young woman

FRIS ▶ **friska**

FRISBEE n tradename of a light plastic disc, thrown with a spinning motion for recreation or in competition

FRISE n fabric with a long normally uncut nap used for upholstery and rugs

FRISEE n endive

FRISEES ▶ **frisee**

FRISES ▶ **fris**

FRISEUR n hairdresser

FRISK vb move or leap playfully ▷ n playful movement

FRISKA n (in Hungarian music) the fast movement of a piece

FRISKAS ▶ **friska**

FRISKED ▶ **frisk**

FRISKER ▶ **frisk**

FRISKET n light rectangular frame, attached to the tympan of a hand printing press, that carries a parchment sheet to protect the nonprinting areas

FRISKS ▶ **frisk**

FRISKY adj lively or high-spirited

FRISSON n shiver of fear or excitement

FRIST archaic word for ▷ postpone

FRISTED ▶ **frist**

FRISTS ▶ **frist**

FRISURE n styling the hair into curls

FRIT n basic materials, partially or wholly fused, for making glass, glazes for pottery, enamel, etc ▷ vb fuse (materials) in making frit

FRITES pl n chipped potatoes

FRITFLY n type of small black fly whose larvae are destructive to grain crops

FRITH same as ▶ **firth**

FRITHS ▶ **frith**

FRITS ▶ **frit**

FRITT same as ▶ **frit**

FRITTED ▶ **frit**

FRITTER n piece of food fried in batter ▷ vb waste or squander

FRITTS ▶ **fritt**

FRITURE archaic word for ▶ **fritter**

FRITZ n as in **on the fritz** state of disrepair

FRIVOL vb behave frivolously

FRIVOLS ▶ **frivol**

FRIZ same as ▶ **frizz**

FRIZE n coarse woollen fabric ▷ vb freeze

FRIZED ▶ **frize**

FRIZER n person who gives nap to cloth

FRIZERS ▶ **frizer**

FRIZES ▶ **frize**

FRIZING ▶ **frize**

FRIZZ vb form (hair) into stiff wiry curls ▷ n hair that has been frizzed

FRIZZED ▶ **frizz**

FRIZZER ▶ **frizz**

FRIZZES ▶ **frizz**

FRIZZLE vb cook or heat until crisp and shrivelled ▷ n tight curl

FRIZZLY ▶ **frizzle**

FRIZZY adj (of the hair) in tight crisp wiry curls

FRO adv away ▷ n afro

FROCK n dress ▷ vb invest (a person) with the office or status of a cleric

FROCKED ▶ **frock**

FROCKS ▶ **frock**

FROE n cutting tool with handle and blade at right angles, used for stripping young trees, etc

FROES ▶ **froe**

FROG n smooth-skinned tailless amphibian with long back legs used for jumping

FROGBIT n floating aquatic Eurasian plant

FROGEYE n plant disease

FROGGED adj decorated with frogging

FROGGY adj like a frog

FROGLET n young frog

FROGMAN n swimmer with a rubber suit and breathing equipment for working underwater

FROGMEN ▶ **frogman**

F

FROGS ▸ frog
FROING n as in **toing and froing** going back and forth
FROINGS ▸ froing
FROISE n kind of pancake
FROISES ▸ froise
FROLIC vb run and play in a lively way ▷ n lively and merry behaviour ▷ adj full of merriment or fun
FROLICS ▸ frolic
FROM prep indicating the point of departure, source, distance, cause, change of state, etc
FROMAGE n as in **fromage frais** low-fat soft cheese
FROND n long leaf or leaflike part of a fern, palm, or seaweed
FRONDED adj having fronds
FRONDS ▸ frond
FRONS n anterior cuticular plate on the head of some insects, in front of the clypeus
FRONT n fore part ▷ adj of or at the front ▷ vb face (onto)
FRONTAL adj of, at, or in the front ▷ n decorative hanging for the front of an altar
FRONTED ▸ front
FRONTER ▸ front
FRONTES ▸ frons
FRONTON n wall against which pelota or jai alai is played
FRONTS ▸ front
FRORE adj very cold or frosty
FROREN same as ▸ **frore**
FRORN same as ▸ **frore**
FRORNE same as ▸ **frore**
FRORY adj frozen
FROS ▸ fro
FROSH n freshman
FROSHES ▸ frosh
FROST n white frozen dew or mist ▷ vb become covered with frost
FROSTED adj (of glass) having a rough surface to make it opaque ▷ n type of ice cream dish
FROSTS ▸ frost
FROSTY adj characterized or covered by frost
FROTH n mass of small bubbles ▷ vb foam
FROTHED ▸ froth
FROTHER ▸ froth

FROTHS ▸ froth
FROTHY ▸ froth
FROUGHY adj rancid
FROUNCE vb wrinkle
FROUZY same as ▸ **frowzy**
FROW same as ▸ **froe**
FROWARD adj obstinate
FROWIE same as ▸ **froughy**
FROWIER ▸ frowie
FROWN vb wrinkle one's brows in worry, anger, or thought ▷ n frowning expression
FROWNED ▸ frown
FROWNER ▸ frown
FROWNS ▸ frown
FROWS ▸ frow
FROWST n hot and stale atmosphere ▷ vb abandon oneself to such an atmosphere
FROWSTS ▸ frowst
FROWSTY adj stale or musty
FROWSY same as ▸ **frowzy**
FROWY same as ▸ **froughy**
FROWZY adj dirty or unkempt
FROZE ▸ freeze
FROZEN ▸ freeze
FRUCTAN n type of polymer of fructose, present in certain fruits
FRUCTED adj fruit-bearing
FRUG vb perform the frug, a 1960s dance
FRUGAL adj thrifty, sparing
FRUGGED ▸ frug
FRUGS ▸ frug
FRUICT obsolete variant of ▸ **fruit**
FRUICTS ▸ fruict
FRUIT n part of a plant containing seeds, esp if edible ▷ vb bear fruit
FRUITED ▸ fruit
FRUITER n fruit grower
FRUITS ▸ fruit
FRUITY adj of or like fruit
FRUMP n dowdy woman ▷ vb mock or taunt
FRUMPED ▸ frump
FRUMPLE vb wrinkle or crumple
FRUMPS ▸ frump
FRUMPY adj (of a woman, clothes, etc) dowdy, drab, or unattractive
FRUSH vb break into pieces
FRUSHED ▸ frush
FRUSHES ▸ frush
FRUST n fragment
FRUSTA ▸ frustum

FRUSTS ▸ frust
FRUSTUM n part of a cone or pyramid contained between the base and a plane parallel to the base that intersects the solid
FRUTEX n shrub
FRUTIFY vb malapropism for notify; used for comic effect by Shakespeare
FRY vb cook or be cooked in fat or oil ▷ n dish of fried food
FRYABLE ▸ fry
FRYER n person or thing that fries
FRYERS ▸ fryer
FRYING ▸ fry
FRYINGS ▸ fry
FRYPAN n long-handled shallow pan used for frying
FRYPANS ▸ frypan
FUB vb cheat
FUBAR adj irreparably damaged or bungled
FUBBED ▸ fub
FUBBERY n cheating
FUBBIER ▸ fubby
FUBBING ▸ fub
FUBBY adj chubby
FUBS ▸ fub
FUBSIER ▸ fubsy
FUBSY adj short and stout
FUCHSIA n ornamental shrub with hanging flowers
FUCHSIN n greenish crystalline substance
FUCI ▸ fucus
FUCOID n type of seaweed
FUCOIDS ▸ fucoid
FUCOSE n aldose
FUCOSES ▸ fucose
FUCOUS same as > **fucoidal**
FUCUS n type of seaweed typically with greenish-brown slimy fronds
FUCUSED adj archaic word meaning made up with cosmetics
FUCUSES ▸ fucus
FUD n rabbit's tail
FUDDIES ▸ fuddy
FUDDLE vb cause to be intoxicated or confused ▷ n confused state
FUDDLED ▸ fuddle
FUDDLER ▸ fuddle
FUDDLES ▸ fuddle
FUDDY n old-fashioned person
FUDGE n soft caramel-like sweet ▷ vb make (an issue) less clear deliberately

▷ *interj* mild exclamation of annoyance

FUDGED ▸ fudge

FUDGES ▸ fudge

FUDGING ▸ fudge

FUDS ▸ fud

FUEHRER *n* leader: applied esp to Adolf Hitler

FUEL *n* substance burned or treated to produce heat or power ▷ *vb* provide with fuel

FUELED ▸ fuel

FUELER ▸ fuel

FUELERS ▸ fuel

FUELING ▸ fuel

FUELLED ▸ fuel

FUELLER ▸ fuel

FUELS ▸ fuel

FUERO *n* Spanish code of laws

FUEROS ▸ fuero

FUFF *vb* puff

FUFFED ▸ fuff

FUFFIER ▸ fuffy

FUFFING ▸ fuff

FUFFS ▸ fuff

FUFFY *adj* puffy

FUG *n* hot stale atmosphere ▷ *vb* sit in a fug

FUGAL *adj* of, relating to, or in the style of a fugue

FUGALLY ▸ fugal

FUGATO *adj* in the manner or style of a fugue ▷ *n* movement, section, or piece in this style

FUGATOS ▸ fugato

FUGGED ▸ fug

FUGGIER ▸ fug

FUGGILY ▸ fug

FUGGING ▸ fug

FUGGY ▸ fug

FUGIE *n* runaway

FUGIES ▸ fugie

FUGIO *n* former US copper coin worth one dollar, the first authorized by Congress (1787)

FUGIOS ▸ fugio

FUGLE *vb* act as a fugleman

FUGLED ▸ fugle

FUGLES ▸ fugle

FUGLING ▸ fugle

FUGS ▸ fug

FUGU *n* puffer fish

U is not normally a desirable letter to have on your rack unless you happen to have the Q, and two Us can be trouble. This Japanese fish can help you out.

FUGUE *n* musical composition in which a theme is repeated in different parts ▷ *vb* be in a dreamlike, altered state of consciousness

FUGUED ▸ fugue

FUGUES ▸ fugue

FUGUING ▸ fugue

FUGUIST *n* composer of fugues

FUGUS ▸ fugu

FUHRER *same as* ▸ fuehrer

FUHRERS ▸ fuhrer

FUJI *n* type of African music

FUJIS ▸ fuji

FULCRA ▸ fulcrum

FULCRUM *n* pivot about which a lever turns

FULFIL *vb* bring about the achievement of (a desire or promise)

FULFILL *same as* ▸ fulfil

FULFILS ▸ fulfil

FULGENT *adj* shining brilliantly

FULGID *same as* ▸ fulgent

FULGOR *n* brilliance

FULGORS ▸ fulgor

FULGOUR *same as* ▸ fulgor

FULHAM *n* loaded die

FULHAMS ▸ fulham

FULL *adj* containing as much or as many as possible ▷ *adv* completely ▷ *vb* clean, shrink, and press cloth

FULLAGE *n* price charged for fulling cloth

FULLAM *same as* ▸ fulham

FULLAMS ▸ fullam

FULLAN *same as* ▸ fulham

FULLANS ▸ fullan

FULLED ▸ full

FULLER *n* person who fulls cloth for his living ▷ *vb* forge (a groove) or caulk (a riveted joint) with a fuller

FULLERS ▸ fuller

FULLERY *n* place where fulling is carried out

FULLEST ▸ full

FULLING ▸ full

FULLISH ▸ full

FULLS ▸ full

FULLY *adv* greatest degree or extent

FULMAR *n* Arctic sea bird

FULMARS ▸ fulmar

FULMINE *vb* fulminate

FULNESS ▸ full

FULSOME *adj* distastefully excessive or insincere

FULVID *same as* ▸ fulvous

FULVOUS *adj* of a dull brownish-yellow colour

FUM *n* phoenix, in Chinese mythology

FUMADO *n* salted, smoked fish

FUMADOS ▸ fumado

FUMAGE *n* hearth money

FUMAGES ▸ fumage

FUMARIC *adj as in* **fumaric acid** colourless crystalline acid with a fruity taste, found in some plants and manufactured from benzene

FUMBLE *vb* handle awkwardly ▷ *n* act of fumbling

FUMBLED ▸ fumble

FUMBLER ▸ fumble

FUMBLES ▸ fumble

FUME *vb* be very angry ▷ *pl n* pungent smoke or vapour

FUMED *adj* (of wood, esp oak) having a dark colour and distinctive grain from exposure to ammonia fumes

FUMER ▸ fume

FUMERS ▸ fume

FUMES ▸ fume

FUMET *n* strong-flavoured liquor from cooking fish, meat, or game: used to flavour sauces

FUMETS ▸ fumet

FUMETTE *same as* ▸ fumet

FUMETTI ▸ fumetto

FUMETTO *n* speech balloon in a comic or cartoon

FUMIER ▸ fume

FUMIEST ▸ fume

FUMING ▸ fume

FUMOUS ▸ fume

FUMS ▸ fum

FUMULI ▸ fumulus

FUMULUS *n* smokelike cloud

FUMY ▸ fume

FUN *n* enjoyment or amusement ▷ *vb* trick

FUNCKIA *n* type of plant resembling the lily

FUNCTOR *n* performer of a function

FUND *n* stock of money for a special purpose ▷ *vb* provide money to

FUNDED ▸ fund

FUNDER ▸ fund

FUNDERS ▸ fund

FUNDI *n* expert or boffin

FUNDIC ▸ fundus

FUNDIE n fundamentalist Christian

FUNDIES ▸ fundie

FUNDING ▸ fund

FUNDIS ▸ fundi

FUNDS pl n money that is readily available

FUNDUS n base of an organ or the part farthest away from its opening

FUNDY n fundamentalist

FUNEBRE adj funereal or mournful

FUNERAL n ceremony of burying or cremating a dead person

FUNEST adj lamentable

FUNFAIR n entertainment with machines to ride on and stalls

FUNFEST n enjoyable time

FUNG same as ▸ **funk**

FUNGAL adj of, derived from, or caused by a fungus or fungi ▷ n fungus or fungal infection

FUNGALS ▸ fungal

FUNGI ▸ fungus

FUNGIC ▸ fungus

FUNGO n in baseball, act of tossing and hitting the ball ▷ vb toss and hit a ball

FUNGOES ▸ fungo

FUNGOID adj resembling a fungus

FUNGOUS adj appearing suddenly and spreading quickly like a fungus

FUNGS ▸ fung

FUNGUS n plant without leaves, flowers, or roots, such as a mushroom or mould

FUNICLE n stalk that attaches an ovule or seed to the wall of the ovary

FUNK n style of dance music with a strong beat ▷ vb avoid (doing something) through fear

FUNKED ▸ funk

FUNKER ▸ funk

FUNKERS ▸ funk

FUNKIA n hosta

FUNKIAS ▸ funkia

FUNKIER ▸ funky

FUNKILY ▸ funky

FUNKING ▸ funk

FUNKS ▸ funk

FUNKY adj (of music) having a strong beat

FUNNED ▸ fun

FUNNEL n cone-shaped tube for pouring liquids into a narrow opening ▷ vb (cause to) move through or as if through a funnel

FUNNELS ▸ funnel

FUNNER ▸ fun

FUNNEST ▸ fun

FUNNIER ▸ funny

FUNNIES pl n comic strips in a newspaper

FUNNILY ▸ funny

FUNNING ▸ fun

FUNNY adj comical, humorous ▷ n joke or witticism

FUNPLEX n large amusement centre

FUNS ▸ fun

FUNSTER n funnyman

FUR n soft hair of a mammal ▷ vb cover or become covered with fur

FURAL n furfural

FURALS ▸ fural

FURAN n colourless flammable toxic liquid heterocyclic compound

FURANE same as ▸ **furan**

FURANES ▸ furane

FURANS ▸ furan

FURBISH vb smarten up

FURCA n any forklike structure, esp in insects

FURCAE ▸ furca

FURCAL ▸ furca

FURCATE vb divide into two parts ▷ adj forked, branching

FURCULA n any forklike part or organ, esp the fused clavicles (wishbone) of birds

FURDER same as ▸ **further**

FUREUR n rage or anger

FUREURS ▸ fureur

FURFAIR same as ▸ **furfur**

FURFUR n scurf or scaling of the skin

FURFURS ▸ furfur

FURIES ▸ fury

FURIOSO adv in a frantically rushing manner ▷ n passage or piece to be performed in this way

FURIOUS adj very angry

FURKID n companion animal

FURKIDS ▸ furkid

FURL vb roll up and fasten (a sail, umbrella, or flag) ▷ n act or an instance of furling

FURLANA same as ▸ **forlana**

FURLED ▸ furl

FURLER ▸ furl

FURLERS ▸ furl

FURLESS ▸ fur

FURLING ▸ furl

FURLONG n unit of length equal to 220 yards (201.168 metres)

FURLS ▸ furl

FURMETY same as > **frumenty**

FURMITY same as > **frumenty**

FURNACE n enclosed chamber containing a very hot fire ▷ vb burn in a furnace

FURNISH vb provide (a house or room) with furniture

FUROL same as > **furfural**

FUROLE same as > **furfural**

FUROLES ▸ furole

FUROLS ▸ furol

FUROR same as ▸ **furore**

FURORE n very excited or angry reaction

FURORES ▸ furore

FURORS ▸ furore

FURPHY n rumour or fictitious story

FURR vb furrow

FURRED same as ▸ **furry**

FURRIER n dealer in furs

FURRIES ▸ furry

FURRILY ▸ furry

FURRING ▸ fur

FURROW n trench made by a plough ▷ vb make or become wrinkled

FURROWS ▸ furrow

FURROWY ▸ furrow

FURRS ▸ furr

FURRY adj like or covered with fur or something furlike ▷ n child's fur-covered toy animal

FURS ▸ fur

FURTH adv out

FURTHER adv in addition ▷ adj more distant ▷ vb promote

FURTIVE adj sly and secretive

FURY n wild anger

FURZE n gorse

FURZES ▸ furze

FURZIER ▸ furze

FURZY ▸ furze

FUSAIN n fine charcoal pencil or stick made from the spindle tree

FUSAINS ▸ fusain

FUSARIA > fusarium

FUSAROL same as > fusarole

FUSBALL > foosball

FUSC adj dark or dark-brown

FUSCOUS adj of a brownish-grey colour

FUSE n cord containing an explosive for detonating a bomb ▷ vb (cause to) fail as a result of a blown fuse

FUSED > fuse

FUSEE n (in early clocks and watches) a spirally grooved spindle, functioning as an equalizing force on the unwinding of the mainspring

FUSEES > fusee

FUSEL n mixture of amyl alcohols, propanol, and butanol: a by-product in the distillation of fermented liquors used as a source of amyl alcohols

FUSELS > fusel

FUSES > fuse

FUSHION n spirit

FUSIBLE adj capable of being melted

FUSIBLY > fusible

FUSIDIC adj as in fusidic acid kind of acid

FUSIL n light flintlock musket

FUSILE adj easily melted

FUSILLI n spiral-shaped pasta

FUSILS > fusil

FUSING > fuse

FUSION n melting ▷ adj of a style of cooking that combines traditional Western techniques and ingredients with those used in Eastern cuisine

FUSIONS > fusion

FUSS n needless activity or worry ▷ vb make a fuss

FUSSED > fuss

FUSSER > fuss

FUSSERS > fuss

FUSSES > fuss

FUSSIER > fussy

FUSSILY > fussy

FUSSING > fuss

FUSSPOT n person who is difficult to please and complains often

FUSSY adj inclined to fuss

FUST vb become mouldy

FUSTED > fust

FUSTET n wood of the Venetian sumach shrub

FUSTETS > fustet

FUSTIAN n (formerly) a hard-wearing fabric of cotton mixed with flax or wool ▷ adj cheap

FUSTIC n large tropical American tree

FUSTICS > fustic

FUSTIER > fusty

FUSTILY > fusty

FUSTING > fust

FUSTOC same as > fustic

FUSTOCS > fustoc

FUSTS > fust

FUSTY adj stale-smelling

FUSUMA n Japanese sliding door

FUTCHEL n timber support in a carriage

FUTHARC same as > futhark

FUTHARK n phonetic alphabet consisting of runes

FUTHORC same as > futhark

FUTHORK same as > futhark

FUTILE adj unsuccessful or useless

FUTILER > futile

FUTON n Japanese-style bed

FUTONS > futon

FUTSAL n form of association football, played indoors with five players on each side

FUTSALS > futsal

FUTTOCK n one of the ribs in the frame of a wooden vessel

FUTURAL adj relating to the future

FUTURE n time to come ▷ adj yet to come or be

FUTURES pl n commodities bought or sold at an agreed price for delivery at a specified future date

FUTZ vb fritter time away

FUTZED > futz

FUTZES > futz

FUTZING > futz

FUZE same as > fuse

FUZED > fuze

FUZEE same as > fusee

FUZEES > fuzee

FUZES > fuze

FUZIL same as > fusil

FUZILS > fuzil

FUZING > fuze

FUZZ n mass of fine or curly hairs or fibres ▷ vb make or become fuzzy

FUZZBOX n device that distorts the sound of eg an electric guitar

FUZZED > fuzz

FUZZES > fuzz

FUZZIER > fuzzy

FUZZILY > fuzzy

FUZZING > fuzz

FUZZLE vb make drunk

FUZZLED > fuzzle

FUZZLES > fuzzle

FUZZY adj of, like, or covered with fuzz

FY same as > fie

FYCE same as > fice

FYCES > fyce

FYKE n fish trap consisting of a net suspended over a series of hoops, laid horizontally in the water ▷ vb catch fish in this manner

FYKED > fyke

FYKES > fyke

FYKING > fyke

FYLE same as > file

FYLES > fyle

FYLFOT rare word for > swastika

FYLFOTS > fylfot

FYNBOS n area of low-growing, evergreen vegetation

FYRD n local militia of an Anglo-Saxon shire, in which all freemen had to serve

FYRDS > fyrd

FYTTE n song

FYTTES > fytte**

Gg

Only three two-letter words begin with **G** (**gi**, **go** and **gu**). Knowing these will save you worrying about other possibilities. There are quite a few short words beginning with **G** that use **Y**, which can prove very useful. These include **gay, gey, goy** and **guy** (7 points each), as well as **gym** and **gyp** (9 points each). And don't forget the very useful **gox** for 11 points.

GAB *vb* talk or chatter ▷ *n* hook or open notch in a rod or lever that drops over the spindle of a valve to form a temporary connection for operating the valve

GABBA *n* type of electronic dance music

GABBARD *same as* ▷ **gabbart**

GABBART *n* Scottish sailing barge

GABBAS ▸ **gabba**

GABBED ▸ **gab**

GABBER ▸ **gab**

GABBERS ▸ **gab**

GABBIER ▸ **gabby**

GABBING ▸ **gab**

GABBLE *vb* speak rapidly and indistinctly ▷ *n* rapid indistinct speech

GABBLED ▸ **gabble**

GABBLER ▸ **gabble**

GABBLES ▸ **gabble**

GABBRO *n* dark coarse-grained basic plutonic igneous rock consisting of plagioclase feldspar, pyroxene, and often olivine

GABBROS ▸ **gabbro**

GABBY *adj* talkative

GABELLE *n* salt tax levied until 1790

GABFEST *n* prolonged gossiping or conversation

GABIES ▸ **gaby**

GABION *n* cylindrical metal container filled with stones, used in the construction of underwater foundations

GABIONS ▸ **gabion**

GABLE *n* triangular upper part of a wall between sloping roofs

GABLED ▸ **gable**

GABLES ▸ **gable**

GABLET *n* small gable

GABLETS ▸ **gablet**

GABLING ▸ **gable**

GABNASH *n* chatter

GABOON *n* dark wood from a western and central African tree, used in plywood, for furniture, and as a veneer

GABOONS ▸ **gaboon**

GABS ▸ **gab**

GABY *n* simpleton

GAD *vb* go about in search of pleasure ▷ *n* carefree adventure

GADDED ▸ **gad**

GADDER ▸ **gad**

GADDERS ▸ **gad**

GADDI *n* cushion on an Indian prince's throne

GADDING ▸ **gad**

GADDIS ▸ **gaddi**

GADE *same as* ▸ **gad**

GADES ▸ **gade**

GADFLY *n* fly that bites cattle

GADGE *n* man

GADGES ▸ **gadge**

GADGET *n* small mechanical device or appliance

GADGETS ▸ **gadget**

GADGETY ▸ **gadget**

GADGIE *n* fellow

GADGIES ▸ **gadgie**

GADI *n* Indian throne

GADID *n* type of marine fish of the family which includes the cod, haddock, whiting, and pollack

GADIDS ▸ **gadid**

GADIS ▸ **gadi**

GADJE *same as* ▸ **gadgie**

GADJES ▸ **gadje**

GADJO ▸ **gorgio**

GADLING *n* vagabond

GADOID *adj* of the cod family of marine fishes ▷ *n* gadoid fish

GADOIDS ▸ **gadoid**

GADROON *n* moulding composed of a series of convex flutes and curves joined to form a decorative pattern, used esp as an edge to silver articles

GADS ▸ **gad**

GADSMAN *n* person who uses a gad when driving animals

GADSMEN ▸ **gadsman**

GADSO *n* archaic expression of surprise

GADWALL *n* type of duck related to the mallard

GAE *Scots word for* ▸ **go**

GAED ▸ **gae**

GAEING ▸ **gae**

GAEN ▸ **gae**

GAES ▸ **gae**

GAFF *n* stick with an iron hook for landing large fish ▷ *vb* hook or land (a fish) with a gaff

GAFFE *n* social blunder

GAFFED ▸ **gaff**

GAFFER *n* foreman or boss

GAFFERS ▸ **gaffer**

GAFFES ▸ **gaffe**

GAFFING ▸ **gaff**

GAFFS ▸ **gaff**

GAG *vb* choke or retch ▷ *n* cloth etc put into or tied across the mouth

GAGA adj senile
GAGAKU n type of traditional Japanese music
GAGAKUS ▸ gagaku
GAGE vb gauge ▷ n (formerly) a glove or other object thrown down to indicate a challenge to fight
GAGED ▸ gage
GAGER same as ▸ **gauger**
GAGERS ▸ gager
GAGES ▸ gage
GAGGED ▸ gag
GAGGER n person or thing that gags
GAGGERS ▸ gagger
GAGGERY n practice of telling jokes
GAGGING ▸ gag
GAGGLE n disorderly crowd ▷ vb (of geese) to cackle
GAGGLED ▸ gaggle
GAGGLES ▸ gaggle
GAGING ▸ gage
GAGMAN n person who writes gags for a comedian
GAGMEN ▸ gagman
GAGS ▸ gag
GAGSTER n standup comedian
GAHNITE n dark green mineral of the spinel group consisting of zinc aluminium oxide
GAID same as ▸ **gad**
GAIDS ▸ gaid
GAIETY n cheerfulness
GAIJIN n (in Japan) a foreigner
GAILY adv merrily
GAIN vb acquire or obtain ▷ n profit or advantage ▷ adj straight or near
GAINED ▸ gain
GAINER n person or thing that gains
GAINERS ▸ gainer
GAINEST ▸ gain
GAINFUL adj useful or profitable
GAINING ▸ gain
GAINLY adj graceful or well-formed ▷ adv conveniently or suitably
GAINS pl n profits or winnings
GAINSAY vb deny or contradict
GAINST short for ▸ **against**
GAIR n strip of green grass on a hillside
GAIRS ▸ gair
GAIT n manner of walking

▷ vb teach (a horse) a particular gait
GAITA n type of bagpipe played in Spain and Portugal
GAITAS ▸ gaita
GAITED ▸ gait
GAITER n cloth or leather covering for the lower leg
GAITERS ▸ gaiter
GAITING ▸ gait
GAITS ▸ gait
GAITT Scots word for ▸ **gate**
GAITTS ▸ gaitt
GAJO same as ▸ **gorgio**
GAJOS ▸ gajo
GAK n (slang) cocaine
GAKS ▸ gak
GAL n girl
GALA n festival
GALABEA same as ▸ **djellaba**
GALABIA same as ▸ **djellaba**
GALAGE same as ▸ **galosh**
GALAGES ▸ galage
GALAGO another name for ▸ **bushbaby**
GALAGOS ▸ galago
GALAH n Australian cockatoo with grey wings, back, and crest and a pink body
GALAHS ▸ galah
GALANGA same as ▸ **galingale**
GALANT n 18th-century style of music characterized by homophony and elaborate ornamentation
GALANTY n as in **galanty show** pantomime shadow play, esp one in miniature using figures cut from paper
GALAS ▸ gala
GALATEA n strong twill-weave cotton fabric, striped or plain, for clothing
GALAX n coltsfoot
GALAXES ▸ galax
GALAXY n system of stars
GALE n strong wind
GALEA n part or organ shaped like a helmet or hood, such as the petals of certain flowers
GALEAE ▸ galea
GALEAS ▸ galea
GALEATE ▸ galea
GALENA n soft bluish-grey mineral consisting of lead sulphide: the chief source of lead
GALENAS ▸ galena

GALENIC ▸ galena
GALERE n group of people having a common interest, esp a coterie of undesirable people
GALERES ▸ galere
GALES ▸ gale
GALETTE n type of savoury pancake
GALILEE n porch or chapel at the entrance to some medieval churches and cathedrals in England
GALIOT n small swift galley formerly sailed on the Mediterranean
GALIOTS ▸ galiot
GALIPOT n resin obtained from several species of pine
GALL n impudence ▷ vb annoy
GALLANT adj brave and noble ▷ n young man who tried to impress women with his fashionable clothes or daring acts ▷ vb court or flirt (with)
GALLATE n salt of gallic acid
GALLED ▸ gall
GALLEIN n type of dyestuff
GALLEON n large three-masted sailing ship of the 15th–17th centuries
GALLERY n room or building for displaying works of art ▷ vb tunnel; form an underground gallery
GALLET vb (in roofing) use small pieces of slate mixed with mortar to support an upper slate
GALLETA n low-growing, coarse grass
GALLETS ▸ gallet
GALLEY n kitchen of a ship or aircraft
GALLEYS ▸ galley
GALLFLY n any of several small insects that produce galls in plant tissues, such as the gall wasp and gall midge
GALLIC adj of or containing gallium in the trivalent state
GALLICA n variety of rose
GALLIED ▸ gally
GALLIES ▸ gally
GALLING adj annoying or bitterly humiliating
GALLIOT same as ▸ **galiot**
GALLISE vb add water and sugar to unfermented

grape juice to increase the quantity of wine produced

GALLIUM n soft grey metallic element used in semiconductors

GALLIZE same as ▸ **gallise**

GALLNUT n type of plant gall that resembles a nut

GALLOCK adj left-handed

GALLON n liquid measure of eight pints, equal to 4.55 litres

GALLONS ▸ **gallon**

GALLOON n narrow band of cord, embroidery, silver or gold braid, etc, used on clothes and furniture

GALLOOT same as ▸ **galoot**

GALLOP n horse's fastest pace ▷ vb go or ride at a gallop

GALLOPS ▸ **gallop**

GALLOUS adj of or containing gallium in the divalent state

GALLOW vb frighten

GALLOWS n wooden structure used for hanging criminals

GALLS ▸ **gall**

GALLUS adj bold ▷ n suspender for trousers

GALLY vb frighten

GALOCHE same as ▸ **galosh**

GALOOT n clumsy or uncouth person

GALOOTS ▸ **galoot**

GALOP n 19th-century dance in quick duple time ▷ vb dance a galop

GALOPED ▸ **galop**

GALOPIN n boy who ran errands for a cook

GALOPS ▸ **galop**

GALORE adv in abundance ▷ adj in abundance ▷ n abundance

GALORES ▸ **galore**

GALOSH n waterproof overshoe ▷ vb cover with galoshes

GALOSHE same as ▸ **galosh**

GALS ▸ **gal**

GALUMPH vb leap or move about clumsily

GALUT same as ▸ **galuth**

GALUTH n exile of Jews from Palestine

GALUTHS ▸ **galuth**

GALUTS ▸ **galut**

GALVO n instrument for measuring electric current

GALVOS ▸ **galvo**

GALYAC same as ▸ **galyak**

GALYACS ▸ **galyac**

GALYAK n smooth glossy fur obtained from the skins of newborn or premature lambs and kids

GALYAKS ▸ **galyak**

GAM n school of whales ▷ vb (of whales) form a school

GAMA n tall perennial grass

GAMAS ▸ **gama**

GAMASH n type of gaiter

GAMAY n red grape variety, or the wine made from it

GAMAYS ▸ **gamay**

GAMB n in heraldry, the whole foreleg of a beast

GAMBA n second-largest member of the viol family

GAMBADE same as ▸ **gambado**

GAMBADO n leap or gambol; caper ▷ vb perform a gambado

GAMBAS ▸ **gamba**

GAMBE same as ▸ **gamb**

GAMBES ▸ **gambe**

GAMBET n tattler

GAMBETS ▸ **gambet**

GAMBIA same as ▸ **gambier**

GAMBIAS ▸ **gambia**

GAMBIER n astringent resinous substance obtained from a tropical Asian climbing plant

GAMBIR same as ▸ **gambier**

GAMBIRS ▸ **gambir**

GAMBIST n person who plays the (viola da) gamba

GAMBIT n opening line or move intended to secure an advantage ▷ vb sacrifice a chess piece, in opening, to gain a better position

GAMBITS ▸ **gambit**

GAMBLE vb play games of chance to win money ▷ n risky undertaking

GAMBLED ▸ **gamble**

GAMBLER ▸ **gamble**

GAMBLES ▸ **gamble**

GAMBO n farm cart

GAMBOES ▸ **gambo**

GAMBOGE n gum resin used as a yellow pigment and purgative

GAMBOL vb jump about playfully, frolic ▷ n frolic

GAMBOLS ▸ **gambol**

GAMBREL n hock of a horse or similar animal

GAMBS ▸ **gamb**

GAME n amusement or pastime ▷ vb gamble ▷ adj brave

GAMED ▸ **game**

GAMELAN n type of percussion orchestra common in the East Indies

GAMELY adv in a brave or sporting manner

GAMER n person who plays computer games

GAMERS ▸ **gamer**

GAMES ▸ **game**

GAMEST ▸ **game**

GAMESY adj sporty

GAMETAL ▸ **gamete**

GAMETE n reproductive cell

GAMETES ▸ **gamete**

GAMETIC ▸ **gamete**

GAMEY adj having the smell or flavour of game

GAMGEE n as in gamgee tissue type of wound-dressing

GAMIC adj (esp of reproduction) requiring the fusion of gametes

GAMIER ▸ **gamey**

GAMIEST ▸ **gamey**

GAMILY ▸ **gamey**

GAMIN n street urchin

GAMINE n slim boyish young woman

GAMINES ▸ **gamine**

GAMING n gambling

GAMINGS ▸ **gaming**

GAMINS ▸ **gamin**

GAMMA n third letter of the Greek alphabet

GAMMAS ▸ **gamma**

GAMME n musical scale

GAMMED ▸ **gam**

GAMMES ▸ **gamme**

GAMMING ▸ **gam**

GAMMOCK vb clown around

GAMMON n cured or smoked ham ▷ vb score a double victory in backgammon over

GAMMONS ▸ **gammon**

GAMONE n any chemical substance secreted by a gamete that attracts another gamete during sexual reproduction

GAMONES ▸ **gamone**

GAMP n umbrella

GAMPISH adj bulging

GAMPS ▸ **gamp**

GAMS ▸ **gam**

GAMUT n whole range or scale (of music, emotions, etc)

GAMUTS ▸ gamut
GAMY same as ▸ **gamey**
GAN vb go
GANACHE n rich icing or filling made of chocolate and cream
GANCH vb impale
GANCHED ▸ ganch
GANCHES ▸ ganch
GANDER n male goose ▷ vb look
GANDERS ▸ gander
GANDY adj as in **gandy dancer** railway track maintenance worker
GANE ▸ gangue
GANEF n unscrupulous opportunist who stoops to sharp practice
GANEFS ▸ ganef
GANEV same as ▸ **ganef**
GANEVS ▸ ganev
GANG n (criminal) group ▷ vb become or act as a gang
GANGED ▸ gang
GANGER n foreman of a gang of labourers
GANGERS ▸ ganger
GANGING ▸ gang
GANGLIA > ganglion
GANGLY same as ▸ **gangling**
GANGREL n wandering beggar
GANGS ▸ gang
GANGSTA n member of a street gang
GANGUE n valueless material in an ore
GANGUES ▸ gangue
GANGWAY same as > **gangplank**
GANJA n highly potent form of cannabis, usually used for smoking
GANJAH same as ▸ **ganja**
GANJAHS ▸ ganjah
GANJAS ▸ ganja
GANNED ▸ gan
GANNET n large sea bird
GANNETS ▸ gannet
GANNING ▸ gan
GANOF same as ▸ **ganef**
GANOFS ▸ ganof
GANOID adj (of the scales of certain fishes) consisting of an inner bony layer covered with an enamel-like substance ▷ n ganoid fish
GANOIDS ▸ ganoid
GANOIN n substance of which the outer layer of fish scales is composed

GANOINE same as ▸ **ganoin**
GANOINS ▸ ganoin
GANS ▸ gan
GANSEY n jersey or pullover
GANSEYS ▸ gansey
GANT vb yawn
GANTED ▸ gant
GANTING ▸ gant
GANTLET n section of a railway where two tracks overlap ▷ vb make railway tracks form a gantlet
GANTRY n structure supporting something such as a crane or rocket
GANTS ▸ gant
GAOL same as ▸ **jail**
GAOLED ▸ gaol
GAOLER ▸ gaol
GAOLERS ▸ gaol
GAOLING ▸ gaol
GAOLS ▸ gaol
GAP n break or opening
GAPE vb stare in wonder ▷ n act of gaping
GAPED ▸ gape
GAPER n person or thing that gapes
GAPERS ▸ gaper
GAPES n disease of young domestic fowl, characterized by gaping or gasping for breath and caused by gapeworms
GAPIER ▸ gapes
GAPIEST ▸ gapes
GAPING adj wide open ▷ n state of having a gaping mouth
GAPINGS ▸ gaping
GAPLESS ▸ gap
GAPO n forest near a river, regularly flooded in the rainy season
GAPOS ▸ gapo
GAPOSIS n gap between closed fastenings on a garment
GAPPED ▸ gap
GAPPER n in British English, person taking a year out between school and further education
GAPPERS ▸ gapper
GAPPIER ▸ gap
GAPPING n the act of taking a gap year
GAPPY ▸ gap
GAPS ▸ gap
GAPY ▸ gapes
GAR same as ▸ **garpike**
GARAGE n building used to house cars ▷ vb put or keep

a car in a garage
GARAGED ▸ garage
GARAGES ▸ garage
GARAGEY adj (of music) in a garage style
GARB n clothes ▷ vb clothe
GARBAGE n rubbish
GARBAGY ▸ garbage
GARBE n in heraldry, a wheat-sheaf
GARBED ▸ garb
GARBES ▸ garbe
GARBING ▸ garb
GARBLE vb jumble (a story, quotation, etc), esp unintentionally ▷ n act of garbling
GARBLED adj (of a story etc) jumbled and confused
GARBLER ▸ garble
GARBLES ▸ garble
GARBO n dustman
GARBOIL n confusion or disturbance
GARBOS ▸ garbo
GARBS ▸ garb
GARBURE n thick soup from Bearn in France
GARCON n waiter
GARCONS ▸ garcon
GARDA n member of the police force of the Republic of Ireland
GARDAI ▸ garda
GARDANT same as > **guardant**
GARDEN n piece of land for growing flowers, fruit, or vegetables ▷ vb cultivate a garden
GARDENS ▸ garden
GARE n filth
GARFISH same as ▸ **garpike**
GARGET n inflammation of the mammary gland of domestic animals, esp cattle
GARGETS ▸ garget
GARGETY ▸ garget
GARGLE vb wash the throat with (a liquid) by breathing out slowly through the liquid ▷ n liquid used for gargling
GARGLED ▸ gargle
GARGLER ▸ gargle
GARGLES ▸ gargle
GARI n thinly sliced pickled ginger, often served with sushi
GARIAL same as ▸ **gavial**
GARIALS ▸ garial
GARIGUE n open shrubby

vegetation of dry Mediterranean regions, consisting of spiny or aromatic dwarf shrubs interspersed with colourful ephemeral species

GARIS ▸ gari

GARISH adj crudely bright or colourful ▹ vb heal

GARJAN same as ▸ **gurjun**

GARJANS ▸ garjan

GARLAND n wreath of flowers worn or hung as a decoration ▹ vb decorate with garlands

GARLIC n pungent bulb of a plant of the onion family, used in cooking

GARLICS ▸ garlic

GARMENT n article of clothing ▹ vb cover or clothe

GARNER vb collect or store ▹ n place for storage or safekeeping

GARNERS ▸ garner

GARNET n red semiprecious stone

GARNETS ▸ garnet

GARNI adj garnished

GARNISH vb decorate (food) ▹ n decoration for food

GAROTE same as ▸ **garrotte**

GAROTED ▸ garote

GAROTES ▸ garote

GAROTTE same as ▸ **garrotte**

GAROUPA in Chinese and SE Asian cookery, another name for ▸ **groper**

GARPIKE n primitive N and Central American freshwater bony fish with very long toothed jaws and thick scales

GARRAN same as ▸ **garron**

GARRANS ▸ garran

GARRE vb compel

GARRED ▸ gar

GARRES ▸ garre

GARRET n attic in a house

GARRETS ▸ garret

GARRING ▸ gar

GARRON n small sturdy pony bred and used chiefly in Scotland and Ireland

GARRONS ▸ garron

GARROT n goldeneye duck

GARROTE same as ▸ **garrotte**

GARROTS ▸ garrot

GARRYA n N American

ornamental catkin-bearing evergreen shrub

GARRYAS ▸ garrya

GARS ▸ gar

GART vb compel

GARTER n band worn round the leg to hold up a sock or stocking ▹ vb secure with a garter

GARTERS ▸ garter

GARTH n courtyard surrounded by a cloister

GARTHS ▸ garth

GARUDA n Hindu god

GARUDAS ▸ garuda

GARUM n fermented fish sauce

GARUMS ▸ garum

GARVEY n small flat-bottomed yacht

GARVEYS ▸ garvey

GARVIE n sprat

GARVIES ▸ garvie

GARVOCK n sprat

GAS n airlike substance that is not liquid or solid ▹ vb poison or render unconscious with gas

GASAHOL n mixture of petrol and alcohol used as fuel

GASBAG n person who talks too much ▹ vb talk in a voluble way, esp about unimportant matters

GASBAGS ▸ gasbag

GASCON n boaster

GASCONS ▸ gascon

GASEITY n state of being gaseous

GASEOUS adj of or like gas

GASES ▸ gas

GASH vb make a long deep cut in ▹ n long deep cut ▹ adj surplus to requirements ▹ adj witty

GASHED ▸ gash

GASHER ▸ gash

GASHES ▸ gash

GASHEST ▸ gash

GASHFUL adj full of gashes

GASHING ▸ gash

GASHLY adv wittily

GASIFY vb change into a gas

GASKET n piece of rubber etc placed between the faces of a metal joint to act as a seal

GASKETS ▸ gasket

GASKIN n lower part of a horse's thigh, between the hock and the stifle

GASKING same as ▸ **gasket**

GASKINS ▸ gaskin

GASLESS ▸ gas

GASLIT adj lit by gas

GASMAN n man employed to read household gas meters and install or repair gas fittings, etc

GASMEN ▸ gasman

GASOHOL n mixture of 80% or 90% petrol with 20% or 10% ethyl alcohol, for use as a fuel in internal-combustion engines

GASP vb draw in breath sharply or with difficulty ▹ n convulsive intake of breath

GASPED ▸ gasp

GASPER n person who gasps

GASPERS ▸ gasper

GASPIER ▸ gasp

GASPING ▸ gasp

GASPS ▸ gasp

GASPY ▸ gasp

GASSED ▸ gas

GASSER n drilling or well that yields natural gas

GASSERS ▸ gasser

GASSES ▸ gas

GASSIER ▸ gassy

GASSILY ▸ gassy

GASSING ▸ gas

GASSY adj filled with gas

GAST vb frighten

GASTED ▸ gast

GASTER ▸ gast

GASTERS ▸ gast

GASTING ▸ gast

GASTRAL adj relating to the stomach

GASTREA same as ▸ **gastraea**

GASTRIC adj of the stomach

GASTRIN n polypeptide hormone secreted by the stomach: stimulates secretion of gastric juice

GASTS ▸ gast

GAT n pistol or revolver

GATE n movable barrier, usu hinged, in a wall or fence ▹ vb provide with a gate or gates

GATEAU n rich elaborate cake

GATEAUS ▸ gateau

GATEAUX ▸ gateau

GATED ▸ gate

GATELEG adj (of a table) with one or two drop leaves that are supported when in use by a hinged leg swung out from the frame

GATEMAN n gatekeeper
GATEMEN ▸ **gateman**
GATER same as ▸ **gator**
GATERS ▸ **gater**
GATES ▸ **gate**
GATEWAY n entrance with a gate
GATH n (in Indian music) second section of a raga
GATHER vb assemble ▷ n act of gathering
GATHERS ▸ **gather**
GATHS ▸ **gath**
GATING ▸ **gate**
GATINGS ▸ **gate**
GATLING n as in **gatling gun** kind of machinegun
GATOR shortened form of ▸ **alligator**
GATORS ▸ **gator**
GATS ▸ **gat**
GATVOL adj in South African English, fed up
GAU n district set up by the Nazi Party during the Third Reich
GAUCHE adj socially awkward
GAUCHER ▸ **gauche**
GAUCHO n S American cowboy
GAUCHOS ▸ **gaucho**
GAUCIE same as ▸ **gaucy**
GAUCIER ▸ **gaucy**
GAUCY adj plump or jolly
GAUD n article of cheap finery ▷ vb decorate gaudily
GAUDED ▸ **gaud**
GAUDERY n cheap finery or display
GAUDGIE same as ▸ **gadgie**
GAUDIER ▸ **gaudy**
GAUDIES ▸ **gaudy**
GAUDILY ▸ **gaudy**
GAUDING ▸ **gaud**
GAUDS ▸ **gaud**
GAUDY adj vulgarly bright or colourful ▷ n celebratory festival or feast held at some schools and colleges
GAUFER n wafer
GAUFERS ▸ **gaufer**
GAUFFER same as ▸ **goffer**
GAUFRE same as ▸ **gaufer**
GAUFRES ▸ **gaufre**
GAUGE vb estimate or judge ▷ n measuring instrument ▷ adj (of a pressure measurement) measured on a pressure gauge that registers zero at atmospheric pressure

GAUGED ▸ **gauge**
GAUGER n person or thing that gauges
GAUGERS ▸ **gauger**
GAUGES ▸ **gauge**
GAUGING ▸ **gauge**
GAUJE same as ▸ **gadgie**
GAUJES ▸ **gauje**
GAULT n stiff compact clay or thick heavy clayey soil
GAULTER n person who digs gault
GAULTS ▸ **gault**
GAUM vb understand
GAUMED ▸ **gaum**
GAUMIER ▸ **gaumy**
GAUMING ▸ **gaum**
GAUMS ▸ **gaum**
GAUMY adj clogged
GAUN ▸ **go**
GAUNCH same as ▸ **ganch**
GAUNT adj lean and haggard ▷ vb yawn
GAUNTED ▸ **gaunt**
GAUNTER ▸ **gaunt**
GAUNTLY ▸ **gaunt**
GAUNTRY same as ▸ **gantry**
GAUNTS ▸ **gaunt**
GAUP same as ▸ **gawp**
GAUPED ▸ **gaup**
GAUPER ▸ **gaup**
GAUPERS ▸ **gaup**
GAUPING ▸ **gaup**
GAUPS ▸ **gaup**
GAUPUS same as ▸ **gawpus**
GAUR n large wild member of the cattle tribe, inhabiting mountainous regions of S Asia
GAURS ▸ **gaur**
GAUS ▸ **gau**
GAUSS n cgs unit of magnetic flux density
GAUSSES ▸ **gauss**
GAUZE n transparent loosely-woven fabric, often used for surgical dressings
GAUZES ▸ **gauze**
GAUZIER ▸ **gauzy**
GAUZILY ▸ **gauzy**
GAUZY adj resembling gauze
GAVAGE n forced feeding by means of a tube inserted into the stomach through the mouth
GAVAGES ▸ **gavage**
GAVE ▸ **give**
GAVEL n small hammer banged on a table by a judge, auctioneer, or chairman to call for attention ▷ vb use a gavel

to restore order
GAVELED ▸ **gavel**
GAVELS ▸ **gavel**
GAVIAL n as in **false gavial** small crocodile
GAVIALS ▸ **gavial**
GAVOT same as ▸ **gavotte**
GAVOTS ▸ **gavot**
GAVOTTE n old formal dance ▷ vb dance a gavotte
GAW n as in **weather gaw** partial rainbow
GAWCIER ▸ **gawcy**
GAWCY same as ▸ **gaucy**
GAWD same as ▸ **gaud**
GAWDS ▸ **gawd**
GAWK vb stare stupidly ▷ n clumsy awkward person
GAWKED ▸ **gawk**
GAWKER ▸ **gawk**
GAWKERS ▸ **gawk**
GAWKIER ▸ **gawky**
GAWKIES ▸ **gawky**
GAWKILY ▸ **gawky**
GAWKING ▸ **gawk**
GAWKISH same as ▸ **gawky**
GAWKS ▸ **gawk**
GAWKY adj clumsy or awkward ▷ n simpleton
GAWP vb stare stupidly
GAWPED ▸ **gawp**
GAWPER ▸ **gawp**
GAWPERS ▸ **gawp**
GAWPING ▸ **gawp**
GAWPS ▸ **gawp**
GAWPUS n silly person
GAWS ▸ **gaw**
GAWSIE same as ▸ **gaucy**
GAWSIER ▸ **gawsie**
GAWSY same as ▸ **gaucy**
GAY adj homosexual ▷ n homosexual
GAYAL n type of ox of India and Myanmar, black or brown with white stockings
GAYALS ▸ **gayal**
GAYDAR n supposed ability of a homosexual person to determine whether or not another person is homosexual
GAYDARS ▸ **gaydar**
GAYER ▸ **gay**
GAYEST ▸ **gay**
GAYETY same as ▸ **gaiety**
GAYLY ▸ **gay**
GAYNESS ▸ **gay**
GAYS ▸ **gay**
GAYSOME adj full of merriment
GAZABO n fellow or companion

GAZABOS ▸ **gazabo**

GAZAL same as ▸ **ghazal**

GAZALS ▸ **gazal**

GAZANIA n S African plant grown for its variegated flowers

GAZAR n type of silk cloth

GAZARS ▸ **gazar**

GAZE vb look fixedly ▹ n fixed look

GAZEBO n summerhouse with a good view

GAZEBOS ▸ **gazebo**

GAZED ▸ **gaze**

GAZEFUL adj gazing

GAZELLE n small graceful antelope

GAZER ▸ **gaze**

GAZERS ▸ **gaze**

GAZES ▸ **gaze**

GAZETTE n official publication containing announcements ▹ vb announce or report (facts or an event) in a gazette

GAZIER ▸ **gazy**

GAZIEST ▸ **gazy**

GAZING ▸ **gaze**

GAZINGS ▸ **gaze**

GAZON n sod used to cover a parapet in a fortification

GAZONS ▸ **gazon**

GAZOO n kazoo

GAZOOKA same as ▸ **gazoo**

GAZOON same as ▸ **gazon**

GAZOONS ▸ **gazoon**

GAZOOS ▸ **gazoo**

GAZUMP vb raise the price of a property after verbally agreeing it with (a prospective buyer) ▹ n act or an instance of gazumping

GAZUMPS ▸ **gazump**

GAZY adj prone to gazing

GEAL vb congeal

GEALED ▸ **geal**

GEALING ▸ **geal**

GEALOUS Spenserian spelling of ▸ **jealous**

GEALS ▸ **geal**

GEAN n white-flowered tree of Europe, W Asia, and N Africa, the ancestor of cultivated sweet cherries

GEANS ▸ **gean**

GEAR n set of toothed wheels connecting with another or with a rack to change the direction or speed of transmitted motion ▹ vb prepare or organize for something

GEARBOX n case enclosing a set of gears in a motor vehicle

GEARE Spenserian spelling of ▸ **jeer**

GEARED ▸ **gear**

GEARES ▸ **geare**

GEARING n system of gears designed to transmit motion

GEARS ▸ **gear**

GEASON adj wonderful

GEAT n in casting, the channel through which molten metal runs into a mould

GEATS ▸ **geat**

GEBUR n tenant farmer

GEBURS ▸ **gebur**

GECK vb beguile

GECKED ▸ **geck**

GECKING ▸ **geck**

GECKO n small tropical lizard

GECKOES ▸ **gecko**

GECKOS ▸ **gecko**

GECKS ▸ **geck**

GED Scots word for ▸ **pike**

GEDACT n flutelike stopped metal diapason organ pipe

GEDACTS ▸ **gedact**

GEDDIT interj exclamation meaning do you understand it?

GEDECKT same as ▸ **gedact**

GEDS ▸ **ged**

GEE interj mild exclamation of surprise, admiration, etc ▹ vb move (an animal, esp a horse) ahead

GEEBUNG n Australian tree or shrub with an edible but tasteless fruit

GEECHEE n Black person from the southern states of the US

GEED ▸ **gee**

GEEGAW same as ▸ **gewgaw**

GEEGAWS ▸ **geegaw**

GEEING ▸ **gee**

GEEK n boring, unattractive person

GEEKDOM ▸ **geek**

GEEKED adj highly excited

GEEKIER ▸ **geek**

GEEKS ▸ **geek**

GEEKY ▸ **geek**

GEELBEK n edible marine fish

GEEP n cross between a goat and a sheep

GEEPS ▸ **geep**

GEES ▸ **gee**

GEESE ▸ **goose**

GEEST n area of sandy heathland in N Germany and adjacent areas

GEESTS ▸ **geest**

GEEZ interj expression of surprise

GEEZAH variant spelling of ▸ **geezer**

GEEZAHS ▸ **geezah**

GEEZER n man

GEEZERS ▸ **geezer**

GEFILTE adj as in **gefilte fish** dish of fish stuffed with various ingredients

GEGGIE Scottish, esp Glaswegian, slang word for the ▸ **mouth**

GEGGIES ▸ **geggie**

GEISHA n (in Japan) professional female companion for men

GEISHAS ▸ **geisha**

GEIST n spirit

GEISTS ▸ **geist**

GEIT n border on clothing

GEITS ▸ **geit**

GEL n jelly-like substance, esp one used to secure a hairstyle ▹ vb form a gel

GELABLE adj capable of forming a gel

GELADA n NE African baboon with a dark brown mane over the shoulders, a bare red chest, and a ridge muzzle

GELADAS ▸ **gelada**

GELANDE adj as in **gelande jump** jump made in downhill skiing

GELANT same as ▸ **gellant**

GELANTS ▸ **gelant**

GELATE vb form a gel

GELATED ▸ **gelate**

GELATES ▸ **gelate**

GELATI n layered dessert of frozen custard and ice cream

GELATIN same as > **gelatine**

GELATIS ▸ **gelati**

GELATO n Italian frozen dessert, similar to ice cream

GELATOS ▸ **gelato**

GELCAP n dose of medicine enclosed in a soluble case of gelatine

GELCAPS ▸ **gelcap**

GELD vb castrate ▹ n tax on land levied in late Anglo-Saxon and Norman England

GELDED ▸ **geld**

GELDER ▸ **geld**
GELDERS ▸ **geld**
GELDING ▸ **geld**
GELDS ▸ **geld**
GELEE n jelly
GELEES ▸ **gelee**
GELID adj very cold, icy, or frosty
GELIDER ▸ **gelid**
GELIDLY ▸ **gelid**
GELLANT n compound that forms a solid structure
GELLED ▸ **gel**
GELLIES ▸ **gelly**
GELLING ▸ **gel**
GELLY same as > **gelignite**
GELOSY Spenserian spelling of > **jealousy**
GELS ▸ **gel**
GELT ▸ **geld**
GELTS ▸ **geld**
GEM n precious stone or jewel ▷ vb set or ornament with gems
GEMCLIP n paperclip
GEMEL n in heraldry, parallel bars
GEMELS ▸ **gemel**
GEMFISH n Australian food fish with a delicate flavour
GEMINAL adj occurring in pairs
GEMINI n expression of surprise
GEMINY n pair
GEMLIKE ▸ **gem**
GEMMA n small asexual reproductive structure in liverworts, mosses, etc, that becomes detached from the parent and develops into a new individual
GEMMAE ▸ **gemma**
GEMMAN dialect form of > **gentleman**
GEMMATE adj (of some plants and animals) having or reproducing by gemmae ▷ vb produce or reproduce by gemmae
GEMMED ▸ **gem**
GEMMEN ▸ **gemman**
GEMMERY n gems collectively
GEMMIER ▸ **gem**
GEMMILY ▸ **gem**
GEMMING ▸ **gem**
GEMMULE n cell or mass of cells produced asexually by sponges and developing into a new individual
GEMMY ▸ **gem**

GEMONY same as ▸ **jiminy**
GEMOT n (in Anglo-Saxon England) a legal or administrative assembly of a community, such as a shire or hundred
GEMOTE same as ▸ **gemot**
GEMOTES ▸ **gemote**
GEMOTS ▸ **gemot**
GEMS ▸ **gem**
GEMSBOK same as ▸ **oryx**
GEN n information ▷ vb gain information
GENA n cheek
GENAL ▸ **gena**
GENAPPE n smooth worsted yarn used for braid, etc
GENAS ▸ **gena**
GENDER n state of being male or female ▷ vb have sex
GENDERS ▸ **gender**
GENE n part of a cell which determines inherited characteristics
GENERA ▸ **genus**
GENERAL adj common or widespread ▷ n very senior army officer ▷ vb act as a general
GENERIC adj of a class, group, or genus ▷ n drug, food product, etc that does not have a trademark
GENES ▸ **gene**
GENESES ▸ **genesis**
GENESIS n beginning or origin
GENET n type of agile catlike mammal of Africa and S Europe, with an elongated head, thick spotted fur, and a very long tail
GENETIC adj of genes or genetics
GENETS ▸ **genet**
GENETTE same as ▸ **genet**
GENEVA n gin
GENEVAS ▸ **geneva**
GENIAL adj cheerful and friendly
GENIC adj of or relating to a gene or genes
GENIE n (in fairy tales) servant who appears by magic and grants wishes
GENIES ▸ **genie**
GENII ▸ **genius**
GENIP same as ▸ **genipap**
GENIPAP n evergreen Caribbean tree with reddish-brown edible

orange-like fruits
GENIPS ▸ **genip**
GENISTA n any member of the broom family
GENITAL adj of the sexual organs or reproduction
GENITOR n biological father as distinguished from the pater or legal father
GENIUS n (person with) exceptional ability in a particular field
GENIZAH n repository (usually in a synagogue) for books and other sacred objects which can no longer be used but which may not be destroyed
GENIZOT ▸ **genizah**
GENLOCK n generator locking device
GENNED ▸ **gen**
GENNEL same as ▸ **ginnel**
GENNELS ▸ **gennel**
GENNET n female donkey or ass
GENNETS ▸ **gennet**
GENNIES ▸ **genny**
GENNING ▸ **gen**
GENNY same as ▸ **genoa**
GENOA n large triangular jib sail, often with a foot that extends as far aft as the clew of the mainsail
GENOAS ▸ **genoa**
GENOISE n rich sponge cake
GENOM same as ▸ **genome**
GENOME n full complement of genetic material within an organism
GENOMES ▸ **genome**
GENOMIC ▸ **genome**
GENOMS ▸ **genom**
GENRE n style of literary, musical, or artistic work
GENRES ▸ **genre**
GENRO n group of highly respected elder statesmen in late 19th- and early 20th-century Japan
GENROS ▸ **genro**
GENS n (in ancient Rome) any of a group of aristocratic families, having a common name and claiming descent from a common ancestor in the male line
GENSENG same as ▸ **ginseng**
GENT n gentleman
GENTEEL adj affectedly proper and polite

GENTES ▸ gens

GENTIAN n mountain plant with deep blue flowers

GENTIER ▸ genty

GENTIL adj gentle

GENTILE n non-Jewish (person) ▷ adj denoting an adjective or proper noun used to designate a place or the inhabitants of a place

GENTLE adj mild or kindly ▷ vb tame or subdue (a horse) ▷ n maggot, esp when used as bait in fishing

GENTLED ▸ gentle

GENTLER ▸ gentle

GENTLES ▸ gentle

GENTLY ▸ gentle

GENTOO n grey-backed penguin

GENTOOS ▸ gentoo

GENTRY n informal, often derogatory term for people just below the nobility in social rank

GENTS n men's public toilet

GENTY adj neat

GENU n any knee-like bend in a structure or part

GENUA ▸ genu

GENUINE adj not fake, authentic

GENUS n group into which a family of animals or plants is divided

GENUSES ▸ genus

GEO n (esp in Shetland) a small fjord or gully

GEODE n cavity, usually lined with crystals, within a rock mass or nodule

GEODES ▸ geode

GEODESY n study of the shape and size of the earth

GEODIC ▸ geode

GEODUCK n king clam

GEOFACT n rock shaped by natural forces, as opposed to a manmade artefact

GEOGENY same as ▸ geogony

GEOGONY n science of the earth's formation

GEOID n hypothetical surface that corresponds to mean sea level and extends at the same level under the continents

GEOIDAL ▸ geoid

GEOIDS ▸ geoid

GEOLOGY n study of the earth's origin, structure, and composition

GEOMANT n geomancer

GEORGIC adj agricultural ▷ n poem about rural or agricultural life

GEOS ▸ geo

GER n portable Mongolian dwelling

GERAH n ancient Hebrew unit of weight

GERAHS ▸ gerah

GERBE same as ▸ garbe

GERBERA n type of plant grown, usually as a greenhouse plant, for its large brightly coloured daisy-like flowers

GERBES ▸ garbe

GERBIL n burrowing desert rodent of Asia and Africa

GERBILS ▸ gerbil

GERE Spenserian spelling of ▸ gear

GERENT n person who rules or manages

GERENTS ▸ gerent

GERENUK n slender E African antelope with a long thin neck and backward-curving horns

GERES ▸ gear

GERLE Spenserian spelling of ▸ girl

GERLES ▸ gerle

GERM n microbe, esp one causing disease ▷ vb sprout

GERMAIN same as ▸ germen

GERMAN n dance consisting of complicated figures and changes of partners ▷ adj having the same parents as oneself

GERMANE adj relevant

GERMANS ▸ german

GERMED ▸ germ

GERMEN n mass of undifferentiated cells that gives rise to the germ cells

GERMENS ▸ germen

GERMIER ▸ germy

GERMIN same as ▸ germen

GERMINA ▸ germen

GERMING ▸ germ

GERMINS ▸ germin

GERMS ▸ germ

GERMY adj full of germs

GERNE vb grin

GERNED ▸ gerne

GERNES ▸ gerne

GERNING ▸ gerne

GERS ▸ ger

GERT adv in dialect, great or very big

GERTCHA interj get out of here!

GERUND n noun formed from a verb

GERUNDS ▸ gerund

GESSE Spenserian spelling of ▸ guess

GESSED ▸ gesse

GESSES ▸ gesse

GESSING ▸ gesse

GESSO n plaster used for painting or in sculpture ▷ vb apply gesso to

GESSOED ▸ gesso

GESSOES ▸ gesso

GEST n notable deed or exploit

GESTALT n perceptual pattern or structure possessing qualities as a whole that cannot be described merely as a sum of its parts

GESTANT adj laden

GESTAPO n any secret state police organization

GESTATE vb carry (developing young) in the uterus during pregnancy

GESTE same as ▸ gest

GESTES ▸ geste

GESTIC adj consisting of gestures

GESTS ▸ gest

GESTURE n movement to convey meaning ▷ vb gesticulate

GET vb obtain or receive

GETA n type of Japanese wooden sandal

GETABLE ▸ get

GETAS ▸ geta

GETAWAY n used in escape

GETS ▸ get

GETTER n person or thing that gets ▷ vb remove (a gas) by the action of a getter

GETTERS ▸ getter

GETTING ▸ get

GETUP n outfit

GETUPS ▸ getup

GEUM n type of herbaceous plant with compound leaves and red, orange, or white flowers

GEUMS ▸ geum

GEWGAW n showy but valueless trinket ▷ adj showy and valueless

GEWGAWS ▸ gewgaw

GEY adv extremely ▷ adj gallant

GEYAN adv somewhat

GEYER ▸ gey

GEYEST ▸ gey

GEYSER n spring that discharges steam and hot water

GEYSERS ▸ geyser

GHARIAL same as ▸ gavial

GHARRI same as ▸ gharry

GHARRIS ▸ gharri

GHARRY n (in India) horse-drawn vehicle available for hire

GHAST vb terrify

GHASTED ▸ ghast

GHASTLY adj unpleasant ▷ adv unhealthily

GHASTS ▸ ghast

GHAT n (in India) steps leading down to a river

GHATS ▸ ghat

GHAUT n small cleft in a hill through which a rivulet runs down to the sea

GHAUTS ▸ ghaut

GHAZAL n Arabic love poem

GHAZALS ▸ ghazal

GHAZEL same as ▸ ghazal

GHAZELS ▸ ghazel

GHAZI n Muslim fighter against infidels

GHAZIES ▸ ghazi

GHAZIS ▸ ghazi

GHEE n (in Indian cookery) clarified butter

GHEES ▸ ghee

GHERAO n form of industrial action in India in which workers imprison their employers on the premises until their demands are met ▷ vb trap an employer in his office, to indicate the workforce's discontent

GHERAOS ▸ gherao

GHERKIN n small pickled cucumber

GHESSE Spenserian spelling of ▸ guess

GHESSED ▸ ghesse

GHESSES ▸ ghesse

GHEST ▸ ghesse

GHETTO n slum area inhabited by a deprived minority ▷ vb ghettoize

GHETTOS ▸ ghetto

GHI same as ▸ ghee

GHIBLI n fiercely hot wind of North Africa

GHIBLIS ▸ ghibli

GHILGAI same as ▸ gilgai

GHILLIE n type of

tongueless shoe with lacing up the instep, originally worn by the Scots ▷ vb act as a g(h)illie

GHIS ▸ ghi

GHOST n disembodied spirit of a dead person ▷ vb ghostwrite

GHOSTED ▸ ghost

GHOSTLY adj frightening in appearance or effect

GHOSTS ▸ ghost

GHOSTY adj pertaining to ghosts

GHOUL n person with morbid interests

GHOULIE n goblin

GHOULS ▸ ghoul

GHRELIN n hormone that stimulates appetite

GHUBAR adj as in ghubar numeral type of numeral

GHYLL same as ▸ gill

GHYLLS ▸ ghyll

GI n loose-fitting white suit worn in judo, karate, and other martial arts

GIANT n mythical being of superhuman size ▷ adj huge

GIANTLY adj giantlike

GIANTRY n collective term for giants

GIANTS ▸ giant

GIARDIA n species of parasite

GIB n metal wedge, pad, or thrust bearing, esp a brass plate let into a steam engine crosshead ▷ vb fasten or supply with a gib

GIBBED ▸ gib

GIBBER vb speak or utter rapidly and unintelligibly ▷ n boulder

GIBBERS ▸ gibber

GIBBET n gallows for displaying executed criminals ▷ vb put to death by hanging on a gibbet

GIBBETS ▸ gibbet

GIBBING ▸ gib

GIBBON n agile tree-dwelling ape of S Asia

GIBBONS ▸ gibbon

GIBBOSE same as ▸ gibbous

GIBBOUS adj (of the moon) more than half but less than fully illuminated

GIBE vb make jeering or scoffing remarks (at) ▷ n derisive or provoking remark

GIBED ▸ gibe

GIBEL n Prussian carp

GIBELS ▸ gibel

GIBER ▸ gibe

GIBERS ▸ gibe

GIBES ▸ gibe

GIBING ▸ gibe

GIBLET ▸ giblets

GIBLETS pl n gizzard, liver, heart, and neck of a fowl

GIBLI same as ▸ ghibli

GIBLIS ▸ gibli

GIBS ▸ gib

GIBSON n martini garnished with onion

GIBSONS ▸ gibson

GIBUS n collapsible top hat operated by a spring

GIBUSES ▸ gibus

GID n disease of sheep characterized by an unsteady gait and staggering

GIDDAP interj exclamation used to make a horse go faster

GIDDAY interj expression of greeting

GIDDIED ▸ giddy

GIDDIER ▸ giddy

GIDDIES ▸ giddy

GIDDILY ▸ giddy

GIDDUP same as ▸ giddyup

GIDDY adj having or causing a feeling of dizziness ▷ vb make giddy

GIDDYAP same as ▸ giddyup

GIDDYUP interj exclamation used to make a horse go faster

GIDGEE n small acacia tree, which at times emits an unpleasant smell

GIDGEES ▸ gidgee

GIDJEE same as ▸ gidgee

GIDJEES ▸ gidjee

GIDS ▸ gid

GIE Scots word for ▸ give

GIED ▸ give

GIEING ▸ give

GIEN ▸ give

GIES ▸ give

GIF obsolete word for ▸ if

GIFT n present ▷ vb make a present of

GIFTED adj talented

GIFTEE n person given a gift

GIFTEES ▸ giftee

GIFTING ▸ gift

GIFTS ▸ gift

GIG n single performance by pop or jazz musicians ▷ vb play a gig or gigs

GIGA same as ▸ **gigue**
GIGABIT n unit of information in computing
GIGAS ▸ **giga**
GIGATON n unit of explosive force
GIGGED ▸ **gig**
GIGGING ▸ **gig**
GIGGIT vb move quickly
GIGGITS ▸ **giggit**
GIGGLE vb laugh nervously or foolishly ▸ n such a laugh
GIGGLED ▸ **giggle**
GIGGLER ▸ **giggle**
GIGGLES ▸ **giggle**
GIGGLY ▸ **giggle**
GIGHE ▸ **giga**
GIGLET n flighty girl
GIGLETS ▸ **giglet**
GIGLOT same as ▸ **giglet**
GIGLOTS ▸ **giglot**
GIGMAN n one who places great importance on respectability
GIGMEN ▸ **gigman**
GIGOLO n man paid by an older woman to be her escort or lover
GIGOLOS ▸ **gigolo**
GIGOT n leg of lamb or mutton
GIGOTS ▸ **gigot**
GIGS ▸ **gig**
GIGUE n piece of music, usually in six-eight time and often fugal, incorporated into the classical suite
GIGUES ▸ **gigue**
GILA n large venomous brightly coloured lizard
GILAS ▸ **gila**
GILBERT n unit of magnetomotive force
GILCUP same as ▸ **giltcup**
GILCUPS ▸ **gilcup**
GILD vb put a thin layer of gold on
GILDED ▸ **gild**
GILDEN adj gilded
GILDER ▸ **gild**
GILDERS ▸ **gild**
GILDING ▸ **gild**
GILDS ▸ **gild**
GILET n waist- or hip-length garment, usually sleeveless, fastening up the front
GILETS ▸ **gilet**
GILGAI n natural water hole
GILGAIS ▸ **gilgai**
GILGIE n type of freshwater crayfish
GILGIES ▸ **gilgie**

GILL n radiating structure beneath the cap of a mushroom ▸ vb catch (fish) or (of fish) to be caught in a gill net
GILLED ▸ **gill**
GILLER ▸ **gill**
GILLERS ▸ **gill**
GILLET n mare
GILLETS ▸ **gillet**
GILLIE n (in Scotland) attendant for hunting or fishing ▸ vb act as a gillie
GILLIED ▸ **gillie**
GILLIES ▸ **gilly**
GILLING ▸ **gill**
GILLION n (no longer in technical use) one thousand million
GILLNET n net designed to catch fish by the gills ▸ vb fish using a gillnet
GILLS pl n breathing organs in fish and other water creatures
GILLY vb act as a gillie
GILPEY n mischievous, frolicsome boy or girl
GILPEYS ▸ **gilpey**
GILPIES ▸ **gilpey**
GILPY same as ▸ **gilpey**
GILT ▸ **gild**
GILTCUP n buttercup
GILTS ▸ **gild**
GIMBAL vb support on gimbals
GIMBALS pl n set of pivoted rings which allow nautical instruments to remain horizontal at sea
GIMEL n third letter of the Hebrew alphabet
GIMELS ▸ **gimel**
GIMLET n small tool with a screwlike tip for boring holes in wood ▸ adj penetrating or piercing ▸ vb make holes in (wood) using a gimlet
GIMLETS ▸ **gimlet**
GIMMAL n ring composed of interlocking rings ▸ vb provide with gimmals
GIMMALS ▸ **gimmal**
GIMME interj give me! ▸ n short putt that one is excused by one's opponent from playing because it is considered too easy to miss
GIMMER n year-old ewe
GIMMERS ▸ **gimmer**
GIMMES ▸ **gimme**
GIMMICK n something

designed to attract attention or publicity ▸ vb make gimmicky
GIMMIE n in golf, an easy putt conceded to one's opponent
GIMMIES ▸ **gimmie**
GIMMOR n mechanical device
GIMMORS ▸ **gimmor**
GIN n spirit flavoured with juniper berries ▸ vb free (cotton) of seeds with an engine; begin
GING n child's catapult
GINGAL n type of musket mounted on a swivel
GINGALL same as ▸ **gingal**
GINGALS ▸ **gingal**
GINGE n person with ginger hair
GINGELI same as ▸ **gingili**
GINGELY same as ▸ **gingili**
GINGER n root of a tropical plant, used as a spice ▸ adj light reddish-brown ▸ vb add the spice ginger to (a dish)
GINGERS ▸ **ginger**
GINGERY adj like or tasting of ginger
GINGES ▸ **ginge**
GINGHAM n cotton cloth, usu checked or striped
GINGILI n oil obtained from sesame seeds
GINGIVA same as ▸ **gum**
GINGKO same as ▸ **gingko**
GINGKOS ▸ **gingko**
GINGLE same as ▸ **jingle**
GINGLES ▸ **gingle**
GINGS ▸ **ging**
GINK n man or boy, esp one considered to be odd
GINKGO n ornamental Chinese tree
GINKGOS ▸ **ginkgo**
GINKS ▸ **gink**
GINN same as ▸ **jinn**
GINNED ▸ **gin**
GINNEL n narrow passageway between buildings
GINNELS ▸ **ginnel**
GINNER ▸ **gin**
GINNERS ▸ **gin**
GINNERY another word for ▸ **ginhouse**
GINNIER ▸ **ginny**
GINNING ▸ **gin**
GINNY adj relating to the spirit gin
GINS ▸ **gin**

GINSENG n (root of) a plant believed to have tonic and energy-giving properties

GINSHOP n tavern

GIO same as ▸ **geo**

GIOCOSO adv (of music) to be expressed joyfully or playfully

GIOS ▸ **gio**

GIP same as ▸ **gyp**

GIPON another word for ▸ **jupon**

GIPONS ▸ **gipon**

GIPPED ▸ **gip**

GIPPER ▸ **gip**

GIPPERS ▸ **gip**

GIPPIES ▸ **gippy**

GIPPING ▸ **gip**

GIPPO same as ▸ **gippy**

GIPPOES ▸ **gippo**

GIPPOS ▸ **gippo**

GIPPY n starling

GIPS ▸ **gip**

GIPSEN obsolete word for ▸ **gypsy**

GIPSENS ▸ **gipsen**

GIPSIED ▸ **gipsy**

GIPSIES ▸ **gipsy**

GIPSY n member of a nomadic people scattered throughout Europe and North America ▸ vb live like a gypsy

GIRAFFE n African ruminant mammal with a spotted yellow skin and long neck and legs

GIRASOL n type of opal that has a red or pink glow in bright light

GIRD vb put a belt round ▸ n blow or stroke

GIRDED ▸ **gird**

GIRDER n large metal beam

GIRDERS ▸ **girder**

GIRDING ▸ **gird**

GIRDLE n woman's elastic corset ▸ vb surround or encircle

GIRDLED ▸ **girdle**

GIRDLER n person or thing that girdles

GIRDLES ▸ **girdle**

GIRDS ▸ **gird**

GIRKIN same as ▸ **gherkin**

GIRKINS ▸ **girkin**

GIRL n female child

GIRLIE adj (of a magazine, calendar, etc) featuring pictures of naked or scantily clad women ▸ n little girl

GIRLIER ▸ **girly**

GIRLIES ▸ **girlie**

GIRLISH adj of or like a girl in looks, behaviour, innocence, etc

GIRLOND obsolete word for ▸ **garland**

GIRLS ▸ **girl**

GIRLY same as ▸ **girlie**

GIRN vb snarl

GIRNED ▸ **girn**

GIRNEL n large chest for storing meal

GIRNELS ▸ **girnel**

GIRNER ▸ **girn**

GIRNERS ▸ **girn**

GIRNIE adj peevish

GIRNIER ▸ **girnie**

GIRNING ▸ **girn**

GIRNS ▸ **girn**

GIRO n (in some countries) system of transferring money within a post office or bank directly from one account to another

GIROLLE n chanterelle mushroom

GIRON n charge consisting of the lower half of a diagonally divided quarter, usually in the top left corner of the shield

GIRONIC ▸ **giron**

GIRONNY adj divided into segments from the fesse point

GIRONS ▸ **giron**

GIROS ▸ **giro**

GIROSOL same as ▸ **girasol**

GIRR same as ▸ **gird**

GIRRS ▸ **girr**

GIRSH n currency unit of Saudi Arabia

GIRSHES ▸ **girsh**

GIRT vb gird; bind

GIRTED ▸ **gird**

GIRTH n measurement round something ▸ vb fasten a girth on (a horse)

GIRTHED ▸ **girth**

GIRTHS ▸ **girth**

GIRTING ▸ **gird**

GIRTS ▸ **girt**

GIS ▸ **gi**

GISARME n long-shafted battle-axe with a sharp point on the back of the axe head

GISMO same as ▸ **gizmo**

GISMOS ▸ **gismo**

GIST n substance or main point of a matter

GISTS ▸ **gist**

GIT n contemptible person ▸ vb dialect version of get

GITANA n female gypsy

GITANAS ▸ **gitana**

GITANO n male gypsy

GITANOS ▸ **gitano**

GITE n self-catering holiday cottage for let in France

GITES ▸ **gite**

GITS ▸ **git**

GITTED ▸ **git**

GITTERN n obsolete medieval stringed instrument resembling the guitar ▸ vb play the gittern

GITTIN n Jewish divorce

GITTING ▸ **git**

GIUST same as ▸ **joust**

GIUSTED ▸ **giust**

GIUSTO adv observed strictly

GIUSTS ▸ **giust**

GIVABLE ▸ **give**

GIVE vb present (something) to another person ▸ n resilience or elasticity

GIVED same as ▸ **gyved**

GIVEN n assumed fact

GIVENS ▸ **given**

GIVER ▸ **give**

GIVERS ▸ **give**

GIVES ▸ **give**

GIVING ▸ **give**

GIVINGS ▸ **give**

GIZMO n device

GIZMOS ▸ **gizmo**

GIZZ n wig

GIZZARD n part of a bird's stomach

GIZZEN vb (of wood) to warp

GIZZENS ▸ **gizzen**

GIZZES ▸ **gizz**

GJETOST n type of Norwegian cheese

GJU n type of violin used in Shetland

This unusual word for a Shetland fiddle is great for disposing of awkward letters for a good score.

GJUS ▸ **gju**

GLACE adj preserved in a thick sugary syrup ▸ vb ice or candy (cakes, fruits, etc)

GLACEED ▸ **glace**

GLACES ▸ **glace**

GLACIAL adj of ice or glaciers ▸ n ice age

GLACIER n slow-moving mass of ice formed by accumulated snow

GLACIS n slight incline

GLAD adj pleased and happy

▷ vb become glad ▷ n gladiolus

GLADDED ▸ **glad**

GLADDEN vb make glad

GLADDER ▸ **glad**

GLADDIE same as ▸ **glad**

GLADDON n stinking iris

GLADE n open space in a forest

GLADES ▸ **glade**

GLADFUL adj full of gladness

GLADIER ▸ **glade**

GLADIUS n short sword used by Roman legionaries

GLADLY ▸ **glad**

GLADS ▸ **glad**

GLADY ▸ **glade**

GLAIK n prank

GLAIKET same as ▸ **glaikit**

GLAIKIT adj foolish

GLAIKS ▸ **glaik**

GLAIR n white of egg, esp when used as a size, glaze, or adhesive, usually in bookbinding ▷ vb apply glair to (something)

GLAIRE same as ▸ **glair**

GLAIRED ▸ **glaire**

GLAIRES ▸ **glaire**

GLAIRIN n viscous deposit found in some mineral waters

GLAIRS ▸ **glair**

GLAIRY ▸ **glair**

GLAIVE archaic word for ▸ **sword**

GLAIVED adj armed with a sword

GLAIVES ▸ **glaive**

GLAM n magical illusion ▷ vb make oneself look glamorous

GLAMMED ▸ **glam** vb

GLAMMY adj glamorous

GLAMOR same as ▸ **glamour**

GLAMORS ▸ **glamor**

GLAMOUR n alluring charm or fascination ▷ vb bewitch

GLAMS ▸ **glam**

GLANCE vb look rapidly or briefly ▷ n brief look

GLANCED ▸ **glance**

GLANCER n log or pole used to protect standing trees from damage

GLANCES ▸ **glance**

GLAND n organ that produces and secretes substances in the body

GLANDES ▸ **glans**

GLANDS ▸ **gland**

GLANS n any small rounded body or glandlike mass, such as the head of the penis

GLARE vb stare angrily ▷ n angry stare ▷ adj smooth and glassy

GLAREAL adj (of a plant) growing in cultivated land

GLARED ▸ **glare**

GLARES ▸ **glare**

GLARIER ▸ **glare**

GLARING adj conspicuous

GLARY ▸ **glare**

GLASS n hard brittle, usu transparent substance consisting of metal silicates or similar compounds ▷ vb cover with, enclose in, or fit with glass

GLASSED ▸ **glass**

GLASSEN adj glassy

GLASSES pl n pair of lenses for correcting faulty vision, in a frame that rests on the nose and hooks behind the ears

GLASSIE same as ▸ **glassy**

GLASSY adj like glass ▷ n glass marble

GLAUM vb snatch

GLAUMED ▸ **glaum**

GLAUMS ▸ **glaum**

GLAUR n mud or mire

GLAURS ▸ **glaur**

GLAURY ▸ **glaur**

GLAZE vb fit or cover with glass ▷ n transparent coating

GLAZED ▸ **glaze**

GLAZEN adj glazed

GLAZER ▸ **glaze**

GLAZERS ▸ **glaze**

GLAZES ▸ **glaze**

GLAZIER n person who fits windows with glass

GLAZILY ▸ **glaze**

GLAZING n surface of a glazed object

GLAZY ▸ **glaze**

GLEAM n small beam or glow of light ▷ vb emit a gleam

GLEAMED ▸ **gleam**

GLEAMER n mirror used to cheat in card games

GLEAMS ▸ **gleam**

GLEAMY ▸ **gleam**

GLEAN vb gather (facts etc) bit by bit

GLEANED ▸ **glean**

GLEANER ▸ **glean**

GLEANS ▸ **glean**

GLEAVE same as ▸ **sword**

GLEAVES ▸ **gleave**

GLEBA n mass of spores

GLEBAE ▸ **gleba**

GLEBE n land granted to a member of the clergy as part of his or her benefice

GLEBES ▸ **glebe**

GLEBIER ▸ **gleby**

GLEBOUS adj gleby

GLEBY adj relating to a glebe

GLED n kite

GLEDE same as ▸ **gled**

GLEDES ▸ **glede**

GLEDGE vb glance sideways

GLEDGED ▸ **gledge**

GLEDGES ▸ **gledge**

GLEDS ▸ **gled**

GLEE n triumph and delight ▷ vb be full of glee

GLEED n burning ember or hot coal

GLEEDS ▸ **gleed**

GLEEFUL adj merry or joyful, esp over someone else's mistake or misfortune

GLEEING ▸ **glee**

GLEEK vb jeer

GLEEKED ▸ **gleek**

GLEEKS ▸ **gleek**

GLEEMAN n minstrel

GLEEMEN ▸ **gleeman**

GLEENIE n guinea fowl

GLEES ▸ **glee**

GLEET n inflammation of the urethra with a slight discharge of thin pus and mucus: a stage of chronic gonorrhoea ▷ vb discharge gleet

GLEETED ▸ **gleet**

GLEETS ▸ **gleet**

GLEETY ▸ **gleet**

GLEG adj quick

GLEGGER ▸ **gleg**

GLEGLY ▸ **gleg**

GLEI same as ▸ **gley**

GLEIS ▸ **glei**

GLEN n deep narrow valley, esp in Scotland

GLENOID adj resembling or having a shallow cavity ▷ n shallow cavity

GLENS ▸ **glen**

GLENT same as ▸ **glint**

GLENTED ▸ **glent**

GLENTS ▸ **glent**

GLEY n bluish-grey compact sticky soil occurring in certain humid regions ▷ vb squint

GLEYED ▸ **gley**

GLEYING ▸ gley

GLEYS ▸ gley

GLIA *n* delicate web of connective tissue that surrounds and supports nerve cells

GLIADIN *n* protein of cereals, esp wheat, with a high proline content: forms a sticky mass with water that binds flour into dough

GLIAL ▸ glia

GLIAS ▸ glia

GLIB *adj* fluent but insincere or superficial ▹ *vb* castrate

GLIBBED ▸ glib

GLIBBER ▸ glib

GLIBLY ▸ glib

GLIBS ▸ glib

GLID *adj* moving smoothly and easily

GLIDDER ▸ glid

GLIDE *vb* move easily and smoothly ▹ *n* smooth easy movement

GLIDED ▸ glide

GLIDER *n* flying phalanger

GLIDERS ▸ glider

GLIDES ▸ glide

GLIDING *n* sport of flying gliders

GLIFF *n* slap

GLIFFS ▸ gliff

GLIFT *n* moment

GLIFTS ▸ glift

GLIKE *same as* ▸ **gleek**

GLIKES ▸ glike

GLIM *n* light or lamp

GLIME *vb* glance sideways

GLIMED ▸ glime

GLIMES ▸ glime

GLIMING ▸ glime

GLIMMER *vb* shine faintly, flicker ▹ *n* faint gleam

GLIMPSE *n* brief or incomplete view ▹ *vb* catch a glimpse of

GLIMS ▸ glim

GLINT *vb* gleam brightly ▹ *n* bright gleam

GLINTED ▸ glint

GLINTS ▸ glint

GLINTY ▸ glint

GLIOMA *n* tumour of the brain and spinal cord, composed of neuroglia cells and fibres

GLIOMAS ▸ glioma

GLIOSES ▸ gliosis

GLIOSIS *n* process leading to scarring in the central nervous system

GLISK *n* glimpse

GLISKS ▸ glisk

GLISTEN *vb* gleam by reflecting light ▹ *n* gleam or gloss

GLISTER *archaic word for* ▸ **glitter**

GLIT *n* slimy matter

GLITCH *n* small problem that stops something from working properly

GLITCHY ▸ glitch

GLITS ▸ glit

GLITTER *vb* shine with bright flashes ▹ *n* sparkle or brilliance

GLITZ *n* ostentatious showiness ▹ *vb* make something more attractive

GLITZED ▸ glitz

GLITZES ▸ glitz

GLITZY *adj* showily attractive

GLOAM *n* dusk

GLOAMS ▸ gloam

GLOAT *vb* regard one's own good fortune or the misfortune of others with smug or malicious pleasure ▹ *n* act of gloating

GLOATED ▸ gloat

GLOATER ▸ gloat

GLOATS ▸ gloat

GLOB *n* rounded mass of thick fluid

GLOBAL *adj* worldwide

GLOBATE *adj* shaped like a globe

GLOBBY *adj* thick and lumpy

GLOBE *n* sphere with a map of the earth on it ▹ *vb* form or cause to form into a globe

GLOBED ▸ globe

GLOBES ▸ globe

GLOBI ▸ globus

GLOBIN *n* protein component of the pigments myoglobin and haemoglobin

GLOBING ▸ globe

GLOBINS ▸ globin

GLOBOID *adj* shaped approximately like a globe ▹ *n* globoid body, such as any of those occurring in certain plant granules

GLOBOSE *adj* spherical or approximately spherical ▹ *n* globose object

GLOBOUS *same as* ▸ **globose**

GLOBS ▸ glob

GLOBULE *n* small round drop

GLOBUS *n* any spherelike structure

GLOBY *adj* round

GLOCHID *n* barbed spine on a plant

GLODE ▸ glide

GLOGG *n* hot alcoholic mixed drink, originally from Sweden, consisting of sweetened brandy, red wine, bitters or other flavourings, and blanched almonds

GLOGGS ▸ glogg

GLOIRE *n* glory

GLOIRES ▸ gloire

GLOM *vb* attach oneself to or associate oneself with

GLOMERA ▸ glomus

GLOMMED ▸ glom

GLOMS ▸ glom

GLOMUS *n* small anastomosis in an artery or vein

GLONOIN *n* nitroglycerin

GLOOM *n* melancholy or depression ▹ *vb* look sullen or depressed

GLOOMED ▸ gloom

GLOOMS ▸ gloom

GLOOMY *adj* despairing or sad

GLOOP *vb* cover with a viscous substance

GLOOPED ▸ gloop

GLOOPS ▸ gloop

GLOOPY ▸ gloop

GLOP *vb* cover with a viscous substance

GLOPPED ▸ glop

GLOPPY ▸ glop

GLOPS ▸ glop

GLORIA *n* silk, wool, cotton, or nylon fabric used esp for umbrellas

GLORIAS ▸ gloria

GLORIED ▸ glory

GLORIES ▸ glory

GLORIFY *vb* make (something) seem more worthy than it is

GLORY *n* praise or honour ▹ *vb* triumph or exalt

GLOSS *n* surface shine or lustre ▹ *vb* make glossy

GLOSSA *n* paired tonguelike lobe in the labium of an insect

GLOSSAE ▸ glossa

GLOSSAL ▸ glossa

GLOSSAS ▸ glossa

GLOSSED ▸ gloss

GLOSSER ▸ gloss

GLOSSES ▸ gloss

GLOSSY adj smooth and shiny ▷ n expensively produced magazine

GLOST n lead glaze used for pottery

GLOSTS ▸ glost

GLOTTAL adj of the glottis

GLOTTIC adj of or relating to the tongue or the glottis

GLOTTIS n vocal cords and the space between them

GLOUT vb look sullen

GLOUTED ▸ glout

GLOUTS ▸ glout

GLOVE n covering for the hand with individual sheaths for each finger and the thumb

GLOVED ▸ glove

GLOVER n person who makes or sells gloves

GLOVERS ▸ glover

GLOVES ▸ glove

GLOVING ▸ glove

GLOW n emit light and heat without flames ▷ n glowing light

GLOWED ▸ glow

GLOWER n scowl ▷ vb stare angrily

GLOWERS ▸ glower

GLOWFLY n firefly

GLOWING adj full of praise

GLOWS ▸ glow

GLOZE vb explain away ▷ n flattery or deceit

GLOZED ▸ gloze

GLOZES ▸ gloze

GLOZING ▸ gloze

GLUCAN n any polysaccharide consisting of a polymer of glucose, such as cellulose or starch

GLUCANS ▸ glucan

GLUCINA n oxide of glucinum

GLUCOSE n kind of sugar found in fruit

GLUE n natural or synthetic sticky substance used as an adhesive ▷ vb fasten with glue

GLUED ▸ glue

GLUEING ▸ glue

GLUEPOT n container for holding glue

GLUER ▸ glue

GLUERS ▸ glue

GLUES ▸ glue

GLUEY ▸ glue

GLUG n word representing a gurgling sound, as of liquid being poured from a bottle or swallowed ▷ vb drink noisily, taking big gulps

GLUGGED ▸ glug

GLUGS ▸ glug

GLUIER ▸ glue

GLUIEST ▸ glue

GLUILY ▸ glue

GLUING ▸ glue

GLUISH ▸ glue

GLUM adj sullen or gloomy

GLUME n one of a pair of dry membranous bracts at the base of the spikelet of grasses

GLUMES ▸ glume

GLUMLY ▸ glum

GLUMMER ▸ glum

GLUMPS n state of sulking

GLUMPY adj sullen

GLUMS n gloomy feelings

GLUNCH vb look sullen

GLUON n hypothetical particle believed to be exchanged between quarks in order to bind them together to form particles

GLUONS ▸ gluon

GLURGE n stories, often sent by email, that are supposed to be true and uplifting, but which are often fabricated and sentimental

GLURGES ▸ glurge

GLUT n excessive supply ▷ vb oversupply

GLUTAEI ▸ glutaeus

GLUTE n same as ▸ gluteus

GLUTEAL ▸ gluteus

GLUTEI ▸ gluteus

GLUTEN n protein found in cereal grain

GLUTENS ▸ gluten

GLUTES ▸ glute

GLUTEUS n any of the three muscles of the buttock

GLUTS ▸ glut

GLUTTED ▸ glut

GLUTTON n greedy person

GLYCAN n polysaccharide

GLYCANS ▸ glycan

GLYCIN same as ▸ glycine

GLYCINE n nonessential amino acid occurring in most proteins

GLYCINS ▸ glycin

GLYCOL n another name (not in technical usage) for or a diol

GLYCOLS ▸ glycol

GLYCOSE n any of various monosaccharides

GLYCYL n radical of glycine

GLYCYLS ▸ glycyl

GLYPH n carved channel or groove, esp a vertical one as used on a Doric frieze

GLYPHIC ▸ glyph

GLYPHS ▸ glyph

GLYPTAL n alkyd resin obtained from polyhydric alcohols and polybasic organic acids or their anhydrides

GLYPTIC adj of or relating to engraving or carving, esp on precious stones

GNAMMA same as ▸ namma

GNAR same as ▸ gnarl

GNARL n any knotty protuberance or swelling on a tree ▷ vb knot or cause to knot

GNARLED adj rough, twisted, and knobbly

GNARLS ▸ gnarl

GNARLY adj good

GNARR same as ▸ gnarl

GNARRED ▸ gnar

GNARRS ▸ gnarr

GNARS ▸ gnar

GNASH vb grind (the teeth) together in anger or pain ▷ n act of gnashing the teeth

GNASHED ▸ gnash

GNASHER n tooth

GNASHES ▸ gnash

GNAT n small biting two-winged fly

GNATHAL same as ▸ gnathic

GNATHIC adj of or relating to the jaw

GNATS ▸ gnat

GNATTY adj infested with gnats

GNAW vb bite or chew steadily ▷ n act or an instance of gnawing

GNAWED ▸ gnaw

GNAWER ▸ gnaw

GNAWERS ▸ gnaw

GNAWING ▸ gnaw

GNAWN ▸ gnaw

GNAWS ▸ gnaw

GNEISS n coarse-grained metamorphic rock

GNOCCHI n dumplings made of pieces of semolina pasta, or sometimes potato, used to garnish soup or served alone with sauce

GNOMAE ▸ gnome

GNOME n imaginary creature like a little old man

GNOMES ▸ gnome

GNOMIC adj of pithy sayings

GNOMISH ▸ gnome

GNOMIST n writer of pithy sayings

GNOMON n stationary arm that projects the shadow on a sundial

GNOMONS ▸ gnomon

GNOSES ▸ gnosis

GNOSIS n supposedly revealed knowledge of various spiritual truths, esp that said to have been possessed by ancient Gnostics

GNOSTIC adj of, relating to, or possessing knowledge, esp esoteric spiritual knowledge ▷ n one who knows

GNOW n Australian wild bird

GNOWS ▸ gnow

GNU n ox-like S African antelope

GNUS ▸ gnu

GO vb move to or from a place ▷ n attempt

GOA n Tibetan gazelle with a brownish-grey coat and backward-curving horns

GOAD vb provoke (someone) to take some kind of action, usu in anger ▷ n spur or provocation

GOADED ▸ goad

GOADING ▸ goad

GOADS ▸ goad

GOAF n waste left in old mine workings

GOAFS ▸ goaf

GOAL n posts through which the ball or puck has to be propelled to score ▷ vb in rugby, to convert a try into a goal

GOALED ▸ goal

GOALIE n goalkeeper

GOALIES ▸ goalie

GOALING ▸ goal

GOALS ▸ goal

GOANNA n large Australian lizard

GOANNAS ▸ goanna

GOARY variant spelling of ▸ gory

GOAS ▸ goa

GOAT n sure-footed ruminant animal with horns

GOATEE n pointed tuft-like beard

GOATEED ▸ goatee

GOATEES ▸ goatee

GOATIER ▸ goat

| This means more like a goat: it may seem a silly sort of word but because it uses such common letters the chance to play it as a bonus comes up very frequently.

GOATISH adj of, like, or relating to a goat

GOATS ▸ goat

GOATY ▸ goat

GOB n lump of a soft substance ▷ vb spit

GOBAN n board on which go is played

GOBANG n Japanese board-game

GOBANGS ▸ gobang

GOBANS ▸ goban

GOBAR adj as in gobar numeral kind of numeral

GOBBED ▸ gob

GOBBET n lump, esp of food

GOBBETS ▸ gobbet

GOBBI ▸ gobbo

GOBBIER ▸ gobby

GOBBING ▸ gob

GOBBLE vb eat hastily and greedily ▷ n rapid gurgling cry of the male turkey ▷ interj imitation of this sound

GOBBLED ▸ gobble

GOBBLER n turkey

GOBBLES ▸ gobble

GOBBO n hunchback

GOBBY adj loudmouthed and offensive

GOBI n (in Indian cookery) cauliflower

GOBIES ▸ goby

GOBIID n member of the genus Gobius

GOBIIDS ▸ gobiid

GOBIOID n type of spiny-finned fish of the suborder which includes the goby and mudskipper

GOBIS ▸ gobi

GOBLET n drinking cup without handles

GOBLETS ▸ goblet

GOBLIN n (in folklore) small malevolent creature

GOBLINS ▸ goblin

GOBO n shield placed around a microphone to exclude unwanted sounds

GOBOES ▸ gobo

GOBONEE same as ▸ gobony

GOBONY adj in heraldry, composed of a row of small, alternately-coloured, squares

GOBOS ▸ gobo

GOBS ▸ gob

GOBURRA n kookaburra

GOBY n small spiny-finned fish

GOD n spirit or being worshipped as having supernatural power ▷ vb deify

GODDAM vb damn

GODDAMN interj oath expressing anger, surprise, etc ▷ adj extremely ▷ vb damn

GODDAMS ▸ goddam

GODDED ▸ god

GODDEN n evening greeting

GODDENS ▸ godden

GODDESS n female divinity

GODDING ▸ god

GODET n triangular piece of material inserted into a garment, such as into a skirt to create a flare

GODETIA n plant with showy flowers

GODETS ▸ godet

GODHEAD n essential nature and condition of being a god

GODHOOD n state of being divine

GODLESS adj wicked or unprincipled

GODLIER ▸ godly

GODLIKE adj resembling or befitting a god or God

GODLILY ▸ godly

GODLING n little god

GODLY adj devout or pious

GODOWN n (in East Asia and India) warehouse

GODOWNS ▸ godown

GODROON same as ▸ gadroon

GODS ▸ god

GODSEND n something unexpected but welcome

GODSHIP n divinity

GODSLOT n time in a television or radio schedule traditionally reserved for religious broadcasts

GODSO same as ▸ gadso

GODSON n male godchild

GODSONS ▸ godson

GODWARD adv towards God

GODWIT n shore bird with long legs and an upturned bill

GODWITS ▸ godwit

GOE same as ▸ **go**

GOEL n in Jewish law, blood-avenger

GOELS ▸ goel

GOER n person who attends something regularly

GOERS ▸ goer

GOES ▸ go

GOEST vb archaic 2nd person sing present of go

GOETH vb archaic 3rd person sing present of go

GOETIC ▸ goety

GOETIES ▸ goety

GOETY n witchcraft

GOEY adj go-ahead

GOFER n employee or assistant whose duties include menial tasks such as running errands

GOFERS ▸ gofer

GOFF obsolete variant of ▸ **golf**

GOFFED ▸ goff

GOFFER vb press pleats into (a frill) ▷ n ornamental frill made by pressing pleats

GOFFERS ▸ goffer

GOFFING ▸ goff

GOFFS ▸ goff

GOGGA n any small insect

GOGGAS ▸ gogga

GOGGLE vb (of the eyes) bulge ▷ n fixed or bulging stare

GOGGLED ▸ goggle

GOGGLER n big-eyed scad

GOGGLES ▸ goggle

GOGGLY ▸ goggle

GOGLET n long-necked water-cooling vessel of porous earthenware, used esp in India

GOGLETS ▸ goglet

GOGO n disco

GOGOS ▸ gogo

GOIER ▸ goey

GOIEST ▸ goey

GOING ▸ go

GOINGS ▸ go

GOITER same as ▸ **goitre**

GOITERS ▸ goiter

GOITRE n swelling of the thyroid gland in the neck

GOITRED ▸ goitre

GOITRES ▸ goitre

GOJI > wolfberry

GOJIS ▸ goji

GOLD n yellow precious metal ▷ adj made of gold

GOLDARN euphemistic variant of ▸ **goddamn**

GOLDBUG n American beetle with a bright metallic lustre

GOLDEN adj made of gold ▷ vb gild

GOLDENS ▸ golden

GOLDER ▸ gold

GOLDEST ▸ gold

GOLDEYE n N American fish with yellowish eyes, silvery sides, and a dark blue back

GOLDIER ▸ goldy

GOLDISH ▸ gold

GOLDS ▸ gold

GOLDURN same as ▸ **goddamn**

GOLDY adj gold-like

GOLE obsolete spelling of ▸ **goal**

GOLEM n (in Jewish legend) artificially created human being brought to life by supernatural means

GOLEMS ▸ golem

GOLES ▸ gole

GOLF n outdoor game in which a ball is struck with clubs into a series of holes ▷ vb play golf

GOLFED ▸ golf

GOLFER n person who plays golf

GOLFERS ▸ golfer

GOLFING ▸ golf

GOLFS ▸ golf

GOLIARD n one of a number of wandering scholars in 12th- and 13th-century Europe famed for their riotous behaviour, intemperance, and composition of satirical and ribald Latin verse

GOLIAS vb behave outrageously

GOLIATH n giant

GOLLAN n yellow flower

GOLLAND same as ▸ **gollan**

GOLLANS ▸ gollan

GOLLAR same as ▸ **goller**

GOLLARS ▸ gollar

GOLLER vb roar

GOLLERS ▸ goller

GOLLIED ▸ golly

GOLLIES ▸ golly

GOLLOP vb eat or drink (something) quickly or greedily

GOLLOPS ▸ gollop

GOLLY interj exclamation of mild surprise ▷ n short for golliwog: used chiefly by children ▷ vb spit

GOLOSH same as ▸ **galosh**

GOLOSHE same as ▸ **galosh**

GOLP same as ▸ **golpe**

GOLPE n in heraldry, a purple circle

GOLPES ▸ golpe

GOLPS ▸ golp

GOMBEEN n usury

GOMBO same as ▸ **gumbo**

GOMBOS ▸ gombo

GOMBRO same as ▸ **gumbo**

GOMBROS ▸ gombro

GOMER n unwanted hospital patient

GOMERAL same as ▸ **gomeril**

GOMEREL same as ▸ **gomeril**

GOMERIL n slow-witted or stupid person

GOMERS ▸ gomer

GOMOKU another word for ▸ **gobang**

GOMOKUS ▸ gomoku

GOMPA n Tibetan monastery

GOMPAS ▸ gompa

GOMUTI n E Indian feather palm whose sweet sap is a source of sugar

GOMUTIS ▸ gomuti

GOMUTO same as ▸ **gomuti**

GOMUTOS ▸ gomuto

GON n geometrical grade

GONAD n organ producing reproductive cells, such as a testicle or ovary

GONADAL ▸ gonad

GONADIC ▸ gonad

GONADS ▸ gonad

GONDOLA n long narrow boat used in Venice

GONE ▸ go

GONEF same as ▸ **ganef**

GONEFS ▸ gonef

GONER n person or thing beyond help or recovery

GONERS ▸ goner

GONG n rimmed metal disc that produces a note when struck ▷ vb sound a gong

GONGED ▸ gong

GONGING ▸ gong

GONGS ▸ gong

GONGYO n (in Nichiren Buddhism) ceremony, performed twice a day, involving reciting parts of the Lotus Sutra and chanting the Daimoku to the Gohonzon

GONGYOS ▸ gongyo

GONIA ▸ gonion

GONIDIA > gonidium

GONIDIC > gonidium

GONIF *same as* ▸ **ganef**

GONIFF *same as* ▸ **ganef**

GONIFFS ▸ goniff

GONIFS ▸ gonif

GONION *n* point or apex of the angle of the lower jaw

GONIUM *n* immature reproductive cell

GONK *n* stuffed toy, often used as a mascot

GONKS ▸ gonk

GONNA *vb* going to

GONOF *same as* ▸ **ganef**

GONOFS ▸ ganof

GONOPH *same as* ▸ **ganef**

GONOPHS ▸ gonoph

GONOPOD *n* either member of a pair of appendages that are the external reproductive organs of insects and some other arthropods

GONS ▸ gon

GONYS *n* lower outline of a bird's bill

GONYSES ▸ gonys

GONZO *adj* wild or crazy

GOO *n* sticky substance

GOOBER *another name for* ▸ **peanut**

GOOBERS ▸ goober

GOOBIES ▸ gooby

GOOBY *n* spittle

GOOD *adj* giving pleasure ▷ *n* benefit

GOODBY *same as* ▸ **goodbye**

GOODBYE *n* expression used on parting ▷ *interj* expression used on parting ▷ *sentence substitute* farewell: a conventional expression used at leave-taking or parting with people and at the loss or rejection of things or ideas

GOODBYS ▸ goodby

GOODIE *same as* ▸ **goody**

GOODIER ▸ goody

GOODIES ▸ goody

GOODISH ▸ good

GOODLY *adj* considerable

GOODMAN *n* husband

GOODMEN ▸ goodman

GOODS ▸ good

GOODY *n* hero in a book or film ▷ *interj* child's exclamation of pleasure ▷ *adj* smug and sanctimonious

GOOEY *adj* sticky and soft

GOOF *n* mistake ▷ *vb* make a mistake

GOOFED ▸ goof

GOOFIER ▸ goofy

GOOFILY ▸ goofy

GOOFING ▸ goof

GOOFS ▸ goof

GOOFY *adj* silly or ridiculous

GOOG *n* egg

GOOGLE *vb* search for (something) on the internet using a search engine

GOOGLED ▸ google

GOOGLES ▸ google

GOOGLY *n* ball that spins unexpectedly from off to leg on the bounce

GOOGOL *n* number represented as one followed by 100 zeros (10^{100})

GOOGOLS ▸ googol

GOOGS ▸ goog

GOOIER ▸ gooey

GOOIEST ▸ gooey

GOOILY ▸ gooey

GOOKY *adj* sticky and messy

GOOL *n* corn marigold

GOOLD *Scots word for* ▸ **gold**

GOOLDS ▸ goold

GOOLS ▸ gool

GOOMBAH *n* patron or mentor

GOOMBAY *n* Bahamian soft drink

GOON *n* stupid person

GOONDA *n* (in India) habitual criminal

GOONDAS ▸ goonda

GOONEY *n* albatross

GOONEYS ▸ gooney

GOONIE *Scots word for a* ▸ **gown**

GOONIER ▸ goon

GOONIES ▸ goonie

GOONS ▸ goon

GOONY ▸ goon

GOOP *n* rude or ill-mannered person

GOOPED *adj as in* **gooped up** sticky with goop

GOOPIER ▸ goop

GOOPS ▸ goop

GOOPY ▸ goop

GOOR *same as* ▸ **gur**

GOORAL *same as* ▸ **goral**

GOORALS ▸ gooral

GOORIE ▸ kuri

GOORIES ▸ goorie

GOOROO *same as* ▸ **guru**

GOOROOS ▸ gooroo

GOORS ▸ goor

GOORY ▸ kuri

GOOS ▸ goo

GOOSE *n* web-footed bird like a large duck ▷ *vb* prod (someone) playfully in the bottom

GOOSED ▸ goose

GOOSERY *n* place for keeping geese

GOOSES ▸ goose

GOOSEY *same as* ▸ **goosy**

GOOSEYS ▸ goosey

GOOSIER ▸ goosy

GOOSIES ▸ goosy

GOOSING ▸ goose

GOOSY *adj* of or like a goose

GOPAK *n* spectacular high-leaping Russian peasant dance for men

GOPAKS ▸ gopak

GOPHER *n* American burrowing rodent ▷ *vb* burrow

GOPHERS ▸ gopher

GOPIK *n* money unit of Azerbaijan

GOPIKS ▸ gopik

GOPURA *n* gateway tower of an Indian temple

GOPURAM *same as* ▸ **gopura**

GOPURAS ▸ gopura

GOR *interj* God!

GORA *n* (in informal Indian English) White or fair-skinned male

GORAL *n* small S Asian goat antelope with a yellowish-grey and black coat and small conical horns

GORALS ▸ goral

GORAMY ▸ gourami

GORAS ▸ gora

GORCOCK *n* male of the red grouse

GORCROW *n* carrion crow

GORDITA *n* small thick tortilla

GORE *n* blood from a wound ▷ *vb* pierce with horns

GORED ▸ gore

GORES ▸ gore

GORGE *n* deep narrow valley ▷ *vb* eat greedily

GORGED ▸ gorge

GORGER ▸ gorge

GORGERS ▸ gorge

GORGES ▸ gorge

GORGET n collar-like piece of armour to protect the throat

GORGETS ▸ gorget

GORGIA n improvised sung passage

GORGIAS ▸ gorgia

GORGING ▸ gorge

GORGIO n word used by gypsies for a non-gypsy

GORGIOS ▸ gorgio

GORGON n terrifying or repulsive woman

GORGONS ▸ gorgon

GORHEN n female red grouse

GORHENS ▸ gorhen

GORI n in informal Indian English, a White or fair-skinned female

GORIER ▸ gory

GORIEST ▸ gory

GORILLA n largest of the apes, found in Africa

GORILY ▸ gory

GORING ▸ gore

GORINGS ▸ gore

GORIS ▸ gori

GORM n foolish person ▹ vb understand

GORMAND same as > **gourmand**

GORMED ▸ gorm

GORMIER ▸ gormy

GORMING ▸ gorm

GORMS ▸ gorm

GORMY adj gormless

GORP same as ▸ **gawp**

GORPED ▸ gawp

GORPING ▸ gawp

GORPS ▸ gawp

GORSE n prickly yellow-flowered shrub

GORSEDD n meeting of bards and druids held daily before an eisteddfod

GORSES ▸ gorse

GORSIER ▸ gorse

GORSOON n young boy

GORSY ▸ gorse

GORY adj horrific or bloodthirsty

GOS ▸ go

GOSH interj exclamation of mild surprise or wonder

GOSHAWK n large hawk

GOSHT n Indian meat dish

GOSHTS ▸ gosht

GOSLET n pygmy goose

GOSLETS ▸ goslet

GOSLING n young goose

GOSPEL n any of the first four books of the New Testament ▹ adj denoting a kind of religious music originating in the churches of the Black people in the Southern US ▹ vb teach the gospel

GOSPELS ▸ gospel

GOSPODA > gospodin

GOSPORT n aeroplane communication device

GOSS vb spit

GOSSAN n oxidised portion of a mineral vein in rock

GOSSANS ▸ gossan

GOSSE same as ▸ **gorse**

GOSSED ▸ goss

GOSSES ▸ gosse

GOSSIB n gossip

GOSSIBS ▸ gossib

GOSSING ▸ goss

GOSSIP n idle talk, esp about other people ▹ vb engage in gossip

GOSSIPS ▸ gossip

GOSSIPY ▸ gossip

GOSSOON n boy, esp a servant boy

GOSTER vb laugh uncontrollably

GOSTERS ▸ goster

GOT ▸ get

GOTCHA adj as in **gotcha lizard** Australian name for a crocodile

GOTCHAS ▸ gotcha

GOTH n aficionado of Goth music and fashion

GOTHIC adj of or relating to a literary style characterized by gloom, the grotesque, and the supernatural ▹ n family of heavy script typefaces

GOTHICS ▸ gothic

GOTHITE same as > **goethite**

GOTHS ▸ goth

GOTTA vb got to

GOTTEN past participle of ▸ **get**

GOUACHE n (painting using) watercolours mixed with glue

GOUCH vb become drowsy or lethargic under the influence of narcotics

GOUCHED ▸ gouch

GOUCHES ▸ gouch

GOUGE vb scoop or force out ▹ n hole or groove

GOUGED ▸ gouge

GOUGER n person or tool that gouges

GOUGERE n choux pastry flavoured with cheese

GOUGERS ▸ gouger

GOUGES ▸ gouge

GOUGING ▸ gouge

GOUJON n small strip of fish or chicken, coated in breadcrumbs and deep-fried

GOUJONS ▸ goujon

GOUK same as ▸ **gowk**

GOUKS ▸ gouk

GOULASH n rich stew seasoned with paprika

GOURA n large, crested ground pigeon found in New Guinea

GOURAMI n large SE Asian labyrinth fish used for food and (when young) as an aquarium fish

GOURAS ▸ goura

GOURD n fleshy fruit of a climbing plant

GOURDE n standard monetary unit of Haiti, divided into 100 centimes

GOURDES ▸ gourde

GOURDS ▸ gourd

GOURDY adj (of horses) swollen-legged

GOURMET n connoisseur of food and drink

GOUSTY adj dismal

GOUT n disease causing inflammation of the joints

GOUTFLY n fly whose larvae infect crops

GOUTIER ▸ gout

GOUTILY ▸ gout

GOUTS ▸ gout

GOUTTE n in heraldry, charge shaped like a drop of liquid

GOUTTES ▸ goutte

GOUTY ▸ gout

GOV n boss

GOVERN vb rule, direct, or control ▹ n ability to be governed

GOVERNS ▸ govern

GOVS ▸ gov

GOWAN n any of various yellow or white flowers growing in fields, esp the common daisy

GOWANED ▸ gowan

GOWANS ▸ gowan

GOWANY ▸ gowan

GOWD Scots word for ▸ **gold**

GOWDER ▸ gowd

GOWDEST ▸ gowd

GOWDS ▸ gowd

GOWF vb strike
GOWFED ▸ gowf
GOWFER ▸ gowf
GOWFERS ▸ gowf
GOWFING ▸ gowf
GOWFS ▸ gowf
GOWK n stupid person
GOWKS ▸ gowk
GOWL n substance often found in the corner of the eyes after sleep ▸ vb howl
GOWLAN same as ▸ gollan
GOWLAND same as ▸ gollan
GOWLANS ▸ gowlan
GOWLED ▸ gowl
GOWLING ▸ gowl
GOWLS ▸ gowl
GOWN n woman's long formal dress ▸ vb supply with or dress in a gown
GOWNBOY n foundationer schoolboy who wears a gown
GOWNED ▸ gown
GOWNING ▸ gown
GOWNMAN n professional person, such as a lawyer, who wears a gown
GOWNMEN ▸ gownman
GOWNS ▸ gown
GOWPEN n pair of cupped hands
GOWPENS ▸ gowpen
GOX n gaseous oxygen

> **Gox** is gaseous oxygen, especially useful if you can use it to hit a bonus square.

GOXES ▸ gox
GOYLE n ravine
GOYLES ▸ goyle
GOZZAN same as ▸ gossan
GOZZANS ▸ gozzan
GRAAL n holy grail
GRAALS ▸ graal
GRAB vb grasp suddenly, snatch ▸ n sudden snatch
GRABBED ▸ grab
GRABBER ▸ grab
GRABBLE vb scratch or feel about with the hands
GRABBY adj greedy or selfish
GRABEN n elongated trough of land produced by subsidence of the earth's crust between two faults
GRABENS ▸ graben
GRABS ▸ grab
GRACE n beauty and elegance ▸ vb honour
GRACED ▸ grace
GRACES ▸ grace

GRACILE adj gracefully thin or slender
GRACING ▸ grace
GRACKLE n American songbird with a dark iridescent plumage
GRAD n graduate
GRADATE vb change or cause to change imperceptibly, as from one colour, tone, or degree to another
GRADDAN vb dress corn
GRADE n place on a scale of quality, rank, or size ▸ vb arrange in grades
GRADED ▸ grade
GRADELY adj fine
GRADER n person or thing that grades
GRADERS ▸ grader
GRADES ▸ grade
GRADIN n ledge above or behind an altar on which candles, a cross, or other ornaments stand
GRADINE same as ▸ gradin
GRADING ▸ grade
GRADINI ▸ gradino
GRADINO n step above an altar
GRADINS ▸ gradin
GRADS ▸ grad
GRADUAL adj occurring, developing, or moving in small stages ▸ n antiphon or group of several antiphons, usually from the Psalms, sung or recited immediately after the epistle at Mass
GRADUS n book of études or other musical exercises arranged in order of increasing difficulty
GRAFF same as ▸ graft
GRAFFED ▸ graff
GRAFFS ▸ graff
GRAFT n surgical transplant of skin or tissue ▸ vb transplant (living tissue) surgically
GRAFTED ▸ graft
GRAFTER ▸ graft
GRAFTS ▸ graft
GRAHAM n made of graham flour
GRAHAMS ▸ graham
GRAIL n any desired ambition or goal
GRAILE same as ▸ grail
GRAILES ▸ graile
GRAILS ▸ grail

GRAIN n seedlike fruit of a cereal plant ▸ vb paint in imitation of the grain of wood or leather
GRAINE n eggs of the silkworm
GRAINED ▸ grain
GRAINER ▸ grain
GRAINES ▸ graine
GRAINS ▸ grain
GRAINY adj resembling, full of, or composed of grain
GRAIP n long-handled gardening fork
GRAIPS ▸ graip
GRAITH vb clothe
GRAITHS ▸ graith
GRAKLE same as ▸ grackle
GRAKLES ▸ grakle
GRAM n metric unit of mass equal to one thousandth of a kilogram
GRAMA n type of grass of W North America and S America, often used as a pasture grass
GRAMARY same as > gramarye
GRAMAS ▸ grama
GRAMASH n type of gaiter
GRAME n sorrow
GRAMES ▸ grame
GRAMMA n pasture grass of the South American plains
GRAMMAR n branch of linguistics dealing with the form, function, and order of words
GRAMMAS ▸ gramma
GRAMME same as ▸ grame
GRAMMES ▸ gram
GRAMP n grandfather
GRAMPA same as ▸ grandpa
GRAMPAS ▸ grampa
GRAMPS ▸ gramp
GRAMPUS n dolphin-like mammal
GRAMS ▸ gram
GRAN n grandmother
GRANA ▸ granum
GRANARY n storehouse for grain
GRAND adj large or impressive, imposing ▸ n thousand pounds or dollars
GRANDAD n grandfather
GRANDAM n archaic word for grandmother
GRANDE feminine form of ▸ grand
GRANDEE n Spanish nobleman of the highest rank

GRANDER ▸ **grand**

GRANDLY ▸ **grand**

GRANDMA n grandmother

GRANDPA n grandfather

GRANDS ▸ **grand**

GRANFER n grandfather

GRANGE n country house with farm buildings

GRANGER n keeper or member of a grange

GRANGES ▸ **grange**

GRANITA n Italian iced drink

GRANITE n very hard igneous rock often used in building

GRANNAM n old woman

GRANNIE vb defeat (in a game or contest) so that one's opponent does not score a single point

GRANNOM n type of caddis fly esteemed as a bait by anglers

GRANNY n grandmother ▸ vb defeat (in a game or contest) so that one's opponent does not score a single point

GRANOLA n muesli-like breakfast cereal

GRANS ▸ **gran**

GRANT vb consent to fulfil (a request) ▸ n sum of money provided by a government for a specific purpose, such as education

GRANTED ▸ **grant**

GRANTEE n person to whom a grant is made

GRANTER ▸ **grant**

GRANTOR n person who makes a grant

GRANTS ▸ **grant**

GRANULE n small grain

GRANUM n membrane layers in a chloroplast

GRAPE n small juicy green or purple berry, eaten raw or used to produce wine, raisins, currants, or sultanas ▸ vb grope

GRAPED ▸ **grape**

GRAPERY n building where grapes are grown

GRAPES n abnormal growth, resembling a bunch of grapes, on the fetlock of a horse

GRAPEY ▸ **grape**

GRAPH n drawing showing the relation of different numbers or quantities

plotted against a set of axes ▸ vb draw or represent in a graph

GRAPHED ▸ **graph**

GRAPHIC adj vividly descriptive

GRAPHS ▸ **graph**

GRAPIER ▸ **grape**

GRAPING ▸ **grape**

GRAPLE same as ▸ **grapple**

GRAPLES ▸ **graple**

GRAPLIN same as ▸ **grapnel**

GRAPNEL n device with several hooks, used to grasp or secure things

GRAPPA n spirit distilled from the fermented remains of grapes after pressing

GRAPPAS ▸ **grappa**

GRAPPLE vb try to cope with (something difficult) ▸ n grapnel

GRAPY ▸ **grape**

GRASP vb grip something firmly ▸ n grip or clasp

GRASPED ▸ **grasp**

GRASPER ▸ **grasp**

GRASPS ▸ **grasp**

GRASS n common type of plant with jointed stems and long narrow leaves, including cereals and bamboo ▸ vb cover with grass

GRASSED ▸ **grass**

GRASSER n police informant

GRASSES ▸ **grass**

GRASSUM n in Scots law, lump sum paid when taking up a lease

GRASSY adj covered with, containing, or resembling grass

GRASTE archaic past participle of ▸ **grace**

GRAT ▸ **greet**

GRATE vb rub into small bits on a rough surface ▸ n framework of metal bars for holding fuel in a fireplace

GRATED ▸ **grate**

GRATER n tool with a sharp surface for grating food

GRATERS ▸ **grater**

GRATES ▸ **grate**

GRATIFY vb satisfy or please ▸ adj giving one satisfaction or pleasure

GRATIN n crust of browned breadcrumbs

GRATINE adj cooked au gratin

GRATING adj harsh or rasping ▸ n framework of metal bars covering an opening

GRATINS ▸ **gratin**

GRATIS adj free, for nothing

GRAUNCH vb crush or destroy

GRAUPEL n soft hail or snow pellets

GRAV n unit of acceleration equal to the standard acceleration of free fall

GRAVE n hole for burying a corpse ▸ adj causing concern ▸ vb cut, carve, sculpt, or engrave ▸ adv to be performed in a solemn manner

GRAVED ▸ **grave**

GRAVEL n mixture of small stones and coarse sand ▸ vb cover with gravel

GRAVELS ▸ **gravel**

GRAVELY ▸ **gravel**

GRAVEN ▸ **grave**

GRAVER n any of various engraving, chasing, or sculpting tools, such as a burin

GRAVERS ▸ **graver**

GRAVES ▸ **grave**

GRAVEST ▸ **grave**

GRAVID adj pregnant

GRAVIDA n pregnant woman

GRAVIES ▸ **gravy**

GRAVING ▸ **grave**

GRAVIS as in **myasthenia gravis** chronic muscle-weakening disease

GRAVITY n force of attraction of one object for another, esp of objects to the earth

GRAVLAX n dry-cured salmon, marinated in salt, sugar, and spices, as served in Scandinavia

GRAVS ▸ **grav**

GRAVURE n method of intaglio printing using a plate with many small etched recesses

GRAVY n juices from meat in cooking

GRAY same as ▸ **grey**

GRAYED ▸ **gray**

GRAYER ▸ **gray**

GRAYEST ▸ **gray**

GRAYFLY n trumpet fly

GRAYING ▸ gray

GRAYISH ▸ gray

GRAYLAG same as ▸ greylag

GRAYLE n holy grail

GRAYLES ▸ grayle

GRAYLY ▸ gray

GRAYOUT n in aeronautics, impairment of vision due to lack of oxygen

GRAYS ▸ gray

GRAZE vb feed on grass ▷ n slight scratch or scrape

GRAZED ▸ graze

GRAZER ▸ graze

GRAZERS ▸ graze

GRAZES ▸ graze

GRAZIER n person who feeds cattle for market

GRAZING n land on which grass for livestock is grown

GREASE n soft melted animal fat ▷ vb apply grease to

GREASED ▸ grease

GREASER n mechanic, esp of motor vehicles

GREASES ▸ grease

GREASY adj covered with or containing grease ▷ n shearer

GREAT adj large in size or number ▷ n distinguished person

GREATEN vb make or become great

GREATER ▸ great

GREATLY ▸ great

GREATS ▸ great

GREAVE n piece of armour for the shin ▷ vb grieve

GREAVED ▸ greave

GREAVES pl n residue left after the rendering of tallow

GREBE n diving water bird

GREBES ▸ grebe

GREBO ▸ greebo

GREBOS ▸ greebo

GRECE n flight of steps

GRECES ▸ grece

GRECIAN same as ▸ grece

GRECISE same as > graecize

GRECIZE same as ▸ graecize

GRECQUE n ornament of Greek origin

GREE n superiority or victory ▷ vb come or cause to come to agreement or harmony

GREEBO n unkempt or dirty-looking young man

GREECE same as ▸ grece

GREECES ▸ greece

GREED n excessive desire for food, wealth, etc

GREEDS ▸ greed

GREEDY adj having an excessive desire for something, such as food or money

GREEING ▸ gree

GREEK vb represent text as grey lines on a computer screen

GREEKED ▸ greek

GREEN adj of a colour between blue and yellow ▷ n colour between blue and yellow ▷ vb make or become green

GREENED ▸ green

GREENER n recent immigrant

GREENIE n conservationist

GREENLY ▸ green

GREENS ▸ green

GREENTH n greenness

GREENY ▸ green

GREES ▸ gree

GREESE same as ▸ grece

GREESES ▸ greese

GREET vb meet with expressions of welcome ▷ n weeping

GREETE same as ▸ greet

GREETED ▸ greet

GREETER n person who greets people at the entrance of a shop, restaurant, casino, etc

GREETES ▸ greete

GREETS ▸ greet

GREGALE n northeasterly wind occurring in the Mediterranean

GREGE vb make heavy

GREGO n short, thick jacket

GREGOS ▸ grego

GREIGE adj (of a fabric or material) not yet dyed ▷ n unbleached or undyed cloth or yarn

GREIGES ▸ greige

GREIN vb desire fervently

GREINED ▸ grein

GREINS ▸ grein

GREISEN n light-coloured metamorphic rock consisting mainly of quartz, white mica, and topaz formed by the pneumatolysis of granite

GREISLY same as ▸ grisly

GREMIAL n cloth spread upon the lap of a bishop when seated during Mass

GREMLIN n imaginary being blamed for mechanical malfunctions

GREMMIE n young surfer

GREMMY same as ▸ gremmie

GREN same as ▸ grin

GRENADE n small bomb thrown by hand or fired from a rifle

GRENNED ▸ gren

GRENS ▸ gren

GRESE same as ▸ grece

GRESES ▸ grese

GREVE same as ▸ greave

GREVES ▸ greve

GREW vb shudder

GREWED ▸ grow

GREWING ▸ grow

GREWS ▸ grow

GREX n group of plants that has arisen from the same hybrid parent group

GREXES ▸ grex

GREY adj of a colour between black and white ▷ n grey colour ▷ vb become or make grey

GREYED ▸ grey

GREYER ▸ grey

GREYEST ▸ grey

GREYHEN n female of the black grouse

GREYING ▸ grey

GREYISH ▸ grey

GREYLAG n large grey goose

GREYLY ▸ grey

GREYS ▸ grey

GRIBBLE n type of small marine crustacean which bores into and damages submerged wooden structures such as wharves

GRICE vb (of a railway enthusiast) to collect objects or visit places connected with trains and railways ▷ n object collected or place visited by a railway enthusiast

GRICED ▸ grice

GRICER ▸ grice

GRICERS ▸ grice

GRICES ▸ grice

GRICING ▸ grice

GRID n network of horizontal and vertical lines, bars, etc

GRIDDED ▸ grid

GRIDDER n American football player

GRIDDLE n flat iron plate for cooking ▷ vb cook (food) on a griddle

GRIDE vb grate or scrape harshly ▷ n harsh or piercing sound

GRIDED ▸ gride

GRIDES ▸ gride

GRIDING ▸ gride

GRIDS ▸ grid

GRIECE same as ▸ grece

GRIECED ▸ griece

GRIECES ▸ griece

GRIEF n deep sadness

GRIEFER n online game player who intentionally spoils the game for other players

GRIEFS ▸ grief

GRIESIE same as ▸ grisy

GRIESLY same as ▸ grisy

GRIESY same as ▸ grisy

GRIEVE vb (cause to) feel grief ▷ n farm manager or overseer

GRIEVED ▸ grieve

GRIEVER ▸ grieve

GRIEVES ▸ grieve

GRIFF n information

GRIFFE n carved ornament at the base of a column, often in the form of a claw

GRIFFES ▸ griffe

GRIFFIN n mythical monster with an eagle's head and wings and a lion's body

GRIFFON same as ▸ griffin

GRIFFS ▸ griff

GRIFT vb swindle

GRIFTED ▸ grift

GRIFTER ▸ grift

GRIFTS ▸ grift

GRIG n lively person ▷ vb fish for grigs

GRIGGED ▸ grig

GRIGRI n African talisman, amulet, or charm

GRIGRIS ▸ grigri

GRIGS ▸ grig

GRIKE n solution fissure, a vertical crack about 0.5 m wide formed by the dissolving of limestone by water, that divides an exposed limestone surface into sections or clints

GRIKES ▸ grike

GRILL n device on a cooker that radiates heat downwards ▷ vb cook under a grill

GRILLE n grating over an opening

GRILLED adj cooked on a grill or gridiron

GRILLER ▸ grill

GRILLES ▸ grille

GRILLS ▸ grill

GRILSE n salmon on its first return from the sea to fresh water

GRILSES ▸ grilse

GRIM adj stern

GRIMACE n ugly or distorted facial expression of pain, disgust, etc ▷ vb make a grimace

GRIME n ingrained dirt ▷ vb make very dirty

GRIMED ▸ grime

GRIMES ▸ grime

GRIMIER ▸ grime

GRIMILY ▸ grime

GRIMING ▸ grime

GRIMLY ▸ grim

GRIMMER ▸ grim

GRIMY ▸ grime

GRIN vb smile broadly, showing the teeth ▷ n broad smile

GRINCH n person whose lack of enthusiasm or bad temper has a depressing effect on others

GRIND vb crush or rub to a powder ▷ n hard work

GRINDED obsolete past participle of ▸ grind

GRINDER n device for grinding substances

GRINDS ▸ grind

GRINNED ▸ grin

GRINNER ▸ grin

GRINS ▸ grin

GRIOT n (in Western Africa) member of a caste responsible for maintaining an oral record of tribal history in the form of music, poetry, and storytelling

GRIOTS ▸ griot

GRIP n firm hold or grasp ▷ vb grasp or hold tightly

GRIPE vb complain persistently ▷ n complaint

GRIPED ▸ gripe

GRIPER ▸ gripe

GRIPERS ▸ gripe

GRIPES ▸ gripe

GRIPEY adj causing gripes

GRIPIER ▸ gripey

GRIPING ▸ gripe

GRIPLE same as ▸ gripple

GRIPMAN n cable-car operator

GRIPMEN ▸ gripman

GRIPPE former name for ▸ influenza

GRIPPED ▸ grip

GRIPPER ▸ grip

GRIPPES ▸ grippe

GRIPPLE adj greedy ▷ n hook

GRIPPY adj having grip

GRIPS ▸ grip

GRIPT archaic variant of ▸ gripped

GRIPY same as ▸ gripey

GRIS same as ▸ grece

GRISE vb shudder

GRISED ▸ grise

GRISELY same as ▸ grisly

GRISES ▸ grise

GRISING ▸ grise

GRISKIN n lean part of a loin of pork

GRISLED another word for ▸ grizzled

GRISLY adj horrifying or ghastly ▷ n large American bear

GRISON n type of mammal of Central and S America with a greyish back and black face and underparts

GRISONS ▸ grison

GRIST n grain for grinding

GRISTER n device for grinding grain

GRISTLE n tough stringy animal tissue found in meat

GRISTLY ▸ gristle

GRISTS ▸ grist

GRISY adj grim

GRIT n rough particles of sand ▷ vb spread grit on (an icy road etc) ▷ adj great

GRITH n security, peace, or protection, guaranteed either in a certain place, such as a church, or for a period of time

GRITHS ▸ grith

GRITS ▸ grit

GRITTED ▸ grit

GRITTER n vehicle that spreads grit on the roads in icy weather

GRITTY adj courageous and tough

GRIVET n E African monkey with long white tufts of hair on either side of the face

GRIVETS ▸ grivet

GRIZE same as ▸ grece

GRIZES ▸ grize

GRIZZLE vb whine or complain ▷ n grey colour

GRIZZLY n large American bear ▷ adj somewhat grey

GROAN n deep sound of grief or pain ▷ vb utter a groan

GROANED ▸ groan

GROANER n person or thing that groans

GROANS ▸ groan

GROAT n fourpenny piece

GROATS pl n hulled and crushed grain of various cereals

GROCER n shopkeeper selling foodstuffs

GROCERS ▸ grocer

GROCERY n business or premises of a grocer

GROCKED ▸ grokked

GROCKLE n tourist, esp one from the Midlands or the North of England

GRODIER ▸ grody

GRODY adj unpleasant

GROG n spirit, usu rum, and water ▷ vb drink grog

GROGGED ▸ grog

GROGGY adj faint, shaky, or dizzy

GROGRAM n coarse fabric of silk, wool, or silk mixed with wool or mohair, often stiffened with gum, formerly used for clothing

GROGS ▸ grog

GROIN n place where the legs join the abdomen ▷ vb provide or construct with groins

GROINED ▸ groin

GROINS ▸ groin

GROK vb understand completely and intuitively

GROKED ▸ grokked

GROKING > grokking

GROKKED ▸ grok

GROKS ▸ grok

GROMA n Roman surveying instrument

GROMAS ▸ groma

GROMET same as ▸ grommet

GROMETS ▸ gromet

GROMMET n ring or eyelet

GRONE obsolete word for ▸ groan

GRONED ▸ grone

GRONES ▸ grone

GRONING ▸ grone

GROOF n face, or front of the body

GROOFS ▸ groof

GROOLY adj gruesome

GROOM n person who looks after horses ▷ vb make or keep one's clothes and appearance neat and tidy

GROOMED ▸ groom

GROOMER ▸ groom

GROOMS ▸ groom

GROOVE n long narrow channel in a surface

GROOVED ▸ groove

GROOVER n device that makes grooves

GROOVES ▸ groove

GROOVY adj attractive or exciting

GROPE vb feel about or search uncertainly ▷ n instance of groping

GROPED ▸ grope

GROPER n type of large fish of warm and tropical seas

GROPERS ▸ groper

GROPES ▸ grope

GROPING ▸ grope

GROSER n gooseberry

GROSERS ▸ groser

GROSERT another word for ▸ groser

GROSET another word for ▸ groser

GROSETS ▸ groset

GROSS adj flagrant ▷ n twelve dozen ▷ vb make as total revenue before deductions ▷ interj exclamation indicating disgust

GROSSED ▸ gross

GROSSER ▸ gross

GROSSES ▸ gross

GROSSLY ▸ gross

GROSZ n Polish monetary unit worth one hundredth of a zloty

GROSZE ▸ grosz

GROSZY ▸ grosz

GROT n rubbish

GROTS ▸ grot

GROTTO n small picturesque cave

GROTTOS ▸ grotto

GROTTY adj nasty or in bad condition

GROUCH vb grumble or complain ▷ n person who is always complaining

GROUCHY adj bad-tempered

GROUF same as ▸ groof

GROUFS ▸ grouf

GROUGH n natural channel or fissure in a peat moor

GROUGHS ▸ grough

GROUND n surface of the earth ▷ adj on or of the ground ▷ vb base or establish

GROUNDS ▸ ground

GROUP n number of people or things regarded as a unit ▷ vb place or form into a group

GROUPED ▸ group

GROUPER n large edible sea fish

GROUPIE n ardent fan of a celebrity or of a sport or activity

GROUPS ▸ group

GROUPY same as ▸ groupie

GROUSE n stocky game bird ▷ vb grumble or complain ▷ adj fine or excellent ▷ adj excellent

GROUSED ▸ grouse

GROUSER ▸ grouse

GROUSES ▸ grouse

GROUT n thin mortar ▷ vb fill up with grout

GROUTED ▸ grout

GROUTER ▸ grout

GROUTS pl n sediment or grounds, as from making coffee

GROUTY adj sullen or surly

GROVE n small group of trees

GROVED ▸ grove

GROVEL vb behave humbly in order to win a superior's favour

GROVELS ▸ grovel

GROVES ▸ grove

GROVET n wrestling hold in which a wrestler in a kneeling position grips the head of his kneeling opponent with one arm and forces his shoulders down with the other

GROVETS ▸ grovet

GROW vb develop physically

GROWER n person who grows plants

GROWERS ▸ grower

GROWING ▸ grow

GROWL vb make a low rumbling sound ▷ n growling sound

GROWLED ▸ growl

GROWLER n person, animal, or thing that growls

GROWLS ▸ growl

GROWLY ▸ growl

GROWN ▸ grow

GROWNUP n adult

GROWS ▸ grow

GROWTH n growing ▷ adj of or relating to growth

GROWTHS ▸ growth

GROWTHY adj rapid-growing

GROYNE n wall built out from the shore to control erosion

GROYNES ▸ groyne

GROZING adj as in **grozing iron** iron for smoothing joints between lead pipes

GRRL n as in **riot grrl** young woman who plays or enjoys an aggressively feminist style of punk rock music

This slang term for a girl who likes loud rock music can come in useful when you are short of vowels. And it can also be spelt **grrrl**.

GRRLS ▸ grrl

GRRRL n as in **riot grrrl** young woman who plays or enjoys an aggressively feminist style of punk rock music

GRRRLS ▸ grrrl

GRUB n legless insect larva ▷ vb search carefully for something by digging or by moving things about

GRUBBED ▸ grub

GRUBBER n person who grubs

GRUBBLE same as ▸ grabble

GRUBBY adj dirty

GRUBS ▸ grub

GRUDGE vb be unwilling to give or allow ▷ n resentment ▷ adj planned or carried out in order to settle a grudge

GRUDGED ▸ grudge

GRUDGER ▸ grudge

GRUDGES ▸ grudge

GRUE n shiver or shudder ▷ vb shiver or shudder

GRUED ▸ grue

GRUEING ▸ grue

GRUEL n thin porridge ▷ vb subject to exhausting experiences

GRUELED ▸ gruel

GRUELER ▸ gruel

GRUELS ▸ gruel

GRUES ▸ grue

GRUFE same as ▸ groof

GRUFES ▸ grufe

GRUFF adj rough or surly in manner or voice ▷ vb talk gruffly

GRUFFED ▸ gruff

GRUFFER ▸ gruff

GRUFFLY ▸ gruff

GRUFFS ▸ gruff

GRUFFY adj gruff

GRUFTED adj dirty

GRUGRU n tropical American palm with a spiny trunk and leaves and edible nuts

GRUGRUS ▸ grugru

GRUING ▸ grue

GRUM adj surly

GRUMBLE vb complain ▷ n complaint

GRUMBLY ▸ grumble

GRUME n clot

GRUMES ▸ grume

GRUMLY ▸ grum

GRUMMER ▸ grum

GRUMMET same as ▸ grommet

GRUMOSE same as ▸ grumous

GRUMOUS adj (esp of plant parts) consisting of granular tissue

GRUMP n surly or bad-tempered person ▷ vb complain or grumble

GRUMPED ▸ grump

GRUMPH vb grunt

GRUMPHS ▸ grumph

GRUMPHY same as ▸ grumphie

GRUMPS ▸ grump

GRUMPY adj bad-tempered

GRUND n as in **grund mail** payment for right of burial

GRUNGE n style of rock music with a fuzzy guitar sound

GRUNGER n fan of grunge music

GRUNGES ▸ grunge

GRUNGEY adj messy or dirty

GRUNGY adj squalid or seedy

GRUNION n Californian marine fish that spawns on beaches

GRUNT vb make a low short gruff sound, like a pig ▷ n pig's sound

GRUNTED ▸ grunt

GRUNTER n person or animal that grunts, esp a pig

GRUNTLE vb grunt or groan

GRUNTS ▸ grunt

GRUSHIE adj healthy and strong

GRUTCH vb grudge

GRUTTEN ▸ greet

GRUYERE n hard flat whole-milk cheese with holes

GRYCE same as ▸ grice

GRYCES ▸ gryce

GRYDE same as ▸ gride

GRYDED ▸ gryde

GRYDES ▸ gryde

GRYDING ▸ gryde

GRYESY adj grey

GRYFON same as ▸ griffin

GRYFONS ▸ gryfon

GRYKE same as ▸ grike

GRYKES ▸ gryke

GRYPE same as ▸ gripe

GRYPES ▸ gripe

GRYPHON same as ▸ griffin

GRYPT archaic form of ▸ gripped

GRYSBOK n small antelope of central and S Africa with small straight horns

GRYSELY same as ▸ grisly

GRYSIE same as ▸ grisy

GU same as ▸ gju

GUACO n any of several tropical American plants whose leaves are used as an antidote to snakebite

GUACOS ▸ guaco

GUAIAC same as > guaiacum

GUAIACS > guaiacum

GUAN n type of bird of Central and S America

GUANA another word for ▸ iguana

GUANACO n S American animal related to the llama

GUANAS ▸ guana

GUANASE n enzyme that converts guanine to xanthine by removal of an amino group

GUANAY n type of cormorant

GUANAYS ▸ guanay

GUANGO n rain tree

GUANGOS ▸ guango

GUANIN same as ▸ guanine

GUANINE n white almost insoluble compound: one of the purine bases in nucleic acids

GUANINS ▸ guanine

GUANO n dried sea-bird manure, used as fertilizer

GUANOS ▸ guano

GUANS ▸ guan

GUANXI n Chinese social concept based on the exchange of favours

GUANXIS ▸ guanxi

GUAR n Indian plant grown as a fodder crop and for the gum obtained from its seeds

GUARANA n type of shrub native to Venezuela

GUARANI n standard monetary unit of Paraguay, divided into 100 céntimos

GUARD vb watch over to protect or to prevent escape ▸ n person or group that guards

GUARDED adj cautious or noncommittal

GUARDEE n guardsman, esp considered as representing smartness and dash

GUARDER ▸ guard

GUARDS ▸ guard

GUARISH vb heal

GUARS ▸ guar

GUAVA n yellow-skinned tropical American fruit

GUAVAS ▸ guava

GUAYULE n bushy shrub of the southwestern US

GUB n white man ▸ vb hit or defeat

GUBBAH same as ▸ **gub**

GUBBAHS ▸ gubbah

GUBBED ▸ gub

GUBBING ▸ gub

GUBBINS n object of little or no value

GUBS ▸ gub

GUCK n slimy matter

GUCKIER ▸ gucky

GUCKS ▸ guck

GUCKY adj slimy and mucky

GUDDLE vb catch (fish) by groping with the hands under the banks or stones of a stream ▸ n muddle

GUDDLED ▸ guddle

GUDDLES ▸ guddle

GUDE Scots word for ▸ **good**

GUDEMAN n male householder

GUDEMEN ▸ gudeman

GUDES n goods

GUDGEON n small freshwater fish ▸ vb trick or cheat

GUE same as ▸ **gju**

GUELDER adj as in **guelder rose** kind of shrub

GUENON n slender Old World monkey of Africa with long hind limbs and tail and long hair surrounding the face

GUENONS ▸ guenon

GUERDON n reward or payment ▸ vb give a guerdon to

GUEREZA n handsome colobus monkey of the mountain forests of Ethiopia

GUERITE n turret used by a sentry

GUES ▸ gue

GUESS vb estimate or draw a conclusion without proper knowledge ▸ n estimate or conclusion reached by guessing

GUESSED ▸ guess

GUESSER ▸ guess

GUESSES ▸ guess

GUEST n person entertained at another's house or at another's expense ▸ vb appear as a visiting player or performer

GUESTED ▸ guest

GUESTEN vb stay as a guest in someone's house

GUESTS ▸ guest

GUFF n nonsense

GUFFAW n crude noisy laugh ▸ vb laugh in this way

GUFFAWS ▸ guffaw

GUFFIE Scots word for ▸ **pig**

GUFFIES ▸ guffie

GUFFS ▸ guff

GUGA n gannet chick

GUGAS ▸ guga

GUGGLE vb drink making a gurgling sound

GUGGLED ▸ guggle

GUGGLES ▸ guggle

GUGLET same as ▸ **goglet**

GUGLETS ▸ guglet

GUICHET n grating, hatch, or small opening in a wall, esp a ticket-office window

GUID Scots word for ▸ **good**

GUIDAGE n guidance

GUIDE n person who conducts tour expeditions ▸ vb act as a guide for

GUIDED ▸ guide

GUIDER ▸ guide

GUIDERS ▸ guide

GUIDES ▸ guide

GUIDING ▸ guide

GUIDON n small pennant, used as a marker or standard, esp by cavalry regiments

GUIDONS ▸ guidon

GUIDS n possessions

GUILD n organization or club

GUILDER n former monetary unit of the Netherlands

GUILDRY n in Scotland, corporation of merchants in a burgh

GUILDS ▸ guild

GUILE n cunning or deceit ▸ vb deceive

GUILED ▸ guile

GUILER n deceiver

GUILERS ▸ guiler

GUILES ▸ guile

GUILING ▸ guile

GUILT n fact or state of having done wrong

GUILTS ▸ guilt

GUILTY adj responsible for an offence or misdeed

GUIMP same as ▸ **guimpe**

GUIMPE n short blouse with sleeves worn under a pinafore dress ▸ vb make with gimp

GUIMPED ▸ guimpe

GUIMPES ▸ guimpe

GUIMPS ▸ guimp

GUINEA n former British monetary unit worth 21 shillings (1.05 pounds)

GUINEAS ▸ guinea

GUIPURE n heavy lace that has its pattern connected by threads, rather than supported on a net mesh

GUIRO n percussion instrument made from a hollow gourd

GUIROS ▸ guiro

GUISARD n guiser

GUISE n false appearance ▸ vb disguise or be disguised in fancy dress

GUISED ▸ guise

GUISER n mummer, esp at Christmas or Halloween revels

GUISERS ▸ guiser

GUISES ▸ guise

GUISING ▸ guise

GUITAR n stringed instrument with a flat back and a long neck, played by plucking or strumming

GUITARS ▸ guitar

GUIZER same as ▸ **guiser**

GUIZERS ▸ guizer

GUL n design used in oriental carpets

GULA n gluttony

GULAG n forced-labour camp

GULAGS ▸ gulag

GULAR adj of, relating to, or situated in the throat or oesophagus

GULAS ▸ gula

GULCH n deep narrow valley ▷ vb swallow fast

GULCHED ▸ gulch

GULCHES ▸ gulch

GULDEN same as ▸ **guilder**

GULDENS ▸ gulden

GULE Scots word for > **marigold**

GULES n red in heraldry

GULET n wooden Turkish sailing boat

GULETS ▸ gulet

GULF n large deep bay ▷ vb swallow up

GULFED ▸ gulf

GULFIER ▸ gulf

GULFING ▸ gulf

GULFS ▸ gulf

GULFY ▸ gulf

GULL n long-winged sea bird ▷ vb cheat or deceive

GULLED ▸ gull

GULLER n deceiver

GULLERS ▸ guller

GULLERY n breeding-place for gulls

GULLET n muscular tube through which food passes from the mouth to the stomach

GULLETS ▸ gullet

GULLEY same as ▸ **gully**

GULLEYS ▸ gulley

GULLIED ▸ gully

GULLIES ▸ gully

GULLING ▸ gull

GULLISH adj stupid

GULLS ▸ gull

GULLY n channel cut by running water ▷ vb make (channels) in (the ground, sand, etc)

GULP vb swallow hastily ▷ n gulping

GULPED ▸ gulp

GULPER ▸ gulp

GULPERS ▸ gulp

GULPH archaic word for ▸ **gulf**

GULPHS ▸ gulph

GULPIER ▸ gulp

GULPING ▸ gulp

GULPS ▸ gulp

GULPY ▸ gulp

GULS ▸ gul

GULY adj relating to gules

GUM n firm flesh in which the teeth are set ▷ vb stick with gum

GUMBALL n round piece of chewing gum

GUMBO n mucilaginous pods of okra

GUMBOIL n abscess on the gum

GUMBOOT n rubber boot

GUMBOS ▸ gumbo

GUMDROP n hard jelly-like sweet

GUMLESS ▸ gum

GUMLIKE ▸ gum

GUMLINE n line where gums meet teeth

GUMMA n rubbery tumour characteristic of advanced syphilis, occurring esp on the skin, liver, brain or heart

GUMMAS ▸ gumma

GUMMATA ▸ gumma

GUMMED ▸ gum

GUMMER n punch-cutting tool

GUMMERS ▸ gummer

GUMMIER ▸ gummy

GUMMIES ▸ gummy

GUMMILY ▸ gummy

GUMMING ▸ gum

GUMMITE n orange or yellowish amorphous secondary mineral consisting of hydrated uranium oxides

GUMMOSE same as ▸ **gummous**

GUMMOUS adj resembling or consisting of gum

GUMMY adj toothless ▷ n type of small crustacean-eating shark whose mouth has bony ridges resembling gums

GUMNUT n hardened seed container of the gumtree

GUMNUTS ▸ gumnut

GUMP vb guddle

GUMPED ▸ gump

GUMPING ▸ gump

GUMPS ▸ gump

GUMS ▸ gum

GUMSHOE n waterproof overshoe ▷ vb act stealthily

GUMTREE n any of various trees that yield gum, such as the eucalyptus, sweet gum, and sour gum

GUMWEED n any of several American yellow-flowered plants that have sticky flower heads

GUMWOOD same as ▸ **gumtree**

GUN n weapon with a metal tube from which missiles are fired by explosion ▷ vb cause (an engine) to run at high speed

GUNBOAT n small warship

GUNDIES ▸ gundy

GUNDOG n dog trained to work with a hunter or gamekeeper

GUNDOGS ▸ gundog

GUNDY n toffee

GUNFIRE n repeated firing of guns

GUNG adj as in **gung ho** extremely or excessively enthusiastic about something

GUNGE n sticky unpleasant substance ▷ vb block or encrust with gunge

GUNGED ▸ gunge

GUNGES ▸ gunge

GUNGIER ▸ gunge

GUNGING ▸ gunge

GUNGY ▸ gunge

GUNITE n cement-sand mortar that is sprayed onto formwork, walls, or rock by a compressed air ejector giving a very dense strong concrete layer: used to repair reinforced concrete, to line tunnel walls or mine airways, etc

GUNITES ▸ gunite

GUNK n slimy or filthy substance

GUNKIER ▸ gunk

GUNKS ▸ gunk

GUNKY ▸ gunk

GUNLESS ▸ gun

GUNLOCK n mechanism in some firearms that causes the charge to be exploded

GUNMAN n armed criminal

GUNMEN ▸ gunman

GUNNAGE n number of guns carried by a warship

GUNNED ▸ gun

GUNNEL same as ▸ **gunwale**

GUNNELS ▸ gunnel

GUNNEN ▸ gun

GUNNER n artillery soldier

GUNNERA n type of herbaceous plant found throughout the S hemisphere and cultivated for its large leaves

GUNNERS ▸ gunner

GUNNERY n use or science of large guns

GUNNIES ▸ gunny

GUNNING ▸ gun

GUNNY n strong coarse fabric used for sacks

GUNPLAY n use of firearms, as by criminals

GUNPORT n porthole, or other, opening for a gun

GUNROOM n (esp in the Royal Navy) the mess allocated to subordinate or junior officers

GUNS ▸ gun

GUNSEL n catamite

GUNSELS ▸ gunsel

GUNSHIP n ship or helicopter armed with heavy guns

GUNSHOT n shot or range of a gun

GUNTER n type of gaffing in which the gaff is hoisted parallel to the mast

GUNTERS ▸ gunter

GUNWALE n top of a ship's side

GUNYAH n hut or shelter in the bush

GUNYAHS ▸ gunyah

GUP n gossip

GUPPIES ▸ guppy

GUPPY n small colourful aquarium fish

GUPS ▸ gup

GUQIN n type of Chinese zither

GUQINS ▸ guqin

GUR n unrefined cane sugar

GURAMI same as ▸ gourami

GURAMIS ▸ gurami

GURGE vb swallow up

GURGED ▸ gurge

GURGES ▸ gurge

GURGING ▸ gurge

GURGLE n bubbling noise ▷ vb (of water) to make low bubbling noises when flowing

GURGLED ▸ gurgle

GURGLES ▸ gurgle

GURGLET same as ▸ goglet

GURJUN n S or SE Asian tree that yields a resin

GURJUNS ▸ gurjun

GURL vb snarl

GURLED ▸ gurl

GURLET n type of pickaxe

GURLETS ▸ gurlet

GURLIER ▸ gurly

GURLING ▸ gurl

GURLS ▸ gurl

GURLY adj stormy

GURN variant spelling of ▸ girn

GURNARD n spiny armour-headed sea fish

GURNED ▸ gurn

GURNET same as ▸ gurnard

GURNETS ▸ gurnard

GURNEY n wheeled stretcher for transporting hospital patients

GURNEYS ▸ gurney

GURNING ▸ gurn

GURNS ▸ gurn

GURRAH n type of coarse muslin

GURRAHS ▸ gurrah

GURRIER n low-class tough ill-mannered person

GURRIES ▸ gurry

GURRY n dog-fight

GURS ▸ gur

GURSH n unit of currency in Saudi Arabia

GURSHES ▸ gursh

GURU n Hindu or Sikh religious teacher or leader

GURUDOM n state of being a guru

GURUISM ▸ guru

GURUS ▸ guru

GUS ▸ gu

GUSH vb flow out suddenly and profusely ▷ n sudden copious flow

GUSHED ▸ gush

GUSHER n spurting oil well

GUSHERS ▸ gusher

GUSHES ▸ gush

GUSHIER ▸ gushy

GUSHILY ▸ gushy

GUSHING ▸ gush

GUSHY adj displaying excessive admiration or sentimentality

GUSLA n Balkan single-stringed musical instrument

GUSLAR n player of the gusla

GUSLARS ▸ guslar

GUSLAS ▸ gusla

GUSLE same as ▸ gusla

GUSLES ▸ gusle

GUSLI n Russian harp-like musical instrument

GUSLIS ▸ gusli

GUSSET n piece of material sewn into a garment to strengthen it ▷ vb put a gusset in (a garment)

GUSSETS ▸ gusset

GUSSIE n young pig

GUSSIED ▸ gussy

GUSSIES ▸ gussy

GUSSY vb dress elaborately

GUST n sudden blast of wind ▷ vb blow in gusts

GUSTED ▸ gust

GUSTFUL adj tasty

GUSTIE adj tasty

GUSTIER ▸ gusty

GUSTILY ▸ gusty

GUSTING ▸ gust

GUSTO n enjoyment or zest

GUSTOES ▸ gusto

GUSTOS ▸ gusto

GUSTS ▸ gust

GUSTY adj blowing or occurring in gusts or characterized by blustery weather

GUT n intestine ▷ vb remove the guts from ▷ adj basic or instinctive

GUTCHER n grandfather

GUTFUL n bellyful

GUTFULS ▸ gutful

GUTLESS adj cowardly

GUTLIKE ▸ gut

GUTROT n diarrhoea

GUTROTS ▸ gutrot

GUTS vb devour greedily

GUTSED ▸ guts

GUTSER n as in come a gutser fall heavily to the ground

GUTSERS ▸ gutser

GUTSES ▸ guts

GUTSFUL n bellyful

GUTSIER ▸ gutsy

GUTSILY ▸ gutsy

GUTSING ▸ guts

GUTSY adj courageous

GUTTA n one of a set of small drop-like ornaments, esp as used on the architrave of a Doric entablature ▷ n rubber substance obtained from the coagulated latex of the guttapercha tree

GUTTAE ▸ gutta

GUTTAS ▸ gutta

GUTTATE adj (esp of plants) covered with small drops or drop-like markings, esp oil glands ▷ vb exude droplets of liquid

GUTTED ▸ gut

GUTTER n shallow channel for carrying away water from a roof or roadside ▷ vb (of a candle) burn

unsteadily, with wax running down the sides
GUTTERS ▸ gutter
GUTTERY ▸ gutter
GUTTIER ▸ gutty
GUTTIES ▸ gutty
GUTTING ▸ gut
GUTTLE vb eat greedily
GUTTLED ▸ guttle
GUTTLER ▸ guttle
GUTTLES ▸ guttle
GUTTY n urchin or delinquent ▷ adj courageous
GUTZER n bad fall
GUTZERS ▸ gutzer
GUV informal name for ▸ governor
GUVS ▸ guv
GUY n man or boy ▷ vb make fun of
GUYED ▸ guy
GUYING ▸ guy
GUYLE same as ▸ guile
GUYLED ▸ guyle
GUYLER ▸ guyle
GUYLERS ▸ guyle
GUYLES ▸ guyle
GUYLINE n guy rope
GUYLING ▸ guyle
GUYOT n flat-topped submarine mountain, common in the Pacific Ocean, usually an extinct volcano whose summit did not reach above the sea surface
GUYOTS ▸ guyot
GUYS ▸ guy
GUYSE same as ▸ guise
GUYSES ▸ guyse
GUZZLE vb eat or drink greedily
GUZZLED ▸ guzzle
GUZZLER n person or thing that guzzles
GUZZLES ▸ guzzle
GWEDUC same as ▸ geoduck
GWEDUCK same as ▸ geoduck
GWEDUCS ▸ gweduck
GWINE dialect form of ▸ going
GWINIAD n powan
GWYNIAD n type of freshwater white fish occurring in Lake Bala in Wales
GYAL same as ▸ gayal
GYALS ▸ gyal
GYBE vb (of a fore-and-aft sail) swing suddenly from

one side to the other ▷ n instance of gybing
GYBED ▸ gybe
GYBES ▸ gybe
GYBING ▸ gybe
GYELD n guild
GYELDS ▸ gyeld
GYLDEN adj golden
GYM n gymnasium
GYMBAL same as ▸ gimbal
GYMBALS ▸ gymbal
GYMMAL same as ▸ gimmal
GYMMALS ▸ gymmal
GYMNAST n expert in gymnastics
GYMNIC adj gymnastic
GYMPIE n tall tree with stinging hairs on its leaves
GYMPIES ▸ gympie
GYMS ▸ gym
GYMSLIP n tunic or pinafore formerly worn by schoolgirls
GYNAE adj gynaecological ▷ n gynaecology
GYNAES ▸ gynae
GYNECIA > gynecium
GYNECIC adj relating to the female sex
GYNIE n gynaecology
GYNIES ▸ gynie
GYNNEY n guinea hen
GYNNEYS ▸ gynney
GYNNIES ▸ gynny
GYNNY same as ▸ gynney
GYNY n gynaecology
GYOZA n Japanese fried dumpling
GYOZAS ▸ gyoza
GYP vb swindle, cheat, or defraud ▷ n act of cheating

⎪ This little word, meaning
⎪ to swindle, can be useful
⎪ when you are short of
⎪ vowels.

GYPLURE n synthetic version of the gypsy moth sex pheromone
GYPPED ▸ gyp
GYPPER ▸ gyp
GYPPERS ▸ gyp
GYPPIE same as ▸ gippy
GYPPIES ▸ gyppy
GYPPING ▸ gyp
GYPPY same as ▸ gippy
GYPS ▸ gyp
GYPSIED ▸ gypsy
GYPSIES ▸ gypsy
GYPSTER n swindler
GYPSUM n chalklike mineral used to make plaster of Paris
GYPSUMS ▸ gypsum

GYPSY n member of a nomadic people scattered throughout Europe and North America ▷ vb live like a gypsy
GYRAL adj having a circular, spiral, or rotating motion
GYRALLY ▸ gyral
GYRANT adj gyrating
GYRASE n topoisomerase enzyme
GYRASES ▸ gyrase
GYRATE vb rotate or spiral about a point or axis ▷ adj curved or coiled into a circle
GYRATED ▸ gyrate
GYRATES ▸ gyrate
GYRATOR n electronic circuit that inverts the impedance
GYRE n circular or spiral movement or path ▷ vb whirl
GYRED ▸ gyre
GYRENE n nickname for a member of the US Marine Corps
GYRENES ▸ gyrene
GYRES ▸ gyre
GYRI ▸ gyrus
GYRING ▸ gyre
GYRO n gyrocompass: nonmagnetic compass that uses a motor-driven gyroscope to indicate true north
GYROCAR n two-wheeled car
GYRON same as ▸ giron
GYRONIC ▸ gyron
GYRONNY same as ▸ gironny
GYRONS ▸ gyron
GYROS ▸ gyro
GYROSE adj marked with sinuous lines
GYROUS adj gyrose
GYRUS n convolution
GYRUSES ▸ gyrus
GYTE n spoilt child
GYTES ▸ gyte
GYTRASH n spirit that haunts lonely roads
GYTTJA n sediment on lake bottom
GYTTJAS ▸ gyttja
GYVE vb shackle or fetter ▷ n fetters
GYVED ▸ gyve
GYVES ▸ gyve
GYVING ▸ gyve

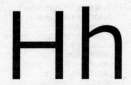

Hh

H forms a two-letter word in front of every vowel except **U** (and you can make **uh** with **U**), making it a versatile tile when you want to form words in more than one direction. It also goes with **M** to make **hm**. As **H** is worth 4 points on its own, you can earn some very high scores by doing this: even **ha, he, hi** and **ho** will give 5 points each. There are lots of good short words beginning with **H**, like **haw, hew, how, hay, hey** and **hoy** (9 each), while **hyp** can be useful if you are short of vowels. More high-scoring words with **H** include **haj, hex** and **hox** for 13 points each, and never forget the invaluable **zho** for 15 points.

H

HA *interj* exclamation expressing triumph, surprise, or scorn

HAAF *n* deep-sea fishing ground off the Shetland and Orkney Islands

HAAFS ▸ haaf

HAAR *n* cold sea mist or fog off the North Sea

HAARS ▸ haar

HABDABS *n* highly nervous state

HABILE *adj* skilful

HABIT *n* established way of behaving ▷ *vb* clothe

HABITAN *same as* **▸ habitant**

HABITAT *n* natural home of an animal or plant

HABITED *adj* dressed in a habit

HABITS ▸ habit

HABITUE *n* frequent visitor to a place

HABITUS *n* general physical state, esp with regard to susceptibility to disease

HABLE *old form of* **▸ able**

HABOOB *n* sandstorm

HABOOBS ▸ haboob

HABU *n* large venomous snake

HABUS ▸ habu

HACEK *n* pronunciation symbol in Slavonic language

HACEKS ▸ hacek

HACHIS *n* hash

HACHURE *n* shading of short lines drawn on a map to indicate the degree of steepness of a hill ▷ *vb* mark or show by hachures

HACK *vb* cut or chop violently ▷ *n* (inferior) writer or journalist ▷ *adj* unoriginal or of a low standard

HACKBUT *n* another word for **> arquebus**

HACKED ▸ hack

HACKEE *n* chipmunk

HACKEES ▸ hackee

HACKER *n* computer enthusiast, esp one who breaks into the computer system of a company or government

HACKERS ▸ hacker

HACKERY *n* journalism

HACKIE *n* US word meaning cab driver

HACKIES ▸ hackie

HACKING ▸ hack

HACKLE *same as* **▸ heckle**

HACKLED ▸ hackle

HACKLER ▸ hackle

HACKLES *pl n* hairs on the back of the neck and the back of a dog, cat, etc, which rise when the animal is angry or afraid

HACKLET *n* kittiwake

HACKLY *adj* rough or jagged

HACKMAN *n* taxi driver

HACKMEN ▸ hackman

HACKNEY *n* taxi ▷ *vb* make commonplace and banal by too frequent use

HACKS ▸ hack

HACKSAW *n* small saw for cutting metal ▷ *vb* cut with a hacksaw

HAD *vb* Scots form of hold

HADAL *adj* of, relating to, or constituting very deep zones of the oceans

HADARIM ▸ heder

HADAWAY *sentence substitute* exclamation urging the hearer to refrain from delay in the execution of a task

HADDEN ▸ have

HADDEST *same as* **▸ hadst**

HADDIE *n* finnan haddock

HADDIES ▸ haddie

HADDING ▸ have

HADDOCK *n* edible sea fish of N Atlantic

HADE *n* angle made to the vertical by the plane of a fault or vein ▷ *vb* incline from the vertical

HADED ▸ hade

HADEDAH *n* large grey-green S African ibis

HADES ▸ hade

HADING ▸ hade

HADITH *n* body of tradition and legend about Mohammed and his followers, used as a basis of Islamic law

HADITHS ▸ hadith

HADJ *same as* **▸ hajj**

HADJEE *same as* **▸ hadji**

HADJEES ▸ hadjee

HADJES ▸ hadj

HADJI same as ▸ hajji

HADJIS ▸ hadji

HADROME n part of xylem

HADRON n any elementary particle capable of taking part in a strong nuclear interaction and therefore excluding leptons and photons

HADRONS ▸ hadron

HADS ▸ have

HADST singular form of the past tense (indicative mood) of ▸ have

HAE Scots variant of ▸ have

HAED ▸ hae

HAEING ▸ hae

HAEM n complex red organic pigment containing ferrous iron, present in haemoglobin

HAEMAL adj of the blood

HAEMIC same as > haematic

HAEMIN n haematin chloride

HAEMINS ▸ haemin

HAEMOID same as > haematoid

HAEMONY n plant mentioned in Milton's poetry

HAEMS ▸ haem

HAEN ▸ hae

HAERES same as ▸ heres

HAES ▸ hae

HAET n whit

HAETS ▸ haet

HAFF n lagoon

HAFFET n side of head

HAFFETS ▸ haffet

HAFFIT same as ▸ haffet

HAFFITS ▸ haffit

HAFFLIN same as > halfling

HAFFS ▸ haff

HAFIZ n title for a person who knows the Koran by heart

HAFIZES ▸ hafiz

HAFNIUM n metallic element found in zirconium ores

HAFT n handle of an axe, knife, or dagger ▷ vb provide with a haft

HAFTARA same as > haftarah

HAFTED ▸ haft

HAFTER ▸ haft

HAFTERS ▸ haft

HAFTING ▸ haft

HAFTS ▸ haft

HAG n ugly old woman ▷ vb hack

HAGADIC > haggadic

HAGBOLT same as > hackbolt

HAGBORN adj born of a witch

HAGBUSH same as > arquebus

HAGBUT > arquebus

HAGBUTS ▸ hagbut

HAGDEN same as > hackbolt

HAGDENS ▸ hagden

HAGDON same as > hackbolt

HAGDONS ▸ hagdon

HAGDOWN same as > hackbolt

HAGFISH n any of various primitive eel-like marine vertebrates

HAGG n boggy place

HAGGADA same as > haggadah

HAGGARD adj looking tired and ill ▷ n hawk that has reached maturity before being caught

HAGGED ▸ hag

HAGGING ▸ hag

HAGGIS n Scottish dish made from sheep's offal, oatmeal, suet, and seasonings, boiled in a bag made from the sheep's stomach

HAGGISH ▸ hag

HAGGLE vb bargain or wrangle over a price

HAGGLED ▸ haggle

HAGGLER ▸ haggle

HAGGLES ▸ haggle

HAGGS ▸ hagg

HAGLET same as ▸ hacklet

HAGLETS ▸ haglet

HAGLIKE ▸ hag

HAGRIDE vb torment or obsess

HAGRODE ▸ hagride

HAGS ▸ hag

HAH same as ▸ ha

HAHA n wall or other boundary marker that is set in a ditch so as not to interrupt the landscape

HAHAS ▸ haha

HAHNIUM n transuranic element artificially produced from californium

HAHS ▸ hah

HAICK same as ▸ haik

HAICKS ▸ haick

HAIDUK n rural brigand

HAIDUKS ▸ haiduk

HAIK n Arab's outer garment of cotton, wool, or silk, for the head and body

HAIKA ▸ haik

HAIKAI same as ▸ haiku

HAIKS ▸ haik

HAIKU n Japanese verse form in 17 syllables

HAIKUS ▸ haiku

HAIL n (shower of) small pellets of ice ▷ vb fall as or like hail ▷ sentence substitute exclamation of greeting

HAILED ▸ hail

HAILER ▸ hail

HAILERS ▸ hail

HAILIER ▸ hail

HAILING ▸ hail

HAILS ▸ hail

HAILY ▸ hail

HAIMISH same as ▸ heimish

HAIN vb Scots word meaning save

HAINCH Scots form of ▸ haunch

HAINED ▸ hain

HAINING ▸ hain

HAINS ▸ hain

HAINT same as ▸ haunt

HAINTS ▸ haint

HAIQUE same as ▸ haik

HAIQUES ▸ haik

HAIR n threadlike growth on the skin ▷ vb provide with hair

HAIRCAP n type of moss

HAIRCUT n act or an instance of cutting the hair

HAIRDO n hairstyle

HAIRDOS ▸ hairdo

HAIRED adj with hair

HAIRIER ▸ hairy

HAIRIF another name for > cleavers

HAIRIFS ▸ hairif

HAIRING ▸ hair

HAIRNET n any of several kinds of light netting worn over the hair to keep it in place

HAIRPIN n U-shaped wire used to hold the hair in place

HAIRS ▸ hair

HAIRST Scots form of ▸ harvest

HAIRSTS ▸ hairst

HAIRY adj covered with hair

HAITH interj Scots oath

HAJ same as ▸ hadj

A **haj** is a Muslim pilgrimage to Mecca, and one of the key words to remember for using the J. It can also be spelt **hadj** or **hajj**, and one who makes a haj is called a **hadjee, hadji, haji** or **hajji.**

HAJES ▸ haj
HAJI same as ▸ **hajji**
HAJIS ▸ haji
HAJJ n pilgrimage a Muslim makes to Mecca
HAJJAH n Muslim woman who has made a pilgrimage to Mecca
HAJJAHS ▸ hajjah
HAJJES ▸ hajj
HAJJI n Muslim who has made a pilgrimage to Mecca
HAJJIS ▸ hajji
HAKA n ceremonial Maori dance with chanting
HAKAM n text written by a rabbi
HAKAMS ▸ hakam
HAKARI n Maori ritual feast
HAKARIS ▸ hakari
HAKAS ▸ haka
HAKE n edible sea fish of N hemisphere
HAKEA n Australian tree or shrub with hard woody fruit
HAKEAS ▸ hakea
HAKEEM same as ▸ **hakim**
HAKEEMS ▸ hakeem
HAKES ▸ hake
HAKIM n Muslim judge, ruler, or administrator
HAKIMS ▸ hakim
HAKU in New Zealand English, same as ▸ **kingfish**
HAKUS ▸ haku
HALACHA n Jewish religious law
HALAKAH same as ▸ **halacha**
HALAKHA same as ▸ **halacha**
HALAKIC ▸ halakha
HALAL n meat from animals slaughtered according to Muslim law ▷ adj of or relating to such meat ▷ vb kill (animals) in this way
HALALA n money unit in Saudi Arabia
HALALAH same as ▸ **halala**
HALALAS ▸ halala
HALALS ▸ halal

HALAVAH same as ▸ **halvah**
HALBERD n spear with an axe blade
HALBERT same as ▸ **halberd**
HALCYON adj peaceful and happy ▷ n (in Greek mythology) fabulous bird associated with the winter solstice
HALE adj healthy, robust ▷ vb pull or drag
HALED ▸ hale
HALER same as ▸ **heller**
HALERS ▸ haler
HALERU ▸ haler
HALES ▸ hale
HALEST ▸ hale
HALF n either of two equal parts ▷ adj denoting one of two equal parts ▷ adv to the extent of half
HALFA n African grass
HALFAS ▸ halfa
HALFEN ▸ half
HALFLIN same as > **halfling**
HALFS ▸ half
HALFWAY adj at or to half the distance
HALFWIT n foolish or stupid person
HALIBUT n large edible flatfish of N Atlantic
HALID same as ▸ **halide**
HALIDE n binary compound containing a halogen atom or ion in combination with a more electropositive element
HALIDES ▸ halide
HALIDOM n holy place or thing
HALIDS ▸ halid
HALIMOT n court held by lord
HALING ▸ hale
HALITE n colourless or white mineral sometimes tinted by impurities, found in beds as an evaporite
HALITES ▸ halite
HALITUS n vapour
HALL n entrance passage
HALLAH variant spelling of ▸ **challah**
HALLAHS ▸ hallah
HALLAL same as ▸ **halal**
HALLALI n bugle call
HALLALS ▸ hallal
HALLAN n partition in cottage
HALLANS ▸ hallan
HALLEL n (in Judaism) section of the liturgy

consisting of Psalms 113–18, read during the morning service on festivals, Chanukah, and Rosh Chodesh
HALLELS ▸ hallel
HALLIAN same as ▸ **hallion**
HALLING n Norwegian country dance
HALLION n lout
HALLO same as ▸ **halloo**
HALLOA same as ▸ **halloo**
HALLOAS ▸ halloa
HALLOED ▸ hallo
HALLOES ▸ hallo
HALLOO interj shout used to call hounds at a hunt ▷ sentence substitute shout to attract attention, esp to call hounds at a hunt ▷ vb shout (something) to (someone)
HALLOOS ▸ halloo
HALLOS ▸ hallo
HALLOT ▸ hallah
HALLOTH same as ▸ **challah**
HALLOW vb consecrate or set apart as being holy
HALLOWS ▸ hallow
HALLS ▸ hall
HALLUX n first digit on the hind foot of a mammal, bird, reptile, or amphibian
HALLWAY n entrance area
HALLYON same as ▸ **hallion**
HALM same as ▸ **haulm**
HALMA n board game in which players attempt to transfer their pieces from their own to their opponents' bases
HALMAS ▸ halma
HALMS ▸ halm
HALO n ring of light round the head of a sacred figure ▷ vb surround with a halo
HALOED ▸ halo
HALOES ▸ halo
HALOGEN n any of a group of nonmetallic elements including chlorine and iodine
HALOID adj resembling or derived from a halogen ▷ n compound containing halogen atoms in its molecules
HALOIDS ▸ haloid
HALOING ▸ halo
HALON n any of a class of chemical compounds derived from hydrocarbons by replacing one or more

hydrogen atoms by bromine atoms and other hydrogen atoms by other halogen atoms (chlorine, fluorine, or iodine). Halons are stable compounds that are used in fire extinguishers, although they may contribute to depletion of the ozone layer

HALONS ▶ halon

HALOS ▶ halo

HALOUMI *same as* **> halloumi**

HALSE *vb* embrace

HALSED ▶ halse

HALSER ▶ halse

HALSERS ▶ halse

HALSES ▶ halse

HALSING ▶ halse

HALT *vb* come or bring to a stop ▷ *n* temporary stop ▷ *adj* lame

HALTED ▶ halt

HALTER *n* strap round a horse's head with a rope to lead it with ▷ *vb* put a halter on (a horse)

HALTERE *n* one of a pair of short projections in dipterous insects that are modified hind wings, used for maintaining equilibrium during flight

HALTERS ▶ halter

HALTING ▶ halt

HALTS ▶ halt

HALUTZ *variant spelling of* **> chalutz**

HALVA *same as* **> halvah**

HALVAH *n* Eastern Mediterranean, Middle Eastern, or Indian sweetmeat made of honey and containing sesame seeds, nuts, rose water, saffron, etc

HALVAHS ▶ halvah

HALVAS ▶ halva

HALVE *vb* divide in half

HALVED ▶ halve

HALVER ▶ halve

HALVERS ▶ halve

HALVES ▶ halve

HALVING ▶ halve

HALYARD *n* rope for raising a ship's sail or flag

HAM *n* smoked or salted meat from a pig's thigh ▷ *vb* overact

HAMADA *n* rocky plateau in desert

HAMADAS ▶ hamada

HAMAL *n* (in Middle Eastern countries) a porter, bearer, or servant

HAMALS ▶ hamal

HAMATE *adj* hook-shaped ▷ *n* small bone in the wrist

HAMATES ▶ hamate

HAMAUL *same as* **▶ hamal**

HAMAULS ▶ hamaul

HAMBLE *vb* mutilate

HAMBLED ▶ hamble

HAMBLES ▶ hamble

HAMBONE *vb* strike body to provide percussion

HAMBURG *same as* **> hamburger**

HAME *n* either of the two curved bars holding the traces of the harness, attached to the collar of a draught animal

HAMED ▶ hame

HAMES ▶ hame

HAMING ▶ hame

HAMLET *n* small village

HAMLETS ▶ hamlet

HAMMADA *same as* **▶ hamada**

HAMMAL *same as* **▶ hamal**

HAMMALS ▶ hammal

HAMMAM *n* bathing establishment, such as a Turkish bath

HAMMAMS ▶ hammam

HAMMED ▶ ham

HAMMER *n* tool with a heavy metal head and a wooden handle, used to drive in nails etc ▷ *vb* hit (as if) with a hammer

HAMMERS ▶ hammer

HAMMIER ▶ hammy

HAMMILY ▶ hammy

HAMMING ▶ ham

HAMMOCK *same as* **▶ hummock**

HAMMY *adj* (of an actor) overacting or tending to overact

HAMOSE *adj* shaped like a hook

HAMOUS *same as* **▶ hamose**

HAMPER *vb* make it difficult for (someone or something) to move or progress ▷ *n* large basket with a lid

HAMPERS ▶ hamper

HAMS ▶ ham

HAMSTER *n* small rodent with a short tail and cheek pouches

HAMULAR ▶ hamulus

HAMULI ▶ hamulus

HAMULUS *n* hook or hooklike process at the end of some bones or between the fore and hind wings of a bee or similar insect

HAMZA *n* sign used in Arabic to represent the glottal stop

HAMZAH *same as* **▶ hamza**

HAMZAHS ▶ hamzah

HAMZAS ▶ hamza

HAN *archaic inflected form of* **> have**

HANAP *n* medieval drinking cup

HANAPER *n* small wickerwork basket, often used to hold official papers

HANAPS ▶ hanap

HANCE *same as* **▶ haunch**

HANCES ▶ hance

HANCH *vb* try to bite

HANCHED ▶ hanch

HANCHES ▶ hanch

HAND *n* part of the body at the end of the arm, consisting of a palm, four fingers, and a thumb ▷ *vb* pass, give

HANDAX *n* small axe held in one hand

HANDBAG *n* woman's small bag for carrying personal articles in

HANDCAR *n* small railway vehicle propelled by hand-pumped mechanism

HANDED ▶ hand

HANDER ▶ hand

HANDERS ▶ hand

HANDFED > handfeed

HANDFUL *n* amount that can be held in the hand

HANDGUN *n* firearm that can be held, carried, and fired with one hand, such as a pistol

HANDIER ▶ handy

HANDILY *adv* in a handy way or manner

HANDING ▶ hand

HANDISM *n* discrimination against people on the grounds of whether they are left-handed or right-handed

HANDJAR *n* Persian dagger

HANDLE *n* part of an object that is held so that it can be used ▷ *vb* hold, feel, or move with the hands

HANDLED ▶ handle

HANDLER n person who controls an animal

HANDLES ▸ handle

HANDOFF n (in rugby) act of warding off an opposing player with the open hand

HANDOUT n clothing, food, or money given to a needy person

HANDS ▸ hand

HANDSAW n any saw for use in one hand only

HANDSEL n gift for good luck at the beginning of a new year, new venture, etc ▷ vb give a handsel to (a person)

HANDSET n telephone mouthpiece and earpiece in a single unit

HANDY adj convenient, useful

HANG vb attach or be attached at the top with the lower part free

HANGAR n large shed for storing aircraft ▷ vb put in a hangar

HANGARS ▸ hangar

HANGDOG adj guilty, ashamed ▷ n furtive or sneaky person

HANGED ▸ hang

HANGER n curved piece of wood, wire, or plastic, with a hook, for hanging up clothes

HANGERS ▸ hanger

HANGI n Maori oven consisting of a hole in the ground filled with hot stones

HANGING ▸ hang

HANGIS ▸ hangi

HANGMAN n man who executes people by hanging

HANGMEN ▸ hangman

HANGOUT n place where one lives or that one frequently visits

HANGS ▸ hang

HANGTAG n attached label

HANGUL n Korean language

HANGUP n emotional or psychological preoccupation or problem

HANGUPS ▸ hangup

HANIWA n Japanese funeral offering

HANJAR same as ▸ handjar

HANJARS ▸ hanjar

HANK n coil, esp of yarn ▷ vb

attach (a sail) to a stay by hanks

HANKED ▸ hank

HANKER vb desire intensely

HANKERS ▸ hanker

HANKIE same as ▸ hanky

HANKIES ▸ hanky

HANKING ▸ hank

HANKS ▸ hank

HANKY n handkerchief

HANSA same as ▸ hanse

HANSAS ▸ hansa

HANSE n medieval guild of merchants

HANSEL same as ▸ handsel

HANSELS ▸ hansel

HANSES ▸ hanse

HANSOM n formerly, a two-wheeled one-horse carriage with a fixed hood

HANSOMS ▸ hansom

HANT same as ▸ haunt

HANTED ▸ hant

HANTING ▸ hant

HANTLE n good deal

HANTLES ▸ hantle

HANTS ▸ hant

HANUMAN n type of monkey

HAO n monetary unit of Vietnam, worth one tenth of a dông

HAOMA n type of ritual drink

HAOMAS ▸ haoma

HAOS ▸ hao

HAP n luck ▷ vb cover up

HAPAX n word that only appears once in a work of literature, or in a body of work by a particular author

HAPAXES ▸ hapax

HAPKIDO n Korean martial art

HAPLESS adj unlucky

HAPLITE same as ▸ aplite

HAPLOID adj denoting a cell or organism with unpaired chromosomes ▷ n haploid cell or organism

HAPLONT n organism, esp a plant, that has the haploid number of chromosomes in its somatic cells

HAPLY archaic word for ▸ perhaps

HAPPED ▸ hap

HAPPEN vb take place, occur

HAPPENS ▸ happen

HAPPIED ▸ happy

HAPPIER ▸ happy

HAPPIES ▸ happy

HAPPILY ▸ happy

HAPPING ▸ hap

HAPPY adj feeling or causing joy ▷ vb make happy

HAPS ▸ hap

HAPTEN n incomplete antigen that can stimulate antibody production only when it is chemically combined with a particular protein

HAPTENE same as ▸ hapten

HAPTENS ▸ hapten

HAPTIC adj relating to or based on the sense of touch

HAPTICS n science of sense of touch

HAPU n subtribe

HAPUKA another name for ▸ groper

HAPUKAS ▸ hapuka

HAPUKU same as ▸ hapuka

HAPUKUS ▸ hapuku

HAPUS ▸ hapu

HARAM n anything that is forbidden by Islamic law

HARAMS ▸ haram

HARASS vb annoy or trouble constantly

HARBOR same as ▸ harbour

HARBORS ▸ harbor

HARBOUR n sheltered port ▷ vb maintain secretly in the mind

HARD adj firm, solid, or rigid ▷ adv with great energy or effort

HARDASS n tough person

HARDEN vb make or become hard ▷ n rough fabric made from hards

HARDENS ▸ harden

HARDER ▸ hard

HARDEST ▸ hard

HARDHAT n hat made of a hard material for protection, worn esp by construction workers, equestrians, etc ▷ adj (in US English) characteristic of the presumed conservative attitudes and prejudices typified by construction workers

HARDIER ▸ hardy

HARDIES ▸ hardy

HARDILY adv in a hardy manner

HARDISH ▸ hard

HARDLY adv scarcely or not at all

HARDMAN n tough,

H

ruthless, or violent man

HARDMEN ▸ hardman

HARDOKE n burdock

HARDPAN n hard impervious layer of clay below the soil, resistant to drainage and root growth

HARDS pl n coarse fibres and other refuse from flax and hemp

HARDSET adj in difficulties

HARDTOP n car equipped with a metal or plastic roof that is sometimes detachable

HARDY adj able to stand difficult conditions ▷ n any blacksmith's tool made with a square shank so that it can be lodged in a square hole in an anvil

HARE n animal like a large rabbit, with longer ears and legs ▷ vb run (away) quickly

HARED ▸ hare

HAREEM same as ▸ harem

HAREEMS ▸ hareem

HARELD n long-tailed duck

HARELDS ▸ hareld

HARELIP n slight split in the upper lip

HAREM n (apartments of) a Muslim man's wives and concubines

HAREMS ▸ harem

HARES ▸ hare

HARIANA n Indian breed of cattle

HARICOT n variety of French bean with light-coloured edible seeds, which can be dried and stored

HARIJAN n member of an Indian caste once considered untouchable

HARIM same as ▸ harem

HARIMS ▸ harim

HARING ▸ hare

HARIRA n Moroccan soup made from a variety of vegetables with lentils, chickpeas, and coriander

HARIRAS ▸ harira

HARISH adj like hare

HARISSA n hot paste made from chilli peppers, tomatoes, spices, and olive oil

HARK vb listen

HARKED ▸ hark

HARKEN same as ▸ hearken

HARKENS ▸ harken

HARKING ▸ hark

HARKS ▸ hark

HARL same as ▸ herl

HARLED ▸ harl

HARLING ▸ harl

HARLOT n prostitute ▷ adj of or like a harlot

HARLOTS ▸ harlot

HARLS ▸ harl

HARM vb injure physically, mentally, or morally ▷ n physical, mental, or moral injury

HARMALA n African plant

HARMAN n constable

HARMANS ▸ harman

HARMED ▸ harm

HARMEL same as ▸ harmala

HARMELS ▸ harmel

HARMER ▸ harm

HARMERS ▸ harm

HARMFUL adj causing or tending to cause harm, esp to a person's health

HARMIN same as > harmalin

HARMINE same as > harmalin

HARMING ▸ harm

HARMINS ▸ harmin

HARMONY n peaceful agreement and cooperation

HARMOST n Spartan governor

HARMS ▸ harm

HARN n coarse linen

HARNESS n arrangement of straps for attaching a horse to a cart or plough ▷ vb put a harness on

HARNS ▸ harn

HARO interj cry meaning alas

HAROS ▸ haro

HAROSET n Jewish dish eaten at Passover

HARP n large triangular stringed instrument played with the fingers ▷ vb play the harp

HARPED ▸ harp

HARPER ▸ harp

HARPERS ▸ harp

HARPIES ▸ harpy

HARPIN n type of protein

HARPING ▸ harp

HARPINS same as > harpings

HARPIST ▸ harp

HARPOON n barbed spear attached to a rope used for hunting whales ▷ vb spear with a harpoon

HARPS ▸ harp

HARPY n nasty or bad-tempered woman

HARRIED ▸ harry

HARRIER n cross-country runner

HARRIES ▸ harry

HARROW n implement used to break up lumps of soil ▷ vb draw a harrow over

HARROWS ▸ harrow

HARRY vb keep asking (someone) to do something, pester

HARSH adj severe and difficult to cope with ▷ vb ruin or end a state of elation

HARSHED ▸ harsh

HARSHEN vb make harsh

HARSHER ▸ harsh

HARSHES ▸ harsh

HARSHLY ▸ harsh

HARSLET same as ▸ haslet

HART n adult male deer

HARTAL n (in India) the act of closing shops or suspending work, esp in political protest

HARTALS ▸ hartal

HARTELY archaic spelling of > heartily

HARTEN same as ▸ hearten

HARTENS ▸ harten

HARTS ▸ hart

HARUMPH same as > harrumph

HARVEST n (season for) the gathering of crops ▷ vb gather (a ripened crop)

HAS ▸ have

HASBIAN n former lesbian who has become heterosexual or bisexual

HASH n dish of diced cooked meat and vegetables reheated ▷ vb chop into small pieces

HASHED ▸ hash

HASHES ▸ hash

HASHIER ▸ hash

HASHING ▸ hash

HASHISH n drug made from the cannabis plant, smoked for its intoxicating effects

HASHY ▸ hash

HASK n archaic name for a basket for transporting fish

HASKS ▸ hask

HASLET n loaf of cooked minced pig's offal, eaten cold

HASLETS ▸ haslet
HASP n clasp that fits over a staple and is secured by a bolt or padlock, used as a fastening ▸ vb secure (a door, window, etc) with a hasp
HASPED ▸ hasp
HASPING ▸ hasp
HASPS ▸ hasp
HASS n as in **white hass** oatmeal pudding made with sheep's gullet
HASSAR n South American catfish
HASSARS ▸ hassar
HASSEL same as ▸ hassle
HASSELS ▸ hassel
HASSES ▸ hass
HASSIUM n element synthetically produced in small quantities by high-energy ion bombardment
HASSLE n trouble, bother ▸ vb bother or annoy
HASSLED ▸ hassle
HASSLES ▸ hassle
HASSOCK n cushion for kneeling on in church
HAST singular form of the present tense (indicative mood) of ▸ have
HASTA Spanish for ▸ until
HASTATE adj (of a leaf) having a pointed tip and two outward-pointing lobes at the base
HASTE n (excessive) quickness ▸ vb hasten
HASTED ▸ haste
HASTEN vb (cause to) hurry
HASTENS ▸ hasten
HASTES ▸ haste
HASTIER ▸ hasty
HASTILY ▸ hasty
HASTING ▸ haste
HASTY adj (too) quick
HAT n covering for the head, often with a brim ▸ vb supply (a person) with a hat or put a hat on (someone)
HATABLE ▸ hate
HATBAND n band or ribbon around the base of the crown of a hat
HATBOX n box or case for a hat or hats
HATCH vb (cause to) emerge from an egg ▸ n hinged door covering an opening in a floor or wall
HATCHED ▸ hatch

HATCHEL same as ▸ heckle
HATCHER ▸ hatch
HATCHES ▸ hatch
HATCHET n small axe
HATE vb dislike intensely ▸ n intense dislike
HATED ▸ hate
HATEFUL adj causing or deserving hate
HATER ▸ hate
HATERS ▸ hate
HATES ▸ hate
HATFUL n amount a hat will hold
HATFULS ▸ hatful
HATH form of the present tense (indicative mood) of ▸ have
HATHA n as in **hatha yoga** form of yoga
HATING ▸ hate
HATLESS ▸ hat
HATLIKE ▸ hat
HATPEG n peg to hang hat on
HATPEGS ▸ hatpeg
HATPIN n sturdy pin used to secure a woman's hat to her hair, often having a decorative head
HATPINS ▸ hatpin
HATRACK n rack for hanging hats on
HATRED n intense dislike
HATREDS ▸ hatred
HATS ▸ hat
HATSFUL ▸ hatful
HATTED ▸ hat
HATTER n person who makes and sells hats ▸ vb annoy
HATTERS ▸ hatter
HATTING ▸ hat
HATTOCK n small hat
HAUBERK n long sleeveless coat of mail
HAUBOIS same as ▸ hautboy
HAUD Scots word for ▸ hold
HAUDING ▸ haud
HAUDS ▸ haud
HAUF Scots word for ▸ half
HAUFS ▸ hauf
HAUGH n low-lying often alluvial riverside meadow
HAUGHS ▸ haugh
HAUGHT same as ▸ haughty
HAUGHTY adj proud, arrogant
HAUL vb pull or drag with effort ▸ n hauling
HAULAGE n (charge for) transporting goods

HAULD Scots word for ▸ hold
HAULDS ▸ hauld
HAULED ▸ haul
HAULER same as ▸ haulier
HAULERS ▸ hauler
HAULIER n firm or person that transports goods by road
HAULING ▸ haul
HAULM n stalks of beans, peas, or potatoes collectively
HAULMS ▸ haulm
HAULMY adj having haulms
HAULS ▸ haul
HAULST same as ▸ halse
HAULT same as ▸ haughty
HAUNCH n human hip or fleshy hindquarter of an animal ▸ vb in archaic usage, cause (an animal) to come down on its haunches
HAUNT vb visit in the form of a ghost ▸ n place visited frequently
HAUNTED adj frequented by ghosts
HAUNTER ▸ haunt
HAUNTS ▸ haunt
HAUSE same as ▸ halse
HAUSED ▸ hause
HAUSEN n variety of sturgeon
HAUSENS ▸ hausen
HAUSES ▸ hause
HAUSING ▸ hause
HAUT same as ▸ haughty
HAUTBOY n type of strawberry
HAUTE adj French word meaning high
HAUTEUR n haughtiness
HAUYNE n blue mineral containing calcium
HAUYNES ▸ hauyne
HAVARTI n Danish cheese
HAVE vb possess, hold
HAVEN n place of safety ▸ vb secure or shelter in or as if in a haven
HAVENED ▸ haven
HAVENS ▸ haven
HAVEOUR same as ▸ havior
HAVER vb talk nonsense ▸ n nonsense
HAVERED ▸ haver
HAVEREL n fool
HAVERS ▸ haver
HAVES ▸ have
HAVING ▸ have
HAVINGS ▸ have
HAVIOR same as ▸ haviour
HAVIORS ▸ havior

HAVIOUR n possession
HAVOC n disorder and confusion ▷ vb lay waste
HAVOCS ▸ havoc
HAW n hawthorn berry ▷ vb make an inarticulate utterance
HAWALA n Middle Eastern system of money transfer
HAWALAS ▸ hawala
HAWBUCK n bumpkin
HAWED ▸ haw
HAWING ▸ haw
HAWK n bird of prey with a short hooked bill and very good eyesight ▷ vb offer (goods) for sale in the street or door-to-door
HAWKBIT n any of three perennial plants with yellow dandelion-like flowers
HAWKED ▸ hawk
HAWKER n person who travels from place to place selling goods
HAWKERS ▸ hawker
HAWKEY same as ▸ hockey
HAWKEYS ▸ hawkey
HAWKIE n cow with white stripe on face
HAWKIES ▸ hawkie
HAWKING another name for > falconry
HAWKISH adj favouring the use or display of force rather than diplomacy to achieve foreign policy goals
HAWKIT adj having a white streak
HAWKS ▸ hawk
HAWM vb be idle and relaxed
HAWMED ▸ hawm
HAWMING ▸ hawm
HAWMS ▸ hawm
HAWS ▸ haw
HAWSE vb of boats, pitch violently when at anchor
HAWSED ▸ hawse
HAWSER n large rope used on a ship
HAWSERS ▸ hawser
HAWSES ▸ hawse
HAWSING ▸ hawse
HAY n grass cut and dried as fodder ▷ vb cut, dry, and store (grass, clover, etc) as fodder
HAYBAND n rope made by twisting hay together
HAYBOX n airtight box full of hay or other insulating material used to keep partially cooked food warm and allow cooking by retained heat
HAYCOCK n small cone-shaped pile of hay left in the field until dry enough to carry to the rick or barn
HAYED ▸ hay
HAYER n person who makes hay
HAYERS ▸ hayer
HAYEY ▸ hay
HAYFORK n long-handled fork with two long curved prongs, used for moving or turning hay
HAYIER ▸ hayey
HAYIEST ▸ hayey
HAYING ▸ hay
HAYINGS ▸ hay
HAYLAGE n type of hay for animal fodder
HAYLE n welfare
HAYLES ▸ hayle
HAYLOFT n loft for storing hay
HAYMOW n part of a barn where hay is stored
HAYMOWS ▸ haymow
HAYRACK n rack for holding hay for feeding to animals
HAYRAKE n large rake used to collect hay
HAYRICK same as > haystack
HAYRIDE n pleasure trip in hay wagon
HAYS ▸ hay
HAYSEED n seeds or fragments of grass or straw
HAYSEL n season for making hay
HAYSELS ▸ haysel
HAYWARD n parish officer in charge of enclosures and fences
HAYWIRE adj (of things) not functioning properly ▷ n wire for binding hay
HAZAN same as > cantor
HAZANIM ▸ hazan
HAZANS ▸ hazan
HAZARD n something that could be dangerous ▷ vb put in danger
HAZARDS ▸ hazard
HAZE n mist, often caused by heat ▷ vb make or become hazy
HAZED ▸ haze
HAZEL n small tree producing edible nuts ▷ adj (of eyes) greenish-brown
HAZELLY ▸ hazel
HAZELS ▸ hazel
HAZER ▸ haze
HAZERS ▸ haze
HAZES ▸ haze
HAZIER ▸ hazy
HAZIEST ▸ hazy
HAZILY ▸ hazy
HAZING ▸ haze
HAZINGS ▸ haze
HAZMAT n hazardous material
HAZMATS ▸ hazmat
HAZY adj not clear, misty
HAZZAN same as ▸ cantor
HAZZANS ▸ hazzan
HE pron male person or animal ▷ n male person or animal ▷ interj expression of amusement or derision
HEAD n upper or front part of the body, containing the sense organs and the brain ▷ adj chief, principal ▷ vb be at the top or front of
HEADAGE n payment to farmer based on number of animals kept
HEADED adj having a head or heads
HEADEND n facility from which cable television is transmitted
HEADER n striking a ball with the head
HEADERS ▸ header
HEADFUL n amount head will hold
HEADIER ▸ heady
HEADILY ▸ heady
HEADING same as ▸ head
HEADMAN n chief or leader
HEADMEN ▸ headman
HEADPIN another word for ▸ kingpin
HEADRIG n edge of ploughed field
HEADS adv with the side of a coin which has a portrait of a head on it uppermost
HEADSET n pair of headphones, esp with a microphone attached
HEADWAY same as > headroom
HEADY adj intoxicating or exciting
HEAL vb make or become well
HEALD same as ▸ heddle
HEALDED ▸ heald
HEALDS ▸ heald

HEALED ▸ heal

HEALEE *n* person who is being healed

HEALEES ▸ healee

HEALER ▸ heal

HEALERS ▸ heal

HEALING ▸ heal

HEALS ▸ heal

HEALTH *n* normal (good) condition of someone's body ▷ *interj* exclamation wishing someone good health as part of a toast

HEALTHS ▸ health

HEALTHY *adj* having good health

HEAME *old form of* ▸ **home**

HEAP *n* pile of things one on top of another ▷ *vb* gather into a pile

HEAPED ▸ heap

HEAPER ▸ heap

HEAPERS ▸ heap

HEAPIER ▸ heapy

HEAPING *adj* (of a spoonful) heaped

HEAPS ▸ heap

HEAPY *adj* having many heaps

HEAR *vb* perceive (a sound) by ear

HEARD *same as* ▸ **herd**

HEARDS ▸ herd

HEARE *old form of* ▸ **hair**

HEARER ▸ hear

HEARERS ▸ hear

HEARES ▸ heare

HEARIE *old form of* ▸ **hairy**

HEARING ▸ hear

HEARKEN *vb* listen

HEARS ▸ hear

HEARSAY *n* gossip, rumour

HEARSE *n* funeral car used to carry a coffin ▷ *vb* put in hearse

HEARSED ▸ hearse

HEARSES ▸ hearse

HEARSY *adj* like a hearse

HEART *n* organ that pumps blood round the body ▷ *vb* (of vegetables) form a heart

HEARTED ▸ heart

HEARTEN *vb* encourage, make cheerful

HEARTH *n* floor of a fireplace

HEARTHS ▸ hearth

HEARTLY *adv* vigorously

HEARTS *n* card game in which players must avoid winning tricks containing hearts or the queen of spades

HEARTY *adj* substantial, nourishing ▷ *n* comrade, esp a sailor

HEAST *same as* ▸ **hest**

HEASTE *same as* ▸ **hest**

HEASTES ▸ heaste

HEASTS ▸ heast

HEAT *vb* make or become hot ▷ *n* state of being hot

HEATED *adj* angry and excited

HEATER *n* device for supplying heat

HEATERS ▸ heater

HEATH *n* area of open uncultivated land

HEATHEN *n* (of) a person who does not believe in an established religion ▷ *adj* of or relating to heathen peoples

HEATHER *n* low-growing plant with small purple, pinkish, or white flowers, growing on heaths and mountains ▷ *adj* of a heather colour

HEATHS ▸ heath

HEATHY ▸ heath

HEATING *n* device or system for supplying heat, esp central heating, to a building

HEATS ▸ heat

HEAUME *n* (in the 12th and 13th centuries) a large helmet reaching and supported by the shoulders

HEAUMES ▸ heaume

HEAVE *vb* lift with effort ▷ *n* heaving

HEAVED ▸ heave

HEAVEN *n* place believed to be the home of God, where good people go when they die

HEAVENS ▸ heaven

HEAVER ▸ heave

HEAVERS ▸ heave

HEAVES ▸ heave

HEAVIER ▸ heavy

HEAVIES ▸ heavy

HEAVILY ▸ heavy

HEAVING ▸ heave

HEAVY *adj* of great weight

HEBE *n* any of various flowering shrubs

HEBEN *old form of* ▸ **ebony**

HEBENON *n* source of poison

HEBENS ▸ heben

HEBES ▸ hebe

HEBETIC *adj* of or relating to puberty

HEBONA *same as* ▸ **hebenon**

HEBONAS ▸ hebona

HECH *interj* expression of surprise

HECHT *same as* ▸ **hight**

HECHTS ▸ hecht

HECK *interj* mild exclamation of surprise, irritation, etc ▷ *n* frame for obstructing the passage of fish in a river

HECKLE *vb* interrupt (a public speaker) with comments, questions, or taunts ▷ *n* instrument for combing flax or hemp

HECKLED ▸ heckle

HECKLER ▸ heckle

HECKLES ▸ heckle

HECKS ▸ heck

HECTARE *n* one hundred ares or 10 000 square metres (2.471 acres)

HECTIC *adj* rushed or busy ▷ *n* hectic fever or flush

HECTICS ▸ hectic

HECTOR *vb* bully ▷ *n* blustering bully

HECTORS ▸ hector

HEDDLE *n* one of a set of frames of vertical wires on a loom, each wire having an eye through which a warp thread can be passed ▷ *vb* pass thread through heddle

HEDDLED ▸ heddle

HEDDLES ▸ heddle

HEDER *variant spelling of* ▸ **cheder**

HEDERA ▸ ivy

HEDERAL ▸ hedera

HEDERAS ▸ hedera

HEDERS ▸ heder

HEDGE *n* row of bushes forming a barrier or boundary ▷ *vb* be evasive or noncommittal

HEDGED ▸ hedge

HEDGER ▸ hedge

HEDGERS ▸ hedge

HEDGES ▸ hedge

HEDGIER ▸ hedge

HEDGING ▸ hedge

HEDGY ▸ hedge

HEDONIC ▸ hedonism

HEED *n* careful attention ▷ *vb* pay careful attention to

HEEDED ▸ heed

HEEDER ▸ heed

HEEDERS ▸ heed

HEEDFUL ▸ heed

HEEDING ▸ heed

HEEDS ▸ heed

HEEDY ▸ heed

HEEHAW *interj* representation of the braying sound of a donkey ▷ *vb* make braying sound

HEEHAWS ▸ heehaw

HEEL *n* back part of the foot ▷ *vb* repair the heel of (a shoe)

HEELBAR *n* small shop or counter where shoes are repaired

HEELED ▸ heel

HEELER *n* dog that herds cattle by biting at their heels

HEELERS ▸ heeler

HEELING ▸ heel

HEELS ▸ heel

HEELTAP *n* layer of leather, etc, in the heel of a shoe

HEEZE *Scots word for* ▸ **hoist**

HEEZED ▸ heeze

HEEZES ▸ heeze

HEEZIE *n* act of lifting

HEEZIES ▸ heezie

HEEZING ▸ heeze

HEFT *vb* assess the weight of (something) by lifting ▷ *n* weight

HEFTE *same as* ▸ **heave**

HEFTED ▸ heft

HEFTER ▸ heft

HEFTERS ▸ heft

HEFTIER ▸ hefty

HEFTILY ▸ hefty

HEFTING ▸ heft

HEFTS ▸ heft

HEFTY *adj* large, heavy, or strong

HEGARI *n* African sorghum

HEGARIS ▸ hegari

HEGEMON *n* person in authority

HEGIRA *n* emigration escape or flight

HEGIRAS ▸ hegira

HEGUMEN *n* head of a monastery of the Eastern Church

HEH *interj* exclamation of surprise or inquiry

HEHS ▸ heh

HEID *Scots word for* ▸ **head**

HEIDS ▸ heid

HEIFER *n* young cow

HEIFERS ▸ heifer

HEIGH *same as* ▸ **hey**

HEIGHT *n* distance from base to top

HEIGHTH *obsolete form of*

▸ height

HEIGHTS ▸ height

HEIL *vb* give a German greeting

HEILED ▸ heil

HEILING ▸ heil

HEILS ▸ heil

HEIMISH *adj* comfortable

HEINIE *n* buttocks

HEINIES ▸ heinie

HEINOUS *adj* evil and shocking

HEIR *n* person entitled to inherit property or rank ▷ *vb* inherit

HEIRDOM *n* succession by right of blood

HEIRED ▸ heir

HEIRESS *n* woman who inherits or expects to inherit great wealth

HEIRING ▸ heir

HEIRS ▸ heir

HEISHI *n* Native American shell jewellery

HEIST *n* robbery ▷ *vb* steal or burgle

HEISTED ▸ heist

HEISTER ▸ heist

HEISTS ▸ heist

HEITIKI *n* Maori neck ornament of greenstone

HEJAB *same as* ▸ **hijab**

HEJABS ▸ hejab

HEJIRA *same as* ▸ **hegira**

HEJIRAS ▸ hejira

HEJRA *same as* ▸ **hegira**

HEJRAS ▸ hejra

HEKTARE *same as* ▸ **hectare**

HELCOID *adj* having ulcers

HELD ▸ hold

HELE *vb as in* **hele in** dialect expression meaning insert (cuttings, shoots, etc) into soil before planting to keep them moist

HELED ▸ hele

HELES ▸ hele

HELIAC *same as* ▸ **heliacal**

HELIAST *n* ancient Greek juror

HELIBUS *n* helicopter carrying passengers

HELICAL *adj* spiral

HELICES ▸ helix

HELICON *n* bass tuba made to coil over the shoulder of a band musician

HELIMAN *n* helicopter pilot

HELIMEN ▸ heliman

HELING ▸ hele

HELIO *n* instrument for sending messages in Morse code by reflecting the sun's rays

HELIOS ▸ helio

HELIPAD *n* place for helicopters to land and take off

HELIUM *n* very light colourless odourless gas

HELIUMS ▸ helium

HELIX *n* spiral

HELIXES ▸ helix

HELL *n* place believed to be where wicked people go when they die ▷ *vb* act wildly

HELLBOX *n* (in printing) container for broken type

HELLCAT *n* spiteful fierce-tempered woman

HELLED ▸ hell

HELLER *n* monetary unit of the Czech Republic and Slovakia

HELLERI *n* Central American fish

HELLERS ▸ heller

HELLERY *n* wild or mischievous behaviour

HELLIER *n* slater

HELLING ▸ hell

HELLION *n* rough or rowdy person, esp a child

HELLISH *adj* very unpleasant ▷ *adv* (intensifier)

HELLO *interj* expression of greeting or surprise ▷ *n* act of saying 'hello' ▷ *sentence substitute* expression of greeting used on meeting a person or at the start of a telephone call ▷ *vb* say hello

HELLOED ▸ hello

HELLOES ▸ hello

HELLOS ▸ hello

HELLOVA *same as* ▸ **helluva**

HELLS ▸ hell

HELLUVA *adj* (intensifier)

HELM *n* tiller or wheel for steering a ship ▷ *vb* direct or steer

HELMED ▸ helm

HELMER *n* film director

HELMERS ▸ helmer

HELMET *n* hard hat worn for protection

HELMETS ▸ helmet

HELMING ▸ helm

HELMS ▸ helm

HELO *n* helicopter

HELOS ▸ helo

HELOT *n* serf or slave

HELOTRY n serfdom or slavery

HELOTS ▸ helot

HELP vb make something easier, better, or quicker for (someone) ▷ n assistance or support

HELPED ▸ help

HELPER ▸ help

HELPERS ▸ help

HELPFUL adj giving help

HELPING n single portion of food

HELPS ▸ help

HELVE n handle of a hand tool such as an axe or pick ▷ vb fit a helve to (a tool)

HELVED ▸ helve

HELVES ▸ helve

HELVING ▸ helve

HEM n bottom edge of a garment, folded under and stitched down ▷ vb provide with a hem

HEMAGOG same as > hemagogue

HEMAL same as ▸ haemal

HEMATAL same as ▸ hemal

HEMATIC same as > haematic

HEMATIN same as > haematin

HEME same as ▸ haem

HEMES ▸ heme

HEMIC > haematic

HEMIN same as ▸ haemin

HEMINA n old liquid measure

HEMINAS ▸ hemina

HEMINS ▸ hemin

HEMIOLA n rhythmic device involving the superimposition of, for example, two notes in the time of three

HEMIONE same as > hemionus

HEMIPOD same as > hemipode

HEMLINE n level to which the hem of a skirt hangs

HEMLOCK n poison made from a plant with spotted stems and small white flowers

HEMMED ▸ hem

HEMMER n attachment on a sewing machine for hemming

HEMMERS ▸ hemmer

HEMMING ▸ hem

HEMOID same as > haematoid

HEMP n Asian plant with tough fibres

HEMPEN ▸ hemp

HEMPIE same as ▸ hempy

HEMPIER ▸ hempy

HEMPIES ▸ hempy

HEMPS ▸ hemp

HEMPY adj of or like hemp ▷ n rogue

HEMS ▸ hem

HEN n female domestic fowl ▷ vb lose one's courage

HENBANE n poisonous plant with sticky hairy leaves

HENBIT n European plant with small dark red flowers

HENBITS ▸ henbit

HENCE adv from this time ▷ interj begone! away!

HENCOOP n cage for poultry

HEND vb seize

HENDED ▸ hend

HENDING ▸ hend

HENDS ▸ hend

HENGE n circular monument, often containing a circle of stones, dating from the Neolithic and Bronze Ages

HENGES ▸ henge

HENLEY n type of sweater

HENLEYS ▸ henley

HENLIKE ▸ hen

HENNA n reddish dye made from a shrub or tree ▷ vb dye (the hair) with henna

HENNAED ▸ henna

HENNAS ▸ henna

HENNED ▸ hen

HENNER n challenge

HENNERS ▸ henner

HENNERY n place or farm for keeping poultry

HENNIER ▸ henny

HENNIES ▸ henny

HENNIN n former women's hat

HENNING ▸ hen

HENNINS ▸ hennin

HENNISH ▸ hen

HENNY adj like hen ▷ n cock that looks like hen

HENOTIC adj acting to reconcile

HENPECK vb (of a woman) to harass or torment (a man, esp her husband) by persistent nagging

HENRIES ▸ henry

HENRY n unit of electrical inductance

HENRYS ▸ henry

HENS ▸ hen

HENT vb seize ▷ n anything that has been grasped, esp by the mind

HENTED ▸ hent

HENTING ▸ hent

HENTS ▸ hent

HEP same as ▸ hip

HEPAR n compound containing sulphur

HEPARIN n polysaccharide, containing sulphate groups, present in most body tissues: an anticoagulant used in the treatment of thrombosis

HEPARS ▸ hepar

HEPATIC adj of the liver ▷ n any of various drugs for use in treating diseases of the liver

HEPCAT n person who is hep, esp a player or admirer of jazz and swing in the 1940s

HEPCATS ▸ hepcat

HEPPER ▸ hep

HEPPEST ▸ hep

HEPS ▸ hep

HEPSTER same as ▸ hipster

HEPT archaic spelling of ▸ heaped

HEPTAD n group or series of seven

HEPTADS ▸ heptad

HEPTANE n alkane found in petroleum and used as an anaesthetic

HEPTOSE n any monosaccharide that has seven carbon atoms per molecule

HER pron refers to a female person or animal or anything personified as feminine when the object of a sentence or clause ▷ adj belonging to her ▷ determiner of, belonging to, or associated with her

HERALD n person who announces important news ▷ vb signal the approach of

HERALDS ▸ herald

HERB n plant used for flavouring in cookery, and in medicine

HERBAGE n herbaceous plants collectively, esp those on which animals graze

HERBAL *adj* of or relating to herbs, usually culinary or medicinal herbs ▷ *n* book describing and listing the properties of plants
HERBALS ▶ **herbal**
HERBAR *same as* ▶ **herbary**
HERBARS ▶ **herbar**
HERBARY *n* herb garden
HERBED *adj* flavoured with herbs
HERBIER ▶ **herby**
HERBIST *same as* > **herbalist**
HERBLET *n* little herb
HERBOSE *same as* ▶ **herbous**
HERBOUS *adj* with abundance of herbs
HERBS ▶ **herb**
HERBY *adj* abounding in herbs
HERD *n* group of animals feeding and living together ▷ *vb* collect into a herd
HERDBOY *n* boy who looks after herd
HERDED ▶ **herd**
HERDEN *n* type of coarse cloth
HERDENS ▶ **herden**
HERDER *same as* > **herdsman**
HERDERS ▶ **herder**
HERDESS *n* female herder
HERDIC *n* small horse-drawn carriage with a rear entrance and side seats
HERDICS ▶ **herdic**
HERDING ▶ **herd**
HERDMAN *same as* > **herdsman**
HERDMEN ▶ **herdman**
HERDS ▶ **herd**
HERE *adv* in, at, or to this place or point ▷ *n* this place
HEREAT *adv* because of this
HEREBY *adv* by means of or as a result of this
HEREDES ▶ **heres**
HEREIN *adv* in this place, matter, or document
HEREOF *adv* of or concerning this
HEREON *archaic word for* > **hereupon**
HERES ▶ **here**
HERESY *n* opinion contrary to accepted opinion or belief
HERETIC *n* person who holds unorthodox opinions
HERETO *adv* this place,

matter, or document
HERIED ▶ **hery**
HERIES ▶ **hery**
HERIOT *n* (in medieval England) a death duty paid by villeins and free tenants to their lord, often consisting of the dead man's best beast or chattel
HERIOTS ▶ **heriot**
HERISSE *adj* with bristles
HERITOR *n* person who inherits
HERL *n* barb or barbs of a feather, used to dress fishing flies
HERLING *n* Scots word for a type of fish
HERLS ▶ **herl**
HERM *n* (in ancient Greece) a stone head of Hermes surmounting a square stone pillar
HERMA *same as* ▶ **herm**
HERMAE ▶ **herma**
HERMAI ▶ **herma**
HERMIT *n* person living in solitude, esp for religious reasons
HERMITS ▶ **hermit**
HERMS ▶ **herm**
HERN *archaic or dialect word for* ▶ **heron**
HERNIA *n* protrusion of an organ or part through the lining of the surrounding body cavity
HERNIAE ▶ **hernia**
HERNIAL ▶ **hernia**
HERNIAS ▶ **hernia**
HERNS ▶ **hern**
HERO *n* principal character in a film, book, etc
HEROES ▶ **hero**
HEROIC *adj* courageous
HEROICS *pl n* extravagant behaviour
HEROIN *n* highly addictive drug derived from morphine
HEROINE *n* principal female character in a novel, play, etc
HEROINS ▶ **heroin**
HEROISE *same as* ▶ **heroize**
HEROISM *n* great courage and bravery
HEROIZE *vb* make into hero
HERON *n* long-legged wading bird
HERONRY *n* colony of breeding herons
HERONS ▶ **heron**

HEROON *n* temple or monument dedicated to hero
HEROONS ▶ **heroon**
HEROS ▶ **hero**
HERPES *n* any of several inflammatory skin diseases, including shingles and cold sores
HERRIED ▶ **herry**
HERRIES ▶ **herry**
HERRING *n* important food fish of northern seas
HERRY *vb* harry
HERS *pron* something belonging to her
HERSALL *n* rehearsal
HERSE *n* harrow
HERSED *adj* arranged like a harrow
HERSELF *pron* feminine singular reflexive form
HERSES ▶ **herse**
HERSHIP *n* act of plundering
HERTZ *n* unit of frequency
HERTZES ▶ **hertz**
HERY *vb* praise
HERYE *same as* ▶ **hery**
HERYED ▶ **herye**
HERYES ▶ **herye**
HERYING ▶ **hery**
HES ▶ **he**
HESP *same as* ▶ **hasp**
HESPED ▶ **hesp**
HESPING ▶ **hesp**
HESPS ▶ **hesp**
HESSIAN *n* coarse jute fabric
HESSITE *n* black or grey metallic mineral consisting of silver telluride in cubic crystalline form
HEST *archaic word for* ▶ **behest**
HESTS ▶ **hest**
HET *n* short for heterosexual ▷ *adj* Scots word for hot
HETAERA *n* (esp in ancient Greece) a female prostitute, esp an educated courtesan
HETAIRA *same as* ▶ **hetaera**
HETE *same as* ▶ **hight**
HETERO *n* short for heterosexual
HETEROS ▶ **hetero**
HETES ▶ **hete**
HETH *n* eighth letter of the Hebrew alphabet
HETHER *same as* ▶ **hither**
HETHS ▶ **heth**
HETING ▶ **hete**
HETMAN *another word for*

▶ **ataman**
HETMANS ▶ **hetman**
HETS ▶ **het**
HETTIE n slang term for a heterosexual
HETTIES ▶ **hettie**
HEUCH Scots word for ▶ **crag**
HEUCHS ▶ **heuch**
HEUGH same as ▶ **heuch**
HEUGHS ▶ **heugh**
HEUREKA same as ▶ **eureka**
HEURISM n use of logic
HEVEA n rubber-producing South American tree
HEVEAS ▶ **hevea**
HEW vb cut with an axe
HEWABLE ▶ **hew**
HEWED ▶ **hew**
HEWER ▶ **hew**
HEWERS ▶ **hew**
HEWGH interj sound made to imitate the flight of an arrow
HEWING ▶ **hew**
HEWINGS ▶ **hew**
HEWN ▶ **hew**
HEWS ▶ **hew**
HEX adj of or relating to hexadecimal notation ▷ n evil spell ▷ vb bewitch

> This word, meaning to bewitch, is a really useful one for using the X.

HEXACT n part of a sponge with six rays
HEXACTS ▶ **hexact**
HEXAD n group or series of six
HEXADE same as ▶ **hexad**
HEXADES ▶ **hexade**
HEXADIC ▶ **hexad**
HEXADS ▶ **hexad**
HEXAGON n geometrical figure with six sides
HEXANE n liquid alkane existing in five isomeric forms that are found in petroleum and used as solvents
HEXANES ▶ **hexane**
HEXAPLA n edition of the Old Testament compiled by Origen, containing six versions of the text
HEXAPOD n six-footed arthropod
HEXARCH adj (of plant) with six veins
HEXED ▶ **hex**
HEXENE same as ▶ **hexylene**
HEXENES ▶ **hexene**
HEXER ▶ **hex**
HEXEREI n witchcraft

HEXERS ▶ **hex**
HEXES ▶ **hex**
HEXING ▶ **hex**
HEXINGS ▶ **hex**
HEXONE n colourless insoluble liquid ketone used as a solvent for organic compounds
HEXONES ▶ **hexone**
HEXOSAN n any of a group of polysaccharides that yield hexose on hydrolysis
HEXOSE n monosaccharide, such as glucose, that contains six carbon atoms per molecule
HEXOSES ▶ **hexose**
HEXYL adj of, consisting of, or containing the group of atoms C_6H_{13}, esp the isomeric form of this group, $CH_3(CH_2)_4CH_2-$
HEXYLIC ▶ **hexyl**
HEXYLS ▶ **hexyl**
HEY interj expression of surprise or for catching attention ▷ vb perform a country dance
HEYDAY n time of greatest success, prime
HEYDAYS ▶ **heyday**
HEYDEY same as ▶ **heyday**
HEYDEYS ▶ **heydey**
HEYDUCK same as ▶ **haiduk**
HEYED ▶ **hey**
HEYING ▶ **hey**
HEYS ▶ **hey**
HI interj hello
HIANT adj gaping
HIATAL ▶ **hiatus**
HIATUS n pause or interruption in continuity
HIBACHI n portable brazier for heating and cooking food
HIC interj representation of the sound of a hiccup
HICATEE same as ▶ **hiccatee**
HICCUP n spasm of the breathing organs with a sharp coughlike sound ▷ vb make a hiccup
HICCUPS ▶ **hiccup**
HICCUPY ▶ **hiccup**
HICK n unsophisticated country person
HICKEY n object or gadget: used as a name when the correct name is forgotten, etc
HICKEYS ▶ **hickey**
HICKIE same as ▶ **hickey**
HICKIES ▶ **hickie**

HICKISH ▶ **hick**
HICKORY n N American nut-bearing tree
HICKS ▶ **hick**
HID ▶ **hide**
HIDABLE ▶ **hide**
HIDAGE n former tax on land
HIDAGES ▶ **hidage**
HIDALGA n Spanish noblewoman
HIDALGO n member of the lower nobility in Spain
HIDDEN ▶ **hide**
HIDDER n young ram
HIDDERS ▶ **hidder**
HIDE vb put (oneself or an object) somewhere difficult to see or find ▷ n place of concealment, esp for a bird-watcher
HIDED ▶ **hide**
HIDEOUS adj ugly, revolting
HIDEOUT n hiding place, esp a remote place used by outlaws, etc; hideaway
HIDER ▶ **hide**
HIDERS ▶ **hide**
HIDES ▶ **hide**
HIDING ▶ **hide**
HIDINGS ▶ **hide**
HIDLING n hiding place
HIDLINS same as ▶ **hidlings**
HIE vb hurry
HIED ▶ **hie**
HIEING ▶ **hie**
HIELAND adj characteristic of Highlanders, esp alluding to their supposed gullibility or foolishness in towns or cities
HIEMAL less common word for > **hibernal**
HIEMS n winter
HIES ▶ **hie**
HIGGLE less common word for ▶ **haggle**
HIGGLED ▶ **higgle**
HIGGLER ▶ **higgle**
HIGGLES ▶ **higgle**
HIGH adj being a relatively great distance from top to bottom; tall ▷ adv at or to a height ▷ n a high place or level ▷ vb hie
HIGHBOY n tall chest of drawers in two sections, the lower section being a lowboy
HIGHED ▶ **high**
HIGHER n advanced level of the Scottish Certificate of Education ▷ vb raise up

H

HIGHERS ▸ higher
HIGHEST ▸ high
HIGHING ▸ high
HIGHISH ▸ high
HIGHLY adv extremely
HIGHMAN n dice weighted to make it fall in particular way
HIGHMEN ▸ highman
HIGHS ▸ high
HIGHT vb archaic word for name or call
HIGHTED ▸ hight
HIGHTH old form of ▸ **height**
HIGHTHS ▸ highth
HIGHTOP n top of ship's mast
HIGHTS ▸ hight
HIGHWAY n main road
HIJAB n covering for the head and face, worn by Muslim women
HIJABS ▸ hijab
HIJACK vb seize control of (an aircraft or other vehicle) while travelling ▷ n instance of hijacking
HIJACKS ▸ hijack
HIJINKS n lively enjoyment
HIJRA same as ▸ **hijrah**
HIJRAH same as ▸ **hegira**
HIJRAHS ▸ hijrah
HIJRAS ▸ hijra
HIKE n long walk in the country, esp for pleasure ▷ vb go for a long walk
HIKED ▸ hike
HIKER ▸ hike
HIKERS ▸ hike
HIKES ▸ hike
HIKING ▸ hike
HIKOI n walk or march, esp a Maori protest march ▷ vb take part in such a march
HIKOIED ▸ hikoi
HIKOIS ▸ hikoi
HILA ▸ hilum
HILAR ▸ hilus
HILCH vb hobble
HILCHED ▸ hilch
HILCHES ▸ hilch
HILD same as ▸ **hold**
HILDING n coward
HILI ▸ hilus
HILL n raised part of the earth's surface, less high than a mountain ▷ vb form into a hill or mound
HILLED ▸ hill
HILLER ▸ hill
HILLERS ▸ hill
HILLIER ▸ hill
HILLING ▸ hill

HILLMEN same as ▸ **hillfolk**
HILLO same as ▸ **hello**
HILLOA same as ▸ **halloa**
HILLOAS ▸ hilloa
HILLOCK n small hill
HILLOED ▸ hillo
HILLOES ▸ hillo
HILLOS ▸ hillo
HILLS ▸ hill
HILLTOP n top of hill
HILLY ▸ hill
HILT n handle of a sword or knife ▷ vb supply with a hilt
HILTED ▸ hilt
HILTING ▸ hilt
HILTS ▸ hilt
HILUM n scar on a seed marking its point of attachment to the seed vessel
HILUS rare word for ▸ **hilum**
HIM pron refers to a male person or animal when the object of a sentence or clause ▷ n male person
HIMATIA ▸ himation
HIMS ▸ him
HIMSELF pron masculine singular reflexive form
HIN n Hebrew unit of capacity equal to about 12 pints or 3.5 litres
HINAU n New Zealand tree
HINAUS ▸ hinau
HIND adj situated at the back ▷ n female deer
HINDER vb get in the way of ▷ adj situated at the back
HINDERS ▸ hinder
HINDGUT n part of the vertebrate digestive tract comprising the colon and rectum
HINDLEG n back leg
HINDS ▸ hind
HING n asafoetida
HINGE n device for holding together two parts so that one can swing freely ▷ vb depend (on)
HINGED ▸ hinge
HINGER n tool for making hinges
HINGERS ▸ hinger
HINGES ▸ hinge
HINGING ▸ hinge
HINGS ▸ hing
HINKIER ▸ hinky
HINKY adj strange
HINNIED ▸ hinny
HINNIES ▸ hinny
HINNY n offspring of a male horse and a female donkey

▷ vb whinny
HINS ▸ hin
HINT n indirect suggestion ▷ vb suggest indirectly
HINTED ▸ hint
HINTER ▸ hint
HINTERS ▸ hint
HINTING ▸ hint
HINTS ▸ hint
HIOI n New Zealand plant of the mint family
HIOIS ▸ hioi
HIP n either side of the body between the pelvis and the thigh ▷ adj aware of or following the latest trends ▷ interj exclamation used to introduce cheers
HIPBONE n either of the two bones that form the sides of the pelvis
HIPLESS ▸ hip
HIPLIKE ▸ hip
HIPLINE n widest part of a person's hips
HIPLY ▸ hip
HIPNESS ▸ hip
HIPPED adj having a hip or hips
HIPPEN n baby's nappy
HIPPENS ▸ hippen
HIPPER ▸ hip
HIPPEST ▸ hip
HIPPIC adj of horses
HIPPIE same as ▸ **hippy**
HIPPIER ▸ hippy
HIPPIES ▸ hippy
HIPPIN same as ▸ **hippen**
HIPPING same as ▸ **hippen**
HIPPINS ▸ hippin
HIPPISH adj in low spirits
HIPPO n hippopotamus
HIPPOS ▸ hippo
HIPPUS n spasm of eye
HIPPY n (esp in the 1960s) person whose behaviour and dress imply a rejection of conventional values ▷ adj having large hips
HIPS ▸ hip
HIPSHOT adj having a dislocated hip
HIPSTER n enthusiast of modern jazz
HIPT ▸ hip
HIRABLE ▸ hire
HIRAGE n fee for hiring
HIRAGES ▸ hirage
HIRCINE adj of or like a goat, esp in smell
HIRE vb pay to have temporary use of ▷ n hiring
HIREAGE same as ▸ **hirage**

HIRED ▸ hire
HIREE n hired person
HIREES ▸ hiree
HIRER ▸ hire
HIRERS ▸ hire
HIRES ▸ hire
HIRING ▸ hire
HIRINGS ▸ hire
HIRLING n Scots word for a type of fish
HIRPLE vb limp ▷ n limping gait
HIRPLED ▸ hirple
HIRPLES ▸ hirple
HIRSEL vb sort into groups
HIRSELS ▸ hirsel
HIRSLE vb wriggle or fidget
HIRSLED ▸ hirsle
HIRSLES ▸ hirsle
HIRSTIE adj dry
HIRSUTE adj hairy
HIRUDIN n anticoagulant extracted from the mouth glands of leeches
HIS adj belonging to him
HISH same as ▸ hiss
HISHED ▸ hish
HISHES ▸ hish
HISHING ▸ hish
HISN dialect form of ▸ his
HISPID adj covered with stiff hairs or bristles
HISS n sound like that of a long s (as an expression of contempt) ▷ vb utter a hiss ▷ interj exclamation of derision or disapproval
HISSED ▸ hiss
HISSELF dialect form of ▸ himself
HISSER ▸ hiss
HISSERS ▸ hiss
HISSES ▸ hiss
HISSIER ▸ hissy
HISSIES ▸ hissy
HISSING ▸ hiss
HISSY n temper tantrum ▷ adj sound similar to a hiss
HIST interj exclamation used to attract attention or as a warning to be silent ▷ vb make hist sound
HISTED ▸ hist
HISTIE same as ▸ hirstie
HISTING ▸ hist
HISTOID adj (esp of a tumour)
HISTONE n any of a group of basic proteins present in cell nuclei and implicated in the spatial organization of DNA
HISTORY n (record or

account of) past events and developments
HISTRIO n actor
HISTS ▸ hist
HIT vb strike, touch forcefully ▷ n hitting
HITCH n minor problem ▷ vb obtain (a lift) by hitchhiking
HITCHED ▸ hitch
HITCHER ▸ hitch
HITCHES ▸ hitch
HITCHY ▸ hitch
HITHE n small harbour
HITHER adv or towards this place ▷ vb come
HITHERS ▸ hither
HITHES ▸ hithe
HITLESS ▸ hit
HITMAN n professional killer
HITMEN ▸ hitman
HITS ▸ hit
HITTER n boxer who has a hard punch rather than skill or finesse
HITTERS ▸ hitter
HITTING ▸ hit
HIVE n structure in which social bees live and rear their young ▷ vb cause (bees) to collect or (of bees) to collect inside a hive
HIVED ▸ hive
HIVER n person who keeps beehives
HIVERS ▸ hiver
HIVES n allergic reaction in which itchy red or whitish patches appear on the skin
HIVING ▸ hive
HIYA sentence substitute informal term of greeting
HIZEN n type of Japanese porcelain
HIZENS ▸ hizen
HIZZ same as ▸ hiss
HIZZED ▸ hizz
HIZZES ▸ hizz
HIZZING ▸ hizz
HM interj sound made to express hesitation or doubt
HMM same as ▸ hm

┃ This variant of **hm**, like
┃ its shorter form, can be
┃ useful when you have a
┃ shortage of vowels.

HOAGIE n sandwich made with long bread roll
HOAGIES ▸ hoagie
HOAGY same as ▸ hoagie
HOAR adj covered with hoarfrost ▷ vb make hoary
HOARD n store hidden

away for future use ▷ vb save or store
HOARDED ▸ hoard
HOARDER ▸ hoard
HOARDS ▸ hoard
HOARED ▸ hoar
HOARIER ▸ hoary
HOARILY ▸ hoary
HOARING ▸ hoar
HOARS ▸ hoar
HOARSE adj (of a voice) rough and unclear
HOARSEN vb make or become hoarse
HOARSER ▸ hoarse
HOARY adj grey or white(-haired)
HOAST n cough ▷ vb cough
HOASTED ▸ hoast
HOASTS ▸ hoast
HOATZIN n South American bird with a brownish plumage and very small crested head
HOAX n deception or trick ▷ vb deceive or play a trick upon
HOAXED ▸ hoax
HOAXER ▸ hoax
HOAXERS ▸ hoax
HOAXES ▸ hoax
HOAXING ▸ hoax
HOB n flat top part of a cooker, or a separate flat surface, containing gas or electric rings for cooking on ▷ vb cut or form with a hob
HOBBED ▸ hob
HOBBER n machine used in making gears
HOBBERS ▸ hobber
HOBBIES ▸ hobby
HOBBING ▸ hob
HOBBISH adj like a clown
HOBBIT n one of an imaginary race of half-size people living in holes
HOBBITS ▸ hobbit
HOBBLE vb walk lamely ▷ n strap, rope, etc, used to hobble a horse
HOBBLED ▸ hobble
HOBBLER ▸ hobble
HOBBLES ▸ hobble
HOBBY n activity pursued in one's spare time
HOBDAY vb alleviate (a breathing problem in certain horses) by the surgical operation of removing soft tissue ventricles to pull back the vocal fold

HOBDAYS ▸ hobday
HOBJOB *vb* do odd jobs
HOBJOBS ▸ hobjob
HOBLIKE ▸ hob
HOBNAIL *n* short nail with a large head for protecting the soles of heavy footwear ▷ *vb* provide with hobnails
HOBNOB *vb* be on friendly terms (with)
HOBNOBS ▸ hobnob
HOBO *n* tramp or vagrant ▷ *vb* live as hobo
HOBODOM ▸ hobo
HOBOED ▸ hobo
HOBOES ▸ hobo
HOBOING ▸ hobo
HOBOISM ▸ hobo
HOBOS ▸ hobo
HOBS ▸ hob
HOC *adj* Latin for this
HOCK *n* joint in the back leg of an animal such as a horse that corresponds to the human ankle ▷ *vb* pawn
HOCKED ▸ hock
HOCKER ▸ hock
HOCKERS ▸ hock
HOCKEY *n* team game played on a field with a ball and curved sticks
HOCKEYS ▸ hockey
HOCKING ▸ hock
HOCKLE *vb* spit
HOCKLED ▸ hockle
HOCKLES ▸ hockle
HOCKS ▸ hock
HOCUS *vb* take in
HOCUSED ▸ hocus
HOCUSES ▸ hocus
HOD *n* open wooden box attached to a pole, for carrying bricks or mortar ▷ *vb* bob up and down
HODAD *n* person who pretends to be a surfer
HODADDY *same as* ▸ **hodad**
HODADS ▸ hodad
HODDED ▸ hod
HODDEN *n* coarse homespun cloth produced in Scotland: hodden grey is made by mixing black and white wools
HODDENS ▸ hodden
HODDIN *same as* ▸ **hodden**
HODDING ▸ hod
HODDINS ▸ hoddin
HODDLE *vb* waddle
HODDLED ▸ hoddle
HODDLES ▸ hoddle
HODJA *n* respectful Turkish form of address

HODJAS ▸ hodja
HODMAN *n* hod carrier
HODMEN ▸ hodman
HODS ▸ hod
HOE *n* long-handled tool used for loosening soil or weeding ▷ *vb* scrape or weed with a hoe
HOECAKE *n* maize cake
HOED ▸ hoe
HOEDOWN *n* boisterous square dance
HOEING ▸ hoe
HOELIKE ▸ hoe
HOER ▸ hoe
HOERS ▸ hoe
HOES ▸ hoe
HOG *n* castrated male pig ▷ *vb* take more than one's share of
HOGAN *n* wooden dwelling covered with earth, typical of the Navaho Indians of N America
HOGANS ▸ hogan
HOGBACK *n* narrow ridge that consists of steeply inclined rock strata
HOGEN *n* strong alcoholic drink
HOGENS ▸ hogen
HOGFISH *n* type of fish
HOGG *same as* ▸ **hog**
HOGGED ▸ hog
HOGGER ▸ hog
HOGGERS ▸ hog
HOGGERY *n* hogs collectively
HOGGET *n* sheep up to the age of one year that has yet to be sheared
HOGGETS ▸ hogget
HOGGIN *n* finely sifted gravel containing enough clay binder for it to be used in its natural form for making paths or roads
HOGGING *same as* ▸ **hoggin**
HOGGINS ▸ hoggin
HOGGISH *adj* selfish, gluttonous, or dirty
HOGGS ▸ hogg
HOGH *n* ridge of land
HOGHOOD *n* condition of being hog
HOGHS ▸ hogh
HOGLIKE ▸ hog
HOGMANE *n* short stiff mane
HOGNOSE *n* *as in* **hognose snake** puff adder
HOGNUT *another name for* ▸ **pignut**

HOGNUTS ▸ hognut
HOGS ▸ hog
HOGTIE *vb* tie together the legs or the arms and legs of
HOGTIED ▸ hogtie
HOGTIES ▸ hogtie
HOGWARD *n* person looking after hogs
HOGWASH *n* nonsense
HOGWEED *n* any of several coarse weedy umbelliferous plants, esp cow parsnip
HOHA *adj* bored or annoyed
HOI *same as* ▸ **hoy**
HOICK *vb* raise abruptly and sharply
HOICKED ▸ hoick
HOICKS *interj* cry used to encourage hounds to hunt ▷ *vb* shout hoicks
HOIDEN *same as* ▸ **hoyden**
HOIDENS ▸ hoiden
HOIK *same as* ▸ **hoick**
HOIKED ▸ hoik
HOIKING ▸ hoik
HOIKS ▸ hoik
HOISE *same as* ▸ **hoist**
HOISED ▸ hoise
HOISES ▸ hoise
HOISIN *n* Chinese sweet spicy reddish-brown sauce made from soya beans, sugar, vinegar, and garlic
HOISING ▸ hoise
HOISINS ▸ hoisin
HOIST *vb* raise or lift up ▷ *n* device for lifting things
HOISTED ▸ hoist
HOISTER ▸ hoist
HOISTS ▸ hoist
HOKA *n* red cod
HOKAS ▸ hoka
HOKE *vb* overplay (a part, etc)
HOKED ▸ hoke
HOKES ▸ hoke
HOKEY *adj* corny
HOKI *n* fish of New Zealand waters
HOKIER ▸ hokey
HOKIEST ▸ hokey
HOKILY ▸ hokey
HOKING ▸ hoke
HOKIS ▸ hoki
HOKKU *same as* ▸ **haiku**
HOKONUI *n* illicit whisky
HOKUM *n* rubbish, nonsense
HOKUMS ▸ hokum
HOLARD *n* amount of water contained in soil
HOLARDS ▸ holard
HOLD *vb* keep or support in

or with the hands or arms ▷ *vb* act or way of holding

HOLDALL *n* large strong travelling bag

HOLDEN *past participle of* ▷ **hold**

HOLDER *n* person or thing that holds

HOLDERS ▸ **holder**

HOLDING ▸ **hold**

HOLDOUT *n* (in US English) person, country, organization, etc, that continues to resist or refuses to change

HOLDS ▸ **hold**

HOLDUP *n* robbery, esp an armed one

HOLDUPS ▸ **holdup**

HOLE *n* area hollowed out in a solid ▷ *vb* make holes in

HOLED ▸ **hole**

HOLES ▸ **hole**

HOLESOM *same as* > **holesome**

HOLEY *adj* full of holes

HOLEYER ▸ **holey**

HOLIBUT *same as* ▸ **halibut**

HOLIDAY *n* time spent away from home for rest or recreation ▷ *vb* spend a holiday

HOLIER ▸ **holy**

HOLIES ▸ **holy**

HOLIEST ▸ **holy**

HOLILY *adv* in a holy, devout, or sacred manner

HOLING ▸ **hole**

HOLINGS ▸ **hole**

HOLISM *n* view that a whole is greater than the sum of its parts

HOLISMS ▸ **holism**

HOLIST ▸ **holism**

HOLISTS ▸ **holism**

HOLK *vb* dig

HOLKED ▸ **holk**

HOLKING ▸ **holk**

HOLKS ▸ **holk**

HOLLA *same as* ▸ **hollo**

HOLLAED ▸ **holla**

HOLLAND *n* coarse linen cloth, used esp for furnishing

HOLLAS ▸ **holla**

HOLLER *n* shout, yell ▷ *vb* shout or yell

HOLLERS ▸ **holler**

HOLLIES ▸ **holly**

HOLLO *interj* cry for attention, or of encouragement ▷ *vb* shout

HOLLOA *same as* ▸ **hollo**

HOLLOAS ▸ **holloa**

HOLLOED ▸ **hollo**

HOLLOES ▸ **hollo**

HOLLOO *same as* ▸ **halloo**

HOLLOOS ▸ **hollo**

HOLLOS ▸ **hollo**

HOLLOW *adj* having a hole or space inside ▷ *n* cavity or space ▷ *vb* form a hollow in

HOLLOWS ▸ **hollow**

HOLLY *n* evergreen tree with prickly leaves and red berries

HOLM *n* island in a river, lake, or estuary

HOLMIA *n* oxide of holmium

HOLMIAS ▸ **holmia**

HOLMIC *adj* of or containing holmium

HOLMIUM *n* silver-white metallic element, the compounds of which are highly magnetic

HOLMS ▸ **holm**

HOLON *n* autonomous self-reliant unit, esp in manufacturing

HOLONIC ▸ **holon**

HOLONS ▸ **holon**

HOLP *past tense of* ▸ **help**

HOLPEN *past participle of* ▸ **help**

HOLS *pl n* holidays

HOLSTER *n* leather case for a pistol, hung from a belt ▷ *vb* return (a pistol) to its holster

HOLT *n* otter's lair

HOLTS ▸ **holt**

HOLY *adj* of God or a god

HOLYDAM *same as* ▸ **halidom**

HOLYDAY *n* day on which a religious festival is observed

HOM *n* sacred plant of the Parsees and ancient Persians

HOMA *same as* ▸ **hom**

HOMAGE *n* show of respect or honour towards someone or something ▷ *vb* render homage to

HOMAGED ▸ **homage**

HOMAGER ▸ **homage**

HOMAGES ▸ **homage**

HOMAS ▸ **homa**

HOMBRE *slang word for* ▸ **man**

HOMBRES ▸ **hombre**

HOMBURG *n* man's soft felt hat with a dented crown and a stiff upturned brim

HOME *n* place where one lives ▷ *adj* of one's home, birthplace, or native country ▷ *adv* to or at home ▷ *vb* direct towards (a point or target)

HOMEBOY *n* close friend

HOMED ▸ **home**

HOMELY *adj* simple, ordinary, and comfortable

HOMELYN *n* species of ray

HOMER *n* homing pigeon ▷ *vb* score a home run in baseball

HOMERED ▸ **homer**

HOMERS ▸ **homer**

HOMES ▸ **home**

HOMEY *same as* ▸ **homy**

HOMEYS ▸ **homey**

HOMIE *short for* ▸ **homeboy**

HOMIER ▸ **homy**

HOMIES ▸ **homie**

HOMIEST ▸ **homy**

HOMILY *n* speech telling people how they should behave

HOMINES ▸ **homo**

HOMING *adj* denoting the ability to return home after travelling great distances ▷ *n* relating to the ability to return home after travelling great distances

HOMINGS ▸ **homing**

HOMINID *n* man or any extinct forerunner of man ▷ *adj* of or belonging to this family

HOMININ *n* member of zoological family that includes humans and direct ancestors

HOMINY *n* coarsely ground maize prepared as a food by boiling in milk or water

HOMME *French word for* ▸ **man**

HOMMES ▸ **homme**

HOMMOCK *same as* ▸ **hummock**

HOMMOS *same as* ▸ **hummus**

HOMO *n* homogenized milk

HOMOLOG *same as* > **homologue**

HOMONYM *n* word spelt or pronounced the same as another, but with a different meaning

HOMOS ▸ **homo**

HOMOSEX *n* sexual activity between homosexuals

HOMS ▸ hom
HOMY adj like a home
HON short for ▸ **honey**
HONAN n silk fabric of rough weave
HONANS ▸ honan
HONCHO n person in charge ▷ vb supervise or be in charge of
HONCHOS ▸ honcho
HOND old form of ▸ **hand**
HONDA n loop through which rope is threaded to make a lasso
HONDAS ▸ honda
HONDLE vb negotiate on price
HONDLED ▸ hondle
HONDLES ▸ hondle
HONDS ▸ hond
HONE vb sharpen ▷ n fine whetstone used for sharpening edged tools and knives
HONED ▸ hone
HONER ▸ hone
HONERS ▸ hone
HONES ▸ hone
HONEST adj truthful and moral
HONESTY n quality of being honest
HONEY n sweet edible sticky substance made by bees from nectar; term of endearment ▷ vb sweeten with or as if with honey
HONEYED ▸ honey
HONEYS ▸ honey
HONG n (in China) a factory, warehouse, etc ▷ vb archaic form of hang
HONGI n Maori greeting in which people touch noses ▷ vb touch noses
HONGIED ▸ hongi
HONGIES ▸ hongi
HONGING ▸ hong
HONGIS ▸ hongi
HONGS ▸ hong
HONIED ▸ honey
HONING ▸ hone
HONK n sound made by a car horn ▷ vb (cause to) make this sound
HONKED ▸ honk
HONKER n person or thing that honks
HONKERS ▸ honker
HONKING ▸ honk
HONKS ▸ honk
HONOR same as ▸ **honour**
HONORED ▸ honor

HONOREE same as ▸ **honorand**
HONORER ▸ honour
HONORS same as ▸ **honours**
HONOUR n sense of honesty and fairness ▷ vb give praise and attention to
HONOURS ▸ honour
HONS ▸ hon
HOO interj expression of joy, excitement, etc
HOOCH n alcoholic drink, esp illicitly distilled spirits
HOOCHES ▸ hooch
HOOCHIE n immoral woman
HOOD n head covering, often attached to a coat or jacket ▷ vb cover with or as if with a hood
HOODED adj (of a garment) having a hood
HOODIA n any of several southern African succulent plants whose sap has appetite-suppressing properties
HOODIAS ▸ hoodia
HOODIE n hooded sweatshirt
HOODIER ▸ hood
HOODIES ▸ hoodie
HOODING ▸ hood
HOODLUM n violent criminal, gangster
HOODMAN n blindfolded person in blindman's buff
HOODMEN ▸ hoodman
HOODOO n (cause of) bad luck ▷ vb bring bad luck to
HOODOOS ▸ hoodoo
HOODS ▸ hood
HOODY ▸ hood
HOOEY n nonsense ▷ interj nonsense
HOOEYS ▸ hooey
HOOF n horny covering of the foot of a horse, deer, etc ▷ vb kick or trample with the hooves
HOOFED adj having a hoof or hoofs
HOOFER n professional dancer
HOOFERS ▸ hoofer
HOOFING ▸ hoof
HOOFROT n disease of hoof
HOOFS ▸ hoof
HOOK n curved piece of metal, plastic, etc, used to hang, hold, or pull something ▷ vb fasten or

catch (as if) with a hook
HOOKA same as ▸ **hookah**
HOOKAH n oriental pipe in which smoke is drawn through water and a long tube
HOOKAHS ▸ hookah
HOOKAS ▸ hooka
HOOKED adj bent like a hook
HOOKER n prostitute
HOOKERS ▸ hooker
HOOKEY same as ▸ **hooky**
HOOKEYS ▸ hookey
HOOKIER ▸ hooky
HOOKIES ▸ hooky
HOOKING ▸ hook
HOOKLET n little hook
HOOKS ▸ hook
HOOKUP n contact of an aircraft in flight with the refuelling hose of a tanker aircraft
HOOKUPS ▸ hookup
HOOKY n truancy, usually from school (esp in the phrase play hooky) ▷ adj hooklike
HOOLEY n lively party
HOOLEYS ▸ hooley
HOOLIE same as ▸ **hooley**
HOOLIER ▸ hooly
HOOLIES ▸ hoolie
HOOLOCK n Indian gibbon
HOOLY adj careful or gentle
HOON n loutish youth who drives irresponsibly ▷ vb drive irresponsibly
HOONED ▸ hoon vb
HOONING ▸ hoon vb
HOONS ▸ hoon
HOOP n rigid circular band, used esp as a child's toy or for animals to jump through in the circus ▷ vb surround with or as if with a hoop
HOOPED ▸ hoop
HOOPER rare word for ▸ **cooper**
HOOPERS ▸ hooper
HOOPING ▸ hoop
HOOPLA n fairground game in which hoops are thrown over objects in an attempt to win them
HOOPLAS ▸ hoopla
HOOPOE n bird with a pinkish-brown plumage and a fanlike crest
HOOPOES ▸ hoopoe
HOOPOO same as ▸ **hoopoe**
HOOPOOS ▸ hoopoo

HOOPS ▸ hoop

HOOR n unpleasant or difficult thing

HOORAH same as ▸ hurrah

HOORAHS ▸ hoorah

HOORAY same as ▸ hurrah

HOORAYS ▸ hooray

HOORD same as ▸ hoard

HOORDS ▸ hoord

HOOROO same as ▸ hurrah

HOORS ▸ hoor

HOOSGOW ▸ jail

HOOSH vb shoo away

HOOSHED ▸ hoosh

HOOSHES ▸ hoosh

HOOT n sound of a car horn ▷ vb sound (a car horn) ▷ interj exclamation of impatience or dissatisfaction: a supposed Scotticism

HOOTCH same as ▸ hooch

HOOTED ▸ hoot

HOOTER n device that hoots

HOOTERS ▸ hooter

HOOTIER ▸ hoot

HOOTING ▸ hoot

HOOTS same as ▸ hoot

HOOTY ▸ hoot

HOOVE same as ▸ heave

HOOVED ▸ hoove

HOOVEN ▸ hoove

HOOVER vb vacuum-clean (a carpet, furniture, etc)

HOOVERS ▸ hoover

HOOVES ▸ hoof

HOOVING ▸ hoove

HOP vb jump on one foot ▷ n instance of hopping

HOPBIND n stalk of the hop

HOPBINE same as ▸ hopbind

HOPDOG n species of caterpillar

HOPDOGS ▸ hopdog

HOPE vb want (something) to happen or be true ▷ n expectation of something desired

HOPED ▸ hope

HOPEFUL adj having, expressing, or inspiring hope ▷ n person considered to be on the brink of success

HOPER ▸ hope

HOPERS ▸ hope

HOPES ▸ hope

HOPHEAD n heroin or opium addict

HOPING ▸ hope

HOPLITE n (in ancient Greece) a heavily armed infantryman

HOPPED ▸ hop

HOPPER n container for storing substances such as grain or sand

HOPPERS ▸ hopper

HOPPIER ▸ hoppy

HOPPING ▸ hop

HOPPLE same as ▸ hobble

HOPPLED ▸ hopple

HOPPLER ▸ hopple

HOPPLES ▸ hopple

HOPPUS adj as in **hoppus foot** unit of volume for round timber

HOPPY adj tasting of hops

HOPS ▸ hop

HOPSACK n roughly woven fabric of wool, cotton, etc, used for clothing

HOPTOAD n toad

HORA n traditional Israeli or Romanian circle dance

HORAH same as ▸ hora

HORAHS ▸ horah

HORAL less common word for ▸ hourly

HORARY adj relating to the hours

HORAS ▸ hora

HORDE n large crowd ▷ vb form, move in, or live in a horde

HORDED ▸ horde

HORDEIN n simple protein, rich in proline, that occurs in barley

HORDES ▸ horde

HORDING ▸ horde

HORDOCK same as ▸ hardoke

HORE same as ▸ hoar

HORIZON n apparent line that divides the earth and the sky

HORKEY same as ▸ hockey

HORKEYS ▸ horkey

HORME n (in the psychology of C. G. Jung) fundamental vital energy

HORMES ▸ horme

HORMIC ▸ horme

HORMONE n substance secreted by certain glands which stimulates certain organs of the body

HORN n one of a pair of bony growths sticking out of the heads of cattle, sheep, etc ▷ vb provide with a horn or horns

HORNBUG n stag beetle

HORNED adj having a horn, horns, or hornlike parts

HORNER n dealer in horn

HORNERS ▸ horner

HORNET n large wasp with a severe sting

HORNETS ▸ hornet

HORNFUL n amount a horn will hold

HORNIER ▸ horny

HORNILY ▸ horny

HORNING ▸ horn

HORNISH adj like horn

HORNIST n horn player

HORNITO n small vent in volcano

HORNLET n small horn

HORNS ▸ horn

HORNY adj of or like horn

HOROEKA n New Zealand tree

HORRENT adj bristling

HORRID adj disagreeable, unpleasant

HORRIFY vb cause to feel horror or shock

HORROR n (thing or person causing) terror or hatred ▷ adj having a frightening subject, usually concerned with the supernatural

HORRORS pl n fit of depression or anxiety ▷ interj expression of dismay, sometimes facetious

HORS adv as in **hors d'oeuvre** appetizer

HORSE n large animal with hooves, a mane, and a tail, used for riding and pulling carts etc ▷ vb provide with a horse

HORSED ▸ horse

HORSES ▸ horse

HORSEY adj very keen on horses

HORSIER ▸ horsy

HORSILY ▸ horsey

HORSING ▸ horse

HORSON same as ▸ whoreson

HORSONS ▸ horson

HORST n ridge of land that has been forced upwards between two parallel faults

HORSTE same as ▸ horst

HORSTES ▸ horste

HORSTS ▸ horst

HORSY same as ▸ horsey

HOSANNA interj exclamation of praise to God ▷ n act of crying "hosanna" ▷ vb cry hosanna

HOSE n flexible pipe for

H

conveying liquid ▷ vb water with a hose

HOSED ▶ hose

HOSEL n socket in head of golf club

HOSELS ▶ hosel

HOSEMAN n fireman in charge of hose

HOSEMEN ▶ hoseman

HOSEN ▶ hose

HOSER n person who swindles or deceives others

HOSERS ▶ hoser

HOSES ▶ hose

HOSEY vb claim possession

HOSEYED ▶ hosey

HOSEYS ▶ hosey

HOSIER n person who sells stockings, etc

HOSIERS ▶ hosier

HOSIERY n stockings, socks, and tights collectively

HOSING ▶ hose

HOSPICE n nursing home for the terminally ill

HOSS n horse

HOSSES ▶ hoss

HOST n person who entertains guests, esp in his own home ▷ vb be the host of

HOSTA n ornamental plant

HOSTAGE n person who is illegally held prisoner until certain demands are met by other people

HOSTAS ▶ hosta

HOSTED ▶ host

HOSTEL n building providing accommodation at a low cost for a specific group of people such as students, travellers, homeless people, etc ▷ vb stay in hostels

HOSTELS ▶ hostel

HOSTESS n woman who receives and entertains guests, esp in her own house ▷ vb act as hostess

HOSTIE n informal Australian word for an air hostess

HOSTIES ▶ hostie

HOSTILE adj unfriendly ▷ n hostile person

HOSTING ▶ host

HOSTLER another name (esp Brit) for ▶ ostler

HOSTLY ▶ host

HOSTRY n lodging

HOSTS ▶ host

HOT adj having a high temperature

HOTBED n any place encouraging a particular activity

HOTBEDS ▶ hotbed

HOTBOX n closed room where marijuana is smoked

HOTCAKE n pancake

HOTCH vb jog

HOTCHED ▶ hotch

HOTCHES ▶ hotch

HOTDOG vb perform a series of manoeuvres in skiing, surfing, etc, esp in a showy manner

HOTDOGS ▶ hotdog

HOTE ▶ hight

HOTEL n commercial establishment providing lodging and meals

HOTELS ▶ hotel

HOTEN ▶ hight

HOTFOOT adv quickly and eagerly ▷ vb move quickly

HOTHEAD n excitable or fiery person

HOTLINE n direct telephone link for emergency use

HOTLINK n area on website connecting to another site

HOTLY ▶ hot

HOTNESS ▶ hot

HOTPOT n casserole of meat and vegetables, topped with potatoes

HOTPOTS ▶ hotpot

HOTROD n car with an engine that has been radically modified to produce increased power

HOTRODS ▶ hotrod

HOTS pl n as in the hots feeling of lust

HOTSHOT n important person or expert, esp when showy

HOTSPOT n place where wireless broadband services are provided through a wireless local area network

HOTSPUR n impetuous or fiery person

HOTTED ▶ hot

HOTTER vb simmer

HOTTERS ▶ hotter

HOTTEST ▶ hot

HOTTIE n sexually attractive person

HOTTIES ▶ hottie

HOTTING n practice of stealing fast cars and

putting on a show of skilful but dangerous driving

HOTTISH adj fairly hot

HOTTY same as ▶ hottie

HOUDAH same as ▶ howdah

HOUDAHS ▶ houdah

HOUDAN n breed of light domestic fowl originally from France, with a distinctive full crest

HOUDANS ▶ houdan

HOUF same as ▶ howf

HOUFED ▶ houf

HOUFF same as ▶ howf

HOUFFED ▶ houff

HOUFFS ▶ houff

HOUFING ▶ houf

HOUFS ▶ houf

HOUGH n in Scotland, a cut of meat corresponding to shin ▷ vb hamstring (cattle, horses, etc)

HOUGHED ▶ hough

HOUGHS ▶ hough

HOUHERE n small evergreen New Zealand tree

HOUMMOS same as ▶ hummus

HOUMOUS ▶ hummus

HOUMUS same as ▶ hummus

HOUND n hunting dog ▷ vb pursue relentlessly

HOUNDED ▶ hound

HOUNDER ▶ hound

HOUNDS ▶ hound

HOUNGAN n voodoo priest

HOUR n twenty-fourth part of a day, sixty minutes

HOURI n any of the nymphs of paradise

HOURIS ▶ houri

HOURLY adv (happening) every hour ▷ adj of, occurring, or done once every hour ▷ n something that is done by the hour; someone who is paid by the hour

HOURS pl n indefinite time

HOUSE n building used as a home ▷ vb give accommodation to ▷ adj (of wine) sold in a restaurant at a lower price than wines on the wine list

HOUSED ▶ house

HOUSEL vb give the Eucharist to (someone)

HOUSELS ▶ housel

HOUSER ▶ house

HOUSERS ▸ house
HOUSES ▸ house
HOUSEY adj of or like house music
HOUSIER ▸ housey
HOUSING n (providing of) houses
HOUT same as ▸ hoot
HOUTED ▸ hout
HOUTING n type of fish that lives in salt water but spawns in freshwater lakes and is valued for its edible flesh
HOUTS ▸ hout
HOVE ▸ heave
HOVEA n Australian plant with purple flowers
HOVEAS ▸ hovea
HOVED ▸ heave
HOVEL n small dirty house or hut ▷ vb shelter or be sheltered in a hovel
HOVELED ▸ hovel
HOVELS ▸ hovel
HOVEN ▸ heave
HOVER vb (of a bird etc) remain suspended in one place in the air ▷ n act of hovering
HOVERED ▸ hover
HOVERER ▸ hover
HOVERS ▸ hover
HOVES ▸ heave
HOVING ▸ heave
HOW adv in what way, by what means ▷ n the way a thing is done ▷ sentence substitute greeting supposed to be or have been used by American Indians and often used humorously
HOWBE same as ▸ howbeit
HOWBEIT adv in archaic usage, however
HOWDAH n canopied seat on an elephant's back
HOWDAHS ▸ howdah
HOWDIE n midwife
HOWDIED ▸ howdy
HOWDIES ▸ howdy
HOWDY vb greet someone
HOWE n depression in the earth's surface, such as a basin or valley
HOWES ▸ howe
HOWEVER adv nevertheless
HOWF n haunt, esp a public house ▷ vb visit place frequently
HOWFED ▸ howf
HOWFF vb visit place frequently

HOWFFED ▸ howff
HOWFFS ▸ howff
HOWFING ▸ howf
HOWFS ▸ howf
HOWK vb dig (out or up)
HOWKED ▸ howk
HOWKER ▸ howk
HOWKERS ▸ howk
HOWKING ▸ howk
HOWKS ▸ howk
HOWL n loud wailing cry ▷ vb utter a howl
HOWLED ▸ howl
HOWLER n stupid mistake
HOWLERS ▸ howler
HOWLET another word for ▸ owl
HOWLETS ▸ howlet
HOWLING adj great
HOWLS ▸ howl
HOWRE same as ▸ hour
HOWRES ▸ howre
HOWS ▸ how
HOWSO same as > howsoever
HOWZAT ▸ how
HOWZIT informal word for ▸ hello
HOX vb hamstring
This is a word found in Shakespeare's plays, and means to cut a horse's hamstring; it's one of the many short words with X that can get you a high score.
HOXED ▸ hox
HOXES ▸ hox
HOXING ▸ hox
HOY interj cry used to attract someone's attention ▷ n freight barge ▷ vb drive animal with cry
HOYA n any of various E Asian or Australian plants
HOYAS ▸ hoya
HOYDEN n wild or boisterous girl ▷ vb behave like a hoyden
HOYDENS ▸ hoyden
HOYED ▸ hoy
HOYING ▸ hoy
HOYLE n archer's mark used as a target
HOYLES ▸ hoyle
HOYS ▸ hoy
HRYVNA n standard monetary unit of Ukraine, divided into 100 kopiykas
HRYVNAS ▸ hryvna
HRYVNIA n money unit of Ukraine
HRYVNYA same as ▸ hryvna

HUANACO same as ▸ guanaco
HUB n centre of a wheel, through which the axle passes
HUBBIES ▸ hubby
HUBBLY adj having an irregular surface
HUBBUB n confused noise of many voices
HUBBUBS ▸ hubbub
HUBBY n husband
HUBCAP n metal disc that fits on to and protects the hub of a wheel, esp on a car
HUBCAPS ▸ hubcap
HUBRIS n pride, arrogance
HUBS ▸ hub
HUCK same as ▸ huckle
HUCKED ▸ huck
HUCKERY adj ugly
HUCKING ▸ huck
HUCKLE n hip or haunch ▷ vb force out or arrest roughly
HUCKLED ▸ huckle vb
HUCKLES ▸ huckle
HUCKS ▸ huck
HUDDEN ▸ haud
HUDDLE vb hunch (oneself) through cold or fear ▷ n small group
HUDDLED ▸ huddle
HUDDLER ▸ huddle
HUDDLES ▸ huddle
HUDDUP interj get up
HUDNA n truce or ceasefire for a fixed duration
HUDNAS ▸ hudna
HUDUD n set of laws and punishments specified by Allah in the Koran
HUDUDS ▸ hudud
HUE n colour, shade
HUED adj having a hue or colour as specified
HUELESS ▸ hue
HUER n pilchard fisherman
HUERS ▸ huer
HUES ▸ hue
HUFF n passing mood of anger or resentment ▷ vb blow or puff heavily
HUFFED ▸ huff
HUFFER ▸ huffing
HUFFERS ▸ huffing
HUFFIER ▸ huff
HUFFILY ▸ huff
HUFFING n practice of inhaling toxic fumes from glue and other household products for their intoxicating effects

H

HUFFISH ▸ huff
HUFFKIN n type of muffin
HUFFS ▸ huff
HUFFY ▸ huff
HUG vb clasp tightly in the arms, usu with affection ▷ n tight or fond embrace
HUGE adj very big
HUGELY adv very much
HUGEOUS same as ▸ huge
HUGER ▸ huge
HUGEST ▸ huge
HUGGED ▸ hug
HUGGER ▸ hug
HUGGERS ▸ hug
HUGGIER ▸ huggy
HUGGING ▸ hug
HUGGY adj sensitive and caring
HUGS ▸ hug
HUGY same as ▸ huge
HUH interj exclamation of derision, bewilderment, or inquiry
HUHU n type of hairy New Zealand beetle
HUHUS ▸ huhu
HUI n meeting of Maori people
HUIA n extinct bird of New Zealand, prized by early Maoris for its distinctive tail feathers
HUIAS ▸ huia
HUIC interj in hunting, a call to hounds
HUIPIL n Mayan woman's blouse
HUIPILS ▸ huipil
HUIS ▸ hui
HUITAIN n verse of eighteen lines
HULA n swaying Hawaiian dance
HULAS ▸ hula
HULE same as ▸ ule
HULES ▸ hule
HULK n body of an abandoned ship ▷ vb move clumsily
HULKED ▸ hulk
HULKIER ▸ hulky
HULKING adj bulky, unwieldy
HULKS ▸ hulk
HULKY same as ▸ hulking
HULL n main body of a boat ▷ vb remove the hulls from
HULLED ▸ hull
HULLER ▸ hull
HULLERS ▸ hull
HULLIER ▸ hully
HULLING ▸ hull

HULLO same as ▸ hello
HULLOA same as ▸ halloa
HULLOAS ▸ hulloa
HULLOED ▸ hullo
HULLOES ▸ hullo
HULLOO same as ▸ halloo
HULLOOS ▸ hulloo
HULLOS ▸ hullo
HULLS ▸ hull
HULLY adj having husks
HUM vb make a low continuous vibrating sound ▷ n humming sound
HUMA n mythical bird
HUMAN adj of or typical of people ▷ n human being
HUMANE adj kind or merciful
HUMANER ▸ humane
HUMANLY adv by human powers or means
HUMANS ▸ human
HUMAS ▸ huma
HUMATE n decomposed plants used as fertilizer
HUMATES ▸ humate
HUMBLE adj conscious of one's failings ▷ vb cause to feel humble, humiliate
HUMBLED ▸ humble
HUMBLER ▸ humble
HUMBLES ▸ humble
HUMBLY ▸ humble
HUMBUG n hard striped peppermint sweet ▷ vb cheat or deceive (someone)
HUMBUGS ▸ humbug
HUMBUZZ n type of beetle
HUMDRUM adj ordinary, dull ▷ n monotonous routine, task, or person
HUMECT vb make moist
HUMECTS ▸ humect
HUMEFY same as ▸ humify
HUMERAL adj of or relating to the humerus ▷ n silk shawl worn by a priest at High Mass; humeral veil
HUMERI ▸ humerus
HUMERUS n bone from the shoulder to the elbow
HUMF same as ▸ humph
HUMFED ▸ humf
HUMFING ▸ humf
HUMFS ▸ humf
HUMHUM n Indian cotton cloth
HUMHUMS ▸ humhum
HUMIC adj of, relating to, derived from, or resembling humus
HUMID adj damp and hot
HUMIDER ▸ humid

HUMIDEX n system of measuring discomfort showing the combined effect of humidity and temperature
HUMIDLY ▸ humid
HUMIDOR n humid place or container for storing cigars, tobacco, etc
HUMIFY vb convert or be converted into humus
HUMINT n human intelligence
HUMINTS ▸ humint
HUMITE n mineral containing magnesium
HUMITES ▸ humite
HUMLIE n hornless cow
HUMLIES ▸ humlie
HUMMAUM same as ▸ hammam
HUMMED ▸ hum
HUMMEL adj (of cattle) hornless ▷ vb remove horns from
HUMMELS ▸ hummel
HUMMER ▸ hum
HUMMERS ▸ hum
HUMMING ▸ hum
HUMMLE adj as in hummle bonnet type of Scottish cap
HUMMOCK n very small hill ▷ vb form into a hummock or hummocks
HUMMUM same as ▸ hammam
HUMMUMS ▸ hummum
HUMMUS n creamy dip originating in the Middle East, made from puréed chickpeas
HUMOGEN n type of fertilizer
HUMOR same as ▸ humour
HUMORAL adj denoting or relating to a type of immunity caused by free antibodies circulating in the blood
HUMORED ▸ humor
HUMORS ▸ humor
HUMOUR n ability to say or perceive things that are amusing ▷ vb be kind and indulgent to
HUMOURS ▸ humour
HUMOUS same as ▸ humus
HUMP n raised piece of ground ▷ vb carry or heave
HUMPED ▸ hump
HUMPEN n old German drinking glass
HUMPENS ▸ humpen

HUMPER ▸ hump

HUMPERS ▸ hump

HUMPH *interj* exclamation of annoyance or scepticism ▹ *vb* exclaim humph

HUMPHED ▸ humph

HUMPHS ▸ humph

HUMPIER ▸ humpy

HUMPIES ▸ humpy

HUMPING ▸ hump

HUMPS ▸ hump

HUMPTY *n* low padded seat

HUMPY *adj* full of humps ▹ *n* primitive hut

HUMS ▸ hum

HUMUS *n* decomposing vegetable and animal mould in the soil

HUMUSES ▸ humus

HUMUSY ▸ humus

HUMVEE *n* military vehicle

HUMVEES ▸ humvee

HUN *n* member of any of several Asiatic nomadic peoples speaking Mongoloid or Turkic languages

HUNCH *n* feeling or suspicion not based on facts ▹ *vb* draw (one's shoulders) up or together

HUNCHED ▸ hunch

HUNCHES ▸ hunch

HUNDRED *n* ten times ten ▹ *adj* amounting to a hundred

HUNG ▸ hang

HUNGAN *same as* ▸ **houngan**

HUNGANS ▸ hungan

HUNGER *n* discomfort or weakness from lack of food ▹ *vb* want very much

HUNGERS ▸ hunger

HUNGRY *adj* desiring food

HUNH *same as* ▸ **huh**

HUNK *n* large piece

HUNKER *vb* squat

HUNKERS *pl n* haunches

HUNKIER ▸ hunky

HUNKS *n* crotchety old person

HUNKSES ▸ hunks

HUNKY *adj* excellent

HUNNISH ▸ hun

HUNS ▸ hun

HUNT *vb* seek out and kill (wild animals) for food or sport ▹ *n* hunting

HUNTED *adj* harassed and worn

HUNTER *n* person or animal that hunts wild animals for food or sport

HUNTERS ▸ hunter

HUNTING *n* pursuit and killing or capture of game and wild animals, regarded as a sport

HUNTS ▸ hunt

HUP *vb* cry hup to get a horse to move

HUPIRO *in New Zealand English, same as* ▸ **stinkwood**

HUPIROS ▸ hupiro

HUPPAH *variant spelling of* ▸ **chuppah**

HUPPAHS ▸ huppah

HUPPED ▸ hup

HUPPING ▸ hup

HUPPOT ▸ huppah

HUPPOTH ▸ huppot

HUPS ▸ hup

HURDEN *same as* ▸ **harden**

HURDENS ▸ hurden

HURDIES *pl n* buttocks or haunches

HURDLE *n* light barrier for jumping over in some races ▹ *vb* jump over (something)

HURDLED ▸ hurdle

HURDLER ▸ hurdle

HURDLES ▸ hurdle

HURDS *same as* ▸ **hards**

HURL *vb* throw or utter forcefully ▹ *n* act or an instance of hurling

HURLBAT *same as* ▸ **whirlbat**

HURLED ▸ hurl

HURLER ▸ hurl

HURLERS ▸ hurl

HURLEY *n* another word for the game of hurling

HURLEYS ▸ hurley

HURLIES ▸ hurly

HURLING *n* Irish game like hockey

HURLS ▸ hurl

HURLY *n* wheeled barrow

HURRA *same as* ▸ **hurrah**

HURRAED ▸ hurra

HURRAH *interj* exclamation of joy or applause ▹ *n* cheer of joy or victory ▹ *vb* shout "hurrah"

HURRAHS ▸ hurrah

HURRAS ▸ hurra

HURRAY *same as* ▸ **hurrah**

HURRAYS ▸ hurray

HURRIED *adj* done quickly or too quickly

HURRIER ▸ hurry

HURRIES ▸ hurry

HURRY *vb* (cause to) move or act very quickly ▹ *n* doing something quickly or the need to do something quickly

HURST *n* wood

HURSTS ▸ hurst

HURT *vb* cause physical or mental pain to ▹ *n* physical or mental pain ▹ *adj* injured or pained

HURTER ▸ hurt

HURTERS ▸ hurt

HURTFUL *adj* unkind

HURTING ▸ hurt

HURTLE *vb* move quickly or violently

HURTLED ▸ hurtle

HURTLES ▸ hurtle

HURTS ▸ hurt

HUSBAND *n* woman's partner in marriage ▹ *vb* use economically

HUSH *vb* make or be silent ▹ *n* stillness or silence ▹ *interj* plea or demand for silence

HUSHABY *interj* used in quietening a baby or child to sleep ▹ *n* lullaby ▹ *vb* quieten to sleep

HUSHED ▸ hush

HUSHER *same as* ▸ **usher**

HUSHERS ▸ husher

HUSHES ▸ hush

HUSHFUL *adj* quiet

HUSHIER ▸ hushy

HUSHING ▸ hush

HUSHY *adj* secret

HUSK *n* outer covering of certain seeds and fruits ▹ *vb* remove the husk from

HUSKED ▸ husk

HUSKER ▸ husk

HUSKERS ▸ husk

HUSKIER ▸ husky

HUSKIES ▸ husky

HUSKILY ▸ husky

HUSKING ▸ husk

HUSKS ▸ husk

HUSKY *adj* slightly hoarse ▹ *n* Arctic sledge dog with thick hair and a curled tail

HUSO *n* sturgeon

HUSOS ▸ huso

HUSS *n* flesh of the European dogfish, when used as food

HUSSAR *n* lightly armed cavalry soldier

HUSSARS ▸ hussar

HUSSES ▸ huss

HUSSIES ▸ hussy

HUSSIF *n* sewing kit**

HUSSIFS ▸ hussif

HUSSY n immodest or promiscuous woman

HUSTLE vb push about, jostle ▷ n lively activity or bustle

HUSTLED ▸ hustle

HUSTLER ▸ hustle

HUSTLES ▸ hustle

HUSWIFE same as > housewife

HUT n small house, shelter, or shed

HUTCH n cage for pet rabbits etc ▷ vb store or keep in or as if in a hutch

HUTCHED ▸ hutch

HUTCHES ▸ hutch

HUTCHIE n groundsheet draped over an upright stick, used as a temporary shelter

HUTIA n rodent of West Indies

HUTIAS ▸ hutia

HUTLIKE ▸ hut

HUTMENT n number or group of huts

HUTS ▸ hut

HUTTED ▸ hut

HUTTING ▸ hut

HUTZPA same as ▸ hutzpah

HUTZPAH variant spelling of > chutzpah

HUTZPAS ▸ hutzpa

HUZOOR n person of rank in India

HUZOORS ▸ huzoor

HUZZA same as ▸ huzzah

HUZZAED ▸ huzza

HUZZAH archaic word for ▸ hurrah

HUZZAHS ▸ huzzah

HUZZAS ▸ huzza

HUZZIES ▸ huzzy

HUZZY same as ▸ hussy

HWAN another name for ▸ won

HWYL n emotional fervour, as in the recitation of poetry

This Welsh word can come in very useful for dealing with a consonant-heavy rack.

HWYLS ▸ hwyl

HYACINE same as > hyacinth

HYAENA same as ▸ hyena

HYAENAS ▸ hyaena

HYAENIC ▸ hyaena

HYALIN n glassy translucent substance, such as occurs in certain degenerative skin conditions or in hyaline cartilage

HYALINE adj clear and translucent, with no fibres or granules ▷ n glassy transparent surface

HYALINS ▸ hyalin

HYALITE n clear and colourless variety of opal in globular form

HYALOID adj clear and transparent ▷ n delicate transparent membrane enclosing the vitreous humour of the eye

HYBRID n offspring of two plants or animals of different species ▷ adj of mixed origin

HYBRIDS ▸ hybrid

HYBRIS same as ▸ hubris

HYDATID n cyst containing tapeworm larvae

HYDRA n mythical many-headed water serpent

HYDRAE ▸ hydra

HYDRANT n outlet from a water main with a nozzle for a hose

HYDRAS ▸ hydra

HYDRASE n enzyme that removes water

HYDRATE n chemical compound of water with another substance ▷ vb treat or impregnate with water

HYDRIA n (in ancient Greece and Rome) a large water jar

HYDRIAE ▸ hydria

HYDRIC adj of or containing hydrogen

HYDRID same as ▸ hydroid

HYDRIDE n compound of hydrogen with another element

HYDRIDS ▸ hydrid

HYDRO n hotel offering facilities for hydropathy ▷ adj electricity as supplied to a residence, business, etc

HYDROID adj of or relating to an order of colonial hydrozoan coelenterates that have the polyp phase dominant ▷ n hydroid colony or individual

HYDROMA same as ▸ hygroma

HYDROPS n anaemia in a fetus

HYDROS ▸ hydro

HYDROUS adj containing water

HYDROXY adj (of a chemical compound) containing one or more hydroxyl groups

HYDYNE n type of rocket fuel

HYDYNES ▸ hydyne

HYE same as ▸ hie

HYED ▸ hye

HYEING ▸ hye

HYEN same as ▸ hyena

HYENA n scavenging doglike mammal of Africa and S Asia

HYENAS ▸ hyena

HYENIC ▸ hyena

HYENINE adj of hyenas

HYENOID adj of or like hyenas

HYENS ▸ hyen

HYES ▸ hye

HYETAL adj of or relating to rain, rainfall, or rainy regions

HYGEIST same as > hygienist

HYGIENE n principles and practice of health and cleanliness

HYGROMA n swelling in the soft tissue that occurs over a joint, usually caused by repeated injury

HYING ▸ hie

HYKE same as ▸ haik

HYKES ▸ hyke

HYLA n type of tropical American tree frog

HYLAS ▸ hyla

HYLDING same as ▸ hilding

HYLE n wood

HYLEG n dominant planet when someone is born

HYLEGS ▸ hyleg

HYLES ▸ hyle

HYLIC adj solid

HYLISM same as > hylicism

HYLISMS ▸ hylism

HYLIST ▸ hylism

HYLISTS ▸ hylism

HYLOIST n materialist

HYMEN n membrane partly covering the opening of a girl's vagina, which breaks before puberty or at the first occurrence of sexual intercourse

HYMENAL ▸ hymen

HYMENIA > hymenium
HYMENS ▸ hymen
HYMN n Christian song of praise sung to God or a saint ▷ vb express (praises, thanks, etc) by singing hymns
HYMNAL n book of hymns ▷ adj of, relating to, or characteristic of hymns
HYMNALS ▸ hymnal
HYMNARY same as ▸ hymnal
HYMNED ▸ hymn
HYMNIC ▸ hymn
HYMNING ▸ hymn
HYMNIST n person who composes hymns
HYMNODY n composition or singing of hymns
HYMNS ▸ hymn
HYNDE same as ▸ hind
HYNDES ▸ hynde
HYOID adj of or relating to the hyoid bone ▷ n horseshoe-shaped bone that lies at the base of the tongue and above the thyroid cartilage
HYOIDAL adj of or relating to the hyoid bone
HYOIDS ▸ hyoid
HYP n short for hypotenuse
HYPATE n string of lyre
HYPATES ▸ hypate
HYPE n intensive or exaggerated publicity or

sales promotion ▷ vb promote (a product) using intensive or exaggerated publicity
HYPED ▸ hype
HYPER ▸ hype
HYPERON n any baryon that is not a nucleon
HYPERS ▸ hype
HYPES ▸ hype
HYPHA n any of the filaments that constitute the body (mycelium) of a fungus
HYPHAE ▸ hypha
HYPHAL ▸ hypha
HYPHEN n punctuation mark (-) indicating that two words or syllables are connected ▷ vb hyphenate
HYPHENS ▸ hyphen
HYPHIES ▸ hyphy
HYPHY n type of hip-hop music
HYPING ▸ hype
HYPINGS ▸ hype
HYPNIC n sleeping drug
HYPNICS ▸ hypnic
HYPNOID adj of or relating to a state resembling sleep or hypnosis
HYPNONE n sleeping drug
HYPNUM n species of moss
HYPNUMS ▸ hypnum
HYPO vb inject with a hypodermic syringe
HYPOED ▸ hypo

HYPOGEA > hypogeum
HYPOID adj as in **hypoid gear** gear having a tooth form generated by a hypocycloidal curve; used extensively in motor vehicle transmissions to withstand a high surface loading
HYPOING ▸ hypo
HYPONEA same as > hypopnea
HYPONYM n word whose meaning is included in that of another word
HYPOS ▸ hypo
HYPOXIA n deficiency in the amount of oxygen delivered to the body tissues
HYPOXIC ▸ hypoxia
HYPPED ▸ hyp
HYPPING ▸ hyp
HYPS ▸ hyp
HYPURAL adj below the tail
HYRACES ▸ hyrax
HYRAX n type of hoofed rodent-like animal of Africa and Asia
HYRAXES ▸ hyrax
HYSON n Chinese green tea
HYSONS ▸ hyson
HYSSOP n sweet-smelling herb used in folk medicine
HYSSOPS ▸ hyssop
HYTE adj insane
HYTHE same as ▸ hithe
HYTHES ▸ hythe

H

I i

The letter **I** can prove a difficult tile to use effectively in Scrabble. It's one of the most common tiles in the game, so you often end up with two or more on your rack, but it can be hard to get rid of. Where **I** does come in very useful, though, is in the number of everyday short words that can be formed from it, which are very helpful when you need to form short words in addition to the main word that you want to play. These words include **in, is, it** (2 points each), **id** (3) and **if** (5). Other handy words are **icy** (8), **ivy** (9) and **imp** (7). Don't forget the three-letter words that use **K**: **ilk, ink** and **irk** (7 each), while **iwi** for 6 points can be very useful in getting rid of a surplus of **I**s.

IAMB *n* metrical foot of two syllables, a short one followed by a long one
IAMBI ▸ **iambus**
IAMBIC *adj* written in metrical units of one short and one long syllable ▸ *n* iambic foot, line, or stanza
IAMBICS ▸ **iambic**
IAMBIST *n* one who writes iambs
IAMBS ▸ **iamb**
IAMBUS *same as* ▸ **iamb**
IATRIC *adj* relating to medicine or physicians
IBADAH *n* following of Islamic beliefs and practices
IBADAT ▸ **ibadah**
IBERIS *n* plant with white or purple flowers
IBEX *n* wild goat with large backward-curving horns
IBEXES ▸ **ibex**
IBICES ▸ **ibex**
IBIDEM *adv* in the same place
IBIS *n* large wading bird with long legs
IBISES ▸ **ibis**
IBRIK ▸ **cezve**
IBRIKS ▸ **ibrik**
ICE *n* water in the solid state, formed by freezing liquid water ▸ *vb* form or cause to form ice
ICEBALL *n* ball of ice
ICEBERG *n* large floating mass of ice
ICEBOAT *n* boat that breaks up bodies of ice in water
ICEBOX *n* refrigerator
ICECAP *n* mass of ice permanently covering an area
ICECAPS ▸ **icecap**
ICED *adj* covered with icing
ICEFALL *n* very steep part of a glacier that has deep crevasses and resembles a frozen waterfall
ICELESS ▸ **ice**
ICELIKE ▸ **ice**
ICEMAN *n* person who sells or delivers ice
ICEMEN ▸ **iceman**
ICEPACK *n* bag or folded cloth containing ice, applied to a part of the body, esp the head, to cool, reduce swelling, etc
ICER *n* person who ices cakes
ICERS ▸ **icer**
ICES ▸ **ice**
ICEWINE *n* dessert wine made from grapes that have frozen before being harvested
ICH *archaic form of* ▸ **eke**

> A Shakespearean spelling of **eke**, this is a useful little word worth remembering because of its unusual combination of letters and relatively high score.

ICHABOD *interj* the glory has departed

ICHED ▸ **ich**
ICHES ▸ **ich**
ICHING ▸ **ich**
ICHNITE *n* trace fossil
ICHOR *n* fluid said to flow in the veins of the gods
ICHORS ▸ **ichor**
ICHS ▸ **ich**
ICHTHIC *same as* > **ichthyic**
ICHTHYS *n* early Christian emblem
ICICLE *n* tapering spike of ice hanging where water has dripped
ICICLED *adj* covered with icicles
ICICLES ▸ **icicle**
ICIER ▸ **icy**
ICIEST ▸ **icy**
ICILY *adv* in an icy or reserved manner
ICINESS *n* condition of being icy or very cold
ICING *n* mixture of sugar and water etc, used to cover and decorate cakes
ICINGS ▸ **icing**
ICK *interj* expression of disgust

> An interjection expressing disgust, this is one of the highest-scoring three-letter words beginning with I. It does not take an S, but it does take a Y to make **icky**.

ICKER *n* ear of corn
ICKERS ▸ **icker**

ICKIER ▸ icky
ICKIEST ▸ icky
ICKILY ▸ icky
ICKLE *ironically childish word for* ▸ **little**
ICKLER ▸ ickle
ICKLEST ▸ ickle
ICKY *adj* sticky
ICON *n* picture of Christ or another religious figure, regarded as holy in the Orthodox Church
ICONES ▸ icon
ICONIC *adj* relating to, resembling, or having the character of an icon
ICONIFY *vb* render as an icon
ICONISE *same as* ▸ **iconize**
ICONIZE *vb* render as an icon
ICONS ▸ icon
ICTAL ▸ ictus
ICTERIC ▸ icterus
ICTERID *n* bird of the oriole family
ICTERUS *n* yellowing of plant leaves, caused by excessive cold or moisture
ICTIC ▸ ictus
ICTUS *n* metrical or rhythmic stress in verse feet, as contrasted with the stress accent on words
ICTUSES ▸ ictus
ICY *adj* very cold
ID *n* mind's instinctive unconscious energies
IDANT *n* chromosome
IDANTS ▸ idant
IDE *n* silver orfe fish
IDEA *n* plan or thought formed in the mind ▸ *vb* have or form an idea
IDEAED ▸ idea
IDEAL *adj* most suitable ▸ *n* conception of something that is perfect
IDEALLY ▸ ideal
IDEALS ▸ ideal
IDEAS ▸ idea
IDEATA ▸ ideatum
IDEATE *vb* form or have an idea of
IDEATED ▸ ideate
IDEATES ▸ ideate
IDEATUM *n* objective reality with which human ideas are supposed to correspond
IDEE *n* idea
IDEES ▸ idee
IDEM *adj* same: used to refer

to an article, chapter, or book already quoted
IDENT *n* short visual image employed between television programmes that works as a logo to locate the viewer to the channel
IDENTIC *adj* (esp of opinions expressed by two or more governments) having the same wording or intention regarding another power
IDENTS ▸ ident
IDES *n* (in the Ancient Roman calendar) the 15th of March, May, July, or October, or the 13th of other months
IDIOCY *n* utter stupidity
IDIOM *n* group of words which when used together have a different meaning from the words individually
IDIOMS ▸ idiom
IDIOT *n* foolish or stupid person
IDIOTCY *same as* ▸ **idiocy**
IDIOTIC *adj* of or resembling an idiot
IDIOTS ▸ idiot
IDLE *adj* not doing anything ▸ *vb* spend (time) doing very little
IDLED ▸ idle
IDLER *n* person who idles
IDLERS ▸ idler
IDLES ▸ idle
IDLESSE ▸ idle
IDLEST ▸ idle
IDLING ▸ idle
IDLY ▸ idle
IDOL *n* object of excessive devotion
IDOLA ▸ idolum
IDOLISE *same as* ▸ **idolize**
IDOLISM ▸ idolize
IDOLIST ▸ idolize
IDOLIZE *vb* love or admire excessively
IDOLON *n* mental image
IDOLS ▸ idol
IDOLUM *n* mental picture
IDS ▸ id
IDYL *same as* ▸ **idyll**
IDYLIST *same as* > **idyllist**
IDYLL *n* scene or time of great peace and happiness
IDYLLIC *adj* of or relating to an idyll
IDYLLS ▸ idyll
IDYLS ▸ idyl
IF *n* uncertainty or doubt

IFF *conj* in logic, a shortened form of if and only if

> This word is one of the highest-scoring three-letter words beginning with I, and of course provides a useful extension to **if**.

IFFIER ▸ iffy
IFFIEST ▸ iffy
IFFY *adj* doubtful, uncertain
IFS ▸ if
IFTAR *n* meal eaten by Muslims to break their fast after sunset every day during Ramadan
IFTARS ▸ iftar
IGAD *same as* ▸ **egad**
IGAPO *n* flooded forest
IGAPOS ▸ igapo
IGARAPE *n* canoe route
IGG *vb* antagonize
IGGED ▸ igg
IGGING ▸ igg
IGGS ▸ igg
IGLOO *n* dome-shaped Inuit house made of snow and ice
IGLOOS ▸ igloo
IGLU *same as* ▸ **igloo**
IGLUS ▸ iglu
IGNARO *n* ignoramus
IGNAROS ▸ ignaro
IGNATIA *n* dried seed
IGNEOUS *adj* (of rock) formed as molten rock cools and hardens
IGNIFY *vb* turn into fire
IGNITE *vb* catch fire or set fire to
IGNITED ▸ ignite
IGNITER *n* person or thing that ignites
IGNITES ▸ ignite
IGNITOR *same as* ▸ **igniter**
IGNOBLE *adj* dishonourable
IGNOBLY ▸ ignoble
IGNOMY *Shakespearean variant of* > **ignominy**
IGNORE *vb* refuse to notice, disregard deliberately ▸ *n* disregard
IGNORED ▸ ignore
IGNORER ▸ ignore
IGNORES ▸ ignore
IGUANA *n* large tropical American lizard
IGUANAS ▸ iguana
IGUANID *same as* ▸ **iguana**
IHRAM *n* customary white robes worn by Muslim pilgrims to Mecca, symbolizing a sacred or consecrated state

IHRAMS ▸ ihram
IJTIHAD n effort of a Muslim scholar to derive a legal ruling from the Koran
IKAN n (in Malaysia) fish used esp in names of cooked dishes
IKANS ▸ ikan
IKAT n method of creating patterns in fabric by tie-dyeing the yarn before weaving
IKATS ▸ ikat
IKEBANA n Japanese art of flower arrangement
IKON same as ▸ **icon**
IKONS ▸ ikon
ILEA ▸ ileum

> This is the plural of **ileum**, part of the small intestine, and is often useful as a rack-balancing play when you have too many vowels.

ILEAC adj of or relating to the ileum
ILEAL same as ▸ **ileac**
ILEITIS n inflammation of the ileum
ILEUM n lowest part of the small intestine
ILEUS n obstruction of the intestine, esp the ileum, by mechanical occlusion or as the result of distension of the bowel following loss of muscular action
ILEUSES ▸ ileus
ILEX n any of a genus of trees or shrubs that includes holly
ILEXES ▸ ilex
ILIA ▸ ilium
ILIAC adj of or relating to the ilium
ILIACUS n iliac
ILIAD n epic poem
ILIADS ▸ iliad
ILIAL ▸ ilium
ILICES ▸ ilex
ILIUM n uppermost and widest of the three sections of the hipbone
ILK n type ▷ determiner each
ILKA same as ▸ **ilk**
ILKADAY n every day
ILKS ▸ ilk
ILL adj not in good health ▷ n evil, harm ▷ adv badly
ILLAPSE vb slide in
ILLEGAL adj against the law ▷ n person who has entered or attempted to enter a country illegally
ILLER ▸ ill
ILLEST ▸ ill
ILLIAD n wink
ILLIADS ▸ illiad
ILLICIT adj illegal
ILLIPE n Asian tree
ILLIPES ▸ illipe
ILLITE n clay mineral of the mica group, found in shales and mudstones
ILLITES ▸ illite
ILLITIC ▸ illite
ILLNESS n disease or indisposition
ILLOGIC n reasoning characterized by lack of logic
ILLS ▸ ill
ILLTH n condition of poverty or misery
ILLTHS ▸ illth
ILLUDE vb trick or deceive
ILLUDED ▸ illude
ILLUDES ▸ illude
ILLUME vb illuminate
ILLUMED ▸ illume
ILLUMES ▸ illume
ILLUPI same as ▸ **illipe**
ILLUPIS ▸ illupi
ILLUVIA > illuvium
ILLY adv badly
IMAGE n mental picture of someone or something ▷ vb picture in the mind
IMAGED ▸ image
IMAGER n device that produces images
IMAGERS ▸ imager
IMAGERY n images collectively, esp in the arts
IMAGES ▸ image
IMAGINE vb form a mental image of ▷ sentence substitute exclamation of surprise
IMAGING ▸ image
IMAGISM n poetic movement in England and America between 1912 and 1917
IMAGIST ▸ imagism
IMAGO n sexually mature adult insect
IMAGOES ▸ imago
IMAGOS ▸ imago
IMAM n leader of prayers in a mosque
IMAMATE n region or territory governed by an imam
IMAMS ▸ imam
IMARET n (in Turkey) a hospice for pilgrims or travellers
IMARETS ▸ imaret
IMARI n Japanese porcelain
IMARIS ▸ imari
IMAUM same as ▸ **imam**
IMAUMS ▸ imaum
IMBALM same as ▸ **embalm**
IMBALMS ▸ imbalm
IMBAR vb bar in
IMBARK vb cover in bark
IMBARKS ▸ imbark
IMBARS ▸ imbar
IMBASE vb degrade
IMBASED ▸ imbase
IMBASES ▸ imbase
IMBATHE vb bathe
IMBED same as ▸ **embed**
IMBEDS ▸ imbed
IMBIBE vb drink (alcoholic drinks)
IMBIBED ▸ imbibe
IMBIBER ▸ imbibe
IMBIBES ▸ imbibe
IMBIZO n meeting, esp a gathering of the Zulu people called by the king or a traditional leader
IMBIZOS ▸ imbizo
IMBLAZE vb depict heraldically
IMBODY same as ▸ **embody**
IMBOSK vb conceal
IMBOSKS ▸ imbosk
IMBOSOM vb hold in one's heart
IMBOSS same as ▸ **emboss**
IMBOWER vb enclose in a bower
IMBRAST Spenserian past participle of ▸ **embrace**
IMBREX n curved tile
IMBROWN vb make brown
IMBRUE vb stain, esp with blood
IMBRUED ▸ imbrue
IMBRUES ▸ imbrue
IMBRUTE vb reduce to a bestial state
IMBUE vb fill or inspire with (ideals or principles)
IMBUED ▸ imbue
IMBUES ▸ imbue
IMBUING ▸ imbue
IMBURSE vb pay
IMID n immunomodulatory drug
IMIDE n any of a class of organic compounds
IMIDES ▸ imide
IMIDIC ▸ imide
IMIDO ▸ imide
IMIDS ▸ imid

IMINE n any of a class of organic compounds
IMINES ▸ imine
IMINO ▸ imine
IMITANT same as > imitation
IMITATE vb take as a model
IMMANE adj monstrous
IMMASK vb disguise
IMMASKS ▸ immask
IMMENSE adj extremely large
IMMERGE archaic word for ▸ immerse
IMMERSE vb involve deeply, engross
IMMESH same as ▸ enmesh
IMMEW vb confine
IMMEWED ▸ immew
IMMEWS ▸ immew
IMMIES ▸ immy
IMMIT vb insert
IMMITS ▸ immit
IMMIX vb mix in
IMMIXED ▸ immix
IMMIXES ▸ immix
IMMORAL adj morally wrong, corrupt
IMMUNE adj protected against a specific disease ▷ n immune person or animal
IMMUNES ▸ immune
IMMURE vb imprison
IMMURED ▸ immure
IMMURES ▸ immure
IMMY n image-orthicon camera
IMP n (in folklore) mischievous small creature with magical powers ▷ vb insert (new feathers) into the stumps of broken feathers in order to repair the wing of a hawk or falcon
IMPACT n strong effect ▷ vb have a strong effect on
IMPACTS ▸ impact
IMPAINT vb paint
IMPAIR vb weaken or damage
IMPAIRS ▸ impair
IMPALA n southern African antelope
IMPALAS ▸ impala
IMPALE vb pierce with a sharp object
IMPALED ▸ impale
IMPALER ▸ impale
IMPALES ▸ impale
IMPANEL variant spelling (esp US) of ▸ empanel

IMPARK vb make into a park
IMPARKS ▸ impark
IMPARL vb parley
IMPARLS ▸ imparl
IMPART vb communicate (information)
IMPARTS ▸ impart
IMPASSE n situation in which progress is impossible
IMPASTE vb apply paint thickly to
IMPASTO n technique of applying paint thickly, so that brush marks are evident ▷ vb apply impasto
IMPAVE vb set in a pavement
IMPAVED ▸ impave
IMPAVES ▸ impave
IMPAVID adj fearless
IMPAWN vb pawn
IMPAWNS ▸ impawn
IMPEACH vb charge with a serious crime against the state
IMPEARL vb adorn with pearls
IMPED ▸ imp
IMPEDE vb hinder in action or progress
IMPEDED ▸ impede
IMPEDER ▸ impede
IMPEDES ▸ impede
IMPEDOR n component, such as an inductor or resistor, that offers impedance
IMPEL vb push or force (someone) to do something
IMPELS ▸ impel
IMPEND vb (esp of something threatening) to be about to happen
IMPENDS ▸ impend
IMPERIA > imperium
IMPERIL vb put in danger
IMPETUS n incentive, impulse
IMPHEE n African sugar cane
IMPHEES ▸ imphee
IMPI n group of Zulu warriors
IMPIES ▸ impi
IMPIETY n lack of respect or religious reverence
IMPING ▸ imp
IMPINGE vb affect or restrict
IMPINGS ▸ imp
IMPIOUS adj showing a lack of respect or reverence
IMPIS ▸ impi

IMPISH adj mischievous
IMPLANT n something put into someone's body, usu by surgical operation ▷ vb put (something) into someone's body, usu by surgical operation
IMPLATE vb sheathe
IMPLEAD vb sue or prosecute
IMPLED ▸ implead
IMPLETE vb fill
IMPLEX n part of an arthropod
IMPLIED adj hinted at or suggested
IMPLIES ▸ imply
IMPLODE vb collapse inwards
IMPLORE vb beg earnestly
IMPLY vb indicate by hinting, suggest
IMPONE vb impose
IMPONED ▸ impone
IMPONES ▸ impone
IMPORT vb bring in (goods) from another country ▷ n something imported
IMPORTS ▸ import
IMPOSE vb force the acceptance of
IMPOSED ▸ impose
IMPOSER ▸ impose
IMPOSES ▸ impose
IMPOSEX n imposition of male sexual characteristics on female gastropods, caused by pollutants
IMPOST n tax, esp a customs duty ▷ vb classify (imported goods) according to the duty payable on them
IMPOSTS ▸ impost
IMPOT n slang term for the act of imposing
IMPOTS ▸ impot
IMPOUND vb take legal possession of, confiscate
IMPOWER less common spelling of ▸ empower
IMPREGN vb impregnate
IMPRESA n heraldic device
IMPRESE same as ▸ impresa
IMPRESS vb affect strongly, usu favourably ▷ n impressing
IMPREST n fund of cash from which a department or other unit pays incidental expenses, topped up periodically from central funds

IMPRINT n mark made by printing or stamping ▷ vb produce (a mark) by printing or stamping

IMPROV n improvisational comedy

IMPROVE vb make or become better

IMPROVS ▸ improv

IMPS ▸ imp

IMPUGN vb challenge the truth or validity of

IMPUGNS ▸ impugn

IMPULSE vb give an impulse to ▷ n sudden urge to do something

IMPURE adj having dirty or unwanted substances mixed in

IMPURER ▸ impure

IMPUTE vb attribute responsibility to

IMPUTED ▸ impute

IMPUTER ▸ impute

IMPUTES ▸ impute

IMSHI interj go away!

IMSHY same as ▸ imshi

IN prep indicating position inside, state or situation, etc ▷ adv indicating position inside, entry into, etc ▷ adj fashionable ▷ n way of approaching or befriending a person ▷ vb to take in

INANE adj senseless, silly ▷ n something that is inane

INANELY ▸ inane

INANER ▸ inane

INANES ▸ inane

INANEST ▸ inane

INANGA n common type of New Zealand grass tree

INANGAS ▸ inanga

INANITY n lack of intelligence or imagination

INAPT adj not apt or fitting

INAPTLY ▸ inapt

INARCH vb graft (a plant) by uniting stock and scion while both are still growing independently

INARM vb embrace

INARMED ▸ inarm

INARMS ▸ inarm

INBEING n existence in something else

INBENT adj bent inwards

INBOARD adj (of a boat's engine) inside the hull ▷ adv within the sides of or towards the centre of a vessel or aircraft

INBORN adj existing from birth, natural

INBOUND vb pass into the playing area from outside it ▷ adj coming in

INBOX n folder which stores in-coming email messages

INBOXES ▸ inbox

INBREAK n breaking in

INBRED n inbred person or animal ▷ adj produced as a result of inbreeding

INBREDS ▸ inbred

INBREED vb breed from closely related individuals

INBRING vb bring in

INBUILT adj present from the start

INBURST n irruption

INBY adv into the house or an inner room ▷ adj located near or nearest to the house

INBYE adv near the house

INCAGE vb confine in or as in a cage

INCAGED ▸ incage

INCAGES ▸ incage

INCANT vb chant (a spell)

INCANTS ▸ incant

INCASE variant spelling of ▸ encase

INCASED ▸ incase

INCASES ▸ incase

INCAVE vb hide

INCAVED ▸ incave

INCAVES ▸ incave

INCAVI ▸ incavo

INCAVO n incised part of a carving

INCEDE vb advance

INCEDED ▸ incede

INCEDES ▸ incede

INCENSE vb make very angry ▷ n substance that gives off a sweet perfume when burned

INCENT vb provide incentive

INCENTS ▸ incent

INCEPT vb (of organisms) to ingest (food) ▷ n rudimentary organ

INCEPTS ▸ incept

INCEST n sexual intercourse between two people too closely related to marry

INCESTS ▸ incest

INCH n unit of length equal to one twelfth of a foot or 2.54 centimetres ▷ vb move slowly and gradually

INCHASE same as ▸ enchase

INCHED ▸ inch

INCHER n something measuring given amount of inches

INCHERS ▸ incher

INCHES ▸ inch

INCHING ▸ inch

INCHPIN n cervine sweetbread

INCIPIT n Latin introductory phrase

INCISAL adj relating to the cutting edge of incisors and cuspids

INCISE vb cut into with a sharp tool

INCISED ▸ incise

INCISES ▸ incise

INCISOR n front tooth, used for biting into food

INCITE vb stir up, provoke

INCITED ▸ incite

INCITER ▸ incite

INCITES ▸ incite

INCIVIL archaic form of ▸ uncivil

INCLASP vb clasp

INCLE same as ▸ inkle

INCLES ▸ incle

INCLINE vb lean, slope ▷ n slope

INCLIP vb embrace

INCLIPS ▸ inclip

INCLOSE less common spelling of ▸ enclose

INCLUDE vb have as part of the whole

INCOG n incognito

INCOGS ▸ incog

INCOME n amount of money earned from work, investments, etc

INCOMER n person who comes to live in a place in which he or she was not born

INCOMES ▸ income

INCONIE adj fine or delicate

INCONNU n whitefish of Arctic waters

INCONY adj fine or delicate

INCROSS n plant or animal produced by continued inbreeding ▷ vb inbreed or produce by inbreeding

INCRUST same as ▸ encrust

INCUBI ▸ incubus

INCUBUS n (in folklore) demon believed to have sex with sleeping women

INCUDAL ▸ incus

INCUDES ▸ incus

INCULT adj (of land) uncultivated

INCUR vb cause (something unpleasant) to happen
INCURS ▸ incur
INCURVE vb curve or cause to curve inwards
INCUS n central of the three small bones in the middle ear of mammals
INCUSE n design stamped or hammered onto a coin ▷ vb impress (a design) in a coin or to impress (a coin) with a design by hammering or stamping ▷ adj stamped or hammered onto a coin
INCUSED ▸ incuse
INCUSES ▸ incuse
INCUT adj cut or etched in
INDABA n (among native peoples of southern Africa) a meeting to discuss a serious topic
INDABAS ▸ indaba
INDAMIN same as ▸ **indamine**
INDART vb dart in
INDARTS ▸ indart
INDEED adv really, certainly ▷ interj expression of indignation or surprise
INDENE n colourless liquid hydrocarbon extracted from petroleum and coal tar and used in making synthetic resins
INDENES ▸ indene
INDENT vb make a dent in
INDENTS ▸ indent
INDEW same as ▸ **indue**
INDEWED ▸ indew
INDEWS ▸ indew
INDEX n alphabetical list of names or subjects dealt with in a book ▷ vb provide (a book) with an index
INDEXAL ▸ index
INDEXED ▸ index
INDEXER ▸ index
INDEXES ▸ index
INDIA n code word for the letter I
INDIAS ▸ india
INDICAN n compound secreted in the urine, usually in the form of its potassium salt
INDICES plural of ▸ **index**
INDICIA > **indicium**
INDICT vb formally charge with a crime
INDICTS ▸ indict
INDIE adj (of rock music)

released by an independent record company ▷ n independent record company
INDIES ▸ indie
INDIGEN same as > **indigene**
INDIGN adj undeserving
INDIGO adj deep violet-blue ▷ n dye of this colour
INDIGOS ▸ indigo
INDITE vb write
INDITED ▸ indite
INDITER ▸ indite
INDITES ▸ indite
INDIUM n soft silvery-white metallic element
INDIUMS ▸ indium
INDOL same as ▸ **indole**
INDOLE n white or yellowish crystalline heterocyclic compound extracted from coal tar and used in perfumery, medicine, and as a flavouring agent
INDOLES ▸ indole
INDOLS ▸ indol
INDOOR adj inside a building
INDOORS adj inside or into a building
INDORSE variant spelling of ▸ **endorse**
INDOW archaic variant of ▸ **endow**
INDOWED ▸ indow
INDOWS ▸ indow
INDOXYL n yellow water-soluble crystalline compound occurring in woad as its glucoside and in urine as its ester
INDRAFT same as > **indraught**
INDRAWN adj drawn or pulled in
INDRI same as ▸ **indris**
INDRIS n large Madagascan arboreal lemuroid primate
INDUCE vb persuade or influence
INDUCED ▸ induce
INDUCER ▸ induce
INDUCES ▸ induce
INDUCT vb formally install (someone, esp a clergyman) in office
INDUCTS ▸ induct
INDUE variant spelling of ▸ **endue**
INDUED ▸ indue
INDUES ▸ indue
INDUING ▸ indue

INDULGE vb allow oneself pleasure
INDULIN same as > **induline**
INDULT n faculty granted by the Holy See allowing a specific deviation from the Church's common law
INDULTS ▸ indult
INDUNA n (in South Africa) a Black African overseer in a factory, mine, etc
INDUNAS ▸ induna
INDUSIA > **indusium**
INDWELL vb (of a spirit, principle, etc) to inhabit
INDWELT ▸ indwell
INEARTH poetic word for ▸ **bury**
INEDITA pl n unpublished writings
INEPT adj clumsy, lacking skill
INEPTER ▸ inept
INEPTLY ▸ inept
INERM adj without thorns
INERT n inert thing ▷ adj without the power of motion or resistance
INERTER ▸ inert
INERTIA n feeling of unwillingness to do anything

> This is not the easiest of words to see, but its combination of common letters makes it one of the most frequently played of 7-letter bonuses, while its plurals, which can be **inertiae** or **inertias**, are among the 8-letter bonus words that come up most often.

INERTLY ▸ inert
INERTS ▸ inert
INEXACT adj not exact or accurate
INFALL vb move towards a black hole, etc, under the influence of gravity
INFALLS ▸ infall
INFAME vb defame
INFAMED ▸ infame
INFAMES ▸ infame
INFAMY n state of being infamous
INFANCY n early childhood
INFANT n very young child ▷ adj of, relating to, or designed for young children
INFANTA n (formerly)

daughter of a king of Spain or Portugal

INFANTE n (formerly) any son of a king of Spain or Portugal, except the heir to the throne

INFANTS ▸ infant

INFARCT n localized area of dead tissue (necrosis) resulting from obstruction of the blood supply to that part, esp by an embolus ▷ vb obstruct the blood supply to part of a body

INFARE vb enter

INFARES ▸ infare

INFAUNA n animals that live in ocean and river beds

INFAUST adj unlucky

INFECT vb affect with a disease ▷ adj contaminated or polluted with or as if with a disease

INFECTS ▸ infect

INFEFT vb give possession of heritable property

INFEFTS ▸ infeft

INFELT adj heartfelt

INFEOFF same as ▸ enfeoff

INFER vb work out from evidence

INFERE adv together

INFERNO n intense raging fire

INFERS ▸ infer

INFEST vb inhabit or overrun in unpleasantly large numbers

INFESTS ▸ infest

INFIDEL n person with no religion ▷ adj of unbelievers or unbelief

INFIELD n area of the field near the pitch

INFIGHT vb box at close quarters

INFILL vb fill in ▷ n act of filling in or closing gaps, etc, in something, such as a row of buildings

INFILLS ▸ infill

INFIMA ▸ infimum

INFIMUM n greatest lower bound

INFIRM vb make infirm ▷ adj physically or mentally weak

INFIRMS ▸ infirm

INFIX vb fix firmly in ▷ n affix inserted into the middle of a word

INFIXED ▸ infix

INFIXES ▸ infix

INFLAME vb make angry or excited

INFLATE vb expand by filling with air or gas

INFLECT vb change (the voice) in tone or pitch

INFLICT vb impose (something unpleasant) on

INFLOW n something, such as liquid or gas, that flows in ▷ vb flow in

INFLOWS ▸ inflow

INFLUX n arrival or entry of many people or things

INFO n information

INFOLD variant spelling of ▸ enfold

INFOLDS ▸ infold

INFORCE same as ▸ enforce

INFORM vb tell ▷ adj without shape

INFORMS ▸ inform

INFOS ▸ info

INFRA adv (esp in textual annotation) below

INFRACT vb violate or break (a law, an agreement, etc)

INFULA same as ▸ infulae

INFULAE pl n two ribbons hanging from the back of a bishop's mitre

INFUSE vb fill (with an emotion or quality)

INFUSED ▸ infuse

INFUSER n any device used to make an infusion, esp a tea maker

INFUSES ▸ infuse

ING n meadow near a river

INGAN Scots word for ▸ onion

INGANS ▸ ingan

INGATE n entrance

INGATES ▸ ingate

INGENER Shakespearean form of ▸ engineer

INGENU n artless or inexperienced boy or young man

INGENUE n artless or inexperienced girl or young woman

INGENUS ▸ ingenu

INGEST vb take (food or liquid) into the body

INGESTA pl n nourishment taken into the body through the mouth

INGESTS ▸ ingest

INGINE n genius

INGINES ▸ ingine

INGLE n fire in a room or a fireplace

INGLES ▸ ingle

INGLOBE vb shape as a sphere

INGO n a reveal

INGOES ▸ ingo

INGOING same as ▸ ingo

INGOT n oblong block of cast metal ▷ vb shape (metal) into ingots

INGOTED ▸ ingot

INGOTS ▸ ingot

INGRAFT variant spelling of ▸ engraft

INGRAIN vb impress deeply on the mind or nature ▷ adj (of carpets) made of dyed yarn or of fibre that is dyed before being spun into yarn ▷ n carpet made from ingrained yarn

INGRAM adj ignorant

INGRATE n ungrateful person ▷ adj ungrateful

INGRESS n entrance

INGROSS archaic form of ▸ engross

INGROUP n highly cohesive and relatively closed social group

INGROWN adj (esp of a toenail) grown abnormally into the flesh

INGRUM adj ignorant

INGS ▸ ing

INGULF variant spelling of ▸ engulf

INGULFS ▸ ingulf

INGULPH archaic form of ▸ engulf

INHABIT vb live in

INHALE vb breathe in (air, smoke, etc)

INHALED ▸ inhale

INHALER n container for an inhalant

INHALES ▸ inhale

INHAUL n line for hauling in a sail

INHAULS ▸ inhaul

INHAUST vb drink in

INHERCE same as ▸ inhearse

INHERE vb be an inseparable part (of)

INHERED ▸ inhere

INHERES ▸ inhere

INHERIT vb receive (money etc) from someone who has died

INHIBIN n peptide hormone

INHIBIT vb restrain (an impulse or desire)

INHOOP vb confine

INHOOPS ▸ inhoop
INHUMAN adj cruel or brutal
INHUME vb inter
INHUMED ▸ inhume
INHUMER ▸ inhume
INHUMES ▸ inhume
INIA ▸ inion
INION n most prominent point at the back of the head, used as a point of measurement in craniometry
INIONS ▸ inion
INISLE vb put on or make into an island
INISLED ▸ inisle
INISLES ▸ inisle
INITIAL adj first, at the beginning ▷ n first letter, esp of a person's name ▷ vb sign with one's initials
INJECT vb put (a fluid) into the body with a syringe
INJECTS ▸ inject
INJELLY vb place in jelly
INJERA n white Ethiopian flatbread, similar to a crepe
INJERAS ▸ injera
INJOINT vb join
INJUNCT vb issue a legal injunction against (a person)
INJURE vb hurt physically or mentally
INJURED ▸ injure
INJURER ▸ injure
INJURES ▸ injure
INJURY n physical hurt
INK n coloured liquid used for writing or printing ▷ vb mark in ink (something already marked in pencil)
INKBLOT n abstract patch of ink, one of ten commonly used in the Rorschach test
INKED ▸ ink
INKER ▸ ink
INKERS ▸ ink
INKHORN n (formerly) a small portable container for ink, usually made from horn
INKHOSI n Zulu clan chief
INKIER ▸ inky
INKIEST ▸ inky
INKING ▸ ink
INKJET adj of a method of printing streams of electrically charged ink
INKLE n kind of linen tape used for trimmings ▷ vb to hint

INKLED ▸ inkle
INKLES ▸ inkle
INKLESS ▸ ink
INKLIKE ▸ ink
INKLING n slight idea or suspicion
INKOSI ▸ inkhosi
INKOSIS ▸ inkhosi
INKPAD n ink-soaked pad used for rubber-stamping or fingerprinting
INKPADS ▸ inkpad
INKPOT n ink-bottle
INKPOTS ▸ inkpot
INKS ▸ ink
INKSPOT n ink stain
INKWELL n small container for ink, often fitted into the surface of a desk
INKWOOD n type of tree
INKY adj dark or black
INLACE variant spelling of ▸ enlace
INLACED ▸ inlace
INLACES ▸ inlace
INLAID ▸ inlay
INLAND adv in or towards the interior of a country, away from the sea ▷ adj of or in the interior of a country or region, away from a sea or border ▷ n interior of a country or region
INLANDS ▸ inland
INLAY n inlaid substance or pattern ▷ vb decorate (an article, esp of furniture) by inserting pieces of wood, ivory, or metal so that the surfaces are smooth and flat
INLAYER ▸ inlay
INLAYS ▸ inlay
INLET n narrow strip of water extending from the sea into the land ▷ vb insert or inlay
INLETS ▸ inlet
INLIER n outcrop of rocks that is entirely surrounded by younger rocks
INLIERS ▸ inlier
INLOCK vb lock up
INLOCKS ▸ inlock
INLY adv inwardly
INLYING adj situated within or inside
INMATE n person living in an institution such as a prison
INMATES ▸ inmate
INMESH variant spelling of

▸ enmesh
INMOST adj innermost
INN n pub or small hotel, esp in the country ▷ vb stay at an inn
INNAGE n measurement from bottom of container to surface of liquid
INNAGES ▸ innage
INNARDS pl n internal organs
INNATE adj being part of someone's nature, inborn
INNED ▸ inn
INNER adj happening or located inside ▷ n red innermost ring on a target
INNERLY ▸ inner
INNERS ▸ inner
INNERVE vb supply with nervous energy
INNING n division of cricket consisting of a turn at batting and a turn in the field for each side
INNINGS ▸ inning
INNIT interj isn't it
INNLESS adj without inns
INNS ▸ inn
INNYARD n courtyard of an inn
INOCULA > inoculum
INORB vb enclose in or as if in an orb
INORBED ▸ inorb
INORBS ▸ inorb
INOSINE n type of molecule making up cell
INOSITE same as ▸ inositol
INPHASE adj in the same phase
INPOUR vb pour in
INPOURS ▸ inpour
INPUT n resources put into a project etc ▷ vb enter (data) in a computer
INPUTS ▸ input
INQILAB n (in India, Pakistan, etc) revolution
INQUERE Spenserian form of ▸ inquire
INQUEST n official inquiry into a sudden death
INQUIET vb disturb
INQUIRE vb seek information or ask (about)
INQUIRY n question
INRO n Japanese seal-box
INROAD n invasion or hostile attack
INROADS ▸ inroad
INRUN n slope down which ski jumpers ski

INRUNS ▸ inrun

INRUSH n sudden and overwhelming inward flow

INS ▸ in

INSANE adj mentally ill

INSANER ▸ insane

INSANIE n insanity

INSCAPE n essential inner nature of a person, an object, etc

INSCULP vb engrave

INSEAM vb contain

INSEAMS ▸ inseam

INSECT n small animal with six legs and two wings, such as an ant or fly

INSECTS ▸ insect

INSEEM vb cover with grease

INSEEMS ▸ inseem

INSERT vb put inside or include ▷ n something inserted

INSERTS ▸ insert

INSET n small picture inserted within a larger one ▷ vb place in or within ▷ adj decorated with something inserted

INSETS ▸ inset

INSHELL vb retreat, as into a shell

INSHIP vb travel or send by ship

INSHIPS ▸ inship

INSHORE adj close to the shore ▷ adv towards the shore

INSIDE prep in or to the interior of ▷ adj on or of the inside ▷ adv on, in, or to the inside, indoors ▷ n inner side, surface, or part

INSIDER n member of a group who has privileged knowledge about it

INSIDES ▸ inside

INSIGHT n deep understanding

INSIGNE same as > **insignia**

INSINEW vb connect or strengthen, as with sinews

INSIPID adj lacking interest, spirit, or flavour

INSIST vb demand or state firmly

INSISTS ▸ insist

INSNARE less common spelling of ▸ **ensnare**

INSOFAR adv to the extent

INSOLE n inner sole of a shoe or boot

INSOLES ▸ insole

INSOOTH adv indeed

INSOUL same as ▸ **ensoul**

INSOULS ▸ insoul

INSPAN vb harness (animals) to (a vehicle)

INSPANS ▸ inspan

INSPECT vb check closely or officially

INSPIRE vb fill with enthusiasm, stimulate

INSTAL same as ▸ **install**

INSTALL vb put in and prepare (equipment) for use

INSTALS ▸ instal

INSTANT n very brief time ▷ adj happening at once

INSTAR vb decorate with stars ▷ n stage in the development of an insect between any two moults

INSTARS ▸ instar

INSTATE vb place in a position or office

INSTEAD adv as a replacement or substitute

INSTEP n part of the foot forming the arch between the ankle and toes

INSTEPS ▸ instep

INSTIL vb introduce (an idea etc) gradually into someone's mind

INSTILL same as ▸ **instil**

INSTILS ▸ instil

INSULA n pyramid-shaped area of the brain within each cerebral hemisphere beneath parts of the frontal and temporal lobes

INSULAE ▸ insula

INSULAR adj not open to new ideas, narrow-minded ▷ n islander

INSULIN n hormone produced in the pancreas that controls the amount of sugar in the blood

INSULSE adj stupid

INSULT vb behave rudely to, offend ▷ n insulting remark or action

INSULTS ▸ insult

INSURE vb protect by insurance

INSURED adj covered by insurance ▷ n person, persons, or organization covered by an insurance policy

INSURER n person or company that sells insurance

INSURES ▸ insure

INSWEPT adj narrowed towards the front

INSWING n movement of a bowled ball from off to leg through the air

INTACT adj not changed or damaged in any way

INTAGLI > intaglio

INTAKE n amount or number taken in

INTAKES ▸ intake

INTEGER n positive or negative whole number or zero

INTEL n US military intelligence

INTELS ▸ intel

INTEND vb propose or plan (to do something)

INTENDS ▸ intend

INTENSE adj of great strength or degree

INTENT n intention ▷ adj paying close attention

INTENTS ▸ intent

INTER vb bury (a corpse)

INTERIM adj temporary, provisional, or intervening ▷ n intervening time ▷ adv meantime

INTERN vb imprison, esp during a war ▷ n trainee doctor in a hospital

INTERNE same as ▸ **intern**

INTERNS ▸ intern

INTERS ▸ inter

INTHRAL archaic form of ▸ **enthral**

INTI n former monetary unit of Peru

INTIL Scots form of ▸ **into**

INTIMA n innermost layer of an organ or part, esp of a blood vessel

INTIMAE ▸ intima

INTIMAL ▸ intima

INTIMAS ▸ intima

INTIME adj intimate

INTINE n inner wall of a pollen grain or a spore

INTINES ▸ intine

INTIRE archaic form of ▸ **entire**

INTIS ▸ inti

INTITLE archaic form of ▸ **entitle**

INTO prep indicating motion towards the centre, result of a change, division, etc

INTOED adj having inward-turning toes

INTOMB same as ▸ **entomb**

INTOMBS ▸ intomb
INTONE vb speak or recite in an unvarying tone of voice
INTONED ▸ intone
INTONER ▸ intone
INTONES ▸ intone
INTORT vb twist inward
INTORTS ▸ intort
INTOWN adj infield
INTRA prep within
INTRADA n prelude
INTRANT n one who enters
INTREAT archaic spelling of ▸ entreat
INTRO n introduction
INTROFY vb increase the wetting properties
INTROIT n short prayer said or sung as the celebrant is entering the sanctuary to celebrate Mass
INTROLD same as ▸ entrold
INTRON n stretch of DNA that interrupts a gene and does not contribute to the specification of a protein
INTRONS ▸ intron
INTROS ▸ intro
INTRUDE vb come in or join in without being invited
INTRUST same as ▸ entrust
INTUIT vb know or discover by intuition
INTUITS ▸ intuit
INTURN n inward turn
INTURNS ▸ inturn
INTUSE n contusion
INTUSES ▸ intuse
INTWINE less common spelling of ▸ entwine
INTWIST vb twist together
INULA n plant of the elecampane genus
INULAS ▸ inula
INULASE n enzyme that hydrolyses inulin to fructose
INULIN n fructose polysaccharide present in the tubers and rhizomes of some plants
INULINS ▸ inulin
INURE vb cause to accept or become hardened to
INURED ▸ inure
INURES ▸ inure
INURING ▸ inure
INURN vb place (esp cremated ashes) in an urn
INURNED ▸ inurn
INURNS ▸ inurn
INUST adj burnt in
INUTILE adj useless

INVADE vb enter (a country) by military force
INVADED ▸ invade
INVADER ▸ invade
INVADES ▸ invade
INVALID n disabled or chronically ill person ▷ vb dismiss from active service because of illness or injury ▷ adj having no legal force
INVAR n alloy made from iron and nickel
INVARS ▸ invar
INVEIGH vb criticize strongly
INVENIT sentence substitute (he or she) designed it: used formerly on objects such as pocket watches next to the designer's name
INVENT vb think up or create (something new)
INVENTS ▸ invent
INVERSE vb make something opposite or contrary in effect ▷ adj reversed in effect, sequence, direction, etc ▷ n exact opposite
INVERT vb turn upside down or inside out ▷ n homosexual
INVERTS ▸ invert
INVEST vb spend (money, time, etc) on something with the expectation of profit
INVESTS ▸ invest
INVEXED adj concave
INVIOUS adj without paths or roads
INVITAL adj not vital
INVITE vb request the company of ▷ n invitation
INVITED ▸ invite
INVITEE n one who is invited
INVITER ▸ invite
INVITES ▸ invite
INVOICE n (present with) a bill for goods or services supplied ▷ vb present (a customer) with an invoice
INVOKE vb put (a law or penalty) into operation
INVOKED ▸ invoke
INVOKER ▸ invoke
INVOKES ▸ invoke
INVOLVE vb include as a necessary part
INWALL vb surround with a wall
INWALLS ▸ inwall

INWARD adj directed towards the middle ▷ adv towards the inside or middle ▷ n inward part
INWARDS adv towards the inside or middle of something
INWEAVE vb weave together into or as if into a design, fabric, etc
INWICK vb perform a curling stroke in which the stone bounces off another stone
INWICKS ▸ inwick
INWIND vb wind or coil around
INWINDS ▸ inwind
INWIT n conscience
INWITH adv within
INWITS ▸ inwit
INWORK vb work in
INWORKS ▸ inwork
INWORN adj worn in
INWOUND ▸ inwind
INWOVE ▸ inweave
INWOVEN ▸ inweave
INWRAP less common spelling of ▸ enwrap
INWRAPS ▸ inwrap
INYALA n antelope
INYALAS ▸ inyala
IO interj an exclamation expressing joy, triumph, grief etc ▷ n a cry of "io"
IODATE same as ▸ iodize
IODATED ▸ iodate
IODATES ▸ iodate
IODIC adj of or containing iodine
IODID same as ▸ iodide
IODIDE n compound containing an iodine atom, such as methyl iodide
IODIDES ▸ iodide
IODIDS ▸ iodid
IODIN same as ▸ iodine
IODINE n bluish-black element used in medicine and photography
IODINES ▸ iodine
IODINS ▸ iodin
IODISE same as ▸ iodize
IODISED ▸ iodise
IODISER ▸ iodise
IODISES ▸ iodise
IODISM n poisoning induced by ingestion of iodine or its compounds
IODISMS ▸ iodism
IODIZE vb treat with iodine
IODIZED ▸ iodize
IODIZER ▸ iodize

IODIZES ▸ iodize

IODOUS adj of or containing iodine, esp in the trivalent state

IODURET n iodide

IOLITE n grey or violet-blue dichroic mineral

IOLITES ▸ iolite

ION n electrically charged atom

IONIC adj of or in the form of ions

IONICS pl n study of ions

IONISE same as ▸ **ionize**

IONISED ▸ ionise

IONISER same as ▸ **ionizer**

IONISES ▸ ionise

IONIUM n naturally occurring radioisotope of thorium

IONIUMS ▸ ionium

IONIZE vb change into ions

IONIZED ▸ ionize

IONIZER n person or thing that ionizes, esp an electrical device used within a room to refresh its atmosphere by restoring negative ions

IONIZES ▸ ionize

IONOGEN n compound that exists as ions when dissolved

IONOMER n thermoplastic with ionic bonding between polymer chains

IONONE n yellowish liquid mixture of two isomers with an odour of violets

IONONES ▸ ionone

IONS ▸ ion

IOS ▸ io

IOTA n ninth letter in the Greek alphabet

This word for a Greek letter is another of those that often come in handy when you are trying to rid your rack of too many vowels.

IOTAS ▸ iota

IPECAC n type of S American shrub

IPECACS ▸ ipecac

IPOMOEA n tropical or subtropical convolvulaceous plant

IPPON n winning point awarded in a judo or karate competition

IPPONS ▸ ippon

IRACUND adj easily angered

IRADE n written edict of a Muslim ruler

IRADES ▸ irade

IRATE adj very angry

IRATELY ▸ irate

IRATER ▸ irate

IRATEST ▸ irate

IRE vb anger ▷ n anger

IRED ▸ ire

IREFUL ▸ ire

IRELESS ▸ ire

IRENIC adj tending to conciliate or promote peace

IRENICS n that branch of theology that is concerned with unity between Christian sects and denominations

IRES ▸ ire

IRID n type of iris

IRIDAL ▸ irid

IRIDEAL ▸ irid

IRIDES ▸ iris

IRIDIAL ▸ irid

IRIDIAN ▸ irid

IRIDIC adj of or containing iridium, esp in the tetravalent state

IRIDISE vb make iridescent

IRIDIUM n very hard corrosion-resistant metal

IRIDIZE vb make iridescent

IRIDS ▸ irid

IRING ▸ ire

IRIS n coloured circular membrane of the eye containing the pupil ▷ vb display iridescence

IRISATE vb make iridescent

IRISED ▸ iris

IRISES ▸ iris

IRISING ▸ iris

IRITIC ▸ iritis

IRITIS n inflammation of the iris of the eye

Since a plague of Is tends to afflict every Scrabble player's rack at regular intervals, it is well worth knowing words like this one, meaning inflammation of the iris, which use several of the wretched letter!

IRK vb irritate, annoy

IRKED ▸ irk

IRKING ▸ irk

IRKS ▸ irk

IRKSOME adj irritating, annoying

IROKO n tropical African hardwood tree

IROKOS ▸ iroko

IRON n strong silvery-white metallic element, widely used for structural and engineering purposes ▷ adj made of iron ▷ vb smooth (clothes or fabric) with an iron

IRONE n fragrant liquid

You may surprise your opponent by adding an E to **iron** if you know this word for a kind of aromatic oil.

IRONED ▸ iron

IRONER ▸ iron

IRONERS ▸ iron

IRONES ▸ irone

IRONIC adj using irony

IRONIER ▸ irony

IRONIES ▸ irony

IRONING n clothes to be ironed

IRONISE same as ▸ **ironize**

IRONIST ▸ ironize

IRONIZE vb use or indulge in irony

IRONMAN n very strong man

IRONMEN ▸ ironman

IRONS ▸ iron

IRONY n mildly sarcastic use of words to imply the opposite of what is said ▷ adj of, resembling, or containing iron

IRREAL adj unreal

IRRUPT vb enter forcibly or suddenly

IRRUPTS ▸ irrupt

IS third person singular present tense of ▸ **be**

ISABEL n brown yellow colour

ISABELS ▸ isabel

ISAGOGE n academic introduction to a specialized subject field or area of research

ISATIN n yellowish-red crystalline compound soluble in hot water, used for the preparation of vat dyes

ISATINE same as ▸ **isatin**

ISATINS ▸ isatin

ISBA n log hut

ISBAS ▸ isba

ISCHIA ▸ ischium

ISCHIAL ▸ ischium

ISCHIUM n one of the three sections of the hipbone, situated below the ilium

ISH n issue

An **ish** is a word for an issue in Scots law. If you have I, S and H on your rack, remember that as well as adding **ish** to the end of many words, you can also play those letters as a word in its own right.

ISHES ▸ ish

ISIT sentence substitute expression used to seek confirmation of something or show one is listening

ISLAND n piece of land surrounded by water ▸ vb cause to become an island

ISLANDS ▸ island

ISLE vb make an isle of ▸ n island

ISLED ▸ isle

ISLEMAN n islander

ISLEMEN ▸ isleman

ISLES ▸ isle

ISLET n small island

ISLETED adj having islets

ISLETS ▸ islet

ISLING ▸ isle

ISM n doctrine, system, or practice

While **ism** can be added to the ends of many words as a suffix, it's worth remembering as a word in its own right.

ISMATIC adj following fashionable doctrines

ISMS ▸ ism

ISNA vb is not

ISNAE same as ▸ isna

ISO n short segment of film that can be replayed easily

ISOAMYL n as in **isoamyl acetate** colourless volatile compound used as a solvent for cellulose lacquers and as a flavouring

ISOBAR n line on a map connecting places of equal atmospheric pressure

ISOBARE same as ▸ isobar

ISOBARS ▸ isobar

ISOBASE n line connecting points of equal land upheaval

ISOBATH n line on a map connecting points of equal underwater depth

ISOCHOR n line on a graph showing the variation of the temperature of a fluid with its pressure, when the volume is kept constant

ISODICA ▸ isodicon

ISODOMA ▸ isodomon

ISODONT n animal in which the teeth are of similar size

ISODOSE n dose of radiation applied to a part of the body in radiotherapy that is equal to the dose applied to a different part

ISOETES n quillwort

ISOFORM n protein similar in function but not form to another

ISOGAMY n (in some algae and fungi) sexual fusion of gametes of similar size and form

ISOGENY ▸ isogenous

ISOGON n equiangular polygon

ISOGONE same as ▸ isogonic

ISOGONS ▸ isogon

ISOGONY ▸ isogonic

ISOGRAM same as ▸ isopleth

ISOGRIV n line connecting points of equal angular difference between magnetic north and grid north

ISOHEL n line on a map connecting places with an equal period of sunshine

ISOHELS ▸ isohel

ISOHYET n line on a map connecting places having equal rainfall

ISOKONT same as ▸ isokontan

ISOLATE vb place apart or alone ▸ n isolated person or group

ISOLEAD n line on a ballistic graph

ISOLEX n isogloss marking off the area in which a particular item of vocabulary is found

ISOLINE same as ▸ isopleth

ISOLOG ▸ isologous

ISOLOGS ▸ isologous

ISOMER n substance whose molecules contain the same atoms as another but in a different arrangement

ISOMERE same as ▸ isomer

ISOMERS ▸ isomer

ISONOME n line on a chart connecting points of equal abundance values of a plant species sampled in different sections of an area

ISONOMY n equality before the law of the citizens of a state

ISOPACH n line on a map connecting points below which a particular rock stratum has the same thickness

ISOPOD n type of crustacean including woodlice and pill bugs ▸ adj of this type of crustacean

ISOPODS ▸ isopod

ISOS ▸ iso

ISOSPIN n internal quantum number used in the classification of elementary particles

ISOTACH n line on a map connecting points of equal wind speed

ISOTONE n one of two or more atoms of different atomic number that contain the same number of neutrons

ISOTOPE n one of two or more atoms with the same number of protons in the nucleus but a different number of neutrons

ISOTOPY ▸ isotope

ISOTRON n device for separating small quantities of isotopes by ionizing them and separating the ions by a mass spectrometer

ISOTYPE n presentation of statistical information in a row of diagrams

ISOZYME n any of a set of structural variants of an enzyme occurring in different tissues in a single species

ISSEI n first-generation Japanese immigrant

ISSEIS ▸ issei

ISSUANT adj emerging or issuing

ISSUE n topic of interest or discussion ▸ vb make (a statement etc) publicly

ISSUED ▸ issue

ISSUER ▸ issue

ISSUERS ▸ issue

ISSUES ▸ issue

ISSUING ▸ issue

ISTANA n (in Malaysia) a royal palace

ISTANAS ▸ istana

ISTHMI ▸ isthmus
ISTHMIC ▸ isthmus
ISTHMUS n narrow strip of land connecting two areas of land
ISTLE n fibre obtained from various tropical American agave and yucca trees used in making carpets, cord, etc
ISTLES ▸ istle
IT pron refers to a nonhuman, animal, plant, or inanimate object ▷ n player whose turn it is to catch the others in children's games
ITA n type of palm
ITACISM n pronunciation of the Greek letter eta as in Modern Greek
ITALIC adj (of printing type) sloping to the right ▷ n style of printing type modelled on this, chiefly used to indicate emphasis, a foreign word, etc
ITALICS ▸ italic
ITAS ▸ ita
ITCH n skin irritation causing a desire to scratch ▷ vb have an itch
ITCHED ▸ itch

ITCHES ▸ itch
ITCHIER ▸ itch
ITCHILY ▸ itch
ITCHING ▸ itch
ITCHY ▸ itch
ITEM n single thing in a list or collection ▷ adv likewise ▷ vb itemize
ITEMED ▸ item
ITEMING ▸ item
ITEMISE same as ▸ itemize
ITEMIZE vb make a list of
ITEMS ▸ item
ITERANT ▸ iterate
ITERATE vb repeat
ITERUM adv again
ITHER Scots word for ▸ other
ITS pron belonging to it ▷ adj of or belonging to it
ITSELF pron reflexive form of it
IURE adv by law
IVIED adj covered with ivy
IVIES ▸ ivy
IVORIED ▸ ivory
IVORIES pl n keys of a piano
IVORIST n worker in ivory
IVORY n hard white bony substance forming the tusks of elephants ▷ adj yellowish-white
IVRESSE n drunkenness

IVY n evergreen climbing plant
IVYLIKE ▸ ivy
IWI n Maori tribe
> This Maori word for a tribe is a great one for getting rid of an awkward combination of letters.

IWIS archaic word for > certainly
IXIA n southern African plant of the iris family with showy ornamental funnel-shaped flowers
IXIAS ▸ ixia
IXODID n hard-bodied tick
IXODIDS ▸ ixodid
IXORA n flowering shrub
IXORAS ▸ ixora
IXTLE same as ▸ istle
IXTLES ▸ ixtle
IZAR n long garment worn by Muslim women
IZARD n type of goat-antelope
IZARDS ▸ izard
IZARS ▸ izar
IZZARD n letter Z
IZZARDS ▸ izzard
IZZAT n honour or prestige
IZZATS ▸ izzat

Jj

J, being worth 8 points on its own, is a good tile for scoring well with, especially as it combines well with **Z** to make **jiz** and with **X** to make great words like **jeux**, **jinx** and **jynx**. However, **J** is a difficult letter when it comes to making bonus words scoring that extra 50 points, so you will normally want to play it off fairly quickly. There are two two-letter words that begin with **J**: **ja** and **jo**. As **J** has such a high value, look out for double- and triple-letter squares when playing these. There are plenty of good three-letter words starting with **J**: **jab** (12 points), **jak** (14), **jam** (12), **jar** (10), **jaw** (13), **jay** (13), **jet** (10), **jib** (12), **jig** (11), **job** (12), **jog** (11), **jot** (10), **joy** (13), **jug** (11) and **jut** (10).

JA interj yes ▷ sentence substitute yes

JAB vb poke sharply ▷ n quick punch or poke

JABBED ▸ jab

JABBER vb talk rapidly or incoherently ▷ n rapid or incoherent talk

JABBERS ▸ jabber

JABBING ▸ jab

JABBLE vb ripple

JABBLED ▸ jabble

JABBLES ▸ jabble

JABERS interj Irish exclamation

JABIRU n large white-and-black Australian stork

JABIRUS ▸ jabiru

JABOT n frill or ruffle on the front of a blouse or shirt

JABOTS ▸ jabot

JABS ▸ jab

JACAL n Mexican daub hut

JACALES ▸ jacal

JACALS ▸ jacal

JACAMAR n tropical American bird with an iridescent plumage

JACANA n long-legged long-toed bird of tropical and subtropical marshy regions

JACANAS ▸ jacana

JACARE another name for ▸ cayman

JACARES ▸ jacare

JACCHUS n small monkey

JACENT adj lying

JACINTH another name for > hyacinth

JACK n device for raising a motor vehicle or other heavy object ▷ vb lift or push (an object) with a jack

JACKAL n doglike wild animal of Africa and Asia ▷ vb behave like a jackal

JACKALS ▸ jackal

JACKASS n fool

JACKDAW n black-and-grey Eurasian bird of the crow family

JACKED ▸ jack

JACKEEN n slick self-assertive lower-class Dubliner

JACKER n labourer

JACKERS ▸ jacker

JACKET n short coat ▷ vb put a jacket on (someone or something)

JACKETS ▸ jacket

JACKING ▸ jack

JACKLEG n unskilled worker

JACKMAN n retainer

JACKMEN ▸ jackman

JACKPOT n largest prize that may be won in a game

JACKS n game in which metal, bone, or plastic pieces are thrown and then picked up between throws of a small ball

JACOBIN n variety of fancy pigeon with a hood of feathers swept up over and around the head

JACOBUS n English gold coin minted in the reign of James I

JACONET n light cotton fabric used for clothing, bandages, etc

JACUZZI n bath or pool equipped with a system of underwater jets

JADE n ornamental semiprecious stone, usu dark green ▷ adj bluish-green ▷ vb exhaust or make exhausted from work or use

JADED adj tired and unenthusiastic

JADEDLY ▸ jaded

JADEITE n usually green or white mineral, found in igneous and metamorphic rocks

JADERY n shrewishness

JADES ▸ jade

JADING ▸ jade

JADISH ▸ jade

JADITIC ▸ jade

JAEGER n marksman in certain units of the German or Austrian armies

JAEGERS ▸ jaeger

JAFFA n (in cricket) well-bowled ball that is practically unplayable

JAFFAS ▸ jaffa

JAG n period of uncontrolled indulgence in an activity ▷ vb cut unevenly

JAGA n guard ▷ vb guard or watch

JAGAED ▸ jaga
JAGAING ▸ jaga
JAGAS ▸ jaga
JAGER same as ▸ jaeger
JAGERS ▸ jager
JAGG same as ▸ jag
JAGGARY same as ▸ jaggery
JAGGED ▸ jag
JAGGER n pedlar
JAGGERS ▸ jagger
JAGGERY n coarse brown sugar made in the East Indies from the sap of the date palm
JAGGIER ▸ jaggy
JAGGIES ▸ jaggy
JAGGING ▸ jag
JAGGS ▸ jagg
JAGGY adj prickly ▷ n jagged computer image
JAGHIR n Indian regional governance
JAGHIRE n Indian regional governance
JAGHIRS ▸ jaghir
JAGIR n Indian regional governance
JAGIRS ▸ jagir
JAGLESS ▸ jag
JAGRA n Hindu festival
JAGRAS ▸ jagra
JAGS ▸ jag
JAGUAR n large S American spotted cat
JAGUARS ▸ jaguar
JAI interj victory (to)
JAIL n prison ▷ vb send to prison
JAILED ▸ jail
JAILER n person in charge of a jail
JAILERS ▸ jailer
JAILING ▸ jail
JAILOR same as ▸ jailer
JAILORS ▸ jailor
JAILS ▸ jail
JAK ▸ jack
JAKE adj slang word meaning all right
JAKES n human excrement
JAKESES ▸ jakes
JAKS ▸ jack
JALABIB ▸ jilbab
JALAP n Mexican convolvulaceous plant
JALAPIC ▸ jalap
JALAPIN n purgative resin
JALAPS ▸ jalap
JALOP same as ▸ jalap
JALOPPY same as ▸ jalopy
JALOPS ▸ jalop
JALOPY n old car

JALOUSE vb suspect
JAM vb pack tightly into a place ▷ n fruit preserve or hold-up of traffic
JAMAAT n Islamic council
JAMAATS ▸ jamaat
JAMADAR n Indian army officer
JAMB n side post of a door or window frame ▷ vb climb up a crack in rock
JAMBART same as ▸ greave
JAMBE same as ▸ jamb
JAMBEAU another word for ▸ greave
JAMBED ▸ jamb
JAMBEE n light cane
JAMBEES ▸ jambee
JAMBER same as ▸ greave
JAMBERS ▸ jamber
JAMBES ▸ jambe
JAMBEUX ▸ jambeau
JAMBIER n greave
JAMBING ▸ jamb
JAMBIYA n curved dagger
JAMBO sentence substitute E African salutation
JAMBOK same as ▸ sjambok
JAMBOKS ▸ jambok
JAMBONE n type of play in the card game euchre
JAMBOOL same as ▸ jambolan
JAMBS ▸ jamb
JAMBU same as ▸ jambolan
JAMBUL same as ▸ jambolan
JAMBULS ▸ jambul
JAMBUS ▸ jambu
JAMDANI n patterned muslin
JAMES n jemmy
JAMESES ▸ james
JAMJAR n container for preserves
JAMJARS ▸ jamjar
JAMLIKE ▸ jam
JAMMED ▸ jam
JAMMER ▸ jam
JAMMERS ▸ jam
JAMMIER ▸ jammy
JAMMIES informal word for ▸ pyjamas
JAMMING ▸ jam
JAMMY adj lucky
JAMON n as in jamon serrano cured ham from Spain
JAMPAN n type of sedan chair used in India
JAMPANI same as ▸ jampanee
JAMPANS ▸ jampan

JAMPOT n container for preserves
JAMPOTS ▸ jampot
JAMS ▸ jam
JANE n girl or woman
JANES ▸ jane
JANGLE vb (cause to) make a harsh ringing noise ▷ n harsh ringing noise
JANGLED ▸ jangle
JANGLER ▸ jangle
JANGLES ▸ jangle
JANGLY adj making a jangling sound
JANITOR n caretaker of a school or other building
JANIZAR n > Turkish soldier
This is an old word for a Turkish soldier, combining J and Z. If your opponent plays it, remember that you can add not only an S to it to form the plural, but also a Y, making the variant spelling **janizary**.
JANKER n device for transporting logs
JANKERS ▸ janker
JANN n lesser jinn
JANNIES ▸ janny
JANNOCK same as ▸ jonnock
JANNS ▸ jann
JANNY n janitor
JANSKY n unit of flux density used predominantly in radio and infrared astronomy
JANSKYS ▸ jansky
JANTEE archaic version of ▸ jaunty
JANTIER ▸ janty
JANTIES ▸ janty
JANTY n petty officer ▷ adj (in archaic usage) jaunty
JAP vb splash
JAPAN n very hard varnish, usu black ▷ vb cover with this varnish ▷ adj relating to or varnished with japan
JAPANS ▸ japan
JAPE n joke or prank ▷ vb joke or jest (about)
JAPED ▸ jape
JAPER ▸ jape
JAPERS ▸ jape
JAPERY ▸ jape
JAPES ▸ jape
JAPING ▸ jape
JAPINGS ▸ jape
JAPPED ▸ jap
JAPPING ▸ jap

JAPS ▸ jap
JAR n wide-mouthed container, usu round and made of glass ▷ vb have a disturbing or unpleasant effect
JARFUL same as ▸ **jar**
JARFULS ▸ jarful
JARGON n specialized technical language of a particular subject ▷ vb use or speak in jargon
JARGONS ▸ jargon
JARGONY ▸ jargon
JARGOON same as ▸ **jargon**
JARHEAD n US Marine
JARINA n South American palm tree
JARINAS ▸ jarina
JARK n seal or pass
JARKMAN n forger of passes or licences
JARKMEN ▸ jarkman
JARKS ▸ jark
JARL n Scandinavian chieftain or noble
JARLDOM ▸ jarl
JARLS ▸ jarl
JAROOL n Indian tree
JAROOLS ▸ jarool
JARP vb strike or smash, esp to break the shell of (an egg) at Easter
JARPED ▸ jarp
JARPING ▸ jarp
JARPS ▸ jarp
JARRAH n Australian eucalyptus yielding valuable timber
JARRAHS ▸ jarrah
JARRED ▸ jar
JARRING ▸ jar
JARS ▸ jar
JARSFUL ▸ jarful
JARTA n heart
JARTAS ▸ jarta
JARUL same as ▸ **jarool**
JARULS ▸ jarul
JARVEY n hackney coachman
JARVEYS ▸ jarvey
JARVIE same as ▸ **jarvey**
JARVIES ▸ jarvie
JASEY n wig
JASEYS ▸ jasey
JASIES ▸ jasey
JASMIN same as ▸ **jasmine**
JASMINE n shrub with sweet-smelling yellow or white flowers
JASMINS ▸ jasmin
JASP another word for ▸ **jasper**

JASPE adj resembling jasper ▷ vb subtly striped woven fabric
JASPER n red, yellow, dark green, or brown variety of quartz
JASPERS ▸ jasper
JASPERY ▸ jasper
JASPES ▸ jaspe
JASPIS archaic word for ▸ **jasper**
JASPS ▸ jasp
JASS obsolete variant of ▸ **jazz**
JASSES ▸ jass
JASSID n leafhopper
JASSIDS ▸ jassid
JASY n wig
JATAKA n text describing the birth of Buddha
JATAKAS ▸ jataka
JATO n jet-assisted takeoff
JATOS ▸ jato
JAUK vb dawdle
JAUKED ▸ jauk
JAUKING ▸ jauk
JAUKS ▸ jauk
JAUNCE vb prance
JAUNCED ▸ jaunce
JAUNCES ▸ jaunce
JAUNSE same as ▸ **jaunce**
JAUNSED ▸ jaunse
JAUNSES ▸ jaunse
JAUNT n short journey for pleasure ▷ vb make such a journey
JAUNTED ▸ jaunt
JAUNTEE old spelling of ▸ **jaunty**
JAUNTIE old spelling of ▸ **jaunty**
JAUNTS ▸ jaunt
JAUNTY adj sprightly and cheerful ▷ n master-at-arms on a naval ship
JAUP same as ▸ **jarp**
JAUPED ▸ jaup
JAUPING ▸ jaup
JAUPS ▸ jaup
JAVA n coffee or a variety of it
JAVAS ▸ java
JAVEL adj as in **javel water** aqueous solution containing sodium hypochlorite and some sodium chloride, used as a bleach and disinfectant
JAVELIN n light spear thrown in sports competitions ▷ vb spear with a javelin
JAVELS ▸ javel
JAW n one of the bones in

which the teeth are set ▷ vb talk lengthily
JAWAN n (in India) a soldier
JAWANS ▸ jawan
JAWARI n variety of sorghum
JAWARIS ▸ jawari
JAWBONE n lower jaw of a person or animal ▷ vb try to persuade or bring pressure to bear (on) by virtue of one's high office or position, esp in urging compliance with official policy
JAWBOX n metal sink

> This Scots word for a sink combines the J and X, and of course its plural **jawboxes**, earning an extra 50 points, would be even better.

JAWED ▸ jaw
JAWFALL n depression
JAWHOLE n cesspit
JAWING ▸ jaw
JAWINGS ▸ jaw
JAWLESS ▸ jaw
JAWLIKE ▸ jaw
JAWLINE n outline of the jaw
JAWS ▸ jaw
JAY n bird with a pinkish body and blue-and-black wings
JAYBIRD ▸ jay
JAYCEE n member of a Junior Chamber of Commerce
JAYCEES ▸ jaycee
JAYGEE n lieutenant junior grade in the US army
JAYGEES ▸ jaygee
JAYS ▸ jay
JAYVEE n junior varsity sports team
JAYVEES ▸ jayvee
JAYWALK vb cross or walk in a street recklessly or illegally
JAZIES ▸ jazy
JAZY n wig

> This means a wig and is a wonderfully useful little word, combining J and Z for a high score.

JAZZ n kind of music with an exciting rhythm, usu involving improvisation ▷ vb play or dance to jazz music
JAZZBO n jazz musician or fan
JAZZBOS ▸ jazzbo

J

JAZZED ▸ jazz
JAZZER ▸ jazz
JAZZERS ▸ jazz
JAZZES ▸ jazz
JAZZIER ▸ jazzy
JAZZILY ▸ jazzy
JAZZING ▸ jazz
JAZZMAN ▸ jazz
JAZZMEN ▸ jazz
JAZZY adj flashy or showy
JEALOUS adj fearful of losing a partner or possession to a rival
JEAN n tough twill-weave cotton fabric used for hard-wearing trousers, overalls, etc
JEANED adj wearing jeans
JEANS pl n casual denim trousers
JEAT n jet
JEATS ▸ jeat
JEBEL n hill or mountain in an Arab country
JEBELS ▸ jebel
JEDI n person claiming to live according to a philosophy based on that of the fictional Jedi, from the StarWars films
JEDIS ▸ jedi
JEE same as ▸ gee
JEED ▸ jee
JEEING ▸ jee
JEEL vb make into jelly
JEELED ▸ jeel
JEELIE same as ▸ jeely
JEELIED ▸ jeely
JEELIES ▸ jeely
JEELING ▸ jeel
JEELS ▸ jeel
JEELY n jelly ▷ vb make into jelly
JEEP n small military four-wheel drive road vehicle ▷ vb travel in a jeep
JEEPED ▸ jeep
JEEPERS interj mild exclamation of surprise
JEEPING ▸ jeep
JEEPNEY n Filipino bus converted from a jeep
JEEPS ▸ jeep
JEER vb scoff or deride ▷ n cry of derision
JEERED ▸ jeer
JEERER ▸ jeer
JEERERS ▸ jeer
JEERING ▸ jeer
JEERS ▸ jeer
JEES ▸ jee
JEEZ interj expression of surprise or irritation

JEFE n (in Spanish-speaking countries) a military or political leader
JEFES ▸ jefe
JEFF vb downsize or close down (an organization)
JEFFED ▸ jeff
JEFFING ▸ jeff
JEFFS ▸ jeff
JEHAD same as ▸ jihad
JEHADI same as ▸ jihadi
JEHADIS ▸ jehadi
JEHADS ▸ jehad
JEHU n fast driver
JEHUS ▸ jehu
JEJUNA ▸ jejunum
JEJUNAL ▸ jejunum
JEJUNE adj simple or naive
JEJUNUM n part of the small intestine between the duodenum and the ileum
JELAB same as ▸ jellaba
JELABS ▸ jelab
JELL vb form into a jelly-like substance
JELLABA n loose robe with a hood, worn by some Arab men
JELLED ▸ jell
JELLIED ▸ jelly
JELLIES ▸ jelly
JELLIFY vb make into or become jelly
JELLING ▸ jell
JELLO n (in US English) fruit-flavoured clear dessert set with gelatine
JELLOS ▸ jello
JELLS ▸ jell
JELLY n fruit-flavoured clear dessert set with gelatine ▷ vb jellify
JEMADAR n native junior officer belonging to a locally raised regiment serving as mercenaries in India, esp with the British Army (until 1947)
JEMBE n hoe
JEMBES ▸ jembe
JEMIDAR same as ▸ jemadar
JEMIMA n boot with elastic sides
JEMIMAS ▸ jemima
JEMMIED ▸ jemmy
JEMMIER ▸ jemmy
JEMMIES ▸ jemmy
JEMMY n short steel crowbar used by burglars ▷ vb prise (something) open with a jemmy ▷ adj neat

JENNET n female donkey or ass
JENNETS ▸ jennet
JENNIES ▸ jenny
JENNY same as ▸ jennet
JEOFAIL n oversight in legal pleading
JEON n Korean pancake
JEOPARD vb put in jeopardy
JERBIL variant spelling of ▸ gerbil
JERBILS ▸ jerbil
JERBOA n small mouselike rodent with long hind legs
JERBOAS ▸ jerboa
JEREED same as ▸ jerid
JEREEDS ▸ jereed
JERID n wooden javelin used in Muslim countries in military displays on horseback
JERIDS ▸ jerid
JERK vb move or throw abruptly ▷ n sharp or abruptly stopped movement
JERKED ▸ jerk
JERKER ▸ jerk
JERKERS ▸ jerk
JERKIER ▸ jerky
JERKIES ▸ jerky
JERKILY ▸ jerky
JERKIN n sleeveless jacket
JERKING ▸ jerk
JERKINS ▸ jerkin
JERKS ▸ jerk
JERKY adj characterized by jerks ▷ n type of cured meat
JERQUE vb search for contraband

> To **jerque** is to search a vessel for stolen goods, and if you have the right additional letters to make **jerqued, jerquer, jerques** or **jerquing**, using all your letters, you would get a really great score.

JERQUED ▸ jerque
JERQUER ▸ jerque
JERQUES ▸ jerque
JERREED variant spelling of ▸ jerid
JERRID n blunt javelin
JERRIDS ▸ jerrid
JERRIES ▸ jerry
JERRY short for ▸ jeroboam
JERSEY n knitted jumper
JERSEYS ▸ jersey
JESS n short leather strap, one end of which is permanently attached to

the leg of a hawk or falcon while the other can be attached to a leash ▷ *vb* put jesses on (a hawk or falcon)

JESSAMY *n* fop

JESSANT *adj* emerging

JESSE *same as* ▸ **jess**

JESSED ▸ **jess**

JESSES ▸ **jess**

JESSIE *n* effeminate, weak, or cowardly boy or man

JESSIES ▸ **jessie**

JESSING ▸ **jess**

JEST *vb* joke ▷ *n* something done or said for amusement

JESTED ▸ **jest**

JESTEE *n* person about whom a joke is made

JESTEES ▸ **jestee**

JESTER *n* professional clown at court

JESTERS ▸ **jester**

JESTFUL ▸ **jest**

JESTING ▸ **jest**

JESTS ▸ **jest**

JESUS *n* French paper size

JET *n* aircraft driven by jet propulsion ▷ *vb* fly by jet aircraft

JETBEAD *n* ornamental shrub

JETE *n* step in which the dancer springs from one leg and lands on the other

JETES ▸ **jete**

JETFOIL *n* type of hydrofoil that is propelled by water jets

JETLAG *n* tiredness caused by crossing timezones in jet flight

JETLAGS ▸ **jetlag**

JETLIKE ▸ **jet**

JETON *n* gambling chip

JETONS ▸ **jeton**

JETPORT *n* airport for jet planes

JETS ▸ **jet**

JETSAM *n* goods thrown overboard to lighten a ship

JETSAMS ▸ **jetsam**

JETSOM *same as* ▸ **jetsam**

JETSOMS ▸ **jetsom**

JETSON *archaic form of* ▸ **jetsam**

JETSONS ▸ **jetson**

JETTED ▸ **jet**

JETTIED ▸ **jetty**

JETTIER ▸ **jetty**

JETTIES ▸ **jetty**

JETTING ▸ **jet**

JETTON *n* counter or token, esp a chip used in such gambling games as roulette

JETTONS ▸ **jetton**

JETTY *n* small pier ▷ *adj* of or resembling jet, esp in colour or polish ▷ *vb* equip with a cantilevered floor

JETWAY *n* tradename of a mobile elevated gangway connecting an aircraft to a departure gate, allowing passengers to board and disembark

JETWAYS ▸ **jetway**

JEU *n* game

> **Jeu** is the French word for game or play. The plural form, **jeux**, is a great little word, using both J and X, particularly if you can play it on a double- or triple-word square.

JEUNE *adj* young

JEUX ▸ **jeu**

JEWEL *n* precious or semiprecious stone ▷ *vb* fit or decorate with a jewel or jewels

JEWELED ▸ **jewel**

JEWELER *same as* ▸ **jeweller**

JEWELRY *same as* ▸ **jewellery**

JEWELS ▸ **jewel**

JEWFISH *n* freshwater catfish

JEWIE *n* jewfish

JEWIES ▸ **jewie**

JEZAIL *n* Afghan musket

> A **jezail** is a kind of Afghan musket, and if you have an S to go with it, earning the extra 50 points, so much the better.

JEZAILS ▸ **jezail**

JEZEBEL *n* shameless or scheming woman

JHALA *n* Indian musical style

JHALAS ▸ **jhala**

JHATKA *n* slaughter of animals for food according to Sikh law

JHATKAS ▸ **jhatka**

JIAO *n* Chinese currency unit

JIAOS ▸ **jiao**

JIB *same as* ▸ **jibe**

JIBB *same as* ▸ **jibe**

JIBBA *n* long, loose coat worn by Muslim men

JIBBAH *same as* ▸ **jubbah**

JIBBAHS ▸ **jibbah**

JIBBAS ▸ **jibba**

JIBBED ▸ **jibb**

JIBBER *same as* ▸ **gibber**

JIBBERS ▸ **jibber**

JIBBING ▸ **jibb**

JIBBONS *pl n* spring onions

JIBBOOM *n* spar forming an extension of the bowsprit

JIBBS ▸ **jibb**

JIBE *vb* taunt or jeer ▷ *n* insulting or taunting remark

JIBED ▸ **jibe**

JIBER ▸ **jibe**

JIBERS ▸ **jibe**

JIBES ▸ **jibe**

JIBING ▸ **jibe**

JIBS ▸ **jib**

JICAMA *n* pale brown turnip with crisp sweet flesh, originating in Mexico

JICAMAS ▸ **jicama**

JIFF *same as* ▸ **jiffy**

JIFFIES ▸ **jiffy**

JIFFS ▸ **jiff**

JIFFY *n* very short period of time

JIG *n* type of lively dance ▷ *vb* dance a jig

JIGAJIG *vb* engage in sexual intercourse

JIGAJOG *same as* ▸ **jigajig**

JIGGED ▸ **jig**

JIGGER *n* small whisky glass ▷ *vb* interfere or alter

JIGGERS ▸ **jigger**

JIGGIER ▸ **jiggy**

JIGGING ▸ **jig**

JIGGISH ▸ **jig**

JIGGLE *vb* move up and down with short jerky movements ▷ *n* short jerky motion

JIGGLED ▸ **jiggle**

JIGGLES ▸ **jiggle**

JIGGLY ▸ **jiggle**

JIGGY *adj* resembling a jig

JIGJIG *same as* ▸ **jigajig**

JIGJIGS ▸ **jigjig**

JIGLIKE ▸ **jig**

JIGOT *same as* ▸ **gigot**

JIGOTS ▸ **jigot**

JIGS ▸ **jig**

JIGSAW *n* picture cut into interlocking pieces, which the user tries to fit together again ▷ *vb* cut with a jigsaw

JIGSAWN ▸ **jigsaw**

JIGSAWS ▸ **jigsaw**

JIHAD *n* Islamic holy war

against unbelievers

JIHADI n person who takes part in a jihad

JIHADIS ▸ jihadi

JIHADS ▸ jihad

JILBAB n long robe worn by Muslim women

JILBABS ▸ jilbab

JILGIE n freshwater crayfish

JILGIES ▸ jilgie

JILL variant spelling of ▸ gill

JILLET n wanton woman

JILLETS ▸ jillet

JILLION n extremely large number or amount

JILLS ▸ jill

JILT vb leave or reject (one's lover) ▷ n woman who jilts a lover

JILTED ▸ jilt

JILTER ▸ jilt

JILTERS ▸ jilt

JILTING ▸ jilt

JILTS ▸ jilt

JIMINY interj expression of surprise

JIMJAM ▸ jimjams

JIMJAMS pl n state of nervous tension, excitement, or anxiety

JIMMIE same as ▸ jimmy

JIMMIED ▸ jimmy

JIMMIES ▸ jimmy

JIMMINY interj expression of surprise

JIMMY same as ▸ jemmy

JIMP adj handsome

JIMPER ▸ jimp

JIMPEST ▸ jimp

JIMPIER ▸ jimpy

JIMPLY adv neatly

JIMPSON ▸ jimson

JIMPY adj neat and tidy

JIMSON n as in **jimson weed** type of poisonous plant with white flowers and shiny fruits

JIN n Chinese unit of weight

JINGAL n swivel-mounted gun

JINGALL same as ▸ jingal

JINGALS ▸ jingal

JINGKO same as ▸ gingko

JINGLE n catchy verse or song used in a radio or television advert ▷ vb (cause to) make a gentle ringing sound

JINGLED ▸ jingle

JINGLER ▸ jingle

JINGLES ▸ jingle

JINGLET n sleigh-bell clapper

JINGLY ▸ jingle

JINGO n loud and bellicose patriot; chauvinism

JINGOES ▸ jingo

JINJILI n type of sesame

JINK vb move quickly or jerkily in order to dodge someone ▷ n jinking movement

JINKED ▸ jink

JINKER n vehicle for transporting timber, consisting of a tractor and two sets of wheels for supporting the logs ▷ vb carry or transport in a jinker

JINKERS ▸ jinker

JINKING ▸ jink

JINKS ▸ jink

JINN ▸ jinni

JINNE interj South African exclamation expressing surprise, admiration, shock, etc

JINNEE same as ▸ jinni

JINNI n spirit in Muslim mythology

JINNIS ▸ jinni

JINNS ▸ jinni

JINS ▸ jin

JINX n person or thing bringing bad luck ▷ vb be or put a jinx on

JINXED ▸ jinx

JINXES ▸ jinx

JINXING ▸ jinx

JIPYAPA same as > jipijapa

JIRBLE vb pour carelessly

JIRBLED ▸ jirble

JIRBLES ▸ jirble

JIRD n gerbil

JIRDS ▸ jird

JIRGA n Afghan council

JIRGAS ▸ jirga

JIRRE same as ▸ jinne

JITNEY n small bus that carries passengers for a low price, originally five cents

JITNEYS ▸ jitney

JITTER vb be anxious or nervous

JITTERS ▸ jitter

JITTERY adj nervous

JIVE n lively dance of the 1940s and '50s ▷ vb dance the jive

JIVEASS adj misleading or phoney

JIVED ▸ jive

JIVER ▸ jive

JIVERS ▸ jive

JIVES ▸ jive

JIVEY ▸ jive

JIVIER ▸ jive

JIVIEST ▸ jive

JIVING ▸ jive

JIVY ▸ jive

JIZ n wig

When you find yourself with J and Z but nothing else that looks promising, there may well be an I on the board around which you can form **jiz**, which means a wig.

JIZZ n term for the total combination of characteristics that serve to identify a particular species of bird or plant

JIZZES ▸ jizz

JNANA n type of yoga

JNANAS ▸ jnana

JO n Scots word for sweetheart

JOANNA n piano

JOANNAS ▸ joanna

JOANNES same as > johannes

JOB n occupation or paid employment ▷ vb work at casual jobs

JOBBED ▸ job

JOBBER n person who jobs

JOBBERS ▸ jobber

JOBBERY n practice of making private profit out of a public office

JOBBIE n piece of excrement

JOBBIES ▸ jobbie

JOBBING adj doing individual jobs for payment ▷ n act of seeking work

JOBE vb scold

JOBED ▸ jobe

JOBES ▸ jobe

JOBING ▸ jobe

JOBLESS pl n unemployed people ▷ adj unemployed

JOBNAME n title of position

JOBS ▸ job

JOCK n athlete

JOCKEY n person who rides horses in races, esp as a profession or for hire ▷ vb ride (a horse) in a race

JOCKEYS ▸ jockey

JOCKISH adj macho

JOCKO n chimpanzee

JOCKOS ▸ jocko

JOCKS ▸ jock

JOCO adj relaxed

JOCOSE adj playful or humorous

JOCULAR adj fond of joking

JOCUND adj merry or cheerful

JODEL same as ▸ **yodel**

JODELS ▸ **jodel**

JODHPUR n as in **jodhpur boots** ankle-length leather riding boots

JOE same as ▸ **jo**

JOES ▸ **joe**

JOEY n young kangaroo

JOEYS ▸ **joey**

JOG vb run at a gentle pace, esp for exercise ▷ n slow run

JOGGED ▸ **jog**

JOGGER n person who runs at a jog trot over some distance for exercise, usually regularly

JOGGERS ▸ **jogger**

JOGGING ▸ **jog**

JOGGLE vb shake or move jerkily ▷ n act of joggling

JOGGLED ▸ **joggle**

JOGGLER ▸ **joggle**

JOGGLES ▸ **joggle**

JOGS ▸ **jog**

JOGTROT n easy bouncy gait, esp of a horse, midway between a walk and a trot

JOHN n toilet

JOHNNIE same as ▸ **johnny**

JOHNNY n chap

JOHNS ▸ **john**

JOIN vb become a member (of) ▷ n place where two things are joined

JOINDER n act of joining, esp in legal contexts

JOINED ▸ **join**

JOINER n maker of finished woodwork

JOINERS ▸ **joiner**

JOINERY n joiner's work

JOINING ▸ **join**

JOINS ▸ **join**

JOINT adj shared by two or more ▷ n place where bones meet but can move ▷ vb divide meat into joints

JOINTED adj having a joint or joints

JOINTER n tool for pointing mortar joints, as in brickwork

JOINTLY ▸ **joint**

JOINTS ▸ **joint**

JOIST n horizontal beam that helps support a floor or ceiling ▷ vb construct (a floor, roof, etc) with joists

JOISTED ▸ **joist**

JOISTS ▸ **joist**

JOJOBA n shrub of SW North America whose seeds yield oil used in cosmetics

JOJOBAS ▸ **jojoba**

JOKE n thing said or done to cause laughter ▷ vb make jokes

JOKED ▸ **joke**

JOKER n person who jokes

JOKERS ▸ **joker**

JOKES ▸ **joke**

JOKEY adj intended as a joke

JOKIER ▸ **jokey**

JOKIEST ▸ **jokey**

JOKILY ▸ **joke**

JOKING ▸ **joke**

JOKOL Shetland word for ▸ **yes**

JOKY same as ▸ **jokey**

JOL n party ▷ vb have a good time

JOLE vb knock

JOLED ▸ **jole**

JOLES ▸ **jole**

JOLING ▸ **jole**

JOLL same as ▸ **jole**

JOLLED ▸ **jol**

JOLLER n person who has a good time

JOLLERS ▸ **joller**

JOLLEY same as ▸ **jolly**

JOLLEYS ▸ **jolley**

JOLLIED ▸ **jolly**

JOLLIER n joker

JOLLIES ▸ **jolly**

JOLLIFY vb be or cause to be jolly

JOLLILY ▸ **jolly**

JOLLING ▸ **jol**

JOLLITY n condition of being jolly

JOLLOP n cream or unguent

JOLLOPS ▸ **jollop**

JOLLS ▸ **joll**

JOLLY adj full of good humour ▷ adv extremely ▷ vb try to make or keep (someone) cheerful ▷ n festivity or celebration

JOLLYER ▸ **jolly**

JOLS ▸ **jol**

JOLT n unpleasant surprise or shock ▷ vb surprise or shock

JOLTED ▸ **jolt**

JOLTER ▸ **jolt**

JOLTERS ▸ **jolt**

JOLTIER ▸ **jolt**

JOLTILY ▸ **jolt**

JOLTING ▸ **jolt**

JOLTS ▸ **jolt**

JOLTY ▸ **jolt**

JOMO same as ▸ **zo**

JOMON n particular era in Japanese history

JOMOS ▸ **jomo**

JONES vb desire

JONESED ▸ **jones**

JONESES ▸ **jones**

JONG n friend, often used in direct address

JONGS ▸ **jong**

JONNOCK adj genuine ▷ adv honestly

JONQUIL n fragrant narcissus

JONTIES ▸ **jonty**

JONTY n petty officer

JOOK vb poke or puncture (the skin) ▷ n jab or the resulting wound

JOOKED ▸ **jook**

JOOKERY n mischief

JOOKING ▸ **jook**

JOOKS ▸ **jook**

JOR n movement in Indian music

JORAM same as ▸ **jorum**

JORAMS ▸ **joram**

JORDAN n chamber pot

JORDANS ▸ **jordan**

JORS ▸ **jor**

JORUM n large drinking bowl or vessel or its contents

JORUMS ▸ **jorum**

JOSEPH n woman's floor-length riding coat with a small cape, worn esp in the 18th century

JOSEPHS ▸ **joseph**

JOSH vb tease ▷ n teasing or bantering joke

JOSHED ▸ **josh**

JOSHER ▸ **josh**

JOSHERS ▸ **josh**

JOSHES ▸ **josh**

JOSHING ▸ **josh**

JOSKIN n bumpkin

JOSKINS ▸ **joskin**

JOSS n Chinese deity worshipped in the form of an idol

JOSSER n simpleton

JOSSERS ▸ **josser**

JOSSES ▸ **joss**

JOSTLE vb knock or push against ▷ n act of jostling

JOSTLED ▸ **jostle**

JOSTLER ▸ **jostle**

JOSTLES ▸ **jostle**

JOT vb write briefly ▷ n very small amount

JOTA n Spanish dance with castanets in fast triple time, usually to a guitar and voice accompaniment

JOTAS ▸ jota

JOTS ▸ jot

JOTTED ▸ jot

JOTTER n notebook

JOTTERS ▸ jotter

JOTTIER ▸ jotty

JOTTING ▸ jot

JOTTY ▸ jot

JOTUN n giant

JOTUNN same as ▸ jotun

JOTUNNS ▸ jotunn

JOTUNS ▸ jotun

JOUAL n nonstandard variety of Canadian French

JOUALS ▸ joual

JOUGS pl n iron ring, fastened by a chain to a wall, post, or tree, in which an offender was held by the neck

JOUK vb duck or dodge ▷ n sudden evasive movement

JOUKED ▸ jouk

JOUKERY same as ▸ jookery

JOUKING ▸ jouk

JOUKS ▸ jouk

JOULE n unit of work or energy ▷ vb knock

JOULED ▸ joule

JOULES ▸ joule

JOULING ▸ joule

JOUNCE vb shake or jolt or cause to shake or jolt ▷ n jolting movement

JOUNCED ▸ jounce

JOUNCES ▸ jounce

JOUNCY ▸ jounce

JOUR n day

JOURNAL n daily newspaper or magazine ▷ vb record in a journal

JOURNEY n act or process of travelling from one place to another ▷ vb travel

JOURNO n journalist

JOURNOS ▸ journo

JOURS ▸ jour

JOUST n combat with lances between two mounted knights ▷ vb fight on horseback using lances

JOUSTED ▸ joust

JOUSTER ▸ joust

JOUSTS ▸ joust

JOVIAL adj happy and cheerful

JOW vb ring (a bell)

JOWAR n variety of sorghum

JOWARI same as ▸ jowar

JOWARIS ▸ jowar

JOWARS ▸ jowar

JOWED ▸ jow

JOWING ▸ jow

JOWL n lower jaw ▷ vb knock

JOWLED ▸ jowl

JOWLER n dog with prominent jowls

JOWLERS ▸ jowler

JOWLIER ▸ jowl

JOWLING ▸ jowl

JOWLS ▸ jowl

JOWLY ▸ jowl

JOWS ▸ jow

JOY n feeling of great delight or pleasure ▷ vb feel joy

JOYANCE n joyous feeling or festivity

JOYED ▸ joy

JOYFUL adj feeling or bringing great joy

JOYING ▸ joy

JOYLESS adj feeling or bringing no joy

JOYOUS adj extremely happy and enthusiastic

JOYPAD n computer games console consisting of buttons on a pad

JOYPADS ▸ joypad

JOYPOP vb take addictive drugs occasionally without becoming addicted

JOYPOPS ▸ joypop

JOYRIDE n drive in a car one has stolen ▷ vb take such a ride

JOYRODE ▸ joyride

JOYS ▸ joy

JUBA n lively African-American dance developed in the southern US

JUBAS ▸ juba

JUBATE adj possessing a mane

JUBBAH n long loose outer garment with wide sleeves, worn by Muslim men and women, esp in India

JUBBAHS ▸ jubbah

JUBE n gallery or loft over the rood screen in a church or cathedral

JUBES ▸ jube

JUBHAH same as ▸ jubbah

JUBHAHS ▸ jubhah

JUBILE same as ▸ jubilee

JUBILEE n special anniversary, esp 25th or 50th

JUBILES ▸ jubile

JUCO n junior college in America

JUCOS ▸ juco

JUD n large block of coal

JUDAS n peephole or a very small window in a door

JUDASES ▸ judas

JUDDER vb vibrate violently ▷ n violent vibration

JUDDERS ▸ judder

JUDDERY adj shaky

JUDGE n public official who tries cases and passes sentence in a court of law ▷ vb act as a judge

JUDGED ▸ judge

JUDGER ▸ judge

JUDGERS ▸ judge

JUDGES ▸ judge

JUDGING ▸ judge

JUDIES ▸ judy

JUDO n sport in which two opponents try to throw each other to the ground

JUDOGI n white two-piece cotton costume worn during judo contests

JUDOGIS ▸ judogi

JUDOIST ▸ judo

JUDOKA n competitor or expert in judo

JUDOKAS ▸ judoka

JUDOS ▸ judo

JUDS ▸ jud

JUDY n woman

JUG n container for liquids, with a handle and small spout ▷ vb stew or boil (meat, esp hare) in an earthenware container

JUGA ▸ jugum

JUGAL adj of or relating to the zygomatic bone ▷ n cheekbone

JUGALS ▸ jugal

JUGATE adj (esp of compound leaves) having parts arranged in pairs

JUGFUL same as ▸ jug

JUGFULS ▸ jugful

JUGGED ▸ jug

JUGGING ▸ jug

JUGGINS n silly person

JUGGLE vb throw and catch (several objects) so that most are in the air at the same time ▷ n act of juggling

JUGGLED ▸ juggle

JUGGLER n person who juggles, esp a professional entertainer

JUGGLES ▸ juggle

JUGHEAD n clumsy person

JUGLET n small jug

JUGLETS ▸ juglet

JUGS ▸ jug
JUGSFUL ▸ jugful
JUGULA ▸ jugulum
JUGULAR *n* one of three large veins of the neck that return blood from the head to the heart
JUGULUM *n* lower throat
JUGUM *n* small process at the base of each forewing in certain insects by which the forewings are united to the hindwings during flight
JUGUMS ▸ jugum
JUICE *n* liquid part of vegetables, fruit, or meat ▷ *vb* extract juice from fruits and vegetables
JUICED ▸ juice
JUICER *n* kitchen appliance, usually operated by electricity, for extracting juice from fruits and vegetables
JUICERS ▸ juicer
JUICES ▸ juice
JUICIER ▸ juicy
JUICILY ▸ juicy
JUICING ▸ juice
JUICY *adj* full of juice
JUJITSU *n* Japanese art of wrestling and self-defence
JUJU *n* W African magic charm or fetish
JUJUBE *n* chewy sweet made of flavoured gelatine
JUJUBES ▸ jujube
JUJUISM ▸ juju
JUJUIST ▸ juju
JUJUS ▸ juju
JUJUTSU *same as* ▸ **jujitsu**
JUKE *vb* dance or play dance music
JUKEBOX *n* coin-operated machine on which records, CDs, or videos can be played
JUKED ▸ juke
JUKES ▸ juke
JUKING ▸ juke
JUKSKEI *n* game in which a peg is thrown over a fixed distance at a stake fixed into the ground
JUKU *n* Japanese martial art
JUKUS ▸ juku
JULEP *n* sweet alcoholic drink
JULEPS ▸ julep
JULIET *n* code word for the letter J
JULIETS ▸ juliet
JUMAR *n* clamp with a handle that can move freely up a rope on which it is clipped but locks when downward pressure is applied ▷ *vb* climb (up a fixed rope) using jumars
JUMARED ▸ jumar
JUMARS ▸ jumar
JUMART *n* mythical offspring of a bull and a mare
JUMARTS ▸ jumart
JUMBAL *same as* ▸ **jumble**
JUMBALS ▸ jumbal
JUMBIE *n* Caribbean ghost
JUMBIES ▸ jumbie
JUMBLE *n* confused heap or state ▷ *vb* mix in a disordered way
JUMBLED ▸ jumble
JUMBLER ▸ jumble
JUMBLES ▸ jumble
JUMBLY ▸ jumble
JUMBO *adj* very large ▷ *n* large jet airliner
JUMBOS ▸ jumbo
JUMBUCK *n* sheep
JUMBY *n* Caribbean ghost
JUMELLE *n* paired objects
JUMP *vb* leap or spring into the air using the leg muscles ▷ *n* act of jumping
JUMPED ▸ jump
JUMPER *n* sweater or pullover
JUMPERS ▸ jumper
JUMPIER ▸ jumpy
JUMPILY ▸ jumpy
JUMPING ▸ jump
JUMPOFF *n* extra round in a showjumping contest when two or more horses are equal first, the fastest round deciding the winner
JUMPS ▸ jump
JUMPY *adj* nervous
JUN *same as* ▸ **chon**
JUNCATE *same as* ▸ **junket**
JUNCO *n* North American bunting
JUNCOES ▸ junco
JUNCOS ▸ junco
JUNCUS *n* type of rush
JUNGLE *n* tropical forest of dense tangled vegetation
JUNGLED *adj* covered with jungle
JUNGLES ▸ jungle
JUNGLI *n* uncultured person
JUNGLIS ▸ jungli
JUNGLY ▸ jungle
JUNIOR *adj* of lower standing ▷ *n* junior person
JUNIORS ▸ junior

JUNIPER *n* evergreen shrub with purple berries
JUNK *n* discarded or useless objects ▷ *vb* discard as junk
JUNKED ▸ junk
JUNKER *n* (formerly) young German nobleman
JUNKERS ▸ junker
JUNKET *n* excursion by public officials paid for from public funds ▷ *vb* (of a public official, committee, etc) to go on a junket
JUNKETS ▸ junket
JUNKIE *n* drug addict
JUNKIER ▸ junky
JUNKIES ▸ junky
JUNKING ▸ junk
JUNKMAN *n* man who buys and sells discarded clothing, furniture, etc
JUNKMEN ▸ junkman
JUNKS ▸ junk
JUNKY *n* drug addict ▷ *adj* of low quality
JUNTA *n* group of military officers holding power in a country, esp after a coup
JUNTAS ▸ junta
JUNTO *same as* ▸ **junta**
JUNTOS ▸ junto
JUPATI *n* type of palm tree
JUPATIS ▸ jupati
JUPE *n* sleeveless jacket
JUPES ▸ jupe
JUPON *n* short close-fitting sleeveless padded garment, used in the late 14th and early 15th centuries with armour
JUPONS ▸ jupon
JURA ▸ jus
JURAL *adj* of or relating to law or to the administration of justice
JURALLY ▸ jural
JURANT *n* person taking oath
JURANTS ▸ jurant
JURAT *n* statement at the foot of an affidavit, naming the parties, stating when, where, and before whom it was sworn, etc
JURATS ▸ jurat
JURE *adv* by legal right
JUREL *n* edible fish found in warm American Atlantic waters
JURELS ▸ jurel
JURIDIC *same as* > **juridical**
JURIED ▸ jury
JURIES ▸ jury

J

JURIST _n_ expert in law

JURISTS ▸ jurist

JUROR _n_ member of a jury

JURORS ▸ juror

JURY _n_ group of people sworn to deliver a verdict in a court of law ▷ _adj_ makeshift ▷ _vb_ evaluate by jury

JURYING ▸ jury

JURYMAN _n_ member of a jury, esp a man

JURYMEN ▸ juryman

JUS _n_ right, power, or authority

JUSSIVE _n_ mood of verbs used for giving orders; imperative

JUST _adv_ very recently ▷ _adj_ fair or impartial in action or judgment ▷ _vb_ joust

JUSTED ▸ just

JUSTER ▸ just

JUSTERS ▸ just

JUSTEST ▸ just

JUSTICE _n_ quality of being just

JUSTIFY _vb_ prove right or reasonable

JUSTING ▸ joust

JUSTLE _less common word for_ ▸ jostle

JUSTLED ▸ justle

JUSTLES ▸ justle

JUSTLY ▸ just

JUSTS _same as_ ▸ joust

JUT _vb_ project or stick out ▷ _n_ something that juts out

JUTE _n_ plant fibre, used for rope, canvas, etc

JUTES ▸ jute

JUTS ▸ jut

JUTTED ▸ jut

JUTTIED ▸ jutty

JUTTIES ▸ jutty

JUTTING ▸ jut

JUTTY _vb_ project beyond

JUVE _same as_ > **juvenile**

JUVENAL _variant spelling (esp US) of_ > **juvenile**

JUVES ▸ juve

JUVIE _n_ juvenile detention centre

JUVIES ▸ juvie

JYMOLD _adj_ having a hinge

JYNX _n_ wryneck

> This unusual word, another name for the bird known as a wryneck, is unique in combining J, Y and X without using any vowels.

JYNXES ▸ jynx

Kk

Worth 5 points, **K** is a valuable tile to have in your rack. However, it's not the most useful tile for forming bonus words scoring that extra 50 points, so, as with the **J**, you will normally want to play it off fairly quickly. There are four two-letter words beginning with **K**: **ka**, **ki**, **ko** and **ky**. When it comes to three-letter words, remember **keg** (8 points), **ken** (7), **key** (10), **kex** (14), **kid** (8), **kin** (7), **kip** (9) and **kit** (7). Other three-letter words with **K** well worth remembering are **jak** (14) and **zek** (16).

KA *n* (in ancient Egypt) attendant spirit supposedly dwelling as a vital force in a man or statue ▷ *vb* (in archaic usage) help

KAAL *adj* naked

KAAMA *n* large African antelope with lyre-shaped horns

KAAMAS ▸ **kaama**

KAAS *n* Dutch cabinet or wardrobe

KAB *variant spelling of* ▸ **cab**

KABAB *same as* ▸ **kebab**

KABABS ▸ **kabab**

KABADDI *n* game in which players try to touch opposing players but avoid being captured by them

KABAKA *n* any of the former rulers of the Baganda people of S Uganda

KABAKAS ▸ **kabaka**

KABALA *same as* > **kabbalah**

KABALAS ▸ **kabala**

KABAR *archaic form of* ▸ **caber**

KABARS ▸ **kabar**

KABAYA *n* tunic

KABAYAS ▸ **kabaya**

KABBALA *same as* > **kabbalah**

KABELE *same as* ▸ **kebele**

KABELES ▸ **kabele**

KABIKI *n* fruit tree found in India

KABIKIS ▸ **kabiki**

KABOB *same as* ▸ **kebab**

KABOBS ▸ **kabob**

KABS ▸ **kab**

KABUKI *n* form of Japanese drama based on popular legends and characterized by elaborate costumes, stylized acting, and the use of male actors for all roles

KABUKIS ▸ **kabuki**

KACCHA *n* trousers worn traditionally by Sikhs

KACCHAS ▸ **kaccha**

KACHA *adj* crude

KACHCHA *same as* ▸ **kacha**

KACHERI *same as* > **kachahri**

KACHINA *n* any of the supernatural beings believed by the Hopi Indians to be the ancestors of living humans

KADDISH *n* ancient Jewish liturgical prayer

KADE *same as* ▸ **ked**

KADES ▸ **kade**

KADI *variant spelling of* ▸ **cadi**

KADIS ▸ **kadi**

KAE *n* dialect word for jackdaw or jay ▷ *vb* (in archaic usage) help

KAED ▸ **kae**

KAEING ▸ **kae**

KAES ▸ **kae**

KAF *n* letter of the Hebrew alphabet

KAFFIR *n* Southern African variety of sorghum, cultivated in dry regions for its grain and as fodder

KAFFIRS ▸ **kaffir**

KAFILA *n* caravan

KAFILAS ▸ **kafila**

KAFIR *same as* ▸ **kaffir**

KAFIRS ▸ **kafir**

KAFS ▸ **kaf**

KAFTAN *n* long loose Eastern garment

KAFTANS ▸ **kaftan**

KAGO *n* Japanese sedan chair

KAGOOL *variant spelling of* ▸ **cagoule**

KAGOOLS ▸ **kagool**

KAGOS ▸ **kago**

KAGOUL *variant spelling of* ▸ **cagoule**

KAGOULE *same as* ▸ **kagoul**

KAGOULS ▸ **kagoul**

KAGU *n* crested nocturnal bird of New Caledonia with a red bill and greyish plumage

KAGUS ▸ **kagu**

KAHAL *n* Jewish community

KAHALS ▸ **kahal**

KAHAWAI *n* food and game fish of New Zealand

KAHUNA *n* Hawaiian priest, shaman, or expert

KAHUNAS ▸ **kahuna**

KAI *n* food

KAIAK *same as* ▸ **kayak**

KAIAKED ▸ **kaiak**

KAIAKS ▸ **kaiak**

KAID *n* North African chieftan or leader

KAIDS ▸ **kaid**

KAIE *archaic form of* ▸ **key**

KAIES ▸ **kaie**

KAIF *same as* ▸ **kif**

KAIFS ▸ **kaif**

KAIK *same as* ▸ **kainga**

KAIKA *same as* ▸ **kainga**

KAIKAI *n* food

KAIKAIS ▸ **kaikai**

KAIKAS ▸ **kaika**

KAIKS ▸ **kaik**

KAIL *same as* ▸ **kale**

KAILS ▸ **kail**

KAIM same as ▸ **kame**
KAIMS ▸ **kaim**
KAIN variant spelling of ▸ **cain**
KAING ▸ **ka**
KAINGA n (in New Zealand) a Maori village or small settlement
KAINGAS ▸ **kainga**
KAINIT same as ▸ **kainite**
KAINITE n white mineral consisting of potassium chloride and magnesium sulphate: a fertilizer and source of potassium salts
KAINITS ▸ **kainit**
KAINS ▸ **kain**
KAIS ▸ **kai**
KAISER n German or Austro-Hungarian emperor
KAISERS ▸ **kaiser**
KAIZEN n philosophy of continuous improvement of working practices that underlies total quality management and just-in-time business techniques
KAIZENS ▸ **kaizen**
KAJAWAH n type of seat or panier used on a camel
KAJEPUT n variety of Australian melaleuca
KAKA n parrot of New Zealand
KAKAPO n ground-living nocturnal New Zealand parrot that resembles an owl
KAKAPOS ▸ **kakapo**
KAKAS ▸ **kaka**
KAKI n Asian persimmon tree
KAKIS ▸ **kaki**
KAKODYL variant spelling of ▸ **cacodyl**
KAKURO n crossword-style puzzle with numbers
KAKUROS ▸ **kakuro**
KALAM n discussion and debate, especially relating to Islamic theology
KALAMS ▸ **kalam**
KALE n cabbage with crinkled leaves
KALENDS same as ▸ **calends**
KALES ▸ **kale**
KALI another name for > **saltwort**
KALIAN another name for ▸ **hookah**
KALIANS ▸ **kalian**

KALIF variant spelling of ▸ **caliph**
KALIFS ▸ **kalif**
KALIMBA n musical instrument
KALIPH variant spelling of ▸ **caliph**
KALIPHS ▸ **kaliph**
KALIS ▸ **kali**
KALIUM n Latin for potassium
KALIUMS ▸ **kalium**
KALMIA n N American evergreen ericaceous shrub with showy clusters of white or pink flowers
KALMIAS ▸ **kalmia**
KALONG n fruit bat
KALONGS ▸ **kalong**
KALOOKI n version of contract rummy popular in Jamaica
KALPA n (in Hindu cosmology) period in which the universe experiences a cycle of creation and destruction
KALPAC same as ▸ **calpac**
KALPACS ▸ **kalpac**
KALPAK variant spelling of ▸ **calpac**
KALPAKS ▸ **kalpak**
KALPAS ▸ **kalpa**
KALPIS n Greek water jar
KALUKI ▸ **kalooki**
KALUKIS ▸ **kaluki**
KAM Shakespearean word for ▸ **crooked**
KAMA n large African antelope with lyre-shaped horns
KAMAHI n tall New Zealand hardwood tree with pinkish flowers
KAMAHIS ▸ **kamahi**
KAMALA n East Indian tree
KAMALAS ▸ **kamala**
KAMAS ▸ **kama**
KAME n irregular mound or ridge of gravel, sand, etc, deposited by water derived from melting glaciers
KAMEES ▸ **kameez**
KAMEEZ n long tunic worn in the Indian subcontinent, often with shalwar
KAMELA same as ▸ **kamala**
KAMELAS ▸ **kamela**
KAMERAD interj shout of surrender ▷ vb surrender
KAMES ▸ **kame**
KAMI n divine being or spiritual force in Shinto

KAMICHI n South American bird
KAMIK n traditional Inuit boot made of caribou hide or sealskin
KAMIKS ▸ **kamik**
KAMILA same as ▸ **kamala**
KAMILAS ▸ **kamila**
KAMIS same as ▸ **kameez**
KAMISES ▸ **kamis**
KAMME same as ▸ **kam**
KAMPONG n (in Malaysia) village
KAMSEEN same as ▸ **khamsin**
KAMSIN same as ▸ **kamseen**
KAMSINS ▸ **kamsin**
KANA n Japanese syllabary, which consists of two written varieties
KANAE n grey mullet
KANAES ▸ **kanae**
KANAKA n Australian word for any native of the South Pacific islands, esp (formerly) one abducted to work in Australia
KANAKAS ▸ **kanaka**
KANAS ▸ **kana**
KANBAN n just-in-time manufacturing process in which the movements of materials through a process are recorded on specially designed cards
KANBANS ▸ **kanban**
KANDIES ▸ **kandy**
KANDY same as ▸ **candie**
KANE n Hawaiian man or boy
KANEH n 6-cubit Hebrew measure
KANEHS ▸ **kaneh**
KANES ▸ **kane**
KANG n Chinese heatable platform used for sleeping and sitting on
KANGA n piece of gaily decorated thin cotton cloth used as a garment by women in E Africa
KANGAS ▸ **kanga**
KANGHA n comb traditionally worn by Sikhs as a symbol of their religious and cultural loyalty
KANGHAS ▸ **kangha**
KANGS ▸ **kang**
KANJI n Japanese writing system using characters mainly derived from Chinese ideograms

KANJIS ▸ kanji
KANS n Indian wild sugar cane
KANSES ▸ kans
KANT archaic spelling of ▸ cant
KANTAR n unit of weight used in E Mediterranean countries, equivalent to 100 pounds or 45 kilograms but varying from place to place
KANTARS ▸ kantar
KANTED ▸ kant
KANTELA same as ▸ kantele
KANTELE n Finnish stringed instrument
KANTEN same as ▸ agar
KANTENS ▸ kanten
KANTHA n Bengali embroidered quilt
KANTHAS ▸ kantha
KANTING ▸ kant
KANTS ▸ kant
KANUKA n New Zealand myrtaceous tree
KANUKAS ▸ kanuka
KANZU n long garment, usually white, with long sleeves, worn by E African men
KANZUS ▸ kanzu
KAOLIN n fine white clay used to make porcelain and in some medicines
KAOLINE same as ▸ kaolin
KAOLINS ▸ kaolin
KAON n meson that has a positive or negative charge and a rest mass of about 966 electron masses, or no charge and a rest mass of 974 electron masses
KAONIC ▸ kaon
KAONS ▸ kaon
KAPA n Hawaiian cloth made from beaten mulberry bark
KAPAS ▸ kapa
KAPH n 11th letter of the Hebrew alphabet
KAPHS ▸ kaph
KAPOK n fluffy fibre from a tropical tree, used to stuff cushions etc
KAPOKS ▸ kapok
KAPPA n tenth letter in the Greek alphabet
KAPPAS ▸ kappa
KAPUKA same as ▸ broadleaf
KAPUKAS ▸ kapuka
KAPUT adj ruined or broken

KAPUTT same as ▸ kaput
KARA n steel bangle traditionally worn by Sikhs as a symbol of their religious and cultural loyalty
KARAISM n beliefs and doctrines of a Jewish sect rejecting Rabbinism
KARAIT same as ▸ krait
KARAITS ▸ krait
KARAKA n New Zealand tree
KARAKAS ▸ karaka
KARAKIA n prayer
KARAKUL n sheep of central Asia, the lambs of which have soft curled dark hair
KARAMU n small New Zealand tree with glossy leaves and orange fruit
KARAMUS ▸ karamu
KARANGA n call or chant of welcome, sung by a female elder ▷ vb perform a karanga
KARAOKE n form of entertainment in which people sing over a prerecorded backing tape
KARAS ▸ kara
KARAT n measure of the proportion of gold in an alloy, expressed as the number of parts of gold in 24 parts of the alloy
KARATE n Japanese system of unarmed combat using blows with the feet, hands, elbows, and legs
KARATES ▸ karate
KARATS ▸ karat
KARENGO n edible type of Pacific seaweed
KARITE n shea tree
KARITES ▸ karite
KARK variant spelling of ▸ cark
KARKED ▸ kark
KARKING ▸ kark
KARKS ▸ kark
KARMA n person's actions affecting his or her fate in the next reincarnation
KARMAS ▸ karma
KARMIC ▸ karma
KARN old word for ▸ cairn
KARNS ▸ karn
KARO n small New Zealand tree or shrub with sweet-smelling brown flowers

KAROO n high arid plateau
KAROOS ▸ karoo
KARORO n large seagull with black feathers on its back
KAROROS ▸ karoro
KAROS ▸ karo
KAROSHI n (in Japan) death caused by overwork
KAROSS n blanket made of animal skins sewn together
KARRI n Australian eucalypt
KARRIS ▸ karri
KARROO same as ▸ karoo
KARROOS ▸ karroo
KARSEY variant spelling of ▸ khazi
KARSEYS ▸ karsey
KARSIES ▸ karsy
KARST n denoting the characteristic scenery of a limestone region, including underground streams, gorges, etc
KARSTIC ▸ karst
KARSTS ▸ karst
KARSY variant spelling of ▸ khazi
KART n light low-framed vehicle with small wheels and engine used for recreational racing
KARTER ▸ kart
KARTERS ▸ kart
KARTING ▸ kart
KARTS ▸ kart
KARYON n nucleus of a cell
KARYONS ▸ karyon
KARZIES ▸ karzy
KARZY variant spelling of ▸ khazi
KAS ▸ ka
KASBAH n citadel of any of various North African cities
KASBAHS ▸ kasbah
KASHA n dish originating in Eastern Europe, consisting of boiled or baked buckwheat
KASHAS ▸ kasha
KASHER vb make fit for use
KASHERS ▸ kasher
KASHMIR variant spelling of ▸ cashmere
KASHRUS same as ▸ kashruth
KASHRUT same as ▸ kashruth
KASME interj (in Indian English) I swear
KAT same as ▸ khat
KATA n exercise consisting of a sequence of the specific

K

K

movements of a martial art, used in training and designed to show skill in technique

KATAL n SI unit of catalytic activity

KATALS ▸ **katal**

KATANA n Japanese samurai sword

KATANAS ▸ **katana**

KATAS ▸ **kata**

KATCINA variant spelling of ▸ **kachina**

KATHAK n form of N Indian classical dancing that tells a story

KATHAKS ▸ **kathak**

KATHODE variant spelling of ▸ **cathode**

KATI variant spelling of ▸ **catty**

KATION variant spelling of ▸ **cation**

KATIONS ▸ **kation**

KATIPO n small poisonous New Zealand spider

KATIPOS ▸ **katipo**

KATIS ▸ **kati**

KATORGA n labour camp in Imperial Russia or the Soviet Union

KATS ▸ **kat**

KATSURA n Asian tree

KATTI variant spelling of ▸ **catty**

KATTIS ▸ **katti**

KATYDID n large green grasshopper of N America

KAUGH same as ▸ **kiaugh**

KAUGHS ▸ **kaugh**

KAUPAPA n strategy, policy, or cause

KAURI n large NZ conifer that yields valuable timber and resin

KAURIES ▸ **kauri**

KAURIS ▸ **kauri**

KAURU n edible stem of the cabbage tree

KAURUS ▸ **kauru**

KAURY variant spelling of ▸ **kauri**

KAVA n Polynesian shrub

KAVAL n type of flute played in the Balkans

KAVALS ▸ **kaval**

KAVAS ▸ **kava**

KAVASS n armed Turkish constable

KAW variant spelling of ▸ **caw**

KAWA n protocol or etiquette, particularly in a Maori tribal meeting place

KAWAS ▸ **kawa**

KAWAU n New Zealand name for black shag

KAWAUS ▸ **kawau**

KAWED ▸ **kaw**

KAWING ▸ **kaw**

KAWS ▸ **kaw**

KAY n name of the letter K

KAYAK n Inuit canoe made of sealskins stretched over a frame ▷ vb travel by kayak

KAYAKED ▸ **kayak**

KAYAKER ▸ **kayak**

KAYAKS ▸ **kayak**

KAYLE n one of a set of ninepins

KAYLES pl n ninepins

KAYLIED adj (in British slang) intoxicated or drunk

KAYO another term for > **knockout**

KAYOED ▸ **kayo**

KAYOES ▸ **kayo**

KAYOING ▸ **kayo**

KAYOS ▸ **kayo**

KAYS ▸ **kay**

KAZI variant spelling of ▸ **khazi**

KAZIS ▸ **kazi**

KAZOO n cigar-shaped metal musical instrument that produces a buzzing sound when the player hums into it

KAZOOS ▸ **kazoo**

KBAR n kilobar

KBARS ▸ **kbar**

KEA n large brownish-green parrot of NZ

KEAS ▸ **kea**

KEASAR archaic variant of ▸ **kaiser**

KEASARS ▸ **keasar**

KEAVIE n archaic or dialect word for a type of crab

KEAVIES ▸ **keavie**

KEB vb Scots word meaning miscarry or reject a lamb

KEBAB n dish of small pieces of meat grilled on skewers ▷ vb skewer

KEBABS ▸ **kebab**

KEBAR n Scots word for beam or rafter

KEBARS ▸ **kebar**

KEBBED ▸ **keb**

KEBBIE n Scots word for shepherd's crook

KEBBIES ▸ **kebbie**

KEBBING ▸ **keb**

KEBBOCK n Scots word for a cheese

KEBBUCK same as

▸ **kebbock**

KEBELE n Ethiopian local council

KEBELES ▸ **kebele**

KEBLAH same as ▸ **kiblah**

KEBLAHS ▸ **keblah**

KEBOB same as ▸ **kebab**

KEBOBS ▸ **kebob**

KEBS ▸ **keb**

KECK vb retch or feel nausea

KECKED ▸ **keck**

KECKING ▸ **keck**

KECKLE Scots variant of ▸ **cackle**

KECKLED ▸ **keckle**

KECKLES ▸ **keckle**

KECKS pl n trousers

KECKSES ▸ **kecks**

KECKSY n dialect word meaning hollow plant stalk

KED n as in **sheep ked** sheep tick

KEDDAH same as ▸ **kheda**

KEDDAHS ▸ **keddah**

KEDGE vb move (a ship) along by hauling in on the cable of a light anchor ▷ n light anchor used for kedging

KEDGED ▸ **kedge**

KEDGER n small anchor

KEDGERS ▸ **kedger**

KEDGES ▸ **kedge**

KEDGIER ▸ **kedgy**

KEDGING ▸ **kedge**

KEDGY adj dialect word for happy or lively

KEDS ▸ **ked**

KEECH n old word for lump of fat

KEECHES ▸ **keech**

KEEF same as ▸ **kif**

KEEFS ▸ **keef**

KEEK Scots word for ▸ **peep**

KEEKED ▸ **keek**

KEEKER ▸ **keek**

KEEKERS ▸ **keek**

KEEKING ▸ **keek**

KEEKS ▸ **keek**

KEEL n main lengthways timber or steel support along the base of a ship ▷ vb mark with this stain

KEELAGE n fee charged by certain ports to allow a ship to dock

KEELED ▸ **keel**

KEELER n bargeman

KEELERS ▸ **keeler**

KEELIE n kestrel

KEELIES ▸ **keelie**

KEELING ▸ **keel**

KEELMAN n bargeman

KEELMEN ▸ keelman
KEELS ▸ keel
KEELSON n lengthways beam fastened to the keel of a ship for strength
KEEMA n (in Indian cookery) minced meat
KEEMAS ▸ keema
KEEN adj eager or enthusiastic ▷ vb wail over the dead ▷ n lament for the dead
KEENED ▸ keen
KEENER ▸ keen
KEENERS ▸ keen
KEENEST ▸ keen
KEENING ▸ keen
KEENLY ▸ keen
KEENO same as ▸ keno
KEENOS ▸ keeno
KEENS ▸ keen
KEEP vb have or retain possession of ▷ n cost of food and everyday expenses
KEEPER n person who looks after animals in a zoo
KEEPERS ▸ keeper
KEEPING ▸ keep
KEEPNET n cylindrical net strung on wire hoops and sealed at one end, suspended in water by anglers to keep alive the fish they have caught
KEEPS ▸ keep
KEESTER same as ▸ keister
KEET short for ▸ parakeet
KEETS ▸ keet
KEEVE n tub or vat
KEEVES ▸ keeve
KEF same as ▸ kif
KEFFEL dialect word for ▸ horse
KEFFELS ▸ keffel
KEFIR n effervescent drink of the Caucasus made from fermented milk
KEFIRS ▸ kefir
KEFS ▸ kef
KEG n small metal beer barrel ▷ vb put in kegs
KEGELER same as ▸ kegler
KEGGED ▸ keg
KEGGER ▸ keg
KEGGERS ▸ keg
KEGGING ▸ keg
KEGLER n participant in a game of tenpin bowling
KEGLERS ▸ kegler
KEGLING n bowling
KEGS ▸ keg
KEHUA n ghost or spirit
KEHUAS ▸ kehua

KEIGHT ▸ ketch
KEIR same as ▸ kier
KEIREN n type of track cycling event
KEIRENS ▸ keiren
KEIRIN n cycling race originating in Japan
KEIRINS ▸ keirin
KEIRS ▸ keir
KEISTER n rump
KEITLOA n southern African black two-horned rhinoceros
KEKENO n New Zealand fur seal
KEKENOS ▸ kekeno
KEKS same as ▸ kecks
KEKSYE same as ▸ kex
KEKSYES ▸ keksye
KELEP n large ant found in Central and South America
KELEPS ▸ kelep
KELIM same as ▸ kilim
KELIMS ▸ kelim
KELL dialect word for ▸ hairnet
KELLAUT same as ▸ khilat
KELLIES ▸ kelly
KELLS ▸ kell
KELLY n part of a drill system
KELOID n hard smooth pinkish raised growth of scar tissue at the site of an injury, tending to occur more frequently in dark-skinned races
KELOIDS ▸ keloid
KELP n large brown seaweed ▷ vb burn seaweed to make a type of ash used as a source for iodine and potash
KELPED ▸ kelp
KELPER n Falkland Islander
KELPERS ▸ kelper
KELPIE n Australian sheepdog with a smooth coat and upright ears
KELPIES ▸ kelpy
KELPING ▸ kelp
KELPS ▸ kelp
KELPY same as ▸ kelpie
KELSON same as ▸ keelson
KELSONS ▸ kelson
KELT n salmon that has recently spawned
KELTER same as ▸ kilter
KELTERS ▸ kelter
KELTIE variant spelling of ▸ kelty
KELTIES ▸ kelty
KELTS ▸ kelt

KELTY n old Scots word for an extra drink imposed on someone not thought to be drinking enough
KELVIN n SI unit of temperature
KELVINS ▸ kelvin
KEMB old word for ▸ comb
KEMBED ▸ kemb
KEMBING ▸ kemb
KEMBLA n small change
KEMBLAS ▸ kembla
KEMBO same as ▸ kimbo
KEMBOED ▸ kembo
KEMBOS ▸ kembo
KEMBS ▸ kemb
KEMP n coarse hair or strand of hair, esp one in a fleece that resists dyeing ▷ vb dialect word meaning to compete or try to come first
KEMPED ▸ kemp
KEMPER ▸ kemp
KEMPERS ▸ kemp
KEMPIER ▸ kempy
KEMPING ▸ kemp
KEMPLE n variable Scottish measure for hay or straw
KEMPLES ▸ kemple
KEMPS ▸ kemp
KEMPT adj (of hair) tidy
KEMPY ▸ kemp
KEN vb know ▷ n range of knowledge or perception
KENAF another name for ▸ ambary
KENAFS ▸ kenaf
KENCH n bin for salting and preserving fish
KENCHES ▸ kench
KENDO n Japanese sport of fencing using wooden staves
KENDOS ▸ kendo
KENNED ▸ ken
KENNEL n hutlike shelter for a dog ▷ vb put or go into a kennel
KENNELS ▸ kennel
KENNER ▸ ken
KENNERS ▸ ken
KENNET n old word for a small hunting dog
KENNETS ▸ kennet
KENNETT vb spoil or destroy ruthlessly
KENNING ▸ ken
KENO n game of chance similar to bingo
KENOS ▸ keno
KENOSES ▸ kenosis
KENOSIS n Christ's

voluntary renunciation of certain divine attributes, in order to identify himself with mankind

KENOTIC ▸ **kenosis**

KENS ▸ **ken**

KENT *dialect word for* ▸ **punt**

KENTE *n* brightly coloured handwoven cloth of Ghana, usually with some gold thread

KENTED ▸ **kent**

KENTES ▸ **kente**

KENTIA *n* plant name formerly used to include palms now allotted to several different genera

KENTIAS ▸ **kentia**

KENTING ▸ **kent**

KENTS ▸ **kent**

KEP *vb* catch

KEPHIR *same as* ▸ **kefir**

KEPHIRS ▸ **kephir**

KEPI *n* French military cap with a flat top and a horizontal peak

KEPIS ▸ **kepi**

KEPPED ▸ **kep**

KEPPEN ▸ **kep**

KEPPING ▸ **kep**

KEPPIT ▸ **kep**

KEPS ▸ **kep**

KEPT ▸ **keep**

KERAMIC *rare variant of* ▸ **ceramic**

KERATIN *n* fibrous protein found in the hair and nails

KERB *n* edging to a footpath ▷ *vb* provide with or enclose with a kerb

KERBAYA *n* blouse worn by Malay women

KERBED ▸ **kerb**

KERBING *n* material used for a kerb

KERBS ▸ **kerb**

KERCHOO *interj* atishoo

KEREL *n* chap or fellow

KERELS ▸ **kerel**

KERERU *n* New Zealand pigeon

KERERUS ▸ **kereru**

KERF *n* cut made by a saw, an axe, etc ▷ *vb* cut

KERFED ▸ **kerf**

KERFING ▸ **kerf**

KERFS ▸ **kerf**

KERKIER ▸ **kerky**

KERKY *adj* stupid

KERMA *n* quotient of the sum of the initial kinetic energies of all the charged particles liberated by

indirectly ionizing radiation in a volume element of a material divided by the mass of the volume element

KERMAS ▸ **kerma**

KERMES *n* dried bodies of female scale insects, used as a red dyestuff

KERMESS *same as* ▸ **kermis**

KERMIS *n* (formerly, esp in Holland and Northern Germany) annual country festival or carnival

KERN *n* part of the character on a piece of printer's type that projects beyond the body ▷ *vb* furnish (a typeface) with a kern

KERNE *same as* ▸ **kern**

KERNED ▸ **kerne**

KERNEL *n* seed of a nut, cereal, or fruit stone ▷ *vb* form kernels

KERNELS ▸ **kernel**

KERNES ▸ **kerne**

KERNING *n* adjustment of space between the letters of words to improve the appearance of text matter

KERNISH *adj* of, belonging to, or resembling an armed foot soldier or peasant

KERNITE *n* light soft colourless or white mineral consisting of a hydrated sodium borate in monoclinic crystalline form: an important source of borax and other boron compounds

KERNS ▸ **kern**

KERO *short for* ▸ **kerosene**

KEROGEN *n* solid organic material found in some rocks, such as oil shales, that produces hydrocarbons similar to petroleum when heated

KEROS ▸ **kero**

KERRIA *n* type of shrub with yellow flowers

KERRIAS ▸ **kerria**

KERRIES ▸ **kerry**

KERRY *n* breed of dairy cattle

KERSEY *n* smooth woollen cloth used for overcoats, etc

KERSEYS ▸ **kersey**

KERVE *dialect word for* ▸ **carve**

KERVED ▸ **kerve**

KERVES ▸ **kerve**

KERVING ▸ **kerve**

KERYGMA *n* essential news of Jesus, as preached by the early Christians to elicit faith rather than to educate or instruct

KESAR *old variant of* ▸ **kaiser**

KESARS ▸ **kesar**

KESH *n* beard and uncut hair, covered by the turban, traditionally worn by Sikhs as a symbol of their religious and cultural loyalty

KESHES ▸ **kesh**

KEST *old form of* ▸ **cast**

KESTING ▸ **kest**

KESTREL *n* type of small falcon

KESTS ▸ **kest**

KET *n* dialect word for carrion

KETA *n* type of salmon

KETAS ▸ **keta**

KETCH *n* two-masted sailing vessel ▷ *vb* (in archaic usage) catch

KETCHES ▸ **ketch**

KETCHUP *n* thick cold sauce, usu made of tomatoes

KETE *n* basket woven from flax

KETENE *n* colourless irritating toxic gas used as an acetylating agent in organic synthesis

KETENES ▸ **ketene**

KETES ▸ **kete**

KETMIA *n as in* **bladder ketmia** plant with pale yellow flowers and a bladder-like calyx

KETMIAS ▸ **ketmia**

KETO *adj as in* **keto form** form of tautomeric compounds when they are ketones rather than enol

KETOL *n* nitrogenous substance

KETOLS ▸ **ketol**

KETONE *n* type of organic solvent

KETONES ▸ **ketone**

KETONIC ▸ **ketone**

KETOSE *n* any monosaccharide that contains a ketone group

KETOSES ▸ **ketosis**

KETOSIS *n* high concentration of ketone

bodies in the blood

KETOTIC ▸ ketosis

KETS ▸ ket

KETTLE n container with a spout and handle used for boiling water

KETTLES ▸ kettle

KETUBAH n contract that states the obligations within Jewish marriage

KETUBOT ▸ ketubah

KEVEL n strong bitt or bollard for securing heavy hawsers

KEVELS ▸ kevel

KEVIL old variant of ▸ kevel

KEVILS ▸ kevil

KEWL nonstandard variant spelling of ▸ cool

KEWLER ▸ kewl

KEWLEST ▸ kewl

KEWPIE n type of brightly coloured doll, commonly given as a prize at a carnival

KEWPIES ▸ kewpie

KEX n any of several large hollow-stemmed umbelliferous plants, such as cow parsnip and chervil

This is another of the great high-scoring three-letter words that use X.

KEXES ▸ kex

KEY n device for operating a lock by moving a bolt ▷ adj of great importance ▷ vb enter (text) using a keyboard

KEYCARD n card with an electronic strip or code on it that allows it to open a corresponding keycard-operated door

KEYED ▸ key

KEYHOLE n opening for inserting a key into a lock

KEYING ▸ key

KEYINGS ▸ key

KEYLESS ▸ key

KEYLINE n outline image of something on artwork or plans to show where it is to be placed

KEYNOTE adj central or dominating ▷ n dominant idea of a speech etc ▷ vb deliver a keynote address to (a political convention, etc)

KEYPAD n small panel with a set of buttons for operating a Teletext system, electronic calculator, etc

KEYPADS ▸ keypad

KEYPAL n person with whom one regularly exchanges emails for fun

KEYPALS ▸ keypal

KEYRING adj of a type of computer drive

KEYS interj children's cry for truce or respite from the rules of a game

KEYSET n set of computer keys used for a particular purpose

KEYSETS ▸ keyset

KEYSTER same as ▸ keister

KEYWAY n longitudinal slot cut into a component to accept a key that engages with a similar slot on a mating component to prevent relative motion of the two components

KEYWAYS ▸ keyway

KEYWORD n word or phrase that a computer will search for in order to locate the information or file that the computer user has requested

KGOTLA n (in South African English) meeting place for village assemblies, court cases, and meetings of village leaders

KGOTLAS ▸ kgotla

KHADDAR n cotton cloth of plain weave, produced in India

KHADI same as ▸ khaddar

KHADIS ▸ khadi

KHAF n letter of the Hebrew alphabet

KHAFS ▸ khaf

KHAKI adj dull yellowish-brown ▷ n hard-wearing fabric of this colour used for military uniforms

KHAKIS ▸ khaki

KHALAT same as ▸ khilat

KHALATS ▸ khalat

KHALIF variant spelling of ▸ caliph

KHALIFA same as ▸ caliph

KHALIFS ▸ khalif

KHAMSIN n hot southerly wind blowing from about March to May, esp in Egypt

KHAN n title of respect in Afghanistan and central Asia

KHANATE n territory ruled by a khan

KHANDA n double-edged

sword that appears as the emblem on the Sikh flag and is used in the Amrit ceremony to stir the amrit

KHANDAS ▸ khanda

KHANGA same as ▸ kanga

KHANGAS ▸ khanga

KHANJAR n type of dagger

KHANS ▸ khan

KHANUM feminine form of ▸ khan

KHANUMS ▸ khanum

KHAPH n letter of the Hebrew alphabet

KHAPHS ▸ khaph

KHARIF n (in Pakistan, India, etc) crop that is harvested at the beginning of winter

KHARIFS ▸ kharif

KHAT n white-flowered evergreen shrub of Africa and Arabia whose leaves have narcotic properties

KHATS ▸ khat

KHAYA n type of African tree

KHAYAL n kind of Indian classical vocal music

KHAYALS ▸ khayal

KHAYAS ▸ khaya

KHAZEN same as ▸ chazan

KHAZENS ▸ khazen

KHAZI n lavatory

KHAZIS ▸ khazi

KHEDA n (in India, Myanmar, etc) enclosure into which wild elephants are driven to be captured

KHEDAH same as ▸ kheda

KHEDAHS ▸ khedah

KHEDAS ▸ kheda

KHEDIVA n khedive's wife

KHEDIVE n viceroy of Egypt under Ottoman suzerainty

KHET n Thai district

KHETH same as ▸ heth

KHETHS ▸ kheth

KHETS ▸ khet

KHI n letter of the Greek alphabet

This is a letter of the Greek alphabet, also spelt **chi**. It is worth remembering as one of the higher-scoring three-letter words starting with K.

KHILAT n (in the Middle East) robe or other gift given to someone by a superior as a mark of honour

KHILATS ▸ khilat

K

KHILIM *same as* ▸ **kilim**

KHILIMS ▸ **khilim**

KHIMAR *n* type of headscarf worn by Muslim women

KHIMARS ▸ **khimar**

KHIRKAH *n* dervish's woollen or cotton outer garment

KHIS ▸ **khi**

KHODJA *same as* ▸ **khoja**

KHODJAS ▸ **khodja**

KHOJA *n* teacher in a Muslim school

KHOJAS ▸ **khoja**

KHOR *n* watercourse

KHORS ▸ **khor**

KHOTBAH *same as* ▸ **khutbah**

KHOTBEH *same as* ▸ **khutbah**

KHOUM *n* Mauritanian monetary unit

KHOUMS ▸ **khoum**

KHUD *n* Indian ravine

KHUDS ▸ **khud**

KHURTA *same as* ▸ **kurta**

KHURTAS ▸ **khurta**

KHUTBAH *n* sermon in a Mosque, especially on a Friday

KI *n* vital energy

KIAAT *n* tropical African leguminous tree

KIAATS ▸ **kiaat**

KIANG *n* variety of wild ass that occurs in Tibet and surrounding regions

KIANGS ▸ **kiang**

KIAUGH *n* (in Scots) anxiety

KIAUGHS ▸ **kiaugh**

KIBBE *n* Middle Eastern dish made with minced meat and bulgur

KIBBEH *same as* ▸ **kibbe**

KIBBEHS ▸ **kibbeh**

KIBBES ▸ **kibbe**

KIBBI *same as* ▸ **kibbe**

KIBBIS ▸ **kibbi**

KIBBITZ *same as* ▸ **kibitz**

KIBBLE *n* bucket used in wells or in mining for hoisting ▷ *vb* grind into small pieces

KIBBLED ▸ **kibble**

KIBBLES ▸ **kibble**

KIBBUTZ *n* communal farm or factory in Israel

KIBE *n* chilblain, esp an ulcerated one on the heel

KIBEI *n* someone of Japanese ancestry born in the US and educated in Japan

KIBEIS ▸ **kibei**

KIBES ▸ **kibe**

KIBITKA *n* (in Russia) covered sledge or wagon

KIBITZ *vb* interfere or offer unwanted advice, esp as a spectator at a card game

KIBLA *same as* ▸ **kiblah**

KIBLAH *n* direction of Mecca, to which Muslims turn in prayer, indicated in mosques by a niche (mihrab) in the wall

KIBLAHS ▸ **kiblah**

KIBLAS ▸ **kibla**

KIBOSH *vb* put a stop to

KICK *vb* drive, push, or strike with the foot ▷ *n* thrust or blow with the foot

KICKBOX *vb* box with hands and feet

KICKED ▸ **kick**

KICKER *n* person or thing that kicks

KICKERS ▸ **kicker**

KICKIER ▸ **kicky**

KICKING ▸ **kick**

KICKOFF *n* kick from the centre of the field that starts a game of football

KICKOUT *n* (in basketball) instance of kicking the ball

KICKS ▸ **kick**

KICKUP *n* fuss

KICKUPS ▸ **kickup**

KICKY *adj* excitingly unusual and different

KID *n* child ▷ *vb* tease or deceive (someone) ▷ *adj* younger

KIDDED ▸ **kid**

KIDDER ▸ **kid**

KIDDERS ▸ **kid**

KIDDIE *same as* ▸ **kiddy**

KIDDIED ▸ **kiddy**

KIDDIER *n* old word for a market trader

KIDDIES ▸ **kiddy**

KIDDING ▸ **kid**

KIDDISH ▸ **kid**

KIDDLE *n* device, esp a barrier constructed of nets and stakes, for catching fish in a river or in the sea

KIDDLES ▸ **kiddle**

KIDDO *n* very informal term of address for a young person

KIDDOES ▸ **kiddo**

KIDDOS ▸ **kiddo**

KIDDUSH *n* (in Judaism) special blessing said before a meal on sabbaths and festivals

KIDDY *n* affectionate word for a child ▷ *vb* tease or deceive

KIDEL *same as* ▸ **kiddle**

KIDELS ▸ **kidel**

KIDGE *dialect word for* ▸ **lively**

KIDGIE *adj* dialect word for friendly and welcoming

KIDGIER ▸ **kidgie**

KIDLET *n* humorous word for small child

KIDLETS ▸ **kidlet**

KIDLIKE ▸ **kid**

KIDLING *n* young kid

KIDNAP *vb* seize and hold (a person) to ransom

KIDNAPS ▸ **kidnap**

KIDNEY *n* either of the pair of organs that filter waste products from the blood to produce urine

KIDNEYS ▸ **kidney**

KIDS ▸ **kid**

KIDSKIN *n* soft smooth leather made from the hide of a young goat

KIDULT *n* adult who is interested in forms of entertainment such as computer games, television programmes, etc that are intended for children ▷ *adj* aimed at or suitable for kidults, or both children and adults

KIDULTS ▸ **kidult**

KIDVID *n* informal word for children's video or television

KIDVIDS ▸ **kidvid**

KIEF *same as* ▸ **kif**

KIEFS ▸ **kief**

KIEKIE *n* climbing bush plant of New Zealand

KIEKIES ▸ **kiekie**

KIER *n* vat in which cloth is bleached

KIERIE *n* South African cudgel

KIERIES ▸ **kierie**

KIERS ▸ **kier**

KIESTER *same as* ▸ **keister**

KIEV *n* chicken breast filled with garlic butter and coated in breadcrumbs

KIEVE *same as* ▸ **keeve**

KIEVES ▸ **kieve**

KIEVS ▸ **kiev**

KIF *n* any drug or agent that when smoked is capable of producing a euphoric condition

KIFF adj South African slang for excellent

KIFS ▸ **kif**

KIGHT n archaic spelling of kite, the bird of prey

KIGHTS ▸ **kight**

KIKOI n piece of cotton cloth with coloured bands, worn wrapped around the body

KIKOIS ▸ **kikoi**

KIKUMON n chrysanthemum emblem of the imperial family of Japan

KIKUYU n type of grass

KIKUYUS ▸ **kikuyu**

KILD old spelling of ▸ **killed**

KILERG n 1000 ergs

KILERGS ▸ **kilerg**

KILEY same as ▸ **kylie**

KILEYS ▸ **kiley**

KILIM n pileless woven rug of intricate design made in the Middle East

KILIMS ▸ **kilim**

KILL vb cause the death of ▷ n act of killing

KILLAS n Cornish clay slate

KILLCOW n important person

KILLDEE same as ▸ **killdeer**

KILLED ▸ **kill**

KILLER n person or animal that kills, esp habitually

KILLERS ▸ **killer**

KILLICK n small anchor, esp one made of a heavy stone

KILLIE same as ▸ **killifish**

KILLIES ▸ **killie**

KILLING adj very tiring ▷ n sudden financial success

KILLJOY n person who spoils others' pleasure

KILLOCK same as ▸ **killick**

KILLS ▸ **kill**

KILLUT same as ▸ **khilat**

KILLUTS ▸ **killut**

KILN n oven for baking, drying, or processing pottery, bricks, etc ▷ vb fire or process in a kiln

KILNED ▸ **kiln**

KILNING ▸ **kiln**

KILNS ▸ **kiln**

KILO n code word for the letter k

KILOBAR n 1000 bars

KILOBIT n 1024 bits

KILORAD n 1000 rads

KILOS ▸ **kilo**

KILOTON n one thousand tons

KILP dialect form of ▸ **kelp**

KILPS ▸ **kilp**

KILT n knee-length pleated tartan skirt-like garment worn orig. by Scottish Highlanders ▷ vb put pleats in (cloth)

KILTED ▸ **kilt**

KILTER n working order or alignment

KILTERS ▸ **kilter**

KILTIE n someone wearing a kilt

KILTIES ▸ **kiltie**

KILTING ▸ **kilt**

KILTS ▸ **kilt**

KILTY same as ▸ **kiltie**

KIMBO vb place akimbo

KIMBOED ▸ **kimbo**

KIMBOS ▸ **kimbo**

KIMCHEE same as ▸ **kimchi**

KIMCHI n Korean dish made from fermented cabbage or other vegetables, garlic, and chillies

KIMCHIS ▸ **kimchi**

KIMMER same as ▸ **cummer**

KIMMERS ▸ **kimmer**

KIMONO n loose wide-sleeved Japanese robe, fastened with a sash

KIMONOS ▸ **kimono**

KIN n person's relatives collectively ▷ adj related by blood

KINA n standard monetary unit of Papua New Guinea, divided into 100 toea

KINARA n African candle holder

KINARAS ▸ **kinara**

KINAS ▸ **kina**

KINASE n any enzyme that can convert an inactive zymogen to the corresponding enzyme

KINASES ▸ **kinase**

KINCHIN old slang word for ▸ **child**

KINCOB n fine silk fabric embroidered with threads of gold or silver, of a kind made in India

KINCOBS ▸ **kincob**

KIND adj considerate, friendly, and helpful ▷ n class or group with common characteristics ▷ vb old word for beget or father

KINDA adv very informal shortening of kind of

KINDED ▸ **kind**

KINDER adj more kind ▷ n kindergarten or nursery school

KINDERS ▸ **kind**

KINDEST ▸ **kind**

KINDIE same as ▸ **kindy**

KINDIES ▸ **kindy**

KINDING ▸ **kind**

KINDLE vb set (a fire) alight

KINDLED ▸ **kindle**

KINDLER ▸ **kindle**

KINDLES ▸ **kindle**

KINDLY adj having a warm-hearted nature ▷ adv in a considerate way

KINDRED adj having similar qualities ▷ n blood relationship

KINDS ▸ **kind**

KINDY n kindergarten

KINE pl n cows or cattle ▷ n Japanese pestle

KINEMA same as ▸ **cinema**

KINEMAS ▸ **kinema**

KINES n ▸ **kine**

KINESES ▸ **kinesis**

KINESIC adj of or relating to kinesics

KINESIS n nondirectional movement of an organism or cell in response to a stimulus, the rate of movement being dependent on the strength of the stimulus

KINETIC adj relating to or caused by motion

KINETIN n plant hormone

KINFOLK another word for ▸ **kinsfolk**

KING n male ruler of a monarchy ▷ vb make king

KINGCUP n yellow-flowered plant

KINGDOM n state ruled by a king or queen

KINGED ▸ **king**

KINGING ▸ **king**

KINGLE n Scots word for a type of hard rock

KINGLES ▸ **kingle**

KINGLET n king of a small or insignificant territory

KINGLY adj appropriate to a king ▷ adv in a manner appropriate to a king

KINGPIN n most important person in an organization

KINGS ▸ **king**

KININ n any of a group of polypeptides in the blood that cause dilation of the blood vessels and make

smooth muscles contract
KININS ▸ kinin
KINK *n* twist or bend in rope, wire, hair, etc ▷ *vb* form or cause to form a kink
KINKED ▸ kink
KINKIER ▸ kinky
KINKILY ▸ kinky
KINKING ▸ kink
KINKLE *n* little kink
KINKLES ▸ kinkle
KINKS ▸ kink
KINKY *adj* given to unusual sexual practices
KINLESS *adj* without any relatives
KINO *same as* ▸ **keno**
KINONE *n* benzoquinone, a yellow crystalline water-soluble ketone used in the production of dyestuffs
KINONES ▸ kinone
KINOS ▸ kino
KINRED *old form of* ▸ **kindred**
KINREDS ▸ kinred
KINS ▸ kin
KINSHIP *n* blood relationship
KINSMAN *n* relative
KINSMEN ▸ kinsman
KIORE *n* small brown rat native to New Zealand
KIORES ▸ kiore
KIOSK *n* small booth selling drinks, cigarettes, newspapers, etc
KIOSKS ▸ kiosk
KIP *vb* sleep ▷ *n* sleep or slumber
KIPE *n* dialect word for a basket for catching fish
KIPES ▸ kipe
KIPP *uncommon variant of* ▸ **kip**
KIPPA *n* skullcap worn by orthodox male Jews at all times and by others for prayer, esp a crocheted one worn by those with a specifically religious Zionist affiliation
KIPPAGE *n* Scots word for a state of anger or excitement
KIPPAS ▸ kippa
KIPPED ▸ kip
KIPPEN ▸ kep
KIPPER *n* cleaned, salted, and smoked herring ▷ *vb* cure (a herring) by salting and smoking it

KIPPERS ▸ kipper
KIPPING ▸ kip
KIPPS ▸ kipp
KIPS ▸ kip
KIPSKIN *same as* ▸ **kip**
KIPUNJI *n* Tanzanian species of monkey
KIR *n* drink made from dry white wine and cassis
KIRANA *n* small family-owned shop in India
KIRANAS ▸ kirana
KIRBEH *n* leather bottle
KIRBEHS ▸ kirbeh
KIRBY *n as in* **kirby grip** hairgrip consisting of a piece of wire bent back on itself and partly bent into ridges
KIRIMON *n* Japanese imperial crest
KIRK *Scots word for* ▸ **church**
KIRKED ▸ kirk
KIRKING ▸ kirk
KIRKMAN *n* member or strong upholder of the Kirk
KIRKMEN ▸ kirkman
KIRKS ▸ kirk
KIRKTON *n* village or town with a parish church
KIRMESS *same as* ▸ **kermis**
KIRN *dialect word for* ▸ **churn**
KIRNED ▸ kirn
KIRNING ▸ kirn
KIRNS ▸ kirn
KIRPAN *n* short sword traditionally carried by Sikhs as a symbol of their religious and cultural loyalty
KIRPANS ▸ kirpan
KIRRI *n* Hottentot stick
KIRRIS ▸ kirri
KIRS ▸ kir
KIRSCH *n* cherry brandy
KIRTAN *n* devotional singing, usually accompanied by musical instruments
KIRTANS ▸ kirtan
KIRTLE *n* woman's skirt or dress ▷ *vb* dress with a kirtle
KIRTLED ▸ kirtle
KIRTLES ▸ kirtle
KIS ▸ ki
KISAN *n* peasant or farmer
KISANS ▸ kisan
KISH *n* graphite formed on the surface of molten iron that contains a large amount of carbon
KISHES ▸ kish

KISHKA *same as* ▸ **kishke**
KISHKAS ▸ kishka
KISHKE *n* beef or fowl intestine or skin stuffed with flour, onion, etc, and boiled and roasted
KISHKES ▸ kishke
KISMAT *same as* ▸ **kismet**
KISMATS ▸ kismat
KISMET *n* fate or destiny
KISMETS ▸ kismet
KISS *vb* touch with the lips in affection or greeting ▷ *n* touch with the lips
KISSED ▸ kiss
KISSEL *n* Russian dessert of sweetened fruit purée thickened with arrowroot
KISSELS ▸ kissel
KISSER *n* mouth or face
KISSERS ▸ kisser
KISSES ▸ kiss
KISSIER ▸ kissy
KISSING ▸ kiss
KISSY *adj* showing exaggerated affection, esp by frequent touching or kissing
KIST *n* large wooden chest ▷ *vb* place in a coffin
KISTED ▸ kist
KISTFUL ▸ kist
KISTING ▸ kist
KISTS ▸ kist
KIT *n* outfit or equipment for a specific purpose ▷ *vb* fit or provide
KITBAG *n* bag for a soldier's or traveller's belongings
KITBAGS ▸ kitbag
KITCHEN *n* room used for cooking ▷ *vb* (in archaic usage) provide with food
KITE *n* light frame covered with a thin material flown on a string in the wind ▷ *vb* soar and glide
KITED ▸ kite
KITENGE *n* thick cotton cloth
KITER ▸ kite
KITERS ▸ kite
KITES ▸ kite
KITH *n* one's friends and acquaintances
KITHARA *same as* ▸ **cithara**
KITHE *same as* ▸ **kythe**
KITHED ▸ kithe
KITHES ▸ kithe
KITHING ▸ kithe
KITHS ▸ kith
KITING ▸ kite
KITINGS ▸ kite

K

KITLING dialect word for
► **kitten**
KITS ► **kit**
KITSCH n art or literature with popular sentimental appeal ▷ n object or art that is tawdry, vulgarized, oversentimental or pretentious
KITSCHY ► **kitsch**
KITSET n New Zealand word for a piece of furniture supplied in pieces for the purchaser to assemble
KITSETS ► **kitset**
KITTED ► **kit**
KITTEL n white garment worn for certain Jewish rituals or burial
KITTELS ► **kittel**
KITTEN n young cat ▷ vb (of cats) give birth
KITTENS ► **kitten**
KITTENY ► **kitten**
KITTIES ► **kitty**
KITTING ► **kit**
KITTLE adj capricious and unpredictable ▷ vb be troublesome or puzzling to (someone)
KITTLED ► **kittle**
KITTLER ► **kittle**
KITTLES ► **kittle**
KITTLY Scots word for
> **ticklish**
KITTUL n type of palm from which jaggery sugar comes
KITTULS ► **kittul**
KITTY n communal fund
KITUL ► **kittul**
KITULS ► **kitul**
KIVA n large underground or partly underground room in a Pueblo Indian village, used chiefly for religious ceremonies
KIVAS ► **kiva**
KIWI n New Zealand flightless bird with a long beak and no tail
KIWIS ► **kiwi**
KLANG n (in music) kind of tone
KLANGS ► **klang**
KLAP vb slap or spank
KLAPPED ► **klap**
KLAPS ► **klap**
KLATCH n gathering, especially over coffee
KLATSCH same as ► **klatch**
KLAVERN n local Ku Klux Klan group
KLAVIER same as ► **clavier**

KLAXON n loud horn used on emergency vehicles as a warning signal ▷ vb hoot with a klaxon
KLAXONS ► **klaxon**
KLEAGLE n person with a particular rank in the Ku Klux Klan
KLEENEX n tradename for a kind of soft paper tissue, used esp as a handkerchief
KLEPHT n any of the Greeks who fled to the mountains after the 15th-century Turkish conquest of Greece and whose descendants survived as brigands into the 19th century
KLEPHTS ► **klepht**
KLEPTO n compulsive thief
KLEPTOS ► **klepto**
KLETT n lightweight climbing boot
KLETTS ► **klett**
KLEZMER n Jewish folk musician, usually a member of a small band
KLICK n kilometre
KLICKS ► **klick**
KLIEG n as in **klieg light** intense carbon-arc light used for illumination in producing films
KLIK US military slang word for > **kilometre**
KLIKS ► **klik**
KLINKER n type of brick used in paving
KLIPDAS n rock hyrax
KLISTER n type of ski dressing for improving grip on snow
KLONG n type of canal in Thailand
KLONGS ► **klong**
KLOOCH same as
> **kloochman**
KLOOF n mountain pass or gorge
KLOOFS ► **kloof**
KLOOTCH same as
> **kloochman**
KLUDGE n untidy solution involving a variety of cobbled-together elements ▷ vb cobble something together
KLUDGED ► **kludge**
KLUDGES ► **kludge**
KLUDGEY ► **kludge**
KLUDGY ► **kludge**
KLUGE same as ► **kludge**
KLUGED ► **kluge**

KLUGES ► **kluge**
KLUGING ► **kluge**
KLUTZ n clumsy or stupid person
KLUTZES ► **klutz**
KLUTZY ► **klutz**
KNACK n skilful way of doing something ▷ vb dialect word for crack or snap
KNACKED adj broken or worn out
KNACKER n buyer of old horses for killing ▷ vb exhaust
KNACKS ► **knack**
KNACKY adj old or dialect word for cunning or artful
KNAG n knot in wood
KNAGGY adj knotty
KNAGS ► **knag**
KNAIDEL same as ► **kneidel**
KNAP n crest of a hill ▷ vb hit, hammer, or chip
KNAPPED ► **knap**
KNAPPER ► **knap**
KNAPPLE old word for
► **nibble**
KNAPS ► **knap**
KNAR old spelling of ► **gnar**
KNARL old spelling of ► **gnarl**
KNARLS ► **knarl**
KNARLY same as ► **gnarly**
KNARRED ► **knar**
KNARRY ► **knar**
KNARS ► **knar**
KNAUR variant form of
► **knur**
KNAURS ► **knaur**
KNAVE n jack at cards
KNAVERY n dishonest behaviour
KNAVES ► **knave**
KNAVISH ► **knave**
KNAWE same as ► **knawel**
KNAWEL n type of Old World plant with heads of minute petal-less flowers
KNAWELS ► **knawel**
KNAWES ► **knawe**
KNEAD vb work (dough) into a smooth mixture with the hands
KNEADED ► **knead**
KNEADER ► **knead**
KNEADS ► **knead**
KNEE n joint between thigh and lower leg ▷ vb strike or push with the knee
KNEECAP nontechnical name for ► **patella**
KNEED ► **knee**
KNEEING ► **knee**

K

KNEEL *vb* fall or rest on one's knees ▷ *n* act or position of kneeling

KNEELED ▸ **kneel**

KNEELER ▸ **kneel**

KNEELS ▸ **kneel**

KNEEPAD *n* any of several types of protective covering for the knees

KNEEPAN another word for ▸ **patella**

KNEES ▸ **knee**

KNEIDEL *n* (in Jewish cookery) small dumpling, usually served in chicken soup

KNELL *n* sound of a bell, esp at a funeral or death ▷ *vb* ring a knell

KNELLED ▸ **knell**

KNELLS ▸ **knell**

KNELT ▸ **kneel**

KNESSET *n* parliament or assembly

KNEVELL *vb* old Scots word meaning beat

KNEW ▸ **know**

KNICKER *n* woman's or girl's undergarment covering the lower trunk and having legs or legholes

KNICKS *pl n* knickers

KNIFE *n* cutting tool or weapon consisting of a sharp-edged blade with a handle ▷ *vb* cut or stab with a knife

KNIFED ▸ **knife**

KNIFER ▸ **knife**

KNIFERS ▸ **knife**

KNIFES ▸ **knife**

KNIFING ▸ **knife**

KNIGHT *n* man who has been given a knighthood ▷ *vb* award a knighthood to

KNIGHTS ▸ **knight**

KNISH *n* piece of dough stuffed with potato, meat, or some other filling and baked or fried

KNISHES ▸ **knish**

KNIT *vb* make (a garment) by interlocking a series of loops in wool or other yarn ▷ *n* fabric made by knitting

KNITCH dialect word for ▸ **bundle**

KNITS ▸ **knit**

KNITTED ▸ **knit**

KNITTER ▸ **knit**

KNITTLE *n* old word for string or cord

KNIVE rare variant of ▸ **knife**

KNIVED ▸ **knive**

KNIVES ▸ **knife**

KNIVING ▸ **knive**

KNOB *n* rounded projection, such as a switch on a radio ▷ *vb* supply with knobs

KNOBBED ▸ **knob**

KNOBBER *n* two-year-old male deer

KNOBBLE *n* small knob ▷ *vb* dialect word meaning strike

KNOBBLY adj covered with small bumps

KNOBBY ▸ **knob**

KNOBS ▸ **knob**

KNOCK *vb* give a blow or push to ▷ *n* blow or rap

KNOCKED ▸ **knock**

KNOCKER *n* metal fitting for knocking on a door

KNOCKS ▸ **knock**

KNOLL *n* small rounded hill ▷ *vb* (in archaic or dialect usage) knell

KNOLLED ▸ **knoll**

KNOLLER ▸ **knoll**

KNOLLS ▸ **knoll**

KNOLLY ▸ **knoll**

KNOP *n* knob, esp an ornamental one

KNOPPED ▸ **knop**

KNOPS ▸ **knop**

KNOSP *n* budlike architectural feature

KNOSPS ▸ **knosp**

KNOT *n* fastening made by looping and pulling tight strands of string, cord, or rope ▷ *vb* tie with or into a knot

KNOTS ▸ **knot**

KNOTTED ▸ **knot**

KNOTTER ▸ **knot**

KNOTTY adj full of knots

KNOUT *n* stout whip used formerly in Russia as an instrument of punishment ▷ *vb* whip

KNOUTED ▸ **knout**

KNOUTS ▸ **knout**

KNOW *vb* be or feel certain of the truth of (information etc)

KNOWE same as ▸ **knoll**

KNOWER ▸ **know**

KNOWERS ▸ **know**

KNOWES ▸ **knowe**

KNOWHOW *n* ingenuity, knack, or skill

KNOWING ▸ **know**

KNOWN ▸ **know**

KNOWNS ▸ **know**

KNOWS ▸ **know**

KNUB dialect word for ▸ **knob**

KNUBBLE *vb* dialect word for beat or pound using one's fists

KNUBBLY adj having small lumps or protuberances

KNUBBY adj knub

KNUBS ▸ **knub**

KNUCKLE *n* bone at the finger joint

KNUCKLY ▸ **knuckle**

KNUR *n* knot or protuberance in a tree trunk or in wood

KNURL *n* small ridge, often one of a series ▷ *vb* impress with a series of fine ridges or serrations

KNURLED ▸ **knurl**

KNURLS ▸ **knurl**

KNURLY rare word for ▸ **gnarled**

KNURR same as ▸ **knur**

KNURRS ▸ **knurr**

KNURS ▸ **knur**

KNUT *n* dandy

KNUTS ▸ **knut**

KO *n* (in New Zealand) traditional digging tool

KOA *n* Hawaiian leguminous tree

KOALA *n* tree-dwelling Australian marsupial with dense grey fur

KOALAS ▸ **koala**

KOAN *n* (in Zen Buddhism) problem or riddle that admits no logical solution

KOANS ▸ **koan**

KOAS ▸ **koa**

KOB *n* any of several waterbuck-like species of African antelope

KOBAN *n* old oval-shaped Japanese gold coin

KOBANG same as ▸ **koban**

KOBANGS ▸ **kobang**

KOBANS ▸ **koban**

KOBO *n* Nigerian monetary unit, worth one hundredth of a naira

KOBOLD *n* mischievous household sprite

KOBOLDS ▸ **kobold**

KOBOS ▸ **kobo**

KOBS ▸ **kob**

KOCHIA *n* any of several plants whose foliage turns dark red in late summer

KOCHIAS ▸ **kochia**

KOEKOEA *n* long-tailed cuckoo of New Zealand

KOEL *n* any of several parasitic cuckoos of S and SE Asia and Australia

KOELS ▸ koel

KOFF *n* Dutch masted merchant vessel

KOFFS ▸ koff

KOFTA *n* Indian dish of seasoned minced meat shaped into small balls and cooked

KOFTAS ▸ kofta

KOFTGAR *n* (in India) person skilled in the art of inlaying steel with gold

KOGAL *n* (in Japan) teenage girl noted for her busy social life and trendy purchases

KOGALS ▸ kogal

KOHA *n* gift or donation, esp of cash

KOHANIM ▸ kohen

KOHAS ▸ koha

KOHEN *n* member of the Jewish priestly caste

KOHL *n* cosmetic powder used to darken the edges of the eyelids

KOHLS ▸ kohl

KOI *n* any of various ornamental forms of the common carp

KOINE *n* common language among speakers of different languages

KOINES ▸ koine

KOIS ▸ koi

KOJI *n* Japanese steamed rice

KOJIS ▸ koji

KOKA *n* former type of score in judo

KOKAKO *n* dark grey long-tailed wattled crow of New Zealand

KOKAKOS ▸ kokako

KOKANEE *n* freshwater salmon of lakes and rivers in W North America

KOKAS ▸ koka

KOKER *n* Guyanese sluice

KOKERS ▸ koker

KOKIRI *n* type of rough-skinned New Zealand triggerfish

KOKIRIS ▸ kokiri

KOKOBEH *adj* (of certain fruit) having a rough skin

KOKOPU *n* any of several small freshwater fish of New Zealand

KOKOPUS ▸ kokopu

KOKOWAI *n* type of clay

used in decoration because of its red colour

KOKRA *n* type of wood

KOKRAS ▸ kokra

KOKUM *n* tropical tree

KOKUMS ▸ kokum

KOLA *n as in* **kola nut** caffeine-containing seed used in medicine and soft drinks

KOLACKY *n* sweet bun with a fruit, jam, or nut filling

KOLAS ▸ kola

KOLBASI *same as* ▸ **kolbassi**

KOLHOZ *same as* ▸ **kolkhoz**

KOLHOZY *same as* ▸ **kolkhoz**

KOLKHOS *same as* ▸ **kolkhoz**

KOLKHOZ *n* (formerly) collective farm in the Soviet Union

KOLKOZ *same as* ▸ **kolkhoz**

KOLKOZY ▸ kolkoz

KOLO *n* Serbian folk dance in which a circle of people dance slowly around one or more dancers in the centre

KOLOS ▸ kolo

KOMATIK *n* sledge with wooden runners and crossbars bound with animal hides

KOMBU *n* dark brown seaweed, the leaves of which are dried and used esp in Japanese cookery

KOMBUS ▸ kombu

KON *old word for* ▸ **know**

KONAKI *same as* ▸ **koneke**

KONAKIS ▸ konaki

KONBU *same as* ▸ **kombu**

KONBUS ▸ konbu

KOND ▸ kon

KONDO *n* (in Uganda) thief or armed robber

KONDOS ▸ kondo

KONEKE *n* farm vehicle with runners in front and wheels at the rear

KONEKES ▸ koneke

KONFYT *n* South African fruit preserve

KONFYTS ▸ konfyt

KONGONI *n* E African hartebeest

KONINI *n* edible dark purple berry of the kotukutuku or tree fuchsia

KONINIS ▸ konini

KONK *same as* ▸ **conk**

KONKED ▸ konk

KONKING ▸ konk

KONKS ▸ konk

KONNING ▸ kon

KONS ▸ kon

KOODOO *same as* ▸ **kudu**

KOODOOS ▸ koodoo

KOOK *n* eccentric person ▷ *vb* dialect word for vanish

KOOKED ▸ kook

KOOKIE *same as* ▸ **kooky**

KOOKIER ▸ kooky

KOOKILY ▸ kooky

KOOKING ▸ kook

KOOKS ▸ kook

KOOKY *adj* crazy, eccentric, or foolish

KOOLAH *old form of* ▸ **koala**

KOOLAHS ▸ koolah

KOORI *n* Australian Aborigine

KOORIES ▸ koori

KOORIS ▸ koori

KOP *n* prominent isolated hill or mountain in southern Africa

KOPECK *n* former Russian monetary unit, one hundredth of a rouble

KOPECKS ▸ kopeck

KOPEK *same as* ▸ **kopeck**

KOPEKS ▸ kopek

KOPH *n* 19th letter in the Hebrew alphabet

KOPHS ▸ koph

KOPIYKA *n* monetary unit of Ukraine, worth one hundredth of a hryvna

KOPIYOK ▸ kopiyka

KOPJE *n* small hill

KOPJES ▸ kopje

KOPPA *n* consonantal letter in the Greek alphabet pronounced like kappa (K) with the point of articulation further back in the throat

KOPPAS ▸ koppa

KOPPIE *same as* ▸ **kopje**

KOPPIES ▸ koppie

KOPS ▸ kop

KOR *n* ancient Hebrew unit of capacity

KORA *n* West African instrument with twenty-one strings, combining features of the harp and the lute

KORAI ▸ kore

KORARI *n* native New Zealand flax plant

KORARIS ▸ korari

KORAS ▸ kora

KORAT *n as in* **korat cat** rare blue-grey breed of cat with brilliant green eyes

KORATS ▸ **korat**

KORE n ancient Greek statue of a young woman wearing clothes

KORERO n talk or discussion ▸ vb speak or converse

KOREROS ▸ **korero**

KORES ▸ **kore**

KORKIR n variety of lichen used in dyeing

KORKIRS ▸ **korkir**

KORMA n type of mild Indian dish consisting of meat or vegetables cooked in water, yoghurt, or cream

KORMAS ▸ **korma**

KORO n elderly Maori man

KORORA n small New Zealand penguin

KORORAS ▸ **korora**

KOROS ▸ **koro**

KOROWAI n decorative woven cloak worn by a Maori chief

KORS ▸ **kor**

KORU n stylized curved pattern used esp in carving

KORUN ▸ **koruna**

KORUNA n standard monetary unit of the Czech Republic and Slovakia, divided into 100 hellers

KORUNAS ▸ **koruna**

KORUNY ▸ **koruna**

KORUS ▸ **koru**

KOS n Indian unit of distance having different values in different localities

KOSES ▸ **kos**

KOSHER adj conforming to Jewish religious law, esp (of food) to Jewish dietary law ▸ n kosher food ▸ vb prepare in accordance with Jewish dietary rules

KOSHERS ▸ **kosher**

KOSMOS variant form of ▸ **cosmos**

KOSS same as ▸ **kos**

KOSSES ▸ **koss**

KOTARE n small greenish-blue kingfisher found in New Zealand, Australia, and some Pacific islands to the north

KOTARES ▸ **kotare**

KOTO n Japanese stringed instrument, consisting of a rectangular wooden body over which are stretched silk strings, which are

plucked with plectrums or a nail-like device

KOTOS ▸ **koto**

KOTOW same as ▸ **kowtow**

KOTOWED ▸ **kotow**

KOTOWER ▸ **kotow**

KOTOWS ▸ **kotow**

KOTUKU n white heron with brilliant white plumage, black legs and yellow eyes and bill

KOTUKUS ▸ **kotuku**

KOTWAL n senior police officer or magistrate in an Indian town

KOTWALS ▸ **kotwal**

KOULAN same as ▸ **kulan**

KOULANS ▸ **koulan**

KOUMIS same as ▸ **kumiss**

KOUMISS same as ▸ **kumiss**

KOUMYS same as ▸ **kumiss**

KOUMYSS same as ▸ **kumiss**

KOUPREY n large wild SE Asian ox

KOURA n New Zealand freshwater crayfish

KOURAS ▸ **koura**

KOUROI ▸ **kouros**

KOUROS n ancient Greek statue of a young man

KOUSSO n Abyssinian tree whose flowers have useful antiparasitic properties

KOUSSOS ▸ **kousso**

KOW old variant of ▸ **cow**
This dialect variant of **cow** scores well for a three-letter word, and can be a good one to form when playing in more than one direction.

KOWHAI n New Zealand tree with clusters of yellow flowers

KOWHAIS ▸ **kowhai**

KOWS ▸ **kow**

KOWTOW vb be servile (towards) ▸ n act of kowtowing

KOWTOWS ▸ **kowtow**

KRAAL n S African village surrounded by a strong fence ▸ adj denoting or relating to the tribal aspects of the Black African way of life ▸ vb enclose (livestock) in a kraal

KRAALED ▸ **kraal**

KRAALS ▸ **kraal**

KRAB same as ▸ **karabiner**

KRABS ▸ **krab**

KRAFT n strong wrapping paper, made from pulp

processed with a sulphate solution

KRAFTS ▸ **kraft**

KRAIT n brightly coloured venomous snake of S and SE Asia

KRAITS ▸ **krait**

KRAKEN n legendary sea monster

KRAKENS ▸ **kraken**

KRANG n dead whale from which the blubber has been removed

KRANGS ▸ **krang**

KRANS n sheer rock face

KRANSES ▸ **krans**

KRANTZ same as ▸ **krans**

KRANZ same as ▸ **krans**

KRANZES ▸ **krans**

KRATER same as ▸ **crater**

KRATERS ▸ **krater**

KRAUT n sauerkraut

KRAUTS ▸ **kraut**

KREEP n lunar substance that is high in potassium, rare earth elements, and phosphorus

KREEPS ▸ **kreep**

KREESE same as ▸ **kris**

KREESED ▸ **kreese**

KREESES ▸ **kreese**

KREMLIN n citadel of any Russian city

KRENG same as ▸ **krang**

KRENGS ▸ **kreng**

KREUZER same as ▸ **kreutzer**

KREWE n club taking part in New Orleans carnival parade

KREWES ▸ **krewe**

KRILL n small shrimplike sea creature

KRILLS ▸ **krill**

KRIMMER n tightly curled light grey fur obtained from the skins of lambs from the Crimean region

KRIS n Malayan and Indonesian stabbing or slashing knife with a scalloped edge ▸ vb stab or slash with a kris

KRISED ▸ **kris**

KRISES ▸ **kris**

KRISING ▸ **kris**

KRONA n standard monetary unit of Sweden

KRONE n standard monetary unit of Norway and Denmark

KRONEN ▸ **krone**

KRONER ▸ **krone**

KRONOR ▸ krona

KRONUR ▸ krona

KROON n standard monetary unit of Estonia, divided into 100 senti

KROONI ▸ kroon

KROONS ▸ kroon

KRUBI n aroid plant with an unpleasant smell

KRUBIS ▸ krubi

KRUBUT same as ▸ krubi

KRUBUTS ▸ krubut

KRULLER variant spelling of ▸ cruller

KRUMPER > krumping

KRUNK n style of hip-hop music

KRUNKED ▸ crunked

KRUNKS ▸ krunk

KRYPSES ▸ krypsis

KRYPSIS n idea that Christ made secret use of his divine attributes

KRYPTON n colourless gas present in the atmosphere and used in fluorescent lights

KRYTRON n type of fast electronic gas-discharge switch, used as a trigger in nuclear weapons

KSAR old form of ▸ tsar

KSARS ▸ ksar

KUCCHA ▸ kaccha

KUCCHAS ▸ kuccha

KUCHCHA same as ▸ kacha

KUCHEN n breadlike cake containing apple, nuts, and sugar, originating from Germany

KUCHENS ▸ kuchen

KUDLIK n Inuit soapstone seal-oil lamp

KUDLIKS ▸ kudlik

KUDO same as ▸ kudos

KUDOS n fame or credit

KUDOSES ▸ kudos

KUDU n African antelope with spiral horns

KUDUS ▸ kudu

KUDZU n hairy leguminous climbing plant of China and Japan, with trifoliate leaves and purple fragrant flowers

KUDZUS ▸ kudzu

KUE n name of the letter Q

KUEH n (in Malaysia) any cake of Malay, Chinese, or Indian origin

KUES ▸ kue

KUFI n cap for Muslim man

KUFIS ▸ kufi

KUFIYAH same as > keffiyeh

KUGEL n baked pudding in traditional Jewish cooking

KUGELS ▸ kugel

KUIA n Maori female elder or elderly woman

KUIAS ▸ kuia

KUKRI n heavy, curved knife used by Gurkhas

KUKRIS ▸ kukri

KUKU n mussel

KUKUS ▸ kuku

KULA n ceremonial gift exchange practised among a group of islanders in the W Pacific, used to establish relations between islands

KULAK n (formerly) property-owning Russian peasant

KULAKI ▸ kulak

KULAKS ▸ kulak

KULAN n Asiatic wild ass of the Russian steppes, probably a variety of kiang or onager

KULANS ▸ kulan

KULAS ▸ kula

KULBASA ▸ kielbasa

KULFI n Indian dessert made by freezing milk which has been concentrated by boiling away some of the water in it, and flavoured with nuts and cardamom seeds

KULFIS ▸ kulfi

KULTUR n German civilization

KULTURS ▸ kultur

KUMARA n tropical root vegetable with yellow flesh

KUMARAS ▸ kumara

KUMARI n (in Indian English) maiden

KUMARIS ▸ kumari

KUMERA same as ▸ kumara

KUMERAS ▸ kumera

KUMISS n drink made from fermented mare's or other milk, drunk by certain Asian tribes, esp in Russia or used for dietetic and medicinal purposes

KUMITE n freestyle sparring or fighting

KUMITES ▸ kumite

KUMMEL n German liqueur flavoured with aniseed and cumin

KUMMELS ▸ kummel

KUMQUAT n citrus fruit resembling a tiny orange

KUMYS same as ▸ kumiss

KUMYSES ▸ kumys

KUNA n standard monetary unit of Croatia, divided into 100 lipa

KUNE ▸ kuna

KUNJOOS adj (in Indian English) mean or stingy

KUNKAR n type of limestone

KUNKARS ▸ kunkar

KUNKUR same as ▸ kunkar

KUNKURS ▸ kunkur

KUNZITE n pink-coloured transparent variety of the mineral spodumene: a gemstone

KURBASH vb whip with a hide whip

KURGAN n Russian burial mound

KURGANS ▸ kurgan

KURI n mongrel dog

KURIS ▸ kuri

KURRE old variant of ▸ cur

KURRES ▸ kurre

KURSAAL n public room at a health resort

KURTA n long loose garment like a shirt without a collar worn in India

KURTAS ▸ kurta

KURU n degenerative disease of the nervous system, restricted to certain tribes in New Guinea, marked by loss of muscular control and thought to be caused by a slow virus

> This word for a kind of sickness found in New Guinea can give you something to laugh about when you have two Us to dispose of.

KURUS ▸ kuru

KURVEY vb (in old South African English) transport goods by ox cart

KURVEYS ▸ kurvey

KUSSO variant spelling of ▸ kousso

KUSSOS ▸ kusso

KUTA n (in Indian English) male dog

KUTAS ▸ kuta

KUTCH same as ▸ catechu

KUTCHA adj makeshift or not solid

KUTCHES ▸ kutch

KUTI n (in Indian English) female dog or bitch

KUTIS ▸ kuti

KUTU n body louse

KUTUS ▸ kutu

KUVASZ n breed of dog from Hungary

KUZU same as ▸ kudzu

> A Japanese climbing plant. This can be a great word for getting a high score out of a difficult rack.

KUZUS ▸ kuzu

KVAS same as ▸ kvass

KVASES ▸ kvas

KVASS n alcoholic drink of low strength made in Russia and E Europe from cereals and stale bread

KVASSES ▸ kvass

KVELL vb US word meaning be happy

KVELLED ▸ kvell

KVELLS ▸ kvell

KVETCH vb complain or grumble

KVETCHY adj tending to grumble or complain

KWACHA n standard monetary unit of Zambia, divided into 100 ngwee

KWACHAS ▸ kwacha

KWAITO n type of South African pop music with lyrics spoken over an instrumental backing usually consisting of slowed-down house music layered with African percussion and melodies

KWAITOS ▸ kwaito

KWANZA n standard monetary unit of Angola, divided into 100 lwei

KWANZAS ▸ kwanza

KWELA n type of pop music popular among the Black communities of South Africa

KWELAS ▸ kwela

KY pl n Scots word for cows

KYACK n type of panier

KYACKS ▸ kyack

KYAK same as ▸ kayak

KYAKS ▸ kyak

KYANG same as ▸ kiang

KYANGS ▸ kyang

KYANISE same as ▸ kyanize

KYANITE n grey, green, or blue mineral consisting of aluminium silicate in triclinic crystalline form

KYANIZE vb treat (timber) with corrosive sublimate to make it resistant to decay

KYAR same as ▸ coir

KYARS ▸ kyar

KYAT n standard monetary unit of Myanmar, divided into 100 pyas

KYATS ▸ kyat

KYBO n temporary lavatory constructed for use when camping

KYBOS ▸ kybo

KYBOSH same as ▸ kibosh

KYDST ▸ kythe

KYE n Korean fundraising meeting

KYES ▸ kye

KYLE n narrow strait or channel

KYLES ▸ kyle

KYLICES ▸ kylix

KYLIE n boomerang that is flat on one side and convex on the other

KYLIES ▸ kylie

KYLIKES ▸ kylix

KYLIN n (in Chinese art) mythical animal of composite form

KYLINS ▸ kylin

KYLIX n shallow two-handled drinking vessel used in ancient Greece

KYLOE n breed of small long-horned long-haired beef cattle from NW Scotland

KYLOES ▸ kyloe

KYND old variant of ▸ kind

KYNDE old variant of ▸ kind

KYNDED ▸ kynd

KYNDES ▸ kynde

KYNDING ▸ kynd

KYNDS ▸ kynd

KYNE pl n archaic word for cows

KYOGEN n type of Japanese drama

KYOGENS ▸ kyogen

KYPE n hook on the lower jaw of a mature male salmon

KYPES ▸ kype

KYRIE n type of prayer

KYRIES ▸ kyrie

KYTE n belly

KYTES ▸ kyte

KYTHE vb appear

KYTHED ▸ kythe

KYTHES ▸ kythe

KYTHING ▸ kythe

KYU n (in judo) one of the five student grades for inexperienced competitors

> This means a novice grade in judo, and its unusual combination of letters makes it a useful word to remember when you have an unpromising set of letters on your rack.

KYUS ▸ kyu

LI

L can be a difficult letter to use well, especially when you need to play short words. Just three two-letter words begin with L: **la**, **li** and **lo**. Knowing this will save you valuable time in a game, especially when you are trying to fit words into a crowded board. There aren't very many three-letter words either, but don't forget common words like **lab** (5 points), **law** (6), **lay** (6), **low** (6) and **lye** (6). Try to remember the three-letter words that combine L with **X**: **lax**, **lex**, **lox** and **lux** (10 points each). These are particularly useful towards the end of a game if you have an **X** but little opportunity to play it. There is also the very useful **luz** for 12 points.

LA n exclamation of surprise or emphasis ▷ n the sixth note of the musical scale

LAAGER n (in Africa) a camp defended by a circular formation of wagons ▷ vb form (wagons) into a laager

LAAGERS ▶ laager

LAARI same as ▶ lari

LAARIS ▶ laari

LAB n laboratory

LABARA ▶ labarum

LABARUM n standard or banner carried in Christian religious processions

LABDA same as ▶ lambda

LABDAS ▶ labda

LABEL n piece of card or other material fixed to an object to show its ownership, destination, etc ▷ vb give a label to

LABELED ▶ label

LABELER ▶ label

LABELLA > labellum

LABELS ▶ label

LABIA ▶ labium

LABIAL adj of the lips ▷ n speech sound that involves the lips

LABIALS ▶ labial

LABIATE n any of a family of plants with square stems, aromatic leaves, and a two-lipped flower, such as mint or thyme ▷ adj of this family

LABILE adj (of a compound) prone to chemical change

LABIS n cochlear

LABISES ▶ labis

LABIUM n lip or liplike structure

LABLAB n twining leguminous plant

LABLABS ▶ lablab

LABOR same as ▶ labour

LABORED same as > laboured

LABORER same as > labourer

LABORS ▶ labor

LABOUR n physical work or exertion ▷ vb work hard

LABOURS ▶ labour

LABRA ▶ labrum

LABRAL adj of or like a lip

LABRET n piece of bone, shell, etc

LABRETS ▶ labret

LABRID same as ▶ labroid

LABRIDS ▶ labrid

LABROID n type of fish ▷ adj of or relating to such fish

LABROSE adj thick-lipped

LABRUM n lip or liplike part

LABRUMS ▶ labrum

LABRYS n type of axe

LABS ▶ lab

LAC same as ▶ lakh

LACE n delicate loosely woven decorative fabric ▷ vb fasten with shoelaces, cords, etc

LACED ▶ lace

LACER ▶ lace

LACERS ▶ lace

LACES ▶ lace

LACET n braidwork

LACETS ▶ lacet

LACEY same as ▶ lacy

LACHES n negligence or unreasonable delay in pursuing a legal remedy

LACIER ▶ lacy

LACIEST ▶ lacy

LACILY ▶ lacy

LACING ▶ lace

LACINGS ▶ lace

LACINIA n narrow fringe on petal

LACK n shortage or absence of something needed or wanted ▷ vb need or be short of (something)

LACKED ▶ lack

LACKER variant spelling of ▶ lacquer

LACKERS ▶ lacker

LACKEY n servile follower ▷ vb act as a lackey (to)

LACKEYS ▶ lackey

LACKING ▶ lack

LACKS ▶ lack

LACMUS n old form of litmus

LACONIC adj using only a few words, terse

LACQUER n hard varnish for wood or metal ▷ vb apply lacquer to

LACQUEY same as ▶ lackey

LACS ▶ lac

LACTAM n any of a group of inner amides

LACTAMS ▶ lactam

LACTARY adj relating to milk

LACTASE n any of a group of enzymes that hydrolyse lactose to glucose and galactose

LACTATE vb (of mammals)

to secrete milk ▷ *n* ester or
salt of lactic acid

LACTEAL *adj* of or like milk
▷ *n* any of the lymphatic
vessels that convey chyle
from the small intestine to
the blood

LACTEAN another word for
> **lacteous**

LACTIC *adj* of or derived
from milk

LACTONE *n* any of a class of
organic compounds

LACTOSE *n* white
crystalline sugar found in
milk

LACUNA *n* gap or missing
part, esp in a document or
series

LACUNAE ▸ **lacuna**

LACUNAL ▸ **lacuna**

LACUNAR *n* ceiling, soffit,
or vault having coffers ▷ *adj*
of, relating to, or
containing a lacuna or
lacunas

LACUNAS ▸ **lacuna**

LACUNE *n* hiatus

LACUNES ▸ **lacune**

LACY *adj* fine, like lace

LAD *n* boy or young man

LADANUM same as
> **labdanum**

LADDER *n* frame of two
poles connected by
horizontal steps used for
climbing ▷ *vb* have or cause
to have such a line of
undone stitches

LADDERS ▸ **ladder**

LADDERY ▸ **ladder**

LADDIE *n* familiar term for a
male, esp a young man

LADDIES ▸ **laddie**

LADDISH *adj* informal word
for behaving in a macho or
immature manner

LADDISM *n* laddish
attitudes and behaviour

LADE *vb* put cargo on board
(a ship) or (of a ship) to take
on cargo ▷ *n* watercourse,
esp a millstream

LADED ▸ **lade**

LADEN *adj* loaded ▷ *vb* load
with cargo

LADENED ▸ **laden**

LADENS ▸ **laden**

LADER ▸ **lade**

LADERS ▸ **lade**

LADES ▸ **lade**

LADETTE *n* young woman
whose social behaviour is

similar to that of male
adolescents or young men

LADHOOD ▸ **lad**

LADIES *n* women's public
toilet

LADIFY same as ▸ **ladyfy**

LADING ▸ **lade**

LADINGS ▸ **lade**

LADINO *n* Italian variety of
white clover

LADINOS ▸ **ladino**

LADLE *n* spoon with a long
handle and a large bowl,
used for serving soup etc
▷ *vb* serve out

LADLED ▸ **ladle**

LADLER *n* person who
serves with a ladle

LADLERS ▸ **ladler**

LADLES ▸ **ladle**

LADLING ▸ **ladle**

LADRON same as ▸ **ladrone**

LADRONE *n* thief

LADRONS ▸ **ladron**

LADS ▸ **lad**

LADY *n* woman regarded as
having characteristics of
good breeding or high rank
▷ *adj* female

LADYBOY *n* transvestite or
transsexual, esp one from
the Far East

LADYBUG same as
▸ **ladybird**

LADYCOW another word for
> **ladybird**

LADYFLY another word for
> **ladybird**

LADYFY *vb* make a lady of
(someone)

LADYISH ▸ **lady**

LADYISM ▸ **lady**

LADYKIN *n* endearing form
of lady

LAER another word for
▸ **laager**

LAERED ▸ **laer**

LAERING ▸ **laer**

LAERS ▸ **laer**

LAESIE old form of ▸ **lazy**

LAETARE *n* fourth Sunday
of Lent

LAEVO *adj* on the left

LAG *vb* go too slowly, fall
behind ▷ *n* delay between
events

LAGAN *n* goods or wreckage
on the sea bed, sometimes
attached to a buoy to
permit recovery

LAGANS ▸ **lagan**

LAGENA *n* bottle with a
narrow neck

LAGENAS ▸ **lagena**

LAGEND same as ▸ **lagan**

LAGENDS ▸ **lagend**

LAGER *n* light-bodied beer
▷ *vb* ferment into lager

LAGERED ▸ **lager**

LAGERS ▸ **lager**

LAGGARD *n* person who
lags behind ▷ *adj* sluggish,
slow, or dawdling

LAGGED ▸ **lag**

LAGGEN *n* spar of a barrel

LAGGENS ▸ **laggen**

LAGGER *n* person who lags
pipes

LAGGERS ▸ **lagger**

LAGGIN same as ▸ **laggen**

LAGGING ▸ **lag**

LAGGINS ▸ **laggin**

LAGOON *n* body of water
cut off from the open sea by
coral reefs or sand bars

LAGOONS ▸ **lagoon**

LAGS ▸ **lag**

LAGUNA *n* lagoon

LAGUNAS ▸ **laguna**

LAGUNE same as ▸ **lagoon**

LAGUNES ▸ **lagune**

LAH *n* (in tonic sol-fa) sixth
degree of any major scale

LAHAR *n* landslide of
volcanic debris and water

LAHARS ▸ **lahar**

LAHS ▸ **lah**

LAIC *adj* laical ▷ *n* layman

LAICAL *adj* secular

LAICH *n* low-lying piece of
land

LAICHS ▸ **laich**

LAICISE same as ▸ **laicize**

LAICISM ▸ **laic**

LAICITY *n* state of being
laical

LAICIZE *vb* withdraw
clerical or ecclesiastical
character or status from
(an institution, building,
etc)

LAICS ▸ **laic**

LAID Scots form of ▸ **load**

LAIDED ▸ **laid**

LAIDING ▸ **laid**

LAIDLY *adj* very ugly

LAIDS ▸ **laid**

LAIGH *adj* low-lying ▷ *n*
area of low-lying ground

LAIGHER ▸ **laigh**

LAIGHS ▸ **laigh**

LAIK *vb* play (a game, etc)

LAIKA *n* type of small dog

LAIKAS ▸ **laika**

LAIKED ▸ **laik**

LAIKER ▸ **laik**

LAIKERS ▸ laik

LAIKING ▸ laik

LAIKS ▸ laik

LAIN ▸ lie

LAIPSE vb beat soundly

LAIPSED ▸ laipse

LAIPSES ▸ laipse

LAIR n resting place of an animal ▷ vb (esp of a wild animal) to retreat to or rest in a lair

LAIRAGE n accommodation for farm animals, esp at docks or markets

LAIRD n Scottish landowner

LAIRDLY adj pertaining to laird or lairds

LAIRDS ▸ laird

LAIRED ▸ lair

LAIRIER ▸ lairy

LAIRING ▸ lair

LAIRISE same as ▸ lairize

LAIRIZE vb show off

LAIRS ▸ lair

LAIRY adj gaudy or flashy

LAISSE n type of rhyme scheme

LAISSES ▸ laisse

LAITH Scots form of ▸ loath

LAITHLY same as ▸ laidly

LAITIES ▸ laity

LAITY n people who are not members of the clergy

LAKE n expanse of water entirely surrounded by land ▷ vb take time away from work

LAKEBED n bed of lake

LAKED ▸ lake

LAKELET n small lake

LAKER n cargo vessel used on lakes

LAKERS ▸ laker

LAKES ▸ lake

LAKH n (in India) 100 000, esp referring to this sum of rupees

LAKHS ▸ lakh

LAKIER ▸ laky

LAKIEST ▸ laky

LAKIN short form of ▸ ladykin

LAKING ▸ lake

LAKINGS ▸ lake

LAKINS ▸ lakin

LAKISH adj similar to poetry of Lake poets

LAKSA n (in Malaysia) a dish of Chinese origin consisting of rice noodles served in curry or hot soup

LAKSAS ▸ laksa

LAKY adj of the reddish colour of the pigment lake

LALANG n coarse weedy Malaysian grass

LALANGS ▸ lalang

LALDIE n great gusto

LALDIES ▸ laldie

LALDY same as ▸ laldie

LALIQUE n type of ornamental glass

LALL vb make imperfect 'l' or 'r' sounds

LALLAN n literary version of the English spoken in Lowland Scotland

LALLAND same as ▸ lallan

LALLANS ▸ lallan

LALLED ▸ lall

LALLING ▸ lall

LALLS ▸ lall

LAM vb attack vigorously

LAMA n Buddhist priest in Tibet or Mongolia

LAMAS ▸ lama

LAMB n young sheep ▷ vb (of sheep) give birth to a lamb or lambs

LAMBADA n erotic Brazilian dance

LAMBAST vb beat or thrash

LAMBDA n 11th letter of the Greek alphabet

LAMBDAS ▸ lambda

LAMBED ▸ lamb

LAMBENT adj (of a flame) flickering softly

LAMBER n person that attends to lambing ewes

LAMBERS ▸ lamber

LAMBERT n cgs unit of illumination, equal to 1 lumen per square centimetre

LAMBIE same as ▸ lambkin

LAMBIER ▸ lamby

LAMBIES ▸ lambie

LAMBING n birth of lambs at the end of winter

LAMBKIN n small or young lamb

LAMBOYS n skirt-like piece of armour made from metal strips

LAMBS ▸ lamb

LAMBY adj lamb-like

LAME adj having an injured or disabled leg or foot ▷ vb make lame ▷ n fabric interwoven with gold or silver threads

LAMED n 12th letter in the Hebrew alphabet

LAMEDH same as ▸ lamed

LAMEDHS ▸ lamedh

LAMEDS ▸ lamed

LAMELLA n thin layer, plate, or membrane, esp any of the calcified layers of which bone is formed

LAMELY ▸ lame

LAMENT vb feel or express sorrow (for) ▷ n passionate expression of grief

LAMENTS ▸ lament

LAMER ▸ lame

LAMES ▸ lame

LAMEST ▸ lame

LAMETER Scots form of ▸ lamiger

LAMIA n one of a class of female monsters depicted with a snake's body and a woman's head and breasts

LAMIAE ▸ lamia

LAMIAS ▸ lamia

LAMIGER n disabled person

LAMINA n thin plate, esp of bone or mineral

LAMINAE ▸ lamina

LAMINAL n consonant articulated with blade of tongue

LAMINAR ▸ lamina

LAMINAS ▸ lamina

LAMING ▸ lame

LAMININ n type of protein

LAMISH adj rather lame

LAMITER same as ▸ lameter

LAMMED ▸ lam

LAMMER Scots word for ▸ amber

LAMMERS ▸ lammer

LAMMIE same as ▸ lammy

LAMMIES ▸ lammy

LAMMING ▸ lam

LAMMY n thick woollen jumper

LAMP n device which produces light from electricity, oil, or gas ▷ vb go quickly with long steps

LAMPAD n candlestick

LAMPADS ▸ lampad

LAMPAS n swelling of the mucous membrane of the hard palate of horses

LAMPED ▸ lamp

LAMPER n lamprey

LAMPERN n migratory European lamprey

LAMPERS ▸ lamper

LAMPING ▸ lamp

LAMPION n oil-burning lamp

LAMPLIT adj lit by lamps

LAMPOON n humorous satire ridiculing someone

▷ *vb* satirize or ridicule
LAMPREY *n* eel-like fish with a round sucking mouth
LAMPS ▸ lamp
LAMPUKA *same as* ▸ **lampuki**
LAMPUKI *n* type of fish
LAMS ▸ lam
LAMSTER *n* fugitive
LANA *n* wood from genipap tree
LANAI *Hawaiian word for* ▸ **veranda**
LANAIS ▸ lanai
LANAS ▸ lana
LANATE *adj* having or consisting of a woolly covering of hairs
LANATED *same as* ▸ **lanate**
LANCE *n* long spear used by a mounted soldier ▷ *vb* pierce (a boil or abscess) with a lancet
LANCED ▸ lance
LANCER *n* formerly, cavalry soldier armed with a lance
LANCERS *n* quadrille for eight or sixteen couples
LANCES ▸ lance
LANCET *n* pointed two-edged surgical knife
LANCETS ▸ lancet
LANCH *obsolete form of* ▸ **launch**
LANCHED ▸ lanch
LANCHES ▸ lanch
LANCING ▸ lance
LAND *n* solid part of the earth's surface ▷ *vb* come or bring to earth after a flight, jump, or fall
LANDAU *n* four-wheeled carriage with two folding hoods
LANDAUS ▸ landau
LANDE *n* type of moorland in SW France
LANDED *adj* possessing or consisting of lands
LANDER *n* spacecraft designed to land on a planet or other body
LANDERS ▸ lander
LANDES ▸ lande
LANDING *n* floor area at the top of a flight of stairs
LANDLER *n* Austrian country dance in which couples spin and clap
LANDMAN *n* person who lives and works on land
LANDMEN ▸ landman

LANDS *pl n* holdings in land
LANE *n* narrow road
LANELY *Scots form of* ▸ **lonely**
LANES ▸ lane
LANEWAY *n* lane
LANG *Scots word for* ▸ **long**
LANGAHA *n* type of Madagascan snake
LANGAR *n* dining hall in a gurdwara
LANGARS ▸ langar
LANGEST ▸ lang
LANGLEY *n* unit of solar radiation
LANGREL *same as* > **langrage**
LANGUE *n* language considered as an abstract system or a social institution
LANGUED *adj* having a tongue
LANGUES ▸ langue
LANGUET *n* anything resembling a tongue in shape or function
LANGUID *adj* lacking energy or enthusiasm
LANGUOR *n* state of dreamy relaxation
LANGUR *n* type of arboreal Old World monkey
LANGURS ▸ langur
LANIARD *same as* ▸ **lanyard**
LANIARY *adj* (esp of canine teeth) adapted for tearing ▷ *n* tooth adapted for tearing
LANITAL *n* fibre used in production of synthetic wool
LANK *adj* (of hair) straight and limp ▷ *vb* become or cause to become lank
LANKED ▸ lank
LANKER ▸ lank
LANKEST ▸ lank
LANKIER ▸ lanky
LANKILY ▸ lanky
LANKING ▸ lank
LANKLY ▸ lank
LANKS ▸ lank
LANKY *adj* ungracefully tall and thin
LANNER *n* large falcon of Mediterranean regions, N Africa, and S Asia
LANNERS ▸ lanner
LANOLIN *n* grease from sheep's wool used in ointments etc
LANOSE *same as* ▸ **lanate**

LANT *n* stale urine
LANTANA *n* shrub with orange or yellow flowers, considered a weed in Australia
LANTERN *n* light in a transparent protective case ▷ *vb* supply with lantern
LANTS ▸ lant
LANUGO *n* layer of fine hairs, esp the covering of the human fetus before birth
LANUGOS ▸ lanugo
LANX *n* dish; plate
LANYARD *n* cord worn round the neck to hold a knife or whistle
LAOGAI *n* forced labour camp in China
LAOGAIS ▸ laogai
LAP *n* part between the waist and knees of a person when sitting ▷ *vb* overtake an opponent so as to be one or more circuits ahead
LAPDOG *n* small pet dog
LAPDOGS ▸ lapdog
LAPEL *n* part of the front of a coat or jacket folded back towards the shoulders
LAPELED ▸ lapel
LAPELS ▸ lapel
LAPFUL *same as* ▸ **lap**
LAPFULS ▸ lapful
LAPHELD *adj* (esp of a personal computer) small enough to be used on one's lap
LAPIDES ▸ lapis
LAPILLI > **lapillus**
LAPIN *n* castrated rabbit
LAPINS ▸ lapin
LAPIS *n as in* **lapis lazuli** brilliant blue mineral used as a gemstone
LAPISES ▸ lapis
LAPJE *same as* ▸ **lappie**
LAPJES ▸ lapje
LAPPED ▸ lap
LAPPEL *same as* ▸ **lapel**
LAPPELS ▸ lappel
LAPPER *n* one that laps ▷ *vb* curdle
LAPPERS ▸ lapper
LAPPET *n* small hanging flap or piece of lace
LAPPETS ▸ lappet
LAPPIE *n* rag
LAPPIES ▸ lappie
LAPPING ▸ lap
LAPS ▸ lap
LAPSANG *n* smoky-tasting

Chinese tea

LAPSE n temporary drop in a standard, esp through forgetfulness or carelessness ▷ vb drop in standard

LAPSED ▸ lapse

LAPSER ▸ lapse

LAPSERS ▸ lapse

LAPSES ▸ lapse

LAPSING ▸ lapse

LAPSUS n lapse or error

LAPTOP adj small enough to fit on a user's lap ▷ n computer small enough to fit on a user's lap

LAPTOPS ▸ laptop

LAPTRAY n tray with a cushioned underside, designed to rest in a person's lap while supporting reading material, etc

LAPWING n plover with a tuft of feathers on the head

LAPWORK n work with lapping edges

LAR n boy or young man

LARCENY n theft

LARCH n deciduous coniferous tree

LARCHEN adj of larch

LARCHES ▸ larch

LARD n soft white fat obtained from a pig ▷ vb insert strips of bacon in (meat) before cooking

LARDED ▸ lard

LARDER n storeroom for food

LARDERS ▸ larder

LARDIER ▸ lardy

LARDING ▸ lard

LARDON n strip or cube of fat or bacon used in larding meat

LARDONS ▸ lardon

LARDOON same as ▸ lardon

LARDS ▸ lard

LARDY adj fat

LARE another word for ▸ lore

LAREE n Asian fish-hook formerly used as currency

LAREES ▸ laree

LARES ▸ lare

LARGE adj great in size, number, or extent ▷ n formerly, musical note of particular length

LARGELY adv principally

LARGEN another word for ▸ enlarge

LARGENS ▸ largen

LARGER ▸ large

LARGES ▸ large

LARGESS same as ▸ largesse

LARGEST ▸ large

LARGISH adj fairly large

LARGO adv in a slow and dignified manner ▷ n piece or passage to be performed in a slow and stately manner

LARGOS ▸ largo

LARI n standard monetary unit of Georgia, divided into 100 tetri

LARIAT n lasso ▷ vb tether with lariat

LARIATS ▸ lariat

LARINE adj of, relating to, or resembling a gull

LARIS ▸ lari

LARK n small brown songbird, skylark ▷ vb have a good time by frolicking

LARKED ▸ lark

LARKER ▸ lark

LARKERS ▸ lark

LARKIER ▸ larky

LARKING ▸ lark

LARKISH ▸ lark

LARKS ▸ lark

LARKY adj frolicsome or mischievous

LARMIER n pouch under lower eyelid of deer

LARN vb learn

LARNAX n coffin made of terracotta

LARNED ▸ larn

LARNEY n white person ▷ adj (of clothes) smart

LARNEYS ▸ larney

LARNIER ▸ larney

LARNING ▸ larn

LARNS ▸ larn

LAROID adj relating to Larus genus of gull family

LARRUP vb beat or flog

LARRUPS ▸ larrup

LARS ▸ lar

LARUM archaic word for ▸ alarm

LARUMS ▸ larum

LARVA n insect in an immature stage, often resembling a worm

LARVAE ▸ larva

LARVAL ▸ larva

LARVAS ▸ larva

LARVATE adj masked; concealed

LARYNX n part of the throat containing the vocal cords

LAS ▸ la

LASAGNA same as ▸ lasagne

LASAGNE n pasta in wide flat sheets

LASCAR n East Indian seaman

LASCARS ▸ lascar

LASE vb (of a substance, such as carbon dioxide or ruby) to be capable of acting as a laser

LASED ▸ lase

LASER n device that produces a very narrow intense beam of light, used for cutting very hard materials and in surgery etc

LASERS ▸ laser

LASES ▸ lase

LASH n eyelash ▷ vb hit with a whip

LASHED ▸ lash

LASHER ▸ lash

LASHERS ▸ lash

LASHES ▸ lash

LASHING ▸ lash

LASHINS same as ▸ lashings

LASHKAR n troop of Indian men with weapons

LASING ▸ lase

LASINGS ▸ lase

LASKET n loop at the foot of a sail onto which an extra sail may be fastened

LASKETS ▸ lasket

LASQUE n flat-cut diamond

LASQUES ▸ lasque

LASS n girl

LASSES ▸ lass

LASSI n cold drink made with yoghurt or buttermilk and flavoured with sugar, salt, or a mild spice

LASSIE n little lass

LASSIES ▸ lassie

LASSIS ▸ lassi

LASSO n rope with a noose for catching cattle and horses ▷ vb catch with a lasso

LASSOCK another word for ▸ lass

LASSOED ▸ lasso

LASSOER ▸ lasso

LASSOES ▸ lasso

LASSOS ▸ lasso

LASSU n slow part of csárdás folk dance

LASSUS ▸ lassu

LAST adv coming at the end or after all others ▷ adj only remaining ▷ n last person or thing ▷ vb continue

LASTAGE n space for storing goods in ship

LASTED ▶ last

LASTER ▶ last

LASTERS ▶ last

LASTING adj existing or remaining effective for a long time ▷ n strong durable closely woven fabric used for shoe uppers, etc

LASTLY adv at the end or at the last point

LASTS ▶ last

LAT n former coin of Latvia

LATAH n psychological condition in which a traumatized individual becomes anxious and suggestible

LATAHS ▶ latah

LATAKIA n type of Turkish tobacco

LATCH n fastening for a door with a bar and lever ▷ vb fasten with a latch

LATCHED ▶ latch

LATCHES ▶ latch

LATCHET n shoe fastening, such as a thong or lace

LATE adj after the normal or expected time ▷ adv after the normal or expected time

LATED archaic word for ▶ belated

LATEEN adj denoting a rig with a triangular sail bent to a yard hoisted to the head of a low mast

LATEENS ▶ lateen

LATELY adv in recent times

LATEN vb become or cause to become late

LATENCE ▶ latent

LATENCY ▶ latent

LATENED ▶ laten

LATENS ▶ laten

LATENT adj hidden and not yet developed ▷ n fingerprint that is not visible to the eye

LATENTS ▶ latent

LATER adv afterwards

LATERAD adv towards the side

LATERAL adj of or relating to the side or sides ▷ n lateral object, part, passage, or movement ▷ vb pass laterally

LATEST n the most recent news, fashion, etc

LATESTS ▶ latest

LATEX n milky fluid found in some plants, esp the rubber tree, used in making rubber

LATEXES ▶ latex

LATH n thin strip of wood used to support plaster, tiles, etc ▷ vb attach laths to (a ceiling, roof, floor, etc)

LATHE n machine for turning wood or metal while it is being shaped ▷ vb shape, bore, or cut a screw thread in or on (a workpiece) on a lathe

LATHED ▶ lathe

LATHEE same as ▶ lathi

LATHEES ▶ lathee

LATHEN adj covered with laths

LATHER n froth of soap and water ▷ vb make frothy

LATHERS ▶ lather

LATHERY ▶ lather

LATHES ▶ lathe

LATHI n long heavy wooden stick used as a weapon in India, esp by the police

LATHIER ▶ lathy

LATHING ▶ lathe

LATHIS ▶ lathi

LATHS ▶ lath

LATHY adj resembling a lath, esp in being tall and thin

LATI ▶ lat

LATICES ▶ latex

LATIGO n strap on horse's saddle

LATIGOS ▶ latigo

LATILLA n stick making up part of ceiling

LATINA n female inhabitant of the US who is of Latin American origin

LATINAS ▶ latina

LATINO n male inhabitant of the US who is of Latin American origin

LATINOS ▶ latino

LATISH adv rather late ▷ adj rather late

LATITAT n writ presuming that person accused was hiding

LATKE n crispy Jewish pancake

LATKES ▶ latke

LATOSOL n type of deep, well-drained soil

LATRANT adj barking

LATRIA n adoration that may be offered to God alone

LATRIAS ▶ latria

LATRINE n toilet in a barracks or camp

LATRON n bandit

LATRONS ▶ latron

LATS ▶ lat

LATTE n coffee made with hot milk

LATTEN n metal or alloy, esp brass, made in thin sheets

LATTENS ▶ latten

LATTER adj second of two

LATTES ▶ latte

LATTICE n framework of intersecting strips of wood, metal, etc ▷ vb make, adorn, or supply with a lattice

LATTIN n brass alloy beaten into a thin sheet

LATTINS ▶ lattin

LATU ▶ lat

LAUAN n type of wood used in furniture-making

LAUANS ▶ lauan

LAUCH Scots form of ▶ laugh

LAUCHS ▶ lauch

LAUD vb praise or glorify ▷ n praise or glorification

LAUDED ▶ laud

LAUDER ▶ laud

LAUDERS ▶ laud

LAUDING ▶ laud

LAUDS n traditional morning prayer of the Western Church, constituting with matins the first of the seven canonical hours

LAUF n run in bobsleighing

LAUFS ▶ lauf

LAUGH vb make inarticulate sounds with the voice expressing amusement, merriment, or scorn ▷ n act or instance of laughing

LAUGHED ▶ laugh

LAUGHER ▶ laugh

LAUGHS ▶ laugh

LAUGHY adj tending to laugh a lot

LAUNCE old form of ▶ lance

LAUNCED ▶ launce

LAUNCES ▶ launce

LAUNCH vb put (a ship or boat) into the water, esp for the first time ▷ n launching

LAUND n open grassy space

LAUNDER vb wash and iron (clothes and linen) ▷ n water trough, esp one used for washing ore in mining

LAUNDRY n clothes etc for washing or which have recently been washed

LAUNDS ▸ **laund**

LAURA n group of monastic cells

LAURAE ▸ **laura**

LAURAS ▸ **laura**

LAUREL n glossy-leaved shrub, bay tree ▹ vb crown with laurel

LAURELS ▸ **laurel**

LAURIC adj as in **lauric acid** dodecanoic acid

LAURYL n as in **lauryl alcohol** crystalline solid used to make detergents

LAURYLS ▸ **lauryl**

LAUWINE ▸ avalanche

LAV short for ▹ **lavatory**

LAVA n molten rock thrown out by volcanoes, which hardens as it cools

LAVABO n ritual washing of the celebrant's hands after the offertory at Mass

LAVABOS ▸ **lavabo**

LAVAGE n washing out of a hollow organ by flushing with water

LAVAGES ▸ **lavage**

LAVAS ▸ **lava**

LAVASH n Armenian flat bread

LAVE archaic word for ▸ **wash**

LAVED ▸ **lave**

LAVEER vb (in sailing) tack

LAVEERS ▸ **laveer**

LAVER n large basin of water used by priests for ritual ablutions

LAVERS ▸ **laver**

LAVES ▸ **lave**

LAVING ▸ **lave**

LAVISH adj great in quantity or richness ▹ vb give or spend generously

LAVOLT same as ▸ **lavolta**

LAVOLTA n Italian dance of the 16th and 17th centuries ▹ vb dance the lavolta

LAVOLTS ▸ **lavolt**

LAVRA same as ▸ **laura**

LAVRAS ▸ **lavra**

LAVROCK same as ▸ **laverock**

LAVS ▸ **lav**

LAVVIES ▸ **lavvy**

LAVVY n lavatory

LAW n rule binding on a community ▹ vb prosecute ▹ adj (in archaic usage) low

LAWBOOK n book on subject of law

LAWED ▸ **law**

LAWER ▸ **law**

LAWEST ▸ **law**

LAWFARE n use of the law by a country against its enemies

LAWFUL adj allowed by law

LAWIN n bill or reckoning

LAWINE n avalanche

LAWINES ▸ **lawine**

LAWING same as ▸ **lawin**

LAWINGS ▸ **lawing**

LAWINS ▸ **lawin**

LAWK interj used to show surprise

LAWKS same as ▸ **lawk**

LAWLAND same as ▸ **lowland**

LAWLESS adj breaking the law, esp in a violent way

LAWLIKE ▸ **law**

LAWMAN n officer of the law, such as a policeman or sheriff

LAWMEN ▸ **lawman**

LAWN n area of tended and mown grass

LAWNED adj having a lawn

LAWNIER ▸ **lawn**

LAWNS ▸ **lawn**

LAWNY ▸ **lawn**

LAWS ▸ **law**

LAWSUIT n court case brought by one person or group against another

LAWYER n professionally qualified legal expert ▹ vb act as lawyer

LAWYERS ▸ **lawyer**

LAX adj not strict ▹ n laxative

LAXATOR n muscle that loosens body part

LAXER ▸ **lax**

LAXES ▸ **lax**

LAXEST ▸ **lax**

LAXISM ▸ **laxist**

LAXISMS ▸ **laxist**

LAXIST n lenient or tolerant person

LAXISTS ▸ **laxist**

LAXITY ▸ **lax**

LAXLY ▸ **lax**

LAXNESS ▸ **lax**

LAY ▸ **lie**

LAYAWAY n merchandise reserved for future delivery

LAYBACK n technique for climbing cracks by pulling on one side of the crack with the hands and pressing on the other with the feet ▹ vb in climbing, use layback technique

LAYDEEZ pl n jocular spelling of ladies, as pronounced in a mid-Atlantic accent

LAYED ▸ **lay**

LAYER n single thickness of some substance, as a cover or coating on a surface ▹ vb form a layer

LAYERED ▸ **layer**

LAYERS ▸ **layer**

LAYETTE n clothes for a newborn baby

LAYIN n basketball score made by dropping ball into basket

LAYING ▸ **lay**

LAYINGS ▸ **lay**

LAYINS ▸ **layin**

LAYLOCK old form of ▸ **lilac**

LAYMAN n person who is not a member of the clergy

LAYMEN ▸ **layman**

LAYOFF n act of suspending employees

LAYOFFS ▸ **layoff**

LAYOUT n arrangement, esp of matter for printing or of a building

LAYOUTS ▸ **layout**

LAYOVER n break in a journey

LAYS ▸ **lie**

LAYTIME n time allowed for loading cargo

LAYUP n period of incapacity through illness

LAYUPS ▸ **layup**

LAZAR archaic word for ▸ **leper**

LAZARET same as ▸ **lazaretto**

LAZARS ▸ **lazar**

LAZE vb be idle or lazy ▹ n time spent lazing

LAZED ▸ **laze**

LAZES ▸ **laze**

LAZIED ▸ **lazy**

LAZIER ▸ **lazy**

LAZIES ▸ **lazy**

LAZIEST ▸ **lazy**

LAZILY ▸ **lazy**

LAZING ▸ **laze**

LAZO another word for ▸ **lasso**

LAZOED ▸ **lazo**

LAZOES ▸ **lazo**

LAZOING ▸ **lazo**

LAZOS ▸ **lazo**

LAZULI n lapis lazuli

LAZULIS ▸ **lazuli**

LAZY vb laze ▹ adj not

inclined to work or exert oneself

LAZYING ▸ lazy

LAZYISH ▸ lazy

LAZZI ▸ lazzo

LAZZO n comic routine in the commedia dell'arte

LEA n meadow

LEACH vb remove or be removed from a substance by a liquid passing through it ▸ n act or process of leaching

LEACHED ▸ leach

LEACHER ▸ leach

LEACHES ▸ leach

LEACHY adj porous

LEAD vb guide or conduct ▸ n first or most prominent place ▸ adj acting as a leader or lead

LEADED adj (of windows) made from many small panes of glass held together by lead strips

LEADEN adj heavy or sluggish ▸ vb become or cause to become leaden

LEADENS ▸ leaden

LEADER n person who leads

LEADERS ▸ leader

LEADIER ▸ leady

LEADING ▸ lead

LEADMAN n man who leads

LEADMEN ▸ leadman

LEADOFF n initial move or action

LEADS ▸ lead

LEADY adj like lead

LEAF n flat usu green blade attached to the stem of a plant ▸ vb turn (pages) cursorily

LEAFAGE n leaves of plants

LEAFBUD n bud producing leaves rather than flowers

LEAFED ▸ leaf

LEAFERY n foliage

LEAFIER ▸ leafy

LEAFING ▸ leaf

LEAFLET n sheet of printed matter for distribution ▸ vb distribute leaflets (to)

LEAFS ▸ leaf

LEAFY adj covered with leaves

LEAGUE n association promoting the interests of its members

LEAGUED ▸ league

LEAGUER vb harass; beset ▸ n encampment, esp of besiegers

LEAGUES ▸ league

LEAK n hole or defect that allows the escape or entrance of liquid, gas, radiation, etc ▸ vb let liquid etc in or out

LEAKAGE n act or instance of leaking

LEAKED ▸ leak

LEAKER ▸ leak

LEAKERS ▸ leak

LEAKIER ▸ leaky

LEAKILY ▸ leaky

LEAKING ▸ leak

LEAKS ▸ leak

LEAKY adj leaking or tending to leak

LEAL adj loyal

LEALER ▸ leal

LEALEST ▸ leal

LEALLY ▸ leal

LEALTY ▸ leal

LEAM vb shine

LEAMED ▸ leam

LEAMING ▸ leam

LEAMS ▸ leam

LEAN vb rest (against) ▸ adj thin but healthy-looking ▸ n lean part of meat

LEANED ▸ lean

LEANER ▸ lean

LEANERS ▸ lean

LEANEST ▸ lean

LEANING ▸ lean

LEANLY ▸ lean

LEANS ▸ lean

LEANT ▸ lean

LEANY old form of ▸ **lean**

LEAP vb make a sudden powerful jump ▸ n sudden powerful jump

LEAPED ▸ leap

LEAPER ▸ leap

LEAPERS ▸ leap

LEAPING ▸ leap

LEAPS ▸ leap

LEAPT ▸ leap

LEAR vb instruct

LEARE same as ▸ **lear**

LEARED ▸ lear

LEARES ▸ leare

LEARIER ▸ leary

LEARING ▸ lear

LEARN vb gain skill or knowledge by study, practice, or teaching

LEARNED ▸ learn

LEARNER n someone who is learning something

LEARNS ▸ learn

LEARNT ▸ learn

LEARS ▸ lear

LEARY same as ▸ **leery**

LEAS ▸ lea

LEASE n contract by which land or property is rented for a stated time by the owner to a tenant ▸ vb let or rent by lease

LEASED ▸ lease

LEASER ▸ lease

LEASERS ▸ lease

LEASES ▸ lease

LEASH n lead for a dog ▸ vb control by a leash

LEASHED ▸ leash

LEASHES ▸ leash

LEASING ▸ lease

LEASOW vb pasture

LEASOWE same as ▸ **leasow**

LEASOWS ▸ leasow

LEAST n smallest amount ▸ adj smallest ▸ n smallest one ▸ adv in the smallest degree

LEASTS ▸ least

LEASURE old form of ▸ **leisure**

LEAT n trench or ditch that conveys water to a mill wheel

LEATHER n material made from specially treated animal skins ▸ adj made of leather ▸ vb beat or thrash

LEATS ▸ leat

LEAVE vb go away from ▸ n permission to be absent from work or duty

LEAVED adj with leaves

LEAVEN n substance that causes dough to rise ▸ vb raise with leaven

LEAVENS ▸ leaven

LEAVER ▸ leave

LEAVERS ▸ leave

LEAVES ▸ leaf

LEAVIER ▸ leavy

LEAVING ▸ leave

LEAVY same as ▸ **leafy**

LEAZE same as ▸ **lease**

LEAZES ▸ leaze

LEBBEK n type of timber tree

LEBBEKS ▸ lebbek

LEBEN n semiliquid food made from curdled milk in N Africa and the Levant

LEBENS ▸ leben

LECCIES ▸ leccy

LECCY n electricity

LECH vb behave lecherously (towards) ▸ n lecherous act or indulgence

LECHAIM interj drinking toast ▸ n small drink with

which to toast something or someone

LECHED ▶ lech

LECHER n man who has or shows excessive sexual desire ▷ vb behave lecherously

LECHERS ▶ lecher

LECHERY n unrestrained and promiscuous sexuality

LECHES ▶ lech

LECHING ▶ lech

LECHWE n African antelope

LECHWES ▶ lechwe

LECTERN n sloping reading desk, esp in a church

LECTIN n type of protein possessing high affinity for a specific sugar

LECTINS ▶ lectin

LECTION n variant reading of a passage in a particular copy or edition of a text

LECTOR n lecturer or reader in certain universities

LECTORS ▶ lector

LECTURE n informative talk to an audience on a subject ▷ vb give a talk

LECTURN old form of ▶ lectern

LECYTHI > lecythus

LED ▶ lead

LEDDEN n language; speech

LEDDENS ▶ ledden

LEDGE n narrow shelf sticking out from a wall

LEDGED ▶ ledge

LEDGER n book of debit and credit accounts of a firm ▷ vb fish using a wire trace that allows the bait to float freely while the weight sinks

LEDGERS ▶ ledger

LEDGES ▶ ledge

LEDGIER ▶ ledge

LEDGY ▶ ledge

LEDUM n evergreen shrub

LEDUMS ▶ ledum

LEE n sheltered side ▷ vb Scots for lie

LEEAR Scots form of ▶ liar

LEEARS ▶ leear

LEECH n species of bloodsucking worm ▷ vb use leeches to suck the blood of

LEECHED ▶ leech

LEECHEE same as ▶ litchi

LEECHES ▶ leech

LEED ▶ lee

LEEING ▶ lee

LEEK n vegetable of the onion family with a long bulb and thick stem

LEEKS ▶ leek

LEEP vb boil; scald

LEEPED ▶ leep

LEEPING ▶ leep

LEEPS ▶ leep

LEER vb look or grin at in a sneering or suggestive manner ▷ n sneering or suggestive look or grin

LEERED ▶ leer

LEERIER ▶ leery

LEERILY ▶ leery

LEERING ▶ leer

LEERS ▶ leer

LEERY adj suspicious or wary (of)

LEES pl n sediment of wine

LEESE old form of ▶ loose

LEESES ▶ leese

LEESING ▶ leese

LEET n list of candidates for an office

LEETLE form of ▶ little

LEETS ▶ leet

LEEWARD n lee side ▷ adv towards this side ▷ adj of, in, or moving in the direction towards which the wind blows

LEEWAY n room for free movement within limits

LEEWAYS ▶ leeway

LEEZE adj as in leeze me Scots for lief is me, an expression of affection

LEFT adj on the opposite side from right ▷ n left side

LEFTE old past tense of ▶ lift

LEFTER ▶ left

LEFTEST ▶ left

LEFTIE same as ▶ lefty

LEFTIES ▶ lefty

LEFTISH ▶ left

LEFTISM ▶ leftist

LEFTIST adj (person) of the political left ▷ n person who supports the political left

LEFTS ▶ left

LEFTY n left-winger

LEG n one of the limbs on which a person or animal walks, runs, or stands

LEGACY n thing left in a will

LEGAL adj established or permitted by law ▷ n legal expert

LEGALLY ▶ legal

LEGALS ▶ legal

LEGATE n messenger or representative, esp from the Pope ▷ vb leave as legacy

LEGATED ▶ legate

LEGATEE n recipient of a legacy

LEGATES ▶ legate

LEGATO adv (piece to be played) smoothly ▷ n style of playing with no gaps between notes

LEGATOR n person who gives a legacy or makes a bequest

LEGATOS ▶ legato

LEGEND n traditional story or myth

LEGENDS ▶ legend

LEGER same as ▶ ledger

LEGERS ▶ leger

LEGES ▶ lex

LEGGE vb lighten or lessen

LEGGED ▶ leg

LEGGER n man who moves barge through tunnel using legs

LEGGERS ▶ legger

LEGGES ▶ legge

LEGGIE n (in cricket) leg spin bowler

LEGGIER ▶ leggy

LEGGIES ▶ leggie

LEGGIN same as ▶ legging

LEGGING n extra outer covering for the lower leg

LEGGINS ▶ leggin

LEGGISM n blacklegging

LEGGY adj having long legs

LEGHORN n type of Italian wheat straw that is woven into hats

LEGIBLE adj easily read

LEGIBLY ▶ legible

LEGION n large military force ▷ adj very large or numerous

LEGIONS ▶ legion

LEGIST n person versed in the law

LEGISTS ▶ legist

LEGIT n legitimate or professionally respectable drama ▷ adj legitimate

LEGITIM n amount of inheritance due to children from father

LEGITS ▶ legit

LEGLAN same as ▶ leglin

LEGLANS ▶ leglan

LEGLEN same as ▶ leglin

LEGLENS ▶ leglen

LEGLESS adj without legs

LEGLET n jewellery worn

around the leg

LEGLETS ▸ leglet

LEGLIKE ▸ leg

LEGLIN n milk-pail

LEGLINS ▸ leglin

LEGMAN n newsman who reports on news stories from the scene of action or original source

LEGMEN ▸ legman

LEGONG n Indonesian dance

LEGONGS ▸ legong

LEGROOM n space to move one's legs comfortably, as in a car

LEGS ▸ leg

LEGSIDE n part of a cricket field to the left of a right-handed batsman as he faces the bowler

LEGUAAN n large S African lizard

LEGUAN ▸ leguaan

LEGUANS ▸ leguan

LEGUME n pod of a plant of the pea or bean family

LEGUMES ▸ legume

LEGUMIN n protein obtained mainly from the seeds of leguminous plants

LEGWEAR n clothing worn on the legs

LEGWORK n work that involves travelling on foot or as if on foot

LEHAIM same as ▸ lechaim

LEHAIMS ▸ lehaim

LEHAYIM same as ▸ lehaim

LEHR n long tunnel-shaped oven used for annealing glass

LEHRS ▸ lehr

LEHUA n flower of Hawaii

LEHUAS ▸ lehua

LEI ▸ leu

LEIDGER same as ▸ ledger

LEIGER same as ▸ ledger

LEIGERS ▸ leiger

LEIPOA n Australian bird

LEIPOAS ▸ leipoa

LEIR same as ▸ lear

LEIRED ▸ leir

LEIRING ▸ leir

LEIRS ▸ leir

LEIS ▸ leu

LEISH adj agile

LEISHER ▸ leish

LEISLER n small bat

LEISTER n spear with three or more prongs for spearing fish, esp salmon ▷ vb spear (a fish) with a leister

LEISURE n time for relaxation or hobbies ▷ vb have leisure

LEK n area where birds gather for sexual display and courtship ▷ vb (of birds) gather at lek

LEKE old form of ▸ leak

LEKKED ▸ lek

LEKKER adj attractive or nice

LEKKING ▸ lek

LEKS ▸ lek

LEKU ▸ lek

LEKVAR n prune or apricot pie filling

LEKVARS ▸ lekvar

LEKYTHI > lekythos

LEMAN n beloved

LEMANS ▸ leman

LEME same as ▸ leam

LEMED ▸ leme

LEMEL n metal filings

LEMELS ▸ lemel

LEMES ▸ leme

LEMING ▸ leme

LEMMA n subsidiary proposition, proved for use in the proof of another proposition

LEMMAS ▸ lemma

LEMMATA ▸ lemma

LEMMING n rodent of arctic regions, reputed to run into the sea and drown during mass migrations

LEMON n yellow oval fruit that grows on trees ▷ adj pale-yellow ▷ vb flavour with lemon

LEMONED ▸ lemon

LEMONS ▸ lemon

LEMONY adj having or resembling the taste or colour of a lemon

LEMPIRA n standard monetary unit of Honduras, divided into 100 centavos

LEMUR n nocturnal animal like a small monkey, found in Madagascar

LEMURES pl n spirits of the dead

LEMURS ▸ lemur

LEND vb give the temporary use of

LENDER ▸ lend

LENDERS ▸ lend

LENDING ▸ lend

LENDS ▸ lend

LENES ▸ lenis

LENG vb linger ▷ adj long

LENGED ▸ leng

LENGER ▸ leng

LENGEST ▸ leng

LENGING ▸ leng

LENGS ▸ leng

LENGTH n extent or measurement from end to end

LENGTHS ▸ length

LENGTHY adj very long or tiresome

LENIENT adj tolerant, not strict or severe ▷ n lenient person

LENIFY vb make lenient

LENIS adj (of a consonant) pronounced with little muscular tension ▷ n consonant pronounced like this

LENITE vb undergo lenition

LENITED ▸ lenite

LENITES ▸ lenite

LENITY n mercy or clemency

LENO n (in textiles) a weave in which the warp yarns are twisted together in pairs between the weft or filling yarns

LENOS ▸ leno

LENS n piece of glass or similar material with one or both sides curved, used to bring together or spread light rays in cameras, spectacles, telescopes, etc

LENSE same as ▸ lens

LENSED adj incorporating a lens

LENSES ▸ lens

LENSING n materials which colour and diffuse light

LENSMAN n camera operator

LENSMEN ▸ lensman

LENT ▸ lend

LENTEN adj of or relating to Lent

LENTI ▸ lento

LENTIC adj of, relating to, or inhabiting still water

LENTIGO technical name for a ▸ freckle

LENTIL n edible seed of a leguminous Asian plant

LENTILS ▸ lentil

LENTISC ▸ lentisk

LENTISK n mastic tree

LENTO adv slowly ▷ n movement or passage performed slowly

LENTOID adj lentiform ▷ n lentiform object

LENTOR n lethargy
LENTORS ▶ lentor
LENTOS ▶ lento
LENTOUS adj lethargic
LENVOY another word for
▶ envoy
LENVOYS ▶ lenvoy
LEONE n standard
monetary unit of Sierra
Leone, divided into 100
cents
LEONES ▶ leone
LEONINE adj like a lion
LEOPARD n large spotted
carnivorous animal of the
cat family
LEOTARD n tight-fitting
garment covering the
upper body, worn for
dancing or exercise
LEP dialect word for ▶ leap
LEPER n person suffering
from leprosy
LEPERS ▶ leper
LEPID adj amusing
LEPORID adj of, relating to,
or belonging to the family
of mammals that includes
rabbits and hares ▷ n any
animal belonging to this
family
LEPPED ▶ lep
LEPPING ▶ lep
LEPRA n leprosy
LEPRAS ▶ lepra
LEPROSE adj having or
denoting a whitish scurfy
surface
LEPROSY n disease
attacking the nerves and
skin, resulting in loss of
feeling in the affected parts
LEPROUS adj having leprosy
LEPS ▶ lep
LEPT ▶ leap
LEPTA ▶ lepton
LEPTIN n protein, produced
by fat cells in the body, that
acts on the brain to
regulate the amount of
additional fat laid down in
the body
LEPTINS ▶ leptin
LEPTOME n tissue of plant
conducting food
LEPTON n any of a group of
elementary particles with
weak interactions
LEPTONS ▶ lepton
LEQUEAR same as ▶ lacunar
LERE same as ▶ lear
LERED ▶ lere
LERES ▶ lere

LERING ▶ lere
LERP n crystallized
honeydew
LERPS ▶ lerp
LESBIAN n homosexual
woman ▷ adj of
homosexual women
LESBIC adj relating to
lesbians
LESION n structural change
in an organ of the body
caused by illness or injury
▷ vb cause lesions
LESIONS ▶ lesion
LESS n smaller amount ▷ adj
smaller in extent, degree, or
duration ▷ pron smaller
part or quantity ▷ adv
smaller extent or degree
▷ prep after deducting,
minus
LESSEE n person to whom a
lease is granted
LESSEES ▶ lessee
LESSEN vb make or become
smaller or not as much
LESSENS ▶ lessen
LESSER adj not as great in
quantity, size, or worth
LESSES ▶ less
LESSON n class or single
period of instruction in a
subject ▷ vb censure or
punish
LESSONS ▶ lesson
LESSOR n person who
grants a lease of property
LESSORS ▶ lessor
LEST conj so as to prevent
any possibility that ▷ vb
listen
LESTED ▶ lest
LESTING ▶ lest
LESTS ▶ lest
LET n act of letting property
▷ vb obstruct
LETCH same as ▶ lech
LETCHED ▶ letch
LETCHES ▶ letch
LETDOWN n
disappointment
LETHAL adj deadly ▷ n
weapon, etc capable of
causing death
LETHALS ▶ lethal
LETHE n forgetfulness
LETHEAN ▶ lethe
LETHEE n life-blood
LETHEES ▶ lethee
LETHES ▶ lethe
LETHIED adj forgetful
LETS ▶ let
LETTED ▶ let

LETTER n written message,
usu sent by post ▷ vb
inscribe letters on
LETTERN another word for
▶ lectern
LETTERS pl n literary
knowledge or ability
LETTING ▶ let
LETTRE n letter
LETTRES ▶ lettre
LETTUCE n plant with large
green leaves used in salads
LETUP n lessening or
abatement
LETUPS ▶ letup
LEU n standard monetary
unit of Romania and
Moldova, divided into 100
bani
LEUCH ▶ lauch
LEUCHEN ▶ lauch
LEUCIN same as ▶ leucine
LEUCINE n essential amino
acid found in many proteins
LEUCINS ▶ leucin
LEUCITE n grey or white
mineral consisting of
potassium aluminium
silicate
LEUCO n as in leuco base
colourless compound
formed by reducing a dye
LEUCOMA n white opaque
scar of the cornea
LEUD Scots word for
▶ breadth
LEUDES ▶ leud
LEUDS ▶ leud
LEUGH ▶ lauch
LEUGHEN ▶ lauch
LEUKOMA same as
▶ leucoma
LEUKON n white blood cell
count
LEUKONS ▶ leukon
LEV n standard monetary
unit of Bulgaria, divided
into 100 stotinki
LEVA ▶ lev
LEVANT n type of leather
made from the skins of
goats, sheep, or seals ▷ vb
bolt or abscond, esp to
avoid paying debts
LEVANTS ▶ levant
LEVATOR n any of various
muscles that raise a part of
the body
LEVE adj darling ▷ adv
gladly
LEVEE n natural or artificial
river embankment ▷ vb go
to the reception of

LEVEED ▷ **levee**

LEVEES ▷ **levee**

LEVEL adj horizontal ▷ vb make even or horizontal ▷ n horizontal line or surface

LEVELED ▷ **level**

LEVELER same as > **leveller**

LEVELLY ▷ **level**

LEVELS ▷ **level**

LEVER n handle used to operate machinery ▷ vb prise or move with a lever

LEVERED ▷ **lever**

LEVERET n young hare

LEVERS ▷ **lever**

LEVES ▷ **leve**

LEVIED ▷ **levy**

LEVIER ▷ **levy**

LEVIERS ▷ **levy**

LEVIES ▷ **levy**

LEVIN archaic word for > **lightning**

LEVINS ▷ **levin**

LEVIS n jeans

LEVITE n Christian clergyman

LEVITES ▷ **levite**

LEVITIC ▷ **levite**

LEVITY n inclination to make a joke of serious matters

LEVO adj anticlockwise

LEVULIN n substance obtained from certain bulbs

LEVY vb impose and collect (a tax) ▷ n imposition or collection of taxes

LEVYING ▷ **levy**

LEW adj tepid

LEWD adj lustful or indecent

LEWDER ▷ **lewd**

LEWDEST ▷ **lewd**

LEWDLY ▷ **lewd**

LEWDSBY another word for > **lewdster**

LEWIS n lifting device for heavy stone or concrete blocks

LEWISES ▷ **lewis**

LEWISIA n type of herb

LEX n system or body of laws

LEXEME n minimal meaningful unit of language, the meaning of which cannot be understood from that of its component morphemes

LEXEMES ▷ **lexeme**

LEXEMIC ▷ **lexeme**

LEXES ▷ **lex**

LEXICA ▷ **lexicon**

LEXICAL adj relating to the vocabulary of a language

LEXICON n dictionary

LEXIS n totality of vocabulary items in a language, including all forms having lexical meaning or grammatical function

LEXISES ▷ **lexis**

LEY n land temporarily under grass

LEYS ▷ **ley**

LI n Chinese measurement of distance

LIABLE adj legally obliged or responsible

LIAISE vb establish and maintain communication (with)

LIAISED ▷ **liaise**

LIAISES ▷ **liaise**

LIAISON n communication and contact between groups

LIANA n climbing plant in tropical forests

LIANAS ▷ **liana**

LIANE same as ▷ **liana**

LIANES ▷ **liane**

LIANG n Chinese unit of weight

LIANGS ▷ **liang**

LIANOID ▷ **liana**

LIAR n person who tells lies

LIARD adj grey ▷ n former small coin of various European countries

LIARDS ▷ **liard**

LIARS ▷ **liar**

LIART Scots form of ▷ **liard**

LIAS n lowest series of rocks of the Jurassic system

LIASES ▷ **lias**

LIATRIS n type of North American plant with small white flowers

LIB n informal, sometimes derogatory word for liberation ▷ vb geld

LIBANT adj touching lightly

LIBATE vb offer as gift to the gods

LIBATED ▷ **libate**

LIBATES ▷ **libate**

LIBBARD another word for ▷ **leopard**

LIBBED ▷ **lib**

LIBBING ▷ **lib**

LIBEL n published statement falsely damaging a person's reputation ▷ vb falsely damage the reputation of (someone)

LIBELED ▷ **libel**

LIBELEE same as > **libellee**

LIBELER ▷ **libel**

LIBELS ▷ **libel**

LIBER n tome or book

LIBERAL adj having social and political views that favour progress and reform ▷ n person who has liberal ideas or opinions

LIBERO another name for ▷ **sweeper**

LIBEROS ▷ **libero**

LIBERS ▷ **liber**

LIBERTY n freedom

LIBIDO n psychic energy

LIBIDOS ▷ **libido**

LIBKEN n lodging

LIBKENS ▷ **libken**

LIBLAB n 19th century British liberal

LIBLABS ▷ **liblab**

LIBRA n ancient Roman unit of weight corresponding to 1 pound, but equal to about 12 ounces

LIBRAE ▷ **libra**

LIBRARY n room or building where books are kept

LIBRAS ▷ **libra**

LIBRATE vb oscillate or waver

LIBRI ▷ **liber**

LIBS ▷ **lib**

LICE ▷ **louse**

LICENCE n document giving official permission to do something ▷ vb (in the US) give permission to

LICENSE vb grant or give a licence for

LICENTE adj permitted; allowed

LICH n dead body

LICHEE same as ▷ **litchi**

LICHEES ▷ **lichee**

LICHEN n small flowerless plant forming a crust on rocks, trees, etc ▷ vb cover with lichen

LICHENS ▷ **lichen**

LICHES ▷ **lich**

LICHI same as ▷ **litchi**

LICHIS ▷ **lichi**

LICHT Scots word for ▷ **light**

LICHTED ▷ **licht**

LICHTER ▷ **licht**

LICHTLY vb treat discourteously

LICHTS ▷ **licht**

LICHWAY n path used to carry coffin into church

LICIT adj lawful, permitted

LICITLY ▸ licit

LICK vb pass the tongue over ▹ n licking

LICKED ▸ lick

LICKER ▸ lick

LICKERS ▸ lick

LICKING n beating

LICKS ▸ lick

LICTOR n one of a group of ancient Roman officials

LICTORS ▸ lictor

LID n movable cover

LIDAR n radar-type instrument

LIDARS ▸ lidar

LIDDED ▸ lid

LIDDING n lids

LIDGER variant form of ▸ ledger

LIDGERS ▸ ledger

LIDLESS adj having no lid or top

LIDO n open-air centre for swimming and water sports

LIDOS ▸ lido

LIDS ▸ lid

LIE vb make a deliberately false statement ▹ n deliberate falsehood

LIED n setting for solo voice and piano of a poem

LIEDER ▸ lied

LIEF adv gladly ▹ adj ready ▹ n beloved person

LIEFER ▸ lief

LIEFEST ▸ lief

LIEFLY ▸ lief

LIEFS ▸ lief

LIEGE adj bound to give or receive feudal service ▹ n lord

LIEGER same as ▸ ledger

LIEGERS ▸ lieger

LIEGES ▸ liege

LIEN n right to hold another's property until a debt is paid

LIENAL adj of or relating to the spleen

LIENS ▸ lien

LIER n person who lies down

LIERNE n short secondary rib that connects the intersections of the primary ribs, esp as used in Gothic vaulting

LIERNES ▸ lierne

LIERS ▸ lier

LIES ▸ lie

LIEU n stead

LIEUS ▸ lieu

LIEVE same as ▸ leve

LIEVER ▸ lieve

LIEVES ▸ lieve

LIEVEST ▸ lieve

LIFE n state of living beings, characterized by growth, reproduction, and response to stimuli

LIFEFUL adj full of life

LIFER n prisoner sentenced to imprisonment for life

LIFERS ▸ lifer

LIFES pl n as in still lifes paintings or drawings of inanimate objects

LIFEWAY n way of life

LIFT vb move upwards in position, status, volume, etc ▹ n cage raised and lowered in a vertical shaft to transport people or goods

LIFTBOY n person who operates a lift, esp in large public or commercial buildings and hotels

LIFTED ▸ lift

LIFTER ▸ lift

LIFTERS ▸ lift

LIFTING ▸ lift

LIFTMAN same as ▸ liftboy

LIFTMEN ▸ liftman

LIFTOFF n moment a rocket leaves the ground ▹ vb (of a rocket) to leave its launch pad

LIFTS ▸ lift

LIFULL obsolete form of ▸ lifeful

LIG n (esp in the media) a function with free entertainment and refreshments ▹ vb attend such a function

LIGAN same as ▸ lagan

LIGAND n atom, molecule, radical, or ion forming a complex with a central atom

LIGANDS ▸ ligand

LIGANS ▸ ligan

LIGASE n any of a class of enzymes

LIGASES ▸ ligase

LIGATE vb tie up or constrict (something) with a ligature

LIGATED ▸ ligate

LIGATES ▸ ligate

LIGER n hybrid offspring of a female tiger and a male lion

LIGERS ▸ liger

LIGGE obsolete form of ▸ lie

LIGGED ▸ lig

LIGGER ▸ lig

LIGGERS ▸ lig

LIGGES ▸ ligge

LIGGING ▸ lig

LIGHT n electromagnetic radiation by which things are visible ▹ adj bright ▹ vb ignite ▹ adv with little equipment or luggage

LIGHTED ▸ light

LIGHTEN vb make less dark

LIGHTER n device for lighting cigarettes etc ▹ vb convey in a type of flat-bottomed barge

LIGHTLY adv in a light way ▹ vb belittle

LIGHTS ▸ light

LIGNAGE another word for ▸ lineage

LIGNAN n beneficial substance found in plants

LIGNANS ▸ lignan

LIGNE n unit of measurement

LIGNES ▸ ligne

LIGNIFY vb make or become woody as a result of the deposition of lignin in the cell walls

LIGNIN n complex polymer occurring in certain plant cell walls making the plant rigid

LIGNINS ▸ lignin

LIGNITE n woody textured rock used as fuel

LIGNOSE n explosive compound

LIGNUM n wood

LIGNUMS ▸ lignum

LIGROIN n volatile fraction of petroleum that is used as a solvent

LIGS ▸ lig

LIGULA same as ▸ ligule

LIGULAE ▸ ligula

LIGULAR ▸ ligula

LIGULAS ▸ ligula

LIGULE n membranous outgrowth at the junction between the leaf blade and sheath in many grasses and sedges

LIGULES ▸ ligule

LIGURE n any of the 12 precious stones used in the breastplates of high priests

LIGURES ▸ ligure

LIKABLE adj easy to like

LIKABLY ▸ likable

LIKE adj similar ▹ vb find enjoyable ▹ n favourable

feeling, desire, or preference
LIKED ▸ like
LIKELY adj tending or inclined ▷ adv probably
LIKEN vb compare
LIKENED ▸ liken
LIKENS ▸ liken
LIKER ▸ like
LIKERS ▸ like
LIKES ▸ like
LIKEST ▸ like
LIKIN n historically, Chinese tax
LIKING n fondness
LIKINGS ▸ liking
LIKINS ▸ likin
LIKUTA n (formerly) a coin used in Zaire
LILAC n shrub with pale mauve or white flowers ▷ adj light-purple
LILACS ▸ lilac
LILIED adj decorated with lilies
LILIES ▸ lily
LILL obsolete form of ▸ loll
LILLED ▸ lill
LILLING ▸ lill
LILLS ▸ lill
LILO n trademark for a type of inflatable plastic mattress
LILOS ▸ lilo
LILT n pleasing musical quality in speaking ▷ vb speak with a lilt
LILTED ▸ lilt
LILTING ▸ lilt
LILTS ▸ lilt
LILY n plant which grows from a bulb and has large, often white, flowers
LIMA n type of edible bean
LIMACEL n small shell inside some kinds of slug
LIMACES ▸ limax
LIMACON n heart-shaped curve
LIMAIL same as ▸ lemel
LIMAILS ▸ limail
LIMAN n lagoon
LIMANS ▸ liman
LIMAS ▸ lima
LIMAX n slug
LIMB n arm, leg, or wing ▷ vb dismember
LIMBA n type of African tree
LIMBAS ▸ limba
LIMBATE adj having an edge or border of a different colour from the rest
LIMBEC obsolete form of

▸ **alembic**
LIMBECK obsolete form of ▸ alembic
LIMBECS ▸ limbec
LIMBED ▸ limb
LIMBER vb loosen stiff muscles by exercising ▷ adj pliant or supple ▷ n part of a gun carriage, consisting of an axle, pole, and two wheels
LIMBERS ▸ limber
LIMBI ▸ limbus
LIMBIC ▸ limbus
LIMBIER ▸ limby
LIMBING ▸ limb
LIMBO n supposed region intermediate between Heaven and Hell for the unbaptized
LIMBOS ▸ limbo
LIMBOUS adj with overlapping edges
LIMBS ▸ limb
LIMBUS n border
LIMBY adj with long legs, stem, branches, etc
LIME n calcium compound used as a fertilizer or in making cement ▷ vb spread a calcium compound upon (land) ▷ adj having the flavour of lime fruit
LIMEADE n drink made from sweetened lime juice and plain or carbonated water
LIMED ▸ lime
LIMELIT > limelight
LIMEN another term for > threshold
LIMENS ▸ limen
LIMEPIT n pit containing lime in which hides are placed to remove the hair
LIMES n fortified boundary of the Roman Empire
LIMEY n British person ▷ adj British
LIMEYS ▸ limey
LIMIER ▸ limy
LIMIEST ▸ limy
LIMINA ▸ limen
LIMINAL adj relating to the point (or threshold) beyond which a sensation becomes too faint to be experienced
LIMING ▸ lime
LIMINGS ▸ lime
LIMIT n ultimate extent, degree, or amount of something ▷ vb restrict or confine

LIMITED adj having a limit ▷ n limited train, bus, etc
LIMITER n electronic circuit that produces an output signal whose positive or negative amplitude, or both, is limited to some predetermined value above which the peaks become flattened
LIMITES ▸ limes
LIMITS ▸ limit
LIMMA n semitone
LIMMAS ▸ limma
LIMMER n scoundrel
LIMMERS ▸ limmer
LIMN vb represent in drawing or painting
LIMNED ▸ limn
LIMNER ▸ limn
LIMNERS ▸ limn
LIMNIC adj relating to lakes
LIMNING ▸ limn
LIMNS ▸ limn
LIMO short for > limousine
LIMOS ▸ limo
LIMOSES ▸ limosis
LIMOSIS n excessive hunger
LIMOUS adj muddy
LIMP vb walk with an uneven step ▷ n limping walk ▷ adj without firmness or stiffness
LIMPA n type of rye bread
LIMPAS ▸ limpa
LIMPED ▸ limp
LIMPER ▸ limp
LIMPERS ▸ limp
LIMPEST ▸ limp
LIMPET n shellfish which sticks tightly to rocks ▷ adj denoting certain weapons that are magnetically attached to their targets and resist removal
LIMPETS ▸ limpet
LIMPID adj clear or transparent
LIMPING ▸ limp
LIMPKIN n rail-like wading bird
LIMPLY ▸ limp
LIMPS ▸ limp
LIMPSEY same as ▸ limpsy
LIMPSY adj limp
LIMULI ▸ limulus
LIMULUS n type of horseshoe crab
LIMY adj of, like, or smeared with birdlime
LIN vb cease
LINABLE ▸ line
LINAC n linear accelerator

LINACS ▸ linac
LINAGE n number of lines in written or printed matter
LINAGES ▸ linage
LINALOL same as ▸ linalool
LINCH n ledge
LINCHES ▸ linch
LINCHET another word for ▸ linch
LINCTUS n syrupy cough medicine
LIND same as ▸ linden
LINDANE n white poisonous crystalline powder
LINDEN n large tree with heart-shaped leaves and fragrant yellowish flowers
LINDENS ▸ linden
LINDIES ▸ lindy
LINDS ▸ lind
LINDY n lively dance
LINE n long narrow mark ▷ vb mark with lines
LINEAGE n descent from an ancestor
LINEAL adj in direct line of descent
LINEAR adj of or in lines
LINEATE adj marked with lines
LINECUT n method of relief printing
LINED ▸ line
LINEMAN same as ▸ linesman
LINEMEN ▸ lineman
LINEN n cloth or thread made from flax
LINENS ▸ linen
LINENY ▸ linen
LINER n large passenger ship or aircraft
LINERS ▸ liner
LINES ▸ line
LINEUP n row or arrangement of people or things
LINEUPS ▸ lineup
LINEY ▸ line
LING n slender food fish
LINGA same as ▸ lingam
LINGAM n (in Sanskrit grammar) the masculine gender
LINGAMS ▸ lingam
LINGAS ▸ linga
LINGCOD n type of food fish
LINGEL n strong shoemaker's thread
LINGELS ▸ lingel
LINGER vb delay or prolong departure

LINGERS ▸ linger
LINGIER ▸ lingy
LINGLE same as ▸ lingel
LINGLES ▸ lingle
LINGO n foreign or unfamiliar language or jargon
LINGOES ▸ lingo
LINGOT n ingot
LINGOTS ▸ lingot
LINGS ▸ ling
LINGUA n any tongue-like structure
LINGUAE ▸ lingua
LINGUAL adj of the tongue ▷ n lingual consonant, such as Scots (r)
LINGUAS ▸ lingua
LINGULA n small tongue
LINGY adj heather-covered
LINHAY n farm building with an open front
LINHAYS ▸ linhay
LINIER ▸ line
LINIEST ▸ line
LININ n network of viscous material in the nucleus of a cell that connects the chromatin granules
LINING n layer of cloth attached to the inside of a garment etc
LININGS ▸ lining
LININS ▸ linin
LINISH vb polish metal
LINK n any of the rings forming a chain ▷ vb connect with or as if with links
LINKAGE n act of linking or the state of being linked
LINKBOY n (formerly) a boy who carried a torch for pedestrians in dark streets
LINKED ▸ link
LINKER n person or thing that links
LINKERS ▸ linker
LINKIER ▸ linky
LINKING ▸ link
LINKMAN same as ▸ linkboy
LINKMEN ▸ linkman
LINKROT n state or condition of having expired hyperlinks on a website
LINKS ▸ link
LINKUP n establishing of a connection or union between objects, groups, organizations, etc
LINKUPS ▸ linkup
LINKY adj (of countryside) consisting of links

LINN n waterfall or a pool at the foot of it
LINNED ▸ lin
LINNET n songbird of the finch family
LINNETS ▸ linnet
LINNEY same as ▸ linhay
LINNEYS ▸ linney
LINNIES ▸ linny
LINNING ▸ lin
LINNS ▸ linn
LINNY same as ▸ linhay
LINO same as ▸ linoleum
LINOCUT n design cut in relief in linoleum mounted on a block of wood
LINOS ▸ lino
LINS ▸ lin
LINSANG n any of several forest-dwelling viverrine mammals
LINSEED n seed of the flax plant
LINSEY n type of cloth
LINSEYS ▸ linsey
LINT n shreds of fibre, etc ▷ vb shed or remove lint
LINTED adj having lint
LINTEL n horizontal beam at the top of a door or window
LINTELS ▸ lintel
LINTER n machine for stripping the short fibres of ginned cotton seeds
LINTERS ▸ linter
LINTIE Scots word for ▸ linnet
LINTIER ▸ lint
LINTIES ▸ lintie
LINTING ▸ lint vb
LINTOL same as ▸ lintel
LINTOLS ▸ lintel
LINTS ▸ lint
LINTY ▸ lint
LINUM n type of plant of temperate regions
LINUMS ▸ linum
LINURON n type of herbicide
LINUX n nonproprietary computer operating system suitable for use on personal computers
LINUXES ▸ linux
LINY ▸ line
LION n large animal of the cat family, the male of which has a shaggy mane
LIONCEL n (in heraldry) small lion
LIONEL same as ▸ lioncel
LIONELS ▸ lionel
LIONESS n female lion

LIONET n young lion
LIONETS ▸ lionet
LIONISE same as ▸ **lionize**
LIONISM n lion-like appearance of leprosy
LIONIZE vb treat as a celebrity
LIONLY ▸ lion
LIONS ▸ lion
LIP n either of the fleshy edges of the mouth ▷ vb touch with the lips
LIPA n monetary unit of Croatia worth one hundredth of a kuna
LIPAS ▸ lipa
LIPASE n any of a group of enzymes that digest fat
LIPASES ▸ lipase
LIPE ▸ lipa
LIPEMIA same as ▸ **lipaemia**
LIPID n any of a group of organic compounds including fats, oils, waxes, and sterols
LIPIDE same as ▸ **lipid**
LIPIDES ▸ lipide
LIPIDIC ▸ lipid
LIPIDS ▸ lipid
LIPIN n family of nuclear proteins
LIPINS ▸ lipin
LIPLESS ▸ lip
LIPLIKE ▸ lip
LIPO n liposuction
LIPOIC adj as in lipoic acid sulphur-containing fatty acid
LIPOID n fatlike substance, such as wax
LIPOIDS ▸ lipoid
LIPOMA n benign tumour composed of fatty tissue
LIPOMAS ▸ lipoma
LIPOS ▸ lipo
LIPPED ▸ lip
LIPPEN vb trust
LIPPENS ▸ lippen
LIPPER Scots word for ▸ **ripple**
LIPPERS ▸ lipper
LIPPIE same as ▸ **lippy**
LIPPIER ▸ lippy
LIPPIES ▸ lippie
LIPPING ▸ lip
LIPPY adj insolent or cheeky ▷ n lipstick
LIPREAD vb follow what someone says by watching their lips
LIPS ▸ lip
LIPURIA n presence of fat in the urine

LIQUATE vb separate one component of (an alloy, impure metal, or ore) by heating so that the more fusible part melts
LIQUEFY vb make or become liquid
LIQUEUR n flavoured and sweetened alcoholic spirit ▷ vb flavour with liqueur
LIQUID n substance in a physical state which can change shape but not size ▷ adj of or being a liquid
LIQUIDS ▸ liquid
LIQUIFY same as ▸ **liquefy**
LIQUOR n alcoholic drink, esp spirits ▷ vb steep (malt) in warm water to form wort in brewing
LIQUORS ▸ liquor
LIRA n monetary unit of Turkey, Malta, and formerly of Italy
LIRAS ▸ lira
LIRE ▸ lira
LIRI ▸ lira
LIRIOPE n grasslike plant
LIRK vb wrinkle
LIRKED ▸ lirk
LIRKING ▸ lirk
LIRKS ▸ lirk
LIROT ▸ lira
LIROTH ▸ lira
LIS n fleur-de-lis
LISENTE ▸ sente
LISK Yorkshire dialect for ▸ **groin**
LISKS ▸ lisk
LISLE n strong fine cotton thread or fabric
LISLES ▸ lisle
LISP n speech defect in which s and z are pronounced th ▷ vb speak or utter with a lisp
LISPED ▸ lisp
LISPER ▸ lisp
LISPERS ▸ lisp
LISPING ▸ lisp
LISPS ▸ lisp
LISPUND same as ▸ **lispound**
LISSES ▸ lis
LISSOM adj supple, agile
LISSOME same as ▸ **lissom**
LIST n item-by-item record of names or things, usu written one below another ▷ vb make a list of
LISTED ▸ list
LISTEE n person on list
LISTEES ▸ listee
LISTEL another name for

▸ **fillet**
LISTELS ▸ listel
LISTEN vb concentrate on hearing something
LISTENS ▸ listen
LISTER n plough with a double mouldboard designed to throw soil to either side of a central furrow
LISTERS ▸ lister
LISTETH ▸ list
LISTFUL adj paying attention
LISTING n list or an entry in a list
LISTS pl n field of combat in a tournament
LIT n archaic word for dye or colouring
LITAI ▸ litas
LITANY n prayer with responses from the congregation
LITAS n standard monetary unit of Lithuania, divided into 100 centai
LITCHI n Chinese sapindaceous tree cultivated for its round edible fruits
LITCHIS ▸ litchi
LITE same as ▸ **light**
LITED ▸ light
LITER same as ▸ **litre**
LITERAL adj according to the explicit meaning of a word or text, not figurative ▷ n misprint or misspelling in a text
LITERS ▸ liter
LITES ▸ lite
LITH n limb or joint
LITHATE n salt of uric acid
LITHE adj flexible or supple, pliant ▷ vb listen
LITHED ▸ lithe
LITHELY ▸ lithe
LITHER ▸ lithe
LITHES ▸ lithe
LITHEST ▸ lithe
LITHIA n lithium present in mineral waters as lithium salts
LITHIAS ▸ lithia
LITHIC adj of, relating to, or composed of stone
LITHIFY vb turn into rock
LITHING ▸ lithe
LITHITE n part of cell with sensory element
LITHIUM n chemical element, the lightest

LITHO n lithography ▷ vb print using lithography

LITHOED ▸ litho

LITHOID adj resembling stone or rock

LITHOPS n fleshy-leaved plant

LITHOS ▸ litho

LITHS ▸ lith

LITING ▸ lite

LITMUS n blue dye turned red by acids and restored to blue by alkalis

LITORAL same as ▸ littoral

LITOTES n ironical understatement used for effect

LITOTIC ▸ litotes

LITRE n unit of liquid measure equal to 1000 cubic centimetres or 1.76 pints

LITRES ▸ litre

LITS ▸ lit

LITTEN adj lighted

LITTER n untidy rubbish dropped in public places ▷ vb strew with litter

LITTERS ▸ litter

LITTERY adj covered in litter

LITTLE adj small or smaller than average ▷ adv not a lot ▷ n small amount, extent, or duration

LITTLER ▸ little

LITTLES ▸ little

LITTLIE n young child

LITTLIN same as ▸ littling

LITU ▸ litas

LITURGY n prescribed form of public worship

LITUUS n type of curved trumpet

LIVABLE adj tolerable or pleasant to live (with)

LIVE vb be alive ▷ adj living, alive ▷ adv in the form of a live performance

LIVED ▸ live

LIVEDO n reddish discoloured patch on the skin

LIVEDOS ▸ livedo

LIVELOD n livelihood

LIVELY adj full of life or vigour

LIVEN vb make or become lively

LIVENED ▸ liven

LIVENER ▸ liven

LIVENS ▸ liven

LIVER n person who lives in

a specified way

LIVERED adj having liver

LIVERS ▸ liver

LIVERY n distinctive dress, esp of a servant or servants ▷ adj of or resembling liver

LIVES ▸ life

LIVEST ▸ live

LIVEYER n (in Newfoundland) a full-time resident

LIVID adj angry or furious

LIVIDER ▸ livid

LIVIDLY ▸ livid

LIVIER same as ▸ liveyer

LIVIERS ▸ livier

LIVING adj possessing life, not dead or inanimate ▷ n condition of being alive

LIVINGS ▸ living

LIVOR another word for ▸ lividity

LIVORS ▸ livor

LIVRE n former French unit of money of account, equal to 1 pound of silver

LIVRES ▸ livre

LIVYER same as ▸ liveyer

LIVYERS ▸ livyer

LIXIVIA ▸ lixivium

LIZARD n four-footed reptile with a long body and tail

LIZARDS ▸ lizard

LIZZIE n as in tin lizzie an old or decrepit car

LIZZIES ▸ lizzie

LLAMA n woolly animal of the camel family used as a beast of burden in S America

LLAMAS ▸ llama

LLANERO n native of llanos

LLANO n extensive grassy treeless plain, esp in South America

LLANOS ▸ llano

LO interj look!

LOACH n carplike freshwater fish

LOACHES ▸ loach

LOAD n burden or weight ▷ vb put a load on or into

LOADED adj (of a question) containing a hidden trap or implication

LOADEN vb load

LOADENS ▸ loaden

LOADER n person who loads a gun or other firearm

LOADERS ▸ loader

LOADING n load or burden

LOADS pl n lots or a lot

LOAF n shaped mass of baked bread ▷ vb idle, loiter

LOAFED ▸ loaf

LOAFER n person who avoids work

LOAFERS ▸ loafer

LOAFING ▸ loaf

LOAFS ▸ loaf

LOAM n fertile soil ▷ vb cover, treat, or fill with loam

LOAMED ▸ loam

LOAMIER ▸ loam

LOAMING ▸ loam

LOAMS ▸ loam

LOAMY ▸ loam

LOAN n money lent at interest ▷ vb lend

LOANED ▸ loan

LOANEE n sportsperson who is loaned from one organization to another

LOANEES ▸ loanee

LOANER ▸ loan

LOANERS ▸ loan

LOANING ▸ loan

LOANS ▸ loan

LOAST ▸ lose

LOATH adj unwilling or reluctant (to)

LOATHE vb hate, be disgusted by

LOATHED ▸ loathe

LOATHER ▸ loathe

LOATHES ▸ loathe

LOATHLY adv with reluctance

LOATHY obsolete form of ▸ loathsome

LOAVE vb make into the form of a loaf

LOAVED ▸ loave

LOAVES ▸ loaf

LOAVING ▸ loave

LOB n ball struck or thrown in a high arc ▷ vb strike or throw (a ball) in a high arc

LOBAR adj of or affecting a lobe

LOBATE adj with or like lobes

LOBATED same as ▸ lobate

LOBBED ▸ lob

LOBBER n one who lobs

LOBBERS ▸ lobber

LOBBIED ▸ lobby

LOBBIES ▸ lobby

LOBBING ▸ lob

LOBBY n corridor into which rooms open ▷ vb try to influence (legislators) in the formulation of policy

LOBBYER ▸ lobby

LOBE n rounded projection

LOBED ▸ lobe

LOBEFIN n type of fish

LOBELET n small lobe

LOBELIA n garden plant with blue, red, or white flowers

LOBES ▸ lobe

LOBI ▸ lobus

LOBING n formation of lobes

LOBINGS ▸ lobing

LOBIPED adj with lobed toes

LOBO n timber wolf

LOBOLA n (in African custom) price paid by a bridegroom's family to his bride's family

LOBOLAS ▸ lobola

LOBOLO same as ▸ lobola

LOBOLOS ▸ lobolo

LOBOS ▸ lobo

LOBOSE another word for ▸ lobate

LOBS ▸ lob

LOBSTER n shellfish with a long tail and claws, which turns red when boiled ▷ vb fish for lobsters

LOBULAR ▸ lobule

LOBULE n small lobe or a subdivision of a lobe

LOBULES ▸ lobule

LOBULI ▸ lobulus

LOBULUS n small lobe

LOBUS n lobe

LOBWORM same as ▸ lugworm

LOCA ▸ locus

LOCAL adj of or existing in a particular place ▷ n person belonging to a particular district

LOCALE n scene of an event

LOCALES ▸ locale

LOCALLY adv within a particular area or place

LOCALS ▸ local

LOCATE vb discover the whereabouts of

LOCATED ▸ locate

LOCATER ▸ locate

LOCATES ▸ locate

LOCATOR n part of index that indicates where to look for information

LOCH n lake

LOCHAN n small inland loch

LOCHANS ▸ lochan

LOCHIA n vaginal discharge of cellular debris, mucus, and blood following childbirth

LOCHIAL ▸ lochia

LOCHS ▸ loch

LOCI ▸ locus

LOCK n appliance for fastening a door, case, etc ▷ vb fasten or become fastened securely

LOCKAGE n system of locks in a canal

LOCKBOX n system of collecting funds from companies by banks

LOCKED ▸ lock

LOCKER n small cupboard with a lock

LOCKERS ▸ locker

LOCKET n small hinged pendant for a portrait etc

LOCKETS ▸ locket

LOCKFUL n sufficient to fill a canal lock

LOCKING ▸ lock

LOCKJAW n tetanus

LOCKMAN n lock-keeper

LOCKMEN ▸ lockman

LOCKNUT n supplementary nut screwed down upon a primary nut to prevent it from shaking loose

LOCKOUT n closing of a workplace by an employer to force workers to accept terms

LOCKRAM n type of linen cloth

LOCKS ▸ lock

LOCKSET n hardware used to lock door

LOCKUP n prison

LOCKUPS ▸ lockup

LOCO n locomotive ▷ adj insane ▷ vb poison with locoweed

LOCOED ▸ loco

LOCOES ▸ loco

LOCOING ▸ loco

LOCOISM n disease of cattle, sheep, and horses caused by eating locoweed

LOCOMAN n railwayman, esp an engine-driver

LOCOMEN ▸ locoman

LOCOS ▸ loco

LOCULAR adj divided into compartments by septa

LOCULE n any of the chambers of an ovary or anther

LOCULED adj having locules

LOCULES ▸ locule

LOCULI ▸ loculus

LOCULUS same as ▸ locule

LOCUM n temporary stand-in for a doctor or clergyman

LOCUMS ▸ locum

LOCUS n area or place where something happens

LOCUST n destructive insect that flies in swarms and eats crops ▷ vb ravage, as locusts

LOCUSTA n flower cluster unit in grasses

LOCUSTS ▸ locust

LOD n type of logarithm

LODE n vein of ore

LODEN n thick heavy waterproof woollen cloth with a short pile, used to make garments, esp coats

LODENS ▸ loden

LODES ▸ lode

LODGE n gatekeeper's house ▷ vb live in another's house at a fixed charge

LODGED ▸ lodge

LODGER n person who pays rent in return for accommodation in someone else's home

LODGERS ▸ lodger

LODGES ▸ lodge

LODGING n temporary residence

LODS ▸ lod

LOERIE same as ▸ lourie

LOERIES ▸ loerie

LOESS n fine-grained soil, found mainly in river valleys, originally deposited by the wind

LOESSAL ▸ loess

LOESSES ▸ loess

LOESSIC adj relating to or consisting of loess

LOFT n space between the top storey and roof of a building ▷ vb strike, throw, or kick (a ball) high into the air

LOFTED ▸ loft

LOFTER n type of golf club

LOFTERS ▸ lofter

LOFTIER ▸ lofty

LOFTILY ▸ lofty

LOFTING ▸ loft

LOFTS ▸ loft

LOFTY adj of great height

LOG n portion of a felled tree stripped of branches ▷ vb saw logs from a tree

LOGAN another name for ▸ bogan

LOGANIA n type of Australian plant

LOGANS ▸ logan
LOGBOOK n book recording the details about a car or a ship's journeys
LOGE n small enclosure or box in a theatre or opera house
LOGES ▸ loge
LOGGAT n small piece of wood
LOGGATS ▸ loggat
LOGGED ▸ log
LOGGER n tractor or crane for handling logs
LOGGERS ▸ logger
LOGGETS n old-fashioned game played with sticks
LOGGIA n covered gallery at the side of a building
LOGGIAS ▸ loggia
LOGGIE ▸ loggia
LOGGIER ▸ loggy
LOGGING ▸ log
LOGGISH ▸ log
LOGGY adj slow, sluggish, or listless
LOGIA ▸ logion
LOGIC n philosophy of reasoning
LOGICAL adj of logic
LOGICS ▸ logic
LOGIE n fire-place of a kiln
LOGIER ▸ logy
LOGIES ▸ logie
LOGIEST ▸ logy
LOGILY ▸ logy
LOGIN n process by which a computer user logs on
LOGINS ▸ login
LOGION n saying of Christ regarded as authentic
LOGIONS ▸ logion
LOGJAM n blockage caused by the crowding together of a number of logs floating in a river ▸ vb cause a logjam
LOGJAMS ▸ logjam
LOGLINE n synopsis of screenplay
LOGLOG n logarithm of a logarithm (in equations, etc)
LOGLOGS ▸ loglog
LOGO same as ▸ logotype
LOGOFF n process by which a computer user logs out
LOGOFFS ▸ logoff
LOGOI ▸ logos
LOGON same as ▸ login
LOGONS ▸ logon
LOGOS n reason or the rational principle expressed in words and things,

argument, or justification
LOGOUT same as ▸ logoff
LOGOUTS ▸ logout
LOGROLL vb use logrolling in order to procure the passage of (legislation)
LOGS ▸ log
LOGWAY another name for ▸ gangway
LOGWAYS ▸ logway
LOGWOOD n leguminous tree of the Caribbean and Central America
LOGY adj dull or listless
LOHAN another word for ▸ arhat
LOHANS ▸ lohan
LOID vb open (a lock) using a celluloid strip
LOIDED ▸ loid
LOIDING ▸ loid
LOIDS ▸ loid
LOIN n part of the body between the ribs and the hips
LOINS pl n hips and the inner surface of the legs where they join the body
LOIPE n cross-country skiing track
LOIPEN ▸ loipe
LOIR n large dormouse
LOIRS ▸ loir
LOITER vb stand or wait aimlessly or idly
LOITERS ▸ loiter
LOKE n track
LOKES ▸ loke
LOKSHEN pl n noodles
LOLIGO n type of squid
LOLIGOS ▸ loligo
LOLIUM n type of grass
LOLIUMS ▸ lolium
LOLL vb lounge lazily ▸ n act or instance of lolling
LOLLED ▸ loll
LOLLER ▸ loll
LOLLERS ▸ loll
LOLLIES ▸ lolly
LOLLING ▸ loll
LOLLOP vb move clumsily
LOLLOPS ▸ lollop
LOLLOPY ▸ lollop
LOLLS ▸ loll
LOLLY n lollipop or ice lolly
LOLOG same as ▸ loglog
LOLOGS ▸ lolog
LOMA n lobe
LOMAS ▸ loma
LOMATA ▸ loma
LOME vb cover with lome
LOMED ▸ lome
LOMEIN n Chinese dish

LOMEINS ▸ lomein
LOMENT n pod of certain leguminous plants
LOMENTA > lomentum
LOMENTS ▸ loment
LOMES ▸ lome
LOMING ▸ lome
LOMPISH another word for ▸ lumpish
LONE adj solitary
LONELY adj sad because alone
LONER n person who prefers to be alone
LONERS ▸ loner
LONG adj having length, esp great length, in space or time ▸ adv for a certain time ▸ vb have a strong desire (for)
LONGA n long note
LONGAN n sapindaceous tree of tropical and subtropical Asia
LONGANS ▸ longan
LONGAS ▸ longa
LONGBOW n large powerful bow
LONGE n rope used in training a horse ▸ vb train using a longe
LONGED ▸ long
LONGER n line of barrels on a ship
LONGERS ▸ longer
LONGES ▸ longe
LONGEST ▸ long
LONGIES n long johns
LONGING n yearning ▸ adj having or showing desire
LONGISH adj rather long
LONGLY ▸ long
LONGS pl n full-length trousers
LOO n informal word meaning lavatory ▸ vb Scots word meaning love
LOOBIER ▸ looby
LOOBIES ▸ looby
LOOBILY ▸ looby
LOOBY adj foolish ▸ n foolish or stupid person
LOOED ▸ loo
LOOEY n lieutenant
LOOEYS ▸ looey
LOOF n part of ship's side
LOOFA same as ▸ loofah
LOOFAH n sponge made from the dried pod of a gourd
LOOFAHS ▸ loofah
LOOFAS ▸ loofa
LOOFFUL n handful**

L

LOOFS ▸ loof
LOOIE same as ▸ **looey**
LOOIES ▸ looie
LOOING ▸ loo
LOOK vb direct the eyes or attention (towards) ▷ n instance of looking
LOOKED ▸ look
LOOKER n person who looks
LOOKERS ▸ looker
LOOKING ▸ look
LOOKISM n discrimination against a person on the grounds of physical appearance
LOOKIST ▸ lookism
LOOKOUT n act of watching for danger or for an opportunity ▷ vb be careful
LOOKS ▸ look
LOOKUP n act of looking up information, esp on the internet
LOOKUPS ▸ lookup
LOOM n machine for weaving cloth ▷ vb appear dimly
LOOMED ▸ loom
LOOMING ▸ loom
LOOMS ▸ loom
LOON n diving bird
LOONEY same as ▸ **loony**
LOONEYS ▸ loony
LOONIE n Canadian dollar coin with a loon bird on one of its faces
LOONIER ▸ loony
LOONIES ▸ loony
LOONILY ▸ loony
LOONING n cry of the loon
LOONS ▸ loon
LOONY adj foolish or insane ▷ n foolish or insane person
LOOP n rounded shape made by a curved line or rope crossing itself ▷ vb form or fasten with a loop
LOOPED ▸ loop
LOOPER n person or thing that loops or makes loops
LOOPERS ▸ looper
LOOPIER ▸ loopy
LOOPILY ▸ loopy
LOOPING ▸ loop
LOOPS ▸ loop
LOOPY adj slightly mad or crazy
LOOR ▸ lief
LOORD obsolete word for ▸ **lout**
LOORDS ▸ loord

LOOS ▸ loo
LOOSE adj not tight, fastened, fixed, or tense ▷ adv in a loose manner ▷ vb free
LOOSED ▸ loose
LOOSELY ▸ loose
LOOSEN vb make loose
LOOSENS ▸ loosen
LOOSER ▸ loose
LOOSES ▸ loose
LOOSEST ▸ loose
LOOSIE n informal word for loose forward
LOOSIES pl n cigarettes sold individually
LOOSING n celebration of one's 21st birthday
LOOT vb pillage ▷ n goods stolen during pillaging
LOOTED ▸ loot
LOOTEN Scots past form of ▸ **let**
LOOTER ▸ loot
LOOTERS ▸ loot
LOOTING ▸ loot
LOOTS ▸ loot
LOOVES ▸ loof
LOP vb cut away (twigs and branches) ▷ n part or parts lopped off, as from a tree
LOPE vb run with long easy strides ▷ n loping stride
LOPED ▸ lope
LOPER ▸ lope
LOPERS ▸ lope
LOPES ▸ lope
LOPING ▸ lope
LOPPED ▸ lop
LOPPER n tool for lopping ▷ vb curdle
LOPPERS ▸ lopper
LOPPIER ▸ loppy
LOPPIES ▸ loppy
LOPPING ▸ lop
LOPPY adj floppy ▷ n man employed to do maintenance tasks on a ranch
LOPS ▸ lop
LOQUAT n ornamental evergreen rosaceous tree
LOQUATS ▸ loquat
LOR interj exclamation of surprise or dismay
LORAL adj of part of side of bird's head
LORAN n radio navigation system operating over long distances
LORANS ▸ loran
LORATE adj like a strap
LORCHA n junk-rigged vessel

LORCHAS ▸ lorcha
LORD n person with power over others, such as a monarch or master ▷ vb act in a superior manner
LORDED ▸ lord
LORDING n gentleman
LORDKIN n little lord
LORDLY adj imperious, proud ▷ adv in the manner of a lord
LORDOMA same as > **lordosis**
LORDS ▸ lord
LORDY interj exclamation of surprise or dismay
LORE n body of traditions on a subject
LOREAL adj concerning or relating to lore
LOREL another word for ▸ **losel**
LORELS ▸ lorel
LORES ▸ lore
LORETTE n concubine
LORGNON n monocle or pair of spectacles
LORIC ▸ lorica
LORICA n hard outer covering of rotifers, ciliate protozoans, and similar organisms
LORICAE ▸ lorica
LORICS ▸ lorica
LORIES ▸ lory
LORIMER n (formerly) a person who made bits, spurs, and other small metal objects
LORINER same as ▸ **lorimer**
LORING n teaching
LORINGS ▸ loring
LORIOT n golden oriole (bird)
LORIOTS ▸ loriot
LORIS n any of several omnivorous nocturnal slow-moving prosimian primates
LORISES ▸ loris
LORN adj forsaken or wretched
LORRELL obsolete word for ▸ **losel**
LORRIES ▸ lorry
LORRY n large vehicle for transporting loads by road
LORY n any of various small brightly coloured parrots of Australia and Indonesia
LOS n approval
LOSABLE ▸ loose
LOSE vb part with or come

to be without

LOSED ▸ lose

LOSEL n worthless person ▷ adj (of a person) worthless, useless, or wasteful

LOSELS ▸ losel

LOSEN ▸ loose

LOSER n person or thing that loses

LOSERS ▸ loser

LOSES ▸ loose

LOSH interj lord

LOSING ▸ lose

LOSINGS pl n losses, esp money lost in gambling

LOSS n losing

LOSSES ▸ loss

LOSSIER ▸ lossy

LOSSY adj (of a dielectric material, transmission line, etc) designed to have a high attenuation

LOST adj missing

LOT pron great number ▷ n collection of people or things ▷ vb draw lots for

LOTA n globular water container, usually of brass, used in India, Myanmar, etc

LOTAH same as ▸ lota

LOTAHS ▸ lotah

LOTAS ▸ lota

LOTE another word for ▸ lotus

LOTES ▸ lote

LOTH same as ▸ loath

LOTHER ▸ loth

LOTHEST ▸ loth

LOTI n standard monetary unit of Lesotho, divided into 100 lisente

LOTIC adj of, relating to, or designating natural communities living in rapidly flowing water

LOTION n medical or cosmetic liquid for use on the skin

LOTIONS ▸ lotion

LOTO same as ▸ lotto

LOTOS same as ▸ lotus

LOTOSES ▸ lotos

LOTS ▸ lot

LOTTE n type of fish

LOTTED ▸ lot

LOTTER n someone who works an allotment

LOTTERS ▸ lotter

LOTTERY n method of raising money by selling tickets that win prizes by chance

LOTTES ▸ lotte

LOTTING ▸ lot

LOTTO n game of chance like bingo

LOTTOS ▸ lotto

LOTUS n legendary plant whose fruit induces forgetfulness

LOTUSES ▸ lotus

LOU Scots word for ▸ love

LOUCHE adj shifty or disreputable

LOUCHER ▸ louche

LOUD adj relatively great in volume

LOUDEN vb make or become louder

LOUDENS ▸ louden

LOUDER ▸ loud

LOUDEST ▸ loud

LOUDISH adj fairly loud

LOUDLY ▸ loud

LOUED ▸ lou

LOUGH n loch

LOUGHS ▸ lough

LOUIE same as ▸ looey

LOUIES ▸ louie

LOUING ▸ lou

LOUIS n former French gold coin

LOUMA n weekly market in rural areas of developing countries

LOUMAS ▸ louma

LOUN same as ▸ lown

LOUND same as ▸ loun

LOUNDED ▸ lound

LOUNDER vb beat severely

LOUNDS ▸ lound

LOUNED ▸ loun

LOUNGE n living room in a private house ▷ vb sit, lie, or stand in a relaxed manner

LOUNGED ▸ lounge

LOUNGER n comfortable sometimes adjustable couch or extending chair designed for someone to relax on

LOUNGES ▸ lounge

LOUNGEY n suggestive of a lounge bar or easy-listening music

LOUNGY adj casual; relaxed

LOUNING ▸ loun

LOUNS ▸ loun

LOUP Scots word for ▸ leap

LOUPE n magnifying glass used by jewellers, horologists, etc

LOUPED ▸ loup

LOUPEN ▸ loup

LOUPES ▸ loupe

LOUPING ▸ loup

LOUPIT ▸ loup

LOUPS ▸ loup

LOUR vb (esp of the sky, weather, etc) to be overcast, dark, and menacing ▷ n menacing scowl or appearance

LOURE n slow, former French dance

LOURED ▸ lour

LOURES ▸ loure

LOURIE n type of African bird with either crimson or grey plumage

LOURIER ▸ loury

LOURIES ▸ lourie

LOURING ▸ lour

LOURS ▸ lour

LOURY adj sombre

LOUS ▸ lou

LOUSE n wingless parasitic insect ▷ vb ruin or spoil

LOUSED ▸ louse

LOUSER n mean nasty person

LOUSERS ▸ louser

LOUSES ▸ louse

LOUSIER ▸ lousy

LOUSILY ▸ lousy

LOUSING ▸ louse

LOUSY adj mean or unpleasant

LOUT n crude, oafish, or aggressive person ▷ vb bow or stoop

LOUTED ▸ lout

LOUTING ▸ lout

LOUTISH adj characteristic of a lout

LOUTS ▸ lout

LOUVAR n large silvery whalelike scombroid fish

LOUVARS ▸ louvar

LOUVER same as ▸ louvre

LOUVERS ▸ louver

LOUVRE n one of a set of parallel slats slanted to admit air but not rain

LOUVRED adj (of a window, door, etc) having louvres

LOUVRES ▸ louvre

LOVABLE adj attracting or deserving affection

LOVABLY ▸ lovable

LOVAGE n European plant used for flavouring food

LOVAGES ▸ lovage

LOVAT n yellowish-green or bluish-green mixture, esp in tweeds or woollens

LOVATS ▸ lovat

LOVE vb have a great

affection for ▷ *n* great
affection
LOVEBUG *n* small US flying
insect
LOVED ▶ **love**
LOVELY *adj* very attractive
▷ *n* attractive woman
LOVER *n* person having a
sexual relationship outside
marriage
LOVERED *adj* having a lover
LOVERLY *adj* loverlike
LOVERS ▶ **lover**
LOVES ▶ **love**
LOVEY *another word for*
▶ **love**
LOVEYS ▶ **lovey**
LOVING *adj* affectionate,
tender
LOVINGS ▶ **loving**
LOW *adj* not tall, high, or
elevated ▷ *adv* in or to a low
position, level, or degree
▷ *n* low position, level, or
degree ▷ *vb* moo
LOWAN *n* type of Australian
bird
LOWANS ▶ **lowan**
LOWBALL *vb* deliberately
under-charge
LOWBORN *adj* of ignoble or
common parentage
LOWBOY *n* table fitted with
drawers
LOWBOYS ▶ **lowboy**
LOWBRED *same as*
▶ **lowborn**
LOWBROW *adj* with
nonintellectual tastes and
interests ▷ *n* person with
uncultivated or
nonintellectual tastes
LOWDOWN *n* inside
information
LOWE *same as* ▶ **low**
LOWED ▶ **low**
LOWER *adj* below one or
more other things ▷ *vb*
cause or allow to move
down
LOWERED ▶ **lower**
LOWERS ▶ **lower**
LOWERY *adj* sombre
LOWES ▶ **lowe**
LOWEST ▶ **low**
LOWING ▶ **low**
LOWINGS ▶ **low**
LOWISH ▶ **low**
LOWLAND *n* low-lying
country ▷ *adj* of a lowland
or lowlands
LOWLIER ▶ **lowly**
LOWLIFE *n* member or

members of the
underworld
LOWLILY ▶ **lowly**
LOWLY *adj* modest, humble
▷ *adv* in a low or lowly
manner
LOWN *vb* calm
LOWND *same as* ▶ **lown**
LOWNDED ▶ **lownd**
LOWNDS ▶ **lownd**
LOWNE *same as* ▶ **loon**
LOWNED ▶ **lown**
LOWNES ▶ **lowne**
LOWNESS ▶ **low**
LOWNING ▶ **lown**
LOWNS ▶ **lown**
LOWP *same as* ▶ **loup**
LOWPED ▶ **lowp**
LOWPING ▶ **lowp**
LOWPS ▶ **lowp**
LOWRIE *another name for*
▶ **lory**
LOWRIES ▶ **lowry**
LOWRY *another name for*
▶ **lory**
LOWS ▶ **low**
LOWSE *vb* release or loose
▷ *adj* loose
LOWSED ▶ **lowse**
LOWSER ▶ **lowse**
LOWSES ▶ **lowse**
LOWSEST ▶ **lowse**
LOWSING ▶ **lowse**
LOWSIT ▶ **lowse**
LOWT *same as* ▶ **lout**
LOWTED ▶ **lowt**
LOWTING ▶ **lowt**
LOWTS ▶ **lowt**
LOWVELD *n* low ground in S
Africa
LOX *vb* load fuel tanks of
spacecraft with liquid
oxygen ▷ *n* kind of smoked
salmon

| This is another good
word when you have an X
to dispose of.

LOXED ▶ **lox**
LOXES ▶ **lox**
LOXING ▶ **lox**
LOXYGEN *n* liquid oxygen
LOY *n* narrow spade with a
single footrest
LOYAL *adj* faithful to one's
friends, country, or
government
LOYALER ▶ **loyal**
LOYALLY ▶ **loyal**
LOYALTY *n* quality of being
loyal
LOYS ▶ **loy**
LOZELL *obsolete form of*
▶ **losel**

LOZELLS ▶ **lozell**
LOZEN *n* window pane
LOZENGE *n* medicated
tablet held in the mouth
until it dissolves
LOZENGY *adj* divided by
diagonal lines to form a
lattice
LOZENS ▶ **lozen**
LUACH *n* calendar that
shows the dates of festivals
and, usually, the times of
start and finish of the
Sabbath
LUAU *n* feast of Hawaiian
food
LUAUS ▶ **luau**
LUBBARD *same as* ▶ **lubber**
LUBBER *n* big, awkward, or
stupid person
LUBBERS ▶ **lubber**
LUBE *n* lubricating oil ▷ *vb*
lubricate with oil
LUBED ▶ **lube**
LUBES ▶ **lube**
LUBFISH *n* type of fish
LUBING ▶ **lube**
LUBRA *n* Aboriginal woman
LUBRAS ▶ **lubra**
LUBRIC *adj* slippery
LUCARNE *n* type of dormer
window
LUCE *another name for* ▶ **pike**
LUCENCE ▶ **lucent**
LUCENCY ▶ **lucent**
LUCENT *adj* brilliant,
shining, or translucent
LUCERN *same as* ▶ **lucerne**
LUCERNE *n* alfalfa
LUCERNS ▶ **lucern**
LUCES ▶ **luce**
LUCHOT ▶ **luach**
LUCHOTH ▶ **luach**
LUCID *adj* clear and easily
understood
LUCIDER ▶ **lucid**
LUCIDLY ▶ **lucid**
LUCIFER *n* friction match
LUCIGEN *n* lamp burning oil
mixed with hot air
LUCITE *n* brand name of a
type of transparent
acrylic-based plastic
LUCITES ▶ **lucite**
LUCK *n* fortune, good or bad
▷ *vb* have good fortune
LUCKED ▶ **luck**
LUCKEN *adj* shut
LUCKIE *same as* ▶ **lucky**
LUCKIER ▶ **lucky**
LUCKIES ▶ **luckie**
LUCKILY ▶ **lucky**
LUCKING ▶ **luck**

LUCKS ▸ luck

LUCKY adj having or bringing good luck ▷ n old woman

LUCRE n money or wealth

LUCRES ▸ lucre

LUCUMA n type of S American tree

LUCUMAS ▸ lucuma

LUCUMO n Etruscan king

LUCUMOS ▸ lucumo

LUD n lord ▷ interj exclamation of dismay or surprise

LUDE n slang word for drug for relieving anxiety

LUDES ▸ lude

LUDIC adj playful

LUDO n game played with dice and counters on a board

LUDOS ▸ ludo

LUDS ▸ lud

LUDSHIP ▸ lud

LUES n any venereal disease

LUETIC ▸ lues

LUETICS ▸ lues

LUFF vb sail (a ship) towards the wind ▷ n leading edge of a fore-and-aft sail

LUFFA same as ▸ loofah

LUFFAS ▸ luffa

LUFFED ▸ luff

LUFFING ▸ luff

LUFFS ▸ luff

LUG vb carry or drag with great effort ▷ n projection serving as a handle

LUGE n racing toboggan on which riders lie on their backs, descending feet first ▷ vb ride on a luge

LUGED ▸ luge

LUGEING ▸ luge

LUGER n tradename for a type of German automatic pistol

LUGERS ▸ luger

LUGES ▸ luge

LUGGAGE n suitcases, bags, etc

LUGGED ▸ lug

LUGGER n small working boat with an oblong sail

LUGGERS ▸ lugger

LUGGIE n wooden bowl with handles

LUGGIES ▸ luggie

LUGGING ▸ lug

LUGHOLE informal word for ▸ ear

LUGING ▸ luge

LUGINGS ▸ luge

LUGS ▸ lug

LUGSAIL n four-sided sail bent and hoisted on a yard

LUGWORM n large worm used as bait

LUIT Scots past form of ▸ let

LUITEN ▸ let

LUKE same as ▸ lukewarm

LULIBUB obsolete form of ▸ lollipop

LULL vb soothe (someone) by soft sounds or motions ▷ n brief time of quiet in a storm etc

LULLABY n quiet song to send a child to sleep ▷ vb quiet or soothe with or as if with a lullaby

LULLED ▸ lull

LULLER ▸ lull

LULLERS ▸ lull

LULLING ▸ lull

LULLS ▸ lull

LULU n person or thing considered to be outstanding in size, appearance, etc

LULUS ▸ lulu

LUM n chimney

LUMA n a monetary unit of Armenia worth one hundredth of a dram

LUMAS ▸ luma

LUMBAGO n pain in the lower back

LUMBANG n type of tree

LUMBAR adj of the part of the body between the lowest ribs and the hipbones ▷ n old-fashioned kind of ship

LUMBARS ▸ lumbar

LUMBER n unwanted disused household articles ▷ vb burden with something unpleasant

LUMBERS ▸ lumber

LUMEN n derived SI unit of luminous flux

LUMENAL ▸ lumen

LUMENS ▸ lumen

LUMINA ▸ lumen

LUMINAL ▸ lumen

LUMINE vb illuminate

LUMINED ▸ lumine

LUMINES ▸ lumine

LUMME interj exclamation of surprise or dismay

LUMMIER ▸ lummy

LUMMOX n clumsy or stupid person

LUMMY interj exclamation of surprise ▷ adj excellent

LUMP n shapeless piece or mass ▷ vb consider as a single group

LUMPED ▸ lump

LUMPEN adj stupid or unthinking ▷ n member of underclass

LUMPENS ▸ lumpen

LUMPER n stevedore

LUMPERS ▸ lumper

LUMPIER ▸ lumpy

LUMPILY ▸ lumpy

LUMPING ▸ lump

LUMPISH adj stupid or clumsy

LUMPKIN n lout

LUMPS ▸ lump

LUMPY adj full of or having lumps

LUMS ▸ lum

LUNA n type of large American moth

LUNACY n foolishness

LUNAR adj relating to the moon ▷ n lunar distance

LUNARS ▸ lunar

LUNARY n moonwort herb

LUNAS ▸ luna

LUNATE adj shaped like a crescent ▷ n crescent-shaped bone forming part of the wrist

LUNATED same as ▸ lunate

LUNATES ▸ lunate

LUNATIC adj foolish and irresponsible ▷ n foolish or annoying person

LUNCH n meal taken in the middle of the day ▷ vb eat lunch

LUNCHED ▸ lunch

LUNCHER ▸ lunch

LUNCHES ▸ lunch

LUNE same as ▸ lunette

LUNES ▸ lune

LUNET n small moon or satellite

LUNETS ▸ lunet

LUNETTE n anything that is shaped like a crescent

LUNG n organ that allows an animal or bird to breathe air

LUNGAN same as ▸ longan

LUNGANS ▸ lungan

LUNGE n sudden forward motion ▷ vb move with or make a lunge

LUNGED ▸ lunge

LUNGEE same as ▸ lungi

LUNGEES ▸ lungee

LUNGER ▸ lunge

LUNGERS ▸ lunge

LUNGES ▸ lunge
LUNGFUL ▸ lung
LUNGI n long piece of cotton cloth worn as a loincloth, sash, or turban by Indian men or as a skirt
LUNGIE n guillemot
LUNGIES ▸ lungie
LUNGING ▸ lunge
LUNGIS ▸ lungi
LUNGS ▸ lung
LUNGYI same as ▸ **lungi**
LUNGYIS ▸ lungyi
LUNIER ▸ luny
LUNIES ▸ luny
LUNIEST ▸ luny
LUNK n awkward, heavy, or stupid person
LUNKER n very large fish, esp bass
LUNKERS ▸ lunker
LUNKS ▸ lunk
LUNT vb produce smoke
LUNTED ▸ lunt
LUNTING ▸ lunt
LUNTS ▸ lunt
LUNULA n white crescent-shaped area at the base of the human fingernail
LUNULAE ▸ lunula
LUNULAR same as > **lunulate**
LUNULE same as ▸ **lunula**
LUNULES ▸ lunule
LUNY same as ▸ **loony**
LUNYIE same as ▸ **lungie**
LUNYIES ▸ lunyie
LUPANAR n brothel
LUPIN n garden plant with tall spikes of flowers
LUPINE adj like a wolf ▷ n lupin
LUPINES ▸ lupine
LUPINS ▸ lupin
LUPOID adj suffering from lupus
LUPOUS adj relating to lupus
LUPPEN Scots past form of ▸ **leap**
LUPULIN n resinous powder extracted from the female flowers of the hop plant
LUPUS n ulcerous skin disease
LUPUSES ▸ lupus
LUR n large bronze musical horn found in Danish peat bogs
LURCH vb tilt or lean suddenly to one side ▷ n lurching movement

LURCHED ▸ lurch
LURCHER n crossbred dog trained to hunt silently
LURCHES ▸ lurch
LURDAN n stupid or dull person ▷ adj dull or stupid
LURDANE same as ▸ **lurdan**
LURDANS ▸ lurdan
LURDEN same as ▸ **lurdan**
LURDENS ▸ lurden
LURE vb tempt or attract by the promise of reward ▷ n person or thing that lures
LURED ▸ lure
LURER ▸ lure
LURERS ▸ lure
LURES ▸ lure
LUREX n thin glittery thread
LUREXES ▸ lurex
LURGI same as ▸ **lurgy**
LURGIES ▸ lurgy
LURGIS ▸ lurgi
LURGY n any undetermined illness
LURID adj vivid in shocking detail, sensational
LURIDER ▸ lurid
LURIDLY ▸ lurid
LURING ▸ lure
LURINGS ▸ luring
LURK vb lie hidden or move stealthily, esp for sinister purposes
LURKED ▸ lurk
LURKER ▸ lurk
LURKERS ▸ lurk
LURKING adj lingering but almost unacknowledged
LURKS ▸ lurk
LURRIES ▸ lurry
LURRY n confused jumble
LURS ▸ lur
LURVE n love
LURVES ▸ lurve
LUSER n user of a computer system, as considered by a systems administator or other member of a technical support team
LUSERS ▸ luser
LUSH adj (of grass etc) growing thickly and healthily ▷ n alcoholic ▷ vb drink (alcohol) to excess
LUSHED ▸ lush
LUSHER adj more lush ▷ n drunkard
LUSHERS ▸ lusher
LUSHES ▸ lush
LUSHEST ▸ lush
LUSHIER ▸ lushy
LUSHING ▸ lush
LUSHLY ▸ lush

LUSHY adj slightly intoxicated
LUSK vb lounge around
LUSKED ▸ lusk
LUSKING ▸ lusk
LUSKISH adj lazy
LUSKS ▸ lusk
LUST n strong sexual desire ▷ vb have passionate desire (for)
LUSTED ▸ lust
LUSTER same as ▸ **lustre**
LUSTERS ▸ luster
LUSTFUL adj driven by lust
LUSTICK obsolete word for ▸ **lusty**
LUSTIER ▸ lusty
LUSTILY ▸ lusty
LUSTING ▸ lust
LUSTRA ▸ lustrum
LUSTRAL adj of or relating to a ceremony of purification
LUSTRE n gloss, sheen ▷ vb make, be, or become lustrous
LUSTRED ▸ lustre
LUSTRES ▸ lustre
LUSTRUM n period of five years
LUSTS ▸ lust
LUSTY adj vigorous, healthy
LUSUS n freak, mutant, or monster
LUSUSES ▸ lusus
LUTE n ancient guitar-like musical instrument with a body shaped like a half pear ▷ vb seal (a joint or surface) with a mixture of cement and clay
LUTEA adj yellow
LUTEAL adj relating to or characterized by the development of the corpus luteum
LUTED ▸ lute
LUTEIN n xanthophyll pigment that has a light-absorbing function in photosynthesis
LUTEINS ▸ lutein
LUTEOUS adj of a light to moderate greenish-yellow colour
LUTER n lute player
LUTERS ▸ luter
LUTES ▸ lute
LUTEUM adj yellow
LUTFISK same as > **lutefisk**
LUTHERN another name for ▸ **dormer**
LUTHIER n lute-maker

LUTING n mixture of cement and clay

LUTINGS ▸ luting

LUTIST same as > lutenist

LUTISTS ▸ lutist

LUTITE another name for ▸ pelite

LUTITES ▸ lutite

LUTTEN ▸ loot

LUTZ n jump in which the skater takes off from the back outside edge of one skate, makes one, two, or three turns in the air, and lands on the back outside edge of the other skate

LUTZES ▸ lutz

LUV n love

LUVS ▸ love

LUVVIE n person who is involved in acting or the theatre

LUVVIES ▸ luvvy

LUVVY same as ▸ luvvie

LUX n unit of illumination

A **lux** is a unit of illumination, and is another of the key words using X.

LUXATE vb put (a shoulder, knee, etc) out of joint

LUXATED ▸ luxate

LUXATES ▸ luxate

LUXE n as in **de luxe** rich, elegant, or sumptuous

LUXES ▸ luxe

LUXURY n enjoyment of rich, very comfortable living ▷ adj of or providing luxury

LUZ n supposedly indestructible bone of the human body

This very unusual word, meaning a supposedly indestructible bone in the human body, is very useful for playing the Z.

LUZERN n alfalfa

LUZERNS ▸ luzern

LUZZES ▸ luz

LWEI n Angolan monetary unit

LWEIS ▸ lwei

LYAM n leash

LYAMS ▸ lyam

LYARD same as ▸ liard

LYART same as ▸ liard

LYASE n any enzyme that catalyses the separation of two parts of a molecule

LYASES ▸ lyase

LYCEA ▸ lyceum

LYCEE n secondary school

LYCEES ▸ lycee

LYCEUM n public building for events such as concerts and lectures

LYCEUMS ▸ lyceum

LYCH same as ▸ lich

LYCHEE same as ▸ litchi

LYCHEES ▸ lychee

LYCHES ▸ lych

LYCHNIS n type of plant with red, pink, or white five-petalled flowers

LYCOPOD n type of moss

LYCRA n tradename for a type of synthetic elastic fabric and fibre used for tight-fitting garments, such as swimming costumes

LYCRAS ▸ lycra

LYDDITE n explosive consisting chiefly of fused picric acid

LYE n caustic solution obtained by leaching wood ash

LYES ▸ lye

LYFULL obsolete form of ▸ lifeful

LYING ▸ lie

LYINGLY ▸ lie

LYINGS ▸ lie

LYM obsolete form of ▸ lyam

LYME n as in **lyme grass** type of perennial dune grass

LYMES ▸ lyme

LYMITER same as ▸ limiter

LYMPH n colourless bodily fluid consisting mainly of white blood cells

LYMPHAD n ancient rowing boat

LYMPHS n lymph

LYMS ▸ lym

LYNAGE obsolete form of ▸ lineage

LYNAGES ▸ lynage

LYNCEAN adj of or resembling a lynx

LYNCH vb put to death without a trial

LYNCHED ▸ lynch

LYNCHER ▸ lynch

LYNCHES ▸ lynch

LYNCHET n terrace or ridge formed in prehistoric or medieval times by ploughing a hillside

LYNE n flax

LYNES ▸ lyne

LYNX n animal of the cat family with tufted ears and a short tail

LYNXES ▸ lynx

LYOPHIL same as > lyophilic

LYRA n as in **lyra viol** lutelike musical instrument of the 16th and 17th centuries

LYRATE adj shaped like a lyre

LYRATED same as ▸ lyrate

LYRE n ancient musical instrument like a U-shaped harp

LYRES ▸ lyre

LYRIC adj (of poetry) expressing personal emotion in songlike style ▷ n short poem in a songlike style

LYRICAL same as ▸ lyric

LYRICON n wind synthesizer

LYRICS ▸ lyric

LYRISM n art or technique of playing the lyre

LYRISMS ▸ lyrism

LYRIST same as > lyricist

LYRISTS ▸ lyrist

LYSATE n material formed by lysis

LYSATES ▸ lysate

LYSE vb undergo or cause to undergo lysis

LYSED ▸ lyse

LYSES ▸ lysis

LYSIN n any of a group of antibodies that cause dissolution of cells against which they are directed

LYSINE n essential amino acid that occurs in proteins

LYSINES ▸ lysine

LYSING ▸ lyse

LYSINS ▸ lysin

LYSIS n destruction or dissolution of cells by the action of a particular lysin

LYSOGEN n lysis-inducing agent

LYSOL n tradename for a solution used as an antiseptic and disinfectant

LYSOLS ▸ lysol

LYSSA less common word for ▸ rabies

LYSSAS ▸ lyssa

LYTE vb dismount

LYTED ▸ lyte

LYTES ▸ lyte

LYTHE *n* type of fish
LYTHES ▸ lythe
LYTIC *adj* relating to, causing, or resulting from lysis

LYTING ▸ lyte
LYTTA *n* rodlike mass of cartilage beneath the tongue in the dog and other carnivores

LYTTAE ▸ lytta
LYTTAS ▸ lytta

L

Mm

M is a very useful letter when you need to form short words as it starts a two-letter word with every vowel, as well as with **Y** and with another **M**. Remembering this allows you to use **M** effectively when you're forming a word parallel to, and in contact with, a word that is already on the board. **M** also combines well with **X** and **Z**, so there is a lot of potential for high-scoring words. Keep **max, mix** and **mux** (12 points each) in mind, as well as **miz** and **muz** (14 each). It's also worth remembering the three-letter words ending in **W: maw, mew** and **mow** (8 points each). **Myc** is another useful word to remember when you are short of vowels.

MA n mother
MAA vb (of goats) bleat
MAAED ▶ maa
MAAING ▶ maa
MAAR n coneless volcanic crater that has been formed by a single explosion
MAARE ▶ maar
MAARS ▶ maar
MAAS n thick soured milk
MAASES ▶ maas
MAATJES n pickled herring
MABE n type of pearl
MABELA n ground kaffir corn used for making porridge
MABELAS ▶ mabela
MABES ▶ mabe
MAC n macintosh
MACABER same as ▶ macabre
MACABRE adj strange and horrible, gruesome
MACACO n type of lemur
MACACOS ▶ macaco
MACADAM n road surface of pressed layers of small broken stones
MACAQUE n monkey of Asia and Africa with cheek pouches and either a short tail or no tail
MACAW n large tropical American parrot
MACAWS ▶ macaw
MACCHIA n thicket in Italy
MACCHIE ▶ macchia
MACE n club, usually having a spiked metal head, used esp in the Middle Ages ▷ vb use a mace

MACED ▶ mace
MACER n macebearer, esp (in Scotland) an official who acts as usher in a court of law
MACERAL n any of the organic units that constitute coal: equivalent to any of the mineral constituents of a rock
MACERS ▶ macer
MACES ▶ mace
MACH n ratio of the speed of a body in a particular medium to the speed of sound in that medium
MACHAIR n (in the western Highlands of Scotland) a strip of sandy, grassy, often lime-rich land just above the high-water mark at a sandy shore: used as grazing or arable land
MACHAN n (in India) a raised platform used in tiger hunting
MACHANS ▶ machan
MACHE n papier-mâché
MACHER n important or influential person: often used ironically
MACHERS ▶ macher
MACHES ▶ mache
MACHETE n broad heavy knife used for cutting or as a weapon
MACHI n as in machi chips in Indian English, fish and chips
MACHINE n apparatus, usu powered by electricity,

designed to perform a particular task ▷ vb make or produce by machine
MACHO adj strongly or exaggeratedly masculine ▷ n strong or exaggerated masculinity
MACHOS ▶ macho
MACHREE n Irish form of address meaning my dear
MACHS ▶ mach
MACHZOR n Jewish prayer book containing prescribed holiday rituals
MACING ▶ mace
MACK same as ▶ mac
MACKLE n double or blurred impression caused by shifting paper or type ▷ vb mend hurriedly or in a makeshift way
MACKLED ▶ mackle
MACKLES ▶ mackle
MACKS ▶ mack
MACLE n crystal consisting of two parts
MACLED ▶ macle
MACLES ▶ macle
MACON n red or white wine from the Mâcon area, heavier than the other burgundies
MACONS ▶ macon
MACOYA n South American tree
MACOYAS ▶ macoya
MACRAME n ornamental work of knotted cord
MACRAMI same as ▶ macrame
MACRO n close-up lens

M

M

MACRON n mark placed over a letter to represent a long vowel
MACRONS ▶ macron
MACROS ▶ macro
MACS ▶ mac
MACULA n small spot or area of distinct colour, such as a freckle
MACULAE ▶ macula
MACULAR ▶ macula
MACULAS ▶ macula
MACULE same as ▶ mackle
MACULED ▶ macule
MACULES ▶ macule
MACUMBA n religious cult in Brazil that combines Christian and voodoo elements
MAD adj mentally deranged, insane ▷ vb make mad
MADAFU n coconut milk
MADAFUS ▶ madafu
MADAM n polite term of address for a woman ▷ vb call someone madam
MADAME n French title equivalent to Mrs
MADAMED ▶ madam
MADAMES ▶ madame
MADAMS ▶ madam
MADCAP adj foolish or reckless ▷ n impulsive or reckless person
MADCAPS ▶ madcap
MADDED ▶ mad
MADDEN vb infuriate or irritate
MADDENS ▶ madden
MADDER n type of rose
MADDERS ▶ madder
MADDEST ▶ mad
MADDING ▶ mad
MADDISH ▶ mad
MADDOCK same as ▶ mattock
MADE ▶ make
MADEFY vb make moist
MADEIRA n kind of rich sponge cake
MADGE n type of hammer
MADGES ▶ madge
MADID adj wet
MADISON n type of cycle relay race
MADLING n insane person
MADLY adv with great speed and energy
MADMAN n person who is insane
MADMEN ▶ madman
MADNESS n insanity

MADONNA n picture or statue of the Virgin Mary
MADOQUA n Ethiopian antelope
MADRAS n medium-hot curry
MADRASA same as > madrasah
MADRE Spanish word for ▶ mother
MADRES ▶ madre
MADRONA n N American evergreen tree or shrub with white flowers and red berry-like fruits
MADRONE same as ▶ madrona
MADRONO same as ▶ madrona
MADS ▶ mad
MADTOM n species of catfish
MADTOMS ▶ madtom
MADURO adj (of cigars) dark and strong ▷ n cigar of this type
MADUROS ▶ maduro
MADWORT n low-growing Eurasian plant with small blue flowers
MADZOON same as ▶ matzoon
MAE adj more
MAELID n mythical spirit of apple
MAELIDS ▶ maelid
MAENAD n female disciple of Dionysus, the Greek god of wine
MAENADS ▶ maenad
MAERL n type of red coralline algae
MAERLS ▶ maerl
MAES ▶ mae
MAESTRI ▶ maestro
MAESTRO n outstanding musician or conductor
MAFFIA same as ▶ mafia
MAFFIAS ▶ maffia
MAFFICK vb celebrate extravagantly and publicly
MAFFLED adj baffled
MAFFLIN n half-witted person
MAFIA n international secret organization founded in Sicily, probably in opposition to tyranny. It developed into a criminal organization and in the late 19th century was carried to the US by Italian immigrants

MAFIAS ▶ mafia
MAFIC n collective term for minerals present in igneous rock
MAFICS ▶ mafic
MAFIOSI ▶ mafioso
MAFIOSO n member of the Mafia
MAFTED adj suffering under oppressive heat
MAFTIR n final section of the weekly Torah reading
MAFTIRS ▶ maftir
MAG vb talk ▷ n talk
MAGALOG same as ▶ magalogue
MAGE archaic word for > magician
MAGENTA adj deep purplish-red ▷ n deep purplish red that is the complementary colour of green and, with yellow and cyan, forms a set of primary colours
MAGES ▶ mage
MAGG same as ▶ mag
MAGGED ▶ mag
MAGGIE n magpie
MAGGIES ▶ maggie
MAGGING ▶ mag
MAGGOT n larva of an insect
MAGGOTS ▶ maggot
MAGGOTY adj relating to, resembling, or ridden with maggots
MAGGS ▶ magg
MAGI ▶ magus
MAGIAN ▶ magus
MAGIANS ▶ magus
MAGIC n supposed art of invoking supernatural powers to influence events ▷ vb to transform or produce by or as if by magic ▷ adj of, using, or like magic
MAGICAL ▶ magic
MAGICS ▶ magic
MAGILP same as ▶ megilp
MAGILPS ▶ magilp
MAGISM ▶ magus
MAGISMS ▶ magus
MAGLEV n type of high-speed train that runs on magnets supported by a magnetic field generated around the track
MAGLEVS ▶ maglev
MAGMA n molten rock inside the earth's crust
MAGMAS ▶ magma
MAGMATA ▶ magma

MAGNATE n influential or wealthy person, esp in industry

MAGNES n magnetic iron ore

MAGNET n piece of iron or steel capable of attracting iron and pointing north when suspended

MAGNETO n apparatus for ignition in an internal-combustion engine

MAGNETS ▸ magnet

MAGNIFY vb increase in apparent size, as with a lens

MAGNON n short for Cro-Magnon

MAGNONS ▸ magnon

MAGNOX n alloy composed mainly of magnesium, used in fuel elements of some nuclear reactors

MAGNUM n large wine bottle holding about 1.5 litres

MAGNUMS ▸ magnum

MAGNUS adj as in **magnus hitch** knot similar to a clove hitch but having one more turn

MAGOT n Chinese or Japanese figurine in a crouching position, usually grotesque

MAGOTS ▸ magot

MAGPIE n black-and-white bird

MAGPIES ▸ magpie

MAGS ▸ mag

MAGSMAN n raconteur

MAGSMEN ▸ magsman

MAGUEY n tropical American agave plant

MAGUEYS ▸ maguey

MAGUS n Zoroastrian priest of the ancient Medes and Persians

MAGYAR adj of or relating to a style of sleeve cut in one piece with the bodice

MAHA n as in **maha yoga** form of yoga

MAHATMA n person revered for holiness and wisdom

MAHEWU n (in South Africa) fermented liquid mealie-meal porridge, used as a stimulant, esp by Black Africans

MAHEWUS ▸ mahewu

MAHJONG n game of Chinese origin, usually

played by four people, in which tiles bearing various designs are drawn and discarded until one player has an entire hand of winning combinations

MAHMAL n litter used in Muslim ceremony

MAHMALS ▸ mahmal

MAHOE n New Zealand tree

MAHOES ▸ mahoe

MAHONIA n Asian and American evergreen shrub cultivated for its ornamental spiny leaves and clusters of small yellow flowers

MAHOUT n (in India and the East Indies) elephant driver or keeper

MAHOUTS ▸ mahout

MAHSEER n large freshwater Indian fish

MAHSIR same as ▸ **mahseer**

MAHSIRS ▸ mahsir

MAHUA n Indian tree

MAHUANG n herbal medicine from shrub

MAHUAS ▸ mahua

MAHWA same as ▸ **mahua**

MAHWAS ▸ mahwa

MAHZOR same as ▸ **machzor**

MAHZORS ▸ mahzor

MAID n female servant ▷ vb work as maid

MAIDAN n (in Pakistan, India, etc) an open space used for meetings, sports, etc

MAIDANS ▸ maidan

MAIDED ▸ maid

MAIDEN n young unmarried woman ▷ adj unmarried

MAIDENS ▸ maiden

MAIDING ▸ maid

MAIDISH ▸ maid

MAIDISM n pellagra

MAIDS ▸ maid

MAIGRE adj not containing flesh, and so permissible as food on days of religious abstinence ▷ n species of fish

MAIGRES ▸ maigre

MAIHEM same as ▸ **mayhem**

MAIHEMS ▸ maihem

MAIK n old halfpenny

MAIKO n apprentice geisha

MAIKOS ▸ maiko

MAIKS ▸ maik

MAIL n letters and packages

transported and delivered by the post office ▷ vb send by mail

MAILBAG n large bag for transporting or delivering mail

MAILBOX n box into which letters and parcels are delivered

MAILCAR same as ▸ **mailcoach**

MAILE n halfpenny

MAILED ▸ mail

MAILER n person who addresses or mails letters, etc

MAILERS ▸ mailer

MAILES ▸ maile

MAILING ▸ mail

MAILL n Scots word meaning rent

MAILLOT n tights worn for ballet, gymnastics, etc

MAILLS ▸ maill

MAILMAN n postman

MAILMEN ▸ mailman

MAILS ▸ mail

MAILVAN n vehicle used to transport post

MAIM vb cripple or mutilate ▷ n injury or defect

MAIMED ▸ maim

MAIMER ▸ maim

MAIMERS ▸ maim

MAIMING ▸ maim

MAIMS ▸ maim

MAIN adj chief or principal ▷ n principal pipe or line carrying water, gas, or electricity ▷ vb lower sails

MAINED ▸ main

MAINER ▸ main

MAINEST ▸ main

MAINING ▸ main

MAINLY adv for the most part, chiefly

MAINOR n act of doing something

MAINORS ▸ mainor

MAINOUR same as ▸ **mainor**

MAINS ▸ main

MAINTOP n top or platform at the head of the mainmast

MAIR Scots form of ▸ **more**

MAIRE n New Zealand tree

MAIRES ▸ maire

MAIRS ▸ mair

MAISE n measure of herring

MAISES ▸ maise

MAIST Scots word for ▸ **most**

MAISTER Scots word for ▸ **master**

M

MAISTRY ▶ maister

MAISTS ▶ maist

MAIZE n type of corn with spikes of yellow grains

MAIZES ▶ maize

MAJAGUA same as ▶ **mahoe**

MAJESTY n stateliness or grandeur

MAJLIS n (in various N African and Middle Eastern countries) an assembly; council

MAJOR adj greater in number, quality, or extent ▷ n middle-ranking army officer ▷ vb do one's principal study in (a particular subject)

MAJORAT n estate, the right to which is that of the first born child of a family

MAJORED ▶ major

MAJORLY adv very

MAJORS ▶ major

MAK Scots word for ▶ **make**

MAKABLE ▶ make

MAKAR same as ▶ **maker**

MAKARS ▶ makar

MAKE vb create, construct, or establish ▷ n brand, type, or style

MAKER n person or company that makes something

MAKERS ▶ maker

MAKES ▶ make

MAKEUP n cosmetics, such as powder, lipstick, etc, applied to the face to improve its appearance ▷ vb devise, construct, or compose, sometimes with the intent to deceive

MAKEUPS ▶ makeup

MAKI n in Japanese cuisine, rice and other ingredients wrapped in a short seaweed roll

MAKING ▶ make

MAKINGS pl n potentials, qualities, or materials

MAKIS ▶ maki

MAKO n powerful shark of the Atlantic and Pacific Oceans

MAKOS ▶ mako

MAKS ▶ mak

MAKUTA plural of ▶ **likuta**

MAKUTU n Polynesian witchcraft ▷ vb cast a spell on

MAKUTUS ▶ makutu

MAL n illness

MALA n string of beads or knots, used in praying and meditating

MALACCA n stem of the rattan palm

MALACIA n pathological softening of an organ or tissue, such as bone

MALADY n disease or illness

MALAISE n something wrong which affects a section of society or area of activity

MALAM same as ▶ **mallam**

MALAMS ▶ malam

MALANGA same as ▶ **cocoyam**

MALAR n cheekbone ▷ adj of or relating to the cheek or cheekbone

MALARIA n infectious disease caused by the bite of some mosquitoes

MALARKY same as > **malarkey**

MALARS ▶ malar

MALAS ▶ mala

MALATE n any salt or ester of malic acid

MALATES ▶ malate

MALAX vb soften

MALAXED ▶ malax

MALAXES ▶ malax

MALE adj of the sex which can fertilize female reproductive cells ▷ n male person or animal

MALEATE n any salt or ester of maleic acid

MALEFIC adj causing evil

MALEIC adj as in **maleic acid** colourless soluble crystalline substance used to synthesize other compounds

MALES ▶ male

MALFED adj having malfunctioned

MALGRE same as ▶ **maugre**

MALGRED ▶ malgre

MALGRES ▶ malgre

MALI n member of an Indian caste

MALIBU n as in **malibu board** lightweight surfboard

MALIC adj as in **malic acid** colourless crystalline compound occurring in apples and other fruit

MALICE n desire to cause harm to others ▷ vb wish harm to

MALICED ▶ malice

MALICES ▶ malice

MALICHO n mischief

MALIGN vb slander or defame ▷ adj evil in influence or effect

MALIGNS ▶ malign

MALIK n person of authority in India

MALIKS ▶ malik

MALINE n stiff net

MALINES ▶ maline

MALIS ▶ mali

MALISM n belief that evil dominates world

MALISMS ▶ malism

MALISON archaic or poetic word for ▶ **curse**

MALIST ▶ malism

MALKIN archaic or dialect name for a ▶ **cat**

MALKINS ▶ malkin

MALL n street or shopping area closed to vehicles ▷ vb maul

MALLAM n (in Islamic W Africa) a man learned in Koranic studies

MALLAMS ▶ mallam

MALLARD n wild duck

MALLED ▶ mall

MALLEE n low-growing eucalypt in dry regions

MALLEES ▶ mallee

MALLEI ▶ malleus

MALLET n (wooden) hammer

MALLETS ▶ mallet

MALLEUS n outermost and largest of the three small bones in the middle ear of mammals

MALLING ▶ mall

MALLOW n plant with pink or purple flowers

MALLOWS ▶ mallow

MALLS ▶ mall

MALM n soft greyish limestone that crumbles easily

MALMAG n Asian monkey

MALMAGS ▶ malmag

MALMIER ▶ malmy

MALMS ▶ malm

MALMSEY n sweet Madeira wine

MALMY adj looking like malm

MALODOR same as > **malodour**

MALONIC adj as in **malonic acid** colourless crystalline compound occurring in sugar beet

MALOTI plural of ▸ **loti**

MALS ▸ **mal**

MALT n grain, such as barley, prepared for use in making beer or whisky ▷ vb make into or make with malt

MALTASE n enzyme that hydrolyses maltose and similar glucosides to glucose

MALTED ▸ **malt**

MALTEDS ▸ **malty**

MALTESE adj as in **maltese cross** cross-shaped part of a film projector

MALTHA n any of various naturally occurring mixtures of hydrocarbons, such as ozocerite

MALTHAS ▸ **maltha**

MALTIER ▸ **malty**

MALTING n building in which malt is made or stored

MALTMAN same as ▸ **maltster**

MALTMEN ▸ **maltman**

MALTOL n food additive

MALTOLS ▸ **maltol**

MALTOSE n sugar formed by the action of enzymes on starch

MALTS ▸ **malt**

MALTY adj of, like, or containing malt

MALVA n mallow plant

MALVAS ▸ **malva**

MALWA n Ugandan drink brewed from millet

MALWARE n computer program designed to cause damage or disruption to a system

MALWAS ▸ **malwa**

MAM same as ▸ **mother**

MAMA n mother

MAMAGUY vb deceive or tease, either in jest or by deceitful flattery ▷ n instance of such deception or flattery

MAMAKAU same as ▸ **mamaku**

MAMAKO same as ▸ **mamaku**

MAMAKOS ▸ **mamako**

MAMAKU n tall edible New Zealand tree fern

MAMAKUS ▸ **mamaku**

MAMAS ▸ **mama**

MAMBA n deadly S African snake

MAMBAS ▸ **mamba**

MAMBO n Latin American dance resembling the rumba ▷ vb perform this dance

MAMBOED ▸ **mambo**

MAMBOES ▸ **mambo**

MAMBOS ▸ **mambo**

MAMEE same as ▸ **mamey**

MAMEES ▸ **mamee**

MAMELON n small rounded hillock

MAMEY n tropical tree

MAMEYES ▸ **mamey**

MAMEYS ▸ **mamey**

MAMIE n tropical tree

MAMIES ▸ **mamie**

MAMILLA n nipple or teat

MAMLUK same as > **mameluke**

MAMLUKS ▸ **mamluk**

MAMMA n buxom and voluptuous woman

MAMMAE ▸ **mamma**

MAMMAL n animal of the type that suckles its young

MAMMALS ▸ **mammal**

MAMMARY adj of the breasts or milk-producing glands

MAMMAS ▸ **mamma**

MAMMATE adj having breasts

MAMMATI > **mammatus**

MAMMEE same as ▸ **mamey**

MAMMEES ▸ **mammee**

MAMMER vb hesitate

MAMMERS ▸ **mammer**

MAMMET same as ▸ **maumet**

MAMMETS ▸ **mammet**

MAMMEY same as ▸ **mamey**

MAMMEYS ▸ **mammey**

MAMMIE same as ▸ **mammy**

MAMMIES ▸ **mammy**

MAMMOCK n fragment ▷ vb tear or shred

MAMMON n wealth regarded as a source of evil

MAMMONS ▸ **mammon**

MAMMOTH n extinct elephant-like mammal ▷ adj colossal

MAMMY n Black woman employed as a nurse or servant to a White family

MAMPARA n foolish person, idiot

MAMPOER n home-distilled brandy made from peaches, prickly pears, etc

MAMS ▸ **mam**

MAMZER n child of an incestuous or adulterous union

MAMZERS ▸ **mamzer**

MAN n adult male ▷ vb supply with sufficient people for operation or defence

MANA n authority, influence

MANACLE vb handcuff or fetter ▷ n metal ring or chain put round the wrists or ankles, used to restrict the movements of a prisoner or convict

MANAGE vb succeed in doing

MANAGED ▸ **manage**

MANAGER n person in charge of a business, institution, actor, sports team, etc

MANAGES ▸ **manage**

MANAIA n common figure in Māori carving consisting of a human body and a bird-like head

MANAIAS ▸ **manaia**

MANAKIN same as ▸ **manikin**

MANANA n tomorrow ▷ adv tomorrow

MANANAS ▸ **manana**

MANAS ▸ **mana**

MANAT n standard monetary unit of Azerbaijan, divided into 100 gopik

MANATEE n large tropical plant-eating aquatic mammal

MANATI same as ▸ **manatee**

MANATIS ▸ **manati**

MANATS ▸ **manat**

MANATU n large flowering deciduous New Zealand tree

MANATUS ▸ **manatu**

MANAWA in New Zealand, same as ▸ **mangrove**

MANAWAS ▸ **manawa**

MANCALA n African and Asian board game

MANCHE n long sleeve

MANCHES ▸ **manche**

MANCHET n type of bread

MANCUS n former English coin

MAND ▸ **man**

M

MANDALA n circular design symbolizing the universe

MANDATE n official or authoritative command ▷ vb give authority to

MANDI n (in India) a big market

MANDIOC same as ▶ manioc

MANDIR n Hindu or Jain temple

MANDIRA same as ▶ mandir

MANDIRS ▶ mandir

MANDIS ▶ mandi

MANDOLA n early type of mandolin

MANDOM n mankind

MANDOMS ▶ mandom

MANDORA n ancestor of mandolin

MANDREL n shaft on which work is held in a lathe

MANDRIL same as ▶ mandrel

MANE n long hair on the neck of a horse, lion, etc

MANED ▶ mane

MANEGE n art of training horses and riders ▷ vb train horse

MANEGED ▶ manege

MANEGES ▶ manege

MANEH same as ▶ mina

MANEHS ▶ maneh

MANENT ▶ manet

MANES pl n spirits of the dead, often revered as minor deities

MANET vb theatre direction, remain on stage

MANFUL adj determined and brave

MANG vb speak

MANGA n type of Japanese comic book with an adult theme

MANGABY same as > mangabey

MANGAL n Turkish brazier

MANGALS ▶ mangal

MANGAS ▶ manga

MANGE n skin disease of domestic animals

MANGEAO n small New Zealand tree with glossy leaves

MANGED ▶ mang

MANGEL n Eurasian variety of the beet plant with a large yellowish root, cultivated as a cattle food

MANGELS ▶ mangel

MANGER n eating trough in a stable or barn

MANGERS ▶ manger

MANGES ▶ mange

MANGEY same as ▶ mangy

MANGIER ▶ mangy

MANGILY ▶ mangy

MANGING ▶ mang

MANGLE vb destroy by crushing and twisting ▷ n machine with rollers for squeezing water from washed clothes

MANGLED ▶ mangle

MANGLER ▶ mangle

MANGLES ▶ mangle

MANGO n tropical fruit with sweet juicy yellow flesh

MANGOES ▶ mango

MANGOLD n type of root vegetable

MANGOS ▶ mango

MANGS ▶ mang

MANGY adj having mange

MANHOLE n hole with a cover, through which a person can enter a drain or sewer

MANHOOD n state or quality of being a man or being manly

MANHUNT n organized search, usu by police, for a wanted man or a fugitive

MANI n place to pray

MANIA n extreme enthusiasm

MANIAC n mad person

MANIACS ▶ maniac

MANIAS ▶ mania

MANIC adj extremely excited or energetic ▷ n person afflicted with mania

MANICS ▶ manic

MANIES ▶ many

MANIHOC variation of ▶ manioc

MANIHOT n tropical American plant

MANIKIN n little man or dwarf

MANILA n strong brown paper used for envelopes

MANILAS ▶ manila

MANILLA n early currency in W Africa in the form of a small bracelet

MANILLE n (in ombre and quadrille) the second best trump

MANIOC same as ▶ cassava

MANIOCA same as ▶ manioc

MANIOCS ▶ manioc

MANIPLE n (in ancient Rome) a unit of 120 to 200 foot soldiers

MANIS n pangolin

MANITO same as ▶ manitou

MANITOS ▶ manito

MANITOU n (among the Algonquian Indians) a deified spirit or force

MANITU same as ▶ manitou

MANITUS ▶ manitu

MANJACK n single individual

MANKIER ▶ manky

MANKIND n human beings collectively

MANKINI n a revealing man's swimming costume

MANKY adj worthless, rotten, or in bad taste

MANLESS ▶ man

MANLIER ▶ manly

MANLIKE adj resembling or befitting a man

MANLILY ▶ manly

MANLY adj (possessing qualities) appropriate to a man

MANMADE adj made or produced by man

MANNA n miraculous food which sustained the Israelites in the wilderness

MANNAN n drug derived from mannose

MANNANS ▶ mannan

MANNAS ▶ manna

MANNED ▶ man

MANNER n way a thing happens or is done

MANNERS pl n person's social conduct viewed in the light of whether it is regarded as polite or acceptable or not

MANNING ▶ man

MANNISH adj (of a woman) like a man

MANNITE same as > mannitol

MANNOSE n hexose sugar

MANO n stone for grinding grain

MANOAO n New Zealand shrub

MANOAOS ▶ manoao

MANOR n large country house and its lands

MANORS ▶ manor

MANOS ▶ mano

MANPACK n load carried by one person

MANQUE *adj* would-be

MANRED *n* homage

MANREDS ▸ manred

MANRENT *same as* ▸ **manred**

MANROPE *n* rope railing

MANS ▸ man

MANSARD *n* roof with two slopes on both sides and both ends, the lower slopes being steeper than the upper

MANSE *n* house provided for a minister in some religious denominations

MANSES ▸ manse

MANSION *n* large house

MANTA *n* type of large ray with very wide winglike pectoral fins

MANTAS ▸ manta

MANTEAU *n* cloak or mantle

MANTEEL *n* cloak

MANTEL *n* structure round a fireplace ▸ *vb* construct a mantel

MANTELS ▸ mantel

MANTES ▸ mantis

MANTIC *adj* of or relating to divination and prophecy

MANTID *same as* ▸ **mantis**

MANTIDS ▸ mantid

MANTIES ▸ manty

MANTIS *n* carnivorous insect like a grasshopper

MANTLE *same as* ▸ **mantel**

MANTLED ▸ mantle

MANTLES ▸ mantle

MANTLET *same as* > **mantelet**

MANTO *same as* ▸ **manteau**

MANTOES ▸ manto

MANTOS ▸ manto

MANTRA *n* any sacred word or syllable used as an object of concentration

MANTRAM *same as* ▸ **mantra**

MANTRAP *n* snare for catching people, esp trespassers

MANTRAS ▸ mantra

MANTRIC ▸ mantra

MANTUA *n* loose gown of the 17th and 18th centuries, worn open in front to show the underskirt

MANTUAS ▸ mantua

MANTY *Scots variant of* ▸ **mantua**

MANUAL *adj* of or done with the hands ▸ *n* handbook

MANUALS ▸ manual

MANUARY *same as* ▸ **manual**

MANUKA *n* New Zealand tree with strong elastic wood and aromatic leaves

MANUKAS ▸ manuka

MANUL *n* Asian wildcat

MANULS ▸ manul

MANUMEA *n* pigeon of Samoa

MANUMIT *vb* free from slavery

MANURE *n* animal excrement used as a fertilizer ▸ *vb* fertilize (land) with this

MANURED ▸ manure

MANURER ▸ manure

MANURES ▸ manure

MANUS *n* wrist and hand

MANWARD *adv* towards humankind

MANWISE *adv* in human way

MANY *adj* numerous ▸ *n* large number

MANYATA *same as* > **manyatta**

MAOMAO *n* fish of New Zealand seas

MAOMAOS ▸ maomao

MAORMOR *same as* ▸ **mormaor**

MAP *n* representation of the earth's surface or some part of it, showing geographical features ▸ *vb* make a map of

MAPAU *n* small New Zealand tree with reddish bark, aromatic leaves, and dark berries

MAPAUS ▸ mapau

MAPLE *n* tree with broad leaves, a variety of which yields sugar

MAPLES ▸ maple

MAPLESS ▸ map

MAPLIKE ▸ map

MAPPED ▸ map

MAPPER ▸ map

MAPPERS ▸ map

MAPPERY *n* making of maps

MAPPING ▸ map

MAPPIST ▸ map

MAPS ▸ map

MAPWISE *adv* like map

MAQUI *n* Chilean shrub

MAQUILA *n* US-owned factory in Mexico

MAQUIS *n* French underground movement

that fought against the German occupying forces in World War II

MAR *vb* spoil or impair ▸ *n* disfiguring mark

MARA *n* harelike S American rodent inhabiting the pampas of Argentina

MARABI *n* kind of music popular in S African townships in the 1930s

MARABIS ▸ marabi

MARABOU *n* large black-and-white African stork

MARACA *n* shaken percussion instrument made from a gourd containing dried seeds etc

MARACAS ▸ maraca

MARAE *n* enclosed space in front of a Māori meeting house

MARAES ▸ marae

MARAH *n* bitterness

MARAHS ▸ marah

MARANTA *n* tropical American plant, some species of which are grown as pot plants for their showy variegated leaves

MARARI *n* eel-like blennoid food fish

MARARIS ▸ marari

MARAS ▸ mara

MARASCA *n* European cherry tree with red acid-tasting fruit from which maraschino is made

MARAUD *vb* wander or raid in search of plunder

MARAUDS ▸ maraud

MARBLE *n* kind of limestone with a mottled appearance, which can be highly polished ▸ *vb* mottle with variegated streaks in imitation of marble

MARBLED ▸ marble

MARBLER ▸ marble

MARBLES *n* game in which marble balls are rolled at one another

MARBLY ▸ marble

MARC *n* remains of grapes or other fruit that have been pressed for wine-making

MARCATO *adj* (of notes) heavily accented ▸ *adv* with each note heavily accented ▸ *n* a heavily accented note

M

MARCEL n hairstyle characterized by repeated regular waves, popular in the 1920s ▷ vb make such waves in (the hair) with special hot irons

MARCELS ▷ marcel

MARCH vb walk with a military step ▷ n action of marching

MARCHED ▷ march

MARCHEN n German story

MARCHER n person who marches

MARCHES ▷ march

MARCONI vb communicate by wireless

MARCS ▷ marc

MARD ▷ mar

MARDIED ▷ mardy

MARDIER ▷ mardy

MARDIES ▷ mardy

MARDY adj (of a child) spoilt ▷ vb behave in mardy way

MARE n female horse or zebra

MAREMMA n marshy unhealthy region near the shore, esp in Italy

MAREMME ▷ maremma

MARENGO adj browned in oil and cooked with tomatoes, mushrooms, garlic, wine, etc

MARERO n member of a C American organized criminal gang

MAREROS ▷ marero

MARES ▷ mare

MARG short for ▷ margarine

MARGAY n feline mammal of Central and S America with a dark-striped coat

MARGAYS ▷ margay

MARGE n margarine

MARGENT same as ▷ margin

MARGES ▷ marge

MARGIN n edge or border ▷ vb provide with a margin

MARGINS ▷ margin

MARGOSA n Indian tree

MARGS ▷ marg

MARIA ▷ mare

MARID n spirit in Muslim mythology

MARIDS ▷ marid

MARIES ▷ mary

MARIMBA n Latin American percussion instrument resembling a xylophone

MARINA n harbour for yachts and other pleasure boats

MARINAS ▷ marina

MARINE adj of the sea or shipping ▷ n (esp in Britain and the US) soldier trained for land and sea combat

MARINER n sailor

MARINES ▷ marine

MARISH n marsh

MARITAL adj relating to marriage

MARK n line, dot, scar, etc visible on a surface ▷ vb make a mark on

MARKA n unit of currency introduced as an interim currency in Bosnia-Herzegovina

MARKAS ▷ marka

MARKED adj noticeable

MARKER n object used to show the position of something

MARKERS ▷ marker

MARKET n assembly or place for buying and selling ▷ vb offer or produce for sale

MARKETS ▷ market

MARKHOR n large wild Himalayan goat with a reddish-brown coat and large spiralled horns

MARKING n arrangement of colours on an animal or plant

MARKKA n former standard monetary unit of Finland, divided into 100 penniä

MARKKAA ▷ markka

MARKKAS ▷ markka

MARKMAN n person owning land

MARKMEN ▷ markman

MARKS ▷ mark

MARKUP n percentage or amount added to the cost of a commodity to provide the seller with a profit and to cover overheads, costs, etc

MARKUPS ▷ markup

MARL n soil formed of clay and lime, used as fertilizer ▷ vb fertilize (land) with marl

MARLE same as ▷ marvel

MARLED ▷ marl

MARLES ▷ marle

MARLIER ▷ marly

MARLIN same as ▷ marline

MARLINE n light rope, usually tarred, made of two strands laid left-handed

MARLING same as ▷ marline

MARLINS ▷ marlin

MARLITE n type of marl that contains clay and calcium carbonate and is resistant to the decomposing action of air

MARLS ▷ marl

MARLY adj marl-like

MARM same as ▷ madam

MARMEM n as in marmem alloy type of alloy

MARMITE n large cooking pot

MARMOSE n South American opossum

MARMOT n burrowing rodent

MARMOTS ▷ marmot

MARMS ▷ marm

MARON n freshwater crustacean

MARONS ▷ maron

MAROON adj reddish-purple ▷ vb abandon ashore, esp on an island ▷ n exploding firework or flare used as a warning signal

MAROONS ▷ maroon

MAROR n Jewish ceremonial dish of bitter herbs

MARORS ▷ maror

MARPLOT n person interfering with plot

MARQUE n brand of product, esp of a car

MARQUEE n large tent used for a party or exhibition

MARQUES ▷ marque

MARQUIS n (in some European countries) nobleman of the rank above a count

MARRAM n as in marram grass any of several grasses of the genus that grow on sandy shores and can withstand drying

MARRAMS ▷ marram

MARRANO n Spanish or Portuguese Jew of the late Middle Ages who was converted to Christianity, esp one forcibly converted but secretly adhering to Judaism

MARRED ▷ mar

MARRELS same as ▷ merils

MARRER ▷ mar

MARRERS ▷ mar

MARRI n W Australian

eucalyptus widely cultivated for its coloured flowers

MARRIED ▸ marry

MARRIER ▸ marry

MARRIES ▸ marry

MARRING ▸ mar

MARRIS ▸ marri

MARRON n large edible sweet chestnut

MARRONS ▸ marron

MARROW n fatty substance inside bones ▷ vb be mate to

MARROWS ▸ marrow

MARROWY ▸ marrow

MARRUM same as ▸ marram

MARRUMS ▸ marrum

MARRY vb take as a husband or wife ▷ interj exclamation of surprise or anger

MARS ▸ mar

MARSALA n dark sweet dessert wine made in Sicily

MARSE same as ▸ master

MARSES ▸ marse

MARSH n low-lying wet land

MARSHAL n officer of the highest rank ▷ vb arrange in order

MARSHES ▸ marsh

MARSHY adj of, involving, or like a marsh

MART n market ▷ vb sell or trade

MARTED ▸ mart

MARTEL n hammer-shaped weapon ▷ vb use such a weapon

MARTELS ▸ martel

MARTEN n weasel-like animal

MARTENS ▸ marten

MARTEXT n preacher who makes many mistakes

MARTIAL adj of war, warlike

MARTIAN n inhabitant of Mars

MARTIN n bird with a slightly forked tail

MARTING ▸ mart

MARTINI n cocktail of vermouth and gin

MARTINS ▸ martin

MARTLET n footless bird often found in coats of arms, standing for either a martin or a swallow

MARTS ▸ mart

MARTYR n person who dies

or suffers for his or her beliefs ▷ vb make a martyr of

MARTYRS ▸ martyr

MARTYRY n shrine or chapel erected in honour of a martyr

MARVEL vb be filled with wonder ▷ n wonderful thing

MARVELS ▸ marvel

MARVER vb roll molten glass on slab

MARVERS ▸ marver

MARVIER ▸ marvy

MARVY shortened form of > marvelous

MARY n woman

MARYBUD n bud of marigold

MAS ▸ ma

MASA n Mexican maize dough

MASALA n mixture of spices ground into a paste ▷ adj spicy

MASALAS ▸ masala

MASAS ▸ masa

MASCARA n cosmetic for darkening the eyelashes

MASCLE n charge consisting of a lozenge with a lozenge-shaped hole in the middle

MASCLED ▸ mascle

MASCLES ▸ mascle

MASCON n any of several lunar regions of high gravity

MASCONS ▸ mascon

MASCOT n person, animal, or thing supposed to bring good luck

MASCOTS ▸ mascot

MASCULY ▸ mascle

MASE vb function as maser

MASED ▸ mase

MASER n device for amplifying microwaves

MASERS ▸ maser

MASES ▸ mase

MASH n soft pulpy mass ▷ vb crush into a soft mass

MASHED ▸ mash

MASHER ▸ mash

MASHERS ▸ mash

MASHES ▸ mash

MASHIE n (formerly) a club, corresponding to the modern No. 5 or No. 6 iron, used for approach shots

MASHIER ▸ mashy

MASHIES ▸ mashie

MASHING ▸ mash

MASHLAM same as ▸ maslin

MASHLIM same as ▸ maslin

MASHLIN same as ▸ maslin

MASHLUM same as ▸ maslin

MASHMAN n brewery worker

MASHMEN ▸ mashman

MASHUA n South American plant

MASHUAS ▸ mashua

MASHUP n piece of recorded or live music in which a producer or DJ blends together two or more tracks, often of contrasting genres

MASHUPS ▸ mashup

MASHY adj like mash

MASING ▸ mase

MASJID same as ▸ mosque

MASJIDS ▸ masjid

MASK n covering for the face, as a disguise or protection ▷ vb cover with a mask

MASKED adj disguised or covered by or as if by a mask

MASKEG n North American bog

MASKEGS ▸ maskeg

MASKER n person who wears a mask or takes part in a masque

MASKERS ▸ masker

MASKING n act or practice of masking

MASKS ▸ mask

MASLIN n mixture of wheat, rye or other grain

MASLINS ▸ maslin

MASON n person who works with stone ▷ vb construct or strengthen with masonry

MASONED ▸ mason

MASONIC adj of, characteristic of, or relating to Freemasons or Freemasonry

MASONRY n stonework

MASONS ▸ mason

MASQUE n 16th–17th-century form of dramatic entertainment

MASQUER same as ▸ masker

MASQUES ▸ masque

MASS n coherent body of matter ▷ adj large-scale ▷ vb form into a mass

M

MASSA old fashioned variant of ▶ **master**

MASSAGE n rubbing and kneading of parts of the body to reduce pain or stiffness ▷ vb give a massage to

MASSAS ▶ **massa**

MASSE n stroke made by hitting the cue ball off centre with the cue held nearly vertically, esp so as to make the ball move in a curve around another ball before hitting the object ball

MASSED ▶ **mass**

MASSES pl n body of common people

MASSEUR n person who gives massages

MASSIER ▶ **massy**

MASSIF n connected group of mountains

MASSIFS ▶ **massif**

MASSING ▶ **mass**

MASSIVE adj large and heavy ▷ n group of friends or associates

MASSY literary word for ▶ **massive**

MAST n tall pole for supporting something, esp a ship's sails

MASTABA n mud-brick superstructure above tombs in ancient Egypt

MASTED ▶ **mast**

MASTER n person in control, such as an employer or an owner of slaves or animals ▷ vb acquire knowledge of or skill in

MASTERS ▶ **master**

MASTERY n expertise

MASTFUL ▶ **mast**

MASTIC n gum obtained from certain trees

MASTICH same as ▶ **mastic**

MASTICS ▶ **mastic**

MASTIER ▶ **mast**

MASTIFF n large dog

MASTING ▶ **mast**

MASTIX n type of gum

MASTOID n projection of the bone behind the ear ▷ adj shaped like a nipple or breast

MASTS ▶ **mast**

MASTY ▶ **mast**

MASU n Japanese salmon

MASULA same as

> **masoolah**

MASULAS ▶ **masula**

MASUS ▶ **masu**

MAT n piece of fabric used as a floor covering or to protect a surface ▷ vb tangle or become tangled into a dense mass ▷ adj having a dull, lustreless, or roughened surface

MATADOR n man who kills the bull in bullfights

MATAI n New Zealand tree, the wood of which is used for timber for building

MATAIS ▶ **matai**

MATATA same as > **fernbird**

MATATAS ▶ **matata**

MATATU n type of shared taxi used in Kenya

MATATUS ▶ **matatu**

MATCH n contest in a game or sport ▷ vb be exactly like, equal to, or in harmony with

MATCHED ▶ **match**

MATCHER ▶ **match**

MATCHES ▶ **match**

MATCHET same as ▶ **machete**

MATCHUP n sports match

MATE n friend ▷ vb pair (animals) or (of animals) be paired for reproduction

MATED ▶ **mate**

MATELOT n sailor

MATER n mother: often used facetiously

MATERS ▶ **mater**

MATES ▶ **mate**

MATEY adj friendly or intimate ▷ n friend or fellow: usually used in direct address

MATEYS ▶ **matey**

MATH same as ▶ **maths**

MATHS same as ▶ **math**

MATICO n Peruvian shrub

MATICOS ▶ **matico**

MATIER ▶ **maty**

MATIES ▶ **maty**

MATIEST ▶ **maty**

MATILDA n bushman's swag

MATILY ▶ **maty**

MATIN adj of or relating to matins

MATINAL same as ▶ **matin**

MATINEE n afternoon performance in a theatre or cinema

MATING ▶ **mate**

MATINGS ▶ **mate**

MATINS pl n early morning service in various Christian Churches

MATIPO n New Zealand shrub

MATIPOS ▶ **matipo**

MATJES same as ▶ **maatjes**

MATLESS ▶ **mat**

MATLO same as ▶ **matelot**

MATLOS ▶ **matlo**

MATLOW same as ▶ **matelot**

MATLOWS ▶ **matlow**

MATOKE n (in Uganda) the flesh of bananas, boiled and mashed as a food

MATOKES ▶ **matoke**

MATOOKE same as ▶ **matoke**

MATRASS n long-necked glass flask, used for distilling, dissolving substances, etc

MATRES ▶ **mater**

MATRIC n matriculation

MATRICE same as ▶ **matrix**

MATRICS ▶ **matric**

MATRIX n substance or situation in which something originates, takes form, or is enclosed

MATRON n staid or dignified married woman

MATRONS ▶ **matron**

MATROSS n gunner's assistant

MATS ▶ **mat**

MATSAH same as ▶ **matzo**

MATSAHS ▶ **matsah**

MATSURI n Japanese religious ceremony

MATT adj dull, not shiny

MATTE same as ▶ **matt**

MATTED ▶ **mat**

MATTER n substance of which something is made ▷ vb be of importance

MATTERS ▶ **matter**

MATTERY adj discharging pus

MATTES ▶ **matte**

MATTIE n young herring

MATTIES ▶ **mattie**

MATTIFY vb make (the skin of the face) less oily or shiny using cosmetics

MATTIN same as ▶ **matin**

MATTING ▶ **mat**

MATTINS same as ▶ **matins**

MATTOCK n large pick with one of its blade ends flattened for loosening soil

MATTOID n person

displaying eccentric behaviour and mental characteristics that approach the psychotic

MATTS ▸ matt

MATURE adj fully developed or grown-up ▷ vb make or become mature

MATURED ▸ mature

MATURER ▸ mature

MATURES ▸ mature

MATWEED n grass found on moors

MATY same as ▸ **matey**

MATZA same as ▸ **matzo**

MATZAH same as ▸ **matzo**

MATZAHS ▸ matzah

MATZAS ▸ matza

MATZO n large very thin biscuit of unleavened bread, traditionally eaten by Jews during Passover

MATZOH same as ▸ **matzo**

MATZOHS ▸ matzoh

MATZOON n fermented milk product similar to yogurt

MATZOS ▸ matzo

MATZOT ▸ matzo

MATZOTH ▸ matzoh

MAUBIES ▸ mauby

MAUBY n (in the E Caribbean) a bittersweet drink made from the bark of a rhamnaceous tree

MAUD n shawl or rug of grey wool plaid formerly worn in Scotland

MAUDLIN adj foolishly or tearfully sentimental

MAUDS ▸ maud

MAUGER same as ▸ **maugre**

MAUGRE prep in spite of ▷ vb behave spitefully towards

MAUGRED ▸ maugre

MAUGRES ▸ maugre

MAUL vb handle roughly ▷ n loose scrum

MAULED ▸ maul

MAULER ▸ maul

MAULERS pl n hands

MAULGRE same as ▸ **maugre**

MAULING ▸ maul

MAULS ▸ maul

MAULVI n expert in Islamic law

MAULVIS ▸ maulvi

MAUMET n false god

MAUMETS ▸ maumet

MAUN dialect word for ▸ **must**

MAUND n unit of weight used in Asia, esp India, having different values in different localities. A common value in India is 82 pounds or 37 kilograms ▷ vb beg

MAUNDED ▸ maund

MAUNDER vb talk or act aimlessly or idly

MAUNDS ▸ maund

MAUNDY n ceremonial washing of the feet of poor persons in commemoration of Jesus' washing of his disciples' feet (John 13:4–34) re-enacted in some churches on Maundy Thursday

MAUNGY adj (esp of a child) sulky, bad-tempered, or peevish

MAUNNA vb Scots term meaning must not

MAURI n soul

MAURIS ▸ mauri

MAUT same as ▸ **mahout**

MAUTHER n girl

MAUTS ▸ maut

MAUVAIS adj bad

MAUVE adj pale purple ▷ n any of various pale to moderate pinkish-purple or bluish-purple colours

MAUVEIN same as > **mauveine**

MAUVER ▸ mauve

MAUVES ▸ mauve

MAUVEST ▸ mauve

MAUVIN same as > **mauveine**

MAUVINE same as > **mauveine**

MAUVINS ▸ mauvin

MAVEN n expert or connoisseur

MAVENS ▸ maven

MAVIE n type of thrush

MAVIES ▸ mavie

MAVIN same as ▸ **maven**

MAVINS ▸ mavin

MAVIS n song thrush

MAVISES ▸ mavis

MAW n animal's mouth, throat, or stomach ▷ vb eat or bite

MAWED ▸ maw

MAWGER adj (of persons or animals) thin or lean

MAWING ▸ maw

MAWK n maggot

MAWKIER ▸ mawk

MAWKIN n slovenly woman

MAWKINS ▸ mawkin

MAWKISH adj foolishly sentimental

MAWKS ▸ mawk

MAWKY ▸ mawk

MAWMET same as ▸ **maumet**

MAWMETS ▸ mawmet

MAWN ▸ maw

MAWPUS same as ▸ **mopus**

MAWR same as ▸ **mauther**

MAWRS ▸ mawr

MAWS ▸ maw

MAWSEED n poppy seed

MAWTHER same as ▸ **mauther**

MAX vb reach the full extent

> Max is a short form of **maximum**, and can also be a verb giving **maxed, maxes** and **maxing**. Another of the key words using X, and it can be extended to **maxi**.

MAXED ▸ max

MAXES ▸ max

MAXI adj (of a garment) very long ▷ n type of large racing yacht

MAXILLA n upper jawbone of a vertebrate

MAXIM n general truth or principle

MAXIMA ▸ maximum

MAXIMAL adj maximum ▷ n maximum

MAXIMIN n highest of a set of minimum values

MAXIMS ▸ maxim

MAXIMUM n greatest possible (amount or number) ▷ adj of, being, or showing a maximum or maximums

MAXIMUS n method rung on twelve bells

MAXING ▸ max

MAXIS ▸ maxi

MAXIXE n Brazilian dance in duple time, a precursor of the tango

MAXIXES ▸ maxixe

MAXWELL n cgs unit of magnetic flux

MAY vb used as an auxiliary to express possibility, permission, opportunity, etc ▷ vb gather may

MAYA n illusion, esp the material world of the senses regarded as illusory

MAYAN ▸ maya

MAYAS ▸ maya

M

MAYBE adv perhaps, possibly ▷ sentence substitute possibly

MAYBES ▶ maybe

MAYBIRD n American songbird

MAYBUSH n flowering shrub

MAYDAY n international radiotelephone distress signal

MAYDAYS ▶ mayday

MAYED ▶ may

MAYEST same as ▶ mayst

MAYFLY n short-lived aquatic insect

MAYHAP archaic word for ▶ perhaps

MAYHEM n violent destruction or confusion

MAYHEMS ▶ mayhem

MAYING ▶ may

MAYINGS ▶ maying

MAYO n mayonnaise

MAYOR n head of a municipality

MAYORAL ▶ mayor

MAYORS ▶ mayor

MAYOS ▶ mayo

MAYPOLE n pole set up for dancing round on the first day of May to celebrate spring

MAYPOP n American wild flower

MAYPOPS ▶ maypop

MAYS ▶ may

MAYST singular form of the present tense of ▶ may

MAYSTER same as ▶ master

MAYVIN same as ▶ maven

MAYVINS ▶ mayvin

MAYWEED n widespread Eurasian weedy plant, having evil-smelling leaves and daisy-like flower heads

MAZARD same as ▶ mazer

MAZARDS ▶ mazard

MAZE n complex network of paths or lines designed to puzzle

MAZED ▶ maze

MAZEDLY adv in a bewildered way

MAZEFUL ▶ maze

MAZER n large hardwood drinking bowl

MAZERS ▶ mazer

MAZES ▶ maze

MAZEY adj dizzy

MAZHBI n low-caste Sikh

MAZHBIS ▶ mazhbi

MAZIER ▶ mazy

MAZIEST ▶ mazy

MAZILY ▶ mazy

MAZING ▶ maze

MAZOUT same as ▶ mazut

MAZOUTS ▶ mazout

MAZUMA n money

MAZUMAS ▶ mazuma

MAZURKA n lively Polish dance

MAZUT n residue left after distillation of petrol

MAZUTS ▶ mazut

MAZY adj of or like a maze

MAZZARD same as ▶ mazard

MBIRA n African musical instrument consisting of tuned metal strips attached to a resonating box, which are plucked with the thumbs

MBIRAS ▶ mbira

ME n (in tonic sol-fa) third degree of any major scale ▷ pron refers to the speaker or writer

MEACOCK n timid person

MEAD n alcoholic drink made from honey

MEADOW n piece of grassland

MEADOWS ▶ meadow

MEADOWY ▶ meadow

MEADS ▶ mead

MEAGER same as ▶ meagre

MEAGRE adj scanty or insufficient ▷ n Mediterranean fish

MEAGRER ▶ meagre

MEAGRES ▶ meagre

MEAL n occasion when food is served and eaten ▷ vb cover with meal

MEALED ▶ meal

MEALER n person eating but not lodging at boarding house

MEALERS ▶ mealer

MEALIE n maize

MEALIER ▶ mealy

MEALIES South African word for ▶ maize

MEALING ▶ meal

MEALS ▶ meal

MEALY adj resembling meal

MEAN vb intend to convey or express ▷ adj miserly, ungenerous, or petty ▷ n middle point between two extremes

MEANDER vb follow a winding course ▷ n winding course

MEANE vb moan

MEANED ▶ meane

MEANER ▶ mean

MEANERS ▶ mean

MEANES ▶ meane

MEANEST ▶ mean

MEANIE n unkind or miserly person

MEANIES ▶ meany

MEANING n what something means

MEANLY ▶ mean

MEANS ▶ mean

MEANT ▶ mean

MEANY same as ▶ meanie

MEARE same as ▶ mere

MEARES ▶ meare

MEARING adj forming boundary

MEASE vb assuage

MEASED ▶ mease

MEASES ▶ mease

MEASING ▶ mease

MEASLE vb infect with measles

MEASLED adj (of cattle, sheep, or pigs) infested with tapeworm larvae

MEASLES n infectious disease producing red spots

MEASLY adj meagre

MEASURE n size or quantity ▷ vb determine the size or quantity of

MEAT n animal flesh as food

MEATAL ▶ meatus

MEATAXE n meat cleaver

MEATED adj fattened

MEATH same as ▶ mead

MEATHE same as ▶ mead

MEATHES ▶ meathe

MEATHS ▶ meath

MEATIER ▶ meaty

MEATILY ▶ meaty

MEATMAN n meat seller

MEATMEN ▶ meatman

MEATS ▶ meat

MEATUS n natural opening or channel, such as the canal leading from the outer ear to the eardrum

MEATY adj (tasting) of or like meat

MEAWES same as ▶ mews

MEAZEL same as ▶ mesel

MEAZELS ▶ meazel

MEBOS n South African dish of dried apricots

MEBOSES ▶ mebos

MECCA n place that attracts many visitors

MECCAS ▶ mecca

MECK same as ▶ maik

MECKS ▶ meck

MECONIC adj derived from poppies

MECONIN n substance found in opium

MED n doctor

MEDACCA n Japanese freshwater fish

MEDAKA same as ▶ medacca

MEDAKAS ▶ medaka

MEDAL n piece of metal with an inscription etc, given as a reward or memento ▷ vb honour with a medal

MEDALED ▶ medal

MEDALET n small medal

MEDALS ▶ medal

MEDDLE vb interfere annoyingly

MEDDLED ▶ meddle

MEDDLER ▶ meddle

MEDDLES ▶ meddle

MEDEVAC n evacuation of casualties from forward areas to the nearest hospital or base ▷ vb transport (a wounded or sick person) to hospital by medevac

MEDFLY n Mediterranean fruit fly

MEDIA n a medium of cultivation, conveyance, or expression

MEDIACY n quality or state of being mediate

MEDIAD adj situated near the median line or plane of an organism

MEDIAE ▶ medium

MEDIAL adj of or in the middle ▷ n speech sound between being fortis and lenis

MEDIALS ▶ medial

MEDIAN n middle (point or line) ▷ adj of, relating to, situated in, or directed towards the middle

MEDIANS ▶ median

MEDIANT n third degree of a major or minor scale

MEDIAS ▶ medium

MEDIATE vb intervene in a dispute to bring about agreement ▷ adj occurring as a result of or dependent upon mediation

MEDIC n doctor or medical student

MEDICAL adj of the science of medicine ▷ n medical examination

MEDICK n type of small leguminous plant with yellow or purple flowers and trifoliate leaves

MEDICKS ▶ medick

MEDICO n doctor or medical student

MEDICOS ▶ medico

MEDICS ▶ medic

MEDIGAP n private health insurance

MEDII ▶ medius

MEDINA n ancient quarter of any of various North African cities

MEDINAS ▶ medina

MEDIUM adj midway between extremes, average ▷ n middle state, degree, or condition

MEDIUMS pl n medium-dated gilt-edged securities

MEDIUS n middle finger

MEDIVAC variant spelling of ▶ medevac

MEDLAR n apple-like fruit of a small tree, eaten when it begins to decay

MEDLARS ▶ medlar

MEDLE same as ▶ meddle

MEDLED ▶ medle

MEDLES ▶ medle

MEDLEY n miscellaneous mixture ▷ adj of, being, or relating to a mixture or variety

MEDLEYS ▶ medley

MEDLING ▶ medle

MEDRESA ▶ madrasah

MEDRESE same as ▶ madrasah

MEDS ▶ med

MEDULLA n marrow, pith, or inner tissue

MEDUSA n jellyfish

MEDUSAE ▶ medusa

MEDUSAL ▶ medusa

MEDUSAN ▶ medusa

MEDUSAS ▶ medusa

MEE n Malaysian noodle dish

MEED n recompense

MEEDS ▶ meed

MEEK adj submissive or humble

MEEKEN vb make meek

MEEKENS ▶ meeken

MEEKER ▶ meek

MEEKEST ▶ meek

MEEKLY ▶ meek

MEEMIE n hysterical person

MEEMIES ▶ meemie

MEER same as ▶ mere

MEERCAT same as ▶ meerkat

MEERED ▶ meer

MEERING ▶ meer

MEERKAT n S African mongoose

MEERS ▶ meer

MEES ▶ mee

MEET vb come together (with) ▷ n meeting, esp a sports meeting ▷ adj fit or suitable

MEETER ▶ meet

MEETERS ▶ meet

MEETEST ▶ meet

MEETING ▶ meet

MEETLY ▶ meet

MEETS ▶ meet

MEFF dialect word for ▶ tramp

MEFFS ▶ meff

MEG short for ▶ megabyte

MEGA adj extremely good, great, or successful

MEGABAR n unit of million bars

MEGABIT n one million bits

MEGAFOG n amplified fog signal

MEGAHIT n great success

MEGAPOD same as ▶ megapode

MEGARA ▶ megaron

MEGARAD n unit of million rads

MEGARON n tripartite rectangular room containing a central hearth surrounded by four pillars, found in Bronze Age Greece and Asia Minor

MEGASS another name for ▶ bagasse

MEGASSE same as ▶ megass

MEGATON n explosive power equal to that of one million tons of TNT

MEGILLA same as ▶ megillah

MEGILP n oil-painting medium of linseed oil mixed with mastic varnish or turpentine

MEGILPH same as ▶ megilp

MEGILPS ▶ megilp

MEGOHM n one million ohms

MEGOHMS ▶ megohm

MEGRIM n caprice

MEGRIMS n fit of depression

M

MEGS ▶ meg

MEH *interj* expression of indifference or boredom

MEHNDI *n* (esp in India) the practice of painting designs on the hands, feet, etc using henna

MEHNDIS ▶ mehndi

MEIKLE *adj* Scots word meaning large

MEIN *Scots word for* ▶ moan

MEINED ▶ mein

MEINEY *same as* ▶ meiny

MEINEYS ▶ meiney

MEINIE *same as* ▶ meiny

MEINIES ▶ meiny

MEINING ▶ mein

MEINS ▶ mein

MEINT *same as* ▶ ming

MEINY *n* retinue or household

MEIOSES ▶ meiosis

MEIOSIS *n* type of cell division in which reproductive cells are produced, each containing half the chromosome number of the parent nucleus

MEIOTIC ▶ meiosis

MEISHI *n* business card in Japan

MEISHIS ▶ meishi

MEISTER *n* person who excels at a particular activity

MEITH *n* landmark

MEITHS ▶ meith

MEJLIS *same as* ▶ majlis

MEKKA *same as* ▶ mecca

MEKKAS ▶ mekka

MEL *n* pure form of honey formerly used in pharmaceutical products

MELA *n* Asian cultural or religious fair or festival

MELAMED *n* Hebrew teacher

MELANGE *n* mixture

MELANIC *adj* relating to melanism or melanosis ▷ *n* darker form of creature

MELANIN *n* dark pigment found in the hair, skin, and eyes of humans and animals

MELANO *n* person with abnormally dark skin

MELANOS ▶ melano

MELAS ▶ mela

MELBA *adj* relating to a type of dessert sauce or toast

MELD *vb* merge or blend ▷ *n* act of melding

MELDED ▶ meld

MELDER ▶ meld

MELDERS ▶ meld

MELDING ▶ meld

MELDS ▶ meld

MELEE *n* noisy confused fight or crowd

MELEES ▶ melee

MELENA *n* excrement or vomit stained by blood

MELENAS ▶ melena

MELIC *adj* (of poetry, esp ancient Greek lyric poems) intended to be sung ▷ *n* type of grass

MELICK *n* either of two pale green perennial grasses

MELICKS ▶ melick

MELICS ▶ melic

MELIK *same as* ▶ malik

MELIKS ▶ melik

MELILOT *n* Old World leguminous plant with narrow clusters of small white or yellow fragrant flowers

MELISMA *n* expressive vocal phrase or passage consisting of several notes sung to one syllable

MELL *vb* mix

MELLAY *same as* ▶ melee

MELLAYS ▶ mellay

MELLED ▶ mell

MELLING ▶ mell

MELLITE *n* soft yellow mineral

MELLOW *adj* soft, not harsh ▷ *vb* make or become mellow

MELLOWS ▶ mellow

MELLOWY *same as* ▶ mellow

MELLS ▶ mell

MELODIA *same as* > melodica

MELODIC *adj* of melody

MELODY *n* series of musical notes which make a tune

MELOID *n* type of long-legged beetle of the family which includes the blister beetles and oil beetles

MELOIDS ▶ meloid

MELON *n* large round juicy fruit with a hard rind

MELONS ▶ melon

MELS ▶ mel

MELT *vb* (cause to) become liquid by heat ▷ *n* act or process of melting

MELTAGE *n* process or result of melting or the amount melted

MELTED ▶ melt

MELTEMI *n* northerly wind in the northeast Mediterranean

MELTER ▶ melt

MELTERS ▶ melt

MELTIER ▶ melty

MELTING ▶ melt

MELTITH *n* meal

MELTON *n* heavy smooth woollen fabric with a short nap, used esp for overcoats

MELTONS ▶ melton

MELTS ▶ melt

MELTY *adj* tending to melt

MEM *n* 13th letter in the Hebrew alphabet, transliterated as *m*

MEMBER *n* individual making up a body or society ▷ *adj* (of a (country or group) belonging to an organization or alliance

MEMBERS ▶ member

MEMBRAL *adj* of limbs

MEME *n* idea or element of social behaviour (passed on through generations in a culture, esp by imitation

MEMENTO *n* thing serving to remind, souvenir

MEMES ▶ meme

MEMETIC *adj* of or relating to a meme

MEMO *n* memorandum

MEMOIR *n* biography or historical account based on personal knowledge

MEMOIRS *pl n* collection of reminiscences about a period or series of events, written from personal experience

MEMORY *n* ability to remember

MEMOS ▶ memo

MEMS ▶ mem

MEN ▶ man

MENACE *n* threat ▷ *vb* threaten, endanger

MENACED ▶ menace

MENACER ▶ menace

MENACES ▶ menace

MENAD *same as* ▶ maenad

MENADS ▶ menad

MENAGE *old form of* ▶ manage

MENAGED ▶ menage

MENAGES ▶ menage

MENAZON *n* type of insecticide

MEND vb repair or patch ▷ n mended area

MENDED ▶ mend

MENDER ▶ mend

MENDERS ▶ mend

MENDIGO n Spanish beggar or vagrant

MENDING n something to be mended, esp clothes

MENDS ▶ mend

MENE Scots form of ▶ moan

MENED ▶ mene

MENEER n S African title of address

MENEERS ▶ meneer

MENES ▶ mene

MENFOLK pl n men collectively, esp the men of a particular family

MENG vb mix

MENGE same as ▶ meng

MENGED ▶ meng

MENGES ▶ menge

MENGING ▶ meng

MENGS ▶ meng

MENHIR n single upright prehistoric stone

MENHIRS ▶ menhir

MENIAL adj involving boring work of low status ▷ n person with a menial job

MENIALS ▶ menial

MENING ▶ mene

MENINX n one of three membranes that envelop the brain and spinal cord

MENISCI > meniscus

MENO adv (esp preceding a dynamic or tempo marking) to be played less quickly, less softly, etc

MENORAH n seven-branched candelabrum used as an emblem of Judaism

MENSA n faint constellation in the S hemisphere lying between Hydrus and Volans and containing part of the Large Magellanic Cloud

MENSAE n star of the mensa constellation

MENSAL adj monthly

MENSAS ▶ mensa

MENSCH n decent person

MENSCHY ▶ mensch

MENSE vb grace

MENSED ▶ mense

MENSES n menstruation

MENSH vb mention

MENSHED ▶ mensh

MENSHEN n Chinese door god

MENSHES ▶ mensh

MENSING ▶ mense

MENSUAL same as ▶ mensal

MENT same as ▶ ming

MENTA ▶ mentum

MENTAL adj of, in, or done by the mind

MENTEE n person trained by mentor

MENTEES ▶ mentee

MENTHOL n organic compound found in peppermint, used medicinally

MENTION vb refer to briefly ▷ n brief reference to a person or thing

MENTO n Jamaican song

MENTOR n adviser or guide ▷ vb act as a mentor to (someone) ▷ vb act as mentor for

MENTORS ▶ mentor

MENTOS ▶ mento

MENTUM n chin

MENU n list of dishes to be served, or from which to order

MENUDO n Mexican soup

MENUDOS ▶ menudo

MENUS ▶ menu

MENYIE same as ▶ meinie

MENYIES ▶ menyie

MEOU same as ▶ meow

MEOUED ▶ meou

MEOUING ▶ meou

MEOUS ▶ meou

MEOW vb (of a cat) to make a characteristic crying sound ▷ interj imitation of this sound

MEOWED ▶ meow

MEOWING ▶ meow

MEOWS ▶ meow

MERANTI n wood from any of several Malaysian trees

MERC n mercenary

MERCAT Scots word for ▶ market

MERCATS ▶ mercat

MERCER n dealer in textile fabrics and fine cloth

MERCERS ▶ mercer

MERCERY ▶ mercer

MERCES ▶ merc

MERCH n merchandise

MERCHES ▶ merch

MERCHET n (in feudal England) a fine paid by a tenant, esp a villein, to his lord for allowing the marriage of his daughter

MERCIES ▶ mercy

MERCIFY vb show mercy to

MERCS ▶ merc

MERCURY n silvery liquid metal

MERCY n compassionate treatment of an offender or enemy who is in one's power

MERDE French word for > excrement

MERDES ▶ merde

MERE adj nothing more than ▷ n lake ▷ vb old form of survey

MERED adj forming a boundary

MEREL same as ▶ meril

MERELL same as ▶ meril

MERELLS same as ▶ merils

MERELS ▶ merils

MERELY adv only

MERER ▶ mere

MERES ▶ mere

MEREST ▶ mere

MERFOLK n mermaids and mermen

MERGE vb combine or blend

MERGED ▶ merge

MERGEE n business taken over by merger

MERGEES ▶ mergee

MERGER n combination of business firms into one

MERGERS ▶ merger

MERGES ▶ merge

MERGING ▶ merge

MERI n Māori war club

MERIL n counter used in merils

MERILS n old board game

MERING ▶ mere

MERINGS ▶ mering

MERINO n breed of sheep with fine soft wool

MERINOS ▶ merino

MERIS ▶ meri

MERISES ▶ merisis

MERISIS n growth by division of cells

MERISM n duplication of biological parts

MERISMS ▶ merism

MERIT n excellence or worth ▷ vb deserve

MERITED ▶ merit

MERITS ▶ merit

MERK n old Scots coin

MERKIN n artificial hairpiece for the pudendum

MERKINS ▶ merkin

MERKS ▶ merk

MERL same as ▶ merle

M

MERLE adj (of a dog, esp a collie) having a bluish-grey coat with speckles or streaks of black

MERLES ▶ merle

MERLIN n small falcon

MERLING n whiting

MERLINS ▶ merlin

MERLON n solid upright section in a crenellated battlement

MERLONS ▶ merlon

MERLOT n black grape grown in France and now throughout the wine-producing world, used, often in a blend, for making wine

MERLOTS ▶ merlot

MERLS ▶ merl

MERMAID n imaginary sea creature with the upper part of a woman and the lower part of a fish

MERMAN n male counterpart of the mermaid

MERMEN ▶ merman

MEROME same as > merosome

MEROMES ▶ merome

MERONYM n part of something used to refer to the whole

MEROPIA n partial blindness

MEROPIC ▶ meropia

MERRIER ▶ merry

MERRIES ▶ merry

MERRILY ▶ merry

MERRY adj cheerful or jolly ▷ n gean

MERSE n low level ground by a river or shore, often alluvial and fertile

MERSES ▶ merse

MERSION n dipping in water

MES ▶ me

MESA n flat-topped hill found in arid regions

MESAIL n visor

MESAILS ▶ mesail

MESAL same as ▶ mesial

MESALLY ▶ mesal

MESARCH adj (of a xylem strand) having the first-formed xylem surrounded by that formed later, as in fern stems

MESAS ▶ mesa

MESCAL n spineless globe-shaped cactus of Mexico and the SW of the USA

MESCALS ▶ mescal

MESCLUM same as ▶ mesclun

MESCLUN n type of green salad

MESE n middle string on lyre

MESEEMS vb it seems to me

MESEL n leper

MESELED adj afflicted by leprosy

MESELS ▶ mesel

MESES ▶ mese

MESETA n plateau in Spain

MESETAS ▶ meseta

MESH n network or net ▷ vb (of gear teeth) engage ▷ adj made from mesh

MESHED ▶ mesh

MESHES ▶ mesh

MESHIER ▶ mesh

MESHING ▶ mesh

MESHUGA adj crazy

MESHY ▶ mesh

MESIAD adj relating to or situated at the middle or centre

MESIAL another word for ▶ medial

MESIAN same as ▶ mesial

MESIC ▶ meson

MESNE adj in Law, intermediate or intervening: used esp of any assignment of property before the last

MESNES ▶ mesne

MESON n elementary atomic particle

MESONIC ▶ meson

MESONS ▶ meson

MESQUIN adj mean

MESQUIT same as > mesquite

MESS n untidy or dirty confusion ▷ vb muddle or dirty

MESSAGE n communication sent ▷ vb send as a message

MESSAN Scots word for ▶ dog

MESSANS ▶ messan

MESSED ▶ mess

MESSES ▶ mess

MESSIAH n exceptional or hoped for liberator of a country or people

MESSIAS same as ▶ messiah

MESSIER ▶ messy

MESSILY ▶ messy

MESSING ▶ mess

MESSMAN n sailor working in ship's mess

MESSMEN ▶ messman

MESSY adj dirty, confused, or untidy

MESTEE same as ▶ mustee

MESTEES ▶ mestee

MESTER n master: used as a term of address for a man who is the head of a house

MESTERS ▶ mester

MESTESO n Spanish music genre

MESTINO n person of mixed race

MESTIZA ▶ mestizo

MESTIZO n person of mixed parentage, esp the offspring of a Spanish American and an American Indian

MESTO adj sad

MESTOM same as ▶ mestome

MESTOME n conducting tissue associated with parenchyma

MESTOMS ▶ mestom

MET n meteorology

META adj in a self-parodying style

METAGE n official measuring of weight or contents

METAGES ▶ metage

METAL n chemical element, such as iron or copper, that is malleable and capable of conducting heat and electricity ▷ adj made of metal ▷ vb fit or cover with metal

METALED ▶ metal

METALLY adj like metal

METALS ▶ metal

METAMER n any of two or more isomeric compounds exhibiting metamerism

METATAG n element of HTML describing the contents of a web page and used by search engines to index pages by subject

METATE n stone for grinding grain on

METATES ▶ metate

METAYER n farmer who pays rent in kind

METAZOA > metazoan

METCAST n weather forecast

METE vb deal out as punishment ▷ n (to) measure

METED ▶ mete

METEOR n small fast-moving heavenly body, visible as a streak of incandescence if it enters the earth's atmosphere

METEORS ▶ meteor

METEPA n type of pesticide

METEPAS ▶ metepa

METER same as ▶ metre

METERED ▶ meter

METERS ▶ meter

METES ▶ mete

METH n variety of amphetamine

METHANE n colourless inflammable gas

METHINK same as ▶ methinks

METHO n methylated spirits

METHOD n way or manner

METHODS ▶ method

METHOS ▶ metho

METHOXY n steroid drug

METHS n methylated spirits

METHYL n compound containing a saturated hydrocarbon group of atoms

METHYLS ▶ methyl

METIC n (in ancient Greece) an alien having some rights of citizenship in the city in which he lives

METICAL n money unit in Mozambique

METICS ▶ metic

METIER n profession or trade

METIERS ▶ metier

METIF n person of mixed race

METIFS ▶ metif

METING ▶ mete

METIS n person of mixed parentage

METISSE ▶ metis

METOL n colourless soluble organic substance used, (in the form of its sulphate, as a photographic developer

METOLS ▶ metol

METONYM n word used in a metonymy

METOPAE ▶ metope

METOPE n square space between two triglyphs in a Doric frieze

METOPES ▶ metope

METOPIC adj of or relating to the forehead

METOPON n painkilling drug

METRE n basic unit of length equal to about 1.094 yards (100 centimetres) ▷ vb express in poetry

METRED ▶ metre

METRES ▶ metre

METRIC adj of the decimal system of weights and measures based on the metre

METRICS n art of using poetic metre

METRIFY vb render into poetic metre

METRING ▶ metre

METRIST n person skilled in the use of poetic metre

METRO n underground railway system, esp in Paris

METROS ▶ metro

METS ▶ met

METTLE n courage or spirit

METTLED adj spirited, courageous, or valiant

METTLES ▶ mettle

METUMP n band for carrying a load or burden

METUMPS ▶ metump

MEU another name for ▶ spignel

MEUS ▶ meu

MEUSE n gap (in fence, wall etc) through which an animal passed ▷ vb go through this gap

MEUSED ▶ meuse

MEUSES ▶ meuse

MEUSING ▶ meuse

MEVE same as ▶ move

MEVED ▶ meve

MEVES ▶ meve

MEVING ▶ meve

MEVROU n S African title of address

MEVROUS ▶ mevrou

MEW n cry of a cat ▷ vb utter this cry

MEWED ▶ mew

MEWING ▶ mew

MEWL vb (esp of a baby) to cry weakly ▷ n weak or whimpering cry

MEWLED ▶ mewl

MEWLER ▶ mewl

MEWLERS ▶ mewl

MEWLING ▶ mewl

MEWLS ▶ mewl

MEWS same as ▶ meuse

MEWSED ▶ mews

MEWSES ▶ mews

MEWSING ▶ mews

MEYNT ▶ ming

MEZAIL same as ▶ mesail

MEZAILS ▶ mezail

MEZCAL variant spelling of ▶ mescal

MEZCALS ▶ mezcal

MEZE n type of hors d'oeuvre eaten esp with an apéritif or other drink in Greece and the Near East

MEZES ▶ meze

MEZQUIT same as ▶ mesquite

> A **mezquit** is a kind of American tree, and makes a great bonus to play. Remember also that it takes an E to form the variant spelling **mezquite**.

MEZUZA same as ▶ mezuzah

MEZUZAH n piece of parchment inscribed with biblical passages and fixed to the doorpost of the rooms of a Jewish house

MEZUZAS ▶ mezuza

MEZUZOT ▶ mezuzah

MEZZ same as ▶ mezzanine

MEZZE same as ▶ meze

MEZZES ▶ mezze

MEZZO adv moderately

MEZZOS ▶ mezzo

MGANGA n witch doctor

MGANGAS ▶ mganga

MHO former name for ▶ siemens

MHORR n African gazelle

MHORRS ▶ mhorr

MHOS ▶ mho

MI n (in tonic sol-fa) the third degree of any major scale

MIAOU same as ▶ meow

MIAOUED ▶ miaou

> These 7-letter words using all of the vowels may not be easy to see on your rack, but they come in useful so often that it's well worth paying them special attention.

MIAOUS ▶ miaou

MIAOW same as ▶ meow

MIAOWED ▶ miaow

MIAOWS ▶ miaow

MIASM same as ▶ miasma

MIASMA n unwholesome or foreboding atmosphere

MIASMAL ▶ miasma

MIASMAS ▶ miasma

MIASMIC ▶ miasma

MIASMS ▶ miasm

MIAUL same as ▶ meow

M

MIAULED ▸ miaul
MIAULS ▸ miaul
MIB n marble used in games
MIBS ▸ mib
MIBUNA n type of Japanese leafy vegetable
MIBUNAS ▸ mibuna
MIC n microphone
MICA n glasslike mineral used as an electrical insulator
MICAS ▸ mica
MICATE vb add mica to
MICATED ▸ micate
MICATES ▸ micate
MICE ▸ mouse
MICELL same as ▸ **micelle**
MICELLA same as ▸ **micelle**
MICELLE n charged aggregate of molecules of colloidal size in a solution
MICELLS ▸ micell
MICH same as ▸ **mitch**
MICHAEL n as in **take the michael** teasing
MICHE same as ▸ **mich**
MICHED ▸ mich
MICHER ▸ mich
MICHERS ▸ mich
MICHES ▸ mich
MICHING ▸ mich
MICHT n Scots word for might
MICHTS ▸ micht
MICKERY n waterhole, esp in a dry riverbed
MICKEY n young bull, esp one that is wild and unbranded ▸ vb drug person's drink
MICKEYS ▸ mickey
MICKIES ▸ micky
MICKLE adj large or abundant ▸ adv much ▸ n great amount
MICKLER ▸ mickle
MICKLES ▸ mickle
MICKY same as ▸ **mickey**
MICO n marmoset
MICOS ▸ mico
MICRA ▸ micron
MICRIFY vb make very small
MICRO n small computer
MICROBE n minute organism, esp one causing disease
MICROHM n millionth of ohm
MICRON n unit of length equal to 10⁻⁶ metre
MICRONS ▸ micron
MICROS ▸ micro
MICS ▸ mic

MICTION n urination
MID adj intermediate, middle ▸ n middle ▸ prep amid
MIDAIR n some point above ground level, in the air
MIDAIRS ▸ midair
MIDBAND adj (of telecommunication transmissions) using a range of frequencies between narrowband and broadband
MIDCAP adj (of investments) involving medium-sized amounts of capital
MIDCULT n middlebrow culture
MIDDAY n noon
MIDDAYS ▸ midday
MIDDEN n dunghill or rubbish heap
MIDDENS ▸ midden
MIDDEST adj in middle
MIDDIE n glass or bottle containing 285ml of beer
MIDDIES ▸ middy
MIDDLE adj equidistant from two extremes ▸ n middle point or part ▸ vb place in the middle
MIDDLED ▸ middle
MIDDLER n pupil in middle years at school
MIDDLES ▸ middle
MIDDY n middle-sized glass of beer
MIDGE n small mosquito-like insect
MIDGES ▸ midge
MIDGET n very small person or thing ▸ adj much smaller than normal
MIDGETS ▸ midget
MIDGIE n informal word for a small winged biting insect such as the midge or sandfly
MIDGIER ▸ midge
MIDGIES ▸ midgie
MIDGUT n middle part of the digestive tract of vertebrates, including the small intestine
MIDGUTS ▸ midgut
MIDGY ▸ midge
MIDI adj (of a skirt, coat, etc) reaching to below the knee or midcalf ▸ n a skirt, coat, etc reaching to below the knee or midcalf
MIDIRON n club, usually a

No. 5, 6, or 7 iron, used for medium-length approach shots
MIDIS ▸ midi
MIDLAND n middle part of a country
MIDLEG n middle of leg
MIDLEGS ▸ midleg
MIDLIFE n middle age
MIDLINE n line at middle of something
MIDLIST n books in publisher's range that sell reasonably well
MIDMOST adv in the middle or midst ▸ n the middle or midst
MIDNOON n noon
MIDRASH n homily on a scriptural passage derived by traditional Jewish exegetical methods and consisting usually of embellishment of the scriptural narrative
MIDRIB n main vein of a leaf, running down the centre of the blade
MIDRIBS ▸ midrib
MIDRIFF n middle part of the body
MIDS ▸ mid
MIDSHIP adj in, of, or relating to the middle of a vessel ▸ n middle of a vessel
MIDSIZE adj medium-sized
MIDSOLE n layer between the inner and the outer sole of a shoe, contoured for absorbing shock
MIDST See ▸ **amid**
MIDSTS ▸ midst
MIDTERM n middle of a term in a school, university, etc
MIDTOWN n centre of a town
MIDWAY adv halfway ▸ adj in or at the middle of the distance ▸ n place in a fair, carnival, etc, where sideshows are located
MIDWAYS ▸ midway
MIDWEEK n middle of the week
MIDWIFE n trained person who assists at childbirth ▸ vb act as midwife
MIDWIVE vb act as midwife
MIDYEAR n middle of the year
MIELIE same as ▸ **mealie**
MIELIES ▸ mielie

MIEN n person's bearing, demeanour, or appearance

MIENS ▶ mien

MIEVE same as ▶ move

MIEVED ▶ mieve

MIEVES ▶ mieve

MIEVING ▶ mieve

MIFF vb take offence or offend ▷ n petulant mood

MIFFED ▶ miff

MIFFIER ▶ miffy

MIFFILY ▶ miffy

MIFFING ▶ miff

MIFFS ▶ miff

MIFFY adj easily upset

MIFTY same as ▶ miffy

MIG n marble used in games

MIGG same as ▶ mig

MIGGLE n US word for playing marble

MIGGLES ▶ miggle

MIGGS ▶ migg

MIGHT ▶ may

MIGHTS ▶ may

MIGHTST ▶ may

MIGHTY adj powerful ▷ adv very

MIGNON adj small and pretty ▷ n tender boneless cut of meat

MIGNONS ▶ mignon

MIGRANT n person or animal that moves from one place to another ▷ adj moving from one place to another

MIGRATE vb move from one place to settle in another

MIGS ▶ mig

MIHA n young fern frond which has not yet opened

MIHAS ▶ miha

MIHI n Māori ceremonial greeting ▷ vb greet

MIHIED ▶ mihi

MIHIING ▶ mihi

MIHIS ▶ mihi

MIHRAB n niche in a mosque showing the direction of Mecca

MIHRABS ▶ mihrab

MIKADO n Japanese emperor

MIKADOS ▶ mikado

MIKE n microphone

MIKED ▶ mike

MIKES ▶ mike

MIKING ▶ mike

MIKRA ▶ mikron

MIKRON same as ▶ micron

MIKRONS ▶ mikron

MIKVAH n pool used esp by women for ritual purification after their monthly period

MIKVAHS ▶ mikvah

MIKVEH same as ▶ mikvah

MIKVEHS ▶ mikveh

MIKVOS ▶ mikveh

MIKVOT ▶ mikveh

MIKVOTH ▶ mikveh

MIL n unit of length equal to one thousandth of an inch

MILADI same as ▶ milady

MILADIS ▶ miladi

MILADY n (formerly) a continental title for an English gentlewoman

MILAGE same as ▶ mileage

MILAGES ▶ milage

MILCH adj (of a cow) giving milk

MILCHIG same as ▶ milchik

MILCHIK adj containing or used in the preparation of milk products and so not to be used with meat products

MILD adj not strongly flavoured ▷ n dark beer flavoured with fewer hops than bitter ▷ vb become gentle

MILDED ▶ mild

MILDEN vb make or become mild or milder

MILDENS ▶ milden

MILDER ▶ mild

MILDEST ▶ mild

MILDEW same as ▶ mould

MILDEWS ▶ mildew

MILDEWY ▶ mildew

MILDING ▶ mild

MILDLY ▶ mild

MILDS ▶ mild

MILE n unit of length equal to 1760 yards or 1.609 kilometres

MILEAGE n distance travelled in miles

MILER n athlete, horse, etc, that specializes in races of one mile

MILERS ▶ miler

MILES ▶ mile

MILFOIL same as ▶ yarrow

MILIA ▶ milium

MILIARY adj resembling or relating to millet seeds

MILIEU n environment or surroundings

MILIEUS ▶ milieu

MILIEUX ▶ milieu

MILITAR same as > military

MILITIA n military force of trained citizens for use in emergency only

MILIUM n pimple

MILK n white fluid produced by female mammals to feed their young ▷ vb draw milk from

MILKED ▶ milk

MILKEN adj of or like milk

MILKER n cow, goat, etc, that yields milk, esp a specified quality or amount

MILKERS ▶ milker

MILKIER ▶ milky

MILKILY ▶ milky

MILKING ▶ milk

MILKMAN n man who delivers milk to people's houses

MILKMEN ▶ milkman

MILKO informal name for ▶ milkman

MILKOS ▶ milko

MILKS ▶ milk

MILKSOP n feeble man

MILKY adj of or like milk

MILL n factory ▷ vb grind, press, or process in or as if in a mill

MILLAGE adj American tax rate calculated in thousandths per dollar

MILLDAM n dam built in a stream to raise the water level sufficiently for it to turn a millwheel

MILLE French word for > thousand

MILLED adj crushed or ground in a mill

MILLER n person who works in a mill

MILLERS ▶ miller

MILLES ▶ mille

MILLET n type of cereal grass

MILLETS ▶ millet

MILLIER n metric weight of million grams

MILLIME same as > millieme

MILLINE n measurement of advertising space

MILLING n act or process of grinding, cutting, pressing, or crushing in a mill

MILLION n one thousand thousands

MILLRUN same as > millrace

MILLS ▶ mill

MILNEB n type of pesticide

MILNEBS ▶ milneb

MILO n any of various early-growing cultivated varieties of sorghum with heads of yellow or pinkish

M

seeds resembling millet

MILOR same as ▶ **milord**

MILORD n (formerly) a continental title used for an English gentleman

MILORDS ▶ **milord**

MILORS ▶ **milor**

MILOS ▶ **milo**

MILPA n form of subsistence agriculture in Mexico

MILPAS ▶ **milpa**

MILREIS n former monetary unit of Portugal and Brazil, divided into 1000 reis

MILS ▶ **mil**

MILSEY n milk strainer

MILSEYS ▶ **milsey**

MILT n sperm of fish ▷ vb fertilize (the roe of a female fish) with milt, esp artificially

MILTED ▶ **milt**

MILTER n male fish that is mature and ready to breed

MILTERS ▶ **milter**

MILTIER ▶ **milty**

MILTING ▶ **milt**

MILTS ▶ **milt**

MILTY adj full of milt

MILTZ same as ▶ **milt**

MILTZES ▶ **miltz**

MILVINE adj of kites and related birds

MIM adj prim, modest, or demure

MIMBAR n pulpit in mosque

MIMBARS ▶ **mimbar**

MIME n acting without the use of words ▷ vb act in mime

MIMED ▶ **mime**

MIMEO vb mimeograph

MIMEOED ▶ **mimeo**

MIMEOS ▶ **mimeo**

MIMER ▶ **mime**

MIMERS ▶ **mime**

MIMES ▶ **mime**

MIMESES ▶ **mimesis**

MIMESIS n imitative representation of nature or human behaviour

MIMETIC adj imitating or representing something

MIMIC vb imitate (a person or manner), esp for satirical effect ▷ n person or animal that is good at mimicking ▷ adj of, relating to, or using mimicry

MIMICAL ▶ **mimic**

MIMICRY n act or art of copying or imitating closely

MIMICS ▶ **mimic**

MIMING ▶ **mime**

MIMMER ▶ **mim**

MIMMEST ▶ **mim**

MIMMICK same as ▶ **minnick**

MIMOSA n shrub with fluffy yellow flowers and sensitive leaves

MIMOSAE ▶ **mimosa**

MIMOSAS ▶ **mimosa**

MIMSEY same as ▶ **mimsy**

MIMSIER ▶ **mimsy**

MIMSY adj prim, underwhelming, and ineffectual

MIMULUS n plants cultivated for their yellow or red flowers

MINA n ancient unit of weight and money, used in Asia Minor, equal to one sixtieth of a talent

MINABLE ▶ **mine**

MINAE ▶ **mina**

MINAR n tower

MINARET n tall slender tower of a mosque

MINARS ▶ **minar**

MINAS ▶ **mina**

MINBAR same as ▶ **mimbar**

MINBARS ▶ **minbar**

MINCE vb cut or grind into very small pieces ▷ n minced meat

MINCED ▶ **mince**

MINCER n machine for mincing meat

MINCERS ▶ **mincer**

MINCES ▶ **mince**

MINCEUR adj (of food) low-fat

MINCIER ▶ **mincy**

MINCING adj affected in manner

MINCY adj effeminate

MIND n thinking faculties ▷ vb take offence at

MINDED adj having an inclination as specified

MINDER n aide or bodyguard

MINDERS ▶ **minder**

MINDFUL adj heedful

MINDING ▶ **mind**

MINDS ▶ **mind**

MINDSET n ideas and attitudes with which a person approaches a situation, esp when these are seen as being difficult to alter

MINE pron belonging to me ▷ n deep hole for digging

out coal, ores, etc ▷ vb dig for minerals

MINED ▶ **mine**

MINEOLA same as > **minneola**

MINER n person who works in a mine

MINERAL n naturally occurring inorganic substance, such as metal ▷ adj of, containing, or like minerals

MINERS ▶ **miner**

MINES ▶ **mine**

MINETTE n type of rock

MINEVER same as ▶ **miniver**

MING vb mix

MINGED ▶ **ming**

MINGIER ▶ **mingy**

MINGING adj unattractive or unpleasant

MINGLE vb mix or blend

MINGLED ▶ **mingle**

MINGLER ▶ **mingle**

MINGLES ▶ **mingle**

MINGS ▶ **ming**

MINGY adj miserly

MINI same as > **minidress**

MINIATE vb paint with minium

MINIBAR n selection of drinks and confectionery provided in a hotel room

MINIBUS n small bus

MINICAB n ordinary car used as a taxi

MINICAM n portable television camera

MINICAR n small car

MINICOM n device used by deaf and hard-of-hearing people, allowing typed telephone messages to be sent and received

MINIER ▶ **miny**

MINIEST ▶ **miny**

MINIFY vb minimize or lessen the size or importance of (something)

MINIKIN n small, dainty, or affected person or thing ▷ adj dainty, prim, or affected

MINILAB n equipment for processing photographic film

MINIM n note half the length of a semibreve ▷ adj very small

MINIMA ▶ **minimum**

MINIMAL adj minimum ▷ n small surfboard

MINIMAX n lowest of a set of maximum values ▷ vb make maximum as low as possible

MINIMS ▸ minim

MINIMUM n least possible (amount or number) ▷ adj of, being, or showing a minimum or minimums

MINIMUS adj youngest: sometimes used after the surname of a schoolboy having elder brothers at the same school

MINING n act, process, or industry of extracting coal or ores from the earth

MININGS ▸ mining

MINION n servile assistant ▷ adj dainty, pretty, or elegant

MINIONS ▸ minion

MINIS ▸ mini

MINISH vb diminish

MINISKI n short ski

MINIUM n bright red poisonous insoluble oxide of lead usually obtained as a powder by heating litharge in air

MINIUMS ▸ minium

MINIVAN n small van, esp one with seats in the back for carrying passengers

MINIVER n white fur, used in ceremonial costumes

MINIVET n brightly coloured tropical Asian cuckoo shrike

MINK n stoatlike animal

MINKE n as in **minke whale** type of small whalebone whale or rorqual

MINKES ▸ minke

MINKS ▸ mink

MINNICK vb behave in fussy way

MINNIE n mother

MINNIES ▸ minnie

MINNOCK same as ▸ minnick

MINNOW n small freshwater fish

MINNOWS ▸ minnow

MINNY same as ▸ minnie

MINO same as ▸ mynah

MINOR adj lesser ▷ n person regarded legally as a child ▷ vb take a minor

MINORCA n breed of light domestic fowl with glossy white, black, or blue plumage

MINORED ▸ minor

MINORS ▸ minor

MINOS ▸ mino

MINSTER n cathedral or large church

MINT n plant with aromatic leaves used for seasoning and flavouring ▷ vb make (coins)

MINTAGE n process of minting

MINTED ▸ mint

MINTER ▸ mint

MINTERS ▸ mint

MINTIER ▸ mint

MINTING ▸ mint

MINTS ▸ mint

MINTY ▸ mint

MINUEND n number from which another number is to be subtracted

MINUET n stately dance

MINUETS ▸ minuet

MINUS adj indicating subtraction ▷ n sign (-) denoting subtraction or a number less than zero ▷ prep reduced by the subtraction of

MINUSES ▸ minus

MINUTE n 60th part of an hour or degree ▷ vb record in the minutes ▷ adj very small

MINUTED ▸ minute

MINUTER ▸ minute

MINUTES pl n official record of the proceedings of a meeting or conference

MINUTIA singular noun of > minutiae

MINX n bold or flirtatious girl

MINXES ▸ minx

MINXISH ▸ minx

MINY adj of or like mines

MINYAN n number of persons required by Jewish law to be present for a religious service, namely, at least ten males over thirteen years of age

MINYANS ▸ minyan

MIOCENE adj of, denoting, or formed in the fourth epoch of the Tertiary period, between the Oligocene and Pliocene epochs, which lasted for 19 million years

MIOMBO n (in E Africa) a dry wooded area with sparse deciduous growth

MIOMBOS ▸ miombo

MIOSES ▸ miosis

MIOSIS n excessive contraction of the pupil of the eye, as in response to drugs

MIOTIC ▸ miosis

MIOTICS ▸ miosis

MIPS n million instructions per second: a unit used to express the speed of a computer's central processing unit

MIR n peasant commune in prerevolutionary Russia

MIRABLE adj wonderful

MIRACLE n wonderful supernatural event

MIRADOR n window, balcony, or turret

MIRAGE n optical illusion, esp one caused by hot air

MIRAGES ▸ mirage

MIRBANE n substance used in perfumes

MIRCHI Indian English word for ▸ hot

MIRE n swampy ground ▷ vb sink or be stuck in a mire

MIRED ▸ mire

MIRES ▸ mire

MIREX n type of insecticide

MIREXES ▸ mirex

MIRI ▸ mir

MIRIER ▸ mire

MIRIEST ▸ mire

MIRIFIC adj achieving wonderful things

MIRIN n Japanese rice wine

MIRING ▸ mire

MIRINS ▸ mirin

MIRITI n South American palm

MIRITIS ▸ miriti

MIRK same as ▸ murk

MIRKER ▸ mirk

MIRKEST ▸ mirk

MIRKIER ▸ mirk

MIRKILY ▸ mirk

MIRKS ▸ mirk

MIRKY ▸ mirk

MIRLIER ▸ mirly

MIRLY same as ▸ marly

MIRO n tall New Zealand tree

MIROS ▸ miro

MIRROR n coated glass surface for reflecting images ▷ vb reflect in or as if in a mirror

MIRRORS ▸ mirror

MIRS ▸ mir

M

MIRTH n laughter, merriment, or gaiety

MIRTHS ▸ mirth

MIRV n missile that has several warheads, each one being directed to different enemy targets ▸ vb arm with mirvs

MIRVED ▸ mirv

MIRVING ▸ mirv

MIRVS ▸ mirv

MIRY ▸ mire

MIRZA n title of respect placed before the surname of an official, scholar, or other distinguished man

MIRZAS ▸ mirza

MIS ▸ mi

MISACT vb act wrongly

MISACTS ▸ misact

MISADD vb add badly

MISADDS ▸ misadd

MISAIM vb aim badly

MISAIMS ▸ misaim

MISALLY vb form unsuitable alliance

MISATE ▸ miseat

MISAVER vb claim wrongly

MISBIAS vb prejudice wrongly

MISBILL vb present inaccurate bill

MISBIND vb bind wrongly

MISBORN adj abortive

MISCALL vb call by the wrong name

MISCAST vb cast (a role or actor) in (a play or film) inappropriately

MISCH adj as in **misch metal** alloy of cerium and other rare earth metals, used esp as a flint in cigarette lighters

MISCITE vb cite wrongly

MISCODE vb code wrongly

MISCOIN vb coin wrongly

MISCOOK vb cook badly

MISCOPY vb copy badly

MISCUE n faulty stroke in which the cue tip slips off the cue ball or misses it altogether ▸ vb make a miscue

MISCUED ▸ miscue

MISCUES ▸ miscue

MISCUT n cut wrongly

MISCUTS ▸ miscut

MISDATE vb date (a letter, event, etc) wrongly

MISDEAL vb deal out cards incorrectly ▸ n faulty deal

MISDEED n wrongful act

MISDEEM vb form bad opinion of

MISDIAL vb dial telephone number incorrectly

MISDID ▸ misdo

MISDIET n wrong diet

MISDO vb do badly or wrongly

MISDOER ▸ misdo

MISDOES ▸ misdo

MISDONE adj done badly

MISDRAW vb draw poorly

MISDREW ▸ misdraw

MISE n issue in the obsolete writ of right

MISEASE n unease

MISEAT vb eat unhealthy food

MISEATS ▸ miseat

MISEDIT vb edit badly

MISER n person who hoards money and hates spending it

MISERE n call in solo whist and other card games declaring a hand that will win no tricks

MISERES ▸ misere

MISERLY adj of or resembling a miser

MISERS ▸ miser

MISERY n great unhappiness

MISES ▸ mise

MISFALL vb happen as piece of bad luck

MISFARE vb get on badly

MISFED ▸ misfeed

MISFEED vb feed wrongly

MISFELL ▸ misfall

MISFILE vb file (papers, records, etc) wrongly

MISFIRE vb (of a firearm or engine) fail to fire correctly ▸ n act or an instance of misfiring

MISFIT n person not suited to his or her social environment ▸ vb fail to fit or be fitted

MISFITS ▸ misfit

MISFORM vb form badly

MISGAVE ▸ misgive

MISGIVE vb make or be apprehensive or suspicious

MISGO vb go wrong way

MISGOES ▸ misgo

MISGONE ▸ misgo

MISGREW ▸ misgrow

MISGROW vb grow in unsuitable way

MISHAP n minor accident ▸ vb happen as bad luck

MISHAPS ▸ mishap

MISHAPT same as **▸ misshapen**

MISHEAR vb hear (what someone says) wrongly

MISHIT n faulty shot, kick, or stroke ▸ vb hit or kick a ball with a faulty stroke

MISHITS ▸ mishit

MISHMEE n root of Asian plant

MISHMI n evergreen perennial plant

MISHMIS ▸ mishmi

MISJOIN vb join badly

MISKAL n unit of weight in Iran

MISKALS ▸ miskal

MISKEEP vb keep wrongly

MISKEN vb be unaware of

MISKENS ▸ misken

MISKENT ▸ misken

MISKEPT ▸ miskeep

MISKEY vb key wrongly

MISKEYS ▸ miskey

MISKICK vb fail to kick properly

MISKNEW vb ▸ **misknow**

MISKNOW vb have wrong idea about

MISLAID ▸ mislay

MISLAIN ▸ mislay

MISLAY vb lose (something) temporarily

MISLAYS ▸ mislay

MISLEAD vb give false or confusing information to

MISLED ▸ mislead

MISLIE vb lie wrongly

MISLIES ▸ mislie

MISLIKE vb dislike ▸ n dislike or aversion

MISLIT ▸ mislight

MISLIVE vb live wickedly

MISLUCK vb have bad luck

MISMADE ▸ mismake

MISMAKE vb make badly

MISMARK vb mark wrongly

MISMATE vb mate wrongly

MISMEET vb fail to meet

MISMET ▸ mismeet

MISMOVE vb move badly

MISNAME vb name badly

MISO n thick brown salty paste made from soya beans, used to flavour savoury dishes, esp soups

MISOS ▸ miso

MISPAGE vb page wrongly

MISPART vb part wrongly

MISPEN vb write wrongly

MISPENS ▸ mispen

MISPLAN vb plan badly or wrongly

MISPLAY vb play badly or wrongly in games or sports ▷ n wrong or unskilful play

MISPLED > misplead

MISRATE vb rate wrongly

MISREAD vb misinterpret (a situation etc)

MISRELY vb rely wrongly

MISRULE vb govern inefficiently or unjustly ▷ n inefficient or unjust government

MISS vb fail to notice, hear, hit, reach, find, or catch ▷ n fact or instance of missing

MISSA n Roman Catholic mass

MISSAE > missa

MISSAID > missay

MISSAL n book containing the prayers and rites of the Mass

MISSALS > missal

MISSAW > missee

MISSAY vb say wrongly

MISSAYS > missay

MISSEAT vb seat wrongly

MISSED > miss

MISSEE vb see wrongly

MISSEEM vb be unsuitable for

MISSEEN > missee

MISSEES > missee

MISSEL adj as in missel thrush large European thrush with a brown back and spotted breast, noted for feeding on mistletoe berries

MISSELL vb sell (a product, esp a financial one) misleadingly

MISSELS > missel

MISSEND vb send wrongly

MISSENT > missend

MISSES > miss

MISSET vb set wrongly

MISSETS > misset

MISSHOD adj badly shod

MISSIER > missy

MISSIES > missy

MISSILE n rocket with an exploding warhead, used as a weapon

MISSING adj lost or absent

MISSION n specific task or duty ▷ vb direct a mission to or establish a mission in (a given region)

MISSIS same as > missus

MISSISH adj like a schoolgirl

MISSIVE n letter ▷ adj sent or intended to be sent

MISSOLD > missell

MISSORT vb sort wrongly

MISSOUT n someone who has been overlooked

MISSTEP n false step ▷ vb take a false step

MISSTOP vb stop wrongly

MISSUIT vb be unsuitable for

MISSUS n one's wife or the wife of the person addressed or referred to

MISSY n affectionate or disparaging form of address to a girl ▷ adj missish

MIST n thin fog ▷ vb cover or be covered with mist

MISTAKE n error or blunder ▷ vb misunderstand

MISTAL n cow shed

MISTALS > mistal

MISTBOW same as > fogbow

MISTED > mist

MISTELL vb tell wrongly

MISTEND vb tend wrongly

MISTER n informal form of address for a man ▷ vb call (someone) mister

MISTERM vb term badly

MISTERS > mister

MISTERY same as > mystery

MISTEUK Scots variant of > mistook

MISTFUL > mist

MISTICO n small Mediterranean sailing ship

MISTIER > misty

MISTILY > misty

MISTIME vb do (something) at the wrong time

MISTING n application of a fake suntan by spray

MISTLE same as > mizzle

MISTLED > mistle

MISTLES > mistle

MISTOLD > mistell

MISTOOK past tense of > mistake

MISTRAL n strong dry northerly wind of S France

MISTS > mist

MISTUNE vb fail to tune properly

MISTY adj full of mist

MISTYPE vb type badly

MISUSE n incorrect, improper, or careless use ▷ vb use wrongly

MISUSED > misuse

MISUSER n abuse of some right, privilege, office, etc, such as one that may lead to its forfeiture

MISUSES > misuse

MISUST > misuse

MISWEEN vb assess wrongly

MISWEND vb become lost

MISWENT > miswend

MISWORD vb word badly

MISWRIT > miswrite

MISYOKE vb join wrongly

MITCH vb play truant from school

MITCHED > mitch

MITCHES > mitch

MITE n very small spider-like animal

MITER same as > mitre

MITERED > miter

MITERER > miter

MITERS > miter

MITES > mite

MITHER vb fuss over or moan about something

MITHERS > mither

MITIER > mity

MITIEST > mity

MITIS n malleable iron, fluid enough for casting, made by adding a small amount of aluminium to wrought iron

MITISES > mitis

MITOGEN n any agent that induces mitosis

MITOSES > mitosis

MITOSIS n type of cell division in which the nucleus divides into two nuclei which each contain the same number of chromosomes as the original nucleus

MITOTIC > mitosis

MITRAL adj of or like a mitre

MITRE n bishop's pointed headdress ▷ vb join with a mitre joint

MITRED > mitre

MITRES > mitre

MITRING > mitre

MITSVAH same as > mitzvah

MITT same as > mitten

MITTEN n glove with one section for the thumb and one for the four fingers together

MITTENS > mitten

MITTS > mitt

MITUMBA n used clothes imported for sale in African countries

M

MITY adj having mites

MITZVAH n commandment or precept, esp one found in the Bible

MIURUS n type of rhythm in poetry

MIX vb combine or blend into one mass ▷ n mixture

MIXABLE ▶ mix

MIXDOWN n (in sound recording) the transfer of a multitrack master mix to two-track stereo tape

MIXED adj formed or blended together by mixing

MIXEDLY ▶ mixed

MIXEN n dunghill

MIXENS ▶ mixen

MIXER n kitchen appliance used for mixing foods

MIXERS ▶ mixer

MIXES ▶ mix

MIXIBLE ▶ mix

MIXIER ▶ mix

MIXIEST ▶ mix

MIXING ▶ mix

MIXT ▶ mix

MIXTE adj of or denoting a type of bicycle frame, usually for women, in which angled twin lateral tubes run back to the rear axle

MIXTION n amber-based mixture used in making gold leaf

MIXTURE n something mixed

MIXUP n something that is mixed up

MIXUPS ▶ mixup

MIXY adj mixed

MIZ shortened form of ▶ misery

Miz is an informal short form of **misery**, very useful as a Z word. But . you'll need a blank tile for the second Z if you want to form the plural **mizzes**.

MIZEN same as ▶ mizzen

MIZENS ▶ mizen

MIZMAZE n maze

MIZUNA n Japanese variety of lettuce having crisp green leaves

MIZUNAS ▶ mizuna

MIZZ same as ▶ miz

MIZZEN n sail set on a mizzenmast ▷ adj of or relating to any kind of gear used with a mizzenmast

MIZZENS ▶ mizzen

MIZZES ▶ miz

MIZZLE vb decamp

MIZZLED ▶ mizzle

MIZZLES ▶ mizzle

MIZZLY ▶ mizzle

MIZZY adj as in mizzy maze dialect expression meaning state of confusion

MM interj expression of enjoyment of taste or smell

MNA same as ▶ mina

MNAS ▶ mna

MNEME n ability to retain memory

MNEMES ▶ mneme

MNEMIC ▶ mneme

MNEMON n unit of memory

MNEMONS ▶ mnemon

MO n moment

MOA n large extinct flightless New Zealand bird

MOAI n any of the gigantic carved stone figures found on Easter Island (Rapa Nui)

MOAN n low cry of pain ▷ vb make or utter with a moan

MOANED ▶ moan

MOANER ▶ moan

MOANERS ▶ moan

MOANFUL ▶ moan

MOANING ▶ moan

MOANS ▶ moan

MOAS ▶ moa

MOAT n deep wide ditch, esp round a castle ▷ vb surround with or as if with a moat

MOATED ▶ moat

MOATING ▶ moat

MOATS ▶ moat

MOB n disorderly crowd ▷ vb surround in a mob to acclaim or attack

MOBBED ▶ mob

MOBBER ▶ mob

MOBBERS ▶ mob

MOBBIE same as ▶ mobby

MOBBIES ▶ mobby

MOBBING ▶ mob

MOBBISH ▶ mob

MOBBISM n behaviour as mob

MOBBLE same as ▶ moble

MOBBLED ▶ mobble

MOBBLES ▶ mobble

MOBBY n West Indian drink

MOBCAP n woman's 18th-century cotton cap with a pouched crown

MOBCAPS ▶ mobcap

MOBCAST vb create and upload a podcast directly from a mobile phone

MOBE n mobile phone

MOBES ▶ mobe

MOBEY ▶ moby

MOBEYS ▶ mobey

MOBIE n mobile phone

MOBIES ▶ moby

MOBILE adj able to move ▷ n hanging structure designed to move in air currents

MOBILES ▶ mobile

MOBLE vb muffle

MOBLED ▶ moble

MOBLES ▶ moble

MOBLING ▶ moble

MOBLOG n chronicle, which may be shared with others, of someone's thoughts and experiences recorded in the form of mobile phone calls, text messages, and photographs

MOBLOGS ▶ moblog

MOBS ▶ mob

MOBSMAN n person in mob

MOBSMEN ▶ mobsman

MOBSTER n member of a criminal organization

MOBY n mobile phone

MOC shortening of > moccasin

MOCCIES pl n informal Australian word for moccasins

MOCH n spell of humid weather

MOCHA n kind of strong dark coffee

MOCHAS ▶ mocha

MOCHELL same as ▶ much

MOCHIE adj damp or humid

MOCHIER ▶ mochie

MOCHILA n South American shoulder bag

MOCHS ▶ moch

MOCHY same as ▶ mochie

MOCK vb make fun of ▷ adj sham or imitation ▷ n act of mocking

MOCKADO n imitation velvet

MOCKAGE same as ▶ mockery

MOCKED ▶ mock

MOCKER vb dress up

MOCKERS ▶ mocker

MOCKERY n derision

MOCKING ▶ mock

MOCKNEY n person who affects a cockney accent ▷ adj denoting an affected cockney accent or a person who has one

MOCKS ▸ mock

MOCKUP n working full-scale model of a machine, apparatus, etc, for testing, research, etc

MOCKUPS ▸ mockup

MOCOCK n Native American birchbark container

MOCOCKS ▸ mocock

MOCS ▸ moc

MOCUCK same as ▸ mocock

MOCUCKS ▸ mocuck

MOD n member of a group of young people, orig. in the mid-1960s, who were very clothes-conscious and rode motor scooters ▷ vb modify (a piece of software or hardware)

MODAL adj of or relating to mode or manner ▷ n modal word

MODALLY ▸ modal

MODALS ▸ modal

MODDED ▸ mod vb

MODDER n person who modifies a piece of hardware or software

MODDERS ▸ modder

MODDING n practice of modifying a car to alter its appearance or performance

MODE n method or manner

MODEL n (miniature) representation ▷ adj excellent or perfect ▷ vb make a model of

MODELED ▸ model

MODELER ▸ model

MODELLI ▸ modello

MODELLO n artist's preliminary sketch or model

MODELS ▸ model

MODEM n device for connecting two computers by a telephone line ▷ vb send or receive by modem

MODEMED ▸ modem

MODEMS ▸ modem

MODENA n popular variety of domestic fancy pigeon originating in Modena

MODENAS ▸ modena

MODER n intermediate layer in humus

MODERN adj of present or recent times ▷ n contemporary person

MODERNE n the style of architecture and design, prevalent in Europe and the US in the late 1920s and 1930s, typified by the use of straight lines, tubular chromed steel frames, contrasting inlaid woods, etc ▷ adj of or relating to this style of architecture and design

MODERNS ▸ modern

MODERS ▸ moder

MODES ▸ mode

MODEST adj not vain or boastful

MODESTY n quality or condition of being modest

MODGE vb do shoddily

MODGED ▸ modge

MODGES ▸ modge

MODGING ▸ modge

MODI ▸ modus

MODICA ▸ modicum

MODICUM n small quantity

MODIFY vb change slightly

MODII ▸ modius

MODIOLI > modiolus

MODISH adj in fashion

MODIST n follower of fashion

MODISTE n fashionable dressmaker or milliner

MODISTS ▸ modist

MODIUS n ancient Roman quantity measure

MODS ▸ mod

MODULAR adj of, consisting of, or resembling a module or modulus ▷ n thing comprised of modules

MODULE n self-contained unit, section, or component with a specific function

MODULES ▸ module

MODULI ▸ modulus

MODULO adv with reference to modulus

MODULUS n coefficient expressing a specified property, for instance elasticity, of a specified substance

MODUS n way of doing something

MOE adv more ▷ n a wry face

MOELLON n rubble

MOER n in South Africa, slang word for the womb ▷ vb in South Africa, attack (someone or something) violently

MOERED ▸ moer

MOERING ▸ moer

MOERS ▸ moer

MOES ▸ moe

MOFETTE n opening in a region of nearly extinct volcanic activity, through which carbon dioxide, nitrogen, and other gases pass

MOFFIE n homosexual ▷ adj homosexual

MOFFIES ▸ moffie

MOG vb go away

MOGGAN n stocking without foot

MOGGANS ▸ moggan

MOGGED ▸ mog

MOGGIE same as ▸ moggy

MOGGIES ▸ moggy

MOGGING ▸ mog

MOGGY n cat

MOGHUL same as ▸ mogul

MOGHULS ▸ moghul

MOGS ▸ mog

MOGUL n important or powerful person

MOGULED adj having moguls

MOGULS ▸ mogul

MOHAIR n fine hair of the Angora goat

MOHAIRS ▸ mohair

MOHALIM same as ▸ mohelim

MOHAWK n half turn from either edge of either skate to the corresponding edge of the other skate

MOHAWKS ▸ mohawk

MOHEL n man qualified to conduct circumcisions

MOHELIM ▸ mohel

MOHELS ▸ mohel

MOHICAN n punk hairstyle

MOHR same as ▸ mhorr

MOHRS ▸ mohr

MOHUA n small New Zealand bird with a yellow head and breast

MOHUAS ▸ mohua

MOHUR n former Indian gold coin worth 15 rupees

MOHURS ▸ mohur

MOI ▸ me

MOIDER same as ▸ moither

MOIDERS ▸ moider

MOIDORE n former Portuguese gold coin

MOIETY n half

MOIL vb moisten or soil or become moist, soiled, etc ▷ n toil

MOILED ▸ moil

MOILER ▶ moil
MOILERS ▶ moil
MOILING ▶ moil
MOILS ▶ moil
MOINEAU n small fortification

> Meaning part of a fortification, this is another of those very useful 7-letter vowel dumps.

MOIRA n fate
MOIRAI ▶ moira
MOIRE adj having a watered or wavelike pattern ▷ n any fabric that has such a pattern
MOIRES ▶ moire
MOISER n informer
MOISERS ▶ moiser
MOIST adj slightly wet ▷ vb moisten
MOISTED ▶ moist
MOISTEN vb make or become moist
MOISTER ▶ moist
MOISTLY ▶ moist
MOISTS ▶ moist
MOIT same as ▶ mote
MOITHER vb bother or bewilder
MOITS ▶ moit
MOJARRA n tropical American sea fish
MOJITO n cocktail consisting of rum, lime, mint, and soda water
MOJITOS ▶ mojito
MOJO n charm or magic spell
MOJOES ▶ mojo
MOJOS ▶ mojo
MOKE n donkey
MOKES ▶ moke
MOKI n edible sea fish of New Zealand
MOKIHI n Māori raft
MOKIHIS ▶ mokihi
MOKIS ▶ moki
MOKO n Māori tattoo or tattoo pattern
MOKORO n (in Botswana) the traditional dugout canoe of the people of the Okavango Delta
MOKOROS ▶ mokoro
MOKOS ▶ moko
MOKSHA n freedom from the endless cycle of transmigration into a state of bliss
MOKSHAS ▶ moksha
MOL n the SI unit mole

MOLA another name for ▶ sunfish
MOLAL adj of or consisting of a solution containing one mole of solute per thousand grams of solvent
MOLAR n large back tooth used for grinding ▷ adj of any of these teeth
MOLARS ▶ molar
MOLAS ▶ mola
MOLASSE n soft sediment produced by the erosion of mountain ranges after the final phase of mountain building
MOLD same as ▶ mould
MOLDED ▶ mold
MOLDER same as ▶ moulder
MOLDERS ▶ molder
MOLDIER ▶ moldy
MOLDING same as > moulding
MOLDS ▶ mold
MOLDY same as ▶ mouldy
MOLE n small dark raised spot on the skin
MOLES ▶ mole
MOLEST vb interfere with sexually
MOLESTS ▶ molest
MOLIES ▶ moly
MOLIMEN n effort needed to perform bodily function
MOLINE adj (of a cross) having arms of equal length, forked and curved back at the ends ▷ n moline cross
MOLINES ▶ moline
MOLINET n stick for whipping chocolate
MOLL n gangster's female accomplice
MOLLA same as ▶ mollah
MOLLAH same as ▶ mullah
MOLLAHS ▶ mollah
MOLLAS ▶ molla
MOLLIE same as ▶ molly
MOLLIES ▶ molly
MOLLIFY vb pacify or soothe
MOLLS ▶ moll
MOLLUSC n soft-bodied, usu hard-shelled, animal, such as a snail or oyster
MOLLUSK same as ▶ mollusc
MOLLY n brightly coloured tropical or subtropical American freshwater fish
MOLOCH n spiny Australian

desert-living lizard that feeds on ants
MOLOCHS ▶ moloch
MOLOSSI > molossus
MOLS ▶ mol
MOLT same as ▶ moult
MOLTED ▶ molt
MOLTEN ▶ melt
MOLTER ▶ molt
MOLTERS ▶ molt
MOLTING ▶ molt
MOLTO adv very
MOLTS ▶ molt
MOLY n magic herb given by Hermes to Odysseus to nullify the spells of Circe
MOM same as ▶ mother
MOME n fool
MOMENT n short space of time
MOMENTA > momentum
MOMENTO same as ▶ memento
MOMENTS ▶ moment
MOMES ▶ mome
MOMI same as ▶ mom
MOMISM n excessive domination of a child by his or her mother
MOMISMS ▶ momism
MOMMA same as ▶ mamma
MOMMAS ▶ momma
MOMMET same as ▶ mammet
MOMMETS ▶ mommet
MOMMIES ▶ mommy
MOMMY same as ▶ mom
MOMS ▶ mom
MOMSER same as ▶ momzer
MOMSERS ▶ momser
MOMUS n person who ridicules
MOMUSES ▶ momus
MOMZER same as ▶ mamzer
MOMZERS ▶ momzer
MON dialect variant of ▶ man
MONA n W African guenon monkey with dark fur on the back and white or yellow underparts
MONACID same as > monoacid
MONACT adj (of sponge) with single-spiked structures in skeleton
MONAD n any fundamental singular metaphysical entity
MONADAL ▶ monad
MONADES ▶ monas

M

MONADIC *adj* being or relating to a monad

MONADS ▸ **monad**

MONAL *n* S Asian pheasant, the male of which has a brilliantly coloured plumage

MONALS ▸ **monal**

MONARCH *n* sovereign ruler of a state

MONARDA *n* mintlike N American plant

MONAS *same as* ▸ **monad**

MONASES ▸ **monas**

MONAUL *same as* ▸ **monal**

MONAULS ▸ **monaul**

MONAXON *n* type of sponge

MONDAIN *n* man who moves in fashionable society ▸ *adj* characteristic of fashionable society

MONDE *n* French word meaning world or society

MONDES ▸ **monde**

MONDIAL *adj* of or involving the whole world

MONDO *n* Buddhist questioning technique

MONDOS ▸ **mondo**

MONEME *less common word for* > **morpheme**

MONEMES ▸ **moneme**

MONER *n* hypothetical simple organism

MONERA ▸ **moner**

MONERAN *n* type of bacterium

MONERON *same as* ▸ **moner**

MONETH *same as* ▸ **month**

MONETHS ▸ **moneth**

MONEY *n* medium of exchange, coins or banknotes

MONEYED *adj* rich

MONEYER *n* person who coins money

MONEYS ▸ **money**

MONGED *adj* under the influence of drugs

MONGER *n* trader or dealer ▸ *vb* deal in

MONGERS ▸ **monger**

MONGERY ▸ **monger**

MONGO *same as* ▸ **mungo**

MONGOE *same as* ▸ **mongo**

MONGOES ▸ **mongoe**

MONGOS ▸ **mongo**

MONGREL *n* animal, esp a dog, of mixed breed ▸ *adj* of mixed breed or origin

MONGST *short for*

▸ **amongst**

MONIAL *n* mullion

MONIALS ▸ **monial**

MONIE *Scots word for* ▸ **many**

MONIED *same as* ▸ **moneyed**

MONIES ▸ **money**

MONIKER *n* person's name or nickname

MONILIA *n* type of fungus

MONISH *same as* > **admonish**

MONISM *n* doctrine that reality consists of only one basic substance or element, such as mind or matter

MONISMS ▸ **monism**

MONIST ▸ **monism**

MONISTS ▸ **monism**

MONITOR *n* person or device that checks, controls, warns, or keeps a record of something ▸ *vb* watch and check on

MONK *n* member of an all-male religious community bound by vows

MONKEY *n* long-tailed primate ▸ *vb* meddle or fool

MONKEYS ▸ **monkey**

MONKISH *adj* of, relating to, or resembling a monk or monks

MONKS ▸ **monk**

MONO *n* monophonic sound

MONOAO *n* New Zealand plant with rigid leaves

MONOAOS ▸ **monoao**

MONOCLE *n* eyeglass for one eye only

MONOCOT *n* type of flowering plant with a single embryonic seed leaf, such as grasses, lilies, palms, and orchids

MONODIC ▸ **monody**

MONODY *n* (in Greek tragedy) an ode sung by a single actor

MONOECY *same as* > **monoecism**

MONOFIL *n* synthetic thread or yarn composed of a single strand rather than twisted fibres

MONOLOG *same as* > **monologue**

MONOMER *n* compound whose molecules can join together to form a polymer

MONONYM *n* person who

is famous enough to be known only by one name, usually the first name

MONOPOD *same as* > **monopode**

MONOS ▸ **mono**

MONOSES ▸ **monosis**

MONOSIS *n* abnormal separation

MONOSKI *n* wide ski on which the skier stands with both feet ▸ *vb* ski on a monoski

MONOSY *same as* ▸ **monosis**

MONS ▸ **mon**

MONSOON *n* seasonal wind of SE Asia

MONSTER *n* imaginary, usu frightening, beast ▸ *adj* huge ▸ *vb* criticize (a person or group) severely

MONTAGE *n* (making of) a picture composed from pieces of others ▸ *vb* make as a montage

MONTAN *adj* as in **montan wax** hard wax obtained from lignite and peat used in polishes and candles

MONTANE *n* area of mountain dominated by vegetation ▸ *adj* of or inhabiting mountainous regions

MONTANT *n* vertical part in woodwork

MONTE *n* gambling card game of Spanish origin

MONTEM *n* former money-raising practice at Eton school

MONTEMS ▸ **montem**

MONTERO *n* round cap with a flap at the back worn by hunters, esp in Spain in the 17th and 18th centuries

MONTES ▸ **monte**

MONTH *n* one of the twelve divisions of the calendar year

MONTHLY *adj* happening or payable once a month ▸ *adv* once a month ▸ *n* monthly magazine

MONTHS ▸ **month**

MONTIES ▸ **monty**

MONTRE *n* pipes of organ

MONTRES ▸ **montre**

MONTURE *n* mount or frame

MONTY *n* complete form of something

M

MONURON n type of weedkiller

MONY Scots word for ▶ **many**

MOO n long deep cry of a cow ▷ vb make this noise ▷ interj instance or imitation of this sound

MOOBS pl n overdeveloped breasts on a man, caused by excess weight or lack of exercise

MOOCH vb loiter about aimlessly

MOOCHED ▶ mooch

MOOCHER ▶ mooch

MOOCHES ▶ mooch

MOOD n temporary (gloomy) state of mind

MOODIED ▶ moody

MOODIER ▶ moody

MOODIES ▶ moody

MOODILY ▶ moody

MOODS ▶ mood

MOODY adj sullen or gloomy ▷ vb flatter

MOOED ▶ moo

MOOI adj pleasing or nice

MOOING ▶ moo

MOOKTAR same as ▶ mukhtar

MOOL same as ▶ mould

MOOLA same as ▶ moolah

MOOLAH slang word for ▶ money

MOOLAHS ▶ moolah

MOOLAS ▶ moola

MOOLED ▶ mool

MOOLEY same as ▶ mooly

MOOLEYS ▶ mooley

MOOLI n type of large white radish

MOOLIES ▶ mooly

MOOLING ▶ mool

MOOLIS ▶ mooli

MOOLOO n person from the Waikato

MOOLOOS ▶ mooloo

MOOLS ▶ mool

MOOLVI same as ▶ moolvie

MOOLVIE n (esp in India) a Muslim doctor of the law, teacher, or learned man also used as a title of respect

MOOLVIS ▶ moolvi

MOOLY same as ▶ muley

MOON n natural satellite of the earth ▷ vb be idle in a listless or dreamy way

MOONBOW n rainbow made by moonlight

MOONED adj decorated with a moon

MOONER ▶ moon

MOONERS ▶ moon

MOONEYE n N American large-eyed freshwater fish

MOONG n as in moong bean kind of bean

MOONIER ▶ moony

MOONIES ▶ moony

MOONILY ▶ moony

MOONING ▶ moon

MOONISH ▶ moon

MOONLET n small moon

MOONLIT adj illuminated by the moon

MOONS ▶ moon

MOONSET n moment when the moon disappears below the horizon

MOONY adj dreamy or listless ▷ n crazy or foolish person

MOOP same as ▶ moup

MOOPED ▶ moop

MOOPING ▶ moop

MOOPS ▶ moop

MOOR n tract of open uncultivated ground covered with grass and heather ▷ vb secure (a ship) with ropes etc

MOORAGE n place for mooring a vessel

MOORED ▶ moor

MOORHEN n small black water bird

MOORIER ▶ moor

MOORILL n disease of cattle on moors

MOORING n place for mooring a ship

MOORISH adj of or relating to the Moor people of North Africa

MOORLOG n rotted wood below the surface of a moor

MOORMAN n person living on a moor

MOORMEN ▶ moorman

MOORS ▶ moor

MOORVA same as ▶ murva

MOORVAS ▶ moorva

MOORY ▶ moor

MOOS ▶ moo

MOOSE n large N American deer

MOOT adj debatable ▷ vb bring up for discussion ▷ n (in Anglo-Saxon England) a local administrative assembly

MOOTED ▶ moot

MOOTER ▶ moot

MOOTERS ▶ moot

MOOTEST ▶ moot

MOOTING ▶ moot

MOOTMAN n person taking part in a moot

MOOTMEN ▶ mootman

MOOTS ▶ moot

MOOVE same as ▶ move

MOOVED ▶ moove

MOOVES ▶ moove

MOOVING ▶ moove

MOP n long stick with twists of cotton or a sponge on the end, used for cleaning ▷ vb clean or soak up with or as if with a mop

MOPANE same as ▶ mopani

MOPANES ▶ mopane

MOPANI n S African tree that is highly resistant to drought and produces very hard wood

MOPANIS ▶ mopani

MOPE vb be gloomy and apathetic ▷ n gloomy person

MOPED n light motorized cycle

MOPEDS ▶ moped

MOPER ▶ mope

MOPERS ▶ mope

MOPERY n gloominess

MOPES ▶ mope

MOPEY ▶ mope

MOPHEAD n person with shaggy hair

MOPIER ▶ mope

MOPIEST ▶ mope

MOPILY ▶ mopy

MOPING ▶ mope

MOPISH ▶ mope

MOPOKE n species of owl

MOPOKES ▶ mopoke

MOPPED ▶ mop

MOPPER ▶ mop

MOPPERS ▶ mop

MOPPET same as ▶ poppet

MOPPETS ▶ moppet

MOPPIER ▶ moppy

MOPPING ▶ mop

MOPPY adj drunk

MOPS ▶ mop

MOPSIES ▶ mopsy

MOPSY n untidy or dowdy person

MOPUS n person who mopes

MOPUSES ▶ mopus

MOPY ▶ mope

MOR n layer of acidic humus formed in cool moist areas where decomposition is slow

MORA n quantity of a short syllable in verse

MORAE ▶ mora

MORAINE n accumulated mass of debris deposited by a glacier

MORAL adj concerned with right and wrong conduct ▷ n lesson to be obtained from a story or event ▷ vb moralize

MORALE n degree of confidence or hope of a person or group

MORALES ▶ morale

MORALL same as ▶ mural

MORALLS ▶ morall

MORALLY ▶ moral

MORALS ▶ moral

MORAS ▶ mora

MORASS n marsh

MORASSY ▶ morass

MORAT n drink containing mulberry juice

MORATS ▶ morat

MORAY n large voracious eel

MORAYS ▶ moray

MORBID adj unduly interested in death or unpleasant events

MORBUS n disease

MORCEAU n fragment or morsel

MORCHA n (in India) a hostile demonstration against the government

MORCHAS ▶ morcha

MORDANT adj sarcastic or scathing ▷ n substance used to fix dyes ▷ vb treat (a fabric, yarn, etc) with a mordant

MORDENT n melodic ornament consisting of the rapid alternation of a note with a note one degree lower than it

MORE adj greater in amount or degree ▷ adv greater extent ▷ pron greater or additional amount or number

MOREEN n heavy, usually watered, fabric of wool or wool and cotton, used esp in furnishing

MOREENS ▶ moreen

MOREISH adj (of food) causing a desire for more

MOREL n edible mushroom with a pitted cap

MORELLE n nightshade

MORELLO n variety of small very dark sour cherry

MORELS ▶ morel

MORENDO adv (in music) dying away

MORES pl n customs and conventions embodying the fundamental values of a community

MORGAN n American breed of small compact saddle horse

MORGANS ▶ morgan

MORGAY n small dogfish

MORGAYS ▶ morgay

MORGEN n South African unit of area, equal to about two acres or 0.8 hectare

MORGENS ▶ morgen

MORGUE same as ▶ mortuary

MORGUES ▶ morgue

MORIA n folly

MORIAS ▶ moria

MORICHE same as ▶ miriti

MORION n 16th-century helmet with a brim and wide comb

MORIONS ▶ morion

MORISCO n a morris dance

MORISH same as ▶ moreish

MORKIN n animal dying in accident

MORKINS ▶ morkin

MORLING n sheep killed by disease

MORMAOR n former high-ranking Scottish nobleman

MORN n morning

MORNAY adj served with a cheese sauce

MORNAYS ▶ mornay

MORNE same as ▶ mourn

MORNED ▶ morne

MORNES ▶ morne

MORNING n part of the day before noon

MORNS ▶ morn

MOROCCO n goatskin leather

MORON n foolish or stupid person

MORONIC ▶ moron

MORONS ▶ moron

MOROSE adj sullen or moody

MOROSER ▶ morose

MORPH n phonological representation of a morpheme ▷ vb undergo or cause to undergo morphing

MORPHED ▶ morph

MORPHEW n blemish on skin

MORPHIA same as ▶ morphine

MORPHIC adj as in **morphic resonance** idea that, through a telepathic effect or sympathetic vibration, an event or act can lead to similar events or acts in the future or an idea conceived in one mind can then arise in another

MORPHIN variant form of ▶ morphine

MORPHO n type of butterfly

MORPHOS ▶ morpho

MORPHS ▶ morph

MORRA same as ▶ mora

MORRAS ▶ morra

MORRELL n tall SW Australian eucalyptus with pointed buds

MORRHUA n cod

MORRICE same as ▶ morris

MORRION same as ▶ morion

MORRIS vb perform morris dance

MORRO n rounded hill or promontory

MORROS ▶ morro

MORROW n next day

MORROWS ▶ morrow

MORS ▶ mor

MORSAL ▶ morsure

MORSE n clasp or fastening on a cope

MORSEL n small piece, esp of food ▷ vb divide into morsels

MORSELS ▶ morsel

MORSES ▶ morse

MORSURE n bite

MORT n call blown on a hunting horn to signify the death of the animal hunted

MORTAL adj subject to death ▷ n human being

MORTALS ▶ mortal

MORTAR n small cannon with a short range ▷ vb fire on with mortars

MORTARS ▶ mortar

MORTARY adj of or like mortar

MORTICE same as ▶ mortise

MORTIFY vb humiliate

MORTISE n slot or recess, usually rectangular, cut into a piece of wood, stone,

M

M

etc, to receive a matching projection (tenon) of another piece, or a mortise lock ▷ vb cut a slot or recess in (a piece of wood, stone, etc)

MORTS ▶ mort

MORULA n solid ball of cells resulting from cleavage of a fertilized ovum

MORULAE ▶ morula

MORULAR ▶ morula

MORULAS ▶ morula

MORWONG n food fish of Australasian coastal waters

MORYAH interj exclamation of annoyance, disbelief, etc

MOS ▶ mo

MOSAIC n design or decoration using small pieces of coloured stone or glass

MOSAICS ▶ mosaic

MOSE vb have glanders

MOSED ▶ mose

MOSELLE n German white wine from the Moselle valley

MOSES ▶ mose

MOSEY vb walk in a leisurely manner

MOSEYED ▶ mosey

MOSEYS ▶ mosey

MOSH n type of dance, performed to loud rock music, in which people throw themselves about in a frantic and violent manner ▷ vb dance in this manner

MOSHAV n cooperative settlement in Israel, consisting of a number of small farms

MOSHED ▶ mosh

MOSHER ▶ mosh

MOSHERS ▶ mosh

MOSHES ▶ mosh

MOSHING ▶ mosh

MOSING ▶ mose

MOSK same as ▶ mosque

MOSKS ▶ mosk

MOSQUE n Muslim temple

MOSQUES ▶ mosque

MOSS n small flowerless plant growing in masses on moist surfaces ▷ vb gather moss

MOSSED ▶ moss

MOSSER ▶ moss

MOSSERS ▶ moss

MOSSES ▶ moss

MOSSIE n common sparrow

MOSSIER ▶ moss

MOSSIES ▶ mossie

MOSSING ▶ moss

MOSSO adv to be performed with rapidity

MOSSY ▶ moss

MOST n greatest number or degree ▷ adj greatest in number or degree ▷ adv in the greatest degree

MOSTE ▶ mote

MOSTEST ▶ most

MOSTLY adv for the most part, generally

MOSTS ▶ most

MOT n girl or young woman, esp one's girlfriend

MOTE n tiny speck ▷ vb may or might

MOTED adj containing motes

MOTEL n roadside hotel for motorists

MOTELS ▶ motel

MOTEN ▶ mote

MOTES ▶ mote

MOTET n short sacred choral song

MOTETS ▶ motet

MOTETT same as ▶ motet

MOTETTS ▶ motet

MOTEY adj containing motes

MOTH n nocturnal insect like a butterfly

MOTHED adj damaged by moths

MOTHER n female parent ▷ adj native or inborn ▷ vb look after as a mother

MOTHERS ▶ mother

MOTHERY ▶ mother

MOTHIER ▶ mothy

MOTHS ▶ moth

MOTHY adj ragged

MOTIER ▶ motey

MOTIEST ▶ motey

MOTIF n (recurring) theme or design

MOTIFIC adj causing motion

MOTIFS ▶ motif

MOTILE adj capable of independent movement ▷ n person whose mental imagery strongly reflects movement, esp his own

MOTILES ▶ motile

MOTION n process, action, or way of moving ▷ vb direct (someone) by gesture

MOTIONS ▶ motion

MOTIVE n reason for a

course of action ▷ adj causing motion ▷ vb motivate

MOTIVED ▶ motive

MOTIVES ▶ motive

MOTIVIC adj of musical motif

MOTLEY adj miscellaneous ▷ n costume of a jester

MOTLEYS ▶ motley

MOTLIER ▶ motley

MOTMOT n tropical American bird with a long tail and blue and brownish-green plumage

MOTMOTS ▶ motmot

MOTOR n engine, esp of a vehicle ▷ vb travel by car ▷ adj of or relating to cars and other vehicles powered by petrol or diesel engines

MOTORED ▶ motor

MOTORIC ▶ motor

MOTORS ▶ motor

MOTORY ▶ motor

MOTS ▶ mot

MOTSER n large sum of money, esp a gambling win

MOTSERS ▶ motser

MOTT n clump of trees

MOTTE n mound on which a castle was built

MOTTES ▶ motte

MOTTIER ▶ motty

MOTTIES ▶ motty

MOTTLE vb colour with streaks or blotches of different shades ▷ n mottled appearance, as of the surface of marble

MOTTLED ▶ mottle

MOTTLER n paintbrush for mottled effects

MOTTLES ▶ mottle

MOTTO n saying expressing an ideal or rule of conduct

MOTTOED adj having motto

MOTTOES ▶ motto

MOTTOS ▶ motto

MOTTS ▶ mott

MOTTY n target at which coins are aimed in pitch-and-toss ▷ adj containing motes

MOTUCA n Brazilian fly

MOTUCAS ▶ motuca

MOTZA same as ▶ motser

MOTZAS ▶ motza

MOU Scots word for ▶ mouth

MOUCH same as ▶ mooch

MOUCHED ▶ mouch

MOUCHER ▶ mouch

MOUCHES ▶ mouch

MOUE n disdainful or pouting look

MOUES ▶ moue

MOUFLON n wild short-fleeced mountain sheep of Corsica and Sardinia

MOUGHT ▶ mote

MOUILLE adj palatalized, as in the sounds represented by Spanish ll or ñ

MOUJIK same as ▶ muzhik

MOUJIKS ▶ moujik

MOULAGE n mould making

MOULD n hollow container in which metal etc is cast ▷ vb shape

MOULDED ▶ mould

MOULDER vb decay into dust ▷ n person who moulds or makes moulds

MOULDS ▶ mould

MOULDY adj stale or musty

MOULIN n vertical shaft in a glacier, maintained by a constant descending stream of water and debris

MOULINS ▶ moulin

MOULS Scots word for ▶ mould

MOULT vb shed feathers, hair, or skin to make way for new growth ▷ n process of moulting

MOULTED ▶ moult

MOULTEN adj having moulted

MOULTER ▶ moult

MOULTS ▶ moult

MOUND n heap, esp of earth or stones ▷ vb gather into a mound

MOUNDED ▶ mound

MOUNDS ▶ mound

MOUNT vb climb or ascend ▷ n backing or support on which something is fixed

MOUNTED adj riding horses

MOUNTER ▶ mount

MOUNTS ▶ mount

MOUP n nibble

MOUPED ▶ moup

MOUPING ▶ moup

MOUPS ▶ moup

MOURN vb feel or express sorrow for (a dead person or lost thing)

MOURNED ▶ mourn

MOURNER n person attending a funeral

MOURNS ▶ mourn

MOUS ▶ mou

MOUSAKA same as
> moussaka

MOUSE n small long-tailed rodent ▷ vb stalk and catch mice

MOUSED ▶ mouse

MOUSER n cat used to catch mice

MOUSERS ▶ mouser

MOUSERY n place infested with mice

MOUSES ▶ mouse

MOUSEY same as ▶ mousy

MOUSIE n little mouse

MOUSIER ▶ mousy

MOUSIES ▶ mousie

MOUSILY ▶ mousy

MOUSING n lashing, shackle, etc, for closing off a hook to prevent a load from slipping off

MOUSLE vb handle roughly

MOUSLED ▶ mousle

MOUSLES ▶ mousle

MOUSME n Japanese girl

MOUSMEE same as ·
▶ mousme

MOUSMES ▶ mousme

MOUSSE n dish of flavoured cream whipped and set ▷ vb apply mousse to

MOUSSED ▶ mousse

MOUSSES ▶ mousse

MOUST same as ▶ must

MOUSTED ▶ moust

MOUSTS ▶ moust

MOUSY adj like a mouse, esp in hair colour

MOUTAN n variety of peony

MOUTANS ▶ moutan

MOUTER same as ▶ multure

MOUTERS ▶ mouter

MOUTH n opening in the head for eating and issuing sounds ▷ vb form (words) with the lips without speaking

MOUTHED ▶ mouth

MOUTHER ▶ mouth

MOUTHS ▶ mouth

MOUTHY adj bombastic

MOUTON n sheepskin processed to resemble the fur of another animal, esp beaver or seal

MOUTONS ▶ mouton

MOVABLE adj able to be moved or rearranged ▷ n movable article, esp a piece of furniture

MOVABLY ▶ movable

MOVE vb change in place or position ▷ n moving

MOVED ▶ move

MOVER n person or animal that moves in a particular way

MOVERS ▶ mover

MOVES ▶ move

MOVIE n cinema film

MOVIES ▶ movie

MOVING adj arousing or touching the emotions

MOVIOLA n viewing machine used in cutting and editing film

MOW vb cut (grass or crops) ▷ n part of a barn where hay, straw, etc, is stored

MOWA same as ▶ mahua

MOWAS ▶ mowa

MOWBURN vb heat up in mow

MOWDIE Scots words for
▶ mole

MOWDIES ▶ mowdie

MOWED ▶ mow

MOWER ▶ mow

MOWERS ▶ mow

MOWING ▶ mow

MOWINGS ▶ mow

MOWN ▶ mow

MOWRA same as ▶ mahua

MOWRAS ▶ mowra

MOWS ▶ mow

MOXA n downy material obtained from various plants and used in Oriental medicine by being burned on the skin as a cauterizing agent or counterirritant for the skin

MOXAS ▶ moxa

MOXIE n courage, nerve, or vigour

MOXIES ▶ moxie

MOY n coin

MOYA n mud emitted from a volcano

MOYAS ▶ moya

MOYITY same as ▶ moiety

MOYL same as ▶ moyle

MOYLE vb toil

MOYLED ▶ moyle

MOYLES ▶ moyle

MOYLING ▶ moyle

MOYLS ▶ moyl

MOYS ▶ moy

MOZ n hex

This unusual word, Australian slang for bad luck, is another of the very useful short words that use the Z, and it can be extended to **moze** or **mozo**.

MOZE vb give nap to

M

MOZED ▶ moze

MOZES ▶ moze

MOZETTA same as > mozzetta

MOZETTE ▶ mozzetta

MOZING ▶ moze

MOZO n porter in southwest USA

MOZOS ▶ mozo

MOZZ same as ▶ moz

MOZZES ▶ mozz

MOZZIE same as ▶ mossie

MOZZIES ▶ mozzie

MOZZLE n luck

MOZZLES ▶ mozzle

MPRET n former Albanian ruler

MPRETS ▶ mpret

MRIDANG n drum used in Indian music

MU n 12th letter in the Greek alphabet, a consonant, transliterated as m

MUCATE n salt of mucic acid

MUCATES ▶ mucate

MUCH adj large amount or degree of ▷ n large amount or degree ▷ adv great degree

MUCHEL same as ▶ much

MUCHELL same as ▶ much

MUCHELS ▶ muchel

MUCHES ▶ much

MUCHLY ▶ much

MUCHO adv Spanish for very

MUCIC adj as in mucic acid colourless crystalline solid carboxylic acid found in milk sugar and used in the manufacture of pyrrole

MUCID adj mouldy, musty, or slimy

MUCIGEN n substance present in mucous cells that is converted into mucin

MUCIN n any of a group of nitrogenous mucoproteins occurring in saliva, skin, tendon, etc, that produce a very viscous solution in water

MUCINS ▶ mucin

MUCK n dirt, filth

MUCKED ▶ muck

MUCKER n person who shifts broken rock or waste ▷ vb hoard

MUCKERS ▶ mucker

MUCKIER ▶ mucky

MUCKILY ▶ mucky

MUCKING ▶ muck

MUCKLE same as ▶ mickle

MUCKLES ▶ muckle

MUCKS ▶ muck

MUCKY adj dirty or muddy

MUCLUC same as ▶ mukluk

MUCLUCS ▶ mucluc

MUCOID adj of the nature of or resembling mucin ▷ n substance like mucin

MUCOIDS ▶ mucoid

MUCOR n type of fungus which comprises many common moulds

MUCORS ▶ mucor

MUCOSA n mucous membrane: mucus-secreting membrane that lines body cavities or passages that are open to the external environment

MUCOSAE ▶ mucosa

MUCOSAL ▶ mucosa

MUCOSAS ▶ mucosa

MUCOSE same as ▶ mucous

MUCOUS adj of, resembling, or secreting mucus

MUCRO n short pointed projection from certain parts or organs, as from the tip of a leaf

MUCROS ▶ mucro

MUCUS n slimy secretion of the mucous membranes

MUCUSES ▶ mucus

MUD n wet soft earth ▷ vb cover in mud

MUDBATH n medicinal bath in heated mud

MUDBUG n crayfish

MUDBUGS ▶ mudbug

MUDCAP vb use explosive charge in blasting

MUDCAPS ▶ mudcap

MUDCAT n any of several large North American catfish living in muddy rivers, esp in the Mississippi valley

MUDCATS ▶ mudcat

MUDDED ▶ mud

MUDDER n horse that runs well in mud

MUDDERS ▶ mudder

MUDDIED ▶ muddy

MUDDIER ▶ muddy

MUDDIES ▶ muddy

MUDDILY ▶ muddy

MUDDING ▶ mud

MUDDLE vb confuse ▷ n state of confusion

MUDDLED ▶ muddle

MUDDLER n person who muddles or muddles through

MUDDLES ▶ muddle

MUDDLY ▶ muddle

MUDDY adj covered or filled with mud ▷ vb make muddy

MUDEJAR n Spanish Moor, esp one permitted to stay in Spain after the Christian reconquest ▷ adj of or relating to a style of architecture originated by Mudéjares

MUDEYE n larva of the dragonfly, commonly used as a fishing bait

MUDEYES ▶ mudeye

MUDFISH n any of various fishes, such as the bowfin and cichlids, that live at or frequent the muddy bottoms of rivers, lakes, etc

MUDFLAP n flap above wheel to deflect mud

MUDFLAT n tract of low muddy land, esp near an estuary, that is covered at high tide and exposed at low tide

MUDFLOW n flow of soil or fine-grained sediment mixed with water down a steep unstable slope

MUDGE vb speak vaguely

MUDGED ▶ mudge

MUDGER ▶ mudge

MUDGERS ▶ mudge

MUDGES ▶ mudge

MUDGING ▶ mudge

MUDHEN n water bird living in muddy place

MUDHENS ▶ mudhen

MUDHOLE n hole with mud at bottom

MUDHOOK n anchor

MUDIR n local governor

MUDIRIA n province of mudir

MUDIRS ▶ mudir

MUDLARK n street urchin ▷ vb play in mud

MUDPACK n cosmetic paste applied to the face to improve the complexion

MUDRA n any of various ritual hand movements in Hindu religious dancing

MUDRAS ▶ mudra

MUDROCK n type of sedimentary rock

MUDROOM n room where muddy shoes may be left

MUDS ▶ mud
MUDSCOW n boat for travelling over mudflats
MUDSILL n support for building at or below ground
MUDWORT n plant growing in mud
MUEDDIN same as ▶ muezzin
MUESLI n mixture of grain, nuts, and dried fruit, eaten with milk
MUESLIS ▶ muesli
MUEZZIN n official who summons Muslims to prayer
MUFF n tube-shaped covering to keep the hands warm ▷ vb bungle (an action)
MUFFED ▶ muff
MUFFIN n light round flat yeast cake
MUFFING ▶ muff
MUFFINS ▶ muffin
MUFFISH ▶ muff
MUFFLE vb wrap up for warmth or to deaden sound ▷ n something that muffles
MUFFLED ▶ muffle
MUFFLER n scarf
MUFFLES ▶ muffle
MUFFS ▶ muff
MUFLON same as ▷ moufflon
MUFLONS ▶ muflon
MUFTI n civilian clothes worn by a person who usually wears a uniform
MUFTIS ▶ mufti
MUG n large drinking cup ▷ vb attack in order to rob
MUGFUL same as ▶ mug
MUGFULS ▶ mugful
MUGG same as ▶ mug
MUGGA n Australian eucalyptus tree with dark bark and pink flowers
MUGGAR same as ▶ mugger
MUGGARS ▶ muggar
MUGGAS ▶ mugga
MUGGED ▶ mug
MUGGEE n mugged person
MUGGEES ▶ muggee
MUGGER n person who commits robbery with violence, esp in the street
MUGGERS ▶ mugger
MUGGIER ▶ muggy
MUGGILY ▶ muggy
MUGGING ▶ mug
MUGGINS n stupid or gullible person

MUGGISH same as ▶ muggy
MUGGS ▶ mug
MUGGUR same as ▶ mugger
MUGGURS ▶ muggur
MUGGY adj (of weather) damp and stifling
MUGHAL same as ▶ mogul
MUGHALS ▶ mughal
MUGS ▶ mug
MUGSHOT n police photograph of person's face
MUGWORT n N temperate herbaceous plant with aromatic leaves and clusters of small greenish-white flowers
MUGWUMP n neutral or independent person, esp in politics
MUHLIES ▶ muhly
MUHLY n American grass
MUID n former French measure of capacity
MUIDS ▶ muid
MUIL same as ▶ mule
MUILS ▶ muil
MUIR same as ▶ moor
MUIRS ▶ muir
MUIST same as ▶ must
MUISTED ▶ muist
MUISTS ▶ muist
MUJIK same as ▶ muzhik
MUJIKS ▶ mujik
MUKHTAR n lawyer in India
MUKLUK n soft boot, usually of sealskin, worn in the American Arctic
MUKLUKS ▶ mukluk
MUKTUK n thin outer skin of the beluga, used as food
MUKTUKS ▶ muktuk
MULATTA n female mulatto
MULATTO n child of one Black and one White parent ▷ adj of a light brown colour
MULCH n mixture of wet straw, leaves, etc, used to protect the roots of plants ▷ vb cover (land) with mulch
MULCHED ▶ mulch
MULCHES ▶ mulch
MULCT vb cheat or defraud ▷ n fine or penalty
MULCTED ▶ mulct
MULCTS ▶ mulct
MULE n offspring of a horse and a donkey ▷ vb strike coin with different die on each side
MULED ▶ mule
MULES vb surgically remove folds of skin from a sheep

MULESED ▶ mules
MULESES ▶ mules
MULETA n small cape attached to a stick used by the matador during the final stages of a bullfight
MULETAS ▶ muleta
MULEY adj (of cattle) having no horns ▷ n any hornless cow
MULEYS ▶ muley
MULGA n Australian acacia shrub growing in desert regions
MULGAS ▶ mulga
MULING ▶ mule
MULISH adj obstinate
MULL vb think (over) or ponder ▷ n promontory or headland
MULLA same as ▶ mullah
MULLAH n Muslim scholar, teacher, or religious leader
MULLAHS ▶ mullah
MULLAS ▶ mulla
MULLED ▶ mull
MULLEIN n type of European plant
MULLEN same as ▶ mullein
MULLENS ▶ mullen
MULLER n flat heavy implement of stone or iron used to grind material against a slab of stone ▷ vb beat up or defeat thoroughly
MULLERS ▶ muller
MULLET n edible sea fish
MULLETS ▶ mullet
MULLEY same as ▶ muley
MULLEYS ▶ muley
MULLING ▶ mull
MULLION n vertical dividing bar in a window ▷ vb furnish (a window, screen, etc) with mullions
MULLITE n colourless mineral
MULLOCK n waste material from a mine
MULLS ▶ mull
MULMUL n muslin
MULMULL same as ▶ mulmul
MULMULS ▶ mulmul
MULSE n drink containing honey
MULSES ▶ mulse
MULSH same as ▶ mulch
MULSHED ▶ mulsh
MULSHES ▶ mulsh
MULTUM n substance used in brewing
MULTUMS ▶ multum

M

MULTURE n fee formerly paid to a miller for grinding grain ▷ vb take multure

MUM n mother ▷ vb act in a mummer's play

MUMBLE vb speak indistinctly, mutter ▷ n indistinct utterance

MUMBLED ▶ mumble

MUMBLER ▶ mumble

MUMBLES ▶ mumble

MUMBLY ▶ mumble

MUMM same as ▶ mum

MUMMED ▶ mum

MUMMER n actor in a traditional English folk play or mime

MUMMERS ▶ mummer

MUMMERY n performance by mummers

MUMMIA n mummified flesh used as medicine

MUMMIAS ▶ mummia

MUMMIED ▶ mummy

MUMMIES ▶ mummy

MUMMIFY vb preserve the body of (a human or animal) as a mummy

MUMMING ▶ mum

MUMMOCK same as ▶ mammock

MUMMS ▶ mumm

MUMMY n body embalmed and wrapped for burial in ancient Egypt ▷ vb mummify

MUMP vb be silent

MUMPED ▶ mump

MUMPER ▶ mump

MUMPERS ▶ mump

MUMPING ▶ mump

MUMPISH ▶ mumps

MUMPS n infectious disease with swelling in the glands of the neck

MUMS ▶ mum

MUMSIER ▶ mumsy

MUMSY adj out of fashion

MUMU n oven in Papua New Guinea

MUMUS ▶ mumu

MUN same as ▶ maun

MUNCH vb chew noisily and steadily

MUNCHED ▶ munch

MUNCHER ▶ munch

MUNCHES ▶ munch

MUNDANE adj everyday

MUNDIC n iron pyrites

MUNDICS ▶ mundic

MUNDIFY vb cleanse

MUNG vb process (computer data)

MUNGA n army canteen

MUNGAS ▶ munga

MUNGE vb modify a password into an unguessable state

MUNGED ▶ mung

MUNGES ▶ mung

MUNGING ▶ mung

MUNGO n cheap felted fabric made from waste wool

MUNGOES ▶ mungo

MUNGOS ▶ mungo

MUNGS ▶ mung

MUNI n municipal radio broadcast

MUNIFY vb fortify

MUNIS ▶ muni

MUNITE vb strengthen

MUNITED ▶ munite

MUNITES ▶ munite

MUNNION archaic word for ▶ mullion

MUNS ▶ mun

MUNSHI n secretary in India

MUNSHIS ▶ munshi

MUNSTER same as ▶ muenster

MUNTIN n supporting or strengthening bar for a glass window, door, etc

MUNTING same as ▶ muntin

MUNTINS ▶ muntin

MUNTJAC n small Asian deer of the genus typically with a chestnut-brown coat, small antlers, and a barklike cry

MUNTJAK same as ▶ muntjac

MUNTRIE n Australian shrub with green-red edible berries

MUON n positive or negative elementary particle with a mass 207 times that of an electron

MUONIC ▶ muon

MUONIUM n form of hydrogen

MUONS ▶ muon

MUPPET n stupid person

MUPPETS ▶ muppet

MURA n group of people living together in Japanese countryside

MURAENA n moray eel

MURAGE n tax levied for the construction or maintenance of town walls

MURAGES ▶ murage

MURAL n painting on a wall ▷ adj of or relating to a wall

MURALED same as ▶ muralled

MURALS ▶ mural

MURAS ▶ mura

MURDER n unlawful intentional killing of a human being ▷ vb kill in this way

MURDERS ▶ murder

MURE archaic or literary word for ▶ immure

MURED ▶ mure

MUREIN n polymer found in cells

MUREINS ▶ murein

MURENA same as ▶ muraena

MURENAS ▶ murena

MURES ▶ mure

MUREX n type of spiny-shelled marine gastropod formerly used as a source of the dye Tyrian purple

MUREXES ▶ murex

MURGEON vb grimace at

MURIATE obsolete name for a ▶ chloride

MURICES ▶ murex

MURID n animal of mouse family

MURIDS ▶ murid

MURINE n type of animal belonging to the Old World family of rodents that includes rats and mice

MURINES ▶ murine

MURING ▶ mure

MURK n thick darkness ▷ adj dark or gloomy

MURKER ▶ murk

MURKEST ▶ murk

MURKIER ▶ murky

MURKILY ▶ murky

MURKISH ▶ murk

MURKLY ▶ murk

MURKS ▶ murk

MURKY adj dark or gloomy

MURL vb crumble

MURLAIN n type of basket

MURLAN same as ▶ murlain

MURLANS ▶ murlan

MURLED ▶ murl

MURLIER ▶ murl

MURLIN same as ▶ murlain

MURLING ▶ murl

MURLINS ▶ murlin

MURLS ▶ murl

MURLY ▶ murl

MURMUR vb speak or say in a quiet indistinct way ▷ n continuous low indistinct sound

MURMURS ▶ murmur

MURPHY dialect or informal word for ▸ **potato**

MURR n former name for a cold

MURRA same as ▸ **murrhine**

MURRAGH n type of large caddis fly

MURRAIN n cattle plague

MURRAM n type of gravel

MURRAMS ▸ **murram**

MURRAS ▸ **murra**

MURRAY n large Australian freshwater fish

MURRAYS ▸ **murray**

MURRE n type of guillemot

MURREE n native Australian

MURREES ▸ **murree**

MURREN same as ▸ **murrain**

MURRENS ▸ **murren**

MURRES ▸ **murre**

MURREY adj mulberry colour

MURREYS ▸ **murrey**

MURRHA same as ▸ **murra**

MURRHAS ▸ **murrha**

MURRI same as ▸ **murree**

MURRIES ▸ **murry**

MURRIN same as ▸ **murrain**

MURRINE same as > **murrhine**

MURRINS ▸ **murrin**

MURRION same as ▸ **murrain**

MURRIS ▸ **murri**

MURRS ▸ **murr**

MURRY same as ▸ **moray**

MURTHER same as ▸ **murder**

MURTI n image of a deity, which itself is considered divine once consecrated

MURTIS ▸ **murti**

MURVA n type of hemp

MURVAS ▸ **murva**

MUS ▸ **mu**

MUSANG n catlike animal of Malaysia

MUSANGS ▸ **musang**

MUSAR n rabbinic literature concerned with ethics, right conduct, etc

MUSARS ▸ **musar**

MUSCA n small constellation in the S hemisphere lying between the Southern Cross and Chamaeleon

MUSCAE ▸ **musca**

MUSCAT same as > **muscatel**

MUSCATS ▸ **muscat**

MUSCID n type of fly of the family which includes the housefly and tsetse fly

MUSCIDS ▸ **muscid**

MUSCLE n tissue in the body which produces movement by contracting ▸ vb force one's way (in)

MUSCLED ▸ **muscle**

MUSCLES ▸ **muscle**

MUSCLY ▸ **muscle**

MUSCOID adj of family of plants

MUSCONE same as ▸ **muskone**

MUSCOSE adj like moss

MUSCOVY adj as in **muscovy duck** a kind of duck

MUSE vb ponder quietly ▸ n state of abstraction

MUSED ▸ **muse**

MUSEFUL ▸ **muse**

MUSER ▸ **muse**

MUSERS ▸ **muse**

MUSES ▸ **muse**

MUSET same as ▸ **musit**

MUSETS ▸ **muset**

MUSETTE n type of bagpipe with a bellows popular in France during the 17th and 18th centuries

MUSEUM n building where natural, artistic, historical, or scientific objects are exhibited and preserved

MUSEUMS ▸ **museum**

MUSH n soft pulpy mass ▸ interj order to dogs in a sled team to start up or go faster ▸ vb travel by or drive a dogsled

MUSHA interj Irish exclamation of surprise

MUSHED ▸ **mush**

MUSHER ▸ **mush**

MUSHERS ▸ **mush**

MUSHES ▸ **mush**

MUSHIER ▸ **mushy**

MUSHILY ▸ **mushy**

MUSHING ▸ **mush**

MUSHY adj soft and pulpy

MUSIC n art form using a melodious and harmonious combination of notes ▸ vb play music

MUSICAL adj of or like music ▸ n play or film with songs and dancing

MUSICK same as ▸ **music**

MUSICKS ▸ **musick**

MUSICS ▸ **music**

MUSIMON same as > **moufflon**

MUSING ▸ **muse**

MUSINGS ▸ **muse**

MUSIT n gap in fence

MUSITS ▸ **musit**

MUSIVE adj mosaic

MUSJID same as ▸ **masjid**

MUSJIDS ▸ **musjid**

MUSK n scent obtained from a gland of the musk deer or produced synthetically ▸ vb perfume with musk

MUSKED ▸ **musk**

MUSKEG n area of undrained boggy land

MUSKEGS ▸ **muskeg**

MUSKET n long-barrelled gun

MUSKETS ▸ **musket**

MUSKIE n large North American freshwater game fish

MUSKIER ▸ **muskie**

MUSKIES ▸ **muskie**

MUSKILY ▸ **musky**

MUSKING ▸ **musk**

MUSKIT same as > **mesquite**

MUSKITS ▸ **muskit**

MUSKLE same as ▸ **mussel**

MUSKLES ▸ **muskle**

MUSKONE n substance in musk

MUSKOX n large Canadian mammal

MUSKRAT n N American beaver-like rodent

MUSKS ▸ **musk**

MUSKY same as ▸ **muskie**

MUSLIN n fine cotton fabric

MUSLINS ▸ **muslin**

MUSMON same as ▸ **musimon**

MUSMONS ▸ **musmon**

MUSO n musician, esp a pop musician, regarded as being overconcerned with technique rather than musical content or expression

MUSOS ▸ **muso**

MUSPIKE n Canadian freshwater fish

MUSROL n part of bridle

MUSROLS ▸ **musrol**

MUSS vb make untidy ▸ n state of disorder

MUSSE same as ▸ **muss**

MUSSED ▸ **muss**

MUSSEL n edible shellfish with a dark hinged shell

MUSSELS ▸ **mussel**

MUSSES ▸ **muss**

MUSSIER ▸ **mussy**

MUSSILY ▸ **mussy**

M

MUSSING ▶ muss
MUSSY adj untidy or disordered
MUST vb used as an auxiliary to express obligation, certainty, or resolution ▷ n essential or necessary thing
MUSTANG n wild horse of SW USA
MUSTARD n paste made from the powdered seeds of a plant, used as a condiment ▷ adj brownish-yellow
MUSTED ▶ must
MUSTEE n offspring of a White and a quadroon
MUSTEES ▶ mustee
MUSTER vb summon up (strength, energy, or support) ▷ n assembly of military personnel
MUSTERS ▶ muster
MUSTH n state of frenzied sexual excitement in the males of certain large mammals, esp elephants, associated with discharge from a gland between the ear and eye
MUSTHS ▶ musth
MUSTIER ▶ musty
MUSTILY ▶ musty
MUSTING ▶ must
MUSTS ▶ must
MUSTY adj smelling mouldy and stale
MUT another word for ▶ **em**
MUTABLE adj liable to change
MUTABLY ▶ mutable
MUTAGEN n any substance that can induce genetic mutation
MUTANDA > mutandum
MUTANT n mutated animal, plant, etc ▷ adj of or resulting from mutation
MUTANTS ▶ mutant
MUTASE n type of enzyme
MUTASES ▶ mutase
MUTATE vb (cause to) undergo mutation
MUTATED ▶ mutate
MUTATES ▶ mutate
MUTCH n close-fitting linen cap formerly worn by women and children in Scotland ▷ vb cadge
MUTCHED ▶ mutch
MUTCHES ▶ mutch
MUTE adj silent ▷ n person

who is unable to speak ▷ vb reduce the volume or soften the tone of a musical instrument by means of a mute or soft pedal
MUTED adj (of sound or colour) softened
MUTEDLY ▶ muted
MUTELY ▶ mute
MUTER ▶ mute
MUTES ▶ mute
MUTEST ▶ mute
MUTI n medicine, esp herbal medicine
MUTINE vb mutiny
MUTINED ▶ mutine
MUTINES ▶ mutine
MUTING ▶ mute
MUTINY n rebellion against authority, esp by soldiers or sailors ▷ vb commit mutiny
MUTIS ▶ muti
MUTISM n state of being mute
MUTISMS ▶ mutism
MUTON n part of gene
MUTONS ▶ muton
MUTS ▶ mut
MUTT n mongrel dog
MUTTER vb utter or speak indistinctly ▷ n muttered sound or grumble
MUTTERS ▶ mutter
MUTTON n flesh of sheep, used as food
MUTTONS ▶ mutton
MUTTONY ▶ mutton
MUTTS ▶ mutt
MUTUAL adj felt or expressed by each of two people about the other ▷ n mutual company
MUTUALS ▶ mutual
MUTUCA same as ▶ **motuca**
MUTUCAS ▶ mutuca
MUTUEL n system of betting in which those who have bet on the winners of a race share in the total amount wagered less a percentage for the management
MUTUELS ▶ mutuel
MUTULAR ▶ mutule
MUTULE n one of a set of flat blocks below the corona of a Doric cornice
MUTULES ▶ mutule
MUTUUM n contract for loan of goods
MUTUUMS ▶ mutuum
MUUMUU n loose brightly-coloured dress

worn by women in Hawaii
MUUMUUS ▶ muumuu
MUX vb spoil
This word meaning to spoil or botch is very useful not only because it contains an X, but because its verb forms can enable you to clear your rack of unpromising letters.
MUXED ▶ mux
MUXES ▶ mux
MUXING ▶ mux
MUZAKY adj having a bland sound
MUZHIK n Russian peasant, esp under the tsars
MUZHIKS ▶ muzhik
MUZJIK same as ▶ **muzhik**
Meaning a Russian peasant, this is a wonderful high-scoring word, combining Z, J and K, and if you can play the plural using all of your tiles, you'll get a bonus of 50 points.
MUZJIKS ▶ muzjik
MUZZ vb make (something) muzzy
MUZZED ▶ muzz
MUZZES ▶ muzz
MUZZIER ▶ muzzy
MUZZILY ▶ muzzy
MUZZING ▶ muzz
MUZZLE n animal's mouth and nose ▷ vb prevent from being heard or noticed
MUZZLED ▶ muzzle
MUZZLER ▶ muzzle
MUZZLES ▶ muzzle
MUZZY adj confused or muddled
MVULE n tropical African tree
MVULES ▶ mvule
MWAH interj representation of the sound of a kiss
MWALIMU n teacher
MY adj belonging to me ▷ interj exclamation of surprise or awe
MYAL ▶ myalism
MYALGIA n pain in a muscle or a group of muscles
MYALGIC ▶ myalgia
MYALISM n kind of witchcraft, similar to obi, practised esp in the Caribbean
MYALIST ▶ myalism
MYALL n Australian acacia

with hard scented wood

MYALLS ▸ myall

MYASES ▸ myasis

MYASIS same as ▸ **myiasis**

MYC n oncogene that aids the growth of tumorous cells

MYCELE n microscopic spike-like structure in mucus

MYCELES ▸ mycele

MYCELIA > mycelium

MYCELLA n blue-veined Danish cream cheese, less strongly flavoured than Danish blue

MYCETES n fungus

MYCOSES ▸ mycosis

MYCOSIS n any infection or disease caused by fungus

MYCOTIC ▸ mycosis

MYCS ▸ myc

MYELIN n white tissue forming an insulating sheath around certain nerve fibres

MYELINE same as ▸ **myelin**

MYELINS ▸ myelin

MYELOID adj of or relating to the spinal cord or the bone marrow

MYELOMA n tumour of the bone marrow

MYELON n spinal cord

MYELONS ▸ myelon

MYGALE n large American spider

MYGALES ▸ mygale

MYIASES ▸ myiasis

MYIASIS n infestation of the body by the larvae of flies

MYLAR n tradename for a kind of strong polyester film

MYLARS ▸ mylar

MYLODON n prehistoric giant sloth

MYNA same as ▸ **mynah**

MYNAH n tropical Asian starling which can mimic human speech

MYNAHS ▸ mynah

MYNAS ▸ myna

MYNHEER n Dutch title of address

MYOGEN n albumin found in muscle

MYOGENS ▸ myogen

MYOGRAM n tracings of muscular contractions

MYOID adj like muscle

MYOLOGY n branch of medical science concerned with the structure and diseases of muscles

MYOMA n benign tumour composed of muscle tissue

MYOMAS ▸ myoma

MYOMATA ▸ myoma

MYOPE n any person afflicted with myopia

MYOPES ▸ myope

MYOPIA n short-sightedness

MYOPIAS ▸ myopia

MYOPIC n shortsighted person

MYOPICS ▸ myopic

MYOPIES ▸ myopy

MYOPS same as ▸ **myope**

MYOPSES ▸ myops

MYOPY same as ▸ **myopia**

MYOSES ▸ myosis

MYOSIN n chief protein of muscle that interacts with actin to form actomyosin during muscle contraction

MYOSINS ▸ myosin

MYOSIS same as ▸ **miosis**

MYOSOTE same as > **myosotis**

MYOTIC ▸ miosis

MYOTICS ▸ miosis

MYOTOME n any segment of embryonic mesoderm that develops into skeletal muscle in the adult

MYOTUBE n cylindrical cell in muscle

MYRBANE same as ▸ **mirbane**

MYRIAD adj innumerable ▷ n large indefinite number

MYRIADS ▸ myriad

MYRICA n dried root bark of the wax myrtle, used as a tonic and to treat diarrhoea

MYRICAS ▸ myrica

MYRINGA n eardrum

MYRRH n aromatic gum used in perfume, incense, and medicine

MYRRHIC ▸ myrrh

MYRRHOL n oil of myrrh

MYRRHS ▸ myrrh

MYRTLE n flowering evergreen shrub

MYRTLES ▸ myrtle

MYSELF pron reflexive form of I or me

MYSID n small shrimplike crustacean

MYSIDS ▸ mysid

MYSOST n Norwegian cheese

MYSOSTS ▸ mysost

MYSPACE vb search for (someone) on the MySpace website

MYSTERY n strange or inexplicable event or phenomenon

MYSTIC n person who seeks spiritual knowledge ▷ adj mystical

MYSTICS ▸ mystic

MYSTIFY vb bewilder or puzzle

MYTH n tale with supernatural characters, usu of how the world and mankind began

MYTHI ▸ mythus

MYTHIC same as > **mythical**

MYTHIER ▸ mythy

MYTHISE same as ▸ **mythize**

MYTHISM same as > **mythicism**

MYTHIST ▸ mythism

MYTHIZE same as > **mythicize**

MYTHOI ▸ mythos

MYTHOS n complex of beliefs, values, attitudes, etc, characteristic of a specific group or society

MYTHS ▸ myth

MYTHUS same as ▸ **mythos**

MYTHY adj of or like myth

MYXO n infectious and usually fatal viral disease of rabbits characterized by swelling of the mucous membranes and formation of skin tumours

MYXOID adj containing mucus

MYXOMA n tumour composed of mucous connective tissue, usually situated in subcutaneous tissue

MYXOMAS ▸ myxoma

MYXOS ▸ myxo

MZEE n old person ▷ adj advanced in years

MZEES ▸ mzee

MZUNGU n White person

MZUNGUS ▸ mzungu

M

Nn

Along with **R** and **T**, **N** is one of the most common consonants in Scrabble. As you'll often have it on your rack, it's well worth learning what **N** can do in different situations. **N** is useful when you need short words, as it begins two-letter words with every vowel except **I**, and with **Y** as well. There are plenty of three-letter words starting with **N**, but there aren't many high-scoring ones apart from **nix** and **nox** for 10 points each and **nek** for 7 points. Remember words like **nab** (5 points), **nag** (4), **nap** (5), **nay** (6), **new** (6), **nib** (5), **nob** (5), **nod** (4) and **now** (6).

NA same as ▶ **nae**

NAAM same as ▶ **nam**

NAAMS ▶ **naam**

NAAN n slightly leavened flat Indian bread

NAANS ▶ **naan**

NAARTJE same as > **naartjie**

NAB vb arrest (someone)

NABBED ▶ **nab**

NABBER n thief

NABBERS ▶ **nabber**

NABBING ▶ **nab**

NABE n Japanese hotpot

NABES ▶ **nabe**

NABIS n Parisian art movement

NABK n edible berry

NABKS ▶ **nabk**

NABLA another name for ▶ **del**

NABLAS ▶ **nabla**

NABOB same as ▶ **nawab**

NABOBS ▶ **nabob**

NABS ▶ **nab**

NACARAT n red-orange colour

NACELLE n streamlined enclosure on an aircraft, esp one housing an engine

NACH n Indian dance

NACHAS n pleasure

NACHE n rump

NACHES ▶ **nache**

NACHO n snack of a piece of tortilla topped with cheese, peppers, etc

NACHOS ▶ **nacho**

NACKET n light lunch, snack

NACKETS ▶ **nacket**

NACRE n mother of pearl

NACRED ▶ **nacre**

NACRES ▶ **nacre**

NACRITE n mineral

NACROUS ▶ **nacre**

NADA n nothing

NADAS ▶ **nada**

NADIR n point in the sky opposite the zenith

NADIRAL ▶ **nadir**

NADIRS ▶ **nadir**

NADORS n thirst brought on by excessive consumption of alcohol

NAE Scots word for ▶ **no**

NAEBODY Scots variant of ▶ **nobody**

NAEVE n birthmark

NAEVES ▶ **naevus**

NAEVI ▶ **naevus**

NAEVOID ▶ **naevus**

NAEVUS n birthmark or mole

NAFF adj lacking quality or taste ▷ vb go away

NAFFED ▶ **naff**

NAFFER ▶ **naff**

NAFFEST ▶ **naff**

NAFFING ▶ **naff**

NAFFLY ▶ **naff**

NAFFS ▶ **naff**

NAG vb scold or find fault constantly ▷ n person who nags

NAGA n cobra

NAGANA n disease of all domesticated animals of central and southern Africa

NAGANAS ▶ **nagana**

NAGAPIE n bushbaby

NAGARI n set of scripts used as the writing systems for several languages of India

NAGARIS ▶ **nagari**

NAGAS ▶ **naga**

NAGGED ▶ **nag**

NAGGER ▶ **nag**

NAGGERS ▶ **nag**

NAGGIER ▶ **nag**

NAGGING ▶ **nag**

NAGGY ▶ **nag**

NAGMAAL n Communion

NAGOR another name for > **reedbuck**

NAGORS ▶ **nagor**

NAGS ▶ **nag**

NAH same as ▶ **no**

NAHAL n agricultural settlement run by an Israeli military youth organization

NAHALS ▶ **nahal**

NAIAD n nymph living in a lake or river

NAIADES ▶ **naiad**

NAIADS ▶ **naiad**

NAIANT adj swimming

NAIF less common word for ▶ **naive**

NAIFER ▶ **naif**

NAIFEST ▶ **naif**

NAIFLY ▶ **naive**

NAIFS ▶ **naif**

NAIK n chief

NAIKS ▶ **naik**

NAIL n pointed piece of metal with a head, hit with a hammer to join two objects together ▷ vb attach (something) with nails

NAILED ▶ **nail**

NAILER ▶ **nail**

NAILERS ▶ **nail**

NAILERY n nail factory

NAILING ▶ **nail**

NAILS ▶ **nail**

NAILSET n punch for driving the head of a nail below the surrounding surface

NAIN adj own

NAIRA n standard monetary unit of Nigeria, divided into 100 kobo

NAIRAS ▶ naira

NAIRU n Non-Accelerating Inflation Rate of Unemployment

NAIRUS ▶ nairu

NAIVE adj innocent and gullible ▷ n person who is naive, esp in artistic style

NAIVELY ▶ naive

NAIVER ▶ naive

NAIVES ▶ naive

NAIVEST ▶ naive

NAIVETE same as ▶ naivety

NAIVETY n state or quality of being naive

NAIVIST ▶ naive

NAKED adj without clothes

NAKEDER ▶ naked

NAKEDLY ▶ naked

NAKER n one of a pair of small kettledrums used in medieval music

NAKERS ▶ naker

NAKFA n standard currency unit of Eritrea

NAKFAS ▶ nakfa

NALA n ravine

NALAS ▶ nala

NALED n type of insecticide

NALEDS ▶ naled

NALLA n ravine

NALLAH same as ▶ nalla

NALLAHS ▶ nallah

NALLAS ▶ nalla

NAM n distraint

NAMABLE ▶ name

NAMASTE n Indian greeting

NAME n word by which a person or thing is known ▷ vb give a name to

NAMED ▶ name

NAMELY adv that is to say

NAMER ▶ name

NAMERS ▶ name

NAMES ▶ name

NAMETAG n identification badge

NAMING ▶ name

NAMINGS ▶ name

NAMMA adj as in namma hole Australian word for a natural well in rock

NAMS ▶ nam

NAMU n black New Zealand sandfly

NAMUS ▶ namu

NAN n grandmother

NANA same as ▶ nan

NANAS ▶ nana

NANDIN n type of shrub

NANDINA n type of shrub

NANDINE n African palm civet

NANDINS ▶ nandin

NANDOO ▶ nandu

NANDOOS ▶ nandoo

NANDU n type of ostrich

NANDUS ▶ nandu

NANE Scots word for ▶ none

NANG adj excellent; cool

NANISM n dwarfism

NANISMS ▶ nanism

NANITE n microscopically small machine or robot

NANITES ▶ nanite

NANKEEN n hard-wearing buff-coloured cotton fabric

NANKIN same as ▶ nankeen

NANKINS ▶ nankin

NANNA same as ▶ nan

NANNAS ▶ nanna

NANNIE same as ▶ nanny

NANNIED ▶ nanny

NANNIES ▶ nanny

NANNY n woman whose job is looking after young children ▷ vb be too protective towards

NANOBE n microbe that is smaller than the smallest known bacterium

NANOBES ▶ nanobe

NANOBOT n microscopically small robot

NANODOT n microscopic cluster of several hundred nickel atoms used to store large amounts of data in a computer chip

NANOOK n polar bear

NANOOKS ▶ nanook

NANS ▶ nan

NANUA same as ▶ moki

NANUAS ▶ nanua

NAOI ▶ naos

> The plural of **naos**, the inner cell of a temple. A very useful word for ridding your rack of unwanted vowels.

NAOS n ancient classical temple

NAOSES ▶ naos

NAP n short sleep ▷ vb have a short sleep

NAPA n type of leather

NAPALM n highly inflammable jellied petrol, used in bombs ▷ vb attack (people or places) with napalm

NAPALMS ▶ napalm

NAPAS ▶ napa

NAPE n back of the neck ▷ vb attack with napalm

NAPED ▶ nape

NAPERY n household linen, esp table linen

NAPES ▶ nape

NAPHTHA n liquid mixture distilled from coal tar or petroleum, used as a solvent and in petrol

NAPHTOL same as > naphthol

NAPING ▶ nape

NAPKIN same as ▶ nappy

NAPKINS ▶ napkin

NAPLESS adj threadbare

NAPOO vb kill

NAPOOED ▶ napoo

NAPOOS ▶ napoo

NAPPA n soft leather, used in gloves and clothes, made from sheepskin, lambskin, or kid

NAPPAS ▶ nappa

NAPPE n large sheet or mass of rock that has been thrust from its original position by earth movements

NAPPED ▶ nappe

NAPPER n person or thing that raises the nap on cloth

NAPPERS ▶ napper

NAPPES ▶ nappe

NAPPIE same as ▶ nappy

NAPPIER ▶ nappy

NAPPIES ▶ nappy

NAPPING ▶ nap

NAPPY n piece of absorbent material fastened round a baby's lower torso to absorb urine and faeces ▷ adj having a nap

NAPRON same as ▶ apron

NAPRONS ▶ napron

NAPS ▶ nap

NARAS same as ▶ narras

NARASES ▶ naras

NARC n narcotics agent

NARCEEN same as > narceine

NARCEIN same as > narceine

NARCISM n exceptional admiration for oneself

NARCIST n narcissist

NARCO n officer working in the area of anti-drug operations

NARCOMA n coma caused by intake of narcotic drugs

NARCOS *n* drug smugglers

NARCOSE *same as* > **narcosis**

NARCS ▸ **narc**

NARD *n* any of several plants whose aromatic roots were formerly used in medicine ▷ *vb* anoint with nard oil

NARDED ▸ **nard**

NARDINE ▸ **nard**

NARDING ▸ **nard**

NARDOO *n* any of certain cloverlike ferns which grow in swampy areas

NARDOOS ▸ **nardoo**

NARDS ▸ **nard**

NARE *n* nostril

NARES *pl n* nostrils

NARGILE *same as* > **narghile**

NARGILY *same as* > **narghile**

NARIAL *adj* of or relating to the nares

NARIC ▸ **nare**

NARINE *same as* ▸ **narial**

NARIS ▸ **nares**

NARK *vb* annoy ▷ *n* informer or spy

NARKED ▸ **nark**

NARKIER ▸ **narky**

NARKING ▸ **nark**

NARKS ▸ **nark**

NARKY *adj* irritable or complaining

NARRAS *n* type of shrub

NARRATE *vb* tell (a story)

NARRE *adj* nearer

NARROW *adj* small in breadth in comparison to length ▷ *vb* make or become narrow

NARROWS *pl n* narrow part of a strait, river, or current

NARTHEX *n* portico at the west end of a basilica or church

NARTJIE *same as* > **naartjie**
> This word for a small sweet orange is one to look out for when you have the J with the good letters of 'retain'. And it has alternative spellings **naartje** and **naartjie**.

NARWAL *same as* ▸ **narwhal**

NARWALS ▸ **narwal**

NARWHAL *n* arctic whale with a long spiral tusk

NARY *adv* not

NAS *vb* has not

NASAL *adj* of the nose ▷ *n* nasal speech sound, such as

English *m*, *n*, or *ng*

NASALLY ▸ **nasal**

NASALS ▸ **nasal**

NASARD *n* organ stop

NASARDS ▸ **nasard**

NASCENT *adj* starting to grow or develop

NASHGAB *n* chatter

NASHI *n* fruit of the Japanese pear

NASHIS ▸ **nashi**

NASIAL ▸ **nasion**

NASION *n* craniometric point where the top of the nose meets the ridge of the forehead

NASIONS ▸ **nasion**

NASTIC *adj* (of movement of plants) independent of the direction of the external stimulus

NASTIER ▸ **nasty**

NASTIES ▸ **nasty**

NASTILY ▸ **nasty**

NASTY *adj* unpleasant ▷ *n* something unpleasant

NASUTE *n* type of termite

NASUTES ▸ **nasute**

NAT *n* supporter of nationalism

NATAL *adj* of or relating to birth

NATANT *adj* (of aquatic plants) floating on the water

NATCH *sentence substitute* naturally ▷ *n* notch

NATCHES ▸ **natch**

NATES *pl n* buttocks

NATHEMO *same as* > **nathemore**

NATION *n* people of one or more cultures or races organized as a single state

NATIONS ▸ **nation**

NATIS ▸ **nates**

NATIVE *adj* relating to a place where a person was born ▷ *n* person born in a specified place

NATIVES ▸ **native**

NATRIUM *obsolete name for* ▸ **sodium**

NATRON *n* whitish or yellow mineral

NATRONS ▸ **natron**

NATS ▸ **nat**

NATTER *vb* talk idly or chatter ▷ *n* long idle chat

NATTERS ▸ **natter**

NATTERY *adj* irritable

NATTIER ▸ **natty**

NATTILY ▸ **natty**

NATTY *adj* smart and spruce

NATURA *n* nature

NATURAE ▸ **natura**

NATURAL *adj* normal or to be expected ▷ *n* person with an inborn talent or skill

NATURE *n* whole system of the existence, forces, and events of the physical world that are not controlled by human beings

NATURED *adj* having a certain disposition

NATURES ▸ **nature**

NAUCH *same as* ▸ **nautch**

NAUCHES ▸ **nauch**

NAUGHT *n* nothing ▷ *adv* not at all

NAUGHTS ▸ **naught**

NAUGHTY *adj* disobedient or mischievous ▷ *n* act of sexual intercourse

NAUNT *n* aunt

NAUNTS ▸ **naunt**

NAUPLII > **nauplius**

NAUSEA *n* feeling of being about to vomit

NAUSEAS ▸ **nausea**

NAUTCH *n* intricate traditional Indian dance performed by professional dancing girls

NAUTIC *same as* > **nautical**

NAUTICS ▸ **nautic**

NAUTILI > **nautilus**

NAVAID *n* navigational aid

NAVAIDS ▸ **navaid**

NAVAL *adj* of or relating to a navy or ships

NAVALLY ▸ **naval**

NAVAR *n* system of air navigation

NAVARCH *n* admiral

NAVARHO *n* aircraft navigation system

NAVARIN *n* stew of mutton or lamb with root vegetables

NAVARS ▸ **navar**

NAVE *n* long central part of a church

NAVEL *n* hollow in the middle of the abdomen where the umbilical cord was attached

NAVELS ▸ **navel**

NAVES ▸ **nave**

NAVETTE *n* gem cut

NAVEW *another name for* ▸ **turnip**

NAVEWS ▸ **navew**

NAVIES ▸ **navy**

NAVVIED ▸ navvy

NAVVIES ▸ navvy

NAVVY n labourer employed on a road or a building site ▷ vb work as a navvy

NAVY n branch of a country's armed services comprising warships with their crews and organization ▷ adj navy-blue

NAW same as ▸ **no**

NAWAB n (formerly) a Muslim ruler or powerful landowner in India

NAWABS ▸ nawab

NAY interj no ▷ n person who votes against a motion ▷ adv used for emphasis ▷ sentence substitute no

NAYS ▸ nay

NAYSAID ▸ naysay

NAYSAY vb say no

NAYSAYS ▸ naysay

NAYWARD n towards denial

NAYWORD n proverb

NAZE n flat marshy headland

NAZES ▸ naze

NAZI n person who thinks or acts in a brutal or dictatorial way

NAZIFY vb make nazi in character

NAZIR n Muslim official

NAZIRS ▸ nazir

NAZIS ▸ nazi

NE conj nor

NEAFE same as ▸ **nieve**

NEAFES ▸ neafe

NEAFFE same as ▸ **nieve**

NEAFFES ▸ neaffe

NEAL same as ▸ **anneal**

NEALED ▸ neal

NEALING ▸ neal

NEALS ▸ neal

NEANIC adj of or relating to the early stages in the life cycle of an organism

NEAP adj of, relating to, or constituting a neap tide ▷ vb be grounded by a neap tide

NEAPED ▸ neap

NEAPING ▸ neap

NEAPS ▸ neap

NEAR adj indicating a place or time not far away ▷ vb draw close (to) ▷ prep at or to a place or time not far away from ▷ adv at or to a place or time not far away

▷ n left side of a horse or vehicle

NEARBY adj not far away ▷ adv close at hand

NEARED ▸ near

NEARER ▸ near

NEAREST ▸ near

NEARING ▸ near

NEARLY adv almost

NEARS ▸ near

NEAT adj tidy and clean ▷ n domestic bovine animal

NEATEN vb make neat

NEATENS ▸ neaten

NEATER ▸ neat

NEATEST ▸ neat

NEATH short for ▸ **beneath**

NEATLY ▸ neat

NEATNIK n very neat and tidy person

NEATS ▸ neat

NEB n beak of a bird or the nose of an animal ▷ vb look around nosily

NEBBED ▸ neb

NEBBICH same as ▸ **nebbish**

NEBBING ▸ neb

NEBBISH n unfortunate simpleton

NEBBUK n type of shrub

NEBBUKS ▸ nebbuk

NEBECK same as ▸ **nebbuk**

NEBECKS ▸ nebeck

NEBEK same as ▸ **nebbuk**

NEBEKS ▸ nebek

NEBEL n Hebrew musical instrument

NEBELS ▸ nebel

NEBISH same as ▸ **nebbish**

NEBRIS n fawn-skin

NEBS ▸ neb

NEBULA n hazy cloud of particles and gases

NEBULAE ▸ nebula

NEBULAR ▸ nebula

NEBULAS ▸ nebula

NEBULE n cloud

NEBULES ▸ nebule

NEBULY adj wavy

NECK n part of the body joining the head to the shoulders ▷ vb kiss and cuddle

NECKED ▸ neck

NECKER ▸ neck

NECKERS ▸ neck

NECKING n activity of kissing and embracing passionately

NECKLET n ornament worn round the neck

NECKS ▸ neck

NECKTIE same as ▸ **tie**

NECROSE vb cause or undergo necrosis

NECTAR n sweet liquid collected from flowers by bees

NECTARS ▸ nectar

NECTARY n any of various glandular structures secreting nectar in a plant

NEDDIER ▸ neddy

NEDDIES ▸ neddy

NEDDISH ▸ neddy

NEDDY n donkey ▷ adj of or relating to neds

NEE prep indicating the maiden name of a married woman ▷ adj indicating the maiden name of a married woman

NEED vb require or be in want of ▷ n condition of lacking something

NEEDED ▸ need

NEEDER ▸ need

NEEDERS ▸ need

NEEDFUL adj necessary or required

NEEDIER ▸ needy

NEEDILY ▸ needy

NEEDING ▸ need

NEEDLE n thin pointed piece of metal with an eye through which thread is passed for sewing ▷ vb goad or provoke

NEEDLED ▸ needle

NEEDLER n needle maker

NEEDLES ▸ needle

NEEDLY ▸ needle

NEEDS adv necessarily ▷ pl n what is required

NEEDY adj poor, in need of financial support

NEELD same as ▸ **needle**

NEELDS ▸ neeld

NEELE same as ▸ **needle**

NEELES ▸ neele

NEEM n type of large Indian tree

NEEMB same as ▸ **neem**

NEEMBS ▸ neemb

NEEMS ▸ neem

NEEP dialect name for ▸ **turnip**

NEEPS ▸ neep

NEESE same as ▸ **neeze**

NEESED ▸ neese

NEESES ▸ neese

NEESING ▸ neese

NEEZE vb sneeze

NEEZED ▸ neeze

NEEZES ▸ neeze

NEEZING ▸ neeze

N

NEF *n* church nave
NEFAST *adj* wicked
NEFS ▸ nef
NEG *n* photographic negative
NEGATE *vb* invalidate
NEGATED ▸ negate
NEGATER ▸ negate
NEGATES ▸ negate
NEGATON *same as* > negatron
NEGATOR ▸ negate
NEGLECT *vb* take no care of ▷ *n* neglecting or being neglected
NEGLIGE *same as* > negligee
NEGRONI *n* type of cocktail
NEGS ▸ neg
NEGUS *n* hot drink of port and lemon juice, usually spiced and sweetened
NEGUSES ▸ negus
NEIF *same as* ▸ nieve
NEIFS ▸ neif
NEIGH *n* loud high-pitched sound made by a horse ▷ *vb* make this sound
NEIGHED ▸ neigh
NEIGHS ▸ neigh
NEINEI *n* type of plant
NEINEIS ▸ neinei
NEIST *Scots variant of* ▸ next
NEITHER *pron* not one nor the other ▷ *adj* not one nor the other (of two)
NEIVE *same as* ▸ nieve
NEIVES ▸ neive
NEK *n* mountain pass
NEKS ▸ nek
NEKTON *n* population of free-swimming animals that inhabits the middle depths of a sea or lake
NEKTONS ▸ nekton
NELIES *same as* ▸ nelis
NELIS *n* type of pear
NELLIE *n* effeminate man
NELLIES ▸ nellie
NELLY *n as in* **not on your nelly** not under any circumstances
NELSON *n* type of wrestling hold
NELSONS ▸ nelson
NELUMBO *n* type of aquatic plant
NEMA *n* filament
NEMAS ▸ nema
NEMATIC *adj* (of a substance) existing in or having a mesomorphic state in which a linear orientation of the

molecules causes anisotropic properties
NEMESES ▸ nemesis
NEMESIA *n* type of southern African plant
NEMESIS *n* retribution or vengeance
NEMN *vb* name
NEMNED ▸ nemn
NEMNING ▸ nemn
NEMNS ▸ nemn
NEMORAL *adj* of a wood
NEMPT *adj* named
NENE *n* rare black-and-grey short-winged Hawaiian goose
NENES ▸ nene
NEOCON *n* supporter of conservative politics
NEOCONS ▸ neocon
NEOGENE *adj* of, denoting, or formed during the Miocene and Pliocene epochs
NEOLITH *n* Neolithic stone implement
NEOLOGY *same as* > neologism
NEON *n* colourless odourless gaseous element used in illuminated signs and lights ▷ *adj* of or illuminated by neon
NEONATE *n* newborn child, esp in the first week of life and up to four weeks old
NEONED *adj* lit with neon
NEONS ▸ neon
NEOSOUL *n* type of popular music combining soul with other genres
NEOTENY *n* persistence of larval or fetal features in the adult form of an animal
NEOTYPE *n* specimen selected to replace a type specimen that has been lost or destroyed
NEP *n* catmint
NEPER *n* unit expressing the ratio of two quantities
NEPERS ▸ neper
NEPETA *same as* ▸ catmint
NEPETAS ▸ nepeta
NEPHEW *n* son of one's sister or brother
NEPHEWS ▸ nephew
NEPHRIC *adj* renal
NEPHRON *n* minute urine-secreting tubule in the kidney
NEPIT *n* a unit of information equal to 1.44 bits

NEPITS ▸ nepit
NEPOTIC > nepotism
NEPS ▸ nep
NERAL *n* isomer of citral
NERALS ▸ neral
NERD *n* boring person obsessed with a particular subject
NERDIC > geekspeak
NERDICS ▸ nerdic
NERDIER ▸ nerd
NERDISH ▸ nerd
NERDS ▸ nerd
NERDY ▸ nerd
NEREID *n* sea nymph in Greek mythology
NEREIDS ▸ nereid
NEREIS *n* type of marine worm
NERINE *n* type of S African plant related to the amaryllis
NERINES ▸ nerine
NERITE *n* type of sea snail
NERITES ▸ nerite
NERITIC *adj* of or formed in the region of shallow seas near a coastline
NERK *n* fool
NERKA *n* type of salmon
NERKAS ▸ nerka
NERKS ▸ nerk
NEROL *n* scented liquid
NEROLI *n* brown oil used in perfumery
NEROLIS ▸ neroli
NEROLS ▸ nerol
NERTS *interj* nuts
NERTZ *same as* ▸ nerts
NERVAL ▸ nerve
NERVATE *adj* (of leaves) with veins
NERVE *n* cordlike bundle of fibres that conducts impulses between the brain and other parts of the body ▷ *vb* give courage to oneself
NERVED ▸ nerve
NERVER ▸ nerve
NERVERS ▸ nerve
NERVES ▸ nerve
NERVIER ▸ nervy
NERVILY ▸ nervy
NERVINE *adj* having a soothing or calming effect upon the nerves ▷ *n* nervine drug or agent
NERVING ▸ nerve
NERVOUS *adj* apprehensive or worried
NERVULE *n* small vein
NERVURE *n* any of the stiff rods that form the

supporting framework of an insect's wing

NERVY adj excitable or nervous

NESH adj sensitive to the cold

NESHER ▸ nesh

NESHEST ▸ nesh

NESS n headland, cape

NESSES ▸ ness

NEST n place or structure in which birds or certain animals lay eggs or give birth to young ▷ vb make or inhabit a nest

NESTED ▸ nest

NESTER ▸ nest

NESTERS ▸ nest

NESTFUL ▸ nest

NESTING ▸ nest

NESTLE vb snuggle

NESTLED ▸ nestle

NESTLER ▸ nestle

NESTLES ▸ nestle

NESTOR n wise old man

NESTORS ▸ nestor

NESTS ▸ nest

NET n fabric of meshes of string, thread, or wire with many openings ▷ vb catch (a fish or animal) in a net ▷ adj left after all deductions

NETBALL n team game in which a ball has to be thrown through a net hanging from a ring at the top of a pole

NETE n lyre string

NETES ▸ nete

NETFUL ▸ net

NETFULS ▸ net

NETHEAD n person who is enthusiastic about or an expert on the internet

NETHER adj lower

NETIZEN n person who regularly uses the internet

NETLESS ▸ net

NETLIKE ▸ net

NETOP n friend

NETOPS ▸ netop

NETROOT n political activist who promotes a cause via the internet

NETS ▸ net

NETSUKE n (in Japan) a carved toggle worn dangling from the waist

NETT same as ▸ **net**

NETTED ▸ net

NETTER n person that makes nets

NETTERS ▸ netter

NETTIE n habitual and enthusiastic user of the internet

NETTIER ▸ net

NETTIES ▸ netty

NETTING ▸ net

NETTLE n plant with stinging hairs on the leaves ▷ vb bother or irritate

NETTLED ▸ nettle

NETTLER ▸ nettle

NETTLES ▸ nettle

NETTLY ▸ nettle

NETTS ▸ nett

NETTY n lavatory, originally an earth closet

NETWORK n system of intersecting lines, roads, etc ▷ vb broadcast (a programme) over a network

NEUK Scots word for ▸ **nook**

NEUKS ▸ neuk

NEUM same as ▸ **neume**

NEUME n one of a series of notational symbols used before the 14th century

NEUMES ▸ neume

NEUMIC ▸ neume

NEUMS ▸ neum

NEURAL adj of a nerve or the nervous system

NEURINE n poisonous alkaloid

NEURISM n nerve force

NEURITE n biological cell component

NEUROID adj nervelike

NEUROMA n any tumour composed of nerve tissue

NEURON same as ▸ **neurone**

NEURONE n cell specialized to conduct nerve impulses

NEURONS ▸ neuron

NEURULA n stage of embryonic development

NEUSTIC ▸ neuston

NEUSTON n organisms, similar to plankton, that float on the surface film of open water

NEUTER adj belonging to a particular class of grammatical inflections in some languages ▷ vb castrate (an animal) ▷ n neuter gender

NEUTERS ▸ neuter

NEUTRAL adj taking neither side in a war or dispute ▷ n neutral person or nation

NEUTRON n electrically neutral elementary particle of about the same mass as a proton

NEVE n mass of porous ice, formed from snow, that has not yet become frozen into glacier ice

NEVEL vb beat with the fists

NEVELS ▸ nevel

NEVER adv at no time ▷ sentence substitute at no time ▷ interj surely not!

NEVES ▸ neve

NEVI ▸ nevus

NEVOID ▸ nevus

NEVUS same as ▸ **naevus**

NEW adj not existing before ▷ adv recently ▷ vb make new

NEWBIE n person new to a job, club, etc

NEWBIES ▸ newbie

NEWBORN adj recently or just born ▷ n newborn baby

NEWCOME ▸ newcomer

NEWED ▸ new

NEWEL n post at the top or bottom of a flight of stairs that supports the handrail

NEWELL n new thing

NEWELLS ▸ newell

NEWELS ▸ newel

NEWER ▸ new

NEWEST ▸ new

NEWIE n fresh idea or thing

NEWIES ▸ newie

NEWING ▸ new

NEWISH adj fairly new

NEWLY adv recently

NEWMOWN adj freshly cut

NEWNESS ▸ new

NEWS n important or interesting new happenings ▷ vb report

NEWSBOY n boy who sells or delivers newspapers

NEWSED ▸ news

NEWSES ▸ news

NEWSIE same as ▸ **newsy**

NEWSIER ▸ newsy

NEWSIES ▸ newsie

NEWSING ▸ news

NEWSMAN n male newsreader or reporter

NEWSMEN ▸ newsman

NEWSY adj full of news ▷ n newsagent

NEWT n small amphibious creature with a long slender body and tail

NEWTON n unit of force

NEWTONS ▸ newton

NEWTS ▶ newt

NEXT adv immediately following ▷ n next person or thing

NEXTLY ▶ next

NEXTS ▶ next

NEXUS n connection or link

NEXUSES ▶ nexus

NGAI n clan or tribe

NGAIO n small New Zealand tree

NGAIOS ▶ ngaio

NGANA same as ▶ nagana

NGANAS ▶ ngana

NGARARA n lizard found in New Zealand

NGATI n (occurring as part of the tribe name) a tribe or clan

NGATIS ▶ ngati

NGOMA n type of drum

NGOMAS ▶ ngoma

NGWEE n Zambian monetary unit worth one hundredth of a kwacha

NHANDU n type of spider

NHANDUS ▶ nhandu

NIACIN n vitamin of the B complex that occurs in milk, liver, and yeast

NIACINS ▶ niacin

NIB n writing point of a pen ▷ vb provide with a nib

NIBBED ▶ nib

NIBBING ▶ nib

NIBBLE vb take little bites (of) ▷ n little bite

NIBBLED ▶ nibble

NIBBLER n person, animal, or thing that nibbles

NIBBLES ▶ nibble

NIBLICK n (formerly) a club, a No. 9 iron, giving a great deal of lift

NIBLIKE ▶ nib

NIBS ▶ nib

NICAD n rechargeable dry-cell battery

NICADS ▶ nicad

NICE adj pleasant

NICEISH ▶ nice

NICELY ▶ nice

NICER ▶ nice

NICEST ▶ nice

NICETY n subtle point

NICHE n hollow area in a wall ▷ adj of or aimed at a specialist group or market ▷ vb place (a statue) in a niche

NICHED ▶ niche

NICHER vb snigger

NICHERS ▶ nicher

NICHES ▶ niche

NICHING ▶ niche

NICHT Scots word for ▶ night

NICHTS ▶ nicht

NICISH ▶ nice

NICK vb make a small cut in ▷ n small cut

NICKAR n hard seed

NICKARS ▶ nickar

NICKED ▶ nick

NICKEL n silvery-white metal often used in alloys ▷ vb plate with nickel

NICKELS ▶ nickel

NICKER n pound sterling ▷ vb (of a horse) to neigh softly

NICKERS ▶ nicker

NICKING ▶ nick

NICKLE same as ▶ nickel

NICKLED ▶ nickle

NICKLES ▶ nickle

NICKS ▶ nick

NICKUM n mischievous person

NICKUMS ▶ nickum

NICOISE adj prepared with tomatoes, black olives, garlic and anchovies

NICOL n device for producing plane-polarized light

NICOLS ▶ nicol

NICOTIN same as > **nicotine**

NICTATE same as > **nictitate**

NID same as ▶ nide

NIDAL ▶ nidus

NIDATE vb undergo nidation

NIDATED ▶ nidate

NIDATES ▶ nidate

NIDDICK n nape of the neck

NIDE vb nest

NIDED ▶ nide

NIDES ▶ nide

NIDGET n fool

NIDGETS ▶ nidget

NIDI ▶ nidus

NIDIFY vb (of a bird) to make or build a nest

NIDING n coward

NIDINGS ▶ niding

NIDOR n cooking smell

NIDORS ▶ nidor

NIDS ▶ nid

NIDUS n nest in which insects or spiders deposit their eggs

NIDUSES ▶ nidus

NIE archaic spelling of ▶ nigh

NIECE n daughter of one's sister or brother

NIECES ▶ niece

NIED ▶ nie

NIEF same as ▶ nieve

NIEFS ▶ nief

NIELLI ▶ niello

NIELLO n black compound of sulphur and silver, lead, or copper ▷ vb decorate or treat with niello

NIELLOS ▶ niello

NIES ▶ nie

NIEVE n closed hand

NIEVES ▶ nieve

NIFE n earth's core, thought to be composed of nickel and iron

NIFES ▶ nife

NIFF n stink ▷ vb stink

NIFFED ▶ niff

NIFFER vb barter

NIFFERS ▶ niffer

NIFFIER ▶ niff

NIFFING ▶ niff

NIFFS ▶ niff

NIFFY ▶ niff

NIFTIER ▶ nifty

NIFTIES ▶ nifty

NIFTILY ▶ nifty

NIFTY adj neat or smart ▷ n nifty thing

NIGELLA n type of plant the Mediterranean and W Asia

NIGGARD n stingy person ▷ adj miserly ▷ vb act in a niggardly way

NIGGLE vb worry slightly ▷ n small worry or doubt

NIGGLED ▶ niggle

NIGGLER ▶ niggle

NIGGLES ▶ niggle

NIGGLY ▶ niggle

NIGH prep near ▷ adv nearly ▷ adj near ▷ vb approach

NIGHED ▶ nigh

NIGHER ▶ nigh

NIGHEST ▶ nigh

NIGHING ▶ nigh

NIGHLY ▶ nigh

NIGHS ▶ nigh

NIGHT n time of darkness between sunset and sunrise ▷ adj of, occurring, or working at night

NIGHTED adj darkened

NIGHTIE same as > **nightgown**

NIGHTLY adv (happening) each night ▷ adj happening each night

NIGHTS adv at night or on most nights

NIGHTY same as ▶ nightie

NIGIRI n small oval block of cold rice, wasabi and fish, sometimes held together by a seaweed band

NIGIRIS ▸ nigiri

NIGRIFY vb blacken

NIHIL n nil

NIHILS ▸ nihil

NIHONGA n Japanese form of painting

NIKAB ▸ niqab

NIKABS ▸ nikab

NIKAH n Islamic marriage contract

NIKAHS ▸ nikah

NIKAU n palm tree native to New Zealand

NIKAUS ▸ nikau

NIL n nothing, zero

NILGAI n large Indian antelope

NILGAIS ▸ nilgai

NILGAU same as ▸ nilghau

NILGAUS ▸ nilgau

NILGHAI same as ▸ nilgai

NILGHAU same as ▸ nilgai

NILL vb be unwilling

NILLED ▸ nill

NILLING ▸ nill

NILLS ▸ nill

NILS ▸ nil

NIM n game in which two players alternately remove one or more small items from one of several rows or piles ▷ vb steal

NIMB n halo

NIMBED ▸ nimb

NIMBI ▸ nimbus

NIMBLE adj agile and quick

NIMBLER ▸ nimble

NIMBLY ▸ nimble

NIMBS ▸ nimb

NIMBUS n dark grey rain cloud

NIMIETY rare word for ▸ excess

NIMIOUS ▸ nimiety

NIMMED ▸ nim

NIMMER ▸ nim

NIMMERS ▸ nim

NIMMING ▸ nim

NIMONIC adj as in **nimonic alloy** type of nickel-based alloy used at high temperature

NIMPS adj easy

NIMROD n hunter

NIMRODS ▸ nimrod

NIMS ▸ nim

NINCOM same as ▸ nicompoop

NINCOMS ▸ nincom

NINCUM same as ▸ nicompoop

NINCUMS ▸ nincum

NINE n one more than eight

NINEPIN n skittle used in ninepins

NINES ▸ nine

NINETY n ten times nine ▷ determiner amounting to ninety

NINJA n person skilled in ninjutsu

NINJAS ▸ ninja

NINNIES ▸ ninny

NINNY n stupid person

NINON n fine strong silky fabric

NINONS ▸ ninon

NINTH n (of) number nine in a series ▷ adj coming after the eighth in counting order, position, time, etc ▷ adv after the eighth person, position, event, etc

NINTHLY same as ▸ ninth

NINTHS ▸ ninth

NIOBATE n type of salt crystal

NIOBIC adj of or containing niobium in the pentavalent state

NIOBITE another name for ▸ columbite

NIOBIUM n white superconductive metallic element

NIOBOUS adj of or containing niobium in the trivalent state

NIP vb hurry ▷ n pinch or light bite

NIPA n palm tree of S and SE Asia

NIPAS ▸ nipa

NIPPED ▸ nip

NIPPER n small child ▷ vb secure with rope

NIPPERS pl n instrument or tool for snipping, pinching, or squeezing

NIPPIER ▸ nippy

NIPPILY ▸ nippy

NIPPING ▸ nip

NIPPLE n projection in the centre of a breast ▷ vb provide with a nipple

NIPPLED ▸ nipple

NIPPLES ▸ nipple

NIPPY adj frosty or chilly

NIPS ▸ nip

NIPTER n type of religious ceremony

NIPTERS ▸ nipter

NIQAB n type of veil worn by some Muslim women

> One of those invaluable words allowing you to play the Q without a U. It can also be spelt **nikab**.

NIQABS ▸ niqab

NIRL vb shrivel

NIRLED ▸ nirl

NIRLIE same as ▸ nirly

NIRLIER ▸ nirly

NIRLING ▸ nirl

NIRLIT ▸ nirl

NIRLS ▸ nirl

NIRLY adj shrivelled

NIRVANA n absolute spiritual enlightenment and bliss

NIS n friendly goblin

NISEI n native-born citizen of the US or Canada whose parents were Japanese immigrants

NISEIS ▸ nisei

NISGUL n smallest and weakest bird in a brood of chickens

NISGULS ▸ nisgul

NISH n nothing

NISHES ▸ nish

NISI adj (of a court order) coming into effect on a specified date

NISSE same as ▸ nis

NISSES ▸ nisse

NISUS n impulse towards or striving after a goal

NIT n egg or larva of a louse

NITE same as ▸ night

NITER same as ▸ nitre

NITERIE n nightclub

NITERS ▸ niter

NITERY ▸ niter

NITES ▸ nite

NITHER vb shiver

NITHERS ▸ nither

NITHING n coward

NITID adj bright

NITINOL n metal alloy

NITON less common name for ▸ radon

NITONS ▸ niton

NITPICK vb criticize unnecessarily

NITRATE n compound of nitric acid, used as a fertilizer ▷ vb treat with nitric acid or a nitrate

NITRE n potassium nitrate

NITRES ▸ nitre

NITRIC adj of or containing nitrogen

NITRID same as ▸ nitride

N

NITRIDE n compound of nitrogen with a more electropositive element ▷ vb make into a nitride

NITRIDS ▶ **nitrid**

NITRIFY vb treat (a substance) or cause (a substance) to react with nitrogen

NITRIL same as ▶ **nitrile**

NITRILE n any one of a particular class of organic compounds

NITRILS ▶ **nitril**

NITRITE n salt or ester of nitrous acid

NITRO n nitroglycerine

NITROS ▶ **nitro**

NITROSO adj of a particular monovalent group

NITROUS adj derived from or containing nitrogen in a low valency state

NITROX n mixture of nitrogen and oxygen used in diving instead of air

NITRY adj nitrous

NITRYL n chemical compound

NITRYLS ▶ **nitryl**

NITS ▶ **nit**

NITTIER ▶ **nitty**

NITTY adj infested with nits

NITWIT n stupid person

NITWITS ▶ **nitwit**

NIVAL adj of or growing in or under snow

NIVEOUS adj resembling snow, esp in colour

NIX sentence substitute be careful! watch out! ▷ n rejection or refusal ▷ vb veto, deny, reject, or forbid (plans, suggestions, etc)

> This is a handy little word, combining X with two of the most common tiles in the game.

NIXE n water sprite

NIXED ▶ **nix**

NIXER n spare-time job

NIXERS ▶ **nixer**

NIXES ▶ **nix**

NIXIE n female water sprite, usually unfriendly to humans

NIXIES ▶ **nixie**

NIXING ▶ **nix**

NIXY same as ▶ **nixie**

NIZAM n (formerly) a Turkish regular soldier

NIZAMS ▶ **nizam**

NKOSI n term of address to a superior

NKOSIS ▶ **nkosi**

NO interj expresses denial, disagreement, or refusal ▷ adj not any, not a ▷ adv not at all ▷ n answer or vote of 'no'

NOAH n shark

NOAHS ▶ **noah**

NOB n person of wealth or social distinction

NOBBIER ▶ **nob**

NOBBILY ▶ **nob**

NOBBLE vb attract the attention of (someone) in order to talk to him or her

NOBBLED ▶ **nobble**

NOBBLER ▶ **nobble**

NOBBLES ▶ **nobble**

NOBBUT adv nothing but

NOBBY ▶ **nob**

NOBLE adj showing or having high moral qualities ▷ n member of the nobility

NOBLER ▶ **noble**

NOBLES ▶ **noble**

NOBLEST ▶ **noble**

NOBLY ▶ **noble**

NOBODY pron no person ▷ n person of no importance

NOBS ▶ **nob**

NOCAKE n Indian meal made from dried corn

NOCAKES ▶ **nocake**

NOCENT n guilty person

NOCENTS ▶ **nocent**

NOCHEL ▶ **notchel**

NOCHELS ▶ **nochel**

NOCK n notch on an arrow or a bow for the bowstring ▷ vb fit (an arrow) on a bowstring

NOCKED ▶ **nock**

NOCKET same as ▶ **nacket**

NOCKETS ▶ **nocket**

NOCKING ▶ **nock**

NOCKS ▶ **nock**

NOCTUA n type of moth

NOCTUAS ▶ **noctua**

NOCTUID n type of nocturnal moth ▷ adj of or relating to this type of moth

NOCTULE n any of several large Old World insectivorous bats

NOCTURN n any of the main sections of the office of matins

NOCUOUS adj harmful

NOD vb lower and raise (one's head) briefly in agreement or greeting ▷ n act of nodding

NODAL adj of or like a node

NODALLY ▶ **nodal**

NODATED adj knotted

NODDED ▶ **nod**

NODDER ▶ **nod**

NODDERS ▶ **nod**

NODDIER ▶ **noddy**

NODDIES ▶ **noddy**

NODDING ▶ **nod**

NODDLE n head ▷ vb nod (the head), as through drowsiness

NODDLED ▶ **noddle**

NODDLES ▶ **noddle**

NODDY n tropical tern with a dark plumage ▷ adj very easy to use or understand

NODE n point on a plant stem from which leaves grow

NODES ▶ **node**

NODI ▶ **nodus**

NODICAL adj of or relating to the nodes of a celestial body, esp of the moon

NODOSE adj having nodes or knotlike swellings

NODOUS same as ▶ **nodose**

NODS ▶ **nod**

NODULAR ▶ **nodule**

NODULE n small knot or lump

NODULED ▶ **nodule**

NODULES ▶ **nodule**

NODUS n problematic idea, situation, etc

NOEL n Christmas

NOELS ▶ **noel**

NOES ▶ **no**

NOESES ▶ **noesis**

NOESIS n exercise of reason, esp in the apprehension of universal forms

NOETIC adj of or relating to the mind, esp to its rational and intellectual faculties

NOG same as ▶ **nogging**

NOGAKU n Japanese style of drama

NOGG same as ▶ **nog**

NOGGED adj built with timber and brick

NOGGIN n head

NOGGING n short horizontal timber member used between the studs of a framed partition

NOGGINS ▶ **noggin**

NOGGS ▶ **nogg**

NOGS ▶ **nog**

NOH *n* stylized classic drama of Japan

NOHOW *adv* under any conditions

NOIL *n* short or knotted fibres that are separated from the long fibres by combing

NOILIER ▶ **noily**

NOILS ▶ **noil**

NOILY ▶ **noil**

NOINT *vb* anoint

NOINTED ▶ **noint**

NOINTER *n* mischievous child

NOINTS ▶ **noint**

NOIR *adj* (of a film) showing characteristics of a *film noir*, in plot or style ▷ *n* film noir

NOIRISH ▶ **noir**

NOIRS ▶ **noir**

NOISE *n* sound, usu a loud or disturbing one

NOISED ▶ **noise**

NOISES ▶ **noise**

NOISIER ▶ **noisy**

NOISILY ▶ **noisy**

NOISING ▶ **noise**

NOISOME *adj* (of smells) offensive

NOISY *adj* making a lot of noise

NOLE *same as* ▶ **noll**

NOLES ▶ **nole**

NOLL *n* head

NOLLS ▶ **noll**

NOLO *vb as in* **nolo contendere** plea indicating that the defendant does not wish to contest the case

NOLOS ▶ **nolo**

NOM *n* name

NOMA *n* gangrenous inflammation of the mouth, esp one affecting malnourished children

NOMAD *n* member of a tribe with no fixed dwelling place, wanderer

NOMADE *same as* ▶ **nomad**

NOMADES ▶ **nomade**

NOMADIC *adj* relating to or characteristic of nomads or their way of life

NOMADS ▶ **nomad**

NOMADY *n* practice of living like nomads

NOMARCH *n* head of an ancient Egyptian nome

NOMAS ▶ **noma**

NOMBLES *variant spelling of*

▶ **numbles**

NOMBRIL *n* point on a shield between the fesse point and the lowest point

NOME *n* any of the former provinces of modern Greece

NOMEN *n* ancient Roman's second name, designating his gens or clan

NOMES ▶ **nome**

NOMIC *adj* normal or habitual

NOMINA ▶ **nomen**

NOMINAL *adj* in name only ▷ *n* nominal element

NOMINEE *n* candidate

NOMISM *n* adherence to a law or laws as a primary exercise of religion

NOMISMS ▶ **nomism**

NOMOI ▶ **nomos**

NOMOS *n* convention

NOMS ▶ **nom**

NON *adv* not

NONA *n* sleeping sickness

NONACID *adj* not acid ▷ *n* nonacid substance

NONAGE *n* state of being under full legal age for various actions

NONAGED ▶ **nonage**

NONAGES ▶ **nonage**

NONAGON *n* geometric figure with nine sides

NONANE *n* type of chemical compound

NONANES ▶ **nonane**

NONART *n* something that does not constitute art

NONARTS ▶ **nonart**

NONARY *adj* based on the number nine

NONAS ▶ **nones**

NONBANK *n* business or institution that is not a bank but provides similar services

NONBODY *n* nonphysical nature of a person

NONBOOK *n* book with little substance

NONCASH *adj* other than cash

NONCE *n* present time or occasion

NONCES ▶ **nonce**

NONCOLA *n* soft drink other than cola

NONCOM *n* person not involved in combat

NONCOMS ▶ **noncom**

NONCORE *adj* not central or essential

NONDRIP *adj* (of paint) specially formulated to minimize dripping during application

NONDRUG *adj* not involving the use of drugs

NONE *pron* not any

NONEGO *n* everything that is outside one's conscious self, such as one's environment

NONEGOS ▶ **nonego**

NONES *n* (in the Roman calendar) the ninth day before the ides of each month

NONET *n* piece of music composed for a group of nine instruments

NONETS ▶ **nonet**

NONETTE *same as* ▶ **nonet**

NONETTI *same as* ▶ **nonet**

NONETTO *same as* ▶ **nonet**

NONFACT *n* event or thing not provable

NONFAN *n* person who is not a fan

NONFANS ▶ **nonfan**

NONFARM *adj* not connected with a farm

NONFAT *adj* fat free

NONFOOD *n* item that is not food

NONFUEL *adj* not relating to fuel

NONG *n* stupid or incompetent person

NONGAME *adj* not pursued for competitive sport purposes

NONGAY *n* person who is not gay

NONGAYS ▶ **nongay**

NONGS ▶ **nong**

NONHEME *adj* of dietary iron, obtained from vegetable foods

NONHERO *n* person who is not a hero

NONHOME *adj* not of the home

NONI *n* type of tree of SE Asia and the Pacific islands whose fruit provides a possibly health-promoting juice

NONIRON *adj* not requiring ironing

NONIS ▶ **noni**

NONJURY *n* trial without a jury

NONLIFE *n* matter which is not living

NONMAN *n* being that is not a man

NONMEAT *n* not containing meat

NONMEN ▷ **nonman**

NONNEWS *adj* not concerned with news

NONNIES ▷ **nonny**

NONNY *n* meaningless word

NONOILY *adj* not oily

NONORAL *adj* not oral

NONPAID *adj* without payment

NONPAR *adj* nonparticipating

NONPAST *n* grammatical term

NONPEAK *n* period of low demand

NONPLAY *n* social behaviour that is not classed as play

NONPLUS *vb* put at a loss ▷ *n* state of utter perplexity prohibiting action or speech

NONPOOR *adj* not poor

NONPROS *vb* enter a judgment of non prosequitur against a plaintiff

NONSELF *n* foreign molecule in the body

NONSKED *n* non-scheduled aeroplane

NONSKID *adj* designed to reduce skidding

NONSLIP *adj* designed to prevent slipping

NONSTOP *adv* without a stop ▷ *adj* without a stop ▷ *n* nonstop flight

NONSUCH *same as* > **nonesuch**

NONSUIT *n* order of a judge dismissing a suit when the plaintiff fails to show a good cause of action or to produce any evidence ▷ *vb* order the dismissal of the suit of (a person)

NONTAX *n* tax that has little real effect

NONUPLE *adj* ninefold ▷ *n* ninefold number

NONUSE *n* failure to use

NONUSER ▷ **nonuse**

NONUSES ▷ **nonuse**

NONWAGE *adj* not part of wages

NONWAR *n* state of nonviolence

NONWARS ▷ **nonwar**

NONWOOL *adj* not wool

NONWORD *n* series of letters not recognised as a word

NONWORK *adj* not involving work

NONYL *n* type of chemical

NONYLS ▷ **nonyl**

NONZERO *adj* not equal to zero

NOO *n* type of Japanese musical drama

NOOB ▷ **newbie**

NOOBS ▷ **noob**

NOODGE *vb* annoy persistently

NOODGED ▷ **noodge**

NOODGES ▷ **noodge**

NOODLE *n* simpleton ▷ *vb* improvise aimlessly on a musical instrument

NOODLED ▷ **noodle**

NOODLES ▷ **noodle**

NOOGIE *n* act of inflicting pain by rubbing someone's head hard

NOOGIES ▷ **noogie**

NOOIT *interj* South African exclamation of pleased or shocked surprise

NOOK *n* corner or recess

NOOKS ▷ **nook**

NOOLOGY *n* study of intuition

NOON *n* twelve o'clock midday ▷ *vb* take a rest at noon

NOONDAY *adj* happening at noon ▷ *n* middle of the day

NOONED ▷ **noon**

NOONER *n* sexual encounter during a lunch hour

NOONERS ▷ **nooner**

NOONING *n* midday break for rest or food

NOONS ▷ **noon**

NOOP *n* point of the elbow

NOOPS ▷ **noop**

NOOSE *n* loop in the end of a rope, tied with a slipknot

NOOSED ▷ **noose**

NOOSER *n* person who uses a noose

NOOSERS ▷ **nooser**

NOOSES ▷ **noose**

NOOSING ▷ **noose**

NOPAL *n* type of cactus

NOPALES ▷ **nopal**

NOPALS ▷ **nopal**

NOPE *interj* no

NOPLACE *same as* ▷ **nowhere**

NOR *prep* and not

NORDIC *adj* of competitions in cross-country racing and ski-jumping

NORI *n* edible seaweed often used in Japanese cookery, esp for wrapping sushi or rice balls

NORIA *n* water wheel with buckets attached to its rim for raising water from a stream into irrigation canals

NORIAS ▷ **noria**

NORIMON *n* Japanese passenger vehicle

NORIS ▷ **nori**

NORITE *n* variety of gabbro composed mainly of hypersthene and labradorite feldspar

NORITES ▷ **norite**

NORITIC ▷ **norite**

NORK *n* female breast

NORKS ▷ **nork**

NORLAND *n* north part of a country or the earth

NORM *n* standard that is regarded as normal

NORMA *n* norm or standard

NORMAL *adj* usual, regular, or typical ▷ *n* usual or regular state, degree or form

NORMALS ▷ **normal**

NORMAN *n* post used for winding on a ship

NORMANS ▷ **norman**

NORMAS ▷ **norma**

NORMED *n* mathematical term

NORMS ▷ **norm**

NORSEL *vb* fit with short lines for fastening hooks

NORSELS ▷ **norsel**

NORTENA *same as* ▷ **norteno**

NORTENO *n* type of Mexican music

NORTH *n* direction towards the North Pole, opposite south ▷ *adj* in or in the north ▷ *adv* in, to, or towards the north ▷ *vb* move north

NORTHED ▷ **north**

NORTHER *n* wind or storm from the north ▷ *vb* move north

NORTHS ▷ **north**

NORWARD *same as* > **northward**

NOS ▶ no

NOSE *n* organ of smell, used also in breathing ▷ *vb* move forward slowly and carefully

NOSEAN *n* type of mineral

NOSEANS ▶ nosean

NOSEBAG *n* bag containing feed fastened round a horse's head

NOSED ▶ nose

NOSEGAY *n* small bunch of flowers

NOSER *n* strong headwind

NOSERS ▶ noser

NOSES ▶ nose

NOSEY *adj* prying or inquisitive ▷ *n* nosey person

NOSEYS ▶ nosey

NOSH *n* food ▷ *vb* eat

NOSHED ▶ nosh

NOSHER ▶ nosh

NOSHERS ▶ nosh

NOSHERY *n* restaurant or other place where food is served

NOSHES ▶ nosh

NOSHING ▶ nosh

NOSIER ▶ nosy

NOSIES ▶ nosy

NOSIEST ▶ nosy

NOSILY ▶ nosy

NOSING *n* edge of a step or stair tread that projects beyond the riser

NOSINGS ▶ nosing

NOSODE *n* homeopathic remedy

NOSODES ▶ nosode

NOSTOC *n* type of bacterium occurring in moist places

NOSTOCS ▶ nostoc

NOSTOI ▶ nostos

NOSTOS *n* story of a return home

NOSTRIL *n* one of the two openings at the end of the nose

NOSTRO *adj as in* **nostro account** bank account conducted by a British bank with a foreign bank

NOSTRUM *n* quack medicine

NOSY *adj* prying or inquisitive

NOT *adv* expressing negation, refusal, or denial

NOTA ▶ notum

NOTABLE *adj* worthy of being noted, remarkable ▷ *n* person of distinction

NOTABLY *adv* particularly or especially

NOTAEUM *n* back of a bird's body

NOTAIRE *n* (in France) notary

NOTAL ▶ notum

NOTANDA > notandum

NOTARY *n* person authorized to witness the signing of legal documents

NOTATE *vb* write (esp music) in notation

NOTATED ▶ notate

NOTATES ▶ notate

NOTCH *n* V-shaped cut ▷ *vb* make a notch in

NOTCHED ▶ notch

NOTCHEL *vb* refuse to pay another person's debts

NOTCHER *n* person who cuts notches

NOTCHES ▶ notch

NOTCHY *adj* (of a motor vehicle gear mechanism) requiring careful gear-changing

NOTE *n* short letter ▷ *vb* notice, pay attention to

NOTED *adj* well-known

NOTEDLY ▶ noted

NOTELET *n* small folded card with a design on the front, used for writing informal letters

NOTEPAD *n* number of sheets of paper fastened together along one edge

NOTER *n* person who takes notes

NOTERS ▶ noter

NOTES *pl n* short descriptive or summarized jottings taken down for future reference

NOTHER *same as* ▶ **other**

NOTHING *pron* not anything ▷ *adv* not at all ▷ *n* person or thing of no importance

NOTICE *n* observation or attention ▷ *vb* observe, become aware of

NOTICED ▶ notice

NOTICER *n* person who takes notice

NOTICES ▶ notice

NOTIFY *vb* inform

NOTING ▶ note

NOTION *n* idea or opinion

NOTIONS *pl n* pins, cotton, ribbon, and similar wares used for sewing

NOTITIA *n* register or list, esp of ecclesiastical districts

NOTOUR *adj* notorious

NOTT *same as* ▶ **not**

NOTUM *n* cuticular plate covering the dorsal surface of a thoracic segment of an insect

NOUGAT *n* chewy sweet containing nuts and fruit

NOUGATS ▶ nougat

NOUGHT *n* figure o

NOUGHTS ▶ nought

NOUL *same as* ▶ **noll**

NOULD *vb* would not

NOULDE *same as* ▶ **nould**

NOULE *same as* ▶ **noll**

NOULES ▶ noule

NOULS ▶ noul

NOUMENA > noumenon

NOUN *n* word that refers to a person, place, or thing

NOUNAL ▶ noun

NOUNIER ▶ nouny

NOUNS ▶ noun

NOUNY *adj* nounlike

NOUP *n* steep headland

NOUPS ▶ noup

NOURICE *n* nurse

NOURISH *vb* feed

NOURSLE *vb* nurse

NOUS *n* common sense

NOUSELL *vb* foster

NOUSES ▶ nous

NOUSLE *vb* nuzzle

NOUSLED ▶ nousle

NOUSLES ▶ nousle

NOUT *same as* ▶ **nought**

NOUVEAU *adj* having recently become the thing specified

NOVA *n* star that suddenly becomes brighter and then gradually decreases to its original brightness

NOVAE ▶ nova

NOVALIA *n* newly reclaimed land

NOVAS ▶ nova

NOVATE *vb* substitute one thing (esp a legal contract) in place of another

NOVATED *adj as in* **novated lease** Australian system of employer-aided car purchase

NOVATES ▶ novate

NOVEL *n* long fictitious story in book form ▷ *adj* fresh, new, or original

NOVELLA *n* short novel

NOVELLE ▶ novella

NOVELLY ▶ novel

N

NOVELS ▶ novel
NOVELTY n newness
NOVENA n set of prayers or services on nine consecutive days
NOVENAE ▶ novena
NOVENAS ▶ novena
NOVICE n beginner
NOVICES ▶ novice
NOVITY n novelty
NOVUM n game played with dice
NOVUMS ▶ novum
NOW adv at or for the present time
NOWAY adv in no manner ▷ sentence substitute used to make an emphatic refusal, denial etc
NOWAYS same as ▶ noway
NOWED adj knotted
NOWHERE adv not anywhere ▷ n nonexistent or insignicant place
NOWISE another word for ▶ noway
NOWL n crown of the head
NOWLS ▶ nowl
NOWN same as ▶ own
NOWNESS ▶ nown
NOWS ▶ now
NOWT n nothing
NOWTIER ▶ nowty
NOWTS ▶ nowt
NOWTY adj bad-tempered
NOWY adj having a small projection at the centre (of a cross)
NOX n nitrogen oxide

Meaning nitrogen oxide, this is another of those very useful short words containing X.

NOXAL adj relating to damage done by something belonging to another
NOXES ▶ nox
NOXIOUS adj poisonous or harmful
NOY vb harrass
NOYADE n execution by drowning
NOYADES ▶ noyade
NOYANCE n nuisance
NOYAU n liqueur made from brandy flavoured with nut kernels
NOYAUS ▶ noyau
NOYED ▶ noy
NOYES archaic form of ▶ noise
NOYESES ▶ noyes
NOYING ▶ noy

NOYOUS ▶ noy
NOYS ▶ noy
NOYSOME ▶ noy
NOZZER n new recruit (in the Navy)
NOZZERS ▶ nozzer
NOZZLE n projecting spout through which fluid is discharged
NOZZLES ▶ nozzle
NTH adj of an unspecified number

A good word to remember for awkward situations on the board, as it's one of very few three-letter words that doesn't contain a vowel.

NU n 13th letter in the Greek alphabet
NUANCE n subtle difference in colour, meaning, or tone ▷ vb give subtle differences to
NUANCED ▶ nuance
NUANCES ▶ nuance
NUB n point or gist (of a story etc) ▷ vb hang from the gallows
NUBBED ▶ nub
NUBBIER ▶ nubby
NUBBIN n something small or undeveloped, esp a fruit or ear of corn
NUBBING ▶ nub
NUBBINS ▶ nubbin
NUBBLE n small lump
NUBBLED ▶ nubble
NUBBLES ▶ nubble
NUBBLY ▶ nubble
NUBBY adj having small lumps or protuberances
NUBIA n fleecy scarf for the head, worn by women
NUBIAS ▶ nubia
NUBILE adj sexually attractive
NUBS ▶ nub
NUBUCK n type of leather with a velvety finish
NUBUCKS ▶ nubuck
NUCELLI > nucellus
NUCHA n back or nape of the neck
NUCHAE ▶ nucha
NUCHAL n scale on a reptile's neck
NUCHALS ▶ nuchal
NUCLEAL ▶ nucleus
NUCLEAR adj of nuclear weapons or energy
NUCLEI ▶ nucleus
NUCLEIC adj as in nucleic

acid type of complex compound that is a vital constituent of living cells
NUCLEIN n any of a group of proteins that occur in the nuclei of living cells
NUCLEON n proton or neutron
NUCLEUS n centre, esp of an atom or cell
NUCLIDE n species of atom characterized by its atomic number and its mass number
NUCULE n small seed
NUCULES ▶ nucule
NUDDIES ▶ nuddy
NUDDY n as in in the nuddy in the nude
NUDE adj naked ▷ n naked figure in painting, sculpture, or photography
NUDELY ▶ nude
NUDER ▶ nude
NUDES ▶ nude
NUDEST ▶ nude
NUDGE vb push gently, esp with the elbow ▷ n gentle push or touch
NUDGED ▶ nudge
NUDGER ▶ nudge
NUDGERS ▶ nudge
NUDGES ▶ nudge
NUDGING ▶ nudge
NUDIE n film, show, or magazine depicting nudity
NUDIES ▶ nudie
NUDISM n practice of not wearing clothes
NUDISMS ▶ nudism
NUDIST ▶ nudism
NUDISTS ▶ nudism
NUDITY n state or fact of being nude
NUDNICK same as ▶ nudnik
NUDNIK n boring person
NUDNIKS ▶ nudnik
NUDZH same as ▶ nudge
NUDZHED ▶ nudzh
NUDZHES ▶ nudzh
NUFF slang form of ▶ enough
NUFFIN slang form of ▶ nothing
NUFFINS ▶ nuffin
NUFFS ▶ nuff
NUGAE n jests
NUGGAR n sailing boat used to carry cargo on the Nile
NUGGARS ▶ nuggar
NUGGET n small lump of gold in its natural state ▷ vb

polish footwear
NUGGETS ▸ nugget
NUGGETY adj of or resembling a nugget
NUKE vb attack with nuclear weapons ▷ n nuclear weapon
NUKED ▸ nuke
NUKES ▸ nuke
NUKING ▸ nuke
NULL adj without legal force ▷ vb make negative
NULLA same as ▸ nullah
NULLAH n stream or drain
NULLAHS ▸ nullah
NULLAS ▸ nulla
NULLED ▸ null
NULLIFY vb make ineffective
NULLING n knurling
NULLITY n state of being null
NULLS ▸ null
NUMB adj without feeling, as through cold, shock, or fear ▷ vb make numb
NUMBAT n small Australian marsupial with a long snout and tongue
NUMBATS ▸ numbat
NUMBED ▸ numb
NUMBER n sum or quantity ▷ vb count
NUMBERS ▸ number
NUMBEST ▸ numb
NUMBING ▸ numb
NUMBLES pl n heart, lungs, liver, etc, of a deer or other animal, cooked for food
NUMBLY ▸ numb
NUMBS ▸ numb
NUMDAH n coarse felt made esp in India
NUMDAHS ▸ numdah
NUMEN n (esp in ancient Roman religion) a deity or spirit presiding over a thing or place
NUMERAL n word or symbol used to express a sum or quantity ▷ adj of, consisting of, or denoting a number
NUMERIC n number or numeral
NUMINA plural of ▸ numen
NUMMARY adj of or relating to coins
NUMNAH same as ▸ numdah
NUMNAHS ▸ numnah
NUMPTY n stupid person
NUN n female member of a religious order

NUNATAK n isolated mountain peak projecting through the surface of surrounding glacial ice
NUNCIO n pope's ambassador
NUNCIOS ▸ nuncio
NUNCLE archaic or dialect word for ▸ uncle
NUNCLES ▸ nuncle
NUNDINE n market day
NUNHOOD n condition, practice, or character of a nun
NUNLIKE ▸ nun
NUNNERY n convent
NUNNISH ▸ nun
NUNNY n as in nunny bag small sealskin haversack used in Canada
NUNS ▸ nun
NUNSHIP ▸ nun
NUPTIAL adj relating to marriage
NUR n wooden ball
NURAGHE n Sardinian round tower
NURAGHI ▸ nuraghe
NURD same as ▸ nerd
NURDIER ▸ nerd
NURDISH ▸ nerd
NURDLE vb score runs in cricket by deflecting the ball rather than striking it hard
NURDLED ▸ nurdle
NURDLES ▸ nurdle
NURDS ▸ nurd
NURDY ▸ nurd
NURHAG n Sardinian round tower
NURHAGS ▸ nurhag
NURL same as ▸ knurl
NURLED ▸ nurl
NURLING ▸ nurl
NURLS ▸ nurl
NURR n wooden ball
NURRS ▸ nurr
NURS ▸ nur
NURSE n person employed to look after sick people, usu in a hospital ▷ vb look after (a sick person)
NURSED ▸ nurse
NURSER n person who treats something carefully
NURSERS ▸ nurser
NURSERY n room where children sleep or play
NURSES ▸ nurse
NURSING n practice or profession of caring for the

sick and injured
NURSLE vb nuzzle
NURSLED ▸ nursle
NURSLES ▸ nursle
NURTURE n act or process of promoting the development of a child or young plant ▷ vb promote or encourage the development of
NUS ▸ nu
NUT n fruit consisting of a hard shell and a kernel ▷ vb to gather nuts
NUTANT adj having the apex hanging down
NUTATE vb nod
NUTATED ▸ nutate
NUTATES ▸ nutate
NUTGALL n nut-shaped gall caused by gall wasps on the oak and other trees
NUTJOB n crazy person
NUTJOBS ▸ nutjob
NUTLET n any of the one-seeded portions of a fruit that fragments when mature
NUTLETS ▸ nutlet
NUTLIKE ▸ nut
NUTMEAL n type of grain
NUTMEAT n kernel of a nut
NUTMEG n spice made from the seed of a tropical tree ▷ vb kick or hit the ball between the legs of (an opposing player)
NUTMEGS ▸ nutmeg
NUTPICK n tool used to dig the meat from nuts
NUTRIA n fur of the coypu
NUTRIAS ▸ nutria
NUTS ▸ nut
NUTTED ▸ nut
NUTTERY n place where nut trees grow
NUTTIER ▸ nutty
NUTTILY ▸ nutty
NUTTING n act of gathering nuts
NUTTY adj containing or resembling nuts
NUTWOOD n any of various nut-bearing trees, such as walnut
NUZZER n present given to a superior in India
NUZZERS ▸ nuzzer
NUZZLE vb push or rub gently with the nose or snout
NUZZLED ▸ nuzzle
NUZZLER n person or thing

N

that nuzzles
NUZZLES ▸ nuzzle
NY *same as* ▸ **nigh**
NYAFF *n* small or
contemptible person ▷ *vb*
yelp like a small dog
NYAFFED ▸ nyaff
NYAFFS ▸ nyaff
NYALA *n* spiral-horned
southern African antelope
NYALAS ▸ nyala
NYANZA *n* (in E Africa) a
lake
NYANZAS ▸ nyanza
NYAS *n* young hawk
NYASES ▸ nyas

NYBBLE *n* small byte
NYBBLES ▸ nybble
NYE *n* flock of pheasants
▷ *vb* near
NYED ▸ nye
NYES ▸ nye
NYING ▸ nye
NYLGHAI *same as* ▸ **nilgai**
NYLGHAU *same as* ▸ **nilgai**
NYLON *n* synthetic material
used for clothing etc
NYLONS *pl n* stockings
made of nylon
NYMPH *n* mythical spirit of
nature, represented as a
beautiful young woman

NYMPHA *n* either one of the
labia minora
NYMPHAE ▸ nympha
NYMPHAL ▸ nymph
NYMPHET *n* sexually
precocious young girl
NYMPHIC ▸ nymph
NYMPHLY ▸ nymph
NYMPHO *n* nymphomaniac
NYMPHOS ▸ nympho
NYMPHS ▸ nymph
NYS ▸ ny
NYSSA *n* type of tree
NYSSAS ▸ nyssa

N

Oo

With eight **O**s in the bag, you're likely to have at least one on your rack during a game. There are plenty of good two-letter words starting with **O**. It's worth knowing that **O** will form a two-letter word in front of every other vowel except **A**, as well as in front of **Y**. **O** also combines well with **X**, with **ox** (9 points) as the obvious starting point, and several words that refer to **oxygen** (17), including **oxo** (10) and **oxy** (13). Don't forget the short everyday words that begin with **O**. While **on** and **or** (2 each) won't earn you many points, they can be very helpful when you are trying to score in more than one direction at a time. **Of** and **oh** (5 each) can also prove very useful.

OAF *n* stupid or clumsy person
OAFISH ▶ **oaf**
OAFS ▶ **oaf**
OAK *n* deciduous forest tree
OAKED *adj* relating to wine that is stored for a time in oak barrels prior to bottling
OAKEN *adj* made of the wood of the oak
OAKER *same as* ▶ **ochre**
OAKERS ▶ **oaker**
OAKIER ▶ **oaky**
OAKIES ▶ **oaky**
OAKIEST ▶ **oaky**
OAKLIKE ▶ **oak**
OAKLING *n* young oak
OAKMOSS *n* type of lichen
OAKS ▶ **oak**
OAKUM *n* fibre obtained by unravelling old rope
OAKUMS ▶ **oakum**
OAKY *adj* hard like the wood of an oak ▷ *n* ice cream
OAR *n* pole with a broad blade, used for rowing a boat ▷ *vb* propel with oars
OARAGE *n* use or number of oars
OARAGES ▶ **oarage**
OARED *adj* equipped with oars
OARFISH *n* very long ribbonfish with long slender ventral fins
OARIER ▶ **oary**
OARIEST ▶ **oary**
OARING ▶ **oar**
OARLESS ▶ **oar**
OARLIKE ▶ **oar**
OARLOCK *n* swivelling device attached to the gunwale of a boat that holds an oar in place
OARS ▶ **oar**
OARSMAN *n* person who rows
OARSMEN ▶ **oarsman**
OARWEED *n* type of brown seaweed
OARY *adj* of or like an oar
OASES ▶ **oasis**
OASIS *n* fertile area in a desert
OAST *n* oven for drying hops
OASTS ▶ **oast**
OAT *n* hard cereal grown as food
OATCAKE *n* thin flat biscuit of oatmeal
OATEN *adj* made of oats or oat straw
OATER *n* film about the American Wild West
OATERS ▶ **oater**
OATH *n* solemn promise, esp to be truthful in court
OATHS ▶ **oath**
OATIER ▶ **oaty**
OATIEST ▶ **oaty**
OATLIKE ▶ **oat**
OATMEAL *n* coarse flour made from oats ▷ *adj* pale brownish-cream
OATS ▶ **oat**
OATY *adj* of, like, or containing oats
OAVES ▶ **oaf**
OB *n* expression of opposition
OBA *n* (in W Africa) a Yoruba chief or ruler

OBANG *n* former Japanese coin
OBANGS ▶ **obang**
OBAS ▶ **oba**
OBCONIC *adj* (of a fruit or similar part) shaped like a cone and attached at the pointed end
OBDURE *vb* make obdurate
OBDURED ▶ **obdure**
OBDURES ▶ **obdure**
OBE *n* ancient Laconian village
OBEAH *vb* cast spell on
OBEAHED ▶ **obeah**
OBEAHS ▶ **obeah**
OBECHE *n* African tree
OBECHES ▶ **obeche**
OBEISM *n* belief in obeah
OBEISMS ▶ **obeism**
OBELI ▶ **obelus**
OBELIA *n* type of jellyfish
OBELIAS ▶ **obelia**
OBELION *n* area of skull
OBELISE *same as* ▶ **obelize**
OBELISK *n* four-sided stone column tapering to a pyramid at the top
OBELISM *n* practice of marking passages in text
OBELIZE *vb* mark (a word or passage) with an obelus
OBELUS *n* mark used in editions of ancient documents to indicate spurious words or passages
OBENTO *n* Japanese lunch box
OBENTOS ▶ **obento**
OBES ▶ **obe**
OBESE *adj* very fat

OBESELY ▶ obese

OBESER ▶ obese

OBESEST ▶ obese

OBESITY ▶ obese

OBEY vb carry out instructions or orders

OBEYED ▶ obey

OBEYER ▶ obey

OBEYERS ▶ obey

OBEYING ▶ obey

OBEYS ▶ obey

OBI n broad sash tied in a large flat bow at the back, worn by Japanese women and children ▷ vb bewitch

OBIA same as ▶ obeah

OBIAS ▶ obia

OBIED ▶ obi

OBIING ▶ obi

OBIISM ▶ obi

OBIISMS ▶ obi

OBIIT vb died

OBIS ▶ obi

OBIT n memorial service

OBITAL adj of obits

OBITER adv by the way

OBITS ▶ obit

OBITUAL adj of obits

OBJECT n physical thing ▷ vb express disapproval

OBJECTS ▶ object

OBJET n object

OBJETS ▶ objet

OBJURE vb put on oath

OBJURED ▶ objure

OBJURES ▶ objure

OBLAST n administrative division of the constituent republics of Russia

OBLASTI ▶ oblast

OBLASTS ▶ oblast

OBLATE adj (of a sphere) flattened at the poles ▷ n person dedicated to a monastic or religious life

OBLATES ▶ oblate

OBLIGE vb compel (someone) morally or by law to do something

OBLIGED ▶ oblige

OBLIGEE n person in whose favour an obligation, contract, or bond is created

OBLIGER ▶ oblige

OBLIGES ▶ oblige

OBLIGOR n person who binds himself by contract to perform some obligation

OBLIQUE adj slanting ▷ n symbol (/) ▷ vb take or have an oblique direction

OBLONG adj having two long sides, two short sides,

and four right angles ▷ n oblong figure

OBLONGS ▶ oblong

OBLOQUY n verbal abuse

OBO n ship carrying oil and ore

OBOE n double-reeded woodwind instrument

OBOES ▶ oboe

OBOIST ▶ oboe

OBOISTS ▶ oboe

OBOL same as ▶ obolus

OBOLARY adj very poor

OBOLE n former weight unit in pharmacy

OBOLES ▶ obole

OBOLI ▶ obolus

OBOLS ▶ obol

OBOLUS n modern Greek unit of weight equal to one tenth of a gram

OBOS ▶ obo

OBOVATE adj (of a leaf) shaped like the longitudinal section of an egg with the narrower end at the base

OBOVOID adj (of a fruit) egg-shaped with the narrower end at the base

OBS ▶ ob

OBSCENE adj portraying sex offensively

OBSCURE adj not well known ▷ vb make (something) obscure

OBSEQUY singular of > obsequies

OBSERVE vb see or notice

OBSESS vb preoccupy (someone) compulsively

OBSIGN vb confirm

OBSIGNS ▶ obsign

OBTAIN vb acquire intentionally

OBTAINS ▶ obtain

OBTECT adj (of a pupa) encased in a hardened secretion

OBTEND vb put forward

OBTENDS ▶ obtend

OBTEST vb beg (someone) earnestly

OBTESTS ▶ obtest

OBTRUDE vb push oneself or one's ideas on others

OBTUND vb deaden or dull

OBTUNDS ▶ obtund

OBTUSE adj mentally slow

OBTUSER ▶ obtuse

OBVERSE n opposite way of looking at an idea ▷ adj facing or turned towards the observer

OBVERT vb deduce the obverse of (a proposition)

OBVERTS ▶ obvert

OBVIATE vb make unnecessary

OBVIOUS adj easy to see or understand, evident

OCA n any of various South American herbaceous plants

OCARINA n small oval wind instrument

OCAS ▶ oca

OCCAM n computer programming language

OCCAMS ▶ occam

OCCAMY n type of alloy

OCCIES ▶ occy

OCCIPUT n back of the head

OCCLUDE vb obstruct

OCCULT adj relating to the supernatural ▷ vb (of a celestial body) to hide (another celestial body) from view

OCCULTS ▶ occult

OCCUPY vb live or work in (a building)

OCCUR vb happen

OCCURS ▶ occur

OCCY n as in **all over the occy** dialect expression meaning in every direction

OCEAN n vast area of sea between continents

OCEANIC adj of or relating to the ocean

OCEANID n ocean nymph in Greek mythology

OCEANS ▶ ocean

OCELLAR ▶ ocellus

OCELLI ▶ ocellus

OCELLUS n simple eye of insects and some other invertebrates

OCELOID adj of or like an ocelot

OCELOT n American wild cat with a spotted coat

OCELOTS ▶ ocelot

OCH interj expression of surprise, annoyance, or disagreement

OCHE n (in darts) mark on the floor behind which a player must stand

OCHER same as ▶ ochre

OCHERED ▶ ocher

OCHERS ▶ ocher

OCHERY ▶ ocher

OCHES ▶ oche

OCHONE interj expression of sorrow or regret

OCHRE n brownish-yellow earth ▷ adj moderate yellow-orange to orange ▷ vb colour with ochre

OCHREA n cup-shaped structure that sheathes the stems of certain plants

OCHREAE ▶ ochrea

OCHRED ▶ ochre

OCHRES ▶ ochre

OCHREY ▶ ochre

OCHRING ▶ ochre

OCHROID ▶ ochre

OCHROUS ▶ ochre

OCHRY ▶ ochre

OCICAT n breed of large short-haired cat with a spotted coat

OCICATS ▶ ocicat

OCKER n uncultivated or boorish Australian

OCKERS ▶ ocker

OCREA same as ▶ ochrea

OCREAE ▶ ocrea

OCREATE adj possessing an ocrea

OCTA same as ▶ okta

OCTAD n group or series of eight

OCTADIC ▶ octad

OCTADS ▶ octad

OCTAGON n geometric figure with eight sides

OCTAL n number system with a base 8

OCTALS ▶ octal

OCTAN n illness that occurs weekly

OCTANE n hydrocarbon found in petrol

OCTANES ▶ octane

OCTANOL n alcohol containing eight carbon atoms

OCTANS ▶ octan

OCTANT n any of the eight parts into which the three planes containing the Cartesian coordinate axes divide space

OCTANTS ▶ octant

OCTAPLA n book with eight texts

OCTAS ▶ octa

OCTAVAL ▶ octave

OCTAVE n (interval between the first and) eighth note of a scale ▷ adj consisting of eight parts

OCTAVES ▶ octave

OCTAVO n book size in which the sheets are folded into eight leaves

OCTAVOS ▶ octavo

OCTET n group of eight performers

OCTETS ▶ octet

OCTETT same as ▶ octet

OCTETTE same as ▶ octet

OCTETTS ▶ octett

OCTOFID adj divided into eight

OCTOPI ▶ octopus

OCTOPOD n type of mollusc ▷ adj of these molluscs

OCTOPUS n sea creature with a soft body and eight tentacles

OCTROI n duty on various goods brought into certain European towns

OCTROIS ▶ octroi

OCTUOR n octet

OCTUORS ▶ octuor

OCTUPLE n quantity or number eight times as great as another ▷ adj eight times as much or as many ▷ vb multiply by eight

OCTUPLY adv by eight times

OCTYL n group of atoms

OCTYLS ▶ octyl

OCULAR adj relating to the eyes or sight ▷ n lens in an optical instrument

OCULARS ▶ ocular

OCULATE adj possessing eyes

OCULI ▶ oculus

OCULIST n ophthalmologist

OCULUS n round window

OD n hypothetical force formerly thought to be responsible for many natural phenomena

ODA n room in a harem

ODAH same as ▶ oda

ODAHS ▶ odah

ODAL same as ▶ udal

ODALISK same as > odalisque

ODALLER ▶ odal

ODALS ▶ odal

ODAS ▶ oda

ODD adj unusual

ODDBALL n eccentric person ▷ adj strange or peculiar

ODDER ▶ odd

ODDEST ▶ odd

ODDISH ▶ odd

ODDITY n odd person or thing

ODDLY ▶ odd

ODDMENT n odd piece or thing

ODDNESS ▶ odd

ODDS pl n (ratio showing) the probability of something happening

ODDSMAN n umpire

ODDSMEN ▶ oddsman

ODE n lyric poem, usu addressed to a particular subject

ODEA ▶ odeum

ODEON same as ▶ odeum

ODEONS ▶ odeon

ODES ▶ ode

ODEUM n (esp in ancient Greece and Rome) a building for musical performances

ODEUMS ▶ odeum

ODIC ▶ od

ODIOUS adj offensive

ODISM ▶ od

ODISMS ▶ od

ODIST ▶ od

ODISTS ▶ od

ODIUM n widespread dislike

ODIUMS ▶ odium

ODONATE n dragonfly or related insect

ODONTIC adj of teeth

ODOR same as ▶ odour

ODORANT n something with a strong smell

ODORATE adj having a strong smell

ODORED same as ▶ odoured

ODORFUL same as > odourful

ODORISE same as ▶ odorize

ODORIZE vb give an odour to

ODOROUS adj having or emitting a characteristic smell or odour

ODORS ▶ odor

ODOUR n particular smell

ODOURED adj having odour

ODOURS ▶ odour

ODS ▶ od

ODSO n cry of suprise

ODYL same as ▶ od

ODYLE same as ▶ od

ODYLES ▶ odyle

ODYLISM ▶ odyl

ODYLS ▶ odyl

ODYSSEY n long eventful journey

ODZOOKS interj cry of surprise

OE n grandchild

OECIST n colony founder

OECISTS ▶ oecist

OEDEMA *n* abnormal swelling

OEDEMAS ▸ oedema

OEDIPAL *adj* relating to an Oedipus complex, whereby a male child wants to replace his father

OENOMEL *n* drink made of wine and honey

OERSTED *n* cgs unit of magnetic field strength

OES ▸ oe

OESTRAL ▸ oestrus

OESTRIN *obsolete term for* > oestrogen

OESTRUM *same as* ▸ oestrus

OESTRUS *n* regularly occurring period of fertility and sexual receptivity in most female mammals

OEUVRE *n* work of art, literature, music, etc

OEUVRES ▸ oeuvre

OF *prep* belonging to

OFF *prep* away from ▷ *adv* away ▷ *adj* not operating ▷ *n* side of the field to which the batsman's feet point ▷ *vb* kill

OFFAL *n* edible organs of an animal, such as liver or kidneys

OFFALS ▸ offal

OFFBEAT *adj* unusual or eccentric ▷ *n* any of the normally unaccented beats in a bar

OFFCAST *n* cast-off

OFFCUT *n* piece remaining after the required parts have been cut out

OFFCUTS ▸ offcut

OFFED ▸ off

OFFENCE *n* (cause of) hurt feelings or annoyance

OFFEND *vb* hurt the feelings of, insult

OFFENDS ▸ offend

OFFENSE *same as* ▸ offence

OFFER *vb* present (something) for acceptance or rejection ▷ *n* something offered

OFFERED ▸ offer

OFFEREE *n* person to whom an offer is made

OFFERER ▸ offer

OFFEROR ▸ offer

OFFERS ▸ offer

OFFHAND *adj* casual, curt ▷ *adv* without preparation

OFFICE *n* room or building where people work at desks

OFFICER *n* person in authority in the armed services ▷ *vb* furnish with officers

OFFICES ▸ office

OFFIE *n* off-licence

OFFIES ▸ offie

OFFING *n* area of the sea visible from the shore

OFFINGS ▸ offing

OFFISH *adj* aloof or distant in manner

OFFKEY *adj* out of tune

OFFLINE *adj* disconnected from a computer or the internet

OFFLOAD *vb* pass responsibilty for (something unpleasant) to someone else

OFFPEAK *adj* relating to times outside periods of intensive use

OFFPUT *n* act of putting off

OFFPUTS ▸ offput

OFFRAMP *n* road allowing traffic to leave a motorway

OFFS ▸ off

OFFSCUM *n* scum

OFFSET *vb* cancel out, compensate for ▷ *n* printing method in which the impression is made onto a surface which transfers it to the paper

OFFSETS ▸ offset

OFFSIDE *adv* (positioned) illegally ahead of the ball ▷ *n* side of a vehicle nearest the centre of the road

OFFTAKE *n* act of taking off

OFFY ▸ offie

OFLAG *n* German prisoner-of-war camp for officers in World War II

OFLAGS ▸ oflag

OFT *adv* often

OFTEN *adv* frequently, much of the time

OFTENER ▸ often

OFTER ▸ oft

OFTEST ▸ oft

OGAM *same as* ▸ ogham

OGAMIC ▸ ogam

OGAMS ▸ ogam

OGDOAD *n* group of eight

OGDOADS ▸ ogdoad

OGEE *n* moulding having a cross section in the form of a letter S

OGEED *adj* (of an arch or moulding) having an ogee

OGEES ▸ ogee

OGGIN *n* sea

OGGINS ▸ oggin

OGHAM *n* ancient alphabetical writing system used by the Celts in Britain and Ireland

OGHAMIC ▸ ogham

OGHAMS ▸ ogham

OGIVAL ▸ ogive

OGIVE *n* diagonal rib or groin of a Gothic vault

OGIVES ▸ ogive

OGLE *vb* stare at (someone) lustfully ▷ *n* flirtatious or lewd look

OGLED ▸ ogle

OGLER ▸ ogle

OGLERS ▸ ogle

OGLES ▸ ogle

OGLING ▸ ogle

OGLINGS ▸ ogle

OGMIC ▸ ogam

OGRE *n* giant that eats human flesh

OGREISH ▸ ogre

OGREISM ▸ ogre

OGRES ▸ ogre

OGRESS ▸ ogre

OGRISH ▸ ogre

OGRISM ▸ ogre

OGRISMS ▸ ogre

OH *interj* exclamation of surprise, pain, etc ▷ *vb* say oh

OHED ▸ oh

OHIA *n* Hawaiian plant

OHIAS ▸ ohia

OHING ▸ oh

OHM *n* unit of electrical resistance

OHMAGE *n* electrical resistance in ohms

OHMAGES ▸ ohmage

OHMIC *adj* of or relating to a circuit element

OHMS ▸ ohm

OHO *n* exclamation expressing surprise, exultation, or derision

OHONE *same as* ▸ ochone

OHS ▸ oh

OI *interj* shout to attract attention ▷ *n* grey-faced petrel

OIDIA ▸ oidium

OIDIOID ▸ oidium

OIDIUM *n* type of fungal spore

OIKIST *same as* ▸ oecist

OIKISTS ▸ oikist

OIL *n* viscous liquid, insoluble in water and usu

OGEES ▸ ogee

flammable ▷ vb lubricate (a machine) with oil

OILBIRD n type of nocturnal gregarious cave-dwelling bird

OILCAMP n camp for oilworkers

OILCAN n container with a long nozzle for applying oil to machinery

OILCANS ▶ oilcan

OILCUP n cup-shaped oil reservoir in a machine providing continuous lubrication for a bearing

OILCUPS ▶ oilcup

OILED ▶ oil

OILER n person, device, etc, that lubricates or supplies oil

OILERS ▶ oiler

OILERY n oil business

OILGAS n gaseous mixture of hydrocarbons used as a fuel

OILHOLE n hole for oil

OILIER ▶ oily

OILIEST ▶ oily

OILILY ▶ oily

OILING ▶ oil

OILLET same as ▶ eyelet

OILLETS ▶ oillet

OILMAN n person who owns or operates oil wells

OILMEN ▶ oilman

OILNUT n nut from which oil is extracted

OILNUTS ▶ oilnut

OILS ▶ oil

OILSEED n seed from which oil is extracted

OILSKIN n (garment made from) waterproof material

OILWAY n channel for oil

OILWAYS ▶ oilway

OILY adj soaked or covered with oil

OINK n grunt of a pig or an imitation of this ▷ interj imitation or representation of the grunt of a pig ▷ vb make noise of pig

OINKED ▶ oink

OINKING ▶ oink

OINKS ▶ oink

OINOMEL same as ▶ oenomel

OINT vb anoint

OINTED ▶ oint

OINTING ▶ oint

OINTS ▶ oint

OIS ▶ oi

OJIME n Japanese bead used

to secure cords

OJIMES ▶ ojime

OKA n unit of weight used in Turkey

OKAPI n African animal related to the giraffe but with a shorter neck

OKAPIS ▶ okapi

OKAS ▶ oka

OKAY adj satisfactory ▷ vb approve or endorse ▷ n approval or agreement ▷ interj expression of approval

OKAYED ▶ okay

OKAYING ▶ okay

OKAYS ▶ okay

OKE same as ▶ oka

OKEH same as ▶ okay

OKEHS ▶ okeh

OKES ▶ oke

OKIMONO n Japanese ornamental item

OKRA n tropical plant with edible green pods

OKRAS ▶ okra

OKTA n unit used in meteorology to measure cloud cover

OKTAS ▶ okta

OLD adj having lived or existed for a long time ▷ n earlier or past time

OLDE adj old-world or quaint, used facetiously

OLDEN adj old ▷ vb grow old

OLDENED ▶ olden

OLDENS ▶ olden

OLDER adj having lived or existed longer

OLDEST ▶ old

OLDIE n old but popular song or film

OLDIES ▶ oldie

OLDISH ▶ old

OLDNESS ▶ old

OLDS ▶ old

OLDSTER n older person

OLDWIFE n any of various fishes, esp the menhaden or the alewife

OLDY same as ▶ oldie

OLE interj exclamation of approval or encouragement customary at bullfights ▷ n cry of olé

OLEA ▶ oleum

OLEARIA n daisy bush

OLEATE n any salt or ester of oleic acid

OLEATES ▶ oleate

OLEFIN same as ▶ olefine

OLEFINE another name for ▶ alkene

OLEFINS ▶ olefin

OLEIC adj as in oleic acid colourless oily liquid used in making soap

OLEIN another name for > triolein

OLEINE same as ▶ olein

OLEINES ▶ oleine

OLEINS ▶ olein

OLENT adj having smell

OLEO n as in oleo oil oil extracted from beef fat

OLEOS ▶ oleo

OLES ▶ ole

OLESTRA n trademark term for an artificial fat

OLEUM n type of sulphuric acid

OLEUMS ▶ oleum

OLFACT vb smell something

OLFACTS ▶ olfact

OLICOOK n doughnut

OLID adj foul-smelling

OLIGIST n type of iron ore

OLINGO n South American mammal

OLINGOS ▶ olingo

OLIO n dish of many different ingredients

OLIOS ▶ olio

OLITORY n kitchen garden

OLIVARY adj shaped like an olive

OLIVE n small green or black fruit used as food or pressed for its oil ▷ adj greyish-green

OLIVER n as in Bath oliver type of unsweetened biscuit

OLIVERS ▶ oliver

OLIVES ▶ olive

OLIVET n button shaped like olive

OLIVETS ▶ olivet

OLIVINE n olive-green mineral of the olivine group

OLLA n cooking pot

OLLAMH n old Irish term for a wise man

OLLAMHS ▶ ollamh

OLLAS ▶ olla

OLLAV same as ▶ ollamh

OLLAVS ▶ ollav

OLLER n waste ground

OLLERS ▶ oller

OLLIE n (in skateboarding and snowboarding) a jump into the air executed by stamping on the tail of the board

O

OLLIES ▶ ollie

OLM n pale blind eel-like salamander

OLMS ▶ olm

OLOGIES ▶ ology

OLOGIST n scientist

OLOGOAN vb complain loudly without reason

OLOGY n science or other branch of knowledge

OLOROSO n golden-coloured sweet sherry

OLPAE ▶ olpe

OLPE n ancient Greek jug

OLPES ▶ olpe

OLYCOOK same as ▶ olykoek

OLYKOEK n American type of doughnut

OM n sacred syllable in Hinduism

OMASA ▶ omasum

OMASAL ▶ omasum

OMASUM n compartment in the stomach of a ruminant animal

OMBER same as ▶ ombre

OMBERS ▶ omber

OMBRE n 18th-century card game

OMBRES ▶ ombre

OMBU n South American tree

OMBUS ▶ ombu

OMEGA n last letter in the Greek alphabet

OMEGAS ▶ omega

OMELET same as ▶ omelette

OMELETS ▶ omelet

OMEN n happening or object thought to foretell success or misfortune ▷ vb portend

OMENED ▶ omen

OMENING ▶ omen

OMENS ▶ omen

OMENTA ▶ omentum

OMENTAL ▶ omentum

OMENTUM n double fold of the peritoneum connecting the stomach with other abdominal organs

OMER n ancient Hebrew unit of dry measure equal to one tenth of an ephah

OMERS ▶ omer

OMERTA n conspiracy of silence

OMERTAS ▶ omerta

OMICRON n 15th letter in the Greek alphabet

OMIGOD interj exclamation of surprise, pleasure,
dismay, etc

OMIKRON same as ▶ omicron

OMINOUS adj worrying, seeming to foretell misfortune

OMIT vb leave out

OMITS ▶ omit

OMITTED ▶ omit

OMITTER ▶ omit

OMLAH n staff team in India

OMLAHS ▶ omlah

OMMATEA > ommateum

OMNEITY n state of being all

OMNIANA n miscellaneous collection

OMNIBUS n several books or TV or radio programmes made into one ▷ adj consisting of or dealing with several different things at once

OMNIETY same as ▶ omneity

OMNIFIC adj creating all things

OMNIFY vb make something universal

OMNIUM n total value

OMNIUMS ▶ omnium

OMOV n one member one vote: a voting system in which each voter has one vote to cast

OMOVS ▶ omov

OMPHALI > omphalos

OMRAH n Muslim noble

OMRAHS ▶ omrah

OMS ▶ om

ON prep indicating position above, attachment, closeness, etc ▷ adv in operation ▷ adj operating ▷ n side of the field on which the batsman stands ▷ vb go on

ONAGER n wild ass of Persia

ONAGERS ▶ onager

ONAGRI ▶ onager

ONANISM n withdrawal in sexual intercourse before ejaculation

ONANIST ▶ onanism

ONBEAT n first and third beats in a bar of four-four time

ONBEATS ▶ onbeat

ONBOARD adj on a ship or other craft

ONCE adv on one occasion ▷ n one occasion

ONCER n (formerly) a
one-pound note

ONCERS ▶ oncer

ONCES ▶ once

ONCET dialect form of ▶ once

ONCOGEN n substance causing tumours to form

ONCOME n act of coming on

ONCOMES ▶ oncome

ONCOST same as > overheads

ONCOSTS ▶ oncost

ONCUS same as ▶ onkus

ONDATRA same as > musquash

ONDINE same as ▶ undine

ONDINES ▶ ondine

ONDING Scots word for ▶ onset

ONDINGS ▶ onding

ONE adj single, lone ▷ n number or figure 1 ▷ pron any person

ONEFOLD adj simple

ONEIRIC adj of or relating to dreams

ONELY same as ▶ only

ONENESS n unity

ONER n single continuous action

ONERIER ▶ onery

ONEROUS adj (of a task) difficult to carry out

ONERS ▶ oner

ONERY same as ▶ ornery

ONES ▶ one

ONESELF pron reflexive form of one

ONETIME adj at some time in the past

ONEYER old form of ▶ one

ONEYERS ▶ oneyer

ONEYRE same as ▶ oneyer

ONEYRES ▶ oneyre

ONFALL n attack or onset

ONFALLS ▶ onfall

ONFLOW n flowing on

ONFLOWS ▶ onflow

ONGOING adj in progress, continuing

ONIE variant spelling of ▶ ony

ONION n strongly flavoured edible bulb ▷ vb add onion to

ONIONED ▶ onion

ONIONS ▶ onion

ONIONY ▶ onion

ONIRIC same as ▶ oneiric

ONIUM n as in onium compound type of chemical salt

ONIUMS ▶ onium

ONKUS adj bad

ONLAY n artificial veneer for a tooth
ONLAYS ▶ onlay
ONLIEST same as ▶ **only**
ONLINE adj connected to a computer or the internet
ONLINER n person who uses the internet regularly
ONLOAD vb load files on to a computer
ONLOADS ▶ onload
ONLY adj alone of its kind ▷ adv exclusively
ONNED ▶ on
ONNING ▶ on
ONO n Hawaiian fish
ONOS ▶ ono
ONRUSH n forceful forward rush or flow
ONS ▶ on
ONSET n beginning
ONSETS ▶ onset
ONSHORE adv towards the land
ONSIDE adv (of a player in various sports) in a legal position ▷ adj taking one's part or side ▷ n part of cricket field where a batsman stands
ONSIDES ▶ onside
ONST same as ▶ **once**
ONSTAGE adj visible by audience
ONSTEAD Scots word for ▷ **farmstead**
ONTIC adj having real existence
ONTO prep a position on
ONUS n responsibility or burden
ONUSES ▶ onus
ONWARD same as ▶ **onwards**
ONWARDS adv at or towards a point or position ahead, in advance, etc
ONY Scots word for ▶ **any**
ONYCHA n part of mollusc
ONYCHAS ▶ onycha
ONYCHIA n inflammation of the nails or claws of animals
ONYMOUS adj (of a book) bearing its author's name
ONYX n type of quartz with coloured layers
ONYXES ▶ onyx
OO Scots word for ▶ **wool**
OOBIT n hairy caterpillar
OOBITS ▶ oobit
OOCYST n type of zygote
OOCYSTS ▶ oocyst

OOCYTE n immature female germ cell that gives rise to an ovum
OOCYTES ▶ oocyte
OODLES pl n great quantities
OODLINS same as ▶ **oodles**
OOF n money
OOFIER ▶ oof
OOFIEST ▶ oof
OOFS ▶ oof
OOFTISH n money
OOFY ▶ oof
OOGAMY n sexual reproduction involving a small motile male gamete and a large much less motile female gamete
OOGENY same as ▷ **oogenesis**
OOGONIA ▷ oogonium
OOH interj exclamation of surprise, pleasure, pain, etc ▷ vb say ooh
OOHED ▶ ooh
OOHING ▶ ooh
OOHS ▶ ooh
OOIDAL adj shaped like egg
OOLAKAN same as ▷ **eulachon**
OOLITE n limestone made up of tiny grains of calcium carbonate
OOLITES ▶ oolite
OOLITH n any of the tiny spherical grains of sedimentary rock of which oolite is composed
OOLITHS ▶ oolith
OOLITIC ▶ oolite
OOLOGIC ▶ oology
OOLOGY n branch of ornithology concerned with the study of birds' eggs
OOLONG n kind of dark tea that is partly fermented before being dried
OOLONGS ▶ oolong
OOM n title of respect used to refer to an elderly man
OOMIAC same as ▶ **umiak**
OOMIACK same as ▶ **umiak**
OOMIACS ▶ oomiac
OOMIAK same as ▶ **umiak**
OOMIAKS ▶ oomiak
OOMPAH n representation of the sound made by a deep brass instrument ▷ vb make the noise of a brass instrument
OOMPAHS ▶ oompah
OOMPH n enthusiasm, vigour, or energy

OOMPHS ▶ oomph
OOMS ▶ oom
OON Scots word for ▶ **oven**
OONS ▶ oon
OONT n camel
OONTS ▶ oont
OOP vb Scots word meaning to bind
OOPED ▶ oop
OOPHYTE n gametophyte in mosses, liverworts, and ferns
OOPING ▶ oop
OOPS interj exclamation of surprise or apology
OOR Scots form of ▶ **our**
OORALI n member of Indian people
OORALIS ▶ oorali
OORIAL n Himalayan sheep
OORIALS ▶ oorial
OORIE adj Scots word meaning shabby

> This Scots word is one of the classic 5-letter vowel dumps. It has almost equally useful variants **ourie** and **owrie**.

OORIER ▶ oorie
OORIEST ▶ oorie
OOS ▶ oo
OOSE n dust
OOSES ▶ oose
OOSIER ▶ oose
OOSIEST ▶ oose
OOSPERM n fertilized ovum
OOSPORE n thick-walled sexual spore that develops from a fertilized oosphere
OOSY ▶ oose
OOT Scots word for ▶ **out**
OOTHECA n capsule containing eggs that is produced by some insects and molluscs
OOTID n immature female gamete that develops into an ovum
OOTIDS ▶ ootid
OOTS ▶ oot
OOZE vb flow slowly ▷ n sluggish flow
OOZED ▶ ooze
OOZES ▶ ooze
OOZIER ▶ oozy
OOZIEST ▶ oozy
OOZILY ▶ oozy
OOZING ▶ ooze
OOZY adj moist or dripping
OP n operation
OPACIFY vb become or make opaque
OPACITY n state or quality

of being opaque
OPACOUS same as
▶ **opaque**
OPAH n large soft-finned
deep-sea fish
OPAHS ▶ **opah**
OPAL n iridescent precious
stone
OPALED adj made like opal
OPALINE adj opalescent ▷ n
opaque or semiopaque
whitish glass
OPALS ▶ **opal**
OPAQUE adj not able to be
seen through, not
transparent ▷ n opaque
pigment used to block out
particular areas on a
negative ▷ vb make opaque
OPAQUED ▶ **opaque**
OPAQUER ▶ **opaque**
OPAQUES ▶ **opaque**
OPCODE n computer code
containing operating
instructions
OPCODES ▶ **opcode**
OPE archaic or poetic word for
▶ **open**
OPED ▶ **ope**
OPEN adj not closed ▷ vb
(cause to) become open ▷ n
competition which all may
enter
OPENED ▶ **open**
OPENER n tool for opening
cans and bottles
OPENERS ▶ **opener**
OPENEST ▶ **open**
OPENING n beginning ▷ adj
first
OPENLY ▶ **open**
OPENS ▶ **open**
OPEPE n African tree
OPEPES ▶ **opepe**
OPERA n drama in which
the text is sung to an
orchestral accompaniment
OPERAND n quantity,
variable, or function upon
which an operation is
performed
OPERANT adj producing
effects ▷ n person or thing
that operates
OPERAS ▶ **opera**
OPERATE vb (cause to)
work
OPERON n group of
adjacent genes in bacteria
functioning as a unit
OPERONS ▶ **operon**
OPEROSE adj laborious
OPES ▶ **ope**

OPHITE n any of several
greenish mottled rocks
OPHITES ▶ **ophite**
OPHITIC adj having small
elongated feldspar crystals
enclosed
OPHIURA n sea creature
like a starfish
OPIATE n narcotic drug
containing opium ▷ adj
containing or consisting of
opium ▷ vb treat with an
opiate
OPIATED ▶ **opiate**
OPIATES ▶ **opiate**
OPINE vb express an opinion
OPINED ▶ **opine**
OPINES ▶ **opine**
OPING ▶ **ope**
OPINING ▶ **opine**
OPINION n personal belief
or judgment
OPIOID n substance that
resembles morphine in its
physiological or
pharmacological effect
OPIOIDS ▶ **opioid**
OPIUM n addictive narcotic
drug made from poppy
seeds
OPIUMS ▶ **opium**
OPORICE n former
medicine made from fruit
OPOSSUM n small
marsupial of America or
Australasia
OPPIDAN adj of a town ▷ n
person living in a town
OPPO n counterpart in
another organization
OPPOS ▶ **oppo**
OPPOSE vb work against
OPPOSED ▶ **oppose**
OPPOSER ▶ **oppose**
OPPOSES ▶ **oppose**
OPPRESS vb control by
cruelty or force
OPPUGN vb call into
question
OPPUGNS ▶ **oppugn**
OPS ▶ **op**
OPSIN n type of protein
OPSINS ▶ **opsin**
OPSONIC ▶ **opsonin**
OPSONIN n constituent of
blood serum
OPT vb show a preference,
choose
OPTANT n person who opts
OPTANTS ▶ **optant**
OPTED ▶ **opt**
OPTER ▶ **opt**
OPTERS ▶ **opt**

OPTIC adj relating to the
eyes or sight
OPTICAL adj of or involving
light or optics
OPTICS n science of sight
and light
OPTIMA ▶ **optimum**
OPTIMAL adj best or most
favourable
OPTIME n mathematics
student at Cambridge
University
OPTIMES ▶ **optime**
OPTIMUM n best possible
conditions ▷ adj most
favourable
OPTING ▶ **opt**
OPTION n choice ▷ vb
obtain an option on
OPTIONS ▶ **option**
OPTS ▶ **opt**
OPULENT adj having or
indicating wealth
OPULUS n flowering shrub
OPUNTIA n type of cactus
OPUS n artistic creation,
esp a musical work
OPUSCLE same as
> **opuscule**
OPUSES ▶ **opus**
OQUASSA n American trout
OR prep before ▷ adj of the
metal gold ▷ n gold
ORA ▶ **os**
ORACH same as ▶ **orache**
ORACHE n type of plant
ORACHES ▶ **orache**
ORACIES ▶ **oracy**
ORACLE n shrine of an
ancient god ▷ vb utter as
an oracle
ORACLED ▶ **oracle**
ORACLES ▶ **oracle**
ORACY n capacity to
express oneself in and
understand speech
ORAD adv towards the
mouth
ORAL adj spoken ▷ n
spoken examination
ORALISM n oral method of
communicating with deaf
people
ORALIST ▶ **oralism**
ORALITY n state of being
oral
ORALLY ▶ **oral**
ORALS ▶ **oral**
ORANG n orangutan
ORANGE n reddish-yellow
citrus fruit ▷ adj
reddish-yellow
ORANGER ▶ **orange**

ORANGES ▶ orange
ORANGEY ▶ orange
ORANGS ▶ orang
ORANGY ▶ orange
ORANT n artistic representation of worshipper
ORANTS ▶ orant
ORARIA ▶ orarium
ORARIAN n person who lives on the coast
ORARION n garment worn by Greek clergyman
ORARIUM n handkerchief
ORATE vb make or give an oration
ORATED ▶ orate
ORATES ▶ orate
ORATING ▶ orate
ORATION n formal speech
ORATOR n skilful public speaker
ORATORS ▶ orator
ORATORY n art of making speeches
ORATRIX n female orator
ORB n ceremonial decorated sphere with a cross on top, carried by a monarch ▷ vb make or become circular or spherical
ORBED ▶ orb
ORBIER ▶ orby
ORBIEST ▶ orby
ORBING ▶ orb
ORBIT n curved path of a planet, satellite, or spacecraft around another body ▷ vb move in an orbit around
ORBITA same as ▶ orbit
ORBITAL adj of or denoting an orbit ▷ n region surrounding an atomic nucleus
ORBITAS ▶ orbita
ORBITED ▶ orbit
ORBITER n spacecraft or satellite designed to orbit a planet without landing on it
ORBITS ▶ orbit
ORBITY n bereavement
ORBLESS ▶ orb
ORBS ▶ orb
ORBY adj orb-shaped
ORC n any of various whales, such as the killer and grampus
ORCA n killer whale
ORCAS ▶ orca
ORCEIN n brown crystalline material

ORCEINS ▶ orcein
ORCHARD n area where fruit trees are grown
ORCHAT same as ▶ orchard
ORCHATS ▶ orchat
ORCHEL same as ▶ orchil
ORCHELS ▶ orchel
ORCHID n plant with flowers that have unusual lip-shaped petals
ORCHIDS ▶ orchid
ORCHIL n any of various lichens
ORCHILS ▶ orchil
ORCHIS n type of orchid
ORCIN same as ▶ orcinol
ORCINE same as ▶ orcinol
ORCINES ▶ orcine
ORCINOL n colourless crystalline water-soluble solid
ORCINS ▶ orcin
ORCS ▶ orc
ORD n pointed weapon
ORDAIN vb make (someone) a member of the clergy
ORDAINS ▶ ordain
ORDEAL n painful or difficult experience
ORDEALS ▶ ordeal
ORDER n instruction to be carried out ▷ vb give an instruction to
ORDERED ▶ order
ORDERER ▶ order
ORDERLY adj well-organized ▷ n hospital attendant ▷ adv according to custom or rule
ORDERS ▶ order
ORDINAL adj denoting a certain position in a sequence of numbers ▷ n book containing the forms of services for the ordination of ministers
ORDINAR Scots word for > ordinary
ORDINEE n person being ordained
ORDINES ▶ ordo
ORDO n religious order
ORDOS ▶ ordo
ORDS ▶ ord
ORDURE n excrement
ORDURES ▶ ordure
ORE n (rock containing) a mineral which yields metal
OREAD n mountain nymph
OREADES ▶ oread
OREADS ▶ oread
ORECTIC adj of or relating

to the desires
OREGANO n sweet-smelling herb used in cooking
OREIDE same as ▶ oroide
OREIDES ▶ oreide
ORES ▶ ore
OREWEED n seaweed
OREXIN n hormone that promotes wakefulness and stimulates the appetite
OREXINS ▶ orexin
OREXIS n appetite
ORF n infectious disease of sheep and sometimes goats and cattle
ORFE n small slender European fish
ORFES ▶ orfe
ORFRAY same as ▶ orphrey
ORFRAYS ▶ orfray
ORFS ▶ orf
ORGAN n part of an animal or plant that has a particular function
ORGANA ▶ organon
ORGANDY same as > organdie
ORGANIC adj of or produced from animals or plants ▷ n substance that is derived from animal or vegetable matter
ORGANON n system of logical or scientific rules, esp that of Aristotle
ORGANS ▶ organ
ORGANUM same as ▶ organon
ORGANZA n thin stiff fabric of silk, cotton, or synthetic fibre
ORGASM n most intense point of sexual pleasure ▷ vb experience orgasm
ORGASMS ▶ orgasm
ORGEAT n drink made from barley or almonds, and orange flower water
ORGEATS ▶ orgeat
ORGIA same as ▶ orgy
ORGIAC ▶ orgy
ORGIAS ▶ orgia
ORGIAST n participant in orgy
ORGIC ▶ orgy
ORGIES ▶ orgy
ORGONE n substance claimed to be needed in people for sexual activity and mental health
ORGONES ▶ orgone
ORGUE n number of stakes

lashed together

ORGUES ▶ **orgue**

ORGY n party involving promiscuous sexual activity

ORIBI n small African antelope

ORIBIS ▶ **oribi**

ORIEL n type of bay window

ORIELS ▶ **oriel**

ORIENCY n state of being orient

ORIENT vb position (oneself) according to one's surroundings ▷ n eastern sky or the dawn ▷ adj eastern

ORIENTS ▶ **orient**

ORIFEX same as ▶ **orifice**

ORIFICE n opening or hole

ORIGAMI n Japanese decorative art of paper folding

ORIGAN another name for ▶ **marjoram**

ORIGANE same as ▶ **origan**

ORIGANS ▶ **origan**

ORIGIN n point from which something develops

ORIGINS ▶ **origin**

ORIHOU n small New Zealand tree

ORIHOUS ▶ **orihou**

ORIOLE n tropical or American songbird

ORIOLES ▶ **oriole**

ORISHA n any of the minor gods or spirits of traditional Yoruba religion

ORISHAS ▶ **orisha**

ORISON another word for ▶ **prayer**

ORISONS ▶ **orison**

ORIXA same as ▶ **orisha**

ORIXAS ▶ **orixa**

ORLE n border around a shield

ORLEANS n type of fabric

ORLES ▶ **orle**

ORLON n tradename for a crease-resistant acrylic fibre or fabric used for clothing, furnishings, etc

ORLONS ▶ **orlon**

ORLOP n (in a vessel with four or more decks) the lowest deck

ORLOPS ▶ **orlop**

ORMER n edible marine mollusc

ORMERS ▶ **ormer**

ORMOLU n gold-coloured alloy used for decoration

ORMOLUS ▶ **ormolu**

ORNATE adj highly decorated, elaborate

ORNATER ▶ **ornate**

ORNERY adj stubborn or vile-tempered

ORNIS less common word for ▶ **avifauna**

ORNISES ▶ **ornis**

OROGEN n part of earth subject to orogeny

OROGENS ▶ **orogen**

OROGENY n formation of mountain ranges by intense upward displacement of the earth's crust

OROIDE n alloy containing copper, tin, and other metals, used as imitation gold

OROIDES ▶ **oroide**

OROLOGY same as ▶ **orography**

OROPESA n float used in minesweeping

OROTUND adj (of the voice) resonant and booming

ORPHAN n child whose parents are dead ▷ vb deprive of parents

ORPHANS ▶ **orphan**

ORPHIC adj mystical or occult

ORPHISM n style of abstract art

ORPHREY n richly embroidered band or border

ORPIN same as ▶ **orpine**

ORPINE n type of plant

ORPINES ▶ **orpine**

ORPINS ▶ **orpin**

ORRA adj odd or unmatched

ORRAMAN n man who does odd jobs

ORRAMEN ▶ **orraman**

ORRERY n mechanical model of the solar system

ORRICE same as ▶ **orris**

ORRICES ▶ **orrice**

ORRIS n kind of iris

ORRISES ▶ **orris**

ORS ▶ **or**

ORT n fragment

ORTHIAN adj having high pitch

ORTHO n type of photographic plate

ORTHOS ▶ **ortho**

ORTHROS n canonical hour in the Greek Church

ORTOLAN n small European

songbird eaten as a delicacy

ORTS pl n scraps or leavings

ORVAL n plant of sage family

ORVALS ▶ **orval**

ORYX n large African antelope

ORYXES ▶ **oryx**

ORZO n pasta in small grain shapes

ORZOS ▶ **orzo**

OS n mouth or mouthlike part or opening

OSAR ▶ **os**

OSCAR n cash

OSCARS ▶ **oscar**

OSCHEAL adj of scrotum

OSCINE n songbird ▷ adj of songbirds

OSCINES ▶ **oscine**

OSCULA ▶ **osculum**

OSCULAR adj of or relating to an osculum

OSCULE n small mouth or opening

OSCULES ▶ **oscule**

OSCULUM n mouthlike aperture

OSE same as ▶ **esker**

OSES ▶ **ose**

OSETRA n type of caviar

OSETRAS ▶ **osetra**

OSHAC n plant smelling of ammonia

OSHACS ▶ **oshac**

OSIER n willow tree

OSIERED adj covered with osiers

OSIERS ▶ **osier**

OSIERY n work done with osiers

OSMATE n salt of osmic acid

OSMATES ▶ **osmate**

OSMATIC adj relying on sense of smell

OSMIATE same as ▶ **osmate**

OSMIC adj of or containing osmium in a high valence state

OSMICS n science of smell

OSMIOUS same as ▶ **osmous**

OSMIUM n heaviest known metallic element

OSMIUMS ▶ **osmium**

OSMOL same as ▶ **osmole**

OSMOLAL ▶ **osmole**

OSMOLAR adj containing one osmole per litre

OSMOLE n unit of osmotic pressure

OSMOLES ▶ **osmole**

OSMOLS ▶ **osmol**

OSMOSE vb undergo or cause to undergo osmosis

OSMOSED ▸ osmose

OSMOSES ▸ osmose

OSMOSIS n movement of a liquid through a membrane from a lower to a higher concentration

OSMOTIC ▸ osmosis

OSMOUS adj of or containing osmium in a low valence state

OSMUND same as ▸ osmunda

OSMUNDA n type of fern

OSMUNDS ▸ osmund

OSPREY n large fish-eating bird of prey

OSPREYS ▸ osprey

OSSA ▸ os

OSSEIN n protein that forms the organic matrix of bone

OSSEINS ▸ ossein

OSSELET n growth on knee of horse

OSSEOUS adj consisting of or like bone

OSSETER n sturgeon

OSSETRA same as ▸ osetra

OSSIA conj (in music) or

OSSICLE n small bone, esp one of those in the middle ear

OSSIFIC adj making something turn to bone

OSSIFY vb (cause to) become bone, harden

OSSUARY n any container for the burial of human bones, such as an urn or vault

OSTEAL adj of or relating to bone or to the skeleton

OSTENT n appearance

OSTENTS ▸ ostent

OSTEOID adj of or resembling bone ▸ n bony deposit

OSTEOMA n benign tumour composed of bone or bonelike tissue

OSTIA ▸ ostium

OSTIAL ▸ ostium

OSTIARY another word for ▸ porter

OSTIATE adj having ostium

OSTIOLE n pore in the reproductive bodies of certain algae and fungi through which spores pass

OSTIUM n any of the pores in sponges through which water enters the body

OSTLER n stableman at an inn

OSTLERS ▸ ostler

OSTMARK n currency of the former East Germany

OSTOMY n surgically made opening connecting organ to surface of body

OSTOSES ▸ ostosis

OSTOSIS n formation of bone

OSTRACA ▸ ostracon

OSTRAKA ▸ ostrakon

OSTRICH n large African bird that runs fast but cannot fly

OTAKU n Japanese computer geeks

OTALGIA technical name for ▸ earache

OTALGIC ▸ otalgia

OTALGY same as ▸ otalgia

OTARIES ▸ otary

OTARINE ▸ otary

This means like an otary or eared seal, and is perhaps the most commonly played of all 7-letter bonus words, so well worth learning for that extra 50 points it can give you.

OTARY n seal with ears

OTHER adj remaining in a group of which one or some have been specified ▸ n other person or thing

OTHERS ▸ other

OTIC adj of or relating to the ear

OTIOSE adj not useful

OTITIC ▸ otitis

OTITIS n inflammation of the ear

OTOCYST n embryonic structure in vertebrates that develops into the inner ear in the adult

OTOLITH n granule of calcium carbonate in the inner ear of vertebrates

OTOLOGY n branch of medicine concerned with the ear

OTTAR same as ▸ attar

OTTARS ▸ ottar

OTTAVA n interval of an octave

OTTAVAS ▸ ottava

OTTER n small brown freshwater mammal that eats fish ▸ vb fish using an otter board

OTTERED ▸ otter

OTTERS ▸ otter

OTTO another name for ▸ attar

OTTOMAN n storage chest with a padded lid for use as a seat

OTTOS ▸ otto

OU interj expressing concession ▸ n man, bloke, or chap

OUABAIN n poisonous white crystalline glycoside

OUAKARI n South American monkey

OUBAAS n man in authority

OUBIT n hairy caterpillar

OUBITS ▸ oubit

OUCH interj exclamation of sudden pain ▸ n brooch or clasp set with gems ▸ vb say ouch

OUCHED ▸ ouch

OUCHES ▸ ouch

OUCHING ▸ ouch

OUCHT Scots word for ▸ anything

OUCHTS ▸ oucht

OUD n Arabic stringed musical instrument resembling a lute or mandolin

OUDS ▸ oud

OUENS ▸ ou

OUGHLY same as ▸ ugly

OUGHT vb have an obligation ▸ n zero

OUGHTED ▸ ought

OUGHTS ▸ ought

OUGLIE same as ▸ ugly

OUGLIED ▸ ouglie

OUGLIES ▸ ouglie

OUGUIYA n standard monetary unit of Mauritania

OUIJA n tradename for a board through which spirits supposedly answer questions

OUIJAS ▸ ouija

OUK Scots word for ▸ week

OUKS ▸ ouk

OULAKAN same as ▸ eulachon

OULD Scots or Irish form of ▸ old

OULDER ▸ ould

OULDEST ▸ ould

OULK Scots form of ▸ week

OULKS ▸ oulk

OULONG same as ▸ oolong

OULONGS ▸ oulong

OUMA n grandmother,

often as a title with a surname

OUMAS ▸ ouma

OUNCE n unit of weight equal to one sixteenth of a pound

OUNCES ▸ ounce

OUNDY adj wavy

OUP same as ▸ **oop**

OUPA n grandfather, often as a title with a surname

OUPAS ▸ oupa

OUPED ▸ oup

OUPH same as ▸ **oaf**

OUPHE same as ▸ **oaf**

OUPHES ▸ ouphe

OUPHS ▸ ouph

OUPING ▸ oup

OUPS ▸ oup

OUR adj belonging to us ▷ determiner of, belonging to, or associated in some way with us

OURALI n plant from which curare comes

OURALIS ▸ ourali

OURANG same as ▸ **orang**

OURANGS ▸ ourang

OURARI same as ▸ **ourali**

OURARIS ▸ ourari

OUREBI same as ▸ **oribi**

OUREBIS ▸ ourebi

OURIE same as ▸ **oorie**

OURIER ▸ ourie

OURIEST ▸ ourie

OURN dialect form of ▸ **our**

OURS pron thing(s) belonging to us

OURSELF pron formal word for myself used by monarchs

OUS ▸ ou

OUSEL same as ▸ **ouzel**

OUSELS ▸ ousel

OUST vb force (someone) out, expel

OUSTED ▸ oust

OUSTER n act or instance of forcing someone out of a position

OUSTERS ▸ ouster

OUSTING ▸ oust

OUSTITI n device for opening locked door

OUSTS ▸ oust

OUT adj denoting movement or distance away from ▷ vb name (a public figure) as being homosexual

OUTACT vb surpass in acting

OUTACTS ▸ outact

OUTADD vb beat or surpass at adding

OUTADDS ▸ outadd

OUTAGE n period of power failure

OUTAGES ▸ outage

OUTASK vb declare wedding banns

OUTASKS ▸ outask

OUTATE ▸ outeat

OUTBACK n remote bush country of Australia

OUTBAKE vb bake more or better than

OUTBAR vb keep out

OUTBARK vb bark more or louder than

OUTBARS ▸ outbar

OUTBAWL vb bawl more or louder than

OUTBEAM vb beam more or brighter than

OUTBEG vb beg more or better than

OUTBEGS ▸ outbeg

OUTBID vb offer a higher price than

OUTBIDS ▸ outbid

OUTBOX vb surpass in boxing

OUTBRAG vb brag more or better than

OUTBRED > outbreed

OUTBULK vb exceed in bulk

OUTBURN vb burn longer or brighter than

OUTBUY vb buy more than

OUTBUYS ▸ outbuy

OUTBY adv outside

OUTBYE same as ▸ **outby**

OUTCALL n visit to customer's home by professional

OUTCAST n person rejected by a particular group ▷ adj rejected, abandoned, or discarded

OUTCHID > outchide

OUTCITY n anywhere outside a city's confines

OUTCOME n result

OUTCOOK vb cook more or better than

OUTCROP n part of a rock formation that sticks out of the earth ▷ vb (of rock strata) to protrude through the surface of the earth

OUTCROW vb exceed in crowing

OUTCRY n vehement or widespread protest ▷ vb cry louder or make more

noise than (someone or something)

OUTDARE vb be more brave than

OUTDATE vb make or become old-fashioned or obsolete

OUTDID ▸ outdo

OUTDO vb surpass in performance

OUTDOER ▸ outdo

OUTDOES ▸ outdo

OUTDONE ▸ outdo

OUTDOOR adj taking place, existing, or intended for use in the open air

OUTDRAG vb beat in drag race

OUTDRAW vb draw (a gun) faster than

OUTDREW ▸ outdraw

OUTDROP same as ▸ **outcrop**

OUTDUEL vb defeat in duel

OUTDURE vb last longer than

OUTEARN vb earn more than

OUTEAT vb eat more than

OUTEATS ▸ outeat

OUTECHO vb echo more than

OUTED ▸ out

OUTEDGE n furthest limit

OUTER adj on the outside ▷ n white outermost ring on a target

OUTERS ▸ outer

OUTFACE vb subdue or disconcert (someone) by staring

OUTFALL n mouth of a river or drain

OUTFAST vb fast longer than

OUTFAWN vb exceed in fawning

OUTFEEL vb exceed in feeling

OUTFELT ▸ outfeel

OUTFIND vb exceed in finding

OUTFIRE vb exceed in firing

OUTFISH vb catch more fish than

OUTFIT n matching set of clothes ▷ vb furnish or be furnished with an outfit, equipment, etc

OUTFITS ▸ outfit

OUTFLEW ▸ outfly

OUTFLOW n anything that flows out, such as liquid or

money ▷ vb flow faster than

OUTFLY vb fly better or faster than

OUTFOOL vb be more foolish than

OUTFOOT vb (of a boat) to go faster than (another boat)

OUTFOX vb defeat or foil (someone) by being more cunning

OUTGAIN vb gain more than

OUTGAS vb undergo the removal of adsorbed or absorbed gas from solids

OUTGATE n way out

OUTGAVE ▷ outgive

OUTGAZE vb gaze beyond

OUTGIVE vb exceed in giving

OUTGLOW vb glow more than

OUTGNAW vb exceed in gnawing

OUTGO vb exceed or outstrip ▷ n cost

OUTGOER ▷ outgo

OUTGOES ▷ outgo

OUTGONE ▷ outgo

OUTGREW ▷ outgrow

OUTGRIN vb exceed in grinning

OUTGROW vb become too large or too old for

OUTGUN vb surpass in fire power

OUTGUNS ▷ outgun

OUTGUSH vb gush out

OUTHAUL n line or cable for tightening the foot of a sail

OUTHEAR vb exceed in hearing

OUTHER same as ▷ other

OUTHIRE vb hire out

OUTHIT vb hit something further than (someone else)

OUTHITS ▷ outhit

OUTHOWL vb exceed in howling

OUTHUNT vb exceed in hunting

OUTHYRE same as ▷ outhire

OUTING n leisure trip

OUTINGS ▷ outing

OUTJEST vb exceed in jesting

OUTJET n projecting part

OUTJETS ▷ outjet

OUTJINX vb exceed in jinxing

If someone else plays **jinx**, you can outjinx them by adding O, U and T! And if you can form the whole word using all of your letters, you'll get a 50-point bonus.

OUTJUMP vb jump higher or farther than

OUTJUT vb jut out ▷ n projecting part

OUTJUTS ▷ outjut

OUTKEEP vb beat or surpass at keeping

OUTKEPT ▷ outkeep

OUTKICK vb exceed in kicking

OUTKILL vb exceed in killing

OUTKISS vb exceed in kissing

OUTLAID ▷ outlay

OUTLAIN ▷ outlay

OUTLAND adj outlying or distant ▷ n outlying areas of a country or region

OUTLASH n sudden attack

OUTLAST vb last longer than

OUTLAW n criminal deprived of legal protection, bandit ▷ vb make illegal

OUTLAWS ▷ outlaw

OUTLAY n expenditure ▷ vb spend (money)

OUTLAYS ▷ outlay

OUTLEAD vb be better leader than

OUTLEAP vb leap higher or farther than

OUTLED ▷ outlead

OUTLER n farm animal kept out of doors

OUTLERS ▷ outler

OUTLET n means of expressing emotion

OUTLETS ▷ outlet

OUTLIE vb lie outside a particular place

OUTLIED ▷ outlie

OUTLIER n outcrop of rocks that is entirely surrounded by older rocks

OUTLIES ▷ outlie

OUTLINE n short general explanation ▷ vb summarize

OUTLIVE vb live longer than

OUTLOOK n attitude ▷ vb look out

OUTLOVE vb exceed in loving

OUTMAN vb surpass in manpower

OUTMANS ▷ outman

OUTMODE vb make unfashionable

OUTMOST another word for > **outermost**

OUTMOVE vb move faster or better than

OUTNAME vb be more notorious than

OUTNESS n state or quality of being external

OUTPACE vb go faster than (someone)

OUTPART n remote region

OUTPASS vb exceed in passing

OUTPEEP vb peep out

OUTPEER vb surpass

OUTPITY vb exceed in pitying

OUTPLAN vb exceed in planning

OUTPLAY vb perform better than one's opponent in a sport or game

OUTPLOD vb exceed in plodding

OUTPLOT vb exceed in plotting

OUTPOLL vb win more votes than

OUTPORT n isolated fishing village, esp in Newfoundland

OUTPOST n outlying settlement

OUTPOUR n act of flowing or pouring out ▷ vb pour or cause to pour out freely or rapidly

OUTPRAY vb exceed in praying

OUTPULL vb exceed in pulling

OUTPUSH vb exceed in pushing

OUTPUT n amount produced ▷ vb produce (data) at the end of a process

OUTPUTS ▷ output

OUTRACE vb surpass in racing

OUTRAGE n great moral indignation ▷ vb offend morally

OUTRAN ▷ outrun

OUTRANG ▷ outring

OUTRANK vb be of higher

rank than (someone)

OUTRATE vb offer better rate than

OUTRAVE vb outdo in raving

OUTRE adj shockingly eccentric

OUTREAD vb outdo in reading

OUTRED vb be redder than

OUTREDS ▶ outred

OUTRIDE vb outdo by riding faster, farther, or better than ▷ n extra unstressed syllable within a metrical foot

OUTRIG vb supply with outfit

OUTRIGS ▶ outrig

OUTRING vb exceed in ringing

OUTRO n instrumental passage that concludes a piece of music

OUTROAR vb roar louder than

OUTROCK vb outdo in rocking

OUTRODE ▶ outride

OUTROLL vb exceed in rolling

OUTROOP n auction

OUTROOT vb root out

OUTROPE same as ▶ outroop

OUTROS ▶ outro

OUTROW vb outdo in rowing

OUTROWS ▶ outrow

OUTRUN vb run faster than

OUTRUNG ▶ outring

OUTRUNS ▶ outrun

OUTRUSH n flowing or rushing out ▷ vb rush out

OUTS ▶ out

OUTSAID ▶ outsay

OUTSAIL vb sail better than

OUTSANG ▶ outsing

OUTSAT ▶ outsit

OUTSAW ▶ outsee

OUTSAY vb say something out loud

OUTSAYS ▶ outsay

OUTSEE vb exceed in seeing

OUTSEEN ▶ outsee

OUTSEES ▶ outsee

OUTSELL vb be sold in greater quantities than

OUTSERT another word for > wraparound

OUTSET n beginning

OUTSETS ▶ outset

OUTSHOT n projecting part

OUTSIDE adv indicating movement to or position on the exterior ▷ adj unlikely ▷ n external area or surface

OUTSIN vb sin more than

OUTSING vb sing better or louder than

OUTSINS ▶ outsin

OUTSIT vb sit longer than

OUTSITS ▶ outsit

OUTSIZE adj larger than normal ▷ n outsize garment

OUTSOAR vb fly higher than

OUTSOLD ▶ outsell

OUTSOLE n outermost sole of a shoe

OUTSPAN vb relax

OUTSPED > outspeed

OUTSTAY vb overstay

OUTSTEP vb step farther than

OUTSULK vb outdo in sulking

OUTSUM vb add up to more than

OUTSUMS ▶ outsum

OUTSUNG ▶ outsing

OUTSWAM ▶ outswim

OUTSWIM vb outdo in swimming

OUTSWUM ▶ outswim

OUTTAKE n unreleased take from a recording session, film, or TV programme ▷ vb take out

OUTTALK vb talk more, longer, or louder than (someone)

OUTTASK vb assign task to staff outside organization

OUTTELL vb make known

OUTTOLD ▶ outtell

OUTTOOK ▶ outtake

OUTTOP vb rise higher than

OUTTOPS ▶ outtop

OUTTROT vb exceed at trotting

OUTTURN same as ▶ output

OUTVIE vb outdo in competition

OUTVIED ▶ outvie

OUTVIES ▶ outvie

OUTVOTE vb defeat by getting more votes than

OUTWAIT vb wait longer than

OUTWALK vb walk farther or longer than

OUTWAR vb surpass or

exceed in warfare

OUTWARD same as > outwards

OUTWARS ▶ outwar

OUTWASH n mass of gravel carried and deposited by the water derived from melting glaciers

OUTWEAR vb use up or destroy by wearing

OUTWEED vb root out

OUTWEEP vb outdo in weeping

OUTWELL vb pour out

OUTWENT ▶ outgo

OUTWEPT ▶ outweep

OUTWICK vb move one curling stone by striking with another

OUTWILE vb surpass in cunning

OUTWILL vb demonstrate stronger will than

OUTWIN vb get out of

OUTWIND vb unwind

OUTWING vb surpass in flying

OUTWINS ▶ outwin

OUTWISH vb surpass in wishing

OUTWIT vb get the better of (someone) by cunning

OUTWITH prep outside

OUTWITS ▶ outwit

OUTWON ▶ outwin

OUTWORE ▶ outwear

OUTWORK n defences which lie outside main defensive works ▷ vb work better, harder, etc, than

OUTWORN adj no longer in use

OUTWRIT > outwrite

OUTYELL vb outdo in yelling

OUTYELP vb outdo in yelping

OUVERT adj open

OUVERTE feminine form of ▶ ouvert

OUVRAGE n work

OUVRIER n worker

OUZEL n type of bird

OUZELS ▶ ouzel

OUZO n strong aniseed-flavoured spirit from Greece

OUZOS ▶ ouzo

OVA ▶ ovum

OVAL adj egg-shaped ▷ n anything that is oval in shape

OVALITY ▶ oval

OVALLY ▶ oval

OVALS ▶ oval

OVARIAL ▸ ovary

OVARIAN ▸ ovary

OVARIES ▸ ovary

OVARY *n* female egg-producing organ

OVATE *adj* shaped like an egg ▷ *vb* give ovation

OVATED ▸ ovate

OVATELY ▸ ovate

OVATES ▸ ovate

OVATING ▸ ovate

OVATION *n* enthusiastic round of applause

OVATOR ▸ ovate

OVATORS ▸ ovate

OVEL *n* mourner, esp during the first seven days after a death

OVELS ▸ ovel

OVEN *n* heated compartment or container for cooking or for drying or firing ceramics ▷ *vb* cook in an oven

OVENED ▸ oven

OVENING ▸ oven

OVENS ▸ oven

OVER *adv* indicating position on the top of, amount greater than, etc ▷ *adj* finished ▷ *n* (in cricket) series of six balls bowled from one end ▷ *vb* jump over

OVERACT *vb* act in an exaggerated way

OVERAGE *adj* beyond a specified age ▷ *n* amount beyond given limit

OVERALL *adv* in total ▷ *n* coat-shaped protective garment ▷ *adj* from one end to the other

OVERAPT *adj* tending excessively

OVERARM *adv* with the arm above the shoulder ▷ *adj* bowled, thrown, or performed with the arm raised above the shoulder ▷ *vb* throw (a ball) overarm

OVERATE ▸ overeat

OVERAWE *vb* affect (someone) with an overpowering sense of awe

OVERBED *adj* fitting over bed

OVERBET *vb* bet too much

OVERBID *vb* bid for more tricks than one can expect to win ▷ *n* bid higher than someone else's bid

OVERBIG *adj* too big

OVERBUY *vb* buy too much or too many

OVERBY *adv* Scots expression meaning over the road or across the way

OVERCOY *adj* too modest

OVERCUT *vb* cut too much

OVERDID ▸ overdo

OVERDO *vb* do to excess

OVERDOG *n* person or side in an advantageous position

OVERDRY *vb* dry too much

OVERDUB *vb* add (new sounds) to a tape so that the old and the new sounds can be heard ▷ *n* sound or series of sounds added by this method

OVERDUE *adj* still due after the time allowed

OVERDYE *vb* dye (a fabric, yarn, etc) excessively

OVEREAT *vb* eat more than is necessary or healthy

OVERED ▸ over

OVEREGG *vb* exaggerate absurdly

OVEREYE *vb* survey

OVERFAR *adv* too far

OVERFAT *adj* too fat

OVERFED > overfeed

OVERFIT *adj* too fit

OVERFLY *vb* fly over (a territory) or past (a point)

OVERGET *vb* overtake

OVERGO *vb* go beyond

OVERGOT ▸ overget

OVERHIT *vb* hit too strongly

OVERHOT *adj* too hot

OVERING ▸ over

OVERJOY *vb* give great delight to

OVERLAP *vb* share part of the same space or period of time (as) ▷ *n* area overlapping

OVERLAX *adj* too lax

OVERLAY *vb* cover with a thin layer ▷ *n* something that is laid over something else

OVERLET *vb* let to too many

OVERLIE *vb* lie on or cover (something or someone)

OVERLIT > overlight

OVERLY *adv* excessively

OVERMAN *vb* provide with too many staff ▷ *n* man who oversees others

OVERMEN ▸ overman

OVERMIX *vb* mix too much

OVERNET *vb* cover with net

OVERNEW *adj* too new

OVERPAY *vb* pay (someone) at too high a rate

OVERPLY *vb* ply too much

OVERRAN ▸ overrun

OVERRED *vb* paint over in red

OVERREN *same as* **▸ overrun**

OVERRUN *vb* conquer rapidly ▷ *n* act or an instance of overrunning

OVERS ▸ over

OVERSAD *adj* too sad

OVERSAW ▸ oversee

OVERSEA *same as* **> overseas**

OVERSEE *vb* watch over from a position of authority

OVERSET *vb* disturb or upset

OVERSEW *vb* sew (two edges) with stitches that pass over them both

OVERSOW *vb* sow again after first sowing

OVERSUP *vb* sup too much

OVERT *adj* open, not hidden

OVERTAX *vb* put too great a strain on

OVERTIP *vb* give too much money as a tip

OVERTLY ▸ overt

OVERTOP *vb* exceed in height

OVERUSE *vb* use excessively ▷ *n* excessive use

OVERWET *vb* make too wet

OVIBOS *n* type of ox

OVICIDE *n* killing of sheep

OVIDUCT *n* tube through which eggs are conveyed from the ovary

OVIFORM *adj* shaped like an egg

OVINE *adj* of or like a sheep ▷ *n* member of sheep family

OVINES ▸ ovine

OVIPARA *n* all oviparous animals

OVISAC *n* capsule or sac, such as an ootheca, in which egg cells are produced

OVISACS ▸ ovisac

OVIST *n* person believing ovum contains all subsequent generations

OVISTS ▸ ovist

OVOID *adj* egg-shaped ▷ *n* something that is ovoid

OVOIDAL *adj* ovoid ▷ *n* something that is ovoid

O

OVOIDS ▶ ovoid

OVOLI ▶ ovolo

OVOLO n convex moulding having a cross section in the form of a quarter of a circle or ellipse

Two Os on your rack can normally be dealt with; three can get a bit much, but this word for a kind of architectural moulding can handle them. Note that the plural can be **ovolos** or **ovoli**.

OVOLOS ▶ ovolo

OVONIC adj using particular electronic storage batteries

OVONICS n science of ovonic equipment

OVULAR ▶ ovule

OVULARY ▶ ovule

OVULATE vb produce or release an egg cell from an ovary

OVULE n plant part that contains the egg cell and becomes the seed after fertilization

OVULES ▶ ovule

OVUM n unfertilized egg cell

OW interj exclamation of pain

OWCHE same as ▶ ouch

OWCHES ▶ owche

OWE vb be obliged to pay (a sum of money) to (a person)

OWED ▶ owe

OWELTY n equality, esp in financial transactions

OWER Scots word for ▶ over

OWERBY adv over there

OWES ▶ owe

OWING ▶ owe

OWL n night bird of prey ▷ vb act like an owl

OWLED ▶ owl

OWLER vb smuggler

OWLERS ▶ owler

OWLERY n place where owls live

OWLET n young or nestling owl

OWLETS ▶ owlet

OWLIER ▶ owly

OWLIEST ▶ owly

OWLING ▶ owl

OWLISH adj like an owl

OWLLIKE ▶ owl

OWLS ▶ owl

OWLY same as ▶ owlish

OWN adj used to emphasize possession ▷ pron thing(s)

belonging to a particular person ▷ vb possess

OWNABLE adj able to be owned

OWNED ▶ own

OWNER n person who owns

OWNERS ▶ owner

OWNING ▶ own

OWNS ▶ own

OWRE same as ▶ ower

OWRELAY Scots form of ▶ overlay

OWRES ▶ owre

OWRIE same as ▶ oorie

OWRIER ▶ owrie

OWRIEST ▶ owrie

OWSE Scots form of ▶ ox

OWSEN Scots word for ▶ oxen

OWT dialect word for > anything

OWTS ▶ owt

OX n castrated bull

OXALATE n salt or ester of oxalic acid ▷ vb treat with oxalate

OXALIC adj as in **oxalic acid** poisonous acid found in many plants

OXALIS n type of plant

OXAZINE n type of chemical compound

OXBLOOD n dark reddish-brown colour ▷ adj of this colour

OXBOW n U-shaped piece of wood fitted around the neck of a harnessed ox and attached to the yoke

OXBOWS ▶ oxbow

OXCART n cart pulled by ox

OXCARTS ▶ oxcart

OXEN ▶ ox

OXER n high fence

OXERS ▶ oxer

OXES ▶ ox

OXEYE n daisy-like flower

OXEYES ▶ oxeye

OXFORD n type of stout laced shoe with a low heel

OXFORDS ▶ oxford

OXGANG n old measure of farmland

OXGANGS ▶ oxgang

OXGATE same as ▶ oxgang

OXGATES ▶ oxgate

OXHEAD n head of an ox

OXHEADS ▶ oxhead

OXHEART n heart-shaped cherry

OXHIDE n leather made from the hide of an ox

OXHIDES ▶ oxhide

OXID same as ▶ oxide

OXIDANT n substance that acts or is used as an oxidizing agent

OXIDASE n any of a group of enzymes that bring about biological oxidation

OXIDATE another word for ▶ oxidize

OXIDE n compound of oxygen and one other element

OXIDES ▶ oxide

OXIDIC ▶ oxide

OXIDISE same as ▶ oxidize

OXIDIZE vb combine chemically with oxygen, as in burning or rusting

OXIDS ▶ oxid

OXIES ▶ oxy

OXIM same as ▶ oxime

OXIME n type of chemical compound

OXIMES ▶ oxime

OXIMS ▶ oxim

OXLAND same as ▶ oxgang

OXLANDS ▶ oxland

OXLIKE ▶ ox

OXLIP n type of woodland plant with small drooping pale yellow flowers

OXLIPS ▶ oxlip

OXO n as in **oxo acid** acid that contains oxygen

OXONIUM n as in **oxonium compound** type of salt derived from an organic ether

OXSLIP same as ▶ oxlip

OXSLIPS ▶ oxslip

OXTAIL n tail of an ox, used in soups and stews

OXTAILS ▶ oxtail

OXTER n armpit ▷ vb grip under arm

OXTERED ▶ oxter

OXTERS ▶ oxter

OXY ▶ oxo

OXYACID n any acid that contains oxygen

OXYGEN n gaseous element essential to life and combustion

OXYGENS ▶ oxygen

OXYMEL n mixture of vinegar and honey

OXYMELS ▶ oxymel

OXYMORA > oxymoron

OXYNTIC adj of or denoting stomach cells that secrete acid

OXYPHIL n type of cell found in glands

OXYSALT *n* any salt of an oxyacid

OXYSOME *n* group of molecules

OXYTONE *adj* having an accent on the final syllable ▷ *n* oxytone word

OY *n* grandchild

OYE *same as* ▶ **oy**

OYER *n* (in the 13th century) an assize

OYERS ▶ **oyer**

OYES *same as* ▶ **oyez**

OYESES ▶ **oyes**

OYESSES ▶ **oyes**

OYEZ *interj* shouted three times by a public crier calling for attention before a proclamation ▷ *n* such a cry

OYEZES ▶ **oyez**

OYS ▶ **oy**

OYSTER *n* edible shellfish ▷ *vb* dredge for, gather, or raise oysters

OYSTERS ▶ **oyster**

OZAENA *n* inflammation of nasal mucous membrane

OZAENAS ▶ **ozaena**

OZALID *n* method of duplicating writing or illustrations

OZALIDS ▶ **ozalid**

OZEKI *n* sumo wrestling champion

OZEKIS ▶ **ozeki**

OZONATE *vb* add ozone to

OZONE *n* strong-smelling form of oxygen

OZONES ▶ **ozone**

OZONIC ▶ **ozone**

OZONIDE *n* type of unstable explosive compound

OZONISE *same as* ▶ **ozonize**

OZONIZE *vb* convert (oxygen) into ozone

OZONOUS ▶ **ozone**

OZZIE *n* hospital

OZZIES ▶ **ozzie**

O

Pp

P forms a two-letter word in front of every vowel except **U**, which makes it very useful for joining a new word to one already on the board. It also forms several three-letter words with **X**: **pax, pix, pox** (12 points each) and **pyx** (15). Other three-letter words with **P** well worth remembering are **zap, zep** and **zip** for 14 points each and **jap** for 12 points.

PA n (formerly) fortified Māori settlement

PAAL n stake driven into the ground

PAALS ▶ **paal**

PAAN n leaf of the betel tree

PAANS ▶ **paan**

PABLUM same as ▶ **pabulum**

PABLUMS ▶ **pablum**

PABULAR ▶ **pabulum**

PABULUM n food

PAC n soft shoe

PACA n large burrowing hystricomorph rodent of Central and South America

PACABLE adj easily appeased

PACAS ▶ **paca**

PACE n single step in walking ▷ vb walk up and down, esp in anxiety ▷ prep with due respect to: used to express polite disagreement

PACED ▶ **pace**

PACEMAN n (in cricket) fast bowler

PACEMEN ▶ **paceman**

PACER n horse trained to move at a special gait, esp for racing

PACERS ▶ **pacer**

PACES ▶ **pace**

PACEWAY n racecourse for trotting and pacing

PACEY adj fast-moving, quick, lively

PACHA same as ▶ **pasha**

PACHAK n fragrant roots of Asian plant

PACHAKS ▶ **pachak**

PACHAS ▶ **pacha**

PACHISI n Indian game somewhat resembling backgammon, played on a

cruciform board using six cowries as dice

PACHUCO n young Mexican living in the US, esp one of low social status who belongs to a street gang

PACIER ▶ **pacy**

PACIEST ▶ **pacy**

PACIFIC adj tending to bring peace

PACIFY vb soothe, calm

PACING ▶ **pace**

PACK vb put (clothes etc) together in a suitcase or bag ▷ n bag carried on a person's or animal's back

PACKAGE same as ▶ **packet**

PACKED adj completely filled

PACKER n person or company whose business is to pack goods, esp food

PACKERS ▶ **packer**

PACKET n small container (and contents) ▷ vb wrap up in a packet or as a packet

PACKETS ▶ **packet**

PACKING n material, such as paper or plastic, used to protect packed goods

PACKLY ▶ **pack**

PACKMAN n person carrying pack

PACKMEN ▶ **packman**

PACKS ▶ **pack**

PACKWAX n neck ligament

PACKWAY n path for pack animals

PACO n S American mammal

PACOS ▶ **paco**

PACS ▶ **pac**

PACT n formal agreement

PACTA ▶ **pactum**

PACTION vb concur with

PACTS ▶ **pact**

PACTUM n pact

PACY same as ▶ **pacey**

PAD n piece of soft material used for protection, support, absorption of liquid, etc ▷ vb protect or fill with soft material

PADANG n (in Malaysia) playing field

PADANGS ▶ **padang**

PADAUK n tropical African or Asian leguminous tree with reddish wood

PADAUKS ▶ **padauk**

PADDED ▶ **pad**

PADDER n highwayman who robs on foot

PADDERS ▶ **padder**

PADDIES ▶ **paddy**

PADDING ▶ **pad**

PADDLE n short oar with a broad blade at one or each end ▷ vb move (a canoe etc) with a paddle

PADDLED ▶ **paddle**

PADDLER ▶ **paddle**

PADDLES ▶ **paddle**

PADDOCK n small field or enclosure for horses ▷ vb place (a horse) in a paddock

PADDY n fit of temper

PADELLA n type of candle

PADI same as ▶ **paddy**

PADIS ▶ **padi**

PADKOS n snacks and provisions for a journey

PADLE another name for > **lumpfish**

PADLES ▶ **padle**

PADLOCK n detachable lock with a hinged hoop fastened over a ring on the object to be secured ▷ vb fasten (something) with a padlock

PADMA n type of lotus

PADMAS ▶ padma

PADNAG n ambling horse

PADNAGS ▶ padnag

PADOUK same as ▶ **padauk**

PADOUKS ▶ padouk

PADRE n chaplain to the armed forces

PADRES ▶ padre

PADRI ▶ padre

PADRONE n owner or proprietor of an inn, esp in Italy

PADRONI ▶ padrone

PADS ▶ pad

PADSAW n small narrow saw used for cutting curves

PADSAWS ▶ padsaw

PADSHAH same as
> **padishah**

PAEAN n song of triumph or thanksgiving

PAEANS ▶ paean

PAEDO n paedophile

PAEDOS ▶ paedo

PAELLA n Spanish dish of rice, chicken, shellfish, and vegetables

PAELLAS ▶ paella

PAENULA n ancient Roman cloak

PAEON n metrical foot of four syllables, with one long one and three short ones in any order

PAEONIC ▶ paeon

PAEONS ▶ paeon

PAEONY same as ▶ **peony**

PAESAN n fellow countryman

PAESANI ▶ paesano

PAESANO n Italian-American man

PAESANS ▶ paesan

PAGAN adj not belonging to one of the world's main religions ▷ n pagan person

PAGANS ▶ pagan

PAGE n (one side of) sheet of paper forming a book etc ▷ vb summon (someone) by bleeper or loudspeaker, in order to pass on a message

PAGEANT n parade or display of people in costume, usu illustrating a scene from history

PAGEBOY n hairstyle in which the hair is smooth and the same medium length with the ends curled under

PAGED ▶ page

PAGEFUL n amount (of text,

etc) that a page will hold

PAGER n small electronic device, capable of receiving short messages

PAGERS ▶ pager

PAGES ▶ page

PAGINAL adj page-for-page

PAGING ▶ page

PAGINGS ▶ page

PAGLE same as ▶ **paigle**

PAGLES ▶ pagle

PAGOD n oriental idol

PAGODA n pyramid-shaped Asian temple or tower

PAGODAS ▶ pagoda

PAGODS ▶ pagod

PAGRI n type of turban

PAGRIS ▶ pagri

PAGURID same as
> **pagurian**

PAH same as ▶ **pa**

PAHLAVI n Iranian coin

PAHS ▶ pah

PAID ▶ pay

PAIDLE Scots variant of **paddle** n

PAIDLES ▶ paidle

PAIGLE n cowslip

PAIGLES ▶ paigle

PAIK vb thump or whack

PAIKED ▶ paik

PAIKING ▶ paik

PAIKS ▶ paik

PAIL n bucket

PAILFUL same as ▶ **pail**

PAILLON n thin leaf of metal

PAILS ▶ pail

PAIN n physical or mental suffering ▷ vb cause (someone) mental or physical suffering

PAINCH Scots variant of ▶ **paunch**

PAINED adj having or suggesting pain or distress

PAINFUL adj causing pain or distress

PAINIM n heathen or pagan

PAINIMS ▶ painim

PAINING ▶ pain

PAINS pl n care or trouble

PAINT n coloured substance, spread on a surface with a brush or roller ▷ vb colour or coat with paint

PAINTED ▶ paint

PAINTER n rope at the front of a boat, for tying it up

PAINTS ▶ paint

PAINTY ▶ paint

PAIOCK obsolete word for ▶ **peacock**

PAIOCKE obsolete word for ▶ **peacock**

PAIOCKS ▶ paiock

PAIR n set of two things matched for use together ▷ vb group or be grouped in twos

PAIRE obsolete spelling of ▶ **pair**

PAIRED ▶ pair

PAIRER ▶ pair

PAIRES ▶ paire

PAIREST ▶ pair

PAIRIAL same as ▶ **prial**

PAIRING ▶ pair

PAIRS ▶ pair

PAIS n country

PAISA n monetary unit of Bangladesh, Bhutan, India, Nepal, and Pakistan worth one hundredth of a rupee

PAISAN n fellow countryman

PAISANA n female peasant

PAISANO n friend

PAISANS ▶ paisan

PAISAS ▶ paisa

PAISE ▶ paisa

PAISLEY n pattern of small curving shapes with intricate detailing, usually printed in bright colours

PAJAMA same as ▶ **pyjama**

PAJAMAS ▶ pajama

PAJOCK obsolete word for ▶ **peacock**

PAJOCKE obsolete word for ▶ **peacock**

PAJOCKS ▶ pajock

PAKAHI n acid land that is unsuitable for cultivation

PAKAHIS ▶ pakahi

PAKAPOO n Chinese lottery with betting slips marked with Chinese characters

PAKEHA n person of European descent, as distinct from a Māori

PAKEHAS ▶ pakeha

PAKFONG same as
> **packfong**

PAKIHI n area of swampy infertile land

PAKIHIS ▶ pakihi

PAKKA same as ▶ **pukka**

PAKOKO n small freshwater fish

PAKOKOS ▶ pakoko

PAKORA n Indian dish consisting of pieces of vegetable, chicken, etc, dipped in a spiced batter and deep-fried

P

PAKORAS ▸ pakora
PAKTONG same as > **pakthong**
PAL n friend ▷ vb associate as friends
PALABRA n word
PALACE n residence of a king, bishop, etc
PALACED adj having palaces
PALACES ▸ palace
PALADIN n knight who did battle for a monarch
PALAGI n (in Samoa) European
PALAGIS ▸ palagi
PALAIS n dance hall
PALAMA n webbing on bird's feet
PALAMAE ▸ palama
PALAPA n open-sided tropical building
PALAPAS ▸ palapa
PALAS n East Indian tree
PALASES ▸ palas
PALATAL adj of or relating to the palate ▷ n bony plate that forms the palate
PALATE n roof of the mouth ▷ vb perceive by taste
PALATED ▸ palate
PALATES ▸ palate
PALAVER n time-wasting fuss ▷ vb (often used humorously) have a conference
PALAY n type of rubber
PALAYS ▸ palay
PALAZZI ▸ palazzo
PALAZZO n Italian palace
PALE adj light, whitish ▷ vb become pale ▷ n wooden or metal post used in fences
PALEA n inner of two bracts surrounding each floret in a grass spikelet
PALEAE ▸ palea
PALEAL ▸ palea
PALEATE adj having scales
PALED ▸ pale
PALELY ▸ pale
PALER ▸ pale
PALES ▸ pale
PALEST ▸ pale
PALET n perpendicular band on escutcheon
PALETOT n loose outer garment
PALETS ▸ palet
PALETTE n artist's flat board for mixing colours on
PALFREY n light saddle horse, esp ridden by women

PALIER ▸ paly
PALIEST ▸ paly
PALIKAR n Greek soldier in the war of independence against Turkey
PALING n wooden or metal post used in fences
PALINGS ▸ paling
PALINKA n type of apricot brandy, originating in Central and Eastern Europe
PALISH adj rather pale
PALKEE n covered Oriental litter
PALKEES ▸ palkee
PALKI same as ▸ **palkee**
PALKIS ▸ palki
PALL n cloth spread over a coffin ▷ vb become boring
PALLA n ancient Roman cloak
PALLAE ▸ palla
PALLAH n S African antelope
PALLAHS ▸ pallah
PALLED ▸ pall
PALLET same as ▸ **palette**
PALLETS ▸ pallet
PALLIA ▸ pallium
PALLIAL adj relating to cerebral cortex
PALLID adj pale, esp because ill or weak
PALLIED ▸ pally
PALLIER ▸ pally
PALLIES ▸ pally
PALLING ▸ pall
PALLIUM n garment worn by men in ancient Greece or Rome, made by draping a large rectangular cloth about the body
PALLONE n Italian ball game
PALLOR n paleness of complexion, usually because of illness, shock, or fear
PALLORS ▸ pallor
PALLS ▸ pall
PALLY adj on friendly terms ▷ vb as in **pally up** to become friends with
PALM n inner surface of the hand ▷ vb conceal in or about the hand, as in sleight-of-hand tricks
PALMAR adj of or relating to the palm of the hand
PALMARY adj worthy of praise
PALMATE adj shaped like an open hand

PALMED ▸ palm
PALMER n (in Medieval Europe) pilgrim bearing a palm branch as a sign of his visit to the Holy Land
PALMERS ▸ palmer
PALMFUL n amount that can be held in the palm of a hand
PALMIE n palmtop computer
PALMIER ▸ palmy
PALMIES ▸ palmie
PALMIET n South African rush
PALMING ▸ palm
PALMIST > palmistry
PALMS ▸ palm
PALMTOP adj small enough to be held in the hand ▷ n computer small enough to be held in the hand
PALMY adj successful, prosperous and happy
PALMYRA n tall tropical Asian palm
PALOLO n polychaete worm of the S Pacific Ocean
PALOLOS ▸ palolo
PALOOKA n stupid or clumsy boxer or other person
PALP n either of a pair of sensory appendages that arise from the mouthparts of crustaceans and insects ▷ vb feel
PALPAL ▸ palp
PALPATE vb examine (an area of the body) by touching ▷ adj of, relating to, or possessing a palp or palps
PALPED ▸ palp
PALPI ▸ palpus
PALPING ▸ palp
PALPS ▸ palp
PALPUS same as ▸ **palp**
PALS ▸ pal
PALSHIP n state of being pals
PALSIED ▸ palsy
PALSIER ▸ palsy
PALSIES ▸ palsy
PALSY n paralysis ▷ vb paralyse ▷ adj friendly
PALTER vb act or talk insincerely
PALTERS ▸ palter
PALTRY adj insignificant
PALUDAL adj of, relating to, or produced by marshes
PALUDIC adj of malaria

PALY adj vertically striped

PAM n knave of clubs

PAMPA n grassland area

PAMPAS pl n vast grassy plains in S America

PAMPEAN ▶ pampas

PAMPER vb treat (someone) with great indulgence, spoil

PAMPERO n dry cold wind in South America blowing across the pampas from the south or southwest

PAMPERS ▶ pamper

PAMPOEN n pumpkin

PAMS ▶ pam

PAN n wide long-handled metal container used in cooking ▷ vb sift gravel from (a river) in a pan to search for gold

PANACEA n remedy for all diseases or problems

PANACHE n confident elegant style

PANADA n mixture of flour, water, etc, or of breadcrumbs soaked in milk, used as a thickening

PANADAS ▶ panada

PANAMA n hat made of the plaited leaves of the jipijapa plant

PANAMAS ▶ panama

PANARY n storehouse for bread

PANAX n genus of perennial herbs

PANAXES ▶ panax

PANCAKE n thin flat circle of fried batter ▷ vb cause (an aircraft) to make a pancake landing or (of an aircraft) to make a pancake landing

PANCE n pansy

PANCES ▶ pance

PANCHAX n brightly coloured tropical Asian cyprinodont fish

PAND n valance

PANDA n large black-and-white bearlike mammal from China

PANDANI n tropical tree

PANDAR vb act as a pimp

PANDARS ▶ pandar

PANDAS ▶ panda

PANDECT n treatise covering all aspects of a particular subject

PANDER vb indulge (a person his or her desires) ▷ n person who procures a sexual partner for someone

PANDERS ▶ pander

PANDIED ▶ pandy

PANDIES ▶ pandy

PANDIT same as ▶ pundit

PANDITS ▶ pandit

PANDOOR same as ▶ pandour

PANDORA n handsome red sea bream

PANDORE another word for ▶ bandore

PANDOUR n one of an 18th-century force of Croatian soldiers in the Austrian service, notorious for their brutality

PANDS ▶ pand

PANDURA n ancient stringed instrument

PANDY n (in schools) stroke on the hand with a strap as a punishment ▷ vb punish with such strokes

PANE n sheet of glass in a window or door ▷ adj (of fish, meat, etc) dipped or rolled in breadcrumbs before cooking

PANED ▶ pane

PANEER n soft white cheese, used in Indian cookery

PANEERS ▶ paneer

PANEITY n state of being bread

PANEL n flat distinct section of a larger surface, for example in a door ▷ vb cover or decorate with panels ▷ adj of a group acting as a panel

PANELED ▶ panel

PANELS ▶ panel

PANES ▶ pane

PANFISH n small food fish

PANFRY vb fry in a pan

PANFUL ▶ pan

PANFULS ▶ pan

PANG n sudden sharp feeling of pain or sadness ▷ vb cause pain

PANGA n broad heavy knife of E Africa, used as a tool or weapon

PANGAMY n unrestricted mating

PANGAS ▶ panga

PANGED ▶ pang

PANGEN same as ▶ pangene

PANGENE n hypothetical particle of protoplasm

PANGENS ▶ pangen

PANGING ▶ pang

PANGRAM n sentence incorporating all the letters of the alphabet

PANGS ▶ pang

PANIC n sudden overwhelming fear, often affecting a whole group of people ▷ vb feel or cause to feel panic ▷ adj of or resulting from such terror

PANICK old word for ▶ panic

PANICKS ▶ panick

PANICKY ▶ panic

PANICLE n loose, irregularly branched cluster of flowers

PANICS ▶ panic

PANICUM n type of grass

PANIER same as ▶ pannier

PANIERS ▶ panier

PANIM n heathen or pagan

PANIMS ▶ panim

PANING ▶ pane

PANINI ▶ panino

PANINIS ▶ panini

PANINO n Italian sandwich

PANISC n faun; attendant of Pan

PANISCS ▶ panisc

PANISK same as ▶ panisc

PANISKS ▶ panisk

PANKO n flaky breadcrumbs used as a coating in Japanese cookery

PANKOS ▶ panko

PANNAGE n pasturage for pigs, esp in a forest

PANNE n lightweight velvet fabric

PANNED ▶ pan

PANNER ▶ pan

PANNERS ▶ pan

PANNES ▶ panne

PANNICK old spelling of the noun ▶ panic

PANNIER n bag fixed on the back of a cycle

PANNING ▶ pan

PANNOSE adj like felt

PANNUS n inflammatory fleshy lesion on the surface of the eye

PANOCHA n coarse grade of sugar made in Mexico

PANOCHE n type of dark sugar

PANOPLY n magnificent array

PANPIPE n wind instrument

PANS ▶ pan

PANSIED adj covered with pansies

PANSIES ▶ pansy

PANSY n small garden

P

flower with velvety purple, yellow, or white petals

PANT vb breathe quickly and noisily during or after exertion ▷ n act of panting

PANTED ▶ pant

PANTER n person who pants

PANTERS ▶ panter

PANTHER n leopard, esp a black one

PANTIE same as ▶ panty

PANTIES pl n women's underpants

PANTILE n roofing tile with an S-shaped cross section ▷ vb tile roof with pantiles

PANTINE n pasteboard puppet

PANTING ▶ pant

PANTLER n pantry servant

PANTO same as > pantomime

PANTON n type of horseshoe

PANTONS ▶ panton

PANTOS ▶ panto

PANTOUM n verse form

PANTRY n small room or cupboard for storing food

PANTS pl n undergarment for the lower part of the body

PANTUN n Malayan poetry

PANTUNS ▶ pantun

PANTY n woman's undergarment

PANZER n German tank

PANZERS ▶ panzer

PAOLI ▶ paolo

PAOLO n Italian silver coin

PAP n soft food for babies or invalids ▷ vb (of the paparazzi) to follow and photograph (a famous person) ▷ vb feed with pap

PAPA n father

PAPABLE adj suitable for papacy

PAPACY n position or term of office of a pope

PAPADAM same as > poppadom

PAPADOM same as > poppadom

PAPADUM same as > poppadom

PAPAIN n proteolytic enzyme occurring in the unripe fruit of the papaya tree

PAPAINS ▶ papain

PAPAL adj of the pope

PAPALLY ▶ papal

PAPAS ▶ papa

PAPAUMA n New Zealand word for broadleaf

PAPAW same as ▶ papaya

PAPAWS ▶ papaw

PAPAYA n large sweet West Indian fruit

PAPAYAN ▶ papaya

PAPAYAS ▶ papaya

PAPE n spiritual father

PAPER n material made in sheets from wood pulp or other fibres ▷ vb cover (walls) with wallpaper

PAPERED ▶ paper

PAPERER ▶ paper

PAPERS ▶ paper

PAPERY adj like paper, esp in thinness, flimsiness, or dryness

PAPES ▶ pape

PAPHIAN n prostitute

PAPILIO n butterfly

PAPILLA n small projection of tissue at the base of a hair, tooth, or feather

PAPOOSE n Native American child

PAPPED ▶ pap

PAPPI ▶ pappus

PAPPIER ▶ pappy

PAPPIES ▶ pappy

PAPPING ▶ pap

PAPPOSE ▶ pappus

PAPPOUS ▶ pappus

PAPPUS n ring of fine feathery hairs surrounding the fruit in composite plants, such as the thistle

PAPPY adj resembling pap

PAPRICA same as ▶ paprika

PAPRIKA n mild powdered seasoning made from red peppers

PAPS ▶ pap

PAPULA same as ▶ papule

PAPULAE ▶ papula

PAPULAR ▶ papule

PAPULE n small solid usually round elevation of the skin

PAPULES ▶ papule

PAPYRAL ▶ papyrus

PAPYRI ▶ papyrus

PAPYRUS n tall water plant

PAR n usual or average condition ▷ vb play (a golf hole) in par

PARA n paratrooper

PARABEN n carcinogenic ester

PARABLE n story that illustrates a religious teaching ▷ vb write parable

PARACME n phase where fever lessens

PARADE n procession or march ▷ vb display or flaunt

PARADED ▶ parade

PARADER ▶ parade

PARADES ▶ parade

PARADOR n state-run hotel in Spain

PARADOS n bank behind a trench or other fortification, giving protection from being fired on from the rear

PARADOX n person or thing made up of contradictory elements

PARAE n type of fish

PARAFLE same as > paraffle

PARAGE n type of feudal land tenure

PARAGES ▶ parage

PARAGON n model of perfection ▷ vb equal or surpass

PARAMO n high plateau in the Andes between the tree line and the permanent snow line

PARAMOS ▶ paramo

PARANG n short stout straight-edged knife used by the Dyaks of Borneo

PARANGS ▶ parang

PARANYM n euphemism

PARAPET n low wall or railing along the edge of a balcony or roof ▷ vb provide with a parapet

PARAPH n flourish after a signature, originally to prevent forgery ▷ vb embellish signature

PARAPHS ▶ paraph

PARAS ▶ para

PARASOL n umbrella-like sunshade

PARATHA n (in Indian cookery) flat unleavened bread, resembling a small nan bread, that is fried on a griddle

PARAZOA > parazoan

PARBAKE vb partially bake

PARBOIL vb boil until partly cooked

PARCEL n something wrapped up, package ▷ vb wrap up

PARCELS ▶ parcel

PARCH vb make very hot and dry
PARCHED ▸ **parch**
PARCHES ▸ **parch**
PARD n leopard or panther
PARDAH same as ▸ **purdah**
PARDAHS ▸ **pardah**
PARDAL variant spelling of ▸ **pardale**
PARDALE n leopard
PARDALS same as ▸ **pardal**
PARDED adj having spots
PARDEE adv certainly
PARDI same as ▸ **pardee**
PARDIE same as ▸ **pardee**
PARDINE adj spotted
PARDNER n friend or partner: used as a term of address
PARDON vb forgive, excuse ▷ n forgiveness ▷ interj sorry ▷ sentence substitute sorry
PARDONS ▸ **pardon**
PARDS ▸ **pard**
PARDY same as ▸ **pardee**
PARE vb cut off the skin or top layer of
PARED ▸ **pare**
PAREIRA n root of a South American menispermaceous climbing plant
PARELLA n type of lichen
PARELLE same as ▸ **parella**
PARENT n father or mother ▷ vb raise offspring
PARENTS ▸ **parent**
PAREO same as ▸ **pareu**
PAREOS ▸ **pareu**
PARER ▸ **pare**
PARERA n New Zealand duck with grey-edged brown feathers
PARERAS ▸ **parera**
PARERGA > **parergon**
PARERS ▸ **pare**
PARES ▸ **pare**
PARESES ▸ **paresis**
PARESIS n incomplete or slight paralysis of motor functions
PARETIC ▸ **paresis**
PAREU n rectangle of fabric worn by Polynesians as a skirt or loincloth
PAREUS ▸ **pareu**
PAREV adj containing neither meat nor milk products and so fit for use with either milk or meat dishes
PAREVE same as ▸ **parev**

PARFAIT n dessert consisting of layers of ice cream, fruit, and sauce, topped with whipped cream, and served in a tall glass
PARGANA n Indian sub-district
PARGE vb coat with plaster
PARGED ▸ **parge**
PARGES ▸ **parge**
PARGET n plaster, mortar, etc, used to line chimney flues or cover walls ▷ vb cover or decorate with parget
PARGETS ▸ **parget**
PARGING ▸ **parge**
PARGO n sea bream
PARGOS ▸ **pargo**
PARIAH n social outcast
PARIAHS ▸ **pariah**
PARIAL n pair royal of playing cards
PARIALS ▸ **parial**
PARIAN n type of marble or porcelain
PARIANS ▸ **parian**
PARIES n wall of an organ or bodily cavity
PARING n piece pared off
PARINGS ▸ **paring**
PARIS n type of herb
PARISES ▸ **paris**
PARISH n area that has its own church and a priest or pastor
PARISON n unshaped mass of glass before it is moulded into its final form
PARITOR n official who summons witnesses
PARITY n equality or equivalence
PARK n area of open land for recreational use by the public ▷ vb stop and leave (a vehicle) temporarily
PARKA n large waterproof jacket with a hood
PARKADE n building used as a car park
PARKAS ▸ **parka**
PARKED ▸ **park**
PARKEE n Eskimo outer garment
PARKEES ▸ **parkee**
PARKER ▸ **park**
PARKERS ▸ **park**
PARKI same as ▸ **parka**
PARKIE n park keeper
PARKIER ▸ **parky**
PARKIES ▸ **parkie**

PARKIN n moist spicy ginger cake usually containing oatmeal
PARKING ▸ **park**
PARKINS ▸ **parkin**
PARKIS ▸ **parki**
PARKISH adj like a park
PARKLY adj having many parks or resembling a park
PARKOUR n sport of running in urban areas performing gymnastics on manmade obstacles
PARKS ▸ **park**
PARKWAY n (in the US and Canada) wide road planted with trees, turf, etc
PARKY adj (of the weather) chilly
PARLAY vb stake (winnings from one bet) on a subsequent wager ▷ n bet in which winnings from one wager are staked on another, or a series of such bets
PARLAYS ▸ **parlay**
PARLE vb speak
PARLED ▸ **parle**
PARLES ▸ **parle**
PARLEY n meeting between leaders or representatives of opposing forces to discuss terms ▷ vb have a parley
PARLEYS ▸ **parley**
PARLIES pl n small Scottish biscuits
PARLING ▸ **parle**
PARLOR same as ▸ **parlour**
PARLORS ▸ **parlor**
PARLOUR n living room for receiving visitors
PARLOUS adj dire ▷ adv extremely
PARLY n short form of parliament
PARODIC ▸ **parody**
PARODOI n path leading to Greek theatre
PARODOS n ode sung by Greek chorus
PARODY n exaggerated and amusing imitation of someone else's style ▷ vb make a parody of
PAROL n (formerly) pleadings in an action when expressed by word of mouth ▷ adj (of a contract, lease, etc) made orally or in writing but not under seal
PAROLE n early freeing of a

P

prisoner on condition that he or she behaves well ▷ *vb* put on parole

PAROLED ▶ **parole**

PAROLEE ▶ **parole**

PAROLES ▶ **parole**

PAROLS ▶ **parol**

PARONYM *n* cognate word

PARORE *n* type of fish found around Australia and New Zealand

PARORES ▶ **parore**

PAROTIC *adj* situated near the ear

PAROTID *adj* relating to or situated near the parotid gland ▷ *n* parotid gland

PAROTIS *n* parotid gland

PAROUS *adj* having given birth

PARP *vb* make a honking sound

PARPANE *n* parapet on bridge

PARPED ▶ **parp**

PARPEN *same as* ▶ **parpend**

PARPEND *same as* ▶ **perpend**

PARPENS ▶ **parpen**

PARPENT *n* parapet on bridge

PARPING ▶ **parp**

PARPS ▶ **parp**

PARQUET *n* floor covering made of wooden blocks arranged in a geometric pattern ▷ *vb* cover with parquet

PARR *n* salmon up to two years of age

PARRA *n* tourist or non-resident on a beach

PARRAL *same as* ▶ **parrel**

PARRALS ▶ **parral**

PARRAS ▶ **parra**

PARRED ▶ **par**

PARREL *n* ring that holds the jaws of a boom to the mast but lets it slide up and down

PARRELS ▶ **parrel**

PARRIED ▶ **parry**

PARRIER ▶ **parry**

PARRIES ▶ **parry**

PARRING ▶ **par**

PARROCK *vb* put (an animal) in a small field

PARROT *n* tropical bird with a short hooked beak and an ability to imitate human speech ▷ *vb* repeat (someone else's words) without thinking

PARROTS ▶ **parrot**

PARROTY *adj* like a parrot; chattering

PARRS ▶ **parr**

PARRY *vb* ward off (an attack) ▷ *n* parrying

PARS ▶ **par**

PARSE *vb* analyse (a sentence) in terms of grammar

PARSEC *n* unit of astronomical distance

PARSECS ▶ **parsec**

PARSED ▶ **parse**

PARSER *n* program or part of a program that interprets input to a computer by recognizing key words or analysing sentence structure

PARSERS ▶ **parser**

PARSES ▶ **parse**

PARSING ▶ **parse**

PARSLEY *n* herb used for seasoning and decorating food ▷ *vb* garnish with parsley

PARSNEP *same as* ▶ **parsnip**

PARSNIP *n* long tapering cream-coloured root vegetable

PARSON *n* Anglican parish priest

PARSONS ▶ **parson**

PART *n* one of the pieces that make up a whole ▷ *vb* divide or separate

PARTAKE *vb* take (food or drink)

PARTAN *Scottish word for* ▶ **crab**

PARTANS ▶ **partan**

PARTED *adj* divided almost to the base

PARTER *n* thing that parts

PARTERS ▶ **parter**

PARTI *n* concept of architectural design

PARTIAL *adj* not complete ▷ *n* any of the component tones of a single musical sound, including both those that belong to the harmonic series of the sound and those that do not ▷ *vb* remove (a factor) from a set of statistics

PARTIED ▶ **party**

PARTIER *n* person who parties

PARTIES ▶ **party**

PARTIM *adv* in part

PARTING *same as* ▶ **part**

PARTIS ▶ **parti**

PARTITA *n* type of suite

PARTITE *adj* composed of or divided into a specified number of parts

PARTLET *n* woman's garment covering the neck and shoulders

PARTLY *adv* not completely

PARTNER *n* either member of a couple in a relationship or activity ▷ *vb* be the partner of

PARTON *n* hypothetical elementary particle postulated as a constituent of neutrons and protons

PARTONS ▶ **parton**

PARTOOK ▶ **partake**

PARTS *pl n* abilities or talents

PARTURE *n* departure

PARTWAY *adv* some of the way

PARTY *n* social gathering for pleasure ▷ *vb* celebrate, have fun ▷ *adj* (of a shield) divided vertically into two colours, metals, or furs

PARTYER *n* person who parties

PARULIS *another name for* ▶ **gumboil**

PARURA *same as* ▶ **parure**

PARURAS ▶ **parura**

PARURE *n* set of jewels or other ornaments

PARURES ▶ **parure**

PARVE *same as* ▶ **parev**

PARVENU *n* person newly risen to a position of power or wealth ▷ *adj* of or characteristic of a parvenu

PARVIS *n* court or portico in front of a building, esp a church

PARVISE *same as* ▶ **parvis**

PARVO *n* disease of cattle and dogs

PARVOS ▶ **parvo**

PAS *n* dance step or movement, esp in ballet

PASCAL *n* unit of pressure

PASCALS ▶ **pascal**

PASCHAL *adj* of the Passover or Easter ▷ *n* Passover or Easter

PASCUAL *adj* relating to pasture

PASE *n* movement of the cape or muleta by a matador to attract the bull's attention and guide its attack

PASEAR vb go for a rambling walk

PASEARS ▶ pasear

PASELA same as ▶ bonsela

PASELAS ▶ pasela

PASEO n bullfighters' procession

PASEOS ▶ paseo

PASES ▶ pase

PASH n infatuation ▷ vb throw or be thrown and break or be broken to bits

PASHA n high official of the Ottoman Empire

PASHAS ▶ pasha

PASHED ▶ pash

PASHES ▶ pash

PASHIM same as ▶ pashm

PASHIMS ▶ pashm

PASHING ▶ pash

PASHKA n rich Russian dessert made of cottage cheese, cream, almonds, currants, etc

PASHKAS ▶ pashka

PASHM n underfur of various Tibetan animals, esp goats, used for cashmere shawls

PASHMS ▶ pashm

PASPIES ▶ paspy

PASPY n piece of music in triple time

PASQUIL n abusive lampoon or satire ▷ vb ridicule with pasquil

PASS vb go by, past, or through ▷ n successful result in a test or examination

PASSADE n act of moving back and forth in the same place

PASSADO n forward thrust with sword

PASSAGE n channel or opening providing a way through ▷ vb move or cause to move at a passage

PASSANT adj (of a beast) walking, with the right foreleg raised

PASSATA n sauce made from sieved tomatoes, often used in Italian cookery

PASSE adj out-of-date

PASSED ▶ pass

PASSEE adj out of fashion

PASSEL n group or quantity of no fixed number

PASSELS ▶ passel

PASSER n person or thing that passes

PASSERS ▶ passer

PASSES ▶ pass

PASSIM adv everywhere, throughout

PASSING adj brief or transitory ▷ n death

PASSION n intense sexual love ▷ vb give passionate character to

PASSIVE adj not playing an active part ▷ n passive form of a verb

PASSKEY n private key

PASSMAN n student who passes without honours

PASSMEN ▶ passman

PASSOUT n (in ice hockey) pass by an attacking player from behind the opposition goal line

PASSUS n (esp in medieval literature) division or section of a poem, story, etc

PAST adj of the time before the present ▷ n period of time before the present ▷ adv ago ▷ prep beyond

PASTA n type of food, such as spaghetti, that is made in different shapes from flour and water

PASTAS ▶ pasta

PASTE n moist soft mixture, such as toothpaste ▷ vb fasten with paste

PASTED ▶ paste

PASTEL n coloured chalk crayon for drawing ▷ adj pale and delicate in colour

PASTELS ▶ pastel

PASTER n person or thing that pastes

PASTERN n part of a horse's foot between the fetlock and the hoof

PASTERS ▶ paster

PASTES ▶ paste

PASTEUP n assembly of typeset matter, illustrations, etc, pasted on a sheet of paper or board

PASTIE n decorative cover for nipple

PASTIER ▶ pasty

PASTIES ▶ pasty

PASTIL same as > pastille

PASTILS ▶ pastil

PASTILY ▶ pasty

PASTIME n activity that makes time pass pleasantly

PASTINA n small pieces of pasta

PASTING n heavy defeat

PASTIS n anise-flavoured alcoholic drink

PASTOR n member of the clergy in charge of a congregation ▷ vb act as a pastor

PASTORS ▶ pastor

PASTRY n baking dough made of flour, fat, and water

PASTS ▶ past

PASTURE n grassy land for farm animals to graze on ▷ vb cause (livestock) to graze or (of livestock) to graze (a pasture)

PASTY adj (of a complexion) pale and unhealthy ▷ n round of pastry folded over a savoury filling

PAT vb tap lightly ▷ n gentle tap or stroke ▷ adj quick, ready, or glib

PATACA n monetary unit of Macao

PATACAS ▶ pataca

PATAGIA > patagium

PATAKA n building on stilts, used for storing provisions

PATAKAS ▶ pataka

PATAMAR n type of boat

PATBALL n game like squash but using hands instead of rackets

PATCH n piece of material sewn on a garment ▷ vb mend with a patch

PATCHED ▶ patch

PATCHER ▶ patch

PATCHES ▶ patch

PATCHY adj of uneven quality or intensity

PATE n head

PATED ▶ pate

PATELLA n kneecap

PATEN n plate, usually made of silver or gold, used for the bread at Communion

PATENCY n condition of being obvious

PATENS ▶ paten

PATENT n document giving the exclusive right to make or sell an invention ▷ adj open to public inspection ▷ vb obtain a patent for

PATENTS ▶ patent

PATER n father

PATERA n shallow ancient Roman bowl

P

PATERAE ▶ patera
PATERS ▶ pater
PATES ▶ pate
PATH n surfaced walk or track ▷ vb make a path
PATHED ▶ path
PATHIC n catamite ▷ adj of or relating to a catamite
PATHICS ▶ pathic
PATHING ▶ path
PATHOS n power of arousing pity or sadness
PATHS ▶ path
PATHWAY n path
PATIBLE adj endurable
PATIENT adj enduring difficulties or delays calmly ▷ n person receiving medical treatment ▷ vb make calm
PATIKI n New Zealand sand flounder or dab
PATIKIS ▶ patiki
PATIN same as ▶ paten
PATINA n fine layer on a surface
PATINAE ▶ patina
PATINAS ▶ patina
PATINE vb cover with patina
PATINED ▶ patine
PATINES ▶ patine
PATINS ▶ patin
PATIO n paved area adjoining a house
PATIOS ▶ patio
PATKA n head covering worn by Sikh men in place of or under a turban
PATKAS ▶ patka
PATLY adv fitly
PATNESS n appropriateness
PATOIS n regional dialect, esp of French
PATONCE adj (of cross) with limbs which broaden from centre
PATRIAL n (in Britain, formerly) person with a right by statute to live in the United Kingdom, and so not subject to immigration control
PATRICK n former Irish coin
PATRICO n fraudulent priest
PATRIOT n person who loves his or her country and supports its interests
PATROL n regular circuit by a guard ▷ vb go round on guard, or reconnoitring
PATROLS ▶ patrol
PATRON n person who gives financial support to

charities, artists, etc
PATRONS ▶ patron
PATROON n Dutch land-holder in New Netherland and New York with manorial rights in the colonial era
PATS ▶ pat
PATSIES ▶ patsy
PATSY n person who is easily cheated, victimized, etc
PATTE n band keeping belt in place
PATTED ▶ pat
PATTEE adj (of a cross) having triangular arms widening outwards
PATTEN n wooden clog or sandal on a raised wooden platform or metal ring ▷ vb wear pattens
PATTENS ▶ patten
PATTER vb make repeated soft tapping sounds ▷ n quick succession of taps
PATTERN n arrangement of repeated parts or decorative designs ▷ vb model
PATTERS ▶ patter
PATTES ▶ patte
PATTIE same as ▶ patty
PATTIES ▶ patty
PATTING ▶ pat
PATTLE dialect for ▶ paddle
PATTLES ▶ pattle
PATTY n small flattened cake of minced food
PATU n short Māori club, now used ceremonially
PATULIN n toxic antibiotic
PATUS ▶ patu
PATY adj (of cross) having arms of equal length
PATZER n novice chess player
PATZERS ▶ patzer
PAUA n edible shellfish of New Zealand, which has a pearly shell used for jewellery
PAUAS ▶ paua
PAUCAL n grammatical number occurring in some languages for words in contexts where a few of their referents are described or referred to ▷ adj relating to or inflected for this number
PAUCALS ▶ paucal
PAUCITY n scarcity

PAUGHTY Scots word for ▶ haughty
PAUL same as ▶ pawl
PAULIN n tarpaulin
PAULINS ▶ paulin
PAULS ▶ paul
PAUNCE n pansy
PAUNCES ▶ paunce
PAUNCH n protruding belly ▷ vb stab in the stomach
PAUNCHY adj having a protruding belly or abdomen
PAUPER n very poor person ▷ vb reduce to beggary
PAUPERS ▶ pauper
PAUSAL ▶ pause
PAUSE vb stop for a time ▷ n stop or rest in speech or action
PAUSED ▶ pause
PAUSER ▶ pause
PAUSERS ▶ pause
PAUSES ▶ pause
PAUSING ▶ pause
PAV short for ▶ pavlova
PAVAGE n tax towards paving streets, or the right to levy such a tax
PAVAGES ▶ pavage
PAVAN same as ▶ pavane
PAVANE n slow and stately dance of the 16th and 17th centuries
PAVANES ▶ pavane
PAVANS ▶ pavan
PAVE vb form (a surface) with stone or brick ▷ n paved surface, esp an uneven one
PAVED ▶ pave
PAVEED adj (of jewels) set close together
PAVEN same as ▶ pavane
PAVENS ▶ paven
PAVER ▶ pave
PAVERS ▶ pave
PAVES ▶ pave
PAVID adj fearful
PAVIN same as ▶ pavane
PAVING n paved surface ▷ adj of or for a paved surface or pavement
PAVINGS ▶ paving
PAVINS ▶ pavin
PAVIOR same as ▶ paviour
PAVIORS ▶ pavior
PAVIOUR n person who lays paving
PAVIS n large square shield, developed in the 15th century, at first portable but later heavy and set up in

a permanent position

PAVISE *same as* ▶ **pavis**

PAVISER *n* soldier holding pavise

PAVISES ▶ **pavise**

PAVISSE *same as* ▶ **pavis**

PAVLOVA *n* meringue cake topped with whipped cream and fruit

PAVONE *n* peacock

PAVONES ▶ **pavone**

PAVS ▶ **pav**

PAW *n* animal's foot with claws and pads ▷ *vb* scrape with the paw or hoof

PAWA *old word for* ▶ **peacock**

PAWAS ▶ **pawa**

PAWAW *vb* recite N American incantation

PAWAWED ▶ **pawaw**

PAWAWS ▶ **pawaw**

PAWED ▶ **paw**

PAWER *n* person or animal that paws

PAWERS ▶ **pawer**

PAWING ▶ **paw**

PAWK *Scots word for* ▶ **trick**

PAWKIER ▶ **pawky**

PAWKILY ▶ **pawky**

PAWKS ▶ **pawk**

PAWKY *adj* having a or characterized by a dry wit

PAWL *n* pivoted lever shaped to engage with a ratchet to prevent motion in a particular direction

PAWLS ▶ **pawl**

PAWN *vb* deposit (an article) as security for money borrowed ▷ *n* chessman of the lowest value

PAWNAGE ▶ **pawn**

PAWNCE *old word for* ▶ **pansy**

PAWNCES ▶ **pawnce**

PAWNED ▶ **pawn**

PAWNEE *n* one who accepts goods in pawn

PAWNEES ▶ **pawnee**

PAWNER *n* one who pawns his or her possessions

PAWNERS ▶ **pawner**

PAWNING ▶ **pawn**

PAWNOR *same as* ▶ **pawner**

PAWNORS ▶ **pawnor**

PAWNS ▶ **pawn**

PAWPAW *same as* ▶ **papaw**

PAWPAWS ▶ **pawpaw**

PAWS ▶ **paw**

PAX *n* peace ▷ *interj* call signalling a desire to end hostilities

Latin for peace, this is yet another of those very useful short words containing X.

PAXES ▶ **pax**

PAXIUBA *n* tropical tree

PAXWAX *n* strong ligament in the neck of many mammals, which supports the head

PAY *vb* give money etc in return for goods or services ▷ *n* wages or salary

PAYABLE *adj* due to be paid

PAYABLY ▶ **payable**

PAYBACK *n* return on an investment

PAYDAY *n* day on which wages or salaries are paid

PAYDAYS ▶ **payday**

PAYED ▶ **pay**

PAYEE *n* person to whom money is paid or due

PAYEES ▶ **payee**

PAYER *n* person who pays

PAYERS ▶ **payer**

PAYFONE *US spelling of* > **payphone**

PAYING ▶ **pay**

PAYINGS ▶ **pay**

PAYLIST *n* list of people to be paid

PAYLOAD *n* passengers or cargo of an aircraft

PAYMENT *n* act of paying

PAYNIM *n* heathen or pagan

PAYNIMS ▶ **paynim**

PAYOFF *n* final settlement, esp in retribution

PAYOFFS ▶ **payoff**

PAYOLA *n* bribe to get special treatment, esp to promote a commercial product

PAYOLAS ▶ **payola**

PAYOR *same as* ▶ **payer**

PAYORS ▶ **payor**

PAYOUT *n* sum of money paid out

PAYOUTS ▶ **payout**

PAYROLL *n* list of employees who receive regular pay

PAYS ▶ **pay**

PAYSAGE *n* landscape

PAYSD *Spenserian form of* ▶ **poised**

PAYSLIP *n* note of payment given to employee

PAZAZZ *same as* ▶ **pizzazz**

PAZZAZZ *same as* ▶ **pizzazz**

PE *n* 17th letter of the Hebrew alphabet,

transliterated as *p*

PEA *n* climbing plant with seeds growing in pods

PEACE *n* calm, quietness

PEACED ▶ **peace**

PEACES ▶ **peace**

PEACH *n* soft juicy fruit with a stone and a downy skin ▷ *adj* pinkish-orange ▷ *vb* inform against an accomplice

PEACHED ▶ **peach**

PEACHER ▶ **peach**

PEACHES ▶ **peach**

PEACHY *adj* of or like a peach, esp in colour or texture

PEACING ▶ **peace**

PEACOAT *n* woollen jacket

PEACOCK *n* large male bird with a brilliantly coloured fanlike tail ▷ *vb* display (oneself) proudly

PEACOD *same as* ▶ **peapod**

PEACODS ▶ **peacod**

PEAFOWL *n* peacock or peahen

PEAG *n* (formerly) money used by North American Indians, made of cylindrical shells strung or woven together

PEAGE *same as* ▶ **peag**

PEAGES ▶ **peage**

PEAGS ▶ **peag**

PEAHEN ▶ **peacock**

PEAHENS ▶ **peacock**

PEAK *n* pointed top, esp of a mountain ▷ *vb* form or reach a peak ▷ *adj* of or at the point of greatest demand

PEAKED *adj* having a peak

PEAKIER ▶ **peak**

PEAKING ▶ **peak**

PEAKISH *adj* sickly

PEAKS ▶ **peak**

PEAKY ▶ **peak**

PEAL *n* long loud echoing sound, esp of bells or thunder ▷ *vb* sound with a peal or peals

PEALED ▶ **peal**

PEALIKE ▶ **pea**

PEALING ▶ **peal**

PEALS ▶ **peal**

PEAN ▶ **peen** (sense 2)

PEANED ▶ **pean**

PEANING ▶ **pean**

PEANS ▶ **pean**

PEANUT *n* pea-shaped nut that ripens underground

PEANUTS ▶ **peanut**

P

PEAPOD n pod of the pea plant
PEAPODS ▶ peapod
PEAR n sweet juicy fruit with a narrow top and rounded base
PEARCE old spelling of ▶ pierce
PEARCED ▶ pearce
PEARCES ▶ pearce
PEARE obsolete spelling of ▶ pear
PEARES ▶ peare
PEARL same as ▶ purl
PEARLED ▶ pearl
PEARLER n person who dives for or trades in pearls ▷ adj excellent
PEARLIN n type of lace used to trim clothes
PEARLS ▶ pearl
PEARLY adj resembling a pearl, esp in lustre ▷ n London costermonger who wears on ceremonial occasions a traditional dress of dark clothes covered with pearl buttons
PEARS ▶ pear
PEARST archaic variant of ▶ pierced
PEART adj lively
PEARTER ▶ peart
PEARTLY ▶ peart
PEAS ▶ pea
PEASANT n person working on the land, esp in poorer countries or in the past
PEASCOD same as ▶ cod
PEASE n archaic or dialect word for pea ▷ vb appease
PEASED ▶ pease
PEASEN obsolete plural of ▶ pease
PEASES ▶ pease
PEASING ▶ pease
PEASON obsolete plural of ▶ pease
PEAT n decayed vegetable material found in bogs, used as fertilizer or fuel
PEATARY n area covered with peat
PEATERY same as ▶ peatary
PEATIER ▶ peat
PEATMAN n person who collects peat
PEATMEN ▶ peatman
PEATS ▶ peat
PEATY ▶ peat
PEAVEY n wooden lever with a metal pointed end

and a hinged hook, used for handling logs
PEAVEYS ▶ peavey
PEAVIES ▶ peavy
PEAVY same as ▶ peavey
PEAZE same as ▶ pease
PEAZED ▶ peaze
PEAZES ▶ peaze
PEAZING ▶ peaze
PEBA n type of armadillo
PEBAS ▶ peba
PEBBLE n small roundish stone ▷ vb cover with pebbles
PEBBLED ▶ pebble
PEBBLES ▶ pebble
PEBBLY ▶ pebble
PEBRINE n disease of silkworms
PEC n pectoral muscle
PECAN n edible nut of a N American tree
PECANS ▶ pecan
PECCANT adj guilty of an offence
PECCARY n piglike animal of American forests
PECCAVI n confession of guilt
PECH Scottish word for ▶ pant
PECHAN Scots word for ▶ stomach
PECHANS ▶ pechan
PECHED ▶ pech
PECHING ▶ pech
PECHS ▶ pech
PECK vb strike or pick up with the beak ▷ n pecking movement
PECKE n quarter of bushel
PECKED ▶ peck
PECKES ▶ pecke
PECKIER ▶ pecky
PECKING ▶ peck
PECKISH adj slightly hungry
PECKS ▶ peck
PECKY adj discoloured
PECS pl n pectoral muscles
PECTASE n enzyme occurring in certain ripening fruits
PECTATE n salt or ester of pectic acid
PECTEN n comblike structure in the eye of birds and reptiles
PECTENS ▶ pecten
PECTIC ▶ pectin
PECTIN n substance in fruit that makes jam set
PECTINS ▶ pectin
PECTISE same as ▶ pectize

PECTIZE vb change into a jelly
PECTOSE n insoluble carbohydrate found in the cell walls of unripe fruit that is converted to pectin by enzymic processes
PECULIA > peculium
PED n pannier
PEDAGOG same as > pedagogue
PEDAL n foot-operated lever used to control a vehicle or machine, or to modify the tone of a musical instrument ▷ vb propel (a bicycle) by using its pedals ▷ adj of or relating to the foot or the feet
PEDALED ▶ pedal
PEDALER ▶ pedal
PEDALO n pleasure craft driven by pedal-operated paddle wheels
PEDALOS ▶ pedalo
PEDALS ▶ pedal
PEDANT n person who is excessively concerned with details and rules, esp in academic work
PEDANTS ▶ pedant
PEDATE adj (of a plant leaf) divided into several lobes arising at a common point, the lobes often being stalked and the lateral lobes sometimes divided into smaller lobes
PEDDER old form of ▶ pedlar
PEDDERS ▶ pedder
PEDDLE vb sell (goods) from door to door
PEDDLED ▶ peddle
PEDDLER same as ▶ pedlar
PEDDLES ▶ peddle
PEDES ▶ pes
PEDESES ▶ pedesis
PEDESIS n random motion of small particles
PEDETIC adj of feet
PEDICAB n pedal-operated tricycle, available for hire, with an attached seat for one or two passengers
PEDICEL n stalk bearing a single flower of an inflorescence
PEDICLE n any small stalk
PEDLAR n person who sells goods from door to door
PEDLARS ▶ pedlar
PEDLARY same as ▶ pedlery

PEDLER same as ▶ **pedlar**
PEDLERS ▶ **pedler**
PEDLERY n business of pedler
PEDOCAL n type of zonal soil that is rich in lime and characteristic of relatively dry areas
PEDRAIL n device replacing wheel on rough surfaces
PEDRERO n type of cannon
PEDRO n card game
PEDROS ▶ **pedro**
PEDS ▶ **ped**
PEE vb urinate ▷ n urine
PEEBEEN n type of large evergreen
PEECE obsolete variant of ▶ **piece**
PEECES ▶ **peece**
PEEK n peep or glance ▷ vb glance quickly or secretly
PEEKABO same as ▶ **peekaboo**
PEEKED ▶ **peek**
PEEKING ▶ **peek**
PEEKS ▶ **peek**
PEEL vb remove the skin or rind of (a vegetable or fruit) ▷ n rind or skin
PEELED ▶ **peel**
PEELER n special knife or mechanical device for peeling vegetables, fruit, etc
PEELERS ▶ **peeler**
PEELING n strip of skin, rind, bark, etc, that is peeled off
PEELS ▶ **peel**
PEEN n end of a hammer head opposite the striking face, often rounded or wedge-shaped ▷ vb strike with the peen of a hammer or with a stream of metal shot in order to bend or shape (a sheet of metal)
PEENED ▶ **peen**
PEENGE vb complain
PEENGED ▶ **peenge**
PEENGES ▶ **peenge**
PEENING ▶ **peen**
PEENS ▶ **peen**
PEEOY n homemade firework
PEEOYS ▶ **peeoy**
PEEP vb look slyly or quickly ▷ n peeping look
PEEPE old spelling of ▶ **pip**
PEEPED ▶ **peep**
PEEPER n person who peeps
PEEPERS ▶ **peeper**

PEEPES archaic spelling of ▶ **peeps**
PEEPING ▶ **peep**
PEEPS ▶ **peep**
PEEPUL n Indian moraceous tree
PEEPULS ▶ **peepul**
PEER n (in Britain) member of the nobility ▷ vb look closely and intently
PEERAGE n whole body of peers
PEERED ▶ **peer**
PEERESS n (in Britain) woman holding the rank of a peer
PEERIE n spinning top ▷ adj small
PEERIER ▶ **peerie**
PEERIES ▶ **peerie**
PEERING ▶ **peer**
PEERS ▶ **peer**
PEERY n child's spinning top
PEES ▶ **pee**
PEEVE vb irritate or annoy ▷ n something that irritates
PEEVED ▶ **peeve**
PEEVER n hopscotch
PEEVERS ▶ **peever**
PEEVES ▶ **peeve**
PEEVING ▶ **peeve**
PEEVISH adj fretful or irritable
PEEWEE same as ▶ **pewee**
PEEWEES ▶ **peewee**
PEEWIT same as ▶ **lapwing**
PEEWITS ▶ **peewit**
PEG n pin or clip for joining, fastening, marking, etc ▷ vb fasten with pegs
PEGASUS n winged horse
PEGBOX n part of stringed instrument that holds tuning pegs
PEGGED ▶ **peg**
PEGGIES ▶ **peggy**
PEGGING ▶ **peg**
PEGGY n type of small warbler
PEGH same as ▶ **pech**
PEGHED ▶ **pegh**
PEGHING ▶ **pegh**
PEGHS ▶ **pegh**
PEGLESS ▶ **peg**
PEGLIKE ▶ **peg**
PEGS ▶ **peg**
PEH ▶ **pe**
PEHS ▶ **peh**
PEIN same as ▶ **peen**
PEINCT vb paint
PEINCTS ▶ **peinct**
PEINED ▶ **pein**
PEINING ▶ **pein**

PEINS ▶ **pein**
PEISE same as ▶ **peize**
PEISED ▶ **peise**
PEISES ▶ **peise**
PEISHWA n Indian leader
PEISING ▶ **peise**
PEIZE vb weight or poise
PEIZED ▶ **peize**
PEIZES ▶ **peize**
PEIZING ▶ **peize**
PEKAN n large North American marten
PEKANS ▶ **pekan**
PEKE n Pekingese dog
PEKEPOO same as ▶ **peekapoo**
PEKES ▶ **peke**
PEKIN n silk fabric
PEKINS ▶ **pekin**
PEKOE n high-quality tea made from the downy tips of the young buds of the tea plant
PEKOES ▶ **pekoe**
PEL n pixel
PELA n insect living on wax
PELAGE n coat of a mammal, consisting of hair, wool, fur, etc
PELAGES ▶ **pelage**
PELAGIC adj of or relating to the open sea ▷ n any pelagic creature
PELAS ▶ **pela**
PELE Spenserian variant of ▶ **peal**
PELES ▶ **pele**
PELF n money or wealth
PELFS ▶ **pelf**
PELHAM n horse's bit for a double bridle, less severe than a curb but more severe than a snaffle
PELHAMS ▶ **pelham**
PELICAN n large water bird with a pouch beneath its bill for storing fish
PELISSE n cloak or loose coat which is usually fur-trimmed
PELITE n any argillaceous rock such as shale
PELITES ▶ **pelite**
PELITIC ▶ **pelite**
PELL n hide of an animal
PELLACH same as ▶ **pellack**
PELLACK n porpoise
PELLET n small ball of something ▷ vb strike with pellets
PELLETS ▶ **pellet**
PELLOCK n porpoise
PELLS ▶ **pell**

PELLUM n dust
PELLUMS ▶ **pellum**
PELMA n sole of the foot
PELMAS ▶ **pelma**
PELMET n ornamental drapery or board, concealing a curtain rail
PELMETS ▶ **pelmet**
PELOID n mud used therapeutically
PELOIDS ▶ **peloid**
PELON adj hairless
PELORIA n abnormal production of actinomorphic flowers in a plant of a species that usually produces zygomorphic flowers
PELORIC ▶ **peloria**
PELORUS n sighting device used in conjunction with a magnetic compass or a gyrocompass for measuring the relative bearings of observed points
PELORY n floral mutation
PELOTA n game played by two players who use a basket strapped to their wrists or a wooden racket to propel a ball against a specially marked wall
PELOTAS ▶ **pelota**
PELOTON n main field of riders in a road race
PELS ▶ **pel**
PELT vb throw missiles at ▷ n skin of a fur-bearing animal
PELTA n small ancient shield
PELTAE ▶ **pelta**
PELTAS ▶ **pelta**
PELTAST n (in ancient Greece) lightly armed foot soldier
PELTATE adj (of leaves) having the stalk attached to the centre of the lower surface
PELTED ▶ **pelt**
PELTER vb rain heavily
PELTERS ▶ **pelt**
PELTING ▶ **pelt**
PELTRY n pelts of animals collectively
PELTS ▶ **pelt**
PELVES ▶ **pelvis**
PELVIC adj of, near, or relating to the pelvis ▷ n pelvic bone
PELVICS ▶ **pelvic**
PELVIS n framework of bones at the base of the

spine, to which the hips are attached
PEMBINA n type of cranberry
PEMICAN same as > **pemmican**
PEMPHIX n type of crustacean
PEN n instrument for writing in ink ▷ vb write or compose
PENAL adj of or used in punishment
PENALLY ▶ **penal**
PENALTY n punishment for a crime or offence
PENANCE n voluntary self-punishment to make amends for wrongdoing ▷ vb (of ecclesiastical authorities) impose a penance upon (a sinner)
PENANG same as ▶ **pinang**
PENANGS ▶ **penang**
PENATES pl n household gods
PENCE ▶ **penny**
PENCEL n small pennon, originally one carried by a knight's squire
PENCELS ▶ **pencel**
PENCES ▶ **penny**
PENCIL n thin cylindrical instrument containing graphite, for writing or drawing ▷ vb draw, write, or mark with a pencil
PENCILS ▶ **pencil**
PEND vb await judgment or settlement ▷ n archway or vaulted passage
PENDANT n ornament worn on a chain round the neck
PENDED ▶ **pend**
PENDENT adj hanging ▷ n pendant
PENDING prep while waiting for ▷ adj not yet decided or settled
PENDS ▶ **pend**
PENDU adj in informal Indian English, culturally backward
PENDULE n manoeuvre by which a climber on a rope from above swings in a pendulum-like series of movements to reach another line of ascent
PENE same as ▶ **peen**
PENED ▶ **pene**
PENES ▶ **penis**

PENFOLD same as ▶ **pinfold**
PENFUL n contents of pen
PENFULS ▶ **penful**
PENGO n standard monetary unit of Hungary, replaced by the forint in 1946
PENGOS ▶ **pengo**
PENGUIN n flightless black-and-white sea bird of the southern hemisphere
PENI old spelling of ▶ **penny**
PENIAL ▶ **penis**
PENICIL n small pad for wounds
PENIE old spelling of ▶ **penny**
PENIES ▶ **penie**
PENILE adj of or relating to the penis
PENILL > **penillion**
PENING ▶ **pene**
PENIS n organ of copulation and urination in male mammals
PENISES ▶ **penis**
PENK n small fish
PENKS ▶ **penk**
PENLITE same as > **penlight**
PENMAN n person skilled in handwriting
PENMEN ▶ **penman**
PENNA n any large feather that has a vane and forms part of the main plumage of a bird
PENNAE ▶ **penna**
PENNAL n first-year student of Protestant university
PENNALS ▶ **pennal**
PENNAME n author's pseudonym
PENNANT same as ▶ **pendant**
PENNATE adj having feathers, wings, or winglike structures
PENNE n pasta in the form of short tubes
PENNED ▶ **pen**
PENNER n person who writes
PENNERS ▶ **penner**
PENNES ▶ **penne**
PENNI n former Finnish monetary unit worth one hundredth of a markka
PENNIA ▶ **penni**
PENNIED adj having money
PENNIES ▶ **penny**
PENNILL n stanza in a Welsh poem
PENNINE n mineral found in the Pennine Alps

PENNING ▶ pen

PENNIS ▶ penni

PENNON n triangular or tapering flag

PENNONS same as ▶ **pennon**

PENNY n British bronze coin worth one hundredth of a pound

PENOCHE n type of fudge

PENS ▶ pen

PENSEE n thought put down on paper

PENSEES ▶ pensee

PENSEL same as ▶ **pencel**

PENSELS ▶ pensel

PENSIL same as ▶ **pencel**

PENSILE adj designating or building a hanging nest

PENSILS ▶ pensil

PENSION n regular payment to people above a certain age, retired employees, widows, etc ▶ vb grant a pension to

PENSIVE adj deeply thoughtful, often with a tinge of sadness

PENSTER n writer

PENSUM n school exercise

PENSUMS ▶ pensum

PENT n penthouse

PENTACT n sponge spicule with five rays

PENTAD n group or series of five

PENTADS ▶ pentad

PENTANE n alkane hydrocarbon with three isomers

PENTENE n colourless flammable liquid alkene with several straight-chained isomeric forms

PENTHIA n child born fifth

PENTICE vb accommodate in a penthouse

PENTISE same as ▶ **pentice**

PENTITI ▶ pentito

PENTITO n person involved in organized crime who offers information to the police in return for immunity from prosecution

PENTODE n electronic valve having five electrodes: a cathode, anode, and three grids

PENTOSE n monosaccharide containing five atoms of carbon per molecule

PENTS ▶ pent

PENTYL n one of a particular chemical group

PENTYLS ▶ pentyl

PENUCHE same as ▶ **panocha**

PENUCHI same as ▶ **panocha**

PENULT n last syllable but one in a word

PENULTS ▶ penult

PENURY n extreme poverty

PEON n Spanish-American farm labourer or unskilled worker

PEONAGE n state of being a peon

PEONES ▶ peon

PEONIES ▶ peony

PEONISM same as ▶ **peonage**

PEONS ▶ peon

PEONY n garden plant with showy red, pink, or white flowers

PEOPLE pl n persons generally ▶ vb provide with inhabitants

PEOPLED ▶ people

PEOPLER n settler

PEOPLES ▶ people

PEP n high spirits, energy, or enthusiasm ▶ vb liven by imbuing with new vigour

PEPFUL adj full of vitality

PEPINO n purple-striped yellow fruit

PEPINOS ▶ pepino

PEPLA ▶ peplum

PEPLOS n (in ancient Greece) top part of a woman's attire, caught at the shoulders and hanging in folds to the waist

PEPLUM same as ▶ **peplos**

PEPLUMS ▶ peplum

PEPLUS same as ▶ **peplos**

PEPO n fruit such as the melon, squash, cucumber, or pumpkin

PEPOS ▶ pepo

PEPPED ▶ pep

PEPPER n sharp hot condiment made from the fruit of an East Indian climbing plant ▶ vb season with pepper

PEPPERS ▶ pepper

PEPPERY adj tasting of pepper

PEPPIER ▶ peppy

PEPPILY ▶ peppy

PEPPING ▶ pep

PEPPY adj full of vitality

PEPS ▶ pep

PEPSIN n enzyme produced in the stomach, which, when activated by acid, breaks down proteins

PEPSINE same as ▶ **pepsin**

PEPSINS ▶ pepsin

PEPTALK n talk meant to inspire ▶ vb give a peptalk to

PEPTIC adj relating to digestion or the digestive juices ▶ n substance that aids digestion

PEPTICS ▶ peptic

PEPTID same as ▶ **peptide**

PEPTIDE n compound consisting of two or more amino acids linked by chemical bonding between the amino group of one and the carboxyl group of another

PEPTIDS ▶ peptid

PEPTISE same as ▶ **peptize**

PEPTIZE vb disperse (a substance) into a colloidal state, usually to form a sol

PEPTONE n any of a group of compounds that form an intermediary group in the digestion of proteins to amino acids

PER prep for each

PERACID n acid, such as perchloric acid, in which the element forming the acid radical exhibits its highest valency

PERAEA ▶ peraeon

PERAEON same as ▶ **pereion**

PERAI another name for ▶ **piranha**

PERAIS ▶ perai

PERCALE n close-textured woven cotton fabric, plain or printed, used esp for sheets

PERCASE adv perchance

PERCE obsolete word for ▶ **pierce**

PERCED ▶ perce

PERCEN ▶ perce

PERCENT n percentage or proportion

PERCEPT n concept that depends on recognition by the senses, such as sight, of some external object or phenomenon

PERCES ▶ perce

PERCH n resting place for a bird ▶ vb alight, rest, or

P

place on or as if on a perch

PERCHED ▶ perch

PERCHER ▶ perch

PERCHES ▶ perch

PERCINE adj of perches

PERCING ▶ perce

PERCOCT adj well-cooked

PERCOID n type of spiny-finned teleost fish

PERCUSS vb strike sharply, rapidly, or suddenly

PERDIE adv certainly

PERDU adj (of a soldier) placed on hazardous sentry duty ▷ n soldier placed on hazardous sentry duty

PERDUE same as ▶ perdu

PERDUES ▶ perdue

PERDURE vb last for long time

PERDUS ▶ perdu

PERDY adv certainly

PERE n addition to a French surname to specify the father rather than the son of the same name

PEREA ▶ pereon

PEREGAL adj equal ▷ n equal

PEREIA ▶ pereion

PEREION n thorax of some crustaceans

PEREIRA n bark of a South American apocynaceous tree

PERENTY same as > perentie

PEREON same as ▶ pereion

PEREONS ▶ pereon

PERES ▶ pere

PERFAY interj by my faith

PERFECT adj having all the essential elements ▷ n perfect tense ▷ vb improve

PERFET obsolete variant of ▶ perfect

PERFIDY n perfidious act

PERFIN former name for ▶ spif

PERFING n practice of taking early retirement, with financial compensation, from the police force

PERFINS ▶ perfin

PERFORM vb carry out (an action)

PERFUME n liquid cosmetic worn for its pleasant smell ▷ vb give a pleasant smell to

PERFUMY adj like perfume

PERFUSE vb permeate (a liquid, colour, etc) through

or over (something)

PERGOLA n arch or framework of trellis supporting climbing plants

PERHAPS adv possibly, maybe ▷ sentence substitute it may happen, be so, etc ▷ n something that might have happened

PERI n (in Persian folklore) one of a race of beautiful supernatural beings

PERIAPT n charm or amulet

PERICON n Argentinian dance

PERIDIA > peridium

PERIDOT n pale green transparent gemstone

PERIGEE n point in the orbit of the moon or a satellite that is nearest the earth

PERIGON n angle of 360°

PERIL n great danger ▷ vb expose to danger

PERILED ▶ peril

PERILLA n type of mint

PERILS ▶ peril

PERINEA > perineum

PERIOD n particular portion of time ▷ adj (of furniture, dress, a play, etc) dating from or in the style of an earlier time ▷ vb divide into periods

PERIODS ▶ period

PERIOST n thick fibrous two-layered membrane covering the surface of bones

PERIQUE n strong highly-flavoured tobacco cured in its own juices and grown in Louisiana

PERIS ▶ peri

PERISH vb be destroyed or die

PERITI ▶ peritus

PERITUS n Catholic theology consultant

PERIWIG same as ▶ peruke

PERJINK adj prim or finicky

PERJURE vb render (oneself) guilty of perjury

PERJURY n act or crime of lying while under oath in a court

PERK n incidental benefit gained from a job, such as a company car ▷ adj pert ▷ vb (of coffee) percolate

PERKED ▶ perk

PERKIER ▶ perky

PERKILY ▶ perky

PERKIN same as ▶ parkin

PERKING ▶ perk

PERKINS ▶ perkin

PERKISH adj perky

PERKS ▶ perk

PERKY adj lively or cheerful

PERLITE n variety of obsidian consisting of masses of small pearly globules

PERLOUS same as > perilous

PERM n long-lasting curly hairstyle produced by treating the hair with chemicals ▷ vb give (hair) a perm

PERMED ▶ perm

PERMIAN adj of, denoting, or formed in the last period of the Palaeozoic era

PERMIE n person, esp an office worker, employed by a firm on a permanent basis

PERMIES ▶ permie

PERMING ▶ perm

PERMIT vb give permission, allow ▷ n document giving permission to do something

PERMITS ▶ permit

PERMS ▶ perm

PERMUTE vb change the sequence of

PERN n type of buzzard

PERNIO n chilblain

PERNOD n aniseed-flavoured aperitif from France

PERNODS ▶ pernod

PERNS ▶ pern

PEROGI n type of Polish dumpling

PERONE n fibula

PERONES ▶ perone

PERORAL adj administered through mouth

PEROXID same as > peroxide

PEROXO n type of acid

PEROXY adj containing the peroxide group

PERP n informal US and Canadian word for someone who has committed a crime

PERPEND n large stone that passes through a wall from one side to the other ▷ vb ponder

PERPENT same as ▶ perpend

PERPLEX vb puzzle, bewilder

PERPS ▶ perp
PERRIER n short mortar
PERRIES ▶ perry
PERRON n external flight of steps, esp one at the front entrance of a building
PERRONS ▶ perron
PERRY n alcoholic drink made from fermented pears
PERSALT n any salt of a peracid
PERSANT adj piercing
PERSE old variant of ▶ pierce
PERSES ▶ perse
PERSICO same as ▶ persicot
PERSING ▶ perse
PERSIST vb continue to be or happen, last
PERSON n human being
PERSONA n someone's personality as presented to others
PERSONS ▶ person
PERSPEX n tradename for any of various clear acrylic resins, used chiefly as a substitute for glass
PERST adj perished
PERSUE obsolete form of ▶ pursue
PERSUED ▶ persue
PERSUES ▶ persue
PERT adj saucy and cheeky ▷ n pert person
PERTAIN vb belong or be relevant (to)
PERTAKE obsolete form of ▶ partake
PERTER ▶ pert
PERTEST ▶ pert
PERTLY ▶ pert
PERTOOK ▶ pertake
PERTS ▶ pert
PERTURB vb disturb greatly
PERTUSE adj having holes
PERUKE n wig for men worn in the 17th and 18th centuries
PERUKED adj wearing wig
PERUKES ▶ peruke
PERUSAL ▶ peruse
PERUSE vb read in a careful or leisurely manner
PERUSED ▶ peruse
PERUSER ▶ peruse
PERUSES ▶ peruse
PERV n pervert ▷ vb give a person an erotic look
PERVADE vb spread right through (something)
PERVE same as ▶ perv
PERVED ▶ perv

PERVERT vb use or alter for a wrong purpose ▷ n person who practises sexual perversion
PERVES ▶ perv
PERVIER ▶ pervy
PERVING ▶ perv
PERVS ▶ perv
PERVY adj perverted
PES n animal part corresponding to the human foot
PESADE n position in which the horse stands on the hind legs with the forelegs in the air
PESADES ▶ pesade
PESANT obsolete spelling of ▶ peasant
PESANTE adv to be performed clumsily
PESANTS ▶ pesant
PESAUNT obsolete spelling of ▶ peasant
PESETA n former monetary unit of Spain
PESETAS ▶ peseta
PESEWA n Ghanaian monetary unit worth one hundredth of a cedi
PESEWAS ▶ pesewa
PESHWA same as ▶ peishwa
PESHWAS ▶ peshwa
PESKIER ▶ pesky
PESKILY ▶ pesky
PESKY adj troublesome
PESO n monetary unit of Argentina, Mexico, etc
PESOS ▶ peso
PESSARY n appliance worn in the vagina, either to prevent conception or to support the womb
PESSIMA n lowest point
PEST n annoying person
PESTER vb annoy or nag continually
PESTERS ▶ pester
PESTFUL adj causing annoyance
PESTIER ▶ pesty
PESTLE n club-shaped implement for grinding things to powder in a mortar ▷ vb pound (a substance or object) with or as if with a pestle
PESTLED ▶ pestle
PESTLES ▶ pestle
PESTO n sauce for pasta, consisting of basil leaves, pine nuts, garlic, oil, and Parmesan cheese, all

crushed together
PESTOS ▶ pesto
PESTS ▶ pest
PESTY adj persistently annoying
PET n animal kept for pleasure and companionship ▷ adj kept as a pet ▷ vb treat as a pet
PETAL n one of the brightly coloured outer parts of a flower
PETALED ▶ petal
PETALS ▶ petal
PETAR obsolete variant of ▶ petard
PETARA n clothes basket
PETARAS ▶ petara
PETARD n device containing explosives used to breach a wall, doors, etc
PETARDS ▶ petard
PETARS ▶ petar
PETARY n weapon for hurling stones
PETASOS same as ▶ petasus
PETASUS n broad-brimmed hat worn by the ancient Greeks
PETCOCK n small valve for checking the water level in a steam boiler or draining condensed steam from the cylinder of a steam engine
PETER vb fall (off) in volume, intensity, etc, and finally cease ▷ n act of petering
PETERED ▶ peter
PETERS ▶ peter
PETHER old variant of ▶ pedlar
PETHERS ▶ pether
PETIOLE n stalk which attaches a leaf to a plant
PETIT adj of little or lesser importance
PETITE adj (of a woman) small and dainty ▷ n clothing size for small women
PETITES ▶ petite
PETNAP vb steal pet
PETNAPS ▶ petnap
PETRALE n type of sole
PETRARY n weapon for hurling stones
PETRE same as ▶ saltpetre
PETREL n sea bird with a hooked bill and tubular nostrils
PETRELS ▶ petrel
PETRES ▶ petre

P

PETRI *n as in* **petri dish** shallow glass dish used for cultures of bacteria

PETRIFY *vb* frighten severely

PETROL *n* flammable liquid obtained from petroleum, used as fuel in internal-combustion engines ▷ *vb* supply with petrol

PETROLS ▶ **petrol**

PETROUS *adj* denoting the dense part of the temporal bone that surrounds the inner ear

PETS ▶ **pet**

PETSAI *n* Chinese cabbage

PETSAIS ▶ **petsai**

PETTED ▶ **pet**

PETTER ▶ **pet**

PETTERS ▶ **pet**

PETTI ▶ **petto**

PETTIER ▶ **petty**

PETTIES ▶ **petti**

PETTILY ▶ **petty**

PETTING ▶ **pet**

PETTISH *adj* peevish or fretful

PETTLE *vb* pat animal

PETTLED ▶ **pettle**

PETTLES ▶ **pettle**

PETTO *n* breast of animal

PETTY *adj* unimportant, trivial

PETUNIA *n* garden plant with funnel-shaped flowers

PEW *n* fixed benchlike seat in a church

PEWEE *n* small N American flycatcher with a greenish-brown plumage

PEWEES ▶ **pewee**

PEWIT *another name for* ▶ **lapwing**

PEWITS ▶ **pewit**

PEWS ▶ **pew**

PEWTER *n* greyish metal made of tin and lead

PEWTERS ▶ **pewter**

PEYOTE *another name for* ▶ **mescal**

PEYOTES ▶ **peyote**

PEYOTL *same as* ▶ **peyote**

PEYOTLS ▶ **peyotl**

PEYSE *vb* weight or poise

PEYSED ▶ **peyse**

PEYSES ▶ **peyse**

PEYSING ▶ **peyse**

PEYTRAL *same as* ▶ **peytrel**

PEYTREL *n* breastplate of horse's armour

PEZANT *obsolete spelling of* ▶ **peasant**

PEZANTS ▶ **pezant**

PFENNIG *n* former German monetary unit worth one hundredth of a mark

PFFT *interj* sound indicating sudden disappearance of something

PFUI *interj* phooey

PHACOID *adj* lentil- or lens-shaped

PHAEIC *adj* (of animals) having dusky coloration

PHAEISM ▶ **phaeic**

PHAETON *n* light four-wheeled horse-drawn carriage with or without a top

PHAGE *n* virus that is parasitic in a bacterium and multiplies within its host, which is destroyed when the new viruses are released

PHAGES ▶ **phage**

PHALANX *n* closely grouped mass of people

PHALLI ▶ **phallus**

PHALLIC *adj* of or resembling a phallus

PHALLIN *n* poisonous substance from mushroom

PHALLUS *n* penis, esp as a symbol of reproductive power in primitive rites

PHANG *old variant spelling of* ▶ **fang**

PHANGED ▶ **phang**

PHANGS ▶ **phang**

PHANTOM *n* ghost ▷ *adj* deceptive or unreal

PHARAOH *n* ancient Egyptian king

PHARE *n* beacon tower

PHARES ▶ **phare**

PHARM *vb* redirect (a website user) to another, bogus website for fraudulent purposes

PHARMA *n* pharmaceutical companies considered together as an industry

PHARMAS ▶ **pharma**

PHARMED ▶ **pharm**

PHARMS ▶ **pharm**

PHAROS *n* lighthouse

PHARYNX *n* cavity forming the back part of the mouth

PHASE *n* any distinct or characteristic stage in a development or chain of events ▷ *vb* arrange or carry out in stages or to coincide with something else

PHASEAL ▶ **phase**

PHASED ▶ **phase**

PHASES ▶ **phase**

PHASIC ▶ **phase**

PHASING *n* tonal sweep achieved by varying the phase relationship of two similar audio signals by mechanical or electronic means

PHASIS *another word for* ▶ **phase**

PHASMID *n* stick insect or leaf insect

PHASOR *n* rotating vector representing a quantity, such as an alternating current or voltage, that varies sinusoidally

PHASORS ▶ **phasor**

PHAT *adj* terrific

PHATIC *adj* (of speech, esp of conversational phrases) used to establish social contact and to express sociability rather than specific meaning

PHATTER ▶ **phat**

PHEAZAR *old variant of* ▶ **vizier**

PHEER *same as* ▶ **fere**

PHEERE *same as* ▶ **fere**

PHEERES ▶ **pheere**

PHEERS ▶ **pheer**

PHEESE *vb* worry

PHEESED ▶ **pheese**

PHEESES ▶ **pheese**

PHEEZE *same as* ▶ **pheese**

PHEEZED ▶ **pheeze**

PHEEZES ▶ **pheeze**

PHELLEM *technical name for* ▶ **cork**

PHENATE *n* ester or salt of phenol

PHENE *n* genetically determined characteristic of organism

PHENES ▶ **phene**

PHENIC *adj* of phenol

PHENIX *same as* ▶ **phoenix**

PHENOL *n* chemical used in disinfectants and antiseptics

PHENOLS ▶ **phenol**

PHENOM *n* person or thing of outstanding abilities or qualities

PHENOMS ▶ **phenom**

PHENOXY *modifier as in* **phenoxy resin** any of a class of resins derived from polyhydroxy ethers

PHENYL *n* chemical substance

PHENYLS ▸ phenyl

PHEON *n* barbed iron head of dart

PHEONS ▸ pheon

PHESE *same as* ▸ **pheese**

PHESED ▸ phese

PHESES ▸ phese

PHESING ▸ phese

PHEW *interj* exclamation of relief, surprise, etc

PHI *n* 21st letter in the Greek alphabet

PHIAL *n* small bottle for medicine etc ▹ *vb* put in phial

PHIALS ▸ phial

PHILTER *vb* drink supposed to arouse love, desire, etc ▹ *vb* arouse sexual or romantic feelings by means of a philter

PHILTRA > philtrum

PHILTRE *n* magic drink supposed to arouse love in the person who drinks it ▹ *vb* mix with love potion

PHIS ▸ phi

PHIZ *n* face or a facial expression

PHIZES ▸ phiz

PHIZOG *same as* ▸ **phiz**

PHIZOGS ▸ phizog

PHIZZES ▸ phiz

PHLEGM *n* thick yellowish substance formed in the nose and throat during a cold

PHLEGMS ▸ phlegm

PHLEGMY ▸ phlegm

PHLOEM *n* plant tissue that acts as a path for the distribution of food substances to all parts of the plant

PHLOEMS ▸ phloem

PHLOMIS *n* plant of Phlomis genus

PHLOX *n* flowering garden plant

PHLOXES ▸ phlox

PHO *n* Vietnamese noodle soup

PHOBIA *n* intense and unreasoning fear or dislike

PHOBIAS ▸ phobia

PHOBIC *adj* of, relating to, or arising from a phobia ▹ *n* person suffering from a phobia

PHOBICS ▸ phobic

PHOBISM *n* phobia

PHOBIST ▸ phobism

PHOCA *n* genus of seals

PHOCAE ▸ phoca

PHOCAS ▸ phoca

PHOCINE *adj* of, relating to, or resembling a seal

PHOEBE *n* greyish-brown North American flycatcher

PHOEBES ▸ phoebe

PHOEBUS *n* sun

PHOENIX *n* legendary bird said to set fire to itself and rise anew from its ashes

PHOH *same as* ▸ **foh**

PHOLAS *n* type of bivalve mollusc

PHON *n* unit of loudness

PHONAL *adj* relating to voice

PHONATE *vb* articulate speech sounds, esp to cause the vocal cords to vibrate in the execution of a voiced speech sound

PHONE *vb* telephone ▹ *n* single uncomplicated speech sound

PHONED ▸ phone

PHONEME *n* one of the set of speech sounds in any given language that serve to distinguish one word from another

PHONER *n* person making a telephone call

PHONERS ▸ phoner

PHONES ▸ phone

PHONEY *adj* not genuine ▹ *n* phoney person or thing ▹ *vb* fake

PHONEYS ▸ phoney

PHONIC ▸ phonics

PHONICS *n* method of teaching people to read by training them to associate letters with their phonetic values

PHONIED ▸ phony

PHONIER ▸ phony

PHONIES ▸ phony

PHONILY ▸ phony

PHONING ▸ phone

PHONO *n* phonograph

PHONON *n* quantum of vibrational energy in the acoustic vibrations of a crystal lattice

PHONONS ▸ phonon

PHONOS ▸ phono

PHONS ▸ phon

PHONY *vb* fake

PHOOEY *interj* exclamation of scorn or contempt

PHORATE *n* type of insecticide

PHORESY *n* association in which one animal clings to another to ensure movement from place to place, as some mites use some insects

PHOS ▸ pho

PHOSSY *adj as in* **phossy jaw** gangrenous condition of the lower jawbone caused by prolonged exposure to phosphorus fumes

PHOT *n* unit of illumination equal to one lumen per square centimetre

PHOTIC *adj* of or concerned with light

PHOTICS *n* science of light

PHOTISM *n* sensation of light or colour caused by stimulus of another sense

PHOTO *n* photograph ▹ *vb* take a photograph of

PHOTOED ▸ photo

PHOTOG *n* photograph

PHOTOGS ▸ photog

PHOTON *n* quantum of electromagnetic radiation energy, such as light, having both particle and wave behaviour

PHOTONS ▸ photon

PHOTOS ▸ photo

PHOTS ▸ phot

PHPHT *interj* expressing irritation or reluctance

PHRASAL *adj* of, relating to, or composed of phrases

PHRASE *n* group of words forming a unit of meaning, esp within a sentence ▹ *vb* express in words

PHRASED ▸ phrase

PHRASER ▸ phrase

PHRASES ▸ phrase

PHRASY *adj* containing phrases

PHRATRY *n* group of people within a tribe who have a common ancestor

PHREAK *vb* hack into a telecommunications system

PHREAKS ▸ phreak

PHRENIC *adj* of or relating to the diaphragm ▹ *n* (a nerve, blood vessel, etc) located in the diaphragm

PHRENSY *obsolete spelling of* ▸ **frenzy**

PHT *same as* ▸ **phpht**

It is easy to overlook this little word, that may offer a way out when your rack seems hopelessly clogged with consonants.

PHUT vb make muffled explosive sound
PHUTS ▶ phut
PHUTTED ▶ phut
PHWOAR ▶ phwoar
PHWOAR interj expression of sexual interest or attraction
PHYLA ▶ phylum
PHYLAE ▶ phyle
PHYLAR ▶ phylum
PHYLE n tribe or clan of an ancient Greek people such as the Ionians
PHYLIC ▶ phyle
PHYLLID n leaf of a liverwort or moss
PHYLLO same as ▶ **filo**
PHYLLOS ▶ phyllo
PHYLON n tribe
PHYLUM n major taxonomic division of animals and plants that contains one or more classes
PHYSED n physical education
PHYSEDS ▶ physed
PHYSES ▶ physis
PHYSIC n medicine or drug, esp a cathartic or purge ▷ vb treat (a patient) with medicine
PHYSICS n science of the properties of matter and energy
PHYSIO n physiotherapy
PHYSIOS ▶ physio
PHYSIS n part of bone responsible for lengthening
PHYTANE n hydrocarbon found in some fossilised plant remains
PHYTIN n substance from plants used as an energy supplement
PHYTINS ▶ phytin
PHYTOID adj resembling plant
PHYTOL n alcohol used to synthesize some vitamins
PHYTOLS ▶ phytol
PHYTON n unit of plant structure, usually considered as the smallest part of the plant that is capable of growth when

detached from the parent plant
PHYTONS ▶ phyton
PI n sixteenth letter in the Greek alphabet ▷ vb spill and mix (set type) indiscriminately
PIA n innermost of the three membranes that cover the brain and the spinal cord
PIAFFE n passage done on the spot ▷ vb strut on the spot
PIAFFED ▶ piaffe
PIAFFER ▶ piaffe
PIAFFES ▶ piaffe
PIAL adj relating to pia mater
PIAN n contagious tropical skin disease
PIANI ▶ piano
PIANIC adj of piano
PIANINO n small upright piano
PIANISM n technique, skill, or artistry in playing the piano
PIANIST n person who plays the piano
PIANO n musical instrument with strings which are struck by hammers worked by a keyboard ▷ adv quietly
PIANOS ▶ piano
PIANS ▶ pian
PIARIST n member of a Roman religious order
PIAS ▶ pia
PIASABA same as > **piassava**
PIASAVA same as > **piassava**
PIASTER same as ▶ **piastre**
PIASTRE n standard monetary unit of South Vietnam, divided into 100 cents
PIAZZA n square or marketplace, esp in Italy
PIAZZAS ▶ piazza
PIAZZE ▶ piazza
PIBAL n method of measuring wind
PIBALS ▶ pibal
PIBROCH n form of bagpipe music
PIC n photograph or illustration
PICA n abnormal craving to ingest substances such as clay, dirt, and hair
PICACHO n pointed solitary mountain

PICADOR n mounted bullfighter with a lance
PICAL adj relating to pica
PICAMAR n hydrocarbon extract of beechwood tar
PICANTE adj spicy
PICARA n female adventurer
PICARAS ▶ picara
PICARO n roguish adventurer
PICAROS ▶ picaro
PICAS ▶ pica
PICCATA adj sautéed and served in a sauce containing lemon, butter, parsley and spices
PICCIES ▶ piccy
PICCOLO n small flute
PICCY n picture or photograph
PICE n former Indian coin worth one sixty-fourth of a rupee
PICENE n type of hydrocarbon
PICENES ▶ picene
PICEOUS adj of, relating to, or resembling pitch
PICINE adj relating to woodpeckers
PICK vb choose ▷ n choice
PICKAX same as ▶ **pickaxe**
PICKAXE n large pick ▷ vb use a pickaxe on (earth, rocks, etc)
PICKED ▶ pick
PICKEER vb make raid for booty
PICKER n person or thing that picks, esp that gathers fruit, crops, etc
PICKERS ▶ picker
PICKERY n petty theft
PICKET n person or group standing outside a workplace to deter would-be workers during a strike ▷ vb form a picket outside (a workplace)
PICKETS ▶ picket
PICKIER ▶ picky
PICKILY ▶ picky
PICKIN n small child
PICKING ▶ pick
PICKINS ▶ pickin
PICKLE n food preserved in vinegar or salt water ▷ vb preserve in vinegar or salt water
PICKLED adj (of food) preserved
PICKLER ▶ pickle

PICKLES ▶ pickle
PICKMAW n type of gull
PICKOFF n baseball play
PICKS ▶ pick
PICKUP n small truck with an open body and low sides
PICKUPS ▶ pickup
PICKY adj fussy
PICNIC n informal meal out of doors ▷ vb have a picnic
PICNICS ▶ picnic
PICOLIN same as ▶ picoline
PICONG n any teasing or satirical banter, originally a verbal duel in song
PICONGS ▶ picong
PICOT n any of pattern of small loops, as on lace ▷ vb decorate material with small loops
PICOTE adj (of material) picoted
PICOTED ▶ picot
PICOTEE n type of carnation having pale petals edged with a darker colour, usually red
PICOTS ▶ picot
PICQUET vb provide early warning of attack
PICRA n powder of aloes and canella
PICRAS ▶ picra
PICRATE n any salt or ester of picric acid, such as sodium picrate
PICRIC adj as in **picric acid** toxic sparingly soluble crystalline yellow acid
PICRITE n coarse-grained ultrabasic igneous rock consisting of olivine and augite with small amounts of plagioclase feldspar
PICS ▶ pic
PICTURE n drawing or painting ▷ vb visualize, imagine
PICUL n unit of weight, used in China, Japan, and SE Asia
PICULET n small tropical woodpecker with a short tail
PICULS ▶ picul
PIDDLE vb urinate
PIDDLED ▶ piddle
PIDDLER ▶ piddle
PIDDLES ▶ piddle
PIDDLY adj trivial
PIDDOCK n marine bivalve that bores into rock, clay, or wood
PIDGEON same as ▶ pidgin

PIDGIN n language, not a mother tongue, made up of elements of two or more other languages
PIDGINS ▶ pidgin
PIE n dish of meat, fruit, etc baked in pastry
PIEBALD adj (horse) with irregular black-and-white markings ▷ n black-and-white horse
PIECE n separate bit or part
PIECED ▶ piece
PIECEN vb join broken threads
PIECENS ▶ piecen
PIECER n person who mends, repairs, or joins something, esp broken threads on a loom
PIECERS ▶ piecer
PIECES ▶ piece
PIECING ▶ piece
PIED ▶ pi
PIEDISH n container for baking pies
PIEFORT same as ▶ piedfort
PIEHOLE n person's mouth
PIEING ▶ pie
PIEMAN n seller of pies
PIEMEN ▶ pieman
PIEND n a salient angle
PIENDS ▶ piend
PIER n platform on stilts sticking out into the sea
PIERAGE n accommodation for ships at piers
PIERCE vb make a hole in or through with a sharp instrument
PIERCED ▶ pierce
PIERCER ▶ pierce
PIERCES ▶ pierce
PIERID n type of butterfly
PIERIDS ▶ pierid
PIERIS n American or Asiatic shrub
PIEROGI n Polish dumpling
PIERROT n clown or masquerader with a whitened face, white costume, and pointed hat
PIERS ▶ pier
PIERST archaic spelling of ▶ pierced
PIERT n small plant with small greenish flowers
PIERTS ▶ piert
PIES ▶ pie
PIET n magpie
PIETA n sculpture, painting, or drawing of the dead Christ, supported by the Virgin Mary

PIETAS ▶ pieta
PIETIES ▶ piety
PIETISM n exaggerated piety
PIETIST ▶ pietism
PIETS ▶ piet
PIETY n deep devotion to God and religion
PIEZO adj piezoelectric
PIFFERO n small rustic flute
PIFFLE n nonsense ▷ vb talk or behave feebly
PIFFLED ▶ piffle
PIFFLER n talker of nonsense
PIFFLES ▶ piffle
PIG n animal kept and killed for pork, ham, and bacon ▷ vb eat greedily
PIGBOAT n submarine
PIGEON n bird with a heavy body and short legs, sometimes trained to carry messages ▷ vb pigeonhole
PIGEONS ▶ pigeon
PIGFACE n creeping succulent plant with bright-coloured flowers and red fruits
PIGFEED n food for pigs
PIGFISH n grunting fish of the North American Atlantic coast
PIGGED ▶ pig
PIGGERY n place for keeping and breeding pigs
PIGGIE same as ▶ piggy
PIGGIER ▶ piggy
PIGGIES ▶ piggy
PIGGIN n small wooden bucket or tub
PIGGING ▶ pig
PIGGINS ▶ piggin
PIGGISH adj like a pig, esp in appetite or manners
PIGGY n child's word for a pig, esp a piglet ▷ adj like a pig, esp in appetite
PIGHT vb pierce
PIGHTED ▶ pight
PIGHTLE n small enclosure
PIGHTS ▶ pight
PIGLET n young pig
PIGLETS ▶ piglet
PIGLIKE ▶ pig
PIGLING n young pig
PIGMEAN same as ▶ pygmaean
PIGMEAT less common name for ▶ pork
PIGMENT n colouring matter, paint or dye ▷ vb

P

colour with pigment

PIGMIES ▶ pigmy

PIGMOID adj of pygmies

PIGMY same as ▶ pygmy

PIGNOLI same as > **pignolia**

PIGNORA ▶ pignus

PIGNUS n pawn or pledge

PIGNUT n bitter nut of any of several North American hickory trees

PIGNUTS ▶ pignut

PIGOUT n binge

PIGOUTS ▶ pigout

PIGPEN same as ▶ **pigsty**

PIGPENS ▶ pigpen

PIGS ▶ pig

PIGSKIN n skin of the domestic pig ▷ adj made of pigskin

PIGSNEY same as ▶ **pigsny**

PIGSNIE same as ▶ **pigsny**

PIGSNY n former pet name for girl

PIGSTY same as ▶ **pigpen**

PIGTAIL n plait of hair hanging from the back or either side of the head

PIGWASH n wet feed for pigs

PIGWEED n coarse North American amaranthaceous weed

PIING ▶ pi

PIKA n burrowing lagomorph mammal of mountainous regions of North America and Asia

PIKAKE n type of Asian vine

PIKAKES ▶ pikake

PIKAS ▶ pika

PIKAU n pack, knapsack, or rucksack

PIKAUS ▶ pikau

PIKE n large predatory freshwater fish ▷ vb stab or pierce using a pike ▷ adj (of the body position of a diver) bent at the hips but with the legs straight

PIKED ▶ pike

PIKELET n small thick pancake

PIKEMAN n (formerly) soldier armed with a pike

PIKEMEN ▶ pikeman

PIKER n shirker

PIKERS ▶ piker

PIKES ▶ pike

PIKI n bread made from blue cornmeal

PIKING ▶ pike

PIKINGS ▶ pike

PIKIS ▶ piki

PIKUL same as ▶ **picul**

PIKULS ▶ pikul

PILA n pillar-like anatomical structure

PILAF same as ▶ **pilau**

PILAFF same as ▶ **pilau**

PILAFFS ▶ pilaff

PILAFS ▶ pilaf

PILAO same as ▶ **pilau**

PILAOS ▶ pilao

PILAR adj relating to hair

PILAU n Middle Eastern dish of meat, fish, or poultry boiled with rice, spices, etc

PILAUS ▶ pilau

PILAW same as ▶ **pilau**

PILAWS ▶ pilaw

PILCH n outer garment, originally one made of skin

PILCHER n scabbard for sword

PILCHES ▶ pilch

PILCORN n type if oat

PILCROW n paragraph mark

PILE n number of things lying on top of each other ▷ vb collect into a pile

PILEA n artillery or gunpowder plant, which releases a cloud of pollen when shaken

PILEAS ▶ pilea

PILEATE adj (of birds) having a crest

PILED ▶ pile

PILEI ▶ pileus

PILEOUS adj hairy

PILER n placer of things on pile

PILERS ▶ piler

PILES pl n swollen veins in the rectum, haemorrhoids

PILEUM n top of a bird's head from the base of the bill to the occiput

PILEUP n multiple collision of vehicles

PILEUPS ▶ pileup

PILEUS n upper cap-shaped part of a mushroom or similar spore-producing body

PILFER vb steal in small quantities

PILFERS ▶ pilfer

PILFERY n theft

PILGRIM n person who journeys to a holy place

PILI n Philippine tree with edible seeds resembling almonds

PILING n act of driving piles

PILINGS ▶ piling

PILINUT n type of nut found in the Philippines

PILIS ▶ pili

PILL n small ball of medicine swallowed whole ▷ vb peel or skin (something)

PILLAGE vb steal property by violence in war ▷ n violent seizure of goods, esp in war

PILLAR n upright post, usu supporting a roof ▷ vb provide or support with pillars

PILLARS ▶ pillar

PILLAU same as ▶ **pilau**

PILLAUS ▶ pillau

PILLBOX n small box for pills

PILLED ▶ pill

PILLIE n pilchard

PILLIES ▶ pillie

PILLING ▶ pill

PILLION n seat for a passenger behind the rider of a motorcycle ▷ adv on a pillion ▷ vb ride pillion

PILLOCK n stupid or annoying person

PILLORY n frame with holes for the head and hands in which an offender was locked and exposed to public abuse ▷ vb ridicule publicly

PILLOW n stuffed cloth bag for supporting the head in bed ▷ vb rest as if on a pillow

PILLOWS ▶ pillow

PILLOWY ▶ pillow

PILLS ▶ pill

PILOSE adj covered with fine soft hairs

PILOT n person qualified to fly an aircraft or spacecraft ▷ adj experimental and preliminary ▷ vb act as the pilot of

PILOTED ▶ pilot

PILOTIS pl n posts raising a building up from the ground

PILOTS ▶ pilot

PILOUS same as ▶ **pilose**

PILOW same as ▶ **pilau**

PILOWS ▶ pilow

PILSNER n type of pale beer with a strong flavour of hops

PILULA n pill

PILULAE ▶ pilula

PILULAR ▶ pilule

PILULAS ▸ pilula
PILULE n small pill
PILULES ▸ pilule
PILUM n ancient Roman javelin
PILUS ▸ pili
PILY adj like wool or pile
PIMA n type of cotton
PIMAS ▸ pima
PIMENT n wine flavoured with spices
PIMENTO same as
> pimiento
PIMENTS ▸ piment
PIMP n man who gets customers for a prostitute in return for a share of his or her earnings ▷ vb act as a pimp
PIMPED ▸ pimp
PIMPING ▸ pimp
PIMPLE n small pus-filled spot on the skin
PIMPLED ▸ pimple
PIMPLES ▸ pimple
PIMPLY ▸ pimple
PIMPS ▸ pimp
PIN n short thin piece of stiff wire with a point and head, for fastening things ▷ vb fasten with a pin
PINA n cone of silver amalgam
PINANG n areca tree
PINANGS ▸ pinang
PINAS ▸ pina
PINATA n papier-mâché party decoration filled with sweets, hung up during parties, and struck with a stick until it breaks open
PINATAS ▸ pinata
PINBALL vb ricochet
PINBONE n part of sirloin
PINCASE n case for holding pins
PINCER vb grip with pincers
PINCERS pl n tool consisting of two hinged arms, for gripping
PINCH vb squeeze between finger and thumb ▷ n act of pinching
PINCHED ▸ pinch
PINCHER ▸ pinch
PINCHES ▸ pinch
PINDAN n desert region of Western Australia
PINDANS ▸ pindan
PINDARI n former irregular Indian horseman
PINDER n person who impounds

PINDERS ▸ pinder
PINDOWN n wrestling manoeuvre
PINE n evergreen coniferous tree ▷ vb feel great longing (for)
PINEAL adj resembling a pine cone ▷ n pineal gland
PINEALS ▸ pineal
PINED ▸ pine
PINENE n isomeric terpene found in many essential oils
PINENES ▸ pinene
PINERY n place, esp a hothouse, where pineapples are grown
PINES ▸ pine
PINESAP n red herb of N America
PINETA ▸ pinetum
PINETUM n area of land where pine trees and other conifers are grown
PINEY ▸ pine
PINFALL another name for
▸ fall
PINFISH n small porgy of the SE North American coast of the Atlantic
PINFOLD n pound for stray cattle ▷ vb gather or confine in or as if in a pinfold
PING n short high-pitched sound ▷ vb make such a noise
PINGED ▸ ping
PINGER n device, esp a timer, that makes a pinging sound
PINGERS ▸ pinger
PINGING ▸ ping
PINGLE vb enclose small area of ground
PINGLED ▸ pingle
PINGLER ▸ pingle
PINGLES ▸ pingle
PINGO n mound of earth or gravel formed through pressure from a layer of water trapped between newly frozen ice and underlying permafrost in Arctic regions
PINGOES ▸ pingo
PINGOS ▸ pingo
PINGS ▸ ping
PINGUID adj fatty, oily, or greasy
PINGUIN same as ▸ penguin
PINHEAD n head of a pin
PINHOLE n small hole made with or as if with a pin
PINIER ▸ piny

PINIES ▸ piny
PINIEST ▸ piny
PINING ▸ pine
PINION n bird's wing ▷ vb immobilize (someone) by tying or holding his or her arms
PINIONS ▸ pinion
PINITE n greyish-green or brown mineral containing amorphous aluminium and potassium sulphates
PINITES ▸ pinite
PINITOL n compound found in pinewood
PINK n pale reddish colour ▷ adj of the colour pink ▷ vb (of an engine) make a metallic noise because not working properly, knock
PINKED ▸ pink
PINKEN vb turn pink
PINKENS ▸ pinken
PINKER n something that pinks
PINKERS ▸ pinker
PINKEST ▸ pink
PINKEY n type of ship
PINKEYE n acute contagious inflammation of the conjunctiva of the eye
PINKEYS ▸ pinkey
PINKIE n little finger
PINKIER ▸ pinky
PINKIES ▸ pinkie
PINKING ▸ pink
PINKISH ▸ pink
PINKLY ▸ pink
PINKO n person regarded as mildly left-wing
PINKOES ▸ pinko
PINKOS ▸ pinko
PINKS ▸ pink
PINKY adj of a pink colour
PINNA n external part of the ear
PINNACE n ship's boat
PINNAE ▸ pinna
PINNAL ▸ pinna
PINNAS ▸ pinna
PINNATE adj (of compound leaves) having leaflets growing opposite each other in pairs
PINNED ▸ pin
PINNER n person or thing that pins
PINNERS ▸ pinner
PINNET n pinnacle
PINNETS ▸ pinnet
PINNIE same as ▸ pinny
PINNIES ▸ pinnie

PINNING ▶ pin
PINNOCK n small bird
PINNOED adj held or bound by the arms
PINNULA same as ▶ pinnule
PINNULE n any of the lobes of a leaflet of a pinnate compound leaf, which is itself pinnately divided
PINNY informal or child's name for ▶ pinafore
PINOCLE same as ▶ pinochle
PINOLE n (in the southwestern United States) flour made of parched ground corn, mesquite beans, sugar, etc
PINOLES ▶ pinole
PINON n low-growing pine
PINONES ▶ pinon
PINONS ▶ pinon
PINOT n any of several grape varieties
PINOTS ▶ pinot
PINS ▶ pin
PINT n liquid measure, 1/8 gallon (.568 litre)
PINTA n pint of milk
PINTADA same as ▶ pintado
PINTADO n species of seagoing petrel
PINTAIL n greyish-brown duck with a pointed tail
PINTANO n tropical reef fish
PINTAS ▶ pinta
PINTLE n pin or bolt forming the pivot of a hinge
PINTLES ▶ pintle
PINTO adj marked with patches of white ▷ n pinto horse
PINTOES ▶ pinto
PINTOS ▶ pinto
PINTS ▶ pint
PINUP n picture of a sexually attractive person, esp when partially or totally undressed
PINUPS ▶ pinup
PINWALE n fabric with narrow ridges
PINWEED n herb with tiny flowers
PINWORK n (in needlepoint lace) fine raised stitches
PINWORM n parasitic nematode worm
PINXIT vb (he or she) painted (it): used formerly on paintings next to the artist's name
PINY same as ▶ peony
PINYIN n system of

romanized spelling for the Chinese language
PINYON n low-growing pine
PINYONS ▶ pinyon
PIOLET n type of ice axe
PIOLETS ▶ piolet
PION n any of three subatomic particles which are classified as mesons
PIONED adj abounding in marsh marigolds
PIONEER n explorer or early settler of a new country ▷ vb be the pioneer or leader of
PIONER obsolete spelling of ▶ pioneer
PIONERS ▶ pioner
PIONEY same as ▶ peony
PIONEYS ▶ pioney
PIONIC ▶ pion
PIONIES ▶ piony
PIONING n work of pioneers
PIONS ▶ pion
PIONY same as ▶ peony
PIOPIO n New Zealand thrush, thought to be extinct
PIOPIOS ▶ piopio
PIOSITY n grandiose display of piety
PIOTED adj pied
PIOUS adj deeply religious, devout
PIOUSLY ▶ pious
PIOY same as ▶ peeoy
PIOYE same as ▶ peeoy
PIOYES ▶ pioye
PIOYS ▶ pioy
PIP n small seed in a fruit ▷ vb chirp
PIPA n tongueless S American toad that carries its young in pits in the skin of its back
PIPAGE n pipes collectively
PIPAGES ▶ pipage
PIPAL same as ▶ peepul
PIPALS ▶ pipal
PIPAS ▶ pipa
PIPE n tube for conveying liquid or gas ▷ vb play on a pipe
PIPEAGE same as ▶ pipage
PIPED ▶ pipe
PIPEFUL ▶ pipe
PIPER n player on a pipe or bagpipes
PIPERIC > piperine
PIPERS ▶ piper
PIPES ▶ pipe
PIPET same as ▶ pipette
PIPETS ▶ pipet

PIPETTE n slender glass tube used to transfer or measure fluids ▷ vb transfer or measure out (a liquid) using a pipette
PIPI n edible mollusc often used as bait
PIPIER ▶ pipe
PIPIEST ▶ pipe
PIPING n system of pipes
PIPINGS ▶ piping
PIPIS ▶ pipi
PIPIT n small brownish songbird
PIPITS ▶ pipit
PIPKIN same as ▶ piggin
PIPKINS ▶ pipkin
PIPLESS ▶ pip
PIPPED ▶ pip
PIPPIER ▶ pippy
PIPPIN n type of eating apple
PIPPING ▶ pip
PIPPINS ▶ pippin
PIPPY adj containing many pips
PIPS ▶ pip
PIPUL n Indian fig tree
PIPULS ▶ pipul
PIPY ▶ pipe
PIQUANT adj having a pleasant spicy taste
PIQUE n feeling of hurt pride, baffled curiosity, or resentment ▷ vb hurt the pride of
PIQUED ▶ pique
PIQUES ▶ pique
PIQUET n card game for two ▷ vb play game of piquet
PIQUETS ▶ piquet
PIQUING ▶ pique
PIR n Sufi master
PIRACY n robbery on the seas
PIRAGUA same as ▶ pirogue
PIRAI n large S American fish
PIRAIS ▶ pirai
PIRANA same as ▶ piranha
PIRANAS ▶ pirana
PIRANHA n small fierce freshwater fish of tropical America
PIRATE n sea robber ▷ vb sell or reproduce (artistic work etc) illegally
PIRATED ▶ pirate
PIRATES ▶ pirate
PIRATIC ▶ pirate
PIRAYA same as ▶ pirai
PIRAYAS ▶ piraya
PIRL n ripple in water

PIRLS ▶ pirl

PIRN n reel or bobbin

PIRNIE n stripy nightcap

PIRNIES ▶ pirnie

PIRNIT adj striped

PIRNS ▶ pirn

PIROG n large pie filled with meat, vegetables, etc

PIROGEN n turnovers made from kneaded dough

PIROGHI ▶ pirog

PIROGI ▶ pirog

PIROGUE n any of various kinds of dugout canoes

PIROJKI same as ▶ piroshki

PIROQUE same as ▶ pirogue

PIRS ▶ pir

PIS ▶ pi

PISCARY n place where fishing takes place

PISCINA n stone basin, with a drain, in a church or sacristy where water used at Mass is poured away

PISCINE n pond or pool

PISCO n S American brandy

PISCOS ▶ pisco

PISE n rammed earth or clay used to make floors or walls

PISES ▶ pise

PISH interj exclamation of impatience or contempt ▷ vb make this exclamation at (someone or something)

PISHED ▶ pish

PISHEOG > pishogue

PISHER n Yiddish term for small boy

PISHERS ▶ pisher

PISHES ▶ pish

PISHING ▶ pish

PISHOGE same as > pishogue

PISKIES ▶ pisky

PISKY n Cornish fairy

PISMIRE archaic or dialect word for ▶ ant

PISO n peso of the Philippines

PISOS ▶ piso

PISTE n ski slope

PISTES ▶ piste

PISTIL n seed-bearing part of a flower

PISTILS ▶ pistil

PISTOL n short-barrelled handgun ▷ vb shoot with a pistol

PISTOLE n any of various gold coins of varying value, formerly used in Europe

PISTOLS ▶ pistol

PISTON n cylindrical part in an engine that slides to and fro in a cylinder

PISTONS ▶ piston

PISTOU n French sauce

PISTOUS ▶ pistou

PIT n deep hole in the ground ▷ vb mark with small dents or scars

PITA n any of several agave plants yielding a strong fibre

PITAPAT adv with quick light taps ▷ n such taps ▷ vb make quick light taps or beats

PITARA same as ▶ petara

PITARAH same as ▶ petara

PITARAS ▶ pitara

PITAS ▶ pita

PITAYA same as > pitahaya

PITAYAS ▶ pitaya

PITCH vb throw, hurl ▷ n area marked out for playing sport

PITCHED ▶ pitch

PITCHER n large jug with a narrow neck

PITCHES ▶ pitch

PITCHY adj full of or covered with pitch

PITEOUS adj arousing pity

PITFALL n hidden difficulty or danger

PITH n soft white lining of the rind of oranges etc ▷ vb destroy the brain and spinal cord of (a laboratory animal) by piercing or severing

PITHEAD n top of a mine shaft and the buildings and hoisting gear around it

PITHED ▶ pith

PITHFUL ▶ pith

PITHIER ▶ pithy

PITHILY ▶ pithy

PITHING ▶ pith

PITHOI ▶ pithos

PITHOS n large ceramic container for oil or grain

PITHS ▶ pith

PITHY adj short and full of meaning

PITIED ▶ pity

PITIER ▶ pity

PITIERS ▶ pity

PITIES ▶ pity

PITIETH vb as in **it pitieth me** archaic inflection of 'pity'

PITIFUL adj arousing pity

PITMAN n coal miner ▷ n connecting rod (in a machine)

PITMANS ▶ pitman

PITMEN ▶ pitman

PITON n metal spike used in climbing to secure a rope

PITONS ▶ piton

PITPROP n support beam in mine shaft

PITS ▶ pit

PITSAW n large saw formerly used for cutting logs into planks, operated by two men, one standing on top of the log and the other in a pit underneath it

PITSAWS ▶ pitsaw

PITTA n small brightly coloured ground-dwelling tropical bird

PITTAS ▶ pitta

PITTED ▶ pit

PITTEN adj having been put

PITTER vb make pattering sound

PITTERS ▶ pitter

PITTING ▶ pit

PITTITE n occupant of a theatre pit

PITUITA n thick nasal secretion

PITUITE n mucus

PITURI n Australian solanaceous shrub

PITURIS ▶ pituri

PITY n sympathy or sorrow for others' suffering ▷ vb feel pity for

PITYING ▶ pity

PIU adv more (quickly, softly, etc)

PIUM n stinging insect

PIUMS ▶ pium

PIUPIU n skirt made from the leaves of the New Zealand flax, worn by Māoris on ceremonial occasions

PIUPIUS ▶ piupiu

PIVOT n central shaft on which something turns ▷ vb provide with or turn on a pivot

PIVOTAL adj of crucial importance

PIVOTED ▶ pivot

PIVOTER ▶ pivot

PIVOTS ▶ pivot

PIX less common spelling of ▶ pyx

PIXEL n any of a number of very small picture elements that make up a picture, as on a visual display unit

PIXELS ▶ pixel

P

PIXES ▶ pix
PIXIE n (in folklore) fairy
PIXIES ▶ pixy
PIXY same as ▶ pixie
PIXYISH ▶ pixy
PIZAZZ same as ▶ pizzazz
PIZAZZY ▶ pizazz
PIZE vb strike (someone a blow)
PIZED ▶ pize
PIZES ▶ pize
PIZING ▶ pize
PIZZA n flat disc of dough covered with a wide variety of savoury toppings and baked
PIZZAS ▶ pizza
PIZZAZ same as ▶ pzazz
PIZZAZZ n attractive combination of energy and style
PIZZLE n penis of an animal, esp a bull
PIZZLES ▶ pizzle
PLAAS n farm
PLAASES ▶ plaas
PLACARD n notice that is carried or displayed in public ▷ vb attach placards to
PLACATE vb make (someone) stop feeling angry or upset
PLACCAT same as ▶ placket
PLACE n particular part of an area or space ▷ vb put in a particular place
PLACEBO n sugar pill etc given to an unsuspecting patient instead of an active drug
PLACED ▶ place
PLACER n surface sediment containing particles of gold or some other valuable mineral
PLACERS ▶ placer
PLACES ▶ place
PLACET n vote or expression of assent by saying the word placet
PLACETS ▶ placet
PLACID adj not easily excited or upset, calm
PLACING n method of issuing securities to the public using an intermediary, such as a stockbroking firm
PLACIT n decree or dictum
PLACITA > placitum
PLACITS ▶ placit
PLACK n small former Scottish coin

PLACKET n opening at the waist of a dress or skirt for buttons or zips or for access to a pocket
PLACKS ▶ plack
PLACOID adj platelike or flattened ▷ n fish with placoid scales
PLAFOND n ceiling, esp one having ornamentation
PLAGAL adj (of a cadence) progressing from the subdominant to the tonic chord, as in the Amen of a hymn
PLAGE n bright patch in the sun's chromosphere
PLAGES ▶ plage
PLAGIUM n crime of kidnapping
PLAGUE n fast-spreading fatal disease ▷ vb trouble or annoy continually
PLAGUED ▶ plague
PLAGUER ▶ plague
PLAGUES ▶ plague
PLAGUEY same as ▶ plaguy
PLAGUY adj disagreeable or vexing ▷ adv disagreeably or annoyingly
PLAICE n edible European flatfish
PLAICES ▶ plaice
PLAID n long piece of tartan cloth worn as part of Highland dress ▷ vb weave cloth into plaid
PLAIDED ▶ plaid
PLAIDS ▶ plaid
PLAIN adj easy to see or understand ▷ n large stretch of level country ▷ adv clearly or simply ▷ vb complain
PLAINED ▶ plain
PLAINER ▶ plain
PLAINLY ▶ plain
PLAINS pl n extensive tracts of level or almost level treeless countryside
PLAINT n complaint or lamentation
PLAINTS ▶ plaint
PLAIT n intertwined length of hair ▷ vb intertwine separate strands in a pattern
PLAITED ▶ plait
PLAITER ▶ plait
PLAITS ▶ plait
PLAN n way thought out to do or achieve something ▷ vb arrange beforehand

PLANAR adj of or relating to a plane
PLANATE adj having been flattened
PLANCH vb cover with planks
PLANCHE same as ▶ planch
PLANE n aeroplane ▷ adj perfectly flat or level ▷ vb glide or skim
PLANED ▶ plane
PLANER n machine with a cutting tool that makes repeated horizontal strokes across the surface of a workpiece
PLANERS ▶ planer
PLANES ▶ plane
PLANET n large body in space that revolves round the sun or another star
PLANETS ▶ planet
PLANING ▶ plane
PLANISH vb give a final finish to (metal) by hammering or rolling to produce a smooth surface
PLANK n long flat piece of sawn timber ▷ vb cover or provide (an area) with planks
PLANKED ▶ plank
PLANKS ▶ plank
PLANNED ▶ plan
PLANNER n person who makes plans, esp for the development of a town, building, etc
PLANS ▶ plan
PLANT n living organism that grows in the ground and has no power to move ▷ vb put in the ground to grow
PLANTA n sole of foot
PLANTAE ▶ planta
PLANTAR adj of, relating to, or occurring on the sole of the foot or a corresponding part
PLANTAS ▶ planta
PLANTED ▶ plant
PLANTER n owner of a plantation
PLANTS ▶ plant
PLANULA n ciliated free-swimming larva of hydrozoan coelenterates such as the hydra
PLANURY another name for > planuria
PLANXTY n Celtic melody for harp

PLAP *same as* ▶ **plop**
PLAPPED ▶ **plap**
PLAPS ▶ **plap**
PLAQUE *n* inscribed commemorative stone or metal plate
PLAQUES ▶ **plaque**
PLASH *same as* ▶ **pleach**
PLASHED ▶ **plash**
PLASHER *n* type of farm tool
PLASHES ▶ **plash**
PLASHET *n* small pond
PLASHY *adj* wet or marshy
PLASM *same as* ▶ **plasma**
PLASMA *n* clear liquid part of blood
PLASMAS ▶ **plasma**
PLASMIC ▶ **plasma**
PLASMID *n* small circle of bacterial DNA that is independent of the main bacterial chromosome
PLASMIN *n* proteolytic enzyme that causes fibrinolysis in blood clots
PLASMON *n* sum total of plasmagenes in a cell
PLASMS ▶ **plasm**
PLAST *archaic past participle of* ▶ **place**
PLASTE *archaic past participle of* ▶ **place**
PLASTER *n* mixture of lime, sand, etc for coating walls ▷ *vb* cover with plaster
PLASTIC *n* synthetic material that can be moulded when soft but sets in a hard long-lasting shape ▷ *adj* made of plastic
PLASTID *n* any of various small particles in the cytoplasm of the cells of plants and some animals
PLAT *n* small area of ground
PLATAN *n* plane tree
PLATANE *same as* ▶ **platan**
PLATANS ▶ **platan**
PLATE *n* shallow dish for holding food ▷ *vb* cover with a thin coating of gold, silver, or other metal
PLATEAU *n* area of level high land ▷ *vb* remain stable for a long period
PLATED *adj* coated with a layer of metal
PLATEN *n* roller of a typewriter, against which the paper is held
PLATENS ▶ **platen**
PLATER *n* person or thing

that plates
PLATERS ▶ **plater**
PLATES ▶ **plate**
PLATIER ▶ **platy**
PLATIES ▶ **platy**
PLATINA *n* alloy of platinum and several other metals, including palladium, osmium, and iridium
PLATING *n* coating of metal
PLATOON *n* smaller unit within a company of soldiers ▷ *vb* organise into platoons
PLATS ▶ **plat**
PLATTED ▶ **plat**
PLATTER *n* large dish
PLATY *adj* of, relating to, or designating rocks the constituents of which occur in flaky layers ▷ *n* small brightly coloured freshwater cyprinodont fish
PLATYPI > **platypus**
PLATYS ▶ **platy**
PLAUDIT *n* expression of enthusiastic approval
PLAY *vb* occupy oneself in (a game or recreation) ▷ *n* story performed on stage or broadcast
PLAYA *n* (in the US) temporary lake, or its dry often salty bed, in a desert basin
PLAYACT *vb* pretend or make believe
PLAYAS ▶ **playa**
PLAYBOY *n* rich man who lives only for pleasure
PLAYDAY *n* day given to play
PLAYED ▶ **play**
PLAYER *n* person who plays a game or sport
PLAYERS ▶ **player**
PLAYFUL *adj* lively
PLAYING > **play** *vb*
PLAYLET *n* short play
PLAYOFF *n* extra contest to decide the winner when two or more competitors are tied
PLAYPEN *n* small portable enclosure in which a young child can safely be left to play
PLAYS ▶ **play**
PLAZA *n* open space or square
PLAZAS ▶ **plaza**
PLEA *n* serious or urgent

request, entreaty ▷ *vb* entreat
PLEACH *vb* interlace the stems or boughs of (a tree or hedge)
PLEAD *vb* ask urgently or with deep feeling
PLEADED ▶ **plead**
PLEADER ▶ **plead**
PLEADS ▶ **plead**
PLEAED ▶ **plea**
PLEAING ▶ **plea**
PLEAS ▶ **plea**
PLEASE *vb* give pleasure or satisfaction to ▷ *adv* polite word of request
PLEASED ▶ **please**
PLEASER ▶ **please**
PLEASES ▶ **please**
PLEAT *n* fold made by doubling material back on itself ▷ *vb* arrange (material) in pleats
PLEATED ▶ **pleat**
PLEATER *n* attachment on a sewing machine that makes pleats
PLEATS ▶ **pleat**
PLEB *n* common vulgar person
PLEBBY *adj* common or vulgar
PLEBE *n* member of the lowest class at the US Naval Academy or Military Academy
PLEBEAN *old variant of* > **plebeian**
PLEBES ▶ **plebe**
PLEBIFY *vb* make plebeian
PLEBS *n* common people
PLECTRA > **plectrum**
PLECTRE *same as* > **plectrum**
PLED ▶ **plead**
PLEDGE *n* solemn promise ▷ *vb* promise solemnly
PLEDGED ▶ **pledge**
PLEDGEE *n* person to whom a pledge is given
PLEDGER *same as* ▶ **pledgor**
PLEDGES ▶ **pledge**
PLEDGET *n* small flattened pad of wool, cotton, etc, esp for use as a pressure bandage to be applied to wounds or sores
PLEDGOR *n* person who gives or makes a pledge
PLEIAD *n* brilliant or talented group, esp one with seven members
PLEIADS ▶ **pleiad**

P

PLENA ▸ **plenum**

PLENARY *adj* (of a meeting) attended by all members ▷ *n* book of the gospels or epistles and homilies read at the Eucharist

PLENCH *n* tool combining wrench and pliers

PLENIPO *n* plenipotentiary diplomat

PLENISH *vb* fill, stock; or resupply

PLENISM *n* philosophical theory

PLENIST ▸ **plenism**

PLENTY *n* large amount or number ▷ *adj* very many ▷ *adv* more than adequately

PLENUM *n* enclosure containing gas at a higher pressure than the surrounding environment

PLENUMS ▸ **plenum**

PLEON *n* abdomen of crustacean

PLEONAL *adj* of the abdomen of a crustacean

PLEONIC ▸ **pleon**

PLEONS ▸ **pleon**

PLEOPOD another name for > **swimmeret**

PLERION *n* filled-centre supernova remnant in which radiation is emitted by the centre as well as the shell

PLEROMA *n* abundance

PLEROME *n* central column in growing stem or root

PLESH *n* small pool

PLESHES ▸ **plesh**

PLESSOR same as ▸ **plexor**

PLEUCH same as ▸ **pleugh**

PLEUCHS ▸ **pleuch**

PLEUGH Scottish word for ▸ **plough**

PLEUGHS ▸ **pleugh**

PLEURA ▸ **pleuron**

PLEURAE ▸ **pleuron**

PLEURAL ▸ **pleuron**

PLEURAS ▸ **pleuron**

PLEURON *n* part of the cuticle of arthropods that covers the lateral surface of a body segment

PLEW *n* (formerly in Canada) beaver skin used as a standard unit of value in the fur trade

PLEWS ▸ **plew**

PLEX *n* shortening of multiplex

PLEXAL ▸ **plexus**

PLEXES ▸ **plex**

PLEXOR *n* small hammer with a rubber head for use in percussion of the chest and testing reflexes

PLEXORS ▸ **plexor**

PLEXURE *n* act of weaving together

PLEXUS *n* complex network of nerves or blood vessels

PLIABLE *adj* easily bent

PLIABLY ▸ **pliable**

PLIANCY ▸ **pliant**

PLIANT *adj* pliable

PLICA *n* folding over of parts, such as a fold of skin, muscle, peritoneum, etc

PLICAE ▸ **plica**

PLICAL ▸ **plica**

PLICATE *adj* having or arranged in parallel folds or ridges ▷ *vb* arrange into parallel folds

PLIE *n* classic ballet practice posture with back erect and knees bent

PLIED ▸ **ply**

PLIER *n* person who plies a trade

PLIERS *pl n* tool with hinged arms and jaws for gripping

PLIES ▸ **ply**

PLIGHT *n* difficult or dangerous situation

PLIGHTS ▸ **plight**

PLIM *vb* swell with water

PLIMMED ▸ **plim**

PLIMS ▸ **plim**

PLIMSOL same as > **plimsole**

PLING *n* (in computer jargon) an exclamation mark

PLINGS ▸ **pling**

PLINK *n* short sharp often metallic sound as of a string on a musical instrument being plucked or a bullet striking metal ▷ *vb* make such a noise

PLINKED ▸ **plink**

PLINKER ▸ **plink**

PLINKS ▸ **plink**

PLINKY *adj* (of a sound) short, sharp, and often metallic

PLINTH *n* slab forming the base of a statue, column, etc

PLINTHS ▸ **plinth**

PLISKIE *n* practical joke

PLISKY same as > **pliskie**

PLISSE *n* fabric with a wrinkled finish, achieved by treatment involving caustic soda

PLISSES ▸ **plisse**

PLOAT *vb* thrash

PLOATED ▸ **ploat**

PLOATS ▸ **ploat**

PLOD *vb* walk with slow heavy steps ▷ *n* act of plodding

PLODDED ▸ **plod**

PLODDER *n* person who plods, esp one who works in a slow and persevering but uninspired manner

PLODGE *vb* wade in water, esp the sea ▷ *n* act of wading

PLODGED ▸ **plodge**

PLODGES ▸ **plodge**

PLODS ▸ **plod**

PLOIDY *n* number of copies of set of chromosomes in cell

PLONG obsolete variant of ▸ **plunge**

PLONGD ▸ **plong**

PLONGE ▸ **plunge** *vb*

PLONGED ▸ **plonge**

PLONGES ▸ **plonge**

PLONGS ▸ **plong**

PLONK *vb* put (something) down heavily and carelessly ▷ *n* cheap inferior wine ▷ *interj* exclamation imitative of this sound

PLONKED ▸ **plonk**

PLONKER *n* stupid person

PLONKO *n* alcoholic, esp one who drinks wine

PLONKOS ▸ **plonko**

PLONKS ▸ **plonk**

PLONKY ▸ **plonk**

PLOOK same as ▸ **plouk**

PLOOKIE same as ▸ **plouky**

PLOOKS ▸ **plook**

PLOOKY ▸ **plook**

PLOP *n* sound of an object falling into water without a splash ▷ *vb* make this sound ▷ *interj* exclamation imitative of this sound

PLOPPED ▸ **plop**

PLOPS ▸ **plop**

PLOSION *n* sound of an abrupt break or closure, esp the audible release of a stop

PLOSIVE *adj* pronounced with a sudden release of breath ▷ *n* plosive consonant

PLOT *n* secret plan to do something illegal or wrong

▷ *vb* plan secretly, conspire

PLOTFUL ▸ **plot**

PLOTS ▸ **plot**

PLOTTED ▸ **plot**

PLOTTER *same as* ▸ **plouter**

PLOTTIE *n* hot spiced drink

PLOTTY *adj* intricately plotted

PLOTZ *vb* faint or collapse

PLOTZED ▸ **plotz**

PLOTZES ▸ **plotz**

PLOUGH *n* agricultural tool for turning over soil ▷ *vb* turn over (earth) with a plough

PLOUGHS ▸ **plough**

PLOUK *n* pimple

PLOUKIE ▸ **plouk**

PLOUKS ▸ **plouk**

PLOUKY ▸ **plouk**

PLOUTER *same as* ▸ **plowter**

PLOVER *n* shore bird with a straight bill and long pointed wings

PLOVERS ▸ **plover**

PLOVERY ▸ **plover**

PLOW *same as* ▸ **plough**

PLOWBOY *same as* > **ploughboy**

PLOWED ▸ **plow**

PLOWER ▸ **plow**

PLOWERS ▸ **plow**

PLOWING ▸ **plow**

PLOWMAN *same as* > **ploughman**

PLOWMEN ▸ **plowman**

PLOWS ▸ **plow**

PLOWTER *vb* work or play in water or mud ▷ *n* act of plowtering

PLOY *n* manoeuvre designed to gain an advantage ▷ *vb* form a column from a line of troops

PLOYED ▸ **ploy**

PLOYING ▸ **ploy**

PLOYS ▸ **ploy**

PLU *same as* ▸ **plew**

PLUCK *vb* pull or pick off ▷ *n* courage

PLUCKED ▸ **pluck**

PLUCKER ▸ **pluck**

PLUCKS ▸ **pluck**

PLUCKY *adj* brave

PLUE *same as* ▸ **plew**

PLUES ▸ **plue**

PLUFF *vb* expel in puffs

PLUFFED ▸ **pluff**

PLUFFS ▸ **pluff**

PLUFFY ▸ **pluff**

PLUG *n* thing fitting into

and filling a hole ▷ *vb* block or seal (a hole or gap) with a plug

PLUGGED ▸ **plug**

PLUGGER ▸ **plug**

PLUGOLA *n* plugging of products on television

PLUGS ▸ **plug**

PLUM *n* oval usu dark red fruit with a stone in the middle ▷ *adj* dark purplish-red

PLUMAGE *n* bird's feathers

PLUMATE *adj* of, relating to, or possessing one or more feathers or plumes

PLUMB *vb* understand (something obscure) ▷ *adv* exactly ▷ *n* weight, usually of lead, suspended at the end of a line and used to determine water depth or verticality

PLUMBED ▸ **plumb**

PLUMBER *n* person who fits and repairs pipes and fixtures for water and drainage systems

PLUMBIC *adj* of or containing lead in the tetravalent state

PLUMBS ▸ **plumb**

PLUMBUM *n* obsolete name for lead (the metal)

PLUMCOT *n* hybrid of apricot and plum

PLUME *n* feather, esp one worn as an ornament ▷ *vb* adorn or decorate with feathers or plumes

PLUMED ▸ **plume**

PLUMERY *n* plumes collectively

PLUMES ▸ **plume**

PLUMIER ▸ **plumy**

PLUMING ▸ **plume**

PLUMIST *n* person who makes plumes

PLUMMER ▸ **plum**

PLUMMET *vb* plunge downward ▷ *n* weight on a plumb line or fishing line

PLUMMY *adj* of, full of, or like plums

PLUMOSE *same as* ▸ **plumate**

PLUMOUS *adj* having plumes or feathers

PLUMP *adj* moderately or attractively fat ▷ *vb* sit or fall heavily and suddenly ▷ *n* heavy abrupt fall or the sound of this ▷ *adv*

suddenly or heavily

PLUMPED ▸ **plump**

PLUMPEN *vb* make or become plump

PLUMPER *n* pad carried in the mouth by actors to round out the cheeks

PLUMPIE *same as* ▸ **plumpy**

PLUMPLY ▸ **plump**

PLUMPS ▸ **plump**

PLUMPY *adj* plump

PLUMS ▸ **plum**

PLUMULA *n* down feather

PLUMULE *n* embryonic shoot of seed-bearing plants

PLUMY *adj* like a feather

PLUNDER *vb* take by force, esp in time of war ▷ *n* things plundered, spoils

PLUNGE *vb* put or throw forcibly or suddenly (into) ▷ *n* plunging dive

PLUNGED ▸ **plunge**

PLUNGER *n* rubber suction cup used to clear blocked pipes

PLUNGES ▸ **plunge**

PLUNK *vb* pluck the strings of (a banjo etc) to produce a twanging sound ▷ *n* act or sound of plunking ▷ *interj* exclamation imitative of the sound of something plunking ▷ *adv* exactly

PLUNKED ▸ **plunk**

PLUNKER ▸ **plunk**

PLUNKS ▸ **plunk**

PLUNKY *adj* sounding like plucked banjo string

PLURAL *adj* of or consisting of more than one ▷ *n* word indicating more than one

PLURALS ▸ **plural**

PLURRY *euphemism for* ▸ **bloody**

PLUS *vb* make or become greater in value

PLUSAGE *same as* > **plussage**

PLUSED ▸ **plus**

PLUSES ▸ **plus**

PLUSH *n* fabric with long velvety pile ▷ *adj* luxurious

PLUSHER ▸ **plush**

PLUSHES ▸ **plush**

PLUSHLY ▸ **plush**

PLUSHY *same as* ▸ **plush**

PLUSING ▸ **plus**

PLUSSED ▸ **plus**

PLUSSES ▸ **plus**

PLUTEAL ▸ **pluteus**

PLUTEI ▸ **pluteus**

P

PLUTEUS n larva of sea urchin

PLUTON n any mass of igneous rock that has solidified below the surface of the earth

PLUTONS ▸ pluton

PLUVIAL adj of or caused by the action of rain ▹ n of or relating to rainfall or precipitation

PLUVIAN n crocodile bird

PLUVIUS adj as in **pluvius insurance** insurance against rain

PLY vb work at (a job or trade) ▹ n thickness of wool, fabric, etc

PLYER n person who plies trade

PLYERS ▸ plyer

PLYING ▸ ply

PLYWOOD n board made of thin layers of wood glued together

PNEUMA n person's vital spirit, soul, or creative energy

PNEUMAS ▸ pneuma

PO n chamber pot

POA n type of grass

POACH vb catch (animals) illegally on someone else's land

POACHED ▸ poach

POACHER n person who catches animals illegally on someone else's land

POACHES ▸ poach

POACHY adj (of land) wet and soft

POAKA n type of stilt (bird) native to New Zealand

POAKAS ▸ poaka

POAKE n waste matter from tanning of hides

POAKES ▸ poake

POAS ▸ poa

POBLANO n variety of chilli pepper

POBOY n New Orleans sandwich

POBOYS ▸ poboy

POCHARD n European diving duck

POCHAY n post chaise: a closed horse-drawn four-wheeled coach

POCHAYS ▸ pochay

POCHOIR n print made from stencils

POCK n pus-filled blister resulting from smallpox

▹ vb mark with scars

POCKARD same as ▸ **pochard**

POCKED ▸ pock

POCKET n small bag sewn into clothing for carrying things ▹ vb put into one's pocket ▹ adj small

POCKETS ▸ pocket

POCKIER ▸ pock

POCKIES pl n woollen mittens

POCKILY ▸ pock

POCKING ▸ pock

POCKPIT n mark left on skin after a pock has gone

POCKS ▸ pock

POCKY ▸ pock

POCO adv little

POCOSEN same as ▸ **pocosin**

POCOSIN n swamp in US upland coastal region

POCOSON same as ▸ **pocosin**

POD n long narrow seed case of peas, beans, etc ▹ vb remove the pod from

PODAGRA n gout of the foot or big toe

PODAL adj relating to feet

PODALIC adj relating to feet

PODCAST n audio file similar to a radio broadcast, which can be downloaded and listened to on a computer or MP3 player ▹ vb make available in this format

PODDED ▸ pod

PODDIE n user of or enthusiast for the iPod, a portable digital music player

PODDIER ▸ poddy

PODDIES ▸ poddy

PODDING ▸ pod

PODDLE vb move or travel in a leisurely manner

PODDLED ▸ poddle

PODDLES ▸ poddle

PODDY n handfed calf or lamb ▹ adj fat

PODESTA n (in modern Italy) subordinate magistrate in some towns

PODEX n posterior

PODEXES ▸ podex

PODGE n short chubby person

PODGES ▸ podge

PODGIER ▸ podgy

PODGILY ▸ podgy

PODGY adj short and fat

PODIA ▸ podium

PODIAL ▸ podium

PODITE n crustacean leg

PODITES ▸ podite

PODITIC adj similar to the limb segment of an arthropod

PODIUM n small raised platform for a conductor or speaker

PODIUMS ▸ podium

PODLEY n young coalfish

PODLEYS ▸ podley

PODLIKE ▸ pod

PODS ▸ pod

PODSOL same as ▸ **podzol**

PODSOLS ▸ podsol

PODZOL n type of soil characteristic of coniferous forest regions having a greyish-white colour in its upper leached layers

PODZOLS ▸ podzol

POEM n imaginative piece of writing in rhythmic lines

POEMS ▸ poem

POEP n emission of gas from the anus

POEPS ▸ poep

POESIED ▸ poesy

POESIES ▸ poesy

POESY n poetry ▹ vb write poems

POET n writer of poems

POETESS n female poet

POETIC adj of or like poetry

POETICS n principles and forms of poetry or the study of these, esp as a form of literary criticism

POETISE same as ▸ **poeticize**

POETIZE same as ▸ **poeticize**

POETRY n poems

POETS ▸ poet

POFFLE n small piece of land

POFFLES ▸ poffle

POGEY n financial or other relief given to the unemployed by the government

POGEYS ▸ pogey

POGGE n European marine scorpaenoid fish

POGGES ▸ pogge

POGIES ▸ pogy

POGO vb jump up and down in one spot, as in a punk dance of the 1970s

POGOED ▸ pogo

POGOER ▸ pogo

POGOERS ▸ pogo

POGOING ▸ **pogo**

POGONIA n orchid with pink or white fragrant flowers

POGONIP n icy winter fog

POGOS ▸ **pogo**

POGROM n organized persecution and massacre ▷ vb carry out a pogrom

POGROMS ▸ **pogrom**

POGY same as ▸ **pogey**

POH interj exclamation expressing contempt or disgust

POHIRI variant spelling of ▸ **powhiri**

POHIRIS ▸ **pohiri**

POI n ball of woven flax swung rhythmically by Māori women during poi dances

POILU n infantryman in the French Army, esp one in the front lines in World War I

POILUS ▸ **poilu**

POINADO old variant of ▸ **poniard**

POIND vb take (property of a debtor) in execution or by way of distress

POINDED ▸ **poind**

POINDER ▸ **poind**

POINDS ▸ **poind**

POINT n main idea in a discussion, argument, etc ▷ vb show the direction or position of something or draw attention to it by extending a finger or other pointed object towards it

POINTE n tip of the toe

POINTED adj having a sharp end

POINTEL n engraver's tool

POINTER n helpful hint

POINTES ▸ **pointe**

POINTS ▸ **point**

POINTY adj having a sharp point or points

POIS ▸ **poi**

POISE n calm dignified manner ▷ vb be balanced or suspended

POISED adj absolutely ready

POISER n balancing organ of some insects

POISERS ▸ **poiser**

POISES ▸ **poise**

POISHA n monetary unit of Bangladesh

POISING ▸ **poise**

POISON n substance that kills or injures when swallowed or absorbed ▷ vb give poison to

POISONS ▸ **poison**

POISSON n fish

POITIN variant spelling of ▸ **poteen**

POITINS ▸ **poitin**

POITREL n breastplate of horse's armour

POKABLE ▸ **poke**

POKAL n tall drinking cup

POKALS ▸ **pokal**

POKE vb jab or prod with one's finger, a stick, etc ▷ n poking

POKED ▸ **poke**

POKEFUL n contents of small bag

POKER n metal rod for stirring a fire

POKERS ▸ **poker**

POKES ▸ **poke**

POKEY same as ▸ **pokie**

POKEYS ▸ **pokey**

POKIE n poker machine

POKIER ▸ **poky**

POKIES ▸ **poky**

POKIEST ▸ **poky**

POKILY ▸ **poky**

POKING ▸ **poke**

POKY adj small and cramped

POL n political campaigner

POLACCA same as ▸ **polacre**

POLACRE n three-masted sailing vessel used in the Mediterranean

POLAR adj of or near either of the earth's poles ▷ n type of line in geometry

POLARON n kind of electron

POLARS ▸ **polar**

POLDER n land reclaimed from the sea, esp in the Netherlands ▷ vb reclaim land from the sea

POLDERS ▸ **polder**

POLE n long rounded piece of wood etc ▷ vb strike or push with a pole

POLEAX same as ▸ **poleaxe**

POLEAXE vb hit or stun with a heavy blow ▷ n axe formerly used in battle or used by a butcher

POLECAT n small animal of the weasel family

POLED ▸ **pole**

POLEIS ▸ **polis**

POLEMIC n fierce attack on or defence of a particular opinion, belief, etc ▷ adj of or involving dispute or controversy

POLENTA n thick porridge made in Italy, usually from maize

POLER n person or thing that poles, esp a punter

POLERS ▸ **poler**

POLES ▸ **pole**

POLEY adj (of cattle) hornless or polled ▷ n animal with horns removed

POLEYN n piece of armour for protecting the knee

POLEYNS ▸ **poleyn**

POLEYS ▸ **poley**

POLICE n organized force in a state which keeps law and order ▷ vb control or watch over with police or a similar body

POLICED ▸ **police**

POLICER n computer device controlling use

POLICES ▸ **police**

POLICY n plan of action adopted by a person, group, or state

POLIES ▸ **poly**

POLING ▸ **pole**

POLINGS ▸ **pole**

POLIO n acute viral disease

POLIOS ▸ **polio**

POLIS n ancient Greek city-state

POLISES ▸ **polis**

POLISH vb make smooth and shiny by rubbing ▷ n substance used for polishing

POLITE adj showing consideration for others in one's manners, speech, etc

POLITER ▸ **polite**

POLITIC adj wise and likely to prove advantageous

POLITY n politically organized state, church, or society

POLJE n large elliptical depression in karst regions, sometimes containing a marsh or small lake

POLJES ▸ **polje**

POLK vb dance a polka

POLKA n lively 19th-century dance ▷ vb dance a polka

POLKAED ▸ **polka**

POLKAS ▸ **polka**

POLKED ▸ **polk**

POLKING ▸ **polk**

POLKS ▸ **polk**

POLL n questioning of a

random sample of people to find out general opinion ▷ vb receive (votes)

POLLACK n food fish related to the cod, found in northern seas

POLLAN n whitefish that occurs in lakes in Northern Ireland

POLLANS ▷ pollan

POLLARD n animal that has shed its horns or has had them removed ▷ vb cut off the top of (a tree) to make it grow bushy

POLLAXE ▷ poleaxe

POLLED adj (of animals, esp cattle) having the horns cut off or being naturally hornless

POLLEE ▷ poll

POLLEES ▷ poll

POLLEN n fine dust produced by flowers to fertilize other flowers ▷ vb collect pollen

POLLENS ▷ pollen

POLLENT adj strong

POLLER ▷ poll

POLLERS ▷ poll

POLLEX n first digit of the forelimb of amphibians, reptiles, birds, and mammals, such as the thumb of man and other primates

POLLICY obsolete spelling of ▷ policy

POLLIES ▷ polly

POLLING n casting or registering of votes at an election

POLLIST n one advocating the use of polls

POLLMAN n one passing a degree without honours

POLLMEN ▷ pollman

POLLOCK same as ▷ pollack

POLLS ▷ poll

POLLUTE vb contaminate with something poisonous or harmful

POLLY n politician

POLO n game like hockey played by teams of players on horseback

POLOIST n devotee of polo

POLONIE same as ▷ polony

POLONY n bologna sausage

POLOS ▷ polo

POLS ▷ pol

POLT n thump or blow ▷ vb strike

POLTED ▷ polt

POLTING ▷ polt

POLTS ▷ polt

POLY n polytechnic

POLYACT adj (of a sea creature) having many tentacles or limb-like protrusions

POLYCOT n plant that has or appears to have more than two cotyledons

POLYENE n chemical compound containing a chain of alternating single and double carbon-carbon bonds

POLYGAM n plant of the Polygamia class

POLYGON n geometrical figure with three or more angles and sides

POLYMER n chemical compound with large molecules made of simple molecules of the same kind

POLYNIA same as ▷ polynya

POLYNYA n stretch of open water surrounded by ice, esp near the mouths of large rivers, in arctic seas

POLYNYI ▷ polynya

POLYOL n type of alcohol

POLYOLS ▷ polyol

POLYOMA n type of tumour caused by virus

POLYP n small simple sea creature with a hollow cylindrical body

POLYPE same as ▷ polyp

POLYPED same as ▷ polypod

POLYPES ▷ polype

POLYPI ▷ polypus

POLYPOD adj (esp of insect larvae) having many legs or similar appendages ▷ n animal of this type

POLYPS ▷ polyp

POLYPUS same as ▷ polyp

POLYS ▷ poly

POLYZOA n small mosslike aquatic creatures

POMACE n apple pulp left after pressing for juice

POMACES ▷ pomace

POMADE n perfumed oil put on the hair to make it smooth and shiny ▷ vb put pomade on

POMADED ▷ pomade

POMADES ▷ pomade

POMATO n hybrid of tomato and potato

POMATUM same as ▷ pomade

POMBE n any alcoholic drink

POMBES ▷ pombe

POME n fleshy fruit of the apple and related plants, consisting of an enlarged receptacle enclosing the ovary and seeds

POMELO n edible yellow fruit, like a grapefruit, of a tropical tree

POMELOS ▷ pomelo

POMEROY n bullet used to down airships

POMES ▷ pome

POMFRET n small black rounded liquorice sweet

POMMEE adj (of cross) having end of each arm ending in disk

POMMEL same as ▷ pummel

POMMELE adj having a pommel

POMMELS ▷ pommel

POMO n postmodernism

POMOS ▷ pomo

POMP n stately display or ceremony

POMPANO n deep-bodied carangid food fish

POMPELO n large Asian citrus fruit

POMPEY vb mollycoddle

POMPEYS ▷ pompey

POMPIER adj slavishly conventional

POMPION n pumpkin

POMPOM n decorative ball of tufted wool, silk, etc

POMPOMS ▷ pompom

POMPON same as ▷ pompom

POMPONS ▷ pompon

POMPOON same as ▷ pompom

POMPOUS adj foolishly serious and grand, self-important

POMPS ▷ pomp

POMROY same as ▷ pomeroy

POMROYS ▷ pomroy

POMS ▷ pom

PONCEAU n scarlet red

PONCHO n loose circular cloak with a hole for the head

PONCHOS ▷ poncho

POND n small area of still water ▷ vb hold back

(flowing water)

PONDAGE n water held in reservoir

PONDED ▷ pond

PONDER vb think thoroughly or deeply (about)

PONDERS ▷ ponder

PONDING ▷ pond

PONDOK n (in southern Africa) crudely made house or shack

PONDOKS ▷ pondok

PONDS ▷ pond

PONE n bread made of maize

PONENT adj westerly

PONES ▷ pone

PONEY same as ▷ pony

PONEYS ▷ poney

PONG n strong unpleasant smell ▷ vb give off a strong unpleasant smell

PONGA n tall New Zealand tree fern with large leathery leaves

PONGAS ▷ ponga

PONGED ▷ pong

PONGEE n thin plain-weave silk fabric from China or India, left in its natural colour

PONGEES ▷ pongee

PONGID n primate of the family which includes the gibbons and the great apes

PONGIDS ▷ pongid

PONGIER ▷ pong

PONGING ▷ pong

PONGO n anthropoid ape, esp an orang-utan or (formerly) a gorilla

PONGOES ▷ pongo

PONGOS ▷ pongo

PONGS ▷ pong

PONGY ▷ pong

PONIARD n small slender dagger ▷ vb stab with a poniard

PONIED ▷ pony

PONIES ▷ pony

PONK n evil spirit ▷ vb stink

PONKED ▷ ponk

PONKING ▷ ponk

PONKS ▷ ponk

PONS n bridge of connecting tissue

PONT n (in South Africa) river ferry, esp one that is guided by a cable from one bank to the other

PONTAGE n tax paid for repairing bridge

PONTAL adj of or relating to the pons

PONTES ▷ pons

PONTIC adj of or relating to the pons

PONTIE same as ▷ ponty

PONTIES ▷ ponty

PONTIFF n Pope

PONTIFY vb speak or behave in a pompous or dogmatic manner

PONTIL same as ▷ punty

PONTILE adj relating to pons ▷ n metal bar used in glass-making

PONTILS ▷ pontil

PONTINE adj of or relating to bridges

PONTON same as ▷ pontoon

PONTONS ▷ ponton

PONTOON n floating platform supporting a temporary bridge ▷ vb cross a river using pontoons

PONTS ▷ pont

PONTY n rod used for shaping molten glass

PONY n small horse ▷ vb settle bill or debt

PONYING ▷ pony

PONZU n type of Japanese dipping sauce made from orange juice, sake, sugar, soy sauce, and red pepper

PONZUS ▷ ponzu

POO vb defecate

POOCH n slang word for dog ▷ vb bulge or protrude

POOCHED ▷ pooch

POOCHES ▷ pooch

POOD n unit of weight, used in Russia, equal to 36.1 pounds or 16.39 kilograms

POODLE n dog with curly hair often clipped fancifully

POODLES ▷ poodle

POODS ▷ pood

POOED ▷ poo

POOGYE n Hindu nose-flute

POOGYES ▷ poogye

POOH interj exclamation of disdain, contempt, or disgust ▷ vb make such an exclamation

POOHED ▷ pooh

POOHING ▷ pooh

POOHS ▷ pooh

POOING ▷ poo

POOJA same as ▷ puja

POOJAH same as ▷ puja

POOJAHS ▷ poojah

POOJAS ▷ pooja

POOK vb pluck

POOKA n malevolent Irish spirit

POOKAS ▷ pooka

POOKING ▷ pook

POOKIT ▷ pook

POOKS ▷ pook

POOL n small body of still water ▷ vb put in a common fund

POOLED ▷ pool

POOLER n person taking part in pool

POOLERS ▷ pooler

POOLING ▷ pool

POOLS pl n organized nationwide principally postal gambling pool betting on the result of football matches

POON n SE Asian tree with lightweight hard wood and shiny leathery leaves

POONAC n coconut residue

POONACS ▷ poonac

POONS ▷ poon

POOP n raised part at the back of a sailing ship ▷ vb (of a wave or sea) break over the stern of (a vessel)

POOPED ▷ poop

POOPER n as in **party pooper** person whose behaviour or personality spoils other people's enjoyment

POOPERS ▷ pooper

POOPING ▷ poop

POOPS ▷ poop

POOR adj having little money and few possessions

POORER ▷ poor

POOREST ▷ poor

POORI n unleavened Indian bread

POORIS ▷ poori

POORISH ▷ poor

POORLY adv in a poor manner ▷ adj not in good health

POORT n (in South Africa) steep narrow mountain pass, usually following a river or stream

POORTS ▷ poort

POOS ▷ poo

POOT vb break wind

POOTED ▷ poot

POOTER ▷ poot

POOTERS ▷ poot

POOTING ▷ poot

POOTLE vb travel or go in a relaxed or leisurely manner

P

POOTLED ▸ pootle
POOTLES ▸ pootle
POOTS ▸ poot
POP vb make or cause to make a small explosive sound ▷ n small explosive sound ▷ adj popular
POPADUM same as > poppadom
POPCORN n grains of maize heated until they puff up and burst
POPE n bishop of Rome as head of the Roman Catholic Church
POPEDOM n office or dignity of a pope
POPERA n music drawing on opera or classical music and aiming for popular appeal
POPERAS ▸ popera
POPERIN n kind of pear
POPES ▸ pope
POPETTE n young female fan or performer of pop music
POPEYED adj staring in astonishment
POPGUN n toy gun that fires a pellet or cork by means of compressed air
POPGUNS ▸ popgun
POPJOY vb amuse oneself
POPJOYS ▸ popjoy
POPLAR n tall slender tree
POPLARS ▸ poplar
POPLIN n ribbed cotton material
POPLINS ▸ poplin
POPOVER n individual Yorkshire pudding, often served with roast beef
POPPA same as ▸ papa
POPPAS ▸ poppa
POPPED ▸ pop
POPPER n press stud
POPPERS ▸ popper
POPPET n term of affection for a small child or sweetheart
POPPETS ▸ poppet
POPPIED adj covered with poppies
POPPIER ▸ poppy
POPPIES ▸ poppy
POPPING ▸ pop
POPPISH adj like pop music
POPPIT n bead used to form necklace
POPPITS ▸ poppit
POPPLE vb (of boiling water

or a choppy sea) to heave or toss
POPPLED ▸ popple
POPPLES ▸ popple
POPPLY adj covered in small bumps
POPPY n plant with a large red flower ▷ adj reddish-orange
POPRIN same as ▸ poperin
POPS ▸ pop
POPSIE same as ▸ popsy
POPSIES ▸ popsy
POPSOCK n women's knee-length nylon stocking
POPSTER n pop star
POPSY n attractive young woman
POPULAR adj widely liked and admired ▷ n cheap newspapers with mass circulation
PORAE n large edible sea fish of New Zealand waters
PORAES ▸ porae
PORAL adj relating to pores
PORANGI adj crazy
PORCH n covered approach to the entrance of a building
PORCHES ▸ porch
PORCINE adj of or like a pig
PORCINI ▸ porcino
PORCINO n edible woodland fungus
PORE n tiny opening in the skin or in the surface of a plant ▷ vb make a close intent examination or study (of a book, map, etc)
PORED ▸ pore
PORER n person who pores
PORERS ▸ pore
PORES ▸ pore
PORGE vb cleanse (slaughtered animal) ceremonially
PORGED ▸ porge
PORGES ▸ porge
PORGIE same as ▸ porgy
PORGIES ▸ porgy
PORGING ▸ porge
PORGY n any of various sparid fishes, many of which occur in American Atlantic waters
PORIER ▸ pory
PORIEST ▸ pory
PORIFER n type of invertebrate
PORINA n larva of a moth which causes damage to grassland

PORINAS ▸ porina
PORING ▸ pore
PORISM n type of mathematical proposition, the meaning of which is now obscure
PORISMS ▸ porism
PORK vb to eat ravenously ▷ n the flesh of pigs used as food
PORKED ▸ pork
PORKER n pig raised for food
PORKERS ▸ porker
PORKIER ▸ porky
PORKIES ▸ porky
PORKING ▸ pork
PORKPIE n hat with a round flat crown and a brim that can be turned up or down
PORKS ▸ pork
PORKY adj of or like pork ▷ n lie
PORLOCK vb interrupt or intrude at an awkward moment
PORN n pornography
PORNIER ▸ porny
PORNO same as ▸ porn
PORNOS ▸ porno
PORNS ▸ porn
PORNY adj pornographic
POROSE adj pierced with small pores
POROSES ▸ porosis
POROSIS n porous condition of bones
POROUS adj allowing liquid to pass through gradually
PORPESS n type of fish
PORRECT adj extended forwards ▷ vb stretch forward
PORRIGO n disease of the scalp
PORT same as > porthole
PORTA n aperture in an organ, such as the liver, esp one providing an opening for blood vessels
PORTAGE n (route for) transporting boats and supplies overland between navigable waterways ▷ vb transport (boats and supplies) in this way
PORTAL n large imposing doorway or gate
PORTALS ▸ portal
PORTAS ▸ porta
PORTATE adj diagonally athwart escutcheon
PORTED ▸ port

PORTEND vb be a sign of

PORTENT n sign of a future event

PORTER n man who carries luggage ▷ vb carry luggage

PORTERS ▶ porter

PORTESS same as > portesse

PORTHOS same as ▶ portesse

PORTICO n porch or covered walkway with columns supporting the roof

PORTIER ▶ port

PORTING ▶ port

PORTION n part or share ▷ vb divide (something) into shares

PORTLY adj rather fat

PORTMAN n inhabitant of port

PORTMEN ▶ portman

PORTOUS same as > portesse

PORTRAY vb describe or represent by artistic means, as in writing or film

PORTS ▶ port

PORTY adj like port

PORY adj containing pores

POS ▶ po

POSABLE ▶ pose

POSADA n inn in a Spanish-speaking country

POSADAS ▶ posada

POSAUNE n organ chorus reed

POSE vb place in or take up a particular position to be photographed or drawn ▷ n position while posing

POSED ▶ pose

POSER n puzzling question

POSERS ▶ poser

POSES ▶ pose

POSEUR n person who behaves in an affected way to impress others

POSEURS ▶ poseur

POSEUSE n female poseur

POSEY adj (of a place) for, characteristic of, or full of posers

POSH adj smart, luxurious ▷ adv in a manner associated with the upper class ▷ vb make posh

POSHED ▶ posh

POSHER ▶ posh

POSHES ▶ posh

POSHEST ▶ posh

POSHING ▶ posh

POSHLY ▶ posh

POSHO n corn meal

POSHOS ▶ posho

POSIER ▶ posy

POSIES ▶ posy

POSIEST ▶ posy

POSING ▶ pose

POSINGS ▶ pose

POSIT vb lay down as a basis for argument ▷ n fact, idea, etc, that is posited

POSITED ▶ posit

POSITIF n (on older organs) manual controlling soft stops

POSITON n part of chromosome

POSITS ▶ posit

POSNET n small basin or dish

POSNETS ▶ posnet

POSOLE n hominy

POSOLES ▶ posole

POSS vb wash (clothes) by agitating them with a long rod, pole, etc

POSSE n group of men organized to maintain law and order

POSSED ▶ poss

POSSER n short stick used for stirring clothes in a washtub

POSSERS ▶ posser

POSSES ▶ posse

POSSESS vb have as one's property

POSSET n drink of hot milk curdled with ale, beer, etc, flavoured with spices, formerly used as a remedy for colds ▷ vb treat with a posset

POSSETS ▶ posset

POSSIE n place

POSSIES ▶ possie

POSSING ▶ poss

POSSUM vb pretend to be dead, asleep, ignorant, etc, to deceive an opponent

POSSUMS ▶ possum

POST n official system of delivering letters and parcels ▷ vb send by post

POSTAGE n charge for sending a letter or parcel by post

POSTAL adj of a Post Office or the mail-delivery service ▷ n postcard

POSTALS ▶ postal

POSTBAG n postman's bag

POSTBOX n box into which mail is put for collection by the postal service

POSTBOY n man or boy who brings the post round to offices

POSTBUS n (in Britain, esp in rural districts) vehicle carrying the mail that also carries passengers

POSTDOC n postdoctoral degree

POSTED ▶ post

POSTEEN n Afghan leather jacket

POSTER n large picture or notice stuck on a wall ▷ vb cover with posters

POSTERN n small back door or gate ▷ adj situated at the rear or the side

POSTERS ▶ poster

POSTFIX vb add or append at the end of something

POSTIE n postman

POSTIES ▶ postie

POSTIL n commentary or marginal note, as in a Bible ▷ vb annotate (a biblical passage)

POSTILS ▶ postil

POSTIN same as ▶ posteen

POSTING n job to which someone is assigned by his or her employer which involves moving to a particular town or country

POSTINS ▶ postin

POSTMAN n person who collects and delivers post

POSTMEN ▶ postman

POSTOP n person recovering from surgery

POSTOPS ▶ postop

POSTS ▶ post

POSTTAX adj of the period after tax is paid

POSTURE n position or way in which someone stands, walks, etc ▷ vb behave in an exaggerated way to get attention

POSTWAR adj occurring or existing after a war

POSY n small bunch of flowers

POT n round deep container ▷ vb plant in a pot

POTABLE adj drinkable ▷ n something fit to drink

POTAE n hat

POTAES ▶ potae

POTAGE n thick soup

POTAGER n small kitchen garden

POTAGES ▸ potage

POTALE n residue from a grain distillery, used as animal feed

POTALES ▸ potale

POTAMIC adj of or relating to rivers

POTASH n white powdery substance obtained from ashes and used as fertilizer ▷ vb treat with potash

POTASS abbreviated form of > **potassium**

POTASSA n potassium oxide

POTATO n roundish starchy vegetable that grows underground

POTBOIL vb boil in a pot

POTBOY n (esp formerly) youth or man employed at a public house to serve beer, etc

POTBOYS ▸ potboy

POTCH n inferior quality opal used in jewellery for mounting precious opals

POTCHE vb stab

POTCHED ▸ potche

POTCHER ▸ potche

POTCHES ▸ potch

POTE vb push

POTED ▸ pote

POTEEN n (in Ireland) illegally made alcoholic drink

POTEENS ▸ poteen

POTENCE same as ▸ **potency**

POTENCY n state or quality of being potent

POTENT adj having great power or influence ▷ n potentate or ruler

POTENTS ▸ potent

POTES ▸ pote

POTFUL n amount held by a pot

POTFULS ▸ potful

POTGUN n pot-shaped mortar

POTGUNS ▸ potgun

POTHEAD n habitual user of cannabis

POTHEEN rare variant of ▸ **poteen**

POTHER n fuss or commotion ▷ vb make or be troubled or upset

POTHERB n plant whose leaves, flowers, or stems

are used in cooking

POTHERS ▸ pother

POTHERY adj stuffy

POTHOLE n hole in the surface of a road

POTHOOK n S-shaped hook for suspending a pot over a fire

POTHOS n climbing plant

POTICHE n tall vase or jar, as of porcelain, with a round or polygonal body that narrows towards the neck and a detached lid or cover

POTIN n bronze alloy with high tin content

POTING ▸ pote

POTINS ▸ potin

POTION n dose of medicine or poison

POTIONS ▸ potion

POTJIE n three-legged iron pot used for cooking

POTJIES ▸ potjie

POTLACH same as > **potlatch**

POTLIKE ▸ pot

POTLINE n row of electrolytic cells for reducing metals

POTLUCK n whatever food happens to be available without special preparation

POTMAN same as ▸ **potboy**

POTMEN ▸ potman

POTOO n nocturnal tropical bird

POTOOS ▸ potoo

POTOROO n Australian leaping rodent

POTPIE n meat and vegetable stew with a pie crust on top

POTPIES ▸ potpie

POTS ▸ pot

POTSHOP n public house

POTSHOT n chance shot taken casually, hastily, or without careful aim

POTSIE same as ▸ **potsy**

POTSIES ▸ potsy

POTSY n hopscotch

POTT old variant of ▸ **pot**

POTTAGE n thick soup or stew

POTTED ▸ pot

POTTEEN same as ▸ **poteen**

POTTER same as ▸ **putter**

POTTERS ▸ potter

POTTERY n articles made from baked clay

POTTIER ▸ potty

POTTIES ▸ potty

POTTING ▸ pot

POTTLE n liquid measure equal to half a gallon

POTTLES ▸ pottle

POTTO n short-tailed prosimian primate

POTTOS ▸ potto

POTTS ▸ pott

POTTY adj crazy or silly ▷ n bowl used by a small child as a toilet

POTZER same as ▸ **patzer**

POTZERS ▸ potzer

POUCH n small bag ▷ vb place in or as if in a pouch

POUCHED ▸ pouch

POUCHES ▸ pouch

POUCHY ▸ pouch

POUDER obsolete spelling of ▸ **powder**

POUDERS ▸ pouder

POUDRE old spelling of ▸ **powder**

POUDRES ▸ poudre

POUF n large solid cushion used as a seat ▷ vb pile up hair into rolled puffs

POUFED ▸ pouf

POUFF same as ▸ **pouf**

POUFFE same as ▸ **pouf**

POUFFED ▸ pouffe

POUFFES ▸ pouffe

POUFFS ▸ pouff

POUFING ▸ pouf

POUFS ▸ pouf

POUK Scots variant of ▸ **poke**

POUKE n mischievous spirit

POUKES ▸ pouke

POUKING ▸ pouk

POUKIT ▸ pouk

POUKS ▸ pouk

POULARD n hen that has been spayed for fattening

POULDER obsolete spelling of **powder** n

POULDRE archaic spelling of ▸ **powder**

POULE n fowl suitable for slow stewing

POULES ▸ poule

POULP n octopus

POULPE same as ▸ **poulp**

POULPES ▸ poulpe

POULPS ▸ poulp

POULT n young of a gallinaceous bird, esp of domestic fowl

POULTER n poultry dealer

POULTRY n domestic fowls

POULTS ▸ poult

POUNCE vb spring upon suddenly to attack or capture ▷ n pouncing

POUNCED ▷ pounce

POUNCER ▷ pounce

POUNCES ▷ pounce

POUNCET n box with a perforated top used for perfume

POUND n monetary unit of Britain and some other countries ▷ vb hit heavily and repeatedly

POUNDAL n fps unit of force

POUNDED ▷ pound

POUNDER ▷ pound

POUNDS ▷ pound

POUPE vb make sudden blowing sound

POUPED ▷ poupe

POUPES ▷ poupe

POUPING ▷ poupe

POUPT ▷ poupe

POUR vb flow or cause to flow out in a stream

POURED ▷ pour

POURER ▷ pour

POURERS ▷ pour

POURIE n jug

POURIES ▷ pourie

POURING ▷ pour

POURS ▷ pour

POURSEW obsolete spelling of ▷ **pursue**

POURSUE obsolete spelling of ▷ **pursue**

POUSADA n traditional Portuguese hotel

POUSSE same as ▷ **pease**

POUSSES ▷ pousse

POUSSIE old variant of ▷ **pussy**

POUSSIN n young chicken reared for eating

POUT vb thrust out one's lips, look sulky ▷ n pouting look

POUTED ▷ pout

POUTER n pigeon that can puff out its crop

POUTERS ▷ pouter

POUTFUL adj tending to pout

POUTHER Scots variant of ▷ **powder**

POUTIER ▷ pout

POUTINE n dish of chipped potatoes topped with curd cheese and a tomato-based sauce

POUTING ▷ pout

POUTS ▷ pout

POUTY ▷ pout

POVERTY n state of being without enough food or money

POW interj exclamation to indicate that a collision or explosion has taken place ▷ n head or a head of hair

POWAN n type of freshwater whitefish occurring in some Scottish lakes

POWANS ▷ powan

POWDER n substance in the form of tiny loose particles ▷ vb apply powder to

POWDERS ▷ powder

POWDERY ▷ powder

POWER n ability to do or act ▷ vb give or provide power to

POWERED ▷ power

POWERS ▷ power

POWHIRI n Māori ceremony of welcome, esp to a marae

POWIN n peacock

POWINS ▷ powin

POWN same as ▷ **powin**

POWND obsolete spelling of ▷ **pound**

POWNDED ▷ pownd

POWNDS ▷ pownd

POWNEY old Scots spelling of ▷ **pony**

POWNEYS ▷ powney

POWNIE old Scots spelling of ▷ **pony**

POWNIES ▷ pownie

POWNS ▷ pown

POWNY old Scots spelling of ▷ **pony**

POWRE obsolete spelling of ▷ **power**

POWRED ▷ powre

POWRES ▷ powre

POWRING ▷ powre

POWS ▷ pow

POWTER vb scrabble about

POWTERS ▷ powter

POWWAW interj expression of disbelief or contempt

POWWOW n talk or conference ▷ vb hold a powwow

POWWOWS ▷ powwow

POX n disease in which skin pustules form ▷ vb infect with pox

POXED ▷ pox

POXES ▷ pox

POXIER ▷ poxy

POXIEST ▷ poxy

POXING ▷ pox

POXY adj having or having had syphilis

POYNANT old variant of ▷ **poignant**

POYNT obsolete spelling of ▷ **point**

POYNTED ▷ poynt

POYNTS ▷ poynt

POYOU n type of armadillo

POYOUS ▷ poyou

POYSE obsolete variant of ▷ **poise**

POYSED ▷ poyse

POYSES ▷ poyse

POYSING ▷ poyse

POYSON obsolete spelling of ▷ **poison**

POYSONS ▷ poyson

POZ adj positive

> **Poz** is an old-fashioned short form of **positive**, and one of the most frequently played short Z words.

POZOLE same as ▷ **posole**

POZOLES ▷ pozole

POZZ adj positive

POZZIES ▷ pozzy

POZZY same as ▷ **possie**

PRAAM same as ▷ **pram**

PRAAMS ▷ praam

PRABBLE same as ▷ **brabble**

PRACTIC adj practical ▷ n practice

PRAD n horse

PRADS ▷ prad

PRAESES n Roman governor

PRAETOR n (in ancient Rome) senior magistrate ranking just below the consuls

PRAHU same as ▷ **proa**

PRAHUS ▷ prahu

PRAIRIE n large treeless area of grassland, esp in N America and Canada

PRAISE vb express approval or admiration of (someone or something) ▷ n something said or written to show approval or admiration

PRAISED ▷ praise

PRAISER ▷ praise

PRAISES ▷ praise

PRAJNA n wisdom or understanding considered as the goal of Buddhist contemplation

PRAJNAS ▷ prajna

PRALINE n sweet made of nuts and caramelized sugar

PRAM n four-wheeled

carriage for a baby, pushed by hand

PRAMS ▶ pram

PRANA n (in Oriental medicine, martial arts, etc) cosmic energy believed to come from the sun and connecting the elements of the universe

PRANAS ▶ prana

PRANCE vb walk with exaggerated bouncing steps ▷ n act of prancing

PRANCED ▶ prance

PRANCER ▶ prance

PRANCES ▶ prance

PRANCK obsolete variant of ▶ **prank**

PRANCKE obsolete variant of ▶ **prank**

PRANCKS ▶ pranck

PRANG n crash in a car or aircraft ▷ vb crash or damage (an aircraft or car)

PRANGED ▶ prang

PRANGS ▶ prang

PRANK n mischievous trick ▷ vb dress or decorate showily or gaudily

PRANKED ▶ prank

PRANKLE obsolete variant of ▶ **prance**

PRANKS ▶ prank

PRANKY ▶ prank

PRAO same as ▶ **proa**

PRAOS ▶ prao

PRASE n light green translucent variety of chalcedony

PRASES ▶ prase

PRAT n stupid person

PRATE vb talk idly and at length ▷ n chatter

PRATED ▶ prate

PRATER ▶ prate

PRATERS ▶ prate

PRATES ▶ prate

PRATIE n potato

PRATIES ▶ pratie

PRATING ▶ prate

PRATS ▶ prat

PRATT n buttocks ▷ vb hit on the buttocks

PRATTED ▶ pratt

PRATTLE vb chatter in a childish or foolish way ▷ n childish or foolish talk

PRATTS ▶ pratt

PRATY obsolete variant of ▶ **pretty**

PRAU same as ▶ **proa**

PRAUNCE obsolete variant of ▶ **prance**

PRAUS ▶ prau

PRAVITY n moral degeneracy

PRAWLE n Shakespearian phonetic spelling of "brawl" meant to indicate that the speaker is Welsh

PRAWLES ▶ prawle

PRAWLIN same as ▶ **praline**

PRAWN n edible shellfish like a large shrimp ▷ vb catch prawns

PRAWNED ▶ prawn

PRAWNER ▶ prawn

PRAWNS ▶ prawn

PRAXES ▶ praxis

PRAXIS n practice as opposed to theory

PRAY vb say prayers ▷ adv I beg you ▷ interj I beg you

PRAYED ▶ pray

PRAYER n thanks or appeal addressed to one's God

PRAYERS ▶ prayer

PRAYING ▶ pray

PRAYS ▶ pray

PRE prep before

PREACE obsolete variant of ▶ **press**

PREACED ▶ preace

PREACES ▶ preace

PREACH vb give a talk on a religious theme as part of a church service

PREACHY adj inclined to or marked by preaching

PREACT vb act beforehand

PREACTS ▶ preact

PREAGED adj treated to appear older

PREAMP n electronic amplifier used to improve the signal-to-noise ratio of an electronic device

PREAMPS ▶ preamp

PREANAL adj situated in front of anus

PREARM vb arm beforehand

PREARMS ▶ prearm

PREASE vb crowd or press

PREASED ▶ prease

PREASES ▶ prease

PREASSE obsolete spelling of ▶ **press**

PREAVER vb aver in advance

PREBADE ▶ prebid

PREBAKE vb bake before further cooking

PREBEND n allowance paid by a cathedral or collegiate church to a canon or

member of the chapter

PREBID vb bid beforehand

PREBIDS ▶ prebid

PREBILL vb issue an invoice before the service has been provided

PREBIND vb bind a book in a hard-wearing binding

PREBOIL vb boil beforehand

PREBOOK vb book well in advance

PREBOOM adj of the period before an economic boom

PREBORN adj unborn

PREBUY vb buy in advance

PREBUYS ▶ prebuy

PRECAST adj (esp of concrete when employed as a structural element in building) cast in a particular form before being used ▷ vb cast (concrete) in a particular form before use

PRECAVA n superior vena cava

PRECEDE vb go or be before

PRECENT vb issue a command or law

PRECEPT n rule of behaviour

PRECES pl n prayers

PRECESS vb undergo or cause to undergo precession

PRECIPE n type of legal document

PRECIS n short written summary of a longer piece ▷ vb make a precis of

PRECISE adj exact, accurate in every detail

PRECODE vb code beforehand

PRECOOK vb cook (food) beforehand

PRECOOL vb cool in advance

PRECOUP adj of the period before a coup

PRECURE vb cure in advance

PRECUT vb cut in advance

PRECUTS ▶ precut

PREDATE vb occur at an earlier date than

PREDAWN n period before dawn

PREDIAL same as ▶ **praedial**

PREDICT vb tell about in advance, prophesy

PREDIED ▶ predy

PREDIES ▶ predy

PREDIVE adj happening

before a dive

PREDOOM vb pronounce (someone or something's) doom beforehand

PREDRY vb dry beforehand

PREDUSK n period before dawn

PREDY vb prepare for action

PREE vb try or taste

PREED ▶ pree

PREEDIT vb edit beforehand

PREEING ▶ pree

PREEMIE n premature infant

PREEMPT vb acquire in advance of or to the exclusion of others

PREEN vb (of a bird) clean or trim (feathers) with the beak ▷ n pin, esp a decorative one

PREENED ▶ preen

PREENER ▶ preen

PREENS ▶ preen

PREES ▶ pree

PREEVE old form of ▶ prove

PREEVED ▶ preeve

PREEVES ▶ preeve

PREFAB n prefabricated house ▷ vb manufacture sections of (building) in factory

PREFABS ▶ prefab

PREFACE n introduction to a book ▷ vb serve as an introduction to (a book, speech, etc)

PREFADE vb fade beforehand

PREFARD vb old form of preferred

PREFECT n senior pupil in a school, with limited power over others

PREFER vb like better

PREFERS ▶ prefer

PREFILE vb file beforehand

PREFIRE vb fire beforehand

PREFIX n letter or group of letters put at the beginning of a word to make a new word, such as un- in unhappy ▷ vb put as an introduction or prefix (to)

PREFORM vb form beforehand

PREFUND vb pay for in advance

PREGAME adj of the period before a sports match ▷ n such a period

PREGGY informal word for > pregnant

PREHEAT vb heat (an oven, grill, pan, etc) beforehand

PREHEND vb take hold of

PREIF old form of ▶ proof

PREIFE old form of ▶ proof

PREIFES ▶ preife

PREIFS ▶ preif

PREJINK same as ▶ perjink

PRELACY n office or status of a prelate

PRELATE n bishop or other churchman of high rank

PRELATY n prelacy

PRELAW adj before taking up study of law

PRELECT vb lecture or discourse in public

PRELIFE n life lived before one's life on earth

PRELIM n event which precedes another

PRELIMS pl n pages of a book, such as the title page and contents, which come before the main text

PRELOAD vb load beforehand

PRELUDE n introductory movement in music ▷ vb act as a prelude to (something)

PRELUDI > preludio

PREM n informal word for a premature infant

PREMADE adj made in advance

PREMAN n a hominid

PREMEAL adj of the period before a meal

PREMED n premedical student

PREMEDS ▶ premed

PREMEET adj happening before a meet

PREMEN ▶ preman

PREMIA ▶ premium

PREMIE same as ▶ preemie

PREMIER n prime minister ▷ adj chief, leading

PREMIES ▶ premie

PREMISE n statement assumed to be true and used as the basis of reasoning ▷ vb state or assume (a proposition) as a premise in an argument, theory, etc

PREMISS same as ▶ premise

PREMIUM n additional sum of money, as on a wage or charge

PREMIX vb mix beforehand

PREMIXT ▶ premix

PREMOLD vb mold in advance

PREMOLT adj happening in the period before an animal molts

PREMOVE vb prompt to action

PREMS ▶ prem

PREMUNE adj having immunity to a disease as a result of latent infection

PREMY same as ▶ preemie

PRENAME n forename

PRENEED adj arranged in advance of eventual requirements

PRENOON adj of the period before noon

PRENT Scots variant of ▶ print

PRENTED ▶ prent

PRENTS ▶ prent

PRENUP n prenuptial agreement

PRENUPS ▶ prenup

PRENZIE adj Shakespearian word, possibly a mistake, supposed by some to mean "princely"

PREON n (in particle physics) hypothetical subcomponent of a quark

PREONS ▶ preon

PREOP n patient being prepared for surgery

PREOPS ▶ preop

PREORAL adj situated in front of mouth

PREP vb prepare

PREPACK vb pack in advance of sale

PREPAID ▶ prepay

PREPARE vb make or get ready

PREPAVE vb pave beforehand

PREPAY vb pay for in advance

PREPAYS ▶ prepay

PREPILL adj of the period before the contraceptive pill became available

PREPLAN vb plan beforehand

PREPONE vb bring forward to an earlier time

PREPOSE vb place before

PREPPED ▶ prep

PREPPIE same as ▶ preppy

PREPPY adj characteristic of or denoting a fashion style of neat, understated, and often expensive clothes ▷ n

P

person exhibiting such style

PREPREG n material already impregnated with synthetic resin

PREPS ▶ prep

PREPUCE n foreskin

PREPUPA n insect in stage of life before pupa

PREQUEL n film or book about an earlier stage of a story or a character's life, released because the later part of it has already been successful

PRERACE adj of the period before a race

PRERIOT adj of the period before a riot

PREROCK adj of the era before rock music

PRERUPT adj abrupt

PRESA n sign or symbol used in a canon, round, etc, to indicate the entry of each part

PRESAGE vb be a sign or warning of ▷ n omen

PRESALE n practice of arranging the sale of a product before it is available

PRESE ▶ presa

PRESELL vb promote (a product, entertainment, etc) with publicity in advance of its appearance

PRESENT adj being in a specified place ▷ n present time or tense ▷ vb introduce formally or publicly

PRESES same as ▶ **praeses**

PRESET vb set the timer so that it starts to work at a specific time ▷ adj (of equipment) with the controls set in advance ▷ n control, such as a variable resistor, that is not as accessible as the main controls and is used to set initial conditions

PRESETS ▶ preset

PRESHIP vb ship in advance

PRESHOW vb show in advance

PRESIDE vb be in charge, esp of a meeting

PRESIFT vb sift beforehand

PRESOAK vb soak beforehand

PRESOLD ▶ presell

PRESONG adj of the period before a song is sung

PRESORT vb sort in advance

PRESS vb apply force or weight to ▷ n printing machine

PRESSED ▶ press

PRESSER ▶ press

PRESSES ▶ press

PRESSIE informal word for ▶ **present**

PRESSOR n something that produces an increase in blood pressure

PREST adj prepared for action or use ▷ n loan of money ▷ vb give as a loan

PRESTED ▶ prest

PRESTER ▶ prest

PRESTO adv very quickly ▷ n passage to be played very quickly

PRESTOS ▶ presto

PRESTS ▶ prest

PRESUME vb suppose to be the case

PRETAPE vb tape in advance

PRETAX adj before tax

PRETEEN n boy or girl approaching his or her teens

PRETELL vb predict

PRETEND vb claim or give the appearance of (something untrue) to deceive or in play ▷ adj fanciful

PRETERM n premature baby

PRETEST vb test (something) before presenting it to its intended public or client ▷ n act or instance of pretesting

PRETEXT n false reason given to hide the real one ▷ vb get personal information under false pretences

PRETOLD ▶ pretell

PRETOR same as ▶ **praetor**

PRETORS ▶ pretor

PRETRIM vb trim in advance

PRETTY adj pleasing to look at ▷ adv fairly, moderately ▷ vb pretty

PRETYPE vb type in advance

PRETZEL n brittle salted biscuit

PREVAIL vb gain mastery

PREVE vb prove

PREVED ▶ preve

PREVENE vb come before

PREVENT vb keep from happening or doing

PREVERB n particle preceding preverb of verb

PREVES ▶ preve

PREVIEW n advance showing of a film or exhibition before it is shown to the public ▷ vb view in advance

PREVING ▶ preve

PREVISE vb predict or foresee

PREVUE same as ▶ **preview**

PREVUED ▶ prevue

PREVUES ▶ prevue

PREWAR adj relating to the period before a war, esp before World War I or II

PREWARM vb warm beforehand

PREWARN vb warn in advance

PREWASH vb give a preliminary wash to (clothes), esp in a washing machine ▷ n preliminary wash, esp in a washing machine

PREWIRE vb wire beforehand

PREWORK vb work in advance

PREWORN adj (of clothes) second-hand

PREWRAP vb wrap in advance

PREWYN obsolete spelling of ▶ **prune**

PREWYNS ▶ prewyn

PREX same as ▶ **prexy**

PREXES ▶ prex

PREXIES ▶ prexy

PREXY n US college president

PREY n animal hunted and killed for food by another animal ▷ vb hunt or seize food by killing other animals

PREYED ▶ prey

PREYER ▶ prey

PREYERS ▶ prey

PREYFUL adj rich in prey

PREYING ▶ prey

PREYS ▶ prey

PREZ n president

PREZES ▶ prez

PREZZIE same as ▶ **pressie**

PRIAL n pair royal of cards

PRIALS ▶ prial

PRIAPI ▶ priapus

PRIAPIC adj phallic

PRIAPUS n representation of the penis

PRIBBLE same as ▸ **prabble**

PRICE n amount of money for which a thing is bought or sold ▸ vb fix or ask the price of

PRICED ▸ **price**

PRICER ▸ **price**

PRICERS ▸ **price**

PRICES ▸ **price**

PRICEY adj expensive

PRICIER ▸ **pricy**

PRICILY ▸ **pricey**

PRICING ▸ **price**

PRICK vb pierce lightly with a sharp point ▸ n sudden sharp pain caused by pricking

PRICKED ▸ **prick**

PRICKER n person or thing that pricks

PRICKET n male deer in the second year of life having unbranched antlers

PRICKLE n thorn or spike on a plant ▸ vb have a tingling or pricking sensation

PRICKLY adj having prickles

PRICKS ▸ **prick**

PRICKY adj covered with pricks

PRICY same as ▸ **pricey**

PRIDE n feeling of pleasure and satisfaction when one has done well

PRIDED ▸ **pride**

PRIDES ▸ **pride**

PRIDIAN adj relating to yesterday

PRIDING ▸ **pride**

PRIED ▸ **pry**

PRIEF obsolete variant of **proof** n

PRIEFE obsolete variant of ▸ **proof**

PRIEFES ▸ **priefe**

PRIEFS ▸ **prief**

PRIER n person who pries

PRIERS ▸ **prier**

PRIES ▸ **pry**

PRIEST n (in the Christian church) person who can administer the sacraments and preach ▸ vb make a priest

PRIESTS ▸ **priest**

PRIEVE obsolete variant of ▸ **proof**

PRIEVED ▸ **prieve**

PRIEVES ▸ **prieve**

PRIG n self-righteous person who acts as if superior to others

PRIGGED ▸ **prig**

PRIGGER n thief

PRIGS ▸ **prig**

PRILL vb convert (a material) into a granular free-flowing form ▸ n prilled material

PRILLED ▸ **prill**

PRILLS ▸ **prill**

PRIM adj formal, proper, and rather prudish ▸ vb make prim

PRIMA same as ▸ **primo**

PRIMACY n state of being first in rank, grade, etc

PRIMAGE n tax added to customs duty

PRIMAL adj of basic causes or origins

PRIMARY adj chief, most important ▸ n person or thing that is first in position, time, or importance

PRIMAS ▸ **prima**

PRIMATE n member of an order of mammals including monkeys and humans

PRIME adj main, most important ▸ n time when someone is at his or her best or most vigorous ▸ vb give (someone) information in advance to prepare them for something

PRIMED ▸ **prime**

PRIMELY ▸ **prime**

PRIMER n special paint applied to bare wood etc before the main paint

PRIMERO n 16th- and 17th-century card game

PRIMERS ▸ **primer**

PRIMES ▸ **prime**

PRIMEUR n anything (esp fruit) produced early

PRIMI ▸ **primo**

PRIMINE n integument surrounding an ovule or the outer of two such integuments

PRIMING same as ▸ **primer**

PRIMLY ▸ **prim**

PRIMMED ▸ **prim**

PRIMMER ▸ **prim**

PRIMO n upper or right-hand part in a piano duet

PRIMOS ▸ **primo**

PRIMP vb tidy (one's hair or clothes) fussily

PRIMPED ▸ **primp**

PRIMPS ▸ **primp**

PRIMS ▸ **prim**

PRIMSIE Scots variant of ▸ **prim**

PRIMULA n type of primrose with brightly coloured flowers

PRIMUS n presiding bishop in the Synod

PRIMY adj prime

PRINCE vb act the prince

PRINCED ▸ **prince**

PRINCES ▸ **prince**

PRINCOX n pert youth

PRINK vb dress (oneself) finely

PRINKED ▸ **prink**

PRINKER ▸ **prink**

PRINKS ▸ **prink**

PRINT vb reproduce (a newspaper, book, etc) in large quantities by mechanical or electronic means ▸ n printed words etc

PRINTED ▸ **print**

PRINTER n person or company engaged in printing

PRINTS ▸ **print**

PRION n dovelike petrel with a serrated bill

PRIONS ▸ **prion**

PRIOR adj earlier ▸ n head monk in a priory

PRIORLY ▸ **prior**

PRIORS ▸ **prior**

PRIORY n place where certain orders of monks or nuns live

PRISAGE n customs duty levied until 1809 upon wine imported into England

PRISE same as ▸ **pry**

PRISED ▸ **prise**

PRISER ▸ **prise**

PRISERE n primary sere or succession from bare ground to the community climax

PRISERS ▸ **prise**

PRISES ▸ **prise**

PRISING ▸ **prise**

PRISM n transparent block usu with triangular ends and rectangular sides, used to disperse light into a spectrum or refract it in optical instruments

PRISMS ▸ **prism**

PRISMY ▸ **prism**

P

PRISON n building where criminals and accused people are held ▷ vb imprison

PRISONS ▶ **prison**

PRISS n prissy person ▷ vb act prissily

PRISSED ▶ **priss**

PRISSES ▶ **priss**

PRISSY adj prim, correct, and easily shocked ▷ n prissy person

PRITHEE interj pray thee

PRIVACY n condition of being private

PRIVADO n close friend

PRIVATE adj for the use of one person or group only ▷ n soldier of the lowest rank

PRIVET n bushy evergreen shrub used for hedges

PRIVETS ▶ **privet**

PRIVIER ▶ **privy**

PRIVIES ▶ **privy**

PRIVILY adv in a secret way

PRIVITY n legally recognized relationship existing between two parties, such as that between lessor and lessee and between the parties to a contract

PRIVY adj sharing knowledge of something secret ▷ n toilet, esp an outside one

PRIZE n reward given for success in a competition etc ▷ adj winning or likely to win a prize ▷ vb value highly

PRIZED ▶ **prize**

PRIZER n contender for prize

PRIZERS ▶ **prizer**

PRIZES ▶ **prize**

PRIZING ▶ **prize**

PRO prep in favour of ▷ n professional ▷ adv in favour of a motion etc

PROA n any of several kinds of canoe-like boats used in the South Pacific, esp one equipped with an outrigger and sails

PROAS ▶ **proa**

PROB n problem

PROBALL adj believable

PROBAND n first patient to be investigated in a family study, to whom all relationships are referred

PROBANG n long flexible rod, often with a small sponge at one end, for inserting into the oesophagus, as to apply medication

PROBATE n process of proving the validity of a will ▷ vb establish officially the authenticity and validity of (a will)

PROBE vb search into or examine closely ▷ n surgical instrument used to examine a wound, cavity, etc

PROBED ▶ **probe**

PROBER ▶ **probe**

PROBERS ▶ **probe**

PROBES ▶ **probe**

PROBING ▶ **probe**

PROBIT n statistical measurement

PROBITS ▶ **probit**

PROBITY n honesty, integrity

PROBLEM n something difficult to deal with or solve ▷ adj of a literary work that deals with difficult moral questions

PROBS ▶ **prob**

PROCARP n female reproductive organ in red algae

PROCEED vb start or continue doing

PROCESS n series of actions or changes ▷ vb handle or prepare by a special method of manufacture

PROCTAL adj relating to the rectum

PROCTOR n member of the staff of certain universities having duties including the enforcement of discipline ▷ vb invigilate (an examination)

PROCURE vb get, provide

PROD vb poke with something pointed ▷ n prodding

PRODDED ▶ **prod**

PRODDER ▶ **prod**

PRODIGY n person with some marvellous talent

PRODRUG n compound that is itself biologically inactive but is metabolized in the body to produce an active therapeutic drug

PRODS ▶ **prod**

PRODUCE vb bring into existence ▷ n food grown for sale

PRODUCT n something produced

PROEM n introduction or preface

PROEMS ▶ **proem**

PROETTE n female golfing professional

PROF short for ▶ **professor**

PROFACE interj much good may it do you

PROFANE adj showing disrespect for religion or holy things ▷ vb treat (something sacred) irreverently, desecrate

PROFESS vb state or claim (something as true), sometimes falsely

PROFFER vb offer ▷ n act of proffering

PROFILE n outline, esp of the face, as seen from the side ▷ vb draw, write, or make a profile of

PROFIT n money gained ▷ vb gain or benefit

PROFITS ▶ **profit**

PROFS ▶ **prof**

PROFUSE adj plentiful

PROG vb prowl about for or as if for food or plunder ▷ n food obtained by begging

PROGENY n children

PROGGED ▶ **prog**

PROGGER n fan of progressive rock

PROGRAM same as ▶ **programme**

PROGS ▶ **prog**

PROGUN adj in favour of public owning firearms

PROIGN same as ▶ **proin**

PROIGNS ▶ **proign**

PROIN vb trim or prune

PROINE same as ▶ **proin**

PROINED ▶ **proin**

PROINES ▶ **proine**

PROINS ▶ **proin**

PROJECT n planned scheme to do or examine something over a period ▷ vb make a forecast based on known data

PROJET n draft of a proposed treaty

PROJETS ▶ **projet**

PROKE vb thrust or poke

PROKED ▶ **proke**

PROKER ▶ **proke**

PROKERS ▶ **proke**

PROKES ▶ proke

PROKING ▶ proke

PROLAN n constituent of human pregnancy urine

PROLANS ▶ prolan

PROLATE adj having a polar diameter which is longer than the equatorial diameter ▷ vb pronounce or utter

PROLE old form of ▶ prowl

PROLED ▶ prole

PROLEG n any of the short paired unjointed appendages on each abdominal segment of a caterpillar and any of certain other insect larvae

PROLEGS ▶ proleg

PROLER n prowler

PROLERS ▶ proler

PROLES ▶ prole

PROLINE n nonessential amino acid that occurs in protein

PROLING ▶ prole

PROLIX adj (of speech or a piece of writing) overlong and boring

PROLL vb prowl or search

PROLLED ▶ proll

PROLLER ▶ proll

PROLLS ▶ proll

PROLOG same as ▶ prologue

PROLOGS ▶ prolog

PROLONG vb make (something) last longer

PROM n formal dance held at a high school or college

PROMINE n substance promoting cell growth

PROMISE vb say that one will definitely do or not do something ▷ n undertaking to do or not to do something

PROMMER n spectator at promenade concert

PROMO vb promote (something)

PROMOED ▶ promo

PROMOS ▶ promo

PROMOTE vb help to make (something) happen or increase

PROMPT vb cause (an action) ▷ adj done without delay ▷ adv exactly ▷ n anything that serves to remind

PROMPTS ▶ prompt

PROMS ▶ prom

PRONAOI ▶ pronaos

PRONAOS n inner area of the portico of a classical temple

PRONATE vb turn (a limb, hand, or foot) so that the palm or sole is directed downwards

PRONE n sermon

PRONELY ▶ prone

PRONER ▶ prone

PRONES ▶ prone

PRONEST ▶ prone

PRONEUR n flatterer

PRONG n one spike of a fork or similar instrument ▷ vb prick or spear with or as if with a prong

PRONGED ▶ prong

PRONGS ▶ prong

PRONK vb jump straight up

PRONKED ▶ pronk

PRONKS ▶ pronk

PRONOTA ▶ pronotum

PRONOUN n word, such as she or it, used to replace a noun

PRONTO adv at once

PROO interj (to a horse) stop!

PROOF n evidence that shows that something is true or has happened ▷ adj able to withstand ▷ vb take a proof from (type matter)

PROOFED ▶ proof

PROOFER n reader of proofs

PROOFS ▶ proof

PROOTIC n bone in front of ear

PROP vb support (something) so that it stays upright or in place ▷ n pole, beam, etc used as a support

PROPAGE vb propagate

PROPALE vb publish (something)

PROPANE n flammable gas found in petroleum and used as a fuel

PROPEL vb cause to move forward

PROPELS ▶ propel

PROPEND vb be inclined or disposed

PROPENE n colourless gaseous alkene obtained by cracking petroleum

PROPER adj real or genuine ▷ n service or psalm regarded as appropriate to a specific day, season, etc

PROPERS ▶ proper

PROPHET n person

supposedly chosen by God to spread His word

PROPINE vb to drink a toast to

PROPJET another name for > **turboprop**

PROPMAN n member of the stage crew in charge of the stage props

PROPMEN ▶ propman

PROPONE vb propose or put forward, esp before a court

PROPOSE vb put forward for consideration

PROPPED ▶ prop

PROPRIA > proprium

PROPS ▶ prop

PROPYL n of, consisting of, or containing the monovalent group of atoms C_3H_7-

PROPYLA > propylon

PROPYLS ▶ propyl

PRORATE vb divide, assess, or distribute (something) proportionately

PRORE n forward part of ship

PRORES ▶ prore

PROS ▶ pro

PROSAIC adj lacking imagination, dull

PROSE n ordinary speech or writing in contrast to poetry ▷ vb speak or write in a tedious style

PROSECT vb dissect a cadaver for a public demonstration

PROSED ▶ prose

PROSER n writer of prose

PROSERS ▶ proser

PROSES ▶ prose

PROSIER ▶ prosy

PROSIFY vb write prose

PROSILY ▶ prosy

PROSING ▶ prose

PROSIT interj good health! cheers!

PROSO n millet

PROSODY n study of poetic metre and techniques

PROSOMA n head and thorax of an arachnid

PROSOS ▶ proso

PROSPER vb be successful

PROSS n prostitute

PROSSES ▶ pross

PROSSIE n prostitute

PROST same as ▶ **prosit**

PROSTIE n prostitute

PROSY adj dull and long-winded

PROTEA n African shrub with showy flowers

PROTEAN adj constantly changing ▷ n creature that can change shape

PROTEAS ▶ protea

PROTECT vb defend from trouble, harm, or loss

PROTEGE n person who is protected and helped by another

PROTEI ▶ proteus

PROTEID n protein

PROTEIN n any of a group of complex organic compounds that are essential for life

PROTEND vb hold out or stretch

PROTEST n declaration or demonstration of objection ▷ vb object, disagree

PROTEUS n aerobic bacterium

PROTHYL same as ▶ protyle

PROTIST n organism belonging to the kingdom which comprises protozoans, unicellular algae, and simple fungi

PROTIUM n most common isotope of hydrogen

PROTO n as in proto team relating to a team of people trained to deal with underground rescues, etc

PROTON n positively charged particle in the nucleus of an atom

PROTONS ▶ proton

PROTORE n primary mineral deposit

PROTYL same as ▶ protyle

PROTYLE n hypothetical primitive substance from which the chemical elements were supposed to have been formed

PROTYLS ▶ protyl

PROUD adj feeling pleasure and satisfaction

PROUDER ▶ proud

PROUDLY ▶ proud

PROUL same as ▶ prowl

PROULED ▶ proul

PROULER Scots variant of ▶ prowler

PROULS ▶ proul

PROVAND n food

PROVANT adj supplied with provisions

PROVE vb establish the validity of

PROVED ▶ prove

PROVEN ▶ prove

PROVEND same as ▶ provand

PROVER ▶ prove

PROVERB n short saying that expresses a truth or gives a warning ▷ vb utter or describe (something) in the form of a proverb

PROVERS ▶ prove

PROVES ▶ prove

PROVIDE vb make available

PROVINE vb plant branch of vine in ground for propagation

PROVING ▶ prove

PROVISO n condition, stipulation

PROVOKE vb deliberately anger

PROVOST n head of certain university colleges in Britain

PROW n bow of a vessel ▷ adj gallant

PROWAR adj in favour of or supporting war

PROWER ▶ prow

PROWESS n superior skill or ability

PROWEST ▶ prow

PROWL vb move stealthily around a place as if in search of prey or plunder ▷ n prowling

PROWLED ▶ prowl

PROWLER ▶ prowl

PROWLS ▶ prowl

PROWS ▶ prow

PROXIES ▶ proxy

PROXIMO adv in or during the next or coming month

PROXY n person authorized to act on behalf of someone else

PROYN obsolete spelling of ▶ prune

PROYNE obsolete spelling of ▶ prune

PROYNED ▶ proyn

PROYNES ▶ proyne

PROYNS ▶ proyn

PRUDE n person who is excessively modest, prim, or proper

PRUDENT adj cautious, discreet, and sensible

PRUDERY ▶ prude

PRUDES ▶ prude

PRUDISH ▶ prude

PRUH same as ▶ proo

PRUINA n woolly white covering on some lichens

PRUINAS ▶ pruina

PRUINE obsolete spelling of ▶ prune

PRUINES ▶ pruine

PRUNE n dried plum ▷ vb cut off dead parts or excessive branches from (a tree or plant)

PRUNED ▶ prune

PRUNER ▶ prune

PRUNERS ▶ prune

PRUNES ▶ prune

PRUNING ▶ prune

PRUNT n glass ornamentation

PRUNTED ▶ prunt

PRUNTS ▶ prunt

PRUNUS n type of ornamental tree or shrub

PRURIGO n chronic inflammatory disease of the skin characterized by the formation of papules and intense itching

PRUSIK n sliding knot that locks under pressure and can be used to form a loop in which a climber can place his or her foot in order to stand or ascend a rope ▷ vb climb (up a standing rope) using prusiks

PRUSIKS ▶ prusik

PRUSSIC adj as in prussic acid weakly acidic extremely poisonous aqueous solution of hydrogen cyanide

PRUTA same as ▶ prutah

PRUTAH n former Israeli coin

PRUTOT ▶ prutah

PRUTOTH ▶ prutah

PRY vb make an impertinent or uninvited inquiry into a private matter ▷ n act of prying

PRYER same as ▶ prier

PRYERS ▶ pryer

PRYING ▶ pry

PRYINGS ▶ pry

PRYS old variant of ▶ price

PRYSE old variant of ▶ price

PRYSED ▶ pryse

PRYSES ▶ pryse

PRYSING ▶ pryse

PRYTHEE same as ▶ prithee

PSALM n sacred song ▷ vb sing a psalm

PSALMED ▶ psalm

PSALMIC ▶ psalm

PSALMS ▶ psalm

PSALTER n devotional or liturgical book containing a version of Psalms

PSALTRY same as ▸ **psaltery**

PSAMMON n community of microscopic life forms living between grains of sand on shores

PSCHENT n ancient Egyptian crown

PSEUD n pretentious person

PSEUDO n pretentious person

PSEUDOS ▸ **pseudo**

PSEUDS ▸ **pseud**

PSHAW n exclamation of disgust, impatience, disbelief, etc ▷ vb make this exclamation

PSHAWED ▸ **pshaw**

PSHAWS ▸ **pshaw**

PSI n 23rd letter of the Greek alphabet

PSION n type of elementary particle

PSIONIC > **psionics**

PSIONS ▸ **psion**

PSIS ▸ **psi**

PSOAE ▸ **psoas**

PSOAI ▸ **psoas**

PSOAS n either of two muscles of the loins that aid in flexing and rotating the thigh

PSOASES ▸ **psoas**

PSOATIC ▸ **psoas**

PSOCID n tiny wingless insect

PSOCIDS ▸ **psocid**

PSORA n itching skin complaint

PSORAS ▸ **psora**

PSORIC ▸ **psora**

PSST interj sound made to attract someone's attention, esp without others noticing

PST interj sound made to attract someone's attention

You would need to be fairly desperate to use good letters to play this exclamation, but sometimes with no vowels on your rack things can be that desperate.

PSYCH vb psychoanalyse

PSYCHE same as ▸ **psych**

PSYCHED ▸ **psych**

PSYCHES ▸ **psych**

PSYCHIC adj having mental

powers which cannot be explained by natural laws ▷ n person with psychic powers

PSYCHS ▸ **psych**

PSYLLA same as ▸ **psyllid**

PSYLLAS ▸ **psylla**

PSYLLID n type of insect of the family which comprises the jumping plant lice

PSYOP n psychological operation

PSYOPS ▸ **psyop**

PSYWAR n psychological warfare

PSYWARS ▸ **psywar**

PTARMIC n material that causes sneezing

PTERIA ▸ **pterion**

PTERIN n compound such as folic acid

PTERINS ▸ **pterin**

PTERION n point on the side of the skull where a number of bones meet

PTEROIC adj as in **pteroic acid** a kind of acid found in spinach

PTERYLA n any of the tracts of skin that bear contour feathers, arranged in lines along the body of a bird

PTISAN n grape juice drained off without pressure

PTISANS ▸ **ptisan**

PTOMAIN same as > **ptomaine**

PTOOEY interj imitation of the sound of spitting

PTOSES ▸ **ptosis**

PTOSIS n prolapse or drooping of a part, esp the eyelid

PTOTIC ▸ **ptosis**

PTUI same as ▸ **ptooey**

PTYALIN n amylase secreted in the saliva of man and other animals

PTYXES ▸ **ptyxis**

PTYXIS n folding of a leaf in a bud

PUB n building with a bar licensed to sell alcoholic drinks ▷ vb visit a pub or pubs

PUBBED ▸ **pub**

PUBBING ▸ **pub**

PUBCO n company operating a chain of pubs

PUBCOS ▸ **pubco**

PUBE n pubic hair

PUBERAL adj relating to puberty

PUBERTY n beginning of sexual maturity

PUBES ▸ **pube**

PUBIC adj of the lower abdomen

PUBIS n one of the three sections of the hipbone that forms part of the pelvis

PUBISES ▸ **pubis**

PUBLIC adj of or concerning the people as a whole ▷ n community, people in general

PUBLICS ▸ **public**

PUBLISH vb produce and issue (printed matter) for sale

PUBS ▸ **pub**

PUCAN n traditional Connemara open sailing boat

PUCANS ▸ **pucan**

PUCCOON n N American plant that yields a red dye

PUCE adj purplish-brown ▷ n colour varying from deep red to dark purplish-brown

PUCELLE n maid or virgin

PUCER ▸ **puce**

PUCES ▸ **puce**

PUCEST ▸ **puce**

PUCK n mischievous or evil spirit ▷ vb strike (the ball) in hurling

PUCKA same as ▸ **pukka**

PUCKED ▸ **puck**

PUCKER vb gather into wrinkles ▷ n wrinkle or crease

PUCKERS ▸ **pucker**

PUCKERY adj (of wine) high in tannins

PUCKING ▸ **puck**

PUCKISH ▸ **puck**

PUCKLE n early type of machine gun

PUCKLES ▸ **puckle**

PUCKOUT n (in hurling) free hit made by the goalkeeper

PUCKS ▸ **puck**

PUD short for ▸ **pudding**

PUDDEN dialect spelling of ▸ **pudding**

PUDDENS ▸ **pudden**

PUDDER vb make bother or fuss

PUDDERS ▸ **pudder**

PUDDIES ▸ **puddy**

PUDDING n dessert, esp a cooked one served hot

PUDDLE n small pool of water, esp of rain ▷ vb

make (clay etc) into puddle
PUDDLED ▶ **puddle**
PUDDLER ▶ **puddle**
PUDDLES ▶ **puddle**
PUDDLY ▶ **puddle**
PUDDOCK same as
▶ **paddock**
PUDDY n paw
PUDENCY n modesty, shame, or prudishness
PUDENDA > **pudendum**
PUDENT adj lacking in ostentation; humble
PUDGE same as ▶ **podge**
PUDGES ▶ **pudge**
PUDGIER ▶ **pudgy**
PUDGILY ▶ **pudgy**
PUDGY adj podgy
PUDIC > **pudendum**
PUDOR n sense of shame
PUDORS ▶ **pudor**
PUDS ▶ **pud**
PUDSEY same as ▶ **pudsy**
PUDSIER ▶ **pudsy**
PUDSY adj plump
PUDU n diminutive Andean antelope with short straight horns and reddish-brown spotted coat
PUDUS ▶ **pudu**
PUEBLO n communal village, built by certain Indians of the southwestern US and parts of Latin America, consisting of one or more flat-roofed stone or adobe houses
PUEBLOS ▶ **pueblo**
PUER vb steep hides in an alkaline substance from the dung of dogs
PUERED ▶ **puer**
PUERILE adj silly and childish
PUERING ▶ **puer**
PUERS ▶ **puer**
PUFF n (sound of) short blast of breath, wind, etc ▷ vb blow or breathe in short quick draughts
PUFFED ▶ **puff**
PUFFER n person or thing that puffs
PUFFERS ▶ **puffer**
PUFFERY n exaggerated praise, esp in publicity or advertising
PUFFIER ▶ **puffy**
PUFFILY ▶ **puffy**
PUFFIN n black-and-white sea bird with a brightly-coloured beak

PUFFING ▶ **puff**
PUFFINS ▶ **puffin**
PUFFS ▶ **puff**
PUFFY adj short of breath
PUG n small snub-nosed dog ▷ vb mix or knead (clay) with water to form a malleable mass or paste
PUGAREE same as
▶ **puggree**
PUGGED ▶ **pug**
PUGGERY same as
▶ **puggree**
PUGGIE n Scottish word for fruit machine
PUGGIER ▶ **puggy**
PUGGIES ▶ **puggie**
PUGGING ▶ **pug**
PUGGISH ▶ **pug**
PUGGLE vb stir up by poking
PUGGLED ▶ **puggle**
PUGGLES ▶ **puggle**
PUGGREE n scarf, usually pleated, around the crown of some hats, esp sun helmets
PUGGRY same as ▶ **puggree**
PUGGY adj sticky, claylike ▷ n term of endearment
PUGH interj exclamation of disgust
PUGIL n pinch or small handful
PUGILS ▶ **pugil**
PUGMARK n trail of an animal
PUGREE same as ▶ **puggree**
PUGREES ▶ **pugree**
PUGS ▶ **pug**
PUH interj exclamation expressing contempt or disgust
PUHA n sow thistle
PUHAS ▶ **puha**
PUIR Scottish word for ▶ **poor**
PUIRER ▶ **puir**
PUIREST ▶ **puir**
PUISNE adj (esp of a subordinate judge) of lower rank ▷ n judge of lower rank
PUISNES ▶ **puisne**
PUISNY adj younger or inferior
PUJA n ritual in honour of the gods, performed either at home or in the mandir (temple)
PUJAH same as ▶ **puja**
PUJAHS ▶ **pujah**
PUJARI n Hindu priest
PUJARIS ▶ **pujari**
PUJAS ▶ **puja**

PUKA in New Zealand English, same as ▶ **broadleaf**
PUKAS ▶ **puka**
PUKATEA n aromatic New Zealand tree, valued for its high-quality timber
PUKE vb vomit ▷ n act of vomiting
PUKED ▶ **puke**
PUKEKO n brightly coloured New Zealand wading bird
PUKEKOS ▶ **pukeko**
PUKER n person who vomits
PUKERS ▶ **puker**
PUKES ▶ **puke**
PUKEY adj of or like vomit
PUKIER ▶ **pukey**
PUKIEST ▶ **pukey**
PUKING ▶ **puke**
PUKKA adj properly done, constructed, etc
PUKU n belly or stomach
PUKUS ▶ **puku**
PUKY ▶ **pukey**
PUL n Afghan monetary unit worth one hundredth of an afghani
PULA n standard monetary unit of Botswana, divided into 100 thebe
PULAO same as ▶ **pilau**
PULAOS ▶ **pulao**
PULAS ▶ **pula**
PULDRON same as
> **pauldron**
PULE vb whine or whimper
PULED ▶ **pule**
PULER ▶ **pule**
PULERS ▶ **pule**
PULES ▶ **pule**
PULI ▶ **pul**
PULIER ▶ **puly**
PULIEST ▶ **puly**
PULIK ▶ **pul**
PULING ▶ **pule**
PULINGS ▶ **pule**
PULIS ▶ **pul**
PULK same as ▶ **pulka**
PULKA n reindeer-drawn sleigh
PULKAS ▶ **pulka**
PULKHA same as ▶ **pulka**
PULKHAS ▶ **pulkha**
PULKS ▶ **pulk**
PULL vb exert force on (an object) to move it towards the source of the force ▷ n act of pulling
PULLED ▶ **pull**
PULLER ▶ **pull**
PULLERS ▶ **pull**
PULLET n young hen

PULLETS ▶ **pullet**

PULLEY n wheel with a grooved rim in which a belt, chain, or piece of rope runs in order to lift weights by a downward pull

PULLEYS ▶ **pulley**

PULLI ▶ **pullus**

PULLING ▶ **pull**

PULLMAN n luxurious railway coach, esp a sleeping car

PULLOUT n removable section of a magazine, etc

PULLS ▶ **pull**

PULLUP n exercise in which the body is raised up by the arms pulling on a horizontal bar fixed above the head

PULLUPS ▶ **pullup**

PULLUS n technical term for a chick or young bird

PULMO n lung

PULP n soft wet substance made from crushed or beaten matter ▷ vb reduce to pulp

PULPAL ▶ **pulp**

PULPED ▶ **pulp**

PULPER ▶ **pulp**

PULPERS ▶ **pulp**

PULPIER ▶ **pulpy**

PULPIFY vb reduce to pulp

PULPILY ▶ **pulpy**

PULPING ▶ **pulp**

PULPIT n raised platform for a preacher

PULPITS ▶ **pulpit**

PULPOUS n soft and yielding

PULPS ▶ **pulp**

PULPY adj having a soft or soggy consistency

PULQUE n light alcoholic drink from Mexico made from the juice of various agave plants, esp the maguey

PULQUES ▶ **pulque**

PULS ▶ **pul**

PULSANT adj vibrant

PULSAR n small dense star which emits regular bursts of radio waves

PULSARS ▶ **pulsar**

PULSATE vb throb, quiver

PULSE n regular beating of blood through the arteries at each heartbeat ▷ vb beat, throb, or vibrate

PULSED ▶ **pulse**

PULSER n thing that pulses

PULSERS ▶ **pulser**

PULSES ▶ **pulse**

PULSING ▶ **pulse**

PULSION n act of driving forward

PULTAN n native Indian regiment

PULTANS ▶ **pultan**

PULTON same as ▶ **pultan**

PULTONS ▶ **pultan**

PULTOON same as ▶ **pultan**

PULTUN same as ▶ **pultan**

PULTUNS ▶ **pultun**

PULTURE n food and drink claimed by foresters as their right from anyone within the limits of a given forest

PULU n substance from Hawaiian ferns, used for stuffing cushions, etc

PULUS ▶ **pulu**

PULVER vb make into powder

PULVERS ▶ **pulver**

PULVIL vb apply perfumed powder

PULVILS ▶ **pulvil**

PULVINI > **pulvinus**

PULWAR n light Indian river boat

PULWARS ▶ **pulwar**

PULY adj whiny

PUMA n large American wild cat with a greyish-brown coat

PUMAS ▶ **puma**

PUMELO same as ▶ **pomelo**

PUMELOS ▶ **pomelo**

PUMICE n light porous stone used for scouring ▷ vb rub or polish with pumice

PUMICED ▶ **pumice**

PUMICER ▶ **pumice**

PUMICES ▶ **pumice**

PUMIE n small stone

PUMIES ▶ **pumie**

PUMMEL vb strike repeatedly with or as if with the fists

PUMMELO same as ▶ **pomelo**

PUMMELS ▶ **pummel**

PUMP n machine used to force a liquid or gas to move in a particular direction ▷ vb raise or drive with a pump

PUMPED ▶ **pump**

PUMPER ▶ **pump**

PUMPERS ▶ **pump**

PUMPING ▶ **pump**

PUMPION archaic word for ▶ **pumpkin**

PUMPKIN n large round fruit with an orange rind, soft flesh, and many seeds

PUMPS ▶ **pump**

PUMY adj large and round

PUN n use of words to exploit double meanings for humorous effect ▷ vb make puns

PUNA n high cold dry plateau, esp in the Andes

PUNALUA n marriage between the sisters of one family to the brothers of another

PUNAS ▶ **puna**

PUNCE n kick ▷ vb kick

PUNCED ▶ **punce**

PUNCES ▶ **punce**

PUNCH vb strike at with a clenched fist ▷ n blow with a clenched fist

PUNCHED ▶ **punch**

PUNCHER ▶ **punch**

PUNCHES ▶ **punch**

PUNCHY adj forceful

PUNCING ▶ **punce**

PUNCTA ▶ **punctum**

PUNCTO n tip of a fencing sword

PUNCTOS ▶ **puncto**

PUNCTUM n tip or small point

PUNDIT n expert who speaks publicly on a subject

PUNDITS ▶ **pundit**

PUNG n horse-drawn sleigh with a boxlike body on runners

PUNGA variant spelling of ▶ **ponga**

PUNGAS ▶ **punga**

PUNGENT adj having a strong sharp bitter flavour

PUNGLE vb make payment

PUNGLED ▶ **pungle**

PUNGLES ▶ **pungle**

PUNGS ▶ **pung**

PUNIER ▶ **puny**

PUNIEST ▶ **puny**

PUNILY ▶ **puny**

PUNISH vb cause (someone) to suffer or undergo a penalty for some wrongdoing

PUNJI n sharpened bamboo stick

PUNJIS ▶ **punji**

PUNK n anti-Establishment youth movement and style of rock music of the late 1970s ▷ adj relating to the

P

punk youth movement of the late 1970s

PUNKA n fan made of a palm leaf or leaves

PUNKAH same as ▶ **punka**

PUNKAHS ▶ **punkah**

PUNKAS ▶ **punka**

PUNKER ▶ **punk**

PUNKERS ▶ **punk**

PUNKEST ▶ **punk**

PUNKEY n small winged insect

PUNKEYS ▶ **punkey**

PUNKIE same as ▶ **punkey**

PUNKIER ▶ **punky**

PUNKIES ▶ **punkey**

PUNKIN same as ▶ **pumpkin**

PUNKINS ▶ **punkin**

PUNKISH ▶ **punk**

PUNKS ▶ **punk**

PUNKY adj of punk music

PUNNED ▶ **pun**

PUNNER ▶ **pun**

PUNNERS ▶ **pun**

PUNNET n small basket for fruit

PUNNETS ▶ **punnet**

PUNNIER ▶ **punny**

PUNNING ▶ **pun**

PUNNY adj of puns

PUNS ▶ **pun**

PUNSTER n person who is fond of making puns

PUNT n open flat-bottomed boat propelled by a pole ▷ vb travel in a punt

PUNTED ▶ **punt**

PUNTEE same as ▶ **punty**

PUNTEES ▶ **puntee**

PUNTER n person who bets

PUNTERS ▶ **punter**

PUNTIES ▶ **punty**

PUNTING ▶ **punt**

PUNTO n hit in fencing

PUNTOS ▶ **punto**

PUNTS ▶ **punt**

PUNTY n long iron rod used in the finishing process of glass-blowing

PUNY adj small and feeble

PUP n young of certain animals, such as dogs and seals ▷ vb (of dogs, seals, etc) to give birth to pups

PUPA n insect at the stage of development between a larva and an adult

PUPAE ▶ **pupa**

PUPAL ▶ **pupa**

PUPARIA > **puparium**

PUPAS ▶ **pupa**

PUPATE vb (of an insect larva) to develop into a pupa

PUPATED ▶ **pupate**

PUPATES ▶ **pupate**

PUPFISH n type of small fish

PUPIL n person who is taught by a teacher

PUPILAR ▶ **pupil**

PUPILS ▶ **pupil**

PUPPED ▶ **pup**

PUPPET n small doll or figure moved by strings or by the operator's hand

PUPPETS ▶ **puppet**

PUPPIED ▶ **puppy**

PUPPIES ▶ **puppy**

PUPPING ▶ **pup**

PUPPY n young dog ▷ vb have puppies

PUPS ▶ **pup**

PUPU n Hawaiian dish

PUPUNHA n fruit of a type of palm tree

PUPUS ▶ **pupu**

PUR same as ▶ **purr**

PURANA n any of a class of Sanskrit writings not included in the Vedas, characteristically recounting the birth and deeds of Hindu gods and the creation, destruction, or recreation of the universe

PURANAS ▶ **purana**

PURANIC ▶ **purana**

PURDA same as ▶ **purdah**

PURDAH n Muslim and Hindu custom of keeping women in seclusion, with clothing that conceals them completely when they go out

PURDAHS ▶ **purdah**

PURDAS ▶ **purda**

PURE adj unmixed, untainted ▷ vb make pure

PURED ▶ **pure**

PUREE n smooth thick pulp of cooked and sieved fruit, vegetables, meat, or fish ▷ vb make (cooked foods) into a puree

PUREED ▶ **puree**

PUREES ▶ **puree**

PURELY adv in a pure manner

PURER ▶ **pure**

PURES ▶ **pure**

PUREST ▶ **pure**

PURFLE n ruffled or curved ornamental band, as on clothing, furniture, etc ▷ vb decorate with such a band or bands

PURFLED ▶ **purfle**

PURFLER ▶ **purfle**

PURFLES ▶ **purfle**

PURFLY ▶ **purfle**

PURGE vb rid (a thing or place) of (unwanted things or people) ▷ n purging

PURGED ▶ **purge**

PURGER ▶ **purge**

PURGERS ▶ **purge**

PURGES ▶ **purge**

PURGING ▶ **purge**

PURI n unleavened flaky Indian bread, that is deep-fried in ghee and served hot

PURIFY vb make or become pure

PURIN same as ▶ **purine**

PURINE n colourless crystalline solid that can be prepared from uric acid

PURINES ▶ **purine**

PURING ▶ **pure**

PURINS ▶ **purin**

PURIRI n forest tree of New Zealand

PURIRIS ▶ **puriri**

PURIS ▶ **puri**

PURISM n strict insistence on the correct usage or style, such as in grammar or art

PURISMS ▶ **purism**

PURIST ▶ **purism**

PURISTS ▶ **purism**

PURITAN n person who follows strict moral or religious principles ▷ adj of or like a puritan

PURITY n state or quality of being pure

PURL n stitch made by knitting a plain stitch backwards ▷ vb knit in purl

PURLED ▶ **purl**

PURLER n headlong or spectacular fall

PURLERS ▶ **purler**

PURLIEU n land on the edge of a royal forest

PURLIN n horizontal beam that supports the rafters of a roof

PURLINE same as ▶ **purlin**

PURLING ▶ **purl**

PURLINS ▶ **purlin**

PURLOIN vb steal

PURLS ▶ **purl**

PURPIE old Scots word for > **purslane**

PURPIES ▶ **purpie**

PURPLE n colour between

red and blue ▷ adj of a colour between red and blue ▷ vb make purple

PURPLED ▸ purple

PURPLER ▸ purple

PURPLES ▸ purple

PURPLY ▸ purple

PURPORT vb claim (to be or do something) ▷ n apparent meaning, significance

PURPOSE n reason for which something is done or exists

PURPURA n any of several blood diseases causing purplish spots or patches on the skin due to subcutaneous bleeding

PURPURE n purple

PURPY same as ▸ purpie

PURR vb (of cats) make low vibrant sound, usu when pleased ▷ n this sound

PURRED ▸ purr

PURRING ▸ purr

PURRS ▸ purr

PURS ▸ pur

PURSE n small bag for money ▷ vb draw (one's lips) together into a small round shape

PURSED ▸ purse

PURSER n ship's officer who keeps the accounts

PURSERS ▸ purser

PURSES ▸ purse

PURSEW archaic spelling of ▸ pursue

PURSEWS ▸ pursew

PURSIER ▸ pursy

PURSILY ▸ pursy

PURSING ▸ purse

PURSUAL n act of pursuit

PURSUE vb chase

PURSUED ▸ pursue

PURSUER ▸ pursue

PURSUES ▸ pursue

PURSUIT n pursuing

PURSY adj short-winded

PURTIER ▸ purty

PURTY adj pretty

PURVEY vb supply (provisions) ▷ n food and drink laid on at a wedding reception, etc

PURVEYS ▸ purvey

PURVIEW n scope or range of activity or outlook

PUS n yellowish matter produced by infected tissue

PUSES ▸ pus

PUSH vb move or try to move by steady force ▷ n act of pushing

PUSHED adj short of

PUSHER n person who sells illegal drugs

PUSHERS ▸ pusher

PUSHES ▸ push

PUSHFUL ▸ push

PUSHIER ▸ pushy

PUSHILY ▸ pushy

PUSHING prep almost or nearly (a certain age, speed, etc) ▷ adj aggressively ambitious ▷ adv almost or nearly (a certain age, speed, etc)

PUSHPIN n pin with a small ball-shaped head

PUSHPIT n safety rail at the stern of a boat

PUSHROD n metal rod transmitting the reciprocating motion that operates the valves of an internal-combustion engine having the camshaft in the crankcase

PUSHUP n exercise in which the body is alternately raised from and lowered to the floor by the arms only, the trunk being kept straight with the toes and hands resting on the floor

PUSHUPS ▸ pushup

PUSHY adj too assertive or ambitious

PUSLE old spelling of ▸ puzzle

PUSLED ▸ pusle

PUSLES ▸ pusle

PUSLEY same as > purslane

PUSLEYS ▸ pusley

PUSLIKE ▸ pus

PUSLING ▸ pusle

PUSS same as ▸ pussy

PUSSEL n slatternly woman

PUSSELS ▸ pussel

PUSSER n naval purser

PUSSERS ▸ pusser

PUSSES ▸ puss

PUSSIER ▸ pussy

PUSSIES ▸ pussy

PUSSLEY n weedy trailing herb

PUSSLY same as ▸ pussley

PUSSY n cat ▷ adj containing or full of pus

PUSTULE n pimple containing pus

PUT vb cause to be (in a position, state, or place) ▷ n throw in putting the shot

PUTAMEN n hard endocarp or stone of fruits such as the peach, plum, and cherry

PUTCHER n trap for catching salmon

PUTCHUK same as ▸ pachak

PUTDOWN n snub or insult

PUTEAL n enclosure around a well

PUTEALS ▸ puteal

PUTELI n (in India) type of boat

PUTELIS ▸ puteli

PUTID adj having an unpleasant odour

PUTLOCK same as ▸ putlog

PUTLOG n short horizontal beam that with others supports the floor planks of a scaffold

PUTLOGS ▸ putlog

PUTOFF n pretext or delay

PUTOFFS ▸ putoff

PUTOIS n brush to paint pottery

PUTON n hoax or piece of mockery

PUTONS ▸ puton

PUTOUT n baseball play in which the batter or runner is put out

PUTOUTS ▸ putout

PUTREFY vb rot and produce an offensive smell

PUTRID adj rotten and foul-smelling

PUTS ▸ put

PUTSCH n sudden violent attempt to remove a government from power

PUTT n stroke on the putting green to roll the ball into or near the hole ▷ vb strike (the ball) in this way

PUTTED ▸ putt

PUTTEE n (esp as part of a military uniform) strip of cloth worn wound around the leg from the ankle to the knee

PUTTEES ▸ puttee

PUTTEN old Scots past participle of ▸ put

PUTTER n golf club for putting ▷ vb busy oneself in a desultory though agreeable manner

PUTTERS ▸ putter

PUTTI ▸ putto

PUTTIE same as ▸ puttee

PUTTIED ▸ putty

PUTTIER n glazier

P

PUTTIES ▸ putty

PUTTING ▸ put

PUTTO n representation of a small boy, a cherub or cupid, esp in baroque painting or sculpture

PUTTOCK n type of bird of prey

PUTTS ▸ putt

PUTTY n stiff paste of whiting and linseed oil ▷ vb fill, fix, or coat with putty

PUTURE n claim of foresters for food for men, horses, hawks, and hounds, within the bounds of the forest

PUTURES ▸ puture

PUTZ n despicable or stupid person ▷ vb waste time

PUTZED ▸ putz

PUTZES ▸ putz

PUTZING ▸ putz

PUY n small volcanic cone

PUYS ▸ puy

PUZEL same as ▸ pucelle

PUZELS ▸ puzel

PUZZEL n prostitute

PUZZELS ▸ puzzel

PUZZLE vb perplex and confuse or be perplexed or confused ▷ n problem that cannot be easily solved

PUZZLED ▸ puzzle

PUZZLER n person or thing that puzzles

PUZZLES ▸ puzzle

PYA n monetary unit of Myanmar worth one hundredth of a kyat

PYAEMIA n blood poisoning with pus-forming microorganisms in the blood

PYAEMIC ▸ pyaemia

PYAS ▸ pya

PYAT n magpie ▷ adj pied

PYATS ▸ pyat

PYCNIC same as **pyknic** adj

PYCNITE n variety of topaz

PYCNON old word for > semitone

PYCNONS ▸ pycnon

PYE same as ▸ pie

PYEBALD same as ▸ piebald

PYEING ▸ pye

PYEMIA same as ▸ pyaemia

PYEMIAS ▸ pyemia

PYEMIC ▸ pyaemia

PYES ▸ pye

PYET same as ▸ pyat

PYETS ▸ pyet

PYGAL n rear part

PYGALS ▸ pygal

PYGARG n type of horned mammal

PYGARGS ▸ pygarg

PYGIDIA > pygidium

PYGMEAN ▸ pygmy

PYGMIES ▸ pygmy

PYGMOID adj of or like pygmies

PYGMY n something that is a very small example of its type ▷ adj very small

PYIC adj relating to pus

PYIN n constituent of pus

PYINS ▸ pyin

PYJAMA same as ▸ pyjamas

PYJAMAS pl n loose-fitting trousers and top worn in bed

PYKNIC adj (of a physical type) characterized by a broad squat fleshy physique with a large chest and abdomen ▷ n person with this physical type

PYKNICS ▸ pyknic

PYLON n steel tower-like structure supporting electrical cables

PYLONS ▸ pylon

PYLORI ▸ pylorus

PYLORIC ▸ pylorus

PYLORUS n small circular opening at the base of the stomach through which partially digested food (chyme) passes to the duodenum

PYNE archaic variant of ▸ pine

PYNED ▸ pyne

PYNES ▸ pyne

PYNING ▸ pyne

PYOID adj resembling pus

PYONER old variant of ▸ pioneer

PYONERS ▸ pyoner

PYOSES ▸ pyosis

PYOSIS n formation of pus

PYOT same as ▸ pyat

PYOTS ▸ pyot

PYRAL ▸ pyre

PYRALID n tropical moth

PYRALIS same as ▸ pyralid

PYRAMID n solid figure with a flat base and triangular sides sloping upwards to a point ▷ vb build up or be arranged in the form of a pyramid

PYRAMIS n pyramid-shaped structure

PYRAN n unsaturated heterocyclic compound having a ring containing five carbon atoms and one oxygen atom and two double bonds

PYRANS ▸ pyran

PYRE n pile of wood for burning a corpse on

PYRENE n solid polynuclear aromatic hydrocarbon extracted from coal tar

PYRENES ▸ pyrene

PYRES ▸ pyre

PYRETIC adj of, relating to, or characterized by fever

PYREX n tradename for any of a variety of borosilicate glasses that have low coefficients of expansion, making them suitable for heat-resistant glassware used in cookery and chemical apparatus

PYREXES ▸ pyrex

PYREXIA technical name for ▸ fever

PYREXIC ▸ pyrexia

PYRIC adj of or relating to burning

PYRIDIC > pyridine

PYRITE n yellow mineral consisting of iron sulphide in cubic crystalline form

PYRITES same as ▸ pyrite

PYRITIC ▸ pyrite

PYRO n pyromaniac

PYROGEN n any of a group of substances that cause a rise in temperature in an animal body

PYROLA n evergreen perennial

PYROLAS ▸ pyrola

PYRONE n type of heterocyclic compound

PYRONES ▸ pyrone

PYROPE n deep yellowish-red garnet that consists of magnesium aluminium silicate and is used as a gemstone

PYROPES ▸ pyrope

PYROPUS same as ▸ pyrope

PYROS ▸ pyro

PYROSES ▸ pyrosis

PYROSIS technical name for > heartburn

PYRRHIC n metrical foot of two short or unstressed syllables ▷ adj of or relating to such a metrical foot

PYRROL same as ▸ pyrrole

PYRROLE n colourless insoluble toxic liquid with a

five-membered ring containing one nitrogen atom

PYRROLS ▶ pyrrol

PYRUVIC *adj as in* **pyruvic acid** colourless pleasant-smelling liquid

PYTHIUM *n* type of fungi

PYTHON *n* large nonpoisonous snake that crushes its prey

PYTHONS ▶ python

PYURIA *n* any condition characterized by the presence of pus in the urine

PYURIAS ▶ pyuria

PYX *n* any receptacle for the Eucharistic Host ▷ *vb* put (something) in a pyx

> This word can also be spelt **pix**. It's a great word to know as it can earn a good score from a rack that is short of vowels.

PYXED ▶ pyx

PYXES ▶ pyx

PYXIDES ▶ pyxis

PYXIDIA > pyxidium

PYXIE *n* creeping evergreen shrub of the eastern US with small white or pink star-shaped flowers

PYXIES ▶ pyxie

PYXING ▶ pyx

PYXIS *same as* ≥ **pyxidium**

PZAZZ *same as* ▶ **pizzazz**

PZAZZES ▶ pzazz

Qq

With a value of 10 points, **Q** can help you to some good scores, but it can also be a very awkward tile, making it difficult to get bonus words scoring that extra 50 points, and you will normally want to play it off quickly. Often you will not have a **U** to go with it, so it's a good idea to remember the short words beginning with **Q** that don't need a **U**. This is easy, as there's only one two-letter word starting with **Q**: **qi** (11 points). There are four three-letter words, only one of which needs a **U**: **qua** (12). The other three are **qat**, **qin** and **qis** (12 each). If you do have a **U**, remember **quiz** (22), which is a very useful word, and can take an **S** at the front to make **squiz**. Don't forget **quartz** (24) either, while the useful **suq** (12 points) is easily overlooked.

QABALA *same as* > **kabbalah**

QABALAH *same as* > **kabbalah**

QABALAS ▶ **qabala**

QADI *variant spelling of* ▶ **cadi**

QADIS ▶ **qadi**

QAID *n* chief
An Arabic word, this and its variant **qadi** are two of the most frequently played words in Scrabble. There are also alternative spellings **cadi, caid, kadi** and **kaid**.

QAIDS ▶ **qaid**

QANAT *n* underground irrigation channel
This word comes up many times as one of the words allowing you to play the Q without a U.

QANATS ▶ **qanat**

QASIDA *n* Arabic verse form

QASIDAS ▶ **qasida**

QAT *variant spelling of* ▶ **khat**
The leaves of this shrub are chewed as a stimulant, and it's certainly been a stimulus for Scrabble, being one of the three three-letter words that can be played without a U: the others are **qin** and **qis**.

QATS ▶ **qat**

QAWWAL *n* qawwali singer

QAWWALI *n* Islamic religious song, esp in Asia

QAWWALS ▶ **qawwal**

QI *same as* ▶ **ki**

QIBLA *same as* ▶ **kiblah**
The direction in which Muslims turn to pray, a useful word allowing the Q to be played without the U. It can also be spelt **keblah, kibla** and **kiblah**.

QIBLAS ▶ **qibla**

QIGONG *n* system of breathing and exercise designed to benefit both physical and mental health

QIGONGS ▶ **qigong**

QIN *n* Chinese stringed instrument related to the zither
This Chinese musical instrument is another indispensable word as, like **qat**, it combines Q with two of the most common letters in the game.

QINDAR *n* Albanian monetary unit worth one hundredth of a lek

QINDARS ▶ **qindar**

QINS ▶ **qin**

QINTAR *same as* ▶ **qindar**

QINTARS ▶ **qintar**

QIS ▶ **qi**

QIVIUT *n* soft muskox wool

QIVIUTS ▶ **qiviut**

QOPH *same as* ▶ **koph**
A letter of the Hebrew alphabet, also spelt **koph**. The Hebrew alphabet, like the Greek alphabet, is well worth studying from the Scrabble point of view, as it gives us many other useful short words like **ayin, beth, heth, kaph** and **lamedh**.

QOPHS ▶ **qoph**

QORMA *variant spelling of* ▶ **korma**

QORMAS ▶ **qorma**

QUA *prep* in the capacity of
This is the only three-letter word beginning with Q that needs a U. It is played so often that it is well worth mastering all the hooks to this: it takes A at the front to make **aqua** and D, G, I, T and Y at the back to make **quad, quag, quai, quat** and **quay**.

QUACK *vb* (of a duck) utter a harsh guttural sound ▷ *n* an unqualified person who claims medical knowledge

QUACKED ▶ **quack**

QUACKER ▶ **quack**

QUACKLE *same as* ▶ **quack**

QUACKS ▶ **quack**

QUACKY ▶ **quack**

QUAD *n* quadrangle

QUADDED *adj* formed of multiple quads

QUADRAT *n* area of vegetation, often one square metre, marked out for study of the plants in the surrounding area

QUADRIC adj having or characterized by an equation of the second degree, usually in two or three variables ▷ n quadric curve, surface, or function

QUADS ▶ quad

QUAERE n query or question ▷ interj ask or inquire: used esp to introduce a question ▷ vb ask

QUAERED ▶ quaere

QUAERES ▶ quaere

QUAFF vb drink heartily or in one draught

QUAFFED ▶ quaff

QUAFFER ▶ quaff

QUAFFS ▶ quaff

QUAG another word for > quagmire

QUAGGA n recently extinct zebra, striped only on the head and shoulders

QUAGGAS ▶ quagga

QUAGGY adj resembling a marsh or quagmire

QUAGS ▶ quag

QUAHAUG same as ▶ quahog

QUAHOG n edible clam

QUAHOGS ▶ quahog

QUAI same as ▶ quay

QUAICH n small shallow drinking cup, usually with two handles

QUAICHS ▶ quaich

QUAIGH same as ▶ quaich

QUAIGHS ▶ quaich

QUAIL n small game bird of the partridge family ▷ vb shrink back with fear

QUAILED ▶ quail

QUAILS ▶ quail

QUAINT adj attractively unusual, esp in an old-fashioned style

QUAIR n book

QUAIRS ▶ quair

QUAIS ▶ quai

QUAKE vb shake or tremble with or as if with fear ▷ n earthquake

QUAKED ▶ quake

QUAKER ▶ quake

QUAKERS ▶ quake

QUAKES ▶ quake

QUAKIER ▶ quaky

QUAKILY ▶ quaky

QUAKING ▶ quake

QUAKY adj inclined to quake

QUALE n essential property or quality

QUALIA ▶ quale

QUALIFY vb provide or be provided with the abilities necessary for a task, office, or duty

QUALITY n degree or standard of excellence ▷ adj excellent or superior

QUALM n pang of conscience

QUALMS ▶ qualm

QUALMY ▶ qualm

QUAMASH another name for ▶ camass

QUANGO n quasi-autonomous nongovernmental organization: any partly independent official body set up by a government

QUANGOS ▶ quango

QUANNET n flat file with handle at one end

QUANT n long pole for propelling a boat, esp a punt, by pushing on the bottom of a river or lake ▷ vb propel (a boat) with a quant

QUANTA ▶ quantum

QUANTAL adj of or relating to a quantum or an entity that is quantized

QUANTED ▶ quant

QUANTIC n mathematical function

QUANTS ▶ quant

QUANTUM n desired or required amount, esp a very small one ▷ adj of or designating a major breakthrough or sudden advance

QUARE adj remarkable or strange

QUARER ▶ quare

QUAREST ▶ quare

QUARK n subatomic particle thought to be the fundamental unit of matter

| This subatomic particle appears in the Scrabble cloud-chamber fairly often, and when it does, remember that you can put an S on the front of it to make **squark**.

QUARKS ▶ quark

QUARREL n angry disagreement ▷ vb have a disagreement or dispute

QUARRY n place where stone is dug from the surface of the earth ▷ vb extract (stone) from a quarry

QUART n unit of liquid measure equal to two pints (1.136 litres)

QUARTAN adj (esp of a malarial fever) occurring every third day ▷ n quartan malaria

QUARTE n fourth of eight basic positions from which a parry or attack can be made in fencing

QUARTER n one of four equal parts of something ▷ vb divide into four equal parts ▷ adj being or consisting of one of four equal parts

QUARTES ▶ quarte

QUARTET n group of four performers

QUARTIC n biquadratic equation

QUARTO n book size in which the sheets are folded into four leaves

QUARTOS ▶ quarto

QUARTS ▶ quart

QUARTZ n hard glossy mineral

QUARTZY ▶ quartz

QUASAR n extremely distant starlike object that emits powerful radio waves

QUASARS ▶ quasar

QUASH vb annul or make void

QUASHED ▶ quash

QUASHEE same as ▶ quashie

QUASHER ▶ quash

QUASHES ▶ quash

QUASHIE n in the Caribbean, an unsophisticated or gullible male Black peasant

QUASI adv as if

QUASS same as ▶ kvass

QUASSES ▶ quass

QUASSIA n tropical American tree, the wood of which yields a substance used in insecticides

QUASSIN n bitter crystalline substance

QUAT n spot

QUATCH vb move

QUATE n fortune

QUATRE *n* playing card with four pips

QUATRES ▸ quatre

QUATS ▸ quat

QUAVER *vb* (of a voice) quiver or tremble ▸ *n* note half the length of a crotchet

QUAVERS ▸ quaver

QUAVERY ▸ quaver

QUAY *n* wharf built parallel to the shore

QUAYAGE *n* system of quays

QUAYD *archaic past participle of* ▸ **quail**
> a Spenserian word meaning daunted, that makes a surprising hook for **quay**.

QUAYS ▸ quay

QUAZZY *adj* unwell

QUBIT *n* quantum bit

QUBITS ▸ qubit

QUBYTE *n* unit of eight qubits

QUBYTES ▸ qubyte

QUEACH *n* thicket

QUEACHY *adj* unwell

QUEAN *n* boisterous, impudent, or disreputable woman

QUEANS ▸ quean

QUEASY *adj* having the feeling that one is about to vomit

QUEAZY *same as* ▸ **queasy**

QUEBEC *n* code word for the letter Q

QUEBECS ▸ quebec

QUEECHY *same as* ▸ **queachy**

QUEEN *n* female sovereign who is the official ruler or head of state ▸ *vb* flaunt one's homosexuality

QUEENED ▸ queen

QUEENIE *n* scallop

QUEENLY *adj* resembling or appropriate to a queen ▸ *adv* in a manner appropriate to a queen

QUEENS ▸ queen

QUEENY *adj* effeminate

QUEER *adj* not normal or usual ▸ *n* derogatory name for a homosexual person ▸ *vb* spoil or thwart

QUEERED ▸ queer

QUEERER ▸ queer

QUEERLY ▸ queer

QUEERS ▸ queer

QUEEST *n* wood pigeon

QUEESTS ▸ queest

QUEINT *same as* ▸ **quaint**

QUELCH *same as* ▸ **squelch**

QUELEA *n* East African weaver bird

QUELEAS ▸ quelea

QUELL *vb* suppress

QUELLED ▸ quell

QUELLER ▸ quell

QUELLS ▸ quell

QUEME *vb* please

QUEMED ▸ queme

QUEMES ▸ queme

QUEMING ▸ queme

QUENA *n* Andean flute

QUENAS ▸ quena

QUENCH *vb* satisfy (one's thirst)

QUEP *interj* expression of derision

QUERIDA *n* sweetheart

QUERIED ▸ query

QUERIER ▸ query

QUERIES ▸ query

QUERIST *n* person who makes inquiries or queries

QUERN *n* stone hand mill for grinding corn

QUERNS ▸ quern

QUERY *n* question, esp one raising doubt ▸ *vb* express uncertainty, doubt, or an objection concerning (something)

QUEST *n* long and difficult search ▸ *vb* go in search of

QUESTED ▸ quest

QUESTER ▸ quest

QUESTOR *same as* > **quaestor**

QUESTS ▸ quest

QUETCH *vb* move

QUETHE *vb* say

QUETHES ▸ quethe

QUETSCH *n* plum brandy

QUETZAL *n* crested bird of Central and N South America
> This is a great word if you can get the tiles for it, so it's well worth remembering both spellings – it can also be **quezal** – and the four plural forms, which are **quetzals** or **quetzales** and **quezals** or **quezales**.

QUEUE *n* line of people or vehicles waiting for something ▸ *vb* form or remain in a line while waiting

QUEUED ▸ queue

QUEUER ▸ queue

QUEUERS ▸ queue

QUEUES ▸ queue

QUEUING ▸ queue

QUEY *n* young cow

QUEYN *n* girl

QUEYNIE *same as* ▸ **queyn**

QUEYNS ▸ queyn

QUEYS ▸ quey

QUEZAL *same as* ▸ **quetzal**

QUEZALS ▸ quezal

QUIBBLE *vb* make trivial objections ▸ *n* trivial objection

QUIBLIN *same as* ▸ **quibble**

QUICH *vb* move

QUICHE *n* savoury flan with an egg custard filling to which vegetables etc are added

QUICHED ▸ quich

QUICHES ▸ quiche

QUICK *adj* speedy, fast ▸ *n* area of sensitive flesh under a nail ▸ *adv* in a rapid manner

QUICKEN *vb* make or become faster ▸ *n* rowan tree

QUICKER ▸ quick

QUICKIE *n* anything done or made hurriedly ▸ *adj* made or done rapidly

QUICKLY ▸ quick

QUICKS ▸ quick

QUICKY *n* hastily arranged divorce

QUID *n* pound (sterling)

QUIDAM *n* specified person

QUIDAMS ▸ quidam

QUIDDIT *same as* > **quiddity**

QUIDDLE *vb* waste time

QUIDS ▸ quid

QUIESCE *vb* quieten

QUIET *adj* with little noise ▸ *n* quietness ▸ *vb* make or become quiet

QUIETED ▸ quiet

QUIETEN *vb* make or become quiet

QUIETER ▸ quiet

QUIETLY ▸ quiet

QUIETS ▸ quiet

QUIETUS *n* release from life

QUIFF *n* tuft of hair brushed up above the forehead

QUIFFS ▸ quiff

QUIGHT *vb* quit

QUIGHTS ▸ quight

QUILL *n* pen made from the feather of a bird's wing or tail ▸ *vb* wind (thread, yarn, etc) onto a spool or bobbin

QUILLAI *another name for* > **soapbark**

QUILLED ▶ **quill**

QUILLET *n* quibble or subtlety

QUILLON *n* either half of the extended crosspiece of a sword or dagger

QUILLS ▶ **quill**

QUILT *n* padded covering for a bed ▷ *vb* stitch together two layers of (fabric) with padding between them

QUILTED ▶ **quilt**

QUILTER ▶ **quilt**

QUILTS ▶ **quilt**

QUIN *short for* > **quintuplet**

QUINA *n* quinine

QUINARY *adj* consisting of fives or by fives ▷ *n* set of five

QUINAS ▶ **quina**

QUINATE *adj* arranged in or composed of five parts

QUINCE *n* acid-tasting pear-shaped fruit

QUINCES ▶ **quince**

QUINCHE *vb* move

QUINE *same as* ▶ **quean**

QUINELA *same as* > **quinella**

QUINES ▶ **quine**

QUINIC *adj as in* **quinic acid** white crystalline soluble optically active carboxylic acid

QUINIE *n* girl

QUINIES ▶ **quinie**

QUININ *same as* ▶ **quinine**

QUININA *same as* ▶ **quinine**

QUININE *n* bitter drug used as a tonic and formerly to treat malaria

QUININS ▶ **quinin**

QUINNAT *n* Pacific salmon

QUINO *same as* ▶ **keno**

QUINOA *n* type of grain high in nutrients

QUINOAS ▶ **quinoa**

QUINOID *same as* > **quinonoid**

QUINOL *n* white crystalline soluble phenol used as a photographic developer

QUINOLS ▶ **quinol**

QUINONE *n* yellow crystalline water-soluble unsaturated ketone

QUINOS ▶ **quino**

QUINS ▶ **quin**

QUINSY *n* inflammation of the throat or tonsils

QUINT *same as* ▶ **quin**

QUINTA *n* Portuguese vineyard where grapes for wine or port are grown

QUINTAL *n* unit of weight equal to (esp in Britain) 112 pounds (50.85 kg) or (esp in US) 100 pounds (45.36 kg)

QUINTAN *adj* (of a fever) occurring every fourth day ▷ *n* quintan fever

QUINTAR *n* Albanian unit of currency

QUINTAS ▶ **quinta**

QUINTE *n* fifth of eight basic positions from which a parry or attack can be made in fencing

QUINTES ▶ **quinte**

QUINTET *n* group of five performers

QUINTIC *adj* of or relating to the fifth degree ▷ *n* mathematical function

QUINTIN *same as* > **quintain**

QUINTS ▶ **quint**

QUINZE *n* card game with rules similar to those of vingt-et-un, except that the score aimed at is 15 rather than 21

> This card game, deriving from the French word for fifteen, makes a high-scoring word that you may well get to play, and if you can use all of your tiles to form the plural, you'll get a 50-point bonus.

QUINZES ▶ **quinze**

QUIP *n* witty saying ▷ *vb* make a quip

QUIPO *same as* ▶ **quipu**

QUIPOS ▶ **quipo**

QUIPPED ▶ **quip**

QUIPPER ▶ **quip**

QUIPPU *same as* ▶ **quipu**

QUIPPUS ▶ **quippu**

QUIPPY ▶ **quip**

QUIPS ▶ **quip**

QUIPU *n* device of the Incas of Peru used to record information, consisting of an arrangement of variously coloured and knotted cords attached to a base cord

QUIPUS ▶ **quipu**

QUIRE *n* set of 24 or 25 sheets of paper ▷ *vb* arrange in quires

QUIRED ▶ **quire**

QUIRES ▶ **quire**

QUIRING ▶ **quire**

QUIRK *n* peculiarity of character ▷ *vb* quip

QUIRKED ▶ **quirk**

QUIRKS ▶ **quirk**

QUIRKY ▶ **quirk**

QUIRT *n* whip with a leather thong at one end ▷ *vb* strike with a quirt

QUIRTED ▶ **quirt**

QUIRTS ▶ **quirt**

QUIST *n* wood pigeon

QUISTS ▶ **quist**

QUIT *vb* stop (doing something) ▷ *adj* free (from)

QUITCH *vb* move

QUITE *archaic form of* ▶ **quit**

QUITED ▶ **quite**

QUITES ▶ **quite**

QUITING ▶ **quite**

QUITS ▶ **quit**

QUITTAL *n* repayment of an action with a similar action

QUITTED ▶ **quit**

QUITTER *n* person who lacks perseverance

QUITTOR *n* infection of the cartilages on the side of a horse's foot, characterized by inflammation and the formation of pus

QUIVER *vb* shake with a tremulous movement ▷ *n* shaking or trembling

QUIVERS ▶ **quiver**

QUIVERY ▶ **quiver**

QUIXOTE *n* impractical idealist

> Using the Q and X, this word for an impractical dreamer has a reasonable chance of coming up, so keeping an eye open for it is not that quixotic!

Q

QUIZ *n* entertainment in which the knowledge of the players is tested by a series of questions ▷ *vb* investigate by close questioning

QUIZZED ▶ **quiz**

QUIZZER ▶ **quiz**

QUIZZES ▶ **quiz**

QUOAD *adv* as far as

QUOD *n* jail ▷ *vb* say

QUODDED ▶ **quod**

QUODLIN *n* cooking apple

QUODS ▶ **quod**

QUOHOG *n* edible clam

QUOHOGS ▶ **quohog**

QUOIF *vb* arrange (the hair)

QUOIFED ▶ **quoif**

QUOIFS ▸ quoif
QUOIN n external corner of a building ▸ vb wedge
QUOINED ▸ quoin
QUOINS ▸ quoin
QUOIST n wood pigeon
QUOISTS ▸ quoist
QUOIT n large ring used in the game of quoits ▸ vb throw as a quoit
QUOITED ▸ quoit
QUOITER ▸ quoit
QUOITS n game in which quoits are tossed at a stake in the ground in attempts to encircle it
QUOKKA n small Australian wallaby
QUOKKAS ▸ quokka
QUOLL n Australian catlike carnivorous marsupial
QUOLLS ▸ quoll
QUOMODO n manner
QUONDAM adj of an earlier time
QUONK vb make an accidental noise while broadcasting
QUONKED ▸ quonk
QUONKS ▸ quonk
QUOOKE archaic past participle of ▸ quake
QUOP vb pulsate or throb
QUOPPED ▸ quop
QUOPS ▸ quop
QUORATE adj having or being a quorum
QUORUM n minimum number of people required to be present at a meeting before any transactions can take place
QUORUMS ▸ quorum
QUOTA n share that is due from, due to, or allocated to a group or person
QUOTAS n quota
QUOTE vb repeat (words) exactly from (an earlier work, speech, or conversation) ▸ n quotation ▸ interj expression used parenthetically to indicate that the words that follow it form a quotation
QUOTED ▸ quote
QUOTER ▸ quote
QUOTERS ▸ quote
QUOTES ▸ quote
QUOTH vb said
QUOTHA interj expression of mild sarcasm, used in picking up a word or phrase used by someone else
QUOTING ▸ quote
QUOTUM same as ▸ quota
QUOTUMS ▸ quotum
QURSH same as ▸ qursh
QURSHES ▸ qursh
QURUSH n Saudi Arabian currency unit
QUYTE same as ▸ quit
QUYTED ▸ quyte
QUYTES ▸ quyte
QUYTING ▸ quyte
QWERTY n standard English-language typewriter or computer keyboard
QWERTYS ▸ qwerty

Rr

R is one of the most common consonants in Scrabble, along with **N** and **T**. Despite this, however, there is only one two-letter word beginning with **R**: **re** (2 points). This is worth remembering, as you won't need to waste time trying to think of others. There are some good three-letter words with **R**, however, some of which are quite unusual: **raj, rax, rex** (10 each), **rez** and **riz** (12 each). Also, don't forget common words like **raw, ray** and **row** (6 each).

RABANNA n Madagascan woven raffia

RABAT vb rotate so that the plane rotated coincides with another

RABATO n wired or starched collar, often of intricate lace, that stood up at the back and sides: worn in the 17th century

RABATOS ▶ rabato

RABATS ▶ rabat

RABATTE same as ▶ rabat

RABBET n recess, groove, or step, usually of rectangular section, cut into a surface or along the edge of a piece of timber to receive a mating piece ▷ vb cut or form a rabbet in (timber)

RABBETS ▶ rabbet

RABBI n Jewish spiritual leader

RABBIES ▶ rabbi

RABBIN same as ▶ rabbi

RABBINS ▶ rabbin

RABBIS ▶ rabbi

RABBIT n small burrowing mammal with long ears ▷ vb talk too much

RABBITO same as > rabbitoh

RABBITS ▶ rabbit

RABBITY adj rabbitlike

RABBLE n disorderly crowd of noisy people ▷ vb stir, mix, or skim (the molten charge) in a roasting furnace

RABBLED ▶ rabble

RABBLER n iron tool or device for stirring, mixing, or skimming a molten

charge in a roasting furnace

RABBLES ▶ rabble

RABBONI n very respectful Jewish title or form of address

RABI n (in Pakistan, India, etc) a crop that is harvested at the end of winter

RABIC ▶ rabies

RABID adj fanatical

RABIDER ▶ rabid

RABIDLY ▶ rabid

RABIES n usu fatal viral disease transmitted by dogs and certain other animals

RABIS ▶ rabi

RACA adj biblical word meaning worthless or empty-headed

RACCOON n small N American mammal with a long striped tail

RACE n contest of speed ▷ vb compete with in a race

RACED ▶ race

RACEME n cluster of flowers along a central stem, as in the foxglove

RACEMED adj with or in racemes

RACEMES ▶ raceme

RACEMIC adj of, concerned with, or being a mixture of equal amounts of enantiomers and consequently having no optical activity

RACER n person, animal, or machine that races

RACERS ▶ racer

RACES ▶ race

RACEWAY n racetrack, esp

one for banger racing

RACH n scent hound

RACHE same as ▶ rach

RACHES ▶ rach

RACHET same as ▶ ratchet

RACHETS ▶ rachet

RACHIAL ▶ rachis

RACHIS n main axis or stem of an inflorescence or compound leaf

RACIAL adj relating to the division of the human species into races

RACIER ▶ racy

RACIEST ▶ racy

RACILY ▶ racy

RACING adj denoting or associated with horse races ▷ n practice of engaging horses (or sometimes greyhounds) in contests of speed

RACINGS ▶ racing

RACINO n combined racetrack and casino

RACINOS ▶ racino

RACISM n hostile attitude or behaviour to members of other races, based on a belief in the innate superiority of one's own race

RACISMS ▶ racism

RACIST ▶ racism

RACISTS ▶ racism

RACK n framework for holding particular articles, such as coats or luggage ▷ vb cause great suffering to

RACKED ▶ rack

RACKER ▶ rack

RACKERS ▶ rack

RACKET n bat with strings stretched in an oval frame, used in tennis etc ▷ vb to strike with a racket

RACKETS n ball game played in a paved walled court

RACKETT n early double-reeded wind instrument

RACKETY adj involving noise, commotion and excitement

RACKFUL ▶ rack

RACKING ▶ rack

RACKLE adj dialect word meaning rash

RACKS ▶ rack

RACLOIR n scraper

RACON n radar beacon

RACONS ▶ racon

RACOON same as ▶ raccoon

RACOONS ▶ racoon

RACQUET same as racket n

RACY adj slightly shocking

RAD n former unit of absorbed ionizing radiation dose equivalent to an energy absorption per unit mass of 0.01 joule per kilogram of irradiated material. 1 rad is equivalent to 0.01 gray ▷ vb fear ▷ adj slang term for great

RADAR n device for tracking distant objects by bouncing high-frequency radio pulses off them

RADARS ▶ radar

RADDED ▶ rad

RADDER ▶ rad

RADDEST ▶ rad

RADDING ▶ rad

RADDLE same as ▶ ruddle

RADDLED adj (of a person) unkempt or run-down in appearance

RADDLES ▶ raddle

RADE (in Scots dialect) past tense of ▶ ride

RADGE adj angry or uncontrollable ▷ n person acting in such a way

RADGER ▶ radge

RADGES ▶ radge

RADGEST ▶ radge

RADIAL adj spreading out from a common central point ▷ n radial-ply tyre

RADIALE n bone in the wrist

RADIALS ▶ radial

RADIAN n unit for measuring angles, equal to 57.296°

RADIANS ▶ radian

RADIANT adj looking happy ▷ n point or object that emits radiation, esp the part of a heater that gives out heat

RADIATA adj as in radiata pine type of pine tree

RADIATE vb spread out from a centre ▷ adj having rays or a radial structure

RADICAL adj fundamental ▷ n person advocating fundamental (political) change

RADICEL n very small root

RADICES ▶ radix

RADICLE n small or developing root

RADII ▶ radius

RADIO n use of electromagnetic waves for broadcasting, communication, etc ▷ vb transmit (a message) by radio ▷ adj of, relating to, or using radio

RADIOED ▶ radio

RADIOS ▶ radio

RADISH n small hot-flavoured root vegetable eaten raw in salads

RADIUM n radioactive metallic element

RADIUMS ▶ radium

RADIUS n (length of) a straight line from the centre to the circumference of a circle

RADIX n any number that is the base of a number system or of a system of logarithms

RADIXES ▶ radix

RADOME n protective housing for a radar antenna made from a material that is transparent to radio waves

RADOMES ▶ radome

RADON n radioactive gaseous element

RADONS ▶ radon

RADS ▶ rad

RADULA n horny tooth-bearing strip on the tongue of molluscs that is used for rasping food

RADULAE ▶ radula

RADULAR ▶ radula

RADULAS ▶ radula

RAFALE n burst of artillery fire

RAFALES ▶ rafale

RAFF n rubbish

RAFFIA n prepared palm fibre for weaving mats etc

RAFFIAS ▶ raffia

RAFFISH adj slightly disreputable

RAFFLE n lottery with goods as prizes ▷ vb offer as a prize in a raffle

RAFFLED ▶ raffle

RAFFLER ▶ raffle

RAFFLES ▶ raffle

RAFFS ▶ raff

RAFT n floating platform of logs, planks, etc ▷ vb convey on or travel by raft, or make a raft from

RAFTED ▶ raft

RAFTER n one of the main beams of a roof ▷ vb to fit with rafters

RAFTERS ▶ rafter

RAFTING ▶ raft

RAFTMAN same as ▶ raftsman

RAFTMEN ▶ raftman

RAFTS ▶ raft

RAG n fragment of cloth ▷ vb tease ▷ adj (in British universities and colleges) of various events organized to raise money for charity

RAGA n any of several conventional patterns of melody and rhythm that form the basis for freely interpreted compositions. Each pattern is associated with different aspects of religious devotion

RAGAS ▶ raga

RAGBAG n confused assortment, jumble

RAGBAGS ▶ ragbag

RAGBOLT n bolt that has angled projections on it to prevent it working loose once it has been driven home

RAGDE archaic past form of ▶ rage

RAGE n violent anger or passion ▷ vb speak or act with fury

RAGED ▶ rage

RAGEE same as ▶ ragi

RAGEES ▶ ragee

RAGEFUL ▶ rage

RAGER ▸rage

RAGERS ▸rage

RAGES ▸rage

RAGG same as > **ragstone**

RAGGA n dance-oriented style of reggae

RAGGAS ▸ragga

RAGGED ▸rag

RAGGEDY adj somewhat ragged

RAGGEE same as ▸ragi

RAGGEES ▸raggee

RAGGERY n rags

RAGGIER ▸raggy

RAGGIES ▸raggy

RAGGING ▸rag

RAGGLE n thin groove cut in stone or brickwork, esp to hold the edge of a roof ▷ vb cut a raggle in

RAGGLED ▸raggle

RAGGLES ▸raggle

RAGGS ▸ragg

RAGGY adj raglike ▷ n cereal grass cultivated in Africa and Asia for its edible grain

RAGI n cereal grass cultivated in Africa and Asia for its edible grain

RAGING ▸rage

RAGINGS ▸rage

RAGINI n Indian musical form related to a raga

RAGINIS ▸ragini

RAGIS ▸ragi

RAGLAN adj (of a sleeve) joined to a garment by diagonal seams from the neck to the underarm ▷ n coat with sleeves that continue to the collar instead of having armhole seams

RAGLANS ▸raglan

RAGMAN n rag-and-bone man

RAGMANS ▸ragman

RAGMEN ▸ragman

RAGMENT n statute, roll, or list

RAGOUT n richly seasoned stew of meat and vegetables ▷ vb make into a ragout

RAGOUTS ▸ragout

RAGS ▸rag

RAGTAG n disparaging term for common people

RAGTAGS ▸ragtag

RAGTIME n style of jazz piano music

RAGTOP n informal word for a car with a folding or removable roof

RAGTOPS ▸ragtop

RAGU n Italian meat and tomato sauce

RAGULED same as ▸raguly

RAGULY adj (in heraldry) having toothlike or stublike projections

RAGUS ▸ragu

RAGWEED n any of several plants regarded as weeds, some of which produce a large amount of hay-fever-causing pollen

RAGWORK n weaving or needlework using rags

RAGWORM n type of worm that lives chiefly in burrows in sand or mud

RAGWORT n plant with ragged leaves and yellow flowers

RAH informal US word for ▸cheer

RAHED ▸rah

RAHING ▸rah

RAHS ▸rah

RAHUI n Māori prohibition

RAHUIS ▸rahui

RAI n type of Algerian popular music based on traditional Algerian music influenced by modern Western pop

RAIA same as ▸rayah

RAIAS ▸raia

RAID n sudden surprise attack or search ▷ vb make a raid on

RAIDED ▸raid

RAIDER ▸raid

RAIDERS ▸raid

RAIDING ▸raid

RAIDS ▸raid

RAIK n wander ▷ vb wander

RAIKED ▸raik

RAIKING ▸raik

RAIKS ▸raik

RAIL n horizontal bar, esp as part of a fence or track ▷ vb complain bitterly or loudly

RAILAGE n cost of transporting goods by rail

RAILBED n ballast layer supporting the sleepers of a railway track

RAILBUS n buslike vehicle for use on railway lines

RAILCAR n passenger-carrying railway vehicle consisting of a single coach with its own power unit

RAILE archaic spelling of ▸rail

RAILED ▸rail

RAILER ▸rail

RAILERS ▸rail

RAILES ▸raile

RAILING n fence made of rails supported by posts

RAILLY old word for ▸mock

RAILMAN n railway employee

RAILMEN ▸railman

RAILS ▸rail

RAILWAY n track of iron rails on which trains run

RAIMENT n clothing

RAIN n water falling in drops from the clouds ▷ vb fall or pour down as rain

RAINBOW n arch of colours in the sky

RAINE archaic spelling of ▸reign

RAINED ▸rain

RAINES ▸raine

RAINIER ▸rainy

RAINILY ▸rainy

RAINING ▸rain

RAINOUT n radioactive fallout or atmospheric pollution carried to the earth by rain

RAINS ▸rain

RAINY adj characterized by a large rainfall

RAIRD same as ▸reird

RAIRDS ▸raird

RAIS ▸rai

RAISE vb lift up ▷ n increase in pay

RAISED ▸raise

RAISER ▸raise

RAISERS ▸raise

RAISES ▸raise

RAISIN n dried grape

RAISING n rule that moves a constituent from an embedded clause into the main clause

RAISINS ▸raisin

RAISINY ▸raisin

RAIT same as ▸ret

RAITA n Indian dish of chopped cucumber, mint, etc, in yogurt, served with curries

RAITAS ▸raita

RAITED ▸rait

RAITING ▸rait

RAITS ▸rait

RAIYAT same as ▸ryot

RAIYATS ▸raiyat

RAJ n (in India) government

R

This Indian word for rule or empire is one of the essential short words that use a J. Remember that it can extended to **raja**.

RAJA same as ▶ **rajah**

RAJAH n (in India, formerly) a ruler or landlord: sometimes used as a form of address or as a title preceding a name

RAJAHS ▶ **rajah**

RAJAS ▶ **raja**

RAJES ▶ **raj**

RAKE n tool with a long handle and a crosspiece with teeth, used for smoothing earth or gathering leaves, hay, etc ▷ vb gather or smooth with a rake

RAKED ▶ **rake**

RAKEE same as ▶ **raki**

RAKEES ▶ **rakee**

RAKEOFF n share of profits, esp one that is illegal or given as a bribe

RAKER n person who rakes

RAKERS ▶ **raker**

RAKERY n rakish behaviour

RAKES ▶ **rake**

RAKI n strong spirit distilled in Turkey, the former Yugoslavia, etc, from grain, usually flavoured with aniseed or other aromatics

RAKIA n strong fruit-based alcoholic drink popular in the Balkans

RAKIAS ▶ **rakia**

RAKIJA ▶ **rakia**

RAKIJAS ▶ **rakija**

RAKING n offence committed when a player deliberately scrapes an opponent's leg, arm, etc with the studs of his or her boots

RAKINGS ▶ **raking**

RAKIS ▶ **raki**

RAKISH adj dashing or jaunty

RAKSHAS same as > **rakshasa**

RAKU n type of Japanese pottery

RAKUS ▶ **raku**

RALE n abnormal coarse crackling sound heard on auscultation of the chest, usually caused by the accumulation of fluid in the lungs

RALES ▶ **rale**

RALLIED ▶ **rally**

RALLIER ▶ **rally**

RALLIES ▶ **rally**

RALLINE adj relating to a family of birds that includes the rails, crakes, and coots

RALLY n large gathering of people for a meeting ▷ vb bring or come together after dispersal or for a common cause

RALLYE US variant of ▶ **rally**

RALLYES ▶ **rallye**

RAM n male sheep ▷ vb strike against with force

RAMADA n outdoor eating area with roof but open sides

RAMADAS ▶ **ramada**

RAMAKIN same as ▶ **ramekin**

RAMAL adj relating to a branch or branches

RAMATE adj with branches

RAMBLA n dried-up riverbed

RAMBLAS ▶ **rambla**

RAMBLE vb walk without a definite route ▷ n walk, esp in the country

RAMBLED ▶ **ramble**

RAMBLER n person who rambles

RAMBLES ▶ **ramble**

RAMCAT n dialect word for a male cat

RAMCATS ▶ **ramcat**

RAMEAL same as ▶ **ramal**

RAMEE same as ▶ **ramie**

RAMEES ▶ **ramee**

RAMEKIN n small ovenproof dish for a single serving of food

RAMEN n Japanese dish consisting of a clear broth containing thin white noodles and sometimes vegetables, meat, etc

RAMENS ▶ **ramen**

RAMENTA > **ramentum**

RAMEOUS same as ▶ **ramal**

RAMET n any of the individuals in a group of clones

RAMETS ▶ **ramet**

RAMI same as ▶ **ramie**

RAMIE n woody Asian shrub with broad leaves and a stem that yields a flaxlike fibre

RAMIES ▶ **ramie**

RAMIFY vb become complex

RAMILIE same as > **ramillie**

RAMIN n swamp-growing tree found in Malaysia and Indonesia

RAMINS ▶ **ramin**

RAMIS ▶ **rami**

RAMJET n type of jet engine in which fuel is burned in a duct using air compressed by the forward speed of the aircraft

RAMJETS ▶ **ramjet**

RAMMED ▶ **ram**

RAMMEL n discarded or waste matter

RAMMELS ▶ **rammel**

RAMMER ▶ **ram**

RAMMERS ▶ **ram**

RAMMIER ▶ **rammish**

RAMMIES ▶ **rammish**

RAMMING ▶ **ram**

RAMMISH adj like a ram, esp in being lustful or foul-smelling

RAMMLE n collection of items saved in case they become useful

RAMMLES ▶ **rammle**

RAMMY n noisy disturbance or free-for-all ▷ vb make a rammy

RAMONA same as > **sagebrush**

RAMONAS ▶ **ramona**

RAMOSE adj having branches

RAMOUS same as ▶ **ramose**

RAMP n slope joining two level surfaces ▷ vb (esp of animals) to rush around in a wild excited manner

RAMPAGE vb dash about violently

RAMPANT adj growing or spreading uncontrollably

RAMPART n mound or wall for defence ▷ vb provide with a rampart

RAMPED ▶ **ramp**

RAMPER ▶ **ramp**

RAMPERS ▶ **ramp**

RAMPICK same as ▶ **rampike**

RAMPIKE n US or dialect word for a dead tree

RAMPING ▶ **ramp**

RAMPION n European and Asian plant that has clusters of bluish flowers and an edible white tuberous root used in salads

RAMPIRE archaic variant of ▸**rampart**

RAMPOLE same as ▸**rampike**

RAMPS ▸**ramp**

RAMROD n long thin rod used for cleaning the barrel of a gun or forcing gunpowder into an old-fashioned gun ▹ adj (of someone's posture) very straight and upright ▹ vb drive

RAMRODS ▸**ramrod**

RAMS ▸**ram**

RAMSON n type of garlic

RAMSONS ▸**ramson**

RAMSTAM adv headlong ▹ adj headlong

RAMTIL n African plant grown in India esp for its oil

RAMTILS ▸**ramtil**

RAMULAR adj relating to a branch or branches

RAMULI ▸**ramulus**

RAMULUS n small branch

RAMUS n barb of a bird's feather

RAN ▸**run**

RANA n genus of frogs

RANAS ▸**rana**

RANCE Scots word for ▸**prop**

RANCED ▸**rance**

RANCEL vb (in Shetland and Orkney) carry out a search

RANCELS ▸**rancel**

RANCES ▸**rance**

RANCH n large cattle farm in the American West ▹ vb run a ranch

RANCHED ▸**ranch**

RANCHER n person who owns, manages, or works on a ranch

RANCHES ▸**ranch**

RANCHO n hut or group of huts for housing ranch workers

RANCHOS ▸**rancho**

RANCID adj (of butter, bacon, etc) stale and having an offensive smell

RANCING ▸**rance**

RANCOR same as ▸**rancour**

RANCORS ▸**rancor**

RANCOUR n deep bitter hate

RAND n monetary unit of South Africa; leather strip on the heel of a shoe ▹ vb cut into rands

RANDAN n boat rowed by three people, in which the person in the middle uses two oars and the people fore and aft use one oar each

RANDANS ▸**randan**

RANDED ▸**rand**

RANDEM adv with three horses harnessed together as a team ▹ n carriage or team of horses so driven

RANDEMS ▸**randem**

RANDIE same as ▸**randy**

RANDIER ▸**randy**

RANDIES ▸**randy**

RANDILY ▸**randy**

RANDING ▸**rand**

RANDOM adj made or done by chance or without plan ▹ n (in mining) the course of a vein of ore

RANDOMS ▸**random**

RANDON old variant of ▸**random**

RANDONS ▸**randon**

RANDS ▸**rand**

RANDY adj sexually aroused ▹ n rude or reckless person

RANEE same as ▸**rani**

RANEES ▸**ranee**

RANG ▸**ring**

RANGE n limits of effectiveness or variation ▹ vb vary between one point and another

RANGED ▸**range**

RANGER n official in charge of a nature reserve etc

RANGERS ▸**ranger**

RANGES ▸**range**

RANGI n sky

RANGIER ▸**rangy**

RANGILY ▸**rangy**

RANGING ▸**range**

RANGIS ▸**rangi**

RANGOLI n traditional Indian ground decoration using coloured sand or chalks

RANGY adj having long slender limbs

RANI n wife or widow of a rajah

RANID n frog

RANIDS ▸**ranid**

RANINE adj relating to frogs

RANIS ▸**rani**

RANK n relative place or position ▹ vb have a specific rank or position ▹ adj complete or absolute

RANKE archaic variant of ▸**rank**

RANKED ▸**rank**

RANKER n soldier in the ranks

RANKERS ▸**ranker**

RANKES ▸**ranke**

RANKEST ▸**rank**

RANKING adj prominent ▹ n position on a scale

RANKISH adj old word meaning rather rank

RANKISM n discrimination against people on the grounds of rank

RANKLE vb continue to cause resentment or bitterness

RANKLED ▸**rankle**

RANKLES ▸**rankle**

RANKLY ▸**rank**

RANKS ▸**rank**

RANPIKE same as ▸**rampike**

RANSACK vb search thoroughly

RANSEL same as ▸**rancel**

RANSELS ▸**ransel**

RANSOM n money demanded in return for the release of someone who has been kidnapped ▹ vb pay money to obtain the release of a captive

RANSOMS ▸**ransom**

RANT vb talk in a loud and excited way ▹ n loud excited speech

RANTED ▸**rant**

RANTER ▸**rant**

RANTERS ▸**rant**

RANTING ▸**rant**

RANTS ▸**rant**

RANULA n saliva-filled cyst that develops under the tongue

RANULAR adj of a cyst under the tongue

RANULAS ▸**ranula**

RANZEL same as ▸**rancel**

RANZELS ▸**ranzel**

RAOULIA n flowering plant of New Zealand

RAP vb hit with a sharp quick blow ▹ n quick sharp blow

RAPE vb force to submit to sexual intercourse ▹ n act of raping

RAPED ▸**rape**

RAPER ▸**rape**

RAPERS ▸**rape**

RAPES ▸**rape**

R

RAPHAE ▶ raphe

RAPHE n elongated ridge of conducting tissue along the side of certain seeds

RAPHES ▶ raphe

RAPHIA same as ▶ raffia

RAPHIAS ▶ raphia

RAPHIDE n any of numerous needle-shaped crystals, usually of calcium oxalate, that occur in many plant cells as a metabolic product

RAPHIS same as ▶ raphide

RAPID adj quick, swift

RAPIDER ▶ rapid

RAPIDLY ▶ rapid

RAPIDS pl n part of a river with a fast turbulent current

RAPIER n fine-bladed sword

RAPIERS ▶ rapier

RAPINE n pillage or plundering

RAPINES ▶ rapine

RAPING ▶ rape

RAPINI pl n type of leafy vegetable

RAPIST n person who commits rape

RAPISTS ▶ rapist

RAPLOCH n Scots word for homespun woollen material ▷ adj Scots word meaning coarse or homemade

RAPPE n Arcadian dish of grated potatoes and pork or chicken

RAPPED ▶ rap

RAPPEE n moist English snuff of the 18th and 19th centuries

RAPPEES ▶ rappee

RAPPEL n (formerly) a drumbeat to call soldiers to arms ▷ vb abseil

RAPPELS ▶ rappel

RAPPEN n Swiss coin equal to one hundredth of a franc

RAPPER n something used for rapping, such as a knocker on a door

RAPPERS ▶ rapper

RAPPES ▶ rappe

RAPPING ▶ rap

RAPPINI same as ▶ rapini

RAPPORT n harmony or agreement

RAPS ▶ rap

RAPT adj engrossed or spellbound

RAPTLY ▶ rapt

RAPTOR n any bird of prey

RAPTORS ▶ raptor

RAPTURE n ecstasy ▷ vb entrance

RARE adj uncommon ▷ vb rear

RAREBIT n as in **Welsh rarebit** dish made from melted cheese and sometimes milk and seasonings and served on toast

RARED ▶ rare

RAREE n as in **raree show** street show or carnival

RAREFY vb make or become rarer or less dense

RARELY adv seldom

RARER ▶ rare

RARES ▶ rare

RAREST ▶ rare

RARIFY same as ▶ rarefy

RARING adj ready

RARITY n something that is valuable because it is unusual

RARK vb as in **rark up** informal New Zealand expression meaning reprimand severely

RARKED ▶ rark

RARKING ▶ rark

RARKS ▶ rark

RAS n headland

RASBORA n often brightly coloured tropical fish

RASCAL n rogue ▷ adj belonging to the mob or rabble

RASCALS ▶ rascal

RASCHEL n type of loosely knitted fabric

RASE same as ▶ raze

RASED ▶ rase

RASER ▶ rase

RASERS ▶ rase

RASES ▶ rase

RASH adj hasty, reckless, or incautious ▷ n eruption of spots or patches on the skin ▷ vb (in old usage) cut

RASHED ▶ rash

RASHER n thin slice of bacon

RASHERS ▶ rasher

RASHES ▶ rash

RASHEST ▶ rash

RASHIE n Australian word for a shirt worn by surfers as protection against sunburn, heat rash, etc

RASHIES ▶ rashie

RASHING ▶ rash

RASHLY ▶ rash

RASING ▶ rase

RASP n harsh grating noise ▷ vb speak in a grating voice

RASPED ▶ rasp

RASPER ▶ rasp

RASPERS ▶ rasp

RASPIER ▶ raspy

RASPING adj (esp of a noise) harsh or grating

RASPISH ▶ rasp

RASPS ▶ rasp

RASPY same as ▶ rasping

RASSE n small S Asian civet

RASSES ▶ rasse

RASSLE dialect variant of ▶ wrestle

RASSLED ▶ rassle

RASSLES ▶ rassle

RAST archaic past form of ▶ race

RASTA adj of a member of a particular Black religious movement

RASTER n image consisting of rows of pixel information, such as a JPEG, GIF etc ▷ vb use web-based technology to turn a digital image into a large picture composed of a grid of black and white dots

RASTERS ▶ raster

RASTRUM n pen for drawing the five lines of a musical stave simultaneously

RASURE n scraping

RASURES ▶ rasure

RAT n small rodent ▷ vb inform (on)

RATA n New Zealand hard-wood forest tree with crimson flowers

RATABLE adj able to be rated or evaluated

RATABLY ▶ ratable

RATAFEE same as ▶ ratafia

RATAFIA n liqueur made from fruit

RATAL n amount on which rates are assessed ▷ adj of or relating to rates (local taxation)

RATALS ▶ ratal

RATAN same as ▶ rattan

RATANS ▶ ratan

RATANY n flowering desert shrub

RATAS ▶ rata

RATATAT n sound of knocking on a door

RATBITE n as in **ratbite**

fever acute infectious disease that can be caught from the bite of an infected rat

RATCH same as ▶ **ratchet**

RATCHED ▶ **ratch**

RATCHES ▶ **ratch**

RATCHET n set of teeth on a bar or wheel allowing motion in one direction only ▷ vb move using or as if using a ratchet system

RATE n degree of speed or progress ▷ vb consider or value

RATED ▶ **rate**

RATEEN same as ▶ **ratine**

RATEENS ▶ **rateen**

RATEL n large African and S Asian musteline mammal

RATELS ▶ **ratel**

RATER ▶ **rate**

RATERS ▶ **rate**

RATES pl n (in some countries) a tax on property levied by a local authority

RATFINK n contemptible or undesirable person

RATFISH n deep-sea fish with a whiplike tail

RATH same as ▶ **rathe**

RATHA n (in India) a four-wheeled carriage drawn by horses or bullocks

RATHAS ▶ **ratha**

RATHE adj blossoming or ripening early in the season

RATHER adv some extent ▷ interj expression of strong affirmation ▷ sentence substitute expression of strong affirmation, often in answer to a question

RATHEST adv dialect or archaic word meaning soonest

RATHOLE n rat's hiding place or burrow

RATHS ▶ **rath**

RATIFY vb give formal approval to

RATINE n coarse loosely woven cloth

RATINES ▶ **ratine**

RATING n valuation or assessment

RATINGS ▶ **rating**

RATIO n relationship between two numbers or amounts expressed as a proportion

RATION n fixed allowance of food etc ▷ vb limit to a

certain amount per person

RATIONS pl n fixed daily allowance of food, esp to military personnel or when supplies are limited

RATIOS ▶ **ratio**

RATITE adj (of flightless birds) having a breastbone that lacks a keel for the attachment of flight muscles ▷ n bird, such as an ostrich, kiwi, or rhea, that belongs to this group

RATITES ▶ **ratite**

RATLIKE ▶ **rat**

RATLIN same as ▶ **ratline**

RATLINE n any of a series of light lines tied across the shrouds of a sailing vessel for climbing aloft

RATLING n young rat

RATLINS ▶ **ratlin**

RATO n rocket-assisted take-off

RATOO same as ▶ **ratu**

RATOON n new shoot that grows from near the root or crown of crop plants, esp the sugar cane, after the old growth has been cut back ▷ vb propagate or cause to propagate by such a growth

RATOONS ▶ **ratoon**

RATOOS ▶ **ratoo**

RATOS ▶ **rato**

RATPACK n members of the press who pursue celebrities and give wide coverage of their private lives

RATS ▶ **rat**

RATTAIL n type of fish

RATTAN n climbing palm with jointed stems used for canes

RATTANS ▶ **rattan**

RATTED ▶ **rat**

RATTEEN same as ▶ **ratine**

RATTEN vb sabotage or steal tools in order to disrupt the work of

RATTENS ▶ **ratten**

RATTER n dog or cat that catches and kills rats

RATTERS ▶ **ratter**

RATTERY n rats' dwelling area

RATTIER ▶ **ratty**

RATTILY ▶ **ratty**

RATTING ▶ **rat**

RATTISH adj of, resembling, or infested with rats

RATTLE vb give out a succession of short sharp sounds ▷ n short sharp sound

RATTLED ▶ **rattle**

RATTLER n something that rattles

RATTLES ▶ **rattle**

RATTLIN same as ▶ **ratline**

RATTLY adj having a rattle

RATTON n dialect word for a little rat

RATTONS ▶ **ratton**

RATTOON same as ▶ **ratoon**

RATTRAP n device for catching rats

RATTY adj bad-tempered, irritable

RATU n title used by Fijian chiefs or nobles

RATUS ▶ **ratu**

RAUCID adj raucous

RAUCITY ▶ **raucous**

RAUCLE adj Scots word for rough or tough

RAUCLER ▶ **raucle**

RAUCOUS adj hoarse or harsh

RAUGHT archaic past form of ▶ **reach**

RAUN n fish roe or spawn

RAUNCH n lack of polish or refinement ▷ vb behave in a raunchy manner

RAUNCHY adj earthy, sexy

RAUNGE archaic word for ▶ **range**

RAUNGED ▶ **raunge**

RAUNGES ▶ **raunge**

RAUNS ▶ **raun**

RAUPATU n confiscation or seizure of land

RAUPO n New Zealand bulrush

RAUPOS ▶ **raupo**

RAURIKI n sow thistle, any of various plants with prickly leaves, milky juice and yellow heads

RAV n Hebrew word for rabbi

RAVAGE vb cause extensive damage to ▷ n destructive action

RAVAGED ▶ **ravage**

RAVAGER ▶ **ravage**

RAVAGES ▶ **ravage**

RAVE vb talk wildly or with enthusiasm ▷ n enthusiastically good review

RAVED ▶ **rave**

RAVEL vb tangle or become

entangled ▷ n tangle or complication

RAVELED ▸ ravel

RAVELER ▸ ravel

RAVELIN n outwork having two embankments at a salient angle

RAVELLY ▸ ravel

RAVELS ▸ ravel

RAVEN n black bird like a large crow ▷ adj (of hair) shiny black ▷ vb seize or seek (plunder, prey, etc)

RAVENED ▸ raven

RAVENER ▸ raven

RAVENS ▸ raven

RAVER n person who leads a wild or uninhibited social life

RAVERS ▸ raver

RAVES ▸ rave

RAVIN archaic spelling of ▸ raven

RAVINE n narrow steep-sided valley worn by a stream

RAVINED ▸ ravin

RAVINES ▸ ravin

RAVING adj delirious ▷ n frenzied, irrational, or wildly extravagant talk or utterances

RAVINGS ▸ raving

RAVINS ▸ ravin

RAVIOLI n small squares of pasta with a savoury filling

RAVISH vb enrapture

RAVS ▸ rav

RAW as in **in the raw** without clothes adj uncooked

RAWARU n New Zealand name for blue cod

RAWARUS ▸ rawaru

RAWBONE archaic variant of > **rawboned**

RAWER ▸ raw

RAWEST ▸ raw

RAWHEAD n bogeyman

RAWHIDE n untanned hide ▷ vb whip

RAWIN n monitoring of winds in the upper atmosphere using radar and a balloon

RAWING (in dialect) same as ▸ rowen

RAWINGS ▸ rawing

RAWINS ▸ rawin

RAWISH ▸ raw

RAWLY ▸ raw

RAWN (in dialect) same as ▸ rowen

RAWNESS ▸ raw

RAWNS ▸ rawn

RAWS ▸ raw

RAX vb stretch or extend ▷ n act of stretching or straining

> A dialect word meaning to stretch or strain, and one of the essential short words to know for using the X.

RAXED ▸ rax

RAXES ▸ rax

RAXING ▸ rax

RAY n single line or narrow beam of light ▷ vb (of an object) to emit (light) in rays or (of light) to issue in the form of rays

RAYA same as ▸ rayah

RAYAH n (formerly) a non-Muslim subject of the Ottoman Empire

RAYAHS ▸ rayah

RAYAS ▸ raya

RAYED ▸ ray

RAYING ▸ ray

RAYLE archaic spelling of ▸ rail

RAYLED ▸ rayle

RAYLES ▸ rayle

RAYLESS adj dark

RAYLET n small ray

RAYLETS ▸ raylet

RAYLIKE adj resembling a ray

RAYLING ▸ rayle

RAYNE archaic spelling of ▸ reign

RAYNES ▸ rayne

RAYON n (fabric made of) a synthetic fibre

RAYONS ▸ rayon

RAYS ▸ ray

RAZE vb destroy (buildings or a town) completely

RAZED ▸ raze

RAZEE n sailing ship that has had its upper deck or decks removed ▷ vb remove the upper deck or decks of (a sailing ship)

RAZEED ▸ razee

RAZEES ▸ razee

RAZER ▸ raze

RAZERS ▸ raze

RAZES ▸ raze

RAZING ▸ raze

RAZOO n imaginary coin

RAZOOS ▸ razoo

RAZOR n sharp instrument for shaving ▷ vb cut or shave with a razor

RAZORED ▸ razor

RAZORS ▸ razor

RAZURE same as ▸ rasure

RAZURES ▸ razure

RAZZ vb make fun of

RAZZED ▸ razz

RAZZES ▸ razz

RAZZIA n raid for plunder or slaves, esp one carried out by Moors in North Africa

RAZZIAS ▸ razzia

RAZZING ▸ razz

RAZZLE n as in **on the razzle** out enjoying oneself or celebrating

RAZZLES ▸ razzle

RE prep concerning ▷ n the second note of the musical scale

REACH vb arrive at ▷ n distance that one can reach

REACHED ▸ reach

REACHER ▸ reach

REACHES ▸ reach

REACT vb act in response (to)

REACTED ▸ react

REACTOR n apparatus in which a nuclear reaction is maintained and controlled to produce nuclear energy

REACTS ▸ react

READ vb look at and understand or take in (written or printed matter) ▷ n matter suitable for reading

READAPT vb adapt again

READD vb add again

READDED ▸ readd

READDS ▸ readd

READER n person who reads

READERS ▸ reader

READIED ▸ ready

READIER ▸ ready

READIES pl n ready money

READILY adv promptly

READING ▸ read

README n document which accompanies computer files or software

READMIT vb let (a person, country, etc) back into a place or organization

READOPT vb adopt again

READORN vb adorn again

READOUT n act of retrieving information from a computer memory or storage device

READS ▸ read

READY adj prepared for use

or action ▷ vb prepare
REAFFIX vb affix again
REAGENT n chemical substance that reacts with another, used to detect the presence of the other
REAGIN n type of antibody that is formed against an allergen and is attached to the cells of a tissue. The antigen-antibody reaction that occurs on subsequent contact with the allergen causes tissue damage, leading to the release of histamine and other substances responsible for an allergic reaction
REAGINS ▶ reagin
REAK same as ▶ reck
REAKED ▶ reak
REAKING ▶ reak
REAKS ▶ reak
REAL adj existing in fact ▷ n name of a former small Spanish or Spanish-American silver coin as well as of the standard monetary unit of Brazil
REALER ▶ real
REALES ▶ real
REALEST ▶ real
REALGAR n rare orange-red soft mineral consisting of arsenic sulphide in monoclinic crystalline form
REALIA pl n real-life facts and material used in teaching
REALIGN vb change or put back to a new or former place or position
REALISE same as ▶ realize
REALISM n awareness or acceptance of things as they are
REALIST n person who is aware of and accepts the physical universe, events, etc, as they are
REALITY n state of things as they are
REALIZE vb become aware or grasp the significance of
REALLIE old or dialect variant of ▶ really
REALLOT vb allot again
REALLY adv very ▷ interj exclamation of dismay, doubt, or surprise ▷ vb (in archaic usage) rally
REALM n kingdom
REALMS ▶ realm

REALO n member of the German Green party with moderate views

> A **realo** is a member of the less radical section of the German Green party. It is important to know not because it scores well, but because it provides an easily overlooked 'hook', by allowing you to add O to **real**.

REALOS ▶ realo
REALS ▶ real
REALTER vb alter again
REALTIE n archaic word meaning sincerity
REALTOR n estate agent
REALTY n immovable property
REAM n twenty quires of paper, generally 500 sheets ▷ vb enlarge (a hole) by use of a reamer
REAME archaic variant of ▶ realm
REAMED ▶ ream
REAMEND vb amend again
REAMER n steel tool with a cylindrical or tapered shank around which longitudinal teeth are ground, used for smoothing the bores of holes accurately to size
REAMERS ▶ reamer
REAMES ▶ reame
REAMIER ▶ reamy
REAMING ▶ ream
REAMS ▶ ream
REAMY Scots for ▶ creamy
REAN same as ▶ reen
REANNEX vb annex again
REANS ▶ rean
REAP vb cut and gather (a harvest)
REAPED ▶ reap
REAPER n person who reaps or machine for reaping
REAPERS ▶ reaper
REAPING ▶ reap
REAPPLY vb put or spread (something) on again
REAPS ▶ reap
REAR n back part ▷ vb care for and educate (children)
REARED ▶ rear
REARER ▶ rear
REARERS ▶ rear
REARGUE vb argue again
REARING ▶ rear
REARISE vb arise again

REARLY old word for ▶ early
REARM vb arm again
REARMED ▶ rearm
REARMS ▶ rearm
REAROSE ▶ rearise
REARS ▶ rear
REASON n cause or motive ▷ vb think logically in forming conclusions
REASONS ▶ reason
REAST same as ▶ reest
REASTED ▶ reast
REASTS ▶ reast
REASTY adj (in dialect) rancid
REATA n lasso
REATAS ▶ reata
REATE n type of crowfoot
REATES ▶ reate
REAVAIL vb avail again
REAVE vb carry off (property, prisoners, etc) by force
REAVED ▶ reave
REAVER ▶ reave
REAVERS ▶ reave
REAVES ▶ reave
REAVING ▶ reave
REAVOW vb avow again
REAVOWS ▶ reavow
REAWAKE vb awake again
REAWOKE ▶ reawake
REB n Confederate soldier in the American Civil War (1861–65)
REBACK vb provide with a new back, backing, or lining
REBACKS ▶ reback
REBADGE vb relaunch (a product) under a new name, brand, or logo
REBAIT vb bait again
REBAITS ▶ rebait
REBAR n rod providing reinforcement in concrete structures
REBARS ▶ rebar
REBATE n discount or refund ▷ vb cut a rabbet in
REBATED ▶ rebate
REBATER ▶ rebate
REBATES ▶ rebate
REBATO same as ▶ rabato
REBATOS ▶ rebato
REBBE n individual's chosen spiritual mentor
REBBES ▶ rebbe
REBEC n medieval stringed instrument resembling the violin but having a lute-shaped body
REBECK same as ▶ rebec
REBECKS ▶ rebeck

R

REBECS ▶ rebec
REBEGAN ▶ rebegin
REBEGIN vb begin again
REBEGUN ▶ rebegin
REBEL vb revolt against the ruling power ▷ n person who rebels ▷ adj rebelling
REBELS ▶ rebel
REBID vb bid again
REBIDS ▶ rebid
REBILL vb bill again
REBILLS ▶ rebill
REBIND vb bind again
REBINDS ▶ rebind
REBIRTH n revival or renaissance
REBIT ▶ rebite
REBITE vb (in printing) to give another application of acid in order to cause further cutting of a plate
REBITES ▶ rebite
REBLEND vb blend again
REBLENT same as ▶ reblend
REBLOOM vb bloom again
REBOANT adj resounding or reverberating
REBOARD vb board again
REBODY vb give a new body to
REBOIL vb boil again
REBOILS ▶ reboil
REBOOK vb book again
REBOOKS ▶ rebook
REBOOT vb shut down and then restart (a computer system)
REBOOTS ▶ reboot
REBOP same as ▶ bebop
REBOPS ▶ rebop
REBORE n boring of a cylinder to restore its true shape ▷ vb carry out this process
REBORED ▶ rebore
REBORES ▶ rebore
REBORN adj active again after a period of inactivity
REBOUND vb spring back ▷ n act of rebounding
REBOZO n long wool or linen scarf covering the shoulders and head, worn by Latin American women
REBOZOS ▶ rebozo
REBRACE vb brace again
REBRAND vb change or update the image of (an organization or product)
REBRED ▶ rebreed
REBREED vb breed again
REBS ▶ reb
REBUFF vb reject or snub

▷ n blunt refusal, snub
REBUFFS ▶ rebuff
REBUILD vb build (a building or town) again, after severe damage
REBUILT ▶ rebuild
REBUKE vb scold sternly ▷ n stern scolding
REBUKED ▶ rebuke
REBUKER ▶ rebuke
REBUKES ▶ rebuke
REBURY vb bury again
REBUS n puzzle consisting of pictures and symbols representing words or syllables
REBUSES ▶ rebus
REBUT vb prove that (a claim) is untrue
REBUTS ▶ rebut
REBUY vb buy again
REBUYS ▶ rebuy
REC n short for recreation
RECAL same as ▶ recall
RECALL vb recollect or remember ▷ n ability to remember
RECALLS ▶ recall
RECALS ▶ recall
RECANE vb cane again
RECANED ▶ recane
RECANES ▶ recane
RECANT vb withdraw (a statement or belief) publicly
RECANTS ▶ recant
RECAP vb recapitulate ▷ n recapitulation
RECAPS ▶ recap
RECARRY vb carry again
RECAST vb organize or set out in a different way
RECASTS ▶ recast
RECATCH vb catch again
RECCE vb reconnoitre ▷ n reconnaissance
RECCED ▶ recce
RECCEED ▶ recce
RECCES ▶ recce
RECCIED ▶ reccy
RECCIES ▶ reccy
RECCO same as ▶ recce
RECCOS ▶ recco
RECCY same as ▶ recce
RECEDE vb move to a more distant place
RECEDED ▶ recede
RECEDES ▶ recede
RECEIPT n written acknowledgment of money or goods received ▷ vb acknowledge payment of (a bill), as by marking it

RECEIVE vb take, accept, or get
RECENCY ▶ recent
RECENSE vb revise
RECENT adj having happened lately
RECEPT n idea or image formed in the mind by repeated experience of a particular pattern of sensory stimulation
RECEPTS ▶ recept
RECESS n niche or alcove ▷ vb place or set (something) in a recess
RECHART vb chart again
RECHATE same as ▶ recheat
RECHEAT n (in a hunt) sounding of the horn to call back the hounds ▷ vb sound the horn to call back the hounds
RECHECK vb check again
RECHEW vb chew again
RECHEWS ▶ rechew
RECHIE adj smoky
RECHIP vb put a new chip into (a stolen mobile phone) so it can be reused
RECHIPS ▶ rechip
RECHOSE > rechoose
RECIPE n directions for cooking a dish
RECIPES ▶ recipe
RECIT n narrative
RECITAL n musical performance by a soloist or soloists
RECITE vb repeat (a poem, story, etc) aloud to an audience
RECITED ▶ recite
RECITER ▶ recite
RECITES ▶ recite
RECITS ▶ recit
RECK vb mind or care about (something)
RECKAN adj strained, tormented, or twisted
RECKED ▶ reck
RECKING ▶ reck
RECKON vb consider or think
RECKONS ▶ reckon
RECKS ▶ reck
RECLAD vb cover in a different substance
RECLADS ▶ reclad
RECLAIM vb regain possession of ▷ n act of reclaiming or state of being reclaimed

RECLAME n public acclaim or attention

RECLASP vb clasp again

RECLEAN vb clean again

RECLIMB vb climb again

RECLINE vb rest in a leaning position

RECLOSE vb close again

RECLUSE n person who avoids other people ▷ adj solitary

RECOAL vb supply or be supplied with fresh coal

RECOALS ▶ recoal

RECOAT vb coat again

RECOATS ▶ recoat

RECOCK vb cock again

RECOCKS ▶ recock

RECODE vb put into a new code

RECODED ▶ recode

RECODES ▶ recode

RECOIL vb jerk or spring back ▷ n backward jerk

RECOILS ▶ recoil

RECOIN vb coin again

RECOINS ▶ recoin

RECOLOR vb give a new colour to

RECOMB vb comb again

RECOMBS ▶ recomb

RECON vb to make a preliminary survey

RECONS ▶ recon

RECOOK vb cook again

RECOOKS ▶ recook

RECOPY vb copy again

RECORD n document or other thing that preserves information ▷ vb put in writing

RECORDS ▶ record

RECORK vb cork again

RECORKS ▶ recork

RECOUNT vb tell in detail

RECOUP vb regain or make good (a loss)

RECOUPE vb (in law) keep back or withhold

RECOUPS ▶ recoupe

RECOURE archaic variant of ▶ recover

RECOVER vb become healthy again

RECOWER archaic variant of ▶ recover

RECOYLE archaic spelling of ▶ recoil

RECRATE vb crate again

RECROSS vb move or go across (something) again

RECROWN vb crown again

RECRUIT vb enlist (new soldiers, members, etc) ▷ n newly enlisted soldier

RECS ▶ rec

RECTA ▶ rectum

RECTAL adj of the rectum

RECTI ▶ rectus

RECTIFY vb put right, correct

RECTION n (in grammar) the determination of the form of one word by another word

RECTO n right-hand page of a book

RECTOR n clergyman in charge of a parish

RECTORS ▶ rector

RECTORY n rector's house

RECTOS ▶ recto

RECTRIX n any of the large stiff feathers of a bird's tail, used in controlling the direction of flight

RECTUM n final section of the large intestine

RECTUMS ▶ rectum

RECTUS n straight muscle, esp either of two muscles of the anterior abdominal wall

RECUILE archaic variant of ▶ recoil

RECULE archaic variant of ▶ recoil

RECULED ▶ recule

RECULES ▶ recule

RECUR vb happen again

RECURE vb archaic word for cure or recover

RECURED ▶ recure

RECURES ▶ recure

RECURS ▶ recur

RECURVE vb curve or bend (something) back or down or (of something) to be so curved or bent

RECUSAL n withdrawal of a judge from a case

RECUSE vb (in law) object to or withdraw (a judge)

RECUSED ▶ recuse

RECUSES ▶ recuse

RECUT vb cut again

RECUTS ▶ recut

RECYCLE vb reprocess (used materials) for further use ▷ n repetition of a fixed sequence of events

RED adj of a colour varying from crimson to orange and seen in blood, fire, etc ▷ n red colour

REDACT vb compose or draft (an edict, proclamation, etc)

REDACTS ▶ redact

REDAN n fortification of two parapets at a salient angle

REDANS ▶ redan

REDATE vb change date of

REDATED ▶ redate

REDATES ▶ redate

REDBACK n small venomous Australian spider

REDBAIT vb harass those with leftwing leanings

REDBAY n type of tree

REDBAYS ▶ redbay

REDBIRD n type of bird, the male of which is distinguished by its bright red plumage and black wings

REDBONE n type of American dog

REDBUD n American leguminous tree with heart-shaped leaves and small budlike pink flowers

REDBUDS ▶ redbud

REDBUG another name for ▶ chigger

REDBUGS ▶ redbug

REDCAP n military policeman

REDCAPS ▶ redcap

REDCOAT n British soldier

REDD vb bring order to ▷ n act or an instance of redding

REDDED ▶ redd

REDDEN vb make or become red

REDDENS ▶ redden

REDDER ▶ redd

REDDERS ▶ redd

REDDEST ▶ red

REDDIER ▶ reddy

REDDING ▶ redd

REDDISH adj somewhat red

REDDLE same as ▶ ruddle

REDDLED ▶ reddle

REDDLES ▶ reddle

REDDS ▶ redd

REDDY adj reddish

REDE n advice or counsel ▷ vb advise

REDEAL vb deal again

REDEALS ▶ redeal

REDEALT ▶ redeal

REDEAR n variety of sunfish with a red flash above the gills

REDEARS ▶ redear

R

REDED ▶ **rede**
REDEEM vb make up for
REDEEMS ▶ **redeem**
REDEFY vb defy again
REDENY vb deny again
REDES ▶ **rede**
REDEYE n inferior whiskey
REDEYES ▶ **redeye**
REDFIN n any of various small fishes with reddish fins that are popular aquarium fishes
REDFINS ▶ **redfin**
REDFISH n male salmon that has recently spawned
REDFOOT n fatal disease of newborn lambs of unknown cause in which the horny layers of the feet become separated, exposing the red laminae below
REDHEAD n person with reddish hair
REDIA n parasitic larva of flukes that has simple locomotory organs, pharynx, and intestine and gives rise either to other rediae or to a different larva (the cercaria)
REDIAE ▶ **redia**
REDIAL vb dial (a telephone number) again
REDIALS ▶ **redial**
REDIAS ▶ **redia**
REDID ▶ **redo**
REDING ▶ **rede**
REDIP vb dip again
REDIPS ▶ **redip**
REDIPT archaic past form of ▶ **redip**
REDLINE vb (esp of a bank or group of banks) to refuse a loan to (a person or country) because of the presumed risks involved
REDLY ▶ **red**
REDNESS ▶ **red**
REDO vb do over again in order to improve ▷ n instance of redoing something
REDOCK vb dock again
REDOCKS ▶ **redock**
REDOES ▶ **redo**
REDOING ▶ **redo**
REDON vb don again
REDONE ▶ **redo**
REDONS ▶ **redon**
REDOS ▶ **redo**
REDOUBT n small fort defending a hilltop or pass

▷ vb fear
REDOUND vb cause advantage or disadvantage (to)
REDOUT n reddened vision and other symptoms caused by a rush of blood to the head in response to negative gravitational stresses
REDOUTS ▶ **redout**
REDOWA n Bohemian folk dance similar to the waltz
REDOWAS ▶ **redowa**
REDOX n chemical reaction in which one substance is reduced and the other is oxidized
REDOXES ▶ **redox**
REDPOLL n mostly grey-brown finch with a red crown and pink breast
REDRAFT vb write a second copy of (a letter, proposal, essay, etc) ▷ n second draft
REDRAW vb draw or draw up (something) again or differently
REDRAWN ▶ **redraw**
REDRAWS ▶ **redraw**
REDREAM vb dream again
REDRESS vb make amends for ▷ n compensation or amends
REDREW ▶ **redraw**
REDRIED ▶ **redry**
REDRIES ▶ **redry**
REDRILL vb drill again
REDRIVE vb drive again
REDROOT n yellow-flowered bog plant of E North America whose roots yield a red dye
REDROVE ▶ **redrive**
REDRY vb dry again
REDS ▶ **red**
REDSEAR same as > **redshort**
REDTAIL n variety of bird with red colouring on its tail
REDTOP n sensationalist tabloid newspaper
REDTOPS ▶ **redtop**
REDUB vb fix or repair
REDUBS ▶ **redub**
REDUCE vb bring down, lower
REDUCED ▶ **reduce**
REDUCER n chemical solution used to lessen the density of a negative or print by oxidizing some of the blackened silver to

soluble silver compounds
REDUCES ▶ **reduce**
REDUIT n fortified part from which a garrison may fight on once an enemy has taken outworks
REDUITS ▶ **reduit**
REDUX adj brought back or returned
REDWARE another name for ▶ **kelp**
REDWING n small European thrush
REDWOOD n giant Californian conifer with reddish bark
REDYE vb dye again
REDYED ▶ **redye**
REDYES ▶ **redye**
REE n Scots word for walled enclosure
REEARN vb earn again
REEARNS ▶ **reearn**
REEBOK same as ▶ **rhebok**
REEBOKS ▶ **reebok**
REECH vb (in dialect) smoke
REECHED ▶ **reech**
REECHES ▶ **reech**
REECHIE same as ▶ **reechy**
REECHO vb echo again
REECHY adj (in dialect) smoky
REED n tall grass that grows in swamps and shallow water
REEDBED n area of wetland with reeds growing in it
REEDE obsolete variant of ▶ **red**
REEDED ▶ **reed**
REEDEN adj of or consisting of reeds
REEDER n thatcher
REEDERS ▶ **reeder**
REEDES ▶ **reede**
REEDIER ▶ **reedy**
REEDIFY vb edify again or rebuild
REEDILY ▶ **reedy**
REEDING n set of small semicircular architectural mouldings
REEDIT vb edit again
REEDITS ▶ **reedit**
REEDMAN n musician who plays a wind instrument that has a reed
REEDMEN ▶ **reedman**
REEDS ▶ **reed**
REEDY adj harsh and thin in tone
REEF n ridge of rock or coral near the surface of the sea

▷ *vb* roll up part of a sail
REEFED ▸ reef
REEFER *n* short thick jacket worn esp by sailors
REEFERS ▸ reefer
REEFIER ▸ reefy
REEFING ▸ reef
REEFS ▸ reef
REEFY *adj* with reefs
REEJECT *vb* eject again
REEK *vb* smell strongly ▷ *n* strong unpleasant smell
REEKED ▸ reek
REEKER ▸ reek
REEKERS ▸ reek
REEKIE *same as* ▸ **reeky**
REEKIER ▸ reek
REEKING ▸ reek
REEKS ▸ reek
REEKY *adj* steamy or smoky
REEL *n* cylindrical object on which film, tape, thread, or wire is wound ▷ *vb* stagger, sway, or whirl
REELECT *vb* elect again
REELED ▸ reel
REELER ▸ reel
REELERS ▸ reel
REELING ▸ reel
REELMAN *n* (formerly) member of a beach life-saving team operating a winch
REELMEN ▸ reelman
REELS ▸ reel
REEMIT *vb* emit again
REEMITS ▸ reemit
REEN *n* ditch, esp a drainage channel
REENACT *vb* enact again
REENDOW *vb* endow again
REENJOY *vb* enjoy again
REENS ▸ reen
REENTER *vb* enter again
REENTRY *n* return of a spacecraft into the earth's atmosphere
REEQUIP *vb* equip again
REERECT *vb* erect again
REES ▸ ree
REEST *vb* (esp of horses) to be noisily uncooperative
REESTED ▸ reest
REESTS ▸ reest
REESTY *same as* ▸ **reasty**
REEVE *n* local representative of the king in a shire until the early 11th century ▷ *vb* pass (a rope or cable) through an eye or other narrow opening
REEVED ▸ reeve
REEVES ▸ reeve

REEVING ▸ reeve
REEVOKE *vb* evoke again
REEXPEL *vb* expel again
REF *n* referee in sport ▷ *vb* referee
REFACE *vb* repair or renew the facing of (a wall)
REFACED ▸ reface
REFACES ▸ reface
REFALL *vb* fall again
REFALLS ▸ refall
REFECT *vb* archaic word for restore or refresh with food and drink
REFECTS ▸ refect
REFED ▸ refeed
REFEED *vb* feed again
REFEEDS ▸ refeed
REFEEL *vb* feel again
REFEELS ▸ refeel
REFEL *vb* refute
REFELL ▸ refall
REFELS ▸ refel
REFELT ▸ refeel
REFENCE *vb* fence again
REFER *vb* allude (to)
REFEREE *n* umpire in sports, esp soccer or boxing ▷ *vb* act as referee of
REFERS ▸ refer
REFFED ▸ ref
REFFING ▸ ref
REFIGHT *vb* fight again ▷ *n* second or new fight
REFILE *vb* file again
REFILED ▸ refile
REFILES ▸ refile
REFILL *vb* fill again ▷ *n* second or subsequent filling
REFILLS ▸ refill
REFILM *vb* film again
REFILMS ▸ refilm
REFIND *vb* find again
REFINDS ▸ refind
REFINE *vb* purify
REFINED *adj* cultured or polite
REFINER *n* person, device, or substance that removes impurities, sediment, or other unwanted matter from something
REFINES ▸ refine
REFIRE *vb* fire again
REFIRED ▸ refire
REFIRES ▸ refire
REFIT *vb* make ready for use again by repairing or re-equipping ▷ *n* repair or re-equipping for further use
REFITS ▸ refit
REFIX *vb* fix again

REFIXED ▸ refix
REFIXES ▸ refix
REFLAG *vb* flag again
REFLAGS ▸ reflag
REFLATE *vb* inflate or be inflated again
REFLECT *vb* throw back, esp rays of light, heat, etc
REFLET *n* iridescent glow or lustre, as on ceramic ware
REFLETS ▸ reflet
REFLEW ▸ refly
REFLEX *n* involuntary response to a stimulus or situation ▷ *adj* (of a muscular action) involuntary ▷ *vb* bend, turn, or reflect backwards
REFLIES ▸ refly
REFLOAT *vb* float again
REFLOOD *vb* flood again
REFLOW *vb* flow again
REFLOWN ▸ refly
REFLOWS ▸ reflow
REFLUX *vb* boil or be boiled in a vessel attached to a condenser, so that the vapour condenses and flows back into the vessel ▷ *n* act of refluxing
REFLY *vb* fly again
REFOCUS *vb* focus again or anew
REFOLD *vb* fold again
REFOLDS ▸ refold
REFOOT *vb* foot again
REFOOTS ▸ refoot
REFORGE *vb* forge again
REFORM *n* improvement ▷ *vb* improve
REFORMS ▸ reform
REFOUND *vb* found again
REFRACT *vb* change the course of (light etc) passing from one medium to another
REFRAIN *n* frequently repeated part of a song ▷ *vb* abstain (from action)
REFRAME *vb* support or enclose (a picture, photograph, etc) in a new or different frame
REFRESH *vb* revive or reinvigorate, as through food, drink, or rest
REFRIED ▸ refry
REFRIES ▸ refry
REFRONT *vb* put a new front on
REFROZE > refreeze
REFRY *vb* fry again
REFS ▸ ref

R

REFT ▶ reave
REFUEL vb supply or be supplied with fresh fuel
REFUELS ▶ refuel
REFUGE n (source of) shelter or protection ▷ vb take refuge or give refuge to
REFUGED ▶ refuge
REFUGEE n person who seeks refuge, esp in a foreign country
REFUGES ▶ refuge
REFUGIA > refugium
REFUND vb pay back ▷ n return of money
REFUNDS ▶ refund
REFUSAL n denial of anything demanded or offered
REFUSE vb decline, deny, or reject ▷ n rubbish or useless matter
REFUSED ▶ refuse
REFUSER ▶ refuse
REFUSES ▶ refuse
REFUTAL n act or process of refuting
REFUTE vb disprove
REFUTED ▶ refute
REFUTER ▶ refute
REFUTES ▶ refute
REG n large expanse of stony desert terrain
REGAIN vb get back or recover ▷ n process of getting something back, esp lost weight
REGAINS ▶ regain
REGAL adj of or like a king or queen ▷ n portable organ equipped only with small reed pipes, popular from the 15th century and recently revived for modern performance
REGALE vb entertain (someone) with stories etc ▷ n feast
REGALED ▶ regale
REGALER ▶ regale
REGALES ▶ regale
REGALIA pl n ceremonial emblems of royalty or high office
REGALLY ▶ regal
REGALS ▶ regal
REGAR same as ▶ regur
REGARD vb consider ▷ n respect or esteem
REGARDS ▶ regard
REGARS ▶ regar
REGATTA n meeting for yacht or boat races

REGAUGE vb gauge again
REGAVE ▶ regive
REGEAR vb readjust
REGEARS ▶ regear
REGENCE old variant of ▶ regency
REGENCY n status or period of office of a regent
REGENT n ruler of a kingdom during the absence, childhood, or illness of its monarch ▷ adj ruling as a regent
REGENTS ▶ regent
REGES ▶ rex
REGEST n archaic word for register
REGESTS ▶ regest
REGGAE n style of Jamaican popular music with a strong beat
REGGAES ▶ reggae
REGGO same as ▶ rego
REGGOS ▶ reggo
REGIE n government-directed management or government monopoly
REGIES ▶ regie
REGIFT vb give (a previously received gift) to someone else
REGIFTS ▶ regift
REGILD vb gild again
REGILDS ▶ regild
REGILT archaic past form of ▶ regild
REGIME n system of government
REGIMEN n prescribed system of diet etc
REGIMES ▶ regime
REGINA n queen
REGINAE ▶ regina
REGINAL adj queenly
REGINAS ▶ regina
REGION n administrative division of a country
REGIONS ▶ region
REGIUS adj as in **regius professor** Crown-appointed holder of a university chair
REGIVE vb give again or back
REGIVEN ▶ regive
REGIVES ▶ regive
REGLAZE vb glaze again
REGLET n flat narrow architectural moulding
REGLETS ▶ reglet
REGLOSS vb gloss again or give a new gloss to
REGLOW vb glow again

REGLOWS ▶ reglow
REGLUE vb glue again
REGLUED ▶ reglue
REGLUES ▶ reglue
REGMA n type of fruit with cells that break open and break away when ripe
REGMATA ▶ regma
REGNA ▶ regnum
REGNAL adj of a sovereign, reign, or kingdom
REGNANT adj reigning
REGNUM n reign or rule
REGO n registration of a motor vehicle
REGORGE vb vomit up
REGOS ▶ rego
REGOSOL n type of azonal soil consisting of unconsolidated material derived from freshly deposited alluvium or sands
REGRADE vb grade again
REGRAFT vb graft again
REGRANT vb grant again
REGRATE vb buy up (commodities) in advance so as to raise their price for profitable resale
REGREDE vb go back
REGREEN vb green again
REGREET vb greet again or return greetings of
REGRESS vb revert to a former worse condition ▷ n return to a former and worse condition
REGRET vb feel sorry about ▷ n feeling of repentance, guilt, or sorrow
REGRETS ▶ regret
REGREW ▶ regrow
REGRIND vb grind again
REGROOM vb groom again
REGROUP vb reorganize (military forces) after an attack or a defeat
REGROW vb grow or be grown again after having been cut or having died or withered
REGROWN ▶ regrow
REGROWS ▶ regrow
REGS ▶ reg
REGULA n rule
REGULAE ▶ regula
REGULAR adj normal, customary, or usual ▷ n regular soldier
REGULI ▶ regulus
REGULO n any of a number of temperatures to which a

gas oven may be set

REGULOS ▶ regulo

REGULUS *n* impure metal forming beneath the slag during the smelting of ores

REGUR *n* black loamy Indian soil

REGURS ▶ regur

REH *n* (in India) salty surface crust on the soil

REHAB *vb* help (addict, disabled person, prisoner, etc) to readapt to society or a new job ▷ *n* treatment or help given to an addict, disabled person, or prisoner, etc

REHABS ▶ rehab

REHANG *vb* hang again

REHANGS ▶ rehang

REHASH *vb* rework or reuse ▷ *n* old ideas presented in a new form

REHEAR *vb* hear again

REHEARD ▶ rehear

REHEARS ▶ rehear

REHEAT *vb* heat or be heated again

REHEATS ▶ reheat

REHEEL *vb* put a new heel or new heels on

REHEELS ▶ reheel

REHEM *vb* hem again

REHEMS ▶ rehem

REHINGE *vb* put a new hinge or new hinges on

REHIRE *vb* hire again

REHIRED ▶ rehire

REHIRES ▶ rehire

REHOME *vb* find a new home for (esp a pet)

REHOMED ▶ rehome

REHOMES ▶ rehome

REHOUSE *vb* provide with a new (and better) home

REHS ▶ reh

REHUNG ▶ rehang

REI *n* name for a former Portuguese coin, more properly called a real

REIF *n* Scots word meaning robbery or plunder

REIFIED ▶ reify

REIFIER ▶ reify

REIFIES ▶ reify

REIFS ▶ reif

REIFY *vb* consider or make (an abstract idea or concept) real or concrete

REIGN *n* period of a sovereign's rule ▷ *vb* rule (a country)

REIGNED ▶ reign

REIGNS ▶ reign

REIK *Scots word for* ▶ **smoke**

REIKI *n* form of therapy in which the practitioner is believed to channel energy into the patient in order to encourage healing or restore wellbeing

REIKIS ▶ reiki

REIKS ▶ reik

REIMAGE *vb* image again

REIN *vb* check or manage with reins

REINCUR *vb* incur again

REINDEX *vb* index again

REINED ▶ rein

REINING ▶ rein

REINK *vb* ink again

REINKED ▶ reink

REINKS ▶ reink

REINS *pl n* narrow straps attached to a bit to guide a horse

REINTER *vb* inter again

REIRD *Scots word for* ▶ **din**

REIRDS ▶ reird

REIS ▶ rei

REISES ▶ rei

REISSUE *n* book, record, etc, that is published or released again after being unavailable for a time ▷ *vb* publish or release (a book, record, etc) again after a period of unavailability

REIST *same as* ▶ **reest**

REISTED ▶ reist

REISTS ▶ reist

REITBOK *same as* ▶ **reedbuck**

REITER *n* soldier in the German cavalry

REITERS ▶ reiter

REIVE *vb* go on a plundering raid

REIVED ▶ reive

REIVER ▶ reive

REIVERS ▶ reive

REIVES ▶ reive

REIVING ▶ reive

REJECT *vb* refuse to accept or believe ▷ *n* person or thing rejected as not up to standard

REJECTS ▶ reject

REJIG *vb* re-equip (a factory or plant) ▷ *n* act or process of rejigging

REJIGS ▶ rejig

REJOICE *vb* feel or express great happiness

REJOIN *vb* join again

REJOINS ▶ rejoin

REJON *n* bullfighting lance

REJONEO *n* bullfighting activity in which a mounted bullfighter spears the bull with lances

REJONES ▶ rejon

REJOURN *vb* archaic word meaning postpone or adjourn

REJUDGE *vb* judge again

REKE *same as* ▶ **reck**

REKED ▶ reke

REKES ▶ reke

REKEY *vb* key again

REKEYED ▶ rekey

REKEYS ▶ rekey

REKING ▶ reke

REKNIT *vb* knit again

REKNITS ▶ reknit

REKNOT *vb* knot again

REKNOTS ▶ reknot

RELABEL *vb* label again

RELACE *vb* lace again

RELACED ▶ relace

RELACES ▶ relace

RELACHE *n* break

RELAID ▶ relay

RELAND *vb* land again

RELANDS ▶ reland

RELAPSE *vb* fall back into bad habits, illness, etc ▷ *n* return of bad habits, illness, etc

RELATA ▶ relatum

RELATE *vb* establish a relation between

RELATED *adj* linked by kinship or marriage

RELATER ▶ relate

RELATES ▶ relate

RELATOR *n* person who relates a story

RELATUM *n* one of the objects between which a relation is said to hold

RELAX *vb* make or become looser, less tense, or less rigid

RELAXED ▶ relax

RELAXER *n* person or thing that relaxes, esp a substance used to straighten curly hair

RELAXES ▶ relax

RELAXIN *n* mammalian polypeptide hormone secreted by the corpus luteum during pregnancy, which relaxes the pelvic ligaments

RELAY *n* fresh set of people or animals relieving others ▷ *vb* pass on (a message)

R

RELAYED ▶ **relay**
RELAYS ▶ **relay**
RELEARN vb learn (something previously known) again
RELEASE vb set free ▷ n setting free
RELEND vb lend again
RELENDS ▶ **relend**
RELENT vb give up a harsh intention, become less severe
RELENTS ▶ **relent**
RELET vb let again
RELETS ▶ **relet**
RELEVE n dance move in which heels are off the ground
RELEVES ▶ **releve**
RELIANT > **reliance**
RELIC n something that has survived from the past
RELICS ▶ **relic**
RELICT n relic
RELICTS ▶ **rclict**
RELIDE archaic past form of ▶ **rely**
RELIE archaic spelling of ▶ **rely**
RELIED ▶ **rely**
RELIEF n gladness at the end or removal of pain, distress, etc
RELIEFS ▶ **relief**
RELIER ▶ **rely**
RELIERS ▶ **rely**
RELIES ▶ **rely**
RELIEVE vb bring relief to
RELIEVO same as ▶ **relief**
RELIGHT vb ignite or cause to ignite again
RELINE vb line again or anew
RELINED ▶ **reline**
RELINES ▶ **reline**
RELINK vb link again
RELINKS ▶ **relink**
RELIQUE archaic spelling of ▶ **relic**
RELISH vb enjoy, like very much ▷ n liking or enjoyment
RELIST vb list again
RELISTS ▶ **relist**
RELIT ▶ **relight**
RELIVE vb experience (a sensation etc) again, esp in the imagination
RELIVED ▶ **relive**
RELIVER vb deliver up again
RELIVES ▶ **relive**
RELLENO n Mexican dish of stuffed vegetable

RELLIE n relative
RELLIES pl n relatives or relations
RELLISH (in music) same as ▶ **relish**
RELOAD vb put fresh ammunition into (a firearm)
RELOADS ▶ **reload**
RELOAN vb loan again
RELOANS ▶ **reloan**
RELOCK vb lock again
RELOCKS ▶ **relock**
RELOOK vb look again
RELOOKS ▶ **relook**
RELUCT vb struggle or rebel
RELUCTS ▶ **reluct**
RELUME vb light or brighten again
RELUMED ▶ **relume**
RELUMES ▶ **relume**
RELY vb depend (on)
RELYING ▶ **rely**
REM n dose of ionizing radiation that produces the same effect in man as one roentgen of x- or gamma-radiation
REMADE n object that has been reconstructed from original materials
REMADES ▶ **remade**
REMAIL vb mail again
REMAILS ▶ **remail**
REMAIN vb continue
REMAINS pl n relics, esp of ancient buildings
REMAKE vb make again in a different way ▷ n new version of an old film
REMAKER ▶ **remake**
REMAKES ▶ **remake**
REMAN vb man again or afresh
REMAND vb send back into custody or put on bail before trial
REMANDS ▶ **remand**
REMANET n something left over
REMANIE n fragments and fossils of older origin found in a more recent deposit
REMANS ▶ **reman**
REMAP vb map again
REMAPS ▶ **remap**
REMARK vb make a casual comment (on) ▷ n observation or comment
REMARKS ▶ **remark**
REMARRY vb marry again following a divorce or the death of one's previous

husband or wife
REMATCH n second or return game or contest between two players ▷ vb match (two contestants) again
REMATE vb mate again ▷ n finishing pass in bullfighting
REMATED ▶ **remate**
REMATES ▶ **remate**
REMBLAI n earth used for an embankment or rampart
REMBLE dialect word for ▶ **remove**
REMBLED ▶ **remble**
REMBLES ▶ **remble**
REMEAD archaic or dialect word for ▶ **remedy**
REMEADS ▶ **remead**
REMEDE archaic or dialect word for ▶ **remedy**
REMEDED ▶ **remede**
REMEDES ▶ **remede**
REMEDY n means of curing pain or disease ▷ vb put right
REMEET vb meet again
REMEETS ▶ **remeet**
REMEID archaic or dialect word for ▶ **remedy**
REMEIDS ▶ **remeid**
REMELT vb melt again
REMELTS ▶ **remelt**
REMEN n ancient Egyptian measurement unit
REMEND vb mend again
REMENDS ▶ **remend**
REMENS ▶ **remen**
REMERCY vb archaic word for thank
REMERGE vb merge again
REMET ▶ **remeet**
REMEX n any of the large flight feathers of a bird's wing
REMIGES ▶ **remex**
REMIND vb cause to remember
REMINDS ▶ **remind**
REMINT vb mint again
REMINTS ▶ **remint**
REMISE vb give up or relinquish (a right, claim, etc) ▷ n second thrust made on the same lunge after the first has missed
REMISED ▶ **remise**
REMISES ▶ **remise**
REMISS adj negligent or careless
REMIT vb send (money) for

goods, services, etc, esp by post ▷ n area of competence or authority

REMITS ▶ remit

REMIX vb change the relative prominence of each performer's part of (a recording) ▷ n remixed version of a recording

REMIXED ▶ remix

REMIXES ▶ remix

REMIXT informal past form of ▶ remix

REMNANT n small piece, esp of fabric, left over ▷ adj remaining

REMODEL vb give a different shape or form to ▷ n something that has been remodelled

REMOLD US spelling of ▶ remould

REMOLDS ▶ remold

REMORA n spiny-finned fish

REMORAS ▶ remora

REMORID ▶ remora

REMORSE n feeling of sorrow and regret for something one did

REMOTE adj far away, distant ▷ n (in informal usage) remote control

REMOTER ▶ remote

REMOTES ▶ remote

REMOUD Spenserian variant of ▶ removed

REMOULD vb change completely ▷ n renovated tyre

REMOUNT vb get on (a horse, bicycle, etc) again ▷ n fresh horse, esp (formerly) to replace one killed or injured in battle

REMOVAL n removing, esp changing residence

REMOVE vb take away or off ▷ n degree of difference

REMOVED adj very different or distant

REMOVER ▶ remove

REMOVES ▶ remove

REMS ▶ rem

REMUAGE n (in the making of sparkling wine) process of turning the bottles to let the sediment out

REMUDA n stock of horses enabling riders to change mounts

REMUDAS ▶ remuda

REMUEUR n (in the making

of sparkling wine) person carrying out remuage, or the turning of bottles

REN archaic variant of ▶ run

RENAGUE same as ▶ renege

RENAIL vb nail again

RENAILS ▶ renail

RENAL adj of the kidneys

RENAME vb change the name of (someone or something)

RENAMED ▶ rename

RENAMES ▶ rename

RENAY vb archaic word meaning renounce

RENAYED ▶ renay

RENAYS ▶ renay

REND vb tear or wrench apart

RENDED ▶ rend

RENDER vb cause to become ▷ n first thin coat of plaster applied to a surface

RENDERS ▶ render

RENDING ▶ rend

RENDS ▶ rend

RENEGE vb go back (on a promise etc)

RENEGED ▶ renege

RENEGER ▶ renege

RENEGES ▶ renege

RENEGUE same as ▶ renege

RENEST vb nest again or form a new nest

RENESTS ▶ renest

RENEW vb begin again

RENEWAL n act of renewing or state of being renewed

RENEWED ▶ renew

RENEWER ▶ renew

RENEWS ▶ renew

RENEY same as ▶ renay

RENEYED ▶ reney

RENEYS ▶ reney

RENGA n type of collaborative poetry found in Japan

RENGAS ▶ renga

RENIED ▶ reny

RENIES ▶ reny

RENIG same as ▶ renege

RENIGS ▶ renig

RENIN n proteolytic enzyme secreted by the kidneys, which plays an important part in the maintenance of blood pressure

RENINS ▶ renin

RENK adj unpleasant

RENKER ▶ renk

RENKEST ▶ renk

RENNASE same as ▶ rennin

RENNE archaic variant of ▶ run

RENNED ▶ ren

RENNES ▶ renne

RENNET n substance for curdling milk to make cheese

RENNETS ▶ rennet

RENNIN n enzyme that occurs in gastric juice and is a constituent of rennet. It coagulates milk by converting caseinogen to casein

RENNING ▶ ren

RENNINS ▶ rennin

RENOWN n widespread good reputation ▷ vb make famous

RENOWNS ▶ renown

RENS ▶ ren

RENT n payment made by a tenant to a landlord or owner of a property ▷ vb grant the right to use one's property for payment

RENTAL n sum payable as rent ▷ adj of or relating to rent

RENTALS ▶ rental

RENTE n annual income from capital investment

RENTED ▶ rent

RENTER n person who lets his property in return for rent, esp a landlord

RENTERS ▶ renter

RENTES ▶ rente

RENTIER n person who lives off unearned income such as rents or interest

RENTING ▶ rent

RENTS ▶ rent

RENVOI n referring of a dispute or other legal question to a jurisdiction other than that in which it arose

RENVOIS ▶ renvoi

RENVOY old variant of ▶ renvoi

RENVOYS ▶ renvoy

RENY same as ▶ renay

RENYING ▶ reny

REO n a New Zealand language

REOCCUR vb happen, take place, or come about again

REOFFER vb offer again

REOIL vb oil again

REOILED ▶ reoil

REOILS ▶ reoil

REOPEN vb open again after

a period of being closed or suspended

REOPENS ▸ reopen

REORDER vb change the order of

REOS ▸ reo

REP n sales representative ▷vb work as a representative

REPACK vb place or arrange (articles) in (a container) again or in a different way

REPACKS ▸ repack

REPAID ▸ repay

REPAINT vb apply a new or fresh coat of paint

REPAIR vb restore to good condition, mend ▷n act of repairing

REPAIRS ▸ repair

REPAND adj having a wavy margin

REPANEL vb panel again or anew

REPAPER vb paper again or afresh

REPARK vb park again

REPARKS ▸ repark

REPASS vb pass again

REPAST n meal ▷vb feed (on)

REPASTS ▸ repast

REPATCH vb patch again

REPAVE vb pave again

REPAVED ▸ repave

REPAVES ▸ repave

REPAY vb pay back, refund

REPAYS ▸ repay

REPEAL vb cancel (a law) officially ▷n act of repealing

REPEALS ▸ repeal

REPEAT vb say or do again ▷n act or instance of repeating

REPEATS ▸ repeat

REPEG vb peg again

REPEGS ▸ repeg

REPEL vb be disgusting to

REPELS ▸ repel

REPENT vb feel regret for (a deed or omission) ▷adj lying or creeping along the ground

REPENTS ▸ repent

REPERK vb perk again

REPERKS ▸ reperk

REPIN vb pin again

REPINE vb fret or complain

REPINED ▸ repine

REPINER ▸ repine

REPINES ▸ repine

REPINS ▸ repin

REPIQUE n score of 30 points made from the cards held by a player before play begins ▷vb score a repique against (someone)

REPLA ▸ replum

REPLACE vb substitute for

REPLAN vb plan again

REPLANS ▸ replan

REPLANT vb plant again

REPLATE vb plate again

REPLAY n immediate reshowing on TV of an incident in sport, esp in slow motion ▷vb play (a match, recording, etc) again

REPLAYS ▸ replay

REPLEAD vb plead again

REPLED ▸ replead

REPLETE adj filled or gorged ▷vb fill again

REPLEVY vb recover possession of (goods) by replevin

REPLICA n exact copy

REPLIED ▸ reply

REPLIER ▸ reply

REPLIES ▸ reply

REPLOT vb plot again

REPLOTS ▸ replot

REPLOW vb plow again

REPLOWS ▸ replow

REPLUM n internal separating wall in some fruits

REPLUMB vb plumb again

REPLY vb answer or respond ▷n answer or response

REPO n act of repossessing

REPOINT vb repair the joints of (brickwork, masonry, etc) with mortar or cement

REPOLL vb poll again

REPOLLS ▸ repoll

REPOMAN n informal word for a man employed to repossess goods in cases of non-payment

REPOMEN ▸ repoman

REPONE vb restore (someone) to his former status, office, etc

REPONED ▸ repone

REPONES ▸ repone

REPORT vb give an account of ▷n account or statement

REPORTS ▸ report

REPOS ▸ repo

REPOSAL n repose

REPOSE n peace ▷vb lie or

lay at rest

REPOSED ▸ repose

REPOSER ▸ repose

REPOSES ▸ repose

REPOSIT vb put away, deposit, or store up

REPOST vb post again

REPOSTS ▸ repost

REPOT vb put (a house plant) into a new usually larger pot

REPOTS ▸ repot

REPOUR vb pour back or again

REPOURS ▸ repour

REPOWER vb put new engine in

REPP same as ▸ rep

REPPED ▸ rep

REPPING ▸ rep

REPPS ▸ repp

REPRESS vb keep (feelings) in check

REPRICE vb price again

REPRIME vb prime again

REPRINT vb print further copies of (a book) ▷n reprinted copy

REPRISE n repeating of an earlier theme ▷vb repeat an earlier theme

REPRIVE archaic spelling of > reprieve

REPRIZE archaic spelling of ▸ reprise

REPRO n imitation or facsimile of a work of art; reproduction

REPROBE vb probe again

REPROOF n severe blaming of someone for a fault ▷vb treat (a coat, jacket, etc) so as to renew its texture, waterproof qualities, etc

REPROS ▸ repro

REPROVE vb speak severely to (someone) about a fault

REPRYVE archaic spelling of > reprieve

REPS ▸ rep

REPTANT adj creeping, crawling, or lying along the ground

REPTILE n cold-blooded egg-laying vertebrate with horny scales or plates, such as a snake or tortoise ▷adj creeping, crawling, or squirming

REPUGN vb oppose or conflict (with)

REPUGNS ▸ repugn

REPULP vb pulp again

REPULPS ▸ repulp

REPULSE vb be disgusting to ▸ n driving back

REPUMP vb pump again

REPUMPS ▸ repump

REPUNIT n any number that consists entirely of the same repeated digits, such as 111 or 55,555

REPURE vb archaic word meaning make pure again

REPURED ▸ repure

REPURES ▸ repure

REPUTE n reputation ▸ vb consider (a person or thing) to be as specified

REPUTED adj supposed

REPUTES ▸ repute

REQUERE archaic variant of ▸ require

REQUEST vb ask ▸ n asking

REQUIEM n Mass celebrated for the dead

REQUIN vb type of shark

REQUINS ▸ requin

REQUIRE vb want or need

REQUIT vb quit again

REQUITE vb return to someone (the same treatment or feeling as received)

REQUITS ▸ requit

REQUOTE vb quote again

RERACK vb rack again

RERACKS ▸ rerack

RERAIL vb put back on a railway line

RERAILS ▸ rerail

RERAISE vb raise again

RERAN ▸ rerun

REREAD vb read (something) again

REREADS ▸ reread

REREDOS n ornamental screen behind an altar

REREMAI n New Zealand word for the basking shark

RERENT vb rent again

RERENTS ▸ rerent

RERIG vb rig again

RERIGS ▸ rerig

RERISE vb rise again

RERISEN ▸ rerise

RERISES ▸ rerise

REROLL vb roll again

REROLLS ▸ reroll

REROOF vb put a new roof or roofs on

REROOFS ▸ reroof

REROSE ▸ rerise

REROUTE vb send or direct by a different route

RERUN n film or programme that is broadcast again, repeat ▸ vb put on (a film or programme) again

RERUNS ▸ rerun

RES informal word for ▸ residence

RESAID ▸ resay

RESAIL vb sail again

RESAILS ▸ resail

RESALE n selling of something purchased earlier

RESALES ▸ resale

RESAT ▸ resit

RESAW vb saw again

RESAWED ▸ resaw

RESAWN ▸ resaw

RESAWS ▸ resaw

RESAY vb say again or in response

RESAYS ▸ resay

RESCALE vb resize

RESCIND vb annul or repeal

RESCORE vb score afresh

RESCUE vb deliver from danger or trouble, save ▸ n rescuing

RESCUED ▸ rescue

RESCUER ▸ rescue

RESCUES ▸ rescue

RESEAL vb close or secure tightly again

RESEALS ▸ reseal

RESEAT vb show (a person) to a new seat

RESEATS ▸ reseat

RESEAU n mesh background to a lace or other pattern

RESEAUS ▸ reseau

RESEAUX ▸ reseau

RESECT vb cut out part of (a bone, an organ, or other structure or part)

RESECTS ▸ resect

RESEDA n plant that has small spikes of grey-green flowers ▸ adj of a greyish-green colour

RESEDAS ▸ reseda

RESEE vb see again

RESEED vb form seed and reproduce naturally, forming a constant plant population

RESEEDS ▸ reseed

RESEEK vb seek again

RESEEKS ▸ reseek

RESEEN ▸ resee

RESEES ▸ resee

RESEIZE vb seize again

RESELL vb sell (something) one has previously bought

RESELLS ▸ resell

RESEND vb send again

RESENDS ▸ resend

RESENT vb feel bitter about

RESENTS ▸ resent

RESERVE vb set aside, keep for future use ▸ n something, esp money or troops, kept for emergencies

RESES ▸ res

RESET vb set again (a broken bone, matter in type, a gemstone, etc) ▸ n act or an instance of setting again

RESETS ▸ reset

RESEW vb sew again

RESEWED ▸ resew

RESEWN ▸ resew

RESEWS ▸ resew

RESH n 20th letter of the Hebrew alphabet

RESHAPE vb shape (something) again or differently

RESHAVE vb shave again

RESHES ▸ resh

RESHINE vb shine again

RESHIP vb ship again

RESHIPS ▸ reship

RESHOD ▸ reshoe

RESHOE vb put a new shoe or shoes on

RESHOED ▸ reshoe

RESHOES ▸ reshoe

RESHONE ▸ reshine

RESHOOT vb shoot again

RESHOT ▸ reshoot

RESHOW vb show again

RESHOWN ▸ reshow

RESHOWS ▸ reshow

RESIANT archaic word for ▸ resident

RESID n residual oil left over from the petroleum distillation process

RESIDE vb dwell permanently

RESIDED ▸ reside

RESIDER ▸ reside

RESIDES ▸ reside

RESIDS ▸ resid

RESIDUA ▸ residuum

RESIDUE n what is left, remainder

RESIFT vb sift again

RESIFTS ▸ resift

RESIGHT vb sight again

RESIGN vb give up office, a job, etc

RESIGNS ▸ resign

R

RESILE vb spring or shrink back

RESILED ▶ resile

RESILES ▶ resile

RESILIN n substance found in insect bodies

RESIN n sticky substance from plants, esp pines ▷ vb treat or coat with resin

RESINED ▶ resin

RESINER n applier or collector of resin

RESINS ▶ resin

RESINY adj resembling, containing or covered with resin

RESIST vb withstand or oppose ▷ n substance used to protect something, esp a coating that prevents corrosion

RESISTS ▶ resist

RESIT vb take (an exam) again ▷ n exam that has to be taken again

RESITE vb move to a different site

RESITED ▶ resite

RESITES ▶ resite

RESITS ▶ resit

RESIZE vb change size of

RESIZED ▶ resize

RESIZES ▶ resize

RESKEW archaic spelling of ▶ rescue

RESKEWS ▶ reskew

RESKILL vb train (workers) to acquire new skills

RESKUE archaic spelling of ▶ rescue

RESKUED ▶ reskue

RESKUES ▶ reskue

RESLATE vb slate again

RESMELT vb smelt again

RESOAK vb soak again

RESOAKS ▶ resoak

RESOD vb returf

RESODS ▶ resod

RESOJET n type of jet engine

RESOLD ▶ resell

RESOLE vb put a new sole or new soles on

RESOLED ▶ resole

RESOLES ▶ resole

RESOLVE vb decide with an effort of will ▷ n absolute determination

RESORB vb absorb again

RESORBS ▶ resorb

RESORT vb have recourse (to) for help etc ▷ n place for holidays

RESORTS ▶ resort

RESOUND vb echo or ring with sound

RESOW vb sow again

RESOWED ▶ resow

RESOWN ▶ resow

RESOWS ▶ resow

RESPACE vb change the spacing of

RESPADE vb dig over

RESPEAK vb speak further

RESPECT n consideration ▷ vb treat with esteem

RESPELL vb spell again

RESPELT ▶ respell

RESPIRE vb breathe

RESPITE n pause, interval of rest ▷ vb grant a respite to

RESPLIT vb split again

RESPOKE ▶ respeak

RESPOND vb answer ▷ n pilaster or an engaged column that supports an arch or a lintel

RESPOOL vb rewind onto spool

RESPOT vb (in billiards) replace on one of the spots

RESPOTS ▶ respot

RESPRAY n new coat of paint applied to a car, van, etc ▷ vb spray (a car, wheels, etc) with a new coat of paint

REST n freedom from exertion etc ▷ vb take a rest

RESTACK vb stack again

RESTAFF vb staff again

RESTAGE vb produce or perform a new production of (a play)

RESTAMP vb stamp again

RESTART vb commence (something) or set (something) in motion again ▷ n act or an instance of starting again

RESTATE vb state or affirm (something) again or in a different way

RESTED ▶ rest

RESTEM vb stem again

RESTEMS ▶ restem

RESTER ▶ rest

RESTERS ▶ rest

RESTFUL adj relaxing or soothing

RESTIER ▶ resty

RESTIFF same as ▶ restive

RESTING ▶ rest

RESTIVE adj restless or impatient

RESTO n restored antique, vintage car, etc

RESTOCK vb replenish stores or supplies

RESTOKE vb stoke again

RESTORE vb return (a building, painting, etc) to its original condition

RESTOS ▶ resto

RESTS ▶ rest

RESTUDY vb study again

RESTUFF vb put new stuffing in

RESTUMP vb provide with new stumps

RESTY adj restive

RESTYLE vb style again

RESULT n outcome or consequence ▷ vb be the outcome or consequence (of)

RESULTS ▶ result

RESUME vb begin again ▷ n summary

RESUMED ▶ resume

RESUMER ▶ resume

RESUMES ▶ resume

RESURGE vb rise again from or as if from the dead

RET vb moisten or soak (flax, hemp, jute, etc) to promote bacterial action in order to facilitate separation of the fibres from the woody tissue by beating

RETABLE n ornamental screenlike structure above and behind an altar, esp one used as a setting for a religious picture or carving

RETACK vb tack again

RETACKS ▶ retack

RETAG vb tag again

RETAGS ▶ retag

RETAIL n selling of goods individually or in small amounts to the public ▷ adj of or engaged in such selling ▷ adv by retail ▷ vb sell or be sold retail

RETAILS ▶ retail

RETAIN vb keep in one's possession

Perhaps the most important word in Scrabble, because its letters combine with every other letter apart from A, Q, V, X, Y and Z to form a 7-letter bonus word that will score you an extra 50 points, so if you have these six letters on your rack you know that a bonus is either available or very close. And if you have an S as well, so much the better, because not only does this rack offer you 11 different words to choose from, but if none of those can be fitted in then RETAINS combines with every other letter except for Q, V, X, Y and Z to form at least one eight-letter word.

RETAINS ▶ retain

RETAKE vb recapture ▷ n act of rephotographing a scene

RETAKEN ▶ retake

RETAKER ▶ retake

RETAKES ▶ retake

RETALLY vb count up again

RETAMA n type of shrub

RETAMAS ▶ retama

RETAPE vb tape again

RETAPED ▶ retape

RETAPES ▶ retape

RETARD vb delay or slow (progress or development) ▷ n offensive term for a retarded person

RETARDS ▶ retard

RETASTE vb taste again

RETAX vb tax again

RETAXED ▶ retax

RETAXES ▶ retax

RETCH vb try to vomit ▷ n involuntary spasm of the stomach

RETCHED ▶ retch

RETCHES ▶ retch

RETE n any network of nerves or blood vessels

RETEACH vb teach again

RETEAM vb team up again

RETEAMS ▶ reteam

RETEAR vb tear again

RETEARS ▶ retear

RETELL vb relate (a story, etc) again or differently

RETELLS ▶ retell

RETEM n type of shrub

RETEMS ▶ retem

RETENE n yellow crystalline hydrocarbon found in tar oils from pine wood and in certain fossil resins

RETENES ▶ retene

RETEST vb test (something) again or differently

RETESTS ▶ retest

RETHINK vb consider again, esp with a view to changing one's tactics ▷ n act or an

instance of thinking again

RETIA ▶ rete

RETIAL ▶ rete

RETIARY adj of, relating to, or resembling a net or web

RETICLE n network of fine lines, wires, etc, placed in the focal plane of an optical instrument to assist measurement of the size or position of objects under observation

RETIE vb tie again

RETIED ▶ retie

RETIES ▶ retie

RETILE vb put new tiles in or on

RETILED ▶ retile

RETILES ▶ retile

RETIME vb time again or alter time of

RETIMED ▶ retime

RETIMES ▶ retime

RETINA n light-sensitive membrane at the back of the eye

RETINAE ▶ retina

RETINAL adj of or relating to the retina ▷ n aldehyde form of the polyene retinol (vitamin A) that associates with the protein opsin to form the visual purple pigment rhodopsin

RETINAS ▶ retina

RETINE n chemical found in body cells that slows cell growth and division

RETINES ▶ retine

RETINOL n another name for vitamin A and rosin oil

RETINT vb tint again or change tint of

RETINTS ▶ retint

RETINUE n band of attendants

RETIRAL n act of retiring from office, one's work, etc

RETIRE vb (cause to) give up office or work, esp through age

RETIRED adj having retired from work etc

RETIREE n person who has retired from work

RETIRER ▶ retire

RETIRES ▶ retire

RETITLE vb give a new title to

RETOLD ▶ retell

RETOOK ▶ retake

RETOOL vb replace, re-equip, or rearrange the

tools in (a factory, etc)

RETOOLS ▶ retool

RETORE ▶ retear

RETORN ▶ retear

RETORT vb reply quickly, wittily, or angrily ▷ n quick, witty, or angry reply

RETORTS ▶ retort

RETOTAL vb add up again

RETOUCH vb restore or improve by new touches, esp of paint ▷ n art or practice of retouching

RETOUR vb (in Scottish law) to return as heir

RETOURS ▶ retour

RETRACE vb go back over (a route etc) again

RETRACK vb track again

RETRACT vb withdraw (a statement etc)

RETRAIN vb train to do a new or different job

RETRAIT archaic form of ▶ **retreat**

RETRAL adj at, near, or towards the back

RETRATE archaic form of ▶ **retreat**

RETREAD n remould ▷ vb remould

RETREAT vb move back from a position, withdraw ▷ n act of or military signal for retiring or withdrawal

RETREE n imperfectly made paper

RETREES ▶ retree

RETRIAL n second trial of a case or defendant in a court of law

RETRIED ▶ retry

RETRIES ▶ retry

RETRIM vb trim again

RETRIMS ▶ retrim

RETRO adj associated with or revived from the past ▷ n a retro style of art

RETROD ▶ retread

RETROS ▶ retro

RETRY vb try again (a case already determined)

RETS ▶ ret

RETSINA n Greek wine flavoured with resin

RETTED ▶ ret

RETTERY n flax-retting place

RETTING ▶ ret

RETUND vb weaken or blunt

RETUNDS ▶ retund

RETUNE vb tune (a musical

R

instrument) differently or again

RETUNED ▸ retune

RETUNES ▸ retune

RETURF vb turf again

RETURFS ▸ returf

RETURN vb go or come back ▷ n returning ▷ adj of or being a return

RETURNS ▸ return

RETUSE adj having a rounded apex and a central depression

RETWIST vb twist again

RETYING ▸ retie

RETYPE vb type again

RETYPED ▸ retype

RETYPES ▸ retype

REUNIFY vb bring together again something previously divided

REUNION n meeting of people who have been apart

REUNITE vb bring or come together again after a separation

REURGE vb urge again

REURGED ▸ reurge

REURGES ▸ reurge

REUSE vb use again ▷ n act of using something again

REUSED ▸ reuse

REUSES ▸ reuse

REUSING ▸ reuse

REUTTER vb utter again

REV n revolution (of an engine) ▷ vb increase the speed of revolution of (an engine)

REVALUE vb adjust the exchange value of (a currency) upwards

REVAMP vb renovate or restore ▷ n something that has been renovated or revamped

REVAMPS ▸ revamp

REVEAL vb make known ▷ n vertical side of an opening in a wall, esp the side of a window or door between the frame and the front of the wall

REVEALS ▸ reveal

REVEL vb take pleasure (in) ▷ n occasion of noisy merrymaking

REVELED ▸ revel

REVELER ▸ revel

REVELRY n festivity

REVELS ▸ revel

REVENGE n retaliation for

wrong done ▷ vb make retaliation for

REVENUE n income, esp of a state

REVERB n electronic device that creates artificial acoustics ▷ vb reverberate

REVERBS ▸ reverb

REVERE vb be in awe of and respect greatly

REVERED ▸ revere

REVERER ▸ revere

REVERES ▸ revere

REVERIE n absent-minded daydream

REVERS n turned back part of a garment, such as the lapel

REVERSE vb turn upside down or the other way round ▷ n opposite ▷ adj opposite or contrary

REVERSI n game played on a draughtboard with 64 pieces, black on one side and white on the other. When pieces are captured they are turned over to join the capturing player's forces

REVERSO another name for ▸ verso

REVERT vb return to a former state

REVERTS ▸ revert

REVERY same as ▸ reverie

REVEST vb restore (former power, authority, status, etc, to a person) or (of power, authority, etc) to be restored

REVESTS ▸ revest

REVET vb face (a wall or embankment) with stones

REVETS ▸ revet

REVEUR n daydreamer

REVEURS ▸ reveur

REVEUSE n female daydreamer

REVIE vb archaic cards term meaning challenge by placing a larger stake

REVIED ▸ revie

REVIES ▸ revie

REVIEW n critical assessment of a book, concert, etc ▷ vb hold or write a review of

REVIEWS ▸ review

REVILE vb be abusively scornful of

REVILED ▸ revile

REVILER ▸ revile

REVILES ▸ revile

REVISAL ▸ revise

REVISE vb change or alter ▷ n act, process, or result of revising

REVISED ▸ revise

REVISER ▸ revise

REVISES ▸ revise

REVISIT vb visit again

REVISOR ▸ revise

REVIVAL n reviving or renewal

REVIVE vb bring or come back to life, vigour, use, etc

REVIVED ▸ revive

REVIVER ▸ revive

REVIVES ▸ revive

REVIVOR n means of reviving a lawsuit that has been suspended owing to the death or marriage of one of the parties

REVOICE vb utter again

REVOKE vb cancel (a will, agreement, etc) ▷ n act of revoking

REVOKED ▸ revoke

REVOKER ▸ revoke

REVOKES ▸ revoke

REVOLT n uprising against authority ▷ vb rise in rebellion

REVOLTS ▸ revolt

REVOLVE vb turn round, rotate ▷ n circular section of a stage that can be rotated by electric power to provide a scene change

REVOTE vb decide or grant again by a new vote

REVOTED ▸ revote

REVOTES ▸ revote

REVS ▸ rev

REVUE n theatrical entertainment with topical sketches and songs

REVUES ▸ revue

REVUIST ▸ revue

REVVED ▸ rev

REVVING ▸ rev

REVYING ▸ revie

REW archaic spelling of ▸ rue

REWAKE vb awaken again

REWAKED ▸ rewake

REWAKEN vb awaken again

REWAKES ▸ rewake

REWAN archaic past form of ▸ rewin

REWARD n something given in return for a service ▷ vb pay or give something to (someone) for a service, information, etc

REWARDS ▶ reward

REWARM vb warm again

REWARMS ▶ rewarm

REWASH vb wash again

REWATER vb water again

REWAX vb wax again

REWAXED ▶ rewax

REWAXES ▶ rewax

REWEAR vb wear again

REWEARS ▶ rewear

REWEAVE vb weave again

REWED vb wed again

REWEDS ▶ rewed

REWEIGH vb weigh again

REWELD vb weld again

REWELDS ▶ reweld

REWET vb wet again

REWETS ▶ rewet

REWIDEN vb widen again

REWIN vb win again

REWIND vb wind again

REWINDS ▶ rewind

REWINS ▶ rewin

REWIRE vb provide (a house, engine, etc) with new wiring

REWIRED ▶ rewire

REWIRES ▶ rewire

REWOKE ▶ rewake

REWOKEN ▶ rewake

REWON ▶ rewin

REWORD vb alter the wording of

REWORDS ▶ reword

REWORE ▶ rewear

REWORK vb improve or bring up to date

REWORKS ▶ rework

REWORN ▶ rewear

REWOUND ▶ rewind

REWOVE ▶ reweave

REWOVEN ▶ reweave

REWRAP vb wrap again

REWRAPS ▶ rewrap

REWRAPT ▶ rewrap

REWRITE vb write again in a different way ▷ n something rewritten

REWROTE ▶ rewrite

REWS ▶ rew

REWTH archaic variant of ▶ ruth

REWTHS ▶ rewth

REX n king

> Rex is a Latin word for king, a very commonly played X word.

REXES ▶ rex

REXINE n tradename for a form of artificial leather

REXINES ▶ rexine

REYNARD n fox

REZ n informal word for an instance of reserving; reservation

> Rez is a short informal word for reservation, and is one of the most commonly played Z words.

REZERO vb reset to zero

REZEROS ▶ rezero

REZONE vb zone again

REZONED ▶ rezone

REZONES ▶ rezone

REZZES ▶ rez

RHABDOM n (in insect anatomy) any of many similar rodlike structures found in the eye

RHABDUS n sponge spicule

RHACHIS same as ▶ rachis

RHAMNUS n buckthorn

RHANJA n Indian English word for a male lover

RHANJAS ▶ rhanja

RHAPHAE ▶ rhaphe

RHAPHE same as ▶ raphe

RHAPHES ▶ rhaphe

RHAPHIS same as ▶ raphide

RHATANY n South American leguminous shrub

RHEA n S American three-toed ostrich

RHEAS ▶ rhea

RHEBOK n woolly brownish-grey southern African antelope

RHEBOKS ▶ rhebok

RHEME n constituent of a sentence that adds most new information, in addition to what has already been said in the discourse. The rheme is usually, but not always, associated with the subject

RHEMES ▶ rheme

RHENIUM n silvery-white metallic element with a high melting point

RHESUS n macaque monkey

RHETOR n teacher of rhetoric

RHETORS ▶ rhetor

RHEUM n watery discharge from the eyes or nose

RHEUMED adj rheumy

RHEUMIC adj of or relating to rheum

RHEUMS ▶ rheum

RHEUMY adj of the nature of rheum

RHEXES ▶ rhexis

RHEXIS n rupture

RHIES ▶ rhy

RHIME old spelling of ▶ rhyme

RHIMES ▶ rhime

RHINAL adj of or relating to the nose

RHINE n dialect word for a ditch

RHINES ▶ rhine

RHINO n rhinoceros

RHINOS ▶ rhino

RHIZIC adj of or relating to the root of an equation

RHIZINE same as ▶ rhizoid

RHIZOID n any of various slender hairlike structures that function as roots in the gametophyte generation of mosses, ferns, and related plants

RHIZOMA same as ▶ rhizome

RHIZOME n thick underground stem producing new plants

RHIZOPI > rhizopus

RHO n 17th letter in the Greek alphabet, a consonant transliterated as r or rh

> It's useful to remember words that start with RH, as there are quite a few that can come in useful. If you or someone else plays rho, which is a Greek letter, remember that it could be expanded to, for example, **rhody, rhomb, rhodium, rhombus** or **rhomboid**.

RHODIC adj of or containing rhodium, esp in the tetravalent state

RHODIE same as ▶ rhody

RHODIES ▶ rhody

RHODIUM n hard metallic element

RHODORA n type of shrub

RHODOUS adj of or containing rhodium (but proportionally more than a rhodic compound)

RHODY n rhododendron

RHOMB same as ▶ rhombus

RHOMBI ▶ rhombus

RHOMBIC adj relating to or having the shape of a rhombus

RHOMBOI ▶ rhomboid

RHOMBOS n wooden slat attached to a thong that

makes a roaring sound when the thong is whirled

RHOMBS ▶ rhomb

RHOMBUS *n* parallelogram with sides of equal length but no right angles, diamond-shaped figure

RHONCHI > rhonchus

RHONE *same as* ▶ **rone**

RHONES ▶ rhone

RHOS ▶ rho

RHOTIC *adj* denoting or speaking a dialect of English in which postvocalic r s are pronounced

RHUBARB *n* garden plant of which the fleshy stalks are cooked as fruit ▷ *interj* noise made by actors to simulate conversation, esp by repeating the word *rhubarb* ▷ *vb* simulate conversation in this way

RHUMB *n as in* **rhumb line** imaginary line on the surface of a sphere, such as the earth, that intersects all meridians at the same angle

RHUMBA *same as* ▶ **rumba**

RHUMBAS ▶ rhumba

RHUMBS ▶ rhumb

RHUS *n* genus of shrubs and small trees, several species of which are cultivated as ornamentals for their colourful autumn foliage

RHUSES ▶ rhus

RHY *archaic spelling of* ▶ **rye** This alternative spelling of **rye** can come in useful when you are short of vowels.

RHYME *n* sameness of the final sounds at the ends of lines of verse, or in words ▷ *vb* make a rhyme

RHYMED ▶ rhyme

RHYMER *same as* > **rhymester**

RHYMERS ▶ rhymer

RHYMES ▶ rhyme

RHYMING ▶ rhyme

RHYMIST ▶ rhyme

RHYNE *same as* ▶ **rhine**

RHYNES ▶ rhyne

RHYTA ▶ rhyton

RHYTHM *n* any regular movement or beat

RHYTHMI > rhythmus

RHYTHMS ▶ rhythm

RHYTINA *n* type of sea cow

RHYTON *n* (in ancient Greece) a horn-shaped drinking vessel with a hole in the pointed end through which to drink

RHYTONS ▶ rhyton

RIA *n* long narrow inlet of the seacoast, being a former valley that was submerged by a rise in the level of the sea. Rias are found esp on the coasts of SW Ireland and NW Spain

RIAD *n* traditional Moroccan house with an interior garden

RIADS ▶ riad

RIAL *n* standard monetary unit of Iran

RIALS ▶ rial

RIALTO *n* market or exchange

RIALTOS ▶ rialto

RIANCY ▶ riant

RIANT *adj* laughing

RIANTLY ▶ riant

RIAS ▶ ria

RIATA *same as* ▶ **reata**

RIATAS ▶ riata

RIB *n* one of the curved bones forming the framework of the upper part of the body ▷ *vb* provide or mark with ribs

RIBA *n* (in Islam) interest or usury, as forbidden by the Koran

RIBALD *adj* humorously or mockingly rude or obscene ▷ *n* ribald person

RIBALDS ▶ ribald

RIBAND *n* ribbon awarded for some achievement

RIBANDS ▶ riband

RIBAS ▶ riba

RIBAUD *archaic variant of* ▶ **ribald**

RIBAUDS ▶ ribaud

RIBBAND *same as* ▶ **riband**

RIBBED ▶ rib

RIBBER *n* someone who ribs

RIBBERS ▶ ribber

RIBBIER ▶ ribby

RIBBING ▶ rib

RIBBON *n* narrow band of fabric used for trimming, tying, etc ▷ *vb* adorn with a ribbon or ribbons

RIBBONS ▶ ribbon

RIBBONY ▶ ribbon

RIBBY *adj* with noticeable ribs

RIBCAGE *n* bony structure

of ribs enclosing the lungs

RIBES *n* genus of shrubs that includes currants

RIBEYE *n* beefsteak cut from the outer side of the rib section

RIBEYES ▶ ribeye

RIBIBE *n* rebeck

RIBIBES ▶ ribibe

RIBIBLE *same as* ▶ **ribibe**

RIBIER *n* variety of grape

RIBIERS ▶ ribier

RIBLESS ▶ rib

RIBLET *n* small rib

RIBLETS ▶ riblet

RIBLIKE ▶ rib

RIBOSE *n* pentose sugar that is an isomeric form of arabinose and that occurs in RNA and riboflavin

RIBOSES ▶ ribose

RIBS ▶ rib

RIBSTON *n* variety of apple

RIBWORK *n* work or structure involving ribs

RIBWORT *n* Eurasian plant with lancelike ribbed leaves and a dense spike of small white flowers

RICE *n* cereal plant grown on wet ground in warm countries ▷ *vb* sieve (potatoes or other vegetables) to a coarse mashed consistency

RICED ▶ rice

RICER *n* kitchen utensil with small holes through which cooked potatoes and similar soft foods are pressed to form a coarse mash

RICERS ▶ ricer

RICES ▶ rice

RICEY *adj* resembling or containing rice

RICH *adj* owning a lot of money or property, wealthy ▷ *vb* (in archaic usage) enrich

RICHED ▶ rich

RICHEN *vb* enrich

RICHENS ▶ richen

RICHER ▶ rich

RICHES *pl n* wealth

RICHEST ▶ rich

RICHING ▶ rich

RICHLY *adv* elaborately

RICHT *adj, adv, n, vb* right

RICHTED ▶ richt

RICHTER ▶ richt

RICHTS ▶ richt

RICIER ▶ ricy

RICIEST ▸ ricy

RICIN n highly toxic protein, a lectin, derived from castor-oil seeds: used in experimental cancer therapy

RICING ▸ rice

RICINS ▸ ricin

RICINUS n genus of plants

RICK n stack of hay etc ▷ vb wrench or sprain (a joint)

RICKED ▸ rick

RICKER n young kauri tree of New Zealand

RICKERS ▸ ricker

RICKET n mistake

RICKETS n disease of children marked by softening of the bones, bow legs, etc, caused by vitamin D deficiency

RICKETY adj shaky or unstable

RICKEY n cocktail consisting of gin or vodka, lime juice, and soda water, served iced

RICKEYS ▸ rickey

RICKING ▸ rick

RICKLE n unsteady or shaky structure, esp a dilapidated building

RICKLES ▸ rickle

RICKLY adj archaic word for run-down or rickety

RICKS ▸ rick

RICKSHA same as > rickshaw

RICOTTA n soft white unsalted Italian cheese made from sheep's milk

RICRAC same as > rickrack

RICRACS ▸ ricrac

RICTAL ▸ rictus

RICTUS n gape or cleft of an open mouth or beak

RICY same as ▸ ricey

RID vb clear or relieve (of)

RIDABLE ▸ ride

RIDDED ▸ rid

RIDDEN ▸ ride

RIDDER ▸ rid

RIDDERS ▸ rid

RIDDING ▸ rid

RIDDLE n question made puzzling to test one's ingenuity ▷ vb speak in riddles

RIDDLED ▸ riddle

RIDDLER ▸ riddle

RIDDLES ▸ riddle

RIDE vb sit on and control or propel (a horse, bicycle, etc)

▷ n journey on a horse etc, or in a vehicle

RIDENT adj laughing, smiling, or gay

RIDER n person who rides

RIDERED ▸ rider

RIDERS ▸ rider

RIDES ▸ ride

RIDGE n long narrow hill ▷ vb form into a ridge or ridges

RIDGED ▸ ridge

RIDGEL same as > ridgeling

RIDGELS ▸ ridgel

RIDGER n plough used to form furrows and ridges

RIDGERS ▸ ridger

RIDGES ▸ ridge

RIDGIER ▸ ridge

RIDGIL same as > ridgeling

RIDGILS ▸ ridgil

RIDGING ▸ ridge

RIDGY ▸ ridge

RIDING ▸ ride

RIDINGS ▸ ride

RIDLEY n marine turtle

RIDLEYS ▸ ridley

RIDOTTO n entertainment with music and dancing, often in masquerade: popular in 18th-century England

RIDS ▸ rid

RIEL n standard monetary unit of Cambodia, divided into 100 sen

RIELS ▸ riel

RIEM n strip of hide

RIEMPIE n leather thong or lace used mainly to make chair seats

RIEMS ▸ riem

RIEVE n archaic word for rob or plunder

RIEVER n archaic word for robber or plunderer

RIEVERS ▸ riever

RIEVES ▸ rieve

RIEVING ▸ rieve

RIF vb lay off

RIFE adj widespread or common

RIFELY ▸ rife

RIFER ▸ rife

RIFEST ▸ rife

RIFF n short repeated melodic figure ▷ vb play or perform riffs in jazz or rock music

RIFFAGE n (in jazz or rock music) act or an instance of playing a short series of chords

RIFFED ▸ riff

RIFFING ▸ riff

RIFFLE vb flick through (pages etc) quickly ▷ n rapid in a stream

RIFFLED ▸ riffle

RIFFLER n file with a curved face for filing concave surfaces

RIFFLES ▸ riffle

RIFFOLA n use of an abundance of dominant riffs

RIFFS ▸ riff

RIFLE n firearm with a long barrel ▷ vb cut spiral grooves inside the barrel of a gun

RIFLED ▸ rifle

RIFLER ▸ rifle

RIFLERS ▸ rifle

RIFLERY n rifle shots

RIFLES ▸ rifle

RIFLING n cutting of spiral grooves on the inside of a firearm's barrel

RIFLIP n genetic difference between two individuals

RIFLIPS ▸ riflip

RIFS ▸ rif

RIFT n break in friendly relations ▷ vb burst or cause to burst open

RIFTE archaic word for ▸ rift

RIFTED ▸ rift

RIFTIER ▸ rift

RIFTING ▸ rift

RIFTS ▸ rift

RIFTY ▸ rift

RIG vb arrange in a dishonest way ▷ n apparatus for drilling for oil and gas

RIGG n type of fish

RIGGALD same as > ridgeling

RIGGED ▸ rig

RIGGER n workman who rigs vessels, etc

RIGGERS ▸ rigger

RIGGING ▸ rig

RIGGISH adj dialect word meaning wanton

RIGGS ▸ rigg

RIGHT adj just ▷ adv correctly ▷ n claim, title, etc allowed or due ▷ vb bring or come back to a normal or correct state

RIGHTED ▸ right

RIGHTEN vb set right

RIGHTER ▸ right

RIGHTLY adv in accordance

R

with the true facts or justice

RIGHTO *interj* expression of agreement or compliance

RIGHTS ▸ right

RIGHTY *n* informal word for a right-winger

RIGID *adj* inflexible or strict ▷ *adv* completely or excessively ▷ *n* strict and unbending person

RIGIDER ▸ rigid

RIGIDLY ▸ rigid

RIGIDS ▸ rigid

RIGLIN *same as* **▸ ridgeling**

RIGLING *same as* **▸ ridgeling**

RIGLINS ▸ riglin

RIGOL *n* (in dialect) ditch or gutter

RIGOLL *same as* **▸ rigol**

RIGOLLS ▸ rigoll

RIGOLS ▸ rigol

RIGOR *same as* **▸ rigour**

RIGORS ▸ rigor

RIGOUR *n* harshness, severity, or strictness

RIGOURS ▸ rigour

RIGOUT *n* person's clothing

RIGOUTS ▸ rigout

RIGS ▸ rig

RIKISHA *same as* **> rickshaw**

RIKISHI *n* sumo wrestler

RIKSHAW *same as* **> rickshaw**

RILE *vb* anger or annoy

RILED ▸ rile

RILES ▸ rile

RILEY *adj* cross or irritable

RILIER ▸ riley

RILIEST ▸ riley

RILIEVI ▸ rilievo

RILIEVO *same as* **▸ relief**

RILING ▸ rile

RILL *n* small stream ▷ *vb* trickle

RILLE *same as* **▸ rill**

RILLED ▸ rill

RILLES ▸ rille

RILLET *n* little rill

RILLETS ▸ rillet

RILLING ▸ rill

RILLS ▸ rill

RIM *n* edge or border ▷ *vb* put a rim on (a pot, cup, wheel, etc)

RIMA *n* long narrow opening

RIMAE ▸ rima

RIMAYE *n* crevasse at the head of a glacier

RIMAYES ▸ rimaye

RIME *same as* **▸ rhyme**

RIMED ▸ rime

RIMER *same as* **▸ rhymester**

RIMERS ▸ rimer

RIMES ▸ rime

RIMFIRE *adj* (of a cartridge) having the primer in the rim of the base ▷ *n* cartridge of this type

RIMIER ▸ rimy

RIMIEST ▸ rimy

RIMING ▸ rime

RIMLAND *n* area situated on the outer edges of a region

RIMLESS ▸ rim

RIMMED ▸ rim

RIMMER *n* tool for shaping the edge of something

RIMMERS ▸ rimmer

RIMMING ▸ rim

RIMOSE *adj* (esp of plant parts) having the surface marked by a network of intersecting cracks

RIMOUS *same as* **▸ rimose**

RIMPLE *vb* crease or wrinkle

RIMPLED ▸ rimple

RIMPLES ▸ rimple

RIMROCK *n* rock forming the boundaries of a sandy or gravelly alluvial deposit

RIMS ▸ rim

RIMSHOT *n* deliberate simultaneous striking of skin and rim of drum

RIMU *n* New Zealand tree whose wood is used for building and furniture

RIMUS ▸ rimu

RIMY *adj* coated with rime

RIN *Scots variant of* **▸ run**

RIND *n* tough outer coating of fruits, cheese, or bacon ▷ *vb* take the bark off

RINDED ▸ rind

RINDIER ▸ rindy

RINDING ▸ rind

RINDS ▸ rind

RINDY *adj* with a rind or rindlike skin

RINE *archaic variant of* **▸ rind**

RINES ▸ rine

RING *vb* give out a clear resonant sound, as a bell ▷ *n* ringing

RINGBIT *n* type of bit worn by a horse

RINGED ▸ ring

RINGENT *adj* (of the corolla of plants such as the snapdragon) consisting of two distinct gaping lips

RINGER *n* person or thing

apparently identical to another

RINGERS ▸ ringer

RINGGIT *n* standard monetary unit of Malaysia, divided into 100 sen

RINGING ▸ ring

RINGLET *n* curly lock of hair

RINGMAN *n* (in dialect) ring finger

RINGMEN ▸ ringman

RINGS ▸ ring

RINGTAW *n* game of marbles in which the aim is to knock other players' marbles out of a ring

RINGWAY *n* bypass

RINK *n* sheet of ice for skating or curling ▷ *vb* skate on a rink

RINKED ▸ rink

RINKING ▸ rink

RINKS ▸ rink

RINNING ▸ rin

RINS ▸ rin

RINSE *vb* remove soap from (washed clothes, hair, etc) by applying clean water ▷ *n* rinsing

RINSED ▸ rinse

RINSER ▸ rinse

RINSERS ▸ rinse

RINSES ▸ rinse

RINSING ▸ rinse

RIOJA *n* red or white Spanish wine with a vanilla bouquet and flavour

RIOJAS ▸ rioja

RIOT *n* disorderly unruly disturbance ▷ *vb* take part in a riot

RIOTED ▸ riot

RIOTER ▸ riot

RIOTERS ▸ riot

RIOTING ▸ riot

RIOTISE *n* archaic word for riotous behaviour and excess

RIOTIZE *same as* **▸ riotise**

RIOTOUS *adj* unrestrained

RIOTRY *n* riotous behaviour

RIOTS ▸ riot

RIP *vb* tear violently ▷ *n* split or tear

RIPCORD *n* cord pulled to open a parachute

RIPE *adj* ready to be reaped, eaten, etc ▷ *vb* ripen

RIPECK *same as* **▸ ryepeck**

RIPECKS ▸ ripeck

RIPED ▸ ripe

RIPELY ▸ ripe

RIPEN *vb* grow ripe

RIPENED ▸ ripen

RIPENER ▸ ripen

RIPENS ▸ ripen

RIPER adj more ripe ▷ n old Scots word meaning plunderer

RIPERS ▸ riper

RIPES ▸ ripe

RIPEST ▸ ripe

RIPIENI ▸ ripieno

RIPIENO n (in baroque concertos and concerti grossi) the full orchestra, as opposed to the instrumental soloists

RIPING ▸ ripe

RIPOFF n grossly overpriced article

RIPOFFS ▸ ripoff

RIPOST same as ▸ riposte

RIPOSTE n verbal retort ▷ vb make a riposte

RIPOSTS ▸ ripost

RIPP n old Scots word for a handful of grain

RIPPED ▸ rip

RIPPER n person who rips

RIPPERS ▸ ripper

RIPPIER n archaic word for fish seller

RIPPING ▸ rip

RIPPLE n slight wave or ruffling of a surface ▷ vb flow or form into little waves (on)

RIPPLED ▸ ripple

RIPPLER ▸ ripple

RIPPLES ▸ ripple

RIPPLET n tiny ripple

RIPPLY ▸ ripple

RIPPS ▸ ripp

RIPRAP vb deposit broken stones in or on

RIPRAPS ▸ riprap

RIPS ▸ rip

RIPSAW n handsaw for cutting along the grain of timber ▷ vb saw with a ripsaw

RIPSAWN ▸ ripsaw

RIPSAWS ▸ ripsaw

RIPSTOP n tear-resistant cloth

RIPT archaic past form of ▸ rip

RIPTIDE n stretch of turbulent water in the sea, caused by the meeting of currents or abrupt changes in depth

RISE vb get up from a lying, sitting, or kneeling position ▷ n rising

RISEN ▸ rise

RISER n person who rises, esp from bed

RISERS ▸ riser

RISES ▸ rise

RISHI n Indian seer or sage

RISHIS ▸ rishi

RISIBLE adj causing laughter, ridiculous

RISIBLY ▸ risible

RISING ▸ rise

RISINGS ▸ rise

RISK n chance of disaster or loss ▷ vb act in spite of the possibility of (injury or loss)

RISKED ▸ risk

RISKER ▸ risk

RISKERS ▸ risk

RISKFUL ▸ risk

RISKIER ▸ risky

RISKILY ▸ risky

RISKING ▸ risk

RISKS ▸ risk

RISKY adj full of risk, dangerous

RISORII ▸ risorius

RISOTTO n dish of rice cooked in stock with vegetables, meat, etc

RISP vb Scots word meaning rasp

RISPED ▸ risp

RISPING ▸ risp

RISPS ▸ risp

RISQUE n risk

RISQUES ▸ risque

RISSOLE n cake of minced meat, coated with breadcrumbs and fried

RISTRA n string of dried chilli peppers

RISTRAS ▸ ristra

RISUS n involuntary grinning expression

RISUSES ▸ risus

RIT vb Scots word for cut or slit

RITARD n (in music) a slowing down

RITARDS ▸ ritard

RITE n formal practice or custom, esp religious

RITES ▸ rite

RITS ▸ rit

RITT same as ▸ rit

RITTED ▸ rit

RITTER n knight or horseman

RITTERS ▸ ritter

RITTING ▸ rit

RITTS ▸ ritt

RITUAL n prescribed order of rites ▷ adj concerning rites

RITUALS ▸ ritual

RITZ modifier as in **put on the ritz** assume a superior air or make an ostentatious display

RITZES ▸ ritz

RITZIER ▸ ritzy

RITZILY ▸ ritzy

RITZY adj luxurious or elegant

RIVA n rock cleft

RIVAGE n bank, shore, or coast

RIVAGES ▸ rivage

RIVAL n person or thing that competes with or equals another for favour, success, etc ▷ adj in the position of a rival ▷ vb (try to) equal

RIVALED ▸ rival

RIVALRY n keen competition

RIVALS ▸ rival

RIVAS ▸ riva

RIVE vb split asunder

RIVED ▸ rive

RIVEL vb archaic word meaning wrinkle

RIVELS ▸ rivel

RIVEN ▸ rive

RIVER n large natural stream of water

RIVERED adj with a river or rivers

RIVERET n archaic word for rivulet or stream

RIVERS ▸ river

RIVERY adj riverlike

RIVES ▸ rive

RIVET n bolt for fastening metal plates, the end being put through holes and then beaten flat ▷ vb fasten with rivets

RIVETED ▸ rivet

RIVETER ▸ rivet

RIVETS ▸ rivet

RIVIERA n coastline resembling the Mediterranean Riviera

RIVIERE n necklace the diamonds or other precious stones of which gradually increase in size up to a large centre stone

RIVING ▸ rive

RIVLIN n Scots word for rawhide shoe

RIVLINS ▸ rivlin

RIVO interj (in the past) an informal toast

RIVULET n small stream

R

RIYAL n standard monetary unit of Qatar, divided into 100 dirhams

RIYALS ▷ riyal

RIZ (in some dialects) past form of ▷ rise

| This unusual past tense of **rise** is one of the essential Z words.

RIZA n partial icon cover made from precious metal

RIZARD n redcurrant

RIZARDS ▷ rizard

RIZAS ▷ riza

RIZZAR n Scots word for red currant ▷ vb Scots word for sun-dry

RIZZARS ▷ rizzar

RIZZART n Scots word for red currant

RIZZER same as ▷ rizzar

RIZZERS ▷ rizzer

RIZZOR vb dry

RIZZORS ▷ rizzor

ROACH n Eurasian freshwater fish ▷ vb clip (mane) short so that it stands upright

ROACHED adj arched convexly, as the back of certain breeds of dog, such as the whippet

ROACHES ▷ roach

ROAD n way prepared for passengers, vehicles, etc

ROADBED n material used to make a road

ROADEO n competition in which drivers or other road users put their skills on the road to the test

ROADEOS ▷ roadeo

ROADIE n person who transports and sets up equipment for a band

ROADIES ▷ roadie

ROADING n road building

ROADMAN n someone involved in road repair or construction

ROADMEN ▷ roadman

ROADS ▷ road

ROADWAY n part of a road used by vehicles

ROAM vb wander about ▷ n act of roaming

ROAMED ▷ roam

ROAMER ▷ roam

ROAMERS ▷ roam

ROAMING ▷ roam

ROAMS ▷ roam

ROAN adj (of a horse) having a brown or black coat sprinkled with white hairs ▷ n roan horse

ROANS ▷ roan

ROAR vb make or utter a loud deep hoarse sound like that of a lion ▷ n such a sound

ROARED ▷ roar

ROARER ▷ roar

ROARERS ▷ roar

ROARIE Scots word for ▷ noisy

ROARIER ▷ roary

ROARING ▷ roar

ROARS ▷ roar

ROARY adj roarlike or tending to roar

ROAST vb cook by dry heat, as in an oven ▷ n roasted joint of meat ▷ adj roasted

ROASTED ▷ roast

ROASTER n person or thing that roasts

ROASTS ▷ roast

ROATE archaic form of ▷ rote

ROATED ▷ roate

ROATES ▷ roate

ROATING ▷ roate

ROB vb steal from

ROBALO n tropical fish

ROBALOS ▷ robalo

ROBAND n piece of marline used for fastening a sail to a spar

ROBANDS ▷ roband

ROBBED ▷ rob

ROBBER ▷ rob

ROBBERS ▷ rob

ROBBERY n stealing of property from a person by using or threatening to use force

ROBBIN same as ▷ roband

ROBBING ▷ rob

ROBBINS ▷ robbin

ROBE n long loose outer garment ▷ vb put a robe on

ROBED ▷ robe

ROBES ▷ robe

ROBIN n small brown bird with a red breast

ROBING ▷ robe

ROBINGS ▷ robe

ROBINIA n type of leguminous tree

ROBINS ▷ robin

ROBLE n oak tree

ROBLES ▷ roble

ROBOT n automated machine, esp one performing functions in a human manner

ROBOTIC ▷ robot

ROBOTRY ▷ robot

ROBOTS ▷ robot

ROBS ▷ rob

ROBUST adj very strong and healthy

ROBUSTA n species of coffee tree

ROC n monstrous bird of Arabian mythology

ROCH same as ▷ rotch

ROCHES ▷ rotch

ROCHET n white surplice with tight sleeves, worn by bishops, abbots, and certain other Church dignitaries

ROCHETS ▷ rochet

ROCK n hard mineral substance that makes up part of the earth's crust, stone ▷ vb (cause to) sway to and fro ▷ adj of or relating to rock music

ROCKABY same as ▷ rockabye

ROCKED ▷ rock

ROCKER n rocking chair

ROCKERS ▷ rocker

ROCKERY n mound of stones in a garden for rock plants

ROCKET n self-propelling device powered by the burning of explosive contents (used as a firework, weapon, etc) ▷ vb move fast, esp upwards, like a rocket

ROCKETS ▷ rocket

ROCKIER ▷ rocky

ROCKIES archaic or dialect word for rock pigeon

ROCKILY ▷ rocky

ROCKING ▷ rock

ROCKLAY same as ▷ rokelay

ROCKOON n rocket carrying scientific equipment for studying the upper atmosphere, fired from a balloon at high altitude

ROCKS ▷ rock

ROCKY adj having many rocks

ROCOCO adj (of furniture, architecture, etc) having much elaborate decoration in an early 18th-century style ▷ n style of architecture and decoration that originated in France in the early 18th century, characterized by elaborate but graceful, light, ornamentation, often containing asymmetrical motifs

ROCOCOS ▶ **rococo**

ROCQUET n another name for the salad plant rocket

ROCS ▶ **roc**

ROD n slender straight bar, stick ▷ vb clear with a rod

RODDED ▶ **rod**

RODDING ▶ **rod**

RODE vb (of the male woodcock) to perform a display flight at dusk during the breeding season

RODED ▶ **rode**

RODENT n animal with teeth specialized for gnawing, such as a rat, mouse, or squirrel

RODENTS ▶ **rodent**

RODEO n display of skill by cowboys, such as bareback riding ▷ vb take part in a rodeo

RODEOED ▶ **rodeo**

RODEOS ▶ **rodeo**

RODES ▶ **rode**

RODEWAY archaic spelling of ▶ **roadway**

RODING ▶ **rode**

RODINGS ▶ **rode**

RODLESS ▶ **rod**

RODLIKE ▶ **rod**

RODMAN n someone who uses or fishes with a rod

RODMEN ▶ **rodman**

RODS ▶ **rod**

RODSMAN same as ▶ **rodman**

RODSMEN ▶ **rodsman**

RODSTER n angler

ROE n mass of eggs in a fish, sometimes eaten as food

ROEBUCK n male of the roe deer

ROED adj with roe inside

ROEMER n drinking glass, typically having an ovoid bowl on a short stem

ROEMERS ▶ **roemer**

ROES ▶ **roe**

ROESTI ▶ **rosti**

ROESTIS ▶ **roesti**

ROGALLO n flexible fabric delta wing, originally designed as a possible satellite retrieval vehicle but actually developed in the 1960s as the first successful hang-glider

ROGNON n isolated rock outcrop on a glacier

ROGNONS ▶ **rognon**

ROGUE n dishonest or unprincipled person ▷ adj (of a wild beast) having a savage temper and living apart from the herd ▷ vb rid (a field or crop) of plants that are inferior, diseased, or of an unwanted variety

ROGUED ▶ **rogue**

ROGUER n rogue

ROGUERS ▶ **roguer**

ROGUERY n dishonest or immoral behaviour

ROGUES ▶ **rogue**

ROGUING ▶ **rogue**

ROGUISH adj dishonest or unprincipled

ROGUY same as ▶ **roguish**

ROIL vb make (a liquid) cloudy or turbid by stirring up dregs or sediment

ROILED ▶ **roil**

ROILIER ▶ **roily**

ROILING ▶ **roil**

ROILS ▶ **roil**

ROILY adj cloudy or muddy

ROIN same as ▶ **royne**

ROINED ▶ **roin**

ROINING ▶ **roin**

ROINISH same as ▶ **roynish**

ROINS ▶ **roin**

ROIST archaic variant of ▶ **roister**

ROISTED ▶ **roist**

ROISTER vb make merry noisily or boisterously

ROISTS ▶ **roist**

ROJAK n (in Malaysia) a salad dish served in chilli sauce

ROJAKS ▶ **rojak**

ROJI n Japanese tea garden or its path of stones

ROJIS ▶ **roji**

ROK same as ▶ **roc**

> **Rok** is an alternative spelling of **roc**, the mythical bird. Other spellings are **ruc** and **rukh**.

ROKE vb (in dialect) steam or smoke

ROKED ▶ **roke**

ROKELAY n type of cloak

ROKER n variety of ray

ROKERS ▶ **roker**

ROKES ▶ **roke**

ROKIER ▶ **roky**

ROKIEST ▶ **roky**

ROKING ▶ **roke**

ROKKAKU n hexagonal Japanese kite

ROKS ▶ **rok**

ROKY adj (in dialect) steamy or smoky

ROLAG n roll of carded wool ready for spinning

ROLAGS ▶ **rolag**

ROLE n task or function

ROLES ▶ **role**

ROLF vb massage following a particular technique

ROLFED ▶ **rolf**

ROLFER ▶ **rolf**

ROLFERS ▶ **rolf**

ROLFING ▶ **rolf**

ROLFS ▶ **rolf**

ROLL vb move by turning over and over ▷ n act of rolling over or from side to side

ROLLBAR n bar that reinforces the frame of a car, esp one used for racing, rallying, etc, to protect the driver if the car should turn over

ROLLED ▶ **roll**

ROLLER n rotating cylinder used for smoothing or supporting a thing to be moved, spreading paint, etc

ROLLERS ▶ **roller**

ROLLICK vb behave in a carefree, frolicsome, or boisterous manner ▷ n boisterous or carefree escapade or event

ROLLING ▶ **roll**

ROLLMOP n herring fillet rolled round onion slices and pickled

ROLLOCK same as ▶ **rowlock**

ROLLOUT n presentation to the public of a new aircraft, product, etc; launch

ROLLS ▶ **roll**

ROLLTOP n as in **rolltop desk** desk having a slatted wooden panel that can be pulled down over the writing surface when not in use

ROLLWAY n incline down which logs are rolled

ROM n male gypsy

ROMA n gypsy

ROMAGE archaic variant of ▶ **rummage**

ROMAGES ▶ **romage**

ROMAIKA n Greek dance

ROMAINE n usual US and

R

Canadian name for 'cos' (lettuce)

ROMAJI n Roman alphabet as used to write Japanese

ROMAJIS ▸ romaji

ROMAL same as ▸ **rumal**

ROMALS ▸ romal

ROMAN adj in or relating to the vertical style of printing type used for most printed matter ▷ n roman type

ROMANCE n love affair ▷ vb exaggerate or fantasize

ROMANO n hard light-coloured sharp-tasting cheese

ROMANOS ▸ romano

ROMANS ▸ roman

ROMANZA n short instrumental piece of song-like character

ROMAUNT n verse romance

ROMCOM n film or television comedy based around the romantic relationships of the characters

ROMCOMS ▸ romcom

ROMEO n ardent male lover

ROMEOS ▸ romeo

ROMNEYA n bushy type of poppy

ROMP vb play wildly and joyfully ▷ n boisterous activity

ROMPED ▸ romp

ROMPER n playful or boisterous child

ROMPERS pl n child's overalls

ROMPING ▸ romp

ROMPISH ▸ romp

ROMPS ▸ romp

ROMS ▸ rom

RONDE n round dance

RONDEAU n poem consisting of 13 or 10 lines with the opening words of the first line used as a refrain

RONDEL n rondeau consisting of three stanzas of 13 or 14 lines with a two-line refrain appearing twice or three times

RONDELS ▸ rondel

RONDES ▸ ronde

RONDINO n short rondo

RONDO n piece of music with a leading theme continually returned to

RONDOS ▸ rondo

RONDURE n circle or curve

RONE n drainpipe or gutter for carrying rainwater from a roof

RONEO vb duplicate (a document) from a stencil ▷ n document reproduced by this process

RONEOED ▸ roneo

RONEOS ▸ roneo

RONES ▸ rone

RONG archaic past participle of ▸ **ring**

RONIN n lordless samurai, esp one whose feudal lord had been deprived of his territory

RONINS ▸ ronin

RONIONS ▸ ronion

RONNE archaic form of ▸ **run**

RONNEL n type of pesticide

RONNELS ▸ ronnel

RONNIE n Dublin slang word for moustache

RONNIES ▸ ronnie

RONNING ▸ ronne

RONT archaic variant of ▸ **runt**

RONTE archaic variant of ▸ **runt**

RONTES ▸ ronte

RONTGEN variant spelling of > **roentgen**

RONTS ▸ ront

RONZ n rest of New Zealand

RONZER n New Zealand word for a New Zealander not from Auckland

RONZERS ▸ ronzer

ROO n kangaroo

ROOD n Cross

ROODS ▸ rood

ROOF n outside upper covering of a building, car, etc ▷ vb put a roof on

ROOFED ▸ roof

ROOFER ▸ roof

ROOFERS ▸ roof

ROOFIE n tablet of sedative drug

ROOFIER ▸ roofy

ROOFIES ▸ roofie

ROOFING n material used to build a roof

ROOFS ▸ roof

ROOFTOP n outside part of the roof of a building

ROOFY adj with roofs

ROOIBOS n tea prepared from the dried leaves of an African plant

ROOIKAT n South African lynx

ROOK n Eurasian bird of the

crow family ▷ vb swindle

ROOKED ▸ rook

ROOKERY n colony of rooks, penguins, or seals

ROOKIE n new recruit

ROOKIER ▸ rooky

ROOKIES ▸ rookie

ROOKING ▸ rook

ROOKISH ▸ rook

ROOKS ▸ rook

ROOKY adj abounding in rooks

ROOM n enclosed area in a building ▷ vb occupy or share a room

ROOMED ▸ room

ROOMER ▸ room

ROOMERS ▸ room

ROOMFUL n number or quantity sufficient to fill a room

ROOMIE n roommate

ROOMIER ▸ roomy

ROOMIES ▸ roomie

ROOMILY ▸ roomy

ROOMING ▸ room

ROOMS ▸ room

ROOMY adj spacious

ROON n Scots word for shred or strip

ROONS ▸ roon

ROOP same as ▸ **roup**

ROOPED ▸ roop

ROOPIER ▸ roopy

ROOPING ▸ roop

ROOPIT same as ▸ **roopy**

ROOPS ▸ roop

ROOPY adj (in dialect) hoarse

ROOS ▸ roo

ROOSA n type of grass

ROOSAS ▸ roosa

ROOSE vb flatter

ROOSED ▸ roose

ROOSER ▸ roose

ROOSERS ▸ roose

ROOSES ▸ roose

ROOSING ▸ roose

ROOST n perch for fowls ▷ vb perch

ROOSTED ▸ roost

ROOSTER n domestic cock

ROOSTS ▸ roost

ROOT n part of a plant that grows down into the earth obtaining nourishment ▷ vb establish a root and start to grow

ROOTAGE n root system

ROOTCAP n layer of cells at root tip

ROOTED ▸ root

ROOTER ▸ root

ROOTERS ▶ root

ROOTIER ▶ root

ROOTIES ▶ rooty

ROOTING ▶ root

ROOTKIT n set of programs used to gain unauthorized access to a computer system

ROOTLE same as ▶ root

ROOTLED ▶ rootle

ROOTLES ▶ rootle

ROOTLET n small root or branch of a root

ROOTS adj (of popular music) going back to the origins of a style, esp in being unpretentious

ROOTSY ▶ roots

ROOTY adj rootlike ▷ n (in military slang) bread

ROPABLE adj capable of being roped

ROPE n thick cord

ROPED ▶ rope

ROPER n someone who makes ropes

ROPERS ▶ roper

ROPERY n place where ropes are made

ROPES ▶ rope

ROPEWAY n type of aerial lift

ROPEY adj inferior or inadequate

ROPIER ▶ ropy

ROPIEST ▶ ropy

ROPILY ▶ ropey

ROPING ▶ rope

ROPINGS ▶ rope

ROPY ▶ as in ▶ ropey

ROQUE n game developed from croquet, played on a hard surface with a resilient surrounding border from which the ball can rebound

ROQUES ▶ roque

ROQUET vb drive one's ball against (another person's ball) in order to be allowed to croquet ▷ n act of roqueting

ROQUETS ▶ roquet

RORAL archaic word for ▶ dewy

RORE archaic spelling of ▶ roar

RORES ▶ rore

RORIC same as ▶ roral

RORID same as ▶ roral

RORIE same as ▶ roary

RORIER ▶ rory

RORIEST ▶ rory

RORQUAL n toothless whale with a dorsal fin

RORT n dishonest scheme ▷ vb take unfair advantage of something

RORTED ▶ rort

RORTER n small-scale confidence trickster

RORTERS ▶ rorter

RORTIER ▶ rort

RORTING ▶ rort

RORTS ▶ rort

RORTY ▶ rort

RORY same as ▶ roary

ROSACE another name for ▶ rosette

ROSACEA n chronic inflammatory disease causing the skin of the face to become abnormally flushed and sometimes pustular

ROSACES ▶ rosace

ROSAKER archaic word for ▶ realgar

ROSALIA n melody which is repeated but at a higher pitch each time

ROSARIA > rosarium

ROSARY n series of prayers

ROSBIF n term used in France for an English person

ROSBIFS ▶ rosbif

ROSCID adj dewy

ROSCOE slang word for ▶ gun

ROSCOES ▶ roscoe

ROSE ▶ rise

ROSEAL adj rosy or roselike

ROSEATE adj rose-coloured

ROSEBAY n as in rosebay willowherb perennial plant with spikes of deep pink flowers

ROSEBUD n rose which has not yet fully opened

ROSED ▶ rise

ROSEHIP n berry-like fruit of a rose plant

ROSELLA n type of Australian parrot

ROSELLE n Indian flowering plant

ROSEOLA n feverish condition of young children that lasts for some five days during the last two of which the patient has a rose-coloured rash. It is caused by the human herpes virus

ROSERY n bed or garden of roses

ROSES ▶ rise

ROSET n Scots word meaning rosin ▷ vb rub rosin on

ROSETED ▶ roset

ROSETS ▶ roset

ROSETTE n rose-shaped ornament, esp a circular bunch of ribbons

ROSETTY ▶ roset

ROSETY ▶ roset

ROSHI n teacher of Zen Buddhism

ROSHIS ▶ roshi

ROSIED ▶ rosy

ROSIER archaic word for > rosebush

ROSIERE archaic word for > rosebush

ROSIERS ▶ rosier

ROSIES ▶ rosy

ROSIEST ▶ rosy

ROSILY ▶ rosy

ROSIN n resin used for treating the bows of violins etc ▷ vb apply rosin to

ROSINED ▶ rosin

ROSINER n strong alcoholic drink

ROSING ▶ rise

ROSINOL n yellowish fluorescent oily liquid obtained from certain resins, used in the manufacture of carbon black, varnishes, and lacquers

ROSINS ▶ rosin

ROSINY ▶ rosin

ROSIT same as ▶ roset

ROSITED ▶ rosit

ROSITS ▶ rosit

ROSOLIO n type of cordial

ROSSER n bark-removing machine

ROSSERS ▶ rosser

ROST archaic spelling of ▶ roast

ROSTED ▶ rost

ROSTER n list of people and their turns of duty ▷ vb place on a roster

ROSTERS ▶ roster

ROSTI n cheese-topped fried Swiss dish consisting of grated potato and, optionally, onion

ROSTING ▶ rost

ROSTIS ▶ rosti

ROSTRA ▶ rostrum

ROSTRAL adj of or like a beak or snout

ROSTRUM n platform or stage

R

ROSTS ▶ rost

ROSULA n rosette

ROSULAS ▶ rosula

ROSY adj pink-coloured ▷ vb redden or make pink

ROSYING ▶ rosy

ROT vb decompose or decay ▷ n decay

ROTA n list of people who take it in turn to do a particular task

ROTAL adj of or relating to wheels or rotation

ROTAN another name for ▶ rattan

ROTANS ▶ rotan

ROTARY adj revolving ▷ n traffic roundabout

ROTAS ▶ rota

ROTATE vb (cause to) move round a centre or on a pivot ▷ adj designating a corolla the united petals of which radiate from a central point like the spokes of a wheel

ROTATED ▶ rotate

ROTATES ▶ rotate

ROTATOR n person, device, or part that rotates or causes rotation

ROTCH n little auk

ROTCHE same as ▶ rotch

ROTCHES ▶ rotch

ROTCHIE same as ▶ rotch

ROTE n mechanical repetition ▷ vb learn by rote

ROTED ▶ rote

ROTES ▶ rote

ROTGUT n alcoholic drink of inferior quality

ROTGUTS ▶ rotgut

ROTHER dialect word for ▶ ox

ROTHERS ▶ rother

ROTI n (in India and the Caribbean) a type of unleavened bread

ROTIFER n minute aquatic multicellular invertebrate

ROTING ▶ rote

ROTIS ▶ roti

ROTL n unit of weight used in Muslim countries, varying in value between about one and five pounds

ROTLS ▶ rotl

ROTO n printing process using a cylinder etched with many small recesses, from which ink is transferred to a moving web of paper, plastic, etc, in a rotary press

ROTOLO n (in Italian cuisine) a roll

ROTOLOS ▶ rotolo

ROTON n quantum of vortex motion

ROTONS ▶ roton

ROTOR n revolving portion of a dynamo, motor, or turbine

ROTORS ▶ rotor

ROTOS ▶ roto

ROTS ▶ rot

ROTTAN n (in dialect) a rat

ROTTANS ▶ rottan

ROTTE n ancient stringed instrument

ROTTED ▶ rot

ROTTEN adj decaying ▷ adv extremely ▷ n (in dialect) a rat

ROTTENS ▶ rotten

ROTTER n despicable person

ROTTERS ▶ rotter

ROTTES ▶ rotte

ROTTING ▶ rot

ROTULA n kneecap

ROTULAE ▶ rotula

ROTULAS ▶ rotula

ROTUND adj round and plump ▷ vb make round

ROTUNDA n circular building or room, esp with a dome

ROTUNDS ▶ rotund

ROUBLE n monetary unit of Russia, Belarus, and Tajikistan

ROUBLES ▶ rouble

ROUCHE same as ▶ ruche

ROUCHES ▶ rouche

ROUCOU another name for ▶ annatto

ROUCOUS ▶ roucou

ROUE n man given to immoral living

ROUEN n breed of duck

ROUENS ▶ rouen

ROUES ▶ roue

ROUGE n red cosmetic used to colour the cheeks ▷ vb apply rouge to

ROUGED ▶ rouge

ROUGES ▶ rouge

ROUGH adj uneven or irregular ▷ vb make rough ▷ n rough state or area

ROUGHED ▶ rough

ROUGHEN vb make or become rough

ROUGHER n person that does the rough preparatory

work on something ▷ adj more rough

ROUGHIE n small food fish found in southern and western Australian waters

ROUGHLY adv without being exact or fully authenticated

ROUGHS ▶ rough

ROUGHT archaic past form of ▶ reach

ROUGHY spelling variant of ▶ roughie

ROUGING ▶ rouge

ROUILLE n kind of sauce

ROUL archaic form of ▶ roll

ROULADE n slice of meat rolled, esp around a stuffing, and cooked

ROULE archaic form of ▶ roll

ROULEAU n roll of paper containing coins

ROULES ▶ roule

ROULS ▶ roul

ROUM archaic spelling of ▶ room

ROUMING n pasture given for an animal

ROUMS ▶ roum

ROUNCE n handle that is turned to move paper and plates on a printing press

ROUNCES ▶ rounce

ROUNCY archaic word for ▶ horse

ROUND adj spherical, cylindrical, circular, or curved ▷ prep indicating an encircling movement, presence on all sides, etc ▷ vb move round ▷ n round shape

ROUNDED adj round or curved

ROUNDEL same as ▷ roundelay

ROUNDER n run round all four bases after one hit in rounders

ROUNDLE same as ▶ roundel

ROUNDLY adv thoroughly

ROUNDS ▶ round

ROUNDUP n act of gathering together livestock, people, facts, etc

ROUP n any of various chronic respiratory diseases of birds, esp poultry ▷ vb sell by auction

ROUPED ▶ roup

ROUPET adj Scots word meaning hoarse or croaky

ROUPIER ▶ roup

ROUPILY ▶ roup

ROUPING ▶ roup

ROUPIT *same as* ▶ **roupet**

ROUPS ▶ roup

ROUPY ▶ roup

ROUSANT *adj* (in heraldry) rising

ROUSE *same as* > **reveille**

ROUSED ▶ rouse

ROUSER *n* person or thing that rouses people, such as a stirring speech or compelling rock song

ROUSERS ▶ rouser

ROUSES ▶ rouse

ROUSING *adj* lively, vigorous

ROUST *vb* rout or stir, as out of bed

ROUSTED ▶ roust

ROUSTER *n* unskilled labourer on an oil rig

ROUSTS ▶ roust

ROUT *n* overwhelming defeat ▷ *vb* defeat and put to flight

ROUTE *n* roads taken to reach a destination ▷ *vb* send by a particular route

ROUTED ▶ route

ROUTER *n* device that allows data to be moved efficiently between two points on a network

ROUTERS ▶ router

ROUTES ▶ route

ROUTH *n* abundance ▷ *adj* abundant

ROUTHIE *adj* abundant, plentiful, or well filled

ROUTHS ▶ routh

ROUTINE *n* usual or regular method of procedure ▷ *adj* ordinary or regular

ROUTING ▶ rout

ROUTOUS ▶ rout

ROUTS ▶ rout

ROUX *n* fat and flour cooked together as a basis for sauces

ROVE ▶ reeve

ROVED ▶ reeve

ROVEN ▶ reeve

ROVER *n* wanderer, traveller

ROVERS ▶ rover

ROVES ▶ reeve

ROVING ▶ rove

ROVINGS ▶ rove

ROW *n* straight line of people or things ▷ *vb* propel (a boat) by oars

ROWABLE ▶ row

ROWAN *n* tree producing bright red berries, mountain ash

ROWANS ▶ rowan

ROWBOAT *n* small boat propelled by one or more pairs of oars

ROWDIER ▶ rowdy

ROWDIES ▶ rowdy

ROWDILY ▶ rowdy

ROWDY *adj* disorderly, noisy, and rough ▷ *n* person like this

ROWED ▶ row

ROWEL *n* small spiked wheel on a spur ▷ *vb* goad (a horse) using a rowel

ROWELED ▶ rowel

ROWELS ▶ rowel

ROWEN *another word for* > **aftermath**

ROWENS ▶ rowen

ROWER ▶ row

ROWERS ▶ row

ROWING ▶ row

ROWINGS ▶ row

ROWLOCK *n* device on a boat that holds an oar in place

ROWME *archaic variant of* ▶ **room**

ROWMES ▶ rowme

ROWND *archaic variant of* ▶ **round**

ROWNDED ▶ rownd

ROWNDS ▶ rownd

ROWOVER *n* act of winning a rowing race unopposed, by rowing the course

ROWS ▶ row

ROWT *archaic variant of* ▶ **rout**

ROWTED ▶ rowt

ROWTH *same as* ▶ **routh**

ROWTHS ▶ rowth

ROWTING ▶ rowt

ROWTS ▶ rowt

ROYAL *adj* of, befitting, or supported by a king or queen ▷ *n* member of a royal family

ROYALET *n* minor king

ROYALLY ▶ royal

ROYALS ▶ royal

ROYALTY *n* royal people

ROYNE *archaic word for* ▶ **gnaw**

ROYNED ▶ royne

ROYNES ▶ royne

ROYNING ▶ royne

ROYNISH *archaic word for* ▶ **mangy**

ROYST *same as* ▶ **roist**

ROYSTED ▶ royst

ROYSTER *same as* ▶ **roister**

ROYSTS ▶ royst

ROZELLE *same as* ▶ **roselle**

ROZET *same as* ▶ **roset**

ROZETED ▶ rozet

ROZETS ▶ rozet

ROZIT *same as* ▶ **roset**

ROZITED ▶ rozit

ROZITS ▶ rozit

ROZZER *n* policeman

ROZZERS ▶ rozzer

RUANA *n* woollen wrap resembling a poncho

RUANAS ▶ ruana

RUB *vb* apply pressure and friction to (something) with a circular or backwards-and-forwards movement ▷ *n* act of rubbing

RUBABOO *n* soup or stew made by boiling pemmican with, if available, flour and vegetables

RUBACE *same as* ▶ **rubasse**

RUBACES ▶ rubace

RUBAI *n* verse form of Persian origin consisting of four-line stanzas

RUBASSE *n* type of quartz containing red haematite

RUBATI ▶ rubato

RUBATO *n* (with) expressive flexibility of tempo ▷ *adv* be played with a flexible tempo

RUBATOS ▶ rubato

RUBBED ▶ rub

RUBBER *n* strong waterproof elastic material, orig. made from the dried sap of a tropical tree, now usu synthetic ▷ *adj* made of or producing rubber ▷ *vb* provide with rubber coating

RUBBERS ▶ rubber

RUBBERY *adj* having the texture of or resembling rubber, esp in flexibility or toughness

RUBBET *old Scots past form of* ▶ **rob**

RUBBIDY *same as* ▶ **rubbity**

RUBBIES ▶ rubby

RUBBING ▶ rub

RUBBISH *n* waste matter ▷ *vb* criticize

RUBBIT *old Scots past form of* ▶ **rob**

RUBBITY *n* pub

R

RUBBLE n fragments of broken stone, brick, etc ▷ vb turn into rubble

RUBBLED ▶ rubble

RUBBLES ▶ rubble

RUBBLY ▶ rubble

RUBBY n rubbing alcohol, esp when mixed with cheap wine for drinking

RUBDOWN n act of drying or cleaning vigorously

RUBEFY vb make red, esp (of a counterirritant) to make the skin go red

RUBEL n currency unit of Belarus

RUBELLA n mild contagious viral disease characterized by cough, sore throat, and skin rash

RUBELS ▶ rubel

RUBEOLA technical name for ▶ measles

RUBICON n point of no return ▷ vb (in bezique) to beat before the loser has managed to gain as many as 1000 points

RUBIDIC > rubidium

RUBIED ▶ ruby

RUBIER ▶ ruby

RUBIES ▶ ruby

RUBIEST ▶ ruby

RUBIFY same as ▶ rubefy

RUBIGO old Scots word for ▶ penis

RUBIGOS ▶ rubigo

RUBIN archaic word for ▶ ruby

RUBINE archaic word for ▶ ruby

RUBINES ▶ rubine

RUBINS ▶ rubin

RUBIOUS adj of the colour ruby

RUBLE same as ▶ rouble

RUBLES ▶ ruble

RUBOFF n resulting effect on something else; consequences

RUBOFFS ▶ ruboff

RUBOUT n killing or elimination

RUBOUTS ▶ rubout

RUBRIC n set of rules for behaviour ▷ adj written, printed, or marked in red

RUBRICS ▶ rubric

RUBS ▶ rub

RUBUS n fruit-bearing genus of shrubs

RUBY n red precious gemstone ▷ adj deep red

▷ vb redden

RUBYING ▶ ruby

RUC same as ▶ roc

RUCHE n pleat or frill of lace etc as a decoration ▷ vb put a ruche on

RUCHED ▶ ruche

RUCHES ▶ ruche

RUCHING n material used for a ruche

RUCK n rough crowd of common people ▷ vb wrinkle or crease

RUCKED ▶ ruck

RUCKING ▶ ruck

RUCKLE another word for ▶ ruck

RUCKLED ▶ ruckle

RUCKLES ▶ ruckle

RUCKMAN n person who plays in the ruck

RUCKMEN ▶ ruckman

RUCKS ▶ ruck

RUCKUS n uproar

RUCOLA n another name for the salad plant rocket

RUCOLAS ▶ rucola

RUCS ▶ ruc

RUCTION n uproar

RUD n red or redness ▷ vb redden

RUDAS n Scots word for a coarse, rude old woman

RUDASES ▶ rudas

RUDD n European freshwater fish

RUDDED ▶ rud

RUDDER n vertical hinged piece at the stern of a boat or at the rear of an aircraft, for steering

RUDDERS ▶ rudder

RUDDIED ▶ ruddy

RUDDIER ▶ ruddy

RUDDIES ▶ ruddy

RUDDILY ▶ ruddy

RUDDING ▶ rud

RUDDLE n red ochre, used esp to mark sheep ▷ vb mark (sheep) with ruddle

RUDDLED ▶ ruddle

RUDDLES ▶ ruddle

RUDDOCK dialect name for the ▶ robin

RUDDS ▶ rudd

RUDDY adj of a fresh healthy red colour ▷ adv bloody ▷ vb redden

RUDE archaic spelling of ▶ rood

RUDELY ▶ rude

RUDER ▶ rude

RUDERAL n plant that

grows on waste ground ▷ adj growing in waste places

RUDERY ▶ rude

RUDES ▶ rude

RUDESBY n archaic word for rude person

RUDEST ▶ rude

RUDIE n member of a youth movement originating in the 1960s

RUDIES ▶ rudie

RUDISH adj somewhat rude

RUDS ▶ rud

RUE vb feel regret for ▷ n plant with evergreen bitter leaves

RUED ▶ rue

RUEDA n type of Cuban round dance

RUEDAS ▶ rueda

RUEFUL adj regretful or sorry

RUEING ▶ rue

RUEINGS ▶ rue

RUELLE n area between bed and wall, at one time used by French ladies of standing for receiving visitors

RUELLES ▶ ruelle

RUELLIA n genus of plants

RUER ▶ rue

RUERS ▶ rue

RUES ▶ rue

RUFF n circular pleated, gathered, or fluted collar of lawn, muslin, etc, often starched or wired, worn by both men and women in the 16th and 17th centuries ▷ vb trump

RUFFE n European freshwater fish

RUFFED ▶ ruff

RUFFES ▶ ruffe

RUFFIAN n violent lawless person ▷ vb act like a ruffian

RUFFIN archaic name for ▶ ruffe

RUFFING ▶ ruff

RUFFINS ▶ ruffin

RUFFLE vb disturb the calm of ▷ n frill or pleat

RUFFLED ▶ ruffle

RUFFLER n person or thing that ruffles

RUFFLES ▶ ruffle

RUFFLY adj ruffled

RUFFS ▶ ruff

RUFIYAA n standard monetary unit of the Maldives, divided into 100 laari

RUFOUS *adj* reddish-brown
RUG *n* small carpet ▷ *vb* (in dialect) tug
RUGA *n* fold, wrinkle, or crease
RUGAE ▶ ruga
RUGAL *adj* (in anatomy) with ridges or folds
RUGATE *same as* ▶ rugose
RUGBIES ▶ rugby
RUGBY *n* form of football played with an oval ball which may be handled by the players
RUGGED *adj* rocky or steep
RUGGER *same as* ▶ rugby
RUGGERS ▶ rugger
RUGGIER ▶ ruggy
RUGGING ▶ rug
RUGGY *adj* (in dialect) rough or rugged
RUGLIKE ▶ rug
RUGOLA *n* another name for the salad plant rocket
RUGOLAS ▶ rugola
RUGOSA *n* any of various shrubs descended from a particular type of wild rose
RUGOSAS ▶ rugosa
RUGOSE *adj* wrinkled
RUGOUS *same as* ▶ rugose
RUGS ▶ rug
RUIN *vb* destroy or spoil completely ▷ *n* destruction or decay
RUINATE *vb* archaic word for bring or come to ruin
RUINED ▶ ruin
RUINER ▶ ruin
RUINERS ▶ ruin
RUING ▶ rue
RUINGS ▶ rue
RUINING ▶ ruin
RUINOUS *adj* causing ruin
RUINS ▶ ruin
RUKH *same as* ▶ roc
RUKHS ▶ rukh
RULABLE ▶ rule
RULE *n* statement of what is allowed, for example in a game or procedure ▷ *vb* govern
RULED ▶ rule
RULER *n* person who governs ▷ *vb* punish by hitting with a ruler
RULERED ▶ ruler
RULERS ▶ ruler
RULES ▶ rule
RULESSE *adj* archaic word meaning ruleless or without rules
RULIER ▶ ruly

RULIEST ▶ ruly
RULING *n* formal decision ▷ *adj* controlling or exercising authority
RULINGS ▶ ruling
RULLION *n* Scots word for rawhide shoe
RULLOCK *same as* ▶ rowlock
RULY *adj* orderly
RUM *n* alcoholic drink distilled from sugar cane ▷ *adj* odd, strange
RUMAKI *n* savoury of chicken liver and sliced water chestnut wrapped in bacon
RUMAKIS ▶ rumaki
RUMAL *n* handkerchief or type of cloth
RUMALS ▶ rumal
RUMBA *n* lively ballroom dance of Cuban origin ▷ *vb* dance the rumba
RUMBAED ▶ rumba
RUMBAS ▶ rumba
RUMBLE *vb* make a low continuous noise ▷ *n* deep resonant sound
RUMBLED ▶ rumble
RUMBLER ▶ rumble
RUMBLES ▶ rumble
RUMBLY *adj* rumbling or liable to rumble
RUMBO *n* rum-based cocktail
RUMBOS ▶ rumbo
RUME *archaic form of* ▶ rheum
RUMEN *n* first compartment of the stomach of ruminants, behind the reticulum, in which food is partly digested before being regurgitated as cud
RUMENS ▶ rumen
RUMES ▶ rume
RUMINA ▶ rumen
RUMINAL ▶ rumen
RUMKIN *n* archaic term for a drinking vessel
RUMKINS ▶ rumkin
RUMLY ▶ rum
RUMMAGE *vb* search untidily and at length ▷ *n* untidy search through a collection of things
RUMMER ▶ rum
RUMMERS ▶ rum
RUMMEST ▶ rum
RUMMIER ▶ rummy
RUMMIES ▶ rummy

RUMMILY ▶ rummy
RUMMISH *adj* rather strange, peculiar or odd
RUMMY *n* card game in which players try to collect sets or sequences ▷ *adj* of or like rum in taste or smell
RUMNESS ▶ rum
RUMOR *same as* ▶ rumour
RUMORED ▶ rumor
RUMORS ▶ rumor
RUMOUR *n* unproved statement ▷ *vb* pass around or circulate in the form of a rumour
RUMOURS ▶ rumour
RUMP *n* buttocks ▷ *vb* turn back on
RUMPED ▶ rump
RUMPIES ▶ rumpy
RUMPING ▶ rump
RUMPLE *vb* make untidy, crumpled, or dishevelled ▷ *n* wrinkle, fold, or crease
RUMPLED ▶ rumple
RUMPLES ▶ rumple
RUMPLY ▶ rumple
RUMPS ▶ rump
RUMPUS *n* noisy commotion
RUMPY *n* tailless Manx cat ▷ *adj* with a large or noticeable rump
RUMS ▶ rum
RUN *vb* move with a more rapid gait than walking ▷ *n* act or spell of running
RUNANGA *n* Māori assembly or council
RUNAWAY *n* person or animal that runs away
RUNBACK *n* (in tennis) the areas behind the baselines of the court
RUNCH *n* another name for white charlock
RUNCHES ▶ runch
RUND *same as* ▶ roon
RUNDALE *n* (formerly) the name given, esp in Ireland and earlier in Scotland, to the system of land tenure in which each land-holder had several strips of land that were not contiguous
RUNDLE *n* rung of a ladder
RUNDLED *adj* rounded
RUNDLES ▶ rundle
RUNDLET *n* liquid measure, generally about 15 gallons
RUNDOWN *adj* tired; exhausted ▷ *n* brief review, résumé, or summary

R

RUNDS ▶ rund

RUNE n any character of the earliest Germanic alphabet

RUNED n with runes on

RUNES ▶ rune

RUNFLAT adj having a safety feature that prevents tyres becoming dangerous or liable to damage when flat

RUNG ▶ ring

RUNGS ▶ ring

RUNIC ▶ rune

RUNKLE vb (in dialect) crease or wrinkle

RUNKLED ▶ runkle

RUNKLES ▶ runkle

RUNLESS ▶ run

RUNLET n cask for wine, beer, etc

RUNLETS ▶ runlet

RUNNEL n small brook

RUNNELS ▶ runnel

RUNNER n competitor in a race

RUNNERS ▶ runner

RUNNET dialect word for ▶ **rennet**

RUNNETS ▶ runnet

RUNNIER ▶ runny

RUNNING ▶ run

RUNNY adj tending to flow

RUNOFF n extra race to decide the winner after a tie

RUNOFFS ▶ runoff

RUNOUT n dismissal of a batsman by running him out

RUNOUTS ▶ runout

RUNOVER n incident in which someone is run over by a vehicle

RUNRIG same as ▶ **rundale**

RUNRIGS ▶ runrig

RUNS ▶ run

RUNT n smallest animal in a litter

RUNTED adj stunted

RUNTIER ▶ runt

RUNTISH ▶ runt

RUNTS ▶ runt

RUNTY ▶ runt

RUNWAY n hard level roadway where aircraft take off and land

RUNWAYS ▶ runway

RUPEE n monetary unit of India and Pakistan

RUPEES ▶ rupee

RUPIA n type of skin eruption

RUPIAH n standard monetary unit of Indonesia,

divided into 100 sen

RUPIAHS ▶ rupiah

RUPIAS ▶ rupia

RUPTURE n breaking, breach ▷ vb break, burst, or sever

RURAL adj in or of the countryside ▷ n country dweller

RURALLY ▶ rural

RURALS ▶ rural

RURBAN adj part country, part urban

RURP n very small piton

RURPS ▶ rurp

RURU another name for ▶ **mopoke**

RURUS ▶ ruru

RUSA n type of deer with a mane

RUSALKA n water nymph or spirit

RUSAS ▶ rusa

RUSCUS n type of shrub

RUSE n stratagem or trick

RUSES ▶ ruse

RUSH vb move or do very quickly ▷ n sudden quick or violent movement ▷ adj done with speed, hasty

RUSHED ▶ rush

RUSHEE n someone interested in gaining fraternity or sorority membership

RUSHEES ▶ rushee

RUSHEN adj made of rushes

RUSHER ▶ rush

RUSHERS ▶ rush

RUSHES pl n (in film-making) the initial prints of a scene or scenes before editing, usually prepared daily

RUSHIER ▶ rushy

RUSHING ▶ rush

RUSHY adj full of rushes

RUSINE adj of or relating to rusa deer

RUSK n hard brown crisp biscuit, used esp for feeding babies

RUSKS ▶ rusk

RUSMA n Turkish depilatory

RUSMAS ▶ rusma

RUSSE adj as in **charlotte russe** cold dessert made from whipped cream, custard, etc, surrounded by sponge fingers

RUSSEL n type of woollen fabric

RUSSELS ▶ russel

RUSSET adj reddish-brown ▷ n apple with rough reddish-brown skin ▷ vb become russet-coloured

RUSSETS ▶ russet

RUSSETY ▶ russet

RUSSIA n Russia leather

RUSSIAS ▶ russia

RUSSIFY vb cause to become Russian in character

RUSSULA n type of fungus, typically of toadstool shape and often brightly coloured

RUST n reddish-brown coating formed on iron etc that has been exposed to moisture ▷ adj reddish-brown ▷ vb become coated with rust

RUSTED ▶ rust

RUSTIC adj of or resembling country people ▷ n person from the country

RUSTICS ▶ rustic

RUSTIER ▶ rusty

RUSTILY ▶ rusty

RUSTING ▶ rust

RUSTLE n (make) a low whispering sound ▷ vb steal (cattle)

RUSTLED ▶ rustle

RUSTLER n cattle thief

RUSTLES ▶ rustle

RUSTRE n (in heraldry) lozenge with a round hole in the middle showing the background colour

RUSTRED ▶ rustre

RUSTRES ▶ rustre

RUSTS ▶ rust

RUSTY adj coated with rust

RUT n furrow made by wheels ▷ vb be in a period of sexual excitability

RUTH n pity

RUTHFUL adj full of or causing sorrow or pity

RUTHS ▶ ruth

RUTILE n black, yellowish, or reddish-brown mineral

RUTILES ▶ rutile

RUTIN n bioflavonoid found in various plants including rue

RUTINS ▶ rutin

RUTS ▶ rut

RUTTED ▶ rut

RUTTER n (in history) type of cavalry soldier

RUTTERS ▶ rutter

RUTTIER ▶ rutty

RUTTILY ▶ rutty

RUTTING ▶ **rut**
RUTTISH *adj* (of an animal) in a condition of rut
RUTTY *adj* full of ruts or holes
RYA *n* type of rug originating in Scandinavia
RYAL *n* one of several old coins
RYALS ▶ **ryal**
RYAS ▶ **rya**
RYBAT *n* polished stone piece forming the side of a window or door
RYBATS ▶ **rybat**

RYE *n* kind of grain used for fodder and bread
RYEPECK *n* punt-mooring pole
RYES ▶ **rye**
RYFE *archaic variant of* ▶ **rife**
RYKE *Scots variant of* ▶ **reach**
RYKED ▶ **ryke**
RYKES ▶ **ryke**
RYKING ▶ **ryke**
RYMME *same as* ▶ **rim**
RYMMED ▶ **rymme**
RYMMES ▶ **rymme**
RYMMING ▶ **rymme**

RYND *n* (in milling) crossbar piece forming part of the support structure of the upper millstone
RYNDS ▶ **rynd**
RYOKAN *n* traditional Japanese inn
RYOKANS ▶ **ryokan**
RYOT *n* (in India) a peasant or tenant farmer
RYOTS ▶ **ryot**
RYPE *n* ptarmigan
RYPECK *same as* ▶ **ryepeck**
RYPECKS ▶ **rypeck**
RYPER ▶ **rype**

R

Ss

S begins only four two-letter words, **sh** (5 points), **si**, **so** and **st** (2 each). These are easy to remember, and it's worth noting that two of them, **sh** and **st**, don't use any vowels. Interestingly, there are quite a few three-letter words beginning with **S** that don't contain vowels. These are **shh** (9), **shy** (9), **sky** (10), **sly** (6), **sny** (6), **spy** (8), **sty** (6), **swy** (9) and **syn** (6). **S** also forms a number of three-letter words with **X**. These are easy to remember as they use every vowel except **U**: **sax, sex, six** and **sox** (10 each). When it comes to **Z**, you will find **saz, sez** and **soz** (12 each) very useful, and the same applies to **suq** (12 points).

SAAG *n* (in Indian cookery) spinach

SAAGS ▶ **saag**

SAB *n* person engaged in direct action to prevent a targeted activity taking place ▷ *vb* take part in such action

SABAL *n* variety of palm tree

SABALS ▶ **sabal**

SABATON *n* foot covering in suit of armour

SABAYON *n* dessert or sweet sauce made with egg yolks, sugar, and wine beaten together over heat till thick

SABBAT *n* midnight meeting of witches

SABBATH *n* period of rest

SABBATS ▶ **sabbat**

SABBED ▶ **sab**

SABBING ▶ **sab**

SABE *n* very informal word meaning sense or savvy ▷ *vb* very informal word meaning know or savvy

SABED ▶ **sabe**

SABEING ▶ **sabe**

SABELLA *n* marine worm

SABER *same as* ▶ **sabre**

SABERED ▶ **saber**

SABERS ▶ **saber**

SABES ▶ **sabe**

SABHA *n* set of Muslim prayer beads

SABHAS ▶ **sabha**

SABIN *n* unit of acoustic absorption equal to the absorption resulting from one square foot of a perfectly absorbing surface

SABINE *same as* ▶ **savin**

SABINES ▶ **sabine**

SABINS ▶ **sabin**

SABIR *n* member of ancient Turkic people

SABIRS ▶ **sabir**

SABKHA *n* flat coastal plain with a salt crust, common in Arabia

SABKHAH *n* sabkha

SABKHAS ▶ **sabkha**

SABKHAT *n* sabkha

SABLE *n* dark fur from a small weasel-like Arctic animal ▷ *adj* black

SABLED ▶ **sable**

SABLES ▶ **sable**

SABLING ▶ **sable**

SABOT *n* wooden shoe traditionally worn by peasants in France

SABOTS ▶ **sabot**

SABRA *n* native-born Israeli Jew

SABRAS ▶ **sabra**

SABRE *n* curved cavalry sword ▷ *vb* injure or kill with a sabre

SABRED ▶ **sabre**

SABRES ▶ **sabre**

SABREUR *n* person wielding sabre

SABRING ▶ **sabre**

SABS ▶ **sab**

SABURRA *n* granular deposit

SAC *n* pouchlike structure in an animal or plant

SACATON *n* coarse grass of the southwestern US and Mexico, grown for hay and pasture

SACBUT *n* medieval trombone

SACBUTS ▶ **sacbut**

SACCADE *n* movement of the eye when it makes a sudden change of fixation, as in reading

SACCATE *adj* in the form of a sac

SACCOI ▶ **saccos**

SACCOS *n* bishop's garment in the Orthodox Church

SACCULE *n* small sac

SACCULI > **sacculus**

SACELLA > **sacellum**

SACHEM *same as* > **sagamore**

SACHEMS ▶ **sachem**

SACHET *n* small envelope or bag containing a single portion

SACHETS ▶ **sachet**

SACK *n* large bag made of coarse material ▷ *vb* dismiss

SACKAGE *n* act of sacking a place

SACKBUT *n* medieval form of trombone

SACKED ▶ **sack**

SACKER ▶ **sack**

SACKERS ▶ **sack**

SACKFUL ▶ **sack**

SACKING *n* rough woven material used for sacks

SACKS ▶ **sack**

SACLESS *adj* old word meaning unchallengeable

SACLIKE ▶ **sac**

SACQUE same as ▶ **sack**

SACQUES ▶ **sacque**

SACRA ▶ **sacrum**

SACRAL adj of or associated with sacred rites ▷ n sacral vertebra

SACRALS ▶ **sacral**

SACRED adj holy

SACRIFY vb old form of sacrifice

SACRING n act or ritual of consecration, esp of the Eucharist or of a bishop

SACRIST same as > **sacristan**

SACRUM n wedge-shaped bone at the base of the spine

SACRUMS ▶ **sacrum**

SACS ▶ **sac**

SAD adj sorrowful, unhappy ▷ vb New Zealand word meaning express sadness or displeasure strongly

SADDED ▶ **sad**

SADDEN vb make (someone) sad

SADDENS ▶ **sadden**

SADDER ▶ **sad**

SADDEST ▶ **sad**

SADDHA same as ▶ **sadhu**

SADDHUS ▶ **saddhu**

SADDIE ▶ **saddo**

SADDIES ▶ **saddie**

SADDING ▶ **sad**

SADDISH ▶ **sad**

SADDLE n rider's seat on a horse or bicycle ▷ vb put a saddle on (a horse)

SADDLED ▶ **saddle**

SADDLER n maker or seller of saddles

SADDLES ▶ **saddle**

SADDO vb make sad ▷ n socially inadequate or pathetic person

SADDOES ▶ **saddo**

SADDOS ▶ **saddo**

SADE same as ▶ **sadhe**

SADES ▶ **sade**

SADHANA n one of a number of spiritual practices or disciplines which lead to perfection, these being contemplation, asceticism, worship of a god, and correct living

SADHE n 18th letter in the Hebrew alphabet

SADHES ▶ **sadhe**

SADHU n Hindu wandering holy man

SADHUS ▶ **sadhu**

SADI same as ▶ **sadhe**

SADIRON n heavy iron pointed at both ends, for pressing clothes

SADIS ▶ **sadi**

SADISM n gaining of (sexual) pleasure from inflicting pain

SADISMS ▶ **sadism**

SADIST ▶ **sadism**

SADISTS ▶ **sadism**

SADLY ▶ **sad**

SADNESS ▶ **sad**

SADO same as ▶ **chado**

SADOS ▶ **sado**

SADS ▶ **sad**

SADZA n southern African porridge

SADZAS ▶ **sadza**

SAE Scots word for ▶ **so**

SAETER n upland pasture in Norway

SAETERS ▶ **saeter**

SAFARI n expedition to hunt or observe wild animals, esp in Africa ▷ vb go on safari

SAFARIS ▶ **safari**

SAFE adj secure, protected ▷ n strong lockable container ▷ vb make safe

SAFED ▶ **safe**

SAFELY ▶ **safe**

SAFER ▶ **safe**

SAFES ▶ **safe**

SAFEST ▶ **safe**

SAFETY n state of being safe ▷ vb make safe

SAFFIAN n leather tanned with sumach and usually dyed a bright colour

SAFFRON n orange-coloured flavouring obtained from a crocus ▷ adj orange

SAFING ▶ **safe**

SAFROL n oily liquid obtained from sassafras

SAFROLE n colourless or yellowish oily water-insoluble liquid

SAFROLS ▶ **safrol**

SAFT Scots word for ▶ **soft**

SAFTER ▶ **saft**

SAFTEST ▶ **saft**

SAG vb sink in the middle ▷ n droop

SAGA n legend of Norse heroes

SAGAMAN n person reciting Norse sagas

SAGAMEN ▶ **sagaman**

SAGAS ▶ **saga**

SAGATHY n type of light fabric

SAGBUT n medieval trombone

SAGBUTS ▶ **sagbut**

SAGE n very wise man ▷ adj wise

SAGELY ▶ **sage**

SAGENE n fishing net

SAGENES ▶ **sagene**

SAGER ▶ **sage**

SAGES ▶ **sage**

SAGEST ▶ **sage**

SAGGAR n clay box in which fragile ceramic wares are placed for protection during firing ▷ vb put in a saggar

SAGGARD n saggar

SAGGARS ▶ **saggar**

SAGGED ▶ **sag**

SAGGER same as ▶ **saggar**

SAGGERS ▶ **sagger**

SAGGIER ▶ **saggy**

SAGGING ▶ **sag**

SAGGY adj tending to sag

SAGIER ▶ **sagy**

SAGIEST ▶ **sagy**

SAGITTA n sine of an arc

SAGO n starchy cereal from the powdered pith of the sago palm tree

SAGOIN n South American monkey

SAGOINS ▶ **sagoin**

SAGOS ▶ **sago**

SAGOUIN n South American monkey

SAGRADA adj as in **cascara sagrada** dried bark of the cascara buckthorn, used as a stimulant and laxative

SAGS ▶ **sag**

SAGUARO n giant cactus of desert regions of Arizona, S California, and Mexico

SAGUIN n South American monkey

SAGUINS ▶ **saguin**

SAGUM n Roman soldier's cloak

SAGY adj like or containing sage

SAHEB same as ▶ **sahib**

SAHEBS ▶ **saheb**

SAHIB n Indian term of address placed after a man's name as a mark of respect

SAHIBA n respectful Indian term of address for woman

SAHIBAH n sahiba

SAHIBAS ▶ **sahiba**

SAHIBS ▸ sahib

SAHIWAL n breed of cattle in India

SAHUARO same as ▸ saguaro

SAI n South American monkey

SAIC n boat of eastern Mediterranean

SAICE same as ▸ syce

SAICES ▸ saice

SAICK n boat of eastern Mediterranean

SAICKS ▸ saick

SAICS ▸ saic

SAID same as ▸ sayyid

SAIDEST ▸ say

SAIDS ▸ said

SAIDST ▸ say

SAIGA n either of two antelopes of the plains of central Asia

SAIGAS ▸ saiga

SAIKEI n Japanese ornamental miniature landscape

SAIKEIS ▸ saikei

SAIL n sheet of fabric stretched to catch the wind for propelling a sailing boat ▷ vb travel by water

SAILED ▸ sail

SAILER n vessel, esp one equipped with sails, with specified sailing characteristics

SAILERS ▸ sailer

SAILING n practice, art, or technique of sailing a vessel

SAILOR n member of a ship's crew

SAILORS ▸ sailor

SAILS ▸ sail

SAIM Scots word for ▸ lard

SAIMIN n Hawaiian dish of noodles

SAIMINS ▸ saimin

SAIMIRI n South American monkey

SAIMS ▸ saim

SAIN vb make the sign of the cross over so as to bless or protect from evil or sin

SAINE vb old form of say

SAINED ▸ sain

SAINING ▸ sain

SAINS ▸ sain

SAINT n person venerated after death as specially holy ▷ vb canonize

SAINTED adj formally recognized by a Christian Church as a saint

SAINTLY adj behaving in a very good, patient, or holy way

SAINTS ▸ saint

SAIQUE n boat in eastern Mediterranean

SAIQUES ▸ saique

SAIR Scots word for ▸ sore

SAIRED ▸ sair

SAIRER ▸ sair

SAIREST ▸ sair

SAIRING ▸ sair

SAIRS ▸ sair

SAIS ▸ sai

SAIST ▸ say

SAITH form of the present tense (indicative mood) of ▸ say

SAITHE n dark-coloured food fish found in northern seas

SAITHES ▸ saithe

SAITHS ▸ saith

SAIYID n Muslim descended from Mohammed's grandson

SAIYIDS ▸ saiyid

SAJOU n South American monkey

SAJOUS ▸ sajou

SAKAI n Malaysian aborigine

SAKAIS ▸ sakai

SAKE n benefit

SAKER n large falcon of E Europe and central Asia

SAKERET n male saker

SAKERS ▸ saker

SAKES ▸ sake

SAKI same as ▸ sake

SAKIA n water wheel in Middle East

SAKIAS ▸ sakia

SAKIEH n water wheel in Middle East

SAKIEHS ▸ sakieh

SAKIS ▸ saki

SAKIYEH n water wheel in Middle East

SAKKOI ▸ sakkos

SAKKOS n bishop's garment in Orthodox Church

SAKSAUL n Asian tree

SAL pharmacological term for ▸ salt

SALAAM n low bow of greeting among Muslims ▷ vb make a salaam

SALAAMS ▸ salaam

SALABLE same as ▸ saleable

SALABLY > saleably

SALAD n dish of raw vegetables, eaten as a meal or part of a meal

SALADE same as ▸ sallet

SALADES ▸ salade

SALADS ▸ salad

SALAL n North American shrub

SALALS ▸ salal

SALAMI n highly spiced sausage

SALAMIS ▸ salami

SALAMON n word used in old oaths

SALARY n fixed regular payment, usu monthly, to an employee ▷ vb pay a salary to

SALBAND n coating of mineral

SALCHOW n type of figure-skating jump

SALE n exchange of goods for money

SALEP n dried ground starchy tubers of various orchids, used for food and formerly as drugs

SALEPS ▸ salep

SALES ▸ sale

SALET same as ▸ sallet

SALETS ▸ salet

SALEWD ▸ salue

SALFERN n plant of borage family

SALIC adj (of rocks and minerals) having a high content of silica and alumina

SALICES ▸ salix

SALICET n soft-toned organ stop

SALICIN n colourless or white crystalline water-soluble glucoside

SALIENT adj prominent, noticeable ▷ n projecting part of a front line

SALIFY vb treat, mix with, or cause to combine with a salt

SALIGOT n water chestnut

SALINA n salt marsh, lake, or spring

SALINAS ▸ salina

SALINE adj containing salt ▷ n solution of sodium chloride and water

SALINES ▸ saline

SALIVA n liquid that forms in the mouth, spittle

SALIVAL ▸ saliva

SALIVAS ▸ saliva

SALIX n plant or tree of willow family

SALL archaic form of ▸ **shall**

SALLAD old spelling of ▸ **salad**

SALLADS ▸ **sallad**

SALLAL n North American shrub

SALLALS ▸ **sallal**

SALLE n hall

SALLEE n SE Australian eucalyptus with a pale grey bark

SALLEES ▸ **sallee**

SALLES ▸ **salle**

SALLET n light round helmet extending over the back of the neck

SALLETS ▸ **sallet**

SALLIED ▸ **sally**

SALLIER ▸ **sally**

SALLIES ▸ **sally**

SALLOW adj of an unhealthy pale or yellowish colour ▷ vb make sallow ▷ n any of several small willow trees

SALLOWS ▸ **sallow**

SALLOWY ▸ **sallow**

SALLY n violent excursion ▷ vb set or rush out

SALMI n ragout of game stewed in a rich brown sauce

SALMIS same as ▸ **salmi**

SALMON n large fish with orange-pink flesh valued as food ▷ adj orange-pink

SALMONS ▸ **salmon**

SALMONY adj of or like a salmon

SALOL n white sparingly soluble crystalline compound with a slight aromatic odour, used as a preservative and to absorb light in sun-tan lotions, plastics, etc

SALOLS ▸ **salol**

SALON n commercial premises of a hairdresser, beautician, etc

SALONS ▸ **salon**

SALOON n closed car with four or more seats

SALOONS ▸ **saloon**

SALOOP n infusion of aromatic herbs or other plant parts formerly used as a tonic or cure

SALOOPS ▸ **saloop**

SALOP same as ▸ **saloop**

SALOPS ▸ **salop**

SALP n minute animal floating in sea

SALPA n any of various minute floating animals of warm oceans

SALPAE ▸ **salpa**

SALPAS ▸ **salpa**

SALPIAN n minute animal floating in sea

SALPID n minute animal floating in sea

SALPIDS ▸ **salpid**

SALPINX n Fallopian tube or Eustachian tube

SALPS ▸ **salp**

SALS ▸ **sal**

SALSA n lively Puerto Rican dance ▷ vb dance the salsa

SALSAED ▸ **salsa**

SALSAS ▸ **salsa**

SALSE n volcano expelling mud

SALSES ▸ **salse**

SALSIFY n Mediterranean plant with a long white edible root

SALT n white crystalline substance used to season food ▷ vb season or preserve with salt

SALTANT adj (of an organism) differing from others of its species because of a saltation ▷ n saltant organism

SALTATE vb go through saltation

SALTATO n saltando

SALTBOX n box for salt with a sloping lid

SALTCAT n salty medicine for pigeons

SALTED adj seasoned, preserved, or treated with salt

SALTER n person who deals in or manufactures salt

SALTERN n place where salt is obtained from pools of evaporated sea water

SALTERS ▸ **salter**

SALTEST ▸ **salt**

SALTIE n saltwater crocodile

SALTIER ▸ **saltire**

SALTIES ▸ **saltie**

SALTILY ▸ **salty**

SALTINE n salty biscuit

SALTING n area of low ground regularly inundated with salt water

SALTIRE n diagonal cross on a shield

SALTISH ▸ **salt**

SALTLY ▸ **salt**

SALTO n daring jump ▷ vb perform a daring jump

SALTOED ▸ **salto**

SALTOS ▸ **salto**

SALTPAN n shallow basin containing salt, gypsum, etc, that was deposited from an evaporated salt lake

SALTS ▸ **salt**

SALTUS n break in the continuity of a sequence, esp the omission of a necessary step in a logical argument

SALTY adj of, tasting of, or containing salt

SALUE vb old word meaning salute

SALUED ▸ **salue**

SALUES ▸ **salue**

SALUING ▸ **salue**

SALUKI n type of tall hound with a smooth coat

SALUKIS ▸ **saluki**

SALUTE n motion of the arm as a formal sign of respect ▷ vb greet with a salute

SALUTED ▸ **salute**

SALUTER ▸ **salute**

SALUTES ▸ **salute**

SALVAGE n saving of a ship or other property from destruction ▷ vb save from destruction or waste

SALVE n healing or soothing ointment ▷ vb soothe or appease

SALVED ▸ **salve**

SALVER same as ▸ **salvor**

SALVERS ▸ **salver**

SALVES ▸ **salve**

SALVETE n Latin greeting

SALVIA n plant with blue or red flowers

SALVIAS ▸ **salvia**

SALVING ▸ **salve**

SALVO n simultaneous discharge of guns etc ▷ vb attack with a salvo

SALVOED ▸ **salvo**

SALVOES ▸ **salvo**

SALVOR n person instrumental in salvaging a vessel or its cargo

SALVORS ▸ **salvor**

SALVOS ▸ **salvo**

SALWAR n as in **salwar kameez** long tunic worn over a pair of baggy trousers, usually worn by women, esp in Pakistan

SALWARS ▸ **salwar**

SAM vb collect

S

SAMA n Japanese title of respect

SAMAAN n South American tree

SAMAANS ▶ samaan

SAMADHI n state of deep meditative contemplation which leads to higher consciousness

SAMAN n South American tree

SAMANS ▶ saman

SAMARA n dry indehiscent one-seeded fruit with a winglike extension to aid dispersal

SAMARAS ▶ samara

SAMAS ▶ sama

SAMBA n lively Brazilian dance ▷ vb perform such a dance

SAMBAED ▶ samba

SAMBAL n Malaysian dish

SAMBALS ▶ sambal

SAMBAR n S Asian deer with three-tined antlers

SAMBARS ▶ sambar

SAMBAS ▶ samba

SAMBHAR n Indian dish

SAMBHUR n Asian deer

SAMBUCA n Italian liqueur

SAMBUKE n ancient Greek stringed instrument

SAMBUR same as ▶ sambar

SAMBURS ▶ sambur

SAME adj identical, not different, unchanged ▷ n something identical

SAMECH n letter in Hebrew alphabet

SAMECHS ▶ samech

SAMEK same as ▶ samekh

SAMEKH n 15th letter in the Hebrew alphabet, transliterated as s

SAMEKHS ▶ samekh

SAMEKS ▶ samek

SAMEL adj of brick, not sufficiently fired

SAMELY adj the same

SAMEN old Scots form of ▶ same

SAMES ▶ same

SAMEY adj monotonous

SAMFOO n style of casual dress worn by Chinese women, consisting of a waisted blouse and trousers

SAMFOOS ▶ samfoo

SAMFU ▶ samfoo

SAMFUS ▶ samfu

SAMIEL same as ▶ simoom

SAMIELS ▶ samiel

SAMIER ▶ samey

SAMIEST ▶ samey

SAMISEN n Japanese plucked stringed instrument with a long neck, an unfretted fingerboard, and a rectangular soundbox

SAMITE n heavy fabric of silk, often woven with gold or silver threads, used in the Middle Ages for clothing

SAMITES ▶ samite

SAMITHI same as ▶ samiti

SAMITI n (in India) an association, esp one formed to organize political activity

SAMITIS ▶ samiti

SAMLET n young salmon

SAMLETS ▶ samlet

SAMLOR n motor vehicle in Thailand

SAMLORS ▶ samlor

SAMMED ▶ sam

SAMMIES ▶ sammy

SAMMING ▶ sam

SAMMY n (in South Africa) an Indian fruit and vegetable vendor who goes from house to house

SAMOSA n (in Indian cookery) a small fried triangular spiced meat or vegetable pasty

SAMOSAS ▶ samosa

SAMOVAR n Russian tea urn

SAMOYED n Siberian breed of dog of the spitz type, having a dense white or cream coat with a distinct ruff, and a tightly curled tail

SAMP n crushed maize used for porridge

SAMPAN n small boat with oars used in China

SAMPANS ▶ sampan

SAMPI n old Greek number character

SAMPIRE n samphire

SAMPIS ▶ sampi

SAMPLE n part taken as representative of a whole ▷ vb take and test a sample of

SAMPLED ▶ sample

SAMPLER n piece of embroidery showing the embroiderer's skill

SAMPLES ▶ sample

SAMPS ▶ samp

SAMS ▶ sam

SAMSARA n endless cycle of birth, death, and rebirth

SAMSHOO n Chinese alcoholic drink

SAMSHU n alcoholic drink from China that is made from fermented rice and resembles sake

SAMSHUS ▶ samshu

SAMURAI n member of an ancient Japanese warrior caste

SAN n sanatorium

SANCAI n glaze in Chinese pottery

SANCAIS ▶ sancai

SANCHO n African stringed instrument

SANCHOS ▶ sancho

SANCTA ▶ sanctum

SANCTUM n sacred place

SAND n substance consisting of small grains of rock, esp on a beach or in a desert ▷ vb smooth with sandpaper

SANDAL n light shoe consisting of a sole attached by straps ▷ vb put sandals on

SANDALS ▶ sandal

SANDBAG n bag filled with sand, used as protection against gunfire or flood water ▷ vb protect with sandbags

SANDBAR n ridge of sand in a river or sea, often exposed at low tide

SANDBOX n container on a railway locomotive from which sand is released onto the rails to assist the traction

SANDBOY n as in happy as a sandboy very happy or high-spirited

SANDBUR n variety of wild grass

SANDDAB n type of small Pacific flatfish

SANDED ▶ sand

SANDEK n man who holds a baby being circumcised

SANDEKS ▶ sandek

SANDER n power tool for smoothing surfaces

SANDERS ▶ sander

SANDFLY n any of various small mothlike dipterous flies: the bloodsucking females transmit diseases including leishmaniasis

SANDHI n modification of the form or sound of a word under the influence of an adjacent word

SANDHIS ▸ **sandhi**

SANDHOG n person who works in underground or underwater construction projects

SANDIER ▸ **sandy**

SANDING ▸ **sand**

SANDLOT n area of vacant ground used by children for playing baseball and other games

SANDMAN n (in folklore) a magical person supposed to put children to sleep by sprinkling sand in their eyes

SANDMEN ▸ **sandman**

SANDPIT n shallow pit or container holding sand for children to play in

SANDS ▸ **sand**

SANDY adj covered with sand

SANE adj of sound mind ▸ vb heal

SANED ▸ **sane**

SANELY ▸ **sane**

SANER ▸ **sane**

SANES ▸ **sane**

SANEST ▸ **sane**

SANG Scots word for ▸ **song**

SANGA n Ethiopian ox

SANGAR n breastwork of stone or sods

SANGARS ▸ **sangar**

SANGAS ▸ **sanga**

SANGEET n Indian pre-wedding celebration

SANGER n sandwich

SANGERS ▸ **sanger**

SANGH n Indian union or association

SANGHA n Buddhist monastic order or community

SANGHAS ▸ **sangha**

SANGHAT n fellowship or assembly, esp a local Sikh community or congregation

SANGHS ▸ **sangh**

SANGO same as ▸ **sanger**

SANGOMA n witch doctor or herbalist

SANGOS ▸ **sango**

SANGRIA n Spanish drink of red wine and fruit

SANGS ▸ **sang**

SANICLE n type of plant

with clusters of small white flowers and oval fruits with hooked bristles

SANIES n thin greenish foul-smelling discharge from a wound, etc, containing pus and blood

SANIFY vb make healthy

SANING ▸ **sane**

SANIOUS ▸ **sanies**

SANITY n state of having a normal healthy mind

SANJAK n (in the Turkish Empire) a subdivision of a vilayet

SANJAKS ▸ **sanjak**

SANK ▸ **sink**

SANKO n African stringed instrument

SANKOS ▸ **sanko**

SANNIE Scots word for ▸ **sandshoe**

SANNIES ▸ **sannie**

SANNOP n Native American married man

SANNOPS ▸ **sannop**

SANNUP n Native American married man

SANNUPS ▸ **sannup**

SANPAN n sampan

SANPANS ▸ **sanpan**

SANPRO n sanitary-protection products, collectively

SANPROS ▸ **sanpro**

SANS archaic word for ▸ **without**

SANSA n African musical instrument

SANSAR n name of a wind that blows in Iran

SANSARS ▸ **sansar**

SANSAS ▸ **sansa**

SANSEI n American whose parents were Japanese immigrants

SANSEIS ▸ **sansei**

SANT n devout person in India

SANTAL n sandalwood

SANTALS ▸ **santal**

SANTERA n priestess of santeria

SANTERO n priest of santeria

SANTIMI ▸ **santims**

SANTIMS n money unit in Latvia

SANTIMU same as ▸ **santims**

SANTIR n Middle Eastern stringed instrument

SANTIRS ▸ **santir**

SANTO n saint or representation of one

SANTOL n fruit from Southeast Asia

SANTOLS ▸ **santol**

SANTON n French figurine

SANTONS ▸ **santon**

SANTOOR same as ▸ **santir**

SANTOS ▸ **santo**

SANTOUR n Middle Eastern stringed instrument

SANTS ▸ **sant**

SANTUR n Middle Eastern stringed instrument

SANTURS ▸ **santur**

SANYASI same as ▸ **sannyasi**

SAOLA n small, very rare bovine mammal of Vietnam and Laos

SAOLAS ▸ **saola**

SAOUARI n tropical American tree

SAP n moisture that circulates in plants ▸ vb undermine

SAPAJOU n capuchin monkey

SAPAN n tropical tree

SAPANS ▸ **sapan**

SAPEGO n skin disease

SAPELE n type of W African tree

SAPELES ▸ **sapele**

SAPFUL adj full of sap

SAPHEAD n simpleton, idiot, or fool

SAPHENA n either of two large superficial veins of the legs

SAPID adj having a pleasant taste

SAPIENS adj relating to or like modern human beings

SAPIENT adj wise, shrewd ▸ n wise person

SAPLESS ▸ **sap**

SAPLING n young tree

SAPONIN n any of a group of plant glycosides

SAPOR n quality in a substance that is perceived by the sense of taste

SAPORS ▸ **sapor**

SAPOTA same as ▸ **sapodilla**

SAPOTAS ▸ **sapota**

SAPOTE n Central American tree

SAPOTES ▸ **sapote**

SAPOUR same as ▸ **sapor**

SAPOURS ▸ **sapour**

SAPPAN n tropical tree

SAPPANS ▸ **sappan**

S

SAPPED ▸ sap

SAPPER n soldier in an engineering unit

SAPPERS ▸ sapper

SAPPHIC adj lesbian ▷ n verse written in a particular form

SAPPIER ▸ sappy

SAPPILY ▸ sappy

SAPPING ▸ sap

SAPPLE vb Scots word meaning wash in water

SAPPLED ▸ sapple

SAPPLES ▸ sapple

SAPPY adj (of plants) full of sap

SAPROBE n organism that lives on decaying organisms

SAPS ▸ sap

SAPSAGO n hard greenish Swiss cheese made with sour skimmed milk and coloured and flavoured with clover

SAPWOOD n soft wood, just beneath the bark in tree trunks, that consists of living tissue

SAR n marine fish ▷ vb Scots word meaning savour

SARAFAN n Russian woman's cloak

SARAN n any one of a class of thermoplastic resins

SARANGI n stringed instrument of India played with a bow

SARANS ▸ saran

SARAPE n serape

SARAPES ▸ sarape

SARCASM n (use of) bitter or wounding ironic language

SARCINA n type of bacterium

SARCODE n material making up living cell

SARCOID adj of, relating to, or resembling flesh ▷ n tumour resembling a sarcoma

SARCOMA n malignant tumour beginning in connective tissue

SARCOUS adj (of tissue) muscular or fleshy

SARD n orange, red, or brown variety of chalcedony, used as a gemstone

SARDANA n Catalan dance

SARDAR n title used before the name of Sikh men

SARDARS ▸ sardar

SARDEL n small fish

SARDELS ▸ sardel

SARDINE n small fish of the herring family, usu preserved tightly packed in tins ▷ vb cram together

SARDIUS same as ▸ sard

SARDS ▸ sard

SARED ▸ sar

SAREE same as ▸ sari

SAREES ▸ saree

SARGE n sergeant

SARGES ▸ sarge

SARGO same as ▸ sargus

SARGOS same as ▸ sargus

SARGUS n species of sea fish

SARI n long piece of cloth draped around the body and over one shoulder, worn by Hindu women

SARIN n chemical used in warfare as a lethal nerve gas producing asphyxia

SARING ▸ sar

SARINS ▸ sarin

SARIS ▸ sari

SARK n shirt or (formerly) chemise

SARKIER ▸ sarky

SARKILY ▸ sarky

SARKING n flat planking supporting the roof cladding of a building

SARKS ▸ sark

SARKY adj sarcastic

SARMENT n thin twig

SARMIE n sandwich

SARMIES ▸ sarmie

SARNEY n sandwich

SARNEYS ▸ sarney

SARNIE n sandwich

SARNIES ▸ sarnie

SAROD n Indian stringed musical instrument that may be played with a bow or plucked

SARODE n Indian stringed instrument

SARODES ▸ sarode

SARODS ▸ sarod

SARONG n long piece of cloth tucked around the waist or under the armpits, worn esp in Malaysia

SARONGS ▸ sarong

SARONIC ▸ saros

SAROS n cycle of about 18 years 11 days in which eclipses of the sun and moon occur in the same sequence

SAROSES ▸ saros

SARS ▸ sar

SARSAR same as ▸ sansar

SARSARS ▸ sarsar

SARSDEN n sarsen

SARSEN n boulder of silicified sandstone found in large numbers in S England

SARSENS ▸ sarsen

SARSNET n type of silk

SARTOR humorous or literary word for ▸ tailor

SARTORS ▸ sartor

SARUS n Indian bird of crane family

SARUSES ▸ sarus

SASER n device for amplifying ultrasound, working on a similar principle to a laser

SASERS ▸ saser

SASH n decorative strip of cloth worn round the waist or over one shoulder ▷ vb furnish with a sash, sashes, or sash windows

SASHAY vb move or walk in a casual or showy manner

SASHAYS ▸ sashay

SASHED ▸ sash

SASHES ▸ sash

SASHIMI n Japanese dish of thin fillets of raw fish

SASHING ▸ sash

SASIN another name for ▸ blackbuck

SASINE n granting of legal possession of feudal property

SASINES ▸ sasine

SASINS ▸ sasin

SASS n insolent or impudent talk or behaviour ▷ vb talk or answer back in such a way

SASSABY n African antelope of grasslands and semideserts

SASSE n old word meaning canal lock

SASSED ▸ sass

SASSES ▸ sass

SASSIER ▸ sassy

SASSIES ▸ sassy

SASSILY ▸ sassy

SASSING ▸ sass

SASSY adj insolent, impertinent ▷ n W African leguminous tree with poisonous bark

SASTRA same as ▸ shastra

SASTRAS ▸ sastra

SAT ▸ sit

SATAI same as ▸ satay

SATAIS ▸ satai

SATANG n monetary unit of Thailand worth one hundredth of a baht

SATANGS ▸ satang

SATANIC adj of Satan

SATARA n type of cloth

SATARAS ▸ satara

SATAY n Indonesian and Malaysian dish consisting of pieces of chicken, pork, etc, grilled on skewers and served with peanut sauce

SATAYS ▸ satay

SATCHEL n bag, usu with a shoulder strap, for carrying books

SATE vb satisfy (a desire or appetite) fully

SATED ▸ sate

SATEEN n glossy linen or cotton fabric, woven in such a way that it resembles satin

SATEENS ▸ sateen

SATEM adj denoting or belonging to a particular group of Indo-European languages

SATES ▸ sate

SATI n Indian widow suicide

SATIATE vb provide with more than enough, so as to disgust

SATIETY n feeling of having had too much

SATIN n silky fabric with a glossy surface on one side ▷ adj like satin in texture ▷ vb cover with satin

SATINED ▸ satin

SATINET n thin or imitation satin

SATING ▸ sate

SATINS ▸ satin

SATINY ▸ satin

SATIRE n use of ridicule to expose vice or folly

SATIRES ▸ satire

SATIRIC same as ▸ satirical

SATIS ▸ sati

SATISFY vb please, content

SATIVE adj old word meaning cultivated

SATORI n state of sudden indescribable intuitive enlightenment

SATORIS ▸ satori

SATRAP n (in ancient Persia) a provincial governor or subordinate ruler

SATRAPS ▸ satrap

SATRAPY n province, office,

or period of rule of a satrap

SATSUMA n kind of small orange

SATYR n woodland god, part man, part goat

SATYRA n female satyr

SATYRAL n mythical beast in heraldry

SATYRAS ▸ satyra

SATYRIC ▸ satyr

SATYRID n butterfly with typically brown or dark wings with paler markings

SATYRS ▸ satyr

SAU archaic past tense of ▸ see

SAUBA n South American ant

SAUBAS ▸ sauba

SAUCE n liquid added to food to enhance flavour ▷ vb prepare (food) with sauce

SAUCED ▸ sauce

SAUCER n small round dish put under a cup

SAUCERS ▸ saucer

SAUCES ▸ sauce

SAUCH n sallow or willow

SAUCHS ▸ sauch

SAUCIER n chef who makes sauces

SAUCILY ▸ saucy

SAUCING ▸ sauce

SAUCY adj impudent

SAUGER n small North American pikeperch

SAUGERS ▸ sauger

SAUGH same as ▸ sauch

SAUGHS ▸ saugh

SAUGHY adj Scots word meaning made of willow

SAUL Scots word for ▸ soul

SAULGE n old word for sage plant

SAULGES ▸ saulge

SAULIE n Scots word meaning professional mourner

SAULIES ▸ saulie

SAULS ▸ saul

SAULT n waterfall in Canada

SAULTS ▸ sault

SAUNA n Finnish-style steam bath ▷ vb have a sauna

SAUNAED ▸ sauna

SAUNAS ▸ sauna

SAUNT Scots form of ▸ saint

SAUNTED ▸ saunt

SAUNTER vb walk in a leisurely manner, stroll ▷ n leisurely walk

SAUNTS ▸ saunt

SAUREL n type of mackerel

SAURELS ▸ saurel

SAURIAN n lizard

SAURIES ▸ saury

SAUROID adj like a lizard

SAURY n type of fish of tropical and temperate seas, having an elongated body and long toothed jaws

SAUSAGE n minced meat in an edible tube-shaped skin

SAUT Scots word for ▸ salt

SAUTE vb fry quickly in a little fat ▷ n dish of sautéed food ▷ adj sautéed until lightly brown

SAUTED ▸ saut

SAUTEED ▸ saute

SAUTES ▸ saute

SAUTING ▸ saut

SAUTOIR n long necklace or pendant

SAUTS ▸ saut

SAV short for ▸ saveloy

SAVABLE ▸ save

SAVAGE adj wild, untamed ▷ n uncivilized person ▷ vb attack ferociously

SAVAGED ▸ savage

SAVAGER ▸ savage

SAVAGES ▸ savage

SAVANNA n open grasslands, usually with scattered bushes or trees, characteristic of much of tropical Africa

SAVANT n learned person

SAVANTE ▸ savant

SAVANTS ▸ savant

SAVARIN n type of cake

SAVATE n form of boxing in which blows may be delivered with the feet as well as the hands

SAVATES ▸ savate

SAVE vb rescue or preserve from harm, protect ▷ n act of preventing a goal ▷ prep except

SAVED ▸ save

SAVELOY n spicy smoked sausage

SAVER ▸ save

SAVERS ▸ save

SAVES ▸ save

SAVEY vb understand

SAVEYED ▸ savey

SAVEYS ▸ savey

SAVIN n small spreading juniper bush of Europe, N Asia, and North America

SAVINE same as ▸ savin

S

SAVINES ▶ savine

SAVING n economy ▷ prep except ▷ adj tending to save or preserve

SAVINGS ▶ saving

SAVINS ▶ savin

SAVIOR same as ▶ saviour

SAVIORS ▶ savior

SAVIOUR n person who rescues another

SAVIOURS ▶ saviour

SAVOR same as ▶ savour

SAVORED ▶ savor

SAVORER ▶ savor

SAVORS ▶ savor

SAVORY same as ▶ savoury

SAVOUR vb enjoy, relish ▷ n characteristic taste or odour

SAVOURS ▶ savour

SAVOURY adj salty or spicy ▷ n savoury dish served before or after a meal

SAVOY n variety of cabbage

SAVOYS ▶ savoy

SAVS ▶ sav

SAVVEY vb understand

SAVVEYS ▶ savvey

SAVVIED ▶ savvy

SAVVIER ▶ savvy

SAVVIES ▶ savvy

SAVVILY ▶ savvy

SAVVY vb understand ▷ n understanding, intelligence ▷ adj shrewd

SAW n hand tool for cutting wood and metal ▷ vb cut with a saw

SAWAH n paddyfield

SAWAHS ▶ sawah

SAWBILL n type of hummingbird

SAWBUCK n sawhorse, esp one having an X-shaped supporting structure

SAWDER n flattery ▷ vb flatter

SAWDERS ▶ sawder

SAWDUST n fine wood fragments made in sawing ▷ vb cover with sawdust

SAWED ▶ saw

SAWER ▶ saw

SAWERS ▶ saw

SAWFISH n fish with a long toothed snout

SAWFLY n any of various hymenopterous insects

SAWING ▶ saw

SAWINGS ▶ saw

SAWLIKE ▶ saw

SAWLOG n log suitable for sawing

SAWLOGS ▶ sawlog

SAWMILL n mill where timber is sawn into planks

SAWN past participle of ▶ saw

SAWPIT n pit above which a log is sawn into planks

SAWPITS ▶ sawpit

SAWS ▶ saw

SAWYER n person who saws timber for a living

SAWYERS ▶ sawyer

SAX same as ▶ saxophone

SAXAUL n Asian tree

SAXAULS ▶ saxaul

SAXE adj as in saxe blue light greyish-blue colour

SAXES ▶ sax

SAXHORN n valved brass instrument used chiefly in brass and military bands

SAXONY n fine 3-ply yarn used for knitting and weaving

SAXTUBA n bass saxhorn

SAY vb speak or utter ▷ n right or chance to speak

SAYABLE ▶ say

SAYED same as ▶ sayyid

SAYEDS ▶ sayed

SAYER ▶ say

SAYERS ▶ say

SAYEST ▶ say

SAYID same as ▶ sayyid

SAYIDS ▶ sayid

SAYING ▶ say

SAYINGS ▶ say

SAYNE ▶ say

SAYON n type of tunic

SAYONS ▶ sayon

SAYS ▶ say

SAYST ▶ say

SAYYID n Muslim claiming descent from Mohammed's grandson Husain

SAYYIDS ▶ sayyid

SAZ n Middle Eastern stringed instrument

> This musical instrument is one of the most frequently played Z words.

SAZERAC n mixed drink of whisky, Pernod, syrup, bitters, and lemon

SAZES ▶ saz

SAZHEN n Russian measure of length

SAZHENS ▶ sazhen

SAZZES ▶ saz

SBIRRI ▶ sbirro

SBIRRO n Italian police officer

SCAB n crust formed over a wound ▷ vb become covered with a scab

SCABBED ▶ scab

SCABBLE vb shape (stone) roughly

SCABBY adj covered with scabs

SCABIES n itchy skin disease

SCABRID adj having a rough or scaly surface

SCABS ▶ scab

SCAD n any of various carangid fishes

SCADS pl n large amount or number

SCAFF n Scots word meaning food

SCAFFIE n Scots word meaning street cleaner

SCAFFS ▶ scaff

SCAG n tear in a garment or piece of cloth ▷ vb make a tear in (cloth)

SCAGGED ▶ scag

SCAGLIA n type of limestone

SCAGS ▶ scag

SCAIL vb Scots word meaning disperse

SCAILED ▶ scail

SCAILS ▶ scail

SCAITH vb old word meaning injure

SCAITHS ▶ scaith

SCALA n passage inside the cochlea

SCALADE short for > escalade

SCALADO same as ▶ scalade

SCALAE ▶ scala

SCALAGE n percentage deducted from the price of goods liable to shrink or leak

SCALAR adj (variable quantity) having magnitude but no direction ▷ n quantity, such as time or temperature, that has magnitude but not direction

SCALARE another name for > angelfish

SCALARS ▶ scalar

SCALD same as ▶ skald

SCALDED ▶ scald

SCALDER ▶ scald

SCALDIC ▶ skald

SCALDS ▶ skald

SCALE n one of the thin overlapping plates covering

fishes and reptiles ▷ *vb* remove scales from

SCALED ▷ **scale**

SCALENE *adj* (of a triangle) with three unequal sides

SCALENI > **scalenus**

SCALER *n* person or thing that scales

SCALERS ▷ **scaler**

SCALES ▷ **scale**

SCALEUP *n* increase

SCALIER ▷ **scaly**

SCALING > **scale** *vb*

SCALL *n* disease of the scalp characterized by itching and scab formation

SCALLED ▷ **scall**

SCALLOP *n* edible shellfish with two fan-shaped shells ▷ *vb* decorate (an edge) with scallops

SCALLS ▷ **scall**

SCALLY *n* rascal

SCALP *n* skin and hair on top of the head ▷ *vb* cut off the scalp of

SCALPED ▷ **scalp**

SCALPEL *n* small surgical knife

SCALPER ▷ **scalp**

SCALPS ▷ **scalp**

SCALY *adj* resembling or covered in scales

SCAM *n* dishonest scheme ▷ *vb* swindle (someone) by means of a trick

SCAMBLE *vb* scramble

SCAMEL *n* Shakespearian word of uncertain meaning

SCAMELS ▷ **scamel**

SCAMMED ▷ **scam**

SCAMMER *n* person who perpetrates a scam

SCAMP *n* mischievous child ▷ *vb* perform without care

SCAMPED ▷ **scamp**

SCAMPER *vb* run about hurriedly or in play ▷ *n* scampering

SCAMPI *pl n* large prawns

SCAMPIS ▷ **scampi**

SCAMPS ▷ **scamp**

SCAMS ▷ **scam**

SCAMTO *n* argot of urban South African Blacks

SCAMTOS ▷ **scamto**

SCAN *vb* scrutinize carefully ▷ *n* scanning

SCAND ▷ **scan**

SCANDAL *n* disgraceful action or event ▷ *vb* disgrace

SCANDIA *n* scandium oxide

SCANDIC *adj* of or containing scandium

SCANNED ▷ **scan**

SCANNER *n* electronic device used for scanning

SCANS ▷ **scan**

SCANT *adj* barely sufficient, meagre ▷ *vb* limit in size or quantity ▷ *adv* scarcely

SCANTED ▷ **scant**

SCANTER ▷ **scant**

SCANTLE *vb* stint

SCANTLY ▷ **scant**

SCANTS ▷ **scant**

SCANTY *adj* barely sufficient or not sufficient

SCAPA *same as* ▷ **scarper**

SCAPAED ▷ **scapa**

SCAPAS ▷ **scapa**

SCAPE *n* leafless stalk in plants that arises from a rosette of leaves and bears one or more flowers ▷ *vb* archaic word for escape

SCAPED ▷ **scape**

SCAPES ▷ **scape**

SCAPI ▷ **scapus**

SCAPING ▷ **scape**

SCAPOSE ▷ **scape**

SCAPPLE *vb* shape roughly

SCAPULA *n* shoulder blade

SCAPUS *n* flower stalk

SCAR *n* mark left by a healed wound ▷ *vb* mark or become marked with a scar

SCARAB *n* sacred beetle of ancient Egypt

SCARABS ▷ **scarab**

SCARCE *adj* insufficient to meet demand

SCARCER ▷ **scarce**

SCARE *vb* frighten or be frightened ▷ *n* fright, sudden panic ▷ *adj* causing (needless) fear or alarm

SCARED ▷ **scare**

SCARER ▷ **scare**

SCARERS ▷ **scare**

SCARES ▷ **scare**

SCAREY *adj* frightening

SCARF *n* piece of material worn round the neck, head, or shoulders ▷ *vb* join in this way

SCARFED ▷ **scarf**

SCARFER ▷ **scarf**

SCARFS ▷ **scarf**

SCARIER ▷ **scary**

SCARIFY *vb* scratch or cut slightly all over

SCARILY ▷ **scary**

SCARING ▷ **scare**

SCARLET *n* brilliant red

▷ *adj* bright red ▷ *vb* make scarlet

SCARP *n* steep slope ▷ *vb* wear or cut so as to form a steep slope

SCARPA *vb* run away

SCARPAS ▷ **scarpa**

SCARPED ▷ **scarp**

SCARPER *vb* run away ▷ *n* hasty departure

SCARPH *vb* join with scarf joint

SCARPHS ▷ **scarph**

SCARPS ▷ **scarp**

SCARRE *n* Shakespearian word of unknown meaning

SCARRED ▷ **scar**

SCARRES ▷ **scarre**

SCARRY ▷ **scar**

SCARS ▷ **scar**

SCART *vb* scratch or scrape ▷ *n* scratch or scrape

SCARTED ▷ **scart**

SCARTH *Scots word for* > **cormorant**

SCARTHS ▷ **scarth**

SCARTS ▷ **scart**

SCARVES ▷ **scarf**

SCARY *adj* frightening

SCAT *vb* go away ▷ *n* jazz singing using improvised vocal sounds instead of words

SCATCH *same as* ▷ **stilt**

SCATH *vb* old word meaning injure

SCATHE *vb* attack with severe criticism ▷ *n* harm

SCATHED ▷ **scathe**

SCATHES ▷ **scathe**

SCATHS ▷ **scath**

SCATOLE *n* substance found in coal

SCATS ▷ **scat**

SCATT *n* old word meaning tax ▷ *vb* tax

SCATTED ▷ **scat**

SCATTER *vb* throw about in various directions ▷ *n* scattering

SCATTS ▷ **scatt**

SCATTY *adj* empty-headed

SCAUD *Scots word for* ▷ **scald**

SCAUDED ▷ **scaud**

SCAUDS ▷ **scaud**

SCAUP *same as* ▷ **scalp**

SCAUPED ▷ **scaup**

SCAUPER *same as* ▷ **scorper**

SCAUPS ▷ **scaup**

SCAUR *same as* ▷ **scar**

SCAURED ▷ **scaur**

SCAURS ▷ **scaur**

S

SCAURY *n* young seagull

SCAVAGE *n* old word meaning toll

SCAW *n* headland

SCAWS ▸ scaw

SCAZON *n* metre in poetry

SCAZONS ▸ scazon

SCEAT *n* Anglo-Saxon coin

SCEATT *n* Anglo-Saxon coin

SCEDULE *old spelling of* > schedule

SCENA *n* scene in an opera, usually longer than a single aria

SCENARY *n* scenery

SCENAS ▸ scena

SCEND *vb* (of a vessel) to surge upwards in a heavy sea ▷ *n* upward heaving of a vessel pitching

SCENDED ▸ scend

SCENDS ▸ scend

SCENE *n* place of action of a real or imaginary event ▷ *vb* set in a scene

SCENED ▸ scene

SCENERY *n* natural features of a landscape

SCENES ▸ scene

SCENIC *adj* picturesque ▷ *n* something scenic

SCENICS ▸ scenic

SCENING ▸ scene

SCENT *n* pleasant smell ▷ *vb* detect by smell

SCENTED ▸ scent

SCENTS ▸ scent

SCEPSIS *n* doubt

SCEPTER *same as* ▸ sceptre

SCEPTIC *n* person who habitually doubts generally accepted beliefs ▷ *adj* of or relating to sceptics

SCEPTRE *n* ornamental rod symbolizing royal power ▷ *vb* invest with authority

SCEPTRY *adj* having sceptre

SCERNE *vb* old word meaning discern

SCERNED ▸ scerne

SCERNES ▸ scerne

SCHANSE *n* stones heaped to shelter soldier in battle

SCHANZE *same as* **schanse**

SCHAPPE *n* yarn or fabric made from waste silk

SCHAV *n* Polish soup

SCHAVS ▸ schav

SCHELLY *n* freshwater whitefish of the English Lake District

SCHELM *n* South African word meaning rascal

SCHELMS ▸ schelm

SCHEMA *n* overall plan or diagram

SCHEMAS ▸ schema

SCHEME *n* systematic plan ▷ *vb* plan in an underhand manner

SCHEMED ▸ scheme

SCHEMER ▸ scheme

SCHEMES ▸ scheme

SCHERZI ▸ scherzo

SCHERZO *n* brisk lively piece of music

SCHISM *n* (group resulting from) division in an organization

SCHISMA *n* musical term

SCHISMS ▸ schism

SCHIST *n* crystalline rock which splits into layers

SCHISTS ▸ schist

SCHLEP *vb* drag or lug (oneself or an object) with difficulty ▷ *n* stupid or clumsy person

SCHLEPP *vb* schlep

SCHLEPS ▸ schlep

SCHLICH *n* finely crushed ore

SCHLOCK *n* goods or produce of cheap or inferior quality ▷ *adj* cheap, inferior, or trashy

SCHLOSS *n* castle

SCHLUB *n* coarse or contemptible person

SCHLUBS ▸ schlub

SCHLUMP *vb* move in lazy way

SCHMALZ *same as* > schmaltz

SCHMEAR *n* situation, matter, or affair ▷ *vb* spread or smear

SCHMECK *n* taste

SCHMEER *same as* ▸ schmear

SCHMELZ *n* ornamental glass

SCHMICK *adj* (in Australia) excellent, elegant, or stylish

SCHMO *n* dull, stupid, or boring person

SCHMOCK *n* stupid person

SCHMOE *n* stupid person

SCHMOES ▸ schmo

SCHMOOS *same as* > schmoose

SCHMOOZ *n* chat

SCHMOS ▸ schmo

SCHMUCK *n* stupid or contemptible person

SCHNAPS *same as* > schnapps

SCHNELL *adj* German word meaning quick

SCHNOOK *n* stupid or gullible person

SCHNORR *vb* beg

SCHNOZ *n* nose

SCHNOZZ *n* nose

SCHOLAR *n* learned person

SCHOLIA > scholium

SCHOOL *n* place where children are taught or instruction is given in a subject ▷ *vb* educate or train

SCHOOLE *n* old form of shoal

SCHOOLS ▸ school

SCHORL *n* type of black tourmaline

SCHORLS ▸ schorl

SCHOUT *n* council officer in Netherlands

SCHOUTS ▸ schout

SCHRIK *same as* ▸ skrik

SCHRIKS ▸ schrik

SCHROD *n* young cod

SCHRODS ▸ schrod

SCHTICK *same as* ▸ shtick

SCHTIK *n* schtick

SCHTIKS ▸ schtik

SCHTOOK *n* trouble

SCHTOOM *adj* silent

SCHTUCK *n* trouble

SCHTUM *adj* silent or dumb

SCHUIT *n* Dutch boat with flat bottom

SCHUITS ▸ schuit

SCHUL *same as* ▸ shul

SCHULN ▸ schul

SCHULS ▸ schul

SCHUSS *n* straight high-speed downhill run ▷ *vb* perform a schuss

SCHUYT *n* Dutch boat with flat bottom

SCHUYTS ▸ schuyt

SCHWA *n* central vowel representing the sound that occurs in unstressed syllables in English

SCHWAS ▸ schwa

SCIARID *n* small fly

SCIATIC *adj* of the hip ▷ *n* sciatic part of the body

SCIENCE *n* systematic study and knowledge of natural or physical phenomena

SCIENT *adj* old word meaning scientific

SCILLA *n* a plant with small bell-shaped flowers

SCILLAS ▸ scilla

SCIOLTO adv musical direction meaning freely

SCION n descendant or heir

SCIONS ▸ scion

SCIROC n hot Mediterranean wind

SCIROCS ▸ sciroc

SCIRRHI > scirrhus

SCISSEL n waste metal left over from sheet metal after discs have been punched out of it

SCISSIL n scissel

SCISSOR vb cut (an object) with scissors

SCIURID n squirrel or related rodent

SCLAFF vb cause (the club) to hit (the ground behind the ball) when making a stroke ▸ n sclaffing stroke or shot

SCLAFFS ▸ sclaff

SCLATE vb Scots word meaning slate

SCLATES ▸ sclate

SCLAVE n old form of slave

SCLAVES ▸ sclave

SCLERA n tough white substance that forms the outer covering of the eyeball

SCLERAE ▸ sclera

SCLERAL ▸ sclera

SCLERAS ▸ sclera

SCLERE n supporting anatomical structure, esp a sponge spicule

SCLERES ▸ sclere

SCLIFF n Scots word for small piece

SCLIFFS ▸ scliff

SCLIM vb Scots word meaning climb

SCLIMS ▸ sclim

SCODIER ▸ scody

SCODY adj unkempt

SCOFF vb express derision ▸ n mocking expression

SCOFFED ▸ scoff

SCOFFER ▸ scoff

SCOFFS ▸ scoff

SCOG vb shelter

SCOGGED ▸ scog

SCOGS ▸ scog

SCOLD vb find fault with, reprimand ▸ n person who scolds

SCOLDED ▸ scold

SCOLDER ▸ scold

SCOLDS ▸ scold

SCOLEX n headlike part of a tapeworm

SCOLIA ▸ scolion

SCOLION n ancient Greek drinking song

SCOLLOP same as ▸ scallop

SCONCE n bracket on a wall for holding candles or lights ▸ vb challenge (a fellow student) on the grounds of a social misdemeanour to drink a large quantity of beer without stopping

SCONCED ▸ sconce

SCONCES ▸ sconce

SCONE n small plain cake baked in an oven or on a griddle

SCONES ▸ scone

SCOOBY n clue; notion

SCOOCH vb compress one's body into smaller space

SCOOG vb shelter

SCOOGED ▸ scoog

SCOOGS ▸ scoog

SCOOP n shovel-like tool for ladling or hollowing out ▸ vb take up or hollow out with or as if with a scoop

SCOOPED ▸ scoop

SCOOPER ▸ scoop

SCOOPS ▸ scoop

SCOOSH vb squirt ▸ n squirt or rush of liquid

SCOOT vb leave or move quickly ▸ n act of scooting

SCOOTCH same as ▸ scooch

SCOOTED ▸ scoot

SCOOTER n child's vehicle propelled by pushing on the ground with one foot

SCOOTS ▸ scoot

SCOP n (in Anglo-Saxon England) a bard or minstrel

SCOPA n tuft of hairs on the abdomen or hind legs of bees, used for collecting pollen

SCOPAE ▸ scopa

SCOPATE adj having tuft

SCOPE n opportunity for using abilities ▸ vb look at or examine carefully

SCOPED ▸ scope

SCOPES ▸ scope

SCOPING ▸ scope

SCOPS ▸ scop

SCOPULA n small tuft of dense hairs on the legs and chelicerae of some spiders

SCORCH vb burn on the surface ▸ n slight burn

SCORE n points gained in a game or competition ▸ vb gain (points) in a game

SCORED ▸ score

SCORER ▸ score

SCORERS ▸ score

SCORES ▸ score

SCORIA n mass of solidified lava containing many cavities

SCORIAC ▸ scoria

SCORIAE ▸ scoria

SCORIFY vb remove (impurities) from metals by forming scoria

SCORING n act or practice of scoring

SCORN n open contempt ▸ vb despise

SCORNED ▸ scorn

SCORNER ▸ scorn

SCORNS ▸ scorn

SCORPER n kind of fine chisel with a square or curved tip

SCORSE vb exchange

SCORSED ▸ scorse

SCORSER ▸ scorse

SCORSES ▸ scorse

SCOT n payment or tax

SCOTCH vb put an end to ▸ n gash

SCOTER n type of sea duck

SCOTERS ▸ scoter

SCOTIA n deep concave moulding

SCOTIAS ▸ scotia

SCOTOMA n blind spot

SCOTOMY n dizziness

SCOTS ▸ scot

SCOTTIE n type of small sturdy terrier

SCOUG vb shelter

SCOUGED ▸ scoug

SCOUGS ▸ scoug

SCOUP vb Scots word meaning jump

SCOUPED ▸ scoup

SCOUPS ▸ scoup

SCOUR vb clean or polish by rubbing with something rough ▸ n scouring

SCOURED ▸ scour

SCOURER ▸ scour

SCOURGE n person or thing causing severe suffering ▸ vb cause severe suffering to

SCOURIE n young seagull

SCOURS ▸ scour

SCOURSE vb exchange

SCOUSE n stew from left-over meat

SCOUSER n inhabitant of Liverpool

SCOUSES ▸ scouse

SCOUT n person sent out to reconnoitre ▷ vb act as a scout

SCOUTED ▶ scout

SCOUTER ▶ scout

SCOUTH n Scots word meaning plenty of scope

SCOUTHS ▶ scouth

SCOUTS ▶ scout

SCOW n unpowered barge used for carrying freight ▷ vb transport by scow

SCOWDER vb Scots word meaning scorch

SCOWED ▶ scow

SCOWING ▶ scow

SCOWL n, vb (have an) angry or sullen expression

SCOWLED ▶ scowl

SCOWLER n person who scowls

SCOWLS ▶ scowl

SCOWP vb Scots word meaning jump

SCOWPED ▶ scowp

SCOWPS ▶ scowp

SCOWRER n old word meaning hooligan

SCOWRIE n young seagull

SCOWS ▶ scow

SCOWTH n Scots word meaning plenty of scope

SCOWTHS ▶ scowth

SCOZZA n rowdy person, esp one who drinks a lot of alcohol

SCOZZAS ▶ scozza

SCRAB vb scratch

SCRABS ▶ scrab

SCRAE Scots word for ▶ scree

SCRAES ▶ scrae

SCRAG n thin end of a neck of mutton ▷ vb wring the neck of

SCRAGGY adj thin, bony

SCRAGS ▶ scrag

SCRAICH vb Scots word meaning scream

SCRAIGH vb Scots word meaning scream

SCRAM vb go away quickly ▷ n emergency shutdown of a nuclear reactor

SCRAMB vb scratch with nails or claws

SCRAMBS ▶ scramb

SCRAMS ▶ scram

SCRAN n food

SCRANCH vb crunch

SCRANNY adj scrawny

SCRANS ▶ scran

SCRAP n small piece ▷ vb discard as useless

SCRAPE vb rub with something rough or sharp ▷ n act or sound of scraping

SCRAPED ▶ scrape

SCRAPER ▶ scrape

SCRAPES ▶ scrape

SCRAPIE n disease of sheep and goats

SCRAPPY adj fragmentary, disjointed

SCRAPS ▶ scrap

SCRAT vb scratch

SCRATCH vb mark or cut with claws, nails, or anything rough or sharp ▷ n wound, mark, or sound made by scratching ▷ adj put together at short notice

SCRATS ▶ scrat

SCRAUCH vb squawk

SCRAUGH vb squawk

SCRAW n sod from the surface of a peat bog or from a field

SCRAWL vb write carelessly or hastily ▷ n scribbled writing

SCRAWLS ▶ scrawl

SCRAWLY ▶ scrawl

SCRAWM vb dialect word meaning scratch

SCRAWMS ▶ scrawm

SCRAWNY adj thin and bony

SCRAWP vb scratch (the skin) to relieve itching

SCRAWPS ▶ scrawp

SCRAWS ▶ scraw

SCRAY n tern

SCRAYE n tern

SCRAYES ▶ scraye

SCRAYS ▶ scray

SCREAK vb screech or creak ▷ n screech or creak

SCREAKS ▶ screak

SCREAKY ▶ screak

SCREAM vb utter a piercing cry, esp of fear or pain ▷ n shrill piercing cry

SCREAMO n type of emo music featuring screaming vocals

SCREAMS ▶ scream

SCREE n slope of loose shifting stones

SCREECH n (utter) a shrill cry ▷ vb utter a shrill cry

SCREED n long tedious piece of writing ▷ vb rip

SCREEDS ▶ screed

SCREEN n surface of a television set, VDU, etc, on which an image is formed ▷ vb shelter or conceal with or as if with a screen

SCREENS ▶ screen

SCREES ▶ scree

SCREET vb shed tears ▷ n act or sound of crying

SCREETS ▶ screet

SCREEVE vb write

SCREICH same as ▶ screigh

SCREIGH Scots word for ▶ screech

SCREW n metal pin with a spiral ridge along its length, twisted into materials to fasten them together ▷ vb turn (a screw)

SCREWED adj fastened by a screw or screws

SCREWER ▶ screw

SCREWS ▶ screw

SCREWUP n something done badly

SCREWY adj crazy or eccentric

SCRIBAL ▶ scribe

SCRIBE n person who copies documents ▷ vb to score a line with a pointed instrument

SCRIBED ▶ scribe

SCRIBER n pointed steel tool used to score materials as a guide to cutting, etc

SCRIBES ▶ scribe

SCRIECH vb Scots word meaning screech

SCRIED ▶ scry

SCRIENE n old form of screen

SCRIES ▶ scry

SCRIEVE vb Scots word meaning write

SCRIKE vb old word meaning shriek

SCRIKED ▶ scrike

SCRIKES ▶ scrike

SCRIM n open-weave muslin or hessian fabric, used in upholstery, lining, building

SCRIMP vb be very economical

SCRIMPS ▶ scrimp

SCRIMPY ▶ scrimp

SCRIMS ▶ scrim

SCRINE n old form of shrine

SCRINES ▶ scrine

SCRIP n certificate representing a claim to stocks or shares

SCRIPS ▶ scrip

SCRIPT n text of a film, play,

or TV programme ▷ vb write a script for

SCRIPTS ▶ **script**

SCRITCH vb screech

SCRIVE Scots word for ▶ **write**

SCRIVED ▶ **scrive**

SCRIVES ▶ **scrive**

SCROBE n groove

SCROBES ▶ **scrobe**

SCROD n young cod or haddock, esp one split and prepared for cooking

SCRODS ▶ **scrod**

SCROG n Scots word meaning small tree

SCROGGY same as > **scroggie**

SCROGS ▶ **scrog**

SCROLL n roll of parchment or paper ▷ vb move (text) up or down on a VDU screen

SCROLLS ▶ **scroll**

SCROME vb crawl or climb, esp using the hands to aid movement

SCROMED ▶ **scrome**

SCROMES ▶ **scrome**

SCROOCH vb scratch (the skin) to relieve itching

SCROOGE same as ▶ **scrouge**

SCROOP vb emit a grating or creaking sound ▷ n such a sound

SCROOPS ▶ **scroop**

SCRORP n deep scratch or weal

SCRORPS ▶ **scrorp**

SCROTA ▶ **scrotum**

SCROTAL ▶ **scrotum**

SCROTUM n pouch of skin containing the testicles

SCROUGE vb crowd or press

SCROW n scroll

SCROWL vb old form of scroll

SCROWLE vb old form of scroll

SCROWLS ▶ **scrowl**

SCROWS ▶ **scrow**

SCROYLE n old word meaning wretch

SCRUB vb clean by rubbing, often with a hard brush and water ▷ n scrubbing ▷ adj stunted or inferior

SCRUBBY adj covered with scrub

SCRUBS ▶ **scrub**

SCRUFF same as ▶ **scum**

SCRUFFS ▶ **scruff**

SCRUFFY adj unkempt or shabby

SCRUM n restarting of play in which opposing packs of forwards push against each other to gain possession of the ball ▷ vb form a scrum

SCRUMMY adj delicious

SCRUMP vb steal (apples) from an orchard or garden

SCRUMPS ▶ **scrump**

SCRUMPY n rough dry cider

SCRUMS ▶ **scrum**

SCRUNCH vb crumple or crunch or be crumpled or crunched ▷ n act or sound of scrunching

SCRUNT n Scots word meaning stunted thing

SCRUNTS ▶ **scrunt**

SCRUNTY ▶ **scrunt**

SCRUPLE n doubt produced by one's conscience or morals ▷ vb have doubts on moral grounds

SCRUTO n trapdoor on stage

SCRUTOS ▶ **scruto**

SCRUZE vb old word meaning squeeze

SCRUZED ▶ **scruze**

SCRUZES ▶ **scruze**

SCRY vb divine, esp by crystal gazing

SCRYDE ▶ **scry**

SCRYER ▶ **scry**

SCRYERS ▶ **scry**

SCRYING ▶ **scry**

SCRYNE n old form of shrine

SCRYNES ▶ **scry**

SCUBA n apparatus used in skin diving, consisting of cylinders containing compressed air attached to a breathing apparatus ▷ vb dive using scuba equipment

SCUBAED ▶ **scuba**

SCUBAS ▶ **scuba**

SCUCHIN n old form of scutcheon

SCUD vb move along swiftly ▷ n act of scudding

SCUDDED ▶ **scud**

SCUDDER ▶ **scud**

SCUDDLE vb scuttle

SCUDI ▶ **scudo**

SCUDLER n Scots word meaning leader of festivities

SCUDO n any of several former Italian coins

SCUDS ▶ **scud**

SCUFF vb drag (the feet) while walking ▷ n mark caused by scuffing

SCUFFED ▶ **scuff**

SCUFFER n type of sandal

SCUFFLE vb fight in a disorderly manner ▷ n disorderly struggle

SCUFFS ▶ **scuff**

SCUFT n dialect word meaning nape of neck

SCUFTS ▶ **scuft**

SCUG vb shelter

SCUGGED ▶ **scug**

SCUGS ▶ **scug**

SCUL n old form of school

SCULCH n rubbish

SCULK vb old form of skulk

SCULKED ▶ **sculk**

SCULKER ▶ **sculk**

SCULKS ▶ **sculk**

SCULL n small oar ▷ vb row (a boat) using sculls

SCULLE n old form of school

SCULLED ▶ **scull**

SCULLER ▶ **scull**

SCULLES ▶ **sculle**

SCULLS ▶ **scull**

SCULP same as > **sculpture**

SCULPED ▶ **sculp**

SCULPIN n type of fish of the family which includes bullheads and sea scorpions

SCULPS ▶ **sculp**

SCULPT same as > **sculpture**

SCULPTS ▶ **sculpt**

SCULS ▶ **scul**

SCULTCH same as ▶ **sculch**

SCUM n impure or waste matter on the surface of a liquid ▷ vb remove scum from

SCUMBER vb old word meaning defecate

SCUMBLE vb soften or blend (an outline or colour) with a thin upper coat of opaque colour ▷ n upper layer of colour applied in this way

SCUMMED ▶ **scum**

SCUMMER ▶ **scum**

SCUMMY adj of, resembling, consisting of, or covered with scum

SCUMS ▶ **scum**

SCUNGE vb borrow ▷ n dirty or worthless person

SCUNGED ▶ **scunge**

SCUNGES ▶ **scunge**

SCUNGY adj sordid or dirty

SCUNNER vb feel aversion ▷ n strong aversion

SCUP n common sparid fish

S

of American coastal regions of the Atlantic

SCUPPER vb defeat or ruin ▷ n drain in the side of a ship

SCUPS ▶ scup

SCUR n small unattached growth of horn at the site of a normal horn in cattle

SCURF n flaky skin on the scalp

SCURFS ▶ scurf

SCURFY ▶ scurf

SCURRED ▶ scur

SCURRIL adj old word meaning vulgar

SCURRY vb move hastily ▷ n act or sound of scurrying

SCURS ▶ scur

SCURVY n disease caused by lack of vitamin C ▷ adj mean and despicable

SCUSE shortened form of ▶ excuse

SCUSED ▶ scuse

SCUSES ▶ scuse

SCUSING ▶ scuse

SCUT n short tail of the hare, rabbit, or deer

SCUTA ▶ scutum

SCUTAGE n payment sometimes exacted by a lord from his vassal in lieu of military service

SCUTAL ▶ scute

SCUTATE adj (of animals) having or covered with large bony or horny plates

SCUTCH vb separate the fibres from the woody part of (flax) by pounding ▷ n tool used for this

SCUTE n horny or chitinous plate that makes up part of the exoskeleton in armadillos, etc

SCUTES ▶ scute

SCUTS ▶ scut

SCUTTER informal word for ▶ scurry

SCUTTLE n fireside container for coal ▷ vb run with short quick steps

SCUTUM n middle of three plates into which the notum of an insect's thorax is divided

SCUZZ n dirt

SCUZZES ▶ scuzz

SCUZZY adj unkempt, dirty, or squalid

SCYBALA > scybalum

SCYE n Scots word meaning

sleeve-hole

SCYES ▶ scye

SCYPHI ▶ scyphus

SCYPHUS n ancient Greek two-handled drinking cup without a footed base

SCYTALE n coded message in ancient Sparta

SCYTHE n long-handled tool with a curved blade for cutting grass ▷ vb cut with a scythe

SCYTHED ▶ scythe

SCYTHER ▶ scythe

SCYTHES ▶ scythe

SDAINE vb old form of disdain

SDAINED ▶ sdaine

SDAINES ▶ sdaine

SDAYN vb old form of disdain

SDAYNED ▶ sdayn

SDAYNS ▶ sdayn

SDEIGN vb old form of disdain

SDEIGNE vb old form of disdain

SDEIGNS ▶ sdeign

SDEIN vb old form of disdain

SDEINED ▶ sdein

SDEINS ▶ sdein

SEA n mass of salt water covering three quarters of the earth's surface

SEABAG n canvas bag for holding a sailor's belongings

SEABAGS ▶ seabag

SEABANK n sea shore

SEABED n bottom of sea

SEABEDS ▶ seabed

SEABIRD n bird that lives on the sea

SEABOOT n sailor's waterproof boot

SEACOCK n valve in the hull of a vessel below the water line for admitting sea water or for pumping out bilge water

SEADOG another word for ▶ fogbow

SEADOGS ▶ seadog

SEAFOLK n people who sail sea

SEAFOOD n edible saltwater fish or shellfish

SEAFOWL n seabird

SEAGIRT adj surrounded by the sea

SEAGULL n gull

SEAHAWK n skua

SEAHOG n porpoise

SEAHOGS ▶ seahog

SEAKALE n European coastal plant

SEAL n piece of wax, lead, etc with a special design impressed upon it, attached to a letter or document as a mark of authentication ▷ vb close with or as if with a seal

SEALANT n any substance used for sealing

SEALCH Scots word for ▶ seal

SEALCHS ▶ sealch

SEALED adj (of a road) having a hard surface

SEALER n person or thing that seals

SEALERS ▶ sealer

SEALERY n occupation of hunting seals

SEALGH Scots word for ▶ seal

SEALGHS ▶ sealgh

SEALIFT vb transport by ship

SEALINE n company running regular sailings

SEALING ▶ seal

SEALS ▶ seal

SEALWAX n sealing wax

SEAM n line where two edges are joined, as by stitching ▷ vb mark with furrows or wrinkles

SEAMAID n mermaid

SEAMAN n sailor

SEAMARK n aid to navigation, such as a conspicuous object on a shore used as a guide

SEAME n old word meaning grease

SEAMED ▶ seam

SEAMEN ▶ seaman

SEAMER n fast bowler who makes the ball bounce on its seam so that it will change direction

SEAMERS ▶ seamer

SEAMES ▶ seame

SEAMIER ▶ seamy

SEAMING ▶ seam

SEAMS ▶ seam

SEAMSET n tool for flattening seams in metal

SEAMY adj sordid

SEAN vb fish with seine net

SEANCE n meeting at which spiritualists attempt to communicate with the dead

SEANCES ▶ seance

SEANED ▶ sean**

SEANING ▸ **sean**

SEANS ▸ **sean**

SEAPORT *n* town or city with a harbour for boats and ships

SEAR *vb* scorch, burn the surface of ▸ *n* mark caused by searing ▸ *adj* dried up

SEARAT *n* pirate

SEARATS ▸ **searat**

SEARCE *vb* sift

SEARCED ▸ **searce**

SEARCES ▸ **searce**

SEARCH *vb* examine closely in order to find something ▸ *n* searching

SEARE *adj* old word meaning dry and withered

SEARED ▸ **sear**

SEARER ▸ **sear**

SEAREST ▸ **sear**

SEARING ▸ **sear**

SEARS ▸ **sear**

SEAS ▸ **sea**

SEASE *vb* old form of seize

SEASED ▸ **sease**

SEASES ▸ **sease**

SEASICK *adj* suffering from nausea caused by the motion of a ship

SEASIDE *n* area, esp a holiday resort, on the coast

SEASING ▸ **sease**

SEASON *n* one of four divisions of the year, each of which has characteristic weather conditions ▸ *vb* flavour with salt, herbs, etc

SEASONS ▸ **season**

SEASURE *n* old form of seizure

SEAT *n* thing designed or used for sitting on ▸ *vb* cause to sit

SEATED ▸ **seat**

SEATER *n* person or thing that seats

SEATERS ▸ **seater**

SEATING *n* supply or arrangement of seats ▸ *adj* of or relating to the provision of places to sit

SEATS ▸ **seat**

SEAWALL *n* wall built to prevent encroachment or erosion by the sea

SEAWAN *n* shell beads, usually unstrung, used by certain North American Indians as money

SEAWANS ▸ **seawan**

SEAWANT *n* Native American name for silver coins

SEAWARD *same as* > **seawards**

SEAWARE *n* any of numerous large coarse seaweeds

SEAWAY *n* waterway giving access to an inland port, navigable by ocean-going ships

SEAWAYS ▸ **seaway**

SEAWEED *n* plant growing in the sea

SEAWIFE *n* variety of sea fish

SEAWORM *n* marine worm

SEAZE *vb* old form of seize

SEAZED ▸ **seaze**

SEAZES ▸ **seaze**

SEAZING ▸ **seaze**

SEBACIC *adj* derived from sebacic acid, a white crystalline acid

SEBASIC *same as* ▸ **sebacic**

SEBATE *n* salt of sebacic acid

SEBATES ▸ **sebate**

SEBIFIC *adj* producing fat

SEBUM *n* oily substance secreted by the sebaceous glands

SEBUMS ▸ **sebum**

SEBUNDY *n* irregular soldier in India

SEC *same as* ▸ **secant**

SECANT *n* (in trigonometry) the ratio of the length of the hypotenuse to the length of the adjacent side in a right-angled triangle

SECANTS ▸ **secant**

SECCO *n* wall painting done on dried plaster with tempera or pigments ground in limewater

SECCOS ▸ **secco**

SECEDE *vb* withdraw formally from a political alliance or federation

SECEDED ▸ **secede**

SECEDER ▸ **secede**

SECEDES ▸ **secede**

SECERN *vb* (of a gland or follicle) to secrete

SECERNS ▸ **secern**

SECESH *n* secessionist in US Civil War

SECH *n* hyperbolic secant

SECHS ▸ **sech**

SECKEL *same as* ▸ **seckle**

SECKELS ▸ **seckle**

SECKLE *n* type of pear

SECKLES ▸ **seckle**

SECLUDE *vb* keep (a person) from contact with others

SECO *adj* (of wine) dry

SECONAL *n* tradename for secobarbital

SECOND *adj* coming directly after the first ▸ *n* person or thing coming second ▸ *vb* express formal support for (a motion proposed in a meeting)

SECONDE *n* second of eight positions from which a parry or attack can be made in fencing

SECONDI ▸ **secondo**

SECONDO *n* left-hand part in a piano duet

SECONDS ▸ **second**

SECPAR *n* distance unit in astronomy

SECPARS ▸ **secpar**

SECRECY *n* state of being secret

SECRET *adj* kept from the knowledge of others ▸ *n* something kept secret

SECRETA *n* secretions

SECRETE *vb* (of an organ, gland, etc) produce and release (a substance)

SECRETS ▸ **secret**

SECS ▸ **sec**

SECT *n* often disparaging term for a subdivision of a religious or political group, esp one with extreme beliefs

SECTARY *n* member of a sect

SECTILE *adj* able to be cut smoothly

SECTION *n* part cut off ▸ *vb* cut or divide into sections

SECTOR *n* part or subdivision ▸ *vb* divide into sectors

SECTORS ▸ **sector**

SECTS ▸ **sect**

SECULAR *adj* worldly, as opposed to sacred ▸ *n* member of the secular clergy

SECULUM *n* age in astronomy

SECUND *adj* having or designating parts arranged on or turned to one side of the axis

SECURE *adj* free from danger ▸ *vb* obtain

SECURED ▸ **secure**

S

SECURER ▶ secure

SECURES ▶ secure

SED old spelling of ▶ said

SEDAN same as ▶ saloon

SEDANS ▶ sedan

SEDARIM ▶ seder

SEDATE adj calm and dignified ▷ vb give a sedative drug to

SEDATED ▶ sedate

SEDATER ▶ sedate

SEDATES ▶ sedate

SEDENT adj seated

SEDER n Jewish ceremonial meal held on the first night or first two nights of Passover

SEDERS ▶ seder

SEDES Latin word for ▶ seat

SEDGE n coarse grasslike plant growing on wet ground

SEDGED adj having sedge

SEDGES ▶ sedge

SEDGIER ▶ sedge

SEDGY ▶ sedge

SEDILE n seat for clergy in church

SEDILIA n group of three seats where the celebrant and ministers sit at certain points during High Mass

SEDUCE vb persuade into sexual intercourse

SEDUCED ▶ seduce

SEDUCER n person who entices, allures, or seduces

SEDUCES ▶ seduce

SEDUM n rock plant

SEDUMS ▶ sedum

SEE vb perceive with the eyes or mind ▷ n diocese of a bishop

SEEABLE ▶ see

SEED n mature fertilized grain of a plant ▷ vb sow with seed

SEEDBED n area of soil prepared for the growing of seedlings before they are transplanted

SEEDBOX n part of plant that contains seeds

SEEDED ▶ seed

SEEDER n person or thing that seeds

SEEDERS ▶ seeder

SEEDIER ▶ seedy

SEEDILY ▶ seedy

SEEDING ▶ seed

SEEDLIP n basket holding seeds to be sown

SEEDMAN n seller of seeds

SEEDMEN ▶ seedman

SEEDPOD n carpel enclosing the seeds of a flowering plant

SEEDS ▶ seed

SEEDY adj shabby

SEEING ▶ see

SEEINGS ▶ see

SEEK vb try to find or obtain

SEEKER ▶ seek

SEEKERS ▶ seek

SEEKING ▶ seek

SEEKS ▶ seek

SEEL vb sew up the eyelids of (a hawk or falcon) so as to render it quiet and tame

SEELD adj old word meaning rare

SEELED ▶ seel

SEELIE pl n good benevolent fairies

SEELIER ▶ seely

SEELING ▶ seel

SEELS ▶ seel

SEELY adj old word meaning happy

SEEM vb appear to be

SEEMED ▶ seem

SEEMER ▶ seem

SEEMERS ▶ seem

SEEMING adj apparent but not real ▷ n outward or false appearance

SEEMLY adj proper or fitting ▷ adv properly or decorously

SEEMS ▶ seem

SEEN ▶ see

SEEP vb trickle through slowly, ooze ▷ n small spring or place where water, oil, etc, has oozed through the ground

SEEPAGE n act or process of seeping

SEEPED ▶ seep

SEEPIER ▶ seepy

SEEPING ▶ seep

SEEPS ▶ seep

SEEPY adj tending to seep

SEER n person who sees

SEERESS ▶ seer

SEERS ▶ seer

SEES ▶ see

SEESAW n plank balanced in the middle so that two people seated on either end ride up and down alternately ▷ vb move up and down

SEESAWS ▶ seesaw

SEETHE vb be very agitated ▷ n act or state of seething

SEETHED ▶ seethe

SEETHER ▶ seethe

SEETHES ▶ seethe

SEEWING n suing

SEFER n scrolls of the Law

SEG n metal stud on shoe sole

SEGAR n cigar

SEGARS ▶ segar

SEGETAL adj (of weeds) growing amongst crops

SEGGAR n box in which pottery is baked

SEGGARS ▶ seggar

SEGHOL n pronunciation mark in Hebrew

SEGHOLS ▶ seghol

SEGMENT n one of several sections into which something may be divided ▷ vb divide into segments

SEGNI ▶ segno

SEGNO n sign at the beginning or end of a section directed to be repeated

SEGNOS ▶ segno

SEGO n American variety of lily

SEGOL same as ▶ seghol

SEGOLS ▶ segol

SEGOS ▶ sego

SEGS ▶ seg

SEGUE vb proceed from one section or piece of music to another without a break ▷ n practice or an instance of playing music in this way

SEGUED ▶ segue

SEGUES ▶ segue

SEHRI n meal eaten before sunrise by Muslims fasting during Ramadan

SEHRIS ▶ sehri

SEI n type of rorqual

SEICHE n periodic oscillation of the surface of an enclosed or semienclosed body of water

SEICHES ▶ seiche

SEIDEL n vessel for drinking beer

SEIDELS ▶ seidel

SEIF n long ridge of blown sand in a desert

SEIFS ▶ seif

SEIK Scots word for ▶ sick

SEIKER ▶ seik

SEIKEST ▶ seik

SEIL vb dialect word meaning strain

SEILED ▶ seil

SEILING ▶ seil

SEILS ▶ seil

SEINE n large fishing net that hangs vertically from floats ▷ vb catch (fish) using this net

SEINED ▶ seine

SEINER ▶ seine

SEINERS ▶ seine

SEINES ▶ seine

SEINING ▶ seine

SEIR n fish of Indian seas

SEIRS ▶ seir

SEIS ▶ sei

SEISE vb put into legal possession of (property, etc)

SEISED ▶ seise

SEISER ▶ seise

SEISERS ▶ seise

SEISES ▶ seise

SEISIN n feudal possession of an estate in land

SEISING ▶ seise

SEISINS ▶ seisin

SEISM n earthquake

SEISMAL adj of earthquakes

SEISMIC adj relating to earthquakes

SEISMS ▶ seism

SEISOR n person who takes seisin

SEISORS ▶ seisor

SEISURE n act of seisin

SEITAN same as ▶ seiten

SEITANS ▶ seitan

SEITEN n gluten from wheat

SEITENS ▶ seiten

SEITIES ▶ seity

SEITY n selfhood

SEIZE vb take hold of forcibly or quickly

SEIZED ▶ seize

SEIZER ▶ seize

SEIZERS ▶ seize

SEIZES ▶ seize

SEIZIN same as ▶ seisin

SEIZING n binding used for holding together two ropes, two spars, etc, esp by lashing with a separate rope

SEIZINS ▶ seizin

SEIZOR n person who takes seisin

SEIZORS ▶ seizor

SEIZURE n sudden violent attack of an illness

SEJANT adj (of a beast) shown seated

SEJEANT same as ▶ sejant

SEKOS n holy place

SEKOSES ▶ sekos

SEKT n German sparkling wine

SEKTS ▶ sekt

SEL Scots word for ▶ self

SELAH n Hebrew word of unknown meaning occurring in the Old Testament psalms, and thought to be a musical direction

SELAHS ▶ selah

SELD adj old word meaning rare

SELDOM adv not often, rarely

SELE n old word meaning happiness

SELECT vb pick out or choose ▷ adj chosen in preference to others

SELECTA n disc jockey

SELECTS ▶ select

SELENIC adj of or containing selenium, esp in the hexavalent state

SELES ▶ sele

SELF n distinct individuality or identity of a person or thing ▷ pron myself, yourself, himself, or herself ▷ vb reproduce by oneself

SELFDOM n selfhood

SELFED ▶ self

SELFING ▶ self

SELFISH adj caring too much about oneself and not enough about others

SELFISM n emphasis on self

SELFIST ▶ selfism

SELFS ▶ self

SELKIE same as ▶ silkie

SELKIES ▶ selkie

SELL vb exchange (something) for money ▷ n manner of selling

SELLA n area of bone in body

SELLAE ▶ sella

SELLAS ▶ sella

SELLE n old word meaning seat

SELLER n person who sells

SELLERS ▶ seller

SELLES ▶ selle

SELLING n the act of providing (e.g. goods or services) to customers in exchange for money

SELLOFF n act of selling cheaply

SELLOUT n performance of a show etc for which all the tickets are sold

SELLS ▶ sell

SELS ▶ sel

SELSYN same as ▶ synchro

SELSYNS ▶ selsyn

SELTZER n natural effervescent water containing minerals

SELVA n dense equatorial forest characterized by tall broad-leaved evergreen trees, lianas, etc

SELVAGE n edge of cloth, woven so as to prevent unravelling ▷ vb edge or border

SELVAS ▶ selva

SELVES ▶ self

SEMATIC adj (of the conspicuous coloration of certain animals) acting as a warning, esp to potential predators

SEMBLE vb seem

SEMBLED ▶ semble

SEMBLES ▶ semble

SEME adj dotted (with)

SEMEE same as ▶ seme

SEMEED adj seme

SEMEIA ▶ semeion

SEMEION n unit of metre in ancient poetry

SEMEME n meaning of a morpheme

SEMEMES ▶ sememe

SEMEMIC ▶ sememe

SEMEN n sperm-carrying fluid produced by male animals

SEMENS ▶ semen

SEMES ▶ seme

SEMI n semidetached house

SEMIDRY adj partly dry

SEMIE n historical name for a student in second year at a Scottish university

SEMIES ▶ semie

SEMIFIT adj not fully fit

SEMILOG adj semilogarithmic

SEMIMAT adj semimatt

SEMINA ▶ semen

SEMINAL adj original and influential

SEMINAR n meeting of a group of students for discussion

SEMIPED n measure in poetic metre

SEMIPRO n semiprofessional

SEMIRAW adj not fully cooked or processed

SEMIS ▶ semi

S

SEMISES ▶ **semi**
SEMITAR old spelling of ▶ **scimitar**
SEMMIT n vest
SEMMITS ▶ **semmit**
SEMPER adv Latin word meaning always
SEMPLE adj Scots word meaning simple
SEMPLER ▶ **semple**
SEMPRE adv (preceding a tempo or dynamic marking) always
SEMSEM n sesame
SEMSEMS ▶ **semsem**
SEN n monetary unit of Brunei, Cambodia, Indonesia, Malaysia, and formerly of Japan
SENA n (in India) the army: used in the names of certain paramilitary political organizations
SENARII ▶ **senarius**
SENARY adj of or relating to the number six
SENAS ▶ **sena**
SENATE n main governing body at some universities
SENATES ▶ **senate**
SENATOR n member of a senate
SEND vb cause (a person or thing) to go to or to be taken or transmitted to a place
SENDAL n fine silk fabric used, esp in the Middle Ages, for ceremonial clothing, etc
SENDALS ▶ **sendal**
SENDED vb old word meaning sent
SENDER ▶ **send**
SENDERS ▶ **send**
SENDING ▶ **send**
SENDOFF n demonstration of good wishes at a person's departure ▷ vb dispatch (something, such as a letter)
SENDS ▶ **send**
SENDUP n parody or imitation
SENDUPS ▶ **sendup**
SENE n money unit in Samoa
SENECA same as ▶ **senega**
SENECAS ▶ **seneca**
SENECIO n type of plant of the genus which includes groundsels and ragworts
SENEGA n milkwort plant of the eastern US, with small

white flowers
SENEGAS ▶ **senega**
SENES ▶ **sene**
SENGI n African shrew
SENHOR n Portuguese term of address for man
SENHORA n Portuguese term of address for woman
SENHORS ▶ **senhor**
SENILE adj mentally or physically weak because of old age ▷ n senile person
SENILES ▶ **senile**
SENIOR adj superior in rank or standing ▷ n senior person
SENIORS ▶ **senior**
SENITI n money unit in Tonga
SENNA n tropical plant
SENNAS ▶ **senna**
SENNET n fanfare: used as a stage direction in Elizabethan drama
SENNETS ▶ **sennet**
SENNIT n flat braided cordage used on ships
SENNITS ▶ **sennit**
SENOPIA n short-sightedness in old age
SENOR n Spanish term of address equivalent to sir or Mr
SENORA n Spanish term of address equivalent to madam or Mrs
SENORAS ▶ **senora**
SENORES ▶ **senor**
SENORS ▶ **senor**
SENRYU n Japanese short poem
SENS ▶ **sen**
SENSA ▶ **sensum**
SENSATE adj perceived by the senses ▷ vb make sensate
SENSE n any of the faculties of perception or feeling ▷ vb perceive
SENSED ▶ **sense**
SENSEI n martial arts teacher
SENSEIS ▶ **sensei**
SENSES ▶ **sense**
SENSI same as ▶ **sensei**
SENSILE adj capable of feeling
SENSING ▶ **sense**
SENSIS ▶ **sensi**
SENSISM n theory that ideas spring from senses
SENSIST ▶ **sensism**
SENSOR n device that

detects or measures the presence of something, such as radiation
SENSORS ▶ **sensor**
SENSORY adj of the senses or sensation
SENSUAL adj giving pleasure to the body and senses rather than the mind
SENSUM n sensation detached from the information it conveys and also from its source in the external world
SENT n former monetary unit of Estonia
SENTE n money unit in Lesotho
SENTED ▶ **send**
SENTI ▶ **sent**
SENTIMO n money unit in Philippines
SENTING ▶ **send**
SENTRY n soldier on watch
SENTS ▶ **sent**
SENVIES ▶ **senvy**
SENVY n mustard
SENZA prep without
SEPAD vb suppose
SEPADS ▶ **sepad**
SEPAL n leaflike division of the calyx of a flower
SEPALED ▶ **sepal**
SEPALS ▶ **sepal**
SEPHEN n stingray
SEPHENS ▶ **sephen**
SEPIA n reddish-brown pigment ▷ adj dark reddish-brown, like the colour of very old photographs
SEPIAS ▶ **sepia**
SEPIC adj of sepia
SEPIOST n cuttlefish bone
SEPIUM n cuttlefish bone
SEPIUMS ▶ **sepium**
SEPMAG adj designating a film or television programme for which the sound is recorded on separate magnetic material and run in synchronism with the picture
SEPOY n (formerly) Indian soldier in the service of the British
SEPOYS ▶ **sepoy**
SEPPUKU n Japanese ritual suicide
SEPS n species of lizard
SEPSES ▶ **sepsis**
SEPSIS n poisoning caused by pus-forming bacteria

SEPT n clan, esp in Ireland or Scotland

SEPTA ▸ **septum**

SEPTAGE n waste removed from septic tank

SEPTAL adj of or relating to a septum

SEPTATE adj divided by septa

SEPTET n group of seven performers

SEPTETS ▸ **septet**

SEPTIC adj (of a wound) infected ▸ n infected wound

SEPTICS ▸ **septic**

SEPTIME n seventh of eight basic positions from which a parry can be made in fencing

SEPTS ▸ **sept**

SEPTUM n dividing partition between two cavities in the body

SEPTUMS ▸ **septum**

SEPTUOR n group of seven musicians

SEQUEL n novel, play, or film that continues the story of an earlier one

SEQUELA n any abnormal bodily condition or disease related to or arising from a pre-existing disease

SEQUELS ▸ **sequel**

SEQUENT adj following in order or succession ▸ n something that follows

SEQUIN n small ornamental metal disc on a garment ▸ vb apply sequins

SEQUINS ▸ **sequin**

SEQUOIA n giant Californian coniferous tree

> This word for a redwood tree is one of the most frequently played bonuses using the Q, a great one to remember as it also clears out a surplus of vowels.

SER n unit of weight used in India, usually taken as one fortieth of a maund

SERA ▸ **serum**

SERAC n pinnacle of ice among crevasses on a glacier, usually on a steep slope

SERACS ▸ **serac**

SERAFIN n old silver coin of Goa

SERAI n (in the East) a caravanserai or inn

SERAIL same as ▸ **seraglio**

SERAILS ▸ **serail**

SERAIS ▸ **serai**

SERAL ▸ **sere**

SERANG n native captain of a crew of sailors in the East Indies

SERANGS ▸ **serang**

SERAPE n blanket-like shawl often of brightly-coloured wool worn by men in Latin America

SERAPES ▸ **serape**

SERAPH n member of the highest order of angels

SERAPHS ▸ **seraph**

SERDAB n secret chamber in an ancient Egyptian tomb

SERDABS ▸ **serdab**

SERE adj dried up or withered ▸ n series of changes occurring in the ecological succession of a particular community ▸ vb sear

SERED ▸ **sere**

SEREIN n fine rain falling from a clear sky after sunset, esp in the tropics

SEREINS ▸ **serein**

SERENE adj calm, peaceful ▸ vb make serene

SERENED ▸ **serene**

SERENER ▸ **serene**

SERENES ▸ **serene**

SERER ▸ **sere**

SERES ▸ **sere**

SEREST ▸ **sere**

SERF n medieval farm labourer who could not leave the land he worked on

SERFAGE ▸ **serf**

SERFDOM ▸ **serf**

SERFISH ▸ **serf**

SERFS ▸ **serf**

SERGE n strong woollen fabric

SERGED adj with sewn seam

SERGER n sewing machine attachment for finishing seams

SERGERS ▸ **serger**

SERGES ▸ **serge**

SERGING n type of sewing

SERIAL n story or play produced in successive instalments ▸ adj of or forming a series

SERIALS ▸ **serial**

SERIATE adj forming a series

▸ vb form into a series

SERIC adj of silk

SERICIN n gelatinous protein found on the fibres of raw silk

SERICON n solution used in alchemy

SERIEMA n either of two cranelike South American birds

SERIES n group or succession of related things, usu arranged in order

SERIF n small line at the extremities of a main stroke in a type character

SERIFED adj having serifs

SERIFS ▸ **serif**

SERIN n any of various small yellow-and-brown finches

SERINE n sweet-tasting amino acid

SERINES ▸ **serine**

SERING ▸ **sere**

SERINGA n any of several trees that yield rubber

SERINS ▸ **serin**

SERIOUS adj giving cause for concern

SERIPH same as ▸ **serif**

SERIPHS ▸ **seriph**

SERK Scots word for ▸ **shirt**

SERKALI n government in Africa

SERKS ▸ **serk**

SERMON n speech on a religious or moral subject by a clergyman in a church service ▸ vb deliver a sermon

SERMONS ▸ **sermon**

SERON n crate

SERONS ▸ **seron**

SEROON n crate

SEROONS ▸ **seroon**

SEROPUS n liquid consisting of serum and pus

SEROSA n one of the thin membranes surrounding the embryo in an insect's egg

SEROSAE ▸ **serosa**

SEROSAL ▸ **serosa**

SEROSAS ▸ **serosa**

SEROUS adj of, containing, or like serum

SEROVAR n subdivision of species

SEROW n either of two antelopes of mountainous regions of S and SE Asia

SEROWS ▸ **serow**

S

SERPENT *n* snake
SERPIGO *n* any progressive skin eruption, such as ringworm or herpes
SERR *vb* press close together
SERRA *n* sawlike part or organ
SERRAE ▶ serra
SERRAN *n* species of fish
SERRANO *n* type of Spanish ham
SERRANS ▶ serran
SERRAS ▶ serra
SERRATE *adj* (of leaves) having a margin of forward pointing teeth ▷ *vb* make serrate
SERRATI > serratus
SERRE *vb* press close together
SERRED ▶ serre
SERRES ▶ serre
SERRIED *adj* in close formation
SERRIES ▶ serry
SERRING ▶ serre
SERRS ▶ serr
SERRY *vb* close together
SERS ▶ ser
SERUEWE *vb* old word meaning survey
SERUM *n* watery fluid left after blood has clotted
SERUMAL ▶ serum
SERUMS ▶ serum
SERVAL *n* feline African mammal
SERVALS ▶ serval
SERVANT *n* person employed to do household work for another ▷ *vb* work as a servant
SERVE *vb* work for (a person, community, or cause) ▷ *n* act of serving the ball
SERVED ▶ serve
SERVER *n* player who serves in racket games
SERVERS ▶ server
SERVERY *n* room from which food is served
SERVES ▶ serve
SERVEWE *vb* old word meaning survey
SERVICE *n* serving ▷ *adj* serving the public rather than producing goods ▷ *vb* provide a service or services to
SERVILE *adj* too eager to obey people, fawning

▷ *n* servile person
SERVING *n* portion of food
SERVLET *n* small program that runs on a web server often accessing databases in response to client input
SERVO *n* servomechanism ▷ *adj* of a servomechanism
SERVOS ▶ servo
SESAME *n* plant cultivated for its seeds and oil, which are used in cooking
SESAMES ▶ sesame
SESE *interj* exclamation found in Shakespeare
SESELI *n* garden plant
SESELIS ▶ seseli
SESEY *interj* exclamation found in Shakespeare
SESH *short for* ▶ **session**
SESHES ▶ sesh
SESS *n* old word meaning tax
SESSA *interj* exclamation found in Shakespeare
SESSES ▶ sess
SESSILE *adj* (of flowers or leaves) having no stalk
SESSION *n* period spent in an activity
SESTET *n* last six lines of a sonnet
SESTETS ▶ sestet
SESTETT *n* group of six
SESTINA *n* elaborate verse form of Italian origin
SESTINE *n* poem of six lines
SESTON *n* type of plankton
SESTONS ▶ seston
SET *vb* put in a specified position or state ▷ *n* setting or being set ▷ *adj* fixed or established beforehand
SETA *n* (in invertebrates and some plants) any bristle or bristle-like appendage
SETAE ▶ seta
SETAL ▶ seta
SETBACK *n* anything that delays progress
SETLINE *n* any of various types of fishing line
SETNESS ▶ set
SETOFF *n* counterbalance
SETOFFS ▶ setoff
SETON *n* surgical thread inserted below the skin
SETONS ▶ seton
SETOSE *adj* covered with setae
SETOUS ▶ seta
SETOUT *n* beginning or outset

SETOUTS ▶ setout
SETS ▶ set
SETT *n* badger's burrow
SETTEE *n* couch
SETTEES ▶ settee
SETTER *n* long-haired gun dog ▷ *vb* treat with a piece of setterwort
SETTERS ▶ setter
SETTING ▶ set
SETTLE *vb* arrange or put in order ▷ *n* long wooden bench with high back and arms
SETTLED ▶ settle
SETTLER *n* colonist
SETTLES ▶ settle
SETTLOR *n* person who settles property on someone
SETTS ▶ sett
SETUALE *n* valerian
SETULE *n* small bristle
SETULES ▶ setule
SETUP *n* way in which anything is organized or arranged
SETUPS ▶ setup
SETWALL *n* valerian
SEVEN *n* one more than six ▷ *adj* amounting to seven ▷ *determiner* amounting to seven
SEVENS *n* Rugby Union match or series of matches played with seven players on each side
SEVENTH *n* (of) number seven in a series ▷ *adj* coming after the sixth and before the eighth ▷ *adv* after the sixth person, position, event, etc
SEVENTY *n* ten times seven ▷ *adj* amounting to seventy ▷ *determiner* amounting to seventy
SEVER *vb* cut through or off
SEVERAL *adj* some, a few ▷ *n* individual person
SEVERE *adj* strict or harsh
SEVERED ▶ sever
SEVERER ▶ severe
SEVERS ▶ sever
SEVERY *n* part of vaulted ceiling
SEVICHE *n* Mexican fish dish
SEVRUGA *n* species of sturgeon
SEW *vb* join with thread repeatedly passed through with a needle
SEWABLE ▶ sew

SEWAGE n waste matter or excrement carried away in sewers

SEWAGES ▸ sewage

SEWAN same as ▸ **seawan**

SEWANS ▸ sewan

SEWAR n Asian dagger

SEWARS ▸ sewar

SEWED ▸ sew

SEWEL n scarecrow

SEWELS ▸ sewel

SEWEN same as ▸ **sewin**

SEWENS ▸ sewen

SEWER n drain to remove waste water and sewage ▷ vb provide with sewers

SEWERED ▸ sewer

SEWERS ▸ sewer

SEWIN n sea trout

SEWING ▸ sew

SEWINGS ▸ sew

SEWINS ▸ sewin

SEWN ▸ sew

SEWS ▸ sew

SEX n state of being male or female ▷ vb find out the sex of ▷ adj of sexual matters

SEXED adj having a specified degree of sexuality

SEXER n person checking sex of chickens

SEXERS ▸ sexer

SEXES ▸ sex

SEXFID adj split into six

SEXFOIL n flower with six petals or leaves

SEXIER ▸ sexy

SEXIEST ▸ sexy

SEXILY ▸ sexy

SEXING ▸ sex

SEXINGS ▸ sexing

SEXISM n discrimination on the basis of a person's sex

SEXISMS ▸ sexism

SEXIST ▸ sexism

SEXISTS ▸ sexism

SEXLESS adj neither male nor female

SEXPERT n person who professes a knowledge of sexual matters

SEXPOT n person, esp a young woman, considered as being sexually very attractive

SEXPOTS ▸ sexpot

SEXT n fourth of the seven canonical hours of the divine office or the prayers prescribed for it: originally the sixth hour of the day (noon)

SEXTAIN same as ▸ **sestina**

SEXTAN adj (of a fever) marked by paroxysms that recur after an interval of five days

SEXTANS n Roman coin

SEXTANT n navigator's instrument for measuring angles to calculate one's position

SEXTET n group of six performers

SEXTETS ▸ sextet

SEXTETT n sextet

SEXTILE n one of five values of a variable dividing its distribution into six groups with equal frequencies

SEXTO same as ▸ **sixmo**

SEXTON n official in charge of a church and churchyard

SEXTONS ▸ sexton

SEXTOS ▸ sexto

SEXTS ▸ sext

SEXTUOR n sextet

SEXUAL adj of or characterized by sex

SEXY adj sexually exciting or attractive

SEY n Scots word meaning part of cow carcase

SEYEN n old form of scion

SEYENS ▸ seyen

SEYS ▸ sey

SEYSURE n old form of seizure

SEZ vb informal spelling of 'says'

| **Sez** is a short informal form of **says**, very useful for disposing of the Z.

SFERICS same as > **spherics**

SFUMATO n gradual transition between areas of different colour in painting

SH interj hush

SHA interj be quiet

SHABASH interj (in Indian English) bravo or well done

SHABBLE n Scots word meaning old sword

SHABBY adj worn or dilapidated in appearance

SHACK n rough hut ▷ vb evade (work or responsibility)

SHACKED ▸ shack

SHACKLE n metal ring for securing a person's wrists or ankles ▷ vb fasten with shackles

SHACKO same as ▸ **shako**

SHACKOS ▸ shacko

SHACKS ▸ shack

SHAD n herring-like fish

SHADE n relative darkness ▷ vb screen from light

SHADED ▸ shade

SHADER ▸ shade

SHADERS ▸ shade

SHADES pl n gathering darkness at nightfall

SHADFLY American name for ▸ **mayfly**

SHADIER ▸ shady

SHADILY ▸ shady

SHADING n graded areas of tone indicating light and dark in a painting or drawing

SHADOOF n mechanism for raising water, esp as used in Egypt and the Near East

SHADOW n dark shape cast on a surface when something stands between a light and the surface ▷ vb cast a shadow over

SHADOWS ▸ shadow

SHADOWY adj (of a place) full of shadows

SHADS ▸ shad

SHADUF same as ▸ **shadoof**

SHADUFS ▸ shaduf

SHADY adj situated in or giving shade

SHAFT n long narrow straight handle of a tool or weapon ▷ vb treat badly

SHAFTED ▸ shaft

SHAFTER ▸ shaft

SHAFTS ▸ shaft

SHAGGY adj covered with rough hair or wool

SHAH n formerly, ruler of Iran

SHAHADA n Islamic declaration of faith, repeated daily by Muslims

SHAHDOM ▸ shah

SHAHEED ▸ shahid

SHAHID n Muslim martyr

SHAHIDS ▸ shahid

SHAHS ▸ shah

SHAIKH n sheikh

SHAIKHS ▸ shaikh

SHAIRD n Scots word meaning shred

SHAIRDS ▸ shaird

SHAIRN Scots word for ▸ **dung**

SHAIRNS ▸ shairn

SHAITAN n (in Muslim countries) an evil spirit

SHAKE vb move quickly up and down or back and forth ▷ n shaking

SHAKED vb old form of shook

SHAKEN ▶ shake

SHAKER n container in which drinks are mixed or from which powder is shaken

SHAKERS ▶ shaker

SHAKES ▶ shake

SHAKEUP n radical reorganization

SHAKIER ▶ shaky

SHAKILY ▶ shaky

SHAKING ▶ shake

SHAKO n tall cylindrical peaked military hat with a plume

SHAKOES ▶ shako

SHAKOS ▶ shako

SHAKT vb old form of shook

SHAKUDO n Japanese alloy of copper and gold

SHAKY adj unsteady

SHALE n flaky sedimentary rock

SHALED ▶ shale

SHALES ▶ shale

SHALEY ▶ shale

SHALIER ▶ shale

SHALING ▶ shale

SHALL vb used as an auxiliary to make the future tense

SHALLI n type of fabric

SHALLIS ▶ shalli

SHALLON n American shrub

SHALLOP n light boat used for rowing in shallow water

SHALLOT n kind of small onion

SHALLOW adj not deep ▷ n shallow place in a body of water ▷ vb make or become shallow

SHALM n old woodwind instrument

SHALMS ▶ shalm

SHALOM n Jewish greeting meaning 'peace be with you'

SHALOMS ▶ shalom

SHALOT n shallot

SHALOTS ▶ shalot

SHALT singular form of the present tense (indicative mood) of ▶ shall

SHALWAR n pair of loose-fitting trousers tapering to a narrow fit around the ankles, worn in the Indian subcontinent, often with a kameez

SHALY ▶ shale

SHAM n thing or person that is not genuine ▷ adj not genuine ▷ vb fake, feign

SHAMA n Indian songbird

SHAMAL n hot northwesterly wind that blows across Iraq and the Persian Gulf

SHAMALS ▶ shamal

SHAMAN n priest of shamanism

SHAMANS ▶ shaman

SHAMAS ▶ shama

SHAMBA n (in E Africa) any field used for growing crops

SHAMBAS ▶ shamba

SHAMBLE vb walk in a shuffling awkward way ▷ n awkward or shuffling walk

SHAMBLY ▶ shamble

SHAME n painful emotion caused by awareness of having done something dishonourable or foolish ▷ vb cause to feel shame

SHAMED ▶ shame

SHAMER n cause of shame

SHAMERS ▶ shame

SHAMES ▶ shame

SHAMINA n wool blend of pashm and shahtoosh

SHAMING ▶ shame

SHAMMAS same as ▶ shammes

SHAMMED ▶ sham

SHAMMER ▶ sham

SHAMMES n official acting as the beadle, sexton, and caretaker of a synagogue

SHAMMOS same as ▶ shammes

SHAMMY n piece of chamois leather ▷ vb rub with a shammy

SHAMOIS n chamois

SHAMOS same as ▶ shammes

SHAMOY n chamois ▷ vb rub with a shamoy

SHAMOYS ▶ shamoy

SHAMPOO n liquid soap for washing hair, carpets, or upholstery ▷ vb wash with shampoo

SHAMS ▶ sham

SHAMUS n police or private detective

SHAN same as ▶ shand

SHAND n old word meaning fake coin

SHANDRY n light horse-drawn cart

SHANDS ▶ shand

SHANDY n drink made of beer and lemonade

SHANK n lower leg ▷ vb (of fruits, roots, etc) to show disease symptoms, esp discoloration

SHANKED ▶ shank

SHANKS ▶ shank

SHANNY n European blenny of rocky coastal waters

SHANS ▶ shan

SHANTEY same as ▶ shanty

SHANTI n peace

SHANTIH same as ▶ shanti

SHANTIS ▶ shanti

SHANTY n shack or crude dwelling

SHAPE n outward form of an object ▷ vb form or mould

SHAPED ▶ shape

SHAPELY adj having an attractive shape

SHAPEN vb old form of shaped

SHAPER ▶ shape

SHAPERS ▶ shape

SHAPES ▶ shape

SHAPEUP n system of hiring dockers for a day's work

SHAPING ▶ shape

SHAPS n leather over-trousers worn by cowboys

SHARD n broken piece of pottery or glass

SHARDED adj old word meaning hidden under dung

SHARDS ▶ shard

SHARE n part of something that belongs to or is contributed by a person ▷ vb give or take a share of (something)

SHARED ▶ share

SHARER ▶ share

SHARERS ▶ share

SHARES ▶ share

SHARIA n body of doctrines that regulate the lives of Muslims

SHARIAH same as ▶ sharia

SHARIAS ▶ sharia

SHARIAT n Islamic religious law

SHARIF same as ▶ sherif

SHARIFS ▶ sharif

SHARING ▶ share

SHARK n large usu predatory sea fish ▷ vb obtain (something) by

cheating or deception
SHARKED ▶ shark
SHARKER n shark hunter
SHARKS ▶ shark
SHARN Scots word for
▶ dung
SHARNS ▶ sharn
SHARNY ▶ sharn
SHARON n as in sharon
fruit persimmon
SHARP adj having a keen
cutting edge or fine point
▷ adv promptly ▷ n symbol
raising a note one semitone
above natural pitch ▷ vb
make sharp
SHARPED ▶ sharp
SHARPEN vb make or
become sharp or sharper
SHARPER n person who
cheats
SHARPIE n member of a
teenage group having short
hair and distinctive clothes
SHARPLY ▶ sharp
SHARPS ▶ sharp
SHARPY n swindler
SHASH vb old form of sash
SHASHED ▶ shash
SHASHES ▶ shash
SHASLIK n type of kebab
SHASTER same as ▶ shastra
SHASTRA n any of the
sacred writings of
Hinduism
SHATTER vb break into
pieces ▷ n fragment
SHAUGH n old word
meaning small wood
SHAUGHS ▶ shaugh
SHAUL vb old form of shawl
SHAULED ▶ shaul
SHAULS ▶ shaul
SHAVE vb remove (hair)
from (the face, head, or
body) with a razor or shaver
▷ n shaving
SHAVED ▶ shave
SHAVEN adj closely shaved
or tonsured
SHAVER n electric razor
SHAVERS ▶ shaver
SHAVES ▶ shaul
SHAVIE n Scots word
meaning trick
SHAVIES ▶ shavie
SHAVING ▶ shave
SHAW n small wood ▷ vb
show
SHAWED ▶ shaw
SHAWING ▶ shaw
SHAWL n piece of cloth
worn over a woman's

shoulders or wrapped
around a baby ▷ vb cover
with a shawl
SHAWLED ▶ shawl
SHAWLS ▶ shawl
SHAWM n medieval form of
the oboe with a conical
bore and flaring bell
SHAWMS ▶ shawm
SHAWN same as ▶ shawm
SHAWS ▶ shaw
SHAY dialect word for
▶ chaise
SHAYA n Indian plant
SHAYAS ▶ shaya
SHAYS ▶ shay
SHAZAM interj magic
slogan
SHCHI n Russian cabbage
soup
SHCHIS ▶ shchi
SHE pron female person or
animal previously
mentioned ▷ n female
person or animal
SHEA n tropical African tree
SHEAF n bundle of papers
▷ vb tie into a sheaf
SHEAFED ▶ sheaf
SHEAFS ▶ sheaf
SHEAFY ▶ sheaf
SHEAL vb old word meaning
shell
SHEALED ▶ sheal
SHEALS ▶ sheal
SHEAR vb clip hair or wool
from ▷ n breakage caused
through strain or twisting
SHEARED ▶ shear
SHEARER ▶ shear
SHEARS ▶ shear
SHEAS ▶ shea
SHEATH n close-fitting
cover, esp for a knife or
sword
SHEATHE vb put into a
sheath
SHEATHS ▶ sheath
SHEATHY ▶ sheathe
SHEAVE vb gather or bind
into sheaves ▷ n wheel
with a grooved rim, esp one
used as a pulley
SHEAVED ▶ sheave
SHEAVES ▶ sheaf
SHEBANG n situation,
matter, or affair
SHEBEAN same as
▶ shebeen
SHEBEEN n place where
alcohol is sold illegally ▷ vb
run a shebeen
SHED n building used for

storage or shelter or as a
workshop ▷ vb get rid of
SHEDDED ▶ shed
SHEDDER n person or thing
that sheds
SHEDFUL n quantity or
amount contained in a shed
SHEDS ▶ shed
SHEEL vb old word meaning
shell
SHEELED ▶ sheel
SHEELS ▶ sheel
SHEEN n glistening
brightness on the surface of
something ▷ adj shining
and beautiful ▷ vb give a
sheen to
SHEENED ▶ sheen
SHEENS ▶ sheen
SHEEP n ruminant animal
bred for wool and meat
SHEEPLE pl n informal
derogatory word for people
who follow the majority in
matters of opinion, taste,
etc
SHEEPO n person employed
to bring sheep to the
catching pen in a shearing
shed
SHEEPOS ▶ sheepo
SHEEPY ▶ sheep
SHEER adj absolute,
complete ▷ adv steeply
▷ vb change course
suddenly ▷ n any
transparent fabric used for
making garments
SHEERED ▶ sheer
SHEERER ▶ sheer
SHEERLY ▶ sheer
SHEERS ▶ sheer
SHEESH interj exclamation
of surprise or annoyance
SHEESHA n Oriental
water-pipe for smoking
tobacco
SHEET n large piece of cloth
used as an inner bed cover
▷ vb provide with, cover, or
wrap in a sheet
SHEETED ▶ sheet
SHEETER ▶ sheet
SHEETS ▶ sheet
SHEETY ▶ sheet
SHEEVE n part of mine
winding gear
SHEEVES ▶ sheeve
SHEHITA n slaughter of
animal according to Jewish
religious law
SHEIK same as ▶ sheikh
SHEIKH n Arab chief

S

SHEIKHA n chief wife of sheikh

SHEIKHS ▶ sheikh

SHEIKS ▶ sheik

SHEILA n girl or woman

SHEILAS ▶ sheila

SHEITAN n Muslim demon

SHEKEL n monetary unit of Israel

SHEKELS ▶ shekel

SHELF n board fixed horizontally for holding things ▷ vb put on a shelf

SHELFED ▶ shelf

SHELFS ▶ shelf

SHELFY ▶ shelf

SHELL n hard outer covering of an egg, nut, or certain animals ▷ vb take the shell from

SHELLAC n resin used in varnishes ▷ vb coat with shellac

SHELLED ▶ shell

SHELLER ▶ shell

SHELLS ▶ shell

SHELLY ▶ shell

SHELTA n secret language used by some traveling people in Britain and Ireland

SHELTAS ▶ shelta

SHELTER n structure providing protection from danger or the weather ▷ vb give shelter to

SHELTIE n small dog similar to a collie

SHELTY same as ▶ sheltie

SHELVE vb put aside or postpone

SHELVED ▶ shelve

SHELVER ▶ shelve

SHELVES ▶ shelf

SHELVY adj having shelves

SHEMALE n male who has acquired female physical characteristics through surgery

SHEND vb put to shame

SHENDS ▶ shend

SHENT ▶ shend

SHEOL n hell

SHEOLS ▶ sheol

SHEQEL same as ▶ shekel

SHEQELS ▶ sheqel

SHERANG n person in charge

SHERBET n fruit-flavoured fizzy powder

SHERD same as ▶ shard

SHERDS ▶ sherd

SHERE old spelling of ▶ sheer

SHEREEF same as ▶ sherif

SHERIA same as ▶ sharia

SHERIAS ▶ sheria

SHERIAT n Muslim religious law

SHERIF n descendant of Mohammed through his daughter Fatima

SHERIFF n (in the US) chief law enforcement officer of a county

SHERIFS ▶ sherif

SHEROOT n cheroot

SHERPA n official who assists at a summit meeting

SHERPAS ▶ sherpa

SHERRIS n old form of sherry

SHERRY n pale or dark brown fortified wine

SHES ▶ she

SHET vb old form of shut

SHETS ▶ shet

SHEUCH n ditch or trough ▷ vb dig

SHEUCHS ▶ sheuch

SHEUGH same as ▶ sheuch

SHEUGHS ▶ sheugh

SHEVA n mark in Hebrew writing

SHEVAS ▶ sheva

SHEW archaic spelling of ▶ show

SHEWED ▶ shew

SHEWEL n old word meaning scarecrow

SHEWELS ▶ shewel

SHEWER ▶ shew

SHEWERS ▶ shew

SHEWING ▶ shew

SHEWN ▶ shew

SHEWS ▶ shew

SHH interj sound made to ask for silence

SHIAI n judo contest

SHIAIS ▶ shiai

SHIATSU n massage in which pressure is applied to the same points of the body as in acupuncture

SHIATZU n shiatsu

SHIBAH n Jewish period of mourning

SHIBAHS ▶ shibah

SHICKER n alcoholic drink

SHIDDER n old word meaning female animal

SHIED ▶ shy

SHIEL vb sheal

SHIELD n piece of armour carried on the arm to protect the body from blows or missiles ▷ vb protect

SHIELDS ▶ shield

SHIELED ▶ shiel

SHIELS ▶ shiel

SHIER n horse that shies habitually

SHIERS ▶ shier

SHIES ▶ shy

SHIEST ▶ shy

SHIFT vb move ▷ n shifting

SHIFTED ▶ shift

SHIFTER ▶ shift

SHIFTS ▶ shift

SHIFTY adj evasive or untrustworthy

SHIKAR n hunting, esp big-game hunting ▷ vb hunt (game, esp big game)

SHIKARI n (in India) a hunter

SHIKARS ▶ shikar

SHIKKER n Yiddish term for drunk person

SHILL n confidence trickster's assistant ▷ vb act as a shill

SHILLED ▶ shill

SHILLS ▶ shill

SHILPIT adj puny

SHILY ▶ shy

SHIM n thin strip of material placed between two close surfaces to fill a gap ▷ vb fit or fill up with a shim

SHIMAAL n hot Middle Eastern wind

SHIMMED ▶ shim

SHIMMER n (shine with) a faint unsteady light ▷ vb shine with a faint unsteady light

SHIMMEY n chemise

SHIMMY n American ragtime dance with much shaking of the hips and shoulders ▷ vb dance the shimmy

SHIMS ▶ shim

SHIN n front of the lower leg ▷ vb climb by using the hands or arms and legs

SHINDIG n noisy party

SHINDY n quarrel or commotion

SHINDYS ▶ shindy

SHINE vb give out or reflect light; cause to gleam ▷ n brightness or lustre

SHINED ▶ shine

SHINER n black eye

SHINERS ▶ shiner

SHINES ▶ shine

SHINESS ▶ shy
SHINGLE n wooden roof tile ▷ vb cover (a roof) with shingles
SHINGLY ▶ shingle
SHINIER ▶ shiny
SHINIES ▶ shiny
SHINILY ▶ shiny
SHINING ▶ shine
SHINJU n (formerly, in Japan) a ritual double suicide of lovers
SHINJUS ▶ shinju
SHINKIN n worthless person
SHINNE n old form of chin
SHINNED ▶ shin
SHINNES ▶ shinne
SHINNEY vb climb with hands and legs
SHINNY same as ▶ shinty
SHINS ▶ shin
SHINTY n game like hockey ▷ vb play shinty
SHINY adj bright and polished
SHIP n large seagoing vessel ▷ vb send or transport by carrier, esp a ship
SHIPFUL n amount carried by ship
SHIPLAP n method of constructing ship hull
SHIPMAN n master or captain of a ship
SHIPMEN ▶ shipman
SHIPPED ▶ ship
SHIPPEN n dialect word for cattle shed
SHIPPER n person or company that ships
SHIPPIE n prostitute who solicits at a port
SHIPPO n Japanese enamel work
SHIPPON n dialect word for cattle shed
SHIPPOS ▶ shippo
SHIPS ▶ ship
SHIPWAY n structure on which a vessel is built, then launched
SHIR n gathering in material
SHIRE n county ▷ vb refresh or rest
SHIRED ▶ shire
SHIRES ▶ shire
SHIRING ▶ shire
SHIRK vb avoid (duty or work) ▷ n person who shirks
SHIRKED ▶ shirk
SHIRKER ▶ shirk

SHIRKS ▶ shirk
SHIRR vb gather (fabric) into two or more parallel rows to decorate a dress, etc ▷ n series of gathered rows decorating a dress, blouse, etc
SHIRRA old Scots word for ▶ sheriff
SHIRRAS ▶ shirra
SHIRRED ▶ shirr
SHIRRS ▶ shirr
SHIRS ▶ shir
SHIRT n garment for the upper part of the body ▷ vb put a shirt on
SHIRTED ▶ shirt
SHIRTS ▶ shirt
SHIRTY adj bad-tempered or annoyed
SHISH adj as in shish kebab dish of meat and vegetables threaded onto skewers and grilled
SHISHA same as ▶ hookah
SHISHAS ▶ shisha
SHISO n Asian plant with aromatic leaves that are used in cooking
SHISOS ▶ shiso
SHIST n schist
SHISTS ▶ shist
SHITAKE same as > shiitake
SHITTAH n tree mentioned in the Old Testament
SHITTIM ▶ shittah
SHITZU n breed of small dog with long, silky fur
SHITZUS ▶ shitzu
SHIUR n lesson in which a passage of the Talmud is studied together by a group of people
SHIURIM ▶ shiur
SHIV variant spelling of ▶ chiv
SHIVA same as ▶ shivah
SHIVAH n Jewish period of formal mourning
SHIVAHS ▶ shivah
SHIVAS ▶ shiva
SHIVE n flat cork or bung for wide-mouthed bottles
SHIVER vb tremble, as from cold or fear ▷ n shivering
SHIVERS ▶ shiver
SHIVERY adj inclined to shiver or tremble
SHIVES ▶ shive
SHIVITI n Jewish decorative plaque with religious message
SHIVOO n Australian word

meaning rowdy party
SHIVOOS ▶ shivoo
SHIVS ▶ shiv
SHIVVED ▶ shiv
SHLEP vb schlep
SHLEPP vb schlep
SHLEPPS ▶ shlepp
SHLEPS ▶ shlep
SHLOCK n something of poor quality
SHLOCKS ▶ shlock
SHLOCKY ▶ shlock
SHLUB same as ▶ schlub
SHLUBS ▶ shlub
SHLUMP vb move in lazy way
SHLUMPS ▶ shlump
SHLUMPY ▶ shlump
SHMALTZ n schmaltz
SHMATTE n rag
SHMEAR n set of things
SHMEARS ▶ shmear
SHMEK n smell
SHMEKS ▶ shmek
SHMO same as ▶ schmo
SHMOCK n despicable person
SHMOCKS ▶ shmock
SHMOES ▶ shmo
SHMOOSE same as > schmooze
SHMOOZE same as > schmooze
SHMOOZY adj talking casually, gossipy
SHMUCK n despicable person
SHMUCKS ▶ schmuck
SHNAPPS same as > schnapps
SHNAPS ▶ schnapps
SHNOOK n stupid person
SHNOOKS ▶ shnook
SHOAL n large number of fish swimming together ▷ vb make or become shallow ▷ adj (of the draught of a vessel) drawing little water
SHOALED ▶ shoal
SHOALER ▶ shoal
SHOALS ▶ shoal
SHOALY adj shallow
SHOAT n piglet that has recently been weaned
SHOATS ▶ shoat
SHOCHET n (in Judaism) a person who has been specially trained and licensed to slaughter animals and birds in accordance with the laws of shechita

S

SHOCK vb horrify, disgust, or astonish ▷ n sudden violent emotional disturbance ▷ adj bushy

SHOCKED ▶ shock

SHOCKER n person or thing that shocks or horrifies

SHOCKS ▶ shock

SHOD ▶ shoe

SHODDEN vb old form of shod

SHODDY adj made or done badly ▷ n yarn or fabric made from wool waste or clippings

SHODER n skins used in making gold leaf

SHODERS ▶ shoder

SHOE n outer covering for the foot, ending below the ankle ▷ vb fit with a shoe or shoes

SHOEBOX n cardboard box for shoes

SHOED ▶ shoe

SHOEING ▶ shoe

SHOEPAC n waterproof boot

SHOER n person who shoes horses

SHOERS ▶ shoer

SHOES ▶ shoe

SHOFAR n ram's horn sounded in the synagogue daily during the month of Elul and repeatedly on Rosh Hashanah

SHOFARS ▶ shofar

SHOG vb shake

SHOGGED ▶ shog

SHOGGLE vb shake

SHOGGLY ▶ shoggle

SHOGI n Japanese chess

SHOGIS ▶ shogi

SHOGS ▶ shog

SHOGUN n Japanese chief military commander

SHOGUNS ▶ shogun

SHOJI n Japanese rice-paper screen in a sliding wooden frame

SHOJIS ▶ shoji

SHOLA n Indian plant

SHOLAS ▶ shola

SHOLOM n Hebrew greeting

SHOLOMS ▶ sholom

SHONE ▶ shine

SHONEEN n Irishman who imitates English ways

SHONKY adj unreliable or unsound

SHOO interj go away! ▷ vb

drive away as by saying 'shoo'

SHOOED ▶ shoo

SHOOFLY n as in **shoofly pie** US dessert similar to treacle tart

SHOOGIE vb Scots word meaning swing

SHOOGLE vb shake, sway, or rock back and forth ▷ n rocking motion

SHOOGLY ▶ shoogle

SHOOING ▶ shoo

SHOOK n set of parts ready for assembly

SHOOKS ▶ shook

SHOOL dialect word for ▶ shovel

SHOOLE dialect word for ▶ shovel

SHOOLED ▶ shool

SHOOLES ▶ shoole

SHOOLS ▶ shool

SHOON plural of ▶ shoe

SHOORA same as ▶ shura

SHOORAS ▶ shoora

SHOOS ▶ shoo

SHOOT vb hit, wound, or kill with a missile fired from a weapon ▷ n new branch or sprout of a plant

SHOOTER n person or thing that shoots

SHOOTS ▶ shoot

SHOP n place for sale of goods and services ▷ vb visit a shop or shops to buy goods

SHOPBOT n price-comparison website

SHOPBOY n boy working in shop

SHOPE n old form of shape

SHOPFUL n amount stored in shop

SHOPHAR same as ▶ shofar

SHOPMAN n man working in shop

SHOPMEN ▶ shopman

SHOPPE old-fashioned spelling of ▶ shop

SHOPPED ▶ shop

SHOPPER n person who buys goods in a shop

SHOPPES ▶ shoppe

SHOPPY adj of a shop

SHOPS ▶ shop

SHORAN n short-range radar system

SHORANS ▶ shoran

SHORE n edge of a sea or lake ▷ vb prop or support

SHORED ▶ shore

SHORER ▶ shore

SHORERS ▶ shore

SHORES ▶ shore

SHORING ▶ shore

SHORL n black mineral

SHORLS ▶ shorl

SHORN past participle of ▶ shear

SHORT adj not long ▷ adv abruptly ▷ n drink of spirits ▷ vb short-circuit

SHORTED ▶ short

SHORTEN vb make or become shorter

SHORTER ▶ short

SHORTIA n American flowering plant

SHORTIE n person or thing that is extremely short

SHORTLY adv soon

SHORTS pl n trousers reaching the top of the thigh or partway to the knee

SHORTY same as ▶ shortie

SHOT vb load with shot

SHOTE same as ▶ shoat

SHOTES ▶ shote

SHOTGUN n gun for firing a charge of shot at short range ▷ adj involving coercion or duress ▷ vb shoot or threaten with or as if with a shotgun

SHOTS ▶ shot

SHOTT n shallow temporary salt lake or marsh in the North African desert

SHOTTE n old form of shoat

SHOTTED ▶ shot

SHOTTEN adj (of fish, esp herring) having recently spawned

SHOTTES ▶ shotte

SHOTTLE n small drawer

SHOTTS ▶ shott

SHOUGH n old word meaning lapdog

SHOUGHS ▶ shough

SHOULD ▶ shall

SHOUSE n toilet ▷ adj unwell or in poor spirits

SHOUSES ▶ shouse

SHOUT n loud cry ▷ vb cry out loudly

SHOUTED ▶ shout

SHOUTER ▶ shout

SHOUTS ▶ shout

SHOUTY adj characterized by or involving shouting

SHOVE vb push roughly ▷ n rough push

SHOVED ▶ shove

SHOVEL n tool for lifting or moving loose material ▷ vb lift or move as with a shovel

SHOVELS ▶ shovel

SHOVER ▶ shove

SHOVERS ▶ shove

SHOVES ▶ shove

SHOVING n act of pushing hard

SHOW vb make, be, or become noticeable or visible ▷ n public exhibition

SHOWBIZ n entertainment industry including theatre, films, and TV

SHOWBOX n box containing showman's material

SHOWD vb rock or sway to and fro ▷ n rocking motion

SHOWDED ▶ showd

SHOWDS ▶ showd

SHOWED ▶ show

SHOWER n kind of bath in which a person stands while being sprayed with water ▷ vb wash in a shower

SHOWERS ▶ shower

SHOWERY ▶ shower

SHOWGHE n old word meaning lapdog

SHOWIER ▶ showy

SHOWILY ▶ showy

SHOWING ▶ show

SHOWMAN n man skilled at presenting anything spectacularly

SHOWMEN ▶ showman

SHOWN ▶ show

SHOWOFF n person who makes a vain display of himself or herself

SHOWS ▶ show

SHOWY adj gaudy

SHOYU n Japanese variety of soy sauce

SHOYUS ▶ shoyu

SHRANK ▶ shrink

SHRED n long narrow strip torn from something ▷ vb tear to shreds

SHREDDY ▶ shred

SHREDS ▶ shred

SHREEK old spelling of ▶ shriek

SHREEKS ▶ shreek

SHREIK old spelling of ▶ shriek

SHREIKS ▶ shreik

SHREW n small mouselike animal ▷ vb curse or damn

SHREWD adj clever and perceptive

SHREWED ▶ shrew

SHREWS ▶ shrew

SHRI n Indian title of respect

SHRIECH old spelling of ▶ shriek

SHRIEK n shrill cry ▷ vb utter (with) a shriek

SHRIEKS ▶ shriek

SHRIEKY ▶ shriek

SHRIEVE archaic word for ▶ sheriff

SHRIFT n act or an instance of shriving or being shriven

SHRIFTS ▶ shrift

SHRIGHT n old word meaning shriek

SHRIKE n songbird with a heavy hooked bill ▷ vb archaic word for shriek

SHRIKED ▶ shrike

SHRIKES ▶ shrike

SHRILL adj (of a sound) sharp and high-pitched ▷ vb utter shrilly

SHRILLS ▶ shrill

SHRILLY ▶ shrill

SHRIMP n small edible shellfish ▷ vb fish for shrimps

SHRIMPS ▶ shrimp

SHRIMPY ▶ shrimp

SHRINAL ▶ shrine

SHRINE n place of worship associated with a sacred person or object ▷ vb enshrine

SHRINED ▶ shrine

SHRINES ▶ shrine

SHRINK vb become or make smaller ▷ n psychiatrist

SHRINKS ▶ shrink

SHRIS ▶ shri

SHRITCH vb old word meaning shriek

SHRIVE vb hear the confession of (a penitent)

SHRIVED ▶ shrive

SHRIVEL vb shrink and wither

SHRIVEN ▶ shrive

SHRIVER ▶ shrive

SHRIVES ▶ shrive

SHROFF n (in China and Japan) expert employed to separate counterfeit money from the genuine ▷ vb test (money) and separate out the counterfeit and base

SHROFFS ▶ shroff

SHROOM n slang for magic mushroom ▷ vb take magic mushrooms

SHROOMS ▶ shroom

SHROUD n piece of cloth used to wrap a dead body ▷ vb conceal

SHROUDS ▶ shroud

SHROUDY ▶ shroud

SHROVE vb dialect word meaning to observe Shrove-tide

SHROVED ▶ shrove

SHROVES ▶ shrove

SHROW vb old form of shrew

SHROWD adj old form of shrewd

SHROWED ▶ shrow

SHROWS ▶ shrow

SHRUB n woody plant smaller than a tree ▷ vb plant shrubs

SHRUBBY adj consisting of, planted with, or abounding in shrubs

SHRUBS ▶ shrub

SHRUG vb raise and then drop (the shoulders) as a sign of indifference or doubt ▷ n shrugging

SHRUGS ▶ shrug

SHRUNK ▶ shrink

SHTCHI n Russian cabbage soup

SHTCHIS ▶ shtchi

SHTETEL n Jewish community in Eastern Europe

SHTETL n (formerly) a small Jewish community in Eastern Europe

SHTETLS ▶ shtetl

SHTICK n comedian's routine

SHTICKS ▶ shtick

SHTICKY ▶ shtick

SHTIK n shtick

SHTIKS ▶ shtik

SHTOOK n trouble

SHTOOKS ▶ shtook

SHTOOM adj silent

SHTUCK n trouble

SHTUCKS ▶ shtuck

SHTUM adj silent

SHTUMM adj silent

SHTUP vb have sex (with)

SHTUPS ▶ shtup

SHUCK n outer covering of something ▷ vb remove the shucks from

SHUCKED ▶ shuck

SHUCKER ▶ shuck

SHUCKS pl n something of little value ▷ interj exclamation of disappointment, annoyance, etc

SHUDDER vb shake or tremble violently, esp with horror ▷ n shaking or trembling

SHUFFLE vb walk without lifting the feet ▷ n shuffling

SHUFTI same as ▶ **shufty**

SHUFTIS ▶ **shufti**

SHUFTY n look

SHUGGY n swing, as at a fairground

SHUL Yiddish word for > synagogue

SHULE vb saunter

SHULED ▶ **shule**

SHULES ▶ **shule**

SHULING ▶ **shule**

SHULN ▶ **shul**

SHULS ▶ **shul**

SHUN vb avoid

SHUNNED ▶ **shun**

SHUNNER ▶ **shun**

SHUNS ▶ **shun**

SHUNT vb move (objects or people) to a different position ▷ n shunting

SHUNTED ▶ **shunt**

SHUNTER n small railway locomotive used for manoeuvring coaches

SHUNTS ▶ **shunt**

SHURA n consultative council or assembly

SHURAS ▶ **shura**

SHUSH interj be quiet! ▷ vb quiet by saying 'shush'

SHUSHED ▶ **shush**

SHUSHER ▶ **shush**

SHUSHES ▶ **shush**

SHUT vb bring together or fold, close

SHUTE same as ▶ **chute**

SHUTED ▶ **shute**

SHUTES ▶ **shute**

SHUTEYE n sleep

SHUTING ▶ **shute**

SHUTOFF n device that shuts something off, esp a machine control

SHUTOUT n game in which the opposing team does not score ▷ vb keep out or exclude

SHUTS ▶ **shut**

SHUTTER n hinged doorlike cover for closing off a window ▷ vb close or equip with a shutter

SHUTTLE n bobbin-like device used in weaving ▷ vb move by or as if by a shuttle

SHWA same as ▶ **schwa**

SHWAS ▶ **shwa**

SHY adj not at ease in company ▷ vb start back in fear ▷ n throw

SHYER ▶ **shy**

SHYERS ▶ **shy**

SHYEST ▶ **shy**

SHYING ▶ **shy**

SHYISH ▶ **shy**

SHYLOCK vb lend money at an exorbitant rate of interest

SHYLY ▶ **shy**

SHYNESS ▶ **shy**

SHYPOO n liquor of poor quality

SHYPOOS ▶ **shypoo**

SHYSTER n person, esp a lawyer or politician, who uses discreditable or unethical methods

SI same as ▶ **te**

SIAL n silicon-rich and aluminium-rich rocks of the earth's continental upper crust

SIALIC ▶ **sial**

SIALID n species of fly

SIALIDS ▶ **sialid**

SIALOID adj resembling saliva

SIALON n type of ceramic

SIALONS ▶ **sialon**

SIALS ▶ **sial**

SIAMANG n large black gibbon

SIAMESE same as ▶ **siameze**

SIAMEZE vb join together

SIB n blood relative

SIBB n sib

SIBBS ▶ **sibb**

SIBLING n brother or sister

SIBS ▶ **sib**

SIBSHIP n group of children of the same parents

SIBYL n (in ancient Greece and Rome) prophetess

SIBYLIC ▶ **sibyl**

SIBYLS ▶ **sibyl**

SIC adv thus ▷ vb attack

SICCAN adj Scots word meaning such

SICCAR adj sure

SICCED ▶ **sic**

SICCING ▶ **sic**

SICCITY n dryness

SICE same as ▶ **syce**

SICES ▶ **sice**

SICH adj old form of such

SICHT Scots word for ▶ **sight**

SICHTED ▶ **sicht**

SICHTS ▶ **sicht**

SICK adj vomiting or likely to vomit ▷ n vomit ▷ vb vomit

SICKBAY n room for the treatment of sick people, for example on a ship

SICKBED n bed where sick person lies

SICKED ▶ **sick**

SICKEE n person off work through illness

SICKEES ▶ **sickee**

SICKEN vb make nauseated or disgusted

SICKENS ▶ **sicken**

SICKER ▶ **sick**

SICKEST ▶ **sick**

SICKIE n day of sick leave from work

SICKIES ▶ **sickie**

SICKING ▶ **sick**

SICKISH ▶ **sick**

SICKLE n tool with a curved blade for cutting grass or grain ▷ vb cut with a sickle

SICKLED ▶ **sickle**

SICKLES ▶ **sickle**

SICKLY adj unhealthy, weak ▷ adv suggesting sickness ▷ vb make sickly

SICKO n person who is mentally disturbed or perverted ▷ adj perverted or in bad taste

SICKOS ▶ **sicko**

SICKOUT n form of industrial action in which all workers in a workplace report sick simultaneously

SICKS ▶ **sick**

SICLIKE adj Scots word meaning suchlike

SICS ▶ **sic**

SIDA n Australian hemp plant

SIDAS ▶ **sida**

SIDDHA n (in Hinduism) person who has achieved perfection

SIDDHAS ▶ **siddha**

SIDDHI n (in Hinduism) power attained with perfection

SIDDHIS ▶ **siddhi**

SIDDUR n Jewish prayer book

SIDDURS ▶ **siddur**

SIDE n line or surface that borders anything ▷ adj at or on the side

SIDEARM n weapon worn on belt

SIDEBAR n small

newspaper article beside larger one

SIDECAR *n* small passenger car on the side of a motorcycle

SIDED ▸ **side**

SIDEMAN *n* member of a dance band or a jazz group other than the leader

SIDEMEN ▸ **sideman**

SIDER *n* one who sides with another

SIDERAL *adj* from the stars

SIDERS ▸ **sider**

SIDES ▸ **side**

SIDEWAY *same as* > **sideways**

SIDH *pl n* fairy people

SIDHA *n* (in Hinduism) person who has achieved perfection

SIDHAS ▸ **sidha**

SIDHE *pl n* inhabitants of fairyland

SIDING *n* short stretch of railway track on which trains are shunted from the main line

SIDINGS ▸ **siding**

SIDLE *vb* walk in a furtive manner ▸ *n* sideways movement

SIDLED ▸ **sidle**

SIDLER ▸ **sidle**

SIDLERS ▸ **sidle**

SIDLES ▸ **sidle**

SIDLING ▸ **sidle**

SIECLE *n* century, period, or era

SIECLES ▸ **siecle**

SIEGE *n* surrounding and blockading of a place ▸ *vb* lay siege to

SIEGED ▸ **siege**

SIEGER *n* person who besieges

SIEGERS ▸ **sieger**

SIEGES ▸ **siege**

SIEGING ▸ **siege**

SIELD *vb* old word meaning given a ceiling

SIEMENS *n* SI unit of electrical conductance

SIEN *n* old word meaning scion

SIENITE *n* type of igneous rock

SIENNA *n* reddish- or yellowish-brown pigment made from natural earth

SIENNAS ▸ **sienna**

SIENS ▸ **sien**

SIENT *n* old word meaning scion

SIENTS ▸ **sient**

SIERRA *n* range of mountains in Spain or America with jagged peaks

SIERRAN ▸ **sierra**

SIERRAS ▸ **sierra**

SIES *interj* in South Africa, an exclamation of disgust

SIESTA *n* afternoon nap, taken in hot countries

SIESTAS ▸ **siesta**

SIETH *n* old form of scythe

SIETHS ▸ **sieth**

SIEUR *n* French word meaning lord

SIEURS ▸ **sieur**

SIEVE *n* utensil with mesh through which a substance is sifted or strained ▸ *vb* sift or strain through a sieve

SIEVED ▸ **sieve**

SIEVERT *n* derived SI unit of dose equivalent, equal to 1 joule per kilogram

SIEVES ▸ **sieve**

SIEVING ▸ **sieve**

SIF *adj* South African slang for disgusting

SIFAKA *n* either of two large rare arboreal lemuroid primates

SIFAKAS ▸ **sifaka**

SIFFLE *vb* whistle

SIFFLED ▸ **siffle**

SIFFLES ▸ **siffle**

SIFREI ▸ **sefer**

SIFT *vb* remove the coarser particles from a substance with a sieve

SIFTED ▸ **sift**

SIFTER ▸ **sift**

SIFTERS ▸ **sift**

SIFTING ▸ **sift**

SIFTS ▸ **sift**

SIGANID *n* tropical fish

SIGH *n* long audible breath expressing sadness, tiredness, relief, or longing ▸ *vb* utter a sigh

SIGHED ▸ **sigh**

SIGHER ▸ **sigh**

SIGHERS ▸ **sigh**

SIGHFUL ▸ **sigh**

SIGHING ▸ **sigh**

SIGHS ▸ **sigh**

SIGHT *n* ability to see ▸ *vb* catch sight of

SIGHTED *adj* not blind

SIGHTER *n* any of six practice shots allowed to

each competitor in a tournament

SIGHTLY *adj* pleasing or attractive to see

SIGHTS ▸ **sight**

SIGIL *n* seal or signet

SIGILS ▸ **sigil**

SIGLA *n* list of symbols used in a book

SIGLAS ▸ **sigla**

SIGLOI ▸ **siglos**

SIGLOS *n* silver coin of ancient Persia worth one twentieth of a daric

SIGLUM *n* symbol used in book

SIGMA *n* 18th letter in the Greek alphabet

SIGMAS ▸ **sigma**

SIGMATE *adj* shaped like the Greek letter sigma or the Roman S ▸ *n* sigmate thing ▸ *vb* add a sigma

SIGMOID *adj* shaped like the letter S ▸ *n* S-shaped bend in the final portion of the large intestine

SIGN *n* indication of something not immediately or outwardly observable ▸ *vb* write (one's name) on (a document or letter) to show its authenticity or one's agreement

SIGNA *pl n* symbols

SIGNAGE *n* signs collectively, esp street signs or signs giving directions

SIGNAL *n* sign or gesture to convey information ▸ *adj* very important ▸ *vb* convey (information) by signal

SIGNALS ▸ **signal**

SIGNARY *n* set of symbols

SIGNED ▸ **sign**

SIGNEE *n* person signing document

SIGNEES ▸ **signee**

SIGNER *n* person who signs something

SIGNERS ▸ **signer**

SIGNET *n* small seal used to authenticate documents ▸ *vb* stamp or authenticate with a signet

SIGNETS ▸ **signet**

SIGNEUR *old spelling of* ▸ **senior**

SIGNIFY *vb* indicate or suggest

SIGNING *n* system of communication using hand

S

and arm movements, such as one used by deaf people

SIGNIOR same as ▶ **signor**

SIGNOR n Italian term of address equivalent to sir or Mr

SIGNORA n Italian term of address equivalent to madam or Mrs

SIGNORE n Italian man: a title of respect equivalent to sir

SIGNORI ▶ **signore**

SIGNORS ▶ **signor**

SIGNORY same as > **seigniory**

SIGNS ▶ **Sign**

SIJO n Korean poem

SIJOS ▶ **sijo**

SIK adj excellent

SIKA n Japanese forest-dwelling deer

SIKAS ▶ **sika**

SIKE n small stream

SIKER adj old spelling of sicker

SIKES ▶ **sike**

SILAGE n fodder crop harvested while green and partially fermented in a silo ▷ vb make silage

SILAGED ▶ **silage**

SILAGES ▶ **silage**

SILANE n gas containing silicon

SILANES ▶ **silane**

SILD n any of various small young herrings, esp when prepared and canned in Norway

SILDS ▶ **sild**

SILE vb pour with rain

SILED ▶ **sile**

SILEN n god of woodland

SILENCE n absence of noise or speech ▷ vb make silent

SILENE n type of plant with mostly red or pink flowers, often grown as a garden plant

SILENES ▶ **silene**

SILENI ▶ **silenus**

SILENS ▶ **silen**

SILENT adj tending to speak very little ▷ n silent film

SILENTS ▶ **silent**

SILENUS n woodland deity

SILER n strainer

SILERS ▶ **siler**

SILES ▶ **sile**

SILESIA n twill-weave fabric of cotton or other fibre

SILEX n type of heat-resistant glass made from fused quartz

SILEXES ▶ **silex**

SILICA n hard glossy mineral found as quartz and in sandstone

SILICAS ▶ **silica**

SILICIC adj of, concerned with, or containing silicon or an acid obtained from silicon

SILICLE same as > **silicula**

SILICON n brittle nonmetallic element widely used in chemistry and industry ▷ adj denoting an area of a country that contains much high-technology industry

SILING ▶ **sile**

SILIQUA n long dry dehiscent fruit of cruciferous plants such as the wallflower

SILIQUE same as ▶ **siliqua**

SILK n fibre made by the larva of a certain moth ▷ vb (of maize) develop long hairlike styles

SILKED ▶ **silk**

SILKEN adj made of silk ▷ vb make like silk

SILKENS ▶ **silken**

SILKIE n Scots word for a seal

SILKIER ▶ **silky**

SILKIES ▶ **silkie**

SILKILY ▶ **silky**

SILKING ▶ **silk**

SILKS ▶ **silk**

SILKY adj of or like silk

SILL n ledge at the bottom of a window or door

SILLER n silver ▷ adj silver

SILLERS ▶ **siller**

SILLIER ▶ **silly**

SILLIES ▶ **silly**

SILLILY ▶ **silly**

SILLOCK n young coalfish

SILLS ▶ **sill**

SILLY adj foolish ▷ n foolish person

SILO n pit or airtight tower for storing silage or grains ▷ vb put in a silo

SILOED ▶ **silo**

SILOING ▶ **silo**

SILOS ▶ **silo**

SILPHIA > **silphium**

SILT n mud deposited by moving water ▷ vb fill or be choked with silt

SILTED ▶ **silt**

SILTIER ▶ **silt**

SILTING ▶ **silt**

SILTS ▶ **silt**

SILTY ▶ **silt**

SILURID n type of freshwater fish of the family which includes catfish

SILVA same as ▶ **sylva**

SILVAE ▶ **silva**

SILVAN same as ▶ **sylvan**

SILVANS ▶ **silvan**

SILVAS ▶ **silva**

SILVER n white precious metal ▷ adj made of or of the colour of silver ▷ vb coat with silver

SILVERN adj silver

SILVERS ▶ **silver**

SILVERY adj like silver

SILVEX n type of weedkiller

SILVICS n study of trees

SIM n computer game that simulates an activity such as flying or playing a sport

SIMA n silicon-rich and magnesium-rich rocks of the earth's oceanic crust

SIMAR variant spelling of ▶ **cymar**

SIMARRE n woman's loose gown

SIMARS ▶ **simar**

SIMAS ▶ **sima**

SIMATIC ▶ **sima**

SIMBA E African word for ▶ **lion**

SIMBAS ▶ **simba**

SIMI n East African sword

SIMIAL adj of apes

SIMIAN n a monkey or ape ▷ adj of or resembling a monkey or ape

SIMIANS ▶ **simian**

SIMILAR adj alike but not identical

SIMILE n figure of speech comparing one thing to another, using 'as' or 'like'

SIMILES ▶ **simile**

SIMILOR n alloy used in cheap jewellery

SIMIOID adj of apes

SIMIOUS adj of apes

SIMIS ▶ **simi**

SIMITAR same as > **scimitar**

SIMKIN word used in India for > **champagne**

SIMKINS ▶ **simkin**

SIMLIN n American variety of squash plant

SIMLINS ▶ **simlin**

SIMMER vb cook gently at just below boiling point ▷ n state of simmering

SIMMERS ▷ **simmer**

SIMNEL n as in simnel cake fruit cake with marzipan eaten at Easter

SIMNELS ▷ **simnel**

SIMONY n practice of buying or selling Church benefits such as pardons

SIMOOM n hot suffocating sand-laden desert wind

SIMOOMS ▷ **simoom**

SIMOON same as ▷ **simoom**

SIMOONS ▷ **simoon**

SIMORG n bird in Persian myth

SIMORGS ▷ **simorg**

SIMP short for > **simpleton**

SIMPAI n Indonesian monkey

SIMPAIS ▷ **simpai**

SIMPER vb smile in a silly or affected way ▷ n simpering smile

SIMPERS ▷ **simper**

SIMPKIN word used in India for > **champagne**

SIMPLE adj easy to understand or do ▷ n simpleton ▷ vb archaic word meaning to look for medicinal herbs

SIMPLED ▷ **simple**

SIMPLER ▷ **simple**

SIMPLES ▷ **simple**

SIMPLEX adj permitting the transmission of signals in only one direction in a radio circuit ▷ n simple word not a compound word

SIMPLY adv in a simple manner

SIMPS ▷ **simp**

SIMS ▷ **sim**

SIMUL adj simultaneous ▷ n simultaneous broadcast

SIMULAR n person or thing that simulates or imitates ▷ adj fake

SIMULS ▷ **simul**

SIMURG n bird in Persian myth

SIMURGH n bird in Persian myth

SIMURGS ▷ **simurg**

SIN n offence or transgression ▷ vb commit a sin

SINCE prep during the period of time after ▷ adv from that time

SINCERE adj without pretence or deceit

SIND same as ▷ **syne**

SINDED ▷ **sind**

SINDING ▷ **sind**

SINDON n type of cloth

SINDONS ▷ **sindon**

SINDS ▷ **sind**

SINE ▷ **syne**

SINED ▷ **sine**

SINES ▷ **sine**

SINEW n tough fibrous tissue joining muscle to bone ▷ vb make strong

SINEWED adj having sinews

SINEWS ▷ **sinew**

SINEWY adj lean and muscular

SINFUL adj guilty of sin

SING vb make musical sounds with the voice ▷ n act or performance of singing

SINGE vb burn the surface of ▷ n superficial burn

SINGED ▷ **singe**

SINGER n person who sings, esp professionally

SINGERS ▷ **singer**

SINGES ▷ **singe**

SINGING ▷ **sing**

SINGLE adj one only ▷ n single thing ▷ vb pick out from others

SINGLED ▷ **single**

SINGLES pl n match played with one person on each side

SINGLET n sleeveless vest

SINGLY adv one at a time

SINGS ▷ **sing**

SINGULT n old word meaning sob

SINH n hyperbolic sine

SINHS ▷ **sinh**

SINICAL ▷ **sine**

SINING ▷ **sine**

SINK vb submerge (in liquid) ▷ n fixed basin with a water supply and drainage pipe

SINKAGE n act of sinking or degree to which something sinks or has sunk

SINKER n weight for a fishing line

SINKERS ▷ **sinker**

SINKIER ▷ **sinky**

SINKING ▷ **sink**

SINKS ▷ **sink**

SINKY adj giving underfoot

SINLESS adj free from sin or guilt

SINNED ▷ **sin**

SINNER n person that sins ▷ vb behave like a sinner

SINNERS ▷ **sin**

SINNET n braided rope

SINNETS ▷ **sinnet**

SINNING ▷ **sin**

SINOPIA n pigment made from iron ore

SINOPIE ▷ **sinopia**

SINOPIS n pigment made from iron ore

SINS ▷ **sin**

SINSYNE adv Scots word meaning since

SINTER n whitish porous incrustation that is deposited from hot springs ▷ vb form large particles from (metal powders or powdery ores) by heating or pressure

SINTERS ▷ **sinter**

SINTERY ▷ **sinter**

SINUATE vb wind

SINUOSE adj sinuous

SINUOUS adj full of turns or curves

SINUS n hollow space in a bone, esp an air passage opening into the nose

SINUSES ▷ **sinus**

SIP vb drink in small mouthfuls ▷ n amount sipped

SIPE vb soak

SIPED ▷ **sipe**

SIPES ▷ **sipe**

SIPHON n bent tube which uses air pressure to draw liquid from a container ▷ vb draw off thus

SIPHONS ▷ **siphon**

SIPING ▷ **sipe**

SIPPED ▷ **sip**

SIPPER ▷ **sip**

SIPPERS ▷ **sip**

SIPPET n small piece of toast eaten with soup or gravy

SIPPETS ▷ **sippet**

SIPPING ▷ **sip**

SIPPLE vb sip

SIPPLED ▷ **sipple**

SIPPLES ▷ **sipple**

SIPPY adj as in sippy cup infant's drinking cup with a tight-fitting lid and perforated spout

SIPS ▷ **sip**

SIR n polite term of address for a man ▷ vb call someone 'sir'

SIRCAR n government in India

SIRCARS ▶ sircar
SIRDAR *same as* ▶ sardar
SIRDARS ▶ sirdar
SIRE *n* male parent of a horse or other domestic animal ▷ *vb* father
SIRED ▶ sire
SIREE *emphasized form of* ▶ sir
SIREES ▶ siree
SIREN *n* device making a loud wailing noise as a warning
SIRENIC ▶ siren
SIRENS ▶ siren
SIRES ▶ sire
SIRGANG *n* Asian bird
SIRI *n* betel
SIRIH *n* betel
SIRIHS ▶ sirih
SIRING ▶ sire
SIRINGS ▶ siring
SIRIS ▶ siri
SIRKAR *n* government in India
SIRKARS ▶ sirkar
SIRLOIN *n* prime cut of loin of beef
SIRNAME *vb* old form of surname
SIROC *n* sirocco
SIROCCO *n* hot wind blowing from N Africa into S Europe
SIROCS ▶ siroc
SIROSET *adj* of the chemical treatment of woollen fabrics to give a permanent-press effect
SIRRA *disrespectful form of* ▶ sir
SIRRAH *n* contemptuous term used in addressing a man or boy
SIRRAHS ▶ sirrah
SIRRAS ▶ sirra
SIRRED ▶ sir
SIRREE *n* form of 'sir' used for emphasis
SIRREES ▶ sirree
SIRRING ▶ sir
SIRS ▶ sir
SIRTUIN *n* protein that regulates cell metabolism and ageing
SIRUP *same as* ▶ syrup
SIRUPED ▶ sirup
SIRUPS ▶ sirup
SIRUPY ▶ sirup
SIS *n* sister
SISAL *n* (fibre of) plant used in making ropes
SISALS ▶ sisal

SISES ▶ sis
SISKIN *n* yellow-and-black finch
SISKINS ▶ siskin
SISS *shortening of* ▶ sister
SISSES ▶ siss
SISSIER ▶ sissy
SISSIES ▶ sissy
SISSOO *n* Indian tree
SISSOOS ▶ sissoo
SISSY *n* weak or cowardly (person) ▷ *adj* effeminate, weak, or cowardly
SIST *vb* Scottish law term meaning stop
SISTED ▶ sist
SISTER *n* girl or woman with the same parents as another person ▷ *adj* closely related, similar ▷ *vb* be or be like a sister
SISTERS ▶ sister
SISTING ▶ sist
SISTRA ▶ sistrum
SISTRUM *n* musical instrument of ancient Egypt consisting of a metal rattle
SISTS ▶ sist
SIT *vb* rest one's body upright on the buttocks
SITAR *n* Indian stringed musical instrument
SITARS ▶ sitar
SITCOM *n* situation comedy
SITCOMS ▶ sitcom
SITE *n* place where something is, was, or is intended to be located ▷ *vb* provide with a site
SITED ▶ site
SITELLA *n* type of small generally black-and-white bird
SITES ▶ site
SITFAST *n* sore on a horse's back caused by rubbing of the saddle
SITH *archaic word for* ▶ since
SITHE *vb* old form of scythe
SITHED ▶ sithe
SITHEE *interj* look here! listen!
SITHEN *adv* old word meaning since
SITHENS *adv* old word meaning since
SITHES ▶ sithe
SITHING ▶ sithe
SITING ▶ site
SITKA *modifier as in* **sitka spruce** tall North American spruce tree

SITREP *n* military situation report
SITREPS ▶ sitrep
SITS ▶ sit
SITTAR *n* sitar
SITTARS ▶ sittar
SITTEN *adj* dialect word for in the saddle
SITTER *n* baby-sitter
SITTERS ▶ sitter
SITTINE *adj* of nuthatch bird family
SITTING ▶ sit
SITUATE *vb* place ▷ *adj* (now used esp in legal contexts) situated
SITULA *n* bucket-shaped container, usually of metal or pottery and often richly decorated
SITULAE ▶ situla
SITUP *n* exercise in which the body is brought into a sitting position from one lying on the back
SITUPS ▶ situp
SITUS *n* position or location, esp the usual or right position of an organ or part of the body
SITUSES ▶ situs
SITZ *n as in* **sitz bath** bath in which the buttocks and hips are immersed in hot water
SIVER *same as* ▶ syver
SIVERS ▶ siver
SIWASH *vb* (in the Pacific Northwest) to camp out with only natural shelter
SIX *n* one more than five
SIXAIN *n* stanza or poem of six lines
SIXAINE *n* six-line stanza of poetry
SIXAINS ▶ sixain
SIXER *same as* ▶ six
SIXERS ▶ sixer
SIXES ▶ six
SIXFOLD *adj* having six times as many or as much ▷ *adv* by six times as many or as much
SIXMO *n* book size resulting from folding a sheet of paper into six leaves or twelve pages, each one sixth the size of the sheet
SIXMOS ▶ sixmo
SIXTE *n* sixth of eight basic positions from which a parry or attack can be made in fencing

SIXTEEN *n* six and ten ▷ *adj* amounting to sixteen ▷ *determiner* amounting to sixteen

SIXTES ▶ **sixte**

SIXTH *n* (of) number six in a series ▷ *adj* coming after the fifth and before the seventh in numbering order ▷ *adv* after the fifth person, position, etc

SIXTHLY *same as* ▶ **sixth**

SIXTHS ▶ **sixth**

SIXTIES ▶ **sixty**

SIXTY *n* six times ten ▷ *adj* amounting to sixty

SIZABLE *adj* quite large

SIZABLY ▶ **sizable**

SIZAR *n* (at certain universities) an undergraduate receiving a maintenance grant from the college

SIZARS ▶ **sizar**

SIZE *n* dimensions, bigness ▷ *vb* arrange according to size

SIZED *adj* of a specified size

SIZEISM *n* discrimination on the basis of a person's size, esp against people considered to be overweight

SIZEIST ▶ **sizeism**

SIZEL *n* scrap metal clippings

SIZELS ▶ **sizel**

SIZER ▶ **size**

SIZERS ▶ **size**

SIZES ▶ **size**

SIZIER ▶ **size**

SIZIEST ▶ **size**

SIZING ▶ **size**

SIZINGS ▶ **size**

SIZISM *n* discrimination against people because of weight

SIZISMS ▶ **sizism**

SIZIST ▶ **sizism**

SIZISTS ▶ **sizism**

SIZY ▶ **size**

SIZZLE *vb* make a hissing sound like frying fat ▷ *n* hissing sound

SIZZLED ▶ **sizzle**

SIZZLER *n* something that sizzles

SIZZLES ▶ **sizzle**

SJAMBOK *n* whip or riding crop made of hide ▷ *vb* beat with a sjambok

SJOE *interj* South African exclamation of surprise,

admiration, exhaustion, etc

SKA *n* type of West Indian pop music of the 1960s

SKAG *same as* ▶ **scag**

SKAGS ▶ **skag**

SKAIL *vb* Scots word meaning disperse

SKAILED ▶ **skail**

SKAILS ▶ **skail**

SKAITH *vb* Scots word meaning injure

SKAITHS ▶ **skaith**

SKALD *n* (in an ancient Scandinavia) a bard or minstrel

SKALDIC ▶ **skald**

SKALDS ▶ **skald**

SKANK *n* fast dance to reggae music ▷ *vb* perform this dance

SKANKED ▶ **skank**

SKANKER ▶ **skank**

SKANKS ▶ **skank**

SKANKY *adj* dirty or unattractive

SKART *Scots word for* > **cormorant**

SKARTH *Scots word for* > **cormorant**

SKARTHS ▶ **skarth**

SKARTS ▶ **skart**

SKAS ▶ **ska**

SKAT *n* three-handed card game using 32 cards, popular in German-speaking communities

SKATE *n* boot with a steel blade or sets of wheels attached to the sole for gliding over ice or a hard surface ▷ *vb* glide on or as if on skates

SKATED ▶ **skate**

SKATER *n* person who skates

SKATERS ▶ **skater**

SKATES ▶ **skate**

SKATING ▶ **skate**

SKATOL *n* skatole

SKATOLE *n* white or brownish crystalline solid

SKATOLS ▶ **skatol**

SKATS ▶ **skat**

SKATT *n* dialect word meaning throw

SKATTS ▶ **skatt**

SKAW *same as* ▶ **scaw**

SKAWS ▶ **skaw**

SKEAN *n* kind of double-edged dagger formerly used in Ireland and Scotland

SKEANE *same as* ▶ **skein**

SKEANES ▶ **skeane**

SKEANS ▶ **skean**

SKEAR *dialect form of* ▶ **scare**

SKEARED ▶ **skear**

SKEARS ▶ **skear**

SKEARY *dialect form of* ▶ **scary**

SKEE *variant spelling of* ▶ **ski**

SKEED ▶ **skee**

SKEEF *adj, adv* South African slang for at an oblique angle

SKEEING ▶ **skee**

SKEELY *adj* Scots word meaning skilful

SKEEN *n* type of ibex

SKEENS ▶ **skeen**

SKEER *dialect form of* ▶ **scare**

SKEERED ▶ **skeer**

SKEERS ▶ **skeer**

SKEERY *dialect form of* ▶ **scary**

SKEES ▶ **skee**

SKEET *n* form of clay-pigeon shooting

SKEETER *informal word for* > **mosquito**

SKEETS ▶ **skeet**

SKEG *n* reinforcing brace between the after end of a keel and the rudderpost

SKEGG *n* skeg

SKEGGER *n* young salmon

SKEGGS ▶ **skegg**

SKEGS ▶ **skeg**

SKEIGH *adj* Scots word meaning shy

SKEIN *n* yarn wound in a loose coil ▷ *vb* wind into a skein

SKEINED ▶ **skein**

SKEINS ▶ **skein**

SKELDER *vb* beg

SKELF *n* splinter of wood, esp when embedded accidentally in the skin

SKELFS ▶ **skelf**

SKELL *n* homeless person

SKELLIE *adj* skelly

SKELLS ▶ **skell**

SKELLUM *n* rogue

SKELLY *n* whitefish of certain lakes in the Lake District ▷ *vb* look sideways or squint ▷ *adj* cross-eyed

SKELM *n* villain or crook

SKELMS ▶ **skelm**

SKELP *vb* slap ▷ *n* slap

SKELPED ▶ **skelp**

SKELPIT *vb* Scots word meaning skelped

S

SKELPS ▸ **skelp**

SKELTER vb scurry

SKELUM n Scots word meaning rascal

SKELUMS ▸ **skelum**

SKEN vb squint or stare

SKENE n Scots word meaning dagger

SKENES ▸ **skene**

SKENNED ▸ **sken**

SKENS ▸ **sken**

SKEO n Scots dialect word meaning hut

SKEOS ▸ **skeo**

SKEP n beehive, esp one constructed of straw ▷ vb gather into a hive

SKEPFUL n amount skep will hold

SKEPPED ▸ **skep**

SKEPS ▸ **skep**

SKEPSIS n doubt

SKEPTIC same as ▸ **sceptic**

SKER vb scour

SKERRED ▸ **sker**

SKERRY n rocky island or reef

SKERS ▸ **sker**

SKET vb splash (water)

SKETCH n rough drawing ▷ vb make a sketch (of)

SKETCHY adj incomplete or inadequate

SKETS ▸ **sket**

SKETTED ▸ **sket**

SKEW vb make slanting or crooked ▷ adj slanting or crooked ▷ n slanting position

SKEWED ▸ **skew**

SKEWER n pin to hold meat together during cooking ▷ vb fasten with a skewer

SKEWERS ▸ **skewer**

SKEWEST ▸ **skew**

SKEWING ▸ **skew**

SKEWS ▸ **skew**

SKI n one of a pair of long runners fastened to boots for gliding over snow or water ▷ vb travel on skis

SKIABLE ▸ **ski**

SKIBOB n vehicle made of two short skis for gliding down snow slopes

SKIBOBS ▸ **skibob**

SKID vb (of a moving vehicle) slide sideways uncontrollably ▷ n skidding

SKIDDED ▸ **skid**

SKIDDER ▸ **skid**

SKIDDOO vb go away quickly

SKIDDY ▸ **skid**

SKIDLID n crash helmet

SKIDOO n snowmobile ▷ vb travel on a skidoo

SKIDOOS ▸ **skidoo**

SKIDPAN n area made slippery so that vehicle drivers can practise controlling skids

SKIDS ▸ **skid**

SKIDWAY n platform on which logs ready for sawing are piled

SKIED ▸ **sky**

SKIER ▸ **ski**

SKIERS ▸ **ski**

SKIES ▸ **sky**

SKIEY adj of the sky

SKIEYER ▸ **skiey**

SKIFF n small boat ▷ vb travel in a skiff

SKIFFED ▸ **skiff**

SKIFFLE n style of popular music of the 1950s, played chiefly on guitars and improvised percussion instruments ▷ vb play this style of music

SKIFFS ▸ **skiff**

SKIING ▸ **ski**

SKIINGS ▸ **ski**

SKILFUL adj having or showing skill

SKILL n special ability or expertise

SKILLED adj possessing or demonstrating accomplishment, skill, or special training

SKILLET n small frying pan or shallow cooking pot

SKILLS ▸ **skill**

SKILLY n thin soup or gruel ▷ adj skilled

SKIM vb remove floating matter from the surface of (a liquid) ▷ n act or process of skimming

SKIMMED ▸ **skim**

SKIMMER n person or thing that skims

SKIMMIA n shrub of S and SE Asia grown for its ornamental red berries and evergreen foliage

SKIMP vb not invest enough time, money, material, etc

SKIMPED ▸ **skimp**

SKIMPS ▸ **skimp**

SKIMPY adj scanty or insufficient

SKIMS ▸ **skim**

SKIN n outer covering of the body ▷ vb remove the skin of

SKINFUL n sufficient alcoholic drink to make one drunk

SKINK n type of lizard with reduced limbs and smooth scales ▷ vb serve a drink

SKINKED ▸ **skink**

SKINKER ▸ **skink**

SKINKS ▸ **skink**

SKINNED ▸ **skin**

SKINNER n person who prepares or deals in animal skins

SKINNY adj thin ▷ n information

SKINS ▸ **skin**

SKINT adj having no money

SKINTER ▸ **skint**

SKIO n Scots dialect word meaning hut

SKIOS ▸ **skio**

SKIP vb leap lightly from one foot to the other ▷ n skipping

SKIPPED ▸ **skip**

SKIPPER vb captain ▷ n captain of a ship or aircraft

SKIPPET n small round box for preserving a document or seal

SKIPPY adj in high spirits

SKIPS ▸ **skip**

SKIRL n sound of bagpipes ▷ vb (of bagpipes) to give out a shrill sound

SKIRLED ▸ **skirl**

SKIRLS ▸ **skirl**

SKIRR vb move, run, or fly rapidly ▷ n whirring or grating sound, as of the wings of birds in flight

SKIRRED ▸ **skirr**

SKIRRET n umbelliferous Old World plant

SKIRRS ▸ **skirr**

SKIRT n woman's garment hanging from the waist ▷ vb border

SKIRTED ▸ **skirt**

SKIRTER n man who skirts fleeces

SKIRTS ▸ **skirt**

SKIS ▸ **ski**

SKIT n brief satirical sketch

SKITCH vb (of a dog) to attack

SKITE n, vb boast

SKITED ▸ **skite**

SKITES ▸ **skite**

SKITING ▸ **skite**

SKITS ▸ **skit**

SKITTER vb move or run rapidly or lightly

SKITTLE n bottle-shaped object used as a target in some games ▷ vb play skittles

SKIVE vb evade work or responsibility

SKIVED ▸ **skive**

SKIVER n tanned outer layer split from a skin ▷ vb cut leather

SKIVERS ▸ **skiver**

SKIVES ▸ **skive**

SKIVIE adj old Scots word meaning disarranged

SKIVIER ▸ **skivie**

SKIVING ▸ **skive**

SKIVVY n female servant who does menial work ▷ vb work as a skivvy

SKIVY ▸ **skive**

SKIWEAR n clothes for skiing in

SKLATE Scots word for ▸ **slate**

SKLATED ▸ **sklate**

SKLATES ▸ **sklate**

SKLENT Scots word for ▸ **slant**

SKLENTS ▸ **sklent**

SKLIFF n Scots word meaning little piece

SKLIFFS ▸ **skliff**

SKLIM vb Scots word meaning climb

SKLIMS ▸ **sklim**

SKOAL same as ▸ **skol**

SKOALED ▸ **skoal**

SKOALS ▸ **skoal**

SKOFF vb eat greedily

SKOFFED ▸ **skoff**

SKOFFS ▸ **skoff**

SKOL sentence substitute good health! (a drinking toast) ▷ vb down (an alcoholic drink) in one go

SKOLIA ▸ **skolion**

SKOLION n ancient Greek drinking song

SKOLLED ▸ **skol**

SKOLLIE same as ▸ **skolly**

SKOLLY n hooligan, usually one of a gang

SKOLS ▸ **skol**

SKOOKUM adj strong or brave

SKOOL ironically illiterate or childish spelling of ▸ **school**

SKOOLS ▸ **skool**

SKOOSH vb Scots word meaning squirt

SKORT n pair of shorts with a front panel which gives the appearance of a skirt

SKORTS ▸ **skort**

SKOSH n little bit

SKOSHES ▸ **skosh**

SKRAN n food

SKRANS ▸ **skran**

SKREEGH vb Scots word meaning screech

SKREEN n screen

SKREENS ▸ **skreen**

SKREIGH vb Scots word meaning screech

SKRIECH vb Scots word meaning screech

SKRIED ▸ **skry**

SKRIEGH vb Scots word meaning screech

SKRIES ▸ **skry**

SKRIK n South African word meaning fright

SKRIKE vb cry

SKRIKED ▸ **skrike**

SKRIKES ▸ **skrike**

SKRIKS ▸ **skrik**

SKRIMP vb steal apples

SKRIMPS ▸ **skrimp**

SKRONK n type of dissonant, grating popular music

SKRONKS ▸ **skronk**

SKRUMP vb steal apples

SKRUMPS ▸ **skrump**

SKRY vb try to tell future

SKRYER ▸ **skry**

SKRYERS ▸ **skry**

SKRYING ▸ **skry**

SKUA n large predatory gull

SKUAS ▸ **skua**

SKUDLER n Scots word meaning leader of festivities

SKUG vb shelter

SKUGGED ▸ **skug**

SKUGS ▸ **skug**

SKULK vb move stealthily ▷ n person who skulks

SKULKED ▸ **skulk**

SKULKER ▸ **skulk**

SKULKS ▸ **skulk**

SKULL n bony framework of the head ▷ vb strike on the head

SKULLED ▸ **skull**

SKULLS ▸ **skull**

SKULPIN n North American fish

SKUMMER vb defecate

SKUNK n small black-and-white N American mammal which emits a foul-smelling fluid when attacked ▷ vb defeat overwhelmingly in a game

SKUNKED ▸ **skunk**

SKUNKS ▸ **skunk**

SKUNKY ▸ **skunk**

SKURRY vb scurry

SKUTTLE vb scuttle

SKY n upper atmosphere as seen from the earth ▷ vb hit high in the air

SKYBORN adj born in heaven

SKYBOX n luxurious suite high up in the stand of a sports stadium

SKYCAP n luggage porter at American airport

SKYCAPS ▸ **skycap**

SKYCLAD adj naked

SKYDIVE vb take part in skydiving

SKYDOVE ▸ **skydive**

SKYED ▸ **sky**

SKYER n cricket ball hit up into air

SKYERS ▸ **skyer**

SKYEY adj of the sky

SKYF n South African slang for a cigarette or substance for smoking ▷ vb smoke a cigarette

SKYFED ▸ **skyf**

SKYFING ▸ **skyf**

SKYFS ▸ **skyf**

SKYHOME n Australian slang for a sub-penthouse flat in a tall building

SKYHOOK n hook hung from helicopter

SKYIER ▸ **skyey**

SKYIEST ▸ **skyey**

SKYING ▸ **sky**

SKYISH ▸ **sky**

SKYJACK vb hijack (an aircraft)

SKYLAB n orbiting space station

SKYLABS ▸ **skylab**

SKYLARK n lark that sings while soaring at a great height ▷ vb play or frolic

SKYLESS adj having no sky

SKYLIKE ▸ **sky**

SKYLINE n outline of buildings, trees, etc against the sky

SKYLIT adj having skylight

SKYMAN n paratrooper

SKYMEN ▸ **skyman**

SKYPHOI ▸ **skyphos**

SKYPHOS n ancient Greek drinking cup

SKYR n Scandinavian cheese

SKYRE vb Scots word

S

meaning shine

SKYRED ▶ **skyre**

SKYRES ▶ **skyre**

SKYRING ▶ **skyre**

SKYRS ▶ **skyr**

SKYSAIL n square sail set above the royal on a square-rigger

SKYSURF vb perform freefall aerobatics

SKYTE vb Scots word meaning slide

SKYTED ▶ **skyte**

SKYTES ▶ **skyte**

SKYTING ▶ **skyte**

SKYWALK n tightrope walk at great height

SKYWARD adj towards the sky ▷ adv towards the sky

SKYWAY n air route

SKYWAYS ▶ **skyway**

SLAB n broad flat piece ▷ vb cut or make into a slab or slabs

SLABBED ▶ **slab**

SLABBER vb dribble from the mouth

SLABBY ▶ **slab**

SLABS ▶ **slab**

SLACK same as ▶ **slake**

SLACKED ▶ **slack**

SLACKEN vb make or become slack

SLACKER n person who evades work or duty

SLACKLY ▶ **slack**

SLACKS pl n casual trousers

SLADANG n Malayan tapir

SLADE n little valley

SLADES ▶ **slade**

SLAE Scots word for ▶ **sloe**

SLAES ▶ **slae**

SLAG n waste left after metal is smelted ▷ vb criticize

SLAGGED ▶ **slag**

SLAGGY ▶ **slag**

SLAGS ▶ **slag**

SLAID vb Scots word for 'slid'

SLAIN ▶ **slay**

SLAINTE interj cheers!

SLAIRG Scots word for ▶ **spread**

SLAIRGS ▶ **slairg**

SLAKE vb satisfy (thirst or desire)

SLAKED ▶ **slake**

SLAKER ▶ **slake**

SLAKERS ▶ **slake**

SLAKES ▶ **slake**

SLAKING ▶ **slake**

SLALOM n skiing or canoeing race over a winding course ▷ vb take part in a slalom

SLALOMS ▶ **slalom**

SLAM vb shut, put down, or hit violently and noisily ▷ n act or sound of slamming

SLAMMED ▶ **slam**

SLAMMER n prison

SLAMS ▶ **slam**

SLANDER n false and malicious statement about a person ▷ vb utter slander about

SLANE n spade for cutting turf

SLANES ▶ **slane**

SLANG n very informal language ▷ vb use insulting language to (someone)

SLANGED ▶ **slang**

SLANGER n street vendor

SLANGS ▶ **slang**

SLANGY ▶ **slang**

SLANK dialect word for ▶ **lank**

SLANT vb lean at an angle, slope ▷ n slope

SLANTED ▶ **slant**

SLANTER same as ▶ **slinter**

SLANTLY ▶ **slant**

SLANTS ▶ **slant**

SLANTY adj slanting

SLAP n blow with the open hand or a flat object ▷ vb strike with the open hand or a flat object

SLAPPED ▶ **slap**

SLAPPER ▶ **slap**

SLAPS ▶ **slap**

SLART vb spill (something)

SLARTED ▶ **start**

SLARTS ▶ **start**

SLASH vb cut with a sweeping stroke ▷ n sweeping stroke

SLASHED ▶ **slash**

SLASHER n tool or tractor-drawn machine used for cutting scrub or undergrowth in the bush

SLASHES ▶ **slash**

SLAT n narrow strip of wood or metal ▷ vb provide with slats

SLATCH n slack part of rope

SLATE n rock which splits easily into thin layers ▷ vb cover with slates ▷ adj dark grey

SLATED ▶ **slate**

SLATER n person trained in laying roof slates

SLATERS ▶ **slater**

SLATES ▶ **slate**

SLATEY adj slightly mad

SLATHER vb spread quickly or lavishly

SLATIER ▶ **slaty**

SLATING n act or process of laying slates

SLATS ▶ **slat**

SLATTED ▶ **slat**

SLATTER vb be slovenly

SLATY adj consisting of or resembling slate

SLAVE n person owned by another for whom he or she has to work ▷ vb work like a slave

SLAVED ▶ **slave**

SLAVER n person or ship engaged in the slave trade ▷ vb dribble saliva from the mouth

SLAVERS ▶ **slaver**

SLAVERY n state or condition of being a slave

SLAVES ▶ **slave**

SLAVEY n female general servant

SLAVEYS ▶ **slavey**

SLAVING ▶ **slave**

SLAVISH adj of or like a slave

SLAW short for ▶ **coleslaw**

SLAWS ▶ **slaw**

SLAY vb kill

SLAYED ▶ **slay**

SLAYER ▶ **slay**

SLAYERS ▶ **slay**

SLAYING ▶ **slay**

SLAYS ▶ **slay**

SLEAVE n tangled thread ▷ vb disentangle (twisted thread, etc)

SLEAVED ▶ **sleave**

SLEAVES ▶ **sleave**

SLEAZE n behaviour in public life considered immoral, dishonest, or disreputable

SLEAZES ▶ **sleaze**

SLEAZO n sleazy person

SLEAZY adj run-down or sordid

SLEB n celebrity

SLEBS ▶ **sleb**

SLED same as ▶ **sledge**

SLEDDED ▶ **sled**

SLEDDER ▶ **sled**

SLEDED ▶ **sled**

SLEDGE n carriage on runners for sliding on snow ▷ vb travel by sledge

SLEDGED ▶ **sledge**

SLEDGER ▶ **sledge**

SLEDGES ▶ **sledge**

SLEDS ▶ sled
SLEE Scots word for ▶ **sly**
SLEECH n slippery mud
SLEECHY ▶ sleech
SLEEK adj glossy, smooth, and shiny ▷ vb make smooth and glossy, as by grooming, etc
SLEEKED ▶ sleek
SLEEKEN vb make sleek
SLEEKER ▶ sleek
SLEEKIT adj smooth
SLEEKLY ▶ sleek
SLEEKS ▶ sleek
SLEEKY ▶ sleek
SLEEP n state of rest characterized by unconsciousness ▷ vb be in or as if in a state of sleep
SLEEPER n railway car fitted for sleeping in
SLEEPRY Scots word for ▶ **sleepy**
SLEEPS ▶ sleep
SLEEPY adj needing sleep
SLEER ▶ slee
SLEEST ▶ slee
SLEET n rain and snow or hail falling together ▷ vb fall as sleet
SLEETED ▶ sleet
SLEETS ▶ sleet
SLEETY ▶ sleet
SLEEVE n part of a garment which covers the arm
SLEEVED ▶ sleeve
SLEEVER n old beer measure
SLEEVES ▶ sleeve
SLEEZY adj sleazy
SLEIDED adj old word meaning separated
SLEIGH same as ▶ **sledge**
SLEIGHS ▶ sleigh
SLEIGHT n skill or cunning
SLENDER adj slim
SLENTER same as ▶ **slinter**
SLEPT ▶ sleep
SLEUTH n detective ▷ vb track or follow
SLEUTHS ▶ sleuth
SLEW vb twist sideways, esp awkwardly
SLEWED ▶ slew
SLEWING ▶ slew
SLEWS ▶ slew
SLEY n weaver's tool for separating threads
SLEYS ▶ sley
SLICE n thin flat piece cut from something ▷ vb cut into slices
SLICED ▶ slice

SLICER ▶ slice
SLICERS ▶ slice
SLICES ▶ slice
SLICING ▶ slice
SLICK adj persuasive and glib ▷ n patch of oil on water ▷ vb make smooth or sleek
SLICKED ▶ slick
SLICKEN vb make smooth
SLICKER n slip or untrustworthy person
SLICKLY ▶ slick
SLICKS ▶ slick
SLID ▶ slide
SLIDDEN ▶ slide
SLIDDER vb slip
SLIDE vb slip smoothly along (a surface) ▷ n sliding
SLIDED ▶ slide
SLIDER ▶ slide
SLIDERS ▶ slide
SLIDES ▶ slide
SLIDING ▶ slide
SLIER ▶ sly
SLIEST ▶ sly
SLIEVE n Irish mountain
SLIEVES ▶ slieve
SLIGHT adj small in quantity or extent ▷ n snub ▷ vb insult (someone) by behaving rudely
SLIGHTS ▶ slight
SLILY ▶ sly
SLIM adj not heavy or stout, thin ▷ vb make or become slim by diet and exercise
SLIME n unpleasant thick slippery substance ▷ vb cover with slime
SLIMED ▶ slime
SLIMES ▶ slime
SLIMIER ▶ slimy
SLIMILY ▶ slimy
SLIMING ▶ slime
SLIMLY ▶ slim
SLIMMED ▶ slim
SLIMMER ▶ slim
SLIMPSY adj thin and flimsy
SLIMS ▶ slim
SLIMSY adj frail
SLIMY adj of, like, or covered with slime
SLING n bandage hung from the neck to support an injured hand or arm ▷ vb throw
SLINGER ▶ sling
SLINGS ▶ sling
SLINK vb move furtively or guiltily ▷ n animal, esp a calf, born prematurely
SLINKED ▶ slink

SLINKER ▶ slink
SLINKS ▶ slink
SLINKY adj (of clothes) figure-hugging
SLINTER n dodge, trick, or stratagem
SLIOTAR n ball used in hurling
SLIP vb lose balance by sliding ▷ n slipping
SLIPE n wool removed from the pelt of a slaughtered sheep by immersion in a chemical bath ▷ vb remove skin
SLIPED ▶ slipe
SLIPES ▶ slipe
SLIPING ▶ slipe
SLIPOUT n instance of slipping out
SLIPPED ▶ slip
SLIPPER n light shoe for indoor wear ▷ vb hit or beat with a slipper
SLIPPY adj slippery
SLIPS ▶ slip
SLIPT vb old form of slipped
SLIPUP n mistake or mishap
SLIPUPS ▶ slipup
SLIPWAY n launching slope on which ships are built or repaired
SLISH n old word meaning cut
SLISHES ▶ slish
SLIT n long narrow cut or opening ▷ vb make a long straight cut in
SLITHER vb slide unsteadily ▷ n slithering movement
SLITS ▶ slit
SLITTED ▶ slit
SLITTER ▶ slit
SLITTY ▶ slit
SLIVE vb slip
SLIVED ▶ slive
SLIVEN ▶ slive
SLIVER n small thin piece ▷ vb cut into slivers
SLIVERS ▶ sliver
SLIVES ▶ slive
SLIVING ▶ slive
SLOAN n severe telling-off
SLOANS ▶ sloan
SLOB n lazy and untidy person
SLOBBER vb dribble or drool ▷ n liquid or saliva spilt from the mouth
SLOBBY ▶ slob
SLOBS ▶ slob
SLOCKEN vb Scots word meaning slake**

S

SLOE n sour blue-black fruit

SLOES ► sloe

SLOG vb work hard and steadily ▷ n long and exhausting work or walk

SLOGAN n catchword or phrase used in politics or advertising

SLOGANS ► slogan

SLOGGED ► slog

SLOGGER ► slog

SLOGS ► slog

SLOID n Swedish woodwork

SLOIDS ► sloid

SLOJD n Swedish woodwork

SLOJDS ► slojd

SLOKEN vb Scots word meaning slake

SLOKENS ► sloken

SLOOM vb slumber

SLOOMED ► sloom

SLOOMS ► sloom

SLOOMY ► sloom

SLOOP n small single-masted ship

SLOOPS ► sloop

SLOOSH vb wash with water

SLOOT n ditch for irrigation or drainage

SLOOTS ► sloot

SLOP vb splash or spill ▷ n spilt liquid

SLOPE vb slant ▷ n sloping surface

SLOPED ► slope

SLOPER ► slope

SLOPERS ► slope

SLOPES ► slope

SLOPIER ► slope

SLOPING ► slope

SLOPPED ► slop

SLOPPY adj careless or untidy

SLOPS ► slop

SLOPY ► slope

SLORM vb wipe carelessly

SLORMED ► slorm

SLORMS ► slorm

SLOSH vb pour carelessly ▷ n splashing sound

SLOSHED ► slosh

SLOSHES ► slosh

SLOSHY ► slosh

SLOT n narrow opening for inserting something ▷ vb make a slot or slots in

SLOTH n slow-moving animal of tropical America ▷ vb be lazy

SLOTHED ► sloth

SLOTHS ► sloth

SLOTS ► slot

SLOTTED ► slot

SLOTTER ► slot

SLOUCH vb sit, stand, or move with a drooping posture ▷ n drooping posture

SLOUCHY adj slouching

SLOUGH n bog ▷ vb (of a snake) shed (its skin)

SLOUGHI n N African breed of dog resembling a greyhound

SLOUGHS ► slough

SLOUGHY ► slough

SLOVE ► slive

SLOVEN n habitually dirty or untidy person

SLOVENS ► sloven

SLOW adj taking a longer time than is usual or expected ▷ adv slowly ▷ vb reduce the speed (of)

SLOWED ► slow

SLOWER ► slow

SLOWEST ► slow

SLOWING ► slow

SLOWISH ► slow

SLOWLY ► slow

SLOWS ► slow

SLOYD n Swedish woodwork

SLOYDS ► sloyd

SLUB n lump in yarn or fabric, often made intentionally to give a knobbly effect ▷ vb draw out and twist (a sliver of fibre) preparatory to spinning ▷ adj (of material) having an irregular appearance

SLUBB same as ► slub

SLUBBED ► slub

SLUBBER vb smear

SLUBBS ► slubb

SLUBBY ► slub

SLUBS ► slub

SLUDGE n thick mud ▷ vb to convert into sludge

SLUDGED ► sludge

SLUDGES ► sludge

SLUDGY adj consisting of, containing, or like sludge

SLUE same as ► slew

SLUED ► slue

SLUEING ► slue

SLUES ► slue

SLUFF same as ► slough

SLUFFED ► sluff

SLUFFS ► sluff

SLUG n land snail with no shell ▷ vb hit hard

SLUGGED ► slug

SLUGGER n (esp in boxing, baseball, etc) a person who strikes hard

SLUGS ► slug

SLUICE n channel that carries a rapid current of water ▷ vb drain water by means of a sluice

SLUICED ► sluice

SLUICES ► sluice

SLUICY ► sluice

SLUING ► slue

SLUIT n water channel in South Africa

SLUITS ► sluit

SLUM n squalid overcrowded house or area ▷ vb temporarily and deliberately experience poorer places or conditions than usual

SLUMBER n sleep ▷ vb sleep

SLUMBRY same as > slumbery

SLUMGUM n material left after wax is extracted from honeycomb

SLUMISM n existence of slums

SLUMMED ► slum

SLUMMER ► slum

SLUMMY ► slum

SLUMP vb (of prices or demand) decline suddenly ▷ n sudden decline in prices or demand

SLUMPED ► slump

SLUMPS ► slump

SLUMPY adj boggy

SLUMS ► slum

SLUNG ► sling

SLUNK ► slink

SLUR vb pronounce or utter (words) indistinctly ▷ n slurring of words

SLURB n suburban slum

SLURBAN ► slurb

SLURBS ► slurb

SLURP vb eat or drink noisily ▷ n slurping sound

SLURPED ► slurp

SLURPER ► slurp

SLURPS ► slurp

SLURPY adj making a slurping noise

SLURRED ► slur

SLURRY n muddy liquid mixture ▷ vb spread slurry

SLURS ► slur

SLUSE same as ► sluice

SLUSES ► sluice

SLUSH n watery muddy substance ▷ vb make one's

way through or as if through slush
SLUSHED ▸ slush
SLUSHES ▸ slush
SLUSHY adj of, resembling, or consisting of slush ▷ n unskilled kitchen assistant
SLUTCH n mud
SLUTCHY ▸ slutch
SLY adj crafty
SLYER ▸ sly
SLYEST ▸ sly
SLYISH ▸ sly
SLYLY ▸ sly
SLYNESS ▸ sly
SLYPE n covered passageway in a church that connects the transept to the chapterhouse
SLYPES ▸ slype
SMA Scots word for ▸ **small**
SMAAK vb South African slang for like or love
SMAAKED ▸ smaak
SMAAKS ▸ smaak
SMACK vb slap sharply ▷ n sharp slap ▷ adv squarely or directly
SMACKED ▸ smack
SMACKER n loud kiss
SMACKS ▸ smack
SMAIK n Scots word meaning rascal
SMAIKS ▸ smaik
SMALL adj not large in size, number, or amount ▷ n narrow part of the lower back ▷ adv into small pieces ▷ vb make small
SMALLED ▸ small
SMALLER ▸ small
SMALLS ▸ small
SMALM same as ▸ **smarm**
SMALMED ▸ smalm
SMALMS ▸ smalm
SMALMY same as ▸ **smarmy**
SMALT n type of silica glass coloured deep blue with cobalt oxide
SMALTI ▸ smalto
SMALTO n coloured glass, etc, used in mosaics
SMALTOS ▸ smalto
SMALTS ▸ smalt
SMARAGD n any green gemstone, such as the emerald
SMARM vb bring (oneself) into favour (with) ▷ n obsequious flattery
SMARMED ▸ smarm
SMARMS ▸ smarm

SMARMY adj unpleasantly suave or flattering
SMART adj well-kept and neat ▷ vb feel or cause stinging pain ▷ n stinging pain ▷ adv in a smart manner
SMARTED ▸ smart
SMARTEN vb make or become smart
SMARTER ▸ smart
SMARTIE same as ▸ **smarty**
SMARTLY ▸ smart
SMARTS pl n know-how, intelligence, or wits
SMARTY n would-be clever person
SMASH vb break violently and noisily ▷ n act or sound of smashing ▷ adv with a smash
SMASHED adj completely intoxicated with alcohol
SMASHER n attractive person or thing
SMASHES ▸ smash
SMASHUP n bad collision of cars
SMATCH less common word for ▸ **smack**
SMATTER n smattering ▷ vb prattle
SMAZE n smoky haze, less damp than fog
SMAZES ▸ smaze
SMEAR vb spread with a greasy or sticky substance ▷ n dirty mark or smudge
SMEARED ▸ smear
SMEARER ▸ smear
SMEARS ▸ smear
SMEARY adj smeared, dirty
SMEATH n duck
SMEATHS ▸ smeath
SMECTIC adj (of a substance) existing in state in which the molecules are oriented in layers
SMEDDUM n any fine powder
SMEE n duck
SMEECH Southwest English dialect form of ▸ **smoke**
SMEEK vb smoke
SMEEKED ▸ smeek
SMEEKS ▸ smeech
SMEES ▸ smee
SMEETH n duck
SMEETHS ▸ smeeth
SMEGMA n whitish sebaceous secretion that accumulates beneath the prepuce

SMEGMAS ▸ smegma
SMEIK ▸ smeke
SMEIKED ▸ smeked
SMEIKS ▸ smeik
SMEKE n smoke ▷ vb smoke
SMEKED ▸ smeke (sense 2)
SMEKES ▸ smeke
SMEKING > smeke (sense 2)
SMELL vb perceive (a scent or odour) by means of the nose ▷ n ability to perceive odours by the nose
SMELLED ▸ smell
SMELLER ▸ smell
SMELLS ▸ smell
SMELLY adj having a nasty smell
SMELT vb extract metal from an ore
SMELTED ▸ smell
SMELTER n industrial plant where smelting is carried out
SMELTS ▸ smell
SMERK same as ▸ **smirk**
SMERKED ▸ smerk
SMERKS ▸ smerk
SMEUSE n way through hedge
SMEUSES ▸ smeuse
SMEW n duck of N Europe and Asia
SMEWS ▸ smew
SMICKER vb look at someone amorously
SMICKET n smock
SMICKLY adv amorously
SMIDDY Scots word for ▸ **smithy**
SMIDGE n very small amount or part
SMIDGEN n very small amount or part
SMIDGES ▸ smidge
SMIDGIN same as ▸ **smidgen**
SMIGHT same as ▸ **smite**
SMIGHTS ▸ smight
SMILAX n type of climbing shrub
SMILE n turning up of the corners of the mouth to show pleasure or friendliness ▷ vb give a smile
SMILED ▸ smile
SMILER ▸ smile
SMILERS ▸ smile
SMILES ▸ smile
SMILET n little smile
SMILETS ▸ smilet
SMILEY n symbol depicting a smile or other facial

S

expression, used in e-mail ▷ *adj* cheerful
SMILEYS ▶ smiley
SMILIER ▶ smiley
SMILING ▶ smile
SMIR *n* drizzly rain ▷ *vb* drizzle lightly
SMIRCH *n* stain ▷ *vb* disgrace
SMIRK *n* smug smile ▷ *vb* give a smirk
SMIRKED ▶ smirk
SMIRKER ▶ smirk
SMIRKS ▶ smirk
SMIRKY ▶ smirk
SMIRR *same as* ▶ smir
SMIRRED ▶ smirr
SMIRRS ▶ smirr
SMIRRY ▶ smirr
SMIRS ▶ smir
SMIT ▶ smite
SMITE *vb* strike hard
SMITER ▶ smite
SMITERS ▶ smite
SMITES ▶ smite
SMITH *n* worker in metal ▷ *vb* work in metal
SMITHED ▶ smith
SMITHS ▶ smith
SMITHY *n* blacksmith's workshop ▷ *vb* work as a smith
SMITING ▶ smite
SMITS ▶ smit
SMITTED ▶ smit
SMITTEN ▶ smite
SMITTLE *adj* infectious
SMOCK *n* loose overall ▷ *vb* gather (material) by sewing in a honeycomb pattern
SMOCKED ▶ smock
SMOCKS ▶ smock
SMOG *n* mixture of smoke and fog
SMOGGY ▶ smog
SMOGS ▶ smog
SMOILE *same as* ▶ smile
SMOILED ▶ smoile
SMOILES ▶ smoile
SMOKE *n* cloudy mass that rises from something burning ▷ *vb* give off smoke or treat with smoke
SMOKED ▶ smoke
SMOKEHO *same as* ▶ smoko
SMOKER *n* person who habitually smokes tobacco
SMOKERS ▶ smoker
SMOKES ▶ smoke
SMOKEY *same as* ▶ smoky
SMOKIE *n* smoked haddock
SMOKIER ▶ smoky

SMOKIES ▶ smoky
SMOKILY ▶ smoky
SMOKING ▶ smoke
SMOKO *n* short break from work for tea or a cigarette
SMOKOS ▶ smoko
SMOKY *adj* filled with or giving off smoke, sometimes excessively ▷ *n* haddock that has been smoked
SMOLDER *same as* > smoulder
SMOLT *n* young salmon at the stage when it migrates to the sea
SMOLTS ▶ smolt
SMOOCH *vb* kiss and cuddle ▷ *n* smooching
SMOOCHY *adj* romantic
SMOODGE *same as* ▶ smooch
SMOOGE *same as* ▶ smooch
SMOOGED ▶ smooge
SMOOGES ▶ smooge
SMOOR *vb* Scots word meaning put out fire
SMOORED ▶ smoor
SMOORS ▶ smoor
SMOOSH *vb* paint to give softened look
SMOOT *vb* work as printer
SMOOTED ▶ smoot
SMOOTH *adj* even in surface, texture, or consistency ▷ *vb* make smooth ▷ *adv* in a smooth manner ▷ *n* smooth part of something
SMOOTHS ▶ smooth
SMOOTHY *same as* > smoothie
SMOOTS ▶ smoot
SMORE *same as* ▶ smoor
SMORED ▶ smore
SMORES ▶ smore
SMORING ▶ smore
SMOTE ▶ smite
SMOTHER *vb* suffocate or stifle ▷ *n* anything, such as a cloud of smoke, that stifles
SMOUCH *vb* kiss
SMOUSE *vb* South African word meaning peddle
SMOUSED ▶ smouse
SMOUSER ▶ smouse
SMOUSES ▶ smouse
SMOUT *n* child or undersized person ▷ *vb* creep or sneak
SMOUTED ▶ smout
SMOUTS ▶ smout

SMOWT *same as* ▶ smout
SMOWTS ▶ smowt
SMOYLE *same as* ▶ smile
SMOYLED ▶ smoyle
SMOYLES ▶ smoyle
SMRITI *n* class of Hindu sacred literature derived from the Vedas
SMRITIS ▶ smriti
SMUDGE *vb* make or become smeared or soiled ▷ *n* dirty mark
SMUDGED ▶ smudge
SMUDGER ▶ smudge
SMUDGES ▶ smudge
SMUDGY *adj* smeared, blurred, or soiled, or likely to become so
SMUG *adj* self-satisfied ▷ *vb* make neat
SMUGGED ▶ smug
SMUGGER ▶ smug
SMUGGLE *vb* import or export (goods) secretly and illegally
SMUGLY ▶ smug
SMUGS ▶ smug
SMUR *same as* ▶ smir
SMURRED ▶ smur
SMURRY ▶ smur
SMURS ▶ smur
SMUSH *vb* crush
SMUSHED ▶ smush
SMUSHES ▶ smush
SMUT *n* obscene jokes, pictures, etc ▷ *vb* mark or become marked or smudged, as with soot
SMUTCH *vb* smudge ▷ *n* mark
SMUTCHY ▶ smutch
SMUTS ▶ smut
SMUTTED ▶ smut
SMUTTY ▶ smut
SMYTRIE *n* Scots word meaning collection
SNAB *same as* ▶ snob
SNABBLE *same as* ▶ snaffle
SNABS ▶ snab
SNACK *n* light quick meal ▷ *vb* eat a snack
SNACKED ▶ snack
SNACKER ▶ snack
SNACKS ▶ snack
SNAFFLE *n* jointed bit for a horse ▷ *vb* steal
SNAFU *n* confusion or chaos regarded as the normal state ▷ *adj* confused or muddled up, as usual ▷ *vb* throw into chaos
SNAFUED ▶ snafu
SNAFUS ▶ snafu

SNAG n difficulty or disadvantage ▷ vb catch or tear on a point

SNAGGED ▶ **snag**

SNAGGY adj having sharp protuberances

SNAGS ▶ **snag**

SNAIL n slow-moving mollusc with a spiral shell ▷ vb move slowly

SNAILED ▶ **snail**

SNAILS ▶ **snail**

SNAILY ▶ **snail**

SNAKE n long thin scaly limbless reptile ▷ vb move in a winding course like a snake

SNAKED ▶ **snake**

SNAKES ▶ **snake**

SNAKEY same as ▶ **snaky**

SNAKIER ▶ **snaky**

SNAKILY ▶ **snaky**

SNAKING ▶ **snake**

SNAKISH ▶ **snake**

SNAKY adj twisted or winding

SNAP vb break suddenly ▷ n act or sound of snapping ▷ adj made on the spur of the moment ▷ adv with a snap

SNAPPED ▶ **snap**

SNAPPER n food fish of Australia and New Zealand ▷ vb stumble

SNAPPY adj irritable

SNAPS ▶ **snap**

SNAPTIN n container for food

SNAR same as ▶ **snarl**

SNARE n trap with a noose ▷ vb catch in or as if in a snare

SNARED ▶ **snare**

SNARER ▶ **snare**

SNARERS ▶ **snare**

SNARES ▶ **snare**

SNARF vb eat or drink greedily

SNARFED ▶ **snarf**

SNARFS ▶ **snarf**

SNARIER ▶ **snare**

SNARING ▶ **snare**

SNARK n imaginary creature in Lewis Carroll's poetry

SNARKS ▶ **snark**

SNARKY adj unpleasant and scornful

SNARL vb (of an animal) growl with bared teeth ▷ n act or sound of snarling

SNARLED ▶ **snarl**

SNARLER ▶ **snarl**

SNARLS ▶ **snarl**

SNARLY ▶ **snarl**

SNARRED ▶ **snar**

SNARS ▶ **snar**

SNARY ▶ **snare**

SNASH vb Scots word meaning speak cheekily

SNASHED ▶ **snash**

SNASHES ▶ **snash**

SNASTE n candle wick

SNASTES ▶ **snaste**

SNATCH vb seize or try to seize suddenly ▷ n snatching

SNATCHY adj disconnected or spasmodic

SNATH n handle of a scythe

SNATHE same as ▶ **snath**

SNATHES ▶ **snathe**

SNATHS ▶ **snath**

SNAW Scots variant of ▶ **snow**

SNAWED ▶ **snaw**

SNAWING ▶ **snaw**

SNAWS ▶ **snaw**

SNAZZY adj stylish and flashy

SNEAD n scythe handle

SNEADS ▶ **snead**

SNEAK vb move furtively ▷ n cowardly or underhand person ▷ adj without warning

SNEAKED ▶ **sneak**

SNEAKER n soft shoe

SNEAKS ▶ **sneak**

SNEAKY ▶ **sneak**

SNEAP vb nip

SNEAPED ▶ **sneap**

SNEAPS ▶ **sneap**

SNEATH same as ▶ **snath**

SNEATHS ▶ **sneath**

SNEB same as ▶ **snib**

SNEBBE same as ▶ **snub**

SNEBBED ▶ **sneb**

SNEBBES ▶ **snebbe**

SNEBS ▶ **sneb**

SNECK n small squared stone used in a rubble wall to fill spaces between stones ▷ vb fasten (a latch)

SNECKED ▶ **sneck**

SNECKS ▶ **sneck**

SNED vb prune or trim

SNEDDED ▶ **sned**

SNEDS ▶ **sned**

SNEE vb cut

SNEED ▶ **snee**

SNEEING ▶ **snee**

SNEER n contemptuous expression or remark ▷ vb show contempt by a sneer

SNEERED ▶ **sneer**

SNEERER ▶ **sneer**

SNEERS ▶ **sneer**

SNEERY adj contemptuous or scornful

SNEES ▶ **snee**

SNEESH n Scots word meaning pinch of snuff

SNEEZE vb expel air from the nose suddenly, involuntarily, and noisily ▷ n act or sound of sneezing

SNEEZED ▶ **sneeze**

SNEEZER ▶ **sneeze**

SNEEZES ▶ **sneeze**

SNEEZY ▶ **sneeze**

SNELL adj biting ▷ vb attach hook to fishing line

SNELLED ▶ **snell**

SNELLER ▶ **snell**

SNELLS ▶ **snell**

SNELLY ▶ **snell**

SNIB n catch of a door or window ▷ vb bolt or fasten (a door)

SNIBBED ▶ **snib**

SNIBS ▶ **snib**

SNICK n (make) a small cut or notch ▷ vb make a small cut or notch in (something)

SNICKED ▶ **snick**

SNICKER same as ▶ **snigger**

SNICKET n passageway between walls or fences

SNICKS ▶ **snick**

SNIDE adj critical in an unfair and nasty way ▷ n sham jewellery ▷ vb fill or load

SNIDED ▶ **snide**

SNIDELY ▶ **snide**

SNIDER ▶ **snide**

SNIDES ▶ **snide**

SNIDEST ▶ **snide**

SNIDEY same as ▶ **snide**

SNIDIER ▶ **snidey**

SNIDING ▶ **snide**

SNIES ▶ **sny**

SNIFF vb inhale through the nose in short audible breaths ▷ n act or sound of sniffing

SNIFFED ▶ **sniff**

SNIFFER n device for detecting hidden substances such as drugs or explosives, esp by their odour

SNIFFLE vb sniff repeatedly, as when suffering from a cold ▷ n slight cold

SNIFFLY ▶ **sniffle**

SNIFFS ▶ **sniff**

S

SNIFFY *adj* contemptuous or scornful

SNIFT *same as* ▸ **sniff**

SNIFTED ▸ **snift**

SNIFTER *n* small quantity of alcoholic drink ▸ *vb* sniff

SNIFTS ▸ **snift**

SNIFTY *adj* slang word meaning excellent

SNIG *vb* drag (a felled log) by a chain or cable

SNIGGED ▸ **snig**

SNIGGER *n* a sly laugh ▸ *vb* laugh slyly

SNIGGLE *vb* fish for eels by dangling or thrusting a baited hook into cavities ▸ *n* baited hook used for sniggling eels

SNIGLET *n* invented word

SNIGS ▸ **snig**

SNIP *vb* cut in small quick strokes with scissors or shears ▸ *n* bargain ▸ *interj* representation of the sound of scissors or shears closing

SNIPE *n* wading bird with a long straight bill ▸ *vb* shoot at (a person) from cover

SNIPED ▸ **snipe**

SNIPER *n* person who shoots at someone from cover

SNIPERS ▸ **sniper**

SNIPES ▸ **snipe**

SNIPIER ▸ **snipy**

SNIPING ▸ **snipe**

SNIPPED ▸ **snip**

SNIPPER ▸ **snip**

SNIPPET *n* small piece

SNIPPY *adj* scrappy

SNIPS ▸ **snip**

SNIPY *adj* like a snipe

SNIRT *n* Scots word meaning suppressed laugh

SNIRTLE *vb* Scots word meaning snicker

SNIRTS ▸ **snirt**

SNIT *n* fit of temper

SNITCH *vb* act as an informer ▸ *n* informer

SNITCHY *adj* bad-tempered or irritable

SNITS ▸ **snit**

SNIVEL *vb* cry in a whining way ▸ *n* act of snivelling

SNIVELS ▸ **snivel**

SNOB *n* person who judges others by social rank

SNOBBY ▸ **snob**

SNOBS ▸ **snob**

SNOD *vb* Scots word meaning make tidy

SNODDED ▸ **snod**

SNODDER ▸ **snod**

SNODDIT ▸ **snod**

SNODS ▸ **snod**

SNOEK *n* edible marine fish

SNOEKS ▸ **snoek**

SNOEP *adj* mean or tight-fisted

SNOG *vb* kiss and cuddle ▸ *n* act of kissing and cuddling

SNOGGED ▸ **snog**

SNOGS ▸ **snog**

SNOKE *same as* ▸ **snook**

SNOKED ▸ **snoke**

SNOKES ▸ **snoke**

SNOKING ▸ **snoke**

SNOOD *n* pouch, often of net, loosely holding a woman's hair at the back ▸ *vb* hold (the hair) in a snood

SNOODED ▸ **snood**

SNOODS ▸ **snood**

SNOOK *n* any of several large game fishes ▸ *vb* lurk

SNOOKED ▸ **snook**

SNOOKER *n* game played on a billiard table ▸ *vb* leave (a snooker opponent) in a position such that another ball blocks the target ball

SNOOKS ▸ **snook**

SNOOL *vb* Scots word meaning dominate

SNOOLED ▸ **snool**

SNOOLS ▸ **snool**

SNOOP *vb* pry ▸ *n* snooping

SNOOPED ▸ **snoop**

SNOOPER *n* person who snoops

SNOOPS ▸ **snoop**

SNOOPY ▸ **snoop**

SNOOT *n* nose ▸ *vb* look contemptuously at

SNOOTED ▸ **snoot**

SNOOTS ▸ **snoot**

SNOOTY *adj* haughty

SNOOZE *vb* take a brief light sleep ▸ *n* brief light sleep

SNOOZED ▸ **snooze**

SNOOZER ▸ **snooze**

SNOOZES ▸ **snooze**

SNOOZLE *vb* cuddle and sleep

SNOOZY ▸ **snooze**

SNORE *vb* make snorting sounds while sleeping ▸ *n* sound of snoring

SNORED ▸ **snore**

SNORER ▸ **snore**

SNORERS ▸ **snore**

SNORES ▸ **snore**

SNORING ▸ **snore**

SNORKEL *n* tube allowing a swimmer to breathe while face down on the surface of the water ▸ *vb* swim using a snorkel

SNORT *vb* exhale noisily through the nostrils ▸ *n* act or sound of snorting

SNORTED ▸ **snort**

SNORTER *n* person or animal that snorts

SNORTS ▸ **snort**

SNORTY ▸ **snort**

SNOT *n* mucus from the nose ▸ *vb* blow one's nose

SNOTRAG *n* handkerchief

SNOTS ▸ **snot**

SNOTTED ▸ **snot**

SNOTTER *vb* breathe through obstructed nostrils

SNOTTIE *n* midshipman

SNOTTY *adj* covered with mucus from the nose

SNOUT *n* animal's projecting nose and jaws ▸ *vb* have or give a snout

SNOUTED ▸ **snout**

SNOUTS ▸ **snout**

SNOUTY ▸ **snout**

SNOW *n* frozen vapour falling from the sky in flakes ▸ *vb* fall as or like snow

SNOWCAP *n* cap of snow on top of a mountain

SNOWCAT *n* tracked vehicle for travelling over snow

SNOWED *adj* under the influence of narcotic drugs

SNOWIER ▸ **snowy**

SNOWILY ▸ **snowy**

SNOWING ▸ **snow**

SNOWISH *adj* like snow

SNOWK *same as* ▸ **snook**

SNOWKED ▸ **snowk**

SNOWKS ▸ **snowk**

SNOWMAN *n* figure shaped out of snow

SNOWMEN ▸ **snowman**

SNOWS ▸ **snow**

SNOWY *adj* covered with or abounding in snow

SNUB *vb* insult deliberately ▸ *n* deliberate insult ▸ *adj* (of a nose) short and blunt

SNUBBE *n* stub

SNUBBED ▸ **snub**

SNUBBER ▸ **snub**

SNUBBES ▸ **snubbe**

SNUBBY ▸ **snub**

SNUBFIN *adj* as in **snubfin dolphin** Australian dolphin with a small dorsal fin

SNUBS ▸ **snub**

SNUCK *past tense and past participle of* ▸ **sneak**

SNUDGE *vb* be miserly

SNUDGED ▸ **snudge**

SNUDGES ▸ **snudge**

SNUFF *n* powdered tobacco for sniffing into the nostrils ▹ *vb* extinguish (a candle)

SNUFFED ▸ **snuff**

SNUFFER ▸ **snuff**

SNUFFLE *vb* breathe noisily or with difficulty ▹ *n* act or the sound of snuffling

SNUFFLY ▸ **snuffle**

SNUFFS ▸ **snuff**

SNUFFY *adj* of, relating to, or resembling snuff

SNUG *adj* warm and comfortable ▹ *n* (in Britain and Ireland) small room in a pub ▹ *vb* make or become comfortable and warm

SNUGGED ▸ **snug**

SNUGGER ▸ **snug**

SNUGGLE *vb* nestle into a person or thing for warmth or from affection ▹ *n* act of snuggling

SNUGLY ▸ **snug**

SNUGS ▸ **snug**

SNUSH *vb* take snuff

SNUSHED ▸ **snush**

SNUSHES ▸ **snush**

SNUZZLE *vb* root in ground

SNY *same as* ▸ **snye**

> A side channel of a river, that can be useful when you are short of vowels. And note that it can be extended to form **snye**.

SNYE *n* side channel of a river

SNYES ▸ **snye**

SO *adv* such an extent ▹ *interj* exclamation of surprise, triumph, or realization ▹ *n* the fifth note of the musical scale

SOAK *vb* make wet ▹ *n* soaking

SOAKAGE *n* process or a period in which a permeable substance is soaked in a liquid

SOAKED ▸ **soak**

SOAKEN ▸ **soak**

SOAKER ▸ **soak**

SOAKERS ▸ **soak**

SOAKING ▸ **soak**

SOAKS ▸ **soak**

SOAP *n* compound of alkali and fat, used with water as a cleaning agent ▹ *vb* apply soap to

SOAPBOX *n* crate used as a platform for speech-making ▹ *vb* deliver a speech from a soapbox

SOAPED ▸ **soap**

SOAPER *n* soap opera

SOAPERS ▸ **soaper**

SOAPIE *n* soap opera

SOAPIER ▸ **soapy**

SOAPIES ▸ **soapie**

SOAPILY ▸ **soapy**

SOAPING ▸ **soap**

SOAPS ▸ **soap**

SOAPY *adj* covered with soap

SOAR *vb* rise or fly upwards ▹ *n* act of soaring

SOARE *n* young hawk

SOARED ▸ **soar**

SOARER ▸ **soar**

SOARERS ▸ **soar**

SOARES ▸ **soare**

SOARING ▸ **soar**

SOARS ▸ **soar**

SOAVE *n* dry white Italian wine

SOAVES ▸ **soave**

SOB *vb* weep with convulsive gasps ▹ *n* act or sound of sobbing

SOBA *n* (in Japanese cookery) noodles made from buckwheat flour

SOBAS ▸ **soba**

SOBBED ▸ **sob**

SOBBER ▸ **sob**

SOBBERS ▸ **sob**

SOBBING ▸ **sob**

SOBEIT *conj* provided that

SOBER *adj* not drunk ▹ *vb* make or become sober

SOBERED ▸ **sober**

SOBERER ▸ **sober**

SOBERLY ▸ **sober**

SOBERS ▸ **sober**

SOBFUL *adj* tearful

SOBOLE *n* creeping underground stem that produces roots and buds

SOBOLES ▸ **sobole**

SOBS ▸ **sob**

SOC *n* feudal right to hold court

SOCA *n* mixture of soul and calypso music popular in the E Caribbean

SOCAGE *n* tenure of land by certain services, esp of an agricultural nature

SOCAGER ▸ **socage**

SOCAGES ▸ **socage**

SOCAS ▸ **soca**

SOCCAGE *same as* ▸ **socage**

SOCCER *n* football played by two teams of eleven kicking a spherical ball

SOCCERS ▸ **soccer**

SOCIAL *adj* living in a community ▹ *n* informal gathering

SOCIALS ▸ **social**

SOCIATE *n* associate

SOCIETY *n* human beings considered as a group

SOCK *n* knitted covering for the foot ▹ *vb* hit hard

SOCKED ▸ **sock**

SOCKET *n* hole or recess into which something fits ▹ *vb* furnish with or place into a socket

SOCKETS ▸ **socket**

SOCKEYE *n* Pacific salmon with red flesh

SOCKING ▸ **sock**

SOCKMAN *same as* ▸ **socman**

SOCKMEN ▸ **sockman**

SOCKO *adj* excellent

SOCKS ▸ **sock**

SOCLE *another name for* ▸ **plinth**

SOCLES ▸ **socle**

SOCMAN *n* tenant holding land by socage

SOCMEN ▸ **socman**

SOCS ▸ **soc**

SOD *n* (piece of) turf ▹ *vb* cover with sods

SODA *n* compound of sodium

SODAIC *adj* containing soda

SODAIN *same as* ▸ **sudden**

SODAINE *same as* ▸ **sudden**

SODAS ▸ **soda**

SODDED ▸ **sod**

SODDEN *adj* soaked ▹ *vb* make or become sodden

SODDENS ▸ **sodden**

SODDIER ▸ **soddy**

SODDIES ▸ **soddy**

SODDING ▸ **sod**

SODDY *adj* covered with turf

SODGER *dialect variant of* ▸ **soldier**

SODGERS ▸ **sodger**

SODIC *adj* containing sodium

SODIUM *n* silvery-white metallic element

SODIUMS ▸ **sodium**

SODOM *n* person who performs sodomy

SODOMS ▸ **sodom**

SODOMY *n* anal intercourse

S

SODS ▷ sod

SOEVER adv in any way at all

SOFA n couch

SOFABED n sofa that converts into a bed

SOFAR n system for determining a position at sea

SOFARS ▷ sofar

SOFAS ▷ sofa

SOFFIT n underside of a part of a building or a structural component

SOFFITS ▷ soffit

SOFT adj easy to shape or cut ▷ adv softly ▷ vb soften

SOFTA n Muslim student of divinity and jurisprudence, esp in Turkey

SOFTAS ▷ softa

SOFTED ▷ soft

SOFTEN vb make or become soft or softer

SOFTENS ▷ soften

SOFTER ▷ soft

SOFTEST ▷ soft

SOFTIE n person who is easily upset

SOFTIES ▷ softy

SOFTING ▷ soft

SOFTISH ▷ soft

SOFTLY ▷ soft

SOFTS ▷ soft

SOFTY same as ▷ **softie**

SOG vb soak

SOGER same as ▷ **sodger**

SOGERS ▷ soger

SOGGED ▷ sog

SOGGIER ▷ soggy

SOGGILY ▷ soggy

SOGGING ▷ sog

SOGGY adj soaked

SOGS ▷ sog

SOH n (in tonic sol-fa) fifth degree of any major scale

SOHO interj exclamation announcing the sighting of a hare

SOHS ▷ soh

SOHUR ▷ suhur

SOHURS ▷ sohur

SOIGNE adj well-groomed, elegant

SOIGNEE same as ▷ **soigne**

SOIL n top layer of earth ▷ vb make or become dirty

SOILAGE n green fodder, esp when freshly cut and fed to livestock in a confined area

SOILED ▷ soil

SOILIER ▷ soil

SOILING ▷ soil

SOILS ▷ soil

SOILURE n act of soiling or the state of being soiled

SOILY ▷ soil

SOIREE n evening party or gathering

SOIREES ▷ soiree

SOJA same as ▷ **soya**

SOJAS ▷ soja

SOJOURN n temporary stay ▷ vb stay temporarily

SOKAH same as ▷ **soca**

SOKAHS ▷ sokah

SOKAIYA n Japanese extortionist

SOKE n right to hold a local court

SOKEMAN same as ▷ **socman**

SOKEMEN ▷ sokeman

SOKEN n feudal district

SOKENS ▷ soken

SOKES ▷ soke

SOKOL n Czech gymnastic association

SOKOLS ▷ sokol

SOL n liquid colloidal solution

SOLA ▷ solum

SOLACE vb comfort in distress ▷ n comfort in misery or disappointment

SOLACED ▷ solace

SOLACER ▷ solace

SOLACES ▷ solace

SOLAH n Indian plant

SOLAHS ▷ solah

SOLAN archaic name for ▷ **gannet**

SOLAND n solan goose

SOLANDS ▷ soland

SOLANIN same as > **solanine**

SOLANO n hot wind in Spain

SOLANOS ▷ solano

SOLANS ▷ solan

SOLANUM n any plant of the mainly tropical genus that includes the potato, aubergine, and certain nightshades

SOLAR adj of the sun

SOLARIA > **solarium**

SOLARS ▷ solum

SOLAS ▷ solum

SOLATE vb change from gel to liquid

SOLATED ▷ solate

SOLATES ▷ solate

SOLATIA > **solatium**

SOLD n obsolete word for salary

SOLDADO n soldier

SOLDAN archaic word for ▷ **sultan**

SOLDANS ▷ soldan

SOLDE n wages

SOLDER n soft alloy used to join two metal surfaces ▷ vb join with solder

SOLDERS ▷ solder

SOLDES ▷ solde

SOLDI ▷ soldo

SOLDIER n member of an army ▷ vb serve in an army

SOLDO n former Italian copper coin worth one twentieth of a lira

SOLDS ▷ sold

SOLE adj one and only ▷ n underside of the foot ▷ vb provide (a shoe) with a sole

SOLED ▷ sole

SOLEI ▷ soleus

SOLEIN same as ▷ **sullen**

SOLELY adv only, completely

SOLEMN adj serious, deeply sincere

SOLER same as ▷ **sole**

SOLERA n system for aging sherry and other fortified wines

SOLERAS ▷ solera

SOLERET n armour for foot

SOLERS ▷ soler

SOLES ▷ sole

SOLEUS n muscle in calf of leg

SOLFEGE same as > **solfeggio**

SOLGEL adj changing between sol and gel

SOLI adv (of a piece or passage) to be performed by or with soloists

SOLICIT vb request

SOLID adj (of a substance) keeping its shape ▷ n three-dimensional shape

SOLIDER ▷ solid

SOLIDI ▷ solidus

SOLIDLY ▷ solid

SOLIDS ▷ solid

SOLIDUM n part of pedestal

SOLIDUS same as ▷ **slash**

SOLING ▷ sole

SOLION n amplifier used in chemistry

SOLIONS ▷ solion

SOLIPED n animal whose hooves are not cloven

SOLITO adv musical instruction meaning play in usual manner

SOLITON n type of isolated particle-like wave

SOLIVE n type of joist

SOLIVES ▶ solive

SOLLAR n archaic word meaning attic

SOLLARS ▶ sollar

SOLLER same as ▶ sollar

SOLLERS ▶ soller

SOLO n music for one performer ▷ adj done alone ▷ adv by oneself, alone ▷ vb undertake a venture alone, esp to operate an aircraft alone or climb alone

SOLOED ▶ solo

SOLOING ▶ solo

SOLOIST n person who performs a solo

SOLON n US congressman

SOLONS ▶ solon

SOLOS ▶ solo

SOLS ▶ sol

SOLUBLE adj able to be dissolved ▷ n soluble substance

SOLUBLY ▶ soluble

SOLUM n upper layers of the soil profile, affected by climate and vegetation

SOLUMS ▶ solum

SOLUNAR adj relating to sun and moon

SOLUS adj alone

SOLUTAL adj relating to a solute

SOLUTE n substance in a solution that is dissolved ▷ adj loose or unattached

SOLUTES ▶ solute

SOLVATE vb undergo, cause to undergo, or partake in solvation

SOLVE vb find the answer to (a problem)

SOLVED ▶ solve

SOLVENT adj having enough money to pay one's debts ▷ n liquid capable of dissolving other substances

SOLVER ▶ solve

SOLVERS ▶ solve

SOLVES ▶ solve

SOLVING ▶ solve

SOM n currency of Kyrgyzstan and Uzbekistan

SOMA n body of an organism, esp an animal, as distinct from the germ cells

SOMAN n organophosphorus compound developed as a nerve gas in Germany during World War II

SOMANS ▶ soman

SOMAS ▶ soma

SOMATA ▶ soma

SOMATIC adj of the body, as distinct from the mind

SOMBER adj (in the US) sombre ▷ vb (in the US) make sombre

SOMBERS ▶ somber

SOMBRE adj dark, gloomy ▷ vb make sombre

SOMBRED ▶ sombre

SOMBRER ▶ sombre

SOMBRES ▶ sombre

SOME adj unknown or unspecified ▷ pron certain unknown or unspecified people or things ▷ adv approximately ▷ determiner (a) certain unknown or unspecified

SOMEDAY adv at some unspecified time in the future

SOMEHOW adv in some unspecified way

SOMEONE pron somebody ▷ n significant or important person

SOMEWAY adv in some unspecified manner

SOMEWHY adv for some reason

SOMITAL ▶ somite

SOMITE n any of a series of dorsal paired segments of mesoderm occurring along the notochord in vertebrate embryos

SOMITES ▶ somite

SOMITIC ▶ somite

SOMNIAL adj of dreams

SOMONI n monetary unit of Tajikistan

SOMS ▶ som

SOMY ▶ som

SON n male offspring

SONANCE ▶ sonant

SONANCY ▶ sonant

SONANT n voiced sound able to form a syllable or syllable nucleus ▷ adj denoting a voiced sound like this

SONANTS ▶ sonant

SONAR n device for detecting underwater objects by the reflection of sound waves

SONARS ▶ sonar

SONATA n piece of music in several movements for one instrument with or without piano

SONATAS ▶ sonata

SONCE n Scots word meaning good luck

SONCES ▶ sonce

SONDAGE n deep trial trench for inspecting stratigraphy

SONDE n rocket, balloon, or probe used for observing in the upper atmosphere

SONDELI n Indian shrew

SONDER n yacht category

SONDERS ▶ sonder

SONDES ▶ sonde

SONE n subjective unit of loudness

SONERI n Indian cloth of gold

SONERIS ▶ soneri

SONES ▶ sone

SONG n music for the voice

SONGFUL adj tuneful

SONGKOK n (in Malaysia and Indonesia) a kind of oval brimless hat, resembling a skull

SONGMAN n singer

SONGMEN ▶ songman

SONGS ▶ song

SONHOOD ▶ son

SONIC adj of or producing sound

SONICS n study of mechanical vibrations in matter

SONLESS ▶ son

SONLIKE ▶ son

SONLY adj like a son

SONNE same as ▶ son

SONNES ▶ sonne

SONNET n fourteen-line poem with a fixed rhyme scheme ▷ vb compose sonnets

SONNETS ▶ sonnet

SONNIES ▶ sonny

SONNY n term of address to a boy

SONOVOX n device used to alter sound of human voice in music recordings

SONS ▶ son

SONSE same as ▶ sonce

SONSES ▶ sonse

SONSHIP ▶ son

SONSIE same as ▶ sonsy

SONSIER ▶ sonsy

SONSY adj plump

SONTAG n type of knitted women's cape

SONTAGS ▶ sontag

S

SONTIES n Shakespearian oath

SOOEY interj call used to summon pigs

SOOGEE vb clean ship using a special solution

SOOGEED ▶ soogee

SOOGEES ▶ soogee

SOOGIE ▶ soogee

SOOGIED ▶ soogie

SOOGIES ▶ soogie

SOOJEY same as ▶ soogee

SOOJEYS ▶ soojey

SOOK n baby ▷ vb suck

SOOKED ▶ sook

SOOKING ▶ sook

SOOKS ▶ sook

SOOL vb incite (a dog) to attack

SOOLE same as ▶ sool

SOOLED ▶ sool

SOOLES ▶ soole

SOOLING ▶ sool

SOOLS ▶ sool

SOOM Scots word for ▶ swim

SOOMED ▶ soom

SOOMING ▶ soom

SOOMS ▶ soom

SOON adv in a short time

SOONER adv rather ▷ n an idler or shirker

SOONERS ▶ sooner

SOONEST adv as soon as possible

SOOP Scots word for ▶ sweep

SOOPED ▶ soop

SOOPING ▶ soop

SOOPS ▶ soop

SOOT n black powder formed by the incomplete burning of an organic substance ▷ vb cover with soot

SOOTE n sweet

SOOTED ▶ soot

SOOTES ▶ soot

SOOTH n truth or reality ▷ adj true or real

SOOTHE vb make calm

SOOTHED ▶ soothe

SOOTHER vb flatter

SOOTHES ▶ soothe

SOOTHLY ▶ sooth

SOOTHS ▶ sooth

SOOTIER ▶ sooty

SOOTILY ▶ sooty

SOOTING ▶ soot

SOOTS ▶ soot

SOOTY adj covered with soot

SOP n concession to pacify someone ▷ vb mop up or absorb (liquid)

SOPH shortened form of ▶ sophomore

SOPHIES ▶ sophy

SOPHISM n argument that seems reasonable but is actually false and misleading

SOPHIST n person who uses clever but invalid arguments

SOPHS ▶ soph

SOPHY n title of the Persian monarchs

SOPITE vb lull to sleep

SOPITED ▶ sopite

SOPITES ▶ sopite

SOPOR n abnormally deep sleep

SOPORS ▶ sopor

SOPPED ▶ sop

SOPPIER ▶ soppy

SOPPILY ▶ soppy

SOPPING ▶ sop

SOPPY adj oversentimental

SOPRA adv musical instruction meaning above

SOPRANI ▶ soprano

SOPRANO n singer with the highest female or boy's voice ▷ adj of a musical instrument that is the highest or second highest pitched in its family

SOPS ▶ sop

SORA n North American rail with a yellow bill

SORAGE n first year in hawk's life

SORAGES ▶ sorage

SORAL ▶ sorus

SORAS ▶ sora

SORB n any of various related trees, esp the mountain ash ▷ vb absorb or adsorb

SORBATE n salt of sorbic acid

SORBED ▶ sorb

SORBENT ▶ sorb

SORBET same as ▶ sherbet

SORBETS ▶ sorbet

SORBIC ▶ sorb

SORBING ▶ sorb

SORBITE n mineral found in steel

SORBO n as in **sorbo rubber** spongy form of rubber

SORBOSE n sweet-tasting hexose sugar derived from the berries of the mountain ash

SORBS ▶ sorb

SORBUS n rowan or related tree

SORCERY n witchcraft or magic

SORD n flock of mallard ducks

SORDA n deaf woman

SORDES pl n dark incrustations on the lips and teeth of patients with prolonged fever

SORDID adj dirty, squalid

SORDINE same as ▶ sordino

SORDINI ▶ sordino

SORDINO n mute for a stringed or brass musical instrument

SORDO n deaf man

SORDOR n sordidness

SORDORS ▶ sordor

SORDS ▶ sord

SORE adj painful ▷ n painful area on the body ▷ adv greatly ▷ vb make sore

SORED ▶ sore

SOREDIA > soredium

This is the plural of **soredium**, a reproductive body in lichens. It is a very frequently played bonus, and it has a 'twin' **roadies**. It is a good idea to become familiar with at least the higher probability twin sevens and eights, since the thought of one will often prompt the other, and it may well be that one twin will fit on the board where the other would not.

SOREE same as ▶ sora

SOREES ▶ soree

SOREHON n old Irish feudal right

SOREL same as ▶ sorrel

SORELL same as ▶ sorrel

SORELLS ▶ sorell

SORELS ▶ sorel

SORELY adv greatly

SORER ▶ sore

SORES ▶ sore

SOREST ▶ sore

SOREX n shrew or related animal

SOREXES ▶ sorex

SORGHO same as ▶ sorgo

SORGHOS ▶ sorgho

SORGHUM n kind of grass cultivated for grain

SORGO n any of several varieties of sorghum that have watery sweet juice

SORGOS ▶ sorgo

SORI ▶ sorus

SORING ▶ sore

SORINGS ▶ sore

SORITES n polysyllogism in which the premises are arranged so that intermediate conclusions are omitted, being understood, and only the final conclusion is stated

SORITIC ▶ sorites

SORN vb obtain food, lodging, etc, from another person by presuming on his or her generosity

SORNED ▶ sorn

SORNER ▶ sorn

SORNERS ▶ sorn

SORNING ▶ sorn

SORNS ▶ sorn

SOROBAN n Japanese abacus

SOROCHE n altitude sickness

SORORAL adj of sister

SOROSES ▶ sorosis

SOROSIS n fleshy multiple fruit

SORRA Irish word for ▶ sorrow

SORRAS ▶ sorra

SORREL n bitter-tasting plant

SORRELS ▶ sorrel

SORRIER ▶ sorry

SORRILY ▶ sorry

SORROW n grief or sadness ▷ vb grieve

SORROWS ▶ sorrow

SORRY adj feeling pity or regret ▷ interj exclamation expressing apology or asking someone to repeat what he or she has said

SORT n group all sharing certain qualities or characteristics ▷ vb arrange according to kind

SORTA adv phonetic representation of 'sort of'

SORTAL n type of logical or linguistic concept

SORTALS ▶ sortal

SORTED interj exclamation of satisfaction, approval, etc ▷ adj possessing the desired recreational drugs

SORTER ▶ sort

SORTERS ▶ sort

SORTES n divination by opening book at random

SORTIE n relatively short return trip ▷ vb make a sortie

SORTIED ▶ sortie

SORTIES ▶ sortie

SORTING ▶ sort

SORTS ▶ sort

SORUS n cluster of sporangia on the undersurface of certain fern leaves

SOS ▶ so

SOSATIE n skewer of curried meat pieces

SOSS vb make dirty or muddy

SOSSED ▶ soss

SOSSES ▶ soss

SOSSING ▶ soss

SOT n habitual drunkard ▷ adv indeed: used to contradict a negative statement ▷ vb be a drunkard

SOTH archaic variant of ▶ sooth

SOTHS ▶ soth

SOTOL n American plant related to agave

SOTOLS ▶ sotol

SOTS ▶ sot

SOTTED ▶ sot

SOTTING ▶ sot

SOTTISH ▶ sot

SOU n former French coin

SOUARI n tree of tropical America

SOUARIS ▶ souari

SOUBISE n purée of onions mixed into a thick white sauce and served over eggs, fish, etc

SOUCAR n Indian banker

SOUCARS ▶ soucar

SOUCE same as ▶ souse

SOUCED ▶ souce

SOUCES ▶ souce

SOUCING ▶ souce

SOUCT ▶ souce

SOUDAN obsolete variant of ▶ sultan

SOUDANS ▶ soudan

SOUFFLE n light fluffy dish made with beaten egg whites and other ingredients ▷ adj made light and puffy, as by beating and cooking

SOUGH vb (of the wind) make a sighing sound ▷ n soft continuous murmuring sound

SOUGHED ▶ sough

SOUGHS ▶ sough

SOUGHT ▶ seek

SOUK same as ▶ sook

SOUKED ▶ souk

SOUKING ▶ souk

SOUKOUS n style of African popular music characterized by syncopated rhythms and intricate contrasting guitar melodies

SOUKS ▶ souk

SOUL n spiritual and immortal part of a human being

SOULDAN same as ▶ soldan

SOULED adj having soul

SOULFUL adj full of emotion

SOULS ▶ soul

SOUM vb decide how many animals can graze particular pasture

SOUMED ▶ soum

SOUMING ▶ soum

SOUMS ▶ soum

SOUND n something heard, noise ▷ vb make or cause to make a sound ▷ adj in good condition ▷ adv soundly

SOUNDED ▶ sound

SOUNDER n electromagnetic device formerly used in telegraphy to convert electric signals into audible sounds

SOUNDLY ▶ sound

SOUNDS ▶ sound

SOUP n liquid food made from meat, vegetables, etc ▷ vb give soup to

SOUPCON n small amount

SOUPED ▶ soup

SOUPER n person dispensing soup

SOUPERS ▶ souper

SOUPFIN n Pacific requiem shark valued for its fins

SOUPIER ▶ soupy

SOUPING ▶ soup

SOUPLE same as ▶ supple

SOUPLED ▶ souple

SOUPLES ▶ souple

SOUPS ▶ soup

SOUPY adj having the appearance or consistency of soup

SOUR adj sharp-tasting ▷ vb make or become sour

SOURCE n origin or starting point ▷ vb establish a supplier of (a product, etc)

SOURCED ▶ source

SOURCES ▶ source

SOURED ▶ sour

S

SOURER ▶ sour

SOUREST ▶ sour

SOURING ▶ sour

SOURISH ▶ sour

SOURLY ▶ sour

SOUROCK *n* Scots word for sorrel plant

SOURS ▶ sour

SOURSE *same as* ▶ source

SOURSES ▶ sourse

SOURSOP *n* small West Indian tree

SOUS ▶ sou

SOUSE *vb* plunge (something) into liquid ▷ *n* liquid used in pickling

SOUSED ▶ souse

SOUSES ▶ souse

SOUSING ▶ souse

SOUSLIK *same as* ▶ suslik

SOUT *same as* ▶ soot

SOUTANE *n* Roman Catholic priest's cassock

SOUTAR *same as* ▶ souter

SOUTARS ▶ soutar

SOUTER *n* shoemaker or cobbler

SOUTERS ▶ souter

SOUTH *n* direction towards the South Pole, opposite north ▷ *adj* or in the south ▷ *adv* in, to, or towards the south ▷ *vb* turn south

SOUTHED ▶ south

SOUTHER *n* strong wind or storm from the south ▷ *vb* turn south

SOUTHS ▶ south

SOUTS ▶ sout

SOV *shortening of* > **sovereign**

SOVIET *n* formerly, elected council at various levels of government in the USSR ▷ *adj* of the former USSR

SOVIETS ▶ soviet

SOVKHOZ *n* (in the former Soviet Union) a large mechanized farm owned by the state

SOVRAN *literary word for* > **sovereign**

SOVRANS ▶ sovran

SOVS ▶ sov

SOW *vb* scatter or plant (seed) in or on (the ground) ▷ *n* female adult pig

SOWABLE ▶ sow

SOWANS *same as* ▶ sowens

SOWAR *n* Indian cavalryman

SOWARRY *same as* > **sowarree**

SOWARS ▶ sowar

SOWBACK *another name for* ▶ hogback

SOWCAR *same as* ▶ soucar

SOWCARS ▶ sowcar

SOWCE *same as* ▶ souse

SOWCED ▶ sowce

SOWCES ▶ sowce

SOWCING ▶ sowce

SOWDER ▶ sawder *n*

SOWDERS ▶ sowder

SOWED ▶ sow

SOWENS *n* pudding made from oatmeal husks steeped and boiled

SOWER ▶ sow

SOWERS ▶ sow

SOWF *same as* ▶ sowth

SOWFED ▶ sowf

SOWFF *same as* ▶ sowth

SOWFFED ▶ sowff

SOWFFS ▶ sowff

SOWFING ▶ sowf

SOWFS ▶ sowf

SOWING ▶ sow

SOWINGS ▶ sow

SOWL *same as* ▶ sole

SOWLE *same as* ▶ sole

SOWLED ▶ sowl

SOWLES ▶ sowle

SOWLING ▶ sowl

SOWLS ▶ sowl

SOWM *same as* ▶ soum

SOWMED ▶ sowm

SOWMING ▶ sowm

SOWMS ▶ sowm

SOWN ▶ sow

SOWND *vb* wield

SOWNDED ▶ sownd

SOWNDS ▶ sownd

SOWNE *same as* ▶ sound

SOWNES ▶ sowne

SOWP *n* spoonful

SOWPS ▶ sowp

SOWS ▶ sow

SOWSE *same as* ▶ souse

SOWSED ▶ sowse

SOWSES ▶ sowse

SOWSING ▶ sowse

SOWSSE *same as* ▶ souse

SOWSSED ▶ sowsse

SOWSSES ▶ sowsse

SOWTER *same as* ▶ souter

SOWTERS ▶ sowter

SOWTH *vb* Scots word meaning whistle

SOWTHED ▶ sowth

SOWTHS ▶ sowth

SOX *pl n* informal spelling of 'socks'

This informal word for **socks** is one of the key short words to remember for using the X.

SOY *n as in* **soy sauce** salty dark brown sauce made from soya beans, used in Chinese and Japanese cookery

SOYA *n* plant whose edible bean is used for food and as a source of oil

SOYAS ▶ soya

SOYBEAN *n* soya bean

SOYLE *n* body

SOYLES ▶ soyle

SOYMILK *n* milk substitute made from soya

SOYS ▶ soy

SOYUZ *n* Russian spacecraft used to ferry crew to and from space stations

SOYUZES ▶ soyuz

SOZ *interj* (slang) sorry

SOZIN *n* form of protein

SOZINE *same as* ▶ sozin

SOZINES ▶ sozine

SOZINS ▶ sozin

SOZZLE *vb* make wet

SOZZLED *adj* drunk

SOZZLES ▶ sozzle

SOZZLY *adj* wet

SPA *n* resort with a mineral-water spring ▷ *vb* visit a spa

SPACE *n* unlimited expanse in which all objects exist and move ▷ *vb* place at intervals

SPACED ▶ space

SPACER *n* piece of material used to create or maintain a space between two things

SPACERS ▶ spacer

SPACES ▶ space

SPACEY *adj* vague and dreamy, as if under the influence of drugs

SPACIAL *same as* ▶ spatial

SPACIER ▶ spacey

SPACING *n* arrangement of letters, words, etc, on a page in order to achieve legibility

SPACKLE *vb* fill holes in plaster

SPACY *same as* ▶ spacey

SPADE *n* tool for digging

SPADED ▶ spade

SPADER ▶ spade

SPADERS ▶ spade

SPADES ▶ spade

SPADGER *n* sparrow

SPADING ▶ spade

SPADIX *n* spike of small flowers on a fleshy stem

SPADO *n* neutered animal

SPADOES ▸ spado
SPADOS ▸ spado
SPAE vb foretell (the future)
SPAED ▸ spae
SPAEING ▸ spae
SPAEMAN n man who foretells future
SPAEMEN ▸ spaeman
SPAER ▸ spae
SPAERS ▸ spae
SPAES ▸ spae
SPAG vb (of a cat) to scratch (a person) with the claws ▸ n Australian offensive slang for an Italian
SPAGGED ▸ spag
SPAGS ▸ spag
SPAHEE same as ▸ spahi
SPAHEES ▸ spahee
SPAHI n (formerly) an irregular cavalryman in the Turkish armed forces
SPAHIS ▸ spahi
SPAIL Scots word for ▸ spall
SPAILS ▸ spail
SPAIN same as ▸ spane
SPAINED ▸ spain
SPAING ▸ spa
SPAINGS ▸ spa
SPAINS ▸ spain
SPAIRGE Scots word for ▸ sparge
SPAIT same as ▸ spate
SPAITS ▸ spait
SPAKE past tense of ▸ speak
SPALD same as ▸ spauld
SPALDS ▸ spald
SPALE Scots word for ▸ spall
SPALES ▸ spale
SPALL n splinter or chip of ore, rock, or stone ▸ vb split or cause to split into such fragments
SPALLE same as ▸ spauld
SPALLED ▸ spall
SPALLER ▸ spall
SPALLES ▸ spalle
SPALLS ▸ spall
SPALT vb split
SPALTED ▸ spalt
SPALTS ▸ spalt
SPAM vb send unsolicited e-mail simultaneously to a number of newsgroups on the internet ▸ n unsolicited electronic mail or text messages sent in this way
SPAMBOT n computer programme that identifies email addresses to send spam to
SPAMMED ▸ spam
SPAMMER ▸ spam

SPAMMIE n love bite
SPAMMY adj bland
SPAMS ▸ spam
SPAN n space between two points ▸ vb stretch or extend across
SPANCEL n length of rope for hobbling an animal, esp a horse or cow ▸ vb hobble (an animal) with a loose rope
SPANDEX n type of synthetic stretch fabric made from polyurethane fibre
SPANE vb Scots word meaning wean
SPANED ▸ spane
SPANES ▸ spane
SPANG adv exactly, firmly, or straight ▸ vb dash
SPANGED ▸ spang
SPANGLE n small shiny metallic ornament ▸ vb decorate with spangles
SPANGLY ▸ spangle
SPANGS ▸ spang
SPANIEL n dog with long ears and silky hair
SPANING ▸ spane
SPANK vb slap with the open hand, on the buttocks or legs ▸ n such a slap
SPANKED ▸ spank
SPANKER n fore-and-aft sail or a mast that is aftermost in a sailing vessel
SPANKS ▸ spank
SPANNED ▸ span
SPANNER n tool for gripping and turning a nut or bolt
SPANS ▸ span
SPAR n pole used as a ship's mast, boom, or yard ▸ vb box or fight using light blows for practice
SPARD ▸ spare
SPARE adj extra ▸ n duplicate kept in case of damage or loss ▸ vb refrain from punishing or harming
SPARED ▸ spare
SPARELY ▸ spare
SPARER ▸ spare
SPARERS ▸ spare
SPARES ▸ spare
SPAREST ▸ spare
SPARGE vb sprinkle or scatter (something)
SPARGED ▸ sparge
SPARGER ▸ sparge
SPARGES ▸ sparge

SPARID n type of marine percoid fish ▸ adj of or belonging to this family of fish
SPARIDS ▸ sparid
SPARING adj economical
SPARK n fiery particle thrown out from a fire or caused by friction ▸ vb give off sparks
SPARKE n weapon
SPARKED ▸ spark
SPARKER ▸ spark
SPARKES ▸ sparke
SPARKIE n electrician
SPARKLE vb glitter with many points of light ▸ n sparkling points of light
SPARKLY adj sparkling ▸ n sparkling thing
SPARKS n electrician
SPARKY adj lively
SPAROID same as ▸ sparid
SPARRE same as ▸ spar
SPARRED ▸ spar
SPARRER ▸ spar
SPARRES ▸ sparre
SPARROW n small brownish bird
SPARRY adj (of minerals) containing, relating to, or resembling spar
SPARS ▸ spar
SPARSE adj thinly scattered
SPARSER ▸ sparse
SPART n esparto
SPARTAN adj strict and austere ▸ n disciplined or brave person
SPARTH n type of battle-axe
SPARTHE same as ▸ sparth
SPARTHS ▸ sparth
SPARTS ▸ spart
SPAS ▸ spa
SPASM n involuntary muscular contraction ▸ vb go into spasm
SPASMED ▸ spasm
SPASMIC ▸ spasm
SPASMS ▸ spasm
SPAT vb have a quarrel
SPATE n large number of things happening within a period of time
SPATES ▸ spate
SPATHAL ▸ spathe
SPATHE n large sheathlike leaf enclosing a flower cluster
SPATHED ▸ spathe
SPATHES ▸ spathe
SPATHIC adj (of minerals) resembling spar, esp in

having good cleavage

SPATIAL adj of or in space

SPATS ▶ spat

SPATTED ▶ spat

SPATTEE n type of gaiter

SPATTER vb scatter or be scattered in drops over (something) ▷ n spattering sound

SPATULA n utensil with a broad flat blade for spreading or stirring

SPATULE n spatula

SPATZLE same as > spaetzle

SPAUL same as ▶ spauld

SPAULD n shoulder

SPAULDS ▶ spauld

SPAULS ▶ spaul

SPAVIE Scots variant of ▶ spavin

SPAVIES ▶ spavie

SPAVIET adj Scots word meaning spavined

SPAVIN n enlargement of the hock of a horse by a bony growth

SPAVINS ▶ spavin

SPAW same as ▶ spa

SPAWL vb spit

SPAWLED ▶ spawl

SPAWLS ▶ spawl

SPAWN n jelly-like mass of eggs of fish, frogs, or molluscs ▷ vb (of fish, frogs, or molluscs) lay eggs

SPAWNED ▶ spawn

SPAWNER ▶ spawn

SPAWNS ▶ spawn

SPAWNY adj like spawn

SPAWS ▶ spaw

SPAY vb remove the ovaries from (a female animal)

SPAYAD n male deer

SPAYADS ▶ spayad

SPAYD same as ▶ spayad

SPAYDS ▶ spayd

SPAYED ▶ spay

SPAYING ▶ spay

SPAYS ▶ spay

SPAZA adj as in spaza shop South African slang for a small shop in a township

SPEAK vb say words, talk

SPEAKER n person who speaks, esp at a formal occasion

SPEAKS ▶ speak

SPEAL same as ▶ spule

SPEALS ▶ speal

SPEAN same as ▶ spane

SPEANED ▶ spean

SPEANS ▶ spean

SPEAR n weapon consisting

of a long shaft with a sharp point ▷ vb pierce with or as if with a spear

SPEARED ▶ spear

SPEARER ▶ spear

SPEARS ▶ spear

SPEARY ▶ spear

SPEAT same as ▶ spate

SPEATS ▶ speat

SPEC vb set specifications

SPECCED ▶ spec

SPECCY n person wearing spectacles

SPECIAL adj distinguished from others of its kind ▷ n product, programme, etc which is only available at a certain time ▷ vb advertise and sell (an item) at a reduced price

SPECIE n coins as distinct from paper money

SPECIES n group of plants or animals that are related closely enough to interbreed naturally

SPECIFY vb refer to or state specifically

SPECK n small spot or particle ▷ vb mark with specks or spots

SPECKED ▶ speck

SPECKLE n small spot ▷ vb mark with speckles

SPECKS ▶ speck

SPECKY same as ▶ speccy

SPECS pl n spectacles

SPECTER same as ▶ spectre

SPECTRA > spectrum

SPECTRE n ghost

SPECULA > speculum

SPED ▶ speed

SPEECH n act, power, or manner of speaking ▷ vb make a speech

SPEED n swiftness ▷ vb go quickly

SPEEDED ▶ speed

SPEEDER ▶ speed

SPEEDO n speedometer

SPEEDOS ▶ speedo

SPEEDS ▶ speed

SPEEDUP n acceleration

SPEEDY adj prompt

SPEEL n splinter of wood ▷ vb Scots word meaning climb

SPEELED ▶ speel

SPEELER ▶ speel

SPEELS ▶ speel

SPEER same as ▶ speir

SPEERED ▶ speir

SPEERS ▶ speir

SPEIL dialect word for ▶ climb

SPEILED ▶ speil

SPEILS ▶ speil

SPEIR vb ask

SPEIRED ▶ speir

SPEIRS ▶ speir

SPEISE same as ▶ speiss

SPEISES ▶ speise

SPEISS n arsenides and antimonides that form when ores containing arsenic or antimony are smelted

SPEK n bacon, fat, or fatty pork used for larding venison or other game

SPEKS ▶ spek

SPELD vb Scots word meaning spread

SPELDED ▶ speld

SPELDER same as ▶ speld

SPELDIN n fish split and dried

SPELDS ▶ speld

SPELEAN same as > spelaean

SPELK n splinter of wood

SPELKS ▶ spelk

SPELL vb give in correct order the letters that form (a word) ▷ n formula of words supposed to have magic power

SPELLED ▶ spell

SPELLER n person who spells words in the manner specified

SPELLS ▶ spell

SPELT ▶ spell

SPELTER n impure zinc, usually containing about 3 per cent of lead and other impurities

SPELTS ▶ spell

SPELTZ n wheat variety

SPELUNK vb explore caves

SPENCE n larder or pantry

SPENCER n short fitted coat or jacket

SPENCES ▶ spence

SPEND vb pay out (money)

SPENDER n person who spends money in a manner specified

SPENDS ▶ spend

SPENDY adj expensive

SPENSE same as ▶ spence

SPENSES ▶ spense

SPENT ▶ spend

SPEOS n (esp in ancient Egypt) a temple or tomb cut into a rock face

SPEOSES ▶ speos

S

SPERM n male reproductive cell released in semen during ejaculation

SPERMIC same as > **spermatic**

SPERMS ▶ **sperm**

SPERRE vb bolt

SPERRED ▶ **sperre**

SPERRES ▶ **sperre**

SPERSE vb disperse

SPERSED ▶ **sperse**

SPERSES ▶ **sperse**

SPERST ▶ **sperse**

SPERTHE same as ▶ **sparth**

SPET same as ▶ **spit**

SPETCH n piece of animal skin

SPETS ▶ **spet**

SPEUG n sparrow

SPEUGS ▶ **speug**

SPEW vb vomit ▷ n something ejected from the mouth

SPEWED ▶ **spew**

SPEWER ▶ **spew**

SPEWERS ▶ **spew**

SPEWIER ▶ **spewy**

SPEWING ▶ **spew**

SPEWS ▶ **spew**

SPEWY adj marshy

SPHAER same as ▶ **sphere**

SPHAERE same as ▶ **sphere**

SPHAERS ▶ **sphaere**

SPHEAR same as ▶ **sphere**

SPHEARE same as ▶ **sphere**

SPHEARS ▶ **sphear**

SPHENE n brown, yellow, green, or grey lustrous mineral

SPHENES ▶ **sphene**

SPHENIC adj having the shape of a wedge

SPHERAL adj of or shaped like a sphere

SPHERE n perfectly round solid object ▷ vb surround or encircle

SPHERED ▶ **sphere**

SPHERES ▶ **sphere**

SPHERIC same as > **spherical**

SPHERY adj resembling a sphere

SPHINX n one of the huge statues built by the ancient Egyptians, with the body of a lion and the head of a man

SPHYNX n breed of cat

SPIAL n observation

SPIALS ▶ **spial**

SPICA n spiral bandage formed by a series of overlapping figure-of-eight turns

SPICAE ▶ **spica**

SPICAS ▶ **spica**

SPICATE adj having, arranged in, or relating to spikes

SPICE n aromatic substance used as flavouring ▷ vb flavour with spices

SPICED ▶ **spice**

SPICER ▶ **spice**

SPICERS ▶ **spice**

SPICERY n spices collectively

SPICES ▶ **spice**

SPICEY same as ▶ **spicy**

SPICIER ▶ **spicy**

SPICILY ▶ **spicy**

SPICING ▶ **spice**

SPICULA > **spiculum**

SPICULE n small slender pointed structure or crystal

SPICY adj flavoured with spices

SPIDER n small eight-legged creature which spins a web to catch insects for food

SPIDERS ▶ **spider**

SPIDERY adj thin and angular like a spider's legs

SPIE same as ▶ **spy**

SPIED ▶ **spy**

SPIEGEL n manganese-rich pig iron

SPIEL n speech made to persuade someone to do something ▷ vb deliver a prepared spiel

SPIELED ▶ **spiel**

SPIELER ▶ **spiel**

SPIELS ▶ **spiel**

SPIER same as ▶ **speir**

SPIERED ▶ **spier**

SPIERS ▶ **spier**

SPIES ▶ **spy**

SPIF n postage stamp perforated with the initials of a firm to avoid theft by employees

SPIFF vb make smart

SPIFFED ▶ **spiff**

SPIFFS ▶ **spiff**

SPIFFY adj smart ▷ n smart thing or person ▷ vb to smarten

SPIFS ▶ **spif**

SPIGHT same as ▶ **spite**

SPIGHTS ▶ **spight**

SPIGNEL n European umbelliferous plant

SPIGOT n stopper for, or tap fitted to, a cask

SPIGOTS ▶ **spigot**

SPIKE n sharp point ▷ vb put spikes on

SPIKED ▶ **spike**

SPIKER ▶ **spike**

SPIKERS ▶ **spike**

SPIKERY n High-Church Anglicanism

SPIKES ▶ **spike**

SPIKEY same as ▶ **spiky**

SPIKIER ▶ **spiky**

SPIKILY ▶ **spiky**

SPIKING ▶ **spike**

SPIKY adj resembling a spike

SPILE n heavy timber stake or pile ▷ vb provide or support with a spile

SPILED ▶ **spile**

SPILES ▶ **spile**

SPILING ▶ **spile**

SPILITE n type of igneous rock

SPILL vb pour from or as if from a container ▷ n fall

SPILLED ▶ **spill**

SPILLER ▶ **spill**

SPILLS ▶ **spill**

SPILT ▶ **spill**

SPILTH n something spilled

SPILTHS ▶ **spilth**

SPIM n unsolicited commercial communications received on a computer via an instant-messaging system

SPIMS ▶ **spim**

SPIN vb revolve or cause to revolve rapidly ▷ n revolving motion

SPINA n spine

SPINACH n dark green leafy vegetable

SPINAE ▶ **spina**

SPINAGE same as ▶ **spinach**

SPINAL adj of the spine ▷ n anaesthetic administered in the spine

SPINALS ▶ **spinal**

SPINAR n fast-spinning star

SPINARS ▶ **spinar**

SPINAS ▶ **spina**

SPINATE adj having a spine

SPINDLE n rotating rod that acts as an axle ▷ vb form into a spindle or equip with spindles

SPINDLY adj long, slender, and frail

SPINE n backbone

SPINED ▶ **spine**

SPINEL n any of a group of hard glassy minerals of variable colour

SPINELS ▶ spinel
SPINES ▶ spine
SPINET n small harpsichord
SPINETS ▶ spinet
SPINIER ▶ spiny
SPINK n finch
SPINKS ▶ spink
SPINNER n bowler who specializes in spinning the ball to make it change direction when it bounces or strikes the bat
SPINNET same as ▶ spinet
SPINNEY n small wood
SPINNY same as ▶ spinney
SPINODE another name for ▶ cusp
SPINOFF n development derived incidentally from an existing enterprise
SPINONE n as in Italian spinone wiry-coated gun dog
SPINONI ▶ spinone
SPINOR n type of mathematical object
SPINORS ▶ spinor
SPINOSE adj (esp of plants) bearing many spines
SPINOUS adj resembling a spine or thorn
SPINOUT n spinning skid that causes a car to run off the road
SPINS ▶ spin
SPINTO n lyrical singing voice
SPINTOS ▶ spinto
SPINULA n small spine
SPINULE n very small spine, thorn, or prickle
SPINY adj covered with spines
SPIRAEA n plant with small white or pink flowers
SPIRAL n continuous curve formed by a point winding about a central axis at an ever-increasing distance from it ▷ vb move in a spiral ▷ adj having the form of a spiral
SPIRALS ▶ spiral
SPIRANT n fricative consonant
SPIRE n pointed part of a steeple ▷ vb assume the shape of a spire
SPIREA same as ▶ spiraea
SPIREAS ▶ spirea
SPIRED ▶ spire
SPIREM same as ▶ spireme
SPIREME n tangled mass of

chromatin threads into which the nucleus of a cell is resolved at the start of mitosis
SPIREMS ▶ spirem
SPIRES ▶ spire
SPIRIC n type of curve
SPIRICS ▶ spiric
SPIRIER ▶ spire
SPIRING ▶ spire
SPIRIT n nonphysical aspect of a person concerned with profound thoughts ▷ vb carry away mysteriously
SPIRITS ▶ spirit
SPIRITY adj spirited
SPIROID adj resembling a spiral or displaying a spiral form
SPIRT same as ▶ spurt
SPIRTED ▶ spirt
SPIRTLE same as ▶ spurtle
SPIRTS ▶ spirt
SPIRULA n tropical cephalopod mollusc
SPIRY ▶ spire
SPIT vb eject (saliva or food) from the mouth ▷ n saliva
SPITAL n hospital, esp for the needy sick
SPITALS ▶ spital
SPITE n deliberate nastiness ▷ vb annoy or hurt from spite
SPITED ▶ spite
SPITES ▶ spite
SPITING ▶ spite
SPITS ▶ spit
SPITTED ▶ spit
SPITTEN ▶ spit
SPITTER ▶ spit
SPITTLE n fluid produced in the mouth, saliva
SPITZ n stockily built dog with a pointed face, erect ears, and a tightly curled tail
SPITZES ▶ spitz
SPIV n smartly dressed man who makes a living by shady dealings
SPIVS ▶ spiv
SPIVVY ▶ spiv
SPLAKE n type of hybrid trout bred by Canadian zoologists
SPLAKES ▶ splake
SPLASH vb scatter liquid on (something) ▷ n splashing sound
SPLASHY adj having irregular marks
SPLAT n wet slapping sound

▷ vb make wet slapping sound
SPLATCH vb splash
SPLATS ▶ splat
SPLAY vb spread out, with ends spreading in different directions ▷ adj spread out ▷ n surface of a wall that forms an oblique angle to the main flat surfaces
SPLAYED ▶ splay
SPLAYS ▶ splay
SPLEEN n abdominal organ which filters bacteria from the blood
SPLEENS ▶ spleen
SPLEENY ▶ spleen
SPLENIA > splenium
SPLENIC adj of, relating to, or in the spleen
SPLENII > splenius
SPLENT same as ▶ splint
SPLENTS ▶ splent
SPLICE vb join by interweaving or overlapping ends
SPLICED ▶ splice
SPLICER ▶ splice
SPLICES ▶ splice
SPLIFF n cannabis, used as a drug
SPLIFFS ▶ spliff
SPLINE n type of narrow key around a shaft that fits into a corresponding groove ▷ vb provide (a shaft, part, etc) with splines
SPLINED ▶ spline
SPLINES ▶ spline
SPLINT n rigid support for a broken bone ▷ vb apply a splint to (a broken arm, etc)
SPLINTS ▶ splint
SPLISH vb splash
SPLIT vb break into separate pieces ▷ n splitting
SPLITS ▶ split
SPLODGE n large uneven spot or stain ▷ vb mark (something) with a splodge or splodges
SPLODGY ▶ splodge
SPLOG n spam blog
SPLOGS ▶ splog
SPLOOSH vb splash or cause to splash about uncontrollably ▷ n instance or sound of splooshing
SPLORE n revel
SPLORES ▶ splore
SPLOSH vb scatter (liquid) vigorously about in blobs

▷ n instance or sound of sploshing

SPLOTCH vb splash, daub

SPLURGE vb spend money extravagantly ▷ n bout of extravagance

SPLURGY ▸ **splurge**

SPOD adj boring, unattractive, or overstudious

SPODDY ▸ **spod**

SPODE n type of English china or porcelain

SPODES ▸ **spode**

SPODIUM n black powder

SPODS ▸ **spod**

SPOFFY same as ▸ **spoffish**

SPOIL vb damage

SPOILED ▸ **spoil**

SPOILER n device on an aircraft or car to increase drag

SPOILS ▸ **spoil**

SPOILT ▸ **spoil**

SPOKE n radial member of a wheel ▷ vb equip with spokes

SPOKED ▸ **spoke**

SPOKEN ▸ **speak**

SPOKES ▸ **spoke**

SPOKING ▸ **spoke**

SPONDEE n metrical foot of two long syllables

SPONDYL n vertebra

SPONGE n sea animal with a porous absorbent skeleton ▷ vb wipe with a sponge

SPONGED ▸ **sponge**

SPONGER n person who sponges on others

SPONGES ▸ **sponge**

SPONGIN n fibrous horny protein that forms the skeletal framework of the bath sponge and related sponges

SPONGY adj of or resembling a sponge

SPONSAL n marriage

SPONSON n outboard support for a gun enabling it to fire fore and aft

SPONSOR n person who promotes something ▷ vb act as a sponsor for

SPOOF n mildly satirical parody ▷ vb fool (a person) with a trick or deception

SPOOFED ▸ **spoof**

SPOOFER ▸ **spoof**

SPOOFS ▸ **spoof**

SPOOFY ▸ **spoof**

SPOOK n ghost ▷ vb frighten

SPOOKED ▸ **spook**

SPOOKS ▸ **spook**

SPOOKY adj ghostly or eerie

SPOOL n cylinder round which something can be wound ▷ vb wind or be wound onto a spool or reel

SPOOLED ▸ **spool**

SPOOLER ▸ **spool**

SPOOLS ▸ **spool**

SPOOM vb sail fast before wind

SPOOMED ▸ **spoom**

SPOOMS ▸ **spoom**

SPOON n shallow bowl attached to a handle for eating, stirring, or serving food ▷ vb lift with a spoon

SPOONED ▸ **spoon**

SPOONEY same as ▸ **spoony**

SPOONS ▸ **spoon**

SPOONY adj foolishly or stupidly amorous ▷ n fool or silly person, esp one in love

SPOOR n trail of an animal ▷ vb track (an animal) by following its trail

SPOORED ▸ **spoor**

SPOORER ▸ **spoor**

SPOORS ▸ **spoor**

SPOOT n razor shell

SPOOTS ▸ **spoot**

SPORAL ▸ **spore**

SPORE n minute reproductive body of some plants ▷ vb produce, carry, or release spores

SPORED ▸ **spore**

SPORES ▸ **spore**

SPORING ▸ **spore**

SPORK n spoon-shaped piece of cutlery with tines like a fork

SPORKS ▸ **spork**

SPOROID adj of or like a spore

SPORRAN n pouch worn in front of a kilt

SPORT n activity for pleasure, competition, or exercise ▷ vb wear proudly

SPORTED ▸ **sport**

SPORTER ▸ **sport**

SPORTIF adj sporty

SPORTS adj of or used in sports ▷ n meeting held at a school or college for competitions in athletic events

SPORTY adj (of a person) interested in sport ▷ n young person who typically wears sportswear, is competitive about sport, and takes an interest in his or her fitness

SPORULE n spore, esp a very small spore

SPOSH n slush

SPOSHES ▸ **sposh**

SPOSHY ▸ **sposh**

SPOT n small mark on a surface ▷ vb notice

SPOTLIT > **spotlight**

SPOTS ▸ **spot**

SPOTTED ▸ **spot**

SPOTTER n person whose hobby is watching for and noting numbers or types of trains or planes

SPOTTIE n young deer of up to three months of age

SPOTTY adj with spots

SPOUSAL n marriage ceremony ▷ adj of or relating to marriage

SPOUSE n husband or wife ▷ vb marry

SPOUSED ▸ **spouse**

SPOUSES ▸ **spouse**

SPOUT vb pour out in a stream or jet ▷ n projecting tube or lip for pouring liquids

SPOUTED ▸ **spout**

SPOUTER ▸ **spout**

SPOUTS ▸ **spout**

SPOUTY ▸ **spout**

SPRACK adj vigorous

SPRAD ▸ **spread**

SPRAG n chock or steel bar used to prevent a vehicle from running backwards on an incline ▷ vb use sprag to prevent vehicle from moving

SPRAGS ▸ **sprag**

SPRAID vb chapped

SPRAIN vb injure (a joint) by a sudden twist ▷ n such an injury

SPRAINS ▸ **sprain**

SPRAINT n piece of otter's dung

SPRANG n branch

SPRANGS ▸ **sprang**

SPRAT n small sea fish

SPRATS ▸ **sprat**

SPRAWL vb lie or sit with the limbs spread out ▷ n part of a city that has spread untidily over a large area

SPRAWLS ▶ sprawl

SPRAWLY ▶ sprawl

SPRAY n (device for producing) fine drops of liquid ▷ vb scatter in fine drops

SPRAYED ▶ spray

SPRAYER ▶ spray

SPRAYEY ▶ spray

SPRAYS ▶ spray

SPREAD vb open out or be displayed to the fullest extent ▷ n spreading ▷ adj extended or stretched out, esp to the fullest extent

SPREADS ▶ spread

SPREAGH n cattle raid

SPREAZE same as > spreathe

SPRED same as ▶ spread

SPREDD same as ▶ spread

SPREDDE same as ▶ spread

SPREDDS ▶ spredd

SPREDS ▶ spred

SPREE n session of overindulgence, usu in drinking or spending money ▷ vb go on a spree

SPREED ▶ spree

SPREES ▶ spree

SPREEZE same as > spreathe

SPRENT > sprinkle

SPREW same as ▶ sprue

SPREWS ▶ sprew

SPRIER ▶ spry

SPRIEST ▶ spry

SPRIG n twig or shoot ▷ vb fasten or secure with sprigs

SPRIGGY ▶ sprig

SPRIGHT same as ▶ sprite

SPRIGS ▶ sprig

SPRING vb move suddenly upwards or forwards in a single motion, jump ▷ n season between winter and summer

SPRINGE n type of snare for catching small wild animals or birds ▷ vb set such a snare

SPRINGS ▶ spring

SPRINGY adj elastic

SPRINT n short race run at top speed ▷ vb run a short distance at top speed

SPRINTS ▶ sprint

SPRIT n small spar set diagonally across a sail to extend it

SPRITE n elf

SPRITES ▶ sprite

SPRITS ▶ sprit

SPRITZ vb spray liquid

SPROD n young salmon

SPRODS ▶ sprod

SPROG n child

SPROGS ▶ sprog

SPRONG ▶ spring

SPROUT vb put forth shoots ▷ n shoot

SPROUTS ▶ sprout

SPRUCE n kind of fir ▷ adj neat and smart

SPRUCED ▶ spruce

SPRUCER ▶ spruce

SPRUCES ▶ spruce

SPRUCY ▶ spruce

SPRUE n vertical channel in a mould through which plastic or molten metal is poured

SPRUES ▶ sprue

SPRUG n sparrow

SPRUGS ▶ sprug

SPRUIK vb speak in public (used esp of a showman or salesman)

SPRUIKS ▶ spruik

SPRUIT n small tributary stream or watercourse

SPRUITS ▶ spruit

SPRUNG ▶ spring

SPRUSH Scots form of ▶ spruce

SPRY adj active or nimble

SPRYER ▶ spry

SPRYEST ▶ spry

SPRYLY ▶ spry

SPUD n potato ▷ vb remove (bark) or eradicate (weeds) with a spud

SPUDDED ▶ spud

SPUDDER same as ▶ spud

SPUDDLE n feeble movement

SPUDDY adj short and fat

SPUDS ▶ spud

SPUE same as ▶ spew

SPUED ▶ spue

SPUEING ▶ spue

SPUER ▶ spue

SPUERS ▶ spue

SPUES ▶ spue

SPUG same as ▶ spuggy

SPUGGY n house sparrow

SPUGS ▶ spug

SPUING ▶ spue

SPULE Scots word for > shoulder

SPULES ▶ spule

SPULYE same as > spuilzie

SPULYED ▶ spulye

SPULYES ▶ spulye

SPULYIE same as > spuilzie

SPULZIE same as > spuilzie

SPUME vb froth ▷ n foam or froth on the sea

SPUMED ▶ spume

SPUMES ▶ spume

SPUMIER ▶ spumy

SPUMING ▶ spume

SPUMONE n creamy Italian ice cream

SPUMONI same as ▶ spumone

SPUMOUS ▶ spume

SPUMY ▶ spume

SPUN ▶ spin

SPUNGE same as ▶ sponge

SPUNGES ▶ spunge

SPUNK n courage, spirit ▷ vb catch fire

SPUNKED ▶ spunk

SPUNKIE n will-o'-the-wisp

SPUNKS ▶ spunk

SPUNKY ▶ spunk

SPUR n stimulus or incentive ▷ vb urge on, incite (someone)

SPURGE n plant with milky sap

SPURGES ▶ spurge

SPURIAE n type of bird feathers

SPURN vb reject with scorn ▷ n instance of spurning

SPURNE vb spur

SPURNED ▶ spurn

SPURNER ▶ spurn

SPURNES ▶ spurne

SPURNS ▶ spurn

SPURRED ▶ spur

SPURRER ▶ spur

SPURREY n any of several low-growing European plants

SPURRY n spurrey ▷ adj resembling a spur

SPURS ▶ spur

SPURT vb gush or cause to gush out in a jet ▷ n short sudden burst of activity or speed

SPURTED ▶ spurt

SPURTER ▶ spurt

SPURTLE n wooden spoon for stirring porridge

SPURTS ▶ spurt

SPURWAY n path used by riders

SPUTA ▶ sputum

SPUTNIK n early Soviet artificial satellite

SPUTTER n splutter ▷ vb splutter

SPUTUM n spittle, usu mixed with mucus

SPY n person employed to

obtain secret information ▷ *vb* act as a spy

SPYAL *n* spy

SPYALS ▸ spyal

SPYCAM *n* camera used for covert surveillance

SPYCAMS ▸ spycam

SPYHOLE *n* small hole in a door, etc through which one may watch secretly

SPYING ▸ spy

SPYINGS ▸ spy

SPYRE *same as* ▸ **spire**

SPYRES ▸ spyre

SPYWARE *n* software installed via the internet on a computer without the user's knowledge and used to gain information about the user

SQUAB *n* young bird yet to leave the nest ▷ *adj* (of birds) recently hatched and still unfledged ▷ *vb* fall

SQUABBY ▸ squab

SQUABS ▸ squab

SQUACCO *n* S European heron

SQUAD *n* small group of people working or training together ▷ *vb* set up squads

SQUADDY *same as* > **squaddie**

SQUADS ▸ squad

SQUAIL *vb* throw sticks at

SQUAILS ▸ squail

SQUALID *adj* dirty and unpleasant

SQUALL *n* sudden strong wind ▷ *vb* cry noisily, yell

SQUALLS ▸ squall

SQUALLY ▸ squall

SQUALOR *n* disgusting dirt and filth

SQUAMA *n* scale or scalelike structure

SQUAMAE ▸ squama

SQUAME *same as* ▸ **squama**

SQUAMES ▸ squama

SQUARE *n* geometric figure with four equal sides and four right angles ▷ *adj* square in shape ▷ *vb* multiply (a number) by itself ▷ *adv* squarely, directly

SQUARED ▸ square

SQUARER ▸ square

SQUARES ▸ square

SQUARK *n* hypothetical boson partner of a quark

SQUARKS ▸ squark

SQUASH *vb* crush flat ▷ *n*

sweet fruit drink diluted with water

SQUASHY *adj* soft and easily squashed

SQUAT *vb* crouch with the knees bent and the weight on the feet ▷ *n* place where squatters live ▷ *adj* short and broad

SQUATLY ▸ squat

SQUATS ▸ squat

SQUATTY *adj* short and broad

SQUAWK *n* loud harsh cry ▷ *vb* utter a squawk

SQUAWKS ▸ squawk

SQUAWKY ▸ squawk

SQUEAK *n* short shrill cry or sound ▷ *vb* make or utter a squeak

SQUEAKS ▸ squeak

SQUEAKY ▸ squeak

SQUEAL *n* long shrill cry or sound ▷ *vb* make or utter a squeal

SQUEALS ▸ squeal

SQUEEZE *vb* grip or press firmly ▷ *n* squeezing

SQUEEZY ▸ squeeze

SQUEG *vb* oscillate

SQUEGS ▸ squeg

SQUELCH *vb* make a wet sucking sound, as by walking through mud ▷ *n* squelching sound

SQUIB *n* small firework that hisses before exploding

SQUIBS ▸ squib

SQUID *n* sea creature with a long soft body and ten tentacles ▷ *vb* (of a parachute) to assume an elongated squidlike shape owing to excess air pressure

SQUIDGE *vb* squash

SQUIDGY *adj* soft, moist, and squashy

SQUIDS ▸ squid

SQUIER *same as* ▸ **squire**

SQUIERS ▸ squier

SQUIFF *same as* ▸ **squiffy**

SQUIFFY *adj* slightly drunk

SQUILL *n* Mediterranean plant of the lily family

SQUILLA *n* type of mantis shrimp

SQUILLS ▸ squill

SQUINCH *n* small arch across an internal corner of a tower, used to support a superstructure such as a spire ▷ *vb* squeeze

SQUINNY *vb* squint ▷ *adj* squint

SQUINT *vb* have eyes which face in different directions ▷ *n* squinting condition of the eye ▷ *adj* crooked

SQUINTS ▸ squint

SQUINTY ▸ squint

SQUINY *same as* ▸ **squinny**

SQUIRE *n* country gentleman, usu the main landowner in a community ▷ *vb* (of a man) escort (a woman)

SQUIRED ▸ squire

SQUIRES ▸ squire

SQUIRM *vb* wriggle, writhe ▷ *n* wriggling movement

SQUIRMS ▸ squirm

SQUIRMY *adj* moving with a wriggling motion

SQUIRR *same as* ▸ **skirr**

SQUIRRS ▸ squirr

SQUIRT *vb* force (a liquid) or (of a liquid) be forced out of a narrow opening ▷ *n* jet of liquid

SQUIRTS ▸ squirt

SQUISH *n* (make) a soft squelching sound ▷ *vb* crush (something) with a soft squelching sound

SQUISHY *adj* soft and yielding to the touch

SQUIT *n* insignificant person

SQUITCH *n* couch grass

SQUITS ▸ squit

SQUIZ *n* look or glance, esp an inquisitive one

The word **quiz** comes up surprisingly often, so it is useful to remember that you can put an S on the front of it to form this Australian slang word for a quick look.

SQUOOSH *vb* squash

SQUUSH *same as* ▸ **squoosh**

SRADDHA *n* Hindu offering to ancestor

SRADHA *same as* ▸ **sraddha**

SRADHAS ▸ sradha

SRI *n* title of respect used when addressing a Hindu

SRIS ▸ sri

ST *interj* exclamation to attract attention

STAB *vb* pierce with something pointed ▷ *n* stabbing

STABBED ▸ stab

STABBER ▸ stab

S

STABILE n stationary abstract construction, usually of wire, metal, wood, etc ▷ adj fixed

STABLE n building in which horses are kept ▷ vb put or keep (a horse) in a stable ▷ adj firmly fixed or established

STABLED ▷ **stable**

STABLER n stable owner

STABLES ▷ **stable**

STABLY ▷ **stable**

STABS ▷ **stab**

STACHYS n type of plant of the genus which includes lamb's ears and betony

STACK n ordered pile ▷ vb pile in a stack

STACKED ▷ **stack**

STACKER ▷ **stack**

STACKET n fence of wooden posts

STACKS ▷ **stack**

STACKUP n number of aircraft waiting to land

STACTE n one of several sweet-smelling spices used in incense

STACTES ▷ **stacte**

STADDA n type of saw

STADDAS ▷ **stadda**

STADDLE n type of support or prop

STADE same as ▷ **stadium**

STADES ▷ **stade**

STADIA n instrument used in surveying

STADIAL n stage in development of glacier

STADIAS ▷ **stadia**

STADIUM n sports arena with tiered seats for spectators

STAFF n people employed in an organization ▷ vb supply with personnel

STAFFED ▷ **staff**

STAFFER n member of staff, esp, in journalism, of editorial staff

STAFFS ▷ **staff**

STAG n adult male deer ▷ adv without a female escort ▷ vb apply for (shares in a new issue) with the intention of selling them for a quick profit

STAGE n step or period of development ▷ vb put (a play) on stage

STAGED ▷ **stage**

STAGER n person of experience

STAGERS ▷ **stager**

STAGERY n theatrical effects or techniques

STAGES ▷ **stage**

STAGEY same as ▷ **stagy**

STAGGED ▷ **stag**

STAGGER vb walk unsteadily ▷ n staggering

STAGGIE n little stag

STAGGY ▷ **stag**

STAGIER ▷ **stagy**

STAGILY ▷ **stagy**

STAGING n temporary support used in building

STAGS ▷ **stag**

STAGY adj too theatrical or dramatic

STAID adj sedate, serious, and rather dull

STAIDER ▷ **staid**

STAIDLY ▷ **staid**

STAIG Scots variant of ▷ **stag**

STAIGS ▷ **staig**

STAIN vb discolour, mark ▷ n discoloration or mark

STAINED ▷ **stain**

STAINER ▷ **stain**

STAINS ▷ **stain**

STAIR n one step in a flight of stairs

STAIRED adj having stairs

STAIRS pl n flight of steps between floors, usu indoors

STAITH same as ▷ **staithe**

STAITHE n wharf

STAITHS ▷ **staith**

STAKE n pointed stick or post driven into the ground as a support or marker ▷ vb support or mark out with stakes

STAKED ▷ **stake**

STAKES ▷ **stake**

STAKING ▷ **stake**

STALAG n German prisoner-of-war camp in World War II

STALAGS ▷ **stalag**

STALE adj not fresh ▷ vb make or become stale ▷ n urine of horses or cattle

STALED ▷ **stale**

STALELY ▷ **stale**

STALER ▷ **stale**

STALES ▷ **stale**

STALEST ▷ **stale**

STALING ▷ **stale**

STALK n plant's stem ▷ vb follow or approach stealthily

STALKED ▷ **stalk**

STALKER ▷ **stalk**

STALKO n idle gentleman

STALKS ▷ **stalk**

STALKY adj like a stalk

STALL n small stand for the display and sale of goods ▷ vb stop (a motor vehicle or engine) or (of a motor vehicle or engine) stop accidentally

STALLED ▷ **stall**

STALLS ▷ **stall**

STAMEN n pollen-producing part of a flower

STAMENS ▷ **stamen**

STAMINA n enduring energy and strength

STAMMEL n coarse woollen cloth in former use for undergarments

STAMMER vb speak or say with involuntary pauses or repetition of syllables ▷ n tendency to stammer

STAMNOI ▷ **stamnos**

STAMNOS n ancient Greek jar

STAMP n piece of gummed paper stuck to an envelope or parcel to show that the postage has been paid ▷ vb bring (one's foot) down forcefully

STAMPED ▷ **stamp**

STAMPER ▷ **stamp**

STAMPS ▷ **stamp**

STANCE n attitude

STANCES ▷ **stance**

STANCH vb stem the flow of (a liquid, esp blood) ▷ adj loyal and dependable

STANCK adj faint

STAND vb be in, rise to, or place in an upright position ▷ n stall for the sale of goods

STANDBY n person or thing that is ready for use

STANDEE n person who stands, esp when there are no vacant seats

STANDEN ▷ **stand**

STANDER ▷ **stand**

STANDS ▷ **stand**

STANDUP n comedian who performs solo

STANE Scots word for ▷ **stone**

STANED ▷ **stane**

STANES ▷ **stane**

STANG vb sting

STANGED ▷ **stang**

STANGS ▷ **stang**

S

STANIEL n kestrel
STANINE n scale of nine levels
STANING ▶ stane
STANK vb dam
STANKED ▶ stink
STANKS ▶ stink
STANNEL same as ▶ staniel
STANNIC adj of or containing tin, esp in the tetravalent state
STANNUM n tin (the metal)
STANOL n drug taken to prevent heart disease
STANOLS ▶ stanol
STANYEL same as ▶ staniel
STANZA n verse of a poem
STANZAS ▶ stanza
STANZE same as ▶ stanza
STANZES ▶ stanze
STANZO same as ▶ stanza
STANZOS ▶ stanzo
STAP same as ▶ stop
STAPES n stirrup-shaped bone that is the innermost of three small bones in the middle ear of mammals
STAPH n staphylococcus
STAPHS ▶ staph
STAPLE n U-shaped piece of metal used to fasten papers or secure things ▷ vb fasten with staples ▷ adj of prime importance, principal
STAPLED ▶ staple
STAPLER n small device for fastening papers together
STAPLES ▶ staple
STAPPED ▶ stap
STAPPLE same as ▶ stopple
STAPS ▶ stap
STAR n hot gaseous mass in space, visible in the night sky as a point of light ▷ vb feature or be featured as a star ▷ adj leading, famous
STARCH n carbohydrate forming the main food element in bread, potatoes, etc, and used mixed with water for stiffening fabric ▷ vb stiffen (fabric) with starch ▷ adj (of a person) formal
STARCHY adj containing starch
STARDOM n status of a star in the entertainment or sports world
STARE vb look or gaze fixedly (at) ▷ n fixed gaze
STARED ▶ stare
STARER ▶ stare

STARERS ▶ stare
STARES ▶ stare
STARETS n Russian holy man
STARETZ same as ▶ starets
STARING ▶ stare
STARK adj harsh, unpleasant, and plain ▷ adv completely ▷ vb stiffen
STARKED ▶ stark
STARKEN vb become or make stark
STARKER ▶ stark
STARKLY ▶ stark
STARKS ▶ stark
STARLET n young actress presented as a future star
STARLIT same as > starlight
STARN same as ▶ stern
STARNED ▶ starn
STARNIE n Scots word for little star
STARNS ▶ starn
STARR n (in Judaism) release from a debt
STARRED ▶ star
STARRS ▶ starr
STARRY adj full of or like stars
STARS ▶ star
START vb take the first step, begin ▷ n first part of something
STARTED ▶ start
STARTER n first course of a meal
STARTLE vb slightly surprise or frighten
STARTLY same as > startlish
STARTS ▶ start
STARTSY ▶ starets
STARTUP n business enterprise that has been launched recently
STARVE vb die or suffer or cause to die or suffer from hunger
STARVED ▶ starve
STARVER ▶ starve
STARVES ▶ starve
STASES ▶ stasis
STASH vb store in a secret place ▷ n secret store
STASHED ▶ stash
STASHES ▶ stash
STASHIE same as ▶ stushie
STASIMA > stasimon
STASIS n stagnation in the normal flow of bodily fluids, such as the blood or urine
STAT n statistic
STATAL adj of a federal state
STATANT adj (of an animal)

in profile with all four feet on the ground
STATE n condition of a person or thing ▷ adj of or concerning the State ▷ vb express in words
STATED adj (esp of a sum) determined by agreement
STATELY adj dignified or grand ▷ adv in a stately manner
STATER n any of various usually silver coins of ancient Greece
STATERS ▶ stater
STATES ▶ state
STATIC adj stationary or inactive ▷ n crackling sound or speckled picture caused by interference in radio or television reception
STATICE n plant name formerly used for both thrift and sea lavender
STATICS n branch of mechanics dealing with the forces producing a state of equilibrium
STATIM adv right away
STATIN n type of drug that lowers the levels of low-density lipoproteins in the blood
STATING ▶ state
STATINS ▶ statin
STATION n place where trains stop for passengers ▷ vb assign (someone) to a particular place
STATISM n theory or practice of concentrating economic and political power in the state
STATIST n advocate of statism ▷ adj of, characteristic of, advocating, or relating to statism
STATIVE adj denoting a verb describing a state rather than an activity, act, or event ▷ n stative verb
STATOR n stationary part of a rotary machine or device, esp a motor or generator
STATORS ▶ stator
STATS ▶ stat
STATTO n person preoccupied with the facts and figures of a subject
STATTOS ▶ statto
STATUA same as ▶ statue

S

STATUAS ▸ statue

STATUE n large sculpture of a human or animal figure

STATUED adj decorated with or portrayed in a statue or statues

STATUES ▸ statue

STATURE n person's height

STATUS n social position

STATUSY adj conferring or having status

STATUTE n written law

STAUN Scots word for ▸ **stand**

STAUNCH same as ▸ **stanch**

STAUNS ▸ staun

STAVE same as ▸ **staff**

STAVED ▸ stave

STAVES ▸ stave

STAVING ▸ stave

STAW Scots form of ▸ **stall**

STAWED ▸ staw

STAWING ▸ staw

STAWS ▸ staw

STAY vb remain in a place or condition ▷ n period of staying in a place

STAYED ▸ stay

STAYER n person or thing that stays

STAYERS ▸ stayer

STAYING ▸ stay

STAYNE same as ▸ **stain**

STAYNED ▸ stayne

STAYNES ▸ stayne

STAYRE same as ▸ **stair**

STAYRES ▸ stayre

STAYS pl n old-fashioned corsets with bones in them

STEAD n place or function that should be taken by another ▷ vb help or benefit

STEADED ▸ stead

STEADS ▸ stead

STEADY adj not shaky or wavering ▷ vb make steady ▷ adv in a steady manner

STEAK n thick slice of meat, esp beef

STEAKS ▸ steak

STEAL vb take unlawfully or without permission

STEALE n handle

STEALED ▸ steal

STEALER n person who steals something

STEALES ▸ steale

STEALS ▸ steal

STEALT ▸ steal

STEALTH n moving carefully and quietly ▷ adj (of technology) able to render

an aircraft almost invisible to radar ▷ vb approach undetected

STEAM n vapour into which water changes when boiled ▷ vb give off steam

STEAMED ▸ steam

STEAMER n steam-propelled ship ▷ vb travel by steamer

STEAMIE n public wash house

STEAMS ▸ steam

STEAMY adj full of steam

STEAN n earthenware vessel

STEANE same as ▸ **steen**

STEANED ▸ steane

STEANES ▸ steane

STEANS ▸ stean

STEAR same as ▸ **steer**

STEARD ▸ stear

STEARE same as ▸ **steer**

STEARED ▸ steare

STEARES ▸ steare

STEARIC adj of or relating to suet or fat

STEARIN n colourless crystalline ester of glycerol and stearic acid

STEARS ▸ stear

STED same as ▸ **stead**

STEDD same as ▸ **stead**

STEDDE same as ▸ **stead**

STEDDED ▸ sted

STEDDES ▸ stedde

STEDDS ▸ stedd

STEDDY same as ▸ **steady**

STEDE same as ▸ **stead**

STEDED ▸ stede

STEDES ▸ stede

STEDING ▸ stede

STEDS ▸ sted

STEED same as ▸ **stead**

STEEDED ▸ steed

STEEDS ▸ steed

STEEDY same as ▸ **steady**

STEEK vb Scots word meaning shut

STEEKED ▸ steek

STEEKIT ▸ steek

STEEKS ▸ steek

STEEL n hard malleable alloy of iron and carbon ▷ vb prepare (oneself) for something unpleasant

STEELD ▸ steel

STEELED ▸ steel

STEELIE n steel ball bearing used as marble

STEELS pl n shares and bonds of steel companies

STEELY ▸ steel

STEEM same as ▸ **esteem**

STEEMED ▸ steem

STEEMS ▸ steem

STEEN vb line with stone

STEENED ▸ steen

STEENS ▸ steen

STEEP adj sloping sharply ▷ vb soak or be soaked in liquid ▷ n instance or the process of steeping or the condition of being steeped

STEEPED ▸ steep

STEEPEN vb become or cause (something) to become steep or steeper

STEEPER ▸ steep

STEEPLE same as ▸ **spire**

STEEPLY ▸ steep

STEEPS ▸ steep

STEEPUP adj very steep

STEEPY same as ▸ **steep**

STEER vb direct the course of (a vehicle or ship) ▷ n castrated male ox

STEERED ▸ steer

STEERER ▸ steer

STEERS ▸ steer

STEERY n commotion

STEEVE n spar having a pulley block at one end, used for stowing cargo on a ship ▷ vb stow (cargo) securely in the hold of a ship

STEEVED ▸ steeve

STEEVER ▸ steeve

STEEVES ▸ steeve

STEIL same as ▸ **steal**

STEILS ▸ steil

STEIN same as ▸ **steen**

STEINED ▸ stein

STEINS ▸ stein

STELA same as ▸ **stele**

STELAE ▸ stele

STELAI ▸ stele

STELAR ▸ stele

STELE n upright stone slab or column decorated with figures or inscriptions

STELENE ▸ stele

STELES ▸ stele

STELIC ▸ stele

STELL n shelter for cattle or sheep built on moorland or hillsides ▷ vb position or place

STELLA n star or something star-shaped

STELLAR adj of stars

STELLAS ▸ stella

STELLED ▸ stell

STELLIO n as in **stellio lizard** denoting type of lizard

STELLS ▶ **stell**

STEM vb stop (the flow of something) ▷ n main axis of a plant, which bears the leaves, axillary buds, and flowers

STEMBOK same as > **steenbok**

STEME same as ▶ **steam**

STEMED ▶ **steme**

STEMES ▶ **steme**

STEMING ▶ **steme**

STEMLET n little stem

STEMMA n family tree

STEMMAS ▶ **stemma**

STEMME archaic variant of ▶ **stem**

STEMMED ▶ **stem**

STEMMER ▶ **stem**

STEMMES ▶ **stemme**

STEMMY adj (of wine) young and raw

STEMPEL n timber support

STEMPLE same as ▶ **stempel**

STEMS ▶ **stem**

STEMSON n curved timber scarfed into or bolted to the stem and keelson at the bow of a wooden vessel

STEN vb stride

STENCH n foul smell ▷ vb cause to smell

STENCHY ▶ **stench**

STENCIL n thin sheet with cut-out pattern through which ink or paint passes to form the pattern on the surface below ▷ vb make (a pattern) with a stencil

STEND vb Scots word meaning bound

STENDED ▶ **stend**

STENDS ▶ **stend**

STENGAH same as ▶ **stinger**

STENNED ▶ **sten**

STENO n stenographer

STENOKY n life and survival that is dependent on conditions remaining within a narrow range of variables

STENOS ▶ **steno**

STENS ▶ **sten**

STENT n surgical implant used to keep an artery open ▷ vb assess

STENTED ▶ **stent**

STENTOR n person with an unusually loud voice

STENTS ▶ **stent**

STEP vb move and set down the foot, as when walking

▷ n stepping

STEPNEY n spare wheel

STEPPE n extensive grassy plain usually without trees

STEPPED ▶ **step**

STEPPER n person who or animal that steps, esp a horse or a dancer

STEPPES ▶ **steppe**

STEPS ▶ **step**

STEPSON n son of one's husband or wife by an earlier relationship

STEPT ▶ **step**

STERE n unit used to measure volumes of stacked timber

STEREO n stereophonic record player ▷ adj (of a sound system) using two or more separate microphones to feed two or more loudspeakers through separate channels ▷ vb make stereophonic

STEREOS ▶ **stereo**

STERES ▶ **stere**

STERIC adj of or caused by the spatial arrangement of atoms in a molecule

STERILE adj free from germs

STERLET n small sturgeon of seas and rivers in N Asia and E Europe

STERN adj severe, strict ▷ n rear part of a ship ▷ vb row boat backward

STERNA ▶ **sternum**

STERNAL ▶ **sternum**

STERNED ▶ **stern**

STERNER ▶ **stern**

STERNLY ▶ **stern**

STERNS ▶ **stern**

STERNUM n long flat bone in the front of the body, to which the collarbone and most of the ribs are attached

STEROID n organic compound containing a carbon ring system, such as many hormones

STEROL n natural insoluble alcohol such as cholesterol and ergosterol

STEROLS ▶ **sterol**

STERTOR n laborious or noisy breathing caused by obstructed air passages

STERVE same as ▶ **starve**

STERVED ▶ **sterve**

STERVES ▶ **sterve**

STET interj instruction to

ignore an alteration previously made by a proofreader ▷ vb indicate to a printer that certain deleted matter is to be kept ▷ n. word or mark indicating that certain deleted written matter is to be retained

STETS ▶ **stet**

STETSON n cowboy hat

STETTED ▶ **stet**

STEVEN n voice

STEVENS ▶ **steven**

STEW n food cooked slowly in a closed pot ▷ vb cook slowly in a closed pot

STEWARD n person who looks after passengers on a ship or aircraft ▷ vb act as a steward (of)

STEWBUM n drunkard

STEWED adj (of food) cooked by stewing

STEWER ▶ **stew**

STEWERS ▶ **stew**

STEWIER ▶ **stew**

STEWING ▶ **stew**

STEWPAN n pan used for making stew

STEWPOT n pot used for making stew

STEWS ▶ **stew**

STEWY ▶ **stew**

STEY adj Scots word meaning steep

STEYER ▶ **stey**

STEYEST ▶ **stey**

STHENIA n abnormal strength

STHENIC adj abounding in energy or bodily strength

STIBBLE Scots form of ▶ **stubble**

STIBIAL ▶ **stibium**

STIBINE n colourless slightly soluble poisonous gas

STIBIUM obsolete name for > **antimony**

STICH n line of poetry

STICHIC ▶ **stich**

STICHOI ▶ **stichos**

STICHOS n line of poem

STICHS ▶ **stich**

STICK n long thin piece of wood ▷ vb push (a pointed object) into (something)

STICKED ▶ **stick**

STICKER n adhesive label or sign ▷ vb put stickers on

STICKIT Scots form of ▶ **stuck**

STICKLE vb dispute

S

stubbornly, esp about minor points
STICKS ▶ stick
STICKUM n adhesive
STICKUP n robbery at gun-point
STICKY adj covered with an adhesive substance ▷ vb make sticky ▷ n inquisitive look or stare
STIDDIE same as ▶ stithy
STIE same as ▶ sty
STIED ▶ sty
STIES ▶ sty
STIEVE same as ▶ steeve
STIEVER ▶ stieve
STIFF adj not easily bent or moved ▷ n corpse ▷ adv completely or utterly ▷ vb fail completely
STIFFED ▶ stiff
STIFFEN vb make or become stiff
STIFFER ▶ stiff
STIFFLY ▶ stiff
STIFFS ▶ stiff
STIFFY n erection of the penis
STIFLE vb suppress ▷ n joint in the hind leg of a horse, dog, etc, between the femur and tibia
STIFLED ▶ stifle
STIFLER ▶ stifle
STIFLES ▶ stifle
STIGMA n mark of social disgrace
STIGMAL adj of part of insect wing
STIGMAS ▶ stigma
STIGME n dot in Greek punctuation
STIGMES ▶ stigme
STILB n unit of luminance equal to 1 candela per square centimetre
STILBS ▶ stilb
STILE same as ▶ style
STILED ▶ stile
STILES ▶ stile
STILET same as ▶ stylet
STILETS ▶ stilet
STILING ▶ stile
STILL adv now or in the future as before ▷ adj motionless ▷ n calmness; apparatus for distillation ▷ vb make still
STILLED ▶ still
STILLER ▶ still
STILLS ▶ still
STILLY adv quietly or calmly ▷ adj still, quiet, or calm

STILT n either of a pair of long poles with footrests for walking raised from the ground ▷ vb raise or place on or as if on stilts
STILTED adj stiff and formal in manner
STILTER ▶ stilt
STILTS ▶ stilt
STILTY ▶ stilt
STIM n very small amount
STIME same as ▶ styme
STIMED ▶ stime
STIMES ▶ stime
STIMIE same as ▶ stymie
STIMIED ▶ stimie
STIMIES ▶ stimie
STIMING ▶ stime
STIMS ▶ stim
STIMULI > stimulus
STIMY same as ▶ stymie
STING vb (of certain animals or plants) wound by injecting with poison ▷ n wound or pain caused by or as if by stinging
STINGED ▶ sting
STINGER n person, plant, animal, etc, that stings or hurts
STINGO n strong alcohol
STINGOS ▶ stingo
STINGS ▶ sting
STINGY adj mean or miserly ▷ n stinging nettle
STINK n strong unpleasant smell ▷ vb give off a strong unpleasant smell
STINKER n difficult or unpleasant person or thing
STINKO adj drunk
STINKS ▶ stink
STINKY adj having a foul smell
STINT vb be miserly with (something) ▷ n allotted amount of work
STINTED ▶ stint
STINTER ▶ stint
STINTS ▶ stint
STINTY ▶ stint
STIPA n variety of grass
STIPAS ▶ stipa
STIPE n stalk in plants that bears reproductive structures
STIPED same as > stipitate
STIPEL n small paired leaflike structure at the base of certain leaflets
STIPELS ▶ stipel
STIPEND n regular allowance or salary, esp

that paid to a clergyman
STIPES n second maxillary segment in insects and crustaceans
STIPPLE vb paint, draw, or engrave using dots ▷ n technique of stippling or a picture produced by or using stippling
STIPULE n small paired usually leaflike outgrowth occurring at the base of a leaf or its stalk
STIR vb mix up (a liquid) by moving a spoon etc around in it ▷ n stirring
STIRE same as ▶ steer
STIRED ▶ stire
STIRES ▶ stire
STIRING ▶ stire
STIRK n heifer of 6 to 12 months old
STIRKS ▶ stirk
STIRP same as ▶ stirps
STIRPES ▶ stirps
STIRPS n line of descendants from an ancestor
STIRRA same as ▶ sirra
STIRRAH same as ▶ sirrah
STIRRAS ▶ stirra
STIRRE same as ▶ steer
STIRRED ▶ stir
STIRRER n person who deliberately causes trouble
STIRRES ▶ stirre
STIRRUP n metal loop attached to a saddle for supporting a rider's foot
STIRS ▶ stir
STISHIE same as ▶ stushie
STITCH n link made by drawing thread through material with a needle ▷ vb sew
STITHY n forge or anvil ▷ vb forge on an anvil
STIVE vb stifle
STIVED ▶ stive
STIVER n former Dutch coin worth one twentieth of a guilder
STIVERS ▶ stiver
STIVES ▶ stive
STIVIER ▶ stivy
STIVING ▶ stive
STIVY adj stuffy
STOA n covered walk that has a colonnade on one or both sides, esp as used in ancient Greece
STOAE ▶ stoa
STOAI ▶ stoa

S

STOAS ▶ **stoa**

STOAT n small mammal of the weasel family, with brown fur that turns white in winter

STOATS ▶ **stoat**

STOB same as ▶ **stab**

STOBBED ▶ **stob**

STOBIE adj as in **stobie pole** steel and concrete pole for supporting electricity wires

STOBS ▶ **stob**

STOCK n total amount of goods available for sale in a shop ▷ adj kept in stock, standard ▷ vb keep for sale or future use

STOCKED ▶ **stock**

STOCKER ▶ **stock**

STOCKS pl n instrument of punishment consisting of a heavy wooden frame with holes in which the feet, hands, or head of an offender were locked

STOCKY adj (of a person) broad and sturdy

STODGE n heavy starchy food ▷ vb stuff (oneself or another) with food

STODGED ▶ **stodge**

STODGER n dull person

STODGES ▶ **stodge**

STODGY adj (of food) heavy and starchy

STOEP n verandah

STOEPS ▶ **stoep**

STOGEY same as ▶ **stogy**

STOGEYS ▶ **stogey**

STOGIE same as ▶ **stogy**

STOGIES ▶ **stogy**

STOGY n any long cylindrical inexpensive cigar

STOIC n person who suffers hardship without showing his or her feelings ▷ adj suffering hardship without showing one's feelings

STOICAL adj suffering great difficulties without showing one's feelings

STOICS ▶ **stoic**

STOIT vb bounce

STOITED ▶ **stoit**

STOITER vb stagger

STOITS ▶ **stoit**

STOKE vb feed and tend (a fire or furnace)

STOKED adj very pleased

STOKER n person employed to tend a furnace on a ship or train powered by steam

STOKERS ▶ **stoker**

STOKES n cgs unit of kinematic viscosity

STOKING ▶ **stoke**

STOKVEL n (in S Africa) informal savings pool or syndicate

STOLE n long scarf or shawl

STOLED adj wearing a stole

STOLEN ▶ **steal**

STOLES ▶ **stole**

STOLID adj showing little emotion or interest

STOLLEN n rich sweet bread containing nuts, raisins, etc

STOLN ▶ **steal**

STOLON n long horizontal stem that grows along the surface of the soil and propagates by producing roots and shoots at the nodes or tip

STOLONS ▶ **stolon**

STOMA n pore in a plant leaf that controls the passage of gases into and out of the plant

STOMACH n organ in the body which digests food ▷ vb put up with

STOMACK n as in **have a stomack** (in E Africa) be pregnant

STOMAL ▶ **stoma**

STOMAS ▶ **stoma**

STOMATA ▶ **stoma**

STOMATE n opening on leaf through which water evaporates

STOMIA ▶ **stomium**

STOMIUM n part of the sporangium of ferns that ruptures to release the spores

STOMP vb tread heavily ▷ n rhythmic stamping jazz dance

STOMPED ▶ **stomp**

STOMPER n rock or jazz song with a particularly strong and danceable beat

STOMPIE n cigarette butt

STOMPS ▶ **stomp**

STOND same as ▶ **stand**

STONDS ▶ **stond**

STONE n material of which rocks are made ▷ vb throw stones at

STONED adj under the influence of alcohol or drugs

STONEN adj of stone

STONER n device for removing stones from fruit

STONERN same as ▶ **stonen**

STONERS ▶ **stoner**

STONES ▶ **stone**

STONEY same as ▶ **stony**

STONG ▶ **sting**

STONIED ▶ **stony**

STONIER ▶ **stony**

STONIES ▶ **stony**

STONILY ▶ **stony**

STONING ▶ **stone**

STONISH same as > **astonish**

STONK vb bombard (soldiers, buildings, etc) with artillery ▷ n concentrated bombardment by artillery

STONKED ▶ **stonk**

STONKER vb destroy

STONKS ▶ **stonk**

STONN same as ▶ **stun**

STONNE same as ▶ **stun**

STONNED ▶ **stonne**

STONNES ▶ **stonne**

STONNS ▶ **stonn**

STONY adj of or like stone ▷ vb astonish

STOOD ▶ **stand**

STOODEN ▶ **stand**

STOOGE n actor who feeds lines to a comedian or acts as the butt of his jokes ▷ vb act as a stooge

STOOGED ▶ **stooge**

STOOGES ▶ **stooge**

STOOK n number of sheaves set upright in a field to dry with their heads together ▷ vb set up (sheaves) in stooks

STOOKED ▶ **stook**

STOOKER ▶ **stook**

STOOKIE n stucco

STOOKS ▶ **stook**

STOOL n chair without arms or back ▷ vb (of a plant) send up shoots from the base of the stem

STOOLED ▶ **stool**

STOOLIE n police informer

STOOLS ▶ **stool**

STOOP vb bend forward and downward

STOOPE same as ▶ **stoup**

STOOPED ▶ **stoop**

STOOPER ▶ **stoop**

STOOPES ▶ **stoope**

STOOPS ▶ **stoop**

STOOR same as ▶ **stour**

STOORS ▶ **stoor**

STOOZE vb borrow money at 0% interest rate on a

S

credit card then invest it to make a profit

STOOZED ▶ **stooze**

STOOZER n person who borrows money at 0% interest rate on a credit card then invests it to make a profit

STOOZES ▶ **stooze**

STOP vb cease or cause to cease from doing (something) ▷ n stopping or being stopped

STOPE n steplike excavation made in a mine to extract ore ▷ vb mine (ore, etc) by cutting stopes

STOPED ▶ **stope**

STOPER n drill used in mining

STOPERS ▶ **stoper**

STOPES ▶ **stope**

STOPGAP n temporary substitute

STOPING n process by which country rock is broken up and engulfed by the upward movement of magma

STOPOFF n break in a journey

STOPPED ▶ **stop**

STOPPER n plug for closing a bottle etc ▷ vb close or fit with a stopper

STOPPLE same as ▶ **stopper**

STOPS ▶ **stop**

STOPT ▶ **stop**

STORAGE n storing

STORAX n type of tree or shrub with drooping showy white flowers

STORE vb collect and keep (things) for future use ▷ n shop

STORED ▶ **store**

STORER ▶ **store**

STORERS ▶ **store**

STORES pl n supply or stock of food and other essentials for a journey

STOREY n floor or level of a building

STOREYS ▶ **storey**

STORGE n affection

STORGES ▶ **storge**

STORIED ▶ **story**

STORIES ▶ **story**

STORING ▶ **store**

STORK n large wading bird

STORKS ▶ **stork**

STORM n violent weather with wind, rain, or snow

▷ vb attack or capture (a place) suddenly

STORMED ▶ **storm**

STORMER n outstanding example of its kind

STORMS ▶ **storm**

STORMY adj characterized by storms

STORY n narration of a chain of events ▷ vb decorate with scenes from history

STOSS adj (of the side of a hill) facing the onward flow of a glacier ▷ n hillside facing glacier flow

STOSSES ▶ **stoss**

STOT n bullock ▷ vb bounce or cause to bounce

STOTIN n monetary unit of Slovenia, worth one hundredth of a tolar

STOTINS ▶ **stotin**

STOTS ▶ **stot**

STOTT same as ▶ **stot**

STOTTED ▶ **stot**

STOTTER same as ▶ **stot**

STOTTIE n wedge of bread cut from a flat round loaf that has been split and filled with meat, cheese, etc

STOTTS ▶ **stott**

STOTTY n type of flat, round loaf made in NE England

STOUN same as ▶ **stun**

STOUND n short while ▷ vb ache

STOUNDS ▶ **stound**

STOUNS ▶ **stoun**

STOUP n small basin for holy water

STOUPS ▶ **stoup**

STOUR n turmoil or conflict

STOURE same as ▶ **stour**

STOURES ▶ **stoure**

STOURIE same as ▶ **stoury**

STOURS ▶ **stour**

STOURY adj dusty

STOUSH vb hit or punch (someone) ▷ n fighting or violence

STOUT adj fat ▷ n strong dark beer

STOUTEN vb make or become stout

STOUTER ▶ **stout**

STOUTH n Scots word meaning theft

STOUTHS ▶ **stouth**

STOUTLY ▶ **stout**

STOUTS ▶ **stout**

STOVE n apparatus for cooking or heating ▷ vb

process (ceramics, metalwork, etc) by heating in a stove

STOVED ▶ **stove**

STOVER n fodder

STOVERS ▶ **stover**

STOVES ▶ **stove**

STOVIES pl n potatoes stewed with onions

STOVING ▶ **stove**

STOW vb pack or store

STOWAGE n space or charge for stowing goods

STOWED ▶ **stow**

STOWER ▶ **stow**

STOWERS ▶ **stow**

STOWING ▶ **stow**

STOWN ▶ **steal**

STOWND same as ▶ **stound**

STOWNDS ▶ **stownd**

STOWP same as ▶ **stoup**

STOWPS ▶ **stowp**

STOWRE same as ▶ **stour**

STOWRES ▶ **stowre**

STOWS ▶ **stow**

STRACK vb archaic past tense form of strike

STRAD n violin made by Stradivarius

STRADS ▶ **strad**

STRAE Scots form of ▶ **straw**

STRAES ▶ **strae**

STRAFE vb attack (an enemy) with machine guns from the air ▷ n act or instance of strafing

STRAFED ▶ **strafe**

STRAFER ▶ **strafe**

STRAFES ▶ **strafe**

STRAFF same as ▶ **strafe**

STRAFFS ▶ **straff**

STRAG n straggler

STRAGS ▶ **strag**

STRAIK Scots word for ▶ **stroke**

STRAIKS ▶ **straik**

STRAIN vb subject to mental tension ▷ n tension or tiredness

STRAINS ▶ **strain**

STRAINT n pressure

STRAIT n narrow channel connecting two areas of sea ▷ adj (of spaces, etc) affording little room ▷ vb tighten

STRAITS ▶ **strait**

STRAK vb archaic past tense form of strike

STRAKE n curved metal plate forming part of the metal rim on a wooden wheel

STRAKED adj having a strake

STRAKES ▶ strake

STRAMP Scots variant of ▶ **tramp**

STRAMPS ▶ stramp

STRAND vb run aground ▷ n shore

STRANDS ▶ strand

STRANG dialect variant of ▶ **strong**

STRANGE adj odd or unusual ▷ n odd or unfamiliar person or thing

STRAP n strip of flexible material for lifting or holding in place ▷ vb fasten with a strap or straps

STRAPPY adj having straps

STRAPS ▶ strap

STRASS another word for ▶ **paste**

STRATA ▶ stratum

STRATAL ▶ stratum

STRATAS ▶ stratum

STRATH n flat river valley

STRATHS ▶ strath

STRATI ▶ stratus

STRATUM n layer, esp of rock

STRATUS n grey layer cloud

STRAW n dried stalks of grain ▷ vb spread around

STRAWED ▶ straw

STRAWEN adj of straw

STRAWN ▶ strew

STRAWS ▶ straw

STRAWY adj containing straw, or like straw in colour or texture

STRAY vb wander ▷ adj having strayed ▷ n stray animal

STRAYED ▶ stray

STRAYER ▶ stray

STRAYS ▶ stray

STRAYVE vb wander aimlessly

STREAK n long band of contrasting colour or substance ▷ vb mark with streaks

STREAKS ▶ streak

STREAKY adj marked with streaks

STREAM n small river ▷ vb flow steadily

STREAMS ▶ stream

STREAMY adj (of an area, land, etc) having many streams

STREEK Scots word for ▶ **stretch**

STREEKS ▶ streek

STREEL n slovenly woman ▷ vb trail

STREELS ▶ streel

STREET n public road, usu lined with buildings ▷ vb lay out a street or streets

STREETS ▶ street

STREETY adj of streets

STRENE same as ▶ **strain**

STRENES ▶ strene

STREP n streptococcus

STREPS ▶ strep

STRESS n tension or strain ▷ vb emphasize

STRETCH vb extend or be extended ▷ n stretching

STRETTA same as ▶ **stretto**

STRETTE ▶ stretta

STRETTI ▶ stretto

STRETTO n (in a fugue) the close overlapping of two parts or voices

STREW vb scatter (things) over a surface

STREWED ▶ strew

STREWER ▶ strew

STREWN ▶ strew

STREWS ▶ strew

STREWTH interj expression of surprise or alarm

STRIA n scratch or groove on the surface of a rock crystal

STRIAE ▶ stria

STRIATA > striatum

STRIATE adj marked with striae ▷ vb mark with striae

STRICH n screech owl

STRICK n any bast fibres preparatory to being made into slivers

STRICKS ▶ strick

STRICT adj stern or severe

STRIDE vb walk with long steps ▷ n long step

STRIDER ▶ stride

STRIDES ▶ stride

STRIDOR n high-pitched whistling sound made during respiration

STRIFE n conflict, quarrelling

STRIFES ▶ strife

STRIFT n struggle

STRIFTS ▶ strift

STRIG vb remove stalk from

STRIGA same as ▶ **stria**

STRIGAE ▶ striga

STRIGIL n curved blade used by the ancient Romans and Greeks to scrape the body after bathing

STRIGS ▶ strig

STRIKE vb cease work as a protest ▷ n stoppage of work as a protest

STRIKER n striking worker

STRIKES ▶ strike

STRIM vb cut (grass) using a strimmer

STRIMS ▶ strim

STRING n thin cord used for tying ▷ vb provide with a string or strings

STRINGS ▶ string

STRINGY adj like string

STRIP vb take (the covering or clothes) off ▷ n act of stripping

STRIPE n long narrow band of contrasting colour or substance ▷ vb mark (something) with stripes

STRIPED adj marked or decorated with stripes

STRIPER n officer who has a stripe or stripes on his uniform, esp in the navy

STRIPES ▶ stripe

STRIPEY same as ▶ **stripy**

STRIPS ▶ strip

STRIPT ▶ strip

STRIPY adj marked by or with stripes

STRIVE vb make a great effort

STRIVED ▶ strive

STRIVEN ▶ strive

STRIVER ▶ strive

STRIVES ▶ strive

STROAM vb wander

STROAMS ▶ stroam

STROBE n high intensity flashing beam of light ▷ vb give the appearance of slow motion by using a strobe

STROBED ▶ strobe

STROBES ▶ strobe

STROBIC adj spinning or appearing to spin

STROBIL n scaly multiple fruit

STRODE ▶ stride

STRODLE same as > **straddle**

STROKE vb touch or caress lightly with the hand ▷ n light touch or caress with the hand

STROKED ▶ stroke

STROKEN ▶ strike

STROKER ▶ stroke

STROKES ▶ stroke

STROLL vb walk in a leisurely manner ▷ n

S

leisurely walk

STROLLS ▸ stroll

STROMA n gel-like matrix of chloroplasts and certain cells

STROMAL ▸ stroma

STROMB n shellfish like a whelk

STROMBS ▸ stromb

STROND same as ▸ strand

STRONDS ▸ strond

STRONG adj having physical power

STROOK ▸ strike

STROOKE n stroke

STROP n leather strap for sharpening razors ▸ vb sharpen (a razor, etc) on a strop

STROPHE n first of two movements made by a chorus during the performance of a choral ode

STROPPY adj angry or awkward

STROPS ▸ strop

STROUD n coarse woollen fabric

STROUDS ▸ stroud

STROUP Scots word for ▸ spout

STROUPS ▸ stroup

STROUT vb bulge

STROUTS ▸ strout

STROVE ▸ strive

STROW archaic variant of ▸ strew

STROWED ▸ strow

STROWER ▸ strow

STROWN ▸ strow

STROWS ▸ strow

STROY archaic variant of ▸ destroy

STROYED ▸ stroy

STROYER ▸ stroy

STROYS ▸ stroy

STRUCK ▸ strike

STRUDEL n thin sheet of filled dough rolled up and baked, usu with an apple filling

STRUM vb play (a guitar or banjo) by sweeping the thumb or a plectrum across the strings

STRUMA n abnormal enlargement of the thyroid gland

STRUMAE ▸ struma

STRUMAS ▸ struma

STRUMS ▸ strum

STRUNG ▸ string

STRUNT Scots word for ▸ strut

STRUNTS ▸ strunt

STRUT vb walk pompously, swagger ▸ n bar supporting a structure

STRUTS ▸ strut

STUB n short piece left after use ▸ vb strike (the toe) painfully against an object

STUBBED ▸ stub

STUBBIE same as ▸ stubby

STUBBLE n short stalks of grain left in a field after reaping

STUBBLY ▸ stubble

STUBBY adj short and broad ▸ n small bottle of beer

STUBS ▸ stub

STUCCO n plaster used for coating or decorating walls ▸ vb apply stucco to (a building)

STUCCOS ▸ stucco

STUCK n thrust

STUCKS ▸ stuck

STUD n small piece of metal attached to a surface for decoration ▸ vb set with studs

STUDDED ▸ stud

STUDDEN ▸ stand

STUDDIE Scots word for ▸ anvil

STUDDLE n post

STUDE vb past tense and past participle of staun (Scots form of stand)

STUDENT n person who studies a subject, esp at university

STUDIED adj carefully practised

STUDIER ▸ study

STUDIES ▸ study

STUDIO n workroom of an artist or photographer

STUDIOS ▸ studio

STUDLY adj strong and virile

STUDS ▸ stud

STUDY vb be engaged in learning (a subject) ▸ n act or process of studying

STUFF n substance or material ▸ vb pack, cram, or fill completely

STUFFED ▸ stuff

STUFFER ▸ stuff

STUFFS ▸ stuff

STUFFY adj lacking fresh air

STUGGY adj stout

STUIVER same as ▸ stiver

STULL n timber prop or

platform in a stope

STULLS ▸ stull

STULM n shaft

STULMS ▸ stulm

STUM n partly fermented wine added to fermented wine as a preservative ▸ vb preserve (wine) by adding stum

STUMBLE vb trip and nearly fall ▸ n stumbling

STUMBLY adj tending to stumble

STUMER n forgery or cheat

STUMERS ▸ stumer

STUMM same as ▸ shtoom

STUMMED ▸ stum

STUMMEL n bowl of pipe

STUMP n base of a tree left when the main trunk has been cut away ▸ vb baffle

STUMPED ▸ stump

STUMPER ▸ stump

STUMPS ▸ stump

STUMPY adj short and thick ▸ n stumpy thing

STUMS ▸ stum

STUN vb shock or overwhelm ▸ n state or effect of being stunned

STUNG ▸ sting

STUNK ▸ stink

STUNNED ▸ stun

STUNNER n beautiful person or thing

STUNS ▸ stun

STUNT vb prevent or impede the growth of ▸ n acrobatic or dangerous action

STUNTED ▸ stunt

STUNTS ▸ stunt

STUPA n domed edifice housing Buddhist or Jain relics

STUPAS ▸ stupa

STUPE n hot damp cloth applied to the body to relieve pain ▸ vb treat with a stupe

STUPED ▸ stupe

STUPEFY vb make insensitive or lethargic

STUPENT adj astonished

STUPES ▸ stupe

STUPID adj lacking intelligence ▸ n stupid person

STUPIDS ▸ stupid

STUPING ▸ stupe

STUPOR n dazed or unconscious state

STUPORS ▸ stupor

STURDY adj healthy and robust ⊳ n disease of sheep
STURE same as ▸ **stoor**
STURMER n type of eating apple with pale green skin
STURNUS n bird of starling family
STURT vb bother
STURTED ▸ **sturt**
STURTS ▸ **sturt**
STUSHIE n commotion, rumpus, or row
STUTTER vb speak with repetition of initial consonants ⊳ n tendency to stutter
STY vb climb
STYE n inflammation at the base of an eyelash
STYED ▸ **stye**
STYES ▸ **stye**
STYGIAN adj dark, gloomy, or hellish
STYING ▸ **sty**
STYLAR ▸ **stylus**
STYLATE adj having style
STYLE n shape or design ⊳ vb shape or design
STYLED ▸ **style**
STYLEE ▸ **style**
STYLEES ▸ **stylee**
STYLER ▸ **style**
STYLERS ▸ **style**
STYLES ▸ **style**
STYLET n wire for insertion into a flexible cannula or catheter to maintain its rigidity during passage
STYLETS ▸ **stylet**
STYLI ▸ **stylus**
STYLIE adj fashion-conscious
STYLIER ▸ **stylie**
STYLING ▸ **style**
STYLISE same as ▸ **stylize**
STYLISH adj smart, elegant, and fashionable
STYLIST n hairdresser
STYLITE n one of a class of recluses who in ancient times lived on the top of high pillars
STYLIZE vb cause to conform to an established stylistic form
STYLO n type of fountain pen
STYLOID adj resembling a stylus ⊳ n spiny growth
STYLOPS n type of insect that lives as a parasite in other insects
STYLOS ▸ **stylo**

STYLUS n needle-like device on a record player that rests in the groove of the record and picks up the sound signals
STYME vb peer
STYMED ▸ **styme**
STYMES ▸ **styme**
STYMIE vb hinder or thwart
STYMIED ▸ **stymy**
STYMIES ▸ **stymy**
STYMING ▸ **styme**
STYMY same as ▸ **stymie**
STYPSIS n action, application, or use of a styptic
STYPTIC adj (drug) used to stop bleeding ⊳ n styptic drug
STYRAX n type of tropical or subtropical tree
STYRE same as ▸ **stir**
STYRED ▸ **styre**
STYRENE n colourless oily volatile flammable water-insoluble liquid
STYRES ▸ **styre**
STYRING ▸ **styre**
STYTE vb bounce
STYTED ▸ **styte**
STYTES ▸ **styte**
STYTING ▸ **styte**
SUABLE adj liable to be sued in a court
SUABLY ▸ **suable**
SUASION n persuasion
SUASIVE ▸ **suasion**
SUASORY ▸ **suasion**
SUAVE adj smooth and sophisticated in manner
SUAVELY ▸ **suave**
SUAVER ▸ **suave**
SUAVEST ▸ **suave**
SUAVITY ▸ **suave**
SUB n subeditor ⊳ vb act as a substitute
SUBA n shepherd's cloak
SUBACID adj (esp of some fruits) moderately acid or sour
SUBACT vb subdue
SUBACTS ▸ **subact**
SUBADAR n (formerly) the chief native officer of a company of Indian soldiers in the British service
SUBAH same as ▸ **subadar**
SUBAHS ▸ **subah**
SUBALAR adj below a wing
SUBAQUA adj of or relating to underwater sport
SUBAREA n area within a larger area

SUBARID adj receiving slightly more rainfall than arid regions
SUBAS ▸ **suba**
SUBATOM n part of an atom
SUBBASE same as ▸ **subbass**
SUBBASS another name for ▸ **bourdon**
SUBBED ▸ **sub**
SUBBIE n subcontractor
SUBBIES ▸ **subbie**
SUBBING ▸ **sub**
SUBBY same as ▸ **subbie**
SUBCELL n cell within a larger cell
SUBCLAN n clan within a larger clan
SUBCODE n computer tag identifying data
SUBCOOL vb make colder
SUBCULT n cult within larger cult
SUBDEAN n deputy of dean
SUBDEB n young woman who is not yet a debutante
SUBDEBS ▸ **subdeb**
SUBDEW same as ▸ **subdue**
SUBDEWS ▸ **subdew**
SUBDUAL ▸ **subdue**
SUBDUCE vb withdraw
SUBDUCT vb draw or turn (the eye, etc) downwards
SUBDUE vb overcome
SUBDUED adj cowed, passive, or shy
SUBDUER ▸ **subdue**
SUBDUES ▸ **subdue**
SUBECHO n echo resonating more quietly than another echo
SUBEDAR same as ▸ **subadar**
SUBEDIT vb edit and correct (written or printed material)
SUBER n cork
SUBERIC same as ▸ **suberose**
SUBERIN n fatty or waxy substance that is present in the walls of cork cells
SUBERS ▸ **suber**
SUBFEU vb grant feu to vassal
SUBFEUS ▸ **subfeu**
SUBFILE n file within another file
SUBFIX n suffix
SUBFUSC adj devoid of brightness or appeal ⊳ n (at Oxford University) formal academic dress

S

SUBFUSK same as ▸**subfusc**

SUBGOAL n secondary goal

SUBGUM n Chinese dish

SUBGUMS ▸**subgum**

SUBHA n string of beads used in praying and meditating

SUBHAS ▸**subha**

SUBHEAD n heading of a subsection in a printed work

SUBIDEA n secondary idea

SUBITEM n item that is less important than another item

SUBITO adv (preceding or following a dynamic marking, etc) suddenly

SUBJECT n person or thing being dealt with or studied ▸ adj being under the rule of a monarch or government ▸ vb cause to undergo

SUBJOIN vb add or attach at the end of something spoken, written, etc

SUBLATE vb deny

SUBLET vb rent out (property rented from someone else) ▸ n sublease

SUBLETS ▸**sublet**

SUBLIME adj of high moral, intellectual, or spiritual value ▸ vb change from a solid to a vapour without first melting

SUBLINE n secondary headline

SUBLOT n subdivision of a lot

SUBLOTS ▸**sublot**

SUBMAN n primitive form of human

SUBMEN ▸**subman**

SUBMENU n further list of options within computer menu

SUBMISS adj docile

SUBMIT vb surrender

SUBMITS ▸**submit**

SUBNET n part of network

SUBNETS ▸**subnet**

SUBORAL adj not quite oral

SUBORN vb bribe or incite (a person) to commit a wrongful act

SUBORNS ▸**suborn**

SUBOVAL adj not quite oval

SUBPAR adj not up to standard

SUBPART n part within another part

SUBPENA same as >**subpoena**

SUBPLOT n secondary plot in a novel, play, or film

SUBRACE n race of people considered to be inferior

SUBRENT n rent paid to renter who rents to another

SUBRING n mathematical ring that is a subset of another ring

SUBRULE n rule within another rule

SUBS ▸**sub**

SUBSALE n sale carried out within the process of a larger sale

SUBSEA adj undersea

SUBSECT n sect within a larger sect

SUBSERE n secondary sere arising when the progress of a sere towards its climax has been interrupted

SUBSET n mathematical set contained within a larger set

SUBSETS ▸**subset**

SUBSIDE vb become less intense

SUBSIDY n financial aid

SUBSIST vb manage to live

SUBSITE n location within a website

SUBSOIL n earth just below the surface soil ▸ vb plough (land) to a depth below the normal ploughing level

SUBSONG n subdued form of birdsong modified from the full territorial song

SUBSUME vb include (an idea, case, etc) under a larger classification or group

SUBTACK Scots word for >**sublease**

SUBTASK n task that is part of a larger task

SUBTAXA ▸**subtaxon**

SUBTEEN n young person who has not yet become a teenager

SUBTEND vb be opposite (an angle or side)

SUBTEST n test that is part of larger test

SUBTEXT n underlying theme in a piece of writing

SUBTIL same as ▸**subtle**

SUBTILE rare spelling of ▸**subtle**

SUBTLE adj not

immediately obvious

SUBTLER ▸**subtle**

SUBTLY ▸**subtle**

SUBTONE n subdivision of a tone

SUBTYPE n secondary or subordinate type or genre

SUBUNIT n distinct part or component of something larger

SUBURB n residential area on the outskirts of a city

SUBURBS ▸**suburb**

SUBVENE vb happen in such a way as to be of assistance, esp in preventing something

SUBVERT vb overthrow the authority of

SUBWAY n passage under a road or railway ▸ vb travel by subway

SUBWAYS ▸**subway**

SUBZERO adj lower than zero

SUBZONE n subdivision of a zone

SUCCADE n piece of candied fruit

SUCCAH same as ▸**sukkah**

SUCCAHS ▸**succah**

SUCCEED vb accomplish an aim

SUCCES French word for ▸**success**

SUCCESS n achievement of something attempted

SUCCI ▸**succus**

SUCCISE adj ending abruptly, as if cut off

SUCCOR same as ▸**succour**

SUCCORS ▸**succor**

SUCCORY another name for ▸**chicory**

SUCCOS same as ▸**succoth**

SUCCOSE ▸**succus**

SUCCOT same as ▸**sukkoth**

SUCCOTH same as ▸**sukkoth**

SUCCOUR n help in distress ▸ vb give aid to (someone in time of difficulty)

SUCCOUS ▸**succus**

SUCCUBA same as >**succubus**

SUCCUBI >**succubus**

SUCCUMB vb give way (to something overpowering)

SUCCUS n fluid

SUCCUSS vb shake (a patient) to detect the sound of fluid in the thoracic or another bodily cavity

SUCH adj of the kind specified ▷ pron such things

SUCK vb draw (liquid or air) into the mouth ▷ n sucking

SUCKED ▶ **suck**

SUCKEN Scots word for > **district**

SUCKENS ▶ **sucken**

SUCKER n person who is easily deceived or swindled ▷ vb strip off the suckers from (a plant)

SUCKERS ▶ **sucker**

SUCKET same as ▶ **succade**

SUCKETS ▶ **sucket**

SUCKIER ▶ **sucky**

SUCKING adj not yet weaned

SUCKLE vb feed at the breast

SUCKLED ▶ **suckle**

SUCKLER ▶ **suckle**

SUCKLES ▶ **suckle**

SUCKS interj expression of disappointment

SUCKY adj despicable

SUCRASE another name for > **invertase**

SUCRE n former standard monetary unit of Ecuador

SUCRES ▶ **sucre**

SUCRIER n small container for sugar at table

SUCROSE same as ▶ **sugar**

SUCTION n sucking ▷ vb subject to suction

SUD singular of ▶ **suds**

SUDAMEN n small cavity in the skin

SUDARIA ▶ **sudarium**

SUDARY same as > **sudarium**

SUDATE vb sweat

SUDATED ▶ **sudate**

SUDATES ▶ **sudate**

SUDD n floating masses of reeds and weeds that occur on the White Nile

SUDDEN adj done or occurring quickly and unexpectedly

SUDDENS ▶ **sudden**

SUDDER n supreme court in India

SUDDERS ▶ **sudder**

SUDDS ▶ **sudd**

SUDOR technical name for ▶ **sweat**

SUDORAL ▶ **sudor**

SUDORS ▶ **sudor**

SUDS pl n froth of soap and water, lather ▷ vb wash in suds

SUDSED ▶ **suds**

SUDSER n soap opera

SUDSERS ▶ **sudser**

SUDSES ▶ **suds**

SUDSIER ▶ **suds**

SUDSING ▶ **suds**

SUDSY ▶ **suds**

SUE vb start legal proceedings against

SUEABLE ▶ **sue**

SUED ▶ **sue**

SUEDE n leather with a velvety finish on one side ▷ vb give a suede finish to

SUEDED ▶ **suede**

SUEDES ▶ **suede**

SUEDING ▶ **suede**

SUENT adj smooth

SUER ▶ **sue**

SUERS ▶ **sue**

SUES ▶ **sue**

SUET n hard fat obtained from sheep and cattle, used in cooking

SUETIER ▶ **suet**

SUETS ▶ **suet**

SUETTY ▶ **suet**

SUETY ▶ **suet**

SUFFARI same as ▶ **safari**

SUFFECT adj additional

SUFFER vb undergo or be subjected to

SUFFERS ▶ **suffer**

SUFFETE n official in ancient Carthage

SUFFICE vb be enough for a purpose

SUFFIX n letter or letters added to the end of a word to form another word ▷ vb add (a letter or letters) to the end of a word to form another word

SUFFUSE vb spread through or over (something)

SUG vb sell a product while pretending to conduct market research

SUGAN n straw rope

SUGANS ▶ **sugan**

SUGAR n sweet crystalline carbohydrate used to sweeten food and drinks ▷ vb sweeten or cover with sugar

SUGARED adj made sweeter or more appealing with or as with sugar

SUGARER ▶ **sugar**

SUGARS ▶ **sugar**

SUGARY adj of, like, or containing sugar

SUGGED ▶ **sug**

SUGGEST vb put forward (an idea) for consideration

SUGGING n practice of selling products under the pretence of conducting market research

SUGH same as ▶ **sough**

SUGHED ▶ **sugh**

SUGHING ▶ **sugh**

SUGHS ▶ **sugh**

SUGO n Italian pasta sauce

SUGOS ▶ **sugo**

SUGS ▶ **sug**

SUHUR n meal eaten before sunrise by Muslims fasting during Ramadan

SUHURS ▶ **suhur**

SUI adj of itself

SUICIDE n killing oneself intentionally ▷ vb commit suicide

SUID n pig or related animal

SUIDIAN ▶ **suid**

SUIDS ▶ **suid**

SUING ▶ **sue**

SUINGS ▶ **sue**

SUINT n water-soluble substance found in the fleece of sheep

SUINTS ▶ **suint**

SUIPLAP n South African slang for a drunkard

SUIT n set of clothes designed to be worn together ▷ vb be appropriate for

SUITE n set of connected rooms in a hotel

SUITED ▶ **suit**

SUITER n piece of luggage for carrying suits and dresses

SUITERS ▶ **suiter**

SUITES ▶ **suite**

SUITING n fabric used for suits

SUITOR n man who is courting a woman ▷ vb act as a suitor

SUITORS ▶ **suitor**

SUITS ▶ **suit**

SUIVEZ vb musical direction meaning follow

SUJEE same as ▶ **soogee**

SUJEES ▶ **sujee**

SUK same as ▶ **souk**

SUKH same as ▶ **souk**

SUKHS ▶ **sukh**

SUKKAH n temporary structure with a roof of branches in which orthodox Jews eat and, if possible, sleep during the

S

festival of Sukkoth
SUKKAHS ▶ sukkah
SUKKOS same as **▶ sukkoth**
SUKKOT same as **▶ sukkoth**
SUKKOTH n eight-day Jewish harvest festival
SUKS ▶ suk
SUKUK n financial certificate conforming to Islam lending principles
SUKUKS ▶ sukuk
SULCAL ▶ sulcus
SULCATE adj marked with longitudinal parallel grooves
SULCI ▶ sulcus
SULCUS n linear groove, furrow, or slight depression
SULDAN same as **▶ sultan**
SULDANS ▶ suldan
SULFA same as **▶ sulpha**
SULFAS ▶ sulfa
SULFATE same as **▶ sulphate**
SULFID same as **> sulphide**
SULFIDE same as **▶ sulphide**
SULFIDS ▶ sulfid
SULFITE same as **▶ sulphite**
SULFO same as **▶ sulphonic**
SULFONE same as **> sulphone**
SULFUR same as **▶ sulphur**
SULFURS ▶ sulfur
SULFURY ▶ sulfur
SULK vb be silent and sullen because of resentment or bad temper ▷ n resentful or sullen mood
SULKED ▶ sulk
SULKER same as **▶ sulk**
SULKERS ▶ sulker
SULKIER ▶ sulky
SULKIES ▶ sulky
SULKILY ▶ sulky
SULKING ▶ sulk
SULKS ▶ sulk
SULKY adj moody or silent because of anger or resentment ▷ n light two-wheeled vehicle for one person, usually drawn by one horse
SULLAGE n filth or waste, esp sewage
SULLEN adj unwilling to talk or be sociable ▷ n sullen mood
SULLENS ▶ sullen
SULLIED ▶ sully
SULLIES ▶ sully
SULLY vb ruin (someone's reputation) ▷ n stain
SULPH n amphetamine sulphate

SULPHA n any of a group of sulphonamides that prevent the growth of bacteria
SULPHAS ▶ sulpha
SULPHID same as **> sulphide**
SULPHS ▶ sulph
SULPHUR n pale yellow nonmetallic element ▷ vb treat with sulphur
SULTAN n sovereign of a Muslim country
SULTANA n kind of raisin
SULTANS ▶ sultan
SULTRY adj (of weather or climate) hot and humid
SULU n type of sarong worn in Fiji
SULUS ▶ sulu
SUM n result of addition, total ▷ vb add or form a total of (something)
SUMAC same as **▶ sumach**
SUMACH n type of temperate or subtropical shrub or small tree
SUMACHS ▶ sumach
SUMACS ▶ sumac
SUMATRA n violent storm blowing from the direction of Sumatra
SUMLESS adj uncountable
SUMMA n compendium of theology, philosophy, or canon law, or sometimes of all three together
SUMMAE ▶ summa
SUMMAND n number or quantity forming part of a sum
SUMMAR Scots variant of **▶ summer**
SUMMARY n brief account giving the main points of something ▷ adj done quickly, without formalities
SUMMAS ▶ summa
SUMMAT pron something ▷ n impressive or important person or thing
SUMMATE vb add up
SUMMATS ▶ summat
SUMMED ▶ sum
SUMMER n warmest season of the year, between spring and autumn ▷ vb spend the summer (at a place)
SUMMERS ▶ summer
SUMMERY ▶ summer
SUMMING ▶ sum
SUMMIST n writer of summae

SUMMIT n top of a mountain or hill ▷ vb reach summit
SUMMITS ▶ summit
SUMMON vb order (someone) to come
SUMMONS n command summoning someone ▷ vb order (someone) to appear in court
SUMO n Japanese style of wrestling
SUMOIST ▶ sumo
SUMOS ▶ sumo
SUMP n container in an internal-combustion engine into which oil can drain
SUMPH n stupid person
SUMPHS ▶ sumph
SUMPIT n Malay blowpipe
SUMPITS ▶ sumpit
SUMPS ▶ sump
SUMPTER n packhorse, mule, or other beast of burden
SUMS ▶ sum
SUMY pl n the monetary units of Uzbekistan
SUN n star around which the earth and other planets revolve ▷ vb expose (oneself) to the sun's rays
SUNBACK adj (of dress) cut low at back
SUNBAKE vb sunbathe, esp in order to become tanned ▷ n period of sunbaking
SUNBATH n exposure of the body to the sun to get a suntan
SUNBEAM n ray of sun
SUNBEAT adj exposed to sun
SUNBED n machine for giving an artificial tan
SUNBEDS ▶ sunbed
SUNBELT n southern states of the US
SUNBIRD n type of small songbird with a bright plumage in the males
SUNBOW n bow of prismatic colours similar to a rainbow, produced when sunlight shines through spray
SUNBOWS ▶ sunbow
SUNBURN n painful reddening of the skin caused by overexposure to the sun ▷ vb become sunburnt

SUNDAE n ice cream topped with fruit etc

SUNDAES ▶ sundae

SUNDARI n Indian tree

SUNDECK n upper open deck on a passenger ship

SUNDER vb break apart

SUNDERS ▶ sunder

SUNDEW n type of bog plant with leaves covered in sticky hairs that trap and digest insects

SUNDEWS ▶ sundew

SUNDIAL n device showing the time by means of a pointer that casts a shadow on a marked dial

SUNDOG n small rainbow or halo near the horizon

SUNDOGS ▶ sundog

SUNDOWN same as ▶ sunset

SUNDRA same as ▶ sundari

SUNDRAS ▶ sundra

SUNDRI same as ▶ sundari

SUNDRIS ▶ sundri

SUNDRY adj several, various

SUNFAST adj not fading in sunlight

SUNFISH n large sea fish with a rounded body

SUNG ▶ sing

SUNGAR same as ▶ sangar

SUNGARS ▶ sungar

SUNGLOW n pinkish glow often seen in the sky before sunrise or after sunset

SUNHAT n hat that shades the face and neck from the sun

SUNHATS ▶ sunhat

SUNI n S African dwarf antelope

SUNIS ▶ suni

SUNK n bank or pad

SUNKEN adj unhealthily hollow

SUNKET n something good to eat

SUNKETS ▶ sunket

SUNKIE n little stool

SUNKIES ▶ sunkie

SUNKS ▶ sunk

SUNLAMP n lamp that generates ultraviolet rays

SUNLAND n sunny area

SUNLESS adj without sun or sunshine

SUNLIKE ▶ sun

SUNLIT > sunlight

SUNN n leguminous plant of the East Indies, having yellow flowers

SUNNA n body of traditional Islamic law

SUNNAH same as ▶ sunna

SUNNAHS ▶ sunnah

SUNNAS ▶ sunna

SUNNED ▶ sun

SUNNIER ▶ sunny

SUNNIES pl n pair of sunglasses

SUNNILY ▶ sunny

SUNNING ▶ sun

SUNNS ▶ sunn

SUNNY adj full of or exposed to sunlight

SUNRAY n ray of light from the sun

SUNRAYS ▶ sunray

SUNRISE n daily appearance of the sun above the horizon

SUNROOF n panel in the roof of a car that opens to let in air

SUNROOM n room or glass-enclosed porch designed to display beautiful views

SUNS ▶ sun

SUNSET n daily disappearance of the sun below the horizon

SUNSETS ▶ sunset

SUNSPOT n dark patch appearing temporarily on the sun's surface

SUNSTAR n type of starfish with up to 13 arms radiating from a central disc

SUNSUIT n child's outfit consisting of a brief top and shorts or a short skirt

SUNTAN n browning of the skin caused by exposure to the sun

SUNTANS ▶ suntan

SUNTRAP n very sunny sheltered place

SUNUP same as ▶ sunrise

SUNUPS ▶ sunup

SUNWARD same as > sunwards

SUNWISE adv moving in the same direction as the sun

SUP same as ▶ supine

SUPAWN same as ▶ suppawn

SUPAWNS ▶ supawn

SUPE n superintendent

SUPER adj excellent ▷ n superannuation ▷ interj enthusiastic expression of approval or assent ▷ vb

work as superintendent

SUPERB adj excellent, impressive, or splendid

SUPERED ▶ super

SUPERS ▶ super

SUPES ▶ supe

SUPINE adj lying flat on one's back ▷ n noun form derived from a verb in Latin

SUPINES ▶ supine

SUPLEX n wrestling hold in which a wrestler grasps his opponent round the waist from behind and carries him backwards

SUPPAWN n kind of porridge

SUPPED ▶ sup

SUPPER n light evening meal ▷ vb eat supper

SUPPERS ▶ supper

SUPPING ▶ sup

SUPPLE adj (of a person) moving and bending easily and gracefully ▷ vb make or become supple

SUPPLED ▶ supple

SUPPLER ▶ supple

SUPPLES ▶ supple

SUPPLY vb provide with something required ▷ n supplying ▷ adj acting as a temporary substitute ▷ adv in a supple manner

SUPPORT vb bear the weight of ▷ n supporting

SUPPOSE vb presume to be true

SUPRA adv above, esp referring to earlier parts of a book etc

SUPREMA > supremum

SUPREME adj highest in authority, rank, or degree ▷ n rich velouté sauce made with a base of veal or chicken stock, with cream or egg yolks added

SUPREMO n person in overall authority

SUPS ▶ sup

SUQ same as ▶ souk

> This unusual word for an Arab market-place is easy to overlook because we tend not to think of words ending in Q. It can also be spelt **sook, souk, suk** or **sukh**.

SUQS ▶ suq

SUR prep above

SURA n any of the 114 chapters of the Koran

SURAH n twill-weave fabric of silk or rayon, used for dresses, blouses, etc

SURAHS ▸ surah

SURAL adj of or relating to the calf of the leg

SURAMIN n drug used in treating sleeping sickness

SURANCE same as ▸ assurance

SURAS ▸ sura

SURAT n (formerly) a cotton fabric from the Surat area of India

SURATS ▸ surat

SURBASE n uppermost part, such as a moulding, of a pedestal, base, or skirting

SURBATE vb make feet sore through walking

SURBED vb put something on its edge

SURBEDS ▸ surbed

SURBET ▸ surbate

SURCOAT n tunic worn by a knight over his armour during the Middle Ages

SURCULI ▸ surculus

SURD n number that cannot be expressed in whole numbers ▷ adj of or relating to a surd

SURDITY n deafness

SURDS ▸ surd

SURE adj free from uncertainty or doubt ▷ interj certainly ▷ vb archaic form of sewer

SURED ▸ sure

SURELY adv it must be true that

SURER ▸ sure

SURES ▸ sure

SUREST ▸ sure

SURETY n person who takes responsibility for the fulfilment of another's obligation ▷ vb be surety for

SURF n foam caused by waves breaking on the shore ▷ vb take part in surfing

SURFACE n outside or top of an object ▷ vb become apparent

SURFED ▸ surf

SURFEIT n excessive amount ▷ vb supply or feed excessively

SURFER ▸ surfing

SURFERS ▸ surfing

SURFIE n young person whose main interest is in surfing

SURFIER ▸ surf

SURFIES ▸ surfie

SURFING n sport of riding towards the shore on a surfboard on the crest of a wave

SURFMAN n sailor skilled in sailing through surf

SURFMEN ▸ surfman

SURFS ▸ surf

SURFY ▸ surf

SURGE n sudden powerful increase ▷ vb increase suddenly

SURGED ▸ surge

SURGENT ▸ surge

SURGEON n doctor who specializes in surgery

SURGER ▸ surge

SURGERS ▸ surge

SURGERY n treatment in which the patient's body is cut open in order to treat the affected part

SURGES ▸ surge

SURGIER ▸ surge

SURGING ▸ surge

SURGY ▸ surge

SURIMI n blended seafood product made from precooked fish, restructured into stick shapes

SURIMIS ▸ surimi

SURING ▸ sure

SURLIER ▸ surly

SURLILY ▸ surly

SURLOIN same as ▸ sirloin

SURLY adj ill-tempered and rude

SURMISE n guess, conjecture ▷ vb guess (something) from incomplete or uncertain evidence

SURNAME n family name ▷ vb furnish with or call by a surname

SURPASS vb be greater than or superior to

SURPLUS n amount left over in excess of what is required ▷ adj extra ▷ vb be left over in excess of what is required

SURRA n tropical febrile disease of animals

SURRAS ▸ surra

SURREAL adj bizarre ▷ n atmosphere or qualities evoked by surrealism

SURREY n light four-wheeled horse-drawn carriage having two or four seats

SURREYS ▸ surrey

SURTAX n extra tax on incomes above a certain level ▷ vb assess for liability to surtax

SURTOUT n man's overcoat resembling a frock coat, popular in the late 19th century

SURVEIL same as ▸ surveille

SURVEY vb view or consider in a general way ▷ n surveying

SURVEYS ▸ survey

SURVIEW vb survey

SURVIVE vb continue to live or exist after (a difficult experience)

SUS same as ▸ suss

SUSES ▸ sus

SUSHI n Japanese dish of small cakes of cold rice with a topping of raw fish

SUSHIS ▸ sushi

SUSLIK n central Eurasian ground squirrel

SUSLIKS ▸ suslik

SUSPECT vb believe (someone) to be guilty without having any proof ▷ adj not to be trusted ▷ n person who is suspected

SUSPEND vb hang from a high place

SUSPENS same as ▸ suspense

SUSPIRE vb sigh or utter with a sigh

SUSS vb attempt to work out (a situation, etc), using one's intuition ▷ n sharpness of mind

SUSSED ▸ suss

SUSSES ▸ suss

SUSSING ▸ suss

SUSTAIN vb maintain or prolong ▷ n prolongation of a note, by playing technique or electronics

SUSU n (in the Caribbean) savings fund shared by friends

SUSUS ▸ susu

SUTILE adj involving sewing

SUTLER n (formerly) a merchant who accompanied an army in order to sell provisions to the soldiers

SUTLERS ▸ sutler
SUTLERY ▸ sutler
SUTOR n cobbler
SUTORS ▸ sutor
SUTRA n Sanskrit sayings or collections of sayings
SUTRAS ▸ sutra
SUTTA n Buddhist scripture
SUTTAS ▸ sutta
SUTTEE n former Hindu custom whereby a widow burnt herself to death on her husband's funeral pyre
SUTTEES ▸ suttee
SUTTLE vb work as sutler
SUTTLED ▸ suttle
SUTTLES ▸ suttle
SUTTLY ▸ subtle
SUTURAL ▸ suture
SUTURE n stitch joining the edges of a wound ▷ vb join (the edges of a wound, etc) by means of sutures
SUTURED ▸ suture
SUTURES ▸ suture
SVARAJ same as ▸ swaraj
SVELTE adj attractively or gracefully slim
SVELTER ▸ svelte
SWAB n small piece of cotton wool used to apply medication, clean a wound, etc ▷ vb clean (a wound) with a swab
SWABBED ▸ swab
SWABBER n person who uses a swab
SWABBIE same as ▸ swabby
SWABBY n seaman
SWABS ▸ swab
SWACK adj flexible
SWACKED adj in a state of intoxication, stupor, or euphoria induced by drugs or alcohol
SWAD n loutish person
SWADDIE same as ▸ swaddy
SWADDLE vb wrap (a baby) in swaddling clothes ▷ n swaddling clothes
SWADDY n private soldier
SWADS ▸ swad
SWAG n stolen property ▷ vb sway from side to side
SWAGE n shaped tool or die used in forming cold metal by hammering ▷ vb form (metal) with a swage
SWAGED ▸ swage
SWAGER ▸ swage
SWAGERS ▸ swage
SWAGES ▸ swage

SWAGGED ▸ swag
SWAGGER vb walk or behave arrogantly ▷ n arrogant walk or manner ▷ adj elegantly fashionable
SWAGGIE same as ▸ swagger
SWAGING ▸ swage
SWAGMAN n tramp who carries his belongings in a bundle on his back
SWAGMEN ▸ swagman
SWAGS ▸ swag
SWAIL same as ▸ swale
SWAILS ▸ swail
SWAIN n suitor
SWAINS ▸ swain
SWALE n moist depression in a tract of land, usually with rank vegetation ▷ vb sway
SWALED ▸ swale
SWALES ▸ swale
SWALIER ▸ swale
SWALING ▸ swale
SWALLET n hole where water goes underground
SWALLOW vb cause to pass down one's throat ▷ n swallowing
SWALY ▸ swale
SWAM ▸ swim
SWAMI n Hindu religious teacher
SWAMIES ▸ swami
SWAMIS ▸ swami
SWAMP n watery area of land, bog ▷ vb cause (a boat) to fill with water and sink
SWAMPED ▸ swamp
SWAMPER n person who lives or works in a swampy region, esp in the southern US
SWAMPS ▸ swamp
SWAMPY ▸ swamp
SWAMY same as ▸ swami
SWAN n large usu white water bird with a long graceful neck ▷ vb wander about idly
SWANG ▸ swing
SWANK vb show off or boast ▷ n showing off or boasting
SWANKED ▸ swank
SWANKER ▸ swank
SWANKEY same as ▸ swanky
SWANKIE same as ▸ swanky
SWANKS ▸ swank

SWANKY adj expensive and showy, stylish ▷ n lively person
SWANNED ▸ swan
SWANNIE n (in NZ) type of all-weather heavy woollen shirt
SWANNY adj swanlike
SWANPAN n Chinese abacus
SWANS ▸ swan
SWAP vb exchange (something) for something else ▷ n exchange
SWAPPED ▸ swap
SWAPPER ▸ swap
SWAPS ▸ swap
SWAPT ▸ swap
SWARAJ n (in British India) self-government
SWARD n stretch of short grass ▷ vb cover or become covered with grass
SWARDED ▸ sward
SWARDS ▸ sward
SWARDY adj covered with sward
SWARE ▸ swear
SWARF n material removed by cutting tools in the machining of metals, stone, etc ▷ vb faint
SWARFED ▸ swarf
SWARFS ▸ swarf
SWARM n large group of bees or other insects ▷ vb move in a swarm
SWARMED ▸ swarm
SWARMER ▸ swarm
SWARMS ▸ swarm
SWART adj swarthy
SWARTH same as ▸ swart
SWARTHS ▸ swarth
SWARTHY adj dark-complexioned
SWARTY ▸ swart
SWARVE same as ▸ swarf
SWARVED ▸ swarf
SWARVES ▸ swarf
SWASH n rush of water up a beach following each break of the waves ▷ vb (esp of water or things in water) to wash or move with noisy splashing
SWASHED ▸ swash
SWASHER n braggart
SWASHES ▸ swash
SWASHY adj slushy
SWAT vb strike or hit sharply ▷ n swatter
SWATCH n sample of cloth
SWATH n width of one

S

sweep of a scythe or of the blade of a mowing machine

SWATHE vb bandage or wrap completely ▷ n bandage or wrapping

SWATHED ▶ swathe

SWATHER ▶ swathe

SWATHES ▶ swathe

SWATHS ▶ swath

SWATHY ▶ swath

SWATS ▶ swat

SWATTED ▶ swat

SWATTER n device for killing insects, esp a meshed flat attached to a handle ▷ vb splash

SWATTY ▶ swotty

SWAY vb swing to and fro or from side to side ▷ n power or influence

SWAYED ▶ sway

SWAYER ▶ sway

SWAYERS ▶ sway

SWAYFUL ▶ sway

SWAYING ▶ sway

SWAYL same as ▶ sweal

SWAYLED ▶ swayl

SWAYLS ▶ swayl

SWAYS ▶ sway

SWAZZLE n small metal instrument used to produce a shrill voice

SWEAL vb scorch

SWEALED ▶ sweal

SWEALS ▶ sweal

SWEAR vb use obscene or blasphemous language

SWEARD same as ▶ sword

SWEARDS ▶ sweard

SWEARER ▶ swear

SWEARS ▶ swear

SWEARY adj inclined to swear or characterized by swear-words

SWEAT n salty liquid given off through the pores of the skin ▷ vb have sweat coming through the pores

SWEATED adj made by exploited labour

SWEATER n (woollen) garment for the upper part of the body

SWEATS ▶ sweat

SWEATY adj covered with sweat

SWEDE n kind of turnip

SWEDES ▶ swede

SWEDGER n Scots dialect word for sweet

SWEE vb sway

SWEED ▶ swee

SWEEING ▶ swee

SWEEL same as ▶ sweal

SWEELED ▶ sweel

SWEELS ▶ sweel

SWEENEY n police flying squad

SWEENY n wasting of the shoulder muscles of a horse

SWEEP vb remove dirt from (a floor) with a broom ▷ n sweeping

SWEEPER n device used to sweep carpets, consisting of a long handle attached to a revolving brush

SWEEPS ▶ sweep

SWEEPY ▶ sweep

SWEER same as ▶ sweir

SWEERED ▶ sweer

SWEERS ▶ sweer

SWEERT ▶ sweer

SWEES ▶ swee

SWEET adj tasting of or like sugar ▷ n shaped piece of food consisting mainly of sugar ▷ vb sweeten

SWEETED ▶ sweet

SWEETEN vb make (food or drink) sweet or sweeter

SWEETER ▶ sweet

SWEETIE n lovable person

SWEETLY ▶ sweet

SWEETS ▶ sweet

SWEETY same as ▶ sweetie

SWEIR vb swear ▷ adj lazy

SWEIRED ▶ sweir

SWEIRER ▶ sweir

SWEIRS ▶ sweir

SWEIRT ▶ sweir

SWELL vb expand or increase ▷ n swelling or being swollen ▷ adj excellent or fine

SWELLED ▶ swell

SWELLER ▶ swell

SWELLS ▶ swell

SWELT vb die

SWELTED ▶ swelt

SWELTER vb feel uncomfortably hot ▷ n hot and uncomfortable condition

SWELTRY adj sultry

SWELTS ▶ swelt

SWEPT ▶ sweep

SWERF same as ▶ swarf

SWERFED ▶ swerf

SWERFS ▶ swerf

SWERVE vb turn aside from a course sharply or suddenly ▷ n swerving

SWERVED ▶ swerve

SWERVER ▶ swerve

SWERVES ▶ swerve

SWEVEN n vision or dream

SWEVENS ▶ sweven

SWEY same as ▶ swee

SWEYED ▶ swey

SWEYING ▶ swey

SWEYS ▶ swey

SWIDDEN n area of land where slash-and-burn techniques have been used to prepare it for cultivation

SWIES ▶ swy

SWIFT adj moving or able to move quickly ▷ n fast-flying bird with pointed wings ▷ adv swiftly or quickly ▷ vb make tight

SWIFTED ▶ swift

SWIFTER n line run around the ends of capstan bars to prevent their falling out of their sockets

SWIFTIE n trick, ruse, or deception

SWIFTLY ▶ swift

SWIFTS ▶ swift

SWIFTY same as ▶ swiftie

SWIG n large mouthful of drink ▷ vb drink in large mouthfuls

SWIGGED ▶ swig

SWIGGER ▶ swig

SWIGS ▶ swig

SWILER n (in Newfoundland) a seal hunter

SWILERS ▶ swiler

SWILL vb drink greedily ▷ n sloppy mixture containing waste food, fed to pigs

SWILLED ▶ swill

SWILLER ▶ swill

SWILLS ▶ swill

SWIM vb move along in water by movements of the limbs ▷ n act or period of swimming

SWIMMER ▶ swim

SWIMMY adj dizzy

SWIMS ▶ swim

SWINDGE same as ▶ swinge

SWINDLE vb cheat (someone) out of money ▷ n instance of swindling

SWINE n contemptible person

SWINERY n pig farm

SWINES ▶ swine

SWING vb move to and fro, sway ▷ n swinging

SWINGBY n act of spacecraft passing close to planet

SWINGE vb beat, flog, or punish

SWINGED ▸ swinge

SWINGER n person regarded as being modern and lively

SWINGES ▸ swinge

SWINGLE n flat-bladed wooden instrument used for beating and scraping flax ▷ vb use a swingle on

SWINGS ▸ swing

SWINGY adj lively and modern

SWINISH ▸ swine

SWINK vb toil or drudge ▷ n toil or drudgery

SWINKED ▸ swink

SWINKER ▸ swink

SWINKS ▸ swink

SWINNEY same as ▸ sweeny

SWIPE vb strike (at) with a sweeping blow ▷ n hard blow

SWIPED ▸ swipe

SWIPER ▸ swipe

SWIPERS ▸ swipe

SWIPES pl n beer, esp when poor or weak

SWIPEY adj drunk

SWIPIER ▸ swipey

SWIPING ▸ swipe

SWIPLE same as ▸ swipple

SWIPLES ▸ swiple

SWIPPLE n part of a flail that strikes the grain

SWIRE n neck

SWIRES ▸ swire

SWIRL vb turn with a whirling motion ▷ n whirling motion

SWIRLED ▸ swirl

SWIRLS ▸ swirl

SWIRLY ▸ swirl

SWISH vb move with a whistling or hissing sound ▷ n whistling or hissing sound ▷ adj fashionable, smart

SWISHED ▸ swish

SWISHER ▸ swish

SWISHES ▸ swish

SWISHY adj moving with a swishing sound

SWISS n type of muslin

SWISSES ▸ swiss

SWITCH n device for opening and closing an electric circuit ▷ vb change abruptly

SWITCHY ▸ switch

SWITH adv swiftly

SWITHE same as ▸ swith

SWITHER vb hesitate or be indecisive ▷ n state of hesitation or uncertainty

SWITHLY ▸ swith

SWITS same as ▸ switch

SWITSES ▸ swits

SWIVE vb have sexual intercourse with (a person)

SWIVED ▸ swive

SWIVEL vb turn on a central point ▷ n coupling device that allows an attached object to turn freely

SWIVELS ▸ swivel

SWIVES ▸ swive

SWIVET n nervous state

SWIVETS ▸ swivet

SWIVING ▸ swive

SWIZ n swindle or disappointment

SWIZZ same as ▸ swiz

SWIZZED ▸ swizz

SWIZZES ▸ swizz

SWIZZLE n unshaken cocktail ▷ vb stir a swizzle stick in (a drink)

SWOB less common word for ▸ swab

SWOBBED ▸ swob

SWOBBER ▸ swob

SWOBS ▸ swob

SWOFFER > swoffing

SWOLLEN ▸ swell

SWOLN ▸ swell

SWOON n faint ▷ vb faint because of shock or strong emotion

SWOONED ▸ swoon

SWOONER ▸ swoon

SWOONS ▸ swoon

SWOONY adj romantic or sexy

SWOOP vb sweep down or pounce on suddenly ▷ n swooping

SWOOPED ▸ swoop

SWOOPER ▸ swoop

SWOOPS ▸ swoop

SWOOPY ▸ swoop

SWOOSH vb make a swirling or rustling sound when moving or pouring out ▷ n swirling or rustling sound or movement

SWOP same as ▸ swap

SWOPPED ▸ swop

SWOPPER ▸ swop

SWOPS ▸ swop

SWOPT ▸ swop

SWORD n weapon with a long sharp blade ▷ vb bear a sword

SWORDED ▸ sword

SWORDER n fighter with sword

SWORDS ▸ sword

SWORE ▸ swear

SWORN ▸ swear

SWOT vb study (a subject) intensively ▷ n person who studies hard

SWOTS ▸ swot

SWOTTED ▸ swot

SWOTTER same as ▸ swot

SWOTTY adj given to studying hard, esp to the exclusion of other activities

SWOUN same as ▸ swoon

SWOUND same as ▸ swoon

SWOUNDS less common spelling of ▸ zounds

SWOUNE same as ▸ swoon

SWOUNED ▸ swoune

SWOUNES ▸ swoune

SWOUNS ▸ swoun

SWOWND same as ▸ swoon

SWOWNDS ▸ swownd

SWOWNE same as ▸ swoon

SWOWNES ▸ swowne

SWOZZLE same as ▸ swazzle

SWUM ▸ swim

SWUNG ▸ swing

SWY n Australian gambling game involving two coins

A type of card-game, that can be useful in helping you to clear a difficult rack.

SYBBE same as ▸ sib

SYBBES ▸ sybbe

SYBIL same as ▸ sibyl

SYBILS ▸ sybil

SYBO n spring onion

SYBOE same as ▸ sybo

SYBOES ▸ syboe

SYBOTIC adj of a swineherd

SYBOW same as ▸ sybo

SYBOWS ▸ sybow

SYCE n (formerly, in India) a servant employed to look after horses, etc

SYCEE n silver ingots formerly used as a medium of exchange in China

SYCEES ▸ sycee

SYCES ▸ syce

SYCONIA > syconium

SYCOSES ▸ sycosis

SYCOSIS n chronic inflammation of the hair follicles

SYE vb strain

SYED ▸ sye

SYEING ▸ sye**

SYEN same as ▶ scion
SYENITE n light-coloured coarse-grained plutonic igneous rock
SYENS ▶ syen
SYES ▶ sye
SYKE same as ▶ sike
SYKER adv surely
SYKES ▶ syke
SYLI n Finnish unit of volume
SYLIS ▶ syli
SYLLABI ▶ syllabus
SYLLOGE n collection or summary
SYLPH n slender graceful girl or woman
SYLPHIC ▶ sylph
SYLPHID n little sylph
SYLPHS ▶ sylph
SYLPHY ▶ sylph
SYLVA n trees growing in a particular region
SYLVAE ▶ sylva
SYLVAN adj relating to woods and trees ▷ n inhabitant of the woods, esp a spirit
SYLVANS ▶ sylvan
SYLVAS ▶ sylva
SYLVIA n songbird
SYLVIAS ▶ sylvia
SYLVIN same as ▶ sylvite
SYLVINE same as ▶ sylvite
SYLVINS ▶ sylvin
SYLVITE n soluble colourless, white, or coloured mineral
SYMAR same as ▶ cymar
SYMARS ▶ symar
SYMBION same as > symbiont
SYMBIOT same as > symbiont
SYMBOL n sign or thing that stands for something else ▷ vb be a symbol
SYMBOLE same as ▶ cymbal
SYMBOLS ▶ symbol
SYMITAR same as > scimitar
SYMPTOM n sign indicating the presence of an illness
SYN Scots word for ▶ since
SYNAGOG same as > synagogue
SYNANON n type of therapy given to drug addicts
SYNAPSE n gap where nerve impulses pass between two nerve cells ▷ vb create a synapse
SYNAPTE n litany in Greek Orthodox Church

SYNAXES ▶ synaxis
SYNAXIS n early Christian meeting
SYNC n synchronization ▷ vb synchronize
SYNCARP n fleshy multiple fruit
SYNCED ▶ sync
SYNCH same as ▶ sync
SYNCHED ▶ synch
SYNCHRO n type of electrical device .
SYNCHS ▶ synch
SYNCING ▶ sync
SYNCOM n communications satellite in stationary orbit
SYNCOMS ▶ syncom
SYNCOPE n omission of one or more sounds or letters from the middle of a word
SYNCS ▶ sync
SYND same as ▶ syne
SYNDED ▶ synd
SYNDET n synthetic detergent
SYNDETS ▶ syndet
SYNDIC n business or legal agent of some universities or other institutions
SYNDICS ▶ syndic
SYNDING ▶ synd
SYNDS ▶ synd
SYNE vb rinse ▷ n rinse ▷ adv since
SYNED ▶ syne
SYNERGY n working together of two or more people, substances, or things to produce an effect greater than the sum of their individual effects
SYNES ▶ syne
SYNESES ▶ synesis
SYNESIS n grammatical construction in which the inflection or form of a word is conditioned by the meaning rather than the syntax
SYNFUEL n synthetic fuel
SYNGAMY n sexual reproduction
SYNGAS n mixture of carbon monoxide and hydrogen
SYNING ▶ syne
SYNOD n church council
SYNODAL adj of or relating to a synod ▷ n money paid to a bishop by less senior members of the clergy at a synod

SYNODIC adj relating to or involving a conjunction or two successive conjunctions of the same star, planet, or satellite
SYNODS ▶ synod
SYNONYM n word with the same meaning as another
SYNOVIA n clear thick fluid that lubricates the body joints
SYNROC n titanium-ceramic substance that can incorporate nuclear waste in its crystals
SYNROCS ▶ synroc
SYNTAGM same as > syntagma
SYNTAN n synthetic tanning substance
SYNTANS ▶ syntan
SYNTAX n way in which words are arranged to form phrases and sentences
SYNTENY n presence of two or more genes on the same chromosome
SYNTH n type of electrophonic musical instrument operated by a keyboard and pedals
SYNTHON n molecule used in synthesis
SYNTHS ▶ synth
SYNTONY n matching of frequencies
SYNURA n variety of microbe
SYNURAE ▶ synura
SYPE same as ▶ sipe
SYPED ▶ sype
SYPES ▶ sype
SYPH shortening of > syphilis
SYPHER vb lap (a chamfered edge of one plank over that of another) in order to form a flush surface
SYPHERS ▶ sypher
SYPHON same as ▶ siphon
SYPHONS ▶ syphon
SYPHS ▶ syph
SYPING ▶ sype
SYRAH n type of French red wine
SYRAHS ▶ syrah
SYREN same as ▶ siren
SYRENS ▶ syren
SYRETTE n small disposable syringe
SYRINGA n mock orange or lilac
SYRINGE n device for withdrawing or injecting

fluids, consisting of a hollow cylinder, a piston, and a hollow needle ▷ *vb* wash out or inject with a syringe

SYRINX *n* vocal organ of a bird, which is situated in the lower part of the trachea

SYRPHID *n* type of fly

SYRTES ▶ **syrtis**

SYRTIS *n* area of quicksand

SYRUP *n* solution of sugar in water ▷ *vb* bring to the consistency of syrup

SYRUPED ▶ **syrup**

SYRUPS ▶ **syrup**

SYRUPY *adj* thick and sweet

SYSOP *n* person who runs a system or network

SYSOPS ▶ **sysop**

SYSTEM *n* method or set of methods

SYSTEMS ▶ **system**

SYSTOLE *n* regular contraction of the heart as it pumps blood

SYSTYLE *n* building with different types of columns

SYTHE *same as* ▶ **sith**

SYTHES ▶ **sythe**

SYVER *n* street drain or the grating over it

SYVERS ▶ **syver**

SYZYGAL ▶ **syzygy**

SYZYGY *n* either of the two positions of a celestial body when sun, earth, and the body lie in a straight line

S

Tt

T is one of the most common consonants in Scrabble. There are only four two-letter words that begin with **T**, but they are easy to remember as there is one for every vowel except **U**. Like **S**, **T** begins a number of three-letter words that don't use vowels, which are well worth remembering. These are: **thy** (6 points), **try** (6), **tsk** (7), **twp** (8) and **tyg** (7). There are also some useful three-letter words using **X**: **tax**, **tex**, **tix** and **tux** (10 each). If you have an **X** during a game, remember words like **text** (11), **texts** (12), **textile** (14), **textual** (14) and **texture** (14). The last three of these have seven letters, and so will earn you 50-point bonuses if you use all your tiles to form them. Other threes well worth remembering are **taj** (10) and **tik** (7).

TA interj thank you ▷ n thank you

TAAL n language: usually, by implication, Afrikaans

TAALS ▶ taal

TAATA child's word for ▶ father

> This East African word for a father is one of those short words that can help you dispose of a surplus of As.

TAATAS ▶ taata

TAB n small flap or projecting label ▷ vb supply with a tab

TABANID n stout-bodied fly, the females of which have mouthparts specialized for sucking blood

TABARD n short sleeveless tunic decorated with a coat of arms, worn in medieval times

TABARDS ▶ tabard

TABARET n hard-wearing fabric of silk or similar cloth with stripes of satin or moire, used esp for upholstery

TABBED ▶ tab

TABBIED ▶ tabby

TABBIES ▶ tabby

TABBING ▶ tab

TABBIS n silken cloth

TABBY vb make (eg a material) appear wavy ▷ n female domestic cat

TABEFY vb emaciate or become emaciated

TABER old variant of ▶ tabor

TABERD same as ▶ tabard

TABERDS ▶ taberd

TABERED ▶ taber

TABERS ▶ taber

TABES n wasting of a bodily organ or part

TABETIC ▶ tabes

TABI n thick-soled Japanese sock, worn with sandals

TABID adj emaciated

TABINET n type of tabbied fabric

TABLA n one of a pair of Indian drums played with the hands

TABLAS ▶ tabla

TABLE n piece of furniture with a flat top supported by legs ▷ vb submit (a motion) for discussion by a meeting

TABLEAU n silent motionless group arranged to represent some scene

TABLED ▶ table

TABLES ▶ table

TABLET n medicinal pill ▷ vb make (something) into a tablet

TABLETS ▶ tablet

TABLIER n (formerly) part of a dress resembling an apron

TABLING ▶ table

TABLOID n small-sized newspaper with many photographs and a concise, usu sensational style

TABOO n prohibition resulting from religious or social conventions ▷ adj forbidden by a taboo ▷ vb place under a taboo

TABOOED ▶ taboo

TABOOS ▶ taboo

TABOR vb play the tabor

TABORED ▶ tabor

TABORER ▶ tabor

TABORET n low stool, originally in the shape of a drum

TABORIN same as ▶ taboret

TABORS ▶ tabor

TABOULI same as > tabbouleh

TABOUR same as ▶ tabor

TABOURS ▶ tabour

TABRERE same as ▶ tabor

TABRET n smaller version of a tabor

TABRETS ▶ tabret

TABS ▶ tab

TABU same as ▶ taboo

TABUED ▶ tabu

TABUING ▶ tabu

TABULA n tablet for writing on

TABULAE ▶ tabula

TABULAR adj arranged in a table

TABULI same as > tabbouleh

TABULIS ▶ tabuli

TABUN n organic compound used in chemical warfare as a lethal nerve gas

TABUNS ▶ tabun

TABUS ▶ tabu

TACAN n electronic ultrahigh-frequency navigation system for aircraft which gives a continuous indication of bearing and distance from a transmitting station

TACANS ▶ **tacan**

TACE same as ▶ **tasset**

TACES ▶ **tace**

TACET n direction on a musical score indicating that a particular instrument or singer does not take part in a movement or part of a movement

TACH n device for measuring speed

TACHE n buckle, clasp, or hook

TACHES ▶ **tache**

TACHINA n as in **tachina fly** bristly fly

TACHISM same as > **tachisme**

TACHIST ▶ **tachism**

TACHO same as > **tachogram**

TACHOS ▶ **tacho**

TACHS ▶ **tach**

TACHYON n hypothetical elementary particle capable of travelling faster than the velocity of light

TACIT adj implied but not spoken

TACITLY ▶ **tacit**

TACK n short nail with a large head ▷ vb fasten with tacks

TACKED ▶ **tack**

TACKER ▶ **tack**

TACKERS ▶ **tack**

TACKET n nail, esp a hobnail

TACKETS ▶ **tacket**

TACKETY ▶ **tacket**

TACKEY same as ▶ **tacky**

TACKIER ▶ **tacky**

TACKIES pl n tennis shoes or plimsolls

TACKIFY vb give (eg rubber) a sticky feel

TACKILY ▶ **tacky**

TACKING ▶ **tack**

TACKLE vb deal with (a task) ▷ n act of tackling an opposing player

TACKLED ▶ **tackle**

TACKLER ▶ **tackle**

TACKLES ▶ **tackle**

TACKS ▶ **tack**

TACKY adj slightly sticky

TACNODE n in maths, point at which two branches of a curve have a common

tangent, each branch extending in both directions of the tangent

TACO n tortilla fried until crisp, served with a filling

TACOS ▶ **taco**

TACRINE n drug used to treat Alzheimer's disease

TACT n skill in avoiding giving offence

TACTFUL ▶ **tact**

TACTIC n method or plan to achieve an end

TACTICS n art of directing military forces in battle

TACTILE adj of or having the sense of touch

TACTION n act of touching

TACTISM another word for ▶ **taxis**

TACTS ▶ **tact**

TACTUAL adj caused by touch

TAD n small bit or piece

TADDIE short for ▶ **tadpole**

TADDIES ▶ **taddie**

TADPOLE n limbless tailed larva of a frog or toad

TADS ▶ **tad**

TAE Scots form of the verb ▶ **toe**

TAED ▶ **tae**

TAEDIUM archaic spelling of ▶ **tedium**

TAEING ▶ **tae**

TAEL n unit of weight, used in the Far East, having various values between one to two and a half ounces

TAELS ▶ **tael**

TAENIA n (in ancient Greece) a narrow fillet or headband for the hair

TAENIAE ▶ **taenia**

> This is the plural of **taenia**, a kind of hairband worn in ancient Greece. It's difficult to see on your rack, but those letters come up so often that it is well worth making the effort to master it.

TAENIAS ▶ **taenia**

TAES ▶ **tae**

TAFFETA n shiny silk or rayon fabric

TAFFETY same as ▶ **taffeta**

TAFFIA same as ▶ **tafia**

TAFFIAS ▶ **taffia**

TAFFIES ▶ **taffy**

TAFFY same as ▶ **toffee**

TAFIA n type of rum, esp

from Guyana or the Caribbean

TAFIAS ▶ **tafia**

TAG n label bearing information ▷ vb attach a tag to

TAGETES n any of a genus of plants with yellow or orange flowers, including the French and African marigolds

TAGGANT n microscopic material added to substance to identify it

TAGGED ▶ **tag**

TAGGEE n one who has been made to wear a tag

TAGGEES ▶ **taggee**

TAGGER n one who marks with a tag

TAGGERS ▶ **tagger**

TAGGIER ▶ **taggy**

TAGGING ▶ **tag**

TAGGY adj (of wool, hair, etc) matted

TAGINE n large, heavy N African cooking pot with a conical lid

TAGINES ▶ **tagine**

TAGLESS adj having no tag

TAGLIKE adj resembling a tag

TAGLINE n funny line of joke

TAGMA n distinct region of the body of an arthropod, such as the head, thorax, or abdomen of an insect

TAGMATA ▶ **tagma**

TAGMEME n class of speech elements all of which may fulfil the same grammatical role in a sentence

TAGRAG same as ▶ **ragtag**

TAGRAGS ▶ **tagrag**

TAGS ▶ **tag**

TAGUAN n large nocturnal flying squirrel of high forests in the East Indies that uses its long tail as a rudder

TAGUANS ▶ **taguan**

TAHA n type of South African bird

TAHAS ▶ **taha**

TAHINA same as ▶ **tahini**

TAHINAS ▶ **tahina**

TAHINI n paste made from ground sesame seeds, used esp in Middle Eastern cookery

TAHINIS ▶ **tahini**

TAHR n goatlike bovid mammal of mountainous

T

regions of S and SW Asia, having a shaggy coat and curved horns

TAHRS ▶ **tahr**

TAHSIL n administrative division of a zila in certain states in India

TAHSILS ▶ **tahsil**

TAI n a type of sea bream

TAIAHA n carved weapon in the form of a staff, now used in Māori ceremonial oratory

TAIAHAS ▶ **taiaha**

TAIGA n belt of coniferous forest extending across much of subarctic North America, Europe, and Asia

TAIGAS ▶ **taiga**

TAIGLE vb entangle or impede

TAIGLED ▶ **taigle**

TAIGLES ▶ **taigle**

TAIHOA interj hold on! no hurry!

TAIKO n large Japanese drum

TAIKOS ▶ **taiko**

TAIL n rear part of an animal's body, usu forming a flexible appendage ▷ adj at the rear ▷ vb follow (someone) secretly

TAILARD n one having a tail

TAILED ▶ **tail**

TAILER n one that tails

TAILERS ▶ **tailer**

TAILFAN n fanned structure at the hind end of a lobster or related crustacean, formed from the telson and uropods

TAILFIN n decorative projection at back of car

TAILFLY n in angling, the lowest fly on a wet-fly cast

TAILING n part of a beam, rafter, projecting brick or stone, etc, embedded in a wall

TAILLE n (in France before 1789) a tax levied by a king or overlord on his subjects

TAILLES ▶ **taille**

TAILLIE n (in law) the limitation of an estate or interest to a person and the heirs of his body

TAILOR n person who makes men's clothes ▷ vb cut or style (a garment) to specific requirements

TAILORS ▶ **tailor**

TAILS adv with the side of a coin that does not have a portrait of a head on it uppermost

TAILYE same as ▶ **taillie**

TAILYES ▶ **tailye**

TAILZIE same as ▶ **taillie**

TAIN n tinfoil used in backing mirrors

TAINS ▶ **tain**

TAINT vb spoil with a small amount of decay, contamination, or other bad quality ▷ n something that taints

TAINTED ▶ **taint**

TAINTS ▶ **taint**

TAIPAN n large poisonous Australian snake

TAIPANS ▶ **taipan**

TAIRA same as ▶ **tayra**

TAIRAS ▶ **taira**

TAIS ▶ **tai**

TAISCH n (in Scotland) apparition of a person whose death is imminent

TAISH same as ▶ **taisch**

TAISHES ▶ **taish**

TAIT same as ▶ **tate**

TAITS ▶ **tait**

TAIVER same as ▶ **taver**

TAIVERS ▶ **taiver**

TAIVERT adj Scots word meaning confused or bewildered

TAJ n tall conical cap worn as a mark of distinction by Muslims

> This word for a Muslim's cap is one of the key words to remember for using the J.

TAJES ▶ **taj**

TAJINE same as ▶ **tagine**

TAJINES ▶ **tajine**

TAK Scots variant spelling of ▶ **take**

TAKA n standard monetary unit of Bangladesh, divided into 100 paise

TAKABLE ▶ **take**

TAKAHE n very rare flightless New Zealand bird

TAKAHES ▶ **takahe**

TAKAS ▶ **taka**

TAKE vb remove from a place ▷ n one of a series of recordings from which the best will be used

TAKEN ▶ **take**

TAKEOFF n act or process of making an aircraft airborne

TAKEOUT n shop or

restaurant that sells such food

TAKER n person who agrees to take something that is offered

TAKERS ▶ **taker**

TAKES ▶ **take**

TAKEUP n the claiming or acceptance of something, esp a state benefit, that is due or available

TAKEUPS ▶ **takeup**

TAKHI n type of wild Mongolian horse

TAKHIS ▶ **takhi**

TAKI ▶ **takhi**

TAKIER ▶ **taky**

TAKIEST ▶ **taky**

TAKIN n massive bovid mammal of mountainous regions of S Asia, having a shaggy coat, short legs, and horns that point backwards and upwards

TAKING ▶ **take**

TAKINGS ▶ **take**

TAKINS ▶ **takin**

TAKIS ▶ **tak**

TAKKIES same as ▶ **tackies**

TAKS ▶ **tak**

TAKY adj appealing

TALA n standard monetary unit of Samoa, divided into 100 sene

TALAK same as ▶ **talaq**

TALAKS ▶ **talak**

TALANT old variant of ▶ **talon**

TALANTS ▶ **talant**

TALAQ n Muslim form of divorce

> In Islamic law, a word for divorce: easy to miss because one tends not to think of words ending in Q.

TALAQS ▶ **talaq**

TALAR n ankle-length robe

TALARIA pl n winged sandals, such as those worn by Hermes

TALARS ▶ **talar**

TALAS ▶ **tala**

TALAUNT old variant of ▶ **talon**

TALAYOT n ancient Balearic stone tower

TALBOT n (formerly) an ancient breed of large hound, usually white or light-coloured, having pendulous ears and strong powers of scent

TALBOTS ▸ talbot

TALC n talcum powder ▷ vb apply talc to ▷ adj of, or relating to, talc

TALCED ▸ talc

TALCIER ▸ talcy

TALCING ▸ talc

TALCKED ▸ talcky

TALCKY same as ▸ **talcy**

TALCOSE ▸ talc

TALCOUS ▸ talc

TALCS ▸ talc

TALCUM n white, grey, brown, or pale green mineral, found in metamorphic rocks. It is used in the manufacture of talcum powder and electrical insulators

TALCUMS ▸ talcum

TALCY adj like, containing, or covered in talc

TALE n story

TALEA n rhythmic pattern in certain mediaeval choral compositions

TALEAE ▸ talea

TALEFUL adj having many tales

TALENT n natural ability

TALENTS ▸ talent

TALER same as ▸ **thaler**

TALERS ▸ taler

TALES n group of persons summoned from among those present in court or from bystanders to fill vacancies on a jury panel

TALI ▸ talus

TALION n system or legal principle of making the punishment correspond to the crime

TALIONS ▸ talion

TALIPAT same as ▸ **talipot**

TALIPED adj having a club foot ▷ n club-footed person

TALIPES n congenital deformity of the foot by which it is twisted in any of various positions

TALIPOT n palm tree of the East Indies, having large leaves that are used for fans, thatching houses, etc

TALK vb express ideas or feelings by means of speech ▷ n speech or lecture

TALKBOX n voice box

TALKED ▸ talk

TALKER ▸ talk

TALKERS ▸ talk

TALKIE n early film with a soundtrack

TALKIER ▸ talky

TALKIES ▸ talkie

TALKING n speech; the act of speaking

TALKS ▸ talk

TALKY adj containing too much dialogue or inconsequential talk

TALL adj higher than average

TALLAGE n tax levied by the Norman and early Angevin kings on their Crown lands and royal towns ▷ vb levy a tax (upon)

TALLAT same as ▸ **tallet**

TALLATS ▸ tallat

TALLBOY n high chest of drawers

TALLENT n plenty

TALLER ▸ tall

TALLEST ▸ tall

TALLET n loft

TALLETS ▸ tallet

TALLIED ▸ tally

TALLIER ▸ tally

TALLIES ▸ tally

TALLIS same as ▸ **tallith**

TALLISH adj quite tall

TALLIT same as ▸ **tallith**

TALLITH n white shawl with fringed corners worn over the head and shoulders by Jewish males during religious services

TALLITS ▸ tallit

TALLOL n oily liquid used for making soaps, lubricants, etc

TALLOLS ▸ tallol

TALLOT same as ▸ **tallet**

TALLOTS ▸ tallot

TALLOW n hard animal fat used to make candles ▷ vb cover or smear with tallow

TALLOWS ▸ tallow

TALLOWY ▸ tallow

TALLS ▸ tall

TALLY vb (of two things) correspond ▷ n record of a debt or score

TALLYHO n cry of a participant at a hunt to encourage the hounds when the quarry is sighted ▷ vb to make the cry of tallyho

TALMA n short cloak

TALMAS ▸ talma

TALMUD n primary source of Jewish religious law, consisting of the Mishnah and the Gemara

TALMUDS ▸ talmud

TALON n bird's hooked claw

TALONED ▸ talon

TALONS ▸ talon

TALOOKA same as ▸ **taluk**

TALPA n sebaceous cyst

TALPAE ▸ talpa

TALPAS ▸ talpa

TALUK n subdivision of a district

TALUKA same as ▸ **taluk**

TALUKAS ▸ taluka

TALUKS ▸ taluk

TALUS n bone of the ankle that articulates with the leg bones to form the ankle joint

TALUSES ▸ talus

TALWEG same as ▸ **thalweg**

TALWEGS ▸ talweg

TAM n type of hat

TAMABLE ▸ tame

TAMAL same as ▸ **tamale**

TAMALE n Mexican dish made of minced meat mixed with crushed maize and seasonings, wrapped in maize husks and steamed

TAMALES ▸ tamale

TAMALS ▸ tamal

TAMANDU same as > tamandua

TAMANU n poon tree

TAMANUS ▸ tamanu

TAMARA n powder consisting of cloves, cinnamon, fennel, coriander, etc, used in certain cuisines

TAMARAO same as ▸ tamarau

TAMARAS ▸ tamara

TAMARAU n small rare member of the cattle tribe of lowland areas of Mindoro in the Philippines

TAMARI n Japanese variety of soy sauce

TAMARIN n small monkey of South and Central American forests

TAMARIS ▸ tamari

TAMASHA n (in India) a show

TAMBAC same as ▸ **tombac**

TAMBACS ▸ tambac

TAMBAK same as ▸ **tombac**

TAMBAKS ▸ tambak

TAMBALA n unit of Malawian currency

TAMBER same as ▶ **timbre**

TAMBERS ▶ **tamber**

TAMBOUR n embroidery frame, consisting of two hoops over which the fabric is stretched while being worked ▷ vb embroider (fabric or a design) on a tambour

TAMBUR n old Turkish stringed instrument

TAMBURA n Middle-Eastern stringed instrument with a long neck, related to the tambur

TAMBURS ▶ **tambur**

TAME adj (of animals) brought under human control ▷ vb make tame

TAMED ▶ **tame**

TAMEIN n Burmese skirt

TAMEINS ▶ **tamein**

TAMELY ▶ **tame**

TAMER ▶ **tame**

TAMERS ▶ **tame**

TAMES ▶ **tame**

TAMEST ▶ **tame**

TAMIN n thin woollen fabric

TAMINE same as ▶ **tamin**

TAMINES ▶ **tamine**

TAMING n act of making (something) tame

TAMINGS ▶ **taming**

TAMINS ▶ **tamin**

TAMIS same as ▶ **tammy**

TAMISE n type of thin cloth

TAMISES ▶ **tamis**

TAMMAR n small scrub wallaby of Australia, with a thick dark-coloured coat

TAMMARS ▶ **tammar**

TAMMIE n short for tam-o'-shanter, a traditional Scottish hat

TAMMIED ▶ **tammy**

TAMMIES ▶ **tammy**

TAMMY n glazed woollen or mixed fabric, used for linings, undergarments, etc ▷ vb (esp formerly) to strain (sauce, soup, etc) through a tammy

TAMP vb pack down by repeated taps

TAMPALA n Asian plant (Amaranthus tricolor), eaten as food

TAMPAN n biting mite

TAMPANS ▶ **tampan**

TAMPED ▶ **tamp**

TAMPER vb interfere ▷ n person or thing that tamps, esp an instrument for

packing down tobacco in a pipe

TAMPERS ▶ **tamper**

TAMPING adj very angry ▷ n act or instance of tamping

TAMPION n plug placed in a gun's muzzle when the gun is not in use to keep out moisture and dust

TAMPON n absorbent plug of cotton wool inserted into the vagina during menstruation ▷ vb use a tampon

TAMPONS ▶ **tampon**

TAMPS ▶ **tamp**

TAMS ▶ **tam**

TAN n brown coloration of the skin from exposure to sunlight ▷ vb (of skin) go brown from exposure to sunlight ▷ adj yellowish-brown

TANA n small Madagascan lemur

TANADAR n commanding officer of an Indian police station

TANAGER n American songbird with a short thick bill and a brilliantly coloured male plumage

TANAGRA n type of tanager

TANAS ▶ **tana**

TANBARK n bark of certain trees, esp the oak and hemlock, used as a source of tannin

TANDEM n bicycle for two riders, one behind the other

TANDEMS ▶ **tandem**

TANDOOR n type of Indian clay oven

TANE old Scottish variant of ▶ **taken**

TANG n strong taste or smell ▷ vb cause to ring

TANGA n triangular loincloth worn by indigenous peoples in tropical America

TANGAS ▶ **tanga**

TANGED ▶ **tang**

TANGELO n hybrid produced by crossing a tangerine tree with a grapefruit tree

TANGENT n line that touches a curve without intersecting it

TANGHIN n strong poison formerly used in Madagascar to determine

the guilt or otherwise of crime suspects

TANGI n Māori funeral ceremony

TANGIE n water spirit of Orkney, appearing as a figure draped in seaweed, or as a seahorse

TANGIER ▶ **tangy**

TANGIES ▶ **tangie**

TANGING ▶ **tang**

TANGIS ▶ **tangi**

TANGLE n confused mass or situation ▷ vb twist together in a tangle

TANGLED ▶ **tangle**

TANGLER ▶ **tangle**

TANGLES ▶ **tangle**

TANGLY ▶ **tangle**

TANGO n S American dance ▷ vb dance a tango

TANGOED ▶ **tango**

TANGOS ▶ **tango**

TANGRAM n Chinese puzzle in which a square, cut into a parallelogram, a square, and five triangles, is formed into figures

TANGS ▶ **tang**

TANGUN n small and sturdy Tibetan pony

TANGUNS ▶ **tangun**

TANGY adj having a pungent, fresh, or briny flavour or aroma

TANH n hyperbolic tangent

TANHS ▶ **tanh**

TANIST n heir apparent of a Celtic chieftain chosen by election during the chief's lifetime: usually the worthiest of his kin

TANISTS ▶ **tanist**

TANIWHA n mythical Māori monster that lives in water

TANK n container for liquids or gases ▷ vb put or keep in a tank

TANKA n Japanese verse form consisting of five lines, the first and third having five syllables, the others seven

TANKAGE n capacity or contents of a tank or tanks

TANKARD n large beer-mug, often with a hinged lid

TANKAS ▶ **tanka**

TANKED ▶ **tank**

TANKER n ship or truck for carrying liquid in bulk

TANKERS ▶ **tanker**

TANKFUL n quantity contained in a tank

TANKIA n type of boat used in Canton

TANKIAS ▸ **tankia**

TANKIES ▸ **tanky**

TANKING n heavy defeat

TANKINI n woman's two-piece swimming costume consisting of a vest or camisole top and bikini briefs

TANKS ▸ **tank**

TANKY n die-hard communist

TANLING n suntanned person

TANNA n Indian police station or army base

TANNAGE n act or process of tanning

TANNAH same as ▸ **tanna**

TANNAHS ▸ **tannah**

TANNAS ▸ **tanna**

TANNATE n any salt or ester of tannic acid

TANNED ▸ **tan**

TANNER ▸ **tan**

TANNERS ▸ **tan**

TANNERY n place where hides are tanned

TANNEST ▸ **tan**

TANNIC adj of, containing, or produced from tannin or tannic acid

TANNIE n in S Africa, title of respect used to refer to an elderly woman

TANNIES ▸ **tannie**

TANNIN n vegetable substance used in tanning

TANNING ▸ **tan**

TANNINS ▸ **tannin**

TANNISH ▸ **tan**

TANNOY n sound-amplifying apparatus used as a public-address system esp in a large building, such as a university ▷ vb announce (something) using a Tannoy system

TANNOYS ▸ **tannoy**

TANREC same as ▸ **tenrec**

TANRECS ▸ **tanrec**

TANS ▸ **tan**

TANSIES ▸ **tansy**

TANSY n yellow-flowered plant

TANTARA n blast, as on a trumpet or horn

TANTI adj old word for worthwhile

TANTIVY adv at full speed

▷ interj hunting cry, esp at full gallop

TANTO adv too much

TANTONY n runt

TANTRA n sacred books of Tantrism, written between the 7th and 17th centuries AD, mainly in the form of a dialogue between Siva and his wife

TANTRAS ▸ **tantra**

TANTRIC ▸ **tantra**

TANTRUM n childish outburst of temper

TANUKI n animal similar to a raccoon, found in Japan

TANUKIS ▸ **tanuki**

TANYARD n part of a tannery

TAO n (in Confucian philosophy) the correct course of action

TAONGA n treasure

TAONGAS ▸ **taonga**

TAOS ▸ **tao**

TAP vb knock lightly and usu repeatedly ▷ n light knock

TAPA n inner bark of the paper mulberry

TAPALO n Latin American scarf, often patterned and brightly coloured

TAPALOS ▸ **tapalo**

TAPAS pl n (in Spanish cookery) light snacks or appetizers, usually eaten with drinks

TAPE n narrow long strip of material ▷ vb record on magnetic tape

TAPED ▸ **tape**

TAPEN adj made of tape

TAPER ▸ **tape**

TAPERED ▸ **tape**

TAPERER ▸ **tape**

TAPERS ▸ **tape**

TAPES ▸ **tape**

TAPET n example of tapestry

TAPETA ▸ **tapetum**

TAPETAL ▸ **tapetum**

TAPETI n forest rabbit of Brazil

TAPETIS ▸ **tapeti**

TAPETS ▸ **tapet**

TAPETUM n layer of nutritive cells in the sporangia of ferns and anthers of flowering plants that surrounds developing spore cells

TAPHOLE n hole in a furnace

for running off molten metal or slag

TAPING ▸ **tape**

TAPIOCA n beadlike starch made from cassava root, used in puddings

TAPIR n piglike mammal of tropical America and SE Asia, with a long snout

TAPIRS ▸ **tapir**

TAPIS n tapestry or carpeting, esp as formerly used to cover a table in a council chamber

TAPISES ▸ **tapis**

TAPIST n person who records (read out) printed matter in an audio format for the benefit of visually impaired people

TAPISTS ▸ **tapist**

TAPLASH n dregs of beer

TAPPA same as ▸ **tapa**

TAPPAS ▸ **tappa**

TAPPED ▸ **tap**

TAPPER n person who taps

TAPPERS ▸ **tapper**

TAPPET n short steel rod in an engine, transferring motion from one part to another

TAPPETS ▸ **tappet**

TAPPICE vb hide

TAPPING ▸ **tap**

TAPPIT adj crested; topped

TAPROOM n public bar in a hotel or pub

TAPROOT n main root of a plant, growing straight down

TAPS ▸ **tap**

TAPSMAN n old word for a barman

TAPSMEN ▸ **tapsman**

TAPSTER n barman

TAPSTRY adj relating to tapestry

TAPU adj sacred ▷ n Māori religious or superstitious restriction on something ▷ vb put a tapu on something

TAPUED ▸ **tapu**

TAPUING ▸ **tapu**

TAPUS ▸ **tapu**

TAR n thick black liquid distilled from coal etc ▷ vb coat with tar

TARA same as ▸ **taro**

TARAIRE n type of New Zealand tree

TARAMA n cod roe

TARAMAS ▸ **tarama**

T

TARAMEA n variety of New Zealand speargrass

TARAND n northern animal of legend, now supposed to have been the reindeer

TARANDS ▸ **tarand**

TARAS ▸ **tara**

TARBOY n boy who applies tar to the skin of sheep cut during shearing

TARBOYS ▸ **tarboy**

TARBUSH same as > **tarboosh**

TARCEL same as ▸ **tarsel**

TARCELS ▸ **tarcel**

TARDIED ▸ **tardy**

TARDIER ▸ **tardy**

TARDIES ▸ **tardy**

TARDILY ▸ **tardy**

TARDIVE adj tending to develop late

TARDO adj (of music) slow; to be played slowly

TARDY adj slow or late ▷ vb delay or impede (something or someone)

TARDYON n particle travelling slower than the speed of light

TARE n weight of the wrapping or container of goods ▷ vb weigh (a package, etc) in order to calculate the amount of tare

TARED ▸ **tare**

TARES ▸ **tare**

TARGA n as in **targa top** denotes removable hard roof on a car

TARGE vb interrogate

TARGED ▸ **targe**

TARGES ▸ **targe**

TARGET n object or person a missile is aimed at ▷ vb aim or direct

TARGETS ▸ **target**

TARGING ▸ **targe**

TARIFF n tax levied on imports ▷ vb impose punishment for a criminal offence

TARIFFS ▸ **tariff**

TARING ▸ **tare**

TARINGS ▸ **tare**

TARMAC See also ▸ **macadam**

TARMACS ▸ **tarmac**

TARN n small mountain lake

TARNAL adj damned ▷ adv extremely

TARNISH vb make or become stained or less bright ▷ n discoloration or blemish

TARNS ▸ **tarn**

TARO n plant with a large edible rootstock

TAROC old variant of ▸ **tarot**

TAROCS ▸ **taroc**

TAROK old variant of ▸ **tarot**

TAROKS ▸ **tarok**

TAROS ▸ **taro**

TAROT n special pack of cards used mainly in fortune-telling ▷ adj relating to tarot cards

TAROTS ▸ **tarot**

TARP informal word for > **tarpaulin**

TARPAN n European wild horse common in prehistoric times but now extinct

TARPANS ▸ **tarpan**

TARPON n large silvery clupeoid game fish found in warm Atlantic waters

TARPONS ▸ **tarpon**

TARPS ▸ **tarp**

TARRAS same as ▸ **trass**

TARRE vb old word meaning to provoke or goad

TARRED ▸ **tar**

TARRES ▸ **tarre**

TARRIED ▸ **tarry**

TARRIER ▸ **tarry**

TARRIES ▸ **tarry**

TARRING ▸ **tar**

TARROCK n seabird

TARROW vb exhibit reluctance

TARROWS ▸ **tarrow**

TARRY vb linger or delay ▷ n stay ▷ adj covered in or resembling tar

TARS ▸ **tar**

TARSAL adj of the tarsus or tarsi ▷ n tarsal bone

TARSALS ▸ **tarsal**

TARSEAL n bitumen surface of a road

TARSEL same as ▸ **tercel**

TARSELS ▸ **tarsel**

TARSI ▸ **tarsus**

TARSIA another term for > **intarsia**

TARSIAS ▸ **tarsia**

TARSIER n small nocturnal primate of the E Indies, which has very large eyes

TARSUS n bones of the heel and ankle collectively

TART n pie or flan with a sweet filling ▷ adj sharp or bitter ▷ adj (of a flavour, food, etc) sour, acid, or astringent ▷ vb (of food, drink, etc) become tart (sour)

TARTAN n design of straight lines crossing at right angles, esp one associated with a Scottish clan

TARTANA n small Mediterranean sailing boat

TARTANE same as ▸ **tartana**

TARTANS ▸ **tartan**

TARTAR n hard deposit on the teeth

TARTARE n mayonnaise sauce mixed with hard-boiled egg yolks, chopped herbs, capers, and gherkins

TARTARS ▸ **tartar**

TARTED ▸ **tart**

TARTER ▸ **tart**

TARTEST ▸ **tart**

TARTIER ▸ **tarty**

TARTILY ▸ **tarty**

TARTINE n slice of bread with butter or jam spread on it

TARTING ▸ **tart**

TARTISH ▸ **tart**

TARTLET n individual pastry case with a filling of fruit or other sweet or savoury mixture

TARTLY ▸ **tart**

TARTS ▸ **tart**

TARTUFE same as > **tartuffe**

TARTUFO n Italian mousse-like chocolate dessert

TARTY adj resembling a promiscuous woman; provocative in a cheap and bawdy way

TARWEED n resinous Californian plant with a pungent scent

TARZAN n man with great physical strength, agility, and virility

TARZANS ▸ **tarzan**

TAS ▸ **ta** n

TASAR same as ▸ **tussore**

TASARS ▸ **tasar**

TASBIH n form of Islamic prayer

TASBIHS ▸ **tasbih**

TASER vb use a Taser (trademark) stun gun on (someone)

TASERED ▸ **taser**

TASERS ▸ **taser**

TASH vb stain or besmirch

TASHED ▶ tash

TASHES ▶ tash

TASHING ▶ tash

TASK *n* piece of work to be done ▷ *vb* give someone a task to do

TASKBAR *n* area of computer screen showing what programs are running

TASKED ▶ task

TASKER ▶ task

TASKERS ▶ task

TASKING ▶ task

TASKS ▶ task

TASLET *same as* ▶ **tasset**

TASLETS ▶ taslet

TASS *n* cup, goblet, or glass

TASSE *same as* ▶ **tasset**

TASSEL *n* decorative fringed knot of threads ▷ *vb* adorn with a tassel or tassels

TASSELL *same as* ▶ **tassel**

TASSELS ▶ tassel

TASSES ▶ tasse

TASSET *n* piece of armour consisting of one or more plates fastened on to the bottom of a cuirass to protect the thigh

TASSETS ▶ tasset

TASSIE *same as* ▶ **tass**

TASSIES ▶ tassie

TASTE *n* sense by which the flavour of a substance is distinguished in the mouth ▷ *vb* distinguish the taste of (a substance)

TASTED ▶ taste

TASTER *n* person employed to test the quality of food or drink by tasting it

TASTERS ▶ taster

TASTES ▶ taste

TASTIER ▶ tasty

TASTILY ▶ tasty

TASTING ▶ taste

TASTY *adj* pleasantly flavoured

TAT *n* tatty or tasteless article(s) ▷ *vb* make (something) by tatting

TATAMI *n* thick rectangular mat of woven straw, used as a standard to measure a Japanese room

TATAMIS ▶ tatami

TATAR *n* brutal person

TATARS ▶ tatar

TATE *n* small tuft of fibre

TATER *n* potato

TATERS ▶ tater

TATES ▶ tate

TATH *vb* (of cattle) to defecate

TATHED ▶ tath

TATHING ▶ tath

TATHS ▶ tath

TATIE *same as* ▶ **tattie**

TATIES ▶ tatie

TATLER *old variant of* ▶ **tattler**

TATLERS ▶ tatler

TATOU *n* armadillo

TATOUAY *n* large armadillo of South America

TATOUS ▶ tatou

TATS ▶ tat

TATSOI *n* variety of Chinese cabbage

TATSOIS ▶ tatsoi

TATT *same as* ▶ **tat**

TATTED ▶ tat

TATTER *vb* make or become torn

TATTERS ▶ tatter

TATTERY *same as* > **tattered**

TATTIE *Scots or dialect word for* ▶ **potato**

TATTIER ▶ tatty

TATTIES ▶ tattie

TATTILY ▶ tatty

TATTING ▶ tat

TATTLE *n* gossip or chatter ▷ *vb* gossip or chatter

TATTLED ▶ tattle

TATTLER *n* person who tattles

TATTLES ▶ tattle

TATTOO *n* pattern made on the body by pricking the skin and staining it with indelible inks ▷ *vb* make such a pattern on the skin

TATTOOS ▶ tattoo

TATTOW *old variant of* ▶ **tattoo**

TATTOWS ▶ tattow

TATTS ▶ tatt

TATTY *adj* worn out, shabby, tawdry, or unkempt

TATU *old variant of* ▶ **tattoo**

TATUED ▶ tatu

TATUING ▶ tatu

TATUS ▶ tatu

TAU *n* 19th letter in the Greek alphabet

TAUBE *n* type of German aeroplane

TAUBES ▶ taube

TAUGHT ▶ teach

TAUHINU *New Zealand name for* ▶ **poplar**

TAUHOU *same as* > **silvereye**

TAUHOUS ▶ tauhou

TAUIWI *n* Māori term for the non-Māori people of New Zealand

TAUIWIS ▶ tauiwi

TAULD *vb* old Scots variant of told

TAUNT *vb* tease with jeers ▷ *n* jeering remark ▷ *adj* (of the mast or masts of a sailing vessel) unusually tall

TAUNTED ▶ taunt

TAUNTER ▶ taunt

TAUNTS ▶ taunt

TAUON *n* negatively charged elementary particle

TAUONS ▶ tauon

TAUPATA *n* New Zealand shrub or tree, with shiny dark green leaves

TAUPE *adj* brownish-grey ▷ *n* brownish-grey colour

TAUPES ▶ taupe

TAUPIE *same as* ▶ **tawpie**

TAUPIES ▶ taupie

TAUREAN *adj* born under or characteristic of Taurus

TAURIC *same as* ▶ **taurean**

TAURINE *adj* of, relating to, or resembling a bull ▷ *n* derivative of the amino acid, cysteine, obtained from the bile of animals

TAUS ▶ tau

TAUT *adj* drawn tight ▷ *vb* Scots word meaning to tangle

TAUTAUG *same as* ▶ **tautog**

TAUTED ▶ taut

TAUTEN *vb* make or become taut

TAUTENS ▶ tauten

TAUTER ▶ taut

TAUTEST ▶ taut

TAUTING ▶ taut

TAUTIT *adj* Scots word meaning tangled

TAUTLY ▶ taut

TAUTOG *n* large dark-coloured wrasse, used as a food fish

TAUTOGS ▶ tautog

TAUTS ▶ taut

TAV *n* 23rd and last letter in the Hebrew alphabet

TAVA *n* thick Indian frying pan

TAVAH *same as* ▶ **tava**

TAVAHS ▶ tavah

TAVAS ▶ tava

TAVER *vb* wander about

TAVERED ▶ taver

TAVERN *n* pub

T

TAVERNA n (in Greece) a guesthouse that has its own bar

TAVERNS ▶ tavern

TAVERS ▶ taver

TAVERT adj bewildered or confused

TAVS ▶ tav

TAW vb convert skins into leather

TAWA n tall timber tree from New Zealand, with edible purple berries

TAWAI n New Zealand beech

TAWAIS ▶ tawai

TAWAS ▶ tawa

TAWDRY adj cheap, showy, and of poor quality ▷ n gaudy finery of poor quality

TAWED ▶ taw

TAWER ▶ taw

TAWERS ▶ taw

TAWERY n place where tawing is carried out

TAWHAI same as ▶ tawai

TAWHAIS ▶ tawhai

TAWHIRI n small New Zealand tree with wavy green glossy leaves

TAWIE adj easily persuaded or managed

TAWIER ▶ tawie

TAWIEST ▶ tawie

TAWING ▶ taw

TAWINGS ▶ taw

TAWNEY same as ▶ tawny

TAWNEYS ▶ tawney

TAWNIER ▶ tawny

TAWNIES ▶ tawny

TAWNILY ▶ tawny

TAWNY adj yellowish-brown ▷ n light brown to brownish-orange colour

TAWPIE n foolish or maladroit girl

TAWPIES ▶ tawpie

TAWS same as ▶ tawse

TAWSE n leather strap with one end cut into thongs, formerly used by schoolteachers to hit children who had misbehaved ▷ vb punish (someone) with or as if with a tawse

TAWSED ▶ tawse

TAWSES ▶ tawse

TAWSING ▶ tawse

TAWT same as ▶ taut

TAWTED ▶ tawt

TAWTIE ▶ tawt

TAWTIER ▶ tawt

TAWTING ▶ tawt

TAWTS ▶ tawt

TAX n compulsory payment levied by a government on income, property, etc to raise revenue ▷ vb levy a tax on

TAXA ▶ taxon

TAXABLE adj capable of being taxed ▷ n person, income, property, etc, that is subject to tax

TAXABLY ▶ taxable

TAXED ▶ tax

TAXEME n any element of speech that may differentiate one utterance from another with a different meaning

TAXEMES ▶ taxeme

TAXEMIC ▶ taxeme

TAXER ▶ tax

TAXERS ▶ tax

TAXES ▶ tax

TAXI n car with a driver that may be hired to take people to any specified destination ▷ vb (of an aircraft) run along the ground before taking off or after landing

TAXICAB same as ▶ taxi

TAXIED ▶ taxi

TAXIES ▶ taxis

TAXIING ▶ taxi

TAXIMAN n taxi driver

TAXIMEN ▶ taximan

TAXING adj demanding, onerous

TAXINGS ▶ tax

TAXIS n movement of a cell or organism in a particular direction in response to an external stimulus ▷ n ancient Greek army unit

TAXITE n type of volcanic rock

TAXITES ▶ taxite

TAXITIC ▶ taxite

TAXIWAY n marked path along which aircraft taxi to or from a runway, parking area, etc

TAXLESS ▶ tax

TAXMAN n collector of taxes

TAXMEN ▶ taxman

TAXOL n trademarked anti-cancer drug

TAXOLS ▶ taxol

TAXON n any taxonomic group or rank

TAXONS ▶ taxon

TAXOR ▶ tax

TAXORS ▶ tax

TAXPAID adj (of taxable products, esp wine) having had the applicable tax paid already

TAXUS n genus of conifers

TAXWISE adv regarding tax

TAXYING ▶ taxi

TAY Irish dialect word for ▶ tea

TAYRA n large arboreal musteline mammal, of Central and South America, with a dark brown body and paler head

TAYRAS ▶ tayra

TAYS ▶ tay

TAZZA n wine cup with a shallow bowl and a circular foot

TAZZAS ▶ tazza

TAZZE ▶ tazza

TCHICK vb make a click by creating a vacuum in the mouth with the tongue pressed againt the palate then suddenly breaking the seal by withdrawing part of the tongue from the palate

TCHICKS ▶ tchick

TE n (in tonic sol-fa) seventh degree of any major scale

TEA n drink made from infusing the dried leaves of an Asian bush in boiling water ▷ vb take tea

TEABAG n porous bag of tea leaves for infusion

TEABAGS ▶ teabag

TEABOWL n small bowl used (instead of a teacup) for serving tea

TEABOX n box for storing tea

TEACAKE n flat bun, usually eaten toasted and buttered

TEACART n trolley from which tea is served

TEACH vb tell or show (someone) how to do something

TEACHER n person who teaches, esp in a school

TEACHES ▶ teach

TEACHIE old form of ▶ tetchy

TEACUP n cup out of which tea may be drunk

TEACUPS ▶ teacup

TEAD old word for ▶ torch

TEADE same as ▶ tead

TEADES ▶ teade

TEADS ▶ tead

TEAED ▸ tea

TEAGLE vb raise or hoist using a tackle

TEAGLED ▸ teagle

TEAGLES ▸ teagle

TEAING ▸ tea

TEAK n very hard wood of an E Indian tree

TEAKS ▸ teak

TEAL n kind of small duck

TEALIKE adj resembling tea

TEALS ▸ teal

TEAM n group of people forming one side in a game ▸ vb make or cause to make a team

TEAMED ▸ team

TEAMER ▸ team

TEAMERS ▸ team

TEAMING ▸ team

TEAMS ▸ team

TEAPOT n container with a lid, spout, and handle for making and serving tea

TEAPOTS ▸ teapot

TEAPOY n small table or stand with a tripod base

TEAPOYS ▸ teapoy

TEAR n drop of fluid appearing in and falling from the eye ▸ vb rip a hole in ▸ vb shed tears

TEARED ▸ tear

TEARER ▸ tear

TEARERS ▸ tear

TEARFUL adj weeping or about to weep

TEARGAS n gas or vaopr that makes the eyes smart and water ▸ vb deploy teargas against

TEARIER ▸ teary

TEARILY ▸ teary

TEARING ▸ tear

TEAROOM same as ▸ teashop

TEARS ▸ tear

TEARY adj characterized by, covered with, or secreting tears

TEAS ▸ tea

TEASE vb make fun of (someone) in a provoking or playful way ▸ n person who teases

TEASED ▸ tease

TEASEL n plant with prickly leaves and flowers ▸ vb tease (a fabric)

TEASELS ▸ teasel

TEASER n annoying or difficult problem

TEASERS ▸ teaser

TEASES ▸ tease

TEASHOP n restaurant where tea and light refreshments are served

TEASING ▸ tease

TEAT n nipple of a breast or udder

TEATED ▸ teat

TEATIME n late afternoon

TEATS ▸ teat

TEAWARE n implements and vessels for brewing and serving tea

TEAZE old variant of ▸ tease

TEAZED ▸ teaze

TEAZEL same as ▸ teasel

TEAZELS ▸ teazel

TEAZES ▸ teaze

TEAZING ▸ teaze

TEAZLE same as ▸ teasel

TEAZLED ▸ teazle

TEAZLES ▸ teazle

TEBBAD n sandstorm

TEBBADS ▸ tebbad

TEC short for ▸ detective

TECH n technical college

TECHED adj showing slight insanity

TECHIE n person who is skilled in the use of technology ▸ adj relating to or skilled in the use of technology

TECHIER ▸ techy

TECHIES ▸ techie

TECHILY ▸ techy

TECHNIC another word for ▸ technique

TECHNO n type of electronic dance music with a very fast beat

TECHNOS ▸ techno

TECHS ▸ tech

TECHY same as ▸ techie

TECKEL n dachshund

TECKELS ▸ teckel

TECS ▸ tec

TECTA ▸ tectum

TECTAL ▸ tectum

TECTITE same as ▸ tektite

TECTRIX another name for ▸ covert

TECTUM n any roof-like structure in the body, esp the dorsal area of the midbrain

TECTUMS ▸ tectum

TED vb shake out (hay), so as to dry it

TEDDED ▸ ted

TEDDER n machine equipped with a series of small rotating forks for tedding hay

TEDDERS ▸ tedder

TEDDIE same as ▸ teddy

TEDDIES ▸ teddy

TEDDING ▸ ted

TEDDY n teddy bear

TEDIER ▸ tedy

TEDIEST ▸ tedy

TEDIOUS adj causing fatigue or boredom

TEDIUM n monotony

TEDIUMS ▸ tedium

TEDS ▸ ted

TEDY same as ▸ tedious

TEE n small peg from which a golf ball can be played at the start of each hole ▸ vb position (the ball) ready for striking, or as if on a tee

TEED ▸ tee

TEEING ▸ tee

TEEK adj in Indian English, well

TEEL same as ▸ sesame

TEELS ▸ teel

TEEM vb be full of

TEEMED ▸ teem

TEEMER ▸ teem

TEEMERS ▸ teem

TEEMFUL ▸ teem

TEEMING ▸ teem

TEEMS ▸ teem

TEEN n affliction or woe ▸ n teenager or boredom ▸ vb set alight

TEENAGE adj (of a person) aged between 13 and 19 ▸ n this period of time

TEEND same as ▸ tind

TEENDED ▸ teend

TEENDS ▸ teend

TEENE same as ▸ teen

TEENED ▸ teen

TEENER ▸ teen

TEENERS ▸ teen

TEENES ▸ teene

TEENFUL ▸ teen

TEENIER ▸ teeny

TEENING ▸ teen

TEENS ▸ teen

TEENSY same as ▸ teeny

TEENTSY same as ▸ teeny

TEENTY same as ▸ teeny

TEENY adj extremely small

TEEPEE same as ▸ tepee

TEEPEES ▸ teepee

TEER vb smear; daub

TEERED ▸ teer

TEERING ▸ teer

TEERS ▸ teer

TEES ▸ tee

TEETER vb wobble or move unsteadily

TEETERS ▶ teeter
TEETH ▶ tooth
TEETHE vb (of a baby) grow his or her first teeth
TEETHED ▶ teethe
TEETHER n object for an infant to bite on during teething
TEETHES ▶ teethe
TEF n annual grass, of NE Africa, grown for its grain
TEFF same as ▶ tef
TEFFS ▶ teff
TEFLON n a trademark for polytetrafluoroethylene when used in nonstick cooking vessels
TEFLONS ▶ teflon
TEFS ▶ tef
TEG n two-year-old sheep
TEGG same as ▶ teg
TEGGS ▶ tegg
TEGMEN n either of the leathery forewings of the cockroach and related insects
TEGMINA ▶ tegmen
TEGS ▶ teg
TEGU n large South American lizard
TEGUA n type of moccasin
TEGUAS ▶ tegua
TEGULA n one of a pair of coverings of the forewings of certain insects
TEGULAE ▶ tegula
TEGULAR adj of, relating to, or resembling a tile or tiles
TEGUMEN same as ▶ tegmen
TEGUS ▶ tegu
TEHR same as ▶ tahr
TEHRS ▶ tehr
TEHSIL n administrative region in some S Asian countries
TEHSILS ▶ tehsil
TEIID n member of the Teiidae family of lizards
TEIIDS ▶ teiid
TEIL n lime tree
TEILS ▶ teil
TEIN n monetary unit of Kazakhstan
TEIND Scots and northern English word for ▶ tithe
TEINDED ▶ teind
TEINDS ▶ teind
TEINS ▶ tein
TEKKIE same as ▶ techie
TEKKIES ▶ tekkie
TEKTITE n small dark glassy object found in several areas around the world, thought to be a product of meteorite impact
TEL same as ▶ tell
TELA n any delicate tissue or weblike structure
TELAE ▶ tela
TELAMON n column in the form of a male figure, used to support an entablature
TELARY adj capable of spinning a web
TELCO n telecommunications company
TELCOS ▶ telco
TELD same as ▶ tauld
TELE same as ▶ telly
TELECOM n telecommunications
TELEDU n badger of SE Asia and Indonesia, having dark brown hair with a white stripe along the back and producing a fetid secretion from the anal glands when attacked
TELEDUS ▶ teledu
TELEFAX another word for ▶ fax
TELEGA n rough four-wheeled cart used in Russia
TELEGAS ▶ telega
TELEMAN n noncommissioned officer in the US navy, usually charged with communications duties
TELEMEN ▶ teleman
TELEOST n bony fish with rayed fins and a swim bladder ▷ adj of, relating to, or belonging to this type of fish
TELEPIC n feature-length film made for television
TELERAN n electronic navigational aid in which the image of a ground-based radar system is televised to aircraft in flight so that a pilot can see the position of his aircraft in relation to others
TELERGY n name for the form of energy supposedly transferred during telepathy
TELES ▶ tele
TELESES ▶ telesis
TELESIS n purposeful use of natural and social processes to obtain specific social goals
TELESM n talisman
TELESMS ▶ telesm
TELETEX n international means of communicating text between a variety of terminals
TELEX n international communication service using teleprinters ▷ vb transmit by telex
TELEXED ▶ telex
TELEXES ▶ telex
TELFER n an overhead transport system
TELFERS ▶ telfer
TELFORD n road built using a method favoured by Thomas Telford (1757-1834)
TELIA ▶ telium
TELIAL ▶ telium
TELIC adj directed or moving towards some goal
TELIUM n spore-producing body of some rust fungi in which the teliospores are formed
TELL vb make known in words ▷ n large mound resulting from the accumulation of rubbish on a long-settled site, esp one with mudbrick buildings, particularly in the Middle East
TELLAR same as ▶ tiller
TELLARS ▶ tellar
TELLEN same as ▶ tellin
TELLENS ▶ tellen
TELLER n narrator ▷ vb (of a plant) to produce tillers
TELLERS ▶ teller
TELLIES ▶ telly
TELLIN n slim marine bivalve molluscs that live in intertidal sand
TELLING ▶ tell
TELLINS ▶ tellin
TELLS ▶ tell
TELLUS n earth
TELLY n television
TELLYS ▶ telly
TELNET n computer system allowing one user to access remotely other computers on the same network ▷ vb use a telnet system
TELNETS ▶ telnet
TELOI ▶ telos
TELOME n fundamental unit of a plant's structure

TELOMES ▸ telome

TELOMIC ▸ telome

TELOS n objective; ultimate purpose

TELPHER same as > telferage

TELS ▸ tel

TELSON n last segment or an appendage on the last segment of the body of crustaceans and arachnids

TELSONS ▸ telson

TELT same as ▸ tauld

TEMBLOR n earthquake or earth tremor

TEME old variant of ▸ team

TEMED ▸ teme

TEMENE ▸ temenos

TEMENOS n sacred area, esp one surrounding a temple

TEMES ▸ teme

TEMP same as > temporary

TEMPED ▸ temp

TEMPEH n fermented soya beans

TEMPEHS ▸ tempeh

TEMPER n outburst of anger ▷ vb make less extreme

TEMPERA n painting medium for powdered pigments

TEMPERS ▸ temper

TEMPEST n violent storm ▷ vb agitate or disturb violently

TEMPI ▸ tempo

TEMPING ▸ temp

TEMPLAR n lawyer, esp a barrister, who lives or has chambers in the Inner or Middle Temple in London

TEMPLE n building for worship

TEMPLED ▸ temple

TEMPLES ▸ temple

TEMPLET same as > template

TEMPO n rate or pace

TEMPORE adv in the time of

TEMPOS ▸ tempo

TEMPS ▸ temp

TEMPT vb entice (a person) to do something wrong

TEMPTED ▸ tempt

TEMPTER ▸ tempt

TEMPTS ▸ tempt

TEMPURA n Japanese dish of seafood or vegetables dipped in batter and deep-fried, often at the table

TEMS same as ▸ temse

TEMSE vb sieve

TEMSED ▸ temse

TEMSES ▸ temse

TEMSING ▸ temse

TEN n one more than nine ▷ adj amounting to ten

TENABLE adj able to be upheld or maintained

TENABLY ▸ tenable

TENACE n holding of two nonconsecutive high cards of a suit, such as the ace and queen

TENACES ▸ tenace

TENAIL same as > tenaille

TENAILS ▸ tenail

TENANCY n temporary possession or use of lands or property owned by somebody else, in return for payment

TENANT n person who rents land or a building ▷ vb hold (land or property) as a tenant

TENANTS ▸ tenant

TENCH n freshwater game fish of the carp family

TENCHES ▸ tench

TEND vb be inclined

TENDED ▸ tend

TENDENZ same as > tendency

TENDER adj not tough ▷ vb offer ▷ n such an offer

TENDERS ▸ tender

TENDING ▸ tend

TENDON n strong tissue attaching a muscle to a bone

TENDONS ▸ tendon

TENDRE n care

TENDRES ▸ tendre

TENDRIL n slender stem by which a climbing plant clings

TENDRON n shoot

TENDS ▸ tend

TENDU n position in ballet

TENDUS ▸ tendu

TENE same as ▸ teen

TENES ▸ tene

TENET n doctrine or belief

TENETS ▸ tenet

TENFOLD n one tenth

TENGE n standard monetary unit of Kazakhstan, divided into 100 tiyn

TENGES ▸ tenge

TENIA same as ▸ taenia

TENIAE ▸ tenia

> This plural of **tenia**, a kind of hair-ribbon, is another of those 6-letter words which come in useful for dumping a surplus of vowels.

TENIAS ▸ tenia

TENIOID ▸ tenia

TENNE n tawny colour

TENNER n ten-pound note

TENNERS ▸ tenner

TENNES ▸ tenne

TENNIES ▸ tenny

TENNIS n game in which players use rackets to hit a ball back and forth over a net

TENNIST n tennis player

TENNO n formal title of the Japanese emperor, esp when regarded as a divine religious leader

TENNOS ▸ tenno

TENNY same as ▸ tenne

TENON n projecting end on a piece of wood fitting into a slot in another ▷ vb form a tenon on (a piece of wood)

TENONED ▸ tenon

TENONER ▸ tenon

TENONS ▸ tenon

TENOR n (singer with) the second highest male voice ▷ adj (of a voice or instrument) between alto and baritone

TENORS ▸ tenor

TENOUR old variant of ▸ tenor

TENOURS ▸ tenour

TENPIN n one of the pins used in tenpin bowling

TENPINS ▸ tenpin

TENREC n small mammal resembling hedgehogs or shrews

TENRECS ▸ tenrec

TENS ▸ ten

TENSE adj emotionally strained ▷ vb make or become tense ▷ n form of a verb showing the time of action

TENSED ▸ tense

TENSELY ▸ tense

TENSER ▸ tense

TENSES ▸ tense

TENSEST ▸ tense

TENSILE adj of tension

TENSING ▸ tense

TENSION n hostility or suspense ▷ vb tighten

T

TENSITY rare word for ▸tension

TENSIVE adj of or causing tension or strain

TENSON n type of French lyric poem

TENSONS ▸tenson

TENSOR n any muscle that can cause a part to become firm or tense

TENSORS ▸tensor

TENT n portable canvas shelter ▷ vb camp in a tent

TENTAGE n tents collectively

TENTED ▸tent

TENTER ▸tent

TENTERS ▸tent

TENTFUL n number of people or objects that can fit in a tent

TENTH n (of) number ten in a series ▷ adj coming after the ninth in numbering or counting order, position, time, etc ▷ adv after the ninth person, position, event, etc

TENTHLY same as ▸tenth

TENTHS ▸tenth

TENTIE adj wary

TENTIER ▸tentie

TENTIGO n morbid preoccupation with sex

TENTING ▸tent

TENTS ▸tent

TENTY same as ▸tentie

TENUE n deportment

TENUES ▸tenuis

TENUIS n (in the grammar of classical Greek) any of the voiceless stops as represented by kappa, pi, or tau (k, p, t)

TENUITY ▸tenuous

TENUOUS adj slight or flimsy

TENURE n (period of) the holding of an office or position ▷ vb to assign a tenured position to

TENURED adj having tenure of office

TENURES ▸tenure

TENUTI ▸tenuto

TENUTO adv (of a note) to be held for or beyond its full time value ▷ vb note sustained thus

TENUTOS ▸tenuto

TENZON same as ▸tenson

TENZONS ▸tenzon

TEOPAN n enclosure surrounding a teocalli

TEOPANS ▸teopan

TEPA n type of tree native to South America

TEPAL n any of the subdivisions of a perianth that is not clearly differentiated into calyx and corolla

TEPALS ▸tepal

TEPAS ▸tepa

TEPEE n cone-shaped tent, formerly used by Native Americans

TEPEES ▸tepee

TEPEFY vb make or become tepid

TEPHRA n solid matter ejected during a volcanic eruption

TEPHRAS ▸tephra

TEPID adj slightly warm

TEPIDER ▸tepid

TEPIDLY ▸tepid

TEPOY same as ▸teapoy

TEPOYS ▸tepoy

TEQUILA n Mexican alcoholic drink

TERAI n felt hat with a wide brim worn in subtropical regions

TERAIS ▸terai

TERAOHM n unit of resistance equal to 10^{12} ohms

TERAPH n any of various small household gods or images venerated by ancient Semitic peoples

TERAS n monstrosity; teratism

TERATA ▸teras

TERBIA n amorphous white insoluble powder

TERBIAS ▸terbia

TERBIC ▸terbium

TERBIUM n rare metallic element

TERCE n third of the seven canonical hours of the divine office, originally fixed at the third hour of the day, about 9 am

TERCEL n male falcon or hawk, esp as used in falconry

TERCELS ▸tercel

TERCES ▸terce

TERCET n group of three lines of verse that rhyme together or are connected by rhyme with adjacent groups of three lines

TERCETS ▸tercet

TERCIO n regiment of Spanish or Italian infantry

TERCIOS ▸tercio

TEREBIC adj as in **terebic acid** white crystalline carboxylic acid produced by the action of nitric acid on turpentin

TEREBRA n ancient Roman device used for boring holes in defensive walls

TEREDO n marine mollusc that bores into and destroys submerged timber

TEREDOS ▸teredo

TEREFA same as ▸tref

TEREFAH same as ▸tref

TEREK n type of sandpiper

TEREKS ▸terek

TERES n shoulder muscle

TERETE adj (esp of plant parts) smooth and usually cylindrical and tapering

TERETES ▸terete

TERF old variant of ▸turf

TERFE old variant of ▸turf

TERFES ▸terfe

TERFS ▸terf

TERGA ▸tergum

TERGAL ▸tergum

TERGITE n constituent part of a tergum

TERGUM n cuticular plate covering the dorsal surface of a body segment of an arthropod

TERM n word or expression ▷ vb name or designate

TERMED ▸term

TERMER same as ▸termor

TERMERS ▸termer

TERMING ▸term

TERMINI > terminus

TERMITE n white antlike insect that destroys timber

TERMLY n publication issued once a term

TERMOR n person who holds an estate for a term of years or until he dies

TERMORS ▸termor

TERMS ▸term

TERN n gull-like sea bird with a forked tail and pointed wings

TERNAL ▸tern

TERNARY adj consisting of three parts ▷ n group of three

TERNATE adj (esp of a leaf) consisting of three leaflets or other parts

TERNE n alloy of lead containing tin (10–20 per cent) and antimony (1.5–2 per cent) ▷ vb coat with this alloy

TERNED ▶ terne

TERNES ▶ terne

TERNING ▶ terne

TERNION n group of three

TERNS ▶ tern

TERPENE n any one of a class of unsaturated hydrocarbons, such as the carotenes, that are found in the essential oils of many plants

TERRA n (in legal contexts) earth or land

TERRACE n row of houses built as one block ▷ vb form into or provide with a terrace

TERRAE ▶ terra

TERRAIN same as ▶ terrane

TERRANE n series of rock formations, esp one having a prevalent type of rock

TERRAS same as ▶ trass

TERREEN old variant of ▶ tureen

TERRENE adj of or relating to the earth ▷ n land

TERRET n either of the two metal rings on a harness saddle through which the reins are passed

TERRETS ▶ terret

TERRIER n any of various breeds of small active dog

TERRIES ▶ terry

TERRIFY vb fill with fear

TERRINE n earthenware dish with a lid

TERRIT same as ▶ terret

TERRITS ▶ territ

TERROIR n combination of factors, including soil, climate, and environment, that gives a wine its distinctive character

TERROR n great fear

TERRORS ▶ terror

TERRY n fabric with small loops covering both sides, used esp for making towels

TERSE adj neat and concise

TERSELY ▶ terse

TERSER ▶ terse

TERSEST ▶ terse

TERSION n action of rubbing off or wiping

TERTIA same as ▶ tercio

TERTIAL same as > **tertiary**

TERTIAN adj (of a fever or the symptoms of a disease, esp malaria) occurring every other day ▷ n tertian fever or symptoms

TERTIAS ▶ tertia

TERTIUM adj as in **tertium quid** unknown or indefinite thing related in some way to two known or definite things, but distinct from both

TERTIUS n third (in a group)

TERTS n card game using 32 cards

TES ▶ te

TESLA n derived SI unit of magnetic flux density equal to a flux of 1 weber in an area of 1 square metre.

TESLAS ▶ tesla

TESSERA n small square tile used in mosaics

TEST vb try out to ascertain the worth, capability, or endurance of ▷ n critical examination

TESTA n hard outer layer of a seed

TESTACY ▶ testate

TESTAE ▶ testa

TESTATE adj having left a valid will ▷ n person who dies and leaves a legally valid will

TESTE n witness

TESTED ▶ test

TESTEE n person subjected to a test

TESTEES ▶ testee

TESTER n person or thing that tests or is used for testing

TESTERN vb give (someone) a teston

TESTERS ▶ tester

TESTES ▶ testis

TESTIER ▶ testy

TESTIFY vb give evidence under oath

TESTILY ▶ testy

TESTING ▶ test

TESTIS same as > **testicle**

TESTON n French silver coin of the 16th century

TESTONS ▶ teston

TESTOON same as ▶ teston

TESTRIL same as > **testril**

TESTS ▶ test

TESTUDO n form of shelter used by the ancient Roman Army for protection against attack from above, consisting either of a mobile arched structure or of overlapping shields held by the soldiers over their heads

TESTY adj irritable or touchy

TET same as ▶ teth

TETANAL ▶ tetanus

TETANIC adj of, relating to, or producing tetanus or the spasms of tetanus ▷ n tetanic drug or agent

TETANUS n acute infectious disease producing muscular spasms and convulsions

TETANY n abnormal increase in the excitability of nerves and muscles resulting in spasms of the arms and legs, caused by a deficiency of parathyroid secretion

TETCHED same as ▶ teched

TETCHY adj cross and irritable

TETE n elaborate hairstyle

TETES ▶ tete

TETH n ninth letter of the Hebrew alphabet transliterated as t and pronounced more or less like English t with pharyngeal articulation

TETHER n rope or chain for tying an animal to a spot ▷ vb tie up with rope

TETHERS ▶ tether

TETHS ▶ teth

TETOTUM same as > **teetotum**

TETRA n brightly coloured tropical freshwater fish

TETRACT n sponge spicule with four rays

TETRAD n group or series of four

TETRADS ▶ tetrad

TETRAS ▶ tetra

TETRI n currency unit of Georgia

TETRIS ▶ tetri

TETRODE n electronic valve having four electrodes, namely a cathode, control grid, screen grid, and anode

TETRYL n yellow crystalline explosive solid used in detonators

TETRYLS ▶ tetryl

TETS ▶ tet

TETTER n blister or pimple ▷ vb cause a tetter to erupt (on)

TETTERS ▶ tetter
TETTIX n cicada
TEUCH Scots variant of ▶ tough
TEUCHAT Scots variant of ▶ tewit
TEUCHER ▶ teuch
TEUGH same as ▶ teuch
TEUGHER ▶ teugh
TEUGHLY ▶ teugh
TEW vb work hard
TEWART same as ▶ tuart
TEWARTS ▶ tewart
TEWED ▶ tew
TEWEL n horse's rectum
TEWELS ▶ tewel
TEWHIT same as ▶ tewit
TEWHITS ▶ tewhit
TEWING ▶ tew
TEWIT n lapwing
TEWITS ▶ tewit
TEWS ▶ tew
TEX n unit of weight used to measure yarn density
TEXAS n structure on the upper deck of a paddle-steamer containing the officers' quarters and the wheelhouse
TEXASES ▶ texas
TEXES ▶ tex
TEXT n main body of a book as distinct from illustrations etc ▷ vb send a text message to (someone)
TEXTED ▶ text
TEXTER n person who communicates by text messaging
TEXTERS ▶ texter
TEXTILE n fabric or cloth, esp woven ▷ adj of (the making of) fabrics
TEXTING ▶ text
TEXTS ▶ text
TEXTUAL adj of, based on, or relating to, a text or texts
TEXTURE n structure, feel, or consistency ▷ vb give a distinctive texture to (something)
THACK Scots word for ▶ thatch
THACKED ▶ thack
THACKS ▶ thack
THAE Scots word for ▶ those
THAGI same as ▶ thuggee
THAGIS ▶ thagi
THAIM Scots variant of ▶ them
THAIRM n catgut
THAIRMS ▶ thairm
THALAMI > thalamus

THALE n as in thale cress a cruciferous wall plant
THALER n former German, Austrian, or Swiss silver coin
THALERS ▶ thaler
THALI n meal consisting of several small meat or vegetable dishes accompanied by rice, bread, etc, and sometimes by a starter or a sweet
THALIAN adj of or relating to comedy
THALIS ▶ thali
THALLI ▶ thallus
THALLIC adj of or containing thallium, esp in the trivalent state
THALLUS n undifferentiated vegetative body of algae, fungi, and lichens
THALWEG n longitudinal outline of a riverbed from source to mouth
THAN prep used to introduce the second element of a comparison ▷ n old variant of "then" (that time)
THANA same as ▶ tana
THANAGE n state of being a 'thane
THANAH same as ▶ tana
THANAHS ▶ thanah
THANAS ▶ thana
THANE n Anglo-Saxon or medieval Scottish nobleman
THANES ▶ thane
THANG n thing
THANGKA n (in Tibetan Buddhism) a religious painting on a scroll
THANGS ▶ thang
THANK vb express gratitude to
THANKED ▶ thank
THANKEE interj thank you
THANKER ▶ thank
THANKIT adj as in be thankit thank God
THANKS pl n words of gratitude ▷ interj polite expression of gratitude
THANNA same as ▶ tana
THANNAH same as ▶ tana
THANNAS ▶ thanna
THANS ▶ than
THAR same as ▶ tahr
THARM n stomach
THARMS ▶ tharm

THARS ▶ thar
THAT pron used to refer to something already mentioned or familiar, or further away
THATCH n roofing material of reeds or straw ▷ vb roof (a house) with reeds or straw
THATCHT old variant of > thatched
THATCHY ▶ thatch
THAW vb make or become unfrozen ▷ n thawing
THAWED ▶ thaw
THAWER ▶ thaw
THAWERS ▶ thaw
THAWIER ▶ thawy
THAWING ▶ thaw
THAWS ▶ thaw
THAWY adj tending to thaw
THE determiner definite article, used before a noun
THEATER same as ▶ theatre
THEATRE n place where plays etc are performed
THEAVE n young ewe
THEAVES ▶ theave
THEBE n inner satellite of Jupiter discovered in 1979
THEBES ▶ thebe
THECA n enclosing organ, cell, or spore case, esp the capsule of a moss
THECAE ▶ theca
THECAL ▶ theca
THECATE ▶ theca
THEE pron refers to the person addressed: used mainly by members of the Society of Friends ▷ vb use the word "thee"
THEED ▶ thee
THEEING ▶ thee
THEEK Scots variant of ▶ thatch
THEEKED ▶ theek
THEEKS ▶ theek
THEELIN trade name for ▶ estrone
THEELOL n estriol
THEES ▶ thee
THEFT n act or an instance of stealing
THEFTS ▶ theft
THEGN same as ▶ thane
THEGNLY ▶ thegn
THEGNS ▶ thegn
THEIC n person who drinks excessive amounts of tea
THEICS ▶ theic
THEIN old variant of ▶ thane
THEINE another name for

> **caffeine**

THEINES ▶ **theine**

THEINS ▶ **thein**

THEIR *determiner* of, belonging to, or associated in some way with them

THEIRS *pron* (thing or person) belonging to them

THEISM *n* belief in a God or gods

THEISMS ▶ **theism**

THEIST ▶ **theism**

THEISTS ▶ **theism**

THELF *n* old contraction of "the element"

THELVES ▶ **thelf**

THEM *pron* refers to people or things other than the speaker or those addressed

THEMA *n* theme

THEMATA ▶ **thema**

THEME *n* main idea or subject being discussed ▷ *vb* design, decorate, arrange, etc, in accordance with a theme

THEMED ▶ **theme**

THEMES ▶ **theme**

THEMING ▶ **theme**

THEN *adv* at that time ▷ *pron* that time ▷ *adj* existing or functioning at that time ▷ *n* that time

THENAGE old variant of ▶ **thanage**

THENAL *adj* of or relating to the thenar

THENAR *n* palm of the hand ▷ *adj* of or relating to the palm or the region at the base of the thumb

THENARS ▶ **thenar**

THENCE *adv* from that place or time

THENS ▶ **then**

THEOCON *n* person who believes that religion should play a greater role in politics

THEOLOG same as > **theologue**

THEORBO *n* obsolete form of the lute, having two necks, one above the other, the second neck carrying a set of unstopped sympathetic bass strings

THEOREM *n* proposition that can be proved by reasoning

THEORIC *n* theory; conjecture

THEORY *n* set of ideas to

explain something

THEOW *n* slave in Anglo-Saxon Britain

THEOWS ▶ **theow**

THERAPY *n* curing treatment

THERE *adv* in or to that place ▷ *n* that place

THEREAT *adv* at that point or time

THEREBY *adv* by that means

THEREIN *adv* in or into that place or thing

THEREOF *adv* of or concerning that or it

THEREON *archaic word for* > **thereupon**

THERES ▶ **there**

THERETO *adv* that or it

THERIAC *n* ointment or potion of varying composition, used as an antidote to a poison

THERIAN *n* animal of the class Theria, a subclass of mammals

THERM *n* unit of measurement of heat ▷ *n* public bath

THERMAE *pl n* public baths or hot springs, esp in ancient Greece or Rome

THERMAL *adj* of heat ▷ *n* rising current of warm air

THERME old variant of ▶ **therm**

THERMEL *n* type of thermometer measuring temperature by means of thermoelectric current

THERMES ▶ **therme**

THERMIC same as ▶ **thermal**

THERMIT same as > **thermite**

THERMOS *n* trademark term for a type of stoppered vacuum flask used to preserve the temperature of its contents

THERMS ▶ **therm**

THEROID *adj* of, relating to, or resembling a beast

THESE *determiner* form of this used before a plural noun

THESES ▶ **thesis**

THESIS *n* written work submitted for a degree

THESP *short for* > **thespian**

THESPS ▶ **thesp**

THETA *n* eighth letter of the

Greek alphabet

THETAS ▶ **theta**

THETCH old variant spelling of ▶ **thatch**

THETE *n* member of the lowest order of freeman in ancient Athens

THETES ▶ **thete**

THETHER old variant of ▶ **thither**

THETIC *adj* (in classical prosody) of, bearing, or relating to a metrical stress

THEURGY *n* intervention of a divine or supernatural agency in the affairs of man

THEW *n* muscle, esp if strong or well-developed

THEWED *adj* strong; muscular

THEWES ▶ **thew**

THEWIER ▶ **thew**

THEWS ▶ **thew**

THEWY ▶ **thew**

THEY *pron* people or things other than the speaker or people addressed

THIAMIN same as > **thiamine**

THIASUS *n* congregation of people who have gathered to sing and dance in honour of a god

THIAZIN same as > **thiazine**

THIAZOL same as > **thiazole**

THIBET *n* coloured woollen cloth

THIBETS ▶ **thibet**

THIBLE *n* stick for stirring porridge

THIBLES ▶ **thible**

THICK *adj* of great or specified extent from one side to the other ▷ *vb* thicken

THICKED ▶ **thick**

THICKEN *vb* make or become thick or thicker

THICKER ▶ **thick**

THICKET *n* dense growth of small trees

THICKLY ▶ **thick**

THICKS ▶ **thick**

THIEF *n* person who steals

THIEVE *vb* steal

THIEVED ▶ **thieve**

THIEVES ▶ **thieve**

THIG *vb* beg

THIGGER ▶ **thig**

THIGGIT *Scots inflection of* ▶ **thig**

THIGH *n* upper part of the human leg

THIGHED adj having thighs

THIGHS ▶ thigh

THIGS ▶ thig

THILK pron that same

THILL another word for ▶ **shaft**

THILLER n horse that goes between the thills of a (cart

THILLS ▶ thill

THIMBLE n cap protecting the end of the finger (when sewing ▷ vb use a thimble

THIN adj not thick ▷ vb make or become thin ▷ adv in order to produce something thin

THINE adj (something) of or associated with you (thou) ▷ pron something belonging to you (thou) ▷ determiner of, belonging to, or associated in some way with you (thou)

THING n material object

THINGS ▶ thing

THINGY adj existing in reality; actual

THINK vb consider, judge, or believe

THINKER ▶ think

THINKS ▶ think

THINLY ▶ thin

THINNED ▶ thin

THINNER ▶ thin

THINS ▶ thin

THIO adj of, or relating to, sulphur

THIOL n any of a class of sulphur-containing organic compounds with the formula RSH, where R is an organic group

THIOLIC ▶ thiol

THIOLS ▶ thiol

THIONIC adj of, relating to, or containing sulphur

THIONIN same as > **thionine**

THIONYL n of, consisting of, or containing the divalent group SO

THIR Scots word for ▶ **these**

THIRAM n antifungal agent

THIRAMS ▶ thiram

THIRD adj of number three in a series ▷ n one of three equal parts ▷ adv in the third place ▷ vb divide (something) by three

THIRDED ▶ third

THIRDLY ▶ third

THIRDS ▶ third

THIRL vb bore or drill

THIRLED ▶ thirl

THIRLS ▶ thirl

THIRST n desire to drink ▷ vb feel thirst

THIRSTS ▶ thirst

THIRSTY adj feeling a desire to drink

THIRTY n three times ten ▷ adj amounting to thirty ▷ determiner amounting to thirty

THIS pron used to refer to a thing or person nearby, just mentioned, or about to be mentioned ▷ adj used to refer to the present time

THISTLE n prickly plant with dense flower heads

THISTLY ▶ thistle

THITHER adv or towards that place

THIVEL same as ▶ **thible**

THIVELS ▶ thivel

THO short for ▶ **though**

THOFT n bench (in a boat) upon which a rower sits

THOFTS ▶ thoft

THOLE n wooden pin set in the side of a rowing boat to serve as a fulcrum for rowing ▷ vb bear or put up with

THOLED ▶ thole

THOLES ▶ thole

THOLI ▶ tholus

THOLING ▶ thole

THOLOI ▶ tholos

THOLOS n dry-stone beehive-shaped tomb associated with the Mycenaean culture of Greece in the 16th to the 12th century BC

THOLUS n domed tomb

THON Scots word for ▶ **yon**

THONDER Scots word for ▶ **yonder**

THONG n thin strip of leather etc

THONGED adj fastened with a thong

THONGS ▶ thong

THORAX n part of the body between the neck and the abdomen

THORIA ▶ thorium

THORIAS ▶ thorium

THORIC ▶ thorium

THORITE n yellow, brownish, or black radioactive mineral consisting of tetragonal thorium silicate. It occurs in coarse granite and is a

source of thorium

THORIUM n radioactive metallic element

THORN n prickle on a plant ▷ vb jag or prick (something) as if with a thorn

THORNED ▶ thorn

THORNS ▶ thorn

THORNY adj covered with thorns

THORO (nonstandard) variant spelling of > **thorough**

THORON n radioisotope of radon that is a decay product of thorium

THORONS ▶ thoron

THORP n small village

THORPE same as ▶ **thorp**

THORPES ▶ thorpe

THORPS ▶ thorp

THOSE determiner form of that used before a plural noun

THOTHER pron old contraction of the other

THOU pron used when talking to one person ▷ n one thousandth of an inch ▷ vb use the word thou

THOUED ▶ thou

THOUGH adv nevertheless

THOUGHT ▶ think

THOUING ▶ thou

THOUS ▶ thou

THOWEL old variant of ▶ **thole**

THOWELS ▶ thowel

THOWL old variant of ▶ **thole**

THOWLS ▶ thowel

THRAE same as ▶ **frae**

THRALL n state of being in the power of another person ▷ vb enslave or dominate

THRALLS ▶ thrall

THRANG n throng ▷ vb throng ▷ adj crowded

THRANGS ▶ thrang

THRASH vb beat, esp with a stick or whip ▷ n party

THRAVE n twenty-four sheaves of corn

THRAVES ▶ thrave

THRAW vb twist (something); make something thrawn

THRAWED ▶ thraw

THRAWN adj crooked or twisted

THRAWS ▶ thraw

THREAD n fine strand or

yarn ▷ *vb* pass thread through

THREADS slang word for ▷ **clothes**

THREADY *adj* of, relating to, or resembling a thread or threads

THREAP *vb* scold

THREAPS ▶ **threap**

THREAT *n* declaration of intent to harm

THREATS ▶ **threat**

THREAVE *same as* ▶ **thrave**

THREE *n* one more than two ▷ *adj* amounting to three ▷ *determiner* amounting to three

THREEP *same as* ▶ **threap**

THREEPS ▶ **threep**

THREES ▶ **three**

THRENE *n* dirge; threnody

THRENES ▶ **threne**

THRENOS *n* threnody; lamentation

THRESH *vb* beat (wheat etc) to separate the grain from the husks and straw ▷ *n* act of threshing

THRETTY *nonstandard variant of* ▶ **thirty**

THREW ▶ **throw**

THRICE *adv* three times

THRID *old variant of* ▶ **thread**

THRIDS ▶ **thrid**

THRIFT *n* wisdom and caution with money

THRIFTS ▶ **thrift**

THRIFTY *adj* not wasteful with money

THRILL *n* sudden feeling of excitement ▷ *vb* (cause to) feel a thrill

THRILLS ▶ **thrill**

THRILLY *adj* causing thrills

THRIMSA *same as* ▶ **thrymsa**

THRIP *same as* ▶ **thrips**

THRIPS *n* small slender-bodied insect with piercing mouthparts that feeds on plant sap

THRIST *old variant of* ▶ **thirst**

THRISTS ▶ **thrist**

THRISTY ▶ **thrist**

THRIVE *vb* flourish or prosper

THRIVED ▶ **thrive**

THRIVEN ▶ **thrive**

THRIVER ▶ **thrive**

THRIVES ▶ **thrive**

THRO *same as* ▶ **through**

THROAT *n* passage from the mouth and nose to the stomach and lungs ▷ *vb* vocalize in the throat

THROATS ▶ **throat**

THROATY *adj* (of the voice) hoarse

THROB *vb* pulsate repeatedly ▷ *n* throbbing

THROBS ▶ **throb**

THROE *n* pang or pain ▷ *n* endure throes

THROED ▶ **throe**

THROES *pl n* violent pangs or pains

THROMBI > **thrombus**

THRONE *n* ceremonial seat of a monarch or bishop ▷ *vb* place or be placed on a throne

THRONED ▶ **throne**

THRONES ▶ **throne**

THRONG *vb* crowd ▷ *n* great number of people or things crowded together ▷ *adj* busy

THRONGS ▶ **throng**

THROUGH *prep* from end to end or side to side of ▷ *adj* finished

THROVE ▶ **thrive**

THROW *vb* hurl through the air ▷ *n* throwing

THROWE *old variant of* ▶ **throe**

THROWER ▶ **throw**

THROWES ▶ **throwe**

THROWN ▶ **throw**

THROWS ▶ **throw**

THRU *same as* ▶ **through**

THRUM *vb* strum rhythmically but without expression on (a musical instrument) ▷ *n* in textiles, unwoven ends of wap thread

THRUMMY *adj* made of thrums

THRUMS ▶ **thrum**

THRUPUT *n* quantity of raw material or information processed in a given period

THRUSH *n* brown songbird

THRUST *vb* push forcefully ▷ *n* forceful stab

THRUSTS ▶ **thrust**

THRUTCH *n* narrow, fast-moving stream ▷ *vb* thrust

THRUWAY *n* thoroughfare

THRYMSA *n* gold coin used in Anglo-Saxon England

THUD *n* dull heavy sound

▷ *vb* make such a sound

THUDDED ▶ **thud**

THUDS ▶ **thud**

THUG *n* violent man, esp a criminal

THUGGEE *n* methods and practices of the thugs of India

THUGGO *n* tough and violent person

THUGGOS ▶ **thuggo**

THUGS ▶ **thug**

THUJA *n* coniferous tree of North America and East Asia, with scalelike leaves, small cones, and an aromatic wood

THUJAS ▶ **thuja**

THULIA *n* oxide of thulium

THULIAS ▶ **thulia**

THULITE *n* rose-coloured zoisite sometimes incorporated into jewellery

THULIUM *n* malleable ductile silvery-grey element

THUMB *n* short thick finger set apart from the others ▷ *vb* touch or handle with the thumb

THUMBED ▶ **thumb**

THUMBS ▶ **thumb**

THUMBY *adj* clumsy; uncoordinated

THUMP *n* (sound of) a dull heavy blow ▷ *vb* strike heavily

THUMPED ▶ **thump**

THUMPER ▶ **thump**

THUMPS ▶ **thump**

THUNDER *n* loud noise accompanying lightning ▷ *vb* rumble with thunder

THUNK *another word for* ▶ **thud**

THUNKED ▶ **thunk**

THUNKS ▶ **thunk**

THURIFY *vb* burn incense near or before an altar, shrine, etc

THURL *same as* ▶ **thirl**

THURLS ▶ **thurl**

THUS *adv* in this manner ▷ *n* aromatic gum resin

THUSES ▶ **thus**

THUSLY *adv* in such a way; thus

THUYA *same as* ▶ **thuja**

THUYAS ▶ **thuya**

THWACK *n* whack ▷ *vb* beat with something flat ▷ *interj* exclamation imitative of this sound

THWACKS ▶ **thwack**

T

THWAITE n piece of land cleared from forest or reclaimed from wasteland

THWART vb foil or frustrate ▷ n seat across a boat ▷ adj passing or being situated across ▷ adv across

THWARTS ▶ thwart

THY adj of or associated with you (thou) ▷ determiner belonging to or associated in some way with you (thou)

THYINE adj of relating to the sandarac tree

THYLOSE old variant of ▶ tylosis

THYME n aromatic herb

THYMES ▶ thyme

THYMEY ▶ thyme

THYMI ▶ thymus

THYMIC adj of or relating to the thymus

THYMIER ▶ thyme

THYMINE n white crystalline pyrimidine base found in DNA

THYMOL n substance obtained from thyme, used as an antiseptic

THYMOLS ▶ thymol

THYMUS n small gland at the base of the neck

THYMY ▶ thyme

THYROID n (of) a gland in the neck controlling body growth ▷ adj of or relating to the thyroid gland

THYRSE n type of inflorescence, occurring in the lilac and grape, in which the main branch is racemose and the lateral branches cymose

THYRSES ▶ thyrse

THYRSI ▶ thyrsus

THYRSUS same as ▶ thyrse

THYSELF pron reflexive form of thou

TI same as ▶ te

TIAN n traditional French vegetable stew or earthenware dish it is cooked in

TIANS ▶ tian

TIAR same as ▶ tiara

TIARA n semicircular jewelled headdress

TIARAED ▶ tiara

TIARAS ▶ tiara

TIARS ▶ tiar

TIBIA n inner bone of the lower leg

TIBIAE ▶ tibia

TIBIAL ▶ tibia

TIBIAS ▶ tibia

TIC n spasmodic muscular twitch

TICAL n former standard monetary unit of Thailand, replaced by the baht in 1928

TICALS ▶ tical

TICCA adj (of a thing or the services of a person) having been acquired for temporary use in exchange for payment

TICCED ▶ tic

TICCING ▶ tic

TICE vb tempt or allure; entice

TICED ▶ tice

TICES ▶ tice

TICH same as ▶ titch

TICHES ▶ tich

TICHIER ▶ tichy

TICHY same as ▶ titchy

TICING ▶ tice

TICK n mark (✔) used to check off or indicate the correctness of something ▷ vb mark with a tick

TICKED ▶ tick

TICKEN same as ▶ ticking

TICKENS ▶ ticken

TICKER n heart

TICKERS ▶ ticker

TICKET n card or paper entitling the holder to admission, travel, etc ▷ vb attach or issue a ticket to

TICKETS pl n death or ruin

TICKEY n South African threepenny piece, which was replaced by the five-cent coin in 1961

TICKEYS ▶ tickey

TICKIES ▶ ticky

TICKING n strong material for mattress covers

TICKLE vb touch or stroke (a person) to produce laughter ▷ n tickling

TICKLED ▶ tickle

TICKLER n difficult or delicate problem

TICKLES ▶ tickle

TICKLY ▶ tickle

TICKS ▶ tick

TICKY same as ▶ tickey

TICS ▶ tic

TICTAC same as > ticktack

TICTACS ▶ tictac

TICTOC same as > ticktock

TICTOCS ▶ tictoc

TID n girl

TIDAL adj (of a river, lake, or sea) having tides

TIDALLY ▶ tidal

TIDBIT same as ▶ titbit

TIDBITS ▶ tidbit

TIDDIER ▶ tiddy

TIDDIES ▶ tiddy

TIDDLE vb busy oneself with inconsequential tasks

TIDDLED ▶ tiddle

TIDDLER n very small fish

TIDDLES ▶ tiddle

TIDDLEY same as ▶ tiddly

TIDDLY adj tiny ▷ n alcoholic beverage

TIDDY n four of trumps in the card game gleek

TIDE n rise and fall of the sea caused by the gravitational pull of the sun and moon ▷ vb carry or be carried with or as if with the tide

TIDED ▶ tide

TIDERIP same as ▶ riptide

TIDES ▶ tide

TIDEWAY n strong tidal current or its channel, esp the tidal part of a river

TIDIED ▶ tidy

TIDIER ▶ tidy

TIDIERS ▶ tidy

TIDIES ▶ tidy

TIDIEST ▶ tidy

TIDILY ▶ tidy

TIDING ▶ tide

TIDINGS pl n news

TIDS ▶ tid

TIDY adj neat and orderly ▷ vb put in order ▷ n small container for odds and ends

TIDYING ▶ tidy

TIE vb fasten or be fastened with string, rope, etc ▷ n long narrow piece of material worn knotted round the neck

TIEBACK n length of cord, ribbon, or other fabric used for tying a curtain to one side

TIED ▶ tie

TIEING same as ▶ tie

TIELESS ▶ tie

TIEPIN n ornamental pin used to pin the two ends of a tie to a shirt

TIEPINS ▶ tiepin

TIER n one of a set of rows placed one above and behind the other ▷ vb be or arrange in tiers

TIERCE same as ▶ terce

TIERCED adj (of a shield)

divided into three sections of similar size but different colour

TIERCEL same as ▶ **tercel**

TIERCES ▶ **tierce**

TIERCET same as ▶ **tercet**

TIERED ▶ **tier**

TIERING ▶ **tier**

TIERS ▶ **tier**

TIES ▶ **tie**

TIETAC n fastener for holding a tie in place

TIETACK same as ▶ **tietac**

TIETACS ▶ **tietac**

TIFF n petty quarrel ▷ vb have or be in a tiff

TIFFANY n sheer fine gauzy fabric

TIFFED ▶ **tiff**

TIFFIN n (in India) a light meal, esp at midday ▷ vb take tiffin

TIFFING ▶ **tiff**

TIFFINS ▶ **tiffin**

TIFFS ▶ **tiff**

TIFOSI ▶ **tifoso**

TIFOSO n fanatical fan (esp an Italian F1 fan)

TIFT Scots variant of ▶ **tiff**

TIFTED ▶ **tift**

TIFTING ▶ **tift**

TIFTS ▶ **tift**

TIG n child's game

TIGE n trunk of an architectural column

TIGER n large yellow-and-black striped Asian cat

TIGERLY adj of or like a tiger

TIGERS ▶ **tiger**

TIGERY ▶ **tiger**

TIGES ▶ **tige**

TIGGED ▶ **tig**

TIGGING ▶ **tig**

TIGHT adj stretched or drawn taut ▷ adv in a close, firm, or secure way

TIGHTEN vb make or become tight or tighter

TIGHTER ▶ **tight**

TIGHTLY ▶ **tight**

TIGHTS pl n one-piece clinging garment covering the body from the waist to the feet

TIGLIC adj as in **tiglic acid** syrupy liquid or crystalline colourless unsaturated carboxylic acid

TIGLON same as ▶ **tigon**

TIGLONS ▶ **tiglon**

TIGON n hybrid offspring of a male tiger and a female lion

TIGONS ▶ **tigon**

TIGRESS n female tiger

TIGRINE adj of, characteristic of, or resembling a tiger

TIGRISH ▶ **tiger**

TIGROID adj resembling a tiger

TIGS ▶ **tig**

TIK n South African slang term for crystal meth

TIKA same as ▶ **tikka**

TIKANGA n Māori ways or customs

TIKAS ▶ **tika**

TIKI n small carving of a grotesque person worn as a pendant ▷ vb take a scenic tour around an area

TIKIED ▶ **tiki**

TIKIING ▶ **tiki**

TIKIS ▶ **tiki**

TIKKA adj marinated in spices and dry-roasted ▷ n act of marking a tikka on the forehead

TIKKAS ▶ **tikka**

TIKS ▶ **tik**

TIL another name for ▶ **sesame**

TILAK n coloured spot or mark worn by Hindus, esp on the forehead, often indicating membership of a religious sect, caste, etc, or (in the case of a woman) marital status

TILAKS ▶ **tilak**

TILAPIA n type of fish

TILBURY n light two-wheeled horse-drawn open carriage, seating two people

TILDE n mark (~) used in Spanish to indicate that the letter 'n' is to be pronounced in a particular way

TILDES ▶ **tilde**

TILE n flat piece of ceramic, plastic, etc used to cover a roof, floor, or wall ▷ vb cover with tiles

TILED ▶ **tile**

TILER ▶ **tile**

TILERS ▶ **tile**

TILERY n place where tiles are produced

TILES ▶ **tile**

TILING n tiles collectively

TILINGS ▶ **tiling**

TILL prep until ▷ vb cultivate (land) ▷ n drawer for money, usu in a cash

register ▷ n unstratified glacial deposit consisting of rock fragments of various sizes

TILLAGE n act, process, or art of tilling

TILLED ▶ **till**

TILLER n on boats, a handle fixed to the top of a rudderpost to serve as a lever in steering ▷ vb use a tiller

TILLERS ▶ **till**

TILLIER ▶ **till**

TILLING ▶ **till**

TILLITE n rock formed from hardened till

TILLS ▶ **till**

TILLY ▶ **till**

TILS ▶ **til**

TILT vb slant at an angle ▷ n slope

TILTED ▶ **tilt**

TILTER ▶ **tilt**

TILTERS ▶ **tilt**

TILTH n (condition of) land that has been tilled

TILTHS ▶ **tilth**

TILTING ▶ **tilt**

TILTS ▶ **tilt**

TIMARAU same as ▶ **tamarau**

TIMBAL n type of kettledrum

TIMBALE n mixture of meat, fish, etc, in a rich sauce, cooked in a mould lined with potato or pastry

TIMBALS ▶ **timbal**

TIMBER n wood as a building material ▷ adj made out of timber ▷ vb provide with timbers ▷ interj lumberjack's shouted warning when a tree is about to fall

TIMBERS ▶ **timber**

TIMBERY ▶ **timber**

TIMBO n Amazonian vine from which a useful insecticide can be derived

TIMBOS ▶ **timbo**

TIMBRAL adj relating to timbre

TIMBRE n distinctive quality of sound of a voice or instrument

TIMBREL n tambourine

TIMBRES ▶ **timbre**

TIME n past, present, and future as a continuous whole ▷ vb note the time taken by

T

TIMED ▶ time

TIMELY adj at the appropriate time ▷ adv at the right or an appropriate time

TIMEOUS adj in good time

TIMEOUT n in sport, interruption in play during which players rest, discuss tactics, or make substitutions

TIMER n device for measuring time, esp a switch or regulator that causes a mechanism to operate at a specific time

TIMERS ▶ timer

TIMES ▶ time

TIMID adj easily frightened

TIMIDER ▶ timid

TIMIDLY ▶ timid

TIMING n ability to judge when to do or say something so as to make the best effect

TIMINGS ▶ timing

TIMIST n one concerned with time

TIMISTS ▶ timist

TIMOLOL n relaxant medicine used (for example) to reduce blood pressure

TIMON n apparatus by which a vessel is steered

TIMONS ▶ timon

TIMOTHY n as in **timothy grass** perennial grass of temperate regions, having erect stiff stems and cylindrical flower spikes: grown for hay and pasture

TIMOUS same as ▶ timeous

TIMPANA n traditional Maltese baked pasta and pastry dish

TIMPANI pl n set of kettledrums

TIMPANO n kettledrum

TIMPS same as ▶ timpani

TIN n soft metallic element ▷ vb put (food) into tins

TINA n (slang) crystal meth

TINAJA n large jar for cooling water

TINAJAS ▶ tinaja

TINAMOU n type of bird of Central and S America, with small wings, a heavy body, and an inconspicuous plumage

TINAS ▶ tina

TINCAL another name for

▶ borax

TINCALS ▶ tincal

TINCHEL n in Scotland, a circle of deer hunters who gradually close in on their quarry

TINCT vb tint ▷ adj tinted or coloured

TINCTED ▶ tinct

TINCTS ▶ tinct

TIND vb set alight

TINDAL n petty officer

TINDALS ▶ tindal

TINDED ▶ tind

TINDER n dry easily-burning material used to start a fire

TINDERS ▶ tinder

TINDERY ▶ tinder

TINDING ▶ tind

TINDS ▶ tind

TINE n prong of a fork or antler ▷ vb lose

TINEA n any fungal skin disease, esp ringworm

TINEAL ▶ tinea

TINEAS ▶ tinea

TINED ▶ tine

TINEID n type of moth of the family which includes the clothes moths

TINEIDS ▶ tineid

TINES ▶ tine

TINFOIL n paper-thin sheet of metal, used for wrapping foodstuffs

TINFUL n contents of a tin or the amount a tin will hold

TINFULS ▶ tinful

TING same as ▶ thing

TINGE n slight tint ▷ vb give a slight tint or trace to

TINGED ▶ tinge

TINGES ▶ tinge

TINGING ▶ tinge

TINGLE n (feel) a prickling or stinging sensation ▷ vb feel a mild prickling or stinging sensation, as from cold or excitement

TINGLED ▶ tingle

TINGLER ▶ tingle

TINGLES ▶ tingle

TINGLY ▶ tingle

TINGS ▶ ting

TINHORN n cheap pretentious person, esp a gambler with extravagant claims ▷ adj cheap and showy

TINIER ▶ tiny

TINIES pl n small children

TINIEST ▶ tiny

TINILY ▶ tiny

TINING ▶ tine

TINK shortened form of ▶ tinker

TINKED ▶ tink

TINKER n derogatory term for travelling mender of pots and pans ▷ vb fiddle with (an engine etc) in an attempt to repair it

TINKERS ▶ tinker

TINKING ▶ tink

TINKLE vb ring with a high tinny sound like a small bell ▷ n this sound or action

TINKLED ▶ tinkle

TINKLER same as ▶ tinker

TINKLES ▶ tinkle

TINKLY ▶ tinkle

TINKS ▶ tink

TINLIKE ▶ tin

TINMAN n one who works with tin or tin plate

TINMEN ▶ tinman

TINNED ▶ tin

TINNER n tin miner

TINNERS ▶ tinner

TINNIE same as ▶ tinny

TINNIER ▶ tinny

TINNIES ▶ tinny

TINNILY ▶ tinny

TINNING ▶ tin

TINNY adj (of sound) thin and metallic ▷ n can of beer

TINPOT adj worthless or unimportant ▷ n pot made of tin

TINPOTS ▶ tinpot

TINS ▶ tin

TINSEL n decorative metallic strips or threads ▷ adj made of or decorated with tinsel ▷ vb decorate with or as if with tinsel

TINSELS ▶ tinsel

TINSEY old variant of ▶ tinsel

TINSEYS ▶ tinsey

TINT n (pale) shade of a colour ▷ vb give a tint to

TINTACK n tin-plated tack

TINTED ▶ tint

TINTER ▶ tint

TINTERS ▶ tint

TINTIER ▶ tinty

TINTING ▶ tint

TINTS ▶ tint

TINTY adj having many tints

TINTYPE another name for > ferrotype

TINWARE n objects made of tin plate

TINWORK n objects made of tin

TINY adj very small

TIP n narrow or pointed end of anything ▷ vb put a tip on

TIPCART n cart that can be tipped to empty out its contents

TIPCAT n game in which a short sharp-ended piece of wood (the cat) is tipped in the air with a stick

TIPCATS ▶ tipcat

TIPI variant spelling of ▶ tepee

TIPIS ▶ tipi

TIPLESS ▶ tip

TIPOFF n warning or hint, esp given confidentially and based on inside information

TIPOFFS ▶ tipoff

TIPPED ▶ tip

TIPPEE n person who receives a tip, esp regarding share prices

TIPPEES ▶ tippee

TIPPER n person who gives or leaves a tip

TIPPERS ▶ tipper

TIPPET n scarflike piece of fur, often made from a whole animal skin, worn, esp formerly, round a woman's shoulders

TIPPETS ▶ tippet

TIPPIER ▶ tippy

TIPPING ▶ tip

TIPPLE vb drink alcohol habitually, esp in small quantities ▷ n alcoholic drink

TIPPLED ▶ tipple

TIPPLER ▶ tipple

TIPPLES ▶ tipple

TIPPY adj extremely fashionable or stylish

TIPS ▶ tip

TIPSIER ▶ tipsy

TIPSIFY vb make tipsy

TIPSILY ▶ tipsy

TIPSTER n person who sells tips about races

TIPSY adj slightly drunk

TIPT ▶ tip

TIPTOE vb walk quietly with the heels off the ground

TIPTOED ▶ tiptoe

TIPTOES ▶ tiptoe

TIPTOP adj of the highest quality or condition ▷ adv of the highest quality or condition ▷ n best in quality ▷ n very top; pinnacle

TIPTOPS ▶ tiptop

TIPULA n crane fly

TIPULAS ▶ tipula

TIPUNA n ancestor

TIPUNAS ▶ tipuna

TIRADE n long angry speech

TIRADES ▶ tirade

TIRAGE n drawing of wine from a barrel prior to bottling

TIRAGES ▶ tirage

TIRASSE n mechanism in an organ connecting two pedals, so that both may be depressed at once

TIRE vb reduce the energy of, as by exertion

TIRED adj exhausted

TIREDER ▶ tired

TIREDLY ▶ tired

TIRES ▶ tire

TIRING ▶ tire

TIRINGS ▶ tire

TIRITI n another name for the Treaty of Waitangi

| A Maori word for treaty. Any 6-letter word that lets you get rid of three Is can't be bad!

TIRITIS ▶ tiriti

TIRL vb turn

TIRLED ▶ tirl

TIRLING ▶ tirl

TIRLS ▶ tirl

TIRO same as ▶ tyro

TIROES ▶ tiro

TIRONIC same as ▶ tyronic

TIROS ▶ tiro

TIRR vb strip or denude

TIRRED ▶ tirr

TIRRING ▶ tirr

TIRRIT n panic; scare

TIRRITS ▶ tirrit

TIRRS ▶ tirr

TIS ▶ ti

TISANE n infusion of dried or fresh leaves or flowers, as camomile

TISANES ▶ tisane

TISICK n splutter; cough

TISICKS ▶ tisick

TISSUAL adj relating to tissue

TISSUE n substance of an animal body or plant ▷ vb weave into tissue

TISSUED ▶ tissue

TISSUES ▶ tissue

TISSUEY ▶ tissue

TISWAS n state of anxiety or excitement

TIT n any of various small songbirds; informal term for a female breast ▷ vb jerk or tug

TITAN n person who is huge, strong, or very important

TITANIA > titanium

TITANIC adj huge or very important

TITANIS n large predatory flightless prehistoric bird

TITANS ▶ titan

TITBIT n tasty piece of food

TITBITS ▶ titbit

TITCH n small person

TITCHES ▶ titch

TITCHY adj very small

TITE adj immediately

TITELY adv immediately

TITER same as ▶ titre

TITERS ▶ titer

TITFER n hat

TITFERS ▶ titfer

TITHE n esp formerly, one tenth of one's income or produce paid to the church as a tax ▷ vb charge or pay a tithe

TITHED ▶ tithe

TITHER ▶ tithe

TITHERS ▶ tithe

TITHES ▶ tithe

TITHING ▶ tithe

TITI n small omnivorous New World monkey of South America, with long beautifully coloured fur and a long nonprehensile tail

TITIAN n reddish gold colour

TITIANS ▶ titian

TITIS ▶ titi

TITLARK another name for ▶ pipit

TITLE n name of a book, film, etc ▷ vb give a title to

TITLED adj aristocratic

TITLER n one who writes titles

TITLERS ▶ title

TITLES ▶ title

TITLING ▶ title

TITLIST n titleholder

TITMAN n (of pigs) the runt of a litter

TITMEN ▶ titman

TITMICE > titmouse

TITMOSE old spelling of > titmouse

TITOKI n New Zealand evergreen tree with a spreading crown and glossy green leaves

TITOKIS ▶ titoki

TITRANT n solution in a titration that is added from

a burette to a measured quantity of another solution

TITRATE *vb* measure the volume or concentration of (a solution) by titration

TITRE *n* concentration of a solution as determined by titration

TITRES ▶ **titre**

TITS ▶ **tit**

TITTED ▶ **tit**

TITTER *vb* laugh in a suppressed way ▷ *n* suppressed laugh

TITTERS ▶ **titter**

TITTIE *n* sister; young woman

TITTIES ▶ **tittie**

TITTING ▶ **tit**

TITTISH *adj* testy

TITTLE *n* very small amount ▷ *vb* chatter; tattle

TITTLED ▶ **tittle**

TITTLES ▶ **tittle**

TITTUP *vb* prance or frolic ▷ *n* caper

TITTUPS ▶ **tittup**

TITTUPY *adj* spritely; lively

TITTY *same as* ▶ **tittie**

TITULAR *adj* in name only ▷ *n* bearer of a title

TITULE *same as* ▶ **title**

TITULED ▶ **titule**

TITULES ▶ **titule**

TITULI ▶ **titulus**

TITULUS *n* (in crucifixion) a sign attached to the top of the cross on which were written the condemned man's name and crime

TITUP *same as* ▶ **tittup**

TITUPED ▶ **titup**

TITUPS ▶ **titup**

TITUPY *same as* ▶ **tittupy**

TIVY *same as* ▶ **tantivy**

TIX *pl n* tickets

> **Tix** is an informal word for **tickets**, and of of the key short words for using the X.

TIYIN *n* monetary unit of Uzbekistan and Kyrgyzstan

TIYINS ▶ **tiyin**

TIZWAS *same as* ▶ **tiswas**

TIZZ *same as* ▶ **tizzy**

TIZZES ▶ **tizz**

TIZZIES ▶ **tizzy**

TIZZY *n* confused or agitated state

TMESES ▶ **tmesis**

TMESIS *n* interpolation of a

word or group of words between the parts of a compound word

TO *prep* indicating movement towards, equality or comparison, etc ▷ *adv* a closed position

TOAD *n* animal like a large frog

TOADIED ▶ **toady**

TOADIES ▶ **toady**

TOADISH ▶ **toad**

TOADS ▶ **toad**

TOADY *n* ingratiating person ▷ *vb* be ingratiating

TOAST *n* sliced bread browned by heat ▷ *vb* brown (bread) by heat

TOASTED ▶ **toast**

TOASTER ▶ **toast**

TOASTIE *same as* ▶ **toasty**

TOASTS ▶ **toast**

TOASTY *n* toasted sandwich ▷ *adj* tasting or smelling like toast

TOAZE *variant spelling of* ▶ **toze**

TOAZED ▶ **toaze**

TOAZES ▶ **toaze**

TOAZING ▶ **toaze**

TOBACCO *n* plant with large leaves dried for smoking

TOBIES ▶ **toby**

TOBY *n* water stopcock at the boundary of a street and house section

TOC *n* in communications code, signal for letter t

TOCCATA *n* rapid piece of music for a keyboard instrument

TOCCATE ▶ **toccata**

TOCHER *n* dowry ▷ *vb* give a dowry to

TOCHERS ▶ **tocher**

TOCK *n* sound made by a clock ▷ *vb* (of a clock) make such a sound

TOCKED ▶ **tock**

TOCKIER ▶ **tocky**

TOCKING ▶ **tock**

TOCKS ▶ **tock**

TOCKY *adj* muddy

TOCO *n* punishment

TOCOS ▶ **toco**

TOCS ▶ **toc**

TOCSIN *n* warning signal

TOCSINS ▶ **tocsin**

TOD *n* unit of weight, used for wool, etc, usually equal to 28 pounds ▷ *vb* produce a tod

TODAY *n* this day ▷ *adv* on this day

TODAYS ▶ **today**

TODDE *same as* ▶ **tod**

TODDED ▶ **tod**

TODDES ▶ **todde**

TODDIES ▶ **toddy**

TODDING ▶ **tod**

TODDLE *vb* walk with short unsteady steps ▷ *n* act or an instance of toddling

TODDLED ▶ **toddle**

TODDLER *n* child beginning to walk

TODDLES ▶ **toddle**

TODDY *n* sweetened drink of spirits and hot water

TODIES ▶ **tody**

TODS ▶ **tod**

TODY *n* small bird of the Caribbean, with a red-and-green plumage and long straight bill

TOE *n* digit of the foot ▷ *vb* touch or kick with the toe

TOEA *n* monetary unit of Papua New Guinea, worth one-hundredth of a kina

> This monetary unit of Papua New Guinea is very often played to rid the rack of a surplus of vowels.

TOEAS ▶ **toea**

TOEBIE *n* South African slang for sandwich

TOEBIES ▶ **toebie**

TOECAP *n* strengthened covering for the toe of a shoe

TOECAPS ▶ **toecap**

TOECLIP *n* clip on a bicycle pedal into which the toes are inserted to prevent the foot from slipping

TOED ▶ **toe**

TOEHOLD *n* small space on a mountain for supporting the toe of the foot in climbing

TOEIER ▶ **toey**

> This is the comparative of **toey**, Australian slang for nervous or edgy, and can come in useful for dumping a surplus of vowels.

TOEIEST ▶ **toey**

TOEING ▶ **toe**

TOELESS *adj* not having toes

TOELIKE ▶ **toe**

TOENAIL *n* thin hard clear

plate covering part of the upper surface of the end of each toe ▷ vb join (beams) by driving nails obliquely

TOES ▶ toe

TOESHOE n ballet pump with padded toes

TOETOE same as ▶ toitoi

TOETOES ▶ toetoe

TOEY adj (of a person) nervous or anxious

TOFF n well-dressed or upper-class person

TOFFEE n chewy sweet made of boiled sugar

TOFFEES ▶ toffee

TOFFIER ▶ toffy

TOFFIES ▶ toffy

TOFFISH adj belonging to or characteristic of the upper class

TOFFS adj like a toff

TOFFY same as ▶ toffee

TOFORE prep before

TOFT n homestead

TOFTS ▶ toft

TOFU n soft food made from soya-bean curd

TOFUS ▶ tofu

TOFUTTI n tradename for any of a variety of nondairy, soya-based food products, esp frozen desserts

TOG n unit for measuring the insulating power of duvets ▷ vb dress oneself, esp in smart clothes

TOGA n garment worn by citizens of ancient Rome ▷ vb wear a toga

TOGAE ▶ toga

TOGAED ▶ toga

TOGAS ▶ toga

TOGATE adj clad in a toga

TOGATED same as ▶ togate

TOGE old variant of ▶ toga

TOGED ▶ toge

TOGES ▶ toge

TOGGED ▶ tog

TOGGER vb play football ▷ n football player

TOGGERS ▶ togger

TOGGERY n clothes

TOGGING ▶ tog

TOGGLE n small bar-shaped button inserted through a loop for fastening ▷ vb supply or fasten with a toggle or toggles

TOGGLED ▶ toggle

TOGGLER ▶ toggle

TOGGLES ▶ toggle

TOGS ▶ tog

TOGUE n large North American freshwater game fish

TOGUES ▶ togue

TOHEROA n large edible mollusc of New Zealand with a distinctive flavour

TOHO n (to a hunting dog) an instruction to stop

TOHUNGA n Māori priest

TOIL n hard work ▷ vb work hard

TOILE n transparent linen or cotton fabric

TOILED ▶ toil

TOILER ▶ toil

TOILERS ▶ toil

TOILES ▶ toile

TOILET n a bowl connected to a drain for receiving and disposing of urine and faeces ▷ vb go to the toilet

TOILETS ▶ toilet

TOILFUL same as > toilsome

TOILING ▶ toil

TOILS ▶ toil

TOING n as in toing and froing state of going back and forth

TOINGS ▶ toing

TOISE n obsolete French unit of length roughly equal to 2m

TOISECH same as > toiseach

TOISES ▶ toise

TOISON n fleece

TOISONS ▶ toison

TOIT vb walk or move in an unsteady manner, as from old age

TOITED ▶ toit

TOITING ▶ toit

TOITOI n tall grasses with feathery fronds

TOITOIS ▶ toitoi

TOITS ▶ toit

TOKAMAK n reactor used in thermonuclear experiments

TOKAY n small gecko of S and SE Asia, having a retractile claw at the tip of each digit

TOKAYS ▶ tokay

TOKE n draw on a cannabis cigarette ▷ vb take a draw on a cannabis cigarette

TOKED ▶ toke

TOKEN n sign or symbol ▷ adj nominal or slight

TOKENED ▶ token

TOKENS ▶ token

TOKER ▶ toke

TOKERS ▶ toke

TOKES ▶ toke

TOKING ▶ toke

TOKO same as ▶ toco

TOKOMAK variant spelling of ▶ tokamak

TOKOS ▶ toko

TOLA n unit of weight, used in India, equal to 180 ser or 180 grains

TOLAN n white crystalline derivative of acetylene

TOLANE same as ▶ tolan

TOLANES ▶ tolane

TOLANS ▶ tolan

TOLAR n standard monetary unit of Slovenia, divided into 100 stotin

TOLARJI ▶ tolar

TOLARS ▶ tolar

TOLAS ▶ tola

TOLD ▶ tell

TOLE same as ▶ toll

TOLED ▶ tole

TOLEDO n type of sword originally made in Toledo

TOLEDOS ▶ toledo

TOLES ▶ tole

TOLIDIN same as > tolidine

TOLING ▶ tole

TOLINGS ▶ tole

TOLL vb ring (a bell) slowly and regularly, esp to announce a death ▷ n tolling

TOLLAGE same as ▶ toll

TOLLBAR n bar blocking passage of a thoroughfare, raised on payment of a toll

TOLLED ▶ toll

TOLLER ▶ toll

TOLLERS ▶ toller

TOLLEY n large shooting marble used in a game of marbles

TOLLEYS ▶ tolley

TOLLIE same as ▶ tolly

TOLLIES ▶ tolly

TOLLING ▶ toll

TOLLMAN n man who collects tolls

TOLLMEN ▶ tollman

TOLLS ▶ toll

TOLLWAY n road on which users must pay tolls to travel

TOLLY n castrated calf

TOLSEL n tolbooth

TOLSELS ▶ tolsel

TOLSEY n tolbooth

TOLSEYS > tolbooth

TOLT n type of obsolete English writ

T

TOLTER vb struggle or move with difficulty, as in mud

TOLTERS ▶ tolter

TOLTS ▶ tolt

TOLU n sweet-smelling balsam obtained from a South American tree, used in medicine and perfume

TOLUATE n any salt or ester of any of the three isomeric forms of toluic acid

TOLUENE n colourless volatile flammable liquid obtained from petroleum and coal tar

TOLUIC adj as in **toluic acid** white crystalline derivative of toluene existing in three isomeric forms

TOLUID n white crystalline derivative of glycocoll

TOLUIDE same as ▶ toluid

TOLUIDS ▶ toluid

TOLUOL another name for ▶ toluene

TOLUOLE another name for ▶ toluene

TOLUOLS ▶ toluol

TOLUS ▶ tolu

TOLUYL n of, consisting of, or containing any of three isomeric groups $CH_3C_6H_4CO-$, derived from a toluic acid by removal of the hydroxyl group

TOLUYLS ▶ toluyl

TOLYL n of, consisting of, or containing any of three isomeric groups, $CH_3C_6H_4-$, derived from toluene

TOLYLS ▶ tolyl

TOLZEY n tolbooth

TOLZEYS ▶ tolzey

TOM n male cat ▷ adj (of an animal) male ▷ vb prostitute oneself

TOMAN n gold coin formerly issued in Persia

TOMANS ▶ toman

TOMATO n red fruit used in salads and as a vegetable

TOMB n grave

TOMBAC n any of various brittle alloys containing copper and zinc and sometimes tin and arsenic: used for making cheap jewellery, etc

TOMBACK variant spelling of ▶ tombac

TOMBACKS ▶ tombac

TOMBAK same as ▶ tombac

TOMBAKS ▶ tombak

TOMBAL adj like or relating to a tomb

TOMBED ▶ tomb

TOMBIC adj of or relating to tombs

TOMBING ▶ tomb

TOMBOC n weapon

TOMBOCS ▶ tomboc

TOMBOLA n lottery with tickets drawn from a revolving drum

TOMBOLO n narrow sand or shingle bar linking a small island with another island or the mainland

TOMBOY n girl who acts or dresses like a boy

TOMBOYS ▶ tomboy

TOMBS ▶ tomb

TOMCAT vb (of a man) to be promiscuous

TOMCATS ▶ tomcat

TOMCOD n small fish resembling the cod

TOMCODS ▶ tomcod

TOME n large heavy book

TOMENTA > tomentum

TOMES ▶ tome

TOMFOOL n fool ▷ vb act the fool

TOMIA ▶ tomium

TOMIAL ▶ tomium

TOMIUM n sharp edge of a bird's beak

TOMMIED ▶ tommy

TOMMIES ▶ tommy

TOMMY n private in the British Army ▷ vb (formerly) to exploit workers by paying them in goods rather than in money

TOMO n shaft formed by the action of water on limestone or volcanic rock

TOMOS ▶ tomo

TOMPION same as ▶ tampion

TOMPON same as ▶ tampon

TOMPONS ▶ tompon

TOMS ▶ tom

TOMTIT n small European bird that eats insects and seeds

TOMTITS ▶ tomtit

TON n unit of weight equal to 2240 pounds or 1016 kilograms (long ton) or, in the US, 2000 pounds or 907 kilograms (short ton); style, distinction

TONAL adj written in a key

TONALLY ▶ tonal

TONANT adj very loud

TONDI ▶ tondo

TONDINI ▶ tondino

TONDINO n small tondo

TONDO n circular easel painting or relief carving

TONDOS ▶ tondo

TONE n sound with reference to its pitch, volume, etc ▷ vb harmonize (with)

TONEARM same as ▶ pickup

TONED ▶ tone

TONEME n phoneme that is distinguished from another phoneme only by its tone

TONEMES ▶ toneme

TONEMIC ▶ toneme

TONEPAD n keypad used to transmit information by generating tones that can be recognised by a central system as corresponding to particular digits

TONER n cosmetic applied to the skin to reduce oiliness

TONERS ▶ toner

TONES ▶ tone

TONETIC adj (of a language) distinguishing words semantically by distinction of tone as well as by other sounds

TONETTE n small musical instrument resembling a recorder

TONEY variant spelling of ▶ tony

TONG n (formerly) a secret society of Chinese Americans ▷ vb gather or seize with tongs ▷ n (formerly) a Chinese secret society

TONGA n light two-wheeled vehicle used in rural areas of India

TONGAS ▶ tonga

TONGED ▶ tong

TONGER n one who uses tongs to gather oysters

TONGERS ▶ tonger

TONGING ▶ tong

TONGMAN another word for ▶ tonger

TONGMEN ▶ tongman

TONGS pl n large pincers for grasping and lifting

TONGUE n muscular organ in the mouth, used in speaking and tasting ▷ vb use the tongue

TONGUED ▸ tongue

TONGUES ▸ tongue

TONIC n medicine to improve body tone ▷ adj invigorating

TONICS ▸ tonic

TONIER ▸ tony

TONIES ▸ tony

TONIEST ▸ tony

TONIGHT n (in or during) the night or evening of this day ▷ adv in or during the night or evening of this day

TONING ▸ tone

TONINGS ▸ tone

TONISH ▸ ton

TONITE n explosive used in quarrying

TONITES ▸ tonite

TONK vb strike with a heavy blow ▷ n effete or effeminate man

TONKA n as in tonka bean tall leguminous tree of tropical America, having fragrant black almond-shaped seeds

TONKED ▸ tonk

TONKER ▸ tonk

TONKERS ▸ tonk

TONKING ▸ tonk

TONKS ▸ tonk

TONLET n skirt of a suit of armour, consisting of overlapping metal bands

TONLETS ▸ tonlet

TONNAG n type of (usually tartan) shawl

TONNAGE n weight capacity of a ship

TONNAGS ▸ tonnag

TONNE same as ▸ ton

TONNEAU n detachable cover to protect the rear part of an open car when it is not carrying passengers

TONNELL old spelling of ▸ tunnel

TONNER n something, for example a vehicle, that weighs one ton

TONNERS ▸ tonne

TONNES ▸ tonne

TONNISH ▸ ton

TONS ▸ ton

TONSIL n small gland in the throat

TONSILS ▸ tonsil

TONSOR n barber

TONSORS ▸ tonsor

TONSURE n shaving of all or the top of the head as a

religious or monastic practice ▷ vb shave the head of

TONTINE n annuity scheme by which several subscribers accumulate and invest a common fund out of which they receive an annuity that increases as subscribers die until the last survivor takes the whole

TONUS n normal tension of a muscle at rest

TONUSES ▸ tonus

TONY adj stylish or distinctive ▷ n stylish or distinctive person

TOO adv also, as well

TOOART variant spelling of ▸ tuart

TOOARTS ▸ tooart

TOOK ▸ take

TOOL n implement used by hand ▷ vb work on with a tool

TOOLBAG n bag for storing or carrying tools

TOOLBAR n horizontal row or vertical column of selectable buttons displayed on a computer screen, allowing the user to select a variety of functions

TOOLBOX n box for storing or carrying tools

TOOLED ▸ tool

TOOLER ▸ tool

TOOLERS ▸ tool

TOOLIE n adult who gatecrashes schools to make advances to the students

TOOLIES ▸ toolie

TOOLING n any decorative work done with a tool, esp a design stamped onto a book cover, piece of leatherwork, etc

TOOLKIT n set of tools designed to be used together or for a particular purpose

TOOLMAN n person who works with tools

TOOLMEN ▸ toolman

TOOLS ▸ tool

TOOLSET n set of predefined tools associated with a particular computer application

TOOM vb empty (something) ▷ adj empty

TOOMED ▸ toom

TOOMER ▸ toom

TOOMEST ▸ toom

TOOMING ▸ toom

TOOMS ▸ toom

TOON n large meliaceous tree of the East Indies and Australia, having clusters of flowers from which a dye is obtained

TOONIE n Canadian two-dollar coin

TOONIES ▸ toonie

TOONS ▸ toon

TOORIE n tassel or bobble on a bonnet

TOORIES ▸ toorie

TOOSHIE adj angry

TOOT n short hooting sound ▷ vb (cause to) make such a sound

TOOTED ▸ toot

TOOTER ▸ toot

TOOTERS ▸ toot

TOOTH n bonelike projection in the jaws of most vertebrates for biting and chewing

TOOTHED adj having a tooth or teeth

TOOTHS ▸ tooth

TOOTHY adj having or showing numerous, large, or prominent teeth

TOOTING ▸ toot

TOOTLE vb hoot softly or repeatedly ▷ n soft hoot or series of hoots

TOOTLED ▸ tootle

TOOTLER ▸ tootle

TOOTLES ▸ tootle

TOOTS Scots version of ▸ tut

TOOTSED ▸ toots

TOOTSES ▸ toots

TOOTSIE same as ▸ tootsy

TOOTSY same as ▸ toots

TOP n highest point or part ▷ adj at or of the top ▷ vb form a top on

TOPARCH n ruler of a small state or realm

TOPAZ n semiprecious stone in various colours

TOPAZES ▸ topaz

TOPCOAT n overcoat

TOPE vb drink alcohol regularly ▷ n small European shark

TOPED ▸ tope

TOPEE n lightweight hat worn in tropical countries

TOPEES ▸ topee

TOPEK same as ▸ tupik

TOPEKS ▸ topek

T

TOPER ▶ **tope**

TOPERS ▶ **tope**

TOPES ▶ **tope**

TOPFUL variant spelling of ▶ **topfull**

TOPFULL adj full to the top

TOPH n variety of sandstone

TOPHE variant spelling of ▶ **toph**

TOPHES ▶ **tophe**

TOPHI ▶ **tophus**

TOPHS ▶ **toph**

TOPHUS n deposit of sodium urate in the helix of the ear or surrounding a joint

TOPI same as ▶ **topee**

TOPIARY n art of trimming trees and bushes into decorative shapes ▷ adj of or relating to topiary

TOPIC n subject of a conversation, book, etc

TOPICAL adj relating to current events

TOPICS ▶ **topic**

TOPING ▶ **tope**

TOPIS ▶ **topi**

TOPKICK n (formerly) sergeant

TOPKNOT n crest, tuft, decorative bow, etc, on the top of the head

TOPLESS adj (of a costume or woman) with no covering for the breasts

TOPLINE vb headline; be the main focus of a newspaper story

TOPMAN n sailor positioned in the rigging of the topsail

TOPMAST n mast next above a lower mast on a sailing vessel

TOPMEN ▶ **topman**

TOPMOST adj highest or best

TOPO n picture of a mountain with details of climbing routes superimposed on it

TOPOI ▶ **topo**

TOPONYM n name of a place

TOPOS ▶ **topo**

TOPPED ▶ **top**

TOPPER n top hat

TOPPERS ▶ **topper**

TOPPIER ▶ **toppy**

TOPPING ▶ **top**

TOPPLE vb (cause to) fall over

TOPPLED ▶ **topple**

TOPPLES ▶ **topple**

TOPPY adj (of audio reproduction) having too many high-frequency sounds

TOPS ▶ **top**

TOPSAIL n square sail carried on a yard set on a topmast

TOPSIDE n lean cut of beef from the thigh containing no bone

TOPSMAN n chief drover

TOPSMEN ▶ **topsman**

TOPSOIL n surface layer of soil ▷ vb spread topsoil on (land)

TOPSPIN n spin imparted to make a ball bounce or travel exceptionally far, high, or quickly, as by hitting it with a sharp forward and upward stroke

TOPWORK vb graft shoots or twigs onto the main branches of (for example, a fruit tree) to modify its yield

TOQUE same as ▶ **tuque**

TOQUES ▶ **toque**

TOQUET same as ▶ **toque**

TOQUETS ▶ **toquet**

TOR n high rocky hill

TORA variant spelling of ▶ **torah**

TORAH n whole body of traditional Jewish teaching, including the Oral Law

TORAHS ▶ **torah**

TORAN n (in Indian architecture) an archway, usually wooden and often ornately carved

TORANA same as ▶ **toran**

TORANAS ▶ **torana**

TORANS ▶ **toran**

TORAS ▶ **tora**

TORC same as ▶ **torque**

TORCH n small portable battery-powered lamp ▷ vb deliberately set (a building) on fire

TORCHED ▶ **torch**

TORCHER ▶ **torch**

TORCHES ▶ **torch**

TORCHON n as in **torchon lace** coarse linen or cotton lace with a simple openwork pattern

TORCHY adj sentimental; maudlin; characteristic of a torch song

TORCS ▶ **torc**

TORDION n old triple-time dance for two people

TORE same as ▶ **torus**

TORERO n bullfighter, esp one on foot

TOREROS ▶ **torero**

TORES ▶ **tore**

TORGOCH n type of char

TORI ▶ **torus**

TORIC adj of, relating to, or having the form of a torus

TORICS ▶ **toric**

TORIES ▶ **tory**

TORII n gateway, esp one at the entrance to a Japanese Shinto temple

TORMENT vb cause (someone) great suffering ▷ n great suffering

TORMINA n complaints

TORN ▶ **tear**

TORNADE same as ▶ **tornado**

TORNADO n violent whirlwind

TORO n bull

TOROID n surface generated by rotating a closed plane curve about a coplanar line that does not intersect the curve

TOROIDS ▶ **toroid**

TOROS ▶ **toro**

TOROSE adj (of a cylindrical part) having irregular swellings

TOROT ▶ **torah**

TOROTH ▶ **torah**

TOROUS same as ▶ **torose**

TORPEDO n self-propelled underwater missile ▷ vb attack or destroy with or as if with torpedoes

TORPEFY n make torpid

TORPID adj sluggish and inactive

TORPIDS n series of boat races held at Oxford University during Lent

TORPOR n torpid state

TORPORS ▶ **torpor**

TORQUE n force causing rotation ▷ vb apply torque to (something)

TORQUED ▶ **torque**

TORQUER ▶ **torque**

TORQUES n distinctive band of hair, feathers, skin, or colour around the neck of an animal

TORR n unit of pressure equal to one millimetre of mercury (133.3 newtons per square metre)

TORREFY vb dry (drugs, ores, etc) by subjection to intense heat

TORRENT n rushing stream ▷ adj like or relating to a torrent

TORRET same as ▶ **terret**

TORRETS ▶ **torret**

TORRID adj very hot and dry

TORRIFY same as ▶ **torrefy**

TORRS ▶ **torr**

TORS ▶ **tor**

TORSADE n ornamental twist or twisted cord, as on hats

TORSE same as ▶ **torso**

TORSEL n wooden beam along the top of a wall for distributing the weight of something laid upon it

TORSELS ▶ **torsel**

TORSES ▶ **torse**

TORSI ▶ **torso**

TORSION n twisting of a part by equal forces being applied at both ends but in opposite directions

TORSIVE adj twisted

TORSK n fish with a single long dorsal fin

TORSKS ▶ **torsk**

TORSO n trunk of the human body

TORSOS ▶ **torso**

TORT n civil wrong or injury for which damages may be claimed

TORTA n (in mining) a flat circular pile of silver ore

TORTAS ▶ **torta**

TORTE n rich cake, originating in Austria, usually decorated or filled with cream, fruit, nuts, and jam

TORTEN ▶ **torte**

TORTES ▶ **torte**

TORTILE adj twisted or coiled

TORTIVE adj twisted

TORTONI n rich ice cream often flavoured with sherry

TORTRIX n type of moth

TORTS ▶ **tort**

TORTURE vb cause (someone) severe pain or mental anguish ▷ n severe physical or mental pain

TORULA n species of fungal microorganisms

TORULAE ▶ **torula**

TORULAS ▶ **torula**

TORULI ▶ **torulus**

TORULIN n vitamin found in yeast

TORULUS n socket in an insect's head in which its antenna is attached

TORUS n large convex moulding approximately semicircular in cross section, esp one used on the base of a classical column

TORY n ultraconservative or reactionary person ▷ adj ultraconservative or reactionary

TOSA n large reddish dog, originally bred for fighting

TOSAS ▶ **tosa**

TOSE same as ▶ **toze**

TOSED ▶ **tose**

TOSES ▶ **tose**

TOSH n nonsense ▷ vb tidy or trim

TOSHACH n military leader of a clan

TOSHED ▶ **tosh**

TOSHER ▶ **tosh**

TOSHERS ▶ **tosh**

TOSHES ▶ **tosh**

TOSHIER ▶ **toshy**

TOSHING ▶ **tosh**

TOSHY adj neat; trim

TOSING ▶ **tose**

TOSS vb throw lightly ▷ n tossing

TOSSED ▶ **toss**

TOSSEN old past participle of ▶ **toss**

TOSSES ▶ **toss**

TOSSIER ▶ **tossy**

TOSSILY ▶ **tossy**

TOSSING ▶ **toss**

TOSSUP n an instance of tossing up a coin

TOSSUPS ▶ **tossup**

TOSSY adj impudent

TOST old past participle of ▶ **toss**

TOSTADA n crispy deep-fried tortilla topped with meat, cheese, and refried beans

TOSTADO same as ▶ **tostada**

TOT n small child ▷ vb total

TOTABLE ▶ **tote**

TOTAL n whole, esp a sum of parts ▷ adj complete ▷ vb amount to

TOTALED ▶ **total**

TOTALLY ▶ **total**

TOTALS ▶ **total**

TOTANUS another name for > **redshank**

TOTARA n tall coniferous forest tree of New Zealand, with a hard durable wood

TOTARAS ▶ **totara**

TOTE vb carry (a gun etc) ▷ n act of or an instance of toting

TOTED ▶ **tote**

TOTEM n tribal badge or emblem

TOTEMIC ▶ **totem**

TOTEMS ▶ **totem**

TOTER ▶ **tote**

TOTERS ▶ **tote**

TOTES ▶ **tote**

TOTHER n other

TOTIENT n quantity of numbers less than, and sharing no common factors with, a given number

TOTING ▶ **tote**

TOTS ▶ **tot**

TOTTED ▶ **tot**

TOTTER vb move unsteadily ▷ n act or an instance of tottering

TOTTERS ▶ **totter**

TOTTERY ▶ **totter**

TOTTIE adj very small

TOTTIER ▶ **totty**

TOTTIES ▶ **totty**

TOTTING ▶ **tot**

TOTTY n people, esp women, collectively considered as sexual objects ▷ adj very small

TOUCAN n tropical American bird with a large bill

TOUCANS ▶ **toucan**

TOUCH vb come into contact with ▷ n sense by which an object's qualities are perceived when they come into contact with part of the body ▷ adj of a non-contact version of particular sport

TOUCHE interj acknowledgment of the striking home of a remark or witty reply

TOUCHED adj emotionally moved

TOUCHER ▶ **touch**

TOUCHES ▶ **touch**

TOUCHUP n renovation or retouching, as of a painting

TOUCHY adj easily offended

TOUGH adj strong or resilient ▷ n rough violent person

T

TOUGHED ▸ tough

TOUGHEN vb make or become tough or tougher

TOUGHER ▸ tough

TOUGHIE n person who is tough

TOUGHLY ▸ tough

TOUGHS ▸ tough

TOUGHY same as ▸ toughie

TOUK same as ▸ tuck

TOUKED ▸ touk

TOUKING ▸ touk

TOUKS ▸ touk

TOUN n town

TOUNS ▸ toun

TOUPEE n small wig

TOUPEED adj wearing a toupee

TOUPEES ▸ toupee

TOUPET same as ▸ toupee

TOUPETS ▸ toupet

TOUR n journey visiting places of interest along the way ▷ vb make a tour (of)

TOURACO n brightly coloured crested arboreal African bird

TOURED ▸ tour

TOURER n large open car with a folding top, usually seating a driver and four passengers

TOURERS ▸ tourer

TOURIE same as ▸ toorie

TOURIES ▸ tourie

TOURING ▸ tour

TOURISM n tourist travel as an industry

TOURIST n person travelling for pleasure ▷ adj of or relating to tourists or tourism

TOURNEY n knightly tournament ▷ vb engage in a tourney

TOURS ▸ tour

TOUSE vb tangle, ruffle, or disarrange; treat roughly

TOUSED ▸ touse

TOUSER ▸ touse

TOUSERS ▸ touse

TOUSES ▸ touse

TOUSIER ▸ tousy

TOUSING ▸ touse

TOUSLE vb make (hair or clothes) ruffled and untidy ▷ n disorderly, tangled, or rumpled state

TOUSLED ▸ tousle

TOUSLES ▸ tousle

TOUSTIE adj irritable; testy

TOUSY adj tousled

TOUT vb seek business in a persistent manner ▷ n person who sells tickets for a popular event at inflated prices

TOUTED ▸ tout

TOUTER ▸ tout

TOUTERS ▸ tout

TOUTIE adj childishly irritable or sullen

TOUTIER ▸ toutie

TOUTING ▸ tout

TOUTS ▸ tout

TOUZE variant spelling of ▸ touse

TOUZED ▸ touze

TOUZES ▸ touze

TOUZIER ▸ touzy

TOUZING ▸ touze

TOUZLE rare spelling of ▸ tousle

TOUZLED ▸ touzle

TOUZLES ▸ touzle

TOUZY variant spelling of ▸ tousy

TOW vb drag, esp by means of a rope ▷ n towing

TOWABLE ▸ tow

TOWAGE n charge made for towing

TOWAGES ▸ towage

TOWARD same as ▸ towards

TOWARDS prep in the direction of

TOWAWAY n vehicle which has been towed away (because, for example, it was illegally parked)

TOWBAR n metal bar on a car for towing vehicles

TOWBARS ▸ towbar

TOWBOAT n another word for tug (the boat)

TOWED ▸ tow

TOWEL n cloth for drying things ▷ vb dry or wipe with a towel

TOWELED ▸ towel

TOWELS ▸ towel

TOWER n tall structure, often forming part of a larger building ▷ vb to be or rise like a tower; loom

TOWERED adj having a tower or towers

TOWERS ▸ tower

TOWERY adj with towers

TOWHEAD n often disparaging term for a person with blond or yellowish hair

TOWHEE n N American

brownish-coloured sparrow

TOWHEES ▸ towhee

TOWIE n truck used for towing

TOWIER ▸ tow

TOWIES ▸ towie

TOWIEST ▸ tow

TOWING ▸ tow

TOWINGS ▸ tow

TOWKAY n sir

TOWKAYS ▸ towkay

TOWLINE same as ▸ towrope

TOWMON same as ▸ towmond

TOWMOND n old word for year

TOWMONS ▸ towmon

TOWMONT same as ▸ towmond

TOWN n group of buildings larger than a village

TOWNEE same as ▸ townie

TOWNEES ▸ townee

TOWNIE n often disparaging term for a resident in a town, esp as distinct from country dwellers

TOWNIER ▸ towny

TOWNIES ▸ towny

TOWNISH ▸ town

TOWNLET n small town

TOWNLY adj characteristic of a town

TOWNS ▸ town

TOWNY adj characteristic of a town

TOWPATH n path beside a canal or river, originally for horses towing boats

TOWROPE n rope or cable used for towing a vehicle or vessel

TOWS ▸ tow

TOWSACK n sack made from tow

TOWSE same as ▸ touse

TOWSED ▸ towse

TOWSER ▸ towse

TOWSERS ▸ towse

TOWSES ▸ towse

TOWSIER ▸ towsy

TOWSING ▸ towse

TOWSY same as ▸ tousy

TOWT vb sulk

TOWTED ▸ towt

TOWTING ▸ towt

TOWTS ▸ towt

TOWY ▸ tow

TOWZE same as ▸ touse

TOWZED ▸ towze

TOWZES ▸ towze
TOWZIER ▸ towzy
TOWZING ▸ towze
TOWZY same as ▸ tousy
TOXEMIA same as > toxaemia
TOXEMIC > toxaemia
TOXIC adj poisonous ▷ n toxic substance
TOXICAL adj toxic
TOXICS ▸ toxic
TOXIN n poison of bacterial origin
TOXINE nonstandard variant spelling of ▸ toxin
TOXINES ▸ toxine
TOXINS ▸ toxin
TOXOID n toxin that has been treated to reduce its toxicity and is used in immunization to stimulate production of antitoxins
TOXOIDS ▸ toxoid
TOY n something designed to be played with ▷ adj designed to be played with ▷ vb play, fiddle, or flirt
TOYED ▸ toy
TOYER ▸ toy
TOYERS ▸ toy
TOYETIC adj (of a film or television franchise) able to generate revenue via spin-off toy products
TOYING ▸ toy
TOYINGS ▸ toy
TOYISH adj resembling a toy
TOYLESS ▸ toy
TOYLIKE ▸ toy
TOYLSOM old spelling of > toilsome
TOYMAN n man who sells toys
TOYMEN ▸ toyman
TOYO n Japanese straw-like material made out of rice paper and used to make hats
TOYON n shrub related to the rose
TOYONS ▸ toyon
TOYOS ▸ toyo
TOYS ▸ toy
TOYSHOP n shop selling toys
TOYSOME adj playful
TOYTOWN adj having an unreal and picturesque appearance
TOZE vb tease out; (of wool, etc) card
TOZED ▸ toze
TOZES ▸ toze

TOZIE n type of shawl
TOZIES ▸ tozie
TOZING ▸ toze
TRABS pl n training shoes
TRACE vb locate or work out (the cause of something) ▷ n track left by something
TRACED ▸ trace
TRACER n projectile which leaves a visible trail
TRACERS ▸ tracer
TRACERY n pattern of interlacing lines
TRACES ▸ trace
TRACEUR n parkour participant
TRACHEA n windpipe
TRACHLE vb (of hair, clothing, etc) make untidy; dishevel; rumple
TRACING n traced copy
TRACK n rough road or path ▷ vb follow the trail or path of
TRACKED ▸ track
TRACKER ▸ track
TRACKS ▸ track
TRACT n wide area ▷ vb track
TRACTED ▸ tract
TRACTOR n motor vehicle with large rear wheels for pulling farm machinery
TRACTS ▸ tract
TRACTUS n anthem sung in some RC masses
TRAD n traditional jazz, as revived in the 1950s
TRADE n buying, selling, or exchange of goods ▷ vb buy and sell ▷ adj intended for or available only to people in industry or business
TRADED ▸ trade
TRADER n person who engages in trade
TRADERS ▸ trader
TRADES ▸ trade
TRADING ▸ trade
TRADS ▸ trad
TRADUCE vb slander
TRAFFIC n vehicles coming and going on a road ▷ vb trade, usu illicitly
TRAGAL ▸ tragus
TRAGEDY n shocking or sad event
TRAGI ▸ tragus
TRAGIC adj of or like a tragedy ▷ n tragedian
TRAGICS ▸ tragic
TRAGULE n mouse deer
TRAGUS n cartilaginous

fleshy projection that partially covers the entrance to the external ear
TRAIK vb trudge; trek with difficulty
TRAIKED ▸ traik
TRAIKIT ▸ traik
TRAIKS ▸ traik
TRAIL n path, track, or road ▷ vb drag along the ground
TRAILED ▸ trail
TRAILER n vehicle designed to be towed by another vehicle ▷ vb use a trailer to advertise (something)
TRAILS ▸ trail
TRAIN vb instruct in a skill ▷ n line of railway coaches or wagons drawn by an engine
TRAINED ▸ train
TRAINEE n person being trained ▷ adj (of a person) undergoing training
TRAINER n person who trains an athlete or sportsman
TRAINS ▸ train
TRAIPSE vb walk wearily ▷ n long or tiring walk
TRAIT n characteristic feature
TRAITOR n person guilty of treason or treachery
TRAITS ▸ trait
TRAJECT vb transport or transmit
TRAM same as ▸ trammel
TRAMCAR same as ▸ tram
TRAMEL variant spelling of ▸ trammel
TRAMELL variant spelling of ▸ trammel
TRAMELS ▸ tramel
TRAMMED ▸ tram
TRAMMEL n hindrance to free action or movement ▷ vb hinder or restrain
TRAMMIE n conductor or driver of a tram
TRAMP vb travel on foot, hike ▷ n homeless person who travels on foot
TRAMPED ▸ tramp
TRAMPER n person who tramps
TRAMPET variant spelling of > trampette
TRAMPLE vb tread on and crush ▷ n action or sound of trampling
TRAMPS ▸ tramp
TRAMPY adj (of woman)

T

disreputable
TRAMS ▶tram
TRAMWAY *same as*
> **tramline**
TRANCE *n* unconscious or dazed state ▷ *vb* put into or as into a trance
TRANCED ▶trance
TRANCES ▶trance
TRANCEY *adj* (of music) characteristic of the trance sub-genre
TRANCHE *n* portion of something large, esp a sum of money
TRANECT *n* ferry
TRANGAM *n* bauble or trinket
TRANGLE *n* (in heraldry) a small fesse
TRANK *n* short form of tranquillizer: drug that calms a person
TRANKS ▶trank
TRANKUM *same as*
▶**trangam**
TRANNIE *n* transistor radio
TRANNY *same as* ▶**trannie**
TRANQ *same as* ▶**trank**

> Short for tranquilliser; another of those useful words allowing you to play the Q without a U.

TRANQS ▶tranq
TRANS *n* short from of translation
TRANSE *n* way through; passage
TRANSES ▶transe
TRANSIT *n* passage or conveyance of goods or people ▷ *vb* make transit
TRANSOM *n* horizontal bar across a window
TRANT *vb* travel from place to place selling goods
TRANTED ▶trant
TRANTER ▶trant
TRANTS ▶trant
TRAP *n* device for catching animals ▷ *vb* catch
TRAPAN *same as* ▶**trepan**
TRAPANS ▶trapan
TRAPE *same as* ▶**traipse**
TRAPED ▶trape
TRAPES *same as* ▶**traipse**
TRAPEZE *n* horizontal bar suspended from two ropes, used by circus acrobats ▷ *vb* swing on a trapeze
TRAPING ▶trape
TRAPPED ▶trap
TRAPPER *n* person who

traps animals for their fur
TRAPPY *adj* having many traps
TRAPS ▶trap
TRAPT *old past participle of*
▶**trap**
TRASH *n* anything worthless ▷ *vb* attack or destroy maliciously
TRASHED *adj* drunk
TRASHER ▶trash
TRASHES ▶trash
TRASHY *adj* cheap, worthless, or badly made
TRASS *n* variety of the volcanic rock tuff, used to make a hydraulic cement
TRASSES ▶trass
TRAT *n* type of fishing line holding a series of baited hooks
TRATS ▶trat
TRATT *short for* > **trattoria**
TRATTS ▶tratt
TRAUMA *n* emotional shock
TRAUMAS ▶trauma
TRAVAIL *n* labour or toil ▷ *vb* suffer or labour painfully, esp in childbirth
TRAVE *n* stout wooden cage in which difficult horses are shod
TRAVEL *vb* go from one place to another, through an area, or for a specified distance ▷ *n* travelling, esp as a tourist
TRAVELS ▶travel
TRAVES ▶trave
TRAVIS *same as* ▶**treviss**
TRAVOIS *n* sled used for dragging logs
TRAWL *n* net dragged at deep levels behind a fishing boat ▷ *vb* fish with such a net
TRAWLED ▶trawl
TRAWLER *n* trawling boat
TRAWLEY *same as* ▶**trolley**
TRAWLS ▶trawl
TRAY *n* flat board, usu with a rim, for carrying things
TRAYBIT *n* threepenny bit
TRAYFUL *n* as many or as much as will fit on a tray
TRAYNE *old spelling of*
▶**train**
TRAYNED ▶train
TRAYNES ▶trayne
TRAYS ▶tray
TREACLE *n* thick dark syrup produced when sugar is

refined ▷ *vb* add treacle to
TREACLY ▶treacle
TREAD *vb* set one's foot on ▷ *n* way of walking or dancing
TREADED ▶tread
TREADER ▶tread
TREADLE *n* lever worked by the foot to turn a wheel ▷ *vb* work (a machine) with a treadle
TREADS ▶tread
TREAGUE *n* agreement to stop fighting
TREASON *n* betrayal of one's sovereign or country
TREAT *vb* deal with or regard in a certain manner ▷ *n* pleasure, entertainment, etc given or paid for by someone else
TREATED ▶treat
TREATER ▶treat
TREATS ▶treat
TREATY *n* signed contract between states
TREBLE *adj* triple ▷ *n* (singer with or part for) a soprano voice ▷ *vb* increase three times
TREBLED ▶treble
TREBLES ▶treble
TREBLY ▶treble
TRECK *same as* ▶**trek**
TRECKED ▶treck
TRECKS ▶treck
TREDDLE *variant spelling of*
▶**treadle**
TREE *n* large perennial plant with a woody trunk
TREED ▶tree
TREEING ▶tree
TREEN *adj* made of wood ▷ *n* art of making treenware
TREENS ▶treen
TREES ▶tree
TREETOP *n* top of a tree
TREEWAX *n* yellowish wax secreted by an oriental scale insect
TREF *adj* in Judaism, ritually unfit to be eaten
TREFA *same as* ▶**tref**
TREFAH *same as* ▶**tref**
TREFOIL *n* plant, such as clover, with a three-lobed leaf
TREHALA *n* edible sugary substance obtained from the pupal cocoon of an Asian weevil
TREIF *same as* ▶**tref**

TREIFA same as ▸ **tref**
TREILLE another word for ▸ **trellis**
TREK n long difficult journey, esp on foot ▷ vb make such a journey
TREKKED ▸ **trek**
TREKKER ▸ **trek**
TREKS ▸ **trek**
TRELLIS n framework of horizontal and vertical strips of wood ▷ vb interweave (strips of wood, etc) to make a trellis
TREMA n mark consisting of two dots placed over the second of two adjacent vowels to indicate it is to be pronounced separately rather than forming a diphthong with the first
TREMAS ▸ **trema**
TREMBLE vb shake or quiver ▷ n trembling
TREMBLY ▸ **tremble**
TREMIE n large metal hopper and pipe used to distribute freshly mixed concrete over an underwater site.
TREMIES ▸ **tremie**
TREMOLO n quivering effect in singing or playing
TREMOR n involuntary shaking ▷ vb tremble
TREMORS ▸ **tremor**
TRENAIL same as ▸ **treenail**
TRENCH n long narrow ditch, esp one used as a shelter in war ▷ adj of or involving military trenches ▷ vb make a trench in (a place)
TREND n general tendency or direction ▷ vb take a certain trend
TRENDED ▸ **trend**
TRENDS ▸ **trend**
TRENDY n consciously fashionable (person) ▷ adj consciously fashionable
TRENISE n one of the figures in a quadrille
TRENTAL n mass said in remembrance of a person 30 days after his or her death
TREPAN same as > **trephine**
TREPANG n any of various large sea cucumbers of tropical Oriental seas, the body walls of which are used as food by the

Japanese and Chinese
TREPANS ▸ **trepan**
TREPID adj trembling
TRES adj very
TRESS n lock of hair, esp a long lock of woman's hair ▷ vb arrange in tresses
TRESSED adj having a tress or tresses as specified
TRESSEL variant spelling of ▸ **trestle**
TRESSES ▸ **tress**
TRESSY ▸ **tress**
TREST old variant of ▸ **trestle**
TRESTLE n board fixed on pairs of spreading legs, used as a support
TRESTS ▸ **trest**
TRET n (formerly) an allowance according to weight granted to purchasers for waste due to transportation
TRETS ▸ **tret**
TREVET same as ▸ **trivet**
TREVETS ▸ **trevet**
TREVIS variant spelling of ▸ **treviss**
TREVISS n partition in a stable for keeping animals apart
TREW old variant spelling of ▸ **true**
TREWS pl n close-fitting tartan trousers
TREY n any card or dice throw with three spots
TREYBIT same as ▸ **traybit**
TREYS ▸ **trey**
TREZ same as ▸ **trey**
TREZES ▸ **trez**
TRIABLE adj liable to be tried judicially
TRIAC n device for regulating the amount of electric current allowed to reach a circuit
TRIACID adj (of a base) capable of reacting with three molecules of a monobasic acid
TRIACS ▸ **triac**
TRIACT adj having three rays
TRIAD n group of three
TRIADIC n something that has the characteristics of a triad
TRIADS ▸ **triad**
TRIAGE n (in a hospital) the principle or practice of sorting emergency patients

into categories of priority for treatment ▷ vb sort (patients) into categories of priority for treatment
TRIAGED ▸ **triage**
TRIAGES ▸ **triage**
TRIAL n investigation of a case before a judge
TRIALS ▸ **trial**
TRIARCH n one of three rulers of a triarchy
TRIATIC n rope between a ship's mastheads
TRIAXON another name for > **triaxial**
TRIAZIN same as ▸ **triazine**
TRIBADE n lesbian, esp one who practises tribadism
TRIBADY another word for > **tribadism**
TRIBAL adj of or denoting a tribe or tribes ▷ n member of a tribal community
TRIBALS > **tribal** n
TRIBBLE n frame for drying paper
TRIBE n group of clans or families believed to have a common ancestor
TRIBES ▸ **tribe**
TRIBLET n spindle or mandrel used in making rings, tubes, etc
TRIBUNE n people's representative, esp in ancient Rome
TRIBUTE n sign of respect or admiration
TRICAR n car with three wheels
TRICARS ▸ **tricar**
TRICE n moment ▷ vb haul up or secure
TRICED ▸ **trice**
TRICEP same as ▸ **triceps**
TRICEPS n muscle at the back of the upper arm
TRICES ▸ **trice**
TRICING ▸ **trice**
TRICK n deceitful or cunning action or plan ▷ vb cheat or deceive
TRICKED ▸ **trick**
TRICKER ▸ **trick**
TRICKIE Scots form of ▸ **tricky**
TRICKLE vb (cause to) flow in a thin stream or drops ▷ n gradual flow
TRICKLY ▸ **trickle**
TRICKS ▸ **trick**
TRICKSY adj playing tricks habitually

T

TRICKY adj difficult, needing careful handling

TRICLAD n type of worm having a tripartite intestine

TRICORN n cocked hat with opposing brims turned back and caught in three places ▷ adj having three horns or corners

TRICOT n thin rayon or nylon fabric knitted or resembling knitting, used for dresses, etc

TRICOTS ▶ **tricot**

TRIDARN n sideboard with three levels

TRIDE old spelling of the past tense of ▶ **try**

TRIDENT n three-pronged spear ▷ adj having three prongs

TRIDUAN adj three days long

TRIDUUM n period of three days for prayer before a feast

TRIE old spelling of ▶ **try**

TRIED ▶ **try**

TRIELLA n three nominated horse races in which the punter bets on selecting the three winners

TRIENE n chemical compound containing three double bonds

TRIENES ▶ **triene**

TRIENS n Byzantine gold goin worth one third of a solidus

TRIER n person or thing that tries

TRIERS ▶ **trier**

TRIES ▶ **try**

TRIFF adj terrific; very good indeed

TRIFFER ▶ **triff**

TRIFFIC adj terrific; very good indeed

TRIFFID n any of a species of fictional plants that supposedly grew to a gigantic size, were capable of moving about, and could kill humans

TRIFID adj divided or split into three parts or lobes

TRIFLE n insignificant thing or amount ▷ vb deal (with) as if worthless

TRIFLED ▶ **trifle**

TRIFLER ▶ **trifle**

TRIFLES ▶ **trifle**

TRIFOLD less common word

for ▶ **triple**

TRIFOLY same as ▶ **trefoil**

TRIFORM adj having three parts

TRIG adj neat or spruce ▷ vb make or become spruce

TRIGAMY n condition of having three spouses

TRIGGED ▶ **trig**

TRIGGER n small lever releasing a catch on a gun or machine ▷ vb set (an action or process) in motion

TRIGLOT n person who can speak three languages

TRIGLY ▶ **trig**

TRIGO n wheat field

TRIGON n (in classical Greece or Rome) a triangular harp or lyre

TRIGONS ▶ **trigon**

TRIGOS ▶ **trigo**

TRIGRAM n three-letter inscription

TRIGS ▶ **trig**

TRIJET n jet with three engines

TRIJETS ▶ **trijet**

TRIKE n tricycle

TRIKES ▶ **trike**

TRILBY n man's soft felt hat

TRILBYS ▶ **trilby**

TRILD old past tense of ▶ **trill**

TRILITH same as > **trilithon**

TRILL n rapid alternation between two notes ▷ vb play or sing a trill

TRILLED ▶ **trill**

TRILLER ▶ **trill**

TRILLO n (in music) a trill

TRILLS ▶ **trill**

TRILOBE n three-lobed thing

TRILOGY n series of three related books, plays, etc

TRIM adj neat and smart ▷ vb cut or prune into good shape ▷ n decoration

TRIMER n polymer or a molecule of a polymer consisting of three identical monomers

TRIMERS ▶ **trimer**

TRIMIX n gas mixture of nitrogen, helium and oxygen used by deep-sea divers

TRIMLY ▶ **trim**

TRIMMED ▶ **trim**

TRIMMER ▶ **trim**

TRIMS ▶ **trim**

TRIMTAB n small control surface attached to the

trailing edge of a main control surface to enable the pilot to balance an aircraft

TRIN n triplet

TRINAL ▶ **trine**

TRINARY adj made up of three parts

TRINDLE vb move heavily on (or as if on) wheels

TRINE n aspect of 120° between two planets, an orb of 8° being allowed ▷ adj of or relating to a trine ▷ vb put in a trine aspect

TRINED ▶ **trine**

TRINES ▶ **trine**

TRINGLE n slim rod

TRINING ▶ **trine**

TRINITY n group of three

TRINKET n small or worthless ornament or piece of jewellery ▷ vb ornament with trinkets

TRINKUM n trinket or bauble

TRINS ▶ **trin**

TRIO n group of three

TRIODE n electronic valve having three electrodes, a cathode, an anode, and a grid

TRIODES ▶ **triode**

TRIOL n any of a class of alcohols that have three hydroxyl groups per molecule

TRIOLET n verse form of eight lines

TRIOLS ▶ **triol**

TRIONES n seven stars of the constellation Ursa Major

TRIONYM another name for > **trinomial**

TRIOR old form of ▶ **trier**

TRIORS ▶ **trior**

TRIOS ▶ **trio**

TRIOSE n simple monosaccharide produced by the oxidation of glycerol

TRIOSES ▶ **triose**

TRIOXID same as > **trioxide**

TRIP n journey to a place and back, esp for pleasure ▷ vb (cause to) stumble

TRIPACK n pack of three

TRIPART adj composed of three parts

TRIPE n stomach of a cow used as food

TRIPERY n place where tripe is prepared

TRIPES ▶ **tripe**

TRIPEY ▶ **tripe**

TRIPIER ▶ **tripe**

TRIPLE adj having three parts ▷ vb increase three times ▷ n something that is, or contains, three times as much as normal

TRIPLED ▶ **triple**

TRIPLES ▶ **triple**

TRIPLET n one of three babies born at one birth

TRIPLEX n building divided into three separate dwellings

TRIPLY vb give a reply to a duply

TRIPOD n three-legged stand, stool, etc

TRIPODS ▶ **tripod**

TRIPODY n metrical unit consisting of three feet

TRIPOLI n lightweight porous siliceous rock derived by weathering and used in a powdered form as a polish, filter, etc

TRIPOS n final examinations for an honours degree at Cambridge University

TRIPPED ▶ **trip**

TRIPPER n tourist

TRIPPET n any mechanism that strikes or is struck at regular intervals, as by a cam

TRIPPLE vb canter

TRIPPY adj suggestive of or resembling the effect produced by a hallucinogenic drug

TRIPS ▶ **trip**

TRIPSES ▶ **tripsis**

TRIPSIS n act of kneading the body to promote circulation, suppleness, etc

TRIPTAN n drug used to treat migraine

TRIPY ▶ **tripe**

TRIREME n ancient Greek warship with three rows of oars on each side

TRISECT vb divide into three parts, esp three equal parts

TRISEME n metrical foot of a length equal to three short syllables

TRISHAW another name for > **rickshaw**

TRISMIC ▶ **trismus**

TRISMUS n state of being unable to open the mouth

because of sustained contractions of the jaw muscles, caused by tetanus

TRISOME n chromosome occurring three times (rather than twice) in a cell

TRISOMY n condition of having one chromosome of the set represented three times in an otherwise diploid organism, cell, etc

TRIST variant spelling of ▶ **triste**

TRISTE adj sad

TRISUL n trident symbol of Siva

TRISULA same as ▶ **trisul**

TRISULS ▶ **trisul**

TRITE adj (of a remark or idea) commonplace and unoriginal ▷ n (on a lyre) the third string from the highest in pitch

TRITELY ▶ **trite**

TRITER ▶ **trite**

TRITES ▶ **trite**

TRITEST ▶ **trite**

TRITIDE n tritium compound

TRITIUM n radioactive isotope of hydrogen

TRITOMA another name for > **kniphofia**

TRITON n any of various chiefly tropical marine gastropod molluscs, having large beautifully-coloured spiral shells

TRITONE n musical interval consisting of three whole tones

TRITONS ▶ **triton**

TRIUMPH n (happiness caused by) victory or success ▷ vb be victorious or successful

TRIUNE adj constituting three in one, esp the three persons in one God of the Trinity ▷ n group of three

TRIUNES ▶ **triune**

TRIVET n metal stand for a pot or kettle

TRIVETS ▶ **trivet**

TRIVIA pl n trivial things or details

TRIVIAL adj of little importance

TRIVIUM n (in medieval learning) the lower division of the seven liberal arts, consisting of grammar, rhetoric, and logic

TRIZONE n area comprising three zones

TROAD same as ▶ **trod**

TROADE same as ▶ **trod**

TROADES ▶ **troade**

TROADS ▶ **troad**

TROAK old form of ▶ **truck**

TROAKED ▶ **troak**

TROAKS ▶ **troak**

TROAT vb (of a rutting buck) to call or bellow

TROATED ▶ **troat**

TROATS ▶ **troat**

TROCAR n surgical instrument for removing fluid from bodily cavities, consisting of a puncturing device situated inside a tube

TROCARS ▶ **trocar**

TROCHAL adj shaped like a wheel

TROCHAR old variant spelling of ▶ **trocar**

TROCHE another name for ▶ **lozenge**

TROCHEE n metrical foot of one long and one short syllable

TROCHES ▶ **troche**

TROCHI ▶ **trochus**

TROCHIL same as > **trochilus**

TROCHUS n hoop (used in exercise)

TROCK same as ▶ **truck**

TROCKED ▶ **trock**

TROCKEN adj dry (used of wine, esp German wine)

TROCKS ▶ **trock**

TROD vb past participle of tread ▷ n path

TRODDEN ▶ **tread**

TRODE same as ▶ **trod**

TRODES ▶ **trode**

TRODS ▶ **trod**

TROELIE same as ▶ **troolie**

TROELY same as ▶ **troolie**

TROFFER n trough-like fixture for holding in place and reflecting light from a fluorescent tube

TROG vb walk, esp aimlessly or heavily

TROGGED ▶ **trog**

TROGGS n loyalty; fidelity

TROGON n bird of tropical and subtropical regions of America, Africa, and Asia. They have a brilliant plumage, short hooked bill, and long tail

TROGONS ▶ **trogon**

TROGS ▸ trog

TROIKA n Russian vehicle drawn by three horses abreast

TROIKAS ▸ troika

TROILUS n type of large butterfly

TROIS Scots form of ▸ troy

TROKE same as ▸ truck

TROKED ▸ troke

TROKES ▸ troke

TROKING ▸ troke

TROLAND n unit of light intensity in the eye

TROLL n giant or dwarf in Scandinavian folklore ▷ vb fish by dragging a lure through the water

TROLLED ▸ troll

TROLLER ▸ troll

TROLLEY n small wheeled table for food and drink ▷ vb transport on a trolley

TROLLS ▸ troll

TROLLY same as ▸ trolley

TROMINO n shape made from three squares, each joined to the next along one full side

TROMMEL n revolving cylindrical sieve used to screen crushed ore

TROMP vb trample

TROMPE n apparatus for supplying the blast of air in a forge, consisting of a thin column down which water falls, drawing in air through side openings

TROMPED ▸ tromp

TROMPES ▸ trompe

TROMPS ▸ tromp

TRON n public weighing machine

TRONA n greyish mineral that consists of hydrated sodium carbonate and occurs in salt deposits

TRONAS ▸ trona

TRONC n pool into which waiters, waitresses, hotel workers, etc, pay their tips

TRONCS ▸ tronc

TRONE same as ▸ tron

TRONES ▸ trone

TRONK n jail

TRONKS ▸ tronk

TRONS ▸ tron

TROOLIE n large palm leaf

TROOP n large group ▷ vb move in a crowd

TROOPED ▸ troop

TROOPER n cavalry soldier

TROOPS ▸ troop

TROOZ same as ▸ trews

TROP adv too, too much

TROPE n figure of speech ▷ vb use tropes (in speech or writing)

TROPED ▸ trope

TROPES ▸ trope

TROPHI pl n collective term for the mandibles and other parts of an insect's mouth

TROPHIC adj of or relating to nutrition

TROPHY n cup, shield, etc given as a prize ▷ adj regarded as a highly desirable symbol of wealth or success ▷ vb award a trophy to (someone)

TROPIC n either of two lines of latitude at $23\frac{1}{2}$°N (tropic of Cancer) or $23\frac{1}{2}$°S (tropic of Capricorn)

TROPICS ▸ tropic

TROPIN n andrenal androgen

TROPINE n white crystalline poisonous hygroscopic alkaloid obtained by heating atropine or hyoscyamine with barium hydroxide

TROPING ▸ trope

TROPINS ▸ tropin

TROPISM n tendency of a plant or animal to turn or curve in response to an external stimulus

TROPIST ▸ tropism

TROPPO adv too much ▷ adj mentally affected by a tropical climate

TROT vb (of a horse) move at a medium pace, lifting the feet in diagonal pairs ▷ n trotting

TROTH n pledge of devotion, esp a betrothal ▷ vb promise to marry (someone)

TROTHED ▸ troth

TROTHS ▸ troth

TROTS ▸ trot

TROTTED ▸ trot

TROTTER n pig's foot

TROTYL n trinitrotoluene; a yellow solid: used chiefly as a high explosive and is also an intermediate in the manufacture of dyestuffs

TROTYLS ▸ trotyl

TROUBLE n (cause of) distress or anxiety ▷ vb

(cause to) worry

TROUCH n rubbish

TROUGH n long open container, esp for animals' food or water ▷ vb eat, consume, or take greedily

TROUGHS ▸ trough

TROULE old variant of ▸ troll

TROULED ▸ troule

TROULES ▸ troule

TROUNCE vb defeat utterly

TROUPE n company of performers ▷ vb (esp of actors) to move or travel in a group

TROUPED ▸ troupe

TROUPER n member of a troupe

TROUPES ▸ troupe

TROUSE pl n close-fitting breeches worn in Ireland

TROUSER adj of trousers ▷ vb take (something, esp money), often surreptitiously or unlawfully ▷ n of or relating to trousers

TROUSES ▸ trouse

TROUT n game fish related to the salmon ▷ vb fish for trout

TROUTER ▸ trout

TROUTS ▸ trout

TROUTY ▸ trout

TROVE n as in treasure-trove valuable articles, such as coins, bullion, etc, found hidden in the earth or elsewhere and of unknown ownership

TROVER n (formerly) the act of wrongfully assuming proprietary rights over personal goods or property belonging to another

TROVERS ▸ trover

TROVES ▸ trove

TROW vb think, believe, or trust

TROWED ▸ trow

TROWEL n hand tool with a wide blade for spreading mortar, lifting plants, etc ▷ vb use a trowel on (plaster, soil, etc)

TROWELS ▸ trowel

TROWING ▸ trow

TROWS ▸ trow

TROWTH variant spelling of ▸ troth

TROWTHS ▸ trowth

TROY n as in troy weight system of weights used for

precious metals and gemstones, based on the grain, which is identical to the avoirdupois grain

TROYS ▸ troy

TRUANCY ▸ truant

TRUANT n pupil who stays away from school without permission ▷ adj being or relating to a truant ▷ vb play truant

TRUANTS ▸ truant

TRUCAGE n art forgery

TRUCE n temporary agreement to stop fighting ▷ vb make a truce

TRUCED ▸ truce

TRUCES ▸ truce

TRUCIAL ▸ truce

TRUCING ▸ truce

TRUCK n railway goods wagon ▷ vb exchange (goods); barter

TRUCKED ▸ truck

TRUCKER n truck driver

TRUCKIE n truck driver

TRUCKLE vb yield weakly or give in ▷ n small wheel

TRUCKS ▸ truck

TRUDGE vb walk heavily or wearily ▷ n long tiring walk

TRUDGED ▸ trudge

TRUDGEN n type of swimming stroke that uses overarm action, as in the crawl, and a scissors kick

TRUDGER ▸ trudge

TRUDGES ▸ trudge

TRUE adj in accordance with facts

TRUED ▸ true

TRUEING ▸ true

TRUEMAN n honest person

TRUEMEN ▸ trueman

TRUER ▸ true

TRUES ▸ true

TRUEST ▸ true

TRUFFE rare word for ▸ truffle

TRUFFES ▸ truffe

TRUFFLE n edible underground fungus ▷ vb hunt for truffles

TRUG n long shallow basket used by gardeners

TRUGO n game similar to croquet, originally improvised in Victoria from the rubber discs used as buffers on railway carriages

TRUGOS ▸ trugo

TRUGS ▸ trug

TRUING ▸ true

TRUISM n self-evident truth

TRUISMS ▸ truism

TRULL n prostitute

TRULLS ▸ trull

TRULY adv in a true manner

TRUMEAU n section of a wall or pillar between two openings

TRUMP adj (card) of the suit outranking the others ▷ vb play a trump card on (another card) ▷ pl n suit outranking the others

TRUMPED ▸ trump

TRUMPET n valved brass instrument with a flared tube ▷ vb proclaim loudly

TRUMPS ▸ trump

TRUNCAL adj of or relating to the trunk

TRUNDLE vb move heavily on wheels ▷ n act or an instance of trundling

TRUNK n main stem of a tree ▷ vb lop or truncate

TRUNKED ▸ trunk

TRUNKS pl n shorts worn by a man for swimming

TRUNNEL same as > treenail

TRUSS vb tie or bind up ▷ n device for holding a hernia, etc in place

TRUSSED ▸ truss

TRUSSER ▸ truss

TRUSSES ▸ truss

TRUST vb believe in and rely on ▷ n confidence in the truth, reliability, etc of a person or thing ▷ adj of or relating to a trust or trusts

TRUSTED ▸ trust

TRUSTEE n person holding property on another's behalf ▷ vb act as a trustee

TRUSTER ▸ trust

TRUSTOR n person who sets up a trust

TRUSTS ▸ trust

TRUSTY adj faithful or reliable ▷ n trustworthy convict to whom special privileges are granted

TRUTH n state of being true

TRUTHS ▸ truth

TRUTHY adj truthful

TRY vb make an effort or attempt ▷ n attempt or effort

TRYE adj very good; select

TRYER same as ▸ trier

TRYERS ▸ tryer

TRYING ▸ try

TRYINGS ▸ try

TRYKE variant spelling of ▸ trike

TRYKES ▸ tryke

TRYMA n drupe produced by the walnut and similar plants, in which the endocarp is a hard shell and the epicarp is dehiscent

TRYMATA ▸ tryma

TRYOUT n a trial or test, as of an athlete or actor

TRYOUTS ▸ tryout

TRYP n parastitic protozoan

TRYPAN modifier as in **trypan blue** dye obtained from tolidine that is absorbed by the macrophages of the reticuloendothelial system and is therefore used for staining cells in biological research

TRYPS ▸ tryp

TRYPSIN n enzyme occurring in pancreatic juice

TRYPTIC ▸ trypsin

TRYSAIL n small fore-and-aft sail set on a sailing vessel to help keep her head to the wind in a storm

TRYST n arrangement to meet ▷ vb meet at or arrange a tryst

TRYSTE variant spelling of ▸ tryst

TRYSTED ▸ tryst

TRYSTER ▸ tryst

TRYSTES ▸ tryste

TRYSTS ▸ tryst

TSADDIK same as ▸ zaddik

TSADDIQ same as ▸ zaddik

TSADE variant spelling of ▸ sadhe

TSADES ▸ tsade

TSADI same as ▸ sadhe

TSADIS ▸ tsadi

TSAMBA n Tibetan dish made from roasted barley and tea

TSAMBAS ▸ tsamba

TSANTSA n (among the Shuar subgroup of the Jivaro people of Ecuador) shrunken head of an enemy kept as a trophy

TSAR n Russian emperor

TSARDOM ▸ tsar

TSARINA n wife of a Russian tsar

TSARISM n system of

government by a tsar, esp in Russia until 1917

TSARIST ▶ **tsarism**

TSARS ▶ **tsar**

TSATSKE same as > tchotchke

TSETSE n any of various bloodsucking African dipterous flies which transmit the pathogens of various diseases

TSETSES ▶ **tsetse**

TSIGANE same as ▶ **tzigane**

TSIMMES variant spelling of ▶ **tzimmes**

TSK vb utter the sound "tsk", usu in disapproval

This can occasionally be useful because it enables you to play K without using vowels.

TSKED ▶ **tsk**

TSKING ▶ **tsk**

TSKS ▶ **tsk**

TSKTSK same as ▶ **tsk**

TSKTSKS ▶ **tsktsk**

TSOORIS same as ▶ **tsuris**

TSORES same as ▶ **tsuris**

TSORIS same as ▶ **tsuris**

TSOTSI n Black street thug or gang member

TSOTSIS ▶ **tsotsi**

TSOURIS same as ▶ **tsuris**

TSUBA n sword guard of a Japanese sword

TSUBAS ▶ **tsuba**

TSUNAMI n tidal wave, usu caused by an earthquake under the sea

TSURIS n grief or strife

TUAN n lord

TUANS ▶ **tuan**

TUART n eucalyptus tree of Australia, yielding a very durable light-coloured timber

TUARTS ▶ **tuart**

TUATARA n large lizard-like New Zealand reptile

TUATERA variant spelling of ▶ **tuatara**

TUATH n territory of an ancient Irish tribe

TUATHS ▶ **tuath**

TUATUA n edible marine bivalve of New Zealand waters

TUATUAS ▶ **tuatua**

TUB n open, usu round container ▷ vb wash (oneself or another) in a tub

TUBA n valved low-pitched brass instrument

TUBAE ▶ **tuba**

TUBAGE n insertion of a tube

TUBAGES ▶ **tubage**

TUBAIST ▶ **tuba**

TUBAL adj of or relating to a tube

TUBAR another word for ▶ **tubular**

TUBAS ▶ **tuba**

TUBATE less common word for ▶ **tubular**

TUBBED ▶ **tube**

TUBBER ▶ **tub**

TUBBERS ▶ **tub**

TUBBIER ▶ **tubby**

TUBBING ▶ **tub**

TUBBISH adj fat

TUBBY adj (of a person) short and fat

TUBE n hollow cylinder

TUBED ▶ **tube**

TUBEFUL n quantity (of something) that a tube can hold

TUBER n fleshy underground root of a plant such as a potato

TUBERS ▶ **tuber**

TUBES ▶ **tube**

TUBFAST n period of fasting and sweating in a tub, intended as a cure for disease

TUBFISH another name for ▶ **gurnard**

TUBFUL n amount a tub will hold

TUBFULS ▶ **tubful**

TUBIFEX n type of small reddish freshwater worm

TUBING n length of tube

TUBINGS ▶ **tubing**

TUBIST ▶ **tuba**

TUBISTS ▶ **tuba**

TUBLIKE ▶ **tub**

TUBS ▶ **tub**

TUBULAR adj of or shaped like a tube

TUBULE n any small tubular structure, esp in an animal or plant

TUBULES ▶ **tubule**

TUBULIN n protein forming the basis of microtubules

TUCHUN n (formerly) a Chinese military governor or warlord

TUCHUNS ▶ **tuchun**

TUCK vb push or fold into a small space ▷ n stitched fold ▷ vb touch or strike

TUCKED ▶ **tuck**

TUCKER n food ▷ vb weary or tire completely

TUCKERS ▶ **tucker**

TUCKET n flourish on a trumpet

TUCKETS ▶ **tucket**

TUCKING ▶ **tuck**

TUCKS ▶ **tuck**

TUFA n porous rock formed as a deposit from springs

TUFAS ▶ **tufa**

TUFF n porous rock formed from volcanic dust or ash

TUFFE old form of ▶ **tuft**

TUFFES ▶ **tuffe**

TUFFET n small mound or seat

TUFFETS ▶ **tuffet**

TUFFS ▶ **tuff**

TUFOLI n type of tubular pasta

TUFT n bunch of feathers, grass, hair, etc held or growing together at the base ▷ vb provide or decorate with a tuft or tufts

TUFTED adj having a tuft or tufts

TUFTER ▶ **tuft**

TUFTERS ▶ **tuft**

TUFTIER ▶ **tuft**

TUFTILY ▶ **tuft**

TUFTING ▶ **tuft**

TUFTS ▶ **tuft**

TUFTY ▶ **tuft**

TUG vb pull hard ▷ n hard pull

TUGBOAT same as ▶ **tug**

TUGGED ▶ **tug**

TUGGER ▶ **tug**

TUGGERS ▶ **tug**

TUGGING ▶ **tug**

TUGHRA n Turkish Sultan's official emblem

TUGHRAS ▶ **tughra**

TUGHRIK same as ▶ **tugrik**

TUGLESS ▶ **tug**

TUGRA same as ▶ **tughra**

TUGRAS ▶ **tugra**

TUGRIK n standard monetary unit of Mongolia, divided into 100 möngös

TUGRIKS ▶ **tugrik**

TUGS ▶ **tug**

TUI n New Zealand honeyeater that mimics human speech and the songs of other birds

TUILLE n (in a suit of armour) hanging plate protecting the thighs

TUILLES ▶ **tuille**

TUILYIE vb fight

TUILZIE *variant form of* ▶ **tuilyie**

TUINA *n* form of massage originating in China

TUINAS ▶ **tuina**

TUIS ▶ **tui**

TUISM *n* practice of putting the interests of another before one's own

TUISMS ▶ **tuism**

TUITION *n* instruction, esp received individually or in a small group

TUKTOO *same as* ▶ **tuktu**

TUKTOOS ▶ **tuktoo**

TUKTU (*in Canada*) another name for ▶ **caribou**

TUKTUS ▶ **tuktu**

TULADI *n* large trout found in Canada and northern areas of the US

TULADIS ▶ **tuladi**

TULBAN *old form of* ▶ **turban**

TULBANS ▶ **tulban**

TULCHAN *n* skin of a calf placed next to a cow to induce it to give milk

TULE *n* type of bulrush found in California

TULES ▶ **tule**

TULIP *n* plant with bright cup-shaped flowers

TULIPS ▶ **tulip**

TULLE *n* fine net fabric of silk etc

TULLES ▶ **tulle**

TULPA *n* being or object created through willpower and visualization techniques

TULPAS ▶ **tulpa**

TULWAR *n* Indian sabre

TULWARS ▶ **tulwar**

TUM *informal or childish word for* ▶ **stomach**

TUMBLE *vb* (cause to) fall, esp awkwardly or violently ▷ *n* fall

TUMBLED ▶ **tumble**

TUMBLER *n* stemless drinking glass

TUMBLES ▶ **tumble**

TUMBREL *n* farm cart for carrying dung, esp one that tilts backwards to deposit its load

TUMBRIL *same as* ▶ **tumbrel**

TUMEFY *vb* make or become tumid

TUMESCE *vb* swell

TUMID *adj* (of an organ or part of the body) enlarged or swollen

TUMIDLY ▶ **tumid**

TUMMIES ▶ **tummy**

TUMMLER *n* comedian or other entertainer employed to encourage audience participation or to encourage guests at a resort to take part in communal activities

TUMMY *n* stomach

TUMOR *same as* ▶ **tumour**

TUMORAL ▶ **tumour**

TUMORS ▶ **tumor**

TUMOUR *n* abnormal growth in or on the body

TUMOURS ▶ **tumour**

TUMP *n* small mound or clump ▷ *vb* make a tump around

TUMPED ▶ **tump**

TUMPHY *n* dolt; fool

TUMPIER ▶ **tump**

TUMPING ▶ **tump**

TUMPS ▶ **tump**

TUMPY ▶ **tump**

TUMS ▶ **tum**

TUMSHIE *n* turnip

TUMULAR *adj* of, relating to, or like a mound

TUMULI ▶ **tumulus**

TUMULT *n* uproar or commotion ▷ *vb* stir up a commotion

TUMULTS ▶ **tumult**

TUMULUS *n* burial mound

TUN *n* large beer cask ▷ *vb* put into or keep in tuns

TUNA *n* large marine food fish

TUNABLE *adj* able to be tuned

TUNABLY ▶ **tunable**

TUNAS ▶ **tuna**

TUND *vb* beat; strike

TUNDED ▶ **tund**

TUNDING ▶ **tund**

TUNDISH *n* type of funnel

TUNDRA *n* vast treeless Arctic region with permanently frozen subsoil

TUNDRAS ▶ **tundra**

TUNDS ▶ **tund**

TUNDUN *n* wooden instrument used by Native Australians in religious rites

TUNDUNS ▶ **tundun**

TUNE *n* (pleasing) sequence of musical notes ▷ *vb* adjust (a musical instrument) so that it is in tune

TUNED ▶ **tune**

TUNEFUL *adj* having a pleasant tune

TUNER *n* part of a radio or television receiver for selecting channels

TUNERS ▶ **tuner**

TUNES ▶ **tune**

TUNEUP *n* adjustments made to an engine to improve its performance

TUNEUPS ▶ **tuneup**

TUNG *n as in* **tung oil** fast-drying oil obtained from the seeds of a central Asian euphorbiaceous tree, used in paints, varnishes, etc, as a drying agent and to give a water-resistant finish

TUNGS ▶ **tung**

TUNIC *n* close-fitting jacket forming part of some uniforms

TUNICA *n* tissue forming a layer or covering of an organ or part, such as any of the tissue layers of a blood vessel wall

TUNICAE ▶ **tunica**

TUNICIN *n* cellulose-like substance found in tunicates

TUNICLE *n* liturgical vestment worn by the subdeacon and bishops at High Mass and other religious ceremonies

TUNICS ▶ **tunic**

TUNIER ▶ **tuny**

TUNIEST ▶ **tuny**

TUNING *n* set of pitches to which the open strings of a guitar, violin, etc, are tuned

TUNINGS ▶ **tuning**

TUNNAGE *same as* ▶ **tonnage**

TUNNED ▶ **tun**

TUNNEL *n* underground passage ▷ *vb* make a tunnel (through)

TUNNELS ▶ **tunnel**

TUNNIES ▶ **tunny**

TUNNING ▶ **tun**

TUNNY *same as* ▶ **tuna**

TUNS ▶ **tun**

TUNY *adj* having an easily discernable melody

TUP *n* male sheep ▷ *vb* cause (a ram) to mate with a ewe, or (of a ram) to mate with (a ewe)

TUPEK *same as* ▶ **tupik**

TUPEKS ▶tupek
TUPELO n large tree of deep swamps and rivers of the southern US
TUPELOS ▶tupelo
TUPIK n tent of seal or caribou skin used for shelter by the Inuit in summer
TUPIKS ▶tupik
TUPLE n row of values in a relational database
TUPLES ▶tuple
TUPPED ▶tup
TUPPING ▶tup
TUPS ▶tup
TUPUNA same as ▶tipuna
TUPUNAS ▶tupuna
TUQUE n knitted cap with a long tapering end
TUQUES ▶tuque
TURACIN n red pigment found in touraco feathers
TURACO same as ▶touraco
TURACOS ▶turaco
TURACOU same as ▶touraco
TURBAN n Muslim, Hindu, or Sikh man's head covering, made by winding cloth round the head
TURBAND old variant of ▶turban
TURBANS ▶turban
TURBANT old variant of ▶turban
TURBARY n land where peat or turf is cut or has been cut
TURBETH same as ▶turpeth
TURBID adj muddy, not clear
TURBINE n machine or generator driven by gas, water, etc turning blades
TURBIT n crested breed of domestic pigeon
TURBITH same as ▶turpeth
TURBITS ▶turbit
TURBO n compressor in an engine
TURBOND old variant of ▶turban
TURBOS ▶turbo
TURBOT n large European edible flatfish
TURBOTS ▶turbot
TURDINE adj of, relating to, or characteristic of thrushes
TURDION same as ▶tordion

TURDOID same as ▶turdine
TUREEN n serving dish for soup
TUREENS ▶tureen
TURF n short thick even grass ▷vb cover with turf
TURFED ▶turf
TURFEN adj made of turf
TURFIER ▶turfy
TURFING ▶turf
TURFITE same as ▶turfman
TURFMAN n person devoted to horse racing
TURFMEN ▶turfman
TURFS ▶turf
TURFSKI n ski down a grassy hill on skis modified with integral wheels
TURFY adj of, covered with, or resembling turf
TURGENT obsolete word for ▶turgid
TURGID adj (of language) pompous
TURGITE n red or black mineral consisting of hydrated ferric oxide
TURGOR n normal rigid state of a cell, caused by pressure of the cell contents against the cell wall or membrane
TURGORS ▶turgor
TURION n perennating bud produced by many aquatic plants
TURIONS ▶turion
TURISTA n traveller's diarrhoea
TURKEY n large bird bred for food
TURKEYS ▶turkey
TURKIES old form of ▷turquoise
TURKIS old form of ▷turquoise
TURKOIS old form of ▷turquoise
TURM n troop of horsemen
TURME same as ▶turm
TURMES ▶turme
TURMOIL n agitation or confusion ▷vb make or become turbulent
TURMS ▶turm
TURN vb change the position or direction (of) ▷n turning
TURNDUN another name for ▶tundun
TURNED ▶turn
TURNER n person or thing that turns, esp a person

who operates a lathe
TURNERS ▶turner
TURNERY n objects made on a lathe
TURNING n road or path leading off a main route
TURNIP n root vegetable with orange or white flesh ▷vb sow (a field) with turnips
TURNIPS ▶turnip
TURNIPY adj like a turnip
TURNKEY n jailer ▷adj denoting a project, as in civil engineering, in which a single contractor has responsibility for the complete job from the start to the time of installation or occupancy
TURNOFF n road or other way branching off from the main
TURNON n something sexually exciting
TURNONS ▶turnon
TURNOUT n number of people appearing at a gathering
TURNS ▶turn
TURNUP n the turned-up fold at the bottom of some trouser legs
TURNUPS ▶turnup
TURPETH n convolvulaceous plant of the East Indies, having roots with purgative properties
TURPS n colourless, flammable liquid
TURRET n small tower
TURRETS ▶turret
TURTLE n sea tortoise
TURTLED ▶turtle
TURTLER ▶turtle
TURTLES ▶turtle
TURVES ▶turf
TUSCHE n substance used in lithography for drawing the design and as a resist in silk-screen printing and lithography
TUSCHES ▶tusche
TUSH interj exclamation of disapproval or contempt ▷n small tusk ▷vb utter the interjection "tush"
TUSHED ▶tush
TUSHERY n use of affectedly archaic language in novels, etc
TUSHES ▶tush

TUSHIE n pair of buttocks
TUSHIES ▶ tushie
TUSHING ▶ tush
TUSHKAR same as
▶ **tuskar**
TUSHKER same as ▶ **tuskar**
TUSHY same as ▶ **tushie**
TUSK n long pointed tooth of an elephant, walrus, etc ▷ vb stab, tear, or gore with the tusks
TUSKAR n peat-cutting spade
TUSKARS ▶ tuskar
TUSKED ▶ tusk
TUSKER n any animal with prominent tusks, esp a wild boar or elephant
TUSKERS ▶ tusker
TUSKIER ▶ tusk
TUSKING ▶ tusk
TUSKS ▶ tusk
TUSKY ▶ tusk
TUSSAC modifier as in **tussac grass** kind of grass
TUSSAH same as ▶ **tussore**
TUSSAHS ▶ tussah
TUSSAL ▶ tussis
TUSSAR same as ▶ **tussore**
TUSSARS ▶ tussar
TUSSEH same as ▶ **tussore**
TUSSEHS ▶ tusseh
TUSSER same as ▶ **tussore**
TUSSERS ▶ tusser
TUSSES ▶ tussis
TUSSIS technical name for a ▶ **cough**
TUSSIVE ▶ tussis
TUSSLE vb fight or scuffle ▷ n energetic fight, struggle, or argument
TUSSLED ▶ tussle
TUSSLES ▶ tussle
TUSSOCK n tuft of grass
TUSSOR same as ▶ **tussore**
TUSSORE n strong coarse brownish Indian silk obtained from the cocoons of an Oriental saturniid silkworm
TUSSORS ▶ tussore
TUSSUCK same as ▶ **tussock**
TUSSUR same as ▶ **tussore**
TUSSURS ▶ tussur
TUT interj an exclamation of mild reprimand, disapproval, or surprise ▷ vb express disapproval by the exclamation of "tut-tut." ▷ n payment system based on measurable work done

rather that time spent doing it
TUTANIA n alloy of low melting point containing tin, antimony, copper and used mostly for decorative purposes
TUTEE n one who is tutored, esp in a university
TUTEES ▶ tutee
TUTELAR same as ▷ **tutelary**
TUTENAG n zinc alloy
TUTMAN n one who does tutwork
TUTMEN ▶ tutman
TUTOR n person teaching individuals or small groups ▷ vb act as a tutor to
TUTORED ▶ tutor
TUTORS ▶ tutor
TUTOYED adj addressed in a familiar way
TUTOYER vb speak to someone on familiar terms
TUTRESS same as ▷ **tutoress**
TUTRIX n female tutor; tutoress
TUTS Scots version of ▶ **tut**
TUTSAN n woodland shrub of Europe and W Asia
TUTSANS ▶ tutsan
TUTSED ▶ tuts
TUTSES ▶ tuts
TUTSING ▶ tuts
TUTTED ▶ tut
TUTTI adv be performed by the whole orchestra or choir ▷ n piece of tutti music
TUTTIES ▶ tutty
TUTTING ▶ tut
TUTTIS ▶ tutti
TUTTY n finely powdered impure zinc oxide obtained from the flues of zinc-smelting furnaces and used as a polishing powder
TUTU n short stiff skirt worn by ballerinas
TUTUED adj wearing tutu
TUTUS ▶ tutu
TUTWORK n work paid using a tut system
TUX short for ▶ **tuxedo**

> **Tux** is a short form of **tuxedo**, and is a very commonly played X word.

TUXEDO n dinner jacket
TUXEDOS ▶ tuxedo
TUXES ▶ tux
TUYER same as ▶ **tuyere**

TUYERE n water-cooled nozzle through which air is blown into a cupola, blast furnace, or forge
TUYERES ▶ tuyere
TUYERS ▶ tuyer
TUZZ n tuft or clump of hair
TUZZES ▶ tuzz
TWA Scots word for ▶ **two**
TWADDLE n silly or pretentious talk or writing ▷ vb talk or write in a silly or pretentious way
TWADDLY ▶ twaddle
TWAE same as ▶ **twa**
TWAES ▶ twae
TWAFALD Scots variant of ▶ **twofold**
TWAIN n two
TWAINS ▶ twain
TWAITE n herring-like food fish
TWAITES ▶ twaite
TWAL n twelve
TWALS ▶ twal
TWANG n sharp ringing sound ▷ vb (cause to) make a twang
TWANGED ▶ twang
TWANGER ▶ twang
TWANGLE vb make a continuous loose twanging sound (on a musical instrument, for example)
TWANGS ▶ twang
TWANGY ▶ twang
TWANK vb make an sharply curtailed twang
TWANKAY n variety of Chinese green tea
TWANKS ▶ twank
TWANKY same as ▶ **twankay**
TWAS ▶ twa
TWASOME same as ▶ **twosome**
TWATTLE rare word for ▶ **twaddle**
TWAY old variant of ▶ **twain**
TWAYS ▶ tway
TWEAK vb pinch or twist sharply ▷ n tweaking
TWEAKED ▶ tweak
TWEAKER n engineer's small screwdriver, used for fine adjustments
TWEAKS ▶ tweak
TWEAKY ▶ tweak
TWEE adj too sentimental, sweet, or pretty
TWEED n thick woollen cloth
TWEEDLE vb improvise

aimlessly on a musical instrument

TWEEDS ▸ tweed

TWEEDY *adj* of or made of tweed

TWEEL *same as* ▸ **twill**

TWEELED ▸ tweel

TWEELS ▸ tweel

TWEELY ▸ twee

TWEEN *same as* ▸ **between**

TWEENER *same as* > **tweenager**

TWEENIE *same as* ▸ **tweeny**

TWEENS ▸ tween

TWEENY *n* maid who assists both cook and housemaid

TWEER *same as* ▸ **twire**

TWEERED ▸ tweer

TWEERS ▸ tweer

TWEEST ▸ twee

TWEET *vb* chirp ▷ *interj* imitation of the thin chirping sound made by small birds

TWEETED ▸ tweet

TWEETER *n* loudspeaker reproducing high-frequency sounds

TWEETS ▸ tweet

TWEEZE *vb* take hold of or pluck (hair, small objects, etc) with or as if with tweezers

TWEEZED ▸ tweeze

TWEEZER *same as* > **tweezers**

TWEEZES ▸ tweeze

TWELFTH *n* (of) number twelve in a series ▷ *adj* of or being number twelve in a series

TWELVE *n* two more than ten ▷ *adj* amounting to twelve ▷ *determiner* amounting to twelve

TWELVES ▸ twelve

TWENTY *n* two times ten ▷ *adj* amounting to twenty ▷ *determiner* amounting to twenty

TWERP *n* silly person

TWERPS ▸ twerp

TWERPY ▸ twerp

TWIBIL *same as* ▸ **twibill**

TWIBILL *n* mattock with a blade shaped like an adze at one end and like an axe at the other

TWIBILS ▸ twibil

TWICE *adv* two times

TWICER *n* someone who does something twice

TWICERS ▸ twicer

TWIDDLE *vb* fiddle or twirl in an idle way ▷ *n* act or instance of twiddling

TWIDDLY ▸ twiddle

TWIER *same as* ▸ **tuyere**

TWIERS ▸ twier

TWIFOLD *same as* ▸ **twofold**

TWIG *n* small branch or shoot ▷ *vb* realize or understand

TWIGGED ▸ twig

TWIGGEN *adj* made of twigs

TWIGGER ▸ twig

TWIGGY *adj* of or relating to a twig or twigs

TWIGHT *old variant of* ▸ **twit**

TWIGHTS ▸ twight

TWIGLET *n* small twig

TWIGLOO *n* temporary shelter made from twigs, branches, leaves, etc

TWIGS ▸ twig

TWILIT > **twilight**

TWILL *n* fabric woven to produce parallel ridges ▷ *adj* (in textiles) of or designating a weave in which the weft yarns are worked around two or more warp yarns to produce an effect of parallel diagonal lines or ribs ▷ *vb* weave in this fashion

TWILLED ▸ twill

TWILLS ▸ twill

TWILLY *n* machine having a system of revolving spikes for opening and cleaning raw textile fibres

TWILT *same as* ▸ **quilt**

TWILTED ▸ twilt

TWILTS ▸ twilt

TWIN *n* one of a pair, esp of two children born at one birth ▷ *vb* pair or be paired

TWINE *n* string or cord ▷ *vb* twist or coil round

TWINED ▸ twine

TWINER ▸ twine

TWINERS ▸ twine

TWINES ▸ twine

TWINGE *n* sudden sharp pain or emotional pang ▷ *vb* have or cause to have a twinge

TWINGED ▸ twinge

TWINGES ▸ twinge

TWINIER ▸ twine

TWINING ▸ twine

TWINJET *n* jet aircraft with two engines

TWINK *n* white correction fluid for deleting written text ▷ *vb* twinkle

TWINKED ▸ twink

TWINKIE *n* stupid person

TWINKLE *vb* shine brightly but intermittently ▷ *n* flickering brightness

TWINKLY ▸ twinkle

TWINKS ▸ twink

TWINNED ▸ twin

TWINS ▸ twin

TWINSET *n* matching jumper and cardigan

TWINTER *n* animal that is 2 years old

TWINY ▸ twine

TWIRE *vb* look intently at with (or as if with) difficulty

TWIRED ▸ twire

TWIRES ▸ twire

TWIRING ▸ twire

TWIRL *vb* turn or spin around quickly ▷ *n* whirl or twist

TWIRLED ▸ twirl

TWIRLER ▸ twirl

TWIRLS ▸ twirl

TWIRLY ▸ twirl

TWIRP *same as* ▸ **twerp**

TWIRPS ▸ twirp

TWIRPY ▸ twirp

TWISCAR *same as* ▸ **tuskar**

TWIST *vb* turn out of the natural position ▷ *n* twisting

TWISTED ▸ twist

TWISTER *n* swindler

TWISTOR *n* variable corresponding to the coordinates of a point in space and time

TWISTS ▸ twist

TWISTY ▸ twist

TWIT *vb* poke fun at (someone) ▷ *n* foolish person

TWITCH *vb* move spasmodically ▷ *n* nervous muscular spasm

TWITCHY *adj* nervous, worried, and ill-at-ease

TWITE *n* N European finch with a brown streaked plumage

TWITES ▸ twite

TWITS ▸ twit

TWITTED ▸ twit

TWITTEN *n* narrow alleyway

TWITTER *vb* (of birds) utter chirping sounds ▷ *n* act or sound of twittering

TWIXT same as ▸ **betwixt**

TWIZZLE vb spin around

TWO n one more than one

TWOCCER > **twoccing**

TWOCKER > **twoccing**

TWOER n (in a game) something that scores two

TWOERS ▸ **twoer**

TWOFER n single ticket allowing the buyer entrance to two events, attractions, etc, for substantially less than the cost were he or she to pay for each individually

TWOFERS ▸ **twofer**

TWOFOLD adj having twice as many or as much ▹ adv by twice as many or as much ▹ n folding piece of theatrical scenery

TWONESS n state or condition of being two

TWONIE same as ▸ **toonie**

TWONIES ▸ **twonie**

TWOONIE same as ▸ **toonie**

TWOS ▸ **two**

TWOSOME n group of two people

TWP adj stupid

This Welsh word for stupid is useful because it contains no vowels, and can thus help when you have an awkward rack full of consonants.

TWYER same as ▸ **tuyere**

TWYERE same as ▸ **tuyere**

TWYERES ▸ **twyere**

TWYERS ▸ **twyer**

TWYFOLD adj twofold

TYCHISM n theory that chance is an objective reality at work in the universe, esp in evolutionary adaptations

TYCOON n powerful wealthy businessman; shogun

TYCOONS ▸ **tycoon**

TYDE old variant of the past participle of ▸ **tie**

TYE n trough used in mining to separate valuable material from dross ▹ vb (in mining) isolate valuable material from dross using a tye

TYED ▸ **tye**

TYEE n large northern Pacific salmon

TYEES ▸ **tyee**

TYEING ▸ **tye**

TYER ▸ **tye**

TYERS ▸ **tye**

TYES ▸ **tye**

TYG n mug with two handles

This old word for a two-handled drinking cup is another key word to know for situations when you are short of vowels.

TYGS ▸ **tyg**

TYIN same as ▸ **tyiyn**

TYING ▸ **tie**

TYIYN n money unit of Kyrgyzstan

TYIYNS ▸ **tyiyn**

TYLER same as ▸ **tiler**

TYLERS ▸ **tyler**

TYLOPOD n mammal with padded feet, such as a camel or llama

TYLOSES ▸ **tylosis**

TYLOSIN n broad spectrum antibiotic

TYLOSIS n bladder-like outgrowth from certain cells in woody tissue that extends into and blocks adjacent conducting xylem cells

TYLOTE n knobbed sponge spicule

TYLOTES ▸ **tylote**

TYMBAL same as ▸ **timbal**

TYMBALS ▸ **tymbal**

TYMP n blast furnace outlet through which molten metal flows

TYMPAN same as > **tympanum**

TYMPANA > **tympanum**

TYMPANI same as ▸ **timpani**

TYMPANO ▸ **tympani**

TYMPANS ▸ **tympan**

TYMPANY n distention of the abdomen

TYMPS ▸ **tymp**

TYND same as ▸ **tind**

TYNDE same as ▸ **tind**

TYNE same as ▸ **tine**

TYNED same as ▸ **tyne**

TYNES ▸ **tyne**

TYNING ▸ **tyne**

TYPABLE ▸ **type**

TYPAL rare word for ▸ **typical**

TYPE n class or category ▹ vb print with a typewriter or word processor

TYPEBAR n one of the bars in a typewriter that carry the type and are operated by keys

TYPED ▸ **type**

TYPES ▸ **type**

TYPESET vb set (text for printing) in type

TYPEY same as ▸ **typy**

TYPHOID adj of or relating to typhoid fever

TYPHON n whirlwind

TYPHONS ▸ **typhon**

TYPHOON n violent tropical storm

TYPHOSE adj relating to typhoid

TYPHOUS ▸ **typhus**

TYPHUS n infectious feverish disease

TYPIC same as ▸ **typical**

TYPICAL adj true to type, characteristic

TYPIER ▸ **typy**

TYPIEST ▸ **typy**

TYPIFY vb be typical of

TYPING n work or activity of using a typewriter or word processor

TYPINGS ▸ **typing**

TYPIST n person who types with a typewriter or word processor

TYPISTS ▸ **typist**

TYPO n typographical error

TYPOS ▸ **typo**

TYPP n unit of thickness of yarn

TYPPS ▸ **typp**

TYPTO vb learn Greek conjugations

TYPTOED ▸ **typto**

TYPTOS ▸ **typto**

TYPY adj (of an animal) typifying the breed

TYRAN vb act as a tyrant

TYRANED ▸ **tyran**

TYRANNE same as ▸ **tyran**

TYRANNY n tyrannical rule

TYRANS ▸ **tyran**

TYRANT n oppressive or cruel ruler ▹ vb act the tyrant

TYRANTS ▸ **tyrant**

TYRE n rubber ring, usu inflated, over the rim of a vehicle's wheel to grip the road ▹ vb fit a tyre or tyres to (a wheel, vehicle, etc)

TYRED ▸ **tyre**

TYRES ▸ **tyre**

TYRING ▸ **tyre**

TYRO n novice or beginner

TYROES ▸ **tyro**

TYRONES ▸ **tyro**

T

TYRONIC ▸ tyro
TYROS ▸ tyro
TYSTIE n black guillemot
TYSTIES ▸ tystie
TYTE variant spelling of ▸ tite
TYTHE same as ▸ tithe
TYTHED ▸ tythe
TYTHES ▸ tythe
TYTHING ▸ tythe
TZADDI ▸ sadhe
TZADDIK same as ▸ zaddik
TZADDIQ same as ▸ zaddik

An unlikely word from Judaism, meaning a person of great piety, but offering a great score played as a bonus.

TZADDIS ▸ tzaddi
TZAR same as ▸ tsar
TZARDOM ▸ tzar
TZARINA same as ▸ tsarina
TZARISM same as ▸ tsarism
TZARIST ▸ tzarism
TZARS ▸ tzar

TZETSE same as ▸ tsetse
TZETSES ▸ tzetse
TZETZE same as ▸ tsetse
TZETZES ▸ tzetze
TZIGANE n type of Gypsy music
TZIGANY same as ▸ tzigane
TZIMMES n traditional Jewish stew
TZITZIS same as > tsitsith
TZITZIT same as > tsitsith
TZURIS same as ▸ tsuris

T

Uu

U can be a difficult tile to use effectively. Although there are quite a few two-letter words beginning with **U**, most of them are quite unusual, and so difficult to remember. Only **up** (4 points) and **us** (2) are immediately obvious, so it's well worth learning words like **ug** (3), **uh** (5), **um** (4), and **un**, **ur** and **ut** (2 each). Three-letter words beginning with **U** can also be difficult to remember. If you are trying to use a **Q**, **X** or **Z**, bear in mind that there aren't any valid three-letter words with these letters that start with **U**. Knowing this can save you valuable time. It's also helpful to remember that there aren't any particularly high-scoring two- or three-letter words starting with **U**, the best being **uke** (7 points) and **uva** (6 points). If you have a surplus of **U**s, it is well worth remembering **ulu**, **umu** and **utu**, which score only 3 points but should improve your rack.

UAKARI *n* type of monkey
UAKARIS ▶ uakari
UBEROUS *adj* abundant
UBERTY *n* abundance
UBIETY *n* condition of being in a particular place
UBIQUE *adv* everywhere
UBUNTU *n* quality of compassion and humanity
UBUNTUS ▶ ubuntu
UCKERS *n* type of naval game
UDAL *n* form of freehold possession of land existing in northern Europe before the introduction of the feudal system and still used in Orkney and Shetland
UDALLER *n* person possessing a udal
UDALS ▶ udal
UDDER *n* large baglike milk-producing gland of cows, sheep, or goats
UDDERED ▶ udder
UDDERS ▶ udder
UDO *n* stout perennial plant of Japan and China with berry-like black fruits and young shoots that are edible when blanched
UDON *n* (in Japanese cookery) large noodles made of wheat flour
UDONS ▶ udon
UDOS ▶ udo
UDS *interj* God's or God save
UEY *n* u-turn

UEYS ▶ uey
UFO *n* flying saucer
UFOLOGY *n* study of UFOs
UFOS ▶ ufo
UG *vb* hate
UGALI *n* type of stiff porridge made by mixing corn meal with boiling water: the basic starch constituent of a meal
UGALIS ▶ ugali
UGGED ▶ ug
UGGING ▶ ug
UGH *interj* exclamation of disgust ▷ *n* sound made to indicate disgust

| Together with **uke**, this is the highest-scoring three-letter word starting with U.

UGHS ▶ ugh
UGLIED ▶ ugly
UGLIER ▶ ugly
UGLIES ▶ ugly
UGLIEST ▶ ugly
UGLIFY *vb* make or become ugly or more ugly
UGLILY ▶ ugly
UGLY *adj* of unpleasant appearance ▷ *vb* make ugly
UGLYING ▶ ugly
UGS ▶ ug
UGSOME *adj* loathsome
UH *interj* used to express hesitation
UHLAN *n* member of a body of lancers first employed in the Polish army and later in

W European armies
UHLANS ▶ uhlan
UHURU *n* national independence

| You won't often have three Us on your rack, but when you do this Swahili word for freedom may get you out of trouble. The only other 5-letter word containing three Us is **urubu**, a kind of vulture.

UHURUS ▶ uhuru
UILLEAN *adj as in* **uillean pipes** bagpipes developed in Ireland and operated by squeezing bellows under the arm
UJAMAA *n as in* **ujamaa village** communally organized village in Tanzania
UJAMAAS ▶ ujamaa
UKASE *n* (in imperial Russia) a decree from the tsar
UKASES ▶ ukase
UKE *short form of* ▶ **ukulele**

| Together with ugh, this is the highest-scoring three-letter word starting with U.

UKELELE *same as* ▶ **ukulele**
UKES ▶ uke
UKULELE *n* small guitar with four strings
ULAMA *n* body of Muslim

U

scholars or religious leaders

ULAMAS ▸ ulama
ULAN same as ▸ **uhlan**
ULANS ▸ ulan
ULCER n open sore on the surface of the skin or mucous membrane. ▷ vb make or become ulcerous
ULCERED ▸ ulcer
ULCERS ▸ ulcer
ULE n rubber tree
ULEMA same as ▸ **ulama**
ULEMAS ▸ ulema
ULES ▸ ule
ULEX n variety of shrub
ULEXES ▸ ulex
ULEXITE n type of mineral
ULICES ▸ ulex
ULICON same as > **eulachon**
ULICONS ▸ ulicon
ULIKON same as > **eulachon**
ULIKONS ▸ ulikon
ULITIS n gingivitis
ULLAGE n volume by which a liquid container falls short of being full ▷ vb create ullage in
ULLAGED ▸ ullage
ULLAGES ▸ ullage
ULLING n process of filling
ULLINGS ▸ ulling
ULMIN n substance found in decaying vegetation
ULMINS ▸ ulmin
ULNA n inner and longer of the two bones of the human forearm
ULNAD adv towards the ulna
ULNAE ▸ ulna
ULNAR ▸ ulna
ULNARE n bone in the wrist
ULNARIA ▸ ulnare
ULNAS ▸ ulna
ULOSES ▸ ulosis
ULOSIS n formation of a scar
ULPAN n Israeli study centre
ULPANIM ▸ ulpan
ULSTER n man's heavy double-breasted overcoat
ULSTERS ▸ ulster
ULTIMA n final syllable of a word
ULTIMAS ▸ ultima
ULTIMO adv in or during the previous month
ULTION n vengeance
ULTIONS ▸ ultion
ULTRA n person who has extreme or immoderate beliefs or opinions ▷ adj extreme or immoderate,

esp in beliefs or opinions
ULTRAS ▸ ultra
ULU n type of knife
ULULANT ▸ ululate
ULULATE vb howl or wail
ULUS ▸ ulu
ULVA n genus of seaweed
ULVAS ▸ ulva
ULYIE Scots variant of ▸ **oil**
ULYIES ▸ ulyie
ULZIE Scots variant of ▸ **oil**
ULZIES ▸ ulzie
UM interj representation of a common sound made when hesitating in speech ▷ vb hesitate while speaking
UMAMI n savoury flavour
UMAMIS ▸ umami
UMBEL n umbrella-like flower cluster with the stalks springing from the central point
UMBELED same as > **umbelled**
UMBELS ▸ umbel
UMBER adj dark brown to reddish-brown ▷ n type of dark brown earth containing ferric oxide (rust) ▷ vb stain with umber
UMBERED ▸ umber
UMBERS ▸ umber
UMBERY ▸ umber
UMBLE adj as in **umble pie** (formerly) a pie made from the heart, entrails, etc, of a deer
UMBLES another term for ▸ **numbles**
UMBO n small hump projecting from the centre of the cap in certain mushrooms
UMBONAL ▸ umbo
UMBONES ▸ umbo
UMBONIC ▸ umbo
UMBOS ▸ umbo
UMBRA n shadow, esp the shadow cast by the moon onto the earth during a solar eclipse
UMBRAE ▸ umbra
UMBRAGE n displeasure or resentment ▷ vb shade
UMBRAL ▸ umbra
UMBRAS ▸ umbra
UMBRE same as > **umbrette**
UMBREL n umbrella
UMBRELS ▸ umbrel
UMBRERE n helmet visor
UMBRES ▸ umbre

UMBRIL same as ▸ **umbrere**
UMBRILS ▸ umbril
UMBROSE same as ▸ **umbrous**
UMBROUS adj shady
UMFAZI n African married woman
UMFAZIS ▸ umfazi
UMIAC same as ▸ **umiak**
UMIACK same as ▸ **umiak**
UMIACKS ▸ umiack
UMIACS ▸ umiac
UMIAK n Inuit boat made of skins
UMIAKS ▸ umiak
UMIAQ same as ▸ **umiak**

> An Inuit word for a type of canoe: easy to miss because one tends automatically to put the Q with the U and not think of a word ending in Q. The many variant spellings of this word include **umiac** and **umiak**.

UMIAQS ▸ umiaq
UMLAUT n mark (¨) placed over a vowel, esp in German, to indicate a change in its sound ▷ vb modify by umlaut
UMLAUTS ▸ umlaut
UMLUNGU n White man: used esp as a term of address
UMM same as ▸ **um**
UMMA n Muslim community
UMMAH ▸ umma
UMMAHS ▸ ummah
UMMAS ▸ umma
UMMED ▸ um
UMMING ▸ um vb
UMP short for ▸ **umpire**
UMPED ▸ ump
UMPH same as ▸ **humph**
UMPIE informal word for ▸ **umpire**
UMPIES ▸ umpy
UMPING ▸ ump
UMPIRE n official who rules on the playing of a game ▷ vb act as umpire in (a game)
UMPIRED ▸ umpire
UMPIRES ▸ umpire
UMPS ▸ ump
UMPTEEN adj very many ▷ determiner very many
UMPTY same as ▸ **umpteen**
UMPY same as ▸ **umpie**
UMRA n pilgrimage to

Mecca that can be made at any time of the year
UMRAH ▸ umra
UMRAHS ▸ umrah
UMRAS ▸ umra
UMS ▸ um
UMU n type of oven
UMUS ▸ umu
UMWELT n environmental factors, collectively, that are capable of affecting the behaviour of an animal or individual
UMWELTS ▸ umwelt
UMWHILE same as
> **umquhile**
UN pron spelling of 'one' intended to reflect a dialectal or informal pronunciation
UNABLE adj lacking the necessary power, ability, or authority (to do something)
UNACTED adj not acted or performed
UNADDED adj not added
UNADEPT adj not adept
UNADULT adj not mature
UNAGED adj not old
UNAGILE adj not agile
UNAGING same as
> **unageing**
UNAI same as ▸ **unau**
UNAIDED adv without any help or assistance ▷ adj without having received any help
UNAIMED adj not aimed or specifically targeted
UNAIRED adj not aired
UNAIS ▸ unai
UNAKIN adj not related
UNAKING Shakespearean form of > **unaching**
UNAKITE n type of mineral
UNALIKE adj not similar
UNALIST n priest holding only one benefice
UNALIVE adj unaware
UNAPT adj not suitable or qualified
UNAPTLY ▸ unapt
UNARM less common word for ▸ **disarm**
UNARMED adj without weapons
UNARMS ▸ unarm
UNARY adj consisting of, or affecting, a single element or component
UNASKED adv without being asked to do

something ▷ adj (of a question) not asked, although sometimes implied
UNAU n two-toed sloth
UNAUS ▸ unau
UNAWAKE adj not awake
UNAWARE adj not aware or conscious ▷ adv by surprise
UNAWED adj not awed
UNAXED adj not axed
UNBAG vb take out of a bag
UNBAGS ▸ unbag
UNBAKED adj not having been baked
UNBALE vb remove from bale
UNBALED ▸ unbale
UNBALES ▸ unbale
UNBAN vb stop banning or permit again
UNBANS ▸ unban
UNBAR vb take away a bar or bars from
UNBARE vb expose
UNBARED ▸ unbare
UNBARES ▸ unbare
UNBARK vb strip bark from
UNBARKS ▸ unbark
UNBARS ▸ unbar
UNBASED adj not having a base
UNBATED adj (of a sword, lance, etc) not covered with a protective button
UNBE vb make non-existent
UNBEAR vb release (horse) from the bearing rein
UNBEARS ▸ unbear
UNBED vb remove from bed
UNBEDS ▸ unbed
UNBEEN ▸ unbe
UNBEGET vb deprive of existence
UNBEGOT adj unbegotten
UNBEGUN adj not commenced
UNBEING n non-existence
UNBELT vb unbuckle the belt of (a garment)
UNBELTS ▸ unbelt
UNBEND vb become less strict or more informal in one's attitudes or behaviour
UNBENDS ▸ unbend
UNBENT adj not bent or bowed
UNBIAS vb free from prejudice
UNBID same as > **unbidden**
UNBIND vb set free from bonds or chains
UNBINDS ▸ unbind

UNBITT vb remove (cable) from the bitts
UNBITTS ▸ unbitt
UNBLENT same as
> **unblended**
UNBLESS vb deprive of a blessing
UNBLEST same as
> **unblessed**
UNBLIND vb rid of blindness
UNBLOCK vb remove a blockage from
UNBLOWN adj (of a flower) still in the bud
UNBOLT vb unfasten a bolt of (a door)
UNBOLTS ▸ unbolt
UNBONE vb remove bone from
UNBONED adj (of meat, fish, etc) not having had the bones removed
UNBONES ▸ unbone
UNBOOT vb remove boots from
UNBOOTS ▸ unboot
UNBORE adj unborn
UNBORN adj not yet born
UNBORNE adj not borne
UNBOSOM vb relieve (oneself) of (secrets or feelings) by telling someone
UNBOUND adj (of a book) not bound within a cover
UNBOWED adj not giving in or submitting
UNBOX vb empty a box
UNBOXED ▸ unbox
UNBOXES ▸ unbox
UNBRACE vb remove tension or strain from
UNBRAID vb remove braids from
UNBRAKE vb stop reducing speed by releasing brake
UNBRED adj not taught or instructed
UNBROKE same as
> **unbroken**
UNBUILD vb destroy
UNBUILT ▸ unbuild
UNBULKY adj not bulky
UNBURNT adj not burnt
UNBURY vb unearth
UNBUSY adj not busy
UNCAGE vb release from a cage
UNCAGED adj at liberty
UNCAGES ▸ uncage
UNCAKE vb remove compacted matter from
UNCAKED ▸ uncake
UNCAKES ▸ uncake

U

UNCANNY *adj* weird or mysterious

UNCAP *vb* remove a cap or top from (a container)

UNCAPE *vb* remove the cape from

UNCAPED ▸ **uncape**

UNCAPES ▸ **uncape**

UNCAPS ▸ **uncap**

UNCARED *adj* *as in* **uncared for** not cared (for)

UNCART *vb* remove from a cart

UNCARTS ▸ **uncart**

UNCASE *vb* display

UNCASED ▸ **uncase**

UNCASES ▸ **uncase**

UNCAST *adj* not cast

UNCATE *same as* > **uncinate**

UNCE *same as* ▸ **ounce**

UNCEDED *adj* not ceded

UNCES ▸ **unce**

UNCHAIN *vb* remove a chain or chains from

UNCHAIR *vb* unseat from chair

UNCHARM *vb* disenchant

UNCHARY *adj* not cautious

UNCHECK *vb* remove check mark from

UNCHIC *adj* not chic

UNCHILD *vb* deprive of children

UNCHOKE *vb* unblock

UNCI ▸ **uncus**

UNCIA *n* twelfth part

UNCIAE ▸ **uncia**

UNCIAL *adj* of or written in letters that resemble modern capitals, as used in Greek and Latin manuscripts of the third to ninth centuries ▷ *n* uncial letter or manuscript

UNCIALS ▸ **uncial**

UNCINAL *same as* > **uncinate**

UNCINI ▸ **uncinus**

UNCINUS *n* small hooked structure, such as any of the hooked chaetae of certain polychaete worms

UNCITED *adj* not quoted

UNCIVIL *adj* impolite, rude or bad-mannered

UNCLAD *adj* having no clothes on

UNCLAMP *vb* remove clamp from

UNCLASP *vb* unfasten the clasp of (something)

UNCLE *n* brother of one's father or mother ▷ *vb* refer to as uncle

UNCLEAN *adj* lacking moral, spiritual, or physical cleanliness

UNCLEAR *adj* confusing or hard to understand

UNCLED ▸ **uncle**

UNCLEFT *adj* not cleft

UNCLES ▸ **uncle**

UNCLEW *vb* undo

UNCLEWS ▸ **unclew**

UNCLING ▸ **uncle**

UNCLIP *vb* remove clip from

UNCLIPS ▸ **unclip**

UNCLIPT *archaic past form of* ▸ **unclip**

UNCLOAK *vb* remove cloak from

UNCLOG *vb* remove an obstruction from (a drain, etc)

UNCLOGS ▸ **unclog**

UNCLOSE *vb* open or cause to open

UNCLOUD *vb* clear clouds from

UNCO *adj* awkward ▷ *n* awkward or clumsy person

UNCOCK *vb* remove from a cocked position

UNCOCKS ▸ **uncock**

UNCODED *adj* not coded

UNCOER ▸ **unco**

UNCOES ▸ **unco**

UNCOEST ▸ **unco**

UNCOIL *vb* unwind or untwist

UNCOILS ▸ **uncoil**

UNCOLT *vb* divest of a horse

UNCOLTS ▸ **uncolt**

UNCOMFY *adj* not comfortable

UNCOMIC *adj* not comical

UNCOOL *adj* unsophisticated

UNCOPE *vb* unmuzzle

UNCOPED ▸ **uncope**

UNCOPES ▸ **uncope**

UNCORD *vb* release from cords

UNCORDS ▸ **uncord**

UNCORK *vb* remove the cork from (a bottle)

UNCORKS ▸ **uncork**

UNCOS ▸ **unco**

UNCOUTH *adj* lacking in good manners, refinement, or grace

UNCOVER *vb* reveal or disclose

UNCOWL *vb* remove hood from

UNCOWLS ▸ **uncowl**

UNCOY *adj* not modest

UNCRATE *vb* remove from a crate

UNCRAZY *adj* not crazy

UNCROSS *vb* cease to cross

UNCROWN *vb* take the crown from

UNCTION *n* act of anointing with oil in sacramental ceremonies

UNCUFF *vb* remove handcuffs from

UNCUFFS ▸ **uncuff**

UNCURB *vb* remove curbs from (a horse)

UNCURBS ▸ **uncurb**

UNCURED *adj* not cured

UNCURL *vb* move or cause to move out of a curled or rolled up position

UNCURLS ▸ **uncurl**

UNCURSE *vb* remove curse from

UNCUS *n* hooked part or process, as in the human cerebrum

UNCUT *adj* not shortened or censored

UNCUTE *adj* not cute

UNDAM *vb* free from a dam

UNDAMS ▸ **undam**

UNDATE *vb* remove date from

UNDATED *adj* (of a manuscript, letter, etc) not having an identifying date

UNDE *same as* ▸ **undee**

UNDEAD *adj* alive

UNDEAF *vb* restore hearing to

UNDEAFS ▸ **undeaf**

UNDEALT *adj* not dealt (with)

UNDEAR *adj* not dear

UNDECK *vb* remove decorations from

UNDECKS ▸ **undeck**

UNDEE *adj* wavy

UNDEIFY *vb* strip of the status of a deity

UNDER *adv* indicating movement to or position beneath the underside or base ▷ *prep* less than

UNDERDO *vb* do (something) inadequately

UNDERGO *vb* experience, endure, or sustain

UNDERN *n* time between sunrise and noon

UNDERNS ▸ **undern**

UNDID ▸ **undo**

UNDIES *pl n* underwear, esp women's

UNDIGHT *vb* remove

UNDINE *n* female water spirit

UNDINES ▶ **undine**

UNDO *vb* open, unwrap

UNDOCK *vb* take out of a dock

UNDOCKS ▶ **undock**

UNDOER ▶ **undo**

UNDOERS ▶ **undo**

UNDOES ▶ **undo**

UNDOING *n* cause of someone's downfall

UNDONE *adj* not done or completed

UNDRAPE *vb* remove drapery from

UNDRAW *vb* open (curtains)

UNDRAWN ▶ **undraw**

UNDRAWS ▶ **undraw**

UNDRESS *vb* take off clothes from (oneself or another) ▷ *n* partial or complete nakedness ▷ *adj* characterized by or requiring informal or normal working dress or uniform

UNDREST *same as* > **undressed**

UNDREW ▶ **undraw**

UNDRIED *adj* not dried

UNDRUNK *adj* not drunk

UNDUE *adj* greater than is reasonable; excessive

UNDUG *adj* not having been dug

UNDULAR > **undulate**

UNDULY *adv* excessively

UNDY *same as* ▶ **undee**

UNDYED *adj* not dyed

UNDYING *adj* never ending, eternal

UNEAGER *adj* nonchalant

UNEARED *adj* not ploughed

UNEARTH *vb* reveal or discover by searching

UNEASE ▶ **uneasy**

UNEASES ▶ **uneasy**

UNEASY *adj* (of a person) anxious or apprehensive

UNEATEN *adj* (of food) not having been consumed

UNEATH *adv* not easily

UNEDGE *vb* take the edge off

UNEDGED ▶ **unedge**

UNEDGES ▶ **unedge**

UNENDED *adj* without end

UNEQUAL *adj* not equal in

quantity, size, rank, value, etc ▷ *person* who is not equal

UNETH *same as* ▶ **uneath**

UNEVEN *adj* not level or flat

UNEYED *adj* unseen

UNFACT *n* event or thing not provable

UNFACTS ▶ **unfact**

UNFADED *adj* not faded

UNFAIR *adj* not right, fair, or just ▷ *vb* disfigure

UNFAIRS ▶ **unfair**

UNFAITH *n* lack of faith

UNFAKED *adj* not faked

UNFAMED *adj* not famous

UNFANCY *vb* consider (a sportsperson or team) unlikely to win or succeed

UNFAZED *adj* not disconcerted

UNFED *adj* not fed

UNFEED *adj* unpaid

UNFELT *adj* not felt

UNFENCE *vb* remove a fence from

UNFEUED *adj* not feued

UNFILDE *archaic form of* ▶ **unfiled**

UNFILED *adj* not filed

UNFINE *adj* not fine

UNFIRED *adj* not fired

UNFIRM *adj* soft or unsteady

UNFIT *adj* unqualified or unsuitable ▷ *vb* make unfit

UNFITLY *adv* in an unfit way

UNFITS ▶ **unfit**

UNFIX *vb* unfasten, detach, or loosen

UNFIXED *adj* not fixed

UNFIXES ▶ **unfix**

UNFIXT *same as* ▶ **unfixed**

UNFLESH *vb* remove flesh from

UNFLUSH *vb* lose the colour caused by flushing

UNFOLD *vb* open or spread out from a folded state

UNFOLDS ▶ **unfold**

UNFOND *adj* not fond

UNFOOL *vb* undeceive

UNFOOLS ▶ **unfool**

UNFORM *vb* make formless

UNFORMS ▶ **unform**

UNFOUND *adj* not found

UNFREE *vb* remove freedom from

UNFREED ▶ **unfree**

UNFREES ▶ **unfree**

UNFROCK *vb* deprive (a priest in holy orders) of his or her priesthood

UNFROZE > **unfreeze**

UNFUMED *adj* not fumigated

UNFUNNY *adj* not funny

UNFURL *vb* unroll or unfold

UNFURLS ▶ **unfurl**

UNFUSED *adj* not fused

UNFUSSY *adj* not characterized by overelaborate detail

UNGAG *vb* restore freedom of speech to

UNGAGS ▶ **ungag**

UNGAIN *adj* inconvenient

UNGATED *adj* without gate

UNGAZED *adj as in* **ungazed at/ungazed upon** not gazed (at or upon)

UNGEAR *vb* disengage

UNGEARS ▶ **ungear**

UNGET *vb* get rid of

UNGETS ▶ **unget**

UNGILD *vb* remove gilding from

UNGILDS ▶ **ungild**

UNGILT ▶ **ungild**

UNGIRD *vb* remove belt from

UNGIRDS ▶ **ungird**

UNGIRT *adj* not belted

UNGIRTH *vb* release from a girth

UNGLAD *adj* not glad

UNGLOVE *vb* remove glove(s)

UNGLUE *vb* remove adhesive from

UNGLUED ▶ **unglue**

UNGLUES ▶ **unglue**

UNGOD *vb* remove status of being a god from

UNGODLY *adj* unreasonable or outrageous

UNGODS ▶ **ungod**

UNGORD *same as* ▶ **ungored**

UNGORED *adj* not gored

UNGOT *same as* > **ungotten**

UNGOWN *vb* remove gown (from)

UNGOWNS ▶ **ungown**

UNGREEN *adj* not environmentally friendly

UNGROWN *adj* not fully developed

UNGUAL *adj* of, relating to, or affecting the fingernails or toenails

UNGUARD *vb* expose (to attack)

UNGUENT *n* ointment

UNGUES ▶ **unguis**

UNGUIS *n* nail, claw, or

hoof, or the part of the digit giving rise to it

UNGULA n truncated cone, cylinder, etc

UNGULAE ▶ ungula

UNGULAR ▶ ungula

UNGULED adj hoofed

UNGUM vb remove adhesive from

UNGUMS ▶ ungum

UNGYVE vb release from shackles

UNGYVED ▶ ungyve

UNGYVES ▶ ungyve

UNHABLE same as ▶ **unable**

UNHAIR vb remove the hair from (a hide)

UNHAIRS ▶ unhair

UNHAND vb release from one's grasp

UNHANDS ▶ unhand

UNHANDY adj not skilful with one's hands

UNHANG vb take down from hanging position

UNHANGS ▶ unhang

UNHAPPY adj sad or depressed ▷ vb make unhappy

UNHARDY adj fragile

UNHASP vb unfasten

UNHASPS ▶ unhasp

UNHASTY adj not speedy

UNHAT vb doff one's hat

UNHATS ▶ unhat

UNHEAD vb remove the head from

UNHEADS ▶ unhead

UNHEAL vb expose

UNHEALS ▶ unheal

UNHEARD adj not listened to

UNHEART vb discourage

UNHEEDY adj not heedful

UNHELE same as ▶ **unheal**

UNHELED ▶ unhele

UNHELES ▶ unhele

UNHELM vb remove the helmet of (oneself or another)

UNHELMS ▶ unhelm

UNHERST archaic past form of ▶ **unhearse**

UNHEWN adj not hewn

UNHINGE vb derange or unbalance (a person or his or her mind)

UNHIP adj not at all fashionable or up to date

UNHIRED adj not hired

UNHITCH vb unfasten or detach

UNHIVE vb remove from a hive

UNHIVED ▶ unhive

UNHIVES ▶ unhive

UNHOARD vb remove from a hoard

UNHOLY adj immoral or wicked

UNHOOD vb remove hood from

UNHOODS ▶ unhood

UNHOOK vb unfasten the hooks of (a garment)

UNHOOKS ▶ unhook

UNHOOP vb remove hoop(s) from

UNHOOPS ▶ unhoop

UNHOPED adj unhoped-for

UNHORSE vb knock or throw from a horse

UNHORSE vb remove from a house

UNHUMAN adj inhuman or not human

UNHUNG ▶ unhang

UNHURT adj not injured in an accident, attack, etc

UNHUSK vb remove the husk from

UNHUSKS ▶ unhusk

UNI n (in informal English) university

UNIBODY adj of a vehicle in which frame and body are one unit

UNIBROW n informal word for eyebrows that meet above the nose

UNICITY n oneness

UNICORN n imaginary horselike creature with one horn growing from its forehead

UNIDEAL adj not ideal

UNIFACE n type of tool

UNIFIC adj unifying

UNIFIED ▶ unify

UNIFIER ▶ unify

UNIFIES ▶ unify

UNIFORM n special identifying set of clothes for the members of an organization, such as soldiers ▷ adj regular and even throughout, unvarying ▷ vb fit out (a body of soldiers, etc) with uniforms

UNIFY vb make or become one

UNION n uniting or being united ▷ adj of a trade union

UNIONS ▶ union

UNIPED n person or thing with one foot

UNIPEDS ▶ uniped

UNIPOD n one-legged support, as for a camera

UNIPODS ▶ unipod

UNIQUE n person or thing that is unique

UNIQUER ▶ unique

UNIQUES ▶ unique

UNIS ▶ uni

UNISEX adj designed for use by both sexes ▷ n condition of seeming not to belong obviously either to one sex or the other from the way one behaves or dresses

UNISIZE adj in one size only

UNISON n complete agreement

UNISONS ▶ unison

UNIT n single undivided entity or whole

UNITAGE ▶ unit

UNITAL ▶ unit

UNITARD n all-in-one skintight suit

UNITARY adj consisting of a single undivided whole

UNITE vb make or become an integrated whole ▷ n English gold coin minted in the Stuart period, originally worth 20 shillings

UNITED adj produced by two or more people or things in combination

UNITER ▶ unite

UNITERS ▶ unite

UNITES ▶ unite

UNITIES ▶ unity

UNITING ▶ unite

UNITION n joining

UNITISE same as ▶ **unitize**

UNITIVE adj tending to unite or capable of uniting

UNITIZE vb convert (an investment trust) into a unit trust

UNITS ▶ unit

UNITY n state of being one

UNJADED adj not jaded

UNJAM vb remove blockage from

UNJAMS ▶ unjam

UNJOINT vb disjoint

UNJUST adj not fair or just

UNKED adj alien

UNKEMPT adj (of the hair) not combed

UNKEND same as ▷ **unkenned**

UNKENT same as
> **unkenned**
UNKEPT adj not kept
UNKET same as ▶ **unked**
UNKID same as ▶ **unked**
UNKIND adj unsympathetic
or cruel
UNKING vb strip of
sovereignty
UNKINGS ▶ **unking**
UNKINK vb straighten out
UNKINKS ▶ **unkink**
UNKISS vb cancel (a
previous action) with a kiss
UNKNIT vb make or become
undone, untied, or
unravelled
UNKNITS ▶ **unknit**
UNKNOT vb disentangle or
undo a knot or knots in
UNKNOTS ▶ **unknot**
UNKNOWN adj not known
▷ n unknown person,
quantity, or thing
UNLACE vb loosen or undo
the lacing of (shoes,
garments, etc)
UNLACED adj not laced
UNLACES ▶ **unlace**
UNLADE less common word
for ▶ **unload**
UNLADED ▶ **unlade**
UNLADEN adj not laden
UNLADES ▶ **unlade**
UNLAID ▶ **unlay**
UNLASH vb untie or
unfasten
UNLAST archaic variant of
▶ **unlaced**
UNLASTE archaic variant of
▶ **unlaced**
UNLATCH vb open or
unfasten or come open or
unfastened by the lifting or
release of a latch
UNLAW vb penalize
UNLAWED ▶ **unlaw**
UNLAWS ▶ **unlaw**
UNLAY vb untwist (a rope
or cable) to separate its
strands
UNLAYS ▶ **unlay**
UNLEAD vb strip off lead
UNLEADS ▶ **unlead**
UNLEAL adj treacherous
UNLEARN vb try to forget
something learnt or to
discard accumulated
knowledge
UNLEASH vb set loose or
cause (something bad)
UNLED adj not led
UNLESS conj except under

the circumstances that
▷ prep except
UNLET adj not rented
UNLEVEL adj not level ▷ vb
make unbalanced
UNLICH Spenserian form of
▶ **unlike**
UNLID vb remove lid from
UNLIDS ▶ **unlid**
UNLIKE adj dissimilar or
different ▷ prep not like or
typical of ▷ n person or
thing that is unlike another
UNLIKED adj not liked
UNLIKES ▶ **unlike**
UNLIME vb detach
UNLIMED ▶ **unlime**
UNLIMES ▶ **unlime**
UNLINE vb remove the
lining from
UNLINED adj not having any
lining
UNLINES ▶ **unline**
UNLINK vb undo the link or
links between
UNLINKS ▶ **unlink**
UNLIT adj (of a fire,
cigarette, etc) not lit and
therefore not burning
UNLIVE vb live so as to
nullify, undo, or live down
(past events or times)
UNLIVED ▶ **unlive**
UNLIVES ▶ **unlive**
UNLOAD vb remove (cargo)
from (a ship, truck, or
plane)
UNLOADS ▶ **unload**
UNLOBED adj without lobes
UNLOCK vb unfasten (a lock
or door)
UNLOCKS ▶ **unlock**
UNLOOSE vb set free or
release
UNLORD vb remove from
position of being lord
UNLORDS ▶ **unlord**
UNLOST adj not lost
UNLOVE vb stop loving
UNLOVED adj not loved by
anyone
UNLOVES ▶ **unlove**
UNLUCKY adj having bad
luck, unfortunate
UNMACHO adj not macho
UNMADE adj (of a bed) with
the bedclothes not
smoothed and tidied
UNMAKE vb undo or
destroy
UNMAKER ▶ **unmake**
UNMAKES ▶ **unmake**
UNMAN vb cause to lose

courage or nerve
UNMANLY adj not
masculine or virile
UNMANS ▶ **unman**
UNMARD same as
> **unmarred**
UNMARRY vb divorce
UNMASK vb remove the
mask or disguise from
UNMASKS ▶ **unmask**
UNMATED adj not mated
UNMEANT adj
unintentional
UNMEEK adj not
submissive
UNMEET adj not meet
UNMERRY adj not merry
UNMESH vb release from
mesh
UNMET adj unfulfilled
UNMETED adj unmeasured
UNMEW vb release from
confinement
UNMEWED ▶ **unmew**
UNMEWS ▶ **unmew**
UNMINED adj not mined
UNMIRY adj not swampy
UNMITER same as
▶ **unmitre**
UNMITRE vb divest of a
mitre
UNMIX vb separate
UNMIXED ▶ **unmix**
UNMIXES ▶ **unmix**
UNMIXT same as ▶ **unmix**
UNMOLD same as
▶ **unmould**
UNMOLDS ▶ **unmold**
UNMOOR vb weigh the
anchor or drop the mooring
of (a vessel)
UNMOORS ▶ **unmoor**
UNMORAL adj outside
morality
UNMOULD vb change
shape of
UNMOUNT vb dismount
UNMOVED adj not affected
by emotion, indifferent
UNMOWN adj not mown
UNNAIL vb unfasten by
removing nails
UNNAILS ▶ **unnail**
UNNAMED adj not
mentioned by name
UNNEATH adj archaic word
for underneath
UNNERVE vb cause to lose
courage, confidence, or
self-control
UNNEST vb remove from a
nest
UNNESTS ▶ **unnest**

U

UNNOBLE vb strip of nobility

UNNOISY adj quiet

UNNOTED adj not noted

UNOAKED adj (of wine) not matured in an oak barrel

UNOFTEN adv infrequently

UNOILED adj not lubricated with oil

UNOPEN adj not open

UNORDER vb cancel an order

UNOWED same as ▶ **unowned**

UNOWNED adj not owned

UNPACED adj without the aid of a pacemaker

UNPACK vb remove the contents of (a suitcase, trunk, etc)

UNPACKS ▶ **unpack**

UNPAGED adj (of a book) having no page numbers

UNPAID adj without a salary or wage

UNPAINT vb remove paint from

UNPANEL vb unsaddle

UNPAPER vb remove paper from

UNPARED adj not pared

UNPAVED adj not covered in paving

UNPAY vb undo

UNPAYS ▶ **unpay**

UNPEG vb remove the peg or pegs from, esp to unfasten

UNPEGS ▶ **unpeg**

UNPEN vb release from a pen

UNPENS ▶ **unpen**

UNPENT archaic past form of ▶ **unpen**

UNPERCH vb remove from a perch

UNPICK vb undo (the stitches) of (a piece of sewing)

UNPICKS ▶ **unpick**

UNPILE vb remove from a pile

UNPILED ▶ **unpile**

UNPILES ▶ **unpile**

UNPIN vb remove a pin or pins from

UNPINKT same as > **unpinked**

UNPINS ▶ **unpin**

UNPLACE same as > **displace**

UNPLAIT vb remove plaits from

UNPLUG vb disconnect (a piece of electrical equipment) by taking the plug out of the socket

UNPLUGS ▶ **unplug**

UNPLUMB vb remove lead from

UNPLUME vb remove feathers from

UNPOPE vb strip of popedom

UNPOPED ▶ **unpope**

UNPOPES ▶ **unpope**

UNPOSED adj not posed

UNPRAY vb withdraw (a prayer)

UNPRAYS ▶ **unpray**

UNPROP vb remove support from

UNPROPS ▶ **unprop**

UNPURE same as ▶ **impure**

UNPURSE vb relax (lips) from pursed position

UNQUEEN vb depose from the position of queen

UNQUIET adj anxious or uneasy ▷ n state of unrest ▷ vb disquiet

UNQUOTE interj expression used to indicate the end of a quotation that was introduced with the word 'quote' ▷ vb close (a quotation), esp in printing

UNRACED adj not raced

UNRAKE vb unearth through raking

UNRAKED adj not raked

UNRAKES ▶ **unrake**

UNRATED adj not rated

UNRAVEL vb reduce (something knitted or woven) to separate strands

UNRAZED adj not razed

UNREAD adj (of a book or article) not yet read

UNREADY adj not ready or prepared

UNREAL adj (as if) existing only in the imagination

UNREAVE vb unwind

UNRED same as ▶ **unread**

UNREDY same as ▶ **unready**

UNREEL vb unwind from a reel

UNREELS ▶ **unreel**

UNREEVE vb withdraw (a rope) from a block, thimble, etc

UNREIN vb free from reins

UNREINS ▶ **unrein**

UNRENT adj not torn

UNREST n rebellious state

of discontent

UNRESTS ▶ **unrest**

UNRID adj unridden

UNRIG vb strip (a vessel) of standing and running rigging

UNRIGHT n wrong

UNRIGS ▶ **unrig**

UNRIMED same as > **unrhymed**

UNRIP vb rip open

UNRIPE adj not fully matured

UNRIPER ▶ **unripe**

UNRIPS ▶ **unrip**

UNRISEN adj not risen

UNRIVEN adj not torn apart

UNRIVET vb remove rivets from

UNROBE same as ▶ **disrobe**

UNROBED ▶ **unrobe**

UNROBES ▶ **unrobe**

UNROLL vb open out or unwind (something rolled or coiled) or (of something rolled or coiled) become opened out or unwound

UNROLLS ▶ **unroll**

UNROOF vb remove the roof from

UNROOFS ▶ **unroof**

UNROOST vb remove from a perch

UNROOT less common word for ▶ **uproot**

UNROOTS ▶ **unroot**

UNROPE vb release from a rope

UNROPED ▶ **unrope**

UNROPES ▶ **unrope**

UNROUGH adj not rough

UNROUND vb release (lips) from a rounded position

UNROVE ▶ **unreeve**

UNROVEN ▶ **unreeve**

UNROYAL adj not royal

UNRUDE adj not rude

UNRUFFE same as ▶ **unrough**

UNRULE n lack of authority

UNRULED adj not ruled

UNRULES ▶ **unrule**

UNRULY adj difficult to control or organize

UNS ▶ **un**

UNSAFE adj dangerous

UNSAFER ▶ **unsafe**

UNSAID adj not said or expressed

UNSAINT vb remove status of being a saint from

UNSATED adj not sated

UNSAVED adj not saved

UNSAWED *same as*
▶ **unsawn**

UNSAWN *adj* not cut with a saw

UNSAY *vb* retract or withdraw (something said or written)

UNSAYS ▶ **unsay**

UNSCALE *same as* ▶ **descale**

UNSCARY *adj* not scary

UNSCREW *vb* loosen (a screw or lid) by turning it

UNSEAL *vb* remove or break the seal of

UNSEALS ▶ **unseal**

UNSEAM *vb* open or undo the seam of

UNSEAMS ▶ **unseam**

UNSEAT *vb* throw or displace from a seat or saddle

UNSEATS ▶ **unseat**

UNSEEL *vb* undo seeling

UNSEELS ▶ **unseel**

UNSEEN *adj* hidden or invisible ▷ *adv* without being seen ▷ *n* passage which is given to students for translation without them having seen it in advance

UNSEENS ▶ **unseen**

UNSELF *vb* remove self-centredness from ▷ *n* lack of self

UNSELFS ▶ **unself**

UNSELL *vb* speak unfavourably of and off-puttingly of (something or someone)

UNSELLS ▶ **unsell**

UNSENSE *vb* remove sense from

UNSENT *adj* not sent

UNSET *adj* not yet solidified or firm ▷ *vb* displace

UNSETS ▶ **unset**

UNSEW *vb* undo stitching of

UNSEWED ▶ **unsew**

UNSEWN ▶ **unsew**

UNSEWS ▶ **unsew**

UNSEX *vb* deprive (a person) of the attributes of his or her sex, esp to make a woman more callous

UNSEXED ▶ **unsex**

UNSEXES ▶ **unsex**

UNSEXY *adj* not sexually attractive

UNSHALE *vb* expose

UNSHAPE *vb* make shapeless

UNSHARP *adj* not sharp

UNSHED *adj* not shed

UNSHELL *vb* remove from a shell

UNSHENT *adj* undamaged

UNSHEWN *adj* unshown

UNSHIFT *vb* release the shift key on a keyboard

UNSHIP *vb* be or cause to be unloaded, discharged, or disembarked from a ship

UNSHIPS ▶ **unship**

UNSHOD *adj* not wearing shoes

UNSHOE *vb* remove shoes from

UNSHOED *same as* ▶ **unshod**

UNSHOES ▶ **unshoe**

UNSHOOT *Shakespearean variant of* ▶ **unshout**

UNSHORN *adj* not cut

UNSHOT *adj* not shot

UNSHOUT *vb* revoke (an earlier statement) by shouting a contrary one

UNSHOWN *adj* not shown

UNSHOWY *adj* not showy

UNSHUT *vb* open

UNSHUTS ▶ **unshut**

UNSIGHT *vb* obstruct vision of

UNSINEW *vb* weaken

UNSIZED *adj* not made or sorted according to size

UNSLAIN *adj* not killed

UNSLICK *adj* not slick

UNSLING *vb* remove or release from a slung position

UNSLUNG ▶ **unsling**

UNSMART *adj* not smart

UNSMOTE *same as* ▶ **unsmitten**

UNSNAG *vb* remove snags from

UNSNAGS ▶ **unsnag**

UNSNAP *vb* unfasten (the snap or catch) of (something)

UNSNAPS ▶ **unsnap**

UNSNARL *vb* free from a snarl or tangle

UNSNECK *vb* unlatch

UNSOBER *adj* not sober

UNSOD *same as* ▶ **unsodden**

UNSOFT *adj* hard

UNSOLD *adj* not sold

UNSOLID *adj* not solid

UNSONCY *same as* ▶ **unsonsy**

UNSONSY *adj* unfortunate

UNSOOTE *adj* not sweet

UNSOUL *vb* cause to be soulless

UNSOULS ▶ **unsoul**

UNSOUND *adj* unhealthy or unstable

UNSOWED *same as* ▶ **unsown**

UNSOWN *adj* not sown

UNSPAR *vb* open

UNSPARS ▶ **unspar**

UNSPEAK *obsolete word for* ▶ **unsay**

UNSPED *adj* not achieved

UNSPELL *vb* release from a spell

UNSPENT *adj* not spent

UNSPIDE *same as* ▶ **unspied**

UNSPIED *adj* unnoticed

UNSPILT *adj* not spilt

UNSPLIT *adj* not split

UNSPOKE ▶ **unspeak**

UNSPOOL *vb* unwind from spool

UNSPUN *adj* not spun

UNSTACK *vb* remove from a stack

UNSTAID *adj* not staid

UNSTATE *vb* deprive of state

UNSTEEL *vb* make (the heart, feelings, etc) more gentle or compassionate

UNSTEP *vb* remove (a mast) from its step

UNSTEPS ▶ **unstep**

UNSTICK *vb* free or loosen (something stuck)

UNSTOCK *vb* remove stock from

UNSTOP *vb* remove the stop or stopper from

UNSTOPS ▶ **unstop**

UNSTOW *vb* remove from storage

UNSTOWS ▶ **unstow**

UNSTRAP *vb* undo the straps fastening (something) in position

UNSTRIP *vb* strip

UNSTUCK *adj* freed from being stuck, glued, fastened, etc

UNSTUFT *same as* ▶ **unstuffed**

UNSTUNG *adj* not stung

UNSUIT *vb* make unsuitable

UNSUITS ▶ **unsuit**

UNSUNG *adj* not acclaimed or honoured

UNSUNK *adj* not sunken

UNSUNNY *adj* not sunny

UNSURE *adj* lacking assurance or self-confidence

U

UNSURED adj not assured
UNSURER ▶ unsure
UNSWEAR vb retract or revoke (a sworn oath)
UNSWEET adj not sweet
UNSWEPT adj not swept
UNSWORE ▶ unswear
UNSWORN ▶ unswear
UNTACK vb remove saddle and harness, etc, from
UNTACKS ▶ untack
UNTAKEN adj not taken
UNTAME vb. undo the taming of
UNTAMED adj not brought under human control
UNTAMES ▶ untame
UNTAX vb stop taxing
UNTAXED adj not subject to taxation
UNTAXES ▶ untax
UNTEACH vb cause to disbelieve (teaching)
UNTEAM vb disband a team
UNTEAMS ▶ unteam
UNTENT vb remove from a tent
UNTENTS ▶ untent
UNTENTY adj inattentive
UNTHAW same as ▶ thaw
UNTHAWS ▶ unthaw
UNTHINK vb reverse one's opinion about
UNTIDY adj messy and disordered ▷ vb make untidy
UNTIE vb open or free (something that is tied)
UNTIED ▶ untie
UNTIES ▶ untie
UNTIL prep in or throughout the period before
UNTILE vb strip tiles from
UNTILED ▶ untile
UNTILES ▶ untile
UNTIMED adj not timed
UNTIN vb remove tin from
UNTINS ▶ untin
UNTIRED adj not tired
UNTO prep to
UNTOLD adj incapable of description
UNTOMB vb exhume
UNTOMBS ▶ untomb
UNTONED adj not toned
UNTORN adj not torn
UNTRACE vb remove traces from
UNTRACK vb remove from track
UNTREAD vb retrace (a course, path, etc)
UNTRIDE same as ▶ untried

UNTRIED adj not yet used, done, or tested
UNTRIM vb deprive of elegance or adornment
UNTRIMS ▶ untrim
UNTROD ▶ untread
UNTRUE adj incorrect or false
UNTRUER ▶ untrue
UNTRULY ▶ untrue
UNTRUSS vb release from or as if from a truss
UNTRUST n mistrust
UNTRUTH n statement that is not true, lie
UNTUCK vb become or cause to become loose or not tucked in
UNTUCKS ▶ untuck
UNTUNE vb make out of tune
UNTUNED ▶ untune
UNTUNES ▶ untune
UNTURF vb remove turf from
UNTURFS ▶ unturf
UNTURN vb turn in a reverse direction
UNTURNS ▶ unturn
UNTWINE vb untwist, unravel, and separate
UNTWIST vb twist apart and loosen
UNTYING ▶ untie
UNURGED adj not urged
UNUSED adj not being or never having been used
UNUSUAL adj uncommon or extraordinary
UNVAIL same as ▶ unveil
UNVAILE same as ▶ unveil
UNVAILS ▶ unvail
UNVEIL vb ceremonially remove the cover from (a new picture, plaque, etc)
UNVEILS ▶ unveil
UNVEXED adj not annoyed
UNVEXT same as ▶ unvexed
UNVISOR vb remove visor from
UNVITAL adj not vital
UNVOCAL adj not vocal
UNVOICE vb pronounce without vibration of the vocal cords
UNWAGED adj (of a person) not having a paid job
UNWAKED same as > unwakened
UNWARE same as ▶ unaware
UNWARES same as > unawares

UNWARIE same as ▶ unwary
UNWARY adj not careful or cautious and therefore likely to be harmed
UNWATER vb dry out
UNWAXED adj not treated with wax, esp of oranges or lemons, not sprayed with a protective coating of wax
UNWAYED adj having no routes
UNWEAL n ill or sorrow
UNWEALS ▶ unweal
UNWEARY adj not weary
UNWEAVE vb undo (weaving)
UNWED adj not wed
UNWELDY same as > unwieldy
UNWELL adj not healthy, ill
UNWEPT adj not wept for or lamented
UNWET adj not wet
UNWHIPT same as > unwhipped
UNWHITE adj not white
UNWILL vb will the reversal of (something that has already occurred)
UNWILLS ▶ unwill
UNWIND vb relax after a busy or tense time
UNWINDS ▶ unwind
UNWIPED adj not wiped
UNWIRE vb remove wiring from
UNWIRED ▶ unwire
UNWIRES ▶ unwire
UNWISE adj foolish
UNWISER ▶ unwise
UNWISH vb retract or revoke (a wish)
UNWIST adj unknown
UNWIT vb divest of wit
UNWITCH vb release from witchcraft
UNWITS ▶ unwit
UNWITTY adj not clever and amusing
UNWIVE vb remove a wife from
UNWIVED ▶ unwive
UNWIVES ▶ unwive
UNWOMAN vb remove womanly qualities from
UNWON adj not won
UNWONT adj unaccustomed
UNWOOED adj not wooed
UNWORK vb destroy (work previously done)
UNWORKS ▶ unwork

UNWORN adj not having deteriorated through use or age

UNWORTH n lack of value

UNWOUND past tense and past participle of ▶ **unwind**

UNWOVE ▶ unweave

UNWOVEN ▶ unweave

UNWRAP vb remove the wrapping from (something)

UNWRAPS ▶ unwrap

UNWRITE vb cancel (what has been written)

UNWROTE ▶ unwrite

UNWRUNG adj not twisted

UNYOKE vb release (an animal, etc) from a yoke

UNYOKED ▶ unyoke

UNYOKES ▶ unyoke

UNYOUNG adj not young

UNZIP vb unfasten the zip of (a garment) or (of a zip or a garment with a zip) to become unfastened

UNZIPS ▶ unzip

UNZONED adj not divided into zones

UP adv indicating movement to or position at a higher place ▷ adj of a high or higher position ▷ vb increase or raise

UPAS n large Javan tree with whitish bark and poisonous milky sap

UPASES ▶ upas

UPBEAR vb sustain

UPBEARS ▶ upbear

UPBEAT adj cheerful and optimistic ▷ n unaccented beat

UPBEATS ▶ upbeat

UPBIND vb bind up

UPBINDS ▶ upbind

UPBLEW ▶ upblow

UPBLOW vb inflate

UPBLOWN ▶ upblow

UPBLOWS ▶ upblow

UPBOIL vb boil up

UPBOILS ▶ upboil

UPBORE ▶ upbear

UPBORNE adj held up

UPBOUND adj travelling upwards

UPBOW n stroke of the bow from its tip to its nut on a stringed instrument

UPBOWS ▶ upbow

UPBRAID vb scold or reproach

UPBRAST same as ▶ upburst

UPBRAY vb shame

UPBRAYS ▶ upbray

UPBREAK vb escape upwards

UPBRING vb rear

UPBROKE ▶ upbreak

UPBUILD vb build up

UPBUILT ▶ upbuild

UPBURST vb burst upwards

UPBY same as ▶ upbye

UPBYE adv yonder

UPCAST n material cast or thrown up ▷ adj directed or thrown upwards ▷ vb throw or cast up

UPCASTS ▶ upcast

UPCATCH vb catch up

UPCHEER vb cheer up

UPCHUCK vb vomit

UPCLIMB vb ascend

UPCLOSE vb close up

UPCOAST adv up the coast

UPCOIL vb make into a coil

UPCOILS ▶ upcoil

UPCOME vb come up

UPCOMES ▶ upcome

UPCOURT adv up basketball court

UPCURL vb curl up

UPCURLS ▶ upcurl

UPCURVE vb curve upwards

UPDART vb dart upwards

UPDARTS ▶ updart

UPDATE vb bring up to date ▷ n act of updating or something that is updated

UPDATED ▶ update

UPDATER ▶ update

UPDATES ▶ update

UPDIVE vb leap upwards

UPDIVED ▶ updive

UPDIVES ▶ updive

UPDO n type of hairstyle

UPDOS ▶ updo

UPDOVE ▶ updive

UPDRAFT n upwards air current

UPDRAG vb drag up

UPDRAGS ▶ updrag

UPDRAW vb draw up

UPDRAWN ▶ updraw

UPDRAWS ▶ updraw

UPDREW ▶ updraw

UPDRIED ▶ updry

UPDRIES ▶ updry

UPDRY vb dry up

UPEND vb turn or set (something) on its end

UPENDED ▶ upend

UPENDS ▶ upend

UPFIELD adj in sport, away from the defending team's goal

UPFILL vb fill up

UPFILLS ▶ upfill

UPFLING vb throw upwards

UPFLOW vb flow upwards

UPFLOWS ▶ upflow

UPFLUNG ▶ upfling

UPFOLD vb fold up

UPFOLDS ▶ upfold

UPFRONT adj open and frank ▷ adv (of money) paid out at the beginning of a business arrangement

UPFURL vb roll up

UPFURLS ▶ upfurl

UPGANG n climb

UPGANGS ▶ upgang

UPGAZE vb gaze upwards

UPGAZED ▶ upgaze

UPGAZES ▶ upgaze

UPGIRD vb belt up

UPGIRDS ▶ upgird

UPGIRT ▶ upgird

UPGO vb ascend

UPGOES ▶ upgo

UPGOING ▶ upgo

UPGONE ▶ upgo

UPGRADE vb promote (a person or job) to a higher rank

UPGREW ▶ upgrow

UPGROW vb grow up

UPGROWN ▶ upgrow

UPGROWS ▶ upgrow

UPGUSH vb flow upwards

UPHAND adj lifted by hand

UPHANG vb hang up

UPHANGS ▶ uphang

UPHAUD Scots variant of ▶ uphold

UPHAUDS ▶ uphaud

UPHEAP vb computing term

UPHEAPS ▶ upheap

UPHEAVE vb heave or rise upwards

UPHELD ▶ uphold

UPHILD archaic past form of ▶ uphold

UPHILL adj sloping or leading upwards ▷ adv up a slope ▷ n difficulty

UPHILLS ▶ uphill

UPHOARD vb hoard up

UPHOIST vb raise

UPHOLD vb maintain or defend against opposition

UPHOLDS ▶ uphold

UPHOORD vb heap up

UPHOVE ▶ upheave

UPHROE variant spelling of ▶ euphroe

UPHROES ▶ uphroe

UPHUNG ▶ uphang

UPHURL vb throw upwards

UPHURLS ▶ uphurl
UPJET vb stream upwards
UPJETS ▶ upjet
UPKEEP n act, process, or cost of keeping something in good repair
UPKEEPS ▶ upkeep
UPKNIT vb bind
UPKNITS ▶ upknit
UPLAID ▶ uplay
UPLAND adj of or in an area of high or relatively high ground ▷ n area of high or relatively high ground
UPLANDS ▶ upland
UPLAY vb stash
UPLAYS ▶ uplay
UPLEAD vb lead upwards
UPLEADS ▶ uplead
UPLEAN vb lean on something
UPLEANS ▶ uplean
UPLEANT ▶ uplean
UPLEAP vb jump upwards
UPLEAPS ▶ upleap
UPLEAPT ▶ upleap
UPLED ▶ uplead
UPLIFT vb raise or lift up ▷ n act or process of improving moral, social, or cultural conditions ▷ adj (of a bra) designed to lift and support the breasts
UPLIFTS ▶ uplift
UPLIGHT n lamp or wall light designed or positioned to cast its light upwards ▷ vb light in an upward direction
UPLINK n transmitter on the ground that sends signals up to a communications satellite ▷ vb send (data) to a communications satellite
UPLINKS ▶ uplink
UPLIT ▶ uplight
UPLOAD vb transfer (data or a program) from one's own computer into the memory of another computer
UPLOADS ▶ upload
UPLOCK vb lock up
UPLOCKS ▶ uplock
UPLOOK vb look up
UPLOOKS ▶ uplook
UPLYING adj raised
UPMAKE vb make up
UPMAKER ▶ upmake
UPMAKES ▶ upmake
UPMOST another word for
▶ uppermost
UPO prep upon

UPON prep on
UPPED ▶ up
UPPER adj higher or highest in physical position, wealth, rank, or status ▷ n part of a shoe above the sole
UPPERS ▶ upper
UPPILE vb pile up
UPPILED ▶ uppile
UPPILES ▶ uppile
UPPING ▶ up
UPPINGS ▶ up
UPPISH adj snobbish, arrogant, or presumptuous
UPPITY adj snobbish, arrogant, or presumptuous
UPPROP vb support
UPPROPS ▶ upprop
UPRAISE vb lift up
UPRAN ▶ uprun
UPRATE vb raise the value, rate, or size of, upgrade
UPRATED ▶ uprate
UPRATES ▶ uprate
UPREACH vb reach up
UPREAR vb lift up
UPREARS ▶ uprear
UPREST n uprising
UPRESTS ▶ uprest
UPRIGHT adj vertical or erect ▷ adv vertically or in an erect position ▷ n vertical support, such as a post ▷ vb make upright
UPRISAL ▶ uprise
UPRISE vb rise up
UPRISEN ▶ uprise
UPRISER ▶ uprise
UPRISES ▶ uprise
UPRIST same as ▶ uprest
UPRISTS ▶ uprist
UPRIVER adv towards or near the source of a river ▷ n area located upstream
UPROAR n disturbance characterized by loud noise and confusion ▷ vb cause an uproar
UPROARS ▶ uproar
UPROLL vb roll up
UPROLLS ▶ uproll
UPROOT vb pull up by or as if by the roots
UPROOTS ▶ uproot
UPROSE ▶ uprise
UPROUSE vb rouse or stir up
UPRUN vb run up
UPRUNS ▶ uprun
UPRUSH n upward rush, as of consciousness ▷ vb rush upwards
UPRYST same as ▶ uprest

UPS ▶ up
UPSCALE adj of or for the upper end of an economic or social scale ▷ vb upgrade
UPSEE n drunken revel
UPSEES ▶ upsee
UPSELL vb persuade a customer to buy a more expensive or additional item
UPSELLS ▶ upsell
UPSEND vb send up
UPSENDS ▶ upsend
UPSENT ▶ upsend
UPSET adj emotionally or physically disturbed or distressed ▷ vb tip over ▷ n unexpected defeat or reversal
UPSETS ▶ upset
UPSEY same as ▶ upsee
UPSEYS ▶ upsey
UPSHIFT vb move up (a gear)
UPSHOOT vb shoot upwards
UPSHOT n final result or conclusion
UPSHOTS ▶ upshot
UPSIDE n upper surface or part
UPSIDES ▶ upside
UPSIES ▶ upsy
UPSILON n 20th letter in the Greek alphabet
UPSIZE vb increase in size
UPSIZED ▶ upsize
UPSIZES ▶ upsize
UPSKILL vb improve the aptitude for work of (a person) by additional training
UPSLOPE adv up a or the slope
UPSOAR vb soar up
UPSOARS ▶ upsoar
UPSOLD ▶ upsell
UPSPAKE ▶ upspeak
UPSPEAK vb speak with rising intonation
UPSPEAR vb grow upwards in a spear-like manner
UPSPOKE ▶ upspeak
UPSTAGE adj at the back half of the stage ▷ vb draw attention to oneself from (someone else) ▷ adv on, at, or to the rear of the stage ▷ n back half of the stage
UPSTAIR same as > upstairs
UPSTAND vb rise
UPSTARE vb stare upwards

UPSTART n person who has risen suddenly to a position of power and behaves arrogantly ▷ vb start up, as in surprise, etc

UPSTATE adv towards, in, from, or relating to the outlying or northern sections of a state, esp of New York State ▷ n outlying, esp northern, sections of a state

UPSTAY vb support

UPSTAYS ▶ upstay

UPSTEP n type of vocal intonation

UPSTEPS ▶ upstep

UPSTIR vb stir up ▷ n commotion

UPSTIRS ▶ upstir

UPSTOOD ▶ upstand

UPSURGE n rapid rise or swell ▷ vb surge up

UPSWAY vb swing in the air

UPSWAYS ▶ upsway

UPSWEEP n curve or sweep upwards ▷ vb sweep, curve, or brush or be swept, curved, or brushed upwards

UPSWELL vb swell up or cause to swell up

UPSWEPT ▶ upsweep

UPSWING n recovery period in the trade cycle ▷ vb swing or move up

UPSWUNG ▶ upswing

UPSY same as ▶ upsee

UPTA same as ▶ upter

UPTAK same as ▶ uptake

UPTAKE n numbers taking up something such as an offer or the act of taking it up ▷ vb take up

UPTAKEN ▶ uptake

UPTAKES ▶ uptake

UPTAKS ▶ uptak

UPTALK n style of speech in which every sentence ends with a rising tone, as if the speaker is always asking a question ▷ vb talk in this manner

UPTALKS ▶ uptalk

UPTEAR vb tear up

UPTEARS ▶ uptear

UPTEMPO adj fast ▷ n uptempo piece

UPTER adj of poor quality

UPTHREW ▶ upthrow

UPTHROW n upward movement of rocks on one side of a fault plane relative to rocks on the other side

▷ vb throw upwards

UPTICK n rise or increase

UPTICKS ▶ uptick

UPTIE vb tie up

UPTIED ▶ uptie

UPTIES ▶ uptie

UPTIGHT adj nervously tense, irritable, or angry

UPTILT vb tilt up

UPTILTS ▶ uptilt

UPTIME n time during which a machine, such as a computer, actually operates

UPTIMES ▶ uptime

UPTOOK ▶ uptake

UPTORE ▶ uptear

UPTORN ▶ uptear

UPTOSS vb throw upwards

UPTOWN adv towards, in, or relating to some part of a town that is away from the centre ▷ n such a part of town, esp a residential part

UPTOWNS ▶ uptown

UPTRAIN vb train up

UPTREND n upward trend

UPTURN n upward trend or improvement ▷ vb turn or cause to turn over or upside down

UPTURNS ▶ upturn

UPTYING ▶ uptie

UPVALUE vb raise the value of

UPWAFT vb waft upwards

UPWAFTS ▶ upwaft

UPWARD same as ▶ upwards

UPWARDS adv from a lower to a higher place, level, condition, etc

UPWELL vb well up

UPWELLS ▶ upwell

UPWENT ▶ upgo

UPWHIRL vb spin upwards

UPWIND adv into or against the wind ▷ adj going against the wind ▷ vb wind up

UPWINDS ▶ upwind

UPWOUND ▶ upwind

UPWRAP vb wrap up

UPWRAPS ▶ upwrap

UR interj hesitant utterance used to fill gaps in talking

URACHI ▶ urachus

URACHUS n cord of tissue connected to the bladder

URACIL n pyrimidine present in all living cells, usually in a combined form, as in RNA

URACILS ▶ uracil

URAEI ▶ uraeus

┃ This plural of **uraeus**, an Egyptian symbol of kingship, is very useful for dumping a surplus of vowels.

URAEMIA n accumulation of waste products, normally excreted in the urine, in the blood: causes severe headaches, vomiting, etc

URAEMIC ▶ uraemia

URAEUS n sacred serpent represented on the headdresses of ancient Egyptian kings and gods

URALI n type of plant

URALIS ▶ urali

URALITE n amphibole mineral, similar to hornblende, that replaces pyroxene in some igneous and metamorphic rocks

URANIA n uranium dioxide

URANIAN adj heavenly

URANIAS ▶ urania

URANIC adj of or containing uranium, esp in a high valence state

URANIDE n any element having an atomic number greater than that of protactinium

URANIN n type of alkaline substance

URANINS ▶ uranin

URANISM n homosexuality

URANITE n any of various minerals containing uranium, esp torbernite or autunite

URANIUM n radioactive silvery-white metallic element, used chiefly as a source of nuclear energy

URANOUS adj of or containing uranium, esp in a low valence state

URANYL n of, consisting of, or containing the divalent ion UO_2^{2+} or the group $-UO_2$

URANYLS ▶ uranyl

URAO n type of mineral

URAOS ▶ urao

URARE same as ▶ urali

URARES ▶ urare

URARI same as ▶ urali

URARIS ▶ urari

URASE same as ▶ urease

URASES ▶ urase

URATE n any salt or ester of uric acid

URATES ▶ **urate**
URATIC ▶ **urate**
URB n urban area
URBAN adj of or living in a city or town
URBANE adj characterized by courtesy, elegance, and sophistication
URBANER ▶ **urbane**
URBIA n urban area
URBIAS ▶ **urbia**
URBS ▶ **urb**
URCEOLI > **urceolus**
URCHIN n mischievous child
URCHINS ▶ **urchin**
URD n type of plant with edible seeds
URDE adj (in heraldry) having points
URDEE ▶ **urde**
URDS ▶ **urd**
URDY n heraldic line pattern
URE same as ▶ **aurochs**
UREA n white soluble crystalline compound found in urine
UREAL ▶ **urea**
UREAS ▶ **urea**
UREASE n enzyme occurring in many plants, esp fungi, that converts urea to ammonium carbonate
UREASES ▶ **urease**
UREDIA ▶ **uredium**
UREDIAL ▶ **uredium**
UREDINE ▶ **uredo**
UREDIUM n spore-producing body of some rust fungi in which uredospores are formed
UREDO less common name for > **urticaria**
UREDOS ▶ **uredo**
UREIC ▶ **urea**
UREIDE n any of a class of organic compounds derived from urea by replacing one or more of its hydrogen atoms by organic groups
UREIDES ▶ **ureide**
UREMIA same as ▶ **uraemia**
UREMIAS ▶ **uremia**
UREMIC ▶ **uremia**
URENA n plant genus
URENAS ▶ **urena**
URENT adj burning
URES ▶ **ure**
URESES ▶ **uresis**
URESIS n urination
URETER n tube that

conveys urine from the kidney to the bladder
URETERS ▶ **ureter**
URETHAN same as > **urethane**
URETHRA n canal that carries urine from the bladder out of the body
URETIC adj of or relating to the urine
URGE n strong impulse, inner drive, or yearning ▷ vb plead with or press (a person to do something)
URGED ▶ **urge**
URGENCE ▶ **urgent**
URGENCY ▶ **urgent**
URGENT adj requiring speedy action or attention
URGER ▶ **urge**
URGERS ▶ **urge**
URGES ▶ **urge**
URGING ▶ **urge**
URGINGS ▶ **urge**
URIAL n type of sheep
URIALS ▶ **urial**
URIC adj of or derived from urine
URICASE n type of enzyme
URIDINE n nucleoside present in all living cells in a combined form, esp in RNA
URINAL n sanitary fitting used by men for urination
URINALS ▶ **urinal**
URINANT adj having the head downwards
URINARY adj of urine or the organs that secrete and pass urine ▷ n reservoir for urine
URINATE vb discharge urine
URINE n pale yellow fluid excreted by the kidneys to the bladder and passed as waste from the body ▷ vb urinate
URINED ▶ **urine**
URINES ▶ **urine**
URINING ▶ **urine**
URINOSE same as ▶ **urinous**
URINOUS adj of, resembling, or containing urine
URITE n part of the abdomen
URITES ▶ **urite**
URMAN n forest
URMANS ▶ **urman**
URN n vase used as a container for the ashes of the dead ▷ vb put in an urn
URNAL ▶ **urn**

URNED ▶ **urn**
URNFUL n capacity of an urn
URNFULS ▶ **urnful**
URNING n homosexual man
URNINGS ▶ **urning**
URNLIKE ▶ **urn**
URNS ▶ **urn**
URODELE n amphibian of the order which includes the salamanders and newts
UROLITH n calculus in the urinary tract
UROLOGY n branch of medicine concerned with the urinary system and its diseases
UROMERE n part of the abdomen
UROPOD n paired appendage that arises from the last segment of the body in lobsters and related crustaceans and forms part of the tail fan
UROPODS ▶ **uropod**
UROSES ▶ **urosis**
UROSIS n urinary disease
UROSOME n abdomen of arthropods
URP dialect word for ▶ **vomit**
URPED ▶ **urp**
URPING ▶ **urp**
URPS ▶ **urp**
URSA n she-bear
URSAE ▶ **ursa**
URSID n meteor
URSIDS ▶ **ursid**
URSINE adj of or like a bear
URSON n type of porcupine
URSONS ▶ **urson**
URTEXT n earliest form of a text as established by linguistic scholars as a basis for variants in later texts still in existence
URTEXTS ▶ **urtext**
URTICA n type of nettle
URTICAS ▶ **urtica**
URUBU n type of bird
URUBUS ▶ **urubu**
URUS another name for the ▶ **aurochs**
URUSES ▶ **urus**
URVA n Indian mongoose
URVAS ▶ **urva**
US pron refers to the speaker or writer and another person or other people
USABLE adj able to be used
USABLY ▶ **usable**
USAGE n regular or constant use

USAGER n person who has the use of something in trust

USAGERS ▸ usager

USAGES ▸ usage

USANCE n period of time permitted by commercial usage for the redemption of foreign bills of exchange

USANCES ▸ usance

USAUNCE same as ▸ **usance**

USE vb put into service or action ▹ n using or being used

USEABLE same as ▸ **usable**

USEABLY ▸ usable

USED adj second-hand

USEFUL adj able to be used advantageously or for several different purposes ▹ n odd-jobman or general factotum

USEFULS ▸ useful

USELESS adj having no practical use

USER n continued exercise, use, or enjoyment of a right, esp in property

USERS ▸ user

USES ▸ use

USHER n official who shows people to their seats, as in a church ▹ vb conduct or escort

USHERED ▸ usher

USHERS ▸ usher

USING ▸ use

USNEA n type of lichen

USNEAS ▸ usnea

USQUE n whisky

USQUES ▸ usque

USTION n burning

USTIONS ▸ ustion

USUAL adj of the most normal, frequent, or regular type ▹ n ordinary or commonplace events

USUALLY adv most often, in most cases

USUALS ▸ usual

USUCAPT > usucapion

USURE vb be involved in usury

USURED ▸ usure

USURER n person who lends funds at an exorbitant rate of interest

USURERS ▸ usurer

USURES ▸ usure

USURESS n female usurer

USURIES ▸ usury

USURING ▸ usure

USUROUS ▸ usury

USURP vb seize (a position or power) without authority

USURPED ▸ usurp

USURPER ▸ usurp

USURPS ▸ usurp

USURY n practice of lending money at an extremely high rate of interest

USWARD adv towards us

USWARDS same as ▸ **usward**

UT n syllable used in the fixed system of solmization for the note C

UTA n side-blotched lizard

UTAS n eighth day of a festival

UTASES ▸ utas

UTE same as ▸ **utility**

UTENSIL n tool or container for practical use

UTERI ▸ uterus

UTERINE adj of or affecting the womb

UTERUS n womb

UTES ▸ ute

UTILE obsolete word for ▸ **useful**

UTILISE same as ▸ **utilize**

UTILITY n usefulness ▹ adj designed for use rather than beauty

UTILIZE vb make practical use of

UTIS n uproar

UTISES ▸ utis

UTMOST n the greatest possible degree or amount ▹ adj of the greatest possible degree or amount

UTMOSTS ▸ utmost

UTOPIA n real or imaginary society, place, state, etc, considered to be perfect or ideal

UTOPIAN adj of or relating to a perfect or ideal existence ▹ n idealistic social reformer

UTOPIAS ▸ utopia

UTOPISM ▸ utopia

UTOPIST ▸ utopia

UTRICLE n larger of the two parts of the membranous labyrinth of the internal ear

UTS ▸ ut

UTTER vb express (something) in sounds or words ▹ adj total or absolute

UTTERED ▸ utter

UTTERER ▸ utter

UTTERLY adv extremely

UTTERS ▸ utter

UTU n reward

UTUS ▸ utu

UVA n grape or fruit resembling this

UVAE ▸ uva

UVAS ▸ uva

UVEA n part of the eyeball consisting of the iris, ciliary body, and choroid

UVEAL ▸ uvea

UVEAS ▸ uvea

UVEITIC ▸ uveitis

UVEITIS n inflammation of the uvea

UVEOUS ▸ uvea

UVULA n small fleshy part of the soft palate that hangs in the back of the throat

UVULAE ▸ uvula

UVULAR adj of or relating to the uvula ▹ n uvular consonant

UVULARS ▸ uvular

UVULAS ▸ uvula

UXORIAL adj of or relating to a wife

U

Vv

If you have a **V** on your rack, the first thing to remember is that there are no valid two-letter words beginning with **V**. In fact, there are no two-letter words that end in **V** either, so you can't form any two-letter words using **V**. Remembering this will stop you wasting time trying to think of some. While **V** is useless for two-letter words, it does start some good three-letter words. **Vex** and **vox** (13 points each) are the best of these, while **vaw, vow** and **vly** (9 each) are also useful.

VAC vb clean with a vacuum cleaner

> Meaning to clean with a vacuum cleaner, this can be a useful short word for dealing with that awkward letter V.

VACANCE n vacant period
VACANCY n unfilled job
VACANT adj (of a toilet, room, etc) unoccupied
VACATE vb cause (something) to be empty by leaving
VACATED ▶ vacate
VACATES ▶ vacate
VACATUR n annulment
VACCINA same as > vaccinia
VACCINE n substance designed to cause a mild form of a disease to make a person immune to the disease itself
VACKED ▶ vac
VACKING ▶ vac
VACS ▶ vac
VACUA ▶ vacuum
VACUATE vb empty
VACUIST n person believing in the existence of vacuums in nature
VACUITY n absence of intelligent thought or ideas
VACUOLE n fluid-filled cavity in the cytoplasm of a cell
VACUOUS adj not expressing intelligent thought
VACUUM n empty space from which all or most air or gas has been removed ▷ vb clean with a vacuum cleaner

VACUUMS ▶ vacuum
VADE vb fade
VADED ▶ vade
VADES ▶ vade
VADING ▶ vade
VADOSE adj of or derived from water occurring above the water table
VAE same as > voe
VAES ▶ vae
VAG n vagrant
VAGAL adj of, relating to, or affecting the vagus nerve
VAGALLY ▶ vagal
VAGARY n unpredictable change
VAGGED ▶ vag
VAGGING ▶ vag
VAGI ▶ vagus
VAGILE adj able to move freely
VAGINA n (in female mammals) passage from the womb to the external genitals
VAGINAE ▶ vagina
VAGINAL ▶ vagina
VAGINAS ▶ vagina
VAGITUS n new-born baby's cry
VAGRANT n person with no settled home ▷ adj wandering
VAGROM same as ▶ vagrant
VAGS ▶ vag
VAGUE adj not clearly explained ▷ vb wander
VAGUED ▶ vague
VAGUELY ▶ vague
VAGUER ▶ vague
VAGUES ▶ vague
VAGUEST ▶ vague

VAGUING ▶ vague
VAGUS n tenth cranial nerve, which supplies the heart, lungs, and viscera
VAHANA n vehicle
VAHANAS ▶ vahana
VAHINE n Polynesian woman
VAHINES ▶ vahine
VAIL vb lower (something, such as a weapon), esp as a sign of deference or submission
VAILED ▶ vail
VAILING ▶ vail
VAILS ▶ vail
VAIN adj excessively proud, esp of one's appearance
VAINER ▶ vain
VAINEST ▶ vain
VAINLY ▶ vain
VAIR n fur, probably Russian squirrel, used to trim robes in the Middle Ages
VAIRE adj of Russian squirrel fur
VAIRIER ▶ vair
VAIRS ▶ vair
VAIRY ▶ vair
VAIVODE n European ruler
VAKAS n Armenian priestly garment
VAKASES ▶ vakas
VAKEEL n ambassador
VAKEELS ▶ vakeel
VAKIL same as ▶ vakeel
VAKILS ▶ vakil
VALANCE n piece of drapery round the edge of a bed ▷ vb provide with a valance
VALE n valley ▷ sentence substitute farewell
VALENCE same as ▶ valency

VALENCY n power of an atom to make molecular bonds

VALERIC adj of, relating to, or derived from valerian

VALES ▸ **vale**

VALET n man's personal male servant ▷ vb act as a valet (for)

VALETA n old-time dance in triple time

VALETAS ▸ **valeta**

VALETE n farewell

VALETED ▸ **valet**

VALETES ▸ **valete**

VALETS ▸ **valet**

VALGOID ▸ **valgus**

VALGOUS same as ▸ **valgus**

VALGUS adj denoting a deformity of a limb ▷ n abnormal position of a limb

VALI n Turkish civil governor

VALIANT adj brave or courageous ▷ n brave person

VALID adj soundly reasoned

VALIDER ▸ **valid**

VALIDLY ▸ **valid**

VALINE n essential amino acid

VALINES ▸ **valine**

VALIS ▸ **vali**

VALISE n small suitcase

VALISES ▸ **valise**

VALIUM n as in **valium picnic** refers to a day on the New York Stock Exchange when business is slow

VALKYR same as ▸ **valkyrie**

VALKYRS ▸ **valkyr**

VALLAR n pertaining to a rampart

VALLARY ▸ **vallar**

VALLATE adj surrounded with a wall

VALLEY n low area between hills, often with a river running through it

VALLEYS ▸ **valley**

VALLUM n Roman rampart or earthwork

VALLUMS ▸ **vallum**

VALONEA same as ▸ **valonia**

VALONIA n acorn cups and unripe acorns of a particular oak

VALOR same as ▸ **valour**

VALORS ▸ **valor**

VALOUR n bravery ▷ n courageous person

VALOURS ▸ **valour**

VALSE another word for

▸ **waltz**

VALSED ▸ **valse**

VALSES ▸ **valse**

VALSING ▸ **valse**

VALUATE vb value or evaluate

VALUE n importance, usefulness ▷ vb assess the worth or desirability of

VALUED ▸ **value**

VALUER ▸ **value**

VALUERS ▸ **value**

VALUES ▸ **value**

VALUING ▸ **value**

VALUTA n value of one currency in terms of its exchange rate with another

VALUTAS ▸ **valuta**

VALVAL same as ▸ **valvular**

VALVAR same as ▸ **valvular**

VALVATE adj furnished with a valve or valves

VALVE n device to control the movement of fluid through a pipe ▷ vb provide with a valve

VALVED ▸ **valve**

VALVES ▸ **valve**

VALVING ▸ **valve**

VALVULA same as ▸ **valvule**

VALVULE n small valve or a part resembling one

VAMOOSE vb leave a place hurriedly

VAMOSE same as

▸ **vamoose**

VAMOSED ▸ **vamose**

VAMOSES ▸ **vamose**

VAMP n sexually attractive woman who seduces men ▷ vb (of a woman) to seduce (a man)

VAMPED ▸ **vamp**

VAMPER ▸ **vamp**

VAMPERS ▸ **vamp**

VAMPIER ▸ **vamp**

VAMPING ▸ **vamp**

VAMPIRE n (in folklore) corpse that rises at night to drink the blood of the living ▷ vb assail

VAMPISH ▸ **vamp**

VAMPS ▸ **vamp**

VAMPY ▸ **vamp**

VAN n motor vehicle for transporting goods ▷ vb send in a van

VANADIC adj of or containing vanadium, esp in a trivalent or pentavalent state

VANDA n type of orchid

VANDAL n person who

deliberately damages property

VANDALS ▸ **vandal**

VANDAS ▸ **vanda**

VANDYKE n short pointed beard ▷ vb cut with deep zigzag indentations

VANE n flat blade on a rotary device such as a weathercock or propeller

VANED ▸ **vane**

VANES ▸ **vane**

VANESSA n type of butterfly

VANG n type of rope or tackle on a sailing ship

VANGS ▸ **vang**

VANILLA n seed pod of a tropical climbing orchid, used for flavouring ▷ adj flavoured with vanilla

VANISH vb disappear suddenly or mysteriously ▷ n second and weaker of the two vowels in a falling diphthong

VANITAS n type of Dutch painting

VANITY n (display of) excessive pride

VANLOAD n amount van will carry

VANMAN n man in control of a van

VANMEN ▸ **vanman**

VANNED ▸ **van**

VANNER n horse used to pull delivery vehicles

VANNERS ▸ **vanner**

VANNING ▸ **van**

VANPOOL n van-sharing group

VANS ▸ **van**

VANT archaic word for

▸ **vanguard**

VANTAGE n state, position, or opportunity offering advantage ▷ vb benefit

VANTS ▸ **vant**

VANWARD adv in or towards the front

VAPID adj lacking character, dull

VAPIDER ▸ **vapid**

VAPIDLY ▸ **vapid**

VAPOR same as ▸ **vapour**

VAPORED ▸ **vapor**

VAPORER ▸ **vapor**

VAPORS ▸ **vapor**

VAPORY ▸ **vapour**

VAPOUR n moisture suspended in air as steam or mist ▷ vb evaporate

VAPOURS ▸ **vapour**

V

VAPOURY ▸ vapour
VAQUERO n cattlehand
VAR n unit of reactive power of an alternating current
VARA n unit of length used in Spain, Portugal, and South America
VARAN n type of lizard
VARANS ▸ varan
VARAS ▸ vara
VARDIES ▸ vardy
VARDY n verdict
VARE n rod
VAREC n ash obtained from kelp
VARECH same as ▸ varec
VARECHS ▸ varech
VARECS ▸ varec
VARES ▸ vare
VAREUSE n type of coat
VARIA n collection or miscellany, esp of literary works
VARIANT adj differing from a standard or type ▸ n something that differs from a standard or type
VARIAS ▸ varia
VARIATE n random variable or a numerical value taken by it ▸ vb vary
VARICES ▸ varix
VARIED ▸ vary
VARIER n person who varies
VARIERS ▸ varier
VARIES ▸ vary
VARIETY n state of being diverse or various
VARIOLA n smallpox
VARIOLE n any of the rounded masses that make up the rock variolite
VARIOUS adj of several kinds
VARIX n tortuous dilated vein
VARLET n menial servant
VARLETS ▸ varlet
VARMENT same as ▸ varmint
VARMINT n irritating or obnoxious person or animal
VARNA n any of the four Hindu castes
VARNAS ▸ varna
VARNISH n solution of oil and resin, put on a surface to make it hard and glossy ▸ vb apply varnish to
VAROOM same as ▸ vroom
VAROOMS same as ▸ varoom
VARROA n small parasite

VARROAS ▸ varroa
VARS ▸ var
VARSAL adj universal
VARSITY n university
VARUS adj denoting a deformity of a limb ▸ n abnormal position of a limb
VARUSES ▸ varus
VARVE n typically thin band of sediment deposited annually in glacial lakes
VARVED adj having layers of sedimentary deposit
VARVEL n piece of falconry equipment
VARVELS ▸ varvel
VARVES ▸ varve
VARY vb change
VARYING ▸ vary
VAS n vessel or tube that carries a fluid
VASA ▸ vas
VASAL ▸ vas
VASCULA > vasculum
VASE n ornamental jar, esp for flowers
VASES ▸ vase
VASSAIL archaic variant of ▸ vassal
VASSAL n man given land by a lord in return for military service ▸ adj of or relating to a vassal ▸ vb vassalize
VASSALS ▸ vassal
VAST adj extremely large ▸ n immense or boundless space
VASTER ▸ vast
VASTEST ▸ vast
VASTIER ▸ vasty
VASTITY ▸ vast
VASTLY ▸ vast
VASTS ▸ vast
VASTY archaic or poetic word for ▸ vast
VAT n large container for liquids ▸ vb place, store, or treat in a vat
VATABLE adj subject to VAT
VATFUL n amount enough to fill a vat
VATFULS ▸ vatful
VATIC adj of, relating to, or characteristic of a prophet
VATICAL same as ▸ vatic
VATMAN n Customs and Excise employee
VATMEN ▸ vatman
VATS ▸ vat
VATTED ▸ vat
VATTER n person who works with vats; blender
VATTERS ▸ vatter

VATTING ▸ vat
VATU n standard monetary unit of Vanuatu
VATUS ▸ vatu
VAU same as ▸ vav
VAUCH vb move fast
VAUCHED ▸ vauch
VAUCHES ▸ vauch
VAUDOO same as ▸ voodoo
VAUDOOS ▸ vaudoo
VAUDOUX same as ▸ voodoo
VAULT n secure room for storing valuables ▸ vb jump over (something) by resting one's hand(s) on it.
VAULTED ▸ vault
VAULTER ▸ vault
VAULTS ▸ vault
VAULTY adj arched
VAUNCE ▸ advance
VAUNCED ▸ vaunce
VAUNCES ▸ vaunce
VAUNT vb describe or display (success or possessions) boastfully ▸ n boast
VAUNTED ▸ vaunt
VAUNTER ▸ vaunt
VAUNTIE same as ▸ vaunty
VAUNTS ▸ vaunt
VAUNTY adj proud
VAURIEN n rascal
VAUS ▸ vau
VAUT same as ▸ vault
VAUTE same as ▸ vault
VAUTED ▸ vaute
VAUTES ▸ vaute
VAUTING ▸ vaut
VAUTS ▸ vaut
VAV n sixth letter of the Hebrew alphabet

It is surprising how often one wants to get rid of two Vs, and when one does, this word, the name of a Hebrew letter, fits the bill nicely. It has an equally useful variant **vaw**.

VAVASOR n (in feudal society) vassal who also has vassals himself
VAVS ▸ vav
VAW n Hebrew letter
VAWARD n vanguard
VAWARDS ▸ vaward
VAWNTIE ▸ vaunty
VAWS ▸ vaw
VAWTE same as ▸ vault
VAWTED ▸ vawte
VAWTES ▸ vawte
VAWTING ▸ vawte

VEAL n calf meat ▷ vb cover with a veil

VEALE same as ▷ **veil**

VEALED ▷ **veal**

VEALER n young bovine animal of up to 14 months old grown for veal

VEALERS ▷ **vealer**

VEALES ▷ **veale**

VEALIER ▷ **veal**

VEALING ▷ **veal**

VEALS ▷ **veal**

VEALY ▷ **veal**

VECTOR n quantity that has size and direction, such as force ▷ vb direct or guide (a pilot) by directions transmitted by radio

VECTORS ▷ **vector**

VEDALIA n Australian ladybird which is a pest of citrus fruits

VEDETTE n small patrol vessel

VEDUTA n painting of a town or city

VEDUTE ▷ **veduta**

VEE n letter 'v'

VEEJAY n video jockey

VEEJAYS ▷ **veejay**

VEENA same as ▷ **vina**

VEENAS ▷ **veena**

VEEP n vice president

VEEPEE n vice president

VEEPEES ▷ **veepee**

VEEPS ▷ **veep**

VEER vb change direction suddenly ▷ n change of course or direction

VEERED ▷ **veer**

VEERIES ▷ **veery**

VEERING ▷ **veer**

VEERS ▷ **veer**

VEERY n tawny brown North American thrush

VEES ▷ **vee**

VEG n vegetable or vegetables ▷ vb relax

> **Veg** is a short form of **vegetable**. If someone plays this, remember that you can add an A or O to it to form **vega** or **vego**.

VEGA n tobacco plantation

VEGAN n person who eats no meat, fish, eggs, or dairy products ▷ adj suitable for a vegan

VEGANIC adj farmed without the use of animal products or byproducts

VEGANS ▷ **vegan**

VEGAS ▷ **vega**

VEGES ▷ **veg**

VEGETAL adj of or relating to plant life ▷ n vegetable

VEGETE adj lively

VEGGED ▷ **veg**

VEGGES ▷ **veg**

VEGGIE n vegetable ▷ adj vegetarian

VEGGIES ▷ **veggie**

VEGGING ▷ **veg**

VEGIE same as ▷ **veggie**

VEGIES ▷ **vegie**

VEGO adj vegetarian ▷ n vegetarian

VEGOS ▷ **vego**

VEHICLE n machine for carrying people or objects

VEHM n type of medieval German court

VEHME ▷ **vehm**

VEHMIC ▷ **vehm**

VEIL n piece of thin cloth covering the head or face ▷ vb cover with or as if with a veil

VEILED adj disguised

VEILER ▷ **veil**

VEILERS ▷ **veil**

VEILIER ▷ **veil**

VEILING n veil or the fabric used for veils

VEILS ▷ **veil**

VEILY ▷ **veil**

VEIN n tube that takes blood to the heart ▷ vb diffuse over or cause to diffuse over in streaked patterns

VEINAL ▷ **vein**

VEINED ▷ **vein**

VEINER n wood-carving tool

VEINERS ▷ **veiner**

VEINIER ▷ **vein**

VEINING n pattern or network of veins or streaks

VEINLET n any small vein or venule

VEINOUS ▷ **vein**

VEINS ▷ **vein**

VEINULE less common spelling of ▷ **venule**

VEINY ▷ **vein**

VELA ▷ **velum**

VELAMEN n thick layer of dead cells that covers the aerial roots of certain orchids

VELAR adj of, relating to, or attached to a velum ▷ n velar sound

VELARIA > **velarium**

VELARIC ▷ **velar**

VELARS ▷ **velar**

VELATE adj having or covered with velum

VELATED same as ▷ **velate**

VELCRO n tradename for a fastening consisting of two strips of nylon fabric that form a strong bond when pressed together

VELCROS ▷ **velcro**

VELD n high grassland in southern Africa

VELDS ▷ **veld**

VELDT same as ▷ **veld**

VELDTS ▷ **veldt**

VELE same as ▷ **veil**

VELES ▷ **vele**

VELETA same as ▷ **valeta**

VELETAS ▷ **veleta**

VELIGER n free-swimming larva of many molluscs

VELITES pl n light-armed troops in ancient Rome, drawn from the poorer classes

VELL vb cut turf

VELLET n velvet

VELLETS ▷ **vellet**

VELLON n silver and copper alloy used in old Spanish coins

VELLONS ▷ **vellon**

VELLS ▷ **vell**

VELLUM n fine calfskin parchment ▷ adj made of or resembling vellum

VELLUMS ▷ **vellum**

VELLUS n as in **vellus hair** short fine unpigmented hair covering the human body

VELOCE adv be played rapidly

VELOUR n fabric similar to velvet

VELOURS same as ▷ **velour**

VELOUTE n rich white sauce or soup made from stock, egg yolks, and cream

VELUM n any of various membranous structures

VELURE n velvet or a similar fabric ▷ vb cover with velure

VELURED ▷ **velure**

VELURES ▷ **velure**

VELVET n fabric with a thick soft pile ▷ vb cover with velvet

VELVETS ▷ **velvet**

VELVETY ▷ **velvet**

VENA n vein in the body

VENAE ▶ vena
VENAL adj easily bribed
VENALLY ▶ venal
VENATIC adj of, relating to, or used in hunting
VENATOR n hunter
VEND vb sell
VENDACE n either of two small whitefish occurring in lakes in Scotland and NW England
VENDAGE n vintage
VENDED ▶ vend
VENDEE n person to whom something, esp real property, is sold
VENDEES ▶ vendee
VENDER same as ▶ vendor
VENDERS ▶ vender
VENDING ▶ vend
VENDIS same as ▶ vendace
VENDISS same as ▶ vendace
VENDOR n person who sells goods such as newspapers or hamburgers from a stall or cart
VENDORS ▶ vendor
VENDS ▶ vend
VENDUE n public sale
VENDUES ▶ vendue
VENEER n thin layer of wood etc covering a cheaper material ▷ vb cover (a surface) with a veneer
VENEERS ▶ veneer
VENEFIC adj having poisonous effects
VENENE n medicine from snake venom
VENENES ▶ venene
VENERER n hunter
VENERY n pursuit of sexual gratification
VENEWE same as ▶ venue
VENEWES ▶ venewe
VENEY n thrust
VENEYS ▶ veney
VENGE vb avenge
VENGED ▶ venge
VENGER ▶ venge
VENGERS ▶ venge
VENGES ▶ venge
VENGING ▶ venge
VENIAL adj (of a sin or fault) easily forgiven
VENIN n any of the poisonous constituents of animal venoms
VENINE same as ▶ venin
VENINES ▶ venine
VENINS ▶ venin

VENIRE n list from which jurors are selected
VENIRES ▶ venire
VENISON n deer meat
VENITE n musical setting for the 95th psalm
VENITES ▶ venite
VENNEL n lane
VENNELS ▶ vennel
VENOM n malice or spite ▷ vb poison
VENOMED ▶ venom
VENOMER ▶ venom
VENOMS ▶ venom
VENOSE adj having veins
VENOUS adj of veins
VENT n outlet releasing fumes or fluid ▷ vb express (an emotion) freely
VENTAGE n small opening
VENTAIL n (in medieval armour) a covering for the lower part of the face
VENTANA n window
VENTED ▶ vent
VENTER ▶ vent
VENTERS ▶ vent
VENTIGE same as ▶ ventage
VENTIL n valve on a musical instrument
VENTILS ▶ ventil
VENTING ▶ vent
VENTOSE adj full of wind
VENTRAL adj relating to the front of the body ▷ n ventral fin
VENTRE same as ▶ venture
VENTRED ▶ ventre
VENTRES ▶ ventre
VENTS ▶ vent
VENTURE n risky undertaking, esp in business ▷ vb do something risky
VENTURI n tube used to control the flow of fluid
VENUE n place where an organized gathering is held
VENUES ▶ venue
VENULAR ▶ venule
VENULE n any of the small branches of a vein
VENULES ▶ venule
VENUS n type of marine bivalve mollusc
VENUSES ▶ venus
VERA adj as in aloe vera plant substance used in skin and hair preparations
VERANDA n porch or portico along the outside of a building
VERB n word that expresses

the idea of action, happening, or being
VERBAL adj spoken ▷ n abuse or invective ▷ vb implicate (someone) in a crime by quoting alleged admission of guilt in court
VERBALS ▶ verbal
VERBENA n plant with sweet-smelling flowers
VERBID n any nonfinite form of a verb or any nonverbal word derived from a verb
VERBIDS ▶ verbid
VERBIFY another word for > verbalize
VERBILE n person who is best stimulated by words
VERBING n use of nouns as verbs
VERBOSE adj speaking at tedious length
VERBS ▶ verb
VERD adj as in verd antique dark green mottled impure variety of serpentine marble
VERDANT adj covered in green vegetation
VERDET n type of verdigris
VERDETS ▶ verdet
VERDICT n decision of a jury
VERDIN n small W North American tit having grey plumage with a yellow head
VERDINS ▶ verdin
VERDIT same as ▶ verdict
VERDITE n type of rock used in jewellery
VERDITS ▶ verdit
VERDOY n floral or leafy shield decoration
VERDURE n flourishing green vegetation
VERGE n grass border along a road ▷ vb move in a specified direction
VERGED ▶ verge
VERGER n church caretaker
VERGERS ▶ verger
VERGES ▶ verge
VERGING ▶ verge
VERGLAS n thin film of ice on rock
VERIDIC same as > veridical
VERIER ▶ very
VERIEST ▶ very
VERIFY vb check the truth or accuracy of
VERILY adv in truth
VERISM n extreme

naturalism in art or literature

VERISMO n school of composition that originated in Italian opera

VERISMS ▶ verism

VERIST ▶ verism

VERISTS ▶ verism

VERITAS n truth

VERITE adj involving a high degree of realism or naturalism ▷ n this kind of realism in film

VERITES ▶ verite

VERITY n true statement or principle

VERLAN n variety of French slang in which the syllables are inverted

VERLANS ▶ verlan

VERLIG adj enlightened

VERMAL ▶ vermis

VERMEIL n gilded silver, bronze, or other metal, used esp in the 19th century ▷ vb decorate with vermeil ▷ adj vermilion

VERMELL same as ▶ vermeil

VERMES ▶ vermis

VERMIAN ▶ vermis

VERMIL same as ▶ vermeil

VERMILS ▶ vermil

VERMILY ▶ vermeil

VERMIN pl n animals, esp insects and rodents, that spread disease or cause damage

VERMINS ▶ vermin

VERMINY ▶ vermin

VERMIS n middle lobe connecting the two halves of the cerebellum

VERMUTH same as ▶ vermouth

VERNAL adj occurring in spring

VERNANT ▶ vernal

VERNIER n movable scale on a graduated measuring instrument for taking readings in fractions

VERNIX n white substance covering the skin of a foetus

VERONAL n a long-acting barbiturate used medicinally

VERRA Scots word for ▶ very

VERREL n ferrule

VERRELS ▶ verrel

VERREY same as ▶ vair

VERRUCA n wart, usu on the foot

VERRUGA same as

▶ verruca

VERRY same as ▶ vair

VERS n verse

VERSAL n embellished letter

VERSALS ▶ versal

VERSANT n side or slope of a mountain or mountain range

VERSE n group of lines forming part of a song or poem ▷ vb write verse

VERSED adj thoroughly knowledgeable (about)

VERSER n versifier

VERSERS ▶ verser

VERSES ▶ verse

VERSET n short, often sacred, verse

VERSETS ▶ verset

VERSIFY vb write in verse

VERSIN same as ▶ versine

VERSINE n mathematical term

VERSING ▶ verse

VERSINS ▶ versin

VERSION n form of something, such as a piece of writing, with some differences from other forms

VERSO n left-hand page of a book

VERSOS ▶ verso

VERST n unit of length used in Russia

VERSTE same as ▶ verst

VERSTES ▶ verste

VERSTS ▶ verst

VERSUS prep in opposition to or in contrast with

VERSUTE adj cunning

VERT n right to cut green wood in a forest ▷ vb turn

VERTED ▶ vert

VERTEX n point on a geometric figure where the sides form an angle

VERTIGO n dizziness, usu when looking down from a high place

VERTING ▶ vert

VERTS ▶ vert

VERTU same as ▶ virtu

VERTUE same as ▶ virtu

VERTUES ▶ vertue

VERTUS ▶ vertu

VERVAIN n plant with spikes of blue, purple, or white flowers

VERVE n enthusiasm or liveliness

VERVEL same as ▶ varvel

VERVELS ▶ vervel

VERVEN same as ▶ vervain

VERVENS ▶ verven

VERVES ▶ verve

VERVET n variety of a South African guenon monkey

VERVETS ▶ vervet

VERY adv more than usually, extremely ▷ adj absolute, exact

VESICA n bladder

VESICAE ▶ vesica

VESICAL adj of or relating to a vesica, esp the urinary bladder

VESICLE n sac or small cavity, esp one containing fluid

VESPA n type of wasp

VESPAS ▶ vespa

VESPER n evening prayer, service, or hymn

VESPERS pl n service of evening prayer

VESPID n insect of the family that includes the common wasp and hornet ▷ adj of or belonging to this family

VESPIDS ▶ vespid

VESPINE adj of, relating to, or resembling a wasp or wasps

VESPOID adj like a wasp

VESSAIL archaic variant of ▶ vessel

VESSEL n container or ship ▷ adj contained in a vessel

VESSELS ▶ vessel

VEST n undergarment worn on the top half of the body ▷ vb give (authority) to (someone)

VESTA n short friction match, usually of wood

VESTAL adj pure, chaste ▷ n chaste woman

VESTALS ▶ vestal

VESTAS ▶ vesta

VESTED adj having an existing right to the immediate or future possession of property

VESTEE n person having a vested interest something

VESTEES ▶ vestee

VESTIGE n small amount or trace

VESTING ▶ vest

VESTRAL ▶ vestry

VESTRY n room in a church used as an office by the priest or minister

V

VESTS ▶ vest

VESTURE *n* garment or something that seems like a garment ▷ *vb* clothe

VET *vb* check the suitability of ▷ *n* military veteran

VETCH *n* climbing plant with a beanlike fruit used as fodder

VETCHES ▶ vetch

VETCHY *adj* consisting of vetches

VETERAN *n* person with long experience in a particular activity, esp military service ▷ *adj* long-serving

VETIVER *n* tall hairless grass of tropical and subtropical Asia

VETKOEK *n* South African cake

VETO *n* official power to cancel a proposal ▷ *vb* enforce a veto against

VETOED ▶ veto

VETOER ▶ veto

VETOERS ▶ veto

VETOES ▶ veto

VETOING ▶ veto

VETS ▶ vet

VETTED ▶ vet

VETTER ▶ vet

VETTERS ▶ vet

VETTING *n as in* **positive vetting** checking a person's background to assess their suitability of an important post

VETTURA *n* Italian mode of transport

VEX *vb* frustrate, annoy

VEXED *adj* annoyed and puzzled

VEXEDLY ▶ vexed

VEXER ▶ vex

VEXERS ▶ vex

VEXES ▶ vex

VEXIL *same as* > **vexillum**

VEXILLA > **vexillum**

VEXILS ▶ vexil

VEXING ▶ vex

VEXINGS ▶ vex

VEXT *same as* ▶ vexed

VEZIR *same as* ▶ vizier

VEZIRS ▶ vezir

VIA *prep* by way of ▷ *n* road

VIABLE *adj* able to be put into practice

VIABLY ▶ viable

VIADUCT *n* bridge over a valley

VIAE ▶ via

VIAL *n* small bottle for liquids ▷ *vb* put into a vial

VIALED ▶ vial

VIALFUL ▶ vial

VIALING ▶ vial

VIALLED ▶ vial

VIALS ▶ vial

VIAND *n* type of food, esp a delicacy

VIANDS ▶ viand

VIAS ▶ via

VIATIC *same as* > **viatical**

VIATICA > **viaticum**

VIATOR *n* traveller

VIATORS ▶ viator

VIBE *n* feeling or flavour of the kind specified

VIBES *pl n* vibrations

VIBEX *n* mark under the skin

VIBEY *adj* lively and vibrant

VIBICES ▶ vibex

VIBIER ▶ vibey

VIBIEST ▶ vibey

VIBIST *n* person who plays a vibraphone in a jazz band or group

VIBISTS ▶ vibist

VIBRANT *adj* vigorous in appearance, energetic ▷ *n* trilled or rolled speech sound

VIBRATE *vb* move back and forth rapidly

VIBRATO *n* rapid fluctuation in the pitch of a note

VIBRIO *n* curved or spiral rodlike bacterium

VIBRION *same as* ▶ vibrio

VIBRIOS ▶ vibrio

VIBS *pl n* type of climbing shoes

VICAR *n* member of the clergy in charge of a parish

VICARLY ▶ vicar

VICARS ▶ vicar

VICARY *n* office of a vicar

VICE *n* immoral or evil habit or action ▷ *adj* serving in place of ▷ *vb* grip (something) with or as if with a vice ▷ *prep* instead of

VICED ▶ vice

VICEROY *n* governor of a colony who represents the monarch

VICES ▶ vice

VICHIES ▶ vichy

VICHY *n* French mineral water

VICIATE *same as* ▶ vitiate

VICINAL *adj* neighbouring

VICING ▶ vice

VICIOUS *adj* cruel and violent

VICOMTE *n* French nobleman

VICTIM *n* person or thing harmed or killed

VICTIMS ▶ victim

VICTOR *n* person who has defeated an opponent, esp in war or in sport

VICTORS ▶ victor

VICTORY *n* winning of a battle or contest

VICTRIX *same as* > **victress**

VICTUAL *vb* supply with or obtain victuals

VICUGNA *same as* ▶ vicuna

VICUNA *n* S American animal like the llama

VICUNAS ▶ vicuna

VID *same as* ▶ video

VIDAME *n* French nobleman

VIDAMES ▶ vidame

VIDE *interj* look

VIDENDA > **videndum**

VIDEO *vb* record (a TV programme or event) on video ▷ *adj* relating to or used in producing television images ▷ *n* recording and showing of films and events using a television set, video tapes, and a video recorder

VIDEOED ▶ video

VIDEOS ▶ video

VIDETTE *same as* ▶ vedette

VIDICON *n* small television camera tube used in closed-circuit television

VIDIMUS *n* inspection

VIDS ▶ vid

VIDUAGE *n* widows collectively

VIDUAL *adj* widowed

VIDUITY *n* widowhood

VIDUOUS *adj* empty

VIE *vb* compete (with someone)

VIED ▶ vie

VIELLE *n* stringed musical instrument

VIELLES ▶ vielle

VIENNA *n as in* **vienna loaf, vienna steak** associated with Vienna

VIER ▶ vie

VIERS ▶ vie

VIES ▶ vie

VIEW *n* opinion or belief ▷ *vb* think of (something) in a particular way

VIEWED ▶ view

VIEWER n person who watches television

VIEWERS ▶ viewer

VIEWIER ▶ viewy

VIEWING n act of watching television

VIEWLY adj pleasant on the eye

VIEWS ▶ view

VIEWY adj having fanciful opinions or ideas

VIFDA same as ▶ vivda

VIFDAS ▶ vifda

VIG n interest on a loan that is paid to a moneylender

VIGA n rafter

VIGAS ▶ viga

VIGIA n navigational hazard marked on a chart although its existence has not been confirmed

VIGIAS ▶ vigia

VIGIL n night-time period of staying awake to look after a sick person, pray, etc

VIGILS ▶ vigil

VIGOR same as ▶ vigour

VIGORO n women's game similar to cricket

VIGOROS ▶ vigoro

VIGORS ▶ vigor

VIGOUR n physical or mental energy

VIGOURS ▶ vigour

VIGS ▶ vig

VIHARA n type of Buddhist temple

VIHARAS ▶ vihara

VIHUELA n obsolete plucked stringed instrument of Spain, related to the guitar

VIKING n Dane, Norwegian, or Swede who raided by sea most of N and W Europe between the 8th and 11th centuries

VIKINGS ▶ viking

VILAYET n major administrative division of Turkey

VILD same as ▶ vile

VILDE same as ▶ vile

VILDLY ▶ vild

VILE adj very wicked

VILELY ▶ vile

VILER ▶ vile

VILEST ▶ vile

VILIACO n scoundrel

VILIAGO same as ▶ viliaco

VILIFY vb attack the character of

VILL n township

VILLA n large house with gardens

VILLAE ▶ villa

VILLAGE n small group of houses in a country area

VILLAIN n wicked person

VILLAN same as ▶ villein

VILLANS ▶ villan

VILLANY same as > villainy

VILLAR ▶ vill

VILLAS ▶ villa

VILLEIN n peasant bound in service to his lord

VILLI ▶ villus

VILLOSE same as ▶ villous

VILLOUS adj (of plant parts) covered with long hairs

VILLS ▶ vill

VILLUS n one of the finger-like projections in the small intestine of many vertebrates

VIM n force, energy

| This word can be helpful when you're stuck with unpromising letters, and gives a reasonable score for a three-letter word.

VIMANA n Indian mythological chariot of the gods

VIMANAS ▶ vimana

VIMEN n long flexible shoot that occurs in certain plants

VIMINA ▶ vimen

VIMINAL ▶ vimen

VIMS ▶ vim

VIN n French wine

VINA n stringed musical instrument related to the sitar

VINAL n type of manmade fibre

VINALS ▶ vinal

VINAS ▶ vina

VINASSE n residue left in a still after distilling spirits, esp brandy

VINCA n type of trailing plant with blue flowers

VINCAS ▶ vinca

VINCULA > vinculum

VINE n climbing plant, esp one producing grapes ▷ vb form like a vine

VINEAL adj relating to wines

VINED ▶ vine

VINEGAR n acid liquid made from wine, beer, or cider ▷ vb apply vinegar to

VINER n vinedresser

VINERS ▶ viner

VINERY n hothouse for growing grapes

VINES ▶ vine

VINEW vb become mouldy

VINEWED ▶ vinew

VINEWS ▶ vinew

VINIC adj of, relating to, or contained in wine

VINIER ▶ vine

VINIEST ▶ vine

VINIFY vb convert into wine

VINING ▶ vine

VINO n wine

VINOS ▶ vino

VINOUS adj of or characteristic of wine

VINS ▶ vin

VINT vb sell (wine)

VINTAGE n wine from a particular harvest of grapes ▷ adj best and most typical ▷ vb gather (grapes) or make (wine)

VINTED ▶ vint

VINTING ▶ vint

VINTNER n dealer in wine

VINTRY n place where wine is sold

VINTS ▶ vint

VINY ▶ vine

VINYL n type of plastic, used in mock leather and records ▷ adj of or containing a particular group of atoms

VINYLIC ▶ vinyl

VINYLS ▶ vinyl

VIOL n early stringed instrument preceding the violin

VIOLA n stringed instrument lower in pitch than a violin

VIOLAS ▶ viola

VIOLATE vb break (a law or agreement) ▷ adj violated or dishonoured

VIOLD archaic or poetic past form of ▶ vial

VIOLENT adj using or involving physical force with the intention of causing injury or destruction ▷ vb coerce

VIOLER n person who plays the viol

VIOLERS ▶ violer

VIOLET n plant with bluish-purple flowers ▷ adj bluish-purple

VIOLETS ▶ violet

VIOLIN n small four-stringed musical

instrument played with a bow

VIOLINS ▶ violin

VIOLIST *n* person who plays the viola

VIOLONE *n* double-bass member of the viol family

VIOLS ▶ viol

VIPER *n* poisonous snake

VIPERS ▶ viper

VIRAGO *n* aggressive woman

VIRAGOS ▶ virago

VIRAL *adj* of or caused by a virus

VIRALLY ▶ viral

VIRANDA *same as* ▶ **veranda**

VIRANDO *same as* ▶ **veranda**

VIRE *vb* turn

VIRED ▶ vire

VIRELAI *same as* ▶ **virelay**

VIRELAY *n* old French verse form

VIREMIA *same as* > **viraemia**

VIREMIC ▶ viremia

VIRENT *adj* green

VIREO *n* American songbird

VIREOS ▶ vireo

VIRES ▶ vire

VIRETOT *n as in* **on the viretot** in a rush

VIRGA *n* wisps of rain or snow that evaporate before reaching the earth

VIRGAS ▶ virga

VIRGATE *adj* long, straight, and thin ▷ *n* obsolete measure of land area, usually taken as equivalent to 30 acres

VIRGE *n* rod

VIRGER *n* rod-bearer

VIRGERS ▶ virger

VIRGES ▶ virge

VIRGIN *n* person, esp a woman, who has not had sexual intercourse ▷ *adj* not having had sexual intercourse ▷ *vb* behave like a virgin

VIRGINS ▶ virgin

VIRGULE *another name for* ▶ **slash**

VIRID *adj* verdant

VIRILE *adj* having the traditional male characteristics of physical strength and a high sex drive

VIRING ▶ vire

VIRINO *n* entity postulated to be the causative agent of BSE

VIRINOS ▶ virino

VIRION *n* virus in infective form, consisting of an RNA particle within a protein covering

VIRIONS ▶ virion

VIRL *same as* ▶ **ferrule**

VIRLS ▶ virl

VIROID *n* any of various infective RNA particles

VIROIDS ▶ viroid

VIROSE *adj* poisonous

VIROSES ▶ virosis

VIROSIS *n* viral disease

VIROUS *same as* ▶ **virose**

VIRTU *n* taste or love for curios or works of fine art

VIRTUAL *adj* having the effect but not the form of

VIRTUE *n* moral goodness

VIRTUES ▶ virtue

VIRTUS ▶ virtu

VIRUS *n* microorganism that causes disease in humans, animals, and plants

VIRUSES ▶ virus

VIS *n* power, force, or strength

VISA *n* permission to enter a country, shown by a stamp on the passport ▷ *vb* enter a visa into (a passport)

VISAED ▶ visa

VISAGE *n* face

VISAGED ▶ visage

VISAGES ▶ visage

VISAING ▶ visa

VISARD *same as* ▶ **vizard**

VISARDS ▶ visard

VISAS ▶ visa

VISCERA *pl n* large abdominal organs

VISCID *adj* sticky

VISCIN *n* sticky substance found on plants

VISCINS ▶ viscin

VISCOID *adj* (of a fluid) somewhat viscous

VISCOSE *same as* ▶ **viscous**

VISCOUS *adj* thick and sticky

VISCUM *n* shrub genus

VISCUMS ▶ viscum

VISCUS *n* internal organ

VISE *vb* advise or award a visa to ▷ *n* (in US English) vice

VISED ▶ vise

VISEED ▶ vise

VISEING ▶ vise

VISES ▶ vise

VISHING *n* telephone scam

used to gain access to credit card numbers or bank details

VISIBLE *adj* able to be seen ▷ *n* visible item of trade

VISIBLY ▶ visible

VISIE *same as* ▶ **vizy**

VISIED ▶ visie

VISIER ▶ visie

VISIERS ▶ visie

VISIES ▶ visie

VISILE *n* person best stimulated by vision

VISILES ▶ visile

VISING ▶ vise

VISION *n* ability to see ▷ *vb* see or show in or as if in a vision

VISIONS ▶ vision

VISIT *vb* go or come to see ▷ *n* instance of visiting

VISITE *n* type of cape

VISITED ▶ visit

VISITEE *n* person who is visited

VISITER *same as* ▶ **visitor**

VISITES ▶ visite

VISITOR *n* person who visits a person or place

VISITS ▶ visit

VISIVE *adj* visual

VISNE *n* neighbourhood

VISNES ▶ visne

VISNOMY *n* method of judging character from facial features

VISON *n* type of mink

VISONS ▶ vison

VISOR *n* transparent part of a helmet that pulls down over the face ▷ *vb* cover, provide, or protect with a visor

VISORED ▶ visor

VISORS ▶ visor

VISTA *n* (beautiful) extensive view ▷ *vb* make into vistas

VISTAED ▶ vista

VISTAL ▶ vista

VISTAS ▶ vista

VISTO *same as* ▶ **vista**

VISTOS ▶ visto

VISUAL *adj* done by or used in seeing ▷ *n* sketch to show the proposed layout of an advertisement, as in a newspaper

VISUALS ▶ visual

VITA *n* curriculum vitae

VITAE ▶ vita

VITAL *adj* essential or highly important ▷ *n* bodily

organs that are necessary to maintain life

VITALLY ▸ **vital**

VITALS ▸ **vital**

VITAMER n type of chemical

VITAMIN n one of a group of substances that are essential in the diet for specific body processes

VITAS ▸ **vita**

VITE adv musical direction

VITELLI > **vitellus**

VITESSE n speed

VITEX n type of herb

VITEXES ▸ **vitex**

VITIATE vb spoil the effectiveness of

VITIOUS adj mistaken

VITRAGE n light fabric

VITRAIL n stained glass

VITRAIN n type of coal occurring as horizontal glassy bands of a nonsoiling friable material

VITRAUX ▸ **vitrail**

VITREUM n vitreous body

VITRIC adj of, relating to, resembling, or having the nature of glass

VITRICS n glassware

VITRIFY vb change or be changed into glass or a glassy substance

VITRINE n glass display case or cabinet for works of art, curios, etc

VITRIOL n language expressing bitterness and hatred ▸ vb attack or injure with or as if with vitriol

VITTA n tubelike cavity containing oil that occurs in the fruits of certain plants

VITTAE ▸ **vitta**

VITTATE ▸ **vitta**

VITTLE obsolete or dialect spelling of ▸ **victual**

VITTLED ▸ **vittle**

VITTLES obsolete or dialect spelling of > **victuals**

VITULAR same as > **vituline**

VIVA interj long live (a person or thing) ▸ n examination in the form of an interview ▸ vb examine (a candidate) in a spoken interview

VIVACE adj, adv (to be performed) in a lively manner ▸ n piece of music to be performed in this way

VIVACES ▸ **vivace**

VIVAED ▸ **viva**

VIVAING ▸ **viva**

VIVARIA > **vivarium**

VIVARY same as > **vivarium**

VIVAS ▸ **viva**

VIVAT interj long live ▸ n expression of acclamation

VIVATS ▸ **vivat**

VIVDA n method of drying meat

VIVDAS ▸ **vivda**

VIVE interj long live

VIVELY adv in a lively manner

VIVENCY n physical or mental energy

VIVER n fish pond

VIVERRA n civet genus

VIVERS ▸ **viver**

VIVES n disease found in horses

VIVID adj very bright

VIVIDER ▸ **vivid**

VIVIDLY ▸ **vivid**

VIVIFIC adj giving life

VIVIFY vb animate, inspire

VIVO adv with life and vigour

VIVRES n provisions

VIXEN n female fox

VIXENLY ▸ **vixen**

VIXENS ▸ **vixen**

VIZARD n means of disguise ▸ vb conceal by means of a disguise

VIZARDS ▸ **vizard**

VIZIED ▸ **vizy**

VIZIER n high official in certain Muslim countries

VIZIERS ▸ **vizier**

VIZIES ▸ **vizy**

VIZIR same as ▸ **vizier**

VIZIRS ▸ **vizir**

VIZOR same as ▸ **visor**

VIZORED ▸ **vizor**

VIZORS ▸ **vizor**

VIZSLA n breed of Hungarian hunting dog with a smooth rusty-gold coat

VIZSLAS ▸ **vizsla**

VIZY vb look

VIZYING ▸ **vizy**

VIZZIE same as ▸ **vizy**

VIZZIED ▸ **vizzie**

VIZZIES ▸ **vizzie**

VLEI n area of low marshy ground, esp one that feeds a stream

VLEIS ▸ **vlei**

VLIES ▸ **vly**

VLOG n video weblog

VLOGGER n person who keeps a video blog

VLOGS ▸ **vlog**

VLY same as ▸ **vlei**

This word for low-lying wet ground can be useful when you are short of vowels. It can also be spelt **vlei**.

VOAR n spring

VOARS ▸ **voar**

VOCAB n vocabulary

VOCABLE n word regarded simply as a sequence of letters or spoken sounds ▸ adj capable of being uttered

VOCABLY ▸ **vocable**

VOCABS ▸ **vocab**

VOCAL adj relating to the voice ▸ n piece of jazz or pop music that is sung

VOCALIC adj of, relating to, or containing a vowel or vowels

VOCALLY ▸ **vocal**

VOCALS ▸ **vocal**

VOCES ▸ **vox**

VOCODER n type of synthesizer that uses the human voice as an oscillator

VOCULAR ▸ **vocule**

VOCULE n faint noise made when articulating certain sounds

VOCULES ▸ **vocule**

VODCAST vb podcast with video

VODDIES ▸ **voddy**

VODDY n vodka

VODKA n (Russian) spirit distilled from potatoes or grain

VODKAS ▸ **vodka**

VODOU same as ▸ **voodoo**

This West Indian word for a kind of black magic may indeed work magic on an unpromising rack. And it has a host of variants, though few people will remember them all: **vaudoo, vaudoux, vodoun, vodun, voodoo, vodoun, voudou** and **voudoun**!

VODOUN same as ▸ **vodun**

VODOUNS ▸ **vodoun**

VODOUS ▸ **vodou**

VODUN n voodoo

VODUNS ▸ **vodun**

VOE n (in Orkney and Shetland) a small bay or narrow creek

VOEMA n vigour or energy

VOEMAS ▶ voema
VOES ▶ voe
VOGIE adj conceited
VOGIER ▶ vogie
VOGIEST ▶ vogie
VOGUE n popular style ▷ adj popular or fashionable ▷ vb bring into vogue
VOGUED ▶ vogue
VOGUER ▶ vogue
VOGUERS ▶ vogue
VOGUES ▶ vogue
VOGUEY ▶ vogue
VOGUIER ▶ vogue
VOGUING same as > vogueing
VOGUISH ▶ vogue
VOICE n (quality of) sound made when speaking or singing ▷ vb express verbally
VOICED adj articulated with accompanying vibration of the vocal cords
VOICER ▶ voice
VOICERS ▶ voice
VOICES ▶ voice
VOICING ▶ voice
VOID adj not legally binding ▷ n feeling of deprivation ▷ vb make invalid
VOIDED adj (of a design) with a hole in the centre of the same shape as the design
VOIDEE n light meal eaten before bed
VOIDEES ▶ voidee
VOIDER ▶ void
VOIDERS ▶ void
VOIDING ▶ void
VOIDS ▶ void
VOILA interj word used to express satisfaction
VOILE n light semitransparent fabric
VOILES ▶ voile
VOIP n voice-over internet protocol
VOIPS ▶ voip
VOITURE n type of vehicle
VOIVODE n type of military leader
VOL n heraldic wings
VOLA n palm of hand or sole of foot
VOLABLE adj quick-witted
VOLAE ▶ vola
VOLAGE adj changeable
VOLANT adj in a flying position
VOLANTE n Spanish horse carriage

VOLAR adj of or relating to the palm of the hand or the sole of the foot
VOLARY n large bird enclosure
VOLATIC adj flying
VOLCANO n mountain with a vent through which lava is ejected
VOLE n small rodent ▷ vb to win by taking all the tricks in a deal
VOLED ▶ vole
VOLENS adj as in nolens volens whether willing or unwilling
VOLERY same as ▶ volary
VOLES ▶ vole
VOLET n type of veil
VOLETS ▶ volet
VOLING ▶ vole
VOLK n people or nation, esp the nation of Afrikaners
VOLKS ▶ volk
VOLLEY n simultaneous discharge of ammunition ▷ vb discharge (ammunition) in a volley
VOLLEYS ▶ volley
VOLOST n (in the former Soviet Union) a rural soviet
VOLOSTS ▶ volost
VOLPINO n Italian breed of dog
VOLS ▶ vol
VOLT n unit of electric potential ▷ vb (in fencing) make a quick movement to avoid a thrust
VOLTA n quick-moving Italian dance popular during the 16th and 17th centuries
VOLTAGE n electric potential difference expressed in volts
VOLTAIC adj producing an electric current
VOLTE same as ▶ volt
VOLTED ▶ volt vb
VOLTES ▶ volte
VOLTI adv musical direction
VOLTING > volt vb
VOLTS ▶ volt
VOLUBIL same as ▶ voluble
VOLUBLE adj talking easily and at length
VOLUBLY ▶ voluble
VOLUME n size of the space occupied by something ▷ vb billow or surge in volume
VOLUMED ▶ volume

VOLUMES ▶ volume
VOLUSPA n Icelandic mythological poem
VOLUTE n spiral or twisting turn, form, or object ▷ adj having the form of a volute
VOLUTED ▶ volute
VOLUTES ▶ volute
VOLUTIN n granular substance found in cells
VOLVA n cup-shaped structure that sheathes the base of the stalk of certain mushrooms
VOLVAE ▶ volva
VOLVAS ▶ volva
VOLVATE ▶ volva
VOLVE vb. turn over
VOLVED ▶ volve
VOLVES ▶ volve
VOLVING ▶ volve
VOLVOX n freshwater protozoan
VOLVULI > volvulus
VOMER n thin flat bone forming part of the separation between the nasal passages in mammals
VOMERS ▶ vomer
VOMICA n pus-containing cavity
VOMICAE ▶ vomica
VOMICAS ▶ vomica
VOMIT vb eject (the contents of the stomach) through the mouth ▷ n matter vomited
VOMITED ▶ vomit
VOMITER ▶ vomit
VOMITO n form of yellow fever
VOMITOS ▶ vomito
VOMITS ▶ vomit
VOMITUS n matter that has been vomited
VONGOLE pl n (in Italian cookery) clams
VOODOO n religion involving ancestor worship and witchcraft ▷ adj of or relating to voodoo ▷ vb affect by or as if by the power of voodoo
VOODOOS ▶ voodoo
VOR vb (in dialect) warn
VORAGO n chasm
VORANT adj devouring
VORLAGE n skiing position
VORPAL adj sharp
VORRED ▶ vor
VORRING ▶ vor
VORS ▶ vor
VORTEX n whirlpool

VOSTRO adj as in **vostro account** bank account held by a foreign bank with a British bank

VOTABLE ▶ **vote**

VOTARY n person dedicated to religion or to a cause ▷ adj ardently devoted to the services or worship of God

VOTE n choice made by a participant in a shared decision ▷ vb make a choice by a vote

VOTED ▶ **vote**

VOTEEN n devotee

VOTEENS ▶ **voteen**

VOTER n person who can or does vote

VOTERS ▶ **voter**

VOTES ▶ **vote**

VOTING ▶ **vote**

VOTINGS ▶ **vote**

VOTIVE adj done or given to fulfil a vow ▷ n votive offering

VOTIVES ▶ **votive**

VOTRESS > **votaress**

VOUCH vb give personal assurance ▷ n act of vouching

VOUCHED ▶ **vouch**

VOUCHEE n person summoned to court to defend a title

VOUCHER n ticket used instead of money to buy specified goods ▷ vb summon someone to court as a vouchee

VOUCHES ▶ **vouch**

VOUDON same as ▶ **voodoo**

VOUDONS ▶ **voudon**

VOUDOU same as ▶ **voodoo**

VOUDOUN same as ▶ **voodoo**

VOUDOUS ▶ **voudou**

VOUGE n form of pike used by foot soldiers in the 14th century and later

VOUGES ▶ **vouge**

VOULGE n type of medieval weapon

VOULGES ▶ **voulge**

VOULU adj deliberate

VOUVRAY n dry white French wine

VOW n solemn and binding promise ▷ vb promise solemnly

VOWED ▶ **vow**

VOWEL n speech sound made without obstructing the flow of breath ▷ vb say as a vowel

VOWELLY ▶ **vowel**

VOWELS ▶ **vowel**

VOWER ▶ **vow**

VOWERS ▶ **vow**

VOWESS n nun

VOWING ▶ **vow**

VOWLESS ▶ **vow**

VOWS ▶ **vow**

VOX n voice or sound

Along with **vex**, this Latin word for voice is the highest-scoring three-letter word beginning with V.

VOXEL n term used in computing imaging

VOXELS ▶ **voxel**

VOYAGE n long journey by sea or in space ▷ vb make a voyage

VOYAGED ▶ **voyage**

VOYAGER ▶ **voyage**

VOYAGES ▶ **voyage**

VOYEUR n person who obtains pleasure from watching people undressing or having sex

VOYEURS ▶ **voyeur**

VOZHD n Russian leader

This unlikely looking word is Russian for a chief or leader, and may provide a great score from an apparently difficult rack.

VOZHDS ▶ **vozhd**

VRAIC n type of seaweed

VRAICS ▶ **vraic**

VRIL n life force

VRILS ▶ **vril**

VROOM interj exclamation imitative of a car engine revving up ▷ vb move noisily and at high speed

VROOMED ▶ **vroom**

VROOMS ▶ **vroom**

VROT adj South African slang for rotten

VROU n Afrikaner woman, esp a married woman

VROUS ▶ **vrou**

VROUW n woman

The heart of any Scrabble player sinks to see a combination of U, V and W on the rack, as there are relatively few words that use even two of these letters. But **vrouw**, a word of Dutch origin for a woman or goodwife, may get you out of the mess.

VROUWS ▶ **vrouw**

VROW same as ▶ **vrouw**

VROWS ▶ **vrow**

VUG n small cavity in a rock or vein, usually lined with crystals

This unusual word of Cornish origin, meaning a cavity in rock, is another that can be useful when you have an uninspiring combination of letters. And it has a variant **vugh** and can be extended to **vuggy** or **vughy.**

VUGG same as ▶ **vug**

VUGGIER ▶ **vug**

VUGGS ▶ **vugg**

VUGGY ▶ **vug**

VUGH same as ▶ **vug**

VUGHIER ▶ **vugh**

VUGHS ▶ **vugh**

VUGHY ▶ **vugh**

VUGS ▶ **vug**

VULCAN n blacksmith

VULCANS ▶ **vulcan**

VULGAR adj showing lack of good taste, decency, or refinement ▷ n common and ignorant person

VULGARS ▶ **vulgar**

VULGATE n commonly recognized text or version ▷ adj generally accepted

VULGO adv generally

VULGUS n the common people

VULN vb wound

VULNED ▶ **vuln**

VULNING ▶ **vuln**

VULNS ▶ **vuln**

VULPINE adj of or like a fox

VULTURE n large bird that feeds on the flesh of dead animals

VULTURN n type of turkey

VULVA n woman's external genitals

VULVAE ▶ **vulva**

VULVAL ▶ **vulva**

VULVAR ▶ **vulva**

VULVAS ▶ **vulva**

VULVATE ▶ **vulva**

VUM vb swear

VUMMED ▶ **vum**

VUMMING ▶ **vum**

VUMS ▶ **vum**

VUTTIER ▶ **vutty**

VUTTY adj dirty

VYING ▶ **vie**

VYINGLY ▶ **vie**

VYINGS ▶ **vie**

V

Ww

W, like V, can be an awkward tile to handle, but at least there are two two-letter words that begin with **W**: **we** and **wo** (5 points each) and two that end with **W**: **aw** and **ow** (5 points each). There are lots of everyday three-letter words that earn good scores: **wiz** (15), **wax** (13) with its two old-fashioned variants **wex** and **wox** (also 13 each) and **way**, **who**, **why**, **wow** and **wry** (9 each). Don't forget **wok** (10) either, which can be as useful on the Scrabble board as in the kitchen!

WAAC *n* (formerly) member of the Women's Auxiliary Army Corp
WAACS ▸ waac
WAB ▸ web *n*
WABAIN *same as* ▸ ouabain
WABAINS ▸ wabain
WABBIT *adj* weary
WABBLE *same as* ▸ wobble
WABBLED ▸ wabble
WABBLER ▸ wabble
WABBLES ▸ wabble
WABBLY ▸ wabble
WABOOM *another word for* > **wagenboom**
WABOOMS ▸ waboom
WABSTER *Scots form of* ▸ webster
WACK *n* friend
WACKE *n* any of various soft earthy rocks that resemble or are derived from basaltic rocks
WACKER *same as* ▸ wack
WACKERS ▸ wacker
WACKES ▸ wacke
WACKEST ▸ wack
WACKIER ▸ wacky
WACKILY ▸ wacky
WACKO *adj* mad or eccentric ▷ *n* mad or eccentric person
WACKOS ▸ wacko
WACKS ▸ wack
WACKY *adj* eccentric or funny
WAD *n* black earthy ore of manganese ▷ *n* small mass of soft material ▷ *vb* form (something) into a wad
WADABLE ▸ wade
WADD *same as* ▸ wad
WADDED ▸ wad

WADDER ▸ wad
WADDERS ▸ wad
WADDIE *same as* ▸ waddy
WADDIED ▸ waddy
WADDIES ▸ waddy
WADDING ▸ wad
WADDLE *vb* walk with short swaying steps ▷ *n* swaying walk
WADDLED ▸ waddle
WADDLER ▸ waddle
WADDLES ▸ waddle
WADDLY ▸ waddle
WADDS ▸ wadd
WADDY *n* heavy wooden club used by Australian Aborigines ▷ *vb* hit with a waddy
WADE *vb* walk with difficulty through water or mud ▷ *n* act or an instance of wading
WADED ▸ wade
WADER *n* long-legged water bird
WADERS *pl n* long waterproof boots which completely cover the legs, worn by anglers for standing in water
WADES ▸ wade
WADI *n* (in N Africa and Arabia) river which is dry except in the wet season
WADIES ▸ wady
WADING ▸ wade
WADINGS ▸ wade
WADIS ▸ wadi
WADMAAL *same as* ▸ wadmal
WADMAL *n* coarse thick woollen fabric, formerly woven esp in Orkney and

Shetland, for outer garments
WADMALS ▸ wadmal
WADMEL *same as* ▸ wadmal
WADMELS ▸ wadmel
WADMOL *same as* ▸ wadmal
WADMOLL *same as* ▸ wadmal
WADMOLS ▸ wadmol
WADS ▸ wad
WADSET *vb* pledge or mortgage
WADSETS ▸ wadset
WADSETT *same as* ▸ wadset
WADT *same as* ▸ wad
WADTS ▸ wadt
WADY *same as* ▸ wadi
WAE *old form of* ▸ woe
WAEFUL *old form of* ▸ woeful
WAENESS *n* sorrow
WAES ▸ wae
WAESOME *adj* sorrowful
WAESUCK *interj* alas
WAFER *n* thin crisp biscuit ▷ *vb* seal, fasten, or attach with a wafer
WAFERED ▸ wafer
WAFERS ▸ wafer
WAFERY ▸ wafer
WAFF *n* gust or puff of air ▷ *vb* flutter or cause to flutter
WAFFED ▸ waff
WAFFIE *n* person regarded as having little worth to society
WAFFIES ▸ waffie
WAFFING ▸ waff
WAFFLE *vb* speak or write in

a vague wordy way ▷ n vague wordy talk or writing
WAFFLED ▶ waffle
WAFFLER ▶ waffle
WAFFLES ▶ waffle
WAFFLY ▶ waffle
WAFFS ▶ waff
WAFT vb drift or carry gently through the air ▷ n something wafted
WAFTAGE ▶ waft
WAFTED ▶ waft
WAFTER n device that causes a draught
WAFTERS ▶ wafter
WAFTING ▶ waft
WAFTS ▶ waft
WAFTURE n act of wafting or waving
WAG vb move rapidly from side to side ▷ n wagging movement
WAGE n payment for work done, esp when paid weekly ▷ vb engage in (an activity)
WAGED ▶ wage
WAGER vb. bet on the outcome of something ▷ n bet on the outcome of an event or activity
WAGERED ▶ wager
WAGERER ▶ wager
WAGERS ▶ wager
WAGES ▶ wage
WAGGA n blanket or bed covering made out of sacks stitched together
WAGGAS ▶ wagga
WAGGED ▶ wag
WAGGER ▶ wag
WAGGERS ▶ wag
WAGGERY n quality of being humorous
WAGGING ▶ wag
WAGGISH adj jocular or humorous
WAGGLE vb move with a rapid shaking or wobbling motion ▷ n rapid shaking or wobbling motion
WAGGLED ▶ waggle
WAGGLER n float only the bottom of which is attached to the fishing line
WAGGLES ▶ waggle
WAGGLY ▶ waggle
WAGGON same as ▶ wagon
WAGGONS ▶ waggon
WAGING ▶ wage
WAGON n four-wheeled vehicle for heavy loads ▷ vb transport by wagon

WAGONED ▶ wagon
WAGONER n person who drives a wagon
WAGONS ▶ wagon
WAGS ▶ wag
WAGSOME another word for ▶ waggish
WAGTAIL n small long-tailed bird
WAGYU n Japanese breed of beef cattle
WAGYUS ▶ wagyu
WAHINE n Māori woman, esp a wife
WAHINES ▶ wahine
WAHOO n food and game fish of tropical seas
WAHOOS ▶ wahoo
WAI n in New Zealand, water
WAIATA n Māori song
WAIATAS ▶ waiata
WAID ▶ weigh
WAIDE ▶ weigh
WAIF n young person who is, or seems, homeless or neglected ▷ vb treat as a waif
WAIFED ▶ waif
WAIFING ▶ waif
WAIFISH ▶ waif
WAIFS ▶ waif
WAIFT n piece of lost property found by someone other than the owner
WAIFTS ▶ waift
WAIL vb cry out in pain or misery ▷ n mournful cry
WAILED ▶ wail
WAILER ▶ wail
WAILERS ▶ wail
WAILFUL ▶ wail
WAILING ▶ wail
WAILS ▶ wail
WAIN vb transport ▷ n farm wagon
WAINAGE n carriages, etc, for transportation of goods
WAINED ▶ wain
WAINING ▶ wain
WAINS ▶ wain
WAIR vb spend
WAIRED ▶ wair
WAIRING ▶ wair
WAIRS ▶ wair
WAIRSH variant spelling of ▶ wersh
WAIRUA n in New Zealand, spirit or soul
WAIRUAS ▶ wairua
WAIS ▶ wai
WAIST n part of the trunk

between the ribs and the hips
WAISTED adj having a waist or waistlike part
WAISTER n sailor performing menial duties
WAISTS ▶ waist
WAIT vb remain inactive in expectation (of something) ▷ n act or period of waiting
WAITE old form of ▶ wait
WAITED ▶ wait
WAITER n man who serves in a restaurant etc ▷ vb serve at table
WAITERS ▶ waiter
WAITES ▶ waite
WAITING ▶ wait
WAITRON n waiter or waitress
WAITS ▶ wait
WAIVE vb refrain from enforcing (a law, right, etc)
WAIVED ▶ waive
WAIVER n act or instance of voluntarily giving up a claim, right, etc
WAIVERS ▶ waiver
WAIVES ▶ waive
WAIVING ▶ waive
WAIVODE same as ▶ voivode
WAIWODE same as ▶ voivode
WAKA n Māori canoe
WAKAME n edible seaweed
WAKAMES ▶ wakame
WAKANDA n supernatural quality said by Native American people to be held by natural objects
WAKAS ▶ waka
WAKE vb rouse from sleep or inactivity ▷ n vigil beside a corpse the night before the funeral
WAKED ▶ wake
WAKEFUL adj unable to sleep
WAKEMAN n watchman
WAKEMEN ▶ wakeman
WAKEN vb wake
WAKENED ▶ waken
WAKENER ▶ waken
WAKENS ▶ waken
WAKER ▶ wake
WAKERS ▶ wake
WAKES ▶ wake
WAKF same as ▶ waqf
WAKFS ▶ wakf
WAKIKI n Melanesian shell currency
WAKIKIS ▶ wakiki

W

WAKING ▶ wake
WAKINGS ▶ wake
WALD Scots form of ▶ weld
WALDO n gadget for manipulating objects by remote control
WALDOES ▶ waldo
WALDOS ▶ waldo
WALDS ▶ wald
WALE same as ▶ weal
WALED ▶ wale
WALER ▶ wale
WALERS ▶ wale
WALES ▶ wale
WALI same as ▶ vali
WALIER ▶ waly
WALIES ▶ waly
WALIEST ▶ waly
WALING ▶ wale
WALIS ▶ wali
WALISE same as ▶ valise
WALISES ▶ walise
WALK vb move on foot with at least one foot always on the ground ▷ n short journey on foot, usu for pleasure
WALKED ▶ walk
WALKER n person who walks
WALKERS ▶ walker
WALKIES pl n as in go walkies a walk
WALKING adj (of a person) considered to possess the qualities of something inanimate as specified ▷ n act of walking
WALKOUT n strike
WALKS ▶ walk
WALKUP n building with stairs to upper floors
WALKUPS ▶ walkup
WALKWAY n path designed for use by pedestrians
WALL n structure of brick, stone, etc used to enclose, divide, or support ▷ vb enclose or seal with a wall or walls
WALLA same as ▶ wallah
WALLABA n type of S American tree
WALLABY n marsupial like a small kangaroo
WALLAH n person involved with or in charge of a specified thing
WALLAHS ▶ wallah
WALLAS ▶ walla
WALLED ▶ wall
WALLER ▶ wall
WALLERS ▶ wall

WALLET n small folding case for paper money, documents, etc
WALLETS ▶ wallet
WALLEYE n fish with large staring eyes
WALLIE same as ▶ wally
WALLIER ▶ wally
WALLIES ▶ wally
WALLING ▶ wall
WALLOP vb hit hard ▷ n hard blow
WALLOPS ▶ wallop
WALLOW vb revel in an emotion ▷ n act or instance of wallowing
WALLOWS ▶ wallow
WALLS ▶ wall
WALLY n stupid person ▷ adj fine, pleasing, or splendid
WALNUT n edible nut with a wrinkled shell ▷ adj made from the wood of a walnut tree
WALNUTS ▶ walnut
WALRUS n large sea mammal with long tusks
WALTIER ▶ walty
WALTY adj (of a ship) likely to roll over
WALTZ n ballroom dance ▷ vb dance a waltz
WALTZED ▶ waltz
WALTZER n person who waltzes
WALTZES ▶ waltz
WALY same as ▶ wally
WAMBLE vb move unsteadily ▷ n unsteady movement
WAMBLED ▶ wamble
WAMBLES ▶ wamble
WAMBLY ▶ wamble
WAME n belly, abdomen, or womb
WAMED ▶ wame
WAMEFOU Scots variant of ▶ wameful
WAMEFUL n bellyful
WAMES ▶ wame
WAMMUL n dog
WAMMULS ▶ wammul
WAMMUS same as ▶ wamus
WAMPEE n type of Asian fruit tree
WAMPEES ▶ wampee
WAMPISH vb wave
WAMPUM n shells woven together, formerly used by Native Americans for money and ornament

WAMPUMS ▶ wampum
WAMPUS same as ▶ wamus
WAMUS n type of cardigan or jacket
WAMUSES ▶ wamus
WAN adj pale and sickly looking ▷ vb make or become wan
WAND n thin rod, esp one used in performing magic tricks
WANDER vb move about without a definite destination or aim ▷ n act or instance of wandering
WANDERS ▶ wander
WANDLE adj supple
WANDOO n eucalyptus tree of W Australia, having white bark and durable wood
WANDOOS ▶ wandoo
WANDS ▶ wand
WANE vb decrease gradually in size or strength
WANED ▶ wane
WANES ▶ wane
WANEY ▶ wane
WANG n cheekbone
WANGAN same as ▶ wanigan
WANGANS ▶ wangan
WANGLE vb get by devious methods ▷ n act or instance of wangling
WANGLED ▶ wangle
WANGLER ▶ wangle
WANGLES ▶ wangle
WANGS ▶ wang
WANGUN same as ▶ wanigan
WANGUNS ▶ wangun
WANHOPE n delusion
WANIER ▶ wany
WANIEST ▶ wany
WANIGAN n provisions for camp
WANING ▶ wane
WANINGS ▶ wane
WANION n vehemence
WANIONS ▶ wanion
WANKLE adj unstable
WANLE same as ▶ wandle
WANLY ▶ wan
WANNA vb spelling of want to intended to reflect a dialectal or informal pronunciation
WANNABE adj wanting to be, or be like, a particular person or thing ▷ n person who wants to be, or be like, a particular person or thing

WANNED ▸ wan
WANNEL same as ▸ wandle
WANNER ▸ wan
WANNESS ▸ wan
WANNEST ▸ wan
WANNING ▸ wan
WANNION ▸ wanion
WANNISH adj rather wan
WANS ▸ wan
WANT vb need or long for ▸ n act or instance of wanting
WANTAGE n shortage
WANTED ▸ want
WANTER ▸ want
WANTERS ▸ want
WANTIES ▸ wanty
WANTING adj lacking ▸ prep without
WANTON adj without motive, provocation, or justification ▸ n sexually unrestrained or immodest woman ▸ vb behave in a wanton manner
WANTONS ▸ wanton
WANTS ▸ want
WANTY adj belt
WANY ▸ wane
WANZE vb wane
WANZED ▸ wanze
WANZES ▸ wanze
WANZING ▸ wanze
WAP vb strike
WAPITI n large N American deer, now also common in New Zealand
WAPITIS ▸ wapiti
WAPPED ▸ wap
WAPPEND adj tired
WAPPER vb blink
WAPPERS ▸ wapper
WAPPING ▸ wap
WAPS ▸ wap
WAQF n endowment in Muslim law

An Arabic word meaning the donation of land, property or money for charitable purposes. As one of the Q words without a U, this comes up surprisingly often. It can also be spelt **wakf**.

WAQFS ▸ waqf
WAR n fighting between nations ▸ adj of, like, or caused by war ▸ vb conduct a war
WARAGI n Ugandan alcoholic drink made from bananas
WARAGIS ▸ waragi

WARATAH n Australian shrub with crimson flowers
WARB n dirty or insignificant person
WARBIER ▸ warb
WARBIRD n vintage military aeroplane
WARBLE vb sing in a trilling voice ▸ n act or an instance of warbling
WARBLED ▸ warble
WARBLER n any of various small songbirds
WARBLES ▸ warble
WARBS ▸ warb
WARBY ▸ warb
WARD n room in a hospital for patients needing a similar kind of care ▸ vb guard or protect
WARDED ▸ ward
WARDEN n person in charge of a building and its occupants ▸ vb act as a warden
WARDENS ▸ warden
WARDER vb guard ▸ n prison officer
WARDERS ▸ warder
WARDIAN n as in wardian case type of glass container for housing delicate plants
WARDING ▸ ward
WARDOG n veteran warrior
WARDOGS ▸ wardog
WARDROP obsolete form of > wardrobe
WARDS ▸ ward
WARE n articles of a specified type or material ▸ vb spend or squander
WARED ▸ ware
WAREHOU n any of several edible saltwater New Zealand fish
WARES pl n goods for sale
WAREZ pl n illegally copied computer software which has had its protection codes de-activated
WARFARE vb engage in war ▸ n fighting or hostilities
WARHEAD n explosive front part of a missile
WARIER ▸ wary
WARIEST ▸ wary
WARILY ▸ wary
WARING ▸ ware
WARISON n (esp formerly) a bugle note used as an order to a military force to attack
WARK Scots form of ▸ work
WARKED ▸ wark

WARKING ▸ wark
WARKS ▸ wark
WARLESS ▸ war
WARLIKE adj of or relating to war
WARLING n one who is not liked
WARLOCK n man who practises black magic
WARLORD n military leader of a nation or part of a nation
WARM adj moderately hot ▸ vb make or become warm ▸ n warm place or area
WARMAN n one experienced in warfare
WARMED ▸ warm
WARMEN ▸ warman
WARMER ▸ warm
WARMERS ▸ warm
WARMEST ▸ warm
WARMING ▸ warm
WARMISH ▸ warm
WARMLY ▸ warm
WARMS ▸ warm
WARMTH n mild heat
WARMTHS ▸ warmth
WARMUP n preparatory exercise routine
WARMUPS ▸ warmup
WARN vb make aware of possible danger or harm
WARNED ▸ warn
WARNER ▸ warn
WARNERS ▸ warn
WARNING n something that warns ▸ adj giving or serving as a warning
WARNS ▸ warn
WARP vb twist out of shape ▸ n state of being warped
WARPAGE ▸ warp
WARPATH n route taken by Native Americans on a warlike expedition
WARPED ▸ warp
WARPER ▸ warp
WARPERS ▸ warp
WARPING ▸ warp
WARPS ▸ warp
WARRAN same as ▸ warrant
WARRAND same as ▸ warrant
WARRANS ▸ warran
WARRANT n (document giving) official authorization ▸ vb make necessary
WARRAY vb wage war on
WARRAYS ▸ warray
WARRE same as ▸ war

W

WARRED ▷ war

WARREN n series of burrows in which rabbits live

WARRENS ▷ warren

WARREY same as ▷ **warray**

WARREYS ▷ warrey

WARRING ▷ war

WARRIOR n person who fights in a war

WARS ▷ war

WARSAW n type of grouper fish

WARSAWS ▷ warsaw

WARSHIP n ship designed and equipped for naval combat

WARSLE dialect word for ▷ **wrestle**

WARSLED ▷ warsle

WARSLER ▷ warsle

WARSLES ▷ warsle

WARST obsolete form of ▷ **worst**

WARSTLE dialect form of ▷ **wrestle**

WART n small hard growth on the skin

WARTED ▷ wart

WARTHOG n wild African pig with heavy tusks, wartlike lumps on the face, and a mane of coarse hair

WARTIER ▷ wart

WARTIME n time of war ▷ adj of or in a time of war

WARTS ▷ wart

WARTY ▷ wart

WARWOLF n Roman engine of war

WARWORK n work contributing to war effort

WARWORN adj worn down by war

WARY adj watchful or cautious

WARZONE n area where a war is taking place or there is some other violent conflict

WAS ▷ be

WASABI n Japanese cruciferous plant cultivated for its thick green pungent root

WASABIS ▷ wasabi

WASE n pad to relieve pressure of load carried on head

WASES ▷ wase

WASH vb clean (oneself, clothes, etc) with water and usu soap ▷ n act or process of washing

WASHDAY n day on which clothes and linen are washed, often the same day each week

WASHED ▷ wash

WASHEN ▷ wash

WASHER n ring put under a nut or bolt or in a tap as a seal ▷ vb fit with a washer

WASHERS ▷ washer

WASHERY n plant at a mine where water or other liquid is used to remove dirt from a mineral, esp coal

WASHES ▷ wash

WASHIER ▷ washy

WASHILY ▷ washy

WASHIN n increase in the angle of attack of an aircraft wing towards the wing tip

WASHING n clothes to be washed

WASHINS ▷ washin

WASHOUT n complete failure

WASHPOT n pot for washing things in

WASHRAG same as > **washcloth**

WASHTUB n tub or large container used for washing anything, esp clothes

WASHUP n outcome of a process

WASHUPS ▷ washup

WASHY adj overdiluted or weak

WASP n stinging insect with a slender black-and-yellow striped body

WASPIE n tight-waisted corset

WASPIER ▷ wasp

WASPIES ▷ waspie

WASPILY ▷ wasp

WASPISH adj bad-tempered

WASPS ▷ wasp

WASPY ▷ wasp

WASSAIL n formerly, festivity when much drinking took place ▷ vb drink health of (a person) at a wassail

WASSUP sentence substitute what is happening?

WAST singular form of the past tense of ▷ **be**

WASTAGE n loss by wear or waste

WASTE vb use pointlessly or thoughtlessly ▷ n act of wasting or state of being wasted ▷ adj rejected as worthless or surplus to requirements

WASTED ▷ waste

WASTEL n fine bread or cake

WASTELS ▷ wastel

WASTER vb waste ▷ n layabout

WASTERS ▷ waster

WASTERY n extravagance

WASTES ▷ waste

WASTING adj reducing the vitality and strength of the body

WASTREL n lazy or worthless person

WASTRIE same as ▷ **wastery**

WASTRY n wastefulness

WASTS ▷ wast

WAT adj wet; drunken

WATAP n stringy thread made by Native Americans from the roots of conifers

WATAPE same as ▷ **watap**

WATAPES ▷ watape

WATAPS ▷ watap

WATCH vb look at closely ▷ n portable timepiece for the wrist or pocket

WATCHED ▷ watch

WATCHER n person who watches

WATCHES ▷ watch

WATCHET n shade of blue

WATE ▷ wit

WATER n clear colourless tasteless liquid that falls as rain and forms rivers etc ▷ vb put water on or into

WATERED ▷ water

WATERER ▷ water

WATERS ▷ water

WATERY adj of, like, or containing water

WATS ▷ wat

WATT n unit of power

WATTAGE n electrical power expressed in watts

WATTAPE same as ▷ **watap**

WATTER ▷ wat

WATTEST ▷ wat

WATTLE n branches woven over sticks to make a fence ▷ adj made of, formed by, or covered with wattle ▷ vb construct from wattle

WATTLED ▷ wattle

WATTLES ▷ wattle

WATTS ▷ watt

WAUCHT same as ▷ **waught**

WAUCHTS ▷ waucht

WAUFF same as ▶ **waff**
WAUFFED ▶ **wauff**
WAUFFS ▶ **wauff**
WAUGH vb bark
WAUGHED ▶ **waugh**
WAUGHS ▶ **waugh**
WAUGHT vb drink in large amounts
WAUGHTS ▶ **waught**
WAUK vb full (cloth)
WAUKED ▶ **wauk**
WAUKER ▶ **wauk**
WAUKERS ▶ **wauk**
WAUKING ▶ **wauk**
WAUKS ▶ **wauk**
WAUL vb cry or wail plaintively like a cat
WAULED ▶ **waul**
WAULING ▶ **waul**
WAULK same as ▶ **wauk**
WAULKED ▶ **waulk**
WAULKER ▶ **waulk**
WAULKS ▶ **waulk**
WAULS ▶ **waul**
WAUR obsolete form of ▶ **war**
WAURED ▶ **waur**
WAURING ▶ **waur**
WAURS ▶ **waur**
WAURST ▶ **waur**
WAVE vb move the hand to and fro as a greeting or signal ▷ n moving ridge on water
WAVED ▶ **wave**
WAVELET n small wave
WAVEOFF n signal or instruction to an aircraft not to land
WAVER vb hesitate or be irresolute ▷ n act or an instance of wavering
WAVERED ▶ **waver**
WAVERER ▶ **waver**
WAVERS ▶ **waver**
WAVERY adj lacking firmness
WAVES ▶ **wave**
WAVESON n goods floating on waves after shipwreck
WAVEY n snow goose or other wild goose
WAVEYS ▶ **wavey**
WAVICLE n origin of wave
WAVIER ▶ **wavy**
WAVIES ▶ **wavy**
WAVIEST ▶ **wavy**
WAVILY ▶ **wavy**
WAVING ▶ **wave**
WAVINGS ▶ **wave**
WAVY adj having curves ▷ n snow goose or other wild goose
WAW another name for ▶ **vav**

WAWA n speech ▷ vb speak
WAWAED ▶ **wawa**
WAWAING ▶ **wawa**
WAWAS ▶ **wawa**
WAWE same as ▶ **waw**
WAWES ▶ **wawe**
WAWL same as ▶ **waul**
WAWLED ▶ **wawl**
WAWLING ▶ **wawl**
WAWLS ▶ **wawl**
WAWS ▶ **waw**
WAX n solid shiny fatty or oily substance used for sealing, making candles, etc ▷ vb coat or polish with wax
WAXABLE ▶ **wax**
WAXBILL n any of various chiefly African finchlike weaverbirds
WAXED ▶ **wax**
WAXEN adj made of or like wax
WAXER ▶ **wax**
WAXERS ▶ **wax**
WAXES ▶ **wax**
WAXEYE n small New Zealand bird with a white circle round its eye
WAXEYES ▶ **waxeye**
WAXIER ▶ **waxy**
WAXIEST ▶ **waxy**
WAXILY ▶ **waxy**
WAXING ▶ **wax**
WAXINGS ▶ **wax**
WAXLIKE ▶ **wax**
WAXWEED n type of wild flower
WAXWING n type of songbird
WAXWORK n lifelike wax model of a (famous) person
WAXWORM n waxmoth larva
WAXY adj resembling wax in colour, appearance, or texture
WAY n manner or method ▷ vb travel
WAYBILL n document stating the nature, origin, and destination of goods being transported
WAYED ▶ **way**
WAYFARE vb travel
WAYGONE adj travel-weary
WAYING ▶ **way**
WAYLAID ▶ **waylay**
WAYLAY vb lie in wait for and accost or attack
WAYLAYS ▶ **waylay**
WAYLESS ▶ **way**
WAYMARK n symbol or

signpost marking the route of a footpath ▷ vb mark out with waymarks
WAYMENT vb express grief
WAYPOST n signpost
WAYS ▶ **way**
WAYSIDE n side of a road
WAYWARD adj erratic, selfish, or stubborn
WAYWODE n Slavonic governor
WAYWORN adj worn or tired by travel
WAZIR another word for ▶ **vizier**
WAZIRS ▶ **wazir**
WAZZOCK n foolish or annoying person
WE pron speaker or writer and one or more others
WEAK adj lacking strength
WEAKEN vb make or become weak or become sickly
WEAKENS ▶ **weaken**
WEAKER ▶ **weak**
WEAKEST ▶ **weak**
WEAKISH ▶ **weak**
WEAKLY adv feebly ▷ adj weak or sickly
WEAKON n subatomic particle
WEAKONS ▶ **weakon**
WEAL n raised mark left on the skin by a blow
WEALD n open or forested country
WEALDS ▶ **weald**
WEALS ▶ **weal**
WEALTH n state of being rich
WEALTHS ▶ **wealth**
WEALTHY adj possessing wealth
WEAMB same as ▶ **wame**
WEAMBS ▶ **weamb**
WEAN vb accustom (a baby or young mammal) to food other than mother's milk
WEANED ▶ **wean**
WEANEL n recently-weaned child or animal
WEANELS ▶ **weanel**
WEANER n person or thing that weans
WEANERS ▶ **weaner**
WEANING ▶ **wean**
WEANS ▶ **wean**
WEAPON vb arm ▷ n object used in fighting
WEAPONS ▶ **weapon**
WEAR vb have on the body as clothing or ornament ▷ n clothes suitable for a

W

WEARED ▸ wear

WEARER ▸ wear

WEARERS ▸ wear

WEARIED ▸ weary

WEARIER ▸ weary

WEARIES ▸ weary

WEARILY ▸ weary

WEARING adj tiring ▷ n act of wearing

WEARISH adj withered

WEARS ▸ wear

WEARY adj tired or exhausted ▷ vb make or become weary

WEASAND former name for the ▸ **trachea**

WEASEL n small carnivorous mammal with a long body and short legs ▷ vb use ambiguous language to avoid speaking directly or honestly

WEASELS ▸ weasel

WEASELY ▸ weasel

WEASON Scots form of ▸ **weasand**

WEASONS ▸ weason

WEATHER n day-to-day atmospheric conditions of a place ▷ vb (cause to) be affected by the weather

WEAVE vb make (fabric) by interlacing (yarn) on a loom

WEAVED ▸ weave

WEAVER n person who weaves, esp as a means of livelihood

WEAVERS ▸ weaver

WEAVES ▸ weave

WEAVING ▸ weave

WEAZAND same as ▸ **weasand**

WEAZEN same as ▸ **wizen**

WEAZENS ▸ weazen

WEB n net spun by a spider ▷ vb cover with or as if with a web

WEBBED ▸ web

WEBBIE n person who is well versed in the use of the World Wide Web

WEBBIER ▸ webby

WEBBIES ▸ webbie

WEBBING n anything that forms a web

WEBBY adj of, relating to, resembling, or consisting of a web

WEBCAM n camera that transmits images over the internet

WEBCAMS ▸ webcam

WEBCAST n broadcast of an event over the internet ▷ vb make such a broadcast

WEBER n SI unit of magnetic flux

WEBERS ▸ weber

WEBFED adj (of printing press) printing from rolls of paper

WEBFEET ▸ webfoot

WEBFOOT n foot having the toes connected by folds of skin

WEBHEAD n person who uses the Internet a lot.

WEBIFY vb convert (information) to a format capable of being displayed on the Internet

WEBINAR n interactive seminar conducted over the World Wide Web

WEBLESS ▸ web

WEBLIKE ▸ web

WEBLISH n shorthand form of English that is used in text messaging, chat rooms, etc

WEBLOG n person's online journal

WEBLOGS ▸ weblog

WEBMAIL n system of electronic mail that allows account holders to access their mail via an internet site rather than downloading it

WEBPAGE n page on website

WEBRING n group of websites organized in a circular structure

WEBS ▸ web

WEBSITE n group of connected pages on the World Wide Web

WEBSTER archaic word for ▸ **weaver**

WEBWORK n work done using the World Wide Web

WEBWORM n type of caterpillar

WEBZINE n magazine published on the Internet

WECHT n agricultural tool

WECHTS ▸ wecht

WED vb marry

WEDDED ▸ wed

WEDDER dialect form of ▸ **weather**

WEDDERS ▸ wedder

WEDDING ▸ wed

WEDEL same as ▸ **wedeln**

WEDELED ▸ wedel

WEDELN n succession of high-speed turns performed in skiing ▷ vb perform a wedeln

WEDELNS ▸ wedeln

WEDELS ▸ wedel

WEDGE n piece of material thick at one end and thin at the other ▷ vb fasten or split with a wedge

WEDGED ▸ wedge

WEDGES ▸ wedge

WEDGIE n wedge-heeled shoe

WEDGIER ▸ wedge

WEDGIES ▸ wedgie

WEDGING ▸ wedge

WEDGY ▸ wedge

WEDLOCK n marriage

WEDS ▸ wed

WEE adj small or short ▷ n instance of urinating ▷ vb urinate

WEED n plant growing where undesired ▷ vb clear of weeds

WEEDED ▸ weed

WEEDER ▸ weed

WEEDERS ▸ weed

WEEDERY n weed-ridden area

WEEDIER ▸ weedy

WEEDILY ▸ weedy

WEEDING ▸ weed

WEEDS pl n widow's mourning clothes

WEEDY adj (of a person) thin and weak

WEEING ▸ wee

WEEK n period of seven days, esp one beginning on a Sunday ▷ adv seven days before or after a specified day

WEEKDAY n any day of the week except Saturday or Sunday

WEEKE same as ▸ **wick**

WEEKEND n Saturday and Sunday ▷ vb spend or pass a weekend

WEEKES ▸ weeke

WEEKLY adv happening, done, etc once a week ▷ n newspaper or magazine published once a week ▷ adj happening once a week or every week

WEEKS ▸ week

WEEL Scots word for ▸ **well**

WEELS ▸ weel

WEEM n underground home

WEEMS ▸ weem
WEEN vb think or imagine (something)
WEENED ▸ ween
WEENIE adj very small ▷ n wiener
WEENIER ▸ weeny
WEENIES ▸ weenie
WEENING ▸ ween
WEENS ▸ ween
WEENSY same as ▸ **weeny**
WEENY adj very small
WEEP vb shed tears ▷ n spell of weeping
WEEPER n person who weeps, esp a hired mourner
WEEPERS ▸ weeper
WEEPIE ▸ weepy
WEEPIER ▸ weepy
WEEPIES ▸ weepy
WEEPILY ▸ weepy
WEEPING adj (of plants) having slender hanging branches
WEEPS ▸ weep
WEEPY adj liable to cry ▷ n sentimental film or book
WEER ▸ wee
WEES ▸ wee
WEEST ▸ wee
WEET dialect form of ▸ **wet**
WEETE same as ▸ **wit**
WEETED ▸ weete
WEETEN same as ▸ **wit**
WEETER ▸ weet
WEETEST ▸ weet
WEETING ▸ weet
WEETS ▸ weet
WEEVER n type of small fish
WEEVERS ▸ weever
WEEVIL n small beetle that eats grain etc
WEEVILS ▸ weevil
WEEVILY another word for ▸ **weevilled**
WEEWEE vb urinate
WEEWEED ▸ weewee
WEEWEES ▸ weewee
WEFT n cross threads in weaving ▷ vb form weft
WEFTAGE n texture
WEFTE n forsaken child
WEFTED ▸ weft
WEFTES ▸ wefte
WEFTING ▸ weft
WEFTS ▸ weft
WEID n sudden illness
WEIDS ▸ weid
WEIGELA n type of shrub
WEIGH vb have a specified weight
WEIGHED ▸ weigh
WEIGHER ▸ weigh

WEIGHS ▸ weigh
WEIGHT n heaviness of an object ▷ vb add weight to
WEIGHTS ▸ weight
WEIGHTY adj important or serious
WEIL n whirlpool
WEILS ▸ weil
WEINER same as ▸ **wiener**
WEINERS ▸ weiner
WEIR vb ward off ▷ n river dam
WEIRD adj strange or bizarre ▷ vb warn beforehand
WEIRDED ▸ weird
WEIRDER ▸ weird
WEIRDIE same as ▸ **weirdo**
WEIRDLY ▸ weird
WEIRDO n peculiar person
WEIRDOS ▸ weirdo
WEIRDS ▸ weird
WEIRDY n weird person
WEIRED ▸ weir
WEIRING ▸ weir
WEIRS ▸ weir
WEISE same as ▸ **wise**
WEISED ▸ weise
WEISES ▸ weise
WEISING ▸ weise
WEIZE same as ▸ **wise**
WEIZED ▸ weize
WEIZES ▸ weize
WEIZING ▸ weize
WEKA n flightless New Zealand rail
WEKAS ▸ weka
WELAWAY same as
> **wellaway**
WELCH same as ▸ **welsh**
WELCHED ▸ welch
WELCHER ▸ welch
WELCHES ▸ welch
WELCOME vb greet with pleasure ▷ n kindly greeting ▷ adj received gladly
WELD vb join (pieces of metal or plastic) by softening with heat ▷ n welded joint
WELDED ▸ weld
WELDER ▸ weld
WELDERS ▸ weld
WELDING ▸ weld
WELDOR ▸ weld
WELDORS ▸ weldor
WELDS ▸ weld
WELFARE n wellbeing
WELK vb wither; dry up
WELKE obsolete form of
▸ **welk**
WELKED ▸ welk

WELKES ▸ welke
WELKIN n sky, heavens, or upper air
WELKING ▸ welk
WELKINS ▸ welkin
WELKS ▸ welk
WELKT adj twisted
WELL adv satisfactorily ▷ adj in good health ▷ interj exclamation of surprise, interrogation, etc ▷ n hole sunk into the earth to reach water, oil, or gas ▷ vb flow upwards or outwards
WELLED ▸ well
WELLIE n wellington boot
WELLIES ▸ welly
WELLING ▸ well
WELLS ▸ well
WELLY n energy or commitment
WELS n type of catfish
WELSH vb fail to pay a debt or fulfil an obligation
WELSHED ▸ welsh
WELSHER ▸ welsh
WELSHES ▸ welsh
WELT same as ▸ **weal**
WELTED ▸ welt
WELTER n jumbled mass ▷ vb roll about, writhe, or wallow
WELTERS ▸ welter
WELTING ▸ welt
WELTS ▸ welt
WEM same as ▸ **wame**
WEMB same as ▸ **wame**
WEMBS ▸ wemb
WEMS ▸ wem
WEN n cyst on the scalp
WENA pron South African word for you
WENCH n young woman ▷ vb frequent the company of prostitutes
WENCHED ▸ wench
WENCHER ▸ wench
WENCHES ▸ wench
WEND vb go or travel
WENDED ▸ wend
WENDIGO n evil spirit or cannibal
WENDING ▸ wend
WENDS ▸ wend
WENGE n type of tree found in central and West Africa
WENGES ▸ wenge
WENNIER ▸ wen
WENNISH ▸ wen
WENNY ▸ wen
WENS ▸ wen
WENT n path
WENTS ▸ went

W

WEPT ▶ weep

WERE vb form of the past tense of **be** used after we, you, they, or a plural noun

WERGELD same as ▶ **wergild**

WERGELT same as ▶ **wergild**

WERGILD n price set on a man's life in successive Anglo-Saxon and Germanic law codes, to be paid as compensation by his slayer

WERO n challenge made by an armed Māori warrior to a visitor to a marae

WEROS ▶ **wero**

WERSH adj tasteless

WERSHER ▶ **wersh**

WERT singular form of the past tense of ▶ **be**

WERWOLF same as > **werewolf**

WESAND same as ▶ **weasand**

WESANDS ▶ **wesand**

WESKIT informal word for > **waistcoat**

WESKITS ▶ **weskit**

WESSAND same as ▶ **weasand**

WEST n part of the horizon where the sun sets ▷ adj or in the west ▷ adv in, to, or towards the west ▷ vb move in westerly direction

WESTED ▶ **west**

WESTER vb move or appear to move towards the west ▷ n strong wind or storm from the west

WESTERN adj of or in the west ▷ n film or story about cowboys in the western US

WESTERS ▶ **wester**

WESTING n movement, deviation, or distance covered in a westerly direction

WESTLIN Scots word for ▶ **western**

WESTS ▶ **west**

WET adj covered or soaked with water or another liquid ▷ n moisture or rain ▷ vb make wet

WETA n type of wingless insect

WETAS ▶ **weta**

WETHER n male sheep, esp a castrated one

WETHERS ▶ **wether**

WETLAND n area of marshy land

WETLY ▶ **wet**

WETNESS ▶ **wet**

WETS ▶ **wet**

WETSUIT n body suit for diving

WETTED ▶ **wet**

WETTER ▶ **wet**

WETTERS ▶ **wet**

WETTEST ▶ **wet**

WETTIE n wetsuit

WETTIES ▶ **wettie**

WETTING ▶ **wet**

WETTISH ▶ **wet**

WETWARE n humorous term for the brain

WEX obsolete form of ▶ **wax**

> Wex is an old word for wax, in the sense of grow. It gives a very good score for a three-letter word, and can be extended to **wexe**.

WEXE obsolete form of ▶ **wax**

WEXED ▶ **wex**

WEXES ▶ **wex**

WEXING ▶ **wex**

WEY n measurement of weight

WEYARD obsolete form of ▶ **weird**

WEYS ▶ **wey**

WEYWARD obsolete form of ▶ **weird**

WEZAND obsolete form of ▶ **weasand**

WEZANDS ▶ **wezand**

WHA Scots form for ▶ **who**

WHACK vb strike with a resounding blow ▷ n such a blow

WHACKED ▶ **whack**

WHACKER ▶ **whack**

WHACKO n mad person

WHACKOS ▶ **whacko**

WHACKS ▶ **whack**

WHACKY variant spelling of ▶ **wacky**

WHAE same as ▶ **wha**

WHAISLE Scots form of ▶ **wheeze**

WHAIZLE same as ▶ **whaisle**

WHALE n large fish-shaped sea mammal ▷ vb hunt for whales

WHALED ▶ **whale**

WHALER n ship or person involved in whaling

WHALERS ▶ **whaler**

WHALERY n whaling

WHALES ▶ **whale**

WHALING n hunting of whales for food and oil ▷ adv extremely

WHALLY adj (of eyes) with light-coloured irises

WHAM interj expression indicating suddenness or forcefulness ▷ n forceful blow or impact or the sound produced by such a blow or impact ▷ vb strike or cause to strike with great force

WHAMMED ▶ **wham**

WHAMMO n sound of a sudden collision

WHAMMOS ▶ **whammo**

WHAMMY n devastating setback

WHAMO same as ▶ **whammo**

WHAMPLE n strike

WHAMS ▶ **wham**

WHANAU n (in Māori societies) a family, esp an extended family

WHANAUS ▶ **whanau**

WHANG vb strike or be struck so as to cause a resounding noise ▷ n resounding noise produced by a heavy blow

WHANGAM n imaginary creature

WHANGED ▶ **whang**

WHANGEE n tall woody grass grown for its stems, which are used for bamboo canes

WHANGS ▶ **whang**

WHAP same as ▶ **whop**

WHAPPED ▶ **whap**

WHAPPER same as ▶ **whopper**

WHAPS ▶ **whap**

WHARE n Māori hut or dwelling place

WHARES ▶ **whare**

WHARF n platform at a harbour for loading and unloading ships ▷ vb put (goods, etc) on a wharf

WHARFED ▶ **wharf**

WHARFIE n person employed to load and unload ships

WHARFS ▶ **wharf**

WHARVE n wooden disc or wheel on a shaft serving as a flywheel or pulley

WHARVES ▶ **wharve**

WHAT pron which thing ▷ interj exclamation of anger, surprise, etc ▷ adv in which way, how much ▷ n part; portion

WHATA n building on stilts or a raised platform for storing provisions

WHATAS ▶ whata

WHATEN adj what; what kind of

WHATNA another word for ▶ whaten

WHATNOT n similar unspecified thing

WHATS ▶ what

WHATSIS US form of ▶ whatsit

WHATSIT n person or thing the name of which is unknown, temporarily forgotten, or deliberately overlooked

WHATSO n of whatever kind

WHATTEN same as ▶ whaten

WHAUP n curlew

WHAUPS ▶ whaup

WHAUR Scots word for ▶ where

WHAURS ▶ whaur

WHEAL same as ▶ weal

WHEALS ▶ wheal

WHEAR obsolete variant of ▶ where

WHEARE obsolete variant of ▶ where

WHEAT n grain used in making flour, bread, and pasta

WHEATEN n type of dog ▷ adj made of the grain or flour of wheat

WHEATS ▶ wheat

WHEATY adj having a wheat-like taste

WHEE interj exclamation of joy, thrill, etc

WHEECH vb move quickly

WHEECHS ▶ wheech

WHEEDLE vb coax or cajole

WHEEL n disc that revolves on an axle ▷ vb push or pull (something with wheels)

WHEELED adj having or equipped with a wheel or wheels

WHEELER n horse or other draught animal nearest the wheel

WHEELIE n manoeuvre on a bike in which the front wheel is raised off the ground

WHEELS ▶ wheel

WHEELY adj resembling a wheel

WHEEN n few

WHEENGE Scots form of ▶ whinge

WHEENS ▶ wheen

WHEEP vb fly quickly and lightly

WHEEPED ▶ wheep

WHEEPLE vb whistle weakly

WHEEPS ▶ wheep

WHEESH vb silence (a person, noise, etc) or be silenced

WHEESHT same as ▶ wheesh

WHEEZE vb breathe with a hoarse whistling noise ▷ n wheezing sound

WHEEZED ▶ wheeze

WHEEZER ▶ wheeze

WHEEZES ▶ wheeze

WHEEZLE vb make hoarse breathing sound

WHEEZY ▶ wheeze

WHEFT same as ▶ waft

WHEFTS ▶ wheft

WHELK n edible snail-like shellfish

WHELKED adj having or covered with whelks

WHELKS ▶ whelk

WHELKY ▶ whelk

WHELM vb engulf entirely with or as if with water

WHELMED ▶ whelm

WHELMS ▶ whelm

WHELP n pup or cub ▷ vb (of an animal) give birth

WHELPED ▶ whelp

WHELPS ▶ whelp

WHEMMLE vb overturn

WHEN adv at what time? ▷ pron at which time ▷ n question of when

WHENAS conj while; inasmuch as

WHENCE n point of origin ▷ adv from what place or source ▷ pron from what place, cause, or origin

WHENCES ▶ whence

WHENS ▶ when

WHENUA n land

WHENUAS ▶ whenua

WHENWE n White immigrant from Zimbabwe, caricatured as being tiresomely over-reminiscent of happier times

WHENWES ▶ whenwe

WHERE adv in, at, or to what place? ▷ pron in, at, or to which place ▷ n question

as to the position, direction, or destination of something

WHEREAS n testimonial introduced by whereas

WHEREAT adv at or to which place

WHEREBY pron by which ▷ adv how? by what means?

WHEREIN adv in what place or respect? ▷ pron in which place or thing

WHEREOF adv of what or which person or thing? ▷ pron of which person or thing

WHEREON adv on what thing or place? ▷ pron on which thing, place, etc

WHERES ▶ where

WHERESO adv in or to unspecified place

WHERETO adv towards what (place, end, etc)? ▷ pron which

WHERRET vb strike (someone) a blow ▷ n blow, esp a slap on the face

WHERRIT vb worry or cause to worry

WHERRY n any of certain kinds of half-decked commercial boats, such as barges, used in Britain ▷ vb travel in a wherry

WHERVE same as ▶ wharve

WHERVES ▶ wherve

WHET vb sharpen (a tool) ▷ n act of whetting

WHETHER conj used to introduce any indirect question

WHETS ▶ whet

WHETTED ▶ whet

WHETTER ▶ whet

WHEUGH same as ▶ whew

WHEUGHS ▶ wheugh

WHEW interj exclamation expressing relief, delight, etc ▷ vb express relief

WHEWED ▶ whew

WHEWING ▶ whew

WHEWS ▶ whew

WHEY n watery liquid that separates from the curd when milk is clotted

WHEYEY ▶ whey

WHEYIER ▶ whey

WHEYISH ▶ whey

WHEYS ▶ whey

WHICH pron used to request or refer to a choice from different possibilities ▷ adj used with a noun in requesting that the particular thing being referred to is further identified or distinguished

WHICKER vb (of a horse) to whinny or neigh

WHID vb move quickly

WHIDAH same as ▶ **whydah**

WHIDAHS ▶ **whidah**

WHIDDED ▶ **whid**

WHIDDER vb move with force

WHIDS ▶ **whid**

WHIFF n puff of air or odour ▷ vb come, convey, or go in whiffs

WHIFFED ▶ **whiff**

WHIFFER ▶ **whiff**

WHIFFET n insignificant person

WHIFFLE vb think or behave in an erratic or unpredictable way

WHIFFS ▶ **whiff**

WHIFFY adj smelly

WHIFT n brief emission of air

WHIFTS ▶ **whift**

WHIG vb go quickly

WHIGGED ▶ **whig**

WHIGS ▶ **whig**

WHILE n period of time

WHILED ▶ **while**

WHILERE adv a while ago

WHILES adv at times

WHILING ▶ **while**

WHILK archaic and dialect word for ▶ **which**

WHILLY vb influence by flattery

WHILOM adv formerly ▷ adj one-time

WHILST same as ▶ **while**

WHIM n sudden fancy ▷ vb have a whim

WHIMMED ▶ **whim**

WHIMMY adj having whims

WHIMPER vb cry in a soft whining way ▷ n soft plaintive whine

WHIMPLE same as ▶ **wimple**

WHIMS ▶ **whim**

WHIMSEY same as ▶ **whimsy**

WHIMSY n capricious idea ▷ adj quaint, comical, or unusual, often in a tasteless way

WHIN n gorse

WHINE n high-pitched plaintive cry ▷ vb make

such a sound

WHINED ▶ **whine**

WHINER ▶ **whine**

WHINERS ▶ **whine**

WHINES ▶ **whine**

WHINEY same as ▶ **whiny**

WHINGE vb complain ▷ n complaint

WHINGED ▶ **whinge**

WHINGER ▶ **whinge**

WHINGES ▶ **whinge**

WHINGY adj complaining peevishly, whining

WHINIER ▶ **whiny**

WHINING ▶ **whine**

WHINNY vb neigh softly ▷ n soft neigh ▷ adj covered in whin

WHINS ▶ **whin**

WHINY adj high-pitched and plaintive

WHIO n New Zealand mountain duck with blue plumage

WHIOS ▶ **whio**

WHIP n cord attached to a handle, used for beating animals or people ▷ vb strike with a whip, strap, or cane

WHIPCAT n tailor

WHIPPED ▶ **whip**

WHIPPER ▶ **whip**

WHIPPET n racing dog like a small greyhound

WHIPPY adj springy

WHIPRAY n stingray

WHIPS ▶ **whip**

WHIPSAW n any saw with a flexible blade, such as a bandsaw ▷ vb saw with a whipsaw

WHIPT old past tense of ▶ **whip**

WHIR n prolonged soft swish or buzz, as of a motor working or wings flapping ▷ vb make or cause to make a whir

WHIRL vb spin or revolve ▷ n whirling movement

WHIRLED ▶ **whirl**

WHIRLER ▶ **whirl**

WHIRLS ▶ **whirl**

WHIRLY adj characterized by whirling

WHIRR same as ▶ **whir**

WHIRRED ▶ **whir**

WHIRRET vb strike with sharp blow

WHIRRS ▶ **whirr**

WHIRRY vb move quickly

WHIRS ▶ **whir**

WHIRTLE same as ▶ **wortle**

WHISH less common word for ▶ **swish**

WHISHED ▶ **whish**

WHISHES ▶ **whish**

WHISHT interj hush! be quiet! ▷ adj silent or still ▷ vb make or become silent

WHISHTS ▶ **whisht**

WHISK vb move or remove quickly ▷ n quick movement

WHISKED ▶ **whisk**

WHISKER n any of the long stiff hairs on the face of a cat or other mammal

WHISKET same as ▶ **wisket**

WHISKEY n Irish or American whisky

WHISKS ▶ **whisk**

WHISKY n spirit distilled from fermented cereals

WHISPER vb speak softly, without vibration of the vocal cords ▷ n soft voice

WHISS vb hiss

WHISSED ▶ **whiss**

WHISSES ▶ **whiss**

WHIST same as ▶ **whisht**

WHISTED ▶ **whist**

WHISTLE vb produce a shrill sound, esp by forcing the breath through pursed lips ▷ n whistling sound

WHISTS ▶ **whist**

WHIT n smallest particle

WHITE adj of the colour of snow ▷ n colour of snow

WHITED adj as in whited sepulchre hypocrite

WHITELY ▶ **white**

WHITEN vb make or become white or whiter

WHITENS ▶ **whiten**

WHITER ▶ **white**

WHITES pl n white clothes, as worn for playing cricket

WHITEST ▶ **white**

WHITHER same as ▶ **wuther**

WHITING n edible sea fish

WHITISH ▶ **white**

WHITLOW n inflamed sore on a finger or toe, esp round a nail

WHITRET n same as > **whittret**

WHITS ▶ **whit**

WHITTAW same as > **whittawer**

WHITTER variant spelling of ▶ **witter**

WHITTLE vb cut or carve

(wood) with a knife ▷ *n* knife, esp a large one

WHIZ same as ▶ **whizz**

WHIZZ *vb* make a loud buzzing sound ▷ *n* loud buzzing sound

WHIZZED ▶ **whizz**

WHIZZER ▶ **whizz**

WHIZZES ▶ **whizz**

WHIZZO ▶ **whizzy**

WHIZZY *adj* using sophisticated technology to produce vivid effects

WHO *pron* which person

WHOA *interj* command used, esp to horses, to stop or slow down

WHOEVER *pron* any person who

WHOLE *adj* containing all the elements or parts ▷ *n* complete thing or system

WHOLES ▶ **whole**

WHOLISM same as ▶ **holism**

WHOLIST same as ▶ **holist**

WHOLLY *adv* completely or totally

WHOM *pron* objective form of *who*

WHOMBLE same as ▶ **whemmle**

WHOMMLE same as ▶ **whemmle**

WHOMP *vb* strike; thump

WHOMPED ▶ **whomp**

WHOMPS ▶ **whomp**

WHOMSO *pron* whom; whomever

WHOOBUB same as ▶ **hubbub**

WHOOF same as ▶ **woof**

WHOOFED ▶ **whoof**

WHOOFS ▶ **whoof**

WHOOP *n* shout or cry to express excitement ▷ *vb* emit a whoop

WHOOPED ▶ **whoop**

WHOOPEE *n* cry of joy

WHOOPER *n* type of swan

WHOOPIE same as ▶ **whoopee**

WHOOPLA *n* commotion; fuss

WHOOPS *interj* exclamation of surprise or of apology

WHOOSH *n* hissing or rushing sound ▷ *vb* make or move with a hissing or rushing sound

WHOOSIS *n* thingamajig

WHOOT obsolete variant of ▶ **hoot**

WHOOTED ▶ **whoot**

WHOOTS ▶ **whoot**

WHOP *vb* strike, beat, or thrash ▷ *n* heavy blow or the sound made by such a blow

WHOPPED ▶ **whop**

WHOPPER *n* anything unusually large

WHOPS ▶ **whop**

WHORE *n* prostitute ▷ *vb* be or act as a prostitute

WHORED ▶ **whore**

WHORES ▶ **whore**

WHORING ▶ **whore**

WHORISH ▶ **whore**

WHORL *n* ring of leaves or petals

WHORLED ▶ **whorl**

WHORLS ▶ **whorl**

WHORT *n* small shrub bearing blackish edible sweet berries

WHORTLE *n* whortleberry

WHORTS ▶ **whort**

WHOSE *pron* of whom or of which ▷ *determiner* of whom? belonging to whom?

WHOSIS *n* thingamajig

WHOSO archaic word for ▶ **whoever**

WHOT obsolete variant of ▶ **hot**

WHOW *interj* wow

WHUMMLE *vb* same as ▶ **whemmle**

WHUMP *vb* make a dull thud ▷ *n* dull thud

WHUMPED ▶ **whump**

WHUMPS ▶ **whump**

WHUP *vb* defeat totally

WHUPPED ▶ **whup**

WHUPS ▶ **whup**

WHY *adv* for what reason ▷ *pron* because of which ▷ *n* reason, purpose, or cause of something

WHYDAH *n* type of black African bird

WHYDAHS ▶ **whydah**

WHYEVER *adv* for whatever reason

WHYS ▶ **why**

WIBBLE *vb* wobble

WIBBLED ▶ **wibble**

WIBBLES ▶ **wibble**

WICCA *n* cult or practice of witchcraft

WICCAN *n* member of wicca

WICCANS ▶ **wiccan**

WICCAS ▶ **wicca**

WICE Scots form of ▶ **wise**

WICH *n* variant of wych

WICHES ▶ **wich**

WICK *n* cord through a lamp or candle which carries fuel to the flame ▷ *adj* lively or active ▷ *vb* (of a material) draw in (water, fuel, etc)

WICKAPE same as ▶ **wicopy**

WICKED *adj* morally bad ▷ *n* wicked person

WICKEDS ▶ **wicked**

WICKEN same as ▶ **quicken**

WICKENS ▶ **wicken**

WICKER *adj* made of woven cane ▷ *n* slender flexible twig or shoot, esp of willow

WICKERS ▶ **wicker**

WICKET *n* set of three cricket stumps and two bails

WICKETS ▶ **wicket**

WICKIES ▶ **wicky**

WICKING ▶ **wick**

WICKIUP *n* crude shelter made of brushwood, mats, or grass and having an oval frame

WICKS ▶ **wick**

WICKY same as ▶ **quicken**

WICKYUP same as ▶ **wickiup**

WICOPY *n* any of various North American trees, shrubs, or herbaceous plants

WIDDER same as ▶ **widow**

WIDDERS ▶ **widder**

WIDDIE same as ▶ **widdy**

WIDDIES ▶ **widdy**

WIDDLE *vb* urinate ▷ *n* urine

WIDDLED ▶ **widdle**

WIDDLES ▶ **widdle**

WIDDY *vb* rope made of twigs

WIDE *adj* large from side to side ▷ *adv* the full extent ▷ *n* (in cricket) a bowled ball ruled to be outside a batsman's reach

WIDELY ▶ **wide**

WIDEN *vb* make or become wider

WIDENED ▶ **widen**

WIDENER ▶ **widen**

WIDENS ▶ **widen**

WIDEOUT *n* footballer who catches passes from the quarterback

WIDER ▶ **wide**

WIDES ▶ **wide**

WIDEST ▶ **wide**

WIDGEON same as ▶ **wigeon**

W

WIDGET n any small device, the name of which is unknown or forgotten

WIDGETS ▸ widget

WIDGIE n female larrikin or bodgie

WIDGIES ▸ widgie

WIDISH ▸ wide

WIDOW n woman whose husband is dead and who has not remarried ▷ vb cause to become a widow

WIDOWED ▸ widow

WIDOWER n man whose wife is dead and who has not remarried

WIDOWS ▸ widow

WIDTH n distance from side to side

WIDTHS ▸ width

WIEL same as ▸ weel

WIELD vb hold and use (a weapon)

WIELDED ▸ wield

WIELDER ▸ wield

WIELDS ▸ wield

WIELDY adj easily handled, used, or managed

WIELS ▸ wiel

WIENER n kind of smoked beef or pork sausage, similar to a frankfurter

WIENERS ▸ wiener

WIENIE same as ▸ wiener

WIENIES ▸ wienie

WIFE n woman to whom a man is married ▷ vb marry

WIFED ▸ wife

WIFEDOM n state of being a wife

WIFELY ▸ wife

WIFES ▸ wife

WIFEY n wife

WIFEYS ▸ wifey

WIFIE n woman

WIFIES ▸ wifie

WIFING ▸ wife

WIFTIER ▸ wifty

WIFTY adj scatterbrained

WIG n artificial head of hair ▷ vb furnish with a wig

WIGAN n stiff fabric

WIGANS ▸ wigan

WIGEON n duck found in marshland

WIGEONS ▸ wigeon

WIGGED ▸ wig

WIGGERY n wigs

WIGGIER ▸ wiggy

WIGGING ▸ wig

WIGGLE vb move jerkily from side to side ▷ n wiggling movement

WIGGLED ▸ wiggle

WIGGLER ▸ wiggle

WIGGLES ▸ wiggle

WIGGLY ▸ wiggle

WIGGY adj eccentric

WIGHT vb blame ▷ n human being ▷ adj strong and brave

WIGHTED ▸ wight

WIGHTLY adv swiftly

WIGHTS ▸ wight

WIGLESS ▸ wig

WIGLET n small wig

WIGLETS ▸ wiglet

WIGLIKE ▸ wig

WIGS ▸ wig

WIGWAG vb move (something) back and forth ▷ n system of communication by flag semaphore

WIGWAGS ▸ wigwag

WIGWAM n Native American's tent

WIGWAMS ▸ wigwam

WIKI n website consisting mainly of user-generated content

WIKIS ▸ wiki

WIKIUP same as ▸ wickiup

WIKIUPS ▸ wikiup

WILCO interj expression in telecommunications etc, indicating that the message just received will be complied with

WILD same as ▸ wield

WILDCAT n European wild animal like a large domestic cat ▷ adj risky and financially unsound ▷ vb drill for petroleum or natural gas in an area having no known reserves

WILDED ▸ wild

WILDER vb lead or be led astray

WILDERS ▸ wilder

WILDEST ▸ wild

WILDING n uncultivated plant, esp the crab apple, or a cultivated plant that has become wild

WILDISH ▸ wild

WILDLY ▸ wild

WILDS ▸ wild

WILE n trickery, cunning, or craftiness ▷ vb lure, beguile, or entice

WILED ▸ wile

WILEFUL adj deceitful

WILES ▸ wile

WILFUL adj headstrong or obstinate

WILGA n small drought-resistant tree of Australia

WILGAS ▸ wilga

WILI n spirit

WILIER ▸ wily

WILIEST ▸ wily

WILILY ▸ wily

WILING ▸ wile

WILIS ▸ wili

WILJA ▸ wiltja

WILJAS ▸ wilja

WILL vb used as an auxiliary to form the future tense or to indicate intention, ability, or expectation ▷ n strong determination

WILLED adj having a will as specified

WILLER ▸ will

WILLERS ▸ will

WILLEST ▸ will

WILLET n large American shore bird

WILLETS ▸ willet

WILLEY same as ▸ willy

WILLEYS ▸ willey

WILLFUL same as ▸ wilful

WILLIAM n as in sweet william flowering plant

WILLIE n informal word for a penis

WILLIED ▸ willy

WILLIES ▸ willy

WILLING adj ready or inclined (to do something)

WILLOW n tree with thin flexible branches ▷ vb (of raw textile fibres) to open and clean in a machine having a system of rotating spikes

WILLOWS ▸ willow

WILLOWY adj slender and graceful

WILLS ▸ will

WILLY vb clean in willowing-machine

WILT vb (cause to) become limp or lose strength ▷ n act of wilting or state of becoming wilted

WILTED ▸ wilt

WILTING ▸ wilt

WILTJA n Aboriginal shelter

WILTJAS ▸ wiltja

WILTS ▸ wilt

WILY adj crafty or sly

WIMBLE n any of a number of hand tools, such as a brace and bit or a gimlet, used for boring holes ▷ vb bore (a hole) with or as if with a wimble

WIMBLED ▶ wimble
WIMBLES ▶ wimble
WIMBREL *same as*
> whimbrel
WIMMIN *n* common
intentional literary
misspelling spelling of
'women'
WIMP *n* feeble ineffectual
person ▷ *vb as in* **wimp out**
fail to complete something
through fear
WIMPED ▶ wimp
WIMPIER ▶ wimp
WIMPING ▶ wimp
WIMPISH ▶ wimp
WIMPLE *n* garment framing
the face, worn by medieval
women and now by nuns
▷ *vb* ripple or cause to ripple
or undulate
WIMPLED ▶ wimple
WIMPLES ▶ wimple
WIMPS ▶ wimp
WIMPY ▶ wimp
WIN *vb* come first in
(a competition, fight, etc)
▷ *n* victory, esp in a game
WINCE *vb* draw back, as if in
pain ▷ *n* wincing
WINCED ▶ wince
WINCER ▶ wince
WINCERS ▶ wince
WINCES ▶ wince
WINCEY *n* plain- or
twill-weave cloth, usually
having a cotton or linen
warp and a wool filling
WINCEYS ▶ wincey
WINCH *n* machine for lifting
or hauling using a cable or
chain wound round a drum
▷ *vb* lift or haul using a winch
WINCHED ▶ winch
WINCHER ▶ winch
WINCHES ▶ winch
WINCING ▶ wince
WIND *n* current of air ▷ *vb*
render short of breath
WINDAC *same as* ▶ windas
WINDACS ▶ windac
WINDAGE *n* deflection of a
projectile as a result of the
effect of the wind
WINDAS *n* windlass
WINDBAG *n* person who
talks much but
uninterestingly
WINDED ▶ wind
WINDER *n* person or device
that winds, as an engine for
hoisting the cages in a mine
shaft

WINDERS ▶ winder
WINDGUN *n* air gun
WINDIER ▶ windy
WINDIGO *same as*
▶ wendigo
WINDILY ▶ windy
WINDING ▶ wind
WINDLE *vb* wind something
round continuously
WINDLED ▶ windle
WINDLES ▶ windle
WINDOCK *same as*
▶ winnock
WINDORE *n* window
WINDOW *n* opening in a
wall to let in light or air ▷ *vb*
furnish with windows
WINDOWS ▶ window
WINDOWY ▶ window
WINDROW *n* long low ridge
or line of hay or a similar
crop, designed to achieve
the best conditions for
drying or curing ▷ *vb* put
(hay or a similar crop) into
windrows
WINDS ▶ wind
WINDSES *pl n* ventilation
shafts within mines
WINDUP *n* prank or hoax
WINDUPS ▶ windup
WINDWAY *n* part of wind
instrument
WINDY *adj* denoting a time
or conditions in which there
is a strong wind
WINE *n* alcoholic drink
made from fermented
grapes ▷ *adj* of a dark
purplish-red colour ▷ *vb*
give wine to
WINED ▶ wine
WINERY *n* place where wine
is made
WINES ▶ wine
WINESAP *n* variety of apple
WINESOP *n* old word for an
alcoholic
WINEY *adj* having the taste
or qualities of wine
WING *n* one of the limbs or
organs of a bird, insect, or
bat that are used for flying
▷ *vb* fly
WINGBOW *n* distinctive
band of colour marking the
wing of a bird
WINGE *same as* ▶ whinge
WINGED *adj* furnished with
wings
WINGER *n* player positioned
on a wing
WINGERS ▶ winger

WINGES ▶ winge
WINGIER ▶ wingy
WINGING ▶ wing
WINGLET *n* small wing
WINGMAN *n* player in the
wing position in Australian
Rules
WINGMEN ▶ wingman
WINGS ▶ wing
WINGTIP *n* outermost edge
of a wing
WINGY *adj* having wings
WINIER ▶ winy
WINIEST ▶ winy
WINING ▶ wine
WINISH ▶ wine
WINK *vb* close and open (an
eye) quickly as a signal ▷ *n*
winking
WINKED ▶ wink
WINKER *n* person or thing
that winks
WINKERS ▶ winker
WINKING ▶ wink
WINKLE *n* shellfish with a
spiral shell ▷ *vb* extract or
prise out
WINKLED ▶ winkle
WINKLER *n* one who forces
person or thing out
WINKLES ▶ winkle
WINKS ▶ wink
WINLESS *adj* not having
won anything
WINN *n* penny
WINNA *vb* will not
WINNARD *n* heron
WINNED ▶ win
WINNER *n* person or thing
that wins
WINNERS ▶ winner
WINNING *adj* (of a person)
charming, attractive, etc
WINNLE *same as* ▶ windle
WINNLES ▶ winnle
WINNOCK *n* window
WINNOW *vb* separate
(chaff) from (grain) ▷ *n*
device for winnowing
WINNOWS ▶ winnow
WINNS ▶ winn
WINO *n* destitute person
who habitually drinks
cheap wine
WINOES ▶ wino
WINOS ▶ wino
WINS ▶ win
WINSEY *same as* ▶ wincey
WINSEYS ▶ winsey
WINSOME *adj* charming or
winning
WINTER *n* coldest season
▷ *vb* spend the winter

W

WINTERS ▸ winter
WINTERY same as ▸ wintry
WINTLE vb reel; stagger
WINTLED ▸ wintle
WINTLES ▸ wintle
WINTRY adj of or like winter
WINY same as ▸ winey
WINZE n steeply inclined shaft, as for ventilation between levels
WINZES ▸ winze
WIPE vb clean or dry by rubbing ▷ n wiping
WIPED ▸ wipe
WIPEOUT n instance of wiping out
WIPER n any piece of cloth, such as a handkerchief, towel, etc, used for wiping
WIPERS ▸ wiper
WIPES ▸ wipe
WIPING ▸ wipe
WIPINGS ▸ wipe
WIPPEN n part of hammer action in piano
WIPPENS ▸ wippen
WIRABLE adj that can be wired
WIRE n thin flexible strand of metal ▷ vb fasten with wire
WIRED adj excited or nervous
WIREMAN n person who installs and maintains electric wiring, cables, etc
WIREMEN ▸ wireman
WIRER n person who sets or uses wires to snare rabbits and similar animals
WIRERS ▸ wirer
WIRES ▸ wire
WIRETAP vb make a connection to a telegraph or telephone wire in order to obtain information secretly
WIREWAY n tube for electric wires
WIRIER ▸ wiry
WIRIEST ▸ wiry
WIRILDA n SE Australian acacia tree with edible seeds
WIRILY ▸ wiry
WIRING n system of wires ▷ adj used in wiring
WIRINGS ▸ wiring
WIRRA interj exclamation of sorrow or deep concern
WIRRAH n Australian saltwater fish with bright blue spots

WIRRAHS ▸ wirrah
WIRY adj lean and tough
WIS vb know or suppose (something)
WISARD obsolete spelling of ▸ wizard
WISARDS ▸ wisard
WISDOM n good sense and judgment
WISDOMS ▸ wisdom
WISE vb guide ▷ adj having wisdom ▷ n manner
WISEASS n person who thinks he or she is being witty or clever
WISED ▸ wise
WISEGUY n person who wants to seem clever
WISELY ▸ wise
WISENT n European bison
WISENTS ▸ wisent
WISER ▸ wise
WISES ▸ wise
WISEST ▸ wise
WISH vb want or desire ▷ n expression of a desire
WISHA interj expression of surprise
WISHED ▸ wish
WISHER ▸ wish
WISHERS ▸ wish
WISHES ▸ wish
WISHFUL adj too optimistic
WISHING ▸ wish
WISHT same as ▸ whisht
WISING ▸ wise
WISKET n basket
WISKETS ▸ wisket
WISP n light delicate streak ▷ vb move or act like a wisp
WISPED ▸ wisp
WISPIER ▸ wispy
WISPILY ▸ wispy
WISPING ▸ wisp
WISPISH ▸ wisp
WISPS ▸ wisp
WISPY adj thin, fine, or delicate
WISS vb urinate
WISSED ▸ wis
WISSES ▸ wis
WISSING ▸ wis
WIST vb know
WISTED ▸ wist
WISTFUL adj sadly longing
WISTING ▸ wist
WISTITI n marmoset
WISTLY adv intently
WISTS ▸ wist
WIT vb detect ▷ n ability to use words or ideas in a clever and amusing way
WITAN n assembly of higher

ecclesiastics and important laymen, including king's thegns, that met to counsel the king on matters such as judicial problems
WITANS ▸ witan
WITCH n person, usu female, who practises (black) magic ▷ vb cause or change by or as if by witchcraft
WITCHED ▸ witch
WITCHEN n rowan tree
WITCHES ▸ witch
WITCHY adj like a witch
WITE vb blame
WITED ▸ wite
WITES ▸ wite
WITGAT n type of S African tree
WITGATS ▸ witgat
WITH prep indicating presence alongside, possession, means of performance, characteristic manner, etc ▷ n division between flues in chimney
WITHAL adv as well
WITHE n strong flexible twig, esp of willow, suitable for binding things together ▷ vb bind with withes
WITHED ▸ withe
WITHER vb wilt or dry up
WITHERS pl n ridge between a horse's shoulder blades
WITHES ▸ withe
WITHIER ▸ withy
WITHIES ▸ withy
WITHIN adv in or inside ▷ prep in or inside ▷ n something that is within
WITHING ▸ withe
WITHINS ▸ within
WITHOUT prep not accompanied by, using, or having ▷ adv outside ▷ n person who is without
WITHS ▸ with
WITHY n willow tree, esp an osier ▷ adj (of people) tough and agile
WITING ▸ wite
WITLESS adj foolish
WITLING n person who thinks himself witty
WITLOOF n chicory
WITNESS n person who has seen something happen ▷ vb see at first hand
WITNEY n type of blanket; heavy cloth

WITNEYS ▸ witney
WITS ▸ wit
WITTED *adj* having wit
WITTER *vb* chatter pointlessly or at unnecessary length ▷ *n* pointless chat
WITTERS ▸ witter
WITTIER ▸ witty
WITTILY ▸ witty
WITTING *adj* deliberate
WITTOL *n* man who tolerates his wife's unfaithfulness
WITTOLS ▸ wittol
WITTY *adj* clever and amusing
WITWALL *n* golden oriole
WIVE *vb* marry (a woman)
WIVED ▸ wive
WIVER another word for ▸ **wivern**
WIVERN *same as* ▸ **wyvern**
WIVERNS ▸ wivern
WIVERS ▸ wiver
WIVES ▸ wife
WIVING ▸ wive
WIZ *shortened form of* ▸ **wizard**

> Wiz is a short form of **wizard**. This is the highest-scoring three-letter word beginning with W, and can be especially useful when there isn't much room to manoeuvre.

WIZARD *n* magician ▷ *adj* superb
WIZARDS ▸ wizard
WIZEN *vb* make or become shrivelled ▷ *n* archaic word for 'weasand' (the gullet)
WIZENED *adj* shrivelled or wrinkled
WIZENS ▸ wizen
WIZES ▸ wiz
WIZIER *same as* ▸ **vizier**
WIZIERS ▸ wizier
WIZZEN *same as* ▸ **wizen**
WIZZENS ▸ wizen
WIZZES ▸ wiz
WO *archaic spelling of* ▸ **woe**
WOAD *n* blue dye obtained from a plant, used by the ancient Britons as a body dye
WOADED *adj* coloured blue with woad
WOADS ▸ woad
WOADWAX *n* small Eurasian leguminous shrub
WOALD *same as* ▸ **weld**

WOALDS ▸ woald
WOBBLE *vb* move unsteadily ▷ *n* wobbling movement or sound
WOBBLED ▸ wobble
WOBBLER ▸ wobble
WOBBLES ▸ wobble
WOBBLY *adj* unsteady ▷ *n* temper tantrum
WOCK *same as* ▸ **wok**
WOCKS ▸ wock
WODGE *n* thick lump or chunk
WODGES ▸ wodge
WOE *n* grief
WOEFUL *adj* extremely sad
WOENESS ▸ woe
WOES ▸ woe
WOESOME *adj* woeful
WOF *n* fool
WOFS ▸ wof
WOFUL *same as* ▸ **woeful**
WOFULLY ▸ woful
WOGGLE *n* ring of leather through which a Scout neckerchief is threaded
WOGGLES ▸ woggle
WOIWODE *same as* ▸ **voivode**
WOK *n* bowl-shaped Chinese cooking pan, used for stir-frying
WOKE ▸ wake
WOKEN ▸ wake
WOKKA *modifier as in* **wokka board** wobble board: a piece of fibreboard used as a musical instrument
WOKS ▸ wok
WOLD *same as* ▸ **weld**
WOLDS ▸ wold
WOLF *n* wild predatory canine mammal ▷ *vb* eat ravenously
WOLFED ▸ wolf
WOLFER *same as* ▸ **wolver**
WOLFERS ▸ wolfer
WOLFING ▸ wolf
WOLFISH ▸ wolf
WOLFKIN *n* young wolf
WOLFRAM another name for ▸ **tungsten**
WOLFS ▸ wolf
WOLLIES ▸ wolly
WOLLY *n* pickled cucumber or olive
WOLVE *vb* hunt for wolves
WOLVED ▸ wolve
WOLVER *n* person who hunts wolves
WOLVERS ▸ wolver
WOLVES ▸ wolf

WOLVING ▸ wolve
WOLVISH *same as* ▸ **wolfish**
WOMAN *n* adult human female ▷ *adj* female ▷ *vb* provide with a woman or women
WOMANED ▸ woman
WOMANLY *adj* having qualities traditionally associated with a woman
WOMANS ▸ woman
WOMB *vb* enclose ▷ *n* hollow organ in female mammals where babies are conceived and develop
WOMBAT *n* small heavily-built burrowing Australian marsupial
WOMBATS ▸ wombat
WOMBED ▸ womb
WOMBIER ▸ womby
WOMBING ▸ womb
WOMBS ▸ womb
WOMBY *adj* hollow; spacious
WOMEN ▸ woman
WOMERA *same as* ▸ **woomera**
WOMERAS ▸ womera
WOMMERA *same as* ▸ **woomera**
WOMMIT *n* foolish person
WOMMITS ▸ wommit
WOMYN *same as* ▸ **woman**
WON *n* standard monetary unit of North Korea, divided into 100 chon ▷ *vb* live or dwell
WONDER *vb* be curious about ▷ *n* wonderful thing ▷ *adj* spectacularly successful
WONDERS ▸ wonder
WONDRED *adj* splendid
WONGA *n* money
WONGAS ▸ wonga
WONGI *vb* talk informally
WONGIED ▸ wongi
WONGIS ▸ wongi
WONING ▸ won
WONINGS ▸ won
WONK *n* person who is obsessively interested in a specified subject
WONKIER ▸ wonky
WONKS ▸ wonk
WONKY *adj* shaky or unsteady
WONNED ▸ won
WONNER ▸ won
WONNERS ▸ won
WONNING ▸ won
WONS ▸ won

W

WONT adj accustomed ▷ n custom ▷ vb become or cause to become accustomed

WONTED adj accustomed or habituated (to doing something)

WONTING ▶ wont

WONTON n dumpling filled with spiced minced pork

WONTONS ▶ wonton

WONTS ▶ wont

WOO vb seek the love or affection of (a woman)

WOOBUT same as ▶ woubit

WOOBUTS ▶ woobut

WOOD n substance trees are made of, used in carpentry and as fuel ▷ adj made of or using wood ▷ vb (of land) plant with trees

WOODBIN n box for firewood

WOODBOX n box for firewood

WOODCUT n (print made from) an engraved block of wood

WOODED adj covered with trees

WOODEN adj made of wood ▷ vb fell or kill (a person or animal)

WOODENS ▶ wooden

WOODHEN another name for ▶ weka

WOODIE n gallows rope

WOODIER ▶ woody

WOODIES ▶ woodie

WOODING ▶ wood

WOODLOT n area restricted to the growing of trees

WOODMAN same as > woodsman

WOODMEN ▶ woodman

WOODRAT n pack-rat

WOODS pl n closely packed trees forming a forest or wood

WOODSIA n type of small fern with tufted rhizomes and wiry fronds

WOODSY adj of, reminiscent of, or connected with woods

WOODWAX same as > woodwaxen

WOODY adj (of a plant) having a very hard stem

WOOED ▶ woo

WOOER ▶ woo

WOOERS ▶ woo

WOOF vb (of dogs) bark or growl

WOOFED ▶ woof

WOOFER n loudspeaker reproducing low-frequency sounds

WOOFERS ▶ woofer

WOOFIER ▶ woofy

WOOFING ▶ woof

WOOFS ▶ woof

WOOFY adj with close, dense texture

WOOHOO interj expression of joy, approval, etc

WOOING ▶ woo

WOOINGS ▶ woo

WOOL n soft hair of sheep, goats, etc

WOOLD vb wind (rope)

WOOLDED ▶ woold

WOOLDER n stick for winding rope

WOOLDS ▶ woold

WOOLED same as ▶ woolled

WOOLEN same as ▶ woollen

WOOLENS ▶ woolen

WOOLER same as ▶ woolder

WOOLERS ▶ wooler

WOOLFAT same as ▶ lanolin

WOOLHAT n poor white person in S States

WOOLIE n wool garment

WOOLIER ▶ wooly

WOOLIES ▶ wooly

WOOLLED adj (of animals) having wool

WOOLLEN adj relating to or consisting partly or wholly of wool ▷ n garment or piece of cloth made wholly or partly of wool, esp a knitted one

WOOLLY adj of or like wool ▷ n knitted woollen garment

WOOLMAN n wool trader

WOOLMEN ▶ woolman

WOOLS ▶ wool

WOOLSEY n cotton and wool blend

WOOLY same as ▶ woolly

WOOMERA n notched stick used by Australian Aborigines to aid the propulsion of a spear

WOON same as ▶ won

WOONED ▶ woon

WOONING ▶ woon

WOONS ▶ woon

WOOPIE n well-off older person

WOOPIES ▶ woopie

WOOPS vb (esp of small child) vomit

WOOPSED ▶ woops

WOOPSES ▶ woops

WOORALI less common name for ▶ curare

WOORARA same as ▶ wourali

WOORARI same as ▶ wourali

WOOS ▶ woo

WOOSE same as ▶ wuss

WOOSEL same as ▶ ouzel

WOOSELL same as ▶ ouzel

WOOSELS ▶ woosel

WOOSES ▶ woose

WOOSH same as ▶ whoosh

WOOSHED ▶ woosh

WOOSHES ▶ woosh

WOOT vb wilt thou?

WOOTZ n Middle-Eastern steel

WOOTZES ▶ wootz

WOOZIER ▶ woozy

WOOZILY ▶ woozy

WOOZY adj weak, dizzy, and confused

WOPPED ▶ wop

WOPPING ▶ wop

WORD n smallest single meaningful unit of speech or writing ▷ vb express in words

WORDAGE n words considered collectively, esp a quantity of words

WORDED ▶ word

WORDIER ▶ wordy

WORDILY ▶ wordy

WORDING n choice and arrangement of words

WORDISH adj talkative

WORDS ▶ word

WORDY adj using too many words

WORE ▶ wear

WORK n physical or mental effort directed to making or doing something ▷ adj of or for work ▷ vb (cause to) do work

WORKBAG n container for implements, tools, or materials, esp sewing equipment

WORKBOX same as ▶ workbag

WORKDAY another word for > workaday

WORKED adj made or decorated with evidence of workmanship

WORKER n person who works in a specified way
WORKERS ▸ worker
WORKFUL adj hardworking
WORKING n operation or mode of operation of something ▷ adj relating to or concerned with a person or thing that works
WORKMAN n manual worker
WORKMEN ▸ workman
WORKOUT n session of physical exercise for training or fitness
WORKS ▸ work
WORKSHY adj not inclined to work
WORKTOP n surface in a kitchen, used for food preparation
WORKUP n medical examination
WORKUPS ▸ workup
WORLD n planet earth ▷ adj of the whole world
WORLDED adj incorporating worlds
WORLDLY adj not spiritual ▷ adv in a worldly manner
WORLDS ▸ world
WORM n small limbless invertebrate animal ▷ vb rid of worms
WORMED ▸ worm
WORMER ▸ worm
WORMERS ▸ worm
WORMERY n piece of apparatus, having a glass side or sides, in which worms are kept for study
WORMFLY n type of lure dressed on a double hook, the barbs of which sit one above the other and back-to-back
WORMIER ▸ wormy
WORMIL n burrowing larva of type of fly
WORMILS ▸ wormil
WORMING ▸ worm
WORMISH ▸ worm
WORMS n disease caused by parasitic worms living in the intestines
WORMY adj infested with or eaten by worms
WORN ▸ wear
WORRAL n type of lizard
WORRALS ▸ worral
WORREL same as ▸ **worral**
WORRELS ▸ worrel
WORRIED ▸ worry

WORRIER ▸ worry
WORRIES ▸ worry
WORRIT vb tease or worry
WORRITS ▸ worrit
WORRY vb (cause to) be anxious or uneasy ▷ n (cause of) anxiety or concern
WORSE vb defeat
WORSED ▸ worse
WORSEN vb make or grow worse
WORSENS ▸ worsen
WORSER archaic or nonstandard word for ▸ **worse**
WORSES ▸ worse
WORSET n worsted fabric
WORSETS ▸ worset
WORSHIP vb show religious devotion to ▷ n act or instance of worshipping
WORSING ▸ worse
WORST n worst thing ▷ vb defeat
WORSTED n type of woollen yarn or fabric
WORSTS ▸ worst
WORT n any of various unrelated plants, esp ones formerly used to cure diseases
WORTH prep having a value of ▷ n value or price ▷ vb happen or betide
WORTHED ▸ worth
WORTHS ▸ worth
WORTHY adj deserving admiration or respect ▷ n notable person ▷ vb make worthy
WORTLE n plate with holes for drawing wire through
WORTLES ▸ wortle
WORTS ▸ wort
WOS ▸ wo
WOSBIRD n illegitimate child
WOST vb wit, to know
WOT vb wit, to know
WOTCHA ▸ wotcher
WOTCHER sentence substitute slang term of greeting
WOTS ▸ wot
WOTTED ▸ wot
WOTTEST ▸ wot
WOTTETH ▸ wot
WOTTING ▸ wot
WOUBIT n type of caterpillar
WOUBITS ▸ woubit

WOULD ▸ will
WOULDS same as ▸ **wouldst**
WOULDST singular form of the past tense of ▸ **will**
WOUND vb injure ▷ n injury
WOUNDED adj suffering from wounds
WOUNDER ▸ wound
WOUNDS ▸ wound
WOUNDY adj extreme
WOURALI n plant from which curare is obtained
WOVE ▸ weave
WOVEN n article made from woven cloth
WOVENS ▸ woven
WOW interj exclamation of astonishment ▷ n astonishing person or thing ▷ vb be a great success with
WOWED ▸ wow
WOWEE stronger form of ▸ **wow**
WOWF adj mad

This is a Scots word meaning crazy: you are not likely to get the chance to play this very often but if your opponent plays **wow** and you have an F you would be wowf to miss the opportunity of the hook!

WOWFER ▸ wowf
WOWFEST ▸ wowf
WOWING ▸ wow
WOWS ▸ wow
WOWSER n puritanical person
WOWSERS ▸ wowser
WOX ▸ wax

Wox is an old past tense of the verb **wax**, to grow, and is another of the key words using X.

WOXEN ▸ wax
WRACK n seaweed ▷ vb strain or shake (something) violently
WRACKED ▸ wrack
WRACKS ▸ wrack
WRAITH n ghost
WRAITHS ▸ wraith
WRANG Scots word for ▸ **wrong**
WRANGED ▸ wrang
WRANGLE vb argue noisily ▷ n noisy argument
WRANGS ▸ wrang
WRAP vb fold (something)

W

round (a person or thing) so as to cover ▷ *n* garment wrapped round the shoulders

WRAPPED ▶ **wrap**

WRAPPER *vb* cover with wrapping ▷ *n* cover for a product

WRAPS ▶ **wrap**

WRAPT *same as* ▶ **rapt**

WRASSE *n* colourful sea fish

WRASSES ▶ **wrasse**

WRASSLE *same as* ▶ **wrestle**

WRAST *same as* ▶ **wrest**

WRASTED ▶ **wrast**

WRASTLE *same as* ▶ **wrestle**

WRASTS ▶ **wrast**

WRATE ▶ **write**

WRATH *n* intense anger ▷ *adj* incensed ▷ *vb* make angry

WRATHED ▶ **wrath**

WRATHS ▶ **wrath**

WRATHY *same as* > **wrathful**

WRAWL *vb* howl

WRAWLED ▶ **wrawl**

WRAWLS ▶ **wrawl**

WRAXLE *vb* wrestle

WRAXLED ▶ **wraxle**

WRAXLES ▶ **wraxle**

WREAK *vb* inflict (vengeance, etc) or to cause (chaos, etc)

WREAKED ▶ **wreak**

WREAKER ▶ **wreak**

WREAKS ▶ **wreak**

WREATH *n* twisted ring or band of flowers or leaves used as a memorial or tribute

WREATHE *vb* form into or take the form of a wreath by intertwining or twisting together

WREATHS ▶ **wreath**

WREATHY *adj* twisted into wreath

WRECK *vb* destroy ▷ *n* remains of something that has been destroyed or badly damaged, esp a ship

WRECKED *adj* in a state of intoxication, stupor, or euphoria, induced by drugs or alcohol

WRECKER *n* formerly, person who lured ships onto the rocks in order to plunder them

WRECKS ▶ **wreck**

WREN *n* small brown songbird

WRENCH *vb* twist or pull violently ▷ *n* violent twist or pull

WRENS ▶ **wren**

WREST *vb* twist violently ▷ *n* act or an instance of wresting

WRESTED ▶ **wrest**

WRESTER ▶ **wrest**

WRESTLE *vb* fight, esp as a sport, by grappling with and trying to throw down an opponent ▷ *n* act of wrestling

WRESTS ▶ **wrest**

WRETCH *n* despicable person

WRETHE *same as* ▶ **wreathe**

WRETHED ▶ **wrethe**

WRETHES ▶ **wrethe**

WRICK *variant spelling* (*chiefly Brit*) *of* ▶ **rick**

WRICKED ▶ **wrick**

WRICKS ▶ **wrick**

WRIED ▶ **wry**

WRIER ▶ **wry**

WRIES ▶ **wry**

WRIEST ▶ **wry**

WRIGGLE *vb* move with a twisting action ▷ *n* wriggling movement

WRIGGLY ▶ **wriggle**

WRIGHT *n* maker

WRIGHTS ▶ **wright**

WRING *vb* twist, esp to squeeze liquid out of

WRINGED ▶ **wring**

WRINGER *same as* ▶ **mangle**

WRINGS ▶ **wring**

WRINKLE *n* slight crease, esp one in the skin due to age ▷ *vb* make or become slightly creased

WRINKLY ▶ **wrinkle**

WRIST *n* joint between the hand and the arm

WRISTS ▶ **wrist**

WRISTY *adj* (of a player's style of hitting the ball in cricket, tennis, etc) characterized by considerable movement of the wrist

WRIT *n* written legal command

WRITE *vb* mark paper etc with symbols or words

WRITER *n* author

WRITERS ▶ **writer**

WRITES ▶ **write**

WRITHE *vb* twist or squirm in or as if in pain ▷ *n* act or an instance of writhing

WRITHED ▶ **writhe**

WRITHEN *adj* twisted

WRITHER ▶ **writhe**

WRITHES ▶ **writhe**

WRITING ▶ **write**

WRITS ▶ **writ**

WRITTEN ▶ **write**

WRIZLED *adj* wrinkled

WROATH *n* unforeseen trouble

WROATHS ▶ **wroath**

WROKE ▶ **wreak**

WROKEN ▶ **wreak**

WRONG *adj* incorrect or mistaken ▷ *adv* in a wrong manner ▷ *n* something immoral or unjust ▷ *vb* treat unjustly

WRONGED ▶ **wrong**

WRONGER ▶ **wrong**

WRONGLY ▶ **wrong**

WRONGS ▶ **wrong**

WROOT *obsolete form of* ▶ **root**

WROOTED ▶ **wroot**

WROOTS ▶ **wroot**

WROTE ▶ **write**

WROTH *adj* angry

WROUGHT *adj* (of metals) shaped by hammering or beating

WRUNG ▶ **wring**

WRY *adj* drily humorous ▷ *vb* twist or contort

WRYBILL *n* New Zealand plover whose bill is bent to one side enabling it to search for food beneath stones

WRYER ▶ **wry**

WRYEST ▶ **wry**

WRYING ▶ **wry**

WRYLY ▶ **wry**

WRYNECK *n* woodpecker that has a habit of twisting its neck round

WRYNESS ▶ **wry**

WRYTHEN *adj* twisted

WUD *Scots form of* ▶ **wood**

W and U are a horrible combination to have on your rack, so this Scots word for wood can be a godsend. And remember that it can also be a verb, meaning to load with wood, so you have **wuds, wudding** and **wudded**.

WUDDED ▶ wud
WUDDING ▶ wud
WUDJULA *n* Australian word for a non-Aboriginal person
WUDS ▶ wud
WUDU *n* practice of ritual washing before daily prayer
WUDUS ▶ wudu
WULL *obsolete form of* ▶ **will**
WULLED ▶ will
WULLING ▶ will
WULLS ▶ will
WUNNER *same as* ▶ **oner**
WUNNERS ▶ wunner
WURLEY *n* Aboriginal hut
WURLEYS ▶ wurley
WURLIE *same as* ▶ **wurley**
WURLIES ▶ wurlie
WURST *n* large sausage, esp of a type made in Germany, Austria, etc
WURSTS ▶ wurst
WURZEL *n* root
WURZELS ▶ wurzel
WUS *n* casual term of address
WUSES ▶ wus
WUSHU *n* Chinese martial arts

WUSHUS ▶ wushu
WUSS *n* feeble or effeminate person
WUSSES ▶ wuss
WUSSIER ▶ wussy
WUSSIES ▶ wussy
WUSSY *adj* feeble or effeminate ▷ *n* feeble person
WUTHER *vb* (of wind) blow and roar
WUTHERS ▶ wuther
WUXIA *n* genre of Chinese fiction and film, concerning the adventures of sword-wielding chivalrous heroes

> This Chinese word for a genre of fiction may get you a decent score from a very difficult-looking rack.

WUXIAS ▶ wuxia
WUZZLE *vb* mix up
WUZZLED ▶ wuzzle
WUZZLES ▶ wuzzle
WYCH *n* type of tree having flexible branches
WYCHES ▶ wych
WYE *n* y-shaped pipe

> If you have W and Y on your rack, look for an E on the board that will allow you to play this name for the letter Y, especially if you can land on a bonus square as a result.

WYES ▶ wye
WYLE *vb* entice
WYLED ▶ wyle
WYLES ▶ wyle
WYLING ▶ wyle
WYN *n* rune equivalent to English 'w'
WYND *n* narrow lane or alley
WYNDS ▶ wynd
WYNN *same as* ▶ **wyn**
WYNNS ▶ wynn
WYNS ▶ wyn
WYTE *vb* blame
WYTED ▶ wyte
WYTES ▶ wyte
WYTING ▶ wyte
WYVERN *n* heraldic beast having a serpent's tail and a dragon's head and a body with wings and two legs
WYVERNS ▶ wyvern

W

Xx

Worth 8 points on its own, **X** is one of the best tiles in the game. It doesn't, however, start many two- and three-letter words. There are only two valid two-letter words, **xi** and **xu** (9 points each) beginning with **X**, and only one three-letter word, **xis**. Therefore, if you have an **X** on your rack and need to play short words, you're probably better off thinking of words that end in **X** or have **X** in them rather than those that start with **X**. Particularly good to remember are **zax, zex** (19 points each) and **kex** (14 points).

XANTHAM *n* acacia gum

XANTHAN *same as*
► **xantham**

XANTHIC *adj* of, containing, or derived from xanthic acid

XANTHIN *n* any of a group of yellow or orange carotene derivatives that occur in the fruit and flowers of certain plants

XEBEC *n* small three-masted Mediterranean vessel with both square and lateen sails, formerly used by Algerian pirates and later used for commerce

> A kind of small boat, and a good high-scoring word that can easily be missed, as we tend to be slow to consider words beginning with X.

XEBECS ► **xebec**

XENIA *n* influence of pollen upon the form of the fruit developing after pollination

XENIAL ► **xenia**

XENIAS ► **xenia**

XENIC *adj* denoting the presence of bacteria

XENIUM *n* diplomatic gift

XENON *n* colourless odourless gas found in very small quantities in the air

XENONS ► **xenon**

XENOPUS *n* African frog

XERAFIN *n* Indian coin

XERARCH *adj* (of a sere) having its origin in a dry habitat

XERASIA *n* dryness of the hair

XERIC *adj* of, relating to, or growing in dry conditions

XEROMA *n* excessive dryness of the cornea

XEROMAS ► **xeroma**

XEROSES ► **xerosis**

XEROSIS *n* abnormal dryness of bodily tissues, esp the skin, eyes, or mucous membranes

XEROTES *same as*
► **xerosis**

XEROTIC ► **xerosis**

XEROX *n* tradename for a machine employing a xerographic copying process ▷ *vb* produce a copy (of a document, etc) using such a machine

XEROXED ► **xerox**

XEROXES ► **xerox**

XERUS *n* ground squirrel

XERUSES ► **xerus**

XI *n* 14th letter in the Greek alphabet

XIPHOID *adj* shaped like a sword ▷ *n* part of the sternum

XIS ► **xi**

XOANA ► **xoanon**

XOANON *n* primitive image of a god, carved, esp originally, in wood, and supposed to have fallen from heaven

> One of the few words starting with X, this means a kind of primitive statue. But be careful: the plural is **xoana** not **xoanons**.

XRAY *n* code word for the letter X

XRAYS ► **xray**

XU *n* Vietnamese currency unit

XYLAN *n* yellow polysaccharide consisting of xylose units: occurs in straw husks and other woody tissue

XYLANS ► **xylan**

XYLEM *n* plant tissue that conducts water and minerals from the roots to all other parts

XYLEMS ► **xylem**

XYLENE *n* type of hydrocarbon

XYLENES ► **xylene**

XYLENOL *n* synthetic resin made from xylene

XYLIC ► **xylem**

XYLIDIN *same as*
> **xylidine**

XYLITOL *n* crystalline alcohol used as sweetener

XYLOGEN *same as*
► **xylem**

XYLOID *adj* of, relating to, or resembling wood

XYLOL *another name (not in technical usage) for*
► **xylene**

XYLOLS ► **xylol**

XYLOMA *n* hard growth in fungi

XYLOMAS ► **xyloma**

XYLONIC *adj* denoting an acid formed from xylose

XYLOSE *n* white crystalline dextrorotatory sugar found in the form of xylan in wood and straw

XYLOSES ► **xylose**

XYLYL *n* group of atoms

XYLYLS ▶ xylyl

XYST *n* long portico, esp one used in ancient Greece for athletics

A kind of court used by ancient Greek athletes for exercises, this is a lovely high-scoring word to play. And if your opponent plays it, remember that you can put an I on it to make **xysti**, as well as an S to make **xysts**.

XYSTER *n* surgical instrument for scraping bone

XYSTERS ▶ xyster

XYSTI ▶ xystus

XYSTOI ▶ xystos

XYSTOS *same as* ▶ xyst

XYSTS ▶ xyst

XYSTUS *same as* ▶ xyst

X

Yy

Y can be a useful tile to have on your rack, particularly if you are short of vowels, but it can make it difficult to find bonus words scoring that extra 50 points, and you will normally want to play it off as soon as a good score offers itself. There are only four two-letter words beginning with **Y**, but these are easy to remember as there's one for every vowel except **I**: **ya, ye, yo** and **yu** (5 points each). There are quite a few useful three-letter words: **yew** (9) and **yob** (8) and remember that **yob** was originally **boy** backwards: if you can't fit in **yob**, you may be able to use **boy** instead. And while his half-brother the **zo** (or **dzo** or **dso** or **zho**) gets all the attention, don't forget that the **yak** (10) earns quite a decent score!

YA pron you

YAAR n in informal Indian English, a friend

YAARS ▶ yaar

YABA n informal word for 'yet another bloody acronym'

YABAS ▶ yaba

YABBA n form of methamphetamine

YABBAS ▶ yabba

YABBER vb talk or jabber ▷ n talk or jabber

YABBERS ▶ yabber

YABBIE same as ▶ yabby

YABBIED ▶ yabby

YABBIES ▶ yabby

YABBY n small freshwater crayfish ▷ vb go out to catch yabbies

YACCA n Australian plant with a woody stem, stiff grasslike leaves, and a spike of small white flowers

YACCAS ▶ yacca

YACHT n large boat with sails or an engine, used for racing or pleasure cruising ▷ vb sail in a yacht

YACHTED ▶ yacht

YACHTER ▶ yacht

YACHTIE n yachtsman

YACHTS ▶ yacht

YACK same as ▶ yak

YACKA same as ▶ yacca

YACKAS ▶ yacka

YACKED ▶ yack

YACKER same as ▶ yakka

YACKERS ▶ yacker

YACKING ▶ yack

YACKS ▶ yack

YAD n hand-held pointer used for reading the sefer torah

YADS ▶ yad

YAE same as ▶ ae

YAFF vb bark

YAFFED ▶ yaff

YAFFING ▶ yaff

YAFFLE n woodpecker with a green back and wings, and a red crown

YAFFLES ▶ yaffle

YAFFS ▶ yaff

YAG n artificial crystal

YAGER same as ▶ jaeger

YAGERS ▶ yager

YAGGER n pedlar

YAGGERS ▶ yagger

YAGI n type of highly directional aerial

YAGIS ▶ yagi

YAGS ▶ yag

YAH interj exclamation of derision or disgust ▷ n affected upper-class person

YAHOO n crude coarse person

YAHOOS ▶ yahoo

YAHS ▶ yah

YAIRD Scots form of ▶ yard

YAIRDS ▶ yaird

YAK n Tibetan ox with long shaggy hair ▷ vb talk continuously about unimportant matters

YAKHDAN n box for carrying ice on a pack animal

YAKKA n work

YAKKAS ▶ yakka

YAKKED ▶ yak

YAKKER same as ▶ yakka

YAKKERS ▶ yakker

YAKKING ▶ yak

YAKOW n animal bred from a male yak and a domestic cow

YAKOWS ▶ yakow

YAKS ▶ yak

YAKUZA n Japanese criminal organization involved in illegal gambling, extortion, gun-running, etc

YALD adj vigorous

YALE n mythical beast with the body of an antelope (or similar animal) and swivelling horns

YALES ▶ yale

YAM n tropical root vegetable

YAMALKA same as ▶ yarmulke

YAMEN n (in imperial China) the office or residence of a public official

YAMENS ▶ yamen

YAMMER vb whine in a complaining manner ▷ n yammering sound

YAMMERS ▶ yammer

YAMPIES ▶ yampy

YAMPY n foolish person

YAMS ▶ yam

YAMULKA same as ▶ yarmulke

YAMUN same as ▶ yamen

YAMUNS ▶ yamun

YANG n (in Chinese

philosophy) one of two complementary principles maintaining harmony in the universe

YANGS ▶ **yang**

YANK *vb* pull or jerk suddenly ▷ *n* sudden pull or jerk

YANKED ▶ **yank**

YANKEE *n* code word for the letter Y

YANKEES ▶ **yankee**

YANKER ▶ **yank**

YANKERS ▶ **yank**

YANKIE *n* shrewish woman

YANKIES ▶ **yankie**

YANKING ▶ **yank**

YANKS ▶ **yank**

YANQUI *n* slang word for American

YANQUIS ▶ **yanqui**

YANTRA *n* diagram used in meditation

YANTRAS ▶ **yantra**

YAOURT *n* yoghurt

YAOURTS ▶ **yaourt**

YAP *vb* bark with a high-pitched sound ▷ *n* high-pitched bark ▷ *interj* imitation or representation of the sound of a dog yapping or people jabbering

YAPOCK *same as* ▶ **yapok**

YAPOCKS ▶ **yapock**

YAPOK *n* type of opossum

YAPOKS ▶ **yapok**

YAPON *same as* ▶ **yaupon**

YAPONS ▶ **yapon**

YAPP *n* type of book binding

YAPPED ▶ **yap**

YAPPER ▶ **yap**

YAPPERS ▶ **yap**

YAPPIE *n* young aspiring professional

YAPPIER ▶ **yap**

YAPPIES ▶ **yappie**

YAPPING ▶ **yap**

YAPPS ▶ **yapp**

YAPPY ▶ **yap**

YAPS ▶ **yap**

YAPSTER ▶ **yap**

YAQONA *n* Polynesian shrub

YAQONAS ▶ **yaqona**

YAR *adj* nimble

YARD *n*. unit of length equal to 36 inches or about 91.4 centimetres ▷ *vb* draft (animals), esp to a saleyard

YARDAGE *n* length measured in yards

YARDANG *n* ridge formed by wind erosion

YARDARM *n* outer end of a ship's yard

YARDED ▶ **yard**

YARDER ▶ **yard**

YARDERS ▶ **yard**

YARDING *n* group of animals displayed for sale

YARDMAN *n* farm overseer

YARDMEN ▶ **yardman**

YARDS ▶ **yard**

YARE *adj* ready, brisk, or eager ▷ *adv* readily or eagerly

YARELY ▶ **yare**

YARER ▶ **yare**

YAREST ▶ **yare**

YARFA *n* peat

YARFAS ▶ **yarfa**

YARK *vb* make ready

YARKED ▶ **yark**

YARKING ▶ **yark**

YARKS ▶ **yark**

YARN *n* thread used for knitting or making cloth ▷ *vb* thread with yarn

YARNED ▶ **yarn**

YARNER ▶ **yarn**

YARNERS ▶ **yarn**

YARNING ▶ **yarn**

YARNS ▶ **yarn**

YARPHA *n* peat

YARPHAS ▶ **yarpha**

YARR *n* wild white flower

YARRAN *n* type of small hardy tree of inland Australia

YARRANS ▶ **yarran**

YARROW *n* wild plant with flat clusters of white flowers

YARROWS ▶ **yarrow**

YARRS ▶ **yarr**

YARTA *Shetland word for* ▶ **heart**

YARTAS ▶ **yarta**

YARTO *same as* ▶ **yarta**

YARTOS ▶ **yarto**

YASHMAC *same as* ▶ **yashmak**

YASHMAK *n* veil worn by a Muslim woman to cover her face in public

YASMAK *same as* ▶ **yashmak**

YASMAKS ▶ **yashmak**

YATAGAN *same as* > **yataghan**

YATE *n* type of small eucalyptus tree yielding a very hard timber

YATES ▶ **yate**

YATTER *vb* talk at length ▷ *n* continuous chatter

YATTERS ▶ **yatter**

YAUD *Scots word for* ▶ **mare**

YAUDS ▶ **yaud**

YAULD *adj* alert, spritely, or nimble

YAUP *variant spelling of* ▶ **yawp**

YAUPED ▶ **yaup**

YAUPER ▶ **yaup**

YAUPERS ▶ **yaup**

YAUPING ▶ **yaup**

YAUPON *n* southern US evergreen holly shrub with spreading branches, scarlet fruits, and oval leaves

YAUPONS ▶ **yaupon**

YAUPS ▶ **yaup**

YAUTIA *n* Caribbean plant cultivated for its edible leaves and underground stems

YAUTIAS ▶ **yautia**

YAW *vb* (of an aircraft or ship) turn to one side or from side to side while moving ▷ *n* act or movement of yawing

YAWED ▶ **yaw**

YAWEY ▶ **yaws**

YAWING ▶ **yaw**

YAWL *n* two-masted sailing boat ▷ *vb* howl, weep, or scream harshly

YAWLED ▶ **yawl**

YAWLING ▶ **yawl**

YAWLS ▶ **yawl**

YAWN *vb* open the mouth wide and take in air deeply, often when sleepy or bored ▷ *n* act of yawning

YAWNED ▶ **yawn**

YAWNER ▶ **yawn**

YAWNERS ▶ **yawn**

YAWNIER ▶ **yawn**

YAWNING ▶ **yawn**

YAWNS ▶ **yawn**

YAWNY ▶ **yawn**

YAWP *vb* gape or yawn, esp audibly ▷ *n* shout, bark, yelp, or cry

YAWPED ▶ **yawp**

YAWPER ▶ **yawp**

YAWPERS ▶ **yawp**

YAWPING ▶ **yawp**

YAWPS ▶ **yawp**

YAWS *n* infectious tropical skin disease

YAWY ▶ **yaws**

YAY *interj* exclamation indicating approval, congratulation, or triumph ▷ *n* cry of approval

YAYS ▶ **yay**

Y

YBET archaic past participle of ▸ **beat**

YBLENT archaic past participle of ▸ **blend**

YBORE archaic past participle of ▸ **bear**

YBOUND archaic past participle of ▸ **bind**

YBRENT archaic past participle of ▸ **burn**

YCLAD archaic past participle of ▸ **clothe**

YCLED archaic past participle of ▸ **clothe**

YCLEEPE archaic form of ▸ **clepe**

YCLEPED same as ▸ **yclept**

YCLEPT adj having the name of

YCOND archaic past participle of ▸ **con**

YDRAD archaic past participle of ▸ **dread**

YDRED archaic past participle of ▸ **dread**

YE pron you ▷ adj the

YEA interj yes ▷ adv indeed or truly ▷ sentence substitute aye ▷ n cry of agreement

YEAD vb proceed

YEADING ▸ **yead**

YEADS ▸ **yead**

YEAH n positive affirmation

YEAHS ▸ **yeah**

YEALDON n fuel

YEALING n person of the same age as oneself

YEALM vb prepare for thatching

YEALMED ▸ **yealm**

YEALMS ▸ **yealm**

YEAN vb (of a sheep or goat) to give birth to (offspring)

YEANED ▸ **yean**

YEANING ▸ **yean**

YEANS ▸ **yean**

YEAR n time taken for the earth to make one revolution around the sun, about 365 days

YEARD vb bury

YEARDED ▸ **yeard**

YEARDS ▸ **yeard**

YEAREND n end of the year

YEARLY adv (happening) every year or once a year ▷ adj occurring, done, or appearing once a year or every year ▷ n publication, event, etc, that occurs once a year

YEARN vb want (something) very much

YEARNED ▸ **yearn**

YEARNER ▸ **yearn**

YEARNS ▸ **yearn**

YEARS ▸ **year**

YEAS ▸ **yea**

YEAST n fungus used to make bread rise and to ferment alcoholic drinks ▷ vb froth or foam

YEASTED ▸ **yeast**

YEASTS ▸ **yeast**

YEASTY adj of, resembling, or containing yeast

YEBO interj yes ▷ sentence substitute expression of affirmation

YECCH same as ▸ **yech**

YECCHS ▸ **yecch**

YECH n expression of disgust

YECHIER ▸ **yechy**

YECHS ▸ **yech**

YECHY ▸ **yech**

YEDE same as ▸ **yead**

YEDES ▸ **yede**

YEDING ▸ **yede**

YEED same as ▸ **yead**

YEEDING ▸ **yeed**

YEEDS ▸ **yeed**

YEELIN n person of the same age as oneself

YEELINS ▸ **yeelin**

YEGG n burglar or safe-breaker

YEGGMAN same as ▸ **yegg**

YEGGMEN ▸ **yeggman**

YEGGS ▸ **yegg**

YEH same as ▸ **yeah**

YELD adj (of an animal) barren or too young to bear young

YELK n yolk of an egg

YELKS ▸ **yelk**

YELL vb shout or scream in a loud or piercing way ▷ n loud cry of pain, anger, or fear

YELLED ▸ **yell**

YELLER ▸ **yell**

YELLERS ▸ **yell**

YELLING ▸ **yell**

YELLOCH vb yell

YELLOW n colour of gold, a lemon, etc ▷ adj of this colour ▷ vb make or become yellow

YELLOWS n any of various fungal or viral diseases of plants, characterized by yellowish discoloration and stunting

YELLOWY ▸ **yellow**

YELLS ▸ **yell**

YELM same as ▸ **yealm**

YELMED ▸ **yelm**

YELMING ▸ **yelm**

YELMS ▸ **yelm**

YELP n a short sudden cry ▷ vb utter a sharp or high-pitched cry of pain

YELPED ▸ **yelp**

YELPER ▸ **yelp**

YELPERS ▸ **yelp**

YELPING ▸ **yelp**

YELPS ▸ **yelp**

YELT n young sow

YELTS ▸ **yelt**

YEMMER southwest English form of ▸ **ember**

YEMMERS ▸ **yemmer**

YEN n monetary unit of Japan ▷ vb have a longing

YENNED ▸ **yen**

YENNING ▸ **yen**

YENS ▸ **yen**

YENTA n meddlesome woman

YENTAS ▸ **yenta**

YENTE same as ▸ **yenta**

YENTES ▸ **yente**

YEOMAN n farmer owning and farming his own land

YEOMEN ▸ **yeoman**

YEP n affirmative statement

YEPS ▸ **yep**

YERBA n stimulating South American drink made from dried leaves

YERBAS ▸ **yerba**

YERD vb bury

YERDED ▸ **yerd**

YERDING ▸ **yerd**

YERDS ▸ **yerd**

YERK vb tighten stitches

YERKED ▸ **yerk**

YERKING ▸ **yerk**

YERKS ▸ **yerk**

YES interj expresses consent, agreement, or approval ▷ n answer or vote of yes ▷ sentence substitute used to express acknowledgment, affirmation, consent, agreement, or approval or to answer when one is addressed ▷ vb reply in the affirmative

YESES ▸ **yes**

YESHIVA n traditional Jewish school devoted chiefly to the study of rabbinic literature and the Talmud

YESK vb hiccup

YESKED ▸ **yesk**

YESKING ▶ yesk
YESKS ▶ yesk
YESSED ▶ yes
YESSES ▶ yes
YESSING ▶ yes
YEST archaic form of ▶ yeast
YESTER adj of or relating to yesterday
YESTERN same as ▶ yester
YESTS ▶ yest
YESTY archaic form of ▶ yeasty
YET adv up until then or now
YETI n large legendary manlike creature alleged to inhabit the Himalayan Mountains
YETIS ▶ yeti
YETT n gate or door
YETTIE n young, entrepreneurial, and technology-based (person)
YETTIES ▶ yettie
YETTS ▶ yett
YEUK vb itch
YEUKED ▶ yeuk
YEUKIER ▶ yeuky
YEUKING ▶ yeuk
YEUKS ▶ yeuk
YEUKY ▶ yeuk
YEVE vb give
YEVEN ▶ yeve
YEVES ▶ yeve
YEVING ▶ yeve
YEW n evergreen tree with needle-like leaves and red berries
YEWEN adj made of yew
YEWS ▶ yew
YEX vb hiccup
  This word meaning to hiccup gives you a good score, and the verb forms offer the chance to expand it if someone else plays it, or if you get the chance later on.
YEXED ▶ yex
YEXES ▶ yex
YEXING ▶ yex
YFERE adv together
YGO archaic past participle of ▶ go
YGOE archaic past participle of ▶ go
YIBBLES adv perhaps
YICKER vb squeal or squeak
YICKERS ▶ yicker
YIDAKI n long wooden wind instrument played by the Aboriginal peoples of Arnhem Land
YIDAKIS ▶ yidaki

YIELD vb produce or bear ▷ n amount produced
YIELDED ▶ yield
YIELDER ▶ yield
YIELDS ▶ yield
YIKE n argument, squabble, or fight ▷ vb argue, squabble, or fight
YIKED ▶ yike
YIKES interj expression of surprise, fear, or alarm
YIKING ▶ yike
YIKKER vb squeal or squeak
YIKKERS ▶ yikker
YILL n ale
YILLS ▶ yill
YIN Scots word for ▶ one
YINCE Scots form of ▶ once
YINDIE n person who combines a lucrative career with non-mainstream tastes
YINDIES ▶ yindie
YINS ▶ yin
YIP n emit a high-pitched bark
YIPE same as ▶ yipes
YIPES interj expression of surprise, fear, or alarm
YIPPED ▶ yip
YIPPEE interj exclamation of joy or pleasure
YIPPER n golfer who suffers from a failure of nerve
YIPPERS ▶ yipper
YIPPIE n young person sharing hippy ideals
YIPPIES ▶ yippie
YIPPING ▶ yip
YIPPY same as ▶ yippie
YIPS ▶ yip
YIRD vb bury
YIRDED ▶ yird
YIRDING ▶ yird
YIRDS ▶ yird
YIRK same as ▶ yerk
YIRKED ▶ yirk
YIRKING ▶ yirk
YIRKS ▶ yirk
YIRR vb snarl, growl, or yell
YIRRED ▶ yirr
YIRRING ▶ yirr
YIRRS ▶ yirr
YIRTH n earth
YIRTHS ▶ yirth
YITE n European bunting with a yellowish head and body and brown streaked wings and tail
YITES ▶ yite
YITIE same as ▶ yite
YITIES ▶ yitie
YITTEN adj frightened

YLEM n original matter from which the basic elements are said to have been formed following the explosion postulated in the big bang theory of cosmology
YLEMS ▶ ylem
YLIKE Spenserian form of ▶ alike
YLKE archaic spelling of ▶ ilk
YLKES ▶ ylke
YMOLT Spenserian past participle of ▶ melt
YMOLTEN Spenserian past participle of ▶ melt
YMPE Spenserian form of ▶ imp
YMPES ▶ ympe
YMPING ▶ ympe
YMPT ▶ ympe
YNAMBU n South American bird
YNAMBUS ▶ ynambu
YO interj expression used as a greeting or to attract someone's attention ▷ sentence substitute expression used as a greeting, to attract someone's attention, etc
YOB n bad-mannered aggressive youth
YOBBERY n behaviour typical of aggressive surly youths
YOBBISH adj typical of aggressive surly youths
YOBBISM ▶ yob
YOBBO same as ▶ yob
YOBBOES ▶ yobbo
YOBBOS ▶ yobbo
YOBS ▶ yob
YOCK vb chuckle
YOCKED ▶ yock
YOCKING ▶ yock
YOCKS ▶ yock
YOD n tenth letter in the Hebrew alphabet
YODE ▶ yead
YODEL vb sing with abrupt changes between a normal and a falsetto voice ▷ n act or sound of yodelling
YODELED ▶ yodel
YODELER ▶ yodel
YODELS ▶ yodel
YODH same as ▶ yod
YODHS ▶ yodh
YODLE variant spelling of ▶ yodel
YODLED ▶ yodle
YODLER ▶ yodle

Y

YODLERS ▶ yodle
YODLES ▶ yodle
YODLING ▶ yodle
YODS ▶ yod
YOGA n Hindu method of exercise and discipline aiming at spiritual, mental, and physical wellbeing
YOGAS ▶ yoga
YOGEE same as ▶ yogi
YOGEES ▶ yogee
YOGH n character used in Old and Middle English to represent a palatal fricative
YOGHS ▶ yogh
YOGHURT same as ▶ yogurt
YOGI n person who practises yoga
YOGIC ▶ yoga
YOGIN same as ▶ yogi
YOGINI ▶ yogi
YOGINIS ▶ yogi
YOGINS ▶ yogin
YOGIS ▶ yogi
YOGISM ▶ yogi
YOGISMS ▶ yogi
YOGURT n slightly sour custard-like food made from milk that has had bacteria added to it, often sweetened and flavoured with fruit
YOGURTS ▶ yogurt
YOHIMBE n bark used in herbal medicine
YOICK vb urge on foxhounds
YOICKED ▶ yoick
YOICKS interj cry used by huntsmen to urge on the hounds to the fox ▷ vb urge on foxhounds
YOJAN n Indian unit of distance
YOJANA same as ▶ yojan
YOJANAS ▶ yojana
YOJANS ▶ yojan
YOK vb chuckle

> A useful short word meaning to laugh, with an alternative spelling **yuk**.

YOKE n wooden bar put across the necks of two animals to hold them together ▷ vb put a yoke on
YOKED ▶ yoke
YOKER vb spit
YOKERED ▶ yoker
YOKERS ▶ yoke
YOKES ▶ yoke
YOKING ▶ yoke
YOKINGS ▶ yoke
YOKKED ▶ yok

YOKKING ▶ yok
YOKS ▶ yok
YOKUL Shetland word for ▶ yes
YOLD archaic past participle of ▶ yield
YOLK n yellow part of an egg that provides food for the developing embryo
YOLKED ▶ yolk
YOLKIER ▶ yolk
YOLKS ▶ yolk
YOLKY ▶ yolk
YOM n day
YOMIM ▶ yom
YOMP vb walk or trek laboriously, esp heavily laden and over difficult terrain
YOMPED ▶ yomp
YOMPING ▶ yomp
YOMPS ▶ yomp
YON adj that or those over there ▷ adv yonder ▷ pron that person or thing
YOND same as ▶ yon
YONDER adv over there ▷ adj situated over there ▷ determiner being at a distance, either within view or as if within view ▷ n person
YONDERS ▶ yonder
YONI n female genitalia, regarded as a divine symbol of sexual pleasure
YONIC adj resembling a vulva
YONIS ▶ yoni
YONKER same as ▶ younker
YONKERS ▶ yonker
YONKS pl n very long time
YONNIE n stone
YONNIES ▶ yonnie
YONT same as ▶ yon
YOOF n non-standard spelling of youth, used humorously or facetiously
YOOFS ▶ yoof
YOOP n sob
YOOPS ▶ yoop
YORE n time long past ▷ adv in the past
YORES ▶ yore
YORK vb bowl or try to bowl (a batsman) by pitching the ball under or just beyond the bat
YORKED ▶ york
YORKER n ball that pitches just under the bat
YORKERS ▶ yorker
YORKIE n Yorkshire terrier

YORKIES ▶ yorkie
YORKING ▶ york
YORKS ▶ york
YORLING n as in yellow yorling yellowhammer
YORP vb shout
YORPED ▶ yorp
YORPING ▶ yorp
YORPS ▶ yorp
YOU pron person or people addressed ▷ n personality of the person being addressed
YOUK vb itch
YOUKED ▶ youk
YOUKING ▶ youk
YOUKS ▶ youk
YOUNG adj in an early stage of life or growth ▷ n young people in general; offspring
YOUNGER ▶ young
YOUNGLY adv youthfully
YOUNGS ▶ young
YOUNGTH n youth
YOUNKER n young man
YOUPON same as ▶ yaupon
YOUPONS ▶ youpon
YOUR adj of, belonging to, or associated with you
YOURN dialect form of ▶ yours
YOURS pron something belonging to you
YOURT same as ▶ yurt
YOURTS ▶ yourt
YOUS pron refers to more than one person including the person or persons addressed but not including the speaker
YOUSE same as ▶ yous
YOUTH n time of being young
YOUTHEN vb render more youthful-seeming
YOUTHLY adv young
YOUTHS ▶ youth
YOUTHY Scots word for ▶ young
YOW vb howl
YOWE Scots word for ▶ ewe
YOWED ▶ yow
YOWES ▶ yowe
YOWIE n legendary Australian apelike creature
YOWIES ▶ yowie
YOWING ▶ yow
YOWL n loud mournful cry ▷ vb produce a loud mournful wail or cry
YOWLED ▶ yowl
YOWLER ▶ yowl
YOWLERS ▶ yowl

YOWLEY n yellowhammer (bird)
YOWLEYS ▸ yowley
YOWLING ▸ yowl
YOWLS ▸ yowl
YOWS ▸ yow
YPERITE n mustard gas
YPIGHT archaic past participle of ▸ pitch
YPLAST archaic past participle of ▸ place
YPLIGHT archaic past participle of ▸ plight
YPSILON same as ▸ upsilon
YRAPT Spenserian form of ▸ rapt
YRENT archaic past participle of ▸ rend
YRIVD archaic past participle of ▸ rive
YRNEH n unit of reciprocal inductance
YRNEHS ▸ yrneh
YSAME Spenserian word for > together
YSHEND Spenserian form of ▸ shend
YSHENDS ▸ yshend
YSHENT ▸ yshend
YSLAKED archaic past participle of ▸ slake
YTOST archaic past participle of ▸ toss
YTTRIA n insoluble solid used mainly in incandescent mantles
YTTRIAS ▸ yttria
YTTRIC ▸ yttrium
YTTRIUM n silvery metallic element used in various alloys
YU n jade
YUAN n standard monetary unit of the People's Republic of China
YUANS ▸ yuan
YUCA same as ▸ yucca
YUCAS ▸ yuca
YUCCA n tropical plant with spikes of white leaves
YUCCAS ▸ yucca
YUCCH interj expression of disgust
YUCH interj expression of disgust

YUCK interj exclamation indicating contempt, dislike, or disgust ▷ vb chuckle
YUCKED ▸ yuck
YUCKER ▸ yuck
YUCKERS ▸ yuck
YUCKIER ▸ yucky
YUCKING ▸ yuck
YUCKO adj disgusting ▷ interj exclamation of disgust
YUCKS ▸ yuck
YUCKY adj disgusting, nasty
YUFT n Russia leather
YUFTS ▸ yuft
YUG same as ▸ yuga
YUGA n (in Hindu cosmology) one of the four ages of mankind
YUGARIE variant spelling of ▸ eugarie
YUGAS ▸ yuga
YUGS ▸ yug
YUK same as ▸ yuck
YUKATA n light kimono
YUKATAS ▸ yukata
YUKE vb itch
YUKED ▸ yuke
YUKES ▸ yuke
YUKIER ▸ yuky
YUKIEST ▸ yuky
YUKING ▸ yuke
YUKKED ▸ yuk
YUKKIER ▸ yukky
YUKKING ▸ yuk
YUKKY same as ▸ yucky
YUKO n score of five points in judo
YUKOS ▸ yuko
YUKS ▸ yuk
YUKY adj itchy
YULAN n Chinese magnolia often cultivated for its showy white flowers
YULANS ▸ yulan
YULE n Christmas, the Christmas season, or Christmas festivities
YULES ▸ yule
YUM interj expression of delight
YUMMIER ▸ yummy
YUMMIES ▸ yummy

YUMMO adj tasty ▷ interj exclamation of delight or approval
YUMMY adj delicious ▷ interj exclamation indicating pleasure or delight, as in anticipation of delicious food ▷ n delicious food item
YUMP vb leave the ground when driving over a ridge
YUMPED ▸ yump
YUMPIE n young upwardly mobile person
YUMPIES ▸ yumpie
YUMPING ▸ yump
YUMPS ▸ yump
YUNX n wryneck
YUNXES ▸ yunx
YUP n informal affirmative statement
YUPON same as ▸ yaupon
YUPONS ▸ yupon
YUPPIE n young highly-paid professional person, esp one who has a materialistic way of life ▷ adj typical of or reflecting the values of yuppies
YUPPIES ▸ yuppy
YUPPIFY vb make yuppie in nature
YUPPY same as ▸ yuppie
YUPS ▸ yup
YUPSTER ▸ yindie
YURT n circular tent consisting of a framework of poles covered with felt or skins, used by Mongolian and Turkic nomads of E and central Asia
YURTA same as ▸ yurt
YURTAS ▸ yurt
YURTS ▸ yurt
YUS ▸ yu
YUTZ n Yiddish word meaning fool
YUTZES ▸ yutz
YUZU n type of citrus fruit
YUZUS ▸ yuzu
YWIS adv certainly
YWROKE archaic past participle of ▸ wreak

Y

Zz

Scoring the same as **Q** but easier to use, **Z** is normally a good tile to have, but it is not the best when it comes to making bonus words scoring that extra 50 points, so you will normally want to play it off as soon as a good score offers itself. There are only two two-letter words beginning with **Z**, **za** and **zo** (11 points), but remembering this will save you wasting time looking for others. There some very good three-letter words starting with **Z**, however. These include another variant of **zo**, **zho** (15), as well as **zax** and **zex**, (19 each) **zap**, (14) **zep**, (14) **zip**, (14) and **zoo** (12).

ZA n pizza
ZABETA n tariff
ZABETAS ▶ zabeta
ZABRA n small sailing vessel
ZABRAS ▶ zabra
ZABTIEH n Turkish police officer
ZACATON n coarse grass
ZACK n Australian five-cent piece
ZACKS ▶ zack
ZADDICK adj righteous
ZADDIK n Hasidic Jewish leader
ZADDIKS ▶ zaddik
ZAFFAR same as ▶ zaffer
ZAFFARS ▶ zaffar
ZAFFER n impure cobalt oxide, used to impart a blue colour to enamels
ZAFFERS ▶ zaffer
ZAFFIR same as ▶ zaffer
ZAFFIRS ▶ zaffir
ZAFFRE same as ▶ zaffer
ZAFFRES ▶ zaffre
ZAFTIG adj ripe or curvaceous
ZAG vb change direction sharply
ZAGGED ▶ zag
ZAGGING ▶ zag
ZAGS ▶ zag
ZAIKAI n Japanese business community
ZAIKAIS ▶ zaikai
ZAIRE n currency used in the former Zaire
ZAIRES ▶ zaire
ZAITECH n investment in financial markets by a company to supplement its main income

ZAKAT n annual tax on Muslims to aid the poor in the Muslim community
ZAKATS ▶ zakat
ZAKUSKA ▶ zakuski
ZAKUSKI pl n hors d'oeuvres, consisting of tiny open sandwiches spread with caviar, smoked sausage, etc
ZAMAN n tropical tree
ZAMANG same as ▶ zaman
ZAMANGS ▶ zamang
ZAMANS ▶ zaman
ZAMARRA n sheepskin coat
ZAMARRO same as ▶ zamarra
ZAMBUCK n St John ambulance attendant, esp at a sports meeting
ZAMBUK same as ▶ zambuck
ZAMBUKS ▶ zambuk
ZAMIA n type of plant of tropical and subtropical America, with a short thick trunk, palmlike leaves, and short stout cones
ZAMIAS ▶ zamia
ZAMOUSE n West African buffalo
ZAMPONE n sausage made from pig's trotters
ZAMPONI ▶ zampone
ZANANA same as ▶ zenana
ZANANAS ▶ zanana
ZANDER n European freshwater pikeperch, valued as a food fish
ZANDERS ▶ zander
ZANELLA n twill fabric
ZANIED ▶ zany

ZANIER ▶ zany
ZANIES ▶ zany
ZANIEST ▶ zany
ZANILY ▶ zany
ZANJA n irrigation canal

> An irrigation canal in Spanish America, notable for combining the J and Z.

ZANJAS ▶ zanja
ZANJERO n irrigation supervisor

> Someone who supervises the distribution of water in a **zanja** or irrigation canal. This has a fair chance of coming up in actual play, and would make a great bonus.

ZANTE n type of wood
ZANTES ▶ zante
ZANY adj comical in an endearing way ▷ n clown or buffoon, esp one in old comedies who imitated other performers with ludicrous effect ▷ vb clown
ZANYING ▶ zany
ZANYISH ▶ zany
ZANYISM ▶ zany
ZANZA same as ▶ zanze
ZANZAS ▶ zanza
ZANZE n African musical instrument
ZANZES ▶ zanze
ZAP vb kill (by shooting) ▷ n energy, vigour, or pep ▷ interj exclamation used to express sudden or swift action
ZAPATA adj (of a

moustache) drooping
ZAPATEO n Cuban folk dance
ZAPPED ▸ zap
ZAPPER n remote control for a television etc
ZAPPERS ▸ zapper
ZAPPIER ▸ zappy
ZAPPING ▸ zap
ZAPPY adj energetic
ZAPS ▸ zap
ZAPTIAH same as ▸ zaptieh
ZAPTIEH n Turkish police officer

> Watch out for this Turkish policeman, who can also be spelt **zabtieh** or **zaptiah**.

ZARAPE n blanket-like shawl
ZARAPES ▸ zarape
ZAREBA n stockade or enclosure of thorn bushes around a village or campsite
ZAREBAS ▸ zareba
ZAREEBA same as ▸ zareba
ZARF n (esp in the Middle East) a holder, usually ornamental, for a hot coffee cup
ZARFS ▸ zarf
ZARI n thread made from fine gold or silver wire
ZARIBA same as ▸ zareba
ZARIBAS ▸ zariba
ZARIS ▸ zari
ZARNEC n sulphide of arsenic
ZARNECS ▸ zarnec
ZARNICH same as ▸ zarnec
ZAS ▸ za
ZATI n type of macaque
ZATIS ▸ zati
ZAX same as ▸ sax

> A chopper for trimming slate, and a great word combining X and Z. It has a variant **zex**.

ZAXES ▸ zax
ZAYIN n seventh letter of the Hebrew alphabet
ZAYINS ▸ zayin
ZAZEN n (in Zen Buddhism) deep meditation undertaken whilst sitting upright with legs crossed
ZAZENS ▸ zazen
ZEA n corn silk
ZEAL n great enthusiasm or eagerness
ZEALANT archaic variant of ▸ zealot

ZEALFUL ▸ zeal
ZEALOT n fanatic or extreme enthusiast
ZEALOTS ▸ zealot
ZEALOUS adj extremely eager or enthusiastic
ZEALS ▸ zeal
ZEAS ▸ zeal
ZEATIN n cytokinin derived from corn
ZEATINS ▸ zeatin
ZEBEC variant spelling of ▸ xebec
ZEBECK same as ▸ zebec
ZEBECKS ▸ zebeck
ZEBECS ▸ zebec
ZEBRA n black-and-white striped African animal of the horse family
ZEBRAIC adj like a zebra
ZEBRANO n type of striped wood
ZEBRAS ▸ zebra
ZEBRASS n offspring of a male zebra and a female ass
ZEBRINA n trailing herbaceous plant
ZEBRINE ▸ zebra
ZEBROID ▸ zebra
ZEBRULA n offspring of a male zebra and a female horse
ZEBRULE same as ▸ zebrula
ZEBU n Asian ox with a humped back and long horns
ZEBUB n large African fly
ZEBUBS ▸ zebub
ZEBUS ▸ zebu
ZECCHIN same as > zecchino
ZECHIN same as > zecchino
ZECHINS ▸ zechin
ZED n British and New Zealand spoken form of the letter z

> A name for the letter Z, and one of the most commonly played Z words.

ZEDOARY n dried rhizome of a tropical Asian plant, used as a stimulant and a condiment
ZEDS ▸ zed
ZEE the US word for ▸ zed

> This word can be very useful because E is the most common tile in Scrabble, so keep it in mind if you draw a Z. Zee scores 12 points.

ZEES ▸ zee

ZEIN n protein occurring in maize and used in the manufacture of plastics
ZEINS ▸ zein
ZEK n Soviet prisoner
ZEKS ▸ zek
ZEL n Turkish cymbal
ZELANT alternative form of ▸ zealant
ZELANTS ▸ zelant
ZELATOR same as > zelatrix
ZELKOVA n type of elm tree
ZELOSO adv with zeal
ZELS ▸ zel
ZEMSTVA ▸ zemstvo
ZEMSTVO n (in tsarist Russia) an elective provincial or district council established in most provinces of Russia by Alexander II in 1864 as part of his reform policy
ZENAIDA n dove
ZENANA n (in the East, esp in Muslim and Hindu homes) part of a house reserved for the women and girls of a household
ZENANAS ▸ zenana
ZENDIK n unbeliever or heretic
ZENDIKS ▸ zendik
ZENITH n highest point of success or power
ZENITHS ▸ zenith
ZEOLITE n any of a large group of glassy secondary minerals
ZEP n type of long sandwich
ZEPHYR n soft gentle breeze
ZEPHYRS ▸ zephyr
ZEPPOLE n Italian fritter
ZEPPOLI ▸ zeppole
ZEPS ▸ zep
ZERDA n fennec
ZERDAS ▸ zerda
ZEREBA same as ▸ zareba
ZEREBAS ▸ zereba
ZERIBA same as ▸ zareba
ZERIBAS ▸ zeriba
ZERK n grease fitting
ZERKS ▸ zerk
ZERO n (symbol representing) the number o ▷ adj having no measurable quantity or size ▷ vb adjust (an instrument or scale) so as to read zero ▷ determiner no (thing) at all
ZEROED ▸ zero
ZEROES ▸ zero
ZEROING ▸ zero

ZEROS ▶ zero

ZEROTH *adj* denoting a term in a series that precedes the term otherwise regarded as the first term

ZEST *n* enjoyment or excitement ▷ *vb* give flavour, interest, or piquancy to

ZESTED ▶ zest

ZESTER *n* kitchen utensil used to scrape fine shreds of peel from citrus fruits

ZESTERS ▶ zester

ZESTFUL ▶ zest

ZESTIER ▶ zest

ZESTILY ▶ zest

ZESTING ▶ zest

ZESTS ▶ zest

ZESTY ▶ zest

ZETA *n* sixth letter in the Greek alphabet, a consonant, transliterated as *z*

ZETAS ▶ zeta

ZETETIC *adj* proceeding by inquiry ▷ *n* investigation

ZEUGMA *n* figure of speech in which a word is used to modify or govern two or more words although appropriate to only one of them or making a different sense with each

ZEUGMAS ▶ zeugma

ZEUXITE *n* ferriferous mineral
This mineral, a kind of tourmaline, makes an excellent bonus.

ZEX *n* tool for cutting roofing slate

ZEXES ▶ zex

ZEZE *n* stringed musical instrument

ZEZES ▶ zeze

ZHO *same as* ▶ **zo**
A cross between a yak and a cow; the other forms are **dso, dzo** and **zo,** and it's worth remembering all of them.

ZHOMO *n* female zho

ZHOMOS ▶ zhomo

ZHOS ▶ zho

ZIBET *n* large civet of S and SE Asia, having tawny fur marked with black spots and stripes

ZIBETH *same as* ▶ **zibet**

ZIBETHS ▶ zibeth

ZIBETS ▶ zibet

ZIFF *n* beard

ZIFFIUS *n* sea monster

ZIFFS ▶ ziff

ZIG *same as* ▶ **zag**

ZIGAN *n* gypsy

ZIGANKA *n* Russian dance

ZIGANS ▶ zigan

ZIGGED ▶ zig

ZIGGING ▶ zig

ZIGS ▶ zig

ZIGZAG *n* line or course having sharp turns in alternating directions ▷ *vb* move in a zigzag ▷ *adj* formed in or proceeding in a zigzag ▷ *adv* in a zigzag manner

ZIGZAGS ▶ zigzag

ZIKURAT *same as* > **ziggurat**

ZILA *n* administrative district in India

ZILAS ▶ zila

ZILCH *n* nothing

ZILCHES ▶ zilch

ZILL *n* finger cymbal

ZILLA *same as* ▶ **zila**

ZILLAH *same as* ▶ **zila**

ZILLAHS ▶ zillah

ZILLAS ▶ zilla

ZILLION *n* extremely large but unspecified number

ZILLS ▶ zill

ZIMB *same as* ▶ **zebub**

ZIMBI *n* cowrie shell used as money

ZIMBIS ▶ zimbi

ZIMBS ▶ zimb

ZIMOCCA *n* bath sponge

ZIN *short form of* > **zinfandel**

ZINC *n* bluish-white metallic element used in alloys and to coat metal ▷ *vb* coat with zinc

ZINCATE *n* any of a class of salts derived from the amphoteric hydroxide of zinc

ZINCED ▶ zinc

ZINCIC ▶ zinc

ZINCIER ▶ zinc

ZINCIFY *vb* coat with zinc

ZINCING ▶ zinc

ZINCITE *n* red or yellow mineral consisting of zinc oxide in hexagonal crystalline form

ZINCKED ▶ zinc

ZINCKY ▶ zinc

ZINCO *n* printing plate made from zincography

ZINCODE *n* positive electrode

ZINCOID ▶ zinc

ZINCOS ▶ zinco

ZINCOUS ▶ zinc

ZINCS ▶ zinc

ZINCY ▶ zinc

ZINE *n* magazine or fanzine

ZINEB *n* organic insecticide

ZINEBS ▶ zineb

ZINES ▶ zine

ZING *n* quality in something that makes it lively or interesting ▷ *vb* make or move with or as if with a high-pitched buzzing sound

ZINGANI ▶ zingano

ZINGANO *n* gypsy

ZINGARA *same as* ▶ **zingaro**

ZINGARE ▶ zingara

ZINGARI ▶ zingaro

ZINGARO *n* Italian Gypsy

ZINGED ▶ zing

ZINGEL *n* small freshwater perch

ZINGELS ▶ zingel

ZINGER ▶ zing

ZINGERS ▶ zing

ZINGIER ▶ zingy

ZINGING ▶ zing

ZINGS ▶ zing

ZINGY *adj* vibrant

ZINKE *n* cornett

ZINKED ▶ zinc

ZINKES ▶ zinke

ZINKIER ▶ zinc

ZINKIFY *vb* coat with zinc

ZINKING ▶ zinc

ZINKY ▶ zinc

ZINNIA *n* plant of tropical and subtropical America, with solitary heads of brightly coloured flowers

ZINNIAS ▶ zinnia

ZINS ▶ zin

ZIP *same as* ▶ **zipper**

ZIPLESS ▶ zip

ZIPLOCK *adj* fastened with interlocking plastic strips ▷ *vb* seal (a ziplock storage bag)

ZIPPED ▶ zip

ZIPPER *n* fastening device operating by means of two parallel rows of metal or plastic teeth on either side of a closure that are interlocked by a sliding tab ▷ *vb* fasten with a zipper

ZIPPERS ▶ zipper

ZIPPIER ▶ zippy

ZIPPING ▶ zip

ZIPPO *n* nothing

ZIPPOS ▶ zippo

ZIPPY *adj* full of energy

ZIPS ▶ zip

ZIPTOP *adj* (of a bag) closed with a zip

ZIRAM *n* industrial fungicide

ZIRAMS ▶ ziram

ZIRCON *n* mineral used as a gemstone and in industry

ZIRCONS ▶ zircon

ZIT *n* spot or pimple

> This little word for a pimple can be very useful for disposing of the Z.

ZITE *same as* ▶ **ziti**

ZITHER *n* musical instrument consisting of strings stretched over a flat box and plucked to produce musical notes

ZITHERN *same as* ▶ **zither**

ZITHERS ▶ zither

ZITI *n* type of pasta

> Another very useful word for disposing of the Z, **ziti** is a type of pasta. It has a variant **zite**. Remember that **ziti** takes an S to form **zitis**, but **zite** does not take an S.

ZITIS ▶ ziti

ZITS ▶ zit

ZIZ *same as* ▶ **zizz**

ZIZANIA *n* aquatic grass

ZIZEL *n* chipmunk

ZIZELS ▶ zizel

ZIZIT *same as* ▶ **zizith**

ZIZITH *variant spelling of* ▶ **tsitsith**

ZIZZ *n* short sleep ▷ *vb* take a short sleep, snooze

ZIZZED ▶ zizz

ZIZZES ▶ zizz

ZIZZING ▶ zizz

ZIZZLE *vb* sizzle

ZIZZLED ▶ zizzle

ZIZZLES ▶ zizzle

ZLOTE ▶ zloty

ZLOTIES ▶ zloty

ZLOTY *n* monetary unit of Poland

ZLOTYCH *same as* ▶ **zloty**

ZLOTYS ▶ zloty

ZO *n* Tibetan breed of cattle, developed by crossing the yak with common cattle

ZOA ▶ zoon

ZOAEA *same as* ▶ **zoea**

ZOAEAE ▶ zoaea

ZOAEAS ▶ zoaea

ZOARIA ▶ zoarium

ZOARIAL ▶ zoarium

ZOARIUM *n* colony of zooids

ZOBO *same as* ▶ **zo**

ZOBOS ▶ zobo

ZOBU *same as* ▶ **zo**

ZOBUS ▶ zobu

ZOCALO *n* plaza in Mexico

ZOCALOS ▶ zocalo

ZOCCO *n* plinth

ZOCCOLO *same as* ▶ **zocco**

ZOCCOS ▶ zocco

ZODIAC *n* imaginary belt in the sky within which the sun, moon, and planets appear to move, divided into twelve equal areas, called signs of the zodiac, each named after a constellation

ZODIACS ▶ zodiac

ZOEA *n* free-swimming larva of a crab or related crustacean, which has well-developed abdominal appendages and may bear one or more spines

> A larval stage in certain crustaceans, and one of the most frequently played words in Scrabble, along with its friends **zoaea** and **zooea** and the various inflections: remember that these words can take an E in the plural as well as S, giving **zoeae**, **zoaeae** and **zooeae**.

ZOEAE ▶ zoea

ZOEAL ▶ zoea

ZOEAS ▶ zoea

ZOECIA ▶ zoecium

ZOECIUM *same as* > **zooecium**

ZOEFORM ▶ zoea

ZOETIC *adj* pertaining to life

ZOFTIG *adj* ripe or curvaceous

ZOIC *adj* relating to or having animal life

ZOISITE *n* grey, brown, or pink mineral

ZOISM *n* belief in magical animal powers

ZOISMS ▶ zoism

ZOIST ▶ zoism

ZOISTS ▶ zoism

ZOL *n* South African slang for a cannabis cigarette

ZOLS ▶ zol

ZOMBI *same as* ▶ **zombie**

ZOMBIE *n* person who appears to be lifeless, apathetic, or totally lacking in independent judgment

ZOMBIES ▶ zombie

ZOMBIFY *vb* turn into a zombie

ZOMBIS ▶ zombi

ZONA *n* zone or belt

ZONAE ▶ zona

ZONAL *adj* of, relating to, or of the nature of a zone

ZONALLY ▶ zonal

ZONARY *same as* ▶ **zonal**

ZONATE *adj* marked with, divided into, or arranged in zones

ZONATED *same as* ▶ **zonate**

ZONDA *n* South American wind

ZONDAS ▶ zonda

ZONE *n* area with particular features or properties ▷ *vb* divide into zones

ZONED ▶ zone

ZONER *n* something which divides other things into zones

ZONERS ▶ zoner

ZONES ▶ zone

ZONING ▶ zone

ZONINGS ▶ zone

ZONK *vb* strike resoundingly

ZONKED *adj* highly intoxicated with drugs or alcohol

ZONKING ▶ zonk

ZONKS ▶ zonk

ZONOID *adj* resembling a zone

ZONULA *n* small zone or belt

ZONULAE ▶ zonula

ZONULAR ▶ zonule

ZONULAS ▶ zonula

ZONULE *n* small zone, band, or area

ZONULES ▶ zonule

ZONULET *n* small belt

ZONURE *n* lizard with ringed tail

ZONURES ▶ zonure

ZOO *n* place where live animals are kept for show

ZOOEA *same as* ▶ **zoea**

ZOOEAE ▶ zooea

ZOOEAL ▶ zooea

ZOOEAS ▶ zooea

ZOOECIA > zooecium

ZOOEY ▶ zoo

ZOOGAMY *n* sexual reproduction in animals

ZOOGENY *n* doctrine of formation of animals

ZOOGLEA *same as* > **zoogloea**

ZOOGONY *same as* ▶ **zoogeny**

Z

ZOOID *n* any independent animal body, such as an individual of a coral colony

ZOOIDAL ▸ zooid

ZOOIDS ▸ zooid

ZOOIER ▸ zoo

ZOOIEST ▸ zoo

ZOOKS *short form of* ▸ gadzooks

ZOOLITE *n* fossilized animal

ZOOLITH *n* fossilized animal

ZOOLOGY *n* study of animals

ZOOM *vb* move or rise very rapidly ▹ *n* sound or act of zooming

ZOOMED ▸ zoom

ZOOMING ▸ zoom

ZOOMS ▸ zoom

ZOON ▸ zoom

ZOONAL ▸ zoon

ZOONED ▸ zoon

ZOONIC *adj* concerning animals

ZOONING ▸ zoon

ZOONITE *n* segment of an articulated animal

ZOONOMY *n* science of animal life

ZOONS ▸ zoon

ZOOPERY *n* experimentation on animals

ZOOS ▸ zoo

ZOOT *n as in* zoot suit man's suit consisting of baggy trousers with tapered bottoms and a long jacket with wide padded shoulders

ZOOTAXY *n* science of the classification of animals

> The science of classifying animals. An unlikely word to appear on your rack, but you never know, and it would make an impressive bonus!

ZOOTIER ▸ zooty

ZOOTOMY *n* branch of zoology concerned with the dissection and anatomy of animals

ZOOTY *adj* showy

ZOOTYPE *n* animal figure used as a symbol

ZOOZOO *n* wood pigeon

ZOOZOOS ▸ zoozoo

ZOPPA *adj* syncopated

ZOPPO *same as* ▸ zoppa

ZORBING *n* activity of travelling downhill inside a large air-cushioned hollow ball

ZORGITE *n* copper-lead selenide

ZORI *n* Japanese sandal

ZORIL *same as* ▸ zorilla

ZORILLA *n* skunk-like African musteline mammal having a long black-and-white coat

ZORILLE *same as* ▸ zorilla

ZORILLO *same as* ▸ zorille

ZORILS ▸ zoril

ZORINO *n* skunk fur

ZORINOS ▸ zorino

ZORIS ▸ zori

ZORRO *n* hoary fox

ZORROS ▸ zorro

ZOS ▸ zo

ZOSTER *n* shingles; herpes zoster

ZOSTERS ▸ zoster

ZOUAVE *n* (formerly) member of a body of French infantry composed of Algerian recruits

ZOUAVES ▸ zouave

ZOUK *n* style of dance music that combines African and Latin American rhythms and uses electronic instruments and modern studio technology

ZOUKS ▸ zouk

ZOUNDS *interj* mild oath indicating surprise or indignation

ZOWIE *interj* expression of pleasurable surprise

ZOYSIA *n* type of grass with short stiffly pointed leaves, often used for lawns

ZOYSIAS ▸ zoysia

ZUFFOLI ▸ zuffolo

ZUFFOLO *same as* ▸ zufolo

ZUFOLI ▸ zufolo

ZUFOLO *n* small flute

ZULU *n* (in the NATO phonetic alphabet) used to represent z

ZULUS ▸ zulu

ZUPA *n* confederation of Serbian villages

ZUPAN *n* head of a zupa

ZUPANS ▸ zupan

ZUPAS ▸ zupa

ZURF *same as* ▸ zarf

ZURFS ▸ zurf

ZUZ *n* ancient Hebrew silver coin

ZUZIM ▸ zuz

ZUZZIM ▸ zuz

ZYDECO *n* type of Black Cajun music

ZYDECOS ▸ zydeco

ZYGA ▸ zygon

ZYGAL ▸ zygon

ZYGOID *same as* ▸ diploid

ZYGOMA *n* slender arch of bone that forms a bridge between the cheekbone and the temporal bone on each side of the skull of mammals

ZYGOMAS ▸ zygoma

ZYGON *n* brain fissure

ZYGOSE ▸ zygosis

ZYGOSES ▸ zygosis

ZYGOSIS *n* (in bacteria) the direct transfer of DNA between two cells that are temporarily joined

ZYGOTE *n* fertilized egg cell

ZYGOTES ▸ zygote

ZYGOTIC ▸ zygote

ZYMASE *n* mixture of enzymes that is obtained as an extract from yeast and ferments sugars

ZYMASES ▸ zymase

ZYME *n* ferment

ZYMES ▸ zyme

ZYMIC ▸ zyme

ZYMITE *n* priest who uses leavened bread during communion

ZYMITES ▸ zymite

ZYMOGEN *n* any of a group of compounds that are inactive precursors of enzymes and are activated by a kinase

ZYMOID *adj* relating to a ferment

ZYMOME *n* glutinous substance that is insoluble in alcohol

ZYMOMES ▸ zymome

ZYMOSAN *n* insoluble carbohydrate found in yeast

ZYMOSES ▸ zymosis

ZYMOSIS *same as* ▸ zymolysis

ZYMOTIC *adj* of, relating to, or causing fermentation ▹ *n* disease

ZYMURGY *n* branch of chemistry concerned with fermentation processes in brewing, etc

ZYTHUM *n* Ancient Egyptian beer

ZYTHUMS ▸ zythum

ZYZZYVA *n* American weevil

ZZZ *n* informal word for sleep

ZZZS ▸ zzz

About the A

Brenda Jackson is a *New York* ~~~~~~~~~~~~~ author of more than 100 romance titles. Brenda lives in Jacksonville, Florida, and divides her time between family, writing and travelling. Email Brenda at authorbrendajackson@gmail.com or visit her on her website at brendajackson.net

Nichole Severn writes romantic suspense with strong heroines, heroes who dare challenge them, and a hell of a lot of guns. When she's not writing, she's injuring herself running and practising yoga.

Born and raised on the Wirral Peninsula in England, **Charlotte Hawkes** is mum to two intrepid boys who love her to play building block games with them, and object loudly to the amount of time she spends on the computer. When she isn't writing – or building with blocks – she is company director for a small Anglo/French construction firm. Charlotte loves to hear from readers, and you can contact her at her website: charlotte-hawkes.com

Romance On Duty

Romance On Duty:

Love in Action

BRENDA JACKSON

NICHOLE SEVERN

CHARLOTTE HAWKES

MILLS & BOON

First Published in Great Britain 2025
by Mills & Boon, an imprint of HarperCollins*Publishers* Ltd
1 London Bridge Street, London, SE1 9GF

www.harpercollins.co.uk

HarperCollins*Publishers*
Macken House, 39/40 Mayor Street Upper,
Dublin 1, D01 C9W8, Ireland

ISBN: 978-0-263-41724-1

HIS SECRET SON

BRENDA JACKSON

Prologue

Bristol Lockett hurriedly moved toward her front door, wondering who would be visiting this late in the afternoon. Although it was still light outside, this particular Paris community was on the other side of town from the famous city center, where most people hung out on Friday nights and weekends. Normally, she would be there herself, but her habits had changed in the last couple of months.

She was one of those pregnant women who experienced morning sickness in the morning and at night. Smells alone would send her running to the nearest bathroom. Most morning sickness lasted until the twelfth week of pregnancy. She was in her sixteenth week and there didn't seem to be an end in sight. Her doctor had even placed her on a special diet to make sure she was getting sufficient nutrients into her body for her baby.

A glance out the peephole indicated her visitor was her best friend, Dionne Burcet. She and Dionne had met when Bristol first arrived in Paris four years ago to attend Académie des Beaux-Arts, which was considered one of the most prestigious and influential art schools in all of France.

Dionne also attended the art academy and with so much in common, they'd hit it off immediately.

Dionne, who'd been born in Paris, had introduced Bristol to French culture, and Bristol had taken Dionne home with her to America last Christmas to meet her aunt Dolly and to experience New Year's Eve in New York. A feeling of sadness fell over Bristol whenever she remembered that was the last holiday she and her aunt had spent together. Her aunt, her only relative, had died a few days later in her sleep.

Bristol opened the door smiling. "Dionne! This is a surprise. I thought you were leaving for—"

"I have something to tell you, Bristol."

Bristol heard the urgency in Dionne's voice, which resonated in her eyes, as well. "Okay, come on in. Would you like a cup of tea? I was just about to make a pot."

"Yes, thanks."

Bristol wondered about Dionne's strange demeanor as she led her friend to the kitchen, which wasn't far from the front door. She loved her studio apartment. It was small but just the right size for her. And it held a lot of memories. Her baby was conceived here, in her bed. She would miss this place when she moved back to the United States next month after graduation.

"Sit and tell me what's wrong. Did you and Mark have a fight?"

Dionne shook her head as she sat down at the table. "No. It's not about me, it's about you."

"Me?" Bristol said in surprise.

"Yes. You remember what you shared with me last month?"

"Yes. I told you I was pregnant." Telling Dionne hadn't been easy but she'd felt the need to confide in someone. The baby's father was a man she'd met one day at a café. He had been a US navy SEAL out with a few of his friends and he'd flirted with her outrageously. She'd done something she had never done before and flirted back. There had been something about Laramie Cooper that had made her behave like a different person and for the next three days, over the Christmas holidays, they had enjoyed a holiday fling. It was a period in her life she would never forget. Her pregnancy made certain of that.

"Yes, from that guy. The American soldier."

"Not just a soldier, Dionne. Laramie was a navy SEAL," Bristol said, smiling proudly.

"Yes, the navy SEAL Laramie Cooper," Dionne said.

From the time they'd been introduced, Bristol had liked his name and he'd said he liked hers. Laramie had told her very little about his work or even about himself. She knew he was an only child and his parents were still living in the US. He hadn't said where.

Bristol regretted that Dionne had been away visiting her grandparents in Marseille for the holidays and hadn't been around to meet Laramie. She believed her friend would have liked him. "What about him?"

"You told me how the two of you spent time together over the holidays and since finding out you were pregnant, you've been trying to locate him to let him know."

Since she'd known very little about Laramie, other than his name and age, she had mailed a letter to him in care of the US Navy. The letter had been returned weeks ago stamped UNABLE TO LOCATE.

"Yes, and like I told you, it doesn't matter to me that our time together was a no-strings affair, I believe he has a right to know about his child. I refused to do to him what my mother did to my father."

For years, Bristol never knew her father and, according to her mother, she never told her father about Bristol. It was information her mother had taken with her to the grave. It was only after her mother's death that Bristol's aunt Dolly had given her the man's name. She had met Randall Lockett at sixteen. He had been surprised to find out about her and had welcomed her into his life.

"Yes, I know. That's why I decided to help you."

Bristol raised a brow. "Help me?"

"Yes."

"How?"

"Remember I told you about that guy—an American—I dated years ago? The one who worked at your embassy?"

"Yes, I remember."

"Well, he was recently reassigned back to the embassy here and I ran into him. I gave him your SEAL's name and asked if he would try locating him and forwarding him a message to contact you."

Happiness eased into Bristol and spread to all parts of her body. Although it might have been nothing more than a holiday fling for Laramie Cooper, it had been a lot more for her. She had fallen in love with him. "Was your friend able to find him?"

Dionne slowly nodded her head. "Yes."

Bristol stared at her friend, knowing there was more. The happiness she felt earlier began dissipating at the sadness she saw in Dionne's eyes. "What is it, Dionne? What did you find out?"

All sorts of things began rushing through her mind. What if Laramie hadn't been the single man he'd claimed to be and had a wife and children somewhere? When Dionne didn't say anything, but looked down at the cup of tea Bristol had placed in front of her, Bristol slouched her shoulders in disappointment. "I think I know why you're hesitating in telling me."

Dionne looked back at her. "Do you?"

"Yes. He's married. Although he told me he wasn't, you found out differently, didn't you?"

"Bristol."

"It doesn't matter. He has a right to know about his child

anyway. If he decides never to be a part of my baby's life, it will be his decision and—"

"That's not it, Bristol," Dionne cut in to say.

Bristol frowned. "Then what is it?"

Dionne took a sip of her tea, hesitating. The dawdling was driving Bristol crazy. "For Pete's sake, Dionne, will you just get it out and tell me what you found out about Laramie?"

Dionne held her gaze and drew in a deep breath. "Some mission he was on went bad and he was killed. He's dead, Bristol."

One

The Naval Amphibious Base Coronado,
San Diego, California, three years later

"Let me get this straight, Lieutenant Cooper. You actually want to give up your holiday leave and remain here and work on base?"

Laramie "Coop" Cooper forced his smile to stay in place while answering his commanding officer's question. "Yes, sir. I actually want to do that."

He wouldn't tell anyone that he'd looked forward to going home for the holidays, because honestly, he hadn't. The phone call he'd gotten from his parents that they would be jet-setting to London again this year was expected. They'd done so every holiday for as long as he could remember. He doubted they'd even canceled those plans that Christmas three years ago when they'd thought him dead.

At thirty-two, he had stopped letting his parents' actions affect him. As far as Ryan and Cassandra Cooper were concerned, the universe revolved around them and nobody else. Especially not a son who, at times, they seemed to forget existed. It wasn't that he thought his parents didn't love him; he knew they did. They just loved each other more. He had long ago accepted that his parents believed there were different degrees of love, and that the love they shared for each other outweighed the love for their child.

In a way, he should be glad that after thirty-five years of marriage his parents were still that into each other. They shared something special, had this unbreakable bond, and some would even say it was the love of a lifetime. But on the other hand, that love never extended to him in the same degree. He knew their lack of affection had nothing to do with his deciding to become a navy SEAL instead of joining his parents' multimillion-dollar manufacturing company. His father had understood Laramie's desire to make his decisions based on what he wanted to do with his life, and he appreciated his dad for accepting that.

More holidays than not, for as far back as Laramie could remember, he'd been packed up and shipped off to his paternal grandparents' ranch in Laredo. Not that he was complaining. His grandparents had been the best and hadn't hesitated to show him the degree of love he'd lacked at home. In fact, he would admit to resenting his parents when they did show up at his grandparents' ranch to get him.

So, here he was volunteering to give up his holiday leave. It wasn't as if he hadn't received invitations from his SEAL teammates to join them and their families for the holidays, because he had. Bane Westmoreland—code name Bane— had been the first to invite Laramie to spend the holidays with his family in Denver. But given the fact that Bane's wife, Crystal, had given birth to triplets six months ago, Laramie didn't want to get underfoot.

Same thing with Thurston McRoy—code name Mac— with his wife, Teri, and their four kids. Gavin Blake—code name Viper—would be celebrating his first Christmas as a married man so Laramie didn't want to intrude there, either. The only other single guy in the group was David

Holloway—code name Flipper. Flipper came from a huge family of four brothers, who were all SEALs, and a father who'd retired as a SEAL commanding officer. Laramie had spent the holidays with Flipper's family last year and didn't want to wear out his welcome.

"I'm denying your request, Lieutenant."

His commanding officer's words recaptured Laramie's attention. He met the man's gaze and tried to keep a frown off his face. "May I ask why, sir?"

"I think you know the reason. SEAL Team Six, of which you are a vital member, has been pretty damn busy this year. I don't have to list all the covert operations success-fully accomplished with very few casualties. You deserve your holiday leave."

"Even if I don't want to take it?"

His commanding officer held his gaze. "Yes, even if you don't want to take it. Military leave is necessary, es-pecially for a SEAL, to recoup both mentally and physi-cally. Don't think I haven't noticed how much you've been pushing yourself. It's like you're trying to make up for the time you were a captive in Syria."

Laramie remembered all eleven months of being held prisoner in that guerilla hellhole. He hadn't known from one day to the next if he'd survive that day. The bastards had done everything in their power to make him think every day would be his last. They'd even played Russian roulette with him a couple of times.

It was on one of those particular days when he'd been rescued. Leave it to Bane, who was a master sniper, to bring down the four men from a distance of over a hundred feet. Laramie was convinced there was no way he would have survived if his SEAL team hadn't shown up.

During those eleven months he'd fought hard to stay sane and the one memory that had sustained him was the face of the woman he'd met in Paris just weeks before the mission.

Bristol Lockett.

It had been a three-day holiday affair. Sadly, there was little he knew about her other than sharing her bed had been the best sexual experience of his life.

"However, since I know you're going to insist," his commanding officer said, reclaiming Laramie's thoughts again, "I've got an important job that I want you to do. However, it means traveling to New York."

Laramie raised a brow. "New York?"

"Yes. An important delivery needs to be made to a member of the United Nations Security Council."

Laramie wondered what kind of delivery. Classified documents no doubt.

He'd heard how beautiful Manhattan was when it was decorated for this time of year. He'd been to the Big Apple a number of times, but never around the holidays. "Once I make the delivery, sir. Then what?"

"That, Lieutenant, is up to you. If you decide to take your holiday leave, then you won't have to report back here until the end of January as scheduled. However, if you still want to give up your leave, then you're free to come back here and I'll find more work for you to do."

Laramie nodded. He might take a week off to enjoy the sights and sounds of New York, but there was no doubt in his mind that he would be returning to San Diego for more work.

Bristol glanced around the art gallery. She always felt a sense of pride and accomplishment whenever she saw one of her paintings on display. Especially here at the Jazlyn Art Gallery of New York. She wanted to pinch herself to make sure she wasn't dreaming.

She had worked so hard for this moment.

"Looks good, doesn't it?"

She glanced up at her manager, Margie Townsend. "Yes, I have to admit that it does."

Margie's tenacious pit bull–like skills had landed Bristol a showing at this gallery, one of the most well-known and highly respected galleries in New York. She and Margie had met last year on the subway and struck up a conversation. When Bristol discovered what Margie did for a living, she felt their chance encounter must have been an omen. She'd invited Margie to her home to see her work, and the excitement reflected in the woman's eyes had been incredible. Margie promised to change Bristol's life. She promised that Bristol would get to the point where she could quit her job as an assistant magazine editor and make her living as the artist she was born to be.

Less than eight months later, Margie had sold one of Bristol's paintings. The buyer had been so taken with her work that he'd also purchased several others. The money had been enough to bring about the change in Bristol's life Margie had guaranteed. She had turned in her resignation and now painted full-time in her home.

Bristol was happy with the direction of her career. She got to spend more time with her son since she kept him with her every day instead of taking him to day care like she used to do.

Her son.

She smiled when she thought about her rambunctious two-year old—the most important person in her life. He was her life. Every decision she made was done with him in mind. She'd already started a college fund for him and couldn't wait to share the holidays with him. Last night they had put up their Christmas tree. Correction, she thought, widening her smile. She had put up the tree. Laramie had gotten in the way with his anxiousness to help.

Laramie…

It was hard not to think of Laramie's father whenever she

thought of her son. She had named him after his biological father, Laramie Cooper, who had died way too young, and without knowing about the child they'd created together. Sometimes she wondered what he would have done had he lived and gotten the letter she'd tried to send him.

Would he have been just as happy as she'd been? Or would he have claimed the child wasn't his? She might not have known Laramie Cooper long, but she wanted to believe he was a man who would have wanted to be a part of his child's life. The way her father had wanted to be a part of hers. The two years she'd shared with the man who'd fathered her had not been enough.

"Are you ready to go? You have a big day tomorrow and I want you well rested."

She chuckled as she tightened her coat around her. "And I will be."

Margie rolled her eyes. "I guess as much as you can be with a two-year-old running around the place."

She knew what Margie was hinting at. Bristol was spending less and less time painting now that Laramie was in the terrible twos. It was also the get-into-everything twos. The only time she really got to paint was during his nap time or while he slept at night.

"Did you give any more thought to what I said?"

Margie had suggested that she send Laramie to day care two to three days a week. "Yes, but I'm thinking of hiring someone to come to my home instead of me having to take him somewhere."

"That might work, but he has to start learning to interact with other kids, Bristol." As they walked toward the waiting private car that was compliments of the gallery, Margie changed the subject. "Have you decided to go out with Steven?"

Bristol shrugged. Steven Culpepper was nice enough, and good-looking, too. However, he was moving too fast.

At least, faster than she liked. They'd met a few weeks ago when she'd closed a huge deal for a commissioned piece. He was the corporation's attorney. He'd asked for her number and, without thinking much about it, she'd given it to him. Since then he'd called constantly, trying to get her to go out with him. So far, she hadn't. She hated pushy men and Steven, she thought, was one of the pushiest.

"No."

"I like him."

Bristol grinned. "You would. You have a thing for wealthy businessmen." She knew Margie had been married to one. Or two. She was on her third marriage and not even fifty yet. But the one thing all three men had in common was the size of their bank accounts.

"Well, I know you still have a thing for Laramie's father and—"

"What makes you think that?"

"Bristol, you make it quite obvious that you haven't gotten over him."

Did she? The only thing she'd told Margie about Laramie's father was that he'd been in the military and had died in the line of duty without knowing he'd fathered a son. She'd even fabricated a tale that Laramie had been her deceased husband and not just her lover.

It had been pretty easy. Dionne's fiancé, Mark, had helped. Mark worked for a judge in Paris and had falsified the papers before Bristol left France. It was a way to make sure her son had his father's last name without people wondering why her last name was different. It wasn't as if she was trying to cash in on her son's father's military benefits or anything.

"If you ask me, I think you should finally move on… with Steven," Margie said, interrupting Bristol's thoughts.

Bristol wanted to say that nobody had asked Margie. But deep down, a part of her knew Margie was right. It was

time for Bristol to move on. However, she doubted very
seriously that it would be with Steven.

A short while later she was entering her home, a beautiful brownstone in Brooklyn that she'd inherited from her
aunt Dolly. She loved the place and knew the neighborhood well. She'd come to live here with her aunt ten years
ago, when she was fifteen. That had been the year her
mother died.

She didn't want to think sad thoughts, especially after
her positive meeting with Maurice Jazlyn, the owner of
the gallery. The man was excited about tomorrow night's
showing and expected a huge crowd. He loved all the artworks she would be exhibiting.

"How did things go tonight?"

She turned toward the older woman coming down the
stairs to the main floor. Charlotte Kramer lived next door
and had been a close friend of her aunt Dolly. With her
four kids grown and living in other parts of New York,
Ms. Charlotte had thought about moving to a condo not
far away, but had decided she'd rather stay put since she'd
lived in the area close to forty years and loved her neighbors. Ms. Charlotte said there were a lot of memories of
Mr. Kramer stored in that house. He'd passed away eight
years ago, a couple of years after Bristol had come to live
with her aunt.

Bristol appreciated that Ms. Charlotte loved watching
Laramie for her whenever she had meetings to attend. And
Ms. Charlotte had offered to watch him again tomorrow
night when Bristol attended the exhibition.

"Everything went well. Everyone is excited about tomorrow. Mr. Jazlyn thinks he'll be able to sell all my paintings."

A huge smile touched Ms. Charlotte's lips. "That's good
news. Dolly would be proud. Candace would be, too."

She doubted the latter. Her mother had never approved

of Bristol becoming an artist. It was only after she died that Bristol learned why. Her father had been an artist who'd broken things off with her mother to study in Paris. It was only after he'd left the country that her mother discovered her pregnancy. She'd known how to reach him but refused to let him know about his child. She had resented him for ending things with her to pursue his dream.

Bristol had been sixteen when she'd met her father for the first time. She would not have met him then if it hadn't been for her aunt's decision to break the promise she'd made to Bristol's mother years ago. Aunt Dolly wanted Bristol to know her father and vice versa. When Bristol was given the man's name, she had been shocked to find that the person whose art she'd admired for years was really her father.

She'd finally gotten the courage to contact him on her sixteenth birthday. Randall Lockett was married with a family when they'd finally met. He had two young sons— ages ten and twelve—with his wife Krista. Bristol was his only daughter and she favored him so much it was uncanny. She was also his only offspring who'd inherited his artistic gift.

When he'd died, he had bequeathed to her full tuition to the school he himself had attended in Paris as well as the vast majority of his paintings. He'd felt she would appreciate them more than anyone, and she had. She'd heard that Krista had remarried and sold off all the artworks that had been left to her and their sons.

Paintings by Randall Lockett were valued in the millions. Art collectors had contacted Bristol on numerous occasions, but she had refused to sell. Instead her father's paintings were on display at the two largest art museums in the world, New York's Metropolitan Museum of Art and the Orsay Museum in Paris.

A few months before her father had died, they had completed a painting together, which was her most cherished possession. It was so uncanny that when it came to art she and her father had possessed identical preferences. They even held their brushes the same way. On those days when she felt down and out, she would look at the portrait over her fireplace and remember the six weeks they'd spent together on his boat while painting it. That was when they'd noticed all the similarities they shared as artists. She hadn't known he was dying of cancer until his final days. He hadn't wanted her to know. He was determined to share every moment he could with her without seeing pity and regret in her eyes.

Forcing those sad thoughts from her mind, she glanced back over at Ms. Charlotte. "Did Laramie behave himself tonight?" she asked, placing her purse on the table.

The older woman chuckled. "Doesn't he always?"

Bristol smiled. "No, but I know you wouldn't tell me even if he was a handful."

"You're right, I wouldn't. Boys will be boys. I know. I raised four of them."

Yes, she had, and to this day Ms. Charlotte's sons looked out for her, making sure she had everything she needed and then some.

After Ms. Charlotte left, Bristol climbed the stairs to her son's room. He was in his bed, sound asleep. Crossing the bedroom floor, she saw he had put away all his toys. That was a good sign that he was learning to follow instructions.

Approaching the bed, she sat on the edge and gently ran her fingers through the curls on his head. He favored his father. Laramie Cooper's features were etched in her memory. Whenever Laramie smiled, he displayed his father's dimples in both cheeks. Then there was the shape of his mouth and the slant of his eyes. Like father, like son. There was no doubt in her mind that one day Laramie would grow up and capture some woman's heart just as quickly and easily as his father had claimed hers.

As she sat there watching her son sleep, she couldn't stop her mind from going back to that time in Paris when she'd met US Navy SEAL Laramie Cooper...

Two

Paris, France, three years ago

Bristol glanced up from her sketch pad when she heard the male voices entering the café. Military men. All five of them. That was easy to deduce, even though they weren't wearing military attire. They were wearing jeans, shirts and dark leather jackets. The five walked confidently and were in perfect physical condition. Boy, were they ever! She wondered what branch of service they represented. It really didn't matter. Whichever one branch it was, they were representing it well.

The group took the table not far away from where she sat and one of the men, as if he felt someone staring at him, glanced over at her. Bam! She'd been caught. She hadn't averted her gaze back to her sketch pad quickly enough. For some reason, she knew without glancing back up that he was still looking at her. She could feel his gaze, just as if it was a physical caress. It made her heart beat faster. It seemed that every single hormone in her body had begun to sizzle. Nothing like that had ever happened to her before.

Okay, Bristol, concentrate on your sketch, she inwardly

admonished herself. Her father hadn't paid her tuition at one of the most prestigious art schools in France for her to get all hot and bothered by a bunch of military men. Although the five were extremely handsome, it was only one of the men who had caught her eye. The one who'd stared back at her.

"Excuse me, miss."

She glanced up and the man was now standing at her table. Up close he was even more gorgeous. Definitely eye candy of the most delectable kind. Hot. Sexy. You name it and this man could definitely claim it. That had to be the reason intense heat was plowing up her spine.

Bristol swallowed deeply before saying, "Yes?"

"I was wondering if…"

When he didn't finish but kept looking at her, she asked. "Wondering what?"

"If I could join you?"

She wished he could but unfortunately, he couldn't. She glanced at her watch then back at him. "Sorry, but I work here and happen to be on my lunch break, which will end in less than five minutes."

"What time do you get off today?"

She tilted her head to look at him. "Excuse me?"

"I asked what time you get off today. I'll wait."

She figured that he had to be kidding, but the look in his eyes showed that he wasn't. "I get off in four hours."

"I'll wait. What's your name?"

This guy was definitely moving fast. But she couldn't ignore the scorching hot attraction between them, even if she wanted to. And for some reason, she didn't want to. She liked it.

"My name is Bristol Lockett."

"The name Bristol is unusual. It suits you well. I like it."

And she liked his voice. It was deep and husky. The sound made heat curl inside her. OMG! What on earth was wrong with her? She'd never thought such outlandish things in her life. She might not have always been prim and proper but she'd been pretty close to it. She'd been in Paris close to four years and although she'd dated, most of the time she did not. She preferred curling up with her sketch pad and working on her watercolors than going out with any man. But now this ultrafine specimen was making her rethink that decision.

"Are you American or French?"

She blinked at his question. "I'm American."

"So am I."

She smiled. And what a good-looking American he was, with a body to die for. She felt as if she could draw her last breath just from looking at him. This guy was tall, at least six foot two or three. And his skin was the color of lightly roasted almonds. His dark eyes appeared somewhat slanted, and as far as she was concerned his lips were perfectly shaped. His hair was cut low on his head and his ears were just the right size for his face. But what captured her attention more than anything were those dimples in his cheeks. Doing absolutely nothing but standing there, he was arousing something within her that no other man ever had.

"And who are you?" she asked, deciding not to let him ask all the questions.

"I'm Laramie," he said, stretching out his hand to her.

She took it and immediately a spike of heat seemed to burst from his fingers and hit her dead center between the thighs. And when she stared into his eyes and saw the dark heat in his pupils, she knew he'd felt something, as well.

"Are you married, Laramie?"

"No. I've never been married. What about you? I approached you because I didn't see a ring on your finger."

At least he didn't hit on married women. Some men didn't care. "No, I'm not married, either, and never have been."

"So, Bristol Lockett, do I have your permission?"

She licked her lips. "For what?"

That sexy smile widened. "To be here when you get off."

Then what? she wondered but decided not to ask. "Sure, if that's what you want."

His chuckle made desire claw at her but it was his next words that sealed her fate. "There are a lot of things I want when it comes to you, Bristol."

Jeez. If he wasn't standing there she would close her eyes and moan. This man presented a temptation she shouldn't even think about yielding to. Too bad her best friend, Dionne, was out of town for the holidays and not around to talk some sense into her.

"What about if we share a drink at one of the pubs first?" she asked, and then frowned. Why had she made it sound as if she would be willing to move to the next stage once they shared a drink?

"That's fine. I'll be back in four hours."

When he walked off she glanced at her watch. Her break was officially over but she knew her encounter with this military man was just beginning.

She hurried behind the counter to put on her apron while watching Mary-Ann, another waitress, head over to the table to serve the five guys. More people entered the café, and Bristol was about to cross the room to serve a couple with a little girl when Mary-Ann stopped her.

"They asked for you," Mary-Ann said, smiling.

"Who?"

"Those soldiers. I've given them menus but they want you to serve their table. That's fine with me. Then I don't have to commit a sin by forgetting I've been married to Joel almost twenty years. Those five are too much temptation," she said, fanning herself. "I hope you can handle it."

Bristol hoped she could handle it as well, as she made her way to the table where all five men sat. Hot and heavy testosterone was thick in the air surrounding them. Drawing in a deep breath she approached them with her notepad in hand. "Have you guys decided what you're having?"

"Apparently, Coop has," one of the men said, grinning at her. "We're still deciding."

She nodded. "Okay, and who is Coop?"

"I am," the guy who had introduced himself to her earlier said.

She met his gaze. "I thought your name was Laramie."

He smiled again and she tried not to feel weak in the knees. "It is. My real name is Laramie Cooper. They call me Coop."

"Oh."

"Let me introduce everyone," Laramie said. "First off, guys, this is Bristol," he said to his friends.

"Hello, Bristol," they all said simultaneously as they stood to their feet, showing they had manners.

"Hello."

"I'm Bane," one of the men said, extending his hand to her.

She smiled at the very handsome military man as she shook his hand. "Hi, Bane."

"Is that a New York accent?" Bane asked.

"Yes, you would think after being in France for almost four years it would not be so easily detected."

Bane's smile widened. "Some things you can't get rid of."

"Apparently," she said, chuckling.

"I'm Flipper," another one of the guys said, offering his hand. He was definitely a hottie, with blond hair and the bluest eyes she'd ever seen. The color reminded her of the ocean and she wondered if that was why his nickname was Flipper.

"Nice meeting you, Flipper," she said, shaking his hand, as well.

"Same here, Bristol."

"I'm Mac," another one of the men said, leaning across to take her hand. This man appeared older than the others by at least three or four years.

"Hi, Mac."

"And I'm Viper."

She glanced at the man who introduced himself as Viper. He was taller than the others and just as handsome. His eyes seemed sharp and penetrating. "Hi, Viper," she said, shaking his hand.

"Hi, Bristol," Viper returned, smiling.

"And you know me," Laramie said, taking her hand.

And just like before, a spike of heat hit her. "Yes, I know you." She quickly pulled her hand away. "It's nice meeting all of you and I like all your nicknames," she said as the men all sat back down.

Bane chuckled. "They aren't nicknames. They're our military code names."

"Oh. And what branch of the military?"

"We're navy SEALs," the one named Flipper said, grinning proudly.

He had every right to feel that way. She'd heard about navy SEALs. Some considered them the American government's secret weapon against any enemy force.

"So, Laramie, I'll start with you. What will you have?" she asked, getting ready to write on her notepad.

"For now I'll take a juicy hamburger, a large order of French fries and a huge malted strawberry shake."

For now? She wondered what he planned to have later. From the way he was looking at her, she had an idea. And why didn't realizing this guy evidently thought she was on his menu bother her?

Bristol went around the table and took everyone's order. Apparently all five were big eaters and she wondered where they would put all that food and how they stayed in such great physical shape. After turning their orders in to the cook, she began waiting on other tables, but felt the heat of Laramie's gaze on her the entire time. Every time she glanced over in his direction, he was staring at her. Blatantly so.

Maybe it hadn't been a good idea for her to agree to have a drink with him when she got off work. She knew nothing about him, other than his name was Laramie Cooper, his military code name was Coop, he loved juicy hamburgers and he was a navy SEAL.

She delivered their food a short while later and watched them eat all of it. She could tell that the five were more than just members of the same military team. They shared a close friendship. That much was obvious from the way they joked around with each other.

Mac was married and had no problem showing her pictures of his wife and kids. It was evident he was proud of them. Bane, she'd discovered, was also married, but from the way the others teased him she could only assume he hadn't seen his wife in a while, which meant the two were separated. Like Laramie, Viper and Flipper were single and from the sound of things they intended to stay that way.

At the end of the meal when they paid their bill, she was shocked at the tip they left her. She would not normally have earned that much tip money in a week. "Thanks, guys."

"No, we want to thank you," Flipper said standing, like the others. "It was nice meeting you, Bristol, and the food was great."

The others shared the same sentiments as they moved to leave the café. Laramie hung back. "I'll be here when you get off work."

She knew now was a good time to tell him that she'd changed her mind about that. However, there was something about Laramie Cooper that made her hold back from doing so. It might have been his smile, or the way he was making her feel, or just the fact that she deserved to have some fun for a change.

For four years she had worked hard at the art academy and come spring she would be graduating. The café would be closing for the holidays and she had the next ten days off work. As far as she was concerned, there was nothing wrong with Laramie being there when she got off. They would just grab drinks at one of the pubs nearby. Besides, after today, she probably wouldn't see him again.

"I'll be waiting," she heard herself say.

She didn't have to wait. Laramie arrived a half hour before she was due to leave work. He ordered a croissant and coffee while he waited for her. She hung up her apron, wished everyone a Merry Christmas and then headed toward the table where he sat. He stood, smiling down at her.

"Ready?" he asked her.

"Yes" was her reply, although she wasn't sure what he had in mind and if she should be ready or not.

He surprised her by taking her hand, as if they both needed to feel the sexual chemistry between them. He led her through the doors and onto the sidewalk. Holiday decorations were everywhere. It was hard to believe tomorrow was Christmas Eve. Last year she had gone home for Christmas and had taken her best friend, Dionne, with her. But not this year. Her aunt Dolly had died in her sleep four days into the New Year.

She needed to stop thinking that she didn't have any living relatives when she had two brothers and a stepmother. She knew they'd only tolerated her while her father was alive and now, with him gone, they had let her know—by not returning her calls or letters—that they didn't have to put up with her anymore. That was fine. She'd adjusted to being a loner. At least she had Dionne and Dionne's family. The thought had even crossed Bristol's mind that she should not return to the United States after graduation and make Paris her home.

"Which pub are we going to?" she asked the man who was walking beside her and still holding her hand.

He smiled down at her. "Which one do you suggest?"

"Charlie's is a good one. It's right around the corner."

They didn't say much as they walked to the pub. They talked about the holidays. He told her that he and his team would be headed out in four days and they were in Paris for a little R and R.

"Your friends are nice," she said.

He smiled down at her as they continued walking. "They said the same thing about you."

She smiled at that, while trying to ignore all that desire she saw in his eyes. She figured if they kept talking it would go away. "The five of you seem close."

"We are. In fact, we're like brothers. Viper, Flipper, Bane and I attended the naval academy together and immediately became the best of friends. Mac is four years older and finished the academy ahead of us. He's been a SEAL longer and likes to think he's looking out for us."

They reached the pub and saw it was crowded with no tables available. It seemed everyone had decided to begin celebrating the holidays early. "I have an idea," Laramie said, tightening his hand on hers.

"What?"

"Let's go someplace private."

An uneasy feeling crept over her, but it was overpowered by exciting sensations that settled in her stomach. Their hands were still joined and his fingers felt warm and reassuring.

"I want to be honest with you about something."

She swallowed. "About what?"

"Usually I spend the holidays alone, but I want to spend them with you."

She held his gaze a minute and then asked, "What about your friends?"

"They'll be in touch with their families."

"But you won't?"

He didn't say anything for a moment and then he said, "My parents are still alive. I'm their only child. But we've never spent the holidays together."

She found that odd. Christmas was the one holiday she never had to worry about being alone. Her mother had always made it special and after her mother's death, her aunt Dolly had been there for her. She'd even spent one Christmas with her father. It had been the first and last holiday they'd spent together. This would be the first Christmas that she had no one. She thought it sad that Laramie had never really spent his holidays with family.

She saw the sincerity in his eyes, in what he'd told her. He wasn't trying to feed her a pity line but was telling her the truth. She felt it in her heart.

"I can think of a place we can go," she suggested.

"Where?"

She knew it would be crazy to invite him, a perfect stranger to her home, but she was about to issue the invitation. "My place. It's not far from here. Just so happens I was going to be alone for the holidays as well and would love some company."

His hand tightened on hers. "You sure?"

Was she? She had never done anything so daring in her life.

She wasn't a child. She knew the obvious signs. Desire was thick between them. Spontaneous combustion as volatile as it could get. She dated infrequently and most guys who'd hit on her had tried to work her. But she would say that Laramie was the first guy who'd tried and managed to elicit her interest. He was also the first guy she was trusting to this degree. She had never invited a man to her home before. There had to be a reason for her doing so now.

"Yes. I'm sure," she said.

From the way his lips spread into a smile, she knew her response had pleased him. "All right then. Lead the way."

That smile made her heart miss a beat as they continued to walk along the sidewalk. Like she'd told him, she didn't live far and they arrived at her studio apartment in no time. "It's small," she said, opening the door. "But it's the right size for me."

She stepped aside and he entered. She immediately thought her apartment might be just the right size for her, but with him inside it, it suddenly appeared small.

"Nice place," he said, glancing around.

Bristol was glad she was a neat freak. There was nothing out of place. "There's a bottle of wine over there if you want to pour us a glass," she said, removing her coat and hanging it in one of the closets.

"Okay," he said, removing his jacket. She took it and hung it in the closet, as well. She tried not to notice how perfect his abs were and what a broad chest he had. She also tried not to notice the sexual chemistry between them, which had increased now that they were alone and behind closed doors.

"Do you need to let your friends know where you are? Won't they be worried when you don't return to your hotel?" she asked him.

He shook his head as he grabbed the wine bottle and glasses off the rack. "No. They'll figure things out."

"Okay." She sat down at the table while he poured the wine into their glasses. And then he joined her there. "I know this isn't champagne but let's make a toast."

"To what?"

"To what I believe will be the best holiday I've ever had."

Deep down she believed it would be the best she ever

had, too. Their glasses clinked and then they took a sip. She met his gaze over the rim and immediately, a deep sexual hunger flared to life in her midsection. From the hot, penetrating look in his eyes, the same hunger hit him, as well.

Bristol placed her glass down the same moment he did. And then he stood and reached out to her. She went into his arms willingly and he lowered his head and captured her mouth in his. The moment she felt his lips on hers, a deep, drugging rush of desire filled her to the core.

He was using his tongue in the most provocative way, making shivers of need course through every part of her. She had never been kissed like this before and he was an expert.

He deepened the kiss and her mouth became locked to his. She couldn't hold back the moan that erupted from deep within her throat. Nor could she hold back the sensations overtaking her. She had been kissed before, but never like this. Never with this much possession, this much overwhelming power.

Moments later he ended the kiss and pulled back slightly to look down at her. A sexy smile touched the corners of his lips and the arms around her tightened, bringing her closer to him. "I wanted to kiss you from the moment I saw you. I had a deep yearning to know how you tasted."

Wow! She wasn't used to having such carnal conversations with a man. "Is that why you kissed me the way you did just now?"

"Partly."

"And the other reason?"

"I just wanted the feel of my tongue in your mouth."

And then as if he hadn't gotten enough of doing that the last time, he lowered his head and captured her mouth again. On a breathless moan she parted her lips, giving him the opening he needed. He slid his tongue inside, mating it with hers, over and over again.

When he finally released her mouth, she looked up at him with glazed eyes. "What are you doing?" she asked, barely able to get the words out. Never had a kiss left her so off balance.

"Starting our celebration of the holidays."

She could feel blood rushing through her veins with his words. She hadn't expected this so soon. She figured they would share a drink today and then tomorrow he could come back for lunch. But it seemed he had other plans, plans she was giving in to. She couldn't help it. So many sexual sensations were taking over her mind and body just from his kiss. She knew there was no way she could stop from wanting him. He sealed her fate when he began kissing her again and she felt herself being lifted into his arms.

He was carrying her someplace and she knew where when he placed her on the bed. What happened next was amazing. In record time he had removed both of their clothes, as if needing to be skin to skin with her was paramount. As if needing to see her naked body was essential.

In a way she understood, since seeing him standing there without a stitch of clothing was doing something to her, as well. He represented such virility and masculinity, and coiling arousal was throbbing deep in her core. Never had she wanted to make love to someone so badly. Never had she felt this filled with need. And she could tell from his huge erection that he wanted her. His desire for her was obvious.

She watched as he put on a condom before heading back to the bed. She reached out and glided her hands up his tight, sculpted abdomen and chest, loving the feel of his skin. Heat curled inside her with the contact.

"You touch me and I will touch you," he warned, grazing his jaw against her ear, while growling low in his throat. It amazed her that he would respond to her touch this way.

"I want you to touch me, Laramie."

She couldn't believe she'd said that. But there was something about Laramie Cooper that she didn't understand. Namely, how he could make her lose her common sense. How he could make her nerves dance and her brain race. How he had the ability to make her want to have things she'd done without in the past. And how he made her want him with a passion.

She needed to make him aware of something. Make him understand and she heard herself saying, "I've never brought a man here before."

She felt the intensity of his gaze all over her body.

"There's a first time for everything, don't you think?" he replied, slowly moving back toward the bed.

With each step he took, she felt her womb contract. He was staring at her with dark, penetrating eyes and her body heated under his intense regard. She'd never had a one-night stand in her life. Always thought she was above that. But at that moment the only thing she wanted was this man, who had the ability to mess with her mind and senses.

There was something else she needed to tell him and it was best if she did it now. "Laramie?"

"Yes?"

"I'm not on any type of birth control."

If she thought that revelation would stop him dead in his tracks, she'd been wrong. He kept moving toward her. "I have condoms. Plenty of them. Around a dozen or so. And if we need more we'll get them," he told her.

Get more? Did he honestly think they would use more than a dozen? Her heart began beating way too fast as she wondered just what kind of stamina he had. Would she be able to keep up?

She was about to find out.

He joined her on the bed and began kissing her again while touching her all over. Sexual excitement churned inside her, sending an intense throb through her veins. She slipped her arms around his muscled back, loving the manly feel of him.

"I'm dying to taste you," he whispered, just moments before shifting his body to place his head between her legs.

She gripped tight to his shoulders as she felt his hot tongue inside her, stroking and licking. He was unwavering in his determination to taste her like he wanted. Sensations she'd never experienced before rushed through her and instinctively, she made sinfully erotic movements with her hips against his mouth.

Over and over he laved her womanly core with greedy intent, making her whisper his name over and over. Suddenly, her body exploded like a volcano erupting and she surrendered to the pleasure he'd given her.

Before the last spasm left her body, he had shifted to position his body over hers, and then she felt him enter her, stretching her to accommodate his size. She inhaled the scent of him—the scent of them—and then used her tongue to lick his shoulder, needing to taste the texture of his skin.

He pushed his shaft as deep inside her as he could go and then he locked their legs together. He began moving, thrusting back and forth, in and out. He established a rhythm that sent sexual undercurrents all through her body.

He looked down at her, held her gaze as he made love to her. She clung to him, holding tight to his shoulders as if they were a lifeline. His languid, deep, hard thrusts were driving her over the edge and making every nerve ending in her body zing brutally to life.

He threw his head back and growled her name as he continued to make love to her, indulging her with his words. Her skin sizzled where their bodies connected and the more he stroked inside her, the more her body awakened to the aching hunger he was feeding.

And then he called her name again. Together they were slammed with another orgasm. He gathered her in his arms, touched the side of her face with his fingers as they rode the tidal waves of ecstasy together.

The next morning it had felt odd waking up with a man in her bed. They had made love practically all evening, only to get up around eight and eat some of the soup she'd made the day before with French bread. Then they had gotten back in bed and made love all over again. All through the night.

No personal information was exchanged. None was needed. She knew the next three days would be considered one and done. Chances were, they would never see each other again. They were taking advantage of the now.

"You're awake?"

She glanced over at him and saw desire in the depths of his dark eyes. "Yes, I'm awake."

"Good."

He got out of bed to put on a condom then returned to her. "And what if I wanted breakfast first?" she asked, grinning.

He grinned back. "And do you want breakfast first?"

She shook her head. "No. I want you, Laramie."

And she did want him. She had to keep telling herself this was just sex and nothing more. When he left here the day after Christmas he wouldn't be coming back, nor would they stay in touch. The only thing she would have were her memories. Regardless, she could not and would not ever regret any time spent with him.

After making love that morning they dressed and went out to grab breakfast. He surprised her with his suggestion that they get a Christmas tree. That meant they had to purchase ornaments, as well. He refused to let her pay for anything. Like kids, they rushed back to the house and decorated the tree. Their tree.

Since most restaurants were closed for the holidays, she decided to prepare Christmas dinner for them. That meant grocery shopping, which she told him she wanted to do alone. She knew from their earlier shopping trip how he liked to spend money and she wanted Christmas dinner to be her treat.

When she returned to her apartment he was waiting for her. The minute she opened the door and glanced over at him, heated sexual attraction consumed them. She couldn't put her grocery bags down fast enough before he was ripping off her clothes, making love to her against the refrigerator.

He surprised her on Christmas Day with a gift, a beautiful scarf and a pair of earrings. The gift touched her deeply. He'd apparently gone shopping when she left to get groceries.

She surprised him with a gift, as well. A pair of gloves, since she'd noticed his were well-worn. He said he enjoyed Christmas dinner, but most of Christmas was spent in bed making love rather than eating.

The next morning, the day after Christmas, she awoke to find him dressed and ready to go. Ready to walk out of her life. She hadn't expected it to be so hard, but it was. She knew she had fallen in love with him. Not with the sex but with the man.

He kissed her deeply, wished her the best in her artistic dreams and thanked her for making this one of the best holidays for him, ever. And then he turned and walked out the door…without looking back.

She'd quickly gotten up and stood at the window to watch him leave. He'd called a cab and, as if he'd known she would be there at the window, before getting into the cab he looked over his shoulder, saw her, blew her a kiss and then waved goodbye.

She blew him a kiss and waved back. And as the cab drove away she knew at that moment that Laramie Cooper had taken a piece of her heart with him.

Three

New York, present day

"I'm glad you guys are finding this entire thing amusing," Laramie said as he moved around the hotel room to dress. He had placed the mobile call on speaker while engaging in a five-way conversation with his teammates.

"Hey, Coop, we can't help but think it's pretty damn funny," Bane Westmoreland said. "I can just imagine the look on your face when you discovered what you were delivering to that member of the Security Council wasn't top secret documents like you thought, but her pet cockatiel."

Laramie couldn't help but smile as he slid on a T-shirt. "No, Bane, you can't imagine."

"Well, just think positive," David Holloway said. "You got a free trip to New York."

"Damn, Flipper, it's cold as the dickens here. I prefer California weather," Laramie said.

"Stop whining, Coop," Gavin Blake said, laughing.

"Kiss it, Viper."

And then he said, "Hey, Mac? You still with us? You're kind of quiet."

"I'm still here," Thurston McRoy said. "I'm trying to keep up with you guys and watch the game, too. In case none of you realized, it's Thursday night football."

That led to a conversation about their predictions for what team would make it to the Super Bowl. By the time Laramie had ended the call, he was completely dressed and ready to leave.

And go where? He figured that since he had a taste for a juicy hamburger, he would grab a meal at Xavier's. Flipper had recommended he dine there and said he wouldn't be disappointed.

A short while later, Laramie entered the restaurant and was shown to a table. It was busy and there had been a fifteen-minute wait but he didn't mind. This wasn't his first visit to Times Square, but he did note a lot of changes since he was here last.

"What would you like tonight?"

He glanced up at the waitress. No one could credit him with being slow and he immediately knew the double meaning behind her question. "A menu would be nice," he said, hoping that would defuse any ideas she had.

Maybe another time, but not tonight. He just wasn't feeling it. He chuckled and wondered if he was running a fever. There hadn't been too many times when he'd turned down sex. And there was no doubt in his mind the woman was offering.

"I'll make sure you get a menu…as well as anything else you might want," she said, smiling.

He smiled back. "Thanks. The menu will do for now and a beer."

She walked off and returned with the menu and his beer. "Thanks."

"You can thank me later." Then she sashayed off.

He wondered why he wasn't taking advantage of those

curves and long gorgeous legs. His excuse had to be that this place sort of reminded him of that café in Paris. The one where Bristol worked.

Bristol.

He'd been thinking about her a lot lately. Maybe because it was around this time—during the holiday season three years ago when they'd met. Whatever the reason, Bristol Lockett was on his mind.

After his rescue from Syria, one of the first places he'd gone had been to Paris to see her, a woman he hadn't meant to ever see again. But something had compelled him to seek her out, only to be told by the manager of the apartment complex where she'd lived that she had returned to the United States a couple of years ago and had not left a forwarding address.

When he noticed the waitress looking over at him, he decided to place his order, eat and then leave. He wasn't up for any female company tonight and didn't want the woman to get any ideas.

An hour or so later, he left the restaurant a pretty satisfied man. The food had been delicious but he'd had a hard time deflating the waitress's flirtation. By the end of his meal, she'd all but placed her apartment key in his hand.

Instead of catching a cab back to his hotel room, he decided to walk off the hamburger and fries he'd eaten. Although he'd complained earlier about the cold weather, it really wasn't too bad. He'd endured worse. Like that time his team had that mission in the Artic.

He was about to cross the street when a sign ahead stopped him. It was an art gallery and the poster said:

TONIGHT
SPECIAL SHOWING OF ART BY BRISTOL

Bristol...

He shook his head. He was losing it. He hadn't thought Bristol was a common name. Was it?

What if it wasn't? Could it be his Bristol?

He dismissed the idea that Bristol was his. She was merely a woman he'd had a three-day fling with while relaxing in Paris before a mission.

Merely a woman he hadn't been able to forget in three years.

The name was unusual. He'd told her so when they'd met. He knew she was an artist. She'd shown him some of her art.

There was no way she could be here.

But then, why not? She was a New Yorker. He'd gathered that much from a conversation she'd had with Bane. Laramie hadn't asked her anything. His main focus had been sleeping with her.

What if the Bristol on the sign was the same Bristol from Paris?

His chest pounded at the possibility. He watched all the well-dressed people getting out of their limos and private cars to enter the gallery. He glanced down at himself. Jeans, pullover shirt, leather jacket, Stetson and boots. Definitely not dressed to mingle with the likes of the high-class crowd entering the gallery. But at that moment, he didn't give a royal damn.

He had to find out if this Bristol was the same woman he hadn't been able to forget.

"Would you like some more wine, Bristol?"

Bristol glanced up at Steven Culpepper, forced a smile and said, "No, thanks. I'm fine."

He nodded. Looking over her shoulder, he said, "Excuse me for a minute. A few of my clients just arrived."

"Sure."

She let out a deep sigh when he walked off. Why was he hanging around as if they were together when they weren't?

She glanced around. There was a huge crowd and she appreciated that. A great number of her paintings had been sold already.

"I see Steven is quite taken with you tonight, Bristol."

She turned to Margie. "I wish he wouldn't be. He's barely left my side."

Margie lifted a brow. "And you see that as a bad thing?"

Bristol shrugged. "I just don't want him getting the wrong idea."

"Oh, I see,"

Bristol doubted it. Margie was determined to play matchmaker.

"A lot of the people here tonight are ones he invited. People with money. Need I say more?" Margie then walked off.

No, in all honesty, Margie didn't have to say anything. Steven had told her several times tonight just how many people were here because of him. It was as if he'd assumed Bristol would not have gotten anyone here on her own. Although he was probably right about that, he didn't have to remind her of it every chance he got.

"Hello, Bristol."

She turned to an older gentleman. His face seemed familiar and after a quick study of his features, she remembered him. "You're Colin Kusac, a close friend of my father's."

He smiled. "Yes, that's right. I haven't seen you since the funeral and the reading of the will."

That was true. Her father had named Colin as executor, and the scene hadn't been nice that day, especially when all her father had left her was revealed. Krista had accused Bristol of looking for her father only to get his money. Her stepmother had been wrong about that.

Her father had told her that he and Colin had attended high school together and over the years had remained the best of friends. Before Randall died, he'd also told her to contact Mr. Kusac if she ever needed anything. Since there was nothing she'd needed, there had been no reason to call him.

"How have you been?" she asked him.

"Fine. And you? I understand you have a son."

She wondered how he'd known that. She lived a quiet life and it hadn't been highly publicized that she was Randall Lockett's daughter. Although, at her father's request, she had taken his last name. At sixteen it had taken a lot of getting used to, going from Bristol Washington to Bristol Lockett.

Although she'd taken her father's name, she'd never flaunted it to influence her own career. And in the art community her father had used the pseudonym Rand, so very few people had made the connection anyway. However, over the years, people had mentioned how much her paintings resembled those of the renowned artist Rand. Although Margie was aware of her father's identity, Bristol had sworn her manager to secrecy. Bristol wanted to make it on her own and not use her father as leverage.

And now she was Bristol Cooper...

"Yes, I have a beautiful two-year-old son. His first name is Laramie, after his father. His middle name is Randall, after my father. He has the names of two good men."

"Randall would have liked that. He would have been proud of his first grandchild." Colin didn't say anything for a minute and then added, "I miss my good friend. He was there for me more times than not. When I first saw your work, I was taken back by just how much you and he painted alike."

She smiled, thinking how wonderful it was that on this very important night, although her father wasn't here, a man she knew to be his closest friend was. "Yes, we discovered that before he died."

"Randall was a gifted artist and so are you."

"Thank you."

"There's a beautiful landscape over there that I'm thinking about buying. I wonder if you can tell me what inspired you."

She knew exactly which one he was talking about. It was the first painting she'd done after her father died and a lot of her pent-up emotions had been poured into it. "Certainly."

And then she and Colin moved toward the huge painting on the wall.

"May I help you, sir?"

Laramie wasn't surprised someone had approached him the minute he walked into the gallery. All he had to do was look around the room to see he seemed obviously out of place. He really wouldn't have to stay a minute longer if the man could answer one question. "The artist on the sign. Bristol. What's her last name?"

When the older man, who he suspected to be someone in charge, gave him a strange look, Laramie added, "I once knew someone by that name."

The man nodded his understanding. "Oh, I see. Her last name is—"

"I will handle this gentleman, Jazlyn," an authoritative voice said behind him.

Laramie didn't turn around. He figured whoever had spoken would make himself known soon enough. Besides, he hadn't liked the emphasis the man had placed on the word *gentleman*. As if he thought Laramie was anything but a gentleman. And what had he meant by "handle him"?

Laramie inwardly smiled. He would like to see that happen.

"Yes, of course, Mr. Culpepper." And then the older man walked off.

The guy who'd spoken came around to stand in front of Laramie and quickly sized him up. Laramie didn't have a problem with that since he was sizing up the other man, as well. And Laramie didn't like the arrogant glint in the man's eyes, like he assumed he was better than Laramie just because he was dressed in a designer suit.

A quick assessment told Laramie what he needed to know. The man was in his upper thirties, probably a Harvard or Yale graduate, a Wall Street type, most likely CEO of his own corporation.

"May I help you, Mr...?"

Evidently no one had explained to this man the proper way to introduce oneself. It wasn't by asking a question. Therefore, Laramie didn't intend to give his name unless this ass gave his. Besides, his name was irrelevant to what he wanted to know. "Like I was saying to the older man a moment ago, before we were interrupted—I once knew a woman name Bristol and was wondering, what is the artist's last name?"

The man's smile didn't quite reach his eyes. Who was this man and what business was it of his that Laramie was inquiring about the artist?

"I'm sure it's not the same person."

How the hell would you know? he wanted to say. Instead he said, "Let me decide that."

He could tell his response hadn't gone over well. The man's eyes darkened in irritation. Evidently, he wasn't used to being put in his place. "I won't let you decide anything. In fact, I'm almost certain Bristol doesn't know you."

Laramie was beginning to read the signs. This man was territorial. Evidently, there was something going on between him and the artist. "You sound sure of that, Mr..."

The man smiled. "Culpepper. Steven Culpepper. And

the reason I sound certain is because I know Bristol. We are well acquainted."

"Obviously. So what's her last name?" He tilted his Stetson back to stare down at the man, wondering why Steven was giving him a hard time.

"What's the name of the woman you're looking for? Just in case you haven't noticed, you're drawing attention."

And he was supposed to give a damn? Laramie drew in a deep breath, tired of playing this cat-and-mouse game. The man was probably right, it wasn't the same Bristol, but there was something about this man's attitude that rubbed Laramie the wrong way. "Lockett. Her name is Bristol Lockett."

The man smiled. "Lockett? Then I was right all along. Her last name isn't Lockett."

"So what is it?"

Evidently tired of this conversation as well, the man said, "It's Cooper. Bristol Cooper."

Laramie frowned. He and the woman had the same last name? What a coincidence. But then there were a lot of Coopers out there. "You're right. It's not the same woman. Sorry I took up so much of your time."

"No problem. Let me see you out."

"No need. I know my way." Laramie had made it to the door when he heard it. That laugh.

It was a distinctive sound that could only come from one woman. He turned and glanced around the room. He didn't see her. Had he only imagined hearing her laughter?

"Is anything wrong?"

That Culpepper guy was back. Laramie looked at him. "Not sure. However, I'd like to meet the artist, Bristol Cooper, after all."

"That's not possible."

Laramie was about to tell the man that with him anything was possible, when he heard the sound again. His gaze sharpened as he looked around the room. The sound had come from another part of the gallery. He was certain he hadn't imagined it twice.

He began moving toward the sound, not caring that people were staring at him.

"Wait a minute! You need to leave now."

When Laramie kept walking, he heard the Culpepper guy call out, "Mr. Jazlyn, I suggest you call for security."

They could call for security all they wanted. He wasn't leaving until he made sure...

He entered another area of the gallery and immediately felt it...that undisguised pang of longing and desire he hadn't felt in three years. He swallowed hard against the deep yearning in his throat as his gaze swept around the room.

And then he saw her.

Her back was to him. She stood beside an older gentleman as the two of them studied a landscape. Laramie knew without even seeing her face that the woman was his Bristol.

He'd only spent three days with her, but he knew that body, even if it was now draped in a beautiful gown. There were a few curves that hadn't been there before, but he was certain everything else belonged to Bristol Lockett, right, front and center. Especially that shapely backside.

He remembered the feel of his hand on that backside as well as the brush of his fingers along her inner thighs. He felt an immediate tightening in his gut at the memory.

Every muscle in his body tensed as he quickly moved in her direction. When he came within a few feet of her, he inhaled her scent. It was the one he remembered from Paris. Hurried footsteps were headed in his direction. Security was coming. Let them come. But not before he made his presence known.

"Bristol?"

She must have heard her name but she seemed almost afraid to face him. And when she slowly turned, she looked as if she was staring at the face of...a ghost?

She took a step forward. She whispered his name. And then she crumpled.

Four

Laramie managed to grab her before she passed out on the floor, sweeping her into his arms. People were staring, some had begun moving in their direction, no doubt wondering what the hell was going on.

"Put her down!"

He recognized Culpepper's voice. Laramie turned to see Culpepper flanked by several security guards and the owner of the gallery. Then suddenly a woman pushed through the crowd. "What happened?"

Laramie thought it was obvious but answered anyway. "She fainted."

"Fainted? How? Why?" She then narrowed her gaze at him. "Who are you?"

"Laramie Cooper."

"Laramie Cooper?" The woman gasped.

He wondered why hearing his name had such an effect on the woman. "Yes, Laramie Cooper. I need to take Bristol somewhere to lie down. And I need someone to get a wet cloth."

"Wait a damn minute," Culpepper was saying. "He has no right to be here. Who is he supposed to be?"

He heard the woman whisper something to the bastard that sounded like "He's her husband."

Laramie wondered why the woman would make such an outlandish claim. He wasn't anyone's husband. Then he recalled what Culpepper had told him earlier. Bristol's last name was Cooper. Now he was more confused than ever and confusion was something he didn't deal with very well.

Suddenly, the older gentleman Bristol had been talking to said, "Will someone do as this man asks and get a wet cloth? Jazlyn, where is your office?"

"Right this way, Mr. Kusac."

"Kusac?"

Laramie ignored the flutter of whispered voices repeating the man's name as if it meant something. Even the woman who was moving ahead of them stopped to look at the man in awe. Who was this guy Kusac? Was he a celebrity or something?

Laramie moved quickly toward the back of the gallery while carrying Bristol in his arms. He recalled the last time he'd carried her, from her kitchen to her bed.

Entering the gallery owner's office, Laramie laid Bristol on the sofa. The man who'd been identified as Kusac closed the office door, only admitting the three of them along with the woman. Laramie couldn't determine who she was studying more, him or Kusac. There was a knock on the door and Kusac opened it. Wet cloths were handed to him and he passed them over to Laramie.

"Is she all right?" the woman asked nervously.

"Yes" was Laramie's response as he began wiping Bristol's face with a cloth.

"By the way, Mr. Kusac, I'm Margie Townsend, Bristol's manager. I appreciate you coming out tonight and giving your support. You and Bristol seem to know each other."

"We do. I was a close friend of her father's."

"Oh." And then out the corner of his eye, Laramie noted

the woman moving closer to him. "And are you really Laramie Cooper?" she asked.

He didn't take his gaze off Bristol as he continued to wipe her face. She was even more beautiful than he'd remembered. Her chocolate brown skin was smooth and soft. He'd always liked the shape of her lips. They had the perfect bow. He recalled kissing them. How he'd licked them with his tongue.

Bristol was three years older now. Twenty-five. But you couldn't tell it by her features. It was as if she hadn't aged at all.

She still was the most beautiful woman he had yet to meet.

He switched his gaze to the woman who'd introduced herself as Bristol's manager and who'd asked him a strange question. "Yes, I'm Laramie Cooper."

"B-but you're supposed to be dead."

Laramie frowned. Bristol must have told her that. But then, how had Bristol known?

Deciding he would get all the answers he wanted from Bristol when she came to, he said, "Yes, I'd been captured, and they presumed I was dead."

"And you decided to show up after all this time?" the woman snapped. "Fine husband you are!"

Before he could ask her what in the hell was she talking about, Bristol made a sound. She whispered his name just moments before her eyes fluttered open.

And then she stared up at him. Tentatively, she reached up and touched his face, as if to make certain he was flesh and blood. Tears fell from her eyes when she whispered, "You're alive."

He nodded. "Yes, I'm alive."

"But they told me you were dead."

He nodded. "They thought so for a while, before I was rescued."

"Rescued?"

"Yes. Almost a year later."

From the look in her eyes, he saw something was bothering her. Maybe it was the fact that she was using his last name and claiming they were married.

"We need to talk privately, Laramie," she said, barely above a whisper.

She was right. They needed to talk. He nodded and then glanced at the other two people in the room. Before he could say anything, Kusac said, "We heard." He opened the door. When Margie Townsend hesitated, Kusac said, "They need time alone."

Margie nodded. "Yes, of course." She then said to Bristol, "If you need me I'll be right outside the door."

When the door closed behind them, Laramie helped Bristol sit up. She drew in a deep breath and stared at him. "I can't believe you are alive."

Laramie didn't say anything. He was trying to make sense of what he'd learned and was failing miserably. He needed answers to help him understand. "How did you know I was supposedly dead?" he asked, sitting beside her on the sofa.

She nervously licked her lips. "I tried to find you. I sent you a letter, through the navy, and it was returned. A friend of mine knew someone who worked in the State Department. They checked into it and that's what I was told."

"When was this?"

"A few months after I last saw you."

He nodded. "I was presumed dead, so the person was right. I was rescued just days before Christmas the following year."

"That was a long time."

"Yes, it was." Only his close friends knew about the nightmares he'd had for months following his rescue. Nightmares he still had at times. His enemies had tried to break him and he'd refused to be broken. But their attempts had become lasting scars.

"Why were you trying to reach me, Bristol?"

Bristol drew in a deep breath, not believing that Laramie was alive, not believing that he'd shown up here tonight. How had he known where she was? Had he been looking for her? If he had, that would make what she was about to tell him easier. But what if he hadn't been looking for her? What if he had forgotten all about her and moved on? For all she knew he could be married, although there was no ring on his finger.

She studied his features. He was even more handsome than she remembered. He looked slightly older and there was a hardness in the lines of his face that hadn't been there before. Instead of taking away from his striking features, the hardness defined them even more. And the look in his eyes reflected experiences she couldn't come close to imagining.

Even if those experiences had changed him, it didn't matter. He still had a right to know about her son. His son. Their son.

He could accept it or question whether Laramie was truly his, but he had a right to know. How he handled the news was up to him.

Drawing in another deep breath, she met his gaze and said, "The reason I tried reaching you was because I wanted to let you know I was pregnant."

Five

Laramie froze. He stared at Bristol. He'd heard what she'd said but he needed to verify it. "You were pregnant?"

"Yes," she said in a soft voice. "And you're free to order a paternity test if you need to confirm that my son is yours."

He had a son?

It took less than a second to go from shock to disbelief. "How?"

She lifted a brow, indicating she'd found his question as stupid as he had, but she answered nonetheless. "Probably from making love almost nonstop for three solid days."

They had definitely done that. Although he'd used a condom each and every time, he knew there was always the possibility something could go wrong. "And, where is he?" he asked, still trying to wrap his mind around the fact that he had a son.

"At home."

Where the hell was that?

It bothered him how little he knew about the woman who'd given birth to his child. At least she'd tried contacting him to let him know. Some women wouldn't have.

If his child had been born nine months after their holiday

fling, that meant he would have turned two in September. Laramie recalled that September. Although it had been hard keeping up with the days while being held hostage, somehow he'd managed, by counting each sunrise. He'd been lucky to be held in a cell with a tiny window.

He hadn't known that while being a pawn in his enemies' game of life and death that somewhere in the world Bristol was giving life.

To his child.

Emotions bombarded him with the impact of a Tomahawk missile. He'd been happy whenever Mac became a father again and had been overjoyed for Bane at the birth of his triplets. And now Laramie was a parent, which meant he had to think about someone other than himself. But then, wasn't he used to looking out for others as a member of his SEAL team?

"Have you gotten married, Laramie?"

He frowned at her question. Marriage was the very last thing on his mind. "No, I'm still single."

She nodded and then said, "I'm not asking you for anything, if that's what you're thinking. I just felt you had a right to know about the baby."

He stared at her while conflicting emotions warred inside him. She wasn't asking him for anything? Did she not know that her bold declaration that he'd fathered her child demanded everything?

"I want to see him."

"And you will. I would never keep Laramie from you."

"You named him Laramie?" Even more emotions swamped him. Her son, their son, had his name?

She hesitated, as if she wasn't sure how he would like her response. "Yes. His first name is Laramie and his middle name is Randall, after my father. I thought you were dead and I wanted him to have your name. So I named him Laramie Randall Cooper."

He didn't say anything for a full minute. Then he asked, "So, what's your reason for giving yourself my name, as well?"

Oh, boy. Bristol wondered why so much was happening to her tonight of all nights. When she'd left home she'd hoped for a great night for the showing of her work at the gallery. She hadn't counted on a lover—specifically, her son's father—coming back from the dead.

And now he wanted answers.

Although she knew he deserved to have them, she wasn't ready to tell him any more than she had already. She just wanted to go home and hug her son. Tomorrow, she would tell her son that the father he thought had become an angel was now a mortal.

She was about to tell him she was tired of talking for now when there was a knock on the door. "I'll get that," he said, standing.

She still appreciated the way he walked. Spine ramrod straight, steps taken in perfect precision with the best-looking tush she'd seen on a man.

When Laramie opened the door he practically blocked the doorway, but she heard Margie's voice. "How is Bristol?"

"I'm fine, Margie," she said. Thankfully, Laramie shifted aside so Margie could see for herself.

"Do you need anything?"

"No, I'll be out in a minute."

"No rush. Most of the people have left anyway. But the good thing is that all your paintings were sold. Tonight was a huge success."

Was it? As far as her manager was concerned, it had been a successful night. But Bristol saw beyond the money her paintings had earned. She saw the man standing by the door. Her heart slammed against her ribs. Already she was wondering what changes were about to be made in her life.

"And Steven is worried about you."

Bristol saw Laramie's body stiffen at the mention of Steven's name and wondered why. She became even more curious when he said, "Tell Culpepper she's fine and is in good hands. Now if you will excuse us, Bristol and I need to finish talking." He then closed the door.

How had Laramie known Steven's last name? Had the two of them met? If so, when?

Laramie slowly turned away from the door to stare at her. It was a good thing she was sitting down because her knees began shaking. The intensity of his gaze sent sensuous chills through her body. How was that possible when she hadn't seen him in three years?

The sexual chemistry that had drawn them to each other from the first was still there. She wanted to deny its existence, but she couldn't. She wanted to break eye contact with him and look away, but she couldn't do that, either. She sat there and endured the moment, hoping it would quickly pass. It didn't. It seemed to extend longer than necessary.

She decided to use it to her advantage; checking him out wasn't a hard thing to do. He wore a pair of jeans, a dark blue pullover shirt, a dark leather jacket, a Stetson and boots. He looked like a cowboy, ready to ride off into the sunset. He seemed to have gotten taller and his body appeared even more fit. Was he still a navy SEAL or had he given it up after that mission that had obviously gone all wrong?

Her gaze moved to his shoulders. She remembered them well. She could easily recall how she clutched tight to them when they made love. How she would cling to them while he thrust inside her. What she remembered the most was that Laramie Cooper was a very physical man, filled with an abundance of strength and virility.

She sighed as her gaze returned to his too-handsome face and stared into his eyes. And she saw it again, that hardness. Pain he refused to show. Ravaged secrets. A wounded heart. A damaged soul.

He probably didn't want her to see any of those things, but for a quick moment, she'd seen them anyway. She wondered what he'd endured during those months when everyone thought he was dead. Would he share the details of that time with her if she were to ask? Was it any of her business?

He didn't say anything as he continued to study her as intensely as she was studying him. What was he seeing? Besides a few extra pounds she hadn't shed after her pregnancy. Some men would think of them as curves. She thought of them as a nuisance that wouldn't go away no matter how much she exercised.

"Are you ready to answer my question?" he asked in a deep, husky voice that seemed to resonate inside her. "Because I have even more."

She'd been afraid of that. She also knew they couldn't stay holed up in Mr. Jazlyn's office forever. She understood she needed to fill Laramie in on so much that had happened but now was not a good time. "I suggest we meet tomorrow and—"

"No. I need to know tonight."

Tonight? "That's not possible," she said, glancing at her watch because she needed to stop looking into his eyes. His dark gaze wasn't just directed at her, it was assessing her in a way she knew too well. During those three days in Paris, she had been able to—most of the time—interpret what he was thinking from his eyes. Namely, she knew when he was ready to make love again by the desire she would see in them.

"Why tonight?" she asked.

"Why not tonight?" he countered.

Drawing in a deep breath, she said, "My neighbor, Ms.

Charlotte, is keeping Laramie and I don't want to get home too late."

He nodded. "And where is home?"

"Brooklyn."

He nodded again as he continued to stare at her. She couldn't help wondering what he was thinking. She found out when he said, "I want to see my son tonight, Bristol."

Why did him saying her name, no matter the tone, make an unexplainable warmth spread through her? "It's past his bedtime and he'll be asleep."

"Doesn't matter. I want to see him."

She eased up off the sofa. "Why?" she asked, not sure she was ready for him to come to her home, invade her space and meet Ms. Charlotte, who was the closest thing to a family she had now. "Don't you believe me?"

"Yes, I do. I just want to see him."

It was similar to her father's wish when she'd first made contact with him. She hadn't known what to expect when she'd first spoken with him. To break the ice, her aunt Dolly had spoken with him first. By the time Bristol had gotten on the phone, he had been eager to talk to her. Nervously, she'd blundered out the words, "I'm your daughter." And he'd said, "I believe you and I want to see you." He'd flown out that same day from Los Angeles and in less than eight hours was knocking on her aunt's door.

Bristol studied Laramie. Noticed his stiff posture. Was he expecting a fight? Hadn't she told him that she wanted him to know about their child? "Fine, you can see him tonight. A private car is taking me home."

She nervously nibbled her bottom lip. There was something she had to tell him before they left the office. It was the answer to the question he'd asked regarding her use of his name. "And to answer your question about me taking your name."

"Yes?"

"Before leaving Paris, I had already made up my mind to name my son after you, first name and last. But I didn't want people asking questions about why we had different last names. My friend Dionne came up with the idea. She had a friend who was an assistant to a judge in Paris who was willing to help with our plan. We did a fake marriage license where I listed you as my husband. It was then filed with the courts in Paris."

He didn't say anything for a minute before he asked, "Giving birth to a child without the benefit of a husband drove you to do that?"

She looked away for a second to figure out how to make him understand. "Yes. More so for Laramie than for me." She paused. "My mom was a single parent and I never knew my father. All my life the stigma of being born illegitimate bothered me because there were those who never let me forget. I got teased a lot about not having a father. I know having kids out of wedlock is more acceptable these days, but still, I didn't want to take a chance and put my child through that."

Although her mother had never said so, Bristol believed it bothered her mother as well, not only for her daughter but for herself. While growing up, there had been organizations Bristol's mother had tried to sign up for that had rejected their application because they hadn't met what was considered normal family dynamics. In other words, she didn't have a father and her mother didn't have a husband.

"I assume your manager believes we're married. She practically accused me of deserting you and my child."

Bristol rubbed her hands down her face, feeling bad about that. "I'm sorry. I'll tell her the truth."

"Don't bother doing that. At least I know why she's been acting like I'm scum. And I also now know why that Culpepper guy was acting like an ass when I asked about you."

"Steven?"

"Yes, I take it he's your boyfriend."

Where would he get an idea like that? "No, he's not my boyfriend. Steven and I have never even gone out on a date."

Laramie held her gaze, apparently finding it odd that the man would act so territorial under those circumstances. "But he has asked you out though, right?"

"Yes, but I've always declined. He's not my type." She checked her watch again and then looked up at him. "Are you going to deny you're my husband? People might question you about it."

"Don't worry. I won't give your secret away."

Six

When they walked out of the office, the first person Laramie noticed was Steven Culpepper and how the man's eyes narrowed when they got closer. If the guy had gotten word that Bristol's supposedly dead husband wasn't dead after all, then what the hell was he still hanging around for?

Laramie detected Bristol's nervousness. Did she think he would rat her out, expose her for lying about their marriage when he'd told her he wouldn't? He slowed his pace and she slowed hers. He glanced down at her. "You okay?"

"Yes. I'm just surprised to see Steven still here."

That made two of them. "You want me to ask him to leave?"

"No. I guess he was concerned. I see Mr. Kusac is still here, too. I can understand his concern since he was a good friend of my father's."

Laramie didn't say anything. He recalled how people had jumped into motion when the man named Kusac had barked out orders earlier. Even the owner of the gallery was quick to do the man's bidding.

Margie left the group to walk toward them, a smile on

her lips. "Well, did the two of you get things straightened out?" she asked.

Laramie answered before Bristol did. "Yes, and we're leaving."

The woman lifted a brow. "Leaving? To go where?"

Laramie was tempted to tell the woman that he didn't think it was any of her business, but Bristol answered, "I'm going home, Margie. Is the car ready to take me there?"

"Yes."

"Good." She then turned to Laramie and said, "I need to say good-night to everyone."

"Okay, let's do that."

Her eyes widened, probably in surprise that he'd included himself in the goodbyes, but she didn't say anything as he walked with her over to the three men. "I would like you to meet Laramie Cooper."

Laramie was sure it didn't go unnoticed how Bristol had introduced him. She hadn't referred to him as her husband. He figured these people assumed he was her back-from-the-dead husband, but she wasn't allowing anyone to presume anything about the nature of their relationship.

She thanked the owner of the gallery for hosting the event and apologized for all the commotion she'd caused by fainting.

Maurice Jazlyn waved off her words and said, "I would have passed out, too, had I thought my husband was dead and then he suddenly appeared out of nowhere."

Laramie didn't speak. If they were waiting for him to explain his absence for the past three years, they could wait on.

Then Jazlyn's face broke into a smile. "But then, I certainly can't complain since every last one of your paintings sold and you being here brought Kusac out tonight. It's been years since I've seen him."

"And I was glad to see him, as well," Bristol said, smiling at the man. "Thanks for coming."

Colin Kusac smiled. "Your first art show in New York—I would not have missed it for the world."

Then Bristol's attention went to Steven Culpepper. Laramie didn't like the vibes he was picking up off the man. He hadn't liked them from the first. "Steven," he heard Bristol say. "Thanks for inviting all those people here tonight. It was a nice turnout thanks to you."

"No need to thank me, but I'd like for us to meet sometime this week. Several of my clients here tonight were impressed with your work and want to see more. A few are willing to commission some of your future projects."

"That's wonderful! I'm sure we can arrange a meeting," Margie said excitedly behind them. "Just give me a call, Steven. I'll work out a date and time when Bristol is available."

A tight smile touched Culpepper's lips. "Yes, of course, Margie." Laramie had a feeling Culpepper had wanted a private meeting with Bristol and her manager had ruined those plans.

"I'll call you tomorrow to discuss your availability, Bristol," Margie said.

"That's fine," Bristol said, smiling. She then turned to him. "I'm ready to go, Laramie."

He nodded and took her hand, leading her toward the door.

"I don't bite, you know."

Bristol glanced across the back seat at Laramie and had to admit there was a lot of space between them. He might not bite but she could vividly recall a lot of other naughty things he could do with his mouth.

Jeez. Why was she remembering that now?

"I know you don't bite, but I figured you would want your space."

She thought the chuckle that ensued from his throat sounded way too sexy for her ears. "Is that a way of letting me know you like yours?"

She shrugged. "I guess I've gotten used to it." No need to tell him that she hadn't had another man in her life since him, serious or otherwise. After her son was born, he had become her whole world and there hadn't been room for anyone else. Some women needed a man to feel like a female; she didn't.

He didn't say anything for a minute and that was fine with her as the private car carried them through the streets of Manhattan and toward the Brooklyn Bridge. When they'd left the gallery she'd noticed the temperature had dropped. Forecasters had predicted a heavy snowfall before Christmas and with this cold snap being less than two weeks before Christmas, she could see it happening.

"Tell me about him. My son."

Laramie's words intruded into her reverie and she glanced over at him. The bright lights from the tall buildings they passed illuminated his features and she could see why she'd been taken with him from the first. Any woman would have been.

In Paris, Laramie Cooper had been handsome and charismatic all rolled into one. He was still handsome, she would give him that, but he had yet to unleash any of the charm that had swept her off her feet and into the nearest bed. But then she figured when a man was told he was the father of a child he hadn't known he had, his secret son, shock might put a damper on the charm.

Bristol settled her body against the leather seat. Talking about her son was one of her favorite subjects. "He's perfect."

There was that sexy chuckle again from him. "Besides

that. How about starting off telling me about your pregnancy. Was it a hard one?"

She could vividly recall all nine months of it. "Not after my sixth month. I was one of those unusual women who had morning sickness in the morning and at night. I could barely keep anything in my stomach, and the smell of some foods would send me rushing for the nearest bathroom."

"Sounds pretty bad."

"I thought so at the time. I had planned to leave Paris in my fifth month but my doctor restricted air travel until I was better. I'd lost a lot of weight. I wasn't eating much and what I was eating my baby was getting. That's why it doesn't surprise me now that Laramie is a big eater."

"When did you leave Paris?"

"In my sixth month. I wanted my baby to be born in the United States. Thank God for online shopping and for Ms. Charlotte, who lives next door to my aunt. The house was cleaned out and baby furniture delivered, which made things easy for me when I finally arrived back in New York. Once the morning sickness stopped and I could retain food, I blew up overnight but the weight gain was mostly all baby. Laramie was born weighing close to nine pounds."

"And during all that time you thought I was dead."

He'd said it not as a question but as a statement. "Yes. I had no reason not to believe what the State Department had reported. A part of me wished I'd known more about you so I could reach out to your parents. I recall you'd mentioned they were alive but you never gave me any personal information about yourself."

"And you never gave me any personal information about yourself, either," he said. "Though I do remember you telling Bane you were from New York."

No, they hadn't exchanged any of those details. She doubted if it would have mattered anyway. It was not like he'd intended to one day pick up where they'd left off.

There was no doubt in her mind that after he'd been rescued he'd gotten on with his life and hadn't given her a second thought.

"How did you stumble across me tonight?" She was certain now that he hadn't been looking for her.

"I came to New York on military business. After dinner I was headed back to my hotel room when I saw the sign at the gallery with your name. I figured there couldn't be too many artists with that name."

"So you came into the gallery on a hunch?"

"Yes, although I knew from the way I was dressed I would stand out like a sore thumb. And then I encountered your Steven Culpepper, who—"

"He's not my Steven."

"He tried to paint the picture that he was. Appeared pretty damn possessive, too. He'd convinced me you weren't the Bristol I was looking for, but then I heard your laugh."

"My laugh?"

"Yes. I was less than a foot from the door when I heard you laugh. Twice."

She nodded. "Colin Kusac was sharing something with me about how he and my father used to get in trouble in high school."

"Your laugh is what let me know you were the same Bristol. I remembered it."

Those three days they'd spent together had been memorable in so many ways. And it hadn't been all about the sex. They'd had fun sharing breakfast in bed, sharing jokes. They'd even watched movies together. She had enjoyed waking up in his arms and going to sleep the same way.

Those memories were what had held her sanity together while she carried his child and believed he'd been lost to her forever. Those memories were what she'd remembered when the labor pains had hit. She'd drawn comfort from them.

The car came to a stop and she glanced out the window. She was home. The place she'd escaped to when she needed to heal from the grief she'd endured when she thought Laramie had died. It was the place where, months later, she had brought her son. Because her baby had been so large, at the last minute she'd had to deliver by C-section. Luckily, Dionne had made plans to be with Bristol as her delivery coach and ended up being a lot more. Her best friend was a godsend during the weeks following the delivery.

The first time Bristol had seen her son she'd been filled with so much love. She'd been given a special gift. She'd immediately noticed how much he looked like his father. It was uncanny. Her son's coloring, the shape of his eyes, the tilt of his mouth, had all come from the older Laramie. And the older her son got the more he looked like his father. Would Laramie notice? There was no way he couldn't.

"Are you okay, Bristol?"

She looked over at him. "Yes, I'm fine." A part of her wondered if that was true.

The driver came around and opened the door. Laramie slid out, and she couldn't help noticing how his masculine jeans-clad thighs slid with ease across the leather. Then he stood by the door and extended his hand out to her, to help her out.

The moment she placed her hand in his, she felt it. That spark, that tingling sensation she'd felt the first time they'd touched. She glanced up at him and met the darkness of his eyes and knew he'd felt it, too. Knew he was remembering.

Then she decided she wasn't fine after all.

Seven

Laramie considered what had passed between him and Bristol a few moments ago. He was fully aware of the strong sexual chemistry that was still between them. Even when they weren't trying, they pushed each other's buttons. No surprise there. But what he found surprising was the intensity of what he'd felt from her touch.

Shoving his hands in his pockets, he turned to look at the line of brownstones, especially the one in front of them. The SEAL in him quickly surveyed his surroundings, took in every nook and cranny. It was a nice neighborhood of older well-kept homes on a tree-lined street with sufficient lighting. Even the sidewalks in front of the homes looked as if they'd been scrubbed clean. It was easy to see this was a block that took pride in their neighborhood.

He followed as Bristol walked ahead of him. Several live plants lined the steps to her front door. Had he told her how nice she looked tonight in that long, flowing black gown with a split on the side? The male in him couldn't help but appreciate how those curves filled out the gown. She was a beautiful woman and he could understand Culpepper's interest. What man wouldn't be interested?

She took the key out of her purse and looked at him. Had she sensed he'd been staring at her backside? "Nice neighborhood," he said, in case she had.

"Yes, it is." She paused. "I will have to tell Ms. Charlotte who you are, as well. She will be shocked."

He nodded. "She also assumes we're married?"

"Yes. The only person who knows the truth is my best friend in Paris. Dionne."

Laramie didn't say anything as she unlocked the door and opened it. Then she stepped aside. "No, after you," he told her. "I'm used to bringing up the rear."

She nodded and entered her home. He followed, closing the door behind him. Her place had a cozy air. It felt small and intimate compared to the monstrosity of a house his parents owned, where he'd grown up as a child.

He stood in a foyer with stairs on one side and a living room on the other. The lit fireplace reminded him of how cold it was outside. The heat in here felt good. She had decorated for the holidays. A Christmas tree sat in front of the windows and he couldn't help noticing that several of the ornaments were the ones he had bought for her in Paris. It made him feel good to know she had kept them.

"Nice place," he said, glancing over at Bristol as he removed his Stetson and placed it on a nearby hat rack.

"Thanks."

"I thought I heard voices. You're home."

An older woman came down the stairs and he figured her to be Ms. Charlotte. She smiled when she saw them. Then suddenly, the smile seemed to freeze on her face and she stopped walking to stare at him.

"Sorry I'm late, Ms. Charlotte. How was Laramie tonight?"

The older woman answered Bristol, without taking her eyes off him. "He was fine as usual."

It was then that Bristol said, "Ms. Charlotte, I'd like to introduce—"

"I know who he is," the older woman said, still staring at him.

The woman's words gave Laramie pause. "How can you know?" he asked, lifting a brow.

"Your son looks just like you."

His son looked like him? "Does he?" he heard himself asking.

"Yes, your spitting image," the older woman said.

"That's one of the first things I noticed after he was born," Bristol added.

The woman finally continued down the stairs. When she reached the bottom step, she said, "I know you're not a ghost, so I can only assume you weren't dead as Bristol thought."

Laramie stared into the older woman's eyes. He admired their sharpness. He had a feeling you couldn't hide much from those eyes. "No, I wasn't dead, although the government thought I was. I was missing in action for almost a year before being recused."

For some reason he felt he should provide her an explanation. She nodded and her lips creased into a smile. "I'm glad you came back alive. You're going to love that little boy up there. He's a sweetheart."

Bristol groaned. "You shouldn't say things that aren't true, Ms. Charlotte. You and I both know he's just gotten the hang of the terrible twos."

"Like I've always said, boys will be boys. I should know after raising four of my own." She then glanced at her watch. "Time for me to leave. I'm sure the two of you have a lot to talk about," she said, heading for the door.

She glanced back at them, specifically at Laramie, and said, "I'm glad you're here." The older woman then opened the door and closed it behind her.

Laramie saw Bristol was focused on the painting that hung over her fireplace. He'd seen it before. In Paris. In her bedroom. It had hung directly over her bed. She'd told him it was one she'd painted with someone. He'd been amazed how the beauty of the Point Arena Lighthouse had been captured so magnificently on canvas. The painting was so vivid it seemed that the waves from the Pacific were hitting the shoreline. He recalled visiting the actual lighthouse years ago with his parents.

"Bristol?"

She switched her gaze to him. "Yes?"

"Are you okay?"

She stood beside a lamp and the light illuminated her. He was thinking then what he'd thought when he'd first seen her. She was beautiful. In the bright light, he could study her. See more. Her dark hair was swept up and away from her face in a way that seemed to make her features even more striking. Especially with those earrings in her ears...

It was then that he remembered. He'd given her the earrings as a gift. It seemed the Christmas ornaments weren't the only thing she'd kept.

"You're ready to see him?"

"Yes."

She nodded. "He's asleep, so whatever you do, try not to wake him. Laramie can be a handful when awakened from his sleep. He doesn't like that very much."

"I won't wake him."

"Okay. Then follow me please."

She headed up the stairs and he followed, feeling his stomach knot with every step. This was crazy. He'd faced bitter enemies without flinching. Yet knowing that at the end of these steps was a child he'd helped to create had nervous tension flowing through him.

The moment they reached the landing she turned to him.

"This way. His bedroom is next to mine so I can hear him at night."

He nodded, inhaling her scent. It was soft, subtle—jasmine. He recalled that was her favorite fragrance and for those three days they'd spent together it had become his.

He hung back when she opened the door and entered the bedroom. She turned on a small lamp. His gaze raked the room. It had bright yellow walls and a mural of zoo animals gathered around an image of someone reading a book.

Then there was the toy box in the corner. He smiled, remembering how he would pull all his toys out of the box at the beginning of the day as a boy, only to have to put them back at the end. His parents always had a full-time housekeeper and undoubtedly, she'd figured the more she taught him to do in his playroom, the less she would have to do.

He watched Bristol move toward the bed. From the doorway he could see the small sleeping form beneath the blanket. A mop of dark curly hair peeped out and he instantly recalled the pictures he'd seen of himself as a child with the same mass of curly hair. His parents hadn't given him his first haircut until he was about four.

When Bristol stopped by the bed, he moved to where she stood as blood pounded in his temples. He looked down and his heart stopped. Suddenly, he was bombarded with emotions he couldn't keep in check. He was looking down at his child. His son.

His son.

A son he and Bristol had made together during their three days of heated passion. Three days he hadn't been able to forget. Three days, the memory of which had helped him maintain his sanity when any normal person would have lost it.

He had expected to feel something. But not this. Not this overflowing of emotions filling him to capacity, taking hold of his mind and heart. He might not have been interested in fathering a child before, but the thought that he'd fathered this one had intense pride tightening his shoulders then spreading all the way down to his gut.

Since his child was lying on his stomach, he could only see one side of his face. That was enough. His mind rang out with the words... *He's mine. All mine.*

Um, not quite, he thought, glancing at the woman by his side. His son was hers, too. That was a fact he couldn't forget.

She met his gaze. At that moment, something passed between them and this time it wasn't sexual in nature. It was an unspoken understanding that no matter what, this child—their child—would always come first. He understood and accepted the pledge.

"Does he sleep through the night?" he whispered. He had to say something. He wanted to know so much. He wanted to know everything.

A smile touched her lips. "If you're hoping he'd awake anytime soon, no such luck," she whispered back. "He usually fights sleep tooth and nail, but when he's out, he's out until the next day."

"May I come back tomorrow to see him? Spend time with him?"

She didn't answer. Why? All he needed was a yes or no, preferably yes. Instead, she whispered, "Let's go back downstairs and talk about it."

Talk about it? Did she think her answer would make him yell and risk waking up his son? What was there to talk about? This was his son. She'd said so. He'd believed her even without seeing all of him. Drawing in a deep breath, he hoped like hell there was not about to be any drama. The only true drama he enjoyed was of the SEALs kind.

He followed her out the door and back down the stairs. "Would you like a cup of coffee or a beer, Laramie?"

"A beer will be fine."

"I'll be right back."

In a way, he was glad she'd left him alone for a few moments to deal with all these emotions. Was she deliberately stalling? Would she try to deny him rights to his son? She'd said the reason she'd tried writing to him three years ago was because she'd wanted him to know she was pregnant. He'd just seen his child. Now what? Did she expect him to walk away? Should he consider obtaining an attorney so he could know his rights as a father? All he knew was that his son had his name. Bristol even had his name, although they weren't legally married.

He rubbed a hand down his face. The hour was late. Was he overthinking things? If he was, it wouldn't be the first time. He was a suspicious bastard by nature. He rarely took anything at face value.

She returned with a beer for him and a cup of tea for herself. He remembered how she would drink a cup of tea every morning and every night before bedtime. He would get all turned on just watching how she sipped her tea.

"Let's sit in there," she said, indicating the living room. "Although I loved my studio apartment in Paris, it's nice to have more room here, especially with Laramie."

She sat down but he remained standing. Her calmness kicked up the uncertainty inside him even more. Was this when she would tell him he could have no part in his child's life or that he would only get whatever part she chose to give him?

He opened his beer and took a huge swig. The cool liquid felt refreshing going down his throat. He glanced over at her and saw she was looking at him. It was as if she wanted to say something but was too nervous to do so. In that case, he needed to just come out and squash whatever ideas were formulating in her head here and now.

"I asked you upstairs if I could come back tomorrow

and you never gave me an answer. So I can only assume you have a problem with me doing so. In that case, I think you need to hear me out, Bristol."

He moved to stand a few feet from where she sat and met her gaze. "I want to see my son again. Every chance I get. I want to know him and I want him to know me. I want to be there for him. I want to be a part of his life. I'm not a man who will walk away from my child. I have rights as a father."

He paused before adding, "And just so you know, if you deny me those rights, I will fight you legally with every penny I have."

Eight

Bristol knew she needed to do something before she began crying. Already it was taking everything within her to fight back the tears glistening in her eyes. She doubted Laramie knew just how much his words meant to her.

A part of her had known that she'd fallen in love with him during their holiday fling for a reason. Although she hadn't gotten to know him in the way she would have liked, in her heart she'd believed he was a man with character. A man of honor. A man who believed in doing the right thing.

When she discovered she was pregnant, letting him know had been automatic because of what her mother had done to her father. But Bristol hadn't known, until this very minute, how Laramie would feel about their son. Whether he would accept him or walk away. Even when he'd said he believed Laramie was his and had wanted to see him, there hadn't been any guarantees as to what his reaction would be. But she could not deny him the right to see his son and if he'd walked out the door after doing so, it would have been his loss. Not hers or her child's.

But from what he'd just said so passionately, he didn't plan to walk out the door. He wanted to be a part of his child's life…just like her father would have wanted to be a part of hers had he known about her sooner. Laramie Cooper was proving there were decent men out there. Just like her father.

Tears she couldn't contain any longer wet her cheeks. Why was she getting so emotional? Especially now? She blamed it on the fact that the man she'd fallen in love with three years ago, the man she'd thought was dead, was not only very much alive but was here, in her home, standing in front of her and accepting his child without any hesitation. Of course that didn't mean he wanted to renew a relationship with her or anything; she understood that. That was fine. The most important thing was that he wanted a relationship with his son.

"Hell, Bristol, you're crying over what I said? Just because I want to be a part of my child's life?" Laramie asked in an incredulous voice.

More tears she couldn't control flooded her eyes, and she saw both anger and confusion in his features. She wasn't handling this very well and now she had him thinking the complete opposite from what she was feeling.

"I need to get some tissue," she said, quickly getting up to go into her kitchen to grab a few. Moments later, when she returned, Laramie was standing in front of her Christmas tree with his back to her. His hands were shoved into the pockets of his jeans. She wondered if he'd noticed the ornaments. She doubted he would ever know how much she'd come to treasure them. How each time she looked at one she was reminded of Paris.

"Laramie?"

He turned around and met her gaze. She could tell from his stance and his brooding expression that he was still angry, even more so. She needed to explain and the only way she could do that was to tell him everything. "I think we need to sit down and talk."

The look in his dark, piercing eyes said that as far as he was concerned, there was nothing to talk about, but he nodded anyway. She took a seat on her sofa again, but he said, "I'd rather stand."

She wished he would sit down. Then she wouldn't have to stare up at him. Wouldn't have to notice just how well-built he still was. How sexy he looked in jeans and a leather jacket. And she wouldn't have to notice how his eyes were trained on her. But she said, "Okay, if you prefer standing."

The room was quiet but she was convinced she could hear the pounding of her heart. "I might have confused you about a few things, Laramie," she said. "I would like to explain and hope in the end you'll understand."

She paused before saying, "Growing up, I never knew my father. Other kids had daddies and I didn't understand why I didn't. It was just me and my mom. One day… I believe I was eight at the time… I asked her about it. I wanted to know where my daddy was. She got angry with me and said I didn't have a daddy, that I didn't need one and not to ever bring up the subject of a father again. Her words were final and I knew it."

Bristol picked up her teacup and took a sip although the tea had cooled. "It was only after my mother died when I was fifteen that I moved from Houston to—"

"You lived in Texas?"

"Yes. I was born in Houston and lived there until I was fifteen."

He nodded. "I'm a Texan, as well. I was born in Austin."

She nodded and then continued her story. "When Mom died, I moved here to New York to live with my aunt Dolly. She was my mother's only sibling."

Bristol took a breath and then continued, "It was only then that I got up enough courage to ask my aunt about my father. I knew nothing about him. I didn't even know his name. But Aunt Dolly did. However, my mother had sworn her to secrecy. According to my aunt, my father and mother dated while in high school in Dallas but he broke things off with my mom to pursue his dream of studying art in Paris. My aunt said he asked my mother to go with him, but she refused, saying she didn't want to live in another country."

"Your father was an artist, as well?" Laramie asked as he leaned against a bookcase.

"Yes." Now might have been a good time to tell him her father was the famous artist known as Rand, but she didn't. Her father's identity wasn't important to this story.

"Imagine how excited I was when I found that out. When I learned where my artistic abilities had come from. It also explained why my mother never wanted me to pursue my art. I guess me doing so reminded her of him. Once I found out who he was, I wanted to connect with the man I never knew. The man my mom had kept from me."

She took another sip of her tea. "According to my aunt, my mother never told my father she had gotten pregnant. He didn't know he had a daughter. The reason Mom kept it from him was because she resented him for choosing Paris over her."

She paused again before saying, "I convinced my aunt that I needed to see my father. To let him know I exist. She prepared me by saying that he might not want a child, that he might question if I was really his. Aunt Dolly didn't want me to get hurt. But I didn't care. I needed to meet him."

She recalled that time and how desperate she'd felt. "One of the men at my aunt's church was a detective with the NYPD. He tracked down my father and discovered he lived in Los Angeles. I made the call to my dad the morning of my sixteenth birthday. Aunt Dolly talked to him first, to break the ice and introduce me. Then she handed the phone to me."

"What did he say?"

No need to tell Laramie it had practically been the same

thing he'd said when she'd told him about their child. "He said that he believed I was his and that he wanted to see me. To prove that point, he flew out immediately. In fact, he knocked on my aunt's door in less than eight hours." She smiled. "That was the best birthday present ever."

She fought back the tears that threatened to fill her eyes again as she said, "On that day, I began what was the happiest two years of my life. He told me that he wrote my mother but she refused to write him back. His letters were returned. She stopped all communication between them. When he returned to Dallas from Paris that first year for the holidays, he'd tried finding my mother but no one knew where she had moved to. Later on, he met someone else. He was still married to that woman when we met. They had two young sons. None of his sons were interested in art and he was glad that I was. We discovered we had quite a lot in common."

"Was he upset that your mom kept your existence from him?"

"Yes, very much so. He saw that as wasted years. Years when I could have been spending time with him. We tried to do everything we could together during those two years because that was all we had."

A bemused look appeared on Laramie's face. "Why was that?"

She swallowed, feeling the lump in her throat. "Because, although I didn't know it, my father was dying of cancer."

She drew in a deep breath as she held Laramie's gaze. "So as you can see, my actions regarding you and my son were based on my own experiences with my dad. That's why I wrote to you as soon as I found out I was pregnant. I didn't want to make the same mistake my mother made. You had a right to know about him, even if you rejected him. It would have been your decision. Your loss."

He didn't say anything for a minute. "I'm sorry about your father."

"Me, too. But we got to spend two years together. He made me feel so loved. So very special. He even asked me to change my last name to his, and I did. He also asked if I would come spend my last two years in high school with him in California. That meant leaving Aunt Dolly and I was torn about doing that, but she was fine with it and encouraged me to go. Although she never said, I think he confided in her and told her he didn't have long to live."

"And nobody told you?"

"No. Very few people knew about his condition. In his final days, I saw him getting weak and asked him about it, but he said he'd caught some kind of a virus. He only told me the truth during his last days. That's when he told me what was wrong and if I ever needed anything to contact Colin Kusac, his close and trusted friend." There was no need to tell him how much her father's wife had resented her presence and how mean she'd been at the reading of her father's will.

"So you ended up in Paris to study like he had?"

"Yes. He made that possible before he died. He wanted me to study at the same art academy." She had worked at that café in Paris not because she had to, but because she had wanted to. Her father had taken care of her tuition as well as provided her with a generous monthly allowance. Then there had been the proceeds from her mother's insurance policies. She had put all the money in a savings account. While growing up, her mother had taught her the importance of being independent and not wasteful.

"I had a wonderful father. I just wish I'd had more time with him."

Laramie didn't say anything for a moment, then he asked, "Do you resent your mother for standing in the way of that happening?"

She drew in a deep breath. "Not now, but for years I did. She wanted to hurt my father by keeping my existence a secret from him. She knew him and had known he would have wanted to become a part of my life, but she never gave him that opportunity. In the end, she not only hurt him but she hurt me, as well. I could never do that to my child. That's why I would never stand in the way of you developing a relationship with Laramie. I know the pain and heartbreak it could cause."

The only noise in the room was the sound of the logs crackling in the fireplace. "Thanks for sharing that with me, Bristol."

Telling him the story of her parents and her relationship with her father had drained her. Slowly standing to her feet, she said, "Now that we've gotten that cleared up, what time would you like to come meet Laramie tomorrow?"

An anxious smile touched Laramie's lips. "How soon can I come?"

She chuckled. "Laramie is an early riser so I'm usually up preparing breakfast around eight. You're welcome to join us if you like."

"I would love to."

She glanced at her watch. It was late. Almost midnight. "Do you want me to call you a cab?"

"No, I should be able to get one on the corner."

"Okay." She walked him to the door and watched as he put on his Stetson, while thinking how much more cowboy than SEAL he looked at that moment. "I'll see you in the morning then."

"Yes. In the morning. Oh, by the way, does Laramie have a favorite toy?"

She shook her head. "No. Like most kids his age he likes stuffed animals. He does have this thing for airplanes and he likes to color so he has a ton of coloring books. For his birthday one of Ms. Charlotte's sons, who also has a two-year-old, gave Laramie an electronic tablet. I'm trying to teach him how to play educational games on it."

He nodded. "What kind of tablet is it?"

Bristol told him the brand. Her heart missed several beats when Laramie stood in front of her, holding her gaze. As if to get her mind off what she was feeling, she thought of something. "It might get confusing with you and Laramie having the same first names. Can I start calling you Coop, or is that name restricted to just your team members?"

"No, it's not restricted so that's no problem."

"Good."

He shoved his hands into his pockets. "If there's a change of plans or if you need me for anything, you can contact me at the Marriott Hotel in Times Square. I'd like for you to have my personal number," he said, pulling out his cell phone. "What's yours so I can call you? That way you can have it."

She rattled off her phone number and when she heard her phone ringing in the purse she'd placed on the table earlier, she said, "I got it."

He nodded. "Now you have mine and I have yours."

She dismissed any significant meaning to that. He was merely providing her his number because of Laramie. "Good night, Laramie... Coop. I am so glad you are alive."

He smiled. "Me, too."

He stood there for a second, staring at her, before saying, "Good night, Bristol. I'll see you in the morning."

He turned and quickly moved down the steps.

Laramie entered his hotel room, feeling a happiness he hadn't felt in a long time. In addition to that, a rush of adrenaline was pumping furiously through his veins. What were the chances of the one woman he thought he would never see again, the one woman he thought about often, the one woman who'd helped him retain his sanity while being held hostage, would be here? In New York? And that he would run into her?

Well, he hadn't exactly run into her, but the circumstances surrounding their chance encounter still seemed unreal. And not only had he found out he had a son tonight, but he'd seen him. What a feeling! It was exhilarating, and he couldn't wait to share it with the guys.

He glanced at his watch. It was late. Almost midnight. But he knew Bane, Viper, Mac and Flipper would be up. However, Bane had triplets and Mac had four kids Laramie didn't want to wake up. To be on the safe side, he would text the four to call him.

Laramie also knew he needed to contact his commanding officer to let him know he would be taking his military leave after all. He wondered what would have happened had he not been in New York tonight. No telling when his and Bristol's paths would have crossed, if ever. He'd already missed two years of his son's life and he didn't plan to miss any more.

At some point he also needed to call his parents to let them know they were grandparents. He wondered how they would feel about that. They'd never hinted one way or the other if they wanted grandchildren. They hadn't ever nagged him about settling down or marrying.

After sending the text off to the guys, he removed his jacket and hung it in the closet before the first call came in. He recognized the number as Bane's. "You okay, Coop?" Bane asked with deep concern in his voice.

"Yes, I'm fine. But I do have some news to share. Hold on, I hear another call coming in."

The others began calling and they connected to their conference number so they could all be on the phone at once. "Okay, Coop, what kind of news do you want to share with us?" Viper asked.

"Don't tell us the commander gave you another top secret job. Another cockatiel for you to deliver to some very important person?" Flipper teased.

"Maybe it will be a dog this time," Mac kidded. "Or maybe a pet monkey."

Laramie took their jokes in stride; nothing could put a damper on his mood. "I ran into Bristol Lockett here in New York."

"Bristol Lockett? That woman we couldn't tear you away from in Paris three years ago?" Viper asked.

"If I recall," Bane said, "you went missing for three days because you were with her."

"And we couldn't wipe that damn smile off your face for almost a month," Mac interjected.

"So how was the reunion?" Flipper asked. "She still look good?"

"Yes, she's the same woman, Viper. I didn't know you were missing me so much during those three days, Bane. I don't recall smiling for almost a month, Mac. If I did, I had a good reason for it. And yes, Flipper, she still looks good and the reunion was great once she recovered from fainting."

"Why did she faint?" Bane asked.

Laramie settled down on the edge of the bed. "Bristol thought she was seeing a ghost. She'd assumed I was dead."

"Why would she assume that? Had she contacted your parents or something?" Viper asked.

"No. I never gave her any information about my family."

"Then why would she assume you were dead? No agency had the authority to release that information. Our mission in Syria was a top secret, highly classified covert operation," Mac said.

"Bristol tried writing to me and the letter was returned. She knew someone who had a friend at the State Department who told her I'd gotten killed in Syria."

"Someone breached classified information?" Flipper asked.

"The person who did it felt she needed to know. Like I said, she was trying to reach me."

"Why was she trying to reach you?" Viper asked.

Laramie paused before saying, "She wanted to let me know she'd gotten pregnant."

Everyone got quiet and Laramie knew why. They were trying to digest what he'd said. A smile touched his lips when he added, "Yes, what you're thinking is right. I have a child. A two-year-old son."

Nine

"Hungry, Mommy."

Standing at the stove while preparing breakfast, Bristol couldn't help but smile. Each morning her son woke up in a good mood. Hungry, but good. It didn't matter that he usually had a bedtime snack. He evidently slept that off every night.

"Mommy is almost done, Laramie. Please color me a picture."

"Okay."

She'd discovered early that Laramie liked marking up things, preferably with his crayon. When her walls became a target, she'd purchased him a coloring book. Now it was the norm for him to color her a picture in the book while he waited for breakfast. And since he was home with her every day, she used any free time she had to teach him things. He already knew his primary colors, how to count to ten and since she knew fluent French, she made that his second language by identifying things in both English and French. So far he was mastering both.

She had just finished cooking the eggs when the doorbell rang. Laramie ceased his chatter long enough to say, "Door, Mommy."

Wiping her hands on a kitchen towel, she turned and said, "Yes, I heard it." And from the way her heart was pounding in her chest, she knew who it was. Laramie… Coop. "I'll be back in a minute, sweetie."

Refusing to acknowledge the fact that she'd taken extra care with her looks this morning, she headed for the door. Coop was here to see Laramie and not her.

Before opening the door, she looked through the peephole. There was no way on earth she could dismiss just how incredibly handsome her son's father was. With his striking masculine looks she found it hard to believe some woman hadn't snatched him up by now. He'd said he wasn't married, but he didn't say whether or not there was a special woman in his life. She tried to push the thought out of her mind; it wasn't any of her business.

Their only connection, the only reason he was standing on her doorstep a little after eight in the morning, was Laramie. And from the looks of it, he was bearing gifts. She had a feeling her son would be getting an early visit from Santa.

Inhaling deeply, she opened the door. "Good morning, Coop."

Bristol looked even more beautiful in the daylight. Today her dark brown hair was flowing down her shoulders. And although she wasn't wearing lipstick, she'd put something on her lips to make them shine. Another thing different from last night was her outfit. Today she was wearing a pair of jeans and a pullover sweater. Was it a coincidence or had she remembered him once telling her that red was his favorite color?

The color really didn't matter because the woman standing in the doorway was too stunningly beautiful for words. He drew in a deep breath and pulled in her scent. She was wearing the same perfume from three years ago, from last night. He tried to keep memories of their holiday fling at bay so he could focus on their son. But then how could he, when the result of that fling was why he was here?

He recalled Mac's lecture. Mac, being the oldest of the group and the one who'd been married the longest, had given him advice last night. If Laramie's only interest in Bristol was his son, then he needed to make that point clear up front. Mac had known a lot of men who hadn't. Because of that, the women in those relationships assumed romance and the baby were a package deal.

As he tried to regain control of his senses, it occurred to Coop that while he'd been checking Bristol out, she'd been doing the same with him. He cleared his throat. "Good morning, Bristol. I hope I'm not too early."

"No, your timing is fine," she said, stepping aside to let him in. "I just finished cooking breakfast. I hope you're hungry."

Boy, was he ever, and it had nothing to do with food. The moment she'd opened the door, he'd felt it. The sizzle of attraction had been bad enough outside, but now, within the cozy confines of her home, it was stronger than ever. Did she feel it, too?

"Yes, I'm hungry."

He couldn't recall ever being swept away by a woman except for once in his life. And she had been that woman.

"Good, because I've made plenty. Laramie is up and as usual for this time of morning, he's in a good mood."

"Is he ever in a bad mood?" he asked, placing the gift-wrapped packages on her sofa.

She smiled and he wished that smile didn't cause a stir-ring in his gut. "Yes, whenever he's sleepy and tries like the dickens to fight it. That's when he becomes cranky."

She took in the numerous gifts he'd brought. "Looks like you went shopping."

He smiled. "I did. I was there when the gift shop at the hotel opened. I plan to do more shopping later today. It's hard to believe Christmas is in less than two weeks."

"Yes, it is."

They reached the kitchen and Coop stopped dead in his tracks. The little boy sitting at the table staring at him was a miniature of himself. The emotions he'd felt when he'd seen his son last night came back to hit him tenfold. Ms. Charlotte and Bristol were right. His son resembled him so much it was uncanny.

They shared the same skin tone, eye color and shape of nose, lips and ears. And then there was that mop of thick curly hair. Although Coop wore his hair cut low now due to military regulations, for years he'd worn it long, even during his teen years. His parents hadn't had a problem with it as long as he kept it looking neat. And he could tell, even though his son was sitting down, that he was taller than most two-year-olds. But then Cooper men were tall. He was six foot two and so was his father. His grandfathers on both sides had been six foot three.

"Who's that?" Laramie asked his mother loudly, pointing at Coop.

"It's not nice to point, Laramie." The little boy put his finger down but kept an I-am-sizing-you-up look on his little face.

"Laramie, this is your daddy. Can you say Daddy?"

"Daddy?" his son asked his mother, as if for clarification.

"Yes, Daddy."

The little boy nodded, looked back over at Coop and said, "Daddy."

Coop's heart missed a beat at hearing his son call him

that for the first time. He watched as Laramie began waving his hand, and then said, "Hi, Daddy."

Coop waved back. "Hi, Laramie."

And then as if Coop was being dismissed, Laramie picked up a crayon and began coloring in the book in front of him.

"You can go ahead and sit down, Coop."

Laramie snatched his head back up and scrunched up his face and said, "He Daddy, Mommy. Not Coop."

Bristol smiled. "You, and only you, can call him Daddy. I can call him Coop. You call him Daddy. Understand?"

Laramie nodded his head up and down. "Yes, Mommy."

Then to explain further she said, "I can also call him Laramie."

Laramie's face scrunched up again. "But that's me."

"Yes, but his name is Laramie, too."

Laramie then looked at his daddy. "You got my name?" he asked.

Coop decided not to say it was the other way around. Instead he would let Bristol handle this since she seemed to know how much their son could understand. "Yes, I have your name."

"But Mommy calls him Coop so he'll know when I am talking to him and not to you. Okay?"

Laramie nodded. "Okay." He then went back to coloring in his book.

Coop moved to the table and sat down. That got his son's attention again. Laramie looked over at him and with a stern face asked, "Clean hands, Daddy?" And to show what he meant, he held his hands out in front of him. "My hands clean."

"Oh." Coop got the message and glanced over at Bristol. "Where can I wash my hands?"

He could tell she was fighting back a smile when she said, "There's a bathroom right off the living room."

He stood. "Thanks." He headed to the bathroom to wash his hands. He had a feeling his two-year old son planned to keep him on his toes.

"Be still my hormones," Bristol muttered under her breath as she watched Coop leave the kitchen and head for the bathroom. Today he was wearing a pair of khakis and a pullover brown sweater. She was convinced that no matter what he put on his body, he was the epitome of sexy. There wasn't a single thing about him that didn't start her heart fluttering and send her female senses into overdrive. Then there was that self-assured walk he'd mastered. The man was true masculinity on legs.

"Daddy gone?"

She glanced over at her son as she placed the plates on the table. Was that sadness she saw in his little eyes? Of course, she had to be imagining things since Laramie had just met Coop. He couldn't have gotten attached already. She'd known Laramie would like Coop since he liked everybody.

"No, Daddy went to wash his hands."

Laramie nodded and then said, "Good." He then added, "Me got clean hands, Mommy." And just like he'd done for Coop, as proof of how clean they were, he held them out and flipped them over a few times.

She smiled and said, "Yes, you have clean hands, Laramie."

At that moment Coop returned and sat back down at the table. "Daddy back," Laramie said, smiling.

Coop returned his son's smile. "Yes, Daddy's back."

"Daddy, want to play some more?"

Coop, who was stretched on the floor, wondered how one little boy could have so much energy. He glanced at his watch. It was almost noon. Had he been here nearly four hours already? Breakfast had been delicious and he'd discovered just what a great cook Bristol was. When he'd complimented her she credited her aunt for making sure her culinary skills were up to par before she'd left New York to live in Paris.

After breakfast he helped Bristol tidy up the kitchen, although she'd said his help was unnecessary. But he'd wanted to help. Laramie had sat at the kitchen table, ignoring them while he colored.

Afterward they had gone to the living room. They'd placed most of the presents under the tree but there had been a few he'd let his son open now. Namely, more coloring books. To give him time alone with Laramie, Bristol had gone upstairs to her studio and closed the door. He felt good knowing she trusted him to take care of Laramie.

For a two-year old, his son was pretty darn smart. He spoke in understandable sentences and even knew how to speak French. During breakfast Bristol would lapse into French with Laramie. Coop appreciated that fact since he himself spoke several different languages, including French, and he enjoyed conversing with them in the language.

"Play games, Daddy."

Coop pulled himself up and looked at Laramie. He knew that his son didn't know the true meaning of the word *daddy*. To him it was just a name, but Coop hoped when Laramie got older it would come to mean a lot more. He wouldn't be around his son 24/7 because of the nature of his work as a SEAL. But he would be with him every chance he got.

That meant after every mission, he would head to New York. It no longer mattered that he liked California's weather better. His son was in New York and that's where he intended to be.

"He hasn't worn you out yet?"

He glanced up and saw a smiling Bristol standing in the entryway to her living room. He chuckled. "No, not yet."

"Well, you get a break since it's lunchtime."

As if Bristol had said a magic word, Laramie jumped up off the floor. "Lunch, Mommy?"

"Yes, Laramie. Lunch."

He was about to race for the kitchen when Coop stopped him and asked, "Clean hands?"

Laramie's small eyes widened. He then looked down at his hands. "No."

Coop nodded. "Come on, let's wash our hands."

Bristol watched them go, walking side by side. Father and son. It was a vision she'd thought she would never see, and seeing it now pulled at her heart. She recalled the telephone call she'd made to Dionne last night, to let her know Laramie was alive. It had taken her a full hour to tell her best friend everything, including how she'd fainted.

Then Dionne had asked her some tough questions. Namely, how she felt about Laramie and if she still loved him. Bristol had to explain that of course she still loved him but now her fears were greater than ever. She had taken news of his death hard and the grief had been so deep she'd sworn never to get that attached to another person again. It seemed all those she loved eventually died. Her mother. Her father. Her aunt Dolly. Was that why she was sometimes overprotective with her son? At least Margie thought that she was.

The work Coop did was dangerous. He risked his life constantly. Most of the time his whereabouts were unknown because the nature of his work was highly classified. There was no way she could make such a person a permanent part of her life. She couldn't imagine going through that sort of grief again. He'd beaten death once but the next time he might not be so lucky.

Dionne had asked Bristol the one question she couldn't answer. How could a woman stop loving a man like Coop?

She had no idea but she was determined to find out. She and Coop hadn't had a chance to sit down and talk, other than the discussion they'd had last night. She had no idea how long he would be in New York or what his plans were while he was here. He had said he wanted to spend as much time with Laramie as he could, and she didn't have a problem with that. She wanted her son to get to know his father.

She needed to get to know him, too. There was a lot of personal information about Coop that she wasn't privy to. She'd just learned last night that he was born in Texas. He rarely spoke of his parents but she knew they were alive. At least they had been alive three years ago.

"Mommy, hands clean now."

Coop and Laramie had returned. Now he was sitting high on Coop's shoulders with a huge grin on his face. "Okay, then, let's head into the kitchen for lunch."

Coop put Laramie down and as soon as his little feet touched the floor he took off toward the kitchen. He paused at the kitchen door long enough to look over his shoulder to say, "Come on, Mommy. Come on, Daddy. Laramie is hungry."

Coop burst out laughing as he walked beside her. "Did I imagine it or did he eat a huge breakfast a few hours ago?"

She chuckled. "No, you didn't imagine it. You'll find out just how much food he consumes. You'll never guess how much I spend on groceries."

He stopped walking and touched her arm. She couldn't contain the surge of sensations that settled in the middle of her stomach from his touch. "I will help you with that."

She shook her head. "Thanks, but I don't need your help. I told you last night that I don't want anything from you and I meant it." All she wanted was for him to have a relationship with his son.

"I don't agree with that."

She frowned, detecting his anger.

"We'll discuss this later, Coop. When Laramie takes his nap."

Coop nodded. "Okay. Do you need help with lunch? I can fix a mean peanut butter and jelly sandwich."

"No, thanks, I've got it covered. Today it's tuna sandwich and chips. He loves anything with seafood."

"So do I."

Bristol wondered if it would be the same way with Coop and Laramie as it was with her and her father. They had discovered so many similarities. She headed for the refrigerator, trying not to notice Coop's sexy walk as he moved to the table, where Laramie was already seated. She couldn't push to the back of her mind how he'd looked stretched out on her living room floor with Laramie. He had made himself at home and removed his sweater. No man had a right to such a sexy chest covered only by a T-shirt. She knew SEALs stayed fit, but he seemed to be working overtime doing so. And she tried not to think about how comfortable it felt having him here in her home with them. It was as if he belonged.

Air was nearly snatched from her lungs at the thought. How could she even think such a thing? There was no way Coop could be a permanent fixture in their lives. At least not hers. He was only here because of Laramie. Had there been more between them, he wouldn't have just stumbled across her the way he had. He would have looked for her after his rescue. But he hadn't. That reinforced her assumption that their holiday fling had been just that, a fling. Afterward he had moved on and not looked back. She knew she'd been out of sight and out of mind. He hadn't expected or probably hadn't wanted to ever see her again.

Like she told him, they would talk when she put Laramie to bed for his nap. There was a lot she and Coop needed to discuss. She had to reiterate that she wanted nothing from him. Hopefully, that would put him at ease that she wasn't going to hit him up for child support payments. However, she had a feeling he would want to pay them anyway, just because of the responsible person he was.

But she didn't intend to let him.

They also had to talk about her fake marriage to him. They needed to resolve that. Yes, she thought, as she began pulling the items out of the refrigerator for lunch. They definitely needed to talk.

Ten

Coop would be the first to admit that he'd been somewhat nervous upon arriving this morning, not sure of how his son would react to him. So far things were going great and he knew he had Bristol to thank for that.

As he settled back on the sofa, he thought about what she'd told him about her childhood. Specifically, growing up without knowing her father. And then only getting to spend a couple of years with him before he'd died.

After hearing her story, he wasn't sure what was worse. Having parents who were bitter toward each other or having parents like his who were obsessively into each other. If he had to choose, it would be the parents who were obsessively into each other. As far as he was concerned, her mother's resentment, bitterness and anger had only hurt Bristol. It was sad how one person's decision could change the lives of so many. He was glad Bristol had learned from her mother's mistake.

He couldn't help but smile when he remembered lunch. Laramie had cleaned his plate in record time. More than once, Bristol had to tell him to slow down so his food could digest. Coop hadn't been sure if Laramie knew what that meant until the boy began taking smaller bites of his sandwich.

It was obvious Bristol and Laramie had a routine. He hadn't put up a fuss when she'd mentioned it was time for his nap. Instead, he'd waved goodbye to Coop. But not before he'd asked if Coop would be there when he woke up. Before Coop could answer, Bristol had told Laramie not to expect him to be there because he had things to do. Was that her way of letting Coop know he was wearing out his welcome?

Hell, he hoped not. He'd placed a call to his commanding officer letting him know that he would be taking his holiday leave and would remain in the New York area. Like he'd told Bristol last night... He planned to spend as much time with his son as he could.

"I think he was asleep before his head hit the pillow. What did you do to tire him out?" Bristol asked, grinning as she returned to the living room.

He looked at her and thought those jeans she wore definitely displayed all her curves. Not all women could wear jeans and exude that kind of effect on a man. The kind that could shoot his libido into overdrive. The kind that made him remember, whether he wanted to or not, how things had been between them in Paris. How easily they'd connected. How insatiable their hunger for each other had been.

With effort, he brought his mind back to the conversation. Coop smiled. "He wanted to play hide-and-seek."

"Oops. I should have warned you about that."

In a way, Coop wished she had. Then he would have given his son restrictions about not hiding in certain areas. Coop hadn't set any rules, and Laramie had found a good place to conceal himself in his mommy's bedroom. He hadn't felt comfortable going into Bristol's room but since she'd left the door open he had seen enough to know it was neat as a pin and decorated in colors of mauve and gray.

And he had seen her bed.

It was the same one she'd had in Paris. Seeing that bed had made him recall everything they'd done and how they'd done it. It also made him realize that his son was conceived in that bed. Or it could have been the time he'd taken her against the refrigerator.

"How many times did you find him?"

Bristol's question interrupted his reverie. "Every single time."

No need to tell her that he'd had to coax Laramie out of his hiding place in her bedroom so he wouldn't have to go in there looking for him. That hadn't been easy. A promise to take him to the park one day soon cinched it.

He watched Bristol sit down on the chair and somehow she did it in a way that was a turn-on. He inhaled deeply, remembering for the umpteenth time that Bristol was off-limits. His presence here had nothing to do with her but everything to do with their son. No matter how many good memories he had of them together, no matter how hard he'd tried to find her in Paris, and no matter how attracted he was to her now, the bottom line was that Laramie was his focus.

A relationship with his son was the only thing that mattered. That meant he and Bristol needed to talk about a few subjects they'd skirted around.

Deciding not to beat around the bush, he said, "So let's talk, Bristol."

He could tell she was nervous. But whatever they discussed would be with the intent of putting their son's needs before their own. Unfortunately, Coop had plenty of needs.

He hadn't bedded a woman since his last assignment nearly eight months ago. No particular reason he hadn't done so other than the fact he'd been too busy trying to hire more men to help run the ranch in Laredo that he'd inherited from his grandparents.

Cooper's Bend was his favorite place in all the world and when he retired from being a SEAL, he planned to move there and make it his permanent home. He could retire after his twenty years with the military, which was what he planned to do. He had less than ten years left. Six more to be exact, since he'd entered the military at eighteen and could officially retire at thirty-eight. Then he would become the full-time rancher his grandfather had been. In the meantime, he had a good group of people running the place and went there from time to time to check on things.

It might be a good idea for him to consider moving there now. That would eliminate his need to find housing in San Diego to accommodate him and Laramie. The ranch, which sat on over six-hundred acres, was plenty big. He would love for Laramie to visit him at the ranch that held so many wonderful childhood memories for him. Hell, when his son got older, he could have his own horse.

"Yes, I think we need to cover a few things and come to an agreement," Bristol said, interrupting his thoughts.

"Okay. What do you want to cover?" he asked her.

She paused and then said, "I meant what I said about not needing anything from you where Laramie is concerned."

Already Coop knew that wouldn't fly. "I can't agree to that because Laramie is my responsibility, too. A responsibility I take seriously."

She opened her mouth to argue the point and he held up his hand to stop her. "Not negotiable, Bristol. It doesn't matter if you're able to take care of him yourself. What sort of man would I be if I didn't contribute to the welfare of my child?"

She didn't say anything and broke eye contact with him to gaze down at the floor. He knew she was thinking, probably of a way to counter what he'd said. As far as he was concerned she could think all she wanted, he wouldn't change his mind. As the only grandchild, he had inherited trust funds from both sets of grandparents. Also, his parents had established an endowment for him that he'd been eligible for when he'd turned thirty. He was yet to touch any one of them. In addition to all that money and the ranch, he was heir to RCC Manufacturing, Inc., a corporation founded by his parents over thirty-five years ago upon their graduation from Harvard. Considering all of that, there was no way in hell he would not contribute to his son's upbringing. In fact, he'd already left a message with his attorney to contact him. He intended to list Laramie's name on all his legal documents as his heir.

"I think we should compromise," she finally said.

He lifted a brow. "Compromise how?"

"You can provide for his future, such as setting up a college fund. I'll take care of any expenses for his well-being now."

Coop shook his head. "No. I still won't agree to that. I want to provide for my child's present and his future."

A frown marred her features. "Why are you being difficult?"

He returned her frown. "Why are you? Most men who father a child and are separated from them are required to pay child support."

"But usually only until they are eighteen. All I'm doing is asking you to start the support at eighteen."

He had news for her. He intended to take care of his child for the rest of his life. The trust funds he planned to establish for Laramie would assure that. The age of eighteen had nothing to do with it. He couldn't believe he was even having this conversation with her. Most women would want his monetary offering. Was he missing something here? "Can I ask you something?"

She nodded slowly, almost reluctantly, before saying, "Yes."

"You said you only met your father at sixteen. I don't

know anything about him, but did he wait until you were eighteen to begin providing for you?"

She stiffened. "He paid my entire tuition at the art school in Paris."

Cooper figured tuition at that school hadn't been cheap. "That's all he did? He actually waited until you were eighteen before doing anything?"

"Of course not."

"Then why would you expect me to? Evidently being an artist has you rolling in dough since you feel you don't need my help. That might be all well and good for you, but not for me. For me it's the principle of the thing. It's about doing my share in providing for a child I helped to create. So please don't ask me to consider doing otherwise."

Bristol's gaze held Coop's and she could tell from the determined look in his eyes that he would not back down on this. She wasn't privy to his income as a SEAL but she was certain he could use his money for better things…

Like what?

She drew in a deep breath when she suddenly accepted something. It was apparent that as far as Coop was concerned, nothing was better than taking care of his son. For Coop, it wasn't about the money. It was about taking care of his own. She'd gotten the impression three years ago that he wasn't extremely close to his family. But what she'd failed to realize was that her son was now his family and he wanted to not only be there for him but also contribute toward his well-being. For Coop, the contribution was essential. She got that now.

He'd been saying it all along, so why hadn't she been listening? Probably because, like her mother, she was determined to be independent and not depend on anyone for anything. She didn't have a problem with Coop being a part of his son's life physically, but she was trying to stop him from being a part of Laramie's life financially. Most men would have jumped at the chance to get out of paying some form of child support. But Coop wasn't one of those men.

Neither was her father.

And Coop was right. Randall Lockett hadn't waited until her eighteenth birthday to be a father to her. He'd immediately stepped in and, like a whirlwind, he'd changed her last name to his, bestowing upon her all the rights of being his offspring. He had taken her under his roof, adding her to his household.

She had enjoyed living with him in Los Angeles, even if it had meant moving out west, attending another school and making new friends. To her it had been worth it just to spend time with her father. He'd made sure she hadn't gone without anything. But the most important thing was the time they'd spent together. Nothing else mattered. Not the closet filled with new clothes, the private school or the international vacations. Not even the new sports car he'd given her.

"Okay, Coop," she finally said.

"Okay, what?"

She released a deep sigh. "Okay, we will share in the cost of raising Laramie."

"You don't have to sound so overjoyed about it."

She narrowed her gaze at him before she saw his lips tilt into a smile. He'd been teasing. Releasing another sigh, she said, "I'm not trying to be difficult, Coop. But when I had Laramie I knew he would be my entire world and that I would be the one he would depend on for everything. I thought you were dead. For the past two years, I've made it work. There hasn't been a decision I made without considering him. Even when I decided to quit my position with that magazine publisher to become an artist full-time. I'm doing okay financially."

No need to tell him about the ridiculously high commissions she received every month from her father's art. "I was raised by a single mother who worked hard and made sure we didn't waste money on frivolous things. I knew the difference between getting the things I really needed and denying myself those things I wanted that weren't essential."

She didn't say anything for a brief moment then added, "The reason I suggested you handle Laramie's future is because I think that's what upset my father the most with my mother...besides her keeping my existence from him. Knowing she hadn't adequately prepared for my future. I had to explain to him that it hadn't been her fault since there was no extra money to set up a college savings account for me. Mom was a teacher, not a six-figure-salary engineer. She had student loans to pay back. But still, we lived in a nice house in a good neighborhood. I thought we lived pretty good."

She smiled. "Mom said we were a team and always would be one. I was happy. I was content. At the time. I really didn't think of life being any better. It was years later that I found out just how complicated life could be."

Coop nodded. "Our son's financial well-being is something you don't have to worry yourself with anymore because I'm here to help." He leaned forward and rested his arms on his thighs. "There is that other item we need to discuss before I leave today, Bristol."

She lifted a brow. "What other item?"

He held her gaze. "The issue of our fake marriage."

Eleven

Coop could tell from the look in Bristol's eyes that she'd forgotten about that complication. That was unfortunate for her, since he clearly remembered. A woman claiming to be your wife was something that pretty much got stuck in your mind.

"I told you why I did it," she said in a defensive tone.

He leaned forward. "Yes, you did. But that doesn't mean we don't need to talk about it. Spinning that tale might have been okay when you assumed I was dead, but as you can see, Bristol, I'm very much alive."

When she didn't say anything, he asked, "What do you think we should do?"

She shrugged. "Why do we have to do anything? It's not as if anyone knows the truth but my best friend, Dionne, and her husband, Mark, who was working for the judge at the time."

"It's a lie, Bristol. And one thing about a lie, it can come back to haunt you when you least expect it."

She stood and began pacing. He watched her, trying to keep his mind on the issue at hand, but found it difficult to do so. Especially when her body was in motion. He should be noticing the sound of the wooden floor creaking beneath her feet or the way her hair brushed against her shoulders as she moved. However, he wasn't attuned to either of those things. Instead his total concentration was on her body. A body he remembered so well.

Coop couldn't watch her move those jeans-clad thighs without recalling a time he'd been between them. Recollecting a time when he'd tasted her. Touched her all over. He was so damn aware of every damn inch of her.

She suddenly stopped pacing and looked over at him. Why? Had she detected him staring? Should he sit there and pretend he hadn't been? He doubted he could, even if he wanted to. That would be trying to do the impossible where she was concerned.

"What do you suggest?" she then asked him.

Right now he thought about suggesting they go upstairs to her bedroom and get it on. Rekindle those days in Paris, if for no other reason than to prove he hadn't imagined it, that it had been as good as he'd remembered.

"There are only two options, Bristol. Either we pretend to get a divorce to end the fake marriage or we make the marriage real."

She came and sat back down. "There's absolutely no reason to make the marriage real, so getting a pretend divorce sounds good to me. All that involves is us saying we're getting a divorce. No paperwork needed." A huge smile touched her lips. "Great! That was an easy solution."

"Not quite."

She lifted a brow. "And why not?"

The muscles in his jaw tightened. "Because in the end you'll emerge smelling like a rose, but I'll be the scumbag. A man who deserted his wife and child for nearly two years, and then who turns around and divorces her."

His harsh description had her lifting a brow, which

meant she knew he didn't appreciate the position she was placing him in. "But I told you why I did it," she said.

"And now you want to take the easy way out."

Coop wondered why he was taunting her, especially when he truly didn't give a royal damn what people thought. They didn't know him. No, it wasn't the people he was concerned about. It was his son. When Laramie grew into manhood, what story would he hear about and believe? No matter how much quality time Coop would spend with his son, he ran the risk of Laramie one day wondering why he hadn't been there for them when it mattered the most. Hadn't Bristol said she'd wondered about it when she didn't know the real deal with her own father?

And, if he was honest, there was another reason he was suddenly thinking this way. It was about those memories he just couldn't shake. It was his attraction to Bristol that had been there from the start. This deep sexual chemistry they'd given in to in Paris.

He'd always prided himself on being a person who exuded total control. His SEAL friends often referred to him as the quiet storm. There was a coolness about him. Always calm. Always composed. Levelheaded to a fault. And beneath all that equanimity, he was watching, waiting, always on the lookout for the unknown. Considering the possibilities while fighting off the restlessness. But when he was provoked, all bets were off and he would kick ass like the best of them. Even more so. When pushed into a corner, he came out fighting.

What if at some point down the road Bristol met someone and decided to marry? How would that impact his relationship with his son? Would he have to stand in line for his son's attention? His affection? Was there a way to assure that didn't happen? Was he being a selfish bastard for wanting to make sure it never did?

"Coop?"

He blinked. Had he been staring at her while all those crazy thoughts rushed through his brain? And were they crazy? His steady gaze held hers. No, they weren't crazy. Irrational, yes. Crazy, no. There was a difference.

When she said his name again he answered, "Yes?"

"Are you okay?"

Now, that was a good question. Was he? To her he said, "I just realized how little we know of each other. How very little information was exchanged between us in Paris."

"We didn't do much talking," she blurted out. From the look on her face he knew she hadn't meant to say that. It didn't matter since what she'd said was true. Her hormones and his testosterone had been working overtime and the only thing they'd wanted to do was assuage the desire flowing between them. He hadn't wanted to know anything about her and she hadn't wanted to know anything about him. For those three days, pleasure had been the name of the game and they'd played it well.

"No, we didn't," he said. "And now we have a son to show for it. I want to get to know you."

"Why?"

"Because you are the mother of my child and there is a lot I don't know."

She lifted a chin. "Don't sweat it. The only thing you truly need to know is that I love him, will always take care of him and put his interests first."

He wondered if that was really all he needed to know. Maybe. Then maybe not. It had been one thing to arrive in New York a few days ago without a care in the world. His only thought had been how soon he could return to California. Now things had changed. He had a son. A real flesh-and-blood son. He also had a fake wife, who was the one woman he desired most. He could admit that no other woman had ignited his passion as quickly and as easily as Bristol.

Thoughts of her had sustained him. He recalled every single time he had touched her. How he had touched her. He remembered tasting her and how she'd tasted. How it felt to experience heaven while inside her. Their bodies locked together and hurtling into one orgasm after another.

"I'm not sure that's the only thing I need to know, Bristol," he said, finally addressing her earlier statement. "I need to know you."

She frowned. "No, you don't."

"Yes, I do. And you need to know me. Laramie needs to know me. He has grandparents that he needs to get to know and vice versa."

"I have no problem with that."

No, she might not. But would everything be on her terms? What if that guy Culpepper decided to come back around sniffing behind her the minute Coop was gone? His mouth pressed into a hard line at the thought.

"Can I ask you something, Coop?"

He looked over at her. "Yes."

"How do you feel about having a son? One you didn't know you had?"

He thought about her question, wanting to answer as honestly as he could. "I always liked kids well enough, Bristol. I get along fine with Mac's four. They call me Uncle Coop and all. But to be quite honest with you, I never intended to have any of my own because marriage wasn't on my radar. And having one out of wedlock was something I never intended to do. But now he's here. I've seen him and knowing he's mine and that you and I made him is so overwhelming. It's caused emotions I didn't think were possible to feel. It's not just about me anymore. Now it's about my child and you."

He saw the frown that touched her lips. "You don't need to concern yourself with me, Coop."

Boy, was she wrong about that. As far as he was concerned, she and his son were a package deal. The kind Mac had warned him about. But them being a package deal was Coop's choice, since it obviously wasn't hers. Nevertheless, he knew better than to try to convince her just yet. They would finish their conversation regarding their fake marriage later.

"When can I come back?"

"You're always welcome here, Coop. You're Laramie's father and like I told you, I would never keep you from sharing a relationship with him."

However, if she were to marry one day, a future husband might. He'd heard stories from Flipper about how one of his brothers had to constantly take his ex-wife to court for visitation rights. Just because this guy she'd married hadn't felt comfortable with Flipper's brother coming around whenever he'd wanted to see his daughter.

Coop didn't want to deal with that kind of problem. "I'd like to take you and Laramie to dinner tonight," he said.

"Dinner?"

"Yes, dinner. Is that a problem?"

"No, but other than McDonald's, I've never taken Laramie out to eat."

He liked the idea that his son's first time going to a restaurant would be with him. "There's a first time for everything, don't you think?"

Bristol recalled another time he'd told her that. It had been in Paris after he'd stripped her naked and she'd told him that no other man had been in her apartment before.

"So will you and Laramie have dinner with me tonight?"

"Where?"

"You pick the place."

She drew in a deep breath. Maybe going out to dinner wouldn't be so bad. "Laramie loves spaghetti and there's an Italian restaurant not far from here."

"I happen to like spaghetti, too, so that will work for me, if it works for you," he said.

"It will work for me if it's early. I need to have Laramie back here with a bath and into his pajamas no later than eight."

He nodded. "Will reservations at five o'clock be okay?"

"Yes. That's the time he usually eats dinner anyway."

Bristol was wondering why on earth she was paying so much attention to Coop's mouth when they should be figuring out details regarding Laramie. Why was she paying so much attention to his captivating eyes? To his masculine body? She saw men all the time but had never focused on any of those things. Why him? She knew the answer. Mainly because she knew how that mouth felt connected to hers.

She knew how it felt to be held within the scope of those eyes while desire streamed through her. And she knew all about that masculine body. How it felt to be beneath it. To feel the weight of it on her. To feel him inside her. Her breathing became choppy and she forced her gaze away from him.

"Are you okay, Bristol?"

Was she? She wanted to think she was, but honestly she wasn't sure. He'd been the last man she had slept with and now all those hot, delicious and wanton thoughts were trying to take over her senses. They really hadn't finished figuring out how to end their fake marriage. For some reason, she found the discussion draining and really didn't want to go back to it right now. There was no doubt in her mind he would bring it back up again.

However, there was something that had been on her mind since last night that she did want to discuss. "I'm fine, Coop, but there is something I've been wondering about."

"What?"

"Your friends. Those four guys I met who were with you in Paris. Mac, Bane, Viper and Flipper. Are they okay?"

A smile touched his lips. "Yes, they're okay. I'm surprised you remembered them."

"They were nice and—" she said, chuckling "—unforgettable. I liked them. I often wondered if they had gotten captured with you and if they'd lost their lives."

"No, in fact they were part of the team that rescued me. If you recall, Mac was married when you met him. He and his wife are doing fine. Bane and his estranged wife renewed their vows and Viper is married now."

"He is?"

"Yes, and happily so. Reminds us of that every chance he gets. Flipper is still Flipper. Happy-go-lucky and cheerfully single. Bane and his wife had triplets this year, almost six months ago."

"Triplets?"

"Yes. Two boys and a girl. They want a huge family so I guess you can say they're off to a good start."

"I'm glad they're all okay. When I got word that you'd been killed, I wondered about them. I take it the five of you are still close friends."

"Yes, and we're closer than ever. Even while I was being held hostage a part of me believed they would find me and get me out. And they did. We stay in contact even when we're not on a mission. I talked to them just last night and told them I had seen you."

"You did?"

"Yes. They remembered you, as well. I also told them I had a son. They're happy for me."

"Even though fatherhood wasn't anything you asked for?"

"Doesn't matter. I used a condom. Close to a dozen if you recall. Evidently one was defective. I regret that." He paused and then said, "But under no circumstances do I regret Laramie."

She nodded. "Neither do I."

He inclined his head and looked at her. Under his close scrutiny she was tempted to cross her arms over her chest. She could feel her nipples hardening. "I keep thinking that things could have been different. You could have made another decision and not had him," he said.

She knew what he was hinting at. "Not having him wasn't an option for me. I admit becoming a mother was the last thing on my mind, but when I found out I was pregnant I knew I would keep my baby. When I mailed that letter to you, I had no idea how you would respond. It really didn't matter. I was doing what I thought was the right thing by letting you know. I was prepared to go solo regardless."

"And now you don't have to because I'm here."

For how long? she wondered. He was still a navy SEAL and could get called away on a mission at any time. A mission he might not return from. She'd already had to deal with news of him dying once; there was no way she could go through it again. That meant she had to fall out of love with him. But how could she do that?

He had made it pretty clear that he wanted to see Laramie as often as he could. So she'd be seeing him often, too. In that case, how could she begin the process of removing him from her heart? There had to be a way and she was determined to find it. She had lost her mother, her father and her aunt. The three most important people in her life were gone. Now she had Laramie. She lived for her son and that would be enough.

"I'll leave now so you can get some things done while Laramie is taking his nap. I'll be back around four-thirty."

"All right."

She moved to walk him to the door, but he just stood

there. Staring at her. More specifically, his gaze was fix-ated on her mouth. She saw it. Felt it. Her lips suddenly felt warm. Sensitive.

She knew she should turn away so her mouth wouldn't be the object of his focus. But the truth was, she couldn't. His assessing gaze was getting to her, and she couldn't do a single thing about it.

Bristol knew what he planned the moment he took a step in her direction but she didn't back up. She couldn't. It was as if she was rooted in place. Then he was stand-ing directly in front of her. His eyes penetrating hers. His features fierce.

"I thought about you a lot, Bristol. During those eleven months while being held hostage."

His words made her heart flip several times. He had thought about her? "You did?"

"Yes. Thinking of you kept me sane…especially dur-ing those times I was being tortured," he told her quietly.

Oh, God! Tortured? There was an intense searing in the pit of her stomach. She couldn't imagine what he'd endured.

"I would close my eyes and remember each and every time I made love to you. Every single time I kissed you. We shared a lot of kisses over those three days."

Yes, they had. They'd shared a lot of things, includ-ing their bodies. He hadn't been the only one who'd re-membered, although her situation hadn't been as difficult as his by any stretch of the imagination. Every time her child, their child, had kicked or moved within her womb, she would think of him. Mourn him. Grieve for him. She would also thank him for giving her his child.

"I need to kiss you," he said in a husky tone, reclaim-ing her attention. "I need to kiss you as much as I need to breathe."

And she needed to kiss him, as well. That was the shock-ing truth. No matter how independent she wanted to be, she needed to kiss him. Her eyes were focused on his lips with the same intensity that his had been on hers. She needed to feel the heat of her body against his.

She was succumbing to everything male that he represented.

"As you wish," Bristol whispered. She was the one who made the first move, standing on tiptoe, leaning in close and placing her mouth against his.

Twelve

Coop wrapped his arms around her and took over the kiss. The moment their tongues touched, getting reacquainted in the most passionate way, liquid heat seemed to spread through, burning him from the inside out.

His body leaped to life. He was now a man very much aware and filled with a yearning so deep it ached. Yet at the same time the yearning calmed the beast within him. Made him accept that Bristol could affect him in ways no other woman could.

He hadn't counted on her kiss being as greedy as his, her need just as insurmountable. Their tongues were mating in ways that sent a crackle of energy escalating between them. From the very first, he'd known she was different. He just hadn't known what role she would eventually play in his life. He had no idea that one day she would become the mother of his child.

He had given more of himself to her than he had to any woman. Even now he felt a need for her in every cell, in every pore. How could she get under his skin this way? To the point where he confessed to thinking of her while being held captive. Remembering her while being in pain.

He'd never shared that much about one of his missions with anyone. There had been no one to tell. His parents hadn't wanted to hear the gory details. And he hadn't been able to open up to the psychiatrist the military had ordered him to see. Only his SEAL teammates had known the hell he'd gone through. And now Bristol knew. Not everything but enough.

They needed to come up for air, so he slowly ended the kiss, pulling his mouth away on a guttural moan. Still needing a connection, he used the tip of his tongue to lick her lips from corner to corner, before grazing his jaw against her ear.

He dropped his hands and couldn't recall at what point his fingers had become buried in her hair. Now it looked unruly. Sexy as hell. The sight of her kiss-swollen lips made him even more aware of how much he wanted her. Desire pulsed through him and he felt hard as a rock.

He took a step back, because otherwise he would be tempted to sweep her off her feet and carry her upstairs to that bedroom he'd refused to enter earlier. "I'll be back to get you and Laramie around four thirty."

And then he headed for the door. He came close to making it out without looking back. But temptation was too much. Overpowering. He stopped and glanced over his shoulder. Bristol was standing there looking more beautiful than any woman he'd ever seen. There was heat in her eyes.

A hungry throb stirred inside him and he drew in a wobbly breath before forcing himself out the door and closing it behind him.

Bristol released a breath before burying her face in her hands. What on earth had she done? What on earth had she started? That kiss had made her come unglued. No, she'd lost her composure long before that kiss. The intensity of

her sexual need had begun to affect her the moment Coop
had walked into her house that morning.

She could no more deny the carnal attraction between
them than she could refrain from breathing. And today,
just a few moments ago in her living room, they'd both unleashed pent-up, held-back desires. Her body knew him, desired him, ached for him. Closing her eyes, she felt a surge
of yearning trying to take over her senses again.

Opening her eyes, she refused to let it. At that moment
she heard her cell phone ring and wondered who was calling. Coop had her number. Would he be calling her? There
was no way he'd made it to the corner already. Maybe he'd
decided dinner wasn't a good idea after all and was cancel-
ing. If that was true then she agreed with him. Sitting in
a restaurant across from him might push temptation to a
new level. She wasn't certain if their son would be enough
of a buffer.

Pulling her phone out of the back pocket of her jeans,
Bristol saw the caller wasn't Coop but Margie. She quickly
clicked it on. "Yes, Margie?"

"You okay? You sound kind of breathless."

She swallowed. Did she? "I'm fine."

"I called to see how things turned out with your soon-
to-be ex."

Bristol frowned, confused. "My soon-to-be ex?"

"Yes. You can divorce him on the grounds of desertion,
you know. I can refer a good attorney you can use."

"Desertion?"

"Yes. At least that's what I call it. You thought he was
dead. Granted I understand the military made a mistake,
but if he had cared anything about you—even if he didn't
know about your son—you were his wife. He should have
moved heaven and earth to find you. Showing up now after
all this time won't cut it."

Bristol didn't like what Margie was saying. But then her

manager didn't know the whole story. "Laramie and I have things to work out."

"What's there to work out? I talked to Steven and he's concerned about a dead husband reappearing. But I explained things to calm him down. I told him it was all a mistake and you would send your ex packing in no time. I assured him that there was no way you would hook up with Laramie again."

Frissons of anger ignited in Bristol's spine. Margie was believing just what Coop said people would believe about him. And it was all her fault. Furthermore, who gave Margie the right to tell Steven anything?

"Look, Margie, I have to go." It was either end the call or end their relationship, Bristol was just that mad.

Her manager didn't say anything for a moment, then added, "You sound upset, Bristol, and I hope it's not with me but with him. I'm aware you loved your husband. And I can understand you having feelings for him now. But I hope you're not thinking about tossing aside a chance with Steven for a man who didn't come looking for you."

Bristol lost it. "I don't know how many times I have to tell you that I'm not interested in Steven. Now goodbye."

She then hung up the phone.

Coop released a deep sigh the moment his hotel room door closed behind him. What a day. It had started out with him enjoying breakfast with his son and then it had ended after lunch with him kissing Bristol like he couldn't get enough of tasting her mouth.

He licked his lips. He still hadn't.

He never knew a woman's taste could mess with your taste buds and block out your other senses. But he had found out today. He just didn't understand it. Once he'd returned to his team to hang out for New Year's, after spending those three days with her, he'd been fine. She hadn't totally consumed his mind.

But he had thought about her...

And he had thought about her even more while being held hostage, because when your thoughts were filled with orgasmic pleasure it could erase the pain. The more those bastards tried to break him, the more he'd thought about Bristol.

Was that why he was so consumed with her now? He had thought about her so much that the memories of the time they'd shared in Paris were now a part of him? He rubbed his hand down his face. Maybe he was thinking way too hard.

He was removing his jacket when his cell phone rang. He recognized the ring tone. It was Bane. He pulled his phone from his pocket, chuckled and said, "With triplets, don't you have more to do with your time these days?"

Bane laughed. "No. That's where the benefits of belonging to a large family kick in. Everyone wants to help out. There haven't been triplets in the family since Quade's babies and everyone's excited. I couldn't tell you the number of visitors we've had. And more of them are planning to visit for the holidays. I told the family about your son. They're ecstatic and want pictures, so I need you to text me a few. You know the routine so get with the program."

Yes, he knew the routine. He had pictures on his phone of Mac's four kids. His phone was also filled with pictures of Bane's triplets. In the beginning, it seemed like Bane would text him a new picture every other day. Now it had decreased to only one a week. "No problem. I'm taking them to dinner and will take a photo then."

"I take it things are going well. I assume you had that talk you said you were going to have with her."

"Yes, I had it. She wasn't keen on the idea of sharing

support for our son. I had to explain that I don't operate that way. She didn't like it but she finally gave in."

"That's good. What did the two of you decide about the fake marriage?"

Coop rubbed the back of his neck when he remembered that particular conversation. "Bristol doesn't want to be married any more than I do. But we have Laramie to consider now. She suggested we just tell everyone we're getting a divorce. That will release her from the fake marriage. She sees that as the easiest and simplest way out."

"Is that what you want?"

Coop dropped down in the wingback chair. "No. But then marriage isn't what I want, either. At least it wasn't until I met my son. At first I convinced myself being a single dad wouldn't be a big deal since I'd be gone on missions most of the time anyway. But then I began thinking about those times I would be around. What if she began seeing someone who didn't want me to have access to my child the way I wanted?"

"You can work out visitation rights with an attorney, so there shouldn't be any problems with that. Why do I get the feeling there's more, Coop?"

Because there was more. It was at times like this that a part of him wished Bane didn't know him so well. He, Bane, Viper, Flipper and another friend by the name of Nick Stover had gone through the naval academy together. Mac had been a SEAL several years before any of them. For the longest time, Mac had come across like the big-brother SEAL looking out for them, like he figured they couldn't take care of themselves. Over time they'd learned how to look out for each other. A few years ago Nick had given up being a SEAL to take a job with Homeland Security after his wife had triplets.

He, Mac, Viper and Flipper had wondered if Bane would do the same thing because of his triplets. But Bane had as-

sured them he wouldn't. Whereas Nick and his wife didn't
have any family to help out, Bane had more family than
the law allowed. Bane's triplets were the third set born in
the Westmoreland family. There were Westmorelands all
over the place. In several states, including Alaska.

Coop was close to all his team members but he and Bane
shared a special bond because they'd been roommates at
the academy.

"Yes, there's more," he finally said. "It's Bristol."

"What about her?"

"I'm more attracted to her than ever, man. She's beautiful. She's also headstrong, independent and a wonderful
mother to Laramie."

"Sounds like you're falling for her all over again."

Coop leaned back in the chair. "To be honest, I don't
think I ever stopped falling. I told you how she was constantly on my mind while I was in Syria and how those
memories of us together were how I held on to my sanity."

"Did you tell her that?"

"Yes."

"And did you tell her that the minute the hospital released you to travel that you headed to Paris, hoping to
see her?"

"No, I didn't tell her that. Maybe one day I will."

"Women like to know they were thought of. Remember how I kept all those cards and letters over the years for
Crystal. It meant a lot to her."

He and Bane talked a little while longer. When they
ended their conversation, he glanced at his watch. He
needed to make another call, namely to his parents. He
also needed to follow up with his attorney. Afterward, he
would go to the hotel's fitness center and work off that delicious breakfast and lunch Bristol had prepared.

He thought about their kiss again. What he'd told Bane
was the truth. He was attracted to her more so than ever.

Visitation rights with his son weren't the only thing he was concerned with. Visitation rights with his son's mother were also on his mind. The thought of her marrying someone else bothered him.

If it bothers you so much, then maybe you should marry her yourself.

What the hell! Why did an idea like that pop into his head? Anyone who knew him would attest to the fact that he wasn't the marrying kind. He liked his freedom. He enjoyed not answering to anyone but himself. He...

Loved his son.

His lips firmed in a straight line. Yes, he loved his son, but what did that have to do with desiring Bristol? Suddenly, he knew the answer. His love for his son affected everything. Even his son's mother.

He groaned in frustration. He had suggested the option of making the marriage real. She had immediately rebuffed it. At the time, it hadn't bothered him one iota. That idea hadn't been at the top of his list anyway.

So why was he thinking about it now?

Once again the answer was the same. He loved his son. Unlike his parents, who believed their love for each other weighed more than the love for their child, he didn't hold such beliefs. Although he'd seen his child for the first time only last night, more love than he thought he could ever have for any other human being had seeped into his heart and it was going to stay there.

He loved his parents. He loved his SEAL teammates as brothers. But the love he had for his child was so amazing that more than once today he'd had to pause to make sure he hadn't dreamed the whole thing.

That little face looked so much like him it was uncanny. Maybe the next time they would have a girl and she would look more like Bristol. Coop went still.

How could he even think what he just had? A daughter? With Bristol as the mother? Jeez.

He stood and began pacing. He was really losing it to even think such a thing. He needed to stay focused. The only person he needed to be thinking about was his son. But how could he think of his son and not think of his son's mother? The woman who'd given birth to him? The woman who made sure he got all the things he needed? The woman who was already teaching him a second language?

Hadn't he decided earlier today that they came as a package deal? But that had only been regarding financial support and nothing more. Hadn't it? Then why was he thinking all crazy? Why was he thinking beyond the financial to something even more? To marriage?

Because she's the woman you want.

Want and not love.

He knew love had nothing to do with it. Whatever feelings he had for Bristol were purely physical. That kiss today proved it, as well as the sexual chemistry surrounding them whenever they were together. That conclusion about the nature of their relationship didn't bother him and he doubted it bothered her.

Coop stood and checked his watch. He needed to go to the fitness center to work off his sexual frustrations, and he had plenty. When he arrived at her house to take them to dinner, maybe he would have worked some sense back into his brain.

Thirteen

"Daddy is back, Mommy?"

Bristol couldn't ignore the excitement in her son's voice. He had been disappointed when he woke up from his nap to find Coop gone. The light had come back into his little eyes only when she'd told him Coop would be back and would take them out to dinner to eat spaghetti.

Laramie had jumped with anticipation when he heard the sound of the doorbell. Now he was right at her heels as she moved toward the door. He was ready and she didn't want to admit it, but so was she. Her lips were still tingling from her and Coop's kiss earlier and she hadn't been able to paint for thinking of him.

And that wasn't good. She needed to get more than a grip. She needed to put things in perspective. When she did, that kiss would be placed on the back burner, where it belonged.

Looking through the peephole, she confirmed it was Coop. He looked handsome, just like the Texan he was proud to say he was. She opened the door and tilted her head to look up at him. Before she could say anything, Laramie, who'd managed to squeeze between her legs, said, "Daddy, you left me."

Her son's words had been spoken with such heartfelt pain that she understood why Coop reached down and pulled Laramie into his arms. She stepped back for him to enter. She was amazed at how quickly Laramie had taken to Coop. Maybe it was a male thing. Maybe he would get attached to any man. She wouldn't know because he rarely saw other men. Ms. Charlotte's sons came around every so often and Bristol hadn't dated since Laramie was born.

"I'll get his coat so we can go," she said, when Laramie sat down on the sofa.

"No rush," Coop said, glancing at her. "We have time."

She started to tell him that he couldn't get all emotional whenever Laramie flashed those sad brown eyes at him. Besides, due to the nature of Coop's job as a SEAL, there would be plenty of times when Laramie wouldn't see him. It was not like this would be Coop's address. He lived heaven knew where. But not here.

She crossed the room to the coatrack to get Laramie's jacket and heard what Coop was telling their son. He was being as honest as he could. "There will be days when Daddy will have to go away. Sometimes for a long time."

"How long?" Laramie asked his father. "This long?" Laramie then stretched his little arms out wide.

"Maybe even this long," Coop said, stretching out his own arms even wider.

"Oh." A disappointed pout curved Laramie's tiny lips.

Coop gathered his son close. "Just remember, I will always come back."

Bristol stopped. She had gone along with everything Coop had said until now. But considering the type of job he did, he couldn't promise that he would always come back. How dare he make such a promise to Laramie?

"Where you go, Daddy?"

"Far away. To keep you safe."

"Keep me safe?"

"Yes. Always."

Of course Laramie had more questions but Bristol had heard enough. She grabbed his coat off the coatrack, determined that she would have a talk with Coop when they returned from dinner, after she put Laramie to bed.

"Here's his coat," she said, returning to the living room to hand the coat to Coop.

There was no need for her to try and put on Laramie's coat since he was determined to stick to Coop like glue. The thought didn't bother her and she wasn't filled with even an ounce of jealousy. There was enough of Laramie to go around for the both of them. She thought it was sad her mother hadn't thought that way when it came to Bristol's father.

"Ready?"

She glanced over at Coop as she buttoned up her own coat. "Yes."

"I rented a car for us to use," Coop said, picking up Laramie.

"Just to go to the restaurant? We could have taken a cab."

"I plan to be in New York for a while and figured I would need one for you and Laramie."

She frowned. "Why would you need it for me and Laramie? If we need to go anywhere, we can take the subway like we always do."

"Not while I'm around," he said, heading for the door with Laramie.

Bristol didn't move for a moment, trying to push feelings of annoyance away. She was not used to depending on anyone except Ms. Charlotte. She should just accept what he'd offered as a kind and thoughtful gesture and let it go. Besides, her mother had always told her to pick her battles. What was foremost on her mind right now was the lie he'd told their son a few moments ago—that promise to always come back.

* * *

"Are you okay?" Coop asked Bristol, after she opened the front door. They were returning from dinner and he was carrying a sleeping Laramie in his arms.

"I'm fine. Why do you ask?"

"You were quiet at dinner."

She shrugged as she closed the door behind them. "I think Laramie did enough talking for the both of us."

Coop couldn't help but chuckle. That was true. His son had definitely been the life of the party. Their waitress had fallen in love with him and had been surprised at how well he conversed for his age. Laramie had eaten all of his spaghetti and clapped his hands afterward, saying how good it was.

Keeping his word to Bane about sending a picture, Coop had given their waitress his cell phone and asked her to take one of them. At first Bristol hadn't wanted to participate, saying it was about him and his son, and that his friends wouldn't want her included. He'd dismissed that assumption by reminding her how much they'd liked her when they'd met her in Paris.

The picture was perfect. They had looked like a family dining out together, enjoying their meal and each other's company. In addition to Bane, Coop had texted the photo to the others. Within minutes, his phone had blown up with their responses. They all thought Laramie was a mini-Coop just as he assumed they would. They also thought Bristol looked good. Really good. And texted him to tell her hello. They also said how good the three of them looked together. Funny, he'd thought the same thing.

He couldn't help but notice how little Bristol had said all evening. Was something bothering her? He knew she hadn't been keen on him renting a car just to have it available for her and Laramie, but surely she wasn't upset because of that.

"You want him upstairs, right?" he asked to make certain.

"Yes. I need to undress him for bed," she said, removing her coat. "It's past his bedtime. He lasted longer than I thought he would."

Carrying their son, he followed her up the stairs, trying not to notice the sway of her hips and the curve of her backside. But he did notice. He was a man after all, and didn't intend to feel guilty about checking her out.

He placed Laramie on the bed then watched while Bristol removed his clothes and put him in pajamas. Laramie opened his eyes once and gave his mother a droopy smile. "Love you, Mommy."

"Love you back, Laramie. See you in the morning." She leaned over and kissed him on the cheek. Then he drifted back to sleep.

Coop felt like an intruder to what was probably a usual bedtime exchange between mother and son. An exchange he was witnessing for the first time, one he felt no part of. He would have loved to dress his son for bed. But he hadn't been asked. Instead, he'd been delegated to the sidelines.

Bristol then glanced over at him and whispered, "We need to talk."

There was something in her tone. Whatever she wanted to talk about, he wasn't going to like it. "Okay."

She moved out of the room and he followed. In spite of his mixed emotions while watching Laramie's bedtime routine, Coop enjoyed walking behind Bristol. She helped keep his libido healthy. He thought now what he'd thought a number of times before. She looked good in jeans. He wondered if his son's birth was the reason behind all those curves that now looked even more delectable to him.

"Coffee or beer?"

Bristol's question thrown over her shoulder drew his attention. He had a feeling he would need something stronger than coffee. Probably even stronger than beer, so he would take the alcohol. "Beer."

She kept walking toward the kitchen while he remained in the living room. With her no longer in sight, he turned his attention to the Christmas tree. He might be wrong but it looked like she'd added more ornaments than were there yesterday. The tree looked all bright and festive, recalling to his mind how perfunctorily the tradition was observed in his own family. His parents, or rather the housekeeper, put up a tree every year. And it remained up until New Year's whether anyone was there to enjoy it or not.

He couldn't help but recall his telephone call to his parents earlier today, to let them know about Laramie. They were surprised he'd been so careless with protection and his father had strongly suggested Coop get a blood test before claiming anyone. His mother had stated that if Laramie was truly his, then they would give the little boy all the love they'd given to Coop. He'd had to chuckle at that.

When his mother asked what was funny, he'd respectfully said nothing. They just didn't get it, but at this point in his life, he didn't care. His parents weren't going to change and he was used to their behavior.

A part of him wondered if he would one day find his soul mate, like his father had. Coop knew well the story of how his parents had met in college and fallen in love, apparently at first sight. He often wondered if his parents had really planned for him, although they claimed they had. One thing was for certain, if Coop ever did meet his soul mate, he wouldn't get so wrapped up in her that he wouldn't love with equal intensity any child they'd made together.

He drew in a deep breath. Why was he thinking about soul mates? As far as he was concerned, one didn't exist for him. Laramie would most likely be his only child. He was satisfied with that.

"Here you are."

He turned and Bristol handed him his beer. It was cold, but what he felt was the warmth of her hand when they touched. She had a beer for herself, as well. This was the first time he'd seen her drink beer instead of tea.

"I didn't know you drank beer," he said, tempted to reach out and touch that lone dimple in one of her cheeks.

"There's a lot you don't know about me, Coop."

She had him there. "What do you want to talk about?" he asked.

She moved past him to sit down on the sofa and, as usual, he watched her movements. He wanted to go sit beside her, but knew he shouldn't. For two people who'd made a baby together, they were as far apart as ever. He felt it. She was upset about something and he couldn't wait to hear what it was. He moved to sit down in the chair across from her.

"I want to talk about what you told Laramie."

He lifted a brow. "And what did I tell Laramie?"

The lamp in the room cast a soft light on her features. She wore her hair up in a ponytail with little curls fanning her face. He remembered her wearing a similar style three years ago. He'd taken the band out of her hair so it could fan around her shoulders. His fingers itched to do the same thing now.

"That you would always come back to him."

"I will."

She frowned. "You don't know that."

Now he was the one who frowned. "Do you think I'd deliberately stay away after seeing him? After getting to know him? You think I'd shuck my responsibilities? Even worse—that I could stop loving him and forget about him?"

"That's not what I'm insinuating, Coop. You're missing the point."

He leaned forward, needing to study her expression. To

try deciphering what the hell she was talking about. "So what is the point? Why don't I know that I will always come back to him?"

"Because."

He lifted a brow. "Because what?"

He watched her bury her face in her hands and draw in a deep breath before looking back up at him. The anguish he saw in her gaze made his insides clench when she said, "Because you could die."

Coop didn't say anything. Flashes of a time when everyone thought he had died, when he'd lived each day extremely close to death, filtered through his mind. He pushed the memories back and concentrated on the real fear he saw in Bristol's eyes. That was what he would address. "Yes, I could die. But so could you."

He saw the shiver pass through her before she lifted her chin. "Don't even try to compare what I do with what you do. I paint. You and others like you carry the weight of the world and all of the country's problems on your shoulders. You constantly put your life in danger, Coop. Do you deny that?"

He shook his head. "No, I don't deny it. But whenever I leave for any mission, I have every intention of coming back. Would you have preferred me to tell my son I won't be coming back?"

"No, but I wish you wouldn't make promises you might not be able to keep. If anything ever happens to you, I will be the one who has to explain what happened."

Why were they talking about him dying? Thanks to his son, he had every reason to live, not that he'd ever taken life lightly. But now he had someone in his life who made living doubly important. "I think you're going to the extreme with this, Bristol."

It was clear his words angered her. "You think I'm going to the extreme? You aren't the one who got word while four months pregnant that the father of her child was dead. Dead, Coop. I thought you'd died like all the others."

He frowned. "What others?"

"It doesn't matter. I prefer you don't make promises to Laramie you might not be able to keep."

He stood, feeling angry now, as well. "Then I suggest you do the same. Stop telling him at bedtime that you'll see him in the morning. Anything can happen to you overnight. You could even die in your sleep."

She narrowed her gaze at him. "Stop being ridiculous."

His jaw tightened. "Then I suggest you stop being ridiculous, too. There are no guarantees in life. People die every day. When your time comes, there's not a damn thing you can do about it."

She took a step forward. Got in his face. "I guess of all people you should know, since you had a chance to beat death."

Not good, he thought, meeting her eyes. He wished she didn't smell so good and he definitely preferred her not standing so close. As if it had a will of its own, his gaze moved from her face to her body. She was beautiful even when she was angry.

"And just what are you looking at?" she all but snapped.

Since she asked, he had no qualms in telling her. "You. Did I tell you how good you looked tonight?"

Fourteen

Bristol suddenly realized she might have made a mistake by getting in Coop's space. How had they gone from discussing his death to how good he thought she looked?

She angrily crossed her arms over her chest and then wished she hadn't when his gaze shifted to her chest. As if on cue her nipples hardened right before his eyes. She drew in a deep breath and took a step back. "I think it's time for you to go."

"Is it?"

"Yes."

"I thought you wanted to talk," he said, reclaiming the distance she'd put between them.

"I think we've said enough for tonight."

"Do you? Have you ever noticed we never seem to resolve anything when we talk?"

"And whose fault is that?" she snapped.

"Both of ours." A smile touched the corners of his mouth. "I agree that we've said enough for tonight."

"Good."

"No, Bristol, this is good." And then before she realized

what he was doing, he pulled her into his arms and lowered his mouth to hers.

Shivers of pleasure, the kind she only experienced with him, shot through every part of Bristol. Her eyelids fluttered shut, too overtaken by desire to remain open. When Coop slipped his tongue into her mouth, tasting of the peppermint candy he'd been sucking on earlier, she shuddered. More enjoyable shivers ran up her spine. Sensations consumed her. When his hands wrapped around her middle, she was pulled close to the fit of his hard, masculine body.

When she felt his engorged erection nestled in the juncture of her thighs, she couldn't help but moan. How could they have been talking about serious stuff one minute and kissing the next?

Heated pleasure nearly melted her where she stood. She should be fighting to hold on to her sanity, but she couldn't. Even thinking of it was almost impossible. His assault on her mouth was sensuous and unhurried. It was mind-blowing. It had awakened needs long ago forgotten. And when she thought she couldn't possibly handle anymore, he deepened the kiss and new sensations overtook her.

Suddenly he broke away and she moaned in protest. Looking into his eyes she saw a naked desire that nearly tripped her pulse. Thickened the blood rushing through her veins. The air shimmered around them with sexual undercurrents.

"I want you, Bristol."

His words, spoken in a deep voice, stroked over her skin like a warm caress. Her breathing became as rapid as her heartbeat. And she knew at that moment that kissing wasn't enough. Especially now that they'd been reminded of how it felt to become so enmeshed in each other. Sexual excitement curled her stomach at the memory. It wasn't about love...at least for him it wouldn't be.

For him, it was physical desire driving what was happening between them.

She, on the contrary, was driven by deep, never-ending love.

Two different drives. One final destination.

No need to deny what she truly wanted. "I want you, too, Coop."

As soon as the words left her lips, she was swept off her feet into strong arms and carried up the stairs.

Coop practically took the stairs two at a time with Bristol in his arms. He'd been unable to endure her form of passion any longer. Desire was clawing at his insides, making his need for her palpable. His need to make love to her was a pulsing, throbbing necessity he couldn't fight.

Entering her room, he went straight to the bed and placed her on it. Then he stood back and began removing his clothes while watching her remove hers. She pulled the sweater over her head and tossed it aside. He inhaled a sharp breath when he saw her breasts encased in a sexy black lace bra. Breasts his tongue had known and wanted to know again.

She unhooked the front clasp of her bra and his erection throbbed harder when the twin globes were freed. He'd always liked her breasts—their shape, size and texture. Coop was convinced if given the chance, he could devour those nipples 24/7.

He stopped taking off his own clothes just to watch Bristol finish taking off hers. He was mesmerized, captivated, so damn fascinated. When she removed her jeans, leaving herself only in undies, his erection got harder. She was wearing black panties that matched the bra.

Three words immediately came to mind. Gorgeous. Hot. Awesome.

"Is there a problem, Coop?"

Her voice snapped him back. He swallowed when he shifted his gaze to her face. "No, there isn't a problem."

"I was just wondering."

He didn't want her to wonder about anything. Especially about him being anxious to make love to her. He was convinced that somehow during those three days they'd spent together in Paris, Bristol had gotten into his blood. That had to be the reason he hadn't been able to forget her. The reason why thinking of her had kept him sane. What other reason could there be?

He quickly removed the rest of his clothes and then pulled out a condom from his wallet. He sheathed himself, knowing she was watching. It wouldn't be the first time she'd seen him do this and he didn't intend for it to be the last.

Bristol frowned when he got closer to the bed. Her fingers touched the scars that hadn't been there the last time they'd made love. From the look on her face he figured she knew where they'd come from. And then she did something he hadn't expected. Something that touched him deeply.

She leaned close and showered kisses over the scars. It was as if she wanted to kiss away any pain they might have caused him. When her mouth came close to his erection, he pulled back. He didn't want a reason to take off his condom. That was probably how she'd gotten pregnant the last time.

"I want to be inside of you, Bristol. I need it," he whispered hoarsely, climbing on the bed to join her.

"And that's where I want you, Coop," she said, wrapping her arms around his neck. "Inside of me."

Maybe she shouldn't have said that, shouldn't have so openly admitted her desire. Maybe she should not have been so brutally honest. But what else could she say when the juncture of her thighs throbbed for him? When her nipples were hard? When her heart was beating fast? When every nerve in her body shrieked with excitement and anticipation? When the moment she'd kissed his scars it was as if they'd become hers?

There was still a lot they didn't agree on and they truly needed to be downstairs talking instead of in her bedroom doing this. But then, maybe this was needed before they could have any sensible discussions. It was hard to sit down and talk like adults when said adults wanted to tear each other's clothes off, roll on the floor in front of the fireplace and mate like rabbits.

There was nothing that could hold her back from this. From giving herself to him like she'd done three years ago. So much had happened since then, but she didn't want to remember any of it…except for the birth of her son. That would always be a spot of joy in her life. But right now, at this instant, she wanted to be transported back in time. She wanted to experience once again how it felt when their bodies joined. When he proved to her just how much vitality he had. How much stamina.

When he showed her just how much he desired her. She could never get enough of that. His open display of need made sexual excitement curl her stomach. She felt light-headed with the effect of his masculine power.

"I plan to take this slow, Bristol."

His words had a shock effect to her system. Slow? He had to be kidding. She was so enthusiastic she was convinced that slow would kill her.

He touched her, using his fingers to unhurriedly skim across her skin, right beneath her breasts. His fingertips elicited sensations that made parts of her tingle. Lighting her up like a flame he intended to let burn gradually before sensuously snuffing it out.

The intensity of his gaze took her breath. She wasn't sure what emotions she saw in his penetrating look—except for one. The sexual vibes between them. They were stronger than they'd been in Paris. That was hard to believe because what they'd shared in Paris had been mind-blowing at minimum.

While his fingers were intent on driving her insane with lust, he increased her pleasure by leaning over and whispering, "I need to taste you."

She knew what he meant. He'd already kissed her. She knew he was referring to tasting her in another way. A way she remembered so well. A way that made the throbbing between her legs intensify. The one thing she remembered about Coop was that he never did anything without telling her beforehand, to make sure she was comfortable with what he wanted to do. He was not a man who exploited a woman's weak moments. There hadn't been any surprises in what he did, only in the magnitude of the pleasure his actions delivered.

She nodded. He took the motion as consent. Before she could draw her next breath, he lowered his head to her chest and slid a nipple into his mouth.

She purred. Of course he would start here, knowing exactly what he was doing to her and how he was making her feel. He was well aware that he could push her into an orgasm just from his mouth devouring her breasts. He'd done it before and, from the feel of things, he intended to do it again.

Suddenly, he pulled his mouth away and looked up at her. "Did you breastfeed our son?"

His question took her by surprise. "Yes."

He smiled as if the thought pleased him. She didn't have the mind to ponder why when his mouth went back to her breasts. Then, as if with renewed energy, he began sucking hard. Her womb contracted with every draw of a nipple into his mouth and her purr got louder.

She needed to touch him. She slid her hands over his shoulders and down his arms before bringing them back to cup the side of his face. Tingling sensations built between her legs. She was certain she was about to be pushed over the edge when he pulled back, lifted his head and said, "Not yet. Remember what I told you. I intend to make this slow so you can remember me for a long time."

She felt his body shift lower. Then he was touching her stomach, caressing it with gentle strokes. His hands moved lower and his fingers stilled when they touched the thin line of a scar.

"Because Laramie weighed so much I had to have a C-section," she said, explaining the bikini cut that was barely visible. Of course someone as observant as him would detect it.

He didn't say anything, but she felt his mouth when his tongue traced a path over the scar. He was kissing her scar like she'd done for his.

The air surrounding them became even more charged. And she was suddenly filled with so many emotions she felt completely out of whack.

Then he lifted her legs to fall over his shoulders while her hips were elevated with his hands. He nudged her knees open and then as if it was the most natural thing to do, eased his face between her legs and slid his tongue inside.

He kissed her with an expertise she found utterly amazing. His tongue went deep. It was thorough. And it was excruciatingly slow. It was as if he had all the time in the world to drive her mad with desire. The more she moaned, the more he tortured her, delving deeper with powerful strokes.

Then she had to fight back a scream when her body exploded into a gigantic orgasm.

Shivers ran through Coop as the thighs encasing his face quivered. He knew what that meant but he refused to stop. In fact, he needed to keep going because her taste was more potent now. Her taste was what he'd remembered, what he'd longed for, yearned for. His shaft throbbed with an urgency he hadn't felt since the last time he'd been with her.

He felt her tremors subside but he refused to let up. Doubted he could even if he wanted to. The taste of her juices flooded him with even more desire. When her thighs began trembling again, he knew she was reaching climax again.

When he'd seen that scar he had been filled with such profound emotion. They both had scars to show from their time apart. Hers had been a celebration of life, his had been a prologue to a death that never happened.

Those days were over. He was free and back in the land of the living. Back in Bristol's bed. The same bed where memories had been made before. The same bed where his son was created. Same bed, same woman.

He couldn't get enough.

When the last of the spasms wore off, Bristol wondered how she'd had mulitple orgasms so close together. Had she been that needy? That greedy? That hard up for sex?

If she'd just wanted sex she would have dated Steven, or any of the other men who'd hit on her over the years. But none of them had enticed her to open herself up this way. To invite them to her bed. To tell them she wanted them inside her. Only with Coop could she behave so boldly. And she knew why.

She was still in love with him.

Coop smiled down at her as his body straddled hers. Surely he didn't think she had the energy for another round of anything. Especially intercourse of the most intense kind. She was so tired she would probably fall asleep in the middle. But then she'd had two orgasms in less than twenty minutes. She owed him something and would fake it if she had to. He deserved his pleasure, as well.

She'd only faked it for one guy, her first time in high school. With Coop she'd never needed to fake a thing. He'd kept her blood pumping. Kept the primal attraction between them so real that she'd been ready whenever he'd been ready. She'd even been tempted to wake him up for more. But not this time. There was no way her body could endure another orgasm tonight. But for him, she would pretend.

"You're not about to go to sleep on me, are you?" he asked her, staring down at her.

She looked into his eyes and her body warmed under his intense regard. She lowered her gaze to his lips. Lips that were wet with her juices. Why did that cause a deep stirring in the pit of her stomach? Maybe it was because she recalled how his tongue had lapped her into consecutive orgasms.

"Ready to taste yourself?" he asked in a low whisper.

Blood rushed through her veins. He'd never asked her anything like that before. Taste herself? She knew how he would do it and imagining it aroused her enough that a low moan escaped her lips.

"Is that a yes?"

A sensual force seemed to overtake her. Where was his sexual aura coming from? Hadn't she thought of faking it just a minute ago? Now he was arousing her all over again with mere words. Laramie Cooper was too compelling for his own good. Definitely too sexy.

She should have known she couldn't fake anything with him because he had the ability to turn her on, even when she thought such a thing wasn't possible.

"Yes," she said.

Then he lowered his mouth to hers. The moment their lips touched, every hormone in her body crackled. She knew it was more than their combined tastes driving her over the edge. It was the masterful way his tongue dominated her mouth.

Her nerves did a pirouette, her brain sprinted and her stomach flipped.

He ended the kiss and looked down at her in a way that made moisture gather between her thighs. "You're ready for me again, Bristol?"

Yes, she was ready, even when she'd thought earlier there was no way she could go another round. Not only could she go, she intended to participate to the fullest and there wouldn't be anything fake about it. "Yes, I'm ready."

Her legs opened automatically, as if her body needed what he was giving. It had been three years since she'd done this and the last time had been with him. She slipped her arms around his neck and felt the large length of his erection touching her feminine mound.

Then he eased inside, inch by inch. His fullness encompassed her as he went deeper, filling her to the hilt. Her body stretched to accommodate him.

"You okay?"

She looked up and met his gaze. "Yes, I'm okay."

And honestly, she was. It was like a homecoming. The man she'd thought lost to her forever, the man she'd believed would never make love to her again, was doing just that. It was more than she could have hoped for.

"Thank you for my son," he whispered hoarsely.

And then he began moving while still holding her gaze, as if daring her to look away. She stared into his eyes while his body thrust inside her with a rhythm that released a sensual throb of desire in her veins. The sinfully erotic movement of his hips drew everything out of her, while at the same time demanding that she take as much of him as she could. Each hard thrust made her moan.

He kept moving at an unhurried pace, as if he wanted her to feel every single stroke. And she did. They were a perfect fit. She felt intense pleasure all the way to her bones.

The undercurrent flowing between them was explosive, hot with passion of the most mind-blowing kind.

Her body moved with his. Her inner muscles tightened around him. Together they were creating a sensual heat like she'd never felt before...not even the last time. She'd thought nothing could be more powerful than what they'd already shared. Bristol was proven wrong.

Then he increased his pace, refined his strokes and pumped into her with a vigor that made her entire body respond. She exploded the same time he did, and he covered her mouth to keep the scream from her lips.

They seemed to flow into each other. Her hips were connected to his. Their bodies were perfectly aligned as they experienced the throes of ecstasy together. When he finally released her mouth, she drew in a deep breath and clung to his shoulders. They rode the waves of pleasure together.

Moments later, he rolled off her and gathered her in his arms. His thumb stroked her cheeks. The last thing Bristol remembered before sleep overtook her was whispering his name.

Fifteen

Coop wasn't sure what awakened him, but he jerked upright in bed and glanced around before remembering where he was. Bristol's bed. He drew in a deep breath and rubbed his hand down his face before looking at the clock. It was three in the morning. The spot beside him was empty. He'd been sleeping so soundly that he hadn't noticed when Bristol got out of bed.

Where was she? He lay back down thinking she was probably in the bathroom. A few minutes later, when she hadn't returned, he got up and checked. She wasn't there. Had she gone to see about Laramie? Coop pulled on his jeans and left the bedroom to go to his son's room. He found his son sleeping, but Bristol wasn't there, either.

He was about to head downstairs when he heard a noise coming from the attic. He knew from playing hide-and-seek with Laramie that she'd converted the attic into her studio and that was where she did most of her painting. Was she painting this time of morning?

Coop walked up the six steps and found the door open. And there she was, standing in front of an easel. Was she wearing anything under that artist's cape? It was short and hit her at midthigh, which gave him a good view of her legs. She had a nice pair and like him, she was in her bare feet. He watched the look of concentration on her face. Her full attention was on whatever she was painting. Considering what they'd done tonight she should be exhausted. Obviously, she had a lot of energy.

She hadn't noticed him and he decided not to disturb her. Coop took in the room. It was huge. There were several built-in cabinets for her supplies. There was also a love seat, as well as a sink and counter that he figured she used as a cleanup station. The room had only one small window and he figured she wanted the least distractions possible while painting.

Coop was about to leave when he noticed several framed photographs on the wall. One was a photo of her and an older man. They favored each other and he figured the man was her father. He studied the man's features and tried to recall why he seemed so familiar.

Coop leaned in the doorway and recalled bits and pieces of what she'd told him about her past. Their son's middle name had been her father's first name. When they'd first met, her last name had been Lockett. He also remembered the story she'd told him about the two years she and her father had spent together before he'd died.

"That's a picture of you and your father, isn't it?"

His words had her swinging around so fast she almost dropped her paint brush. She released a nervous breath. "Coop, you scared me."

"Sorry," he said, entering the room. "I woke up and found you gone and wondered where you'd taken off to." It hadn't been his intention to stay the night at her house, but after making love that first time, they'd slept and had awakened to make love once more. Then they'd fallen asleep again.

She smiled over at him. "I didn't want to wake you. In

addition to painting during Laramie's nap time, I often paint late at night when he's asleep." She then broke eye contact and glanced at the framed photograph. "Yes, that's my father," she said proudly. He could hear the love in her voice.

"Randall Lockett was your father."

She snatched her gaze to him. "How do you know that?"

He could see the surprised look on her face. Was her father's identity supposed to be a secret or something? "I recognize him. I'm familiar with his work thanks to my parents, namely my mother. She owns several of his paintings."

"She does?"

"Yes."

He glanced at her easel and back at her before saying, "I even met him once when he came to Austin for an art show to benefit one of my mother's charities. I liked his work. I should have made the connection in Paris with your last name being Lockett and the two of you having similar styles. But it never crossed my mind." There was no need to tell her that the only thing that had been on his mind was getting her to the nearest bed.

"I can't believe you actually met my father."

He heard the excitement in her voice. "Yes, I was seventeen at the time and a senior in high school. It was the last event my mother sort of forced me to attend with her and my dad. In the end, I'm glad I went. He was a nice man. Very personable. Like I said, Mom has quite a few of your father's paintings and it was nice meeting the man who was getting so much of her money. I'm sure you know his work isn't cheap."

She chuckled. "Yes, I know."

"I remember that time well," he said. "I'd gotten word a few days before of my acceptance into the naval academy and was going away with my parents' blessing. I was relieved they hadn't placed any pressure on me to follow in their footsteps and take part in the family business."

"And what business is that?"

"RCC Manufacturing Company."

She lifted a brow. "RCC? I'm familiar with them. They're a huge operation based in Texas. I order a number of my art supplies through them."

He chuckled. "My parents would be happy to hear that."

"And you decided to become a SEAL instead of going into your family business?"

"Yes, that's right. I knew early on I wasn't cut out for the business-suit-and-tie crowd."

Coop glanced back over at the framed photograph and then back at her. "You seemed surprised that I knew Randall Lockett was your father, like it was supposed to be a secret or something. Was it?"

Bristol looked away from Coop to glance at the picture she'd taken with her father, one that she'd proudly hung on her wall. She wished Coop wouldn't stand there shirtless and in his bare feet. In jeans riding low on his hips and not quite zipped up all the way, with the snap undone. He looked way too sexy for her peace of mind.

She'd yet to answer Coop's question and she realized how little they knew about each other, even with all the intimacy they'd shared. She blamed it on the fact that whenever they were together they did little talking due to all the sexual chemistry surrounding them. Like now. She could feel it and she knew he did, as well.

She hadn't known so much need had been bottled up inside her. All it had taken was Coop unleashing it and she'd become a mad woman wanting to make up for lost time. Luckily for her, he'd been the same way. It was as if they hadn't been able to get enough of each other.

"It's not a secret per se. I just don't go around broadcasting it, so few people know. I don't want to use his name to build my own career as an artist, although I am proud to have been Randall Lockett's daughter."

"And I'm sure he was glad he was Bristol Lockett's father."

His words made her feel good. More than once, her father had told her how proud he was of her and all she'd accomplished. "Thank you for saying that."

"No need to thank me."

He moved around the room, looking at the easels showing various paintings she had done. She wasn't used to anyone invading her space, especially in here. For some reason his presence didn't bother her.

Another thing that didn't bother her, when maybe it should have, was how quickly they'd become intimate again. Had it been just the night before when he'd shown up at the gallery? She had wanted him immediately. Had needed him sexually. And he'd delivered, satisfying her.

It wasn't his fault that she had fallen in love with him years ago. Nor was it any of his concern that she was trying to fall out of love with him now. Sleeping with him hadn't confused the issue for her. She knew he didn't love her back.

She needed to get her mind off Coop, namely off his body, and transfer her thoughts to something else. She walked over to the coffeepot she kept in her studio and poured a cup. She then turned to him. "Would you like some?"

Her insides heated when his gaze roamed over her, making her realize just what she'd asked. She swallowed, thinking he'd had some already. A lot actually. But if he wanted more…she was game.

Drawing in a deep breath, she clarified, "Would you like a cup of coffee, Coop?"

He nodded slowly. "Yes, I'd love a cup."

She poured his coffee and he walked over to take the cup from her hand. Their fingers brushed and her stomach curled with pleasure.

"Thanks," he said.

"You're welcome."

They both took a sip of their coffees. Despite trying not to love him, she wanted to get to know him. Like she'd told him earlier, she was very familiar with his parents' company. It was on the Fortune 500 list, which meant he came from money. He'd said the reason he'd wanted to become a SEAL was that the work was a better fit for his personality. And he'd become a SEAL with his parents' blessing. She knew things didn't always work that way for the sons of important families.

"It's late. I hadn't intended to impose on you by spending the night. I'll leave now if you want me to."

She looked at him over the rim of her cup. Did she want him to leave? No, she didn't. "There's no need, unless you want to go. You'll probably be back in the morning for breakfast anyway."

He chuckled. "Only if I get an invitation."

"You have an invitation, Coop. I told you, you can spend as much time with Laramie as you want."

He nodded and took a sip of his coffee. "In that case, I'd like to ask you something."

"What?" she asked.

"What plans do you and Laramie have for the holidays?"

She thought about his question. "Just a quiet time at home this year. It will be Laramie's first Christmas where he understands that the holidays are special. I've been telling him that if he's a good boy, Santa will bring him something nice. He's been keeping his toys put away and getting better with potty training." She paused before asking, "Why did you want to know about my plans for the holidays?"

"Because I'm hoping I can join the two of you." He drew in a deep breath. "And before you ask, the answer is no. I had no plans to spend Christmas with my folks."

Bristol remembered the last holiday they'd spent together. At that time, he'd given her the impression that he and his parents weren't close. Now was just as good a time as any to ask him about it. After all, his parents were her son's only living grandparents. In fact, the only living relatives Laramie had besides her and Coop, as far as she knew. If anything were to ever happen to her or Coop...

She suddenly needed to know about the people who might one day be responsible for her son. "You're welcome to join us, but I want you to tell me about your parents, Coop. Laramie's grandparents."

He leaned against her art table, avoiding her stacks of supplies. "What do you want to know?"

She shrugged. "Mainly, why you never want to spend the holidays with them?"

A part of Coop wanted to think her question was simple enough. But when it came to his parents, nothing was simple unless you accepted them for who they were. He'd done that a long time ago.

"Come on, let's sit on the sofa and I'll tell you about them."

"Okay."

Together, they sat down. To be on the safe side, since she was too desirable for her own good, he sat at the other end of the sofa. He took a sip of his coffee and said, "I think my parents are swell people who after nearly thirty-five years of marriage still love each other deeply."

He chuckled. "I wouldn't be wrong if I were to say they were obsessed with each other. I was told by both sets of my grandparents—who are deceased now—that it had been that way from the first, when they'd met at Harvard.

Dad was from Laredo, Texas, and Mom from Laramie, Wyoming."

She lifted a brow. "Laramie?"

"Yes, and before you ask, the answer is yes. She named me after the city where she was born. She loved it that much and tried getting my father to move there after they were married. But he was a Texan through and through. He'd come from generations of ranchers, but he gave up that way of life, deciding not to follow in his father's, grandfather's and great-grandfather's footsteps as a rancher. He was the suit-and-tie kind. After college, he and my mom lived in Austin and started a business. Less than a year after graduating from college, the two of them were married. I was born three years later."

"No wonder your parents were so understanding about allowing you to have the career you wanted. They'd faced the same challenge."

"Yes, but my paternal grandparents weren't as understanding. They thought Dad was throwing away his legacy. Especially since my father was their only child."

He paused to take another sip of coffee. "I'm told that my mom's pregnancy with me was difficult. At one point, they thought she would die. My father was even told he might have to choose to either save his wife or his child. He picked his wife. But a top specialist arrived and assured my father he could save us both. He did. However, I think I was still a stark reminder to my dad of how close he came to losing Mom."

Bristol frowned, and he thought it was cute. "Surely, he didn't hold you responsible and mistreat you in any way."

"No, not at all. Dad was good. However, my parents' relationship took a turn. They were always close, but I think nearly losing Mom freaked Dad out. After that he was determined to spend every moment he could with her... for the rest of their lives. They take more trips than I can count every year, and they have a tradition of spending the holidays together somewhere—usually with friends in England. Like I told you before, I've never spent the holidays with my parents. I've always spent them with my grandparents on their ranch. And trust me, I had no complaints. My grandparents were the greatest. I loved being out on their ranch."

"Did you ever feel resentful of your parents for not spending time with you?"

He knew it was hard to understand his relationship with his parents, but for her he wanted to try to explain. "It's not that my parents never spent time with me, Bristol, because they did. They were very active in my life while growing up and there were a number of trips we took together."

He took another sip of coffee. "Thanks to them, I saw most of the world before my sixteenth birthday. There was never a time I didn't think my parents loved me. However, I always knew they loved each other more."

"And you didn't have a problem with that?"

"No. I had friends whose parents didn't even like each other, couldn't stand to be in the same room together. Some of their parents divorced as soon as they finished school and my friends knew they had been the glue that held their parents' unhappy marriages together. That wasn't the case with my parents. There was never any doubt in my mind that Dad and Mom loved each other to the moon and back."

He didn't say anything for a minute, then he added, "When they thought I was dead, they went bonkers. I think they got even closer, if such a thing is possible with them. When I was found alive, they refused to let me out of their sight at first. They even questioned if I should continue being a SEAL. I knew they were worried, but I wasn't used to all the attention, at least not from them. I couldn't wait until I finished my recuperation period to return to work."

She spun her cup in her hands and asked, "What happened to your grandparents' ranch?"

"They willed it to me, although they were fully aware of my career as a SEAL. But my grandparents also knew I would manage the ranch as well as become a SEAL. For the ranch, I hired the right people to take care of it until I retire from the military, which will be in about six years. Some of the men working at the ranch for me used to work for my grandparents and can be trusted."

She nodded. "What kind of ranch is it?"

"It was always a cattle ranch but thanks to Bane's family, the Westmorelands, I've added horses. Several of his family members own a horse breeding and training company. They needed another holding depot before shipping the horses off to be trained. That's where my ranch comes in. So, I guess my ranch is a horse ranch, as well."

"Do you go there often?"

"Not as much as I would like. When I do go there it's mainly to check on things. My men have everything pretty much under control."

"I'm glad."

A part of him believed she was, which made him say, "I want to show you and Laramie my ranch one day." He would tell her that much. He wouldn't tell her yet that he planned to make it his primary home for whenever Laramie visited.

She smiled and he felt a stirring in his stomach. "I'd love to see it, Coop. I know Laramie will, too. He loves horses."

"Then it's settled. I will take the two of you there after the holidays." Standing, he said, "I've kept you from your work long enough."

She smiled, standing, as well. "I'm okay. I was about to come to a stopping point anyway."

"You do this every night? Paint while Laramie sleeps?"

"Not every night. Just whenever the urge hits."

Funny, she should mention urges. At that moment, he was swamped with another urge. "Speaking of urges, Bristol," he said, setting his cup aside.

"What about them?"

"I feel one coming on myself."

She smiled. "You want to try your hand at painting?"

He chuckled. "No. It's not an urge to paint."

"Oh? What kind of urge is it?"

He leaned over and whispered in her ear. She smiled and placed her own coffee cup on the table. She moved closer and wrapped her arms around his neck. "In that case, I think we need to deal with these urges of yours."

"I agree." He swept her off her feet and headed toward her bedroom.

Sixteen

Coop felt something poke him against his nose and he snatched his eyes open. He saw a miniature pair of eyes and a little hand right in his face. "You in my mommy's bed," his son all but accused.

Yes, he was in Laramie's mommy's bed. Before Coop could open his mouth to assure his son that everything was okay, Laramie had pulled himself up on the bed and crawled over him, saying, "Move over, Daddy." The little boy then planted himself in the middle of the bed, unceremoniously separating Coop and Bristol like the parting of the Red Sea.

"Laramie!" Bristol said, quickly sitting up after coming awake. "Be nice."

"He in your bed, Mommy."

Bristol yawned and ran a hand through her son's curls. "I know and it's okay. Good morning, Laramie."

He wrapped his arms around his mother's neck. "Good morning, Mommy."

Then, as if satisfied, Laramie slid beneath the covers and closed his eyes.

Bristol glanced over at Coop and smiled. "Sorry about that."

"Hey, don't apologize. I take it he does this every morning."

She nodded, pushing a mass of hair back from her face. "Yes. And as you can see it's not quite six o'clock. He comes in here, gets in my bed and will go back to sleep for another hour or so, then he'll wake up hungry. That's how we start our day."

For Coop that was a bummer because he'd planned to start his day by making love to her. Now, thanks to their son, those plans would be canned. But son or no son, Coop intended to get a good morning kiss. He leaned over and placed a kiss on her lips. "Good morning, Bristol."

She smiled. "Good morning, Coop."

He returned her smile. He'd liked waking up with her while in Paris and he liked waking up with her now. Even after making love to her multiple times last night, he still had a lot of sexual energy to work off and he knew only one other way to do so besides making love to Bristol.

"I'm going to the fitness center."

She lifted a brow. "The fitness center?"

"Yes, back at the hotel. I'm used to working out every morning." Usually he worked out twice a day. "I'll be back for breakfast if that's okay."

"That's fine. We'll be here."

"I'm counting on it." He leaned over and kissed her again, this time a little longer, before easing out of bed. He slid into his jeans and went into the connecting bathroom. When he returned a few moments later, he saw she had drifted off to sleep with Laramie cuddled close.

As he finished dressing, he couldn't stop looking at them. Something deep tugged at his heart. He wasn't sure how to deal with all these emotions. For years, he'd stayed in control of all relationships he was involved in. Usually, none were for the long-term. He'd been determined that no woman would ever rule his heart.

He liked his freedom. Besides, his work as a SEAL wasn't conducive to a normal family life. He didn't know from one month to the next where a mission might take him or for how long he'd be gone. He'd always enjoyed the adventure, the excitement, the quest and, yes, even the danger. Definitely the danger. It was enough to get your blood pumping and your adrenaline flowing.

But, he thought, studying Bristol while she slept, she got his blood pumping and his adrenaline flowing, as well. And when he thought about what they'd shared last night, he couldn't help but smile. Then his smile widened and he knew why. He was happy. Truly happy. And the two people responsible for his happiness were sleeping in that bed. In the last forty-eight hours, his life had changed.

Already, he could admit he wouldn't want it any other way.

When he finished dressing, he walked back over to the bed to stare down at them. At her. He wondered if she had any idea what she did to him, what she had done to him three years ago. Resisting her hadn't been an option.

Bristol had gotten next to him without much effort and there hadn't been anything he could do about it.

Other than to fall in love with her.

That admission shook him to the core. He hadn't seen that coming. But now that he knew the truth, he had to accept it.

He loved her.

He drew in a deep breath. If he analyzed his behavior over the past three years, he probably would have realized he'd fallen in love with her the moment he and the guys had walked into that café in Paris. He'd seen her staring at him. He was certain he'd lost his heart then and there.

He'd left everyone at the table to approach her, determined to introduce himself before they could. Now his actions made sense. Love explained everything. Including the importance of those memories to his survival as well as why he'd returned to Paris looking for her as soon as he'd recuperated. When he'd accepted that she had been lost to him forever, he'd moved on. He'd been living a satisfied life but not a truly happy one.

There had to be a reason their paths had crossed in New York after all this time, a reason they had a child, who would always be a bond between them. And more than anything he also believed, whether she agreed or not, there was a purpose behind her decision to concoct a fake marriage and take his name.

He wanted Bristol and Laramie to always be a part of his life. He might not have planned for the recent turn of events, but now that he was faced with this little family of his, he had no regrets.

He was well aware that Bristol harbored reservations about making their marriage real, but he intended to get rid of whatever roadblocks stood in their way.

She didn't love him yet, but in the end she would. He was a determined man and when he came to a decision there was no stopping him.

He turned and walked out of her bedroom.

Bristol was in the middle of preparing breakfast when her phone rang. Was it Coop letting her know he wouldn't make it back for breakfast? Upon waking up again, Laramie had seemed a little disappointed that Coop had left. She had to admit, she was, too.

As she put the biscuits in the oven, she thought about how he'd found her in her studio working. He had been a distraction, but a welcome one. They had talked. But the one thing he hadn't said was whether or not he'd told his

Bristol raised a brow. "Was I in a bad mood yesterday?"

parents about Laramie. And about their fake marriage. If so, what did his parents think of all this?

When she grabbed the phone, she saw from the caller ID that it was Margie. "Yes, Margie?"

"Are you in a better mood today?"

Bristol raised a brow. "Was I in a bad mood yesterday?"

"I thought so. I might have upset you with those things I said about your husband. If I did, I'm sorry."

Bristol drew in a deep breath. Margie's words from yesterday had annoyed her. "There is a lot about my relationship with him that you don't know." And one of them was the fact he was not really her husband.

"Then enlighten me. Let's do lunch today."

Bristol nibbled on her bottom lip. Today was not a good day. She didn't like having to ask Ms. Charlotte to keep an eye on Laramie at the last minute. There might be a chance Coop would be available to watch him, but she couldn't depend on that. On top of those conflicts, she and Coop still had more to work through. They needed to decide how to move forward. He wanted to spend the holidays with them and she was fine with that. What she didn't want was what they'd shared last night muddying the waters.

She didn't want him to think that just because she'd allowed him in her bed she'd allow him into her life. That wasn't the case.

"Tomorrow will be better, Margie," she heard herself say.

"Okay, and tomorrow would it be a good time for you and Steven to talk?"

Margie's words got her attention. "Talk about what?"

Margie chuckled. "Honestly, Bristol, have you forgotten he represents a company who's a client? A client who made it possible for you to leave that boring job to stay home with your son and paint every day."

No, she hadn't forgotten, mainly because Margie refused

to let her. She just didn't understand why Margie couldn't see that Bristol and Steven didn't click. "Fine, as long as this is strictly a business meeting, Margie."

"What other kind of meeting would I arrange? You don't like Steven, I get that now, although for Pete's sake, I don't know why. But it's your choice. Call me later and tell me when would be a good time to get together tomorrow."

"All right. I'll talk to you later."

As soon as she clicked off the phone and placed it aside, her doorbell rang. "Daddy's back, Mommy!"

The excitement in her son's voice touched her. At least he wasn't annoyed like he'd been this morning when he'd discovered his favorite spot in her bed already occupied. Once he'd gone to sleep and woken back up, he'd been team Coop all over again. "Yes, sweetheart, I think your daddy is back."

Putting the kitchen towel aside, she left the kitchen and headed toward the door.

"Good morning. I got you this," Coop said, handing her a huge poinsettia. There was a florist shop by the hotel and when he'd seen it this morning he knew he wanted to get it for her.

"Thanks. It's beautiful, Coop."

"You're welcome. I liked it when I saw it. It looks healthy and there are leaves that will be turning red in a few days."

She smiled. "Come on in." She stepped aside. "I just put the biscuits in the oven."

"Biscuits? You can make biscuits?"

"Yes, thanks to Aunt Dolly."

He entered, pulling off his Stetson and hanging his jacket on the coatrack. "I knew you could cook but claiming you can make biscuits has elevated you to another level."

She smiled. "That's good to know."

He watched as she placed the potted plant on a small

table not far from the Christmas tree. It was hard to believe it was a week before Christmas, but in New York it was hard to forget the season. There seemed to be a Santa on every corner and all the light posts were decorated with wreaths.

"So, what do you think?" she asked, turning to stand beside the plant he'd given her.

His focus was on her when he said, "I wish I could have seen you pregnant."

"Where did that come from?" she asked, smiling.

"You asked what I thought and those were my thoughts while seeing you standing there, knowing my son is in the kitchen sitting at the table."

"Coloring."

He chuckled. "Yes, coloring."

She didn't say anything for a minute. "While pregnant, I looked like a blimp."

He crossed the floor to stop in front of her. He cupped her chin in his hand. "I bet you looked beautiful." He leaned down and brushed his lips across hers.

Then, as if she needed time to compose herself, she said, "The biscuits are about ready to come out the oven."

She hurried to the kitchen.

A couple hours later, Bristol stood in front of her easel. The sound of her son's laughter could be heard all the way upstairs, letting her know he was enjoying another day of Coop's company.

Her thoughts shifted back to breakfast. Laramie had been glad to see his father and had talked a mile a minute. Just like yesterday, after breakfast Coop had volunteered to help clean up the kitchen. Although she'd told him his help wasn't needed, he'd given it anyway. And she would inwardly admit there had been something comfortable about him helping with kitchen chores.

Her thoughts shifted to the poinsettia he'd given her. It was big and beautiful and looked like it belonged right in the spot she'd placed it. It had been so thoughtful of him to bring it for her, and it made her feel special, although she wished it didn't. The only other man who'd given her flowers had been her father. He had arrived at their first meeting with flowers and had given her flowers on her birthday ever since. Even after his death the flowers were delivered. They were always a beautiful bouquet and the card always said, "You are forever loved, Dad."

She wiped the tears from her eyes that always sprang up when she thought of her father and the little time they'd had together. But he was still making a positive impact on her life. The same way she believed Coop would make a positive impact on Laramie's life. He was spending time with their son and that meant a lot. Laramie would miss Coop when he left but he would look forward to his father's return.

If he returned…

She drew in a sharp breath as fear gripped her. She didn't want to think of the risk Coop took whenever he left on a covert operation, but she couldn't push it from her mind. Although he'd told her little about his work, he had explained to her in Paris that most of his missions were classified and couldn't be discussed. She wondered how families of navy SEALs dealt with not knowing from one day to the next the whereabouts of their loved ones and when they would return.

The sound of her cell phone snapped her out of her reverie. She grabbed it off the table and smiled when she saw the caller was Dionne. "Hi, what's up?"

"Just calling to check on you. Are you and my godson okay?"

Bristol smiled. "We're fine. Just getting used to having a male presence around." She thought of how Coop had looked, standing on her doorstep that morning wearing a Stetson, jeans, suede jacket and boots. You could take the man out of Texas but you couldn't take Texas out of the man.

"A hot male presence, right?"

She thought about what had taken place in her bed last night and hot was just one adjective she could use. Other descriptions definitely came to mind but since Dionne had said hot… "Um, you can't imagine just how hot."

"*Oui!* Tell me!"

Bristol laughed. "No details for now. I need to prepare Laramie's lunch."

"Okay, but you will tell me later."

"Yes, later."

"You sound happy, Bristol."

Did she? "It's the holidays. Of course I sound happy."

"Usually you're not cheerful this time of year. Those memories of your aunt…"

Yes, there would always be memories of her aunt, who'd died over the holidays. "I know. At least I was here when it happened."

"Yes, I was there, too. I got to meet her. She was so nice."

"She was super."

They talked about other things while Dionne brought Bristol up to date on her family and the other friends Bristol had left behind in Paris. "Bristol?"

"Yes?"

"Have you decided what you're going to do?"

Bristol frowned. "About what?"

"Your fake marriage. We went to a lot of trouble to make it seem real."

Bristol didn't say anything at first. She and Coop still hadn't decided how to proceed. "A fake divorce makes sense then, doesn't it? But then why waste money undoing something that wasn't real anyway?"

"Is that what he wants? To undo it?"

"I don't know what he wants. It only came up once. We need to talk about it again and make a decision," she said. "Everyone here thinks I was a widow and then out of the clear blue sky my husband reappears. It placed him in an awkward situation since he had no idea everyone thought we were married until I told him."

"Why not make it a real marriage under the pretense of renewing your vows?"

"Because there is no love between us."

Bristol knew what Dionne was going to say before she'd even said it. "There is love, Bristol, at least on your part. You loved him after Paris. Remember, I'm the one who told you he had died. I saw what that did to you and the grief you endured. You loved him too much. That much love doesn't just go away. There's no way you don't still love him."

Bristol opened her mouth to say that wasn't true, that she didn't still love Coop, but she couldn't lie to Dionne. "It doesn't matter. I intend to fall out of love with him."

"Why?"

Bristol drew in a deep breath. "You just said the reason. You saw the way I handled the news of his death and the grief I suffered as a result. I couldn't risk going through something like that a second time. I can't and I won't."

Seventeen

For the second night in a row Coop stood aside while Bristol tucked their son into bed. Today had been a full day of activities. After breakfast he'd stretched out on the floor and helped Laramie put Lego blocks together. Then after lunch he had bundled his son up in his boots and coat and they'd walked to the park.

Bristol had invited Coop to stay for dinner and now he couldn't help wondering if she would invite him to stay the night. She really hadn't invited him last night, but their need for each other had pretty much made the decision for them.

There was a strong possibility she might send him packing after they had the little talk he intended for them to have. It was time he forced her hand on a few things.

"Laramie wants to tell you good-night."

Bristol's words broke into Coop's thoughts and he moved from leaning in the doorway to where his son lay, barely able to keep his eyes open. His son, who had captured his heart the moment he'd heard he existed.

"Daddy, you stay. Sleep in Mommy's bed, okay?"

He couldn't help but smile. His son was giving him

permission even though Bristol hadn't done so. Instead of agreeing with Laramie, Coop said, "Good night, Laramie."

"Stay, Daddy. Sleep in Mommy's bed. Okay?"

Evidently Laramie wasn't going to let him off that easy. Was this the same kid who'd pushed his nose in this morning when he discovered Coop was in Bristol's bed? The same little fellow who'd crawled over him to claim his spot beside his mother?

"He will stay, Laramie. Now you need to go to sleep."

He glanced over at Bristol. Was that her way of giving him an invitation? But then all she'd assured their son was that he would stay, not necessarily that he would stay in her bed. Did that mean she planned to make him sleep on the sofa?

He'd tried deciphering her mood today. Although she'd been friendly enough, it had seemed as if she had a lot on her mind. That was fine. He had a lot on his, too. But still, he couldn't help wondering if she regretted the intimacy they'd shared last night. She hadn't mentioned it and neither had he.

"Love you, Mommy."

"Love you back, Laramie. See you in the morning." And just like the night before, Bristol leaned over and kissed him on the cheek. However, unlike last night, before drifting off to sleep Laramie said, "Love you, Daddy."

Coop felt a tug at his heart and a tightness in his throat. It boggled his mind how a child could love so easily. "I love you back, Laramie."

He and Bristol watched as their son drifted off to sleep.

When they left Laramie's room, Coop told her they needed to talk.

Did he regret sleeping with her last night? The morning had started off well…at least she'd thought so, when he'd returned and surprised her with that beautiful plant. However, since then he'd seemed quiet. More than once she'd noticed him studying her like she was a puzzle he was trying to put together. Why?

She looked across the room at him. He was staring at the Christmas tree. What was he thinking? She'd invited him to spend Christmas with her and Laramie. Then what? When would he be leaving New York for his next mission?

"Ready to talk?"

She wondered why he was asking her when he was the one who initiated the meeting. "I'm ready if you are."

He nodded and sat in the chair across from her. He looked at her for a few moments then he said, "I spoke with my attorney today."

"Oh? Why did you feel the need to do that?"

He leaned back in the chair and the fabric of his jeans emphasized his masculine thighs. She wished she didn't notice such things, but she did.

"Laramie is my heir and I wanted to include him in all my important documents."

"I see."

"I also needed legal advice on my rights as his father."

Bristol raised a brow. "Your rights?"

"Yes."

She frowned. "I don't understand. I thought I made it clear that I would never deny you access to Laramie and you could spend as much time with him as you want."

"Yes, but what if you decide to marry one day and your husband feels differently?"

"I don't ever plan to marry, so you have nothing to worry about."

"You don't know that."

"I don't know what?"

"That you never plan to marry. Things happen. You might change your mind."

Her frown deepened. "That won't happen."

"You can't be sure," he countered.

"Yes, I can."

He shook his head. "No, you can't. And because you can't, my attorney suggested that I take steps to protect my rights as Laramie's father by filing for joint custody."

Coop watched her lean forward in her seat, at full attention. Her eyes widened. "Joint custody?"

"Yes."

"That's crazy. You're not in this country most of the time. How can you even think about joint custody?"

"How can I not think about it, Bristol? In a way, it will make things easier on you."

"How do you figure that?" she asked, glaring at him.

"You will know what times during the year he will be with me and when he will be with you. One thing I'd like is to swap holidays every year."

"Swap holidays?" She asked the question like what he was requesting was the craziest thing she'd ever heard.

"Yes. I told you about the ranch I inherited from my grandparents. I want him to spend the holidays with me there next year. That will free you up to do whatever you want to do."

"Free me up? To do. Whatever I want. To do?"

She had enunciated each phrase. He could tell from the sound of her voice that her anger was increasing. "Yes. I figure with me pitching in, you'll be able to paint more. While I'm away as a SEAL, I plan on hiring a full-time nanny who—"

"A full-time nanny? You've got to be kidding." She inhaled and exhaled a few times and he knew she was trying to get her anger under control. "What's going on, Coop? What are you trying to do?"

He had no problem giving her an answer. "I'm trying to give you a reason to make our marriage real."

* * *

Bristol's pulse jumped a few notches as she inhaled deeply. "Why?" she asked him. "Why should we make our marriage real?"

He shifted again in his seat and she wondered if he'd done it on purpose to distract her. Did he have any idea how his movements always increased her hormone level?

"The foremost reason is our son. I just cited complications that could arise if we aren't married. Knowing I have a child is a game changer for me. It was never my intent to father a child until later in life, and like I told you, I don't regret him, Bristol. I appreciate everything you went through to bring him into this world. And just so you know, if the situation had been different and I hadn't been held hostage, if I had gotten your letter, you would not have been alone. I would have come to you. I would have been there for you and for my child."

"But how would you have been there, Coop? You're a part of the military's special services. When you leave on one of your missions you have no idea when you'll get back."

"True, but I would have taken the time off. The entire nine months if I had to. I would have made sure I was there for you. You would not have gone through your pregnancy alone."

He didn't say anything for a few moments. "I believe in accepting my responsibilities, Bristol, but, just so you know, I would not have asked you to marry me just because you were having a baby. I would have done right by my child and by you, but I would not have suggested marriage between us unless I thought it would work."

At least he was honest, she thought. "So given that, why do you think it will work now? We don't even know each other."

"We know enough and over the past couple of days

we've found out more. We could be together for years and not know everything. Besides, I enjoy getting to know you."

He shifted again and her gaze followed the movement. "I know you are a good mother. As far as I'm concerned, you're the best. I can't think of anyone else I'd want to be the mother of my child. I watch you with Laramie and I know how much you love him and will always put him first. A part of me wants to envy that closeness, but I can't. I want to be a part of it, Bristol. You've given Laramie something special. A home."

His words reminded her of something her father had said. Even though her mother had robbed him of time with Bristol, in the end, he couldn't resent her mother when his heart was filled with gratitude to her for shaping Bristol into the woman she was. One who was loyal and independent. Not spoiled or selfish. Although her father had never said so, she knew he'd compared her to his other two kids. After living in their household for almost two years, she could plainly see that his wife's parenting skills had been vastly different from her mother's. Krista Lockett hadn't known how to tell her sons no.

"To me marriage is more than a piece of paper," he said, interrupting her thoughts. "I can't help but believe that, especially when I see my parents together and how they interact with each other. Even if there wasn't all that love, I believe there would still be trust, respect and friendship between them."

Unfortunately, Bristol thought, she'd never witnessed any such thing between a married couple. It had always been just her and her mother, and her mother had rarely dated. The few times she had, Bristol hadn't been introduced to the men. When she'd asked her mother about it, all she'd said was that until she met someone special, there was no reason to introduce her dates to her daughter. Evidently her mother never met anyone special. And as for her father's marriage to Krista, Bristol could honestly say she'd never felt any love in their relationship. They'd shared the same bedroom but that was about all. They'd lived separate lives.

Bristol drew in a deep breath as she thought about what Coop had said. Yes, there was trust and respect between them. She'd trusted him enough three years ago to invite him into her home and she still trusted him. She also respected him. In just two days he had made an impact on his son's life. And there was his love for his country and his willingness to put his life on the line to protect it. There was no doubt in her mind they could be friends as they got to know each other. Sex between them was good.

But what about the love?

That was something he hadn't mentioned. He didn't love her, whereas she'd loved him almost from the start. A part of her truly believed she'd fallen in love with him the moment she'd seen him in Paris. There was no way she would have agreed to an affair if she hadn't loved him.

But none of those feelings mattered because all the love, respect, trust and friendship in the world couldn't erase how she'd felt when she'd thought he'd died. That was a period in her life she couldn't relive. Somehow, she needed to make him understand that.

"What you said might be true, but there's a reason I can't marry you, Coop, and it's one I can't get beyond."

He lifted a brow. "And what reason is that?"

She met his gaze, held it and said, "You might die."

Eighteen

"You might die..."

Coop stared at her, recalling their conversation last night when she'd said the same thing. Why was she so hung up on the possibility of him dying?

Something else he recalled her saying last night was that three years ago she'd thought he'd died like the others. At the time, he'd wondered what others she was talking about. Now he had an idea who they were. Her mother, father and aunt. All the people she'd ever cared about and loved.

His heart pounded hard in his chest. Did that mean she cared deeply for him, that she loved him?

What if he was right? The thought that she could love him as much as he loved her was more than he could have hoped for. There was only one way to find out.

"I vividly remember having this conversation with you last night. Why are you so obsessed with the possibility of me dying, Bristol? Why are you so convinced I won't come back to you and Laramie?"

He watched her closely, saw how she went still, saw the stark look of fear come into her eyes. Their gazes locked for a minute longer and then she rubbed her hand down her face before meeting his eyes again. Then he saw the tears she was fighting to hold back.

"Talk to me, Bristol. Tell me," he said softly.

Bristol's mind shifted to that day when Dionne had arrived at her apartment and told her what she'd found out about Coop. How could she make him understand how she'd felt and why there was no way they could have a real marriage?

There was no way she could go through something like that again.

"When I thought you had died," she said, trying not to choke on the words, "I thought I was going to die, as well. It came as such a shock. I experienced pain like I'd never felt before. It was deeper than when I lost my mom, my dad and Aunt Dolly. And I felt so alone."

She fought back her tears to continue. "Then I suddenly felt my baby…our baby…move for the first time. It was like he was trying to reassure me that things would be all right. But the thought that I'd lost you was more than I could bear. Even when I told myself that I never had you, that all we'd had was a holiday affair and that I probably would not have seen you again anyway, it didn't matter. The thought of you dying like the others nearly destroyed me. It was only when I finally came to grips with the fact that I was having a baby…your baby…a baby that would always be a part of you, that I was able to move on with my life."

Coop stood and walked over to her, extending his hand out to her. She took it and he gently tugged her off the sofa and into his arms. It was only then that she realized she hadn't been able to hold back all her tears. A few were streaming down her face. How awful it was for him to see her like this, crying over a man who'd meant more to her than she'd meant to him. But when he tightened his arms around her, pulling her deeper into the warmth of his embrace, it didn't seem to matter.

"Knowing you cared that much means a lot to me, Bristol. Like I told you, you were never far from my thoughts when I was captured. Thoughts of you are what helped me survive."

"Why?" she asked, wanting to know why he'd thought of her.

"Because during those three days we were together, you made a lasting impression on me."

Like he'd made on her, she thought. However, he'd gone a step further in making her fall in love with him.

He pulled back and looked at her, forcing her to meet his gaze. "And as you can see, I am very much alive. No matter how much torture they inflicted on me, I refused to let those bastards break me—because of you."

She lifted a brow. "Because of me?"

"Yes. I convinced myself that I had to survive for you. That once I was rescued I had to get back to you."

Too bad he hadn't meant that, she thought.

"By the time I made it to Paris, you had left."

Bristol went still as she stared at him. "What did you say?" She was convinced she'd heard him wrong.

"After getting rescued I had to comply with military procedures and get both physical and psychiatric evaluations. That took about three months. Then I flew to Paris to see you. Your landlord said you'd moved back to the States and hadn't left a forwarding address."

Bristol's head began spinning. "You went to Paris looking for me?"

"Yes."

"But why?"

He gently cupped her chin in his hand. "I had to see you again and let you know those three days with you meant everything to me."

"They did?"

"Yes, and I just didn't know the depth of what they meant until I saw you again the other night. But it really hit me this morning when I saw you and Laramie in bed, sleeping. Then I knew for certain."

"What did you know?"

He dropped his hands from her face to wrap them around her waist. "That I had fallen in love with you."

His words made her head spin even more. "What did you just say?"

He smiled down at her. "I said I fell in love with you, during that time in Paris. I tried to convince myself it was about the sex, and maybe it was at first. But by the time I left your place I felt an attachment to you I've never felt to any other woman." A smile touched his lips. "Who knows? Maybe my body knew I'd left something behind with you that I've never left with another woman, my baby."

"Oh, Coop," she said, feeling more tears well in her eyes. "I love you, too, but I'm so afraid I might lose you again."

He pulled her into his arms and tightened his hold on her. "Shh, sweetheart, it's okay. In life there are no guarantees, we know that. That's why it's important to enjoy our time together. If nothing else, being close to death so many times has taught me not to sweat the small stuff and to appreciate life. Living it to the fullest is what I want to do with you and our son. Please don't deny me that."

He paused before adding, "You gave me the hope and the will to live before, which was how I survived that hellhole. And you will continue to give me hope whenever I go out on any covert operation, Bristol. Now I have two people to come back to. Both you and Laramie. The two people I love the most."

His words meant everything. They were what she'd needed to hear. But could she get past the thought of losing him again?

She tightened her arms around him knowing she had to get beyond those fears. For her sake, for his sake and for their son's. She had to be strong and believe there was a reason their lives had reunited after all this time.

She pulled back and went on tiptoe to place her lips to his. The moment their lips touched, intense heat consumed her. She felt it spreading to him. He tightened his hold on her.

His masculine scent invaded her nostrils as he took her mouth with an urgency that made her weak in the knees. When she shifted she felt the hardness of his erection pressing against the juncture of her thighs.

Bristol released pleasured moans with every stroke of his tongue. She needed this. She had to think positively and believe they'd been reunited for a reason. For a purpose. They would do what her parents didn't do and raise their child together.

He deepened the kiss and she felt it all the way to the bone.

Suddenly, he pulled back and looked deep into her eyes. "I need more."

She needed more, too. "Then take more. Give me more."

Nothing else needed to be said. He swept her off her feet and into his arms and carried her up the stairs.

"I love you, sweetheart," Coop said, after making love to Bristol again.

He pulled her into his arms and glanced over at the clock. They'd made love three times since coming upstairs and had gotten little sleep in between. If the other morning was anything to go by, he figured his son would be invading this room in a couple hours, and Coop and Bristol still needed to talk.

Coop knew she was about to drift off to sleep and he needed to get her attention. "Bristol?"

"Um?"

"Will you marry me?"

She didn't say anything at first, then she looked up at him. "I can't let fear have power over me, right?"

He nodded. "Right."

A smile touched the corners of her lips. "Then yes, Coop. I will marry you."

A huge smile touched his features. "How soon?"

She chuckled. "Can we get through the holidays first?"

He shrugged. "I guess we can."

She kissed him on the cheek. "Thanks for being so accommodating." Then she asked, "When do you have to leave for another mission?"

"End of January, and I want us married before I leave."

"That shouldn't be a problem," she said.

"As far as anyone knows, we are renewing our vows. There will only be a few who know the truth."

"Your teammates?"

"Yes, and my parents. I told them I loved you and if nothing else, they understand the love between two people and how strong it can be. They can't wait to meet you and Laramie."

She eyed him skeptically. "You sure about that?"

"I'm positive." And he was. Once the initial shock wore off, his parents had called him back. They were excited and happy to have a grandchild. Coop figured they must have decided Bristol couldn't be all bad since she hadn't shown up trying to claim any of his inheritance on behalf of her child after she'd gotten word he was dead.

"And since we won't have time for a real honeymoon until later, I thought it would be nice if I took you and Laramie to my ranch for a week or two before I head out. We can hire an interior decorator to spruce the place up while I'm gone."

"I'd love that. Would you prefer living there more so than here?" she asked him.

"Wherever you want to live is fine with me. We can even do both if you like."

"Yes, that might be best. But for some reason I think I'm going to like your ranch."

He hoped she did. He wanted Laramie to love Cooper's Bend as much as he had while growing up.

"You will check out of the hotel and move in here with us, right?"

He chuckled. "Yes, I'll move in here with you and Laramie and we will spend the holidays together."

"Good."

He pulled her closer. She was right, all was good, and as long as he had her in his life, everything would continue to be good.

Everything would be perfect.

Epilogue

"I now pronounce you husband and wife. Laramie Cooper, you may kiss your bride."

Coop pulled Bristol into his arms and all he could think about was that she was now truly his. Legally so. When he felt a pull on his pants he broke off the kiss to glance down at his son.

"I want to kiss Mommy, too, Daddy."

Everyone laughed when Coop lifted his son up to kiss Bristol, as well.

He then glanced around. It had been a small wedding at the church Bristol attended. All his teammates had arrived yesterday with their wives, including Bane and Crystal. Coop's parents had gushed all over their grandson and Laramie enjoyed being the center of their attention.

Ms. Charlotte and her four sons attended and Coop was glad to meet them. Bristol hadn't told him that all four worked for the New York Police Department. They assured Coop that whenever he was gone they would keep an eye on Bristol. It wouldn't be a problem since she lived next door to their mother and they routinely checked on her anyway.

Coop's mother had walked into Bristol's home that

morning and her gaze had immediately latched on to the huge painting over her fireplace. When she asked Bristol about it, Bristol confessed it was a painting she and her father had done together. It was then that she'd told his mother who her father was. Coop thought he was going to have to pick his mother up off the floor. His very sophisticated mother had gotten giddy at the thought that her future daughter-in-law was the daughter of the famous artist, Randall Lockett.

The reception would be held in the church's dining hall, and tomorrow the three of them would fly to his ranch in Laredo. He couldn't wait to introduce his wife and son to ranch life at Cooper's Bend.

They would take a honeymoon when he got back from his next mission. Ms. Charlotte had agreed to watch Laramie for a week while they went to Jamaica.

"Ready to go to the reception Ms. Charlotte set up for us?" Bristol asked him.

Holding their son in his arms, Coop smiled at her. "Yes, sweetheart, I am ready. When it comes to you, I will always be ready."

"Thanks for inviting me, Bristol."

She smiled up at Colin Kusac. They had exchanged phone numbers that night at the gallery when she'd reunited with Coop. When Mr. Kusac had called to check up on her a few days later, she'd learned that just as she'd suspected, he was the person carrying out her father's wishes to make sure she got flowers every year on her birthday. He had explained that Randall had asked that of him before he'd died and Mr. Kusac had promised he would do so.

He'd also told her that he'd promised her father he would check on her from time to time. He confided that he knew how she'd been while living in Paris; and that when she returned to the United States to have her baby, he'd known about that, as well. He'd seen that night at the gallery as an opportunity to talk to her himself. She had discovered that Mr. Kusac—Colin—was one of the wealthiest men in New York and had come from old money.

"Thanks for standing in for Dad and giving me away."

"Thanks for asking me. I was honored to do so. Randall would have been proud of you today."

"Thank you."

They talked for a while longer and then the wives of Coop's teammates came up to say hello. She liked all the wives—Crystal, who was married to Bane, Layla, who was married to Viper, and Teri, who had been married to Mac from the start. They assured Bristol that she wasn't the only one with fears—that was part of being a SEAL wife. They would be part of her support team and would be there whenever she needed them. They even invited her to visit them at their homes. Everyone was excited when Viper and Layla announced they would be having a baby come early summer. They exchanged numbers with her and she knew they were women she would get to know as friends.

No sooner had the women walked off than Margie appeared, all smiles. Bristol knew why.

"I can't believe your husband is connected to so much wealth. Who would have thought his parents would be *those* Coopers. And that he's their heir."

"Yes, who would have thought?" Bristol smiled, knowing how Margie's mind worked.

"You did good, choosing him over Steven."

Bristol decided not to say that Steven hadn't even been in the running. When Margie left, Coop appeared at Bristol's side. "A car will be picking us up in a few minutes for the airport."

His parents' jet would fly them to Texas, where they

would stay for a week on a short vacation with Laramie. After Coop had told Laramie about the horses, their son had been bubbling over with excitement to visit the ranch.

Not caring that they had an audience, Coop pulled his wife into his arms and whispered, "I love you."

She smiled up at him. "And I love you, too."

And she meant that from the bottom of her heart.

* * * * *

RULES IN BLACKMAIL

NICHOLE SEVERN

For my husband: couldn't do this without you.

Chapter One

"You have exactly five seconds to talk, or I start shooting." Sullivan Bishop slipped his finger alongside the gun's trigger.

"I'm not armed." The woman in his sights raised her hands to shoulder level, but didn't make another move. She might've been pretty, but in his experience, pretty faces were the best at hiding lies. And the lean dark-haired woman standing in the middle of his office had one of the prettiest faces he'd ever seen. Knowing her, she'd come armed. "I want to talk. Figured this would be the best place to do it."

He balanced his weight between both feet. His heart pumped hard as he tightened his grip around the Glock. How long had it been since Jane Reise—the legendary JAG Corps prosecutor herself—had crossed his mind? Nine months? Ten? Didn't matter. Nobody uninvited strolled into Blackhawk Security and stepped back through those doors without answering for something.

Jane had a lot to answer for.

"And you thought breaking into my private security company after hours was your best plan? How the hell did you get in here?" Sullivan closed in on her one inch at a time while he listened for movement on the rest of the floor. How had she gotten past his security system? Blackhawk Security provided top-of-the-line security measures, including cameras, body-heat sensors, motion detectors and more. Whatever the client needed, they delivered. Sometimes those services included personal protection, investigating, logistical support to the US government and personal recovery. They did it all. But right now, his gut instincts were telling him Jane wasn't standing in his office for some added security around her town house.

"Would you believe me if I said I came to hire you?" She swiped her tongue over her full bottom lip. Dropping her hands to her side, she scanned the rest of the office and widened her stance. Moonlight, coming through the wall of windows looking over downtown Anchorage, splayed across one half of her face. It washed out the brilliant color of her hazel eyes he'd studied from her file all those months ago. She was far more beautiful in person—no argument there— but the cord of tension stiffening her neck darkened her features.

"You're kidding, right?" This was a joke. Had to be. Sullivan stopped no more than five feet from her, a quick burst of laughter rumbling through his chest. The gun grew heavy in his hand. He lowered it to his side but wouldn't holster the Glock until he was certain she'd come unarmed. "I'm the last person on this planet who'd help you."

Jane scanned the office a second time, looking everywhere but at him. Even in the dark, Sullivan swore the color drained from her face.

"I never meant..." She cleared her throat, determination wiping away the momentary fall of her features. "You have every reason to laugh in my face and shove me out the door, but I don't have anywhere else to go. The police don't have any leads, and I can't get the army involved. Not yet."

"Involved in what?" Flipping on the overhead lights, Sullivan saw what she'd tried to hide by sticking to the shadows of his office. She squinted against the onslaught of brightness. Dark circles had taken up residence under her eyes, a sort of hollowness thinning her cheeks. Her normally athletic and lean frame seemed smaller than he remembered from her photos, as though she'd lost not only weight but any muscle she'd gained from her current stint in the army. The white T-shirt and black cargo jacket washed color from her skin but didn't detract from her overall beauty. Still, something was wrong. This wasn't the same woman who'd stood in front of a judge a year ago and ripped apart his family.

"I'm being watched." The corner of her mouth twitched as though she were biting the inside of her cheek. Her shoulders rose on a deep inhale. "Stalked."

The fear in her voice twisted his insides—would twist any man's insides—but Sullivan didn't respond. It was a counterintelligence tactic. Keep your mouth shut, and the target was more likely to fill the silence. If she was lying, he'd know by the way her eyes darted to the left or how she held her arms around her middle.

"They've been in my house and my car. I don't know where else." Jane brushed a piece of short dark hair behind her ear and the strong, confident woman he'd studied from the surveillance photos and video taken during the trial disappeared. "If the army knew about this, they'd limit my security clearance, and I could lose my job. I called in an anonymous tip to the police, but—"

"The case isn't high on their list." He understood the way the Anchorage Police Department worked. Until there was an actual threat on Jane's life, they had more important cases to work. That'd been one of the reasons Sullivan had founded Blackhawk Security in the first place. Aside from providing investigative services for government officials and witnesses to crimes, his team protected victims law enforcement couldn't. Or wouldn't. But taking on Jane's case...

She wasn't lying, at least not from what he could tell, but helping her wasn't exactly high on his priority list either. "Do you have proof?"

With a quick nod of her perfectly angled chin, she drew her cell phone from her jacket pocket, swiping her finger across the screen. A few more clicks and she offered him the phone. "I found this picture of me sleeping in my bed yesterday morning. It's dated two nights ago, around midnight."

He took the phone from her and his index finger brushed against the side of her hand. The lack of warmth in her skin caught his attention, and he pulled back. Studying the photo taken with her own phone, Sullivan fought the urge to tighten his grip on the device. The idea of a man—any man—taking photos of a woman without her permission built pressure behind his sternum. A woman shouldn't be afraid, shouldn't have to look over her shoulder. Not ever. "Any ideas of who could've broken in?"

"No." Her defeated answer wisped out from between her lips, drawing his attention up. Eyes wide, she shook her head slightly. "I live alone."

Then, barring a random break-in, she most definitely had a stalker. Handing the phone back to her, Sullivan ensured his fingers didn't touch hers again. His insides had already caught fire from an intruder breaking into his highly secure office. He didn't need anything else clouding his head. "Does anyone else have a key to your apartment? Maybe an old boyfriend who hasn't gotten the idea you two are over?"

With another shake of her head, her hair swung slightly below her earlobes. "No. I don't..." Jane cocked her head to the side as she shrugged. "I don't have any old boyfriends. Not since I went into the army."

Which was five years ago, according to her military record. Sullivan's fingers twitched at his side. "And what about your case files? Anyone not—" he ground his back teeth "—*happy* with the way you handled their case?"

Aside from him, that was.

Her lips thinned as she rolled them between her teeth. "Not that I know of, but I have all the files for the cases I was assigned back at my house if you want to go through them."

Not going to happen. He shoved the Glock into his shoulder holster, the adrenaline rush draining from his veins. Despite getting past his security system, Jane wasn't a threat. Yet. "That won't be necessary."

"Okay, what then?" She rolled her shoulders back but didn't move otherwise. Did she realize how much he blamed her for what happened and didn't want to take the chance of getting close? He liked to think so. She'd prosecuted dozens of devoted soldiers—men and women who'd sworn to protect this country, men like him—and she wanted his help? The woman was insane.

Captain Jane Reise was responsible for his brother's suicide. She didn't deserve an ounce of pity from him.

Spinning toward his desk, he grabbed a pad of paper and a pen. "This is the name of another security consultant to handle your case. I suggest you give him a call and get out of my office."

"I came here because I need *your* help." Hints of that legendary prosecutor he'd studied bled into her voice. Her sweet scent of vanilla climbed down into his lungs and he forced himself to hold his breath. "Isn't that what Blackhawk Security does? Help people?"

"Yes." Sullivan ripped the note from the pad and handed it to her. He spun away from those far too intelligent eyes and headed for the door. Turning the knob, he swung it open and motioned her out. "But not you."

Crossing her arms, Jane leveled her chin to the floor and sat back against the desk. Every cell in his body stood at attention as fire bled into her gaze. "I'm not leaving until you agree to help me."

"Move. Or I'll throw you over my shoulder and dump you in the hallway." He liked the visual. Far too much. He shouldn't, but damn it he did. All that soft skin, her lean frame wrapped around his, her hair tickling him across his back. Sullivan shut down that line of thought. Didn't matter how fiery or intelligent she was or how much she begged for his help. Wasn't going to happen. Ever. He crossed his arms over his chest, parroting her movement. Even from this distance, he noted her throat constricting on a slow swallow. "Get out."

"I can pay you." She pushed off from the desk. "Anything you want."

"This isn't about money." Sullivan dropped his hold

on the door. Marching across the room, he shortened the space between them until she had to look up at him.

Her chin notched higher as she held her ground.

The woman had stood up to all kinds of criminals and soldiers over the years. She wasn't intimidated. Damn if that wasn't the sexiest thing he'd ever seen. But he knew better than to trust her.

Chest almost pressed against her, he quirked one corner of his mouth. There were other ways to get her out of his office. He pushed his palms on either side of her on the desk, leaning down. "Unless you're talking about something other than money…"

Her lips parted, a sharp exhale of air beating against him. Jane studied his face from top to bottom but didn't move to escape the box he'd created around her. She locked that striking gaze on his, eyes determined and wide. "Dollars and cents, Lieutenant Bishop. Nothing more."

"Then you'll want to leave before I put in a call to your commanding officer and have you disbarred for harassing the family of one of your victims." He shoved himself away from the desk, away from that intoxicating scent of hers, and headed toward the door.

"I can make you help me," she said.

Another rush of heat overwhelmed his control, and he stopped dead in his tracks. What part of his answer didn't she understand? He spun back toward her. If it was a fight she was looking for, fine. He had no problem taking down the woman who'd destroyed his family. He might even enjoy it. "I'd like to see you try."

"All right." Jane straightened her spine as though she was preparing for battle. That same fire he'd caught a glimpse of during his brother's court-martial encroached on the darkness embedded in her features. "I know who you really are. And I know what you've been hiding."

"YOU DON'T KNOW anything about me." Sullivan Bishop seemed so much...*bigger* than he had a moment ago. Caged by his body against the desk, she felt his heat tunnel through her clothing. Hatred had burned in those sea-colored eyes as he'd pressed his chest against hers.

Jane swallowed as he stretched his shoulders wider. What had she been thinking to try to blackmail a man like him? Blackhawk Security's CEO wasn't an administrator over a team of highly trained ex-military operatives. He *was* ex-military. He'd been a SEAL, capable of the worst kind of violence. And she'd just threatened everything he'd ever worked for.

He closed in on her a second time. His clean, fresh scent whispered across the underside of her jaw as he spoke.

The hairs on the back of her neck stood on end. Every word out of his mouth promised she was going to wish she hadn't gone down this path, but Jane didn't have any other choice. Gliding her tongue across her bottom lip—a movement his eyes locked onto—she stood her ground. There was no turning back. He was the best, and she needed his help. One way or another.

"I know Sullivan Bishop isn't your real name." Every muscle in his body tightened in warning, and Jane forced herself to breathe evenly. She pressed her lower back into the desk. "And the people holding your company's military contracts might be interested to know why you changed it. A few of your classified clients, too, I imagine."

"You're blackmailing me?" A low growl reverberated up his throat and hiked her blood pressure higher. The shadows angling across the dark, thick stubble darkening his jaw shifted, but those sea-blue eyes never left hers. The veins in his arms popped as he leaned into her, the butt of the Glock in his shoulder holster pressing into her arm. "Are you sure you want to go down this road, Captain Reise? It won't end well."

"I'm willing to do whatever it takes to survive." A shiver chased up her spine, but Jane held her ground. She couldn't live like this anymore. The late-night phone calls, the feeling of being watched, the sick photo in her cell phone of her sleeping. And there was more. Going back several weeks. "Have you ever been hunted like an animal, Lieutenant Bishop?"

The suffocating bubble of tension he'd built around her disappeared. The edge to his features softened. She breathed a little easier. Putting some distance between them, Sullivan relaxed his hands to his sides, but the strong muscles flexing the length of his arms promised he was fully capable of violence. "Yes."

"Then you know what it's like to constantly be looking over your shoulder, to feel so helpless you don't seem to have any control of your own life." She crossed her arms over her chest, fully aware of the loss of body heat he'd forced through her with his proximity. Her hands shook as the terror she'd tried keeping to herself crept through her. "To feel like every second you're alive could actually be your last."

The lines running from the edge of his nose to those perfectly crafted lips deepened. She couldn't read his expression, but the tension in his neck and shoulders released.

"How did you get through it?" she asked.

Sullivan's chest expanded on a deep inhale. At least he wasn't crowding her anymore. She could actually breathe again, but the cold fist tightened in the pit of her stomach. "I have people I trust to back me up no matter what the situation calls for."

She nodded. That was what she was counting on. Why she was here in the first place. Sullivan had the reputation for committing himself to every job he took on, and while it was a risk to rely on the man she was blackmailing, she hoped his reputation proved true. "Well, I don't have a team. I have you. And if it's going to take blackmail to get you to help me, then so be it."

Silence pressed in on her as Sullivan studied her from head to toe. A scorching trail of awareness skittered across her skin. What did he see? A woman who couldn't protect herself? Or the woman responsible for his brother's death?

"I'll give you twenty-four hours of my time," he said. "After that, you can go back to your cold, empty existence and leave me the hell alone."

He was just like the rest of them: her peers, the men and women she prosecuted to protect citizens of the United States, even her commanding officer. She'd earned her reputation as the Full Metal B, she supposed. Her job required an almost ruthless approach to the cases she'd been assigned, but this was the first time her rib cage tightened at someone's assessment of her. Which didn't make sense. She didn't care what Sullivan Bishop thought of her. She didn't care what any of them thought of her. Her insides twisted. She didn't care. Jane shoved off from the massive desk he'd trapped her against moments before. Uncrossing her arms, she stepped toward him. "So you'll help me?"

"I don't have a choice, do I? Isn't that how blackmail is supposed to work?" Sullivan rounded his desk. The thick muscles across his back flexed through his shirt. She forced her attention to the sway of his gun rather than the way he moved, to prove she could take her eyes off him. Lean waist, strong legs, hints of his trident tattoo peeking out from under his T-shirt. Such a dangerous man shouldn't be that attractive. "We'll take my car."

Jane straightened. Okay. They were doing this. "Where are we going?"

"To your town house. I'll brief my team on the way." He unholstered the Glock from his side and dropped the magazine into his hand. After a glance at the rounds, he replaced it with efficient, sure movements and chambered a round. He raised that piercing gaze to hers. "I have a man on my team who used to work forensics for the NYPD. If your stalker has been in your house like you claim, he'll find the evidence and we can all move on with our lives."

She ran her cold palms over the front of her jeans and took another step toward him. He was actually going to help her find the man trying to destroy her life? A knot of hope pulsed from deep in her chest. "And if he does find evidence? What then?"

Sullivan came around the desk, his wide shoulders blocking out the magnificent view of the Chugach mountain range behind him. Nearly pressing against her, he stared down at her. At six foot four, it wasn't hard, but the intimidation had drained from his body.

He stalked toward the office door. "Then you'll have the proof you need to take to the police."

"What?" Jane wrapped her hand halfway around his massive biceps and spun him around to look at her. He'd let her. She didn't have the strength to move a mountain like him. She was at the end of her rope, and she hadn't come here to admit defeat. Her leave ended in a week, and she'd come no closer to discovering her stalker's identity than she was three months ago. Desperation held her tight.

She glared up into those sea-blue eyes of his, her throat constricting. "I thought I made myself perfectly clear. Either *you* help me find the person stalking me or I go to the government and your clients with what I know about you. And your family."

Facing her, oh-so-slowly, Sullivan towered over her, and she fought the urge to take a step back. He leaned in close, mere centimeters from her mouth, as though he intended to kiss her. "Then let me make myself perfectly clear. The only way you get my help is if we do this my way, and I plan to get you out of my life as soon as I can."

Jane flinched, but he didn't wait for her to answer, heading for the door.

"Let's go," he said.

This was a mistake. She should've known how deep Sullivan's hatred for her flowed, but she'd run out of options. Jane followed on his heels toward the elevator, allowing a good amount of distance between them as they crowded into the small space on the way down to the parking garage. Neither said a word. His clean scent wrapped around her, and she gripped the handrail to clear her head. In less than a minute, he led her out of the elevator and across the empty parking garage toward a black SUV.

Tingling spread across her back—an all-too-familiar feeling—and Jane turned back toward the elevator, heart in her throat. Darkness surrounded them. Everyone in the building had already gone home for the day. She'd made sure. Everyone except Sullivan and a few security guards, but someone else was here. *He* was here, watching her. She felt it.

"Jane." Sullivan's deep timbre flooded her nerves with relief, but she couldn't shake the feeling they were being watched. "Jane," he said again.

She stared at him. It was her imagination. Had to be. There was no way anyone could've followed her here. She'd been too careful, but still, the sensation between her shoulder blades prickled her instincts. "I'm coming."

Sullivan ripped open the driver's-side door of the large black SUV, his eyes sweeping across the parking garage as she moved to the other side. Once she was safely inside the car, the sensation disappeared and Jane breathed a bit easier. Nobody had been watching her. The constant paranoia had just become a habit.

Sullivan slammed the door behind him and started the engine. Black leather and dark interiors gave her a false sense of security, but having him in the driver's seat eased some of the tension on either side of her spine. At the exit, he lowered the window and scanned his key card. Nobody went in or out of the garage without a card. He swung the SUV north through an area of warehouses and railroads, as though he knew exactly where they were headed.

The SUV plowed through the wet streets of downtown Anchorage, spitting up water and snow along the way. The heater chased away the ice that'd built inside her over the past few weeks. She was reminded of Sullivan's heat back in his office. The same heat rolled off him in waves now. She watched him from her peripheral vision. He wore only a T-shirt and jeans in these temperatures, a human furnace. It'd been too long since she'd felt anything but fear.

"I know what you've heard about me, what they called me in Afghanistan. I'm not as cold as you think." Sitting straighter in her seat, Jane stared down into her lap to counteract the need to explain herself to Blackhawk Security's CEO. "I didn't want to dig into your history. I needed—"

"We're not doing this right now," he said, one hand on the wheel. He still wouldn't look at her. Typical alpha male, determined not to talk. Sullivan pressed his foot on the accelerator as they rolled onto the bridge across Knik Arm, the shallow water almost motionless with a few inches of ice across the top.

"All right." She wiped her clammy hands down her thighs. "Tough crowd."

A light falling of snow peppered the windshield. Nothing like the storms Anchorage usually saw this time of year, but just as beautiful as she remembered growing up in Seattle.

The high screech of peeling tires broke their self-imposed silence, and Jane swept her gaze out the window. Blinded by fast-approaching headlights, she shoved away from the door as a truck slammed into her side of the SUV.

Chapter Two

The loud groan of a truck's engine brought Sullivan around.

"Reise?" Pain. In his skull. Everywhere. He blinked to clear his vision and ran his hand over his left cheek. Something warm and sticky coated his hand. Blood. He fought to scan his body for other injuries. Hell. They'd flipped.

Cracks in the windshield spidered out in a dendritic pattern, blocking his view of the other driver. Had they survived? Been injured? He depressed the seat belt button and collapsed onto the SUV's roof. Broken glass from the window cut into him. He pounded his fist into the roof and locked his jaw. "Damn it!"

He swiped blood from his eyes. Where was Jane? Twisting inside the crushed interior, he spotted her. Sullivan crawled through debris and around the middle console, ignoring the pain screaming for his attention. The seat belt held her in the passenger seat, upside down. Couldn't search her for injuries here. They needed to get clear of the wreck. "Captain Reise, can you hear me?"

She didn't respond, unconscious.

Bracing himself, Sullivan released her belt and

caught her just before she hit the SUV's roof. He pressed his palm against the glistening gash across the right side of her head to stop the bleeding, then checked her slender neck for a pulse. Thready, but there.

Burning rubber and exhaust worked down into his lungs. Crouching low to see through the passenger-side window, he kept pressure on her wound. But couldn't hold it for long. The yellow tow truck's tires screeched again as it made another lunge straight for them.

"You've got to be kidding me." His fight-or-flight instinct kicked into high gear. Heaving Jane across the cab, he pulled her through his shattered driver's-side window with everything he had. They cleared the SUV, but his momentum catapulted them down the steep embankment surrounding the shallow water of Knik Arm.

The world spun as snow and mud worked under his clothes and clung tight to his skin and hair. His arms closed around Jane, the movement as natural as breathing as they rolled. They slammed into a nearby tree, mere feet from the ice-cold water of the river. Positioned on top of her, he scanned her once more, panting. His vision split into two and he shook his head.

He leveraged his weight into the palms of his hands to give her more breathing room, his heart pumping hard. "Captain Reise, wake up. We need to—"

The second crash forced Sullivan's gaze up the snow-covered hill. The SUV's headlights flickered a split second before the entire vehicle started to slide down the slope, heading right for them. There was no time to think. He dug his fingertips into Jane's arm and spun them through the snow and weeds to the right as fast as he could. The SUV sped past, breaking through the six inches of solid ice at the edge of the river.

Hell. This wasn't some freak accident. Someone wasn't just stalking Jane. They'd now decided they wanted her dead. He studied the cut across her head, then her sharp features. She'd been telling the truth. Sullivan exhaled hard. Puffs of breath crystallized in front of his mouth. "Come on, Jane. We have to get out of here."

Jane? When had he started calling her by her first name?

Screeching tires above echoed in his ears as the tow truck hauled fast away from the scene. *Damn it.* He hadn't seen the driver at all. He could still catch up. He could—

Jane moaned as she stirred in his arms. Her lips parted. Such soft, pink lips. Pulse now beating steady at the base of her throat, she fought to focus on him. She lifted one hand toward her face, but he wrapped his fingers around her small wrist. "What...happened? My head—" She locked her fuzzy gaze on him. "Did you just call me Jane instead of Captain Reise?"

He swallowed. She'd heard that? "You hit your head pretty hard against the window when the truck slammed into us. Must've heard me wrong."

Sullivan shoved a strand of her hair out of her face to see her wound better. Her features softened as she closed her eyes. She was okay as far as he could tell, but the spike of adrenaline had yet to drain from his system. Whoever had been driving that truck had made a very dangerous enemy. Not only had he gone after an unarmed woman, he'd tried killing the CEO of the government's most resourced private security contractor. No way Sullivan was going to turn Jane's case over to Anchorage PD now. That bastard was his.

"What happened?" Those brilliant hazel eyes swept over the embankment, and he noted exactly when Jane caught sight of the totaled SUV. Every muscle down her spine tightened as she dug her heels into the snow to sit up. "Somebody tried to kill us."

No point in denying the facts. Her stalker had gone from hunting Jane in her own home to outright attempted murder. "Looks that way. Can you stand?"

She nodded, rolling her upper body off the ground, but grabbed for his arm. Stinging heat splintered through his muscles where she touched him, his bare skin exposed to the dropping temperatures.

"It'll be light soon." Sullivan tugged his arm from her grasp as he scanned their surroundings. They hadn't made it too far from downtown, but he couldn't take the chance of taking her back to the office. Her stalker had known exactly where to find them, as if he'd been waiting. Might've been on her tail when Jane had broken into Blackhawk Security. Whoever it was, the guy was willing to kill bystanders to get to her, which meant they couldn't go to her town house either. "We don't want to be caught out here overnight."

"There's nowhere we can hide." Her teeth chattered together as she wrapped her arms around her midsection. She stared at the half-sunken SUV, shaking her head. "I was careful. I made sure no one was following me when I went to your office. I made sure…" Her words left her mouth quick and breathless as she finally looked at him. "He wants me dead."

His insides flipped, and Sullivan reached for her without thinking. He pulled her into his chest. At about five foot three, Jane barely came to his sternum, but she fitted. Fragile, vulnerable, but strong. His back molars clamped together, jaw straining. She'd ripped apart his family. She was even blackmailing him into protecting her, but the fear darkening those eyes had urged him to lock her body against his automatically. Her job might've made her a few enemies, but not even the army's most revered prosecutor deserved to be hunted like an animal. No one did.

Tremors racked through her—most likely shock—but he dropped his hold. Wisps of her sweet scent replaced the smell of exhaust and burned rubber seared into his memory, and he inhaled deeply to clear his system. They had to get moving. "Whoever this guy is, we'll find him."

The shivers simmered. Sliding her hands between their bodies, she placed them above his heart and tilted her head back to look up at him. "Thank you."

Heat worked through his chest, a combination of dropping temperatures and the rage he held for her fighting for his attention. Her nearly dying at the hands of a crazed psychopath wouldn't change the past between them. Nothing could.

"For getting me out of the SUV, I mean." Cuts, scrapes and dried blood marred her otherwise flawless skin, a small bruise forming on the right side of her face. A strand of short black hair slid along the curve of her cheek, but he wouldn't brush it away. "You could've left me there to take care of your blackmail problem, but you didn't. I appreciate that."

He kept his expression tight. Right. Jane Reise had the power to bring down his entire company with one phone call and had made it perfectly clear she was willing to use it. How could he have forgotten?

"Yeah, well, whoever you pissed off tried to kill

me, and you're the only lead I have to hunt him down."
Sullivan put some much-needed space between them.
She'd most certainly lived up to her reputation in the
last hour they'd been forced together. He curled his fingers into his palms to douse the urge to comfort her.
The woman who'd destroyed his family—the woman
blackmailing him for his help—didn't deserve comfort. And she wouldn't get it from him. He had control. Time to use it.

"Right." Jane's throat constricted on a hard swallow.
She shoved her hands into her jacket pockets and sur-
veyed their surroundings. "I'd say call a tow truck, but
I think your SUV is beyond saving."

Cracking ice pulled his attention toward the river.
The SUV was sinking. In less than five minutes, the
entire vehicle would be submerged in the icy Gulf of
Alaska. Treading through six inches of muddy snow
toward the vehicle, Sullivan registered her confident
footsteps behind him. He hauled the tailgate above his
head and tossed the false bottom of the trunk to his
right. "Now we're on foot. Take this." He thrust the
lighter duffel bag from the trunk at Jane. He grabbed a
thick coat and the heavier bag for himself. Boy Scouts,
SEALs and Alaskans all had one motto in common:
Never Get Caught in the Wilderness Unprepared.

She unzipped the bag he'd handed her. "Food and
guns. You're officially the man of my dreams."

She'd meant it as a joke, but, hell, the compliment
forced him to pause.

"Wait until you see what's in this bag. Between us,
we'll be able to survive out here for at least three days."
He didn't bother closing the tailgate. Some civilian
would drive past and put a call in to the cops, or the

SUV would sink. Either way, he and Jane weren't sticking around to find out. He couldn't take the risk of her stalker coming back to the scene to make sure the job was done. "We're heading northeast." He pointed toward the thick outcropping of trees as he pulled on his thick coat. "It's a three-mile hike. We need to leave now in case your stalker realizes he didn't finish the job."

"Where are we going?" She brought up the hood on her cargo jacket. Smart move. The Alaskan wilderness wasn't any place to screw around. They had to stay warm and dry or risk hypothermia.

Sullivan covered his head to conserve body heat. A gust of freezing wind whipped one side of his body as he headed into the forest. "Somewhere no one will find us."

HE'D CALLED HER Jane back on the embankment. Not Captain Reise. She'd heard him clear as day. Because even in the midst of suffocating unconsciousness, Jane had locked on to his voice. The man she was blackmailing had brought her out of the darkness. Why? He had no allegiance to her.

Sullivan cleared a path through the thickest parts of the forest with one of the extra blades from his duffel bag a few feet up ahead of her. Shadows cast across his features from the beam from his flashlight. Snow had worked down into her boots, turning to slush. Her jeans were soaked through. How long had they been out here? An hour? Two? Three miles didn't seem like much until deep snow and freezing temperatures added to the misery. Not to mention it was dark and difficult to see. Her toes had gone numb long ago, fingers following close behind, but Jane kept her mouth shut.

They had to be close, right? She swiped away a few drops of water from her cheek, wincing as pain radiated up toward her temple. The sooner they made it to their destination—wherever that was—the better.

Distraction. She had to keep her mind off her frozen limbs. "Bet you've never had to walk through the Alaskan wilderness with a client to escape a crazed psychopath before."

"You're right." He laughed, a deep guttural rumble she felt down into her bones. It was real, warming. Swinging his arm out, he held back a large branch so she could pass. He stared down at her while she maneuvered around him, those sea-blue eyes brightening in the muted beam from his flashlight. "I usually reserve these kinds of trips for people I've been assigned to hunt down."

"Is that a nice way of putting that you've killed people for a living?" She instantly regretted the words, and her heart rate rocketed. "I mean, I read your military record during the trial. I know you used to be a SEAL, one of the best. You don't have to lie to me or sugarcoat anything."

"Once a SEAL, always a SEAL. You never really retire. It stays in your blood, makes you who you are. Forever." Defensiveness tinted his words as Jane followed in his sunken footsteps. But, faster than she thought possible, he latched onto her arm and spun her into his chest. The hard set to his eyes said Sullivan Bishop could be a very dangerous enemy, but she'd known that before throwing his secrets in his face. Right now, in this moment, her instincts said he wouldn't hurt her. She'd learned to trust those instincts to get her through the past few years. "And, as a prosecutor, you of all people should understand that the best defense against evil men is good men who deal in violence."

Jane took a deep breath. One, two. She couldn't get enough air. Staring up at him, she noted the gash across his cheek he must've suffered during the wreck. He'd protected her back there because she was a lead. Nothing more. He'd said as much, but why did being this close to him change her breathing patterns? "And what about now?"

"What do you mean?" Sullivan narrowed his eyes, his features turning to stone.

"Do you still 'hunt down' people for a living?" she asked.

Seconds ticked by, then a minute. Something in her heart froze. Sullivan was a killer. It'd been part of the job description, part of his past, but Jane couldn't keep track of how long he held her there as snow fell from branches around them. His mesmerizing gaze held hers, but Jane had a feeling he wasn't really seeing her at all. His fingers dug into her, keeping his hold light enough not to bruise. He wasn't trying to hurt her. Maybe…he didn't want to let her go.

"Isn't that why you blackmailed me into helping you?" The demons were evident in his eyes, but Sullivan released his grip on her arm and put a few inches of freezing Alaska air between them as he turned his back on her and pushed forward.

"No. I blackmailed you to find the man doing this to me so we can turn him over to the police." Her skin tingled through her thin coat where he'd latched onto her arm. Phantom sensations. There was no way he could affect her like that. Not in these temperatures. She studied him from behind, the way his back stretched each time he took a step, the way he carried himself as though nothing could get through him if a threat arose. "I'm sorry. I didn't mean to…"

What? Pry into his life? Doubt his reasons for doing what needed to be done overseas and here in the United States?

Pushing on up ahead, he worked to clear branches. After a few seconds, Sullivan halted in his tracks, turning back toward her. Stubble speckled with ice and snow, he swayed on his feet. Good to know she wasn't the only one suffering from exhaustion. He scanned over her from head to toe. "Don't worry about it."

"I appreciate everything you've done for your country and what you're doing now. I'm sure every American does. It's admirable." She fought for a full lungful of air. Despite the dropping temperatures, her skin heated when he looked at her like that. Like she was a threat. She stepped over the remnants of a few branches he'd demolished along the way, nearly losing her footing. In that moment, something between them shifted. An understanding of sorts. No messy blackmail. No psychotic lunatic trying to run them down with his tow truck. Not even security consultant and client. Just two people trying to survive in the middle of the Alaskan wilderness. Together. "You don't have to do all this work yourself, you know. I can help."

"You're more than welcome to…" His mouth went slack as though he couldn't get enough oxygen. Probably couldn't. Freezing temperatures didn't discriminate against SEALs or lawyers. Mother Nature treated everyone equally.

"Are you okay?" she asked. "Sullivan?"

They'd crossed at least two and a half miles of

heavy snow and growth, maybe more. She was tired and couldn't feel her toes, but her instincts urged her to get to him. Now.

Sullivan doubled over, dropping his gear before he collapsed onto his side.

"Sullivan!" Jane discarded the duffel bag and lunged toward him. Her feet felt like frozen blocks of ice, but she fought the piling snow with everything she had. Hands outstretched, she checked his pulse. Weak. "No, no, no, no. Come on. Get up."

Gripping his jawline, she brought one ear to his mouth. Still breathing. Would anyone hear her out here? "Help!"

Sullivan Bishop was a SEAL, for crying out loud. This shouldn't be happening. He'd trained for situations exactly like this. Her heart beat out of control. She dived for the duffel bag he'd been carrying. Food, more guns. There had to be a—

"Yes!" She ripped the first-aid kit from the bag, fought to break the seal on the space blanket, then covered him completely. The hand and foot warmers were easier to open with her stiff fingers, but they wouldn't be enough. One look at Sullivan's normally full, sensual pink lips said she was running out of time. She had to get his body temperature up before hypothermia set in, but the blanket and a few warmers wouldn't cut it.

"You are not allowed to die on me. You hear me? I can't do this without you. You're going to listen to my voice and wake up so I don't have to carry you." Scanning the thick trees ahead of their location, Jane narrowed in on a clearing. And across that? A small cabin set into the other side of the trees. Had to be Sullivan's safe house. Had to be. If not, they'd at least have some protection from the elements while the owners called for help. "You're going to make me drag you there, aren't you?"

She didn't have time to wait for an answer. Leaving the duffel bags, Jane fisted her numb grip into his jacket and pulled. The snow eased the friction underneath him as she hefted Sullivan toward the clearing, but her strength gave out after only a few hundred feet. She collapsed back into the snow, fingers aching, heart racing. Hours upon hours of training kept her in shape in the army, but this? This was different. And the security contractor at her feet wasn't exactly a lightweight. "Come on, Sullivan. Think lighter thoughts."

The trees passed by in a blur. She couldn't focus on anything but shoving one foot back behind the other. Minutes passed, hours it seemed, and they hit the clearing. Only a few hundred more feet and faster than she thought possible, the heels of her boots knocked against the steps leading into the cabin. She tried the door. Locked. Pounding her fists against the door, she listened carefully for movement, but no one answered. In a rush, she searched for a fake rock, anything that would get her inside. She hunted around the bushes and flitted over something that was most certainly not natural: a key taped to one of the thick branches. Shoving the steel into the dead bolt and turning, she sighed in victory.

Heat enveloped her in seconds, thawing her fingers in a rush until they burned. No time. She spun back to Sullivan and slid her grip under his arms. An exhausted groan broke free from her lips as she hauled him inside. Fire. She had to start a fire to get him warm.

"Almost there. Hang on." Throwing off her coat,

Jane ran toward the fireplace and got a small fire going. She'd add more to it in a few minutes, but right now, Sullivan's wet clothes and his own sweat were doing his body more harm than good. She stripped off her coat, socks and jeans, staring down at the peaceful expression settled across his strong, handsome features. Then it was his turn.

"Sorry, Sullivan. You might hate me even more after you wake up." Crouching at his feet, she untied his boot laces and unbuttoned his pants. Jane hefted her own shirt over her head, adding it to the pile of clothes at her feet. Tugging him up into a sitting position, she stripped him down to nothing. "But it's going to save your life."

Chapter Three

Dying hurt like hell.

Heat blistered along his forearms, neck and face. His entire body ached in places he hadn't thought about since his SEAL days. He hadn't been on active duty for over a year now, but Sullivan still trained as though he were. Had to be ready for anything his clients might throw his way. Even the beginning stages of hypothermia. Damn it, he should've known better. Groaning, he cracked open his eyes, stomach still rolling. A fire popped a few feet from him.

At least he knew where he was. The cabin was sparse: one bedroom, one bath, a living room and small kitchen. He mostly came out here when he wanted to be alone, needed to get away from people, the city or both. No neighbors, no one to encroach on his business. And he'd never brought anyone here before. He'd kept this place under his mother's maiden name in case he'd needed a safe house. It couldn't be traced back to him if Jane's stalker—or anyone else—had the inclination to investigate. But how in the hell did he get here?

Sullivan raised his head. He wasn't alone.

Endless amounts of warm, smooth skin stretched out beside him under the heaviest blanket he kept on hand in the cabin. A head of black hair rested against his right arm. Jane? He had to be dreaming. Skimming his fingers across her shoulder blade, he sank into how very real she felt. Nope. Not a dream. But why would she… The lapse in his memory filled almost instantly. The last thing he remembered was the look on her face as he…collapsed. Terrified. Hell. Had she dragged him all the way out here on her own?

Her shoulders rising and falling against him in a slow, even rhythm said she was fast asleep. He couldn't have been out for long. An hour—two, tops—from the amount of moonlight coming through the front room window. He'd messed up out there, but her sultry vanilla scent spared him a few ounces of guilt. It dived into his lungs, and he took a deep breath to keep it in his system as long as possible. His heart rate dropped to a slow, even thump behind his ears. He closed his eyes, all too easily seeing himself burying his nose in her hair for another round.

Nope. Not the time and definitely not this woman.

Sullivan shifted his hips away from her backside. If Jane woke up now, there'd be no hiding what was going on downstairs in that moment. His brain might have control, but with the expanse of soft skin along his front, his body had other ideas. He scanned the living room and spotted his clothes hanging from fishing line around the open rafters by the fireplace. He'd gotten out of some real complicated situations in the navy. There had to be a way to unwind himself from this warm, coldhearted woman without waking her.

He leveraged his weight into his toes and stretched out his arm. A soft, guttural moan worked up Jane's throat. Something primal washed through him. He froze. There was a stalker on the loose and he'd nearly died out in the wilderness, but all Sullivan could think about was what he wouldn't give to hear that sound again.

She shifted against him, wrapping her leg around him as though she sensed he was trying to escape. What the—

The breath Sullivan had been holding crushed from his lungs. He settled back where he'd been, pressed right against her, his front to her back. "You're awake, aren't you?"

Rolling into him, Jane startled him with a wide, gut-clenching grin. The dark, sultry look of her gaze constricted his throat, and a shiver chased down his spine. Her pupils expanded. For an instant, he swore he saw desire blazing in her eyes. Or maybe the hypothermia had done more damage to his brain than he'd originally thought. "I couldn't wait to see your reaction when you woke up and found a naked woman under the blanket with you. Surprise."

"Did I meet your expectations?" Sullivan was proud of the fact his voice sounded steady and calm. Especially considering how very far from calm he felt at the moment. Aware of how naked he was and how she couldn't possibly miss the show going on at her lower back, he held his weight away from her.

"Absolutely priceless. And, as a bonus, I got to see you naked." That amused smile of hers did funny things to his stomach, and he couldn't help but clench the blanket in his grip for some piece of control. Resting her hand on his chest, Jane pushed herself up to a sitting position, taking the blanket with her as she stood. Cool air rushed down his body, prickling his skin along the way. "Don't worry, big guy. It wasn't anything sexual. You were dying and I had to get your body temperature up."

Her long legs peeked out from between the folds of the blanket as she walked, the fire glinting off her bright red toenail polish. Not exactly the color he'd visualized for the woman he'd blamed for his brother's suicide this past year. Black maybe, something to match her soul.

But Jane had saved his life out there. Even if she was only using him to track down her stalker, that counted for something in his world. Her reputation said she was the JAG Corps prosecutor willing to do anything and everything to convict the men and women who interrupted her crusade for justice. He scanned over his clothing hanging from the rafters. The Full Metal Bitch had only kept him alive to fix her stalker problem. Nothing more.

There was a lot he didn't know about her, even more he couldn't trust. One thing he did know? He would've died out there today if it hadn't been for Jane. So, for now, he would choose to see a woman in danger, a woman who'd lost her grip on everything she thought she could control. Not someone who could turn on him at any moment.

She smiled over her shoulder at him as she pulled her clothing from the makeshift laundry lines.

Pulling a pillow from the couch across his hips, Sullivan cleared his throat. "Thank you for saving my life out there. Can't imagine what it took to get me through that door. Couldn't have been easy."

"Guess that makes us even, doesn't it?" Her hair flipped around her head as she headed straight for the single bathroom on the other side of the cabin and shut the door tight. The sound of the lock clicking into place shut down any hint of something between them.

It wasn't going to happen. Not now. Not ever. She might've saved his life out there a few hours ago, but Jane had a lifetime of steel running through her veins, steel that'd gotten his brother killed. She was the reason he didn't have any family left in this world. Besides, she was a client, and Blackhawk Security operatives were never to get involved with their clients. No exceptions.

Which reminded him—he had to fill his team in on their new case. Because even without blackmail hanging over his head, the bastard terrorizing Jane owed Sullivan a new SUV.

He tossed the pillow back onto the couch and dressed in a hurry. She'd hung his clothes up by the fire to dry them out, and the warm fabric chased away the chill of Jane leaving his side. How could he have been so stupid out there? Rule number one when in below-freezing temperatures: stay dry, stay warm. He usually had enough sense to slow down and ensure he wasn't sweating. What had changed?

The bathroom door clicked open and his attention slid toward Jane as she stepped back into the main room. He pulled his shoulders back. There stood his answer. He hadn't exactly been in the right frame of mind after nearly getting run down by a tow truck. He'd wanted to get Jane to safety as fast as possible. Stupid. She'd proved she could take care of herself, had even saved his life in the process. Aside from a few bumps and bruises, she was no worse for wear.

"This is a nice place." She scanned over the small

cabin, fingers stuffed into her jacket as he opened one drawer of his massive desk. "Not great security, though. A key taped to a bush? Thought you security consultants were better than that."

"Sometimes there's beauty in simplicity. Anybody breaking in here would expect some kind of elaborate security system, all the while wasting time looking for it. Gives me time to counter." Another one of those debilitating smiles overwhelmed her features, and he couldn't help but smile back. Sullivan flipped one of the many burner cell phones he'd unearthed from the desk over in his hand. The sensation of lightness disappeared, however, the longer he studied her. Eyes narrowing, he tried justifying the last few hours since she'd broken into his office. Why him? Why now? "What are you doing here, Jane?"

A small burst of laughter escaped from between those rosy lips. She motioned toward the front door. "Well, I couldn't very well leave you here alone after—"

"No." Sullivan closed in on her, the hairs on the back of his neck standing on end. "I mean why did you break into my office tonight? You had other options. Any number of bodyguards or private investigators in Anchorage would've jumped to help you for the right price. After all, you were ready to offer me anything." He halted no more than a foot from her, reading those deep hazel eyes for any sign of hesitation. "Why come to me?"

"Isn't it obvious?" She tried backing away but hit the wall beside the front door. "I had dirt on you and your family, and I knew I could use it to force you to help me. Saved myself a hell of a lot of money in the process."

Heat prickled under Sullivan's skin, crawling up his neck and warming his face. Only Jane crossed her arms across her chest and the strong pulse at the base of her neck beat unevenly. She didn't believe a word she was saying. And, thinking about it now, she'd only pulled the blackmail card when he'd refused to help her the first two times she'd asked. "You're lying."

Color left her features, a telling reaction he'd noted back in his office. Jane curled her fingers into the palms of her hands, stance wide as though she intended to run straight out the front door. Nervousness? Embarrassment? Difficult to tell when she wiped any kind of emotion from her features so fast.

"What do you want from me?" He stalked toward her. No. She wasn't going to hide behind that hardened exterior this time.

"I guess after what happened on the road, you deserve the truth. It seems stupid now, but I didn't have anyone else I could trust." She licked her bottom lip, but Sullivan refused to let the motion distract him this time. Answers. That was all he wanted. He'd risked his life—twice—for her. Now he needed to know why she'd pulled him into this mess. She cocked her head to the side. "I came to you because I saw how protective and dedicated you were to Marrok during his trial. And after I uncovered that photo in my phone yesterday, I needed a little bit of that in my life." Raising that beautiful gaze to his, she let her shoulders deflate and she exhaled hard. "I needed *you*."

"I NEED TO brief my team." His gravelly voice played havoc with her insides, but Sullivan turned away from her, phone in hand. Refused to even look at her.

Every nerve in Jane's body caught fire. That was all he had to say? Watching him, she noted the strain around his eyes, the slightly haggard expression on his features as he spoke into the phone in whispered, clipped responses. She was used to it. In their line of work, she'd learned anybody could be listening in. Phone taps, parabolic mics. Without an idea of who her stalker was, why they'd come after her or what resources they had access to, she and Sullivan couldn't afford to be careless.

She headed into the kitchen. When had she eaten last? Her stomach rumbled. Too long ago. Sullivan turned toward her at the sound. The weight of his gaze slid across her sternum. Head down, she focused on her hunt for anything edible in this place. No luck. He obviously didn't stay here often. The walls were bare, the counters covered in dust. She ran her fingers over the cream granite, but ripped her hand away at the low temperature.

"I sent my forensic investigator, Vincent, to your place with some backup." Sullivan tossed the cell phone he'd been using onto the granite. Exhaustion played across his features, darkening the circles under his eyes. He hadn't gotten much sleep after nearly dying. Neither of them had, but Jane was too wound up and too anxious to figure this mess out. "If your stalker has been there, Vincent will find the evidence and call me back. Could be an hour, could be tomorrow. Just depends."

"Okay. What do we do until then?" She couldn't sit around waiting for some maniac to make the next move. There had to be something in her case files, something in her work for the army that could point them in the right direction to an ID of who'd T-boned them back at the bridge.

"We dig into your cases." Sullivan slid onto the bar stool on the other side of the granite countertop as though using it as a barrier between them. Probably a good idea. Because those heated, confusing minutes of them under the blanket in front of the fire together hadn't exactly gone as Jane had expected. His skin had pressed against hers from chest to toes, his very prominent arousal at her lower back, and the way he'd feathered his fingertips over her shoulder... Jane swallowed back the memories. His touch had felt good, real. Then again, she'd lived the past few months as a hermit and wouldn't know the difference between her own arousal and the simple need for human contact. Jane shivered. No. That wasn't it. She'd recognized the difference. She just hadn't felt that kind of drowning heat in a long time. Her insides burned to close the distance between them for another passing glimpse of it, however fleeting.

But Sullivan's reaction had been simple biology. There'd been a naked woman pressed against him and his body had responded. He didn't want her. Because no matter how many heated moments they shared, how many times they laughed together or how long they talked, Sullivan blamed her for his brother's suicide. Plain and simple.

"I'm already having the files brought from your town house by another operative on my team," he said.

Pressure built behind her sternum. Sullivan might not use all of his training from his military days for Blackhawk Security, but from what she'd read of him, he never missed a clue. She cleared her throat, stuffing her hands into her sweatshirt pockets. "Good idea. I've already gone through most of them, but another set of eyes might uncover something I missed."

Jane's stomach growled again.

"You need to eat and rest before Elliot gets here with the files." Sullivan stood, his wide shoulders blocking her view of the living room and the fire popping and cracking in the fireplace. Muscles flexed across his chest and arms, and Jane swallowed the rush of saliva filling her mouth. "I don't come up here often so I'm sorry to say there's nothing more than a few MREs lying around, but there should be enough in the duffel bags we brought to last us three days." He searched the living room. "Where did you put the bags after I tried to kill myself out there? I'll make us something to eat."

Jane's responding smile to his willingness to feed her disappeared. Exhaling, she ran her hand through her hair. Crap. "I left them outside. I wasn't thinking after I pulled you in—"

"Don't worry about it." He stepped right into her, that massive chest of his brushing against her. Staring down at her, Sullivan bent at the knees to look her right in the eye, his hands posed above her arms as though he didn't dare touch her. And she didn't blame him. The difference in height between them was laughable, but she appreciated the even ground now. His hands rested around her upper arms. Her insides flipped as his body heat spread through her, but she didn't pull away. "You had your priorities straight. You saved my life. I'll get them. About how far did you drop them?"

Good. He'd just go get them. Her breathing eased the longer he kept his grip on her, but it took a few seconds to clear her head of his proximity enough to answer. "Beyond the tree line. I don't think it snowed enough to cover my tracks. You should be able to follow them to the bags."

"All right. And when I get back, we'll call Anchorage PD to have them put an APB out for that tow truck." He dropped his hold on her, spinning toward his discarded gear drying over the fireplace. A shiver rushed through her, but Jane held her ground as Sullivan donned his shoulder holster and thick coat. He reached under the built-in desk where the keyboard drawer clicked into place and removed a Glock, disengaged the magazine and pulled back the slide to check the chamber. He moved in quick, confident steps to reload the magazine and put a round in the chamber as though he'd done the same moves a thousand times before. Which he probably had. "I shouldn't be gone more than five minutes." He checked the batteries in the flashlight next. "If anything happens while I'm out there, use the burner phone to call the last number I dialed. It'll put you directly through to my guy Elliot. He's the closest right now, and he'll get here as fast as he can."

Jane nodded. He wouldn't be gone more than a few minutes, but she pointed toward the gun. "Do you have an extra one of those for me? Just in case." They'd already proved anything could happen. For crying out loud, a tow truck had blindsided them on purpose. She wasn't about to make it easier for this psychopath to get to her.

A smile lit up his features before he turned toward what she assumed was the only bedroom in the cabin. Mere seconds later, he handed her another Glock. "This is my service weapon from the SEALs and my favorite gun. If you have to shoot it outside for any reason, make sure there's no snow in the barrel and that you've warmed it up. Otherwise, it might blow up in your hands."

"I went through weapons training, too, remember? I know how to handle my guns in cold weather." Jane hit the button to disengage the magazine and pulled back the slide to clear the chamber, just as Sullivan had done with his own gun. Faster than she thought possible, the guarded curiosity in Sullivan's eyes changed to something dark, primal. She clenched her lower abdomen. Air stalled in her throat. She focused on the gun in her hand. "Besides, you won't be gone that long. I'm sure I can manage to take care of myself for five minutes."

"Of that—" he secured the Glock he'd taken from under the desk in his shoulder holster, eyes scanning her from head to toe "—I have no doubt." Sullivan disappeared out the door without looking back.

The goose bumps along her forearms receded the longer Jane stared after him. There was no denying it now. She'd seen the way he'd looked at her, the way he'd held on to her earlier. He wanted the intel she'd called in a few favors to get, the one with his real identity inside. Because there was no way that man wanted her for any other reason. No matter how deep he'd buried his past, she'd uncovered the truth and she'd known the second she confronted him with it, she would pay for using blackmail. What was he going to do? Torture her with desire until she gave him everything she had on him and his family?

Jane leaned against the countertop, Sullivan's service weapon comfortable in her grip. Now that she thought about it, torture by desire was one of the better ways to go. Especially with a six-foot-four, muscled, powerfully built SEAL. A smile pulled at her lips. Crap, she imagined that outcome between them all too easily. The heat, the explosion of passion, the—

The front door slammed open and her muscle memory hefted the gun up. She aimed, ready to pull the trigger. Adrenaline pumped fast through her veins as Sullivan swung his head around the thick, wooden door. Jane dropped the gun to her side, heart beating a mile a second. She could've shot him. "You scared me to death. Do you always barge into a room like that?"

Sullivan stomped his boots on the mat at the door, then headed straight for the burner phone on the kitchen counter. He brushed against her, but instead of heat penetrating through her jacket like before, she only felt cold. Something was wrong. Stabbing the pad of his thumb into the keypad, he brought the phone up to his ear, those sea-blue eyes glued on her. Darkness etched into his expression, and Jane took a step back to give him some space. "The bags are gone."

Chapter Four

The guns, extra ammunition, food, tracks, everything was gone. Looked like Jane's mysterious stalker had tracked her back here after all. The phone rang once in his ear before Elliot Dunham, his private investigator, picked up.

"Go for Dunham," Elliot said.

Sullivan checked his watch. "How far out are you?"

"Five minutes."

"Make it three. The bastard knows we're here."

"See you in two." The revving of a car engine echoed in the background before the line disconnected. As an operative on the Blackhawk Security team, Elliot would understand to come in hot—armed and ready for a fight. Sullivan had swiped the private investigator off the Iraqi streets right after Sullivan's discharge from the SEALs. The man had a knack for finding and recovering classified documents, digging into a person's life, discovering those secrets his target didn't want the world to know about. Like a pit bull with his favorite chew toy, Elliot never gave up and never surrendered. Most likely a side effect of his con artist days; each case a long con. With a genius-level IQ, he dug deep, he got personal. At least until the job was done. Then he disappeared to start fresh. It hadn't been difficult to recruit him either. Only a few phone calls that could put Elliot back into an Iraqi jail cell.

His next call was to Anchorage PD to report the tow truck that'd nearly rammed them into the Gulf of Alaska. A minute later, Sullivan tossed the phone onto the counter and rubbed at his face.

"Is Elliot bringing supplies?" Jane stared up at him, arms wrapped around her small midsection. Her shoulders hunched inward as though she felt the weight of someone watching her. Which Sullivan bet was familiar by now.

The same weight pressed in on him, too, but they only had to wait a few more minutes. Then they could get through her case files and find out who exactly had turned Jane into a target. After that, they'd come up with a plan. "I make every member of my team carry extra guns, ammo and food in case of emergency."

"Do you think whoever is after me is out there, right now, watching us?" Jane's voice trembled. She was scared. And rightfully so.

Whoever had taken their bags had wiped any evidence of their existence from the snow. There weren't a whole lot of men who possessed that kind of skill, Sullivan being one of the few. His father had ensured his sons knew how to hunt their prey properly, before the old man had turned into the sick psychopath he became known for. But right now, in this moment, Sullivan wasn't the hunter. He felt like the prey.

A soft ringing reached his ears, and Jane extracted her cell phone from her jacket pocket. Frowning, she put the phone to her ear. "Hello?"

He couldn't hear the response from this distance

and, while eavesdropping on his client's phone calls was technically part of the job, Sullivan wouldn't crowd her. *I needed you.* Those three small words had been circling his brain since they'd left her mouth.

"Who is this?" The color drained from Jane's features.

Sullivan's instincts prickled at the alarm in her voice. He stepped into her personal space, forcing her to meet his gaze, then reached for her phone. He hit the speaker button, holding the phone between them. "Who the hell is this?"

"He can't protect you, Jane," the voice whispered across the line. Her name on the bastard's lips tightened the muscles down Sullivan's spine. "You're going to pay for what you've done."

Memorizing the number on the screen, Sullivan gripped the phone tighter. He couldn't peg an accent due to the whispering, no dialect to pinpoint where her stalker originated from. "Come within three hundred feet of her and I will tear you apart. You tried to kill her once. Won't happen again. Understand?" His voice dropped low—deadly—as he studied the fear skating across Jane's features. "Don't call this number again."

He moved to hang up the call.

"Always the protector... *Sullivan.*" Laughter trickled through the phone.

Sullivan's thumb froze over the end button. A shiver spread across his shoulders. The line went dead, only static and crackling from the fireplace filling the silence.

In a split second, one of the burner phones he kept on hand was at his ear, ringing through to Blackhawk Security's head of network security. The line picked up. "Elizabeth, trace this number." He recited the number he'd memorized from the call. "I want a location as soon as possible. Send it straight to the number I'm calling you from."

"You got it, boss," the former NSA analyst said.

He hung up. Sullivan's gaze lifted from the phone as Jane backed away. The terror etched into her expression urged him toward her. Without hesitation, he reached for her. "Jane…"

Eyes wide, mouth slack, she shut down her expression, and Sullivan dropped his hand. "He's here. He's *watching* me. He knows you're with me."

That had always been a possibility. Stalkers liked to keep tabs on their targets. The bastard had most likely been the one responsible for taking their gear, too. She'd known the risks going into this, but Sullivan wouldn't remind her of them now. In this moment, he needed her head on straight. Focused. "You hired me because I'm good at my job. He's never going to get close to you. You have my word."

"Thank you." Her chin notched higher. Jane shifted her weight onto her toes as though she intended to kiss him, and right then, all too easily, Sullivan imagined how it'd feel to claim that perfect mouth of hers. Would she taste as good as she smelled? Damn it. Why couldn't he keep himself in check around her?

Three knocks on the door ripped him back. The thick wood swung inward, and Sullivan shoved Jane behind him. Her fingers clenched the back of his shirt as he unholstered the Glock at his side. The man hunting Jane most likely wouldn't knock, but maybe there were polite stalkers out there in the world.

"And here I thought I'd get to shoot someone when I got here." Elliot Dunham's wide grin shifted the dark stubble across his jawline. The lines at the edges of his stormy gray eyes deepened. The private investigator holstered his own weapon underneath a thick cargo jacket and kicked the door closed behind him. "Good news for everyone. The perimeter is clear, and I won't get blood on my new shirt."

"We wouldn't want that. I'd have to hear about it all night." Sullivan couldn't help but smile as he clapped Elliot on the back. "Did you bring the files?"

"Got them in the truck along with extra munitions and snacks. But I have to be honest, I ate all the nuts on the way here. This place is in the middle of nowhere." Swiveling his head around Sullivan, Elliot caught sight of their new client. Jane. The con-man-turned-investigator sidestepped his boss, something close to intrigue smoothing out his features. "And you must be Jane. Your picture doesn't do you justice."

"You're kidding, right?" Jane asked. "*That's* your opening line?"

"Oh, I like her." Elliot's smile made another appearance.

Sullivan clamped a hand on his investigator's shoulder. Elliot had absolutely no interest in their new client, but something inside had tightened at the thought of another man coming anywhere near her with that look on his face. What did he care? He'd taken her on as a client, however forced. He didn't have any kind of claim on her. "How about you do your job and get me those files from the truck?"

"Sure thing, boss." Elliot half saluted Jane, then spun back toward the front door and disappeared.

A tri-chimed message tone brought the burner phone back into his hand. Sullivan read Elizabeth's message, then dropped the phone onto the hardwood and stomped on it. The screen cracked under his boots, pieces of plastic skating across the floor. "My team couldn't trace the number. We weren't on the line long enough to get a location."

"And you felt the need to take it out on your phone?" she asked.

"Can't be too careful." In reality, he'd been thinking ahead. If this case went south and the man hunting Jane expanded his crosshairs, Sullivan wouldn't leave any evidence behind that could lead to his team.

"So that's your private investigator." Not a question. Jane's arm brushed his as she passed him heading into the living room. A shot of awareness trailed up Sullivan's arm. He slapped a hand over the oversensitized skin, but she didn't notice. Head in the game. Standing in front of the fire, her bruises and cuts illuminated by the brilliant orange flames, Jane still held her head high. There was a target on her back, but she hadn't fallen apart. She didn't trust him with her emotions. Didn't seem to trust anyone.

"Elliot is the best private investigator in the country." He closed in on her one step at a time, giving in to the urge to have her nearby in case her stalker took a shot through the front windows. He'd already tried to kill her once. No telling what he'd do next. At least for now. "Used to be a con man. Elliot can read people. He has the resources to dig into their lives and a genius-level IQ to see three steps ahead. He'll find whoever's targeting you."

"What if he can't?" Turning toward him, Jane gave him an exhausted smile. Her shoulders sagged as though she'd collapse into a puddle on the floor. "I've been through those files a dozen times. I know them better than anyone, and I couldn't pick out any potential suspects." She massaged her temples with her fingers. "I just want my life back."

"Look at me." Sullivan closed the small space between them. He pushed every ounce of sincerity into his expression, his gaze, his voice, but didn't move to touch her this time. "I don't give my word lightly. You might've blackmailed me into it, but I promised to protect you, and I will." The small muscles in his jaw tightened. "We will figure this out."

She nodded. "I believe you."

"Good." Four hours ago, he'd tried kicking her out of his office. But now... They were in this together. He'd saved her life. She'd saved his. And he wouldn't let some nutjob with a sick obsession get close to her again. No matter how much he blamed her for Marrok's death. "You're dead on your feet. Why don't you go lie down in the bedroom? I'll wake you if we find a lead."

Jane nodded, her eyes brighter than a few moments ago. "I'll also expect that meal you promised when I come out."

A laugh rumbled through his chest as Sullivan watched her disappear into the bedroom. Flashes of those long legs peeking out from under his blanket skittered across his mind, and his gut warmed. He stared after her a few seconds longer, but the weight of being watched pressed between his shoulder blades. His neck heated. *Damn.* "How long have you been standing there?"

"Long enough to see you're going to break your own rule if you're not careful." Elliot dropped the box of Jane's case files and laptop onto the built-in desk and raised his hands in surrender. "Okay, now you look like you want to kill me."

No way was he going to talk about this with his private investigator. Or anybody. Ever. "What did you find when you went through the files?"

"I've narrowed it down to two possibilities within the army after you said the guy erased his tracks after taking off with your supplies. That takes a lot of skill, and not many of the people she has regular contact with have any kind of training like that." Elliot shoved the lid off the box and extracted three manila file folders. "Your girl took some damn fine notes on the cases she worked. Made my job easier."

His girl? Not even close. But Sullivan didn't correct his investigator. He took the files from Elliot and scanned over the extensive notes inside. Must've been Jane's handwriting. Precise, to the point. Nothing fancy. But the purple and pink Post-its stuck through the files surprised him. Just as her red toenail polish had. He scanned over the first file. "Staff Sergeant Marrok Warren."

Something sour swept across his tongue.

"Now, that guy is a piece of work. There's only one problem." Elliot leveraged his weight against the desk and crossed his arms over his chest. "Jane prosecuted him for sexual assault of three female enlisted soldiers, but—"

"He's dead." There it was. Stamped across Jane's case file in big red letters. *Deceased.* Sullivan's ears rang. He discarded the file back into the box, his body strung as tight as a tension spring. His brother might've had the skills to pull off blindsiding them in the SUV and taking their supplies without leaving behind a trace, but it wasn't possible. Marrok Warren was dead. Sullivan had buried him ten months ago almost to the day.

"That would be the problem. I tied him to Jane's case because of the guy's father." Elliot pulled a bag of peanuts from his jacket pocket. "Ever heard of the Anchorage Lumberjack? Killed twelve victims, all with an ax. With Staff Sergeant Warren dead, could be a close family member coming after Jane now, maybe one of those psychopathic groupies I'm always hearing about. Wonder what they're like…"

Sullivan crumpled the files in his hand, the tendons in his neck straining. He locked his attention on Elliot, then took a deep breath, forcing himself to relax. "Who else do you have?"

"We've got her commanding officer." His private investigator nodded toward the second file in Sullivan's hand, ignoring the obvious tension that'd filled the room. "Major Patrick Barnes is Jane's CO. He'd know her daily schedule, her routine, and have access to all of her files. He would know her whereabouts while on tour, and he's the one who grants permission for her to go on leave."

"It's not Major Barnes," a familiar voice said.

Twisting around, Sullivan locked on to Jane, the grip around his rib cage lightening at the sight of her. As long as she was in his sights, she was safe. He tossed the files onto the desk. "You should be resting."

"Couldn't wind down. Besides, this is my case. I should be helping." Jane shoved off from against the doorjamb and sauntered forward. Reaching for Major Barnes's file, she scanned through the pages, her proximity setting Sullivan's nerve endings on high alert.

She tossed the file on top of Marrok Warren's and crossed her arms over her chest. "I owe Barnes my life. He tackled me to the ground after an IED exploded in the parking lot outside my office in Afghanistan two months ago. He wouldn't have done that just to turn around and come after me himself. And he has no motive."

"All right. Then we take a tour of your life outside the army. The only other name that stands out to me is Christopher Menas." Elliot handed the file to Jane, but shifted his gaze to Sullivan before settling back against the desk. Hesitant? "He's won a few hunting awards, but that's about all I know aside from his criminal record. I can't find any employment records, no college degree, no military record, nothing that says he's changed his name, or a death certificate attached to this guy. Menas simply dropped off the grid after skipping bail, but you two had a complicated past and that's why I'm pinning him as a suspect."

"I can't believe this." She stared at the name on the edge of the folder, her eyes panicked and wide. She slipped her index finger between the yellow card stock but didn't move to open the file. "I haven't thought about Christopher in years."

"Jane?" Warning bells rang in Sullivan's head as he closed in on her. "What are you thinking?"

Tearing her attention from the folder, Jane lifted her gaze to his. "It's him. He's the one doing this to me."

CHRISTOPHER MENAS.

Flashes of his face, of those cold brown eyes and dark skin, lit up the back of her eyelids. Jane bolted upright off the bed, out of breath, surrounded by pure darkness. She'd been in love—outright smitten—with the quarterback of the University of Washington Huskies football team. And it'd all been a lie.

She couldn't see anything with the bedroom door shut, but her instincts screamed she wasn't alone. The silhouette of a man shifted in her peripheral vision. She slipped her hand under her pillow, curling her fingers around the gun Sullivan had lent her when she'd gone to bed.

"I'm not armed." A chair creaked to her left before the mattress dipped with added weight. Her hand relaxed from around the Glock. Sullivan. The light on the nightstand flickered to life, bathing his stern features in warmth. "Tell me about Christopher Menas."

"What?" She squinted into the brightness. "What time is it?"

"Just before dawn. You were talking in your sleep earlier. About Christopher Menas." Every muscle in her body tightened at that name. Sullivan's voice remained soft, coaxing. "I read the police report on him. He sexually assaulted two women while you two were dating. Your roommates, right? Right before he came after you."

A shiver chased up her spine. How could this be happening again? She'd moved on with her life, joined the army, made something of herself. She'd left that part of her life—left Christopher and everything that reminded her of him—behind.

"Is that why you went after my brother so aggressively? To make Marrok pay because your college boyfriend got away with his crimes?" Sullivan stared at her, stone-like. The muscles in his jawline flexed as though he was grinding his back molars, but Jane still forced herself to meet his gaze.

"Are you really accusing me of corruption, or is this because I prosecuted your brother for sexual assault?" She regretted the words the second they left her mouth. Clenching the sheets, she steadied her nerves. No. This was his job; this was why she'd blackmailed him in the first place. He got the job done, no matter what it took. And if Christopher was the man behind this, she'd make sure her ex paid this time. With Sullivan's help. "I'll tell you anything you need to know about Christopher, but believe me when I say this has nothing to do with you or your brother."

"How can I trust you?" Sullivan's calm, collected exterior broke around his eyes and mouth. "You charged my brother with these exact same crimes, which led to Marrok committing suicide. You're blackmailing me into helping you now. And you purposefully left out a credible lead."

What? "I never—"

"You told me you didn't have any ex-boyfriends who would hold a grudge against you. You're the one who turned Menas over to the police all those years ago. You knew he'd skipped bail. All this time you didn't think he was the one who might be after you?" Standing, Sullivan ran his hands through his hair. Shadows threw his features into sharper angles and brought out the darkness he'd kept under control up until now. "Damn it, Jane. I could've gotten people on him the second we left my office and none of this would've happened."

"How do you know it's him stalking me or he's the one who ran us off the road? You said it yourself, whoever took the bags didn't leave any evidence, and you never got a look at the driver." Jane threw her legs over the edge of the bed and stood, thankful she'd chosen warmer attire tonight rather than her usual T-shirt and panties. None of this made sense. Why would her ex-boyfriend come after her now? That was a lifetime ago. The statute of limitations had run out on his charges and he'd never gone to prison. What could he possibly hold against her now?

"Weren't you the one who said, 'It's him. He's the one doing this to me,' out there?" Dropping his hands, Sullivan faced her head-on, body still tense.

She didn't know how to respond. The idea of Christopher coming back into her life after all this time…

"Anchorage PD recovered the vehicle. The tow truck that blindsided us was recovered from behind a gas station just inside town." Sullivan pulled a hand through his short hair. "My forensics guy has been working with Anchorage PD. They've confirmed the black paint on the fender is from my SUV. Jane, the registration is filed under Christopher Menas's name."

The air in her throat froze. They had a lead, proof. Christopher had come to Anchorage. For her. Locking her teeth together, Jane tugged her sweatshirt off the edge of the bed, then shoved her feet into her boots. She'd gone into the army because of her ex, learned to protect herself against men like him. But no more running. Christopher wanted revenge? He was going to have to work for it. Heading for the door, she gave into the sudden rush of determination pumping through her. "Then what are we waiting for? Let's go."

"Go where?" he asked.

Wasn't this man a SEAL, trained to think two

steps ahead of everybody else to get the upper hand in any situation? "To Christopher's. He must have a safe house, a hotel room or an apartment—something around here if he's stalking me, right?"

"We can't go barging into the man's private residence, Jane." Sullivan shot to his feet and wrapped his hand around her arm, but she wrenched away. He seemed to be doing a lot of that in the last twenty-four hours, touching her, but now wasn't the time to analyze the contact. Despite the fact he'd accused her of corruption, they had a stalker to find. "We're not the police. We don't have a warrant. The best thing we can do is put surveillance on him for the next couple days. Then we can go from there."

On any other case, she'd agree. She'd taken an oath as a lawyer. She was supposed to play by the book, but this case had turned more personal than she'd imagined. "I don't have a couple of days. I need my life back *now*." Throwing the door open, she stalked straight toward Elliot, who was asleep on the couch. "I need your car keys."

Elliot's feet lifted off the couch as he dropped his arms away from his forehead. A yawn twisted his features as he rubbed sleep from his eyes. "Well, good morning to you, too."

"Keys." Jane extended her hand. "Please."

"I take it you told her about the tow truck," Elliot said to Sullivan over her shoulder. He sat up, digging into his jacket pocket before dangling the car keys in front of her. "Have a nice field trip, sweetheart. Call me if you need me."

She swiped the keys from his hand.

"If we're going—" Sullivan fisted both his hands in

Elliot's jacket and hefted him from the couch "—then you're coming, too."

"We don't have much time. Christopher is smart. He probably left that truck there for us to trace back to him, but I doubt he's going to stick around and risk arrest." Jane took a deep breath to clear her head and handed the keys back to Elliot. A rush of cold air slammed against her as they stepped back into the freezing Alaskan wilderness. It took a few seconds for her lungs to catch up with the change in temperature, but she refused to slow down. They had to catch Christopher by surprise, but the sun would be up soon and they'd lose their cover of night.

Once they were all within the safety of the truck, Elliot put the shifter into Reverse but didn't move. "What exactly is our plan here?"

"You're a private investigator. I assume you already know where Christopher is hiding." Jane buckled herself into the back seat. "I want to surprise him and get some answers. That's the plan for right now."

"And if he's armed?" Sullivan turned around, his gaze glued to her.

"Isn't that why I hired you?" Throwing his own words back in his face wouldn't smooth the tension between them, but Jane still couldn't believe he'd implied she'd had anything personal against his brother during the court-martial. Sure, Marrok's charges were nearly identical to Christopher Menas's, but she'd always strived for compartmentalization and professionalism when prosecuting a case. She couldn't practice law if her emotions got the best of her. Hence that damn nickname. No emotion. No attachment. Jane cringed inwardly and crossed her arms over her chest as they pulled away from the cabin. But that wasn't her. Not anymore.

The truck barreled through the snow as they headed back toward Anchorage without signs of an ambush, but Jane still kept an eye out for any rogue tow trucks waiting for them at signals through town. According to Elliot's research, Christopher Menas had been renting an apartment near Taku Lake. Within twenty minutes, the private investigator parked the pickup two blocks from their destination.

The apartment complex wasn't anything special— two levels, blond-wood balconies with white stucco on the sides. Trees and shrubs gave the complex a lighter feel, but as Jane stepped onto the pavement, a ball of dread fisted at the base of her spine.

"He's in apartment 310." Sullivan stayed on her tail as she headed down the street and for the third building to her right. Dressed for warmer temperatures, he showed off long lengths of muscle down his arms, and the flood of apprehension gripping her disappeared. "May I remind you this isn't a good idea? We have no idea what's waiting for us on the other side of that door."

Right then, she didn't care. "I'm putting an end to this. For good."

Screeching metal filled Jane's ears as Elliot extracted a long steel tube from the bed of his truck. Both Sullivan and Jane spun, staring at him. "What?" He hefted the small battering ram over his shoulder. "It's in case we want to commit a felony."

The breath she'd been holding rushed from her. She couldn't believe any of this. She hadn't thought of Christopher Menas in years. But here she was, climbing up the steps to her ex-boyfriend's apartment to find out why he was trying to kill her.

Sullivan maneuvered in front of her, using his body to shield her from the door. Her throat tightened as his fingers smoothed over her jacket. He couldn't have meant what he'd said back at the cabin, could he? After everything they'd been through the last twenty-four hours, he couldn't think so low of her. She'd saved his life. Didn't that count for something? Pounding on the door, Sullivan stepped back and pulled his weapon. As did Elliot with his free hand.

No answer. No sounds of movement inside.

It was barely sunrise. Surely her stalker could have had the decency to be home when she came to confront him.

Sullivan pounded his fist against the wood again. Nothing. "Are you sure you want to do this?" He nodded toward Menas's front door. "We can still go back, come at this from another angle."

Go back? She couldn't go back. She couldn't walk away now. Jane swallowed the hesitation screaming at the back of her mind. "I'm sure."

"All right. Breaking and entering it is, Counselor. Just promise not to charge us, since you're the one giving the orders." He stepped aside, ushering Elliot forward. "Have at it."

"Once we're in, be sure not to touch anything. Someone's about to call the police." Elliot slammed the head of the battering ram into the thick wood, and the door frame splintered. He hit it a second time, buckling the hinges, and within a minute, they were inside.

"Let's go. We don't have long before the police or a curious neighbor show up." Sullivan stepped inside

first, Glock in his hand, body tense. Like the good security consultant she'd blackmailed him to be.

Jane's insides clenched as she followed close behind
him. Whether it was from their conversation back in
the bedroom or the situation, she couldn't tell. She
hadn't seen Christopher Menas in nearly a decade.

Sullivan flipped on the lights with his elbow, and
Jane leveraged her weight against one wall to clear
her head. The inside of the apartment was…normal.
No foul-smelling decaying bodies, no bloodstained
carpets. The two-bedroom apartment had been decorated in a Southwestern theme—where Christopher
was from—and looked like it'd been that way for a
while. No quick getaway for him. Their suspect intended to stick around.

"Are you sure we have the right information?" Jane
smoothed the hem of her coat sleeve over the back of
the black leather couch. "This place doesn't exactly
scream psychopath."

Searching the kitchen, Sullivan used a napkin to
open drawers, go through receipts and sift through
photos. He held up a business card for her to see, as
Elliot checked out the back bedrooms. "We're in the
right place."

She took the card from him, not entirely stable on
her own two feet. "Menas Towing. Why didn't that
show up in Elliot's research?" Jane scanned the rest
of the apartment, taking anything—everything—in.
There had to be something here that pointed to Jane as
a target. According to the profilers she'd worked with
on dozens of cases for the army, stalkers usually kept
mementos of their victims. Trophies. But from what
Jane could see, they'd made a mistake. There was noth-

ing here. So if Christopher wasn't her stalker, then who was? The only evidence they had to go on was the tow truck registered in his name. "Who would be stupid enough to hit us with their own truck?"

"Nobody." Sullivan locked those mesmerizing eyes on her for the first time since accusing her of corruption. Her heart rate skyrocketed when he looked at her like that, like a puzzle he needed to solve. "Unless we're supposed to be here. What about the voice on the call? Did it sound like Menas?"

"I couldn't tell from the way he was whispering. And it's been so long since I've talked to him, I'm not sure I could identify it as his anyway." She ran through Sullivan's words a second time and half turned toward him. "Do you think somebody is setting Christopher up?"

"Not likely." Elliot stepped back into the main room and hitched a thumb over his shoulder. "You need to see this."

"What did you find?" Jane sprinted after the private investigator, heart in her throat. Had he found the evidence? Found Christopher? The hallway passed in a blur as she hurried after Elliot toward the back bedroom. She halted at the door frame. Her jaw slackened. She couldn't breathe. The world tilted on an axis, but she managed to stay upright.

"What the hell?" Sullivan's words echoed her own thoughts as he brushed past her and moved into the room.

Jane shook her head, clinging to the door frame with everything she had. "I don't think we're in the wrong place anymore."

Chapter Five

No matter where he turned, Jane was there.

"There has to be hundreds of photos of me here." Jane's voice shook as she stepped up to one wall.

Something deep in his chest urged him to reach out for her, but Sullivan stood his ground. This wasn't the time. There were more photos than the one on Jane's phone of her sleeping. These showed her eating. In court. Right outside her home. His insides raged as he scanned over the closest wall a second time. In the shower. From the look of it, the past three months of her life had been documented in pictures taped to four plain white walls. Rage burned hot under his sternum. The sick freak had stolen precious moments from her life—too many to count—and Jane would never get them back.

She slid her fingertips over a handful of photos, seeming not to even breathe.

And he couldn't take staying away any longer. Sullivan took a step toward her, hand outstretched. "Jane—"

"This is my life. He…" Her lips parted on a strong inhale. She dropped her hand, turning toward him, and he froze. Swallowing, Jane covered her mouth. She rushed past him, her vanilla scent thick on the air. "I think I'm going to be sick."

She fled the room. A few seconds later, a door slammed down the hallway and he shut his eyes against the onslaught of surveillance her stalker had collected. One inhale. Two. The protector buried deep inside of him clawed its way to the surface for a breath of fresh air. Christopher Menas was a dead man. Whatever game the bastard had going on with Jane was over. Sullivan was coming for him. Opening his eyes, he spun toward the hallway. "Elliot, document everything. We're leaving."

He had to get Jane out of here. The police were most likely on their way from when Elliot had brought down the door. She couldn't get wrapped up in their investigation. The second the report went live, the army would limit her security clearance and she'd be at risk of losing her job. Stalking down the hall toward the bathroom, gun in hand, he listened for signs of movement. He was sure their suspect wasn't in the apartment, but a man who could cover his tracks in the Alaskan wilderness had to have a few more tricks up his sleeves. And Sullivan wasn't about to make a mistake on this case. Not with Jane's life on the line.

With three light taps on the bathroom door, he leaned against the wood. "Jane?"

No answer.

His heartbeat rocketed into his throat. He squeezed his free hand around the door handle, but didn't move to open it. Yet. Fanning his grip over the Glock, he scanned down the hallway. "Are you okay?"

Still nothing.

"All right." Backing up, Sullivan cradled the gun in

both hands, prepared to kick in the door if he had to, to get to her. "I'm coming in."

The door swung open on silent hinges, and the torn woman in front of him hurried to swipe salty streaks of tears from her face with the back of her hand. In a split second, she locked her emotions away as though she hadn't fallen apart out of his sight. "I'm fine. I just needed a minute."

"You don't have to hide from me, Jane." His throat tightened, but he released his suffocating grip on the gun. Every cell in his body urged him to stand as a pillar of comfort for her, and he straightened. Forget the past. Forget the rules for a few seconds. Jane was falling apart and it was his job to hold his client's life together. Even if she'd blackmailed him into it. Closing in on her slowly, he brushed a stray tear from her face, careful to leave space for her to escape if she wanted. Hesitation shot down his arms and into his chest, but this time he didn't pull away. Didn't feel the need. Those hazel eyes closed as she leaned into him for support, and he set his chin onto the crown of her head. Her short black hair tumbled forward against his chest and his fingers tingled with the urge to shove it behind her ear so she'd look up at him. "I'm sorry you had to see all of that. You don't deserve this."

For the first time since Jane had broken into his office last night, he meant every word. Her body heat tunneled through his jacket, sinking into his muscles, his bones. The tension throughout his body relaxed second by second. All Sullivan could think about in this moment was taking her back to the cabin and shielding her from what was to come. Men willing to kill the object of their obsessions didn't give up easily. But she couldn't run. Not from this.

Sullivan inhaled deep. He smelled…smoke.

"Do you smell that?" Jane pulled back.

"Elliot." Panic wrapped a tight fist around his heart. Clamping his hand around hers, Sullivan tugged Jane after him down the hallway. After discovering Menas's sick collection, he wasn't about to let her out of his sight. Black smoke escaped out from under the second bedroom door. Had he closed it behind him? He dropped his hold on her and kicked in the door. Bright flames climbed up the walls where Jane's photos used to hang. Covering his face and eyes in the crook of his arm, Sullivan avoided the majority of the smoke but couldn't see anything worth a damn. There was too much smoke. Too many flames. "Elliot!"

"Sullivan, there!" Jane latched onto his arm, pointing to one corner of the room. Without waiting for him, she launched herself through the flames consuming the door frame.

"Jane, no!" He grabbed after her but missed her jacket by mere centimeters. She couldn't pull Elliot out of there on her own. Not with flames consuming the walls on every side. The roar of the fire drowned out any sounds of Jane or his private investigator. Lunging into the heart of the fire, he kept low, searching for her, searching for Elliot. "Jane!"

"Over here." A cough led him toward the back of the room. The crackling of the flames nearly drowned out her voice, but he homed in on the uncontrollable coughing coming from his right.

"Jane." Within seconds, he'd wrapped his hands around her arms and shoved her back toward the bedroom door. He covered his mouth and nose with the crook of his arm as smoke worked into his lungs. Squinting from the heat, he fought to see the door. "Get out of here. Get outside."

She'd found Elliot knocked out near the west wall. Hiking his private investigator over his shoulder, Sullivan narrowly avoided a falling rafter as he wound through debris and flames.

Outside, he breathed in as much clean air as his lungs allowed, nearly collapsing as his muscles weakened from oxygen depletion. Jane ran forward, eyes wide, hands outstretched to catch them both. The three of them fell in a pile of limbs and heavy breathing as sirens filled the night. In less than seven minutes, fire crews sprinted to put out the blaze. Staring up at the damage, Sullivan noted the entire building had caught fire.

"How many—" His lungs worked overtime to expel the smoke he'd inhaled. He didn't want to think about the casualties. There was no way the fire had been a coincidence. Christopher Menas had known they were there. The fire had most likely been set to destroy the evidence he'd left behind. Maybe to hurt them, to hurt Jane.

"I got them all out." Jane cradled Elliot's head in her lap, her palms on both sides of his slackened jaw. "When you pushed me out the door, I pulled the fire alarm."

Streaks of soot lined her jaw and forehead, enhancing the bruises and scrapes from the car accident, but Jane had never been more beautiful than right in this moment. She'd charged into that bedroom to save one of his men's lives. And ended up saving many others in the building. What was it about the woman he blamed that compelled her to keep saving lives?

A nasty gash bled freely from the right side of Elliot's head. Knocked unconscious. Damn it. They'd walked straight into Menas's trap.

Sullivan shook his head. He couldn't breathe. Couldn't think. Until he saw the blood streaking down Jane's cargo jacket. Reaching across Elliot's unconscious body for her, he inspected the wound. "Are you okay?"

"Nothing a few stitches won't fix." She twisted her arm so she could see it better. "I'm kind of sad about this jacket, though. It's my favorite."

Squealing tires and red and blue lights claimed his attention. He tightened his hold on Jane, unwilling to let her out of his sight yet. But that gash wouldn't stitch itself.

EMTs rushed to their side, hefting Elliot onto a stretcher and prying his eyes open. But not before Sullivan lifted Elliot's phone from his private investigator's jacket pocket. Elliot had documented Christopher Menas's collection in that bedroom, and the cops weren't about to stick it in some evidence room before Sullivan could review the photos. Evidence tampering be damned.

Elliot was in good hands. Sullivan's instincts said Menas wouldn't come after him. But Jane? That was another story. They couldn't stay here. Menas had been watching them. Could still be watching them. "Are you okay to move?"

"Would you throw me over your shoulder like you did with Elliot if I said no?" Lean muscle flexed down the backs of her thighs as she stood, and Sullivan fought a smile. "I'm fine. Really. And I'm glad those pictures didn't survive."

"You went in that bedroom for Elliot. Looks like I just might owe you again." Freezing gusts of wind beat against him on one side as he hiked himself to his feet, blistering heat from the burning apartment on the other. EMTs closed in on them, two leading Jane to an ambulance and another swinging a light in front of his face. He shoved the technician away. He was fine. Minor case of smoke inhalation. Nothing Sullivan hadn't lived through before. His breath sawed in and out of him as bright orange flames licked up the side of the apartment building.

They could've died in there.

Two Anchorage police units rolled up as Sullivan messaged his team from Elliot's phone. Keeping Jane in his peripheral vision as medics looked her over on the back of the ambulance, he headed toward the officers to give his statement. While Anchorage PD would run their own investigation, he had no intention of leaving Jane's case in their hands. They'd already failed to take her claim seriously. He had far more resources to bring this particular arsonist down.

Within five minutes, another Blackhawk Security SUV pulled into the scene. Sullivan caught sight of his weapons expert as the six-foot-five-inch wall of solid, sunglass-loving muscle stepped out onto the pavement. Anthony Harris surveyed the scene from behind his favorite pair of sunglasses, chest wide, fingers relaxed at his side. The thick beard covering the former Ranger's jawline hid his expression, but Sullivan sensed he was calculating the chances of another attack and where it'd come from. Always ready for the fight, always on alert. That was what made Anthony one of the best men on the Blackhawk Security team. "Need a ride?"

"Jane." Sullivan pushed through the EMTs blocking his path to her and offered her his hand. "We're leaving." Her long fingers slid across his palm without hesitation, and he pulled her to her feet. They had to get her off the street. Most stalkers willing to take out their targets in daylight—in public—loved watching the aftermath of their work. She wasn't safe here, even with three EMTs and two Anchorage PD officers. But his team could protect her. *He* could protect her. "I've got you."

He wasn't sure where the words had come from, but Jane nodded once, setting his racing heart at ease. Hand wrapped tight around hers, he headed toward Anthony and the safety of the SUV. She'd been through hell—again—and he fought the urge to wrap her in his arms. Holding her back in that apartment, just before it'd burned to the ground, had comforted him as much as it had her. He'd overstepped the boundaries he'd set between them. Didn't seem as important then as it did now. Jane. She'd been all that'd mattered.

Shoving her into the back of the SUV, Sullivan climbed in after her. "Go," he ordered Anthony, and the SUV spun around before he shut the door.

"Where are we going? Christopher knew the tow truck would be recovered, and that we would come here." Voice soft, Jane swept her gaze across the back window, knuckles white from her grip on the edge of her seat. "He was waiting for us."

"We're going on lockdown. I've already called in the rest of my team to meet us." Sullivan studied the rooftops as they sped through downtown. Water kicked up along the side of the SUV, but he forced himself to keep his senses on the possible threat rather than the smell of smoke coming off her skin. Unholstering the Glock at his side, he cleared the chamber and loaded another round. Just in case. "Look on the bright side. You didn't have to drag anyone out of that building."

Jane's resulting laugh dissolved the knot of tightness behind his sternum, and it became easier to breathe. His smile vanished. This wasn't right. He shouldn't be trying to make her laugh, to help her cope with the situation. Shouldn't want to hike her into his side like he had some kind of claim.

"We're here." Anthony swung the SUV into Blackhawk Security's parking garage. The gate locked down behind them the second the bumper cleared. Four other vehicles had been parked close to the elevator doors. The rest of the team had already arrived and were waiting for orders. Good. The sooner he wrapped up Jane's case, the better. He might've led some of the blackest operations the US government had ever ordered during his time as a SEAL, but Sullivan only had so much control when it came to the woman determined to surprise him at every turn.

"Stay behind me. Use my body as a shield." He locked his gaze on those beautiful hazel eyes before Jane could climb out of the SUV. "If you feel threatened in any way, run for the emergency exit next to the garage door and don't look back."

"Okay." Her hair hid one side of her face. His fingers itched to put it back where it belonged. But he wouldn't. No matter how many times he'd thought of touching her, getting mixed up with a client—with *her*—only complicated the situation. He wasn't about to take that chance. For her own safety and his brother's memory, he couldn't do it. "What about you?"

Sullivan cleared his head. *Keep her safe. Eliminate the threat. Nothing more.* "Don't worry about me. I can take care of myself."

"As you clearly showed on the way to your cabin." A smile brightened her features.

"I knew you were going to throw that almost dying thing back in my face," he said.

Her smile disappeared. She shot her hand out to rest on his arm before he could climb from the SUV. Sullivan sat paralyzed, hypnotized, as an uncontrollable rush of desire raced up his arm. Despite their past, he was beginning to like it when she touched him. Too much. "Promise me something before we get out of the car."

One hand on the door handle, the other on his weapon, Sullivan narrowed his eyes. "Anything."

He meant it, but he swallowed hard. What was coming his way?

"As a lawyer, I took an oath to uphold the law. Promise me we're going to bring this guy to justice." Determination unlike Sullivan had ever seen sharpened her jawline, and a chill swept down his spine. "Legally."

"That is the one thing I can't promise, Jane." He stepped out onto the pavement. He controlled *his* actions. God-given agency prevented him from doing that for someone else. So whether or not Christopher Menas saw the inside of a jail cell rather than the inside of a coffin was up to him. Not Sullivan.

He took point, with Jane close on his heels and Anthony taking up the rear. They moved as one toward the elevator doors, the only way into the main building from the garage. Blackhawk Security was one of the most protected buildings in the world. Then again, Jane had walked right into his office last night without setting off the alarms.

Which begged the question, how had a JAG Corps prosecutor gotten past his security? And how had she uncovered his true identity to blackmail him in the first place?

SOMETIMES MEMORIES WERE the worst form of torture.

Jane dropped her head against her palm and brought her knees into her chest while she sat on the couch outside Blackhawk Security's main conference room. Sullivan's team had been holed up in there for two hours now. Coming up with a plan. She had wanted to be part of the meeting, but Sullivan wouldn't budge—Blackhawk agents only.

She closed her eyes against the flashes of all those photos on Christopher Menas's wall, photos he'd taken of *her*.

Her stomach rolled. Exhaustion tore at her from the inside, her clothes smelled of smoke and she hadn't eaten in over twenty-four hours. How much more before the nightmare ended? She wanted her life back.

Raised voices—male voices—penetrated through the glass doors. Jane studied movements between the closed blinds just as the door to the conference room swung open. She straightened.

A thin woman with long blond hair and stiletto heels threw her a sad smile as she sauntered down the hallway in her pencil skirt. She carried files with her, but hollowness in the woman's cheeks and the dark circles under her eyes kept Jane from asking if the files pertained to her case. Grief, thick and strong, clung to the woman, and Jane wouldn't stop her in the middle of her escape.

A handful of Sullivan's team trickled past the door frame and down the hall. She'd met Anthony, the tall, silent statue of muscle who wouldn't spare her a glimpse from behind those dark sunglasses of his, but the others weren't familiar. Another woman, this one with shoulder-length brown hair and a strong jawline, kept her head down in her own files as she followed the blonde. Had to be Elizabeth, the NSA analyst Sullivan had called to trace the call to Jane's cell phone. The lone man left behind—muscular, handsome with wild brown hair and tan skin—headed straight toward her.

Sullivan trailed the group out of the conference room, staring at her as she stood. "Jane, this is Vincent Kalani, our forensics expert."

"Nice to finally meet you." His Hawaiian accent surrounded her in a trusting vice as Vincent offered his hand. The peacoat he kept drawn up around his neck attempted to cover the dark tattoos flowing artistically down his neck but failed. Deep lines creased his forehead as he studied her from head to toe. Not sexually, but almost as though he'd been waiting for this moment between them for a long time. "I feel like I know you already."

"Oh?" Jane took his hand. Rough. Worn around the edges. Just like his dark brown eyes. Dropping his grip, she crossed her arms over her midsection. Something about Sullivan's forensics expert raised her defenses. Like he really did know her…and all of her secrets.

"Vincent is the one I sent to your town house to collect evidence your stalker had left behind after breaking in. He worked for the NYPD, so he's familiar with cases like yours." Sullivan maneuvered to her side, his hand planting on her lower back, and she couldn't help the tiny flood of comfort from his touch. "Tell her what you found."

"Aside from the fact you hide massive amounts of chocolate-chip cookie dough in a drawer at the back of your fridge," Vincent said, straight-faced, "nothing."

"What?" Jane uncrossed her arms. Pressure built behind her sternum the longer the forensics expert refused to elaborate. "What do you mean 'nothing'? He was in my house. I have the proof on my phone—"

"Everything in your home has been wiped clean." Handing her a manila file folder, he nodded toward it. "No fingerprints. No hairs. Nothing in your carpets left from shoes. No fibers left around." Vincent shifted his weight as she read the file, lowering his voice. "Not even yours."

"That's not possible." She snapped her head up. Checking the address at the top of Vincent's report, she closed the file. Her gut instincts kicked into overdrive. She didn't have to read the rest of the report to figure out where this was going. It was written all over the forensics expert's face, in the way he'd held her hand a little too tightly a few moments ago, in the way he studied her now, looking for a crack in her expression. She was a lawyer. She'd attended her fair share of interrogations over the years. Pointing the report toward Vincent, she leveled her gaze with his. "You think I'm hiding something."

Not a question. She'd heard part of an argument from outside the conference room while the Blackhawk Security team deliberated what to do about her next. Her grip tightened on the folder, and she slid her attention to Sullivan. Did he trust her? Or Vincent? "And you? I assume you read the report. After everything we've been through the past day and a half, the accident, the fire, what do you think?"

"I can't forget you kept Christopher Menas's name from us." Arms crossed over his chest, stance wide, Sullivan's expression turned defensive. He exhaled hard, but refused to look at her, attention on Vincent's report. "I have to look at every possibility and, as of right now, we don't have the evidence to confirm Christopher Menas is after you. Both the tow truck and the photos could've been used to frame him." His eyes shifted to Vincent. "This could be someone's way to get back at Menas for skipping his sentencing and not paying for what he did ten years ago."

Not someone. Her. An invisible knife twisted in her stomach. Jane held her ground, but she wasn't sure how much longer she could stand there. She rolled her fingers into the center of her palm to keep the betrayal working up her throat at bay. "I see. So I hired someone to T-bone us in that intersection, putting my life at risk, took all those photos of myself and hung them in his apartment, then set the fire while you and Elliot weren't looking?"

"You're a smart woman, Ms. Reise," Vincent said. "Top of your class at University of Washington School of Law, instant promotion during your enlistment. It's not difficult to imagine a scenario where you might want revenge on a man who ran from his crimes." He took a single step toward her, most likely trying to intimidate her with his six-foot-plus frame, but it wouldn't work. She was the Full Metal Bitch. Her gaze flickered to Sullivan, and Jane's insides froze. It wouldn't work. "Is that why you came to Blackhawk Security?"

"It's *Captain* Reise." Jane notched her chin higher, her voice more confident than she felt inside. "And I have no idea what you're talking about. I already told Sullivan why I came to him. He has the skills to catch whoever is doing this to me."

"See, now, I think it's more than that." Vincent shoved his hands into his coat. "As Sullivan has just informed us, you were the lead prosecutor on Marrok Warren's case. You hated the fact Sullivan blamed you for his brother's death, and now you're here to make it look like you're the victim. Or is it a coincidence you moved to Anchorage shortly after Sullivan was discharged from the navy?"

Her jaw wobbled, but Jane clamped it tight. This wasn't about Marrok. This wasn't about her and Sullivan. This was about survival. Turning to Sullivan, Jane pushed every ounce of strength she had left into her voice and stared straight into those sea-blue-colored eyes, the eyes she'd started to trust. Foolishly.

"If blaming victims is how you insist on running your security firm, then I made a mistake in relying on you for help." Jane headed for the elevators down the hall, but stopped alongside a fake ficus tree and turned her attention over her shoulder. "Run my phone records, check my email or get my financials. Do whatever you have to do. Do it and then call me when you figure out who's trying to kill me."

Sullivan's eyes widened a split second before she turned, forcing her feet to slow as she headed toward the elevators. He followed after her. "Where are you going?"

"I'm not standing around here waiting for whoever is after me to find me again. I haven't slept or eaten in over a day." She punched the button for the elevator to take her to the main floor but refused to look back at him. Instead, she watched the red LED lights shift into different numbers and focused on keeping her eyes dry. "I'm going home. Don't follow me."

Chapter Six

Jane wasn't responsible for any of this.

He'd known the second she'd given his team permission to run phone records and financials, and to sift through her laptop. Vincent had pushed too hard, but questioning her motives had been the only way to clear Jane's name from the suspect list. There'd been too many coincidences so far in this case and too many ways it'd gone south. How had Menas known to wait for them at that light? How had he found them at the cabin? And how the hell had he gotten the upper hand on them at the apartment?

A short growl resonated deep in his chest as Sullivan pounded his fist into the door three times, his face square in the peephole's focus. Interrogating Jane had been the last thing on his mind when he'd stepped into that conference room, and he'd made that perfectly clear to his team. But the evidence—or lack thereof—spoke volumes. They were dealing with a professional.

The door ripped open. And time froze. Damn, she was a sight for sore eyes.

"I thought I told you not to follow me." Jane leaned against the door, showing off her lean, athletic shape and a hint of skin from under her T-shirt, which she realized and straightened.

"Can I come in?" His insides vibrated with the need to touch her, to ensure he hadn't broken the trust they'd forged over the last couple days, however ridiculous that sounded.

"Let me guess." She crossed her arms over her chest, accentuating the fact she wasn't wearing a bra, but didn't move to let him past the door. "You're here to tell me you uncovered something else that points to me framing Christopher Menas so I can have my own sick revenge."

"I'm sorry about before." And Sullivan meant it. "You've officially been taken off our suspect list. It won't happen again."

Nodding once, Jane moved aside to let him in.

Mentally punching himself in the face, he pushed past her and scanned the town house for signs of forced entry. A window, the back French doors, anything. But Jane had everything locked up tight. The three-bedroom, two-and-a-half-bathroom rental reflected a vibrant personality. Lots of color, fake flowers, geometric-style pillows. Nothing like the bare walls of his cabin or the emptiness of his office. The thick scent of vanilla surrounded him. The entire house smelled of it. Of her. He spun back toward her, determined to say what he'd come to say and get out before he didn't have the mind to leave. "If it makes you feel any better, I had Elizabeth scour your records, and everything checks out."

A loud beep filled the living room. She brushed against his arm on her way toward the kitchen and opened the microwave. "Someone has tried to kill me

two times in the last two days. Nothing short of my
stash of cookie dough will make me feel better, if Vincent didn't steal it."

Slamming the microwave door closed, she stuck a
fork into whatever she'd nuked and blew on it to cool
it down, which shouldn't seem so damn sexy, but right
here, right now, Jane was home. She looked relaxed in
her sweatpants and T-shirt, hair slightly wet. He'd obviously caught her coming out of the shower. Too bad
his own self-hatred had kept him parked outside her
house until a few minutes ago. He could've—

"How is Elliot doing?" she asked.

"He'll pull through. He's too stubborn to let a little
blow to the head get the best of him, but that's not why
I'm here." Resting his hands on his hips, Sullivan focused on her eyes instead of the way her sweatpants
hung off her hips. "I need to know how you broke into
my office two days ago and where you got your intel
on my real name."

Her gaze snapped to his—alarmed—but she covered her surprise faster than he thought possible for
a woman who chased the truth for a living. "Because
you still think I'm bent on revenge or you're genuinely curious?"

"I've installed a top-of-the-line security system,
rigged hundreds of cameras and have around-the-
clock security on every floor in that building." Sullivan slowly closed the space between them. His heart
rate sped up as though he'd just run a marathon, and he
couldn't slow it down. She held her ground but tilted
her head back to stare straight up at him without giving anything away. Her sweet scent washed over him,
and Sullivan couldn't help but lean into her further.

He'd been shot at, tortured, endured physical nightmares and watched men on his team die right in front of him. All without his pulse raising a single beat. How was it possible Jane affected him like this? "There's no way you could've gotten past that system without triggering one of my alarms. Not to mention I buried the files on my old life and my family so deep, not even the CIA could get their hands on them."

"You're right. You have the best security in the world. It's impossible. But the files? That didn't take very much digging at all." Those hazel eyes stayed glued to him, her voice rich and gravelly with exhaustion. A playful sweep of her fingertips across his shoulder froze the air in his lungs. "But I'm not about to give away all my secrets until I can trust you."

Sullivan straightened his spine. "You seem awfully confident for a woman who was accused of orchestrating her own stalking a few hours ago."

"If you believed Vincent's report that I set this whole thing up, that I moved here to change your mind about me—" the playfulness disappeared from Jane's expression "—then you wouldn't have stood up for me against your team in that conference room."

He couldn't argue with that. The instincts that'd been beaten into him during his enlistment in the navy screamed her innocence. She didn't have anything to do with Christopher Menas or whoever was behind this trying to make her life a living hell. She was the victim here.

"Now, if you're hungry, I have more microwavable mush in the freezer. Unless you're into peanut-butter-and-jelly sandwiches." Putting some distance between them, Jane held up a thin black tray with what looked like chicken nuggets, mashed potatoes and a warm brownie. "That is, if you don't want to go back to sitting in your SUV all night, eating beef jerky."

"You saw me?" Tingling spread across his chest. Another smile pulled at the corners of his mouth as Sullivan drove his hands into his jacket pockets. Of course she'd seen him. This wasn't just any client he was dealing with. This was a woman who'd received death threats every day of her career. That brand of work required her to keep her instincts on alert and a gun under her pillow. *His* kind of woman. "And here I thought I had good surveillance skills."

"I've been stalked across the world by a crazed psychopath for the past three months. I'm bound to notice one of your SUVs parked for a couple hours two blocks down the street. Besides, I'm not stupid. I wouldn't have come home and let my guard down long enough to shower if I hadn't known there'd be backup." Jane shoved a forkful of dessert into her mouth, eyes bright, her delectable mouth curling into a smile. "Would you judge me if I said I only bought these meals for the brownie?"

Sullivan straightened. "Across the world?"

Her smile didn't last long. "Guess I left that part out, didn't I?" Lowering her fork back to the plastic dish, she wiped her fingers across her mouth. "Vincent wasn't totally wrong about my moving to Anchorage." Alarm flooded her features. "I mean, I didn't move here in some sick attempt to get you to forgive me for what happened to Marrok. I came here because I started noticing things missing from my quarters back in Afghanistan. At first, it was little things. One of my hair ties, some pieces of clothing." She set her food on the edge of the small round kitchen table a few feet away and crossed her arms under her breasts. "Then my service weapon was stolen. A .40 Smith & Wesson. I asked to be put on leave for personal reasons and came to find you. And to blackmail you if you wouldn't help."

"Your stalker tracked you down in Afghanistan, then followed you to the States?" Sullivan made a mental note to check Menas's travel records, phone records, credit cards, anything that could put him in the Middle East the same time as Jane. Would've been good information to know from the start, but they hadn't exactly gotten the chance to dive deeper into Menas's life before it'd literally gone up in flames.

"I can't think of anyone who would hate me this much. Aside from you." Jane crossed her arms over her chest once again, the strength in her forearms apparent. The apprehension clouding those beautiful eyes singed him right down to the core. "Hey, maybe you're the one stalking me."

"I tried hating you." Sullivan noted the flash of sadness across her features and locked his jaw tight. "Didn't stick after you saved my life back at the cabin. Then ran into a wall of flames to save my private investigator."

Her features brightened as she picked up her forgotten dinner. "Then since you're not here to turn me into the police and I'm not telling you how I broke into your office or uncovered your real name, why are you still here, Sullivan?"

"You're not safe here. This guy knows you. He knows things he shouldn't—"

"Doesn't seem like I'm safe anywhere right now. At

your cabin, on the move. I might as well find a small bit of comfort in my own house as long as I can." Yellow lighting reflected off the line of water welling in her lower lash line. Her shoulders sagged as she tossed her meal back onto the table. "It doesn't matter where I go. Whoever wants me dead is going to find me."

"Not if I have anything to do with it." The darkness in her beauty compelled him to close the small amount of space between them and he stepped into her. Sullivan framed her sharp features with calloused hands, those troubled eyes of hers widening. His blood pumped hard through his veins as he breathed her in. His last memory of his brother pulsed at the back of his mind. But right then, all he could think about was chasing the shadows from Jane's gaze. Stupid really.

"We should get some sleep." Jane pulled back, mere centimeters between them, breathing heavy. "You're welcome to take the couch and anything in the fridge."

He clamped his grip around her arms, not willing to let her leave yet. She was soft but strong, the kind of woman who could hold her own in a fight. "Even the cookie dough?"

"Sure. I guess you deserve it." Her lips curled into a smile. "But I'm still not telling you how I broke into your office."

Sullivan used every ounce of control left in his body to take a step back. Damn, he was a sucker for pain. Getting involved with a client—with Jane at all—was possibly the worst idea he'd ever had. But the sight of her when she'd opened the door had unleashed everything he'd tried to bury since he'd pulled his gun on her two nights ago. Desire. Hope. Life. "Give me a clue?"

"All right. I'll give you one clue, but that's all you get." She hooked her hands behind his neck and pulled herself into him. Shifting her weight to her toes, Jane raised her mouth to his ear, her exhale tickling his already sensitized skin. "It wasn't as hard as you might think."

JANE ENTERED HER bedroom with slow, determined steps and shut the door behind her. But no amount of space from Sullivan eased her racing heart. Had she really imagined kissing him?

She leaned against the door and thunked her head a little harder than she intended. Pain radiated across the back of her head and down her neck, but still didn't dislodge the rampant desire flooding her veins. Offering Sullivan her couch for the night probably wasn't the best idea. It'd been at least ten minutes since he'd taken her face in his hands, but the heat in her lower abdomen still hadn't cooled.

But she couldn't go down that path. Her life depended on her keeping her emotional distance. She exhaled his clean scent from her system and immediately felt better. Swiping the hair out of her face, Jane wrenched the bifold door of her closet back and punched in the six-digit code to her firearm safe. She'd meant every word when she'd told Sullivan that her stalker would find her.

Because she intended to let him.

It'd been the reason she returned home. Whoever was doing this to her had already shown a willingness to harm bystanders. She only hoped Sullivan had the resources and the manpower to protect her neighbors and to get the job done since she'd vastly underestimated the man coming after her. They both had. But not anymore.

No place was more comfortable and familiar to her than her own home. Yes, her stalker had broken in. Had probably searched the place. But she was the one who lived there and knew every detail of her town house.

It was much better than trying to lay a trap somewhere new.

Wrapping her fingers around the .40 Smith & Wesson—similar to the one her stalker had stolen in Afghanistan—she dropped the magazine out, then slammed it back into place. The drill had been burned into her muscle memory for years. She could strip down and reassemble any weapon in the US military arsenal, but her own personal firearm would have to do for tonight. The steel warmed in her hand. It'd been a long time since she'd had to shoot first and ask questions later, but tonight was about survival.

Not the fact that Sullivan Bishop was downstairs on her couch.

"Keep it together a little while longer, Reise." Jane placed the gun under her pillow, brushed her teeth and climbed into bed. The cold sheets raised goose bumps along her arms. Nothing like Sullivan's hot, hair-raising touch. Her mind raced with different ways she could make that particular fantasy come true. All she had to do was go down to her living room.

Nope. Not going there. Tossing onto her side, Jane stared into the lens of the small camera she'd installed a few minutes before Sullivan pounded on her front door. Her stalker had already broken in once. Wouldn't happen again. Stay awake. Finish this once and for all. Get on with her life. And Sullivan...

She shoved her nose into her T-shirt and inhaled deep, clinging to the remnants of his scent on her clothing. They could cross that road when there wasn't blackmail and a life-threatening stalker hanging over their heads.

Visions of his magnetic blue eyes danced across the back of her eyelids. Exhaustion pulled at her, her body aching for sweet relief. It'd been more than twenty-four hours since she'd had the chance to lie down, but she couldn't give in to sleep yet. The camera would catch her stalker on video—give them concrete evidence Christopher Menas was behind this—but the gun under her pillow would put an end to this sick game.

DEAFENING SILENCE WOKE HER.

Jane rubbed her eyes with the heels of her hands. Crap, she'd fallen asleep. Reaching for the S&W tucked under her pillow, she sat up straight. Fog clouded her brain, but not so much as to not realize what was missing. Where was her gun? She spun for the lamp on the nightstand and twisted the knob, checking the rest of the bed.

A crisp white piece of paper lay beside an all-too-familiar .40 S&W handgun on the pillow. She'd recognize that gun anywhere. Her stolen service weapon.

Her heart hiccuped.

Five words in block letters. "You're going to need this."

He'd been here. In her house. Maybe even touched her.

She couldn't breathe. Couldn't think. Covering her

mouth with the back of her arm, Jane fought the bile climbing up her throat. This was what she'd wanted, why she'd come home, but the reality gutted her from the inside. How had her stalker gotten past Sullivan? Snapping her attention toward the cracked bedroom door, Jane wrapped her hand around the gun and threw off the sheets. "Sullivan."

If something had happened to him, she'd never forgive herself for dragging him into this mess.

The soft echo of the front door closing propelled her out of bed. The intruder was still close by. Grip tight on the gun, Jane ripped out of her room and ran after the shadow disappearing through the front door. He wouldn't slip away this time.

Freezing November air slammed against her, but she pumped her legs hard without missing a beat. No more games. No more fear. Gravel cut into her bare feet as she chased after the figure up ahead. He passed under a streetlamp, heading south. Thick black jacket, Huskies ball cap, short brown hair. She was too far away to get much else and ground her back molars as she pushed herself harder. Her stalker ducked into a short alley between two single-family houses, but he wouldn't lose her that easily. "Christopher!"

The breath that heaved in and out of her lungs crystallized into large, white puffs in front of her mouth as she slowed. Her skin tingled with the sudden change in temperature, but Jane wasn't going back to her town house. Not yet. She pressed herself into the wall outside the alleyway. She'd memorized this neighborhood and every escape route the day she'd moved in. Her stalker obviously hadn't taken the same precautions. The alley ended at the back of a Chinese restaurant with no other access unless he broke into the large factory directly north of there. There was nowhere for him to run.

Jane angled her head around the corner, but moonlight and streetlamps cut off at the top of the houses. She couldn't see anything. Surveying the rest of the street, she took a deep breath. Hints of spicy aftershave hung on the air, pulling at memories of first love, suspicions, then terror. She remembered that aftershave from college, from Christopher's skin. But why come after her now? It didn't make sense.

With another look down the alley, her instincts screamed for her to go back home. No sign of the man who'd run from her. Something wasn't right, like Christopher had lured her to this point for a reason. But why?

"Jane!" Sullivan pounded up the street toward her.

The tension running down her spine lessened. He'd chew her out for running after a crazed stalker on her own, but a small part of her was relieved he'd followed her. And he wasn't hurt.

Lowering her weapon, Jane relaxed in defeat and sunk her weight against the house. She glanced one last time into the alley. Christopher was still just playing games with her. Trying to keep her scared, confused. Vulnerable. And it'd worked. He'd lured her out of the house. She shook her head as though she could rewind the past few minutes. She'd let emotion get in the way of catching the man responsible for turning her world upside down. How could she have been so stupid? Shoving off from the wall, she stepped toward the road to head Sullivan off. "Over here—"

"Hello, Janey." A hand clamped around her mouth,

then another around her waist, pulling her against a wall of muscle.

Jane struggled against her attacker's grip as he dragged her into the depths of the alleyway, darkness closing around her.

Chapter Seven

Sullivan was either going to kill Jane for running out the door with a loaded gun by herself or kiss her. He'd decide when he found her. He stumbled out the front door, gun in hand, but the world tilted on its axis. He hit the ground hard. Whatever drug he'd been injected with still hadn't cleared his system. The intruder had come through the front door. No forced entry—like they'd had a key. Every second played in his mind on slow repeat. Sullivan had shot up from the couch, clicked off the safety on his weapon and took a single step forward. But whoever had broken in had been two steps ahead of him. The syringe had emptied into his neck before he'd even had a chance to counter. He'd crumpled right there on the floor. Paralyzed but alert. His mind had gone to a dark place while he'd watched Jane run out the door and he lay there. Useless.

What the hell had he been shot up with? A mild paralyzer?

Menas had come into Jane's home, had terrorized her for the last three months. The bastard was going to find out exactly what kind of monster Sullivan had kept locked up the past decade.

Adrenaline pumped hard through his veins as he

burst through the foot of snow in Jane's front yard, only the sound of his breathing loud in his ears. A cramp shot up his right calf muscle, curling his toes inside his boots, but he pushed through. Pain, exhaustion and stiffness clawed at him from the inside, his vision blurry, but he wouldn't stop until he found Jane alive.

There were no other options.

Shuffling down one of the alleys to his left claimed his attention. The man behind these mind games wasn't an idiot. He'd known Sullivan would be there to protect his target and had drugged him to keep him out of the fight. Wasn't happening. Sullivan fanned his grip around the gun, index finger planted beside the trigger. Anticipation vibrated down his spine. This was what he did best, what he enjoyed doing. For his country. For his clients. For Jane.

What was it about her that he couldn't seem to hate? After everything she put him through—was *still* putting him through—she deserved it. But he couldn't hate her. Not such a strong, intelligent, vulnerable woman. She needed his help. She needed *him*. And nothing would stop him from getting to her.

Back pressed to one of the houses, Sullivan checked the alleyway. No sign of movement, but that didn't mean anything. Her stalker might've knocked Jane unconscious or— No. Sullivan wouldn't go there. Shoulders pulled back, gun up, he kept low and moved fast. His right foot dragged behind slightly, the last of the paralysis taking its sweet time leaving his system. Would've been easy to finish the job back at the town house with Sullivan unable to fight back, but apparently Jane's stalker didn't want him dead. Which he fully intended to take advantage of.

But where was Jane? Sullivan held his weapon steady, closing in on the alleyway one slow step at a time. "I'll give you three seconds to show your face before I start shooting. There's nowhere left to run. We know who you are and why you're doing this. And I'll hunt you down as long as it takes to put you behind bars."

Another round of shuffling said he was in the right place, and he swung the gun to his right. Pain shot up his neck and spidered throughout the base of his skull. He fought to stay upright and keep his weapon level.

But a wall of flesh slammed into him.

He hit the side of the building, the air knocked from his lungs. The gun slid across the pavement as blow after blow rained down on him from the shadow armed with a metal pipe. Sullivan held his forearm out to block the hits. Heart thundering in his ears, he swept one leg out and unbalanced his attacker.

The man went down, landing on his left arm. The crack of bone filled the few short seconds of silence just before deep groans reverberated off the walls, but it didn't keep his attacker down for long. A glint of metal flashed. The man had traded his pipe for a knife.

Sullivan pushed to his feet, pulling out his own knife, which he kept strapped to his ankle, and flipped the blade outward. He swung it parallel to his wrist and moved in, legs spread, torso angled to make himself a smaller target. His attacker did the same, and Sullivan hesitated.

Christopher Menas didn't have military training according to his records, yet this man almost mirrored Sullivan in his movements. The first swipe came fast, but Sullivan blocked it and shoved his attacker's arm down, striking out with a fist to the man's face. Shadows played across his attacker's black ski mask as Sullivan countered, slicing the blade across the man's chest.

Another groan filled the alleyway, but the injury didn't slow his opponent. He charged at full speed.

Sullivan kicked out, slamming his boot into the man's kneecap to keep from getting tackled. He barely registered the remnants of the drug in his system, but another swipe from his attacker's blade landed home. Stinging pain lanced through his biceps, but disappeared as his body's fight-or-flight response surged through his blood again.

No more games. Jane could be anywhere by now. Could be hurt.

He lunged forward, shoulders low, and hiked his attacker over his shoulder and into the alleyway wall. Hard. An elbow slammed into his spine. Two times. Three. Sullivan's knees buckled, and he forced all of his momentum into rolling his attacker over his head. With one foot planted in the man's stomach, he tossed the masked assailant as far as he could, using his attacker's momentum to roll himself on top.

Only his attacker had the same idea.

Sullivan's vision blurred as he spun, landing pinned under his opponent against the cold, wet asphalt. In the span of half a breath, his attacker plunged the blade down toward Sullivan's sternum, but Sullivan caught his wrist a split second before the knife hit home. His muscles burned as he held the blade above his chest. Sullivan was stronger, but whoever was on top of him leveraged everything he had into putting that blade into his chest. Sweat dripped into his eyes, the air in his lungs frozen.

He wouldn't lose this battle. Not when Jane's life depended on him. Sullivan hiked his right knee into his attacker's rib cage, dislodging the man's hold on him. He slipped out from under the knife and shot to his feet. He wrapped his hand around his opponent's neck, flipped him over and planted his knee into the man's spine. Moonlight glinted off his blade as he placed it at his attacker's throat.

Convulsed breaths echoed throughout the alleyway.

"Where is she? Where is Jane?" The words left his mouth as a growl. The urge to tear, to rip—to protect what was his—surged through his blood. And the man pinned beneath him looked a lot like prey. Sullivan clenched the man's ski mask and ripped it over his head. Pulling his attacker into the circle of light from the streetlamp, he swayed on his feet. He breathed through his nose, slowing down his heart rate to keep his head on straight. His fingers went numb for a moment as he studied the man in his grasp. A hard exhale rushed from him, but he tightened his grip on his attacker. "You're not Christopher Menas. Who the hell are you?"

Bubbling laughter filled the alleyway. An older, darker face, nowhere close to Menas's thirty-four years of age, contorted in pain as the man in his grip fought to look up at Sullivan, a crooked smile spreading across his face. "I don't kill and tell."

"A contract killer. Great." He should've known. No way Menas would've been able to defend himself like that. Jane's stalker was a tow truck operator. No military experience. But none of this made sense. How did

Menas even get in contact with a mercenary? Shoving the blade under the man's throat, Sullivan leaned in close. "Where is Jane?"

A sniper's laser sight slipped over the mercenary's shoulder, and Sullivan reacted by instinct. He dropped the knife and swung the man in his grip around. Two bullets ripped through his attacker's back, the shots rocking Sullivan with two strong thumps.

A glint of moonlight reflected back toward him from the roof of the warehouse across the street, but disappeared a split second later. Another slow exhale worked to bring his heart rate under control. A scope. Had to be another contracted mercenary cleaning up the loose ends. But where did that leave Jane?

Sullivan discarded the man he'd used as a human shield and stepped over the body. Sweeping his weapon into his hand, he stalked toward the factory at the north end of the alleyway. With a single tap on the device lodged in his ear, he had his weapons expert on the other line. "We've got new players. One of them just took a shot at me. Warehouse north of Jane's town house. Bring the shooter to me."

"Done." Anthony hung up. No time to waste.

Loud pops cracked in Sullivan's neck as he wrenched his head from side to side. Didn't matter how many mercenaries Menas had hired to protect himself. The bastard could have an entire army behind him for all Sullivan cared. It wouldn't stop him from getting to Jane.

JANE THREW HER elbow back with as much force as she could but hit solid muscle and Kevlar. Digging her fingernails into her attacker's wrist, she swung her legs wide and threw her weight forward in an attempt to unbalance him. Didn't work. The man squeezing the air from her chest was so much bigger and so much stronger than she was. No amount of escape attempts seemed to faze him as he pulled her across the wide expanse of the factory.

"Did you think you could get away from me that easily? I'm not the man you claimed you loved back in college anymore, Jane. I've changed. Traveled. Killed people. Made some new friends." The eerily familiar voice closed in on her right ear and sent a shiver down her spine. Christopher Menas. "Besides, I've been waiting too long for this chance."

"Christopher, please. It doesn't have to be like this." Her bare heels caught on chunks of broken cement as she struggled to loosen his forearm grip around her collarbone. The sour scent of cigarettes dived deep into her lungs with every panicked inhale. He'd already dragged her halfway through the sheet metal factory, weaving between large pieces of machinery she'd never seen before. Any deeper and Sullivan wouldn't be able to track her. Because he was coming for her. She had to believe that. Stall. Get Christopher to slow down. Give Sullivan a chance.

"Sure it does, Janey." Her insides flipped at the nickname he'd used for her all throughout their relationship, but not in the way it used to. He didn't sound the same, didn't feel the same as she remembered. Christopher pulled up short and swung her around to face him.

His dark brown eyes flashed as a stream of molten metal poured into a base a few feet away. It was late. Usually only a few factory workers kept an eye on operations overnight, but the unhinged mania in Christopher's gaze said it all. He'd kill anyone who got in his way. She couldn't risk dragging innocent lives into this. Sweat glistened down his stern features as he stared at her. He was right. He wasn't the same man she'd given her heart to all those years ago. Familiar angles and planes of his face were still there, but he'd filled out. A lot. The Kevlar vest he'd strapped on struggled to rein in the muscle underneath and intensified the in-depth story of tattoos covering every inch of his now-massive arms. Scars interrupted the thick five-o'clock shadow across his jaw, as well as his eyebrows, and his hair had receded several inches. The man staring her down with hell in his gaze was dangerous. Perhaps psy-chotic. Definitely not the tow truck operator she'd had in mind when she and Sullivan had pinned him as her stalker less than twelve hours ago. "And don't worry about your bodyguard. My friends certainly know how to show a guy like him a good time."

Friends? Her heart sank. *Sullivan.*

"What did you do?" She ripped out of his grasp and, surprisingly, Christopher let her go. No point in run-ning. He'd wound them through a maze of machinery she had no idea how to escape. Probably for that reason alone. He'd catch her without trying, and she'd have wasted precious time in getting to Sullivan.

At least four knives and just as many handguns peeked out from under his jacket and from the pock-ets of his cargo pants. What had her ex turned himself into? A mercenary? Flipping his wrist over, he read his watch. Christopher reached for her again and hauled her into his chest. Her sternum hit his Kevlar with a thud. "We've got such plans for you."

We?

"Are you going to kill me?" *Keep him talking. Keep him distracted.* Jane snaked her hand around to his closest pocket. Loud hissing sounds from the nearest machine drew Christopher's attention to his left and he reached for one of the many sidearms haphazardly packed into his gear. Not in control. Too easy to scare. Dangerous. Her fingertips scraped over the butt of a large blade in his pants, but Jane couldn't wrap her hand around the grip without tipping Christopher off. Her throat tightened, his cigarette breath fanning across her cheek.

"Not yet." He slid back from her. Jane let his own movements draw the knife into her hand. "First—" wrapping his bruising strength around her arm again, he shoved her ahead of him "—we've got a chopper to catch."

"I'm not going anywhere with you." Jane swung fast, arcing the blade straight across Christopher's face. He doubled over to the side as she hit her target, his scream nearly bursting her eardrums. Fleeing, Jane pumped her legs hard, exhaustion from the insufferable heat around her already pulling at her muscles. Grip tight around the knife, she mentally ticked off the different machines Christopher had dragged her past on the way in. There had to be a way out of this maze.

The factory's windows had been blacked out. No sign of an exit. No idea which way they'd come in. She couldn't just run from a crazed maniac until she lucked out with an exit. She needed a plan. The aggressive hissing and movements of the machines covered any sounds Christopher might've made from following her. Jane checked over her shoulder. She couldn't see him but ducked behind one of the larger machines for cover. Air dragged through her windpipe as her heart fought to keep up with the rest of her body. She'd kept in shape over the years, but running on pure adrenaline would only take her so far.

Okay, luring Christopher to her town house hadn't been the best idea. But then again, she hadn't expected him to be a mercenary either. None of Sullivan's or his team's research into her ex had hinted as much. Although, now that she thought about it, there was a piece of her that always believed she'd see his name on the FBI's Most Wanted List someday.

"Janey..." he said, taunting. Her name on his lips pooled dread in her stomach. "That wasn't very nice." He sounded close all of a sudden—too close.

Her spine straightened, and she pressed her back into the machine behind her. Heat seared her skin, but Jane clamped her mouth shut. She couldn't call out, couldn't give away her position. If she had to guess, she'd ended up at the south end of the building. She studied the blade in her hand, the edge tinted red. There wasn't an exit on the south end. At least, not one she'd noted mapping out her neighborhood when she'd first moved in.

Where was Sullivan? She had no doubt the former SEAL could take care of himself, but neither of them had calculated the addition of Christopher's "friends."

Footsteps echoed nearby, and her surroundings came into a sharp focus. She breathed deeply, evenly, as a deadly calm descended over the factory floor. Sweat dripped from her eyebrows. The blade's handle grew slick in her hand. She needed to get to the exit, needed to find Sullivan.

"Janey." A shadow passed in front of her faster than

she thought possible. Christopher knocked the knife from her hand and clamped his grip around her throat. Shoving her hard against the machine at her back, he let the skin across her shoulder blades sizzle from the blistering heat for a few seconds. Searing pain lightninged throughout her upper body, but Jane couldn't scream with her air supply cut off.

She fought for breath, vision blurry, but this close, she realized she'd slashed a deep cut into his right cheekbone. And the look in his near-black eyes along with the hand still around her throat said he intended to make her pay. But the second she gave in would be the end of her. She wasn't getting on whatever chopper he had waiting for her. No matter what. Mentally checking off all the ways to counter an attack, Jane unclamped her hands from around his wrist and went for his eyes. She dug the fingernails of her thumbs into his eye sockets, then kneed him in the groin.

Christopher's grip lightened but didn't let go as another scream ripped up his throat. And before she knew what was coming, his other hand slammed into her jawline. "You shouldn't have done that. I promised to bring you in alive. Not untouched."

She hit the heated cement floor—hard—sparks and hot metal brightening up the dark edges of her vision. His rough exhales drowned out the overwhelming pounding in her head. A single kick to her rib cage pushed the air from her lungs and shut down any other ideas of her fighting back. Jane rolled into the fetal position to prevent another hit, but the damage had already been done. Pain unlike anything she'd experienced washed over her, her vision going white for a few seconds. She couldn't breathe. Couldn't think.

"You've got a lot more spunk in you than I remember." Christopher crouched over her, slipping the blade she'd stolen from his pants back to its rightful place. "Where was this girl when we were dating? I might not have had to go after your roommates if you'd shown me a little bit of a challenge."

Her lungs spasmed out of paralysis from the kick to her midsection, gulping down heated air. She couldn't stop fighting, couldn't let him take her. Because, from the deadly look in his expression, the chances of her getting out alive were not in her favor. A single name crossed her mind as tears welled in her eyes. Where was he? Was he alive? "Sullivan…"

"Dead," he said.

No, no, no, no. Not Sullivan. "No."

"Yes." Christopher's scarred features closed in on her as he slipped a strand of her hair behind her ear. Her mouth filled with bile at the intimate gesture. The world spun as he wrapped his calloused hands around her arms and hiked her over his shoulder. He straightened, locking her knees against him and her hands in his grasp. "Nobody's coming for you, Janey. You're finally mine."

Chapter Eight

When Sullivan finally reached the factory, Jane was slumped over a heavily armed man's shoulder. He'd found her.

Tearing across the slick cement factory floor, Sullivan sprinted harder than he had in years. The navy had trained him for any kind of combat, taught him how to successfully shoot his Glock and hit the target from two hundred yards, but risking Jane's life in the process wasn't an option. Unbearable heat dived deep into his lungs, and he inhaled fast to keep oxygen pumping to his extremities. "Jane!"

Thick doors slammed behind the man with Jane in his arms as they disappeared out the west exit. Sullivan pushed himself harder, sweat dripping into his eyes and down his neck. The longer he lost sight of them, the smaller chance he had of recovering her unharmed. He rammed his left shoulder into the steel, slamming the door open into the concrete wall behind him. His heart pounded behind his ears as his lungs devoured the cold, fresh air.

No sign of Jane.

"Jane!" Sullivan ran a hand across his forehead to dispel the sweat now freezing to his skin. No response.

Damn it. He couldn't have lost her already. It was impossible. The factory's brightly lit parking lot didn't offer anything in the way of cover. Whoever had Jane couldn't have disappeared with a 120-pound woman that fast on foot. Unless...

Headlights drifted over the right side of his face a split second before a black Audi Q7 barreled straight toward him. Sullivan dived for cover, swinging his gun up and over. He squeezed off four rounds, none of which penetrated the SUV's windows. Bulletproof. The SUV sped across the parking lot, heading for the main road.

He tapped the earpiece connected to the most combat-experienced asset on his team and vaulted after the vehicle on foot. He wouldn't get far on his own, but he wasn't about to give up on Jane either. "Forget the shooter. The package is in a black Audi Q7 heading east toward Seward Highway. License plate is—"

A Blackhawk Security GMC screeched to a halt in front of him, and Sullivan lunged inside. Anthony Harris, his resident weapons expert, slammed on the accelerator, not waiting for Sullivan to shut the passenger-side door. He twisted the steering wheel, flipping around. "Your shooter is in that vehicle. Hold on to something."

Momentum pinned Sullivan to the back of his seat, and he braced himself against the roof of the SUV as they raced over the speed bumps set throughout the parking lot. Red taillights flashed at least a quarter mile ahead as the Audi spun onto the highway. "Faster, damn it. We can't lose them."

Anthony didn't answer. Always one for taking orders without question. The GMC's engine growled as he pushed it harder, and within seconds they were approaching the highway. They skidded into oncoming traffic, horns and headlights penetrating through the thick cloud of pressure inside the SUV.

"There." Sullivan pointed at the Audi weaving in and out of both lanes of cars. He leaned forward, hoping to catch a glimpse of Jane's outline through the dark tinted windows. No such luck. Majestic snow-covered mountains edged up against the freeway, but it was too dark to see much of anything else. Something wet and sticky tickled the underside of his arm as they maneuvered through traffic. Blood glistened across his skin with the help of the headlights of other cars.

"There's a first-aid kit under your seat," Anthony said, eyes never leaving the road.

Sullivan put pressure on the wound across his arm with his gun hand. "I'm fine. Just find a way to get me closer to the SUV." He would jump on the car's hood if he had to. Although, shooting out the tires should be enough, as long as they weren't armored, as well.

The Audi cut through two lanes of cars. Motorists swerved to avoid hitting others, effectively causing all traffic to skid to a halt. Anthony slammed on the brakes. Bracing himself for impact, Sullivan kept his focus on the SUV now turning onto International Airport Road, one of the only roads leading to Ted Stevens Anchorage International Airport. If her stalker got Jane onto a plane, Sullivan would never see her again. And that wasn't an option. Not today. Not ever.

Screeching tires filled his ears as the GMC skidded at a twenty-degree angle until his weapons expert veered off-road and cut west.

"They're headed for the airport." Sullivan pushed

the button to release his seat belt and then climbed into the back seat and unearthed the heavy-duty case of ammunition that traveled anywhere Anthony went. Dropping the magazine out of his Glock, he replaced the expended 9 mm rounds he'd wasted on the bulletproof SUV and slammed the magazine back into place. He flipped open another case that stored three black Kevlar vests and geared up. Two more knives and an extra magazine of rounds fitted into the vest. "I'm not going to even ask if you're armed."

"Don't worry about me," Anthony said. "Get ready. We're going in hard."

Through the windshield, Sullivan watched the distance between the two vehicles shrink fast. Anthony closed in on the Audi's bumper, slamming the back driver's-side quarter panel. The hit rocked through the vehicle, and Sullivan pitched forward between the two front seats. "Hit them again."

The GMC lurched forward and cut off any maneuvering the driver of the Audi had in mind. This was it. No way would that SUV reach the airport. Anthony spun the steering wheel and slammed into the Audi. The SUV fishtailed until the vehicle hit the GMC perpendicular. The tires caught on the pavement and the Audi flipped, two times, three. Air rushed from Sullivan's lungs.

Anthony slammed on the brakes to keep from ramming into the underside of the SUV, but Sullivan was out of the vehicle before the GMC came to a full stop.

Boots heavy on the pavement, he palmed the Glock in his right hand and unsheathed a knife with his left. The sounds of broken glass and heavy breathing consumed his attention, as someone fought to leave the vehicle. Jane was strong, a survivor like him, but the hand clawing its way through the debris wasn't hers. He couldn't think about that right now. Mercs were known to shoot first and ask questions later, and he had to do the same. *Neutralize the threat. Then get to her.*

A car door slammed behind him.

Sullivan clicked off the safety of his gun and aimed without looking back at his weapons expert. The former army Ranger could take care of himself and understood the directive: get the client to safety. At any cost.

The first shots forced Sullivan to take cover behind the GMC's open passenger door. He returned fire, hitting the shooter multiple times. The thick tree line on either side of the road provided deep cover, but Sullivan wasn't about to let any strays escape. The shooting stopped. Nothing but the sound of the wind rustling through the trees reached his ears. This wasn't over. Not by a long shot. He maneuvered around the door, weapon raised, muscles tight.

Two more heavily armed men climbed from the wreckage. Neither had the chance to lift their weapons in defense as Anthony closed in on the vehicle. Seconds passed in silence. Minutes. Where was Jane?

Another round of gunfire spread over the pavement, and Sullivan hit the ground.

"Sullivan!" a familiar voice screamed.

He snapped his head up. "Jane."

Tracking the rushed movements of two shadows as they ran down the road—one with short dark hair— Sullivan pushed up from the asphalt and took off after them. Menas's contract killers had nowhere left to run. The tree line was thinning, the airport was still five miles away, and the woman he held on to only slowed him down. His heart thundered in his ears. Or was that something else?

"Boss!" Anthony called.

A pool of light materialized over Jane and her kidnapper, illuminating the road and the mercenary's identity with blinding light. Christopher Menas. Sullivan clenched his jaw and leaned into the run as the black EC725 Super Cougar helicopter descended over its target—Jane.

Choppers. Mercenaries. Who the hell was this guy?

A spread of bullets flew over his head from behind, but Anthony's attempt to keep the helicopter from landing was in vain. Cougars were built for war, made to repel anything weaker than a Hellfire missile.

If Jane got onto that chopper, he couldn't follow. With a three-hundred-mile range at his fingertips, Menas could take her anywhere in the country, and Sullivan would lose her forever. Not an option.

"Jane!" He swung his arms hard, anything to force his legs to go faster. He was within shooting range to stop Menas but wouldn't risk Jane's life in the process.

She swung her elbow up and back into Menas's face, buying Sullivan a few more seconds, but a backhand to her face knocked her out cold onto the pavement.

A growl worked up Sullivan's throat as he lunged for Menas. He collided with solid muscle and Kevlar but held on to his gun. Straddling the enemy, Sullivan pulled the trigger, but Menas shoved his wrist aside. The bullet hit the asphalt next to Menas's head, and a blow to Sullivan's left side wrenched him off her kidnapper.

Menas straightened, blood running down his cheek

from a deep gash. "You must be the great Sullivan Bishop. Heard a lot about you, Frogman."

Sullivan caught the kidnapper's boot as he kicked out and flipped the bastard onto the pavement. Rolling Menas's head between his thighs, he squeezed with as much pressure as he could, taking hit after hit to his kidneys. Outside the pool of light, Anthony collected Jane and ran to the GMC. Mission complete. Time to end this. The pilot of the chopper rushed to help Menas, but Sullivan put one round in each of his legs before the pilot could pull his weapon.

"I have a strict no-abduction policy when it comes to my clients, Menas." Sullivan twisted Menas's arm until a snap sent a shiver down his spine, but, to the bastard's credit, Menas didn't scream. He'd finish this now. For Jane.

A spray of bullets ricocheted off the asphalt at his feet, and Sullivan swung his gun up as he jumped to his feet. He fired three rounds at the second SUV barreling toward the chopper from the other direction. Damn it. Menas must've had another team waiting at the airport. The Glock clicked as he squeezed the trigger. Empty. He discarded the gun across the road and spun for cover. Tires screeched ahead of him as he took position behind the chopper, return fire whizzing past him to his left. Anthony had him covered, but as two mercenaries exited the SUV and closed in on Menas—raining a nonstop storm of bullets on the GMC—Sullivan recognized the window on ending Jane's nightmare closing fast.

Menas remained motionless in the chopper's spotlight as two members of his team clamped on to his arms and dragged their leader across the pavement toward their escape vehicle, all the while spraying rounds right at Sullivan. He didn't have any other weapons, no way to stop Menas from getting away.

The Blackhawk Security GMC rolled up beside him, Anthony positioned out the driver's-side window to keep the mercs at bay in case they returned fire. Sullivan fought to catch his breath, the aches and pains of fighting overwhelming. Doubling over, he clamped a hand over the gash in his arm, then straightened. Satisfied they were in the clear—for now—his weapons expert leaned across the cab and pushed open the passenger-side door. "Boss, we gotta go. She's not looking good."

Sullivan ignored the open door and slid in beside Jane, attention on the second SUV hauling away from the scene. The brake lights dimmed in the darkness. Menas was gone. Wrapping his arms around her, he checked her pulse and wiped the blood from her skin. Her moan rumbled through him, hiking his heart into his throat. She was alive, but this was far from over. "I've got you, Jane. I've got you."

SOFT PULSES OF sound echoed in her ears. Her eyelids felt heavy, like she could sleep for a few more hours. But that beeping...

Jane ran her tongue across her bottom lip. Dry.

Cracking her eyes, she fought against the sudden onslaught of the fluorescent overhead lighting. She blinked to clear her head. White walls. White floors. White bedding. And an IV in her forearm. A strained groan vibrated up her throat. A hospital.

"Hello, gorgeous." Elliot stepped into her clouded vision, a bright smile plastered on his face. "I was hoping you'd wake up on my watch. There's something about those few short seconds of watching someone realize they're not dead after all."

"Hi," she said, her voice gravelly. Putting her hand to her throat, she tried massaging the dryness away, but it hung tight. "When did you get released?"

"Here, this'll help." Handing her a clear cup of water with a straw, he helped her adjust to a sitting position and fluffed her pillows before she relaxed back into the bed. "I checked myself out as soon as I heard about what happened at the sheet metal factory. Couldn't sit there and let you and Sullivan have all the fun."

"Yeah, fun." Stinging pain radiated across her shoulders as she struggled to sit up, and she wrenched forward with a hiss. She angled her head over her shoulder. White gauze and tape covered the burns under the thin hospital gown, but she was all too aware of how they'd gotten there in the first place. Christopher Menas. The sheet metal factory. The helicopter. And Sullivan. She scanned the room for those sea-blue eyes, but her stomach sank. "How long have I been out?"

She took a long, slow sip of water. Her muscles relaxed as the liquid did its job in her throat, and Jane set her head back against the pillows. Couldn't have been more than a day or two, right? Where did that leave them? "Is Christopher dead? Is it over?"

"Not by a long shot, beautiful. But come on now." Elliot sat in a padded chair he'd pulled next to the bed and laced his fingers behind his head, still smiling. He looked awfully chipper for someone who'd had his head nearly smashed in by a tow-truck-operator-turned-mercenary. "You know that's not what you want to ask me."

She didn't dare ask about Sullivan. Asking meant

she'd be breaking one of her own rules that she'd set when she'd decided to blackmail a former navy SEAL: no getting emotionally attached. "How long have I been out?"

"Two days," Elliot said.

Inhaling some of the water, Jane coughed and spit until she cleared her lungs.

Elliot shot forward and took the cup from her, as she covered her mouth with one of the sheets. Sitting back down, he waited until she took a full breath, then sat forward. His deep brown eyes studied her, that infectious smile gone. "He knows what you did, Jane, offering yourself up as bait. He found the camera in your room."

"Oh." She sat back again, swiping one hand through her short hair and running the edge of her sheet under her fingernail with the other. She focused on the bedding and not the disappointment in Elliot's eyes. Why she cared to give Sullivan's private investigator an explanation, she had no idea. But the words fell from her mouth anyway. "We were out of leads, and I needed to know who was doing this to me. It didn't make sense that Christopher might be stalking me all these years later. I'm not a threat to him anymore. The statute of limitations ran out a year ago." She took a deep breath to counteract the painful reminder of her and Christopher's reunion at the factory. "There's something else going on here. Menas said something..." A headache pounded at the base of her skull. "But I can't remember what."

"Elliot, get out," a familiar voice commanded from the door.

"Sullivan." Jane shot her head up. The dread that'd

pooled at the base of her spine spread thin, and she straightened a bit more. Pure rage tightened the small muscles controlling his expression, and he suddenly seemed much more dangerous than she remembered. Didn't matter. He was here. He was okay.

"Hey, look at that, my shift is over. By the way, I've been eating your chocolate pudding for the last two days. I'll pay you back when you're out of here." Elliot somehow gracefully maneuvered around his boss and escaped down the hall as though he'd done this before.

And by the serious lines carved into Sullivan's features, Jane bet he had.

Seconds ticked by, possibly minutes. She couldn't tell. One part of her wished Sullivan would step completely into her room and help her forget the horrible memories of the past few days. The other part demanded she keep her head on straight and remember why she'd blackmailed him in the first place. To bring her stalker to justice.

"You could've been killed." He rolled his fingers into fists. "You almost were."

And he'd been hurt by the look of his arms and knuckles. The air rushed out of her as she scanned the cuts and bruises marring his tanned skin. Christopher Menas had gotten in a few good hits. Because of her. She'd screwed up any chance of catching her stalker by running out her front door without any idea of what waited on the other side. "Sullivan, I'm sorry. I had no idea Christopher would have backup—"

"That's right. You had no idea. We were supposed to investigate the leads together, Jane, but this is what I find instead." He shoved a hand into his jeans pocket and tossed the small camera she'd mounted in her room onto the bed. Broken into several pieces. "You put me and my entire team at risk by going after Menas yourself."

Jane didn't know what else to say, her throat closing as she fought to hold on to the last remnants of her emotional control. She fisted her hands in the sheets. Rolling her lips between her teeth, she bit down to stay in the moment. She couldn't fight Christopher and his team of mercenaries on her own, but she hadn't meant to put the Blackhawk Security team's lives at stake either. They deserved more. Sullivan deserved more. "You're right. I wasn't thinking clearly."

He stalked toward her like a soldier, his grip loose at his sides, ready to go for his weapon at a moment's notice. He walked with power. The edge of her mattress dipped under his weight, his body heat tunneling through the sheets on her bed and down into her bones. Jane couldn't think about her awareness of him right now. Because something had changed. He was looking at her differently. Like he actually would've cared had Christopher gotten her onto that helicopter. "Do you know what would've happened if Menas had killed you?"

The memories flooded in with no one to stop them from overtaking the small amount of control she'd built up. Jane blinked back the tears welling in her lower eyelids. "Well, you definitely wouldn't have had to worry about me blackmailing you anymore."

"That's not my priority right now, Jane. You're a survivor. Like me. Setting up the camera, going after Menas…" He exhaled hard. "As much as I want to be angry at you for it, you did what you felt like you had to do, and I respect you for it. You're strong, you're used to taking care of yourself, but you hired me to protect you, and I can't do that when you're running your own agenda on the side. Understand?" He slid his fingers into her hair, caging her between his massive calloused palms. Those mesmerizing blue eyes bored deep down into her as though he could bare every inch of her with a single look. Sullivan's tone dipped into dangerous territory. "If Menas had gotten you onto that helicopter, I would've spent the rest of my life hunting him and every associate involved until I put them all in the ground."

She blinked to restart her circuits. "I've upended your entire life. Twice. Why would you care what happens to me?"

"Because you put aside your own well-being to save my and Elliot's lives." Sullivan dropped the pad of his thumb to the crack in her bottom lip, and something hot and sensual rushed through her. He thought all that about her? "And because Menas won't stop coming after you, and I'm eager to personally introduce him to a world of disappointment."

He housed shadows—downright darkness sometimes—but he was also honorable. He gave his word and followed through. More than she could say about any other man in her life.

"You think highly of yourself, don't you?" And with damn good reason. SEALs were the principal special operators of the navy. With sea, land and air in their blood, they could operate in any kind of environment, hostile or not. The edges of his dark trident tattoo peeked out from under his T-shirt sleeve. Dryness set up residence in her throat again, and it had nothing to do with the drugs the hospital staff had given her over the last two days. But she sobered almost instantly. "Everyone who gets close to me ends up hurt. All my friends…my family."

No one had understood why she hadn't come back from college the same, why she couldn't move on from what Christopher had done. She didn't have anyone left.

"Then it's a good thing I can take care of myself." Sullivan set one hand beside her hip and leaned in, totally and completely focused on her. He teased her senses in every possible way. His fingertips streaking softly down her bruised jawline, his clean, masculine scent filling her lungs, the sound of his uneven breathing. Every cell in her body stood at attention, wanting him to kiss her, needing him. He traced over the cuts along her arms and collarbone, then pulled away. Air rushed from her lungs, her head clearing fast. "Menas is going to pay. I promise. I have Anthony tracking his movements since his team pulled him off the highway as we speak. We're going after him."

She didn't want to think about that right now, not with him this close, not with him chasing back the pain her body still clung to. Then his words registered. Wait. What? Jane straightened, the burns along her shoulder blades pulling a hiss from her lips. "Sullivan—"

"That's not my name." He pulled away, but the remnants of his touch would stick with her long after they finished their investigation and went their separate ways. "I want to hear my real name on your lips. I need to hear you say it, just once."

Her brows drew inward. "But you're not that man anymore."

"You don't know that," he said. "You don't know anything about me."

A weak smile pulled at the corners of her mouth. If this was some kind of test, proof that she knew who he was and what he'd done, Sullivan Bishop was in for a rude awakening. "All right, *Sebastian Warren*, you want to go after Menas? Fine. But you're taking me with you."

Chapter Nine

Another Fine Navy Day.

Or, in other words, not so much.

Sullivan rolled his head back, stretching the stiff muscles in his neck. The second trip to the cabin hadn't been nearly as exciting as the first. Of course, had Jane been *his* target, he would've struck while she lay unconscious in the hospital. But Menas had to be licking some wounds right about now. His attention drifted to the closed bedroom door. Jane had taken the single bedroom in order to clean up and rest, but he couldn't sleep.

Not with an entire group of mercenaries coming after her.

The stitches in his upper arm stretched as he pushed himself off the couch for yet another perimeter check. He wasn't taking any chances this time. The investigation had gone from gathering intel on a tow truck operator who couldn't let the past die to defending Jane against an armored attack. Sullivan parted the blinds hanging in the front window, his favorite Glock in hand. The gun wasn't his only line of defense this time. He'd made sure Anthony had visited over the last few days to turn the cabin from his getaway spot to a fortified bunker. If Menas and his band of mercenaries came within a hundred yards of the cabin, Sullivan would know.

"Couldn't sleep?" Her husky voice straightened his spine. Those hazel eyes brightened as Sullivan looked her over in the overlarge T-shirt and sweatpants he'd lent her from his dresser drawers. His private investigator had dropped off a duffel bag of clothing and shoes for her but had somehow "forgotten" Jane's sleepwear. Her long fingers stretched around the mug of coffee he'd made her when they'd first arrived. She was the epitome of perfection—more beautiful than he'd imagined—and his mouth went dry. "Me neither."

Sullivan cleared his throat. "How are you feeling?"

"Everything hurts and I'm dying." A rush of laughter burst from her chest, but she grabbed for her bruised jaw. The swelling had gone down, but the pain obviously hadn't subsided just yet. Even so, her smile warmed parts of Sullivan he'd almost forgotten existed. Flashes of threading his fingers through her hair, of bringing that delectable mouth to his, streaked through his mind. "But I can't complain too much. I'm alive, right?"

Thank heaven for that. "It wouldn't bother me if you did." Sullivan replaced the gun in his shoulder holster and rested his hands at his sides. "You've been through a lot the past few days."

"We both have." Setting the mug on the countertop to her left, Jane tucked her short hair behind her ears. Her lean frame drowned in his clothes, but something deep inside him wouldn't dream of dressing her in anything else. Because as he'd watched Menas haul her toward that chopper, he'd realized just how far he was willing to go to keep her safe. She'd gone up against a mercenary alone. And survived. How many of Christopher Menas's victims could say the same?

"Sullivan, listen." One hand leveraged on the counter, the other on her hip, Jane rolled her lips into her mouth, a tell, he'd noted, of when she was nervous. Her gaze rose to his, a hint of pink rising up her neck and into her cheeks. "I can't begin to tell you how sorry I am for what happened at my town house. The camera…" She shook her head, eyes closing briefly as though she could undo everything over the last two days. "It was stupid. The whole thing was stupid. I should've told you what I was doing." She centered on him. "I'm sorry I didn't trust you enough to tell you what I'd been planning. It won't happen again."

Sullivan's fingers twitched at his sides. He'd thought about that particular piece of information a lot over the course of the last two days as he and Elliot took apart Christopher Menas's cover piece by piece. She hadn't trusted him to get the job done, to protect her, but Sullivan wouldn't let the sting sink too deep. Despite her reputation, he saw her distrust for what it really was. Survival. Jane waited for his response, her teeth digging into that split bottom lip of hers. He'd tell her the truth. "If it hadn't been for you luring Menas in, we probably never would've uncovered his real profession."

"As a mercenary." The words left her mouth as a whisper, as though she couldn't believe her college boyfriend was so adept at violence.

"We confirmed it a little while ago. Makes sense when you think about it. You said it yourself. Christopher Menas likes to hurt people. He doesn't have any regard for authority and doesn't believe in the justice system. The sexual assault against your roommates while you two were in college was only the beginning." Sullivan had come across a few mercs during his time as a SEAL, had even been asked if he'd wanted to get in on the ground floor of a new private security company that specialized in Menas's kind of work not too long ago. His brother, Marrok, saw the career potential before he'd died—he swallowed back the tightness in his throat—but Sullivan only killed to survive or protect. Not for a paycheck. "Unfortunately, clients will pay a lot of money for traits like that."

"I take it since you've added a few new security measures to the cabin you still think he's a threat." Jane shifted on her feet. "You were going to kill him, weren't you? Even after I asked you to have him arrested and tried."

"Yes." Plain and simple. She'd asked for the justice system to punish Menas for his crimes, but in those rage-induced seconds of Sullivan fighting for his life— fighting for *hers*—he'd made a choice. He took a deep breath. "Men like Christopher Menas don't give up. They get off by making others suffer. I couldn't watch that happen to you."

"I understand." She ran a hand up and over her shoulder, where the worst of Menas's damage had been cleaned and bandaged. The burned skin would scar but could never detract from Jane's beauty. A weak smile sharpened the angles of her face. "I might not be able to sleep for a few days. But that's nothing new. Christopher's been stalking me for a while. I should be used to it, shouldn't I?"

Sullivan opened his mouth, wanting to assure her

this was the safest place for her to be, that he could protect her from any kind of danger. But he had a sense the fears Jane talked about weren't entirely physical. And he could relate. The brightness in her gaze dimmed slightly, and he couldn't help but close the distance between them. He notched her chin higher to have her look straight at him. "When this is over, the nightmares will get better. It'll just take time."

He studied the slim navy-blue box on the bookshelf over her shoulder, the one with the custom-made pen he'd kept after all these years. A gift from his mother. Identical to the pen she'd given Marrok when he'd turned twelve. "Someday, you'll wake up and they won't be the first thing you think about in the morning. After that, you won't remember them."

"Was that how it was for you?" Nothing but the pure need of reassurance radiated in her eyes. "After what happened with your dad?"

Yes. Violence left a stain, one that took a long time to bleach out. That single incident at age fifteen had changed the course of his life. It'd taken every penny he owned to have a new identity forged. He'd had his birth name declared deceased and gone into the military a few years later, desperate to get away. Joined the SEALs. Founded Blackhawk Security. Dropping his hand to his side, Sullivan focused on the warm, far too intelligent woman in front of him. He wasn't about to tell that particular story. Because it wouldn't end the way she hoped. "You should eat something. Get some rest. We have a lot of work ahead of us."

He turned away.

"You asked me to call you Sebastian in the hospital. Right after you…" She inhaled sharp and clear, the feeling of his hands on her smooth skin still so clear. "Do you remember that?" Soft footsteps padded toward him, and before he was ready, she slid her long fingers over his bare arm to turn him around.

"I remember." He remembered everything since setting sights on her in that damn hospital bed. The way her eyes lit up at the sight of him. The way her lips had creased when he'd slipped his thumb over her mouth. The undeniable rage to tear Christopher Menas to pieces as he'd traced her injuries. Another round of tension stiffened his muscles. No man had the right to hit a woman, but Menas wasn't a real man. He was a gun for hire. Any kind of morality had gone out the window long before their run-in on Seward Highway.

Sullivan closed his eyes. Heat ran up his fingers and into his shoulders. His skin tingled where she touched him. Desire stirred in his gut, kicking up speed the longer Jane held on to him. He turned toward her, nothing but her vanilla scent in his lungs. How could she possibly still smell so good after what she'd been through? "You think I'm not that man anymore."

"Am I wrong?" Jane maneuvered her hand over his chest, her heat tunneling through his T-shirt and down beneath his sternum. Down to the spot where his soul resided. "I read the papers. I know you were only a teenager when you—"

"Killed my father for murdering my mother and eleven other women?" There. He'd said it. He'd drawn blood at the tender age of fifteen and hadn't looked back. Not even for his younger brother. Sullivan squared his shoulders. "Release of that information might lose me the business I've built from the ground up, but the Anchorage Lumberjack was a serial killer who started with women who wouldn't agree to his advances and ended with my mother. So if you're looking for some kind of guilty plea, you're not going to find it, Counselor."

"I'm not looking for a guilty plea." Jane fanned her fingers over his chest. "I just want to get to know the man taking on an entire mercenary ring for me."

Get to know him? This woman wanted to face off with years of his personal demons? A laugh rumbled deep in his chest. Having her this close, with nothing but honesty and desire in her expression, Sullivan couldn't back away. As he should. Never mind that she'd blackmailed him into this mess in the first place, but Jane had single-handedly brought down the only family he'd had left.

But she hadn't forced his brother to commit suicide, had she? Marrok had pulled the trigger himself. And the blackmail… Well, he was a SEAL, damn it. He had held live grenades in his bare hands, had prevented an attack on civilians in the Middle East, could hold his breath for more than three minutes without releasing a single bubble underwater. Blackmail didn't compare to the last twelve years of nonstop training and missions he'd successfully completed. If anyone could battle the monsters hiding in his closet, the Full Metal Bitch had the best chance of survival. "Are you sure you can handle it?"

"I've faced dangerous, military-trained criminals every day of my career, survived two attempts on my life by a mercenary and dragged your deadweight through the Alaskan wilderness by myself." Her mouth turned up into a gut-wrenching smile that clenched his insides and destroyed his excuses. "Why don't you give me a challenge?"

WHY DID HER heart insist on getting involved in things it had no business interfering with? Its job was to pump blood. That was it. Get to know the real Sullivan Bishop? That should've been the last thing on her mind. But at the moment, Jane couldn't remember why. His eyes had settled on her, and the pain, the exhaustion, the alarm bells sounding off in her head all disappeared.

He shouldn't have touched her in the hospital. Because now all she could think about was having those hands on her again. And, hell, if that didn't send her thoughts on tangents everywhere but where it should be: on bringing her stalker to justice.

The shadows across the rough ridge of his nose shifted as Sullivan closed in on her. The action, so simple, set off an explosive chain reaction that stole the air from her lungs. Skin heated, heart racing, her fight-or-flight response kicked into high gear. He'd almost kissed her back in the hospital, but this, the desire raging in his gaze, was something completely different. Like he'd finally come to a decision about her.

Long-dormant longing flooded through her, but she stepped out of Sullivan's range. She had been fed, had rested, felt safe here in his cabin, everything that said she was supposed to be ready for an intimate relationship according to Maslow's hierarchy of needs, but she couldn't do this. At least, not with him.

Take care of the threat. Get her life back.

Mind over matter. That was all it'd take.

They'd only known each other for four days—albeit four of the most intense days of her life—but people got hurt when they insisted on staying in her life.

"Jane?" Confusion chased the desire from his expression. "What's wrong?"

Good question. She'd been with a handful of men in the past. Nothing serious. But it was like riding a bike, right? Except this bike was inexplicably protective of her, had taken on a group of mercenaries to save her life and stared at her as though he intended to devour her. Sullivan was a good man. And despite her original intentions when she'd broken into his office, she wouldn't let him throw away his life for her. Because guilt was the unwanted gift that just kept on giving.

"Everything." Jane ran a hand through her hair, then crossed her arms over her stomach and leaned against the back of the couch for support. Her knees locked to keep her upright when all she wanted to do was collapse into Sullivan. All the oxygen disappeared from the room. The three small lines between his eyebrows deepened, and she clenched her jaw to keep herself in the moment. Why was her chest so tight? "I blackmailed you into helping me, Sullivan, but after what happened with Christopher... I have no idea how to get you out of this."

"Get me out of this?" Sullivan widened his stance, crossing his arms over his chest. "What gave you the idea I'm looking for a way out?"

"You beat Christopher Menas until he was unconscious to save me on the highway. In my experience, mercenaries like him aren't going to forget about something like that and move on. He's turned you into a target, too." She inhaled deep, savoring his masculine, clean scent. "I know what you said about taking care of yourself before, but people who've gotten close to me over the years always end up hurt. And for some stupid reason, I don't want that to happen to you."

Silence stretched between them, a living, breathing thing.

Slowly, dangerously, Sullivan stalked toward her, a predator closing in on his prey. Before Jane had a chance to escape, he caged her between his massive arms against the couch, just as he had back in his office. The ice in his gaze melted, warming every inch of her body. "Do I look like the kind of man who's willing to back down from a fight?"

Not in the least.

"Stop looking at me like that." Jane straightened— at a loss with him practically wrapped around her— but she didn't get far. Didn't he understand? Nothing could happen between them. Ever. Christopher wasn't going to stop. He'd hunt her down until he got whatever kind of revenge he sought from her. There was nowhere she could go that didn't put them both in danger. Clearing her throat, she stood up against him. Fine. He wouldn't back down voluntarily? She'd make him see reason. "You should hate me for what happened with your brother, for what I did to force you to help me."

"I tried. It didn't work." The cage he'd constructed around her disappeared. The muscles in the right side of his jaw ticked off a steady beat. "Do you want me to hate you? Is that it?"

It would sure make them going their separate ways easier after they finished with Christopher and his friends. But what if they never found him? She'd have to leave her job with the JAG Corps. Change her name. Move again. Jane exhaled hard, but the tightness in her chest didn't lessen. What if her stalker got to her again and Sullivan wasn't around the next time? Rapid flashes of what'd happened in the factory took over, and the burns across her back tingled. Without Sullivan, who knew what would've happened to her had Christopher gotten her onto that chopper. Dread curdled in her gut. She didn't want to think about it.

"We've gone up against some of the most violent men in existence, Jane. Men most people would run from. But you…you held your ground. You've fought like hell for yourself and for me since you broke into my office." Sullivan stared down at her. "You might be the Full Metal Bitch, but I can't hate you."

Her insides warmed, relaxing her muscles.

This should've been easy. She'd planned everything down to the letter. She'd blackmail him into tracking down her stalker, the police would take over and she'd have her life back. Sullivan wasn't supposed to take on a clan of mercenaries for her. She wasn't supposed to consider what might happen to them after the job was done.

Oh, no. No, no, no, no. She did not have feelings for him. She couldn't. First rule of blackmail: don't fall in love.

Jane inhaled deep, swiping her tongue across her bottom lip. Her heart pounded loud in her ears. She couldn't get enough air. She took a deep breath to steady her nerves, but it didn't help. "Then where does that leave us?"

"Jane, my brother made his own choices. I honestly don't know what kind of man Marrok turned out to be, or whether or not he assaulted those women, but I do know you. I left that life behind—I left him behind—and while I will regret that for the rest of my life, I have every reason to believe you did your job." Wrapping his strong, calloused fingers around her upper arms, Sullivan slid his thumbs over her skin in comforting circles. Goose bumps prickled down her arms, the combination of cold and hot fighting for her senses. "You might've brought up the charges against Marrok, but nobody forced him to eat his gun. And—" his wide, muscled chest expanded on a deep inhale "—from what I've learned about you over the last few days, I don't think you'd do something like that without cause."

Jane blinked. "You don't?"

"No," he said. "Because we're a team, and I do everything in my power to back up the people on my team. And if you can believe it, that even includes Elliot." His smile vaporized the knot of apprehension that had set up shop in her chest.

Jane sank into him, setting her ear against Sullivan's chest. The steady thump of his heart settled her fried nerve endings, but the silence before the storm wouldn't last long. Christopher was still out there, still hunting her. Sullivan slid his hands up her back, thankfully avoiding the burns across her shoulder blades. "Someday, when all this is over, you're going to have to tell me what Elliot did to land in your good graces."

"Only if you tell me how you got into my office." He set his lips against the crown of her head.

"Did you think it would be that easy?" A laugh escaped from between her lips. How could she have wanted to push Sullivan away? The man was a SEAL for crying out loud. He took on the most dangerous threats to the United States with green paint on his face and a motto on his lips.

All in, all the time. For her.

Chapter Ten

Splashes of pinks, greens and purples wove intricate designs overhead. Aurora borealis. One of the most beautiful things he'd had the privilege of experiencing in his life. But nothing compared to the woman next to him. Three days ago, she'd survived what would probably be the most brutal attack of her life, yet here she sat, stunning as ever.

Puffs of air crystallized in front of his mouth as Sullivan exhaled. The temperature had dropped significantly over the last fifteen minutes, but he didn't dare move. Not with those vibrant colors lighting up the snow before the heavy tree line, and not with Jane bundled this close into his side.

"I've never seen the northern lights this clearly before." A fresh mug of steaming coffee gripped in her hand, she stared up at the sky. Her pupils lit up as the shifts in color played across her face. She huddled deeper into her coat, setting her head against his shoulder. "Never thought I'd get the chance to sit here and enjoy it. It's nice."

Sullivan took a sip of his own black coffee, every high-strung muscle relaxing one by one. There was something about watching the northern lights, enjoying a cup of coffee, feeling a woman's heartbeat against his side that washed the tightness from his chest. When was the last time that'd happened? A year? Two? A decade? There'd been women. Nothing serious. But this—*Jane*—was different.

The Glock he'd strapped under his jacket pressed into him. Well, he wasn't completely relaxed. Menas could show up uninvited anytime, but the merc wouldn't touch another hair on Jane's head. Ever. Sullivan's gaze followed a line of bright pink up and over the thick tree line surrounding his property. "I come out here when I need to get away from everything and everyone, or my back needs actual support from a bed instead of my office sofa night after night. Clears my head." A smile tugged at one corner of his mouth as he took another drink of his coffee. This cabin had saved his life and his sanity more than once over the years, given him the solitude he craved. He lowered his voice. "Now, if I could get rid of you, it'd be perfect."

The muscles around her spine tightened as she rammed her elbow back into his solar plexus, and Sullivan couldn't help but flinch. The woman was strong, a lot stronger than she looked, the kind of woman he'd be proud to have at his side in the middle of a fight. Jane tipped her head back to meet his eyes, a gut-wrenching smile on her lips. "Tell more jokes like that. I've got all night."

"Jokes? What are you talking about? I was completely serious," he said.

"All right." Jane shoved away from him, hurrying across the snow-covered deck as flakes quickly replaced the ones her footsteps disrupted. Doubling over, she scooped up a handful of snow and packed it between her hands. "You want to play it that way? Let's do this."

She wound her arm back and let the snowball fly.

Sullivan saw it coming but couldn't move fast enough without spilling his coffee. He dived to the other side of the bench, but it was too late. Snow plastered against his neck and melted down into his heavy jacket, setting his skin on fire. Coffee surged over the edge of his mug and spilled down his jeans. A small growl reverberated through his chest. Slowly, carefully, he set the coffee down, stood and brushed off the remnants of pure white snow.

"Are you sure you want to go down this path, Captain?" Taking a single step forward, Sullivan mentally prepared his attack, always thinking ahead to the next move and the one after that. "Because I don't know if you're aware of this, but I've been known to handle myself in tough situations. Some fairly recently. And I wouldn't want you to get hurt."

"I played varsity softball in high school and college, even helped win the army's annual softball tournament while on tour. I think I can take care of myself." Jane tossed another ball of snow a few inches up in the air and caught it bare-handed. "Unless you're scared to take me on?"

"Oh, you're going down." Sullivan lunged.

Her eyes widened a split second before she turned tail and ran as fast as she could for the tree line. He appreciated the view as high-pitched laughter drifted over the deep snowbanks she tried plowing through, but Jane couldn't outrun him. Hour after hour, he'd trained in this forest, mentally mapped out every tree, every rock, anywhere the enemy could hide. She didn't have a chance. Snow kicked up around her as she darted toward the trees, and time seemed to slow.

All his life he'd fought for control. Relentless command over his body, his mind, his life. Growing up in a psychopath's house demanded nothing less, especially for Marrok's sake. But it was the military that had beat self-reliance into him. Nobody would control him, no one would hurt him like his father had hurt their family. But the warmth blossoming in his chest right now wasn't under his control. The second Jane had broken into his office, something had changed.

Four days. That was all it'd taken for her to melt his steel heart. Saving his life in the wilderness, putting her own at risk for Elliot when the fire broke out in Menas's apartment... None of it had lined up with her reputation. Could've been intentional, Jane's way of going the extra mile to secure his services, but Sullivan's instincts said that side of her never really existed in the first place. It'd been her defense mechanism, just as solitude had been his. Sullivan took a deep breath. Dozens of men had tried to stop his heart, but Jane could actually hurt him.

The thought knotted a tight fist of anxiety in his chest, but that didn't stop Sullivan from balling a handful of snow and nailing Jane in the middle of the back. The stitches in his arm stretched, but he pushed the discomfort to the back of his mind. She'd started this fight, he'd finish it. Sullivan bent over to gather more snow, but when he'd straightened, Jane had disappeared.

The smile pulling at his mouth vanished. Dead silence surrounded him, the tree line clear. He struggled to level out his racing heartbeat but took a deep breath.

Vanilla infused the light breeze cutting through the trees. She hadn't gone far. Darting for the patch of snow he'd last seen her, Sullivan tracked a set of footsteps toward the tree line. If Menas had gotten a hold of her...

A wall of coat-padded woman tackled him to the ground.

His heart rocketed into his throat as Jane's soft groan transformed into a trail of laughter and eased the tension hardening his muscles. He stared up at her, those sharp features surrounded by pinks, greens and blues in the dancing night sky. How had she managed to sneak up on him like that? He was a SEAL. Nothing got past him.

"Easy there, soldier. You don't want to make any sudden moves." Straddling him, Jane raised a snow-filled hand. Her smile lit up his insides and chased the remnants of the small adrenaline rush from his veins. "This snowball is deadly cold, and I'm prepared to use it."

Scanning the spot where he'd seen her positioned last, Sullivan rested his head into the snow. The sensitive skin on the back of his neck burned as he fought to catch his breath. "Where the hell did you come from?"

"Sneak attack from the trees." She'd lowered her voice as though she were telling him a secret, those perfect, kissable lips spread wide. Straightening, Jane washed the smile from her features. "Silence!"

Setting one hand on his chest, Jane let drops of melted snow fall against his neck. The beads of frigid water panicked his nervous system, and he struggled underneath Jane as though he couldn't bear the thought of torture. "I warned you, Sullivan Bishop. I am very good at this game and I'm serious about winning. Now, it's my turn to ask the questions."

An interrogation. Interesting.

"You got me. I'll tell you everything." Sullivan raised his hands in surrender, but with her strong thighs gripping his hips—every man's dream—he had no intention of cooperating with her demands. No. He was going to drag this out as long as he could.

"Good. And you shall be rewarded for your cooperation." She tossed the snowball to the ground and fitted her hand around his neck. Cold penetrated deep under his jacket as she leaned in close, her lips mere inches from his, but Sullivan didn't dare move. "Tell me, if you could go anywhere in the world right now, where would you go?"

He rested his palms on the tops of her knees, the denim covering her legs thin enough he could feel her body heat. The strong muscles under her clothing urged him to slide his hands higher, but Sullivan kept himself in control. He wasn't an animal. He wouldn't take until she offered. However long that might be. "I'd be stupid to move an inch right now."

"Yes, you would be, but that's not what I asked. And now you must be punished." The edges of her mouth turned upward, and before he understood what she'd meant, she held another handful of snow over his face and neck. Freezing water trailed under his coat and T-shirt, and Sullivan had had enough.

He maneuvered one foot behind hers and bucked with the opposite hip. Jane fell to the side, and he rolled on top of her, pinning her into the snow. He was back in control. And she was his. Snowflakes peppered their clothing, but soon they'd be too cold to do anything but run for the closest hot shower. Maybe together. He held his weight off her, careful of her wounds, grip loose around her wrists, giving her the chance to escape if she wanted. But the surprised look in those hazel eyes said she planned on staying right where she was. "Now it's my turn to ask the questions."

"All right," she said. "Shoot."

"Are you going back into the army when this investigation is over?" He shouldn't have asked, didn't have any right, but Sullivan hadn't been able to think of anything else since he'd checked her out of the hospital a few hours ago.

Any evidence of playfulness disappeared from her features. "I haven't thought about it. After what happened at the factory, I didn't think I'd make it out alive."

Nothing but their combined breathing filled the silence, as a fresh wave of snow fell from the sky. Hell. He hadn't meant to resurrect those memories. The past few minutes with her had put them, and the man responsible, to the back of his mind. Freeing him from responsibility, revenge, rage. Sullivan lightened his hold on her and pulled back to give her some room.

"You are not what has happened to you, Jane." He tamped down on the strange ache growing in the middle of his chest. Sullivan had never been the relationship type, but right now, with Jane pinned underneath him, he could see himself following her down that path when this was over. If she let him. Because the thought of losing her in the middle of that highway had nearly killed him. "You're what you choose to become. Remember that."

Her mouth parted, breathing slightly uneven. "Are we really going after Christopher?"

"I like to finish what I start," he said.

Jane pushed her weight onto her elbows to sit up, with him still straddled across her legs. A shiver rode across her chest. "Do you think we'll survive?"

"I don't know." Better to tell her the truth, but as her features fell, Sullivan let the urge to protect her rage through him. His hands fisted in her thick jacket, pulling her toward him. "But I'm sure as hell not going down without a fight."

SULLIVAN BISHOP WASN'T the knight in shining armor, the one who had never been to war. He was the knight with tarnished and dented armor who knew how to win the fight and keep her safe. He'd taken Christopher and his band of mercenaries down once before. He could do it again.

But what if he couldn't or, worse, didn't survive?

Her gaze snapped to his. Jane clenched her jaw, refusing to let her thoughts sprint down that path. Because, if she was completely honest with herself, she'd rather run from Christopher for the rest of her life than let Sullivan become another casualty in this mess.

"Jane?" Concern deepened his tone.

Forget the frigid temperatures and the falling snow. Her body urged her to close the small space between them. She wanted to kiss him. More than wanted. *Needed* to. Puffs of frozen air solidified in front of her mouth. And the longer Jane studied his shadow of a beard, the sea-blue eyes that revealed his true intensions, the way his forehead creased when he was thinking something over, that need strengthened. "Don't talk. Just…"

Heat spread behind her sternum, lifting her up,

pressing her against him. The burns across her back protested, but the dull sting wouldn't stop her. Only the sound of their combined exhales reached her ears, her heartbeat steady, calm. Cold seeping through her jeans demanded her attention, but anticipation for the feeling of his lips against hers—of finally tasting him—drowned out her body's survival instincts.

Sullivan's patience disappeared.

Gripping the back of her neck, he crushed his mouth to hers. The cold reaching down into her bones melted away as the rich taste of him spread across her tongue. Black coffee, peppermint and something smoother. Like a dark scotch. The elaborate combination heightened her senses to another level. The pressure at the back of her neck lightened, but Jane didn't move away. Tilting her head to the side, she opened wider for him, invited him to take more. Take all of her.

But Sullivan took his time. Nibbling, nuzzling, going slow. So slow. Her insides flooded with need as he nipped at her bottom lip, a spike of desire rushing through her blood. He threaded his fingers through the nap of hair at the base of her neck, pulling her harder against him. Her nerve endings fired in little electric pulses each time his lips moved against hers. The aurora above her, the snow below her, Sullivan around her. Jane never wanted to move.

But the Alaskan wilderness wasn't kind.

A shiver chased across her skin, and Sullivan pulled away. A burst of laughter rumbled deep in his chest. Didn't matter she'd worn her thickest coat from the duffel bag Elliot had dropped off. He ran his palms up and down her arms to generate some heat. "You're freezing."

Danger loomed ahead, but the man straddling her in the middle of his snow-covered property smiled. Her heart rate kicked up, and it had nothing to do with her mind telling her this couldn't happen. Sullivan Bishop, former navy SEAL burdened with years of death and destruction, looked happy for the first time since Jane had broken into his office. Melted snow had penetrated through her clothing but, in that moment, she didn't care. The world had changed. He'd changed. And she couldn't help but smile back. "I don't know how. You're like a furnace. Your body heat could keep us both alive for days."

"Yeah, but it was yours that kept me alive out here the first time." He pushed to his feet, offering her a hand to help her up. "Which I intend to repay you for."

"You've saved my life plenty since I pulled you out of the snow." She reached for him without hesitation, sliding her fingers across his calloused palms. Not harsh, but worked. Like him. The colors of the northern lights blended together as Sullivan pulled her into his chest, but they bled into the dark night sky the longer they stood together. Mother Nature's show had faded, but Jane would never forget these last few minutes. Never forget Sullivan when this ended. She fingered the zipper on his dark coat. "But if you want to pay me back, I have a couple things in mind."

Jane tugged on his jacket until his mouth met hers once again. She wasn't gentle. She wasn't careful. She meant to conquer, to banish the last few days. Pushing every bullet missed, every patch of skin burned, every second she felt like she was being watched into her kiss, Jane reveled in the feeling of lightness overwhelming her body. She breathed easier, sinking into

Sullivan as she broke their connection. "That is, if you're up for it."

"I have a lot of unchecked frustration built up from the last few days. You might be the perfect person to help with that." The predatory desire raging in his eyes bolted straight to her core. Another round of heated arousal flooded her system as Sullivan wrapped his large hand around hers and tugged her after him. Snow kicked up into her boots, but Jane didn't slow as they vaulted up the front porch stairs.

A wall of warm air slammed into her, and Sullivan kicked the door closed behind them. Then his hands were on her. Pulling down the zipper on her coat, shoving the thick layers to the floor. His coat fell next, as Jane kicked off her boots, lost in his masculine scent, the mountain that was his rock-solid body. Her heart pounded loud in her ears, but nothing like in the factory as she'd run for her life. She was safe here. Sullivan was safe.

"You should get out of those wet clothes." He dropped his mouth to her neck, licking, nipping, hiking her arousal to levels she'd never experienced before. Her insides burned, every inch of her skin aware of only one thing: him.

But Jane planted her hand on his chest. All of this, the northern lights, the snowball fight, the kiss, it was everything she could hope for. But what about when it was over? Her leave was due to end in a week, and Sullivan had a business—a team—to run. Neither of those things left much room to explore this beyond tonight, but maybe that didn't have to be a bad thing. Maybe it was for the best. Because no matter how many people she'd cut herself off from, those who got close to her always ended up getting hurt. She stared straight up at him, almost a foot shorter but determined to hold her ground. "Before we do this, I need to know something."

"Ask me." He slid his hand over hers, his calluses scraping against her oversensitized skin. Sincerity cooled the flood of desire in his gaze. "I'll tell you anything you want to know. No more secrets between us. I trust you."

"You do?" Her throat went dry, but the steady thump of his heart against her hand chased the surprise to the back of her mind.

"Yes." Sullivan stared down at her hand on his chest, stroking the back of her hand with his fingers. "You might've blackmailed me into helping you, but I'm glad you did." A laugh rumbled under her hand, and Jane couldn't help but smile. "I can't remember the last time I felt this good." His hand on her hip pinned her in place. "You already know my secrets. I don't have to hide from you like I do from my team. I don't have to be so controlled. It's…freeing."

The backs of her knees weakened, and Jane fisted his shirt to keep her balance. "Wow. You really know how to sweep a woman off her feet."

"That's the plan." A gut-twisting smile deepened the laugh lines around his mouth. Sullivan spread his fingers across the bare skin beneath her T-shirt. His touch battled the waves of debilitating coldness and won. In seconds, he'd warmed her more than an hour-long hot shower ever could have. "But what did you need to ask me?"

Ask him? Right. Shaking her head, Jane fought to focus over the desperate urge to mold herself to him. She pulled her bottom lip between her teeth, that knot of concern holding her tight. People might've gotten hurt because of her in the past, but Sullivan had made it perfectly clear he could take care of himself, had even proved it over the last few days. So maybe letting herself have feelings for the former navy SEAL she'd blackmailed wouldn't get him killed.

Jane checked the distance to the single bathroom over her shoulder, then turned back to him. "I need to know how long it's going to take for you to get me into a hot shower."

Faster than she thought possible, Sullivan buried his forearms behind her knees and lifted her into his arms without regard for the stitches in his arm. The cabin blurred in her vision, but he remained steady, a constant. The warm swirl of desire in his eyes tightened Jane's hold on his T-shirt. "Why don't we find out?"

Chapter Eleven

Jane was asleep in his arms. Warm. Soft. Everything he'd ever imagined when he'd let his mind go down that path. Hope. Unquenched desire. And more. But the sun climbing over the Chugach Mountains claimed his attention. Sullivan dropped his nose to the crown of her head and breathed deep. Last night had been perfect in every regard, but, unfortunately, they were out of time.

He reached for his phone on the nightstand and swiped his thumb across the screen. A knot of tension chased back the peace running through his veins. The latest surveillance from Anthony and Elliot revealed Menas and his mercenaries gearing up in an abandoned construction site just outside the city. Sullivan knew the area but flicked through the brief's attached photos and the official report of Menas's history anyway. After skipping bail for the assault of three women in college, the seasoned hunter had realized he could make a living off doing what he did best: inflicting pain. Anthony's report started with a few jobs Menas had picked up working security for a Seattle company under an assumed name, then sped through the mercenary's climb to the private sector. From there, the money got better, the guns got bigger and Menas had put together his own team of mercenaries.

Right now, he had a team of three remaining, including himself, all highly armed with military-grade weapons and gear. Then again, the chopper landing in the middle of Seward Highway had already given Sullivan a clue. He dropped the phone to the sheets as Jane shifted in his arms, careful not to wake her. He'd had run-ins with mercs before, but not a single one of them had access to the kind of gear Menas had strapped to his hunting party. Despite not having anything to do with the military, Menas must have some kind of inside connection. Because stealing that grade of weapons and ammunition took a lot of bullets and skills that Sullivan would've heard of before now.

Something else must be going on here. Maybe Jane had been right back in the hospital. The statute of limitations to prosecute Menas for sexual assault had run out in the state of Washington several months ago, which meant the mercenary had no reason to come after her now.

Unless Menas and his team were only doing something that they'd been hired to do.

"How long do we have before we have to get out of bed?" The huskiness in Jane's sleep-filled voice raised the hairs on the back of his neck. Along with other things. Her fingers trailed across his chest, resurrecting overused nerve endings and sending a shiver across his chest. There was nothing like her touch. No one had brought his body to the brink over and over again like she had.

He pressed a kiss to her forehead, raptured with those hazel eyes staring up at him. Checking his phone again, he hit the silence button and rolled into her. "We have about fifteen minutes before Elliot walks through the front door."

"Mmm." Jane pressed her lips to his. The kiss was oddly sweet and full of promises he'd die trying to keep. He'd never been the sweet type. But promises? He intended to live up to every single one of them. For her. She maneuvered on top of him, chest to chest, the wrinkled sheets bunching over the small of her back. Soft skin surrounded him from almost every angle, and Sullivan wouldn't budge an inch. Dropping her chin to his sternum, she smiled. "Tell me he doesn't have a key and we can stretch those fifteen minutes out as long as possible."

For the first time in longer than Sullivan could remember, he laughed openly. Wrapping the top of his foot around hers, Sullivan flipped her onto her back and tossed his phone to the floor. He intended to bury himself in her warmth all over again, kissing her with everything he had left. "He most certainly does not have a key."

"Good," she said.

Fifteen minutes later, pounding on the front door pulled Sullivan from heaven. He shoved his legs through his jeans and laced his feet into his boots, closing the door behind him as Jane dressed. His heartbeat returned to a steady rhythm the more he distanced himself from her. Damn, that woman could do things to him with a single look, but last night and this morning? She'd turned his brain to mush and him into a grinning idiot.

"Right on time, Elliot." *Unfortunately.* Sullivan

ripped open the front door, every cell in his body running cold.

Elliot wasn't standing on his porch.

A solid kick to the stomach knocked Sullivan to the floor, but he rebounded fast as adrenaline dumped into his blood. He lunged for the Glock in the shoulder holster hanging off one of the dining table chairs. Two pricks of pain embedded into the muscles along his bare back, then fired with white-hot electricity. Soft clicking reached his ears as the Taser wiped out his central nervous system. His body spasmed, curling his toes in his boots and his fingers into his palms. Jaw clenched, Sullivan fought in vain to reach the gun as current after current of electricity washed over him. The spasms rolled him onto his back, but he failed to dislodge the Taser's probes.

Christopher Menas stalked through the door, two members of his team on his tail, weapons up and fingers on triggers. A cruel smile split open the slash Jane had cut into the mercenary's cheekbone, and Sullivan couldn't help but smile back. Must've hurt like hell. They fanned out into the living room. Searching. "Check the bedroom. She's in here somewhere."

Jane was smart. She would've heard the commotion and gone out the bedroom window as fast as possible. Seconds ticked by. One of Menas's teammates kicked in the bedroom door when he couldn't open it manually, but the resulting silence said there was no sign of Jane. Sullivan kept his attention on the lead mercenary, the uncontrollable spasms lessening. She'd gotten out of the cabin. Relief flooded through him, but it wasn't over. He'd give her the time she needed to escape. Even if she had to leave him behind.

Menas's expression hardened as he focused those dark eyes back onto Sullivan. The mercenary lunged, wrapping a strong hand around his throat, and brought Sullivan to his feet. The probes ripped from his skin as Menas discarded the Taser and replaced the weapon in his hand with the M16 slung over his shoulder. One pull of the trigger, and the best medical examiner in the world would have a difficult time identifying Sullivan's insides. "Where is she?"

"You know something? I'm glad you're armed this time." Sullivan knocked Menas's hand away from his throat and threw a punch right into that gash on his face. The merc doubled over; Menas's trigger finger was too twitchy. Bullets sprayed across the floor, up the far wall and straight through one of his men, who hit the floor. Sullivan kicked the M16 away, but a fist to the right side of his face forced his vision to go dark for a split second.

Another kick to the torso threw him out the open front door and down the two short stairs on the porch. Blistering cold spread across his bare chest as he hit the snow.

Menas charged full force and caught Sullivan around the ribs, hiking him up and over his shoulder.

Sullivan threw two elbows to the spine. Three. Menas dropped him. Clutching the mercenary's jacket, Sullivan pushed the bastard backward, aiming punches for Menas's kidneys along the way. Sullivan blocked the first attempt to knock him out, but not the second. He stumbled back, out of breath, as Menas took a second to compose himself. Snow kicked up around him, but he barely felt the temperatures now as anticipation pumped hard through his veins. The teammate Menas hadn't killed watched on from the porch, weapon aimed to finish the job in case his superior lost the fight. Because this was between him and Christopher Menas.

Menas rolled his fists in a circular motion as though he'd done a few rounds of illegal bare-knuckle boxing before becoming a gun for hire. Wouldn't surprise Sullivan. The mercenary came at him with a straight blow to the head, which Sullivan blocked with his forearm, spinning his attacker ninety degrees and shooting an elbow straight into the back of Menas's knee. The mercenary's screams filled the small clearing as Menas shifted most of his weight to the opposite leg.

Time to end this.

"I warned you not to come after her, Menas." Sullivan clutched the mercenary's jacket, lining him up as he pulled back his elbow for one last hit. Jane wanted her stalker turned over to the authorities, but there was no stopping men like Christopher Menas. He leaned over his attacker. "You should've listened."

"My man over there will shoot you the second my heart stops beating. Then he'll go after Jane." The mercenary stared up at him. A line of blood dripped from his bottom lip but didn't stop him from pulling his mouth up into another crooked smile. "Is that what you want?"

Sullivan glanced toward the assault rifle targeted at him. "Doesn't matter what I want anymore. You went after Jane and tried to kill me in the process. No one is going to remember your name when you're dead."

A glint of sunlight flashed off the blade cutting toward him. Menas moved fast, faster than Sullivan thought possible after the energy they'd both expended, and sliced through muscle along his side. Searing pain spread across the left side of Sullivan's body. Blood seeped down into the waistband of his jeans and stained the bright white snow around him.

Repositioning the blade in his hand, Menas hiked himself higher in order to stab down at him. Sullivan crossed his forearms, barely holding back the blade's tip from his face. Menas was strong, but Sullivan was stronger.

He threw a knee into the mercenary's midsection and watched as the blade landed in a snowbank a few feet away. "Any other surprises you want to try before I break your neck?"

Sullivan's breath heaved in and out of his lungs. He was losing too much blood to keep this up for long, but Menas wasn't recovering as quickly either.

"This isn't over with me, you know." Menas bent at the waist, holding his side. Most likely a few broken ribs. Maybe Sullivan was lucky enough one of them had punctured a lung. "I'm not the only one he hired."

Sullivan's heart stuttered. "What did you just say?"

The mercenary lunged again, and Sullivan widened his stance for the hit.

A single gunshot exploded in the small clearing.

Both Menas and Sullivan turned toward the shooter across the property, as Menas's teammate swung his assault rifle toward Jane.

"Get away from him, Christopher." She held Sullivan's favorite Glock straight up in the air, but, closing a few feet of space between them, she aimed straight for Menas. "This is between you and me."

HER WORDS SOUNDED a whole lot more confident than Jane felt. She held the gun steady, relying on the countless hours she'd forced herself to brush up on her skills at the range. Her heart drummed too fast in her chest. Muscle memory kicked in after a few heartbeats, but these were mercenaries she was dealing with. Not some muscled jock of an ex-boyfriend who hadn't been able to get over the past. He'd turned himself into a professional killer.

"Jane, what are you doing? Get out of here." Sullivan doubled over. Blood dripped from between his fingers on his left side. He was injured. Damn it. What had Christopher done to him? Her protector didn't stay down long. He raised that intense gaze to her, expression stone-like, the muscles in his jaw frozen. "Get out of here. *Now.*"

He was too stubborn and too strong.

But Jane wasn't going anywhere.

"Once again, the army is coming to bail the navy out of trouble." Not a time to make jokes, but her gut instincts were telling her all she needed to do here was stall. Elliot was on his way. Wasn't that what Sullivan had said earlier? She only hoped the private investigator had thought to bring backup.

"No," she continued. "I'm getting you out of this mess. Once and for all." She focused on Christopher. Sullivan had done his job. He'd found her stalker and she could take care of the rest. "Attempted murder. Stalking in the second degree. I could keep going. You have a lifetime of prison ahead of you, Christopher."

"Janey." Christopher limped two steps toward her, hands in the air as though he was about to surrender. Jane knew better. The last thing on the mercenary's mind was giving up. He took one more step. "We both know you're not going to shoot me. You're a lawyer, remember? Not a killer."

Jane dropped the gun a few inches and pulled the trigger. The bullet disappeared into the snow at Christopher's feet. "I might be a lawyer, but I still know how to use a gun." She directed him to the right. "Now, have your friend join you over there by Sullivan and drop your weapons."

Christopher's smile burned straight through her soul. Pure evil. "Janey—"

"Do it!" She fired another round near his right foot. Her hand tingled from the kickback, but Jane was prepared to fire a lot more shots if he forced her.

"Guess we've got to do what the lady says." Shrugging at his teammate, the mercenary tossed his remaining guns and blades into the snow at his feet and maneuvered closer to Sullivan. The second mercenary followed suit, losing his gun in the snow. "What now, sweetheart? Going to wait until the cavalry shows up? Because I've got bad news for you, Janey. This will all be over before they can even get here."

Where the small muscles in her face slackened, she noted all of the wonderful muscle in Sullivan's body went rock hard, even from this distance. His eyes widened. "Jane!"

Strong arms wrapped around her from behind, picking her up off her feet. Jane threw her head back, hitting solid bone, but whoever had her wasn't going to let a broken nose stop him. Sullivan lunged for her, but Christopher landed a hit to the gash in his side, and the SEAL went down. Sullivan's groan echoed all around her. She struggled inside the suffocating grip squeezing the oxygen from her body, her arms and legs fighting her brain's commands. Her vision blurred, and the gun fell from her hand.

"I'm a killer, Jane, and I've been doing this a long time now. I learn from my mistakes," Christopher said. Both mercenaries collected their weapons. Christopher planted a boot along Sullivan's spine, pressing his bare chest into the snow-covered ground, and widened his arms straight out to his sides. "You chose an ex–navy SEAL to protect you. I chose to bring a hell of a lot more men." He brushed the snow from his handgun and pressed a muddy boot into the side of Sullivan's head, taking aim. "And now, because of you, he's going to die."

"No!" Jane rocketed her elbow back into her attacker's stomach and then straight into his face when his grip lightened. She grabbed the fallen Glock at her feet and pumped her legs, the air in her lungs freezing. The mercenary at Christopher's side ran to head her off. The distance between them closed fast. She wasn't strong enough to take him alone, but Jane had run out of options. Sullivan wasn't going to die because of her. Not ever.

A sniper shot echoed from beyond the tree line, then ripped through the oncoming mercenary's collarbone. Jane watched as his face contorted into painful surprise and he dropped to his knees. In her next breath, he fell face-first into the snow, as another bullet took care of the contract killer rushing up behind her.

"Too late, Janey." Christopher squeezed the trigger. Sullivan's body jerked as the mercenary crouched low, desperation to survive bright in his dark eyes.

"Sullivan!" He'd been hit. Jane lunged. Her left shoulder slammed into Christopher, and she pushed as hard as she could to get him off his feet. The world spun as they rolled together through the snow. Once. Twice.

Christopher dug his fingernails into her arms, keeping her close, controlling her movements. She fought to dislodge the gun from his thigh holster, but couldn't get her arms free. He pinned her to the ground and smiled. He had her right where he wanted her, and her stomach revolted. "Just like old times, Janey. Remember?"

"Get your hands off her." Christopher's weight disappeared as Sullivan ripped him back. The mercenary stumbled but straightened fast. Blood dripped down Sullivan's side and from the bullet wound in his opposite shoulder. No normal man could survive that much damage and still have the strength to fight a contract killer.

But Sullivan Bishop was no ordinary man.

He swung, connecting with Christopher's face, his kidneys, his spine. The mercenary kept trying to block the hits, but Sullivan didn't let up, like a boxer who knew it'd be his last fight. Christopher wobbled on his feet, mouth hanging open, one eye swelling shut.

Jane stood, collecting her discarded Glock from the snow. Blood rushed to her head, but she stumbled after them as they neared the tree line. Those sniper shots that'd taken out Christopher's team said the Blackhawk Security team was close. If Sullivan knocked the mercenary out long enough to restrain him, Elliot or Anthony could haul him in while Jane got Sullivan to the hospital. His strength wouldn't last forever. Already, his punches weren't having the same effect, and Christopher realized it.

And then Christopher produced something in his

hand. The mercenary ran forward, shoving a blade up and under Sullivan's rib cage.

"No!" She ran hard as Christopher dropped Sullivan to the ground. No. This wasn't happening. "Sullivan." Her senses sharpened. Jane was already raising the gun. Her finger was on the trigger as Christopher limped toward her, Sullivan's blood on his hands. And she fired, hitting the vulnerable flesh just below his Kevlar vest.

The mercenary froze in his tracks, mouth still open.

She fired again and again and again. Blistering cold worked to freeze the tears streaking down her cheeks, but Jane emptied the magazine until the gun merely clicked in her hand.

Christopher collapsed into the snow. Dead.

Her shoulders dropped. Rushing past his worthless body, she fell at Sullivan's side. He stared straight up into the sky. "No, no, no, no. Sullivan, come on. Stay with me."

"You did it, Jane." His voice strained, something wet and guttural choking his words.

"*We* did it. It's over." She'd pulled him through the Alaskan wilderness once. She could do it again to get him the help he desperately needed. "Come on. We need to get you inside before you freeze to death."

The trees to her left shifted, and Jane raised the gun. She'd emptied the magazine into Christopher. No time to go for Sullivan's stash of weapons in the cabin. Without any rounds left in the Glock, she couldn't stop more attackers in their tracks, but Christopher's men weren't taking her from Sullivan. She might be a lawyer, but she'd kill everyone who tried before leaving him to die here alone. Two figures burst from the tree line, both heavily armed, and Jane's arm sank with the weight of the gun. Elliot and Anthony rushed forward, the weapons expert already barking orders into the radio in his hand.

"Jane." Sullivan wrapped his fingers around hers, his pupils growing bigger until limited amounts of the sea blue she'd started falling in love with remained. Bringing the back of her hand to his mouth, he kissed the sensitive skin there and a chill swept through her. "Go."

"I'm not leaving you." Hot tears fell onto his chest, smudging lines of blood. "This is all my fault."

A soft thumping reverberated across the property, but Jane had attention for only the man who'd nearly died to save her life. The man she'd blackmailed into this. Her hair whipped in front of her face. Where had the wind come from?

"Jane, you need to get out of the way." Rough hands wrapped around her upper arms, but she shrugged them away. She wasn't sure who'd grabbed her. Didn't matter. "The EMTs have to get through."

"Help him." She held on to Sullivan's hand tighter. "Please, help him."

"Jane, come on." Elliot's voice filtered through the fog around her brain. He tugged her free of Sullivan's grip as a team of EMTs closed in a tight circle around him. "You don't want to see this."

"This is all my fault. I'm sorry." Jane couldn't think. Couldn't breathe. Legs weak as Elliot dragged her against him and carried her away, Jane kept her eyes locked on Sullivan's motionless hand against the spreading red snow. "I'm so sorry."

Chapter Twelve

Bullets. Blood. Scars. Some things never changed.

A groan vibrated through Sullivan's chest as he straightened in the hospital bed. Hell, that hurt. But the pain and haziness disappeared as he caught sight of a beautiful head of short black hair sprawled across the white sheets on one side of his bed.

Jane.

He sat forward, brushing a strand of soft hair away from her face. Her breathing sped up, and a smile pulled at one side of his mouth. He'd never get used to the way she reacted to him when he touched her. She'd wrapped her long fingers around his before falling asleep, and he didn't dare pull away. With her fast asleep, the nightmares of the last five days had slipped from her features. The bruise along her cheek had lightened, the cut across her head healing without stitches. Not an ounce of fear pulled her expression taut. She looked peaceful. For once. He'd traveled the world, experienced the most amazing and destructive forces of nature, but Jane Reise was by far the most amazing.

And his.

This isn't over with me, you know. I'm not the only one he hired. Menas. Sullivan tightened his grip around

Jane's hand. The mercenary had deserved every bullet she'd emptied into him, but this was far from over. Whoever had hired Menas and his team wasn't finished. Not until Jane's heart stopped beating, which wouldn't happen. Because he'd take another hundred stabs to the torso by another dozen mercenaries if it meant she got to walk away from this. And she would. They both would.

"I don't think I've ever seen you smile at another human being like that. A piece of chocolate cake, yes. Not a woman." Anthony Harris's forest green eyes—free of sunglasses—locked on to Sullivan. The former Ranger buried his hands deep into his jacket pockets as though he didn't know what to do without a gun in his grip. Which was probably why he kept scanning the room for potential threats. Anthony cleared his throat. "If someone made me happy like that, I'd fight like hell to keep her with me, too."

The number one thing Sullivan could count on his weapons expert for? The blatant truth, even when his trigger-happy best friend should keep his mouth shut. "How long has she been here?"

"She hasn't left your side since the EMTs brought you through the front doors. Wouldn't let the technicians look at her until they got your stats stable." Anthony rolled his wrist to check his watch. "Going on thirty hours. She's been asleep for about two."

Jane. Always putting others first, even when Menas had a gun aimed at her head.

Sullivan swallowed as the memories of the final battle with Menas flashed across his mind. He'd almost lost her. Again. But this time, it'd been his own fault.

"Tell me how we missed the fact Christopher Menas was contracted to come after Jane."

"I've worked with guys like him and his team." Anthony shifted in his seat. "They've got the resources and the motives to create entire identities that hide what they do for a living. Some have two or three they cycle through to keep governments off their backs. Technically, they don't exist. No families. No friends. They're good at what they do. But Menas. Man, this guy is something else."

"He used his real name." Sullivan's gaze flickered to the rise and fall of Jane's chest. Why would a mercenary take the chance of being identified? He rested his head back against the mountain of pillows behind him. "He wanted Jane to know he was coming after her."

To throw off suspicion of the real threat?

"How did Menas manage to escape your and Elliot's detail?" he asked.

"He knew we were there. He sent a four-man team straight at us as he and three others sped from the construction site." Spreading one hand over his beard, Anthony let his eyebrows hike higher, a telling sign of stress. "I tried calling, but you never answered your phone."

Because he'd tossed it to the floor to have a few more minutes with Jane. Damn it. This whole thing could've been avoided had he just been able to keep his hands off her. He'd put her in danger. He'd *failed* her. Sullivan studied the rise and fall of Jane's back. She'd gone up against a mercenary. To save his life. Again. Shaking the disbelief from his thoughts, he dropped the back of his head to the pillows propping him up. He could really fall for this woman. He ran his free hand down his face. Hell, maybe he already had.

"Call Elizabeth. I want a list of Menas's associates, his phone records from the cell you recovered from the cabin, his laptop if you can track it down, travel records and anything else she can get her hands on. Jane said the stalking started while she was on tour. Find out who else on our suspect list has made a visit to Afghanistan." Sullivan ripped the IV out of the catheter in his inner wrist. Stinging pain radiated up his arm, but he pushed it to the back of his mind. He'd survived worse. "Get it to me as soon as possible."

Anthony speed-dialed Blackhawk Security's resident former NSA analyst and shut the door behind him. They wouldn't have the intel for at least another hour. Enough time for Sullivan to put a new plan in place. With Menas's team out of commission, they were back at square one. But the question had changed from who was stalking Jane to who wanted her dead enough to hire a contract killer?

A soft moan whispered from between her lips, and Jane's hold on his hand tightened. He stroked his fingers along the inner line of her wrist, bringing her around slowly. She lifted her head, a smile pulling at the edges of her delicate mouth. Those hazel eyes brightened as she studied him. "You're awake." She pulled her hand from his and pressed her palms into her eye sockets. He'd never tire of the huskiness in her voice when she woke, an experience he intended to live over and over. She sat back in the chair, stretching her neck to one side, then the other. "How are you feeling?"

"I'll live. Thanks to you." He hadn't been okay with her stepping between him and Menas at the time, but without her rushing the mercenary at the last second, Sullivan would've died from high-speed lead poisoning. He owed her his life. Again. "How many times have you saved my life now? Two or three?"

"Three." A flash of straight white teeth deepened the laugh lines around her mouth and Sullivan's heart stuttered. "Should I make another reference to how the army comes in to save the day or let it be this time around?"

"I knew you were going to go there. You grunts never could take a win humbly. Got to let the whole world know you saved the day." He shook his head, but had never felt so relaxed, so…at peace than he did in that moment. Anthony had been right. Jane made him happy, gave him purpose beyond running Blackhawk Security, and a reason to look forward to the future. And he'd fight like hell to keep her.

"You always know what to say." Jane slid her hand back into his, a few cuts and bruises decorating the thin skin along the top of her hand. Her smile disappeared. Connecting that beautiful gaze with his, she rolled her bottom lip between her teeth. Not a good sign. "My leave is due to end in two days, Sullivan. The army was generous enough to give me these last few months off, but with the threat gone—" she inhaled slowly "—with Christopher gone, I need to get back to work. In Afghanistan."

The pad of his thumb stopped midstroke against the back of her hand. *Afghanistan?* "You're leaving."

Not a question. Sullivan rested his head back against the pillow, staring up at the ceiling. How could he have been so stupid? Of course she'd planned on going back to Afghanistan. Her life was there. Her job was there. At least, until she was reassigned.

"Unless…" she said.

He straightened. "Unless, what?"

"Unless I put in to be reassigned here in Anchorage." That gut-wrenching smile of hers returned, and Sullivan couldn't help but hang on every word. "There's an opening at Joint Base Elmendorf-Richardson, and I'm thinking of taking it. It'd be a step down in salary for me, but Anchorage could be my last assignment before I have the option of discharge in about a year. My CO has already said the position's mine. All I have to do is ask."

"Then ask." The words were out of his mouth before he had a chance to think about what he was asking of her. He exhaled hard, but the tendons between his neck and shoulder strained. Sitting up as best he could, Sullivan ignored the pain shooting throughout his torso and brought Jane up onto the bed. Damn if he popped a few stitches. Jane was worth every ounce of agony. "I'm not going to lie. I'm not going to play games with you. I want you to ask for the transfer. I want you to stay here, with me."

Her heart beat fast against the soft column of her throat. He'd caught her off guard. Good. Smoothing her fingers over his arms, she studied him from the waist up. "Great. Because I already put the call in to my CO while you were passed out. He's sending me the papers in the morning."

Sullivan threaded his fingers through her hair and brought her mouth to his. He drank her in, memorized her in ways he'd never experienced before. He kept the kiss soft when all he wanted to do was claim her. She was staying. For him. For them. Tilting her head to the side, she opened her mouth wide, inviting him, nipping at him. She pressed herself against him, but the leads connected to strategic points on his body were determined to block his access to her. The EKG pounded loud in his ears, an echo of his own heart rate, and Sullivan couldn't drown the laugh rumbling through his chest. He gently framed her jaw with both hands, calluses against silk, and put a few small centimeters between them. "Any more of this and the nurses are going to run in here thinking I'm having a heart attack."

His hospital room door opened, but he couldn't focus on anything but her. His Jane.

"As much as I'd like to leave you two to go at it like rabbits," Anthony said, "I've got that new intel you wanted."

Sullivan's stomach sank. Right. The world wouldn't stop just for them. "Anything we can use?"

"New intel?" Jane studied Anthony, then turned back to him, eyebrows drawn inward. She checked the clock on the wall. "Oh. If this is another case, I can go. I'm supposed to give my statement to Anchorage PD in a few minutes anyway." She gathered her jacket in one hand and stood. "Then I need to go home and change."

Sullivan clamped his hand around her arm, staring up at her without any idea how he would tell her the truth. He owed her an answer, owed her far more than that, but his instincts screamed he was about to lose Jane all over again. Right when they'd agreed to give this a shot. But if she discovered the truth on her own? He'd never see her again. "It's not a new case, Jane." He licked his bottom lip, a nervous habit of hers he'd obviously inherited since setting sights on her in his office. "It's your case."

"What do you mean? Christopher is dead. My case is closed." Her eyes narrowed as seconds passed. Confusion slipped over her perfect features. "I shot him seven times, Sullivan. He's officially been declared dead."

"Christopher Menas was paid to take you out, Jane." He clamped his hand around hers, desperate to keep her within arm's reach. Not for her—Jane was strong—but for his own selfish need to hold on to her. "And whoever hired him is still after you."

"WHAT?" PANIC THREATENED to overwhelm her. No. The nightmare was over. She was supposed to get her life back. She'd put in for the transfer to Anchorage to start over. She and Sullivan were going to try to make this work. The room spun and Jane gripped the sheets for balance. Someone had hired Menas to come after her? "Who…who would hire a mercenary team to take me out?"

She was one woman. A lawyer for the army with no record of sending innocent soldiers to their deaths, not someone with a highly politicized agenda. She mostly dealt with divorces, immigration and passport issues, and reenlistment questions when she wasn't assigned to prosecute cases. She wasn't important.

"That's what I'm trying to find out. Anthony has worked with men like Menas before. I'm hoping we can get a hit off a source in one of his circles. I also asked my NSA contact to pull phone records." Sullivan wrapped his strong, steady hand around hers. "Menas would've had contact with whoever hired him. We're going to find out how."

This wasn't happening.

Christopher was dead. Despite her initial intentions to bring him to justice, she'd *killed* him and almost lost Sullivan in the process. Her hands shook as she dropped her hold on the sheets and fisted a handful of her own hair instead. Thirty hours. That was all the relief she'd had with Christopher's death. What was she supposed to do now?

Slivers of blood seeped through Sullivan's bandages. A bullet wound, a knife to the gut and a slash across the arm. She couldn't remember how many stitches the doctor had told her they'd had to sew in to keep him together, but he couldn't go through that again.

"Jane, I need to know what's going through your head, baby." Sullivan rubbed small circles into the back of her hand. The weight of those captivating sea-blue eyes studying her was almost suffocating. "Tell me."

She couldn't go home. Couldn't go back to work. And she couldn't keep putting the man she'd started to fall for in harm's way. Not for her.

Whoever'd hired Christopher Menas and his team had done their research on her, and if Christopher was reporting back, they knew she'd recruited Sullivan to keep her safe. She exhaled hard. Sullivan had done his job. He'd found her stalker. Her muscles tightened. Now she had to learn to protect herself. Jane stood, slipping out of his grasp a little too easily. He'd let her go. Because that was the kind of man he was. Considerate. Caring. Never one to thwart her own agency. She headed for the door. "I have to go."

"For how long?" he asked.

The rough edge to his tone revealed exactly what she'd feared, and Jane stopped cold. He'd either read her mind or read her expression, she didn't know. It didn't matter. She had to get out of here. Away from him. Away from the whole Blackhawk Security team. The nightmare wasn't ever going to end. They were all still in danger as long as she stuck around. Anthony waited in front of the door, capable of keeping her here if Sullivan ordered. But he wouldn't. She had to believe that.

"Jane, we can fight this thing together. You don't have to run." His voice washed over her in comforting waves, and it took everything she had not to turn back around. "Please. I don't want to lose you."

"Then you know exactly how I feel." Jane turned, her heart overriding every logical thought speeding through her mind. She should've kept on walking, should've shoved Anthony out of the way and left this all behind. But she couldn't end things with Sullivan like this. Not after everything they'd been through. Five days, that was all it'd taken for her to fall for him. How was that possible? "Do you know how hard it was for me to watch you bleed out after Christopher was finished with you?"

She fought back the memories, her throat closing.

Sullivan straightened in the bed. "I can imagine."

"Those were the worst two minutes of my life, Sullivan." She hugged her jacket into her middle when all she really wanted to hold on to was lying in a hospital bed only a few feet away. "I warned you what happens to people who get close to me. And look where you are. Look at your body." She motioned to the darkening bandages taped all over his chest and shoulder.

"But how is it going to end the next time? Or the time after that? I care about you, about what you want and need, and this isn't it."

"Jane, I can—"

"Take care of yourself," she finished for him. "I know. But you did your job. Christopher is dead. Now it's time for me to take care of myself." Jane headed toward the door, her insides twisting harder than ever before.

Sullivan hissed behind her, the machines he'd been hooked up to going haywire.

The look on Anthony's face as he lunged for the hospital bed spun her around. Ripping out the catheter and leads, Sullivan fought to stand beside the bed. His weapons expert offered a hand, but the stubborn SEAL brushed him off.

Her eyes widened, but Jane couldn't close the space between them. She'd fought too hard to get even this far. "Sullivan, what are you doing? You're going to rip your stitches out."

"Then I'll rip them out. I'm not letting you do this alone." He used the bed for support and shuffled forward. The hospital gown molded to him, a little too tight and too short for his musculature. "If that means we need to leave now, then we leave now. Anthony, go get the SUV. We'll meet you at the front."

"No. You're not going anywhere." The constant beeping from the machines would call the nurses and doctors in here in a few seconds, but even with their medical orders, Sullivan wouldn't stop until the job was done. Wasn't in his nature. She had to admire him for that, given that was exactly why she'd blackmailed him in the first place, but this time, Jane wouldn't stand by helpless when whoever hunted her caught up. And she wouldn't let Sullivan risk his life for her again, even if she had to go to extremes to stop him. "Do you remember what I said back in your office when you refused to help me?"

Fire consumed his gaze, almost hotter and wilder than when he'd taken on Christopher at the cabin. He fought to stand on his own, leaning against the bed rails, but Sullivan had lost a lot of blood. He wouldn't get far. "You wouldn't."

Jane stepped backward toward the door.

"Jane…" He pushed off from the bed, the muscles in his jawline ticking away with his erratic heartbeat. "Don't do this."

"You did your job, Sullivan. This is the only way to keep you safe. I'm sorry." She ripped open the door and shouted down the hall. "Police!"

Two uniformed Anchorage PD officers spun toward her from the end of the hall. She'd known they'd be there, waiting for her to give her statement. Both sprinted toward the room, hands on the butt of their guns, and hurried inside. "Ma'am?"

"This man isn't who he says he is. His real name is Sebastian Warren." Jane maneuvered closer to the door as they came inside the room, dread pooling at the base of her spine. This was the only way. "There's a warrant out for his arrest for murdering his father, the Anchorage Lumberjack, nineteen years ago."

The officers moved in, but Anthony constructed a barrier of hardened muscle before Sullivan set a tense hand on his weapon expert's shoulder and pushed him back. Fluorescent lighting glinted off a pair of handcuffs as the officers moved Sullivan back into the bed, but the SEAL only had attention for her.

The fire in his eyes had simmered, the remaining ashes full of...heartbreak?

A tight knot of hesitation spread through her, but Jane shoved her arms into her jacket as the officers started questioning Sullivan, and she slipped out the door. The cell phone she'd stolen from one of the officers was in her hand, her eye on the exit. She fought back the tears blurring her vision as she dialed the number she'd memorized for circumstances like this a few months ago. Never could be too careful. Off the grid. Leave everything behind.

"Jane!" Sullivan's voice echoed down the hallway, but she wouldn't turn back.

She unburied her own phone from her jacket pocket and tossed it into the garbage can against the wall. First thing Sullivan would do after posting bail would be to track her through her phone. He wanted to help, but she wouldn't lose him. Not the man who'd given her a reason to fight.

Keep moving. Don't look back. Bringing the stolen phone to her ear, she counted off the rings on the other line. Two. Three. The line picked up.

"Hey, it's me." Jane checked over her shoulder to make sure Sullivan hadn't ordered Anthony to follow her. Two nurses bolted into his room behind the Anchorage police officers as he shouted her name over and over again. She clutched the keys she'd taken off Anthony as he'd rushed to help Sullivan stand and focused on the double glass doors leading to the parking garage. Tears welled in her lower lash line, but Jane pushed them back. Turning him in might solidify her reputation, but her leaving ensured the safety of the one man she couldn't bear to lose. Sullivan. He was all that mattered now. "I need your help."

Chapter Thirteen

"How didn't we see this coming?" Sullivan threw all of the team's research into a file box and shoved it across his desk. Pain shot up into his shoulder and across his rib cage as the box hit the floor and scattered the files from Jane's case across his office. The phone rang for the hundredth time in the last hour since he'd been released from Anchorage PD custody, intensifying the headache at the base of his skull. He pointed a finger at Elliot with the hand not strapped into a sling. "You're the private investigator. You're the one who should've been able to uncover Christopher Menas's true motive before this all blew up in our face."

"The guy was good at his job, Sullivan. I don't know what else you want me to say." Elliot collapsed back in one of the many leather chairs positioned in front of the CEO's massive oak desk, cell phone in hand. The brightness of the screen highlighted the stitches in his forehead from the fire at Menas's apartment, and regret flooded through Sullivan. In reality, they were lucky Elliot hadn't been killed, considering what Menas did for a living. "Besides, I think we all learned something very valuable here. Never trust the system. Everything you need to know is in a person's routines and daily life. Had we surveilled Menas before he'd tried killing us, I could've told you everything you'd needed to know."

"Who screwed up their job the most doesn't matter right now." Elizabeth Dawson, Blackhawk Security's head of network security, tossed a handful of manila file folders onto the gleaming desk between them. "We've got a client on the run, one who's probably scared out of her mind, and we have no idea who is after her. I'd say that qualifies as our first priority." The former NSA analyst nodded toward the pile of research. "Here's everything I could get my hands on for Christopher Menas. Phone records, emails, instant messages, bank accounts, payroll for his team, surveillance photos of Jane. I had to pull a few strings, so you owe me."

Every muscle in Sullivan's body tensed at the sound of her name. Damn it. Now wasn't the time to let emotion rule. His wrist still chafed where the Anchorage PD had cuffed him while they questioned him in that hospital bed for over twenty hours. The only reasons he'd been released after Jane's attempt to keep him off her case were a heavily funded bank account and the high-priced lawyer Blackhawk Security kept on retainer. But the nightmare wasn't over.

He'd killed his father before the psychopath could hurt anyone else. Sullivan had known this day would come. He locked his jaw. But, despite the possibility of spending the rest of his life in prison, he had more important things on his mind. First things first: find Jane. If he could talk to her—

"None of it tells me who might've hired Menas." Elizabeth leveraged her weight onto her hand against the desk, wide brown eyes only giving a hint of the off-the-charts intelligence behind them. "Either Christopher Menas was lying when he told you he'd been contracted to take Jane out, or the guy behind the curtain is one of the best shadow agents I've ever come across. And trust me, I know a few."

"He wasn't lying." Sullivan straightened. Head in the game. Get Jane to safety. "The entire reason he'd used his own name was to throw us off the scent of the real threat. Any word from Anthony?"

"Jane hasn't gone back to the town house, and there's no report from her CO either." Elliot held up his phone, waving it from side to side. "I went back through her bank records. No activity on her credit or debit cards, no withdrawals from her account. She has to be getting some kind of help to stay off the grid this long. As of right now, she's gone."

"Not acceptable." He'd never lost a mission or a client in all his time on this earth, and he wasn't about to start now. "We're just going to have to find the threat responsible for the price on Jane's head—" Sullivan ground his back molars, her name still sweet on his tongue "—before he finds her."

"This woman turned you over to the police and endangered the entire company. She doesn't want you on the case anymore, Sullivan." Vincent Kalani turned around from the other side of the office, uncrossing his arms. The forensics expert hadn't said another word this entire meeting, keeping to himself in the corner, but Sullivan read the resistance across his dark features. Shadows crossed Vincent's stern expression. Of all the men and women Sullivan had hired to create the Blackhawk Security team, Vincent had the uncanny ability to bring him back to earth when he was in over his head. But not this time. "Are you going to put yourself—put *us*—back in this guy's crosshairs to save someone who doesn't want our help and who sold you out?"

"Yes." Because a man never gave up on the woman he loved. Sullivan ignored the burn of pain down his side. He inhaled deep, hoping to catch her vanilla scent in the air, but disappointment gripped him. Jane was running from whoever'd hired Menas, but also from him. She didn't want him in a position that would get him killed, but she didn't understand. He'd been in that position his entire life. First with his father, then the SEALs, now as part of the foremost private security consultancy in the United States. All of those moments had forged him into the man he was now, the man who could save her life. She'd just finally made the risk worth it.

"I built this company—and hired every single one of you—to save lives, and that's exactly what we're going to do. Save a life. Doesn't matter if we trust our clients. Doesn't matter if we like them. We have a responsibility to the people who walk through those doors, and today I only have attention for one of them. Jane Reise." Sullivan shifted his attention to Vincent. "But if you won't do the job I hired you for—" he nodded toward the double glass doors on the other side of his office "—there's the door. I don't have the time to question whether I can rely on you right now."

The phone rang again, attempting to break the tense silence descending between him and his team. Sullivan picked up the receiver and slammed it back down. He didn't have time for distractions either.

"Well, you got my vote, boss." Elliot stood, slapping his hand into Sullivan's. "But mostly because I'm terrified you're going to send me back to the prison you found me in if I don't comply."

A laugh rumbled through Sullivan's chest. "Don't you forget it, con man."

Elizabeth collected the files he'd tossed onto the floor and reorganized them across the desk. "I'll start combing through possible suspects in Jane's life again, targeting military personnel. Do you want me to call in Kate for another profile?"

"No. We can handle this without her." Blackhawk Security's profiler deserved all the time she could get after losing her husband to a random shooting two months ago. Sullivan wouldn't ask her to come back until she was ready. He ran over Elizabeth's words a second time. "Why target military personnel?"

"Someone this good at hiding his identity is a professional. At first I thought whoever hired Christopher Menas might've been former NSA, maybe current, but that doesn't add up. You said Jane was stalked in Afghanistan. The NSA hasn't had any assets there in over a year." Elizabeth brushed a piece of short brown hair behind her ear. Not quite as short as Jane's, but it accentuated her heart-shaped face and warm brown eyes, where Jane's gave the angles of her face more of an edge. "Without contacts within the intelligence community, our target wouldn't have been able to hire a mercenary team. On top of that, he knows her, he knows every detail of her life and has been following her across the globe. She doesn't have any relatives she's close to, so I've narrowed it down to three possibilities." Elizabeth ticked them off on her fingers one by one. "Our suspect is either her commanding officer, another lawyer who's worked with her or a criminal who's been prosecuted by her. All military."

"That's still a giant suspect pool, and Jane swore her CO didn't have anything to do with this when we first brought him up." Sullivan swiped his uninjured hand across his face, then focused on the hundreds of photos of Jane staring up at him from his desk. She'd disappeared twenty-four hours ago. She could be anywhere in the world. And so could her stalker. Hell. Sullivan curled his fingers into his palms, needing the small bite of pain to keep him focused. They didn't have time to make any more mistakes. "It'll take us weeks to sort through them all."

"I'll take her commanding officer." Vincent stepped close to the desk and motioned for Elizabeth to give him the file. The tribal tattoos climbing up his neck and down his arms stretched with the action. "He'd know her routine, her close friends in the JAG Corps and which defendants might want to take revenge. It's as good a place to start as any." He lifted his toffee-colored gaze to Sullivan.

"Thank you." Didn't matter that Jane had sworn up and down her CO had nothing to do with this. They'd run out of leads. Slapping his hand across Vincent's back, maybe a little too hard, he nodded. He rounded the desk and picked up one of the many photos Elliot had recovered from Christopher Menas's apartment before it'd been burned to the ground. "Now that only leaves about fifty more people we need to dig into, and any one of them could already be three steps ahead."

He didn't like those odds.

Sullivan studied the photo in his hand, his eyebrows

drawing inward. It was a photo of Jane in court. Her hair was a little longer, nearly brushing her fatigues emblazoned with the JAG Corps insignia pinned to her chest. The walls were simple, bare, only two flags standing tall on either side of the judge. The American flag and the US Army flag. No other American insignia on the walls, which meant it probably wasn't an American courtroom. Could've been Afghanistan. There was no way to tell for sure, but Christopher Menas hadn't taken the picture. Jane would've recognized him in a heartbeat if her ex-college-boyfriend-turned-mercenary had sat a few feet from her.

"Boss?" Elliot asked. "Everything okay?"

From the angle of the photo, the picture had to have been taken by the defense's side of the courtroom. But why would a defendant or an attorney snap a picture in the middle of court, and where had Menas gotten the picture in the first place? Jane stood near the witness stand, not looking at the person who'd taken the photo. A surveillance photo. His stomach sank, but Sullivan rotated the photo in order to get a good look at the papers sprawled across the desk, any evidence that could point them in the right direction. A name. An official charge. A rank.

Something else caught his eye.

He brought the photo closer. The pen on the desk. Dread pooled at the base of his spine. He'd seen it before. But…

His cell phone chimed, and he read the incoming message from Anthony.

Subject has returned home.

He put the screen to sleep and shoved the phone into his pants pocket.

"I know who hired Christopher Menas." Sullivan snapped his head up. It didn't make sense, but he wasn't about to second-guess his instincts. Setting Jane's photo back onto the desk, he pulled his top desk drawer open and shoved his favorite Glock into his shoulder holster. There wasn't any time left. They had to get to Jane's town house now. "And I know why he's doing this."

CHRISTOPHER MENAS HAD gotten exactly what he'd wanted.

Captain Jane Reise of the United States JAG Corps no longer existed.

She stared down at the new passport, birth certificate, driver's license and Social Security card on her lap, not sure why she hadn't gotten out of the car yet. The photos had been taken from her old passport, but the name, date of birth and address beside it had transformed her into someone completely different, thanks to a friend in the FBI's witness protection program. Sliding the airline ticket out from behind the thin leather, she memorized the information all over again. Her flight out of Ted Stevens International Airport to LAX left in two hours. Enough time to collect the cash she'd stashed beneath the floorboards under the right side of her bed. She couldn't use the money in her accounts. Too easy to trace. With that money, she'd have a fresh start. And there'd be no trace of her old life to follow.

The dropping temperatures were showing her breath, but Jane sat there, surveying the street for the hundredth time. No sign of an intruder, of a mercenary waiting for her to open the door. No sign of another Blackhawk Security vehicle either. Jane exhaled hard as pressure built behind her sternum. Sullivan hadn't come after her.

She pulled back her shoulders. She recalled the details of her new life. Now she was Rita Miller, a criminal defense lawyer from Los Angeles, California, who worked for a large firm right in the center of the city. She had no idea how her friend in the FBI had managed to pull that off, but did it matter?

She craned her head over her shoulder toward the town house again. So, in reality, the rental wasn't even hers anymore. All of the furniture, her clothing, the small possessions she'd collected from her travels over the last few years would be sold off in some estate sale. Her father and his new family wouldn't want them and Jane wasn't allowed to pack and ship them to her new address in California, according to the rules. Leave everything behind. Leave *everyone* behind.

The rules. A small burst of laughter had her setting the crown of her head against the headrest. Frayed wiring dangled from the control panel centered above the rearview mirror. Sullivan really should've been more careful about concealing the tracking devices he'd installed in his vehicles. Or at least have a backup. Staring up at the SUV's ceiling, she closed her eyes. She'd worked her entire life sticking to the rules, bending them to fit her or her clients' needs, but never breaking them, and she'd done a good job.

Until five days ago.

She'd broken the first rule she'd given herself when breaking into Sullivan Bishop's office: don't fall in love. And look where breaking the rules had landed her. Sitting outside her own town house in the middle of the night in freezing temperatures because she couldn't bear the thought of what she might find inside.

Or who.

Her lower lash line burned. She swiped at the runaway tear streaking down her face. This was stupid. Sullivan hadn't followed her. He wasn't waiting inside for her to come home. Jane dropped her chin to her chest, opening her eyes. "Screw the rules."

This was the only way to start over, to save the man she'd blackmailed into protecting her.

She tossed the new passport into the passenger-side seat and jammed her shoulder into the door of the Blackhawk Security SUV she'd borrowed from the hospital garage. She'd take the SUV to the airport, then let Elliot or Anthony know where they could pick it up. There was a good chance she'd change her mind if she talked to Sullivan again. Although, with how she'd left things between them in the hospital, him in handcuffs, her running out the door, he might make it easier than she imagined.

Jane jogged across the street, keeping an eye out for any movement, any glare of headlights coming to life. The key was already in her hand, in case she had to get inside in a hurry. She twisted the key in the lock and pushed the door inward. A wall of hot air rushed against her, relieving some of the tightness in her lower back. She tossed her keys onto the table by the door, as she did every day, and closed the door behind her, locking it. Her throat went dry. It still smelled like him. Her attention shot to the makeshift bed on the couch where Sullivan had slept, and she shuffled toward it.

Slumping down onto the couch, she stared at what remained of the space she used to consider a safe haven.

The town house had been tossed. Clothing, books, photos, all destroyed. She couldn't imagine how many people had trudged through her personal belongings, picked apart her life since she'd run off into the middle of the night after a murderer. Police, Sullivan's team, Christopher Menas. But, here, surrounded by the scent of the man she'd unwillingly surrendered to, her muscles slowly released. It was over. For now. The man who'd turned her life upside down for the past couple of months—who'd tried to kill her—was dead. Of course, someone had hired Christopher's band of mercenaries in the first place, but she couldn't think about that right now. A few more minutes of relief was all she needed. Then she'd get the cash and lock up for good. No looking back. A fresh start.

There should've been some relief in that thought, but all Jane could think about was the look on Sullivan's face when she'd called for the police. Christopher Menas would've killed her had it not been for Sullivan. And she'd thrown it in his face. She'd hurt him— badly—and she wasn't sure if there was any way he'd trust another woman again. Or forgive her.

She rubbed her fingers into her sternum to counteract the pain spreading through her chest. Sullivan had forgiven her for her part in Marrok's suicide, but he had every reason to hate her now. Tears welled in her eyes again, but Jane wiped them away.

She couldn't believe what she was about to do.

She was going to find Sullivan. Witness protection could wait. She had to fix this. No matter how long it took or how many times he slammed the door in her face, she'd make this right.

Because she couldn't imagine another day of her life without Sullivan Bishop—or Sebastian Warren—in it. She loved him. Threading the sheets between her fingers, Jane relaxed back against the couch. She loved him. Why had it taken her so long to realize it? She was an idiot. Of course she'd fallen for him. Sullivan protected people for a living, protected her. He stood against the evil in this world and smiled while doing it. He'd committed himself one hundred percent to the job and refused to stop when the chances of dying skyrocketed. But the best part? The way he'd looked at her while he did it, like he could've loved her back. The way he held her, ready to take a bullet to keep her safe... Jane thunked her head against the back of the couch. And wasn't that a kick to the stomach? She ground her back molars.

She'd made a mistake.

Hefting herself from the couch coated in Sullivan's clean, masculine scent, she stepped over the debris toward her bedroom. The damage extended up the stairs and through to the main bathroom, but Jane didn't have the energy to start cleaning. Wasn't any point now. After she saw Sullivan, she wasn't coming back. Every muscle in her body ached. Take a shower. Call the hospital, the police department, Blackhawk Security, whoever she had to call to track Sullivan down. In that order. She discarded her jacket onto the ottoman at the foot of her bed and turned. She hit a wall of solid muscle.

"Tell me, Captain Reise, does this rag smell like chloroform to you?" a voice from the past asked. A hand clamped a white rag over her mouth as another grabbed the back of her head to keep her in place against his chest. "Shh. It'll all be over soon."

Jane threaded her hands between his arms and looped them wide. The cloth over her mouth disappeared, but an acrid taste spread across her tongue as she lunged for the bedroom door. Her fight-or-flight response kicked into high gear. This wasn't possible. Searing pain spread over her skull as he fisted a handful of her hair and pulled her back into him. Her fingers automatically shot to her head to relieve the pain, and he clamped the soaked rag over her mouth again.

Jane kicked and kneed at him, grabbing onto his wrists to dislodge his hold. But he was strong. Too strong. And she'd lost too much energy over the last few days. She couldn't control her breathing, the poison working down into her system too fast for her to keep up the fight. The edges of her vision darkened. *No. Stay awake. Leave evidence.* Sullivan had to know...

Her grip lightened, her muscles protesting the orders her brain gave. Jane wrapped her left hand around the closest thing she could grab from her attacker's button-down shirt pocket. A single pen. Her legs gave out.

"That's it." He led her to the floor but refused to remove the rag from her mouth. "Just relax. You're in good hands."

Her arm arched up above her head, and she let the pen slip from her hold. It rolled under the bed. Staring up into the face of her attacker, Jane couldn't move, couldn't keep her eyes open as the darkness closed in. The shadows across his sharp, angled jawline shifted as he pressed her into the floor. She'd recognize that face anywhere. Her eyebrows drew inward as she squinted away the blurriness closing in. "Not…you."

"That's right, Jane. Me." He bent low over her, the scars across his eyebrows and chin deeper than she remembered. His breath snaked across the underside of her neck. She tried to pull away, tried to run, but couldn't stay awake. Her eyelids sagged closed. "And now it's my turn to torture *you*."

Chapter Fourteen

Sullivan clutched the only piece of evidence he and his team had recovered from Jane's town house as he sped down the highway: the pen. It'd rolled under her bed, but his instincts screamed that Jane had been trying to leave him a clue as to who'd taken her.

And there was only one place her stalker would hide to get his attention. The cabin.

"I'm coming, Jane. I'm coming." He'd promised to keep her safe, and he intended to keep every promise he'd made to her. Murky water kicked up along the SUV's windows as he pressed his foot harder against the pedal. The wipers crossed the windshield in the same rhythm his heart tried to beat out of his chest. This whole thing hadn't been about Jane, at least not entirely. His past had come back to haunt him, too. He just didn't have all the pieces yet. Sullivan rotated the wheel to the left, taking the SUV down the snow-coated trail. Pain zinged through his arm and side, but he only gripped the steering wheel tighter.

Clouds and short bursts of wind dumped flakes onto the windshield. The closer he got to his destination, the less he could see, nearly everything in sight a complete whiteout. Rubbing the inside of the windshield clear of fog, Sullivan squinted through the snow. He should be coming up on the cabin any second now—

A black blur appeared directly in the SUV's path.

"Damn it!" He spun the SUV to the left, straight into the tree line, and slammed on the brakes. Adrenaline flooded into his veins, heart rate rocketing. The back end of the GMC fishtailed, and time seemed to slow. Sullivan turned into the spin, breath frozen in his throat. He fought to keep control of the vehicle. The back end of the SUV missed an unconscious Jane by mere inches, but he couldn't correct in time.

The GMC slammed into a thick tree, and he hit the steering wheel hard. A cascade of snow fell over the crumpled hood as the engine died. Shoving himself back in his seat, he brushed his fingertips across his forehead. Blood dripped down the side of his face. It was a miracle he hadn't lost consciousness. His breath sawed in and out of his lungs, but he clamped on to the door handle. "Jane."

Shoving his recently stitched shoulder into the door, Sullivan suppressed a scream as agony washed over him. He tumbled out of the SUV. His boots slid along the compacted snow, and he collapsed against the GMC. The pain dissipated, slowly, but he had to push it to the back of his mind. *Get to Jane. Neutralize the threat.* He kept his breathing shallow, even, and opened his eyes.

Hands tied behind the back of a chair, Jane sat slumped over her legs, unconscious, about twenty feet away. She hadn't realized he'd almost killed her coming to save her life. Relief, however fleeting, flooded through him, and he took the magazine out of his Glock and shoved it back into place. But he didn't make a move toward her. Nobody put a victim in the middle of the road like that unless they intended to take the high ground to watch the chaos unfold. Dread coiled a tight fist in the pit of his stomach. There was only one way this could end. Her kidnapper wanted a show? Sullivan would give him one.

"I know you're out there," he shouted over his shoulder. Sullivan pressed his back into the SUV for cover, finger on the trigger. His head throbbed, heart beating loudly, but the soft crunching of snow reached his ears. His target froze in his tracks, approximately ten yards to the southeast, just on the other side of the road. "Let's finish this."

Sullivan bounded away from the SUV and swung his gun up and around.

And froze.

"Hey, big brother." Acrid smoke filled the air around Marrok Warren. He tossed the lit cigar into the snow and stomped it out with his boot, the butt of a gun peeking out from under his jacket. Thick brown hair covered the scars Sullivan had witnessed cut into his younger brother's chin by their father when they'd been younger. Deep lines wrinkled the top of Marrok's forehead as he unholstered the weapon at his side. "Guess you never expected to see me again."

"Not after I buried you next to Mom. No, I did not." His recovery of the pen their mother had given Marrok when he'd turned twelve had told Sullivan exactly what—*who*—to expect on the wrong end of his gun, but Sullivan swallowed hard. He shifted his stance wide and readjusted his grip on the Glock. "You faked your death in order to torture Jane for prosecuting you."

"What's a little revenge among friends? I certainly

had a good time terrorizing her the past three months. Then she hired you, and I had to up the stakes. Playtime was over." Marrok circled to his right, putting him in the center of the road. "Sebastian Warren. My big brother. Always the *savior*. Always the hero."

"So now you're blaming me for keeping you alive for all those years Dad came after you?" A burst of laughter exploded from between Sullivan's teeth. He shook his head, gun still aimed as he counteracted his brother's movements. "You're sick, Marrok. I can get you help."

"Thanks for the offer, big brother, but I wouldn't be the man I am now had it not been for Dad's influence. If I hadn't followed in his footsteps, I wouldn't have the connections or the money I do now. And, let me tell you, it was all worth it. Only difference between Dad and me? My tastes are a little more…" Marrok's dark eyes flickered past Sullivan. To Jane. One scarred edge of his mouth turned upward. "Refined."

The muscles surrounding his spine hardened one by one. Sullivan had buried his brother as a hero, put him to rest next to their mother in their hometown cemetery. He'd believed in his innocence for over a year. "Jane was right about you all along. You assaulted those women while you were on tour."

Marrok drove his hand into his jacket pocket, extracting a small black device. "You can't win this fight, Sebastian. Don't forget, I know you better than anyone else. You're just using a different name now." His younger brother wiggled the device for Sullivan to see, then raised his gun and took aim. At Sullivan's heart. "I know you won't kill me because you can't stand the thought of killing your own brother, but I also know you'd do anything to save an innocent life. Especially one you've been taking to bed."

"I know you, too, little brother. You're not going to shoot me." Sullivan fought to relieve the searing pain spreading down his side. Marrok had been watching them this whole time? A sick feeling rolled through him. His brother was right. He wouldn't kill Marrok, but that didn't mean he couldn't make him pay for what he'd done. He tightened his grip around the gun as he backed up a few feet to where Jane sat. Sullivan tipped her head back and his stomach sank. Pressing his fingers to her throat, he counted off the slow, uneven rhythm in his head. Her lips had turned blue, the blistering cold slowing down her heart rate, but the bomb vest strapped to her chest kicked his up a notch.

"No, Sebastian. You *knew* me. Then you abandoned me for the navy, leaving me behind to deal with the aftermath you caused after killing Dear-Old-Dad, and never looked back. Even changed your name so I couldn't track you down. Now I find you're protecting the one person I hate most in the world. *Jane Reise.*" Her sweet name growled from between Marrok's lips as he nodded toward Jane. "So you're right. I might not put a bullet in you, but I sure as hell won't feel guilty if you're caught in the crossfire."

"Marrok." Sullivan took a single step forward, his ears going numb from the pounding wind. "Everything I did, I did for you, to protect—"

"You can save the speech, big brother. I know the truth. You've always wanted to escape the life we had, and killing our father gave you a way to do it." Marrok held up the device in his hand, pointing it toward Jane. "You're a SEAL. You know what this is and what will happen if you're anywhere close to her when that bomb blows."

"Jane, baby." No answer. He brushed her hair back from her face, then straightened. "Can you hear me?"

"You don't get a choice in this, Sebastian, and you're running out of time." Keeping the gun aimed at Sullivan's chest, Marrok walked backward down the road slowly. "It's over. She gets what she deserves and we all move on with our lives."

"No." The growl reverberated through him. Move on without Jane? A small burst of wind dislodged the piles of snow lining the tree branches, whiting out visibility between them, and Sullivan had his shot.

"Jane *is* my life." He sprinted with every bit of energy his battered body could produce, the icy air filling his lungs. But the wind died too fast, and he found himself out in the open. Still, Sullivan didn't slow.

Eyes wide, Marrok squeezed off one round, which went wide. Then another, hitting Sullivan in the right arm. A third round lodged in his upper thigh. He didn't care. Blood dripped down his fingers, but he wouldn't stop. Because he loved Jane. Didn't matter when it'd happened. Didn't matter how. All that mattered was that it'd happened. He'd fallen in love with the one woman he'd vowed to condemn for the rest of his life.

Sullivan's jaw strained against his body's screams for relief. But without that detonation device, he'd lose everything. He rammed his shoulder under Marrok's ribs, tackling his brother to the ground. He pulled back his elbow, only the slightest hesitation gripping him. Enough time for Marrok to take advantage.

"You shouldn't have gotten involved, big brother." Marrok slammed the butt of his gun into Sullivan's head.

Scalding pain spread over his skull as Marrok kicked him backward. Sullivan hit the ground, cushioned by two feet of snow. Memories of countless nights, of holding a baseball bat or a knife or a gun in the back of their shared closet to protect his younger brother, flashed across his mind. He'd done what he'd had to, to protect his family. But the one person he'd never counted on turning on him had lost his damn mind. His gaze shot to Jane as her head fell to one side. She was coming around. And she needed him to protect her now.

"You were right, though. I don't like the idea of killing you either. There's a reason Menas drugged and Tasered you first." Marrok shifted his finger over the trigger of his gun. "But I will end you now if you choose Jane Reise over your own flesh and blood."

Sullivan pushed to his feet and maneuvered into the middle of the road, right between Marrok and Jane. The gun was pointed straight at him. A blast of wind kicked up snow as it swept across the clearing beside his cabin. His right arm and thigh burned from the two rounds Marrok had squeezed off. No major damage, but enough to pull at his attention. He was a SEAL, hardened and trained in every kind of environment. He didn't need to see the threat to neutralize it. A glint of sunlight off glass caught his attention from the tree line, and a smile pulled at one side of his mouth. "If you know me so well, then you know I don't stop until the job is done. And we're not done."

"I thought you might say something like that." Marrok shrugged, gun in one hand, the detonator in the other. With one click of a button, his younger brother would take everything from him. "Just like I know you brought your team to take me out in case things went south."

Marrok's gaze flickered over his shoulder as Anthony and Elliot burst through the trees, each armed and ready to neutralize the threat on Sullivan's orders. "Well, guess what, big brother? Things are about to go south." Raising the gun to Sullivan's head, Marrok compressed the detonator. "I'll see you in hell, Sebastian."

"No!" Sullivan lunged, focused solely on the detonator and not the gun aimed between his eyes.

As Marrok pulled the trigger.

The gunshots had brought her around. All too familiar.

"Sullivan." His name barely whispered from her lips, her body fighting her brain's commands. Jane struggled against the rope at her wrists and ankles, but couldn't move. The brightness of the snow blinded her. Had Marrok Warren finally killed her?

She had to warn Sullivan.

Her eyelids were heavy, but Jane managed to roll her head to one side. Either hell had frozen over or she was actually strapped to a chair in the middle of the Alaskan wilderness. What had Marrok planned for her? Leave her to the wolves? Not very original.

Catching sight of two dark gray rocks half-buried in the snow beside her, she curled her fingers into her palms. She couldn't move. Couldn't scream from the effects of the chloroform. Couldn't protect herself. But she'd be damned if she didn't go down fighting like Sullivan had taught her.

Get out of the chair. Get to Sullivan. She twisted hard, tipping the chair into the snow. Air crushed from her lungs as she sent flakes above her head. Her fingers brushed against the rough edges of one rock and she stretched her hands as far as they would go to grab it. The ties were too tight, and her body was so tired. Marrok would get what he wanted, and Sullivan… No. She couldn't think about that. Her fingertips brushed against the rough surface of one rock. *There.*

Relief flooded through her as she grabbed the rock and hacked away at the rope. The ties fell from around her wrists, and she maneuvered out from under the chair. Bending to cut through the rope at her ankles, Jane caught a flash of red across her abdomen and, for a moment, she assumed it was blood. But the color was off. Brighter. And the flash disappeared, then reappeared. She squinted at the message glowing from the display, her mouth going dry. *Armed.* More colors claimed her attention. These ones long and thin. Red, blue, green and white. Wires. Oxygen rushed from her lungs as she hastily cut through the rope at her feet.

Marrok had strapped her into a bomb vest? Running her and Sullivan off the road, trying to burn them to ashes in Menas's apartment and sending a mercenary detail after her in the first place hadn't been enough. He had to blow her up, too? All because she'd done her job.

Jane clawed at the vest but couldn't find a zipper or Velcro or anything to get her out of it. A guttural groan reached her ears and she spun toward the sound. Sullivan landed backward in the snow, and the man standing over him… "Marrok."

She didn't have a weapon—unless she counted the new piece of apparel strapped across her chest—but ran toward the fight anyway. The cold had drained energy from her muscles, but she pushed on even as Anthony and Elliot burst through the tree line and surrounded the man behind all of this. Sullivan shoved to his feet, and she nearly collapsed before leveraging her weight onto a nearby tree trunk. Shoving her hair out of her eyes, she breathed a little easier. He was okay. Marrok couldn't escape now. The army would take custody of him, and this whole thing would be over. She'd have her life back. She could go back to being Jane Reise.

But in the blink of an eye, Marrok Warren raised the gun to Sullivan's head. The world stopped spinning. Her hands tightened, her insides churned. No. This wasn't how this was supposed to end. Not him. Not because of her. Jane stumbled forward, closing the vast distance between them as fast as she could. Every cell in her body fought against the desperation clawing up her throat to push herself harder. She'd only taken three steps. "Sul—"

A bullet exploded from the chamber of Marrok's gun as Sullivan reached under his heavy coat. Then two more gunshots echoed throughout the clearing, each stealing more of her hope.

Sullivan dropped his backup weapon into the snow, reaching out for his brother, but it was too late. Marrok Warren collapsed to the ground, his own weapon falling from his grip. The breath she'd been holding rushed from her lungs. She'd seen too many of those kinds of injuries on tour. There was no saving his brother now.

Only the tree beside her kept Jane on her feet. Tears welled in her eyes. Her stomach rolled. Not for Marrok but because of the way Sullivan hovered over his brother's body. Nobody deserved to watch someone they loved die right in front of them. Hadn't Sullivan been betrayed enough? Jane pushed off from the tree, her arms tingling to wrap around him as he grieved.

A series of beeps rang from the vest.

Jane stopped cold. The message stretched across her chest had changed from *Armed* to a series of numbers. And they were counting down. She shot her head up, her survival instincts paralyzed. No. No, no, no, no. This wasn't happening. She wasn't an active bomb. An invisible elephant sat on her chest, and she couldn't think. Couldn't breathe.

"Jane!" Sullivan's features cleared through the fresh tears streaming down her face.

She stumbled back. No. She didn't want to die, but she wasn't going to be responsible for taking his life. Not Sullivan. Jane surveyed the trees. She wasn't an expert with explosives, but she was smart enough to know the closer he got, the more danger he was in. If she could get some distance, he might have a better chance of surviving the blast. Throwing her hands out, she backed toward the tree line. "Stay back! It's armed!"

He didn't listen, running straight at her. Those sea-blue eyes never left her as he closed in fast. "Elliot, get your tools!"

The private investigator ran for one of the Black-hawk Security SUVs.

She stumbled back into the tree she'd used for support mere moments ago and fell. They were going to try to disarm the bomb. They were going to put their lives on the line. For her. Jane checked the display. Less than two minutes. She lifted her gaze back to Sullivan. Blackmailing him, revealing his true identity to the police in an attempt to save his life, it'd all been a mistake. He had to know that. She'd never meant for any of this to happen. "I'm sorry. I'm so sorry."

She didn't know what else to say.

Sullivan dropped to his knees beside her. Darkness consumed his features, and her insides flipped. He moved in close, his hands sliding along the underside of her jaw. He threaded his fingers through the hair at the base of her skull, and goose bumps rose along her skin at his touch. With him this close, the surrounding air filling with his reassuring scent, she wanted nothing more than to sink into his hold. But they were running out of time. Literally. "Are you okay?"

Chaos and concern tinted Sullivan's words. Not a good combination.

"I'm fine." And it was the truth. At least in her last two minutes on earth, Jane had what she wanted. Sullivan Bishop. She framed his jawline with one hand. "But you need to get away from me. This thing—"

"Isn't going to blow with you in it." A growl vibrated through Sullivan's chest. "I promise."

"Okay." Any promise Sullivan made, he kept, but the tightness in her tendons connecting her neck and shoulders refused to believe him. Lacing her fingers between his, Jane nodded. They didn't have much time left before he had to start running. And she wasn't about to make any more mistakes with the man she'd fallen in love with. "I'm sorry. For everything. Breaking into your office, blackmailing you, going after Menas on my own. All of it. I'm sorry I dragged you into this. I'm sorry about Marrok."

Elliot slid onto his knees on her other side, out of breath but smiling. "Hello, gorgeous. Not dead again, I see. Always a plus." He pushed at her shoulder, putting her flat on her back. "Hand me the wire cutters," he said to Sullivan. "I'm going to need you to hold very still. You are literally a ticking time bomb, and any movement could set it off early."

"I'm not sorry." Sullivan thrust the cutters into his private investigator's hands. A slow smile spread across Sullivan's features as he squeezed her hand. "I thought the Full Metal Bitch had broken into my office, but, in reality, it was my future. You're my future, Jane, and I'm not going anywhere."

"I can't think when you're expressing your feelings, boss. It's unnatural." Elliot's voice held a word of caution as he sifted through countless wires and traced them to different points on the vest. "That was beautiful, by the way."

Did that mean Sullivan loved her, too? The remnants of cold drained from her body at his words. But Jane still unwound her fingers from his hand and shoved him back. "You need to run."

"The last time I left your side, my brother strapped you to this damn thing." He wrapped his hand in hers again and kissed the sensitive skin along the back. "I learn from my mistakes. And the police already know who I really am, so you have no other leverage to get rid of me. Ever again."

"There are too many wires." Elliot sat back on his heels. "We've got less than thirty seconds. Boss—"

"Then we're going to cut her out of it." Sullivan reached for the serrated blade tucked inside his boot. The world blurred as they flipped her onto her front. "I'm not giving up."

Blistering cold spread down into her bones as sounds of ripping fabric reached her ears. Adrenaline dumped into her veins and rocketed her heart rate higher as she prepared for the explosion. But she couldn't move on to the afterlife without telling the man she'd blackmailed how she felt. Jane reached for him. "Sullivan, no matter what happens, I need you to know... I love you."

He hesitated for a split second, his gaze softening. Sullivan tugged on the vest, cutting down the back. "I've got it!"

Sullivan hauled her upright. The weight of the vest pulled her to the ground, but she extracted her arms from the sleeve holes. The clock was still counting down. His grip tightened around her arm. He tossed the active vest far into the woods and tugged her after him. "Take cover!"

The rest of the Blackhawk Security team scattered behind the SUVs or the long line of snowbanks. Sullivan dragged her across the road and then pushed her ahead of him. "Get behind the tree line!"

A faint hum echoed through the trees.

Then the explosion erupted. The flames shot out behind them, the blast tossing them into the air. Terror ricocheted through her as Jane hit the ground and rolled. Twice. Three times. Smoke worked deep into her system when she came to a stop. She'd lost sight of Sullivan as darkness closed in around the edges of her vision. She stared up into the trees as mountains of snow fell from the branches above, burying her deeper while blackness closed in.

"Jane..."

Chapter Fifteen

Probation and over two hundred hours of community service. Sullivan might've lost half of Blackhawk Security's clients thanks to Jane having him arrested for murder, but he also had the rest of his life to hold it over her head.

And he intended to do just that.

The hospital's white walls blurred together at the edges of his vision as he stalked toward Jane's room, the only room with an ex-Ranger stationed outside the door. It'd been a precaution in case his psychopathic brother had hired any other hit men who hadn't heard the news: Jane Reise was off-limits. And *his*.

"Hey, man." Nodding at Anthony in acknowledgment, Sullivan wrapped his hand around the doorknob. And froze. His nervous system flipped, a ball of tension gripping his stomach. The stitches in his arm and thigh where Marrok had shot him stretched, but it wasn't the pain keeping him in place. The birth certificate, Social Security card, driver's license and passport with Jane's picture she'd left in the Blackhawk Security SUV all said she'd planned on starting a new life. In California. What if, even after they'd neutralized the threat, even after he'd beaten murder charges, she hadn't changed her mind about leaving?

"I don't think I've seen your skin that shade of white before." Anthony might take refuge behind those sunglasses, but his apparent amusement stretched across his expression. "Boss."

"Do you blame me? Every time I'm around her, someone is either shooting at me or trying to blow me up." Not the truth, but Anthony didn't need to know differently. The possibility of Jane saying no to staying in Anchorage, of her taking back those three words she'd blurted when her life was in danger, constricted his hold on the doorknob. A slight sting in his side from where Christopher Menas had tried to gut him like a fish claimed his attention. He forced a smile. "I never thanked you for watching out for her. I appreciate it."

"You've always said you'd do anything to protect the team, and every one of us feels the same." Anthony shifted his weight and, for the first time, Sullivan noted a beaten gold ring hanging from around Anthony's neck, tucked behind the Kevlar vest. Glennon's ring. Anthony Harris, ex-Ranger and Blackhawk Security weapons expert, had been holding on to the love of his life all this time? He'd never said a word. Sullivan's heart sank. Surveying the hospital corridor, Anthony shoved the gold band under his shirt without making eye contact. "We don't agree with you keeping the fact she blackmailed you into all this from us, but if you love her, Jane Reise is part of this team. And we'll fight for her."

"Thanks again." The knot of tension in his gut dissipated. Not completely, but there was only one way to fix that. Because Sullivan wouldn't hang on to Jane like Anthony held on to the woman who'd walked out on him, never finding closure, always wondering if she was safe, but not being part of her life. He twisted the hospital room door handle, shouldering his way inside.

And all the air rushed from his lungs.

Jane pushed her arms through her jacket beside the hospital bed. He closed the door softly and watched her. The burns and cuts along her creamy skin had started healing, the dark circles he'd noted when they first met lighter than before. Her addictive vanilla scent filled the room, and Sullivan couldn't help but take a deep breath, holding on to her as long as he could. His Jane.

"You can stop staring at me any second now." Leveling that hazel gaze on him from over her shoulder, she smiled. Jane fixed her collar and turned toward him. "Unless you're here to tell me you're busting me out of this place a second time."

"I'm sure something could be arranged." In truth, her doctors had already cleared her to leave, but Sullivan shoved his hands into his jacket pockets and leveraged his weight back against the door. A few more minutes with her. That was all he needed. "Surviving a mercenary and my brother certainly looks good on you."

The brightness in her eyes dimmed for a split second, and that loss resurrected the gutting pain he'd felt when Menas had planted a knife in his rib cage.

"I'm so sorry about Marrok, Sullivan. You have no idea how much I wish he hadn't been involved. I never meant for any of this to happen." She rolled her lips between her teeth, her expression simply lost. She fidgeted with an invisible speck of dirt on her jacket. "You told me you didn't hate me before." She wrapped her arms across her midsection, almost as though she were preparing herself for the worst. "Have you changed your mind?"

"You deserve the truth." Sullivan closed the space between them slowly, giving her a chance to back away if she wanted. He could almost read her mind as the muscles along her spine sagged. Guilt. Shame. Regret. "Everything since that night has changed. For the first time in nineteen years, the world knows who I really am. And what I did. Because of you."

The color drained from her face. Her jaw slackened. Jane swiped at her face, her attention on the door over his shoulder, then moved to maneuver around him. "I understand."

"No, you don't." Sullivan clamped a hand around her arm and spun her into his chest. For the first time, she didn't fight, and he took that as a good sign. Staring down at her, he locked her in his hold. She wasn't going anywhere. At least, not without him. "If you understood, you wouldn't keep running away from me. None of this was your fault, Jane. You can't control other people's behavior. You did your job like you were supposed to."

Spreading his fingers along her jaw, he fought back the memories of Marrok in his final moments. And the thought of almost losing Jane to the bomb his brother had strapped to her chest. It shouldn't have gone down like that, but there'd been no way to see the real threat before discovering his brother's pen in that photo. "As much as I hate to admit what he was capable of, Marrok made his own decisions, and he paid for them."

"And what about the fact I turned you in to the police for murder?" Her voice was so soft, soft and vulnerable, and Sullivan's insides contracted. She refused to look at him, setting her palms against his beating heart. "Is the Full Metal Bitch going to be credited with bringing down Blackhawk Security's CEO? Because…" She picked at his shirt. "I'm not that person anymore, Sullivan, and I don't want you, of all people, to believe I am."

"I'm not in love with a heartless woman who would do anything in her power to bring down hardworking soldiers. I'm in love with *you*, the real Jane Reise." He moved a strand of hair off her cheek, hugging her closer. "You're determined, yes. Willing to do whatever it takes to get what you want, but I think that's what I love about you the most. You're caring and brave. And I can't imagine a better woman by my side."

A smile stretched across her features. "Don't forget saving your life two more times."

"How could I? Lucky for you, the district attorney and I came to an agreement. No prison time, considering the circumstances of who my father was and Marrok's second death." Sullivan breathed a little easier at the thought but still tightened his hold on the woman in his arms. He might never have laid eyes on her again had the DA not taken recent events into account. "He hit me with community service and probation as long I promise not to exact vigilante justice again."

"A little late for that, isn't it?" A small puff of laughter burst from her lips, as she finally looked up at him. Fisting the collar of his jacket in her hands, she shoved against him and pulled him back in. "Is that a promise you think you can keep?"

"I keep all my promises. You know that." He traced his fingertips across her jaw. Jane's breathing pattern changed. Because of him. Because of his touch. And his body hummed with the possibility of experimenting with her reactions for the rest of their lives. "But if I have to break that promise to keep you safe, Jane, I will. Whether there's a possibility of me going to prison or not."

"All right. Then I'll make a promise, too." The darkness in her beauty vanished, replaced with warmth, hope and so much more. The burden she'd hung on to for the last few months had been lifted, and Sullivan loved the effect. "Whatever happens after we walk out those hospital doors, I promise never to blackmail you into helping me again."

Whatever happened? She'd meant it as a joke, but confusion closed in on him, and Sullivan backed off a step. "If by 'whatever happens,' you mean you walking out those doors with me and signing the paperwork for your permanent transfer to Anchorage."

"Sullivan…" Jane let her hands fall to her sides, and everything inside him went cold. "Haven't you learned your lesson yet? Forget prison. Loving me is a *death* sentence. And I'm not going to be the one responsible for taking your life. I think I've screwed it up enough."

She couldn't be serious. Not after everything they'd been through. Sliding his hands through his hair, Sullivan turned away to hide the obvious fire burning through his veins. Because he couldn't stand the thought of her walking away from this. From him. "So saying you loved me when Elliot was trying to disarm that bomb strapped to your chest was some attempt to… What?" He took a deep breath, trying to clear her scent from his system, but she was all around him. She was in his veins. "Put my mind at ease in case you died?"

"No—" she swiped her tongue across her bottom lip, and his heart rate kicked up a notch "—of course not. I—"

"What you do with your life is up to you, Jane. I would never force you into anything you're not comfortable with. If you don't want to stay here in Anchorage, fine. That's your choice." He stalked toward her, craving the feel of her against him, but he caged the desire racking his nervous system. He pushed every ounce of raw passion he held for the woman who'd blackmailed him into his voice. "But just because you're holding on to your guilt with everything you have does not give you the right to make the decision of what I do with my life or who gets to stay in it."

Sullivan rolled his fingers into fists when all he wanted to do was grab her by the arms and commit every inch of her body to memory all over again. His heart worked to beat out of his chest. He took a deep breath. Two. The fire simmered to a slow burn. There, but manageable. He relaxed his hands, trailing the pad of his thumb across her full bottom lip, the one she always licked when she was nervous. "When I said everything has changed since that night under the aurora borealis, it's not that I changed my mind. It's that I'm scared as hell to love you, Jane, but here I am, in love with you anyway."

Sliding one hand into his jacket pocket, he extracted the documents she'd had made under a different name and tossed them onto the bed without taking his eyes off her. "Now all you have to do is stay."

Stay?

Her lips parted as she caught sight of the documents, and her mouth went dry. The pulse at the base of her neck quickened. She closed her eyes for a split second. She'd left them in the Blackhawk Security SUV she'd stolen from Anthony at the hospital. Sullivan's weapons expert must've recovered them and handed them over to his boss after Marrok had taken her.

The hair on the back of her neck stood at attention as the memories flashed across her mind. The bomb's beeping as Marrok had set the countdown into motion played over and over in her head. Pressing her fingers into her eye sockets, she attempted to relieve the pressure building behind her eyes. But the look of horror on Sullivan's face as he realized what his brother had done had ingrained itself into her mind. Forever. "I need…"

What did she need?

"Jane," he said.

His voice slid through her, drowning out the nightmare that'd brought them together, and she couldn't help but step into his arms. His body heat worked down through her clothing, deep into her bones, as she set her ear against his heart. She interlaced her fingers at the small of his back, terrified to let go. "I need…you." Her own words echoed throughout her mind as she recalled her reasons for seeking Sullivan out in the first place. "I need you."

"You have me. But I can't live the rest of my life wondering what would've happened if I let you walk away now. I love you. I want you to stay." He set his cheek against the crown of her head, his clean, masculine scent surrounding her, working down into her pores. "So what is it going to be, Jane?"

The tension hardening the muscles along her spine dissipated as he wrapped his thick arms around her, and she sank further into him. Was this how it would always be between them? This give and take, this passion to keep each other from getting hurt?

From the second she'd broken into Sullivan Bishop's office, she swore not to let her heart rule her decision making, but the rules of blackmail had gone out the window one by one over the past days. He'd saved her life, protected her from a group of mercenaries for crying out loud and put his future at risk. All for her. And in her last perceived moments on this earth, she'd trusted her gut to tell him exactly what her head refused to acknowledge. She loved him.

She wasn't sure when it'd happened, maybe only now, but she'd decided she wanted him more than she was afraid of losing him.

His heart pounded hard against her ear, strong and reliant. He was a SEAL. And he could take care of himself. No matter the threat, Sullivan Bishop protected those he cared about and always seemed to stay alive in the process. Jane tightened her hold on him. And that would have to be enough. "I love you, too."

He pushed her back a few inches, trying to fight the smile curling at the edge of his mouth. Sullivan gripped her around the waist. His eyes brightened as the smile overwhelmed his expression, and Jane's heart stuttered. "Really?"

"Yes. And I'm staying. With you." She nodded. Her gut instincts said this was the right choice. This was where she wanted to be. "Unless you need someone to drag you to safety through the middle of the Alaskan wilderness again, then you're on your own."

Sullivan framed her jawline between his strong hands and crushed his mouth to hers. She tried to breathe around the rush of desire flooding through her. He'd worked his way under her skin, branded himself on her soul, and her body's response to him slipped further and further out of her control. He caressed her lower back and lifted her off her feet, pressing her against him as though he intended to make them one. And she might've had a few ideas herself on how to make that happen. Injuries be damned. This was where she wanted to be.

He swept his tongue inside her mouth, laying claim. He kissed her with a wild, desperate passion and Jane took everything he gave. Arms wrapped around his neck, she clung to him as months of fear and paranoia drained from her muscles.

She had her life back. Because the one man she'd needed the most had kept his promise. Because of Sullivan.

"Is it necessary to hold that woman so tight?" a familiar voice asked.

They turned toward Elliot in the door frame, cheeks pressed together, but Sullivan kept her in his arms. A growl vibrated from deep in Sullivan's chest as he eased her back to her feet. "This better be important."

Pressed against him, Jane enjoyed the funny things that growl did to her insides but wiped at her mouth and pulled her T-shirt down over her jeans' waistband. Heat worked up her neck and into her face the longer the private investigator smiled at them.

"The police want your statements about what went down at the cabin." Elliot hiked a thumb over his shoulder. "Should I tell them to give you another thirty minutes?"

Another growl echoed throughout the room.

"Okay, okay. Forty-five minutes." Blackhawk Security's private investigator spun on his heel and wrenched open the door. How she hadn't heard him come in in the first place, Jane would never know.

"You know, Jane, I was actually worried you would be too late in telling him how you felt, and we were all going to die." Elliot turned back before hitting the hallway, and that crooked smile of his warned Jane she wasn't about to like what came out of his mouth next. "I'm glad everything worked out for the best."

"Come again?" Narrowing his eyes, Sullivan stepped toward the private investigator with fire burning hot in his gaze, but Jane held him back.

"Wait a second. Do you mean to tell me you knew which wire to cut prior to Sullivan cutting me out of the vest? And the only reason you waited was because I hadn't told him how I felt yet?" Heat surged through her. Forget about Sullivan beating Elliot to a pulp. She'd kill him herself. Jane crossed the room. Grabbing the private investigator by the collar, she hauled him close. "Are you insane? We almost died!"

"I knew you'd do the right thing when it came down to the wire. No pun intended." That crooked, cocky smile deepened the laugh lines around Elliot's mouth, but, as his attention shifted over Jane's shoulder—to Sullivan—the smile disappeared.

She didn't have to turn around to know her SEAL was considering ways to use his tightly honed skills in torture on his private investigator. Tension filled the hospital room, and she didn't see any way out for Elliot other than resigning from his job and going into hiding for the rest of his life. Jane unclenched her hold on his collar and moved out of the way. "You better start running now."

Elliot's coffee-colored eyes widened as Sullivan closed in.

"Now, boss, we're friends, right? I owe you my life. I was using the bomb as an incentive." Elliot backed toward the door, hands held up in defense, but Jane didn't hold her SEAL back this time. "Keep in mind I gave you plenty of time to cut her out of the vest in case she didn't want to express how she felt."

"The next time I see you better be on a plane to Iraq, Dunham." Sullivan stalked after him, danger and rage rising in each step.

Elliot ran out the door as fast as he could. No looking back. Probably a good decision on his part. His voice slid through the crack in the door as he bolted down the hallway. "You should be thanking me!"

The tightness remained across Sullivan's back, but Jane couldn't help but thread her arms around his waist.

"Give him a head start before you kill him." A laugh bubbled from her lips as Jane sank into the comfort of Sullivan's strong, muscled back. He spun in her grasp, pinning her with those sea-blue eyes she couldn't get enough of.

"There's still one thing we need to get clear on before we walk out those doors together." His expression sobered as he stared down at her, and Jane tightened her grip on him. "And after what happened with Menas and my brother, I think I have the right to know."

"Are you sure you're up for another interrogation? I seem to recall me winning the last one." Caution narrowed her gaze. She didn't have any more secrets. At least, none that would get them killed. But she trusted him with her life. If he wanted to interrogate her before jumping into the most dangerous assignment of his career—a relationship with her—all he had to do was ask. Echoes from the PA system filtered into the room, but Jane had attention for only the wide expanse of muscle under her fingertips. "I'll tell you anything."

"That's a good start. Because I have ways of making you talk." His voice was deep and dark, and it sent an instinct of warning down her spine. But then Sullivan raised his hand a split second before he dropped a piece of ice down her T-shirt.

Freezing water dripped down her spine. Jane screamed, trying to dislodge the ice cube, but it'd caught in her sports bra. "Where the heck did you get ice?"

"I paid Elliot five dollars to come in and tell you that whole thing about the bomb as a distraction so I could lift a piece of ice from your side table." A gut-wrenching smile spread across Sullivan's features as he wrapped her in his arms.

"So what he said wasn't true?" she asked.

"No." Sullivan shook his head. "I'm pretty sure I would've already broken my promise to the district attorney had any of that been true."

The ice fell from her shirt, and she slapped at his shoulder. "Oh, this isn't over. When we get back to the cabin, you're going to need me to save you from the brink of death in front of the fire again."

"Mmm. I like that idea." He purred into her ear, the

tip of his nose tracing the most sensitive part of her neck. "But, really, tell me how you broke into Blackhawk Security. I've had my network security team run diagnostics on my entire security system—three times—and they haven't come back with a single loophole. Either you paid someone to let you in, which your financials can't prove, or you're more than what you seem, Counselor."

"All right, Frogman, you want to know?" He'd fought like hell for her, nearly died for her—more times than she could count—and lost a brother all over again in the process. At this point, she'd give him anything he asked for. And not just the truth. Everything she had. Everything she was. And she would fight like hell for him for the rest of their lives.

"More than anything," he said.

"It's really eating you up inside, isn't it? Okay then." She crooked her finger at him, putting her mouth right next to Sullivan's ear as he leaned in. His scent washed over her, and she took a deep breath. He wanted answers, but Jane wanted more. She wanted forever. With him. A smile spread her lips thin, and she dropped the ice cube down the back of his shirt. "Did you think it was going to be that easy?"

Sullivan jerked away, his laugh loud enough to echo down the hall. Locking that enthralling blue gaze on her, he stalked toward her, all SEAL, all predator. All hers. "Oh, this is going to be fun."

* * * * *

TEMPTED BY DR. OFF-LIMITS

CHARLOTTE HAWKES

Montgomery and Bartholomew,
my beautiful boys.

Make every step one you believe in, and shine.

xxx

CHAPTER ONE

'HEY, GORGEOUS, THOSE lips of yours look so lonely, do they wanna meet mine?'

It took Elle a moment to realise the cheesy pick-up line had been aimed—or, more accurately, *slurred*—at her. She cringed and hoped that if she ignored him he might get the message, even as a part of her wondered why she didn't make one of the witty, no-nonsense comebacks for which she was renowned among her army colleagues.

Two weeks ago she would have.

In fact, two weeks ago she wouldn't have been sitting on this barstool, having nursed the same warm drink for the last couple of hours. She'd have been tearing up that dance-floor, alone or not.

Then again, two weeks ago she hadn't walked in on her fiancé, Stevie, in bed with not one—as she'd told her best friend, Fliss, in some last desperate grasp at dignity—but two bimbos. Two. As if cheating on her wasn't enough, he had to utterly humiliate her. They were football groupies, who'd then sold their sordid selfies to the tabloids. And in that moment it had been as though Stevie had stripped away all of Elle's self-assurance, the very foundation of her confidence, which had been so carefully cultivated over the last decade or so, leaving her feeling more like the nerdy, geeky outsider of her youth.

The fifteen-year-old girl who had let her new stepmother

bully her when her bereaved father hadn't been around, and her schoolmate peers had pushed her around when her adored teachers hadn't been looking, until the cool, sixteen-year-old rising football star Stevie had taken a shine to her and everyone had reluctantly backed off. They hadn't disappeared altogether but had hovered, waiting for their chance to pounce as soon as Stevie dumped her.

But he hadn't, they'd been together for fifteen years in total. Two kids from a no-shoes-poor background who had dreamed of breaking free. He was the only boy she'd ever kissed, the only man she'd ever slept with. Without his support—both emotional and financial—her deep-seated desire of going to university to study medicine would have remained a pipe dream.

She was only grateful that her photo hadn't appeared within Stevie's double-page spread, including the moment he'd scored the winning goal for his club in the most recent Premier League match. *And surely that in itself was fairly damning?* Her photo hadn't been there because—fifteen years or not—the press had, mercifully, never really known about her. For the first few years of their relationship they'd been practically inseparable, looking for each other in school or at lunch-breaks, and then she'd gone to university and everything had changed. For almost the last decade of her relationship with Stevie she'd tried to keep her life and career as a respected army trauma doctor as far away from his professional footballer lifestyle as she possibly could.

'*Man*, what's a bloke gotta do t'get some attention around here?'

Elle startled as the drunk man next to her lolled over the bar, trying in vain to get the bartender to notice him. She refrained from telling him that she'd seen sober people wait up to about ten minutes to get served; she doubted he'd get anything more to drink from anyone. He seemed to have forgotten about her and she didn't particularly want to engage the bloke when she didn't have to.

She glanced around the bar-cum-club with its Latin dance vibe and sexily dressed patrons and reminded herself why she'd come tonight. In a matter of days she'd be thousands of miles away back on the second half of her latest tour of duty, and after the last fortnight holed up in her hotel room down the road she'd had something of a lightbulb moment. Why was she letting someone else—why she was letting *Stevie*—control her happiness, when it finally occurred to her that aside from the shock and humiliation of walking in on...*that*, she wasn't remotely as devastated as she perhaps should feel. If anything, a tiny part of her actually thought it felt...*relief*? So she'd ended up here, trying to be cool and independent and remind herself of the strong, capable woman she'd finally become, instead of the insecure, frightened girl she'd felt on discovering her fiancé's betrayal.

Instead, she just felt like a fish so far out of water she might as well have been back in the scorching desert she knew so well. It was time for her to cut her losses and go back to her hotel room, indulge in a long soak and snuggle down into that huge, fluffy, pure white bed. In a couple of days she'd be back out on her tour of duty and back into an environment she understood. Some people hated their jobs, but she loved hers. Always had. A small smile of relief tugged at her mouth.

'You took your time, huh, darlin', but I guess your lips liked the idea of meeting mine after all?'

Elle barely had time to snap back to reality to realise that the drunk man was still there, and was now lurching towards her with an excited gleam in his eye, clearly taking it as an invitation to plant a sloppy wet one on her. Apparently ignoring him hadn't worked after all, and now a second guy hovered in the background, grinning inanely at his buddy's apparent good fortune.

'Like I said...' she pulled away hastily, but caught off

guard she was barely able to keep herself from toppling backwards off her barstool '…I'm not interested.'

'Sure you are, hot stuff. You just don't know it yet.'

A grabby hand snagged hers and she had to yank sharply to free it, her attitude changing immediately as she pulled herself back together.

'You're not listening,' Elle ground out coldly. 'I'm *really* not interested.'

'Tell you what…' he leered like he was making some huge concession '…I'll even buy you a drink to help loosen you up.'

'You're not the first man—and I use that term loosely where you're concerned—to offer to buy me a drink this evening and I declined.' A few of them had been pretty good looking, too, and she still hadn't been tempted. 'They were polite about it and took no for an answer. I suggest you do the same.'

If she had to physically defend herself, she knew she could. The army had trained her well enough, even though she'd been fortunate enough never to have to use it in practice. But it didn't mean her stomach wasn't churning in a way that it hadn't been a moment ago, or that she preferred not to make her debut in a bar back in the UK with some inebriated idiot.

'Aw, c'mon, don't be a tease…'

Elle reacted, some of her old self racing back to her in that instant as her hand closed swiftly, efficiently and discreetly over his, exerting just enough pressure on the first joint of his thumb. The words suddenly died on the man's lips, replaced with an audible intake of breath while his eyes bulged slightly. She felt a sliver of pride slip back into place.

Abruptly she became aware of someone stepping up behind her. Her grip still firm, Elle was about to turn around when the look on the drunk man's face changed as his bloodshot eyes attempted to focus just to the right of Elle's shoulder and upwards. And then up again. He clearly didn't like what he saw and she could only assume it was someone coming to her rescue.

Not that she needed rescuing. Stevie might have knocked her confidence as a woman, but he certainly hadn't knocked her confidence in her ability to take care of herself, *thank you very much*. She opened her mouth to tell the unseen stranger that she had it under control when the fine hairs on the back of her neck stood on end and a voice spoke, deeper, smoother and richer than the luxurious one hundred per cent cacao hot chocolate she'd indulged in that afternoon. It positively *oozed* dominance.

'Is everything okay here?'

The drunk man struggled to catch his breath, grunting as he winced.

'Get lost, jerk, I saw her first.'

She could practically *feel* the disdain radiating from the newcomer and unexpectedly something kicked low in her gut.

'Everything is just fine,' Elle countered lightly, determined not to reveal quite how her heart was hammering in her chest, though whether it was adrenalin from the confrontation or the unexpected impact of her would-be rescuer, she couldn't be sure.

'I have the situation under control,' she added quietly.

The dark shadow appeared in her peripheral vision and a decidedly muscular figure moved to insert himself between her and her misguided suitor, but Elle twisted her wrist and pushed her other hand over another barely imperceptible notch so that he went from red to puce. His friend was opening and closing his mouth but not moving to help.

'Like I said,' she repeated firmly, 'it's under control. The gentlemen were just leaving for some much-needed fresh air. Isn't that right, boys?'

'Okay, okay,' he gasped. 'We're leaving.'

Similarly, her would-be hero took a half-step backwards in tacit acknowledgment that she did indeed have matters in hand, though he did remain close as if for back-up should she need it. Elle appreciated both actions, even as the drunk man stumbled backwards, nursing his hand and shooting her a baleful look before appearing to realise he was free again. His eyes gleamed and he stood his ground, jutting his chin out pugnaciously. She opened her mouth to issue another warning, but this time the stranger beat her to it.

'There isn't a problem here, is there, lads?'

It ought to have been a question but it wasn't. The stranger's physical presence only emphasised his strength, and yet somehow he managed to make it do it without actually crowding the men or looking as though he was threatening them.

Her eyes were still firmly locked on the drunken man—something warned her that to look at the stranger directly would be as dangerous as staring straight into the sun. Elle tried to sound disapproving out of the corner of her mouth.

'I really can handle him. But thanks.'

'He's drunk and humiliated. You have no idea which way he'll jump,' the liquid gold voice murmured.

'Besides, that was one impressive thumb-lock you executed back there. I'd fancied myself to have been swooping in here like some modern-day superhero when I saw you almost fall off your stool before. At least throw me this bone now so I don't feel completely impotent.'

There was something utterly secure in the stranger's tone that made Elle smile. She doubted this man had ever felt anything close to impotent in his whole life. In any sense of the word. And his compliment had warmed her far more than it perhaps ought to have.

'Then far be it from me to emasculate you.' She covered her mouth with her hand to hide her sudden, irrepressibly inane grin.

Then, crossing her leather-trouser-clad legs on the bar stool—the brand-new purchase intended to lift her spirits—she gestured discreetly.

'Be my guest.'

Without another word the stranger stepped forward. Goose-bumps coursed along Elle's arms and over her skin and for one long second her gaze lingered on a tight backside and muscular thighs, all wrapped up in black jeans, then slowly travelled upwards. He was tall, very tall, and solidly built, with a black T-shirt seemingly following every contour of his exquisitely hewn torso.

She blinked—*since when did she ogle?*—before forcing herself to focus on what he was saying.

'Well, lads? Didn't you say you were leaving?' he said, offering the men a way of backing down while still allowing them the appearance of keeping their dignity.

It was a pretty impressive skill, which was sadly lost on the drunken duo. One of them craned his head up to glower, swaying precariously.

'D'you wanna fight, or shhomething?'

'I don't, particularly.' The response was even, conversational, but there was no mistaking the ominous tone. 'But if that's really how you'd like to end your evening…?'

For a moment everything seemed to hang. And then, to Elle's relief, the one turned to his mate, muttering something about her not being worth the effort, and slunk away into the crowd. Still, the stranger watched with his arms folded across his chest making his biceps bunch appealingly from behind, and shifted his weight from one foot to the other. Poised, controlled, but ready if they suddenly returned.

'Better?' she asked him, once she was sure the men had left.

Affecting nonchalance, she deliberately plucked a non-existent stray thread from her thigh, wondering who had removed all her internal organs and replaced them with a veritable butterfly pavilion.

'Much, thanks,' he agreed with no trace of embarrassment, pulling a comical pose as he flexed his muscles. 'I feel like a man again.'

She finally made herself look at him properly, and the instant she did she found she couldn't drag her gaze away.

And what a man.

He was strong, fit—Stevie had been fit, his football giving him an enviable physique—but this was something... *more*. A whole different level. The stranger had a dangerous power about him that seemed to emanate from the inside just as much as the view on the outside. He was commanding, impressive, *thrilling*. She'd worked with plenty of majors and colonels and brigadiers in her career, but this guy eclipsed them all.

Was this what she'd been missing all these years?

She barely resisted cocking her head to assess him more thoroughly. Lookswise, his face was inarguably masculine with a defined jawline and a blade of a nose. Not pretty-boy handsome, but far more arresting. The kind of face that would be imprinted in her mind for ever. Greedily she drank in the view. From the honed, squared jaw to the tiny crinkle lines around his eyes, which seemed to add character, it was a face that could have stopped a whole bar full of women and, if the daggers she could feel in her back even now were anything to go in, already had.

Unreadable and intense, his eyes were a smoky blue-grey and were were focussed entirely on her. They drew her in and refused to release her, and so help her she didn't want to go anywhere. Forget the butterflies; now a hundred tiny fireflies had sprung up in her belly like a magical light show on a warm summer evening.

She couldn't decide whether it was thrilling or nerve-racking. She flicked her tongue out to moisten nervous lips.

Something momentarily flared in his eyes, something that sent the fireflies racing for cover as fire spread through her entire torso and her heart pounded so hard it would surely leave black and-blue marks on the inside of her chest.

'Where did you learn to do that thumb-lock, incidentally? Very *Jane Bond*... You're not army, by any chance?'

Something about his tone made Elle hesitate, as if it was more important to him than he would have preferred to let on. Maybe he was one of those blokes who hated the military, or one who got a kick out of a woman in uniform? Either way, tonight she didn't want to be Major Caplin, Dr Caplin, or even Gabriella Caplin. She just wanted to be Elle.

'Self-defence class when I was a uni student,' she answered, not untruthfully.

'Ah.'

She might have been imagining it, but she could have sworn he relaxed. *So, not a military fan, then.*

'Are you okay?'

'Fine,' she croaked out. 'Thanks.'

She was jerking her head like she'd just electrocuted herself.

'Are you always so effective at shooting a guy down?'

'I don't know where that came from.' She shrugged. 'He put his hand on me and I just reacted, but I had tried ignoring him first. I thought he might have gone away.'

The stranger nodded sagely.

'Ah, you see, that's where you went wrong,' he continued deadpan. 'That's a polite woman's logic. A drunken man just thinks, *She hasn't told me to sod off yet, she must be interested.*'

Elle laughed. She couldn't help it. Some of the awkwardness dissipated.

'I see. Well, thanks, I'll remember that for the next time.'

A small smiled tugged at those irrationally tempting lips of his.

'At the risk of a knee to my most valued possessions, can I buy you a drink?'

For the first time that evening, Elle was actually tempted. More than tempted. And it only had a little to do with the devilish grin he'd just flashed, which turned her insides out, and more to do with the man flashing it.

But something made her stall.

It could have been the fact that she'd been about to head for the door before the unpleasant interlude with the drunken duo. But Elle suspected it was more to do with the fact that this man here was ridiculously hot, making her brain turn to treacle and her tongue forget how to function. She'd come here to rediscover herself, not pick someone up. And if she accepted a drink from him, would he think she was some-how...obligated to more? She had no idea, but she was sure *that* wasn't going to happen. Still, what were the rules? How did she go about this flirtation dance stuff? The last time she'd dated had been fourteen years ago.

'I have a drink,' she managed, buying herself time to think.

'Which is no doubt warm and unpleasant since you've been cradling it for the last hour.'

She wasn't sure whether to be feel pleased or creeped out. Something about the guy made her feel more the for-mer than the latter.

'You've been watching me.'

His chuckled. A rich, warm sound that made her stom-ach flip-flop.

'I wouldn't say *watching* exactly, that might sound a bit... off, don't you think? I happened to be getting the drinks in when we first arrived.'

We?

'You're with someone?' She tried to remind herself that she had no right to feel so disappointed.

'Over there.'

She followed the direction he indicated, the ridiculous beam rushing back to her face.

'A lads' night out?'

'I'm glad that delights you so much,' he commented wryly, turning to the bar with a minimal dip of his head to attract the bartender's attention. 'I think I'll take that as a good sign and order you a fresh drink after all.'

Elle gave herself a mental kick. She had some good qualities, she knew that. Her colleagues generally described her as focussed and driven yet also fun and bubbly, and she prided herself on her ability to master a curveball, but she never had mastered the art of flirting. She'd never had to. And right now she felt about as sophisticated as turning up to an officers' garden party wearing jeans and a white tee. Yet somehow the obvious appreciation in his gaze stopped her from feeling too gauche.

She was still trying to work out her next move a few moments later as the bartender carefully removed her tepid half-consumed drink and replaced it with a fresh one.

'How did you do that?' she marvelled, with a glance at the frantically waved notes in the crowd as customers still clamoured for attention. 'It was like magic.'

'No magic, we've just got a tab going. And we tip well.'

'You come here often?'

Oh, Lord, had she really said that?

'Not really, but when we do it's usually an all-out affair.' He grinned, and white-hot attraction seared through her, turning her inside out. Elle swallowed hard, forcing herself to remain nonchalant.

'Celebration?'

'Call it a bit of a…leaving do.'

Moments later a generous glass of dark liquid was set quietly in front of the stranger. Elle glanced at the fizzing bubbles in surprise.

'You're on soft drinks?'

'I don't drink.' He shrugged casually.

'Ah.'

Recovering alcoholic? That explained a lot. Like why a guy who looked like he did was still single. And that unexpected bitterness to his earlier comment about not knowing how the drunken guy was going to react.

'Maybe the odd glass of wine if I'm dining out, but I'm generally happy to be the designated driver on a night out like this,' he added, as if he'd read her mind. 'Easier than trying to get a taxi sometimes.'

Yet she didn't miss the flash of…something that skittered across his face before he shot it down.

So he wasn't the drunk, but maybe someone close to him?

She gave herself a mental shake at her uncharacteristic curiosity.

What did it matter? It wasn't any of her business.

Admittedly, she'd dealt with enough soldiers telling her only half-truths about their injuries in order to get back to their unit quicker. If you knew the give-aways it could be easy to spot when someone was holding back, even if you had no idea *what* they were withholding. But this wasn't the army now. She wasn't at work. This was about play. So if this stranger wanted to keep something private then who was she to pry?

She smiled openly.

'So, you aren't going back to them? Your friends?'

'Do you want me to?'

She should tell him it didn't matter to her either way. Hadn't she been ready to leave anyway for the comforts of her hotel spa bath and downy bed? Instead, she held out her hand by way of silent invitation.

'I'm Elle.'

'*Just* Elle?' He smiled, stretching out his arm.

His fingers brushed hers moments before a strong palm enveloped her hand. Something arced between them, making the air seem to crackle. It was all Elle could do not to snatch her hand back.

Or to lean into him and give in to the rash impulse to press her mouth to those inviting lips.

'Well, then, Just Elle, I'm just Fitz.'

'Touché.'

She couldn't help a soft chuckle from slipping out and the

instant flare of awareness from the stranger—from Fitz—
instilled her with another unexpected boost of confidence.

*The guy who was coveted by a good proportion of the
females in the place actually fancied her? From something
as simple as her laugh?*

'So, Elle, what brings you here tonight? Alone? Only—
and forgive me if this sounds impertinent—aside from your
impressive moves back there with your unwanted admirers,
you've looked a little…uncomfortable all evening.'

She offered a rueful smile.

'Was it that obvious?'

'You mean aside from the ramrod-straight back? Or the
untouched drink? Or the fact that most people are happy
to flirt yet you were oblivious to the five or six other, non-
inebriated men who tried to make a play for you all evening?'

'Are you saying I don't fit in?' She couldn't help teasing
him, firmly quashing the slither of unease that he might
have a point.

'I'm saying you looked a little like you weren't used to it.'

She sighed. She could try to be nonchalant, but it wasn't
likely to work. Maybe she should just be honest? She had
opened her mouth to speak when a commotion on the other
side of the room caught her attention. But as the people jostled she caught sight of a body on the floor, convulsing as
a screaming girl tried to hold it down.

Elle didn't think, she didn't wait, she just glanced at her
watch to note the time and she acted.

CHAPTER TWO

ONE MOMENT ELLE was sitting on the barstool next to him, the next she was thrusting people out of her way as she made a beeline for some hubbub behind him. Call it intuition after fifteen years as an army officer, call it something about Elle's understated purposefulness, but Fitz was compelled to follow even as he strained to see past the throng.

It was only when he saw the young man on the floor, with Elle gently forcing a sobbing girl to release her grip on him, that Fitz realised what was happening. Icy fingers slid the length of his spine, the length of his body, rooting him to the spot. He fought to shut his mind to the memories that threatened to overtake him, but not fast enough. They slammed into him with brutal force, knocking his breath out like a bullet striking body armour.

The last time he'd seen someone having a seizure like this had been over twenty years ago. His baby sister had had seizures from about the age of one. Not often, but still. *How had he forgotten about that?*

Memories crowded his head. Images he'd buried along with her body. Her tiny, five-year-old's coffin next to the adult-size one of their mother. He struggled to shove the unwanted images away and try instead to focus on helping the woman he'd just met who was managing the situation with the same cool efficiency with which she'd dispatched Tweedle-Dum and Tweedle-Dumber earlier.

'Let him go,' Elle was telling the girl, kindly but firmly.

'No. No. I can't.' She shook her head manically and tried to shrug Elle off. 'He's my brother, he's going to hurt himself.'

'How long has your brother suffered from epilepsy?'

'What? No.' The girl shook her head violently. 'He's seventeen, he doesn't have epilepsy. He's *never* had epilepsy. What's wrong with him?'

'Your brother's never had a seizure before?' Elle asked calmly.

The same calmness with which Fitz remembered his mother teaching his eleven-year-old self what to do if his sister ever had a seizure if he was alone with her. Not that he'd ever needed to in the end.

'Of course he's never had one,' the girl was wailing. 'I told you, there's nothing wrong with him.'

'What about anyone else in your family?'

'What? No. I'm his sister, I'd *know* if he had epilepsy.' The girl was practically apoplectic. 'I have to make sure he doesn't hurt himself. Oh, God, what's wrong with him?'

'It's okay.' Taking the girl's head in her hands, Elle forced the kid to look at her. 'I'm a doctor, do you understand me? It's going to be okay but you have to trust me. Let go of your brother. If you try to hold him in place you could end up causing more damage.'

Her soothing tone not only seemed to help the girl but him too, and he began to be able to move past his memories just as she glanced up at the room, her stern, clear voice carrying over the now music-free club.

'Everyone else, can you just back up, please, and give him some room?' She turned back to the girl. 'Okay, now this is what you're going to do. You're going to move that table away for me so your brother doesn't hurt himself by banging it.'

All of a sudden Fitz's legs sprang back into life and, propelling himself forward, he distracted the girl.

'Come on, I'll help you. We need to move everything else out of the way. You move those bottles and glasses onto the table down there and I'll move the table itself, understand? Great, okay, now we should move those chairs and the stool.'

His mind and body acting in slick, smooth unison, the way he'd honed them to ever since he'd joined the army, Fitz eased himself even further away from the unwelcome, debilitating memories. Instead, he concentrated on Elle and trying to pre-empt her needs, passing her a jumper, which she took with a silent nod, balled up and slid under the boy's head to cushion it. Then he placed himself between the peering crowd and the boy.

'That's all, folks,' he said authoritatively. 'If you don't need to be here, I suggest you move away and get back to your own affairs. There's nothing to see here.'

He nodded with satisfaction as the crowd immediately began to dissipate, but he was hardly surprised when there were a few reluctant to leave, one of whom was even reaching for his mobile phone.

'*Now*,' Fitz growled, taking a step closer so that he was invading the guy's personal space without making actual physical contact.

It felt as though ever since he'd seen Elle his night had been one incident after another when usually a night out for him, in the rare downtime he had as a colonel, was fairly uneventful.

What was it about this woman, the emerald-eyed redhead, that seemed to turn his world upside down? She was so damned captivating. But as much as he was loath to admit it, he suspected it wasn't simply about her striking looks, even if they were what had drawn him from almost the first minute his group had walked into the club.

So she was a doctor?

He didn't like to examine quite how relieved that made him feel. Something about her attitude and confidence had seemed so familiar, he'd suspected she might be military.

It wouldn't be surprising. They were close to a mobilisation army barracks, which was how his group of fellow officers knew about the club. It was one they always frequented before they went on a tour of duty. The place was more bar than pub, and, though it had a dance-floor, it was not a nightclub, so as officers they could be comfortable having a night out without risking running into the junior ranks, who typically opted for the pubs and bars in the centre of town, which would be heaving with soldiers over the next few nights.

But the idea of Elle potentially being military had been more of a let-down than it perhaps should have been. That would have been the one obstacle to make him walk away. Not that there was any military reason that would prevent them from getting together, of course—as a doctor she would be a commissioned officer just as he was—but, still, it was a line he had always refused to cross for his own personal reasons. Ever since Janine. But Fitz suspected Elle might have made him consider breaking his unnecessarily strict personal rules.

He wasn't yet prepared to examine why he had been so pleased that the fact that she was a doctor, and not military, meant he didn't have to find out.

'Fitz?' Elle's voice broke into his reverie. 'Can you call for an ambulance? Tell them a seventeen-year-old male is suffering from a seizure with no known history of epilepsy.'

Without waiting for his response, as though trusting him implicitly, she lowered her head to check on the boy then turned back to the girl with a gentle smile.

'What's your name?'

'Lisa.' The girl sniffed.

'Okay, Lisa, can you contact your parents?'

'Our parents? Oh, God, I can't call them, they'll kill us. They'll kill *me*. Adam's only seventeen.'

'Has your brother consumed alcohol?' Fitz heard Elle ask as he slid his mobile from his back pocket. 'Don't worry,

I don't care how old you are, I just need you to tell me the truth so that I can look after him the best way I can.'

'Yes,' Lisa sobbed.

'Okay, that's fine. Do you know how much?'

'A lot. We both had a lot. Oh, this is all my fault, isn't it?'

Fitz stepped away as the emergency services operator came on the line, and gave their location and the details. After a brief check of the boy he made his way over to the bar and asked for a blanket and then made sure the crowd had dissipated. By the time he turned back to Elle, Lisa was just about calming down as her brother was slowly coming around.

'My parents are going to *kill* me.'

'Shh, you're okay, Adam,' Elle soothed, checking her watch again. 'You just had a little seizure, but you're safe and your sister's here.'

'The ambulance is on its way,' Fitz muttered quietly. 'This is for his bladder. I'm going out to check the car, I've probably got spare clothes in my gym bag in the boot.'

Gratefully, Elle took the blanket and laid it over the boy's lap, asking him how he felt and trying to note his clarity of answers through Lisa's panicked interference. It was clearly going to be a lot easier for Elle to make her assessment without Adam's sister wailing and babbling.

'Come with me, Lisa,' Fitz commanded softly, in the tone he used when he needed people to do things he knew they absolutely didn't want to do. 'We'll work it out, but your parents need to know. However mad you think they're going to be, imagine how upset and angry they would feel if you didn't contact them.'

Almost against her will, Lisa backed away from her brother, her eyes still locked on his dazed form.

'I… I guess they'd be even more angry?'

'I think you're probably right. Now, my…friend is going to stay with Adam until the ambulance arrives, but you and I need to call your parents together and let them know what's going on.'

'And tell them Adam's going to need to go to hospital for an EEG,' Elle muttered in a low voice. 'Tell them to meet Lisa and Adam there.'

'Understood.' He turned back to the sister. 'Right, shall we step outside where it's a little quieter?'

The sister flip-flopped again.

'No, no… I *can't*.'

Time to take her properly in hand.

'Lisa, they're going to find out some time,' Fitz informed her sternly. 'Better sooner, don't you think? If you'd prefer, I can call them for you, but someone needs to do it. Now.'

The girl hesitated, then nodded, silently handed over her mobile, and followed him outside.

'Thanks for moving everyone away so quickly,' Elle said forty minutes later as they watched the ambulance pull away from the kerb. 'The last thing that kid needed was to come round to find a bar full of nosy people gawking at him.'

'No problem. You were quite impressive back there. Again.' He smiled. 'Shall we go back inside?'

She shook her head.

'No, I really *do* need to go. But thanks for the drink.'

Her guarded gaze caught him by surprise. He couldn't shake the feeling he was missing something. The sounds of the music thumped sensually into the street from the live band who had taken the stage early to lift the mood of the still stunned crowd, but neither of them made a move.

'Ah, okay. I did find one thing odd, though,' Fitz said, stalling for time. 'His sister really had no idea he was epileptic?'

'He might not be.' Elle cocked her head, apparently happy to be delayed. 'It isn't uncommon to have a single seizure and then for it never to happen again for the rest of his life. Especially because he's seventeen and alcohol can be a trigger. The EEG should help to determine whether or not there is unusual electrical activity in Adam's brain and he'll go from there.'

'And what do you think?' Fitz asked, admiring the way her eyes lit up when she talked about medicine. Clearly being a doctor was more than just a job to her, it was something she loved.

'I don't know without the results, but from everything he said afterwards, I'm thinking he's had a few absence seizures in the past, which he never really thought much about. Then the combination of alcohol, exams in school, finding it hard to sleep at night was a trigger for more. But that's just a guess.' She hunched her shoulders. 'Anyway, from your reactions I'm guessing that isn't the first time you've seen a seizure either?'

'My little sister suffered from epilepsy. From the first year of her life.'

The words were out before Fitz had time to think and he halted abruptly. He never talked about his sister. *Never*.

The last time he'd even talked about his family—other than to trot out the one, practised sentence that his mother and sister had died a long time ago—had been to Janine. And even then he hadn't told her the full story, just enough to satisfy her questions after her colonel father had already told her about the car crash.

He'd certainly never told her about those three years when it had just been his mother, his sister and himself in that tiny, cramped flat. The happiest three years of their lives together until his old man had walked back in that night.

'Suffered? Past tense?' Elle asked. 'Did she grow out of it? I think it's somewhere around ninety percent of children with childhood absence epilepsy can grow out of it by about the age of twelve, although I understand they can sometimes have other types of seizure.'

'No. She died.'

Elle held his gaze steadily, her expression changing.

'I'm so sorry. What happened?'

Old, familiar guilt had resurrected itself, and was pressing on his chest like a flatbed truck was crushing him. Images assailed Fitz. Him getting home, the car gone, the phone lying smashed on the floor, the shattered furniture, leaving the house turned upside down. And everywhere the stench of booze. The stench of *him*. The man who was Fitz's father in name only.

'Car crash. She was six, nearly seven. My mother died too.'

He braced himself for the *look*, pity coupled with discomfort as they quickly changed the topic. Instead, he simply saw quiet empathy, a calmness and genuine interest. It seemed to slice through all the layers of protective armour he'd spent years pulling into place.

'Fitz, how awful for you. So it was just you and your father?'

'He was driving.' Fitz tried to swallow the words. Elle was a stranger and this was no one's business except his. 'Drunk. I was the only one left.'

Instead, they kept pouring out, as if they'd been waiting for this moment—for this woman—for half his lifetime.

'Is that why you wanted to protect me from the drunken bloke who was hassling me at the bar, and his mate?' she asked softly. 'So, how old were you?'

'Sorry?' he stalled.

This was the longest he'd allowed himself to think about it in a long, long time. And he didn't want to. Not here. Not now. Not ever.

'How old were you when your family died?' she repeated steadily.

'You ask a lot of questions for a damsel in distress.'

'I wasn't in distress. I had my thumb-lock, remember?' Another smile that twisted in his gut. 'But that's not to say I didn't appreciate the solid back-up.'

'Well, then, that makes me feel better.' He managed a wry smile.

He should have known better than to distract her. Her gaze never wavered and he was compelled to address her unanswered question.

'Seventeen. But it was the night of my eighteenth.'

He should have had happy memories of the time but all he had was one of his mother and his sister lying in that hospital mortuary. To this day he didn't know which of the mass of bruises over his mother's face had been caused by the crash itself and which had been the result of his drunkard father's cruel fists. Fitz struggled to breathe, let alone regulate his voice, which sounded a million miles away when he spoke.

'Listen, this isn't something I like to talk about.'

A beat passed before Elle answered, but not before reaching out to run a hand over his cheek as if she actually cared. And the oddest thing was, he felt like she did.

'Maybe you *should* talk.'

'I don't need to talk,' he bit out.

She gave an apologetic shrug, but it didn't stop her from continuing.

'I'm sorry. I know it's probably none of my business but I'm a doctor. I can see the signs when someone has repressed things for a long time. Especially soldiers who think they're too tough to need to talk and repress all kinds of bad incidents.'

'What makes you think I'm a soldier?' he asked sharply.

'Those spare gym trousers you gave to the boy in there after his seizure had made him lose bladder control? I couldn't help noticing they were military issue. And there's just something about the way you handle yourself. I'm guessing Infantry?'

The way she smiled, polite but with none of the openness or interest of earlier, made him sure that discovering he was military had put her off. Ironically, his experience with women was that it was usually the other way around.

'Not Infantry but, yes, I'm army. A colonel,' he confirmed, technically not a full colonel, a lieutenant colonel, but he doubted that would make a difference to her.

Neither would the fact that until a couple of months ago he'd been a major in a different Royal Engineers regiment. Now he was at the start of his two-year posting as commanding officer of his very own regiment.

Yet right now all he could think was that something about the army meant that Elle was about to walk away from him, and a part of him desperately wanted her to stay. He wondered if she had a brother, a father who had served and been hurt. Or worse.

'You don't like it that I'm in the army, do you?'

'No, no. It isn't that. It's…complicated.'

'Too complicated to finish that drink with me?'

She sucked in a deep breath, as though trying to make her mind up about something. It was unsettling how much he wanted to spend more time with her. A drink, an hour, maybe the rest of the evening, whatever she was prepared to offer. He couldn't recall the last time he'd ever wanted to spend time with any woman like this. But at least now her determination to leave had faded and she was looking decidedly undecided.

'After the last hour, I'm guessing both of us would benefit from a bit of fun now,' he pressed. 'A bit of a laugh? A drink? Maybe a dance?'

'I don't dance.' She frowned uncertainly but didn't refuse him.

She was torn. He still didn't know exactly what had put her off before but she was clearly as attracted to him as he was to her.

It didn't make sense. He'd had short-term relationships and a handful of one-night stands over the years, all with attractive women of varying intelligence, but there was something different about Elle that seemed to pull at his gut and not just at the other, more…*obvious* part of his anatomy. Something glowed, like a whisper of wind over dying embers, inside Fitz; somewhere that had been a gnawing void for longer than he could remember.

He snorted silently inside his head. It was physical attraction, pure and simple. It was just the unusual circumstances of their meeting that had given rise to such a fanciful notion. The unexpected memory of his baby sister and the life he'd long since forgotten.

He hadn't really wanted to come out tonight, the eighteenth anniversary of his mother and sister's deaths. Its echoes of celebration seemed cruelly hollow. From today, his life had been devoid of their love and laugher and warmth for longer than they had been a part of it. Hardly a night for letting loose.

But he didn't have a choice. It was a long-standing tradition with the men with whom he'd gone through Royal Military Training Academy—officer cadets over a decade earlier—to come on a final night out before a tour of duty. To have reneged on it would have raised questions Fitz didn't want to answer.

And so he'd come, and from the minute he'd walked in and headed to the bar to buy the first round, his gaze had snagged on the arresting woman with the stunning red hair. A glorious, waist-length curtain of vibrant golds and reds and coppers that had evoked long-buried memories of the vivid autumn day over a decade earlier when he'd returned, exhilarated and hooked after his first ever tour of duty. It had tugged at something primal, deep inside him, yet… something he still couldn't quite identify had also held him back from approaching her immediately.

Then those drunken idiots had given him the excuse he'd pretended he hadn't been looking for, only to find that she could take care of herself with aplomb, and he'd been even more intrigued.

Fitz reminded himself that tonight was about fun, having a good time. In a matter of days he'd be thousands of miles away in a geographically hostile—though for once non-combat—environment and neck-deep in responsibility for his engineers' role in a crucial, multi-discipline, hearts-and-minds mission. Tonight was his last chance to blow off some steam.

'I don't believe you can't dance.' He grinned. 'But if that's true, how about I teach you?'

'You dance?'

Her brows knitted together and his stomach pulled tight. *Man, she was cute.* He shoved his hands into his trousers to counter the sudden impulse to take her face in his hands and kiss the frown lines away.

'Not like some of those guys in there who can set the floor on fire.' He lifted his shoulders. 'But I can move my feet and keep a decent beat. So what do you say?'

CHAPTER THREE

FITZ COULD MORE than just hold a decent beat, Elle thought an hour or so later as they took a break from another round of dancing in order to get a much-needed drink. He wasn't competition standard, but he had a few nice moves and she was enjoying herself far more than she could have dreamed a couple of hours ago. She was glad she hadn't left.

She'd been going to when she'd realised he was army. Not that she had to, it wasn't against the rules given their ranks, but it was a complication she wasn't sure she needed. And then he'd told her about his family and she'd felt a connection to him. The patent physical attraction between them only partially explained the draw; he'd trusted her enough to tell her, and that made it easier for her to feel she could trust him too.

Especially after Stevie.

'Water, please.' She nodded gratefully as he asked her what she wanted, trying not to read too much into the fact that his hand was still curled gently around her smaller one. 'Or an orange juice. I could really go for an ice-cold juice right about now. Wait, I'll come with you.'

'Fine,' Fitz agreed. 'Just stay close.'

Her heart hammered even harder than it had been doing all evening as he pulled her casually to him and began to lead her through the throng to the bar. Then, reaching for a free sample of a lurid-coloured shot, he sniffed it warily.

'You sure you just want water? You could try this Diablo's Poison they've been pushing all night. I mean, it looks like some hacked jet engine fuel, smells even worse, and would probably strip your insides for the year, but if you can down it in one go you get a selfie and a photo on their media site. I mean, what's not to love?'

He faked choking and Elle laughed, a rich feeling that seemed to bubble up out of nowhere, washing away the very last vestiges of the grime and sadness of the last few weeks. She was beginning to feel more and more like her old self with every passing moment. Stevie hadn't got the better of her, and she wasn't making quite the fool out of herself with this flirting business, as she'd initially feared. His betrayal had knocked her back but it hadn't devastated her.

If anything, tonight's unexpected turn of events had reminded her that Stevie had nothing to do with all the best qualities she prided herself on having: her skill as a doctor; her ability to take care of herself; her appeal to someone like Fitz. She didn't know what it was about Fitz that seemed to lift her the way he did, she just knew the more time she was in his company the more time she wanted to spend with him.

And the fact that he'd confided in her earlier—things about his family that he didn't tell many people, if any—had allowed her to let her guard down with him. As though she knew him, rather than had just met him. Another side to the man she could easily see as a strong colonel, a dynamic leader, an inspiring mentor.

'You look more relaxed than you were earlier,' Fitz said suddenly, ordering the drinks and then turning to her.

His gaze was unexpectedly more penetrating than before, reminding her that her body was tantalisingly close to his.

Abruptly, she ached for more.

They'd been dancing for over an hour, yet it had been so fast-paced that this was probably the closest she'd been to him for any length of time. And her body seemed acutely aware of it.

'I *feel* more relaxed,' Elle admitted, ignoring the irony as she struggled to regulate her breathing, and control the goose-bumps of anticipation from racing over her skin.

'So, what brought you here tonight?'

She drew in a sharp breath.

'Why ask that now, particularly?' she managed slowly.

His mouth curved up into the seductive smile that she'd already discovered turned her insides out.

'Because, I'd very much like to kiss you.' He didn't let her break the gaze for a moment. Direct and concise, just what she'd come to expect from Fitz. 'But I don't think that's what you were looking for when you first came in here.'

'Astute of you,' Elle murmured, trying to buy herself some time.

It was as though the evening had been leading up to this point from the moment he'd stepped up to her at the bar. Now it was up to her to decide whether dancing, a drink, a laugh were as far as things went, or if she wanted more with Fitz tonight.

He didn't answer. He didn't rush her. He simply waited. And Elle was mesmerised by the way his thumb traced lazy, circular patterns over the back of her hand, as though the two of them had all the time in the world.

With his other hand, he reached between their bodies and picked up her drink from the bar to offer it to her before taking his own.

'Come on,' he muttered, turning and leading her back through the mass of rhythmically throbbing bodies and to a quieter corner of the club.

Then he turned back to face her, his gaze snagging hers as easily as before.

Dragging her eyes away, she took a fortifying gulp of orange juice.

Then a second.

Finally, she lifted her gaze back to Fitz.

'I was in a relationship. Two weeks ago I discovered he'd been cheating on me. I admit that it knocked me. I walked out and have been staying in the hotel up the road ever since. I suppose you might say I've been licking my wounds.'

She offered a rueful smile but Fitz just frowned.

'Long-term relationship?'

'Fourteen years,' she confirmed.

He let out a low whistle.

'That must be tough. You were serious about this guy, then?'

He tailed off and Elle could guess what he was probably thinking.

'Only I don't seem as cut up about it as you'd have thought?'

'I'm not judging.'

She shrugged.

'I was hurt, humiliated. I felt betrayed. I sat in that hotel room and felt like a prize idiot. I felt as though I didn't know who I was.' She'd wondered if she was less of a woman, less sexy, less desirable. Not that she was about to tell Fitz that. 'And then I had what I call my "light-bulb" moment; I realised it was more about my pride being hurt than me actually *being* hurt, and I asked myself why I was letting someone else's actions shake my belief in myself.'

'That's very logical.' Fitz didn't look convinced. 'Very controlled.'

She smiled wistfully.

'Isn't that the point? I realised we'd been growing apart for a very long time. He was a...sportsman.' No need to name names. 'He spent a lot of time training and travelling. And my career is very demanding. I think a part of me was still in love with the idea of childhood sweethearts, when in reality we'd fallen out of love a long time ago. We didn't see each other like regular couples tend to, and we weren't really bothered.'

If she calculated it—which she hadn't been able to stop herself from doing a couple of times over the last fortnight—between multiple tours of duty, training courses and postings around the country, she doubted she'd spent more than thirty long weekends and a handful of week-long or fortnight R&Rs in Stevie's company over the last decade or so. At best a couple of hundred days.

'We didn't even live together. We always had our own homes, blaming it on the distance, but that was just an excuse. As the money rolled in, each apartment became more and more blingy, and they weren't my style. I visited but he never gave me my own key. I never needed one, but I guess I now know why he was afraid I might just pop in unannounced.'

'So that was how you found out? You decided to surprise him with a visit?'

'The doorman recognised me and let me in, sweet old guy who only did a couple of nights to top up his pension. I don't know whether he knew the girls were up there, or if he did but thought it was time I knew what Stevie was up to. First time I'd surprise visited in years. Pretty dumb, huh?'

'Only if you're talking about him.' Fitz's thunderous expression somehow soothed her bruised ego.

Elle wrinkled her nose.

'It wasn't just Stevie's fault. I liked my own space, too. I think in the last ten years we might have seen each other two hundred days. Two hundred days out of three thousand, six hundred and fifty-two-ish.'

Her stomach rolled with guilt.

She'd been pretty much fine with that—they both had, by the end—but in the very beginning how many keys had Stevie offered her? In the beginning how many times had he begged her to visit more? To come to his major league matches? To attend some B-list party? And she'd always found an army-related excuse not to. Then again, where had Stevie been when she'd finally graduated or passed out of her Sandhurst course? Out with his teammates, celebrating his own big wins. Too busy to come to either of the two biggest days in her life.

So what did that tell her about the state of their relationship? They'd had three years as teenagers in the flush of first love unable to stand being apart for even a maths lesson, to adults who hadn't blinked an eye at being apart for three months at a time. Or, at least, *she* hadn't. But, still, she would never have dreamed of cheating on him and it wasn't as though she hadn't had the opportunity over the years.

Yet Stevie had. A wave of sadness washed over her. He hadn't always been that way. He'd changed. Fame had changed him. And, as if to add clichéd insult to even more clichéd injury, his excuse had been that the two bimbos 'meant nothing', that they were 'football groupies', that as a professional footballer he was a 'high-profile target' who had done well to resist their seduction skills as often as he had.

She'd taken time to get her head around *that* prize gem this last fortnight and finally seen it for the bull it was. Finally, he had professed that he couldn't be blamed for being lonely and needing physical comfort given how often her work kept her away from him. And *that* particular knife of guilt had been the one to actually lodge in her back.

She shook her head and took another long drink.

'So why stay in a hotel?' he asked curiously. 'Why not just go back to your own home?'

'I didn't want him to follow me down here. I didn't want him to find me.'

She didn't want to do something stupid like let him cry and beg and guilt her into taking him back.

'Anyway, it's not a subject I want to dwell on. I came here to prove to myself that I could enjoy a night out in my own company. I didn't bank on how eventful it would be, but I've felt more like myself than ever. And I guess meeting you wasn't a bad bonus.'

She managed a deliberately cheeky smile, something tightening in her chest when Fitz finally stopped frowning and laughed with her.

'Okay.' He dipped his head. 'Then what would you like to do now? Another drink? Another dance? I could just walk you back to your hotel if you've had enough.'

There was no hint of suggestion in his tone, not that Elle was expecting there to be any. Fitz was the kind of guy who didn't crowd a girl, and she appreciated it. His interest in her was clear yet at no time this evening had he made her feel under any obligation. He was utterly secure in his own skin in everything he seemed to do, and it was an incredibly attractive quality.

The funny thing was that the more he gave her space, the closer to him she wanted to get.

'I think this is what I'd like to do now.'

Before she could second-guess herself, she stretched up onto her toes and pressed her lips against his.

Vaguely she considered it might have been better if she'd remembered to set her glass down first, but then a crackle of energy shot between them and Elle forgot everything else.

Everything stopped in that instant as he bent his head. Fitz didn't merely kiss her back, he *claimed* her, expertly and devastatingly, licking through her body and firing up senses she'd never even known existed. His hands lifted to cup her head, fingers entangling their way into her hair as though he'd been waiting to touch it—to touch *her*—all evening, and Elle held herself closer to his powerful frame.

His mouth was crushing hers, tasting her, exulting in her and, in its ruthlessly exquisite way, crushing any last doubts that she somehow wasn't enough as a woman. He made her feel beautiful, and desirable, and sexy. Fitz made her feel bolder than she'd ever felt before—at least, outside her work persona—as he helped her to discover a side of herself she'd never dreamed existed. A side of herself that was revelling in every stroke of his sensual tongue.

Her fingers bit into his shoulders and she exulted in the power there. Her entire body rocked against his, almost involuntarily, in a rhythm totally apart from the music's. A rhythm as old as time, yet one that she hadn't felt for a long time. And certainly never, *ever* anything quite like this. She pulsed everywhere. Her head was in a mad spin and her chest felt like a band was being wound tightly around her. Yet however close she pressed her body against his strong, unmistakeably hard frame, it didn't feel enough. She couldn't get close enough.

His kisses were like a heavenly sin. His arms around her, locking her in place, were like a sumptuous jail. She could feel every perfect, chiselled inch of him along every inch of *her*. But it wasn't enough. She wanted more.

Apprehension slithered down her spine, rapidly overtaken by excitement.

She'd never had a one-night stand in her life. And somehow she knew she'd never want one again. No one had ever got under her skin quite the way Fitz had, even in these few hours. And it wasn't just that she'd always been in a relationship in the past while now she was single. That alone didn't explain it. She'd worked with enough male army officers in her career to have seen plenty of impressive examples of a man, in confidence, in charisma, in looks. But even if she'd been single, none of them would have affected her quite the way Fitz did. None of them could have tempted her to do something as completely crazy and impulsive as invite them back to her hotel room.

How did she even begin to go about suggesting it?

'Can we get out of here?' She reluctantly tore her mouth from his, murmuring nervously. She licked her lips. 'Maybe go somewhere quieter?'

He peeled her body away from his and Elle was unprepared for the sudden sense of loss.

One hand on her shoulder, the other on her waist, Fitz

held her away and searched her face, reading her unspoken suggestion.

'You're sure that's what you want?'

She opened her mouth to confirm it, then paused. She
still hadn't told him they were both army, and she didn't
want to. Tonight wasn't a night for talking *Green*, or comparing tours or barracks.

She tried to debate whether she ought to tell him or not.

Military-wise, there nothing compelling her to tell him.
They were both single, both commissioned officers, and
he wasn't even in the same corps as her, let alone unit, so
there was no conflict. He'd mentioned he was heading out
on a tour of duty, that was true, but her tour of duty was a
non-combat one so Fitz could be going to a different country, not just region, from her. And even if he *was* going to
the same area, that would mean he'd probably be based
out of Camp Razorwire, where she'd spent the first three
months of her tour.

But when she returned she would be working in the local
civilian hospital almost a couple of hundred miles and about
an hour's helicopter ride away. She'd be working with a
different field hospital team on the first wave of a twelve-
month hearts-and-minds mission to rebuild the damaged
hospital and train the local doctors to carry out surgical
techniques for the benefit of the population there.

There was no conflict, no issue, no need to tell him. Tonight she really *could* be Just Elle. With a clear conscience.

'Yes, I'm sure that's what I want.' She nodded.

Fitz didn't answer, he didn't move. He just perused her
face again, as if making his own mind up about something.

A horrid thought occurred to her.

'Is that what you want?' she asked abruptly.

'Yes, I want you.' He didn't even hesitate. 'God, I want
you.'

His simple, direct, sure response fanned that fire that

seemed to burn inside her, making her feel almost feverish. The pulsing in her body redirected itself to between her legs.

'I just want to know what that hesitation was. I need to be sure.'

'That wasn't about *this*. But I guess I'll just have to convince you.'

She was proud of herself for keeping the shake out of her tone as she stepped back into his circle of space and ran her finger lightly down his sharp jawline. Then, with a whisper-light touch, she brushed her lips on his. His response was immediate, as she'd hoped it would be.

This time his kiss was hotter, hungrier, and lethally practised. His hands moving over her body trailed sparks in their wake. Her body thrummed beneath his touch and dimly she acknowledged that after sleeping with Fitz there would be no going back. She would never be the same again. *Sex* would never be the same again.

Elle trembled at the mere thought, and it seemed to spur Fitz on as he muttered against her lips.

'Then let's get out of here.'

CHAPTER FOUR

IT WAS ALL Fitz could do to keep a controlled pace, with her boots echoing quickly next to him, their arms entwined. As if he could outpace the niggle of doubt, the wondering if this was a bad idea.

Not because he didn't want her. Because he did. God knew, his body ached for her—literally. And not because he hadn't had one-night stands before. He'd had his share.

But there was something different about Elle.

It had been so subtle that he hadn't really noticed it at first. He'd been drawn in by the attraction, nothing more. The realisation had been more recent, when it was too late to do anything about it; somewhere along the line, Elle had begun to scrape away at something deep inside him. She made him feel more than just physical attraction. She piqued his interest, stirred his soul. She made him feel a connection between the two of them.

Uncovering a truth about himself that he'd buried a long time ago.

And he couldn't afford to let her.

Because the truth was that he couldn't allow himself to feel any connection. He couldn't allow himself emotions. A mutual physical attraction was one thing, but anything more and he'd end up destroying the other person.

Hadn't he learned as much from his mother? His sister? Janine?

All three of them. Crushed. Shattered. Two of them dead. All because he'd let them down, betrayed them.

Fitz had sworn he'd never let himself get close to another person to hurt them like that, and for over ten years he'd managed just that. One-night stands or short-lived relationships had kept that loneliness, that darkness at bay. His career had done the rest and Fitz didn't intend for it to end any time soon, which was easier said than done.

It was part of the natural military order that a good proportion of officers didn't progress to the next rank, with multiple majors all after a handful of lieutenant colonel postings. Fitz's aim was to become a full colonel, then brigadier beyond that. But right now there were multiple new lieutenant colonels like him, all fighting for the same single position. It was a matter of dedicating oneself to rising through the officer ranks with focus, speed and ability, sacrificing personal relationships with barely a second thought.

Now, suddenly, for the first time he found himself standing still for a moment, taking stock and wondering what his life might have been like if he'd made different choices. And he couldn't afford to think that way because there *was* no other choice for him.

He was damaged. Hadn't Janine told him so? And hadn't her father told him that he destroyed lives? Weren't his mother and sister proof of that?

'Fitz? What is it?'

It was only when Elle swung around to face him, stopping him altogether, that Fitz realised he'd slowed down to almost a standstill. He made himself look her in the eye.

It was a mistake. Emerald depths stared unblinkingly back at him, wide and intelligent.

'You understand tonight is all I can offer you?' He barely recognised the raw quality to his voice.

'I know that.'

The almost imperceptible quiver in her response gave her away. He had to force himself to continue, even as his brain was screaming at him that he was just trying to come up with excuses and he couldn't explain why.

'Yes, but do you really understand what that means?'

Elle snorted, but her eyes dropped momentarily from his as though she couldn't bring herself to look at him.

'Of course I do. I'm pretty sure the term *one-night stand* is self-explanatory.'

'And you said yourself that up until two weeks ago you'd been with one man for fourteen years. Are you sure you're prepared for a one-night stand?'

'Are you saying I'm too sweet? Because, believe me, I've heard that before.'

'There are two kinds of sweet, Just Elle: naughty and nice.' Was that really his voice, so thick and carnal? 'I'm trying to work out which one you are.'

He couldn't help himself. Lifting a finger, he traced the velvet-soft skin of her cheek. She swallowed.

'Why don't you kiss me again and find out?'

Before he realised it, he'd hooked his finger under her chin and dropped an obliging, if restrained kiss on those deliciously swollen lips.

Another mistake.

Her eyes were glassy with desire, only serving to stoke the furnace that was already consuming him from the inside out. He wanted her with a ferocity he'd never known before. Not even with Janine.

Elle might look wholesome but she tasted like pure sin, even without that wantonly lithe body pressed so tightly against his. Without knowing it, he'd already memorised everything about her, from the way that autumnal curtain tumbled and bounced past her shoulders and down her back to the way her leather trousers clung so lovingly to her feminine curves and the shimmering, metallic green top that skimmed her waist and swung to reveal a gap at the back, giving tantalisingly discreet glimpses of smooth, bare skin.

And then she stepped into him again and there was nothing discreet about the way the hard buds of her nipples pushed through the thin material, or the way his thumb seared as he slid it into the gap and ran it down her exposed back. Not to mention the seductive heat between her legs, which was pure, full-on sexy.

'What did you decide?' she managed, her breathing rapid and shallow.

That she abraded a deep, black part of himself that he couldn't allow to be exposed. That he should walk away from her now. That he wanted her with a hunger he couldn't seem to control.

'I didn't,' he growled.

'Then let me make it easier for you. Tonight I'm the naughty side of sweet, and I want you. And you said you want me too.'

The husky whisper was his undoing.

Yes, he was toxic. To forget that was to step onto a dangerous track. If he went to Elle's hotel tonight, if he slept with her—and, God, he wanted to—then that had to be it. Like any other time, like any other woman. Sex was simply sex. Whatever it was that she scraped away inside him, he could shut that down. He had to.

Fitz cupped her head in his hands and kissed her fiercely again, as if testing himself, as if proving that the physical could be split out from anything else that had no business swirling around his chest. He kissed her until his head sparked and his body ached with such intensity it was almost agony, until he was finally convinced he was back on solid ground and it was all about the physical again.

And then he grabbed her hand and led her to the hotel and into the lift, barely releasing her long enough to press the button for the floor before pulling her against him, her back up to his chest, sliding that glorious curtain of hair to one side and dipping his head on the other side to kiss the base of her neck, as she leaned back into him and sighed softly. Perfectly.

* * *

They tumbled into her room. The heavy wooden door, restrained by its soft closing mechanism, seemed to close too slowly for Elle, firing up her sense of anticipation. Then, when it finally shut with an audible click, the weight of expectation that accompanied that soft sound was unmistakeable.

For a fraction of a second she froze. She was in a bedroom, with a stranger—a hot, caring, responsible stranger, given his actions all evening, but a stranger nonetheless.

As much as she wanted to, could she really go through with this?

Instantly—impressively, too, given the evidence of his desire was pressed, hard and undeniable, against her body—Fitz pulled back from her. She was shocked at just how bereft that tiny movement made her feel.

'Last chance,' he growled. 'You can still change your mind.'

His rich, low voice thrummed with barely restrained lust, making her pulse thready and her insides turn molten. She'd never felt so desired and so *needy*. And the fact that, even now, he was prepared to stop actually boosted her confidence that final little step.

'I don't want to change my mind,' she whispered, running her hands over the muscles that were still frustratingly covered by the material of his shirt.

'You have to be sure, Elle,' he commanded thickly. 'Because after this, I don't know how much self-control I'll have.'

A giggle escaped her lips. A result of the heady sensation that she could exert such desire in a man like Fitz. She had no doubt that, despite his words, if he had to stop at the very last second, he'd find the superhuman willpower to do so. But the idea that he could want her so urgently was a potent thought.

Carefully concealing the tremble that threatened to play

havoc with her entire body, Elle slid her hand lower to cup the evidence of his need. He flexed under her touch, a rough sound rolling from deep in his throat, the combination doing strange things to her insides.

She didn't want to talk any more, she just wanted him with such an intensity it was almost frightening.

As if reading her mind, Fitz dropped his mouth to hers, his kiss every bit as demanding, skilful and dominating as it had been in the bar. It seared through her and all she could do was cling to his shoulders and let him carry her through the flames. Again and again his tongue met hers in a slow, sensual dance. Exploring, touching, tasting, breaking away frequently to take detours at an agonisingly delicious, leisurely pace, starting at one corner of her mouth, trailing along her jaw before dipping below and down her neck.

Elle shook in his arms as Fitz sprinkled short, hot kisses along her collarbone and to the sensitive hollow in the centre. He took his time, which both reassured Elle and simultaneously drove her wild. It felt as though they'd been engaging in foreplay from the moment they'd met in that bar and, if she thought about it, it was also more foreplay than she'd had in the past year in total.

It had never been like this with Stevie. Never. Not even in the beginning when everything had been new and exciting, but they'd been so inexperienced, and certainly not at the end when he'd grown accustomed to people fawning over him, too many hangers-on only too happy to please him. Both in and out of bed.

She'd never, in her wildest dreams, thought it could ever be this good. And Fitz was just getting started, but as much as this indulgent approach was setting her every nerve ending on fire, she was ready for more. *Much more*.

Then he was kissing lower. Elle wasn't quite sure how it happened, but one moment she was in his arms with both of them fully clothed, and the next they were both naked from the waist up and his skilful mouth was making its way, in a lazily winding path, down between her breasts. He cupped her in each hand, as though testing the weight of her, and then he flicked a rough thumb-pad over one nipple as his tongue played with the other. She cried out, a powerful mix of pleasure, need and relief.

It had been such a very, *very* long time since her body had been so worshipped.

Raw need throbbed between her legs and Elle actually ached to feel Fitz sliding inside her, filling her, assuaging the yawning void that had unexpectedly opened up in her soul. Vaguely she became aware of some part of her syrupy brain struggling to extricate herself, to warn her.

If it had succeeded, it might have reminded her that this was supposed to be about sex, that it had been about proving to herself that her lack of sexual experience hadn't been the problem—more like Stevie's abject failure to keep it in his pants. As it was, that logical side to her brain was drowned out while Elle was lost to the moment, lost to Fitz's touch, lost to her own body's primal reactions. She couldn't think past the hot, urgent, intoxicating sensations that were cascading through her, much less think about her ex-fiancé. She couldn't even think enough to move them to the bedroom itself; instead they stood in the vestibule, her back still against the wall to the adjoining room. To move might mean breaking contact, something she couldn't bear to do. And so Elle stayed in place, her fingers tracing that incredible physique and marvelling at the way it reacted so urgently to her touch.

Over and over he paid homage to her body, his skin slick against her, his hands expertly working their magic and stoking those internal fires until she was sure she couldn't wait any longer. As if reading her mind, Fitz's fingers trailed over the curves of her belly, down to the waistband of her low-slung trousers, and unzipped her in one smooth action before peeling the leather down over her legs.

Glassy-eyed, Elle shucked them, along with her heels,

fully expecting Fitz to stand back up to resume where he'd left off. Instead, he stayed where he was, his fingers tracking up her leg from her calf to the sensitive hollow behind her knee and then sensually caressing her inner thighs. Never rushing, always taking care, inching his way upwards with incredible control.

'Are you getting pleasure in torturing me?' Elle gasped at last.

'A little.' His devilish voice sounded thick with need and the ache between her legs intensified. 'Just as I know you're getting pleasure from me torturing you.'

'Fitz…' She barely recognised her own voice in the strangled plea.

'Hmm?'

He was doing it deliberately, she realised. Teasing her.

'Something you wanted to say, Elle?'

His fingers were there, one more caress away from touching her where she needed him to. One inch higher. She waited, only to realise he'd stopped.

'Elle?' he prompted huskily.

He was going to make her say it.

But of course he was.

'Fitz…please…' She shifted so that his fingers should have come into contact with her.

He was too quick.

'I want you,' she managed self-consciously.

Their interaction, his teasing, it was all so much more than she was used to. And while there was no doubt that she preferred it to the mechanical routine with merely a few grunts as a soundtrack, she still wasn't quite sure what to do with this exhilarating, all-consuming side of sex.

'You want me to touch you?' he questioned wickedly.

'Fitz…'

'Like this?' Without warning he swept a finger over her.

A mere brush over the lacy fabric of her briefs, but it sent shockwaves crashing through her. She gasped, squirmed, sought him out again, but his hand was gone, sliding around to cradle her backside.

'Or like this?' he murmured.

Before she could process what he was doing, she felt his breath on her skin and then his mouth.

Hot. Urgent. Terrifying.

Elle's entire body went rigid, her eyes focussing as she pulled desperately away.

'I don't... I don't do that.'

She could barely bring herself to look at him, crouched down there, and when she did she wished she hadn't. He was frowning up at her, his eyes locking with hers, scanning, assessing, disbelieving. Like she was some kind of...freak.

'You don't *do* that?'

Elle jutted her chin out, ignoring the two bright spots of shame that seemed to be burning holes high in her cheeks.

Strangely, though, it didn't make her want to stop altogether. It didn't make her want to give up on the idea of a night together. It just made her want to get past this moment, this awkwardness, and get on with the rest of what might be to come.

'I don't do that,' she repeated, agitated. 'Can't we just... move onto something else?'

'Why don't you do that?'

Direct but firm, he clearly wasn't going to take any excuses. But, then, Elle wasn't about to give in either.

Images of Stevie crowded her head, making her feel hemmed in. She could count on the fingers of her two hands the number of times he'd done that for her in their entire time together, and always hurried, clearly resenting it, and only ever so that she would do it in return. And his attitude had meant that she, in turn, had hated it. The feel of his hands tight on the back of her head, keeping her on him even when she wanted to move away, the way he'd groaned how good she was just to give himself the excuse that he hadn't had time to pull back at the end.

When she'd hesitantly told him she didn't like that, he'd played the guilt card, claiming that he missed her, that her career took her away too much, that she'd never have become a doctor but for him. So she'd done it, and quickly she'd decided it was too painful to go through the charade of him pretending to do the same for her. But she carried the shame of it with her, even now.

Especially now. She couldn't tell Fitz any of that. She didn't want to be that person tonight. She wanted to be the *new* Elle, the version of herself that she'd decided should be born the moment she'd finally had the courage to walk out of the only relationship with a man she'd ever known. And she wanted to keep this perfect image of Fitz. The way he touched her body and set off fireworks inside her very core, not the way he would change once he gave her cursory attention and then expected her to service him in return.

'I don't like it,' she offered at last, when his piercing gaze refused to let her off. She licked her lips uncomfortably. 'Can't we just go back to where we were before?'

'You don't *like* it?' he said, his scepticism clear.

Elle sighed. She couldn't hoodwink him, he'd never fall for it. She'd have to offer him something more. Enough truth that he would believe her, not so much that she humiliated herself.

She sucked in a deep breath.

'In the past I didn't like it. It...it wasn't very good.'

'Ah...' he murmured, the hard stare instantly softening into something else.

For a fraction of a second, Elle relaxed.

'But you will enjoy it with me,' Fitz declared. 'I can promise you that.'

Before she could move again he hooked her leg over his shoulder and pulled the scrappy fabric to one side, then, locking her in place with his hands on her backside, Fitz simply licked a path to her undoing. Pure, molten heat coursed to Elle's core. With every practised stroke of his tongue, bubbles of fire exploded in her. Still, his rhythm kept on as though he knew exactly what she needed. As though he enjoyed giving it to her. As though he enjoyed *her*.

There was no earthly way she could bring herself to move away again and though a faint voice warned her that she would pay for it sooner than she would like, Elle finally let go of her fears and gave herself up to Fitz's unhurried but unrelenting pace. Expertly bringing her to the brink once. Twice. Then the third time, when she was so wound up with pent-up need, he finally slid his finger deep inside her, his mouth sucking on the very centre of her ache.

Elle fragmented. Her fingers sliding through his hair, her hips bucking of their own accord, she lost herself and cried his name. And still Fitz didn't stop, driving her on again and again, sending another explosion rolling through her entire body. Finally, when she couldn't take any more, he eased back and stood up again, his gentle caresses assuring her that they weren't done yet.

By the time Elle finally started to come down from the incredible high he'd just gifted her, reality had started to kick in. He was going to expect her to return the favour. Part of her knew she would be expected to, but another part of her wanted to hold onto this perfect moment for a little longer. Hold onto the image of a perfect Fitz a little longer. Generous. Unparalleled. Untarnished. She couldn't bear to see him change into Stevie right before her eyes.

Too bad, she owed him. Right?

'Still want to tell me you don't like it?' he asked mildly, a smile toying with the corners of his mouth. As though he wasn't waiting for her to perform her new duty.

She felt the flush from her cheeks to her very toes.

'That was like nothing I've ever known before,' she croaked.

Which was why she really shouldn't begrudge him.

Elle forced a bright smile to her lips as his head bowed to kiss her neck, ignoring the sensations that were flooding through her anew. Placing her hands flat on his chest, she moved him away and dropped down to her knees, her hands searching for his belt buckle as she went.

'What are you doing?'

His voice was sharper than she'd expected. She forced a pleasant, even tone to her words.

'Returning the favour.'

'No.'

Elle startled as his large hands locked tightly around her wrists and he pulled her back to her feet, forcing her to look at him. His dark look was intimidating.

'But you did it for me.' She frowned uncertainly. 'So now it's my turn.'

'That isn't how it works, Elle.'

She stifled her derision.

'Of course it is.'

Fitz couldn't seriously be saying he didn't expect anything in return. No man would, right?

'I don't know how your past relationships—relationship—worked, but that isn't how it should be.'

His clipped tone caught Elle by surprise, making her insides flutter. *Who exactly was he angry with?* He was almost glowering as he stared into her eyes. It was as though he could see right into her soul and she found she couldn't drag her gaze away. The moment seemed to stretch out into eternity. Finally he broke the silence.

'Sex should never be a chore, Elle. You do things because you *want* to. You don't do them because you somehow feel you *owe* the other person.'

It was astonishing how his words seemed to go straight to the root of her fears.

'But—'

'No. There are no "buts" to that simple truth.'

'You don't…?' Elle swallowed, still not quite certain. 'You don't want me to do that for you?'

'I do not,' he confirmed firmly. 'Not when you don't want to.'

'Part of me does,' she whispered sadly, almost by way of apology. But she was surprised to find that abruptly there was a small part of her that really did want to. She dropped her eyes, afraid that she wouldn't be able to say the words if he was still holding her gaze.

'Because it's you.'

Unexpectedly a soft smile chased the darkness from Fitz's face as he hooked a finger under her chin to force her to look back up at him.

'Then I hope for you that one day someone, the *right* guy, will make more than just a part of you feel that comfortable. But for now I suggest we move over to that bed and I show you other ways we can continue this evening.'

His words were bitter-sweet. The realisation that he really wasn't going to allow this one moment to spoil the rest of the night warred with the reminder that he wasn't her right guy, he was just her one and only tonight guy.

When had she started to forget that?

She managed a jerky little nod, reminding herself not to get so carried away for the rest of the night, ignoring the voice that whispered that Fitz might have been the 'right guy' for her if only she'd been a few months, maybe a year down the road.

The right guy but at completely the wrong time.

'Elle?'

Snapping her head back to the present, she tried to remember the last thing he'd said. Something about moving to the bed to continue their evening.

'I'd like that,' she managed.

With a satisfied nod Fitz dropped his hand from her chin and then, before she could react, he'd taken her hand and was leading her over to the bed.

'Then let's get back to having fun.' He grinned wickedly

at her, lowering his head to hers and kissing her as though the ugly moment had never happened.

Incredibly, the further they got from that vestibule and towards the huge inviting bed in the corner the more her mood started to lift. By the time he'd deposited her on the bed, Elle found it easy to kiss him back, some underlying sense of relief lending her a renewed sense of eagerness. As he stood back to finally slide her lacy briefs down, shucking off the last of his own clothing after discreetly throwing a foil square onto the bed, Elle indulged in her first full view of his beautiful physique. He had a stark male beauty that spoke to her very core. And then there was his proud and impossibly generous erection. Her heart flip-flopped and hunger kicked low in her abdomen. Urgent and primal. He was overwhelming, yet he was staring at her as though she was equally breathtaking. As though he were committing every line of her body, every curve to memory.

'Stunning,' he ground out.

His rich, lusty voice seemed to resonate through her very sex, which was still deliciously sensitive after the care he had shown her before. Her long-deflated, crumpled ego began to unfurl and breathe life again.

Tonight might be all they had, but she'd be damned if she wasted it on what-ifs. No, she would thoroughly indulge in every last second of what was left of this night together and then she would hold onto this moment, the memory of this man, for the rest of her life. Pushing herself up onto one elbow, Elle reached for Fitz with a new-found sense of confidence, a warmth spreading though her as he moved onto the bed to join her.

She didn't want to wait another second.

CHAPTER FIVE

FITZ DRANK IN the sight of her, completely naked and laid out on the bed before him looking every bit as enticing and delectable as she had tasted.

'Stunning,' he murmured unconsciously.

God help him, she'd felt better than he'd been imagining all evening. *Hotter, slicker, tighter.* And she was reaching for him as though she couldn't wait any longer.

'We've got all night,' he reminded her, scarcely recognising the raw heat of his own voice.

It was immoral that a woman so bright and sexy and *alive* shouldn't have been lavished every single day with the kind of attention he'd paid to her arresting body, and the realisation that her ex-fiancé had clearly hurt her in this way filled him with inexplicable rage. Yet at the same time Fitz felt an incongruous burst of triumph that *he* should be the one to open her eyes to it. That *he* should have been the one to sweep away her obvious reticence. That *he* had completely erased from her head her unspoken expectation that he'd somehow end up letting her down.

He wanted to take his time, show her more of how it ought to be between two people, even if it was only for one night. But he didn't think he could wait any longer. His erection was so rock-solid it was almost painful. He couldn't remember ever wanting any other woman with such intensity.

She ran her hands over his chest, his sides, his back, exploring every last inch of his torso, and then, her eyes flitting nervously to his, she grazed her nails gently against his skin. Fitz offered a soft groan of appreciation as his mouth fell to plunder hers, and then without warning her hand was moving around to take him in her hand, fitting him to her palm. His groan was instinctive and far more guttural this time, as he flexed against her.

Something seemed to shift in her attitude as she realised the sexual power she had over him. A mischievous glint appeared in her eyes. A hint, perhaps, of the young woman she'd been before something—or someone—had quashed her?

'If we have all night,' she observed, running her thumb around him and then over his tip, 'surely we can slow things down *next* time.'

'You're sure that's what you want?' he managed gruffly.

She lifted her heavy eyelids to look at him, those emerald depths almost black with lust, her breath already shallow and rapid.

'Quite sure.'

He didn't need any further invitation. It took him seconds to open the foil square and roll the condom down his length, ignoring the little voice that taunted him that he'd been so caught up in Elle that he'd only remembered protection when it had fallen out of his pocket as he'd taken off his jeans. The bewitching creature had made him forget the one thing he'd been so fastidious about ever since...well, ever since what had happened with Janine.

The baby he'd never fought for. The baby she had lost at three months because he hadn't taken care of her the way he was supposed to have.

He jerked his head up in frustration. These were the blackest of thoughts he'd locked away in a box over a decade ago, and had thought he'd thrown away the key. The beginnings of memories he didn't want resurfacing, tonight of all nights. He'd slept with his fair share of women over the years and not one of *them* had ever pulled at something deep inside him, the way Elle seemed to.

Angrily, he thrust all thoughts from his head.

Tonight was supposed to be about indulging in a beautiful, intelligent woman. A woman who had made him *crave* her, a woman who seemed to want him with the same dark intensity.

Fitz blocked out his mind and concentrated on Elle.

Gently, he nudged her legs apart and covered her body with his, nestling into her wet heat and revelling in the slickness of their bodies moving over each other. And then he gave in to the aching need and slid inside her.

Sensations rushed him, urging him on. Her soft gasp and low moan only pushed him further but he forced himself to go slowly, to give her a chance to stretch around him, to make sure she was ready. Carefully he moved, languorous slides in and out as he watched her, waiting for her to find his rhythm, to meet him, to match him. Until soon they were moving in perfect synchronicity, and she was arching her hips to draw him in deeper and drive him on. Faster and wilder.

He layered butterfly kisses on her sweetly exposed neck when she let her head fall back, like nectar he had been denying himself for so long. And when he heard her gasp his name, a peculiar sense of euphoria flooded through him. A sense of possession.

As if she were his.

The realisation should have slammed him with more force. It should have set alarm bells clanging wildly in his head. It should have made him feel guilty for beginning this madness. He'd sworn to himself back in the street that whatever it was Elle possessed that seemed to stealthily intrude inside him in a way nothing else ever had, he would control it.

Instead, he was imagining she was *his*. Wondering what it would be like to come back to this strong, characterful, beautiful woman again and again. *Stupid.* Because that could never happen. She could never be his, he had nothing to offer but pain and betrayal. He should never have begun this madness with her. But he hadn't been able to help himself, inexorably drawn to her as though her brilliance, her energy could somehow illuminate the darkness in him.

Then she cried his name a second time and he was lost again, consumed by his need for her. And as her body gripped his and she exploded around him with shudder after shudder of her release, he gave himself up completely to the pleasure of her all around him. Seconds later, he followed.

If this was the start of their night together then he could only wish it would never end. Imagine it would never end. For this one night he could pretend he wasn't damaged, wasn't incomplete, that he was the kind of man who could make a woman like Elle happy in life, not just in bed.

She made him feel like he was more than just a good colonel, a good soldier, a good engineer. Elle made him feel that somewhere deep inside he was good man. And, just this once, he wanted to believe it.

He could deal with the fallout later.

Fitz checked his mobile. Zero-five-hundred. He really should get going, back to barracks. He wasn't required specifically but his visible presence around the barracks would be good for his men's morale, especially for those who hadn't been on operational duty before and especially because this was his new role as their commanding officer.

He eased himself out of the bed, but as he rolled Elle rolled too, as though seeking out his warmth, and so help him he couldn't tear himself away. He didn't want to. He kissed her as she pressed herself against him, his own reaction instantaneous at the feel of her silken skin all along the length of his body.

'I have to leave,' he whispered, making no effort at all to untwine himself from her arms.

'Already?'

Sleepily seductive, she stretched languorously until she realised exactly what she was stretching against. Her eyes flew open wide.

'Morning,' he managed wryly.

She peered at the clock and grumbled good-naturedly.

'Barely. You really have to go?'

'I have time for breakfast.' The words slipped out before his mind had a chance to engage.

'Really?'

No.

'Yes.'

Quickly, quietly she slipped out of bed, unashamedly searching for her clothes as though being with him here the morning after wasn't awkward or strange at all. And he liked it. He liked her confidence, her strength, the certainty that last night hadn't been a mistake.

He pulled his T-shirt over his head, watching as she slipped her feet into tiny ballet pumps from the wardrobe across the room, and then, as she rounded the bed, he reached impulsively for her hand.

'Come on, I know a little bakery nearby. I'll take you there.'

Steadfastly he ignored the part of his brain telling him he should get going. He ignored it as they walked, hand in hand with an intimacy he'd never known before, down the deserted streets. He ignored it as he easily talked his old friend into letting them into the bakery before it was supposed to be open. He ignored it while he listened to Elle's soft voice chatting to him as the early sunlight danced over her animated features and played with the light as it bounced off hair he longed to lose his fingers in again and again. And as she watched him curiously, he couldn't help asking what it was she was thinking.

She hesitated, a shy smile tugging at her lips.

'I didn't think this was what the morning after would

look like.' She ducked her head and concentrated on a few crumbs of her almond croissant, unable to meet his eyes.

'What did you expect?' he heard himself asking, as if him leaving wasn't how he'd expected the early hours to unfold either.

'I thought you'd be gone. Sneaking away in the night. You told me you didn't do relationships.'

'I don't.' He took another sip of his black coffee, aware of the irony.

'Yet here you are.' She finally lifted her head. 'You don't seem as emotionally disconnected as you like people to think.'

Her words should have alarmed him. Instead, he felt immeasurably sad.

'You don't know me.'

'So tell me.'

And instead of shutting her down, he thought of the way she'd opened up to him last night. How she'd bravely told him about her sexual experiences with her ex. He'd thrilled in showing her exactly how good it could be, his own body hardening beyond anything he'd ever experienced at the sound of her coming undone in his arms.

Now the words came from nowhere he recognised. A dark place within him that he'd locked down so many years ago, like a kid with a scary monster in the closet. But the light she shone made everything less frightening.

'My father was army, like me,' he began, hesitantly at first. 'Only he wasn't a commissioned officer, he was a nineteen-year-old corporal with his sights set on staff sergeant and beyond when he met my mother. A couple of months later she found she was pregnant and they got married. He always resented being tied down. He took it out on my mother, usually with his fists, usually when he'd been out drinking, although I didn't know about it for years. My mother had always been terrified he'd hurt me so she did the only thing she felt she could, and took the beatings in silence as long as he left me alone, and later my sister.'

'Fitz!' Elle gasped, and tried to disguise it, but Fitz didn't miss her shock. He fought to shut out the memories, so old and repressed they were like a silent black and white movie in his head now. But they still made his heart thump furiously in his chest, like it was trying to ram its way out. Like it was trying to escape.

'Mum and I used to breathe a sigh of relief every time he walked out that door with his kitbag for another tour, especially if he'd been home a while. Him being away meant months of blissful peace, and if we were lucky and he went somewhere else for R&R, we might even get a full year.'

'Were you close, then? You and your mum?' Elle asked gently.

'Sort of.' He hunched his shoulders. No emotions, just facts. He couldn't explain this urge to talk to Elle, just that it was there. But that didn't mean he was ready to actively *think* about it, *feel* it. Not yet.

'But my mother was as unhappy in her own way as he was. Neither of them had wanted to marry the other, but they'd had no choice. Add to that the fact he beat her, and it made for a fairly unpleasant life. I never lacked for anything in terms of food, clothing, toys. She worked hard, and in her own way she loved me, but she was never exactly the huggy sort of mum from American TV shows. It was never a happy home, not exactly full of love.'

'It's all relative, isn't it?' Elle murmured, almost to herself. 'I thought I had it bad with my stepmother, but at least I got to experience something better before that. I knew it didn't have to be that way.'

Fitz shrugged, unable to answer that.

'Maybe. But maybe it's worse. Sometimes words can hurt as much as fists. If someone says you're worthless, stupid, unwanted often enough, you can start to believe them.'

Elle nodded sadly.

'My stepmother was devious. She'd pretend to be okay when my father was around but when he wasn't, she was spiteful and vindictive. If I hadn't had Stevie, if I'd been a bit younger, I might have let her win. In many ways I got lucky, but then it only added to my guilt later for not loving him.'

'He didn't deserve your love.' A stab of jealousy sliced through him.

'But he deserved my honesty.'

'Words are powerful tools in the right hands,' Fitz said slowly. 'But powerful weapons in the wrong ones.'

Elle met his gaze, thoughtful and open.

'Or else they're meaningless,' she countered. 'Stevie used to tell me he loved me, but all the while he was cheating on me. I think I'd far rather have actions over words.'

Fitz nodded but said nothing. He knew he would too, but he hadn't any right to it. He'd always failed in his actions. In trying to be everything his father hadn't been, he'd ended up acting in precisely the same self-serving way. He couldn't escape his nature, it seemed.

'So what happened, Fitz?' Elle touched his arm sadly and Fitz worked to loosen his tightly clamped jaw.

'When I was fifteen he got injured and he was home for a long while. Things just deteriorated. One night, or at least the early hours of the next morning, he came in steaming drunk. I don't know what she said or did, probably nothing, but he completely lost it. I remember hearing her trying to muffle her screams so she didn't wake me or my two-year-old baby sister. Something snapped in me. One minute I was in my bed and the next I was in my parents' bedroom and my dad was lying flat out on the floor and I was threatening to kill him if he ever touched her again.'

Despite the monochrome background of the rest of the memory, he could still see the bright red stain on the dirty carpet from his father's bloodied nose. And the absolute shock on the old man's face.

'He hit you?'

'He didn't dare,' Fitz snorted bitterly. 'A bully doesn't pick on someone he can't intimidate. But he never touched my mother after that. In fact, he pretty much never returned to their army house after that. They stayed married, at least for appearances, but he took posts that meant he was stationed away. He did courses during his downtime, and on the couple of occasions he really didn't have anywhere else to go, my mother took my sister and me to visit her sister, who was married to a soldier and stationed abroad.'

'So you never really saw him again?'

'Not really. He'd never been interested in a family anyway. His wife and son had been imposed on him. My sister was the product of a married couple who went through the motions. So, no, we didn't really see him again. Not until that last time.'

'What happened the last time, Fitz?' Elle half-whispered, as though a part of her already suspected it wasn't good.

He hunched his shoulders, feeling suddenly chilled in the otherwise pleasant late-afternoon air. Suddenly it wasn't easy to tell her anything more. Suddenly, he wished he'd never started. The words were lodged thick and painful, choking in his throat.

'The night he came back was the night they died.'

'The car crash,' she said quietly.

Guilt, anger, grief, all of which had been simmering barely beneath the surface until now, suddenly rushed Fitz so hard he felt physically winded. It took him several long moments to regulate his breathing enough to answer her.

'Yes,' he bit out. 'I don't want to talk about that any more. I don't usually. Last night was the anniversary of their deaths. It's been eighteen years and I realised that I've now been without them, without her, for longer than I ever had her. I guess it just got to me.'

'It would get to anyone!' Elle exclaimed.

'So let's just close it down now and enjoy the last hour or so we have left.'

It wasn't a request and he could see her biting back whatever she'd been about to say.

'Of course,' she said instead.

So they did. Fitz fought to shrug off the unwanted, alien emotions and the acknowledgement that talking to Elle had been far more cathartic than he could ever have imagined. And he let himself enjoy the last hour as they made their way back to the hotel, and to her room, and he couldn't stop himself from making love to her one more time. This time, when he woke he slid carefully out of the bed, seeing her hair puddled on the white pillow like a splash of light, and dressed in silence. Wishing they had more time.

Not knowing what difference that would have made.

He headed for the door, opening it softly to let himself out, before stepping back inside, crossing the room and snatching up a pen and paper from the desk under the mirror and jotting down his phone number.

Last night had been perfect, like a dream he'd never expected to experience. He'd never felt so connected, so at ease with anyone before. But it was just an illusion. A woman he'd met in a bar. For her, he was a means of putting something between her and her failed engagement. For him, a last indulgence before yet another tour of duty. Not that he begrudged it, he loved his career. It was who he was.

Or at least it was the good part of who he was.

Fitz stared at the phone number in his hands. What was he thinking? This hadn't been a first date. Yes, he dated occasionally, but only women who knew the score from the start. Women who agreed from the start. And he ended it as soon as they began to start talking seriously. And for good reason. He was incapable of loving selflessly. He was damaged, and he hurt people. He'd tried to love when he'd found Janine, but even with her he hadn't been able to make that part of his soul work again. Hurting someone as lovely as Elle would be inevitable if he was selfish enough to pursue her. Worse, it was dangerous, because he couldn't shake the feeling that she would challenge every rule he had for himself.

He would never have set aside his meticulously planned schedule of going in early this morning for any other woman. Not for a croissant and a coffee, and not to spend that last hour in their company talking about long-buried emotions.

Ripping the paper from the pad, he screwed it into a tight ball and launched it into the bin, and still he had to force himself to leave Elle's room without a backward glance.

The soft sound of the door closing finally woke Elle. She sat up, the bed sheet clutched tightly to her constricting chest as she stared around the empty suite with fresh eyes. One night with Fitz and now the hotel room, which had felt like a pleasant refuge for the last few nights, suddenly felt cold and lonely.

She felt cold and lonely.

Dropping the sheet and sliding out of the bed, Elle shook the notion roughly from her head. Last night had been a one-night stand. But as wonderful, as incredible as it had been, it had just been that. One night. No strings. No regrets.

Padding around the suite, Elle forced herself to concentrate on the mundane. To clean her teeth, to get her shower, to dry her hair. But everything felt different. *She* felt different. She sat at the dressing-table mirror and stared at her reflection, almost disappointed that she didn't *look* different too. How could it be that she looked exactly the same as she had last night when inside her it felt as though she had undergone such a seismic shift?

Part of her expected Fitz to walk back in any moment. After the way they'd connected, how was it possible for him to walk away without a second thought? Almost on autopilot, she ran the brush through her hair and chased it with the hairdryer, trying not to remember with such startling clarity the way Fitz had run his fingers through her hair, telling her how beautiful it was, how beautiful *she* was, bit by bit restoring every bit of confidence that Stevie's actions had knocked out of her. Maybe even more.

Elle wasn't quite sure when or how her brain registered the pen and notepaper, no longer at the back of the table where they'd been her entire stay. Her eyes scanned the room for anything she'd missed but she saw nothing and then, almost instinctively, she glanced over to look into the waste basket. It was empty but for one screwed-up ball of white paper. Her heart slammed inside her chest as she stared, immobile. Slowly, very slowly, she reached out with one trembling hand and retrieved the paper.

Now what?

She willed herself to open it but instead sat, her back ramrod straight, her fingers quivering, gazing at the little white ball, unable to act. It might not say anything. It might say something that would spoil the night before. A tiny voice warned her that she might be better dropping it back in the basket and leaving well alone.

The voice was probably right, but she found she simply couldn't. With painstaking precision she smoothed the page and scanned the phone number, her fingers tracing the letters of his name almost of their own volition.

Then, abruptly, her brain roared into life and she screwed the paper back up.

It was a relief to know that he had felt that same connection she had, and he'd been as seduced by it as she had. But then he'd recognised it for what it was. A snapshot. A perfect moment in a perfect night.

Last night she'd been crazy and impulsive, like a role an actor played for a movie. But that wasn't who she was in real life. She wasn't carefree or daring, she was steadfast and focused, a major, a combat doctor in the British army. However perfect last night had seemed, it had been built on foundations that were little more than illusions, and she couldn't help the stab of guilt at her part in that.

But what was done was done. Last night had been about getting closure on a relationship that had actually died years ago, not about the start of something new. She wasn't ready for that, and she didn't want it. However much Fitz might have confused that for her right now.

Fitz had been right to throw his number away, they would only be chasing after something that didn't really exist. Bracing herself, Elle hurled the paper back into the basket before she could change her mind again.

Last night had been perfect. Trying to squeeze anything more out of it would only sully the wonderful memories she now had. *Just Elle* was gone. It was time to get back to Major Gabriella Caplin, army trauma doctor.

CHAPTER SIX

'THIS IS ARI,' the nurse, a corporal who'd been there a month or so longer than Elle, informed her as soon as she came on shift for the morning. 'He's eight and he has a broken leg with an open wound. This is his first visit to us but the team at the main hospital have been trying to treat him for over a month.'

Elle smiled at the boy, receiving a sweet smile in return as he clung onto his mother's hand. Her own fears were masked by a tight smile, too. The nearest hospital was across the border, several hours and a treacherous drive away. It was no wonder that even though this hospital had been intended to be just a training ground for local doctors, with only a few cases while the army got the rebuild under way, the locals were ignoring that and bringing their sick and injured here anyway.

Another reason why getting this hospital back up and running quickly was so essential.

'They've been trying to heal the infected wound before they can attempt to set the bone,' the nurse added.

Elle nodded. Infection really was the enemy out here. Even if they set the bone, it wouldn't heal unless the infection was gone.

'He needs a smaller surgical plates-and-pins kit that I don't have among my army kit,' Elle assessed quickly. 'Neither do Razorwire. But our logistics teams are bringing supplies all the time now we're out here, so I'll put in a requisition for more instruments appropriate for dealing with children. In the meantime, we do need to get the infection under control.'

'He can't tolerate washing the wound without anaesthesia,' the nurse warned. 'And we don't have any here.'

'No, well, without the custom-sized plates and pins to hold the bones together they'll be moving and the pain will be incredible for him. We'll leave the leg in plaster for now and wash the wound as much as Ari can withstand, and always under anaesthetic. As soon as the smaller surgical plates arrive we'll be able to hold the bones together and we'll have more options.'

'Understood,' the nurse confirmed.

'Who's in the next bay?'

'Young boy named Zav. He's only five. He suffers from a severe form of thalassaemia so he needs blood transfusions every five weeks. His family are from a village a little east of here, wealthy by local standards, but they say they can't keep making the journey across the border and want to bring him to this hospital for his transfusions.'

'Right.' Elle nodded grimly. Thalassaemia wasn't uncommon out here, not just as an inherited blood disorder, but also because there was no national plan to tackle the disease. It meant that few health facilities could offer treatment for the more severe cases, and parents weren't educated on its causes, which were mutations in the DNA of cells. They only understood the symptoms of chronic fatigue, anaemia and, ultimately, if she recalled rightly, a life expectancy of around fifteen years in this region. Twenty years across the country.

'I take it infection, bone deformities and slowed growth rates, especially in children, are common.'

'Right,' the nurse agreed. 'We see a lot of abnormal bone structure in the face and skull, broken bones, iron over-

loads and heart problems such as arrhythmias and conges-
tive heart failure.'

Elle nodded. There was little she could say. Treatments
were basically frequent blood transfusions or stem-cell
transplants, usually from a non-affected sibling. Otherwise, affected or carrier parents would be looking at IVF
with embryos pre-tested for genetic defects. Hardly a possibility in a country like this one.

'And in the far bed?' Elle forced herself to move on.

'A two-month-old. Bronchiolitis.'

Again, not uncommon in this region, affecting hundreds
of babies every season. Still, she would be glad when the
rebuild was under way and she could start kitting out dedicated wards with incubators, paediatric kits and equipment
for women in labour. Training the local health profession-
als to be part-doctors, part-nurses, part-surgeons, however,
promised to be no mean feat.

As she flew around the wards—or what passed for wards
in the damaged hospital—Elle considered the best place
to start in terms of the rebuild. She knew that Major Carl
Howes, the officer in command of the troop working at
the hospital itself, was focussed on getting the main infra-
structure up first. Without water and power, everything else
would be doubly hard, but the discovery of an unexpected
aquifer running below the area had thrown their programme
into turmoil, and Carl had told her he'd called in his commanding officer to go through the finer details.

She could only hope Carl's colonel was as much of an
expert as Carl claimed the man was.

She glanced quickly at her watch. There was a joint
regiment briefing in a couple of hours and her own commanding officer had flown in as well. She really didn't
want to keep him waiting so her ward rounds were going
to be postponed. Grabbing a hat for the shade, Elle ducked

outside, seeing the older man straight away and beaming at her mentor.

'Colonel Duggan, thanks for flying in. I take it you've heard about the aquifer?'

Fitz surveyed the vast expanse of nothing beneath the helicopter as it flew the hour or so trip across the barren land, his eyes constantly scanning, more out of habit than anything since they were in a non-combat environment out here.

Part of him was actually relishing the challenge of the unexpected aquifer. Anything to occupy his mind, to distract it from the emerald-eyed, flame-haired beauty who had haunted his dreams—waking and sleeping—for almost a week now. He couldn't shake her from his memory, but every time he tried to work out what made her so special, so unique from any other woman he'd dated, he just seemed to tie himself up in knots.

It was uncharacteristic and he loathed it. Yet he wouldn't have changed it even if he could have.

He'd watched a group of squaddies playing with a deck of cards the previous night and had realised that right now his life, his career had been like a perfectly ordered deck of cards until Elle had given them a playful shuffle. It had taken him all of the last week to re-order them and fit them neatly back into their box.

Still, he had no intention of letting them get messed up again. Not while he was out here on tour, in any case.

Maybe afterwards, once he returned home, if visions of that flame-haired, emerald-eyed temptress still haunted his dreams, he might consider stepping out of his comfort zone and contacting the hotel to see if he couldn't inveigle something—anything—out of them regarding Elle's name.

Anything to sate the gnawing ache she'd left inside him.

Finally the heli landed, and Fitz stepped out to greet

Major Howes, one of the five majors under his direct command.

'Colonel.'

'Major.'

'How was your ride, sir?'

'Fine, thanks. Good to see you again, Major. We missed each other at Razorwire.'

'Yes, sir, I didn't think I'd have to wait long for you to come out and see the hospital site first-hand. I'm glad, too, as I could use someone with your particular specialism right now. I was going to radio HQ to send me someone yesterday but then I heard you were on your way. I'll show you around when you're ready.'

'I'm happy for you to show me around now,' Fitz said as they moved out of the way while soldiers began unloading the several tonnes of materials and equipment from the heli.

Dutifully, Carl instructed a young lance corporal to take Fitz's pack to his office.

'How was the drive out here?' Fitz asked as the two officers slipped easily into conversation.

The convoy had left Razorwire earlier in the week before Fitz had even arrived. He would have preferred to have travelled with them, it was always good to get an idea of the ground, but he had been needed elsewhere.

'Six hours. Not bad.' Carl shrugged. 'The route was long but that's because we still have to go the long way round that valley, and you know what passes for roads around here.'

'You're lucky if they're paved,' Fitz acknowledged. 'So what's the issue you wanted me here to look at? You mentioned an aquifer.'

'Your speciality. It runs directly beneath where we're planning on putting the plant room for the generators. I had a couple of solutions, which I was going through with the medical liaison officer, but I'd like it if you could run over them, too.'

'Okay, when did you schedule the briefing for me today?'

'Zero-nine-hundred hours. Ninety minutes away.'

'Understood. Then don't let me hold you up, let's go.' He followed as Carl led the way around the hospital, mentally orientating himself as they progressed. 'What's the medical colonel running this hospital like? Colonel Duggan, isn't it? I heard he had a good reputation as a surgeon, don't tell me he's making things difficult on our construction side?'

'No, the Colonel is okay,' Carl answered as they made their way through and around the part-damaged, part-derelict hospital. 'He *has* got a good reputation apparently, and he mainly deals with teaching the local doctors. But one of the majors under his command, a Major Caplin, has experience both as a combat doctor *and* of building cottage hospitals back in the UK, so her CO has been happy to pass a lot of the liaison work on to her.'

'Makes sense if she has that kind of experience and he doesn't.' Fitz nodded, thinking how he'd always found that one of the greatest strengths of the British army. 'But not if she's insisting the plant room go above the aquifer without considering the other options.'

As structured and hierarchical as it might appear to an outsider, in reality it was far more nuanced and elastic. A brigadier should be willing to take advice from a lieutenant, or even a sergeant, if that individual had specific expertise that everyone else lacked. For all intents and purposes, he could be answerable to this Major Caplin if her commanding officer Colonel Duggan had passed over administrative and operational command of the hospital rebuild to her. Usually, it worked well and was balanced. But if she was awkward and demanding the hospital be constructed in a way that wasn't feasible then he was prepared to pull rank if required.

'No, she isn't insisting that. She's tough and she knows what she wants, but she also has a good head on her shoulders and she isn't difficult to work with. She's clearly a skilled doctor, too.'

Fitz eyed his old friend shrewdly.

'She's also attractive, isn't she?' he noted wryly. 'I'd forgotten you were one for the females.'

'Only single commissioned females. Usually back home but certainly never in a combat zone,' Carl pointed out with a sheepish grin. 'I'm always discreet and I don't contravene the rules. I *never* dip into the non-commissioned officers pool. I value my career, thanks. Besides, there's no need for us all to be complete monks like you.'

He'd either forgotten about Janine, or deliberately wasn't mentioning her. Janine's father—back then a colonel, now a general—had no doubt made sure of that.

Lost in his own thoughts, Fitz was completely unprepared when he rounded the corner.

Just Elle?

Shock stole over him, taking his breath and leaving him feeling physically winded. She might as well have snatched that perfectly ordered deck of cards he'd imagined earlier out of his hands and hurled them high into the cloudless sky. Now some were fluttering in the breeze while others plummeted, ominously, to land face down in the dust.

Even putting one foot in front of the other suddenly seemed like a mammoth feat.

She couldn't be out here. The woman, the one-night stand he was already struggling to put behind him. Surely it was impossible now?

And yet he *had* to put that night behind him. *Especially now.*

Oblivious, Carl stepped forward and made the formal introductions.

'Colonel Fitzwilliam, this is the medical CO, Colonel Duggan. And one of the majors under his command, Major Caplin.'

'Fitz,' he clarified, holding his hand out to his counterpart, focussing on the older man. But the only person he could see, could focus on, was Elle.

'Phil,' Colonel Duggan responded immediately.

A solid handshake and warm greeting confirmed Carl's assessment of the guy as a secure CO. It was all Fitz could do to keep his eyes from sliding to the side.

But even in his peripheral vision he could see how remarkably stiff Elle was, blood draining from her face to leave two pinched high spots. He got the sense that if she'd been allowed to salute in the field, she would have. Evidently she was as thrown as he was, yet Fitz was helpless against the inexplicable sense of anger welling inside him.

He prided himself on his focus, his drive, his steadiness. And Elle threatened all that. She made him feel unbalanced. He *allowed* her to unsettle him and he didn't know who he was more furious with.

He was only grateful that army protocol gave him some semblance of structure that he might otherwise have felt was lacking.

'Major.'

'Colonel.' She thrust out her hand to take his with no acknowledgement in her expression.

Yet there was no doubting the spark that arced between them as their hands made contact, the hitch in her breath as it grew shallow, the way his chest pounded. Things that only the two of them would notice, but which proved the attraction from that night hadn't dimmed in any way.

If anything, it seemed to have increased.

He had to act. Before she did something stupid like pretend they'd never met. They might not be about to flaunt the exact circumstances of their encounter—that wasn't anyone else's business but their own—but neither did it mean it was anything they should need to hide.

Ignoring the voice in his head challenging why he *really* didn't like the idea of going along with it—the inexplicable sense of possession—Fitz smothered his irrational fury and dipped his head.

'We've already met. Once. Isn't that right, Major?'

She managed a murmur of agreement but he had already turned back to his counterpart. As though that would somehow ground him, as though the more professional he could keep it, the less he could pretend he was affected by her. Until he'd managed to control his frustration.

'Major Howes informs me there's already been a development. An aquifer that wasn't previously identified?'

'That's right,' Colonel Duggan agreed. 'Directly beneath the intended location for the medical gas supply system.'

'But it shouldn't be too much of an issue.' Fitz frowned. 'We can bridge over it or close it in.'

The medical colonel held a hand up with a smile.

'Let me stop you there, Fitz. Major Caplin here has experience in hospital construction so it's better if she runs you through her concerns. My expertise is as a vascular surgeon and I'm mainly based at the field hospital back in Razorwire, so Major Caplin essentially has administrative and operational command of this hospital. Of course, she keeps me updated in her daily sit-rep so I'm always happy to discuss it with you, but it might be easier to speak to the major in the first instance.'

Just what he didn't need.

'Not a problem, Phil.'

'Then, if you'll excuse me, I've got a teaching operation scheduled in about half an hour. I'll send someone to let you know when I'm out and we can go through anything.'

'Appreciate it,' Fitz confirmed, as the man checked with Elle if she needed anything else.

He couldn't blame the man, it was exactly what he would have done. In fact, hadn't he left his second-in-command liaising with brigade back at Razorwire in his absence? Furthermore, Carl was right, Colonel Duggan looked like he would be good to work with. The man was secure enough to acknowledge when it was advantageous to hand off to his more experienced major, but still remain directly responsible.

If only that major wasn't Major Caplin, wasn't Elle. Not that he didn't respect her or admire her—far from it. But he couldn't imagine working with someone whose laugh still jingled in his head and whose body he could taste on his tongue if he closed his eyes.

'Nice to meet you, Colonel,' Colonel Duggan signed off cheerily, and Fitz forced himself back to reality with a pleasant smile.

'Likewise.'

With the medical CO gone, that left him and Carl. And Elle. With Carl gazing at her with respect and a hint of lust, which only an old friend like Fitz himself would have recognised.

Something shot through him. Something which—if he hadn't known better—he might have mistaken for a touch of jealousy and...possession?

But he did know better.

He knew because he'd sworn, after Janine, that he'd never allow himself to blur the lines between personal and professional again. And now that Elle was out here, with him, in this environment, he *had* to stop remembering that night.

He liked things to be distinct, clear, compartmentalised. It avoided messiness.

He didn't date army colleagues. Oh, there was no rule against him and Elle getting together that night, but it was a line he didn't like to cross in his own mind. Just as he didn't *do* long-term relationships.

He wasn't built for them. He was too selfish. Too thoughtless. Too damaged.

The kind of man who'd been too busy celebrating his eighteenth with his mates to take the time out to listen to his voicemail. For the sake of thirty seconds, he'd have heard his mother's desperate, frightened message. Their deaths were on his hands.

The one time he'd thought he could be a better person, he'd thought he could be there for Janine the way he never had been for his family, he'd failed again. The loss of their unborn baby, another death on his conscience.

He couldn't run from it. It was in his DNA.

A good soldier. A good leader.

A destructive family man.

One-night stands and temporary relationships with women who never knew the military side of him meant he never had to deal with complications when they ended. He'd been meticulous about keeping the two sides of his life distinct from each other.

And now here he was. Acutely aware of the woman standing stiffly beside him. A woman who had made him feel the most relaxed and comfortable that he'd been in a long, long time. That night with her he'd actually felt a carefree happiness.

But wanting something more with Elle now, as a fellow officer, would allow his personal life to bleed into his professional one, a no-go in his mind. Or at least it *should* have been a no-go. Yet even now, as his initial shock dulled, he couldn't shake the possibility. As if Elle had the ability to break down whatever barriers he tried to erect between them.

He'd never felt so off-kilter. Elle had sneaked under his skin when he hadn't noticed and all he could think of was how she'd looked in his arms, how she'd tasted when he'd kissed her, and how she'd sounded when he'd made her come apart time and again.

He was hardly surprised when Elle jumped straight in with a determinedly professional expression. And then her eyes locked with his and there was no doubting that she was as unsettled as he was. Both of them striving to remain soldier-like, both of them unable to help homing in on each other as though it was just the two of them in the whole world.

'I understand from Major Howes that the soil on either

side of the aquifer is hard and competent, so it might be possible to bridge it. However, he did mention he wanted to get advice from an aquifer specialist. I didn't know that was you, *sir.*'

Fitz doubted Carl would hear anything but polite respect in her tone. But, then, Carl hadn't got to know the major quite as intimately as he himself had.

'Major Howes is right. It is possible to bridge some aquifers, but I'd need to study this one before I could confirm it in this case. I don't know what the pressure is in the aquifer, and even if the soil either side is hard and competent, if it's made up of over-consolidated silt it could wash away if we have to drive any piles into the ground.'

'He mentioned basal uplift?'

Why wasn't he surprised that Elle had absorbed every bit of information Carl must have given her? And, just like when they'd pulled together so harmoniously back at the bar with the young lad and his sister, Fitz found himself slipping easily back into working with her. Setting aside their unsettled history for the moment.

'That can happen if we excavate the water and soil from on top of the aquifer—which is currently keeping it contained—and the pressure within the aquifer itself bursts, swamping this entire site. That could also happen even if we don't have a blow-out but simply pierce the aquifer.'

'That sounds like a risk we don't want.' She frowned.

'Only if we don't allow for it. We can drill a series of relief wells, even back-up relief wells, and instal pumps to get some draw-down and relieve the pressure. We can also spread the footings of the buildings to avoid piles piercing the aquifer.'

'And what if we moved the plant room altogether, how feasible is that?'

'It depends how extensive the aquifer is. Major Howes and I have already agreed this is a priority discussion.'

'If at all possible, I'd like to consider moving to the other side of the site, to avoid any risk of contaminating the aquifer altogether,' Elle stated firmly. 'In this area the population mainly use groundwater, either from foothill infiltration or from riverbed exfiltration, with little chance of rainwater recharge. And with the population in this region growing exponentially, there is increasing over-exploitation of the scarce water resources.'

He could see exactly where she was heading.

'So you want to tap into this aquifer for the local communities. Perhaps a series of clean water wells?'

'I'm not a ground surveyor like you are, and I certainly don't know anything about aquifers to speak of, but I would think this offers a significant clean water supply to the community, especially when cholera and other water-borne diseases are so prevalent out here. Do you agree, Colonel?'

'I do,' he mused, looking over her shoulder at the basic geological plans Carl had already put together. 'But if you're moving across the site, it will mean redesigning your hospital layout. The main hospital itself, as damaged as it has been over the last decade, is still the best medical resource the local population have.'

The familiar citrusy scent powered into him before he realised it, tightening his chest and stealing his breath away.

'So we need to minimise the impact on them and make as few alterations as possible. Yes, Colonel,' Elle bit out, stiffening abruptly.

Their sudden proximity clearly affected her just as much as it did him. Fitz jerked around to Carl, as much to remind himself of his Major's presence as anything else.

'Any ideas, Major Howes?'

'Working on it, sir.' Carl stepped forward, apparently unaware of the tension Fitz felt was practically sparking between himself and Elle. 'The plant room houses the heat, ventilation and air-conditioning units.'

Fitz made a quick assessment.

'Which means also moving the generators in the next-door unit since they'll be relying on the HVAC plant room to keep them cool, especially in these temperatures.'

'What about moving the medical gas supply system here?' Elle tapped another location on the map, and he stepped close again, so close her fingers accidentally brushed his and his gut kicked in response even as she snatched her hand away.

'The HVAC could go here—' the faint, almost imperceptible quiver in her voice betrayed her '—and the generators could go there.'

'What's on that side of the wall?'

'The ICU.'

'Then no. And, anyway, I'd like the generator-housing unit to have bigger blast walls if we're having to move them closer to the hospital.' Fitz scanned the ground. 'Can we take a walk around? I've studied the plans back at Razorwire, and I had a good aerial view coming in, but I want to see it for myself.'

'Colonel.' Elle and Carl acquiesced simultaneously.

He was used to it, a first-name basis in private but generally formal in public, yet this time it particularly reminded him of how well he and Elle had worked together before. How effortlessly they'd slipped into working together now. How easy she made it.

At every turn she challenged his fears of complications and messiness. She made him wonder whether he could have more after all. More time with her. More *of* her.

The possibility intrigued him.

And the distraction annoyed him.

Forcing himself to focus on the plans in front of him as well as the geography of the site, Fitz tried to forget that Elle was suddenly *here*, and concentrated on mapping it all in his head. It was a sixty-bed hospital, with electricity intermittent. So the back-up generators were vital, as was good access from the road to fuel them. He moved around the site thoughtfully, finally coming back to a possibility in his mind.

'So the proposed ORs were to have been on the other side of this wall?'

'Yes.' Elle nodded. 'On each side of the corridor.'

Fitz consulted the design then glanced over the other end of the site, warming to his work as he always did, and forgetting for a moment that he and Elle had any issues between them.

'So, hypothetically, if we extended that part of the facility to house them on the other side, we'd have to move the recovery areas too?'

'Yes. And building room is tighter on this side so, as you said, we'd have to either create more space between the hospital and the proposed location for the generators, or build thicker blast walls.'

'It could work,' Fitz mused. 'I need to look into it in more detail and understand how your internal layout for the hospital works.'

He'd built plenty of bridges, railheads, electricity plants and more in his time, not to mention demolished or blown up a fair few buildings. But this was the first hospital he'd built.

'I admire your frankness, Colonel.' Elle beamed unexpectedly when he told her as much, and a thousand explosions went off in Fitz's chest, like an unused pyrotechnics display at the end of an army year.

It was impossible not be drawn into those vivid emerald pools.

And that smile.

It was ridiculous that he'd been missing that smile so profoundly. He didn't miss smiles. He didn't miss people.

She made him feel things he'd never felt before and he couldn't afford that. The last time he'd tried to pretend that he was normal, that he wasn't missing fundamental pieces of a human being, he'd ended up causing immeasurable pain. He could still recall the distraught expression on Janine's face, the pain, the hurt, the recrimination in her eyes when she'd screamed at him that she'd have been better off never meeting him in the first place.

He was broken, and his attempts to fix himself had only ever caused more pain to those around him.

He was only here for a few days. How hard could it be to keep himself at arm's length from Elle? To refuse to allow himself to give into temptation and seek her out as though that night had been more than it had been?

'Colonel.' Carl's voice interrupted his thoughts. 'The briefing you scheduled is due to start in forty minutes.'

Had they been that long walking around the place?

'Right.' He jerked his head, forcing himself to focus. 'Thank you, Major.'

'If you don't need me here, I'll go and start setting up, sir.'

'That'll be fine,' Fitz confirmed smoothly, watching Elle twist her hands in discomfort.

This was the moment to put into practice what he'd been thinking. To keep himself at arm's length. To walk away. To let Elle walk away.

He didn't move.

Neither did Elle.

They both knew what was coming. It was inevitable. And unavoidable. They'd fallen into working together with incredible ease but they couldn't ignore their shared night. And, worryingly, he found he didn't want to. So much for it being a one-night stand; he needed to hear her talk about it, to know that she found it as unforgettable as he did. Which only made him all the more irritable.

Fitz waited until Carl had rounded the corner before he began speaking.

'You told me you weren't military.'

'No, I didn't.' She shook her head miserably. 'I told you I was a doctor, I omitted to say I was an army trauma doctor.'

'Yet you knew I was a colonel in the army.'

What was wrong with him that he was blaming her?

It was as though the more frustrated he felt at his own inability to walk away from her, the angrier he felt, and he turned it onto her in some misplaced effort to keep his distance. To stop himself from hauling her into his arms and kissing her senseless. Which, at this instant, was the only thing he ached to do.

Ached.

He'd never wanted anyone like this. Never. It made no damned sense.

'Yes, but I didn't think it would matter.' She swallowed hard. 'Listen, I understand this isn't the most ideal development to our...one-night stand.'

His whole body balked at the sound of the words on her lips. It was *exactly* what that night had been and yet, ludicrously, it seemed a wholly inadequate description.

The ache became a crushing need, the likes of which he'd never experienced.

'*Not the most ideal development* hardly even begins to describe what this is, wouldn't you agree?'

In his effort to stay distant his voice sounded harsher, uglier than he'd like, and she jerked her head up in shock. But he was fighting to make sense of the maelstrom in his head. In his chest. He suspected that if he didn't push her away he might end up kissing her. And he could hardly do that.

'Not ideal, no,' she agreed slowly, tightly. 'But you're acting like it's a scourge on you or something. It isn't. We haven't contravened a single rule. We're both commissioned officers and you aren't my boss. There's no rule against us having slept together.'

'Not here,' he silenced her, glancing hastily around, his tone even more brusque than the jerk of his head.

There was no one about but, still, it didn't hurt to be careful. He strode angrily back to the set of buildings, barely pausing to throw a final command over his shoulder.

'My office.'

CHAPTER SEVEN

THERE WAS NO mistaking the barely restrained fury in his glower. Wordlessly she followed him to the main building, her heart detonating in her chest.

Guilt poured through her.

Wait, was he somehow blaming her for the unforesee-able turn of events?

Disappointment crashed over her, almost painful as it burned within her chest and swamped out everything else. All of the fantasies she'd so absurdly cradled this past week, all of her memories, were torn down in a single instant.

What a fool she was, building him up in her head into a perfect, unrealistic image of a man who had shown her such generosity and selflessness that night together, fault-lessly anticipating her needs, and then exceeding them, over and over again.

In that one night he'd restored her confidence in her-self as a desirable woman. A confidence which had been quashed for so many years—if she'd ever really had it at all. She supposed, whatever happened from here, she should hold onto that memory and be grateful to him for at least such a gift.

Instead, faced with this furious side of Fitz, she wished that night really *had* been all she had. At least that memory would have remained intact. Unblemished by this moment.

Lost in her thoughts, she barely noticed when he stopped

without warning, and she ran into the back of him before she could stop herself.

'My office?' he demanded, this time less of an order and more of a question.

He was clearly irritable that he didn't yet know his way around and, for some reason, that made her feel a little more in control of her skittering emotions.

Yes, all right, perhaps she should have told him she was an army doctor, but how could she possibly have known that Fitz would be the commanding officer of the squadron sent to work alongside a unit from the field hospital? Even so, indignation followed the guilt. He had no right to be so arrogant, as though sleeping with her was a black mark on his reputation.

Still, Elle schooled her thoughts, and her voice, determined not to let him see how much he affected her until she'd worked out exactly what it was she was going to say. For now, she'd resume a professional façade and get him back to his office, and then she'd get as far away from him as was possible in this confined place and try to regroup.

'Your office is this way, *Colonel*,' she emphasised.

Carefully, she manoeuvred past him and strode through the rabbit warren of old, partially damaged corridors, all of which looked the same, with none of her usual tour guide fun. Privately she decided she might even get a tiny, perverse kick out of seeing him get lost for the first couple of days. Finally, she stopped outside a nondescript door.

'Your office, Colonel. The stairs are just there.' She waved to the recess behind her. 'And your sleeping quarters are first floor up and the third door down. Two doors down from mine. Although *sleeping quarters* makes them sound a lot grander than the bare concrete cell-like boxes which they actually are. This place is so rundown there isn't a single one that hasn't fallen into disrepair.'

At least, being a colonel, he had a room to himself while she shared with two other female majors, neither of whom were medical and who she didn't know well enough to relax around.

Despite her admonishments to herself it seemed that the wicked streak Fitz had revealed in her had chosen this moment to reassert itself. Even as a delicious memory rippled through her, Elle mentally kicked herself for allowing Fitz to see precisely how he'd inveigled his way into her subconscious.

'Come in and close the door behind you,' he ordered, heading straight into his office and moving to the ancient, steel-framed industrial desk in the far corner. 'I don't want anyone overhearing our conversation.'

His brittle tone sliced through her, so cold it wounded Elle far more than any words could have done. She jutted her chin out, determined not to let herself lose what little ground she'd made on her self-confidence.

'Is there any need for conversation, *Colonel*?' she emphasised again. 'I think we should just forget that night ever happened. It's only for a couple of days, surely, while you check on your squadron out here, and then you'll be back in Razorwire?'

'Is that why you thought pretending we'd never met was such a bright idea, *Elle*?'

The emphasis of her name made it clear he intended to have this out with her. There was little point in continuing any charade. She exhaled a little shakily.

'I thought it was the easiest solution. I've never been in this situation before.'

'Neither have I,' he bit out. 'But I know that other officers saw us together that night. If we stick as close to the truth as possible then we can't get caught out with people assuming there must have been more to it than there was.'

She couldn't help that his words stung a little, as though the idea that it could have been more was preposterous. But at least the surprise admission that he hadn't been in this

situation before made her feel a little better. So there wasn't
a line of female officers he'd also slept with.

'Fitz, is there really any need for this conversation? I
think we both know what you're going to say.'

'Is that so? And what would that be?'

Elle pursed her lips. It was what they'd both agreed that
night in the hotel.

Yet somehow it didn't make it any easier.

'That we agreed what we had was a…a one-night stand.
That neither of us could have anticipated we'd end up work
colleagues.'

'Couldn't we?' he cut in abruptly. The chillness in his
tone seeped through to her bones despite the forty-degree
heat.

Elle tightened her arms around her body, as though to
offer herself support.

'Say again?'

'Did you really have no idea who I was? I told you I was
a colonel in the Royal Engineers and that we were deploying. Razorwire was an obvious possibility, you must have
put two and two together.'

'Actually,' Elle shocked herself by interrupting haugh-
tily, 'you originally said you and your buddies were on a
leaving do, and it was only after I challenged you about the
army-issue trousers you gave that lad after he had that seizure that you told me you were a colonel, otherwise I doubt
you would have said a word. And you certainly never mentioned you were Royal Engineers. If you're going to berate
me then you should at least be accurate.'

She didn't quite recognise the look that danced over his
striking features. And then it was gone and he was back to
chastising her.

'Fine, then for the sake of *accuracy*,' he underscored, his
jaw locked in disapproval, 'you still deliberately concealed
the fact that you were an army doctor. Nor, when I told you

I was being deployed, did you admit that you were in the middle of your own deployment.'

Elle sucked in a sharp breath. When he put it that way it *did* look bad, but then she already knew that, and while she was prepared to hold her hands up to some of it, she'd be damned if she was going to take the blame for the part for which she was actually innocent.

'You're right. I knew you were an army colonel and I knew you were leaving on a tour of duty, but I didn't say anything. For that, I'm sorry. In my defence, though, how could I possibly have guessed we'd end up in the same place? It isn't like I knew *where* you deploying to. It could have been different areas, different regions, even different countries.'

'Razorwire's a big camp. Plenty of soldiers end up there, you knew it was a possibility,' he bit out, his glare hurled at her with all the pinpoint accuracy of a top athlete throwing a javelin.

Rooted in place, Elle had no choice but to stand her ground, but she knew she was clinging to very shaky distinctions. Still, they were all she had.

'But we aren't actually *at* Razorwire, are we? I couldn't have foreseen that.'

'You lied to me.'

'No,' she began, then stopped abruptly. 'Maybe.'

Elle exhaled heavily, the fight unexpectedly sucked out of her. He was right. She *had* lied to him. Not for the reasons he assumed, but if they were to work efficiently together for the remainder of her tour, then they were going to need some kind of trust.

And he certainly didn't trust her right now.

'Fitz, I honestly didn't intend to deceive you but I really didn't want to talk *green*, or compare tours, or analyse postings. I didn't want to be Major Gabriella Caplin, heck, I didn't even want to be Elle Caplin that night. Like I told you, I'd just left my ex-fiancé who'd been cheating on me and I wanted one night—just one—where I did something a little crazy and out of character. Something Major Caplin would *never* have done.'

The silence was so thick, so cloying that Elle felt like she was suffocating.

'But, at the risk of repeating myself, you're acting as though it's a big deal when it doesn't have to be. We were perfectly entitled to sleep with each other and even now there's no conflict of interest.'

'I'm a colonel,' he bit out, for the first time appearing less sure of himself.

It might be only the merest hint of a chink in his impermeable armour but Elle wasn't about to let that stop her.

'But you're not *my* colonel,' she pointed out. 'You're not *my* CO. Colonel Duggan is. So a relationship between you and me isn't against the rules, but of course you already know that. So what's this about, Fitz?'

She eyed him speculatively. The look of fury in his black eyes didn't make any sense. Quickly, she ran through anything she might be missing.

'Colonel Duggan has administrative and operational command for the running of this hospital, and therefore *I* do when he leaves the site. You have operational command for the construction of the hospital, and therefore Major Howes does when you're not here. You can't re-task me, or tell me how to do my job. And it's not even a combat environment—we're on a peacetime hearts-and-minds mission, so it isn't as though things could suddenly get hostile.'

'It crosses a line,' he ground out.

'Which line?' She threw up her hands, exasperated.

And then an almost paralysing nausea snaked through her mind. She could barely bring herself to ask the question, but she knew she had to.

'Unless you're not single.' The words tasted acrid on her tongue. 'If you're married then it would have crossed a line, it would have contravened army rules.'

'Of course I'm not married,' he bit out instantly.

Elle grabbed the back of the chair, relief making her knees wobble. After what Stevie had done, she couldn't have endured to be the other woman herself. She couldn't have withstood the idea that Fitz had made her that person.

'So which line?' she repeated shakily.

His pulse leapt beneath his jaw. Evidence, not that she needed it, of his irritation. But she couldn't step back; he'd started this personal attack and now she had to know.

'*My* line,' he spat out, at length.

She had no idea whether his disgust was at her or himself.

'I have my professional life and I have my personal one, and I don't blur the lines between the two.'

Why not?

The question lingered. It was on the very tip of her tongue. Yet she couldn't bring herself to ask it. He would fob her off and she didn't want him to do that. He was clearly one of those soldiers who left his civvy life at the door of the barracks and put on his colonel-soldier one and she could understand that, it was usually how she liked to be on operations, especially if she was going into a combat environment. But out here, on this particular mission, things were more relaxed and Fitz didn't need to be quite so rigid. He wasn't protecting anyone.

Except, perhaps, himself.

Should she leave? Stay? She glanced at Fitz, hoping for some kind of response but he was only watching her. Judging her. For not being able to draw a line the way he could.

She bristled and turned to the door, faltered, then stepped back to his desk.

'You have no right to judge me, you don't even know me.'

'I'm not judging you,' he argued. 'I'm trying to protect you.'

'From whom?' she exclaimed. 'From you?'

The bleak look in his eyes caught her off guard. A haunted look that clawed at her insides.

'Fitz, why on earth would you think I need protection from you?'

He shook his head, his lips pulled into a thin line as though he didn't intend to answer. And then he spoke.

'You're bright and vibrant and happy. And I'll destroy it. It's who I am.'

Incredulity spread through her. That was so far removed from the man she'd met that night.

'Why on earth would you say that?'

He shook his head as though he didn't want to say any more but the words kept coming.

'Because I've done it before. Because I'm my father's son.'

This was about the car crash, she realised with a rush, remembering what Fitz had told her that night. Now she realised he felt guilty over his mother's death. Whether he realised it or not, he was likely punishing himself for still being alive while his mother and sister were gone.

She should have seen it earlier, she should have recognised it. *Guilt.* She knew it only too well. Only in her case it was guilt and gratitude. Without Stevie she doubted she would ever have realised her dream of becoming a doctor; she simply couldn't have afforded the university course. It was the reason she'd ignored the little signs that Stevie had been cheating on her for a long time. She'd told herself that it wasn't true, and she'd allowed herself to believe it, until that night she'd said the words out loud to Fitz and realised how unlikely they sounded.

And she couldn't shake the suspicion that it was some form of guilt that made Fitz shut people out, deny himself happiness. As though, somehow, he didn't deserve it.

She stepped towards him, shaking her head gently.

'Your father was a drunk. You were a seventeen-year-old kid. What happened to your mother and sister wasn't your fault.'

He laughed—a humourless bark that splintered inside her.

'You have no idea what was or wasn't my fault.'

'So tell me,' she encouraged softly.

She could actually see the battle raging inside him, etched into every chiselled groove of his face. Some part of Fitz wanted to tell her, she was sure of it. But he was fighting it and she didn't know why.

Still, she forced herself to wrinkle her nose at him coolly. As though her every fantasy since last week hadn't involved Fitz doing deliciously wicked things to her.

And then he said the words she least wanted to hear and it felt as though her heart was shattering. Shredded by shrapnel as if it had been caught in a homemade IED.

'After all, it was just sex, right?'

The root of the pain was so deep she couldn't have pinpointed it if she tried. It snatched her breath away and left her legs feeling weaker than those of a newborn foal.

As though it would have been no hardship to him at all to walk away from her that night. When she knew she would have never been able to resist him.

Fitz was supposed to have been a one-night stand yet somewhere along the line she'd given him the power to hurt her as much as Stevie had because they were both able to dismiss her as inconsequential.

She tried to steel herself, desperately trying not to show Fitz how much that throwaway line had hurt her. But she wasn't fast enough, and she felt too raw.

'God, how do you guys *do* that?' she demanded, her voice little more than a strained whisper.

'Elle…'

He took a step towards her but she backed up, shaking her head, unable to get the words out. Unable to process the inexplicable pain.

This had to be about Stevie. It couldn't be about Fitz, that didn't make sense, he had been just a one-night stand. *Stevie* was the one who had hurt her, betrayed her, made her feel worse than nothing. She was just transferring to Fitz because he was here and her ex wasn't.

Right?

Damn Stevie.

She hated him for making her feel like she somehow wasn't enough. Not sexy enough, not available enough, just not enough. And she hated herself for not being able to act cool and nonchalant. For letting Fitz see how vulnerable she still was. She tried to fight back, to claw back some measure of dignity.

'Don't think this is about you,' she choked out between the unattractive barks of bitter laughter.

'I know that.'

She wasn't prepared for the bleakness, the hollowness of his response. As though he really believed her. As though he hadn't for one minute considered the impact he'd made on her.

Caught up in the emotions roiling inside her, she let her neck fall back to stare at the rough-textured grey concrete ceiling and exhaled hard, her head struggling to make sense of it.

This was a side to Fitz she knew for a fact that no one else saw. His reputation preceded him. A fearsome soldier, an inspiring leader, a caring commander. They didn't know the internal war he waged. Hadn't he told her things that he'd said he'd never told anyone else?

Surely that had to count for something?

'But you still can't treat me like the enemy,' she said tentatively. 'I didn't set out to deceive you.'

There had been something between them that first night. A connection that had gone beyond simple attraction, or sex, though both had helped. They'd both confided in each other, and whether it was the events of that evening, the fact that they'd never expected to meet again, or just the fact that her guard had been lowered and he'd been there, Elle couldn't be sure. But they'd opened themselves up to each other and they couldn't just slam those doors shut now because it was no longer convenient.

'I know that too.' He pulled himself up taller, as though regrouping. 'And I know you're not the enemy. I didn't mean to hurt you with what I said. For what it's worth, it isn't personal. I just don't like to have a crossover between my professional life and my private one.'

'What you mean is that you don't like people knowing too much about you, and certainly not the things you told me that night,' she pushed bravely.

It was how she'd intended that night to go, but deep down she suspected it was that shared vulnerability that had allowed her to sleep with him in the first place. She couldn't have gone through it with anyone else but Fitz. It hadn't just been about the sex, as incredible as that had undeniably been, it had been about the way Fitz had made her feel about herself. After Stevie's betrayal had left her feeling so worthless, Fitz had made her feel good about herself again, and he'd made her laugh out loud.

When was the last time Stevie had made her laugh?

'Maybe,' he answered carefully.

'But I know because you told me, and that unsettles you, doesn't it?'

'Elle…' His low voice held a warning, but some reckless facet of her personality, the one that Fitz himself had been the one to awaken, was taking over her.

'Is it because I make it harder for you to take off your *Fitz* head and put on your CO head?' She was proud of herself for keeping the shake out of her voice. 'Or is it because you're still attracted to me?'

Who was this daring, challenging person? She wanted to think this new, bolder side of herself was a reaction to Stevie. Yet somehow it was less about her ex-fiancé and more about Fitz, the man who had made her feel as though he had her back if she needed him, without eroding her own sense of control or undermining her capability.

Elle snapped her head back to see Fitz had advanced on her, closing the gap between them, and for a moment she wondered if he was about to throw her out of his office.

'I think you know the answer to that one.' Fitz's voice rumbled right through her, down to her very core.

Elle couldn't answer. He was close, so close she could breathe in that all-too-familiar woodsy scent. He was right, she still wanted him as much as she had that night.

Fitz had made her feel wicked and wanton, and all woman. And suddenly Elle wanted to experience that again. If only once more. She tried telling herself it was a fantasy that would never happen, but instead she opened her mouth again. Breathy and seductive and nothing like her usual self.

'I do. So what are we going to do about it?'

CHAPTER EIGHT

HE SHOULD STOP THIS.

He *had* to stop this.

He wanted to pull away but he couldn't, he was rooted to the very spot. Her husky, seductive tone scraped inside him, through him, along his very sex.

It was why he'd closed the gap between them in a move that was infinitely more dangerous than he'd thought. He was drawn to her like a planet to the sun, just as he'd been that night. But it was an illusion. He'd been plagued by ghosts that night, the anniversary of his mother's death, and he'd been looking for something, anything to fill that void and help him stuff back the pain. If it hadn't been Elle, it would have been someone else. The connection they felt wasn't real.

And yet, however many times he told himself that, Elle was all too real.

Which had been part of the magic of that night.

'You were going to leave me your phone number the next morning,' she breathed, playing it like it was her trump card. Which, he supposed, it was. 'I know you wrote it on the hotel notepad before throwing it in the bin.'

He couldn't answer. There was no response that wouldn't confirm everything she already thought. That one night hadn't been enough.

'It was a mistake. That night was all we could have.'

'So tell me to stop,' she whispered. 'And I'll walk out of here and we won't ever speak of it again, if that's what you want.'

He couldn't even bring himself to open his mouth. The way she was staring at him now, so intently, was infinitely better than the way she'd been watching him a few moments earlier. With such an expression of hurt clouding her lovely features that he felt like a complete coward. He hadn't felt that way since Janine's father had ordered him to get out of their house and never return—and he'd been only too happy to oblige.

That was why he didn't get involved. He let people down, he betrayed them. He hurt people. One look back on his past proved it.

He didn't need Elle as further evidence.

And then he'd given himself away and she'd realised it was all a show, she'd seen exactly how rattled he was.

He'd never been rattled before Elle had come along.

The relief on her face had fired everything back up inside him. Seeing how much it mattered to her, that their one-night stand hadn't been meaningless.

But that didn't mean it was *meaningful* either, and that was the problem. He couldn't offer her a future. Even if he wanted to, he lacked the ability; it wasn't the kind of man he could ever be.

'What do you want from me, Elle?' he rasped.

He didn't know whether he was challenging her because if she couldn't say the words then it gave them an out, or because he so urgently wanted to hear them from her lips.

She swallowed.

'One more night.'

One more night. Not a relationship. Not a future. It seemed like such a reasonable demand, and one his whole being ached to consent to.

He'd never wanted any woman the way he'd wanted her from the moment he'd seen that damned thumb-lock. He'd never felt so out of control. His entire career had been built on adhering to rigid rules, whether military or his own. Now he couldn't seem to find a valid reason for either.

But he had to. He had to end this now.

He didn't move.

A slow smile toyed with the corners of her mouth, a game-changer smile, and he knew he'd given too much away. With a deep breath she crossed the room and locked the door, ironically one of the few things in this place still to work. Then, swinging back to face him, she advanced, hesitantly at first.

And then she was standing in front of him, her breathing as ragged and shallow as his felt. They stood, motionless, watching each other for the longest time. Finally, she lifted her hand and placed it on his chest, over his heart. He felt a droplet of emotion swelling inside, and it plinked onto the frozen glacier of his heart. But he knew only too well that the icy block was so big, so compact it would take a river of warm water and more years than he had on this earth to melt it.

And, still, a part of him actually longed to let her try. To see if Elle could be the one person to help him heal the pain of how he'd let his mother and sister die. How he'd let Janine think he didn't care about her, or about their unborn baby before it, too, had been lost. He was selfish, just like his father. He *had* to push Elle away, for her own protection.

He grasped at the only life raft he could see.

'Careful, Major.'

She stopped, blinked. Then shook it off.

'Oh, no, Fitz, that's not fair.' She almost managed to disguise the quiver in her tone, but he was attuned to her. 'You don't get to pick and choose when to follow the rules here. I was ready to show you to your office and walk away, to leave things on a professional footing, on a military footing. But *you* ordered me to come in and *you* made things personal when you brought up our intimate past. You made this about Elle and Fitz, woman and man, not Major and Colonel. So right now you don't get to pull rank like that. If you don't want this then you tell me to stop as Elle. Don't use excuses.'

The air practically crackled around them, tension twisting his insides as the blood pumped around his body. She was unmistakeably determined to stand her ground. So it turned out that life raft was actually an old naval mine.

She was no closer and yet he felt she was all around him. She was all he could see, all he could hear, all he could smell. The more he resisted, the softer she seemed to make her tone. Not harsh, or in his face, but the most feminine of challenges tumbled out of her tempting lips. She didn't have to say the words. He knew it was on him. He could turn around and walk away.

But he didn't. She was so close he could almost taste her.

'Even if I kiss you, it won't change anything.'

'So you say.'

She lifted her other hand. Both palms were flat on his chest and he felt another rush of intoxicating need.

He dipped his head, stopping millimetres before making contact. So close her breath rippled along his cheek.

She tilted her head up a fraction further, angling it perfectly without making contract. A silent power play, but instead of claiming it for themselves they were each offering it to the other.

'Last chance,' she whispered.

He had to push her away now.

Instead, he sneaked one hand around her waist, hauling her to him. Then he dipped his head and claimed her mouth with his, revelling in the sensations that cascaded over him at her touch, her feel, her taste. As if he'd been stranded in the barren wasteland outside for far, far too long, and she was his oasis.

She tasted every bit as heady as he recalled, her body fitting to his like she was made for him, her teeth grazing his bottom lip with the lightest of touches, her soft sighs sending his willpower scattering.

With a low groan, Fitz angled his head, deepening her kiss to something much more urgent and demanding, revelling in the way her lips parted for him, and the soft sound that came from somewhere in the back of her throat. He forgot that he was meant to be warning her to safeguard herself. He forgot that he would inevitably hurt her as his father had hurt those around him.

He forgot everything. He simply indulged. For what seemed like an eternity, his mouth slid over hers. When he pushed, she pushed back. When he held back, Elle sought him. He trailed kisses down her jaw, her collarbone and to the hollow at the base of her neck. Her shivers of pleasure stoked his need. And each time he returned to those plump, pink lips, her mouth reached for his and her tongue met his in the same sinfully sinuous dance.

As he gave himself up to the sensations, as each kiss from Elle threatened to undermine every defence he'd spent years putting in place, the plink of those warm droplets on his ice-block heart grew more insistent.

Before he could help himself, he'd released the curtain of reds and golds from its military bun, inhaling its familiar fresh, floral scent as his hands buried themselves in its luxuriant depths. He could recall exactly how it had felt brushing over his naked skin that night and his body tightened.

She felt it instantly; he could feel the sweet uplift of her smile against his lips, and then she rocked against him.

'Gabriella,' he groaned, unable to make up his mind whether it was a groan or a warning growl.

And still he kissed her, sometimes gently and reverently, other times hard and greedily. As though he never wanted to stop. He didn't know when he backed her up so that she was sitting on his desk with him standing between her legs, or when his fingers crept under the hem of her tee, or when he lifted it over her head and dropped it in a puddle on the plans he was supposed to be going through.

He just knew his hands were sweeping over velvet skin he'd been dreaming about for a week, running over her ribs and circling her body so that his thumbs were grazing the lower swell of her perfect breasts.

He needed to stop. Needed to remind her—remind himself—what kind of a man he was. How he would inevitably hurt her.

'So, what now?' he managed harshly, shocked by the sheer force of his own driving desire. 'We give in to this thing between us? Here, now? Tell me, Elle, do you want it on the uneven floor or on the rusty metal desk?'

Any other woman would have fled, intimidated by the tone, let alone the words. Elle merely sparkled brighter, as though she enjoyed the push-pull of it. He couldn't work it out.

'So this is what the real Fitz looks like,' she murmured, moving her hands down his body. Though he could hear the quiver in her voice. 'Not quite as cool and utterly in control as everyone might think. I like this side of you, the side behind the mask.'

'Elle…'

'I want what you want. One more night.'

It wasn't encouraged or condoned by the army, but they both knew it happened. As long as they were utterly discreet, and, like Elle had pointed out before, they were both commissioned officers and he wasn't her boss.

He glanced at the desk. It wasn't his style. It wasn't her style. But he knew that in that instant they both wanted each other too much to care.

He *had* to put the brakes on it.

It felt as though it took every last bit of strength in his body to move his hands to her upper arms and push her away.

'I can't let this happen.' His voice actually cracked.

'I take responsibility for myself, Fitz,' she told him, her eyes glittering with desire so hot it scorched him.

'It isn't that simple.'

Raw need pulsed between them but he couldn't give in to it.

'I think it is. Why do you have such rigid rules for yourself?' she asked, the soft voice piercing through the heart of his fears better than any arrow could. 'Who are you trying to protect yourself from?'

'I'm trying to protect you.' He gritted his teeth so hard he was surprised his jaw didn't crack.

'From whom? You?' She shook her head. 'Why?'

He didn't want to answer. He'd never volunteered his story to anyone before. And yet under her coaxing the words spilled from his lips and there was nothing he could do to stop them.

'That car crash with my mother and sister was my fault.'

'I didn't think you were there.' She squinted up at him.

'Exactly. I wasn't there, but I should have been. I was too busy enjoying myself on a night out with friends. We were celebrating a week early. My mum had been a barmaid at the local pub for a few years; they treated her a bit like a manager and every time someone didn't turn up for a shift they'd call her and she'd rush over there to fill in.'

Even now he could remember just how aggrieved he'd felt, as though she was deliberately ruining their precious family time together when all she'd been doing had been trying to keep her job so the meagre income would keep the roof over their heads and some food on the table. All he'd ever thought was that it was never enough. He shook off the memories, forcing himself to carry on, to show Elle exactly what kind of man he was.

'I sometimes felt they didn't employ enough staff just because they knew they could turn to her and she'd cover it all. So from the age of about fifteen I became the babysitter. Nights out with schoolfriends were inevitably cancelled because she'd get called in and I'd end up looking after my baby sister. And I began to resent it.'

'So that night you went out?' Elle asked quietly. 'How could you have known any different?'

'Because she phoned me. Fifteen messages, each one more frantic than the last. She called me to tell me my father had found us, that he was drunk and that she'd hidden my sister in the cupboard over the stairs.'

'Fitz...'

He ignored her, determined to carry on. Fighting the overwhelming guilt and regret.

'I saw the missed calls and I turned my phone off. By the time I listened to the calls it was hours later. I raced home but of course I was far too late.'

'Fitz,' she gasped. 'That must have been... I can't imagine how that must have been. But you can't honestly blame yourself. How could you have known? You were seventeen, a kid, you couldn't have foreseen your father had found you.'

'I should have cared enough to listen. I should have taken her call, not shut it down as though she didn't deserve my time.'

'That's ridiculous,' Elle cried, but he ignored the emotions her words threatened to stir in him.

He didn't know why she insisted on seeing him in such a bold, fair light, but she had it wrong.

'You don't understand. I let them down. I wasn't there for them when they needed me. I was thoughtless, selfish, I was just like *him*.'

He practically spat the last word out in disgust, and still Elle looked at him with empathy, and care, as though she understood. As though he wasn't the self-serving young man he'd actually been. But he knew the truth. He knew he could have been there for them. He *should* have been there for them.

Just like with Janine. He should have been there for her and then she would never have lost her baby.

Their baby.

He'd tried to make himself love her. He'd told himself that if he could love her, maybe he wasn't as broken as he'd feared. But he couldn't. Janine was sweet and kind, and she'd loved him. But he'd been unable to feel the same about her. He hadn't been capable of it. He'd ended up using her. She'd been right, she'd have been better off never meeting him.

Just as Elle would be.

He opened his mouth to tell her, then stopped. What if she told him it wouldn't have made a difference? For any of them? He might actually allow himself to believe her. She was so understanding, so empathetic, so damned convincing. She looked at him as though he was a good man and he wanted so much to be the human being she saw.

He was a good leader, a good soldier. But he wasn't a good man.

Another plink and he could swear he felt the tiniest fissure race through the block of ice that surrounded his heart.

It suddenly occurred to him that if she melted it then he would have to feel again.

All that pain he'd stuffed down for so long.

Fear finally galvanised him and he found his voice, as raw and biting as it sounded.

'You don't see it, do you, Elle? It was sex. That's all it was.'

He told himself he didn't regret the flash of hurt his harshness caused in Elle's eyes. That, in the long run, this was the only way to protect her from him. But he knew he was hurting her. He knew the rejection burned her more than anything after the way her ex had already rejected her, betrayed her.

So what kind of a man was he, to play on an insecurity he knew ate away at her? And still he couldn't stop.

'I'm not the man you want me to be.' He rammed the point home before he could change his mind. 'That person is a figment of your imagination.'

'You're lying,' she whispered.

Hopeful.

Pleading.

More than anything he wanted to tell her she was right. She knew him better than she realised. Better than anyone else ever had.

Instead he told himself it was for the best. That whatever hurt she was feeling now was nothing compared to the misery he would inevitably cause her if they let anything happen between them. If he let her down, too.

So he steeled his resolve and kept heading for the door. She'd been right in the first place when she'd wanted to avoid this discussion, but he was the one who had insisted on it.

Why? Because he really had wanted to create a clear division between that night and now? Or because deep down there was a part of him that didn't want to let her slip through his fingers a second time?

As if she'd ever been his to lose.

'I don't have time for nonsense like this. I have a briefing to get to,' he threw over his shoulder, refusing to look back.

Because to do so would mean looking at Elle and if he saw her he wouldn't be able to walk out that door; he'd go straight back to her, take her in his arms and surrender to her instead.

But capitulation wasn't an option. If he didn't end it now, he feared he might end up telling her things he'd never told anyone else. Ever. He might let her into that dark corner of his soul in the hope that her brilliant light might finally make it feel less black. It would open too many old wounds.

And that would only end up laying waste to both of them.

CHAPTER NINE

'YOU SEE THE ulcer lies on the antrum of the patient's stomach?' Elle glanced at her student. 'So what would you suggest?'

'Wedge excision,' Amir said confidently. 'Closure of the consequential defect should be achieved fairly easily without significant deformation of the stomach.'

'Good.' Elle nodded. 'And if the ulcer had instead been along the lesser curvature of the stomach?'

'It would be more problematic. More prone to re-bleeding because of the rich complex of blood vessels from the left gastric artery.'

'Anything else?'

Amir paused, and she couldn't be sure whether it was the language barrier or a gap in his knowledge. Many of the local doctors here were on an extremely steep learning curve but she was continually impressed by their eagerness to soak up everything she and her team were teaching them. And having a CO like Phil, who didn't just have decades of experience as a brilliant surgeon but was also an inspiring teacher, certainly kept Elle at her best. It was a challenge she usually relished.

But not today.

For the past couple of days all she'd wanted to do was stay in her army cot, lick her wounds, and hope that everything looked a little less grim when Fitz finally left the hospital camp and headed back to Razorwire.

That, obviously, hadn't been an option. But at least she'd managed to avoid him since that awful day in his office, to give herself the chance to start thinking straight again. At first she'd vacillated between rage and mortification. Rage that he'd lifted the lid on their attraction and mortification that he'd shut her down so completely.

She dragged her mind back to the present and to Amir.

'Okay, wedge excision of gastric ulcers along the lesser curvature of the stomach is harder to do and is much more likely to result in a deformed J-shaped stomach and luminal obstruction or gastric volvulus, which is rotation of the stomach by more than one hundred and eighty degrees...'

'Yes, yes.' Amir nodded vigorously. 'Inconstant blood loss, obstruction of materials moving through the stomach, and sometimes tissue death.'

'Okay, good.' Elle smiled. 'We'll go over it again, it's something you're likely to come across often here. Right, let's see what we can do for our patient here.'

She worked carefully, talking Amir through each step, until finally she was satisfied, taking half a step back and straightening her spine.

'Did you ask your Colonel Duggan if you can continue here, or return on...what you call it, a *back-to-back* tour when this tour of yours now is over?'

Lifting her head, Elle glanced into the hopeful expression on Amir's face. Having started this tour of duty at Razorwire, once her three months here were up, two more rotations of army doctors would take over during the course of the next twelve months, and Elle had hoped to be able to return on the last one. The fact that Amir also hoped she would return spoke volumes about her teaching style and Elle couldn't help smiling proudly.

'Colonel Duggan, yes. I did chat with him while he was here, unofficially of course. He considered the possibility of me returning within the year was quite high, but there's no guarantee, of course.'

'That's wonderful news. You are so dedicated to your career, you sacrifice greatly to be a soldier doctor, yes? But it is your life, you are single-minded, and you are not needing anything else. It inspires much.'

'Thank you,' Elle managed graciously, trying not to frown. 'Right, you recall the suture technique I demonstrated yesterday? Good. Because I want you to close up now.'

Amir nodded, clearly pleased, and stepped forward, leaving Elle, her eyes still on the surgery, to wonder if she wasn't a little too single-minded.

How else to forge a career like this? Fitz must have done the same. Was that what he'd meant about not being good for her? She could hardly square the Fitz she'd met that night with the Colonel who was out here. It wasn't so much like two sides to the one man as it was two completely different men. The man from that night who had told her things about his past, about his family, had been very different from the man who had stood in front of her the other day and lied to her. She was sure of it.

Clearly Major Howes knew Fitz well from the past and still liked and respected him, and, from what little she could tell, so did the rest of the men in the troop from Fitz's regiment. And surely they should know—he was *their* commanding officer after all. He might only just be at the start of his two-year posting as their colonel but morale among them had certainly appeared boosted in the few days he'd been on site.

She couldn't shake the idea that none of them had ever seen the Fitz *she'd* met that night. Neither could she shake the idea that there had been more between them that night than either of them had realised. Enough for him to tell her things he'd never told anyone. And after the way Stevie had lied to her, she valued honesty more than ever.

Either way it was irrelevant. She shook the thought away irritably. She was never going to get the chance to find out. Fitz had made it more than clear that as much as he was still attracted to her, he wasn't interested in opening himself up to anyone. As for her, she'd obviously let herself get too emotionally involved to be any good at no-strings sex. And the wounds from her years with Stevie were still too fresh, she wasn't ready for another relationship. Not that it was even on the cards with Fitz.

So where did that leave her?

With your career, she reminded herself firmly. When all else failed, she'd always have her role as an army doctor to rely on. She drowned out the little voice that suggested that she might have liked to have known Fitz just a little better. As he'd said, he wasn't the man she'd imagined him to be.

She shrugged off her gloomy thoughts and leaned in to check Amir's sutures.

She might have nothing back home, but she had her career and hadn't that always been the most important thing to her? And right now she had command of a hospital that, partially destroyed or not, brought different cases every day.

While Royal Engineers and logistics units worked on building, rebuilding and refitting the old hospital so that some of the major international charities would send teams out over the coming years, her job was to keep the medical side running in the meantime. Local communities were desperate to be able to use the hospital again, instead of having to make the hazardous four-hour drive across the border to the next closest hospital. No one wanted to risk the drive if they could avoid it, with the unsafe roads and dangerous checkpoint crossing, not to mention the fact that, out here, it was down to the men to allow their wives or children to seek medical help, so the more accessible it was, the easier that would be.

But with so few surgeons and doctors there was no place for specialties and the experience was testing and refreshing her knowledge all the time. Elle found it both exciting and challenging, with patients ranging from babies to the elderly, and from victims who'd stepped on old, forgotten landmines to women having labour problems. In fact, the latter accounted for a huge percentage of her operations, given maternal mortality was so high out here, all of which was a far cry from the combat trauma she'd been doing in other postings over the last few years. She couldn't afford to let Fitz ruin what was otherwise a unique career opportunity for her.

What had Fitz said? That he destroyed everything? That he'd destroy her?

She was beginning to understand just how close to the mark that was.

Shaking the bleak thoughts from her head, Elle concentrated on her task of watching her student work, commenting if necessary but trying to take a step back as much as she could. Amir's work was neat and clean; he picked things up quickly but he also listened well and watched closely. He would likely be a real asset to the hospital in very little time, which was good since he'd have his work cut out for him.

Finally, he was closing up on the perforated ulcer patient.

'Nice job,' she congratulated him. 'How would you feel about heading up a mobile team on your own this time? We're due to carry out a round of measles and polio vaccinations for infants in some of the outlying communities.'

A surprised look crossed the young doctor's face, swiftly replaced by a proud one.

'I'd like that very much.'

'I'm not sure but I heard something about a sandstorm being due in the next couple of days,' one of the voluntary aid nurses interjected apologetically. 'Of course you can never be sure, and there's every chance you might get out and back before it even hits, but...'

'But you can't be too safe.' Elle flashed her a bright smile to reassure her. 'Then we'll hold back for now but pick your team and as soon as we get the all-clear you can go, Amir.'

'Thank you,' he nodded. 'I will.'

'Major?'

Elle craned her neck around as one of the designated liaison soldiers stood at the edge of the privacy screen, evidently having heard the exchange and concluding he wouldn't be disturbing them. He could have been there for any length of time, waiting patiently while they carried out the operation.

For the moment, the simple screen set-up was the only thing to separate the delivery room from the open ward. In a few months it would all look completely different and would be significantly more sterile and high-tech. For now, it was all they had.

'What is it, Corporal?' With a final check on Amir's work, Elle stepped around the screen.

'Colonel Fitzwilliam asked if you were available to go through a couple of design modifications with him and Major Howes for the power and water supplies to the hospital.'

And just like that, her heart slammed against her chest wall. He'd had the presence to include Major Howes in the message but she couldn't work out whether it was a good thing or a bad one. They would have a buffer, true, but there would be even more pressure to act normally—whatever that meant—around Fitz, and she wasn't sure she was enough of an actress to pull it off.

'We're almost done here.' Elle had no idea how the words came out, as strangled as they sounded to her ears.

The corporal, however, didn't seem to notice anything amiss.

'Ma'am.'

'Will you inform the Colonel I'll be there within the half-hour?'

'Yes, Major.'

She watched him leave and stood motionless long after the double doors had closed and stilled behind the lad. Her hands felt sticky, her heart was racing, and none of it was due to the searing temperatures inside that operating area. She'd performed two Caesareans and overseen the perforated ulcer operation pretty much back to back this morning, and yet one mention of Fitz and she was instantly flustered. It didn't bode well for their future working relationship.

Finally, almost jerkily, she managed to get her legs moving again and rounded the screen to help Amir finish up. The last suture was put in place as a strange rattling began and the ground felt like it was shaking beneath their feet.

Earthquake. Not uncommon out here and probably some distance away, but it was certainly a strong one. She grabbed hold of the bed, more concerned that the patient didn't fall to the floor.

It seemed as though the very earth was mirroring her uncertainty out here. She snorted quietly to herself and waited for the quake to end.

'So the Colonel and I thought we could extend this part of the facility...' Carl tapped the plans with the tip of his pencil '...and move the ICU to where the ORs would have been, and therefore demolish the block where the ICU is currently planned to be.'

'That won't work.' Elle shook her head, keeping her focus firmly on Carl, as she had during the entire briefing.

If she allowed herself to look at Fitz, even once, she was afraid she would crumple, but now she could see him in her peripheral vision, moving forward in his chair.

'Why not, Major?' he demanded tightly.

She bristled. That steely part of her core that had been AWOL for the last few days started to hum back into life. She composed herself and faced him.

'The ICU would still connect to the ORs, Colonel,' she acknowledged, 'but that's a long way around for one of the wards. In an emergency it would take too long and I'd end up having to rush men to Theatre through the women's ward, or vice versa.'

'Ah, I see.' She could almost hear his tone relax.

Had he been as apprehensive about this meeting as her?

Somehow, that made her feel a fraction better.

'Then there's another option.' Fitz moved his hand across the plans and she shivered, stopping herself from recalling quite how that strong palm had felt on her skin. 'If we moved the ORs to this location we could put the plant room for the medical gas supply system here. The ICU would go here and the wards could be there, or there. The generators would then go here and we could even tap into the aquifer with a new pipeline to ensure the running water for the facility is as clean as it possibly can be until the government builds a new waste management plant next year.'

Quickly, she ran it over and over in her head. It looked promising, although her sixth sense told her there was one area that could be improved from a medical point of view, but which they couldn't have foreseen as engineers.

'Would that work for you, Major?' Fitz asked.

'It looks like a viable solution and I like the sound of it,' she mused. 'I might like to make a couple of tweaks to the internal layout designs if it's to work optimally. How long do I have to go over it?'

'How long do you need?'

Fitz's voice was so flat she couldn't work out what he was thinking.

'Not long. I'd like to get it back to you by the end of today, as long as we don't get an influx of emergencies. With Colonel Duggan back at Razorwire, we're down a surgeon and a teacher.'

'At the moment we're still going through the hospital itself to make the last structural repairs to the east wing, such as it is.' Carl smiled. 'But I'd like to start on the external foundations this week. I'm heading out with a logistics convoy to inspect the ongoing railhead operation in the north and won't be back until tomorrow, so what if I leave the plans with you overnight and then go through them with you when I return?'

Her body numbed.

If Carl was going off-site then it meant that if there were any issues needing immediate discussion or resolution she'd have to deal with Fitz directly. The thought of having to work on anything *one on one* with him set her stomach churning with fear.

'I'm heading a medical convoy out into the communities myself tomorrow.' She sent out a silent apology to Amir for taking his place after she'd just offered it to him. 'I'll be gone for a few days.' She feigned apology. 'I could look at it tonight and then pass it to my second-in-command to go through it with you?'

Fitz spoke before Carl could answer.

'Major Howes, if you could ask Staff Sergeant Bell to start on that area of ground we discussed this morning?'

'Colonel.' Carl dipped his head, heading quickly out of the door.

Fitz waited for it to close before confronting her.

'Why are you taking a mobile medical unit into the communities?'

Elle raised her eyebrow. They both knew the question wasn't within his remit as commanding officer of the Royal Engineers. She could have challenged him, but instead she chose to play it straight down the line as strictly professional.

'I have a wave of IPVs to administer.'

'IPVs?'

'Inactivated polio vaccines. Part of the medical role out here is to ensure every child under the age of ten has been vaccinated against polio and measles. We can't guarantee the husbands will make the trip to me for their children so until the charities arrive to begin the grandmothers' health groups, we stand more chance of getting the men to agree if we go to them.'

'And the grandmothers' health groups are…?'

'Like many of the places the charities have worked, out here it's down to the men to decide whether their wives and children can get medical help. Over the decades they've found that the most effective way to encourage attitude change is to teach the grandmothers. They are some of the most valued and respected people within their communities and they have more influence over their sons and sons-in-law than the young wives do over their husbands.'

'I see. But until we've completed a lot of the rebuild, the charities aren't going to be out here. So going into the communities makes them more amenable?'

'Sure. A lot of it is more about lack of information and advice than anything. Not all families have the means, or inclination, to get to the hospital, so I go to them. We try to educate them on why getting their child immunised is so important, and describe symptoms such as acute flaccid paralysis so that they know what to look out for and when to bring their child to us at the hospital.'

'Which communities?' he bit out.

'Say again?'

'When you head out tomorrow, which direction?'

'South-west.' She frowned. 'I don't see—'

'Is that entirely necessary? The region isn't safe at the moment,' Fitz cut her off, oblivious. 'There are severe dust storms in that area at the moment, advancing walls of dust and debris that can be miles wide and thousands of feet high.'

'Yes, thank you.' She bit her tongue from giving a flippant retort and battled to keep her voice even. 'This isn't my first tour of duty, I *have* come across dust storms before.'

For a moment she thought she saw a flash of concern on Fitz's face. Then it was gone.

'Good, then I shouldn't need to tell you that heading into

the local communities right now is a bad idea. There are wide expanses in that direction, the roads are barely roads and the risk of RTAs is much higher.'

Her irritation, her discomfort all dissolved as a wisp of empathy curled its way up from her stomach. She recalled that haunted look in his eyes from the first night, pained and helpless, when he'd told her how his family had died in a crash. His father, drink-driving. A murmur escaped her lips.

'This is about the crash, isn't it? You're worried about a convoy crash?'

There were units driving in and out of the site all the time, especially logistics convoys as they ferried supplies. So, perhaps more accurately, he was worried about *her* convoy being caught by a rapidly moving wall of dust.

She was absurdly touched, even as his face turned deathly white. Abruptly his eyes burned with fury, searing her to the spot, a snarl twisting the features she'd touched, kissed, tasted.

'Why would you say that?' he rasped, his anger bouncing off the walls, making the tiny room throb.

Anyone else might be intimidated. Elle refused to allow herself to be. Instead, she peered at him.

'You don't remember telling me about your mum and sister?'

'I remember,' he ground out, as if waiting for her to say something else.

She licked her lips, steadying herself.

'I think you feel somehow responsible. Maybe for not being there. Maybe because they died and you lived. But because you couldn't control that situation, you're concerned about my convoy going out tomorrow.'

The silence swelled and the small space felt even more stifled, like a pressurised can left out in the sweltering sun. But she wasn't about to back down.

'That's it?' His bark of laughter rang out, a hollow and unpleasant sound.

'Isn't it enough?' she asked softly.

And then, oddly, she could have sworn *relief* flickered in those eyes, swiftly chased by disdain.

'I suppose it is.' He shrugged. 'But, no, telling you about my family was a combination of factors from that night; let me assure you it wasn't anything special about *you*. I was merely concerned about your team in Colonel Duggan's absence. So, if you've quite finished psychoanalysing me...'

It was all she could do to stay upright. His words were as cutting as if he'd taken her out by the knee, winding her and humiliating her in one smooth strike. *What a fool she was for thinking he'd been worried about her.* When was she going to get it through her head that whatever they'd shared that night, in Fitz's head it was over and done with?

CHAPTER TEN

HE REGRETTED THE words as soon as they'd left his lips but that did little to reduce their efficacy. His low blow had clearly left her reeling and he hated himself for it.

He was supposed to be protecting Elle from himself by keeping her at arm's length so that he wouldn't destroy her. He wasn't supposed to be destroying her in the process.

'I'm sorry. That was...uncalled for,' he told her quietly, sincerely.

She inclined her head stiffly, plainly struggling to compose herself.

'I appreciate your concern for my convoy, Colonel, but it's misplaced. Furthermore, I would respectfully remind you that Colonel Duggan and I are running the medical side of this mission and I have administrative and operational command in his absence. I'm satisfied that the risk of dust storms is no greater than usual in this area. If we get caught out, as convoys frequently do around here, we'll follow protocol and find shelter or at least pull off the road to wait it out.'

So stiff, so formal. He'd really hurt her.

'I did try to warn you, even from that first night, that I wasn't a good man. That I always end up destroying people.'

She pressed her lips together, her back bracing just a fraction.

'I'm sure I don't have to tell you that dust storms in

this area are unpredictable, Colonel, so we're going to have to take a chance at some point. And, to refer to your earlier question, yes, it *is* necessary,' she cut in respectfully but firmly. 'There are refugees crossing the border in their hundreds of thousands, and even though there are vaccination stations at many of the crossings there are still tens of thousands, if not hundreds of thousands, of children and babies who are missing out and who have already moved on and into existing communities. If I can spare children from suffering polio paralysis then I have to go, possible sandstorm or not.'

He almost smiled as her voice changed when she spoke of her work. That passion of hers had been one of the things to attract him in the first place. And the fact that she was desperately clinging to formality and keeping the topic mission-related hadn't gone unnoticed either. Normally, he wouldn't have pushed it—then again, normally he wouldn't have been in this position to start with—but that…tenderness she'd demonstrated moments ago when she'd spoken of his family, of his loss, told him that she'd been touched at the idea he'd been worried for her safety.

He owed her the truth.

'I'm sorry, Elle, but I tried to warn you I wasn't a good man, whatever you might think of me right now.'

Her shoulders actually sagged.

A strange silence descended over them and he had to let her be the one to break it. But when she did, he wasn't prepared for the sadness in her voice as it tore into his chest.

'I never thought you were cruel, Fitz, even without seeing the way your men love and respect you. But you can't keep doing this, flip-flopping between acknowledging this attraction between us one minute and then pushing me away the next.'

'I'm just trying to do the right thing.' He shook his head.

'You create barriers,' she countered. 'You never intended to tell me those secrets of yours that first night, but you decided it didn't matter because we were never going to see each other again; even if I hadn't been set on one crazy night, *you* would have made sure of it. And then when we turned up here together you resented me for it. You've been using army barriers, rules that don't technically exist, to push me away ever since.'

How did she do it? How did she see that side of him that no one else had, and yet fail to see the swirling darkness within him?

'Why do you want to be with me?' he demanded hotly, standing abruptly and rounding the desk so there was nothing between them. 'I'm not a good man. I'm not the responsible, caring man you seem to think I am.'

'Tell that to those men out there who think the world of you!' she exclaimed.

They were so close he could feel her body heat, experience the emotion as it poured off her, her fierceness making his chest ache. Yet, deliberately, neither of them closed the gap any further.

'Tell that to the men they've spoken to back home and at Razorwire who spoke so highly of you, leading from the front in more combat zones than they could remember. Tell that to High Command, who appointed you as one of the youngest lieutenant colonels.'

He wanted to believe her. So much that it hurt.

He couldn't.

'That's just the army. I like the man I am when I'm serving. The responsibility, the care, the life is different. It's easy to be a good leader, I know what's expected of me.'

'No, it's easy because it's who you are.' She heaved out a shaky sigh.

He bowed his head towards hers.

'But that's not the man I am out *there*, away from the structure. Where real feelings are needed. I don't have them. I'm empty, and broken, and toxic.'

Much closer and their heads would have touched. That

last absence of contact was the only thing saving either of
them right now.

'I don't believe that,' she whispered at length. 'Because
that's not the man I met that night. *Just Fitz* opened up to
me because he wanted to. A thoughtful, considerate, sensitive man in the bar with that young lad, and then later with
me, in bed. I couldn't have hoped for anyone more giving
or generous to make me feel respected. You made me feel
desirable again.'

'You wouldn't say that if you knew the things I've done.
The lives I've destroyed. I can't forget my mistakes, I can't
pretend they were okay.'

'Everybody makes mistakes, Fitz. The trick is to learn
from them.'

'Why don't you have the sense to walk away?' He demanded. 'I *have* learned from my mistakes. I learned that
I'm just like my old man. Selfish, joyless, destructive.'

'Funny,' she whispered, 'but that isn't a description I
recognise, and neither would your old friend Major Howes,
who speaks of you so highly.'

'That's because I'm a different person here.'

'Then let me say that it isn't the side of you that I saw
that night.'

Pain expanded in his chest, almost crushing everything
else.

'But it would be. If that night was allowed to be something more.' His voice sounded raw even to his ears. 'That's
why I'm trying to shield you.'

Her whisper was so low he had to strain to hear her.

'See, that's where I have the difficulty. If you're so much
this selfish person, then why would you be trying to shield
me?'

He stiffened, momentarily thrown. She made him *want*
to believe in himself the way she seemed to.

'Because there's worse you don't know about.'

'So, try me.'

Hot. Urgent. Desperate.

And he wanted to. He wanted to tell her everything, to lay every last, ugly truth out there and let her smooth it away, the way he suspected she could.

But if she didn't, if she saw what he'd been trying to hide all along, the mirror image of his father, Fitz didn't think he could bear it.

It was a reminder he needed.

This wasn't about him. This was about Elle. If they hadn't ended up here, at this hospital, in this place, they would never have tried to see each other again. He ignored the voice that reminded him how he'd been considering contacting the hotel about her when he came back off his tour of duty, however unlikely it was they might have assisted. And, yes, it was more than just sex, it felt like there was some kind of connection there. But how long would that last? It would disappear in the end. He'd feel stifled, trapped, just as he had with Janine. And then, despite his best intentions, hurting Elle would be inevitable.

'I have to live with the consequences of my choices every day,' he bit out, firmer now. 'But I *can* make sure I don't hurt a single other person. I *can* make sure I don't destroy you.'

It was for the best.

'Except that you can't, can you?' Elle whispered. 'You keep trying to push me away but then you can't help yourself, you have to reel me back in. You might not mean to but you do. You obviously care about me in some small way when you worry about a dust storm, but when I challenge you, you call me a meaningless fling. How is that not hurting me?'

He froze. As much as he might not want to admit it, there was merit to her words. From the moment they'd met he'd felt some kind of connection with her and he'd found it next to impossible to leave her the next day without also leaving his phone number, even though he'd come to his senses and binned it.

He'd dragged her into his office and dredged it all up that first day he'd turned up to see her, and he'd allowed himself to kiss her, to convey all the confusion neither of them could articulate. And now he'd dragged her here again, dismissed Carl, engineered things to be with her. He should have left days ago. He could have worked on the plans back at Razorwire, but this was where Elle was.

The more he pushed her away, the more aware he seemed to be of her. As though the fact that she was out here on site, yet avoiding him, left him feeling illogically hollow. The more she avoided him, the more she took up residence in his head. Instead of her absence helping to quell his ache for her, it only made him want her all the more. *Crave her.*

And not just physically. He ached to hear her laugh, see her smile, feel the warm glow that accompanied her presence.

Just because she was out of sight it didn't mean he hadn't gathered as much information as he could about her from the other officers around the site, both those who had worked with her for years and those who had just started to get to know her on this mission.

Yet the answers were always the same. She was respected, admired, liked and not infrequently lusted after, though no one but Carl openly admitted it. As a man who was suffering from the same affliction he could recognise the signs, not least because it caused a fresh sense of possession to course through his veins.

He could hear a muffled part of his brain proposing that if pushing her away and distancing himself from Elle wasn't working, then perhaps allowing himself to spend time with her, saturating himself with her presence would do the job. More time with her would allow him to see her as just another woman, flawed like everyone else. He could stop elevating her, could stop seeing her through the sentimental eyes of that first night, when the grim anniversary of his family's deaths had already been stirring long-buried emotions inside him, and which Elle had inadvertently tapped into.

The events of that night had created a false sense of connection with her, and that was what was causing him to lose his head now. It was stopping him from focussing on a job to which he'd never had any issue applying himself in the past.

If he allowed himself to explore being with Elle, then perhaps he would finally be able to shake off this unreasonably acute, distracting need to know her, to understand her.

And if they both knew the rules of any such encounter from the outset, if they both agreed it was temporary, an extension of that one night, then surely he could also set aside his fear that he would hurt her. He'd never worried about that with previous relationships, he'd never let that stop him.

But Elle wasn't like them. She was different. *He* felt different with her.

He needed time to think.

'I'm trying to protect you,' Fitz eventually stated flatly. 'That's the last thing I'm going to say. For now.'

He didn't know how he did it, but he finally tore himself away from her and moved back around the desk.

'When do you leave?' he asked.

The hurt that made her whole body slump almost wrecked him.

'Elle, I'm asking as Fitz. Not as a colonel. I'm not using protocol as an excuse. I know what you said last time.'

It was the only concession he could make to her, and he was relieved when she nodded, dredging up a faint smile, acknowledging it for what it was. He wasn't shutting her down like he had last time. He was buying himself time. And she was prepared to sell it to him.

'We leave at dawn. It's a couple of hours' drive so we'll get most of tomorrow and then all of the following day. We'll head back the day after.'

'Okay.' He nodded.

So tomorrow he'd either be heading back to Razorwire,

putting Elle into his past for good, or staying here and riding this attraction out until he could finally let her go.

He barely had the night to decide.

'He can't be serious?'

Fitz could hear Elle's muttered objection as she stood alone, her back to him, in the deserted square outside the hospital, the sunrise giving an almost halo effect to her flame-red hair. She was far enough from the hospital that she couldn't be heard, but close enough that she could watch the convoy go through its final preparations without standing out against the backdrop of the building.

'Something amiss?' he asked casually as he walked up behind her, and she spun around with a startled cry.

She eyed him cautiously, as though recognising his less controlled, less distant attitude but still uncertain what it meant.

'There's a three-vehicle engineers' convoy alongside my medical one, Colonel,' she said, as she indicated towards where the vehicles were parked, less than a couple of hundred metres away, one of which was a four-by-four towing a boring rig.

'Indeed there is,' he agreed brightly.

Was it wrong that it gave him such a perverse pleasure to beat her at her own game?

She narrowed her eyes a fraction.

'May I ask to what purpose, sir?'

'You may. Although given that there's no one immediately around I think we can dispense with the formality at this time, don't you?' he countered lightly. 'Anyway, I realised that accompanying the mobile medical unit into the local communities could be advantageous to my men. As part of our mission in this area, the Royal Engineers are to be responsible for digging new wells and building schools throughout various communities in the region. After all the conflict over the last few decades, the people here are naturally suspicious of non-locals but they *do* accept the medical units.'

'So you want to accompany us to trade off our good reputation?' she asked slowly.

He grinned, knowing she couldn't fault his logic.

'And gain their trust more easily in order to perform a couple of test drills at each site you visit, yes. Furthermore, padding out your convoy will make you less of a target and mean only one lot of force protection will be required.'

Not that anyone was particularly expecting trouble in a non-combat area but a security detail was more about appearances.

'I see. So…?' she started, then paused, concluding feebly with another, 'I see.'

She still thought it was about his fears over the safety of her convoy after his mother's car crash. She wasn't entirely off the mark, though it wasn't the car crash that haunted him when he thought of Elle. The idea of her being out there, risking some of the most severe dust storms the region had experienced in a decade, brought fear and old demons to assail him. He knew all too well the impact of one of these dust storms on a military convoy. And he was fairly certain that Elle was only heading up that convoy as an excuse to get away from site, from him, for a couple of days. After the way he'd treated her, he could understand it.

If anything happened to Elle the way it had to Janine… all because of him…

'I just… I don't know if we have time,' Elle hazarded. 'Setting up your rig and doing your test drills will take time. We were intending to make this a brief dash. Get out there, vaccinate, head back.'

'Indeed? Only yesterday you gave the impression you might be out there for a couple of days.'

She flushed.

'You know these things are never straightforward.'

'And you appear to have a vehicle loaded up with hens

sent by one of the charities.' He quashed a smile. 'Presumably this is part of the nutrition and economic sustainability initiative? Give each family a couple of hens so that they have free eggs and, as they gain experience, the surplus can be sold at market to give them money to buy other supplies. All of which will take time.'

The corners of her mouth tightened with guilt.

'Yes…well…'

He didn't blame her for pushing him away. He wanted to apologise. To explain. But he couldn't even explain it to himself. Had he really finally stopped pushing her away in some kind of attempt at reverse psychology on himself? It sounded ludicrous even in his own mind.

Not giving her any chance to stammer any further, Fitz adopted a deliberately breezy tone.

'So plenty of time to test drill for suitable watercourses in each location.'

'Yes, but—'

'And you know as well as I do that this country's health status is one of the worst. Lack of education about defecating near the same rivers from which drinking water is collected is a significant issue, and admittedly the wells are only a small part of it, as is the long-term plan to start building new sewer and wastewater treatment plants.'

'Yes, I know—'

'But the wells will still help, not least in reducing diarrhoea and therefore malnourishment, helminth, typhus, kidney diseases, shall I go on?'

A look of defeat skittered over her face.

'I suppose if you put it like that…' She shrugged.

'It's exactly like that.'

He pushed back his sense of triumph, knowing that he was only trying to deceive himself. Accompanying the medical unit into the local communities was an inspired idea, but it was the knowledge that he would therefore have to accompany her that gave him the greater sense of satisfaction.

The entire situation was alien to Fitz and while he knew he would never compromise a mission, or his role, for Elle, the fact remained that he was more than happy at the prospect of being able to combine the two so easily.

Then again, the thought appeared from nowhere, *how many times had he seen a vehicle flip over in front of or behind him?*

The thought came before he had the chance to check himself.

'Now, whose vehicle would you prefer to travel in?'

She looked aghast.

'Say again?'

'I recommend my four-by-four—it's less of a bumpy ride than your ambulance—but it's your choice.'

She sucked in a breath, actually squaring her shoulders as she glared at him.

'I'm not travelling with the engineers.'

They both knew she meant she wasn't travelling with *him*. He smothered a grin. This was a heck of a lot better than the tension of the last week. It felt like a step back to the easy banter they'd enjoyed that first night in the bar, and he was going to enjoy it fully for the next few minutes.

'Is there a medical priority?' he enquired with wry politeness.

She narrowed her eyes at him, quite aware that he was teasing her.

'You know there isn't. But—'

'Good.' Fitz nodded, ignoring her objection. 'Because we still need to talk about the design variations for the hospital and several hours of driving through nothingness, with nothing else to do, is the ideal opportunity.'

CHAPTER ELEVEN

Two and a half hours of pure torture.

Elle squirmed in her seat as the four-by-four finally drew to a halt just outside the buildings of their first local community. It was all she could do not to fling open the door and throw herself out just to get away from Fitz. How was it that in spite of the callous way in which he'd rejected her this last week, she still wanted him? She'd never known it was possible to feel a yearning so intense that it actually physically *hurt*.

And then she'd fallen under his spell all over again. She'd fallen for the idea of something more with him, even if she had precisely zero idea what that would be. Although she was fairly sure it hadn't been being cooped up in the back of a four-by-four with him, jolted around so much that their bodies had been in contact the entire journey, yet unable to talk freely because of the driver.

Really, she should pat herself on the back. For two hours, thirty-one minutes and some seconds she had endured Fitz's solid thigh pressed against her, generating heat that had little to do with the soaring daytime temperatures as it had bounced off each other's bodies, and withstood the sparks of awareness and the tiniest hairs prickling in response. She had spent two hours, thirty-one minutes and some seconds muffling the maddening military tattoo roll over her heart as his deep voice had rumbled into her ear and through her body to ignite a wanton fire in the depth of her core.

And she had forced herself to concentrate on designs and principles and timings for two hours, thirty-one minutes and some seconds, when all her brain had wanted to do was mull over the intoxicating possibilities that his earlier assertions had raised.

She *affected* him. He'd said so. He had rejected and humiliated her, proved to her that he *could* turn it on and off like the twist of a tap, yet her torment was all no longer of her own making.

It had turned out he wasn't so immune to her after all. Even if she still wasn't sure where that left them. When they got back home, did he want to date? Would they be colleagues with benefits? And what did *she* want? Elle wasn't even sure she knew. Realistically, she and Fitz knew so little about each other, perhaps his olive branch to be friends was just about getting to know each other while they were out here.

It was probably a good idea. But one thing she *did* know was that, despite the crushing effect Fitz had on her, she had miraculously found a way to push aside her emotions and discuss steadily, and proficiently, all Fitz's proposed variations to the hospital services layout, even putting forward several improvements of her own. Surprisingly, perhaps even astoundingly, it seemed when it came to working together on their military assignment, she and Fitz made a remarkably strong, united team. A professional team.

She couldn't help liking the idea of that. But just because they had proved once again that they could still work in harmony on a mission level, it didn't give them the green light to make their relationship a sexual one again. Even if her throbbing body was trying to convince her otherwise.

Her internal battle had undoubtedly taken its toll—a battle with her own body, and with her very senses, leaving her mentally and physically spent. As the engines were all finally killed and the occupants began to spill from the various vehicles, Elle opened the door and unfurled her shaky legs, furiously berating her wandering thoughts even as she put some distance between herself and Fitz.

She propelled herself towards the ambulance where the supplies for the community sat ready to go. *This* was what she was here for—helping people, saving lives, health education. In other words, her job as an army doctor. It was what she understood. It was what she was good at.

Reaching for her grab-bag, she slung it over her shoulder and followed their interpreter, and Zi, the sixty-three-year-old widow who had spent nearly a decade volunteering with charities across the border to help educate small villages and communities, and would be working with the army in this region until the charities came in to take over. They were already being eagerly welcomed inside what passed for the community hall, and Elle hurried to catch up. It wasn't always this easy but today of all days she was grateful for the lack of local resistance. Fitz hadn't followed her, his own good grasp of the local language allowing him to quickly begin chatting to some of the local men. He, too, appeared to be meeting very little distrust. If every stop they made was this smooth, they'd be heading back to the hospital in half the time.

Elle's sense of reprieve grew as she looked through the window to see him begin moving around the village to find potential bore sites, and she tasked herself with carrying out the immunisations she was there for. And yet their earlier conversation, his evident thawing towards her, had jump-started previously well-controlled feelings within her, as though the antagonism of the last week was forgotten and they had both been thrown back to the awkward, stumbling yet thrilling feeling of the morning-after-the-night-before.

Not that she'd ever experienced it before for herself, but the way her body was reacting now, like a million teeny-tiny jumping spiders were playing on trampolines in her tummy, it was exactly how she would have imagined it would feel. She felt his presence everywhere, as if the village itself was too small to hold him.

If she'd thought Fitz had got into her head after that first night together, after that incredible sex, after the way he'd made her feel, then it was nothing compared to the way Fitz was cracking open her heart with even the mere hint that he was opening himself up to her on an emotional level.

Looping her stethoscope around her neck, Elle forced herself to quash the tumbling thoughts and beamed at her team.

'Ready, guys? Let's help to save some kids' lives. Look out for anything else we can help with now—diarrhoea, open wounds, you know the drill. Zi will be chatting to the women in the waiting area about latrines, hand washing, basic hygiene—the women are still going to the toilet in the open air so they'll be the first to get a latrine, but the community's waste is still getting into the river where they draw their drinking water. So let's take any opportunity to back up what Zi will be telling them.

'Also, the community have put forward five or six grandmothers, elders who they respect and listen to, so we'll join Zi in a couple of hours to start taking them through health care, mainly focussing on clean water and sanitation procedures, and pregnancy and labour advice. Anything to help prepare the ground for when the charities start running their full programmes in the coming weeks and months.'

To a chorus of enthusiastic agreement, Elle watched her teams filter out to their cubicles, maximising the number of patients they could see as well as administering the polio and measles immunisations. It was proving to be an interesting mission out here, and each day she was more and more convinced that returning on a second back-to-back tour would be a rewarding, if challenging experience.

The rest of Elle's morning passed in something of a blur. At least she and Jools—the staff sergeant and nurse assisting her with the vaccines—went way back. Jools had been one of Elle's closest allies when Elle had just been a lieutenant and the woman had a razor-sharp wit and an innate skill at drawing the local women into the levity, even if they couldn't understand the precise wording. A morning of laughter was just what she needed and, given the nature of the medical units and their work, rank and title were often shunned in favour of a first-name basis, meaning things were less formal and more easygoing.

So when the first lull came a couple of hours later, Elle couldn't help but balk at the thought of Jools suggesting they take their usual leg-stretching walk to get out of the stifling room for a while.

'Maybe it's time we get a small group together and head out to encourage the villagers to attend clinic,' Elle remarked as they set up a new batch of needles while the last set of patients left the room. 'I know Zi is good, and we've been lucky so far this morning, but there are bound to be more families who haven't come down yet.'

'No need.' Jools grinned. 'Have you seen the waiting area?'

Stepping around the cubicle, Elle carefully peered through before spinning back to her colleague in shock.

'It's full out there. I don't understand.'

What was more, many of the women were grouped attentively around Zi, who was educating them and entertaining the children in one easy performance. It was the lack of noise that had prompted Elle to think there weren't many families out there, but the question still remained as to why, since Zi had been indoors all morning, so many of them had come across voluntarily.

It was never usually this easy. They often had to carefully persuade suspicious members of the male population to allow their wives and children to get immunised. It was easier if the charities had been teaching the respected grandmothers about the benefits so *they* could encourage their sons to do the same, but Elle knew her team was the first in the area for a decade.

'They all just attended of their own volition?'

'Colonel Fitzwilliam,' the nurse said dreamily, as though his name in itself was explanation enough.

'Colonel Fitzwilliam?' echoed Elle.

The whimsical gaze only intensified. Elle gritted her teeth. She'd barely managed to stop herself from watching every time he passed, her eyes seeming to lift up at just the right moment to see his robust form striding across the frame of the tiny window with, even more surprisingly, a growing cluster of village men scurrying eagerly after him. Or to see him setting aside his own work to carry out some manual labour or other with the community, winning hearts and minds by actually joining in with something the village had been working on and needed.

And in those moments Elle had seen exactly how Fitz had acquired, and maintained, that impressive physique of his. Not in a gym but in the real world. Not with artificial machines but doing real manual labour. She'd remembered with embarrassing clarity just how he'd felt, driving inside her, claiming her, imprinting himself on her for ever.

Even at this distance, even though appearing no bigger than a matchstick, Fitz dominated entirely.

'I'm not sure what he has to do with the heaving waiting area.' She hadn't intended to sound so prim.

'Well, that's because not everyone is as immune to charm as you, Major I-Only-Have-Eyes-for-My-Childhood-Sweetheart!' Jools laughed. 'And Major Fitzwilliam has charm in spades. Haven't you seen how he's been working out there with the local men? And on more than just the wells. Last time I went for a new batch of vaccines from the mobile unit I heard that the six-tonner he brought with him was loaded with supplies for building hen-houses. Did you know that?'

'We have some basic kits to get them started!' Elle exclaimed. 'The charities gave them to us and they'll do the rest when they come out. He knew that, he even mentioned it to me this morning.'

'Yes, but the Colonel brought better timber and some tools. He's been showing them how to build them to best suit the birds, and which ground is better for siting them. He's been gaining their trust and apparently casually chatting to them about the health benefits of the clinic.'

'So that heaving waiting area is *his* doing?'

'Amazing, isn't he?' Jools sighed. 'I'd love to have your job as liaison officer, having to work with him practically every day and on a one-on-one basis. Getting to travel that awful journey out here cooped up with him. No offence but it's wasted on you.'

Elle resisted the urge to roll her eyes. *How could she criticise Jools's swooning when she herself wasn't much different?*

'Wait, look, he's about to send over some more. A couple of local men just approached him and pointed over here. You'll see.'

Her legs almost carried her back to the window of their own volition as Elle spotted Fitz conferring with his new-found supporters, nodding in agreement as they gesticulated towards her location. Even the interpreter didn't seem to need to do much translating. Moments later, the men crossed the ground and went into various homes or out of sight.

'Give it a few minutes and a group of fresh families will come through our doors,' Jools confirmed. 'There, that's the last of this batch of immunisations set up. Shall I have the next group readied for us?'

'Sure,' Elle replied, still staring thoughtfully through the window at the apparent hero of the hour. 'The quicker we can get through them, the sooner we can move on to help the next village.'

Thanks to Fitz, it seemed they might be able to get to even more communities and help even more locals during this trip.

It was bad enough lusting after the guy, but did he have to make her admire him so much, too?

She needed to get through the next couple of days and then she'd be back at the hospital and could go back to avoiding him. So much for wanting the chill between them to thaw. It seemed that, instead of helping matters, his new openness to her had only confused matters and made her all the more attracted to him.

Clearly, in future, she needed to watch what she wished for.

'There you are. I wondered where you were hiding out.'

Elle clutched her ration-pack hot chocolate in its steel cup—watery and tasteless, but at least wet and welcoming—as the dust storm raged outside. For two days the sky had been perfectly blue as they'd travelled from village to village, some makeshift, some well established. Thanks to Fitz and Zi, they had encountered less resistance than normal and had therefore been able to do more than normal, successfully immunising children, health-checking pregnant mothers and passing on even more valuable sensitisation information than previously planned. Elle had even convinced herself that they would get back to the hospital before the weather turned.

Murphy's law, however, meant that the storm hit just as her team had been loading up the last of their kit. Still, she supposed it was better than if they'd been halfway between two locations and slap-bang in the middle of nowhere. At least this was one of the largest established communities and they had shelter, a safe place to wait it out.

At least, it *had* been safe before *he'd* walked through the door.

'I'm not hiding out,' she lied.

'The rest of the two teams are in the main community hall across the square.'

'And I'd have been with them if I hadn't been packing up the last of my kit when the storm came out of nowhere.'

'I think we both know you had time to get across, if you'd wanted to.'

Elle dipped her head and took another sip of the watery drink. He was right, there was little point in denying it.

'You were avoiding me.'

There was a beat of silence.

'Can you blame me?'

'I thought we'd decided on starting afresh. No antagonism.'

'I know.' Elle rubbed her forehead. 'I'm just…not sure how to be around you. I've never been in this situation before.'

'Neither have I,' he said wryly, turning his back to her and unpacking a small gas stove from his pack.

She watched as he lit it, the flickering flame instantly changing the atmosphere in the low-lit room, and she couldn't help it, she was transported back to that bar the first night.

'Here, try this instead.'

His voice cut into her thoughts as he replaced the cup in her hands with something that felt decidedly more…luxurious. As the decadent scent reached her nostrils she bit back her objection and sniffed appreciatively.

'It's not five-star-hotel hot chocolate,' he murmured. 'But it's better than that ration-pack sludge you were drinking.'

He remembered. The drink she'd ordered when they'd got room service in the early hours. It was such a tiny point but the fact that he'd noted it, and echoed it now, was touching. She couldn't stop it. For an instant she was transported back to that night. Being in this tiny dark, supply room of the stone building, so utterly basic yet the village's beloved town hall, was hardly the same as the relative opulence of her hotel room. And yet they were alone again, and she couldn't help feeling oddly safe. Just as she had with him that first night.

She could keep fighting it, but the attraction wasn't going away.

Her head snapped up to meet his gaze, unprepared for the hard, heated look in his eyes. Dizziness threatened to overtake her and she told herself it was just hunger from the mayhem of the last few days.

She knew that wasn't it.

'I'm still not entirely sure what it is that we're starting over,' she confessed.

If she'd expected him to prevaricate she'd been wrong. He snagged her gaze, pinning her in place, his voice clear, confident.

'Getting to know each other.'

'To what end?'

'Whatever we decide.'

'Okay,' she managed. 'Starting with what?'

'Tell me about Stevie. How you let him hurt you.'

'Low blow,' she muttered.

'Not intentionally.' Fitz shook his head. 'You just don't seem like the type to stand for any nonsense, and yet the things you've told me suggest otherwise.'

'You mean…the sex.' She flushed, thinking of their conversation that first night when Fitz had dropped to his knees and pressed his lips to her sex. And so much more.

'I mean the sex, the cheating. I got the impression you weren't surprised, so I'm guessing it wasn't the first time.'

God, had he really read all that as easily as if she'd been an open book?

She didn't intend to sound defensive, but that was how it came out.

'I suppose you think I was stupid to stay with him?'

'I don't think anything, that's why I'm asking.'

She bit her lip in discomfort, not understanding why it was so important to him.

'Tell me, why do you want to play detective all of a sudden?'

'It isn't all of a sudden,' he muttered. 'I wanted to know from the start.'

The irritation in his tone caught her attention. It wasn't so much that he wanted to know, she realised, as that he *had* to know. He couldn't fathom her and he was intrigued. Which meant he cared. More than he was prepared to admit.

She inhaled deeply, formed her mouth into a perfect O and blew out. Then flashed a bitter, humourless smile. 'The ten-thousand-pound question.'

'You stayed with him for ten thousand pounds?' Fitz's face twisted into a mix of expressions she couldn't identify but which she could easily guess.

'You could put it like that if you like.'

'I don't like.' His jaw locked in irritation and it surprised her that she was beginning to recognise his 'tells' so easily. 'So explain it to me.'

She sighed.

'What would be the point? Apart from satisfying your curiosity? Would it change anything between us? Not, I realise, that there *is* an us.'

'Humour me, Elle.'

She thought for a long time, then dipped her head.

'Short version only.'

'Whatever you prefer. For now.'

She chose to ignore that.

'Stevie and I were childhood sweethearts. I was fourteen, he was fifteen, though we'd known each other all our lives. We were both poor kids from the worst housing estate in the area, but while his dad baled on his mum and her seven kids, my parents were the exception. I can't remember a day when they didn't have a laugh with each other, a joke, a hug, a tease.'

'They never argued?'

The look in his eyes was so fleeting, so inscrutable that Elle wasn't sure if it had simply been her imagination.

'Yeah, they argued. Of course they did. We had no money, and that always created tension. But they always made it up. Every single night. They told us kids we should never go to bed in anger. She was so beautiful, my mum, deep red hair and sparkling green eyes.'

'Like you,' Fitz said softly.

She snorted, trying to conceal how his words affected her.

'No, not like me. I have her basic components, but I'm not stunning like she was.'

'*Just* like your mother,' he murmured again.

He held her gaze and it took everything she had to tear her eyes away.

'And they danced, God, how they loved to dance. They could jive and swing and lindy hop like you wouldn't believe.'

'You told me you couldn't dance that night in the bar.'

She flushed, recalling the feel of Fitz's arms around her, his fingers grazing her skin, his thigh slotted between hers. She swallowed. Hard.

'I can't. It was one of their greatest sources of amusement. But they could and they used to enter competitions and I'd go and watch. Stevie too. The kids around where we lived had no prospects, there was no such thing as a school night, and their idea of recreation was going around the back of the station to drink cider and take drugs...'

'*Their* idea of recreation? Not yours?'

'No. I dreamed of becoming a doctor. Don't ask me where it came from, even my parents never knew, but apparently it started from the age of about five and it was all I ever wanted to be when I grew up. And Stevie, he had his football and he dreamed of making it his way out of that hellhole too.'

'So you and he bonded over being different.'

'Sure, why not?' Elle frowned at his scepticism. 'We were the outliers. The oddballs who didn't fit in. When my mother died, my father was so lonely that he remarried. I think he was trying recapture what he'd lost with Mum, but it wasn't the same. She was cruel, but I suppose when I look back she was jealous of what my parents had had. But Stevie was there. Back then he was loyal, and kind, and generous. He kept telling me to fight for my dream even when she was nasty and told me I had ideas above my station. She told me I was wasting my time getting A Levels when I'd never be able to afford university anyway. She tried to make me get a job in the local factory—everyone got a job in the local factory—and bring a wage in instead of scrounging off her.'

'But you got to uni. You joined the army and got a scholarship and did it by yourself.'

'No.' Elle shook her head. 'I didn't. She was right, I couldn't afford university. I didn't know the army gave bursaries for medical degrees and I knew I didn't stand a hope in hell of making it through. But by then Stevie had made it to professional league football and he wouldn't let me give up on my dream. He used his money and he paid for my degree, my accommodation, my books, my food, he paid for everything.'

'As long as you turned a blind eye to his cheating?'

'No. Not back then. I'm sure of it. The old Stevie wasn't like that. Oh, I don't know. Maybe he did. He certainly never gave me a key to his place in all those years, and I never just turned up apart from that last time. His doorman recognised me and let me in.'

'So he *did* cheat on you.'

'Maybe. But, God, Fitz, you have to understand, we were two kids from nothing. And he was suddenly catapulted into this world where he was idolised. Seems like everybody loves a footballer when they're winning. He had fans, groupies, people who adored him, and he was nineteen with no home life to speak of to keep him grounded. Is it any wonder he let the fame and adulation get to him?'

Fitz sneered.

'You're seriously making excuses for him?'

'No,' she cried. 'I'm the last person who would do that. I'm just saying I can see how it happened. And I wonder if I couldn't have been the one thing to keep him steady… if I'd only cared enough to try. But I didn't. I didn't care enough and I didn't try. We never saw each other, between his training and his matches he didn't have much spare time, and by then I'd got an army bursary and I didn't want to make the time either. So he was pretty much on his own, surrounded by sycophants and girls throwing themselves at him. The cheating started after that and things deteriorated year on year.'

'Yet you still didn't leave?'

'Like I said, I felt guilty.' Elle shrugged. 'Not guilty enough to make an effort, but guilty enough not to leave. I didn't want the responsibility of ending things. I think I was waiting for him to do it. When it all boils down to it, I still felt as though I owed him, that without his help that first year I would never have become a doctor.'

'You'd have found another way.'

'Maybe.' She shrugged. 'But we'll never know. Stevie made sure I never had to risk that.'

'If he was so great, why didn't you love him?'

'I never said he was so great. He was impossibly moody, and he had his father's temper. And I did love him, in the beginning. But it was teenage love, tainted by where we grew up. We got together through circumstance, we were never a good fit. And Stevie was a brilliant footballer but…well, we could never have what you might call an in-depth conversation. If it wasn't about football or movies then forget it.'

'But when he cheated, you still felt guilty?'

'Don't underestimate guilt, Fitz. It can tie you up in knots. You can't understand what it's like.'

'I can,' he muttered unexpectedly. 'More than you think.'

'Your mother and sister?' she guessed hesitantly. 'Or Janine?'

The room was so thick with tension Elle thought the dust storm might as well have entered the building.

'What have you heard about her?'

'Not a lot,' Elle confessed. 'But you're an eligible male around the site. You know what gossip is like. I heard she was a logistics officer and you were once engaged?'

It took a long time before he broke the silence.

'It's complicated.'

'Try me,' Elle asked.

He shook his head but she couldn't let it drop. It was about more than just words.

'Trust me. Please, Fitz. Like I just trusted you.'

This time he didn't reply. The silence in the compact space grew, slowly but surely seeming to suck all the oxygen out of the room until Elle felt she was on the verge of suffocating. When he finally opened his mouth to speak, to break the spell, it wasn't with a murmur but with a growl that seemed to explode in her head.

The sound of a door banging open in the main room outside, interrupting with an urgency that was impossible to ignore, had them both leaping to their feet.

A pregnant young woman, crying out and bloodied, was being carried in by an older man, flanked by at least four others, a long shard of metal debris impaled through the side of her abdomen.

CHAPTER TWELVE

'GET THE INTERPRETER,' Elle instructed quickly as she hurried forward, trying to encourage them to bring the girl through to a gurney.

'No need.'

Grimly Fitz matched her, communicating efficiently with the group as Elle struggled to make out snippets and words in the cacophony of voices. Back and forth the conversation went as Fitz quickly established order, instructing them to bring the woman through to where Elle could examine her and eliciting information.

His face tightened.

'What's wrong?' Elle pressed urgently.

'She's seven months pregnant, and they were travelling on the main road out there when the storm hit. They pulled over to wait it out but another car coming in the opposite direction drove off the road and into them, rolling their car down an embankment into the wadi at the side.'

Elle drew her lips into a thin line, remembering the route from the way in. It was a fair way down, the car could have rolled a couple of times and she doubted the woman had been wearing a seatbelt.

'She's in pain and afraid for the baby.'

His voice broke on the last part and Elle stared at him in shock. His expression was too haunted, too bleak to be solely a reaction to this woman's condition. But there was no time for her to dwell on it. Her priority was the woman and her baby.

'Can you send one of the men to the main building, ask for Jools, and tell her to bring my medical bag?'

'I'll go. I can't send anyone out there,' Fitz managed, his voice filled with pain like nothing she'd ever heard from him before.

Something in her heart broke for him, even if she didn't know why.

'No. I need you here to translate.' Elle stopped him firmly.

He moved to the door, not appearing to hear her.

'Colonel.' She raised her voice firmly. 'Colonel Fitzwilliam. *Fitz.*'

He finally turned at her last bellow.

'You cannot go, do you understand?' Elle said quietly but firmly. 'You need to listen to me, this is a medical situation.'

For a moment she wasn't sure her words were registering, and then he snapped out of it—whatever it was—as quickly as it had started.

'Major,' he acknowledged, turning to the men and issuing the instruction.

There was little need for discussion as two of them promptly volunteered and headed out together. Elle was relieved; there was a degree of safety in numbers. Quickly Elle moved on, turning back to the woman and tapping her own chest as she gave her name, smiling when the woman responded in kind.

'Roshan, good, that's good.' So at least the woman was cognisant enough to process Elle's words.

Her language skills might not be anywhere as fluent as Fitz's, but the army had given her plenty of phrases to assist in everyday and medical situations.

'Colonel,' Elle stated, more to establish order than anything else, 'can you ask the men for their accounts of what happened while I ask Roshan here? Get as much information as possible.'

There was no time now to think about Fitz, but something had spooked him and she didn't think it was just about the crash. She could feel emotion flowing off Fitz, hot then cold, colourless then vivid, still then raging. It seeped into her chest, pulling it tight, and it seeped into her head, making it feel ready to explode. A mass of contradictions, out of control. A mess. And nothing like the man Elle knew. She struggled to make sense of it and then, all of a sudden, it hit her.

Pain.

This was what Fitz had been stuffing down all this time. The barrier that had always stood between them. The wall she'd wanted him to tear down for as long as she could remember. The trench that had stopped him from trusting her, and which had made her feel as though she ought to think it was too soon after Stevie. But finally she couldn't ignore the truth any longer. She was falling for Fitz. She'd probably started falling for him from the minute they'd met.

Fitz had been everything Stevie hadn't been. She'd spent years acknowledging all the ways that Stevie wasn't the right man for her, so when Fitz had come along she—or at least a part of her subconscious—had recognised in an instant all the qualities she knew she wanted in a man.

And now he was hurting and all she wanted to do was help, but there wasn't time. She'd have to get to the bottom of it. Later. With a supreme effort, Elle pushed thoughts of Fitz from her mind and turned back to Roshan to ask where it hurt most and if there had been any blood. Despite the long metal shard in her abdomen, Elle conducted a quick visual triage knowing that the most obvious injury wasn't always the most life-threatening.

As she finished, the interpreter hurried in with Jools. By the looks of them, the worst of the dust storm had passed, but that didn't mean they were free and clear.

'That looks bad. But then again, there isn't much blood,' the interpreter muttered quietly to her. 'What do you want me to tell her?'

'Nothing at the moment. There's no way to know merely by looking. The lack of blood doesn't prove anything. She's breathing and talking, and she's gesticulating so that's good and I want to do a full primary check, but first I'd like to make sure she has no other injuries, specifically neck and back, and what state that penetrating injury is in, so that I can get her onto her left side.'

'They keep telling her to stay on her back.'

'Yes, I can see that, but I need you to explain that uterine compression on the inferior vena cava and aorta can aggravate shock in pregnant women, especially if they're in the third trimester. Put it into whatever terms you need to in order to make them understand.'

She waved Fitz over. A darkness swirled in his eyes, almost mesmerising. But it seemed he still wasn't going to speak. Elle stared in silence, feeling herself being drawn into their dangerous depths. She could drown in those depths and never realise it.

'Can you get me a kit bag from the medical vehicle, blood-pressure monitor, blankets and maybe some kind of screen? Okay.' Elle turned her focus to the mother with a soothing tone. 'Let's look after you.'

There was no point telling the woman everything would be all right. Although there was no evidence of vaginal bleeding or significant external bleeding from the penetration wound, Elle had no idea what was going on inside. The shard may or may not have caused direct trauma to the foetus, ruptured the placenta, damaged organs or caused internal bleeding. Yet the initial check was looking more positive than she'd feared.

By the time Fitz had returned with the bag, Elle was satisfied the woman's pulse was strong, she wasn't clammy or pale, and from the way she was describing the accident, frequently punctuated by sharp pleas to make sure her baby was all right, she didn't seem confused or weak in any way.

'What now?' Fitz appeared suddenly at her shoulder, his voice uncharacteristically tight.

'At this point I'm as satisfied as I can be that Roshan isn't going into hypovolemic shock. Neitherr does she indicate any kind of abdominal pain, even from the metal shard. Now I can only hope the penetration wound isn't as deep as I'd feared, but we still need to pack her carefully for moving her.'

'You're moving her?' Fitz didn't look happy.

'With that shard in her side, I want to check the baby's well-being then do a secondary check on the mother. We'll have to get them to our hospital, Razorwire's too far away or I'd call it in.'

'If the baby's alive, will you need to operate? To save it?'

'A C-section? Not necessarily,' Elle answered grimly. 'Besides, until the hospital is up and running we have no incubators or anything to help. We don't even have the new generators yet. But it's too soon to tell what Roshan or her baby might need.'

Slipping in the earpieces of her portable foetal heart monitor just in case, Elle prepared herself as she searched for the heartbeat, her eyes locked to the screen. It was almost a shock when she found it, slightly slower than she would have preferred but strong and steady.

Clicking for a printout, Elle removed the earphones so that the woman could hear the sound of her baby for herself. She was rewarded with a flood of tears from the mother.

'It's alive,' Fitz bit out.

'Yes, not in any immediate distress.'

'Then you're leaving the metal *in situ*?'

'I'd prefer to, yes,' she confirmed, knowing he would understand that from combat injuries. 'At the moment it doesn't appear to be causing an issue and we'll have more on hand back at the hospital, if anything goes wrong.'

'So now?'

'Now we make sure everyone else is okay.'

'Already done. Jools and your team have taken the rest over to the other building. It's calm outside now. They'll deal with everyone and we've got anyone who needs further attention onto appropriate vehicles. Most look to be only superficial injuries, the only vehicle really damaged was the one carrying the woman and her husband and he has a head wound she wants you to look at.'

'Great.' Elle nodded, those black depths drawing her in again.

She struggled to break free. She *would* drown, that was the point, because Fitz would never throw her a lifeline. Not because he didn't want to but because somehow he didn't think he could. At least, not in his personal life. In his professional life as a leader Fitz not only lived up to but exceeded his responsibilities—she'd seen that for herself over the last couple of weeks. But in his personal life he appeared to have some ridiculous notion that he destroyed life, destroyed people. *He* was the one who needed a lifeline, and Elle couldn't shake the belief that she was the only one who could offer it to him.

'What was that about, Fitz?' she asked softly.

'It was nothing.'

'I see.'

She didn't push it immediately. His very choice of words acknowledged there had been something even as he tried to deny it. She let his unintentional admission sink into his own head.

'It was nothing you should have to be concerned with.'

'If it affects you,' she answered simply, 'I'm concerned.'

She knew he held himself responsible for his mother's death, and his sister's death, even though he hadn't been there. She knew, too, that he held himself responsible for Janine's convoy accident, even though he couldn't possibly have had any influence over it. He was Royal Engineers, she'd been Logistics. None of it seemed to make sense, but the worst of it was that Fitz didn't trust anyone—didn't trust *her*—enough to confide in her.

And that hurt more than anything else.

Worse, because she knew she had no right to expect him to want to confide in her, but it didn't stop her wishing he wanted to. It didn't stop her falling for him.

Working with him over the last couple of months twenty-four seven had been eye-opening. In a job like this, especially in an environment like this, Elle knew only too well how soldiers got to know the people working alongside them in a way no other profession allowed. They lived together, ate together, slept together. There was no escape, no chance to step away for a while.

It had also meant she'd spent more days in Fitz's company than she'd spent with Stevie in probably the last five or six years they'd been together. And she liked the man Fitz was more than she'd ever liked the man Stevie had been turning into.

She couldn't help it. She wanted to be there for Fitz, she wanted to show him he needed her. And he *did* need her. Hadn't he already told her things he'd admitted he'd never told anyone else? Their connection was real, she wasn't imagining it. It wasn't just about the sex that first night.

Fitz spent the entire journey back oscillating between relief and frustration. Relief at the fact that Elle was in the ambulance with Roshan, giving him some much-needed breathing room, and frustration at the realisation that only Elle's presence next to him would have calmed his uncharacteristically jangling nerves.

He'd been shocked when she'd mentioned Janine, but the anger he might have previously expected to flood out of him had gone, replaced by a deep-seated need to talk it through with someone. With Elle.

It was almost torture when she disappeared into the hospital with Roshan and he had to return to his office alone, searching for paperwork to occupy his racing thoughts. Yet at the same time he was immensely grateful to her for saving both the young mum's life and that of her baby. As if somehow it made up for the baby he and Janine had lost.

He had no idea how much time passed until a light knock on his door wrestled him from his dark thoughts.

'I thought you might like to know mother and baby are resting and are fine. I eventually removed the shard and incredibly it had missed the baby entirely and slid into a void between Roshan's internal organs. They both handled the operation well and I'm hoping she'll be able to carry her baby to term.'

'How likely is that?'

'If they get through the night without any complications, I'll be a lot happier,' Elle admitted. 'Besides, the generators are due in the next few days, and as soon as we have them up and running the first incubators will arrive. If Roshan can at least hang on until then, it would be great.'

He took in her wan smile, the strain around her eyes giving her away.

'You must be exhausted,' he said quietly. 'Thank you for coming to tell me.'

She blinked.

'I thought you were going to…talk to me.'

Part of him wanted to. Another part thought he'd dodged that bullet for today.

'I thought you might prefer to get some sleep. I can't imagine you've had more than about ten hours over the last four days or so.'

'Right,' Elle conceded stiffly.

Still, she hesitated as though she wanted to say more. Instead, finally, she dipped her head and stepped towards the door. He should be grateful that she wasn't trying to push the matter.

'Janine was my ex-fiancée,' he announced abruptly,

watching as she froze with her hand on the doorhandle. Slowly, so slowly, she drew her fingers back, listening to him without turning around. 'Not that I think you can call it an engagement really. It lasted less than twenty-four hours and it wasn't exactly planned. There was a baby.'

She twisted her head back over her shoulder.

'I don't understand.'

He didn't blame her. He wasn't sure even he had ever understood it, everything had happened so fast.

'Janine was a fellow officer. We met at Sandhurst. She was kind and generous and quiet, exactly the kind of girl I ought to like. To love. She understood the army and she loved me. I wanted to love her back.'

'You wanted to?'

He could hear the confusion in her voice.

'There was no reason why I shouldn't have loved her. I liked her. But that was it. I couldn't. That was when I realised I was flawed. I'm not like other people, Elle, I don't feel the way other people do. I lack that empathy, that connection.'

'I don't believe that. You just weren't right for each other.'

'No, you don't understand. I felt more for Janine than I have any other person but I couldn't love her. It just wasn't there. I was selfish, just like my father was.'

He watched her expression change from surprise, to shock, to disbelief.

'You are *not* your father. How could you even think that?'

Her faith in him was humbling, the way her eyes stared so deeply into his as if she could somehow show him exactly how she saw him.

But he had to resist. He couldn't fall for it. She knew about his cruel and violent father, she understood about the car crash, she soothed his guilt over not being there for his mother and sister. However, she didn't know about Janine.

And it was time he told her. He owed Elle that much. That hard, unwieldy truth.

'Elle,' he began, 'I don't deserve your kindness. I never did. You think I'm a better man that I am. I wish you were right, but you're not.'

'Fitz—'

'No.' He stood up, cutting her off before she could object. 'You keep insisting I'm this stand-up guy because that's the army guy everyone sees. But you're wrong. All of you. The man I seem to be able to be out here is the person I would like to be. The colonel I would like to be. I like who I am, what I've achieved, how much my men accomplish when inspired. It's why I love my job. I've poured everything I have into my career.'

'I know that,' she began, but he refused to let her steer the conversation.

'But I'm not that same man back home, out of Green, in my personal life. I never have been. God knows, I've tried.'

'You *are* the same man. I saw it that night. You're just too plagued with the demons of your past to see it. You signed up within weeks of that fatal car crash and you used the army to give you a new life, to reinvent yourself. And it worked, but in doing so you never allowed yourself time to grieve. I don't think you ever properly grieved. So every time you go home you're still stuck in the same place. Until you grieve you can't let go, and until you let go you can never let yourself move on.'

Every one of her words slammed into him, like rounds into body armour. He wanted to believe her. But he still hadn't told her everything. He sucked in a sharp breath.

'Elle, stop talking for a minute,' he said simply. 'You need to listen, *really* listen, to what I need to tell you.'

He didn't know why, but he began to move around the desk as she stepped closer. As if it was just him and her. And soon the ugly truth.

A sharp rap on the door startled them both.

'Come in.' It was an effort to conceal his frustration.

'Colonel, we've just had a message from Major Howes.

There's a problem with one of his troops in the Zenghar Valley. He's caught up with a complication at the railhead after the earthquake.'

The switch was immediate for Fitz. It had to be serious if Carl was calling at this hour.

'The troop out there was building a bridge to link the railhead with this hospital.'

'Yes, sir. They think the earthquake has affected the stability of the ground. Major Howes says there's a large local population who live beneath.'

The risk of landslides in that region was already quite high without the additional danger of the aftershocks.

'Potential for multiple fatalities if the ground gives way...' he muttered, almost to himself.

'We understand so, Colonel.'

'Get me Brigade, Corporal,' Fitz ordered quickly, his mind already engaging.

'They're already on the line, sir. In the ops office.'

He didn't hesitate. He was heading out of the door behind the young lad before he remembered Elle, and spun around quickly.

'We *will* talk,' he said quietly, knowing the corporal was too far away to hear.

'Forget it.' She shook her head, as though it didn't matter in the slightest, though he'd seen the initial frustration in her eyes to match his. 'Go.'

Without another glance, he went.

CHAPTER THIRTEEN

'WELL, THAT WAS a really good morning.' Elle congratulated her team with deliberate brightness as they deposited their theatre gloves and gowns in the bins. 'Three back-to-back surgeries, and all of them went better than anyone could have anticipated. Nice work, guys.'

It felt good to have such a high mood after the last couple of days. Elle reached for the hand scrub, content to listen to the chattering of her colleagues. The storm had caused a fair amount of damage in communities far and wide and injury levels had spiked, but it finally felt like they were starting to break the back of the influx of new arrivals without compromising care for existing patients.

Stepping through the doors to the main corridor to check on the wards, Elle knew instantly that something was wrong. The low, tense buzz was unsettling and it didn't take her long to find Jools, already huddled in conversation with a small group.

'What's going on?'

There was no need for preamble, they knew each other too well. Jools's head snapped up in dismay.

'There's been a landslide in the Zenghar Valley. That earthquake we had the other day was closer to them than to us and they think it likely caused the slide. Razorwire are sending out Medical Emergency Response Teams, but there are sixty-three confirmed dead so far.'

Fitz.

A chilling fear stole through Elle, its icy fingers closing painfully tightly in her chest. That was where one of his other units was bridge-building.

'Colonel Fitzwilliam was heading out there to oversee things.'

Jools nodded grimly.

'The engineers were caught in it, too. We know they suffered a couple of fatalities, but that's all we know.'

Elle didn't understand how her jellified legs didn't buckle under her weight. She wasn't certain how she made it across the room and around the curtain to collapse in the chair, away from prying eyes. She couldn't even be sure how her heart remembered to keep beating after initially hanging, frozen in her chest.

What a time to finally realise she was as invested in Fitz as her parents had once been in each other. As though she'd suddenly discovered that tiny last piece of who she was when she hadn't known, all these years, that a piece of her had been missing. And now, at the fear that Fitz had been injured—or worse—it felt like that tiny, new part of her had just been smashed against an invisible wall and was, even now, shattering into tiny, irreparable fragments inside her. She knew she'd begun to care for him, but when had she begun to care so very deeply?

When had she fallen in love with Fitz?

The stark realisation came out of nowhere.

As insane as it was, a part of her had fallen for him that first night. When he'd been happy to take direction from her with the seizure yet had been able to pre-empt all her needs. When he'd opened up about his family dying in the car crash and she'd seen that very first hint of vulnerability.

Fitz had exuded self-assurance, determination and power right from the start. And it had excited and enthralled her; more than that it had intoxicated her. Yet she'd also seen kindness in him, and been privileged enough to glimpse a sensitivity that had intrigued her. Fitz was everything that Stevie wasn't.

Everything she'd dreamed a life partner would be.

And she'd been prepared to let him slip through her fingers without even trying to fight for him, simply because convention suggested her break-up was too recent and Fitz had to be a rebound. Because she'd allowed Stevie's betrayal to remind her of all the mental blows she'd absorbed from her stepmother as a kid, and she'd forgotten to tell herself that she deserved a love that was better than any of that.

It was time she stopped listening to her head and tried listening to her heart.

She leapt up from the chair and rounded the curtain so fast that she almost collided with another body.

'Elle? Where are you hurrying off to?' Jools gasped as she darted backwards.

'To contact Colonel Duggan at Razorwire,' Elle called over her shoulder as she jogged away. 'They're going to need doctors on the ground and I'm a damn sight more use out there than I am here right now.'

'Good.' Pushing off the wall, Jools raced to catch up. 'Then can you count me in, too.'

'Just leave it be,' Fitz grumbled as he tried to snag his arm away from the young medic. 'I'm fine.'

'You need medical attention, Colonel.' The lance corporal stared him down, though his Adam's apple bobbed nervously. 'Given the nature of your injuries, you need to be easing the strain on your body. The fact that you've just single-handedly pulled three people out of the rubble only means the risk of internal injuries is also a factor.'

Fitz glowered. The boy had guts, he'd give him that. He might only be a lance corporal but he knew that in medical matters he had the authority to dictate to a colonel and, boy, was the kid sticking to his guns. He suppressed a smile of admiration.

'With an attitude like that, remind me to tell your CO that you deserve a field promotion,' he muttered as he settled back on the makeshift gurney. 'Just stitch me up and let me get back to my men.'

'Thank you, sir, but you understand you need to be on a MERT back to Razorwire? You can't put any more physical stress on your body.'

'The MERTs have higher priority patients to evacuate than me. I'm walking and talking. I'm fine.'

'Like I said, *Colonel*, we don't know about internal injuries…'

'Son,' Fitz growled abruptly, glancing over to where the latest MERT was landing and teams were already ferrying stretchered patients across the ground. They really needed more trained medical staff on the ground, there were so many injured. 'I'm fine. Now, fix me up as quickly as you can so that I can head back to help my men.'

'Sir…' the boy began, then shifted his glance as soon as he caught sight of Fitz's expression. 'Yes, sir.'

Whatever else the lance corporal might have been about to say was lost on Fitz as his eyes locked on one of the disembarking soldiers.

She couldn't be out here.

Before the medic could finish attending to him Fitz had pushed off the gurney and was striding across the ground, barely even paying attention to his step as he moved past the debris littered all around. As though he couldn't get to her fast enough. As though he was running through the thickest, stickiest treacle.

'What the hell are you doing here?'

'Good to see you too, Colonel,' she muttered, as he realised he'd roared at her, his nose only inches from hers.

He forced himself to lower his voice, though it wasn't as though anyone else could have heard them in the fracas, but he couldn't feel any remorse. Fear splintered through him like an axe cleaving wood, and with it a sense of protectiveness so fierce it was overwhelming, chasing everything else from his head—the landslide, the mission, the chaos around them.

'You can't be here.'

Fitz couldn't explain it, but he felt desperate, panicked, out of control.

Just like he had when he'd finally listened to his mother's terrified messages that night.

He told himself he couldn't see someone else he cared about getting hurt. Because however much he'd tried to dodge it over the last couple of months, he cared about Elle. Deep down, he suspected that was barely scratching the surface of it but he refused to follow that line of thought to its inevitable conclusion. He blinked as he realised she was answering him.

'I'm a trauma doctor.' Outwardly she looked the picture of calm, but he could hear the quiver in her voice. 'And this is an accident site. Where else would I be?'

'You should be back at the hospital. You have patients.'

A silent voice was urging him to send her back where it was safer. Back where even more of the valley couldn't come crashing down over her any second. It had always been a treacherous valley but now no one could be sure exactly how much damage the aftershocks of that earthquake had caused. But that wasn't his call, he wasn't her CO. And thank God, because if he had been, this was exactly why a relationship between them would have been against the rules.

'I should be right here. The relief in place are already taking over in the hospital, and I'm one of Colonel Duggan's first choices to be out here.'

'It isn't safe.' He heard the agony in his words as they were torn from his lips.

Yet the bedlam around them—the confusion that he was here to get a handle on and to calm—was nothing compared to the maelstrom raging deep within his chest right now.

'And that's our job,' she finished softly.

Quiet but steadfast, determined, her jaw set and shoulders squared, ready to stand off against even him if he got in the way of her doing her job. Every inch the professional, driven Elle he'd seen that first night. The Elle he'd so admired, been so drawn to, so attracted to. For several long seconds they stood immobile, and Fitz had the peculiar sensation of everything receding around them.

All the chaos, and the noise, and the dust fell away. It was just him and Elle.

And he finally allowed his brain to acknowledge what his heart and soul had realised a long time ago.

He loved her.

The urge to tell her almost crushed him.

Beautiful, lovely Elle, who always looked for the upside. And if there wasn't one then she created it just by her vibrant spirit and sheer force of will. She was like his morning coffee, like food, like *air*. He'd felt as though he'd almost been holding his breath until he'd seen her each day, and never in his life had he felt such a compulsion to be with someone.

Elle was a woman like no other he'd ever known. The more he knew her, the more he felt he didn't know enough. He wanted to know everything about her, tell her everything about him. He would never get enough of her, this woman who had shone a warm light into even the blackest caverns of his soul.

A woman who resisted the army chefs' chocolate cake if she'd been working in the hospital all day, but could devour two slices if she'd been rushing around the local communities. The woman who loathed drinking her water from a round plastic bottle and always decanted it into a battered square one she refused to throw away. Who had a pink lion token on her pack so she could identify it day or night but had learned a funny little story in the local language to break the ice with the local kids. He knew she always loaded up one of the pockets of her vest with small colouring books and crayons for them.

The thought of losing her actually twisted inside his gut and the urge to tell her almost crushed him.

But this wasn't the place and it certainly wasn't the time.

She was right, it *was* their job out here, and he had always prided himself on his professionalism as an army officer. But more than that, it was who they both were. They'd both chosen this life, they both loved this life and, right now, that had to come first. Besides, Elle's role was certainly vital but there was one thing in his favour.

The noise and pandemonium of their surroundings suddenly raced back to the foreground, crowding in on them.

'Fine.' Fitz blew out a breath. 'But since we aren't back at the hospital and this is *my* site, this is now *my* command. You listen to me, understand?'

'Colonel.' She dipped her head in acknowledgement, a soft smile playing on her lips as the light he so loved tiptoed back into her eyes. 'So where would you like me?'

He thrust the last of his doubts and fear away.

'What have you got? A couple of twelve by twelves?'

'Three of them, so far.'

It took him seconds to glance around the site, years of experience kicking in. There was a decent location a few hundred metres away, safe enough to be out of line of immediate danger but close enough that the injured could be easily carried there to be triaged, treated or prepped for the MERTs, and close to the helicopter landing site.

'You can set up over there.'

'Yes, Colonel,' Elle agreed, snatching her pack up and spinning back around to where her team was offloading kit from the helicopter. He watched her go, irrationally proud of the woman he saw; a woman who was liked and respected everywhere she went.

A woman who had achieved the one thing he'd never expected anyone could ever do so subtly he hadn't even noticed it happening; she'd put the shattered fragments of his heart back together and, more than that, she'd done so with such skill that he almost couldn't believe it had ever been crushed in the first place.

In his life there had been a few people who had known about what had happened to his mother and his sister. The therapist the state had made him visit for that first week before he'd turned eighteen, the army mental health doctor when he'd enlisted a couple of weeks later, even Janine when her father had told her what was in his file about the crash, but he'd never told them some of the things he'd told Elle that first night.

And although all of them had told him it hadn't been his fault, none of them had made him believe it. None of them had known the full story that Elle had known, about the phone messages or the abuse his mother had suffered. Elle had been the one to make him accept that he couldn't have changed anything. That he couldn't have known his mother was calling because his father had reappeared after three years, and that even if he'd raced home after that first call they would already have been gone. Even if he'd called the police, no one could have got there in time.

She'd allowed him to finally accept that the only person to blame that night had been his father, and that it was time for him to let go at last. He'd spent nearly two decades focusing on his army life, his career, throwing himself into it as a way to avoid having to consider what his non-army life had been like. He'd thrown up a wall between his personal life and his professional one, always keeping himself on the side of the latter. But in a matter of months Elle had begun to take down that wall, brick by brick, and now he knew that he could step over what was left of that division if he wanted to. He could finally consider a future that didn't centre on his career. Fitz wasn't yet sure what that future might hold, he only knew it contained Elle.

He just had to convince her of that.

But he could wait. A day, a week, a month, until they had the chance to be alone again. She deserved to know how very incredible, and special, and unique she was. How he couldn't foresee a life without her in it. And how what they had wasn't transitory or a bit of fun, because she was the only woman with whom he could ever—*had* ever—been able to see tantalising glimpses of a future.

Unexpectedly, Elle turned, although he hadn't said a word, and even if he had she could never have heard him over the clamour. It was an instinct that had begun to bind them ever since that first night.

'Colonel?'

He couldn't hear the words but he could read her lips, and still it didn't stop him from speaking aloud, the words swallowed up within the pandemonium, yet that did nothing to diminish the excitement bubbling inside him.

Like he was once again the kid he'd stopped being the night he'd lost his beloved mother.

'Nothing.' He smiled. 'Everything.'

For a moment Elle simply stared, as though trying to be sure that he meant what she thought. And then she responded with a smile of her own, the bright, easy, open Elle-style beam shining as brightly, as warmly as if she could reflect the very sun from the sky.

His Elle. He could spend the rest of his life bathed in the glow of her happiness and be a contented man. And he would willingly spend the rest of his life making sure she felt every bit as treasured, as admired, as loved as she deserved.

CHAPTER FOURTEEN

ANOTHER CHEER WENT up as they finally freed yet another kid from the rubble. Dirty and exhausted but most certainly alive. He lifted the tiny body as the child clung madly to him, his eyes locked on an exhausted Elle as she hurried over to them.

'Bring her this way, we've set up more treatment areas over here...' She indicated. 'And then you need to take a break. When is the last time you ate?'

'When's the last time *you* did?' Fitz challenged, following her as she lifted the rope to the cordoned-off area that allowed her to triage and treat without the pressure of understandably desperate relatives crowding in to see proof for themselves of their missing loved one.

As they slipped inside the tents the little girl was whisked away by Elle's team, what looked to be her mother crying with relief by a waiting bed.

It had been almost twenty hours since they'd started securing the area and finding people to pull free. Even now, they were still finding occasional survivors, the shouts for silence going up any time they thought they heard sounds of a survivor, and marvelling at the resilience of the human spirit. But the death toll, low in the first few hours, was now beginning to race up, the bodies more damaged the deeper they excavated, and Fitz knew he would have to put the local volunteers on three-hour maximums before making them take a compulsory break, and to talk to someone about what they'd seen. His own men could work longer shifts, but it was still back-breaking work that was becoming increasingly demoralising the more time passed and the fewer survivors they found.

'I've just had a break, actually,' Elle said gently, answering his original question.

'Voluntarily?' he couldn't quite picture that. 'You mean someone *made* you take a break.'

Her sheepish expression said it all.

'The point is that you need to stop and eat, regroup,' she admonished anyway.

No one was around to overhear but, still, they both knew it was their way of silently showing each other they cared. In spite of their surroundings, he couldn't help an unexpected wisp of happiness from curling up inside him.

'I will when relief arrives,' he consented eventually.

She glanced up quickly.

'It should have arrived about half an hour ago. Major Howes brought his other two troops and Major Richards brought his squadron.'

'But they haven't reached us?'

'No.'

Fitz frowned.

'Which means it's likely there's been another slide on the other side of the valley, on the way in. I have to go and find out.'

'No,' Elle commanded, stepping inside. 'I'll give this little girl a check-up and then I want to inspect those stitches of yours, to see if they're still holding up. I'm surprised you haven't burst them out there.'

'Is that a medical order, Major?' Fitz cocked his eyebrow.

'It is.' She smiled, ducking into the next tent to retrieve a few medical supplies.

He settled on the edge of the bed, ready to expose the dressing on his shoulder.

'Fitz?'

He stiffened, turned.

It couldn't be.

'Janine?'

He steeled himself for the inevitable guilt but it didn't come.

Instead, in that instant, he finally understood what had happened with Janine. It had barely been a couple of years since the car crash and he'd been so desperate to fix the yearning chasm in his soul after his family's deaths that he'd seen the way this sweet, young girl had loved him and he'd tried to convince himself that if he could love her back then he wouldn't be damaged any more. He wouldn't be alone any more. But Janine, as gentle as she was, could never have helped him rebuild his shattered past enough to move on. Janine would always have needed someone whole, untainted by tragedy, someone *she* could lean on to escape her controlling father. She could never have seen or understood the twisted mess inside him, much less helped him to untangle it. He would always have provided for their baby but in many ways it was a good thing there had never been a child stuck in the middle of them. He would always have been the wrong man for Janine, just as she could never have been the right woman for him. She wasn't Elle.

'Thank God you're here.' She exhaled heavily.

Abruptly, Fitz registered Janine's blanched, preoccupied expression and he forgot all his insignificant personal demons.

'I didn't know your logistics unit was out here.'

'We were bringing the generators through the valley to a new hospital being built when a small slide hit multiple vehicles in the middle of our convoy,' she stated.

'Everyone okay?'

'Mostly, a couple of four-by-fours rolled and there are some bumps and bruises but we got lucky. Fortunately none of the gennies were hit.'

'There should be a couple of my squadrons out there now.' He frowned as Janine nodded.

'They were behind us, they're clearing and securing the area now. They've got better equipment for it and we had to keep going as we have a time constraint for getting the generators to the hospital. There's an MRI coming on our next run.'

It wasn't just the MRI. Fitz thought of the last ancient back-up generator they'd repaired too many times already. It was imperative they get the new generators to the site because if the back-up failed before the new generators were in place, the hospital would have no power at all.

'If Major Howes is dealing with the landslide then you're going to need me to head to the hospital with you,' he decided quickly.

'Major Howes assured me he'd be right behind us.'

'No.' Fitz quickly ran through the route in his head. 'There's a bridge between here and the hospital, we already recced it but that was before the earthquake. I want to make sure it hasn't been weakened and won't collapse under the weight of those gennies.'

Her relief was obvious.

'Thank you.'

He was off the bed and across the tent before Elle's voice, tight and high, halted him.

'Colonel, your arm.'

He turned to see her standing at the back of the tent, supplies in hand, her expression stricken. She'd obviously heard most of the conversation.

Fitz hesitated for a fraction of a second. He wanted to tell her, to explain to her that, as much as he would be doing this anyway to complete a crucial mission, there was also a personal element to it now. Because in helping Janine he felt as though he would finally get closure on his regret from their past. And if he did, then he would finally have a clear conscience. He could at last be free to look to a new, more promising future with Elle. He wanted to tell her all of that, but there was no time. Instead, he invested every bit of meaning he could into his words, hoping she'd understand the message.

'You need to be checked out. Major Caplin will do it. I'll get a team together.'

He also needed to get Carl to bring at least one of the troops to the valley to join the rescue effort here.

'I really *do* need to check that wound, Colonel,' Elle asserted firmly, but he waved her away.

The sooner he completed this mission, the sooner he could consider a future with her.

'Major Caplin, my arm's fine. I have to leave now. Please check over Major Billings here. Pack up your kit and your team and head out as soon as you're ready. Don't wait for me.'

The expression on her face twisted his gut. He'd hurt her. Again. And he couldn't do a thing about it. He would have to be content with seeing her back at the hospital. Then they could finally have a conversation that he now realised was long overdue. Unless she ran, like he suspected she might. And if she did, then he would have no choice but to respect her decision. He would have to let her go.

Don't wait for me.

Elle stared at the heavy-duty canvas tent flap long after Fitz had disappeared and it had dropped heavily back into place. There was no doubt in her mind that Fitz had been trying to tell her something. A message within the words.

She forced herself to turn to the major, dredging up her practised medical smile. She couldn't shake the feeling the woman was watching her shrewdly. Yet another of Fitz's admirers, no doubt.

'Can you sit on the bed, please, Major Billings?'

'Janine,' the woman introduced herself immediately.
Janine.
It hit Elle like a blast wave. Suddenly it all made sense.
Janine.
Fitz was still in love with her.
He'd chosen her over Elle's own medical advice. And,
Elle couldn't help feeling, he'd chosen Janine over her personally. She was second again. Dispensable. Just like she'd
been to Stevie. Only the difference here was that Fitz had
never broken any commitment to her because he'd never
offered her any promises. From the outset he'd told her that
they didn't have a future, that he didn't *do* relationships.

The error had been on her part in allowing herself to believe that he didn't do relationships because he hadn't yet
met the right person, the woman who could help him to get
past the trauma and guilt of his past. And the error had been
in thinking that she could be that woman and ignoring what
had been right under her nose. That Janine had always been
in the forefront of Fitz's head.

Don't wait for me.
As painful and unbearable as it might be, she had to listen to him. Fitz didn't want her. He'd made that clear again
and again, she'd just chosen to read something more into
it. She'd chosen to believe it was because he couldn't find
a way to open up to her, and she'd chosen to believe that
if she loved him enough she could find a way to help him.

She'd been wrong. She would pack up here and finish
up the last few days in Razorwire before returning home.
The hospital didn't need her, the next squadron was out here
already and the relief teams had taken over.

She wouldn't come back as long as Fitz was still out here.
She couldn't bear to work alongside him, loving him but
unable to do a thing about it.

'You know who I am,' Janine said slowly, her eyes watching Elle intently.

She could play it down the line, strictly professional, of course. But they were both grown women, both majors, both equals.

'I know a little,' Elle hedged.

To her surprise, Janine's shoulders sagged and the woman looked defeated.

'So he really is in love with you.'

It was more a comment to herself than to Elle, but still Elle couldn't help snorting with nervous shock.

'You couldn't be more wrong.'

Sharp eyes pierced Elle as Janine jerked her head up.

'You didn't know?'

Elle focussed on her job, unsure what else to say.

'I sensed something between you the moment he saw you come in.' Janine spoke softly, almost wistfully. 'I would have given anything for him to look at me, just once, the way he looked at you at that moment.'

Elle told herself not to listen, not to believe, not to let that little flicker of hope surge so strongly inside her. She told herself it would only hurt all the more when she had to prove Janine was wrong.

And still the hope grew, leaning towards Janine's words the way a tree leaned to the sun. Making her admit things she would never have admitted to anyone, least of all Janine.

'It isn't love. At least, not on Fitz's part.' The words spilled out before she could stop herself.

But instead of Janine using the confession as ammunition, as Elle might have feared, the woman simply offered a sweet, if watery smile.

'Did he tell you about the baby?'

Elle didn't know how to answer.

'He did.' Janine nodded, as if she'd suspected as much. 'Then you're wrong. He loves you very much. I don't think he's ever told anyone about me. About us, such as there ever was an us.'

'He didn't go into detail,' Elle found herself half-apologising, as though she was intruding on someone else's business.

'That sounds like Fitz.' Janine offered another soft, sad smile. 'But the fact that he opened up to you at all should tell you all you need to know about how much he values you. How about his family? Did he tell you about them?'

She should end the conversation. It felt disloyal talking about Fitz behind his back. But a part of her couldn't stop. He'd told her she was the only person he'd ever wanted to talk to about his family. At the time it had made her feel special, valued, as though he wanted her to understand him in a way he never had with anyone else.

It had turned out that was just a lie.

'I know his mother and sister died in the car crash,' Elle said after a moment.

Janine frowned.

'It was his whole family. His poor father, too. It must have been devastating for Fitz, losing his whole family in one single instant, but he never spoke about it.'

Elle hesitated. Didn't Janine know his father had been drinking? Had reappeared out of nowhere? Had abused his mother?

'But he spoke about it with you,' she pointed out cautiously, deliberately focussing on the check-up and avoiding Janine's direct gaze.

'Only because I made him. My father…he was a colonel back then, and when he found out that I'd been pregnant he told me to forget about Fitz, about the car crash. Told me that he was damaged.'

Damaged.

Exactly the words Fitz had used to describe himself that first night.

'Did you ever say that to him?' she demanded, unable to help herself. 'Did you ever tell him he was damaged?'

The woman dropped her head, misery and guilt etched in every crevice and curve.

'I never should have, I know that. But I was hurt and I was grieving. I'd just lost my baby, and Fitz didn't seem bothered. I know now he was probably still numb from finding out in the first place—I'd only told him I was pregnant a few hours earlier...'

'A few hours?' Elle exclaimed.

'He didn't tell you that?'

'He told me you were three months pregnant when you went out on that convoy. That he didn't stop you. That he should have told someone and made sure you were sent home to safety. He holds himself responsible.'

'Fitz does?' Janine twisted around to face Elle. 'How could any of it be his fault? I only told him that morning, before the convoy went out. I knew he was in shock but he immediately told me we'd get married and he would take care of us, just as I'd known he would. My convoy was due back that night and then I was heading home for R&R. I was going to tell my parents then.'

'He never said.' Elle shook her head.

Part of her was still reeling, yet another part of her was absorbing the revelations, sifting them in with the story Fitz had told her, working through how it had impacted on him. Compounding the guilt and helplessness and vulnerability he must already have felt at losing his mother and sister only a few years earlier.

No wonder he had trust issues.

No wonder he found it hard to let her in.

If she really loved him as much as she thought she did, then she had to find a way to prove she wasn't going to let him down or leave him, while giving him the time and space he needed to accept her.

'He thinks he let you down, betrayed your trust,' Elle said at length.

It was a risk, telling Janine something that Fitz had told her in confidence, but Elle decided it was a risk she was prepared to take. Despite everything, there was a part of her that couldn't help liking Janine and feeling sorry for her. She was no doubt a decent enough major, her army father would have drilled that into her, but as a woman Janine seemed a little naïve, a bit young for her age. And yet if anyone could tell her the truth about Fitz, Elle couldn't help feeling it was going to be this woman.

'He never let me down.' Janine hung her head again. 'I let *him* down. I…manipulated him. I'm not proud of it. But I was twenty-two and I was naïve and foolish, and I was desperate to get away from my controlling father. I fell for Fitz the first week of our officer training course, he was different from the other lads. Stronger, more focussed, resolute.

'The longer I spent in his company, the more I fell in love. I thought if I could give him a family—like the one he'd lost—then I could break through those barriers of his and he would love me back. But he never did. He would have married me, he would have taken care of me, of our baby. But he never loved me like I thought I loved him. Yet if I *had* loved him, I suppose I never would have wanted to trap him.'

'Getting pregnant was deliberate?' Elle managed slowly.

'*No!* At least, I don't think so. Maybe. No. I don't know, subconsciously perhaps? And I regret it, more than you can imagine.'

'Why tell me all this?' Elle asked, her curiosity finally getting the better of her.

Janine shrugged.

'I'm not sure. Guilt, I suppose. I've been carrying it around with me all this time, wondering how Fitz is doing. I followed his career for a while but I knew he had a reputation for never getting involved with anyone. Then I stopped. I realised I wasn't doing myself any favours refusing to let go of the past. When I saw you in here, I don't know… I guess I thought it was my chance to make amends.'

'Ironic,' Elle mused softly.

'What is?'

Elle hesitated, wondering whether it was wise to say anything else, then deciding that it was the least she could do after Janine had been so painfully honest with her.

'I could be wrong, but I have a feeling Fitz wanting to be the one to personally take charge of this mission and accompany your convoy is as much about making amends to you and ensuring your safety as it is about ensuring the generator's safety. Maybe he feels he owes you, maybe it's about closure.'

'He doesn't owe me anything,' Janine answered quietly. 'But I'll happily take the closure. So what about you? What are you going to do now?'

Elle was spared any response as a young corporal appeared at the tent door, breathing hard from running.

'Major Billings, Colonel Fitzwilliam told me to inform you that his vehicle is ready when your convoy is cleared to go.'

'Understood.' Janine nodded, turning to Elle as she slid off the bed. 'Am I clear to leave?'

'You seem fine,' confirmed Elle.

'Okay, well…as to the other thing, good luck.'

Elle watched as the woman hurried away. The silence only emphasised the way her heart was beating out a tattoo and the blood was rushing in her ears.

Fitz was just as damaged as he'd tried to tell her, but she hadn't listened. She hadn't really understood. Now she knew more, and she understood better. If she crowded Fitz then she was only going to compound the issue. Especially when her own insecurities were still so close to the surface. She hadn't realised, until she'd seen Fitz and Janine in that first instant and had felt that surge of jealousy that had been so absent when she'd walked in on Stevie, that she'd never allowed herself to heal.

Not just from the obvious pain of being cheated on by her fiancé, but because she'd never allowed herself to mourn the boy who had saved her from the misery of her teenage years as he'd turned into a man she hadn't recognised. Hadn't even liked.

Until she allowed herself to repair a decade of a mentally draining relationship, how could she possibly dive into another one with Fitz? They both needed time to heal, to work out who they were, to go into any new relationship without unnecessary baggage from their respective pasts.

But a tiny part of her was terrified to leave things as they were with Fitz. Because if she walked away, he could close the door on her that final inch and she'd never be able to get back in.

She had absolutely no idea what to do.

CHAPTER FIFTEEN

FITZ TOOK OUT the piece of paper for the hundredth time since he'd found Elle's address and jotted it down.

He didn't think he'd ever forget the despair that had scraped at his insides when he'd discovered she'd spent her last few days at Razorwire and had left without a word.

As though he'd meant nothing.

As though they'd meant nothing.

He'd sworn to himself that he wouldn't follow her. That if she walked away he would let her go. But it had felt so different when it had actually happened.

He'd thrown himself back into his work, into the mission, but at every turn he had been reminded of Elle. Brigade had been more than pleased with the progress they'd already made on the hospital and he'd been forced to remember that much of it had been down to Elle's expertise on the layout, her ability to communicate the hospital's needs, and her capacity for compromise with the engineering priorities. The fact that they had clicked so easily together, working as such a good team, only made it all the harder to push aside the memories of her.

The day he'd received the details of his R&R flight home, he'd known he had to find Elle. To speak to her. To convince her that they should at least try to see if there wasn't some future for them.

And now he was minutes from landing, and it was time

to decide whether to bin the address and let her get on with her life, or visit in the hope of...what? Convincing her to try a relationship with a man who didn't have the faintest idea of how a real one should work? A man who was more than likely going to hurt her despite his best intentions because, when it came to love, his best wouldn't be enough?

Fitz closed his eyes and waited for the plane to begin its final descent, the weight of hope, expectation and uncertainly all pressing down more intensely on his shoulders than even the heaviest of military packs. When the plane finally landed, he still had no idea what he should do. Losing her from his life had been unbearable even for the short time since she'd finished her tour of duty, but convincing her to risk more of herself only to lose her permanently, and no doubt crush her in the process, was unconscionable.

He was still coming to terms with what Janine had told him this last time they'd met.

Fitz was still lost in his thoughts as he split off from the soldiers heading out of the front door for the coaches, and instead strode out of the side door of the hangar, which led to the senior officers' parking area. And then he saw her in front of him, resting, in civvy clothes that reminded with startling clarity of that first night, on the bonnet of her car.

He stopped dead, then slowly, very slowly managed to instruct his legs to work again as he walked up to her.

'Major.'

'Colonel.'

That slight quirk of her mouth tugged at his chest.

'Elle.'

'Fitz.'

She walked around to the driver's door, letting herself in and clipping her seatbelt on. When he still hadn't moved, she lowered the window.

'Are you getting in or not?'

So calm, and cool, as though she knew exactly what she was doing and wasn't plagued by even one of the doubts that collided inside his head. She made him want to believe it would all be okay. She made him want to see himself through her eyes.

She made him want to be the man she saw through her eyes.

The piece of paper with her address on it fluttered in the breeze, still held in his fingers. He smiled wryly and passed it through the window to her before opening the boot and putting his pack in. By the time he slid into the passenger seat, she had already started the engine.

'So,' she asked a few minutes later as she pulled away from the gatehouse and onto the main road, 'were you going to use it?'

'Your address? I honestly don't know,' he answered. 'I kept telling myself to be a better man and let you go, but I suspect I couldn't have stayed away for the entire two weeks.'

She didn't answer at first, then she dipped her head in a simple nod.

'Good.'

He let her drive, watching out of the window thoughtfully. It was only when she pulled up in a quiet road and he saw the house numbers that he realised they matched the address on the paper. She'd brought him to her home.

It gave him an irrational surge of satisfaction.

Her smile was like a beacon of light as she unclipped her seatbelt and, wordlessly, he followed her into her house. He couldn't help taking everything in, from the muted, sophisticated colour scheme on the walls and floor to the vibrant splashes of colour in fun paintings or soft furnishings. It was all so essentially Elle. Every last photograph, every last knick-knack—not that there were many of either—but the selective few only emphasised her personality all the more.

Her home reflected every different facet of her personality, solid and consistent yet quirky and dynamic.

Oddly, it felt like the closest thing to a home he'd ever known, and he'd barely been here for a few minutes.

It only made him want to be with her all the more.

'About Janine—' he began, but Elle silenced him.

'I don't want to know about your past. At least, not right now. You still have stuff to work through and, since I thought about it, so do I. I've already told you that you can't underestimate guilt, Fitz. Believe me, I know how complicated and confusing it can be. But what I want to know is if you want us to work through it together. I want to know if you see a future for us.'

'I don't know *how* to build a future with someone—my whole adult life all I've ever concentrated on is my career, or it was until you came along—but I want to try. For the record, I never said it back that day but I know I love you. I just don't know if love is enough.'

'That's still a great start.' Her breath whooshed out as she took a step towards him.

'But is it enough?'

'Who knows? It will be if we want it to be. It will depend on us, I guess.'

He wanted to believe as she did. More than anything.

'And if it falls apart?' He barely recognised the strangled voice as his, echoing all the fears in his soul. 'If I can't be the man you need, the man you deserve, if it's not in my DNA?'

'I told you, let go of your past.' She took that final step.

Her toes pushed against his, her breath rippled over the skin in the small V of his chest, where his shirt was unbuttoned. Then higher, as she tilted her head to look at him.

'What happens if I hurt you?'

She took his face in her hands and he felt every last inch

of that old, familiar, unwelcome glacier in his chest crack and slide away.

'And what happens if you don't?' she whispered.

His hands came up to hold hers, then hauled her to him. Elle had no idea how long they stood entwined, as though he never wanted to let her go. She only knew she didn't want to move, didn't even want to breathe heavily in case it shattered the perfect moment.

Her little home suddenly felt more alive than she'd ever known it. Fitz filled the space, the air crackling around them, and it felt like the place could barely contain him. Or maybe it could barely contain all that flowed between them. She'd always hated anyone in her home. It had always been her sanctuary, her personal space from the world. Her real life away from the ever-increasing opulence of Stevie's luxury bachelor pads. This had been *her* perfect home, and only her best friend Fliss had ever been welcome.

And now Fitz.

Somehow it felt as though he'd always belonged here.

'I want to promise you everything,' he murmured into her hair, his hand cupping her head like she was the most precious thing in the world to him. 'You make me feel things I never knew existed before. Like what I thought was important isn't as significant any more, and yet things I never gave a second thought to are suddenly vital. Like anything is possible as long as you are by my side.'

He shook his head, still trying to fathom it.

'You make me feel cherished,' she added simply.

Her words humbled him and yet made his chest swell with pride all at once.

'But we've both said in the past that words mean nothing without actions to back them up.'

'So don't say them,' she whispered. 'You've already told me you love me, and that's enough for now. We'll work on the rest through actions, deal?'

'Agreed. But for the record, can I tell you one thing again?' His voice rumbled low against her cheek now, and she shivered in anticipation. 'Because I don't ever want to tire of saying it. I love you, Major Gabriella Caplin.'

'I love you too.' She drew her head back, her smile freezing on her lips, her breath catching in her throat.

She didn't want to talk any more. She wanted something else entirely. Fitz's eyes were dark, intense, hungry. But there was something else, too. Something more. Promises he couldn't yet articulate and she wasn't ready to hear. Like they'd agreed. Actions. Not words.

'Enough talking,' he muttered abruptly, bringing his mouth down to claim hers with a fire she hoped would never be quenched. He kissed her with all the unspoken words that lay between them. He kissed her with all the possession she needed to make her feel wanted. He kissed her with all his flawed yet perfect heart.

And when he finally, reluctantly pulled away, she felt strangely bereft. Just like that first night.

'There was one other thing I brought,' he said suddenly. 'Wait here.'

She watched as he slid the keys from the basket on her hall stand and dashed out to the car. And then he was back and the palm-sized pretty velvet box in his hands made her stomach flip-flop. A tiny bit of excitement, a lot of fear, but mainly with disappointment.

Because he didn't know her at all after all. She wasn't ready for this yet. It wasn't right.

'When did you do this?' she asked nervously, hoping he couldn't tell she was stalling.

'In Razorwire. It's where I got the box. It's odd the things some people send in care packages.'

He was edgy too, she realised. But it didn't help. She licked her lips.

'Fitz, this is—'

'Just open it, Elle,' he insisted quietly.

Heavy-hearted, she pulled at the bow with painstaking hesitation and clicked open the box.

Her entire body soared until her head felt dizzy.

'It's a key!' she exclaimed.

He'd remembered and this was his way of showing her—proving to her—that she could trust him. The first of his actions-not-words promise. Her grin was so wide it was almost uncomfortable. *Had she ever known how it felt to be this happy?*

'To my place,' confirmed Fitz. 'You can call in whenever you want. No invitation necessary.'

'Thank you.' Her voice cracked as she nodded vigorously. 'It's perfect.'

'Like you,' he murmured, pulling her back into his arms. 'Now, where were we?'

Elle could hear the Gurkha piper playing as she and Fitz turned. The honour guard formed outside the doors of the church, fellow officers from both their regiments only too happy to play their part in the big day.

'Happy?' Fitz murmured as they began their walk down the aisle, permanent grins attached to both their faces.

'It doesn't even begin to describe it.' The laughter bubbled up inside her. 'The perfect culmination to a wonderful three years together.'

'It gets better,' a voice chirped up from behind as Elle swung around to grin at Fliss, her heavily pregnant matron of honour.

'If your waters break on my wedding dress train,' Elle teased in a threatening voice, 'well…I won't mind a bit. I'm just relieved you made it through the service.'

And then Fliss disappeared into the background as Fitz wrapped his arm around her—her new husband. It felt so exciting and yet so fitting.

'Come on, Major Fitzwilliam.' Fitz chuckled. 'Or are you sticking with Major Caplin?'

'You already know the answer.' She swatted him gently even as he led her out of the church doors and under the honour guard. 'Definitely Fitzwilliam, but they'd better not call me Fitz.'

'They wouldn't dare. Not the incoming lieutenant colonel of the field hospital, and an OBE to boot.'

He soundest almost prouder of her than she was herself. But, then, that was Fitz. In the last three years he'd never let her down, never put his career ahead of hers. They'd worked together, well and truly buried any last demons, and now they were beginning another new, pristine chapter of their lives together. And Elle couldn't wait.

'Well, I had to do something to keep up with you, Deputy Assistant Chief of Staff for HQ Telridge Command. Although thanks to your new post, starting tomorrow morning, this is going to be the shortest honeymoon in history.'

'I'll make it up to you,' Fitz promised.

'No need.' She turned to him as his arm snaked about her back and he pulled her close. 'Enough talking, more action, soldier.'

And he obliged. As he always did.

* * * * *

COMING SOON!

We really hope you enjoyed reading this book.
If you're looking for more romance
be sure to head to the shops when
new books are available on

Thursday 22nd May

To see which titles are coming soon, please visit
millsandboon.co.uk/nextmonth

MILLS & BOON